ATHLE
2015
THE INTERNATIONAL TRACK AND FIELD ANNUAL

BY PETER MATTHEWS

ASSOCIATION OF TRACK & FIELD STATISTICIANS

Published by SportsBooks Ltd

SportsBooks Limited
9 St Aubyns Place
York
YO24 1EQ
United Kingdom
Tel: 01904 613475
e-mail randall@sportsbooks.ltd.uk
Website www.sportsbooks.ltd.uk

This publication incorporates the ATFS Annual.

Photographs supplied by Mark Shearman, 22 Grovelands Road, Purley, Surrey, CR8 4LA.
Tel: 0208 660 0156: mark@athleticsimages.com

British Library Cataloguing in Publication Data

Athletics: the international track and
field annual – 2015
1. Athletics. Track & Field events –
Serials
1. International athletics annual (London)
796.4'2'05

ISBN 9781907524479

Cover design: Kath Grimshaw

Printed arranged by Jellyfish Solutions, UK

CONTENTS

INTRODUCTION

THE EXERCISE OF putting together this International Athletics Annual in the opening months of every year provides so many memories of the past year in the sport. Personally I can look back on so many rich experiences as I was fortunate to be able to work, providing TV commentary, at such major meetings as the World Indoor Championships in Sopot, the World Relays in Nassau, the Commonwealth Games in Glasgow and the European Championships in Zürich. As ever such events show that there is no substitute for the excitements brought about by meaningful competition. Three of those events are thoroughly well established in the International calendar, but it was great to welcome the newcomer – the World Relays, a meeting that was such an outstanding success, with the citizens of the Bahamas packing the Thomas A. Robinson Stadium in Nassau and bringing intense enthusiasm to the event.

After no global championship outdoors in 2014, we have the major event of 2015 to look forward to as the World Championships. Each and every one of the World Championships since the biennial meeting was introduced at Helsinki in 1983 has been a magnificent event, and one trusts that Beijing will be no exception. Once again it will be fascinating to see which athletes most catch the eye, whether it be the established stars led by Usain Bolt seeking to star for a fourth successive Worlds, Renaud Lavillenie, Valerie Adams, Shelly-Ann Fraser-Pryce, Robert Harting, David Rudisha, Barbara Špotáková and others, or whether it be the new generation of the likes of Katarina Johnson-Thompson, Dafne Schippers, Trayvon Brommell, Ronald Kwemoi and Konrad Bukowiecki, or indeed names yet barely known to the general fan. For one of the great things about athletics is that there is always mix of newcomers and established stars. 2015 will also be a year of administrative and leadership change, with the Presidents of the IAAF and of European Athletics stepping down after years of distinguished service. Lamine Diack, an IAAF Council member from 1976, succeeded Primo Nebiolo at the head of the IAAF after the latter's death in 1990, and Hans-Jörg Wirz has headed European Athletics for 15 years. There will be elections for their successors this year.

I have maintained the structure of the Annual virtually unchanged with all the essential features from the reviews and results of the major meetings in 2014, through to the biographical profiles of some 800 top athletes, world and continental records, all-time lists and the core deep lists for the past year. As ever the Annual is as topical as I can make it with results from March 2015 of the European Indoor Championships and the World Cross-country and indoor lists for the year. One section that has grown over the years is the Obituary. As the years pass so we bid farewell to athletes who competed at a time when the sport was growing fast in worldwide appeal and participation, and so there are more of them to include. But apart from the great athletes, I note the passing in early 2015 of two great international journalists whom I was fortunate to be able to count as friends over several decades, Gustav Schwenk and Jim Dunaway. They both lived to a good age, but will be greatly missed.

Peter Matthews April 2015

Information can be sent to me at 10 Madgeways Close, Great Amwell, Ware, Herts SG12 9RU, England. Email: p.matthews121@btinternet.com

Information or requests re sales, distribution, publication etc. to the publishers, SportsBooks Ltd.
Email: info@sportsbooks.ltd.uk
www.sportsbooks.ltd.uk

ABBREVIATIONS

The following abbreviations have been used for meetings with, in parentheses, the first year that they were held.

AAU (USA) Amateur Athletic Union Championships (1888) (later TAC)
Af-AsG Afro-Asian Games (2003)
AfCh African Championships (1979)
AfG African Games (1965)
Af-J African Junior Championships (1994)
AmCp America's Cup (World Cup Trial) (1977)
APM Adriaan Paulen Memorial, Hengelo
AsiC Asian Championships (1973)
AsiG Asian Games (1951)
Asi-J Asian Junior Championships (1990)
ASV Weltklasse in Köln, ASV club meeting (1934)
Athl Athletissima, Lausanne (1976)
Balk Balkan Games (1929), C – Championships
Barr (Cuba) Barrientos Memorial (1946)
BGP Budapest Grand Prix (1978)
Bisl Bislett Games, Oslo (1965) (Bergen 2004)
Bol G Bolivar Games (1938)
BrGP British Grand Prix
CAC Central American and Caribbean Championships (1967)
CAG Central American and Caribbean Games (1926)
CalR California Relays (1942)
C.Asian Central Asian Championships
CAU Inter-counties, GBR (1934)
CG Commonwealth Games (1930)
C.Cup Continental Cup (2010)
Déca Décanation, Paris (C) (2005)
DL Diamond League (2010)
DNG DN Galan, Stockholm (1966)
Drake Drake Relays (1910)
EAF European Athletics Festival, Bydgoszcz (2001)
EAsG East Asian Games (1993)
EC European Championships (1934)
ECCp European Clubs Cup (1975)
EChall European Challenge (10,000m 1997, Throws 2001)
ECp European Cup – track & field (1965), multi-events (1973)
EI European Indoor Championships (1970, Games 1966-9)
EICp European Indoor Cup (2003)
EJ European Junior Championships (1970)
ET European Team Championships (replaced European Cup, 2009)
EU23 European Under-23 Championships (1997) and European Under-23 Cup (1992-4)
FBK Fanny Blankers-Koen Games, Hengelo (formerly APM) (1981)
FlaR Florida Relays (1939)
FOT (USA) Final Olympic Trials (1920)
Franc Francophone Games (1989)
Gaz Gaz de France meeting, FRA (was BNP) (1968)
GGala Golden Gala, Roma (from 1980), Verona (1988), Pescara (1989), Bologna (1990)
GL Golden League (1998-2009)
GNR Great North Run – Newcastle to South Shields, GBR (1981)
GP Grand Prix
GPF IAAF Grand Prix Final (1985)
GS Golden Spike, Ostrava (1969)
Gugl Zipfer Gugl Grand Prix, Linz (1988)
GWG Goodwill Games (1986)
Gyulai István Gyulai Memorial, Budapest (2011-13), Székesfehérvár (2014)
Hanz Hanzekovic Memorial, Zagreb
Herc Herculis, Monte Carlo, Monaco (1987)
IAAF International Association of Athletics Federations
IAC IAC meeting (1968), formerly Coca-Cola
IAU International Association of Ultrarunners
IbAm Ibero-American Championships (1983)
ISTAF Internationales Stadionfest, Berlin (1921)
Jenner Bruce Jenner Classic, San Jose (1979)
Jerome Harry Jerome Track Classic (1984)
Jordan Payton Jordan U.S. Track & Field Open, Stanford (2004)
JUCO Junior Colleges Championships, USA
KansR Kansas Relays, Lawrence (1923)
Kuso Janusz Kusocinski Memorial (1954)
Kuts Vladimir Kuts Memorial ((1978))
LGP London Grand Prix, Crystal Palace
MAI Malmö AI Galan, Sweden (formerly Idag) (1958)
Mast Masters pole vault, Grenoble (1987), Donetsk
MedG Mediterranean Games (1951)
Mill Millrose Games, New York indoors (1908)
ModR Modesto Relays
MSR Mt. San Antonio College Relays (1959)
NA Night of Athletics, Heusden (2000) formerly Hechtel
NACAC North American, Central American & Caribbean Ch (2003)
NC National Championships
NC-w National Winter Championships
NCAA National Collegiate Athletic Association Championships, USA (1921)
NCAA-r NCAA Regional Championships (2003)
NCp National Cup
Nebiolo Memorial Primo Nebiolo, Torino (2000, originally 1963)
NG National Games
Nik Nikaïa, Nice (1976)
NM Narodna Mladezhe, Sofia (1955)
N.Sch National Schools
Nurmi Paavo Nurmi Games (1957)
NYG New York Games (1989)
OD Olympischer Tag (Olympic Day)
Oda Mikio Oda Memorial Meeting, Hiroshima
Odlozil Josef Odlozil Memorial, Prague (1994) OG Olympic Games (1896)
OT Olympic Trials
Owens Jesse Owens Memorial (1981)
PAm Pan American Games (1951)
PArab Pan Arab Championships (1977) (G- Games 1953)
Pedro Pedro's Cup, Poland (2005)
PennR Pennsylvania Relays (1895)
PTS Pravda Televízia Slovnaft, Bratislava (1957) (later GPB)

Pre Steve Prefontaine Memorial (1976)
RdVin Route du Vin Half Marathon, Luxembourg (1962)
RomIC Romanian International Championships (1948)
RWC Race Walking Challenge Final (2007)
SACh South American Championships (1919)
SAsG South Asian Games (1984)
SEAG South East Asia Games (1959)
SEC Southeast Conference Championships
SGP IAAF Super Grand Prix
Skol Skolimowska Memorial (2010)
Slovn Slovnaft, Bratislava (formerly PTS) (1990)
Spark Sparkassen Cup, Stuttgart (indoor) (1987)
Spart (URS) Spartakiad (1956)
Spitzen Spitzen Leichtathletik Luzern (1987)
Stra Stramilano Half marathon, Milan
Super Super Meet, Japan (Tokyo, Shizuoka, Yokohama, Kawasaki)
Tsik Athens Grand Prix Tsiklitiria (1998)
TexR Texas Relays (1925)
USOF US Olympic Festival
VD Ivo Van Damme Memorial, Brussels (1977)
Veniz Venizélia, Haniá, Crete (1936)
WAC Western Athletic Conference Championships
WAF World Athletics Finals (2003)
WCh World Championships (1983)
WCM World Challenge Meeting (2010)
WCp World Cup – track & field (1977), marathon (1985)
Walking – Lugano Trophy – men (1961), Eschborn Cup – women (1979)
WCT World Championships Trial
WG World Games, Helsinki (1961)
WI World Indoor Championships (1987), World Indoor Games (1985)
WJ World Junior Championships (1986)
WK Weltklasse, Zürich (1962)
WMilG World Military Games (or CISM) (1995)
WUG World University Games (1923)
WY World Youth Championships (1999)
Zat Emil Zátopek Classic, Melbourne
Znam Znamenskiy Brothers Memorial (1958)
-j, -y, -23 Junior, Youth or under-23

Dual and triangular matches are indicated by "v" (versus) followed by the name(s) of the opposition. Quadrangular and larger inter-nation matches are denoted by the number of nations and -N; viz 8-N designates an 8-nation meeting.

Events

CC cross-country
Dec decathlon
DT discus
h hurdles
Hep heptathlon
HJ high jump
HMar half marathon
HT hammer
JT javelin
LJ long jump
Mar marathon
Pen pentathlon
PV pole vault
R relay
SP shot
St steeplechase
TJ triple jump
W walk
Wt weight

Miscellaneous abbreviations

+ Intermediate time in longer race
= Tie (ex-aequo)
A Made at an altitude of 1000m or higher
b date of birth
D Made in decathlon competition
dnf did not finish
dnq did not qualify
dns did not start
exh exhibition
h heat
H Made in heptathlon competition
hr hour
i indoors
kg kilograms
km kilometres
m metres
M mile
m/s metres per second
mx Made in mixed men's and women's race
nh no height
O Made in octathlon competition
P Made in pentathlon competition
pb personal best
Q Made in qualifying round
qf quarter final (or q in lists)
r Race number in a series of races
sf semi final (or s in lists)
w wind assisted
WIR world indoor record
WR world record or best
y yards
* Converted time from yards to metres:
For 200m: 220 yards less 0.11 second
For 400m: 440 yards less 0.26 second
For 110mh: 120yh plus 0.03 second

Countries

(IAAF membership reached 213 in 2008, back to 212 in 2011, but South Sudan accepted as provisional member 2014). IAAF and IOC abbreviations are now identical.

AFG Afghanistan
AHO Netherlands Antilles #
AIA Anguilla
ALB Albania
ALG Algeria
AND Andorra
ANG Angola
ANT Antigua & Barbuda
ARG Argentina
ARM Armenia
ARU Aruba
ASA American Samoa
AUS Australia
AUT Austria
AZE Azerbaijan
BAH Bahamas
BAN Bangladash
BAR Barbados
BDI Burundi
BEL Belgium
BEN Benin
BER Bermuda
BHU Bhutan
BIH Bosnia Herzegovina
BIZ Belize
BLR Belarus
BOL Bolivia
BOT Botswana
BRA Brazil
BRN Bahrain

BRU Brunei
BUL Bulgaria
BUR Burkina Faso
CAF Central African Republic
CAM Cambodia
CAN Canada
CAY Cayman Islands
CGO Congo
CHA Chad
CHI Chile
CHN People's Republic of China
CIV Côte d'Ivoire (Ivory Coast)
CMR Cameroon
COD Democratic Republic of Congo
COK Cook Islands
COL Colombia
COM Comoros
CPV Cape Verde Islands
CRC Costa Rica
CRO Croatia
CUB Cuba
CUR Curaçao
CYP Cyprus
CZE Czech Republic
DEN Denmark
DJI Djibouti
DMA Dominica
DOM Dominican Republic
ECU Ecuador
EGY Egypt
ENG England
ERI Eritrea
ESA El Salvador
ESP Spain
EST Estonia
ETH Ethiopia
FIJ Fiji
FIN Finland
FRA France
FRG Federal Republic of Germany (1948-90)
FSM Micronesia
GAB Gabon
GAM The Gambia
GBR United Kingdom of Great Britain & Northern Ireland
GBS Guinea-Bissau
GDR German Democratic Republic (1948-90)
GEO Georgia
GEQ Equatorial Guinea
GER Germany (pre 1948 and from 1991)
GHA Ghana
GIB Gibraltar
GRE Greece
GRN Grenada
GUA Guatemala
GUI Guinea
GUM Guam
GUY Guyana
HAI Haiti
HKG Hong Kong, China
HON Honduras
HUN Hungary
INA Indonesia
IND India
IRI Iran
IRL Ireland
IRQ Iraq
ISL Iceland
ISR Israel
ISV US Virgin Islands
ITA Italy
IVB British Virgin Islands
JAM Jamaica
JOR Jordan
JPN Japan
KAZ Kazakhstan
KEN Kenya
KGZ Kyrgyzstan
KIR Kiribati
KOR Korea
KSA Saudi Arabia
KUW Kuwait
LAO Laos
LAT Latvia
LBA Libya
LBR Liberia
LCA St Lucia
LES Lesotho
LIB Lebanon
LIE Liechtenstein
LTU Lithuania
LUX Luxembourg
MAC Macao
MAD Madagascar
MAR Morocco
MAS Malaysia
MAW Malawi
MDA Moldova
MDV Maldives
MEX Mexico
MGL Mongolia
MKD Former Yugoslav Republic of Macedonia
MLI Mali
MLT Malta
MNE Montenegro
MNT Montserrat
MON Monaco
MOZ Mozambique
MRI Mauritius
MSH Marshall Islands
MTN Mauritania
MYA Myanmar
NAM Namibia
NCA Nicaragua
NED Netherlands
NEP Nepal
NFI Norfolk Islands
NGR Nigeria
NGU Papua New Guinea
NI Northern Ireland
NIG Niger
NMA Northern Marianas Islands
NOR Norway
NRU Nauru
NZL New Zealand
OMA Oman
PAK Pakistan
PAN Panama
PAR Paraguay
PER Peru
PHI Philippines
PLE Palestine
PLW Palau
PNG Papua New Guinea
POL Poland
POR Portugal
PRK North Korea (DPR Korea)
PUR Puerto Rico
PYF French Polynesia
QAT Qatar
ROU Romania
RSA South Africa
RUS Russia
RWA Rwanda
SAM Samoa
SCG Serbia & Montenegro (to 2006)
SCO Scotland
SEN Sénégal
SEY Seychelles
SIN Singapore
SKN St Kitts & Nevis
SLE Sierra Leone
SLO Slovenia
SMR San Marino
SOL Solomon Islands
SOM Somalia
SRB Serbia
SRI Sri Lanka
STP São Tomé & Principé
SUD Sudan
SUI Switzerland
SUR Surinam
SVK Slovakia
SWE Sweden
SWZ Swaziland
SYR Syria
TAN Tanzania
TCH Czechoslovakia (to 1991)
TGA Tonga
THA Thailand
TJK Tadjikistan
TKM Turkmenistan
TKS Turks & Caicos Islands
TLS East Timor
TOG Togo
TPE Taiwan (Chinese Taipei)
TTO Trinidad & Tobago
TUN Tunisia
TUR Turkey
TUV Tuvalu
UAE United Arab Emirates
UGA Uganda
UKR Ukraine
URS Soviet Union (to 1991)
URU Uruguay
USA United States
UZB Uzbekistan
VAN Vanuatu
VEN Venezuela
VIE Vietnam
VIN St Vincent & the Grenadines
WAL Wales
YEM Republic of Yemen
YUG Yugoslavia (to 2002)
ZAM Zambia
ZIM Zimbabwe

ceased to exist as a separate territory in 2010, and absorbed into the Netherlands.

ACKNOWLEDGEMENTS

ONCE AGAIN I would like to thank all those who have helped me to compile this Annual – whether in a major way or just with a few items of information. As they have throughout the 65-year history of the ATFS Annual, the annual world lists provide the essential core of the book and I have worked up these lists from original compilations by Richard Hymans and Mirko Jalava with reference to those of many other experts. I refer all who want to follow the results of the sport closely to Mirko's superb web site www.tilastopaja.net. I am indebted to Carlos Fernández for his expertise on the road lists and to Ray Herdt for the walks. I circulate draft lists to a number of ATFS experts and receive much valuable information from a worldwide circle of correspondents, most of whom have helped with information from their nations for many years. Of the great Spanish group Juan Mari Iriondo and Miguel Villaseñor checked the biographies and obituaries. Börre Lilloe provided much index data and Ken Nakamura checked distance lists. I am delighted that Bob Phillips has again provided an article in taking a historical perspective of 100 years ago.

Over the years I have come to take on more and more of the work involved on the world lists and, after 31 years of editing this Annual will surely need more assistance in future, so we will welcome volunteers to fill this gap who might like to compile and check world lists, especially for women and juniors. Contact me or the ATFS (see page 10)

Both for this annual and throughout the year with *Athletics International* that I produce with Mel Watman, Winfried Kramer helps with widespread probing for results as do the area experts: Africa: Yves Pinaud, Asia: Heinrich Hubbeling, Central and South America: Eduardo Biscayart and Luis Vinker, and specialists: Records György Csiki, Road racing: Marty Post, Ultrarunning Andy Milroy, Indoors Ed Gordon, Multi events: Hans van Kuijen, Pole vault Kenneth Lindqvist, 800m: Nejat Kök.

Australia: Paul Jenes and David Tarbotton; Austria: Dr Karl Graf; Belgium: André de Hooghe and Alain Monet; Bulgaria: Aleksandar Vangelov; China: Mirko Jalava; Cuba: Alfredo Sánchez; Czech Republic: Milan Urban; Denmark: Erik Laursen; Dominican Republic: Arisnel Rodríguez; Estonia: Erlend Teemägi and Enn Endjärv; Finland: Juhani Jalava, Mirko Jalava, Mikko Nieminen and Matti Hannus; France: Alain Bouillé, Carles Baronet, Patricia Doilin and José Guilloto; Germany: Sven Kuus, Greece: Thomas Konstas and Nikos Kriezis; Hungary: György Csiki; India: Ram. Murali Krishnan; Ireland: Pierce O'Callaghan and Liam Hennessy; Israel: David Eiger; Italy: Raul Leoni; Japan: Yoshimasa Noguchi, Akihiro Onishi and Ken Nakamura; Latvia: Andris Stagis; Lithuania: Stepas Misiunas; Luxembourg: Georges Klepper; Malaysia: Jad Adrian, Montenegro: Ivan Popovic; New Zealand: Murray McKinnon and Tony Hunt; Norway: Tore Johansen, Ole Petter Sandvig and Børre Lilloe; Poland: Zbigniew Jonik, Janusz Rozum and Tadeusz Wolejko; Portugal: Manuel Arons Carvalho; Puerto Rico: Pedro Anibal Diaz; Russia: Sergey Tikhonov,; Serbia: Ozren Karamata and Olga Acic; Slovakia: Alfons Juck; Slovenia: Zdravko Peternelj; South Africa: Danie Cornelius, Riël Hauman; Spain: José Luis Hernández, Carles Baronet and the AEEA team; Sweden: Jonas Hedman and Peter Larsson; Switzerland: Alberto Bordoli and Antonin Hejda; Trinidad: Bernard Linley, Turkey: Nejat Kök, Ukraine: Ivan Kachkivskiy; UK: Tony Miller and Ian Hodge; USA: Tom Casacky, Garry Hill, Sieg Lindstrom, Glen McMicken, Marty Post, Jack Shepherd, Mike Kennedy, and Track Newsletter. Also various national federation lists and to those who post results or ranking lists to various web sites.

Also to Marco Buccellato, Mark Butler, Ottavio Castellini (IAAF), Carole Fuchs, José Maria García, Stan Greenberg, Alan Lindop, Rooney Magnusson (obituaries), Bill Mallon, Pino Mappa, David Monti, Bob Phillips, Zdenek Procházka (hammer), Miguel Villaseñor and Rob Whittingham.

My apologies to anybody whose name I may have missed or who have corresponded with other key ATFS personnel, but all help, however small, is deeply appreciated.

Keep the results flowing

During the year Mel Watman and I publish marks to ATFS standards (150-200 deep on world lists) in Athletics International, of which there are over 35 issues per year by email. This serves as a base from which the lists in this book can be compiled, together with information from web sites, Track & Field News (USA) with its email results spin-off Track Newsletter and newsletters, especially Alfons Juck's EME News and Carles Baronet's Track in Sun blog.

In order to ensure that the record of 2015 is as complete as possible I urge results contribution worldwide to AI, and then in turn our lists in Athletics 2016 will be as comprehensive as we can make them.

THE ASSOCIATION OF TRACK & FIELD STATISTICIANS

The ATFS was founded in Brussels (at the European Championships) in 1950 and ever since has built upon the work of such key founding members as Roberto Quercetani, Don Potts and Fulvio Regli to produce authoritative ranking lists in the International Athletics Annual and elsewhere.

Current Executive Committee

President: Paul Jenes AUS
Vice-President: A.Lennart Julin SWE
Treasurer: Tom Casacky USA
Secretary: Michael J McLaughlin AUS
Past Presidents: Rooney Magnusson SWE, Dr Roberto Quercetani ITA
Committee: Eduardo Biscayart ARG/USA, Riël Hauman RSA, Nejat Kök TUR, Bernard Linley TRI, Giuseppa Mappa ITA, Peter J Matthews GBR, Yoshimasa Noguchi JPN, Yves Pinaud FRA

Website: www.afts.org

Internet – Websites

IAAF	www.iaaf.org
IAU	www.iau-ultramarathon.org
Africa (CAA)	www.webcaa.org
Asian AA	athleticsasia.org
CAC Confederation	www.cacacathletics.org
European AA	www.european-athletics.org
NACAC	www.athleticsnacac.org
Oceania AA	www.athletics-oceania.com
South American Fed.	www.consudatle.org
WMRA	www.wmra.info
World Masters	www.world-masters-athletics.org
Marathon Majors	www.worldmarathonmajors.com
Africa	www.africathle.com
Andorra	www.faa.ad
Argentina	www.cada-atletismo.org
Australia	www.athletics.com.au
Austria	www.oelv.at
Bahamas	www.bahamastrack.com
Belarus	www.bfla.eu
Belgium	www.val.be
Bermuda	www.btfa.bm
Bosnia Hercegovina	www.asbih.org
Brazil	www.cbat.org.br
Bulgaria	www.bfla.org
Canada	www.athletics.ca
Chile	www.fedachi.cl
China	www.athletics.org.cn
Costa Rica	www.fecoa.org
Croatia	www.has.hr
Cyprus	www.koeas.org.cy
Czech Republic	www.atletika.cz
Denmark	www.dansk-atletik.dk
Dominican Republic	www.fedomatle.org
England	www.englandathletics.org
Estonia	www.ekjl.ee
Finland	www.sul.fi
France	www.athle.com
Germany	www.leichtathletik.de
Great Britain	www.britishathletics.org.uk
deep statistics	www.topsinathletics.info
	www.thepowerof10.info
Greece	www.segas.gr
Hong Kong	www.hkaaa.com
Hungary	www.masz.hu
Iceland	www.fri.is
India	www.indianathletics.org
Indonesia	www.indonesia-athletics.org
Ireland	www.athleticsireland.ie
Israel	www.iaa.co.il
Italy	www.fidal.it
Jamaica	www.trackandfieldja.com
Japan	www.jaaf.or.jp
running news	japanrunningnews.blogspot.co.uk
Kazakhstan	www.kazathletics.kz
Kenya	www.athleticskenya.or.ke
Latvia	http://lat-athletics.lv
Lithuania	www.lengvoji.lt
Luxembourg	www.fla.lu
Macedonia	www.afm.org.mk
Malaysia	www.maf.org.my
results	www.adriansprints.com
Mexico	www.fmaa.mx
Moldova	www.fam.com.md
Monaco	www.fma.mc
Montenegro	www.ascg.co.me
Morocco	www.moroccanathletics.com
Netherlands	www.atletiekunie.nl
New Zealand	www.athletics.org.nz
Northern Ireland	www.niathletics.org
Norway	www.friidrett.no
Peru	www.fedepeatle.org
Poland	www.pzla.pl
Portugal	www.fpatletismo.pt
	www.atletismo-estatistica.pt
Puerto Rico	www.atletismofapur.com
	www.pedroanibaldiaz.com
Romania	www.fra.ro
Russia	www.rusathletics.com
Scotland	www.scottishathletics.org.uk
	www.scotstats.net
Serbia	www.ass.org.rs
Singapore	www.singaporeathletics.org.sg
Slovakia	www.atletikasvk.sk
Slovenia	www.atletska-zveza.si
South Africa	www.athletics.org.za
Spain	www.rfea.es
Sweden	www.friidrott.se
Switzerland	www.swiss-athletics.ch
Taiwan	www.cttfa.org.tw
Trinidad & Tobago	www.ttnaaa.org
Turkey	www.taf.org.tr
Ukraine	www.uaf.org.ua
Uruguay	www.atlecau.org.uy
USA	www.usatf.org
collegiate results	www.ustfccca.org
Wales	www.welshathletics.org
	athleticsstatswales.webeden.co.uk

Other recommended sites for statistics and results

AIMS	www.aimsworldrunning.org
ARRS	www.arrs.net
British historical	www.gbrathletics.com
	www.athlos.co.uk
DGLD (German stats)	www.ladgld.de
French history etc.	http://cdm.athle.com
Marathons	www.marathonguide.com
Masters Track & Field	www.mastersathletics.net
Mirko Jalava	www.tilastopaja.org
NUTS/Track Stats	www.nuts.org.uk
Rankings etc	www.all-athletics.com
Runners World	www.runnersworld.com
Tracklion (NED/BEL)	sportslion.net/tracklion.html
Track & Field News	www.trackandfieldnews.com
Track in Sun results	trackinsun.blogspot.co.uk
Ultra marathon stats	statistik.d-u-v.org/index.php
World juniors	www.worldjuniorathleticsnewsnzl.co.nz
Olympic Games	www.aafla.org
	www.sports-reference.com

DIARY OF 2014

by Peter Matthews

A chronological survey of highlights in major events in the world of track and field athletics.
See Championships or National sections for more details. DL = Samsung Diamond League, WCM = World Challenge Meeting.

January

2 **Xiamen**, China. Mare Dibaba recorded a course record 2:21:36 in the 12th C&D International Marathon.

16 **Chelyabinsk**, Russia. Early indications of a fine year for high jumping came with Ivan Ukhov clearing 2.41 and Mariya Kuchina 2.00 indoors.

16 **Boston (Allston)**, USA. Galen Rupp took 5.74 sec. off the North American indoor 5000m record with 13:01.26.

24 **Dubai**, United Arab Emirates. 15th Standard Chartered Marathon. 18 year-old Tsegaye Mekonnen won in 2:04:32, a world junior record on his debut at the distance, and Ethiopians took the first 14 places in the men's race and 9 in the women's, won by Mulu Seboka 2:25:01. Each winner earned $200,000.

24-25 **Boston (Allston)**, USA. Galen Rupp regained the North American indoor 2miles record with 8:07.41 and 17 year-old Mary Cain ran 1 mile in 4:24.11, just 0.01 outside the world junior indoor record.

25 **Rouen**, France. Renaud Lavillenie set a French indoor pole vault record with 6.04 on his first attempt.

26 **Osaka**, Japan. 33rd Women's Marathon. Tetyana Hamera-Shmyrko won in 2:24:37 to repeat her win of 2013.

26 **Glasgow**, GBR. The annual International match at the Emirates Arena was won by the Commonwealth Select team with 62 from GBR 59, USA 53 and Scotland 40.

30 **Düsseldorf**, Germany. Top marks at the PSD Bank meeting came from shot putters David Storl 21.10 and Christina Schwanitz 19.93.

31 **Bydgoszcz**, France. Renaud Lavillenie improved his pole vault record to 6.08 for second to Sergey Bubka on the world all-time list. He cleared first time and had plenty to spare.

February

1 **Karlsruhe**, Germany. Genzebe Dibaba smashed the world indoor record for 1500m, her 3:55.17 taking 4.11 off the old mark. Her splits were 30.56, 31.83, 32.83, 33.74, 31.25, 30.26, 29.72, 14.98; 59.9 last 400m as Sonja Roman led through 62.39 and 2:08.96 before Dibaba picked up the pace to 3:10.47 at 1200m. Sifan Hassan win on her indoor debut with 8:45.32 for 3000m.

2 **Moscow**. Russian Winter meeting (IAAF Permit). Mohammed Aman came close to the world indoor best with 1:15.31 for 600m. Tina Sutej tied her week-old Slovenian indoor record at 4.56 and improved that to 4.61, 4.66 and 4.71, The 2013 world no.1 long jumper Aleksandr Menkov started well with 8.30.

6 **Stockholm**, Sweden. XL Galen. Maintaining her brilliant form, Genzebe Dibaba improved the world indoor 3000m record from 8:23.72 to 8:16.60. The race started out reasonably fast and ended even quicker as the pacemakers left by 1000m; her splits were 1k 2:48.7, 1500m 4:12.0, 2k 5:34.25. Her final 2000m in 5:27.95 was more than 2 sec quicker than the world indoor 2000m record. Only three Chinese woman from their notorious races in 1993 have ever run faster for 3000m (outdoors). Abeba Aregawi ran a European indoor 1500m record of 3:57.91 and Mariya Kuchina high jumped 2.01, a mark that remained unsurpassed in 2014.

7 **Havana**, Cuba. 20 year-old Pedro Pichardo triple jumped 17.76.

8 **Arnstadt**, Germany. Ivan Ukhov won with 2.40 on count-back from Aleksey Dmitrik at the 39th indoor "High Jump with Music" event, the first time ever that two men cleared 2.40 in one competition. In the women's event Kamila Licwinko (née Stepaniuk) became the first Polish woman to clear 2.00.

8 **Boston (Roxbury)**, USA. New Balance GP. An American All Star team of Richard Jones (1:51.01), David Torrence (1:47.46), Duane Solomon (1:47.98) and Erik Sowinski (1:46.66) broke the world indoor record for the 4x800m relay – 7:13.94 by an American squad on this same track in 2000 – with 7:13.11. Excelling as they did in 2013, Mary Cain delighted the fans with a world junior indoor 1000m record of 2:35.80 and Hagos Gebrhiwet set a world year's best 3000m time for the indoor season with 7:34.13.

8-9 **UK Indoor Championships**, Sheffield. Katarina Johnson-Thompson took her high jump best from 1.89 indoors to 1.90, 1.92 and 1.96 for an absolute British record and also won the long jump with 6.75 (from a previous best of 6.56).

9 **Gent, Belgium**. Pawel Maslák set a European 300m best of 32.15 and Anna Rogowska won the pole vault with 4.76, the 2014 season's best.

9 **Donetsk**, Samsung Pole Vault Stars meeting. Renaud Lavillenie cleared 6.16 on his first attempt to remove Sergey Bubka's 6.15 set in this city 21 years earlier from the list of world records. Lavillenie, who had first-time clearances at 5.76 and 5.91 and 6.01 on his third attempt, then tried 6.21 but injured himself (lacerated left heel) at his one attempt. Luke Cutts was 2nd at 5.81 and Thiago Braz da Silva set a South American record 5.76 for third.

15 **Ra's Al Khaymah**, United Arab Emirates. In ideal conditions (13°C at the 7 am start) there was unprecedented depth for a half marathon. Eight men ran inside the hour for the first time ever, although the winning 59:36 by Lelisa Desisa was a little slower than hoped for. Priscah Jeptoo was the women's winner in 67:02, 1:11 ahead of Flomena Cheyech.

15 **Birmingham**, GBR. IAAF Permit Meeting. Genzebe Dibaba set her third world indoor best in 15 days as she ran 9:00.48 for 2 miles, just 1.90 secs short of the world outdoor best. Her 440y splits were 65.7, 2:15.1, 3:23.7, 4:31.7, 5:38.6, 6:46.9 and 7:54.0. Other marks that remained world bests for the season were 60m James Dasaolu 6.47 heat (he won the final in 6.50 but suffered a left hamstring tear with two strides to go, as Jimmy Vicaut, who had won his heat in 6.48, also hobbled over the line 6th in 6.58), and 800m Mohammed Aman 1:44.52, an African indoor record.

15 **New York (Armory)**, USA. 107th Millrose Games. 13 years after his first major record 39 year-old Bernard Lagat set a North American indoor record 4:54.74 for 2000m.

15-16 **Asian Indoor Championships**, Hangzhou, China. Mutaz Essa Barshim excelled with 2.36 at high jump.

16 **Barcelona**, Spain. Florence Kiplagat took 38 seconds off the world record for the women's half marathon with 65:12, passing 10k in 31:08, 15k in 46:35, and 20k in a world record 61:56; she won by over 7 minutes. She had two male pacemakers to 18k.

17-19 **Russian Indoor Championships**, Moscow. Ivan Ukhov continued his fine form with 2.38 in the high jump.

18-19 **Winter Olympic Games**, Sochi, Russia. Lauryn Williams became the first athletics summer Olympics medallist (silver 100m 2004, gold 4x100m 2012) to also win a medal at the Winter Olympics as she took silver at 2-woman bobsleigh for the USA.

21-23 **US Indoor Championships**, Albuquerque. From a previous pb of 4567 Sharon Day-Monroe set a US indoor record 4805 points for pentathlon. The first three in the men's shot all set pbs as Ryan Whiting won with 22.23 (the longest indoor put in the world for six years) from Kurt Roberts 21.50 and Joe Kovacs 21.46, and just 0.008 separated the top four men in the 60m hurdles, won by Omo Osaghae in 7.553.

22 **Balkan Indoor Championships**, Istanbul, Turkey. Romania was the top nation and the best mark was a 6.92 Serbian long jump record by Ivana Spanovic.

22-23 **German Indoor Championships**, Leipzig. Malte Mohr won the pole vault with 5.84.

22-23 **Polish Indoor Championships**, Sopot. Kamila Licwinko cleared 2.00 to equal her national high jump record.

22-23 **Spanish Indoor Championships**, Sabadell. Ruth Beitia (34) won her 13th national indoor title, a Spanish women's record, and cleared 2.00m, her twelfth career competition at that height or above.

23 **Tokyo**, Japan. Dickson Chumba took 1:15 off the course record in the marathon, now one of the Marathon Majors series, with 2:05:18. Tadesse Tola was 2nd in 2:05:57. The first four women, headed by Tirfi Tsegaye 2:22:23 broke the course record, although they did not run as fast as the 2:21:37 that Mizuki Noguchi ran in 2007 in the Tokyo Ladies' Marathon.

25 **Prague** (O2 Arena), Czech Republic. Ivan Ukhov jumped an absolute Russian high jump record with a soaring clearance, achieved on his first attempt with daylight between his torso and the bar, at 2.42, just 1cm below Javier Sotomayor's world indoor record. This was his seventh successive win indoors, all at 2.36 or higher. Blanka Vlasic won the women's event with 2.00 and Germán Lauro improved his South American indoor shot record from 20.53 to 20.68 and 21.04. Pawel Maslák ran a European best of 60.36 for 500m.

27- Mar 1 **Fayetteville**, USA. As usual the SEC Championships provided fast sprinting with world-leading times for 200m from Kamaria Brown 22.51 and 22.50 and for 400m from Deon Lendore, a Trinidadian record 45.03.

March

1 **Berlin**. Germany. There were about 10,500 spectators in the O2 World Arena for the first ISTAF Indoor meeting. They were enthused by world-class wins from Malte Mohr, 5.90 in the pole vault, and David Storl, who maintained his unbeaten run in his seventh competition this year with 21.20 in the shot. The large arena was able to accommodate the discus, won by Martin Wierig with 64.82.

1 **Split**, Croatia. Sandra Perkovic made a brilliant start to her 2014 campaign by throwing national discus records of 69.96 and 70.51 in Spilt. The latter was the world's best since 1992.

7-9 15th **World Indoor Championships**, Sopot, Poland. A great success – well organised with much excellent athletics and enthusiastic crowds filling the 11,000-seat Ergo Arena on the last two days. The final event, the men's 4x400m relay produced the one world indoor and championship record as Kyle Clemons, David Verburg, Kind Butler and Calvin Smith ran consistently well for a final time of 3:02.13 for the USA. Top individual marks came for men from Ashton Eaton, whose 6632 heptathlon score was just a second at 1000m off his world record, and for women from the 6.98 win at 60m by the ever-smiling Shelly-Ann Fraser-Pryce. The star of the indoor season Genzebe Dibaba flowed away from the field after a very slow start to the 3000m with c.4:04 for the second 1500m, and Abeba Aregawi was a class apart in the 1500m as she won by 6.51 sec. in 4:00.61. In all world leads were set in 12 events. The USA with 8 gold, 2 silver and 2 bronze easily headed the medal table. *For leading results see Athletics 2014 p. 81-2.*

13-14 **ODESUR (South American Games)**, Santiago de Chile. Brazil with 14 gold, 13 silver and 13 bronze medals was the most successful nation at this quadrennial multi-sport event. Top marks included Anderson Henriques, 400m 45.03, Irving Saladino, LJ 8.16, and Lorena Arenas, South American record 20,000m walk 1:31:46.9.

14-15 **NCAA Indoor Championships**, Albuquerque, USA. Kendell Williams (18) set personal bests in all five events for a pentathlon total of 4635, adding 100 points to Carolina Klüft's 2002 world junior record. World leading marks were set with 20.32 for 200m by Diondre Batson, 50.46 US record for women's 400m by Phyllis Francis, and 8.39 long jump by Jarrion Lawson (19). Oregon won both men's (helped by a 3000m/5000m double by Edward Cheserek) and women's titles, the latter by just half a point from Texas after Francis came from 0.32 down to win the 4x400 by 0.02.

15 **Jacksonville**, Florida, USA. Shalane Flanagan took 12 secs off Deena Kastor's 2003 US record as she ran 47:03 to take the US 15k title, winning by over two minutes.

15-16 14th **European Cup Winter Throwing**, Leiria, Portugal. Pawel Fajdek beat Krisztián Pars 78.75 to 77.96 in the hammer in what was once again a great competitive opportunity for Europe's throwers. In three events the U23s exceeded the bests of the seniors: men's javelin Maksym Bohdan 83.41, women's discus Shanice Craft 64.16 and javelin Liina Lassama an Estonian record 63.17.

16 **African Cross-Country Championships**, Kampala, Uganda. Kenya dominated, winning all but two individual medals and all eight gold medals (team and individual). Their athletes swept the first five places in the senior men's race, won by Leonard Barsotom, and first four in the senior women's race, won by Faith Kipyegon.

16 **Asian Walks Championships**, Nomi, Japan.

16 **Lugano**. Switzerland. Ruslan Dmytrenko won the men's 20k in 1:20:08 and Liu Hong the women's in 1:27:25 in the first races of the IAAF Walking Challenge for 2014.

16 **New York**, USA. Geoffrey Mutai beat Mo Farah in the City Half Marathon 60:50 to 61.07, but there was drama in the cold weather (-1ºC) as Farah fell heavily nearing the 10k mark and collapsed at the finish, passing out for three minutes. Sally Kipyego made an impressive debut at the distance to be women's winner in a course record 68:31.

18-20 **Copa Cuba**, Havana, Cuba Pedro Pichardo highlighted the national championships with 17.71 in the triple jump.

22 **Melbourne**, Australia (WCM). Kim Mickle added 3cm to the Oceania javelin record with 66.83. Tom Walsh, who had excelled to take the bronze medal with 21.26 at the World Indoor Championships, took Jacko Gill's New Zealand outdoor record with a 20.48, 20.54 and 21.16.

22 **Russian Winter Walks Championships**, Sochi. Heading the usual fast times were winners Aleksandr Ivanov, 20k 1:20:44, Mikhail Ryzhov, 35k 2:28:11, and Anisya Kirdyapkina, women's 20k 1:28:05.

25-30 **World Masters Indoor Championships**, Budapest, Hungary.

26-29 87th **Texas Relays,** Austin, USA. Trayvon Bromell tied the world junior 100m record with 10.01.

29 **World Half Marathon Championships**, Copenhagen, Denmark. Geoffrey Kipsang Kamworor won the individual title in 59:08, but Kenya, team winners on the past six occasions, had to settle for silver behind Eritrea, whose athletes finished 2-4-5-7 and 8. Thus Zersenay Tadesse, who had run this race five times but had six consecutive silver medals as last gained team gold for his 4th place here. Kenya were dominant in the women's race, taking the first five places led by Gladys Cherono 67:29. *For leading results see Athletics 2014 p. 119.*

30 **Berlin**, Germany. Leonard Komon made the fastest ever debut at half marathon as he won in 59:14.

April

3-6 **Australian Championships**, Melbourne. Sally Pearson won the 100m and 100m hurdles double for the sixth time in her career (from 2005) and Dani Samuels added 97cm to her pb with 66.81 for her eighth discus title.

4-5 **Florida Relays**, Gainesville, USA. The Boogie Fast TC team of Nia Ali, Kristi Castlin, Queen Harrison and Tiffany Porter improved the world best time for 4x100m hurdles that they had set here in 2013 from 50.78 to 50.66.

6 **Paris**, France. Kenenisa Bekele won on his marathon debut in 2:05:04 with Limenih Getachew second in 2:06:49, and women's winner was Flomena Cheyech 2:22:44. There was a race record 39,116 finishers (31,091 men and 8024 women from 40,783 starters).

11-12 **South African Championships**, Pretoria (A). Simon Magakwe broke the South African record for 100m with 9.98 and Khotso Mokoena returned to the triple jump and won his first national title at the event since 2006.

13 Virgin **London Marathon**, GBR. Wilson Kipsang repeated his 2012 win and lowered the course record to 2:04:29 to earn him $180,000, with Stanley Biwott second in 2:04:55. Mo Farah was 8th in an English record 2:08:21 on his marathon debut. After being runner-up in the previous two years Edna Kiplagat was the women's winner in 2:20:21, three seconds ahead of Florence Kiplagat. Tirunesh Dibaba made a splendid marathon debut for third in 2:20:35.

13 **Rotterdam Marathon**, Netherlands. Eliud Kipchoge won the 34th running of this race in 2:05:00 despite windy conditions, finishing well clear of Bernard Koech 2:06:08.

17-19 56th **Mt SAC Relays**, Walnut, California, USA. This was again a massive event, meeting records including 1:43.88 for 800m by Duane Solomon and 74.98 for women's hammer by Sultana Frizell. Ashton Eaton made his 400m hurdles debut, running 50.01.

21 118th **Boston Marathon**, USA. Rita Jeptoo broke the course record in one of the fastest races ever with 2:18:57 from Buzunesh Deba 2:19:59, while 39 year-old Meb Keflezighi became the first US winner of the event since 1985 in a lifetime best of 2:08:37, winning by 11 secs from Wilson Chebet. Eleven women under 2:25 beat the previous record of nine and the times from 6th to 11th place were the fastest ever recorded in a women's marathon.

23-26 105th **Drake Relays**, Des Moines, USA. Renewing their rivalry LaShawn Merritt 44.44, Kirani James 44.60 and Luguelin Santos 44.72 finished 1-2-3 in the 400m. Derek Drouin cleared eight heights on his first attempt before tying Charles Austin's 1991 North American high jump record on his third try at 2.40, a new Commonwealth record. Kristi Castlin and Brianna Rollins ran 12.58 for 100m hurdles, but Castlin won by 0.005, thus ending Rollins' winning streak of 35 races since July 2012. Chaunté Lowe, in her first major competition for almost two years following a pregnancy break, won the high jump on count-back at 1.96.

24 **Chula Vista** USA. Greg Rutherford added 16cm to the British long jump record with 8.51.

24-26 120th **Penn Relays**, Philadelphia, USA. Home teams won four of the six USA v The World Relays, but the Bahamas scored a fine 4x400m victory in 3:00.78. Apart from the elite events the Relays featured athletes from 1020 high schools and 252 colleges! A three-day attendance of 108,660 included 49,103 for the final day.

29 **Hiroshima**, Japan. The 48th Mikio Oda Memorial included an improvement from 78.21 to 85.48 in the javelin by Ryohei Arai.

May

2 **Bloomington**, USA. The first of eight scheduled American Track League meetings.

2 The US Anti-Doping Agency announced that **Tyson Gay** would serve a one-year suspension, dated from 23 June 2013, following three positive tests within a short period for a prohibited substance, an exogenous androgenic anabolic steroid and/or its metabolites. The ban would normally be two years but USADA halved the penalty in return for Gay's assistance and his voluntary decision to stop competing while an investigation into the circumstances took place. All of his results from 15 July 2012 were annulled, thus losing his 4th at 100m and silver medal at 4x100m at the 2012 Olympic Games.

3 **Kingston**, Jamaica (WCM). Christian Cantwell, fully recovered at last from elbow surgery on his right (throwing) arm, won the shot with an outdoor world leading 21.85. Francena McCorory won the 400m in 50.24, but strong headwinds marred many sprint times.

3-4 **World Race Walking Cup**, Taicang, China. Mikhail Ryzhov 3:39:05 and Ivan Noskov 3:39:38 led Russia to victory in the 50k, in which 30 men beat 4 hours and 25 of the 48 finishers set pbs with Jesús Ángel García, at 44, competing in the event for the 11th time. There was another sweeping Russian victory with 1, 3 and 4 in the women's 20k won by Anisya Kirdyapkina in 1:26:31. This was the greatest ever women's walk in depth: 24 women broke 1:30, far ahead of the previous record of 15 at the 2012 Olympic Games, there were best ever marks for places 7 and 9 to 50, eight national records and 15 of the top 30 set pbs. Susana Feitor tied the women's record with her tenth World Cup appearance. The men's 20k also had great depth despite rain that got steadily heavier throughout the race, with seven men under 1:20 and 22 under 1:21 (ten in pbs), led home in 1:18:37 by Ruslan Dmytrenko who also helped Ukraine to team victory. Individual and team winners in the junior races were all from China.

4 **Stanford**, USA. As usual there was a plethora of classy distance running performances at the Payton Jordan Cardinal Invitational. Sally Kipyego (in her first track 10k since the 2012 Olympics) 30:42.26, Molly Huddle and Betsy Saina broke 31 minutes in the women's 10,000m and after 27 women broke 33 minutes, there were best ever times for places 28-31 (at least).

9 **Doha**, Qatar (DL). A record six men finished inside 3:31.00 with best ever times for places 5-7 in the 1500m won by Asbel Kiprop in 3:29.18 from Silas Kiplagat 3:29.70 and Ayanleh Souleiman 3:30.16. Hellen Obiri set an African, Commonwealth and Diamond League record of 8:20.68 in the women's 3000m in which Ethiopia's Genzebe Dibaba ran an outdoor pb 8:26.21 that was only good enough for sixth as the first eleven woman ran pbs and there were best ever marks for 6th to 8th. Mohammad Aman beat Nijel Amos 1:44.49 to 1:44.54 in the 800m and top field mark was Ivan Ukhov's high jump 2.41 with a record four men at 2.37 or higher. The biggest surprise came with a 54.59 win at 400m hurdles by Kemi Adekoya.

10 **London (Parliament Hill)**. In her first race since the birth of daughter Emily on 4 Sep 2013 Jo Pavey won the UK 10,000m title in 32:11.04.

10 **Wiesbaden**, Germany. 19th WLV Werfer Cup. Dani Samuels improved her discus best to 67.40 and 67.99.

11 **Tokyo**, Japan (WCM). Golden Grand Prix. Bohdan Bondarenko made an amazing start to his season as he cleared 2.40 in his first high jump competition since September at the end of his epic 2013 campaign. He had one attempt at a WR 2.46 and saw off the challenge of Ivan Ukhov, who failed three times at 2.40 after a clean card up to 2.34.

15-17 **Collegiate Conference Championships**, USA. Top marks included 44.36 for 400m by Deon Lendore (who also anchored Texas A&M to fast relay times of 38.50 and 3:01.19), and an 11.11 100m and 22.23 200m double by Olivia Ekponé in ever-strong sprint times at the SEC (Lexington). A +4.2 wind helped 18 year-old Trayvon Bromell to 9.77w for 100m in the Big 12 at Lubbock, the fastest time ever run by a junior under any conditions, and there Courtney Okolo ran a world-leading and collegiate record 50.03 for 400m.

17 **Manchester**, GBR. Meghan Beesley ran a world auto-timed best for 200mh of 25.05 on the straight track laid in Deansgate.

17-18 **Halle**, Germany. 40th Werfertage. Piotr Malachowski beat Robert Harting, 69.28 to 68.28 in the discus, and Nadine Müller won the women's event with 67.30. Pavel Fajdek edged Dilshod Nazarov 79.59 to 79.49 in the hammer.

18 **Shanghai**, China (DL). Ihab Abdelrahman Sayed set an African javelin record with 89.21, a high improvement on his previous pb of 83.93, and Sandra Perkovic improved her Croatian record by 1cm with 70.52. Emma Coburn surprised the African contingent with a women's steeplechase win in 9:19.80.

18 **Ponce**, Puerto Rico (WCM). World leading marks were set by LaShawn Merritt with 44.14 for 400m and Caterine Ibargüen 14.87 triple jump.

21 **Beijing**, China (WCM). Justin Gatlin maintained his brilliant form with a 9.87 100m win.

23-25 **Havana**, Cuba. Barrientos Memorial. Sally Diago set a CAC junior 800m record of 1:57.74.

24-25 **European Clubs Cup**, Vila Real de Santo António, Portugal. The Italian team Fiamme Gialle won the men's competition for the third successive year and Spanish team Valencia Terra i Mar achieved their first success in the women's, but there was no Russian participation this year.

24-25 **IAAF World Relays**, Nassau, Bahamas. Highly enthusiastic fans filled the Thomas A. Robinson Stadium in beautiful weather (29-30°C) for this inaugural venture – and were rewarded with world records by Jamaica (1:18.63) in the men's 4x200m and Kenya in the men's (14:22.22, 14.01 off the old mark) and women's (16:33.58, 34.59 off the old mark) 4x1500m, and 2014 world bests established in the other seven events. Yohan Blake was timed in his anchor legs in 9.07 for 100m and 19.0 for the 200m. Noise levels were extraordinary, particularly for Chris Brown on the third leg in the men's 4x400m as the Bahamas, a small nation but with a great relay tradition, tried to beat the USA, coming up just short, 2:57.59 to 2:57.25, with LaShawn Merritt bringing home the USA in 43.8. Asbel Kiprop ran a solo 3:32.3 in anchoring the Kenyan men in the 4x1500m. A total of $1.4 million in prize money was awarded, plus $150,000 for the three world records.

29-31 **NCAA Qualifying**, USA. Preliminary rounds for the NCAA Championships were held in Eastern and Western sections at Jacksonville and Fayetteville.

30-31 **Eugene**, USA. 40th Prefontaine Classic (DL). This was a marvellous meeting with a host of world leading performances, The first evening session was dominated by the 10,000m, in which three Kenyans set pbs of inside 27 minutes but victory went to Galen Rupp in the North American and USA record time of 26:44.36. A monumental clash in the 400m resulted in a very narrow victory for Kirani James 43.963 to 43.967 by LaShawn Merritt. David Rudisha was happy to run 1:44.67 for 800m on his return from knee injury, but this left him 7th in the race won by Nijel Amos in 1:43.63 from Mohammed Aman 1:43.99. The Bill Bowerman Mile was won by Ayanleh Souleiman in 3:47.32, tenth on the world all-time list and the world's fastest since 2007, from Silas Kiplagat 3:47.88 and Aman Wote 3:48.60 with the best ever times for places 6 (3:49.56) to 11 (3:52.16). Five women inside 4 minutes at 1500m were headed by Hellen Obiri 3:57.05. Abeba Aregawi was second in 3:58.57, ending a run of 18 consecutive 1500m wins from 2012. Justin Gatlin won the 100m in 9.76w from Mike Rodgers 9.80, and Tori Bowie made a shock breakthrough to win the 200m in 22.18 from lane 1. Best known as a long jumper (pb 6.95) she had improved from 23.99 to 22.57 in April.

31 **Clermont**, USA. Exceptional times were run in a 100m race, headed by Richard Thompson 9.74m but no wind reading was taken, and it is most likely that it would have been over 4 m/s.

31- Jun 1 **Götzis**, Austria. Tree Hardee completed his first decathlon since his Olympic silver in 2012 and won with 8518 points from Kai Kazmirek 8471. Brianne Theisen-Eaton set a Canadian heptathlon record of 6641 but that left her 41 points behind the hugely promising 21 year-old Katarina Johnson-Thompson, whose 6682 included pbs at 200m and 800m. Dafne Schippers broke her Dutch record with 6545 for third.

June

1 **Comrades Marathon**, Pietermaritzburg to Durban, South Africa, The world's largest ultra race had 11,983 finishers (9556 men and 2427 women).

5 **Rome**, Italy. Golden Gala 'Pietro Mennea' (DL). Mutaz Essa Barshim starred with an Asian record 2.41 in the high jump, with about 5cm of daylight between his torso and the bar and clear air between his heels and the apparatus, and there were six close failures at 2.43, three apiece from Barshim and Bohdan Bondarenko, who had passed to then after clearing 2.34. There were world-leading marks in women's events from Genzebe Dibaba, 5000m 14:34.99, Brianna Rollins 100mh 13.53, and Kaliese Spencer, 400mh 53.97. Barbora Spotáková started her come-back season with a 66.43 javelin win and the Eugene form was reversed as Silas Kiplagat beat Ayanleh Souleiman 3:30.44 to 3:31.18 at 1500m, with Asbel Kiprop again third, 3:31.89.

5-7 **Kenyan Championships/Trials**, Nairobi. The Kenyan Commonwealth Games team was substantially chosen from the meeting. 18 year-old Ronald Kwemoi won the 1500m in 3:34.6 from a previous best of 3:42.25.

6-8 **Japanese Championships**, Tokyo. Koji Murofushi won his 20th successive national hammer title with 73.93.

7 **Szczecin**, Poland. Krisztián Pars came out ahead of Pawel Fajdek in their close rivalry, with a 79.35 to 78.15 win in the IAAF Hammer Challenge event held within the 60th Janusz Kusocinski Memorial and Marcel Lomnicky split them with 78.40.

8 **European Cup 10,000m**, Skopje, Macedonia.

8 **Hengelo**, Netherlands. 32nd Fanny Blankers-Koen Games (WCM). Richard Thompson won the 100m in 9.95, but only just as Chijindu Ujah, the 2013 European Junior champion, improved his pb from 10.17 to a startling 9.96.

8 **Marrakech**, Morocco. 7th Mohammed VI meeting (WCM). Tianna Bartoletta, continuing her impressive return to long jumping, recorded an outdoor world-leading 6.93, a 4cm improvement to her pb set when she won the world title in Helsinki in 2005. 17 year-old Dawit Seyaum ran away from the 1500m field to an Ethiopian junior record of 3:59.53 for sixth on the world all-time junior list.

9 **Prague**, Czech Republic. 19th Josef Odlozil Memorial.

11 **Oslo**, Norway (DL). ExxonMobil Bislett Games. The Dream Mile was won for the second year by Ayanleh Souleiman in 3:49.49 from Nick Willis 3:49.83 and Homiyu Tesfaye 3:49.86, with Henrik Ingebrigtsen setting a Norwegian record 3:50.72 in 4th. Other highlights included Tianna Bartoletta, 7.02 long jump for the first 7m leap of the year, Yenew Alamirew gaining revenge over Caleb Ndiku in the 5000m 13:01.57 to 13:02.15, Jairus Birech adding to his rapidly growing reputation with a commanding win in the steeplechase in 8:02.37; and Pascal Martinot-Lagarde taking his second Diamond League 110m hurdles win on the trot, slicing 0.01 off his world-leading time from Eugene with 13.12.

12-15 **Asian Junior Championships**, Taipeh, Taiwan.

14 **New York (Randall's Island)**, USA. adidas GP (DL). There was another great high jump competition as Bohdan Bondarenko equalled the European record to beat Mutaz Essa Barshim (Asian record) on count-back as both cleared 2.42 on their first attempts; both came tantalisingly close to a world record at 2.46. Further world leading marks came in the 200m, Warren Weir 19.82, 400m hurdles, Javier Culson 48.03, and women's pole vault, Fabiana Murer 4.85, and javelin, Linda Stahl 67.32. David Rudisha scored his first victory of 2014 in the 800m with 1:44.63.

11-14 **NCAA Championships**, Eugene, USA. A month short of his 19th birthday, Trayvon Bromell became the first junior to break 10 seconds for 100m with a legal wind as he won in a world junior record 9.97, after 9.92w in his semi. Other top performances included an only just windy 19.91 200m by Dedric Dukes, 13.16 110m hurdles by 19 year-old Devon Allen, whose previous pb was 13.27, and a 50.23 400m by Courtney Okolo (plus a 49.57 anchor leg for Texas in the 4x400m). Oregon were clear winners of the men's title with a record score of 88 points from Florida 70 and Texas A&M 41.5, while the women's title was won by Texas A&M 75 from Texas 66 and Oregon 59. *See USA section for winners*.

16 **Ostrava**, Czech Republic. World-leading hammer marks were produced by Krisztián Pars 81.57 and Betty Heidler 78.00 at the IAAF World Hammer Throw Challenge

competitions held, as usual, on the day before the main Golden Spike meeting. This was Heidler's third best ever performance and in second place Anna Wlodarczyk made a fine start to her season with 76.41.

17 **Ostrava**, Czech Republic. 53rd Golden Spike (WCM). Justin Gatlin shaved 0.01 off his world-leading 100m time 100m with 9.86 into a 0.4 breeze and LaShawn Merritt was inside 44.5 sec for 400m for the seventh time since late April with a seemingly unstraining 44.16 ahead of a Botswana record of 44.83 by Isaac Makwala. Caleb Ndiku scored a runaway win in the Zátopek Memorial 3000m in 7:31.66 with Yomif Kejelcha, apparently still 16, second in 7:36.28, and Genzebe Dibaba ran 5:27.50 for 2000m, an African record and third best of all-time. Vitezslav Vesely won the javelin with 87.38 from Zigismunds Sirmais 86.61 and Dmitriy Tarabin 85.92.

20-22 **Trinidad & Tobago Championships**, Port of Spain. Richard Thompson won the 100m in a national record 9.82 and Michelle-Lee Ahye won the women's race in 10.88 after a 10.85 semi.

21-22 **European Team Championships**, Braunschweig, Germany. The German team ended three years of Russian domination to win the fifth edition of this event with Robert Harting, discus, and Betty Heidler, hammer, achieving fourth successive wins. Andreas Hofmann improved his javelin best by 2.5m to win with 86.13. The First League in Tallinn was won by Belarus, the Second League in Riga by Switzerland and the Third League in Tbilisi by Cyprus.

25-29 **US Championships**, Sacramento. World leading marks for the year were set in four events: Ronnie Ash, 110mh 12.99, Joe Kovacs, shot (held on the lawn of the State Capitol) 22.03 (best outdoors), Trey Hardee, decathlon 8599, and Francena McCorory, 400m 49.48. Will Claye won the triple jump with 17.75 and in 38°C on the final day Jeff Henderson went out to 8.52w and 8.43 in the long jump. Dawn Harper-Nelson just beat Queen Harrison, 12.55 to 12.56 at 100m hurdles. The 19 year-old NCAA champion Devon Allen dipped for a surprise 110mh win in 13.16 ahead of Ryan Wilson (13.16) and David Oliver (13.23), as Ronnie Ash crashed out mid-race in the final, after his 12.99 semi. Inika McPherson, only 1.63m tall, won the high jump with a lifetime best of 2.00 and became the shortest woman ever to clear that height, setting a world best of 37cm for height differential by a woman. Jenn Suhr won her eighth title at pole vault (plus seven indoors), Bernard Lagat his seventh at 5000m and Galen Rupp his sixth consecutive US 10000m title.

26-29 **Jamaican Championships**, Kingston. There was again great depth of sprinting, although times in some finals were affected by adverse winds. Kaliese Spencer ran a world-leading 53.41 to take the 400m hurdles and in the men's race Roxroy Cato ran 48.48 and Annsert Whyte 48.58. Veronica Campbell-Brown showed that she was back in top form with a women's 100m victory in 10.96.

27 **Zhukovskiy**, Russia. 56th Znamenskiy Memorial.

27-29 **UK Championships**, Birmingham. Katarina Johnson-Thompson added 11cm to her outdoor best long jump, winning the title with 6.81. Goldie Sayers (62.75) won her eleventh national javelin title and Dwain Chambers his eighth at 100m.

July

1 **Velenje**, Slovenia. 19th Miners; Day Meet (EA Classic). Pawel Fajdek won the hammer with a pb 82.37 from Krisztián Pars 81.08.

3 **Lausanne**, Switzerland. Athletissima (DL). The men's high jump again made the headlines as Bohdan Bondarenko won with 2.40 and was joined as a 2.40 man by compatriot Andriy Protsenko with the best ever marks for 3rd (tied), 4th and 5th (tied): Ivan Ukhov 2.38, Mutaz Essa Barshim 2.38 and Derek Drouin 2.35. Although LaShawn Merritt ran a season's 400m best of 43.97, he was well beaten by Kirani James 43.74, a CAC and Commonwealth record, and Youssef Al-Masrahi ran an Asian record 44.43 for third and Chris Brown a world age-35 record of 44.59 for fourth. Ronald Kwemoi won the 1500m in 3:31.48, the world's fastest by a junior for ten years, Justin Gatlin won the 100m in 9.80, the second fastest of his career, from Tyson Gay 9.93, and Alonso Edward was back to his best with a 19.84 200m win. Caterine Ibargüen equalled her world leading mark of 14.87 in the triple jump and Valerie Adams in good form in the shot with 20.42 and three of four efforts over 20m; she took her unbeaten run to 51.

5 **Saint-Denis**, France. Areva meeting (DL). Asbel Kiprop dropped down a distance to win the 800m in 1:43.34, finishing clear of Nijel Amos 1:43.70. This was one of five world-leading marks as Edwin Soi became the first this year to dip under 13 minutes for 5000m with 12:59.82, Hansle Parchment set a Jamaican 110m hurdles record of 12.94, Sifan Hassan ran 1500m in a European U23 record 3:57.00 from Jennifer Simpson 3:57.22 with Hellen Obiri, Faith Kipyegon and Shannon Rowbury also under 4 minutes, and Dawn Harper-Nelson clocked 12.44 for 100m hurdles. Sandra Perkovic was only fourth after five rounds of the women's discus, but came through to win with 68.48 from Dani Samuels 67.40.

5-6 **European Cup of Combined Events**. Russia won the Super League at Torun from the Netherlands, who had both individual winners with Eelco Sintnicolaas decathlon 8156 and Nadine Broersen heptathlon 6539, a pb despite dreadful weather on the second day. At Ribeira Brava the Czech Republic won the First League and Romania the Second League.

5-6 **US Junior Championships**, Eugene. Trentavis Friday ran a brilliant 10.00 in his heat of the 100m only to disqualified for a false start in the final, won by Trayvon Bromell, 10.07. Friday came back, however, to win the 200m in 20.03w. 16 year-old Kaylin Whitney set world youth records in both 100m 11.10, and 200m 22.49. She removed previous records set by Chandra Cheeseborough, 11.13 in 1976, and Marion Jones, 22.58 in 1992. Kendall Williams ran a North American junior record for 100m hurdles of 12.87.

6 **La Chaux-de-Fonds**, Switzerland. Isaac Makwala took full advantage of the 997m altitude to reduce his Botswana records for 200m from 20.21 (2013) to 19.96 and for 400m from 44.83 to 44.01, the last also an African record.

8 **Székesfehérvár,** Hungary. 4th István Gyulai Memorial Meeting. The hammer events, part of the IAAF World Challenge, provided highlights. Anita Wlodarczyk beat Betty Heidler, 75.53 to 75.34, and Krisztián Pars added 12cm to Pawel Fajdek's world leading mark for 2014 and 9cm to his own pb with a final round 82.49. Fajdek was second with 80.87 and Dilshod Nazarov, over 80m for the second time this year, third with 80.24. Zoltán Kövágó won his first competition on return from his two-year drugs ban with 64.72 in the discus.

11-12 **Glasgow**, GBR. Sainsbury's Grand Prix (DL). This was the first major meeting to be held on the nine-lane track raised 1.9m above the famous football pitch at Hampden Park, the venue for the forthcoming Commonwealth Games, Once the world's largest stadium with 149,415 spectators attending the Scotland v England football match in 1937, the seating capacity was 44,000. On the first day the most popular winner was Eilidh Child, who won the 400m hurdles in 54.39, fastest this year by a European and close to her Scottish record of 54.22. Tianna Bartoletta won the long jump with 6.97 from the 6.92 pb by Katarina Johnson-Thompson. Javier Culson won the 400m hurdles in 48.35 some 3m clear of fast-finishing Ashton Eaton, who reduced his best to 48.69. There was a shock in the women's discus as Sandra Perkovic was beaten in a DL event for the first time in two years; 35 year-old Gia Lewis-Smallwood threw a pb of 67.59 in the fourth round while Perkovic could manage only 66.30. On day 2 David Rudisha returned to winning form with 1:43.34 for 800m and Hiwot Ayalew ran a world-leading 9:10.64 in the steeplechase as second-placed Emma Coburn set a North American record of 9:11.42. Matthew Hudson-Smith improved his best at 400m from 45.80 to 44.97 for 3rd in a 400m race won by Isaac Makwala 44.71 and Dafne Schippers ran a Dutch 200m record of 22.34 to beat Allyson Felix 22.35.

11-13 **French Championships**, Reims. Cindy Billaud equalled the French record for 100m hurdles with 12.56 in her heat before winning the final in 12.58, Christophe Lemaitre won the sprint double, and Pascal Martinot-Lagarde the 110m hurdles in 13.10. Mélina Robert-Michon won a 14th title in 15 years in the women's discus and Mélanie Skotnik a ninth in ten years at high jump. Yohann Diniz moved to fifth on the world all-time list for 10,000m walk with a French record 38:08.13.

13 **European Mountain Running Championships**, Gap, France. Italy achieved their 19th men's team win in the 20 years of the event and their 12th women's team win.

14 **Linz**, Austria. Justin Gatlin won the 100m at the Gugl Games in 9.82.

15 **Luzern**, Switzerland. The 28th Spitzen Leichtathletik meeting included a 52nd successive shot win by Valerie Adams, 20.42. Michelle-Lee Ahye maintained her season's unbeaten record at 100m with a clear victory over Tianna Bartoletta in 11.09 and completed a fine double by taking the 200m in a pb equalling 22.77, both races being slowed by headwinds.

16 **Liège (Naimette-Xhovément)**, Belgium. Ashton Eaton stepped down to the 110m hurdles, and won in 13.43, and Demetrius Pinder set a Bahamas 300m record at 32.05.

18 **Herculis, Monaco (**DL). As usual this was a magnificent meeting. For instance behind Silas Kiplagat 3:27.64 (fourth all-time), Asbel Kiprop in 3:28.45 and Ronald Kwemoi world junior record 3:28.81 there were the best ever times for places 4 to 10 (Henrik Ingebrigtsen's 3:31.46 Norwegian record). For only the second time (after the 2012 Olympics) five men broke 1:43 in an 800m, as Nijel Amos won in 1:42.45 from Pierre-Ambroise Bosse 1:42.53 French record and Mohammed Aman 1:42.63, Ferguson Cheruiyot 1:42.84 and David Rudisha 1:42.98. Pascal Martinot-Lagarde won the 110m hurdles in a French record 12.95 and further world-leading marks came from Justin Gatlin, 200m 19.68, Tori Bowie, 100m 10.80, Ajee' Wilson, 800m 1:57.67, Genzebe Dibaba, 5000m 14:28.88 holding off a powerful challenge from Almaz Ayana 14:29.19, and Catarine Ibargüen, triple jump 15.31, a huge improvement on her South American record of 14.99A.

18-20 **Italian Championships**, Rovereto. Nicola Vizzoni (75.99) won his 14th hammer title from 1998 and shot putter Chiara Rosa her tenth in succession.

19 **Heusden-Zolder**, Belgium. KBC Night of Athletics. Depth of distance running was as usual the feature here.

19 **Madrid**, Spain (WCM). Dilshod Nazarov was over 80m in the hammer for the third time in 2014 with 80.51.

20 **London**, GBR. The Sainsbury's Anniversary Games was staged on specially constructed tracks and jumping areas in London's Horse Guards Parade. Blanka Vlasic continued her encouraging return with 2.00 in the high jump for the second time this year and David Storl took his season's best and pb from 21.90 to 21.97 in the shot.

22-27 **World Junior Championships**, Eugene, USA. Two world junior records topped the performances: Wilhem Belocian 12.99 for the 99cm 110m hurdles and Anezka Drahotová 42:47.25 for 10000m walk a day before her 19th birthday. 17 year-old Morgan Lake won both the heptathlon, her score of 6148 the highest ever by a youth with the senior specification, and the high jump with 1.93. Even younger was Kaylin Whitney, who won the 200m in 22.82w, and also just before his 17th birthday was Yomif Kejelcha, 5000m winner in 13:25.19. The USA easily topped the medal table with 11 gold, 5 silver and 5 bronze.

23-26 **Russian Championships**, Kazan. Top marks came in the women's field events, from Darya Klishina, LJ 6.90, and Yekaterina Koneva, TJ 14.84w, but with some top names missing performances were solid rather than spectacular.

24-26 **Ukrainian Championships**, Kirovograd. Hanna Hatsko-Fedusova added 4.19 to her pb with a national javelin record 67.29.

25-27 **German Championships**, Ulm. David Storl, in a rich run of form, produced the outstanding performance as he won the shot with 21.87. Sabrina Mockenhaupt won her 13th 5000m title in 14 years and this was her 39th German title at all events. Robert Harting won his eighth discus title and Markus Esser his eighth successive at hammer, but Kathrin Klaas beat Betty Heidler 72.08 to 69.83 to deny the latter a ninth successive hammer title.

26-27 73rd **Balkan Championships**, Pitesti, Romania. Romania came out as easily the top nation.

26-27 **Dutch Championships**, Amsterdam. Dafne Schippers improved the national long jump record to 6.78 as well as winning the 100m in 11.10.

26-27 **Spanish Championships**, Alcobendas. Berta Castells won her 12th successive women's hammer title and Ruth Beitia her tenth at high jump, with the top mark a Spanish record 42:23.37 by Julia Takacs at 10000m walk.

27- Aug 2 **Commonwealth Games**, Glasgow, GBR. Much higher overall standards were achieved than at Delhi 2010 and indeed were better than at Melbourne 2006. Games records were set in ten events – four were by men: the superb Kirani James at 400m, Jonathan Ndiku, who scored an upset victory over Jairus Birech and Ezekiel Kemboi at steeplechase, O'Dayne Richards, who improved his shot pb from 21.11 to a CAC record 21.61 and by the Jamaican 4x100m team, whose 37.58 was a 2014 world-leading time and smashed the previous Games record of 38.20 and for whom Usain Bolt ran a superb anchor leg. Like Bolt, Shelly-Ann Fraser-Pryce brought home the Jamaican team in a world-leading time, 41.83 compared to the previous Games record of 42.44; she did not contest the individual events, won in majestic style by Blessing Okagbare, 100m Games record 10.85 and 200m 22.25. Valerie Adams won her third women's shot title (after silver in 2002), and others to retain their individual titles were Moses Kipsiro at 10,000m, Sally Pearson at 100m hurdles, Alana Boyd in the pole vault, and Sultana Frizell, who improved the Games record for hammer three times. The youngest winner was the 18-year old Eleanor Patterson of the women's high jump. Kenya and Jamaica both won ten gold medals, but England had the most medals in all, 23 (but just three gold), and also topped the points table.

29-31 **Polish Championships**, Szczecin. Tomasz Majewski won his twelfth shot title and Piotr Malachowski his ninth at discus.

August

1-3 16th **Ibero-American Championships**, São Paulo, Brazil. Andrés Silva improved the 400mh record for Uruguay from his 49.11 (2011) to 48.65, but Brazil were easily the most successful nation, with 16 gold, 17 silver and 15 bronze medals.

8-10 **NACAC (U23) Championships**, Kamloops, Canada.

10 **Belém**, Brazil. 30th Grande Premio Brasil Caixa de Atletismo (WCM).

10-14 **African Championships**, Marrakech, Morocco. Nine new championship records were headed by Isaac Makwala, 400m 44.23, Mostafa Al-Gamal, hammer 79.07, Blessing Okagbare, 100m 11.00, and Sunette Viljoen, javelin 65.32. Hua Wilfried Koffi scored an unexpected 100m/200m double in Ivorian records of 10.05 and 20.25. Kabelo Kogosiemang won his sixth African Games or Championships high jump title. Nine Commonwealth Games champions repeated their successes.

12-17 22nd **European Championships**, Zürich, Switzerland. Yohann Diniz took 1.41 off the world record with 3:32:33 for 50km walk and championship records were also set by Christelle Daunay, 2:25:14 marathon, and Anita Wlodarczyk, 78.76 hammer. There were also world-leading marks for discus 71.08 by Sandra Perkovic, winning by a margin of 5.75m, 82.69 hammer by Krisztián Pars, 8616 decathlon by Andrey Kravchenko, 22.03 for 200m by Dafne Schippers and 2.01 (tied) by Ruth Beitia.

Schippers achieved a sprint double (with the 100m in 11.12 into a 1.7 wind) in majestic style and the other individual double champion was Mo Farah, who despite just previous one track run in 2014, produced his renowned sprint finish to devastating effect in both 5000m and 10,000m. Thirteen individual titles were retained and of these Farah (5000m), Robert Harting (discus), Olga Saladukha (triple jump) and Perkovic won three in a row (2010, 2012 and 2014). Jo Pavey became, at 40, the oldest ever European women's champion with her heart-warming victory at 10,000m. Mahiedine Mekissi-Benabbad had his steeplechase gold taken from him as he had taken off his vest in the home straight but returned to win the 1500m with a devastating sprint. Both Britain and France had their most successful ever European Championships, with 23 medals apiece, and 12 and 9 gold medals respectively. Russia were just ahead of them in the points table, but had only three gold medals.

15-16 **Pan-American Sports Festival**, Mexico City. Good depth of performances featured many by Cubans including 64.94 discus by Jorge Fernández and 14.53 triple jump by Mabel Gay.

20-26 2nd **Youth Olympic Games**, Nanjing, China. Jaheel Hyde improved the world youth record for 110m hurdles to 12.96.

21 **Stockholm**, Sweden. 48th DN Galan (DL). Genzebe Dibaba had a 10m lead at the bell in the women's 1500m, but was caught by Sifan Hassan in the home straight. Dibaba held Hassan 4:01.00 to 4:01.62, but both were passed by Jennifer Simpson who won in 4:00.38. Muktar Edris won the 5000m in a world season's best of 12:54.83, holding off the challenge of Thomas Longosiwa 12:56.16 and Caleb Ndiku 12:59.17. Renaud Lavillenie's winning run of 23 pole vault competitions came to an unexpected end as he failed to clear a height in the tricky conditions. He came in at 5.60, a height cleared by the first three. Six men bettered 84m in the javelin, won by Antti Ruuskanen 87.24.

22-24 **Eberstadt**, Germany. Winners at the 36th high jump meeting were Mutaz Essa Barshim 2.41 and Airine Palyste 1.98.

22-31 19th **European Masters Championships**, Izmir, Turkey. Germany topped the medal table with 297 (121G-93S-83B) from Great Britain 158 (67-53-38) and Italy 115 (42-41-32). In all 38 countries won medals.

23 **Warsaw**, Poland. Kamila Skolimowska Memorial Meeting. Usain Bolt won the 100m in 9.98 in just his fourth but last race of 2014 on a specially constructed 100m straight down the side of the infield area of the National Stadium. This was indoors given that the roof was completely closed and another world indoor best came with 13.03 by Orlando Ortega for 110m hurdles. Top mark, however, was a Polish hammer record 83.48 by Pawel Fajdek.

24 **Birmingham**, GBR. Sainsbury's Grand Prix (DL). With mile splits of 4:07.8 and 4:00.1, Mo Farah won the 2 miles in 8:07.85 to break the UK best of 8:13.51 set by Steve Ovett in 1978, and in the women's race Mercy Cherono ran a Kenyan best of 9:11.49. David Rudisha won the 600m in 1:13.71 for fourth on the world all-time list and Liz Gleadle had an upset win over Barbora Spotáková, 64.49 to 62.89, in the javelin. Asbel Kiprop beat Ayanleh Souleiman to win the Emsley Carr Mile in 3:51.89.

28 **Zürich**, Switzerland. Weltklasse. Of the 15 athletes who came to Zürich for part one of the IAAF Diamond League finals as the overall leader in their events (an injured Tori Bowie was unable to compete in the 100m), only seven scored sufficient points to emerge as Diamond Race winners, pocketing $40,000 apiece, and two of those – LaShawn Merritt in the 400m and Sandra Perkovic in the discus – had already won subject to turning up. Those who fell at the final hurdle were Nickel Ashmeade (200m), David Rudisha (800m), Yenew Alamirew (5000m), Will Claye (TJ), Ihab Abdelrahman (JT), Abeba Aregawi (1500m), Queen Harrison (100mh; she fell and broke her left arm) and Blanka Vlasic (tied for the lead in the HJ prior to Zürich). Those who excelled in taking titles included Jenny Simpson, who beat Shannon Rowbury by 0.01 in 3:59.92 for 1500m, Thomas Röhler, pb 87.63 in the javelin, LaShawn Merritt, 44.36 his 11th sub-44.50 mark of the season, and, with season's bests, Christian Taylor, triple jump 17.51, and Reese Hoffa, shot 21.88. Habiba Ghribi won the women's steeplechase in 9:15.23 from the DL 1-2 Hiwot Ayalew and Sofia Assefa; fourth-placed Ruth Chebet (17) set an Asian record of 9:20.55.

29:31 **Finland v Sweden**, Gothenburg, Sweden beat Finland in both men's, 216-193, and women's, 206-204, matches in the annual Finnkampen.

30 **Angers**, France. The USA had a seventh successive win in the annual DécaNation (ten men's and ten women's events) meeting with 114 points, just ahead of France 112 and Russia 108. A 69.17 discus throw by Gia Lewis-Smallwood added 1.43m to the North American record.

31 **Berlin**, Germany. 73rd ISTAF (WCM). Anita Wlodarczyk regained the hammer world record with her second round throw of a magnificent series: 75.29, 79.58, 78.46, 79.04, 78.64, 77.94 (so four of the top ten throws ever). Former record holder Betty Heidler was second with 75.20. Robert Harting thrilled the home crowd with 68.31 for his fifth consecutive ISTAF discus victory, Pawel Wojciechowski won the pole vault with 5.80, his best since 2011 and in a very close finish Mohammed Aman beat Taoufik Makhloufi by 0.01 in a 1:43.52 800m.

September

2 **Rovereto**, Italy. 50th Palio Citta della Quercia meeting.

2 **Zagreb**, Croatia. 64th Boris Hanzekovic Memorial (WCM). Sandra Perkovic starred with a 65.09 discus win.

5 **Brussels**, Belgium. 38th Van Damme Memorial (DL). Star of this DL final meeting was Mutaz Essa Barshim who sealed his victory in the Diamond Race with a beautiful clearance of an Asian record 2.43, a height previously achieved only by Javier Sotomayor in 1988-93, and Bohdan Bondarenko had to settle for second at 2.40. Jairus Birech, already the winner of five DL races, became the 11th man to break 8 minutes for the 3000m steeplechase with 7:58.41; he was followed by Mahiedine Mekissi-Benabbad 8:03.23 and Evan Jager 8:04.71, a North American record. Mercy Cherono won a highly competitive women's 3000m in 8:28.95 from Sifan Hassan 8:29.38 Dutch record, Genzebe Dibaba 8:29.41, Jennifer Simpson 8:29.58 and Shannon Rowbury 8:29.93 with the best ever times for places 9 to 18; 12 women under 8:35 and 16 under 8:40 compared to previous bests of 8 and 10. Silas Kiplagat won the Diamond Race 1500m but with 3:31.80 was second here to Taoufik Makhloufi 3:31.78. Allyson Felix won the 200m in a 2014 world best of 22.02 from Myriam Soumare's pb 22.11 and Dafne Schippers 22.30. Other world leading marks came from Valerie Adams (outdoors), her 20.59 shot win being her 56th in succession, Barbora Spotáková, 67.99 javelin, and Justin Gatlin, 9.77 for 100m. Gatlin returned later for a non-DL 200m race and won in 19.71, thus achieving the best ever 100m/200m one-day double.

7 **Rieti**, Italy (WCM). Pietro Mennea Memorial. Top marks included 9.83 by Justin Gatlin, completing an unbeaten season, and 9.90 by Asafa Powell in separate 100m races, 31.93 Polish record 300m by Karol Zalewski, and 1:43.83 800m by Taoufik Makhloufi. On the preceding day Pawel Fajdek beat Krisztián Pars 81.11 to 80.78 in the final IAAF Hammer Challenge meeting of the year, but they finished in reverse order overall.

7 33rd **Great North Run, Newcastle to South Shields**, GBR. Mary Keitany took 1 second off Paula Radcliffe's course record of 65:39, finishing well clear of runner-up Gemma Steel 68:13. Mo Farah edged Mike Kigen for the men's win as both were timed in 60:00; the drop of 30.5m overall and point-to-point course meant that this was not eligible for a British record. There were 41,923 starters and the race was extra special as it became the first road race – beating New York, London and Boston Marathons – to boast a millionth finisher. The event, the brainchild of Brendan Foster, was first contested in June 1981.

13 **5th Avenue Mile, New York**, USA. Jenny Simpson had her third win in the race in 4:19.4 and a record 14 women broke 4:30 and 9 men, headed by Jordan McNamara 3:51.0, bettered 3:54.

13-14 **IAAF Continental Cup**, Marrakech, Morocco. Europe had the depth of talent to win with 447.5 points from Americas 390, Africa 339 and Asia-Pacific 257.5. There was just one championship (Continental and World Cups) record – by Dawn Harper-Nelson who won the 100m hurdles in 12.47 from Tiffany Porter who recaptured the British record with 12.51. Khotso Mokoena confirmed his successful return to triple jumping with a South African record 17.35 but was beaten by Benjamin Compaoré 17.48. The closest result came in the men's 200m as Alonso Edward beat Rasheed Dwyer 19.972 to 19.974. A total of $2,900,000 in prize money was paid out with each individual winner receiving $30,000. The one disappointment came from very small crowds.

14 30th **WMRA World Mountain Running Championships**, Castette di Massa, Italy. Isaac Kiprop won the men's race with Ugandans finishing 1-2-3 and taking the men's team title. Andrea Mayr won the women's title for a record fifth time, with Italy women's champions for the 11th time in the last 17 years.

20-21 **Talence**, France. Décastar. Carolin Schäfer was the clear winner of the women's heptathlon with 6383 points. This ensured her second place in the IAAF World Combined Events Challenge (to Nadine Broersen) and she set pbs at 200m and 800m. Mikk Pahapill produced a season's best to win the decathlon with 8077 points.

27-Oct 3 **Asian Games**, Incheon, Korea. With 39 medals, 15 of them gold, Chinese athletes were the dominant force and the standard was high with Games records set in 16 events. These included Asian records from Femi Ogunode, 100m 9.93 (and a Games record 200m 20.14), Zhao Qinggang, javelin 89.15 (from a pre-meet best of 81.18) and the Chinese 4x100m team 37.99. In all at least 14 gold medals, 6 silver and 3 bronze medals with five new Games records were set by African-born athletes, including three more double individual champions: Mohamed Al-Garni 5000m and 10,000m, Kemi Adekoya, 400m and 400mh, and Maryam Jamal, 1500m and 5000m, taking her career Asian Games total to five golds, tying the record. Youssef Al-Masrahi just missed his Asian 400m record of 44.43 with 44.46. Zhang Wenxiu threw the hammer a pb of 77.33, but just after the Games came the news that she had failed a drugs test so the title passed to her Chinese colleague Wang Zheng with 74.16.

28 BMW **Berlin Marathon**, Germany. For the sixth time in 12 years a new world record for the marathon was set on this course. Dennis

Kimetto took 26 secs off the ratified mark with 2:02:57 and second-placed Emmanuel Mutai was also inside the old mark with 2:03:13. Third was Abera Kuma 2:05:56. Kimetto had 5k splits of 14:42, 29:24, 44:10, 58:36, 61:45 half, 1:13:08, 1:27:38, 1:41:47, 1:56:29, so he ran halves of 61:45 and 61:12 and became the first to run every 5k interval in 14:45 or faster; he won a total of 120,000 euros in prize and bonus money. The world record for 30k was also broken; pacemaker Wilfred Kirwa led in 1:27:16 but will not be eligible for the record as he did not finish, but 1:27:37 was clocked by Mutai. Tirfi Tsegaye won the women's race in 2:20:18 from Feyse Tadese 2:20:27 and Shalane Flanagan 2:21:14.

October

3-5 **South American U23 Championships**, Montevideo, Uruguay. Brazil easily headed the medal table with 18 gold, 21 silver and 13 bronze medals.

9-12 **São Paulo**, Brazil. 33rd Trofeu Brasil (national championships). Jucilene de Lima set a South American javelin record of 62.89.

9-13 **Chinese Championships**, Suzhou. Top mark was a 1.96 women's high jump by Zheng Xingjuan.

12 37th **Chicago Marathon**, USA. Eliud Kipchoge sped away with a 14:34 5k split between 30 and 35k and ran on smoothly to victory in 2:04:11 (62:11 and 62:00), 17 secs ahead of Sammy Kitwara with Dickson Chumba running the fastest ever third place time of 2:04:32. Kenenisa Bekele was well behind, 4th in 2:05:51. A Kenyan double was achieved as women's winner was Rita Jeptoo in 2:24:35 (72:36 and 71:59) – before news came of her drugs failure.

19 **Amsterdam**, Netherlands. Bernard Kipyego achieved his first marathon success as he won in a pb 2:06:22.

19 **Valencia**, Spain. Abreham Cheroben ran a world-leading half marathon time of 58:48, leading four Kenyans under the hour.

26 **Frankfurt-am-Main**, Germany. 38 year-old Mark Kiptoo won in 2:06:49 by 10 secs from Mike Kigen with women's winner Aberu Kebede 2:22:32 from Sharon Cherop 2:23:44.

November

2 **New York City Marathon**, USA. Cold and windy conditions held back times, but Wilson Kipsang had little problem in winning in 2:10:59 and taking the 2013/14 World Marathon Majors Series title with Lelisa Desisa 2nd in 2:11:07. The women's race was more competitive with Mary Keitany impressing with a fine win in 2:25:07 in her comeback race after the birth of her daughter in 2013. Jemima Jelagat was 2nd in 2:25:10 with Sara Moreira a delighted 3rd in 2:26:00 on her marathon debut. There were a world record 50,432 finishers (30,034 men and 29,398 women).

December

7 **Fukuoka**, Japan. Patrick Makau returned to form to win the 68th Fukuoka International race in 2:08:22. In third place and in his 33rd marathon Serod Bat-Ochir improved his Mongolian record to 2:08:50.

14 **European Cross-Country Championships**, Samokov, Bulgaria. Polat Kemboi Arikan and Ali Kaya led Turkey to the senior men's title and Alemayehu Bezabeh of Spain completed an all-African born top three, while Gemma Steel won a close battle for the senior women's race as they finished well clear of the rest and ensured that Britain won the team title. The British team was again much the most successful nation overall.

Top women athletes who gave birth in 2014 included:

Mariya Abakumova RUS, Kseniya Aksyonova (Ustalova) RUS, Anna Avdeyeva RUS, Stephanie Bruce (Rothstein) USA, Tatyana Chernova RUS, Meseret Defar ETH, Jessica Ennis-Hill GBR, Ariane Friedrich GER, Yuliya Gushchina RUS, Moa Hjelmer SWE, Yelena Isinbayeva RUS, Anastasiya Kapachinskaya RUS, Yuliya Katsura RUS, Antonina Krivoshapka RUS, Anastasiya Mironchik-Ivanova BLR, Natalya Nazarova RUS, Yelena Nevmerzhitskaya BLR, Christina Obergföll GER, Yevgeniya Polyakova RUS, Elisa Rigaudo ITA, Hilary Stellingwerff CAN, Yuliya Zaripova RUS.

Retired in 2014/15

Men: Leon Baptiste GBR, Yuriy Borzakovskiy RUS, Simon Bairu CAN, Jared Connaugton CAN, Giuseppe Gibilisco ITA, David Gillick IRL, Jason Hartmann USA, Steve Hooker AUS, Jukka Keskisalo FIN. Robert Lathouwers NED, Christian Malcolm GBR, Norman Müller GER, Denis Nizhegorodov RUS, Arnoud Okken NED, Christian Reif GER, Viktor Röthlin SUI, Irving Saladino PAN, Matt Scherer USA, Carsten Schlangen GER, Helge Schwarzer GER, Terrence Trammell USA, Andrew Turner GBR, Tobias Unger GER, Alan Webb USA, Günther Weidlinger AUT.

Women: Jitka Bartonícová CZE, Zoë Brown IRL, Diane Cummins CAN, Muriel Hurtis FRA, Yuri Kano JPN, Manuela Levorato ITA, Sávva Líka GRE, Beatrice Lundmark SUI, Lee McConnell GBR, Irina Mikitenko GER, Yipsi Moreno CUB. Jennifer Oeser GER, Derval O'Rourke IRL, Nicola Sanders GBR, Yelena Slesarenko RUS, Svetlana Usovich BLR, Bettie Wade USA

ATHLETES OF 2014

By Peter Matthews

Male Athlete of the Year

EVEN TAKING INTO account the world records for the marathon by Dennis Kimetto and for 50k walk by Yohann Diniz, there can be no doubt that the top performance of 2014 was Renaud Lavillenie's absolute world pole vault record. Few could have imagined that Sergey Bubka's indoor 6.15 at Donetsk, Ukraine 31 years ago would be bettered, but Lavillenie added a centimetre to that. The Frenchman had entered 2014 with a best of 6.03 (indoors in 2011) for joint sixth on the world all-time list. He moved up to second with 6.04 at Rouen on January 24 and 6.08 at Bydgoszcz on January 31 before his first time clearance in front of Bubka at his Stars meeting in Donetsk on February 15. This came after he had cleared 5.86 and 5.91 on his first attempts and 6.01 on his third. Having cleared 6.16 (20ft 2½") he had the bar set at 6.20 (20ft 4½"). Unfortunately he did not get lift off and his pole pushed him back up the track. In the process his left heel clipped the edge of the raised runway and left a 4-inch gash. This injury hampered his preparations for the outdoor season and in that his best was 5.92. Nonetheless he was still a different class to the rest of the world and his 2014 competition record was 6 wins in 6 indoor events and 15 in 16 outdoors. His unbeaten run from August 2013 ended at 23 when he failed to clear his opening height of 5.60 in Stockholm, when he was tired just five days after winning the European title. He was the IAAF Male Athlete of the Year.

Selections for World Top Ten

My selection of the top 10 athletes of 2014 together with the lists compiled by international experts polled by *Track & Field News* and those of *Athletics International* readers:

	PJM	*TFN*	*AI*
Renaud Lavillenie	1	1	1
Bohdan Bondarenko	2	2	3
Mutaz Essa Barshim	3	4	2
Justin Gatlin	4	3	9
Jairus Birech	5	6	10
Nijel Amos	6	8	8
Robert Harting	7	5	6
Dennis Kimetto	8		4
Yohann Diniz	9		5
Kirani James	10		7
Caleb Ndiku	11		-
LaShawn Merritt	12	7	-
Eliud Kipchoge		9	
Krisztián Pars		10	

The most exciting event for fascinating competition in 2014 was the men's high jump. A record six men cleared 2.40 or higher, and Bohdan Bondarenko and Mutaz Essa Barshim, who had done so in 2013, edged their way closer to Javier Sotomayor's 1993 world record of 2.45. Bondarenko had a narrow lead on win-loss, 4-3 v Barshim, but Barshim had the best jump with 2.43 at the DL final in Brussels (when Bondarenko was 2nd with 2.40) while Bondarenko had a best of 2.42 in New York when he won on count-back from Barshim. Bondarenko won 10 of his 13 competitions and Barshim 6 of 11 outdoors and all 4 indoors. The slender Barshim looked perhaps the most likely to go yet higher and at 1.92m/70kg he contrasts with the 1.95/82 for Sotomayor and 1.97/80 for Bondarenko.

World records continue to be very scarce commodities and Lavillenie's vault mark was the only one in 2014 at any standard track and field event, but there were two on the roads. Yohann Diniz has sometimes cracked when attempting a very fast pace, but had no such problem at the Europeans where he took 1 min 41 secs off the old record for 50km walk with 3:32:33. Then Dennis Kimetto ran 2:02:57 to take 26 secs off the marathon mark, the sixth successive world record for the event to be set on the flat course in Berlin.

While many looked askance at his even competing, having served a four-year drugs ban from 2006 to 2010 the most successful in terms of an unbeaten record in 2014 was Justin Gatlin, who won all his 14 competitions at 100m and three at 200m. Galen Rupp at 10,000m and Trey Hardee at decathlon won their two competitions at the event. Other world leaders who got close to unbeaten seasons were Lavillenie, 21 of 22 as noted above, Robert Harting, 13 of 15 at discus, and Kirani James, 4 of 5 at 400m.

Most successful in the Diamond League was six wins by Jairus Birech at steeplechase and Lavillenie at pole vault, and five by LaShawn Merritt at 400m and Pascal Martinot-Lagarde at 110m hurdles from the maximum seven.

Usain Bolt had been the IAAF World Male Athlete of the Year for five time in six years up to 2013, but he had a quiet year in 2014 with just a couple of 100m races and heat and final in ensuring the Jamaica won the Commonwealth Games 4x100m title.

100 Metres

WITH USAIN BOLT running the event just twice, Justin Gatlin was easily the world's top sprinter in 2014, winning all his 15 finals and running 6 of the 8 wind-legal sub-9.90 times headed by 9.77 in the DL final in Brussels and 9.76w at Eugene. The others to run such times were Richard Thompson, 9.82 in the Trinidad & Tobago Champs before fading in the final weeks of the season, and Asafa Powell who returned from his (reduced) drugs ban to add to his record tally of sub-10 runs with 9.87 at Austin, 9.95 for 3rd in Brussels and 9.90 to win in Rieti. US champion Mike Rodgers was clearly world no. 2 with consistently excellent form throughout the year and, having started modestly, Kemar Bailey-Cole followed third to Nickel Ashmeade and Jason Livermore at the Jamaican Champs with Commonwealth Games gold in a run of five wins at big meetings. He was 2-1 v Powell, 3-4 v Nesta Carter (dns Jamaican Champs), and 2-0 with James Dasaolu, who did not run until July but won at the Europeans and Continental Cup. The order at the DL final behind Gatlin was 2 Rodgers, 3 Powell, 4 Bailey-Cole, 5 Dasaolu, 6 Tyson Gay, 7 Carter, 8 Thompson. Gay, also returning from his drugs ban, ran just four times, including 2nd in 9.93 to Gatlin in Lausanne, but only 9th at Zürich. He was 2-0 against the redoubtable 38 year-old Kim Collins, who remarkably improved his national record to 9.96, but did not run at the Commonwealth Games as he remained in dispute with his national federation. Another drugs returnee Femi Ogunode ended the year in style with 3rd in the Continental Cup and 9.93 for gold at the Asian Games. Adam Gemili did not run quite the fast times of other top tenners but was 2nd, 0.02 ahead of Ashmeade, at the Commonwealth Games, where Thompson was only 3rd in his semi. Trayvon Bromell was beaten by Kendal Williams at the World Juniors but had set a world junior record 9.97 to win the NCAA title after an earlier 9.77w. Jimmy Vicaut started in good form, but after just four earlier races had to pull out through a hamstring injury at the Europeans.

The fastest times run indoors at 60m were 6.47 by Dasaolu and 6.48 by Vicaut and US champion Marvin Bracy, but the first two were unable to run at the World Indoors, at which Bracy was surprisingly beaten by Richard Kilty, 6.49 to 6.51with Ogunode 3rd 6.52.

Most times at 10.00/10.05 or faster: Gatlin 9+1w/12+1w, Rodgers 6+2w/9+2w, Bailey-Cole 4+1w/5+1w, Powell 3/4, Carter 2+1w/5+1w, Thompson 2+1w/3+1w, Dasaolu 1/5, Ogunode 1/4, Bromell 1+2w, 3+2w, Vicaut 1+1w/3+1w, Gay 1/3, Ashmeade 1+1w/2+1w.

1. Gatlin, 2. Rodgers, 3. Bailey-Cole, 4. Dasaolu, 5. Powell, 6. Carter, 7. Ogunode, 8. Gemili, 9. Thompson, 10. Ashmeade

200 Metres

GATLIN RAN ONLY three 200m races, but was clearly dominant with the two fastest times of the year, as he ran 19.68 in Monaco with Nickel Ashmeade 2nd in 19.99, and 19.71 in Brussels with Alonso Edward 2nd in 20.26. Edward and Ashmeade went 2-2 in their clashes, as Edward had 9 wins, a 2nd and a 3rd and Ashmeade 2 wins and 4 2nds in their 200m races. Warren Weir was the year's second fastest with 19.82 in New York, but was beaten by over a metre at the Commonwealth Games by Rasheed Dwyer, with whom he was 2-2 overall, Dwyer winning at the Jamaican Champs. Edward won at the Continental Cup from Dwyer, Femi Ogunode and Christophe Lemaitre and Ogunode went on to complete an Asian Games sprint double. Adam Gemili was a brilliant winner in 19.98 despite a head-wind and cool weather at the Europeans from Lemaitre 20.15. Curtis Mitchell was the US champion, but NCAA champion Dedric Dukes was unable to start in the final. Joining the above men in breaking 20 secs in 2014 was Isaac Makwala, but he was well beaten by Hua Wilfried Koffi for the African title and was 6th at the Continental Cup. Aaron

Best one-day sprint doubles, scored on IAAF tables

Name	*Venue*	*Date*	*100m*	*200m*	*Total*
Justin Gatlin	Brussels	5 Sep 14	9.77	19.71	2553
Ato Boldon	Stuttgart	13 Jul 97	9.90	19.77	2497
Ato Boldon	Athens	16 Jun 99	9.86	19.86	2497
Maurice Greene	Athens	16 Jun 99	9.79	20.03	2495
Ato Boldon	Athens	17 Jun 98	9.86	19.88	2494
Ato Boldon	Stockholm	7 Jul 97	9.95	19.82	2472
Ato Boldon	Lausanne	3 Jul 96	9.94	19.85	2471
Ato Boldon	Athens	16 Jun 99	9.97	19.86	2459
Walter Dix	Gainesville	26 May 07	10.05	19.69	2458
Shawn Crawford	Pretoria	12 Apr 02	9.99A	19.85A	2454
Wind assisted					
Maurice Greene	Eugene	31 May 98	9.79w	19.88w	2519
Frank Fredericks	Villeneuve d'Ascq	6 Jul 92	9.91w	19.99w	2460
Steve Mullings	Fort Worth	17 Apr 04	9.96	19.90	2456

Brown was 2nd at the NCAAs in 2002 with a series of other good times. Usain Bolt did not run at 200m this year.

Most times at 20.30 or better: Edward 10, Lemaitre 9, Mitchell, Brown 5+1w, Weir, Ashmeade, Dwyer, Ogunode 5, Dukes 3+2w, Gemili 3, Wallace Spearmon 2+1w.

1. Gatlin, 2. Edward, 3. Ashmeade, 4. Dwyer, 5. Weir, 6. Ogunode, 7. Gemili, 8. Lemaitre, 9. Mitchell, 10. Dukes

400 Metres

The four sub-44 times of 2014 went two apiece to Kirani James and LaShawn Merritt, whose rivalry is developing into one of the greatest in track history *(see table)*. The score this year was 2-1 to James, including the fastest times of the year in Lausanne, where it was 43.74 to 43.92. James went on to won the Commonwealth title but had a limited season of just five races, winning four, whereas Merritt had 16 400m competitions, winning 12 and with 11 of the 19 sub-44.5 times; the only other man to beat him was Luguelín Santos at Kingston in May. The DL races went five to Merritt and two to James. The world's third best was Isaac Makwala, who improved from 45.25 (2012) to an African record 44.01; he surprisingly went out in his semi at the Commonwealth Games, but won the African title and was 2nd to Merritt at the Continental Cup when he was followed as 3rd to 5th by Youssef Al-Masrahi (1st Asian Games), Wayde van Niekerk (2nd CG and African) and Santos. European champion Martyn Rooney (4th CG) was only 7th in that race and, in the absence through a hamstring injury of World Indoor champion Pavel Maslák, was top European. Gil Roberts was the US champion and had strong 2nd places in Monaco and Zürich. Tony McQuay, although never better than 3rd, had a consistent season and although 0-3 to Rooney, was 2-2 with 1 tie against Santos, who had a better set of times. Chris Brown was unable to start the Commonwealth final but was 3-1 v Santos, 3-0 v McQuay, 3-2 v Rooney and 3-1 v Lalonde Gordon (3rd CG). NCAA champion Deon Lendore was unbeaten in four indoor and four outdoor competitions, all in the USA. He was fastest in the world indoors at 45.03 and fourth on the world list outdoor list at 44.46, but did not meet the other top men.

Most sub-45.00 times: Merritt 13, Makwala 7, Al-Masrahi 6, James, Santos 5; Roberts 4, van Niekerk, Brown 3.

1. James, 2, Merritt, 3. Makwala, 4. Al-Masrahi, 5. Roberts, 6. van Niekerk, 7. Brown, 8. Santos, 9. Rooney, 10. Lendore

LaShawn Merritt v Kirani James

Date	Venue	Merritt	James
30 Aug 11	Daegu WCh	44.63-2	44.60-1
8 Sep 11	Zürich WK	44.67-2	44.36-1
2 Jun 12	Eugene Pre	44.91-1	dq/fs*
20 Jul 12	Monaco Herc	dnf	44.76-2
18 May 13	Shanghai DL	44.60-2	44.02-1
1 Jun 13	Eugene Pre	44,32-1	44.39-2
6 Jul 13	Saint-Denis DL	44.09-2	43.96-1
13 Aug 13	Moscow WCh	43.74-1	44.99-7
29 Aug 13	Zürich WK	44.13-1	44.32-2
25 Apr 14	Des Moines Drake R	44.44-1	44.60-2
31 May 14	Eugene Pre	43.97-2	43.97-1
3 Jul 14	Lausanne Athl	43.92-2	43.74-1

* ran under protest and finished 2nd

800 Metres

WHILE DAVID RUDISHA steadily made his way back from a calf injury, top ranking went to the man who had been second in Rudisha's epic Olympic triumph in 2012. Nijel Amos did not have a perfect season as he was 2nd to Mohammed Aman in Doha and to Asbel Kiprop in Saint-Denis before slipping to 5th in Stockholm, but won his seven other races including a complete set of the most prestigious ones of Commonwealth Games, African Champs, DL final in Zürich and Continental Cup. He also won in Monaco in 1:42.45, heading the year's five fastest times as he was followed by Pierre-Ambroise Bosse, Aman, Ferguson Rotich Cheruiyot and Rudisha. Aman was only 8th in Zürich (with Kiprop 11th in his only other 800m race), but was 2nd at the Africans and Continental Cup and had won the World Indoor title from Kszczot. Ayanleh Souleiman ran only four 800m races, but after two wins was 2nd in Stockholm (to Adam Kszczot) and in Zürich. Kszczot, 7th Zürich and 3rd C.Cup, won the European title and was 6-3 against his compatriot Marcin Lewandowski, but the latter was only 5th at the Europeans when, even more surprisingly, Bosse faded to 8th. US champion Duane Solomon was 1-1 and Bosse 2-1 against Cheruiyot, who was 3-1 v Lewandowski but was only 4th in the CG and Africans. Completing the ranking contenders were Taoufik Makhloufi, 3rd at the Africans, and Yeimar López, who each ran two sub-1:44 times, and André Olivier (3rd CG).

Most times sub-1:44.8: Lewandowski 6, Aman 5+1i, Amos, Kszczot 5; Rudisha, Bosse 4; Cheruiyot, Solomon, Souleiman, Job Kinyor 3.

1. Amos, 2. Aman, 3. Rudisha, 4 Souleiman, 5. Kszczot, 6. Bosse, 7. Cheruiyot, 8. Lewandowski, 9. Makhloufi, 10. Solomon

1500 Metres

SILAS KIPLAGAT BEAT Asbel Kiprop 4-3 in 2014 taking their rivalry to Kiplagat 17 Kiprop 12 at 1500m/1M from 2010 to 2014 (plus 1-0 at 3000m). They finished 1st Kiplagat 3:27.64 and 2nd Kiprop 3:28.45 with 18-year-old Ronald Kwemoi 3rd in a world junior record 3:28.81 in Monaco in the three fastest times of the year. Ayanleh Souleiman was 4th in that race in 3:29.58, but he beat Kiprop 5-3 overall for second in the rankings to Kiplagat, who had a 4-2 win-loss advantage over him. Kiplagat won four times and was 2nd five times in his ten races, Souleiman won the World Indoor title and four out of nine outdoors, including the African and Continental Cup races, in both of which Kiprop was 2nd, and Kiprop won three of ten races. The new star Kwemoi won his first five races including the Kenyan title (when he improved from 3:42.25 to 3:34.3) and was 2nd at the Commonwealth Games and 3rd at the African Championships. Also under 3:30 this year for seven men in all were 5th to 7th at Monaco, Abdelaaati Iguider, Aman Wote and Nick Willis (in an Oceania record). Wote was the best of these as he beat Iguider 5-2 and was also 4-3 against Commonwealth champion James Magut. Elijah Manangoi, Magut, Collins Cheboi and Vincent Kibet were 2nd to 5th at the Kenyan Champs and while Manangoi was only 12th at the CG, overall Magut was 5-2 v Cheboi, who was 3-2 v Kibet. Taoufik Makhloufi was 4th in Doha in May behind Kiprop, Kiplagat and Souleiman and ahead of Magut and Wote, but then was 11th in Eugene and 9th in Rome before a major win in the DL final in Brussels, just beating Kiplagat with Souleiman, Cheboi, Wote, Homiyu Tesfaye, Henrik Ingebrigtsen and Vincent Kibet following in 3rd to 8th. In very slow races Mahiedine Mekhissi-Benabbad and Ingebrigtsen were 1-2 at the Europeans (with Tesfaye 5th) and 3-4 at the Continental Cup behind Souleiman and Kiprop. Willis (3rd CG) was 6th in the latter. Matt Centrowitz beat Ingebrigtsen 3-2.

Most times sub-3:34 or 3:51M: Kiplagat 8, Wote 7, Souleiman, Iguider, Cheboi 6, Kiprop, Ingebrigtsen 4, Magut, Centrowitz, Mekonnen Gebremedhin, Tesfaye, Kibet, Johan Cronje 3.

1. Kiplagat, 2. Souleiman, 3. Kiprop, 4. Kwemoi, 5. Wote, 6. Iguider, 7. Magut, 8. Cheboi, 9. Makhloufi, 10. Kibet

3000 Metres/2 Miles

CALEB NDIKU WAS unbeaten. He won his three indoor competitions, including the World Indoors, and ran the year's fastest time outdoors with 7:31.66 at Ostrava before taking the slowly run Continental Cup race. Galen Rupp, later 4th at the World Indoors, set a North American indoor 2 miles record of 8:07.41 at Boston.

5000 Metres

CALEB NDIKU WAS third behind Muktar Edris (12:54.83) and Thomas Longosiwa in the year's fastest 5000m race in Stockholm, but had a clear case for top ranking with wins at the Commonwealth Games, African Champs and DL final in Zürich; he also had three of the top eleven times of the year (in which only four men beat 13 minutes). Yenew Alamirew faded to 5th at the Africans and 12th in Zürich, but before then had three wins and three second places, four of them under 13:05, and was 4-1 v Longosiwa, 4-2 v Edwin Soi and 2-1 v Galen Rupp, who were the other men with the best series of times. Edris was 2nd in Zürich but had been 6th in Marrakech and 8th in Saint-Denis in a race won by Soi from Alamirew, Paul Tanui and Rupp, as they ran the 4th to 7th fastest times of the year. Edris was 2-1 v Longosiwa and Rupp, Rupp 3-1 v Longosiwa and Soi, and Longosiwa 4-2 v Soi. Isiah Koech was beaten 4-0 v Soi, but had an excellent championship record with 2nd at Commonwealth Games and Africans and 1st at the Continental Cup. Augustine Choge, who also won in Berlin, John Kipkoech and NCAA champion Lawi Lalang, who was 6th at Saint-Denis and Zürich, were 1-2-3 at Heusden. Mo Farah had only two races at 5000m, he won in Portland in 13:23.42 and then took his third successive European title in a time outside 14 minutes.

Most times sub 13:08: Ndiku, Alamirew, Rupp, Longosiwa 4, Soi 3

1. Ndiku, 2. Alamirew, 3. Edris, 4. Rupp, 5. Longosiwa, 6. Soi, 7. Koech, 8. Choge, 9. Kipkoech, 10. Tanui

10,000 Metres

THERE WAS ALL too little action at this distance, with, again, no 10,000m at the Van Damme Memorial in Brussels. The top four and sixth best times came at the Prefontaine Classic in Eugene. Winner Galen Rupp in a North American record 26:44.26 was also US champion. After him Kenyans took the next ten places on the world lists, including five at Eugene: Paul Tanui, winner at Kita-Kyushu, Bidan Karoki, also 3rd at Kobe, Stephen Sambu, no other races, Emmanuel Bett, 7th Kenyan Champs, and Kenneth Kipkemoi, no other races. Seventh was El Hassan El Abbassi, later the Asian Games winner. Moses Kipsiro won a close Commonwealth Games final in 27:56.11 from Josphat Bett, Cam Levins and Peter Kirui, but is hard to rank with no other races. Bett and Kirui were 1-2 at the Kenyan Champs and were 3rd and 6th at the African Champs, when the winner was Nguse Tesfaldet (no other races). William Sitonik and Edward Waweru were 1-2 and under 27:30 at Kobe, and each had further wins in Japan, while Sitonik was 5th at the Kenyan Champs, and another Japanese-based Kenyan was Jeremiah Thuku, 2nd in both Kita-Kyushu and Abashiri, where he beat Waweru into 3rd as the winner was James Mwangi. Mo Farah won his second European title but his 28:08.11 put him 66th on the world list.

1. Rupp, 2. Tanui, 3. Karoki, 4. Kipsiro, 5. Bett, 6. Waweru, 7. Sitonik, 8. Sambu, 9. Thuku, 10. Levins

Half Marathon

THE 1 HOUR standard was bettered by 31 men, headed by Abreham Cheroben with 58:48 at Valencia in October after he had been second to Leonard Komon in Berlin in March, both running 59:14. Geoffrey Kamworor won the World title in Copenhagen in March with 59:08; he was followed there by Samuel Tsegay (who had won the Eritrean title in 59:42), Guye Adola and the five-time world champion Zersenay Tadese. Bidan Karoki, winner in Philadelphia and Lisbon, ran two sub-1 hour times and he had a third major win with 60:02 in Gifu. Other major race winners included Lelisa Desisa at Ra's Al-Khaymah, and Mo Farah in the Great North Run, when he just held off Mike Kigen, both men timed at 60:00. Busiest racer was Richard Mengist with five times between 60:11 and 61:06. Eight men under the hour in Ra's Al-Khaymah in February was a record, but was beaten when nine men did so at New Delhi in November, Adola winning from Kamrorer.

Marathon

DENNIS KIMETTO DID not finish at Boston but he was ready for Berlin and there set the sixth successive world record on the course, taking 26 sec off the official mark set the previous year by by Wilson Kipsang, with Emmanuel Mutai also inside the old mark at 2:03:13. For Mutai this was a return to form after he had been only 8th in London, nearly four minutes behind the top two, Kipsang (who also won in New York) and Stanley Biwott. Three men ran two sub-2:06 marathons: Eliud Kipchoge won in Rotterdam in 2:05:00 and in Chicago 2:04:11, Dickson Chumba won in Tokyo in 2:05:42 and was 3rd in Chicago in 2:04:31, and Kenenisa Bekele won in 2:05:04 on his debut at the distance on Paris and was 4th in Chicago in 2:05.51. Second in Chicago in 2:04:28 was Sammy Kitwara who had been 3rd in 2:06:30 in Tokyo, where 2nd was Tadesse Tola, who went on to win in Warsaw. Tsegaye Kebede was 3rd in London, but only 9th in Berlin. Tsegaye Mekonnen was sixth fastest with his Dubai win in 2:04:32 with Markos Geneti 2nd, and this pair went on to 5th London and 8th Boston respectively. Yuki Kawauchi ran a record 13 marathons sub 2:20 (2:09:36 to 2:16:41) and won four of them.

1. Kimetto, 2. Kipchoge, 3. Kipsang.
4. E Mutai, 5. Chumba, 6. Kitwara, 7. Bekele,
8. Biwott, 9, Tola, 10. Kebede

3000 Metres Steeplechase

JULIUS BIRECH STEPPED up from being ranked eighth in 2013 to be clearly top this year. He had six DL wins and after several near misses succeeded in his bid to break 8 minutes in the DL final in Brussels where his 7:58.41 took him to 10th on the world all-time list. There was the usual Kenyan 1-2-3 at the Commonwealth Games, but Birech was surprisingly beaten by Jonathan Ndiku, gaining revenge at the African Champs with the great Ezekiel Kemboi third in both races. Mahiedine Mekhissi-Benabbad had only three steeplechase competitions, but to my mind merits second ranking. He won at Sotteville and was 2nd in Brussels. Yes he took his short off and was disqualified at the Europeans, but he finished well clear of the field. Evan Jager was again the US champion and was 3rd in Brussels and second to Birech at the Continental Cup. Kenyans then dominate the lists, with Ndiku, 2nd at the Kenyan Champs to Birech, 1-1 v Conseslus Kipruto. Outside the championships, Kemboi did not finish in Rome and was 15th in Brussels but was a fine winner in Doha in 8:04.12 ahead of Brimin Kipruto, Paul Kipsiele Koech, Birech, Hillary Yego. Gilbert Kirui and Abel Mutai. Win-loss helps to sort them out: C Kipruto 3-1 v B Kipruto, who was 4-2 v Yego, who was 6-2 v Koech. Dan Huling, US 2nd, was a fine 4th in Brussels, ahead of four of those top Kenyans.

Most times under 8:15: Birech 10, Koech 4, Jager, Yego, Ndiku, B Kipruto 3.

1. Birech, 2. Mekhissi-Benabbad, 3. Jager,
4. Ndiku, 5. C Kipruto, 6. B Kipruto, 7. Yego,
8. Kemboi, 9. Koech, 10. Huling

110 Metres Hurdles

THERE WERE JUST three sub-13 second times in 2014: one each by Hansle Parchment, Pascal Martinot-Lagarde and Ronnie Ash, but Martinot-Lagarde also had another eight times at 13.13 or better (so 9 of top 19 times). Although he slipped to 3rd at the European Team and European Championships he was clearly the world number one, sweeping through to victory in 9 of his 16 competitions, most notably with his 12.95 at Monaco in the midst of winning the last five DL races. He beat European champion Sergey Shubenkov 7-3 and while Shubenkov's best was 13.13, he had a splendidly consistent season as indeed did the European silver medallist William Sharman. Orlando Ortega had 7 of the top 19 times but started with some moderate runs before ending in fine style, including 2nd in Monaco and at the DL final in Brussels; he was 2-2 v Shubenkov. Parchment's season ended through injury in mid-July and, although he beat Ortega and Oliver 3-0, he was beaten 2-0 by Sharman and 3-2 by Andrew Riley, who beat Sharman for the Commonwealth title. Devon Allen was the most exciting newcomer and the American Footballer excelled to win both NCAA and US titles, but did not compete outside the US so is hard to rank. In the US Champs he was followed by Ryan Wilson. David Oliver and Aleec Harris (2nd NCAA) with Ash a heavy faller. Riley was 2-1 v Oliver, who did not match his 2013 form but was very consistent in the 13.21 to 13.38 range in all but one of his finals and was 5-3 v Wilson, while Ash, 2nd to Shubenkov in the Continental Cup, possibly just had the edge on overall form. Harris was 2-1 v Wilson and Xie Wenjun, 4th Continental Cup and 1st Asian Games, beat Wilson 2-0. The last two world record holders Aries Merritt and Dayron Robles had bests of 13.27 and 13.29 respectively for 17= and 19= on the world list.

Indoors US champion Omo Osaghae won the World Indoor title in 7.45 from Martinot-Lagarde 7.46 and Garfield Darien 7.47, and Martinot-Lagarde had five of the 9 times at 7.50 or better, sharing the world lead with 7.45.

Most times under 13.30: Martinot-Lagarde 16, Shubenkov 10, Sharman 9+3w, Oliver 7+1w, Ortega 7, Harris 5+2w, Wilson 5+1w, Parchment 5, Ash, Riley, Wayne Davis 4, Yordan O'Farrill 3.

1. Martinot-Lagarde, 2. Shubenkov, 3. Ortega, 4. Ash, 5. Riley, 6. Oliver, 7. Sharman, 8. Parchment, 9. Allen, 10. Harris

400 Metres Hurdles

THE FASTEST OF the year, 48.03 by Javier Culson in New York, was the slowest world lead for 39 years. The top three men were closely matched. Culson was 4-3 v Cornel Fredericks and 4-4 v Michael Tinsley with Tinsley 4-2 v Fredericks. Tinsley's record was let down by falling in his heat at the US Champs and placing only 7th at the Continental Cup, which was won by Fredericks with Kariem Hussein 2nd and Culson 3rd. Culson and Tinsley each had three wins in Diamond League races, but Fredericks won the final in Zürich from Tinsley and Culson. Hussein made a huge advance from a pre-season best of 49.61 with new bests of 49.33 and 49.08 in June, then 48.96 to win the European title, 48.70 for 4th at Zürich and 48.47 in Marrakech. European runner-up Rasmus Mägi also made a big advance from 49.19 to 48.54 and multi-event great Ashton Eaton made a starting debut at the event, bringing his times down steadily to 48.69 in Glasgow. He was 1-1 against Félix Sánchez, 37 in August, who was beaten 2-0 by Mägi. World champion Jehue Gordon did not get near to his best, but was 2nd to Fredericks at the Commonwealth Games (with Jeffery Gibson 3rd) and 3-0 v Mägi and 2-3 v Sánchez. Roxroy Cato started well and won the Jamaican title in 48.48, for fifth on the world list, but did not beat 49 secs in Europe and was disqualified in his CG heat, and Johnny Dutch won the US title but did not have much to back this up. Overall standards were well down on usual levels.

Most times under 49.00: Culson 10, Tinsley, Fredericks 7; Gibson 4, Hussein, Mägi 3.

1. Culson, 2. Fredericks, 3. Tinsley, 4. Hussein, 5. Mägi, 6. Eaton, 7. Sánchez, 8. Gordon, 9. Cato, 10. Gibson

High Jump

AFTER MANY YEARS in the doldrums, men's high jump is back as a highly competitive and top class event. Bohdan Bondarenko (12) and Mutaz Essa Barshim (5) had several attempts to better Javier Sotomayor's 2.45 world record. Bondarenko (2.42 best) had five and Barshim (2.43) four competitions at 2.40 or higher and also successful with this feat were Ivan Ukhov three (2 indoors, 1 out), and Derek Drouin, who equalled the North American record, Andriy Protsenko and Aleksey Dmitrik (indoors) one each. Although Barshim looked perhaps the man most likely to get that 2.45-plus jump at his best, his outdoor record of 6 wins, two 2nd and two 4ths plus four indoor wins was not as good as 10 wins and 3 seconds by Bondarenko, who lost only to Barshim, but beat him four times; each won three DL events, Bondarenko the European and Continental Cup and Barshim at the Asian Games. Barshim beat Ukhov on count-back at 2.38 for the World Indoor title after Ukhov had tied the European indoor record at 2.42. Ukhov started outdoors with 2.41 at Doha (with Drouin and Erik Kynard tied for 2nd and Barshim 4th, all at 2.37), but was a little inconsistent after that although taking European 3rd and Continental Cup 2nd; he was, however 5-2 v Drouin, who in turn was 6-2 (1 tie) v US champion Kynard. Protsenko improved from a pre-2014 2.32 to 2.40 and was third at the World Indoors and runner-up at the Europeans. Dmitrik had one 2.30 outdoors, far below his indoor form, when he cleared 2.40 behind Ukhov at Arnstadt. Also best indoors were Daniyil Tsyplakov and Marco Fassinotti, 5th and 6th at the World Indoors and both exceeding 2.30 three times. Outdoors they were 5th and 7= at the Europeans but while Fassinotti had bests of 2.30 and 2.28, Tsyplakov had 2.33, 2.32 to win the Russian title and another 2.30. Zhang Guowei was 7th at the World Indoors, had a best of 2.34 and won the Asian Games title with 2.33. There Naoto Tobe was only fifth but he had a consistent season with four competition at 2.30 or more. Tobe was 3rd at Eberstadt behind Barshim and Drouin with 4th Ukhov and 5th Jaroslav Bába, who was 4th at the Europeans and returned to the rankings after missing two years.

Most competitions over 2.35/2.30m (outdoors+in): Bondarenko 11/23, Barshim 9+3i/11+4i, Drouin 4/11, Ukhov 3+8i/10+8i, Kynard 3/11+6i, Protsenko 2+1i/7+3i, Tobe 4, Tsyplakov 3+3i, Zhang 3+1i, Bába 3, Dmitrik 1+5i, Fassinotti 1+3i.

1. Bondarenko, 2. Barshim, 3. Ukhov, 4. Drouin, 5. Kynard, 6. Protsenko, 7. Zhang (10), 8. Bába (-), 9. Tsyplakov (7), 10. Tobe (-). – Dmitrik (8), Fassinotti (9) (Including indoors).

Pole Vault

RENAUD LAVILLENIE WAS top for the fifth successive year. As documented in the introduction he set the absolute world record at 6.16 indoors and remained a class apart from the rest, winning six DL events and at the Continental Cup. Indeed world standards were well down on recent years, not helped by the absence for nearly the whole year of his closest challenger Björn Otto, the inability of Raphael Holzdeppe to do better than 5.53 and the loss of form of Malte Mohr outdoors, although Mohr had jumped 5.90 indoors and was 3rd to Konstadínos Filippídis and Jan Kudlicka at the World Indoors, all clearing 5.80 which was better than anything they managed outdoors. After Lavillenie the best series of marks outdoors was four over 5.80 by Mark Hollis and one 5.80+ clearance was achieved outdoors by Piotr Lisek 5.82, Xue Changrui, Pawel Wojciechowski and Robert Sobera 5.80, but the challengers for rankings from two downwards had very mixed form. For instance Filippídis, who had just one jump at 5.70 before a series of marks 5.60-5.65, beat Hollis 3-1 and Xue, the Asian Games champion and 2nd Continental Cup, 4-0 and Xue was 3-2 v Hollis. Wojciechowski, 3-4 v Hollis, was 2nd at the Europeans where Kudlicka and Kévin Ménaldo tied for 3rd, all at 5.70, and Filippídis only 7th. Amidst all mixed form, one athlete with a near perfect record was Sam Kendricks, who won all his six competitions outdoors including NCAA and US (5.75) titles (the first to do this double since 1996), and five of six indoors, his one loss being to Shawn Barber at the NCAAs. Lisek was 6th but Sobera nh at the Europeans and they went 5-5 outdoors (Sobera 1-0 indoors). Thiago Braz da Silva was another best indoors, 5.76 and 4th at the World Indoors, to outdoors 5.73 before he broke his hand. Steve Lewis beat Luke Cutts on count-back for the Commonwealth title, but Cutts had been much better indoors, with a British record 5.83.

Most competitions over 5.70m (outdoors/in): Lavillenie 14/6i, Hollis 7, Wojciechowski 5/2i, Kudlicka 3/4i, Ménaldo 3/2i, Dilla 3, Filippídis, Mohr, Lisek 1/5i, Sobera 1/2i.

1. Lavillenie, 2. Filippídis, 3. Hollis (5), 4. Wojciechowski (8), 5. Xue Changrui (6), 6. Kudlicka (4), 7. Kendricks (9), 8. Ménaldo (-), 9. Lisek (10), 10. Sobera (-). – Mohr (3), Braz da Silva (7). (Including indoors).

Long Jump

GREG RUTHERFORD 8.51 and Jeffrey Henderson 8.52w (to win the US title) produced the 8.50 plus jumps of 2014. They met twice, Henderson winning 8.31 to 8.29 at Lausanne, one of nine successive wins (including three in DL meetings and all over 8m) that he had at the start of the outdoor season, and Rutherford 4th with 8.04 and Henderson 5th with 8.01 at the Birmingham DL. Rutherford took major honours by winning at the Commonwealth Games and European Champs and in all won 5 of his 9 outdoor competitions; Henderson, who was poor at the World Indoors, ended his season early due to a heel bruise. Next on the world list were Christian Reif with 8.49, but with a next best of 8.20 and 8th at the Europeans, and Li Jinzhe, but his 8.47 was followed by a next best of 8.17 (and 8.23 for 2nd at the World Indoors). Still Li was 2-0 v Loúis Tsátoumas, the European silver medallist and the overall standard in depth was modest. Ignisious Gaisah was as usual inconsistent but he won at the Continental Cup and had a good win-loss record, including 6-1 v Zarck Visser (2nd CG, 1st African, 3 C.Cup) and 3-2 v Khotso Mokoena, who won the DL final and was 6-3 v Visser. Third and fourth at the Europeans were Kafétien Gomis and Eusebio Cáceres, but while Gomis had little other form Cáceres was 2-1 v Gaisah and 1-0 v Mokoena. Mauro da Silva won the World Indoor title with 8.28 (from Li and Michal Tornéus 8.21) but had just one 8m jump (8.08w) outdoors. Will Claye was 2nd at the Continental Cup and Christian Taylor 3rd at the DL final, but both competed sparingly at this event, and next best Americans were perhaps Mike Hartfield, 3rd US Champs and 4th DL final, and Tyron Stewart, US champion indoors and 4th outdoors. The 2013 1-2 Aleksandr Menkov and Luis Rivera competed at a lower level in 2014.

Most competitions over 8.10m (outdoors/in): Henderson 7+1w, Rutherford 5, Tsátoumas 4+3i+1w, Reif 3+1i, Hartfield, Visser, Gao Xinglong 3, Stewart 1+2i+1w, Claye 1+2w.

1. Henderson (3), 2. Rutherford (1), 3. Li Jinzhe (2), 4. Tsátoumas, 5. Gaisah, 6. Cáceres, 7. Mokoena, 8. Reif (9), 9. Hartfield, 10. Visser (-), - Tornéus (8), da Silva (10)

Triple Jump

PEDRO PICHARDO HEADED the world list with 17.76 at Havana in February and also that month won the Cuban title with 17.71, but those were his only outdoor competitions, although he competed three times indoors including 3rd at the World Indoors behind Lyukman Adams and Ernesto Revé. Outdoors there were 15 performances at 17.35 or more, and of these Will Claye and Benjamin Compaoré had four each and Christian Taylor three. Claye jumped 17.75 in beating Taylor for the US title and had a 4-3 advantage over his former University of Florida team-mate, With the best series of marks and three DL wins Claye has a major claim for top ranking, but, after starting the year far behind Claye at Eugene (8th 16.57 to Claye's winning 17.66), Compaoré came though with a splendid series of performances: winning the European title with 17.46, 2nd at Zürich in the DL final with 17.46 (Taylor won with 17.51, Claye 3rd 17.39) and 1st at the Continental Cup 17.48. Claye was third in the last two and down 3-1 to Compaoré overall. Taylor beat Compaoré 2-1.

Revé's season tailed off after starting with 17.50 and 17.58 in February, but other Cubans showed form throughout the year – 16 year-old Lázaro Martínez started with a world youth record of 17.24 and over five months later won the World Junior title with 17.13, and Alexis Copello was consistent at 17m. Khotso Mokoena, after a tentative start, competing at the event for the first time since 2005, was over 17m in winning at the Commonwealth Games and African Champs and 2nd at the Continental Cup with a South African record 17.35. He was also 4th at the DL final in Zurich. Adams, Aleksey Fyodorov, Yoann Rapinier and Marian Oprea were 2nd to 5th at the Europeans, Tosin Oke was Commonwealth and African second plus fourth at the Continental Cup, and fifth there was Cao Shuo who won at the Asian Games.

Most competitions over 17.00: Claye 7, Compaoré, Taylor 6; Martínez 4+2w, Copello 4+1w, Adams 3+2i, Revé 3+1w, Mokoena 3, Fyodorov 2+1w, Oprea 3i.

1. Compaoré, 2. Claye, 3. Taylor, 4. Mokoena (5), 5. Pichardo (4), 6. Revé, 7. Martínez (8), 8. Adams (7), 9. Copello, 10. Fyodorov. (Including indoors).

Shot

TWO MEN EXCEEDED 22m in 2014: Ryan Whiting did so twice indoors, with 22.23 for the US title and 22.05 for the World Indoors, and Joe Kovacs won the US title outdoors with 22.03. Whiting's form fell away outdoors with just one win in 12 competitions. The top two men throughout the year were David Storl, 22 wins in 28 competitions, 2nd at the World Indoors and DL final and winner at the Europeans and Continental Cup, and Reese Hoffa, winner of 10 of his 17 events, four in the DL, including the final. Hoffa was 3-2 v Storl and 9-2 v Kovacs although beaten by Kovacs and Kurt Roberts at the US Champs. Hard to rank are Christian Cantwell, who had four big wins in the 21.33 to 21.85 range followed by 3rd at Eugene with 21.38, but then four competitions declining from 20.38 to 18.92, and Ryan Crouser, who was unbeaten in four competitions indoors and four outdoors, winning NCAA titles indoors and out, but he competed only in the USA and did not meet throwers outside collegiate competition. Cantwell was beaten 5-2 by Tomasz Majewski, all those losses in the second half of his season. O'Dayne Richards and Tom Walsh took gold and silver at the Commonwealth Games after Walsh had made a breakthrough to take the World Indoor bronze. Richards, who improved from 20.97 in 2013 to 21.81, beat Walsh, up from 20.61 to 21.26i, 3-2 outdoors (01-1 indoors) and both were closely matched with other top men, Richards 4-1 v Majewski and 2-3 v Cantwell; Walsh 3-3 v Whiting, 4-4 v Kovacs, 6-1 v Majewski etc.. Amongst the Americans, Kovacs was 5-2 v Roberts, who was 4-1 v Whiting but 0-5 to Cantwell, so overall the situation was very muddled. Borja Vivas and Majewski were 2nd and 3rd at the Europeans.

Most competitions over 20.80: Storl 19+8i, Kovacs 12+2i, Hoffa 12, Roberts 5+1i, Cantwell 5, Whiting 4+5i, Crouser 4+2i, Majewski, Walsh 4+1i, Richards 4, Clarke, Vivas 3, Ivanov 1+3i.

1. Storl, 2. Hoffa, 3. Kovacs, 4. Richards (5), 5. Walsh (6), 6. Cantwell (7), 7. Roberts (9), 8. Whiting (4), 9. Crouser (10), 10. Majewski (8). (Including indoors).

Discus

ROBERT HARTING HAD another great season to rank top for the sixth successive year. His 13 wins included retaining his European title and he lost just twice: 4th in the indoor event in Berlin in March and 2nd in Halle with 68.28 to Piotr Malachowski's yearly best of 69.26. Malachowski beat Gerd Kanter 8-1, the last being as Kanter was 2nd, Robert Urbanek 3rd and Malachowski 4th at the Europeans with Viktor Butenko fifth. The same men took the top four places at the DL final in Brussels, where the order was Harting, Malachowski, Kanter, Urbanek, Martin Wierig (EC 11th), Philip Milanov, Vikas Gowda and Benn Harradine; overall DL wins went 4 to Harting and 3 to Malachowski. Wierig was 5-3 v Urbanek and both men were beaten in their one meeting with Jorge Fernández, who was 2nd in the Continental Cup. Ehsan Hadadi beat Gowda at the Asian Games and Gowda won at the Commonwealth Games with Harradine fourth. My rankings have 1-2-3-5-6-8 in the same places as 2013.

Most competitions over 65m: Harting 15, Malachowski 12, Kanter 10, Wierig 6, Urbanek, Fernández, Frank Casañas, Harradine 3.

1. Harting, 2. Malachowski, 3. Kanter, 4. Fernández, 5. Wierig, 6. Urbanek, 7. Hadadi, 8. Gowda, 9. Harradine, 10. Butenko

Hammer

THERE WERE 19 performances over 80m in 2014, of these 9 were by Krisztián Pars and 6 by Pavel Fajdek with 3 by Dilshod Nazarov and 1 by Mostafa Al-Gamal (African record 81.27). Although Fajdek had the year's best of 83.48 and they went 5-5 in their clashes (plus one to Pars in the exhibition at Wroclaw), Pars is top ranked for the fourth successive year as he beat Fajdek into 2nd and 3rd places in the European Champs and Continental Cup; Pars won 15 times and was 2nd 4 times, Fajdek won 11 with two 2nds and 4 thirds. My rankings reflect the order of the top seven in IAAF World Hammer Challenge with just one exception in that I put Pavel Krivitskiy a place ahead of Marcel Lomnicky with a 3-1 win-loss advantage and 4th to 7th at the Europeans. Lomnicky was 3-1 against European bronze medallist Sergey Litvinov. Al-Gamal improved his best during the year by 3.08m and he won the African title and was 2nd at the Continental Cup, at which 4th was Nazarov who went on to win at the Asian Games and was 4-1 v Al-Gamal. Primoz Kozmus again competed sparingly, but was 6th at the Europeans, a place behind Szymon Ziólkowski and two ahead of David Söderberg, who beat Ziólkowski 2-1. German champion Markus Esser did not compete after July so missed the Europeans but was 5-0 v Ziólkowski.

Most competitions over 80m/78.50m: Pars 9/17, Fajdek 6/14, Nazarov 3/8, Al-Gamal 1/7, Krivitskiy 4, Litvinov 3.

1. Pars, 2. Fajdek, 3. Nazarov, 4. Al-Gamal, 5. Krivitskiy, 6. Lomnicky, 7. Litvinov, 8. Kozmus, 9. Söderberg, 10. Esser

Javelin

IHAB ABDELRAHMAN EL SAYED caused a shock when he improved his best from 83.94 to 89.21 in the first Diamond League meeting of the year for javelin at Shanghai. That remained the year's best mark and the Egyptian continued in fine form; his eight competitions over 80m included a win in his final event, the Continental Cup. Last year's top man Vitezslav Vesely was 2nd in that event with Keshorn Walcott 3rd and Julius Yego 4th. The man with the best set of marks was Tero Pitkämäki who regains the top ranking he had in 2005 and 2007; he had a positive win-loss record against all his rivals, but only one DL win to 2 each by Abdelrahman and Thomas Röhler, and he was 3rd at the Europeans behind Antti Ruuskanen and Vesely. Röhler was only 12th at the Europeans, but finished very strongly with six wins in his last eight competitions including at the DL final in Zürich, where he threw a pb 87.63 to win over Walcott (TTO record 85.77), Pitkämäki, Yego, Vesely, Ruuskanen and Abdelrahman. Röhler was 3-2 v Abdelrahman and 4-3 v Vesely. Yego beat Walcott at the Commonwealth Games and Abdelrahman at the African Champs and was 4-1 v Ruuskanen and 3-3 v Walcott. Zhao Qinggang came to the Asian Games with a best of 83.14 (2013) but proceeded to throw Chinese records of 85.29 and 86.50 before a mighty final round 89.15. But with 81.18 Zhao's only other 80m throw of the year he ranks behind two Europeans with nine and twelve 80m competitions: Dmitriy Tarabin (5th EC) and Ari Mannio, with Lassi Etelätalo and Andres Hoffmann, 4th and 9th EC, close to a ranking.

Most competitions over 84m/82.50m: Pitkämäki 10/12, Abdelrahman 7/9, Röhler 6/9, Yego 5/9, Ruuskanen 4/10, Vesely 4/8, Walcott 3/7, Tarabin -/4.

1. Pitkämäki, 2. Abdelrahman, 3. Röhler, 4. Vesely, 5. Yego, 6. Walcott, 7. Ruuskanen, 8. Tarabin, 9. Mannio, 10. Zhao Qinggang.

Decathlon

ASHTON EATON TOOK a year off from decathlon, and that left the Olympic runner-up Trey Hardee to take top ranking with his wins at Götzis 8518 and US Champs 8599. The top scores of the year, however were achieved at the European Championships by Andrey Kravchenko 8616 and Kevin Mayer 8521 with four more men over 8450: Ilya Shkurenyov, Eelco Sintnicolaas, Arthur Abele and Kai Kazmirek. Kravchenko did not finish his only other decathlon – at Götzis, where 2nd was Kazmirek, 3rd Rico Freimuth and 4th Yordanis García. Freimuth also had an important win at Ratingen from Mayer and Abele and with 7th at the Europeans won the IAAF World Challenge from Sintnicolaas, García and Oleksiy Kasyanov (1st Kladno, 8th Europeans); only three of the world top ten competed in the minimum three decathlons needed to get into the prize money for this. Mikk Pahapill won at Talence from Kasyanov and García. Larbi Bouraada won the African title, Damian Warner the Commonwealth, and Keisuke Ushiro, who won his three other decathlons, the Asian Games.

The top indoor heptathlon scores came at the World Indoors at which Eaton had a clear win with 6632, just 13 short of his world record, from Kravchenko 6303 and Thomas Van Der Plaetsen 6250, Sintnicolaas was 4th at 6198, having scored 6242 to win the Dutch title.

1. Hardee, 2. Kravchenko, 3. Mayer, 4. Kazmirek, 5. Shkurenyov, 6. Sintnicolaas, 7. Freimuth, 8. Abele, 9. García, 10. Ushiro

20 Kilometres Walk

JUST AS IN 2013 it was just about impossible to produce a definitive ranking list for this event with conflicting evidence of form by the leading walkers. The World Cup race, with great depth of performance despite heavy rain, was the most significant, but the European Championships also featured many of the top men and those who did both included Ruslan Dmytrenko (1st WC, 4th EC), Miguel Ángel López (5th and 1st), Aleksandr Ivanov (dq and 2nd) and Denis Strelkov (30th and 3rd). Dmytrenko, who won the IAAF World Race Walking Challenge, also won at Lugano from Cai Zelin, who went on to 2nd World Cup and 4th Asian Games, and Matej Tóth, who had two more important wins but was then only 28th at the World Cup. Further top World Cup places went to: 3 Andrey Ruzavin (4th Russian winter), 4 Yusuke Suzuki (Japanese champion and 2nd at both Asian Champs and Games), 6 Wang Zhen (1st Asian Games), 7 Igor Hlavan (11th Lugano), 8 Omar Segura, 9 Eiki Takahashi (7th Asian Games). Ivanov was dq at the World Cup but won the Russian winter race from Strelkov and Pyotr Trofimov. Suzuki had the best depth of times with four at 1:21:01 or better, and he had two sub-1:20s as also did López, Wang and Strelkov. Towards the end of the year came the news of the possible drugs dq of Ruzavin.

1. Dmytrenko, 2. Suzuki, 3. Cai Zelin, 4. López, 5. Wang Zhen, 6. Ivanov, 7. Strelkov, 8. Takahashi, 9. Tóth, 10. Kim Hyun-sub; drugs dq? Ruzavin (8th).

50 Kilometres Walk

YOHANN DINIZ SET a marvellous world record of 3:32:33 to win the European title by almost four minutes from Matej Tóth. The Russians Ivan Noskov and Mikhail Ryzhov followed in reverse order from their 1-2 at the World Cup, breaking 3:40 in both races. Jared Tallent and Yuriy Andronov followed as 3rd and 4th at the World Cup, both in their only 50ks of the year, before Andronov's drugs disqualification, leaving Aleksey Bartsaykin 4th. Twice faster then them, however, was Takayuki Tanii, who won the Japanese Champs in 3:41:32 and the Asian Games in 3:40:19. Also faster at 3:42:26 to win the Russian title was Aleksandr Yargunkin, but he was 14th at the Europeans, so ranking higher are the 5th Ivan Banzeruk (also 9th World Cup) and 6th Igor Hlavan. Hiroki Arai and Horacio Nava 2nd as a guest in the Russian Champs, also made the top ten on times

1. Diniz, 2. Tóth, 3. Ryzhov, 4. Noskov, 5. Tanui, 6. Tallent, 7. Banzeruk, 8. Hlavan, 9. Yargunkin, 10. Arai

Woman Athlete of the Year

I DOUBT THAT there would be much agreement as to the Woman Athlete of the Year for 2014, as there seems to be no obvious single stand-out candidate, but one can start with two women who went through the year undefeated: Caterine Ibargüen at triple jump, headed by 15.31 for 5th on the all-time list, and Valerie Adams at shot, continuing her long winning streak but not at her best this year due to injuries; she was the IAAF Female Athlete of the Year. Perhaps superior to either, although she lost once, was Anita Wlodarczyk, as she won the major events and set a world record 79.58 at the hammer. Also losing just her opening race of the year but otherwise dominant was Kaliese Spencer at 400m hurdles. Setting world records on the road was Florence Kiplagat with 65:12 for half marathon and 61:56 for 20km en route.

Other world leaders who went through the year undefeated at their events but with limited competition were Anisya Kirdyapkina (two at 20k walk) and Katarina Johnson-Thompson (one heptathlon). Dominant forces at their events were Barbora Spotáková, who won 9 times in 10 javelin competitions, Sandra Perkovic, who won 10 of 12 at discus and with 71.08 to win European gold, the world's best discus throw since 1992, and Eunice Sum, with 11 wins in 14 800m competitions, including Commonwealth Games, African Championships and Continental Cup. Genzebe Dibaba had been clearly the star of the indoor season with world indoor records of 3:55.17 for 1500m and 8:16.60 for 3000m and a world best 9:00.48 for 2 miles. She could not match such form outdoors but was still top ranked at 5000m and she set an African record at 2000m.

Adams won all her seven Diamond League competitions and Spencer, Ibargüen and Perkovic achieved six wins.

Selections for World Top Ten

	PJM	TFN	AI
Anita Wlodarczyk	1	1	2
Caterine Ibargüen	2	3	3
Genzebe Dibaba	3	6	6
Valerie Adams	4	2	1
Sandra Perkovic	5	4	4
Kaliese Spencer	6	5	7
Dafne Schippers	7	9	5
Florence Kiplagat	8	-	-
Barbora Spotáková	9	7	8
Eunice Sum	10	8	9
Dawn Harper-Nelson		10	-
Sifan Hassan			10

Note Track & Field News excludes cross-country and road (apart from marathon) races

100 Metres

SHELLY-ANN FRASER-PRYCE HAD been the clear number one in 2013, but after winning the World Indoor 60m title in 6.98 struggled for form outdoors, when her best for 100m was 11.01 for 6th in Monaco, and there are four women who at one time or other looked to be the best. The most majestic was perhaps Blessing Okagbare in the form of mid-season when she won the Commonwealth Games and African titles. Similarly Michelle Lee Ahye looked terrific when she won her first ten races before succumbing to injury, struggling in her heat at the CG and a well-beaten 2nd at the Continental Cup. Murielle Ahouré, 2nd in the Africans and in the DL final at Zurich, was 3-1 v Okagbare, and Tori Bowie made a great breakthrough with DL wins in Rome, New York and Monaco, the last the year's fastest time of 10.80 but she was a non-finisher with a leg injury in Birmingham and could not race thereafter; she was 2-0 v Ahouré. But in the end top ranking goes to an all-time great, Veronica Campbell-Brown, who although she was beaten by 0.18 secs by Okagbare at the CG, ended 2-1 against the Nigerian with wins in the big end-of-season races, Zürich and Continental Cup after earlier winning the Jamaican title and placing 2nd in Monaco. Ahye beat Ahouré 2-0 and Bowie 1-0, while Ahouré was 3-1 v Okagbare. Dafne Schippers won the European title from Myriam Soumaré (7th Monaco) and this pair was 3rd and 5th at the Continental Cup. Bowie was unable to start the final of the US Champs after 10.91 in her semi, and Tianna Bartoletta, who had been injured in 2013, after 10.92 in her semi won the title from Barbara Pierre, but then concentrated more on long jumping at the major meetings. Kerron Stewart with 2nd Jamaicans, 3rd CG and 5th DL final, was 2-2 v Pierre.

Most times under 11.00/11.10: Campbell-Brown 4/8, Ahye 3/6+2w, Okagbare 3/6, Ahouré 2/5, Stewart, Pierre 4+1w, Soumaré 3+1w.

1. Campbell-Brown, 2. Okagbare, 3. Ahye, 4. Bowie, 5. Ahouré, 6. Schippers, 7. Bartoletta, 8. Fraser-Pryce, 9. Soumaré, 10. Stewart

200 Metres

AS IN THE 100m it was pretty close at the top, with the fastest times coming from Allyson Felix 22.03 and Myriam Soumaré 22.11 in the DL final at Brussels and in between them 22.03 by Dafne Schippers in winning the European title. Schippers beat Felix 22.34 to 22.35 in Glasgow while it became 1-1 between them when Schippers was 3rd in Brussels with 22.30. Tori Bowie was fourth fastest from her 22.18 win in Eugene over Blessing Okagbare, and Okagbare also beat Felix 22.32 to 22.34 at Saint-Denis. Felix had two more DL wins, Oslo and Stockholm, and was 2-2 v Okagbare, as the latter was 3rd in Glasgow and 6th in Brussels. Schippers won at the Continental Cup from Joanna Atkins, who, stepping down from 400m, had a solid season including 3rd at the US Champs and 4th in Brussels, Soumaré and Anthonique Strachan. Just three 200m competitions were had by Bowie, who started the year with a best of 23.99 but improved to 22.57 and 22.18 (she was 2-0 v Atkins), and Murielle Ahouré, who was African champion as well as 4th at Eugene and 5th at Oslo. The US 1-2 had been Jeneba Tarmoh and Kimberlyn Duncan, with Shalonda Solomon 4th. Duncan beat Tarmoh 2-1 but was 1-3 down to Strachan. Okagbare was at her best in winning the CG title from the British trio of Jodie Williams, Bianca Williams and Anyika Onuara and Jodie and Bianca, who had been 1st and 2nd at the UK champs, went on place 2nd and 4th at the Europeans with Soumaré 3rd.

Most times under 22.70: Okagbare 10, Schippers 6, Soumaré 5, Atkins 4+1w, Felix, T Williams, Strachan 4; Duncan 3+4w, Solomon. Tarmoh 3+1w.

1. Felix, 2. Schippers, 3. Okagbare, 4. Soumaré, 5. J Williams, 6. Bowie, 7. Atkins, 8. Ahouré, 9. Strachan, 10. Duncan

400 Metres

THERE WERE FIVE sub-50 sec times in 2014, three by Francena McCorory and two by Sanya Richards-Ross; their top times being 49.48 to 49.66 at the US Champs. McCorory, who started by winning US and World titles indoors and ended the year by winning at the Continental Cup from Novlene Williams-Mills, Libania Grenot and Kabunge Mpopo, just takes the top ranking although she was beaten 4-3 by Williams-Mils, but with win-loss advantage of 4-2 v Richards-Ross, and 5-2 v Stephenie Ann McPherson, who beat Williams-Mills for the Commonwealth title. McCorory was only 7th in the DL final in Brussels, won by Richards-Ross from McPherson and Williams-Mills against whom she was 4-2 and 3-3 respectively. Williams-Mills won four DL races, including the first three. With something of a gap after the top four, next come US 3rd placer Natasha Hastings and CG 3rd Christine Day, who were 6th and 7th in Brussels. Faster than either was NCAA champion Courtney Okolo, who ran only in US collegiate races. Grenot was European champion with Olga Zemlyak (4th Brussels, 5th C.Cup) 2nd. 2nd and 3rd at the NCAAs were Phyllis Francis (dq US Champs) and Kendall Baisden, who went on to win the World Junior title. Of last year's 1-2-3, Amantle Montsho had a shock doping failure after finishing 4th at the Commonwealth Games, Christine Ohuruogu a quiet year with a best when 4th at the Europeans, and Antonina Krivoshapka had a baby.

Most times under 50.80: McPherson, McCorory & Williams-Mills 11; Richards-Ross 6, Hastings, Okolo 4, Montsho 3.

1. McCorory, 2. Richards-Ross, 3. Williams-Mills, 4. McPherson, 5. Hastings, 6. Day, 7. Grenot, 8. Okolo, 9. Zemlyak, 10. Francis

800 Metres

EUNICE SUM TOOK the top ranking in 2013 fairly narrowly, but she was the clear choice in 2014, winning 11 of her 14 800m competitions, including the first four DL races, Commonwealth Games, African Championships and Continental Cup. Two athletes, however, ran faster – Ajee' Wilson with 1:57.67 in Monaco ahead of Sum's best of 1:57.92, and the Cuban junior Sally Diago, 1:57.74 in Havana. Sum's other loss was her 3rd in the DL final in Brussels behind Brenda Martinez and Lynsey Sharp, who had also been second at the CG and at the Europeans behind Marina Arzamasova. Arzamasova, 2-2 v Sharp and 1-2 v Wilson, was 4th in Brussels with Janeth Jepkosgei (sf CG and 2nd Africans) 5th and Wilson 9th. Wilson had won the US title from Chanelle Price, who had earlier won the World Indoor title, Molly Beckwith-Ludlow, Maggie Vessey and Martinez, against whom Wilson was 3-2. Yekaterina Poistogova won at the European Teams and was 4th at the European Champs (3rd Joanna Józwik), and Winnie Nanyondo was 3rd at the CG; they were 5th and 3rd at Monaco with 4th Jepkosgei, who beat Beckwith-Ludlow 3-1. Rose Mary

Almanza was 4-2 v Diago, who was beaten by Margaret Wambui for the World Junior title.

Most times under 1:59.8: Sum 9, Sharp, Poistogova 5, Wilson, Beckwith-Ludlow, Almanza 4; Martinez, Jepkosgei, Nanyondo 3.

1. Sum, 2. Wilson, 3. Martinez, 4. Arzamasova,
5. Sharp, 6. Poistogova. 7. Nanyondo,
8. Almanza, 9. Jepkosgei, 10. Beckwith-Ludlow.

1500 Metres

SEVEN WOMEN BROKE 4 minutes outdoors in 2014 as opposed to four in 2013, but Genzebe Dibaba, who had an outdoor best of 4:01.00 (2nd in Stockholm in her only race at the distance), ran the year's fastest time with a world indoor record of 3:55.17 in Karlsruhe. Running three sub-4 times were Abeba Aregawi (including one indoors) and Jennifer Simpson and both had two DL wins as did Sifan Hassan, who beat Aregawi to win the European title. Simpson had a terrific year and ended with big wins in Stockholm and at the DL final in Zürich; she beat Hassan 4-1 and was 3-3 v Aregawi, who had hamstring problems after her strong start to the year that included winning the World Indoor title by a huge margin. The best depth of times came with five women running sub-4 in Eugene, won by Hellen Obiri in 3:57.05 from Aregawi, Faith Kipyegon, Simpson and Hassan, and in Saint-Denis by Hassan in 3:57.00 from Simpson, Obiri, Kipyegon and Shannon Rowbury. Obiri was 4-1 v Kipyegon, but was only 6th at the Commonwealth Games won by Kipyegon from Laura Weightman, who was also 3rd at the Europeans. Rowbury had a solid set of results ending with 2nd in Zürich and at the Continental Cup behind Hassan and ahead of Dawit Seyaum and Obiri. Seyaum won the World Junior title and was 2nd to Obiri at the Africans (Kipyegon 5th). Mimi Belete broke 4:02 in three DL races and was second to Maryam Jamal at the Asian Games. Kibiwot beat Meraf Bahta 2-0.

Most times under 4:04 (or 4:23.6 mile): Simpson, Hassan 7, Aregawi 6+2i, Rowbury 4, Bahta, Belete, Weightman 3.

1. Simpson, 2. Hassan, 3. Aregawi, 4. Obiri,
5. Kipyegon, 6. Rowbury, 7. Seyaum (8),
8. Kibiwot (9), 9. Belete (10), 10. Weightman (-). – G Dibaba (7) (including indoors).

3000 Metres

GENZEBE DIBABA RAN a world indoor best 8:16.60 indoors at Stockholm and a world indoor 2 miles best 9:04.48 at Birmingham followed by the World Indoor 3000m title, but although she won a slow Continental Cup race at the end of the year, she was unable to quite recapture that form outdoors. She was 6th at Doha in 8:26.21 in a marvellous race won by Hellen Obiri in an African record 8:20.68 from Mercy Cherono, Faith Kipyegon, Viola Kibiwot and Almaz Ayana with Irene Jelagat 7th also under 8:30 and the best ever times set for places 6-8. Even better depth of times came at Brussels, where Cherono was the winner in 8:28.95 from Sifan Hassan, Dibaba, Jennifer Simpson and Shannon Rowbury, all under 8:30 and there were best ever times for places 9-18, with 16 women under 8:40 and 14 of the top 22 outdoor performances of the year. Cherono also had DL wins in New York, Lausanne and Birmingham, where she ran a Commonwealth record 9:11.49 for 2 miles ahead of Kibiwot, Irene Jelagat. Dibaba and Betsy Saina. There was also a good 2 miles at Eugene, won by Cherono in 9:13.27 from Kibiwot, Mimi Belete and Shannon Rowbury.

5000 Metres

THE THREE FASTEST times of the year were run at Monaco, by Genzebe, Almaz Ayana and Viola Kibiwot and five more women broke 14:50: Sally Kipyego (in her only 5000m of the year), Betsy Saina, Molly Huddle, Mercy Cherono and Rowbury, so this race had 8 of the top 12 times of the year. The other seven of the top 15 times came at Rome, where the winner was Dibaba 14:34.99 from Ayana, Kibiwot, Cherono, Janet Kisa, Alemitu Heroye (World Junior champion) and Huddle. But this was far from a vintage year for fast times as the championship races were slow: Cherono won at the Commonwealth Games in 15:07.21 from Kisa, Jo Pavey and Margaret Muriuki, Meraf Bahta beat Sifan Hassan for the European title in 15:31.39, and Ayana was African champion in 15:32.72 from Dibaba, Kisa, Muriuki and Cherono. Ayana also won at the Continental Cup in 15:33.32 followed by Joyce Chepkirui and Pavey. So Dibaba takes top ranking by beating Ayana 2-1. Kibiwot beat Cherono 2-0.

Most times under 15:10: Cherono 4, Huddle, Kisa 3.

1. G Dibaba, 2. Ayana, 3. Kibiwot, 4. M Cherono,
5. Kipyego, 6. Saina, 7. Huddle, 8. Kisa,
9. Bahta, 10. Rowbury

10,000 Metres

SADLY THERE WERE very few top-class 10,000m races. Easily the fastest was at Stanford as there the top three, 6th and 8th to 10th best times of 2014 were set; Sally Kipyego, Molly Huddle and Betsy Saina broke 31 minutes. Turning to the championships races, Joyce Chepkirui stands out; she did not break 32 minutes but was 2nd at the Kenyan Champs and then won the Commonwealth and African titles. Florence Kiplagat ran 31:48.6 in Iten, worth a minute quicker at low altitude, won the Kenyan Champs and was 2nd at the CG, and Emily Chebet was 3rd Kenyan, 3rd CG and 2nd Africans. At the Europeans there was a wonderful win by 40 year-old Jo Pavey, who had earlier won the British title in her year's best of 32:11.04, from Clémence Calvin, European Cup winner in 31:48.17. The world fourth fastest was Selly Chepyego with 31:28.07 at Kobe and she also won in 31:38.54 at Yamaguchi. Jordan Hasay and Kim Conley, the Stanford 4th and 8th went 2-1 at the US Champs. The most prolific racer was Ayumi Hagiwara, with three sub-32 times including 3rd at the Asian Games behind Alia Mohamed Saeed and Ding Changqin.

1. Chepkirui, 2. F Kiplagat, 3. Kipyego,
4. Huddle, 5. Saina, 6. Chepyego, 7. E Chebet,
8. Conley, 9. Hasay, 10. Pavey

Half Marathon

FLORENCE KIPLAGAT SET a world record 65:22 for the distance at Barcelona in February, passing 20k in a world record 61:56 en route. Her time improved not only Mary Keitany's previous record of 65:40 but also times set on the ineligible courses at Lisbon and South Shields, headed by Paula Radcliffe's 65:40, although Kiplagat had male pacemakers. Later in the year Keitany returned to run the second fastest ever time with a splendid Great North Run win in 65:39. Joyce Chepkirui was the third fastest of the year with 66:19 in Prague, and Emily Chebet, later to win in 68:01 at Valencia, was second in 68:28. Priscah Jeptoo won the prestigious annual race at Ra's Al-Khaymah in 67:02. Following these women on the world list were the 1-2-3 at the World Championships: Gladys Cherono, Mercy Wacera and Sally Chepyego, and Cherono had another fast win, 68:16 in Yangzhou.

Marathon

TWO WOMEN BROKE 2:20 in 2014, both on the aided course at Boston: Rita Jeptoo 2:18:57 and Buzunesh Deba 2:19:59 and in that race Mare Dibaba and Jemina Jelagat ran 2:20s, Meselech Melkamu and Aleksandra Duliba 2:21s and Shalane Flanagan 7th in 2:22:02. Jeptoo seemed to have sealed the World Majors prize for 2013/14 with a further win in Chicago, but then came news that she had tested positive for EPO. She defeated a stellar field at Chicago with Mare Dibaba, Florence Kiplagat and Birhane Dibaba 2nd to 4th, but times were slow. Edna Kiplagat ran 2:20:21 to win in London from Florence Kiplagat, Tirunesh Dibaba, Feyse Tadesse and Aberu Kebede, all under 2:23:30 as were the first four in Berlin: Tirfi Tsegaye 2:20:18, Tadesse, Flanagan and Tadelech Bekele. Mare Dibaba had started the year with a win in Xiamen in 2:21:36, so had three races under 2:26 and Tsegaye had another fast win with 2:22:23 in Tokyo. New York rather muddled the issue. Mary Keitany ran well in windy conditions to beat Jelagat, but Deba was 9th and Edna Kiplagat 13th. Mulu Seboka won her three marathons but did not contest the Majors.

1. Tsegaye, 2. E Kiplagat, 3. F Kiplagat,
4. Tadesse, 5. M Dibaba, 6. Deba, 7. Jelagat,
8. Keitany, 9. T Dibaba, 10. Flanagan. dq?,
R Jeptoo

3000 Metres Steeplechase

THERE WAS A fascinating series of races between the top three with top ranking going to Hiwot Ayalew who beat Sofia Assefa to take the African title and was 4-2 overall against her and 5-2 v US champion Emma Coburn, who improved the North American record to 9:11.42. Ayalew, who won three DL races, set her best to win at Glasgow in 9:10.64 and Assefa her best to win at Eugene in 9:11.39. This trio was challenged at the end of the year by Hassiba Ghribi, who after 10th at Eugene and 5th at the Africans, won at the DL final in Zürich in 9:15.23 when she was followed by Ayalew, Assefa, Ruth Chebet and Coburn. Chebet, the 17 year-old World Junior Champion, was third at the Continental Cup behind Coburn and Ayalew and went on to win at the Asian Games. Salima El Ouali Alami was 3rd Africans, 8th Zürich and 6th C.Cup and was 4-2 v Etenesh Diro. Then eighth on the world list was former no.1 Milcah Chemos, but she was beaten 3-0 by Diro and 3-1 by Kenyan champion Purity Kirui. Kirui, Chemos and Joan Rotich made it a Kenyan 1-2-3 at the Commonwealth Games. Third and fourth at the Kenyan Champs were Hyvin Jepkemoi, who was 3-1 v Alami and 2-1 v Diro and Lydia Chepkurui. Antje Möldner-Schmidt won the European title but did not quite make the world top ten.

Most times under 9:30: Ayalew 10, Diro 9, Chemos, Chepkurui 8; Assefa 6, Kirui 4.

1. Ayalew, 2. Coburn, 3. Assefa, 4. Ghribi,
5. Chebet, 6. Jepkemoi, 7. Alami, 8. Diro,
9. Kirui, 10. Chemos Cheywa

100 Metres Hurdles

AFTER RANKING SECOND or third five times in six years, Dawn Harper-Nelson made the top ranking. She had the year's fastest time, 12.44 at Saint-Denis from Queen Harrison 12.46, and ran five of the nine wind-legal times of 12.55 or better. She won at the US Champs, DL final in Zürich and at the Continental Cup and beat US runner-up Harrison 5-3 with each winning three DL races. Sally Pearson started the year with 12.59 in Perth, but was unable to do better than 12.67 thereafter, although she won the Commonwealth title, was 2nd in Zürich and ahead of leading rivals on win-loss: 3-1 v Brianna Rollins and 4-2 v Tiffany Porter. Pearson was, however, beaten 2-0 by Lolo Jones (US 3rd), whose season ended in mid-July. Porter, 5-2 v Rollins, was 2nd at the Commonwealth Games and Continental Cup and 3rd in Zürich and also won the European title from Cindy Billaud and Cindy Roleder. US athletes took 14 of the world top 20 places and others in rankings contention included Jasmin

Stowers, Kristi Castlin, Nia Ali and NCAA champion Sharika Nelvis. Roleder got into the mix, beating Ali 2-1 and 1-1 v Castlin.

At 60m indoors Ali ran 7.80 to win the US title and was a surprise winner of the World Indoor title from Pearson and Porter, while Pearson headed the world lists with two times of 7.79.

Most times at 12.70 or faster: Harrison 12, Harper-Nelson 9, Porter, Jones 5, Rollins, Billaud 4; Pearson 3.

1. Harper-Nelson, 2. Harrison, 3. Jones, 4. Pearson, 5. Porter, 6. Roliins, 7. Billaud, 8. Stowers, 9. Castlin, 10. Roleder

400 Metres Hurdles

AFTER HER DOMINANT season in 2013, Zuzana Hejnová made a gentle return from injury (broken bone in her left instep in January) with a best of 55.86 in two competitions. Meanwhile Kaliese Spencer was dominant this year, as after 2nd to Kemi Adekoya in Doha, she won all her ten races, including six in the Diamond League, and she had eight of the ten fastest times of the year. She beat Eilidh Child, European champion, into second place by 0.92 at the Commonwealth Games and by 0.90 at the Continental Cup. Adekoya was 3rd in the latter and ended the year by winning the Asian Games title; she was 2-2 v Child. Kori Carter ran 53.84 for second on the world list to win the US title, but after that was 8th in Monaco, dnf Birmingham and 7th in Marrakech. Hanna Titimets, Irina Davydova and Denisa Rosolová were the European 2-3-4 and the US 2-3-4 were Georganne Moline, Cassandra Tate and Tiffany Williams; all these athletes were closely matched The DL final in Brussels resulted in 1 Spencer, 2 Rosolová, 3 Child, 4 Titimets, 5 Tate, 6 Moline and 8 Adekoya. Anna Ryzhykova (née Yaroshchuk) won at the European Teams from Child, Davydova and Rosolová, but fell in her heat at the Europeans. Wenda Nel was disqualified at the CG before winning the African title and coming 5th at the Continental Cup.

Most times under 54.0/55.0: Spencer 4/10, Carter 1/2, Child 7, Moline, Adekoya, Titimets 4; Rosolová, Williams, Nel 3.

1. Spencer, 2. Child, 3. Adekoya, 4. Rosolová, 5. Titimets, 6. Moline, 7. Carter, 8. Tate, 9. Nel, 10. Williams

High Jump

THE 2013 NO. 1 Svetlana Shkolina did not compete in 2014 due to a foot problem and it was a non-vintage year with just 7 performances by 5 women outdoors at 2.00 or above and 9 by 4 indoors. Mariya Kuchina won all five competitions indoors and 8 of 11 outdoors with a 2.01 and two 2.00s indoors and two 2.00s outdoors plus three DL wins including the final. She tied with Kamila Licwinko for the World Indoor title, with Ruth Beitia third, all clearing 2.00, and was 2nd at the Europeans with 1.99 behind Beitia 2.01. Blanka Vlasic decided that she was not in the shape to compete at the Europeans, but still had two DL wins, two 2m jumps outdoors and one indoors, where she was 6th at the World Indoors (4th Kaprzycka, 5th Emma Green). In her stead fellow-Croatian Ana Simic progressed to take European bronze at 1.99. Vlasic was 2-1 indoors and 3-2 outdoors v Simic. Inika McPherson set a new women's high jump world record for height differential of 37cm when she cleared 2.00 to win the US title from Chaunté Lowe 1.94 but was later found to have used a prohibited substance, so lost all results from this date; she would otherwise have ranked her 5th outdoors and 7th including indoors behind the Poles Licwinko and Justyna Kaprzycka who had good indoor form. Kaprzycka beat Licwinko 5-2 outdoors, but the latter was 2-1 up indoors. The 2-3 of 2013 had truncated seasons due to injury, Brigitta Barrett with a best of 1.95 and Anna Chicherova started with 2.01 in Eugene for the joint top mark of the year but then managed only 1.90 and 1.75 in her other competitions. Oksana Okunyeva, 6th Europeans and 4= at the DL final in Zürich (with Vlasic, behind Kuchina and Simic), was 3-1 v Svetlana Radzivil, Asian Games champion and 4th at the Continental Cup behind Kuchina, Lowe and Simic, and 2-2 v Marie-Laurence Jungfleisch, 5th Europeans. Green, suffering from back pain, had an outdoor best of 1.93m whereas she had eight competitions had 1.94 or higher indoors. Airine Palsyte had 1.97 indoors and two 1.98s outdoors, but was only 13th at the Europeans and 10= at the World Indoors.

Most competitions over 2.00/1.96m outdoors (+indoors): Kuchina 2+3i/7+3i, Vlasic 2+1i/4+1i, Beitia 1+2i/3+3i, Simic 5, Kasprzycka 3, Licwinko 3i/2+4i, Green 3i, Jungfleisch 2+2i.

1. Kuchina, 2. Beitia, 3. Vlasic, 4. Simic, 5. Kasprzycka, 6. Okunyeva, 7. Radzivil (8), 8. Licwinko (7), 9. Jungfleisch, 10. Palsyte. – Green (10). (Including indoors)

Pole Vault

STANDARDS WERE DOWN this year and the pregnant Yelena Isinbayeva was missed while Jenn Suhr was unable to recapture her 5m form with bests of 4.73 indoors and 4.71 out. As usual nowadays with the vertical jumps much of the best action was indoors (21 of the top 32 performances), but the year's best jump came outdoors – Fabiana Murer 4.80 in New York. Although her season was far from perfect, no height at the Continental Cup for instance, Murer returns to the top ranking she had in 2010 with a 5-2 win-loss advantage over US champion Suhr and four DL wins. The best depth of marks came with four women clearing 4.70 at the World Indoors, count-back settling the result as 1 Yarisley Silva, 2= Anzhelika Sidorova and Jirina Svobodová, 4 Murer, followed by 5= Anna Rogowska and Suhr. and 7 Silke Spiegelburg all 4.65. The last only had three outdoor competitions before suffering a fractured wrist, and both she and Rogowska had outdoor bests of 4.50, while Holly Bleasdale after a 4.73 indoor best did not compete at all outdoors. Three women went over 4.70 in Monaco: 1 Murer 4.76, 2 Suhr 4.71, 3 Ekateríni Stefanídi 4.71. The Russian champion Sidorova won the European title at 4.65, 5cm ahead of Stefanídi 2nd, Angelina Krasnova 3rd and Lisa Ryzih 4th. Silva had a couple of 4.70 jumps and was 2-2 outdoors v Stefanídi, who improved from 4,51 (2012). Other major winners were Alana Boyd, Commonwealth Games, and Li Ling, Continental Cup and Asian Games (but a best of only 4.61). Also in ranking contention were Nikoléta Kiriakopoúlou, 3= with Stefanídi, and Nicole Büchler 5th, all at 4.67 in the DL final in Zürich, that was won by Murer 4.72 from Suhr 4.67.

Most competitions over 4.60m (outdoors/ in): Murer 7/4i, Suhr 7/6i, Silva 6/2i, Stefanidi 6, Sidorova 4/5i, Ryzih 4/1i, Kiriakopoúlou 3/1i, Ptácniková 1/5i; Spiegelburg 5i, Bleasdale, Kylie Hutson, Mary Saxer 4i, Krasnova 3, Rogowska 3i.

1. Murer, 2. Suhr, 3. Stefanídi (5), 4. Silva (3), 5. Sidorova (4), 6. Krasnova (9), 7. Ryzih (10), 8. Kiriakopoúlou (-), 9. Boyd (-), 10. Svobodová (7). – Spiegelburg (6), Bleasdale (8) (Including indoors)

Long Jump

CONCENTRATING ON THE long jump for the first time for several years, Tianna Bartoletta improved her best from the 6.89 with which she had won the 2005 World title as Tianna Madison to 7.02. She also had the next three best jumps of the year at 6.98, 6.94 and 6.93 plus 6.98w, three of them in DL meetings, and takes top ranking outdoors with 6 wins in 12 competitions. It was close, though, as form was mixed. Éloyse Lesueur won the World Indoor and European titles as well as at the Continental Cup and was 3-2 v Bartoletta. Lesueur was, however, only 8th at the DL final in Zürich, where Ivana Spanovic won from Bartoletta, Brittney Reese, Irène Pusterla, Melanie Bauschke and Erica Jarder. Spanovic (2-4 outdoors v Lesueur, 3-2 v Bartoletta and 3rd World Indoors), was 2nd at the Europeans, followed by Russian champion Darya Klishina and Malaika Mihambo. Spanovic beat Klishina 7-1 (1-0 indoors), but was only just (3-2) ahead of Reese on win-loss and the latter, who tried a new run-up this year, was at her best with 6.92 to win the US title from Bartoletta and Funmi Jimoh. Klishina was 2-1 v Mihambo (European Team winner) and Shara Proctor (4th World Indoors), who was 2-2 v Jimoh but had no-jumps in the CG final. The best British jumper, however, was Katarina Johnson-Thompson, who after 2nd at the World Indoors only competed three times at the event outdoors, where she set bests to win the UK title with 6.81 and with 6.92 at Glasgow, 10cm ahead of Proctor. Anna Klyashtornaya (née Nazarova) produced the joint fourth best jump of 2014 with 6.93 in qualifying at the Russian Champs before 2nd in the final, but her next bests were 6.62 and 6.88w and she was 10th at the Europeans. Blessing Okagbare won the opening DL long jump with 6.86 in Shanghai, but did not try the event again.

Most competitions over 6.70m (outdoors/in): Bartoletta 7+1w, Lesueur 6+2w/2i, Spanovic 5/3i, Jimoh 5+1w Mihambo 5, Reese 4+1w, Johnson-Thompson 3/2i, Klishina 3/1i, Proctor, Alina Rotaru, Sosthene Moguenara 3; dq: 3i Biryukova

1. Bartoletta (2), 2. Lesueur (1), 3. Spanovic, 4. Reese, 5. Klishina, 6. Mihambo, 7. Johnson-Thompson, 8. Proctor. 9. Jimoh, 10. Bauschke. (Including indoors)

Triple Jump

CATERINE IBARGÜEN WAS unbeaten just as she was in 2013, her eleven wins (inc. six DL) taking her unbeaten run to 21. She went from 22nd to 5th on the all-time list with her South American record 15.31 in Monaco. As in 2013 Yekaterina Koneva, Olga Saladukha and Kimberley Williams ranked 2-3-4. Koneva beat Saladukha by 1cm for the World Indoor title with Williams a close third, but Saladukha produced easily her best of the year 14.73 to beat Koneva 14.69 for the European title; overall, however, Koneva beat Saladukha 4-2 outdoors and 1-0 indoors. The top four finished in their ranking order at the Continental Cup and the next best were the Cubans Yosiri Urrutia and Mabel Gay, the former having a 2-0 advantage on win-loss. These two came to Europe but two other Cubans with good marks Yarianna Martínez and Dailenis Alcántara competed only in Central America, Martínez ahead 9-2 in their clashes. Alsu Murtazina was seventh on the world list with 14.50 when 2nd to Koneva at the Russian Champs, but the third in that event Irina Gumenyuk went on to 4th at the Europeans, while Murtazina was only 10th. Faring even worse was Patricia Mamona, dnq 13th, but she had four competitions over 14m outdoors and two indoors, including 4th at the World Indoors. At the DL final the order was Ibargüen, Saladukha, Koneva, Williams (1st CG), Urrutia, Gumenyuk, Olga Rypakova (who went on to win the Asian Games title on her return from maternity leave) and Murtazina. Rouguy Diallo showed great promise in taking the World Junior title with 14.44w/14.20 from a pre-meeting best of 13.74.

Most competitions over 14.30m: Ibargüen 11, Saladukha 8+4i, Koneva 8, Gay 6+1i, Urrutia 5, Williams 3+2i, Gumenyuk 2+1w.

1. Ibargüen, 2. Koneva, 3. Saladukha, 4. Williams, 5. Urrutia, 6. Gay, 7. Gumenyuk, 8. Rypakova (9), 9. Mamona (8), 10. Martínez. (Including indoors)

Shot

DESPITE A SERIES of injuries during the year and thus not quite at her best Valerie Adams continued her domination of the event, taking her winning run to 56 with 14 wins in 2014 and is top for the eighth time in nine years. Her best was 20.69 to win her fourth World Indoor title and she had the top five marks outdoors, topped by 20.59 in the final in Brussels to complete a perfect DL season. Michelle Carter got closest, 17cm behind in New York, and then Christina Schwanitz was 41 cm behind in Rome. Schwanitz, winner at the Europeans and Continental Cup (when Adams was a late withdrawal) and 2nd World Indoors, had a fine season, winning 5/6 indoors and 14/18 outdoors, all her losses being second places to Adams and she was over 20m six times (once indoors) to ten by Adams (twice indoors). Carter was 2nd and Gong Lijiao 3rd at the Continental Cup, But Gong beat Carter 3-1 outdoors and 1-0 indoors. Asian Games champion Gong was 2-0 v Yevgeniya Kolodko as well as 3rd to 4th at the World Indoors. Kolodko and Anita Márton (who improved her pb from 18.48 to 19.04) and Yuliya Leontyuk were 2nd, 3rd and 4th at the Europeans and Cleopatra Borel won the Commonwealth silver medal. Second and third at the US Champs were Felisha Johnson and Tia Brooks and though 3-3 on win-loss, Johnson had the better marks. Hanna Obleshchuk only had five outdoor competitions, but was over 19m twice and was 3-0 v Márton , who was 4-0 v Johnson and 3-1 v Brooks.

Most competitions over 19m: Schwanitz 19+7i, Adams 13, Carter 10+1i, Kolodko 8+1i, Gong 8

1. Adams, 2. Schwanitz, 3. Gong, 4. Carter, 5. Kolodko, 6. Borel, 7. Leontyuk, 8. Obleshchuk, 9. Márton, 10. Johnson.

Discus

FOR THE THIRD successive year Sandra Perkovic was top; she won the European title with 71.08 for 18th on the all-time list but this was the world's best throw since 1992 and in all she won ten times including six Diamond League meetings. She lost twice: to Gia Lewis-Smallwood in Glasgow and then to Lewis-Smallwood and Dani Samuels (who were 3-3 against each other) at the Continental Cup. Late developer Lewis-Smallwood, who did not reach 60m until she was 30, threw a North American record 69.17 at the age of 34. Samuels won at the Commonwealth Games, 3.27m ahead of Seema Punia, who went on to win at the Asian Games. Mélina Robert-Michon was 4th at the Continental Cup, won at the European Throws and European Team, and was 2nd at the Europeans. Next in the rankings are four Germans and two Cubans. Shanice Craft, 21 in June, improved her pb from 62.02 to 65.88 and was the German champion ahead of Julia Fischer and Anna Rüh, and this trio came 3rd, 5th and 4th at the Europeans, with Zinaida Sendriute 6th. Nadine Müller only competed in May and June but was 4-1 v Fischer and 2-1 v Rüh. Yaimí Pérez was the Cuban champion but was beaten 10-5 by runner-up Denia Caballero, including at the CAC Games. Craft was 2-1 v Pérez, having beaten her 2nd to 7th at Eugene, but in the other main Cuban-German clash, at Saint-Denis, the order (5th to 9th) was Caballero, Craft, Pérez, Fischer, Rüh.

Most competitions over 63m: Samuels 13, Perkovic 12, Craft 11, Lewis-Smallwood 10, Robert-Michon 9, Pérez, Caballero 6; Müller, Fischer 4; Sendriute, Rüh, Strokova 3

1. Perkovic, 2. Lewis-Smallwood, 3. Samuels, 4. Robert-Michon, 5. Craft, 6. Caballero, 7. Pérez, 8. Müller, 9. Fischer, 10. Rüh

Hammer

OF THE THREE women who had dominated the world rankings in recent years, Tatyana Lysenko called an early halt to her season in June after a best of 70.62, so it was left to Anita Wlodarczyk and Betty Heidler to continue their rivalry. Heidler won at Ostrava, 78.00 to 76.41, but while that remained the German's best of the year, Wlodarczyk went on to win her remaining seven competitions, setting successive season's bests of 78.17, 78.76 (to win the European title) and 79.58 in Berlin to regain the world record that she had last held in 2010. Wlodarczyk had five and Heidler three of the year's performances over 76m, and the only other women at this level were Wang Zheng 77.68 in Chengdu and Zhang Wenxiu 77.33 at the Asian Games, but the latter mark was lost when Zhang failed a drugs test, the title going to Wang. At the European Championships 2nd to 5th places went to Martina Hrasnová, Joanna Fiodorow, Kathrin Klaas and Heidler; Klaas was 4-1 v Hrasnová, who was 5-2 v Fiodorow. Top North Americans contest the middle rankings with these women. Commonwealth champion Sultana Frizell set a North American and Commonwealth record of 75.73 and beat US champion Amanda Bingson 3-1, although Bingson was 2nd at the Continental Cup with Hrasnová 3rd, Wang 4th and Frizell 5th. Bingson was 3-2 v US runner-up Jessica Cosby Toruga, but both were beaten 2-1 by US 3rd Amber Campbell. Both Russian champion Anna Bulgakova and Evá Orbán did not register a throw in the European Champs final.

Most competitions over 73m: Wlodarczyk 9,

Heidler, Klaas 7, Wang Z 6, Zhang W, Hrasnová 5; Frizell, Bingson 4; Cosby Toruga, Bulgakova 3.

1. Wlodarczyk, 2. Heidler, 3. Wang, 4. Klaas, 5. Hrasnová, 6. Frizell, 7. Bingson, 8. Fiodorow, 9. Campbell, 10. Cosby Toruga. Drugs dq? Zhang (4th)

Javelin

AFTER JUST ONE competition in 2013 following the birth of her son, Barbora Spotáková took her seventh top ranking in the past nine years. She won nine times as her only loss was to Liz Gleadle at Birmingham. Her main rivals in recent years Mariya Abakumova and Christina Obergföll sat out the season through pregnancy. The European medals went to Spotáková, Tatjana Jelaca and Linda Stahl followed by Madara Palameika, Tatyana Klododovich and Martina Ratej and the Commonwealth medals to Kimberley Mickle, Sunette Viljoen and Kelsey-Lee Roberts followed by Kathryn Mitchell and Gleadle. Coming together, the order at the Continental Cup was Spotáková, Viljoen, Gleadle, Mickle and Stahl. Only sixth there was Zhang Li, but she improved mightily to win the Asian Games title with 65.47. Spotáková's fourth DL win of the year came in the final when she threw the world's top mark of 67.99. Mickle beat African champion Viljoen 3-1 and Stahl 5-0 to rank second., while although she was 5-4 v Stahl and 2-1 v Viljoen, Ratej is ranked lower through her European 6th and DL final 7th. Mitchell was 3-1 v Palameika, who beat US champion Kara Patterson 4-1. Gleadle, who only competed in one DL event, and Patterson were 1-1. Hanna Hatsko-Fedusova joined Spotáková and Stahl in throwing over 67m, but her next best was 63.10 and she did not qualify for the European final; she was, however, 2-1 v Jelaca.

Most competitions over 62m: Spotáková, Mickle 9; Stahl 8, Viljoen 7, Mitchell, Hatsko-Fedusova 5; Palameika, Gleadle, Patterson 3.

1. Spotáková, 2. Mickle, 3. Viljoen, 4. Stahl, 5. Ratej, 6. Mitchell, 7. Palameika, 8. Gleadle, 9. Hatsko-Fedusova, 10. Jelaca

Heptathlon

KATARINA JOHNSON-THOMSON IS perhaps the most exciting young talent in world athletics, and in 2014 set pbs at 13 different events, including a British record 1.96i at high jump and a world-class 6.92 long jump. She recorded the year's top heptathlon mark with 6682 at Götzis, but then injury ended her season in July and she was unable to bid for further honours. Brianne Theisen-Eaton recorded the second and third best scores – 6641 for 2nd at Götzis and 6597 for 1st at the Commonwealth Games. Most of the world's best competed at Götzis so the order there is vital in determining rankings: with 3 Dafne Schippers (no other heptathlon), 4 Nadine Broersen, 5 Nafissatou Thiam, 6 Carolin Schäfer, 7 Laura Ikauniece-Admidina, 8 Xénia Krizsán, 9 Anouk Vetter, all over 6300 points. Broersen went on to win the European Cup with 6539 and was 2nd at the Europeans with 6498, 53 behind Antoinette Nana Djimou, whose other heptathlons were 2nd in the European Cup and dnf at Talence, with Thiam 3rd. Indeed only four of the world top ten competed in the minimum three heptathlons needed to get into the prize money for the IAAF World Challenge, won by Broersen from Schäfer (4th EC, 1 Talence), Lilli Schwarzkopf (10th Götzis, 1st Ratingen, 5th EC) and Eliska Klucinová (12th Götzis, 1st Kladno, 1 1st Eur Cup 1, dnf Europeans). Ikaunice and Vetter were 6th and 7th at the Europeans. Sharon Day-Monroe won the US title with 6470 in her only serious try at the event.

Most of the best indoor pentathlon scores were achieved at the World Indoors, won by Broersen 4830, from Theisen-Eaton, Alina Fyodorova, Day-Monroe, Claudia Rath, and Maksimova, all over 4650 points. Day-Monroe had the year's second highest score, 4805A at the US Champs and Maksimova had her best 4686 to win the Belarus title.

1. Johnson-Thompson, 2. Theisen-Eaton, 3. Broersen, 4. Nana Djimou, 5. Schippers, 6. Thiam, 7. Schäfer 8. Schwarzkopf, 9. Day-Monroe, 10. Ikauniece-Admidina

20 Kilometres Walk

YELENA LASHMANOVA HAD dominated women's walking for two years, but she joined the horribly long list of Russian walkers from Viktor Chegin's stable in Saransk to receive a drugs ban. So the 2013 2nd and 3rd in the rankings stepped up a place. Anisya Kirdyapkina won her two races – Russian winter and World Cup and Liu Hong won at Lugano and La Coruña with 2nd at the World Cup. Further World Cup placings (with the world's fastest six times of the year coming in this race at Taicang with 24 women under 1:30 and best ever marks for places 7 and 9 to 50) pretty much determined the rankings as 3rd to 10th were: Elmira Alembekova, Vera Sokolova, Eleonora Giorgi, Lu Xiuzhi, Lyudmila Olyanovska, Ana Cabacinha, Antonella Palmisano and Marina Pandakova. Alembekova went on to win the European title from Olyanovska, Anezka Drahotová, Sokolova, Giorgi, Cabecinha and Palmisano. Drahotová set a world junior record for 10,000m on the track with 42:47.25 to take the World Junior title and she was also 3rd at Lugano behind Liu and Giorgi with Agnieszka Dygacz 4th and Olyanovska 5th. The IAAF World Race Walking Challenge was won by Liu from Giorgi and Cabecinha.

1. Kirdyapkina, 2. Liu Hong, 3. Alembekova, 4. Drahotová, 5. Sokolova, 6. Giorgi, 7, Lu Xiuzhi, 8. Olyanovska, 9. Cabecinha, 10. Palmisano

Note abbreviations: CG = Commonwealth Games, C.Cup = Continental Cup, DL = Diamond League, EC = European Championships.

CROSS-COUNTRY - NATIONAL CHAMPIONS 2014

	Men (long distance)	*Women (long distance)*
Algeria	Rabah Aboud	Amina Bettiche
Australia (Aug)	Duer Yoa	Courtney Powell
Austria	Valentin Pfeil	Lisa Perterer
Belgium	Jeroen D'Hoedt	Veerle Dejaeghere
Brazil	Valerio Fabiano	Tatiele de Carvalho
Bulgaria (Oct)	Yolo Nikolov	Yana Georgieva
Canada (Nov)	Chris Winter	Rachel Hannah
Chile	Iván Chávez	Verónica Angel
China	Zhu Rexue	Jing Changqin
Colombia	Javier Andrés Peña	Martha Inés Ronceria
Croatia (Nov)	Dino Bosnjak	Matea Parlov
Czech Republic	Milan Kocourek	Lucie Sekanová
Denmark	Abdi Hakim Ulad	Simone Glad
England	Steve Vernon	Gemma Steel
Eritrea	Samson Gebreyohanes	Weldu Negash
Estonia	Roman Fosti	Jekaterina Patjuk
Ethiopia (Trials)	Yasin Hassen	Genet Ayalew
Finland	Lewis Korir	Sandra Eriksson
France	El Hassane Ben Lkhainouch	Laila Traby
Germany	Richard Ringer	Sabrina Mockenhaupt
Greece	Konstadínos Gelaoúzos	Sofía Ríga
Hungary	Albert Minczer	Anikó Kálovics
Ireland (Nov)	Paul Pollock	Fionnuala Britton
Israel	Yimer Getahun	Azawant Taka
Italy	Stefano La Rosa	Veronica Inglese
Kenya	Wilson Kiprop	Priscah Jeptoo
Korea	Chung Hyo-young	Lim Eun-ha
Lithuania (Spring)	Justinas Berzanskis	Milda Vilcinskaite
(Autumn)	Mykola Yuhimchuk UKR	Diana Lobacevske
Luxembourg	Pol Mellina	Pascale Schmoetten
Moidova (Oct)	Roman Prodius	Olesea Smovjenco
Morocco	Mohamed Reda El Aaraby	Salima El Ouali Alami
Netherlands (Nov)	Khalid Choukoud	Sifan Hassan
New Zealand	Callan Moody	Camille Buscomb
Northern Ireland	Paul Pollock	Elmear Mullan
Norway (Oct)	Sondre Nordstad Moen	Marthe Katrine Myhre
Poland (Nov)	Krzysztof Gosiewski	Iwona Lewandowska
Portugal	Manuel Damião	Ana Dulce Félix
Russia	Yegor Nikolayev	Alla Kulyatina
(Sep)	Igor Maksimov	Yekaterina Sokolenko
Scotland	Callum Hawkins	Rhona Auckland
Serbia	Jasmin Ljajic	Amela Terzic
Slovakia (Nov)	Peter Durec	Lubomira Maniková
Slovenia	Anton Kosmac	Marusa Mismas
South Africa (Sep)	Stephen Mokoka	Lebogang Phalula
Spain	Ayad Lamdassem	Nuria Fernández
Sweden (Oct)	Abraham Adhanon	Meraf Bahta
Switzerland	Rolf Rufenacht	Fabienne Schlumpf
Trinidad & Tobago (Nov)	George Smith	Samantha Shukla
Turkey	Kemal Koyuncu	Esma Aydemir
Uganda	Moses Kipsiro	Linet Chebet
UK (CAU)	Richard Goodman	Lily Partridge
Ukraine (Mar)	Igor Porozov	Natalya Bartak
(Oct)	Igor Heletiy	Tetyana Holovchenko
USA	Chris Derrick	Amy Van Alstine
Wales	Dewi Griffiths	Andrea Whitcombe
Arab	Salah Badri TUN	Amira Ben Amor TUN
Asian	Aweke Yimer BRN	Tejitu Chalchissa BRN
Balkan	Vedat Günen TUR	Özlem Kaya TUR
European Clubs Teams	Atletismo Bikila ESP	Luch Moskva RUS
NACAC	Joe Gray USA	Kellyn Johnson USA
NCAA (Nov)	Edward Chesarek KEN	Kate Avery GBR
Nordic (Nov)	Hans Kristian Fløystad NOR	Veronika Blom NOR
South American	Wellington da Silva BRA	Sueli da Silva BRA
World Military	Abdennassir Fathi MAR	Iwona Lewandowska POL
World Universities	Joshua Cheptegei UGA	Winnie Nanyondo UGA

Short course winners	*Men*	*Women*
Austria	Christian Steinhammer	
Belgium	Pieter-Jan Hannes	Sofie Van Accom
China	Yang Dinghong	Jing Changqin
Czech Republic	Petr Vitner	
Denmark	Thijs Nijhuis	Maja Alm
Finland	Lewis Korir	
France	Florian Carvalho	Clemence Cavin
Norway	Johan Bugge	Karoline Finne
Poland (Nov)	Mateusz Demczyszak	Mariola Slusarczyk
Portugal	Manuel Damião	Carla Rocha
Russia	Aleksey Popov	Lyudmila Lebedeva
Scotland (Nov)	Andrew Butchart	Rhona Auckland
South Africa	Steven Mhlongo	Mamphielo Sibanda
Sweden	Abraham Adhanon	Meraf Bahta
Ukraine	Andriy Melnik	Viktoriya Pogyrelska
World Military	Rabah Aboud ALG	

Winners of EAA and IAAF Permit Cross-Country Races 2014

4 Jan	Antrim (IAAF)	Japheth Korir KEN	Mimi Belete BRN
6 Jan	San Giorgio su Legnano (IAAF)	Albert Rop KEN/BRN	Hiwot Ayalew ETH
11 Jan	Edinburgh (IAAF)	Garrett Heath USA	Gemma Steel GBR
12 Jan	Villa Lagarina (EA)	Robert Ndiwa KEN	Linah Cheruto KEN
12 Jan	Elgóibar (EA)	Timothy Toroitich UGA	Hiwot Ayalew ETH
19 Jan	Santiponce (IAAF)	Paul Tanui KEN	Hiwot Ayalew ETH
26 Jan	San Vittore Olana (IAAF)	Paul Tanui KEN	Faith Kipyegon KEN
26 Jan	Hannut (EA)	Titus Mbishei KEN	Birtukan Adamu ETH
2 Feb	Albufeira (IAAF)	Mohammed Moustaoui MAR	Hiwot Ayalew ETH
2 Feb	Belgrade (EA)	Muamer Hasanovic SRB	Amela Terzic SRB
9 Feb	Diekirch (IAAF)	Alex Kibet KEN	Eleni Gebrehiwot ETH
15 Feb	Nairobi (IAAF)	Bidan Karoki KEN	Faith Kipyegon KEN
16 Nov	Burgos (Atapuerca) (IAAF)	Imane Merga ETH	Belaynesh Oljira ETH
23 Nov	Tilburg (EA)	Khalid Choukoud NED	Sifan Hassan NED
30 Nov	Alobendas (EA)	Timothy Toroitich UGA	Doris Changeiywo KEN
30 Nov	Leffinckroucke (EA)	Birhan Nebebew ETH	Senbera Teferi ETH
30 Nov	Roeselare (EA)	Pieter Jan Hannes BEL	Almensch Belete BEL
21 Dec	Venta de Baños (EA)	Timothy Toroitich UGA	Mimi Belete BRN
21 Dec	Brussels (IAAF)	Abel Kibet KEN	Sheila Chepngetich KEN

African Cross-Country Championships 2014

At Cape Town, South Africa, March 18.

Senior Men (10k)
1. Leonard Barsotom KEN 34:27
2. Cornelius Kangogo KEN 34:57
3. Philemon Rono KEN 35:02
4. Solomon Kirwa Yego KEN 35:15
5. Philip Langat KEN 35:21
6. Moses Kibet UGA 35:26
7. Joseph Kitur KEN 35:43
8. Thomas Ayeko UGA 35:53
9. Abrar Osman ERI 35:57
10. Moses Kipsiro UGA 36:00

Team: 1. KEN 10, 2. UGA 37, 3. ETH 52, 4. ERI 79, 5. TAN 83, 6. RWA 115, 7. ALG 118, 8. SUD 195

Junior Men (8k)
1. Moses Mukono KEN 22:37
2. Andrew Lorot KEN 22:51
3. Berhane Afewerki ETH 22:57
4. John Langat KEN 22:59
5. Hillary Kipkemoi KEN 23:02
6. Emmanuel Bett KEN 23:13

Team: 1. KEN 12, 2. ERI 32, 3. ETH 54, 4. UGA 56, 5. MAR 111, 6. RWA 124

Senior Women (8k)
1. Faith Kipyegon KEN 25:34
2. Janet Kisa KEN 25:42
3. April Aprot KEN 25:47
4. Edith Chelimo KEN 26:03
5. Tadelech Bekele ETH 26:11
6. Yeshaneh Ababel ETH 26:15
7. Ruti Aga ETH 26:33
8. Beatrice Mutai KEN 26:46
9. Linet Chebet UGA 26:50
10. Nazret Weldu ERI 27:04

Team: 1. KEN 10, 2. ETH 29, 3. UGA 57, 4. TAN 71, 5. RWA 98

Junior Women (6k)
1. Agnes Tirop KEN 18:51
2. Alemitu Heroye ETH 19:05
3. Nancy Nzisa KEN 19:17
4. Roseline Chepngetich KEN 19:40
5. Lilian Rengeruk KEN 19:51
6. Alemitu Hawi ETH 19:56

Team: 1 KEN 13, 2. ETH 28, 3. UGA 55, 4. ERI 72, 5. MAR 119, 6. RWA 120.

European Cross-Country Championships 2014

At Samokov, Bulgaria, December 14

Senior Men (10.01k)
1. Polat Kemboi Arikan TUR 32:19
2. Ali Kaya TUR 32:19
3. Alemayehu Bezabeh ESP 32:30
4. Florian Carvalho FRA 32:59
5. Ross Millington GBR 33:00
6. Mohamed Marhoum ESP 33:04
7. Khalid Choukoud NED 33:04
8. Stefano La Rosa ITA 33:17
9. Adam Hickey GBR 33:19
10. Timothée Bommier FRA 33:21
11. Cihat Ulus TUR 33:22
12. Antonio Abadía ESP 33:24
13. Sondre Nordstad Moen NOR 33:25
14. Marouan Razine ITA 33:26
15. Roberto Alaiz ESP 33:26

70 of 75 finished.

Teams: 1. TUR 33, 2. ESP 36, 3. ITA 59, 4. FRA 69, 5. GBR 76, 6. IRL 127, 7. UKR 178, 8. ROU 219, 9. DEN 231.

Under-23 Men (7.78k)
1. Ilgizar Safiulin RUS 25:31
2. Igor Maksimov RUS 25:33
3. Vladimir Nikitin RUS 25:37
4. Johnny Hay GBR 25:46
5. Callum Hawkins GBR 25:49
6. Elmar Engholm SWE 25:52
7. Marc Scott GBR 25:54
8. François Barrer FRA 25:56

66 of 74 finished.

Teams: 1. RUS 16, 2. GBR 31, 3. SWE 62, 4. FRA 93, 5. ESP 110, 10 teams completed.

Junior Men (6.08k)
1. Yemaneberhan Crippa ITA 20:07
2. Carlos Mayo ESP 20:22
3. Said Ettaqy ITA 20:28
4. Ayoub Mokhtar ESP 20:30

5. Yohanes Chiappinelli ITA 20:33
94 of 104 finished.
Teams: 1. ITA 18, 2. ESP 41, 3. TUR 70, 4. FRA 74, 5. GBR 85; 17 completed
Senior Women (7.78k)
1. Gemma Steel GBR 28:27
2. Kate Avery GBR 28:27
3. Meraf Bahta SWE 28:52
4. Almensch Belete BEL 28:52
5. Sophie Duarte FRA 25:58
6. Fionnuala Britton IRL 28:59
7. Stephanie Twell GBR 29:07
8. Iwona Lewandowska POL 29:09
9. Iris Fuentes-Pila ESP 29:19
10. Carla Salomé Rocha POR 29:20
11. Lily Partridge GBR 29:22
12. Sara Treacy IRL 29:23
13. Trihas Gebre ESP 29:25
14. Katarzyna Kowalska POL 29:29
15. Sonia Samuels GBR 29:32
58 of 62 finished.
Teams: 1. GBR 21, 2. ESP 70, 3. IRL 87, 4. FRA 88, 5. ITA 112, 6. DEN 124, 7. ROU 215
Under-23 Women (6.08k)
1. Rhona Auckland GBR 22:23
2. Militsa Mircheva BUL 22:25
3. Gulshat Fazlitdinova RUS 22:28
4. Yekaterina Sokolenko RUS 22:32
5. Maureen Koster NED 22:37
6. Sevilay Eytemis TUR 22:44
7. Louise Carton BEL 22:49
8. Svetlana Aplachkina RUS 22:56.
59 of 60 finished.
Teams: 1. RUS 32, 2. GBR 37, 3. TUR 95, 4. GER 107, 5. BLR 123; 9 completed.
Junior Women (3.85k)
1. Emine Hatun Tuna TUR 14:13
2. Jessica Judd GBR 14:18
3. Lydia Turner GBR 14:25
4. Alina Reh GER 14:34
5. Amy Griffiths GBR 14:38
74 of 76 finished.
Teams: 1. GBR 18, 2. FRA 64, 3. GER 74, 4. TUR 99, 5. ESP 111; 10 completed.
Overall medals: GBR 4 gold-4 silver-1 bronze, RUS & TUR 3-1-2, ITA 2-0-2, ESP 0-4-1, BUL & FRA 0-1-0, SWE 0-0-2, IRL & GER 0-0-1.

2014 WORLD ROAD RACE REVIEW

By Marty Post

FLORENCE KIPLAGAT SET an IAAF world record for the half-marathon of 1:05:12 at Barcelona on February 16. More than that, she broke two significant barriers in that race. She became the first woman to break 62 minutes for 20 kilometres, passing that split in 61:56. In addition she averaged 4:58.6 for the 13.1 miles, the first ever sub-5 minute per mile pace for that distance. Yet she did not have the fastest start of the year in a half-marathon. At Prague, April 5, Kenyan compatriot Joyce Chepkirui covered the first 5 km in 15:16, an astonishing 34 seconds quicker than Kiplagat and equivalent to 164:26 for 21.1 km. Chepkirui could not hold that kind of pace, but she wound her way through the Czech Republic capital in 66:19, a personal best and 29 seconds better than the previous course record. Mary Keitany had the second fastest half-marathon of 2014 and all-time. Moreover her 65:39 at the Great North Run was a noteworthy accomplishment, slicing one second off Paula Radcliffe's former course record which only the year before had narrowly survived a record attempt by Priscah Jeptoo 65:45.

Chepkirui's 10km split of 30:56 at Prague held up as the year's fastest time for more than five months until Betsy Saina posted a 30:46 victory at the Rabobank Tilburg Ladies Run on September 7. In one of the closest races of the year at Berlin on October 12, Chepkirui edged Emily Chebet, both timed in 31:02, as Margaret Wangari ran 31:06, the fastest third place time in history.

Kenyan women put on an awesome display of team running at the IAAF World Half-Marathon Championships in Copenhagen on March 29. All three medal winners – Gladys Cherono, Mary Nguri Wacera and Selly Keptich Chepyego – were under 68 minutes and their total time used to determine the team champion was exactly four minutes faster than the runner-up nation of Ethiopia. For good measure, Kenyans were also fourth and fifth.

There were also two IAAF world records set in 2014 within the same race on the men's side, but with a significant difference: two different men accounted for these two records. At the BMW Berlin Marathon on September 28, Dennis Kimetto set a world record of 2:02:57. However Emmanuel Mutai was one second ahead at the 30km mark at 1:27:37. Mutai went on to finish second and that time was accorded world record recognition. A second runner, Geoffrey Kamworor, also posted a 1:27:37 but as he did complete the full distance, that performance was not a joint world-record. (Peter Kirui also ran 1:27:37 at the 2011 Berlin Marathon, but did not finish that race.)

The fastest 25km of the year also occurred at Berlin but in a different race. Abraham Cheroben won the BIG 25 Berlin on May 4 in 1:11:47, the third fastest time in history. Runner-up Kenneth Kipkemoi moved to eighth all-time at 1:12:32. Cheroben was also the fastest man at the half-marathon in 2014. He was also the only one to break 59 minutes, winning at Valencia on October 19 in 58:48. That made him the equal sixth performer all-time, and his 41:55 at 15km was the best time of the year. At the half-marathon distance, Kipkemoi (59:01) was the second both that day and for the year. The fastest overall half-marathon was at New Delhi on November 23. While Guye Adola won in 59:06, nine men broke the hour mark and best times in history for places fifth through ninth were set.

The IAAF World Championships yielded an abundance of all-time best times for places, including 18th and 20th through 29th inclusive. The contest for the gold medal became a runaway for Geoffrey Kipsang 59:08, an impressive 13 seconds ahead of the field. The battle for the silver and bronze was spirited, as Samuel Tsegaye edged Adola, both time in 59:21.

Stephen Sambu was the 2014 world leader at 10km, 27:25 (Boston, June 22). There were official timers at 8km (not an official IAAF record distance) where Sambu and Geoffrey Mutai went by in 22:01.1, considered a 'world record' by the Association of Road Running Statisticians.

WINNERS OF LEADING 2014 ROAD RACES

Date	Race	Men	Women
12 Jan	Egmond aan Zee HMar	Ayele Abshero ETH 62:52	Guteni Shone ETH 71:55
12 Jan	Valencia 10k	Abel Kipsang KEN 28:34	Marta Esteban ESP 33:15
19 Jan	Santa Pola HMar	Abraham Cheroben KEN 61:25	Bekele Ashefe ETH 71:18
19 Jan	Naples HMar	Kiprono Kurgat KEN 64:02	Caroline Rotich KEN 69:58 *=
24 Jan	Dubai 10k	John Ndungu KEN 28:56	Gladys Jemaiyo KEN 33:41
26 Jan	Marrakech HMar	Guye Adola ETH 61:26	Rkia El Moukim MAR 70:03
1 Feb	Edinburg USA 10k	Leonard Korir KEN 29:06	Alena Shewarge ETH 33:50
2 Feb	Eldoret HMar/10k	Amos Mitei KEN 62:50	Peris Chepkirui KEN 31:54
2 Feb	Granollers HMar	Wilson Kipsang KEN 61:18	Faith Jeruto KEN 74:07
2 Feb	Marugame HMar	Martin Mathathi KEN 60:11	Eri Makikwa JPN 70:27
9 Feb	Coamo HMar	Ghirmay Ghebrselassie ETH 63:53	Gladys Tejeda PER 75:22
10 Feb	Schoorl 10k	Abdi Nageeye NED 29:10	Jip Vastenburg NED 32:49
14 Feb	R'as Al-Khaymah HMar	Lelisa Desisa ETH 59:36	Priscah Jeptoo KEN 67:02
16 Feb	Barcelona HMar	Eliud Kipchoge KEN 60:52	Florence Kiplagat KEN 65:12 WR
16 Feb	Kumamoto 30k	Yuma Hattori JPN 1:28:52	Yuka Takashima JPN 1:44:19
16 Feb	Verona HMar	William Kibor KEN 60:51	Valeria Straneo ITA 69:45
16 Feb	Yamaguchi HMar	Daniel Gatau KEN 60:59	Tomomi Tanaka JPN 69:24
23 Feb	San Juan 10k	Bidan Karoki KEN 28:35	Mary Wacera KEN 32:06
2 Mar	Ostia HMar	Aziz Lahbabi MAR 59:25	Caroline Chepkwony KEN 68:48
2 Mar	Paris HMar	Mulle Wasihun ETH 60:08	Yebrqual Melese ETH 69:23
9 Mar	Den Haag HMar	John Mwangangi KEN 60:26	Jip Vastenburg NED 73:15
9 Mar	Taroudant 10k	Hassan El Abbassi MAR 28:04	Asmae Leghzaoui MAR 32:31
9 Mar	Verbania HMar	Edwin Kibet KEN 60:47	Waganesh Amare ETH 70:08
15 Mar	Jacksonville 15k NC	Ben True USA 43:04	Shalane Flanagan USA 47:00
15 Mar	Kerzera 15k	Thomas Lokomwa KEN 43:13 *	Lucy Wambui Murigi KEN 49:28 *
16 Mar	Lisboa HMar	Bidan Karoki KEN 59:58	Worknesh Degefa ETH 68:46
16 Mar	Matsue HMar	women only	Ayumi Hagiwara JPN 70:17
16 Mar	New Orleans 8k	Isiah Koech KEN 22:09	Rkia El Moukim MAR 25:42
16 Mar	New York City HMar	Geoffrey Mutai KEN 60:50	Sally Kipyego KEN 68:31
22 Mar	Azkoitia HMar	Alex Korio Oloitiptip KEN 59:58	Marta Tigabea ETH 70:32
22 Mar	Laredo 10k	Wilson Too KEN 27:39	Paula González ESP 32:36
22 Mar	Mobile 10k	Julius Kogo KEN 27:58	Janet Bawcom USA 32:03
23 Mar	Milano HMar	Thomas Lokomwa KEN 61:39	Lucy Wambui Murigi KEN 70:52
30 Mar	Berlin HMar	Leonard P Komon KEN 59:14	Tadelech Bekele ETH 70:05
30 Mar	Carlsbad 4.96k	Dejen Gebremeskel ETH 13:13	Julia Bleasdale GBR 15:06
30 Mar	Warszawa HMar	Victor Kipchirchir KEN 60:48 *	Pauline Njeru KEN 69:06 *
5 Apr	Praha HMar	Peter Kirui KEN 59:22	Joyce Chepkirui KEN 66:19 *
6 Apr	Poznan HMar	Mark Kangogo KEN 62:45	Lucy Njeri KEN 71:32
6 Apr	Madrid HMar	Peter Lemuya KEN 62:00	Cynthia Limo KEN 69:40
6 Apr	Sacramento 10M	Shadrack Biwott USA 47:59	Kim Conley USA 54:44 *
6 Apr	Washington DC 10M	Stephen Sambu KEN 45:29	Mamitu Daska ETH 52:05
13 Apr	Vitry-sur-Seine HMar	Charles Ogari KEN 61:22	Leonidah Mosop ETH 71:47
13 Apr	Würzburg 10k	Nicholas Bor KEN 28:18	Margaret Wangari KEN 31:16 *
19 Apr	Boston 5k	Dejen Gebremeskel ETH 13:26 *	Molly Huddle USA 15:12 *=
19 Apr	New Orleans 10k	Leonard P Komon KEN 27:44	Risper Gesabwa KEN 31:43
19 Apr	Paderborn 10k	Frederick Ngeny KEN 28:28	Viola Jepchumba KEN 32:21
19 Apr	Paderborn HMar	Fentahun Hunegnaw ETH 62:16	Letebrhan Gebreslasea ETH 69:45
21 Apr	Dongio 10k	Cornelius Kangogo KEN 28:15	men only
27 Apr	Nice HMar	Kennedy Kipyego KEN 61:31	Janet Kisa KEN 71:01
3 May	Indianapolis HMar	Nelson Oyugi KEN 61:53 *	Lilian Mariita KEN 72:04

3 May	Luzern 8.71k/4.25k	Patrick Ereng KEN 25:02	Cynthia Kosgei KEN 13:17
4 May	Berlin 25k	Abraham Cheroben KEN 1:11:47	Janet Rono KEN 1:24:37
4 May	Philadelphia 10M	Mourad Marofit MAR 47:07	Bertukan Feyisa ETH 55:26
4 May	Spokane 12k	Allan Kiprono KEN 34:11	Mary Wacera KEN 39:36
10 May	Grand Rapids 25k	Samson Gebreyohanes ERI 1:14:08	Kellyn Johnson USA 1:25:26
10 May	New York City 10k	Stephen Sambu KEN 27:39	Joyce Chepkirui KEN 31:17 *
11 May	Sendai HMar	Johana Maina KEN 61:43	Yui Okada JPN 71:27
18 May	Bangalore 10k	Geoffrey Kamworor KEN 27:44 *	Lucy Kabuu KEN 31:46 *
18 May	Bucharest HMar	David Maru KEN 61:43	Vicoty Chepokimoi KEN 72:17
18 May	Cleveland 10k	Julius Koskei KEN 29:06	Lilian Mariita KEN 33:42
18 May	Gifu HMar	Bidan Karoki KEN 60:02 *	Visiline Jepkesho KEN 70:53
18 May	Göteborg HMar	Ghirmay Gebrselassie ERI 60:36	Worknesh Degefa ETH 70:12
18 May	Manchester 10k	Kenenisa Bekele ETH 28:23	Tirunesh Dibaba ETH 31:09
18 May	San Francisco 12k	Geoffrey Kenisi KEN 35:04	Diane Nukuri-Johnson BDI 40:19
18 May	Santos 10k	Joseph Aperumoi KEN 28:17	Nancy Kipron KEN 32:13
24 May	Karlovy Vary HMar	Teshome Mekonen ETH 61:21 *	Christelle Daunay FRA 69:17 *
24 May	Ottawa 10k	Wilson Kiprop KEN 28:01	Mary Keitany KEN 31:22 *
25 May	Casablanca HMar	John Lottang KEN 61:26	Daba Bedada ETH 71:11
25 May	Cobán HMar	Geoffrey Bundi KEN 64:10	Alena Shewarge ETH 78:25
25 May	Den Haag 10k	Edwin Kiprop KEN 28:07	Rose Kosgei KEN 33:30
25 May	Toa Baja 10k	Sammy Kitwara KEN 28:31	Daliris Lopez PUR 38:54
26 May	Boulder 10k (A)	Berhane Afewerki ERI 29:12	Mamitu Daska ETH 32:22
26 May	Huntsville 10k	Kimutai Cheruiyot KEN 29:20	Sophy Jepchirchir KEN 33:46
31 May	Albany 5k	women only	Lucy Kabuu KEN 15:21
1 Jun	San Diego HMar (dh 84m)	Solomon Deksisa ETH 60:12	Birhane Dibaba ETH 69:34
6 Jun	Oelde 10k	Richard Mengich KEN 28:14	Helah Kiprop KEN 32:20
7 Jun	Ceske Budejovice HMar	Geoffrey Kamworor KEN 60:09	Betelhem Moges ETH 72:31
14 Jun	Langueux 10k	Victor Chumo KEN 28:16	Angela Tanui KEN 31:51
14 Jun	New York City 10k	women only	Molly Huddle USA 31:37
14 Jun	Zwolle HMar	Jonathan Maiyo KEN 61:01	Helah Kiprop KEN 69:46
15 Jun	Casablanca 10k	Edwin Rotich KEN 28:13	Khadija Sammah MAR 32:23
21 Jun	Duluth HMar	Julius Koskei KEN 63:36	Cynthia Limo KEN 1:09:50
21 Jun	Olomouc HMar	Geoffrey Ronoh KEN 60:17 *	Edna Kiplagat KEN 1:08:53 *
22 Jun	Boston 10k	Stephen Sambu KEN 27:25	Mamitu Daska ETH 31:04 *
28 Jun	Appingedam 10k	Philip Langat KEN 28:10	Caroline Kilel KEN 32:03
29 Jun	Hamburg HMar	Charles Maina KEN 61:41 *	Agnes Mutune KEN 72:46 *
4 Jul	Atlanta 10km (dh 34m)	Christo Landry USA 28:25	Amy Hastings USA 32:16
4 Jul	Cedar Rapids 8k	Edwin Tabut KEN 24:16	Cynthia Limo KEN 25:48 *
12 Jul	Kingsport 8k	Simon Ndirangu KEN 22:30	Susan Jerotich KEN 26:46
13 Jul	Gateshead 10k	Stephen Kiprotich UGA 29:39	Gemma Steel GBR 32:45
13 Jul	Utica 15k	Geoffrey Bundi KEN 44:18	Mary Wacera KEN 50:14
18 Jul	Buffalo 4M	Yonas Mebrahtu ERI 18:19	Cynthia Limo KEN 20:03 *
26 Jul	Castelbuono 10k	Ghirmay Gebrselassie ERI 30:32	men only
26 Jul	Davenport 7M	Sean Quigley USA 33:28	Molly Huddle USA 36:14
27 Jul	Bogotá HMar (A)	Geoffrey Kamworor KEN 63:18	Rita Jeptoo KEN 73:39
27 Jul	Capitola 6M	Simon Ndirangui KEN 27:34	Caroline Rotich KEN 30:18
2 Aug	Wheeling 5k	Cleophas Ngetich KEN 13:50	Susan Jerotich KEN 15:39 *
3 Aug	Cape Elizabeth 10k	Bedan Karoki KEN 27:37	Gemma Steel GBR 31:27
10 Aug	Sydney 14k	Craig Mottram AUS 41:56	Casey Wood AUS 47:59
16 Aug	Parkersburg HMar	Julius Kogo KEN 62:25	Cynthia Limo KEN 71:12
16 Aug	Schortens 10M	Nicholas Togom KEN 46:32	Rose Kosgei KEN 53:43
17 Aug	Falmouth 7M	Stephen Sambu KEN 31:46	Betsy Saina KEN 35:56
24 Aug	Klagenfurt HMar	Geoffrey Ronoh KEN 59:45 *	Lucy Murigi KEN 71:34
24 Aug	Flint 10M	Julius Kogo KEN 46:36	Aliphine Tuliamuk-Bolton KEN 52:48
31 Aug	Arras 10k	Hillary Kipkemboi KEN 28:48	Rose Chelimo KEN 32:22
31 Aug	Rio de Janeiro HMar	Leul Gebreselassie ETH 63:44	Nancy Kipron KEN 73:13
1 Sep	New Haven 20k	Girma Mecheso ETH 61:26	Molly Huddle USA 68:34
6 Sep	Prague 10k	Geoffrey Ronoh KEN 27:28 *	Goretti Jepkoech KEN 31:05 *
6 Sep	Lille HMar	Mark Korir KEN 60:49	Rael Kiyara KEN 69:29
6 Sep	Luanda HMar	Sammy Kitwara KEN 60:24 *	Eunice Kirwa KEN 68:31 *
7 Sep	Hamburg 10k	Andrew Kimutai KEN 28:24	Rose Chelimo KEN 32:05 *

7 Sep	South Shields HMar (dh 30.5m)		
		Mo Farah GBR 60:00	Mary Keitany KEN 65:39 *
7 Sep	Tilburg 10M/10k	Bernard Koech KEN 45:12	Betsy Saina KEN 30:46
14 Sep	Gaia HMar HMar	Bernard Kipyego KEN 60:38	Purity Rionoripo KEN 70:40
14 Sep	Usti ned Labem HMar	Adugna Takele ETH 60:45	Goretti Jepkoech KEN 69:35
14 Sep	Wachau HMar	Daniel Wanjiru KEN 60:38 *	Joan Chelimo KEN 71:52
21 Sep	Philadelphia HMar	Bidan Karoki KEN 59:23	Aberu Kebede ETH 68:41
21 Sep	Providence 5k	Diego Estrada USA 13:57	Molly Huddle USA 15:10
21 Sep	Zaandam 10M	John Mwangangi KEN 45:45	Linet Masai KEN 53:09
28 Sep	Montbéliard HMar	Mulue Andom ETH 62:03	Peris Jepchirchir KEN 69:12 *
5 Oct	Breda HMar	Richard Mengich KEN 60:11 *	Rose Chelimo KEN 68:40 *
5 Oct	Cardiff HMar	Boniface Kongin KEN 62:02	Joan Chelimo KEN 72:26
5 Oct	Glasgow HMar	Stephen Mokoka KEN 61:25	Edna Kiplagat KEN 67:57 *
5 Oct	Lisboa HMar	Stephen Kibet KEN 61:06	Purity Rionoripo KEN 71:02
12 Oct	Berlin 10k	Kinde Atanew ETH 27:49	Joyce Chepkirui KEN 31:02
12 Oct	Boston HMar	Lelisa Desisa ETH 61:38	Mamitu Daska ETH 68:20 *
12 Oct	Groningen 4M	Abrar Osman ERI 17:33	Viola Kibiwot KEN 19:23
12 Oct	Paris 20k	Muhajr Haredin ETH 58:28	Rose Chelimo KEN 65:01 *
12 Oct	Rennes 10k/5k	Victor Chumo KEN 28:12	Janet Kisa KEN 15:32
13 Oct	Boston 10k	women only	Jordan Hasay USA 31:39
19 Oct	Birmingham HMar	Joel Kimutai KEN 61:39	Pauline Njeru KEN 70:48
19 Oct	Valencia HMar	Abraham Cheroben KEN 58:48 *	Emily Chebet KEN 68:01 *
26 Oct	Portsmouth 10M	James Rungaru KEN 46:31	Belaynesh Oljira ETH 52:40
2 Nov	Kabarnet HMar (A)	Joseph Kiprop KEN 61:25	Cynthia Limo KEN 70:06
9 Nov	Pittsburgh 10M	Leonard Korir KEN 46:52	Sara Hall USA 53:47 *
16 Nov	Alexandria 12k NC	Brian Shrader USA 34:11 *	Molly Huddle USA 38:08
16 Nov	Billancourt HMar	Yitayal Atnafu ETH 61:03	Bekelech Daba ETH 71:10
16 Nov	Nijmegen 15k	Aberu Kuma ETH 42:18	Priscah Jeptoo KEN 46:59
23 Nov	Addis Ababa 10k (A)	Azmeraw Bekele ETH 30:12	Wude Ayalew ETH 34:04
23 Nov	New Delhi HMar	Guye Adola ETH 59:06 *	Florence Kiplagat KEN 70:04
27 Nov	Manchester USA 4.75M	Ben True USA 21:34	Diane Nukuri BDI 24:38
6 Dec	Genève 7.25k/4.79k	Abraham Kipyatich KEN 20:57	Cynthia Kosgei KEN 15:51
7 Dec	Kochi HMar	Bernard Kipyego KEN 62:38 *	Helah Kiprop KEN 71:40 *
7 Dec	Kosa 10M	Jeremiah Karemi KEN 45:51	men only
7 Dec	's-Heerenberg 15k	Hizkial Tewelde ERI 43:27	Askale Merachi ETH 50:44
13 Dec	Sion 7.35k/5.25k	Abraham Kipyatich KEN 19:38	Cynthia Kosgei KEN 16:19
14 Dec	Zurich 9k/6.6k	Abraham Kipyatich KEN 25:40	Cynthia Kosgei KEN 21:27
28 Dec	Houilles 10k	Victor Chumo KEN 28:04	Peris Jepchirchir KEN 31:34
31 Dec	Bolzano 10.05k/5.05k	Muktar Edris ETH 29:08	Janet Kisa KEN 15:50
31 Dec	Luanda 10k	Stephen Kosgei KEN 28:34	Josephine Chepkoech KEN 32:19
31 Dec	Madrid 10km (dh 50m)	Mike Kigen KEN 27:51	Gemma Steel GBR 31:52
31 Dec	São Paulo 15k	Dawit Fikadu ETH 45:04	Wude Ayalew ETH 50:43

* course record

MARATHON REVIEW – 2014

By Marty Post

WHEN GEOFFREY MUTAI crossed the finish line of the 2011 Boston Marathon in two hours three minutes and two seconds many keen athletics observers believed it would be a decade or more before that time would be surpassed. After all it was almost a full minute better than the contemporary world record (2:03:59), and atypically strong tailwinds that day had combined with the downhill course to produce such a startling result.

Not only was that time bettered in less than three and a half years, but with it came the breaking of another historic time barrier. Dennis Kimetto's masterpiece at Berlin reduced the IAAF world record by 26 seconds to two hours two minutes and 57 seconds. It was the sixth straight men's world record set at the German capital, at a race which has managed to combine the maximum set of ingredients to produce surrealistic times. The course is generally flat with few significant turns. The race is held in late September when cool temperatures and low humidity prevail. And most importantly the organization brings in the most proficient pace-makers to set up a record quest.

The 2014 edition had virtually no wind, another bonus, and halfway was reached in 1:01:45, with Kimetto and the other pre-race favourite, Emmanuel Mutai, part of the lead group. Between 30 and 35 kilometres Kimetto blistered a 14:09 (the fastest such interval in history) and yet Mutai responded with a 14:11 and was just two seconds down. Kimetto was able to sustain a slightly faster tempo over that final 7.2 km, as he stretched the final lead to 16 seconds. Mutai ran 2:03:13, ten seconds better than the pre-race world record.

The most inspirational victory of the year – and for many years – occurred at the Boston Marathon in April. After the horror of the bombing there in 2013 what could be more apropos than a win by an American, something that seemed rather farfetched since it hadn't happened in 31 years? Indeed even when Meb Keflezghi, a naturalized U.S. citizen, broke away in the first half of the race, the rest of the elite field let him go, figuring that surely a man a month short of his 39th birthday would falter. But he did not, as he maintained the gap and strode to a stunning triumph, in a personal best 2:08:37 no less, the oldest man to wear the laurel wreath since 41-year-old Clarence DeMar in 1930.

The finest double performance of the year belonged to Wilson Kipsang. Against arguably the strongest field of the year at the Virgin Money London marathon, Kipsang scored a course record of 2:04:29. Six months later he added a victory at New York City making him the first man in history with wins at both of those races plus Berlin. It also earned him the $500,000 award as the winner of the 2013-14 World Marathon Majors competition.

Eliud Kipchoge also produced an impressive double win with a 2:05:00 (Rotterdam) and 2:04:11 (Chicago), a one-year total of 4:09:11, second only to Haile Gebrselassie's 4:08:52 in 2008 for two record-quality courses. Also at Chicago, Dickson Chumba, the winner at Tokyo, ran 2:04:32, the fastest third place time in history.

Ethiopian Tsegaye Mekonnen put his name into the record books, winning the Dubai Marathon in 2:04:32, the fastest time ever for a junior competitor. Mekonnen, five months from his 19th birthday, ran the third best debut on a record eligible course.

The women's elite field at Boston ran aggressively, with a first half split of 1:09:25. Rita Jeptoo ran almost the same pace for the second half and won in a course record 2:18:57. Ten women broke 2:34 as all-time best times were set for fourth through eleventh place. Jeptoo was also the race day winner at the Bank of America Chicago Marathon for the second consecutive year. However, it was later revealed that she had a positive doping test for EPO two weeks before that race when she was in Kenya. Athletics Kenya held a hearing on the matter in mid-January but a determination on a prospective disqualification was not expected for several months.

After earlier unsuccessful attempts Kenyans Edna Kiplagat (2:20:21, London) and Mary Keitany (2:25:07, New York City) made it into the winner's circle at those World Marathon Majors races for the first time. Tirfi Tsegaye was the top Ethiopian woman marathoner for 2014. She won the Tokyo Marathon in a course record 2:22:23 (the fastest time ever for the month of February) and then added another victory at Berlin, taking her personal best to 2:20:18. Her nine second margin over Feyse Tadese was the smallest ever in the history of that race.

There was also a standout age-group record breaking performance in 2014 by Gwen McFarlan. At the Ottawa Marathon the 80-year-old Canadian averaged 9:38.8 per mile for a total time of 4:12:44, almost 19 full minutes faster than any other octogenarian woman had ever run for 26.2 miles.

WINNERS OF 2014 INTERNATIONAL MARATHONS

Date	Race	Men	Time	Women	Time
2 Jan	Xiamen	Mariko Kiplagat KEN	2:08:06	Mare Dibaba ETH	2:21:36*
10 Jan	Tiberias	Tariku Jufar ETH	2:10:33	Divina Jepkosgei KEN	2:34:42
19 Jan	Houston	Bazu Worku ETH	2:07:32	Abebech Bekele ETH	2:25:52
19 Jan	Mumbai	Evans Rutto KEN	2:09:33	Dinknesh Mekash ETH	2:28:08
24 Jan	Dubai	Tsegaye Mekonnen ETH	2:04:32	Mulu Seboka ETH	2:25:01
26 Jan	Marrakech	Deribe Robi ETH	2:08:04	Meseret Kitata ETH	2:31:08
26 Jan	Osaka	women only		Tetyana Hamera-Shmyrko UKR	2:24:37
2 Feb	Beppu-Oita	Abraham Kiplimo UGA	2:09:23	Haruka Yamaguchi JPN	2:41:56
16 Feb	Hong Kong	Feyera Gemeda ETH	2:15:05	Rehima Kedir ETH	2:34:53
23 Feb	Taipei	Moses Kiptoo Kurgat KEN	2:16:21	Mercy Jelimo KEN	2:34:54
23 Feb	Tokyo	Dickson Chumba KEN	2:05:42*	Tirfi Tsegaye ETH	2:22:23*
23 Feb	Sevilla	Cosmas Kiplimo Lagat KEN	2:08:33*	Pamela Rotich KEN	2:35:43

28 Feb	Tel Aviv	Ezekiel Koech KEN	2:14:38	Margaret Njuguna KEN	2:44:22
2 Mar	Otsu	Bazu Worku ETH	2:09:10	men only	
2 Mar	Torreón	Stephen Njorege KEN	2:15:40	Alena Shewarge ETH	2:35:31
9 Mar	Brescia	Haile Tolossa ETH	2:13:24	Zeytuna Arbe ETH	2:35:05
9 Mar	Nagoya	women only		Mariya Konovalova RUS	2:23:43
9 Mar	Santa Monica (dh)	Gebo Burka ETH	2:10:37	Amena Gobena ETH	2:27:37
16 Mar	Barcelona	Getachew Abayu ETH	2:10:45	Frashiah Waithaka KEN	2:32:26
16 Mar	Seoul	Yacob Jarso ETH	2:06:17	Helah Kiprop KEN	2:27:29
23 Mar	Roma	Shume Hailu ETH	2:09:47	Ayelu Lemma ETH	2:34:49
30 Mar	Zhengzhou	William Yegon KEN	2:19:45	Winfrida Kwamboka KEN	2:37:09
6 Apr	Brighton	William Chebor KEN	2:09:25*	Alice Milgo KEN	2:35:33
6 Apr	Daegu	Yemane Tsegay Adhane ETH	2:06:51*	Mulu Seboka ETH	2:25:23
6 Apr	Debno	Cosmas Kyeva KEN	2:09:57	Arleta Meloch POL	2:43:02
6 Apr	Linz	Laban Mutai KEN	2:08:03	Lydia Rutto KEN	2:34:19
6 Apr	Milano	Francis Kiprop KEN	2:08:53	Visiline Jepkesho KEN	2:28:40
6 Apr	Paris	Kenenisa Bekele ETH	2:05:04*	Filomena Cheyech KEN	2:22:44
6 Apr	Santiago de Chile	Eriki Beyene ETH	2:11:50	Alena Shewarge ETH	2:35:30
6 Apr	Zürich	Hayle Lemi Berhanu ETH	2:10:40	Mona Stockhecke GER	2:34:04
13 Apr	London	Wilson Kipsang KEN	2:04:29*	Edna Kiplagat KEN	2:20:21
13 Apr	Lódz	Yared Shegumo POL	2:10:41	Karolina Jarzynska POL	2:28:12
13 Apr	Pyongyang	Pak Chol PRK	2:12:26	Kim Hye-gyong PRK	2:27:05
13 Apr	Rotterdam	Eliud Kipchoge KEN	2:05:00	Abebech Afework ETH	2:27:50
13 Apr	Warszawa	Tadese Tola ETH	2:06:55*	Bizuayehu Ehitu ETH	2:30:30
13 Apr	Wien	Getu Feleke ETH	2:05:41*	Anna Hahner GER	2:28:59
21 Apr	Boston (dh)	Meb Keflezighi USA	2:08:37	Rita Jeptoo KEN	2:18:57*
27 Apr	Düsseldorf	Gilbert Yegon KEN	2:08:07	Annie Bersagel USA	2:28:59
27 Apr	Enschede	Elijah Sang KEN	2:10:22	Reina Visser NED	2:42:07
27 Apr	Hannover	Henry Chirchir KEN	2:11:30	Souad Aït Salem ALG	2:33:09
27 Apr	Madrid	Ezekiel Chebii KEN	2:09:15*	Alem Fikre ETH	2:32:11
1 May	Dongying	Workneh Tiruneth ETH	2:12:02	Mestawet Tufa ETH	2:28:27
4 May	Geneva	Simon Mukun KEN	2:11:00	Milka Jerotich KEN	2:32:34
4 May	Hamburg	Shumi Dechasa ETH	2:06:43	Georgina Rono KEN	2:26:47
4 May	Volgograd	Sergey Rybin RUS	2:16:43	Gulnara Vygovskaya RUS	2:33:47
11 May	Praha	Patrick Terer KEN	2:08:07	Firehiwot Dado ETH	2:23:34
11 May	Skopje	Emmanuel Samal KEN	2:14:26	Lucy Wambui Murigi KEN	2:37:47
18 May	Cleveland	Philip Lagat KEN	2:12:39	Sarah Kiptoo KEN	2:34:58
18 May	København	Julius Mutai KEN	2:17:54	Ayelu Abebe ETH	2:40:02
18 May	Lima	Simon Njoroge KEN	2:13:44	Gladys Ruto KEN	2:46:26
18 May	Riga	Yu Chiba JPN	2:13:44	Tigist Teshome Ayanu ETH	2:36:51*
25 May	Ottawa	Yemane Tsegay ETH	2:06:54*	Tigist Tufa ETH	2:24:31*
31 May	Luxembourg	Johnston Maiyo KEN	2:15:44	Meseret Godana ETH	2:38:56
31 May	Stockholm	Benjamin Bitok KEN	2:13:21	Isabellah Andersson SWE	2:32:28
1 Jun	Lanzhou	Gilbert Chepkwony KEN	2:14:18	Eunice Kirwa KEN	2:31:53
21 Jun	Duluth	Dominic Ondoro KEN	2:09:06*	Pasca Cheruiyot Myers KEN	2:33:45
6 Jul	Gold Coast	Silas Limo TAN	2:09:14*	Asami Kato JPN	2:28:51
27 Jul	Rio de Janeiro	Edmilson dos Reis BRA	2:17:12	Ednah Mukwanah KEN	2:40:32
16 Aug	Helsinki	Justus Kiprono KEN	2:20:42	Natalia Starkova RUS	2:37:56
31 Aug	Ciudad de México	Raul Pacheco PER	2:18:29	Shewarge Alene Amare ETH	2:41:21
31 Aug	Perth	Yuki Kawauchi JPN	2:12:53*	Nancy Rotich KEN	2:43:28
31 Aug	Sapporo	Shigeki Tsuji JPN	2:15:24	Azusa Nojiri JPN	2:30:26
7 Sep	Johannesburg	Ketema Bekele ETH	2:15:05	Florence Jepkosgei KEN	2:36:34
14 Sep	Köln	Anthony Maritim KEN	2:10:26	Shasho Insermu ETH	2:35:36
				drugs dq Julia Mumbi KEN	2:28:00
14 Sep	Münster	Josphat Kiprono KEN	2:10:40	Yenealem Ayano ETH	2:40:40
20 Sep	Hengshui	Markos Geneti ETH	2:07:38	Rebecca Kangogo Chesire KEN	2:27:16
21 Sep	Cape Town	William Kibor KEN	2:10:45	Meseret Mengistu ETH	2:30:56
21 Sep	Sydney	Gebo Burka ETH	2:11:18*	Eshetu Degefa ETH	2:29:42
28 Sep	Berlin	Dennis Kimetto KEN	2:02:57*	Tirfi Tsegaye ETH	2:20:18

28 Sep	Warszawa	Victor Kipchirchir KEN	2:09:59	Svitlana Stanko UKR	2:33:04
5 Oct	Bucharest	Boaz Kipyego KEN	2:13:37	Paula Todoran ROU	2:41:24
5 Oct	Kosice	Gilbert Chepkwony KEN	2:08:26	Lydia Rutto KEN	2:28:48
5 Oct	Lisboa	Samuel Ndungi KEN	2:08:21*	Visiline Jepkesho KEN	2:26:47*
5 Oct	St. Paul	Tyler Pennel USA	2:13:32	Esther Erb USA	2:34:01
12 Oct	Chicago	Eliud Kipchoge KEN	2:04:11	Mare Dibaba ETH	2:25:37
				(dq Rita Jeptoo KEN	2:24:35#)
12 Oct	Eindhoven	Tilahun Regassa ETH	2:06:21	Iwona Lewandowska POL	2:28:33
12 Oct	Kuala Lumpur	Kennedy Kiprop Lilan KEN	2:17:47	Hellen Wanjiku Mugo KEN	2:43:22
12 Oct	Melbourne	Dominic Ondoro KEN	2:11:30	Nikki Chapple AUS	2:31:05
12 Oct	Poznan	Kiprotich Kirui KEN	2:13:28	Irene Chepkirui Makori KEN	2:31:55
19 Oct	Amsterdam	Bernard Kipyego KEN	2:06:22	Bethlehem Moges ETH	2:28:35
19 Oct	Beijing	Birhanu Gebru ETH	2:10:42	Fatuma Sado ETH	2:30:03
19 Oct	Gyeongju	Silas Cheboit KEN	2:07:15	Lim Kyung-hee KOR	2:39:56
19 Oct	Reims	Dejene Kelkilew ETH	2:11:21	Ayantu Hailemaryam ETH	2:33:59
19 Oct	São Paulo	Paul Kangogo KEN	2:14:18	Elizabeth Rumokol KEN	2:42:27
19 Oct	Toronto	Laban Korir KEN	2:08:15	Mulu Seboka ETH	2:23:15
26 Oct	Casablanca	Philemon Rotich KEN	2:10:19	Sarah Kiptoo KEN	2:35:22
26 Oct	Chunchon	Nickson Kurgat KEN	2:07:11	Yeum Ko-eun KOR	2:43:33
26 Oct	Frankfurt	Mark Kiptoo KEN	2:06:59	Aberu Kebede ETH	2:22:21
26 Oct	Jakarta	Julius Seurei KEN	2:14:51	Winfridah Kwamboka KEN	2:40:25*
26 Oct	Ljubljana	Ishmael Bushendich KEN	2:08:25*=	Janet Rono KEN	2:29:16
26 Oct	Nairobi (A)	Peter Kosgei KEN	2:12:24	Edith Irungu KEN	2:32:02
26 Oct	Osaka	Jackson Limo KEN	2:11:43	Maryna Damantsevich BLR	2:33:04
26 Oct	Rennes	Felix Kiprotich KEN	2:08:05*	Olha Kotovska UKR	2:28:47
26 Oct	Toulouse	Raymond Kemboi KEN	2:10:59	Sardana Trofimova RUS	2:28:18
26 Oct	Venezia	Mamo Ketema ETH	2:16:45	Konjit Tilahun ETH	2:40:20
27 Oct	Dublin	Eliud Too KEN	2:14:47	Esther Macharia KEN	2:34:15
2 Nov	New York City	Wilson Kipsang KEN	2:10:59	Mary Keitany KEN	2:25:07
2 Nov	Porto	Workneh Fikre Serbessa ETH	2:13:10	Marta Tigabea ETH	2:31:54
2 Nov	Shanghai	Stephen Mokoka RSA	2:08:43*	Tigist Tufa ETH	2:21:52*
2 Nov	Soweto	Sintayehu Legese ETH	2:17:55	Meseret Mengistu ETH	2:36:02
9 Nov	Athína	Felix Kandie KEN	2:10:37*	Naomi Maiyo KEN	2:41:06
9 Nov	Beirut	Fikadu Girma ETH	2:12:28	Mulahabt Tsega ETH	2:29:17
9 Nov	Nice to Cannes	Sumi Hailu ETH	2:09:27	Rose Chepchumba KEN	2:33:52
9 Nov	Seoul	Feyisa Bekele ETH	2:07:43	Ahn Seul-ki KOR	2:37:47
9 Nov	Xichang	Noah Chepngabit KEN	2:12:48	Eshetu Degega ETH	2:30:26
16 Nov	Hefei	William Yegon KEN	2:10:23	Winfrida Kwamboka KEN	2:33:18
16 Nov	Istanbul	Hafid Chani MOR	2:11:53	Amane Gobena ETH	2:28:46
16 Nov	Torino	Samuel Rutto KEN	2:10:00	Esther Ndiema KEN	2:28:41
16 Nov	Valencia	Jacob Kendagor KEN	2:08:39	Beata Naigambo NAM	2:30:54
16 Nov	Yokohama	women only		Tomomi Tanaka JPN	2:26:57
23 Nov	Guangzhou	Deressa Chimsa ETH	2:13:18	Agnes Barsosio KEN	2:31:17
30 Nov	Firenze	Abel Kipsang KEN	2:09:55	Bizuayehe Ehite ETH	2:31:28
30 Nov	La Rochelle	Afewerk Mesfin ETH	2:12:15	Peninah Arusei KEN	2:33:09
7 Dec	Castellón	Daniel Kosgei KEN	2:10:13	Magdaline Mukunzi KEN	2:35:38
7 Dec	Fukuoka	Patrick Makau KEN	2:08:22	men only	
7 Dec	Makau	Julius Kiplimo Masei KEN	2:14:45	Hellen Mugo KEN	2:33:35
7 Dec	Sacramento (dh)	Jacob Chemtai KEN	2:11:57	Olga Mazuronak BLR	2:27:33*
7 Dec	Singapore	Kenneth Mungara KEN	2:16:42	Waganesh Mekasha ETH	2:46:54
14 Dec	Honolulu	Wilson Chebet KEN	2:15:35	Joyce Chepkirui KEN	2:30:23
14 Dec	Kisumu (short?)	Deklerk Omari KEN	2:13:04	Rebecca Chepchirchir KEN	2:41:00

# see comment in previous narrative. A = altitude over 1000m; * course record,
dh = net downhill >1m/km: Santa Monica 131m. Boston 136m, Sacramento 105m

REVIEW OF ULTRARUNNING 2014

by Andy Milroy

IN SOME WAYS 2014 was a throw back to the years before Ultra World championships were held. There were no 24-hour championships and the 100k championships did not take place until November. To a degree this lack of focus was beneficial, giving elite athletes the freedom to run more local races without pressure, and seek to set records.

For the first time the World 100k was held in the Middle East – in Doha, Qatar. The favourite was probably Steve Way who had run 6:19:20 at Gravesend in May, but it was neither Way nor the leading performer from 2013 Vasiliy Larkin (6:18:26) who were to emerge the winner, but a relatively unknown American, Max King. His 6:27:43 was a new US record and behind him came Jonas Buud SWE 6:32:04 and José Antonio Requejo ESP 6:37:01. The team title went to the USA 20:08:06 from JPN 20:55:09 and GBR 20:57:51. Because King set his best performance in a major international competition, defeating Way, he is the obvious contender for World No. 1.

The winner of the women's race was the Canadian based Ellie Greenwood of Great Britain in the best time of the year, 7:30:48, with the up and coming Japanese talent Chiyuki Mochizuki second in 7:38:23. Third was the former Polish runner, now competing for Great Britain, Joasia Zakrzewski 7:42:02. Great Britain took the team title convincingly with Jo Meek finishing fourth. Their combined times was 22:56:27, from JPN 23:22:32 and the USA 24:05:25. Greenwood is the obvious World No 1. Her second World 100k title followed a win in the tough Comrades Marathon, giving her a unique double that no man or woman had achieved before.

In the other major standard event, the 24 hours, the championship set for Soochow in Taiwan in December was cancelled but with many top runners peaking for this event, there was a proliferation of good 24 hours marks in December.

Before moving on to these, it is worth mentioning that as in 2013 when there were several notable 100 mile times, in 2014 national records for the 200k distance were set on several occasions. Yoshikazu Hara set a Japanese national record of 16:04 (official time not yet available) in December; only Yiannis Kouros has run faster on the track. Zach Bitter also set a US track record of 16:23:28 in 2014. Katalin Nagy, formerly of Hungary but now apparently a US citizen, set two US records at 200k, first 20:01:06 and then 19:29:02 when completing the greatest 24 hour distance for 2014. Using 200k as a useful intermediate target in a 24 hour event is logical.

This experimentation with the 200k makes sense particularly without the added pressure of an international championships. As I said earlier the cancellation of the World 24 hour scheduled for December meant that elite runners peaked for national events that month instead. For much of 2014 the world 24 hour lists were headed by a pair of Australian marks set in Coburg in April. Barry Loveday, formerly of GBR, ran 265.000k and the former Canadian Bernadette Benson 238.261k, and these were not surpassed until December. Then Yoshikazu Hara JPN not only set a new Asian 24 hour track best, a mark unsurpassed by anyone other than Kouros, with 285.366k, and is the obvious World No.1. With no head-to-head competition, the top woman is less certain, but Nagy with her 243.725k is well clear of any opposition.

At the longer 48 hour event the best male mark was set by the Italian Tiziano Marchesi with 407.885k in Athens, Greece, with the best female mark 389.611k by the American 24-hour national team member Traci Falbo indoors on a 400m track in Anchorage, Alaska.

In the classic 6-day event the best male mark was also set indoors on the same track in Anchorage, Joe Fejes running 933.902k. Oliver Chaigne of France was his nearest challenger in term of distance, running 920.771k on the road in Balatonfüred in Hungary. The best female mark was 764.438k on the road in New York by the veteran Catherine (Dipali) Cunningham GBR/AUS resident in the USA.

Actual 1000 mile races are at present rare and far between. The best times in 2014 were achieved in the much longer 3100 mile event in New York, the longest race in the world held on a certified course. Mikhail Ukrainskyi UKR covered 1000M in 14 days 6:15:54 en route to winning in 44 days 6:58:10 and the Australian Sarah Barnett ran 1000 miles in 15 days 15:13:36, going on to be first woman in 50 days 3:55:08.

Although standard distances dominate the sport, there is still room for the classic point-to-point events which are the roots of the sport. The 89.28k Comrades Marathon was won in 5:28:34 by Bongmusa Mthembu RSA from Ludwick

Mamabolo, the defending 'down run' winner from 2012 who recorded a time of 5:33.14; Gift Kelehe, was third in 5:34.39. Ellie Greenwood finally broke the 11-year Russian stranglehold in a spectacular women's race. Her time was 6:18:15 from the Russians Yelena Nurgaliyeva, bidding to win a record ninth crown, 6:23:18, and her twin sister Olesya Nurgaliyeva 6:24:51. For those with long memories the former track star, Zola Budd Pieterse RSA was 7th in 6:55:55.

The other classic point-to-point event is the Spartathlon from Athens to Sparta. The Italian Ivan Cudin won it convincingly for the third time in 22:29:29 from Florian Reus GER 23:57:13 and Andrzej Radzikowski POL way back in third with 25:49:05. Szilvia Lubics HUN took the women's title in 26:53:40 from Nagy 28:55:03 and Eva Esnaola ESP third some way back in 30:52:41.

There was just one extended stage race in 2014 – the Trans Gaule – 19 stages crossing France from Roscoff to Gruissan-Plage covering 1192k. Stéphane Pelissier of France won in an elapsed time of 107:19:44 from the Taiwanese runner Wan-Chun Tsai 112:38:58 and Carmen Hildebrand repeated her women's victory of 2013 in the slightly faster time of 116:15:15.

The 24 hours has long been seen as well suited to the Japanese temperament as the remarkable Mami Kudo has shown with her numerous world bests in the event on both road and track, and in 2014 a Japanese man at last reached his potential at 24 hours with a new Asian record. Yoshikazu Hara's mark perhaps shows that the event is now moving firmly into a post-Kouros era now the great Greek runner is no longer the hugely dominant figure he once was.

The focus on the 200k as a major stepping stone towards stronger 24 hour performances is a positive sign. The 24 hours is a finely judged balancing act where pace judgement, feeding and drink strategies have to be at optimum levels to achieve good results. The growth in interest in the longer 6-day event, as well as the 48 hours, continues. There were thirteen such 6-day events in 2014 up from the ten in 2013.

So it was an intriguing and different year in 2014 as longer events became more popular and new talents emerged.

World Mountain Racing Trophy/Championships

Held annually from 1985. Most titles 1985–2014

Men	6 Jonathan Wyatt NZL 1998, 2000, 2002, 2004–05, 2008
	5 Marco De Gasperi ITA 1997, 1999, 2001, 2003, 2007 (& Junior 1996)
Women	5 Andre Mayr AUT 2006, 2008, 2010, 2012, 2014
	4 Isabelle Guillot FRA 1989, 1991, 1993, 1997
	4 Gudrun Pflüger AUT 1992, 1994–96
Men team	23 Italy, 4 Eritrea
Women team	15 Italy, 4 France & Switzerland

European Mountain Racing Trophy

Most titles 1995–2014

Men	3 Antonio Molinari ITA 1998–9, 2001
Women	3 Andrea Mayr AUT 2005, 2013–14

IAU World 100 Kilometres Challenge/World Cup/Championships

Held annually (except for 2013) from 1987. Most titles 1987–2014

Men	3 Konstantin Santalov RUS 1992–93, 1996
	3 Giorgio Calcaterra ITA 2008, 2011–12
	Fastest: 6:18:09 Valmir Nuñes BRA 1995
Women	3 Tatyana Zhyrkova RUS 2002, 2004, 2008
	Fastest: 7:00:27 Norimi Sakurai JPN 2007
Men team	7 Russia, 4 Italy & Japan
Women team	9 Russia, 4 France

European 100 Kilometres Championships

Most titles 1992–2014

Men	3 Jaroslav Janicki POL 1994–96
	3 Giorgio Calcaterra ITA 2008, 2011–12
	Fastest: 6:23:22 Giorgio Calcaterra ITA 2012
Women	2 by four women
	Fastest: 7:19:51 Tatyana Zhyrkova RUS 2003
Men team	7 Russia, 4 Italy & Japan
Women team	9 Russia, 4 France

EUROPEAN CHAMPIONSHIPS 2014

August 12-17, Zürich, Switzerland

BOTH BRITAIN AND France had their most successful ever European Championships, as success after success came their way and they ended with 23 medals apiece, and 12 and 9 gold medals respectively. Russia were just ahead of them in the points table, but had only three gold medals, while Poland won 12 medals and Germany just 8 although faring better on the in-depth points calculations.

The top performance came from a Frenchman, as it was the remarkable 3:32:33 for 50 kilometres walk by Yohann Diniz, a time that took 1:41 off the world record. The discus throw of 71.08 by Sandra Perkovic, winning by a margin of 5.75m, and hammer 78.76 by Anita Wlodarczyk (with the 50k walk and the women's marathon the only new championship records) headed the other world leading marks: 82.69 hammer by Krisztián Pars, 8616 decathlon by Andrey Kravchenko, 22.03 for 200m by Dafne Schippers and 2.01 by Ruth Beitia that tied the world best of 2014. Schippers achieved a sprint double in majestic style to emulate her compatriot Fanny Blankers-Koen, and the other individual double champion was Mo Farah, who despite just one track run this year prior to the championships, produced his renowned sprint finish to devastating effect in both 5000m and 10,000m. Thirteen individual titles were retained and of these Farah (5000m), Robert Harting (discus), Olga Saladukha (triple jump) and Perkovic won three in a row (2010, 2012 and 2014). Of course this feat is easier in these days with biennial championships. Britain dominated the men's sprints; taking the 100, 200 and 400m titles as well as both relays.

Standards were generally excellent given that the weather was very variable – from

Medals and Points Table

Points: 8 for 1st to 1 for 8th.

Nation	*Men*			*Women*			*Total*			*Points:*	*2014*	*2012*
	G	*S*	*B*	*G*	*S*	*B*	*G*	*S*	*B*	*Medals*		
RUS	1	3	8	2	3	5	3	6	13	22	214	147.5
GBR	8	3	3	4	2	3	12	5	6	23	196	96
FRA	5	3	4	4	5	2	9	8	6	23	191.5	139.5
GER	2	1	-	2	-	3	4	1	3	8	167	199.5
POL	1	5	3	1	-	2	2	5	5	12	132	54.5
ESP	1	1	1	1	-	2	2	1	3	6	86	63
UKR	1	1	1	1	4	-	2	5	1	8	82	143.5
NED	-	-	-	3	2	1	3	2	1	6	73	61
ITA	1	-	-	1	1	-	2	1	-	3	69	58.5
CZE	-	1	1	1	-	1	1	1	2	4	47.5	67.5
BLR	1	-	-	1	-	-	2	-	-	2	43	47
SWE	-	-	-	1	2	-	1	2	-	3	34	35
FIN	1	-	1	-	-	-	1	-	1	2	29	9
SUI	1	-	-	-	-	-	1	-	-	1	26	10
CRO	-	-	-	1	-	1	1	-	1	2	24	8
POR	-	-	-	-	-	1	-	-	1	1	24	38
SVK	-	1	-	-	1	-	-	2	-	2	22	19.5
BEL	-	-	-	-	-	1	-	-	1	1	22	27
SRB	-	-	-	-	2	-	-	2	-	2	23	21
HUN	1	-	-	-	-	1	1	-	1	2	19	19
GRE	-	1	-	-	1	-	1	2	-	2	19	17
EST	-	2	-	-	-	-	-	2	-	2	19	11
TUR	-	-	1	-	-	-	-	-	1	1	19	66.5
IRL	-	-	1	-	-	-	-	-	1	1	16	11

More points
(medals): ROU 15, BUL 13, LAT 12, NOR, (1S) 10, SLO 9, AZE 7, ISR, (1B), DEN 6; LTU 5, BIH 3

As usual I have adjusted the points to cater for ties, thus changing the mathematically incorrect scores issued, as usual, in official results. G = gold, S= silver, B = bronze for medals. Note that several nations did not send full teams to the 2012 edition, when there were also no marathons and walks.

torrential rain and a storm warning that caused a long delay in the decathlon pole vault to overcast conditions much of the time and lovely sunny weather for the first morning and for the final day. The walks were conducted on an up and back course on the banks of the river Limmat and the marathon was on a four-loop course in the centre of the city (with a steep hill incorporated).

The wondrous Jo Pavey became, at 40, the oldest ever European women's champion with her heart-warming victory at 10,000m. Both she and javelin winner Barbora Spotáková had given birth in 2013. Beitia also seems to get better and better with age and at 35 won the high jump with 2.01 and Daunay, marathon victor, was aged 39.

The official attendance for all sessions was given as 148,432 (51,817 morning, 96,615 evening) with a peak of 18,939 for the evening of the fourth day (15 August).

*Dates given in brackets after the heading for each event are those of the final. * Championships record.*

Men

100 Metres (13th) (-0.4)

1. James Dasaolu GBR	10.06
2. Christophe Lemaitre FRA	10.13
3. Harry Aikines-Aryeetey GBR	10.22
4. Dwain Chambers GBR	10.24
5. Lukas Jakubczyk GER	10.25
6. Jaysuma Saidy Ndure NOR	10.35
7. Catalin Cîmpeanu ROU	10.44
8. Yazaldes Nascimento POR	10.46

AFTER LEMAITRE HAD been fastest in the heats with 10.16, he was beaten 10.04 to 10.10 by Dasaolu in the semis, and the margin between these two favourites was slightly more in the final that was run in cold weather and into a slight headwind after half an hour's delay. Aikines-Aryeetey and Chambers, in his fifth European 100m final and his sixth European Championship, made it three British sprinters in the top four.

200 Metres (15th) (-1.6)

1. Adam Gemili GBR	19.98
2. Christophe Lemaitre FRA	20.15
3. Sergiy Smelyk UKR	20.30
4. Churandy Martina NED	20.37
5. Diego Marani ITA	20.43
6. Ramil Guliyev TUR	20.48
7. Lik.-Stefános Tsákonas GRE	20.53
8. Karol Zalewski POL	20.58

GEMILI WAS FASTEST in each round (20.39 heat, 20.23 semi) as Lemaitre, the 100m/200m double champion of 2010, won the other semi in 20.26. Despite the cold (13°C), rain-sodden track and a 1.6m headwind in the straight, Gemili equalled his pb of 19.98 with a brilliant run to beat his French rival clearly. Smelyk set pbs in both semi (20.32) and final.

400 Metres (15th)

1. Martyn Rooney GBR	44.71
2. Matthew Hudson-Smith GBR	44.75
3. Donald Sanford ISR	45.27
4. Jakub Krzewina POL	45.52
5. Conrad Williams GBR	45.53
6. Kamghe Gaba GER	45.83
7. Samuel García ESP	46.35
dns. Jonathan Borlée BEL	-

ROONEY, THIRD IN 2010, at last won a major title and missed his pb by just 0.11, but was chased hard by 19 year-old Hudson-Smith, in his first year concentrating on 400m running, who reduced his pb from 44.97. Sanford set Israeli records in semi (45.39) and final.

800 Metres (15th)

1. Adam Kszczot POL	1:44.15
2. Artur Kuciapski POL	1:44.89
3. Mark English IRL	1:45.03
4. Andreas Bube DEN	1:45.21
5. Marcin Lewandowski POL	1:45.78
6. Amel Tuka BIH	1:46.12
7. Jozef Repcik SVK	1:46.29
8. Pierre-Ambroise Bosse FRA	1:46.55

BOSSE WENT OUT hard and led at 400m in 50.97 and 600m in 1:17.24, but took 29.31 for the last 200m. Kszczot was 6m down at 400/600 but sprinted clear from his unheralded team-mate Kuciapski with 2010 winner Lewandowski completing three Poles in the top five. Bube slipped from second to fourth in the closing stages as English snatched the bronze medal.

1500 Metres (17th)

1. Mahiedine Mekhissi-Benabbad FRA	3:45.60
2. Henrik Ingebrigtsen NOR	3:46.10
3. Chris O'Hare GBR	3:46.18
4. Paul Robinson IRL	3:46.35
5. Homiyu Tesfaye GER	3:46.46
6. David Bustos ESP	3:46.92
7. Timo Benitz GER	3:47.26
8. Tarik Moukrime BEL	3:47.33

TWELVE MEN BEAT 3:40 in the heats, but the final was run at a ridiculously slow pace and inevitably several men fell. There was a savage increase in pace on the third lap (55.55) and O'Hare was in the lead just before the bell, when Mekhissi shot past everyone to open up an extraordinary lead with 12.2 for the next 100m. Despite showboating again (see steeplechase) along the finishing straight, vest in place this time, the 29 year-old Frenchman covered the last lap in 52.17.

5000 Metres (17th)

1. Mohammed Farah GBR	14:05.82
2. Hayle Ibrahimov AZE	14:08.32
3. Andrew Vernon GBR	14:09.48

4. Robert Ringer GER	14:10.92
5. Roberto Alaiz ESP	14:11.47
6. Bouabdellah Tahri FRA	14:11.62
7. Arne Gabius GER	14:11.84
8. Antonio Abadía ESP	14:11.89

FARAH WON HIS third successive 5000m title (after 2nd in 2006). The winning time was the slowest since 1946 but Farah's finishing speed was phenomenal with 58.44 and 52.23 for the last two laps and he won by nearly 20m. Vernon added bronze to his silver at 10,000m.

10,000 Metres (13th)

1. Mohammed Farah GBR	28:08.11
2. Andrew Vernon GBR	28:08.66
3. Ali Kaya TUR	28:08.72
4. Polat Kemboi Arikan TUR	28:11.11
5. Bashir Abdi BEL	28:13.61
6. Daniele Meucci ITA	28:19.79
7. Bouabdellah Tahri FRA	28:25.03
8. Stefano La Rosa ITA	28:49.99

THE RACE WAS slowly run until the ninth kilometre was run in 2:44.58, and then Farah covered the last kilometre in 2:31.57 to regain the title he won in 2010. Vernon came through from fourth at 200m to take silver. 18 of 24 finished.

Marathon (17th)

1. Daniele Meucci ITA	2:11:08
2. Yared Shegumo POL	2:12:00
3. Aleksey Reunkov RUS	2:12:15
4. Javier Guerra ESP	2:12:32
5. Viktor Röthlin SUI	2:13:07
6. Abdellatif Meftah FRA	2:13:16
7. Ruggero Pertile ITA	2:14:18
8. André Pollmächer GER	2:14:51

European Marathon Cup (3 to score): 1. RUS 6:46:04, 2. FRA 6:46:29, 3. SUI 6:46:48, 4. ITA 6:46:58, 5. DEN 6:54:01, 6. UKR 7:00:14, 7. IRL 7:01:02, 8. NED 7:08:25, 9. SWE 7:09:56, 10. ISR 7:19:50.

ONLY 50 OF 70 starters completed the fairly tough course on a sunny (14-17°C) morning. Marcin Chabowski broke away early on and led at halfway in 64:45, but dropped out exhausted about 6k from the finish. Meucci judged his race to perfection to run out an untroubled winner in a pb of 2:11:08 (65:34 for each half).

3000 Metres Steeplechase (14th)

1. Yoann Kowal FRA	8:26.66
2. Krystian Zalewski POL	8:27.11
3. Ángel Mullera ESP	8:29.16
4. Sebastián Martos ESP	8:30.08
5. Ivan Lukyanov RUS	8:32.50
6. Jukka Keskisalo FIN	8:32.70
7. Steffen Uliczka GER	8:32.99
8. Tarik Langat Akdag TUR	8:33.13

MAHIEDINE MEKHISSI-BENABBAD was heading untroubled for a record third European title in this event, when, approaching the final barrier, he celebrated prematurely. He pulled off his vest, stuffed it into his mouth and, milking the crowd's appreciation, crossed the line bare-chested in 8:25.30. But that wasn't the end of the affair. The Spanish camp, on behalf of fourth finisher Mullera, lodged a protest for infringing IAAF rules 143.1 & 143.7 relating to approved clothing and displaying bib numbers. Mekhissi was deleted from first place; the French counter-protested but their appeal was dismissed. The kilometre splits were 2:55.92, 2:49.30 and 2:41.44 (2:40.08 for Mekhissi; 60.9 last lap). Víctor García fell heavily at the final barrier (as he had in the 2012 final!) in his heat and was stretchered off.

110 Metres Hurdles (14th) (0.5)

1. Sergey Shubenkov RUS	13.19
2. William Sharman GBR	13.27
3. Pascal Martinot-Lagarde FRA	13.29
4. Balázs Baji HUN	13.29
5. Petr Svoboda CZE	13.63
6. Artur Noga POL	14.25
dq (3). Dimitri Bascou FRA	(13.28)
dns. Lawrence Clarke GBR	-

IN THE HEATS the three eventual medallists each won in 13.29, then in the semis the first was won by Sharman from Shubenkov, each running 13.19, and the second by favourite Martinot-Lagarde in 13.17. In the final Martinot-Lagarde hit nearly every hurdle and only won a medal because Bascou was disqualified for obstruction, his left arm hitting Baji as he came from lane 8 into lane 7. Sharman hit the seventh hurdle with his trail leg and the eighth with his lead leg and that enabled Shubenkov to win by close to a metre in 13.19. Baji set a Hungarian record in fourth place.

400 Metres Hurdles (15th)

1. Kariem Hussein SUI	48.96
2. Rasmus Mägi EST	49.06
3. Denis Kudryavtsev RUS	49.16
4. Timofey Chalyy RUS	49.56
5. Felix Franz GER	49.83
6. Emir Bekric SRB	49.90
7. Varg Königsmark GER	49.91
8. Oskari Mörö FIN	50.14

HUSSEIN RAN THE race of his life to win despite stumbling a few strides after landing from the last hurdle, holding on against a fast finishing Mägi. Kudryavtsev was fastest in the heats with 49.05 and the three fastest times in the semis came in the third, won by Mägi in an Estonian record 48.54 from Chalyy 48.69 and Franz 48.96, with Hussein and Kudryavtsev the other winners.

High Jump (15th)

1. Bohdan Bondarenko UKR	2.35

2. Andriy Protsenko UKR	2.33
3. Ivan Ukhov RUS	2.30
4. Jaroslav Bába CZE	2.30
5. Daniyil Tsyplakov RUS	2.26
6. Yuriy Krymarenko UKR	2.26
7= Marco Fassinotti ITA	2.26
7= Tihomir Ivanov BUL	2.26
7= Gianmarco Tamberi ITA	2.26

BONDARENKO STARTED WITH a second attempt clearance at 2.30 and sealed gold with 2.35 at his second try before taking one attempt at 2.43. Protsenko went over 2.33 third time as Ukhov and Bába found this beyond them in inclement weather.

Pole Vault (16th)

1. Renaud Lavillenie FRA	5.90
2. Pawel Wojciechowski POL	5.70
3= Jan Kudlicka CZE	5.70
3= Kevin Ménaldo FRA	5.70
5. Aleksandr Gripich RUS	5.65
6. Piotr Lisek POL	5.65
7. Konstadínos Filippídis GRE	5.60
8. Edi Maia POR	5.60

LAVILLENIE EMULATED Wolfgang Nordwig by winning a third title at the event; he cleared 5.65 and 5.80 first time and 5.90 at the second go before failing three times at 6.01. Wojciechowski took silver with a clean card before failing at 5.75.

Long Jump (17th)

1. Greg Rutherford GBR	8.29/-0.4
2. Loúis Tsátoumas GRE	8.15/-0.4
3. Kafétien Gomis FRA	8.14/1.5
4. Eusebio Cáceres ESP	8.11/-0.7
5. Michel Tornéus SWE	8.09/0.1
6. Ignisious Gaisah NED	8.08/-0.6
7. Tomasz Jaszczuk POL	8.07/1.5
8. Christian Reif GER	7.95/0.5

TSÁTOUMAS LED THE qualifiers with 8.19 from Cáceres 8.05 and Rutherford 8.03, and jumped 8.15 in the first round of the final. But he managed only a best of 7.86 thereafter and Rutherford was a class apart with 8.27, 8.18 and 8.29 in rounds 2-4. Cáceres jumped 8.11 in round 2 but was passed by Gomis who jumped 8.13 in round 3 and 8.14 in round 6.

Triple Jump (14th)

1. Benjamin Compaoré FRA	17.46/-0.1
2. Lyukman Adams RUS	17.09/-0.5
3. Aleksey Fyodorov RUS	17.04/1.1
4. Yoann Rapinier FRA	17.01/-0.1
5. Marian Oprea ROU	16.94/0.9
6. Nelson Évora POR	16.78/0.4
7. Fabrizio Donato ITA	16.66/-0.7
8. Pablo Torrijos ESP	16.56/0.0

COMPAORÉ ONLY QUALIFIED on his third attempt of 16.83 after 16.20 and a foul, but produced a pb 17.46 in the first round of the final, followed by 17.18 in round two to have a clear win from Adams who started with 17.09 and finished with 17.06 after topping the qualifiers with 16.97. Daniele Greco ruptured his left Achilles tendon in warm-up.

Shot (12th)

1. David Storl GER	21.41
2. Borja Vivas ESP	20.86
3. Tomasz Majewski POL	20.83
4. Snipe Zunic CRO.	20.68
5. Asmir Kolasinac SRB	20.55
6. Jan Marcell CZE	20.48
7. Marco Fortes POR	20.35
8. Valeriy Kokoyev RUS	20.23

STORL BECAME THE first man to win this event twice at both the European and World Championships. He led the qualifiers with 20.76 and took the gold with his opening 21.41 in the final. Majewski had all six efforts over 20.50, but had to settle for third, 3cm behind Vivas, both men doing their best in round 2. Zunic added 8cm to his pb.

Discus (13th)

1. Robert Harting GER	66.07
2. Gerd Kanter EST	64.75
3. Robert Urbanek POL	63.81
4. Piotr Malachowski POL	63.54
5. Viktor Butenko RUS	62.80
6. Mario Pestano ESP	62.31
7. Daniel Jasinski GER	62.04
8. Frank Casañas ESP	61.47

THE 2006 CHAMPION Virgilijus Alekna was 21st in qualifying with 59.35, but the 2010 champion Malachowski (64.98) and 2012 champion Harting (67.01) had no problem with Kanter second best at 65.79. The final was delayed considerably because of the high wind and eventually took place in the rain with the circle very slippery. Not surprisingly 11 of the 12 men failed to throw as far as in the qualification in which 12 men exceeded 61.50. Harting took the gold with his third round 66.07.

Hammer (16th)

1. Krisztián Pars HUN	82.69
2. Pawel Fajdek POL	82.05
3. Sergey Litvinov RUS	79.35
4. Pavel Krivitskiy BLR	78.50
5. Szymon Ziólkowski POL	78.41
6. Primoz Kozmus SLO	77.46
7. Marcel Lomnicky SVK	76.89
8. David Söderberg FIN	76.55

Defending champion Pars only managed 74.44 (ninth best behind Fajdek 77.45 and Lomnicky 77.06) and two fouls in qualifying but was back in top form in the final. He started with a first round lead at 78.11, then 78.45 behind Fajdek 78.48, and 82.18 in the third round. Pars ended with 81.69 and 82.69, but was pushed by Fajdek's fifth round 82.05, while Litvinov took the bronze with his fifth round throw.

Javelin (17th)

1. Antti Ruuskanen FIN	88.01
2. Vitezslav Vesely CZE	84.79
3. Tero Pitkämäki FIN	84.40
4. Lassi Etelätalo FIN	83.16
5. Dmitriy Tarabin RUS	81.24
6. Risto Mätas EST	80.73
7. Valeriy Iordan RUS	78.40
8. Matija Kranjc SLO	78.27

AFTER LEADING THE qualifiers with 83.87 from Pitkämäki 81.48 and Thomas Röhler 81.24, Ruuskanen was a surprise winner, improving with each of his first three throws: 83.81, 86.85 and 88.01 and all six at 82.37 or better. Vesely took silver with his fifth round throw and Pitkämäki bronze with his second, but Röhler threw only 70.31 for 12th.

Decathlon (12th-13th)

1. Andrey Kravchenko BLR	8616
2. Kevin Mayer FRA	8521
3. Ilya Shkurenyov RUS	8498
4. Eelco Sintnicolaas NED	8478
5. Arthur Abele GER	8477
6. Kai Kazmirek GER	8458
7. Rico Freimuth GER	8308
8. Oleksiy Kasyanov UKR	8231

KAZMIREK LED MOST of the time for the first seven events, but slipped back with a 4.60 vault compared to the best of 5.40 by Sintnicolaas and 5.20 by Shkurenyov and Mayer. But Kravchenko, who had taken the lead on day one after a 2.22 pb high jump, regained the lead with a 5.10 vault and stayed ahead for gold, including a remarkable javelin pb of 68.11 considering that he was carrying multiple leg strappings. Mayer's 4:24.16 for 1500m took him from 6th to 2nd as despite adverse conditions on the second day the standard was excellent with six men over 8450 points and ten over 8150.

4 x 100 Metres (17th)

1. GBR	37.93	Ellington, Aikines-Aryeetey, Kilty, Gemili (ht: 4 Talbot)
2. GER	38.09	Reus, Knipphals, Kosenkow, Jakubczyk
3. FRA	38.47	Vincent, Lemaitre, Tinmar, Bassaw
4. SUI	38.56	6. POL 38.85
5. NED	38.60	dnf. ITA, POR

BRITAIN WON THEIR heat in 38.26 ahead of a Swiss record 38.54 while Germany took the other heat in 38.15 ahead of France, greatly weakened by the absence through injury of Jimmy Vicaut. In the final Britain stormed to a 37.93 clocking with Gemili on the anchor leg taking over just ahead of Germany's Jakubczyk and finishing close to 2m in front. France took bronze, enabling Lemaitre to become the most bemedalled male athlete in European Champs history with 4 gold, 2 silver and 2 bronze.

4 x 400 Metres (17th)

1. GBR	2:58.79	C Williams 44.8, Hudson-Smith 44.5, Bingham 45.61, Rooney 43.93 (Levine and Yousif ran in heat)
2. RUS	2:59.38	Dyldin 45.1e, Ivashko 44.1e, Uglov 45.28, Krasnov 44.83 (Trenikhin ran in heat)
3. POL	2:59.85	Omelko 45.4e, Kozlowski 44.5e, Krawczuk 45.63, Krzewina 44.31 (Pietrzak and Jaros ran in heat)
4. FRA	2:59.89	
5. IRL	3:01.67	7. BEL 3:02.80
6. GER	3:01.70	8. CZE 3:04.56

BRITAIN, AFTER 1-2-5 in the individual 400m, won their heat in 3:00.65 with Rooney ('just jogging') anchoring in 44.50. They duly won the final, but three more teams beat 3 minutes. Conrad Williams ran a fine first leg but then Russia's Pavel Ivashko ran a storming second leg in 44.1e to hold the lead at the halfway mark a metre ahead of Hudson-Smith's 44.5. But even faster was Kevin Borlée who ran 43.6e for Belgium. The consumate relay runner Rooney completed his double gold with an assured 43.93 anchor leg.

20 Kilometres Walk (13th)

1. Miguel Ángel López ESP	1:19:44
2. Aleksandr Ivanov RUS	1:19:45
3. Denis Strelkov RUS	1:19:46
4. Ruslan Dmytrenko UKR	1:19:46
5. Christopher Linke GER	1:21:00
6. Alvaro Martín ESP	1:21:41
7. Andriy Kovenko UKR	1:21:48
8. Giorgio Rubino ITA	1:22:07

AFTER A SLOWISH start the race just got quicker and quicker with halves of 40:43 and 39:01 for the winner. From an opening 2k split 8:19, times tumbled until López covered his final 2k in an amazing 7:28. In the closest ever finish to a major walking event, just 2 sec covered the top four. 28 of 34 men finished.

50 Kilometres Walk (15th)

1. Yohann Diniz FRA	3:32:33*
2. Matej Tóth SVK	3:36:21
3. Ivan Noskov RUS	3:37:41
4. Mikhail Ryzhov RUS	3:39:07
5. Ivan Banzeruk UKR	3:44:49
6. Igor Hlavan UKR	3:45:08
7. Marco De Luca ITA	3:45:25
8. Jesús Ángel García ESP	3:45:41

DINIZ WON AN unprecedented third title in this event and in so doing smashed the world record of 3:34:14 by Russia's Denis Nizhegorodov in 2008. With much of the race conducted in heavy rain, Diniz was accompanied by Ryzhov and Noskov through 10k in 43:44. Diniz and Ryzhov went clear through 20k in 1:26:55 ahead of Noskov and Robert Heffernan 1:27:21 and Tóth 1:27:39. Ryzhov made a great effort to break clear during the third 10k, covered in 42:19, and opened a 6 sec gap over Diniz by 30k (2:09:14 to 2:09:20) with Noskov 2:10:48 and Tóth 2:10:51 scrapping for third. Diniz then kicked in 41:42 to 40k, so that Ryzhov was then 39 sec behind, and 41:21 for his final 10k. Tóth completed a brilliant race in a Slovakian record with Noskov overtaking Ryzhov after about 48k to take bronze, also in a pb. Heffernan was one of 8 non-finishers from the 34 starters.

Women

100 Metres (13th) (-1.7)

1. Dafne Schippers NED 11.12
2. Myriam Soumaré FRA 11.16
3. Ashleigh Nelson GBR 11.22
4. Mujinga Kambundji SUI 11.30
5. Ivet Lalova BUL 11.33
6. Céline Distel-Bonnet FRA 11.38
7. Desiree Henry GBR 11.43
8. Ayodelé Ikuesan FRA 11.54

SOUMARÉ WAS FASTEST in the first round with 11.03 as Schippers ran an easy-looking 11.10, and these two women won their semis in 11.17 and 11.08 respectively with Lalova the third winner in 11.15. Conditions were horrible for the final; pouring rain on a cool evening and a 1.7m headwind. Soumaré got off to a quick start but Schippers was majestic when she got into her running and won by 0.04. Having run a pb 11.19 in her heat, Nelson took the bronze, the first for Britain in this event for 40 years. Kambundji set Swiss records of 11.32 in her heat and 11.20 in her semi.

200 Metres (15th) (-0.5)

1. Dafne Schippers NED 22.03
2. Jodie Williams GBR 22.46
3. Myriam Soumaré FRA 22.58
4. Bianca Wiliiams GBR 22.68
5. Mujinga Kambundji SUI 22.83
6. Jamile Samuel NED 23.31
7. Hanna-Maari Latvala FIN 23.48

dnf. Dina Asher-Smith GBR-J –

SCHIPPERS WAS FASTEST in heat (22.73) and semi (22.48) and completed the sprint double with an awesome run, featuring a sublime bend, and Dutch record time of 22.01. Asher-Smith ran 22.75 and 22.61 in the prelims but pulled up injured in the final, as the former World Youth and Junior champion Jodie Williams took silver in a pb, with namesake Bianca also running a pb. Kambundji's 22.83 was another Swiss record.

400 Metres (15th)

1. Libania Grenot ITA 51.10
2. Olga Zemlyak UKR 51.36
3. Indira Terrero ESP 51.38
4. Christine Ohuruogu GBR 51.38
5. Malgorzata Holub POL 51.84
6. Bianca Razor ROU 51.95
7. Marie Gayot FRA 52.14
8. Aauri Lorena Bokesa ESP 52.39

GRENOT, THE ONLY European to have bettered 51 sec in 2014, duly won the final from Zemlyak, who had run 51.16 in her heat and 51.24 in her semi. In a low-key year for her Ohuruogu ran season's bests of 51.40 heat and 51.38 final.

800 Metres (16th)

1. Marina Arzamasova BLR 1:58.15
2. Lynsey Sharp GBR 1:58.80
3. Joanna Józwik POL 1:59.63
4. Yekaterina Poistogova RUS 1:59.69
5. Svetlana Rogozina RUS 2:00.76
6. Vanya Stambolova BUL 2:00.91
7. Jessica Judd GBR-J 2:01.65
8. Mirela Lavric ROU 2:09.25

THE TWO SEMI-FINAL winners, Arzamasova 2:00.36 and Sharp 2:00.58, had a fine race in the final, both setting pbs. Uncharacteristically Sharp led at 200m, going on to pass 400m in 58.26 and 600m in 1:27.51 but Arzamasova finished very strongly to take gold ahead of Sharp's Scottish record. Józwik was a delighted third.

1500 Metres (15th)

1. Sifan Hassan NED 4:04.18
2. Abeba Aregawi SWE 4:05.08
3. Laura Weightman GBR 4:06.32
4. Renata Plis POL 4:06.65
5. Federica Del Buono ITA 4:07.49
6. Hannah England GBR 4:07.80
7. Anna Shchagina RUS 4:08.05
8. Diana Sujew GER 4:08.63

AFTER SLOW LAPS of 65.95 and 69.17, Weightman stepped up the pace with 62.88 for the third and held on for third place ahead of fast-finishing Plis behind the two Ethiopian-born women, of whom Hassan sprinted past Arigawi at the start of the finishing straight to win with a last lap of 60.81.

5000 Metres (16th)

1. Meraf Bahta SWE 15:31.39
2. Sifan Hassan NED 15:31.79
3. Susan Kuijken NED 15:32.82
4. Yelena Korobkina RUS 15:32.89
5. Nuria Fernández ESP 15:35.59
6. Sara Moreira POR 15:38.13
7. Jo Pavey GBR 15:38.41
8. Giulia Viola ITA 15:38.76

The race was run at a painfully slow tempo with 3000m reached in 9:40.24 before the ex-Eritrean Bahta went ahead, followed by Pavey, a lap later. Hassan made a big move along the back straight and as they entered the final straight it became a duel between Hassan and Bahta, the latter winning with a last lap of 61.66 and kilometre of 2:44.32.

10,000 Metres (12th)

1. Jo Pavey GBR	32:22.39
2. Clémence Calvin FRA	32:23.58
3. Laila Traby FRA	32:26.03
4. Jip Vastenburg NED	32:27.37
5. Sara Moreira POR	32:30.12
6. Sabrina Mockenhaupt GER	32:30.49
7. Olga Mazuronak BLR	32:31.15
8. Fionnuala Britton IRL	32:32.45

THE TIME WAS the slowest winning-time for a European 10,000m, but Pavey achieved a marvellous win for her first major gold medal – at the age of 40, making her the oldest female European champion in any event. The first eight kilometre splits were all over 3:15, before Calvin began a long run for home in the ninth, run in 3:11.27. At the bell she was a stride ahead of Pavey, who drew well clear over the last lap and completed a final kilometre run in 2:55.00. Former Moroccan Traby set a pb in 3rd in just her second track 10k race, as did the 4th finisher, 20 year-old European Junior 5000m champion Vastenburg.

Marathon (16th)

1. Christelle Daunay FRA	2:25:14*
2. Valeria Straneo ITA	2:25:27
3. Jéssica Augusto POR	2:25:41
4. Lisa Nemec (Stublic) CRO	2:28:36
5. Elvan Abeylegesse TUR	2:29:46
6. Anna Incerti ITA	2:29:58
7. Rasa Drazdauskaite LTU	2:30:32
8. Jessica Draskau-Petersson DEN	2:30:53

European Marathon Cup (3 to score): 1. ITA 7:27:59, 2. POR 7:33.06, 3. RUS 7:42:03, 4. LTU 7:45:38, 5. SUI 7:47.01, 6. NED 7:49.55, 7. IRL 7:58:28, 8. TUR 7:59:02, 9. SWE 8:06:51, 10. FRA 8:15:37, 11. EST 8:16:36.

CONDITIONS WERE CONDUCIVE for good times as the race was run mainly in the rain with the temperature at 13°C, and the first three all broke the championship record of 2:26:05. Halfway was reached in 72:33 and the pace remained remarkably even as Daunay and Straneo led at 30k in 1:43:15. Behind them Abeylegesse was dropped on a long uphill stretch and caught and passed by Augusto, who remained an isolated third as the top two raced stride by stride before Daunay got away on a downhill section before 40k (2:17:41). She led then by 3 sec, stretching it to 13 sec at the finish. Estonia's three scorers were the 28 year-old Luik triplets, Llina, Leila and Lily.

3000 Metres Steeplechase (17th)

1. Antje Möldner-Schmidt GER	9:29.43
2. Charlotta Fougberg SWE	9:30.16
3. Diana Martín ESP	9:30.70
4. Svetlana Kudzelich BLR	9:30.99
5. Gesa-Felicitas Krause GER	9:35.46
6. Natalya Vlasova RUS	9:36.99
7. Katarzyna Kowalska POL	9:43.09
8. Silvia Danekova BUL	9:44.81

IN THE FINAL Kudzelich led at 1000m in 3:09.85 and Möldner-Schmidt at 2000m in 6:24.33, before running the final kilometre in 3:05.10 to take the gold medal ahead of Fougberg, who had led with 200m to go.

100 Metres Hurdles (13th)

(-0.7)

1. Tiffany Porter GBR	12.76
2. Cindy Billaud FRA	12.79
3. Cindy Roleder GER	12.82
4. Anne Zagré BEL	12.89
5. Alina Talay BLR	12.97
6. Nadine Hildebrand GER	13.01
7. Rosina Hodde NED	13.08
8. Eline Berings BEL	13.24

PORTER (12.69 and 12.63) and Billaud (12.75 and 12.79) were fastest in the prelims, with Billaud getting closer to the American-born Briton in the final.

400 Metres Hurdles (16th)

1. Eilidh Child GBR	54.48
2. Anna Titimets UKR	54.56
3. Irina Davydova RUS	54.60
4. Denisa Rosolová CZE	54.70
5. Yadisleidy Pedroso ITA	55.90
6. Vera Rudakova RUS	56.22
7. Axelle Dauwens BEL	56.29
8. Joanna Linkiewicz POL	56.59

CHILD WAS FASTEST in heat (55.32) and semi (54.71). In the final she was closely pressed by Rosolová as they turned into the straight but was 2m up at the last hurdle. On the run-in Rosolová went from second to fourth as Titimets and defending champion Davydova stormed past but they couldn't quite catch the 27 year-old Scot. One of the favourites Hanna Ryzhykova fell in her heat.

High Jump (17th)

1. Ruth Beitia ESP	2.01
2. Mariya Kuchina RUS	1.99
3. Ana Simic CRO	1.99
4. Justyna Kasprzycka POL	1.99
5. Marie-Laurence Jungfleisch GER	1.97
6. Oksana Okuneva UKR	1.94
7. Eleriin Haas EST	1.94
8. Daniela Stanciu ROU	1.94

IN HER FIFTH European final Beitia, now 35, retained her title, clearing 2.01 at her first attempt, just 1cm below her Spanish record. Kuchina had a clean card up to 1.99 and, while

Simic and Kasprzycka also cleared on their first attempts at 1.99, medals were determined by previous failures. The excellent standard was shown by five of the top eight setting pbs.

Pole Vault (14th)

1. Anzhelika Sidorova RUS 4.65
2. Ekateríni Stefanidi GRE 4.60
3. Angelina Zhuk-Krasnova RUS 4.60
4. Lisa Ryzih GER 4.60
5. Angelica Bengtsson SWE 4.45
6. Jirina Svobodová CZE 4.45
7= Nikolia Kiriakopoúlou GRE 4.35
7= Alayna Lutkovskaya RUS-J 4.35
7= Minna Nikkanen FIN 4.35

A CLOSE CONTEST was won by Sidorova clearing 4.65 on her third attempt after passing 4.60 and thus leaving her out of the medals at that point. and after the three women successful at 4.60 had all failed three times at 4.65.

Long Jump (13th)

1. Éloyse Lesueur FRA 6.85/-0.3
2. Ivana Spanovic SRB 6.81/-1.6
3. Darya Klishina RUS 6.65/-0.1
4. Malaika Mihambo GER 6.65/0.1
5. Alga Grabuste LAT 6.57/-0.2
6. Melanie Bauschke GER 6.55/0.1
7. Alina Rotaru ROU 6.55/-0.5
8. Erica Jarder SWE 6.39/-2.3

LESUEUR (6.72) AND Mihambo (6.70) led the qualifiers. Spanovic took the lead in the final with a first-round 6.81 and produced further jumps of 6.75 and 6.80, but had to give best to the fourth-round 6.85 of Lesueur, who had only one other valid jump, 6.66. Klishina took bronze on second-best from Mihambo (6.53 to 6.51). Bauschke has a jump measured as 6.79 in the first round, but this was later corrected to 6.55.

Triple Jump (16th)

1. Olga Saladukha UKR 14.73/-0.4
2. Yekaterina Koneva RUS 14.69/1.1
3. Irina Gumenyuk RUS 14.46/-0.2
4. Ruth Ndoumbe ESP 14.14/-0.7
5. Gabriela Petrova BUL 14.13/0.1
6. Dana Veldáková SVK 13.87/-0.2
7. Snezana Vukmirovic SLO 13.82/0.1
8. Susana Costa POR 13.78/-1.0

BOTH SALADUKHA AND Koneva achieved their best jumps in round two of the final after being best at 14.42 and 14.21 respectively in qualifying. Saladukha added other fine jumps of 14.68, 14.59 and 14.63 while Koneva's next best was 14.54.

Shot (17th)

1. Christina Schwanitz GER 19.90
2. Yevgeniya Kolodko RUS 19.39
3. Anita Márton HUN 19.04
4. Yuliya Leontyuk BLR 18.68
5. Chiara Rosa ITA 18.10
6. Irina Tarasova RUS 18.05
7. Alyona Dubitskaya BLR 17.95
8. Lena Urbaniak GER 17.77

SCHWANITZ THREW 19.90 in the second round followed by 19.66, 19.79 and 19.66, so won easily from Kolodko whose best came in the last round. Márton took the bronze with a Hungarian record 19.04 from a previous best of 18.63 indoors. With only 16 entries, just four women were eliminated in qualifying, in which Schwanitz at 19.35 was 1.03m ahead of the next best.

Discus (16th)

1. Sandra Perkovic CRO 71.08
2. Mélina Robert-Michon FRA 65.33
3. Shanice Craft GER 64.33
4. Anna Rüh GER 62.46
5. Julia Fischer GER 61.20
6. Zenaida Sendriute LTU 60.65
7. Sanna Kämäräinen FIN 60.52
8. Yuliya Maltseva RUS 60.40

PERKOVIC LED THE qualifiers with 63.93 from 63.62 by Robert-Michon, and produced a stunning display in the final, starting with 64.58, 67.37 and 68.78 before a Croatian record 71.08 in the fifth round, the longest throw in the world since 1992. Robert-Michon's fourth round 65.33 overtook Craft's second round 64.33 for the silver medal.

Hammer (15th)

1. Anna Wlodarczyk POL 78.76*
2. Martina Hrasnová SVK 74.66
3. Joanna Fiodorow POL 73.67
4. Kathrin Klaas GER 72.89
5. Betty Heidler GER 72.39
6. Alexandra Tavernier FRA 70.32
7. Bianca Perie ROU 69.26
8. Nikola Lomnicka SVK 67.39

WORLD RECORD SETTERS Wlodarczyk (75.73) and Heidler (73.05) were well ahead of the rest in qualifying, but Heidler managed only fifth place in the final, in which Wlodarczyk started with two fouls but then showed her class with 75.88 and 76.16 before adding 32cm to the Polish record that she had set at the 2013 Worlds and 2.09 to the championship record. Hrasnová took silver with a fifth-round 74.66 from Fiodorow whose 73.67 came with her last throw.

Javelin (14th)

1. Barbora Spotáková CZE 64.41
2. Tatjana Jelaca SRB 64.21
3. Linda Stahl GER 63.91
4. Madara Palameika LAT 62.04
5. Tatyana Kholodovich BLR 61.66
6. Marina Ratej SLO 61.58
7. Christin Hussong GER 59.29
8. Goldie Sayers GBR 58.33

SPOTÁKOVÁ ADDED EUROPEAN gold to two Olympic golds and one World title. She was behind Stahl, 62.86 to 63.91, in the first round, but found form with 64.41 in the fourth round just minutes after Jelaca had taken the lead with Serbian record 64.21 in round 4. Ratej had led the qualifiers with 61.87.

Heptathlon (14th-15th)

1. Antoinette Nana Djimou FRA	6551
2. Nadine Broersen NED	6498
3. Nafissatou Thiam BEL	6423
4. Carolin Schäfer GER	6395
5. Lilli Schwarzkopf GER	6332
6. Laura Ikauniece-Admidina LAT	6310
7. Anouk Vetter NED	6281
8. Claudia Rath GER	6225

DEFENDING CHAMPION Nana Djimou had the fastest hurdles time of 13.05. Then Broersen replaced her as leader by high jumping a Dutch record of 1.94 but 19 year-old Thiam zoomed up from 18th to 2nd overall with 1.97. Thiam went ahead after shot and 200m for the overnight lead of 3851 ahead of Schäfer 3845, Broersen 3841 and Nana Djimou 3793. Nand Djimou came through with 54.26 in the javelin with Broersen 52.18 and Thiam also excelling. Nana Djimou (pb 2:15.94) needed to stay very close to Broersen (pb 2:11.11) to ensure victory and she did much better than that, clocking a lifetime best of 2:15.22, over 2 secs ahead of her rival with 3rd and 4th both setting 800m pbs. 15 women exceeded 6000 points.

4 x 100 Metres (17th)

1. GBR	42.24	Philip, Nelson, J Williams, Henry (ht: 3. Onuora)
2. FRA	42.45	Distel-Bonnet, Ikuesan, Soumaré, Akakpo
3. RUS	43.22	Panteleyeva, Rusakova, Savlinis, Sivkova (ht: 3. Vukolova)
4. ITA	43.26	6. SWE 44.36
5. UKR	43.58	dnf. SUI & NED

France couldn't quite replicate their 42.29 heat time and finished a good 2m behind Britain in 42.45, while Russia were far behind in 3rd place. Britain had won their heat in 42.62 before taking 0.19 off the British record (set in 1980) in the final. Misfortune befell both the Netherlands (42.77 heat) and Switzerland (42.98 heat) as Ghafoor fell while trying to pass the baton to Schippers, and Kambundji, the Swiss heroine of the week, suffered the nightmare of knocking the baton out of her hand at the start

4 x 400 Metres Relay (17th)

1. FRA	3:24.27	Gayot 52.0e, Hurtis 50.7e, Raharolahy 51.78, Guei 49.71 (Perrossier and Anacharsis ran in heat)
2. UKR	3:24.32	Pygyda 51.6e, Stuy 51.2e, Ryzhykova 50.82, Zemlyak 50.62 (Prystyupa and Lyakhova ran in heat)
3. GBR	3:24.34	Child 51.3e, Massey 50.9e, Cox 51.26, Adeoye 50.74 (Diamond and V Ohuruogu ran in heat)
4. RUS	3:25.02	
5. POL	3:25.73	7. ITA 3:28.30
6. GER	3:27.69	8. BEL 3:31.82

THIS WAS A terrific race. Child led for Britain on the first leg from Germany and Russia. Then Massey stretched that lead over Russia and France (Hurtis 50.7). Firova (50.5) took over to give Russia the lead after three legs but their final runner Renzhina slipped back to fourth as a marvellous 49.71 leg by Guei took France from a detached fourth (and still 10m behind Britain with 200m to go) to a narrow win over Ukraine and Britain.

20 Kilometres Walk (14th)

1. Elmira Alembekova RUS	1:27:56
2. Lyudmyla Olyanovska UKR	1:28:07
3. Anezka Drahotová CZE-J	1:28:08
4. Vera Sokolova RUS	1:28:24
5. Eleonora Giorgi ITA	1:28:28
6. Ana Cabecinha POR	1:28:40
7. Antonella Palmisano ITA	1:28:43
8. Beatriz Pascual ESP	1:29:02

As is becoming traditional the race steadily got quicker so that the dozen women in the lead pack at 10k in 45:05 was whittled away and Alembekova won with a second half of 42:51. After an opening 2k of 9:16 the Russian had times of 8:18 and 8:20 for her final two 2k laps. Nine women broke 1:30 and only one of the 29 starters was disqualified with three other non-finishers. The junior Drahotová set a Czech record but was overtaken by Olyanovska for silver in the closing few metres.

SEVEN ATHLETES COMPETED at the European Championships for a sixth time. Six matched the men's record of Abdon Pamich 1954-71, Ludvik Danek 1962-78 and Nenad Stekic 1971-90, They were: Virgilijus Alekna and Jesús Ángel García 1994-2010 and 2014, and Dwain Chambers GBR, Sergiy Lebid, Nicola Vizzoni and 1998-2014. And one woman Nuria Fernández 1998-2014 equalled the women's record of Helena Fibingerová 1969-86, Fernanda Ribeiro 1986-2010 and Felicea Tilea/Moldovan 1990-2010.

COMMONWEALTH GAMES 2014

July 27 – August 2, Glasgow, GBR

IN THE DAYS leading up to the start of the athletics the Glasgow weather was glorious but temperatures in the mid-20s then dropped to 16-18°C for most of the athletics programme. This was a big contrast to temperatures of up to 35°C that had been experienced four years earlier in Delhi. Just two days had rain, but it was very heavy for much of the final evening and the women's pole vault was ruined. The winning marks in Glasgow were better than those in Delhi by 35 events (including all men's track) to 8 with one equal. Similarly it was 35-9 for 6th place, with the men 20-2 ahead. The overall standard of competitors was considerably higher than in Delhi, and although there was weakness in depth in some events, nearly all the winners were top world-class athletes. Perhaps more significantly the winning marks in Glasgow were better than those of Melbourne 2006 in 25 events to 17, with one tied

England easily topped the points table with strength in depth. They won 12 silver medals, but three golds was far behind the 10 each won by Kenya and Jamaica. Each had clean sweeps, Jamaica in the men's 200m and Kenya in both steeplechases and women's 10,000m. Only Moses Kipsiro, who won the 10,000m in a thrilling finish, prevented Kenya winning all track events from 1500m upwards.

Games records were set in ten events (four men's and six women's) culminating in splendid 4x100m times by Jamaica, whose top stars ran just the anchor legs for this event. The incomparable Usain Bolt delighted the crowd with his pre-race entertainment and lap of honour, stopping for 'selfies' etc. He ran clear of the field to bring his team home in 37.58, and Shelley-Ann Fraser-Pryce the women's in 41.83; these world-leading times compared to previous Games records of 38.20 and 42.44. Sadly there were no walks events.

Valerie Adams won her third women's shot title (after silver in 2002), and others to retain their individual titles were Kipsiro at 10,000m, Sally Pearson at 100m hurdles, Alana Boyd in the pole vault, and Sultana Frizell at hammer. The youngest winner was the 18-year old Eleanor Patterson of the women's high jump. A strong contender for athlete of the meeting was Blessing Okagbare, with her majestic running for the 100m/200m sprint double.

*Dates given in brackets after the heading for each event are those of the final. * Games record.*

Medals and Points Table

(8 for 1st to 1 for 8th)

Nation	Men			Women			Total			Total	Points:	2010
	G	S	B	G	S	B	G	S	B	Medals		
ENG	3	6	-	-	6	8	3	12	8	23	290	297
KEN	4	6	1	6	4	2	10	10	2	22	205	251
JAM	5	1	3	5	2	3	10	3	6	17	184	84
AUS	1	-	1	5	-	2	6	-	3	9	179	200
CAN	3	-	4	2	1	5	5	1	9	15	148.5	126.5
RSA	2	2	2	-	1	-	2	3	2	7	73	36
NGR	-	1	-	3	2	-	3	3	-	6	70	34
SCO	-	-	1	-	2	-	-	2	1	3	55	58
NZL	-	1	2	1	1	-	1	2	2	5	55	56.5
TTO	-	2	3	-	1	1	-	3	4	7	54	37
BAH	-	1	1	-	-	-	-	1	1	2	54	41
UGA	1	-	1	-	-	1	1	-	2	3	33	30
IND	1	-	1	-	1	-	1	1	1	3	31	142
CYP	-	2	-	-	-	-	-	2	-	2	26	19.5
WAL	-	-	-	-	2	-	-	1	-	1	25.5	53.5
BAR	-	-	1	-	-	-	-	-	1	1	17	0
BOT	1	-	-	-	-	-	1	-	-	1	16.5	21
GRN	1	-	1	-	-	-	1	-	1	2	14	3
GHA	-	-	1	-	1	-	0	1	1	2	16	17

Other nations to score points: LCA 10.5 (1B), CMR 6, ANT, IVB, LES, SKN 5; DMA, SRI, VIN 3; BER 2, JER, TAN, ZAM 1 The above table does not include the six events (three each men and women) for Paralympians included in official standings.

Men

100 Metres (28th) (0.0)

1. Kemar Bailey-Cole JAM 10.00
2. Adam Gemili ENG 10.10
3. Nickel Ashmeade JAM 10.12
4. Antoine Adams SKN 10.16
5. Mark Jelks NGR 10.17
6. Jason Livermore JAM 10.18
7. Warren Fraser BAH 10.20
8. Ramon Gittens BAR 10.25

BAILEY-COLE WON his heat in 10.16 and was fastest in the semis with 10.00 (0.175) into an 0.5m wind. Gemili also impressed with 10.15 into an 0.8m wind in his heat and 10.07 after a slow start in his semi. A surprising elimination in the semis was Richard Thompson, the fastest entrant at 9.82 (& 9.74w) but who could muster only 10.19. Gemili had a much better reaction time than Bailey Cole (0.144 to 0.190) in the final, but the tall Jamaican came through to win by a metre.

200 Metres (31st) (0.5)

1. Rasheed Dwyer JAM 20.14
2. Warren Weir JAM 20.26
3. Jason Livermore JAM 20.32
4. Mosito Lehata LES 20.36
5. Akine Simbine RSA 20.37
6. Daniel Bailey ANT 20.43
7. Danny Talbot ENG 20.45
8. Gavin Smellie CAN 20.55

DWYER WAS FASTEST in the semis at 20.42 and in the final he got the better of Weir after a great battle along the straight. Livermore completed a clean sweep for Jamaica.

400 Metres (30th)

1. Kirani James GRN 44.24*
2. Wayde van Niekerk RSA 44.68
3. Lalonde Gordon TTO 44.78
4. Martyn Rooney ENG 45.15
5. LaToy Williams BAH 45.63
6. Jarrin Solomon TTO 45.82

dnf. Renny Quow TTO –
dns. Chris Brown BAH –

JAMES WAS FASTEST in the semis with 45.14, but Isaac Makwala failed to progress with 45.33. In the final van Niekerk went out very fast and was just ahead entering the final straight where James drew away to win by almost 4m, and Gordon finished strongly for bronze.

800 Metres (31st)

1. Nijel Amos BOT 1:45.18
2. David Rudisha KEN 1:45.48
3. Andre Olivier RSA 1:46.03
4. Ferguson Rotich KEN 1:46.09
5. Jeffrey Riseley AUS 1:46.12
6. Guy Learmonth SCO 1:46.69
7. Michael Rimmer ENG 1:46.71
8. Ronald Musagala UGA 1:47.19
9. Evans Kipkorir KEN 1:47.34

FASTEST IN THE semis were Amos 1:45.65 and Musagala 1:45.98. In the final Rudisha ran from the front, 200m 24.8 (Amos 25.0) but the pace slowed considerably as he reached the bell in 52.71 (Amos 53.0). Rotich moved ahead to 600m in 1:19.77, but Rudisha took over again rounding the final bend to hit the straight with a 5m advantage over Rotich with Amos some 7m behind the leader. Then the latter produced an electrifying finishing burst to sweep past for a clear-cut victory. Olivier moved up late to take bronze.

1500 Metres (2nd)

1. James Magut KEN 3:39.31
2. Ronald Kwemoi KEN-J 3:39.53
3. Nick Willis NZL 3:39.60
4. Johan Cronje RSA 3:39.65
5. Jeffrey Riseley AUS 3:40.27
6. Chris O'Hare SCO 3:40.63
7. Charlie Grice ENG 3:41.58
8. Bazili Baynit TAN 3:41.74

RONALD MUSAGALA (11th 3:42.42) led through the first two laps in 58.64 and 2:00.97 and the entire 12-man field were in close order at the bell, reached in 2:46.1 with Kwemoi and Magut in the lead. Kwemoi led into the final straight, but Magut had the biggest kick and ran the last lap in 53.2, while a spectacular finish by Willis (a disappointed 10th in the 5000m) deprived Cronje of the bronze medal.

5000 Metres (27th)

1. Caleb Ndiku KEN 13:12.07
2. Isiah Koech KEN 13:14.06
3. Zane Robertson NZL 13:16.52
4. Joseph Kitur KEN 13:17.49
5. Mohammed Ahmed CAN 13:18.88
6. Andy Vernon ENG 13:22.32
7. Thomas Farrell ENG 13:23.96
8. Moses Kipsiro UGA 13:28.23

KOECH LED FROM 800m to 3000m (8:04.85). Then the Robertson twins shared the lead, but Jake fell after 4k (10:46.14). Ndiku, who led by just 0.1 at the bell, sped through the final 200m in 26.1, 400m in 54.1 and kilometre in 2:25.93. 24 men contested the race.

10,000 Metres (1st)

1. Moses Kipsiro UGA 27:56.11
2. Josphat Bett KEN 27:56.14
3. Cameron Levins CAN 27:56.23
4, Peter Kirui KEN 27:58.24
5. Charles Cheruiyot KEN 27:59.91
6. Mohammed Ahmed CAN 28:02.96
7. Jake Robertson NZL 28:03.70
8. Timothy Toroitich UGA 28:03.79

KIPSIRO OUTKICKED THE Kenyans, just as he had in his double in Delhi 2010. Kirui led at halfway in 14:07.87 and at 9000m in 25:21.77 as the pace did not pick up until the final kilometre run in 2:34.34. Levins led into the straight but was passed by Kipsiro on the inside and by Bett on the outside. The latter stretched his arms wide, believing he had won, but it was Kipsiro by 0.03.

Marathon (27th)

1. Michael Shelley AUS	2:11:15
2. Stephen Chemlany KEN	2:11:58
3. Abraham Kiplimo UGA	2:12:23
4. Solomon Mutai UGA	2:12:26
5. John Kelai KEN	2:12:41
6. Eric Ndiema KEN	2:13:44
7. Liam Adams AUS	2:13:49
8. Philip Kiplimo UGA	2:14:09

SHELLEY, WHO HAD been 2nd to Kelai in 2010, moved ahead just before the two-hour mark and stretched his lead to 43 secs, the first non-African to win for 20 years. 24 of 26 runners finished.

3000 Metres Steeplechase (1st)

1. Jonathan Ndiku KEN	8:10.44*
2. Jairus Birech KEN	8:12.68
3. Ezekiel Kemboi KEN	8:19.73
4. Matt Hughes CAN	8:21.88
5. James Wilkinson ENG	8:24.98
6. Chris Winter CAN	8:29.83
7. Luke Gunn ENG	8:45.99
8. Stephen Lisgo SCO	9:05.13

THE KENYAN 1-2-3 was their fifth in succession at this event, contested by just ten men. Birech did all the work, covering the first kilometre in a very fast 2:37.17, shadowed by Ndiku while Kemboi allowed his team-mates to open up a 40m gap. The second kilometre slowed to 2:50.16 and at the bell the trio were together, but Ndiku proved much the strongest with a final lap (including water jump) of 61.30. Kemboi's bronze added to his 2006 gold and 2001 and 2010 silver.

110 Metres Hurdles (29th) (-0.3)

1. Andrew Riley JAM	13.32
2. William Sharman ENG	13.36
3. Shane Brathwaite BAR	13.49
4. Nicholas Hough AUS	13.57
5. Ryan Brathwaite BAR	13.63
6. Greggmar Swift BAR	13.74
7. Alex Al-Ameen NGR	13.77
8. Lawrence Clarke ENG	13.84

DEFENDING CHAMPION Andy Turner fell in his heat, won by Riley 13.47, with Ryan Brathwaite also a heat winner in 13.48, 0.01 ahead of Sharman. In the final Sharman was ahead of Riley for most of the race and might have held on had he not hit the eighth hurdle, causing him to twist on landing. He was still just in front over the final barrier but Riley was too fast on the run-in.

400 Metres Hurdles (31st)

1. Cornel Fredericks RSA	48.50
2. Jehue Gordon TTO	48.75
3. Jeffery Gibson BAH	48.78
4. Niall Flannery ENG	49.46
5. Christian Morton NGR	49.65
6. Boniface Mucheru KEN	49.99
7. Richard Yates ENG	50.13
dnf. Annsert Whyte JAM	–

THE 2006 AND 2010 champions L.J. van Zyl and David Greene were far from past form as they were 3rd and 4th in their heat in 50.07 and 50.36 and other favourites Leford Green and Roxroy Cato were disqualified for trailing leg offences. Fredericks was fastest in the heats with 49.26 and held on to a big lead in the final to beat Gordon and fast-finishing Gibson. Whyte fell while second at the eighth hurdle.

High Jump (30th)

1. Derek Drouin CAN	2.31
2. Kyriakos Ioannou CYP	2.28
3. Michael Mason CAN	2.25
4. Chris Baker ENG	2.25
5= Kabelo Kgosiemang BOT	2.21
5= Martyn Bernard ENG	2.21
7. Fernan Djoumessi CMR	2.21
8. Brandon Starc AUS	2.21

DROUIN WON AS expected but poor weather prevented him going higher than 2.31 (he tried 2.37). Ioannou, with a season's best of just 2.20 following hernia surgery, excelled to take silver. 13 men cleared 2.20 in qualifying.

Pole Vault (1st)

1. Steve Lewis ENG	5.55
2. Luke Cutts ENG	5.55
3. Shawn Barber CAN	5.45
4. Jaz Thoirs SCO	5.45
5= Nikandros Stylianou CYP	5.35
5= Paul Walker WAL	5.35
7. Paul Pocklington AUS	5.20
8. K'Don Samuels JAM	5.00

AFTER BRONZE IN 2006 and silver in 2010, Lewis took gold, but only after a tense jump-off with Cutts, both having clean cards up to 5.55. Lewis won at 5.55 after each after four failures at 5.60.

Long Jump (30th)

1. Greg Rutherford ENG	8.20/-0.7
2. Zarck Visser RSA	8.12/-0.4
3. Rushwahl Samaai RSA	8.08/-0.1
4. Fabrice Lapierre AUS	8.00/0.9
5. Chris Tomlinson ENG	7.99/1.4
6. Robbie Crowther AUS	7.96w/2.1
7. J J Jegede ENG	7.81/0.3
8. Tyrone Smith BER	7.79/0.9

RUTHERFORD LED THE qualifiers with 8.05 and jumped 8.12 in round one of the final, a distance matched by Visser in round two, before Rutherford's winning 8.20 came in the third round.

Triple Jump (2nd)

1. Khotso Mokoena RSA 17.20/-0.1
2. Tosin Oke NGR 16.84/0.0
3. Arpinder Singh IND 16.63/1.4
4. Olumide Olamigoke NGR 16.56/0.0
5. Phillips Idowu ENG 16.45/0.0
6. Nathan Fox ENG 16.26/0.6
7. Daniel Lewis JAM 16.09/0.6
8. Yordanys Durañona DMA 15.81/0.1

DEFENDING CHAMPION OKE led the qualifiers with 16.75 from Idowu 16.70 and Mokoena 16.69. In the second round of the final Mokoena, in his first season at the event since 2007, produced a startling 17.20, just 5cm short of a pb dating from 2005, and backed this with 16.99 in the third round as Oke's second round 16.84 was his only valid jump.

Shot (28th)

1. O'Dayne Richards JAM 21.61*
2. Tom Walsh NZL 21.19
3. Tim Nedow CAN 20.59
4. Orazio Cremona RSA 20.13
5. Damien Birkenhead AUS 19.59
6. Om Prakash Singh IND 18.73
7. Dillon Simon DMA 18.66
8. Raymond Brown JAM 18.65

WALSH ADDED 22cm to the Games record with an Oceania record 21.24 in qualifying and he had five throws over 20.73 in the final with best of 21.19 but in round four. But after opening with 20.94 and being second at halfway to Walsh, Richards added half a metre to his pb and 16cm to the CAC record with a Games record 21.61 in round four.

Discus (31st)

1. Vikas Gowda IND 63.64
2. Apostolos Parellis CYP 63.32
3. Jason Morgan JAM 62.34
4. Benn Harradine AUS 61.91
5. Brett Morse WAL 60.48
6. Chad Wright JAM 60.33
7. Carl Myerscough ENG 59.88
8. Zane Duquemin JER 59.39

THE BEST THROWS of the competition came from the qualifying round: Gowda 64.32, Victor Hogan 64.16 and Morgan 63.82, but the final was held in difficult, rainy weather. The lead changed in each of the first three rounds from Morgan 62.18 to Parellis 63.32 and Gowda 63.64, and they remained the medallists but Hogan could manage only two fouls and 56.42 for 10th.

Hammer (29th)

1. James Steacy CAN 74.16
2. Nick Miller ENG 72.99
3. Mark Dry SCO 71.64
4. Alex Smith ENG 70.99
5. Tim Driesen AUS 69.94
6. Amir Williamson ENG 69.38
7. Constantinos Stathelakos CYP 68.22
8. Narayan Singh IND 67.99

MILLER LED THE qualifiers with 72.78 from Smith 72.34, and improved a little in the final, but Steacy took the lead from the first two rounds 72.61 and 74.16, ending with three more throws over 73m.

Javelin (2nd)

1. Julius Yego KEN 83.87
2. Keshorn Walcott TTO 82.67
3. Hamish Peacock AUS 81.75
4. Josh Robinson AUS 79.95
5. Stuart Farquhar NZL 78.14
6. Rocco van Rooyen RSA 76.84
7. Luke Cann AUS 75.93
8. Lee Doran WAL 72.73

THE FAVOURITES WALCOTT, with a national record 85.28, and Yego (82.83) were the only men over 80m in qualifying. Walcott threw a first round 82.13 in rainy weather in the final and Peacock threw 81.75 in round two with Yego in third place with his 79.28 opener before taking the lead with 83.87 in round three. Walcott responded with 81.59 and 83.67 but Yego was Kenya's first ever Commonwealth champion at a throws event.

Decathlon (28-29th)

1. Damien Warner CAN 8282
2. Ashley Bryant ENG 8109
3. Kurt Felix GRN 8070
4. John Lane ENG 7922
5. Stephen Cain AUS 7787
6. Ben Gregory WAL 7725
7. Friedrich Pretorius RSA 7639
8. David Guest WAL 7516

WARNER STARTED WITH 10.29 for 100m and went on to an expected victory. Lane, with three pbs, was in second place after the first day, but Bryant had a much better second day and Felix held his place, adding 8 points to his new national record.

4 x 100 Metres (2nd)

1. JAM	37.58*	Livermore, Bailey-Cole, Ashmeade, Bolt (ht: 1 Roach, 2 Forte)
2. ENG	38.02	Gemili, Aikines-Aryeetey, Kilty, Talbot (ht: 1 Ellington, 4 Robertson)
3. TTO	38.10	Bledman, Burns, Sorrillo, Thompson
4. RSA	38.35	Bruintjies. Magakwe, Titi, Simbine
5. BAH	39.16	7. ANT 40.45
6. NGR	40.17	dnf. CAN –

THE FASTEST QUALIFYING times came in the first heat, won by Trinidad in 38.33 from Canada 38.41 and Bahamas, a national record 38.52, while Jamaica had a problem as first-leg runner Kimmari Roach pulled a muscle at speed and did well to complete his stage, albeit several metres down, but his team came through to win their heat in 38.99. In the final there was little between Jamaica and slick-passing English squad until, racing at full speed for the first time in 2014, Bolt opened up a gap of close to 5m to bring his team home in a world leading 37.58.

4 x 400 Metres (2nd)

1. ENG	3:00.46	C Williams 45.2, Bingham 45.3, Awde 45.38, Hudson-Smith 44.56
2. BAH	3:00.51	L Williams 45.7, Mathieu 45.1, Russell 45.16, Brown 44.39
3. TTO	3:01.51	L Gordon 45.3, Solomon 44.8, Quow 45.34, Hewitt 45.92
4. JAM	3:02.17	7. NGR 3:04.86
5. SCO	3:04.07	8. ZAM 3:10.26
6. AUS	3:04.19	

EVEN WITHOUT Martyn Rooney, England had a fine win with Matthew Hudson-Smith overtaking Zewde Hewitt of Trinidad on the last leg and managing to hold off the redoubtable Chris Brown. Scotland set a national record of 3:03.94 in their heat and Jamie Bowie followed a 45.0 2nd leg then with 45.21 on the 3rd in the final.

Women

100 Metres (28th) (0.3)

1. Blessing Okagbare NGR	10.85*
2. Veronica Campbell-Brown JAM	11.03
3. Kerron Stewart JAM	11.07
4. Asha Philip ENG	11.18
5. Schillonie Calvert JAM	11.21
6. Bianca Williams ENG	11.31
7. Khamica Bingham CAN	11.37
8. Gloria Asumnu NGR	11.41

OSAGBARE STRODE MAJESTICALLY through each round, 11.20 heat, 10.93 semi (easing up) and a Games record 10.85 to win the final, when she ran such a strong second half that she left Campbell-Brown (11.02 semi) two metres behind. Stewart ran a season's best for bronze but Calvert was unable to match her semi-final win in 11.08.

200 Metres (31st) (0.4)

1. Blessing Okagbare NGR	22.25
2. Jodie Williams ENG	22.50
3. Bianca Williams ENG	22.58
4. Anyika Onuora ENG	22.64
5. Anneisha McLaughlin JAM	22.68
6. Schillonie Calvert JAM	22.94
7. Kimberly Hyacinthe CAN	23.11
8. Samantha Henry-Robinson JAM	23.24

OKAGBARE BECAME THE eighth woman to achieve a CG 100m/200m double. Her 22.25 was just 0.02 outsiode her pb and 0.05 off the Games record. She was followed by an English 2-3-4, all finishing strongly in pbs. Fastest in the heats were Bianca Williams 22.97 and Okagbare 22.99 and in the first semi Okagbare won in 22.43 from Jodie Williams 22.64 and McLaughlin 22.79.

400 Metres (29th)

1. Stephenie Ann McPherson JAM	50.67
2. Novlene Williams-Mills JAM	50.86
3. Christine Day JAM	51.09
4. Sade Abugan NGR	52.33
5. Kineke Alexander VIN	52.78
6. Shaunae Miller BAH	53.08
7. Kelly Massey GBR	53.08
dq? 4. Amantle Montsho BOT	51.10

THE JAMAICANS EACH won a semi-final (McPherson 50.69, Williams-Mills 50.73 and Day 50.73) and they swept the medals but the fourth placed finisher, defending champion Montsho, was later provisionally disqualified for failing a drugs test for a stimulant. Williams-Mills went out hard in the final, pursued by Montsho and led into the home straight, but McPherson came through strongly for gold.

800 Metres (1st)

1. Eunice Sum KEN	2:00.31
2. Lynsey Sharp SCO	2:01.34
3. Winnie Nanyondo UGA	2:01.38
4. Jessica Judd ENG-J	2:01.91
5. Angie Smit NZL	2:01.94
6. Jennifer Meadows ENG	2:02.19
7. Nikki Hamblin NZL	2:02.43
8. Melissa Bishop CAN	2:02.61

BISHOP WAS FASTEST in the heats with 2:01.73 and Sum in the semis 2:01.38 at which stage Janeth Jepkosgei was a surprise elimination. Sum led throughout the final, passing 200m in 27.4, 400m 58.24 and 600m 1:29.81. Meadows was second at halfway but faded to 6th as Sharp. ill on the eve of the race, closed strongly.

1500 Metres (29th)

1. Faith Kipyegon KEN	4:08.94
2. Laura Weightman ENG	4:09.24
3. Kate Van Buskirk CAN	4:09.41
4. Nicole Sifuentes CAN	4:10.48
5. Nikki Hamblin NZL	4:10.77
6. Hellen Obiri KEN	4:10.84
7. Hannah England ENG	4:11.10
8. Kaila McKnight AUS	4:12.77

OBIRI SET A Games record of 4:04.43 when winning the first heat from Hamblin 4:05.08, Laura Muir 4:05.19, England 4:05.62, Melissa Duncan 4:05.76 and McKnight 4:06.06 and the second heat was won by Kipyegon in 4:05.77 from Van Buskirk 4:07.74 and Weightman 4:08.58, but all were slower in the final. This had a very slow start as Selah Busienei led through 70.94 and 2:18.95, but the last 300m was fast and furious (last lap 61.20). Weightman led at 1200m in 3:23.25 and then Kipyegon led all down the home straight, initially followed by Obiri who faded to 6th. Muir had her heel clipped rounding the final turn, stumbled and finished 11th in 4:14.21.

5000 Metres (2nd)

1. Mercy Cherono KEN	15:07.21
2. Janet Kisa KEN	15:08.90
3. Jo Pavey ENG	15:08.96
4. Margaret Muriuki KEN	15:10.38
5. Eloise Wellings AUS	15:14.99
6. Laura Whittle SCO	15:33.72
7. Emily Brichacek AUS	15:39.96
8. Emelia Gorecka ENG	15:40.03

THE ABIDING MEMORY of this race will be the wonderful run by the 40-year-old Pavey. After a slow start, Kisa led at 3000m in 9:15.79. Pavey edged ahead to pass 4000m in 12:19.23, and led until Cherono took over with a little under 600m remaining. At the bell, though, it was Pavey in front again (14:04.5), chased by Cherono, Kisa, Muriuki and Wellings. Around the last turn Cherono got away and Pavey was down to 4th and a Kenyan clean sweep looked highly probable but Pavey came again in the straight to snatch 3rd place ahead of Muriuki and very nearly caught silver medallist Kisa. A quite amazing and inspiring display. Cherono ran a 62.6 last lap and a 2:47.98 for the final kilo. The final 3000m was covered in under 8:52 with Pavey not much slower. 17 runners.

10,000 Metres (29th)

1. Joyce Chepkirui KEN	32:09.35
2. Florence Kiplagat KEN	32:09.48
3. Emily Chebet KEN	32:10.82
4. Kate Avery ENG	32:33.35
5. Beth Potter SCO	32:33.36
6. Linet Chebet UGA	32:41.95
7. Sonia Samuels ENG	32:57.96
8. Vanis Chemutai UGA	33:11.98

THIRTEEN WOMEN contested the race, in which the leaders ran the first half in 16:32.26 and the second in 15:37.09 at a constantly changing tempo. In the end the three Kenyans finished well clear with Chepkirui passing Kiplagat just six strides from the finish. The there was a battle between British runners Avery and Potter for 4 and 5.

Marathon (27th)

1. Flomena Cheyech KEN	2:26:45
2. Caroline Kilel KEN	2:27:10
3. Jess Trengove AUS	2:30:12
4. Lanni Marchant CAN	2:31:14
5. Helaria Johannes NAM	2:32:02
6. Susan Partridge SCO	2:32:18
7. Louise Damen ENG	2:32:59
8. Melanie Panayiotou AUS	2:35:01

A LATE WITHDRAWAL by Philes Ongori meant that Kenya had just two contestants in the 20-woman field, but they duly finished 1-2. Cheyech won with halves of 74:26 and 72:19. Trengrove came through for a pb and bronze from 46 sec behind Johannes and 7 sec behind Marchant at halfway.

3000 Metres Steeplechase (30th)

1. Purity Kirui KEN	9:30.96
2. Milcah Chemos Cheywa KEN	9:31.30
3. Joan Kipkemoi Rotich KEN	9:33.34
4. Madeline Heiner AUS	9:34.01
5. Genevieve LaCaze AUS	9:37.04
6. Eilish McColgan SCO	9:44.65
7. Racheal Bamford ENG	9:45.51
8. Philippa Woolven ENG	9:47.97

THE STRONG KENYAN trio repeated their medal sweep of 2010, with Kirui, who led at 1000m in 3:12.91 and 2000m 6:26.70, prevailing in the sprint for the line.

100 Metres Hurdles (1st) (-0.1)

1. Sally Pearson AUS	12.67
2. Tiffany Porter ENG	12.80
3. Angela Whyte CAN	13.02
4. Danielle Williams JAM	13.06
5. Michelle Jenneke AUS	13.36
6. Kierre Beckles BAR	13.38
7. Josanne Lucas TTO	13.41
8. Shannon McCann AUS	13.60

THE TOP TWO were clearly the class of the field. Pearson retained her title, getting way to a cracking start (0.122 reaction time) to win by 0.13 from Porter. They had won their heats in 12.69 and 12.84 respectively.

400 Metes Hurdles (31st)

1. Kaliese Spencer JAM	54.10
2. Eilidh Child SCO	55.02
3. Janieve Russell JAM	55.64
4. Lauren Wells AUS	56.09
5. Noelle Montcalm CAN	56.74
dnf. Chanice Chase CAN	–
dq. Wenda Nel RSA	–
dq. Amaka Ogoebunenam NGR	–

THE CROWD WAS delighted as Child, the 'poster girl' of the Games took the silver medal, but she was some seven metres behind Spencer at the finish. There were just five placers as two women suffered trailing leg disqualifications and Chase failed to finish. Spencer 55.45 and Child 55.56 were fastest in the heats.

High Jump (1st)

1. Eleanor Patterson AUS-J	1.94
2. Isobel Pooley ENG	1.92
3. Lavern Spencer LCA	1.92
4= Leontia Kallenou CYP	1.89
4= Jeanelle Scheper LCA	1.89
6. Hannah Joye AUS-J	1.89

7. Saniel Atkinson-Grier JAM	1.86
8. Sahana Kumari IND	1.86

POOLEY TOOK THE lead by clearing 1.92 on her first attempt, followed by 18-year-old Patterson second time and Spencer on her third, but Patterson took gold with a first-time clearance at 1.94.

Pole Vault (2nd)

1. Alana Boyd AUS	4.50
2. Sally Peake WAL	4.25
3= Alysha Newman CAN	3.80
3= Sally Scott ENG	3.80
six women no height	

THE EVENT WAS ruined by very heavy rain. The start was delayed by 45 minutes and then after frantic clearing of water from the runway, the event started at 3.80. The first two to try the height cleared (and eventually got bronze medals for this), but then the heavy rain returned and the remaining six who entered at this height had no chance of success as failure after failure followed. including athletes such as Zoë Brown, who had gone over 4.42 and 4.45 in her previous competitions. Peake entered at 4.00 and was thrilled to clear it as the rain eased and Boyd came in at 4.15; she hardly got off the ground with her first two tries but succeeded at the third. The rain cleared and defending champion Boyd had first-time successes at 4.35, 4.40 and 4.50 (the bar shaking) before bowing out at a would-be Games record of 4.63.

Long Jump (31st)

1. Ese Brume NGR-J	6.56/0.4
2. Jazmin Sawyers ENG	6.54/1.9
3. Christabel Nettey CAN	6.49/0.4
4. Chantel Malone IVB	6.41/-0.3
5. Lorraine Ugen ENG	6.39/-0.8
6. Margaret Gayen AUS	6.34/1.3
7. Nektaria Panayi CYP	6.33/0.1
8. Bianca Stuart BAH	6.31/0.1

IN QUALIFYING, STUART jumped 6.67, Malone 6.55 and Shara Proctor 6.51, but Proctor pulled up injured on her first jump in the final. Brume scraped into the final with 6.29 for 12th after being 33rd in qualifying with 5.18 at the World Juniors a week earlier, but she was a surprising gold medallist with a third-round 6.56 after Nettey had led with 6.47 and 6.49 from 6.47 by Sawyers 6.47 who jumped 6.54 in the final round to take the silver.

Triple Jump (29th)

1. Kimberly Williams JAM	14.21/-0.9
2. Laura Samuel ENG	14.09/1.5
3, Ayanna Alexander TRI	14.01/0.8
4. Shenieka Thomas JAM	13.85w/2.8
5. Linda Leverton AUS	13.69/0.9
6. Ellen Pettitt AUS	13.54/1.1
7. Joëlle Mbumi Nkouindjin CMR	13.48/-0.9
8. Chioma Matthews ENG	13.46/0.8

AS EXPECTED WILLIAMS led the qualifiers with 13.94 (from Alexander 13.78), and took the lead with 14.11 in the first round of the final, but in round two Samuel got close as she improved her pb from 13.75 to 14.09. After a series of no jumps Samuel added 13.98 in the final round, in which Williams sealed her win with 14.21.

Shot (30th)

1. Valerie Adams NZL	19.88
2. Cleopatra Borel TRI	18.57
3. Julie Labonté CAN	17.58
4. Rachel Wallader ENG	16.83
5. Sophie McKinna ENG	16.59
6. Eden Francis ENG	16.57
7. Auriole Dongmo CMR	16.50
8. Kirsty Yates SCO	16.42

WHILE NOT AT her best, Adams maintained her position as the world's best shot putter. This was her 54th successive victory and her third CG title (after 2nd in 2002). Her series was x, 19.88, 19.58, x, 19.76, 19.79. Borel followed 4th, 3rd and 2nd at previous Games with another silver.

Discus (1st)

1. Dani Samuels AUS	64.88
2. Seema Punia IND	61.61
3. Jade Lally ENG	60.48
4. Siositina Hakeai NZL	58.67
5. Krishna Poonia IND	57.84
6. Kellion Knibb JAM	57.39
7. Eden Francis ENG	55.80
8. Danniel Thomas JAM	55.02

SAMUELS, BRONZE MEDALLIST in 2006, who had missed the 2010 Games, confirmed her status as favourite with 64.53 in qualifying and taking the lead in the final with 62.30 in round one, improving to 64.88 in round 3. Punia (née Antil) moved up a place from 2010, but defending champion Poonia slipped to 5th.

Hammer (29th)

1. Sultana Frizell CAN	71.97*
2. Julia Ratcliffe NZL	69.96
3. Sophie Hitchon ENG	68.72
4. Sarah Holt ENG	65.67
5. Carys Parry WAL	65.37
6. Susan McKelvie SCO	63.76
7. Rachel Hunter SCO	63.29
8. Gabrielle Neighbour AUS	61.84

DEFENDING CHAMPION FRIZELL set three Games records: 68.92 in qualifying and 70.55 and 71.97 in the final, in which she had four throws over 70m. She was followed by Ratcliffe, 67.96 qualifying and five throws over 68m in the final, and Hitchon, who started with 67.59 and whose best came in the last round.

Javelin (30th)

1. Kimberley Mickle AUS 65.96*
2. Sunette Viljoen RSA 63.19
3. Kelsey-Lee Roberts AUS 62.95
4. Kathryn Mitchell AUS 62.59
5. Liz Gleadle CAN 60.69
6. Nadeeka Lakmali SRI 59.04
7. Goldie Sayers ENG 57.68
8. Annu Rani IND 56.37

THE FIRST FOUR all exceeded the old Games record of 62.34. Mickle broke it with her opening throw of 62.97 and improved in the next round to 65.96. That proved out of the reach of the 2006 and 2010 champion Viljoen, who was nonetheless over 62m with all her six throws. Mitchell started with 62.33 but was passed by Roberts, 62.40 round two and 62.95 in the last.

Heptathlon (29-30th)

1. Brianne Theisen-Eaton CAN 6597
2. Jessica Zelinka CAN 6270
3. Jessica Taylor ENG 5826
4. Sophie Stanwell AUS 5754
5. Salcia Slack JAM 5718
6. Jessica Tappin ENG 5695
7. Grace Clements ENG 5512
8. Shianne Smith BER 5187

KATARINA JOHNSON-THOMPSON'S withdrawal meant that one of the most eagerly awaited clashes did not materialise, so Theisen-Eaton was left a clear winner, 327 ahead of Zelinka who won silver as in 2010. Zelinka led with 12.83 for 100mh but a 1.69 HJ left her well behind her compatriot's 1.84. Taylor set a pb for third.

4 x 100 Metres (2nd)

1. JAM 41.83* Stewart, Campbell-Brown, Calvert, Fraser-Pryce (ht: 3 Thompson)
2. NGR 42.92 Asumnu, Okagbare, Duncan, Uzor (ht: 2 P George, 4 Ozoh)
3. ENG 43.10 Philip, B Williams, J Williams, Nelson (ht: 2 Onuora, 3 Bloor)
4. CAN 43.33
5. AUS 44.21
6. BAH 44.25
7. WAL 44.51
8. TTO 44.78

JAMAICA EQUALLED THE Games record of 42.44 in the heats, and for the final they brought in Schillonie Calvert to replace Elaine Thompson on the third leg. With Kerron Stewart and Veronica Campbell-Brown on the first two legs and Shelly-Ann Fraser-Pryce on the anchor the outcome was never in doubt. Campbell-Brown at age 32 finally won her first CG gold medal after silver medals in 2002 (100m & 4x100m), 2006 (200m) and the 100m here in Glasgow. Blessing Okagbare added a silver to her two gold medals.

4 x 400 Metres (2nd)

1. JAM 3:23.82* Day 51.3, Williams-Mills 50.6, Le-Roy 51.52, McPherson 50.33
2. NGR 3:24.71 P George 51.7, R George 50.8, Benjamin 51.06, Abugan 51.07
3. ENG 3:27.24 C Ohuruogu 52.0, Cox 51.7, Massey 51.83, Onuora 51.72
4. AUS 3:30.27
5. CAN 3:32.45
6. TTO 3:33.50
7. BAH 3:34.86
dq. IND –

BOTH JAMAICA AND Nigeria broke the previous Games record of 3:25.63 with England finishing an isolated third.

CHAMPIONSHIPS 2014

World Junior Championships

At Eugene, USA 22-27 July

Men

100m (-0.6)
1. Kendal Williams USA 10.21
2. Trayvon Bromell USA 10.28
3. Yoshihide Kiryu JPN 10.34
4. Levi Cadogan BAR 10.39
5. Cejhae Greene ANT 10.43
6. Ojie Edoburun GBR 10.45
7. Andre Ford-Azoinwanna CAN 10.46
8. Jonathan Farina TTO 10.47

200m (2.3)
1. Trentavis Friday USA 20.04w (*)
2. Divine Oduduru NGR 20.25
3. Michael O'Hara JAM 20.31
4. Yoshihide Koike JPN 20.34
5. Zharnel Hughes AIA 20.73
6. Masaharu Mori JPN 20.84
7. Thomas Somers GBR-Y 20.92
8. Jonathan Farinha TTO 21.09

400m
1. Machel Cedenio TTO 45.13
2. Nobuya Kato JPN 46.17
3. Abbas Abubaker BRN 46.20
4. Alex Sampao KEN 46.55
5. Jack Crosby GBR 46.63
6. Lamar Bruton-Grinnage USA 46.75
7. Kaisei Yui JPN 47.08
8. Tyler Brown USA 47.30

800m
1. Alfred Kipketer KEN 1:43.95
2. Joshua Masikonde KEN 1:45.14
3. Andreas Almgren SWE 1:45.65
4. Thiago André BRA 1:46.06

5. Jena Umar ETH 1:46.23
6. Tre Kinnaird USA 1:47.13
7. Kalle Berglund SWE 1:47.31
8. Kyle Langford GBR 1:55.21

1500m 1. Jonathan Sawe KEN 3:40.02
2. Abdi Waiss Mouhyadin DJI 3:41.38
3. Hillary Ngetich KEN 3:41.61
4. Thiago André BRA 3:42.58
5. Zak Patterson AUS 3:44.21
6. Jan Petrac SLO 3:44.39
7. Julius Lawnik GER 3:44.96
8. Alexis Meillet FRA 3:45.28

5000m 1. Yomif Kejelcha ETH-Y 13:25.19
2. Yasin Haji ETH 13:26.21
3. Moses Mukono KEN 13:28.11
4. Joshua Cheptegei UGA 13:32.84
5. Fredrick Kipkosgei KEN 13:35.39
6. Phillip Kipyeko UGA 13:40.55
7. Tsegay Tuemay ERI 13:50.78
8. Justyn Knight CAN 14:08.93

10,000m 1. Joshua Cheptegei UGA 28:32.86
2. Elvis Cheboi KEN 28:35.20
3. Nicholas Kosimbei KEN 28:38.68
4. Berhane Afewerki ERI 28:45.83
5. Abdallah Mande UGA 28:53.77
6. Yihunilign Adane ETH 28:54.84
7. Keisuke Nakatani JPN 29:11.40
8. Hazuma Hattori JPN 29:12.74

3000mSt 1. Barnabas Kipyego KEN 8:25.57
2. Titus Kibiego KEN 8:26.15
3. Evans Chematot BRN 8:32.61
4. Soufiane El Bakkali MAR 8:34.98
5. Hailemariyam Amare ETH-Y 8:42.00
6. Yohanes Chiappinelli ITA-Y 8:43.18
7. Meresa Kassaye ETH 8:44.15
8. Ali Messaoui ALG 8:45.20

110mh (0.5) 1. Wilhem Belocian FRA 12.99*
2. Tyler Mason JAM 13.06
3. David Omoregie GBR 13.35
4. Wellington Zaza LBR 13.38
5. Benjamin Sedecias FRA 13.47
6. Ruebin Walters TTO 13.52
7. Francisco López ESP 13.55
8. Nick Anderson USA 13.93

400mh 1. Jaheel Hyde JAM-Y 49.29
2. Ali Khamis Abbas BRN 49.55
3. Tim Holmes USA 50.07
4. Jonas Hanssen GER 51.07
5. Yi Sihang CHN 51.32
6. Leandro Zamora CUB 51.49
7. José Luís Gaspar CUB 51.71
dnf. Ruan Mentz RSA

HJ 1. Mikhail Akimenko RUS 2.24
2. Dmitriy Nabokov BLR 2.24
3. Woo Sang-hyeok KOR 2.24
4. Cristoffe Bryan JAM 2.24
5. Falk Wendrich GER 2.22
6. Danyil Lysenko RUS-Y 2.22
7. Chris Kandu GBR 2.20
8. Joel Baden AUS 2.17

PV 1. Axel Chapelle FRA 5.55
2. Danyil Kotov RUS 5.50
3. Oleg Zernikel GER 5.50
4. Devin King USA 5.50
5= Huang Bokai CHN 5.45
5= Leonid Kobelev RUS 5.45
7. Jack Hicking AUS 5.40
8. Adam Hague GBR-Y 5.35

LJ 1. Wang Jianan CHN 8.08/1.5
2. Lin Qing CHN 7.94/ 1.6
3. Shontaro Shiroyama JPN 7.83w/2.4
4. Travonn White USA 7.72w/2.3
5. Kodai Sakuma JPN 7.71/1.7
6. José Luis Despaigne CUB 7.71/1.8
7. Cedric Dufag FRA 7.67w/2.1
8. Thobias Nilsson Montier SWE 7.65w/2.7

TJ 1. Lázaro Martínez CUB-Y 17.13/0.7
2. Max Hess GER 16.55/1.4
3. Mateus de Sá BRA 16.47/1.5
4. Andy Díaz CUB 16.43w/2.1
5. Leyon Aghasyan ARM 16.28w/2.4
6. Fang Yaoqing CHN 16.15/1.4
7. Ryoma Yamamoto JPN 15.89/0.9
8. Alvaro Cortez CHI 15.88/0.4

6kg **SP** 1. Konrad Bukowiecki POL-Y 22.06
2. Denzel Comenentia NED 20.17
3. Braheme Days USA 20.01
4. Hamza Mohamed EGY 19.85
5. Osman Can Özdeveci TUR 19.58
6. Martin Markovic CRO 19.57
7. Amir Ali Patterson USA 19.20
8. Mustafa Amer Ahmed EGY 19.20

1.75kg **DT** 1. Martin Markovic CRO 66.94
2, Henning Prüfer GER 64.18
3. Sven Martin Skagestad NOR 63.21
4. Matt Denny AUS 62.73
5. Ola Stunes Isene NOR 61.83
6. Mitch Cooper AUS 61.77
7. Gian Piero Ragonesi ITA 60.47
8. Ryan Njegovan USA 59.56

6kg **HT** 1. Ashraf Amjad El-Seify QAT 84.71
2. Bence Pásztor HUN 79.99
3. Ilya Terentyev RUS 76.31
4. Alexej Mikhailov GER 75.88
5. Matija Greguric CRO 75.71
6. Igor Yevseyev RUS 74.65
7. Maksim Mitskou BLR 74.11
8. Joaquín Gómez ARG 73.67

JT 1. Gatis Cakss LAT 74.04
2. Matija Muhar SLO 72.97
3. Adrian Mardare MDA 72.81
4. Jonas Bonewit GER 71.62
5. Shakiel Waithe TTO 70.78
6. Edis Matusevicius LTU 70.58
7. Ioánnis Kirioazís GRE 70.38
8. Shu Mori JPN 69.73

Dec 1. Jirí Sykora CZE 8135*
2. Cedric Dubler AUS 8094
3. Tim Nowak GER 7980
4. Yevgeniy Likhanov RUS 7788
5. Roman Kondratyev RUS 7780
6. Harrison Williams USA 7760
7. Friedrich Pretorius RSA 7689
8. Gabriel More USA 7619

4x100m 1. USA (J Miller, T Bromell, K Williams, T Friday) 38.70 (T Jernigan, M Wells ran in ht)
2. JPN (T Kawakami, Y Kiryu, Y Koike, M Mori) 39.02
3. JAM (R Robinson, M O'Hara, E Clarke,

J Minzie) 39.12 (W Williams, R Chambers ran in ht)
4. CHN 39.51
5. NGR 39.66
6. TTO 39.92
7. AUS 40.09
dnf. THA

4x400m 1. USA (J Lyles, T Brown, R Morgan, M Cherry) 3:03.31 (M Parish ran in ht)
2. JPN (J Walsh, K Yui, T Kitagawa, N Kato) 3:04.11
3. JAM (T Crooks, M Manley, N Allen, J Hyde) 3:04.47 (I Henry ran in ht)
4. GBR 3:06.42
5. AUS 3:06.80
6. BAH 3:08.08
dq: BOT, RSA

10,000W 1. Daisuke Matsunaga JPN 39:27.19*
2. Diego García ESP 39:51.59
3. Paolo Yurivilca PER 40:02.07
4. Yuga Yamashita JPN 40:15.27
5. Nikolay Markov RUS 40:22.48
6. Zaharías Tsamoudákis GRE 40:35.89
7. Ricardo Ortíz MEX 40:40.31
8. Wang Rui CHN 40:48.62

Women

100m (-1.0) 1. Dina Asher-Smith GBR 11.23
2. Ángela Tenorio ECU 11.39
3. Kaylin Whitney USA-Y 11.45
4. Desiree Henry GBR 11.56
5. Ewa Swoboda POL-Y 11.59
6. Irene Ekelund SWE-Y 11.61
7. Ariana Washington USA 11.64
8. Andrea Purica VEN 11.76

200m (2.4) 1. Kaylin Whitney USA 22.82w
2. Irene Ekelund SWE-Y 22.97
3. Ángela Tenorio ECU 23.15
4. Shannon Hylton GBR 23.25
5. Jada Martin USA 23.35
6. Arialis Gandulla CUB 23.48
7. Natalliah Whyte JAM-Y 23.48
8. Gina Lückenkemper GER 23.50

400m 1. Kendall Baisden USA 51.85
2. Gilda Casanova CUB 52.59
3. Olivia Baker USA 53.00
4. Laura Müller GER 53.40
5. Yana Glotova RUS 53.63
6. Ofonime Odiong NGR 54.06
7. Christian Brennan CAN 54.15
8. Susanne Walli AUT 54.61

800m 1. Margaret Wambui KEN 2:00.49
2. Sahily Diago CUB 2:02.11
3. Georgia Wassall AUS 2:02.71
4. Georgia Griffith USA 2:04.12
5. Sara Souhi MAR 2:06.16
6. Zeytuna Mohammed ETH 2:09.38
dnf. Aníta Henriksdóttir ISL
dnf. Maximiula Imali KEN

1500m 1. Dawit Seyaum ETH 4:09.86
2. Gudaf Tsegay ETH-Y 4:10.83
3. Sheila Keter KEN 4:11.21
4. Elise Cranny USA 4:12.82
5. Sofia Ennaoui POL 4:13.06
6. Alexa Efraimson USA-Y 4:13.31
7. Winfredah Nzisa KEN 4:13.80
8. Bobby Clay GBR 4:16.47

3000m 1. Mary Cain USA 8:58.48
2. Lilian Rengeruk KEN-Y 9:00.53
3. Valentine Mateiko KEN 9:00.79
4. Nozomi Takamatsu JPN-Y 9:02.85
5. Etagegne Woldu ETH 9:06.42
6. Emine Hatun Tuna TUR 9:06.85
7. Jessica Hull AUS 9:08.85
8. Weini Kelati ERI 9:12.32

5000m 1. Alemitu Haroye ETH 15:10.08
2. Alemitu Hawi ETH 15:10.46
3. Agnes Tirop KEN 15:43.12
4. Stella Chesang KEN 15:53.85
5. Loice Chemnung KEN-Y 15:55.17
6. Miki Izumida JPN 15:55.26
7. Courtney Powell AUS 15:56.00
8. Fuyuka Kimura JPN 15:59.72

3000mSt 1. Ruth Chebet BRN 9:36.74
2. Roseline Chepngetich KEN-Y 9:40.28
3. Daisy Jepkemei KEN 9:47.65
4. Bezuayehu Mohamed ETH 9:48.66
5. Woynshet Ansa ETH 9:59.31
6. Zulema Arenas PER 9:59.38
7. Rosa Flanagan NZL 10:04.01
8. Rosemary Katua BRN 10:18.01

100mh (1.9) 1. Kendell Williams USA 12.89
2. Dior Hall USA 12.92
3. Nadine Visser NED 12.99
4. Yasmin Miller GBR 13.13
5. Genesi Romero VEN 13.26
6. Sarah Missinne BEL 13.29
7. Reetta Hurske FIN 13.69
dnf. Elisa Girard-Mondoloni FRA

400mh 1. Shamier Little USA 55.66
2. Shona Richards GBR 56.16
3. Jade Miller USA 56.22
4. Zurian Hechavarría CUB 56.89
5. Mariam Abdul-Rashid CAN-Y 57.42
6. Genekee Leith JAM 58.33
7. Ayomide Folorunso ITA 58.34
8. Joan Medjid FRA 58.84

HJ 1. Morgan Lake GBR-Y 1.93
2. Michaela Hrubá CZE 1.91
3. Irina Iliyeva RUS 1.88
4. Rachel McCoy USA 1.88
5= Iryna Herashchenko UKR 1.85
5= Cassie Purdon AUS 1.85
7. Erika Furlani ITA 1.85
8. Wang Lin CHN 1.82

PV 1. Alyona Lutkovskaya RUS 4.50*
2. Desiree Freier USA 4.45
3. Eliza McCartney NZL 4.45
4. Nina Kennedy AUS-Y 4.40
5. Anastasiya Sadovnikova RUS 4.25
6. Rebeka Silhanová CZE 4.25
7. Elienor Werner SWE-Y 4.20
8. Reena Koll EST 4.20

LJ 1. Akela Jones BAR 6.34/-2.7
2. Nadia Akpana Assa NOR 6.31/-0.4
3. Maryse Luzolo GER 6.24/-1.5
4. Jogaile Petrokaite LTU 6.13/-2.6
5. Quanesha Burks USA 6.04/0.9
6. Jazmin McCoy USA 6.01/-0.4
7. Rougui Sow FRA 5.98/-1.8
8. Elise Malmberg SWE 5.95/0.0

TJ 1. Rouguy Diallo FRA 14.44w/3.3
2. Liadagmis Povea CUB 14.07w/3.3

3. Li Xiaohong CHN 14.03w/2.6
4. Valeriya Fyodorova RUS 13.96w/3.5
5. Elena Panturoiu ROU 13.73w/3.4
6. Ana Peleteiro ESP 13.71w/3.2
7. Marshay Ryan USA 13.60/1.0
8. Nubia Soares BRA 13.53w/3.5

SP 1. Guo Tianqian CHN 17.71
2. Raven Saunders USA 16.63
3. Emel Dereli TUR 16.55
4. Xu Jiaqi CHN 16.32
5. Klaudia Kardasz POL 16.29
6. Fanny Roos SWE 16.29
7. Yelena Bezruchenko RUS 16.24
8. Lezaan Jordaan RSA 16.15

DT 1. Izabela da Silva BRA 58.03
2. Valarie Allman USA 56.75
3. Navjeet Kaur IND 56.36
4. Liang Yan CHN 56.27
5. Claudine Vita GER 55.58
6. Tetyana Yuryeva UKR 54.35
7. Filoi Aukuso AUS 53.92
8. June Kintana ESP 53.36

HT 1. Alyona Shamotina UKR 66.05
2. Réka Gyurátz HUN 64.68
3. Ilíana Korosídou GRE 63.67
4. Audrey Ciofani FRA 63.30
5. Beatrice Nedberge Llano NOR-Y 63.23
6. Zsofia Bácskay HUN-Y 62.51
7. Katarzyna Furmanek POL 61.93
8. Vanessa Sterckendries BEL 61.63

JT 1. Yekaterina Starygina RUS 56.85
2. Sofi Flink SWE 56.70
3. Sara Kolak CRO 55.74
4. Marcelina Witek POL 54.14
5. Maria Andrejczyk POL 53.66
6. Christine Winkler GER 53.53
7. Marie-Therese Obst NOR 53.19
8. Arantxa Moreno ESP 52.08

Hep 1. Morgan Lake GBR-Y 6148
2. Yorgelis Rodríguez CUB 6006
3. Nadine Visser NED 5948
4. Celina Leffler GER 5746
5. Louisa Grauvogel GER 5621
6. Sofia Linde SWE 5616
7. Georgia Ellenwood CAN 5594
8. Emma Stenlöf SWE 5562

4x100m 1. USA (T Daniels, A Washington, J Martin, K Whitney) 43.46 (K Westbrook ran 4th leg in ht)
2. JAM (S Forbes, K Dallas, S Cameron, N Whyte 43.97 (S Williams & C Bonner ran in ht)
3. GER (L Kwaiye, L Mayer, G Lückenkemper, C Butzek) 44.65
4. TTO 44.75 6. JPN 45.40
5. SUI 45.02 dq. BAH, dnf. BRA

4x400m 1. USA (S Little, O Baker, S Wimbley, K Baisden) 3:30.42 (F Majors, A Barnes ran in ht)
2. GBR (S Richards, L Bleaken, S Bakare, C Hylton) 3:32.00 (L Nielsen, N Campbell-Smith ran in ht)
3. GER (L Müller, H Mergenthaler, Laura Gläsner, A-K Kopf) 3:33.02 (Schonig, E Frommann ran in ht)
4. CAN 3:33.17 7. AUS 3:39.65
5. NGR 3:35.14 dq. JAM
6. POL 3:37.52

10,000mW 1. Anezka Drahotová CZE 42:47.25*
2. Wang Na CHN 44:02.64
3. Ni Yuanyuan CHN 44:16.72
4. Laura García-Cano ESP 44:32.84
5. Mária Pérez ESP 44:57.30
6. Rena Goto JPN 45:54.07
7. Kana Minemura JPN 46:22.88
8. Stefany Coronado BOL 46:42.06

Medals (G-S-B) and points leaders

	G	S	B	Pts		G	S	B	Pts
USA	11	5	5	206	POL	1	-	-	34
KEN	4	5	7	124	BRN	1	1	2	28
GER	-	2	5	87	CZE	2	1	-	26
JPN	1	3	2	83	BRA	1	-	1	25
RUS	3	1	2	80.5	TTO	1	-	-	25
GBR	3	2	1	78	UGA	1	-	-	25
ETH	3	3	-	74	ESP	-	1	-	23
CHN	2	2	2	69.5	NOR	-	1	1	23
CUB	1	4	-	57	CRO	1	-	1	21
AUS	-	1	1	55.5	NED	-	1	2	19
JAM	1	2	3	50	NGR	-	1	-	18
FRA	3	-	-	39	HUN	-	2	-	17

CAN 16, UKR 14.5 (1G), TUR 13 (1B), ECU 13 (1S, 1B), BAR 13 (1G), GRE 11 (1B), SLO 10 (1S), PER 9 (1B), BLR 9 (1S), ITA, MAR 9; QAT, LAT 8 (1G); NZL 8 (1B), LTU, ERI 8; DJI 7 (1S), IND, KOR, MDA 6 (1B); EGY 6; LBR, VEN 5; ANG, ARM, BEL, ROU, SUI 4; BAH, RSA 3; FIN, MEX 2; ALG, ARG, AUT, BOL, CHI, EST 1. 21 nations won gold and 40 nations won medals.

IAAF World Race Walking Cup

At Taicang, China 3-4 May

Men – 20km (4 May)

1. Ruslan Dmytrenko UKR 1:18:37
2. Cai Zelin CHN 1:18:52

dq? 3. Andrey Ruzavin RUS 1:18:59

4. Yusuke Suzuki JPN 1:19:19
5. Miguel Ángel López ESP 1:19:21
6. Wang Zhen CHN 1:19:40
7. Igor Hlavan UKR 1:19:59
8. Omar Segura MEX 1:20:03
9. Eiki Takahashi JPN 1:20:04
10. Nazar Kovalenko UKR 1:20:11
11. Evan Dunfee CAN 1:20:13
12. Inaki Gómez CAN 1:20:18
13. Benjamin Thorne CAN 1:20:19
14. Dane Bird-Smith AUS 1:20:27
15. Chen Ding CHN 1:20:28

100 of 112 finished

Teams: 1. UKR 18, 2. CHN 23, 3. JPN 35, 4. CAN 36, 5. RUS 50, 6. ESP 61, 7. MEX 75, 8. IND 86, 9. ITA 117, 10. FRA 128, 11. AUS 135, 12. SVK 136, 13. BLR 150, 14. POL 164, 15. IRL 180, 16. TUR 257, 17. USA 276.

Men – 50km (3 May)

1. Mikhail Ryzhov RUS 3:39:05
2. Ivan Noskov RUS 3:39:38
3. Jared Tallent AUS 3:42:48
4. Aleksey Bartsaykin RUS 3:46:34
5. Oleksiy Kazanin UKR 3:47:01
6. Omar Zepeda MEX 3:47:35
7. Zhang Lin CHN 3:48:49

8. Ivan Banzeruk UKR 3:49:00
9. Sergiy Budza UKR 3:49:25
10. Chris Erickson AUS 3:49:33
11. Rolando Saquipay ECU 3:50:19
12. Quentin Rew NZL 3:50:22
13. Igor Saharuk UKR 3:50:49
14. Wu Qianlong CHN 3:50:51
15. Jonnathan Caceres ECU 3:50:52
drugs dq 4. Yuriy Andronov RUS 3:43:52
48 of 60 finished
Teams: 1. RUS 7, 2. UKR 25, 3. CHN 40, 4. ESP 76, 5. ITA 85, 6. COL 92, 7. IND 92, 8. GUA 139
Women - 20km (3 May)
1. Anisya Kirdyapkina RUS 1:26:31
2. Liu Hong CHN 1:26:58
3. Elmira Alembekova RUS 1:27:02
4. Vera Sokolova RUS 1:27:03
5. Eleonora Giorgi ITA 1:27:05 rec
6. Lu Xiuzhi CHN 1:27:15
7. Lyudmyla Olyanovska UKR 1:27:27
8. Ana Cabecinha POR 1:27:40
9. Antonella Palmisano ITA 1:27:51
10. Marina Pandakova RUS 1:27:54
11. Vera Santos POR 1:28:02
12. Lina Bikulova RUS 1:28:12
13. Raquel González ESP 1:28:36
14. Nie Jingjing CHN 1:28:43
15. Maria José Poves ESP 1:28:46
82 of 88 finished
Teams: 1. RUS 8, 2. CHN 22, 3. POR 36, 4. ESP 49, 5. ITA 70, 6. UKR 81, 7. LTU 100, 8. GUA 104, 9. POL 109, 10. BLR 121, 11. JPN 160, 12. USA 167, 13. ECU 186, 14. FRA 189, 15. CAN 190, 16. SUI 228
Junior Men - 10km (3 May)
1. Gao Wenkui CHN 39:40*
2. Daisuke Matsunaga JPN 39:45
3. Nikolay Markov RUS 39:55
4. Diego García ESP 40:10
5. Jie Jinzhu CHN 40:46
6. Paolo Yurivilca PER 40:47
33 of 41 finished
Teams: 1. CHN 6, 2. ESP 17, 3. AUS 19, 4. MEX 20, 5. JPN 23, 6. ITA 39, 11 teams scored.
Junior Women - 10km (4 May)
1. Duan Dandan CHN 43:05
2. Yang Jiayu CHN 43:37
3. Anezka Drahotová CZE 43:40
4. Laura García-Caro ESP 45:29
5. Cun Hailu CHN 45:52
6. Klavdiya Afanaseva RUS 45:59
44 of 48 finished
Teams: 1. CHN 3, 2. ESP 13, 3. AUS 20, 4. MEX 25, 5. ITA 29, 6. RUS 29, 14 teams scored
Prize Money: Individual: 1st $30,000, 2nd $15,000, 3rd $10,000, 4th $7000, 5th $5000, 6th $3000, Team: 1st $15,000, 2nd $12,000, 3rd $9,000, 4th $7500, 5th $6000, 6th $3000. Total: $367,500. No prize money for the Junior 10ks. 5 could start, 3 to score on senior teams.

IAAF World Relays

At Nassau, Bahamas 24-25 May

Men
4x100 metres (b)
1. JAM (Nesta Carter, Nickel Ashmeade, Julian Forte, Yohan Blake) 37.77
2. TTO (Keston Bledman, Marc Burns, Rondel Sorrillo, Richard Thompson) 38.04
3. GBR (Richard Kilty, Harry Aikines-Aryeetey, James Ellington, Dwain Chambers) 38.19
4. BRA (de Barros, Lucindo, A da Silva, Vides) 38.40
5. JPN (Oseto, Takase, Kiryu-J, Ilzuka) 38.40
6. CAN (Smellie, Richards-Kwok, Connaughton, J Warner) 38.55
7. GER (Menga, Jakubczyk, Reus, Keller) 38.69
dns, FRA.
B final: 1, UKR (Ibragimov, Smelyk, Bodrov, Korzh) 38.53
2. CUB (Carrero-J, Skyers, Mena-J, Cuéllar) 38.60
4x200 metres (a)
1. JAM (Nickel Ashmeade, Warren Weir, Jermaine Brown, Yohan Blake) 1:18.63
2. SKN (Antoine Adams, Lestrod Roland, B.J. Lawrence, Allistar Clarke) 1:20.51
3. FRA (Christophe Lemaitre, Yannick Fonsat, Ben Bassaw, Ken Romain) 1:20.66
4. BAR (Gittens, Cadogan-J, Hinds, Forde) 1:21.88
5. KEN (Barasa, Nkanata, Chirchir, Moenga) 1:22.35
6. BAH 1:23.19 7. CHN 1:25.83
dq, USA (Maurice Mitchell, Curtis Mitchell, Webb, Spearmon) (1:20.61)
4x400 metres (a-b)
1. USA (David Verburg 44.8, Tony McQuay 44.1, Christian Taylor 44.6, LaShawn Merritt 43.8) 2:57.25
2. BAH (LaToy Williams 45.0, Demetrius Pinder 43.8, Chris Brown 44.2, Michael Mathieu 44.6) 2:57.59
3. TTO (Lalonde Gordon 44.3, Renny Quow 44.6, Machel Cedenio-J 44.5, Jarrin Solomon 44.9) 2:58.34
4. GBR (Bingham 45.4, Williams 44.7, Levine 46.0, Rooney 44.2) 3:00.32
5. CUB (Collazo 45.5, Acea 44.5, Chacón 46.2, Lescay 44.4) 3:00.61
6. VEN (Ramírez 46.0, Bravo 45.0, Meléndez 45.6, Mezones 44.8) 3:01.44
7. BRA 3:03.87 8. JAM 3:10.23
B final: 1, BEL (D Borlée 46.6, J Borlée 45.2, Watrin 46.0, K Borlée 45.2) 3:02.97
2. JPN (Yui-J 46.4, Kanemaru 45.6, Ishitsuka 45.8, Watanabe 45.4) 3:03.24
3. DOM (Cuesta 47.0, L Santos 44.8, Soriano 46.4, J Santos 45.2) 3:03.41
4x800 metres (a)
1. KEN (Ferguson Cheruiyot 1:46.0, Sammy Kirongo 1:45.7, Job Kinyor 1:47.9, Alfred Kipketer-J 1:48.8) 7:08.40
2. POL (Karol Konieczny 1:48.9, Szymon Krawczyk 1:49.1, Marcin Lewandowski 1:45.9, Adam Kszczot 1:44.8) 7:08.69
3. USA (Michael Rutt 1:48.6, Robby Andrews 1:47.2, Brandon Johnson 1:48.1, Duane Solomon 1:45.2) 7:09.06
4. AUS (Ralph 1:49.6, Gregson 1:48.3, Williamsz 1:46.3, West 1:47.3) 7:11.48
5. ESP (K López 1:48.1, Marco 1:49.4, Rodríguez 1:49.5, Roldán 1:52.9) 7:19.90
6. MEX 7:21.12, 7. BER 7:21.87, 8. SVK 7:32.87, 9. UGA 7:53.34

4x1500 metres (b)
1. KEN (Collins Cheboi 3:38.5, Silas Kiplagat 3:32.4, James Magut 3:39.0, Asbel Kiprop 3:32.3) 14:22.22
2. USA (Patrick Casey 3:38.2, David Torrence 3:36.6, Will Leer 3:39.3, Leonel Manzano 3:46.7) 14:40.80
3. ETH (Mekonnen Gebremedhin 3:39.9, Soresa Fida 3:37.5, Zebene Alemayehu 3:46.5, Aman Wote 3:37.3) 14:41.22
4. AUS (Gregson 3:39.1, McEntee 3:44.9, Birmingham 3:38.3, Williamsz 3:43.7) 14:46.04
5. ESP (Mechaal, Rodruez, Alsonso, Imedio) 15:00.69
6. POL 15:05.70, 7. QAT 15:10.77

Women

4x100 metres (a):
1. USA (Tianna Bartoletta, Alex Anderson, Jeneba Tatmoh, Lakeisha Lawson) 41.88
2. JAM (Carrie Russell, Kerron Stewart, Schillonie Calvert, Samantha Henry-Robinson) 42.28
3. TTO (Kamaria Durant, Michelle-Lee Ahye, Reyare Thomas, Kai Selvon) 42.66
4. NGR (Asumnu, Okagbare, Duncan, Okwara) 42.67
5. GBR (Philip, B Williams, J Williams, Henry-J) 42.75
6. GER (Kwadwo, Weit, Pinto, Sailer) 43.38
7. BRA (V dos Santos, Krasucki, E dos Santos, R Santos) 43.67
8. FRA (Lesueur, Distel-Bonnet, Gaydu, Akakpo) 43.76

B final: 1, CAN (Bingham, Hyacinthe, Emmanuel, Davis) 43.33
2. BAH (Robinson, Ferguson, Armbrister, Strachan) 43.46
3. SUI (Cueni, Lavanchy, Kambundji, Sprunger) 43.55

4x200 metres (b):
1. USA (Shalonda Solomon, Tawanna Meadows, Bianca Knight, Kimberlyn Duncan) 1:29.45
2. GBR (Desiree Henry-J, Anyika Onuora, Bianca Williams, Asha Philip) 1:29.61
3. JAM (Simone Facey, Sheri-Ann Brooks, Anneisha McLaughlin, Shelly-Ann Fraser-Pryce) 1:30.04
4. BAH (Ferguson, Strachan, Smith, Armbrister) 1:31.31
5. SUI (Kambundji, Sprunger, Golay, Humair) 1:31.75
6. FRA 1:32.23, 7. NGR 1:33.71, dnf. TTO

4x400 metres (a-b)
1. USA (Deedee Trotter 50.7, Sanya Richards-Ross 50.4, Natasha Hastings 50.0, Joanna Atkins 50.6) 3:21.73
2. JAM (Kaliese Spencer 51.2, Novlene Williams-Mills 49.7, Anastasia Le-Roy 51.2, Shericka Jackson 51.2) 3:23.26
3. NGR (Folasade Abugan 52.1, Regina George 49.6, Omolara Omotoso 50.9, Patience George 50.8) 3:23.41
4. FRA (Gayot 52.2, Guion-Firmin 51.5, Raharolahy 51.8, Guei 50.4) 3:25.84
5. POL (Holub 52.6, Wyciszkiewicz 51.5, Linkiewicz 52.2, Swiety 51.1) 3:27.37
6. ITA (Bazzoni 52.8, Spacca 51.8, Bonfanti 52.6, Grenot 50.2) 3:27.44
7. GBR (Child 52.9, Cox 51.0, C Ohuruogu 53.0, Adeoye 51.1) 3:28.03
8. BRA (J Sousa 53.1, L Barbosa 53.1, de Lima 53.5, Coutinho 51.9) 3:31.59

B final: 1, AUS (Rubie 52.6, Mitchell 52.1, Gulli 53.5, Pekin 52.8) 3:31.01
2. BAH (Clarke 53.4, Amertil 51.4, Henfield 54.8, Byfield 52.1) 3:31.71
3. CAN (Martin 54.1, Muir 52.5, Wells 52.6, Dorr 53.4) 3:32.58

4x800 metres (b)
1. USA (Chanelle Price 2:01.0, Geena Lara 2:02.8, Ajee Wilson 1:59.1, Brenda Martinez 1:58.7) 8:01.58
2. KEN (Agatha Kimaswai 2:03.8, Sylvia Chesebe 2:01.7, Janeth Jepkosgei 1:59.6, Eunice Sum 1:59.2) 8:04.28
3. RUS (Irina Maracheva 2:02.6, Yelena Kobeleva 2:01.9, Tatyana Myazina 2:02.3, Svetlana Rogozina 2:01.4) 8:08.19
4. AUS (McGowan 2:03.6, Buckman 2:01.6, Kajan 2:02.2, Duncan 2:05.9) 8:13.26

IAAF World Combined Events Challenge

Based on the sum of the best scores achieved in any three of the 13 designated competitions during the year.

Men Decathlon

1	Rico Freimuth GER	24,981	8317 Götzis	8356 Ratingen	8308 Europeans
2	Eelco Sintnicolaas NED	24,795	8156 Eur Cup	8478 Europeans	7830 Talence
3	Yordanis García CUB	24,423	8299 Götzis	8179 P.Am Cup	7945 Talence
4	Oleksiy Kasyanov UKR	24,376	8083 Kladno	8231 Europeans	8062 Talence
5	Ashley Bryant GBR	24,052	7802 Firenze	8141 Götzis	8109 Comm G
6	Adam Helcelet CZE	23,945	8001 Götzis	7989 Kladno	7955 Eur Cup 1
7	Eduard Mikhon BLR	23,632	7987 Kladno	8004 Eur Cup	7641 Talence
8	Lars Vikan Rise NOR	23,516	7918 Kladno	7759 Eur Cup 1	7839 Europeans

Women Heptathlon

1	Nadine Broersen NED	19,573	6536 Götzis	6539 Eur Cup	6498 Europeans
2	Carolin Schäfer GER	19,164	6386 Götzis	6395 Europeans	6383 Talence
3	Lilli Schwarzkopf GER	18,973	6215 Götzis	6426 Ratingen	6332 Europeans
4	Eliska Klucinová CZE	18,846	6195 Götzis	6460 Kladno	6191 Eur Cup 1
5	Yana Maksimova BLR	18,525	6163 Götzis	6173 Eur Cup	6189 Talence
6	Xénia Krizsán HUN	18,468	6317 Götzis	6156 Europeans	5995 Talence
7	Anastasiya Mokhnyuk UKR	18,446	6201 Götzis	6025 Europeans	6220 Talence
8	Györgyi Zsivoczky-Farkas HUN	18,351	6020 Götzis	6151 Europeans	6180 Talence

Prize Money: 1st $30,000, 2nd $20,000, 3rd $15,000, 4th $10,000, 5th $8000, 6th $7000, 7th $6000, 8th $5000.

5. JAM (Malcolm 2:04.8, Campbell 2:07.0, Gordon 2:05.5, Goule 2:00.0) 8:17.22
6. FRA (Fedronic 2:02.6, Moh 2:02.8, Blameble 2:08.5, Lamote 2:03.7) 8:17.54
7. ROU 8:23.12, 8. MEX 8:24.45, dnf. TTO

4x1500 (a)
1. KEN (Mercy Cherono 4:07.5, Faith Kipyegon 4:08.5, Irene Jelagat 4:10.5, Hellen Obiri 4:07.1) 16:33.58
2. USA (Heather Kampf 4:09.2, Katie Mackey 4:19.4, Kate Grace 4:16.6, Brenda Martinez 4:10.2) 16:55.33
3. AUS (Zoe Buckman 4:08.0, Bridey Delaney 4:15.6, Brittany McGowan 4:29.1, Melissa Duncan 4:16.0) 17:08.65
4. ROU 17:51.48

Team Standings (8-7-6-5-4-3-2-1:) 1, USA 60; 2, JAM 41; 3, KEN 35; 4, GBR 24; 5, AUS 21; 6, TTO 19; 7, FRA 18; 8, BAH 15; 9, POL 14; 10, NGR 13, 11, BRA 10. 29 teams scored at least 1 point.

IAAF Hammer Throw Challenge

Final standings, top three meetings to score. Prize money from $30,000 for 1st to $500 for 12th.

Men: 1. Krisztián Pars HUN 244.84, 2. Pawel Fajdek POL 241.49, 3. Dilshod Nazarov TJK 241.37, 4. Mostafa Al-Gamel EGY 234.80, 5. Marcel Lomnicky SVK 234.24, 6. Pavel Krivitskiy BLR 232.76, 7. Sergey Litvinov RUS 225.63, 8. Szymon Ziólkowski POL 225.16, 9. Olexiy Sokyrskyy UKR 224.51, 10. Markus Esser GER 223.84; **Women**: 1. Anita Wlodarczyk POL 232.52, 2. Betty Heidler GER 228.54, 3. Kathrin Klaas GER 222.65, 4. Wang Zheng CHN 221.45, 5. Martina Hrasnová SVK 218.84, 6. Amanda Bingson USA 214.29, 7. Joanna Fiodorow POL 213.08, 8. Gwen Berry USA 211.74, 9. Éva Orbán HUN 210.68, 10. Bianca Perie ROU 209.69.

IAAF World Race Walking Challenge

Results of walks at 12 meetings qualified. Walkers needed to compete at three or more of these to qualify and positions were based on the best positions from these races, with a sliding scale of points from three categories. Prize money: 1st $30,000, 2nd $20,000, 3rd $14,000, 4th $9000, 5th $7000, 6th $6000, 7th $4500, 8th $4000, 9th $3000, 10th $2000, 11th $1000, 12th $500.

Overall placings: **Men**: 1, Ruslan Dmytrenko UKR 29, 2. Jared Tallent AUS 23, 3, Caio Bonfim BRA 18, 4, Matej Tóth SVK 17, 5. Erick Barrondo GUA 17, 6, Miguel Ángel López ESP 16, 7. Omar Zepeda MEX 16, 8. Omar Segura MEX 15, 9. Dane Bird-Smith AUS 14, 10. Isamu Fujisawa JPN 11. **Women** – 1. Liu Hong CHN 34, 2. Eleonora Giorgi ITA 23, 3,. Ana Cabecinha POR 22, 4, Inês Henriques POR 17, 5. Anezka Drahotová CZE 14, 6. Lorena Arenas COL 14, 7. Lyudmyla Olyanovska UKR 13, 8. Claudia Balderrama BOL 11, 9. Mirna Ortíz GUA 11, 10. Kelly Ruddick AUS 10.

World Marathon Majors 2013–14

Final Standings

Men: 1. Wilson Kipsang KEN 76, 2. Dennis Kimetto KEN 75, 3=. Tsegaye Kebede ETH, Lelisa Desisa 55; 5. Emmanuel Mutai KEN 45.

Women: *Pending decision on Rita Jeptoo* 1. Rita Jeptoo KEN 100, 2. Edna Kiplagat KEN 65, 3. Tirfi Tsegaye ETH 51, 4. Priscah Jeptoo KEN, Florence Kiplagat KEN 50; 6. Jemima Jelagat Sumgong KEN 35.

Youth Olympic Games

At Nanjing, China 20-26 August

Men: **100m**: Sydney Siame ZAM 10.56, **200m**: Noah Lyles USA 20.80, **400m**: Martin Manley JAM 46.31, **800m**: Myles Marshall USA 1:49.14, **1500m**: Gilbert Kwemoi Soet KEN 3:41.99, **3000m**: Yomit Kejelcha ETH 7:56.20, **2000mSt**: Wogene Sebisibe ETH, 91cm **110H**: Jaheel Hyde JAM 12.96, 84cm **400mh**: Xu Zhihang CHN 50.61, **HJ**: Danyil Lysenko RUS 2.20, **PV**: Noel Del Cerro ESP 5.10, **LJ**: Anatoliy Ryapolov RUS 7.54, **TJ**: Miguel van Assen SUR 16.15, 5kg **SP**: Konrad Bukowiecki POL 23.17, 1.5kg **DT**: Cheng Yulong CHN 64.14, 5kg **HT**: Hlib Piskunov UKR 82.65, 700g **JT**: Lukas Moutarde FRA 74.48, **10,000mW**: Minoru Oganawa JPN 42:03.64; **Women**: **100m**: Liang Xiaojing CHN 11.65, **200m**: Natalliah Whyte JAM 23.55, **400m**: Jessica Thornton AUS 52.50, **800m**: Martha Bissah GHA 2:04.90, **1500m**: Kokebe Tesfaye ETH 4:15.38, **3000m**: Nozomi Takamatsu JPN 9:01.58, **2000mSt**: Rosefline Chepngetich KEN 6:22.67, 76cm **100mh**: Laura Valette FRA 13.34, **400mh**: Gezelle Magerman RSA 57.91, **HJ**: Yuliya Levchenko UKR 1.89, **PV**: Angelica Moser SUI 4.36, **LJ**: Yelizaveta Babiy UKR 6.26, **TJ**: Esmeralda David FRA 13.33, **SP**: Alena Bugakova RUS 18.95, **DT**: Sun Kangping CHN 52.79, **HT**: Xu Xinying CHN 68.35, **JT**: Hanna Tarasyuk BLR 59.52, **5000mW**: Ma Zhenxia CHN 22:22.08. Medal table leaders: CHN 6-0-1, ETH 4-3-2, UKR 3-2-1, RUS 3-2-0, FRA 3-1-1, JAM 3-1-0, KEN 2-2-2, JPN 2-1-1.

6th Asian Indoor Championships

At Hangzhou, China 15-16 February

Men: **60m**: Samuel Francis QAT 6.61, **400m**: Mehdi Zamani IRI 48.25, **800m**: Abdulrahman Musaeb Balla QAT 1:50.27, **1500m/3000m**: Mohamed Al-Garni QAT 3:48.79/8:08.65, **60mh**: Abdulaziz Al-Mandeel KUW 7.80, **HJ**: Mutaz Essa Barshim QAT 2.36, **PV**: Hsieh Chia-Han TPE 5.15, **LJ**: Saleh Al-Haddad KUW 7.94, **TJ**: Fu Haitao CHN 16.11, **SP**: Om Prakash Singh IND 19.07, **Hep**: Dmitriy Karpov KAZ 5752 **4x400m**: KAZ 3:13.94; **Women**: **60m**: Tao Yujia CHN 7.36, **400m**: Maryam Toosi IRI 54.24, **800m**: Tatyana Yurchenko KAZ 2:14.20, **1500m/3000m**: Maryam Jamal BRN 4:19.42/8:43.16*, **60mh**: Wu Shujiao CHN 8.02*, **HJ**: Svetlana Radzivil UZB 1.96*, **PV**: Tomomi Abiko JPN 4.30, **LJ**: Yurina Hiraka JPN 6.34, **TJ**: Anastasiya Juravlyeva UZB 13.60, **SP**: Sofiya Burkhanova UZB 16.80, **Pen**: Wang Qingling 4246, **4x400m**: KAZ

3:42.45. **Medal table leaders**: QAT 5G-3S-0B, CHN 4-7-9, KAZ 4-5-3, UZB 3-3-2, KUW 2-2-1, JPN 2-1-3, IRI 2-1-1, BRN 2-0-0; 15 nations won medals.

Asian Junior Championships

At Taipeh, Taiwan 12-15 June

Men: **100m**: Takuya Kawakami JPN 10.47, **200m**: Mohammad Abareghi IRI 20.69 (20.63* ht), **400m**: Mohamed Nasir Abbas QAT 47.31, **800m:** Mohamed El Nour Mohamed QAT 1:52.73, **1500m**: Idriss Moussa Youssouf QAT 3:53.36, **5000m**: Musaab Adam Ali QAT 14:34.07, **10,000m**: Hazuma Hattori JPN 31:10.60, **3000mSt**: Musaab Adam Ali QAT 9:02.80, **110mh** (99cm): Taio Kanai JPN 13.33*, **400mh**: Yu Chia-Hsu-an TPE 50.49, **HJ**: Bai Jiaxu CHN 2.10, **PV**: Huang Bo-Kai CHN 5.25, **LJ**: Lin Qing CHN 7.99, **TJ**: Fang Yaoq-ing CHN 16.32, 6kg **SP**: Shahin Mehrdelan IRI 18.85, 1.75kg **DT**: Mustafa Al-Saamah IRQ 59.35, 6kg **HT**: Ashraf Amjad El-Seify QAT 79.71, **JT**: Hsu Shui-Chang TPE 67.24, **Dec** (jnr): Wang Chen-Yuan TPE 6566, **10,000mW**: Fumitaka Oikawa 44:08.25, **4x100m**: JPN 39.49, **4x400m**: THA 3:08.89; **Women**: **100m:** Liang Xiaojing CHN 11.58w, **200m**: Dutee Chand IND 23.74, **400m:** Siti Nur Afiqah Abdul Razak MAS 53.93, **800m**: Ryoko Hirano JPN 2:06.75, **1500m**: O Song-mi PRK 4:28.38, **3000m**: Daria Maslova KGZ 9:16.23, **5000m**: Maki Izumida JPN & Daria Maslova KGZ 16:18.35, **3000mSt**: Nguyen Thi Oanh VIE 10:27.29, **100mh**: Mako Fukube JPN 13.98, **400mh**: Akiko Ito JPN 58.80, **HJ**: Wang Lin CHN 1.88, **PV**: Li Chaoqun CHN 4.05, **LJ**: Li Xiaohong CHN 6.27, **TJ**: Wang Rong CHN 13.64, **SP**: Xu Jiaqi CHN 16.50, **DT**: Xie Yuchen CHN 55.65, **HT**: Hung Hsiu-Wen TPE 56.81, **JT**: Shiori Toma JPN 55.75, **Hep**: Kotchakorn Khamrueangsri THA 5290, **10.000mW**: Kaori Kawazoe JPN 50:38.05, **4x100m**: CHN 45.34, **4x400m**: IND 3:40.53.

Medal winners: CHN 12G-10S-2B, JPN 11-5-5, QAT 6-2-1, TPE 4-3-8, , IND 2-5-5, THA 2-5-1, IRI 2-2-5, KGZ 2-0-0, PRK 1-1-2. 22 nations won medals (12 gold).

Asian Games

At Incheon, Korea 27 September – 3 October

Men

100m	1. Femi Ogunode QAT 9.93*
(0.4)	2. Su Bingtian CHN 10.10
	3. Kei Takase JPN 10.15
200m	1. Femi Ogunode QAT 20.14*
(0.3)	2. Fahad Mohamed Al-Subaie KSA 20.74
	3. Yeo Ho-su-ah KOR 20.82
400m	1. Youssef Al-Masrahi KSA 44.46*
	2. Abbas Abubaker BRN-J 45.62
	3. Arokia Rajiv IND 45.92
800m	1. Adnan Taees Akkar IRQ 1:47.48
	2. Teng Haining CHN 1:47.81
	3. Jamal Al-Hayrani QAT 1:48.25
1500m	1. Mohamed Al-Garni QAT 3:40.23
	2. Rashid Ramzi BRN 3:40.95
	3. Adnan Taees Akkar IRQ 3:42.50
5000m	1. Mohamed Al-Garni QAT 13:26.13*
	2. Alemu Bekele BRN 13:27.98
	3. Albert Rop BRN 13:28.08
10,000m	1. El Hassan El Abbassi BRN 28:11.20
	2. Suguru Osako JPN 28:11.94
	3. Isaac Korir BRN 28:45.65
Mar	1. Ali Hassan Mahboob BRN 2:12:38
	2. Kohei Matsumura JPN 2:12:39
	3. Yuki Kawauchi JPN 2:12:42
3000mSt	1. Ali Abubaker Kamal QAT 8:28.72
	2. Tareq Mubarak Taher BRN 8:39.62
	3. Naveen Kumar IND 8:40.39
110mh	1. Xie Wenjun CHN 13.36
(0.4)	2. Kim Byung-jun KOR 13.43
	3. Jumrut Rittidet THA 13.61
400mh	1. Ali Khamis Abbas BRN-J 49.71
	2. Takayuki Kishimoto JPN 49.81
	3. Cheng Wen CHN 50.29
HJ	1. Mutaz Essa Barshim QAT 2.35*
	2. Zhang Guowei CHN 2.33
	3. Muamer Aissa Barshim QAT 2.25
PV	1. Xue Changrui CHN 5.55
	2. Daichi Sawano JPN 5.55
	3. Jin Min-sup KOR 5.45
LJ	1. Li Jinzhe CHN 8.01/-0.7
	2. Kim Duk-hyung KOR 7.90/-0.2
	3. Gao Xinglong CHN 7.86/0.5
TJ	1. Cao Shuo CHN 17.30/-0.2
	2. Dong Bin CHN 16.95/0.9
	3. Kim Duk-hyung 16.93/1.4
SP	1. Sultan Al-Hebshi KSA 19.99
	2. Chang Ming-Huang TPE 19.97
	3. Indrajit Singh IND 19.63
DT	1. Ehsan Hadadi IRI 65.11
	2. Vikas Gowda IND 62.58
	3. Ahmed Mohamed Dheeb QAT 61.25
HT	1. Dilshod Nazarov TJK 76.82
	2. Wang Shizhu CHN 73.65
	3. Wan Yong CHN 73.43
JT	1. Zhao Qinggang CHN 89.15*
	2. Ryohei Arai JPN 84.42
	3. Ivan Zaytsev UZB 83.68
Dec	1. Keisuke Ushiro JPN 8088
	2. Leonid Andreyev UZB 7879
	3. Akihiko Nakamura JPN 7828
4x100m	1. CHN (Chen Shiwei, Xie Zhenye, Su Bingtian, Zhang Peimeng) 37.99*
	2. JPN 38.49
	3. HKG 38.98
4x400m	1. JPN (Kanemaru, Fujimitsu, Iizuka, Kato) 3:01.88
	2. KOR 3:04.03
	3. KSA 3:04.03
20kmW	1. Wang Zhen CHN 1:19:45*
	2. Yusuke Suzuki JPN 1:20:44
	3. Kim Hyun-sub KOR 1:21:37
50kmW	1. Takayuki Tanii JPN 3:40:19*
	2. Park Chil-sung KOR 3:49:15
	3. Wang Zhendong CHN 3:50:52

Women

100m	1. Wei Yongli CHN 11.48
(-0.5)	2. Chisato Fukushima JPN 11.49
	3. Olga Safronova KAZ 11.50
200m	1. Olga Safronova KAZ 23.02
(0.0)	2. Wei Yongli CHN 23.27
	3. Chisato Fukushima JPN 23.45
400m	1. Kemi Adekoya BRN 51.59
	2. Quach Thi Lan VIE-J 52.06
	3. Machettira Raju Poovamma IND 52.36
800m	1. Margarita Mukasheva KAZ 1:59.02*
	2. Tintu Luka IND 1:59.19
	3. Zhao Jing CHN 1:59.48

1500m	1. Maryam Jamal BRN 4:09.90
	2. Mimi Belete BRN 4:11.03
	3. Orchatteri P Jaisha IND 4:13.46
5000m	1. Maryam Jamal BRN 14:59.69
	2. Mimi Belete BRN 15:00.87
	3. Ding Changqin CHN 15:12.51
10,000m	1. Alia Saeed Mohamed UAE 31:51.86
	2. Ding Changqin CHN 31:53.09
	3. Ayumi Hagiwara JPN 31:55.67
Mar	1. Eunice Jepkirui BRN 2:25:37
	2. Ryoko Kizaki JPN 2:25:50
	3. Lishan Dula BRN 2:33:13
3000mSt	1. Ruth Chebet BRN-J 9:31.36*
	2. Li Zhenzhu CHN 9:35.23
	3. Lalita Babar IND 9:35.37
100mh	1. Wu Shuijiao CHN 12.72
(0.0)	2. Sun Yawei CHN 13.05
	3. Ayako Kimura JPN 13.25
400mh	1. Kemi Adekoya BRN 55.77
	2. Satomi Kubokura JPN 56.21
	3. Xiao Xia CHN 56.59
HJ	1. Svetlana Radzivil UZB 1.94
	2. Zheng Xingjuan CHN 1.92
	3. Nadezhda Dusanova UZB 1.89
PV	1. Li Ling CHN 4.35*=
	2. Tomomi Abiko JPN 4.25
	3. Lim Eun-ji KOR 4.15
LJ	1. Maria Natalia Londa INA 6.55/0.3
	2. Bui Thi Thu Thao VIE 6.44/0.9
	3. Jiang Yanfei CHN 6.34/0.3
TJ	1. Olga Rypakova KAZ 14.32/-0.4
	2. Aleksandra Kotlyarova UZB 14.05/0.2
	3. Irina Ektova KAZ 13.77/-0.1
SP	1. Gong Lijiao CHN 19.06
	2. Leyla Rajabi IRI 17.80
	3. Guo Tianqian CHN-J 17.52
DT	1. Seema Punia IND 61.03
	2. Lu Xiaoxin CHN 59.35
	3. Tan Jian CHN 59.03
HT	1. Wang Zheng CHN 74.16*
	2. Manju Bala Singh IND 60.47
	3. Masumi Aya JPN 59.84
	drugs dq (1), Zhang Wenxiu CHN 77.33(*)
JT	1. Zhang Li CHN 65.47*
	2. Li Lingwei CHN 61.43
	3. Annu Rani IND 59.53
Hep	1. Yekaterina Voronina UZB 5912
	2. Wang Qingling CHN 5856
	3. Yuliya Tarasova UZB 5482
4x100m	1. CHN (Tao Yujia, Kong Lingwei, Lin Huijun, Wei Yongli) 42.83*
	2. KAZ 43.90
	3. JPN 44.05
4x400m	1. IND (Panwar, Luka, Kaur, Poovamma) 3:28.68*
	2. JPN 3:30.80
	3. CHN 3:32.02
20kW	1. Lu Xiuzhi CHN 1:31:06
	2. Khushbir Kaur IND 1:33:07
	3. Jeon Yeong-eun KOR 1:33:18

Medal Table Leaders

Nation	*G*	*S*	*B*
CHN	15	13	11
BRN	9	6	3
QAT	6	0	3
JPN	3	12	8
KAZ	3	1	2
IND	2	4	7
UZB	2	2	3
KSA	2	1	1
IRI	1	1	0
IRQ	1	0	1
KOR	0	4	6

in all 18 nations won medals.

Winning at Asian Games in 2006, 2010 and 2014: Maryam Jamal W 1500m (and 800m 2006, 5000m 2014), Ehsan Hadadi DT; Dilshod Nazarov HT (after 7th 1998, 9th 2002); Zhang Wenxiu W HT (until her later dq).

Asian Walks Championships

At Nomi City, Japan 16 March

Men 20k: 1. Kim Hyun-sub KOR 1:19:24, 2. Yusuke Suzuki 1:21:01, 3. Gurmeet Singh IND 1:21:30; **Women 20k**: 1. Zhou Tongmei CHN 1:31:58, 2. Rei Inoue JPN 1:32:56, 3. Khushbir Singh IND 1:33:37.

Balkan Championships

At Pitesti, Romania 26-27 July

Men: **100m/200m**: Ramil Ganiyev TUR 10.24/21.04; **400m**: Yavuz Can TUR 46.50, **800m**: Andréas Dimitrákis GRE 1:49.74; **1500m**: Kemal Koyuncu TUR 3:45.80, **5000m**: Nicolae Soare ROU 14:17.95, **3000mSt**: Mitko Tsenov BUL 8:52.33, **110mh**: Milan Ristic 14.47, **400mh**: Emir Bekric SRB 50.08, **HJ**: Tihomir Ivanov BUL 2.22, **PV**: Ivan Horvat CRO 5.30, **LJ/ TJ**: Marian Oprea ROU 7.78/16.77, **SP**: Georgi Ivanov BUL 19.62; **DT**: Martin Maric 62.91, **HT**: Serghei Marghiev MDA 76.20, **JT**: Fatih Avan TUR 75.98, **Dec**: Darko Pesic MNE 7259, **4x100**: ROU 40.09, **4x400**: TUR 3:07.41; **Women**: **100m**: Andreea Ograzeanu ROU 11.33, **200m**: Inna Eftimova BUL 23.99, **400m**: Bianca Razor ROU 52.24, **800m**: Mirela Lavric ROU 2:04.21; **1500m**: Florina Pierdevara ROU 4:24.95, **5000m**: Esma Aydemir TUR 15:58.25, **3000mSt**: Silva Danekova BUL 9:43.45, **100mh**: Ivana Loncarek CRO 13.37, **400mh**: Angela Morosanu ROU 57.43, **HJ**: Venelina Veneva-Mateeva BUL 1.90, **PV**: Loréla Mánou GRE 4.35, **LJ**: Alina Rotaru ROU 6.72, **TJ**: Cristina Bujin ROU 14.11, **SP**: Radoslava Mavrodieva BUL 17.60, **DT**: Dragana Tomasevic SRB 57.60, **HT**: Bianca Perie ROU 69.42, **JT**: Nicoleta Anghelescu ROU 53.12; **Hep**: Sofía Ifantídou GRE 5724, **4x100**: GRE 44.76, **4x400**: ROU 3:31.02.

Marathon *at Beograd, Serbia 27 April*. **Men:** Vitalie Gheorghita MDA 2:31:24, **Women:** Ana Subotic SRB 2:44:04.

Walks *at Balchik, Bulgaria 12 April*. **Men 20k:** Vladimir Savanovic SRB 1:28:31, **Women 20k:** Déspina Zapounídou GRE 1:34:56.

Central American and Caribbean Games

22nd edition at Xalapa, Mexico, 23-30 November. 1420m altitude

Men

100m	1. Rolando Palacios HON 10.27
(0.9)	2. Levi Cadogan BAR 10.27

	3. Yaniel Carrero CUB 10.28
200m	1. Roberto Skyers CUB 20.47
(-1.8)	2. Reynier Mena CUB 20.54
	3. José Herrera MEX 20.63
400m	1. Raidel Acea CUB 45.36
	2. Yoandis Lescay CUB 45.56
	3. Albert Bravo VEN 45.82
800m	1. Andy González CUB 1:45.73
	2. Rafith Rodríguez COL 1:45.74
	3. Wesley Vázquez PUR 1:46.05
1500m	1. Andy González CUB 3:45.52
	2. Pablo Solares MEX 3:45.62
	3. Christopher Sandoval MEX 3:47.55
5000m	1. Juan Luis Barrios MEX 14:15.98
	2. Iván González COL 14:25.16
	3. Mario Pacay GUA 14:27.34
10,000m	1. Juan Luis Barrios MEX 29:13.63
	2. Juan Romero MEX 29:28.32
	3. Iván González COL 29:41.31
Mar	1. Richer Perez CUB 2:19:33
	2. José García GUA 2:19:45
	3. Daniel Vargas MEX 2:20:27
3000mSt	1. Marvin Blanco VEN 8:43.76
	2. José Gregorio Peña VEN 8:45.04
	3. Luis Ibarra MEX 8:48.42
110mh	1. Yordan O'Farrill CUB 13.46
(0.7)	2. Jhoanis Portilla CUB 13.53
	3. Greggmar Swift BAR 13.59
400mh	1. Omar Cisneros CUB 49.56
	2. Eric Alejandro PUR 50.05
	3. Leslie Murray ISV 50.21
HJ	1. Sergio Mestre CUB 2.27
	2. Eure Yáñez VEN 2.24
	3. Ryan Ingraham BAH 2.24
PV	1. Lázaro Borges CUB 5.30
	2. Yanquier Lara CUB 5.10
	3. Raúl Rios MEX 5.00
LJ	1. David Registe DMA 7.79/-0.2
	2. Abdul Halim ISV 7.75/-0.6
	3. Yunior Díaz CUB 7.66/-0.9
TJ	1. Ernesto Revé CUB 16.94/-0.1
	2. Lázaro Martínez CUB 16.91/-0.6
	3. Yordanis Durañona DMA 16.67/-0.4
SP	1. Mario Cota MEX 19.30
	2. Stephen Sáenz MEX 19.27
	3. Raymond Brown JAM 18.30
DT	1. Jorge Fernández CUB 63.17
	2. Mauricio Ortega COL 60.69
	3. Mario Cota MEX 58.21
HT	1. Roberto Janet CUB 74.11
	2. Reinier Mejías CUB 71.81
	3. Roberto Sawyers CRC 70.66
JT	1. Guillermo Martínez CUB 79.27
	2. Juan Méndez MEX 76.80
	3. Osmani Laffita CUB 76.28
Dec	1. Yordani García CUB 7854
	2. José Ángel Mendieta CUB 7517
	3, Román Garibay MEX 7243
4x100m	1. CUB 38.94
	2. DOM 39.01
	3. VEN 39.22
4x400m	1. CUB 3:00.70*
	2. VEN 3:01.80
	3. COL 3:02.52
20kmW	1. Horacio Nava MEX 1:25:05
	2. Eider Arévalo COL 1:26:03
	3. José Montaña COL 1:27:30
50kmW	1. Erick Barrondo GUA 3:49:40*
	2. Omar Zepeda MEX 3:52:45
	3. Cristian Berdeja MEX 3:53:39
Women	
100m	1. Andrea Purica VEN 11.29
(1.5)	2. Nediam Vargas VEN 11.43
	3. Laverne Jones-Ferrette ISV 11.54
200m	1. Nercely Soto VEN 23.14
(-1.6)	2. María Alejandra Idrobo COL 23.52
	3. Allison Peter ISV 23.54
400m	1. Lisneidy Veitia CUB 51.72
	2. Daysiurami Bonne CUB 52.49
	3. Yennifer Padilla COL 52.95
800m	1. Rose Mary Almanza CUB 2:00.79
	2. Cristina Guevara MEX 2:01.68
	3. Gabriela Medina MEX 2:02.36
1500m	1. Muriel Coneo COL 4:14.84*
	2. Cristina Guevara MEX 4:16.51
	3. Adriana Muñoz CUB 4:20.50
5000m	1. Brenda Flores MEX 16:02.64*
	2. Sandra López MEX 16:13.23
	3. Yanisleidis Castillo CUB 16:16.21
10,000m	1. Brenda Flores MEX 35:54.44
	2. Kathya Garcia MEX 36:23.32
	3. Yudisleyvis Castillo CUB 36:29.04
Mar	1. Margarita Hernández MEX 2:41:16*
	2. Dailín Belmonte CUB 2:42:01
	3. Zuleima Amaya VEN 2:42:27
3000mSt	1. Ángela Figueroa COL 10:05.25
	2. Muriel Coneo COL 10:07.94
	3. Beverly Ramos PUR 10:08.39
100mh	1. Lina Florez COL 13.19
(-0.8)	2. Briggit Merlano COL 13.19
	3. Kierre Beckles BAR 13.47
400mh	1. Zudikey Rodríguez MEX 56.79
	2. Magdalena Mendoza VEN 57.67
	3. Zurian Hechavarría CUB 57.74
HJ	1. Levern Spencer STL 1.89
	2. Priscilla Frederick ANT 1.83
	3. Kashani Ríos PAN 1.80
PV	1. Yarisley Silva CUB 4.60*
	2. Diamara Planell PUR 4.15
	3. Robeilys Peinado VEN 4.15
LJ	1. Chantel Malone BVI 6.46/-0.3
	2. Irisdaymi Herrera CUB 6.36/0.9
	3. Zoila Flores MEX 6.26/1.0
TJ	1. Caterine Ibargüen COL 14.57/-0.4*
	2. Dailenis Alcántara CUB 14.09/-0.3
	3. Yosiri Urrutia COL 13.89/0.3
SP	1. Cleopatra Borel TTO 18.99
	2. Yaniuvis López 17.88
	3. Sandra Lemos COL 17.50
DT	1. Denia Caballero CUB 64.47*
	2. Yaimi Pérez CUB 62.42
	3. Johana Martínez COL 56.27
HT	1. Yipsi Moreno CUB 71.35*
	2. Yirisleydi Ford CUB 69.62
	3. Eli Johana Moreno COL 67.77
JT	1. Flor Denis Ruiz COL 63.80*
	2. Abigail Gómez MEX 57.28
	3. Coralys Ortiz PUR 54.53
Hep	1. Yorgelis Rodríguez CUB 5984*
	2. Yusleidys Mendieta CUB 5819

	3. Alysbeth Félix PUR 5721
4x100m	1. VEN 43.53
	2. COL 44.02
	3. CUB 44.19
4x400m	1. CUB 3:29.69
	2. MEX 3:33.16
	3. COL 3:34.14
20kmW	1. Mirna Ortiz GUA 1:35:43*
	2. Lorena Arenas COL 1:36:29
	3. Ingrid Hernández COL 1:37:11

Medal table of leading nations

Nation	*G*	*S*	*B*
CUB	23	15	8
MEX	8	11	9
COL	5	9	10
VEN	4	5	4
GUA	2	1	2

In all 10 nations won gold medals and 19 won medals.

14th European Cup Winter Throwing

At Leiria, Portugal 15-16 March

Men: **SP:** 1. Aleksandr Lesnoy RUS 21.23, 2. Mario Fortes POR 21.01, 3. Georgi Ivanov BUL 20.59; **DT**: 1. Viktor Butenko RUS 64.38, 2, Erik Cadée NED 63.56, 3. Christoph Harting GER 62.56; **HT**: 1. Pawel Fajdek POL 78.75, 2. Krisztián Pars HUN 77.24, 3. Denis Lukyanov RUS 74.11; **JT**: 1. Zigismunds Sirmais LAT 81.60, 2. Thomas Röhler GER 81.17, 3. Risto Mätas EST 80.58; **U23**: Maksym Bohdan UKR 83.41; **Women: SP:** 1. Yevgeniya Kolodko RUS 18.66, 2. Alena Kopets BLR 18.50, 3. Yuliya Leontyuk BLR 18.55; **DT**: 1. Mélina Robert-Michon FRA 64.20, 2. Anna Rüh GER 63.21, 3. Dragana Tomasevic SRB 59.26; **U23**: Shanice Craft GER 64.16; **HT**: 1. Joanna Fiodorow POL 72.70, 2. Éva Orbán HUN 72.49, 3. Kathrin Klaas GER 70.99; **JT**: 1. Linda Stahl GER 61.20, 2. Kathrin Molitor GER 60.97, 3. Martina Ratej SLO 59.57; U23: Liina Laasma 63.17; **Team: Men**: 1. RUS 4454, 2. BLR 4243, 3. ITA 4222; U23: 1. RUS 4078, 2. FRA 3995, 3. GER 3865; **Women**: 1. GER 4263, 2. RUS 4136, 3. FRA 4128; U23: 1. GER 4164, 2. UKR 3829, 3. RUS 3731.

European Team Championships

Super League *at Braunschweig, Germany 21-22 June*
1. GER 372, 2. RUS 359.5, 3. POL 294; 4. FRA 284*, 5, GBR 282.5; 6, UKR 274; 7, ITA 240.5; 8, ESP 221.5; 9, SWE 214; 10, NED 210; 11, CZE 209.5; 12, TUR 139.5.
* after losing 11 points originally won by hammer thrower Quentin Bigot (drugs dq).

100m	1. Jimmy Vicaut FRA 10.03
(0.7)	2. Danny Talbot GBR 10.30
	3. Ramil Guliyev TUR 10.37
200m	1. Karol Zalewski POL 20.56
(2.0)	2. Ramil Guliyev TUR 20.57
	3. James Ellington GBR 20.60
400m	1. Mame-Ibra Anne FRA 45.71
	2. Pavel Ivashko RUS 45.95
	3. Daniel Awde GBR 46.10
800m	1. Timo Benitz GER 1:46.24
	2. Adam Kszczot POL 1:46.36
	3. Giordano Benedetti ITA 1:46.45
1500m	1. Jakub Holusa CZE 3:37.74
	2. Homiyu Tesfaye GER 3:38.10
	3. Marcin Lewandowski POL 3:38.19
3000m	1. Richard Ringer GER 7:50.99
	2. Jakub Holusa CZE 7:51.43
	3. Antonio Abadia ESP 7:52.22
5000m	1. Arne Gabius GER 13:55.89
	2. Jesús España ESP 13:56.00
	3. Ali Kaya TUR 13:56.64
3000mSt	1. Yoann Kowal FRA 8:25.50
	2. Martin Grau GER 8:29.16
	3. Nikolay Chavkin RUS 8:30.61
110mh	1. Sergey Shubenkov RUS 13.20*
(1.0)	2. William Sharman GBR 13.21
	3. Pascal Martinot Lagarde FRA 13.35
400mh	1. Denis Kudryavtsev RUS 49.38
	2. Silvio Schirrmeister GER 49.80
	3. Richard Yates GBR 50.11
HJ	1. Andriy Protsenko UKR 2.30
	2. Andrey Silnov RUS 2.28
	3. Jaroslav Bába CZE 2.26
PV	1. Renaud Lavillenie FRA 5.62
	2= Aleksandr Gripich RUS 5.62
	2= Jan Kudlicka CZE 5.62
LJ	1. Christian Reif GER 8.13/-0.5
	2. Greg Rutherford GBR 7.99/0.6
	3. Eusebio Cáceres ESP 7.97/0.2
TJ	1. Aleksey Fyodorov RUS 16.95/1.0
	2. Fabrizio Donato ITA 16.82/-1.9
	3. Viktor Kuznetsov UKR 16.63/-1.6
SP	1. David Storl GER 21.20
	2. Tomasz Majewski POL 20.57
	3. Aleksandr Lesnoy RUS 20.24
DT	1. Robert Harting GER 67.42
	2. Piotr Malachowski POL 65.35
	3. Viktor Butenko RUS 62.81
HT	1. Sergey Litvinov RUS 76.34
	2. Pawel Fajdek POL 75.26
	3. Markus Esser GER 74.90
	2dq. Quentin Bigot FRA 76.15
JT	1. Andreas Hofmann GER 86.13
	2. Dmitriy Tarabin RUS 83.40
	3. Maksym Bohdan UKR 80.93
4x100m	1. GBR (Kilty, Aikines-Aryeetey, Ellington, Gemili) 38.51
	2. GER (Blum, Knipphals, Kosenkow, Reus) 38.88
	3 (1B). ITA (Ferraro, Desalu, Marani, Obou) 39.06
4x400m	1. RUS (Dyldin, Mosin, Trenikhin, Krasnov) 3:02.68
	2. FRA (Anne, Venel, Macedot, Jordier) 3:03.05
	3. GER (Rigau, Gaba, Gollnow, Schneider) 3:03.18

Women

100m	1. Myriam Soumaré FRA 11.35
(-0.9)	2. Jamile Samuel NED 11.42
	3. Verena Sailer GER 11.45
200m	1. Dafne Schippers NED 22.74
	2. Nataliya Pogrebnyak UKR 23.13
	3. Amyika Onuora GBR 23.24

400m	1. Alena Tamkova RUS 51.72
	2. Esther Cremer GER 52.23
	3. Olga Zemlyak UKR 52.28
800m	1. Yekaterina Poistogova RUS 2:02.65
	2. Renelle Lamote FRA 2:03.36
	3. Olga Lyakhova UKR 2:03.39
1500m	1. Abeba Aregawi SWE 4:14.20
	2. Anna Shchagina RUS 4:15.04
	3. Nataliya Pryshchepa UKR 4:15.71
3000m	1. Sifan Hassan NED 8:45.24
	2. Yelena Korobkina RUS 8:51.00
	3. Nuria Fernández ESP 8:51.54
5000m	1. Meraf Bahta SWE 15:36.36
	2. Gamze Bulut TUR 15:37.70
	3. Giulia Viola ITA 15:40.30
3000mSt	1. Charlotta Fougberg SWE 9:35.92
	2. Antje Möldner-Schmidt GER 9:40.21
	3. Katarzyna Kowalska POL 9:41.78
100mh	1. Cindy Billaud FRA 12.66*
(1.8)	2. Nadine Hildebrand GER 12.80
	3. Yuliya Kondakova RUS 12.86
400mh	1. Hanna Ryzhykova UKR 55.00
	2. Eilidh Child GBR 55.36
	3. Irina Davydova RUS 55.79
HJ	1. Mariya Kuchina RUS 1.95
	2. Oksana Okunyeva UKR 1.95
	3= Ruth Beitia ESP 1.90
	3= Kamila Licwinko POL 1.90
PV	1. Anzhelika Sidorova RUS 4.65
	2. Jirina Svobodová CZE 4.60
	3. Katharina Bauer GER 4.40
LJ	1. Malaika Mihambo GER 6.90/1.5
	2. Éloyse Lesueur FRA 6.87w/2.3
	3. Erica Jarder SWE 6.67/0.9
TJ	1. Yekaterina Koneva RUS 14.55/-0.9
	2. Olga Saladukha UKR 14.33/1.4
	3. Jenny Elbe GER 14.01/0.6
SP	1. Christina Schwanitz GER 19.43
	2. Irina Tarasova RUS 18.36
	3. Chiara Rosa ITA 17.92
DT	1. Mélina Robert-Michon FRA 675.51
	2. Shanice Craft GER 65.07
	3. Yekaterina Strokova RUS 63.97
HT	1. Betty Heidler GER 74.63
	2. Joanna Fiodorow POL 72.23
	3. Anna Bulgakova RUS 71.83
JT	1. Barbora Spotáková CZE 65.57
	2. Hanna Hatsko-Fedusova UKR 63.01
	3. Linda Stahl GER 61.58
4x100m	1 (1B). NED (Sedney, Schippers, Van Schagen, Samuel) 42.95
	2 (1A). FRA (Distel-Bonnet, Ikuesan, Galais, Akakpo) 43.19
	3 (2A). RUS (Panteleyeva, Rusakova, Savlinis, Chermoshanskaya) 43.45
4x400m	1. UKR (Prystupa, Ryzhykova, Stuy, Zemlyak) 3:27.66
	2. GER (Cremer, Schmidt, Hoffmann, Spelmeyer) 3:28.34
	3. FRA (Diarra, Raharolahy, Perrossier, Guei) 3:28.35

First League *at Tallinn, Estonia 21-22 June*

1. BLR 302.5, 2. NOR 300, 3. FIN 290.5, 4. ROU 281.5, 5. GRE 276.5, 6. EST 275.5, 7. IRL 253.5, 8. POR 251.5, 9. BEL 251, 10. LTU 227, 11. SLO 209.5, 12. HUN 191.

***Winners*: Men**: **100m/200m**: Jaysuma Saidy Ndure NOR 10.12/20.70, **400m**: Brian Gregan IRL 46.54, **800m**: Mark English IRL 1:47.63, **1500m**: Paul Robinson IRL 3:51.05, **3000m**: Henrik Ingebrigtsen NOR 8:16.00, **5000m**: Tiidrek Nurme EST 14:14.92, **3000mSt**: Justinas Berzanskis LTU 8:48.49, **110mh**: Balázs Baji HUN 13.51, **400mh**: Thomas Barr IRL 49.30, **HJ**: Mihai Donisan ROU 2.26, **PV**: Arnaud Art BEL 5.42, **LJ**: Loúis Tsátoumas GRE 8.25w, **TJ**: Marian Oprea ROU 16.68, **SP**: Pavel Lyzhyn BLR 19.74, **DT**: Andrius Gudzius LTU 61.92, **HT**: Krisztián Pars HUN 75.26, **JT**: Antti Ruuskanen 79.62, **4x100m**: NOR 39.97, **4x400m**: BLR 3:09.00.

Women: **100m**: Ezinne Okparaebo NOR 11.41w, **200m**: María Belibasáki GRE 23.12, **400m**: Aghne Serksniené LTU 52.94, **800m**: Marina Arzamasova BLR 2:00.95, **1500m**: Ingvill Måkestad Bovim NOR 4:11.07, **3000m**: Sara Moreira POR 9:07.14, **5000m**: Dulce Félix POR 15:21.32, **3000mSt**: Sandra Eriksson FIN 9:40.36, **100mh**: Isabelle Pedersen NOR 13.18, **400mh**: Angela Morosanu ROU 56.70, **HJ**: Anna Iljustsenko EST 1.84, **PV**: Ekateríni Stefanídi GRE 4.55, **LJ**: Alina Rotaru ROU 6.62, **TJ**: Patricia Mamona POR 14.26w, **SP**: Yuliya Leontyuk BLR 18.48, **DT**: Zinaida Sendriuté LTU 65.83, **HT**: Bianca Perie ROU 71.93, **JT**: Tatyana Kholodovich BLR 58.33, **4x100m**: GRE 44.38, **4x400m**: ROU 3:32.83.

Second League *at Riga, Latvia 21-22 June*

1. SUI 210, 2. LAT 206.5, 3. BUL 191, 4. SRB 185, 5. DEN 173, 6. CRO 168, 7. SVK 157.5, 8. AUT 144.

Winners: **100m**: Pascal Mancini SUI 10.44, **200m**: Alex Wilson SUI 20.93w, **400m**: Nick Ekelund-Arenander DEN 46.12, **800m**: Jozef Repcík SVK 1:51.77, **1500m**: Andreas Vojta AUT 3:45.86, **3000m**: Dmitrijs Jurkevics 8:18.71, **5000m**: Brenton Rowe AUT 14:19.11, **3000mSt**: Mitko Tsenov BUL 8:45.55, **110mh**: Milan Ristic SRB 13.80, **400mh**: Emir Bekric SRB 49.64, **HJ**: Lukás Beer SVK 2.22, **PV**: Mareks Atrents LAT 5.30, **LJ**: Elvis Misans LAT 8.05, **TJ**: Rumen Dimitrov BUL 16.77w, **SP**: Asmir Kolasinac SRB 20.15, **DT**: Gerhard Mayer AUT 59.34, **HT**: Marcel Lomnicky SVK 75.69, **JT**: Rolands Strobinders LAT 78.32, **4x100m**: SUI 39.60, **4x400m**: DEN 3:07.57.

Women: **100m/200m**: Ivet Lalova BUL 11.34/22.93w, **400m**: Gunta Latiseva-Cudare LAT 53.69, **800m**: Vania Stambolova BUL 2:01.41, **1500m/3000m**: Amela Terzic SRB 4:28.99/9:11.64, **5000m**: Fabienne Schlumpf SUI 15:51.06, **3000mSt**: Silvia Danekova BUL 9:43.13, **100mh**: Ivana Loncarek CRO 13.18, **400mh**: Petra Fontanive SUI 57.57, **HJ**: Ana Simic CRO 1.92, **PV**: Caroline Bonde Holm DEN 4.35, **LJ/TJ**: Ivana Spanovic SRB 6.58/13.50, **SP**: Radoslava Mavrodieva BUL 17.80, **DT**: Sandra Perkovic CRO 64.05, **HT**: Martina Hrasnová SVK 71.302, **JT**: Tatjana Jelaca SRB 61.19, **4x100m**: SUI 44.27, **4x400m**: BUL 3:37.04.

Third League *at Tbilisi, Georgia 21-22 June*

1. CYP 495, 2. ISL 487, 3. ISR 471.5, 4. MDA 446, 5. AZE 363, 6. LUX 357, 7. GEO 334.5, 8. BIH 323, 9. MNE 278, 10. MLT 258, 11. ARM 249.5, 12. ALB 164, 13. MKD 162.5, 14. Small States of Europe 150, 15. AND 126.

European Cup Combined Events

Super League *at Torun, Poland 5-6 July*
1. RUS 41,159, 2. NED 41,048, 3. FRA 40,761, 4. BLR 40,152, 5. EST 39,015, 6. GBR 38,516, 7. SUI 38,076, 8. POL 36,879
Men Dec: 1. Eelco Sintnicolaas NED 8156, 2. Eduard Mikhon BLR 8004, 3. Ingmar Vos NED 7959, 4. Sergey Sviridov RUS 7952, 5. Yevgeniy Sarantsev RUS 7917; **Women Hep**: 1. Nadine Broersen NED 6539, 2. Antoinette Nana Djimou FRA 6221, 3. Yana Maksimova BLR 6173, 4. Grit Sadeiko EST 6128, 5. Anna Blank RUS 5990.
First League *at Ribeira Brava, Portugal 5-6 July*
1. CZE 40,384, 2. UKR 40,056, 3. SWE 39,753, 4. ESP 38,962, 5. NOR 38,777, 6. ITA 38,032, 7. FIN 37,845, 8. POR 36,686.
Men Dec: 1. Adam Helcelet CZE 7955, 2. Jirí Sykora CZE 7927, 3. Fabian Rosenquist SWE 7844; **Women Hep:** 1. Eliska Klucinová CZE 6191, 2. Alina Fyodorova UKR 6090, 3. Anastasiya Mokhnyuk UKR 5982
Second League. *at Ribeira Brava, Portugal 5-6 July*
1. ROU 35,532, 2. ISL 34,618, 3. TUR 29,968. **Men Dec:** Niels Pittomvils BEL 8000; **Women Hep:** Sofía Ifantídou GRE 5806.

European Cup 10,000m

At Skopje, Macedonia 8 June
Men: 1, Polat Kemboi Arikan TUR 28:17.14, 2. Ali Kaya TUR 28:17.82, 3, Yassine Mandour FRA 28:22.30; Team: 1, TUR 1:25:30.44, 2. ITA 1:27:36.24, 3. UKR 1:27:57.97. **Women**: 1, Clémence Calvin FRA 31:52.86, 2. Jéssica Augusto POR 31:55.56, 3. Sara Moreira POR 32:01.42; Team: 1, POR 1:36:53.43, 2. FRA 1:39:34.38, 3. ESP 1:40:16.15.

Ibero-American Championships

At São Paulo, Brazil 1-3 August
Men: **100m**: Andy Martínez PER 10.30, **200m**: Jorge Vides BRA 20.42, **400m**: Ánderson Henriques BRA 45.40, **800m**: Rafith Rodríguez COL 1:44.77*, **1500m/3000mSt**: Marvin Blanco VEN 3:43.88/8:35.87, **3000m**: Juan Luis Barrios MEX 7:59.50, **5000m**: Bayron Piedra ECU 13:50.20, **110mh**: Jorge McFarlane PER 13.53, **400mh**: Andrés Silva URU 48.65*, **HJ**: Edgar Rivera MEX 2.28, **PV**: Germán Chiaraviglio ARG 5.20, **LJ**: Luis Rivera MEX 8.24, **TJ**: Jonathan Silva BRA 16.84, **SP/DT**: Germán Lauro ARG 20.14/61.62, **HT**: Wágner Domingos BRA 74.12, **JT**: Dairon Márquez COL 78.80, **Dec**: Felipe dos Santos BRA 7810, **20,000mW**: Iván Garrido COL 1:22:13.74, **4x100m**: BRA 39.35; **4x400m**: DOM 3:02.73. **Women**: **100m**: Ana Cláudia Silva BRA 11.13*, **200m**: Franciela Krasucki BRA 23.41, **400m**: Geisa Coutinho BRA 51.76, **800m**: Gabriela Medina MEX 2:03.17, **1500m**: Muriel Coneo COL 4:14.42, **3000m**: Juliana dos Santos BRA 9:19.80, **5000m**: Inés Melchor PER 15:58.85, **3000mSt**: María Mancebo DOM 9:45.84, **100mh**: Lavonne Idlette DOM 12.99, **400mh**: Zudikey Rodríguez MEX 56.64, **HJ**: Mônica Freitas BRA 1.82, **PV**: Patrícia dos Santos 4.10, **LJ**: Juliet Itoya ESP 6.64, **TJ**: Yosiri Urrutia COL 14.41, **SP**: Natalia Ducó CHI 17.53, **DT**: Karen Gallardo CHI 59.66, **HT**: Jenny Dahlgren ARG 66.84, **JT**: Jucilene de Lima 61.71, **Hep**: Vanessa Spínola 5722, **10,000mW**: Julia Takacs ESP 43:10.95*, **4x100m/4x400m**: BRA 42.92*/3:29.66. **Medal table leaders**: BRA 16G-17S-15B, COL 5-6-4, MEX 5-2-2, ARG 3-2-2, PER 3-2-2.

NACAC (U23) Championships

At Kamloops, Canada 8-10 August
Men: **100m**: Diondre Batson USA 10.08, **200m**: Remontay McClain USA 20.32, **400m**: Brycen Spratling USA 45.18, **800m**: Bryan Martínez MEX 1:47.90, **1500m**: Matt Hillenbrand USA 3:54.85, **5000m**: Edgar Alan García MEX 14:35.00, **10,000m**: Chris Bendtsen USA 31:43.37, **3000mSt**: Chris Dulhanty CAN 8:56.60, **110mh**: Eddie Lovett ISV 13.39w, **400mh**: Trevor Brown USA 49.92, **HJ**: Ryan Ingraham BAH 2.28*, **PV**: Jake Blankenship USA 5.50, **LJ**: Braxton Drummond USA 7.64, **TJ**: Eric Sloan USA 16.20, **SP**: Willy Irwin USA 19.44, **DT**: Rodney Brown USA 63.34*, **HT**: Diego del Real MEX 69.42, **JT**: Michael Shuey USA 76.02, **Dec**: James Turner CAN 7536, **20,000mW**: Benjamin Thorne CAN 1:28:08.64, **4x100m/4x400m**: USA 38.47/3:04.34. **Women**: **100m/200m**: Ciera White USA 11.32/23.05, **400m**: Allison Peter ISV 51.92, **800m**: Shelby Houlihan USA 2:03.00*, **1500m**: Jenna Westaway CAN 4:15.52*, **5000m**: Erin Finn USA 16:06.26*, **10,000m**: Margo Malone USA 36:07.71, **3000mSt**: Rachel Johnson USA 9:46.79*, **100mh**: LeTristan Pledger USA 13.04w, **400mh**: Kiah Seymour USA 56.35, **HJ**: Alyx Treasure CAN 1.85, **PV**: Sandi Morris USA 4.40*, **LJ**: Sha'Keela Saunders USA 6.40, **TJ**: Tori Franklin USA 13.42, **SP/DT**: Kelsey Card USA 17.32/53.82, **HT**: Brooke Pleger USA 64.60, **JT**: Fawn Miller USA 54.90, **Hep**: Niki Oudenaarden CAN 5692, **10,000mW**: Andreina González DOM 52:12.40, **4x100m/4x400m**: USA 43.89/3:35.79.

Pan-American Combined Events Cup

At Ottawa, Canada 17-18 July
Men Dec: 1. Yordani García CUB 8179, 2. José Ángel Mendieta CUB 7559, 3, James Turner CAN 7408. **Women Hep**: 1. Jillian Drouin CAN 5972, 2. Natasha Jackson CAN 5928, 3. Lindsay Schwartz USA 5835.

10th South American Games (ODESUR)

At Santiago de Chile 13-16 March
Men

100m	1. Alonso Edward PAN 10.23*
(1.1)	2. Jefferson Lucindo BRA 10.30
	3. Alex Quiñónez ECU 10.39
200m	1. Aldemir G da Silva BRA 20.32*
(1.9)	2. Alex Quiñónez ECU 20.66
	3. Arturo Ramírez VEN 20.67
400m	1. Anderson Henriques BRA 45.03*
	2. Hugo Sousa BRA 45.09
	3. Freddy Mezones VEN 45.86
800m	1. Kléberson Davide BRA 1:45.30*
	2. Rafith Rodríguez COL 1:45.39
	3. Lutimar Paes BRA 1:47.52

1500m 1. Federico Bruno ARG 3:39.96*
2. Iván López CHI 3:42.62
3. Rafith Rodríguez COL 3:42.75
5000m 1. Víctor Aravena CHI 14:06.02
2. Joílson da Silva BRA 14:07.77
3. Javier Carriqueo ARG 14:11.41
10,000m 1. Bayron Piedra ECU 28:48.31*
2. Giovani dos Santos BRA 28:53.90
3. Diego Colorado COL 29:10.75
3000mSt 1. José Gregorio Peña VEN 8:36.81*
2. Gerard Giraldo COL 8:45.96
3. Mariano Mastromarino ARG 8:48.11
110mh (-0.5) 1. Javier McFarlane PER 13.77
2. Jonathan Mendes BRA 13.81
3. Jorge McFarlane PER 13.83
400mh 1. Andrés Silva URU 49.57*
2. Lucirio Garrido VEN 49.66
3. Mahau Suguimati BRA 50.47
HJ 1. Eure Yáñez VEN 2.21
2. Arturo Chávez PER 2.18
3= Carlos Layoy ARG 2.18
3= Rafael dos Santos BRA 2.18
PV 1. Augusto Dutra de Oliveira BRA 5.40
2. Germán Chiaraviglio ARG 5.35
3. Gonzalo Barroilhet CHI 5.20
LJ 1. Irving Saladino PAN 8.16*/-0.5
2. Emiliano Lasa URU 7.94/0.5
3. Mauro Vinicius da Silva BRA 7.88/0.7
TJ 1. Jonathan Silva BRA 16.51*/-0.6
2. Jefferson Dias Sabino BRA 16.44/0.7
3. Jhon Murillo COL 16.27/0.4
SP 1. Germán Lauro ARG 20.70*
2. Darlan Romani BRA 19.96
3. Aldo González BOL 18.15
DT 1. Mauricio Ortega COL 59.95*
2. Ronald Julião BRA 59.12
3. Germán Lauro ARG 59.36
HT 1. Wágner Domingos BRA 70.62
2. Roberto Sáez CHI 67.38
3. Juan Ignacio Cerra ARG 66.34
JT 1. Víctor Fatecha PAR 76.09
2. Júlio César de Oiiveira BRA 75.98
3. Dayron Márquez COL 75.11
Dec 1. Luiz Alberto de Araújo BRA 7733*
2. Gonzalo Barroilhet CHI 7617
3. Guillermo Ruggeri ARG 7298
4x100m 1. BRA (Feitosa, Lucindo, de Barros, A da Silva) 38.90*
2. VEN 39.85
3. COL 40.26
4x400m 1. BRA (Sousa, Davide, Feitosa, Henriques) 3:03.94*
2. VEN 3:04.17
3. COL 3:10.15
20000mW 1. Eider Arévalo COL 1:22:11.1*
2. José Montaña COL 1:22:14.1
3. Mauricio Arteaga ECU 1:23:19.3

Women

100m (-0.1) 1. Alejandra Idrobo COL 11.62
2. Ángela Tenorio ECU-J 11.64
3. Franciela Krasucki BRA 11.67
200m (-0.4) 1. Nercely Soto VEN 23.25
2. Ángela Tenorio ECU-J 23.66
3. Erika Chávez ECU 23.72
400m 1. Geisa Coutinho BRA 51.81
2. Nercely Soto VEN 52.30
3. Joelma Sousa BRA 52.75
800m 1. Déborah Rodríguez URU 2:06.62
2. Mariana Borelli ARG 2:07.57
3. Christiane dos Santos BRA 2:07.96
1500m 1. Muriel Coneo COL 4:15.66*
2. Andrea Ferris PAN 4:20.81
3. Tatiana Araújo BRA 4:24.59
5000m 1. Inés Melchor PER 15:51.20*
2. Tatiele de Carvalho BRA 16:04.70
3. María Peralta ARG 16:15.01
10,000m 1. Inés Melchor PER 33:10.06*
2. Wilma Arizapana PER 33:26.84
3. Tatiele de Carvalho BRA 33:39.93
3000mSt 1. Muriel Coneo COL 10:05.02*
2. Ángela Figueroa COL 10:07.02
3. Cinthia Paucar PER 10:17.64
100mh (-1.6) 1. Yvette Lewis PAN 13.11*
2. Lina Florez COL 13.29
3. Briggit Merlano COL 13.30
400mh 1. Déborah Rodríguez URU 56.60*
2. Javiera Errázuriz CHI 57.83
3. Liliane Barbosa BRA 59.51
HJ 1. Yulimar Rojas VEN-J 1.79
2. Kashani Rios PAN 1.76
3. Guillercy González VEN 1.76
PV 1. Fabiana Murer BRA 4.40*
2. Robeliys Peinado VEN-Y 4.20
3. Karla da Silva BRA 4.10
LJ 1. Keila Costa BRA 6.35/0.5
2. Jéssica dos Reis BRA 6.32/1.4
3. Yuliana Angulo ECU 6.10/0.5
TJ 1. Keila Costa BRA 13.65/-1.5
2. Gidsele de Oliveira BRA 13.08/0.8
3. Silvana Segura PER 13.07/1.1
SP 1. Natalia Ducó CHI 18.07*
2. Ahymara Espinoza VEN 17.63
3. Sandra Lemus COL 17.20
DT 1. Karen Gallardo CHI 59.65*
2. Rocío Comba ARG 59.29
3. Fernanda Borges BRA 56.08
HT 1. Rosa Rodríguez VEN 68.61*
2. Jennifer Dahlgren ARG 67.94
3. Eli Johana Moreno COL 65.58
JT 1. Flor Denis Ruiz COL 60.59*
2. Jucilene de Lima BRA 60.17
3. Laila e Silva BRA 57.11
Hep 1. Ana Camila Pirelli PAR 5669*
2. Fiorella Chiappe ARG-J 5568
3. Guillercy González VEN 5509
4x100m 1. VEN (Hidalgo, Álvarez, Soto, Villalobos) 45.08
2. CHI 45.09
3. COL 45.13
4x400m 1. BRA (J Sousa, Zavolski, Barbosa, Coutinho) 3:35.07*
2. COL 3:35.96
3. CHI 3:37.42
20000mW 1. Lorena Arenas COL 1:31:46.9*
2. Sandra Galvis COL 1:34:04.4
3. Érica de Sena BRA 1:36:37.3

Medal table: BRA 14G-13S-14B, COL 7-7-10, VEN 6-6-4, CHI 3-5-2, PER 3-2-3, PAN 3-2-0, URU 3-1-0, ARG 2-5-7, PAR 2-0-0. ECU 1-3-4, BOL 0-0-1.

South American Marathon Championships

At Santiago de Chile 6 April

Men: Roberto Carlos Echeverría CHI 2:16:58; **Women**: Erika Olivera CHI 2:36:08.

South American U23 Championships

At Montevideo, Uruguay 3-5 October

Men: **100m:** Andy Martínez PER 10.40, **200m**: Aldemir G da Silva BRA 20.50*, **400m**: José Meléndez VEN 46.05, **800m**: Joseílton Cunha BRA 1:48.47, **1500m**: Carlos Martín Díaz CHI 3:44.52; **5000m/10,000m**: Matías Andrés Silva CHI 13:57.58*/30:13.81, **3000mSt**: Roberto Tello CHI 8:57.49, **110mh**: Jonathas Brito BRA 13.69, **400mh**: Wesley Martins BRA 51.12, **HJ**: Fernando Ferreira BRA 2.24*, **PV**: José Rodolfo Pacho ECU 5.10, **LJ**: Higor Alves BRA 7.60, **TJ**: Kaual Bento BRA 15.77w, **SP**: Willian Braido BRA 18.98, **DT**: Mauricio Ortega COL 60.46*, **HT**: Joaquín Gómez ARG 67.98*, **JT**: Braian Toledo ARG 77.35, **Dec**: Renato dos Santos BRA 7025, **20,000mW**: Manuel Soto COL 1:23:22.7*; **4x100m/4x400m**: BRA 39.74/3:08.95. **Women**: **100m**: Andrea Purica VEN 11.50, **200m**: Bruna Farias BRA 23.61, **400m/800m/400mh**: Déborah Rodríguez URU 52.53*/2:08.65/58.49, **800m**: Jéssica dos Santos BRA 2:07.42, **1500m**: Flávia da Silva BRA 4:21.05*, **5000m**: Soledad Torre PER 16:39.95*, **10,000m**: Giselle Álvarez CHI 35:28.30, **3000mSt**: Zulema Arenas PER 10:06.25*, **100mh**: Nelsibeth Villalobos VEN 14.48, **HJ**: Tamara de Souza BRA 1.82, **PV**: Robeilys Peinado VEN 3.90, **LJ/TJ**: Yulimar Rojas VEN 6.36/13.35, **SP**: Ivanna Gallardo CHI 16.20, **DT**: Izabela da Silva BRA 58.70*, **HT**: Génesis Olivera VEN 63.80, **JT**: Edivania Araújo BRA 53.79, **Hep**: Evelys Aguilar COL 5333, **20,000mW**: Wendy Gabriela Cornejo BOL 1:37:43.1*, **4x100m/4x400m**: BRA 45.44/3:42.07.

Medal Table: BRA 18G-21S-13B, VEN 7-4-1, CHI 6-5-11, PER 3-4-2, COL 3-2-5, URU 3-1-2, ARG 2-3-2, ECU 1-0-4, BOL 1-2-0, PAR 0-2-3, PAN 0-0-2.

IAU World Trophy 50km

At Doha, Qatar 31 October

Men: 1. Collen Mazawa ZIM 3:00:41, 2. Phil Anthony GBR 3:01:26, 3. Harm Sengers NED 3:05:01; **Women**: 1. Emily Harrison USA 3:32:30, 2. Joanna Zakrzewski GBR 3:33:23, 3. Catrin Jones CAN 3:37:57.

IAU 100Km World Championships

At Doha, Qatar 21 November

Men: 1. Max King USA 6:27:43, 2. Jonas Buud SWE 6:32:04, 3. José Antonio Requejo ESP 6:37:01, 4. Hideo Nojo JPN 6:39:21, 5. Yoshiki Takada JPN 6:46:47, 6. Zach Bitter USA 6:48:53, 7. Vasiliy Larkin RUS 6:50:38, 8. Alberico Di Cecco ITA 6:51:14; Team: 1. USA 20:08:05, 2. JPN 20:55:09, 3. GBR 20:57:50, 4. SWE 21:14:01, 5. ITA 21:24.42, 18 team scored, **Women** – 1. Ellie Greenwood GBR 7:30:48, 2. Chiyuki Mochizuki JPN 7:38:23, 3. Joasia Zakrzewski GBR 7:42:02, 4. Jo Meek GBR 7:43:37, 5. Irina Antropova RUS 7:44:26, 6. Shiho Katayama JPN 7:49:41, 7. Veronika Jurisic CRO 7:51:08, 8. Meghan Arbogast USA 7:52:12; Team: 1. GBR 22:56.27, 2. JPN 23:22.32, 3. RUS 23:53.31, 4. USA 24:05.25, 5. CRO 25:41.50, 9 teams scored.

European Mountain Racing Championships

At Gap, France 12 July. 1055m to 1305m A.

Men 12.8k (750m hd): 1. Bernard De Matteis ITA 56:10, 2. Robbie Simpson GBR 56:10, 3. Martin De Matteis ITA (twin) 56:32; Team: 1. ITA 11, 2. GBR 27, 3. FRA 31; **Junior** 8.1k (500m hd): Dominik Sadlo CZE 37:23; Team: 1. ITA 20, 2. CZE 24, 3. TUR 26; **Women** 8.1k (8k (500m hd): 1. Andrea Mayr AUT (previously won in 2005, 2013) 39:43, 2. Mateja Kosovelj SLO 40:53, 3. Sabine Reiner AUT 41:03; Team: 1. ITA 20, 2. GBR 31, 3. AUT 36; **Junior** 4.2k (8k (250m hd): Georgia Malir GBR 22:10; Team: 1. TUR 14, 2. GBR 29, 3. FRA 37.

IAAF DIAMOND LEAGUE

The IAAF's successor to the Golden League, the expanded and more globally widespread Diamond League, was launched in 2010 with 14 meetings spread across Asia, Europe, the Middle East and the USA. The total prize money was increased from $6.63 million (with a $50,000 bonus for any new world record) in 2010 to $8 million from 2011. Winners of each Race receive a Diamond Trophy (4 carats of diamonds) and a $40,000 cash prize.

SAMSUNG DIAMOND LEAGUE

– winners 2014

D Doha May 9, **Sh** Shanghai May 18, **E** Eugene May 31, **R** Rome Jun 5, **O** Oslo Jun 11, **NY** New York Jun 14, **L** Lausanne Jul 3, **P** Paris Saint-Denis Jul 5, **G** Glasgow Jul 11-12; **M** Monaco Jul 18, **St** Stockholm Aug 21; **Bi** Birmingham Aug 24, Finals with double points at: **Z** Zürich Aug 28, **Br** Brussels Sep 65

Men:

100m: Justin Gatlin Sh- 9.92, E- 9.76w, Br- 9.77; Richard Thompson O- 10.02; Mike Rodgers P- 10.00; Nickel Ashmeade G- 9.97; Nesta Carter St- 9.96

200m: Neville Ashmeade D- 20.13, B- 20.33; Alonso Edward R- 20.19, L- 19.84, Z- 19.95; Warren Weir NY- 19.82; Justin Gatlin M- 19.68

400m: LaShawn Merritt D- 44.44, R- 44.48, NY- 44.19, M- 44.30, Z- 44.36; Kirani James L- 43.74, Bi- 44.59

800m: Robert Biwott Sh- 1:44.69, Nijel Amos E- 1:43.63, Z- 1:43.77; David Rudisha NY- 1:44.63, G- 1:43.34; Asbel Kiprop P- 1:43.34; Adam Ksczot St- 1:45.25

1500m/1M: Asbel Kiprop D- 3:29.18, Ayanleh Souleiman E- 3:47.32M, O- 3:49.49M; Silas Kiplagat R- 3:30.44, M- 3:27.64; Ronald Kwemoi L- 3:31.48; Taoufik Makhloufi Br- 3:31.78

5000m: Yenew Alamirew Sh- 13:04.83, O- 13:01.57; Caleb Ndiku E- 13:01.71, Z- 13:07.01; Edwin Soi P- 12:59.82; Hagos Gebrhiwet G- 13:11.09, Muktar Edris St- 12:54.63

3000mSt: Ezekiel Kemboi D- 8:04.12; Joseph Birech

R- 8:06.20, O- 8:02.37, L- 8:03.34, M- 8:03.33, Bi- 8:07.80, Br- 7:58.41
110mh: David Oliver D- 13.23; Xie Wenjun Sh- 13.23; Pascal Martinot-Lagarde E- 13.13, O- 13.12, L- 13.09, M- 12.95, Br- 13.08
400mh: Michael Tinsley Sh- 48.77, P- 48.25, St- 49.60; Javier Culson NY- 48.03, L- 48.32, G- 48.35; Cornel Fredericks Z- 48.25
HJ: Ivan Ukhov D- 2.41; Mutaz Essa Barshim R- 2.41, Bi- 2.39, Br- 2.43; Bohdan Bondarenko NY- 2.42, L- 2.40, M- 2.40
PV: Renaud Lavillenie Sh- 5.92, E- 5.80, O- 5.77, L- 5.87, P- 5.70, Br- 5.93; Konstadínos Filppídis 5.60
LJ: Loúis Tsátoumas D- 8.06; Jeff Henderson NY- 8.33, L- 8.31; Li Jinzhe M- 8.09; Khotso Mokoena St- 8.09, Br- 8.19; Christian Taylor Bi- 8.09
TJ: Lyukman Adams Sh- 17.10; Will Claye E- 17.66, R- 17.14, O- 17.41; Benjamin Compaoré P- 17.12; Christian Taylor G- 17.36, Z- 17.51
SP: Christan Cantwell Sh- 21.73; Reese Hoffa E- 21.64, G- 21.67, St- 21.06, Z- 21.88; Joe Kovacs O- 21.14; David Storl P- 21.41
DT: Piotr Malachowski D- 66.72, L- 66.63, M- 65.84; Robert Harting R- 68.36, NY 68.24, Bi- 67.57, Br- 67.57
JT: Ihab Abdelrahman El Sayed Sh- 89.21, P- 87.10; Vitezslav Vesely E- 73.75; Tero Pitkämäki O- 84.18; Thomas Röhler G- 86.99, Z- 87.63; Antti Ruuskanen St- 87.24

Women

100m: Shelly-Ann Fraser-Pryce D- 11.13; Tori Bowie R- 11.05, NY- 11.07, M- 10.80; Michelle-Lee Ahye L- 10.98; Kerron Stewart 11.22; Veronica Campbell-Brown Z- 11.04
200m: Blessing Okagbare Sh- 22.36, P- 22.32; Tori Bowie E- 22.18; Allyson Felix O- 22.73, St- 22.85, Br- 22.02; Dafne Schippers G- 22.34
400m: Novlene Williams-Mills Sh- 50.31, E- 50.40, O- 50.06, St- 50.09; Sanya Richards-Ross P- 50.10, Br- 49.98; Francena McCorory G- 49.93
800m: Eunice Sum D- 1:59.33, R- 1:59.49, O- 1:59.02, L- 1:58.48; Ajee' Wilson M- 1:57.67; Lynsey Sharp Bi- 1:59.14; Brenda Martinez Br- 1:58.84
1500m: Abeba Aregawi Sh- 3:58.72, NY- 4:00.13; Hellen Obiri E- 3:57.05; Sifan Hassan P- 3:57.00, G- 4:00.67; Jennifer Simpson St- 4:00.38, Z- 3:59.92
3/5000m: Hellen Obiri D- 8:20.68; Genzebe Dibaba R- 14:34.99, M- 14:28.88; Mercy Cherono NY- 8:39.84, L- 8:50.24, Bi- 9:11.49 (2M), Br- 8:28.95
3000mSt: Emma Coburn Sh- 9:19.80; Sofia Assefa E- 9:11.39, NY- 9:18.58; Hiwot Ayalew P- 9:11.65, G- 9:10.64, St- 9:17.04; Habiba Ghribi Z- 9:15.23
100mh: Brianna Rollins R- 12.53; Queen Harrison NY- 12.62, G- 12.58, St- 12.68; Dawn Harper-Nelson P- 12.44, Bi- 12.66, Z 12.58
400mh: Kemi Adekoya D- 54.59; Kaliese Spencer E- 54.29, R- 53.97, O- 54.94, M- 54.09, Bi- 53.80. Br- 54.12
HJ: Ana Simic Sh- 1.97; Anna Chicherova E- 2.01; Mariya Kuchina O- 1.98, St- 1.94, Z- 2.00; Blanka Vlasic P- 2.00, G- 1.96
PV: Nikoléta Kiriakopoúlou D- 4.63; Yarisley Silva D- 4.70; Fabiana Murer NY- 4.80, G- 4.65, M- 4.76, Z- 4.72; Ekateríni Stefanídi Bi- 4.57
LJ: Blessing Okagbare Sh- 6.86; Ivana Spanovic E- 6.88, Z- 6.80; Tianna Bartoletta O- 7.02, G- 6.98, St- 6.98; Éloyse Leseuer P- 6.92
TJ: Caterine Ibargüen D- 14.43, R- 14.48, L- 14.87, M- 15.31, Bi- 14.52, Br- 14.98; Kimberley Williams NY- 14.31w
SP: Valerie Adams D- 20.20, R- 20.01, NY- 19.68, L- 20.41, M- 20.38, Bi-019.96, Br- 20.59
DT: Sandra Perkovic Sh- 70.52, E- 69.32, O- 67.17, P- 68.48, St- 66.74, Z- 68.36; Gia Lewis-Smallwood G- 67.59
JT: Martina Ratej D- 65.48; Barbora Spotáková R- 66.43, L- 66.72, M- 66.96, Br- 67.99; Linda Stahl NY- 67.32; Elizabeth Gleadle Bi- 64.49

FINAL PLACINGS 2014

Diamond Race final placings: 100: 1. Gatlin 16 (3 wins), 2. Rodgers (1), 3. Carter 7 (1); **200:** 1. Edward 19 (3), 2. Ashmeade 18 (2), 3. Lemaitre 4; **400:** 1. Merritt 26 (5), 2. Roberts 6, 3=. Makwala & Masrahi 5; **800:** 1. Amos 14 (2), 2. Rudisha 10 (2), 3. Souleiman 6; **1500:** 1. Kiplagat 16 (2), 2=. Kiprop (2) & Souleiman (1) 11; **3000/5000:** 1. C Ndiku 15 (2), 2. Alamirew 14 (2), 3. Edris 8 (1); **3000SC:** 1. Birech 28 (6), 2. B Kipruto 5, 3=. Kemboi (1). Mekhissi-Benabbad. Jager & C Kipruto 4; **110mh:** 1. Martinot-Lagarde 27 (5), 2. Shubenkov 8, 3. Ortega 6; **400mh:** 1. Tinsley 21 (3), 2. Culson 17 (3), 3. Fredericks 12 (1); **HJ:** 1. Barshim 20 (3), 2. Bondarenko 20 (3), 3. Ukhov 8 (1); **PV:** 1. Lavillenie 28 (6), 2. Filippídis 11 (1), 3=. Sobera & Dutra de Oliveira 4; **LJ:** 1. Mokoena 12 (2), 2. Gaisah 9, 3. Taylor 8 (1); **TJ:** 1. Taylor 20 (2), 2. Claye 16 (3), 3. Compaoré 8 (1); **SP**: 1. Hoffa 23 (4), 2. Storl 13 (1), 3. Kovacs 10 (1); **DT:** 1. Malachowski 22 (3), 2. Harting 20 (4), 3. Kanter 5; **JT:** 1. Röhler 15 (2), 2. Pitkämäki 10 (1), 3=. Abdelrahman (2) & Vesely (1) 8; **Women – 100:** 1. Campbell-Brown 10 (1), 2=. Stewart (1) & Ahouré 7; **200:** 1. Felix 21 (3), 2. Okagbare 11 (2), 3. Schippers 6 (1); **400:** 1. Williams-Mills 20 (4), 2. Richards-Ross 16 (2), 3. McPherson 8; **800:** 1. Sum 22 (4), 2. Martinez 9 (1), 3. Sharp 8 (1); **1500:** 1. Simpson 17 (2), 2. Aregawi 12 (2), 3. Hassan 10 (2); **3000/5000:** 1. Cherono 22 (4), 2. G Dibaba 12 (2), 3. Kibiwot 5; **3000SC:** 1. Ayalew 19 (3), 2. Assefa 13 (2), 3=. Ghribi (1) & Coburn (1) 10; **100mh:** 1. Harper-Nelson 21 (3), 2. Harrison 17 (3), 3. Pearson 6; **400mh:** 1. Spencer 30 (6), 2. Child 7, 3. Adekoya 6 (1); **HJ:** 1. Kuchina 18 (3), 2. Simic 12 (1), 3. Vlasic 10 (2); **PV**: 1. Murer 20 (4), 2= Stefanídi (1) & Suhr 9; **LJ:** 1. Bartoletta 16 (3), 2. Spanovic 16 (2), 3. Lesueur 7 (1); **TJ:** 1. Ibargüen 28 (6), 2. Koneva 8, 3=. Williams (1) & Saladukha; **SP:** 1. Adams 32 (7), 2. Schwanitz 10, 3. Carter 6; **DT:** 1. Perkovic 30 (6), 2. Lewis-Smallwood 13 (1), 3. Samuels 9; **JT:** 1. Spotáková 22 (4), 2. Ratej 10 (1), 3=. Stahl (1) & Viljoen 5.

The Diamond Race winners automatically qualify to compete as wild cards in the 2015 IAAF World Championships.

A TOTAL OF 887 athletes from 85 nations took part in 2014. Renaud Lavillenie is the first five-time Diamond Race winner … Valerie Adams, the only athlete to win her event at all seven meetings in 2014 (the maximum 32 points), has now won a record 24 times and has the most Diamond Race points with 126 … Blessing Okagbare is the most prolific athlete of the IAAF Diamond League since it began in 2010, with 38 appearances.

2014 - THE YEAR OF THE MEN'S HIGH JUMP

THE EVENT OF 2014 was the men's high jump, in which there was great rivalry, especially between the world's top two, Bohdan Bondarenko and Mutaz Essa Barshim. But they were joined at 2.40m plus by four other men, and new standards were set for performances over this height. My table shows the number of performances and number of men over 2.40, 2.35 and 2.32 each year from 1980 to 2014, including indoors and outdoors. It is fascinating to see how there was a great era for the event, headed by Javier Sotomayor from the mid 1980s to the mid 1990s, but how then standards slipped considerably until the renaissance over the past couple of years. Note that there were new record figures in my first three columns, but 18 men over 2.32 in 2014 is still well behind the 26 who did so in 1990.

The first 2.35 jumps came from Jacek Wszola and Dietmar Mögenburg in May 1980, followed by Gerd Wessig who won the 1980 Olympic title in Moscow with a world record 2.36. From those days high jump standards are shown in the table:

Men's High Jump 1980 to 2014

	Over 2.40		*Over 2.35*		*Over 2.32*		
	No.	*Men*	*No.*	*Men*	*No.*	*Men*	*Best*
1980	-	-	3	3	4	3	2.36 Wessig
1981	-	-	-	-	2	2	2.33 Woodard (i), Demyanuk
1982	-	-	-	-	8	7	2.34 Mögenburg
1983	-	-	3	2	17	12	2.38 Zhu Jianhua
1984	-	-	11	6	34	15	2.39 Zhu Jianhua
1985	2	2	15	10	40	20	2.41 Paklin
1986	-	-	8	5	46	18	2.38 Paklin
1987	4	2	27	8	63	18	2.42 Sjöberg
1988	2	2	33	13	93	24	2.43 Sotomayor
1989	5	2	32	9	72	20	2.44 Sotomayor
1990	1	1	24	11	76	26	2.40 Matei
1991	3	3	18	9	45	16	2.40 Conway (i), Sotomayor, Austin
1992	-	-	16	9	55	16	2.38i Sjöberg
1993	5	1	34	12	75	17	2.45 Solomayor
1994	9	1	34	7	83	18	2.42 Solomayor
1995	1	1	26	8	54	19	2.40 Sotomayor
1996	-	-	18	6	46	16	2.39 Austin
1997	-	-	9	6	34	12	2.37 Sotomayor
1998	-	-	4	3	28	14	2.37 Sotomayor
1999	-	-	7	5	29	14	2.37 Voronin
2000	1	1	12	7	54	18	2.40 Voronin
2001	-	-	5	5	22	12	2.37 Voronin
2002	-	-	6	6	29	10	2.37 Freitag
2003	-	-	5	3	30	12	2.36 Holm (i), Walerianczyk
2004	-	-	7	2	39	12	2.37i Holm
2005	1	1	16	7	46	14	2.40i Holm
2006	-	-	10	5	43	14	2.37 Rybakov (i), Ukhov (i), Silnov
2007	-	-	14	9	48	18	2.39i Ukhov
2008	-	-	19	8	57	17	2.38 Rybakov (i), Silnov
2009	1	1	8	5	36	13	2.40i Ukhov
2010	-	-	5	1	25	10	2.38i Ukhov
2011	-	-	11	7	50	17	2.38i Ukhov
2012	-	-	15	7	39	12	2.39 Ukhov, Barshim
2013	3	2	18	7	53	17	2.41 Bondarenko
2014	16	6	46	8	93	18	2.43 Barshim

Javier Sotomayor had a record 30 performances at 2.32 or higher in 1994.

As at 1 April 2015 there have been 131 performances at 2.38 or higher (56 at 2.40 or higher) by: Javier Sotomayor 30 (21), Ivan Ukhov 16 (5), Mutaz Essa Barshim 12 (7), Patrik Sjöberg 12 (4), Bohdan Bondarenko 11 (7), Hollis Conway 6 (1), Igor Paklin 4 (1), Gennadiy Avdeyenko & Yaroslav Rybakov 4 (0), Carlo Thränhardt 3 (2), Charles Austin 3 (1), Stefan Holm, Sorin Matei & Derek Drouin 2 (1), Zhu Jianhua 2 (0), Rudolf Povarnitsyn, Vyacheslav Voronin, Aleksey Dmitrik & Andriy Protsenko 1 (1), 13 men 1 at 2.39 or 2.38.

MAJOR MEETINGS 2014–2015

Diamond League, World Challenge and European Athletics Premium Meetings

DL – Diamond League, WC – World Challenge, EAP European Premium Meeting (EAC Classic).

2014 date		Meeting	2015 date	
22 Mar	WC	Telstra Melbourne Track Classic, AUS	21 Mar	WC
3 May	WC	Jamaica International, KIngston JAM	9 May	WC
9 May	DL	Qatar Super Grand Prix, Doha, QAT	15 May	DL
11 May	WC	Golden Grand Prix, Tokyo 2014, Kawasaki 2015, JPN	10 May	WC
18 May	WC	Ponce Grand Prix, PUR	23 May	WC
18 May	DL	Shanghai Golden Grand Prix, CHN	17 May	DL
21 May	WC	Bejing, CHN	20 May	WC
23 May		Dakar, Sénégal	23 May	WC
1 Jun	DL	Prefontaine Classic, Eugene, Oregon, USA	31 May	DL
2 Jun		European Athletics Festival, Bydgoszcz, POL	7 Jun	
5 Jun	DL	Golden Gala, Rome, ITA	4 Jun	DL
8 Jun	WC	Fanny Blankers-Koen Games, Hengelo, NED	8 Jun	WC
8 Jun	WC	Mohammed VI d'Athlétisme, Marrakech 2014, Rabat 2015, MAR	14 Jun	WC
9 Jun	EAP	Josef Odlozil Memorial, Prague, CZE	8 Jun	EAP
11 Jun	DL	ExxonMobil Bislett Games, Oslo, NOR	11 Jun	DL
11 Jun	WC	Moscow Challenge, RUS	12 Jun	WC
14 Jun	DL	adidas Grand Prix, New York (RI), USA	13 Jun	DL
cancelled	EAP	Memorial Primo Nebiolo, Turin, ITA	18 Jun	EAP
17 Jun	WC	Golden Spike, Ostrava, CZE	26 May	WC
25 Jun	EAP	Paavo Nurmi Games, Turku, Finland	25 Jun	EAP
3 Jul	DL	Athletissima, Lausanne, SUI	3 Jul	DL
5 Jul	DL	Meeting AREVA Paris Saint-Denis, FRA	4 Jul	DL
11/12 Jul	DL	London (OS) 2015, GP Glasgow 2014	24-25 Jul	DL
18 Jul	DL	Herculis, Monaco, MON	17 Jul	DL
19 Jul	WC	Atletismo Madrid, ESP	11 Jul	WC
10 Aug	WC	GP Brasil de Atletismo, Bélem BRA	9 Aug	WC
21 Aug	DL	DN Galan, Stockholm, SWE	30 Jul	DL
22-24 Aug	EASp	Internationales Hochsprung, Eberstadt, GER	1-2 Aug	EASp
24 Aug	DL	British Grand Prix, Birmingham, GBR	7 Jun	DL
28 Aug	DL	Weltklasse, Zürich, SUI	3 Sep	DL
31 Aug	WC	ISTAF, Berlin, GER	6 Sep	WC
2 Sep	WC	Zagreb, CRO	8 Sep	WC
2 Sep	EAP	Palio Citta della Quercia, Rovereto, ITA	8 Sep	EAP
5 Sep	DL	Memorial Van Damme, Brussels, BEL	11 Sep	DL
7 Sep	WC	Rieti, ITA	13 Sep	WC

INDOORS

IAAF and EAA – respective indoor permit meetings; US USATF series in USA.

2014 date		Meeting	2015 date	
19 Jan	EAA	International Games, Reykjavik, ISL	17 Jan	EAA
26 Jan		Sainsbury's International, Glasgow, GBR	24 Jan	EAA
30 Jan	EAA	International PSD Bank, Düsseldorf, GER	29 Jan	EAA
31 Jan	EAA	Pedro's Cup, Bydgoszcz 2014, Lódz 2015, POL	17 Feb	EAA
1 Feb	IAAF	BW-Bank Meeting, Karlsruhe, GER	31 Jan	IAAF
2 Feb	IAAF	Russian Winter, Moscow, RUS	1 Feb	IAAF
	—	Copernicus Cup, Torun, POL	3 Feb	EAA
		Banskobystrica latka, Banská Bystrica, SVK	4 Feb	EAA
6 Feb	IAAF	XL-Galen, Stockholm, SWE	19 Feb	IAAF
6 Feb		Flanders Indoor, Gent, BEL	7 Feb	EAA
7/8 Feb		International Combined Events, Tallinn, EST	6-7 Feb	EAA
8 Feb	US	New Balance Indoor GP, Boston (Roxbury), USA	7 Feb	IAAF/US
9 Feb	EAA	Pole Vault Stars, Donetsk, UKR	—	EAA
15 Feb	IAAF	British Indoor Grand Prix, Birmingham, GBR	21 Feb	IAAF
15 Feb		Millrose Games, New York (Armory), USA	14 Feb	US
25 Feb	EAA	Prague (O2 Arena), CZE	—	
1 Mar		ISTAF Indoor meeting, Berlin, GER	14 Feb	
—		Malmö Games, SWE	25 Feb	EAA
27 Feb-1 Mar	US	USA Indoor Championships. Albuquerque	27 Feb-1 Mar	US

IAAF WORLD COMBINED EVENTS CHALLENGE 2014 & 2015

2/3 May	Multistars, Firenze, ITA	15-16 May
31 May-1 Jun	Hypo-Mehrkampf Meeting, Götzis, AUT	30/31 May
14/15 Jun	TNT Express Meeting, Kladno, CZE	12-13 Jun
	Combined Events Capital Cup, Ottawa, CAN	19-20 Jun
28/29 Jun	Erdgas DLV Mehrkampf, Ratingen, GER	28-28 Jun
20/21 Sep	Decastars, Talence, FRA	19-20 Sep

Plus International Games and Championships
European Athletics Combined Events Permit 2015: Arona 6/7 Jun

IAAF WORLD RACE WALKING CHALLENGE 2014 & 2015

2 Feb	Hobart 2014, Adelaide 2015, AUS	22 Feb
22 Feb	Chihuahua, MEX	7 Mar
16 Mar	Nomi, JPN	15 Mar
22 Mar	Dudince, SVK	21 Mar
—	African Championships, Maurice, MRI	11-12 Apr
5 Apr	Rio Maior, POR	18 Apr
3-4 May	Taicang, CHN (RW Cup in 2014)	1 May
31 May	Gran Premio Cantones de La Coruña, ESP	6 Jun

Plus International Championships

European Athletics Race Walking Permit Meetings 2015

16 Mar	Lugano, SUI	15 Mar
12 Apr	Podebrady, CZE	11 Apr

Both the above were in the iAAF World Challenge in 2014

IAAF HAMMER THROW CHALLENGE 2015

At the foliowing meetings (above): Melbourne AUS, Kawasaki JPN, Beijing CHN, Ponce PUR, Ostrava CZE, Moscow RUS, Rabat MAR, Belém BRA, Rieti ITA

MARATHON MAJORS 2015

Tokyo 22 Feb, Boston 20 Apr, London 26 Apr, Berlin 27 Sep, Chicago 11 Oct, New York 1 Nov

EUROPEAN AA CLASSIC MEETINGS 2014/2015

Kalamáta GRE 31/30 May, Marseille FRA 31 May/6 Jun, Montreuil-sous-Bois FRA 7 Jul/9 Jun, Huelva ESP (Iberoamerican) 12/10 Jun, Bydgoszcz POL 8/14 Jun Sollentuna SWE 26/25 Jun, Velenje SLO 1 Jul/30 Jun, Tomblaine FRA 27 Jun/1 Jul, Sotteville-lès-Rouen FRA 14 Jun/6 Jul, Székesfehérvár HUN (István Gyulai Memorial) 8/7 Jul, Luzern SUI (Spitzen) 15/14 Jul, Heusden-Zolder, BEL 19/18 Jul, Zhukovskiy/Moscow RUS (Znamenskiy Memorial) 27 Jun/18-19 Jul, Karlstad SWE 16/22 Jul, Szczecin POL (Kusocinski) 7 Jun/9 Aug, Göteborg SWE 14 Jun/5 Sep, Padua ITA 6 Jul/6 Sep
2014 only: Linz AUT (Gugl) 14 Jul, Malmö SWE 5 Aug, Cagliari ITA (Terra Sarda) 6 Sep

A further 12 meetings in eight countries have been designated as **European Athletics outdoor area permit meetings**

NORTH AMERICA NACAC MEETINGS 2014/2015

Des Moines (Drake Relays) USA 24 Apr, Philadelphia (Penn Relays) USA 25 Apr, Baie Mahault, Guadeloupe 10/2 May, George Town CAY 7/16 May, Guelph CAN 31/30 May, Tortola IVB 7/6 Jun, Halifax (Alison Meagher International Classic) CAN 14/2 Jun, Vancouver (Harry Jerome International) CAN 11 Jul/8 Jun, Victoria CAN 8 Jul/10 Jun, Port of Spain (Hasely Crawford Classic) TRI 2 May/11 Jul, Edmonton CAN 5/12 Jul

SOUTH AMERICA 2014/2015

18 meetings in 9 countries have been designated as South American Grands Prix in 2015.

MAJOR INTERNATIONAL EVENTS 2013-2020

2015

African Junior Championships – Addis Ababa, Ethiopia (5-8 March)
European Indoor Championships – Prague, Czech Republic (6-8 Mar)
IAAF World Cross Country Championships – Guiyang (A), China (28 Mar)
Carifta Games – Basseterre, St. Kitts Nevis (4-6 Apr)
Asian Youth Championships – Doha, Qatar (1-4 May)
IAAF World Relays – Nassau, Bahamas (2-3 May)
Oceania Championships – Cairns (8-10 May)
Pan-American Race Walking Cup – Arica, Chile (9-10 May)
European Cup Race Walking – Murcia, Spain (17 May)
Pan-American Youth Championships – Cali (A), Colombia (30-31 May)
European Cup 10,000m – Chia, Italy (6 June)
South East Asia Games – Singapore (7-12 June)
European Team Championships – Super League Cheboksary, Russia (20-21 June)

Asian Championships – Wuhan, China (3-7 June)
European Cup Combined Events (4-5 July)
World University Games – Gwangju, Korea (8-12 July)
European U23 Championships – Tallinn, Estonia (9-12 July)
IAAF World Youth Championships – Cali (A), Colombia (15-19 July)
European Junior Championships – Eskilstuna, Sweden (16-19 July)
Pan-American Games – Toronto, Canada (21-26 July)
Pan-American Junior Championships – Edmonton, Canada (31 July – 2 Aug)
All-Africa Games – Brazzaville, Congo
NACAC Championships – San José, Costa Rica (7-9 Aug)
IAAF World Championships – Beijing, China (22-30 Aug)
IAU World & European 100K Championships – Winschoten, Netherlands (12 Sep)
World Mountain Running Championships – Betws y Coed, GBR (19 Sep)
European Cross Country Championships – Toulon-Hyères, France (13 Dec)

2016

World University Cross Country Championships – Monte Cassino, Italy (11-13 March)
IAAF World Indoor Championships – Portland, Oregon, USA (18-20 March)
IAAF World Half Marathon Championships – Cardiff, GBR (26 March)
IAAF Race Walking Team Championships – Cheboksary, Russia (7-8 May)
European Championships – Amsterdam, Netherlands (5-10 July)
European Youth Championships ¬ Tbilisi, Georgia (14-19 July)
IAAF World Junior Championships – Kazan, Russia (19-24 July)
NACAC U23 Championships – Mayagüez, Puerto Rico (July)
Olympic Games – Rio de Janeiro, Brazil (5-12 Aug)

2017

European Indoor Championships – Belgrade, Serbia
IAAF World Cross Country Championships – Kampala, Uganda
IAAF World Youth Championships – Nairobi, Kenya
NACAC Championships
IAAF World Championships – London, GBR (5-13 Aug)
World University Games – Taipeh, Taiwan (20-25 Aug)

2018

IAAF World Indoor Championships – Birmingham, GBR (March)
Commonwealth Games – Gold Coast, Australia (4-15 April)
IAAF World Race Walking Cup – Cheboksary, Russia
Central American & Caribbean Games –
European Championships – Berlin, Germany
Asian Games – Jakarta, Indonesia
IAAF Continental Cup – Ostrava, Czech Republic
Youth Olympic Games – Buenos Aires, Argentina (11-23 Sep)

2019

Pan-American Games ¬ Lima, Peru
World University Games – Brasilia, Brazil
IAAF World Championships – Doha, Qatar (28 Sep – 6 Oct)
Asian Games – Hanoi, Vietnam
Pan-American Games ¬ Lima, Peru
World University Games – Brasilia, Brazil

2020

Olympic Games – Tokyo, Japan (31 July – 9 August)

The IAAF have decided that the name of the **World Race Walking Cup** be changed to the 'IAAF World Race Walking Team Championships.' The new name will apply from the next edition in Cheboksary in 2016. For the **World Youth Championships**, which will be held in Cali, Colombia in 2015, the Medley Relays will be replaced with one mixed 4x400m relay, containing two boys and two girls.

Masters category exhibition events will be held as part of the **2015 IAAF World Championships**; on Saturday August 29. These will be a 400m for women and a 800m for men; neither will have more than eight athletes.

EUROPEAN INDOOR CHAMPIONSHIPS 2015

O2 Arena, Prague, Czech Republic 6-8 March

REAL CHAMPIONSHIP ACTION was splendidly served in these the 33rd European Indoor Championships in athletics. The O2 Arena in Prague provided a splendid setting, although since it is primarily an ice hockey arena, sight lines for spectators and media were far from ideal and the four tiers of seating meant that those at the top were very high above the action. The total number of spectators (excluding media and team seats) was 52,284, possibly the highest ever for a European Indoors.

Hugely enthusiastic spectators gave terrific support for the Czech (and indeed the Slovak) competitors and were richly rewarded with magnificent victories by Pavel Maslák in the 400m and by Jakub Holusa in the 1500m. Holusa judged his effort to perfection with a 26.6 last lap and just came past the tiring William Tanui Özbilen in the closing strides, Maslák's 45.33 was one of three men's Championship records, the others being Renaud Lavillenie's 6.04 pole vault to add a centimetre to his 2011 mark and bring him the title for the fourth successive time, and the 3:02.87 run for 4x400m by Belgium in the final event to bring the meeting to a rousing finish. This was also a European record and Poland, who had led all the way until the brilliantly judged run by Kevin Borlée brought his nation to victory, also beat the old record and the first three teams were all well inside the previous Championship best of 3:05.50. Maslák, Lavillenie and Alina Talay (women's 60m hurdles) were the only athletes to successfully defend their titles.

While Lavillenie was surely the male star of the meeting, then Katarina Johnson-Thompson was that on the women's side. She ended disappointed not to have broken the world record for the pentathlon, but having to run the 800m as a virtually solo effort proved just too much. Nonetheless her Championship record 5000 points was yet further confirmation of her outstanding talent. She started with a 60m hurdles pb of 8.18 and produced world-class performances at high jump 1.95 and long jump 6.89, both indeed good enough for individual event medals. Those two stars set world-leading marks as did Ilya Shkuryenov with a 6353 heptathlon score, Yekaterina Koneva, 14.69 in the women's triple jump, and Dafne Schippers with 7.05 in a closely-contested women's 60m, resolved by her charge through the field to the finish to finish ahead of 19 year-old Asher-Smith who tied the British record with 7.08. Schippers now holds European titles at 60m (indoors) and at 100m and 200m (outdoors) simultaneously.

With only Liechtenstein missing from the 50 European Athletics members, this was a record-breaking championship. Russia, who had a string of successes in the technical events on the final day, easily topped the medal table with six golds, but their eight in all was behind Britain with nine. It was fascinating to see just how close the top nations: Russia, Germany, Britain and Poland were on the placings table.

MEN

60 Metres (7-8-8)

1. Richard Kilty GBR	6.51
2. Christian Blum GER	6.58
3. Julian Reus GER	6.60
4. Michael Tumi ITA	6.61
5. Pascal Mancini SUI	6.62
6. Lucas Jakubczyk GER	6.62
7. Emmanuel Biron FRA	6.72
dq. Chijindu Ujah GBR	

400 Metres (6-6-7)

1. Pavel Maslák CZE	45.33*
2. Dylan Borlée BEL	46.25
3. Rafal Omelko POL	46.26
4. Lukasz Krawczuk POL	46.31
5. Yevhen Hutsol UKR	46.73
6. Matteo Galvan ITA	46.87

800 Metres (6-7-8)

1. Marcin Lewandowski POL	1:46.67
2. Mark English IRL	1:47.20
3. Thijmen Kupers NED	1:47.25
4. Andreas Almgren SWE	1:47.78
5. Robin Schembera GER	1:47.83
6. Guy Learmonth GBR	1:47.84

1500 Metres (7-8)

1. Jakub Holusa CZE	3:37.68
2. Ilham Tanui Özbilen TUR	3:37.74
3. Chris O'Hare GBR	3:38.96
4. Homiyu Tesfaye GER	3:39.08
5. Charlie Grice GBR	3:39.43
6. Henrik Ingebrigtsen NOR	3:39.70
7. John Travers IRL	3:41.50
8. Valentin Smirnov RUS	3:41.88
9. Artur Ostrowski POL	3:44.98

3000 Metres (6-7)

1. Ali Kaya TUR	7:38.42
2. Lee Emanuel GBR	7:44.48
3. Henrik Ingebrigtsen NOR	7:45.54
4. Jesús España ESP	7:47.12
5. Richard Ringer GER	7:48.44
6. Adel Mechaal ESP	7:49.59
7. Lukasz Parszczynski POL	7:50.11
8. Florian Orth GER	7:51.02
9. Philip Hurst GBR	7:51.94
10. Yegor Nikolayev RUS	7:51.99
11. Florian Carvalho FRA	7:57.14
12. Pieter-Jan Hannes BEL	7:59.43

60 Metres Hurdles (6)

1. Pascal Martinot Lagarde FRA	7.49
2. Dimitri Bascou FRA	7.50
3. Wilhem Belocian FRA	7.52
4. Erik Balnuweit GER	7.59
5. Lawrence Clarke GBR	7.63
6. Konstadínos Douvalídis GRE	7.64
7. Balázs Baji HUN	7.65
8. Petr Svoboda CZE	7.67

High Jump (7-8)

1. Daniyil Tsyplakov RUS	2.31
2= Silvano Chesani ITA	2.31
2= Adónios Mástoras GRE	2.31
4. Aleksandr Shustov RUS	2.28
5. Jaroslav Bába CZE	2.28
6. Andriy Protsenko UKR	2.28
7. Gianmarco Tamberi ITA	2.24
nh. Kyriakos Ioannou CYP	–

Pole Vault (6-7)

1. Renaud Lavillenie FRA	6.04*
2. Aleksandr Gripich RUS	5.85
3. Piotr Lisek POL	5.85
4. Robert Sobera POL	5.80
5. Konstadínos Filippídis GRE	5.75
6. Valentin Lavillenie FRA	5.65
7= Anton Ivakin RUS	5.65
7= Jan Kudlicka CZE	5.65
9. Thomas Scherbarth GER	5.45

Long Jump (5-6)

1. Michel Tornéus SWE	8.30
2. Radek Juska CZE	8.10
3. Andeas Otterling SWE	8.06
4. Loúis Tsátoumas GRE	7.98
5. Jean Marie Okutu ESP	7.93
6. Pavel Shalin RUS	7.80
7. Alyn Camara GER	7.70
8. Rain Kask EST	7.24

Triple Jump (6-7)
1. Nelson Évora POR 17.21
2. Pablo Torrijos ESP 17.04
3. Marian Oprea ROU 16.91
4. Aleksey Fyodorov RUS 16.88
5. Georgi Tsonov BUL 16.75
6. Dmitriy Sorokin RUS 16.65
7. Dmitriy Platnitskiy BLR 16.43
8. Rumen Dimitrov BUL 16.36

Shot (5-6)
1. David Storl GER 21.23
2. Asmir Kolasinac SRB 20.90
3. Ladislav Prásil CZE 20.66
4. Borja Vivas ESP 20.59
5. Bob Bertemes LUX 20.48
6. Konrad Bukowiecki POL-J 20.46
7. Stipe Zunic CRO 20.28
8. Tobias Dahm GER 19.58

Heptathlon (7/8)
1. Ilya Shkurenyov RUS 6353
(6.98, 7.78, 13.89, 2.10, 7.86, 5.30, 2:44.84)
2. Arthur Abele GER 6279
3. Eelco Sintnicolaas NED 6185
4. Gaël Quérin FRA 6115
5. Adam Helcelet CZE 6031
6. Bastien Auzeil FRA 6011
7. Jorge Ureña ESP 5941
8. Petter Olson SWE 5869
9. Marek Lukás CZE 5865
10. Artyom Lukyanenko RUS 5857
11. Matthias Brugger GER 5846

4 x 400 Metres (8)
1. BEL 3:02.87
J Watrin 46.88, D Borlée 45.86, J Borlée 45.14, K Borlée 44.99
2. POL 3:02.97
K Zalewski 45.98, R Omelko 45.48, L Krawczuk 45.64, J Krzewina 45.87
3. CZE 3:04.09
D Nemecek 47.06, P Sorm 46.03, J Tesar 45.59, P Maslák 45.41
4. RUS 3:08.00
5. GBR 3:08.56
6. IRL 3:10.61

WOMEN

60 Metres (7-8-8)
1. Dafne Schippers NED 7.05
2. Dina Asher-Smith GBR 7.08
3. Verena Sailer GER 7.09
4. Ezinne Okparaebo NOR 7.10
5. Mujinga Kambundju SUI 7.11
6. Olesya Povh UKR 7.11
7. Jamile Samuel NED 7.19
8. Ewa Swoboda POL-J 7.20

400 Metres (6-6-7)
1. Nataliya Pyhyda UKR 51.96
2. Indira Terrero ESP 52.63
3. Seren Bundy-Davies GBR 52.64
4. Iveta Putalová SVK 52.84
5. Marie Gayot FRA 53.11
6. Denisa Rosolová CZE 53.20

800 Metres (6-7-8)
1. Selina Büchel SUI 2:01.95
2. Yekaterina Poistogova RUS 2:01.99
3. Nataliya Lupu UKR 2:02.25
4. Joanna Józwik POL 2:02.45
5. Anita Hinriksdóttir ISL-J 2:02.74
dns. Jennifer Meadows GBR -

1500 Metres (8)
1. Sifan Hassan NED 4:09.04
2, Angelika Cichocka POL 4:10.53
3. Federica Del Buono ITA 4:11.61
4. Katarzyna Broniatowska POL 4:12.71
5. Gesa-Felicitas Krause GER 4:15.40
6. Rosie Clarke GBR 4:16.49
7. Diana Mezuliáníková CZE 4:16.93
8. Renata Plis POL 4:16.96
9. Florina Pierdevara ROU 4:17.05
10. Sonja Roman SLO 4:20.85
11. Silvia Danekova BUL 4:25.44

3000 Metres (6-7)
1. Yelena Korobkina RUS 8:47.62
2. Svetlana Kudzelich BLR 8:48.02
3. Maureen Koster NED 8:51.64
4. Laura Muir GBR 8:52.44
5. Sandra Eriksson FIN 8:54.06
6. Sofia Ennaoui POL 8:56.77
7. Giulia Viola ITA 8:59.04
8. Marusa Mismas SLO 8:59.51
9. Jennifer Wenth AUT 8:59.84
10. Kristiina Mäki CZE 9:05.95
11. Charlotta Fougberg SWE 9:06.50
12. Emelia Gorecka GBR 9:06.79

60 Metres Hurdles (6)
1. Alina Talay BLR 7.85
2. Lucy Hatton GBR 7.90
3. Serita Solomon GBR 7.93
4. Cindy Roleder GER 7.93
5. Isabelle Pedersen NOR 7.96
6. Nooralotta Neziri FIN 7.97
7. Andrea Ivancevic CRO 8.02
8. Hanna Platitsyna UKR 8.10

High Jump (6-7)
1. Mariya Kuchina RUS 1.97
2. Alessia Trost ITA 1.97
3. Kamila Licwinko POL 1.94
4. Airine Palsyte LTU 1.94
5. Ruth Beitia ESP 1.94
6. Justyna Kasprzycka POL 1.94
7. Venelina Veneva-Mateeva BUL 1.90
8= Michaela Hrubá CZE-Y 1.85
8= Barbara Szabó HUN 1.85

Pole Vault (6-8)
1. Anzhelika Sidorova RUS 4.80
2. Ekateríni Stefanídi GRE 4.75
3. Angelica Bengtsson SWE 4.70
4. Angelina Krasnova RUS 4.60
5= NIkoléta Kiriakopoúlou GRE 4.50
5= Marion Fiack FRA 4.50
nh. Katherina Bauer GER –
dns. Lisa Ryzih GER –

Long Jump (6-7)
1. Ivana Spanovic SRB 6.98
2. Sosthene Moguenara GER 6.83
3. Florentina Marincu ROU-J 6.79
4. Alina Rotaru ROU 6.74
5. Éloyse Lesueur FRA 6.73
6. Melanie Bauschke GER 6.59
7. Karin Melis Mey TUR 6.57
8. Aiga Grabuste LAT 6.54

Triple Jump (7-8)
1. Yekaterina Koneva RUS 14.69
2. Gabriela Petrova BUL 14.52
3. Hanna Minenko ISR 14.49
4. Kristin Gierisch GER 14.46
5. Patricia Mamona POR 14.32
6. Cristina Bujin ROU 13.91
7. Natalya Vyatkina BLR 13.69
8. Kristiina Mäkelä FIN 13.66

Shot (5-7)
1. Anita Márton HUN 19.23
2. Yuliya Leontyuk BLR 18.60
3. Radoslava Mavrodieva BUL 17.83
4. Alena Abramchuk BLR 17.63
5. Paulina Guba POL 17.47
6. Denise Hinrichs GER 17.35
7. Anastasiya Podolskaya RUS 16.81
8. Úrsula Ruíz ESP 16.07

Pentathlon (6)
1. Katarina Johnson-Thompson GBR 5000
(8.18, 1.95, 12.32, 6.89, 2:12.78)
2. Nafissatou Thiam BEL 4696
3. Eliska Klucinová CZE 4687
4. Yana Maksimova BLR 4628
5. Antoinette Nana Djimou FRA 4591
6. Gyorgyi Zsivoczky-Farkas HUN 4564
7. Alina Fyodorova UKR 4563
8. Anouk Vetter NED 4548
9. Morgan Lake GBR-J 4527
10. Aleksandra Butvina RUS 4518
11. Anna Blank RUS 4489
12. Yekaterina Netsvetayeva BLR 4414

4 x 400 Metres (6)
1. FRA 3:31.61
F Guei 52.86, E M Diarra 53.14, A Raharolahy 53.47, M Gayot 52.14
2. GBR 3:31.79
K Massey 53.79, S Bundy-Davies 52.14, L Maddox 54.03, K McAslan 51.83
3. POL 3:31.90
J Linkiewicz 54.09, M Holub 52.38, M Szczesna 53.58, J Swiety 51.85
4. CZE 3:32.08
5. UKR 3:32.39
6. RUS 3:32.53

Leading Nations – Medals & Points

Nation	G	S	B	Points
RUS	6	2	-	95.5
GER	1	3	2	86
GBR	2	4	3	85
POL	1	2	4	83
FRA	3	1	1	65.5
CZE	2	1	3	62.5
ESP	-	2	-	38
NED	2	-	3	37
BLR	1	2	-	36
ITA	-	2	1	32
UKR	1	-	1	31
GRE	-	2	-	30
SWE	1	-	2	26
BEL	1	2	-	22
BUL	-	1	-	20
ROU	-	-	2	20
NOR	-	-	1	18
TUR	1	1	-	17
SUI	1	-	-	16
SRB	1	1	-	15
HUN	1	-	-	14
POR	1	-	-	12
IRL	-	1	-	12

16 nations won gold, 24 medals and 33 placed athletes in top 8.

WORLD CROSS-COUNTRY CHAMPIONSHIPS 2015

At Guiyang, China 28 March

THE WORLD CROSS-COUNTRY was inevitably dominated by Ethiopia and Kenya who came 1st and 2nd in all the team competitions and supplied at least the top four in all four races. Of the other East African nations Uganda were 3rd to 5th in all four races, Eritrea had a 3rd and a 4th and the East African monopoly was maintained by Bahrain, whose runners were all from East Africa, and whose teams took two 3rd places and a 4th. The first non-African born runners were 24th and 16th in the two senior races and 25th and 16th in the junior races.

The senior men's winner was the 2014 World Half Marathon champion Geoffrey Kamworer who became just the third man ever to win both Junior (2011) and senior Cross titles. Kamworer set a very fast pace from the gun and soon the lead pack was formed solely of the men from the East African highlands. After four laps, the eventual top three had got away from the rest and a lap later Edris had had to yield to the two Kenyans who ran together until Kamworer produced a superb sprint finish over the final 300m. Scores for the senior men's teams were 20 for both Ethiopia and Kenya, the former winning their ninth title at the event as their fourth placer came 7th to Kenya's 12th.

Two 19 year-olds were dominant in the senior women's race, with Agnes Tirop, second in 2013, who looked very strong throughout, prevailing as the youngest winner since Zola Budd in 1985. The favourite Emily Chebet, winner in 2010 and 2013, had to settle for 6th place. Ethiopia won their eleventh women's team title, ending a run of four Kenyan successes, by just two points as all six Ethiopians were in the top ten and all six Kenyans in the top 13.

Each race was run over laps of a 1980m course plus a 90m stretch to the finish.

While the overall number of participants was similar to that of 2013, the event continues to be attract far too little support from the Western world, with many traditional cross-country nations ignoring the event or sending just a few runners. Sadly federations, coaches and athletes are failing to recognise to necessity of cross-country running in building distance running ability. This situation is, of course, not helped by holding the event so far away from the mainstays of cross-country.

Senior Men 11.97km

1. Geoffrey Kamworor KEN 34:52
2. Bedan Karoki Muchiri KEN 35:00
3. Muktar Edris ETH 35:06
4. Hagos Gebrhiwet ETH 35:15
5. Leonard Barsoton KEN 35:24
6. Tamirat Tola ETH 35:33
7. Atsedu Tsegay ETH 35:47
8. Moses Kibet UGA 35:53
9. Ismail Juma TAN 35:55
10. Aweke Ayalew BRN 35:56
11. Albert Rop BRN 35:59
12. Phillip Langat KEN 36:05
13. Abrar Osman ERI 36:13
14. Bonsa Dida ETH 36:17
15. El Hassan El Abbassi BRN 36:22
16. Moses Mukono KEN 36:23
17. Teklemariam Medhin ERI 36:24
18. Isaac Korir BRN 36:27
19. Zelalem Bacha BRN 36:30
20. Hassan Chani BRN 36:35
21. Joseph Kiptum KEN 36:37
22. Polat Kemboi Arikan TUR 36:40
23. Goitom Kifle ERI 36:44
24. Chris Derrick USA 36:45
25. Phillip Kipyeko UGA 36:50
26. Tesfaye Abera ETH 36:59
27. Timothy Torootich UGA 37:02
28. Brett Robinson AUS 37:11

108 of 110 finished

Team 4 to score, 15 teams completed

1. ETH	20	10. ALG	189
2. KEN	20	11. AUS	210
3. BRN	54	12. ESP	256
4. ERI	91	13. PER	264
5. UGA	92	14. CHN	285
6. TAN	130	15. GBR	295
7. USA	131	16. ECU	299
8. RWA	153	17. CAN	323
9. RSA	162		

Junior Men 8.01km

1. Yasin Haji ETH 23:42
2. Geoffrey Korir KEN 23:47
3. Alfred Ngeno KEN 23:54
4. Dominic Kiptarus KEN 24:00
5. Evans Chematot BRN 24:03
6. Abraham Habte ERI 24:04
7. Yihunilign Adane ETH 24:05
8. Abe Gashahun ETH 24:08
9. Fred Musobo UGA 24:10
10. Rodgers Chumo KEN 24:11
11. Joshua Cheptegei UGA 24:11
12. Moses Koech KEN 24:11

113 of 118 finished

Team 4 to score. 17 teams completed

1. KEN	19	12. RSA	236
2. ETH	33	13. GBR	243
3. ERI	52	14. ALG	249
4. BRN	70	15. FRA	258
5. UGA	76	16. CAN	278
6. USA	132	17. ESP	315
7. MAR	139	18. BRA	317
8. ITA	176	19. AUS	353
9. JPN	200	20. YEM	380
10. CHN	209	21. QAT	385
11. SUD	215		

Senior Women 8.01km

1. Agnes Tirop KEN 26:01
2. Senbera Teferi ETH 26:06
3. Netsanet Gudeta ETH 26:11
4. Alemitu Heroye ETH 26:14
5. Stacy Ndiwa KEN 26:16
6. Emily Chebet KEN 26:18
7. Irene Cheptai KEN 26:26
8. Mamitu Daska ETH 26:29
9. Belaynesh Olijira ETH 26:29
10. Genet Ayalew ETH 27:00
11. Nazareth Weldu ERI 27:19
12. Janet Kisa KEN 27:22
13. Margaret Kipkemboi KEN 27:32
14. Juliet Chekwel UGA 27:40
15. Trihas Gebre ESP 27:50
16. Ding Changqin CHN 27:52
17. Zhang Xinyan CHN 28:02
18. Gemma Steel GBR 28:14
19. Rhona Auckland GBR 28:17
20. Sara Hall USA 28:19
21. Gladys Tejeda PER 28:22
22. Wu Xufeng CHN 28:24
23. Miho Shimizu JPN 28:26
24. Adero Nyakisi UGA 28:31
25. Rachel Hannah CAN 28:34
26. Amina Bettiche ALG 28:40
27. Natasha Wodak CAN 28:43
28. Nawal Yahi ALG 28:44

80 of 82 finished

Team 4 to score. 15 teams completed

1. ETH	17	7. ESP	139
2. KEN	19	8. PER	156
3. UGA	101	9. JPN	159
4. CHN	122	10. CAN	171
5. USA	128	11. AUS	187
6. ALG	139	12. RSA	192

Junior Women 6.03km

1. Letesenbet Gidey ETH 19:48
2. Dera Dida ETH 19:49
3. Etagegn Woldu ETH 19:53
4. Daisy Jepkemei KEN 19:59
5. Tefera Adhena ETH 20:02
6. Dagmawit Kidane ETH 20:07
7. Gladys Kipkoech KEN 20:13
8. Desi Mokonin BRN 20:17
9. Ruth Chebet BRN 20:20
10. Winfred Nzisa KEN 20:31
11. Stella Chesang UGA 20:37
12. Rosefline Chepngetich KEN 20:38

97 of 100 finished

Team 4 to score, 14 teams completed

1. ETH	11	9. PER	212
2. KEN	33	10. MAR	229
3. BRN	52	11. FRA	229
4. UGA	65	12. AUS	232
5. JPN	98	13. CAN	247
6. CHN	136	14. RSA	279
7. ERI	138	15. GBR	279
8. USA	177	16. KOR	310

Britain, the home of cross-country, had easily its worst ever Championhips, with, for the first time, no team in the top ten, and not even sending a full senior women's team.

WORLD CHAMPIONSHIPS 2015

THE 15th IAAF World Championships will be staged in Beijing, China on 22-30 August 2015.

Previous Championships

ATHLETICS EVENTS at the Olympic Games have had world championship status, but the first championships for athletics alone were staged in 1983. It should, however, be noted that separate World Championships were held for men's 50 kilometres walk in 1976 and for women's 3000m and 400m hurdles in 1980, as those events were not on the Olympic programme in those years.

Year	*Venue*	*Athletes*	*Nations*
1983	Helsinki, FIN	1572	153
1987	Rome, ITA	1741	157
1991	Tokyo, JPN	1551	164
1993	Stuttgart, GER	1624	187
1995	Göteborg, SWE	1804	191
1997	Athens, GRE	1882	198
1999	Seville, ESP	1821	201
2001	Edmonton, CAN	1677	189
2003	Saint-Denis, FRA	1679	198
2005	Helsinki, FIN	1688	189
2007	Osaka, JPN	1800	197
2009	Berlin GER	1895	200
2011	Daegu KOR	1742	199
2013	Moscow, RUS	1784	203

World Championship Records

Men

100m	9.58	Usain Bolt JAM	2009
200m	19.19	Usain Bolt JAM	2009
400m	43.18	Michael Johnson USA	1999
800m	1:43.06	Billy Konchellah KEN	1987
1500m	3:27.65	Hicham El Guerrouj MAR	1999
5000m	12:52.79	Eliud Kipchoge KEN	2003
10,000m	26:46.31	Kenenisa Bekele ETH	2009
Mar	2:06:54	Abel Kirui KEN	2009
3000mSt	8:00.43	Ezekiel Kemboi KEN	2009
110mh	12.91	Colin Jackson GBR	1993
400mh	47.18	Kevin Young USA	1993
HJ	2.41	Bohdan Bondarenko UKR	2013
PV	6.05	Dmitriy Markov AUS	2001
LJ	8.95	Mike Powell USA	1991
TJ	18.29	Jonathan Edwards GBR	1995
SP	22.23	Werner Günthör SUI	1987
DT	70.17	Virgilijus Alekna BLR	2005
HT	83.89	Ivan Tikhon BLR	2005
JT	92.80	Jan Zelezny CZE	2001
Dec	8902	Tomás Dvorák CZE	2001
4x100m	37.04	Jamaica	2011
4x400m	2:54.29	USA	1993
20kmW	1:17:21	Jefferson Pérez ECU	2003
50kmW	3:36:03	Rob. Korzeniowski POL	2003

Women

100m	10.70	Marion Jones USA	1999
200m	21.74	Silke Gladisch GDR	1987
400m	47.99	Jarmila Kratochvílová TCH	1983
800m	1:54.68	Jarmila Kratochvílová TCH	1983
1500m	3:58.52	Tatyana Tomashova RUS	2003
3000m	8:28.71	Qu Yunxia CHN	1993
5000m	14:38.59	Tirunesh Dibaba ETH	2005
10,000m	30:04.18	Berhane Adere ETH	2003
Mar	2:20:57	Paula Radcliffe GBR	2005
3000mSt	9:06.57	Yekaterina Volkova RUS	2007
100mh	12.28	Sally Pearson AUS	2011
400mh	52.42	Melaine Walker JAM	2009
HJ	2.09	Stefka Kostadinova BUL	1987
PV	5.01	Yelena Isinbayeva RUS	2005
LJ	7.36	Jackie Joyner-Kersee USA	1987
TJ	15.50	Inessa Kravets UKR	1995
SP	21.24	Natalya Lisovskaya URS	1987
	21.24	Valerie Adams NZL	2011
DT	71.62	Martina Hellmann GDR	1987
HT	78.80	Tatyana Lysenko RUS	2013
JT	71.99	Marita Abakumova RUS	2011
Hep	7128	Jackie Joyner-Kersee USA	1987
4x100m	41.29	Jamaica	2013
4x400m	3:16.71	USA	1993
20kmW	1:25:41	Olimpiada Ivanova RUS	2005

Winners of the most medals

14 Merlene Ottey JAM gold 4x100m 1991, 200m 1993 & 1995; silver 200m 1983, 100m 1993 & 1995, 4x100m 1995; bronze 4x100m 1983, 100m & 200m 1987 & 1991, 4x100m 1993, 200m 1997

10 Carl Lewis USA gold 100m, LJ & 4x100m 1983; 100m, LJ & 4x100m 1987, 100m & 4x100m 1991; silver LJ 1991; bronze 200m 1993

10 Usain Bolt JAM gold 100m, 200m & 4x100m 2009 & 2013; 200m & 4x100m 2011; silver 200m & 4x100m 2007

10 Allyson Felix USA gold 200m 2005, 2007 & 2009; 4x100m 2007 & 2011; 4x400m 2007, 2009 & 2011; silver 400m & bronze 200m 2011

9 Jearl Miles Clark USA gold 400m 1993, 4x400m 1993, 1995 & 2003; silver 4x400m 1991, 1997, 1999; bronze 400m 1995 & 1997

9 Veronica Campbell-Brown JAM gold 100m 2007, 200m 2011; silver 100m 2005, 2011; 200m 2007, 4x100m 2005, 2007 & 2011, 200m 2009

(8) Michael Johnson USA gold 200m 1991 & 1995, 400m 1993, 1995, 1997 & 1999, 4x400m 1993, 1995 (lost 1999 gold when team dq)

Winners of the most gold medals

8 Michael Johnson, Carl Lewis, Usain Bolt, Allyson Felix – above

6 Sergey Bubka PV 1983, 1987, 1991, 1993, 1995, 1997

5 Gail Devers, Marion Jones, Maurice Greene USA 1997-2001, Lars Riedel GER DT 1991-2001,

Allen Johnson USA 1995-2003, Jeremy Wariner, Kenenisa Bekele ETH 2005-09, Shelly-Ann Fraser-Pryce JAM 2007-13, Tirunesh Dibaba ETH 2003-13

Oldest world champions

Men 37y 258d V. Soldatenko USSR 50kW 1996
Women 40y 268d Ellina Zvereva BLR DT 2001

Oldest medallists

Men 40y 274d Troy Douglas NED 3rd 4x1 2003
40y 71d John Powell USA 2nd DT 1987
Women 40y 268d Ellina Zvereva BLR 1st DT 2001

Youngest gold medallists

Women 17y 248d Merlene Frazer JAM 4x100m (ran in heat) 1991
Men 18y 177d Ismael Kirui KEN 10,000m 1993

Youngest medallists

M: 16y 305d Darrel Brown TRI 4x100m 2001
W: 15y 153d Sally Barsosio KEN 10,000m 1993

Most wins by event

Men inc. all with 3 or more
100m 3 Carl Lewis USA 1983-87-91
3 Maurice Greene USA 1997-99-2001
200m 3 Usain BoltnJAM 2009-11-13
400m 4 Michael Johnson 1993-95-97-99
800m 3 Wilson Kipketer DEN 1995-97-99
1500m: 4 Hicham El Guerrouj MAR 1997-99-01-03
3 Nourredine Morceli ALG 1991-93-95
5000m 2 Ismael Kirui KEN 1993-95
2 Mo Farah GBR 2011-13
10,000m 4 Haile Gebrselasie ETH 1993-95-97-99
4 Kenenisa Bekele ETH 2003-05-07-09
Mar 2 Abel Antón ESP 1997-9
2 Jaouad Gharib MAR 2003-05
2 Abel Kirui KEN 2009-11
3000mSt 3 Moses Kiptanui KEN 1991-93-95
3 Ezekiel Kemboi KEN 2009-11-13
110mh 4 Allen Johnson USA 1995-97-2001-03
3 Greg Foster USA 1983-87-91
400mh 2 Edwin Moses 1983-87; Félix Sánchez DOM 2001-03; Kerron Clement USA 2007-09
HJ 2 Javier Sotomayor CUB 1993-97
PV 6 Sergey Bubka UKR 1983-87-91-93-95-97
LJ 4 Iván Pedroso CUB 1995-97-99-2001
4 Dwght Phillips USA 2003-05-09-11
TJ 2 Jonathan Edwards GBR 1995-2001
SP 3 Werner Günthör SUI 1987-91-93
3 John Godina USA 1995-97-2001
DT 5 Lars Riedel GER 1991-93-95-97-2001
3 Robert Harting GER 2009-11-13
HT 3 Ivan Tikhon BLR 2003-05-07
JT 3 Jan Zelezny CZE 1993-95-2001
Dec 3 Dan O'Brien USA 1991-93-95
3 Tomás Dvorák CZE 1997-99-2001
4x100m 8 USA 1983-87-91-93-99-2001-03-07
4x400m 8 USA 1987-93-95-2005-07-09-11-13
20kmW 3 Jefferson Pérez ECU 2003-05-07
50kmW 3 Rob. Korzeniowski POL 1997-2001-03

Women
100m 2 Marion Jones USA 1997-99
2 Shelly-Ann Fraser-Pryce 2009-13
200m 3 Allyson Felix USA 2005-07-09
400m 2 Cathy Freeman AUS 1997-99
2 Christine Ohurogu GBR 2009-13
800m 3 Maria Mutola MOZ 1993-2001-03
1500m 2 Hassiba Boulmerka ALG 1991-95
2 Tatyana Tomashova RUS 2003-05
2 Maryam Jamal BRN 2007-09
5000m 2 Gabriela Szabo ROU 1997-99
2 Tirunesh Dibaba ETH 2003-05
2 Vivian Cheruiyot KEN 2009-11
2 Meseret Defar ETH 2007-13
10,000m 3 Tirunesh Dibaba ETH 2005-07-13
Mar 2 Catherine Ndereba KEN 2003-07
2 Edna Kiplagat KEN 2011-13
3000mSt 1 by five women
100mh 3 Gail Devers USA 1993-95-99
400mh 2 Nezha Bidouane MAR 1997-2001
HJ 2 Stefka Kostadinova BUL 1987-1995
2 Hestrie Cloete RSA 2001-03
2 Blanka Vlasic CRO 2007-09
PV 3 Yelena Isinbayeva RUS 2005-07-13
LJ 3 Brittney Reese USA 2009-11-13
TJ 2 Tatyana Lebedeva RUS 2001-03
2 Yargelis Savigne CUB 2007-09
SP 4 Valerie Adams NZL 2007-09-11-13
3 Astrid Kumbernuss GER 1995-97-99
DT 3 Franka Dietzsch GER 1999-2005-07
HT 2 Yipsi Moreno CUB 2001-03
2 Tatyana Lysenko RUS 2011-13
JT 2 Trine Hattestad NOR 1993-97
2 Miréla Manjani GRE 1999-2003
2 Osleidys Menéndez CUB 2001-05
Hep 3 Carolina Klüft SWE 2003-5-07
4x100m 5 USA 1995-97-2001-05-07
4x400m 5 USA 1993-95-2003-07-09
20kmW 3 Olga Kaniskina RUS 2007-09-11

Qualifying Standards

Event	*Men*	*Women*
100m	10.16	11.33
200m	20.50	23.20
400m	45.50	52.00
800m	1:46.00	2:01.00
1500m	3:36.20	4:06.50
(or 1M)	3:53.30	4:25.20
5000m	13:23.00	15:20.00
10,000m	27:45.00	32:00.00
Mar	2:18:00	2:44:00
3000mSt	8:28.00	9:44:00
110/100mh	13.00	13.47
400mh	49.50	56.20
HJ	2.28	1.94
PV	5.65	4.50
LJ	8.10	6.70
TJ	16.9	014.20
SP	20.45	17.75
DT	65.00	61.00
HT	76.00	70.00
JT	82.00	61.00
Dec/Hep	8071	6075
20kmW	1:25:00	1:36:00
50kmW	4:06:00	–

The entry and participation principles have been thoroughly reviewed by the IAAF and a new qualification system has been introduced. The key element of this is that the IAAF shall establish the ideal number of athletes (and relay teams) to start in each event of the championships and shall ensure that such ideal numbers are met through a qualification system which, essentially, combines entry standards (only one standard as opposed to A and B standards in the past) and invitations based on rankings. As in the past, there are still some special qualification opportunities and it will still be possible for member federations without any qualified athletes to be represented with one unqualified athlete (subject to certain conditions).

Athletes can also qualify on the finishing position at designated competitions as follows (in these cases the athletes shall also be considered as having achieved the entry standard):

· Area champions in all the individual events (except for the marathons). The member federation of the area champion will have the ultimate authority to enter the athlete or not, based on its own selection criteria.

· For 10,000m: top 15 athletes finishing in the senior men's and women's races at the IAAF World Cross Country Championships, Guiyang 2015.

· For combined events: top three in the 2014 IAAF Combined Events Challenges.

· For 20km and 50km walk:s top three in the 2014 men's and women's IAAF World Race Walking Challenge.

· For marathons: top 10 finishers at the IAAF Gold Label marathons held in the qualification period.

The IAAF will accept the participation of the reigning world outdoor champion and that of the winner of the previous year's IAAF Diamond Race (in the corresponding World Championships events) and Hammer Throw Challenge as wild cards, in each individual event, on the condition that the athlete in question is entered by his or her federation. If both are from the same country, only one of the two can be entered with this wild card.

Complete details are on the IAAF website at:

http://www.iaaf.org/news/iaaf-news/world-championships-qualification-system-2015

Most World Champs Appearances

Men

11 Jesús Ángel García ESP 1993-2011
10 Virgilijus Alekna LTU 1995-2013

Women

11 Susana Feitor POR 1991-2011
10 Franka Dietzsch GER 1991-2009
9 five women

Oldest Competitor

47y 108d Merlene Ottey SLO 100m (1st round) 2007

WORLD YOUTH CHAMPIONSHIPS

The 9th IAAF World Youth (U18) Championships will be in Calí, Colombia on 15-19 July 2015.

Previous Championships

Year	*Venue*	*Athletes*	*Nations*
1999	Bydgoszcz, POL	1055	131
2001	Edmonton, CAN	1262	159
2003	Sherbrooke, CAN	1013	153
2005	Marrakech, MAR	1250	177
2007	Ostrava, CZE	1217	150
2009	Bressanone, ITA	1284	167
2011	Villeneuve d'Ascq FRA	1322	166
2013	Donetsk, UKR	1408	153

World U18 Championship Records

Men			
100m	10.31	Darrel Brown TTO	2001
200m	20.40	Usain Bolt JAM	2003
400m	45.24	Kirani James GRN	2009
800m	1:44.08	Leonard Kosencha KEN	2011
1500m	3:36.77	Robert Biwott KEN	2013
3000m	7:40.10	William Sitonik KEN	2011
2000mSt	5:19.99	Meresa Kassaye ETH	2013
110mh *	13.13	Jaheel Hyde JAM	2013
400mh *	49.01	William Wynne USA	2007
HJ	2.27	Huang Haiqiang CHN	2005
PV	5.26	Nico Weiler GER	2007
LJ	7.95/7.97w	Chris Noffke AUS	2005
TJ	16.63	Héctor Fuentes CUB	2005
	16.63	Lázaro Martínez CUB	2013
SP 5kg	24.35	Jacko Gill NZL	2011
DT 1.5kg	70.67q	Mykyta Nesterenko UKR	2007
HT 5kg	82.30	Bence Pásztor HUN	2011
JT 700g	82.96	Reinhardt van Zyl RSA	2011
Octathlon	6491	Jake Stein AUS	2011
MedleyR	1:49.23	Jamaica	2013
10000mW	40:51.31	Pavel Parshin RUS	2011
Women			
100m	11.31	Jessica Onyepunuka USA	2003
200m	22.92	Irène Ekelund SWE	2013
400m	51.19	Nawal Al-Jack SUD	2005
800m	2:01.13	Anita Henriksdóttir ISL	2013
1500m	4:09.48	Faith Kipyegon KEN	2011
3000m	8:53.94	Mercy Cherono KEN	2007
2000mSt	6:11.83	Korahubish Itaa ETH	2009
100mh *	12.94	Yanique Thompson JAM	2013
400mh	55.96	Ebony Collins USA	2005
HJ	1.92	Irina Kovalenko UKR	2003
PV	4.35	Vicky Parnov AUS	2007
LJ	6.47	Darya Klishina RUS	2007
TJ	13.86	Cristine Spîtaru ROU	2003
SP 3kg	20.09	Emel Dereli TUR	2013
DT	54.93	Ma Xuejun CHN	2001
HT 3kg	73.20	Réke Gyurátz HUN	2013
JT	59.74	Christin Hussong GER	2011
Hep	5875	Tatyana Chernova RUS	2005
4x100m	44.30	Jamaica	1999
MedleyR	2:03.42	Jamaica	2011
5000mW	20:13.91	Olga Shargina RUS	20137

* 110mh 91.4cm, 400mh 84cm, W 100mh 84cm

Mark	Wind	Name		Nat	Born	Pos	Meet	Venue	Date

YOUTH (U18) ALL-TIME LISTS – MEN

100 METRES

10.19	0.5	Yoshihide	Kiryu	JPN	3 Nov 12
10.20	1.4	Darryl	Haraway	USA	14 Jun 14
10.23	0.8	Atorudibo	Tamunosiki	NGR	23 Mar 02
10.23	1.2	Parson	Rynell	USA	21 Jun 01
10.24	0.0	Darrell	Brown	TTO	14 Apr 01
Wind assisted					
10.08	2.2	Prezel	Hardy	USA	6 Jun 09
10.12	5.0	Ivory	Williams	USA	11 May 02
10.13	3.4	Jack	Hale	AUS	6 Dec 14
10.17	3.8	Quincy	Watts	USA	30 May 87

200 METRES

20.10	0.0	Usain	Bolt	JAM	20 Jul 03
20.37	1.6	DaBryan	Blanton	USA	12 May 01
20.37	1.9	Thomas	Somers	GBR	24 Jul 14
20.39	-1.4	Clinton	Davis	USA	1 Aug 82
20.41		Darrel	Brown	TTO	16 May 01
20.28*	wa	Roy	Martin	USA	6 May 83

400 METRES

45.14	Obea	Moore	USA	2 Sep 95
45.15A	Riaan	Dempers	RSA	6 May 94
45.17	William	Reed	USA	20 Jun 87
45.22	Nagmeldin	El Abubakr	SUD	13 Oct 03
45.24	Kirani	James	GRN	10 Jul 09

800 METRES

1:43.37	Mohammed	Aman	ETH	10 Sep 11
1:44.08	Leonard	Kosencha	KEN	9 Jul 11
1:44.98	Timothy	Kitum	KEN	9 Jul 11
1:45.78	Abubaker	Kaki	SUD	10 Jun 06
1:46.25	Benson	Esho	KEN	21 Jul 04

1500 METRES

3:33.72	Nicholas	Kemboi	KEN	18 Aug 06
3:35.16	Cornelius	Chirchir	KEN	3 Sep 00
3:35.53	Abdelaati	Iguider	MAR	15 Jul 04
3:35.54A	Geoffrey	Barusei	KEN	13 May 11
3:35.55	Isaac	Songok	KEN	26 Aug 01
3:35.80	Benson	Esho	KEN	1 Jul 04

3000 METRES

7:32.37	Abreham	Cherkos	ETH	11 Jul 06
7:35.66	Albert	Rop	KEN	10 Sep 11
7:36.28	Yomif	Kejelcha	ETH	17 Jun 14
7:36.82	Augustine	Choge	KEN	5 Sep 04
7:39.22	Hillary	Chenonge	KEN	30 Aug 02

5000 METRES

12:54.19	Abreham	Cherkos	ETH	14 Jul 06
12:57.01	Augustine	Choge	KEN	12 Sep 04
13:06.47	Hillary	Chenonge	KEN	16 Aug 02
13:15.67	Ismael	Kirui	KEN	10 Jul 92

2000 METRES STEEPLECHASE

5:19.99	Meresa	Kassaye	ETH	12 Jul 13
5:20.92	Nicholas	Bett	KEN	12 Jul 13
5:21.36	Nabil	Ouhadi	MAR	16 Jul 06
5:24.69	Abel	Kiprop	KEN	15 Jul 05
5:24.87	Bisluke	Kiplagat Kipkorir	KEN	15 Jul 05

110 METRES HURDLES (91.4m)

12.96	1.3	Jaheel	Hyde	JAM	23 Aug 14
13.12	0.8	Wilhem	Belocian	FRA	21 Jul 12
13.18	0.2	Wayne	Davis	USA	12 Jul 07
13.22	0.0	Konstadínos	Douvalídis	GRE	2 Oct 04
13.25	-0.4		Chu Pengfei	CHN	17 Jul 10

400 METRES HURDLES

48.89	Louis	van Zyl	RSA	19 Jul 02
49.29	Jaheel	Hyde	JAM	25 Jul 14
With 84cm hurdles				
49.01	William	Wynne	USA	15 Jul 07
49.86	Marthinus	Kritzinger	RSA	18 Jul 99
49.91	Jason	Richardson	USA	12 Jul 03

HIGH JUMP

2.33	Javier	Sotomayor	CUB	19 May 84
2.29	Tim	Forsyth	AUS	12 Aug 90
2.28	Dothel	Edwards	USA	9 Jul 83
2.28	Oleksandr	Nartov	UKR	28 May 05
2.28	James	White	USA	21 Apr 09

POLE VAULT

5.51	Germán	Chiaraviglio	ARG	1 May 04
5.50	István	Bagyula	HUN	19 Jun 86
5.45	Grigoriy	Yegorov	KAZ	26 May 84
5.45		Yang Yansheng	CHN	18 Oct 05
5.43	Daniel	Clemens	GER	7 Aug 09

LONG JUMP

8.25	1.9	Luis Alberto	Bueno	CUB	28 Sep 86
8.17	0.5		Zhang Xiaoyi	CHN	23 Apr 06
8.05	1.7	Kareem	Streete-Thompson	CAY	20 Jul 90
8.03	2.0		Wang Cheng	CHN	22 Oct 87
8.02			Cai Peng	CHN	24 May 99

TRIPLE JUMP

17.24	0.7	Lázaro	Martínez	CUB	1 Feb 14
16.89			Gu Junjie	CHN	24 Aug 00
16.68	1.2	Yoelbi	Quesada	CUB	7 Jul 90
16.63	1.4	Héctor	Fuentes	CUB	16 Jul 05
16.56	0.0	Ernesto	Revé	CUB	30 May 09

SHOT 5kg

24.45	Jacko	Gill	NZL	12 Dec 11
24.24i	Konrad	Bukowiecki	POL	30 Dec 14
	23.17			24 Aug 14
23.23	Krzysztof	Brzozowski	POL	23 Aug 10
22.79	Marin	Premeru	CRO	13 Oct 07
22.44	Mykyta	Nesterenko	UKR	20 May 08

DISCUS 1.5kg

77.50	Mykyta	Nesterenko	UKR	19 May 08
69.50	Margus	Hunt	EST	30 Jul 04
68.48	Attila	Horváth	HUN	11 Oct 84
68.44	Werner	Reiterer	AUS	2 Nov 85
68.20	Marin	Premeru	CRO	26 Jul 07

HAMMER 5kg

87.16	Bence	Halász	HUN	31 May 14
85.38	Joaquin	Gómez	ARG	30 Nov 13
85.26	Ashraf Amjad	El-Seify	QAT	20 Jul 11
84.41	Bence	Pásztor	HUN	28 Jul 11
83.28	József	Horváth	HUN	10 May 01

JAVELIN 700g

89.34	Braian	Toledo	ARG	6 Mar 10
83.42	Yuriy	Kushniruk	UKR	29 Jul 11
83.16	Morné	Moolman	RSA	9 Jul 11
83.02	Valeriy	Iordan	RUS	17 May 09
82.96	Reinhard	van Zyl	RSA	10 Jul 11

OCTATHLON

6491	Jake	Stein	AUS	9 Jul 11
6482	Yordani	García	CUB	14 Jul 05
6478	Kevin	Meyer	FRA	9 Jul 09
6456	Andrés	Silva	URU	11 Jul 03
6451	José Ángel	Mendieta	CUB	2 Jul 08
6451	Karsten	Warholm	NOR	11 Jul 13

10,000 METRES TRACK WALK

39:47.20		Chen Ding	CHN	11 Jul 08
40:08.23	Jefferson	Pérez	ECU	10 Aug 90
40:15.1	Maris	Putenis	LAT	8 May 99
40:27.95	Eider	Arévalo	COL	10 Oct 10
40:34.2	Vladimir	Kanaykin	RUS	25 May 02

Mark Wind Name Nat Born Pos Meet Venue Date

WOMEN

100 METRES

Mark	Wind	Name		Nat	Date
11.10	0.9	Kaylin	Whitney	USA	5 Jul 14
11.13	2.0	Chandra	Cheeseborough	USA	21 Jun 76
11.14	1.7	Marion	Jones	USA	6 Jun 92
		11.12w	4.1		31 May 91
11.14	-0.5	Angela	Williams	USA	21 Jun 97
		10.98w	3.8		24 May 97
11.16	1.2	Gabby	Mayo	USA	22 Jun 06

200 METRES

Mark	Wind	Name		Nat	Date
22.49	1.3	Kaylin	Whitney	USA	6 Jul 14
22.58	0.8	Marion	Jones	USA	28 Jun 92
22.74A	2.0	Raelene	Boyle	AUS	18 Oct 68
22.77A	0.0	Chandra	Cheeseborough	USA	16 Oct 75
		22.64w	2.3		24 Jun 76
22.79	2.0	Jodie	Williams	GBR	23 May 10

400 METRES

Mark	Name		Nat	Date
50.01		Li Jing	CHN	18 Oct 97
50.48	Grit	Breuer	GER	22 Jul 89
50.69	Sanya	Richards	USA	22 Jun 02
50.74	Monique	Henderson	USA	3 Jun 00
50.84	Christina	Brehmer	GDR	21 Jun 75

800 METRES

Mark	Name		Nat	Date
1:57.18		Wang Yuan	CHN	8 Sep 93
1:58.16		Lin Na	CHN	22 Oct 97
1:59.51	Mary	Cain	USA	1 Jun 13
1:59.65	Marion	Hübner	GDR	11 Aug 79
1:59.75	Charlotte	Moore	GBR	29 Jul 02

1500 METRES

Mark	Name		Nat	Date
3:54.52		Zhang Ling	CHN	18 Oct 97
3:59.81		Wang Yuan	CHN	11 Sep 93
4:02.83	Gudaf	Tsegay	ETH	21 May 14
4:03.96	Meskerem	Legesse	ETH	24 May 03
4:04.62	Mary	Cain	USA	17 May 13

3000 METRES

Mark	Name		Nat	Date
8:36.45		Ma Ningning	CHN	6 Jun 93
8:39.00	Zola	Budd	RSA	2 Apr 83
8:41.86	Tirunesh	Dibaba	ETH	30 Aug 02
8:44.53	Sally	Barsosio	KEN	16 Aug 95
8:44.54	Purity	Rionoripo	KEN	29 Aug 10

2000 METRES STEEPLECHASE

Mark	Name		Nat	Date
6:11.83	Korahubish	Itaa	KEN	10 Jul 09
6:11.90	Lucia	Muangi	KEN	10 Jul 09
6:12.0A	Roseline	Chepngetich	KEN	11 Jun 13
6:15.12	Daisy	Jepkemei	KEN	14 Jul 13
6:16.41	Norah	Tanui	KEN	10 Jul 11

100 METRES HURDLES

Mark	Wind	Name		Nat	Date
12.95	1.5	Candy	Young	USA	16 Jun 79
13.14	-0.7	Aliuska	López	CUB	18 Jul 86
With 76.2cm hurdles					
12.94	0.0	Yanique	Thompson	JAM	11 Jul 03
13.01	0.0	Dior	Hall	USA	11 Jul 03
13.08	-0.4	Adrianna	Lamalle	FRA	7 Jul 11
13.11	-0.1	Trinity	Wilson	USA	7 Jul 11
13.14	0.5	Sally	Pearson	AUS	11 Jul 03

400 METRES HURDLES

Mark	Name		Nat	Date
55.20	Lesley	Maxie	USA	9 Jun 84
55.30		Li Rui		26 Oct 95
55.43		Li Shuju	CHN	21 Oct 97
55.63	Sydney	McLaughlin	USA	6 Jul 14
55.96	Ebony	Collins	USA	15 Jul 05

HIGH JUMP

Mark	Name		Nat	Date
1.96A	Charmaine	Gale	RSA	4 Apr 81
1.96	Olga	Turchak	UKR	7 Sep 84
1.96	Eleanor	Patterson	AUS	7 Dec 13
1.94	Yelena	Topchina	RUS	28 Aug 83
1.94	Morgan	Lake	GBR	22 Jul 14

POLE VAULT

Mark	Name		Nat	Date
4.47	Angelica	Bengtsson	SWE	22 May 10
4.40	Valeriya	Volik	RUS	8 Jul 06
4.40		Zhang Yingning	CHN	5 May 07
4.40	Vicky	Parnov	AUS	30 Jun 07
4.40	Liz	Parnov	AUS	17 Apr 10
4.40A	Robeilys	Peinado	VEN	25 Aug 13
4.40	Nina	Kennedy	AUS	24 Jul 14

LONG JUMP

Mark	Wind	Name		Nat	Date
6.91	1.0	Heike	Daute	GDR	9 Aug 81
		7.02w	4.0		20 Aug 81
6.82		Natalya	Shevchenko	RUS	17 Jul 83
6.74	1.0		Lu Minjia	CHN	23 Oct 09
6.64	1.3	Anu	Kaljurand	EST	30 May 86
6.63	0.7	Helga	Radtke	GDR	11 Aug 79
6.63	0.5	Oluyinka	Idowu	GBR	21 May 89

TRIPLE JUMP

Mark	Wind	Name		Nat	Date
14.57	0.2		Huang Qiyuan	CHN	19 Oct 97
14.29	1.4		Ren Ruiping	CHN	13 Sep 93
14.25	0.5	Dailenys	Alcántara	CUB	10 Jul 08
14.07	1.4		Yu Shaohua	CHN	14 May 02
14.02	1.4		Li Jiahui	CHN	22 Sep 96
14.02	-1.3	Mabel	Gay	CUB	29 Jul 00

SHOT 4kg

Mark	Name		Nat	Date
19.08	Ilke	Wyludda	GDR	9 Aug 86
18.84	Simone	Michel	GDR	10 Aug 77
18.70		Liu Yingfan	CHN	26 Sep 04
18.63		Wang Yawen	CHN	8 Aug 90
18.58	Heike	Rohrmann	GDR	10 Jul 86
3kg				
20.14	Emel	Dereli	TUR	11 Jul 13
19.60	Alyona	Bugakova	RUS	4 Jul 14

DISCUS

Mark	Name		Nat	Date
65.86	Ilke	Wyludda	GDR	1 Aug 86
63.68	Astrid	Kumbernuss	GDR	28 Jul 87
62.42	Irina	Meszynski	GDR	23 Jun 79
61.96	Larisa	Platonova	UKR	8 Jun 83
60.32		Liu Fengying	CHN	22 Sep 96

HAMMER 3kg

Mark	Name		Nat	Date
76.04	Réka	Gyurátz	HUN	23 Jun 13
74.38	Helga	Völgyi	HUN	23 Jun 13
73.97	Zsófia	Bácskay	HUN	1 Mar 14
71.14	Alex	Hulley	AUS	6 Dec 14
4kg				
70.60		Zhang Wenxiu	CHN	5 Apr 03

JAVELIN 600g

Mark	Name		Nat	Date
62.93		Xue Juan	CHN	27 Oct 03
60.90		Liang Lili	CHN	18 Jun 99
60.14	Vivian	Zimmer	GER	31 Jul 04
59.89		Song Dan	CHN	2 Nov 07
59.74	Christin	Hussong	GER	7 Jul 11

HEPTATHLON

Mark	Name		Nat	Date
6185		Shen Shengfei	CHN	18 Oct 97
6179	Valentina	Savchenko	UKR	5 Aug 84
6148	Morgan	Lake	GBR	23 Jul 14
6081	Beatrice	Mau	GDR	12 Jun 88
6046	Sibylle	Thiele	GDR	20 Jun 82

all above better than ant marks with lower hurdles (76.2cm) now used for U18 heptathlon

5000 METRES TRACK WALK

Mark	Name		Nat	Date
21:11.01	Sabine	Zimmer	GER	12 Jun 98
21:13.16		Cui Yingxi	CHN	30 Oct 88
21:15.9	Oksana	Kirillova	RUS	19 Jun 05
21:20.0		Zhou Tongjie	CHN	16 Oct 06
21:21.14	Irina	Yumanova	RUS	12 Jul 07

OBITUARY 2014

See ATHLETICS 2014 for obituaries from early 2014: Adedoyin ADEGBOYEGA, Ranjit BHATIA, Georges BREITMAN, Christopher CHATAWAY, Jirí DADAK, Jaroslav HALVA, Jerzy HAUSLEBER, Erling HELLE, Rolf HESSELVALL, Andrew HOLDEN, Michal JOACHIMOWSKI, Paavo KOTILA, Pierre LACAZE, Pamela LISORENG, Amadou MEITÉ, Dave POWER, Peter WILKINSON and Bill WOODHOUSE.

Aimo AHO (Finland) (b. 31 May 1951 Reisjärvi) on 10 July in Haapajärvi. A most consistent javelin thrower, he exceeded 80m 14 years in a row (1972-85), all with the old model, with a pb 89.42 in 1977. Finnish champion in 1975 with six silvers and two bronzes, he had 20 international matches 1973-83, winning against Sweden in 1976. 9th Europeans 1974, 10th Olympics 1980, 10th Worlds 1983.

Henry Kiyoyasu **AIHARA** (USA) (b. 7 Apr 1926 Garden Grove, California of Japanese parents) on 14 September in Garden Grove. He won the NCAA long jump for the University of Illinois in 1945 and after army service was 3rd in 1949 and 2nd in 1950 for the University of Southern California. At AAU Championships he was 4th at triple jump in 1945 and 1949 and at long jump 4th in 1945 and 3rd in 1949. He competed for the USA against Scandinavia in 1949. Pbs: LJ 7.54/7.66w (1950), TJ 14.12 (1949).

Colin ANDERSON (USA) (b. 20 Nov 1951) on 10 November. He was a member of the non-competing 1980 US Olympic team with 3rd in the Olympic Trials, having won the 1979 AAU indoor shot and placing 2nd in the 1980 AAU with his pb 21.08. He was a teacher in Minnesota for 33 years. His wife Lynne (née Winbigler), was AAU discus champion in 1976, 1978 & 1979 and also on the non-competing 1980 Olympic team. Their son, Thomas, is a promising shot putter (18.45i in 2014).

Fatima AOUAM (Morocco) (b. 16 Dec 1959) on 27 December in Casablanca. She was African champion at 3000m in 1988 (2nd 1500m), having been 2nd at 1500m and 4th at 800m in 1984, and 2nd at 1500m and 3rd at 800m in 1985. She also competed at the 1988 Olympic Games, 10th 1500m and heats 3000m. She set an African record of 4:05.49 for 1500m in 1986, Moroccan records for 800m 2:00.17 (1986) and 3000m 8:57.48 (1989) and ran a world best of 9:38.44 for 2 miles at Padua on 13 Sep 1987.

Jim BANICH (USA) (b. 12 Sep 1963) on 12 September in Arvada, Colorado. He was 2nd in the NCAA shot for UCLA in 1987. Pbs: His best marks SP 19.91 (1988), DT 60.92 (1986).

Jean Ruth **BARNETT** (née **WALRAVEN)** (USA) (b. 26 Sep 1926 Cleveland) on 17 December. She competed at 80m hurdles and long jump at the 1948 Olympic Games, having best championships placings of second equal in the AAU high jump and second indoor in 1946.

Frantisek BARTOS (Czech Republic) (b. 1 Jan 1947 Lanzhot) on 21 March. At the European Championships he was 12th in 1974 and 7th in 1978 at 3000m steeplechase and he was Czechoslovak champion at 3000m steeplechase in 1975 and 1977-8 and at 10,000m in 1979. Pbs: 5000m 13:35.0 (1978), 10,000m 28:53.5 (1978), 3000mSt 8:30.8 (1976); 14 internationals 1970-81.

Dr. **John** Lavers **BARTRAM** (Australia) (b. 3 Jun 1925 Mount Barker, South Australia) on 20 November. He competed at the 1948 Olympics, when a semi-finalist at 100m, quarter-finalist at 400m and also running in the heats of the 4x100m. He was Australian champion at 220y in 1947 and 1951 and at 440y in 1947 and 1948. Pbs: 100y 9.6 (1947), 100m 10.6 (1948), 220y 21.1 (1949), 440y 48.4 (1948).

Eckart BERKES (Germany) (b. 9 Feb 1949 Worms) on 24 September in Leimen-St. Illgen. European Indoor champion at 60m hurdles in 1971, at 110mh he competed at the 1972 Olympics (heat) and was FRG champion in 1973 (2nd 1972). Pbs: 100m 10.6 (1969), 50mh 6.7i (1969), 60mh 7.6i (1971), 110mh 13.8 (1970), PV 4.51 (1978).

Francis Joseph '**Frank**' **BUDD** (USA) (b. 20 Jul 1939 Long Branch, New Jersey) on 29 April in Marlton, New Jersey. He was 5th at 100m in the Olympic 100m in 1960 (and ran the first leg on the US 4x100m team that was disqualified after finishing first) and in 1961 was the world number one. After twice tying the mark at 9.3, he broke the world record for 100y as he won the AAU title in 9.2 in New York on June 24. He also ranked joint first on the world list for 100m with 10.2 and for 200m with 20.7 plus second to Bob Hayes for 220y straight at 20.2, and he ran the second leg on the US team that took 0.4 off the world 4x100m record with 39.1 in the USA v USSR match in Moscow. He also won the AAU indoor 60y and the NCAA 100y in both 1961 and 1962 and the NCAA 220y in 1961. In 1962 he twice tied the world record for 60y indoors with 6.0 (6.12 with auto timing) and outdoors tied the world record for 220y straight with 20.0 on May 12 at Villanova, where he went to university, graduating in economics. He then had a brief career as a wide receiver for Philadelphia Eagles and Washington Redskins in the NFL and for Calgary Stampeders in the CFL.

Hermann BUHL (GDR/Germany) (b. 31 Oct 1935 Hainsberg) on 22 March in Reith bei Seefeld. He ranked in the world top five at 3000m steeplechase each year 1958-62 and had a best of 8:34.0 in 1966, his fourth GDR record from 8:51.2 (1958). He was 11th in 1958 and 4th in 1962 at the Europeans and went out in his heat at the 1960 Olympics. GDR champion 1958-9 and 1961-2. Other pbs: 800m 1:54.7 (1959), 1000m 2:25.2 (1959), 1500m 3:44.2 (1960), 2000m 5:17.6 (1962), 3000m 7:56.4 (1961), 5000m 13:50.6 (1962), 10000m 30:12.8 (1960); 13 internationals 1958-64. He became a doctor.

Annual progression at 3000mSt: 1955- 9:42.3, 1956- 9:29.4, 1957- 9:07.6, 1958- 8:37.6, 1959- 8:42.6, 1960- 8:34.0, 1961- 8:34.9, 1962- 8:35.4, 1963- 8:37.6, 1964- 8:53.0, 1965- 8:48.8.

Arthur Ernest **'Ernie' BULLARD** (USA) (b. 30 Jul 1977 Safford, Arizona) on 21 August in Stockton, California. He was 5th equal in the NCAA pole vault for Arizona State in 1958; pb 4.38 (1959). He was head coach at San Jose State 1971-84 and at USC 1985-90.

Ulla Kristina **BUUTS** (Sweden) (née ÖBERG) (b. 14 Dec 1942 Eskilstuna) on 22 November. At discus she was Swedish champion 1971-5, represented Sweden on 20 occasions and had pb 52.20 (1974).

Dave CAREY (b. 2 Oct 1939 Glen Ridge, New Jersey) on 1 October in Naperville, Illinois. A long-time member of the ATFS, he co-authored the "Progression of American National Records (1999). A graduate of MIT, he received a PhD from the University of Michigan and worked as a physicist.

Benedict "Rolls Royce" **CAYENNE** (Trinidad & Tobago) (b. 22 Mar 1944 Barrackpore) on 1 November in Philadelphia. He set a national record 1:46.83 in his 800m semi final at the 1968 Olympic Games, but, having needed oxygen after both heat and semi-final, his 51.3 first lap behind Kiplagat`s 51.0 proved too much for him in the thin Mexico City air and he finished 8th and last in the final 1:54.40. In 1966 he was 3rd at 800m and 2nd at 4x400m at the CAC Games. At the Commonwealth Games he was a semi-finalist at 880y in 1966 and won silver at 800m and 4x400m in 1970. At Pan American Games he was a 400m semi-finalist in 1967 and 7th at 800m in 1971. He had been a policeman in Trinidad before enrolling at Maryland University, and was later head coach at Swarthmore College, then a tax preparer in Philadelphia. Pbs: 400m 46.3 (1967), 800m 1:46.83 (1968), 1500m 3:53.2 (1970).

Peter Ronald **CLARK** (GBR) (b.29 Nov 1933) on 11 June in Tooting, London. He made four international appearances for Britain in 1958-9 and was 4th in the European Champs 5000m and 5th in the Commonwealth Games 3 miles in 1958. He ran the second leg (4:06.6) for the England team that set a world record for 4 x 1 mile of 16:30.6 at the White City, London on 27 Sep 1958. Pbs: 800m 1:52.7 (1957), 1000m 2:24.3 (1957), 1500m 3:51.1 (1960), 1M 4:01.7 (1958), 3000m 8:14.2 (1959), 2M 8:37.6 (1958), 3M 13:25.0 (1958), 5000m 13:53.8 (1958). 3rd AAA 3M 1958, Thames Valley Harriers.

Alice COACHMAN (later DAVIS) (USA) (b. 9 Nov 1923 Albany, Georgia) on 14 July in Albany. In 1948 she became the first black female to win an Olympic gold medal at any sport. She won the high jump with an American record 1.68m and then retired to be a teacher. Although her career was restricted by WW II she won a record ten consecutive US high jump titles 1939-48 – and five at 50m 1943-7 and three at 100m 1942, 1945-6. She was high jump indoors in 1941 and 1945-6 and at 50m in 1945-6. Pbs: 50m 6.4 (1944, US record), 100m 12.0 (1945).

Annual progression at HJ: 1939- 1.635, 1941- 1.59, 1942- 1.65, 1943- 1.524, 1944- 1.565, 1945- 1.525, 1946- 1.58, 1947- 1.56, 1948- 1.68.

Philip Ransom **'Phil' CONLEY** (USA) (b. 17 Aug 1934 Madera, California) on 12 March in Santa Rosa, California. In 1956 he won the NCAA javelin for Cal Tech and was 10th in the Olympics. He was 2nd at the Pan-American Games in 1959, 2nd at the 1956 US Olympic Trials (and 6th in 1960) and 3rd at the AAUs each year 1958-60 with nine top six places 1956-65. Pb 79.31 (1964); also a successful veteran.

Attila CSENGER (Hungary) (b. 14 Aug 1930 Budapest), in October. Hungarian champion at 110mh (1954) and 200mh (1952), he had 21 internationals 1950-7. Pbs: 100m 10.9 (1950), 200m 22.6 (1951), 400m 50.4 (1952), 110mh 14.8 (1954), 200mh 24.4 (1954), 400mh 54.2 (1951). In 1991-2 he was the ambassador of Hungary in Bonn.

Csaba CSUTORÁS (Hungary) (b. 13 Sep 1937 Budapest) on 25 August in Budapest. He competed at the Olympic Games in 1960 (200 & 400 heats), and 1964 (200, 400, 4x100 heats), and at the Europeans in 1958 (sf 400m), and 1962 (100m hts, 200m sf, 4x100m 6th). World University Games: 1957 (3rd 400m), 1963 (5th 200m, 1st 4x100m), and 1965 (4th 4x100m, 2nd 4x400m). Hungarian champion at 100m 1961-4, 200m 1959-60, 1962 and 1964, 400m 1958-9 and 1962. 32 internationals 1957-65. He set Hungarian records: 100m (5) from 10.4 in 1962 to 10.3 in 1964, 200m (3) from 21.0 in 1960 to 20.7 in 1964, and 400m (2) 46.8 in 1960 and 46.7 in 1962. Pb 400mh 53.2 (1962).

Valentina Spasova **DIMITROVA** (Bulgaria) (b. 4 May 1956 Kostenets) (née Stoimenova) on 2 November in Sofia. She set six Bulgarian records at pentathlon (to 4650 in 1980) and four at heptathlon to 6453 points (current tables) when 2nd at Götzis in 1983. At pentathlon she was World University Games champion in 1977 and 7th at the 1980 Olympics, and at heptathlon 6th Europeans 1982 and 5th Worlds 1983. She was married to leading coach Georgi Dimitrov and ended her career in 1984 after a serious injury. She had two sons and continued as a coach. Other pbs: 200m 24.59 (1983), 800m 2:08.10 (1983), 100mh 14.02 (1977), HJ 1.88 (1983), LJ 6.30 (1982), SP 16.45 (1983), JT 44.60 (1983).

Kenneth Leslie **DOUBLEDAY** (Australia) (b. 14 Feb 1926) on 8 June in Geelong. He competed at the Olympic Games in 1952: 5th 110mh, quarter-finals 400mh and heats of both relays, and 1956 heats 110mh. At the Commonwealth Games he was a semi-finalist at 440y hurdles in 1950 and did not finish in the 120yh final in 1954. He won Australian titles at 120yh 1954-6, 220yh 1953-4, 440yh 1951 and 1953, and triple jump 1947. Pbs: 120yh 14.2 (1954), 220yh(t) 23.6 (1952), 440yh 54.8 (1950), TJ 14.58 (1947).

Frank EISENBERG (GDR/Germany) (b. 7 Dec 1943 Solmsdorf) on 12 August in Dresden. At 5000m he was 9th at the 1971 Europeans and 1972 Olympics and was GDR champion in 1972. Pbs: 800m 1:52.1 (1971), 1000m 2:23.7 (1972), 1500m 3:39.9 (1971), 3000m 7:55.8 (1971), 5000m 13:29.0 (GDR record 1972), 10000m 29:13.2 (1969), 3000mSt 9:04.0 (1970); 6 internationals 1969-72.

His twin brother Gerd had bests of 1500m 3:40.3 (1971), 5000m 13:32.4 (1972) and 10000m 28:26.78 (1970).

Pertti ERÄKARE (up to 1954 NIEMINEN) (Finland) (b. 24 Jan 1930 Helsinki) on 8 October in Espoo. Chairman of the Finnish Athletics Federation (SUL) in 1981-2 and a bank manager, he had been a top class youth runner with national 800m silver (1955) and bronze (1956), and two 4x800 relay golds on HKV (Helsingin Kisa-Veikot) teams. His pbs of 1:51.2 and 3:46.6 (1500 m) were not good enough for national teams, but he excelled as a hare with excellent pace judgment.

John FAIRGRIEVE (Great Britain) (b. 18 Apr 1926) on 19 July in Slad, Gloucestershire. He competed for Britain at 200m (qf) at the 1948 Olympic Games after 2nd in the AAA 220y in 1947 and 1948. Pbs 100m 10.8 (1947), 200m 21.6 (1947). He also had trials for England and Scotland at rugby union. He studied medicine at Cambridge University and Middlesex Hospital and became a consultant and specialist in vascular surgery, pioneering new techniques. He was also a talented artist.

Jacquilyn Louise **'Jackie' FAIRWEATHER** (Australia) (b. 10 Nov 1967) (née Gallagher) on 1/2 November. Having been a top runner as a junior, and running in the World Cross in 1993, she was joint Australian sportswoman of the year in 1996 when she uniquely won world titles at both triathlon and duathlon, winning a further world duathlon title in 1999 and triathlon silver medals in 1995, 1997 and 1999, but was devastated to miss selection for the 2000 Olympic Games. She then retired from triathlon and remerged as an athlete, running 2:35:46 on her marathon debut in Boston, followed by the Commonwealth Games bronze later that year. She ran her marathon best of 2:32:40 for 9th in Nagoya in 2004 and was Australian champion in 2005. Other pbs: 1500m 4:26.42, 3000m 9:18.8 (1993), 5000m 16:19.43 (2004), 10,000m 33:14.16 (1992), HMar 74:38 (1992). Turning to ultra-running she won Australian titles and set a 100km pb of 7:41:23 in winning the Commonwealth title in 2009, also working as a coach, performance manager and commentator. She graduated from the University of Queensland and took a Masters degree at Eastern Illinois University, USA. She married Simon Fairweather, who won the individual gold medal for archery at the 2000 Olympic Games, in 2004.

Hélène FIZE (Mme. Devèze 1941) (France) (b. 15 Jan 1914 Nîmes) on 1 June at Roquevaire near Marseille. She was French champion at 800m 1938-9 and 1941 and cross-country 1939 and 1945 and set a French record of 2:21.2 for 800m in 1938, improving to 2:19.0 in 1941 (world best for the year). She ran the anchor leg on the French team that set a world record of 7:22.6 for 3x800m at Monaco in 1939.

Erich FUCHS (Germany) (b. 27 Jun 1925 Mühlheim an der Eis) on 26 July in Kaiserslautern. He had 7 internationals 1952-6 and in 1952 was second in the FRG 100m, ran at the Olympics (heats) and set his pb of 10.6, pb 200m 22.2 (1954). He was national coach of the German women's sprint relay team 1960-8 and was a professor at the Pedagogical University in Kaiserslautern.

Luigi GNOCCHI (Italy) (b. 14 Jan 1933 Gallarate, Varese) on 18 October. He tied the Italian record for 100m with 10.4 in 1956, and that year ran on the Italian 4x100m team that was 4th at the Olympic Games (also heat 100m). In 1954 he was 5th at 4x100m at the Europeans and in 1955 won a Mediterranean Games triple (100m/200m/4x100m). Italian 100m champion 1954-6, he had 11 internationals 1953-6.

Penelope **'Penny' GRAY** (Australia) (later Dunbabin) (b. 12 Oct 1958 Launceston, Tasmania) on 21 May. Australian champion at 800m in 1977 and 1500m in 1979, she had pbs of

800m 2:03.93 and 1500m 4:17.09 (both 1979), She was selected at 1500m for the Olympics in 1980, but was unable to go. However, she went to the 1984 Games, playing for Australia at hockey

Frank E. **GREENBERG** (USA) on 29 June in Palm Harbor, Florida. A Philadelphia lawyer, he was a past president of the Athletics Congress and USATF 1988-92, a member of the U.S. Olympic International Competition Committee, and vice chair of the International Doping Commission for the IAAF.

Lars-Erik Börje **GUSTAFSSON** (Sweden) (b. 17 Aug 1938 Visby) on 26 December. He was 8th at 3000m steeplechase at the 1964 Olympic Games, when his 8:34.2 in a heat was a national record and remained his pb. He represented Sweden on 11 further occasions and was Swedish 4km cross country champion in 1961 and at steeplechase in 1962. Other pbs: 800m 1:52.5 (1959), 1500m 3:47.3 (1961), 3000m 8:15.2 (1964), 5000m 14:19.4 (1961), 10000m 30:37.8 (1970).

Alex GUYODO (France) (b. 19 Jun 1922 Mesquer) on 7 April at Saint-Nazaire. At 3000m steeplechase he was 4th at the 1948 Olympics, 5th at the 1950 Europeans and French champion 1949-50. 15 internationals 1946-51. Pbs: 1500m 3:57.6 (1954), 5000m 15:07.0 (1952), 3000mSt 9:11.6 (1948).

Ernst **Göte HAGSTRÖM** (Sweden) (b. 7 Sep 1918 Gagnef) on 5 October in Kvarnsveden. A member of Kvarnsveden GoIF, Borlänge, he won the bronze medal at 3000m steeplechase at the 1948 Olympic Games, completing a clean sweep of the medals for Sweden. He was 2nd in the Swedish Championships that year, after 3rd in 1944-5 and 1947 and second fastest in the world in 1948 with his pb 9:01.0 behind Thore Sjöstrand 8:59.8 in the match against Finland. Other pbs: 1500m 3:54.0 (1948), 2000m 5:23.2 (1940), 3000m 8:27.2 (1942), 5000m 14:36.8 (1942).

Kalle HAKKARAINEN (Finland) (b. 8 Dec 1940 Rautalampi) on 19 May in Suolahti. His 21 marathons 1968-76 included Kosice 2nd 1971 and 3rd 1972, Boston 5th 1970, Karl-Marx-Stadt 3rd 1971 with a pb 2:18:01.2. That year he ran five hard marathons, finishing 9th in the Europeans. He won Nordic silvers in 1969 and 1970 and the Finnish title in 1970 (silver 1971 and two bronzes). Pbs: 10,000m 29:58.4, 25,000m 1:18:38.0. In 1991 aged 50 he ran the marathon in 2:38:16.

Jaroslav HALVA (Slovakia) (b. 20 May 1942 Modry Kamen) on 11 March. He was the first Czechoslovak thrower to exceed 80m with the old specification, with 80.06 in 1970, and national champion 1973; 13 internationals 1970-6. Later he was a successful coach.

Peter HENDERSON (New Zealand) (b. 18 Apr 1926 Gisborne) on 24 November. He was the NZ 100y champion in 1949 and in 1950 was 5th at 100y (pb 9.9 in heat) and bronze medallist at 4x110y at the Empire Games. He played seven times for the All Blacks at rugby union in 1949-50, top scoring with seven tries on their tour of South Africa in 1949 and also playing the last three test matches against the touring British Lions team in 1950. He then turned to rugby league in England, playing for Huddersfield for seven years, scoring 214 tries in 258 appearances.

Xavier HÖGER (Germany) (b. 7 Mar 1930 Grönenbach) on 7 April in Bad Grönenbach. At 10,000m he was 12th at the 1958 Europeans and 17th at the 1960 Olympics, set a German record with 29:19.0 in 1960 and was FRG champion in 1959 (also at forest running 1956); 20 internationals 1954-60. Other pbs: 1500m 3:58.4 (1960), 3000m 8:13.8 (1959), 5000m 14:02.6 (1960), 6M 28:26.2 (1959), Mar 2:51:19 (1987).

Vic HOLCHAK (USA) (b. 10 Aug 1940 Los Angeles) on 5 September in Hollywood. A well-informed radio commentator and journalist, he trained at London's prestigious RADA and was also a theatre and TV actor (standing 6ft 7in/2.01m tall) who appeared in several popular soap operas.

Roy Anselm **HOLLINGSWORTH** (Trinidad /GBR) (b. 28 Dec 1933) on 14 September in Trinidad. He was 10th at discus for the UK at the 1964 Olympic Games and at the Commonwealth Games was 7th at discus and 14th at shot for England in 1962 and 5th DT and 7th SP for Trinidad & Tobago in 1966. At the discus he set UK records with 56.18 and 56.71 in 1963 and was AAA champion in 1964. He was 2nd at shot and won the discus at the 1966 CAC Games. Pbs: SP 15.71 (1967), HT 37.46 (1976). He became Sports Director at the University of West Indies St. Augustine.

Ivan IVANCIC (Croatia) (b. 6 Dec 1937 Grabovac) on 28 August in Zagreb. At the shot for Yugoslavia he won the Mediterranean Games title in 1975, the Balkan Games in 1970-2 and 1983, was 3rd at the European Indoors in 1980 and 1983 and was 12th at the World Championships in 1983. He also competed at the Olympic Games of 1972 and 1976 and European Champs in 1971. He was Yugoslav champion in 1970-5 and 1977 and set six Yugoslav records from 18.98 (1971) to 19.86 (1976).Pbs: SP 20.77 (1983), DT 54.46 (1981). He became a coach, notably of Sandra Perkovic.

Gerhard JEITNER (Germany) (b. 17 Jul 1923 Troppau – now Opava CZE) on 8 July in Leipzig. He set a GDR pole vault record with 4.57 in 1959, and had a pb of 4.60 (1962). Third GDR Champs 1955, 1958 and 1962.

Bertil Leonard (Johansson) **KÄLLEVÅGH** (Sweden) (b. 19 Jul 1931 Järstad) on 2 October. Swedish champion at 5000m 1959, 4km cross country 1959-60. 22 internationals. Pbs: 1500m 3:50.6 (1957), 2000m 5:09.8 (1955), 3000m 8:09.8 (1957), 2 miles 8:56.6 (1959), 5000m 14:13.6 (1959), 10000m 29:45.6 (1962).

Lars Olov Arnold **KARLBOM** (Sweden) (b. 24 Apr 1928 Västland) on 15 June. He set a Swedish triple jump record of 15.43 in 1958 and had pb LJ 7.07 (1954). 19 internationals.

Mia KJØLBERG (later Høyum) (Norway) (b. 29 Mar 1960) on 6 September. A regular walks international 1973-84, she took part in the first three Eschborn Cups in 1979, 1981 and 1983, was Norwegian champion at 3000mW and 5000mW 1983-4, and had walks pbs of 3000m 13:39.2 (1983), NOR record), 5000m 23:27.7 (1983), 10k 48:30 (1980), 20k 1:45:59 (1980).

Dr **Lore KLUTE** (Germany) (b. 16 Sep 1928 Düsseldorf) on 5 April in Bickenbach. She was 7th in the European shot in 1958 and at World University Games was 3rd SP and 2nd DT in 1951, won both SP and DT 1953, 1st SP and 2nd DT 1955. Second FRG DT 1952, SP 1956. Pbs: SP 14.90 (1958), DT 42.79 (1955).

Yago LAMELA (Spain) (b. 24 Jul 1977 Avilés) was found dead at his parents' home in Avilés on 8 May, having suffered from depression and anxiety attacks for several years. He first exceeded 8m in the long jump with 8.04w in 1996 and improved to 8.14/8.20w in 1998. He then had a sensational year in 1999: after Spanish indoor records at 8.20 and 8.22 he set more records at the World Indoor Champs of 8.29, 8.42 and 8.56 when second to Iván Pedroso 8.62. Outdoors Lamela also jumped 8.56 in June (his fifth Spanish outdoor record of the year), won the European U23 title and was second to Pedroso at the outdoor World Champs 8.40 to 8.56. He won the European indoor silver and outdoor bronze in 2002 (after 8th in 1998) and was back at his best to head the world list with 8.53 in 2003, when he was also 2nd at the Worlds Indoors and 3rd outdoors. He had been 4th at the 1996 World Juniors and at the Olympics was dnq 19th in 2000 and 11th in 2004. Spanish champion 1998-2000 and 2003 and Ibero-American 1998. Other pbs: 100m 10.93 (1999), TJ 16.72 (1998). He did not manage to return to competition after an Achilles operation in 2005.

Annual progression at LJ: 1991- 5.98, 1992- 6.69i/6.62, 1993- 7.16i/6.89/7.09w, 1994- 7.27, 1995- 7.75i/7.66, 1996- 7.80/8.04w, 1997- 7.87/7.90w, 1998- 8.14/8.20w, 1999- 8.56, 2000- 8.22, 2001- 8.07, 2002- 8.21/8.25w, 2003- 8.53, 2004- 8.16

Torrin LAWRENCE (USA) (b. 1 Apr 1989 Jacksonville) was killed on July 29 in Cordele when a truck crashed into his car while he was awaiting assistance for a burst tyre. He made a breakthrough from 46.18i in 2009 to 45.03i in 2010 to win the NCAA indoor 400m title for the University of Georgia and set an outdoor best of 45.32 on 12 July 2014 in Kortrijk, Belgium. He had run in the heats for the US 4x400m team at the 2014 World Relays.

John LE MASURIER (GBR) (b. 24 Jul 1917 Guernsey) on 31 August. With fairly modest athletics credentials (440yh 58.5 in 1939) he began coaching that year and after War service (rising to Major in the Royal Marines), he was appointed AAA National Coach for the South of England from 1949 and then joint AAA Principal National Coach with Denis Watts from 1961 to 1978. Hugely respected, his crowning glory was coaching Mary Rand to the 1964 Olympic long jump title and world record.

Walter LEMOS Cándido (Argentina) (b. 23 Mar 1930 Santa Fe) on 10 June in Buenos Aires. At the marathon he was 7th in the 1959 Pan-American Games and 50th in the Olympics in 1960. He was 2nd in the South American Champs at 10000m and half marathon and 3rd at 5000m in 1956, and 2nd at 10,000m and half marathon in 1958. He set South American records for 10,000m with 30:24.0 in 1956 and 29:39.8 in 1957 and Argentinian records for 3000m 8:15.9 (1956), 25,000m 1:20:35.0 and 30,000m 1:37:50.7 (1957). Pb 5000m 14:26.4 (1956).

Prof. Dr. **Karl LENNARTZ** (Germany) (b. 17 Mar 1940 Aachen) on 2 May in Bad Oeynhausen. A most distinguished sports historian, with many books and articles to his credit, particularly in the Olympic Games, he was President of the International Society of Olympic Historians 2004-12. From 1982 he directed the Carl and Liselott Diem Archive. He had pbs: Mar 2:42 16 (1985), 100k 7:50:10 (1986). His daughter Birgit set a European 100k record of 7:17.57 (1990).

Hans Kristian **LILJEKVIST** (Sweden) (b. 3 Jan 1923 Hälsingborg) on 13 June. After a sensational 1:51.9 in 1942, he set in 1943 aged 20, Swedish records at 800m (1:49.2), 880y (1:51.7), 1000m (2:22.6 and 2:21.9 – 0.4 from Harbig's WR) and ran 1500m in 3:51.8; all remained his pbs. His 1:49.2 was against Denmark, 2nd to Niels Holst Sørensen DEN, in a race that had the world's three best times of the year. He was Swedish 800m champion in 1943-5 (3rd in 1947-8); 8 internationals. In 1946 he was temporarily barred from competition in connection with verdicts against Hägg, Andersson and others. In 1947 he ran the first leg for a Swedish 4x880y team that ran 7:29.0, improving the world record by 5.5 seconds but not approved by the IAAF as Liljekvist was then a "national" amateur. Other pb: 400m: 48.8 (1944).

Dr. **Allan** Shanks **LINDSAY** (GBR) (b. 5 Mar 1926 St. Andrews) on 2 April in Norwich.

A triple jumper with a best of 14.37 (1949), he competed at the 1948 Olympic Games (dnq 16=) after 3rd at the AAAs, and was 8th at the 1950 Empire Games. He went to St. Andrews University and was Scottish champion 1947-8.

James **'Jim'** **LINGEL** (USA) (b.) on 22 November 1931 in Buffalo. He was 5th in the AAU 400m and NCAA 440y (in a pb 47.8) while at Cornell University in 1951.

David LITTLEWOOD (GBR) on 16 March at the age of 76. He gave a huge amount to the sport nationally and internationally in many ways; one of the most respected officials, he was chairman, then secretary of the English Schools AA, was an International Track Referee, and the records man for Britain, serving on the IAAF Technical Committee, Rules and Records. He was a long-time member of Hercules Wimbledon AC, treasurer for 43 years and was awarded the MBE in 2010. Pb 100y 10.1 (1959).

Stanko LORGER (Slovenia/Yugoslavia) (b. 14 Nov 1931 Buce) on 25 April in Ljubljana. A consistently strong high hurdler, he was 5th at the 1956 Olympic Games (semi-finalist 1952 and 1960) and at the Europeans was successively 5th 1954, 2nd 1958 and 7th 1962. He won World University Games titles in 1957 and 1959, the Balkan Games 100m 1959 and 110mh 1953-61, and was Yugoslav champion at 100m 1952, 1956 and 1958-61 and at 110mh 1952 and 1954-62, plus indoors at 60m and 60mh 1955-8. He set five Yugoslav records at 100m from 10.5 (1956) to 10,4 (1958/59/60), ten at 110mh from 14.9 (1952) to 13.8 (1958) and 24.7 (1954) for 200mh. Other pb: 200m 21.7 (1955). 41 internationals 1951-62.

Patrick **'Paddy' LOWRY** (Ireland) (b. 19 Dec 1936 Tralee, Kerry) on 18 September in Dublin. He ran at the 1960 Olympics (heats 100m and 200m) and was Irish AAIU champion at 100y 1956 and 1958-9 and 220y 1960 and AAU/NIAA All-Ireland champion at 100y 1960 and 220y 1959-61. Pbs 100y 9.8, 220y 21.8 (both 1960). He became managing director of Sterling-Winthrop Pharmaceuticals.

Werner LUEG (Germany) (b. 16 Sep 1931 Brackwede) on 13 July in Gehrden. Having been the first German to break 3:50 for 1500m with 3:49.4 in 1951, he improved to tie the world record for 1500m with 3:43.0 in Berlin on 29 Jun 1952. A month later he took the Olympic bronze medal. He was 5th in the 1954 Europeans and was FRG champion in 1952-5 (2nd 1951 and 1957). He also set a German record with 2:20.8 for 1000m in 1955 and had other pbs of 800m 1:49.7 (1954), 1M 4:06.4 (1952), 2000m 5:22.6 (1954) and 3000m 8:15.6 (1952). 19 internationals 1951-7.

Annual progression at 1500m (position on world list): 1950- 3:54.4 (44=), 1951- 3:49.4 (10), 1952- 3:43.0 (1), 1953- 3:47.0 (11), 1954- 3:45.4 (9=), 1955- 3:44.4 (10=), 1957- 3:47.9 (59).

Anne Elizabeth **McKENZIE** (South Africa) (née Joubert) (b. 28 Jul 1925 Ceres) on 23 July in Pinelands, Cape Town. A pioneer of middle and long distance running in South Africa, having previously competed as a thrower and hurdler, she set 18 national records at 800m/880y from 2:24.8y in 1962 to 2:06.5m/2:07.4y at age 42 in 1967 plus two at 1500m, 4:48.0 in 1965 and 4:36.0 in 1967 and one at 1M 4:47.2 in 1967. In 1963 she won inaugural RSA titles at 880y (and again in 1964-6) and cross-country (again in 1964 and 1966-7). Over the ensuing years she set 30 world age records at distances from 100m to 1500m and at javelin and won four 50+ titles at the first World Masters Championships in 1975 and three titles at 55+ in 1981. Other pbs: 100m 12.4 (1967), 220y 25.4 (1967), 80mh 11.6 (1963).

Sir Ronald **Thomas** Stewart **MACPHERSON** (GBR) (b. 4 Oct 1920 Edinburgh) on 6 November. 'Tommy' had a very distinguished War, escaping from prison camps and leading Special Operations Executive operations in France, for which he won three Military Crosses and three Croix de Guerre and was awarded a papal knighthood. He then went to Trinity College, Oxford and, as well as excelling at rugby and hockey, won an athletics blue as a miler (2nd UAU 1947), pbs: 1500m 3:57.8, 1M 4:24.0 (both 1947). He had a most successful business career, was awarded the CBE in 1967 and knighted for his services to commerce and industry in 1992. He was president of the Achilles Club for many years.

Dr **Luitpold MAIER** (Germany) (b. 1 May 1930) on 26 January in Munich. At javelin he was 3rd in 1955 and 2nd in 1958 at FRG Championships and won the discus at the unofficial World University Games in 1957. Pbs: LJ 7.06 (1952), DT 48.49 (1955), JT 67.36 (1956), Pen 3510 (1955); 5 internationals 1955-9.

ISTVÁN MAJOR (Hungary) (b. 20 May 1949 Budapest), on 3 May near Toronto, Canada. He won three European Indoor titles 1971-3 (2nd 1974) and outdoors was 5th 1969, 4th 1971, 4th 1974, while at the Olympic Games he was 6th in 1972 (dnq 1976); He was also 2nd at the World University Games in 1973 and 1975 and 6th 1977. Hungarian champion 1973 and 1976-8, he had 41 internationals 1969-81. The first Hungarian to use the Fosbury Flop, he set ten national records from 2.12 in 1969 to 2.24 in 1973 and also jumped 2.24 indoors in 1972. HUN athlete of the year 1971, and 1973-4. He lived in Toronto from 1983.

Todor Khristov **MANOLOV** (Bulgaria) (b. 3 Mar 1951 Varna) on 5 September. He set 11 Bulgarian records at hammer from 67.06 in 1970 to 73.52 in 1976. He became Bulgaria's first official European Junior champion in 1970 and was 21st in qualifying at the 1972 Olympic Games. He was Bulgarian champion in 1973 and 1976 and won the Balkan title in 1974 and 1976.

Phillip John **MAY** (Australia) (b. 20 Sep 1944) on 30 November in Claremont, Western Australia. He was 6th in the Olympic triple jump in a Commonwealth record 17.04 in 1968, won the LJ/TJ double at the Pacific Conference Games in 1969 and was 3rd TJ in 1973. At the Commonwealth Games he was 6th LJ and 10th TJ in 1966, 2nd and 1st in 1970, and 5th at LJ 1974. He was national champion six times at triple jump and four times at long jump and set an Australian record 7.71 for long jump in 1965, improving to 8.04 and 8.15w in 1970. Pbs: 100m 10.4 (1969), 200m 21.1, TJ 17.10w (1971).

János MEDOVARSZKI (Hungary) (b. 27 Oct 1937 Békéscsaba) on 11 September. At high jump he was 3rd at the 1965 World University Games, 10= at the 1966 Europeans and Hungarian champion in 1958 and 1962-6. He set Hungarian records with 2.06 (1961) and 2.09 (1965) and competed in 27 internationals 1957-67. Other pbs: 100m 11.1 (1961), 110mh 14.9 (1964), 200mh 25.8 (1962), 400mh 57.7 (1958), LJ 7.05 (1964), TJ 13.66 (1965), Dec 5366 (1959). He became a leading coach, most recently of Balázs Baji.

Predrag MILOVANOVIC (Serbia) (b. 30 Jul 1973) on 17 May in Kragujevac. He set his long jump pb of 7.81 when winning the Serbian title in 1998; 2 internationals for SRB 1996-8.

Peter MÖRBEL (Germany) (b. 19 Feb 1941) on 3 August in Mainz. At javelin he was 2nd in 1965 and 1970 and 3rd in 1963 and 1975-6 at FRG Championships. He threw over 70m each year 1960-78 and again in 1980, Pbs: SP 14.97 (1963), JT 78.34 (1970); 6 internationals 1965-72.

Charles E **MOSELEY** (USA) (b. 1941) on 8 April in Mobile, Alabama. While at the University of Alabama he was 4th in the NCAA at 120yh and LJ and had pbs of 13.9 and 7.78/7.87w in 1963.

Mbulaeni MULAUDZI (South Africa) (b. 8 Sep 1980 Muduluni Village, Limpopo Province) was killed in a car accident near Johannesburg on 24 October. He won the gold medal at the 1999 African Junior Championships and silver at the 2000 African Championships. He showed his ability to excel in the biggest events with a pb 1:44.81 in the semi-finals before 6th in the final of the 2001 World Championships. A week later he improved his best to 1:44.01 in Zürich. In 2002 he took the gold medal at the Commonwealth Games and was 3rd at the African Champs, again improving at Zürich – to 1:43.81. In 2003 he ran 1:42.89 in Brussels, a week after taking the World bronze medal. He won the World Indoor title in 2004 and despite moderate form in the outdoor season to that date took the Olympic silver medal in 2004. In 2006 he was 2nd at the World Indoors, won at the World Athletics Final and was 3rd at the World Cup, and in 2007 was 2nd at the African Games but disappointed with 7th at the Worlds. He was 2nd in the World Indoor 800m and an Olympic semi-finalist in 2008 before his greatest success – winning the World title in 2009. After that he ran his fastest ever time, 1:42.86 when 3rd at Rieti. South African champion 2001-03, 2005-09 and 2012, African Games silver medallist 2003 and 2007. He ran under 1:45 for 800m for ten successive seasons 2001-10 and his last race was 4th in the New York Diamond League in 2013. Other best times: 400m 46.3 (2007), 600m 1:17.25i (2005), 1000m 2:15.86 (2007, South African record), 1500m 3:38.55 (2009).

Annual progress at 800m: 1998- 1:50.33A, 1999- 1:48.33A; 2000- 1:45.55, 2001- 1:44.01, 2002- 1:43.81, 2003- 1:42.89, 2004- 1:44.56, 2005- 1:44.08, 2006- 1:43.09, 2007- 1:43.74, 2008- 1:43.26, 2009- 1:42.86, 2010- 1:43.29, 2011- 1:45.50, 2012- 1:45.78, 2013- 1:47.46.

Peter Matheka **MUTUKU** (Kenya) (b. 12 Jan 1994) was killed in a road accident in Kenya on 10 July. He won the 2000m steeplechase at the 2010 Youth Olympic Games in 5:37.63 and had a 3000m steeple best of 8:40.2A (2013).

Angéla NÉMETH-RÁNKY (Hungary) (b. 18 Feb 1946 Budapest) on 5 August in Budapest. She won the 1968 Olympic gold medal at javelin in Mexico City with 60.36, the third of her four Hungarian records from 58.60 in 1968 to 60.58 in Budapest in 1969. She was also 13th at the 1972 Olympics, won the European title in 1969 (plus dnq 1966 and 4th 1971) and was 4th at the World University Games in 1965. She was Hungarian champion in 1968-9 and 1971 and had 14 internationals 1965-72. Other pbs: HJ 1.58 (1968), SP 13.35 (1963), DT 43.56 (1964). She became a member of the Hungarian Olympic Committee.

Annual progression at JT (position on world list): 1961- 41.16, 1962- 38.44, 1963- 44.58, 1964- 47.59 (97), 1965- 52.26 (28), 1966- 51.52 (42), 1967- 55.12 (14), 1968- 60.36 (1), 1969- 60.58 (1), 1971- 59.44 (6), 1972- 57.20 (23).

Fritz **Roland NILSSON** (Sweden) (b. 26 Nov 1924 Svanö) on 21 February in Alton, USA. Swedish champion at shot 1946-9, 1952 and 1954 and discus 1952 and 1954. He competed at the Olympic Games in 1948 (dnq SP) and 1952 (5th SP, 7th DT)., and at the Europeans in 1946 (4th SP) and 1954 (4th SP, 5th DT). His absence in other years was due to his living in USA after 1949. In addition to 11 internationals (SP 9 wins, DT 6 wins in 8 matches) he was a member of the Nordic countries team v USA in 1949. He set five Swedish records at shot from 15.93 (1947) to 16.64 (1952), and at discus 53.64 and 54.54 in 1954; unratified were his SP pb 17.00 and DT 53.13 in 1953.

Hugo NISKANEN (Finland) (b. 8 Sep 1920 Kaavi) on 4 December at Outokumpu. At 10,000m he had a best of 30:28.0 (1952), was 19th in the 1952 Olympics and Finnish champion in 1951 (2nd 1952, 3rd 1955).

Gerald Arthur **'Gerry' NORTH** (GBR) (b. 2 May 1936 Chester) on 1 April in Portsmouth. He had one track international for Britain at 10,000m in 1963, but was best known as an outstanding cross-country runner. At the English National CC, he won the Junior race in 1957 and had seven top 10 placings in the senior race in the 1960s, winning in 1962. His best placings in six International CC races were 4th in 1964 and 8th in 1962. Pbs: 2M 8:52.8 (1963), 3M 13:37.0 (1965), 5000m 14:15.0 (1968), 6M 28:08.4 (1967), 10,000m 29:21.0 (1968), 10M 48:38.2 (1962), 1Hr 19,485m (1962). Originally with Blackpool & Fylde AC, he joined Belgrave Harriers in 1962, and later coached at Portsmouth AC. His younger brother Geoff also had one track international for Britain (1966) at 5000m, pb 13:44.4 (1969).

Robert OJO (Nigeria) (b. 29 Apr 1941 Ikare, Owo) on 27 March in Ibadan. He competed at the Olympic Games in 1968 (4x100m & qf 100m) and 1972 (4x400m & qf 400m) and at the 1970 Commonwealth Games (4x100m & qf 200m). Pbs: 100m 10.4 (1968), 400m 46.39 (1972). He retired as a police superintendent.

Heiki Olavi **'Olli' PARTANEN** (Finland) (b. 18 Aug 1922 Kouvola) in Kouvola on June 15. He was third in the discus at the 1950 Europeans and competed in the 1952 Olympic Games (dnq 18). Pb 50.14 (1949).

Melvin Emory **PATTON** (USA) (b. 16 Nov 1924 Los Angeles) on 9 May in Fallbrook, California. After two world record-equalling times of 9.4 for 100 yards, he became the first man to run a 9.3 at the West Coast Relays at Fresno on 15 May 1948, a time that was not beaten until 1961. Later that year, after second at 100m, he won the 200m at the US Olympic Trials at Evanston, tying the world best around a turn of 20.7. The clear Olympic favourite, he disappointed with 5th place at 100m but won gold at 200m and 4x100m relay. A graceful but nervous runner, he never entered the AAU Championships but won each NCAA title he contested for the University of Southern California, the 100y or 100m 1947-9 and 200m/220y 1948-9. In 1949 in the USC-UCLA dual meet he ran the 100y in a wind-assisted 9.1 and then, with the wind below the allowable limit, set a world record for 220 yards straight with 20.2. He also twice ran on USC world record-setting 4 x 220y relay teams in 1949 and only lost three races in his years of sprinting dominance 1947-9. He became a teacher and track coach and later an executive in the aerospace and electronics industries. Other yearly bests: 1942- 21.4w/21.5ySt, 1943- 9.8, 21.2ySt; 1946- 9.6y, 10.7, 21.9*, 21.1y St; 1947- 9.4, 10.5, 20.4ySt; 1948- 10.3, 20.6ySt; 1949- 9.5.

Petar PECELJ (Serbia) (b. 11 July 1927 Ljubinje) on 14 March in Belgrade. He was 6th at 100m and a semi-finalist at 200m at the European Championships of 1950 as well as competing at 4x100m in 1950 and 1954. Yugoslav champion at 100m 1951 & 1953, 200m 1950-2, he set Yugoslav records at 100m 10.7 (1951), 200m 21.7 (1953) and had 22 internationals.

Jean-Pierre PERRINELLE (France) (b. 6 Jul 1949) Versailles, Yvelines) on 30 August. At 400mh he competed (heats) at the Olympic Games of 1972 and 1976, was French champion 1972 and 1976 and had a pb of 50.07 (1976). 50.0 (1972), 11 internationals 1969-76.

Anatoliy PETROV (USSR) (b. 19 Aug 1928) on 1 July in St. Petersburg. He had a pole vault best of 4.45 in 1958, was 11th at the 1956 Olympic Games and at USSR Championships was 2nd in 1956 and 3rd in 1957-8.

Herbert PFEFFER (Germany) (b. 7 Dec 1927 Darmstadt) on 21 September in Darmstadt. At triple jump in 1954 he was 2nd at the FRG Champs and competed at the Europeans (dnq 21st). Pbs 14.59i (1955), 14.54 (1959); 3 internationals 1954-5.

Leonhard **'Leo' POHL** (Germany) (b. 18 Jul 1929 Allenstein, now Olsztyn, Poland) on 23 April in Pfungstadt. He won Olympic bronze at 4x100m in 1956 (semis 200m) and was 4th at 100m at the Europeans in 1954 after 2nd in the FRG 100m and 200m. Pbs: 100m 10.5/10.3w and 200m 21.1 and he ran on the German team that set a European record of 40.0 for 4x100m (all 1956). 27 internationals 1952-7. He was responsible for German television's technical arrangements at the 1972 Olympic Games.

Allan Matthew **POTTS** (New Zealand) (b. 1934) on 8 May in Hastings. NZ 10 mile champion in 1964, he was president of Athletics New Zealand in 2002-03. He coached his wife Sylvia, who competed at 800m or 1500m at the 1968 Olympics and 1970 and 1974 Commonwealth Games, and the NZ team at the 1992 Olympic Games. Appointed an Officer of the New Zealand Order of Merit in 1998. Pbs: 3M 13:41.4 (1962), 6M 29:01.0 (1962), Mar 2:23:22 (1963).

Pierre PRAT (France) (b. 19 Jan 1930 Camlez) on 13 March at Rostrene. He competed (heat) at 3000m steeplechase at the 1952 Olympics and was French champion 1952-4. 10 internationals 1949-55. Pbs: 1500m 4:01.6 (1952), 3000m 8:38.3 (1951), 5000m 15:08.6 (1951), 3000mSt 9:04.8 (1952).

Dieter PROLLIUS (Germany/GDR) (b. 1 Jun 1944 Dresden) on 27 March in Dresden. He had a shot best of 20.24 in 1972 and was GDR champion 1967; 4 internationals 1967-8. Pb DT 54.76 (1969). His son Maik was the European junior shot bronze medallist in 1985.

Lasse RÄIHÄ (Finland) (b. 26 Oct 1925 Kirkkonummi) on 22 August. The Finnish 800m champion in 1949 (2nd 1947), he had three international matches in 1949, including for the Rest of Scandinavia against Sweden in Stockholm, in which he ran his pb 1:52.8. A relay runner par excellence in the Helsingfors IFK team, he won seven Finnish titles at 4x400 (1948-54) and six at 4x800 (1946-7, 1949-52). In 1952-5 he played handball for HIFK in the main national series.

Emma REED (later WRIGHT) (USA) (b. 30 May 1925 Redwood, Mississippi) on 4 April in Washington, DC. She competed at HJ (14=) and LJ (12th) at the 1948 Olympics, having won the US indoor and Olympic Trials long jump, and set pbs of: HJ 1.54 and LJ 5.59.

Miloslava REZKOVÁ/HÜBNEROVÁ (Czech Republic) (b. 22 Jul 1950 Prague) on 19 October in Prague. A straddle jumper, she was the surprise winner of the 1968 Olympic high jump title at the age of 18 when she cleared 1.82 on her third attempt. She then won the European title in 1969 with 5th in 1971 and 1974, and 15th at the 1972 Olympics. After ranking as world number one in 1968 and 1969, she remained in the world top ten but ranked between fifth and ninth each year 1970-4. She set eight Czechoslovak record from 1.80 in 1968 to her eventual pb of 1.87 in 1972 and was national champion in 1968-9, 1972 and 1974 (and indoors 1973). Pb 100mh 14.8/14.6w (1972). In 1970 she married her coach and fellow high jumper Dr Rudolf Hübner (pb 2.18i 1968).

Annual progression at HJ: 1964- 1.46, 1965- 1.55, 1966- 1.60, 1967- 1.66, 1968- 1.82, 1969- 1.84, 1970- 1.85, 1971- 1.85, 1972- 1.87, 1973- 1.85i, 1974- 1.87, 1975- 1.83, 1976- 1.80.

Sándor ROZSNYOI (Hungary) (b. 24 Nov 1930 Zalaegerszeg) 2 September in Sydney, Australia. Starting at 800m he eventually moved up to the steeplechase and joined Mihaly Igloi's group of "Magnificent Magyars", training alongside the likes of Sándor Iharos, István Rózsavölgyi and László Tábori, all world record breakers at distances between 1000m and 10,000m. After 9:46.2 in 1953, his first great success at 3000m steeplechase was winning the 1954 European title in 8:49.6 (the first world record in this event to be officially ratified by the IAAF) and two years later he reclaimed the record with 8:35.6 two months before finishing second at the Olympic Games, also setting Hungarian records at 8:48.0 and 8:45.2 in 1955. He remained in Australia as Hungary had been invaded by the Soviet Union and became a PE teacher and athletics coach in New South Wales. He competed in 15 internationals 1954-6 and was Hungarian 3000mSt champion in 1954-5. Other pbs: 800m 1:54.2 (1953), 1500m 3:46.4 (1956), 3000m 8:05.0 (1956), 5000m 14:14.0 (1956), 10000m 31:05.0 (1956).

Annual progression at 3000mSt: 1953- 9:46.2, 1954- 8:49.6, 1955- 8:45.2, 1956- 8:35,6.

Yoshinori SAKAI (Japan) (b. 6 Aug 1945 Miyoshi, Hiroshima Prefecture) on 10 September in Tokyo, As a 19 year-old he lit the flame at the 1964 Olympic opening ceremony. A promising sprinter at the time, he was chosen for the role as he was born close to Hiroshima on the very day that city was struck by an atomic bomb and he symbolised Japan's post-war reconstruction and peace. He won the Japanese 400m title and took gold (4x400m) and silver (400m in his pb of 47.4) medals at the Asian Games in 1966. He later became a journalist and sports producer with the Fuji Television Network.

Lucio SANGERMANO (Italy) (b. 11 Aug 1932 Florence) in Florence on 27 October. Italian 200m champion 1953, with pbs 100m 10.6 (1954), 200m 21.3 (1953), he ran at the 1952 Olympics (ht 200m) and 1954 Europeans (5th 4x100m). 8 internationals 1951-7. He became a famous lawyer.

Bob SBORDONE (USA) (b. 6 May 1940 Boston) in Mission Viejo, California, on 3 August. He was 4th in the 1961 NCAAs (for USC) and the 1964 US Olympic Trials javelin and had a pb 79.16 in 1965, ranking 26th in the world that year. He obtained a doctorate in psychology from UCLA and became an authority in clinical neuropsychology, traumatic brain damage and post-traumatic stress disorder.

Friedrich Wilhelm Heinrich **'Friedel' SCHIRMER** (Germany) (b. 20 Mar 1926 Stadthagen) on 30 November in Stadthagen. A decathlete who was 8th at the 1952 Olympic Games and 7th at the 1954 Europeans, he became a legendary coach for the event; his pupils including 1964 Olympic champion Willi Holdorf and the 1968 1-2-3 Bill Toomey, Hans-Joachim Walde and Kurt Bendlin and his book 'Zehnkämpfer – Training und Wettkampf' was published in 1965. He then went into politics and was a SPD party member of the Bundestag 1969-83 and president of the Association of German Olympians from 1984. He was FRG champion at decathlon in 1951 and 1953-4 and at pentathlon in 1951. Pbs: Dec 6646 (1956, 1952 tables), 100m 11.0/10.7w (1952), 400m 49.8 (1956), 110mh 15.1 (1956), 200mh 24.7 (1951), 400mh 55.5 (1952), HJ 1.80 (1951), PV 3.60 (1952), LJ 7.11 (1948), SP 14.43 (1956), DT 42.58 (1959), JT 59.40 (1954). 8 internationals 1952-6.

Howard SCHMERTZ (USA) (b. 9 June 1925 Bronx, New York) on 27 March, A lawyer, he acted as unpaid meet director of the famed Millrose Games in New York for 29 years from 1975. The Games were inaugurated in 1908 and for 41 years, from 1934, they were run by Howard's father, Fred Schmertz, and the 18,000-capacity Madison Square Garden venue was invariably sold out during the meet's heyday. However, the public appeal of indoor athletics in New York declined in recent years and after fewer than 10,000 fans watched the 2011 edition the meet transferred to a new home (and a much faster track) at the New Balance Armory Track & Field Center.

Siw **Barbro SCHÖNBORG** (Sweden) (b. 8 Apr 1931 Herrljunga) on 4 March. Swedish discus champion 1952, 1954-6, 1958-9 and 1961 and 2nd in 1951, 1953, 1957, 1960 with seven further medals in SP, JT and Slingball. Represented Sweden on 23 occasions. pbs: SP 11.88 (1956), DT 44.73 (1960), JT 38.00 (1959).

Wolf **Rainer SCHUBERT** (Germany) (b. 12 Oct 1941 Dresden) in Bad Kreuznach on 13 August. He was twice an Olympic finalist at 400m hurdles: 7th in Mexico City 1968 in 49.30 (after a pb 49.15A in his semi-final) and 5th at Munich in 1972 in 49.56. He was FRG champion in 1965 and 1967-9, and set his low altitude pb of 49.35 for 2nd in 1972. Other pbs: 200m 21.4 (1970), 400m 46.3 (1971), 800m 1:51.5 (1966), 110mh 14.5 (1969), LJ 7.07 (1967), Dec 6489 (1964).

Dr **Otey SCRUGGS** (USA) (b. 29 Jun 1929 Vallejo CA), on 14 February in Cranberry Township, Penn. He placed 3rd in the 1950 and 1951 US decathlon championships and was 5th ranked in the world in 1951 with 7178 on the tables then in use (6739 on current tables).

Pekka SIMOLA (Finland) (b. 1 Jan 1920 Turku) on 31 August in Somero. Finnish long jump champion 1943-5 and 1947-8 (2nd 1946), he won 7 of 19 international dual matches 1939-50. His pb 7.40 was first with wind assistance in 1939 aged 19, then legally in 1943 just a few weeks after wounding an arm in Russian front. He bravely continued his sports career in spite of left wrist never working properly again. Controversially, he was not selected to London 1948 Olympic Games. He became a judge, working in the legal sphere for 40 years

Colin George **SMITH** (GBR) (b. 2 Aug 1935 Harlesden, London) on 20 December in Australia. He made 24 international appearances for Britain 1955-67 including at the European Champs in 1958 and 1962 and he achieved his greatest success for England at the Commonwealth Games: 1st in 1958 and 2nd in 1962, when he set his pb of 77.92. He had set three UK records at the javelin in 1957: 71.00 for 2nd AAAs, 72.62 2nd v France and 75.16 to win against West Germany. A member of Thames Valley Harriers, he was AAA champion in 1958-9 and 1963, having been junior champion in 1953.

Viktor SNAJDER (Croatia) (b. 17 Jun 1934) on 14 November in Zagreb. He ran for Yugoslavia at 4x400m at the 1960 Olympics (sf) and in the Europeans in 1962 (also 400m semis 1958). At 400m he was Balkan champion 1958-9, Mediterranean Games 1959 and Yugoslav champion 1958; 21 internationals. He set four Yugoslav records from 48.0 to 47.0 in 1958.

Rainer STENIUS (Finland) (b. 19 Mar 1943 Helsinki) in November in Espoo. An extraordinary long jump talent, he did 6.65 without any training in 1959 aged 16 and 7.47 in 1961. Known for his immensely powerful take-off, he took the 1962 European silver medal behind Igor Ter-Ovanesyan, his 7.85 there remaining the Finnish junior record for 32 years. After studying at Los Angeles State College, USA in January 1963 and an injury-spoiled 1964 he made a great comeback in 1965, equaling Pentti Eskola´s Finnish record 8.04. In 1966, Stenius did 8.16 from a rubber asphalt take-off in Westwood in May, just 19 cm short of Ralph Boston´s WR and no. 4 all-time, and this lasted as the Finnish record until 2005. He was 5th at the 1966 Europeans when there were three Finns in the top eight, but had to retire at the age of 24 due to a serious Achilles tendon problem. After completing his doctoral thesis on biomechanics at the University of Oregon he worked in the USA before returning to Finland in 1997. Finnish champion 1962, 1965-6, NCAA 1966, and Nordic 1965; 11 international matches with 8 wins.

Dragutin **'Drago' STRITOF** (Yugoslavia/ Serbia) (b. 1 Aug 1923 Vucilcevo) on 2 November in Belgrade. Yugoslav champion at 5000m 1955, 1957-8, 3000mSt 1952 & 1956 and CC 1955 and 1958, and Balkan champion at 5000m 1954-5 and CC 1955, he competed at the 1952 Olympics (ht 3000mSt) and at the Europeans of 1950 (dnf 3000mSt), 1954 (ht 5000m) and 1958 (9th 10,000m). He set Yugoslav records at 3000m 8:14.8 (1955), 5000m 14:18.6 and 14:16.4 (1955) and 10,000m 29:36.5 & 29:34.8 (1958). Other pbs: 1500m 3:53.2 (1954), 5000m 14:12.8 (1958), 3000mSt 8:58.4 (1955). He became a coach at his club AC Partizan, Beograd.

Clive John **THOMAS** (GBR) (b. 27 Mar 1947 Bridgend) on 22 September. He competed in three UK internationals 1974-5 (at 1500m and 3000m steeple) and six times for Wales in the International CC Championships 1973-80. He won the AAA 1500m in 1974 and Welsh 1500m 1973. Pbs: 800m 1:51.2 (1971), 1500m 3:43.6 (1974), 1M 4:01.0 (1974), 3000m 8:04.98 (1976), 5000m 13:42.73 (1975), 10,000m 30:13.3 (1981), Mar

2:29:58 (1981), 3000mSt 8:37.8 (1975). Having competed for Thames Valley Harriers, he was a teacher and coached at Wells City Harriers

Dorothy Jennifer Beatrice **TYLER** (GBR) (b. 14 Mar 1920 Stockwell, London) (née Odam) on 25 September at Long Melford, Suffolk. As Dorothy Odam in 1936 and Tyler at the 1948 Olympics she cleared the same height as the high jump winner, respectively (1.60m and 1.68m), only to take 2nd place; under the current rules for settling ties on count-back she would have won in 1936. She was the first British woman to gain an Olympic athletics medal and won the Empire Games title in 1938. She married Richard Tyler in 1940 and after War service and the birth of two sons in 1946-7, she was 2nd in the Europeans and won at the Empire Games in 1950 and was 2nd at the 1954 Commonwealth Games, changing her style from scissors to western roll in 1951. She first jumped over 5ft in 1935 at 15 and was still clearing that height 31 years later, and her 20-year span of competing at Olympic Games is a British women's record for any sport, as she went on to 7th equal in 1952 and 12th equal in 1956. She is the youngest ever British record holder in athletics with her 1.65 high jump in 1936 at 16 years 39 days. This tied the world record, but was not ratified, but her 1.66m in 1939 was, until it was superseded by an earlier, 1938, performance by Dora Ratjen (Germany). However, Ratjen was then shown to have been a man and Tyler's mark was put back in its rightful place in the record books.

Tyler set further British records at 1.66 and 1.68 at the 1948 Olympics. She was WAAA high jump champion eight times outdoors, 1936-9, 1948-9, 1952 and 1956, placing in the first three 14 times over 22 years, and four times indoors 1936-9; and also won the long jump and pentathlon in 1951, the latter in a British record 3953 points (1954 tables). Other bests: 80m hurdles 11.8 (1950), long jump 5.73m (1951), 5.75w (1956). She became a leading coach and was awarded the MBE in the 2002 New Year Honours.

Annual progression at HJ (position on world lists): 1934- 1.524 (18=), 1935- 1.60 (4=), 1936- 1.65 (1), 1937- 1.635 (1), 1938- 1.625 (4), 1939- 1.66 (1), 1945- 1.562 (3), 1946- 1.524 (24=), 1948- 1.68 (1=), 1949- 1.657 (1), 1950- 1.651 (3), 1951- 1.625 (5), 1952- 1.65 (3=), 1953- 1.651 (4=), 1954- 1.63 (9=), 1955- 1.66 (6=), 1956- 1.651 (15=), 1957- 1.575 (86=), 1958- 1.60 (58=), 1959- 1.60 (72=), 1960- 1.575, 1961- 1.63 (62=), 1962- 1.575, 1963- 1.549.

Petrus Karel **'Piet' VAN DER LEEUW** (South Africa) (b. 5 Dec 1931 Ladysmith) on 11 December. He competed for South Africa in 1955 and that year set an RSA record of 1:51.8 for 880y that lasted just seven days. He finished the Comrades Marathon eleven times between 1967 and 1982 with a best of ninth in 1970.

Jane WELZEL Liggett (USA) (b. 24 Apr 1955 Hopkinton, Massachusetts) on 31 August in Fort Collins. She was the 1990 US champion who participated in five US Olympic Marathon Trials. She broke her neck in a car accident in 1984 but returned to become *Runner's World's* Comeback Runner of the Year in 1988. In 1993 she was 19th in the World Champs and 25th in the World Cup; her best time was 2:33:01 when winning in Duluth in 1992.

Jan WERNER (Poland) (b. 25 Jul 1946 Brzeziny) on 21 September in Warsaw. Ranked four times in the world top ten at 400m, at the European Championships he was champion in 1969 and 3rd in 1971 and at 4x400m 1st in 1966, 4th in 1969 and 2nd in 1971, with 4th at 200m in 1966. At the Olympic Games he was a semi-finalist in 1968 and 1972 and 8th in 1976 when he was a silver medallist at 4x400m and he was also 2nd in the European Indoor 400m in 1969. He was European Cup 400m winner in 1970, and Polish champion at 200m in 1967, 1969 and 1971 and at 400m in 1968, 1970-1 and 1976. He set a Polish record with 20.4 for 200m in 1967 and had other pbs of 100m 10.3 (1967) and 400m 45.44 (1976).

Annual progression at 400m: 1965- 48.3, 1966- 45.7, 1967- 45.7, 1968- 45.6, 1969- 45.7, 1970- 45.9, 1971- 45.6, 1972- 45.8, 1974- 46.6, 1975- 46.4, 1976- 45.44.

Alfons WIEGAND (Germany) (b. 29 Apr 1933 Fulda) on 15 September in Frankfurt. At hammer in 1958 he was 3nd at the FRG Champs, competed at the Europeans (dnq 20th) and set his pb of 60.83; 4 internationals 1957-8.

Hywel Lloyd **WILLIAMS** (GBR) (b. 15 Dec 1929 Llanharan) on 30 August. He was the 1957 AAA decathlon champion and represented Wales at shot and discus in the 1954 (11th/5th) & 1958 (12th/7th) Commonwealth Games. He set Welsh records at discus (8) to 47.50 (1959), decathlon (6) to 6050 (1959) (6259 on 1962 tables), and pole vault 3.66 (1952) and was Welsh champion at pole vault 1952, shot 1958, discus 1952-3, 1958-9, and 1963-5, and decathlon 1950-2 and 1959. Pb SP 14.20 (1958), 4 UK internationals 1955-9. He became a successful coach and persuaded Clive Longe, his successor as Welsh record holder and 2nd at the 1966 Commonwealth Games, to switch from basketball to decathlon.

Borys YAKOVLEV (Ukraine) (b. 16 Jul 1945 Petrovsk, Russia) on 23 June. At 20km walk he was 7th in 1969, 7th in 1971 and 4th in 1978 at the European Championships with 2nd at the Lugano Trophy in 1:19:46.0 (short course) in 1979. He also competed at the 1980 Olympic Games (dq 50km walk). Pbs: 20kW 1:21:52 (2001), 50kW 3:51:43 (1982), 3:37:36 short (1980). He became a national coach.

Louis Silvie **ZAMPERINI** (USA) (b. 26 Jan 1917 Olean, New York) on 2 July in Los Angeles. From Torrance High School in California, he competed at the 1936 Olympic Games, coming 8th in the 5000m in 14:46.8, a time that remained his best, gaining four places with a spectacular 56-second last lap. He won a scholarship to the University of Southern California and had pbs of 880y 1:53.2 (1938), 1500m 3:52.6 (1939), 1M 4:08.3 (1938), 2M 9:32.8 (1939), and was 4th in 1938 and 3rd in 1939 in the AAU 1500m, winning the NCAA mile title each year. He served as a bombardier in World War II and crashed in the Pacific Ocean when flying a rescue mission. He was declared dead, but he and his co-pilot were picked up by a Japanese patrol boat after 47 days adrift in a life raft. He then spent the rest of the War in brutal prison camps, receiving the Purple Heart and Distinguished Flying Cross on his return. He became a born-again Christian, influenced by Billy Graham, and became an inspirational speaker. He wrote two books about his experiences and his story was told in *Unbroken* by Laura Hillenbrand, a book published in 2010. A Hollywood movie based on this book, directed by Angelina Jolie was released on December 25.

Died in early 2015

Margaret ARNOLD (née **JOHNSON**) (Australia) (b. 15 Jun 1937) in February. She competed in the long jump (dnq 16th) at the 1956 Olympic Games in Melbourne and was twice third in the Australian Champs – 1954 and 1956 with a best of 5.70 in 1953 (20th in the world that year). Her granddaughter Bronte Barrett won an Olympic swimming gold medal at 4x200m freestyle in 2008.

Dmitriy BAGRYANOV (Russia) (b. 18 Dec 1967) on 4 February. At the long jump he was ranked fifth in the world in 1992, when he set his pb of 8.35, was European Indoor champion, CIS champion and 7th at the Olympic Games. He was also 7th at the World Indoors in 1991 and 6th indoors and 5th outdoors at the 1994 Europeans. Previously he had been a 400m hurdler with a best of 50.19 in 1989.

Daundre BARNABY (Canada) (b. 9 Dec 1990 St. Ann, Jamaica) on 26 March, drowning when caught in an ocean current while at a training camp in St. Kitts. He became a Canadian citizen in 2012 and ran at 400m for Canada at the 2012 Olympics (heat) and 2014 Commonwealth Games (semis). He went to Mississippi State University in the USA, running his best 400m time of 45.47 for them in the NCAA West meeting at Greensboro in 2013. He was Canadian champion and had a best of 45.55 in 2014.

Gordon DICKSON (Canada) (b. 2 Jan 1932 Calgary) on 19 January. He went to Drake University before graduate school at New York University, then returning to Canada, where he won national titles at 6 miles 1958, marathon 1957-60, 1962 and 1964 and cross-country 1957-9. At marathon he was 55th at the 1960 Olympics, 5th in 1958 and 12th in 1962 at the Commonwealth Games and 3rd at the 1959 Pan-American Games; pb Canadian record 2:21:51 (1958). He was 3rd in the 1959 Boston Marathon.

Shane DONNELLY (New Zealand) (b. 23 Oct 1955) on 17 January. He was 50th at 20k walk at the 1983 World Champs and 10th at 30k walk at the 1990 Commonwealth Games and was NZ walks champion at 5000m 1982 and 1984-5, 20k 1981 and 1987, and 30k and 50k in 1984. Pbs: 20kW 1:28:58 (1986), 50kW 4:36:27 (1984).

James **'JIM' DUNAWAY** (USA) (b. 17 Aug 1927 Houston) on 15 March in Austin, Texas. A fine journalist, he covered 14 Olympic Games from 1956, all but one World Championships and all the major US meetings in his career of over 60 years for a wide variety of leading magazines and newspapers. He was inducted in the US National Hall of Fame in 2010. He graduated in science from Penn State and worked in New York City and New Jersey for much of his life before returning in recent years to his home state. He was president of the Track & Field Writers of America in 1999-2001 and 2005-07 and author of the Sports Illustrated Book of Track & Field: Running Events.

Evelyn FURTSCH Ojeda (USA) (b. 17 Apr 1914 San Diego) on 5 March in Santa Ana, California at the age of 100. She won an Olympic gold medal on the US 4x100m at the 1932 Olympic Games. That was the end of her sporting career; she married and had a baby in 1935. Los Angeles AC. 2nd US 100y 1931.

Benjamin Benito **'Benny' GARCIA** (USA) (b. 7 Jul 1933 La Luz, New Mexico) on 17 February. A javelin thrower at Arizona State University, he set a pb of 73.94 in 1956 and, after third in the AAU and in the US Trials, he competed at the Olympic Games (no throws in the final). He worked as a broker.

Harry L **GORDON** (Australia) (b. 9 Nov 1925) on 21 January. He was a notable sports journalist, particularly known as an Olympic historian, writing 15 books, and covering all the Games from 1952 to 2012. He edited the *Sun News-Pictorial* in Melbourne 1968-72, having joined the paper at the age of 16.

John F. **'Jack' HEYWOOD** (GBR) (b. 19 Feb 1932) on 2 January. A member of Herne Hill Harriers, he set a British record for 15 miles on the track with 1:17:25.0 on 20 Oct 1956 at

Walton-on-Thames after completing 19,153m in 1 hour behind the UK record of 19,375m by Fred Norris. He had one international for Britain at 10,000m in 1955 and had other pbs of: 2M 9:02.4 (1955), 3M 13:51.0 (1957), 5000m 14:12.8 (1955), 6M 29:21.6 (1954), 10,000m 31:07.2 (1956), 10M 50:15.4 (1956), 20M 1:48:13 (1955), 2Hr 35,565m (1955).

James Joseph **'Jim' HOGAN** (Ireland/UK) (b. 25 May 1933 Croom, Limerick, né Cregan) on 10 January in Limerick, Ireland. Remembered with great affection by so many, he had his greatest successes in 1966, the first of three years in which he competed for Britain internationally as after running his pb of 2:19:27 for second in the Poly/AAA Marathon he won the European marathon in his usual front-running style in 2:20:04.6 and two months later set a world record for 30,000m on the track with 1:32:25.4. At the time he worked as a groundsman at Chiswick at the grounds of his club Polytechnic Harriers. He was 27th at 10,000m at the 1968 Olympic Games. Earlier he had represented Ireland at the 1962 Europeans (5000m ht and 10,000m) and 1964 Olympics (10,000m and marathon), but failing to finish in each of those races. In the Tokyo Olympic marathon he led with Ron Clarke and Abebe Bikila at 15k, and stayed in second to Bikila to 35k, but had to give up at that point. Other pbs: 3000m 8:14.0 (1967), 2M 8:43.6 (1965), 3M 13:19.6 (1965), 5000m 13:57.0 (1966), 6M 27:32.74 (1968), 10,000m 28:49.66 (1965), 15,000m 45:26.4 (1966), 10M 49:09.0 (1961), 1Hr 19,737m (1966), 20,000m 60:49.6 (1966), 25,000m 1:16:35.4 (1966).

Patrick JOURNOUD (France) (b. 27 Apr 1964 Casablanca, Morocco) on 16 January. At discus he was the 1983 European Junior bronze medallist and competed at the 1987 World Champs (dnq 24th) and 1988 Olympic Games (dnq 18th). He set French discus records with 62.36 (1967) and 63.02 (1988); pb SP 18.20 (1989). He was French champion at discus 1988-90 and indoor shot 1986; 15 internationals 1982-9.

Gerda Johanna Maria **van der KADE-KOUDIJS** (Netherlands) (b. 29 October 1923 Rotterdam) on 19 March Almelo, Netherlands at the age of 91. She ran the third leg for the Dutch team, anchored by Fanny Blankers-Koen, that set a world record for 4x110y with 47.4 at Rijswijk and two weeks later won the 4x100m at the 1948 Olympic Games. She had also run on world record setting relay teams at 4x110y and 4x200m in 1944. At the 1946 Europeans she won gold medals at long jump and 4x100m and was 6th at 100m and dq in her 80mh heat. She was Dutch champion at 200m in 1942-3 and long jump 1943. Pbs: 100m 11.9 (1944), 200m 25.2 (1942-3, 1947), 80mh 11.9 (1944), 11.4w (1946); LJ 5.76 (1947).

Jaroslav KOVÁR (Czech Republic) (b. 12 May 1934) in February. At high jump he won the European bronze medal in 1954, was Czechoslovak champion in 1955-7, set three national records: 2.02 in 1954 and 2.04 and 2.05 in 1955 and had a pb of 2.06 (1957). 15 internationals 1953-9. He became the top Czech high jump coach.

Väinö KUISMA (Finland) (b. 7 Aug 1934 in Vuoksenranta, Karelia, now Russia) on 18 February. At the javelin he was 4th at the Olympic Games in 1960, his then pb 78.40 missing the bronze medal by just 17 cm. He was controversially left out of 1964 Olympic team and set his final pb in October 1965 in Turku with 85.04, then 10th world all-time. In European Championships he was 5th 1958, 10th 1962, 6th 1966. 25 international matches 1957-66. Finnish champion 1958 and 1960 (five 2nd), Nordic silver 1961 and bronze 1965.

Esko LIPSONEN (Finland) (b. 24 Apr 1950 Vilppula) in Jyväskylä on 3 February. For a decade he was a top class distance runner, excelling in road relays during a great Finnish era, but he never made a big championship team in spite of pbs: 3000m 7:55.6 (1976), 5000m 13:39.9 (1979), 10,000m 28:36.4 (1973) and marathon 2:15:42 (on debut in Turku 1972 aged 21). He had two international dual matches, and at Finnish Champs was 2nd cross country 1972 and 1978 and 3rd 1973, 3rd 10,000m 1975 and marathon 1978.

Franjo MIHALIC (Croatia/Yugoslavia (Serbia) (b. 9 Mar 1920 Ludina village, Croatia) on 14 February in Belgrade. One of Yugoslavia's greatest ever athletes, he was the Olympic silver medallist at marathon in 1956, with 18th at 10,000m in 1952 and 12th marathon in 1960. At the Europeans he was 11th in 1950 and 5th in 1954 at 10,000m and dnf marathon 1958 and 1962. He won the Boston Marathon in 1958, Balkan 10000m 1954 and 1957, marathon 1956, cross-country 1958; and was Yugoslav champion at 5000m (1952, 1954), 10,000m (1946-7, 1949-51, 1953, 1955-60), cross-country (1948, 1953-4, 1956-7, 1959-60, 1963) and 25km road run (1956-8, 1960, 1962, 1964). He had also been champion in the war-time Croatia at 5000m 1943 and 10,000m 1943-4 before moving to Belgrade in 1047. Yugoslav records: 5000m (3) 14:20.8 (1952) to 14:19.6 (1954), 10,000m (14) 32:21.0 (1947) to 29:37.6 (1954) as well as (all still Serbian records) at 1 hour 19,214m, 15,000m 46:36.4 and 20,000m 1:02:24.4 (all 1952) and 25,000m 1:19:35.2 (1957). Other pbs: Pbs: 3000m 8:19.6 (1954), 5000m 14:18.8 (1956), 3000mSt 10:12.0 (1946), Marathon 2:21:24 (1957). 53 internationals for Yugoslavia. He became a teacher and athletics coach.

Oleg SAKIRKIN (USSR/Kazakhstan) (b. 23 Jan 1966 Shymkent) 18 March in Shymkent. Competing for the Soviet Union at triple jump. he won the World bronze medal in 1987 with European Indoor gold in 1988 and silver in 1990. He set his pb of 17.58 when 2nd in the USSR Championships in 1989 and that year won at the European Cup. With the splitting up of the USSR, he competed for Kazakhstan, set an Asian record 17.35, won at the Asian Games and was 3rd at the World Cup in 1994, and was 2nd in 1993 and 4th in 1995 at the Asian Champs. He was also dnq 28th at the 2000 Olympic Games, Central Asian champion in 1995 and 1999 and at the World University Games was 3rd in 1989 and 2nd in 1993. He first exceeded 15m in 1983, 16m in 1965 and was over 17m in ten successive years 1986-95, with 16.43 in his final season of 2003. Pb LJ 7.76 (1987).

Gustav SCHWENK (Germany) (b. 17 Dec 1923 Düsseldorf) in Düsseldorf on 11 January. A wonderful man, great athletics expert and marvellous journalist (also reporting handball), he began his career at the "Sport-Informations-Dienst" (sid) news agency in Düsseldorf from 1947 to 1957. In all he reported on 15 Summer Olympic Games, a record number for which he was honoured at the London 2012 Games. He was a founding member of the AIPS Athletics Commission from 1962 and a member of the IAAF Press Commission 1991-2006, as well as a press delegate at numerous World and European events, including nine World Junior Championships. He was honoured by the IAAF as their inaugural World Athletics Journalist in 2009.

Eino SIMELIUS (Finland) (b. 14 Dec 1931 Karijoki) on 12 January in Helsinki. Originally a discus thrower with a pb of 47.40 (1953) and Finnish champs bronze in 1953 and 1954, he changed to high jump, winning Finnish title in 1956 with two silvers and a bronze. Six international matches 1956-7, pb 2.06 (1962).

Lang Joseph **STANLEY** Jr. (USA) (b. 10 Apr 1931 Los Angeles) in March. His pb for 800m was 1:47.6, a time that ranked him 8th in the world in 1955. He won the NCAA 880y title for San Jose Sate in 1953 and at AAU Championships he was 4th in 1954 and 1955 and 3rd in 1957, while just missing out on an Olympic place as he was 4th in the 1956 Trials 800m. He later worked as an insurance broker and as a Veteran Affairs Counselor.

Markku TUOKKO (Finland) (b. 24 Jun 1951 Nurmo) on 20 February in Lohja. A school teacher and rangy discus thrower 196 cm tall, in 1973 he improved by 8m to 65.60, still the Finnish U23 record. Over 60m for 11 consecutive years, his pb was 68.12 in Fresno in May 1979; a Finnish record for 22 years. He was one of the three host country athletes caught for anabolic steroids, the first doping cases in Finnish athletics, at the European Cup final in Helsinki 1977. After a one-year ban he took the 1978 European silver. He was 9th at the Olympic Games in 1980 and 4th World Cup 1977 (later annulled). 19 wins in 29 international matches and 5 European Cups 1972-84. Finnish champion 1977 and 1979-82 (with four silvers). At shot: pb 20.03 (1979), 4th European indoors 1979, two Finnish champs silvers and one bronze.

Charlie (Charles) **THOMAS** (USA) (b. 3 Oct 1931 Fostoria, Texas) on 26 January in Bryan, Texas. He anchored University of Texas teams to a ratified 4x110y world record of 40.5 in May 1954 (and an unratified 40.3 the previous month). He narrowly failed to make the US Olympic team in 1952, clocking 21.2 for 200m (turn) and 20.3w 200m (straight) that year. In 1953 he ran 9.5 for 100y, equal third fastest in the world that season; in 1954 he recorded 21.1 for 220y (turn) and the year's equal quickest straight 220y time of 20.5. He won the NCAA 220y in 1954 and silver in the 1955 Pan American Games 200m; in the AAU he was 2nd at 220y in 1954 and 3rd at 200m in 1951 (straight track) and in 1952. He became head track coach at East Texas State University in 1956 and at Texas A&M in 1959; when he retired in 1990 he had produced eight world record holders, three Olympic champions and two silver medallists, eight American record holders and 22 NCAA individual champions.

Dan TUNSTALL PEDOE (GBR) (b. 30 Dec 1939 Southampton) on 13 February. A distinguished cardiac consultant, he was medical director of the London Marathon from its inception in 1981 to 2008 and was the most experienced doctor in marathon medicine.

Klaus ULONSKA (Germany) (b. 10 Dec 1942 Cologne) in March. He was a gold medallist at 4x100m (and sf 200m) at the 1962 European Championships. 2nd FRG 100m 1961, he had 20 internationals 1961-4 with pbs 100m 10.4 and 200m 20.9 (both 1962).

Add to 2013

Gladys Mary **CLARKE** later PENTLAND (GBR) (b. 15 Feb 1923 West Bromwich) on 10 June in Weston-super-Mare. A member of Birchfield Harriers, she competed at the 1948 Olympic Games (dnq 15th) and in one international in 1950 at javelin; and was WAAA champion in 1945; pb 35.60 (1949).

Vladislavs VAIVADS (Latvia) (b. 11 Sep 1929) on 27 October in Moscow. The first Latvian 60m plus hammer thrower, he was four times Latvian champion and set six national records to 62.05 (1958). He coached in Cuba and in Moscow, returning to Latvia in 1991 and was a long-time IAAF Technical Delegate.

DRUG BANS 2014

AS ANNOUNCED BY IAAF or national governing bodies. Suspension: L - life ban, y = years, m = months, W = warning and disqualification, P = pending hearing

Leading athletes

Men *Name*	*Date*	*Ban*
Yuriy Andronov RUS	3 May	2y
Quentin Bigot FRA	21 Jun	4y
(2 of 4 years suspended)		
Andriy Borodkin UKR	3 Jun	4y
Adil Bouafif SWE		P
Abderrahim El Asri MAR	16 Feb	2y
Abdellah Haidane ITA	23 Feb	4m
Jeremy Hicks USA	1 Apr	1y
Grigoriy Kamulya UZB	14 Jun	20m
Dmitriy Khomutov RUS	14 Jul	2y
Myhaylo Knysh UKR	25 Jul	2y
Rutger Koppelaar NED	31 May	2y
Martin Maric CRO	13 Jul	2y
Edder Moreno COL	16 Feb	2y
Dmytro Mykolaychuk UKR	Jul	2y
Kofi Amoah Prah GER	16 Feb	2y
Andrey Ruzavin RUS	9 Oct	2.5y
Mohammed Shaween KSA		3y
Wallace Spearmon USA	6 Jul	3m
Mihail Stamatóyiannis GRE		P
James Theuri FRA	9 May	1y
Sergiu Ursu ROU	11 Mar	2y
Gareth Warburton GBR	17 Jun	6m
Rhys Williams GBR	11 Jul	4m
Women		
Svetlana Biryukova RUS	26 Feb	2y
Emily Chepkorir KEN	26 Jan	2y
Tatyana Dektyareva RUS	9 Dec	2y
Alyona Dubitskaya BLR	31 Aug	6m
Vanda Gomes BRA	25 Sep	P
Anca Heltne ROU	7 Feb	8y
Adrienne Herzog NED	Mar	2y
Grigoría-Emmanouéla Keramidá GRE		P
Rita Jeptoo KEN	25 Sep	2y
Natalya Kholodilina RUS	13 Sep	P
Joyce Kiplimo KEN	20 Apr	2y
Nataliya Lupu UKR	7 Mar	9m
Inika McPherson USA	29 Jun	21m
Nadezhda Mokayeva RUS-J	23 Mar	2y
Julia Mombi KEN	14 Sep	2y
Amantle Montsho BOT	29 Jul	2y
Nadia Noujani MAR	26 Apr	2y
Mariya Ryemyen UKR	10 Jan	2y
Kseniya Ryzhova (née Vdovina) RUS	7 Mar	9m
Mouna Tabsart MAR	16 Feb	8y
Laïla Traby FRA		P
Yuliya Tutayeva RUS	26 Feb	2y
Irina Yumanova RUS	22 Mar	2y
Ruddy Zang Milama GAB	21 May	7m

8y: Ketki Sethi IND (16 Aug); **4y:** Giuseppe Baldelli ITA (6 Apr); **3y:** Himik Marcin SWE (3 Jun), Dmitriy Sentsov RUS (12 Jul); **2y:** Abror Akramov UZB (14 May), Abdulaziz Aldossary KSA (17 May), Angeeta IND (11 May), Erwan Baqas FRA (29 Jun), Kevin Becerra MEX (17 May), Abdelkri Boubker MAR (23 May), Rodolfo Casanova URU (16 Mar), Cheng Jungzhai CHN (4 Jan), Alexei Cravcenko MDA (12 Aug), Poliuna Dontsova RUS (26 Apr), Mikhail Feropontov RUS (12 Jul), Søren Hammer DEN (26 Mar), Yevgeniya Ivanova RUS (1 Aug), Philip Kandie KEN, Andrey Khizbulin RUS (12 Jul), Naveen Kumar IND (6 Jun), Sunil Kumar IND (6 Jun), Aziz Makhrout MAR (8 Apr), Amit Malik IND (7 Aug), Mikael Malmqvist SWE (17 Jun), Manisha IND (10 Mar), Raja Oomon IND (24 May), Olga & Yelena Paushkina RUS-Y (16 Apr), Graziella Persico ITA (6 Jul), Martinique Potgieter RSA (1 Jun), Catalina Puscasu ROU (30 Aug), Sara Ramadhani TAN (12 Jan), Leidy Ramirez Manase DOM (29 May), Shahin Mehrdelan IRI (13 Jun), Baba Mohammed IND (8 Jul), Stanislav Mokin RUS (25 Apr), Yuliya Nevyantseva RUS (14 Feb), Yelena Ryabenko RUS (14 Jul), Vitaliy Ryzhykov RUS (20 Dec) Sandeep IND (4 Sep), Damir Saurbayev RUS (15 Jul), Viktor Sayenko RUS (30 Mar), Roman Semakin RUS (26 Feb), Vyacheslav Shalamov RUS (16 Apr), Ulyana Sharikova RUS (30 Mar), Sikender IND (7 Aug), Karan Singh IND (2 Sep), Navtejdeep Singh IND (9 May), Stephen Tanui KEN (26 Jan), Yelena Tarakanova RUS (12 Jul), Azaliya Valeyeva RUS (12 Jul), Ioan Vasile ROU 16 Feb, S.Velayutham IND (19 Aug), Anna Yagupova RUS (12 Jul), Sahir Ziaee IRI (20 Jun); **1y:** Kristi Anderson USA (17 Aug); **9m:** Yevgeniy Pantyushin RUIS (13 Sep); **6m:** Parneet Kaur IND (10 Mar), Niklas Lindstedt SWE (22 Mar), Quintaveon Poole USA (27 Jul), Gareth Warburton GBR (17 Jun); **4m:** Paolo Cannas ITA (27 Apr); 4m: Rhys Williams GBR (11 Jul); **3m:** Praveen Kumar IND (10 May), P.K.Prajitha IND (9 May); W: Asli Arik TUR (27 Mar); P: Theópistos Mavrídis GRE

Jon Drummond, coach of Tyson Gay and others, received an 8-year ban from all coaching activity to run from 17 Dec 2014.

Three year 2 month bans for biological passport anomalies for five top Russian walkers were announced in January 2015. These were dated back to late 2009 and are likely to result (subject to IAAF ratification)

in Sergey Kirdyapkin losing 2009 World and 2012 World Cup and Olympic wins – all at 50k; Sergey Bakulin losing 2010 European bronze 2011 World title and 2012 Olympic 5th place – all at 50k, and Olga Kaniskina losing 2009 and 2011 World and 2010 European titles and 2012 Olympic silver. Valeriy Borchin received an 8-year ban and faces losing 2009 and 2011 World titles. Vladimir Kanaykin received a life ban and should lose 2011 World silver and 2012 World Cup bronze at 20k.

Yuliya Zaripova was given a 2 years 6 months ban backdated from 22 July 2013 with results also annulled between 20 Jun 2011 and 20 Aug 2011 and 3 Jul to 3 Sep 2012, thus losing her 2012 Olympic title.

Tatyana Chernova was given a 2 years ban backdated from 22 July 2013 with results also annulled between 15 Aug 2009 and 14 Aug 2011.

Add to Drugs Bans 2013

Men

Aysegül Aniacik TUR	24 Aug	2y
Walter Davis USA	1 Jul	1y
Reggie Dixon USA	16 Dec	1y
Matej Gasaj SVK	13 Oct	2y
Abraham Kiprotich FRA	17 Nov	2y
Asafa Powell JAM	21 Jun	6m
Joshua Ross USA	3 Jul	1.5y
Traves Smikle JAM	22 Jun	2y
Yevgenit Ustavshchikov RUS	22 Dec	2y

Women

Dominique Blake JAM	1 Jul	4.5y
Tatyana Chernova RUS	22 Jul	2y
Agnisezka Gortel POL	13 Oct	2y
Halima Hachlaf MAR	14 Oct	4y
Yevgeniya Pecherina RUS	23 Jun	10y
Allison Randall JAM	21 Jun	2y
Sherone Simpson JAM	21 Jun	6m
Nevin Yanit TUR	8 Feb	3y
Yuliya Zaripova RUS	25 Jul	2.5y

6y: Jagdish Patel IND (28 Aug); **4y**: Alexander Gnezdilov RUS (22 Dec), Lindikhaya Mthangayi RSA (22 Sep); **2y**: Ashwini IND (25 Dec), Andrew Carnes USA (1 Jun), Viola Chelangat Kimetto KEN (1 Dec), Benjamin Kipkurui Cheruiyot (24 Nov), Dipti Chutiya IND (30 Nov), José Roberto de Jesus BRA (3. Nov), Sergio Dias POR (12 Feb), Dilyogi IND (25.Dec), Aleksandra Gulyayeva RUS (22 Dec), Dhamender Kumar IND (26 Dec), Gaurav Kumar IND (23 Sep), Aleksandr Gnezdilov RUS (22 Dec), Surender Kumar IND (6 Dec), Saw Mar Lar New MYA (15 Dec), Udaya Laxmi IND (5 Jun), Sumit Malik IND (5 Dec), Eloita Michiuye BRA (17 Nov); Bianca Moreno COL (8 Dec), Julius Mutai KEN (1 Dec), Ak. Hafiy Tajuddin Rositi BRU (15 Dec), Tsehynesh Tsake AZE (27 Dec); **16m**: Daniela Roman AUS (16 Mar); **1y**: Damar Robinson JAM (16 Jun); **4m**: Hiriut Beyene ETH (5 May).

A suspension given to Kelly-Ann Baptiste TTO was lifted in January 2015 after appeal to the CAS.

Add to Drugs Bans 2012

Men

Hamza Driouch QAT*	2 Aug	2y
Daniel Pineda CHI	30 Jun	2y
Mo Trafeh USA	1 Jan	4y
Sourabh Vij IND	8 Apr	4y

Tyson Gay USA loses all marks from 15 Jul 2012, with a one-year ban from 23 Jun 2013.

Women

Elizabeth Chelagat KEN	2 Dec	2y
Semoy Hackett TTO	9 Jun	2y 4m
Meriem Alaoui Selsouli MAR	6 Jul	8y

2y: Patrick Fakiye AUS (11 Feb), Alice Ndirangu KEN (16 Dec), James Nyankabaria KEN (2 Dec)

Add to Drugs Bans 2011

Men

Mohammed Shahween KSA	12 Nov	3y

Women

Yekaterina Kostetskaya RUS	30 Aug	2y
Binnaz Uslu TUR	30 Aug	L

Add to Drugs Bans 2010

Men

Stanislav Yemelyanov RUS	26 Jul	2y

Women

Natalya Koreyvo BLR*	28 Oct	2y

Add to Drugs Bans 2009

Men

Hussain Al-Hamdah KSA*	26 Mar	2.5y

Women

Anna Alminova RUS*	16 Feb	30m
Liliya Shobukhova RUS	9 Oct	2y

* Athlete Biological Passport Case.

Ivan Tikhon BLR has received a 2-year ban following positive tests (on re-testing) on 23 Aug 2004 and 8 Aug 2005.

Added in March 2015

The anti-doping commission of the All-Russian athletics federation has banned race walkers Andrey Ruzavin (28) and Nina Okhotnikova based on abnormal measures of their biological passports. Ruzavin was banned for two and half year from 9 Oct 2014 and his results in periods 18.12.2011 – 18.02.2012 and 13.09.2013 – 13.11.2013 were cancelled. Okhotnikova was banned for two years starting from 22 January 2015 with results cancellation from 21.6.2011 – 17.11.2011.

WORLD LISTS 1965

= world record.
me auto times are ahown to hundredths of a second

MEN – 100 YARDS

2	Bob Lay AUS	1	Sydney	10 Mar
2	Richard Stebbins USA	1	Baton Rouge	10 Apr
3	George Anderson USA	1	Prairie View	3 Apr
3	George Eriquezzo USA	1	Little Riock	15 Apr
3	Craig Wallace USA	1	Lexington	1 May
3	Darel Newman USA	1	Fresno	1 May
3	Fred Kuller USA	1	Fresno	8 May
3	Larry Questad USA	1	Fresno	1 May
3	Harry Jerome CAN	1	Toronto	10 Jun
3	Mel Pender USA	2	Toronto	10 Jun
5	Jim Freeman USA	1	Elizabeth NJ	20 Aug

th best 9.5, 100th 9.6

2w	Terry Williams USA	1	Hobbs	1 May
3Aw	Zeak Williaims	1	El Paso	30 Mar
3Aw	Bernie Rivers USA	1	Albuquerque	3 Apr
3w	William Hurd USA	1	Memphis	16 Apr
3w	Billy Foster USA	1	Dallas	1 May
3w	Wayne Brandt USA	2	College Station	8 May

100 METRES

.0!	Chen Chua-chuan CHN	1	Chungking	24 Oct
.1A	J-L Ravelonanantsoa MAD	1	Antanarivo	3 Apr
.1	Darel Newman USA	1	Kyiv	31 Jul
.1	Wieslaw Maniak POL	1	Szczecin	13 Aug
.1	Enrique Figuerola CUB	1	Caracas	13 Nov
.2	16 men, 50th best 10.3, 100th 10.4			
.1w	Hideo Iijima JPN	1	Budapest	26 Aug
.1w	George Anderson USA	2	Budapest	26 Aug

200 METRES (* 220y less 0.1 sec.)

.4*	Edwin Roberts TRI	1	Sioux Falls	5 Jun
.5*	Tommie Smith USA	1	San Jose	27 Feb
.5*	Clyde Glosson USA	1	Prairie View	1 May
	20.3*	1	xx	xx
.5A	Clyde Duncan USA	1	Cd. de México	17 Apr
.5*	Richard Stebbins USA	1	Houston	8 May
.5	Claude Piquemal FRA	1	Paris	11 Jun
.5*	Adolph Plummer USA	1	San Diego	27 Jun
0.5	Paul Drayton USA	1	Caracas	13 Nov
0.5	Thomas Randolph USA	2	Caracas	13 Nov
0.5	Enrique Figuerola CUB	1	La Habana	12 Dec

0th best 20.9, 100th 21.0

220 YARDS Straight Track (* 200m +0.1)

0.1*	Tommie Smith USA	1	San Jose	13 Mar
0.0w	Eli Myers USA	1	Gary	1 May

400 METRES (* 440y less 0.3 sec.)

5.5*	Theron Leewis USA	1s2	San Diego	26 Jun
5.6	Andrej Badenski POL	1	Warszawa	7 Aug
5.8*	Ulis Williams USA	1	Tempe	27 Mar
5.8*	Jim Kemp USA	1	Long Beach	12 Jun
5.8*	Ollan Cassell USA	1	San Diego	27 Jun
5.9*	Don Owens USA	2	Houston	8 May
5.9*	Ray Saddler USA	3	Houston	8 May
5.9*	Everett Mason USA	1	Beaumont	22 May
5.9*	Don Payne USA	1	Bakersfield	22 Jun

6.0* Doyle Magee, Bob Tobler, Art Carter, Lyn Saunders, onert Johnson, Forrest Beaty all USA; Wendell Mottley RI; 50th best 46.6, 100th 47.1

800 METRES (* 880y less 0.7 sec.)

:46.3	Jürgen May GBR	1	Potsdam	25 Aug
:46.6	Chris Carter GBR	1	Berlin	5 Sep
:46.7*	John Garrison USA	1	Los Angeles	7 Jul
1:46.8*	Morgan Groth USA	1	Pullman	22 May
:46.8	George Germann USA	1	Kyiv	31 Jul
:47.0*	George Hunt USA	1	Houston	29 May
:47.0*	Dave Perry USA	2	Houston	29 May
1:47.1	Bill Crothers CAN	1	Oslo	14 Jul
1:47.1	Jan Kasal TCH	1	Praha	30 Sep
1:47.1*	Wade Bell USA	2	Pullman	22 May

50th best 1:48.4, 100th 1:49.3

1000 METRES

2:16.2!	Jürgen May GBR	1	Erfurt	20 Jul
2:18.6	Josef Odlozil TCH	1	Stara Boleslav	15 Sep
2:18.9	Siegfried Herrmann GDR	2	Erfurt	20 Jul
2:18.9	Wolf-Dieter Holtz GDR	1	Potsdam	20 Aug
2:18.9	Bernd Dissner GDR	2	Potsdam	20 Aug
2:19.0	Jan Kasal TCH	1	Stara Boleslav	6 Oct

1500 METRES

3:36.4	Jürgen May GBR	1	Erfurt	16 Jul
3:36.6+	Kipchoge Keino KEN	1	Auckland	15 Dec
3:38.4	Michel Jazy FRA	1	Rennes	9 Jun
3:39.0	Jim Grelle USA	1	Köln	7 Jul
3:39.5	Bodo Tummler FRG	2	Köln	7 Jul
3:39.7+	Josef Odlozil TCH	3	London (WC)	30 Aug
3:39.8	Harald Norpoth FRG	3	Köln	7 Jul
3:40.4	Jim Ryun USA	2	Kyiv	1 Aug
3:40.6+	Alan Simpson GBR	4	London (WC)	30 Aug
3:40.7	Bob Schul USA	4	Köln	7 Jul
3:40.7	Dyrol Burleson USA	1	Kouvala	19 Jul

50th best 3:43.9, 100th 3:45.9

1 MILE

3:53.6	Michel Jazy FRA	1	Rennes	9 Jun
3:53.8	Jürgen May GBR	1	Wanganui	11 Dec
3:54.16	Kipchoge Keino KEN	1	London (WC)	30 Aug
3:55.3	Jim Ryun USA	1	San Diego	27 Jun
3:55.4	Jim Grelle USA	1	Vancouver	15 Jun
3:55.4	Peter Snell NZL	2	San Diego	27 Jun
3:55.55	Josef Odlozil TCH	2	London (WC)	30 Aug
3:55.68	Alan Simpson GBR	3	London (WC)	30 Aug
3:56.4	Bob Day USA	1	Bakersfield	12 Jun
3:56.8	John Davies NZL	3	Auckland	17 Nov
3:57.2	Jean Wadoux FRA	2	St. Maur	2 Jun
3:57.4	Witold Baran POL	3	St. Maur	2 Jun

50th best 4:02.7, 100th 4:06.1

2000 METRES

5:01.2!	Josef Odlozil TCH	1	Stara Boleslav	8 Sep

3000 METRES

7:39.6!	Kipchoge Keino KEN	1	Halsingborg	27 Aug
7:46.0!	Siegfried Herrmann GDR	1	Erfurt	5 Aug
7:48.6	Gaston Roelants BEL	1	Heverlee	15 Aug
7:49.0+	Michel Jazy FRA	1	Melun	23 Jun
7:51.0+	Ron Clarke AUS	2	Melun	23 Jun
7:51.0	John Davies NZL	1	Karlovy Vary	11 Jul

2 MILES

8:22.6!	Michel Jazy FRA	1	Melun	23 Jun
8:24.8	Ron Clarke AUS	2	Melun	23 Jun
8:25.2	Kipchoge Keino KEN	1	Sydney	19 Dec

5000 METRES

13:24.2!	Kipchoge Keino KEN	1	Auckland	30 Nov
13:25.0!	Ron Clarke AUS	1	Los Angeles	4 Jun
13:27.6	Michel Jazy FRA	1	Helsinki	30 Jun
13:30.0	Siegfried Herrmann GDR	1	Potsdam	11 Aug
13:35.0	Mike Wiggs GBR	4	Helsinki	30 Jun
13:36.8	Gaston Roelants BEL	3	Stockholm	6 Jul
13:37.4	Thor Helland NOR	5	Helsinki	30 Jun
13:37.8	Bengt Najde SWE	6	Helsinki	30 Jun
13:39.90	Lajos Mecser HUN	1	London (WC)	14 Aug
13:41.4	Billy Mills USA	1	Oslo	15 Jul

50th best 13:57.4, 100th 14:10.2 (14:04.8 inc. 3M equiv.)

3 Miles

12:52.26	Ron Clarke AUS	1	London (WC)	10 Jul
12:58.6+	Kipchoge Keino KEN	1	Auckland	30 Nov
13:04.02	Gerry Lindgren USA	2	London (WC)	10 Jul

13:04.8+	Michel Jazy	1	Helsinki	30 Jun
13:07.54	Lajos Mecser HUN	3	London (WC)	10 Jul
13:08.6+	Mike Wiggs GBR	4	Helsinki	30 Jun
13:08.6+	Gaston Roelants BEL	3	Stockholm	6 Jul
13:10.4	Bob Schul USA	1	San Diego	26 Jun
13:10.8	Neville Scott NZL	2	San Diego	26 Jun

10,000 METRES

27:39.4!	Ron Clarke AUS	1	Oslo	14 Jul
28:10.6	Gaston Roelants BEL	1	Oslo	21 Aug
28:17.6	Billy Mills USA	1	Augsburg	12 Aug
28:22.0	Nikolay Dutov URS	1	Kyiv	21 Jul
28:29.8	Leonid Ivanov URS	2	Kyiv	21 Jul
28:31.2	Lajos Mecser HUN	2	Oslo	21 Aug
28:37.2	Mike Freary GBR	1	Berlin	4 Sep
28:35.6	Lutz Philipp FRG	2	Augsburg	12 Aug
28:45.2	Bernard Maroquin FRA	4	Oslo	21 Aug
28:46.0	Kazimierz Zimny POL	3	Stuttgart	11 Sep
28:47.2	Kestutis Orentas URS	1	Kyiv	5 Aug

50th best 29:20.4, 100th 29:46.6 (29:41.0 inc. 6M equiv.)

6 Miles

26:47.0!	Ron Clarke AUS	1	Oslo	14 Jul
27:11.6!	Billy Mills USA	1	San Diego	27 Jun
27:11.6!	Gerry Lindgren USA	1	San Diego	27 Jun
27:38.12	Mohamed Gammoudi TUN	1	London (WC)	9 Jul
27:40.90	Ron Hill GBR	2	London (WC)	9 Jul
28:43.0+	Mike Freary GBR	1	Berlin	4 Sep
27:43.76	Mike Bullivant GBR	3	London (WC)	9 Jul
27:44.78	Jim Hogan IRL	4	London (WC)	9 Jul

MARATHON

2:12:00!	Mario Shigematsu JPN	1	Chiswick	12 Jun
2:12:41	Toru Terasawa JPN	2	Chiswick	12 Jun
2:14:34	Leonard Edelen USA	3	Chiswick	12 Jun
2:15:37	Takayuki Nakao JPN	2	Beppu	7 Feb
2:16:07.8	Hideaki Shishido JPN	3	Beppu	7 Feb
2:16:26	Yoshikazu Funasako JPN	4	Beppu	7 Feb
2:16:47	Hirokzu Okabe JPN	4	Chiswick	12 Jun
2:16:50	Bill Adcocks GBR	1	Port Talbot	21 Aug
2:16:57	Kazuo Mitsubara JPN	6	Beppu	7 Feb
2:16:57.4	Chang You-cheng CHN	1	Beijing	28 Apr

50th best 2:21:38, 100th 2:24:05

3000m STEEPLECHASE

8:26.4!	Gaston Roelants BEL	1	Bruxelles	7 Aug
8:29.6	Ivan Belyayev URS	1	Moskva	10 Aug
8:31.0	Viktor Kudinsky URS	1	Minsk	4 Jul
8:31.6	Aleksandr Morozov URS	2	Moskva	10 Aug
8:32.6	Adolfas Aleksejunas URS	3	Moskva	10 Aug
8:34.2	Bengt Persson SWE	1	Stockholm	23 Jul
8:36.0	Zoltan Vamos ROU	1	Timosoara	17 Jul
8:36.2	Maurice Herriott GBR	1	Zagreb	22 Aug
8:37.6	Jouko Kuma FIN	1	Stockholm	4 Sep
8:37.8	Victor Caramihai ROU	2	Timosoara	17 Jul

50th best 8:48.4, 100th 8:55.6

110 METRES HURDLES (y = 120yh)

13.5	Willie Davenport USA	1	Kyiv	31 Jul
13.5	Lin Tsui CHN	1	Wuhan	15 Nov
13.5Ay	Gerry Cerulla USA	1	Logan	11 May
13.6A	Roy Hicks USA	1	Cd. de México	17 Apr
13.6	Eddy Ottoz ITA	1	Budapest	29 Aug
13.6	Liang Shih-chiangi CHN	2	Wuhan	15 Nov
13.6y	Don Shy USA	1	Fresno	8 May
13.6Ay	Al Rockwell USA	2	Logan	11 May
13.7	Bobby May USA	1	Eugene	20 Jun
13.7	Blaine Lindgren USA	2	Kyiv	31 Jul
13.7	Anatoliy Mikhailov URS	1	Oslo	21 Aug
13.7y	Roger Morgan USA	1	Natchitoches	14 Apr
	13.6yw	1	Natchitoches	8 May
13.7y	Roger Mann USA	2	Natchitoches	14 Apr
	13.6yw	2	Natchitoches	8 May
13.7y	Arnoldo Bristol PUR	1	Houston	29 May
13.7y	Paul Kerry USA	1	Bakersfield	12 Jun

50th best 14.0, 100th 14.2

200 METRES HURDLES

22.8	Vyach. Skomorokov URS	1	Alma-Ata	17 Sep
22.9	Vasiliy Anisimov	2	Alma-Ata	17 Sep

400 METRES HURDLES (* 440y less 0.3 sec.)

49.5	Vasiliy Anisimov URS	1	Alma-Ata	16 Oct
50.0*	Rex Cawley USA	1	San Diego	26 Jun
50.0	Roberto Frinolli ITA	1	Roma	30 Oct
50.2	Ron Whitney USA	1	Augsburg	12 Aug
50.4*	Gary Knoke AUS	1	Melbourne	14 Feb
50.5*	Jay Luck USA	3	San Diego	26 Jun
50.5	Imants Kuklich URS	1	Kyiv	8 Aug
50.5	Edvins Zageris URS	2	Alma-Ata	16 Oct
50.6*	Roger Johnson NZL	1	Pullman	22 May
50.6	Robert Poirier FRA	1	Oslo	22 Aug

50th best 51.8, 100th 52.5

HIGH JUMP

2.25	Ni Zhiqin CHN	1	Wuhan	20 Nov
2.21i	Valeriy Brumel URS	1	New York	11 Feb
	2.19	1	Oslo	21 Aug
2.19	Lawrie Peckham AUS	1	Melbourne	23 Oct
2.19	Tony Sneazwell AUS	2	Melbourne	23 Oct
2.18i	Eduard Czernik POL	1	New York	25 Feb
	2.17	1	Zielona Gora	10 Oct
2.18	Viktor Bolshov URS	1	Minsk	3 Jul
2.18	Otis Burrell USA	1	Warszawa	8 Aug
2.17	Ed Carruthers USA	1	Norwalk	15 Apr
2.16A	Gene Johnson USA	1	Nairobi	5 May
2.15	Valeriy Skvortsov URS	1	Kyiv	25 Jul

50th best 2.09, 100th 2.06

POLE VAULT

5.18	John Pennel USA	1	San Diego	26 Jun
5.06	John Cramer USA	1	Lahja	22 Aug
5.05	Paul Wilson USA	1	Westminster	22 Mar
5.05	Wolfgang Nordwig GDR	1	Potsdam	11 Aug
5.03i	Billy Pemelton USA	1	Louisville	27 Feb
5.02i	Mel Hein USA	1	San Francisco	26 Feb
5.00i	Wolfgang Reinhardt FRG	1	Kiel	23 Jan
5.00i	Rudolf Tomasek TCH	1	Bratislava	5 Mar
5.00	Gennadiy Bliznyetsov URS	1	Alma-Ata	15 Oct
4.98	Jeff Chase USA	1	Los Angeles	4 Jun
	5.05 exh	-	Wichita	23 Jul
4.98	Bob Seagren USA	3	San Diego	26 Jun

50th best 4.80, 100th 4.68

LONG JUMP

8.35!	Ralph Boston USA	1	Modesto	29 May
8.19	Igor Ter-Ovanesyan URS	1	Budapest	28 Aug
8.16	Clarence Robinson USA	1	Des Monies	23 Apr
8.04	Rainer Stenius FIN	1	Jyväskylä	7 Aug
8.00	Leonid Barkhovskiy URS	3	Kyiv	31 Jul
7.99	Dennis Holland USA	1	Kalamazoo	29 May
7.92A	Wellesley Clayton JAM	1	Albuquerque	3 Apr
7.89	Lynn Davies GBR	2	Budapest	28 Aug
	7.99w	1	Swansea	23 Jun
7.88	Hirromi Yamada JPN	1	Tokyo	8 May
7.86	Darrell Horn USA	4	Kyiv	31 Jul
7.84	Pentti Eskola FIMN	1	Kauhbva	28 Jun

50th best 7.62, 100th 7.51

TRIPLE JUMP

16.74	Józef Schmidt POL	1	London (WC)	30 Jul
16.54	Henrik Kalocsaii HUN	1	Warszawa	20 Jun
16.51	Hans-Jürgen Ruckborn GDR	1	Stuttgart	12 Sep
16.50	Aleksandr Zolotaryev URS	1	Kyiv	1 Aug
16.41	Tien Chao-chung CHN	1	Beijing	15 Sep
16.39	Fred Alsop GBR	4	Stuttgart	12 Sep
	16.65w	1	London (WC)	13 Aug
16.35	Dragan Ivanov HUN	2	Budapest	29 Aug
16.35	Michael Sauer FRG	3	Budapest	29 Aug

34 Art Walker USA 1 Los Angeles 26 Jul
16.56w 1 Modesto 29 May
32 Aleksandr Lazarenko URS 1 Alma-Ata 17 Oct
th best 15.94, 100th 15.61
29w Ian Tomlinson AUS 1 Melbourne 4 Jan

SHOT

.52! Randy Matson USA 1 College Station 8 May
.40i John McGrath USA 1 San Francisco 26 Feb
19.20 1 San Diego 27 Jun
.34 Neal Steinhauer USA 1 Grants Pass 12 Jun
.21i Jay Silvester USA 2 Los Angeles 13 Feb
18.96 1 Walnut 24 Apr
.19 Nikolay Karasyov URS 1 Stuttgart 11 Sep
.14 Dave Price USA 1 Sioux Falls 5 Jun
.10 Vilmos Varju HUN 1 Gyula 23 May
.00 Viktor Lipsnis URS 3 Kyiv 31 Jul
.98 Dave Maggard USA 2 San Diego 27 Jun
.98 Les Mills NZL 1 Rotorua 28 Dec
th best 17.94, 100th 17.29

DISCUS

.22! Ludvik Danek TCH 1 Sokolov 12 Oct
.16 Jay Silvester USA 2 Long Beach 4 Jun
.64 Bill Neville USA 1 Long Beach 27 Feb
.41 Randy Matson USA 1 Waco 14 Apr
.25 Dave Weill USA 2 Sacramento 12 Jun
.49 Zenon Begier POL 1 Warszawa 22 Jul
.41 Rink Babka USA 3 Long Beach 5 Jun
.41 Bob Humphreys USA 1 Long Beach 14 Aug
.32 Edmund Piatkowski POL 1 Szczecin 14 Aug
.00 Parry O'Brien USA 1 Oxnard 25 Jul
th best 55.24, 100th 53.83

HAMMER

.75! Gyula Zsivótzky HUN 1 Debrecen 4 Sep
.26! Hal Connolly USA 1 Walnut 20 Jun
.02 Romuald Klim URS 1 Oslo 21 Aug
.70 Ed Burke USA 2 Walnut 20 Jun
.40 Gennadiy Kondrashov URS 1 Alma-Ata 16 Oct
.10 Aleksey Baltovskiy URS 1 Kherson 4 Sep
.04 Yuriy Nikulin URS 2 Kyiv 18 Jul
.84 Uwe Beyer FRG 1 Kiel 9 Oct
.54 Martin Lotz GDR 1 Leipzig 20 Jun
.02 Anatoliy Shuplyakov URS 1 Leselidze 18 Apr
th best 63.44, 100th 61,09

JAVELIN

.14 Jorma Kinnunen FIN 1 Hyvinkää 8 Jun
.56 Janis Lusis URS 1 Tbilisi 25 Oct
.50 Janusz Sidlo POL 1 Zürich 29 Jun
.04 Vaino Kuisma FIN 1 Turku 3 Oct
4.28 Ari Suppanen FIN 1 Vuohijärvi 26 Sep
4.18 Gergely Kulcsar HUN 1 Oslo 22 Aug
4.05 Maat Paama URS 1 Tartu 25 Sep
3.35 Frank Covelli USA 1 Long Beach 4 Sep
3.28 Manfred Stolle GDR 2 Helsinki 28 Jul
2.91 Larry Stuart USA 1 Long Beach 10 Jul
0th best 77.14, 100th 74.38

DECATHLON (1962 tables)

863 Mikhail Storozhenko URS 1 Kyiv 1 Aug
848 Kurt Bendlin FRG 1 Augsburg 5 Sep
764 Bill Toomey USA 1 Bakersfield 1 Jul
682 Russ Hodge USA 2 Bakersfield 1 Jul
636 Horst Beyer FRG 1 Augsburg 12 Augl
600 Paul Herman USA 2 Walnut 12 Jun
556 Rein Aun URS 3 Kyiv 1 Aug
519 Yuriy Dyachkov URS 1 Alma-Ata 16 Oct
486 Don Shy USA 3 Walnut 12 Jun
486 Frank Vravnik YUG 1 Celje 27 Jun
0th best 7074

20 KILOMETRES WALK

:27:21.8 Hans-Joachim Pathus GDR 1 K-Marx-St 25Jul
1:27:32.4 Hans-Georg Reimann GDR 2 K-Marx-St 25Jul
1:28:09.8 Dieter Lindner GDR 1 Pescara 9 Oct
1:28:47.2 Gerhard Sperling GDR 4 Karl-Marx-St. 25 Jul
1:28:52 Albert Kotov URS 1 Mosyr 16 May
1:29:08.2 Antal Kiss HUN 2 Pescara 9 Oct
1:29:22.8 Georg Gutpelcs URS 1 Minsk 25 May
1:29:23.0 Janis Zveidris URS 2 Minsk 25 May
1:29:23.2 Jaan Poldma URS 3 Minsk 25 May
1:29:24,6 Peter Frenkel GDR 5 Karl-Marx-St 25 Jul
50th best 1:32:10

50 KILOMETRES WALK

3:55:36 Gennadiy Agapov URS 1 Alma-Ata 17 Oct
3:57:28 Aleksandr Scherbina URS 2 Alma-Ata 17 Oct
4:02:08 Grigoriy Klimov URS 3 Alma-Ata 17 Oct
4:03:14 Christophe Höhne GDR 1 Pescara 10 Oct
4:04:15 Mikhail Korchunov URS 4 Alma-Ata 17 Oct
4:06:01.6 Burkhard Leuschke GD 2 Pescara 10 Oct
4:06:40.2 Abdon Pamich ITA 3 Pescara 10 Oct
4:06:43 Vytautas Zurnis URS 5 Alma-Ata 17 Oct
4:09:14.2 Don Thompson GBR 4 Pescara 10 Oct
4:09:47 Sergey Bondarenko URS 2 Moskva 11 Aug
Pescara uncertain course measurement. 50th 4:25:36.2

4 x 100 METRES (* 4x 110y less 0.2 sec.)

39.2 Poland 1 Warszawa 7 Aug
39.2 USSR 1 Colombes 2 Oct
39.3 France 2 Colombes 2 Oct
39.5* Stanford Univ. USA 1 Fresno 8 May
39.5 FR Germany 3 Stuttgart 11 Sep
39.7 Italy 1 Bern 3 Jul

4 x 400 METRES (* 4x 440y less 1.1 sec.)

3:03.4* Southern Univ. USA 1 Modesto 29 May
3:04.8 FRG 2 Augsburg 12 Aug
3:06.6 FR Germany 1 Bern 4 Jul
3:07.6 Poland 1 London (WC) 31 Jul
3:08.1 Italy 2 Roma 21 Aug
3:08.2 England GBR 1 Berlin 5 Sep
3:08.2 GDR 2 Berlin 5 Sep

WOMEN

100 YARDS

10.3! Wyomia Tyus USA 1 Kingston 17 Jul
10.5 Jennifer Lamy AUS 1 Sydney 16 Jan
10.2w 1 Sydney 13 Nov
10.5 Rhonda Bainbridge AUS 2 Sydney 16 Jan
10.3w 2 Sydney 13 Nov
10.5 Debbie Thompson USA 1 Melbourne 10 Mar
10.5 Irena Kirszenstein POL 1= Spala 25 Jul
10.5 Ewa Klobukowska POL 1= Spala 25 Jul

100 METRES

11.1! Ewa Klobukowska POL 1 Praha 9 Jul
11.1! Irena Kirszenstein POL 2 Praha 9 Jul
11.1! Wyomia Tyus USA 1 Kyiv 31 Jul
11.4 Tatyana Talisheva URS 1 Kyiv 12 Jul
11.4 Irina Press URS 1 Kyiv 24 Jul
11.4 Edith McGuire USA 2 Kyiv 31 Jul
11.4 Miguelina Cobian CUB 1h Budapest 15 Aug
11.4 Lyudmila Samotyesova URS 1 Kislovodsk 3 Oct
11.4 Galina Mitrokhina URS 1 Alma-Ata 9 Oct
11.5 five women, 50th best 11.8
11.4w Diane Bowering AUS 1 Adelaide 1 Jan
11.4w Judy Pollock AUS 1 Melbourne 11 Mar
11.4w Beverley Holman AUS 2 Melbourne 11 Mar

200 METRES (* 220y less 0.1 sec.)

22.7! Irena Kirszenstein POL 1 Warszawa 8 Aug
23.0 IEwa Klobukowska POL 2 Warszawa 8 Aug
23.1 Edith McGuire USA 1 Kyiv 1 Aug
23.3 Wyomia Tyus USA 2 Kyiv 1 Aug
23.5 Vyera Popkova URS 3 Kyiv 1 Aug
23.5 Ioana Pettrescu ROU 1 Timisoara 1 Oct
23.6 Lyudmila Samotyesova URS 1s Alma-Ata 10 Oct

23.8*A Johanna Cornelissen RSA 1 Pretoria 3 Apr
23.8* Janet Simpson GBR 1 Stevenage 22 May
23.8 six women. 50th best 24.3

400 METRES

52.1* Judy Pollock AUS 1 Perth 27 Feb
52.9 Maria Itkina URS 1 Alma-Ata 10 Oct
53.5 Lilita Zagere URS 2 Alma-Ata 10 Oct
53.7 Janell Smith USAS 1 Waszawa 7 Aug
53.7 Hilde Slaman NED 1 Groningen 14 Aug
53.8 Gertrud Schmidt GDR 1 Leipzig 22 Aug
54.1 Joy Grieveson GBR 2 London (WC) 30 Jul
54.2* Madelina Manning USA 1 Wichita 23 Jul
54.2 Deirdre Watkinson GBR 2 London (WC) 30 Jul
54.2 Genia Marochkina URS 3 Alma-Ata 10 Oct
50th best 55.7 * 440y less 0.3 sec.

800 METRES

2:04.3 Hannelora Suppe GDR 1 Kassel 19 Sep
2:04.6 Ilja Laman NED 2 Kassel 19 Sep
2:04.7 Antje Gleichfeld FRG 3 Kassel 19 Sep
2:04.9 Zsuzsa Nagy HUN 4 Kassel 19 Sep
2:05.0 Vyera Mukhanova URS 1 Moskva 11 Aug
2:05.3 Anne Smith GBR 1 London (WC) 13 Aug
2:05.9 Tamara Dunayskaya URS 2 Moskva 11 Aug
2:06.1 Tamara Dmitriyeva URS 1 Alma-Ata 13 Oct
2:06.2 Zoya Skobtsova URS 3 Moskva 11 Aug
2:06.2 Laine Eerik URS 1 Budapest 29 Aug
50th best 2:09.3

1500 METRES

4:29.0 Maria Ingrova CZE 1 Gottwaldow 28 Oct

1 MILE

4:46.30 Anne Smith 1 London (WC) 30 Aug
4:51.5 Joyce Snith GBR 1 Dublin 6 Jul

80 METRES HURDLES

10.3! Irina Press URS 1 Tbilisi 24 Oct
10.4 Pamela Kilborn AUS 1 Melbourne 6 Feb
10.3w 1 Melbourne 23 Nov
10.5 Gundula Diel GDR 1 Berlin 4 Sep
10.4w 1 Berlin 28 Aug
10.6 Rimma Larionova URS 1 Chelyabinsk 22 Aug
10.6 Inge Schell FRG 1 Lübeck 10 Sep
10.7 Li Shu-nu CHN 1 Canton 28 Jun
10.7 Tatyana Talisheva RUS 1 Kyiv 13 Jul
10.7 Galina Bystrova URS 2 Kyiv 1 Aug
10.7 Renate Balck FRG 1 Hamburg 18 Aug
10.7 Galina Kuznyetsova URS 2 Chelyabinsk 22 Aug
10.7 Alla Konyakhina URS 3 Chelyabinsk 22 Aug
10.7 Yeh Li-fang CHN 1 Beijing 30 Sep
10.7 Danuta Straszynska POL 1 Kraków 3 Oct
10.6w 1 Budapest 26 Aug
50th best 11.0

100 METRES HURDLES (2'6")

13.3! Chi Cheng TPE 1 Oakland 20 Jun
13.3! Valentina Bolshova URS 1 Alma-Ata 10 Oct

200 METRES HURDLES

27.5! Jennifer Wingerson CAN 1 Columbus 3 Jul
27.7 Mamie Rallins USA 2 Columbus 3 Jul

HIGH JUMP

1.86 Iolanda Balas ROM 1 Bucuresti 2 Sep
1.81 Hsuan Hsaio-mei CHN 1 Beijing 1 Sep
1.80 Wu Fu-shan CHN 1 Beijing 16 May
1.77 Cheng Feng-jung CHN 2 Beijing 14 Sep
1.76 Taisia Chenchik URS 1 Moskva 16 May
1.76 Galina Kostyenko URSA 1 Moskva 6 Sep
1.76 Karin Ruger GDR 1 Leipzig 22 Sep
1.76 Robyn Woodhouse AUS 1 Sydney 6 Feb
1.75 Chang Ching-ying CHN 2 Tsinan 18 May
1.74i Eleanor Montgomery USA 2 Cleveland 19 Mar
1.73 five women. 50th best 1.67

LONG JUMP

6.71 Tatyana Shchelkanova URS 1 Kyiv 1 Aug
6.54 Irena Kirszenstein POL 1 Warszawa 20 Jun
6.52 Viorica Viscopoleanu ROU 1 Constanza 22 Aug
6.44 Hsiao Chieh-ping CHN 1 Beijing 30 Jul
6.44 Willye White USA 1 München 13 Aug
6.41 Tatyana Talisheva RUS 2 Kyiv 1 Aug
6.40 Mary Rand GBR 1 London (WC) 3 Jul
6.40 Berit Berthelsen NOR 1 Oslo 10 Aug
6.33 Helen Frith AUS 1 Sydney 13 Feb
6.30 Ingrid Becker FRG 1P Celje 27 Jun
50th best 6.08
6.36w Ursula Wittman FRG 1 Duisburg 6 Aug

SHOT

18.59! Tamara Press URS 1 Kassel 19 Sep
17.58 Renaye Garisch GDR 1 Berlin 5 Sep
17.56 Nadezhda Chizhova URS 1 Kyiv 18 Jul
17.29 Galina Zybina URS 2 Minsk 3 Jul
17.09 Margarita Helmboldt GDR 2 Berlin 5 Sep
16.92 Maritta Lange GDR 2 Karl-Marx-St. 3 Jul
16.82 Valentina Nazarova URS 3 Minsk 3 Jul
16.68 Ivanka Khristova BUL 1 Sofia 23 May
16.61 Chung Hsih-yung CHN 1 Nanking 17 Oc
16.40 Mariene Klein FRG 1 München 13 Aug
50th best 14.81

DISCUS

59.70! Tamara Press URS 1 Budapest 25 Aug
57.86 Jolán Kleiber HUN 1 Budapest 1 Aug
57.83 Lyud.Shcherbakova URS 1 Krasnodar 9 Sep
56.98 Judit Stugner HUN 2 Budapest 1 Aug
56.20 Anita Henshel GDR 1 Karl-Marx-St. 24 Jul
55.98 Ingrid Lotz GDR 1 Leipzig 28 Aug
55.81 Liesel Westermann FRG 1 Ludwigshafen 26 Sep
55.10 Li Teh-tsui CHN 1 Beijing 28 Aug
55.04 Yevgeniya Kuznyetsova URS 1 Kyiv 7 Aug
55.02 Verzhinia Mikhailova URS 1 Neon Phaleron 10 Sep
50th best 49.72

JAVELIN

59.22 Mihaela Penes ROU 1 Budapest 25 Aug
58.49 Yelena Gorchakova URS 1 Kassel 19 Sep
58.30 Marta Rudas HUN 1 Praha 10 Jul
56.38 Ranae Bair USA 1 Warszawa 7 Aug
56.32 Valentina Popova URS 1 Kyiv 31 Jul
56.20 Ameli Koloska FRG 1 Wolfsburg 1 May
56.12 Marion Graefe GDR 1 Leipzig 16 Jun
55.84 Mariya Dubograyeva URS 1 La Habana 12 Dec
55.27 Galina Visotskaya URS 1 Poltava 13 Jun
55.10 Helgard Richter GDR 1 Karl-Marx-St. 14 Jun
50th best 50.44

PENTATHLON (1954 tables)

5208 Irina Press URS 1 Alma-Ata 11 Oct
4886 Inge Exner GDR 1 Jena 24 Jun
4802 Tatyana Shchelkanova URS 1 Budapest 28 Aug
4785 Mary Rand GBR 1 Berlin 5 Sep
4763 Valentina Tikhomirova URS 1 Kyiv 30 May
4760 Galina Mitrokhina URS 2 Alma-Ata 11 Oct
4751 Valentina Shapkina URS 3 Alma-Ata 11 Oct
4705 Irena Kirszenstein POL 1 Warszawa 6 Jun
4701 Ingrid Becker FRG 1 Celje 27 Jun
4700 Mariya Sizyakova URS 1 Voronezh 15 Jul
50th best 4396

4 x 100 METRES

44.2 Poland 1 Warszawa 7 Aug
44.2 USA 2 Warszawa 7 Aug
44.5 USSR 2 Kyiv 31 Jul
45.1 Great Britain 2 London (WC) 1 Aug
45.4* Jamaica 2 Kingston 15 Jul
45.4 FR Germany 1 Cosntanza 22 Aug
* 4 x 110y less 0.3 sec.

THE WORLD RECORD MILE OF 100 YEARS AGO

By Bob Phillips

WHEN NORMAN TABER broke the world mile record a century ago this year, achieving 4min 12.6sec on 16 July 1915, it was to be by no means the greatest advance in the event in terms of time gained. His time was 1.8 seconds faster than his fellow-American, John Paul Jones, had run two years before, and throughout the remainder of the 20th Century half-a-dozen others were to make more substantial gains: Nurmi in 1923, Andersson in 1943, Bannister in 1954, Elliott (by the widest margin of 2.7 seconds) in 1958, Ryun in 1966 and Morceli in 1993. Yet a strong argument could be made for saying that Taber's achievement was more significant than those of any of his illustrious successors. Taber was the first amateur to improve on the time of 4min 12¾sec set by Walter George as a professional in 1886, and at long last the steadfast belief that professional milers would always be faster than amateurs, which had prevailed for more than 60 years, was laid to rest. The closest that any amateur before Taber had got to George's record was a time of 4min 15.6sec by the Irish-born American, Tommy Conneff, in 1895.

After Conneff, no progress was made in either of the dominant miling nations, Great Britain and the USA, until 1911, when John Paul Jones ran 4:15.4, and the following year Jones was one of seven Americans who lined up for the Olympic 1500 metres final in Stockholm, though they were all beaten by the languid Oxford University undergraduate, Arnold Jackson, with Abel Kiviat leading the American contingent in 2nd place, Taber 3rd and Jones 4th. Kiviat was to live a very long life, reaching the age of 99 to become the USA's oldest surviving Olympian, and was to recall ruefully of the Stockholm race when interviewed in 1985, 'This fellow shot off. I'd never heard of Jackson before. I should have started my sprint sooner.' In 1913 Jones improved his record to 4:14.4, with Taber a full two seconds behind.

Jackson summarised his training régime as nothing more than the occasional walk or round of golf, and even allowing for instinctive English under-statement there seems no reason to disbelieve him. Certainly he was by no means a fully committed athlete and never, for instance, even competed in the English AAA Championships. Instead, he contented himself with winning the mile for Oxford against Cambridge in the Inter-Varsity matches of 1912, 1913 and 1914 and then undertaking more serious duties, serving in the army with great distinction during World War I and becoming the youngest Brigadier General at the age of 27. What a pity that his athletics career was never consummated. Jack Moakley, the respected coach to John Paul Jones, told Jackson that he had the ability to be the first four-minute miler! Jones, incidentally, had run only one more race after his world-record mile and had then graduated from Cornell University with a degree in mechanical engineering and retired from running at the age of merely 22, though that would be a common occurrence in athletics for another 70 or so years to come.

Jackson's casual attitude left the field open for Americans, at least until the USA entered the war in 1916, and the rather more obvious candidate than Taber to break the mile record was the Olympic silver-medallist, Kiviat. He had been born in New York on 23 June 1892, formally named Avraham Richard but always in later life to be known by the nickname, 'Abel', and was the eldest of seven children of Russian-Jewish parents who had escaped to the USA from persecution in their native Bialystok. Still only 20 years of age at the time of the Stockholm Olympics, Kiviat was a high school drop-out who worked each weekday from 8am to 6pm as a sports-goods salesman in Wanamaker's department store in New York, and he was almost as much of a natural running talent as England's Olympic champion, training only once a week under the guidance of the renowned Scots-born coach, Lawson Robertson, though bolstering his fitness by often racing several times at weekends. Kiviat, who was only 5ft 3in (1.60m) tall, had set a world record for 1500 metres of 3:55.8 at the 1912 US Olympic trials and was national (AAU) champion at the mile in 1911, 1912 and 1914. He also raced prolifically indoors and set the fastest times ever for 600 yards, 1000 yards and the mile.

Taber, by contrast, came from a very much more privileged background. Born the year before Kiviat, on 3 September 1891, he was a student at Brown University, in his home town of Providence, Rhode Island. The university had been founded by John Brown and his two brothers in 1764 as 'The College in the English Colony of Rhode Island and Providence Plantations'. John Brown's occupations included that of a slave-trader and he owned the vessel, 'Providence', which was to become the first warship in the American navy during the revolution against British rule and was at one time captained by another hero of that age, John Paul Jones, after whom the miling rival of Taber and Kiviat's had been named. Taber interrupted Kiviat's sequence of AAU wins by taking the mile title in 1913, with the defending champion 3rd, and then went to Oxford University as a Rhodes Scholar, where he was to meet up with Jackson again.

At 5ft 8½in (1.74m) tall and wafer-slim, weighing 115lb (52kg), Taber was much more the classic middle-distance type than was Kiviat and had won an Olympic gold medal in the 3000 metres team race. After placing 2nd to an exceptionally talented Australian undergraduate, George Sproule, in the Inter-Varsity cross-country match of December 1913 contested between Oxford and Cambridge Universities, Taber impressively won the 880 yards at his university sports the following February in a time of 1:57.4, having 'made his own pace practically from the start to the finish', according to the correspondent for *The Times*, who added, 'Taber has not any outstanding beauty of style, but that he is a very fine runner there can be no doubt.' He and Jackson met up in the mile and Jackson won by five yards in 4:23.6, setting a record for the Iffley Road track which had been built and first used in 1876. At the Inter-Varsity track meeting the following month, Jackson duly won the mile again, but Taber was surprisingly and decisively beaten by a dozen yards in the half-mile by Cambridge's ungainly but spirited Rollo Atkinson – the merit of Atkinson's time of 1:56.4 at such an inclement time of the year should be viewed in the context of the existing world record of 1:52.5 by the USA's Olympic 800 metres champion, Ted Meredith. Atkinson subsequently served as an army officer in World War I and was shot dead by a German sniper in 1916.

An Oxford University quartet was entered for the 4x1 mile event at the annual Penn Relays in Philadelphia in April of 1914, and Arnold Jackson, George Sproule and David Gaussen set sail across the Atlantic to join Taber, who was already back home. Sproule ran the first stage, Gaussen (another war victim two years later, who was to die of wounds on active army service) the second, Taber the third and Jackson the anchor. Neither Gaussen nor Taber performed well and Jackson saved the day by making up a dozen yards to win in a desperately close finish. With the onset of war later that summer athletics more or less came to a halt at Oxford and Cambridge, and it was reported from Oxford in *The Times* during February of 1915 that 'of University sports and amusements there were practically none', with the additional note – containing absolutely no sense of irony on the part of the writer – that 'fox-hunting is kept going' because it is 'natural and useful to the soldier at home and abroad'.

Taber's coach at Brown University, Eddie O'Connor, was firmly of the belief that Jones's world record could be beaten and so persuaded Taber to spend the winter of 1914–15 training hard at Oxford, and maybe the distraction was welcome. It was most unusual for an American of that era to continue his running career beyond his active college days, and all credit to both coach and athlete that they were prepared to persevere. For the great majority of athletes in the first half of the 20th Century track and field competition, even at international level, was no more than a brief diversion before settling down to earning a living. It ought to have been a reasonable assumption that had Jones and Taber found the opportunity to continue competing into their late 20s – as, for example, Glenn Cunningham was to do in the 1930s – they would have run several seconds faster. But then, of course, the war would have stifled those ambitions.

Returning home in 1915, Taber came very close to Jones's record with 4:15.2 on 26 June in Boston, and then at the Harvard University stadium in Cambridge, Massachusetts, on 16 July officials of the club to which Taber belonged, the Boston Athletic Association, set up an artfully arranged handicap race as a record-breaking bid. JW Ryan started from the 10-yard mark to set the first-lap pace (58.0). DS Mahoney, off 125 yards, went through halfway in 2:05.0. Taber reached the bell in 3:13.0, and JM Burke, receiving 355 yards, provided the impetus until the home straight, inspiring Taber to run the last quarter in 59.6. Such slow middle laps of 67 and 68 were characteristic of the way mile races were run in those days, and it was only when Paavo Nurmi at last improved Taber's time to 4:10.4 eight years later with laps of 60.3, 62.9, 63.4 and 63.7 that the idea of more even-paced running began to prevail. After his record-breaking mile Taber had then made the five-day trans-America train journey to San Francisco for the AAU Championships, held in September, but was out-kicked by Joie Ray (4:23.2) after leading throughout, with Abel Kiviat placing 4th. Ray would go on to add seven successive titles from 1917 to 1923. Kiviat's competitive career came to an end in 1916 when he was banned for allegedly claiming excess expenses from meeting promoters, but his biographer in 2009, Alan Katchen, claims that Kiviat was singled out and that there was an anti-semitic element to the case.

Taber turned to the serious matter of work and set up his own financial consultancy business, specialising in municipal affairs. He died on 15 July 1952, by which time the mile record had stood to Gunder Hägg at 4:01.4 for the previous seven years, and Taber could have been forgiven for thinking that such an interlude suggested that the ultimate had been reached. Jack Moakley – who had considered the four-minute mile feasible more than 30 years before – lived long enough to hear of its achievement, dying on 21 May 1955, aged 91. Kiviat served in the US army in France in World War I and then was to spend 41 years working as a Federal court clerk in New York, and he far outlived all his contemporaries, dying on 24 August 1991. By then the mile record was Steve Cram's 3:46.32, but the next fastest at the distance from 1988 onwards had been almost three seconds slower. So Kiviat, like Taber before him, might have pondered that substantially less than half-a-minute's progress in eight decades, taking into account all the advantages accruing to athletes over the intervening years, was not all that impressive.

Note: for convenience sake all times are shown as decimals, although they were recorded to the nearest one-fifth of a second in the earlier years of the 20th century.

World Record Splits

Men			*400m*	*800m*	*1200m*	*1600m*	*2000m*	*2400m*	*2800m*	
800m	1:40.91	Rudisha 2010	49.28	1:40.91						(600m 1:14.30)
1000m	2:11.96	Ngeny 1999	49.66	1:44.62						(200m 24.12, 600m 1:17.14)
1500m	3:26.00	El Guerrouj 1998	54.3	1:50.7	2:46.4					(1000m 2:18.8)
1M	3:43.13	El Guerrouj 1999	55.2	1:51.2	2:47.0					(1000m 2:19.2)
2000m	4:44.79	El Guerrouj 1999	57.1	1:55.4	2:52.4	3:49.60				
3000m	7:20.67	Komen 1996	57.6	1:57.0	2:54.9	3:53.6	4:53.4	5:51.3	6:51.2	(1500m 3:38.6)
2M	7:58.61	Komen 1997	58.6	2:00.4		3:58.4	4:58.2	5:56.7	6:57.5	(1M 3:59.2)
5000m	12:37.35	Bekele 2004	kms: 2:33.24, 5:05.47, 7:37.34, 10:07.93, last 400m 57.9							
10,000m	26:17.53	Bekele 2005	kms: 2:40.6, 5:16.4, 7:53.3, 10:30.4, 13:09.4, 15:44.66, 18:23.98, 21:04.63, 23:45.09, 26:17.53, last 400m 57.1							
3kmSt	7:53.63	Shaheen 2004	1000m 2:36.13, 2000m 5:18.09							
Women										
800m	1:53.28	Kratochvílová 1983	56.1	1:53.28						(600m 1:25.0)
1000m	2:28.98	Masterkova 1996	58.3	1:59.8						(200m 28.4, 600m 1:29.1)
1500m	3:50.46	Qu Yunxia 1993	57.2	2:00.8	3:05.2					
1M	4:12.56	Masterkova 1996	62.0	2:06.7	3:12.2					(1000m 2:39.5, 1500m 3:56.77)
2000m	5:25.36	O'Sullivan 1994	64.9	2:07.8	3:14.8	4:23.5	5:25.36			

			1km	2km	3km	4km	5km	6km	7km	8km	9km
3000m	8:06.11	Wang J 1993	2:42.0	5:29.7	(last 400m 62.7)						
2M	8:58.58	Defar 2007	2:48.4	5:37.5	8:24.51 (1M 4:33.07, last 400m 62.6)						
5000m	14:11.15	Dibaba 2008	2:48.3	5:43.8	8:39.0	11:28.44	14:11.15				
10000m	29:31.78	Wang J 1993	2:54.7	5:56.6	8:59.2	12:02.8	15:05.7	18:10.1	21:14.4	23:59.9	26:44.8
3kmSt	8:58.81	Galkina 2008	1000m 2:58.63, 2000m 6:01.20								

REFERENCE BOOKS 2014-15

The Greatest Athletes of the Modern Era, Statistics from Early Years to the Present – Men's Discus and Javelin. A4 140p. This is the tenth in the series by Ari Törmä with detailed statistics from all-time lists as at 31.12.1868 to 75 deep all-time lists at four-yearly intervals to 31.12.2012 plus yearly progressions for top three men on Törmä's scoring system and profiles of his top scorers Adolfo Consolini and Eric Lemming. Published by the Finnish Athletics Archive Society, Suomen Yleisurheiluarkisto, membership of which is euros 65 with 3-5 booklets plus newsletters each year, The price of one book for non-members is 25 euros including postage. Payments to Suomen Yleisurheiluarkisto. IBAN: FI82 1572 3000 406017. SWIFT: NDEAFIHH on in cash or by PayPal. Payment information from mikko.nieminen@dlc.fi. Book information from athletics@aritorma.net

The Early History of Modern Field Athletics (by Ari Törmä (in collaboration with Peter Lovesey) is the 17th in the NURMI series of publications by the Finnish Athletics Archive Association (Suomen Yleisurheiluarkisto, SYUA. For details contact the Chairman of the Board of the society: Mikko Nieminen, mikko.nieminen@dlc.fi or see www.aritorma.net. This book (A4, 128 pp) concentrates mainly on the years between 1826 and 1865, providing articles on the events (principally high jump, pole vault, long jump, triple jump, shot and hammer) and leading athletes for each together with deep lists of performers for each year, adjusting results for weights etc.

Das was der DDR-Leichtathletik 1945-1990 by Karlheinz Peml has been published by the DGLD – the German statistical group, Deutsche Gesellschaft für Leichtathletik-Dokumentation in three parts each of over 500 pages and priced at €30 from Hans Waynberg, Liebigstrasse 9, 41464 Neuss, Germany. hans.waynberg@t-online.de. See the website: www.leichtathletik-dgld.de for further details.

European Athletics Championships Zürich 2014. A 644-page A5 statistics handbook was available to the media at the European Championships, updating the edition that had been published for Helsinki 2012. Edited by Mirko Jalava with assistance from György Csiki (records) and using the previous championships data compiled by the late Jirí Havlín.

3:59.4: The Quest for the Four Minute Mile" by Bob Phillips. This book was fully revised and updated for the 60th anniversary of Roger Bannister's first sub-four minute mile. It has the history of the mile from the 18th Century to 1954, based on contemporary sources and first-hand accounts, plus a detailed summary of the development of the event since. More than 50 photo–graphs and in-depth statistics. Published as an ebook for £4.99, available via Amazon, iBooks, Nook and Kobo. enquiries to www.chequeredflagpublishing.co.uk

A Hundred Years Afoot, A Celebration of a Century of Race Walking, The RWA centenary (actually 2007) publication. £15 plus £3 postage and packing in the UK from Peter Cassidy, Hufflers, Heard's Lane, Shenfield, Brentwood, CM15 0SF. email peter.cassidy@btinternet.com

Cronologia de los Records y Mejores Marcas Españolas de Atletsmo. 248 x 172mm, 563pp. This massive (and weighty) tome compiled by the Spanish statisticians (AEEA) is a most attractive publication with many photographs in colour and black and white to accompany the text that gives details of progressive Spanish records (including full results of races and competitions, split times etc.) at all events indoors and out from 1900. Orders to: José Luis Hernández, Royal Spanish Athletics Federation, Avenida de Valladolid, 81, 1º 28008 Madrid, SPAIN or email: estadistica@rfea.es.

Latvijas Barjherskrejeji. A4 184pp. Andris Stagis has written a most attractive book on the men's 110m hurdles for Latvia (with a chapter on the world scene). the text is in Latvian, but there are a large number of black and white photographs and a very extensive statistical section of 83 pages with progressive records, deep all-time lists, yearly top ten lists, lists of champions etc. plus profiles of the top men, headed by Igors Kazanovs and Stanislavs Olijars.

ANNUALS

L'Athlétisme Africain/African Athletics 2014. A5, 152 pages. By Yves Pinaud. Published by Éditions Polymédias with support from the IAAF, the 33rd edition in this splendid series has 100 deep men's and women's lists for Africa for 2013, with all-time lists, national championships and major meetings results. 20 euro, £18 or US $30 including postage from La Mémoire du Sport, 166 rue de Decize, 03000 Moulins, France. (Also available: booklist with very extensive list of athletics books and magazines for sale).

Asian Athletics 2013 Rankings. A5 97 pages. Heinrich Hubbeling continues his magnificent annual job of compiling Asian statistics. The booklet contains top 30s for 2013 for athletes from Asian nations, with continuation lists for countries other than China and Japan, indicating new national records, and full lists of Asian records. Euro 20/US $30 in cash or by International Money Order from the author, Haydnstrasse 8, 48691 Vreden, Germany. email hhubbeling@t-online.de. Copies also available for 1998, 2007-09, 2011-12 at €15/US $22 each.

Athlérama 2013. A5 720pp. The 51st edition of the French Annual, edited by Patricia Doilin with a strong team of compilers, is again a superb reference book and bigger than ever, accompanied this year by a CD containing a pdf of the contents. Packed with information on French athletics – records, profiles of 81 top athletes, results, deep year lists for 2013 for all age groups plus all-time lists and indexes. Maintaining the sequence there are French top ten lists for 1913 and 1963. 28 euros from the FFA, 33 avenue Pierre de Coubertin, 7540 Paris Cedex 13, France. email Patricia.Doilin@athle.org

British Athletics 2014. A5 432 pages. The 56th NUTS Annual, edited by Rob Whittingham, Peter Matthews, and Tony Miller. Deep UK ranking lists for all age groups in 2013, top 12 merit rankings, all-time lists, results etc. Also a survey of participation trends in British athletics. £18 plus postage (£2 UK & Europe, £5 outside Europe); from Rob Whittingham, 7 Birch Green, Croft Manor, Glossop, Derbyshire SK13 8PR, UK. Cash or sterling cheques.

2014 Combined Events Annual by Hans van Kuijen. The 200 pages contain outdoor and indoor all-time lists, 2014 ranking lists, national records, 50 bests' biographies etc. Cost 30 EUR or 30 GBP or 45 USD (until Dec 10), after that 35 EUR or 35 GBP or 50 USD. For details contact Hans. j.kuijen4@upcmail.nl

Eesti Kergejõustiku Aastaraamat 2015. 266pp. An attractively produced annual with comprehensive Estonian ranking lists indoors and out for 2014, with results and records and many colour photographs. From the Estonian Athletic Federation, Maakri 23, Tallinn 10145, Estonia. ejkl@ejkl.ee

Friidrott 2014. 170 x 240 mm 488 pp, hardback. Edited by Jonas Hedman, text in Swedish. This high quality production reviews world and Scandinavian athletics, including detailed championships and major events results with narrative, world outdoor top 50 year and all-time-lists, top 25 Scandinavian and Swedish year and all-time lists plus indoor top tens and record lists for World, Europe, Scandinavia and Sweden. 495 kronor from TextoGraf Förlag, Jonas Hedman, Springarvägen 14, 142 61 Trångsund, Sweden. See www.textograf.com. Email jonas.hedman@textograf.com

Israeli Athletics Annual 2014/15. 240 x 170mm, 54pp, illustrated. By David Eiger. Records, championship results, 2014 top 20s and all-time lists, with profiles of leading Israeli athletes. 8 euro or US $9 from David Eiger, 10 Ezra Hozsofer Str, Herzliya 46 371, Israel. Past editions from 1986 onwards are also available.

Latvijas Vieglatletikas Gadagramata 2015. A5 240 pp. Comprehensive coverage of Latvian athletics for 2014, including records, results, athlete profiles and year and all-time lists, compiled by Andris Stagis. From the Latvian Athletic Association, Augsiela 1, Riga LV-1009, Latvia. email: lvs@lat-athletics.lv

Annuaire FLA 2014. A4 240p. The Luxembourg Annual, edited by Georges Klepper, is again a magnificent and extraordinarily comprehensive volume, with reviews, results, 2014 and all-time lists, plus many colour photographs. 15 euros locally, by post €18 in Luxembourg, €27 elsewhere to account no. LU32 1111 0200 0321 0000. See www.fla.lu.

Athletics New Zealand 2013 Almanac. A5 178pp. Edited by Steve Hollings and Simon Holroyd. Athletics NZ annual has been expanded by 30 pages this year. It again includes national ranking lists for 2013 up to 50 deep for seniors plus lists for juniors and youths, all-time top 20s, records for the various age groups and results of championships and other major events. For details, see www.athletics.org.nz and go to "Shop". Price: $NZ 24.50 (inc. postage $50 international, $40 Australia & Pacific, $30 New Zealand).

Anuario Athlético Español 2013/2014. 1382 pp. This massive publication with results, 2014 year and all-time lists, with all-time Spanish champions, current biographies and much more is available for downloading in sections at http://www.rfea.es/revista/libros/rfea_rankingAL.htm. There are special studies of athlete of the year Ruth Beitia and of Yago Lamela, who died during the year.

Sverige Bästa 2013. A5 290 pages. Edited by Jonas Hedman. Detailed Swedish lists for seniors (100 deep), and younger age groups (20 deep). $20 (plus postage and shipping) from the Swedish Athletic Association: Svenska Friidrottsförbundet, Heliosgatan 3, 120 30 Stockholm, Sweden. Email: info@friidrott.se

2014 USA Track & Field FAST Annual. General editor Tom Casacky. A5 560pp. The 36th FAST Annual, contains records, 50-deep US lists for 2013 and all-time, with 15-deep junior and college all-time lists. The final index section includes annual progressions and championships details for top American athletes. This year it is not combined with the USATF Media Guide. although published by the USATF. $25 post paid in the USA or $42 or 32 Euros airmail from Tom Casacky, PO Box 192252, San Francisco, CA 94119-2252, USA. Payment is easiest by PayPal (to tom@interis.com).

Yleisurheilu 2014. A5 672pp. The Finnish Yearbook, published by Suomen Urheiluliitto (Finnish Athletics) and compiled by Juhani and Mirko Jalava, contains every conceivable statistic for Finnish athletics (with results and deep year lists) in 2014 and also world indoor, outdoor and junior lists for the year as known at November. 19 euros plus 10 euros for postage and packaging. Orders by e-mail to juhani@tilastopaja.fi.

Statistical Bulletins

TRACK STATS. The NUTS quarterly bulletin, edited by Bob Phillips, includes a wealth of fascinating statistics and articles. A5, 68-80 pages. Annual subscription (4 issues) is £20 (UK), £25 (rest of Europe) or £28 (elsewhere); contact Liz Sissons, 9 Fairoak Lane, Chessington, Surrey KT9 2NS, UK. lizsissons9@gmail.com

Contents of recent issues have included:

Volume 52 No. 2 April 2014 had several articles headed 'Shadows of the Four-Minute Mile' with features on Leslie MacMitchell, John Munski, John Joe Barry, Alex Breckenridge and Ian Boyd. Also on British cross-country runners of the 1940s, Mac Bailey, Cecil Griffiths, David Coleman's Manchester Mile win, Roma Ashby and Alan Turing.

A special issue was entitled **"Scotland the Brave: Impressions of the Commonwealth Games"**. Every aspect of Scottish participation in the Games is covered in this 72-page booklet including a list of all medallists since the inaugural Games in 1930, articles on such champions as Dunky Wright, Alan Hunter and Joe McGhee (1954 marathon), a history of athletics at Hampden Park and recollections of when Ian and Lachie Stewart struck gold in Edinburgh in 1970.

No. 3 October 2014 included a feature on Martin Lauer, the career record of Grete Waitz and an interview with marathon star Ian Thompson.

No. 4 December 2014 included progressive pbs by Katarina Johnson-Thompson. profile of Bertha Crowther and other heptathlon features. Features on Ian Thompson, Violet Piercy, John Freeborn and Robert Stronach, career record of Mary Slaney, International CC 1909 etc/

The Walks – By John Powell and Peter Matthews. A5 128pp. The latest in the NUTS series of Event Booklets deals with British race walking, honouring the rich history of the deeds of British walkers. All British performances in international championships and Games are given, together with British performances in all international matches – senior and junior, men and women – for Britain or England with a directory of all these international walkers. Top sixes are listed for all national and inter-counties championships, with winners of Scottish, Welsh, Northern Irish and English area championships and of other major races in Britain. There are also progressions of British records plus deep all-time lists. Information up to June 2014. On sale for £8 including postage in the UK or £10 in Europe, £12 in the rest of the world. From Don Turner (donturner@btinternet.com), 40 Rosedale Road, Stoneleigh, Epsom, Surrey KT17 2JH, UK. Sterling cheques payable to NUTS. See the NUTS web-site at www.nuts.org.uk/walksbook.htm for Paypal payments from outside the UK (or contact sales@nuts.org.uk).

Don Turner also has stocks of NUTS publications, including back issues of Track Stats from 1998.

Each £5: Event booklets (detailed statistics on UK athletes including results of championships and very detailed all-time lists, profiles etc.): UK women's hurdles (2004), Long Jump (2005), Shot Put (2006), Pole Vault (2008). Also 1930-39 UK men's ranking lists. And **Hammer** by Ian Tempest (2011), 88pp at £8 including postage. **Decathlon** (2011) 120pp by Alan Lindop £9 including postage.

The **DGLD** – the **German** statistical group, Deutsche Gesellschaft für Leichtathletik-Dokumentation produces annual national ranking lists (**Deutsche Bestenliste 2013**, 192 pages) for Germany and impressive bulletins of up to 292 pages, packed with historical articles and statistical compilations. Each issue (three per year) includes statistical profiles of athletes born 70, 75, 80, 85, 90 years ago etc. Membership, with free Deutsche Bestenliste – euro 55 per year. Contact Hans Waynberg, Liebigstrasse 9, 41464 Neuss, Germany; hans.waynberg@t-online.de. Website: www.ladgld.de

No. 68 1 Mar 2014 had 182 pages included articles on the Germany v Switzerland international of 1924 with profiles of all the German team (and results of the first match between the nations in 1921), the Olympic Marathon 1932 with details of races leading up to it and career details of all participants, German men's and women's indoor all-time lists at 31.12.45, German women's javelin top 40s for each age 13 to 19 'athletics and bobsleigh' with detailed statistical profiles of 132 athletes to also have had bobsleigh credentials.

No. 69 1 Jul 2014 228 pages was packed with statistical goodies. These include a survey by Rooney Magnusson of the first IAAF world record list issued in 1914, the Baltic Games of 1914, statistical profiles of athletes born in 1914 (and briefer ones of the 1915-18 births) and an In Memoriam for 1914-18. These are followed by district Championships results of the 1930s and various area lists plus records by Winfried Kramer for all men's and women's of the territories not recognised as separate nations by the IAAF – from the Åland Island to Wallis & Fortuna, including all the constituent parts of the United Kingdom.

No. 70, 1 Nov 2014 250 pages As well as the usual features, the contents include a long article by Volker Kluge on the Luz Long-Jesse Owens story, extensive all-time lists for Germany, generally 100-deep for men and women, as at 1945 (136 pages), and 50-deep 100m women's lists for each age 13 to 19.

The **Spanish group, the AEEA** continues to produce magnificent publications. Membership (four bulletins per year) is 55 euros per year (€61 outside Europe) from AEEA secretary Ignacio Mansilla, C/Encinar del Rey, 18 - 28450 Collado Mediano, Madrid, Spain. email: ranking@rfea.es

Bulletin No. 94 (A5 254 pages) included ranking lists of non-standard events for Spain for men as at 1960 and for all women's events as at 1964, a survey of Spanish athletes in world and European lists 2009-13, complete career details of SP/DT man José Luis Torres 1952-56, deep performer and performance Ibero-American women's rankings as at 31.12.1975, and chronological World, European and Spanish veteran's (35+) records for all men's and women's events.

IAAF Handbooks

IAAF Statistics Handbook 2nd Youth Olympic Games, Nanjing, China, 164 pages by Ottavio Castellini and Félix Capilla, with results and all-time lists can be downloaded from

http://iaaf-ebooks.s3.amazonaws.com/2014/YOG/projet/IAAF-YOG-nanjing-.pdf

The **IAAF Yearbook for 2014**, full of articles, reviews and colour photos in its 128 pages, can be viewed online at http://www.iaaf.org/news/iaaf-news/2014-yearbook-365.

IAAF Statistics Handbook 2nd Youth Olympic Games, Nanjing, China 2014, 164 pages by Ottavio Castellini and Félix Capilla, with results and all-time lists can be downloaded http://iaaf-ebooks.s3.amazonaws.com/2014/YOG/projet/IAAF-YOG-nanjing-.pdf

See www.iaaf.org/about-iaaf/publications for their extensive list of publications and videos for sale at 17 rue Princesse Florestine, BP 359, MC 98007, Monaco. Prices include postage by airmail. Email to: headquarters@iaaf.org. Payment by credit card (Visa, Mastercard or eurocard only), quoting name on card, number of card, expiry date, name and address and signature.

European Athletics Yearbook 2013. As last year, this is split into three parts: The first is the Athletics Review 2013 – a beautifully illustrated 156-page A4 review of the year packed with illustrations and features on competitions and developments. The second is the Statistics Yearbook 2013, A5 480pp with records, championship bests and 100-deep European lists with 50-deep lists for U23s and U20s, 30-deep indoor lists in 2013 and 50-deep all-time lists compiled as usual by Mirko Jalava. The third is a 92-page pocket sized Directory. Statistics Yearbook (with free Athletics Review) 25 euro in Europe, 30 euro elsewhere – see www.European-athletics.org

WORLD LIST TRENDS - MEN

This table shows the 10th and 100th bests in the year lists for the last seven years and 2004, with previous bests.

Men 10th Bests	To 2004	2007	2008	2009	2010	2011	2012	2013	2014
100m	9.98- 97	10.02	9.95	9.97	9.95	**9.89**	9.94	9.96	9.96
200m	**20.03- 00**	20.06	20.17	20.17	20.11	20.16	20.10	20.10	20.08
400m	**44.51- 96**	44.62	44.70	44.81	44.81	44.78	44.77	44.82	44.71
800m	**1:43.66- 96**	1:44.27	1:44.10	1:43.82	1:43.89	1:44.07	1:43.71	1:43.87	1:43.71
1500m	**3:31.10- 04**	3:32.13	3:32.16	3:31.90	3:32.20	3:31.84	3:31.61	3:31.94	3:30.98
5000m	**12:54.99- 03**	13:02.89	13:03.04	12:58.16	12:55.95	12:59.15	12:55.99	13:01.64	13:03.85
10000m	27:14.61- 03	**27:00.30**	27:08.06	27:15.94	27:17.61	26:52.84	27:03.49	27:21.50	27:28.27
Half Mar	60:20- 02	59:32	59:37	59:30	59:40	59:39	**59:15**	59:54	59:21
Marathon	2:06:48- 03	2:07:19	2:06:25	2:06:14	2:05:52	2:05:45!	2:04:54	2:05:16	2:05:13
3000mSt	**8:08.14- 02**	8:09.72	8:12.72	8:10.63	8:09.87	8:08.43	8:10.20	8:08.83	8:11.86
110mh	13.20- 98	13.19	13.24	13.21	13.28	13.23	**13.13**	13.18	13.19
400mh	**48.25- 02**	48.26	48.52	48.30	48.47	48.47	48.41	48.46	48.69
HJ	**2.36- 88**	2.34	2.34	2.33	2.32	2.33	2.32	2.34	2.34
PV	**5.90- 98**	5.83	5.81	5.80	5.80	5.80	5.73	5.80	5.76
LJ	**8.35- 97**	8.26	8.25	8.30	8.25	8.27	8.26	8.29	8.28
TJ	**17.48- 85**	17.39	17.43	17.41	17.29	17.35	17.31	17.26	17.24
SP	**21.63- 84**	20.87	21.19	20.99	21.29	21.16	21.14	21.09	21.37
DT	**68.20- 82**	66.61	67.91	66.19	66.90	67.21	67.50	65.98	66.11
HT	**81.88- 88**	80.00	80.58	79.48	78.73	79.27	79.56	79.16	78.27
JT	**87.12- 96/97**	84.35	85.05	84.24	85.12	84.81	84.72	84.61	85.92
Decathlon	**8526- 98**	8298	8372	8406	8253	8288	8322	8390	8311
20kmW	**1:18:30- 05**	1:19:34	1:19:15	1:19:55	1:20:36	1:19:57	1:19:20	1:19:36	1:19:43
50kmW	3:41:30- 05	3:44:26	3:45:21	3:41:55	3:47:54	3:44:03	**3:41:24**	3:43:38	3:43:02

Peak years shown in bold.

Men 100th Bests	To 2004	2007	2008	2009	2010	2011	2012	2013	2014
100m	10.24- 00	10.25	10.23	10.22	10.26	10.21	10.20	10.21	**10.18**
200m	20.66- 99/00	20.66	20.67	20.68	20.71	20.63	20.57	20.60	**20.51**
400m	45.78- 00	45.91	45.89	45.86	45.92	45.91	45.79	45.87	**45.69**
800m	1:46.54- 99	1:46.99	1:46.70	1:46.88	1:46.76	1:46.50	1:46.56	**1:46.44**	1:46.60
1500m	3:38.42- 97	3:38.66	3:38.57	3:38.60	3:38.47	3:37.77	**3:36.84**	3:37.77	3:38.47
5000m	13:28.62- 00	13:27.48	13:25.05	13:26.90	13:25.88	13:26.29	**13:23.58**	13:27.29	13:28.60
10000m	28:15.98- 00	28:10.73	**28:04.47**	28:18.00	28:21.00	28:15.79	28:06.74	28:18.68	28:20.77
Half Mar	62:00- 00	61:54	61:50	61:28	61:38	61:31	61:19	61:25	**61:17**
Marathon	2:10:38- 03	2:10:43	2:10:22	2:09:53	2:09:31	2:09:19!	**2:08:32**	2:09:06	2:08:58
3000mSt	**8:31.06- 04**	8:32.94	8:32.12	8:35.21	8:35.29	8:35.45	8:31.2	8:34.42	8:35.05
110mh	13.72- 96	13.72	13.67	13.71	13.68	13.67	**13.66**	13.67	13.67
400mh	50.06- 00	50.28	50.33	50.35	50.41	50.28	50.15	50.16	50.21
HJ	**2.24- 84/88/89/92/9**6	2.23	2.23	2.23	2.23	**2.24**	**2.24**	**2.24**	**2.24**
PV	**5.55- 00**	5.50	5.50	5.46	5.42	5.45	5.50	5.50	5.50
LJ	**7.96- 04**	7.90	7.93	7.94	7.91	7.94	7.93	7.92	7.89
TJ	**16.60- 8**8	16.44	16.53	16.46	16.46	16.53	16.49	16.40	16.38
SP	19.48- 84	19.22	19.21	19.15	19.08	19.18	**19.51**	19.41	19.47
DT	**60.96- 84**	59.75	60.77	60.00	59.77	59.98	60.95	60.21	60.64
HT	**73.06- 84**	70.58	70.89	70.66	70.78	70.44	71.22	70.49	70.45
JT	77.14- 91	75.66	76.28	77.03	76.71	77.38	**77.78**	77.10	77.16
Decathlon	**7702- 88**	7545	7594	7623	7526	7678	7648	7586	7559
20kmW	**1:22:48- 0**5	1:23:55	1:23:32	1:23:57	1:24:24	1:23:40	1:23:10	1:22:56	1:23:07
50kmW	4:03:49- 99	4:04:52	4:05:05	4:09:24	4:08:08	4:06:15	**4:03:04**	4:08:33	4:06:22

! From 2011 main marathon lists no longer include Boston or other such excessively downhill races

Number of athletes achieving base level standards for world lists:

Men		2009	2010	2011	2012	2013	2014
100m	10.29	161	133	166	198	187	226
200m	20.79	174	140	175	226	198	242
400m	46.19	163	154	151	184	177	203
800m	1:47.59	154	169	198	220	190	200
1500m	3:39.99	141	152	170	201	185	171
5000m	13:37.0	181	177	193	203	180	169
10000m	28:35.0	159	157	172	199	168	152
HMar	61:59	158	145	147	199	171	199
Mar	2:10:59	160	175	215	233	212	207
3000St	8:39.9	140	135	147	184	141	138
110mh	13.89	171	196	194	214	199	208
400mh	50.79	152	155	171	186	177	191

		2009	2010	2011	2012	2013	2014
HJ	2.20	184	194	192	216	197	210
PV	5.40	151	138	139	177	179	177
LJ	7.80	182	173	186	183	180	181
TJ	16.30	123	139	142	144	120	124
SP	18.50	171	168	163	203	217	210
DT	58.00	164	156	155	177	166	173
HT	68.00	149	158	149	158	146	147
JT	74.00	166	168	173	199	190	187
Dec	7400	150	136	165	173	143	150
20kmW	1:25:00	136	124	154	175	175	151
50kmW	4:10:00	105	103	110	132	106	113
TOTAL	3695	3595	3545	3827	4386	4004	4130

The 2014 numbers compared to those of 2013: for 10th best 9-12 (1T), 100th best 8-11 (3 tie), base level 13-9 (1 tie)

WORLD LIST TRENDS - WOMEN

This table shows the 10th and 100th bests in the year lists for the last seven years and 2004, with previous bests.

10th Bests	To 2004	2004	2007	2008	2009	2010	2011	2012	2013
100m	**10.92- 88**	11.04	10.95	11.04	11.08	11.01	10.99	10.93	11.01
200m	**22.24- 88**	22.49	22.43	22.45	22.49	22.55	22.37	22.40	22.46
400m	**49.74- 84**	50.16	50.11	50.27	50.43	50.67	50.06	50.19	50.74
800m	**1:56.91- 88**	1:58.61	1:57.9	1:58.80	1:58.67	1:58.21	1:57.77	1:58.92	1:58.84
1500m	**3:58.07- 97**	4:02.8	4:02.44	4:00.86	4:00.25	4:01.73	3:59.71	4:01.48	4:00.17
5000m	14:45.35- 00	14:45.22	14:43.89	14:41.62	**14:38.64**	14:39.44	14:50.80	14:47.12	14:52.67
10000m	31:01.07- 03	31:22.80	**30:39.96**	30:51.92	31:29:03	31:10.02	30:59.19	31:04.85	31:48.6
Half Mar	68:23- 00	68:28	68:51	68:14	67:52	68:07	67:42	**67:39**	68:13
Marathon	2:23:33- 02	2:24:23	2:24:14	2:25:06	2:23:44	2:22:43!	**2:20:57**	2:23:00	2:22:30
3000mSt	9:44.95- 03	9:26.63	9:21.76	**9:18.54**	9:24.84	9:25.96	9:23.52	9:27.49	9:23.43
100mh	12.67- 98	12.67	**12.58**	12.67	12.65	12.73	12.62	12.81	12.71
400mh	**53.99- 04**	54.14	54.45	54.49	54.58	54.69	54.21	54.38	54.74
HJ	**2.01- 03**	1.97	1.98	1.98	1.97	1.96	1.96	1.97	1.97
PV	4.60- 02/03	4.70	4.70	4.65	4.66	**4.71**	4.70	**4.71**	**4.71**
LJ	**7.07- 88**	6.89	6.89	6.87	6.89	6.88	6.97	6.91	6.90
TJ	14.76- 03	14.69	**14.84**	14.62	14.48	14.57	14.60	14.50	14.10
SP	**20.85- 87**	19.13	19.29	19.38	19.47	19.26	19.60	18.81	19.03
DT	**70.34- 88**	64.87	64.10	63.89	64.04	63.91	64.45	64.46	65.51
HT	71.12- 03	73.94	74.40	73.07	73.40	72.65	**75.59**	75.02	74/20
JT	64.89- 00	63.58	63.24	63.89	63.36	63.50	**64.91**	63.55	64/50
Heptathlon	**6540- 88**	6327	6465	6323	6204	6338	6466	6345	6395
20kmW	1:27:55- 01	1:28:51	1:27:18	1:28:50	1:29:20	1:28:41	1:27:08	1:27:53	1:27:54
Women 100th Bests									
100m	11.36- 00	11.37	11.36	11.41	11.40	11.36	11.34	11.35	**11.32**
200m	23.21- 00	23.27	23.17	23.26	23.27	23.21	**23.10**	23.19	23.17
400m	52.25- 00	52.14	**52.08**	52.44	52.52	52.33	52.16	52.25	52.36
800m	2:01.50- 84	2:02.25	2:02.50	2:02.13	2:02.14	2:01.86	**2:01.48**	2:02.05	2:02.05
1500m	4:10.22- 84	4:11.67	4:11.64	4:11.06	4:10.50	4:09.88	**4:09.06**	4:09.98	4:10.09
5000m	**15:27.20- 04**	15:33.90	15:27.50	15:37.31	15:37.45	15:31.67	15:32.88	15:35.74	15:33.42
10000m	32:32.47- 00	32:46.28	**32:30.10**	32:54.64	32:57.59	32:53.44	32:38.95	32:48.60	32:43.90
Half Mar	71:29- 01	71:15	71:19	70:57	70:59	71:06	70:48	**70:44**	70:45
Marathon	2:31:05- 01	2:31:25	2:29:53	2:30:08	2:29:36	2:28:32	**2:28:01**	2:29:10	2:29:17
3000mSt	10:23.76- 03	10:03.2	9:56.48	10:02.94	10:03.50	9:59.44	9:53.79	9:56.50	**9:53.19**
100mh	13.22- 00	13.25	13.22	13.28	13.23	13.16	**13.11**	13.19	13.14
400mh	57.48- 00	57.21	57.46	57.45	57.22	57.26	**57.14**	57.40	57.34
HJ	**1.88- 86/87/88/92/93**	1.87	1.86	1.86	1.87	1.86	1.87	1.87	1.86
PV	4.15- 03	4.22	4.25	4.21	4.25	4.30	**4.31**	4.30	4.30
LJ	6.53- 88	6.49	6.52	6.49	6.51	6.50	**6.55**	6.49	6.45
TJ	13.68- 00	13.64	**13.75**	13.65	13.67	13.70	13.71	13.69	13.60
SP	**17.19- 87**	16.54	16.49	16.43	16.46	16.60	16.82	16.65	16.60
DT	**58.50- 92**	55.92	55.43	56.06	55.05	56.12	56.94	55.70	56.27
HT	63.23- 03	64.34	64.81	63.77	64.12	64.79	**65.78**	64.65	64.79
JT	55.55- 00	55.07	54.81	55.16	54.98	55.34	**55.97**	55.10	55.78
Heptathlon	**5741- 88**	5674	5687	5586	5568	5591	5702	5560	5668
20kmW	1:34:11- 05	1:35:57	1:34:30	1:35:54	1:36:32	1:34:52	**1:33:43**	1:33:48	1:35:20

All-time record levels indicated in bold.

! From 2011 main marathon lists no longer include Boston or other such excessively downhill races.

Number of athletes achieving base level standards for world lists:

Women		2009	2010	2011	2012	2013	2014
100m	11.50	185	171	195	217	208	227
200m	23.39	140	135	146	185	187	175
400m	52.99	169	167	187	210	196	190
800m	2:03.50	153	153	176	196	166	183
1500m	4:13.5	154	152	161	197	167	169
5000m	15:45.0	136	139	163	201	167	172
10000m	33:15.0	144	133	146	200	153	174
HMar	72:00	173	156	174	199	204	192
Mar	2:32:00	143	152	165	212	170	171
3000mSt	10:12.0	147	144	177	200	191	201
100mh	13.39	140	154	177	198	175	195

		2009	2010	2011	2012	2013	2014
400mh	58.44	179	169	181	228	193	194
HJ	1.85	136	142	172	164	155	148
PV	4.15	153	156	176	189	181	203
LJ	6.35	181	180	185	212	171	168
TJ	13.30	183	182	191	199	184	171
SP	15.85	159	159	163	180	177	189
DT	53.65	139	144	153	172	159	152
HT	61.00	163	167	181	205	190	193
JT	53.00	154	151	160	177	159	172
Hep	5450	137	126	146	157	140	156
20kmW	1:38:00	137	123	167	173	191	148
TOTAL	3654	3405	3355	3742	4270	3884	3944

The 2014 numbers compared to those of 2013: for 10th best 9-10 (2 tie), 100th best 11-8 (2 ties), base level 14-8

NOTES FROM THE EDITOR

Transfer of Nationality/Allegiance

Name	*From*	*To*	*Noted*	*Eligible*
Men				
Tadesse Abraham	ETH	SUI	10.6.14	19.7.14
Tyron Akins	USA	NGR	2.6.14	
Alex Al-Ameen	GBR	NGR	23.7.14	
Mohsin Anani	EGY	TUN	pending	
Kevin Batt	AUS	IRL	7.5.14	
Johnathan Cabral	USA	CAN	13.3.15	
Hassan Chani	MAR	BRN	21.3.15	
Nicholas Chepseba	KEN	RUS		
Yasmani Copello	CUB	TUR	21.10.13	30.4.14
Shumi Dechasa	ETH	BRN	1.9.13	10.9.14
Jeremy Dodson	USA	SAM	6.11.14	
Monzavour Rae Edwards	USA	NGR	.14	
El Hssan El Abbassi	MAR	BRN	13.8.13	19.7.14
Diego Estrada	MEX	USA	18.11.11	15.5.14
Mamadou Kassé Hann	SEN	FRA	.13	
Abdelilah Haroun	SUD	QAT	2.2.15	1.2.16
Payton Hazzard	USA	GRN	14.7.14	
Mark Jelks	USA	NGR	23.7.14	
Kip Kangogo	KEN	CAN	4.4.14	26.6.14
John Kibet Koech	KEN	BRN	15.9.13	14.9.14
Amos Kibitok	KEN	RUS		
Evans Kiplagat	KEN	RUS		
Daniel Lewis	GBR	JAM	26.6.14	
Ivan Luchianov	MDA	RUS	28.12.13	15.5.14
Conor McCullough	IRL	USA	10.7.14	12.7.14
Calvin Nkanata	USA	KEN		
Tosin Ogunode	NGR	QAT	29.1.15	28.1.16
Yunier Pérez	CUB	TUR	25.7.14	24.7.17
Robert Simmons	USA	NGR	26.6.14	
Abraham Tadesse	ERI	SUI	23.6.14	
Women				
Oluwakemi Adekoya	NGR	BRN	11.9.13	10.9.14
Ebere Agbapuluonwu	NGR	BRN		
Kelsie Ahbe	USA	CAN	13.1.15	
Ruth Chebet	KEN	BRN	19.5.13	19.5.14
Eunice Chumba	KEN	BRN	15.9.13	14.9.14
Biljana Cvijanovic	BIH	SRB	19.8.13	18.8.14
Nicole Denby	USA	NGR	2.3.14	
Margaryta Dorozhon	UKR	ISR	12.1.15	30.4.15
Dominique Duncan	USA	NGR	23.5.14	
Eleni Gebrehiwot	ETH	GER	13.2.14	5.5.14
Amy Harris	GBR	ANT	26.5.14	8.7.14
Eunice Jepkirui Kirwa	KEN	BRN	11.12.13	15.7.14
Valentina Kibalnikova	UZB	RUS	31.12.12	
Ugonna Ndu	USA	NGR	14.6.13	
Francesca Okwara	USA	NGR	23.5.14	
Leonora Petrina (Joy)	NZL	USA	24.9.13	14.7.14
Indira Terrero	CUB	ESP	7.1.14	15.5.14

Change of name and nationality – Men

Jacques Harvey JAM Jak Ali Harvey TUR 25.7.14 24.7.15

Some Recent Marriages

Female	*Male*	
Holly Bleasdale GBR	Paul Bradshaw GBR	25.10.14
Kate Dennison GBR	Martyn Rooney GBR	19.9.14
Amy Hastings USA	Alistair Cragg IRL	8.11.14
Yelena Isinbayeva RUS	Nikita Petinov RUS	.14
Anna Jagaciak POL	Lukasz Michalski POL	.7.14
Chelsea Johnson USA	Trey Hardee USA	13.9.14
Liz McColgan GBR	John Nuttall GBR	18.1.14
Anna Melnychenko UKR	Oleksiy Kasyanov UKR	18.10.14
Ana Paula de Oliviera BRA	Thiago Braz da Silva BRA	13.12.14
Kara Patterson USA	Russ Winger USA	28.9.14
Yevgeniya Polyakova RUS	Lyukman Adams RUS	
Svetlana Rogozina RUS	Ildar Minshin RUS	.8.14

Recent women's name changes

Original	*Married name*
Nina Argunova RUS	Morozova
Karolina Blazej POL	Zawila
Rachel Gair GBR	Wilcockson
Geena Gall USA	Lara
Heidi Gregson AUS	See
Amber Henry USA	Schultz
Natasha Miller CAN	Jackson
Kristina Khalayeva RUS	Ugarova
Lucia Klocová SVK	Hrivnak Klocová
Aleksandra Kuzmina KAZ	Romanova
Natasha LaBeaud CAN	Anzures
Beki Lee AUS	Smith
Jeneva McCall USA	Stevens
Marina Marghieva MDA	Nichisenko
Shaye Maurer USA	Springall
Anna Nazarova RUS	Klashtornaya
Carolin Nytra GER	Dietrich
Melinda Owen USA	Withrow
Sarah Pappas USA	Sheppard
Svetlana Podosyonova RUS	Karamasheva
Kristina Poltavets RUS	Korolyova
Viktoriya Pyayachenko UKR	Kashcheyeva
Susanne Rosenbauer GER	Siebert
Nicole Schappert USA	Tully
Angela Smit NZL	Petty
Kseniya Vdovina RUS	Ryzhova
Anna Yaroshchuk UKR	Ryzhykova
Angelina Zhuk RUS	Krasnova

See also list of recent marriages below

Notes on updates to world All-time list

Men

5000m: first change 45th 12:54.83 Muktar Edris

400mh: Only change to top 100 48.47 Kariem Hussein to 91=

LJ: best performance 8.51 Rutherford was 126= all-time; DT: only in top 100: 67.92 Maric to 60th

Decathlon: only top 50 change: 46th 8521 Mayer

Women

800m: no changes in top 100. 1st change 1:57.67 Ajee' Wilson at 111st

400mh: no change in top 100 performances, only change in top 100 performers: 54.56 Titimets 97=

LJ: top change 53= 7.02 Tianna Bartoletta

SP: Adams best 20.67 is far from making top performances list (100th 21.54) and top new performer is 19.40 Obleshchuk at 123=

Junior W SP: no changes to top 50: 54= 18.08 Guo Tianqian and none to top 80 in Junior W DT

More transfers of allegiance

Stanley Kebenei	KEN	USA	28.8.14 5.3.15
Maksim Korolev	KAZ	USA	22.2.15
Claudio Villanueva	ESP	ECU	19.3.15
Women			
Katie Kirk	GBR	IRL	26.3.15
Valentyna Liashenko	UKR	GEO	3.3.15

AMENDMENTS TO ATHLETICS 2014

p.20 7-8 Sep Sweden v Finland match was in Stockholm
p.76 South East Asia Games: Women 20k: drugs dq Saw, winner was Ngyuyen Thi Thanh Phuc VIE 1:37:08*
p.81-2 World Indoors 2014: W 60m: 1. Shelly-Ann Fraser-Pryce, TJ: 2. Olga Saladukha, Hep: 3. Alina Fyodorova; 800m: drugs dq (5) Lupu, 5 Masná; 4x400m: drugs dq (4) RUS (Ryzhova), so 4. POL, 5. NGR
p.97 Bengt Wikner died on 6 Feb 2014.
p.98 Rolf Hesselvall Swedish champion 1968-9
p.181 Hungarian 2013 champions: HT: Krisztián Pars 80.41
p.239 USA 2013 champions: HMar: Meb Keflezighi 61:22 (drugs dq Mohamed Trafeh 61:17)
p.274-6 World & Continental records set in 2013: 200HSt W Men 35 22.68 Felix SÁNCHEZ DOM Manchester 25 May 13; Indoors: delete M35 SP 21.60 Hoffa (record 21.70 Kevin Toth 2003)
p.316 Women's all-time lists – inadvertently 2013 changes omitted from 100m-400m

2013 World Lists

Men

60m: 6.51 Pérez; **100m**: 9.86 Gay to drugs dq, so 30/9 and adjust (10s) from 10th 9.97; 9.96 Rodgers 1 & 9.97 Collins 2 at Lausanne, 10.07 Patton 2, 10.24w Constantine (J) 24.3.95; **200m**: to drugs dq 19.79w Gay

400m: 44.82 Arman Hall b. 12 Feb 94 (& 200m 20.73/20.71w), 45.10 Clemons 27.12.90, 45.84 Bonavacia CUR/NED; hand 45.5 Williams Collazo; to drugs dq 45.95 Gay

800m: 1:47.30 Echchibani (& 3:39.08 1500m), 1:47.31 Learmonth 20.4.92; Juniors: 1:47.64 Ahmed El Yemni MAR 13.11.95 2 Oudja 23 Mar

1500m: 3:35.47 Dirirsa, 3:37.5A Letting 16.6.93, 3:38.8A Kaptingei 12.8.86, delete 3:37.91 Bett; Jnrs: 3:41.52A Phillip Kipyeko UGA 10.1.95 3 Kampala 11 May

3000m: 7:49.09 Deriba; Jnr: 7:58.84 Kamais

5000m: 13:32.24 Ndegwa 10.10.82, 13:36.26 Ayele

10,000m: 28:35.7A Jairus Chanchima KEN .84 7 Jun, 28:36.5A Bernard Kipyego KEN 16.7.86 24 May, 28:37.0A Kurui; **10k**: 27:59+ Belay .92, 28:02 Kosgei 5.5.85, 28:14+ Behailu ETH-J 19.3.94, 28:23+ Maru 23.1.92, 28:26 Ondoro 3.3.88, 28:29+ Tola 11.8.91

HMar: 60:41 Maru 23.1.92 (& 28:23 10k), 60:50 Kosgei 5.5.85, 60:53 Behailu J 19.3.94 (add to juniors), 60:58 Belay .92, 61:17 Trafeh to drugs dq, 61:22 Keflezighi 1, 61:27 Tola 11.8.91, 61:37 Meketa .92, 61:41 Baday to dugs dq, 61:45 Ondoro 3.3.88 (and 2:08:00 Mar), 61:51 Emmanuel Ngatuny, 61:56 Solomon Yego .87

Mar: 2:09:00 Milaw Assefa 3.1.88, 2:09:20 Chebogut 1.9.85, 2:09:42 G Alemayehu 29.11.87, 2:09:48 P Cheruiyot 12.6.87, 2:09:49 Gilbert Yegon 6.8.88, 2:09:50 B Kiptoo 10.1.79, 2:09:58 Chege .80, 2:10:06 Kipkemei .86, 2:10:26 Tiruneh 30.9.84, 2:10:46 Kangor .88

3000mSt: 8:25.0A Kemboi 15.6.93, 8:31.75 J Koech 22.12.82, 8:38.5A Yego .89. 8:38.8A Peter Bomo 4.8.84 27 Apr; delete 8:38.76 Majdoub (see 8:33.82); Jnrs: 8:41.0A Kapsis 10.5.96 6 27 Apr, 8:43.0A Maina 10.1.94, 8:45.93 Habte Y 14.7.96, 8:49.90A Wakeni

400mh: 50.10 Díaz 1 Marano 14 Sep (from 50.35); this makes 100th best 50.16 O'Shea

HJ: 2.29A Kgosiemang, 2.23 Ghazal 16 Apr (from 2.22), 2.20 JaCorian Duffield; Juniors; Christoffe Bryan

PV: 5.62 Arents 6.8.86; Juniors: 5.30i Sergey Safonov RUS 18.2.95 4 & Dmitriy Lyubushkin RUS 21.3.94 5 both Chelyabinsk 15 Dec

LJ: 7.87A Dylan Cotter RSA 23.8.91 16 Mar

SP: (31/7), 20.46 Kokoyev 22.7.88, 20.06i Chavez 30.7.92; Jnrs 7.26kg: 18.27 Amrou Mohamed Ahmed EGY 16.12.95 1 El Maadi 13 Nov

DT: Juniors: 56.44 Nick Percy GBR 6.12.94 1 Peter-borough 26 Aug; 1.75kg: 62.79 Percy 6.12.94

HT: 73.60 El-Ashry 2 Cairo 26 Apr (delete 75.11), 70.13 Vicet; **JT**: 82.54 Tovarnov 20.1.85

Dec: 7411 McCune 7.4.93. 7406 (w) Kregers

4x100m: 39.87 DOM 7 Apr, hand 39.7A KEN 20 Jun

4x400m: 3:06.29 (not 'A') KEN, 3:07.36 GRE 29 Jun, 3:08.27 ALG 29 Jun; best la: 3:04.26 CUB; Jnr: 3:06.57 USA 1 Chambers

3000mW/10000mW: 18:59.51/39:37.96 Téraoui

5000mW: 19:29.50 López

Women

100m: 11.30A was w Tenorio, so replace by 11.41 -0.8 3 WY Donetsk 11 Jul (also in Juniors list); to drugs dq 11.03 Simpson (best earlier 11.27 0.5 2 Kingston 8 Jun), 11.28dq Hackett; **150mt**: Schippers 16.93

200m: to drugs dq 22.55 Simpson (best earlier 22.83 0.5 4 Kingston 4 May & 22.73w 2.2 2 DL Doha 10 May), 22.98dq Hackett; 23.05 Selvon 2

400m: Hand: 52.6A Janeth Jepkosgei 13.12.82 22 Jun; Indoor: 52.86 Blessing Mayungbe NGR 15.4.92 24 Feb

800m: 2:01.25 Assefa ETH-Y 3.12.96

1000m: Drugs dq 2:40.66i Koreyvo

1500m: Drugs dq 4:02.56 Zaripova (RUS champ becomes Svetlana Podosyonova 4:04.01 1), 4:05.91 Shchagina 3, 4:07.63 Konovalova 5, 4:0.81 Kupina 6, 4:09.98 Tumayeva 7, drugs dq 4:13.09 Koreyvo

3000m: 8:49.5+ Ghribi in 5000 Eugene 1 Jun (from 8:52.06), **5000m**: 15:12.26 mx Belete

10000m: 32:57.0A Yator 30.7.93

HMar: 69:24 Kioko 4.10.87, 70:24 Kiplimo 28.9.89, 70:51 Tufa 26.1.81, 71:03 Shure Demisse ETH-Y 21.1.96 3 Rabat 7 Apr (add to Jnrs), 71:10 Macharia 7.12.87 (& 31:55 10k, 49:51 15k)

Mar: 2:28:22 Lydia Rutto KEN-J .94, 2:28:54 Cheruto 9.11.79, 2:29:20 Johannes, 2:29:35 Kwambai 22.3.86, 2:32:34 Abidi 9.5.86, 2:32:47 Mukwana .85, drugs dq 2:30:28 Gortel ¶

100k: 222.065 Falbo was her second best, so (20) is 220.221

2000mSt: 6:25.18 Ansa 2h2 WY Donetsk 12 Jul (from 6:30.05 top junior)

3000mSt: 9:34.33 Chesang 1.4.86, 9:43.70 Perraux, drugs dq 9:45.22 Uslu; 9:49.84 Özata 1; 10:02.46 Kibor 27.9.94; Jnr: 10:10.45 Drahotová 4

100mh: 13.38 Kibalnikova RUS, 12.66w Zelinka 4

400mh: 58.11 Zurec; **PV**: 4.50i Petrillose 10.12.92, 4.20 Tatyana Polnova RUS 20.4.79 1 Krasnodar 6 Jul

TJ: 13.40w Alvarez only needed in best la.

SP: (31/5), delete repeated marks from 18.77 to 17.88. Juniors: 15.67 Aikhonbare 1 Los Angeles (ER) 4 May (from 15.54)

DT: to drugs dq 58.97 Randall, best earlier 57.95 6 DL New York 25 May; **HT**: 61.70 Byrd 15.3.93

Hep: 5429w Yelena Yermolina

4x100m: 44.38 BLR (4 Gonchar), 44.98 PUR; Jnrs: 43.97A USA 1 Akinosun

4x400m: 3:27.43 (2 Reynolds), 3:32.90 BAH splits 52.7, 52.9, 53.4, 53.9; 3:34.8A KEN Police Koki,

J Jepkosgei, Shikanda, Sum 1 NC Nairobi 20 Jun, 3:36.58 THA, 3:39.45 ESP; mixed: 3:27.09 Arkansas (C Williams, McKnight TTO, Flowers, George NGR)
10000mW: 45:57.91t Zhang Xing CHN 17.8.89 16 May
20kW: 1:33:00 Jie Yefang CHN-Y 4.3.96 1, 1:34:18 Olga Suranova, 1:34:47 Tatyana Korotkova RUS 31.5.82, 1:35:50 Susana Feitor POR 28.1.75 & 1:37:58 Ni Yuanyuan CHN-J 6.4.95 all at Suzhou 11 Nov; to drugs dq: 1:35:03 Saw Mar Lar New; 194 under 1:38:00

Amendments to World Indoor Lists 2014

400m: 45.60A Clemons 27.12.90; **LJ:** 8.22 Crawford 12.12.91; **SP**: 20.06i Chavez 30.7.92; **W 800m:** drugs dq 2:00.65 Lupu, best earlier 2:01.33 2 Moskva 2 Feb; **2000m**: delete 5:37.2+ G Dibaba; **PV:** 4.42 Desiree Freier USA-J 24.7.96 17 Apr; **SP:** 18.88 drugs dq Heltne; **Pen**: 4830 Broersen.

Amendments to Previous World Lists

2012: 100m: to drugs dq: 9.80, 9.83, 9.90 Gay ('legal' best 9.86), 9.88 Bailey 4 OG, (31/7); 10.02 Vicaut 4, 10.08 Atkins 3s3; 200m: 20.21 Gay, 20.43 Bailey 4; 1500m: drugs dq 3:39.42 Shahween; 5000m: drugs dq: Al-Hamdah 13:17.03; Mar: drugs dq, Ahmad Baday 2:09:16; 20k: drugs dq 1:18:29 Yemelyanov, so move up other Sochi pos.

W 800m: Drugs dq 1:57.46 Kostetskaya, 2:02.67i Koreyvo; pos. changes to 2:00.16 Klocová 8, 2:00.24 Martynova 9, 2:00.38 Khalayeva 1B, 2:00.39 Glazkova 2B; 1500m: Drugs dq 3:59.28 Kostetskaya, 4:01.70 Zaripova, 4:02.37 Koreyvo (also loses OG 7th, move rest up); pos. changes to 3:59.49 Martynova 1 (to RUS champion), 3:59.71 Tomasheva 2, 4:00.09 Soboleva 3, 4:01.85 Tevdokimova 4, 4:02.99 Weightman 6s2, 4:02.99 Klocová 7s2, 4:05.03 Buckman 9s2, 4:06.57 Fernández 9s1, 4:08.38 Mikheyeva 9; PV: 4.35i Kazeka 1 Chelyabinsk 28 Dec (from 4.30i)

3000mSt Drugs dq Zaripova 9:05.02, 9:06.72, 9:09.99 (RUS champ becomes Gulnara Galkina 9:25.92)

2011: Drugs dq: Al-Hamdah 5000m 13:12.17, 10,000m 28:33.04; Drugs dq, Ahmad Baday HMar 62:04, Mar 2:10:14; 20kW: Drugs dq 1:19:33 Yemelyanov, so move up all Rio Maior marks 1 pos.; W 800m: Drugs dq 1:57.82 Kostetskaya, so 1:58.50 Vessey 5; 1:59.17 Magiso 3s3, 2:00.71 García 4s1; dq 2:01.88 Koreyvo (also 1000m 2:37.33i, 1500m 4:06.40); 1500m: pos.: 4:06.50 Macias 8, 4:07.28 Chojecka 9, 4:02.29 Moreira 10, 4:09.71 Fuentes-Pila 12

Tatyana Chernova**:** 200m 23.32w, 100mh 13.32 (OK 13.32 0.9 H WCh Daegu 29 Aug). LJ 6.82 (OK 6.61 -0.7 1H Daegu 30 Aug); Yulia Zaripova 3kSt 9:23.82 (RUS champ becomes Lyudmila Kuzmina 9:26.03)

3000mSt: 9:24.06 drugs dq Uslu, best earlier 9:33.50 1 WUG Shenzhen 19 Aug; amend to 2-3-4h1 top 1-2-3h1

2010: Drugs dqs: Ahmad Baday HMar 61:48; Stanislav Yemelyanov 10kW 40:14+ & 20kW 1:20:10 so move rest of EC places up; Anna Alminova 800 2:02.04i, 1000 2:40.33i, 1500 3:57.65 (and 4:00.84, 4:01.53), 3000m 8:47.57i. (RUS 1500 champion to Nataliya Yevdokimova 4:04.56). Tatyana Chernova: 100mh 13.47, HJ 1.86i, LJ 6.77, Hep 6572, 6512 & 6453 (many changes in positions for others).

2010 Indoors: dq Chernova LJ 6.72, Pen 4855

2009: Drugs dq: Al-Hamdah 5000m 13:11.64, 10,000m 28:01.8; W TJ: Taranova-Potapova 14.68 1 Volgograd 24 Jan. Drugs dq Anna Alminova 800 1:57.86, 1500 3:58.38 (and 4:01.15, 4:01.44, 4:01.54); RUS champion to Nataliya Yevdokimova 3:59.66 and adjust other positions, 2000 5:40.99, 3000 8:40.63, W Hep: 6306 dq Chernova.

Liliya Shobukhova – all results annulled from 9 Oct 2009 this including Marathons: 2:25:56 (1) Chicago 11 Oct 09, 2:22:00 (1) London 25 Apr 10, 2:20:25 (1) Chicago 10 Oct 10, 2:20:15 (2) London 17 Apr 11, 2:18:20 (1) Chicago 9 Oct 11, 2:22:59 (4) Chicago 7 Oct 12

Championships Medal Changes

Drugs dqs – move rest up accordingly

2013 European Indoors: W 1500m 4th Koreyvo so 4. Podosyenova, 5. Soboleva, 6. Viola, 7. Muir

2012 Olympics: W 3000mSt: 1st Zaripova so 1. Ghribi, 2. Assefa, 3. Chemos etc.

2012 World Indoors: W 1500m 4th Koreyvo so 4. Dehiba, 5. Bogale, 6. Cichocka, 7. Macias

2011 Worlds: 10000m: 13th Al-Hamdah; 20kW: 5th Yemelyanov, so 5. Kim...; W 800m 5th Kostetskaya so 5. Vessey, 6. Sinclair; 3000mSt: 7th Uslu so 7. Ouhaddou etc.

2010 World Indoors: 3rd Chernova

2010 Continental Cup: revised scores after drugs dqs of Mikhnevich (3 SP) & Bekele (2 W 3000m): 1. Americas 422.5, 2. Europe 417, 3. Africa 293, 4. Asia Pacific 290.5.

2010 Europeans: Hep: 4th Chernova, 20kW 1st Yemelyanov.

2010 European Cup Race Walking (p.75) 1st Yemelyanov

2009 European Indoors: W 1500 1st and 3000 6th Alminova. 1500m to: 1. Natalia Rodríguez ESP 4:08.72, 2. Sonja Roman SLO 4:11.42, 3. Roisin McGettigan IRL4:11.58

2009 European Team: W 1500 1st Alminova, so 1 Fernández, 2 Cusma Piccione, 3. Hannah England GBR 4:09.25.

2009 Gulf Champs. 5000m: James Kwalia QAT 14:10.10; 10,000m: Essa Ismail Rasheed QAT 29:36.2; after Hussein Jamaan Al-Hamdah KSA drugs dq.

Thanks for amendments to year and all-time lists to José María García, Juan Mari Iriondo, Keith Morbey, Yves Pinaud

Corrections and additions to Obituaries in this Annual pages 96-108

Frantisek BARTOS: died in Lanzhot.
Hélène FIZE: also pb national record 400m 1:05.0 (1940).
Stanko LORGER: 13.8 (1958), then 2nd European all-time, behind Martin Lauer.
Alan POTTS: his wife Sylvia ... (1943-99).
Dieter PROLLIUS: his son Maik had pb 19.10 (1986).
Lasse RÄiHÄ: other pbs 400m 50.0, 400mh 56.0 (both in 1950).
Rainer SCHUBERT, 49.15A was FRG record.
Louis ZAMPERINI: his 14:46.8 was world junior best.

Additions to Drugs Bans pages 109-110

In 2014

8y: Harvendra Singh IND (29 Apr); **2y:** Stephen Chelal KEN (2 Mar), Kamaraj Gunasekeran IND (12 Nov); **5m**: Olga Lenskiy ISR (20 Apr); **3m**: Mohammed Lamiri MAR (9 Aug)

In 2013: 2y: Isaac Kemboi Kimaiyo KEN (19 May), Viola Kimetto KEN (1 Dec)

In 2010: 2y: Ahmed Baday MAR (26 Mar)

2014 Men: 100m: 10.21w 3.1 Idrissa Adam CMR 28.12.84 17 May;

2014 Women: 800m: 2:03.25 Siham Halali 2.5.86 17 May; 3000mSt: 10:00.75 Fadwa Sidi Madane MAR 20.11.94 17 May

HALL OF FAME 2015

WE STARTED a Hall of Fame in ATHLETICS 2001. Five athletes are added each year – a mix of past and current stars. Prior to this year 91 athletes have been included (there was a bumper selection in ATHLETICS 2003 following a survey of the best athletes for each event).

Current stars can be included if they have had at least ten years in international competition and this year we include Jeremy Wariner, who slipped out the world top 50 at 400m in 2014 after twelve successive years therein and compiling a record at 400m second only to Michael Johnson.

Saïd AOUITA (Morocco) (b. 2 Nov 1959 Kenitra). Aouita was the world's best 5000 metres runner of the 1980s, when he was unbeaten at that distance for ten years. He won the Olympic title in 1984 and the World title in 1987. His other titles include the World Student Games 1500m 1981, African 1500m 1984 and World Indoor 3000m 1989, and he was the IAAF Grand Prix overall champion in 1986, 1988 and 1989.

His range of distance-running ability was unprecedented, for having run 27:26.11 for 10,000m in 1986 he stepped down to the 800m to take the Olympic bronze in 1988 with a best of 1:43.86. Injury then prevented him from taking part in the 1500m after reaching the semi-finals, and further injury caused him to miss the 1992 Olympics. Thus his 1983 World bronze medal remained his best in a global 1500m final, although he was African champion in 1984, after second in 1982 (and third at 800m). Steve Cram beat him at Nice on 16 Jul 1985 when they became the first and second men to better 3:30 for 1500m, but then Aouita embarked on a sequence of 44 consecutive race wins to September 1987 at distances from 800m to 10,000m. Eleven days after the Nice race he set a 5000m world record at 13:00.40 at Oslo on 27 Jul 1985, then he took the world 1500m record with 3:29.46 in Berlin on 23 Aug 1985. In May 1987 he ran a world best for 2 miles with 8:13.45 and had a superb sequence in July 1987 when he just missed Cram's world mark for the mile with 3:46.76 and then set world records at 2000m (4:50.81), and 5000m (12:58.39). These records were characterised by following a pace exactly on schedule, with a finishing kick to break the previous mark by a small margin, but his final world record came at 3000m in 1989 when his 7:29.45 took 2.65 secs off Henry Rono's 11 year-old mark. He retired at the end of the 1993 season, when he took up the position of technical director of the Moroccan federation but he lasted only six months in that job (he had another five months in this post in 2008–09). He was national distance coach for Australia in 2002–04 but left with many allegations against his conduct in this unhappy period.

Other bests: 1000m 2:15.16 (1988), 3000m Steeple 8:21.92 (1987).

Nina Yavovlevna **DUMBADZE** (USSR) (b. 23 Jan 1919 Tbilisi, Georgia. d. 14 Apr 1983 Tbilisi. Later Dyachkova). Dumbadze revolutionised women's discus throwing in the 1940s with seven improvements on the world record, although the first four of these, from 49.11m in 1939 to 50.50 in 1946, were not put forward for ratification because the USSR were not then members of the IAAF. With their return to international competition she won the European title in 1946 and 1950 and was third in her one Olympics, in 1952 at the age of 33. The IAAF recognised her records of 53.25 in 1948 and 53.37 in 1951. After Nina Romashkova (later Ponomaryova) had thrown 53.61 in 1952, Dumbadze achieved the greatest ever improvement by adding 3.43m to that with her final record of 57.04. This remained unsurpassed for eight years. Eight times Soviet champion, 1939, 1943-4, 1946-50, she was also placed 2nd or 3rd each year 1951-5.

She married Vladimir Dyachkov, later best known as the coach of Valeriy Brunel, and their son Yuriy Dyachkov competed in the 1960 Olympic decathlon.

John Jesus **FLANAGAN** (Ireland/USA) (9 Jan 1873 Kilbreedy, Co. Limerick. d. 4 Jun 1938 Kilmallack, Co. Limerick) The father of modern hammer throwing, Flanagan won three Olympic gold medals, 1900, 1904 and 1908, and set 19 world records. His first world record was 44.46m at Clonmel, Ireland on 9 Sep 1895, and his last 56.18m at New Haven, USA on 24 Jul 1909, when he was 41 years and 196 days. That remains the oldest at which a track and field world record has been set. He was the first man to surpass 45m (in 1897) and 50m (in 1899). He emigrated from his native Ireland to the USA in the autumn of 1896 and dominated the event for the next decade. He returned to Ireland in 1911 and in his final international appearance won the hammer for Ireland against Scotland.

In the USA between 1897 and 1908 he was AAU champion seven times at hammer and six times at 56lb weight, and he won AAA hammer titles in 1896 and 1900. In the 1904 Olympics he also took a silver medal at the 56lb weight throw and was fourth in the discus.

A charming and gentle man, in his early days he was a fine all-round athlete, with second places at both high jump and long jump at the 1895 Irish Championships.

Marlies GÖHR (GDR) (née Oelsner. b. 21 Mar 1958 Gera). Her outstanding sprinting career included a record number of European Cup victories, winning at both 100m and sprint relay at all six finals 1977-87, and five European outdoor gold medals, including a hat-trick of 100m titles, 1978, 1982 and 1986. She won five European Indoor titles at 60m (1977-9, 1982-3) and was also twice second and twice third in that event. The first woman to run a sub 11-second 100 metres, she ran a record 36 such times, including 3 with excess wind assistance, between 1977 and 1988. She set three world records at 100m, 10.88 in 1977 and 1982 and 10.81 in 1983, and for GDR relay teams nine at 4x100m and one at 4x200m. Indoors she set three world bests at 60 metres to 7.10 in 1980.

She started her sprinting career with 100m silver and relay gold at the 1975 European Juniors. In 1976 she was 8th at her first Olympics, and although she took relay gold in 1976 and 1980 she never won an Olympic 100m title as she was 2nd in 1980 and went out in the semi-finals in 1988. At 100m she was World Student champion in 1979 and had World Cup wins in 1977 and 1985.

A compact sprinter at 1.65m tall and 55kg, she ran the 200m only rarely, but was second in the 1978 Europeans and had a best time of 21.74 in 1984, then just 0.03 off the world record. She was GDR champion ten times at 100m, 1977-85, 1988, and twice at 200m, 1978, and 1984. A psychology student she ran for SC Motor Jena. She gave birth to daughter Nadja in 1989.

Jeremy Mathew **WARINER** (USA) (b. 31 Jan 1984 Irving, Texas). When Wariner won the Olympic gold medal for 400m at Athens in 2004 in a personal best time of 44.00 he became, at 20, the youngest winner of the title since 1988 and the first white American to win since Mike Larrabee in 1964. He led a US clean sweep with Otis Harris and Derrick Brew taking silver and bronze and he then teamed up with them and his Baylor University team-mate Darrold Williamson to win 4x400m gold. A year later he improved to 43.94, the world's fastest time for five years to win the World 400m title and again added a second gold at 4x400m. From Lamar High School, Arlington, Texas he followed in the footsteps of the world's greatest ever 400m runner his fellow-Texan Michael Johnson in going to Baylor and being coached by Clyde Hart, and Johnson became his agent and mentor. In 2006 Wariner improved his best to 43.91 and 43.62 and won all eleven 400m races to the World Athletics Final before dropping out in his last race; he shared the Golden League jackpot. He retained his supremacy in 2007, winning all of the ten 400m races he finished, mostly by large margins, including at the World Champs in a pb of 43.45 for third on the world all-time list. In 2008 he had to yield world top ranking to LaShawn Merritt, who beat him 3-2 including the three most important races, US Champs, Olympic Games and World Athletics Finals – in all of which Wariner was second. He had a season's best of 43.82 and ran a solo final leg in 43.18 on the gold medal-winning US 4x400m relay team at the Olympics. Merritt was again well ahead in 2009, but Wariner won the World silver medal and ran a brilliant second leg on the winning US 4x400m team. With Merritt receiving a two-year drugs ban, Wariner was back as world number one in 2010, when he won the Diamond League and Continental Cup at 400m. He was 2nd in the US Championships in 2011, but struggled for top form and was unable through injury to compete at the World Championships, and had moderate seasons in 2012, when he was 6th at the US Olympic Trials, and again in 2013, when he was US indoor champion.

Wariner was US junior champion in 2003 and 2nd at the Pan Am Junior Championships (plus relay gold), improving that year from 45.47 to 45.13 before his most impressive breakthrough to become the world's best in 2004. He was US 400m champion 2004-05 and NCAA champion indoors and out in 2004. Other bests: 200m 20.19 (2006), 300m 31.61 (2008).

Yohann Diniz took 1:41 off the world record for 50km walk with a storming victory at the European Championships.

Anita Wlodarczyk was our Women Athlete of the Year for her great year of hammer throwing culminating in a world record 79.58m.

In a great year for men's high jumping Bohdan Bondarenko (top) and Mutaz Essa Barshim vied for supremacy.

Dafne Schippers emulated Fanny Blankers-Koen with her 100m/200m double at the Europeans, and ranked fifth at heptathlon.

Sandra Perkovic twice produced the best discus throw by a woman since 1992.

Justin Gatlin attracted controversy with his drugs-bans past but was clearly the top sprinter of the year.

Katarina Johnson-Thompson missed the major summer championships through injury but won the World Indoor long jump silver, topped the heptathlon rankings at Götzis, and set pbs at 13 events.

Nijel Amos came to the fore at 800m with a complete set of wins in the most prestigious events: Commonwealth Games, African Champs, DL final in Zürich and Continental Cup.

Jeremy Wariner dropped out of the world top 50 at 400m for the first time since 2001 but we pay tribute to a man who ranked as world number one five times and won three Olympic and five World gold medals.

NATIONAL CHAMPIONS 2014 and BIOGRAPHIES OF LEADING ATHLETES

By Peter Matthews

THIS SECTION incorporates biographical profiles of 798 of the world's top athletes, 425 men and 373 women, listed by nation. Also listed are national champions at standard events in 2014 for the leading countries prominent in athletics (for which I have such details).

The athletes profiled have, as usual, changed quite considerably from the previous year , not only that all entries have been updated, but also that many newcomers have been included to replace those who have retired or faded a little from the spotlight. The choice of who to include is always invidious, but I have concentrated on those who are currently in the world's top 10-15 per event, those who have the best championship records and some up-and-coming athletes who I consider may make notable impact during the coming year.

Since this section was introduced in the 1985 Annual, biographies have been given for a total of 4517 different athletes (2553 men and 1964 women).

The ever continuing high turnover in our sport is reflected in the fact that there are many newcomers to this section (119 in all, 56 men, 63 women), as well as 8 athletes (5 men, 3 women) reinstated from previous Annuals. The athletes to have had the longest continuous stretch herein are Haile Gebrselassie 22 years, Jesús Ángel García 21 years, Virgilijus Alekna and Szymon Ziólkowski 19 years. Athletes who have retired have generally been omitted, although a few have been retained as they had significant achievements in 2014.

No doubt some of those dropped from this compilation will also again make their presence felt; the keen reader can look up their credentials in previous Annuals, and, of course, basic details may be in the athletes' index at the end of this book.

Athletes included in these biographies are identified in the index at the end of this Annual by * for those profiled in this section and by ^ for those who were included in previous Annuals.

The biographical information includes:

a) Name, date and place of birth, height (in metres), weight (in kilograms).
b) Previous name(s) for married women; club or university; occupation.
c) Major championships record – all placings in such events as the Olympic Games, World Championships, European Championships, Commonwealth Games, World Cup and Continental Cup; leading placings in finals of the World Indoor Championships, European or World Junior Championships, European Under-23 Championships and other Continental Championships; and first three to six in European Indoors or World University Games. European Cup/Team Champs and IAAF Grand Prix first three at each event or overall. World Athletics Final (WAF) and Diamond League series (DL) winners
d) National (outdoor) titles won or successes in other major events.
e) Records set: world, continental and national; indoor world records/bests (WIR/WIB).
f) Progression of best marks over the years at each athlete's main event(s).
g) Personal best performances at other events.
h) Other comments.

See Introduction to this Annual for lists of abbreviations used for events and championships.

Information given is as known at 1 April 2015 (to include performances at the European Indoor Championships and World Cross-country Championships as well as some other early indoor and outdoor events of 2015).

I am most grateful to various ATFS members who have helped check these details. Additional information or corrections would be welcomed for next year's Annual.

Peter Matthews

ALGERIA

Governing body: Fédération Algerienne d'Athlétisme, BP n°61, Dely-Ibrahim 160410, Alger. Founded 1963.

National Champions 2014: **Men**: 100m: Abdel-hadi Bouchakour 10.53, 200m:Djamil Skandar Athmani 21.64, 400m: Miloud Laaredj 46.23. 800mYassine Hathat 1:46.52, 1500m: Sami Lafi 3:49.43, 5000m: Mohammed Merbouhi 14:14.52, HMar: Ahmed Messeles 64:24, 3000mSt: Bilal Tabti 8:35.84, 110mh: Lyès Mokdal 13.54, 400mh: Admelmalik Lahoulou 50.27, HJ: Hichem Krim 2.11, PV: Hichem Cherabi 5.00, LJ: Yasser Triki 7.46, TJ: Lauhab Kafia 16.63, 20kW: Hicham Medjber 1:25:21; **Women**. 100m/200m: Souheir Bouali 11.78/24.39, 800m: Nahida Touhami 2:10.26, 1500m: Amina Betiche 4:16.55, 5000m/HMar: Souad Aït Salem 15:52.16/71:34, 3000mSt: Mawal Yahi 10:09.84, 100mh: Dihia Haddar 14.35, 400mh: Samira Messaad 61.79, LJ: Romaissa Belbiod 6.29w, TJ: Katia Oukaci 12.62, SP/HT: Zouina Bouzebra 13.22/57.91.

Larbi BOURAADA b. 10 May 1988 1.87m 84kg.
At Dec (/PV): WCh: '09- 13, '11- 10; AfG: '07- 3, '11- dnf/1; AfCh: '08- 1/2, '10- 1/2, '14- 1.
Two African decathlon records 2009-11, ALG record 2014
Progress at Dec: 2007- 7349, 2008- 7697, 2009- 8171, 2010- 8148A, 2011- 8302, 2012- 8332dq, 2014- 8311. pbs: 60m 6.89i '10, 100m 10.67 '10, 10.61w '11, 10.58dq '12; 400m 46.69 '09, 1000m 2:39.86i '10, 1500m 4:12.15 '09, 60mh 8.05i '10, 110mh 14.33 '14, HJ 2.10 '09, PV 5.00 '11, LJ 7.69 '09, 7.94w '11; SP 14.00i/13.59 '10, 13.64dq '12; DT 40.34 '11, JT 65.53A '10, 67.68dq '12; Hep 5911i '10. Two-years drugs ban from positive test 15 Jun 2012.

Taoufik MAKHLOUFI b. 29 Apr 1988 Souk Ahras 1.81m 66kg.
At (800m)/1500m: OG: '12- 1; WCh: '09/11- sf; AfG: '11- 1/3; AfCh: '10- h, '12- (1), '14- (3).
Progress at 800m, 1500m: 2008- 3:43.4, 2009- 1:49.40, 3:34.34; 2010- 1:48.39, 3:32.94; 2011- 1:46.32, 3:34.4; 2012- 1:43.71, 3:30.80; 2013- 3:36.30, 2014- 1:43.53, 3:30.40. pb 1M 3:52.16 '14.

ARGENTINA

Governing body: Confederación Argentina de Atletismo (CADA), 21 de Noviembre No. 207. 3260 Concepción del Uruguay, Entre Ríos. Founded 1954 (original governing body founded 1919).**National Championships** first held in 1920 (men), 1939 (women). **2014 Champions**: **Men**: 100m: Matías Robledo 10.60, 200m/110mh/LJ: Guillermo Ruggeri 21.75w/14.55/7.05, 400m: Fabio Martínez 48.55, 800m/1500m/Mar: Joaquín Arbe 1:53.14/3:49.93/2:21:01, 5000m/HMar: Gustavo Frencia 14:33.08/66:45, 10000m: Luis Ariel Molina 29:48.47, 3000mSt: Nahuel Luengo 9:08.89, 400mh: Jaime Rodríguez 51.70, HJ: Carlos Layoy 2.10, PV: Germán Chiaraviglio 4.90, TJ: Federico Guerrero 14.92, SP: Hugo Nieto 17.04, DT: Jorge Balliengo 54.63, HT: Juan Cerra 67.61, JT: Braian Toledo 70.57, Dec: Román Gastaldi 7368, 10,000mW: Juan Manuel Cano 40:05.03. **Women**: 100m: Victoria Woodward 11.79, 200m/400m: Valeria Barón 24.38/55.55, 800m: Mariana Borelli 2:11.58, 1500m: Evangelina Thomas 4:30.32, 5000m: María Angélica Ovejero 16:41.63, 10000m: Viviana Chávez 35:01.73, HMar: Rosa Godoy 74:06, Mar: Karina Neipán 2:47:18, 3000mSt: Carolina Lozano 10:38.92, 100mh: Agustina Zerboni 13.84, 400mh: Milagros de la Colina 64.32, HJ: Betsabé Páez 1.75, PV: Valeria Chiaraviglio 4.10, LJ: Josefina Loyza 5.77, TJ: Valeria Paz 11.64, SP/DT: Rocío Comba 13.94/55.64, HT: Jennifer Dahlgren 67.45, JT: Bárbara López 50.63, Hep: Martina Corra 4609, 20,000W: Yenny Ortiz 1:55:33.7.

Germán LAURO b. 2 Apr 1984 Trenque Lauquen, Buenos Aires 1.85m 127kg. Ferro Carril Oeste.
At SP/(DT): OG: '08- dnq 31, '12- 6/dnq 37; WCh: '07-09-11: dnq 23/ nt/20; 13- 7; WI: '12- 6, '14- 6; PAm: '07- 5/4, '11- 3; SAG: '14- 1/3; SACh: '05-06-07-09-11-13: 4/1/1&1/1&1/1&2/1&1. Won S.AmG 2014, IbAm SP & DT 2012, 2014; ARG SP 2005-13, DT 2007-13.
Shot Records: 6 South American indoor 2012-14; 13 Argentinian 2006-13.
Progress at SP: 2001- 15.24, 2002- 15.14, 2003- 16.87, 2004- 17.79, 2005- 18.17, 2006- 19.78, 2007- 19.67, 2008- 19.88, 2009- 19.20, 2010- 20.43, 2011- 20.42, 2012- 20.84, 2013- 21.26, 2014- 21.04i/20.70. pb DT 63.55 '12.
6th in 2012 was best Argentinian placing at Olympics for 56 years.

Women

Jennifer DAHLGREN b. 21 Apr 1984 Buenos Aires 1.80m 115kg. Studied English teaching at the University of Georgia
At HT: OG: '04-08-12: dnq 22/29/nt; WCh: '05-07-09-13: dnq nm/24/17/17, '11- 9; WJ: '00- dnq 23, 02- 5; WY: '01- 4; PAm: '07- 3, '11- 6; SAG: '14- 2; SACh: '05-06-09-11-13: 1/1/3/1/3; CCp: '10- 5; Won SAm-J 2000, PAm-J 2003, NCAA 2006-07, IbAm 2010, 2014; ARG 2008-09, 2011-12, 2014.
14 South American hammer records 2004-10.
Progress at HT: 1999- 46.36, 2000- 56.68, 2001- 57.18, 2002- 59.48, 2003- 61.60, 2004- 66.12, 2005- 67.07, 2006- 72.01, 2007- 72.94, 2008- 66.38, 2009- 72.79, 2010- 73.74, 2011- 73.44, 2012- 72.79, 2013- 72.74, 2014- 71.66. pbs: SP 15.54i '04, 15.03 '03; DT 44.28 '03, Wt 24.04i '06 (S.Am rec).
Her mother Irene Fitzner competed at 100m at the 1972 Olympics and was 2nd in the South American 100m in 1971.

AUSTRALIA

Governing body: Athletics Australia, Suite 22, Fawkner Towers, 431 St.Kilda Rd, Melbourne, Victoria 3004. Founded 1897.

National Championships first held in 1893 (men) (Australasian until 1927), 1930 (women). **2014 Champions: Men**: 100m: Tim Leathart 10.56, 200m: Mangar Chuot 21.08, 400m: Steven Solomon 45.36, 800m: Joshua Ralph 1:46.57, 1500m: Jeff Riseley 3:46.47, 5000m: Collis Birmingham 13:44.55, 10000m: Brett Robinson 28:45.36, Mar: Rowan Walker 2:21:47, 3000mSt: James Nipperess 8:38.87, 110mh: Nicholas Hough 14.12, 400mh: Ian Dewhurst 49.52, HJ: Nik Bojic 2.23, PV: Joel Pocklington 5.25, LJ: Robert Crowther 8.03, TJ: Alwyn Jones 16.37w, SP: Damien Birkenhead 19.04, DT: Benn Harrington 62.23, HT: Timothy Driesen 67.16, JT: Joshua Robinson 82.48, Dec: Jake Stein 7564, 10000mW/20kW: Dane Bird-Smith 38:57.16/ 1:22:39, 50kW: Chris Erickson 3:56:38. **Women**: 100m/100mh: Sally Pearson 11.70/12.72, 200m: Ella Nelson 23.47, 400m: Morgan Mitchell 52.22, 800m: Brittany McGowan 2:02.15, 1500m: Zoe Buckman 4:10.86, 5000m: Emily Brichacek 15:52.65, 10000m: Eloise Wellings 32:22.22, Mar: Tarli Bird 2:43:58, 3000mSt: Victoria Mitchell 9:42.01, 400mh: Lauren Wells 56.76, HJ: Eleanor Patterson 1.92, PV: Liz Parnov 4.20, LJ: Brooke Stratton 6.70, TJ: Linda Leverton 13.93, SP: Kimberley Mulhall 15.00, DT: Dani Samuels 66.81, HT: Lara Nielsen 63.11, JT: Kimberley Mickle 64.28, Hep: Sophie Stanwell 5621, 10000mW: Tanya Holliday 45:08.42, 20kW: Kelly Ruddick 1:34:44.

Benn HARRADINE b. 14 Oct 1982 Newcastle, NSW 1.98m 115kg. Ringwood. Personal trainer.
At DT: OG: '08- dnq 31, '12- 9; WCh: '09- dnq 15, '11- 5, '13- dnq 20; CG: '06-10-14: 8/1/4; CCp: '10- 2, '14- 5. AUS champion 2007-08, 2010-12, 2014.
Five Oceania discus records 2008-13.
Progress at DT: 2000- 51.50, 2001- 54.76, 2002- 57.78, 2003- 55.25, 2004- 57.68, 2005- 63.65, 2006- 60.70, 2007- 62.99, 2008- 66.37, 2009- 64.97, 2010- 66.45, 2011- 66.07, 2012- 67.53, 2013- 68.20, 2014- 65.94. pb SP 15.17 '05.

Jared TALLENT b. 17 Oct 1984 Ballarat 1.78m 60kg. Ballarat YCW. Graduate of University of Canberra.
At 20kW(/50kW): OG: '08- 3/2, '12- 7/2; WCh: '05- 18, '07- dq, '09- 6/7, '11- 25/3, 13- (3); CG: '06- 3, '10- 1; WCp: '06-08-10-12-14: 14/10/(3)/(2)/(3). At 10000mW: WJ: '02- 19; WY: '01- 7. Won AUS 5000mW 2012, 20kW 2008-11, 2013; 30kW 2004, 50kW 2007, 2009, 2011.
Commonwealth 5000m walk record 2009.
Progress at 20kW, 50kW: 2002- 1:40:21, 2003- 1:31:24, 2004- 1:27:02, 2005- 1:22:53, 2006- 1:21:36, 3:55:08; 2007- 1:21:25, 3:44:45, 2008- 1:19:41, 3:39:27; 2009- 1:19:42, 3:38:56; 2010- 1:19:15, 3:54:55; 2011- 1:19:57, 3:43:36; 2012- 1:20:02, 3:36:53; 2013- 1:20:41, 3:40:03; 2014- 1:20:55, 3:42:48. pbs: 3000mW 11:15.07 '09, 5000mW 18:41.83 '09, 10000mW 40:41.5 '06, 10kW 38:29 '10, 30kW 2:10:52 '13, 35kW 2:32:37 '12.
Won IAAF Walks Challenge 2008 and 2013. Married Claire Woods on 30 Aug 2008, she has 20kW pb 1:28:53 '12, 2 CG '10.

Julian WRUCK b. 6 Jul 1991 Brisbane 1.98m 125kg. Sports student at UCLA, previously Texas Tech, USA.
At DT: OG: '12- dnq 13; WCh: '13- 11; CG: '10- 8, '14- 9; WJ: '10- 3. AUS champion 2013, 2015; NCAA 2011 and 2013.
Progress at DT: 2008- 51.89, 2009- 54.74, 2010- 61.02, 2011- 65.74, 2012- 64.84, 2013- 68.16, 2014- 65.54. pb SP 17.01 '13

Women

Alana BOYD b. 10 May 1984 Melbourne 1.71m 61kg. Maroochy AC
At PV: OG: '08- dnq 16=, '21- 11; CG: '10- 1, '14: 1; CCp: '10- 6, '14- 3=. AUS champion 2008-9, 2013, 2015.
Two Oceania pole vault records 2012.
Progress at PV: 2002- 3.15, 2003- 3.85, 2004- 3.65, 2005- 4.30, 2006- 4.40, 2007- 4.55, 2008- 4.56, 2009- 4.35, 2010- 1.73, 2011- 1.82, 2012- 4.76, 2013- 4.50, 2014- 4.65.
Here father and mother were both Olympians. Ray won 12 AUS pole vault titles and after 4th in 1970 and 1974 won at the Commonwealth Games in 1982, Denise (née Robertson) was 7th in the Olympic 200m in 1976 and 1980 and won 8 Commonwealth Games medals (100m/200m/4x100m/4x400m: '74- 3/2/1/-, '78- 3/1/3/2, '82- -/4/4/2). Alana's sister Jacinta (LJ pb 6.64 '06) and brother Matt (PV 5.35 '08) competed at World Youths and Juniors.

Kimberley MICKLE b. 28 Dec 1984 Perth 1.69m 69kg. Mandurah/Rockingham.
At JT: OG: '12- dnq 17; WCh: '09- dnq 15, '11- 6, '13- 2; CG: '06-10-14: 4/2/1; WJ: '02- 9; WY: '01- 1; WCp: '06-10-14: 5/3/4. AUS champion 2005-07, 2009-15.
Oceania javelin record 2014.
Progress at JT: 1999- 45.13, 2000- 45.76, 2001- 51.83, 2002- 52.77, 2003- 48.03, 2004- 50.38, 2005- 58.16, 2006- 58.56, 2007- 59.36, 2008- 57.64, 2009- 63.49, 2010- 61.36, 2011- 63.82, 2012- 64.12, 2013- 66.60, 2014- 66.83, 2015- 66.57.

Kathryn MITCHELL b. 10 Jul 1982 Hamilton, Victoria 1.68m 75kg. Eureka AC.
At JT: OG: '12- 9; WCh: '13- 5; CG: '06-10-14: 6/5/4; AUS champion 2008.
Progress at JT: 1999- 43.17, 2000- 51.44, 2001- 54.98, 2002- 54.72, 2003- 57.11, 2004- 48.10, 2005- 54.87, 2006- 58.81, 2007- 58.61, 2008- 58.77, 2010- 59.68, 2011- 59.47, 2012- 64.34, 2013- 63.77, 2014- 66.10.

Eleanor PATTERSON b. 22 May 1996 Leongatha, Victoria 1.82m 62kg. South Coast Athletics.
At HJ: CG: '14: 1; WY: '13- 1. Won AUS 2014-15. World youth and Oceania junior high jump record 2013.
Progress at HJ: 2010- 1.73, 2011- 1.82, 2012- 1.87, 2013- 1.96, 2014- 1.94, 2015- 1.96.

Sally PEARSON b. 19 Sep 1986 Sydney 1.66m 60kg. née McLellan. Gold Coast Victory. Griffith University.
At (100m)/100mh: OG: '08- 2, '12- 1; WCh: '03- hR, '07- sf/sf, '09-11-13: 5/1/2; CG: '06- 7/fell/3R, '10- dq/1, '14- 1; WJ: '04- 3/4; WY: '03- 1; WCp: '06- 8/4, '10- 1. At 60mh: WI: '12- 1, '14- 2. AUS champion 100m & 100mh 2005-7, 2009, 2011, 2014-15; 200m 2011.
Records: Oceania 100mh (8) 2007-11, 60m 2009 & 60mh indoors (3) 2009-12; Commonwealth 100mh (2) 2011.
Progress at 100mh: 2003- 14.01, 2004- 13.30, 2005- 13.01, 2006- 12.95, 2007- 12.71, 2008- 12.53, 2009- 12.50, 2010- 12.57, 2011- 12.28, 2012- 12.35, 2013- 12.50, 2014- 12.59. pbs: 60m 7.16 '11, 100m 11.14 '07, 150m 16.86 '10, 200m 23.02/22.66w '09, 300m 38.34 '09, 400m 53.86mx '11, 200mh 27.54 '06, 60mh 7.73i '12, 200mh 26.96 '09, 400mh 62.98 '07.
Married Kieran Pearson on 3 April 2010. IAAF female Athlete of the Year 2011.

Dani SAMUELS b. 26 May 1988 Fairfield, Sydney 1.82m 82kg. Westfields, University of Western Sydney.
At DT/(SP): OG: '08- 9, '12- 11; WCh: '07-09-11-13: dnq 13/1/10/10; CG: '06- 3/12, '14- 1; WJ: '06- 1/7; WY: '05- 1/3; WCp: '06- 6; WUG: '07- 2, '09- 1; CCp: '10- 4, '14- 2. AUS champion SP 2006-07, 2009, 2012; DT 2005-11, 2014-15.
Progress at DT: 2001- 39.17, 2002- 45.52, 2003- 47.29, 2004- 52.21, 2005- 58.52, 2006- 60.63, 2007- 60.47, 2008- 62.95, 2009- 65.44, 2010- 65.84, 2011- 62.33, 2012- 63.97, 2013- 64.46, 2014- 67.99. pbs: SP 17.05 '14, HT 45.39 '05.
Sisters Jamie and Casey played basketball for Australia.

AUSTRIA

Governing body: Österreichischer Leichtathletik Verband OLV), 1040 Vienna, Prinz Eugenstrasse 12. Founded 1902.
National Championships first held in 1911 (men), 1918 (women). **2014 Champions**: **Men**: Benjamin Grill 10.63, 200m/400m: Thomas Kain 21.80/47.76, 800m: Andreas Rapatz 1:55.27, 1500m: Andreas Vojta 3:54.61, 5000m: Christian Steinhammer 14:44.89, 10000m/3000mSt: Christoph Sander 31:05.89/9:11.52, HMar: Valentin Pfeil 66:28, Mar: Edwin Kemboi KEN 2:22:00 (Karl Aumayr 2:24:37), 110mh: Dominik Distelberger 14.37, 400mh: Markus Kornfeld 53.53, HJ: Josip Kopic 2.09, PV: Matthias Freinberger 5.05, LJ/TJ: Julian Kellerer 7.55/15.87, SP: Lukas Weisshaidinger 18.42, DT: Gerhard Mayer 59.64, HT: Benjamin Siart 60.94, JT: Matthias Kaserer 69.53, Dec: Dominick Siedlaczek 6904, 20kW/50kW: Franz Kropik 1:53:25/5:22:13. **Women**: 100m: Viola Kleiser 11.88, 200m: Susanne Walli 24.03, 400m: Elisabeth Niedereder 57.10, 800m/400mh: Verena Menapace 2:06.01/59.50, 1500m/HMar: Jennifer Werth 4:27.07/74:46, 5000m: Martina Winter 17:12.51, 10000m: Andrea Mayr 34:41.61, Mar: Karin Freitag 2:49:45, 3000mSt: Stefanie Huber 10:48.15, 100mh: Beate Schrott 13.25, HJ: Yekaterina Kuntsevich RUS 1.85, PV: Kira Grünberg 4.30, LJ: Lisa Felderer 5.69, TJ: Michaele Egger 12.14, SP: Christina Scheffauer 14.03, DT: Veronika Watzek 49.52, HT: Bettina Weber 54.03, JT: Elisabeth Eberl 53.93, Hep: Vreiner Preiner 5417, 20kW: Andrea Zirknitzer 2:05:38.

AZERBAIJAN

Hayle IBRAHIMOV b. 18 Jan 1990 Mek'ele, Tigray, Ethiopia 1.68m 58kg. Baku.
At 5000m: OG: '12- 9; EC: '10- 3, '12- 6; EJ: '09- 1 (1 10000m); WUG: '13- 1. At 3000m: CCp: '14- 2; WI: '14- 6; EI: '11- 2, '13- 1. Eur U23 CC: '12- 8.
AZE records: 3000m (2) 2012-13, 5000m (5) 2010-14.
Progress at 5000m: 2009- 13:53.60, 2010- 13:32.98, 2011- 13:34.54, 2012- 13:11.54, 2013- 13:23.59, 2014- 13:09.17. pbs: 1500m 3:44.76 '10, 3000m 7:34.57 '13, 10000m 30:03.57 '11.
Formerly Haile Desta Hagos of Ethiopia, switched to AZE 1 Feb 2009.

BAHAMAS

Governing body: Bahamas Association of Athletics Associations, P.O.Box SS 5517, Nassau. Founded 1952.
National Champions 2014: **Men**: 100m/200m: Shavez Hart 10.11/20.57, 400m: LaToy Williams 44.97, 800m: Trevino Thompson 1:57.57, 1500m: O'Neil Williams 3:57.83, 5000m: Adelet Elysee 18:36.42, 110mh: Dennis Bain 13.91, 400mh: Jeffrey Gibson 50.97, HJ: Ryan Ingraham 2.28, LJ: Raymond Higgs 7.88, SP: Delron Inniss 15.52, DT: Frederick Laing 45.77, JT: Tre Adderley 51.83. **Women**: 100m: Anthonique Strachan 11.33, 200m: Nivea Smith 23.08, 400m: Shaunae Miller 51.86, 800m: Te'shon Adderley 2:08.00, 1500m: Itsa Smith 5:23.46, 100mh: Yvana Hepburn-Bailey 13.21, 400mh: Katrina Seymour 59.05, LJ: Bianca Stuart 6.65, TJ: Tamara Myers 13.24, SP/DT: Racquel Williams 13.53/44.80.

Christopher BROWN b. 15 Oct 1978 Nassau 1.78m 68kg. Was at Norfolk State University.
At 400m/4x400mR: OG: '00- qf/3R, '04- sf, '08- 4/2R, '12- 4/1R; WCh: '01-03-05-07-09-11-13: h&1R/sf&3R/4&2R/4&2R/5/sf/sf; CG: '02- 7/3R, '06- 4, '14- dns/2R; PAm: '07- 1/1R. '11- 7;

PAm-J: '97- 2R; CAG: '98- 3R, '99- 1R, '03- 2/1R; CCp: '14- 3R; WI: '06-08-10-12-14: 3/3/1/3/2; BAH champion 2002, 2004, 2007-09. At 800m: CG: '98- h.
Bahamas records 400m 2007 & 2008, 800m 1998. CAC & Commonwealth 4x400m record 2012. World M35 400m records indoors and out 2014.
Progress at 400m: 1997- 47.46, 1998- 46.44, 1999- 45.96, 2000- 45.08, 2001- 45.45, 2002- 45.11, 2003- 44.94A/45.16, 2004- 45.09, 2005- 44.48, 2006- 44.80, 2007- 44.45, 2008- 44.40, 2009- 44.81, 2010- 45.05, 2011- 44.79, 2012- 44.67, 2013- 45.18, 2014- 44.59. pbs: 100m 10.26+ '14, 150mSt 15.10 '14, 200m 21.05 '03, 20.56w '06; 300m 32.4+ '12, 800m 1:49.54 '98.
Fourth at four global championships outdoors. Had fastest split (43.42 anchor leg) in 2005 World 4x400m.

Demetrius PINDER b. 13 Feb 1989 Grand Bahama 1.78m 70kg. Studied theatre at Texas A&M University, USA.
At 400m: OG: '12- 7/1R; WCh: '11- sf; WI: '12- 2; BAH champion 2010-12.
CAC & Commonwealth 4x400m record 2012.
Progress at 400m: 2006- 49.03, 2007- 47.48, 2008- 47.34, 2009- 48.21i, 2010- 44.93, 2011- 44.78, 2012- 44.77, 2014- 45.30. pbs: 200m 20.23 '12, 300m 32.3+ '12. Ran fastest leg (43.3) in 2012 Olympic 4x400m final.

Donald THOMAS b. 1 Jul 1984 Freeport 1.90m 75kg. Lindenwood University, USA.
At HJ: OG: '08/12- dnq 21=/30=; WCh: '07-09-11-13: 1/dnq 15/11/6; CG: '06-10-14: 4/1/9=; PAm: '07- 2, '11- 1; CAG: '06- 4=, '10- 1; CCp: '10- 2. Won WAF & NCAA indoors 2007, BAH 2007, 2010-11.
Progress at HJ: 2006- 2.24, 2007- 2.35, 2008- 2.28i/2.26, 2009- 2.30, 2010- 2.32, 2011- 2.32, 2012- 2.27, 2013- 2.32, 2014- 2.33i/2.25.
A basketball player, he made a sensational start by clearing 2.22 indoors in January 2006 with no high jump training since he had jumped at school five years earlier. 19 months later he was world champion.

Women

Shaunae MILLER b. 15 Apr 1994 Nassau 1.85m 69kg. University of Georgia, USA.
At (200m)/400m: OG: '12- ht; WCh: '13- (4); CG: '14- 7; WJ: '10- 1, '12- 4; WY: '11- 1; CCp: '14- (4); WI: '14- 3. Won BAH 400m 2010-11, 2014; NCAA indoor 400m 2013.
CAC junior records 200m 2013, 400m 2013.
Progress at 200m, 400m: 2009- 55.52, 2010- 24.09, 52.45; 2011- 23.70, 51.84; 2012- 22.70, 51.25; 2013- 22.45/22.41w, 50.70; 2014- 22.87, 51.63i/51.86. Pbs: 60m 7.59i '13, 100m 11.40 '14, 300m 36.10i '14.
Great-uncle Leslie Miller set BAH 400m record of 46.99 at 1968 Olympics.

Anthonique STRACHAN b. 22 Aug 1993 Nassau 1.68m 57kg. Going to Auburn University, USA.
At (100m)/200m: OG: '12- sf; WCh: '11/13- sf; WJ: '10- sf, '12- 1/1; PAm-J: '11- 1. Won BAH 100m 2014, 200m 2013.
Two CAC junior 200m records 2011-12.
Progress at 200m: 2009- 23.95, 2010- 23.66, 2011- 22.70, 2012- 22.53, 2013- 22.32, 2014- 22.50. Pbs: 100m 11.20 '12, 400m 54.48 '10.
Won IAAF Female Rising Star Award 2012.

BAHRAIN

Governing body: Bahrain Athletics Association, PO Box 29269, Isa Twon-Manama. Founded 1974.

Albert Kibichii **ROP** b. 17 Jul 1992 Kapsabet, Kenya 1.76m 55kg.
At 5000m: AsiG: '14- 3; CCp: '14- 4; Arab champion 2013. World CC: '15- 11.
Records: 1 Asian, 2 Bahrain 5000m and Bahrain 3000m 2013; 2 Asian indoor 3000m 2014 (if eligible).
Progress at 5000m: 2010- 14:15.81A, 2011- 13:03.70, 2012- 13:01.91, 2013- 12:51.96, 2014- 13:06.12. Pbs: 1500m 3:45.7A '13, 3000m 7:35.53 '13. Bahrain citizen from 2 Apr 2013, international eligibility 1 Apr 2014.

Abraham Kipchirchir **ROTICH** b. 26 Sep 1993 Kenya 1.81m 62kg.
Progress at 800m: 2010- 1:50.76A, 2011- 1:46.4A, 2012- 1:43.13, 2013- 1:44.57, 2014- 1:46.30i/ 1:46.94dq. pb 1000m 2:17.08 '12.
Transferred from Kenya to Bahrain 2 Apr 2013, international eligibility 1 Apr 2014.

Women

Oluwa**kemi ADEKOYA** b. 16 Jan 1993 Nigeria 1.68m 57kg. Accountancy graduate of University of Lagos.
At 400mh: AsiG: '14- 1 (1 400m); CCp: '14- 3.
Progress at 400mh: 2012- 57.16, 2013- 55.30, 2014- 54.59. pbs: 100m 11.55 '14, 400m 51.11 '14.
Bahrain 400m (2) & 400mh records 2014.
Switched nationality from Nigeria to Bahrain from 11 Sep 2013, with international eligibility from 10 Sep 2014.

Mimi BELETE b. 9 Jun 1988 Ethiopia 1.64m 62kg.
At 1500m/(5000m): OG: '12- sf; WCh: '09- sf, '11- 7, '13- sf; AsiG: '10- 3/1, '14- 2/2; AsiC: '09- 6, '13- 2; CCp: '10- 4, '14- 6 (5 3000m); won W.Asian 2010.
Asian 2M record 2014.
Progress at 1500m: 2007- 4:13.55, 2008- 4:06.84, 2009- 4:04.36, 2010- 4:00.25, 2011- 4:03.13, 2012- 4:01.72, 2013- 4:03.63, 2014- 4:00.08. pbs: 800m 2:04.63 '10, 2000m 5:38.0+ '14, 3000m 8:30.00 '14, 2M 9:13.85 '14, 5000m 15:00.87 '14.
From Ethiopia, has lived in Belgium from 2005; BRN from 2009. Younger sister Almensch Belete BEL pbs 1500m 4:06.87 '10, 5000m 15:03.63 '11; 5 EI 3000m 2013.

Ruth CHEBET b. 17 Nov 1996 Kenya 1.65m 49kg.
At 3000mSt: WJ: '14- 5; AsiG: '14- 1; AsiC: '13- 1 but ineligible; CCp: '14- 3. Won Arab 3000m 2014. World CC: '15- 9J.
Asian 3000m steeplechase record 2014.
Progress at 3000mSt: 2013- 9:40.84, 2014- 9:20.55. pbs: 3000m 9:09.8A '13, 5000m 16:16.1A '13, road 10k 32:18 '14, 2000mSt 6:17.33 '13.
Switched nationality from Kenya to Bahrain from 19 May 2013, with international eligibility from 19 May 2014.

Shitaye ESHETE Habtegebrei b. 21 May 1990 Ethiopia 1.59m 46kg.
At (5000m/)10000m: OG: '12- 10/6; WCh: '11- 6, '13- 6; AsiG: '10- 3; AsiC: '11- 1, '13- 1; AfC: '09- (6); CCp: '10- (6). At 3000m: WI: '12- 5. World CC: '10-11-13: 11/12/4. Won Arab 10000m 2013, CC 2010, 2013; Asian CC 2012, Asian indoor 3000m 2012.
Three BRN 10,000m records 2010-12.
Progress at 10000m: 2010- 31:53.27, 2011- 31:21.57, 2012- 30:47.25, 2013- 31:13.79. pbs: 3000m 8:49.27i '12, 5000m 15:03.13 '13.

Maryam Yusuf **JAMAL** b. 16 Sep 1984 Alkesa, Arsi Province, Ethiopia 1.70m 54kg. Stade Lausanne, Switzerland.
At (800m)/1500m: OG: '08- 5, '12- 3; WCh: '05-07-09-11: 5/1/1/11; WI: '06- 3, '08- 2; AsiG: '06- 1/1, '10- 6/1, '14- 1 (1 5000m); WCp: '06- 1. At 3000m: WI: '14- 3. World CC: '09- 9, '11- 23; Won WAF 2005-08, Swiss CC 2003, P.Arab 800m, 1500m & 5000m 2005, Arab 4k CC 2006, Asian indoor 1500m & 3000m 2014, CC 2007, 2009.
Records: Two Asian 1M 2007, 2000m 2009, Bahrain 800m (3), 1500m (3), 2000m, 3000m (3), 5000m 2005-09. Asian indoor 1500m 2006 & 2008, 1M (4:24.71) 2010.
Progress at 800m, 1500m, 5000m: 2003- 4:18.12, 2004- 2:02.18, 4:07.78, 15:19.45mx; 2005- 1:59.69, 3:56.79, 14:51.68; 2006- 1:59.04, 3:56.18, 2007- 3:58.75, 15:20.28; 2008- 1:57.80, 3:59.79i/3:59.84; 2009- 1:59.98, 3:56.55; 2010- 1:59.89, 3:58.93; 2011- 4:00.33, 2012- 2:00.44, 4:01.19; 2013- 4:07.31, 2014- 4:04.10, 14:59.69. pbs: 1M 4:17.75 '07, 2000m 5:31.88 '09, 3000m 8:28.87 '05, 2M 9:33.47 '14, HMar 71:43 '04.
Has a record 16 sub-4 min 1500m times. Formerly Ethiopian Zenebech Kotu Tola, based in Switzerland, ran series of fast times after converting to Jamal of Bahrain in 2005. First Olympic medallist for Bahrain at any sport. Married to Mnashu Taye (now Tareq Yaqoob BRN).

BARBADOS

Governing body: Amateur Athletic Association of Barbados, P.O.Box 46, Bridgetown. Founded 1947.
National Champions 2014: **Men**: 100m: Andrew Hinds 10.19, 200m: Fallon Forde 20.89, 400m: Fabian Norgrove 46.75, 110mh: Shane Brathwaite 13.37, 400mh: Rivaldo Leacock 51.70, LJ: Shamar Rock 7.84, TJ: Hackeem Belle 15.36, JT: Janeil Craigg 69.75. **Women**: 100m/200m: Jade Bailey 11.44/23.19, 400m: Sadé Sealy 53.29, 100mh: Kierre Beckles 13.36, 400m: Tia Adana Belle 58.26, LJ: Akela Jones 6.18.

Ryan BRATHWAITE b. 6 Aug 1988 Bridgetown 1.86m 75kg. Sociology graduate of the University of Mississippi.
At 110mh: OG: '08- sf, '12- 5; WCh: '07-09-11-13: sf/1/h/sf; CG: '14- 5; WY: '05- 2; WJ: '06- h; PAm: '07- 4; CAG: '10- 1; PAm-J: '07- 3; won WAF 2009, CAC-J 2006, BAR 2008-09, 2011, 2013.
Eight Barbados 110mh records 2008-13.
Progress at 110mh: 2005- 14.64, 2006- 14.14, 2007- 13.61, 2008- 13.38, 2009- 13.14/13.05w, 2010- 13.34/13.10w, 2011- 13.54, 2012- 13.23, 2013- 13.14/13.13w, 2014- 13.41A/13.44. pbs: 60m 7.02i '08, 55mh 7.18i '09, 60mh 7.61i '10.
First world medallist for Barbados in athletics.

Shane BRATHWAITE b. 8 Feb 1990 Bridgetown 1.82m 75kg. Was at Texas Tech University, USA.
At 110mh: OG: '14- h; CG: 14- 3, won CAC 2013.
At Oct: WY: '07- 1. At 400mh: WJ: '08- sf.
Progress at 110mh: 2008- 14.54, 2009- 13.83, 2010- 13.71A/13.80w, 2011- 13.58, 2012- 13.31A/13.46/13.43w, 2013- 13.44/13.43w, 2014- 13.24. pbs: 100m 10.43 '09, 200m 20.97 '14, 400m 46.97 '11, 1000m 2:48.01 '07, 55mh 7.15i '13, 60mh 7.77i '12, 400mh 50.90 '12, HJ 1.86 '07, LJ 7.02/7.13w '08. No relation to Ryan Brathwaite.

BELARUS

Governing body: Belarus Athletic Federation, Kalinovskogo Street 111A, Minsk 220119. Founded 1991.
National Champions 2014: **Men**: 100m: Ilya Siratsyuk 10.60, 200m: Aleksandr Linnik 20.96, 400m: Aleksandr Krasovskiy 48.17, 800m: Maksim Yuschenko 1:51.07, 1500m: Sergey Platonov 3:45.91, 5000m: Gennadiy Verkhovodkin 14:21.60, 10000m: Ilya Slavinskiy 29:57.15, 3000mSt: Aleksandr Tereshenko 9:01.32, 110mh: Maksim Lynsha 13.82, 400mh: Sergey Serkov 51.26, HJ: Andrey Churylo 2.24, PV: Stanislav Tikonchik 5.20, LJ: Konstantin Boritsevskiy 7.81w, TJ: Dmitriy Plotnitskiy 16.60, SP/DT: Pavel Lyzhin 19.90/60.19, HT: Pavel Boreysho 76.52, JT: Aleksandr Ashomko 77.51, Dec: Aleksandr Dergachev 7504, 20kW: Denis Simanovich 1:22:44, 50kW: Ivan Trotskiy 4:05:39. **Women**: 100m/200m: Yeketerina Gonchar 11.58/23.74, 400m: Ilona Usovich 52.82, 800m: Olga Rulevich 2:05.34, 1500m/3000mSt: Svetlana Kudzelich 4:10.76/9:43.94, 5000m: Nina Savina 16:28.03, 10000m: Olga Mazurenok 33:02.18, 100mh: Alina Talay 12.99, 400mh: Yekaterina Artyukh 57.10, HJ: Yana Maksimova 1.90, PV: Akina Vishnevskaya 4.00, LJ: Olga Sudareva 6.67, TJ: Natalya Vyatkina 14.35, SP:

Alyona Dubitskaya 19.03, DT: Anastasiya Kashtonova 52.74, HT: Alena Novogrodskaya 68.71, JT: Tatyana Kholodovich 63.61, Hep: Yekaterina Netsvetayeva 6121, 20kW: Alina Matveyuk 1:30:48.

Andrey KRAVCHENKO b. 4 Jan 1986 Petrikov, Gomel region 1.87m 84kg.
At Dec: OG: '08- 2; WCh: '07- dq 100m, '09- 10, 13- 12; EC: '10- 3, '14- 1; WJ: '04- 1; EU23: '07- 1; EJ: 05- 1; ECp: '08-09: 1/1. At Oct: WY: '03- 2. At Hep: WI: '08-10-12-14: 2/4/6/2; EI: '07- 3, '11- 1. World youth record for octathlon (6415) 2003.
Progress at Dec: 2005- 7833, 2006- 8013, 2007- 8617, 2008- 8585, 2009- 8336, 2010- 8370, 2011- 8023, 2013- 8390, 2014- 8616. pbs: 60m 7.03i '08, 100m 10.86 '07, 400m 47.17 '07, 1000m 2:39.80i '11, 1500m 4:24.44 '06, 60mh 7.90i '10, 110mh 13.93 '07, HJ 2.22 '14, PV 5.30i/5.20 '08, LJ 7.90 '07, SP 15.42i/15.19 '14, DT 47.46 '14, JT 68.11 '14, Hep 6303i '13.
Added 604 points to pb to win with European U23 record at Götzis 2007. Won IAAF Combined Events Challenge 2008 and 2013.

Pavel KRIVITSKIY b. 17 Apr 1984 Grodno 1.84m 115kg.
At HT: OG: '12- dnq 28; WCh: '09- 8, '11- 5, '13- dnq 14; EC: '10-12-14: dnq 16/9/4; EU23: '05- 1; ET: '10- 1. Won BLR 2007, 2010-12.
Progress at HT: 2004- 72.05, 2005- 77.51, 2006- 78.62, 2007- 78.61, 2008- 80.02, 2009- 79.48, 2010- 80.44, 2011- 80.67, 2012- 80.25, 2013- 79.36, 2014- 79.21.

Pavel LYZHIN b. 24 Mar 1981 Voronok, Russia 1.89m 110kg. Mogilyov. Army.
At SP(/DT): OG: '04- dnq 16, '08- 4, '12- 8; WCh: '03-05-07-09-11-13: dnq 14/nt/19/6/dnq 15/dnq nt; EC: '02- dnq, '06- 8, '10- 6; WJ: '00- 4/7; EU23: '01- 8, '03- 1; EJ: '99- 4/2; WI: '10- 5; EI: '02- 6, '07- 2; WUG: '03- 2, '05- 5. Won BLR SP 2001, 2004, 2009, 2011-14; DT 20114.
Progress at SP: 1999- 17.98, 2000- 19.12, 2001- 20.12, 2002- 20.15, 2003- 20.86, 2004- 20.92, 2005- 20.38, 2006- 20.85, 2007- 20.82i/20.02, 2008- 20.98, 2009- 20.98, 2010- 21.21, 2011- 20.85, 2012- 20.69, 2013- 20.12, 2014- 20.75. pb DT 61.72 '07.

Yuriy SHAYUNOV b. 22 Oct 1987 Minsk 1.89m 120kg. Minsk.
At HT: WCh: '09- dnq 26, '11- nt, '13- 12; EC: '10-12: dnq 20/17; WJ: '04- dnq 13, '06- 4; EU23: '07- 1, '09- 1; EJ: '05- 3; WUG: '09- 1, '13- 4. BLR champion 2009, 2013.
Progress at HT: 2007- 74.92, 2008- 77.32, 2009- 80.72, 2010- 78.73, 2011- 78.70, 2012- 79.00, 2013- 78.99, 2014- 76.86.

Women

Alena ABRAMCHUK b. 14 Feb 1988 1.78m 84kg. née Kopets. Brest.
At SP: WCh: '13- dnq 13; EC: '14- 4; WJ: '02- 7; EU23: '05- 4; EJ: '03- 2; WUG: '07- 2; WI: '14- 7; EI: '07- 4, '15- 2. BLR champion 2013.
Progress at SP: 2006- 15.88, 2007- 16.32i/16.21, 2008- 16.71i/16.69, 2009- 17.97, 2010- 17.99, 2011- 18.82i/17.71, 2012- 18.90i/17.83, 2013- 19.24, 2014- 18.81. pb DT 54.57 '14.

Marina ARZAMASOVA b. 17 Dec 1987 Minsk 1.73m 57kg. née Kotovich. Minsk.
At 800m: OG: '12- 5; WCh: '11/13- sf; EC: '12- 3, '14- 1; WJ: '06- h; CCp: '14- 3; WI: '14- 3; EI: '13- 3. Won W.MilG 2011, BLR 800m 2008, 2013, 1500m 2013.
Progress at 800m: 2004- 2:09.37, 2005- 2:07.24, 2006- 2:06.39, 2007- 2:04.33, 2008- 2:02.67, 2009- 2:05.53i, 2011- 1:59.30, 2012- 1:59.63, 2013- 1:59.60, 2014- 1:58.15. pbs: 400m 52.81 '12, 600m 1:27.28i '13, 1000m 2:37.93 '11, 1500m 4:15.99 '12.
Parents were Aleksandr Kotovich UKR (HJ 2.35i '85, 2.33 '84; 2 EI 85) and Ravilya Agletdinova BLR (800m 1:56.1 '82, 1500m 3:58.40 '85, 1 EC 86, 4 WCh 83).

Yuliya LEONTYUK b. 31 Jan 1984 1.85m 80kg.. Brest.
At SP: WCh: '13- dnq 16; EC: '14- 4; WJ: '02- 7; WY: '01- 3; EU23: '05- 4; EJ: '03- 2; WUG: '07- 2; ECp: '08- dq (1); WI: '14- 7; EI: '15- 2.
Progress at SP: 2001- 15.16, 2002- 16.47, 2003- 17.44, 2004- 16.37, 2005- 17.91, 2006- 18.86, 2007- 18.86, 2008- 19.79, 2013- 18.47, 2014- 18.87, 2015- 19.00i. pb DT 48.72 '14.
Two-year drugs ban 2008-10.

Oksana MENKOVA b. 28 Mar 1982 Krichev, Mogilev region 1.83m 91kg.
At HT: OG: '08- 1, '12- 7; WCh: '03-07-09-13: dnq 23/nt/13/22; EC: '02/06/14: dnq 27/23/13; EU23: 03- 2; EJ: '01- 5; WUG: '05- 5; ECp: '07- 2, '08- 1. Five Belarus hammer records 2006-12.
Progress at HT: 1999- 47.87, 2000- 56.50, 2001- 59.24, 2002- 66.42, 2003- 67.58, 2004- 70.23, 2005- 70.15, 2006- 76.86, 2007- 73.94, 2008- 77.32, 2009- 76.32, 2010- 67.27, 2011- 67.78, 2012- 78.69, 2013- 75.45, 2014- 71.56.
Had a terrible record at major events and only 11th in qualifying, but took gold with Olympic record 76.34 in 2008. Daughter Anna born on 25 Sep 2010.

Anastasiya MIRONCHIK-IVANOVA b. 13 Apr 1989 Slutsk 1.71m 54kg. Minsk.
At LJ: OG: '12- 7; WCh: '09- 11, '11- 4; EC: '10- 6; WJ: '08- 2; WY: '05- 8; EU23: '09- 2, '11- 6; WI: '12- 5; EI: '11- 6. BLR champion 2007, 2010-12.
Progress at LJ: 2004- 5.90, 2005- 6.10/6.13w, 2007- 6.03i/5.89, 2008- 6.71, 2009- 6.65/6.76w, 2010- 6.84, 2011- 6.85/6.92w, 2012- 7.08/7.22w, 2013- 6.60. pb TJ 14.29 '11. Son born June 2014.

Olga SUDAREVA b. 22 Feb 1984 Gomel 1.76m 63kg. née Serygeyenko. Gomel.
At LJ: OG: '08/12- dnq 32/13; WCh: '13- 4; EC: '12- 2, '14- 11; BLR champion 2008, 2011, 2013-14.
Progress at LJ: 2005- 6.01i/6.00, 2006- 6.33, 2007- 6.46, 2008- 6.72, 2011- 6.40, 2012- 6.85, 2013- 6.82, 2014- 6.67. pbs: 60m 7.86i '08, 200m 24.86 '08.

Alina TALAY b. 14 May 1989 Orsha, Vitebsk 1.64m 54kg.
At 100mh: OG: '12- sf; WCh: '13- sf; EC: '10-12-14: sf/2/5; WJ: '08- 4; EU23: '09- 3, '11- 1; WUG: '13- 2; ET: '11- 2; won W.MilG 2011, BLR 2009-10, 2013-14. At 60mh: WI: '12- 3; EI: '11-13-15: 5/1/1.
Progress at 100mh: 2007- 14.38/14.01w, 2008- 13.31, 2009- 13.07, 2010- 12.87, 2011- 12.91, 2012- 12.71, 2013- 12.78, 2014- 12.89. pbs: 60m 7.35i '13, 100m 11.48 '11, 200m 23.59 '11, 50mh 6.89i '11, 60mh 7.85i '15.

BELGIUM

Governing bodies: Ligue Royale Belge d'Athlétisme, Stade Roi Baudouin, avenue du Marathon 199B, 1020 Bruxelles (KBAB/LRBA). Vlaamse Atletiekliga (VAL); Ligue Belge Francophone d'Athlétisme (LBFA). Original governing body founded 1889.
National Championships first held in 1889 (women 1921). **2014 Champions**: **Men**: 100m: Chamberry Muaka 10.68, 200m: Arnout Matthys 21.23, 400m: Kevin Borlée 45.28, 800m: Ismael Debjani 1:49.51, 1500m: Isaac Kimeli 3:52.34, 5000m/10000m/HMar: Abdelhadi El Hachimi 14:05.36/28:57.89/65:52, Mar: Gino Van Geyte 2:27:21, 3000mSt: Krijn Van Koolwyk 8:57.08, 110mh: Damien Broothaerts 13.85, 400mh: Michaël Bultheel 49.13, HJ: Bram Ghuys 2.15, PV: Arnaud Art 5.35, LJ: Mathias Broothaerts 8.07, TJ: Solomon Commey 15.51, SP: Jurgen Verbrugghe 17.52; DT: Philip Milanov 60.57, HT: Tim De Coster 60.75, JT: Timothy Herman 75.00, Dec: Daan Elsen 6997, 50kW: Daniel Lhoest 5:23:01. **Women**: 100m/200m: Olivia Borlée 11.54/23.50, 400m: Kimberley Efonye 53.57, 800m: Marlies Schils 2:13.82, 1500m: Sofie Van Accom 4:27.29, 5000m: Veerle Van Linden 16:54.17, 10000m/HMar: Karen Van Proeyen 36:57.52/ 78:37, Mar: Clarisse Wagelmans 3:04:23, 3000mSt: Sofie Gallein 10:37.74, 100mh: Eline Berings 12.87, 400mh: Axelle Dauwens 55.81, HJ: Claire Orcel 1.82, PV: Chloé Henry 4.20, LJ: Els De Wael 6.14, TJ: Linda Onana 12.91, SP/HT: Jolien Boumkwo 16.05/66.92, DT: Annelies Peetroons 54.12, HT: Vanessa Sterckendries 59.09, JT: Melissa Dupre 54.13, Hep: Sietske Lenchant 5081, 10kW/20kW: Myriam Nicolas 57:21/1:59:04.

Jonathan BORLÉE b. 22 Feb 1988 Woluwe-Saint Lambert 1.80m 70kg. Was at Florida State University.
At 400m: OG: '08- sf/5R, '12- 6; WCh: '11- 5, '13- 4; EC: '10- 7/3R, '12- 1R, '14- dns; WJ: '06- 4; WY: '05- 5; EJ: '07- h; WI: '10- 2R; EI: '11- 3R, '15- 1R. Won NCAA 2009. At 200m: EC: '12- 4. Won BEL 200m 2012-13, 400m 2006, 2011
Four Belgian 400m records 2009-12, 300m 2012.
Progress at 400m: 2005- 47.50, 2006- 46.06, 2007- 47.85, 2008- 45.11, 2009- 44.78, 2010- 44.71, 2011- 44.78, 2012- 44.43, 2013- 44.54, 2014- 45.37. pbs: 60m 6.81i '07, 100m 10.78 '07, 200m 20.31 '12, 300m 31.87 '12, 500m 1:00.76i '15, 600m 1:18.60i '11.
Twin brother of Kevin Borlée, their sister Olivia (b. 10 Apr 1986) has pbs 100m 11.39 '07, 200m 22.98 '06, 3 WCh '07, 2 OG '08 at 4x100mR. Younger brother **Dylan** (b. 20 Sep 1992) pb 45.80 '13 and 2 EI '15 (the three brothers ran on BEL 4x400m team 5th WCh 2013. 1st EI 2015). Their father Jacques was an international 400m runner (45.4 '79), mother Edith Demartelaere had pbs 200m 23.89 and 400m 54.09 in 1984.

Kévin BORLÉE b. 22 Feb 1988 Woluwe-Saint Lambert 1.80m 71kg. WS. Was at Florida State University.
At 400m: OG: '08- sf/5R, '12- 5; WCh: '09- sf/4R, '11- 3, '13- sf; EC: '10- 1/3R, '12- 1R, '14- sf; WJ: '06- sf; WI: '10- 2R; EI: '11- 3R, '15- 1R; CCp: '10- 4/2R. At 200m: WY: '05- sf. Won DL 2012, BEL 200m 2009, 2011; 400m 2007, 2013.
Belgian 400m records 2008 and 2012.
Progress at 400m: 2005- 47.86, 2006- 46.63, 2007- 46.38, 2008- 44.88, 2009- 45.28, 2010- 45.01, 2011- 44.74, 2012- 44.56, 2013- 44.73, 2014- 45.28. pbs: 60m 6.85i '13, 100m 10.62 '07, 200m 20.72 '11, 300m 32.72i '13, 32.76 '08; 600m 1:15.65i '11.

Thomas VAN DER PLAETSEN b. 24 Dec 1990 Gent 1.88m 82kg. AAC Deinze.
At Dec: WCh: '11- 13, '13- 15; EC: '14- 10; EU23: '11- 1; EJ: '09- 1; WUG: '13- 1; Won BEL PV 2011, 2013; Dec 2010. At Hep: WI: '14- 3; EI: '11- 6.
Belgian decathlon record 2011.
Progress at Dec: 2010- 7564, 2011- 8157, 2013- 8255, 2014- 8184. pbs: 60m 7.13i '14, 100m 11.04 '14, 200m 22.34 '10, 400m 48.64 '11, 1000m 2:40.50i '14, 1500m 4:32.52 '11, 60mh 8.06i '14, 110mh 14.45 '11, HJ 2.17 '11, PV 5.40 '14, LJ 7.80 '13, SP 14.32i/14.12 '14, DT 41.32 '13, JT 65.31 '13, Hep 6259i '14.

Women

Nafissatou THIAM b. 19 Aug 1994 Namur 1.84m 69kg. RFCL. Student of geographical science at University of Liège.
At Hep: WCh: '13- 14; EC: '14- 3; WJ: '12- 14; WY: '11- 4; EJ: '13- 1. At Pen: EI: '13- 6, '15- 2. At HJ: WI: '14- 8=. Won BEL Hep 2012.
Two Belgian heptathlon records 2013-14. World junior heptathlon best 2013.
Progress at HJ, Hep: 2010- 1.74, 2011- 1.81, 2012- 1.88, 5916; 2013- 1.92, 6298, 2014- 1.97, 6508. pbs: 60m 7.81i '13, 200m 24.78 '14, 800m 2:20.79 '14, 60mh 8.42i '15, 100mh 13.81 '14, LJ 6.37 '13, TJ: 12.82 '14, SP 15.03 '14, JT 51.90 '14, Pen 4696i '15.
Tied world best in a heptathlon with 1.97 high jump at EC 2014.

BOTSWANA

Governing body: Botswana Athletics Association, PO Box 2399, Gaborone. Founded 1972.

Nijel AMOS b. 15 Mar 1994 Marobela 1.79m 60kg.
At 800m: OG: '12- 2; CG: '14- 1; WJ: '12- 1, WY: '11- 5; AfCh: 14- 1; CG: '14- 1; WUG: '13- 1. Won DL 2014.
World junior 800m and two Botswana 800m records 2012.
Progress at 800m: 2011- 1:47.28, 2012- 1:41.73, 2013- 1:44.71, 2014- 1:42.45. pbs: 400m 45.56 '14, 600m 1:15.0+ 12.

Isaac MAKWALA b. 29 Sep 1986 Tutume 1.83m 79kg.
At (200m)/400m: OG: '12- h; WCh: '09- h, '13- (h); CG: '10- sf, '14- sf; AfG: '07- sf, '11- 7; AfCh: '08-10-12: 2/sf/1/1 & (2)/1R; CCp: 6/2/1R.
Records: African 400m 2014, Botswana 100m (2) 2013-14200m 2013-14, 400m (3) 2014
Progress at 200m, 400m: 2007- 46.48, 2008- 21.20, 45.64A; 2009- 20.73, 45.56; 2010- 21.33, 46.07; 2011- 21.17, 46.27; 2012- 20.87, 45.25; 2013- 20.21, 45.86; 2014- 19.96/19.7A, 44.01. Pb 100m 10.20A, 10.14wA '14.

Women

Amantle MONTSHO b. 4 Jul 1983 Mabudutsa 1.73m 64kg.
At 400m: OG: '04- h, '08- 8, '12- 4; WCh: '05-07-09-11-13: h/sf/8/1/2; CG: '06-10-14: sf/1/4dq; AfG: '03-07-11: h/1/1; AfCh: '04-06-08-10-12: h/2/1/1/1; WI: '10- 4; CCp: '10- 1/3R. Won DL 2011-13.
Botswana records 100m 2011, 200m 2001-12, 400m 2003-13.
Progress at 400m: 2003- 55.03, 2004- 53.77, 2005- 52.59, 2006- 52.14, 2007- 50.90, 2008- 49.83A/50.54, 2009- 49.89, 2010- 49.89, 2011- 49.56, 2012- 49.54, 2013- 49.33, 2014- 50.37. pbs: 100m 11.60 '11, 200m 22.89 '12, 22.88w '11, 300m 36.33i '10 (African record).
First Botswana woman to win a major title. Positive test at 2014 Commonwealth Games, for which she has received a two-year ban.

BRAZIL

Governing body: Confederação Brasileira de Atletismo (CBAt), Avenida Rio Purus No. 103 - Conj. Vieiralves, Bairro N.Sra das Graças, Manaus, AM 69053-050. Founded 1914 (Confederação 1977).
National Championships first held in 1925. **2014 Champions**: **Men**: 100m: Bruno de Barros 10.48, 200m: Aldemir G da Silva 20.32, 400m: Hugo de Sousa 45.40, 800m: Cleiton Abrão 1:45.59, 1500m: Lutimar Paes 3:40.86, 5000m: Joílson da Silva 14:00.81, 10000m: Giovani dos Santos 28:42.27, 3000mSt: Jean Carlos Machado 8:52.31, 110mh: Jonathan Mendes 13.53, 400mh: Hederson Estefani 49.59, HJ: Fernando Ferreira 2.21, PV: Fábio Gomes da Silva 5.71, LJ: Higor Alves 8.18, TJ: Jonathan Silva 16.53 , SP: Darlan Romani 20.84, DT: Ronald Julião 58.93, HT: Wágner Domingos 75.47, JT: Julio de Oliveira 70.13, Dec: Felipe dos Santos 7952, 20kW: Caio Bonfim 1:26:19, 50kW: Cláudio dos Santos 4:14:18. **Women:** 100m/200m: Ana Cláudia Silva 11.27/ 22.81, 400m: Geisa Coutinho 51.44, 800m: Jéssica dos Santos 2:03.98, 1500m: Flávia da Silva 4:19.15, 5000m/10000m: Cruz da Silva 16:26.31/ 34:59.43, 3000mSt: Sabine Heitling 10:13.33, 100mh: Fabiana Moraes 13.08, 400mh: Jaílma de Lima 57.43, HJ: Mônica de Freitas 1.86, PV: Patrícia dos Santos 4.20, LJ: Keila Costa 6.63, TJ: Nubia Soares 14.22, SP: Keely Medeiros 17.58, DT: Fernanda Borges 61.35, HT: Mariana Marcelino 61.39, JT: Jucilene de Lima 62.89, Hep: Tamara de Souza 5962, 20000mW: Érica de Sena 1:38:59.

Carlos Eduardo CHININ b. 3 May 1985 São Paulo 1.95m 83kg. BM&F Atletismo.
At Dec: OG: '08- dnf; WCh: '07- dnf '13- 6; PAm: '07- 3; SACh: '05-06-09: 4/1/1; WUG: '07- 3; BRA champion 2008, 2010, 2013.
South American records: decathlon 2013, indoor heptathlon 2014.
Progress at Dec: 2005- 7426, 2006- 7261, 2007- 7977, 2008- 7850 2009- 7690, 2010- 7641, 2011- 8068, 2013- 8393, 2014- dnf. pbs: 60m 7.01i '14, 100m 10.78 '13, 400m 48.18 '07, 1000m 2:44.88i '14, 1500m 4:23.99 '07, 60mh 7.99i '14. 110mh 14.05 '13, HJ 2.13 '07, PV 5.10 '13, LJ 7.76 '07, SP 15.28 '13, DT 48.38 '11, JT 59.98 '13, Hep 5951i '14.

Augusto Dutra de OLIVEIRA b. 16 Jul 1990 Marília, São Paulo 1.80m 70kg. BMF Bovespa.
At PV: WCh: '13- 11; WI: '14- 7; SAG: '14- 1; SACh: '11- 4; CCp: '14- 4; won SAm-J '2009.
Two South American pole vault records and two indoors 2013.
Progress at PV: 2008- 4.60, 2009- 5.00, 2010- 5.40, 2011- 5.32, 2012- 5.45, 2013- 5.82, 2014- 5.70.

Mauro Vinícius da SILVA b. 26 Dec 1986 Presidente Prudente 1.83m 69kg.
At LJ: OG: '08- dnq 26, '12- 7; WCh: '13- 5; WI: '12- 1, '14- 1; SAG: '14- 3; SACh: '13- 1. BRA champion 2010, 2012-13.
Progress at LJ: 2005- 7.35/7.73w, 2006- 7.61, 2007- 7.66, 2008- 8.10/8.20w?, 2009- 8.04i/7.94, 2010- 8.12, 2011- 8.27, 2012- 8.28i/8.11, 2013- 8.31, 2014- 8.28i/7.88/8.08w. pbs: 60m 6.76i '09, 100m 10.40 '07, 200m 21.02 '07.
Won World Indoor title with 8.23 but took off behind the board with 24cm to spare.

Thiago Braz da SILVA b. 16 Dec 1993 Marília 1.93m 84kg. Orcampi/Unimed.
At PV: WCh: '13- dnq 14=; WJ: '12- 1; WI: '14- 4; SACh: '13- 1; won Yth Oly 2010, PAm-J '2011.
South American pole vault record 2013, indoors (2) 2014.
Progress at PV: 2009- 4.60, 2010- 5.10, 2011- 5.31, 2012- 5.55, 2013- 5.83, 2014- 5.76i/5.73.
Married Ana Paula de Oliveira (HJ 1.82 '14) on 13 Dec 2014.

Women

Jucilene de LIMA b. 14 Sep 1990 Taperoá, Paraíba 1.74m 63kg. BM&F Atletismo.

At JT: WCh: '13- dnq 26; WJ: '06-nt, '08- 11; WY: '05-dnq 17, '07- 10; PAm: '07- 10; SAG: '14-2; SACh: '07-09-13: 4/2/3. Won IbAm 2013, SAm-J 2007.

Javelin records: South American 2014, BRA (3) 2013-14, S.American junior (5) 2006-09.

Progress at JT: 2004- 48.04, 2005- 48.58, 2006- 54.24, 2007- 54.53, 2008- 51.91, 2009- 56.75, 2010- 55.73, 2011- 55.44, 2012- 57.85, 2013- 61.98, 2014- 62.89.

Fabiana de Almeida **MURER** b. 16 Mar 1981 Campinas, São Paulo 1.72m 64kg. BM&F Atletismo. Degree in physiotherapy.

At PV: OG: '08- 10=, '12- dnq 14; WCh: '05-07-09-11-13: dnq 15/6=/5/1/5=; WJ: '98- dnq 14=, '00- 10; PAm: '99-07-11: 9/1/2; WI: '08-10-14: 3=/1/4; SAG: '14- 1; SACh: '99-01-05-06-07-09-11: 3/6/2/1/1/1/1; WCp: '06-10-14: 2/3/nh. Won DL 2010, 2014; IbAm 2006, 2010; SAmG 2014; SAm-J 1998-2000, BRA 2005-07, 2010, 2013.

13 South American pole vault records, 16 indoors 2006-15, 29 BRA records 1998-2011.

Progress at PV: 1998- 3.66, 1999- 3.81, 2000- 3.90, 2001- 3.91, 2002- 3.70, 2003- 4.06, 2004- 4.25, 2005- 4.40, 2006- 4.66, 2007- 4.66i/4.65, 2008- 4.80, 2009- 4.82, 2010- 4.85, 2011- 4.85, 2012- 4.77, 2013- 4.75, 2014- 4.80, 2015- 4.83i.

Married to coach Élson de Souza (pb 5.02 '89).

BULGARIA

Governing body: Bulgarian Athletics Federation, 75 bl. Vassil Levski, Sofia 1000. Founded 1924.

National Championships first held in 1926 (men), 1938 (women). **2014 Champions**: **Men:** 100m: Denis Dimitrov 10.57, 200m: Petar Kremenski 21.64, 400m: Krasimir Braykov 47.34, 800m/1500m: Sava Todorov 1:56.91/3:52.86, 5000m/10000m/HMar: Yolo Nikolov 14:35.44/32:24.35/72:30, Mar: Shaban Mustafa 2:25:05, 3000mSt: Mitko Tsenov 9:07.62, 110mh: Milan Volkanov 14.75, 400mh: Lazar Katouchev 52.98, HJ: Viktor Ninov 2.26, PV: Atanas Petrov 4.80, LJ: Mikhail Velkov 7.36, TJ: Rumen Dimitrov 16.49, SP/DT: Rosen Karamfilov 16.84/54.10, HT: Aykhan Apti 67.71, JT: Radoslav Ivanov 62.84, Dec: Kiril Zagorski 5252, 20kW: Bozhidar Vasilev 1:49:39. **Women**: 100m: Inna Eftimova 11.52, 200m: Maria Dankova 24.82, 400m/800m: Vania Stambolova 53.83/2:03.64, 1500m: Yana Georgieva 4:22.01, 5000m/3000mSt: Silvia Danekova 16:21.58/9:55.82, 10000m: Dobrinka Shalamanova 36:25.81, HMar/Mar: Milka Mikhaylova 1:23:43/2:58:51, 100mh: Elena Miteva 14.11, 400mh: Teodora Kolarova 60.67, HJ: Mirela Demireva 1.85, PV: Temenuzkha Atanasova 3.00, LJ: Andriana Bânova 6.20, TJ: Maria Dimitrova 13.43, SP/DT: Radoslava Mavrodieva 17.42/43.90, HT: Mikhaela Metodieva 51.50, JT: Khristina Georgieva 46.52, Hep: Iva Alexandrova 4423, 20kW: Radosveta Simeonova 1:56:03.

Georgi IVANOV b. 13 Mar 1985 Sliven 1.87m 130kg. "Pavel Pavlov" Vratsa & Dukla Praha.

At SP: OG: '08- dnq, '12- dnq 22; WCh: '09- dnq 33, '13- 8; EC: '10/12- dnq 21/16, '14- nt; WJ: '02- dnq, '04- 1; WY: '01- 1; WI: '14- 5; EU23: '07- 4; EJ: '03- 3, BUL champion 2007-09, 2011-12; Balkan 2013-14.

Two Bulgarian shot records 2013.

Progress at SP: 2002- 17.98i/16.37, 2003- 18.42i/16.73, 2005- 19.51, 2006- 19.04i/18.96, 2007- 19.42, 2008- 20.02, 2009- 19.41, 2010- 19.90i/19.12, 2011- 19.23i/18.90, 2012- 20.33, 2013- 21.09, 2014- 21.02i/20.91. pb DT 51.96 '04.

Engaged to Andriana Banova (TJ 14.34 '11); their son was born in 2013.

Women

Ivet LALOVA-COLLIO b. 18 May 1984 Sofia 1.68m 56kg. née Lalova. Levski Sofia, Panellínios GRE.

At 100m/(200m): OG: '04- 4/5, '08- sf/qf, '12- sf/sf; WCh: '07- qf, '09- qf/h, '11- 7/sf, '13- sf/sf; EC: '10- h, '12- 1/sf, '14- 5/sf; WJ: '02- sf; WY: '01- h/sf; EJ: '03: 1/1; EI: '05- (1). At 60m: WI: '12- 8; EI: '13- 3. Won BUL 100m 2004-05, 200m 2004; Balkan 100m 2011, 2013.

Bulgarian 100m record 2004.

Progress at 100m, 200m: 1998- 13.0, 27.2; 1999- 12.71, 2000- 12.14, 25.24; 2001- 11.72, 24.03; 2002- 11.59, 24.4; 2003- 11.14, 22.87; 2004- 10.77, 22.51/22.36w; 2005- 11.03, 22.76; 2007- 11.26/11.15w, 23.00; 2008- 11.31/11.28w, 23.13; 2009- 11.48/11.24w, 23.60; 2010- 11.43, 23.71; 2011- 10.96, 22.66; 2012- 11.06/11.01w, 22.98; 2013- 11.04, 22.78; 2014- 11.10, 23.17/22.92w. pbs: 50m 6.23i+ '12, 60m 7.12i '13.

Broke her leg in a warm-up collision with two athletes on 14 Jun 2005. Married Simone Collio (Italy, 60m 6.55 ITA record 2008, 100m 10.06 in 2009) on 20 Sep 2013. Her father Miroslav Lalov had 100m best of 10.4 and was BUL 200m champion in 1966, mother Liliya was a heptathlete.

Vania STAMBOLOVA b. 28 Nov 1983 Varna 1.75m 63kg. SC Kostenets. Student at the Sports Academy of Sofia.

At 400m: EC: '06- 1; WI: '06-10-12: 2/3/4; EI: '11- 4; WCp: '06- 2. At 800m: EC: '14- 6. At 400mh: OG: '12- h; WCh: '05-09-11-13: h/sf/6/sf; EC: '10- 2; WUG: '09- 1; CCp: '10- 3. Won Balkan 400mh 2005, 2011, 2013; 400m 2011; BUL 400m 2009, 2014; 800m 2014, 400mh 2002, 2005-06.

Bulgarian Records: 400m (5) 2006, 400mh (2) 2006-10.

Progress at 400m, 400mh: 1998- 57.91, 64.34; 1999- 57.45, 63.53; 2000- 58.82, 62.72; 2001- 57.86, 61.38; 2002- 58.30, 61.11; 2005- 52.99, 56.29; 2006- 49.53, 54.55; 2009- 51.47, 55.14; 2010- 50.88, 53.82;

2011- 50.98, 53.68; 2012- 50.87, 54.04; 2013- 54.77h, 2014- 52.81. pb 200m 22.81 '06, 22.7 '10; 300m 36.81i '12, 800m 2:00.91 '14, 1000m 2:42.76i '14. Former footballer. Two-year drugs ban 2007-09.

BURUNDI

Francine NIYONSABA b. 5 May 1993 Nkanda Bweru, Ruyiqi 1.61m 56kg.
At 800m: OG: '12- 6; AfCh: '12- 1.
Five Burundi 800m records 2012.
Progress at 800m: 2012- 1:56.59, 2013- 1:56.72. pbs: 400m 54.3 '13, 600m 1:27.6 '12.

CANADA

Governing body: Athletics Canada, Suite B1-110, 2445 S-Laurent Drive, Ottawa, Ontario K1G 6C3. Formed as Canadian AAU in 1884.
National Championships first held in 1884 (men), 1925 (women). **2014 Champions: Men**: 100m: Gavion Smellie 10.37, 200m: Brendon Rodney 20.80w, 400m: Daundre Barnaby 45.96, 800m: Brandon McBride 1:46.69, 1500m: Nathan Brannen 3:42.50, 5000m: Cam Levins 13:25.70, 10000m: Barry Britt 30:10.81, HMar/Mar: Eric Gillis 64:28/2:13:47, 3000mSt: Matt Hughes 8:32.22, 110mh: Damian Warner 13.66, 400mh: Gabriel El Hanbli 51.65, HJ: Derek Drouin 2.28, PV: Shawn Barber 5.55, LJ: Benjamin Warnock 7.49w, TJ: Patrick Hanna 14.86, SP/DT: Tim Nedow 20.60/54.77, HT: James Steacy 74.68, JT: Raymond Dykstra 78.58, Dec: James Turner 7408, 20kW: Evan Dunfee 1:21:57. **Women**: 100m: Crystal Emmanuel 11.46, 200m: Kimberley Hyacinthe 23.46, 400m: Carline Muir 52.13, 800m: Melissa Bishop 2:03.23, 1500m: Kate Van Buskirk 4:10.83, 5000m: Jessica O'Connell 15:47.35, 10000m: Leslie Sexton 37:15.65, HMar: Rachel Hannah 73:38, Mar: Rhiannon Jones 2:47:11, 3000mSt: Jessica Furlan 9:55.71, 100mh: Phylicia George 13.20, 400mh: Noelle Montcalm 56.67, HJ: Alyx Treasure 1.89, PV: Lindsey Bergevin 4.10, LJ: Christabel Nettey 6.64, TJ: Carolina Eberhardt 13.06w, SP/DT: Julie Labonté 17.10/51.94, HT: Sultana Frizell 73.78, JT: Liz Gleadle 60.62, Hep: Jillian Drouin 5972, 20kW: Rachel Seaman 1:32:54.

Dylan ARMSTRONG b. 15 Jan 1981 Kamloop, British Columbia 1.90m 125kg. Dylan BC Athletics. Was at University of Texas.
At SP: OG: '08- 3, '12- 5; WCh: '07-09-11-13: 8/dnq 17/2/3; CG: '10- 1; WI: '10- 3; PAm: '07- 1, '11- 1; PAm-J: '99- 2 (1 HT, 3 DT); CCp: '10- 5. At HT: WCh: '01- dnq 31; WJ: '00- 2 (dnq DT). Won Canadian HT 2001-02, SP 2005-10, 2012; DL SP 2011.
Seven Canadian shot records 2008-11.
Progress at SP: 1999- 16.16, 2000- 16.30, 2001- 18.07, 2004- 19.55, 2005- 19.83, 2006- 20.62, 2007- 20.72, 2008- 21.04, 2009- 20.92, 2010- 21.58, 2011- 22.21, 2012- 21.50, 2013- 21.45. pbs: DT 54.60 '00, HT 71.51 '03, Wt 22.78i '03.

Shawnacy BARBER b. 27 May 1994 Toronto 1.90m 82kg. Student at Akron University, USA.
At PV: WCh: '13- dnq 27; CG: '14- 3; WJ: '12- 3; PAm-J: 13- 1; Canadian champion 2013-14, NCAA indoor 2014.
Three Canadian pole vault records 2013-15, indoors (6) 2014-15.
Progress at PV: 2011- 5.03, 2012- 5.57, 2013- 5.71, 2014- 5.75Ai/5.65, 2015- 5.91i./5.90
His father George vaulted 5.03 in 1985 and in 1983 competed for Canada (nh) at the Worlds and was Canadian champion.

Derek DROUIN b. 6 Mar 1990 Sarnia, Ontario 1.95m 80kg. Student of exercise science at Indiana University.
At HJ: OG: '12- 3=; WCh: '13- 3; CG: '14- 1; WY: '07- 10; CCp: '14- 5. Won PAmJ 2009, CAN 2012-14, NCAA 2013, Franc G 2013.
Commonwealth high jump record 2014, four Canadian high jump records 2013-14.
Progress at HJ: 2007- 2.07, 2008- 2.11, 2009- 2.27, 2010- 2.28i/2.26, 2011- 2.33i/2.23, 2012- 2.31, 2013- 2.38, 2014- 2.40. pbs: 60mh 7.98i '12, 1000m 2:45.06i '13, 110mh 14.04 '13, PV 4.15i '13. 3.65 '11; LJ 7.20i '13, 6.85 '11; Hep 5817i '13.
His sister Jillian (b. 30 Sep 1986) set a heptahlon pb of 5972w to win the Pan-Am Cup in 2014; 6th CG 2010.

Damian WARNER b. 4 Nov 1989 London, Ontario 1.85m 83kg. LWTF.
At Dec: OG: '12- 5; WCh: '11- 18, '13- 3; CG: '14- 1. Won Canadian 110mh 2014, Dec 2011-13. At Hep: WI: '14- 7.
Progress at Dec: 2010- 7449, 2011- 8102A/7832, 2012- 8442, 2013- 8512, 2014- 8282. pbs: 60m 6.74i '10, 100m 10.29 '14, 200m 20.96 '13, 400m 46.36i '15, 47.63 '13; 1000m 2:37.98i '14, 1500m 4:29.85 '12, 60mh 7.66i '15, 110mh 13.50 '14, HJ 2.09 '13, PV 4.80A '12, LJ 7.62 '14, TJ 14.75w '08, SP 14.23 '13, DT 45.90 '12, JT 64.67 '13, Hep: 6129 14.
Made 340 points improvement on pb when 5th at 2012 Olympics, setting six pbs, and 70 more at 2013 Worlds, with three pbs. Won Götzis & Talence 2013.

Women

Sultana FRIZELL b. 24 Oct 1984 Perth, Ontario 1.83m 110kg. Was at University of Georgia.
At HT: OG: '08/12- dnq 33/25; WCh: '09- 10, '13- dnq 16; CG: '10- 1, '14- 1; PAm: '07- 7, '11- 2; PAm-J: '03- 4; CCp: '14- 5; Canadian champion 2007-08, 2010, 2013-14.
Four Commonwealth hammer records 2009-12, North American 2012, seven Canadian 2008-12.
Progress at HT: 2002- 54.75, 2003- 57.95, 2004- 63.36, 2005- 66.42, 2006- 63.39, 2007- 67.92, 2008- 70.94, 2009- 72.07, 2010- 72.24, 2011- 71.46, 2012- 75.04, 2013- 71.57, 2014- 75.73. pbs: SP 15.82 '06, Wt 20.37i '05, JT 46.58 '04.

Christabel NETTEY b. 2 Jun 1991 Brampton, Ontario 1.62m 59kg. Was at Arizona State

University (justice studies).
At LJ: WCh: '13- dnq 20; CG: '14- 3; WY: '07- dnq 14; PAm-J: '09- 2; CCp: '14- 4. At 100mh: WY: '07- 8 (3 MedR). Won CAN LJ 2013-14., NACAC 2012 Four Canadian indoor LJ records 2014-15.
Progress at LJ: 2006- 6.12, 2007- 6.14, 2008- 6.21, 2009- 6.05/6.10w, 2010- 6.42i/6.28, 2011- 6.49/6.55i, 2012- 6.58, 2013- 6.75, 2014- 6.73, 2015- 6.99i. pbs: 100m 12.14 '06, 60mh 8.25i '13, 100mh 13.42 '13, HJ 1.66 '11, TJ 12.80 '12, 12.90w '07; SP 12.16 '11, Hep 5068 '11.
Older sister Sabrina has LJ pbs 6.32i '14, 6.26 '12.

Brianne THEISEN-EATON b. 18 Dec 1988 Humboldt 1.80m 64kg. Sasketchewan. Student at University of Oregon
At Hep: OG: '12- 10; WCh: '09- 15, '13- 2; CG: '14- 1; WJ: '06- 17. Won CAN 2013, PAm-J 2007, NCAA 2009-10, 2012. At Pen: WI: '14- 2.
Canadian heptathlon record 2014
Progress at Hep: 2005- 5181, 2006- 5240, 2007- 5413, 2008- 5738, 2010- 6094, 2012- 6440, 2013- 6530, 2014- 6641. pbs: 200m 23.41 '14, 400m 53.72 '12, 800m 2:09.03 '13, 60mh 8.10i '15, 100mh 13.00 '14, HJ 1.88i '12, 1.87 '14; LJ 6.59 '14, SP 13.92 '14, JT 46.47 '12, Pen 4766i '14.
Won Götzis 2013. Married Ashton Eaton on 15 July 2013.

Angela WHYTE b. 22 May 1980 Edmonton 1.70m 56kg. Graduate in crime and justice studies from University of Idaho, USA.
At 100mh: OG: '04- 6, '08- h; WCh: '01-03-05-07-09-13: h/sf/sf/8/h/6; CG: '02-06-10-14: 5/2/2/3; PAm: '03- 5, '07- 3, '11- 2. Canadian champion 2001, 2013.
Progress at 100mh: 1999- 13.97/13.43Aw, 2000- 13.37A/13.58, 2001- 13.09/12.82w, 2002- 13.03/13.00w, 2003- 12.78, 2004- 12.69, 2005- 12.88, 2006- 12.69, 2007- 12.63/12.55w, 2008- 12.96, 2009- 12.93, 2010- 12.98/12.93w, 2011- 12.88/12.76w, 2012- 12.83/12.75w, 2013- 12.66A/12.76/12.52w. 2014- 12.89. pbs: 60m 7.36i '08, 100m 11.63 '03, 11.37w '04; 200m 23.60 '07, 800m 2:19.91 '03, 55mh 7.48iA '03, 60mh 7.92i '08, 400mh 58.74 '01, HJ 1.69 '14, LJ 6.23 '14, SP 13.26 '14, JT 40.02 '14, Hep 6018 '14.

Jessica ZELINKA b. 3 Sep 1981 London, Ontario 1.72m 62kg. Calgary AB.
At Hep(/100mh): OG: '08- 5, '12- 6/7; WCh: '05-11, '11- 9, '13- (sf); CG: '06-10-14: 4/2/2; PAm: '07- 1; WJ: '00- 5/h. Won CAN Hep 2001, 2004-06, 2008, 2010, 2012; 100mh 2012.
Six Canadian heptathlon records 2006-12.
Progress at 100mh. Hep: 1996- 4700, 1997- 4586, 1998- 14.18/14.13w, 4859; 1999- 14.18, 5059; 2000- 13.81, 5583; 2001- 13.67, 5702; 2002- 5962, 2003- 13.52, 6031; 2004- 13.26/13.10w, 6296; 2005- 13.42/13.15w, 6137; 2006- 13.08, 6314; 2007- 13.25, 6343; 2008- 12.97, 6490; 2010- 13.19, 6204; 2011- 13.01, 6353; 2012- 12.65, 6599A/6480; 2013- 12.86/12.66w, 2014- 12.83, 6270. pbs: 50m 6.56i '02, 60m 7.53i '04, 100m 11.63 '14, 11.36w '13; 200m 23.32 '12, 800m 2:07.95 '08, 60mh 8.19i '06, HJ 1.79 '07, LJ 6.19/6.23w '06, SP 14.97 '07, JT 46.60A '12, Pen 4386i '07

CHILE

Governing body: Federación Atlética de Chile, Calle Santo Toribio No 660, Ñuñoa, Santiago de Chile. Founded 1914.

National Champions 2014: **Men**: 100m: Enrique Polanco 10.56, 200m: Ignacio Rojas 21.46, 400m: Sergio Germain 47.35, 800m: Aquiles Zúñiga 1:52.26, 1500m/10000m: Leslie Encina 3:53.07/30:04.97, 3000m: Carlos Martín Díaz 8:23.66, 5000m: Víctor Aravena 14:36.22, 3000mSt: Mauricio Valdivia Enzo Yáñez 9:04.71, 110mh: Diego Lyon 14.36, 400mh: Alfredo Sepúlveda 52.57, HJ: Rodrigo Arriagada 2.05, PV: Felipe Fuentes 4.90, LJ: Camilo Olivares 7.17, TJ: Randy Hoodf 14.83, SP: Matías López 16.36, DT: Rodrigo Cárdenas 46.42, HT: Roberto Sáez 64.89, JT: Ignacio Guerra 69.51, Dec: Matías Péndola 5866, 20kW: Yerko Araya 1:29:34/1:26:08.5t, 50kW: Jean-Pierre Valenzuela 5:06:30. **Women**: 100m/200m: Cindy Leyton 12.76/26.52, 400m/400mh: Constanza Castillo 58.04/62.24, 800m: Javiera Faletto 2:18.78, 1500m: Geraldine Becerra 4:57.94, 3000m: Jennifer González 10:01.95, 5000m: Yetsemin González 18:11.83, 10000m: Giselle Álvarez 35:37.3, 3000mSt: Margarita Masías 11:01.71, 100mh: Ljubica Milos 14.71, HJ: Marta Evelin Herrera 1.65, PV/TJ: María Victoria Fernández 3.50/12.21, LJ: Carolina Castillo 5.58, SP: Ivanna Gallardo 15.64, DT: Karen Gallardo 52.32, HT: Constanza Ávila 45.55, JT: María Paz Ríos 48.38, 20kW: Cristal Paillalef 1:46:36/1:53:53.5t.

CHINA

Governing body: Athletic Association of the People's Republic of China, 2 Tiyuguan Road, Beijing 100763.

National Championships first held in 1910 (men), 1959 (women). **2014 Champions**: **Men**: 100m/200m: Xie Zhenye 10.36/20.44, 400m: Fang Yuan 46.67, 800m: Ma Junyi 1:53.05, 1500m: Teng Haining 3:48.54, 5000m: Liu Hongliang 14:27.37, 10000m: Qi Zhenfei 29:31.60, Mar: Han Chengcai 2:18:21. 3000mSt: Yang Tao 8:55.19, 110mh: Jiang Fan 13.57, 400mh: Cheng Wen 50.27, HJ: Guo Jinqi 2.24, PV: Zhang Wei 5.60, LJ: Gao Xinglong 8.21w, TJ: Xu Xiaolong 16.82, SP: Liu Yang 18.97, DT: Wu Jian 58.63, HT: Wan Yong 71.85, JT: Zhao Qinggang 76.97, Dec: Hu Yufei 7433. **Women**: 100m: Tao Yujia 11.56, 200m: Lin Huijin 23.59, 400m: Yang Huizhen 52.73, 800m: Wang Mei 2:11.39, 1500m: Zhao Jing 4:16.36, 5000m: Xi Qiuzi 16:01.93, 10000m: Ding Changqin 33:07.62, Mar: Gong Lihua 2:32:23, 3000mSt: Yin Anna 10:17.23, 100mh: Sun Yawei 13.01, 400mh: Wang Huan 57.16, HJ: Zheng Xingjuan 1.96, PV: Li Ling 4.15, LJ: Wang

Wupin 6.40, TJ: Deng Lina 13.71, SP: Gong Lijiao 18.67, DT: Tan Jian 61.07, HT: Wang Zheng 72.61, JT: Li Lingwei 62.56, Hep: Wang Qingling 5873.

CAI Zelin b. 11 Apr 1991 Dali, Yunnan 1.72m 55kg.
At 20kW: OG: '12- 4; WCh: '13- 26; AsiG: '14- 4; WCp: '14- 2. At 10000mW: WJ: '10- 2; WCp: '10- 2J. CHN 20kW champion 2012.
Progress at 20kW: 2010- 1:22:28, 2011- 1:21:07, 2012- 1:18:47, 2013- 1:18:55, 2014- 1:18:52, 2015- 1:20:13. Pbs: 5000mW 19:35.00 '14, 10,000W 38:59.98 '12, 30kmW 2:45:13 '09.

CHEN Ding b. 5 Aug 1992 Dali, Yunnan 1.80m 62kg. Guangdong.
At 20kW: OG: '12- 1; WCh: '13- 2; WCp: '10- 5, '12- 8. At 10000mW: WJ: '08- 2; WCp: '08- 2J.
World youth 10,000m walk record 2008.
Progress at 20kW: 2008- 1:20:16, 2009- 1:21:21, 2010- 1:21:59, 2011- 1:18:52, 2012- 1:17:40, 2013- 1:21:09, 2014- 1:20:48, 2015- 1:21:11. Pbs: 10kW 38:23 '10, 39:47.20t '08; 30kmW 2:12:16 '10.

LI Jianbo b. 14 Nov 1986 Qujing, Yunnan 1.76m 57kg.
At 50kW: OG: '08- 14, '12- 6; WCh: '11- 25, '13- 26. At 20kW: WCh: '09- 12; AsiC: '09- 1. Won Asian walks 50k 2009, Asi-J 10kW 2004, CHN 20kW 2013, 50kW 2012.
Progress at 20kW, 50kW: 2003- 1:26:37, 4:03:08; 2004- 1:26:21, 2005- 1:19:34, 3:45:13; 2006- 1:19:38, 3:43:02; 2007- 1:23:23, 3:53:24; 2008- 1:20:47, 3:52:12; 2009- 1:19:10, 3:44:59; 2010- 1:21:08, 2011- 1:25:45, 3:43:38; 2012- 1:20:55, 3:39:01; 2013- 1:18:52, 3:52:12. pb 35kW 2:34:42 '13.

LI Jinzhe b. 1 Sep 1989 Beijing 1.88m 64kg.
At LJ: OG: '12- dnq 20; WCh: '09- dnq 13, '13- 12; WI: '14- 2; AsiG: '14- 1; AsiC: '09- 1; CCp: '10- 4, '14- 4; won E.Asian 2009, Asian indoors 2012, CHN 2009, CHN NG 2013.
Chinese long jump record 2014.
Progress at LJ: 2006- 7.19i, 2007- 7.85, 2008- 7.79, 2009- 8.18, 2010- 8.12/8.29w, 2011- 8.02, 2012- 8.25, 2013- 8.34, 2014- 8.47.

WANG Zhen b. 24 Aug 1991 Changzhou 1.80m 62kg. Heilongjiang.
At 20kW: OG: '12- 3; WCh: 11- 4, '13- dq; AsiG: '14- 1; WCp: '12- 1, 14- 6; CHN champion 2011, NG 2013. Won World Race Walking Challenge Final 10k 2010, 2012 (2nd 2011).
Walks records: World junior 10k 2010, Asian 20k 2012, 10,000m track 2012 & 2015.
Progress at 20kW: 2008- 1:28:01, 2009- 1:22:10, 2010- 1:20:42, 2011- 1:18:30, 2012- 1:17:36, 2013- 1:19:08, 2014- 1:19:40. 2015- 1:19:29. Pbs: 3000mW 11:23.2 14, 5000mW 18:49.10 '14, 10kW 37:44 '10, 38:23.73 '15; 30kmW 2:08:46 '08, 50kmW 3:53:00 '09.

XIE Wenjun b. 11 Jul 1990 Shanghai 1.88m 77kg, Shanghai
At 110mh: OG: '12- sf; WCh: '13- 1; AsiG: '14- 1; CCp: '14- 4; Won CHN 2012, NG 2013.
Progress at 110mh: 2007- 14.09, 2008- 13.47, 2009- 13.53, 2010- 13.47, 2011- 13.45, 2012- 13.34, 2013- 13.28, 2014- 13.23. pbs: 100m 11.04 '06, 60mh 7.60i '13.

XUE Changrui b. 31 May 1991 Shandong prov. 1.83m 60kg
At PV: WCh: '13- 12; WI: '14- 5, AsiG: '14- 1; AsiC: '13- 1; CCp: '14- 2; Won CHN NG 2013.
Chinese pole vault record 2014,
Progress at PV: 2011- 5.30, 2012- 5.60, 2013- 5.75i/5.65, 2014- 5.80. pb LJ 7.15 '08

ZHANG Guowei b. 4 Jun 1991 Binzhon, Shandong prov. 2.00m 77kg.
At HJ: OG: '12- dnq 21=; WCh: '11- 10, '13- 9; WI: '12- 4=, 14- 7, AsiG: '14- 2; CCp: '14- 6. CHN champion 2011.
Progress at HJ: 2010- 2.23, 2011- 2.31, 2012- 2.31, 2013- 2.32i/2.29, 2014- 2.34.

ZHANG Peimeng b. 13 Mar 1987 Beijing 1.86m 78kg.
At 100m: WCh: '13- sf; AsiG: '14- 4; AsiC: '09-1; WCp: '14- 6; WUG: '07- 2/3R. At 200m: OG: '08- h; WJ: '06- sf. Won Chinese 100m 2007, 200m 2011.
Chinese records 100m (3) and 200m 2013.
Progress at 100m: 2004- 10.80, 2005- 10.53, 2006- 10.64, 2007- 10.27, 2008- 10.23, 2009- 10.28, 2010- 10.31, 2011- 10.21, 2012- 10.28, 2013- 10.00, 2014- 10.18/10.08w. pbs: 60m 6.58i '13, 200m 20.47 '13.
Fastest 100m by Asian-born athlete.

ZHAO Qinggang b. 24 Jul 1985 Dalian 1.84m 93kg.
At JT: WCh: '13- dnq 22; AsiG: '14- 1. CHN champion 2012-14, NG 2013, E.Asian 2013
Asian and three Chinese javelin records 2014.
Progress at JT: 2006- 68.07, 2007- 72.57, 2008- 77.20, 2009- 79.62, 2010- 79.80, 2011- 78.40, 2012- 81.74, 2013- 83.14, 2014- 89.15.
At 2014 Asian Games improved his pb from 83.14 to national records of 85.29 and 86.50 and ended series with Asian record 89.15.

Women

GONG Lijiao b. 24 Jan 1989 Luquan, Hebei Prov. 1.74m 110kg. Hebei.
At SP: OG: '08- 5, '12- 3; WCh: '07-09-11-13: 7/3/4/3; WI: '10- 8, '14- 3; AsiG: '10- 2, '14- 1; AsiC: '09- 1; CCp: '10- 3, '14- 3. Chinese champion 2007-12, 2014; NG 2009, 2013; Asian indoor 2008.
Progress at SP: 2005- 15.41i, 2006- 17.92, 2007- 19.13, 2008- 19.46, 2009- 20.35, 2010- 20.13, 2011- 20.11, 2012- 20.22, 2013- 20.12, 2014- 19.65. pb JT 53.94 '07.

GU Siyu b. 11 Feb 1993 1.82m 80kg.
At DT: WCh: '13- dnq.
Progress at DT: 2008- 47.85, 2009- 50.02, 2010- 53.79, 2011- 56.12, 2012- 60.59, 2013- 67.86, 2014- 60.78. pb SP 16.59 '11.

LI Ling b. 6 Jul 1989 Zhubo, Henan Province 1.80m 65kg. Zhejiang

At PV: OG: '08/12- dnq 27=/30; WCh: '09-11-13: dnq 18/dnq 29/11; WJ: '06- nh; AsiG: '10- 2, '14- 1; AsiC: '11- 2, '13- 1. Won CHN 2008-09, 2011-13, NG 2013, Asian Indoors 2009, 2012.
Asian PV records: 2013, indoor 2015, junior 2008.
Progress at PV: 2005- 3.90i/3.70, 2006- 4.15, 2007- 4.30, 2008- 4.45, 2009- 4.40, 2010- 4.45i/4.40, 2011- 4.40, 2012- 4.50i/4.40, 2013- 4.65, 2014- 4.61, 2015- 4.50i.

LI Yanfeng b. 15 May 1979 Suihua City, Heilongjiang 1.79m 90kg.
At DT: OG: '04- 8, '08- 7, '12- 2; WCh: '11- 1; AsiG: '10- 1; AsiC: '00-02-03-07: 3/1/1/2; WUG: '01- 2, '03- 2; WCp: '02- 4, '10- 1. Won E.Asian G & CHN NG 2009, CHN 2010-11.
Progress at DT: 1997- 56.68, 1998- 57.30, 1999- 63.67, 2000- 60.84, 2001- 61.77, 2002- 62.52, 2003- 61.87, 2004- 64.34, 2005- 61.61, 2007- 62.24, 2008- 63.79, 2009- 66.40, 2010- 66.18, 2011- 67.98, 2012- 67.84, 2013- 63.91. Married on 6 Oct 2013.

LIU Hong b. 12 May 1987 Anfu, Jiangxi Prov. 1.61m 48kg. Guangdong.
At 20kW: OG: '08- 4, '12- 4; WCh: '07-09-11-13: 19/3/2/3; WCp: '06- 6, 14- 2; AsiG: '06- 1, '10- 1; won CHN 2010-11, NG 2009. At 10000mW: WJ: '06- 1; won IAAF Race Walking Challenge 10k 2012, 2014 (2nd 2011).
Asian records 5000m & 20k walk 2012.
Progress at 20kW: 2004- 1:35:04, 2005- 1:29:39, 2006- 1:28:26, 2007- 1:29:41, 2008- 1:27:17, 2009- 1:28:11, 2010- 1:30:06, 2011- 1:27:17, 2012- 1:25:46, 2013- 1:27:06, 2014- 1:26:58, 2015- 1:27:39. pbs: 3000mW 12:18.18 '05, 5000mW 20:34.76 '12, 10kW 42:30R '10, 43:16.68t '12.

LU Huihui b. 26 Jun 1989 Huwan, Henan 1.71m 68kg.
At JT: OG: '12- 5.
Two Asian javelin records 2012-13.
Progress at JT: 2005- 49.62, 2006- 49.96, 2010- 55.35, 2011- 58.72, 2012- 64.95, 2013- 65.62 , 2015- 64.59.

LU Xiuzhi b. 26 Oct 1993 Chuzhou 1.67m 52kg.
At 20kW: OG: '12- 6; AsiG: '14- 1; WCp: '12- 4, 14- 6; 3rd RWC 2012, won CHN NG 2013, Champs 2014.
Asian 20k wak record 2015, junior 2012.
Progress at 20kW: 2011- 1:29:50, 2012- 1:27:01, 2013- 1:27:53, 2014- 1:27:15, 2015- 1:25:12. pb 10kW 43:16 '12.

QIEYANG Shenjie b. 11 Nov 1990 Haiyan, Qinghai Prov. 1.60m 50kg.
At 20kW: OG: '12- 3; WCh: '11- 5, '13- 15; WCp: '12- 15.
Asian 20k walk record 2012.
Progress at 20kW: 2009- 1:35:54, 2010- 1:30:33, 2011- 1:28:04, 2012- 1:25:16, 2013- 1:28:05, 2015- 1:28:37. pbs: 5000mW 20:42.67 '12, 10kW 43:16 '12.
First athlete from Tibet to win an Olympic medal.

SUN Huanhuan b. 15 Mar 1990 1.61m 50kg.
At 20kW: WCh: '13- 4.
Progress at 20kW: 2008- 1:32:11, 2009- 1:32:51, 2010- 1:30:35, 2011- 1:29:46, 2012- 1:30:21, 2013- 1:27:36, 2014- 1:29:20.

TAN Jian b. 20 Jan 1988 Chengdu 1.79m 80kg. Sichuan,
At DT: OG: '12- dnq; WCh: '11- 6, '13- 6; AsiG: '14- 3; WJ: '06- 3. Chinese champion 2012, 2014; NG 2013.
Progress at DT: 2004- 56.00, 2005- 57.01, 2007- 56.99, 2008- 55.04, 2009- 57.40, 2010- 59.65, 2011- 63.72, 2012- 64.45, 2013- 64.40, 2014- 61.07.

WANG Zheng b. 14 Dec 1987 Xian, Shanxi Province 1.74m 108kg.
At HT: OG: '08- dnq 32; WCh: '13: 4; WJ: '06- 9; AsiG: '10- 2, '14- 1; AsiC: '13- 1; CCp: '14- 5; won Asi-J 2006, E.Asian 2009, CHN 2014.
Asian hammer record 2014.
Progress at HT: 2000- 60.30, 2001- 66.30, 2002- 67.13, 2003- 70.60, 2004- 72.42, 2005- 73.24, 2006- 74.15, 2007- 74.86, 2008- 74.32, 2009- 74.25, 2010- 73.83, 2011- 75.65, 2012- 75.72, 2012- 76.99, 2013- 75.58, 2014- 77.68.

XIE Limei b. 27 Jun 1986 Fujian Prov. 1.73m 57kg. Fujian.
At TJ: OG: '08- 12, '12- dnq 23; WCh: '07- 8, '09- 9, '11- dnq 25; WJ: '04- 2; AsiG: '06- 1, '10- 2; AsiC: '05- 1, '11- 1; WI: '08- 8, '10- 7; CCp: '10- 4. Won Asian indoors 2012, CHN 2006-07, 2009-11, 2013; NG 2013.
Asian TJ record 2007.
Progress at TJ: 2002- 13.51, 2003- 13.89, 2004- 14.08, 2005- 14.38, 2006- 14.54, 2007- 14.90, 2008- 14.39, 2009- 14.62, 2010- 14.35, 2011- 14.54/14.62w, 2012- 14.21i/13.82, 2013- 14.39. pb LJ 6.41 '06.

ZHANG Wenxiu b. 22 Mar 1986 Dalian 1.82m 108kg. Army.
At HT: OG: '04- 7, '08- 3, '12- 4; WCh: '01-03-05-07-09-11-13: 11/dnq 14/4/3/5/3/3; WJ: '02- dnq 20; AsiG: '06-10-14: 1/1/dq1; AsiC: '05- 1, '09- 1; WCp: '06- 4, '10- 2. Won Asi-J 2002, CHN 2004, 2006-10, 2012; NG 2003, 2009, 2013.
Nine Asian hammer records 2001-12, world youth 2003, two world junior 2004-05.
Progress at HT: 2000- 60.30, 2001- 66.30, 2002- 67.13, 2003- 70.60, 2004- 72.42, 2005- 73.24, 2006- 74.15, 2007- 74.86, 2008- 74.32, 2009- 74.25, 2010- 73.83, 2011- 75.65, 2012- 76.99, 2013- 75.58, 2014- 77.33dq/75.50.
World age bests at 15-16-18. Lost third Asian Games title with a positive drugs test in 2014.

COLOMBIA

Governing body: Federación Colombiana de Atletismo, Calle 27° No. 25-18, Apartado Aéreo 6024, Santafé de Bogotá. Founded 1937.
National Games Champions 2014: Men: 100m: Isidro Montoya 10.34, 200m/400m: Bernardo Baloyes 20.35w/45.68, 800m: Rafith Rodríguez

1:48.52, 1500m: Iván González 3:53.38, 5000m: José Mauricio González 14:19.78; 10000m: Oscar Robayo 30:09.73, 3000mSt: Gerald Giraldo 9:04.78, 110mh: Cristian Alzate 13.90, 400mh: Jefferson Valencia 50.90, HJ: Carlos Izquierdo 2.11, PV: Yefrey Azcárate 5.00, LJ: Edwin Murillo 7.46, TJ: Jhon Freddy Murillo 16.47, SP: Jhon Freddy Zea 17.21, DT: Mauricio Ortega 62.30, HT: Elías Mauricio Díaz 63.78, JT: Dayron Márquez 78.82, Dec: José Gregorio Lemus 7089, 20kW: Freddy Hernández 1:27:07.5. **Women:** 100m: Eliecet Palacios 11.37, 200m: María Alejandra Idrobo 23.38w, 400m/800m: Zulay Melisa Torres 54.68/2:07.37, 1500m: Muriel Coneo 4:24.81, 5000m/10000m: Carolina Tabares 16:40.40/34:59.67, 3000mSt: Ángela Figueroa 10:18.02, 100mh: Briggit Merlano 13.01w, 400mh: Julieth Caballero 58.45, HJ: Anyi Paola García 1.75, PV: Goseth Montaño 3.80, LJ: Yosiri Urrutia 6.37w, TJ: Caterine Ibargüen 14.98w, SP: Sandra Lemus 17.18, DT: Johana Martínez 53.82, HT: Johana Moreno 65.15, JT: Flor Ruiz 60.09, Hep: Evelys Aguilar 5707, 20000mW: Lorena Arenas 1:39:38.5.

Women

Caterine IBARGÜEN b. 12 Feb 1984 Apartadó, Antioquia 1.81m 65kg. Studying nursing.
At TJ/(LJ): OG: '12- 2; WCh: '11- 3, '13- 1; WJ: '02: dnq 17; PAm: '11- 1/3; SACh: '03- 3/2, '05- 3/3, '06- 2/2, '07- (3), '09- 1, '11- 1/3; CAG: '02-06-10-14: 2/(2)/2/1; CCp: '14- 1. At HJ: OG: '04- dnq 28=; WCh: '09- dnq 28=; PAm: '07- 4; SACh: '99-05-06-07-09: 3/1/1/1/1; CAG: '02- 2, '06- 2. Won DL 2013-14, COL HJ 1999, 2001-03, 2005-12; LJ 2003-04, 2006-08, 2011-12; TJ 2002-05, 2007-12, 2014.
Records: South American triple jump (7) 2011-14, junior HJ 2004. Colombia HJ (7) 2002-05, LJ (7) 2004-11, TJ (14) 2004-11
Progress at TJ: 2001- 12.90, 2002- 13.38A, 2003- 13.23A, 2004- 13.64A, 2005- 13.66A, 2006- 13.91A/13.98Aw, 2007- 12.66A, 2008- 13.79A, 2009- 13.96A/13.93, 2010- 14.29, 2011- 14.99A/ 14.84, 2012- 14.95A/14.85, 2013- 14.85/14.93w, 2014- 15.31. pbs: 200m 25.34 '08, 100mh 14.09 '11, HJ 1.93A '05, LJ 6.73A/6.87Aw/6.63/6.66w '12, SP 13.79 '10, JT 44.81 '09, Hep 5742 '09.
Formely a high jumper, concentrating fully on TJ from 2010. First Colombian woman to win a medal in world champs. Unbeaten in eight competitions in 2013 and in eleven in 2014. She lives in Puerto Rico.

Yosiri URRUTIA b. 26 Jun 1986 Chigorodó Antioquia 1.75m 61kg. Graduated from nursing school at Universidad Metropolitana, Puerto Rico.
At (LJ/)TJ: SACh: 13- 5/2; CAG: '14- 3. Won Ib Am 2014, BolG 2013, COL LJ 2010, 2013.
Progress at TJ: 2005- 12.00, 2007- 12.43A, 2010- 12.94, 2013- 14.08, 2014- 14.58. pbs: 100mh 14.40 '10, LJ 6.53A/6.42 '10.
Previously a long jumper, she focused fully on the triple jump from 2013,

CROATIA

Governing body: Hrvatski Atletski Savez, Trg kralja Petra Svacica 17, 10000 Zagreb. Fd 1912.
National Champions 2014 Men: 100m: Zvonimir Ivaskovic 10.93, 200m: Gregor Kokalovic 21.80, 400m: Mateo Ruzic 46.78, 800m: Martin Srsa 1:52.19, 1500m: Ivan Malic 3:53.06, 5000m/10000m/HMar: Goran Grdenic 15:10.74/31:37.40/68:07, Mar: Matija Grabrovecki 2:41:06, 3000mSt: Zoran Zilic 9:41.16, 110mh: David Sarancic 14.76, 400mh: Yann Senjaric 50.88, HJ: Alen Melon 2.15, PV: Ivan Hirvat 5.30, LJ/TJ: Sanjin Simic 7.44/15.67, TJ: Andro Duzevic 15.21, SP: Nedzad Mulabegovic 20.67, DT: Filip Mihaljevic 58.67, HT: Andras Haklits 71.03, JT: Ante-Roko Zemunik 66.28, Dec: Marin Jurjevic 5819. **Women**: 100m/200m: Lucija Pokos 11.97/ 24.07, 400m: Anita Banovic 53.92, 800m: Anamarija Petres 2:12.94, 1500m/3000m: Matea Parlov 4:26.59/9:50.44. 5000m: Matea Matosevic 19:37.39, 10000n: Lisa Stublic/Nemec 33:17.91, HMar: Barbara Belusic 76:46, Mar: Marija Vrajic 2:57:47, 3000mSt: Kristina Bozic 10:55.34, 100mh: Ivana Loncarek 13.22, 400mh: Nikolina Horvat 59.02, HJ: Lucija Zupcic 1.78, PV: Petra Malkoc 3.70, LJ: Nina Djordjevic 6.46, TJ: Paola Borvic 13.03, SP: Spela Hus 13.83, DT: Tijana Frajtic 46.44, HT: Petra Jakeljic 56.73, JT: Sara Kolak 54.23, Hep: Katarina Gasparovic 4481.

Stipe ZUNIC b. 13 Dec 1990 1.88m 115kg. ASK Split. Sociology student at University of Florida, USA.
At SP: EC: '14- 4; WY: '07- dnq 29; EI: '15- 7; NCAA indoor champion 2015. At JT: WJ: '08- dnq 18; WY: '07- 7; EJ: '09-9 (11 DT); EU23: '11- 11; Croatian champion JT 2009-10.
Progress at SP: 2007- 15.36, 2008- 15.87, 2009- 16.83, 2011- 17.39i/16.60, 2012- 17,30i, 2014- 20.68, 2015- 21.11i. pbs: DT 58.31 '14, JT 77.89 '12
Huge improvement at shot in 2014-15 after switching from javelin. Fortmerly world junior champion at kick-boxing.

Women

Sandra PERKOVIC b. 21 Jun 1990 Zagreb 1.83m 80kg. Zagreb.
At DT(/SP): OG: '12- 1; WCh: '09- 9, '13- 1; EC: '10-12-14: 1/1/1; WJ: '06- dnq 21, '08- 3/dnq 13; WY: '07- 2/dnq 13; EJ: '07- 2, '09- 1/5; CCp: '10- 2, '14- 3. Won DL 2012-14, Med G 2013; CRO SP 2008-10, DT 2010, 2012.
9 Croatian DT records 2009-14, 2 SP 2010-11.
Progress at DT: 2006- 50.11, 2007- 55.42, 2008- 55.89, 2009- 62.79, 2010- 66.93, 2011- 67.96/69.99dq, 2012- 69.11, 2013- 68.96, 2014- 71.08. pb SP 16.99i/16.40 '11.
First woman to win European and Olympic gold for Croatia. Won 11 of 12 competitions in

both 2012 and 2013 and 10 of 12 in 2014. 70.51 and 71.08 to win her third European title in 2014 were the women's world's best discus throws since 1992. Six months drugs ban 2011.

Ana SIMIC b. 5 May 1990 Gradacac, Bosnia 1.77m 58kg. Zagreb.
At HJ: OG: '12- dnq 29=WCh: '13- dnq 19; EC: '10-12: dnq 22=/20, '14- 3; WJ: '08- dnq 14=; WY: '07- dnq 21=; EU23: '11- 7; EJ: '09- dnq 18; CCp: '14- 3; Croatian champion 2006-09, 2011.
Progress at HJ: 2006- 1.78, 2007- 1.73, 2008- 1.82, 2009- 1.87, 2010- 1.92, 2011- 1.92, 2012- 1.91i/1.88, 2013- 1.96, 2014- 1.99.

Blanka VLASIC b. 8 Nov 1983 Split 1.92m 75kg. ASK Split.
At HJ: OG: '00- dnq 17, '04- 11, '08- 2; WCh: '01-03-05-07-09-11: 6/7/dnq 19=/1/1/2; EC: '02- 5=, '06- 4, 10- 1; WJ: '00- 1, '02- 1; WY: '99- 8; EU23: '03- 1; EJ: '01- 7; WI: '03-04-06-08-10-14: 4/3/2/1/1/6; EI: '07- 4, '09- 5=; CCp: '10- 1. Won WAF 2007-09, DL 2010-11, MedG 2001, CRO 2001-02, 2005.
Ten Croatian high jump records 2003-09.
Progress at HJ: 1998- 1.68, 1999- 1.80, 2000- 1.93, 2001- 1.95, 2002- 1.96, 2003- 2.01, 2004- 2.03, 2005- 1.95, 2006- 2.05i/2.03, 2007- 2.07, 2008- 2.06, 2009- 2.08, 2010- 2.06i/2.05, 2011- 2.03, 2013- 2.00, 2014- 2.00.
IAAF Woman Athlete of the Year 2010. Won 5/6 Golden League HJs in both 2007 and 2008. She has had 105 competitions at 2m or higher to the end of 2014 (and 173 jumps over 2m), including 42 successive Jul 2007- Feb 2009, but in 2008 lost on count-back both at Olympic Games (when she won first ever athletics medal for Croatia) and in the final Golden League meeting, thus losing her share of the Jackpot. She had 60 attempts at the world record 2007-10. Her father Josko set the Croatian decathlon record with 7659 (1983) and named Blanka after Casablanca, where he won Mediterranean Games title.

CUBA

Governing body: Federación Cubana de Atletismo, Calle 13 y C, Vedado 601, Zona Postal 4, La Habana 10400. Founded 1922.
National Champions 2014: Men: 100m: Yaniel Carrero 10.1h, 200m: Robert Skyers 20.73, 400m: Yoandys Lescay 46.43, 800m/1500m: Jorge Félix Liranzo 1:46.21/3:50.82, 5000m: Liván Luque 14:29.99, 10000m: Richer Pérez 30:47.55, Mar: Jorge Luis Suárez 2:28:45, 110mh: Yordan O'Farrill 13.53w, 400mh: Amaurys Valle 50.66, HJ: Raudelys Rodríguez 2.22, PV: Eduardo Napoles 4.60, LJ: Junior Díaz 7.74, TJ: Pedro Pablo Pichardo 17.71, SP/DT: Jorge Fernández 16.94/62.06, HT: Roberto Janet 75.35, JT: Guillermo Martínez 77.74, Dec: Manuel A. González 7496, 20kW: Loisel Gutiérrez 1:36:48. **Women**: 100m/200m: Arialis Gandulla 11.57/23.89, 400m: Gilda Casanova 53.13, 800m: Rose Mary Almanza 1:59.76, 1500m: Arletis Thaureaux 4:29.80, 5000m/10000m: Dailín Belmonte 16:49.3/34:48.3, Mar: Misleidys Vargas 3:09:30, 100mh: Belkis Milanés 13.34, 400mh: Zurian Hechavarría 58.39, HJ: Lesyaní Mayor 1.82, PV: *none*, LJ: Irisdaymi Herrera 6.20, TJ: Yarianna Martínez 14.29, SP: Yaniuvis López 19.10, DT: Yaimé Pérez 64.22, HT: Ariannis Vichy 71.07, JT: Lismania Muñoz 58.47, Hep: Yusleidyis Mendieta 6013, 20kW: Misleidys Vargas 1:52:26.

Omar CISNEROS b. 19 Nov 1989 Camagüey 1.86m 80kg.
At 400mh: OG: '12- sf; WCh: '09/11- sf, '13- 4; PAmG: '11- 1/1R; CAG: '14- 1. Won IbAm 2010, Cuban 2009-10, 2013. At 400m: PAm: '07- sf.
Four Cuban 400mh records 2010-13.
Progress at 400mh: 2007- 49.57, 2008- 50.1, 2009- 48.87, 2010- 48.21, 2011- 47.99A/49.26, 2012- 48.23, 2013- 47.93, 2014- 49.56A. pbs: 200m 21.36 '07, 400m 45.47 '12, 600m 1:17.61 '13.

Alexis COPELLO b. 12 Aug 1985 Santiago de Cuba 1.85m 80kg.
At TJ: OG: '08- dnq 13, '12- 8; WCh: '09- 3, '11- 4; WI: '12- 7; PAmG: '11- 1; CAG: '06- 2; CCp: '10- 2. Won IbAm 2010, CAC 2009, Cuban 2009, 2011.
Progress at TJ: 2002- 15.38, 2003- 16.34, 2004- 16.90, 2005- 16.95/17.09w, 2006- 17.38, 2007- 16.87/17.15w, 2008- 17.50, 2009- 17.65/17.69w, 2010- 17.55, 2011- 17.68A/17.47, 2012- 17.17, 2014- 17.05. pb LJ 7.35 '04.
Elder brother Alexander decathlon pb 7359 '02.

Jorge FERNÁNDEZ b. 2 Dec 1987 Matanzas 1.90m 100kg. MTZ.
At DT: OG: '08- dnq 27, '12- 11; WCh: '11- 8, '13- 10; PAmG: '11- 1; CAG: '14- 1; WJ: '06- 5; CCp: '14- 2. Won CAC 2008-09, Cuban 2009-14 (& SP 2014).
Progress at DT: 2005- 53.69, 2006- 54.77, 2007- 57.57, 2008- 63.31, 2009- 63.92, 2010- 66.00, 2011- 65.89, 2012- 66.05, 2013- 65.09, 2014- 66.50. pb SP 16.94 '14.

Yordani GARCÍA b. 21 Nov 1988 San Luis, Pinar del Río 1.93m 88kg.
At Dec: OG: '08- 15, '12- 14; WCh: '07- 8, '09- 8, '11- dnf; PAm: '07- 2, '11- 3; CAG: '14- 1; WJ: '06- 2. At Oct: WY: '05- 1. At Hep: WI: '12- 7. Won Cuban Dec 2006-07, 2010; PV 2011; PAmCp 2009, 2013.
Cuban & CAC junior decathlon record 2007. World youth octathlon record (6482) 2005.
Progress at Dec: 2005- 6765, 2006- 7879h, 2007- 8257, 2008- 7992, 2009- 8496, 2010- 8381h, 2011- 8397, 2012- 8061, 2013- 8157h, 2014- 8337. pbs: 60m 6.89i '09, 6.6 '13; 100m 10.60 '09, 10.5dt '10, 300m 34.4 '13, 400m 48.18 '14, 1000m 2:50.21i '12, 1500m 4:31.40 '11, 60mh 7.80i '10, 110mh 13.89 '09, HJ 2.10 '09, PV 4.90 '10, LJ 7.36 '09, SP 16.50 '09, DT 47.70 '08, JT 69.37 '09, Hep 5905i '09.

Yeimer LÓPEZ b. 20 Aug 1982 Buey Arriba, Granma 1.84m 75kg.

At 800m: OG: '08- 6; WCh: '05/07- h, '09- 10; PAm: '07- 1. At 400m: OG: '04- sf; WCh: '03- sf; PAm: '03- 2; CAG: '06- 1. Won CAC 2005, 2009; IbAm 2010; Cuban 400m 2003, 2006, 800m 2002, 2005, 2007, 2009-10.
Progress at 800m: 2001- 1:50.75, 2002- 1:47.2, 2003- 1:47.94, 2005- 1:46.61, 2006- 1:48.92, 2007- 1:44.48, 2008- 1:43.07, 2009- 1:44.10, 2010- 1:44.18, 2011- 1:45.90, 2012- 1:45.89, 2013- 1:46.90, 2014- 1:43.71. pb 400m 45.11 '03.
Decided to stay in Spain in 2010, so will not be representing Cuba internationally in future. Twin sister Ana María López ran at 2004 OG at 4x100m (pbs 11.1/23.50 '02).

Guillermo MARTÍNEZ b. 28 Jun 1981 Camagüey 1.85m 100kg.
At JT: OG: '12- dnq 16; WCh: '05-07-09-11-13: 10/9/2/3/dnq 15; PAm: '07- 1, '11- 1; CAG: '06- 1, '14- 1. Won CAC 2009, 2011; IbAm 2010, Cuban 2004-07, 2009-14.
Cuban & CAC javelin records 2006 & 2011.
Progress at JT: 1999- 64.66, 2000- 70.82, 2001- 73.50, 2002- 75.90, 2003- 75.35, 2004- 81.45, 2005- 84.06, 2006- 87.17, 2007- 85.93, 2009- 86.41, 2010- 86.38, 2011- 87.20A, 2012- 82.72, 2013- 85.59, 2014- 79.27A.

Lázaro MARTÍNEZ b. 3 Nov 1997 Guantánamo 1.92m 83kg.
At TJ: WJ: '14- 1; WY: '13- 1; CAG: '14- 2.
World youth triple jump record 2014.
Progress at TJ: 2011- 14.62, 2012- 15.38, 2013- 16.63, 2014- 17.24.

Orlando ORTEGA b. 29 Jul 1991 La Habana 1.85m 70kg.
At 110mh: OG: '12- 6; WCh: '13- h; WJ: '10- h; PAm: '11- 3. Cuban champion 2011.
Progress at 110mh: 2009- 14.11, 2010- 13.99, 2011- 13.29/13.1w, 2012- 13.09, 2013- 13.08, 2014- 13.01. pbs: 100m 10.62 '11, 400m 47.84 '09, 50mh 6.66+i '12, 60mh 7.45i '15.
Left Cuba in 2013, becoming ineligible to represent the country internationally. Now living in Guadalajara, Spain and hopes to represent Spain.

Pedro Pablo PICHARDO b. 30 Jun 1993 Santiago de Cuba 1.85m 71kg.
At TJ: WCh: '13- 2; WJ: '12- 1; WI: '14- 3. Won CAC-J 2012, CUB 2014.
Progress at TJ: 2009- 14.55, 2010- 15.35/15.45w, 2011- 16.09, 2012- 16.79, 2013- 17.69, 2014- 17.76.

Ernesto REVÉ b. 26 Feb 1992 Guantánamo 1.81m 65kg.
At TJ: WJ: '10- 2; CAG: '14- 1; WI: '14- 2. Cuban champion 2012-13.
CAC junior triple jump record (=) 2011.
Progress at TJ: 2006- 14.97, 2007- 15.22, 2008- 16.32, 2009- 16.56, 2010- 16.73, 2011- 17.40, 2012- 17.13, 2013- 17.46, 2014- 17.58. pb LJ 7.00 '13.

Dayron ROBLES b. 19 Nov 1986 Guantánamo 1.91m 91kg. AS Monaco.
At 110mh: OG: '08- 1, '12- dq; WCh: '05-07-09-11: sf/4/sf/dq(1); WJ: '04- 2, WY: '03- 6; CAG: '06- 1; PAm: '07- 1, '11- 1; WCp: '06- 3; won PAm-J 2005, WAF 2007, CAC 2009, Cuban 2006-07, DL 2011. At 60mh: WI: '06- 2, '10- 1.
World 110mh record 2008, three Cuban & CAC 2006-08, CAC junior record 2005. Two CAC 60mh indoor records 2008.
Progress at 110mh: 2002- 15.01, 2003- 14.30, 2004- 13.75, 2005- 13.46/13.2/13.41w, 2006- 13.00, 2007- 12.92, 2008- 12.87, 2009- 13.04, 2010- 13.01, 2011- 13.00, 2012- 13.10, 2013- 13.18, 2014- 13.29. pbs: 100m 10.70 '06, 200m 21.85 '06, 50mh 6.39i '08, 60mh 7.33i '08.
Season's record 7 sub-13 second times in 2008. Disqualified for obstructing Liu Xiang after finishing first at 2011 Worlds. Pulled muscle in 2012 Olympic final.

Leonel SUÁREZ b. 1 Sep 1987 Holguín 1.81m 76kg.
At Dec: OG: '08- 3, '12- 3; WCh: '09- 2, '11- 3, '13- 10; PAm: '07- 4, '11- 1. CAC and Cuban champion 2009. At Hep: WI: '10- 7.
CAC decathlon record 2009, four Cuban records 2008-09.
Progress at Dec: 2005- 7267, 2006- 7357, 2007- 8156, 2008- 8527, 2009- 8654, 2010- 8328, 2011- 8501, 2012- 8523, 2013- 8317. pbs: 60m 7.11i '09, 100m 10.90 '08, 10.6w '06; 400m 47.65 '09, 1000m 2:36.12i '10, 1500m 4:16.70 '08, 60mh 7.90i '10, 110mh 14.12 '08, HJ 2.17 '08, PV 5.00 '09, LJ 7.52 '11, SP 15.20 '09, DT 47.32 '11, JT 77.47 '09, Hep 5964i '10.
Won at Talence 2010. Won IAAF Combined Events Challenge 2011.

Women

Rose Mary ALMANZA b. 13 Jul 1992 Camagüey 1.66m 53kg.
At 800m: OG: '12- sf; WCh: '13- sf; WJ: '10- 4; WY: '09- 4; PAm: '11- 4. Won Cuban 800m 2010-11, 2014; 1500m 2013.
Two CAC junior 800m records 2010-11.
Progress at 800m: 2008- 2:11.1, 2009- 2:03.61, 2010- 2:02.04, 2011- 2:00.56, 2012- 1:59.55, 2013- 1:59.4, 2014- 1:59.48. pbs: 400m 54.64 '12, 600m 1:26.33mx '14, 1:26.9 '13; 1000m 2:38.1 '14, 1500m 4:14.53 '14.

Yarelys BARRIOS b. 12 Jul 1983 Pinar del Río 1.72m 98kg.
At DT: OG: '08- 2, '12- 3; WCh: '07-09-11-13: 2/2/3/3; WJ: '02- 7; PAm: '07- 1, '11- 1; CAG: '06- 2; WUG: '07- 1; CCp: '10- 3. Won DL 2010-11, WAF 2008-09, CAC 2005, 2008-09; Cuban 2009-12.
Progress at DT: 2006- 61.01, 2007- 63.90/66.68ex, 2008- 66.13, 2009- 65.86, 2010- 65.96, 2011- 66.40A, 2012- 68.03, 2013- 67.36.

Denia CABALLERO b. 13 Jan 1990 Caibarién, Villa Clara 1.75m 73kg. VCL.
At DT: OG: '12- dnq 26; WCh: '11-9, '13- 8; PAm: 11- 3; CAG: '14- 1.

Progress at DT: 2006- 43.77, 2007- 46.08, 2008- 52.10, 2009- 57.21, 2010- 59.92, 2011- 62.94, 2012- 65.60, 2013- 63.47, 2014- 64.89.

Mabel GAY b. 5 May 1983 Santiago de Cuba 1.85m 69kg.
At TJ: OG: '08- dnq 15; WCh: '03-05-09-11-13: 5/ dnq 18/2/4/5; WJ: '00- 4,'02- 1; WY: '99- 1; PAm: '03-07-11: 1/3/3; PAm-J: '01- 1; CAG: '06- 1; WI: '04-10-12: 9/5/3; Won WAF 2009. CAC 2008, CAC-J 2002, IbAm 2002, Cuban 2003-04, 2006, 2013.
CAC junior TJ record 2002.
Progress at TJ: 1997- 13.00, 1998- 13.48, 1999- 13.82, 2000- 14.02, 2001- 14.05, 2002- 14.29, 2003- 14.52, 2004- 14.57i/14.20, 2005- 14.21/14.44w, 2006- 14.27, 2007- 14.66, 2008- 14.41A/14.39, 2009-14.64, 2010- 14.30i/14.06, 2011- 14.67, 2012- 14.40, 2013- 14.45, 2014- 14.53A/14.42. pb LJ 6.28 '09. World age 17 record in 1999.

Yaimé PÉREZ b. 29 May 1991 Santiago de Cuba 1.74m 78kg.
At DT: OG: '12- dnq 29; WCh: '13- 11; WJ: '10- 1; CAG: '14- 2. Cuban champion 2013-14.
Progress at DT: 2007- 46.29, 2008- 51.80, 2009- 55.23, 2010- 59.30, 2011- 59.26, 2012- 62.50, 2013- 66.01, 2014- 66.03. pbs SP 13.88 '08.

Yargeris SAVIGNE b. 13 Nov 1984 Niceto Pérez, Guantánamo 1.68m 59kg.
At (LJ)/TJ: OG: '08- dnq 17/5, '12- 9; WCh: '05- 3/2, '07- 1, '09- 1, '11- 6; WJ: '02- (dnq); PAm: '03- (3), '07- 3/1, '11- 2; WI: '06- 5/5, '08- 1, '10- 2, '12- 4; CCp: '10- 2/3 Won DL 2010, WAF 2007, CAC TJ 2005, 2009 (LJ 2005,); IbAm 2010, Cuban TJ 2007, 2009, 2011 (LJ 2006-07).
Records: three Cuban TJ 2005-07, two CAC indoor 2008.
Progress at LJ, TJ: 1998- 12.13, 1999- 5.60, 12.65; 2000- 5.92, 12.70; 2001- 6.24, 13.03; 2002- 6.46, 2003- 6.63, 2004- 6.60A/6.52, 2005- 6.77/6.88w, 14.82; 2006- 6.67/6.81w, 14.91; 2007- 6.79i/6.66/ 6.81w, 15.28; 2008- 6.77i/6.49, 15.20; 2009- 6.77, 15.00; 2010- 6.91, 15.09; 2011- 14.99, 2012- 6.30, 14.55i/14.35; 2013- 6.10, 14.05; 2014- 14.01.

Yarisley SILVA b. 1 Jun 1987 Pinar del Rio 1.69m 68kg.
At PV: OG: '08- dnq 27=, '12- 2; WCh: '11- 5, '13- 3; WI: '12- 7, '14- 1; WJ: '06- dnq; PAm: '07- 3, '11- 1; CAG: '14- 1; Won CAC 2009, Cuban 2004, 2006-07, 2009, 2012-13.
Pole vault records: 18 Cuban & CAC 2007-13 (9 in 2011), 8 CAC indoor 2012 & 2013 (to 4.82).
Progress at PV: 2001- 2.50, 2002- 3.10, 2003- 3.70, 2004- 4.00, 2005- 4.10, 2006- 4.20, 2007- 4.30, 2008- 4.50, 2009- 4.50, 2010- 4.40, 2011- 4.75A/4.70, 2012- 4.75, 2013- 4.90, 2014- 4.70.

CYPRUS

Governing body: Amateur Athletic Association of Cyprus, Olympic House, 2025 Strovolos, Nicosia. Founded 1983. **National Championships** first held in 1896, 1952 (women). **2014 Champions**: **Men**: 100m: Charis Koutras 10.59, 200m/400m: Paisios Dimitriades 21.62/48.06, 800m/1500m: Amine Khadiri 1:51.0/3:47.6, 5000m/10000m/3000mSt: Christoforos Protopapas 15:15.53/33:15.6/9:25.27, HMar: Leonidas Ioannou 78:45, 110mh: Milan Trajkovic 13.65, 400mh: Minas Alozidis 52.2, HJ: Kyriakos Ioannou 2.20, PV: Nicandros Stylianou 5.35, LJ: Christodoulos Theofilou 7.34, TJ: Panayiotis Volou 15.61, SP: Georgios Arestis 17.91, DT: Apostolos Parellis 63.71, HT: Constantinos Stathelakos 68.42, JT: Michail Kakotas 65.11, Dec: Andreas Christodoulou 6123. **Women**: 100m/200m: Ramona-Anna Papaioannou 11.50/23.44, 400m: Christiana Katsari 57.04, 800m/1500m: Natalia Evangelidou 2:05.7/ 4:52.6, 5000m: Marilena Sophocleous 18:44.28, HMar/3000mSt: Elpida Christodoulidou 1:28:36/11:21.32, Mar: Liga Apine 3:45:09, 100mh: Natalia Christofi 14.22, 400mh: Iris Theodosiou 63.6, HJ: Stephany Razi 1.64, PV: Maria Aristotelous 3.70, LJ: Philippa Fotopoulo 6.08, TJ: Eleftheria Christofi 12.75, SP: Florentia Kappa 15.63, DT: Androniki Lada 56.39, HT: Paraskevi Theodorou 65.04, JT: Alexandra Tsisiou 51.89, Hep: Polyxeni Irodotou 4301.

CZECH REPUBLIC

Governing body: Cesky atleticky svaz, Diskarská 100, 16900 Praha 6 -Strahov, PO Box 40. AAU of Bohemia founded in 1897.
National Championships first held in 1907 (Bohemia), 1919 (Czechoslovakia), 1993 CZE. **2014 Champions**: **Men**: 100m: Jan Veleba 10.32, 200m: Lukás Stastny 20.95, 400m: Daniel Nemecek 46.09, 800m: Miroslav Burian 1:50.42, 1500m: Petr Vitner 3:49.82, 5000m: Jakub Holusa 14:19.11, 10000m/3000mSt: Milan Kocourek 29:30.00/8:55.41, HMar: Jan Kreisinger 67:50, Mar: Petr Pechek 2:21:43, 110mh: Petr Svoboda 13.50, 400mh: Michal Broz 50.51, HJ: Jaroslav Bába 2.31, PV: Jan Kudlicka 5.72, LJ: Radok Juska 7.94, TJ: Jirí Vondrácek 15.52w, SP: Jan Marcell 20.48, DT: Igor Gondor 57.88, HT: Lukás Melich 72.57, JT: Jakub Vadlejch 81.26, Dec: Marek Lukás 7558, 20kW/50kW: Lukás Gdula 1:29:55/4:01:52. **Women**: 100m: Martina Stychová 11.87, 200m: Martina Schmidová 23.92, 400m: Helena Jiranová 54.29, 800m: Alena Ulrichová 2:10.16, 1500m: Kristiina Mäki 4:27.17, 5000m: Eva Vrabcová 16:28.78, 10000m: Lucie Sekanová 33:22.90; HMar: Petra Pastorová 78:31, Mar: Katerina Kriegelová 2:51:07, 3000mSt: Barbora Jísová 10:41.90, 100mh: Lucie Skrobáková 12.99, 400mh: Denisa Rosolová 54.63, HJ: Oldriska Maresová 1.87, PV: Jirina Svobodová 4.50, LJ: Eliska Klucinová 6.06, TJ: Lucie Májková 13.59, SP: Jana Kárníková 16.56, DT: Eliska Stanková 58.17, HT: Tereza Králová 68.34, JT: Petra Andrejsková 57.48, Hep: Alena Galertová 5186, 20kW: Anezka Drahotová 1:29:43.

Jaroslav BÁBA b. 2 Sep 1984 Karviná 1.96m 82kg. Dukla Praha.
At HJ: OG: '04- 3, '08- 6, '12- dnq 21=; WCh: '03-05-07-09-11-13: 11/5=/8/5=/4/dnq 14=; EC: '10-12-14: 5/8=/4; WJ: '02- 8; WY: '01- 10=; EU23: '05- 1; EJ: '03- 1; WI: '03-04-08: 9/3=/9; EI: '05-11-13-15: 4/2/3/5; ET: '09-11-14: 2/3=/3. Won CZE 2003, 2005, 2009-14.
Czech high jump record 2005.
Progress at HJ: 1997- 1.72i, 1998- 1.81i/1.75, 1999- 1.93i/1.92, 2000- 1.95, 2001- 2.16i/2.15, 2002- 2.27/2.28et, 2003- 2.32i/2.30, 2004- 2.34, 2005- 2.37i/2.36, 2006- 2.28i, 2007- 2.29, 2008- 2.30i/ 2.29, 2009- 2.33, 2010- 2.28, 2011- 2.34i/2.32, 2012- 2.31i/2.28, 2013- 2.31i/2.27, 2014- 2.31. pb TJ 15.43 '03.

Jan KUDLICKA b. 29 Apr 1988 Opava 1.84m 76kg. Dukla Praha.
At PV: OG: '08- 10, '12- 8; WCh: '09: dnq 23=, '11- 9, '13- 7; EC: '10- 12-14: 10/6/3=; WJ: '06- 5=; WY: '05- 6; EU23: '09- 8=; WI: '14- 3; EI: '13- 5, '15- 7=; ET: '14- 2=; Won CZE 2008, 2010-14.
Progress at PV: 2002- 3.65, 2003- 4.21, 2004- 4.80, 2005- 5.09, 2006- 5.30, 2007- 5.61/5.62ex, 2008- 5.70, 2009- 5.62, 2010- 5.65, 2011- 5.81ex/5.65, 2012- 5.73, 2013- 5.83ex/5.77i/5.76, 2014- 5.80i/5.72/5.76ex. pbs: 60m 7.11i '07, HJ 2.05i/2.03 '07, LJ 7.55 '07, TJ 14.41 '07.

Pavel MASLÁK b. 21 Feb 1991 Havírov 1.76m 67kg. Dukla Praha.
At 400m: OG: '12- sf (h 200m); WCh: '13- 5; EC: '12- 1; WY: '07- h; WI: '12- 5, '14- 1; EI: '13- 1/3R, '15- 1/3R. At 200m: WJ: '10- 7; EU23: '11- 3, '13- 3; EJ: '09- 5/2R. At 100m: WJ: '08- h. Won CZE 200m 2012-13, 400m 2011.
European indoor 300m & 500m bests 2014. Czech records: 200m (4) 2012-13, 400m (5) 2012-14.
Progress at 400m: 2006- 50.41, 2007- 48.30, 2008- 47.60, 2009- 47.44, 2010- 46.89, 2011- 47.05i/47.43, 2012- 44.91, 2013- 44.84, 2014- 44.79. pbs: 60m 6.65i '14, 100m 10.36 '13, 200m 20.49 '13, 300m 32.15i '14, 32.34 '13; 500m 1:00.35 '13.
European Athletics Rising Star Award 2012.

Lukás MELICH b. 16 Sep 1980 Jilemnice, Liberecky kraj 1.86m 110kg. Dukla Praha.
At HT: OG: '08- dnq 29, '12- 6; WCh: '05-09: dnq 12/14, '13- 3; WJ: '98- 10; EC: '06-12-14: dnq 16/28/13; EU23: '01- 11; EJ: '99- 5. CZE champion 2003, 2006-10, 2012-14.
Progress at HT: 1996- 52.02, 1997- 59.90, 1998- 64.64, 1999- 68.73, 2000- 69.08, 2001- 71.47, 2002- 70.82, 2003- 76.38, 2004- 76.22, 2005- 79.36, 2006- 77.91, 2007- 74.74, 2008- 76.97, 2009- 78.91, 2010- 73.24, 2011- 75.40, 2012- 79.44, 2013- 80.28, 2014- 75.89. pbs: DT 51.56 '03, Wt 24.75 '06.

Ladislav PRÁSIL b. 17 May 1990 Sternberk 1.98m 125kg. Dukla Praha.
At SP: WCh: '13- 5; EC: '12-14: dnq 19/13; EU23: '11- 5; EJ: '09- 7; EI: '13- 3, '15- 3; Czech champion 2012-13.
Progress at SP: 2007- 14.32i, 2008- 16.82, 2009- 17.67, 2010- 18.26, 2011- 18.41, 2012- 20.14, 2013- 21.47, 2014- 20.82i/20.56.

Vitezslav VESELY b. 27 Feb 1983 Hodonin 1.86m 94kg. Dukla Praha.
At JT: OG: '08- 12, '12- 4; WCh: '09- dnq 28, '11- 4, '13- 1; EC: '10-12-14: 9/1/2; WJ: '02- 9; CCp: '14- 2. Won DL 2012-13, CZE 2008, 2010-12.
Progress at JT: 2001- 66.18, 2002- 73.22, 2003- 66.95, 2004- 72.32, 2005- injured, 2006- 75.98, 2007- 79.45, 2008- 81.20, 2009- 80.35, 2010- 86.45, 2011- 84.11, 2012- 88.34, 2013- 87.68, 2014- 87.38.

Women

Anezka DRAHOTOVÁ b. 22 Jul 1995 Rumburk. USK Praha.
At 20kW: WCh: '13- 7; EC: '14- 3. At 10000mW: WJ: '12- 6, '14- 1; EJ: '11- 13, '13- 1 (9 3000mSt); ECp: '13- 2J. At 5000mW: WY: '11- 6. World Mountain Running: '12- 7J. Won CZE 20kW 2014.
World junior 10000m walk record 2014. Czech records 10000mW 2013, 20kmW (3) 2013-14.
Progress at 20kW: 2013- 1:29:05, 2014- 1:28:08. 2015- 1:28:52. pbs: 1500m 4:24.46i '14, 4:24.89 '13; 3000m 9:26.28 '13, 5000m 16:47.24 '13, 3000mSt 10:10.45 '13, 10kmRd 33:59 '13, 5000mW 21:21.15 '14, 10000mW 42:47.25 '14, HMar 74:25 '14.
19th junior women's world road race at cycling in 2013. Twin Eliska 4/3 EJ 10000mW 2011/2013.

Zuzana HEJNOVÁ b. 19 Dec 1986 Liberec 1.70m 54kg. Dukla Praha.
At 400mh/4x400mR: OG: '08- 7, '12- 3; WCh: '05-07-09- sf, '11- 7, '13- 1; EC: '06- sf, '10- 4, 12- 4/3R; EU23: '07- 3; WJ: '02- 5, '04- 2; EJ: '03- 3; '05- 1; WY: '03- 1; WI: '10- 3R; ET: '09- 3, '11- 1. Won DL 2013. At 400m: EI: '13- 4/3R. At Pen: EI: '11- 7. Won CZE 400m 2006, 2009.
12 Czech 400mh records 2005-13. 3 world bests 300mh 2011 (38.91) and 2013 (38.75 & 38.16).
Progress at 400mh: 2002- 58.42, 2003- 57.54, 2004- 57.44, 2005- 55.89, 2006- 55.83, 2007- 55.04, 2008- 54.96, 2009- 54.90, 2010- 54.13, 2011- 53.29, 2012- 53.38, 2013- 52.83, 2014- 55.86. pbs: 150m 17.66 '13, 200m 23.65 '13, 300m 37.49A/37.80 '13, 400m 51.90/51.27i '13, 600m 1:28.04i '15, 800m 2:03.60i '14, 60mh 8.25i '11, 100mh 13.36 '11, 13.18w '10; 300mh 38.16 '13, HJ 1.80i '11, 1.74 '04; LJ 5.96i '11, 5.76 '07, SP 12.11i '11, JT 36.11 '10, Pen 4453i '11.
Unbeaten season at hurdles in 2013. Sister of Michaela Hejnová (b. 10 Apr 1980) pb Hep 6174w/6065 '04; OG: '04- 26; EC '02- 7; EU23: '01- 5; WJ: '98- 5; EJ: '97- 6/'99- 6 (100mh); WUG: '01- 5, '03- 3.

Eliska KLUCINOVÁ b. 14 Apr 1988 Prague 1.77m 69kg. USK Praha.
At Hep: OG: '12- 17; WCh: '09- 23, '13- 7; EC: '10-12-14: 6/7/dnf; WJ: '06- 8; WY: '05- 8; EU23: '09- 4, EJ: '07- 2; WUG: '13- 4. Won CZE LJ 2012, 2014; Hep 2008-09.
Four CZE heptathlon records 2010-14.

Progress at Hep: 2004- 5006, 2005- 5074, 2006- 5468, 2007- 5844, 2008- 5728, 2009- 6015, 2010- 6268, 2012- 6283, 2013- 6332, 2014- 6460. pbs: 200m 24.56 '12, 800m 2:12.50 '13, 60mh 8.53i '15, 100mh 13.81 '14, HJ 1.90 '14, LJ 6.43 '14, SP 15.07i'15, 14.48 '10; JT 50.75 '10, Pen 4687i '15 (CZE rec).

Jirina PTACNÍKOVÁ b. 20 May 1986 Plzen 1.75m 69kg. Was Svobodová. USK Praha.
At PV: OG: '12- 6=; WCh: '09- dnq 16=, '11- 7, '13- 8=; EC: '06-10-12-14: dnq 27/5/1/6; WJ: '02/04- nh; EJ: '03- 6, '05- 4; WY: '03- 5; WUG: '09- 1; WI: '10-12-14: 5/6/2=; EI: '11- 4=, '13- 4; ET: '09-11-14: 5/3/2. CZE champion 2009-11, 2013.
Czech pole vault record 2013.
Progress at PV: 2001- 3.20, 2002- 4.00, 2003- 4.02, 2004- 4.11i/3.90, 2005- 4.15, 2006- 4.27, 2007- 4.22i/4.00, 2008- 4.28, 2009- 4.55, 2010- 4.66, 2011- 4.65, 2012- 4.72, 2013- 4.76, 2014- 4.71i/4.60. pb LJ 5.85 '10, 5.95i '11.
Father Frantisek Ptacník was Czech indoor record holder at 60m (6.59 '87, 3= EI 1987), pb 100m 10.25 '85. She married Petr Svoboda (1 EI 60mh 2011, CZE 110mh record 13.27 '10) on 19 Sep 2012, but marriage ended two years later.

Denisa ROSOLOVÁ b. 21 Aug 1986 Karvina 1.75m 63kg. née Scerbová. USK Praha.
At 400m/4x400mR: WCh: '11- sf; EC: '10- 5; WI: '10- 3R, '12- 6; EI: '11- 1, '13- 5/3R, '15- 6; ET: '11- 2. At 400mh: OG: '12- 7; WCh: '13- sf; EC: '12- 2/3R, '14- 4. At LJ: OG: '04/08- dnq 24/20; WCh: '07- dnq 13; WJ: '04- 1; WY: '01- 10, '03- 2; EJ: '03- 4, '05- 1; EI: '07- 3. At Hep: OG: '08- dnf; EC: '06- dnf. Won CZE LJ 2004, 2007-08; 200m 2008, 2010-11, 2013; 400mh 2012, 2014.
Progress at 400m, 400mh: 2001- 57.26, 2002- 55.55, 2004- 60.09H, 2007- 54.05i, 2008- 53.61i, 2009- 55.63i, 2010- 50.85, 2011- 50.84, 2012- 52.07, 54.24; 2013- 52.12i, 54.38; 2014- 52.37i, 54.54. pbs: 60m 7.44i '11, 100m 11.61/11.32w '10, 200m 23.03 '10, 300m 36.58 '14, 800m 2:11.70 '08, 60mh 8.20i '08, 100mh 13.32 '08, 200mhSt 25.86 '14, HJ 1.80i/1.77 '06, LJ 6.68 '04, TJ 13.10 '05, SP 12.48 '08, JT 35.12 '07, Pen 4632i '06, Hep 6104 '08.
Divorced from husband tennis player Lukas Rosol, who achieved top fame in 2012 by beating Rafael Nadal at Wimbledon.

Barbora SPOTÁKOVÁ b. 30 Jun 1981 Jablonec nad Nisou 1.82m 80kg. Dukla Praha.
At JT: OG: '04- dnq 23, '08- 1, '12- 1; WCh: '05-07-09-11: dnq 13/1/2/2; EC: '02-06-10-14: dnq 17/2/3/1; EU23: '03- 6; WUG: '03- 4, '05- 1; CCp: '14- 1; ET: '09-11-14: 2/3/1; won DL 2010, 2012, 2014; WAF 2006-08, Czech 2003, 2005-12. At Hep: WJ: '00- 4.
World javelin record 2008, two European records 2008, 11 Czech records 2006-08. World heptathlon javelin best (60.90) in 2012.
Progress at JT: 1996- 31.32, 1997- 37.28, 1998- 44.56, new: 1999- 41.69, 2000- 54.15, 2001- 51.97, 2002- 56.76, 2003- 56.65, 2004- 60.95, 2005- 65.74, 2006- 66.21, 2007- 67.12, 2008- 72.28, 2009- 68.23, 2010- 68.66, 2011- 71.58, 2012- 69.55, 2013- 62.33, 2014- 67.99. pbs: 200m 25.33/25.11w '00, 800m 2:18.29 '00, 60mh 8.68i '07, 100mh 13.99 '00, 400mh 62.68 '98, HJ 1.78 '00, LJ 5.65 '00, SP 14.53 '07, DT 36.80 '02, Hep 5880 '12, Dec 6749 '04.
Son Janek born 24 May 2013.

DENMARK

Governing body: Dansk Athletik Forbund, Idraettens Hus, Brøndby Stadion 20, DK-2605 Brøndby. Founded 1907.

National Championships first held in 1894. **2014 Champions**: **Men**: 100m: Morten Dalgaard Madsen 10.80, 200m/400m: Nick Ekelund-Arenander 21.07/46.36, 800m: Nick Jensen 1:54.10, 1500m: Andreas Bueno 4:06.50, 5000m/HMar: Thijs Nijhuis 14:16.59/67:47, 10000m: Abdi Hakim Ulad 29:53.83, Mar: Henrik Them 2:23:29, 3000mSt: Ole Hesselbjerg 9:32.83, 110mh: Andreas Martinsen 13.81, 400mh: Nicolai Trock Hartling 50.94, HJ: Andreas Jeppesen 2.06, PV: Mikkel Mswrek Nielsen 5.36, LJ: Andreas Trajkovski 7.60w, TJ: Peder Nielsen 15.80, SP: Nick Petersen 17.39, DT: Alexander Berthelsen 49.77, HT: Brian Nielsen 60.50, JT: Lukas Björnvad 65.89, Dec: Christian Laugesen 6695, 5000mW/10000mW/30kW: Andreas W.Nielsen 23:17.44/47:04.2/2:30:38, 50kW: Peer Jensen 5:37:26. **Women**: 100m/100mh: Mathilde U. Kramer 12.10/14.33, 200m: Zarah Buchwald 25.71, 400m: Stina Troast 55.81, 800m/1500m: Maria Larsen 2:09.26/4:28.12, 5000m/10000m/3000mSt: Simone Glad 16:23.79/35:34.04/10:30.34, HMar: Louise Langelund-Batting 75:58, Mar: Rikke Due-Andersen 2:46:41, 400mh: Sara Petersen 56.79, HJ: Sandra Christensen 1.73, PV: Lina Renée Jensen 3.85, LJ: Martha Traore 6.14w, TJ: Janne Nielsen 12.46w, SP: Maria Sløk Hansen 15.80, DT: Kathrine Bebe 50.77, HT: Meiken Greve 57.74, JT: Chriostina Marie Vestergaard 50.90, Hep: Tine Bach Ejlersen 5339, 3000mW: Birgit Klaproth 22:57.73.

DJIBOUTI

Hassan **Ayanleh SOULEIMAN** b. 3 Dec 1992 Djibouti City 1.72m 80kg.
At (800m)/1500m: WCh: '13- 3/sf; WI: '12- 5; AfG: '11- 6; AfCh: '12- 2, '14- 1; CG: '14- 1; WI: '14- 1; won DL 2013, Arab G 2011, Franc G 2013. At 3000m: WY: '09- h.
DJI records: 800m (3) 2012-13, 1000m 2013, 1500m (3) 2011-14, 1M (3) 2012-14, 3000m 2012.
Progress at 800m, 1500m: 2011- 1:51.78A, 3:34.32; 2012- 1:47.45, 3:30.31; 2013- 1:43.63, 3:31.64; 2014- 1:43.69, 3:29.58. pbs: 1000m 2:15.77 '13, 1M 3:47.32 '14, 3000m 7:39.81i '13, 7:42.22 '12.
Djibouti's first ever world champion.

DOMINICAN REPUBLIC

Governing body: Federación Dominicana de

Asociaciones de Atletismo. Avenida J.F. Kennedy, Centro Olímpico "Juan Pablo Duarte". Santo Domingo. Founded 1953.

Félix SÁNCHEZ b. 30 Aug 1977 New York, USA 1.78m 73kg. Was at University of Southern California.
At 400mh: OG: '00- sf, '04- 1, '08- h, '12- 1; WCh: '99-01-03-05-07-09-11-13: ht/1/1/dnf/2/8/4/5; PAm: '99- 4, '03- 1/3R, '07- 4/3R, '11- 3; CAG: '02- 1R, '10- 4; WCp: '02- 1R. Won NCAA 2000, GWG 2001, GP 2002 (3rd overall), WAF 2003.
Three CAC 400mh records 2001-03. DOM records: 400mh (11) 1997-2003, 400m (3) 2001-02.
Progress at 400mh: 1995- 51.33, 1996- 51.19, 1997- 50.01, 1998- 51.30, 1999- 48.60, 2000- 48.33, 2001- 47.38, 2002- 47.35, 2003- 47.25, 2004- 47.63, 2005- 48.24, 2006- 49.10, 2007- 48.01, 2008- 51.10, 2009- 48.34, 2010- 48.17, 2011- 48.74, 2012- 47.63, 2013- 48.10, 2014- 48.91. pbs: 100m 10.45 '05, 200m 20.87 '01, 400m 44.90 '01, 800m 1:49.36 '04, 200mSt 22.61 '14.
Born in New York and raised in California, he first competed for the Dominican Republic, where his parents were born, in 1999 after placing 6th in US 400mh. Took a share of Golden League jackpot in 2002 and won 43 successive 400mh races (including 7 heats) from loss to Dai Tamesue on 2 Jul 2001 until he pulled up in Brussels on 3 Sep 2004. Ran his fastest for eight years to regain Olympic title in 2012, the same time (47.63) with which he had won in 2004.

Luguelín SANTOS b. 12 Nov 1993 Bayaguana 1.73m 61kg. Universidad Interamericana de San Germán, Puerto Rico.
At 400m: OG: '12- 2; WCh: '13- 3 (h 200m); WJ: '10- 6, '12- 1; PAm: '11- 2/2R; CCp: '14- 5; YthOG: '10- 1.
DOM records 200m 2013, 400m (3) 2011-12. CAC indoor 600m best 2015.
Progress at 400m: 2009- 47.88, 2010- 46.19, 2011- 44.71A, 2012- 44.45, 2013- 44.52, 2014- 44.53. pbs: 200m 20.55A '13, 20.73 '12; 300m 32.4+/32.56 '12, 600m 1:15.15 '15, 800m 1:49.18 '14.
Younger broler Juander (b. 7 May 1995) has 400m pb 45.93A '14.

EGYPT

Governing body: Egyptian Amateur Athletic Federation, Sport Federation Building, El Estad El Bahary, Nasr City – Cairo. Founded 1910.

Ihab ABDELRAHMAN El-Sayed b. 1 May 1989 Al-Sharqiyah 1.94m 96kg.
At JT: OG: '12- dnq 29; WCh: '11- dnq 35, '13- 7; AfG: '11- 5; AfCh: '10-12-14: 1//5/2; WJ: '08- 2; Af-J: '07- 3; CCp: '14- 1; Arab champion 2009, 12011, 2013..
African JT record 2014, six Egyptian 2010-14.
Progress at JT: 2007- 71.15, 2008- 76.20, 2009- 78.44, 2010- 81.84, 2011- 78.83, 2012- 82.25, 2013- 83.62, 2014- 89.21.

Mostafa Hicham AL-GAMAL b. 1 Oct 1988 Giza 1.91m 105kg.
At HT: OG: '12- dnq 29; WCh: '11- dnq 30; AfG: '11- 1; AfCh: '08-10-12-14: 2/3/3/1; CCp: '14- 2; Won Med G 2013.
African hammer record 2014.
Progress at HT: 2006- 61.44, 2007- 66.26, 2008- 71.15, 2009- 71.88, 2010- 73.27, 2011- 74.76, 2012- 77.14, 2013- 77.73, 2014- 81.27.

ERITREA

Governing body: Eritrean National Athletics Federation, PO Box 1117, Asmara. F'd 1992.

Teklemariam MEDHIN Weldeselassie b. 24 Jun 1989 Hazega 1.78m 57kg.
At (5000m/)10000m: OG: '08- 32,'12- 7; WCh: '09- 15/12, '13- dnf; WJ: '06- (12). World CC: 2006-07-08-09-10-11-13-15: 13J/14J/23/9/2/14/3/17. African CC: '12- 2.
Progress at 5000m, 10000m: 2006- 14:13.9, 2008- 13:48.18, 27:46.50; 2009- 13:11.01, 27:58.89; 2010- 13:04.55, 28:50.63A; 2011- 13:16.53, 27:37.21; 2012- 13:17.25, 27:16.69; 2013- 13:32.86, 27:19.97; 2014- 27:38.83. pbs: 3000m 7:48.6+ '11, Road 10M 47:11 '09, HMar 61:47 '14.

Zersenay TADESE b. 8 Feb 1982 Adi Bana 1.60m 56kg. C.A. Adidas. Madrid, Spain.
At (5000m)/10000m: OG: '04- 7/3, '08- 5, '12- 6; WCh: '03- (8), '05- 14/6, '07- 4, '09- 2, '11- 4; AfCh: '02- 6, AfG: '07- 1. World CC: 2002-03-04-05-06-07-08-09: 30/9/6/2/4/1/3/3; 20k: '06- 1; HMar: '02-03-07-08-09-10-12-14: 21/7/1/1/1/2/1/4.
Records: World 20km and half marathon 2010. Eritrean 3000m (2), 2M, 5000m (4), 10000m (5) HMar (3) 2003-10.
Progress at 5000m, 10000m, HMar: 2002- 13:48.79, 28:47.29, 63:05; 2003- 13:05.57, 28:42.79, 61:26; 2004- 13:13.74, 27:22.57; 2005- 13:12.23, 27:04.70, 59:05; 2006- 12:59.27, 26:37.25, 59:16; 2007- 27:00.30, 58:59; 2008- 27:05.11, 59:56; 2009- 13:07.02, 26:50.12, 59:35; 2010- 58:23, 2011- 12:59.32, 26:51.09, 58:30; 2012- 27:33.51, 59:34; 2013- 60:10, 2014- 59.38. pbs: 3000m 7:39.93 '05, 2M 8:19.34 '07, Road: 15k 41:27 '05, 10M 45:52 '07, 20k 55:21+ '10, Mar 2:10:41 '12.
Won Eritrea's first medal at Olympics in 2004 and World CC in 2005 and first gold in the World 20k in 2006 before four more at half marathon. 15 wins in 18 half marathons 2002-13; ran 59:05 for the fastest ever to win the Great North Run (slightly downhill overall) in 2005 and won Lisbon 2010-11 in two fastest ever times. Won a national road cycling title in 2001 before taking up athletics. His younger brother **Kidane** (b. 31 Aug 1987) has pbs 5000m 13:11.85 '10, 10,000m 27:06.16 '08; at 5000m/(10000m): OG: '08- 10/12, WCh: '09- h/9; World CC: '12- 6.

Samuel TSEGAY Tesfamriam b. 24 Oct 1988 Kudofelasi 1.76m 55kg.
At 5000m: WCh: '09- h. At 10,000m: WJ: '06- 4.

At HMar: WCh: '09-10-14: 5/5/2. At Mar: WCh: '13- 16. World CC: '06-07-09-10: 8J/8J/16/5. Eritream marathon record 2011.
Progress at HMar, Mar: 2009- 60:17, 2010- 61:13, 2011- 2:07:28, 2012- 61:09, 2:08:06; 2013- 62:34, 2:14:41; 2014- 59:21. pbs: 5000m 13:16.59 '09, 10000m 28:20.96 '09; Road: 15k 41:31 '11, 10M 44:38 '11.

ESTONIA

Governing body: Eesti Kergejôustikuliit, Maakri 23, Tallinn 10145. Founded 1920.
National Championships first held in 1917. **2014**: **Men**: 100m: Rait Veesalu 10.95, 200m/400m: Marek Niit 20.85/46.39, 800m: Andi Noot 1:50.87, 1500m: Tidrek Nurme 3:53.06, 5000m/10000m/HMar: Roman Fosti 15:03.04/30:38.64/65:29, Mar: Ilja Nikolajev 2:21:34, 3000mSt: Priit Aus 8:50.51, 110mh: Andres Raja 14.29, 400mh: Rasmus Mägi 48.77, HJ: Hendrik Lepik 2.16, PV: Veiko Aunapuu 5.00, LJ: Mihkel Saks 7.65, TJ: Igor Syunin 15.83, SP: Kristo Galeta 18.09, DT: Gerd Kanter 66.02, HT: Mart Olman 64.76, JT: Tanel Laanmäe 80.02, Dec: Karel Joevali 7672, 20000mW: Lauri Lelumees 1:38:47.52, 50kW: Margus Luik 4:28:53. **Women**: 100m/200m: Maarja Kalev 11.84/24.51, 400m/400mh: Maris Mägi 54.07/59.79, 800m/1500m: Liina Tsernov 2:07.18/4:29.09, 5000m/3000mSt: Jekaterina Patjuk 16:43.39/10:27.55, 10000m/Mar: Evelin Talts 36:55.75/2:56:26, HMar: Lily Luik 79:49, 100mh/LJ: Grit Sadeiko 13.44/6.28, HJ: Eleriin Haas 1.88, PV: Reena Koll 4.00, TJ: Merilyn Uudmäe 12.36, SP: Kätlin Piirimäe 14.92, DT: Kätlin Töllasson 49.84, HT: Kati Ojaloo 63.33, JT: Helina Karvak 55.36, Hep: Linda Treiel 5469, 10000mW/20kW: Angela Mandel 55:58.13/1:59:23.

Gerd KANTER b. 6 May 1979 Tallinn 1.96m 125kg. Tallinna SS Kalev. Business management graduate.
At DT: OG: '04- dnq 19, '08- 1, '12- 3; WCh: '03-05-07-09-11-13: dnq 25/2/1/3/2/3; EC: '02-06-10-12-14: 12/2/4/2/2; EU23: '01- 5; CCp: '14- 1; WUG: '05- 1. Won WAF 2007-08, DL 2012-13, Estonian 2004-09, 2011-14.
Five Estonian discus records 2004-06.
Progress at DT: 1998- 47.37, 1999- 49.65, 2000- 57.68, 2001- 60.47, 2002- 66.31, 2003- 67.13, 2004- 68.50, 2005- 70.10, 2006- 73.38, 2007- 72.02, 2008- 71.88, 2009- 71.64, 2010- 71.45, 2011- 67.99, 2012- 68.03, 2013- 67.59, 2014- 66.28. pb SP 17.31i '04, 16.11 '00.
Threw over 70m in four rounds at Helsingborg on 4 Sep 2006; a feat matched only by Virgilijus Alekna. Six successive seasons over 70m.

Rasmus MÄGI b. 4 May 1992 Tartu 1.88m 74kg. Tartu University ASK.
At 400mh: OG: '12- h; WCh: '13- sf; EC: '12- 5, '14- 2; WJ: '10- h; EU23: '13- 3; EJ: '11- 4; CCp: '14- 4. Won EST 400m 2012, 400mh 2009, 2014.
Six Estonian 400mh records 2012-14
Progress at 400mh: 2010- 52.79, 2011- 50.14, 2012- 49.54, 2013- 49.19, 2014- 48.54. pbs: 200m 21.90 '11, 400m 46.40 '13, 200mh 24.01 '11, LJ 7.73 '12.
His sister Maris has won 19 Estonian titles in sprints and hurdles, pbs: 400m 52.21 '11, 400mh 56.56 '13 (EST record).

ETHIOPIA

Governing body: Ethiopian Athletic Federation, Addis Ababa Stadium, PO Box 3241, Addis Ababa. Founded 1961.
2014 National Champions: **Men**: 400m: Haji Ture 46.1, 800m: Jena Umar 1:47.0, 1500m: Aman Wote 3:38.2, 5000m: Ibrahim Jeylan 14:02.3, 10000m: Adugna Tekele 28:46.5, 3000mSt: Nesredin Dette 8:48.0. **Women**: 400m: Genet Lire 51.5, 800m: Zeytuna Mohammed 2:01.6, 1500m: Baso Sado 4:13.4, 5000m: AlmazAyana 16:11.4, 10000m: Genet Ayalew 32:45.1, 3000mSt: Tigist Mekonen 10:00.2.

Ayele ABSHERO Biza b. 28 Dec 1990 Yeboda 1.67m 52kg.
At 5000m: Af-J: '09- 4. At Mar: OG: '12- dnf. World CC: '08- 2J, '09- 1J.
Progress at 10000m, Mar: 2009- 27:54.29, 2011- 27:48.94, 2012- 2:04:23, 2013- 2:06:57, 2014- 2:06:31. pbs: 3000m 7:40.08 '10, 5000m 13:11.38 '09; Road: 15k 42:02 '10, 10M 45:33 '10, HMar 59:42 '11.
Second fastest ever debut marathon to win at Dubai in 2012, 3rd London 2013. Elder brother Tessema has marathon pb 2:08:26 '08.

Yenew ALAMIREW b. 27 May 1990 Tilili 1.75m 57kg.
At 5000m: OG: '12- 12; WCh: '13- 9; AfG: '11- 2; AfCh: '14- 5; won DL 2013. At 3000m: WI: '12- 9.
Progress at 5000m: 2010- 13:16.53, 2011- 13:00.46, 2012- 12:48.77, 2013- 12:54.95, 2014- 13:00.21. pbs: 1500m 3:35.09+ '11, 1M 3:50.43 '11, 3000m 7:27.26 '11, Road: 10k 29:26A '10, 15k 42:30 '14.

Mohammed AMAN Geleto b. 10 Jan 1994 Asella 1.69m 55kg.
At 800m: OG: '12- 6; WCh: '11- 8, '13- 1; WY: '11- 2; WI: '12- 1, '14- 1; AfCh: '14- 2; CCp: '14- 2; won DL 2012-13, Afr-J 2011, Yth OG 1000m 2010.
Records: Ethiopian 800m (6) 2011-13, 1000m 2014, world youth 800m indoors and out 2011, world junior 600m indoor 2013 (1:15.60), African indoor 800m 2014.
Progress at 800m: 2008- 1:50.29, 2009- 1:46.34, 2010- 1:48.5A, 2011- 1:43.37, 2012- 1:42.53, 2013- 1:42.37. 2014- 1:42.83. pbs: 600m 1:15.0+ '12, 1000m 2:15.75 '14, 1500m 3:43.52 '11, 1M 3:57.14 '11.
Was disqualified from taking the African Junior 800m gold in 2009 for being under-age (at 15). Youngest ever World Indoor champion at 18 years 60 days in 2012. Beat David Rudishsa in the latter's last races in both 2011 and 2012.

Kenenisa BEKELE b. 13 Jun 1982 near Bekoji, Arsi Province 1.62m 54kg.

At 5000m(/10000m): OG: '04- 2/1, '08- 1/1, '12- (4); WCh: '03- 3/1, '05- (1), '07- (1), '09- 1/1; WJ: '00- 2; AfG: '03- 1; AfCh: '06- 1, '08- 1. At 3000m: WY: '99- 2; WI: '06- 1; WCp: '06- 2. World CC: '99- 9J, 4k: '01- 1J/2 4k, '02-03-04-05-06: all 1/1, '08- 1. Won WAF 3000m 2003, 2009; 5000m 2006. World records: 5000m 2004, 10000m 2004 & 2005, indoor 5000m (12:49.60) 2004, 2000m 2007, 2M 2008; World junior record 3000m 2001.
Progress at 5000m, 10000m, Mar: 2000- 13:20.57, 2001- 13:13.33, 2002- 13:26.58, 2003- 12:52.26, 26:49.57; 2004- 12:37.35, 26:20.31; 2005- 12:40.18, 26:17.53; 2006- 12:48.09, 2007- 12:49.53, 26:46.19; 2008- 12:50.18, 26:25.97; 2009- 12:52.32, 26:46.31; 2011- 13:27e+, 26:43.16; 2012- 12:55.79, 27:02.59; 2013- 13:07.88, 27:12.08; 2014- 2:05:04. pbs: 1000m 2:21.9+ '07, 1500m 3:32.35 '07, 1M 3:56.2+ '07, 2000m 4:49.99i '07, 4:58.40 '09, 3000m 7:25.79 '07, 2M 8:04.35i '08, 8:13.51 '07; Road: 15k 42:42 '01, 10M 46:06 '13, 20k 57:19 '13, HMar 60:09 '13, 25k 1:13:42 '14, 30k 1:28:40 '14.
At cross-country has a record 20 (12 individual, 8 team) world gold medals from his record winning margin of 33 seconds for the World Juniors in 2001, a day after second in senior 4km. The only man to win both World senior races in the same year, he did this five times. Unbeaten in 27 races from Dec 2001 to March 2007 when he did not finish in the Worlds. After winning all his 12 10,000m track races including five major gold medals, from a brilliant debut win over Haile Gebrselassie at Hengelo in June 2003, he had two years out through injury and then dropped out of World 10,000 in 2011 before running the year's fastest time to win at Brussels. 17 successive wins at 5000m 2006-09. Shared Golden League jackpot in 2009. Won Great North Run on half marathon debut 2013. Won in Paris on marathon debut 2014, then 4th Chicago. IAAF Athlete of the Year 2004-05.
His fiancée Alem Techale (b. 13.12.87, the 2003 World Youth 1500m champion) died of a heart attack on 4 Jan 2005. He married film actress Danawit Gebregziabher on 18 Nov 2007.

Tariku BEKELE b. 21 Jan 1987 near Bekoji 1.68m 52kg.
At 5000m: OG: '08- 6; WCh: '05- 7, '07- 5; WJ: '04- 3, '06- 1; AfG: '07- 3; AfCh: '08- 4, '10- 6. At 10000m: OG: '12- 3. At 3000m: WY: '03- 2; WI: '06-08-10: 6/1/4; CCp: '10- 4; won WAF 3000m 2006. World CC: '05- 6J, '06- 3J.
World junior indoor 2M best 2006.
Progress at 5000m, 10000m: 2004- 13:11.97, 2005- 12:59.03, 2006- 12:53.81, 2007- 13:01.60, 2008- 12:52.45, 2010- 12:53.97, 2011- 12:59.25, 2012- 12:54.13, 27:03.24; 2013- 13:13.61, 27:38.15; 2014- 13:28.41. pbs: 1500m 3:37.26 '08, 2000m 5:00.1 '06, 3000m 7:28.70 '10, 2M 8:04.83 '07, Road: 15k 43:35 '11, 10M 46:33 '10, HMar 61:39dh '14.
Younger brother of Kenenisa Bekele.

Deressa CHIMSA Edae b. 21 Nov 1986 Koreodo 1.75m 62kg.
At Mar: WC: '09- dnf. World HMar: '12- 2. Won ETH HMar 2009.
Progress at Mar: 2008- 2:10:16, 2009- 2:07:54, 2010- 2:08:45, 2011- 2:07:39, 2012- 2:05:42, 2013- 2:07:05, 2014- 2:07:40. pbs: HMar 60:51 '12.
Marathon wins: Daegu 2010, Prague 2012, Toronto 2013.

Yigrem DEMELASH b. 28 Jan 1994 1.67m 52kg.
At 10000m: WJ: '12- 1.
Progress at 5000m, 10000m: 2012- 13:03.30, 26:57.56; 2013- 13:13.18, 27:15.51; 2014- 13:11.80. Pb 15k Rd 42:26 '14.

Lelisa DESISA Benti b. 14 Jan 1990 Shewa 1.70m 52kg.
At 10000m: Af-J: '09- 1. At: HMar: WCh: '10- 7, AfG: '11- 1. At Mar: WCh: '13- 2.
Progress at 10000m, HMar, Mar: 2009- 28:46.74, 2010- 59:39; 2011- 59:30, 2012- 27:11.98, 62:50; 2013- 2:04:45, 2014- 59:36, 2:11:06; 2015- 2:05:52. pbs: 5000m 13:22.91 '12, Road: 15k 42:25 '10, 10M 45:36 '11.
Brilliant marathon debut to win Dubai 2013 and then won Boston and 2nd Worlds. 2nd New York 2014, Dubai 2015.

Muktar EDRIS Awel b. 14 Jan 1994 Adio 1.72m 57kg.
At 5000m: WCh: '13- 7; WJ: '12- 1. At 10000m: Af-J: '11- 4. World CC: '11-13-15: 7J/3J/3; AfCC: 12- 1J.
Progress at 5000m: 2012- 13:04.34, 2013- 13:03.69, 2014- 12:54.83. pbs: 3000m 7:46.0 '14, 10000m 28:44.95 '13, 10k Rd 28:11 '13.

Gebre-egziabher GEBREMARIAM b. 10 Sep 1984 Shere, Tigray region 1.78m 56kg.
At 10000m (5000m): OG: '04- (4), '12- 8; WCh: '03- (6), '05- 15, '07- 6, '09- 10; WJ: '02- 1 (3); AfG: '03- 2, '07- 3; AfCh: '08- 1. At Mar: WCh: '11- dnf. World CC: '02-03-04-05-06-08-09-10: 1J/3/2&2/9(4k)/13/17/1/10. Won ETH CC 2003 & 2009, 5000m 2005, 10000m 2005., 2009; E.Afr 2004.
Progress at 5000m, 10000m, Mar: 2001- 14:13.74A, 31:04.61A; 2002- 13:12.14, 27:25.61; 2003- 12:58.08, 28:03.03; 2004- 12:55.59, 26:53.73; 2005- 12:52.80, 27:11.57; 2006- 13:30.95, 27:03.95; 2007- 13:10.29, 26:52.33; 2008- 13:36.67, 27:20.65; 2009- 13:13.20, 27:44.04; 2010- 2:08:14, 2011- 2:04:53wdh/2:08:00, 2012- 13:33.2+, 27:03.58, 2:22:56; 2013- 2:10:28. pbs: 3000m 7:39.48 '05, 2M 9:34.82i '06, HMar 60:25 '10, 3000mSt 8:57.7A '02.
Won New York 2010 on marathon debut (3rd 2014), 3rd Boston 2011 and 2013. Married Worknesh Kidane on 4 Feb 2006. She has 21 World CC medals, he has 16.

Mekonnen GEBREMEDHIN Woldegiorgis b. 11 Oct 1988 Addis Ababa 1.80m 64kg.
At 1500m: OG: '12- 6; WCh: '07-09-11-13: sf/h/7/7; WI: '08-10-12: 6/4/3; AfCh: '10- 3, '14- 4; CCp: '10- 2. At 800m: WJ: '06- sf.

Progress at 1500m: 2004- 3:47.1A, 2006- 3:41.00, 2007- 3:36.04, 2008- 3:35.68, 2009- 3:34.49, 2010- 3:31.57, 2011- 3:31.90, 2012- 3:31.45, 2013- 3:32.43, 2014- 3:32.79. pbs: 800m 1:46.63 '12, 1M 3:49.70 '11, 3000m 7:41.42 '11, 3000mSt 8:59.06 '12.

Dejen GEBREMESKEL b. 24 Nov 1989 Adiqrat, Tigray region 1.78m 53kg.
At 5000m: OG: '12- 2; WCh: '11- 3; WJ: '08- 3; Af-J: '07- 2. At 10000m: WCh: '13- 16. At 3000m: WI: '10- 12-14: 10/5/3. World CC: '08- 18J.
Progress at 5000m, 10000m: 2007- 13:21.05, 2008- 13:08.96, 2009- 13:03.13, 2010- 12:53.56, 2011- 12:55.89, 2012- 12:46.81, 2013- 13:31.02, 26:51.02; 2014- 13:09.73. pbs: 3000m 7:34.14i '12, 7:45.9+ '10, HMar 62:36 '14.
Fastest ever debut 10,000m at Sollentuna 2013.

Hagos GEBRHIWET Berhe b. 11 May 1994 Tsaedaenba, Tigray region 1.67m 55kg. Mesfen Engineering
At 5000m: OG: '12- 11; WCh: '13- 2; AfCh: '14- dnf. At 3000m: WY: '11- 5; WI: '14- 5. World CC: '13- 1J, '15- 4, AfCC: '12- 4J.
World junior records 5000m 2012, indoor 3000m 2013.
Progress at 5000m: 2011- 14:10.0A, 2012- 12:47.53, 2013- 12:55.73, 2014- 13:06.88. pbs: 3000m 7:30.36 '13, 10k Rd 27:57dh '11.

Markos GENETI b. 30 May 1984 Walega 1.75m 55kg.
At 5000m: WJ: '02- 2; AfG: '03- 4. At 3000m: WY: '01- 1; WI: '04- 3. At 1500m: WCh: '05- sf. World CC: '07- 15.
Progress at 5000m: 2001- 13:50.14, 2002- 13:28.83, 2003- 13:11.87, 2004- 13:17.57, 2005- 13:00.25, 2006- 13:13.98, 2007- 13:07.65, 2008- 13:08.22, 2009- 13:31.71i, 2010- 13:18.64i/13:21.99. At Mar: 2011- 2:06:35, 2012- 2:04:54, 2013- 2:12:44, 2014- 2:05:13, 2015- 2:07:25. pbs: 1500m 3:33.83 '05, 1M 4:08.8 '10, 3000m 7:32.69i '07, 7:38.11 '05; 2M 8:08.39i '04, 8:19.61 '06, Road: 10k 29:38 '11, HMar 61:38 '14, 30k 1:28:15 '14.
Won in Los Angeles 2011 in sixth fastest ever debut marathon time. 3/2 Dubai 2012/2014.

Ibrahim JEYLAN Gashu b. 12 Jun 1989 Bale Province 1.68m 57kg. Muger Cement.
At 10000m: WCh: '11- 1, '13- 2; WJ: '06- 1, '08- 3; AfG: '11- 1; AfCh: '08- 2. At 3000m: WY: '05- 2. World CC: '06- 5J, '08- 1J. Won ETH 5000m 2014, 10000m 2006.
Two world youth 10,000m records 2006.
Progress at 5000m, 10000m: 2006- 13:09.38, 27:02.81; 2007- 13:17.99, 27:50.53; 2008- 13:15.12, 27:13.85; 2009- 13:19.70, 27:22.19; 2010- 13:21.29, 27:12.43; 2011- 13:09.95, 27:09.02; 2013- 13:09.16, 27:22.23; 2014- 13:09.67. pbs: 3000m 8:04.21 '05, 15k 43:38 '08, HMar 61:47 '14.

Tsegaye KEBEDE Wordofa b. 15 Jan 1987 Gerar Ber 1.58m 50kg.
At Mar: OG: '08- 3; WCh: '09- 3, '13- 4.
Progress at Mar: 2007- 2:08:16, 2008- 2:06:10, 2009- 2:05:18, 2010- 2:05:19, 2011- 2:07:48, 2012- 2:04:38, 2013- 2:06:04, 2014- 2:06:30, 2015- 2:07:58. pbs: Road: 10k 28:10 '08, HMar 59:35 '08.
Marathon wins: Addis Ababa 2007, Paris 2008, Fukuoka 2008-09, London 2010 & 2013 (2nd 2009, 3rd 2012, 2014), Chicago 2012 (2nd 2010), New York 2013 (3rd 2011). World Marathon Majors winner 2012/13. Has record 12 sub-2:08 and 14 sub-2:09 times. Won Great Ethiopian Run 2007, Great North Run 2008.

Abera KUMA Lema b. 31 Aug 1990 Ambo 1.60m 50kg.
At 5000m: WCh: '11- 5, '13- 5; Af-J: '09- 1. At 3000m: WY: '07- 5.
Tied world 30km record 2014.
Progress at 5000m, 10000m, Mar: 2009- 13:29.40, 2010- 13:07.83, 2011- 13:00.15, 27:22.54; 2012- 13:09.32, 27:18.39; 2013- 26:52.85, 2014- 2:05:56. pbs: 1500m 3:48.73 '09, 3000m 7:39.09i/7:40.85 '12, Road: 15k 42:01 '10, 10M 45:28 '11, HMar 60:19 '12, 25k 1:13:08 '14, 30k 1:27:38 '14.
3rd Berlin Marathon 2014.

Feysa LILESA b. 1 Feb 1990 Tullu Bultuma 1.58m 50kg.
At Mar: WCh: '11- 3, '13- dnf, World CC: 2008-09-10-11-13: 14J/12/25/17/9. Won ETH CC 2013.
Progress at Mar: 2009- 2:09:12, 2010- 2:05:23, 2011- 2:10:32, 2012- 2:04:52, 2013- 2:07:46, 2014- 2:08:26, 2015- 2:06:35. pbs: 5000m 13:34.80 '08, 10000m 27:46.97 '08; Road: 15k 42:15+ '13, 20k 56:19+ '12, HMar 59:22 '12, 25k 1:13:22 '13, 30k 1:28:05 '13.
Marathons won: Dublin 2009, Xiamen 2010. 3rd/2nd Chicago 2010/2012, 4th Rotterdam 2010 in then fastest ever by 20 year-old, 4th London 2013.

Imane MERGA Jida b. 15 Oct 1988 Tulu Bolo, Oromia region 1.74m 61kg. Defence.
At 5000m/(10000m): WCh: '09- (4), '11- dq/3, '13- (12); AfCh: '10- 5, '14- (5); Af-J: '07- (3); CCp: '10- 5; won DL 2010-11, WAF 2009. World CC: '07-11-13: 7J/1/2.
Progress at 5000m, 10000m: 2007- 13:33.52, 30:12.03; 2008- 13:08.20, 27:33.53, 2009- 12:55.66, 27:15.94; 2010- 12:53.58; 2011- 12:54.21, 26:48.35; 2012- 12:59.77, 27:14.02; 2013- 13:09.17, 26:57.33; 2014- 13:11.94, 28:17.75. pbs: 3000m 7:43.59 '14, HMar 59:56 '12.
Disqualified for running inside the kerb after finishing 3rd in World 5000m 2011.

Endeshaw NEGESSE b. 13 Mar 1988 1.70m 54kg.
Progress at Mar: 2012- 2:09:59, 2013- 2:04:52, 2014- 2:08:32, 2015- 2:06:00.
Won Tokyo Marathon 2015.

Tadesse TOLA Woldegeberal b. 31 Oct 1987 Addis Ababa 1.78m 60kg.
At Mar: '13- 3. At 10000m: WCh: '07- 13; AfCh: '06- 5; AfG: '07- 2. World 20k: '06- 7; World CC: '06- 10J, '07- 7, '09- 17.

Progress at 10000m, Mar: 2006- 28:15.16, 2007- 27:04.89, 2008- 27:15.17, 2009- 28:51.4A, 2:15:48; 2010- 2:06:31, 2011- 2:07:13, 2012- 2:05:10, 2013- 2:04:49, 2014- 2:05:57. pbs: 3000m 7:43.70 '07, 5000m 13:18.82 '07, 10000m 27:04.89 '07; Road: 15k 43:49 '08, 20k 57:27 '06, HMar 59:49 '10.
Won Paris Marathon 2010 (2nd 2013), Beijing 2013, Warsaw 2014; 2nd Frankfurt 2010 & Tokyo 2014. Pb when 3rd at Dubai 2013.

Aman WOTE Fete b. 18 Apr 1984 Kabete 1.81m 64kg.
At 1500m: OG: '12- ht; WCh: 13- sf; AfG: '11- 5; AfCh: '10- 7; WI: '12- 4, '14- 2. Won ETH 1500m 2014.
Ethiopian records 1500m (2) & 1M 2014.
Progress at 1500m: 2010- 3:38.89A 2011- 3:35.61, 2012- 3:35:38, 2013- 3:32.65, 2014- 3:29.91. pbs: 800m 1:44.99 '13, 1M 3:48.60 '14, 3000m 7:43.99i '13.

Women

Birtukan ADAMU b. 29 Apr 1992 1.64m 49kg.
At 3000mSt: WCh: '11- 13; WJ: '10-2; AfG: '11- 3; AfCh: '12- 2, Af-J: '11- 1.
World junior 3000m steeplechase record 2011.
Progress at 3000mSt: 2010- 9:31.39, 2011- 9:20.37, 2012- 9:36.40, 2013- 9:43.22, 2014- 9:27.29. pbs: 1500m 4:24.91 '11, 3000m 8:58.73i '12.

Sofia ASSEFA Abebe b. 14 Nov 1987 Tenta District, south Wello 1.71m 58kg. Ethiopian Bank.
At 3000mSt: OG: '08- h, '12- 2; WCh: '09- 13, '11- 6,'13- 3; AfCh: '08-10-14: 4/2/2; CCp: '10- 3.
Ethiopian 3000mSt records 2011 and 2012.
Progress at 3000mSt: 2006- 10:17.48, 2007- 9:48.46, 2008- 9:31.58, 2009- 9:19.91, 2010- 9:20.72, 2011- 9:15.04, 2012- 9:09.00, 2013- 9:12.84, 2014- 9:11.39. pbs: 1000m 2:49.79 '07, 5000m 15:59.74 '07, 2000mSt 6:33.49 '07.

Hiwot AYALEW Yemer b. 6 Mar 1990 Gojam, Amhara 1.73m 51kg. Commercial Bank.
At 3000mSt: OG: '12- 4; WCh: '13- 4; AfG: '11- 2; AfCh: '14- 1; CCp: '14- 2; won DL 2014. At 3000m: WI: '14-11. World CC: '11- 11, '13- 2.
Progress at 3000mSt: 2011- 9:23.88, 2012- 9:09.61, 2013- 9:15.25, 2014- 9:10.64. pbs: 3000m 8:43.29i '14, 2M: 9:21.59i '14, 5000m 14:49.36 '12, 10k Rd 31:47 '14.
Younger sister of Wude Ayalew.

Wude AYALEW Yimer b. 4 Jul 1987 Sekela, Amhara region 1.50m 44kg.
At 10000m: WCh: '09- 3; AfG: '11- 2; AfCh: '08- 3, '10- 4. At 5000m: WJ: '06- 5. World CC: '06-07-09-11: 5/10/5/6. Won ETH CC 2009.
Progress at 5000m, 10000m: 2006- 14:57.23, 33:57.0; 2008- 15:07.65, 31:06.84; 2009- 14:38.44, 30:11.87; 2010- 15:02.47, 32:29.92A; 2011- 14:59.71, 31:24.09; 2013- 31:16.68. pbs: 1500m 4:14.85 '07, 3000m 8:30.93 '09; Road: 10k 31:41+ '08, 15k 48:15 '14, 20k 65:28 '14, HMar 67:58 '09.
Won Great Ethiopian Run 2008. Older sister of Hiyot Ayalew.

Almaz AYANA Eba b. 21 Nov 1991 1.65m 50kg.
At 5000m: WCh: '13- 3; AfCh: '14- 1; CCp: '14- 1. At 3000mSt: WJ: '10- 5; won ETH 5000m 2014, 3000mSt 2013.
World junior 3000m steeplechase record 2010.
Progress at 5000m, 3000mSt: 2009- 10:03.75, 2010- 9:22.51, 2011- 15:12.24, 9:30.23; 2012- 14:57.97, 9:38.62; 2013- 14:25.84, 9:27.49; 2014- 14:29.19. pbs: 2000m 5:37.5+ '14, 3000m 8:24.58 '14, 10k 32:19 '10.

Gelete BURKA Bati b. 15 Feb 1986 Kofele 1.65m 45kg.
At 1500m: OG: '08- h; WCh: '05- 8, '09- 10 (fell), '11- sf, '13- h; WI: '08- 1, '10- 3; AfG: '07- 1; AfCh: '08- 1, '10- 2; CCp: '10- 7. At 3000m: WI: '12- 3. At 5000m: OG: '12- 5; WCh: '07- 10. World CC: '03-05-06-07-08-09: 3J/1J/1 4k/4/6/8. Won ETH 800m 2011, 1500m 2004-05, 2007; 5000m 2005, 4k CC 2006.
African records: 1M 2008, 200m 2009, indoor 1500m 2008, junior 1500m 2005. World youth 1M best (4:30.81) 2003.
Progress at 1500m, 5000m. Mar: 2003- 4:10.82, 16:23.8A, 2004- 4:06.10, 2005- 3:59.60, 14:51.47; 2006- 4:02.68, 14:40.92; 2007- 4:00.48, 14:31.20; 2008- 3:59.75i/4:00.44, 14:45.84; 2009- 3:58.79, 2010- 3:59.28, 2011- 4:03.28, 2012- 14:41.43, 2013- 4:04.36, 14:42.07, 2:30:40; 2014- 2:26:03. pbs: 800m 2:02.89 '10, 1M 4:18.23 '08, 2000m 5:30.19 '09, 3000m 8:25.92 '06; Rd: 10k 32:38+/30:53dh '12, 15k 49:26 '12, HMar 71:10+ 13, 25k 1:25:39 '14, 30k 1:43:03 '14.
Married Taddele Gebrmehden in 2007.

Firehiwot DADO Tufa b. 9 Jan 1984 Assefa, Arsi prov. 1.65m.
Progress at Mar: 2008- 2:37:34, 2009- 2:27:08, 2010- 2:25:28, 2011- 2:23:15, 2012- 2:34:56dh, 2014- 2:23:34. pbs: Road: 10k 31:49 '13, 15k 48:32+ '12, 20k 65:06+ '12, HMar 68:35 '12, 30k 1:40:45 '11.
Marathon wins: New York 2011, Rome 2009-11, Florence 2010, Prague 2014. 3rd Dubai 2014.

Mamitu DASKA Molisa b. 16 Oct 1983 Liteshoa 1.64m 45kg.
At HMar: AfrG: '11- 2. World CC: '09-10-15: 12/8/8. ETH half marathon record 2015.
Progress at Mar: 2009- 2:26:38, 2010- 2:24:19, 2011- 2:21:59, 2012- 2:23:52, 2013- 2:23:23, 2014- 2:29:35. pbs: 10000m 31:36.88 '09. Road: 10k 31:04 '14, 10M 51:54 '14, HMar 66:27 '15, 30k 1:39:46 '11. Marathon wins: Dubai 2010, Houston and Frankfurt 2011.

Buzunesh DEBA Dejene b. 8 Sep 1987 Arsi 1.62m 45kg.
Progress at Mar: 2009- 2:32:17, 2010- 2:27:24, 2011- 2:23:19, 2013- 2:24:26, 2014- 2:19:59dh/ 2:31:40. pbs: 5000m 15:52.33 '04, Road: 10k 32:10 '10, 15k 49:05 '14, HMar 68:59 '14.
Worked Worku Bayi in 2005, lives in Bronx, New York. Marathon wins: Sacramento 2009, Jacksonville, Duluth, St.Paul & Sacramento 2010, Los Angeles & San Diego 2011. 2nd New

York 2011, Houston 2013.

Meseret DEFAR b. 19 Nov 1983 Addis Ababa 1.55m 42kg.
At 5000m(/10000m): OG: '04- 1, '08- 3, '12- 1; WCh: '03- h, '05- 2, '07- 1, '09- 3/5, '11- 3/dnf, '13- 1; WJ: '00- 2, '02- 1; AfG: '03- 1, '07- 1; AfCh: '00-06-08-10: 2/1/2/2; WCp: '06- 1. At 3000m: WJ: '02- 1; WY: '99- 2; WI: '03-04-06-08-10-12: 3/1/1/1/1/2; CCp: '10- 1. Won WAF 3000m 2004-09, 5000m 2005, 2008-09; DL 5000m 2013. World CC: '02- 13J.
Records: World 5000m 2006 & 2007, 2M 2007 (2); indoor 3000m 2007, 2M 2008 (9:10.50) & 2009 (9:06.26), 5000m 2009; African 5000m 2005, Ethiopian 3000m (2) 2006-07. World 5k road best 14:46 Carlsbad 2006.
Progress at 3000m, 5000m, 10000m: 1999- 9:02.08, 33:54.9A; 2000- 8:59.90, 15:08.36; 2001- 8:52.47, 15:08.65; 2002- 8:40.28, 15:26.45; 2003- 8:38.31, 14:40.34; 2004- 8:33.44i/8:36.46, 14:44.81; 2005- 8:30.05i/8:33.57, 14:28.98; 2006- 8:24.66, 14:24.53; 2007- 8:23.72i/8:24.51, 14:16.63; 2008- 8:27.93i/8:34.53, 14:12.88; 2009- 8:26.99i/8:30.15, 14:24.37i/14:36.38, 29:59.20; 2010- 8:24.46i/8:36.09, 14:24.79i/14:38.87; 2011- 8:36.91i/8:50.36+, 14:29.52, 31:05.05; 2012- 8:31.56i/8:46.49, 14:35.85; 2013- 8:30.29, 14:26.90, 30:08.06. pbs: 1500m 4:02.00 '10, 1M: 4:28.5ei '06, 4:33.07+ '07; 2000m 5:34.74i/ 5:38.0 '06, 2M 8:58.58 '07, road 15k 47:30 '13, HMar 66:09 '13.
Married to Teodros Hailu. IAAF woman athlete of the year 2007. Record nine WAF wins. Daughter Gabriella born on 23 June 2014.

Birhane DIBABA b. 11 Sep 1993 Moyagajo 1.59m 44kg.
Progress at Mar: 2012- 2:29:22, 2013- 2:23:01, 2014- 2:22:30, 2015- 2:23:15. pbs: HMar 71:13 '13, 69:34dh '14.
Won Valencia marathon 2012, Tokyo 2015; 2nd São Paulo 2012, Nagoya 2013, Tokyo 2014; 3rd Frankfurt 2013.

Genzebe DIBABA b. 8 Feb 1991 Bekoji. Muger Cement. 1.68m 52kg.
At 1500m: OG: '12- h; WCh: '13- 8; WI: '12- 1. At 3000m: CCp: '14- 1; WI: '14- 1. At 5000m: WCh: '09 -8, '11- 8; AfCh: '14- 2; WJ: '08- 2, '10- 1; Af-J: '09- 1. World CC: '07-08-09-10-11: 5J/1J/1J/11J/9. Won ETH 1500m 2010.
Records: World indoor 1500m, 3000m & 2M 2014, 5000m 2015. Ethiopian 1500m 2012, 2000m 2014.
Progress at 1500m, 5000m: 2007- 15:53.46, 2008- 15:02.41, 2009- 14:55.52, 2010- 4:04.80i/4:06.10, 15:08.06; 2011- 4:05.90, 14:37.56; 2012- 3:57.77, 2013- 3:57.54, 14:37.68; 2014- 3:55.17i/4:01.00, 14:28.88; 2015- 14:18.86i. pbs: 1M 4:22.2e '14, 2000m 5:27.50 '14, 3000m 8:16.60i/8:26.21 '14, 2M 9:00.48i/ 9:14.28 '14.
Younger sister of Ejegayehu (2 OG 10000m 2004, 3 WCh 5000 & 10000m 2005) and Tirunesh Dibaba.

Mare DIBABA Hurssa b. 20 Oct 1989 Sululta 1.60m 42kg.
At Mar: OG: '12- 23. At HMar: AfG: '11- 1. Won AZE 3000m and 5000m 2009.
AZE records (as Mare Ibrahimova) at 3000m and 5000m 2009.
Progress at HMar, Mar: 2008- 70:28, 2009- 68:45, 2010- 67:13, 2:25:27, 2011- 68:39, 2:23:25; 2012- 67:44, 2:19:52; 2014- 68:56, 2:21:36/2:20:35dh; 2015- 2:19:52. pbs: 3000m 9:16.94 '09, 5000m 15:42.83 '09, Road: 10k 31:55+ '10, 15k 48:04+ '10, 10M 51:29+ '10, 20k 63:47+ '10, 30k 1:39:19 '14.
She switched to Azerbaijan in December 2008 but back to Ethiopia as of 1 Feb 2010. Major marathons: won at Xiamen 2014 and 2015, 2nd Chicago 2014, 3rd Dubal 2012, Boston 2014.

Tirunesh DIBABA Kenene b. 1 Oct 1985 Chefa near Bekoji, Arsi region 1.60m 47kg.
At 5000m(/10000m): OG: '04- 3, '08- 1/1, '12- 3/1; WCh: '03- 1, '05- 1/1, '07- (1), '13- (1); WJ: '02- 2; AfG: '03- 4; AfCh: '06- 2, '08- (1), '10- (1). At 3000m: WCp: '06- 1. World CC: '01-02-03-05-06-07-08-10: 5J/2J/1J/1/1/2/1/4; 4k: '03-04-05: 7/2/1. Won WAF 5000m 2006, ETH 4k CC & 5000m 2003. 8k CC 2005.
World records: 5000m 2008, indoor 5000m 2005 (14:32.93) & 2007, junior 5000m 2003-04, indoor 3000m & 5000m 2004, world road 5k best 14:51 2005, 15k 2009. African 10000m record 2008.
Progress at 5000m, 10000m, Mar: 2002- 14:49.90, 2003- 14:39.94, 2004- 14:30.88, 2005- 14:32.42, 30:15.67; 2006- 14:30.40, 2007- 14:27.42i/14:35.67, 31:55.41; 2008- 14:11.15, 29:54.66; 2009- 14:33.65, 2010- 14:34.07, 31:51.39A; 2012- 14:50.80, 30:20.75; 2013- 14:23.68, 30:26.67; 2014- 2:20:35. pbs: 2000m 5:42.7 '05, 3000m 8:29.55 '06, 2M 9:12.23i '10, road 15k 46:28 '09, HMar 66:56 '13, 30k 1:39:14 '14.
In 2003 she became, at 17 years 333 days, the youngest ever world champion at an individual event and in 2005 the first woman to win the 5000m/10000m double (with last laps of 58.19 and 58.4) at a global event after earlier in the year winning both World CC titles. Now has women's record 21 World CC medals. Married Sileshi Sihine on 26 Oct 2008; son Natan Seleshi born 26 Mar 2015. Retained the Olympic 10,000m title and won the Great North Run on half marathon debut in 2012. Third in London on marathon debut 2014. She has run eleven 10,000m track races – and won them all.

Buze DIRIBA Kejela b. 9 Feb 1994 Arsi 1.60m 43kg.
At 5000m: WCh: '13- 5; WJ: '12- 1. World CC: '11- 10J, '13- 9J
Progress at 5000m: 2012- 14:53.06, 2013- 14:50.02, 2014- 15:16.83. pbs: 1500m 4:10.96 '12, 3000m 8:39.65 '12, 2M 9:40.01 '14, 10k Rd 33:52 '12.

Etenesh DIRO Neda b. 10 May 1991 Jeidu, Oromiya 1.69m 47kg.
At 3000mSt: OG: '12- 5; WCh: '13- 5; AfCh: '14- 4.

Progress at 3000mSt: 2011- 9:49.18, 2012- 9:14.07, 2013- 9:16.97, 2014- 9:19.71. pbs: 3000m 9:00.39 '11, 5000m 15:19.77 '12, Road: 10k 33:32A '11, 15k 51:21 '09, HMar 71:35 '10.

Axumawit EMBAYE Abraya b. 18 Oct 1994 1.60m 50kg.
At 1500m: WJ: '12- 7; WI: '14- 2,
Progress at 1500m: 2012- 4:12.92, 2013- 4:05.16, 2014- 4:02.35, 2015- 4:02.92i. pbs: 800m 2:03.27i '15, 1M 4:23.50i '15.

Erba **Tiki GELANA** b. 22 Oct 1987 Bekoji, Oromiya 1.65m 48kg.
At Mar: OG: '12- 1; WCh: '13- dnf.
Ethiopian marathon record 2012.
Progress at Mar: 2009- 2:33:49, 2010- 2:28:28, 2011- 2:22:08, 2012- 2:18:58, 2013- 2:36:55, 2014- 2:26:58, 2015- 2:24:26. pbs: 3000m 8:55.88 '08, 5000m 15:17.74 '08, 10000m 31:27.80 '08; Road: 15k 48:09 '12, 20k 65:06+ '12, HMar 67:48 '12, 30k 1:40:45 '11.
Won Amsterdam Marathon 2011, Rotterdam 2012; 3rd Tokyo 2015.

Aberu KEBEDE Shewaye b. 12 Sep 1989 Shewa 1.63m 50kg.
At Mar: WCh: '11- 12, '13- 13. World HMar: '09- 3; CC: '07- 16J. Won ETH 10000m 2009.
Progress at 10000m, Mar: 2009- 30:48.26, 2010- 32:17.74, 2:23:58; 2011- 2:24:34, 2012- 31:09.28, 2:20:30; 2013- 2:23:28, 2014- 2:22:21, 2015- 2:21:17. pbs: 5km Rd 15:13 '09, HMar 67:39 '09, 30k 1:39:50 '14.
Won Rotterdam and Berlin marathons 2010 after 2nd Dubai on debut, won Berlin again in 2012 and Tokyo and Shanghai 2013.

Fantu MAGISO Manedo b. 9 Jun 1992 Hosana Lenchicho 1.78m 60kg.
At 800m: WCh: '11- sf, '13- h; WI: '12- 4; AfG: '11- 2. At 400m/400mR: WCh; '09- sf; AfCh: '10- 2R; Af-J: '11- 1/3R (2 200m).
Ethiopian records: 200m (4) 2010-11, 400m 2011, 800m (4) 2011-12.
Progress at 800m: 2011- 1:59.17, 2012- 1:57.48, 2013- 2:00.25. pbs: 200m 23.90A '11, 400m 52.09A, 52.23 '11.

Meselech MELKAMU b. 27 Apr 1985 Debre Markos, Amhara region 1.58m 47kg.
At 5000m(/10000m): OG: '08- 8; WCh: '05- 4, '07- 6, '09- 5/2, '11- (5); AfG: '07- 2, '11- (dnf); AfCh: '06- 6, '08- 1, '10- (2); WJ: '04- 1. At Mar: WCh: '13- dnf. At 3000m: WI: '08- 2. World CC: '03-04-05-06-07-08-09-10-11: 4J/1J/4 & 6/3 & 3/3/9/3/3/4 (17 medals). Won ETH 5000m 2004, 4k CC 2005, CC 2006-07.
African 10000m record 2009.
Progress at 5000m, 10000m, Mar: 2003- 15:27.93, 2004- 15:00.02, 2005- 14:38.97, 2006- 14:37.44, 2007- 14:33.83, 2008- 14:38.78, 31:04.93; 2009- 14:34.17, 29:53.80; 2010- 14:31.91, 31:04.52; 2011- 14:39.44, 30:56.55m 2012- 2:21:01, 2013- 2:25:46, 2014- 2:25:23, 2:21:28dh. pbs: 1500m 4:07.52 '07, 1M 4:33.94 '03, 2000m 5:39.2i+, 5:46.3+ '07; 3000m 8:23.74i '07, 8:34.73 '05, Road: HMar 68:05 '13, 25k 1:23:23 '12, 1:22:27dh '14; 30k 1:39:58 '12, 1:39:21dh '14.
Third fastest ever marathon debut to win at Frankfurt 2012. 2nd Dubai 2014.

Aselefech MERGIA b. 23 Jan 1985 Woliso 1.68m 51kg.
At Mar: OG: '12- 42; WCh: '09- 3, '11- dnf. HMar: WCh: '08- 2. World CC: '08- 16.
Ethiopian marathon record 2012.
Progress at HMar, Mar: 2006- 74:13, 2007- 74:50, 2008- 68:17, 2009- 67:48, 2:25:02; 2010- 67:22, 2:22:38; 2011- 67:21, 2:22:45; 2012- 69:42+, 2:19:31; 2014- 73:49, 2015- 2:20:02. pbs: 1500m 4:14.85 '07, 3000m 8:54.42 '08; Road: 10k 31:25+ '08, 15k 47:53 '09, 20k 63:41 '09, 30k 1:41:52 '09.
2nd Paris Marathon 2009 on debut, 2nd London 2010, won Dubai 2011-12 and 2015. Daughter Sena born in July 2013.

Belaynesh OLJIRA Jemane b. 26 Jun 1990 Welek'a, Amhara 1.65m 49kg.
At 10000m: OG: '12- 5; WCh: '13- 3; AfCh: '14- 3. World CC: '11-13-15: 10/3/9; AfCC: '12- 5. Won ETH 10000m 2011. ETH 1500m record 2012.
Progress at 10000m, Mar: 2011- 31:17.80, 2012- 30:26.70, 2013- 30:31.44, 2:25:01; 2014- 32:49.39, 2:24:21dh. pbs: 1500m 4:33.14 '12, 3000m 8:40.73 '10, 2M 9:23.32 '14, 5000m 14:58.16 '10, Road: 15k 49:08 '14, 10M 52:40 '14, HMar 67:27 '11, 30k 1:39:33dh '14.

Mulu SEBOKA Seyfu b. 13 Jan 1984 1.58m 45kg.
World 25k: '06- 25.
Progress at Mar: 2003- 2:43:30, 2004- 2:37:29, 2005- 2:30:54, 2006- 2:30:41, 2007- 2:33:27, 2008- 2:29:06, 2009- 2:29:38, 2010- 2:30:47, 2011- 2:35:14, 2012- 2:25:45, 2013- 2:23:43, 2014- 2:23:15, 2015- 2:21:56. pbs: 15k 48:38 '12, HMar 70:55+ '14, 30k 1:41:13 '14.
Marathon wins: Mumabi 2005-06, Toronto 2008, Melbourne 2010, Guangzhou 2012, Jakarta 2013, Dubai, Daegu & Toronto 2014.

Dawit SEYAUM b. 27 Jul 1996 Tumano 1.m kg.
At 1500m: WJ: '14- 1; WY: '13- 2; AfCh: '14- 2; Af-J: '13- 1; CCp: '14- 3.
Progress at 1500m: 2013- 4:09.00, 2014- 3:59.53. pbs: 1M 4:32.13i '15, 2000m 5:35.46i '15.

Feysa TADESE Boru b. 19 Nov 1988 1.67m 53kg.
At Mar: WCh: '13- dnf. World HMar: '10- 4, '12- 2; CC: '10- 7.
Progress at Mar: 2009- 2:36:57, 2011- 2:25:20, 2012- 2:23:07, 2013- 2:21:06, 2014- 2:20:27. pbs: 10000m 32:29.07 '10, Road: 10k 32:21 '13, 15k 48:51 '12, 20k 65:41 '12, HMar 68:35 '13, 30k 1:39:18 '14.
Four wins in nine marathons: Seoul and Shanghai 2012, Paris 2013, Tokyo 2014; 2nd Berlin 2014.

Senbera TEFERI b. 3 May 1995 1.59m 45kg. Oromiya.
At 1500m: WCh: '13- h; WJ: '12- 3; WY: '11- 2; World CC: '15- 2.
Progress at 1500m: 2011- 16:09.0A, 2012- 15:36.74, 2013- 4:04.55, 2014- 4:08.49. pbs: 2000m 5:34.27 '14, 3000m 8:41.54 '14, 5000m 16:21.0A '13, 5k Rd 15:43 '14.

Tirfi TSEGAYE Beyene b. 25 Nov 1984 Bokoji 1.65m 54kg.
World HMar: '09- 6.
Progress at Mar: 2008- 2:35:32, 2009- 2:28:16, 2010- 2:22:44, 2011- 2:24:12, 2012- 2:21:19, 2013- 2:23:23, 2014- 2:20:18. pbs: 15k 49:48 '14, HMar 67:42 '12, 30k 1:39:17 '14.
Marathon wins: Porto 2008, Paris 2012, Dubai 2013, Tokyo & Berlin 2014.

FINLAND

Governing body: Suomen Urheiluliitto, Radiokatu 20, SF-00240 Helsinki. Founded 1906.
National Championships first held in 1907 (men), 1913 (women). **2014 Champions**: **Men**: 100m/200m: Eetu Rantala 10.58/21.08, 400m/800m: Ville Lampinen 47.85/1:50.45, 1500m: Jukka Keskisalo 3:55.27, 5000m/10000m: Lewis Korir KEN 14:14.70/29:42.98, HMar: Jussi Utriainen 66:47, Mar: Marko Tuokko 2:27:51, 3000mSt: Janne Ukonmaanaho 8:49.05, 110mh: Jussi Kanervo 13.90, 400mh: Oskari Mörö 50.33, HJ: Jussi Viita 2.26, PV: Jouni Marjaniemi 5.20, LJ: Kristian Pulli 7.81, TJ: Aleksi Tammentie 16.55, SP: Arttu Kangas 19.22, DT: Pyri Niskala 60.71, HT: David Söderberg 75.75, JT: Antti Ruuskanen 83.70, Dec: Toomy Barrineau 7609, 20kW: Jarkko Kinnunen 1:27:07. **Women**: 100m/200m: Hanna-Maari Latvala 11.50/23.24, 400m: Katri Mustola 53.20, 800m: Karin Storbacka 2:07.00, 1500m/3000mSt: Sandra Eriksson 4:24.01/9:49.46, 5000m: Johanna Peiponen 16:23.02, 10000m: Minna Lamminen 35:30.31, HMar: Hanna Jantunen 76:42, Mar: Anne-Mari Hyryläinen 2:45:24, 100mh: Nooralotta Neziri 13.03, 400mh: Anniina Laitinen 58.26, HJ: Elina Smolander 1.86, PV: Minna Nikkanen 4.51, LJ: Emmi Mäkinen 6.28, TJ: Elina Torro 13.37, SP/DT: Sanna Kämäräinen 14.92/58.56, HT: Merja Korpela 65.67, JT: Oona Sormunen 56.95, Hep: Jutta Heikkinen 5202, 10kW: Taika Nummi 48:21, 20kW: Anne Halkivaha 1:44:54.

Lassi ETELÄTALO b. 30 Apr 1988 Helsinki 1.93m 90kg. Joemsuun Kataja.
At JT: EC: '14- 4; EU23: '09- 9; EJ: '07- dnq 15.
Progress at JT: 2006- 66.70, 2007- 68.81, 2008- 76.07, 2009-79.70, 2010- 77.58, 2011- 84.41, 2012- 84.06, 2013- 80.39, 2014- 84.98.

Ari MANNIO b. 23 Jul 1987 Lehtimäki 1.85m 104kg. Lehtimäen Jyske.
At JT: OG: '12- 11; WCh: '11- dnq 14; EC: '12- 3; WJ: '04- 6, '06- 2; EU23: '07- 4, '09- 1; EJ: '05- 3; ET: '10- 3. Finnish champion 2011.
Progress at JT: 2004- 70.83, 2005- 76.40, 2006- 79.68, 2007- 80.31, 2008- 81.54, 2009- 85.70, 2010- 85.12, 2011- 85.12, 2012- 84.62, 2013- 84.65, 2014- 83.70.

Tero PITKÄMÄKI b. 19 Dec 1982 Ilmajoki 1.95m 92kg. Nurmon Urheilijat. Electrical engineer.
At JT: OG: '04- 8, '08- 3, '12- 5; WCh: '05-07-09-11-13: 4/1/5/dnq 17/2; EC: '06-10-12-14: 2/3/11/3; EU23: '03- 3; EJ: '01- 6; ECp: '06- 1. Won WAF 2005, 2007; Finnish 2004-07, 2013.
Progress at JT: 1999- 66.83, 2000- 73.75, 2001- 74.89, 2002- 77.24, 2003- 80.45, 2004- 84.64, 2005- 91.53, 2006- 91.11, 2007- 91.23, 2008- 87.70, 2009- 87.79, 2010- 86.92, 2011- 85.33, 2012- 86.98, 2013- 89.03, 2014- 86.63.
Partner is Niina Kelo (b. 26 Mar 1980) pb Hep 5956 (15 EC 2006).

Antti RUUSKANEN b. 21 Feb 1984 Kokkola 1.89m 86kg. Pielaveden Sampo.
At JT: OG: '12- 3; WCh: '09-11-13: 6/9/5; EC: '14- 1; EU23: '05- 2; EJ: '03- 3; CCp: '14- 8. Finnish champion 2012, 2014.
Progress at JT: 2002- 66.08, 2003- 72.87, 2004- 75.84, 2005- 79.75, 2006- 84.10, 2007- 82.71/87.88dh, 2008- 87.33, 2009- 85.39, 2010- 83.45, 2011- 82.29, 2012- 87.79, 2013- 85.70, 2014- 88.01.

FRANCE

Governing body: Fédération Française d'Athlétisme, 33 avenue Pierre de Coubertin, 75640 Paris cedex 13. Founded 1920.
National Championships first held in 1888 (men), 1918 (women). **2014 Champions: Men**: 100m/200m: Christophe Lemaitre 10.14/20.53, 400m: Mame-Ibra Anne 45.80, 800m: Pierre-Ambroise Bosse 1;45.47, 1500m: Mahiédine Mekhissi-Benabbad 3:46.75, 5000m/Mar: Bouabdellah Tahri 14:20.66/2:16:28, 10000m: El Hassane Ben Lkhainouch 28:29.49, HMar: James Theuri 64:39; 3000mSt: Yoann Kowal 8:49.14, 110mh: Pascal Martinot-Lagarde 13.10, 400mh: Adrien Clemenceau 50.05, HJ: Mickaël Hanany 2.25, PV: Renaud Lavillenie 5.80, LJ: Salim Sdiri 7.96, TJ: Yoann Rapinier 17.16, SP: Gaëtan Bucki 20.01, DT: Lolassonn Djouhan 57.90, HT: Jérôme Bortoluzzi 74.01, JT: Jeremy Nicollin 74.41, Dec: Florian Geffrouais 8164, 10000mW: Yohann Diniz 38:08.13, 20kW: Antonin Boyez 1:26:55, 50kW: Cédric Houssaye 3:58:54. **Women**: 100m: Myriam Soumaré 11.08w, 200m: Céline Distel-Bonnet 24.09, 400m: Marie Gayot 52.27, 800m: Renelle Lamote 2:02.01, 1500m: Clémence Calvin 4:16.21, 5000m: Laila Traby 15:59.60, 10000m: Laure Funten 34:58.68, HMar: Patricia Laubertie 74:50, Mar: Élodie Navarro 2:43:56, 3000mSt: Claire Perraux 9:58.09, 100mh: Cindy Billaud 12.58, 400mh: Aurélie Chaboudez 57.36, HJ: Mélanie Skotnik 1.85, PV: Vanessa

Boslak 4.45, LJ: Éloyse Lesueur 6.86, TJ: Nathalie Marie-Nélly 13.91, SP: Jessica Cérival 17.02, DT: Mélina Robert-Michon 61.42, HT: Alexandra Tavernier 66.99, JT: Mathilde Andraud 58.25, Hep: Marissa De Aniceto 5556, 10000mW: Émilie Tissot 46:36.92, 20kW: Émilie Menuet 1:36:52.

Dimitri BASCOU b. 20 Jul 1987 Schoelcher, Martinique 1.82m 79kg. Racing Club de France.
At 110mh: OG: '12- sf; WCh: '09/11- sf; EC: '10- 4, 14- dq; EU23: '07- h, '09- 4; EJ: '05- h; won FRA 2009-11. At 60mh: EI: '11- 6, '15- 2.
Progress at 110mh: 2004- 14.61w, 2005- 14.35, 2006- 14.24, 2007- 13.76, 2008- 13.61/13.39w, 2009- 13.49, 2010- 13.41, 2011- 13.37/13.26w, 2012- 13.34, 2013- 13.51, 2014- 13.25. pbs: 60m 6.88i '14, 100m 10.72 '07, 200m 21.62 '09, 50mh 6.57i '12, 60mh 7.46i '15.
Disqualified after finishing 3rd at the 2014 Europeans.

Wilhem BELOCIAN b. 22 Jun 1995 Guadeloupe 1.79m 70kg. Stade Lamertin.
At 110mh: WJ: '12- 3, '14- 1; WY: '11- (3 Med R); EJ: '13- 1; At 60mh: EI: '15- 3.
World junior record 99cm 110mh 12.99 in 2014, three European JR 2014-14.
Progress at 110mh: 2014- 13.54. pbs: 60m 6.82i '12, 100m 10.73 '13, 60mh 7.52i '15.

Pierre-Ambroise BOSSE b. 11 May 1992 Nantes 1.85m 68kg. UA Gujan Mestras.
At 800m: OG: '12- sf; WCh: '13- 7; EC: '12- 3, '14- 8; WJ: '10- 8; EU23: '13- 1; EJ: '11- 1. French champion 2012, 2014.
French 800m record 2014, European U23 1000m 2014.
Progress at 800m: 2007- 2:02.81, 2008- 1:56.05, 2010- 1:48.38, 2011- 1:46.18, 2012- 1:44.97, 2013- 1:43.76, 2014- 1:42.53. pbs: 400m 48.54 '11, 600m 1:15.63i '13, 1000m 2:15.31 '14, 1500m 3:54.81 '09.

Benjamin COMPAORÉ b. 5 Aug 1987 Bar-le-Duc 1.89m 86kg. Strasbourg AA.
At TJ: OG: '12- 6; WCh: '11- 8; EC: '10- 5, '14- 1; WJ: '06- 1; EJ: '05- 9; CCp: '14- 1; WI: '12- 6. FRA champion 2014.
Progress at TJ: 2003- 14.50, 2004- 15.48, 2005- 16.00/16.12w, 2006- 16.61, 2007- 16.62, 2008- 17.05, 2009- 16.98, 2010- 17.21/17.28w, 2011- 17.31, 2012- 17.17, 2013- 17.07, 2014- 17.48. pbs: 60m 7.13i '08, 100m 10.76 '13, 400m 48.69 '12, 1500m 4:44.43 '12, 110mh 15.72 '12, HJ 1.98 '12, LJ 7.88 '08, Dec 6704 '12.

Yohann DINIZ b. 1 Jan 1978 Epernay 1.85m 69kg. EFS Reims Athlétisme.
At 20kW: ECp: '07- 1; At 50kW: OG: '08- dnf, '12- dq; WCh: '05-07-09-11-13: dq/2/12/dq/10; EC: '06-10-14: 1/1/1; ECp: '05- 4, '13- 1. Won French 10000mW 2010, 2012, 2014; 20kW 2007-09, 50kW 2005.
World walks records: track 50,000m 2011, road 50k 2014, 20k 2015. French records 5000mW (3) 2006-08, 10000mW 2014, 20000mW 2014, 20kW (4) 2005-15, 50kW 2006 & 2009, 1 Hr 2010.
Progress at 20kW, 50kW: 2001- 1:35:05.0t, 2002- 1:30:40, 2003- 1:26:54.99t, 2004- 1:24:25, 3:52:11.0t; 2005- 1:20:20, 3:45:17; 2006- 1:23:19, 3:41:39; 2007- 1:18:58, 3:44:22; 2008- 1:22:31, 2009- 1:22:50, 3:38:45; 2010- 1:20:23, 3:40:37; 2011- 3:35:27.2t, 2012- 1:17:43, 2013- 1:23:17, 3:41:07; 2014- 1:19:42.1t, 3:32:33 ; 2015- 1:17:02. pbs: 3000mW 10:52.44 '08, 5000mW 18:16.76i '14, 18:18.01 '08; 10000mW 38:08.13 '14, 20000mW 1:19:42.1 '14, 1HrW 15,395m '10, 35kW 2:32:24 '12.

Mamadou Kassé HANN b. 6 Mar 1988 Pikine, Dakar 1.90m 73kg. Lives in France.
At 400mh OG: '12- sf; WCh: '13- 7; AfG: '07- h; AfCh: '06-08-10-12: h/h&3R/3/2; CCp: '10- 4.
Progress at 400mh: 2005- 54.41, 2006- 51.82, 2007- 51.26, 2008- 50.22, 2009- 50.63, 2010- 48.89, 2011- 50.38, 2012- 48.80, 2013- 48.50, 2014- 48.86. pbs: 200m 21.23 '10, 400m 46.13 '10.
Switched allegiance to France after the 2014 season.

Yoann KOWAL b. 28 May 1987 Nogent-le-Rotrou 1.72m 58kg. E. Périgueux Sarlat Trélissac.
At 1500m: OG: '12- sf; WCh: '09- h, '11- sf; EC: '10- 5; EU23: '09- 6; ET: '09- 3. At 3000mSt: WCh: '13- 8; EC: '14- 1; WJ: '06- h; EU23: '07- 11; ET: '13- 3, '14- 1. Won FRA 1500m 2008, 2010; 3000mSt 2014.
Progress at 3000mSt: 2006- 8:56.54, 2007- 8:36.11, 2008- 8:34.66, 2009- 9:02.38, 2011- 8:41.07, 2012- 8:21.66, 2013- 8:12.53, 2014- 8:25.50. pbs: 800m 1:47.95 '10, 1000m 2:20.43 '10, 1500m 3:33.75 '11, 2000m 5:04.18 '13, 3000m 7:44.26i '12, 7:56.88 '11; 5000m 14:40.02 '06, 10k Rd 29:01 '11.

Renaud LAVILLENIE b. 18 Sep 1986 Barbezieux-Saint-Hilaire 1.77m 69kg. Clermont Athl. Auvergne.
At PV: OG: '12- 1; WCh: '09- 3, '11- 3, '13- 2; WI: '12- 1; EC: '10-12-14: 1/1/1; EU23: '07- 10; EI: '09-11-13-15: 1/1/1/1; CCp: '10- 2, '14- 1; ET: '09-10-13-14: 1/1/1/1. Won DL 2010-14, French 2010, 2012-14.
World indoor pole vault record 2014. French record (indoors) 2011 and outdoors 2013.
Progress at PV: 2002- 3.40, 2003- 4.30, 2004- 4.60, 2005- 4.81i/4.70, 2006- 5.25i/5.22, 2007- 5.58i/5.45, 2008- 5.81i/5.65, 2009- 6.01, 2010- 5.94, 2011- 6.03i/5.90, 2012- 5.97, 2013- 6.02, 2014- 6.16i/5.93, 2015- 6.04i. pbs: 60m 7.23i '08, 100m 11.04 '11, 60mh 8.41i '08, 100m 11.04 '11, 110mh 14.51 '10, HJ 1.89i '08, 1.87 '07; LJ 7.31 '10, Hep 5363i '08.
Broke Sergey Bubka's 21 year-old absolute world pole vault record indoors in 2014. 23 successive wins 31 Aug 2013 to EC 2014, only man to win all five Diamond League titles from 2010. IAAF Male Athlete of the Year 2014. His brother **Valentin** (b. 16 Jul 1991) has PV pb 5.80i '15, 5.65 '13; 3rd EU23 and nh WCh in 2013; 6 EI '15.

Christophe LEMAITRE b. 11 Jun 1990 Annecy 1.89m 74kg. AS Aix-les-Bains.
At 100m/(200m): OG: '12- (6); WCh: '09- qf, '11- 4/3/2R, '13- 7; EC: '10- 1/1/1R, '12- 1/3R, '14- 2/2/3R; WJ: '08- (1); WY: '07- 4/5; EJ: '09- 1; CCp: '10- 1, '14- 5/4/2R; ET: '10- 2, '11- 1/1, '13- (1). At 60m: EI: '11- 3. Won French 100m 2010-12, 2014; 200m 2010-14.
Records: European 4x200m 2014; French 100m (7) 2010-11, 200m (2) 2010-11, European junior 100m 2009. U23 100m 2010-11, 200m 2011.
Progress at 100m, 200m: 2005- 11.46, 2006- 10.96, 2007- 10.53, 21.08; 2008- 10.26, 20.83; 2009- 10.04/10.03w, 20.68; 2010- 9.97, 20.16; 2011- 9.92, 19.80; 2012- 10.04/9.94w, 19.91; 2013- 10.00/9.98w, 20.07; 2014- 10.10, 20.08. pbs: 60m 6.55i '10, 150m St 14.90 '13.
First Caucasian sub-10.00 100m runner and first to win sprint treble at European Champs; now has men's record eight EC medals.

Pascal MARTINOT-LAGARDE b. 22 Sep 1991 St Maur-des-Fossés 1.90m 80kg. Neuilly Plaisance Sport.
At 110mh: WCh: '13- h; EC: '14- 3; WJ: '10- 1; EU23: '11- h; EJ: '09- 4; ET: '13- 2, '14- 3; won DL 2014, FRA 2014. At 60mh: WI: '12- 3, '14- 2; EI: '13- 3, '15- 1. French 110m hurdles record 2014.
Progress at 110mh: 2008- 15.03, 2009- 14.13, 2010- 13.74, 2011- 13.94, 2012- 13.41/13.30w, 2013- 13.12, 2014- 12.95. pbs: 60m 7.07i '10, 100m 10.94 '13, 60mh 7.45i '14.
His brother **Thomas** (b. 7 Feb 1988) has 110mh pb 13.26, 7 WCh and French champion in 2013.

Kevin MAYER b. 10 Feb 1992 Argenteuil 1.86m 77kg. EA Tain-Tournon.
At Dec: OG: '12- 15; WCh: '13- 4; EC: '12- dnf, '14- 2; WJ: '10- 1; EJ: '11- 1; ECp: '13- 1. At Oct: WY: '09- 1. At Hep: EI: '13- 2.
Progress at Dec: 2011- 7992, 2012- 8447w/8415, 2013- 8446, 2014- 8521. pbs: 60m 7.10i '13, 100m 11.04 '13, 400m 48.66 '11, 1000m 2:37.30i '13, 1500m 4:18.04 '12, 60mh 8.01i '13, 110mh 14.21 '12, HJ 2.10i '10, 2.09 '12; PV 5.20 '12, LJ 7.65 '14, SP 15.16i '13, 15.14 '14; DT 45.37 '13, JT 66.09 '13, Hep 6297i '13.

Mahiédine MEKHISSI-BENABBAD b. 15 Mar 1985 Reims 1.90m 75kg. EFS Reims.
At 3000mSt: OG: '08- 2, '12- 2; WCh: '07/09- h, '11- 3, '13- 3; EC: '10- 1, '12- 1, '14- dq (1 1500m); WJ: '04- h; EU23: '05- h, '07- 1; CCp: '10- 3; ECp: '07- 2, '08- 1. At 1500m: WI: '10- 8; EI: '13- 1; WCp: '06- 7, '14- 3. Won FRA 1500m 2014, 3000mSt 2008, 2012-13.
Records: World best 2000m steeplechase 2010. European 3000mSt 2013, French 1M 2014.
Progress at 3000mSt: 2003- 9:52.07, 2004- 9:01.01, 2005- 8:34.45, 2006- 8:28.25, 2007- 8:14.22, 2008- 8:08.95, 2009- 8:06.98, 2010- 8:02.52, 2011- 8:02.09, 2012- 8:10.90, 2013- 8:00.09, 2014- 8:03.23. pbs: 800m 1:53.61 '04, 1000m 2:17.14 '09, 1500m 3:33.12 '13, 1M 3:51.55 '14, 2000m 4:56.85 '13, 3000m 7:43.72i '13, 7:44.98 '10; 5000m 14:32.9 '05, 2000mSt 5:10.68 '10.
Disqualified after he took his vest off in the finishing straight when finishing well clear in 2014 EC steeplechase.

Yoann RAPINIER b. 29 Sep 1989 Pontoise 1.82m 70kg. Franconville Ermont.
At TJ: WCh: '13- 12; EC: '14- 4; EU23: '09- 9; EI: '11- 4. Won FRA 2014, Franc G 2013.
Progress at TJ: 2004- 12.56i, 2005- 12.83, 2007- 14.04i, 2008- 15.69, 2009- 16.24, 2010- 16.58/16.73w, 2011- 17.23i/16.39/16.46w, 2012- 16.76, 2013- 17.45, 2014- 17.16. pbs: 100m 10.85 '10, 200m 22.16 '10, 400m 47.80 '10, 400mh 54.17 '07, HJ 2.15i/2.08 '08, LJ 7.30 '10.

Bouabdellah 'Bob' TAHRI b. 20 Dec 1978 Metz 1.91m 68kg. Athlétisme Metz Métropole.
At 3000mSt: OG: '00- h, '04- 7, '08- 5; WCh: '99-01-03-05-07-09-11: 12/5/4/8/5/3/4; EC: '98-02-06-10: 10/4/3/2; WJ: '96- 7; WCp: '06- 3; ECp: '00-01-02-04: 1/1/1/1. At 5000m: EC: '14- 6 (7 10000m); EJ: '97- 1; CCp: '10- 3, '14- 6; ECp: '05- 2, '13- 2. At 3000m: WI: '01- 11; EI: '98-07-09: 8/2/2; ECp: '07- 1, '13- 1. At 1500m: WCh: '13- sf. World CC: '97- 22J, '04- 15 4k; Eur CC: '05- 4, '08- 6. Won FRA 1500m 2004, 2006; 5000m & Mar 2014, 3000mSt 1998, 2010-11.
Three European records 3000mSt 2003-09, indoor 5000m (13:11.13) 2010; best 2000mSt 2002 & 2009. World best 2000mSt 2010.
Progress at 3000mSt: 1996- 8:44.65, 1998- 8:19.75, 1999- 8:12.24, 2000- 8:16.14, 2001- 8:09.23, 2002- 8:10.83, 2003- 8:06.91, 2004- 8:14.26, 2005- 8:09.58, 2006- 8:09.53, 2007- 8:09.06, 2008- 8:12.72, 2009- 8:01.18, 2010- 8:03.72, 2011- 8:05.72. pbs: 800m 1:48.96 '01, 1000m 2:20.34 '05, 1500m 3:32.73 '13, 1M 3:52.95 '02, 2000m 4:57.58 '02, 3000m 7:33.18 '09, 5000m 13:12.22 '14, 10000m 27:31.46 '11, 15k Rd 43:49 '12, HMar 63:38 '13, Mar 2:16:28 '14, 2000mSt 5:13.47 '10.
Missed 2012 season through injury and has concentrated on the flat since then.

Teddy TAMGHO b. 15 Jun 1989 Paris 1.87m 82kg. CA Montreuil.
At TJ: WCh: '09- 11, '13- 1; EC: '10- 3; WI: '10- 1; WJ: '08- 1; EJ: '07- 4; EI: '11- 1 (4 LJ); ET: '10- 3, '13- 2. Won DL 2010, French 2009-10, 2013.
Four World indoor triple jump records 2010 (17.90) & 2011, four absolute French records 2009-13; three Eur U23 records 2010.
Progress at TJ: 2004- 12.56, 2005- 14.89, 2006- 15.58, 2007- 16.53i/16.35/16.42w, 2008- 17.19/17.33w, 2009- 17.58i/17.11, 2010- 17.98, 2011- 17.92i/17.91, 2013- 18.04. pbs: 60m 6.92i '06, 100m 10.60 '09, LJ 8.01i '11, 7.81 '13.
2011 season ended when broke ankle in warm-up for European U23s and also missed all of 2012. His 18.04 to win 2013 World title was third best ever and world's best for 17 years. Fractured his shin in November 2013 and missed all the 2014 season.

Jimmy VICAUT b. 27 Feb 1992 Bondy 1.88m 83kg. Paris Avenir Athletic.
At 100m/(200m)/4x100mR: OG: '12- sf; WCh: '11- 6/2R, '13- sf/sf; EC: '10- 1R, '12- 2/3R (res), '14- sf; WJ: '10- 3; WY: '09- 7; EJ: '11- 1/1R; ET: '13- 1, '14- 1. At 60m: EI: '13- 1. Won French 100m 2013.
Progress at 100m: 2005- 13.0, 2006- 12.50, 2007- 11.0, 2008- 10.75/10.69w, 2009- 10.56, 2010- 10.16, 2011- 10.07, 2012- 10.02, 2013- 9.95, 2014- 9.95/ 9.89w. pbs: 60m 6.48i '13, 200m 20.30 '13.
His brother Willi was French U17 shot champion in 2012 and has senior pb of 17.33 '14.

Women

Cindy BILLAUD b. 11 Mar 1986 Nogent-sur-Marne 1.67m 59kg. US Créteil.
At 100mh: WCh: '09- sf, '11- h, '13- 7; EC: '14- 2; WJ: '04- sf; EU23: '07- sf; EJ: '05- 3; ET: '14- 1; FRA champion 2013-14. At 60mh: WI: '14- 4; EI: '09- 7.
French 100mh record 2014.
Progress at 100mh: 2004- 13.48, 2005- 13.57, 2006- 13.49/13.46w, 2007- 13.25, 2008- 12.99/12.97w, 2009- 12.97, 2010- 13.11, 2011- 12.93, 2012- 12.97, 2013- 12.59, 2014- 12.56. pbs: 60m 7.64i '08, 100m 12.00 '05, 200m 24.68 '08, 50mh 7.14+i '12, 60mh 7.87i '14.

Éloyse LESUEUR b. 15 Jul 1988 Créteil 1.79m 65kg. SCO Saint Marguerite, Marseille.
At LJ: OG: '12- 8; WCh: '09- 11-13: dnq 18/26/22; EC: '14- 1; WI: '08- 4, '12- 1; WY: '05- 2 (7 100m); EC: '12- 1; EU23: '09- 3; EJ: '07- 2; EI: '11-13-15: 4/2/5; CCp: '14- 5; ET: '10-11-13-14: 1/3/1/2. Won FRA 2006, 2010-14. At Hep: WJ: '06- dnf.
Progress at LJ: 2002- 5.72, 2003- 5.50, 2004- 5.68, 2005- 6.40, 2006- 6.30/6.47w, 2007- 6.47, 2008- 6.84i/6.50, 2009- 6.64/6.72w, 2010- 6.78, 2011- 6.91, 2012- 6.81/7.04w, 2013- 6.90i/6.78, 2014- 6.92/6.94w. pbs: 60m 7.34i '12, 100m 11.54, 11.52w '14, 200m 24.11 '06, 800m 2:21.67 '06, 100mh 13.89 '06, HJ 1.75 '06, Hep 5370w/5320 '06.

Antoinette NANA DJIMOU Ida b. 2 Aug 1985 Douala, Cameroon 1.74m 69kg. CA Montreuil.
At Hep: OG: '08- 18, '12- 5; WCh: '07-09-11-13: dnf/7/7/8; EC: '06-10-12-14: 21/dnf/1/1; WJ: '04- 4; EU23: '05- 5, '07- 7; ECp: '08- 2, '14- 2. At Pen: WI: '10- 4; EI: '09-11-13-15: 3/1/1/5. Won French LJ 2008, Hep 2006-07.
CMR heptathlon record 2003, French indoor pentathlon record 2011.
Progress at Hep: 2003- 5360, 2004- 5649, 2005- 6089w/5792, 2006- 5981, 2007- 5982, 2008- 6204, 2009- 6323, 2010- 5994, 2011- 6409, 2012- 6576, 2013- 6326, 2014- 6551. pbs: 60m 7.51i '11, 100m 11.78 '08, 200m 24.36 '11, 800m 2:15.22 '14, 60mh 8.11i '10, 100mh 12.96 '12, HJ 1.84i '10, 1.83 '11; LJ 6.44i '09, 6.42 '12, 6.61w '08; SP 15.41i/14.84 '13, JT 57.27 '12, Pen 4723i '11.
Came to France at age 14, naturalised French citizen in 2004. Three pbs when winning European gold in 2012.

Mélina ROBERT-MICHON b. 18 Jul 1979 Voiron 1.80m 85kg. Lyon Athlétisme
At DT: OG: '00/04- dnq 29/30, '08- 8, '12- 5; WCh: '01-03-07-09-13: dnq 20/11/11/8/2; EC: '98-02-06-12-14: dnq 29/12/dnq 16/6/2; WJ: '98- 2; EU23: '99-12, '01- 1; WUG: '01- 3; CCp: '14- 4; ECp: '00-01-02-03-04-06-07-08-09-13-14: 5/6/8/ 2/4/7/5/4/2/1/1. French champion 2000-09, 2011-14; MedG 2009.
Five French discus records 2000-13.
Progress at DT: 1997- 49.10, 1998- 59.27, 1999- 60.17, 2000- 63.19/63.61dh, 2001- 63.87, 2002- 65.78, 2003- 64.27, 2004- 64.54, 2005- 58.01, 2006- 59.89, 2007- 63.48, 2008- 62.21, 2009- 63.04, 2010- 56.52, 2011- 61.07, 2012- 63.98, 2013- 66.28, 2014- 65.51. pbs: SP 15.23 '07, HT 47.92 '02.
Daughter Elyssa born in 2010. Broke her 11 year-old French record in winning 2013 World silver.

Myriam SOUMARÉ b. 29 Oct 1986 Paris 1.67m 57kg. AA Pays de France Athlé 95.
At 100m/(200m): OG: '12- sf/7; WCh: '09- qf, '11-13: sf/sf; EC: '10- 3/1/2R, '12- (3), '14- 2/3/2R; EU23: '07- 3; CCp: '14- 5/3; ET: '13- 2/2, '14- 1. At 4x400m: EJ: '05- 7. At 60m: WI: '10- 7; EI: '11- 7, '13- 2. Won FRA 100m 2009, 2012-14; 200m 2011-13.
Progress at 100m: 2004- 24.66i, 2005- 12.07/ 11.98w, 24.05; 2006- 11.68, 23.78; 2007- 11.50/11.39w, 23.44; 2008- 11.43, 23.64/23.40w; 2009- 11.34, 23.34; 2010- 11.18/11.13w, 22.32; 2011- 11.17/ 11.12w, 22.71; 2012- 11.07, 22.56; 2013- 11.30, 22.83/22.81w; 2014- 11.03, 22.11. pbs: 50m 6.22i '10, 55m 6.86i '13, 60m 7.07i '13, 400m 52.83 '14.
Astonishing breakthrough in final of European 200m 2010 when she improved pb from 23.01 to win in 22.32. Daughter Elyssa born in 2010. Parents came from Mauritania.

GERMANY

Governing body: Deutscher Leichtathletik Verband (DLV), Alsfelder Str. 27, 64289 Darmstadt. Founded 1898.

National Championships first held in 1891. **2014 Champions**: **Men**: 100m: Julian Reus 10.01w; 200m: Robin Erewa 20.61, 400m: Kamghe Gaba 45.82, 800m: Dennis Krüger 1:48.91, 1500m: Tomo Benitz 3:57.53, 5000m/ 10000m: Richard Ringer 13:43.45/28:28.96, HMar: Manuel Stöckert 65:04, Mar: Tobias Schreindl 2:21:50, 3000mSt: Steffen Uliczka 8:35.82, 110mh: Matthias Bühler 13.20w, 400mh: Felix Franz 49.34, HJ: Martin Günther 2.25, PV: Tobias Scharbarth 5.60, LJ: Markus Rehm (prosthetic leg) 8.24, TJ: Manuel Ziegler 16.54, SP: David Storl 21.87, DT: Robert Harting 66.67, HT: Markus Esser 75.18, JT: Thomas Röhler 84.28, Dec: René Stauss 7735, 10000W/20kW: Christopher Linke 39:42.12/1:21:18, 50kW: Nils

Brembach 3:54:47. **Women**: 100m: Tatjana Pinto 11.20, 200m: Rebekka Haase 23.24, 400m: Esther Cremer 52.56, 800m: Christina Hering 2:01.45, 1500m: Maren Kock 4:20.85, 5000m: Sabrina Mockenhaupt 15:49.63, 10000m: Corinna Harrer 32:27.75, HMar: Susanne Hahn 74:29, Mar: Steffi Volke 2:44:40, 3000mSt: Antje Möldner-Schmidt 9:46.86, 100mh: Nadine Hildebrand 12.71, 400mh: Christiane Klopsch 56.13, HJ: Marie-Laurence Jungfleisch 1.90, PV: Lisa Ryzih 4.50, LJ: Melanie Bauschke 6.66, TJ: Kristin Gierisch 14.34w, SP: Christina Schwanitz 19.69, DT: Shanice Craft 65.88, HT: Kathrin Klaas 72.08, JT: Linda Stahl 63.55, Hep: Anna Maiwald 5864; 20kW: Bianca Schenker 1:43:39.

Arthur ABELE b. 30 Jul 1986 Mutlangen, Baden-Württemberg 1.84m 80kg. SSV Ulm 1846.
At Dec: OG: '08- dnf; WCh: '07- 9; EC: '14- 5; WJ: '04- 7; EJ: '05- 2; ECp: '04- 4. German champion 2013. At Hep: '15- 2.
Progress at Dec: 2006- 8012, 2007- 8269, 2008- 8372, 2013- 8251, 2014- 8477. pbs: 60m 6.93i '15, 100m 10.67 '14, 200m 22.41 '14, 400m 47.98 '08, 1000m 2:35.64i '15, 1500m 4:15.35 '08, 60mh 7.67i '15, 110mh 13.55 '14, 400mh 51.71 '04, HJ 2.04 '07, PV 5.01 '14, LJ 7.56i '15, 7.55 '14; SP 15.54i '15, 15.39 '14; DT 44.69 '14, JT 69.53 '13, Hep 6279i '15.
Five individual event absolute bests in European Indoor silver heptathlon 2015.

Sebastian BAYER b. 11 Jun 1986 Aachen 1.89m 79kg. Hamburger SV. Soldier.
At LJ: OG: '08- dnq 23, '12- 5; WCh: '09- dnq 19, '11- 8, '13- 8; EC: '06-12-14: dnq 20/1/dnq 23; WJ: '04- dnq 17; EJ: '05- 2; EI: '09- 1, '11- 1. German champion 2006, 2008-09, 2011-12.
Progress at LJ: 2000- 5.65, 2001- 6.14, 2002- 6.57, 2003- 7.27, 2004- 7.57, 2005- 7.82i/7.73, 2006- 7.95, 2007- 7.88i, 2008- 8.15, 2009- 8.71i/8.49, 2010- 8.06, 2011- 8.17, 2012- 8.34, 2013- 8.04, 2014- 8.05. pbs: 60m 6.80i '09, 100m 10.73 '09, HJ 1.83 '03, JT 50.17 '14.
Sensational improvement at 2009 European Indoors – from pb of 8.17 to 8.29 and then European record 8.71 with final jump.

Pascal BEHRENBRUCH b. 19 Jan 1985 Offenbach 1.96m 94kg. LG Eintracht Frankfurt.
At Dec: OG: '12- 10; WCh: '09- 6, '11- 7, '13- 11; EC: '06- 5, '12- 1; EJ: '03- 10; EU23: '07- 2. At Hep: WI: '14- 8.
Progress at Dec: 2005- 7842, 2006- 8209, 2007- 8239, 2008- 8242, 2009- 8439, 2010- 8202, 2011- 8232, 2012- 8558, 2013- 8514, 2014- 8055. pbs: 60m 7.08i '10, 100m 10.84 '07, 10.73w '13; 400m 48.40 '13, 1000m 2:53.39i '06, 1500m 4:24.16 '06, 60mh 8.10i '10, 110mh 14.02 '09, HJ 2.03 '08, PV 5.00 '12, LJ 7.21 '11, 7.32w '07, SP 16.89 '12, DT 51.31 '09, JT 71.40 '11, Hep 5604i '06.

Markus ESSER b. 3 Feb 1980 Leverkusen 1.80m 105kg. TSV Bayer 04 Leverkusen. Army lieutenant.
At HT: OG: '00-04-08: dnq 35/10/9; WCh: '05-07-09-11-13: 4/8/6/4/10; EC: '02-06-10-12: dnq 29/4/dnq 19/7; WJ: '98- 12; EJ: '99- 3; EU23: '01- 7; ECp: '04-05-07-08-09-10-11-13-14: 2/3/2/3/3/3/1/2/3. German champion 2006-08, 2010-14.
Progress at HT: 1997- 64.78, 1998- 73.10, 1999- 70.29, 2000- 76.66, 2001- 75.69, 2002- 76.94, 2003- 78.13, 2004- 79.01, 2005- 80.00, 2006- 81.10, 2007- 80.68, 2008- 79.97, 2009- 79.43, 2010- 78.87, 2011- 79.69, 2012- 77.93, 2013- 77.99, 2014- 76.64.

Rico FREIMUTH b. 14 Mar 1988 Potsdam 1.96m 92kg. Hallesche LA-Freunde.
At Dec: OG: '12- 6; WCh: '11- dnf, '13- 7; EC: '14- 7; EU23: 09- 10; EJ: '07- 3.
Progress at Dec: 2009- 7689, 2010- 7826, 2011- 8287, 2012- 8322, 2013- 8488w/8382, 2014- 8356. pbs: 60m 6.98i '12, 100m 10.40 '14, 10.36w '13; 200m 21.39 '12, 400m 47.51 '12, 1000m 2:48.22i '12, 1500m 4:34.60 '13, 60mh 7.83i '14, 110mh 13.63 '14, HJ 1.99 '13, PV 4.90 '12, LJ 7.55 '13, SP 15.14 '12, DT 50.37 '14, JT 65.04 '11, Hep 5715i '12.
His father Uwe had decathlon best of 8794 (1984), and was 4th at 1983 Worlds and 1986 Europeans and twice winner at Götzis. Uwe and Rico are the highest scoring father-son combination. His uncle Jörg won the high jump bronze medal at the 1980 Olympic Games in a pb of 2.31.

Robert HARTING b. 18 Oct 1984 Cottbus 2.01m 126kg. SCC Berlin.
At DT: OG: 08- 4, '12- 1; WCh: '07-09-11-13: 2/1/1/1; ECh: '06-10-12-14: dnq 13/2/1/1; CCp: '10- 1; ECp: '07-08-09-10-11-13-14: 2/2/2/1/1/1/1; WJ: '02- dnq 13; WY: '01- 2; EU23: '05- 1. German champion 2007-14.
Progress at DT: 2002- 54.25, 2003- 59.54, 2004- 64.05, 2005- 66.02, 2006- 65.22, 2007- 66.93, 2008- 68.65, 2009- 69.43, 2010- 69.69, 2011- 68.99, 2012- 70.66, 2013- 69.91, 2014- 68.47. pb SP 18.63 '07.
35 successive wins 2011-13. His brother Christoph (b. 4 Oct 1990) has pb 64.99 '13, dnq 13 WCh '13. His father Gert had pbs SP 16.05, DT 42.80 '88, and mother Bettina SP 15.04 and DT 43.06 '80.

Raphael HOLZDEPPE b. 28 Sep 1989 Kaiserslautern 1.81m 78kg. LAZ Zweibrücken.
At PV: OG: 08- 8, '12- 3; WCh: '11- dnq 20, '13- 1; EC '10- 9, '12- 3; WJ: '06- 5, '08- 1; EU23: '09- 1; EJ: '07- dnq; EI: '13- 8.
World junior pole vault record (=) 2008 (and indoors 5.68).
Progress at PV: 2002- 3.45, 2003- 4.25, 2004- 4.50, 2005- 5.00, 2006- 5.42, 2007- 5.50, 2008- 5.80, 2009- 5.65, 2010- 5.80, 2011- 5.72, 2012- 5.91, 2013- 5.91, 2014- 5.53.

Kai KAZMIREK b. 28 Jan 1991 Torgau 1.89m 91kg. LG Rhein-Wied.
At Dec: EC: '14- 6; WJ: '10- 6; EU23: '11- 6, '13- 1; EJ: '09- 3. German champion 2012. At Hep: WI: '14- 6.

Top steeplechaser of 2014 was Jairus Birech who broke 8 minutes and won six of seven Diamond League races.

Caterine Ibargüen was unbeaten at triple jump just as she was in 2013, her eleven wins, including six in the Diamond League, taking her unbeaten run to 21.

The winner Edna Kiplagat and her unrelated namesake Florence who finished first and second in the London Marathon. Florence also set the world record for half marathon in February.

Adam Gemili produced perhaps the best ever run by a British athlete at 200m, when he beat Christophe Lemaitre to win the European title in 19.97 despite adverse conditions.

Genzebe Dibaba was the star of the 2014 indoor season with world indoor records of 3:55.17 for 1500m and 8:16.60 for 3000m and a world best 9:00.48 for 2 miles.

Jo Pavey became, at 40, the oldest ever European women's champion with her first ever gold medal, winning the 10,000m, having earlier thrilled all with her last lap charge to take Commonwealth bronze at 5000m.

Kaliese Spencer was dominant in 2014 at 400m hurdles, including at the Commonwealth Games when she beat Eilidh Child by 0.92 sec.

Greg Rutherford improved the British long jump record to 8.51 and won at both Commonwealth Games and European Championships.

Progress at Dec: 2011- 7802, 2012- 8130, 2013- 8366, 2014- 8471. pbs: 60m 7.01i '15, 100m 10.75 '14, 10.61w '13; 200m 21.40 '12, 400m 46.75 '11, 1000m 2:39.51i '14, 1500m 4:33.78 '14, 60mh 8.00i '14, 110mh 14.05 '14, HJ 2.15 '14, PV 5.20 '13, LJ 7.68 '14, SP 14.34 '14, DT 44.77 '13, JT 63.17 '14, Hep 6173i '13.

Jan Felix KNOBEL b. 16 Jan 1989 Bad Homburg 1.92m 91kg. LG Eintracht Frankfurt. Architecture student.
At Dec: OG: '12- dnf; WCh: '11- 8; WJ: '06- 1; EU23: '11- 19. German champion 2009. At Oct: WY: 05- 5.
Progress at Dec: 2009- 7758, 2010- dnf, 2011- 8288, 2012- 8228, 2013- 8396w. pbs: 60m 7.18i '10, 100m 11.04 '12, 10.85w '13; 400m 48.89 '12, 1000m 2:49.22i '10, 1500m 4:43.12 '11, 60mh 8.20i '14, 110mh 14.59 '13, HJ 2.01 '11, PV 5.03 '12, LJ 7.36 '13, SP 16.06 '11, DT 50.87 '13, JT 76.36 '13, Hep 5778i '10.

Malte MOHR b. 24 Jul 1986 Bochum 1.92m 84kg. TV Wattenscheid.
At PV: OG: '12- 9=; WCh: '09- 14, '11- 5, '13- 5; EC: '10- dnq 17=, '12- 4; WI: '10-12-14: 2/4/2; EI: '11- 3, 13- 3; ET: '09- 2, '11- 2. German champion 2010-12.
Progress at PV: 2003- 4.81, 2004- 5.11i, 2005- 5.30, 2006- 5.71, 2007- 5.31, 2008- 5.76, 2009- 5.80, 2010- 5.90, 2011- 5.86i/5.85, 2012- 5.91, 2013- 5.86, 2014- 5.90i/5.70.
His father (and coach) Wolfgang Mohr had a best of 5.41 in 1976 and his mother Gisela Derksen was a good junior multi-eventer.

Björn OTTO b. 16 Oct 1977 Frechen 1.91m 90kg. ASV Köln. Studied biology at University of Cologne.
At PV: OG: '12- 2; WCh: '07- 5, '09- dnq 18=, '13- 3; EC: '12- 2; WI: '12- 2; EI: '00-05-07-13: 6/4/3/2; WUG: '99-01-03-05: 8/7/3=/1; ET: '13- 3. German champion 2013.
German pole vault record 2012. Two world over-35 records 2013.
Progress at PV: 1991- 3.20, 1992- 3.20, 1993- 4.10, 1994- 4.71, 1995- 5.00, 1996- 5.30i/5.20, 1997- 5.40, 1998- 5.52sq/5.40, 1999- 5.55/5.60ex, 2000- 5.65/5.71ex, 2001- 5.51/5.63ex, 2002- 5.63sq/5.60, 2003- 5.72i/5.70, 2004- 5.82i/5.70, 2005- 5.80, 2006- 5.85, 2007- 5.90, 2008- 5.70, 2009- 5.71, 2010- 5.60i/5.41, 2011- 5.75/5.80ex, 2012- 6.01, 2013- 5.90, 2014- 5.60i.

Christian REIF b. 24 Oct 1984 Speyer 1.96m 84kg. LC Rehlingen. Sports student.
At LJ: OG: '12- dnq 13; WCh: '07- 9, '11- 7, '13- 6; EC: '10- 1, "14- 8; WI: '10- 5, '14- 8; EI: '13- 3; CCp: '10- 3; ET: '14- 1. German champion 2010.
Progress at LJ: 2001- 7.15, 2002- 7.55, 2004- 7.83, 2005- 7.64i, 2006- 7.90, 2007- 8.19, 2008- 7.80, 2009- 8.18, 2010- 8.47, 2011- 8.26/8.38w, 2012- 8.26, 2013- 8.27, 2014- 8.49. pbs: 60m 6.86i '06, 100m 10.68 '06, 200m 21.90 '06.
Tied pb of 8.27 in qualifying, then 8.47 in final of Europeans 2010.

Thomas RÖHLER b. 30 Sep 1991 Jena 1.95m 83kg. LC Jena.
At JT: WCh: '13- dnq 29; EC: '12- dmq 13, '14- 12; WJ: '10- 9; EU23: '11- 7, '13- 3; ET: '13- 2. Won DL 2014, German champion 2012-14.
Progress at JT: 2009- 61.26, 2010- 76.37, 2011- 78.20, 2012- 80.79, 2013- 83.95, 2014- 86.99, 2014- 87.63.

Michael SCHRADER b. 1 Jul 1987 Duisberg-Homburg 1.86m 84kg. TSV Bayer 04 Leverkusen.
At Dec: OG: '08- 10; WCh: '13- 2; EU23: '07- 6. German champion 2010.
Progress at Dec: 2007- 7947, 2008- 8248, 2009- 8522, 2010- 8003, 2013- 8670. pbs: 100m 10.51 '11, 200m 21.70 '09, 400m 47.66 '13, 1500m 4:19.32 '08, 110mh 14.02 '13, HJ 2.00 '12, PV 5.10 '13, LJ 8.05 '09, SP 14.74 '13, DT 46.44 '13, JT 65.67 '13.
Won Götzis decathlon with seven pbs 2009, set three pbs when adding 148 points to pb for World silver 2013. Injured and did not compete in 2014.

David STORL b. 21 Jul 1990 Rochlitz 1.99m 122kg. Leipzig SC DHfK. Federal police officer.
At SP: OG: '12- 2; WCh: '09- dnq 27, '11- 1, '13- 1; EC: '10-12-14: 4/1/1; WJ: '08- 1; WY: '07- 1; EU23: '11- 1; EJ: '09- 1; WI: '10-13-14: 6/2/2; EI: '11- 2, '15- 1; WCp: '14- 1; ET: '11-13-14: 1/1/1. German champion 2011-12, 2014.
World junior shot record and three with 6kg (to 22.73) 2009.
Progress at SP: 2008- 18.46, 2009- 20.43, 2010- 20.77, 2011- 21.78, 2012- 21.88i/21.86, 2013- 21.73, 2014- 21.97.
Nine major international titles plus four second places.

Homiyu TESFAYE Heyi b. 23 Jun 1993 Debre Zeyit, Ethiopia 1.83m 66kg. LG Eintracht Frankfurt.
At 1500m: WCh: '13- 5; EC: '14- 5; WI: '14- 7; EI: '15- 4; ET: '14- 2.
European U23 1500m record 2014.
Progress at 1500m: 2011- 3:46.02, 2012- 3:38.56, 2013- 3:34.18, 2014- 3:31.98, 2015- 3:34.13i. pbs: 800m 1:46.40 '13, 1000m 2:17.56 '14, 1M 3:49.86 '14, 3000m 7:58.09i '14, 8:03.95 '12; 5000m 13:58.73 '13, 10000m 29:08.44 '13.
Claimed asylum in Germany in 2010, and German citizen from 27 Jun 2013.

Martin WIERIG b. 10 Jun 1987 Neindorf 2.02m 108kg. SC Magdeburg. Federal police officer.
At DT: OG: '12- 6; WCh: '11- dnq 18, '13- 4; EC: '10- 12-14: 7/dnq 14/11; WJ: '04- 8, '06- 3; EU23: '07- 1, '09- 3; EJ: '05- 3 (dnq SP).
Progress at DT: 2005- 57.44, 2006- 57.37, 2007- 61.10, 2008- 63.09, 2009- 63.90, 2010- 64.93, 2011- 67.21, 2012- 68.33, 2013- 67.46, 2014- 66.59. pb SP 17.30 '11.

Women

Shanice CRAFT b. 15 May 1993 Mannheim 1.85m 89kg. MTG Mannheim.
At (SP)/DT: EC: '14- 3; WJ: '12- 1/2; WY: '09- 3; EU23: '13- 2/2; EJ: '11- 1; ET: '14- 2. Won GER 2014, Yth Oly 2010,
Progress at DT: 2007- 44.86, 2008- 48.14, 2009- 50.57, 2010- 55.49, 2011- 58.65, 2012- 62.92, 2013- 60.77, 2014- 65.88. Pb SP 17.75 '14.

Julia FISCHER b. 1 Apr 1990 Berlin 1.92m 95kg. SC Charlottenburg.
At DT: OG: '12- dnq 20; WCh: '13- dnq 13; EC: '12- 5, '14- 5; WJ: '08- 2; WY: '07- 1; EU23: '11- 1; EJ: '09- 2; ET: '13- 2.
Progress at DT: 2005- 45.69, 2006- 50.23, 2007- 51.39, 2008- 55.92, 2009- 56.74, 2010- 57.49, 2011- 59.60, 2012- 64.22, 2013- 66.04, 2014- 66.46.

Betty HEIDLER b. 14 Oct 1983 Berlin 1.75m 80kg. LG Eintracht Frankfurt. Federal police officer.
At HT: OG: '04- 4, '08- 9, '12- 3; WCh: '03-05-07-09-11-13: 11/dnq 29/1/2/2/dnq 18; EC: '06-10-12-14: 5/1/dnq 16/5; EU23: '03- 4, '05- 2; WJ: '00/02- dnq 19/17; EJ: '01- 9, WUG: '09- 1; CCp: '10- 4; ECp: '04-07-09-10-11-13-14: 3/1/2/1/1/1/1. Won WAF 2006, 2009; World HT challenge 2010-12, German 2005-13.
World hammer record 2011, seven German records 2004-11.
Progress at HT: 1999- 42.07, 2000- 56.02, 2001- 60.54, 2002- 63.38, 2003- 70.42, 2004- 72.73, 2005- 72.19, 2006- 76.55, 2007- 75.77, 2008- 74.11, 2009- 77.12, 2010- 76.38, 2011- 79.42, 2012- 78.07, 2013- 76.48, 2014- 78.00.

Kathrin KLAAS b. 6 Feb 1984 Haiger 1.68m 72kg. LG Eintracht Frankfurt.
At HT: OG: '08- dnq 24, '12- 5; WCh: '05-07-13: dnq -/ 27/20, '09- 4, '11- 7; EC: '06-10-12-14: 6/ dnq 15/4/4; EJ: '03-8, EU23: '05- 4; WUG: '09- 3. German champion 2014.
Progress at HT: 2000- 44.24, 2001- 50.10, 2002- 57.74, 2003- 63.72, 2004- 68.01, 2005- 70.91, 2006- 71.67, 2007- 73.45, 2008- 70.39, 2009- 74.23, 2010- 74.53, 2011- 75.48, 2012- 76.05, 2013- 72.57, 2014- 74.62.

Gesa Felicitas KRAUSE b. 3 Aug 1992 Ehringshausen 1.67m 55kg. LG Eintracht Frankfurt. Student.
At 3000mSt: OG: '12- 7; WCh: '11- 8, '13- 9; EC: '12- 4, '14- 5; WJ: '10- 4; EU23: '13- 1; EJ: '11- 1. At 2000mSt: WY: '09- 7. At 1500m: EI: '15- 5.
European junior 3000mSt record 2011.
Progress at 3000mSt: 2010- 9:47.78, 2011- 9:32.74, 2012- 9:23.52, 2013- 9:37.11, 2014- 9:35.46. pbs: 800m 2:05.25 '11, 1000m 2:44.68 '10, 1500m 4:11.94 '12, 3000m 9:01.16i '12, 5km Rd 16:15 '11, 2000mSt 6:22.45 '11.

Malaika MIHAMBO b. 3 Feb 1994 Heidelberg 1.70m 52kg. LG Kurpfalz. Political science student at Mannheim University.
At LJ: WCh: '13- dnq 14; EC: '14- 4; WJ: '12- dnq 14; WY: '11- 9; EJ: '13- 1; ET: '14- 1.
Progress at LJ: 2008- 5.55, 2009- 5.81, 2010- 5.96, 2011- 6.40, 2012- 6.45i/6.32/6.50w, 2013- 6.70/6.80w, 2014- 6.90. pbs: 200m 24.20 '11, HJ 1.78i/1.75 '10.
Tanzanian father, German mother.

Sosthene Taroum **MOGUENARA** b. 17 Oct 1989 Sarh, Moyen-Chari, Chad 1.82m 68kg. TV Wattenscheid 01.
At LJ: OG: '12- dnq 20; WCh: '11- dnq 31, '13- 12; EC: '12- 4, '14- 9; EU23: '09- 4, '11- 3; EI: '15- 2. German champion 2013.
Progress at LJ: 2007- 6.22, 2008- 6.37, 2009- 6.61/6.69w, 2010- 6.65, 2011- 6.83, 2012- 6.88, 2013- 7.04, 2014- 6.82, 2015- 6.83i. pbs: 60m 7.66i '08, 100m 11.94 '10, 200m 24.85 '07.
Has lived in Germany from the age of nine.

Antje MÖLDNER-SCHMIDT b. 13 Jun 1984 Babelsberg 1.73m 56kg. SC Potsdam. Police officer.
At 3000mSt: OG: '08- h, '12- 6; WCh: '09- 9, '13- 8; EC: '12- 3; ECp: '09-13-14: 1/3/2. At 1500m: WJ: '02- h, EU23: '05- 3, EJ: '03- 6; EI: '05- 6. Won GER 1500m 2005, 2007; 3000mSt 2008-09, 2012-14. German records 3000mSt (5) 2000mSt (2) 2008-09.
Progress at 3000mSt: 2008- 9:29.86, 2009- 9:18.54, 2012- 9:21.78, 2013- 9:29.27, 2014- 9:29.43. pbs: 800m 2:04.34 '05, 1000m 2:48.36 '07, 1500m 4:08.81 '05, 2000m 5:47.66 '06, 3000m 9:00.74 '05, 5000m 16:05.82 '07, 2000mSt 6:15.90 '09.
Unable to compete in 2010 due to a lymphoid cells disorder.

Katharina MOLITOR b. 8 Nov 1983 Bedurg, Erft 1.82m 76kg. TSV Bayer 04 Leverkusen.
At JT: OG: '08- 8, 12- 6; WCh: '11- 5, '13- dnq 13; EC: '10-12-14: 4/5/9; EU23: '05- 2; WUG: '07- 6, '08- 4. German champion 2010.
Progress at JT: 2000- 42.94, 2001- 48.53, 2002- 49.01, 2003- 48.03, 2004- 50.04, 2005- 57.01, 2006- 57.58, 2007- 58.87, 2008- 61.74, 2009- 62.69, 2010- 64.53, 2011- 64.67, 2012- 63.20, 2013- 63.55, 2014- 63.40. Played volleyball in the Bundesliga.

Nadine MÜLLER b. 21 Nov 1985 Leipzig 1.93m 90kg. Hallesche LA-Freunde. Federal police officer.
At DT: OG: '12- 4; WCh: '07-09-11-13: dnq 23/6/2/4; EC: '10- 8, '12- 2; WJ: '04- 3; EU23: '05- 10, '07- 8; EJ: '03- 2; ET: '10- 1. German champion 2010-13.
Progress at DT: 2000- 36.10, 2001- 46.27, 2002- 48.90, 2003- 53.44, 2004- 57.85, 2005- 59.35, 2006- 58.46, 2007- 62.93, 2008- 61.36, 2009- 63.46, 2010- 67.78, 2011- 66.99, 2012- 68.89, 2013- 66.89, 2014- 67.30.

Christina OBERGFÖLL b. 22 Aug 1981 Lahr (Baden) 1.75m 79kg. LG Offenburg.
At JT: OG: '04- dnq 15, '08- 3, '12- 2; WCh: '05-07-09-11-13: 2/2/5/4/1; EC: '06-10-12: 4/2/2;

EU23: '01- 9, '03- 8; WJ: '00- 8; ECp: '07-09-10-11-13: 1/1/1/1/1. Won DL 2011, 2013; German 2007-08, 2011-12.
European javelin records 2005 & 2007.
Progress at JT: 1997- 49.20, 1998- 48.52, new: 1999- 50.57, 2000- 54.50, 2001- 56.83, 2002- 60.61, 2003- 57.40, 2004- 63.34, 2005- 70.03, 2006- 66.91, 2007- 70.20, 2008- 69.81, 2009- 68.59, 2010- 68.63, 2011- 69.57, 2012- 67.04, 2013- 69.05.
Made a great breakthrough at the 2005 World Champs to take her pb from 64.59 to a European record 70.03 and the silver medal. Married her coach Boris Henry (JT: 90.44 '97; 3rd Worlds 1995 & 2003, Europeans 2002) on 14 Sep 2013; son Marlon born in June 2014.

Claudia RATH b. 25 Apr 1986 Hadamar, Hessen 1.75m 65kg. LG Eintracht Frankfurt.
At Hep: WCh: '11- 4; EC: '10-12-14: 10/6/8. German champion 2010-11. At WI: '14- 5.
Progress at Hep: 2003- 5231, 2004- 5353, 2005- 5323, 2007- 5274, 2008- 5697, 2009- 5941, 2010- 6107, 2011- 6098, 2012- 6210, 2013- 6462, 2014- 6314. pbs: 200m 23.77 '14, 800m 2:06.43 '13, 60mh 8.43i '14, 100mh 13.46 '13, HJ 1.83 '13, LJ 6.67 '13, SP 13.78 '14, JT 43.45 '14, Pen 4681i '14.

Cindy ROLEDER b. 21 Aug 1989 Chemnitz 1.75m 62kg. LAZ Leipzig.
At 100mh: OG: '12- sf, WCh: '11- sf; EC: '10- h,'14- 3; WJ: '08- sf; EU23: '09- sf; EJ: '07- 4; CCp: '14- 3; GER champion 2011. At 60mh: WI: '14- 6; EI: '15- 4.
Progress at 100mh: 2007- 13.49, 2008- 13.72, 2009- 13.38, 2010- 12.97, 2011- 12.91, 2012- 12.91, 2013- 13.03/12.93w, 2014- 12.80. pbs: 60m 7.52i '15, 100m 11.72 '13, 200m 23.97 '14, 800m 2:19.22 '14, 50mh 7.14+i '10, 60mh 7.93i '15, HJ 1.61i/1.60 '14 '14. LJ 6.32i '14. 6.17 '13; SP 12.42 '14, JT 31.32 '14, Pen 4187i '14.

Anna RÜH b. 17 Jun 1993 Greifswald 1.86m 78kg. SC Neubrandenburg.
At SP: DT: '12- 9; EC: '12- 4, '14- 4; WJ: '10- dnq 21, '12- 1; EU23: '13- 1; EJ: '11- 2 (3 SP).
Progress at DT: 2009- 44.43, 2010- 51.67, 2011- 59.97, 2012- 63.38, 2013- 64.33, 2014- 64.17. pb SP 16.58i '15, 16.01 '11.

Elisaveta '**Lisa**' **RYZIH** b. 27 Sep 1988 Omsk, Russia 1.79m 59kg. Formerly Ryshich. ABC Ludwigshafen. Psychology student.
At PV: OG: '12- 6=; WCh: '13- 8=; EC: '10-12-14: 3/7/4; WJ: '04- 1, '06- nh; WY: '03- 1; EU23: '09- 1; EJ: '07- 4; EI: '11- 7; CCp: '10- 2, '14- 3. German champion 2014.
Progress at PV: 2002- 3.92, 2003- 4.10, 2004- 4.30, 2005- 4.15, 2006- 4.35, 2007- 4.35, 2008- 4.52i/4.50, 2009- 4.50, 2010- 4.65, 2011- 4.65i, 2012- 4.65, 2013- 4.55, 2014- 4.71, 2015- 4.72i. pb LJ 5.38w '06.
Set world age bests at 13 in 2002 and 15 in 2004. Her sister 'Nastja' was World Indoor champion in 1999 and set four world junior and five European junior PV records in 1996 to 4.15, and three German records in 1999 to 4.50i/4.44 and had a pb of 4.63 in 2006. Their family left Omsk in Siberia in 1992 to live in Ulm; mother Yekaterina Ryzhikh (née Yefimova b. 20 Jan 1959) had HJ pb 1.91i '85 and 1.89 '81, and father Vladimir is a pole vault coach.

Verena SAILER b. 16 Oct 1985 Illertissen 1.66m 57kg. MTG Mannheim
At 100m: OG: '08- 5R, '12- sf; WCh: '07- qf, '09- sf/3R, '13- sf; EC: '06-10-12-14: sf/1/6&1R/sf; WJ: '04- 5; EU23: '05- 3, '07- 1; EJ: '03- 6; CCp: '10- 4; ECp: '07- 2, '14- 3. At 60m: WI: '14- 8; EI: '09-13-15: 3/7/3. Won German 100m 2006-10, 2012-13.
Progress at 100m: 2001- 12.13, 2002- 11.88, 2003- 11.58, 2004- 11.49. 2005- 11.51, 2006- 11.43, 2007- 11.31, 2008- 11.28, 2009- 11.18/11.11w, 2010- 11.10/11.06w, 2011- 11.63/11.46w, 2012- 11.05, 2013- 11.02, 2014- 11.14/11.02w. pbs: 60m 7.09i '15, 200m 24.01 '06. Former gymnast.

Carolin SCHÄFER b. 5 Dec 1991 Bad Wildungen 1.76m 56kg. TV Friedrichstein-Alt Wildungen.
At Hep: EC: '12- 10, '14- 4; WJ: '08- 1; EU23: '11- 5, '13- 6; EJ: '09- 1. German champion 2013. At WI: '14- 5.
Progress at Hep: 2007- 5545, 2008- 5833, 2009- 5697, 2010- 5333, 2011- 5941, 2012- 6072, 2013- 5972, 2014- 6395. pbs: 60m 7.86i '07, 200m 23.78 '14, 800m 2:15.55 '14, 60mh 8.50i '14, 100mh 13.20 '14, HJ 1.84 '14, LJ 6.30 '14, SP 13.50 '12, JT 49.50 '12, Pen 4098i '09.

Christina SCHWANITZ b. 24 Dec 1985 Dresden 1.80m 103kg. LV 90 Erzebirge. Soldier.
At SP: OG: '08- 11, '12- 10; WCh: '05-09-11-13: 7/12/12/2; EC: '12- 5, '14- 1; WJ: '04- 3; EU23: '05- 2; WI: '08- 6, '14- 2; EI: '11- 2, '13- 1; CCp: '14- 1; ET: '08-13-14: 1/1/1. German champion 2011, 2013-14.
Progress at SP: 2001- 13.57, 2002- 14.26, 2003- 15.25, 2004- 16.98, 2005- 18.84, 2007- 17.06, 2008- 19.68i/19.31, 2009- 19.06, 2010- 18.28, 2011- 19.20, 2012- 19.15i/19.05, 2013- 20.41, 2014- 20.22. pb DT 47.27 '03.

Lilli SCHWARZKOPF b. 28 Aug 1983 Novo Pokrovka, Kyrgyzhstan 1.74m 65kg. LG Rhein-Wied. Student.
At Hep: OG: '08- 8, '12- 2; WCh: '05-07-09-11: 13/5/dnf/6; EC: '06- 3, '14- 5; WJ: '02- 5; EU23: '05- 2. German champion 2004.
Progress at Hep: 2001- 5079, 2002- 5597, 2003- 5735, 2004- 6161, 2005- 6146, 2006- 6420, 2007- 6439, 2008- 6536, 2009- 6355, 2010- 6386, 2011- 6370, 2012- 6649, 2014- 6426. pbs: 100m 12.22 '10, 200m 24.72 '11, 800m 2:09.63 '06, 60mh 8.46i '10, 100mh 13.26 '12, HJ 1.85 '14, LJ 6.35i/6.34 '07, SP 14.89 '11, JT 55.25 '09, Pen 4641i '08.
Has lived in Germany from age 7.

Silke SPIEGELBURG b. 17 Mar 1986 Georgsmarienhütte 1.73m 64kg. TSV Bayer 04 Leverkusen. Economics student.

At PV: OG: '04- 13, '08- 7, '12- 4; WCh: '07-09-11-13: nh/4/9/4; EC: '06-10-12: 6/2/4=; WJ: '02- 8; WY: '01- 1; EU23: '07- 4; EJ: '03- 1, '05- 1; WI: '06-12-14: 8/4/7; EI: '07-09-11: 5/2/2; ECp: '08-09-10-11-13: 3/3/2/2/1; Won WAF 2008, DL 2012-13, German 2005-10, 2012.
PV records: World junior 2005, German 2012.
Progress at PV: 1998- 2.75, 1999- 3.30, 2000- 3.75, 2001- 4.00, 2002- 4.20, 2003- 4.20i/4.15, 2004- 4.40, 2005- 4.48i/4.42, 2006- 4.56, 2007- 4.60, 2008- 4.70, 2009- 4.75i/4.70, 2010- 4.71, 2011- 4.76i/4.75, 2012- 4.82, 2013- 4.79, 2014- 4.72i/4.50.
Brothers: Henrik PV pb 4.80, Christian (b. 15 Apr 1976) 5.51 '98; **Richard** (b. 12 Aug 1977) 5.85 '01; 6= WCh 01, 1 WUG 99.

Linda STAHL b. 2 Oct 1985 Steinheim 1.74m 72kg. TSV Bayer 04 Leverkusen. Medical student.
At JT: OG: '12- 3; WCh: '07-09-11-13: 8/6/dns/4; EC: '10-12-14: 1/3/3; EU23: '07- 1; CCp: '10- 4, '14- 5; ET: '14- 3. German champion 2013-14.
Progress at JT: 2000- 42.94, 2001- 43.96, 2002- 47.23, 2003- 47.32, 2004- 50.11, 2005- 53.94, 2006- 57.17, 2007- 62.80, 2008- 66.06, 2009- 63.86, 2010- 66.81, 2011- 60.78, 2012- 64.91, 2013- 65.76, 2014- 67.32. pb SP 13.91i '06.

Martina STRUTZ b. 4 Nov 1981 Schwerin 1.60m 57kg. SC Neubrandenburg. Police officer.
At PV: OG: '12- 5; WCh: '11- 2; EC: '06- 5, '12- 2; WJ: '00- 5; EU23: '01- 4, '03- 9=; WCp: '06- 4. German champion 2011, 2013.
Two German pole vault records 2011.
Progress at PV: 1996- 3.30, 1997- 3.60i/3.50, 1998- 3.80, 1999- 4.10, 2000- 4.20, 2001- 4.42, 2002- 4.30, 2003- 4.20, 2004- 4.31, 2005- 4.40i/4.35, 2006- 4.50, 2007- 4.45, 2008- 4.52, 2009- 4.40, 2010- 4.30, 2011- 4.80, 2012- 4.60, 2013- 4.65, 2014- 4.46i/4.41.

GREECE

Governing body: Hellenic Amateur Athletic Association (SEGAS), 137 Siggroú Avenue, 171 21 Nea Smirni, Athens. Founded 1897.
National Championships first held in 1896 (men), 1930 (women). **2014 Champions**: 100m/200m: Likoúrgos-Stéfanos Tsákonas 10.38/20.58, 400m: Mihaíl Dardaneliótis 47.73, 800m/1500m: Andréas Dimitrákis 1:49.39/ 3:41.29, 5000m/10000m: Dímos Maggínas 14:24.92/30:23.03, HMar: Mihaíl Parmákis 69:55, Mar: Hristóforos Meroúsis 2:25:15, 3000mSt: Ilías Kássos 9:15.31, 110mh: Konstadínos Douvalídis 13.49, 400mh: Ioánnis Loulás 51.36, HJ: Adónios Mástoras 2.26, PV: Konstadínos Filippídis 5.60, LJ: Loúis Tsátoumas 8.08, TJ: Dimítrios Tsiámis 16.73, SP: Yerásimos Theodórou 17.13, DT: Yeóryios Trémos 58.73, HT: Konstadínos Kostoglídis 68.24, JT: Spirídon Lebésis 76.60, Dec: Panayiótis Mántis 6659, 20kW: Aléxandros Papamihaíl 1:26:06, 50kW: *not held*. **Women**: 100m: Yeoryía Koklóni 11.58, 200m: María Belibasáki 23.27, 400m: Déspina Mourtá 54.70, 800m: Eléni Filándra 2:04.35, 1500m: Eléni Theodorakopoúlou 4:29.64, 5000m: Anastasia Karakatsáni 16:27.27, 10000m: Ouranía Rempouli 34:44.85, HMar: Magdaliní Gazéa 1:22:09, Mar: Sofía Ríga 2:45:38, 3000mSt: María Pardaloú 10:27.69, 100mh: Elisávet Pesirídou 13.36, 400mh: Ekateríni Daláka 59.61, HJ: Tatiána Goúsin 1.83, PV: Nikoléta Kiriakopoúlou 4.40, LJ: Háido Alexoúli 6.29, TJ: Kristína Alvertsiuán 13.12, SP: Florentia Kappa 15.10, DT: Hrisoúla Anagnostopoúlou 53.49, HT: Ekateríni Vamvoukáki 57.80, JT: Vasilikí Kotsovoú 48.25, Hep: Sofía Ifantídou 5622, 20kW: Antigóni Drisbióti 1:35:38.

Konstadínos FILIPÍDDIS b. 26 Nov 1986 Athens 1.88m 73kg. Panellínios YS Athens. Postgraduate student at Athens University of Economics and Business.
At PV: OG: '12- 7; WCh: '05-09-11-13: dnq 14=/ dnq 17/6/10; EC: '06-10: dnq 26/21=, '12-14: 5/7; WJ: '04- 4; WY: '03- 4; EJ: '05- 2; WI: '10-12-14: 4=/7/1; EI: '11-13-15: 5/4/5; WUG: '05- 2; ET: '09/10- 4; Won MedG 2005; Greek champion 2005, 2009-14.
Nine Greek pole vault records 2005-13.
Progress at PV: 2001- 3.70, 2002- 4.80, 2003- 5.22, 2004- 5.50, 2005- 5.75, 2006- 5.55, 2007- 5.35i/5.30/5.40dq, 2009- 5.65, 2010- 5.70i/5.55, 2011- 5.75, 2012- 5.80, 2013- 5.83i/5.82, 2014- 5.80i/5.70.
Two-year drugs ban (reduced to 18 months) from positive test on 16 June 2007.

Loúis TSÁTOUMAS b. 12 Feb 1982 Messíni 1.87m 76kg. Messiniakós YS (Kalamáta).
At LJ: OG: '04-08-12: dnq 22/nj/dnq 29; WCh: '03-09-11-13: 12/11/dnq 14/10; EC: '06-10-14: 8/6/2; WJ: '00- dnq 21; WY: '99- 4; EU23: '03- 1; EJ: '01- 1; WI: '06-12-14: 4/6/4; EI: '07-13-15: 2/5/4; WCp: '06- nj; ECp: '03-07-08-09-13: 1/1/1/3/2; Greek champion 2003-08, 2010-11. 2013-14 (& 8 indoors); MedG 2013.
Greek long jump record 2007.
Progress at LJ: 1996- 6.56, 1997- 7.07, 1998- 7.41/7.43w, 1999- 7.64, 2000- 7.52, 2001- 7.93/7.98w, 2002- 8.17, 2003- 8.34, 2004- 8.19/8.37w, 2005- 8.15i/8.14, 2006- 8.30, 2007- 8.66, 2008- 8.44, 2009- 8.21, 2010- 8.09/8.17w, 2011- 8.26, 2012- 8.05i/7.98, 2013- 8.23/8.24w, 2014- 8.25. pb 200m 22.3 '98.
8.66 is best outdoors by European at sea-level.

Women

Nikoléta KIRIAKOPOÚLOU b. 21 Mar 1986 Athens 1.67m 54kg. AYES Kámiros Rhodes.
At PV: OG: '08/12- dnq 27=/19=; WCh: '09- dnq 19, '11- 8, '13- dnq 13=; EC: '10-12-14: dnq 13/3/7=; WJ: '04- 6; EJ: '05- 7; EI: '11- 9, '15- 5=. Balkan champion 2008, Med G 2009, Greek 2009, 2011-14.
Five Greek pole vault records 2010-11.

Progress at PV: 2001- 2.90, 2002- 3.10, 2003- 3.70, 2004- 4.00, 2005- 4.10, 2006- 3.60, 2007- 4.00i/3.90, 2008- 4.45, 2009- 4.50, 2010- 4.55, 2011- 4.71, 2012- 4.60, 2013- 4.65, 2014- 4.72i/4.67, 2015- 4.80i.

Ekateríni STEFANÍDI b. 4 Feb 1990 Athens 1.72m 63kg. Was at Stanford University, USA and then as a graduate student in cognitive psychology at Arizona State University.
At PV: OG: '12- dnq 24; EC: '12- nh, '14- 2; WJ: '08- 3; WY: '05- 1, '07- 2; EU23: '11- 2; EI: '15- 2; WUG: '11- 3. Greek champion 2012, NCAA 2012.
World youth pole vault best 2005.
Progress at PV: 2002- 3.40, 2003- 3.90, 2004- 4.14, 2005- 4.37i/4.30, 2006- 4.10, 2007- 4.25, 2008- 4.25, 2009- 4.13, 2010- 4.30, 2011- 4.45, 2012- 4.51, 2013- 4.45Ai/4.40, 2014- 4.71, 2015- 4.77Ai.

GRENADA

Governing body: Grenada Athletic Assocation, PO Box 419, St George's. Founded 1924.

Kirani JAMES b. 1 Sep 1992 St George's 1.85m 74kg. Student at University of Alabama, USA
At (200m)/400m: OG: '12- 1; WCh: '11- 1, '13- 7; CG: '14- 1; WJ: '08- 2, '10- 1; WY: '07- 2, '09- 1/1; WI: '12- 6. Won DL 2011, PAm-J 400m 2009, 200m 2011; NCAA 2010-11.
Records: CAC & Commonwealth 400m 2012 & 2014, GRN 200m 2011, 400m (2) 2011-12; Indoor 400m: CAC & Commonwealth 2010 (45.24) &. 2011, World Junior (44.80) 2011.
Progress at 400m: 2007- 46.96, 2008- 45.70, 2009- 45.24, 2010- 45.01, 2011- 44.36, 2012- 43.94, 2013- 43.96, 2014- 43.74. pbs: 200m 20.41A/20.53w '11, 20.76 '10; 300m: 32.0+ '12.
He set world age bests at 14 and 15. In 2011 he became the youngest ever World or Olympic champion at 400m and in 2012 the first Olympic medallist for Grenada at any sport. In January 2012 the 'Kirani James Boulevard' was opened in the Grenadan capital St. George. IAAF Rising Star award 2011.

GUATEMALA

Governing body: Federación Nacional de Atletismo, Palacio de los Deportes, 26 Calle 9-31, Zona 5, Ciudad de Guatemala. Fd 1896.

Érick BARRONDO b. 14 Jun 1991 San Cristóbal Verapaz 1.72m 60kg.
At 20kW(/50kW): OG: '12- 2/dq; WCh: '11- 9, '13- dq; PAm: '11- 1; CAG: '14- (1). Won Bol G 20kW 2013, GUA 50kW 2012.
50k walk records: CAC 2013, GUA 2012-13.
Progress at 20kW, 50kW: 2010- 1:23:16A, 2011- 1:20:58, 2012- 1:18:25, 3:44:59; 2013- 1:20:25, 3:41:09; 2014- 1:21:14, 3:49:40A. pb 10000mW 40:10.73A '13.
Won Guatemala's first Olympic medal at any sport in 2012. His cousin José Alejandro Barrondo has 10000mW pb 42:00.98 '13.

HUNGARY

Governing body: Magyar Atlétikai Szövetség, 1146 Budapest, Istvánmezei út 1-3. Fd 1897.
National Championships first held in 1896 (men), 1932 (women). **2014 Champions. Men**: 100m: Dániel Karlik 10.47w, 200m/400m: Bálint Móricz 21.15/46.63, 800m/1500m: Tamás Kazi 1:48.50/3:52.49, 5000m: Barnabás Bene 14:44.54, 10000m: László Gregor 29:59.74, HMar: Tamás Kovács 67:01, Mar: Tamás Nagy 2:27:15, 3000mSt: Albert Minczér 8:46.10, 110mh: Balázs Baji 13.52, 400mh: Máté Koroknai 50.50, HJ: Péter Bakosi 2.17, PV: Dezsö Szabó 5.10, LJ: István Virovecz 7.74, TJ: Tibor Galambos 15.86w, SP: Tibor Rakovszky 17.62, DT: Zoltán Kövágó 62.66, HT: Krisztián Pars 81.38, JT: Zoltán Magyari 72.91, Dec: Tibor Galambos 6999, 20kW: Máté Helebrandt 1:24:38, 50kW: Dávid Tokodi 4:12:11. **Women**: 100m/200m: Éva Kaptur 11.54w/23.91, 400m/800m: Bianka Kéri 54.24/2:09.01, 1500m: Zsanett Kenesei 4:23.60, 5000m/HMar: Zsófia Erdélyi 16:28.95/77:57, 10000m: Krisztina Papp 32:59.39, Mar: Simona Juhász-Staicu 2:51:08, 3000mSt: Viktória Gyürkés 10:16.33, 100mh: Gréta Kerekes 13.72, 400mh: Mónika Zsiga 60.76, HJ: Barbara Szabó 1.85, PV: Enikö Erös 4.00, LJ: Fanni Schmelcz 6.41w, TJ: Krisztina Hoffer 13.02w, SP/DT: Anita Márton 17.64/55.93, HT: Éva Orbán 70.88, JT: Annabella Bogdán 50.73, Hep: Beatrix Szabó 4548, 20kW: Viktória Madarász 1:35:32.

Balázs BAJI b. 9 Jun 1989 Békéscsaba 1.92m 83kg. Békéscsabai AC.
At 110mh: OG: '12- h; WCh: '11- h, '13- sf; WJ: '08- 7; EC: '10-12-14: h/sf/4; EU23: '09- h,'11- 2; WUG: '11- 6; won HUN 200m 2009, 110mh 2007, 2011-14. At 60mh: EI: '13- 4, '15- 7.
Two Hungarian 110mh records 2014.
Progress at 110mh: 2007- 14.48, 2008- 14.44/14.43w, 2009- 13.96/13.88w, 2010- 13.79, 2011- 13.58, 2012- 13.50, 2013- 13.36, 2014- 13.29. pbs: 60m 6.85i '13, 100m 10.60 '09, 200m 21.35 '13, 400m 49.6 '07, 60mh 7.56i '13, 400mh 56.38 '06.

Zoltán KÖVÁGÓ b. 10 Apr 1979 Szolnok 2.04m 127kg. Szolnoki Honvéd SE. Army lieutenant.
At DT: OG: '00- dnq, '04- 2, '08- dnq 21; WCh: '01-03-05-07-09-11: dnq 20/dnq 19/10/9/6/dnq 15; EC: '02-10-12-14: 7/dnq 21/dq (3)/dnq 14; WJ: '96- 4, '98- 1; EJ: '97- 3; EU23: '99- 6, '01- 1. HUN champion 2001, 2004-05, 2008-11, 2014.
Progress at DT: 1995- 49.78, 1996- 59.70, 1997- 62.16, 1998- 60.27, 1999- 63.23, 2000- 66.76, 2001- 66.93, 2002- 65.98, 2003- 66.03, 2004- 68.93, 2005- 66.00, 2006- 69.95, 2007- 66.42, 2008- 68.17, 2009- 67.64, 2010- 69.69, 2011- 69.50, 2012- 68.21dq, 2014- 65.82. pb SP 15.93 '01.
2-year drugs ban 2012.

Krisztián PARS b. 18 Feb 1982 Körmend 1.88m 113kg. Dobó SE.
At HT: OG: '04- 5, '08- 4, '12- 1; WCh: '05-07-09-

11-13: 6/5/4/2/2; EC: '06-10-12-14: 5/3/1/1; WY: '99- 1; EJ: '01- 1; EU23: '03- 1; CCp: '14- 1. Won HUN 2005-14; World HT challenge 2011-12, 2014. World junior records with 6kg hammer: 80.64 & 81.34 in 2001.
Progress at HT: 1998- 54.00, 1999- 61.92, 2000- 66.80, 2001- 73.09, 2002- 74.18, 2003- 78.81, 2004- 80.90, 2005- 80.03, 2006- 82.45, 2007- 81.40, 2008- 81.96, 2009- 81.43, 2010- 79.64, 2011- 81.89, 2012- 82.28, 2013- 82.40, 2014- 82.69. pbs: SP 15.60 '05, DT 53.80 '06.

Women

Anita MÁRTON b. 15 Jan 1989 Szeged 1.71m 84kg. Békéscsabai AC.
At SP: OG: '12- dnq 23; WCh: '09-11-13: dnq 24/22/20; EC: '10-12-14: 11/7/3; WJ: '06- dnq 15, '08- 7; WY: '05- 11; EU23: '09- 5, '11- 5; EJ: '07- 7; WUG: '13- 4; WI: '14- 6; EI: '15- 1; won HUN SP 2006-14, DT 2008-14.
Hungarian shot record 2014.
Progress at SP: 2004- 13.88, 2005- 14.12i/13.90, 2006- 15.57, 2007- 15.68, 2008- 16.90, 2009- 17.27, 2010- 18.20, 2011- 18.15, 2012- 18.48, 2013- 18.18, 2014- 19.04, 2015- 19.23i. pbs: DT 59.27 '14, HT 48.87 '08. Improved pb from 18.48/18.63i to 19.04 to take EC bronze 2014.

Éva ORBÁN b. 29 Nov 1984 Pápa, Veszprém 1.73m 75kg. VEDAC, Was at University of Southern California, USA.
At HT: OG: '04-08-12: dnq 24/34/16; WCh: '05-09-11: dnq 20/14/12, '13- 8; EC: '06-10-12-14: dnq 25/11/7/nt; WY: '01- 11; EU23: '05- 11; EJ: '03- 6, WUG: '11- 1. HUN champion 2005-06, 2008-11, 2013-14; NCAA 2008..
Three Hungarian hammer records 2011-13.
Progress at HT: 1999- 47.70, 2000- 53.23, 2001- 58.04, 2002- 62.00, 2003- 65.77, 2004- 67.60, 2005- 68.70, 2006- 69.10, 2007- 66.98, 2008- 70.18, 2009- 70.16, 2010- 69.73, 2011- 71.33, 2012- 69.03, 2013- 73.44, 2014- 72.49. pbs: SP 12.93 '05, DT 45.40 '05.

ICELAND

Governing body: Frjálsíthróttasamband Islands, Engjavegur 6, IS-104 Reykjavik. Founded 1947.
National Championships first held in 1927. **2014 National champions: Men:** 100m/200m: Jóhann Björn Sigurbjörnsson 10.77/21.83, 400m/400mh: Ivar Kristinn Jasonarson 49.33/ 54.26, 800m: Kristin Thór Kristinsson 1:53.91, 1500m/5000m: Hlynur Andrésson 3:55.94/ 15:01.69, 110mh/Dec: Einar Dadi Lárusson 14.51w/ 7429, HJ: Hermann Thór Haraldsson 1.96, PV: Krister Blær Jónsson 5.15, LJ: Kristinn Torfason 7.23, TJ: Stefan Pór Jósefsson 12.52, SP: Ódinn Björn Thorsteinsson 17.95, DT: Gudni Valur Gudnason 47.05, HT: Hilmar Örn Jónsson 68.58, JT: Sindri Hrafn Gudmunsson 77.28. **Women:** 100m/200m/400m/LJ/TJ: Hafdís Sigurdardóttir 11.84/24.29/54.16/6.20/12.32, 800m: María Birkisdóttir 2:20.25, 1500m: Anita Hinriksdóttir 4:27.93, 3000m: Andrea Kolbeinsdóttir 10:52.02, 100mh/400mh: Kristín Birna Olafsdóttir-Johnson 14.05/61.03, HJ: Selma Líf Thórólfsdóttir 1.63, PV: Rakel Ósk Dyrförd Björnsdóttir 3.56, SP: Sveinbjörg Zophoníasdóttir 13.64, DT: Thea Imani Sturludóttir 38.42, HT: Vigdis Jónsdóttir 52.70, JT: Ásdis Hjálmsdóttir 55.51; Hep: Póranna Ósk Sigurjónsdóttir 4066.

INDIA

Governing body: Athletics Federation of India, WZ-72, Todapur Main Road, Dev Prakash Shastri Marg, New Delhi - 110012. Fd 1946.
National Championships first held as Indian Games in 1924. **2014 Champions: Men**: 100m/200m Manikanda Arumugam 10.56/ 20.98, 400m: P.P.Kunhu Mohammed 46.97, 800m: Sajeesh Joseph 1:49.91, 1500m: Ajay Kumar Saroj 3:48.53, 5000m: Nitender Singh Rawat 14:16.28, 10000m: T.Gopi 29:32.26, 3000mSt: Jaiveer Singh 8:53.85, 110mh: Kuppusamy Prem Kumar 13.91, 400mh Durgesh Kumar Pal 50.61, HJ: Harshith Shashidhar 2.17, PV: Kundan Singh 5.06, LJ: Ankit Sharma 7.87, TJ: Renjith Maheswary 16.09, SP Kashish Khanna 18.59, DT: Arjun Kumar 56.45, HT: Neeraj Kumar 68.86, JT: Rohit Kumar 72.30, Dec: Nariender 6676, 20000mW: Manish Singh Rawat 1:33:17.0, 20kW: Gurmeet Singh 1:22:58, 50kW: 50kW: Sandeep Kumar 4:08:54. **Women**: 100m: Sharada Narayanan 12.21, 200m: Asha Roy 24.46, 400m: M.R.Poovamma 53.59, 800m: Tintu Luka 2:03.88, 1500m/5000m: Orchatteri P.Jaisha 4:17.80/16:13.61, 10000m: Suriya Loganathan 33:56.05, 3000mSt: Sudha Singh 10:08.50, 100mh: Govindaraj Gayathry 13.71, 400mh: M. Arpitha 59.82, HJ: Steny Michael 1.73, PV: V. Suresh Surekha Renjith 4.15, LJ: Narayanan V.Neena 6.29, TJ: Nellickal V.Sheena 12.99, SP: Manpreet Kaur 16.39, DT: Navjeet Kaur 55.33, HT: Gunjan Singh 58.38, JT: Annu Rani 54.01, Hep: Liksy Joseph 5444, 20000mW: Sapna 1:49:58.0, 20kW: Kushbir Kaur 1:36:25.

Vikas GOWDA b. 5 Jul 1983 Mysore, Karnataka 1.96m 115kg. Studied statistics at University of North Carolina, USA.
At DT: OG: '04/08- 14/22, '12- 8; WCh: '05/07- dnq 14/17, '11- 7, '13- 7; CG: '06-10-14: 6/2/1; AsiG: '06-10-14: 6/3/2; AsiC: 05- 2, '11- 2, '13- 1. Won NCAA 2006.
Three Indian discus records 2005-12
Progress at DT: 2002- 55.28, 2003- 59.32, 2004- 64.35, 2005- 64.69, 2006- 61.76, 2007- 64.96, 2008- 64.83, 2010- 63.69, 2011- 64.91, 2012- 66.28, 2013- 65.82. 2014- 65.62. pb SP 19.62 '06.

IRAN

Governing body: Amateur Athletic Federation of Islamic Republic of Iran, Shahid Keshvari

Sports Complex, Razaneh Junibi St Mirdamad Ave, Tehran. Founded 1936.

Ehsan HADADI b. 21 Jan 1985 Ahvaz 1.93m 125kg.
At DT: OG: '08- dnq 17, '12- 2; WCh: '07- 7, '11- 3; WJ: '04- 1; AsiG: '06-10-14: 1/1/1; AsiC: '03-05-07-09-11: 8/1/1/1/1; AsiJ: '04- 1; WCp: '06- 2, '10- 3. W.Asian champion 2005.
Eight Asian discus records 2005-08.
Progress at DT: 2002- 53.66, 2003- 54.40, 2004- 54.96, 2005- 65.25, 2006- 63.79, 2007- 67.95, 2008- 69.32, 2009- 66.19, 2010- 68.45, 2011- 66.08, 2012- 68.20, 2013- 66.98, 2014- 65.24. pb SP 17.82i '08, 16.00 '06.
First Iranian athlete to win an Olympic medal.

IRELAND

Governing Body: The Athletic Association of Ireland (AAI), Unit 19, Northwood Court, Northwood Business Campus, Santry, Dublin 9. Founded in 1999. Original Irish federation (Irish Champions AC) founded in 1873.
National Championships first held in 1873. **2014 Champions**: **Men**: 100m: Jamie Davis 10.90, 200m: David Hynes 21.42, 400m: Brian Gregan 46.56, 800m: Mark English 1:49.91, 1500m: Ciarán Ó'Lionáird 3:43.85, 5000: Kevin Batt 14:08.23, 10000m/HMar: Mick Clohisey 29:58.31/65:55, Mar: Sergui Ciobanu MDA 2:21:01, 3000mSt: Rory Chesser 8:46.95, 110mh: Gerard O'Donnell 14.57, 400mh: Thomas Barr 50.04, HJ: Liam Zamel-Paez 2.16, PV: Ian Rogers 4.70, LJ: Sam Healy 7.25, TJ: Denis Finnegan 15.34, SP: Seán Breathnach 16.27, DT: Colin Quirke 52.73, HT: Conor McCullough 72.81, JT: Rory Gunning 59.22, Dec: Kourosh Foroughi 6303, 10000mW: Alex Wright 42:09.79, 20kW: Luke Hickey 1:28:13. **Women**: 100m: Amy Foster 11.49, 200m/LJ: Kelly Proper 23.23/6.27, 400m: Mandy Gault 54.24, 800m: Katie Kirk GBR 2:09.01, 1500m: Ciara Mageean 4:15.35, 5000m: Fionnuala Britton 15:39.40, HMar: Sarah Mulligan 76:03, Mar: Maria McCambridge 2:34:19, 3000mSt: Sara Treacy 9:59.75, 100mh: Sarah Lavin 13.48, 400mh: Christine McMahon 57.73, HJ: Cathriona Farrell 1.75, PV: Zoë Brown 4.30, TJ: Caoimhe King 12.44, SP/DT: Claire Fitzgerald 16.20/49.09, HT: Cara Kennedy 56.86, JT: Anita Fitzgibbon 48.62, Hep: Karen Dunne 4058, 5000mW: Sinead Burke 25:17.86.

Robert HEFFERNAN b. 20 Feb 1978 Cork City 1.73m 55kg. Togher AC.
At 20kW/(50kW): OG: '00- 28, '04- dq, '08- 8, '12- 9/4; WCh: '01-05-07-09-13: 14/dq/6/15/(1); EC: '02- 8, '10- 3/4, '14- (dnf); WCp: '08- 9, '12- 11; ECp: '07-09-11-13: 5/4/9/9. At 10000mW: EJ: '97- 14; EU23: '99- 13. Won Irish 10000mW 2001-02, 2004-5, 2007-11; 20kW 2000-02, 2004, 2009; 30kW 2008.
Irish records: 3000mW 2013, 20kW (4) 2001-08, 50kW (3) 2010-12. World M35 3000mW 2013.
Progress at 20kW, 50kW: 1999- 1:26:45, 2000- 1:22:43, 2001- 1:21:11, 2002- 1:20:25, 2003- 1:23:03, 2004- 1:20:55, 2005- 1:24:20, 2006- 1:22:24, 2007- 1:20:15, 2008- 1:19:22, 2009- 1:22:09, 2010- 1:20:45, 3:45:30; 2011- 1:20:54, 3:49:28; 2012- 1:20:18, 3:37.54; 2013- 1:21:59, 3:37:56; 2014- 1:20:57. pbs: 1MW 5:39.75i '14, 3000mW 11:09.08 14, 5000mW 18:51.46i '08, 18:59.37 '07; 10000mW 38:27.57 '08, 30kW 2:07:48 '11, 35kW 2:31:19 '00.
Married to Marian Andrews (b. 16 Apr 1982, Irish 400m champion 2008-09, pb 53.10 '11).

ISRAEL

Governing body: Israeli Athletic Association, PO Box 24190, Tel Aviv 61241. Founded as Federation for Amateur Sport in Palestine 1931.
National Championships first held in 1935. **2014 Champions**: **Men**: 100m: Imri Pressiado 10.50, 200m/400m: Donald Sanford 21.30w/45.65, 800m: Mokat Fatana 1:49.08, 1500m/5000m/10000m: Aimeru Almeya 3:49.77/14:07.56/28:12.87, HMar: Demsew Zegeye 65:33, Mar: Zohar Zimto 2:16:25, 3000mSt: Noam Ne'eman 9:00.15, 110mh: Tomer Almogi 14.81, 400mh: Maor Szeged 52.08, HJ: Dmitriy Kroyter 2.21, PV: Roman Kogan 4.72, LJ: Daniel Butael 7.34, TJ: Yochai Halevi 16.08, SP: Itamar Levi 17.36, DT: Mark Alterman 54.94, HT: Viktor Zaginaiko 58.32, JT: Alan Ferber 69.32, Dec: Kionstantin Krinitzkiy 6579. **Women**: 100m: Rita Pogorelov 11.99, 200m: Diana Weissman 25.04, 400m/400mh: Alexandra Lukshin 56.04/60.91, 800m: Shanie Landen 2:15.98, 1500m/5000m/100000m: Azawant Taka 4:38.94/17:22.14/36:21.59, HMar/Mar: Svetlana Bakhmand 1:21:35/2:52:57, 3000mSt: Meigal Attias 10:56.46, 100mh: Kristina Vanusheva 15.23, HJ: Maayan Shahaf 1.86, PV: Na'ama Bernstein 3.25, LJ/TJ: Hanna Knyazyeva-Minenko 6.52/14.23, SP/DT: Anastasia Muchkaev 14.90/51.62, HT: Yevgeniya Zabolotniy (11th successive title) 53.44, JT: Dorit Naor 44.67 (18th title), Hep: Olga Bronstein 4119 (28th title at 6 different events).

Hanna KNYAZYEVA-MINENKO b. 25 Sep 1989 Periaslav-Khmelnytskyi 1.78m 61kg. Kiev.
At TJ: OG: '12- 4; WCh: '13- 6; WJ: '08- 4; EJ: '07- 2; EU23: '11- 5. Won UKR TJ 2012, ISR LJ 2014, 2013-14.
Five Israeli triple jump records 2013.
Progress at TJ: 2005- 12.87, 2006- 13.28, 2007- 13.85, 2009- 13.81, 2010- 13.65, 2011- 14.20, 2012- 14.71, 2013- 14.58, 2014- 14.29. pb LJ 6.52 '14.
Married Anatoliy Minenko (Dec 7046 '10) in November 2012 and switched from Ukraine to Israel on 12 May 2013.

ITALY

Governing Body: Federazione Italiana di Atletica Leggera (FIDAL), Via Flaminia Nuova 830, 00191 Roma. Constituted 1926. First governing body formed 1896.

National Championships first held in 1897 (one event)/1906 (men), 1927 (women). **2014 Champions**: **Men**: 100m: Delmas Obou 10.33, 200m: Diego Marani 20.47, 400m: Matteo Galvan 45.58, 800m: Giordano Benedetti 1:49.09, 1500m: Mohad Abdikadad 3:46.63, 5000m: Marouan Razine 14:13.88, 10000m: Jamal Chatbi 28:14.87, HMar: Daniele Meucci 62:44, Mar: Danilo Goffi 2:17:20, 3000mSt: Patrick Nasti 8:42.91, 110mh: Hassane Fofana 13.60, 400mh: Leonardo Capotosti 50.17, HJ: Gianmarco Tamberi 2.22, PV: Giorgio Piantella 5.40, LJ: Emanuele Catania 7.98, TJ: Fabrizio Schembri 16.61, SP: Daniele Secci 18.55, DT: Hannes Kirchler 62.73, HT: Nicola Vizzoni 75.99, JT: Norbert Bonvecchio 78.96, Dec: Michele Calvi 7492, 10kW/20kW: Giorgio Rubino 40:13/1:26:57, 50kW: Matteo Giupponi 3:51:49. **Women**: 100m/200m: Irene Siragusa 11.51/23.27, 400m: Libania Grenot 50.55, 800m: Marta Milani 2:05.01, 1500m: Federica Del Buono 4:10.26. 5000m: Giulia Viola 15:55.98, 10000m: Veronica Inglese 32:25.76, HMar: Valeria Straneo 69:45, Mar: Claudia Gelsomino 2:51:22, 3000mSt: Valeria Roffino 9:53.82, 100mh: Marzia Caravelli 13.07, 400mh: Yadisleidy Pedroso 55.84, HJ: Alessia Trost 1.90, PV: Roberta Bruni 4.30, LJ: Tania Vicenzino 6.51, TJ: Daria Derkach 13.10, SP: Chiara Rosa 17.21, DT: Valentina Aniballi 55.54, HT: Micaela Mariani 66.24, JT: Sara Jemai 53.85, Hep: Flavia Nasella 5468, 10kW/20kW: Antonella Palmisano 45:15/1:32:24.

Marco DE LUCA b. 12 May 1981 Rome 1.89m 72kg. Fiamme Gialle.
At 50kW: OG: '08- 19, '12- 16; WCh: 05-'09-11-13: 13/8/12/15; EC: '06-10-14: 7/6/7; WCp: 06-08-10-12: 9/8/14/8; ECp: '07-09-11: 8/8/2. Won Italian 20kW 2011, 50kW 2006, 2009.
Progress at 50kW: 2002- 4:07:06, 2003- 4:13:24, 2004- 4:05:01, 2005- 3:55:30, 2006- 3:48:08, 2007- 3:47:04, 2008- 3:49:21, 2009- 3:46:31, 2010- 3:48:36, 2011- 3:49:40, 2012- 3:47:19, 2013- 3:48:05, 2014- 3:45:25. pbs: 3000mW 12:03.79 '09, 5000mW 19:29.54i '15, 20:03.6 '05, 10000mW 40:48.0 '09, 20kW 1:22:38 '10, 30kW 2:09:37 '04, 35kW 2:28:53 '10.

Fabrizio DONATO b. 14 Aug 1976 Latina 1.89m 82kg. Fiamme Gialle.
At TJ: OG: '00/04/08: dnq 25/21/21, '12- 3; WCh: '03/07-09-13: dnq 13/32/41/15, '11- 10; EC: '02-06-10-12-14: 4/dnq 16/9/1/7; EJ: '95- 5; WI: '01-08-10-12: 6/4/5/4; EI: '00-02-09-11: 6/4/1/2; ECp: '00-02-03-04-06-14: 2/2/1/6/1/2. Won MedG 2001, Italian 2000, 2004, 2006-08, 2010-11.
Italian triple jump record 2000.
Progress at TJ: 1992- 12.88, 1993- 14.36, 1994- 15.27, 1995- 15.81, 1996- 16.35, 1997- 16.40A, 1998- 16.73, 1999- 16.66i/16.53w, 2000- 17.60, 2001- 17.05, 2002- 17.17, 2003- 17.16, 2004- 16.90, 2005- 16.65/16.68w, 2006- 17.33i/17.24, 2007- 16.97/ 17.06w, 2008- 17.27i/16.91/17.29w, 2009- 17.59i/ 15.81, 2010- 17.39i/17.08, 2011- 17.73i/17.17, 2012- 17.53/17.63w, 2013- 16.86, 2014- 16.89/17.24w. pb LJ 8.03i '11, 8.00 '06.
Italian indoor record to win 2009 European Indoor title. Married Patrizia Spuri (400m 51.74 '98, 8 EC 98, 800m 1:59.96 '98) on 27 Sep 2003.

Marco FASSINOTTI b. 29 Apr 1989 Turin 1.90m 71kg. Aeronautica Militare.
At HJ: EC: '10- 9, '14- 7; WJ: '08- 7; EU23: '09- 6, '11- 5; Italian champion 2013.
Progress at HJ: 2005- 1.70, 2006- 1.90, 2007- 2.08, 2008- 2.17, 2009- 2.22, 2010- 2.28, 2011- 2.29i/2.25, 2012- 2.26i/2.24, 2013- 2.27, 2014- 2.34i/2.30, 2015- 2.34i.

Daniele GRECO b. 1 Mar 1989 Nardó, Apulia 1.88m 76kg. Fiamme Oro, Padova.
At TJ: OG: '12- 4; WCh: '09-13: dnq 34/nj; EC: '10-12: dnq 17/24; WJ: '08- 4; EU23: '09- 1, '11- 4; EJ: '07- 12; WI: '12: 5; EI: '13- 1. Won Italian 2012, Med G 2013.
Progress at TJ: 2005- 15.01, 2006- 15.45, 2007- 15.58i/15.54, 2008- 16.41, 2009- 17.20, 2010- 16.95i/16.57, 2011- 16.89, 2012- 17.47/17.67w, 2013- 17.70i/17.25, 2014- 16.84. pbs: 60m 6.75i '09, 100m 10.38 '08, 200m 21.17 '12, 21.14w '09; 300m 33.7, LJ 7.44i '14, 7.25 '07.
Injured in warm-up for EC 2014. Engaged to Francesca Lanciano (b. 3 Apr 1994), 11 WY '11, 12 WJ '12, NJR 13.59 '12.

Giorgio RUBINO b. 15 Apr 1986 Roma 1.74m 56kg. Fiamme Gialle.
At 20kW: OG: '08- 18, '12- 42; WCh: '07-09-11-13: 5/4/dq/28; EC: '06-10-14: 8/4/8; EU23: '07- dq; ECp: '09- 1, '11- 4. At 10000mW: WJ: '04- 10; WY: '03- 4; EJ: '05- 3. Won Italian 10kW 2012, 2014; 20kW 2005, 2014.
Progress at 20kW: 2005- 1:23:58, 2006- 1:22:05, 2007- 1:21:17, 2008- 1:22:11, 2009- 1:19:37, 2010- 1:22:12, 2011- 1:20:44, 2012- 1:20:10, 2013- 1:21:07, 2014- 1:20:44. pbs: 5000mW 19:14.33i '08, 19:38.5 '06; 10000mW 39:43.20 '11, 38:00R '10; 35kW 2:36:50 '09.

Nicola VIZZONI b. 4 Nov 1973 Pietrasanta, Lucca 1.93m 122kg. Fiamme Gialle.
At HT: OG: '00- 2, '04- 10, '08- dnq 13, '12- 8; WCh: '99-01-09-11-13: 7/4/9/8/7, '97-03-05-07- dnq 22/15/24/17; EC: '98-02-06-10-12-14: dnq 17/ dnq 13/9/2/5/11; WJ: '92- 5; EJ: '91- 8; WUG: '97- 5, '99- 5, '01- 1; WCp: '10- 4; ECp: '99-01-02-03-04-05-08-09-10: 4/2/7/5/3/4/2/1/2; EU23Cp: '92- 5. Won Med G 2009, ITA 1998, 2000-07, 2009-11, 2013-14.
Progress at HT: 1991- 66.62, 1992- 69.32, 1993- 70.76, 1994- 71.78, 1995- 74.48, 1996- 75.30, 1997- 77.10, 1998- 77.89, 1999- 79.59, 2000- 79.64, 2001- 80.50, 2002- 78.80, 2003- 77.69, 2004- 76.95, 2005- 74.82, 2006- 76.89, 2007- 78.21, 2008- 78.79, 2009- 79.74, 2010- 79.12, 2011- 80.29, 2012- 76.42, 2013- 77.61, 2014- 75.99.
Left-handed thrower. Engaged to Claudia Coslovich (ITA javelin record 65.30 '00).

Women

Eleonora GIORGI b. 17 Jun 1980 Cuneo 1.63m 52kg. Fiamme Azzurre. Graduated in social-economic law from University "Bocconi" of Milan.
At 20kW: OG: '12- 14; WCh: '13- 10; EC: '14- 5; EU23: '09- 11, '11- 4; WCp: '12- 14, '14- 5; ECp: '13- 6; won MedG 2013. At 10000mW: WJ: '08- 18
World best 5000m walk 2014, Italian records 20k walk 2014 & 2015.
Progress at 20kW: 2009- 1:34:27, 2010- 1:34:00, 2011- 1:33:46, 2012- 1:29:48, 2013- 1:30:01, 2014- 1:27:05, 2015- 1:26:46. pbs: 3000mW 11:50.08i/ 12:05.83 '13, 5000mW 20:01.80 '14, 10kW 44:33.56t '13, 44:14R '14.

Libania GRENOT b. 12 Jul 1983 Santiago de Cuba 1.75m 61kg. Fiamme Galle.
At 400m: OG: '08/12- sf; WCh: '01- hR, '05- h, '09/13- sf; EC: '10-12-14: 4/6/1; WY: '99- 5; PAm: '03- 4; CCp: '10- 6/2R, '14- 3/2R; ET: '10- 1. Won MedG 2009, CUB 2003-05, ITA 400m 2009-10, 2014; 200m 2012.
Four Italian 400m records 2008-09.
Progress at 400m: 1997- 56.2, 1998- 54.9, 1999- 53.87, 2000- 53.79, 2001- 52.91, 2002- 53.34A, 2003- 52.20, 2004- 51.68, 2005- 51.51, 2007- 54.21, 2008- 50.83, 2009- 50.30, 2010- 50.43, 2011- 52.17, 2012- 50.55, 2013- 50.47, 2014- 50.55. pbs: 200m 22.85 '12, 300m 36.82 '14. 500m 1:08.26 '09.
Switched from Cuba to Italy after she married Silvio Scaffetti in 2006 and gained Italian citizenship on 18 Mar 2008.

Elisa RIGAUDO b. 17 Jun 1980 Cuneo 1.68m 56kg. Fiamme Gialle.
At 20kW: OG: '04- 6, '08- 3, '12- 7; WCh: '03-05-07-09-11-13: 10/7/dnf/9/4/5; EC: '06- 3; EU23: '01- 1; WCp: '02-04-06-12: 16/5/10/7; ECp: '05-07-11: 3/4/3. At 5000mW: WJ: '98- 7; EJ: '99-6. Won MedG 20kW 2005, Italian 5000mW 2004, 2007; 10000mW 2013, 20kW 2004-05, 2008.
Progress at 20kW: 1999- 1:42:40. 2000- 1:32:50, 2001- 1:29:54, 2002- 1:30:42, 2003- 1:30:34, 2004- 1:27:49, 2005- 1:29:26, 2006- 1:28:37, 2007- 1:29:15, 2008- 1:27:12, 2009- 1:29:04, 2011- 1:30:44, 2012- 1:27:36, 2013- 1:28:41. pbs: 3000mW 11:57.00i '04, 12:28.92 '02; 5000mW 20:56.29 '02, 10kW 42:29.06t '13.
Won IAAF Walks Challenge 2004. Daughters Elena born in September 2010 and Simone on 8 Sep 2014.

Valeria STRANEO b. 5 Apr 1976 Alessandria 1.68m 44kg. SBV Runner Team 99, Turin.
At Mar: OG: '12- 8; WCh: 13- 2; EC: '14- 2. Eur CC: '11- 10. World HMar: '14- 8. Won MedG HMar 2013, ITA 10000m 2013, HMar 2012, 2014. Italian marathon record 2012.
Progress at Mar: 2009- 2:41:15, 2011- 2:26:33, 2012- 2:23:44, 2013- 2:25:58, 2014- 2:25:27. pbs: 3000m 9:31.10 '11, 10000m 32:15.87 '12; Road: 10k 32:07 '11, HMar 67:46 '12.
2nd Rotterdam Marathon 2012. Won Stramilano 2011. Children Leonardo born 2006 and Arianna 2007. Reached national standard after removal of spleen in 2010.

Alessia TROST b. 8 Mar 1993 Pordenone 1.88m 68kg. Fiamme Gialle.
At HJ: WCh: '13- 7=; EC: '14- 9=; WJ: '12- 1; WY: '09- 1; EU23: '13- 1; EJ: '11- 4; EI: '13- 4=, '15- 2; ET: '13- 2; YthOly: '10- 2. ITA champion 2013-14.
Progress at HJ: 2003- 1.37, 2004- 1.55, 2005- 1.62, 2006- 1.68, 2008- 1.81, 2009- 1.89, 2010- 1.90, 2011- 1.87, 2012- 1.92, 2013- 2.00i/1.98, 2014- 1.96i/1.91, 2015- 1.97i. pbs: 100mh 15.5 '11, LJ 6.01 '14, SP 10.76i '14, Pen 4035i '14.

IVORY COAST

Governing Body: Fédération Ivoirienne d'Athlétisme, Abidjan. Founded 1960.

Murielle AHOURÉ b. 23 Aug 1987 Abidjan 1.67m 57kg. Graduated in criminal law from the University of Miami, USA
At 100m/200m: OG: '12- 7/6; WCh: '13- 2/2; AfCh: '14- 2/1. At 60m: WI: '12- 2, 14- 2. Won NCAA Indoor 200m 2009.
Two African 60m indoor records 2013. CIV records 100m (3) 2009-11, 200m (3) 2012-13.
Progress at 100m: 2005- 11.96, 2006- 11.42, 23.33; 2007- 11.41/11.28w, 23.34; 2008- 11.45, 23.50; 2009- 11.09, 22.78; 2010- 11.41, 2011- 11.06/10.86w, 2012- 10.99, 22.42; 2013- 10.91, 22.24; 2014- 10.97, 22.36. pbs: 60m 6.99i '13, 300m 38.09i '07, 400m 54.77 '08.
Lived in Paris from age 2, then USA from age 12. Won first medals for Ivory Coast at World Champs.

JAMAICA

Governing body: Jamaica Athletics Administrative Association, PO Box 272, Kingston 5. Founded 1932.
2014 Champions: **Men** 100m: Nickel Ashmeade 10.06, 200m: Rasheed Dwyer 20.04, 400m: Akeem Gauntlett 45.00, 800m: Ricardo Cunningham 1:48.10, 1500m: Lenford Adams 4:00.51, 5000m: Demarley Johnson 16:08.64, 110mh: Andrew Riley 13.27, 400mh: Roxroy Cato 48.48, HJ: Christoffe Bryan 2.19, LJ: Damar Forbes 8.10, TJ: Damon McLean 16.15, SP: O'Dayne Richards 20.56, DT: Chad Wright 62.69, JT: Orrin Powell 66.43. **Women**: 100m: Veronica Campbell-Brown 10.96, 200m: Anneisha McLaughlin 22.79, 400m: Novlene Williams-Mills 50.05, 800m: Natoya Goule 2:01.34, 1500m: Sharlene Nickle 4:30.80, 100mh: Monique Morgan 12.96, 400mh: Kaliese Spencer 53.41, HJ: Kimberly Williamson 1.84, LJ: Jovanee Jarrett 6.38, TJ: Kimberly Williams 14.07, SP: Danniel Thomas 16.04, DT: Kellion Knibb 58.88, HT: Natalie Grant 57.90, JT: Kateema Riettie 46.69.

Nickel ASHMEADE b. 7 Apr 1990 Ocho Rios, Saint-Ann 1.84m 87kg.
At 200m/4x100mR (100m): WCh: '11- 5, '13- 4/1R (5); CG: 14- 3/1R; WJ: '08- 2/2R (2 4x400m); WY: '07- 3 (2, 3 MedR); PAm-J: '09- 1; won DL 2012, CAC 2009.
World 4x200m record 2014.
Progress at 100m, 200m: 2006- 10.60, 21.30; 2007- 10.39, 20.76; 2008- 10.34, 20.80/20.16w; 2009- 10.37/ 10.21w, 20.40; 2010- 10.39, 20.63; 2011- 9.96, 19.91; 2012- 9.93, 19.85; 2013- 9.90, 19.93; 2014- 9.97/9.95w, 19.95. pbs: 60m 6.62i '14, 400m 47.19 '12.

Kemar BAILEY-COLE b. 10 Jan 1992 St. Catherine 1.95m 83kg. Racers TC.
At 100m/4x100mR (200m): OG: '12- res (1)R; WCh: '13- 4/1R; CG: '14- 1/1R; WY: '09- sf/sf.
Progress at 100m: 2008- 10.85, 2009- 10.41/10.38w, 2010- 10.53, 2011- 10.28, 2012- 9.97, 2013- 9.93, 2014- 9.96/9.95w. pbs: 150mSt 15.00 '14, 200m 20.83 '12, 400m 47.36 '14.

Yohan BLAKE b. 26 Dec 1989 St. James 1.81m 79kg. Racers TC.
At 100m/4x100mR: OG: '12- 2/2/1R; WCh: '11- 1/1R; WJ: '06- 3/1R, '08- 4/2R; WY: '05- 7; PAm-J: '07- 2 (3 4x400m); won CAC-J 100m & 200m 2006; JAM 100m & 200m 2012.
World record 4x100m 2012, 4x200m 2014.
Progress at 100m, 200m: 2005- 10.56, 22.10; 2006- 10.33, 20.92; 2007- 10.11, 20.62; 2008- 10.27/10.20w, 21.06; 2009- 10.07/9.93dq, 20.60; 2010- 9.89, 19.78; 2011- 9.82/9.80w, 19.26; 2012- 9.69, 19.44; 2013- 20.72, 2014- 10.02, 20.48. pbs: 60m 6.75i '08, 150mSt 14.71 '14, 400m 46.32 '13.
3-month drugs ban from positive test at Jamaican Champs 25 Jun 2009. Cut 200m pb from 20.60 to 19.78 in Monaco 2010 and then to 19.26 in Brussels 2011. Youngest ever World 100m champion at 21 in 2011.

Usain BOLT b. 21 Aug 1986 Sherwood Content, Trelawny 1.96m 88kg. Racers TC.
At (100m)/200m/4x100mR: OG: '04- h, '08 & '12- 1/1/1R; WCh: '05- 8, '07- 2/2R, '09- 1/1/1R, '11- dq/1/1R, '13- 1/1/1R; CG: '14- 1R; WJ: 02- 1/2R/2R; WY: '01- sf, '03- 1; PAm-J: '03- 1/2R; WCp: '06- 2; won WAF 200m 2009, DL 100m 2012, CAC 200m 2005, JAM 100m 2008-09, 2013; 200m 2005, 2007-09.
World records: 100m (3), 200m (2), 4x100m (4) 2008-12, best low altitude 300m 2010, CAC records 100m (4) 2008-09, 200m (3) 2007-09, WJR 200m 2003 & 2004, World U18 200m record 2003.
Progress at 100m, 200m, 400m: 2000- 51.7; 2001- 21.73, 48.28; 2002- 20.58, 47.12; 2003- 20.13, 45.35; 2004- 19.93, 2005- 19.99, 2006- 19.88, 2007- 10.03, 19.75, 45.28; 2008- 9.69, 19.30, 46.94; 2009- 9.58, 19.19, 45.54; 2010- 9.82, 19.56, 45.87; 2011- 9.76, 19.40; 2012- 9.63, 19.32; 2013- 9.77, 19.66, 46.44; 2014- 9.98. pbs: 60m 6.31+ '09, 100y 9.14+ '11, 150m 14.35 straight & 14.44+ turn '09 (world bests), 300m 30.97 '10 (world low altitude best).
Bolt was the sensational superstar of the 2008 Olympics when he won triple gold – all in world records. In 2009 he smashed both the 100m and 200m WRs at the World Champs and after two more golds at the 2011 Worlds (dq for false start at 100m) he repeated his Olympic treble in 2012 and won a further World treble in 2013. Ten World Champs medals matches Carl Lewis. In 2002, after running 20.61 to win the CAC U17 200m title, he became the youngest ever male world junior champion at 15y 332d and set a world age best with 20.58, with further age records for 16 and 17 in 2003-04. Won IAAF 'Rising Star' award for men in 2002 and 2003 and male Athlete of the Year award 2008-09, 2011-12. He has won 39 of his 43 100m finals 2007-14. He was appointed an Ambassador-at-Large for Jamaica.

Nesta CARTER b. 11 Oct 1985 Banana Ground 1.78m 70kg. MVP TC.
At 100m/4x100mR: OG: '08/12- 1R; WCh: '07- sf/2R, '11- 7/1R, '13- 3/1R; CCp: '14- 1R. At 200m: WJ: '04- sf/res (2)R. At 60m: WI: '10-12-14: 7/2/7.
Three world 4x100m records 2008-12.
Progress at 100m: 2004- 10.0/10.56/10.52w, 2005- 10.59, 2006- 10.20, 2007- 10.11, 2008- 9.98, 2009- 9.91, 2010- 9.78, 2011- 9.89, 2012- 9.95, 2013- 9.87, 2014- 9.96/9/89w. pbs: 50m 5.67i '12, 60m 6.49i '12, 200m 20.25 '11, 400m 47.46 '15.

Roxroy CATO b. 25 Apr 1988 Saint Mary 1.83m 76kg.Was at Lincoln University, Missouri, USA.
At 400mh: OG: '12- h; CG: '14- dq h.
Progress at 100m, 200m: 2007- 54.24; 2008- 52.75, 2009- 50.74, 2010- 49.45, 2011- 49.66, 2012- 49.03, 2013- 49.15, 2014- 48.48. pbs: 100m 11.01 '08, 200m 21.36Ai '11, 21.38 '13, 400m 46.97 '14.

Rasheed DWYER b. 29 Jan 1989 St. Mary 1.88m 80kg. G.C.Foster College.
At 200m/4x100mR: CG : '10- sf/2R, '14- 1; WJ: '08- res2R; WUG: '11- 1, '13- 2; CCp: '14- 2.
CAC 4x200m record 2014.
Progress at 200m: 2006- 21.67, 2007- 21.81, 2008- 21.84, 2009- 21.12/20.82w, 2010- 20.49, 2011- 20.20, 2012- 20.59, 2013- 20.15, 2014- 19.98. pbs: 100m 10.20 '13, 400m 47.49 '15.

Jason LIVERMORE b. 25 Apr 1988 Kingston 1.78m 77kg. Akan Track.
At (100m)/200m/4x100mR: WCh: '13- sf; CG: '14- 6/3/1R; PAm: '07-, '11- sf.
CAC 4x200m record 2014.
Progress at 100m, 200m: 2007- 10.64, 22.02; 2008- 10.61, 2009- 10.66, 2010- 10.43, 21.61; 2011- 10.31, 20.73A; 2012- 10.31, 21.00; 2013- 10.07, 20.13; 2014- 10.05, 20.25. pbs: 200m 20.83 '12, 400m 47.36 '14.

Hansle PARCHMENT b. 17 Jun 1990 Saint Thomas 1.96m 90kg. Student of psychology at University of the West Indies.
At 110mh: OG: '12- 3; WCh: '13- sf; CG: '10- 5; WY: '07- sf; WUG: '11- 1. Won JAM 2012.

Three Jamaican 110mh records 2012-13.
Progress at 110mh: 2010- 13.71, 2011- 13.24, 2012- 13.12, 2013- 13.05, 2014- 12.94. Pb 400mh 53.74 '08.

Asafa POWELL b. 23 Nov 1982 St Catherine 1.90m 88kg. MVP. Studied sports medicine at Kingston University of Technology.
At 100m/4x100mR: OG: '04- 5 (dns 200), '08- 5/1R, '12- 7; WCh: '03- qf, '07- 3/2R, '09- 3/1R; CG: '02- sf/2R, '06- 1/1R; PAm-J: '01- 2R. Won JAM 100m 2003-05, 2007, 2011; 200m 2006, 2010; WAF 100m 2004, 2006-08; 200m 2004; DL 100m 2011, GL 2006.
Four world 100m records, five CAC & Commonwealth 2005-07, seven JAM 2004-7; WR 4x100m 2008. Two world bests 100y 2010.
Progress at 100m, 200m: 2001- 10.50, 2002- 10.12, 20.48; 2003- 10.02/9.9, 2004- 9.87, 20.06; 2005- 9.77, 2006- 9.77, 19.90; 2007- 9.74, 20.00; 2008- 9.72, 2009- 9.82, 2010- 9.82/9.72w, 19.97; 2011- 9.78, 20.55; 2012- 9.85, 2013- 9.88, 2014- 9.87. pbs: 50m 5.64i '12, 60m 6.42+ '09, 6.50i '12; 100y 9.07+ '10, 400m 45.94 '09.
Disqualified for false start in World quarters 2003 after fastest time (10.05) in heats. In 2004 he tied the record of nine sub-10 second times in a season and in 2005 he took the world record for 100m at Athens, tying that at Gateshead and Zürich in 2006, when he ran a record 12 sub-10 times and was world athlete of the year. Took record to 9.74 in Rieti 2007 and ran 15 sub-10 times in 2008, including seven sub-9.90 in succession after 5th place at Olympics. Now has record 84 sub-10 times (plus 7w). Withdrew from 2011 Worlds through injury. IAAF Athlete of the Year 2006. He tested positive for a banned stimulant on 21 Jun 2013; an original 18-month ban was reduced to 6 months by the CAS. Elder brother Donovan (b. 31 Oct 1971): at 60m: 6.51i '96 (won US indoors '96, 6 WI '99); 100m 10.07/9.7 '95.

O'Dayne RICHARDS b. 14 Dec 1988 St. Andrew 1.78m 117kg. MVP TC. Data communications graduate.
At SP: WCh: '13- dnq 20; CG: '14- 1; WUG: '11- 1; CCp: '14- 2; won CAC 2011, 2013; JAM 2013-14.
CAC shot record 2014.
Progress at SP: 2008- 16.76, 2009- 18.05, 2010- 18.74, 2011- 19.93, 2012- 20.31, 2013- 20.97, 2014- 21.61. pb DT 58.31 '12.

Andrew RILEY b. 6 Sep 1988 Saint Thomas 1.88m 80kg. Economics graduate of University of Illinois.
At 110mh: OG: '12- h; WCh: '11- sf, '13- 8; CG: 14- 1. Jamaican champion 2011, 2013-14; won NCAA 100m 2012, 110mh 2010 & 2012. At 60mh: WI: '14 dns final.
Progress at 110mh: 2009- 13.74/13.61w, 2010- 13.45, 2011- 13.32, 2012- 13.19, 2013- 13.14, 2014- 13.19. Pbs: 60m 6.57i '12, 100m 10.02 '12, 200m 21.25w '12, 60mh 7.53i '12, HJ 2.10 '08.
First to win NCAA 100m and 110mh double 2012.

Warren WEIR b. 31 Oct 1989 Trelawny 1.78m 75kg. Racers TC.
At 200m/4x100mR: OG: '12- 3; WCh: '13- 2/res 1R; CG: '14- 1; won DL 2013, JAM 2013. At 110mh: WJ: '08- sf.
World 4x200m record 2014.
Progress at 200m: 2008- 22.26, 2009- 21.46w, 2010- 21.52, 2011- 20.43, 2012- 19.84, 2013- 19.79, 2014- 19.82. pbs: 100m 10.02 '13, 400m 46.23 '13, 110mh 13.65 '07, 13.45w '08; 400mh 53.28 '09.

Jason YOUNG b. 21 Mar 1991 1.80m 68kg. Racers TC.
At 200m: WUG: '11- 2.
Progress at 200m: 2007- 22.10, 2008- 21.61, 2009- 21.57, 2011- 20.53, 2012- 19.86, 2013- 19.98/19.96w, 2014- 20.85. pb 100m 10.06 '12.

Women

Schillonie CALVERT b. 27 Jul 1988 Saint James 1.66m 57kg. Racers TC. Univ. of Technology.
At 100m/4x100R: OG: '12- res (2)R; WCh: '13- sf/1R; CG: '14- 5/1R; WJ: '04- 7, '06- sf/3/3R; WY: '05- 3; PAm-J '05- 2, '07-1 (2 200m).
CAC & Commonwealth 4x100m record 2013.
Progress at 100m: 2004- 11.44/11.33w, 2005- 11.40, 2006- 11.21, 2007- 11.35, 2008- 11.23, 2009- 11.19, 2010- 11.36, 2011- 11.05, 2012- 11.05, 2013- 11.07, 2014- 11.08. pbs: 200m 22.55 '11, 400m 53.50 '12.

Veronica CAMPBELL-BROWN b. 15 May 1982 Clarks Town, Trelawny 1.63m 61kg. Adidas. Was at University of Arkansas, USA.
At (100m)/200m/4x100mR: OG: '00- 2R, '04- 3/1/1R, '08- 1, '12- 3/4/2R; WCh: '05- 2/4/2R, '07- 1/2/2R, '09- 4/2, '11- 2/1/2R; CG: '02- (2)/2R, '06- 2, 14- (2)/1R; WJ: '98- (qf), '00- 1/1/2R; WY: '99- (1)/1R; PAm-J: '99- 2R; CCp: '14- (1)/1R. At 60m: WI: '10-12-14: 1/1/5. Won WAF 100m 2004-05, 200m 2004; DL 100m 2014; CAC-J 100m 2000, JAM 100m 2002, 2004-05, 2007, 2011, 2014; 200m 2004-05, 2007-09, 2011.
Three CAC & Commonwealth 4x100m records 2004-12. CAC junior 100m record 2000.
Progress at 100m, 200m: 1999- 11.49, 23.73; 2000- 11.12/11.1, 22.87; 2001- 11.13/22.92; 2002- 11.00, 22.39; 2004- 10.91, 22.05; 2005- 10.85, 22.35/22.29w; 2006- 10.99, 22.51; 2007- 10.89, 22.34; 2008- 10.87/10.85w, 21.74; 2009- 10.89/10.81w, 22.29; 2010- 10.78, 21.98; 2011- 10.76, 22.22; 2012- 10.81, 22.32; 2013- 11.01/10.78w, 22.53/22.18w; 2014- 10.86, 22.94/22.30w. pbs: 50m 6.08i '12, 60m 7.00i '10, 100y 9.91+ '11 (world best), 400m 52.24i '05, 52.25 '11.
In 2000 became the first woman to become World Junior champion at both 100m and 200m. Unbeaten at 200m in 28 finals (42 races in all) from 11 March 2000 to 22 July 2005 (lost to Allyson Felix). Married Omar Brown (1 CG 200m 2006) on 3 Nov 2007. She received a public warning for a positive test for a banned diuret-

ic on 4 May 2013 and was suspended for the season, but the Court of Arbitration for Sport upheld her appeal against the suspension in February 2014.

Christine DAY b. 12 Aug 1986 St. Mary 1.68m 51kg. University of TE.
At 400m/4x400mR: OG: '12- sf/3R; WCh: '09- sf; CG: 14- 3/1R; CCp: '14- 1R.
Progress at 400m: 2006- 55.33, 2007- 53.91, 2008- 53.10, 2009- 51.54, 2010- 52.43, 2011- 52.08, 2012- 50.85, 2013- 50.91, 2014- 50.16. pb 200m 23.73 '13.

Shelly-Ann FRASER-PRYCE b. 27 Dec 1986 Kingston 1.60m 52kg. MVP. Graduate of the University of Technology. née Fraser. Married Jason Pryce on 7 Jan 2011.
At 100m/(200m)/4x100mR: OG: '08- 1, '12- 1/2/2R; WCh: '07- res (2)R, '09- 1/1R, '11- 4/2R, '13- 1/1/1R; CG: '14- 1R. At 60m: WI: '14- 1. Won WAF 2008, DL 100m 2012-13, 200m 2013; JAM 100m 2009, 2012; 200m 2012-13.
CAC and Commonwealth records 100m 2009 & 2012, 4x100m (3) 2011-13; CAC 4x200m 2014
Progress at 100m, 200m: 2002- 11.8, 2003- 11.57, 2004- 11.72, 24.08; 2005- 11.72; 2006- 11.74, 24.8; 2007- 11.31/11.21w, 23.5; 2008- 10.78, 22.15; 2009- 10.73, 22.58; 2010- 10.82dq, 22.47dq; 2011- 10.95, 22.59/22.10w; 2012- 10.70, 22.09; 2013- 10.71, 22.13; 2014- 11.01, 22.53. pb 60m 6.98i '14, 400m 55.67 '15.
Double World and Olympic champion with eight global gold medals (and four silver). Huge improvement in 2008 and moved to joint third on world all-time list for 100m when winning 2009 world 100m title. 6-month ban for positive test for a non-performance enhancing drug on 23 May 2010.

Stephenie Ann McPHERSON b. 25 Nov 1988 1.68m 55kg. MVP. Was at Kingston University of Technology.
At 400m/4x400mR: WCh: '13- 4; CG: 14- 1/1R; CCp: '14- 1R; WI: 14- 2R.
Progress at 400m: 2006- 56.42, 2007- 55.77, 2008- 52.80, 2009- 51.95, 2010- 51.64, 2012- 52.98, 2013- 49.92, 2014- 50.12. pbs: 100m 11.44 '10, 200m 22.93 '14, 800m 2:15.24 '12, 400mh 57.46 '12.

Carrie RUSSELL b. 18 Oct 1990 Cedar Valley, St. Thomas 1.71m 68kg. Univ. of Technology.
At 100m/4x100mR: WCh: '13- 1R; WJ: '06- 3/3R; WUG: '11- 1/3R.
CAC & Commonwealth 4x100m record 2013.
Progress at 100m: 2006- 11.36, 2007- 11.72, 2008- 11.44/11.39w, 2009- 11.27/11.21w, 2010- 11.14, 2011- 11.05, 2012- 11.24, 2013- 10.98, 2014- 11.10. pb: 60m 7.28 '14, 200m 22.62 '13.

Kaliese SPENCER b. 6 May 1987 Westmoreland 1.73m 59kg. Was at University of Texas.
At 400mh/4x400mR: OG: '12- 4; WCh: '07-09-11-13: sf/4&res 2R/4/dq h; CG: 14- 1; WJ: '06- 1/3R; CCp: '14- 1; Won DL 2010-12, 2014; JAM 2011, 2014. At 400m: WI: '14- 2.
Progress at 400mh: 2006- 55.11, 2007- 55.62, 2009- 53.56, 2010- 53.33, 2011- 52.79, 2012- 53.49, 2013- 54.22, 2014- 53.41. pbs: 200m 23.11 '13, 400m 50.19 '13, 800m 2:03.01 '11.

Kerron STEWART b. 16 Apr 1984 Kingston 1.75m 61kg. Adult education student at Auburn University, USA.
At 100m/(200m)/4x100mR: OG: '08- 2=/3, '12- sf/2R; WCh: '07- 7/2R, '09- 2/1R, '11- 6/5/2R, '13- 5/1R; CG: '14- 3/1RWJ: '02- 4/1R; WY: '01- 2/2R. Won NCAA 200m 2007, indoor 60m & 200m 2007; JAM 100m 2008, 2013.
Three CAC & Commonwealth 4x100m records 2011-13.
Progress at 100m, 200m: 2000- 11.89, 24.09w; 2001- 11.70, 23.90; 2002- 11.46, 24.21; 2003- 11.34, 23.50; 2004- 11.40, 23.63i/23.66; 2005- 11.63, 23.77i/24.22/23.46w; 2006- 11.03, 22.65; 2007- 11.03, 22.41; 2008- 10.80, 21.99; 2009- 10.75, 22.42; 2010- 10.96, 22.57/22.34w; 2011- 10.87, 22.63; 2012- 10.92, 22.70; 2013- 10.96, 22.71; 2014- 11.02, 23.64. pbs: 55m 6.71i '06, 60m 7.14i '07, 400m 51.83 '13.

Kimberly WILLIAMS b. 3 Nov 1988 Saint Thomas 1.69m 66kg. Florida State University, USA.
At TJ: OG: '12- 6; WCh: '09/11 dnq 15/14, '13- 4; CG: '14- 1; WJ: '06- dnq 15; WY: '05- dnq; CAG: '10- 1; PAm-J: '07- 2; CCp: '14- 4; WI: '12- 5, '14- 3. Won NCAA LJ & TJ 2009, JAM TJ 2010, 2012-14.
Progress at TJ: 2004- 12.53/12.65w, 2005- 12.63/13.09w, 2006- 13.18, 2007- 13.52, 2008- 13.82i/13.69/13.83w, 2009- 14.08/14.38w, 2010- 14.23, 2011- 14.25, 2012- 14.53, 2013- 14.62/14.78w, 2014- 14.59. pbs: 100m 11.76 '12, 200m 24.55 '11, LJ 6.55i 11, 6.42/6.66w '09.

Novlene WILLIAMS-MILLS b. 26 Apr 1982 Saint Ann 1.70m 57kg. Studied recreation at University of Florida, USA.
At 400m/4x400mR: OG: '04- sf/3R, '08- sf/3R, '12- 5/3R; WCh: '05- 2R, '07- 3/2R, '09- 4/2R, '11- 8/2R, '13- 8; CG: '06- 3, '14- 2/1R; PAm: '03- 6/2R; WI: '06- 5; WCp: '06- 3/1R, '14- 2/1R. Won DL 2014, JAM 400m 2006-07, 2009-14.
Progress at 400m: 1999- 55.62, 2000- 53.90, 2001- 54.99, 2002- 52.05, 2003- 51.93, 2004- 50.59, 2005- 51.09, 2006- 49.63, 2007- 49.66, 2008- 50.11, 2009- 49.77, 2010- 50.04, 2011- 50.05, 2012- 49.78, 2013- 50.01, 2014- 50.05. pbs: 200m 23.25 '10, 500m 1:11.83i '03.
Married 2007. Younger sister Clora Williams (b. 26.11.83) joined her on JAM's 3rd place 4x400m team at 2010 WI; she has 400m pb 51.06 and won NCAA 2006.

Shericka WILLIAMS b. 17 Sep 1985 Black River, St. Elizabeth 1.70m 64kg. MVP. Kingston University of Technology.
At 400m/4x400mR: OG: '08- 2/3R, '12- 3R; WCh: '05- sf/2R, '07- sf/2R, '09- 2/2R, '11- 6/2R; CG: '06- 5; WCp: '06- 1R, '10- 4/1R; won JAM 400m 2005.

Progress at 200m, 400m: 2001- 24.74, 2003- 23.90, 55.44; 2004- 23.96/23.70w, 53.52; 2005- 23.08, 50.97; 2006- 22.55, 50.24; 2007- 23.32, 50.37; 2008- 22.50, 49.69; 2009- 22.57, 49.32; 2010- 23.25, 50.04; 2011- 23.49/23.16w, 50.45; 2012- 23.12, 50.34; 2013- 51.86, 2014- 51.23. pb 100m 11.34 '07, 800m 2:09.17 '07.

JAPAN

Governing body: Nippon Rikujo-Kyogi Renmei, 1-1-1 Jinnan, Shibuya-Ku, Tokyo 150-8050. Founded 1911.

National Championships first held in 1914 (men), 1925 (women). **2014 Champions**: **Men**: 100m: Yoshihide Kiryu 10.22, 200m: Shota Hara 20.62, 400m: Yuzo Kanemaru 45.69, 800m: Sho Kawamoto 1:48.42, 1500m: Keisuke Tanaka 3:43.77, 5000m/10000m: Yuki Sato 13:40.99/ 28:32.07, 3000mSt: Jun Shinoto 8:35.43, 110mh: Genta Masuno 13.58, 400mh: Takayuki Kishimoto 49.49, HJ: Takashi Eto 2.23, PV: Daichi Sawano 5.61, LJ: Kota Minemura 7.94, TJ: Yohei Kajikawa 16.36, SP: Satoshi Hatase 18.50, DT: Yuji Tsutsumi 58.44, HT: Koji Murofushi 73.93, JT: Ryohei Arai 81.97, Dec: Keisuke Ushiro 8308, 20kW: Yusuke Suzuki 1:18:17, 50kW: Takayuki Tanii 3:41:32. **Women**: 100m/200m: Chisato Fukushima 11.69/23.79, 400m: Nanako Matsumoto 54.00, 800m: Fuymika Omori 2:05.05, 1500m: Ayako Jinnouchi 4:17.12, 5000m: Misaki Onishi 15:32.74, 10000m: Kasumi Nishihara 32:37.23, 3000mSt: Misaki Sango 9:49.85, 100mh: Ayako Kimura 13.34, 400mh: Satomi Kubokura 56.39, HJ: Yuki Watanabe 1.75, PV: Megumi Hamana 4.09, LJ: Mao Igarashi 6.19w, TJ: Mayu Yoshida 13.03, SP: Chiaki Yokomizo 15.22, DT: Marika Tokai 51.28, HT: Masumi Aya 61.31, JT: Yuki Ebihara 57.77, Hep: Chie Kiriyama 5500, 20k: Rei Inoue 1:31:48.

Ryohei ARAI b. 1 Feb 1988 1.83m 92kg.
At JT: AsiG: '14- 2.
Progress at JT: 2011- 78.21, 2012- 78.00, 2013- 78.19, 2014- 86.83.

Yukifumi MURAKAMI b. 23 Dec 1979 Ueshima, Ehime 1.86m 102kg. Suzuki Motor, Was at Nihon University.
At JT: OG: '04/08/12- dnq 18/15/24; WCh: '05-07-11-13: dnq 27/21/15/21, '09- 3; WJ: '98- 3; AsiG: 02-06-10: 2/2/1; AsiC: '09- 1, '11- 1; Asi-J: '97- 2; JPN champion 2000-11, 2013.
Progress at JT: 1995- 56.60, 1996- 68.00, 1997- 76.54, 1998- 73.62, 1999- 71.70, 2000- 78.57, 2001- 80.59, 2002- 78.77, 2003- 78.98, 2004- 81.71, 2005- 79.79, 2006- 78.54, 2007- 79.85, 2008- 79.71, 2009- 83.10, 2010- 83.15, 2011- 83.53, 2012- 83.95, 2013- 85.96, 2014- 81.66.

Yusuke SUZUKI b. 1 Feb 1988 Yokohama 1.69m 56kg. Fujitsu.
At 20kW: OG: '12- 36; WCh: '09-11-13: 42/7/12; WCp: '14- 4; AsiG: '10- 5, '14- 2; Asian champion 2013, 2015; JPN 2011, 2013. At 10000mW: WJ: 04-17, '06- 3; WY: '05- 3.
World 20k record 2015, Asian 10000m walk record 2014, Japanese records 10k 2015, 20k (3) 2013-15.
Progress at 20kW: 2007- 1:24:40, 2008- 1:22:34, 2009- 1:22:05, 2010- 1:20:06, 2011- 1:21:13, 2012- 1:22:30, 2013- 1:18:34, 2014- 1:18:17, 2015- 1:18:13. pbs:10kW 38:06 '15, track 38:27.09 '14.

Eiki TAKAHASHI b. 1 Feb 1988 1.75m 58kg.
At 20kW: WCp: '14- 9; AsiG: '14- 7.
Japanese 20k walk record 2015.
Progress at 20kW: 2011- 1:26:16, 2012- 1:22:33, 2013- 1:20:25, 2014- 1:18:41, 2015- 1:18:03. pbs: 5000mW 19:42.35 '12, 10000mW 39:24.42 '14.

Takayuki TANII b. 14 Feb 1983 Namerikawa, Toyama 1.67m 57kg. Sagawa, was at Nihon University.
At (20kW)/50kW: OG: '04- (15), '08- 29; WCh: '05-07-11-13: (23)/(21)/9/9; AsiG: '14- 1; At 10000mW: WJ: '02- 7; WY: '99- 3. Won Asian 20kW 2007, JPN 20kW 2004-05, 50kW 2013-14.
Japanese 50k walk record 2003.
Progress at 50kW: 2003- 3:47:54, 2006- 3:47:23, 2007- 3:50:08, 2008- 3:49:33, 2009- 3:52:22, 2010- 3:53:27, 2011- 3:48:03, 2012- 3:43:56, 2013- 3:44:25, 2014- 3:40:19. pbs: 5000mW 19:36.78 '13, 10000mW 40:03.42 '03, 20kW 1:20:39 '04, 30kW 2:11:34 '14, 35kW 2:33:37 '14.

Yuki YAMAZAKI b. 16 Jan 1984 Toyama 1.77m 65kg. Was at Juntendo University.
At (20kW)/50kW: OG: '04- 16, '08- 11/7, '12- dq; WCh: '05-07-09: 8/dnf/dq; WCp: '10- 6; AsiG: '02- dq/dq, '06- (4), '14- dq; AsiC: '03- (2), '07- 2. At 10000mW: WJ: '00- 20, '02- 5; WY: '01- 4. Won JPN 20kW 2002, 50kW 2004-10, 2012.
Four Japanese 50k walk records 2006-09. World youth 5000m walk best 2001.
Progress at 50kW: 2004- 3:55:20, 2005- 3:50:40, 2006- 3:43:38, 2007- 3:47:40, 2008- 3:41:29, 2009- 3:40:12, 2010- 3:46:46, 2011- 3:44:03, 2012- 3:41:47, 2014- 3:44:23. pbs: 5000mW 19:35.79 '01, 10000mW 39:29.00 '08, 20kW 1:20:38 '03, 30kW 2:11:31 '12, 35kW 2:33:06 '12.

Women

Ryoko KIZAKI b. 21 Jun 1985 Yosano, Kyoto Pref. 1.57m 44kg. Daihatsu.
At Mar: OG: '12- 16; WCh: 13- 4; JPN champion 2013. At HMar: WUG: '05- 2; WCh: '09-10: 12/10, At 10000m: WUG: '07- 2 (4 5000m).
Progress at Mar: 2010- 2:27:34, 2011- 2:26:32, 2012- 2:27:16, 2013- 2:23:34, 2014- 2:25:26. pbs: 1500m 4:23.36 '04, 3000m 9:16.3 '08, 5000m 15:22.87 '11, 10000m 31:38.71 '10, HMar 70:16 '09.
Marathon wins: Yokohama 2011, Nagoya 2013 (3rd 2014).

KAZAKHSTAN

Governing body: Athletic Federation of the Republic of Kazakhstan, Abai Street 48, 480072 Almaty. Founded 1959.

2014 National Champions: Men: 100m: Rakhat Magzamov 10.71, 200m: Omirserik Bekenov 21.49, 400m: Sergey Zaykov 46.70, 800m: Ivan Obeyshik 1:52.51, 1500m: Kudaybergen Zeynollayev 3:57.61, 5000m: Mikhail Krasilov 15:54.73, 10000m: Andrey Leymenov 31:56.7, 3000mSt: Amir Baytukanov 9:30.24, 110mh: Dmitriy Karpov 14.35, 400mh: Dmitriy Koblov 49.40, HJ: Yuriy Dergachov 2.28, PV: Nikita Filippov 5.50, LJ: Konstantin Safronov 7.90, TJ: Yevgeniy Ektov 16.45, SP: Ivan Ivanov 17.43, DT: Yevgeniy Labutov 51.60, HT: Vladimir Torlotov 53.55, JT: Sergey Urov 57.94, Dec: Ilya Kuznetsov 6519, 20kW: Vitaliy Anichkin 1:33:03; **Women**: 100m: Svetlana Ivanchukova 11.62, 200m: Olga Safronova 22.85, 400m: Elina Mikhina 53.02, 800m: Margarita Mukasheva 2:03.52, 1500m: Tatyana Palkina 4:50.48, 5000m/10000m: Irina Smolnikova 17:46.25/37:36.9, 3000mSt: Tatyana Neroznak 11:12.71, 100mh: Anastasiya Pilipenko 12.93, 400mh: Marina Zayko 58.50, HJ: Marina Aitova 1.85, PV: Anna Danilovskaya 3.40, LJ: Yekaterina Ektova 6.25, TJ: Irina Ektova 13.92, SP/DT: Mariya Telushkina 14.10/50.10, JT: Asiya Rabayeva 43.66, Hep: Irina Karpova 50.36, 20kW: Galina Kichigina 1:37:00.

Women

Olga RYPAKOVA b. 30 Nov 1984 Kamenogorsk 1.83m 62kg. née Alekseyeva.
At TJ/(LJ): OG: '08- 4 (dnq 29), '12- 1; WCh: '07- 11, '09- 10, '11- 2; WJ: '00- (dnq 23); AsiG: '06- (3), '10- 1/2, '14- 1; AsiC: '07- 1/1, '09- 1; WI: '08-10-12: 4/1/2; WUG: '07- (1); WCp: '06- (8), '10: 1/3; won DL TJ 2012, Asian Indoor LJ & TJ 2009. At Hep: WJ: '02- 2; WY: '01- 4; AsiG: '06- 1; won C.Asian 2003. Won KAZ LJ 2005, 2008, 2011; TJ 2008, 2011; Hep 2006.
Four Asian TJ records 2008-10, five indoors 2008-10, seven KAZ records 2007-10.
Progress at LJ, TJ: 2000- 6.23, 2001- 6.00, 2002- 6.26, 2003- 6.34i/6.14, 2004- 6.53i, 2005- 6.60, 2006- 6.63, 2007- 6.85, 14.69; 2008- 6.52/6.58w, 15.11; 2009- 6.58i/6.42, 14.53/14.69w; 2010- 6.60, 15.25; 2011- 6.56, 14.96; 2012- 14.98, 2014- 14.37. pbs: 200m 24.83 '02, 800m 2:20.12 '02, 60mh 8.67i '06, 100mh 14.02 '06, HJ 1.92 '06, SP 13.04 '06, JT 41.60 '03, Hep 6122 '06, Pen 4582i '06 (Asian rec).
Former heptathlete, concentrated on long jump after birth of daughter. Four KAZ and three Asian TJ records with successive jumps in Olympic final 2008, three Asian indoor records when won World Indoor gold in 2010. Son born June 2013.

KENYA

Governing body: Kenya Amateur Athletic Association, PO Box 46722, 00100 Nairobi. Founded 1951.

2014 National Champions: **Men**: 100m: Walter Moenga 10.58, 200m: Collins Omae 21.60, 400m/400mh: Boniface Mucheru 45.43/49.25, 800m: Ferguson Cheruiyot, 1500m: Ronald Kwemoi 3:34.6, 5000m: Joseph Kiplimo 13:30.34, 10000m: Josphat Bett 28:06.2, 3000mSt: Jairus Birech 8:18.0, 110mh: Samuel Korir 14.65, HJ: Mathew Sawe 2.10, LJ: Tera Langat 7.96, TJ: Elijah Kimitei 16.40, DT: David Limo 49.41, JT: Julius Yego 80.02, 20kW: David Kimutai 1:23:58. **Women**: 100m: Milicent Ndoro 12.19, 200m: Maureen Thomas 24.17, 400m: Maureen Maiyo 51.78, 800m: Eunice Sum 2:01.82, 1500m: Hellen Obiri 4:04.97, 5000m: Mercy Cherono 15:26.66, 10000m: Florence Kiplagat 32:30.92, 3000mSt: Purity Kirui 9:43.38, 100mh: Caroline Withera 14.60, 400mh: Francisca Koki 57.40, HJ: Caroline Cherotich 1.70, PV: Winnie Langat 3.10, LJ/TJ: Gladys Musyoki 6.17/12.98, SP: Priscilla Isiaho 13.13, DT: Roselyn Rakamba 44.89, HT: Linda Oseso 58.08, JT: Zeddy Cherotich 44.65, 20kW: Grace Njue 1:35:40.

Leonard BARSOTON b. 21 Oct 1994 1.66m 56kg.
World CC: '13- 2J, '15- 5; AfCC: '14- 1.
Progress at 10000m: 2013- 27:33.13, 2014- 27:20.74. pb 5000m 13:19.04 '13.

Emmanuel Kipkemei **BETT** b. 30 Mar 1983 1.70m 55kg.
Progress at 10000m: 2011- 26:51.95, 2012- 26:51.16, 2013- 27:28.71. pbs: 3000m 7:48.8 '14, 2M 8:25.55 '14, 5000m 13:08.35 '12, 15k 43:00+ '11, HMar 60:56 '12.

Josphat Kipkoech **BETT** b. 12 Jun 1990 Kericho 1.73m 60kg.
At 10000m: CG: '14- 2; AfCh: '14- 3; WJ: '10- 1. Kenyan champion 2014.
Progress at 5000m, 10000m: 2008- 13:44.51, 27:30.85; 2009- 12:57.43, 28:21.51; 2010- 13:11.60, 28:05.46A; 2011- 13:11.29, 26:48.99; 2012- 13:32.20i, 27:39.65; 2013- 13:19.46, 27:44.26A; 2014- 13:48.5A, 27:56.14. pbs: 3000m 7:42.38 '09, 10M 46:22 '14, HMar 61:01 '12.

Jairus Kipchoge **BIRECH** b. 14 Dec 1992 Uasin Gishu 1.67m 56kg.
At 3000mSt: CG: '14- 2; AfG: '11- 4; AfCh: '14- 1; Af-J: '11- 2; CCp: '14- 1. Won DL 2014, Kenyan 2014.
Progress at 3000mSt: 2010- 8:50.0A, 2011- 8:11.31, 2012- 8:03.43, 2013- 8:08.72, 2014- 7:58.41. pbs: 2000m 4:58.76 '11, 3000m 7:41.83 '13, 5000m 13:48.0A '14.

Bethwel Kiprotich **BIRGEN** b. 6 Aug 1988 Eldoret 1.78m 64kg.
At 1500m: WCh: '13- sf; WI: '14- 8.
Progress at 1500m: 2010- 3:35.60, 2011- 3:34.59, 2012- 3:31.00, 2013- 3:30.77, 2014- 3:31.22. pbs: 800m 1:48.32 '11, 1M 3:50.42 '13, 3000m 7:37.15 '13, 5000m 14:01.0A '12.

Stanley Kipleting **BIWOTT** b. 21 Apr 1986 1.76m 60kg.
Progress HMar, Mar: 2006- 2:14:25, 2007- 61:20,

2010- 2:09:41, 2011- 60:23, 2:07:03; 2012- 59:44, 2:05:12; 2013- 58:56, 2014- 59:18, 2:04:55; 2015- 59:20. Road pbs: 10k 28:00 '12, 15k 42:13 '13, 20k 56:02 '13, 30k 1:28:06 '12.
Marathon wins: São Paulo 2010, Chunchon 2011, Paris 2012; 2nd London 2014

Collins CHEBOI b. 25 Sep 1987 1.75m 64kg.
At 1500m: AfG: '11- 2.
World 4x1500m record 2014.
Progress at 1500m: 2007- 3:49.0A, 2009- 3:36.24, 2010- 3:34.17, 2011- 3:32.45, 2012- 3:32.08, 2013- 3:31.53, 2014- 3:32.00. pbs: 1M 3:49.56 '14, 2000m 5:00.30+ '12, 3000m 7:51.41 '10, 5000m 13:51.3A '13.

Vincent Kiprop **CHEPKOK** b. 5 Jul 1988 Kapkitony, Keiyo district 1.74m 60kg.
At 5000m: WCh: '09- 9. World CC: '07- 2J, '11- 3. African CC: '12- 5.
Progress at 5000m, 10000m: 2006- 13:17.57, 28:23.46; 2008- 13:06.41, 2009- 12:55.98, 2010- 12:51.45, 2011- 12:55.29, 2012- 12:59.28, 26:51.68; 2013- 13:15.51, 27:17.30. pbs: 1500m 3:40.47 '08, 3000m 7:30.15 '11, Rd 10k 28:12 '12, HMar 60:53 '14, Mar 2:13:21 '14.

Nixon Kiplimo **CHEPSEBA** b. 12 Dec 1990 Keiyo 1.85m 66kg.
At 1500m: OG: '12- 11; WCh: '13- 4; Af-J: '09- 2. Won DL 2011.
Progress at 1500m: 2009- 3:37.2A, 2010- 3:32.42, 2011- 3:30.94, 2012- 3:29.77, 2013- 3:33.15, 2014- 3:34.64. pbs: 800m 1:45.6A '12, 1000m 2:18.61 '09, 1M 3:50.95 '13, 3000m 7:37.64i '11, 5000m 13:26.28 '14.
Married Mercy Kosgei (1500m 4:11.7A '06, 2 WJ 06, 3/2 WJ CC 06/07) on 23 Apr 2011.

Ferguson Rotich CHERUIYOT b. 30 Nov 1989 1.83m 73kg.
At 800m: WCh: '13- sf; CG: '14- 4; AfCh: '14- 4. Kenyan champion 2014.
Progress at 800m: 2013- 1:43.22, 2014- 1:42.84. pb 1000m 2:16.88 '14, 1500m 3:49.0A '14
Changed first name from Simon to Ferguson in honour of Manchester United manager Alex Ferguson.

Augustine Kiprono **CHOGE** b. 21 Jan 1987 Kipsigat, Nandi 1.62m 53kg.
At 5000m: CG: '06- 1; WJ: '04- 1. At 3000m: WY: '03- 1; WI: '10-12-14: 11/2/9. At 1500m: OG: '08- 9; WCh: '05- h, '09- 5. World CC: '03-05-06-08: 4J/1J/7 (4k)/12. Won KEN 1500m 2013, East African Youth 800m/1500m/3000m 2003, Junior 1500m 2004.
Records: World 4x1500m 2009, world youth 5000m 2004, world junior 3000m 2005.
Progress at 1500m, 5000m: 2003- 3:37.48, 13:20.08; 2004- 3:36.64, 12:57.01; 2005- 3:33.99, 12:53.66; 2006- 3:32.48, 12:56.41; 2007- 3:31.73, 2008- 3:31.57, 13:09.75; 2009- 3:29.47, 2010- 3:30.22, 13:04.64; 2011- 3:31.14, 13:21.24; 2012- 3:37.47, 13:15.50; 2013- 3:33.21, 13:05.31; 2014- 3:35.5A, 13:06.12. pbs: 800m 1:44.86 '09, 1000m 2:17.79i '09, 1M 3:50.01 '13, 2000m 4:56.30i '07, 3000m 7:28.00i/7:28.76 '11, 10000m 29:06.5A '02.
At 17 in 2004 he become youngest to break 13 minutes for 5000m.

Dickson Kiptolo **CHUMBA** b. 27 Oct 1986 1.67m 50kg. Nandi.
Progress at Mar: 2010- 2:09:20dh, 2011- 2:07:23, 2012- 2:05:46, 2013- 2:10:15, 2014- 2:04:32, 2015- 2:06:34. pbs: 1500m 3:44.33 '10, 5000m 13:41.34 '10, road: 10k 28:09 '13, HMar 61:34 '12, 60:39dh '14; 30k 1:28:36 '12.
Marathon wins: Rome 2011, Eindhoven 2012, Tokyo 2014; 3rd Chicago 2014, Tokyo 2015.

Geoffrey Kipsang KAMWOROR b. 28 Nov 1992 1.68m 54kg.
World CC: '11- 1J, '15- 1; HMar: '14- 1.
Tied world 30km record 2014.
Progress at 10000m, HMar, Mar: 2011- 27:06.35, 59:31; 2012- 59:26, 2:06:12; 2013- 28:17.0A, 58:54, 2:06:26; 2014- 59:08, 2:06:39. pbs: 1500m 3:48.15 '10, 3000m 7:54.15 '10. 5000m 13:12:23 '11; Road: 15k 42:05 '12, 20k 56:02 '13, 30k 1:27:37 '14.
3rd in Berlin Marathon 2012 (on debut) and 2013 (4th 2014). Won RAK half marathon 2013.

Bidan KAROKI Muchiri b. 21 Aug 1990 Nyandarua 1.69m 53kg. S&B Foods, Japan.
At 10000m: OG: 12- 5; WCh: '13- 6; AfG: '11- 2. World CC: '15- 2. Won Kenyan CC 2012.
Progress at 10000m: 2010- 27:23.62, 2011- 27:13.67, 2012- 27:05.50; 2013- 27:13.12, 2014- 26:52.36. pbs: 1500m 3:50.91 '08, 3000m 7:37.68 '13, 5000m 13:15.25 '14, 15k 42:01 '14, 10M 45:02 '14, HMar 59:23 '14. Went to Japan in 2007.

Ezekiel KEMBOI Cheboi b. 25 May 1982 Matira, near Kapsowar, Marakwet District 1.75m 62kg.
At 3000mSt: OG: '04- 1, '08- 7, '12- 1; WCh: '03-05-07-09-11-13: 2/2/2/1/1/1; CG: '02-06-10-14: 2/1/2/3; AfG: '03- 1, '07- 2; AfCh: '02-06-10-14: 4/dq/2/3; Af-J: '01- 1. Won WAF 2009, Kenyan 2003, 2006-07.
Progress at 3000mSt: 2001- 8:23.66, 2002- 8:06.65, 2003- 8:02.49, 2004- 8:02.98, 2005- 8:09.04, 2006- 8:09.29, 2007- 8:05.50, 2008- 8:09.25, 2009- 7:58.85, 2010- 8:01.74, 2011- 7:55.76, 2012- 8:10.55, 2013- 7:59.03, 2014- 8:04.12. pbs: 1500m 3:40.8A '04, 3000m 7:44.24 '12, 5000m 13:50.61 '11, 10k Rd 28:38 '11.
Five gold and three silver medals from global 3000m steeplechase races.

Stephen Kipkosgei **KIBET** b. 9 Nov 1986.
At HMar: WCh: '12- 5.
Progress at HMar: 2009- 60:34, 2010- 60:09, 2011- 60:20, 2012- 58:54, 2013- 59:59, 2014- 59:21. road pbs: 10k 27:44 '14, 15k 42:01+ '12, 20k 55:55+ '12, Mar 2:08:05 '12.
Six successive half marathon wins 2009-12.

Vincent KIBET b. 6 May 1991 1.70m 57kg.
Progress at 1500m: 2010- 3:46.7A, 2011- 3:42.7A,

2012- 3:40.51A, 2013- 3:35.62, 2014- 3:31.96. pbs: 800m 1:46.71 '14, 1M 3:52.15 '14, 3000m 7:58.9 '14.

Mike Kipruto **KIGEN** b. 15 Jan 1986 Keiyo district 1.70m 54kg.
At 5000m/(10000m): AfCh: '06- 2/2; WCp: '06- 2. World CC: '06- 5. Won Kenyan 5000m 2006.
Progress at 5000m, 10000m: 2005- 13:22.48, 2006- 12:58.58, 28:03.70; 2008- 13:09.84, 2009- 13:04.38, 2011- 13:11.65, 27:30.53; 2012- 13:21.55A, 27:03.49; 2013- 13:36.51, 2014- 13:26.6. pbs: 3000m 7:35.87 '06, 2M 8:20.09 '05, Road: 10M 45:34 '14, HMar 59:58 '11, 25k 1:14:17 '14, 30k 1:29:15 '14, Mar 2:06:59 '14. 2nd Frankfurt marathon 2014.

Dennis Kipruto **KIMETTO** b. 22 Jan 1984 near Kapngetuny.
World records 25km road 2012, marathon 2014.
Progress at Mar: 2012- 2:04:16, 2013- 2:03:45, 2014- 2:02:57. Road pbs: 10k 28:21 '12, 15k 42:46 '11, HMar 59:14 '12, 25k 1:11:18 '12, 30k 1:27:38 '14.
Second Berlin 2012 in fastest ever marathon debut after earlier major road wins at half marathon and 25k in Berlin in 2012. Won Tokyo and Chaicago marathons 2013. Dnf Boston before WR in Berlin marathon 2014.

Eliud KIPCHOGE b. 5 Nov 1984 Kapsisiywa, Nandi 1.67m 52kg.
At 5000m: OG: '04- 3, '08- 2; WCh: '03-05-07-09-11: 1/4/2/5/7; CG: '10- 2. At 3000m: WI: '06- 3. World CC: '02-03-04-05: 5J/1J/4/5; HMar: '12- 6. Won WAF 5000m 2003, 3000m 2004, Kenyan CC 2005.
World junior 5000m record 2003. World road best 4M 17:10 '05.
Progress at 1500m, 5000m, 10000m: 2002- 13:13.03, 2003- 3:36.17, 12:52.61; 2004- 3:33.20, 12:46.53; 2005- 3:33.80, 12:50.22; 2006- 3:36.25i, 12:54.94; 2007- 3:39.98, 12:50.38, 26:49.02; 2008- 13:02.06, 26:54.32; 2009- 12:56.46, 2010- 3:38.36, 12:51.21; 2011- 12:55.72i/12:59.01, 26:53.27; 2012- 12:55.34, 27:11.93. At HMar, Mar: 2012: 59:25, 2013- 60:04, 2:04:05, 2014- 60:52, 2:04:11. pbs: 1M 3:50.40 '04, 2000m 4:59.?+ '04, 3000m 7:27.66 '11, 2M 8:07.39i '12, 8:07.68 '05; Road: 10k 26:55dh '06, 27:34 '05; 25k 1:13:42 '14, 30k 1:28:46 '14.
Kenyan Junior CC champion 2002-03, followed World Junior CC win by winning the World 5000m title, becoming at 18 years 298 days the second youngest world champion. Age 19 bests for 3000m & 5000m 2004. Ran 26:49.02 in 10,000m debut at Hengelo in 2007. Won Hamburg Marathon on debut (2:05:30) then 2nd Berlin in 2013, 1st Rotterdam & Chicago 2014.

Kenneth Kiprop **KIPKEMOI** b. 2 Aug 1984 1.65m 52kg.
At 10000m: WCh: '13- 7; AfCh: '12- 1. Kenyan champion 2012. World HMar: '14- 10.
Progress at 10000m, HMar: 2009- 62:59A, 2011- 27:48.5A, 59:47; 2012- 26:52.65, 59:11; 2013- 27:28.50, 60:45; 2014- 27:30.94, 59:01. pbs: 3000m 7:49.28+ '11, 5000m 13:03.37 '12, 15k 43:22 '12, 25k 1:22:32 '14.

Alfred KIPKETER b. 26 Dec 1996 1.69m 61kg.
At 800m: WJ: '14- 1; WY: '13- 1.
Progress at 800m: 2013- 1:46.2A, 2014- 1:43.95.

John KIPKOECH (also CHEPKWONY) b. 29 Dec 1991 1.60m 52kg.
At 5000m: WCh: '13- h;WJ: '10- 2. World CC: '09- 9J.
Progress at 5000m: 2010- 13:26.03, 2012- 12:49.50, 2013- 13:01.64, 2014- 13:07.60. pbs: 3000m 7:32.72 '10, 10000m 29:14.8A '13, 10k Rd 27:57 '14, HMar 61:38 '14.

Silas KIPLAGAT b. 20 Aug 1989 Siboh village, Marakwet 1.70m 57kg.
At 1500m: OG: '12- 7; WCh: '11- 2, '13- 6; CG: '10- 1; AfCh: '10- 4; WI: '12- 6. Won DL 2012, 2014; Kenyan 2011.
World 4x1500m record 2014.
Progress at 1500m: 2009- 3:39.1A, 2010- 3:29.27, 2011- 3:30.47, 2012- 3:29.63, 2013- 3:30.13, 2014- 3:27.64. pbs: 800m 1:44.8A '12, 1M 3:47.88 '14, 3000m 7:39.94 '10, 5000m 13:55.0A '13, 10k Rd 28:00 '09.

Asbel Kipruto **KIPROP** b. 30 Jun 1989 Uasin Gishu, Eldoret. North Rift 1.86m 70kg.
At (800m)/1500m: OG: '08- 1, '12- 12; WCh: '07- 4, '09- sf/4, '11- 1, '13- 1; AfG: '07- 1; AfCh: '10- 1, '14- 2; CCp: '10- 6, '14- 2; Won DL 2010, Kenyan 2007, 2010. At 800m: AfCh: '08- 3. World CC: '07- 1J.
World 4x1500m record 2014.
Progress at 800m, 1500m: 2007- 3:35.24, 2008- 1:44.71, 3:31.64; 2009- 1:43.17, 3:31.20; 2010- 1:43.45, 3:31.78; 2011- 1:43.15, 3:30.46; 2012- 1:45.91, 3:28.88; 2013- 1:44.8A, 3:27.72; 2014- 1:43.34, 3:28.45; 2015- 1:44.4A. pbs: 1M 3:48.50 '09, 3000m 7:42.32 '07, 5000m 13:59.7A '10.
Father David Kebenei was a 1500m runner.

Wilson KIPROP b. 14 Apr 1987 Soi, Uasin Gishu 1.72m 62kg.
At 10000m: OG: '12- dnf; AfCh: '10- 1. World HMar: '10- 1, '14- 6. Won KEN 10000m 2010, CC 2014.
Progress at 10000m, Mar: 2010- 27:26.93A, 2:09:09; 2011- 27:32.9A; 2012- 27:01.98, 2013- 28:18.0A, 2:19:20. pbs: 5000m 13:30.13i '09, 13:45.38 '08; 1Hr 20756m '09; Road: 15k 43:42 '14, 20k 56:57 '14, HMar 59:15 '12.

Brimin KIPRUTO b. 31 Jul 1985 Korkitony, Marakwet District 1.76m 54kg.
At 3000mSt: OG: '04- 2, '08- 1 '12- 5; WCh: '05-07-09-11: 3/1/7/2; CG: '10- 3; Af-J: '03- 2; KEN champion 2011. At 1500m: WJ: '04- 3. At 2000St: WY: '01- 2. World 4k CC: '06- 18.
Commonwealth & African 3000mSt record 2011.
Progress at 3000mSt: 2002- 8:33.0A, 2003- 8:34.5A, 2004- 8:05.52, 2005- 8:04.22, 2006- 8:08.32, 2007- 8:02.89, 2008- 8:10.26, 2009- 8:03.17,

2010- 8:00.90, 2011- 7:53.64, 2012- 8:01.73, 2013- 8:06.86, 2014- 8:04.64. pbs: 1500m 3:35.23 '06, 2000m 4:58.76i '07, 3000m 7:39.07i '12, 7:47.33 '06; 5000m 13:58.82 '04, 2000mSt 5:36.81 '01.
First name is actually Firmin, but he stayed with the clerical error of Brimin, written when he applied for a birth certificate in 2001.

Conseslus KIPRUTO b. 8 Dec 1994 Eldoret 1.74m 55kg.
At 3000mSt: WCh: '13- 2; WJ: '12- 1; won DL 2013. At 2000St: WY: '11- 1. World CC: 2013- 5J.
Progress at 3000mSt: 2011- 8:27.30, 2012- 8:03.49, 2013- 8:01.16, 2014- 8:09.81. pbs: 800m 1:49.0A '15, 1000m 2:19.85 '12, 1500m 3:39.57 '13, 3000m 7:44.09 '12, 2000mSt 5:28.65 '11.

Wilson KIPSANG Kiprotich b. 15 Mar 1982 Keiyo district 1.78m 59kg.
At Mar: OG: '12- 3; HMar: WCh: '09- 4.
World marathon record 2013.
Progress at HMar, Mar: 2008- 59:16, 2009- 58:59, 2010- 60:04, 2:04:57; 2011- 60:49, 2:03:42; 2012- 59:06, 2:04:44; 2013- 61:02, 2:03:23; 2014- 60:25, 2:04:29. pbs: 5000m 13:55.7A '09, 10000m 28:37.0A '07; Road: 10k 27:42 '09, 15k 41:51+ '11, 10M 44:59+ '11, 20k 56:10+ '12, 25k 1:12:58 '13, 30k 1:28:02 '13.
Eight wins from eleven marathons: third in Paris in 2:07:13 on debut, won Frankfurt in 2010 and 2011, Lake Biwa 2011, London 2012 and 2014, Honolulu 2012, Berlin 2013 and New York 2014. Won World Marathon Majors 2013/14. Has record five marathons inside 2:05. Won Great North Run 2012.

Mark Kosgei **KIPTOO** b. 21 Jun 1976 Lugafri 1.75m 64kg. Kenyan Air Force.
At 5000m: CG: '10- 3; AfG: '07- 9; AfCh: '10- 3, '12- 1 (2 10000m). World CC: '08- 14, '09- 7. Won World Military 5000m & 2nd 10000m 2007, KEN 5000m 2008.
Progress at 5000m, 10000m, Mar: 2007- 13:12.60, 28:22.62; 2008- 13:06.60, 27:14.67; 2009- 12:57.62, 2010- 12:53.46, 28:37.4A; 2011- 12:59.91, 26:54.64; 2012- 13:06.23, 27:18.22; 2013- 13:20.51, 28:24.04A, 2:06:16; 2014- 2:06:49. pbs: 1500m 3:48.0A '05, 3000m 7:32.97 '09, 2M 8:29.96 '12, HMar 60:29 '11
Won Frankfurt Marathon 2014 (2nd 2013 on debut).

Bernard KIPYEGO Kiprop b. 16 Jul 1986 Kapkitony, Keiyo district 1.60m 50kg.
At 10000m: WCh: '09- 5; Af-J: '03- 3. At Mar: WCh: '13- 12. World CC: '05-07-08: 2J/3/10; HMar: '09- 2.
Progress at 10000m, Mar: 2003- 29:29.09, 2004- 28:18.94, 2005- 27:04.45, 2006- 27:19.45, 2007- 26:59.51, 2008- 27:08.06, 2009- 27:18.47, 2010- 2:07:01, 2011- 2:06:29, 2012- 2:06:40, 2013- 28:36.5A, 2:07:19, 2014- 2:06:22. pbs: 3000m 7:54.91 '05, 5000m 13:09.96 '05, Road: 15k 42:34 '11, 10M 45:44 '11, HMar 59:10 '09, 30k 1:29:51 '14.
Won in Berlin on half marathon debut in 59:34 in 2009, 5th Rotterdam on marathon debut 2010, won Amsterdam 2014, 2nd Paris 2011 and Beijing 2013; 3rd Chicago 2011, Tokyo 2013 and Rotterdam 2014.

Michael Kipkorir **KIPYEGO** b. 2 Oct 1983 Kemeloi, Marakwet 1.68m 59kg.
At 3000mSt: WCh: '03- h; WJ: '02- 1; AfCh: '08- 2. At 3000m: WY: '99- 8; Af-J: '01- 2. At Mar: WCh: '13- 25. World CC: '02-03-07: 12J/4 4k/6.
Progress at 3000mSt: 2001- 8:41.26, 2002- 8:22.90, 2003- 8:13.02, 2004- 8:23.14, 2005- 8:10.66, 2006- 8:14.99, 2007- 8:11.62, 2008- 8:09.05, 2009- 8:08.48, 2010- 8:16.46. At Mar: 2011- 2:06:48, 2012- 2:07:37, 2013- 2:06:58, 2014- 2:06:58. pbs: 1500m 3:39.93 '05, 3000m 7:50.03 '09.
Won Tokyo Marathon 2012, 2nd 2013, 4th 2014. Brother of Sally Kipyego.

Abel KIRUI b. 4 Jun 1982 Bornet, Rift Valley 1.77m 62kg. Police.
At Mar: OG: '12- 2; WCh: '09- 1, '11- 1.
Progress at Mar: 2006- 2:15:22, 2007- 2:06:51, 2008- 2:07:38, 2009- 2:05:04, 2010- 2:08:04, 2011- 2:07:38, 2012- 2:07:56, 2014- 2:09:04. pbs: 1500m 3:46.10 '05, 3000m 7:55.90 '06, 5000m 13:52.71 '05, 10000m 28:16.86A '08; Road: 10k 27:59 '09, 15k 42:22 '07, 10M 46:40 '11, HMar 60:11 '07, 25k: 1:13:41 '08, 30k 1:28:25 '08.
Brilliantly retained World marathon title with halves of 65:07 and 62:31 and a fastest 5k split of 14:18. Won Vienna Marathon 2008, 2nd Berlin 2007, 3rd Rotterdam 2009. Uncle Mike Rotich has marathon pb 2:06:33 '03.

Gilbert Kiplangat **KIRUI** b. 22 Jan 1994 1.72m 55kg.
At 3000mSt: WJ: '12- 2; won Af-J 2011. At 2000St: WY: '11- 2.
Progress at 3000mSt: 2010- 8:40.1A, 2011- 8:25.03, 2012- 8:11.27, 2013- 8:06.96, 2014- 8:11.86. pbs: 2000mSt 5:30.49 '11.

Timothy KITUM b. 20 Nov 1994 Marakwet 1.72m 60kg.
At 800m: OG: '12- 3; WJ: '12- 2; WY: '11- 3.
Progress at 800m: 2011- 1:44.98, 2012- 1:42.53, 2013- 1:44.45, 2014- 1:43.65. pbs: 600m 1:14.4A '12, 1000m 2:17.96 '12.

Sammy Kiprop **KITWARA** b. 26 Nov 1986 Sagat village, Marakwet district 1.77m 54kg.
At 10000m: Kenyan champion 2009. World HMar: '09- 10, '10- 3.
Progress at 10,000m, HMar, Mar: 2007- 28:11.6A, 2008- 28:12.26A, 60:54; 2009- 27:44.46A, 58:58; 2010- 28:32.77A, 59:34; 2011- 58:47, 2012- 2:05:54, 2013- 61:53, 2:05:16; 2014- 60:24, 2:04:28. pbs: 5000m 13:34.0A '08, Road: 10k 27:11 '10, 15k 41:54 '09, 10M 45:17 '08, 20k 57:42 '08, 25k 1:13:42 '14, 30k 1:28:46 '14.
2nd Chicago marathon 2014 (4th 2012), 3rd Rotterdam & Chicago 2013, Tokyo 2014

Bernard Kiprop **KOECH** b. 31 Jan 1988 1.65m 50kg.
At Mar: WCh: '13- dnf.

Progress at Mar: 2013- 2:04:53, 2014- 2:06:08. pbs: 1500m 3:44.33 '10, 5000m 13:41.34 '10, road: 10k 27:54 '12, 15k 42:32 '12, 10M 45:12 '14, 20k 56:54 '13, HMar 59:10 '12, 58:42dh '13, 25k 1:13:42 '14, 30k 1:28:47 '14.
Fifth in Dubai on marathon debut (6th fastest ever) and third in Amsterdam in 2013, 2nd Rotterdam 2014.

Isiah Kiplangat **KOECH** b. 19 Dec 1993 Kericho 1.78m 60kg.
At 5000m: OG: '12- 5; WCh: '11- 4, '13- 3; CG: '14- 2; AfCh: '14- 2; CCp: '14- 1; won DL 5000m 2012, Kenyan 2011, 2013. At 3000m: WY: '09- 1. World CC: '10- 4J, '11- 10J.
World junior records indoors: 5000m 2011, 3000m 2011 & 2012.
Progress at 5000m, 10000m: 2010- 13:07.70, 2011- 12:53.29i/12:54.18, 2012- 12:48.64, 27:17.03; 2013- 12:56.08, 2014- 13:07.55. pbs: 1500m 3:38.7A '12, 3000m 7:30.43 '12, 2M 8:14.16 '11.

Paul Kipsiele **KOECH** b. 10 Nov 1981 Cheplanget, Buret District 1.68m 57kg.
At 3000mSt: OG: '04- 3; WCh: '05- 7, '09- 4, '13- 4; AfG: '03- 2; AfCh: '06- 1; WCp: '06- 2; won DL 2010-12, WAF 2005-08. At 3000m: WI: 08- 2.
Progress at 3000mSt: 2001- 8:15.92, 2002- 8:05.44, 2003- 7:57.42, 2004- 7:59.65, 2005- 7:56.37, 2006- 7:59.94, 2007- 7:58.80, 2008- 8:00.57, 2009- 8:01.26, 2010- 8:02.07, 2011- 7:57.32, 2012- 7:54.31, 2013- 8:02.63, 2014- 8:05.47. pbs: 1500m 3:37.92 '07, 2000m 5:00.9+i '08, 5:01.84 '14; 3000m 7:32.78i '10, 7:33.93 '05; 2M 8:06.48i/8:13.31 '08, 5000m 13:02.69i 12, 13:05.18 '10.

Micah Kemboi **KOGO** b. 3 Jun 1986 Burnt Forest, Uasin Gishu 1.70m 60kg.
At 10000m: OG: '08- 3; WCh: '09- 7.
World 10k road record (27:01) 2009.
Progress at 5000m, 10000m: 2004- 14:02.99, 2005- 13:16.31, 2006- 13:00.07, 26:35.63; 2007- 13:10.68, 26:58.42; 2008- 13:03.71, 27:04.11; 2009- 13:01.30, 27:26.33; 2010- 13:07.62, 2011- 13:46.01, 27:50.50. At Mar: 2013- 2:06:56, 2014- 2:17:12. pbs: 2000m 5:03.05 '06, 3000m 7:38.67 '07, 2M 8:20.88 '05; Road: 15k 41:51+ '11, 10M 44:59+ '11, 20k 56:10+ '12, HMar 59:07 '12.
Won Van Damme 10,000m in Brussels in 2006 for 6th world all-time. 2nd Boston on marathon debut 2013, then 4th Chicago.

Daniel Kipchirchir **KOMEN** b. 27 Nov 1984 Chemorgong, Kolbatek district 1.75m 60kg.
At 1500m: WCh: '05- h, '07/11- sf; WI: '06- 2, '08- 2; won WAF 2007. At 5000m: Af-J: '03- 2.
Progress at 1500m, 5000m: 2003- 13:49.20, 2004- 3:34.66, 13:16.26; 2005- 3:29.72, 2006- 3:29.02, 2007- 3:31.75, 2008- 3:31.49, 13:24.39; 2009- 3:34.86i, 2010- 3:32.16, 13:04.02; 2011- 3:32.47A, 13:20.80; 2012- 3:32.98, 13:09.90; 2013- 3:33.05, 2014- 13:33.67. pbs: 800m 1:47.3A '05, 1000m 2:16.9+ '06, 1M 3:48.28 '07, 3000m 7:31.41 '11, Mar 2:14:20 '15.

Leonard Patrick **KOMON** b. 10 Jan 1988 Korungotuny Village, Mt. Eldon District 1.75m 52kg.
World CC: '06-07-08-09-10: 2J/4J/2/4/4.
World road records 10km and 15km 2010.
Progress at 5000m, 10000m: 2006- 13:04.12, 2007- 13:04.79, 2008- 13:17.48, 26:57.08; 2009- 12:58.24, 28:02.24A; 2010- 12:59.15, 2011- 26:55.29, 2012- 27:01.58. pbs: 2000m 5:04.0+ '07, 3000m 7:33.27 '09, 2M 8:22.56 '07, road 10k 26:44 '10, 15k 41:13 '10, 10M 44:27 '11, HMar 59:14 '14.
Ran fastest ever debut half marathon, 59:14 to win at Berlin in 2014.

Japheth Kipyegon **KORIR** b. 30 Jun 1993 Sotik 1.68m 55kg.
At 5000m: 3rd Comm YthG 2008. World CC: 09-10-13: 5J/3J/1; AfCC: 11- 1J, 12- 2J.
Progress at 5000m: 2008- 13:57.2A, 2010- 13:19.43, 2011- 13:17.18, 2012- 13:11.44i, 2013- 13:31.94 pbs: 3000m 7:40.37 '12, 10k Rd 28:43 '12.
Became youngest ever senior men's world cross-country champion in 2013.

James Kipsang **KWAMBAI** b. 28 Feb 1983 Marakwet East district 1.62m 52kg
Commonwealth marathon record 2009.
Progress at Mar: 2006- 2:10:20, 2007- 2:12:25, 2008- 2:05:36, 2009- 2:04:27, 2010- 2:11:31, 2011- 2:08:50, 2012- 2:05:50, 2013- 2:06:25, 2014- 2:07:38. pbs: Road: 10k 28:17 '02, 20k 58:51 '08, HMar 59:09 '09, 30k 1:28:27 '08.
Won Brescia and Beijing marathons 2006, took 4:44 off pb when 2nd in Berlin 2008 and went to joint second all-time when 2nd in Rotterdam 2009. Won Joongang Seoul Marathon 2011-13.

Ronald KWEMOI b. 19 Sep 1995 Mt. Elgon 1.80m 68kg.
At 1500m: CG: '14- 2; AfCh: '14- 3; Kenyan champion 2014. World CC: '13- 9J.
World junior 1500m record 2014.
Progress at 1500m: 2013- 3:45.39, 2014- 3:28.81. pbs: 5000m 13:21.53 '14.

Lawi LALANG b. 15 Jun 1991 Eldoret 1.70m 58kg. University of Arizona.
Won NCAA CC 2011, 5000m 2013 & 10000m 2013; indoor 3000m & 5000m 2013, 1M and 3000m 2013.
Progress at 5000m: 2011- 13:30.64, 2012- 13:18.55, 2013- 13:00.95, 2014- 13:03.85. pbs: 800m 1:48.88 '11, 1500m 3:33.20 '13, 1M 3:52.88i '14, 3000m 7:36.44 '14, 10000m 28:14.63 '13.
Older brother **Boaz** (b. 8 Fen 1989) won CG 800m '10, pb 1:42.95 '10.

Thomas Pkemei **LONGOSIWA** b. 14 Jan 1982 West Pokot 1.75m 57kg. North Rift.
At 5000m: OG: '08- 12, '12- 3; WCh: '11- 6, '13- 4; AfG: '07- 6. World CC: '06- 13J (but dq after birthdate found to be 1982). Won Kenyan 5000m 2007.
Progress at 5000m: 2006- 13:35.3A, 2007- 12:51.95, 2008- 13:14.36, 2009- 13:03.43, 2010- 13:05.60, 2011-

12:56.08, 2012- 12:49.04, 2013- 12:59.81, 2014- 12:56.16. pbs: 1500m 3:41.92 '13, 2000m 5:01.6+ '10, 3000m 7:30.09 '09, 10000m 28:11.3A '06.

James Kiplagat **MAGUT** b. 20 Jul 1990 Nandi 1.80m 64kg.
At 1500m: CG: '10- 2, '14- 1; WJ: '08- 2, AfCh: '12- 3, '14- 5; Af-J: '08- 1.
World 4x1500m record 2014.
Progress at 1500m: 2008- 3:42.3A, 2009- 3:36.8A, 2010- 3:40.47, 2012- 3:33.31, 2013- 3:35.2A, 2014- 3:30.61. pbs: 1000m 2:19.72 '13, 1M 3:49.43 '14.

Patrick MAKAU Musyoki b. 2 Mar 1985 Manyanzwani, Tala Kangundo district 1.73m 57kg.
World HMar: '07- 2, '08- 2.
World 30km and marathon records 2011.
Progress at HMar, Mar: 2005- 62:00, 2006- 62:42, 2007- 58:56, 2008- 59:29, 2009- 58:52, 2:06:14; 2010- 59:51, 2:04:48; 2011- 2:03:38, 2012- 2:06:08, 2013- 2:14:10, 2014- 2:08:22. pbs: 3000m 7:54.50 '07, 5000m 13:42.84 '06. Road: 10k 27:27 '07, 15k 41:30 '09, 10M 45:41 '12, 20k 55:53 '07, 30k 1:27:38 '11.
Second fastest ever debut marathon when 4th Rotterdam 2009 and won there a year later in 2:04:48 for fourth world all-time. Won Berlin 2010 and 2011, Frankfurt 2012, Fukuoka 2014.

Martin Irungu **MATHATHI** b. 25 Dec 1985 Nyahururu 1.67m 52kg. Suzuki, Japan.
At 10000m: OG: '08- 7; WCh: '05- 5, '07- 3, '11- 5. World CC: '06- 3.
Progress at 5000m, 10000m: 2003- 14:09.3A, 27:43.16; 2004- 13:03.84, 27:22.46; 2005- 13:05.99, 27:08.42; 2006- 13:05.55, 27:10.51; 2007- 13:22.13, 27:09.90; 2008- 13:46.87, 27:08.25; 2009- 13:11.46, 26:59.88; 2010- 13:10.94, 2011- 13:15.93, 27:23.85; 2012- 13:27.06, 27:35.16; 2013- 13:41.80, 27:52.65. pbs: 1500m 3:38.57 '06, Road: 10M 44:51 '04 (world junior best), 15k 42:14 '10, 20k 56:44 '10, HMar 58:56dh '11, 59:48 '10; Mar 2:07:16 '13.
Won Great North Run 2011. Won Fukuoka Marathon 2013.

Bernard Nganga MBUGUA b. 17 Jan 1985 1.70m 55kg.
Progress at 3000mSt: 2007- 8:43.0A, 2009- 8:17.94, 2010- 8:16.22, 2011- 8:05.88, 2012- 8:08.33, 2013- 8:19.14, 2014- 8:15.01. pbs: 1500m 3:40.29 '13, 5000m 13:49.19 '11, 2000mSt 5:25.70 '10.

Moses Cheruiyot **MOSOP** b. 17 Jul 1985 Kamasia, Marakwet 1.72m 57kg. Police officer.
At 10000m: OG: '04- 7; WCh: '05- 3. World CC: '02-03-05-07-09: 10J/7J/18/2/11; HMar: '10- 10. Won KEN 10000m 2006, CC 2009.
World records 25,000m and 30,000m 2011.
Progress at 5000m, 10000m: 2002- 29:38.6A, 2003- 13:11.75, 27:13.66; 2004- 13:09.68, 27:30.66; 2005- 13:06.83, 27:08.96; 2006- 12:54.46, 27:17.00; 2007- 13:07.89, 26:49.55. At Mar: 2011- 2:05:37/ 2:03:06wdh, 2012- 2:05:03, 2013- 2:11:19, 2014- 2:06:19. pbs: 3000m 7:36.88 '06, 15k Rd 42:25+ '10, HMar 59:20 '10, 20000m 58:02.2 '11, 25000m 1:12:25.4 '11, 30000m 1:26:47.4 '11.
Second with fastest ever marathon debut at Boston and won at Chicago 2011 and Xiamen 2015. 3rd Rotterdam 2012. Formerly married to Florence Kiplagat.

Abel Kiprop **MUTAI** b. 2 Oct 1988 Nandi 1.72m 73kg.
At 3000mSt: OG: '12- 3; WCh: '13- 7; Af-J: '07- 1; Kenyan champion 2012. At 2000mSt: WY: '05- 1.
Progress at 3000mSt: 2006- 8:35.38, 2007- 8:29.76, 2009- 8:11.40, 2011- 8:21.02, 2012- 8:01.67, 2013- 8:08.83, 2014- 8:15.83. pbs: 3000m 8:05.16 '06, 5000m 14:07.80 '06, 2000mSt 5:24.69 '05.

Emmanuel Kipchirchir **MUTAI** b. 12 Oct 1984 Tulwet, Rift Valley 1.68m 54kg.
At Mar: OG: '12- 17; WCh: '09- 2.
World 30k record in Berlin Marathon 2014.
Progress at Mar: 2007- 2:06:29, 2008- 2:06:15, 2009- 2:06:53, 2010- 2:06:23, 2011- 2:04:40, 2012- 2:08:01, 2013- 2:03:52, 2014- 2:03.13. pbs: 10000m 28:21.14 '06, Road: 10k 27:51 '06, 15k 42:11 '10, 20k 56:44 '10, HMar 59:52 '11, 25k 1:13:08 '14, 30k 1:27:37 '14.
Made marathon debut with 7th in Rotterdam in 2:13:06 in 2007, then won in Amsterdam. London: 4th 2008 & 2009, 2nd 2010 & 2013, 1st 2011. 2nd New York 2010-11, Chicago 2013, Berlin 2014. World Marathon Majors winner 2010/11.

Geoffrey Kiprono **MUTAI** b. 7 Oct 1981 Koibatek District 1.83m 56kg. Policeman.
At 10000m: AfCh: '10- 3. World CC: '11- 5. Won Kenyan 10000m 2013, CC 2011.
Progress at 10000m, Mar: 2007- 2:12:50sh?, 2008- 28:01.74, 2:07:50; 2009- 2:07:01, 2010- 27:27.79A, 2:04:55; 2011- 2:03:02wdh/2:05:06, 2012- 28:23.0A, 2:04:15; 2013- 27:55.3A, 2:08:24; 2014- 2:08:18. pbs: 15k 42:12+ '13, 20k 56:02 '13, HMar 58:58 '13, 25k 1:13: 08 '14, 30k 1:27:37 '14.
Marathons: Won Monte Carlo 2008, Eindhoven 2008 & 2009, Boston 2011, New York 2011 & 2013, Berlin 2012; 2nd Rotterdam and Berlin 2010. World Marathon Majors winner 2011/12.

Caleb Mwangangi **NDIKU** b. 9 Oct 1992 Machakos 1.83m 68kg.
At 1500m: WJ: '10- 1; WY: '09- 2; AfG: '11- 1; AfCh: '12- 1; Kenyan champion 2012. At 3000m: CCp: '14- 1; WI: '14- 1. At 5000m: CG: '14- 1; AfCh: '14- 1; won DL 2014 World CC: '10- 1J.
Progress at 1500m, 5000m: 2009- 3:38.2A, 2010- 3:37.30, 2011- 3:32.02, 2012- 3:32.39, 2013- 3:29.50, 13:03.80; 2014- 3:35.8A, 12:59.17. pbs: 800m 1:52.6A '07, 1M 3:49.77 '11, 3000m 7:30.99 '12, 10000m 28:28.4A '14.
His father David was a javelin thrower.

Jonathan Muia **NDIKU** b. 18 Sep 1991 1.73m 60kg. Team Hitachi Cable, Japan.
At 3000mSt: CG: '14- 1; AfCh: '14- 2; WJ: '08- 1, '10- 1; Af-J: '09- 1. At 2000mSt: WY: '07- 4.
Progress at 3000mSt: 2008- 8:17.28, 2009-

8:28.1A, 2010- 8:19.25A. 2011- 8:07.75, 2012- 8:17.88, 2013- 8:18.78, 2014- 8:10.44. pbs: 1500m 3:39.27 '10, 3000m 7:39.63 '14, 5000m 13:11.99 '09, 10000m 27:37.72 '09, 2000mSt 5:37.30 '07.

Lucas Kimeli **ROTICH** b. 16 Apr 1990 1.71m 57kg.
At 3000mSt: WY: '07- 2. World CC: '08- 3J, '10- 18.
Progress at 5000m, 10000m: 2007- 29:12.5A, 2008- 13:15.54, 2009- 12:58.70, 28:15.0A; 2010- 12:55.06, 27:33.59; 2011- 13:00.02, 26:43.98; 2012- 13:09.58, 27:09.38. pbs: 1500m 3:43.64 '08, 3000m 7:35.57 '11, HMar 59:44 '11, Mar 2:07:18 '14.
2nd Amsterdam Marathon 2014.

David Lekuta **RUDISHA** b. 17 Dec 1988 Kilgoris 1.89m 73kg. Masai.
At 800m: OG: '12- 1; WCh: '09- sf, '11- 1; CG: '14- 2; WJ: '06- 1/4R; AfCh: '08- 1, '10- 1; Af-J: '07- 1; CCp: '10- 1. Won DL 2010-11, WAF 2009, Kenyan 2009-11.
Three world 800m records 2010-12, four African records 2009-10.
Progress at 800m: 2006- 1:46.3A, 2007- 1:44.15, 2008- 1:43.72, 2009- 1:42.01, 2010- 1:41.01, 2011- 1:41.33, 2012- 1:40.91, 2013- 1:43.87, 2014- 1:42.98. pbs: 400m 45.50 '10, 45.2A '13; 600m 1:13.71 '14.
IAAF Male Athlete of the Year 2010, won 26 successive 800m finals 2009-11. His father Daniel won 4x400m silver medal at 1968 Olympics with 440y pb 45.5A '67.

Stephen Kiptoo **SAMBU** b. 3 Jul 1988 Eldoret 1.69m 55kg. Was at University of Arizona.
Progress at 10000m: 2009- 28:37.96, 2010- 29:01.34, 2011- 27:28.64, 2012- 28:06.16, 2014- 26:54.61. pbs: 1500m 3:43.56 '12, 3000m 7:51.59i/8:13.69 '12, 5000m 13:13.74i/13:31.51 '12, 10M Rd 45:29 '14, HMar 60:41 '13.

Edwin Cheruiyot **SOI** b. 3 Mar 1986 Kericho 1.72m 55kg.
At 5000m: OG: '08- 3, '12- h; WCh: '13- 5; AfCh: '10- 1; CCp: '10- 4. At 3000m: WI: '08- 4, '12- 3; won WAF 3000m 2007, 5000m 2007-08. World CC: '06- 8 4k, '07- 9.
Progress at 5000m, 10000m: 2002- 29:06.5A, 2004- 13:22.57, 2005- 13:10.78, 2006- 12:52.40, 27:14.83; 2007- 13:10.21, 2008- 13:06.22, 2009- 12:55.03, 2010- 12:58.91, 2011- 12:59.15, 2012- 12:55.99, 2013- 12:51.34, 26:49.41; 2014- 12:59.82. pbs: 1500m 3:40.52 '13, 2000m 5:01.4+ '10, 3000m 7:27.55 '11, 2M 8:14.10 '11, 10k Rd 28:13 '08.

Paul Kipngetich **TANUI** b. 22 Dec 1990 Chesubeno village, Moio district 1.72m 54kg. Kyudenko Corporation, Japan.
At 10000m: WCh: '11- 9, '13- 3. World CC: '09-10-11: 4J/8/2. Won Kenyan CC 2010.
Progress at 5000m, 10000m: 2008- 13:59.2A, 2009- 13:37.15, 27:25.24; 2010- 13:14.87, 27:17.61; 2011- 13:04.65, 26:50.63; 2012- 13:19.18, 27:27.56; 2013- 13:16.57, 27:21.50, 2014- 13:00.53, 26:49.41. pbs: 1500m 3:43.97 '10, 3000m 7:50.88 '11, HMar 62:48 '14.

Hillary Kipsang **YEGO** b. 2 Apr 1992 1.78m 60kg.
At 2000mSt: WY: '09- 1.
Progress at 3000mSt: 2009- 8:46.8A, 2010- 8:19.50, 2011- 8:07.71, 2012- 8:11.83. 2013- 8:03:57, 2014- 8:09.07. pbs: 1500m 3:43.3 '10, 3000m 7:53.18 '10, 2000mSt 5:25.33 '09, 10k Rd 29:10 '11, Mar 2:13:59 '13.
Won 2013 Athens Classic Marathon on debut at the distance.

Julius Kiplagat **YEGO** b. 4 Jan 1989 Cheptonon, Nandi district1.75m 90kg.
At JT: OG: '12- 12; WCh: '13- 4; CG: '10- 7, '14- 1; AfG: '11- 1; AfCh: '10-12-14: 3/1/1; CCp: '14- 4. Kenyan champion 2008-14.
Five Kenyan javelin records 2011-13.
Progress at JT: 2008- 72.18A, 2009- 74.00A, 2010- 75.44, 2011- 78.34A, 2012- 81.81; 2013- 85.40, 2014- 84.72.

Women

Emily CHEBET Muge b. 18 Feb 1986 Bornet 1.57m 45kg.
At 10000m: WCh: '07- 9, '13- 4; CG: '14- 3; AfCh: '06- 3, '14- 2. World CC: '03-10-13-15: 5J/1/1/6; AfCC: 12- 3.
Progress at 5000m, 10000m: 2006- 31:33.39, 2007- 32:31.21, 2010- 32:49.43A. 2011- 31:30.22, 2013- 14:46.89, 30:47.02; 2014- 32:10.82. pbs: 1500m 4:18.75 '05, 3000m 8:53.46 '05; Road 10k 30:58 '12, 15k 47:32 '14, 20k 64:38 '14, HMar 68:01 '14.
Has daughter Emily. Married to Edward Muge (Kenyan 10000m champion 2008 in pb 27:52.09A).

Milcah CHEMOS Cheywa b. 24 Feb 1986 Bugaa Village, Mt. Elgon district 1.63m 48kg. Police.
At 3000mSt: OG: '12- 3; WCh: '09- 3, '11- 3, '13- 1; CG: '10- 1, '14- 2; AfCh: '10- 1; CCp: '10- 2. Won DL 2010-13, KEN 2010-11.
Commonwealth & African 3000mSt record 2012.
Progress at 3000mSt: 2009- 9:08.57, 2010- 9:11.71, 2011- 9:12.89, 2012- 9:07.14, 2013- 9:11.65, 2014- 9:21.91. pbs: 800m 2:04.35A '11, 1500m 4:12.3A '09, 2000m 5:41.64 '09, 3000m 8:43.92 '09, 2000mSt 6:16.95 '13.
Married to Alex Sang (pb 800m 1:46.84 '08). Started athletics seriously after birth of daughter Lavine Jemutai and in first season, 2008, was 4th in Kenyan 800m. Rapid progress from first steeplechase in April 2009.

Joyce CHEPKIRUI b. 20 Aug 1988 Bureti 1.52m 48kg.
At 10000m: OG: '12- dnf; CG: '14- 1; AfCh: '14- 1. At 5000m: CCp: '14- 2. At 1500m: AfG: '11- 2; Af-J: '07- 5. At HMar: WCh: '10- 5. AfCC: '12- 1. Won Kenyan CC 2012.
Progress at 10000m, HMar: 2007- 75:11, 2009- 71:47, 2010- 69:25, 2011- 31:26.10, 69:04; 2012- 32:34.71A, 67:03; 2013- 68:15, 2014- 32:09.35, 66:19. pbs: 1500m 4:08.80A '11, 5000m 15:58.31 '14,

3000mSt 10:26.7A '08; Road: 10k 30:37 '11, 15k 46:49 '14, 10M 51:33 '13, 20k 62:55 '14, Mar 2:30:23 '13.
Won Honolulu Marathon 2014. Married Erick Kibet, pb HMar 61:10 '10, in 2009.

Lydia Tum **CHEPKURUI** b. 23 Aug 1984 1.70m 52kg.
At 3000mSt: WCh: '13- 2; AfG: '11- 4, Kenyan champion 2013.
Progress at 3000mSt: 2011- 9:30.73, 2012- 9:14.98, 2013- 9:12.55, 2014- 9:24.07. pbs: 1500m 4:14.97 '12, 3000m 8:55.21i '14, 2M 9:45.97i '14.

Gladys CHERONO b. 12 May 1983 Kericho 1.66m 50kg.
At 10000m: WCh: '13- 2; AfCh: '12- 1 (1 5000m). World HMar: '14- 1. Won Kenyan 5000m 2012.
Progress at 5000m, 10000m, Mar: 2005- 16:16.8A, 2007- 16:03.8A, 2008- 15:56.0A, 2012- 15:39.5A, 32:41.40; 2013- 14:47.12, 30:29.23; 2014- 16:49.8A, 34:13.0A; 2015- 2:20:03. pbs: 1500m 4:25.13 '04, 3000m 8:34.05 '13, Road: 15k 47:43 '13, 20k 63:26 '13, HMar 66:48 '13.
Second Dubai Marathon 2015 (third fastest ever debut).

Mercy CHERONO b. 7 May 1991 Kericho 1.68m 54kg.
At (3000m)/5000m: WCh: '11- 5, '13- 2; CG: '14- 1; AfCh: '14- 5; WJ: '08- (1), '10- 1/2; WY: '07- (1); Af-J: '09- 1/2; won DL 2014, KEN 5000m 23014. World CC: '07-09-10: 23J/2J/1J. Won Afr CC 2011. Two world 4x1500m records 2014. Commonwealth 2M best 2014.
Progress at 5000m: 2007- 16:49.13A, 2009- 15:46.74A, 2010- 14:47.13, 2011- 14:35.13, 2012- 14:47.18, 2013- 14:40.33, 2014- 14:43.11. pbs: 800m 2:05.7A '13, 1500m 4:02.31 '11, 2000m 5:35.65 '10, 3000m 8:21.14 '14, 2M 9:11.49 '14, 10000m 34:33.4A '06, 3000mSt 10:41.4A '13.

Sharon Jemutai **CHEROP** b. 16 Mar 1984 Marakwet district 1.57m 45kg.
At Mar: WCh: '11- 3. At 10000m: AfG: '99- 5. At 5000m: WJ: '00- 3. World CC: '02- 10J.
Progress at Mar: 2007- 2:38:45, 2008- 2:39:52, 2009- 2:33:53, 2010- 2:22:43, 2011- 2:22:42wdh/ 2:29:14, 2012- 2:22:39, 2013- 2:22:28, 2014- 2:23:44. pbs: 3000m 9:09.23 '04, 5000m 15:40.7A '00, 10000m 32:03.0A '11, HMar 67:08 '11, 30k 1:39:21dh/1:40:04 '14.
Marathon wins: Toronto & Hamburg 2010, Boston & Turin 2012, Singapore 2013; 2nd Berlin 2013, Frankfurt 2014; 3rd Boston 2011, 2013.

Vivian CHERUIYOT b. 11 Sep 1983 Keiyo 1.55m 38kg.
At 5000m (/10000m): OG: '00- 14, '08- 5, '12- 2/3; WCh: '07- 2, '09- 1, '11- 1/1; CG: '10- 1; WJ: '02- 3; AfG '99- 3; AfCh: '10- 1; CCp: '10- 1; won DL 2010-12. At 3000m: WY: '99- 3; WI: '10- 2. World CC: '98-9-00-01-02-04-06-07-11: 5J/2J/1J/4J/3J/8 4k/8 4k/8/1. Won KEN 1500m 2009, 5000m 2010-11, 10000m 2011-12.
African 2000m record 2009, Commonwealth 5000m 2009 & 2011, indoor 3000m (8:30.53) 2009; Kenyan 5000m 2007 & 2011.
Progress at 5000m, 10000m: 1999- 15:42.79A, 2000- 15:11.11, 2001- 15:59.4A, 2002- 15:49.7A, 2003- 15:44.8A, 2004- 15:13.26, 2006- 14:47.43, 2007- 14:22.51, 2008- 14:25.43, 2009- 14:37.01, 2010- 14:27.41, 2011- 14:20.87, 30:48.98; 2012- 14:35.62, 30:30.44. pbs: 1500m 4:06.6A '12, 2000m 5:31.52 '09, 3000m 8:28.66 '07, 2M 9:12.35i '10.
Laureus Sportswomen of the Year for 2011. Married Moses Kirui on 14 Apr 2012; son Allan born 19 Oct 2013.

Flomena Daniel **CHEYECH** b. 5 Jul 1982 1.65m 49kg..
At Mar: CG: '14- 1.
Progress at Mar: 2006- 2:42:15A, 2012- 2:34:13, 2013- 2:24:34, 2014- 2:22:44, 2015- 2:26:54. pbs: 3000m 9:16.21 '07, 5000m 15:19.47 '09, 10000m 31:58.50 '08, road: 15k 48:26 '13, HMar 67:39 '13, 30k 1:40:33 '14.
Marathon wins: Porto Alegre 2012, Vienna & Toronto 2013, Paris 2014.

Irene JELAGAT b. 10 Dec 1988 Samutet, Nyanza 1.62m 45kg.
At 1500m: OG: '08- h; WCh: '09- h; CG: '10- 6; AfG: '11- 1; AfCh: '08- 5, '10- 4; WJ: '06- 1; WY: '05- dns; WI: '10- 5. At 3000m: WI: 13- 4.
Two world 4x1500m records 2014.
Progress at 1500m: 2005- 4:21.3A, 2006- 4:08.88, 2007- 4:10.27, 2008- 4:04.59, 2009- 4:03.62, 2010- 4:03.76, 2011- 4:02.59, 2014- 4:04.07. pb 800m 2:02.99 '06, 2000m 5:46.4 '14, 3000m 8:28.51 '14, 2M 9:12.90 '14, 5000m 15:01.73 '14.

Jemima Sumgong JELAGAT b. 21 Dec 1984 Eldoret 1.58m 45kg.
Progress at Mar: 2006- 2:35:22, 2007- 2:29:41, 2008- 2:30:18, 2010- 2:32:34, 2011- 2:28:32, 2012- 2:31:52, 2013- 2:20:48, 2014- 2:20:41dh/2:25:10. pbs: 1500m 4:26.95 '15, 5000m 16:51.0A '13, 10000m 33:08.0A '13, Road: 10k 31:15 '06, 15k 47:14 '13, 10M 50:38 '13, 20k 62:32 '13, HMar 68:32 '14, 30k 1:39:20dh '14.
Marathon wins: Las Vegas 2006, Castellón 2011, Rotterdam 2013; 2nd Boston 2012, Chicago 2013 & New York 2014. Married Noah Talam in 2009, daughter born in 2011. Originally given a 2-year ban in 2012, but later cleared by the IAAF.

Hyvin Kiyeng **JEPKEMOI** b. 13 Jan 1992 1.56m 45kg.
At 3000mSt: WCh: '13- 6; AfG: '11- 1 (4 5000m); AfCh: '12- 3.
Progress at 3000mSt: 2011- 10:00.50, 2012- 9:23.53, 2013- 9:22.05, 2014- 9:22.58. pbs: 1500m 4:19.44 '11, 3000m 9:07.51 '11, 5000m 15:42.64 '11, 10000m 35:14.0A '14.

Janeth JEPKOSGEI Busienei b. 13 Dec 1983 Kabirirsang, near Kapsabet 1.67m 47kg. North Rift.

At 800m: OG: '08- 2, '12- 7; WCh: '07- 1, '09- 2, '11- 3; CG: '06- 1, '14- sf; AfCh: '06-10-14: 1/2/2; WJ: '02- 1; WY: '99- h; WCp: '06- 2, '10- 1; won DL 2010, WAF 2007, KEN 2011.
Five Kenyan 800m records 2005-07, Commonwealth & African 4x800m 2014.
Progress at 800m, 1500m: 1999- 2:11.0A, 2001- 2:06.21, 2002- 2:00.80, 2003- 2:03.05, 2004- 2:00.52, 4:11.91; 2005- 1:57.82, 4:15.77; 2006- 1:56.66, 4:15.43; 2007- 1:56.04, 4:14.70; 2008- 1:56.07, 4:08.48; 2009- 1:57.90, 4:13.87; 2010- 1:57.84, 4:04.17; 2011- 1:57.42, 4:02.32; 2012- 1:57.79, 4:07.34; 2013- 1:58.71, 4:12.61; 2014- 1:58.70. pbs: 400m 54.06A '10, 600m 1:25.0+ '08, 1000m 2:37.98 '02, 1M 4:28.72 '08.
Brilliant front-running victory at 2007 Worlds.

Priscah JEPTOO b. 26 Jun 1984 Chemnoet Village, Nandi 1.65m 49kg.
At Mar: OG: '12- 2; WCh: '11- 2. At 10000m: AfG: '99- 5. At 5000m: WJ: '00- 3. Won KEN CC 2014.
Progress at Mar: 2009- 2:30:40, 2010- 2:27:02, 2011- 2:22:55, 2012- 2:20:14, 2013- 2:20:15. pbs: 3000m 9:05.7 '13, road: 10k 31:18 '13, 15k 46:59 '14, 10M 50:38 '13, 20k 62:32 '13, HMar 65:45 '13.
Marathon wins: Porto 2009, Turin 2010, Paris 2011, London 2013 (3rd 2012), New York 2013. World Marathon Majors winner 2012/13. Won Great North Run 2013. Married to Douglas Chepsiro, son born 20 Feb 2009.

Rita Sitienei **JEPTOO** b. 15 Feb 1981 Eldoret 1.65m 48kg.
At Mar: WCh: '05- 7, '07- 7; World 20k: '06- 3; HMar: '04- 14.
African record 20km road 2006.
Progress at Mar: 2004- 2:28:11, 2005- 2:24:22, 2006- 2:23:38, 2007- 2:32:03, 2008- 2:26:34, 2011- 2:25:44, 2012- 2:22:04, 2013- 2:19:57. 2014- 2:18:57dh/2:24:35dq. pbs: 3000m 9:38.13 '98, 5000m 15:56.90 '02, 10000m 33:23.04A '05; Road: 10k 31:17 '13, 15k 47:13+ '13, 20k 63:11 '13, HMar 66:27 '11.
Won marathons at Stockholm and Milan 2004, Boston 2006 & 2013 (3rd 2008), Eldoret 2011; Chicago 2013 (2nd 2012). Would have won World Marathons Major 2013-14 but tested positive for EPO in September 2014 and lost 'win' at Chicago in receiving a 2-year ban. Separated from husband Noah Busienei.

Lucy Wangui KABUU b. 24 Mar 1984 Ichamara, Nyeri region 1.55m 41kg. Suzuki, Japan.
At (5000m)/10000m: OG: '04- 9, '08- 7; CG: '06- 3/1; AfCh: '08- 4. At Mar: WCh: '13- 24. World 4k CC: '05- 5; HMar: '14- 4. Won KEN 10000m 2013.
Progress at 5000m, 10000m, HMar, Mar: 2001- 15:45.04, 2002- 15:33.03, 32:54.70; 2003- 15:10.23, 31:06.20; 2004- 14:47.09, 31:05.90, 69:47; 2005- 15:00.20, 31:22.37; 2006- 14:56.09, 31:29.66; 2007- 14:57.55, 31:32.52; 2008- 14:33.49, 30:39.96; 2009- 16:50.3A, 2011- 67:04, 2012- 2:19:34, 2013- 32:44.1A, 66:09, 2:24:06; 2014- 32:50.37A, 68:37. 2:24:16; 2015- 2:20:21. pbs: 1500m 4:08.6A '12, 3000m 8:46.15 '08. Road 15k 47:13+ 13, 20k 62:48 '13, 25k 1:21:37 '13.
At the marathon set the pace in Osaka 2007, but at her first proper try was 2nd in 2:19:34 at Dubai 2012. 3rd Chicago 2012 and Tokyo 2014. Won Great North Run 2011, RAK half marathon 2013.

Mary Jepkosgei **KEITANY** b. 18 Jan 1982 Kisok, Kabarnet 1.68m 53kg.
At Mar: OG: '12- 4. World HMar: '07- 2, '09- 1.
Records: World 25km 2010, 10M, 20km, half marathon 2011. African and two Kenyan half marathon 2009. Kenyan marathon 2012.
Progress at HMar, Mar: 2000- 72:53, 2002- 73:01, 2003- 73:25, 2004- 71:32, 2005- 70:18, 2006- 69:06, 2007- 66:48, 2009- 66:36, 2010- 67:14, 2:29:01; 2011- 65:50, 2:19:19; 2012- 66:49, 2:18:37; 2014- 65:39, 2:25:07; 2015- 66:02. pbs: 1500m 4:24.33 '99, 10000m 32:18.07 '07; Road: 5k 15:25 '11, 10k 30:45 '11, 15k 46:40 '11, 10M 50:05 '11, 20k 62:36 '11, 25k 1:19:53 '10.
13 wins in 14 half marathons 2006-15 inc. Great North Run 2014, RAK 2011-12, 2015. Marathons: won London 2011-12, New York 2014 (3rd 2010-11). Married to Charles Koech (pbs 10k 27:56 & HMar 61:27 '07), son Jared born in June 2008 and daughter Samantha on 5 Apr 2013.

Sylvia Chibiwott **KIBET** b. 28 Mar 1984 Kapchorwa, Keiyo district 1.57m 44kg. Kenya Police.
At 5000m: OG: '08- 4; WCh: '07- 4, '09- 2, '11- 2; CG: '10- 2; AfG: '07- 3; AfCh: '06- 3. At 3000m: WI: '08-10-12: 4/4/4, won Afr-Y 1998. At 1500m: WY: '99- 2. World CC: '11- 13. Won KEN 5000m 2011.
Progress at 5000m, 10000m: 2006- 15:02.54, 31:39.34; 2007- 14:57.37, 2008- 15:00.03, 2009- 14:37.77, 30:47.20; 2010- 14:31.91, 2011- 14:35.43, 2012- 14:46.73, 2013- 14:58.26. pbs: 1500m 4:05.33i/4:07.87 '10, 3000m 8:37.47 '13, 2M 9:16.62 '07, Road: 15k 48:24 '12, 10M 51:42 '12, HMar 69:32 '15.
Did not compete in 2001-02. Married Erastus Limo in 2003, daughter Britney Jepkosgei born in 2004. Older sister is Hilda Kibet NED and cousin of Lornah Kiplagat NED.

Viola Jelagat **KIBIWOT** b. 22 Dec 1983 Keiyo 1.57m 45kg.
At 1500m: OG: '08- h; WCh: '07- 5, '09/11- sf; CG: '06- 7, '10- 7; WJ: '02- 1. At 5000m: OG: '12- 6; WCh: '13- 4. World CC: '00-01-02-13: 3J/1J/1J/7; AfCC: '11-2.
Progress at 1500m, 5000m: 2003- 15:32.87, 2004- 4:06.64, 2006- 4:08.74, 2007- 4:02.10, 2008- 4:04.17, 14:51.59; 2009- 4:02.70, 2010- 4:03.39, 14:48.57; 2011- 4:05.51, 14:34.86; 2012- 3:59.25, 14:39.53; 2013- 4:00.76, 14:33.48; 2014- 4:00.46, 14:33.73. pbs: 800m 2:04.7A '12, 2000m 5:38.2+ '14, 3000m 8:24.41 '14, 2M 9:12.59 '14, 10k Rd 32:49 '14, HMar 72:18 '14.

Valentine KIPKETER b. 5 Jan 1993 1.50m 40kg.
Progress at Mar: 2012- 2:28:02, 2013- 2:23:02. Pbs: 3000m 9:17.12 '10, 5000m 16:22.83 '10, Road: 10k 33:07 11, HMar 68:21 '11.
Won Mumbai and Amsterdam marathons 2013.

Edna Ngeringwony **KIPLAGAT** b. 15 Nov 1979 Eldoret 1.71m 54kg. Corporal in Kenyan Police.
At Mar: OG: '12- 20; WCh: '11- 1, '13- 1. At 3000m: WJ: '96- 2, '98- 3. World CC: '96-97-06: 5J/4J/13.
African record 30km 2008.
Progress at Mar: 2005- 2:50:20, 2010- 2:25:38, 2011- 2:20:46, 2012- 2:19:50, 2013- 2:21:32, 2014- 2:20:21. pbs: 3000m 8:53.06 '96, 5000m 15:57.3A '06, 10000m 33:27.0A '07; Road: 5k 15:20 '10, 10k 31:18 '10, 15k 47:57 '10, 10M 54:56 '09, HMar 67:41 '12, 30k 1:39:11 '14.
Won Los Angeles and New York Marathons 2010, London 2014 (2nd 2012-13, 3rd 2011). Married to Gilbert Koech (10000m 27:55.30 '01, 10k 27:32 '01, Mar 2:13:45 dh '05, 2:14:39 '09); two children.

Florence Jebet **KIPLAGAT** b. 27 Feb 1987 Kapkitony, Keiyo district 1.55m 42kg.
At 5000m: WJ: '06- 2. At 10000m: WCh: '09- 12; CG: '14- 2. World CC: '07- 5, '09- 1; HMar: '10- 1. Won Kenyan 1500m 2007, 10000m 2014, CC 2007 & 2009.
World records 20k and half marathon 2014 & 2015, 15k 2015.. Kenyan 10000m record 2009.
Progress at 5000m, 10000m, HMar, Mar: 2006- 15:32.34, 2007- 14:40.74, 31:06.20; 2009- 14:40.14, 30:11.53; 2010- 14:52.64, 32:46.99A, 67:40; 2011- 68:02, 2:19:44; 2012- 30:24.85, 66:38, 2:20:57; 2013- 67:13, 2:21:13; 2014- 31:48.6A, 65:12, 2:20:24; 2015- 65:07. pbs: 1500m 4:09.0A '07, 3000m 8:40.72 '10, Road: 15k 46:13 '15, 20k 61:54 '15, 30k 1:39:11 '14.
Won half marathon debut in Lille in 2010, followed a month later by World title. Did not finish in Boston on marathon debut in 2011; won Berlin 2011 and 2013; 2nd London & 3rd Chicago 2014. Formerly married to Moses Mosop, daughter Aisha Chelagat born April 2008. Niece of William Kiplagat (Mar 2:06:50 '99, 8 WCh '07).

Sally Jepkosgei **KIPYEGO** b. 19 Dec 1985 Kapsowar, Marakwet district 1.68m 52kg. Was at Texas Tech University, USA.
At (5000m)/10000m: OG: '12- 4/2; WCh: '11- 2, '13- 7. World CC: '01- 8J. Won record equalling nine NCAA titles 5000m 2008, 10000m 2007, CC 2006-08, indoor 3000m 2007, 5000m 2007-09.
Progress at 5000m, 10000m: 2005- 16:34.90, 2006- 16:13.39, 2007- 15:19.72, 31:56.72; 2008- 15:11.88, 31:25.48; 2009- 15:09.03, 33:44.7A; 2010- 14:38.64, 2011- 14:30.42, 30:38.35; 2012- 14:43.11, 30:26.37; 2014- 14:37.18, 30:42.26. pbs: 800m 2:08.26 '08, 1500m 4:06.23 '11, 1M 4:27.19i/4:29.64 '09, 2000m 5:35.20 '09, 3000m 8:34.18 '14, 2M 9:21.04i, 9:22.10 '14, Road: 15k 48:51 '14, 20k 64:54 '14, HMar 68:31 '14.
Married to Kevin Chelimo (5000m 13:14.57 '12). One of her eight brothers is Mike Kipyego (3000mSt 8:08.48).

Faith Chepngetich **KIPYEGON** b. 10 Jan 1994 Bornet 1.57m 42kg.
At 1500m: OG: '12- h; WCh: '13- 5; CG: '14- 1; AfCh: '14- 5; WJ: '12- 1; WY: '11- 1. World CC: '10-11-13: 4J/1J/1J; AfCC: '12- 1J, '14- 1.
Records: World 4x1500m 2014, Commonwealth, African junior & Kenyan 1500m 2013.
Progress at 1500m: 2010- 4:17.1A, 2011- 4:09.48, 2012- 4:03.82, 2013- 3:56.98, 2014- 3:58.01. pb 800m 2:02.8A '13, 2000m 5:37.8+ '14, 3000m 8:23.55 '14.
Older sister Beatrice Mutai (b. 19 Apr 1987) 11 World CC 2013, HMar 69:30 '14.

Purity Cherotich **KIRUI** b. 13 Aug 1991 Kericho 1.62m 47kg.
At 3000mSt: CG: '14- 1; AfCh: '14- 6; WJ: '10- 1; Kenyan champion 2014.
Progress at 3000mSt: 2008- 10:27.19A, 2009- 10:05.1A, 2010- 9:36.34, 2011- 9:37.85, 2012- 9:35.61, 2013- 9:19.42, 2014- 9:23.43. pbs: 800m 2:07.6A '14, 1500m 4:31.83 '08, 5000m 16:13.42 '11.

Janet KISA b. 5 Mar 1992 1.60m 48kg.
At 3000m: CCp: '14- 4. At 5000m: CG: '14- 2; AfCh: '14- 3; Af-J: '11- 2. World CC: '11-13-15: 5J/6/12; AfCC: '14- 2.
Progress at 5000m: 2010- 16:02.2A, 2011- 15:24.75, 2012- 14:57.68, 2013- 15:05.89, 2014- 14:52.59. pbs: 1500m 4:14.77 '11, 2000m 5:45.9 '14, 3000m 8:32.66 '14, 10k Rd 33:55 '13, HMar 71:01 '14.

Linet Chepkwemoi **MASAI** b. 5 Dec 1989 Kapsokwony, Mount Elgon district 1.70m 55kg.
At (5000m)/10000m: OG: '08- 4; WCh: '09- 1, '11- 6/3; AfCh: '10- 3. World CC: '07-08-09-10-11: 1J/3/2/2/2. Won KEN 10000m 2010, CC 2010-11.
World junior record and Kenyan record at 10000m 2008, World 10 miles road record 2009.
Progress at 5000m, 10000m: 2007- 14:55.50, 2008- 14:47.14, 30:26.50; 2009- 14:34.36, 30:51.24; 2010- 14:31.14, 31:59.36A; 2011- 14:32.95, 30:53.59; 2012- 14:53.93, 2013- 15:02.98, 31:02.89. pbs: 1500m 4:12.26 '09, 2000m 5:33.43 '09, 3000m 8:38.97 '07. Road: 15k 47:21 '09, 10M 50:39 '09, HMar 71:45 '14.
Younger sister of Moses (qv) and Dennis Masai. Younger sister Magdalene (b. 4 Apr 1993) has 5000m pb 15:10.46 '15.

Margaret Wangare **MURIUKI** b. 21 Mar 1986 Nakuru 1.58m 45kg.
At 1500m: AfG: '07- 7; AfCh: '12- 3, At 5000m: WCh: '13- h; CG: '14- 4; AfCh: '14- 4; World CC: 08-10-13: 8/6/5; AfCC: '12- 2. Won KEN CC 2013
Progress at 5000m: 2003- 16:55.7A, 2005- 16:39.6A, 2010- 14:48.94, 2011- 15:19.89, 2013- 14:40.48, 2014- 15:10.38. pbs: 3000m 8:46.6 '14, 2M 9:24.89 '14, road: 10k 31:05 '10, 15k 48:39 '14, HMar 69:02 '14.

Hellen Onsando **OBIRI** b. 13 Dec 1989 Nyangusu, Kisii 1.55m 45kg.
At 1500m: OG: '12- 10; WCh: '11- 10 (fell), '13- 3; CG: '14- 6; AfCh: '14- 1; CCp: '14- 4. At 3000m: WI: '12- 1, '14- 2. Won Kenyan 1500m 2011-14.
Two world 4x1500m records 2014. African & Commonwealth 3000m record 2014.
Progress at 1500m: 2011- 4:02.42, 2012- 3:59.68, 2013- 3:58.58, 2014- 3:57.05. pbs: 800m 2:00.54 '11, 1000m 2:46.00i '12, 2000m 5:37.7+ '14, 3000m 8:20.68 '14, 5000m 15:49.7A '13.

Philes ONGORI b. 19 Jul 1986 Chironge, Kisii district 1.58m 47kg. Based in Sapporo, Japan.
At 10000m: WCh: '07- 8. World HMar: '09- 2.
Progress at 5000m, 10000m, Mar: 2003- 16:11.32, 2004- 15:08.3mx/15:25.50, 2005- 15:09.49, 32:30.83; 2006- 15:19.90, 31:18.85; 2007- 14:50.15, 31:39.11; 2008- 14:46.20mx/14:46.06, 30:29.21mx/ 31:19.73; 2009- 15:12.15, 31:53.46; 2011- 2:24:20, 2013- 2:28:53, 2014- 2:23:22dh/2:26:59. pbs: 800m 2:05.56 '04, 1500m 4:11.90 '04, 3000m 8:47.88 '07, Road: 15k 47:38 '08, HMar 67:38 '09, 30k.
Won Japanese High School 3000m 2004. Won Rotterdam Marathon 2011 on debut, 2nd Yokohama 2014.

Lydia Chebet **ROTICH** b. 8 Aug 1988 Kipkilot, Keiyo District 1.58m 45kg. Kenya Police traffic officer.
At 3000mSt: OG: '12- h; WCh: '11- 5; AfCh: 10- 3.
Progress at 3000mSt: 2007- 10:44.3A, 2008- 9:55.62, 2009- 9:26.51, 2010- 9:18.03, 2011- 9:19.20, 2012- 9:31.09, 2013- 9:26.31. pb 5000m 16:01.0A '12.

Betsy SAINA b. 30 Jun 1988 Sokosik, Nandi 1.63m 48kg. Nike. Graduate of Iowa State University, USA
At 10000m: AfCh: '12- 3. Won NCAA indoor 5000m & CC 2012.
Progress at 5000m, 10000m: 2009- 16:15.74, 36:34.94; 2010- 16:10.69, 33:13.13; 2011- 15:50.74i/16:06.05, 33:13.87; 2012- 15:36.09i, 31:15.97; 2013- 15:12.05, 31:37.22; 2014- 14:39.49, 30:57.30. pbs: 1M 4:40.98i '13, 2000m 5:45.7 '14, 3000m 8:38.01 '14, 2M 9:16.95 '14, Rd 10k 30:46 '14, 10M 51:55 '14, HMar 69:27 '14.

Eunice Jepkoech **SUM** b. 2 Sep 1988 Burnt Forest, Uasin Gishu 1.72m 53kg. Police.
At 800m: WCh: '11- sf, '13- 1; CG: '14- 1; AfCh: '10- h,'12- 2, '14- 1; CCp: '14- 1; won DL 2013-14. At 1500m: OG: '12- h, Won Kenyan 800m 2012, 2014.
World 4x1500m record 2014, Commonwealth & African 4x800m 2014..
Progress at 800m, 1500m: 2009- 2:07.4A, 2010- 2:00.28, 2011- 1:59.66A, 4:12.41; 2012- 1:59.13, 4:04.26; 2013- 1:57.38, 4:02.05; 2014- 1:57.92, 4:01.54. pb 3000m 8:53.12 '12.
Daughter Diana Cheruto born in 2008.

Agnes Jebet **TIROP** b. 23 Oct 1995 1.59m 44kg.
At 5000m: WJ: '12- 3, '14- 3; World CC: '13-15: 2J/1; AfCC: '12- 2J, '14- 1J.
Progress at 5000m: 2011- 16:09.0A, 2012- 15:36.74, 2013- 14:50.36, 2014- 15:00.19. pbs: 1500m 4:12.68 '13, 2000m 5:48.65 '13, 3000m 8:39.13 '13, 3000mSt 10:27.4A '12.

KOREA

Governing body: Korea Athletics Federation, 10 Chamshil Dong, Songpa-Gu, Seoul. Founded 1945. **National Champions 2014**: **Men:** 100m: Kim Kuk-young 10.34, 200m: Yeo Ho-su-ah 20.91, 400m: Park Bong-ko 46.20, 800m: Choi Hyun-ki 1:48.77, 1500m: Shin Sang-min 3:48.56, 5000m: Baek Seung-ho 14:09.78, 10000m: Kim Min 30:17.85, Mar: Lee Du-haeng 2:15:46, 3000mSt: Kim Young-jin 8:54.54, 110mh: Kim Byung-jun 13.82, 400mh: Lee Seung-yun 50.66, HJ: Yoon Sung-hyun 2.25, PV: Jim Min-sup 5.50, LJ/TJ: Kim Duk-hyun 7.66/16.61, SP: Jung Il-woo 18.34, DT: Choi Jong-bum 56.10, HT: Lee Yun-chul 68.60, JT: Kim Ye-ram 78.17, Dec: Bae Sang-hwa 7421, 20kW: Choe Byung-kwang 1:28:26. **Women:** 100m: Lee Sun-ae 11.94, 200m: Jung Han-sol 24.13, 400m: Oh Se-ra 55.59, 800m: Park Young-sun 2:10.32, 1500m: Oh Dal-nim 4:28.50, 5000m/10000m: Kim Do-yeon 16:29.75/35:33.55, Mar: Lim Kyung-hee 2:39:56, 3000mSt: Lee Se-jung 10:26.91, 100mh: Lee Yeon-kyong 13.74, 400mh: Shon Kyong-mi 58.75, HJ: Suk Mi-jung 1.76, PV: Lim Eun-ji 4.10, LJ: Jung Soon-ok 6.32, TJ: Bae Chan-mi 13.57, SP: Lee Mi-young 16.89, DT: Chung Ye-rim 51.24, HT: Kang Na-ru 60.91, JT: Kim Kyong-ae 56.72, Hep: Chung Yeon-ji 5006, 20kW: Jeon Yong-eun 1:38:35.

KIM Hyun-sub b. 31 May 1985 Sokcho 1.75m 53kg.
At 20kW: OG: '08- 23, '12- 17; WCh: '07-09-11-13: 20/34/5/10; AsiG: '06-10-14: 2/3/3; WUG: '05-07-09: 2/6/5. Asian champion 2011, 2014 (2nd 2015); KOR 2005-06, 2008-13. At 10000m/10k-mW: WJ: '04- 3; WCp: '04- 8.
Five Korean 20km road walk records 2008-15.
Progress at 20kW: 2004- 1:24:58, 2005- 1:22:15, 2006- 1:21:45, 2007- 1:20:54, 2008- 1:19:41, 2009- 1:22:00, 2010- 1:19:36, 2011- 1:19:31, 2012- 1:21:36, 2013- 1:21:22, 2014- 1:19:24, 2015- 1:19:13. Pb 10000mW 39:30.56 '09, 38:13R '10.

KUWAIT

Governing body: Kuwait Association of Athletic Federation, PO Box 5499, 13055 Safat, Kuwait. Founded 1957.

Ali **Mohammed AL-ZANKAWI** b. 27 Feb 1984 Kuwait City 1.86m 97kg.
At HT: OG: '04/08/12- dnq 29/18/18; WCh: '05/09/11- dnq 21/13/13, '07- 12; WJ: '02- 2; AsiG: '06- 2, '14- 4; AsiC: '03-05-07-09-11-12: 1/1/1/2/1/4; CCp: '10- 3, '14- 5. Pan-Arab champion 2004-05, 2007, 2009, 2011, 2013; West Asian 2005, 2010, Asian-J 2002.

13 Kuwait hammer records 2004-09, Asian junior record 2003.
Progress at HT: 2001- 64.66, 2002- 66.88, 2003- 72.70, 2004- 76.54, 2005- 76.25, 2006- 76.97, 2007- 77.14, 2008- 77.25, 2009- 79.74, 2010- 78.40, 2011- 79.27, 2012- 75.28, 2013- 76.68, 2014- 75.73.
His father Mohamed Al-Zinkawi competed at 1976, 1980 and 1988 Olympics at shot, best 18.65 '81.

LATVIA

Governing body: Latvian Athletic Association, 1 Augsiela Str, Riga LV-1009. Founded 1921.
National Championships first held in 1920 (men), 1922 (women). **2014 Champions**: **Men** 100m: Ronalds Arajs 10.44, 200m: Janis Mezitis 21.63, 400m: Renars Stepins 48.68, 800m/1500m: Dmitrijs Jurkevics 1:49.33/3:49.53, 3000m: Dmitrijs Serjogins 8:31.38, 5000m/HMar: Valerijs Zolnerovics 14:27.00/65:30, Mar: Rolands Kaimins 2:30:39, 3000mSt: Valters Abolins 10:01.68, 110mh: Kristaps Sietins 14.66, 400mh: Janis Baltuss 51.70, HJ: Martins Sulainis 2.01, PV: Mareks Arents 5.55, LJ: Elvijs Misans 7.72, TJ: Pavels Kovajovs 15.51, SP: Maris Urtans 18.63, DT: Arnis Zvirins 48.64, HT: Igors Sokolovs 71.13, JT: Ainars Kovals 81.75, Dec: Ingus Zarins 6368, 20kW/50kW: Arnis Rumbenieks 1:27:09/4:14:41. **Women**: 100m: Diana Daktere 12.21, 200m: Gunta Latiseva-Cudare 24.55, 400m: Aleksandra Koblence 55.92, 800m/1500m: Jelena Abele 2:08:57/4:23.64, 3000m/HMar: Jelena Prokopcuka 9:14.83/73:32, 5000m/Mar: Jolanta Liepina 17:27.07/3:08:46, 3000mSt: Polina Jelizarova 9:56.53, 100mh: Dace Dreimane 14.81, 400mh: Liga Velvere 57.41, HJ: Madara Onuzane 1.84, PV: Ildze Bortascenoka 3.60, LJ: Aiga Grabuste 6.50, TJ: Santa Matule 13.19, SP: Linda Ozola 13.91, DT: Dace Steinerte 49.73, HT: Karina Orlova 51.67, JT: Madara Palameika 60.15, Hep: Jolanta Kaupe 4929, 20kW: Ilma Mlene 1:59:22.

Zigismunds SIRMAIS b. 6 May 1992 Riga 1.91m 90kg. Riga Arkadija.
At JT: OG: '12- dnq; WCh: '11: dnq 32; EC: '12- dnq 23; WJ: '10- 7; EU23: '13- 1; EJ: '11- 1.
Two world junior javelin records 2011.
Progress at JT: 2009- 65.03, 2010- 82.27, 2011- 84.69, 2012- 84.06, 2013- 82.77, 2014- 86.61.
Sister Katrina Sirma (b. 31 Mar 1994) JT 55.87 '14.

Women

Aiga GRABUSTE b. 24 Mar 1988 Rezekne 1.78m 67kg. Rezeknes BJSS.
At Hep: OG: '08- 19, '12- dnf; WCh: '07- 17, '09- 13, '11- 12; EC: '12- 3; WJ: '06- 9; WY: '05- 27; EJ: '07- 1; EU23: '09- 1. At Pen: WI: '10- 7; EI: '11- 10. At LJ: EC: '14- 5; EI: '15- 8. Won LAT 100mh 2007-08, 2011; LJ 2011, 2014; SP 2010-11, Hep 2009, 2011.
Latvian heptathlon record 2011.
Progress at Hep: 2006- 5443, 2007- 6019, 2008- 6050, 2009- 6396, 2011- 6507(w)/6414, 2012- 6325. Pbs: 60m 7.82i '08, 100m 12.08 '14, 200m 24.42/24.35w '11, 400m 55.43 '11, 800m 2:12.90 '12, 60mh 8.48i '12, 100mh 13.46 '11, HJ 1.79i '11, 1.77 '07; LJ 6.82i '15, 6.69/6.75w '14; SP 14.81i '12, 14.56 '09; JT 48.67 '11, Pen 4463i '09.
Son Arturs born in 2013.

Laura IKAUNIECE-ADMIDINA b. 31 May 1992 Jürmala 1.79m 60kg. Jürmalas SS.
At Hep: OG: '12- 8; WCh: '13- 11; EC: '12- 2, '14- 6; WJ: '10- 6; WY: '09- 2; EJ: '11- 3; WUG: '13- 2. Won LAT 100m 2012-13, 200m 2009, 2013; 100mh & HJ 2010.
Latvian heptathlon record 2012.
Progress at Hep: 2008- 5175, 2010- 5618, 2011- 6063, 2012- 6414, 2013- 6321, 2014- 6320. Pbs: 60m 7.60i '14, 100m 11.96 '14, 11.91w '13; 200m 24.08 '13, 24.06w '14; 800m 2:11.83 '14, 60mh 8.38i '14, 100mh 13.44 '13, HJ 1.85i '12, 1.84 '14; LJ 6.31 '12, SP 13.07 '13, JT 53.73 '12, Hep 4496i '14.
Her mother Vineta Ikauniece set Latvian records at 100m 11.34A '87, 200m 22.49A '87 and 400m 50.71 '88, and her father Aivars Ikaunieks had 110mh bests of 13.71A '87 and 13.4 '84.

Madara PALAMEIKA b. 18 Jun 1987 Valdemarpils 1.85m 76kg. Ventspils.
At JT: OG: '12- 8; WCh: '09-13: dnq 27/27, '11- 11; EC: '10-12-14: 8/8/4; WJ: '06- dnq 16; EU23: '07- 3, '09- 1; EJ: '05- dnq 17. Won LAT 2009-11, 2014.
Latvian javelin records 2009 & 2014.
Progress at JT: 2002- 42.31, 2003- 49.11, 2004- 51.50, 2005- 51.75, 2006- 54.19, 2007- 57.98, 2008- 53.45, 2009- 64.51, 2010- 62.02, 2011- 63.46, 2012- 62.74, 2013- 62.72, 2014- 66.15.

LITHUANIA

Governing body: Athletic Federation of Lithuania, Kareiviu 6, LT-09117 Vilnius. Founded 1921.
National Championships first held in 1921 (women 1922). **2014 Champions: Men:** 100m/200m: Ugnius Savickas 10.73/21.67, 400m: Mantas Rainys 48.47, 800m: Vitalij Kozlov 1:49.62, 1500m: Petras Gliebus 3:52.34, 5000m/HMar: Valdas Dopolskas 14:59.02/67:51, 10000m: Paulius Bieliunas 32:59.11, Mar: Remigijus Kancys 2:23:41, 3000mSt: Justinas Berzanskis 8:45.10, 110mh: Tomas Malakauskas 14.32, 400mh: Arturas Janauskas 53.40, HJ: Raivydas Stanys 2.26, PV: Egidijus Zaniauskas 4.20, LJ: Povilas Mykolaitis 7.86, TJ: Darius Aucyna 16.55, SP: Rimantas Martisauskas 18.85, DT: Andrius Gudzius 63.03, HT: Tomas Juknevicius 59.93, JT: Edvardas Matusevicius 64.53, Dec: Vykintas Dolobauskas 6301, 20kW/50kW: Tadas Suskevicius 1:24:52/3:51.58. **Women**: 100m/200m: Lina Grincikaite 11.58/23.67, 400m: Eva Misiunaite 55.17, 800m: Egle Balciunaite 2:06.66, 1500m: Rasa Drazdauskaite 4:24.54, 5000m/Mar: Vaida Zusinaite 16:44.79/

2:43:13, 10000m: Remalda Kergyte 35:13.99, HMar: Zivile Balciunaite 76:37, 3000mSt: Evelina Usevaite 11:15.41, 100mh: Sonata Tamosaityte 13.31, 400mh: Egle Staisiunaite 56.79, HJ: Airine Palsyte 1.98, PV: Rolanda Demcenko 3.60, LJ: Asta Dauksaite 6.08, TJ: Dovile Dzindzaletaite 14.26w, SP: Ieva Zarankaite 14.49, DT: Zinaida Sendriute 63.11, HT: Aiste Ziginskaite 49.49, JT: Indre Jakubaityte 56.05, Hep: Evelina Auzelyte 4742, 10kW Brigita Virbalyte 44:17, 20kW: Neringa Aidietyte 1:29:01.

Virgilijus ALEKNA b. 13 Feb 1972 Terpeikiai, Kupiskis 2.00m 130kg. Graduate of Lithuanian Academy of Physical Culture. Guard of the Lithuanian president 1995-2010, advisor to the Lithuanian Ministry of the Interior from 2011.
At DT: OG: '96-00-04-08-12: 5/1/1/3/4; WCh: '95-97-99-01-03-05-07-09-11-13: dnq 19/2/4/2/1/1/4/4/6/dnq 16; EC: '94-98-02-06-10-14: dnq 16/3/2/1/5/dnq 21; WCp: '98- 1, '06- 1. Won WAF 2003, 2005-06, 2009; GP 2001 (2nd 1999); DL 2011. LTU champion 1998, 2000-05, 2008-09, 2011-12.
Four Lithuanian discus records 2000. World over-40 record 2012.
Progress at DT: 1990- 52.84, 1991- 57.16, 1992- 60.86, 1993- 62.84, 1994- 64.20, 1995- 62.78, 1996- 67.82, 1997- 67.70, 1998- 69.66A, 1999- 68.25, 2000- 73.88, 2001- 70.99, 2002- 66.90, 2003- 69.69, 2004- 70.97, 2005- 70.67, 2006- 71.08, 2007- 71.56, 2008- 71.25, 2009- 69.59, 2010- 65.33, 2011- 67.90, 2012- 70.28, 2013- 64.66, 2014- 65.76. pb SP: 19.99 '97.
His 72.35 and 73.88 at the 2000 LTU Championships were the second and third longest ever discus throws. His 70.17 to win the 2005 World title (coming from 2nd at 68.10 with the last throw) was the first ever 70m throw at a global championships. He has 20 competitions and 31 throws over 70m. 37 successive wins from August 2005 to 4th at Worlds August 2007. Given IAAF Distinguished Career Award 2014. Married on 4 Mar 2000 Kristina Sablovskyte (pb LJ 6.14 '96, TJ 12.90 '97, sister of Remigija Nazaroviene).

Women

Airine PALSYTE b. 13 Jul 1992 Vilnius 1.86m 62kg. Vilnius.
At HJ: OG: '12- 11; WCh: '13- 12; WJ: '09- 4; WY: '08- dnq 23; EC: '10- dnq 18, '14- 13; EJ: '11- 2; EU23: '13- 2; WUG: '11- 2; EI: '15- 4; Lithuanian champion 2012-14.
Three LTU high jump records 2011-14
Progress at HJ: 2006- 1.71, 2008- 1.80, 2009- 1.85i/1.83, 2010- 1.92, 2011- 1.96, 2012- 64.03, 2013- 65.97, 2014- 1.98, 2015- 1.98i. pb 200m 24.78 '12, TJ 12.70 '12.

Zinaida SENDRIUTE b. 20 Dec 1984 Klaisiai, Skuodas 1.88m 89kg. COSMA.
At DT: OG: '08- dnq 33, '12- 8; WCh: '09- dnq 31, '11- 12, '13- 9; EC: '06-10-12-14: dnq 17/5/dnq 17/6; EJ: '03- 7; EU23: '05- 6; WUG: '11- 2; Lithuanian champion 2003, 2005-08, 2010-14.
Progress at DT: 2000- 33.37, 2001- 40.55, 2002- 48.66, 2003- 50.62, 2004- 51.38, 2005- 55.25, 2006- 57.26, 2007- 56.74, 2008- 59.42, 2009- 60.21, 2010- 60.70, 2011- 62.49, 2012- 64.03, 2013- 65.97, 2014- 65.83. pb SP 14.15 '10.

LUXEMBOURG

Governing body: Fédération Luxembourgeoise d'Athlétisme, 3 Route d'Arlon, L-8009 Strassen, Luxembourg. Founded 1928.

2014 National Champions: Men: 100m/200m: Festus Geraldo 10.90/22.50, 400m: Jacques Frisch 48.35, 800m: Ben Bertemes 1:56.28, 1500m/ 10000m/HMar: Pol Mellina 3:53.07/30:42.85/ 69:01, 5000m: Christian Molitor 15:33.17, Mar: Pascal Groben 2:38:46, 3000mSt: Luc Scheller 9:54.14, 110mh: Claude Godart 14.51, 400mh/ Dec: Wesley Charlet 57.30/5878, HJ/TJ: Ben Kiffer 1.96/13.07w, PV: Joe Seil 4.50, LJ: Tom Hutmacher 6.78, SP: Bob Bertemes 18.76, DT: Sven Forster 50.95, HT: Steve Tonizzo 50.00, JT: Tun Wagner 63.14. **Women**: 100m/400mh: Anais Bauer 12.43/67.03, 200m: Laurence Jones 24.95, 400m/Hep: Kim Reuland 57.01/4580, 800m: Vera Hoffmann 2:18.05, 1500m: Véronique Hansen 4:55.86, 3000m: Martine Mellina 10:24.73, 10000m: Pascale Schmoetten 36:31.11, HMar: Tania Harpes 1:26:01, Mar: Karin Schank 2:58:13, 3000mSt: Liz Weiler 11:24.27, 100m: Victoria Rausch 14.68, HJ: Elodie Tshilumba 1.80, PV: Gina Reuland 4.00, LJ: Laurence Jones 5.64, TJ: Nita Bokomba 11.78, SP: Stéphanie Krumlovsky 13.42, DT: Noémie Pleimling 37.38, HT: Mireille Tonizzo 42.65, JT: Véronique Michel 40.72.

MEXICO

Governing body: Federación Mexicana de Atletismo, Anillo Periférico y Av. del Conscripto, 11200 México D.F. Founded 1933.

National Champions 2014: Men: 100m/200m: José Carlos Herrera 10.21/20.38, 400m: José Martínez 47.26, 800m: James Eichberger 1:47.23, 1500m: Christopher Sandoval 3:44.00, 5000m/ 10000m: Juan Luis Barrios 13:54.02/29:04.64, 3000mSt: Luis Ibarra 8:59.47, 110mh: Genaro Rodríguez 13.76, 400mh: Sergio Rios 50.78, HJ: Edgar Rivera 2.15, PV: Victor Manuel Castillero 5.00, LJ/TJ: Alberto Álvarez 7.62/16.43, SP: Stephen Saenz 18.92, DT: Mario Cota 58.18, HT: Diego del Real 67.74, JT: Juan José Méndez 74.28, 20kW: Horacio Nava 1:23:01, 50k: Cristian Berdeja 4:03:10. **Women:** 100m/200m: Iza Daniela Flores 11.63/24.30, 400m: Natali Brito 53.94, 800m: Gabriela Medina 2:05.07, 1500m: Cristina Guevara 4:19.91, 5000m/10000m: Brenda Flores 16:13.54/35:09.88, 3000mSt: Ana Narvaez 10:25.72, 100mh: Gabriela Santos 13.62,

400mh: Zudikey Rodríguez 57.32, HJ: Fabiola Elizabeth Ayala 1.78, PV: Carmelita Correa 4.05, LJ: Zoila Flores 5.99, TJ: Liliana Hernández 13.47, SP: Laura Pulido 14.92, DT: Iraís Estrada 50.99, HT: Araceli Ibarra 52.30, JT: Abigail Gomez 53.68, 20kW: Monica Equihua 1:36:05.

Jorge **Horacio NAVA** b. 20 Jan 1982 Chihuahua 1.75m 62kg.
At 50kW: OG: '08- 6, '12- 15; WCh: '05-07-09-11-13: 9/9/19/18/32; PAm: '07- 2, '11- 1; CAG: '10- 1; WCp: '06-08-10-12: 7/5/2/11. At 20kW: WCh: '11- 19; CAG: '14- 1. At 10000mW: WY: '99- 5; PAm-J: '01- 2. Won MEX 20000mW 2013, 20kW 2014.
Progress at 50kW: 2005- 3:53:57, 2006- 3:48:22, 2007- 3:52:35, 2008- 3:45:21, 2009- 3:56:26, 2010- 3:54:16, 2011- 3:45:29, 2012- 3:46:59, 2013- 3:58:00, 2014- 3:42:51. pbs: 5000m 18:40.11 '09, 10000mW 40:33.52 '04, 20kW 1:22:04 '12.

Luis RIVERA Morales b. 21 Jun 1987 Agua Prieta, Sonora 1.83m 79kg. Degree in engineering from University of Arizona.
At LJ: OG: '12- dnq 32; WCh: '13- 3; WI: '14- 7; CCp: '14- 6; WUG: '13- 1. Won IbAm LJ 2014, Mexican LJ 2006-07, 2009-10, 2012-13; TJ 2005-07. Two Mexican long jump records 2013.
Progress at LJ: 2006- 7.31/7.47w, 2007- 7.60, 2008- 7.84i/7.61, 2009- 7.99i/7.95, 2010- 7.93, 2011- 7.77Ai/7.32, 2012- 8.22, 2013- 8.46, 2014- 8.24. pbs: 110mh 15.02 '07, TJ 15.97 '09.
Brother Edgar (b. 13 Feb 1991) has HJ pb 2.28 '11 (5 WY 07, 6 WJ 10).

MOROCCO

Governing Body: Fédération Royale Marocaine d'Athlétisme, Complex Sportif Prince Moulay Abdellah, PO Box 1778 R/P, Rabat. Fd. 1957.
2014 National Champions: Men: 100m: Abdelhafid Haddadi 10.64, 200m: Hamza Mlaab 21.49, 400m: Younés Belkaïfa 47.46, 800m: Abdellatif Elguesse 1:48.00; 1500m: Abdelhadi Labali 3:45.56, 5000m: Soufiyan Bouqantar 13:48.54, 10000m: Mustapha El Aziz 28:14.84, 3000mSt: Hamid Ezzine 8:27.6, 110mh: Mohamed Koussi 14.11, 400mh: Abdelhadi Masaoudi 52.37, HJ: Saad Hammouda 2.05, PV: Mouhcine Cheaouri 5.20, LJ: Abdelhakim Mlaab 7.75, TJ: Abderrahim Zahouani 16.13, SP: Mohamed Gharrous 17.08, DT: Nabil Kiram 52.68, HT: Driss Barid 64.79, 10000mW: Ali Daghiri 43:21.74. **Women**: 100m: Assia Raziki 12.22, 400m: Malika Akkaoui 54.67, 800m: Sara Souhi 2:05.80, 1500m: Sultana Aït Hammou 4:10.38, 5000m/10000m: Khadija Sammah 16:01.05/33:24.24, 3000mSt: Salima El Ouali Alami 9:42.2, 100mh: Lamia Lhabz 13.92, 400mh: Hayat Lambarki 57.52, HJ: Ghiziane Siba 1.82, PV: Dinar Nasrine 3.60, LJ/TJ: Jamaa Chnaïk 6.20/13.57, DT: Amina Moudden 49.54, HT: Soukana Zakkour 52.04.

Hamid EZZINE b. 5 Dec 1983 Aït Ali 1.74m 60kg.
At 3000mSt: OG: '08- h. '12- 7; WCh: '05-07-11-13: h/h/9/9; AfCh: 04-06-14: 4/5/6. Won Franc G 2013.
Progress at 3000mSt: 2004- 8:25.10, 2005- 8:21.38, 2006- 8:19.37, 2007- 8:09.72, 2008- 8:13.20, 2011- 8:11.81, 2012- 8:16.93, 2013- 8:13.27, 2014- 8:14.33. pbs: 1500m 3:43.03 '12, 3000m 7:54.65 '11, 5000m 13:51.77 '13.
Two-year drugs ban 2009-11. Older brother Ali set MAR 300mSt record 8:03.57 '00; OG: '00- 3, '04- 8; WCh: '99- 3, '01- 2, '03- 10; WJ: '96- 3.

Abdelaati IGUIDER b. 25 Mar 1987 Errachidia 1.70m 52kg.
At 1500m(/5000m): OG: '08- 5, '12- 3/6; WCh: '07-09-11-13: h/11/5/sf; WJ: '04- 1, '06- 2; WI: '10-12-14: 2/1/3.
Progress at 1500m, 5000m: 2004- 3:35.53, 2005- 3:35.63, 2006- 3:32.68, 2007- 3:32.75, 2008- 3:31.88, 2009- 3:31.47, 2010- 3:34:25, 2011- 3:31.60, 2012- 3:33.99, 13:09.17; 2013- 3:33.29, 2014- 3:29.83. pbs: 800m 1:47.14 '07, 1000m 2:19.14 '07, 1M 3:49.09 '14, 3000m 7:34.92i '13, 7:34.99 '14.

Mohamed MOUSTAOUI b. 2 Apr 1985 Khouribga 1.74m 60kg.
At 1500m: OG: '08/12- sf; WCh: '07-09-11-13: sf/6/6/9; AfCh: '06- 5; WJ: '04- 4; AfJ: '03- 2; Arab champion 2007. World CC: '04- 14J, '05- 14 4k.
Progress at 1500m: 2003- 3:42.9, 2004- 3:37.44, 2005- 3:36.20, 2006- 3:32.51, 2007- 3:32.67, 2008- 3:32.06, 2009- 3:32.60, 2010- 3:36.92+, 2011- 3:31.84, 2012- 3:35.46, 2013- 3:32.08, 2014- 3:35.0i/3:35.21. pbs: 800m 1:45.44 '09, 1000m 2:20.00i '08, 1M 3:50.08 '08, 2000m 5:00.98i '07, 3000m 7:40.00i '14, 7:43.99 '11; 2M 8:26.49i '05, 5000m 13:22.61 '05.

Women

Malika AKKAOUI b. 25 Dec 1987 Zaida, Meknès-Tafilalet 1.60m 46kg.
At 800m: OG: '12- sf; WCh: '13: sf; AfCh: 10-12-14: 3/3/6; WJ: '06- h. At 1500m: WCh: '11- h. Won MAR 400m 2014, 800m 2007-08, MedG 800m 2013.
Progress at 800m: 2004- 2:09.2, 2005- 2:08.1, 2006- 2:06.29, 2007- 2:05.04, 2008- 2:04.25, 2009- 2:02.10, 2010- 2:00.6, 2011- 1:59.75, 2012- 1:59.01i/1:59.54, 2013- 1:57.64, 2014- 2:00.58. pbs: 400m 53.19 '13, 1000m 2:39.86 '13, 1500m 4:04.96 '11.

Salima El Ouali **ALAMI** b. 29 Dec 1983 Karia Ba Mohamed 1.67m 53kg.
At 3000mSt: OG: '12- h; WCh: '11- h, '13- 15; AfCh: '14- 3; CCp: '14- 6.
Progress at 3000mSt: 2010- 10:21.66, 2011- 9:42.51, 2012- 9:31.03, 2013- 9:35.88, 2014- 9:21.24. pbs: 1500m 4:12.25 '12, 3000m 8:55.51 '13, 5000m 16:10.29 '09.

Siham HILALI b. 2 May 1986 Oued Zem 1.61m 58kg.
At 1500m: OG: '08-10, '12- sf; WCh: '07-09-11-13:

h/h/sf/11; AfCh: 10- 10; WJ: '04- 3 (3 3000m); WI: '08- 5, '14- 4. Won MedG 2013. At 3000m: WY: '03- 1.
Progress at 1500m: 2003- 4:15.1, 2004- 4:08.15, 2006- 4:25.82, 2007- 4:04.03, 2008- 4:05.36, 2009- 4:03.74, 2010- 4:03.89, 2011- 4:01.33, 2012- 4:02.59, 2013- 4:02.16, 2014- 4:05.46. pbs: 800m 2:00.15 '13, 2000m 5:47.93 '09, 3000m 8:46.17i '12, 9:03.16 '04.

NETHERLANDS

Governing body: Koninklijke Nederlandse Atletiek Unie (KNAU), Postbus 60100, NL-6800 JC Arnhem. Founded 1901.

National Championships first held in 1910 (men), 1921 (women). **2014 Champions: Men**: 100m/200m: Churandy Martina 10.13/20.62, 200m: Dennis Spillekom 20.96, 400m: Lee-Marvin Bonevacia 45.41, 800m: Thijmen Kupers 1:47.07, 1500m: Mark Nouws 3:51.68, 5000m: Jesper van der Wielen 14:30.71, 10000m: Olfert Molenhuis 30:08.23, HMar: Khalid Choukoud 63:21, Mar: Paul Zwama 2:21:59, 3000mSt: Simon Grannetia 9:14.84, 110mh: Koen Smet 13.78w, 400mh: Cliff Ellsworth 52.32, HJ: Douwe Amels 2.18, PV: Menno Vloon 5.40, LJ: Ignisious Gaisah 7.75, TJ: Sander Hage 15.16, SP: Patrick Cronie 18.66, DT: Erik Cadée 62.72, HT: Sander Stok 59.10, JT: Jurriaan Wouters 77.16, Dec: Bas Markies 7514, 50kW: Rob Tersteeg 4:54:23. **Women**: 100m/LJ: Dafne Schippers 11.10/6.78, 200m: Tessa van Schagen 23.52, 400m: Madiea Ghafoor 52.73, 800m: Sanne Verstegen 2:01.07, 1500m: Susan Kuijken 4:13.09, 5000m/HMar: Jip Vastenburg 15:31.50/73:15, 10000m: Miranda Boonstra 34:56.32, Mar: Jacelyn Gruppen 2:55:43, 3000mSt: Veerle Bakker 10:42.28, 100mh: Sharona Bakker 13.07, 400mh: Bianca Baak 59.01, HJ: Nadine Broersen 1.91, PV: Rianna Galiart 4.20, TJ: Tamara Middelburg 12.78, SP: Melissa Boekelman 16.65, DT: Corinne Nugter 51.54, HT: Wendy Koolhaas 62.44, JT: Lisanne Schol 53.53, Hep: Myrte Goor 5776, 10kW: Anne van Andel 57:55.

Erik CADÉE b. 15 Feb 1984 s'Hertogenbosch 2.01m 120kg. Prins Hendrik, Vught.
At DT: OG: '12- 10; WCh: '07-09-11-13: dnq 23/19/19/14; EC: '10-12-14: nt/10/dnq 14; WJ: '02- dnq 22; EU23: '05- 5; EJ: '03- 1; EYth: '01- 2. Dutch champion 2010, 2012-14.
Progress at DT: 2002- 50.63, 2003- 54.05, 2004- 56.59, 2005- 60.27, 2006- 61.36, 2007- 62.68, 2008- 61.75, 2009- 65.61, 2010- 66.20, 2011- 66.95, 2012- 67.30, 2013- 65.92, 2014- 65.24. pb SP 18.99i, 17.70 '09.

Ignisious GAISAH b. 20 Jun 1983 Kumasi 1.85m 75kg. Formerly known as Anthony Essuman.
At LJ: OG: '04- 6, '12- dnq 18; WCh: '03-05-11-13: 4/2/dnq 17/2; EC: '14- 6; CG: '06- 1, '10- 3; AfG: '03- 1, '11- 2; AfCh: '06- 1, '12- 3; WI: '06-10-12: 1/7/7; WCp: '06- 4, '14- 1. Won WAF 2004, Dutch 2013-14.
Long jump records: Ghana (9) 2003-06, NED 2013, African junior 2002, indoor 2006.
Progress at LJ: 1998- 7.35, 1999- 7.42, 2000- 7.40, 2002- 8.12, 2003- 8.30, 2004- 8.32, 2005- 8.34, 2006- 8.43/8.51w, 2007- 8.08, 2008- 7.78i, 2009- 7.78, 2010- 8.12, 2011- 8.26. 2012- 8.04, 2013- 8.29, 2014- 8.13. pb 100m 11.04 09.
After injury had to switch his take-off leg. Changed from Ghana to Netherlands, where he has lived since 2002, in 2013.

Churandy MARTINA b. 3 Jul 1984 Willemstad, Curaçao 1.78m 75kg. Rotterdam Atletiek. Studied civil engineering at University of Texas at El Paso, USA.
At 100m/(200m): OG: '04- qf, '08- 4/dq, '12- 5/5; WCh: '03- h, '05- qf, '07- 5/5, '09- qf, '11- sf/sf, '13- sf/7; EC: '14- sf/4; WJ: '00- h/h, '02- qf; WY: '99- sf; EC: '12- (1)/1R; PAm: '03- sf, '07- 1; CAG: '06- 1/1R, '10- 1/1/3R; CCp: '10- (2)/1R. Won PAm-J 2003; NED 100m 2011-13, 200m 2011.
Records: AHO 100m (8) 2004-08, 200m (6) 2005-10, 400m 2007; NED 100m (2) 2011-12, 200m (2) 2012.
Progress at 100m, 200m: 2000- 10.73, 21.73; 2001- 10.64A, 21.55; 2002- 10.30, 20.81; 2003- 10.29/ 10.26w, 20.71; 2004- 10.13, 20.75; 2005- 10.13/9.93Aw, 20.32/20.31w; 2006- 10.04A/10.06/ 9.76Aw/9.99w, 20.27A; 2007- 10.06, 20.20; 2008- 9.93, 20.11; 2009- 9.97, 20.76; 2010- 10.03A/10.07/ 9.92w, 20.08; 2011- 10.10, 20.38; 2012- 9.91, 19.85; 2013- 10.03, 20.01; 2014- 10.13, 20.25. pbs: 60m 6.58i '10, 400m 46.13A '07.
At 2008 Olympics set three national records at 100m and one at 200m before crossing line in second place in final in 19.82 only to be disqualified for running out of his lane. Competed for Netherlands Antilles until 2010.

Eelco SINTNICOLAAS b. 7 Apr 1987 Dordrecht 1.86m 81kg. AV '34 (Apeldoorn). Economics student.
At Dec: OG: '12- 11; WCh: '09- dnf, '11- 5, '13- 5; EC: '10- 2, '14- 4; WJ: '06- 8; EU23: '09- 1; EJ: '05- 14; ECp: '14- 1. At Hep: WI: '14- 4; EI: '11-13-15: 4/1/3.
Dutch decathlon record 2012.
Progress at Dec: 2007- 7466, 2008- 7507w, 2009- 8112, 2010- 8436, 2011- 8304, 2012- 8506, 2013- 8391, 2014- 8478. pbs: 60m 6.88i '13, 100m 10.71 '10, 10.69w '08; 200m 21.62 '10, 400m 47.88 '10, 1000m 2:37.42i '06, 1500m 4:22.29 '11, 60mh 7.88i '13, 110mh 13.92/13.89w '13, 400mh 51.59 '10, HJ 2.08i/2.02 '13, PV 5.52i '11, 5.45 '10; LJ 7.65i, 7.76w '09, 7.65 '12; SP 14.66i '14, 14.31 '11; DT 43.38 '14, JT 63.59 '12, Hep 6372i '13.
Set six pbs in improving pb by 277 points for European silver 2010.

Women

Nadine BROERSEN b. 29 Apr 1990 Hoorn 1.71m 62kg. AV Sprint Breda.
At Hep: OG: '12- 12; WCh: '13- 10; EC: '14-

2;EU23: '11- 9; EJ: '09- 5; ECp: '14- 1. At Pen: 14- 1. Won NED HJ 2010-11, 2014; JT 2013.
Four Dutch high jump records 2013-14 and indoors 2014.
Progress at Hep: 2009- 5507, 2010- 5967, 2011- 5932(w)/5854, 2012- 6319, 2013- 6345, 2014- 6539. pbs: 200m 24.57 '14, 800m 2:11.11 '14, 60mh 8.32i '13, 100mh 13.39 '14, HJ 1.94 '14, LJ 6.39 '14, SP 14.93i '14, 14.34 '13; JT 54.97 '12, Pen 4830i '14.
Lost c.200 points in stumbling at last hurdle in first event of 2013 World heptathlon.

Sifan HASSAN b. '1 Jan' 1993 Adama, Ethiopia 1.70m 49kg. Eindhoven Atletiek.
At 1500m/(5000m): EC: '14- 1/2; CCp: '14- 1; EI: 15- 1. At 3000m: WI: '14- 5; ET: '14- 1. Eur CC: 13- 1 U23.
Records: European U23 1500m (2) 2014, Dutch 1500m (2) & 3000m 2014.
Progress at 1500m, 5000m: 2011- 4:20.13, 2012- 4:08.74, 2013- 4:03.73. 2014- 3:57.00, 14:59.23; 2015- 4:00.46i. pbs: 800m 1:59.95 '14, 1000m 2:41.43 '13, 1M 4:29.85 '12, 2000m 5:46.1 '14, 3000m 8:29.38 '14, 10kRd 34:28 '12, HMar 77:10 '11.
Came to the Netherlands as a refugee at age 15. Dutch eligibility from 29 Nov 2013.

Dafne SCHIPPERS b. 15 Jun 1992 Utrecht 1.79m 68kg. Hellas.
At Hep: OG: '12- 11; WCh: '13- 3; WJ: '10- 1; EJ: '09- 4, '11- 1. At 100m/LJ: EU23: '13- 1/3. At (100m)/200m/4x100mR: WCh: '11- sf; EC: 12- 5/2R, '14- 1/1; WJ: '10- 3R; EU23: '13- (1) (3 LJ); CCp: '14- 3/1; ET: '14- 1. At 60m: EI: '13- 4, 15- 1. Won NED 100m 2011-12, 2014; LJ 2012, 2014.
Dutch records: 100m 2014, 200m (4) 2011-14, LJ 2014, Hep 2013 & 2014.
Progress at 100m, 200m, Hep: 2007- 12.09/ 12.08w, 2008- 12.26/12.01w, 2009- 11.79, 24.21, 5507; 2010- 11.56, 23.70/23.41w, 5967; 2011- 11.19/11.13w, 22.69, 6172; 2012- 11.36, 22.70, 6360; 2013- 11.09, 22.84, 6477; 2014- 11.03, 22.03, 6545. pbs: 60m 7.05i '15, 150m 16.93 '13, 800m 2:08.59 '14, 60mh 8.18i '12, 100mh 13.13 '14, HJ 1.80 '12, LJ 6.78 '14, SP 14.19 '11, JT 41.80 '11.
Added 117 points to pb and reduced 800m best from 2:15.52 to 2:08.62 in taking 2013 World heptathlon bronze. First Dutch woman to win a medal in World Championships and emulated Fanny Blankers-Koen (1950) by winning EC sprint double 2014.

NEW ZEALAND

Governing body: Athletics New Zealand, PO Box 305 504, Triton Plaza, Auckland.
National Championships first held in 1887 (men), 1926 (women). **2014 Champions: Men**: 100m/200m: Joseph Millar 10.49/21.15w, 400m: Alex Jortdan 47.83, 800m: Brad Mathas 1:53.71, 1500m: Hamish Carson 3:46.23, 3000m/3000mSt: Daniel Balchin 8:22.19/9:26.28, 5000m: Malcolm Hicks 14:13.47, 10000m: Aaron Pulford 29:47.09, Mar: Phil Costley 2:29:46, 110mh: Mike Cochrane 14.04w, 400mh: Cameron French 50.16, HJ: William Crayford 2.09, Thomas North 4.20, LJ: Matthew Wyatt 7.65, TJ: Phillip Wyatt 15.45w, SP: Tom Walsh 20.79, DT: Marshall Hall 58.25, HT: Philip Jensen (20th title) 61.85, JT: Stuart Farquhar 78.16, Dec: Nicholas Gerrard 7375, 3000mW/20kW: Matthew Holcroft 12:54.37/ 1:42:04, 50kW: Graeme Jones 5:11:11. **Women**: 100m/100mh: Fiona Morrison 11.87w/13.62, 200m/400m: Louise Jones 24.28/53.53, 800m/ 1500m: Angela Smit 2:01.53/4:17.95,, 3000m/ 3000mSt: Rosa Flanagan 9:43.33/9:57.47, 5000m: 16:32.68, 10,000m: Lydia O'Donnell 35:05.53, HMar:, Mar: Sally Gibbs 2:45:58, 400mh: Zoe Ballantyne 59.42, HJ: Sarah Cowley 1.84, PV: Kerry Charlesworth 3.85, LJ: Mariah Ririnui 6.01, TJ: Nneka Okpala 13.24, SP: Valerie Adams 20.46, DT: Siositina Hakeai 58.77, HT: Nicole Bradley 56.06, JT: Tori Peeters 54.45, Hep: Portia Bing 5695, 3000mW/20kW: Courtney Ruske 13:20.12/ 1:46:06, 20kW: Alana Barber 1:39:01.

Jacko GILL b. 20 Dec 1994 Auckland 1.90m 118kg. Takapuna.
At SP: CG: '14- 11; WJ: '10- 1, '12- 1; WY: '11- 1, YthOG: '10- 2. Oceania champion 2014.
Five World youth shot records 5kg 23.86 '10, 24.35 and 24.45 '11; 6kg (4) 21.34 to 22.31, 7.26kg (3) in 2011. World junior 6kg record 23.00 '13. Three NZL records 2011.
Progress at SP: 2010- 18.57, 2011- 20.38, 2012- 20.05, 2014- 20.70, 2015- 20.75.
World age 15 and 16 bests for 5kg, 6kg and 7.26kg shot. His father Walter was NZ champion at SP 1987 & 1989, DT 1975, pbs 16.57 '86 & 53.78 (1975); his mother Nerida (née Morris) had discus best of 51.32 and was NZ champion in 1990.

Zane ROBERTSON b. 14 Nov 1989 Hamilton 1.80m 65kg. Hamilton City Hawks.
At 5000m: WCh: '13- 14; CG: 14- 3 (h 1500m); CCp: '14- 2.
Oceania half marathon record 2015.
Progress at 5000m: 2011- 13:58.37, 2013- 13:13.83, 2014- 13:14.69. pbs: 1500m 3:34.19 '14, 1M 3:53.72 '14, 3000m 7:41.37 '14, 2M 8:22.82 '14, 10k Rd 29:12 '14, HMar 59:47 '15.
Twin brother **Jake** pbs 5000m 13:15.54 '13, 10000m 27:45.46 '13. CG '14: 7 10000m, 9 5000m.

Tomas WALSH b. 1 Mar 1992 Timaru 1.86m 123kg. South Canterbury.
At SP: CG: '14- 2; WJ: '10- dnq 16; WY: '09- 6 (dnq 31 DT), CCp: '14- 4; WI: '14- 3. NZ champion SP 2010-14, DT 2013.
Two New Zealand shot records 2013-14 and two Oceania indoor records 2014.
Progress at SP: 2010- 17.57, 2011- 18.83, 2012- 19.33, 2013- 20.61, 2014- 21.26i/21.16, 2015- 21.37. pb DT 53.58 '14.
Set four NZ indoor shot records at 2014 World Indoors.

Nick WILLIS b. 25 Apr 1983 Lower Hutt 1.83m 68kg. Economics graduate of University of Michigan, USA.
At 1500m: OG: '04- sf, '08- 2, '12- 9; WCh: '05-07-11-13: sf/10/12/sf; CG: '06-1, '10- 3, '14-3 (10 5000m); WJ: '02- 4; WI: '08/14- dq; WCp: '06- 3, '14- 6 (4 3000m). Won NCAA indoor 2005, NZ 1500m 2006, 3000m 2013, 5000m 2011-12.
Records: NZ 1500m (5) 2005-14, 3000m 2014. Oceania 1500m (2) 2012-14 and indoors 1500m (3:35.80) 2010, 1M (3:51.61) 2015..
Progress at 1500m: 2001- 3:43.54, 2002- 3:42.69, 2003- 3:36.58, 2004- 3:32.64, 2005- 3:32.38, 2006-3:32.17, 2007- 3:35.85, 2008- 3:33.51, 2009- 3:38.85i, 2010- 3:35.17, 2011- 3:31.79, 2012- 3:30.35, 2013-3:32.57, 2014- 3:29.91. pbs: 800m 1:45.54 '04, 1000m 2:16.58 '12, 1M 3:49.83 '14, 3000m 7:36.91 '14, 5000m 13:20.33 '14, HMar 67:06 '14.
His brother Steve (b. 25 Apr 1975) had pbs: 1500m 3:40.29 '99, 1M 3:59.04 '00.

Women

Valerie ADAMS b. 6 Oct 1984 Rotorua 1.93m 123kg. Auckland City.
At SP: OG: '04- 7, '08- 1, '12- 1; WCh: '03-05-07-09-11-13: 5/2/1/1/1/1; CG: '02-06-10-14: 2/1/1/1; WJ: '02- 1; WY: '99- 10, '01- 1; WI: '04-08-10-12-14: dnq 10/1/2/1/1; WCp: '02- 6, '06- 1, '10- 1. Won WAF 2005, 2008-09, DL 2011-14, NZL SP 2001-11, 2013-14; DT 2004, HT 2003.
Nine Oceania & Commonwealth shot records 2005-11, 22 NZ 2002-11, 10 OCE indoor 2004-13.
Progress at SP: 1999- 14.83, 2000- 15.72, 2001-17.08, 2002- 18.40, 2003- 18.93, 2004- 19.29, 2005-19.87, 2006- 20.20, 2007- 20.54, 2008- 20.56, 2009-21.07, 2010- 20.86, 2011- 21.24, 2012- 21.11, 2013-20.98i/20.90, 2014- 20.67i/20.59. pbs: DT 58.12 '04, HT 58.75 '02.
NIne senior global shot titles. IAAF Female Athlete of the Year 2014. Matched her age with metres at the shot from 14 to 18 and missed that at 19 by only two months. 28 successive shot wins from September 2007 to World Indoor silver in March 2010, and another 56 from August 2010 to September 2014. Her father came from England and her mother from Tonga. Married New Caledonia thrower Bertrand Vili (SP 17.81 '02, DT 63.66 '09, 4 ECp '07 for France) in November 2004 (divorced in 2010).

NIGERIA

Governing body: The Athletic Federation of Nigeria, P.O.Box 18793, Garki, Abuja. F'd 1944.
2014 National Champions: **Men**: 100m: Mark Jelks 10.23, 200m: Divine Oduduru 20.87, 400m: Isah Salihu 46.15, 800m: Sean Obinwa 1:49.00, 1500: Hamajan Soudi 3:46.94, 5000m/10000m/3000mSt: Ismail Sadjo 14:24.86/30:24.61/9:03.61, 110mh: Ty Akins 13.66, 400mh: Amaechi Morton 49.90, HJ: Obiora Arinze 2.10, LJ: Samson Idiata 7.91, TJ: Tosin Oke 17.21w, SP/DT: Stephen Mozia 18.14/56.39, HT: Ibrahim Baba 52.47, JT: Kenechukwu Ezeofor 70.26. **Women**: 100m/200m: Blessing Okagbare 11.06/22.62, 400m: Sade Abugan 51.39, 800m/1500m: Joy David Abiye 2:06.90/4:30.08, 5000m: Nancy Mathew 17:39.09, 10000m: Lydia Michael 38:12.43, 100mh: Nichole Denby 13.29, 400mh: Amaka Ogoegbunam 56.77, HJ: Chinyere Anslem 1.65, LJ: Ese Brume 6.68, TJ: Blessing Ibrahim 13.45, SP: Nikki Okwelogu 15.40, DT: Chinwe Okoro 55.74, HT: Queen Obisesan 59.66, JT: Patience Okoro 44.63, Hep: Faustina Oguh 52:03.02, 10000mW: Faustina Oguh 52:03.02.

Mark JELKS b. 10 Apr 1984 Gary, Indiana, USA 1.70m 66kg.
At 100m: WCh: '07- h; CG: '14- 5; AfCh: '14-2/1R; CG: '14- 4/3R. Nigerian champion 2014. Won US indoor 60m 2009.
Progress at 100m: 2002- 10.45/10.25w, 2003-10.67, 2004- 10.47, 2005- 10.02/10.10w/9.8w, 2006-10.32, 2007- 10.04/10.03w, 2008- 9.99, 2009-10.04/9.99w, 2010- 9.99w, 2013- 10.28, 2014-10.07/10.05w. pbs: 60m 6.51i '09, 200m 20.28 '09.
Two-year drugs ban 2010-12. Switched allegiance USA to Nigeria from 23 Jul 2014.

Tosin OKE b. 1 Oct 1980 London, UK 1.78m 77kg. Woodford Green, UK. Chemistry graduate of Manchester University.
At TJ: OG: '12- 7; WCh: '09/11- dnq 16/16; EC: '02- nj; CG: '02-10-14: 5/1/2; AfG: '11- 1; AfCh: '10-12-14: 1/1/2; EJ: '99- 1; CCp: '10- 6; '14- 4 ECp: '03- 4. Won UK 2007, NGR 2009-10, 2012-13.
Progress at TJ: 1997- 14.07, 1998- 15.16/15.62w, 1999- 16.57, 2000- 16.04/16.37w, 2001- 16.08i/15.72, 2002- 16.65, 2003- 16.61i/16.59, 2004- 16.49/16.75w, 2005- 16.12/16.30w, 2006- 16.33/16.50w, 2007-16.86, 2008- 16.47/16.63w, 2009- 16.87, 2010-17.22A/17.16, 2011- 17.21, 2012- 17.23, 2013-16.87i/16.64, 2014- 16.97/17.21w. pb LJ 7.31 '05.
Switched allegiance from Britain to Nigeria (grandfather) from 10 Feb 2009.

Women

Blessing OKAGBARE b. 9 Oct 1988 Sapele 1.80m 68kg. Student at University of Texas at El Paso, USA.
At LJ/(100m): OG: '08- 3, '12- dnq 17/8; WCh: '11- dnq 18/5, '13- 2/6 (3 200m); CG: 1 100m & 200m/2R; AfG: '07- 2 (4 TJ), '11- 1/2; AfCh: '10-1/1/1R, '12- 1/2, '14- (1)/1R; WJ: '06- 16 (dnq 17 TJ); CCp: '10- 6/3/3R; Won Nigerian 100m 2009-14, 200m 2013-14, LJ 2008-09, 2011-13; TJ 2008; NCAA 100m & LJ 2010.
Two African 100m records 2013, Nigerian & African junior TJ record 2007.
Progress at 100m, 200m, LJ: 2004- 5.85 irreg, 2006- 6.16, 2007- 6.51, 2008- 23.76A, 6.91; 2009-11.16, 6.73/6.90w; 2010- 11.00/10.98w/10.7Aw, 22.71, 6.88; 2011- 11.08/11.01w, 22.94, 6.78/6.84w; 2012- 10.92, 22.63, 6.97; 2013- 10.79/10.75w, 22.31,

7.00/7.14w; 2014- 10.85, 22.23, 6.86. pbs: 60m 7.18i '10, 300m 37.04 '13, TJ 14.13 '07.
Majestic winner of Commonwealth Games sprint double in 2014. Married football international Jude Igho Otegheri on 7 Nov 2014.

NORWAY

Governing body: Norges Friidrettsforbund, Serviceboks 1, Ullevaal Stadium, 0840 Oslo. Founded 1896.
National Championships first held in 1896 (men), 1947 (women, walks 1937). **2014 Champions**: **Men**: 100m: Jaysuma Saidy Ndure 10.22, 200m: Carl Emil Kåshagen 21.39, 400m: Karsten Warholm 47.03, 800m: Thomas Roth 1:47.97, 1500m: Henrik Ingebrigtsen 3:42.66, 5000m: Marius Vedvik 14:16.34. 10000m: Weldu Gebretsadik ERI 29:32.59, HMar: Ørjan Grønnevig 67:38, Mar: Martin Kjäll-Ohlsson SWE 2:28:54, 3000mSt: Tom Erling Kårbø 9:00.55, 110mh: Vladimir Vukicevic & Karsten Warholm 14.48, 400mh: Øyvind Kjerpeset 51.21, HJ: Ivan Kristoffer Nilsen 2.14, PV: Eirik Dolve 5.20, LJ/TJ: Vetle Utsi Onstad 7.44/15.53, SP: Stian Andersen 17.70, DT: Fredrik Amundgård 58.75, HT: Eivind Henriksen 72.70, JT: Håkon Kveseth 72.34, Dec: Lars Vikan Rise 7635, 5000mW: Erik Tysse 19:24.08, 10000mW: Joakim Sælen 42:57.26, 20kW: Håvard Haukenes 1:26:11. **Women**: 100m: Ezinne Okparaebo 11.36, 200m: Elisabeth Slettum 23.98, 400m: Trine Mjåland 54.03, 800m: Hedda Hynne 2:05.17, 1500m: Ingvill Måkestad Bovim 4:12.34, 5000m: Karoline Bjerkeli Grøvdal 15:47.63, 10000m: Kristin Størmer Steira 33:40.75, HMar: Marthe Katrine Myhre 1:19:10, Mar: Maria Venås 2:46:46, 3000mSt: Heidi Mårtensson 10:25.06, 100mh: Isabelle Pedersen 13.31, 400mh: Vilde Svortevik 59.51, HJ: Tonje Angelsen 1.85, PV: Lene Retzius 3.80, LJ: Nadia Akpana Assa 6.36, TJ: Inger Anne Frøysedal 13.45, SP: Kristin Sundsteigen 14.12, DT: Grete Etholm 53.55, HT: Trude Raad 61.46, JT: Marte Aaltvedt 54.10, Hep: Anna Bogunovic Jakobsen 3822, 3000mW: Merete Helgheim 14:17.95, 5000mW/10kW: Ellen Nordqvist Sjøblom 28:01.46/57:31.

Henrik INGEBRIGTSEN b. 24 Feb 1991 Stavanger 1.80m 69kg. Sandnes IL
At 1500m: OG: '12- 5; WCh: 13- 8; EC: '10-12-14: h/1/2; WJ: '10- h; EU23: '11- h; EJ: '09- h; CCp: '14- 4; EI: '15- 6 (3 3000m). At 5000m: EU23: '13- 1. Won NOR 800m 2013, 1500m 2010, 2012, 2014. Eur U23 CC: '12- 1.
Norwegian records: 1500m (4) 2012-14, 1M (3) 2012-14.
Progress at 1500m: 2004- 4:30.63, 2005- 4:22.48, 2006- 4:04.15, 2007- 3:54.08, 2008- 3:50.63, 2009- 3:44.53, 2010- 3:38.61, 2011- 3:39.50, 2012- 3:35.43, 2013- 3:33.95, 2014- 3:31.46. pbs: 800m 1:48.09 '14, 1M 3:50.72 '14, 3000m 7:42.19 '13, 5000m 14:19.39 '13, 2000mSt 5:41.03 '09, 3000mSt 8:52.56 '09.
Younger brother Filip (b. 20 Apr 1993) 1500m pb 3:38.76 '13 (10 WJ '12, 6 EU23 '13).

Jaysuma SAIDY NDURE b. 1 Jan 1984 Bakau, The Gambia 1.92m 72kg. IL i BUL, Oslo.
At (100m)/200m: OG: '04- qf/qf, '08- qf/sf, '12- h/sf; WCh: '03- h, '05- sf, '09- (sf), '11- sf/4, '13- 8; EC: '10- 6/5, '12- (3), '14- 6/h; CG: '02- qf, '06- sf; WJ: '02- h; AfG: '03- h/sf; AfCh: '04- 3/6; CCp: '10- dnf, ET: '13- 2/2. At 60m: EI: '13- 4. Won WAF 200m 2007, Norwegian 100m 2007-08, 2011, 2014; 200m 2007, 2010, 2012.
Records: Gambian 100m & 200m 2001-06, Norwegian 100m (6) 2007-11, 200m 2007.
Progress at 100m, 200m: 2001- 10.66, 21.27; 2002- 10.73/10.59w, 21.20; 2003- 10.52/10.51w, 21.18; 2004- 10.26, 20.69; 2005- 10.31/10.18w, 20.51/ 20.14w, 2006- 10.27, 20.47; 2007- 10.06, 19.89; 2008- 10.01, 20.45; 2009- 10.10/10.07w, 20.55; 2010- 10.00/9.98w, 20.29; 2011- 9.99, 19.95; 2012- 10.13, 20.34; 2013- 10.07/9.95w, 20.23/20.12w; 2014- 10.11/9.92w, 20.43. pbs: 60m 6.55i '08, 300m 33.76 '09, 400m 48.71 '09.
Having lived in Oslo from 2001, became a Norwegian citizen in November 2006.

Andreas THORKILDSEN b. 1 Apr 1982 Kristiansand 1.88m 90kg. Kristiansands IF.
At JT: OG: '04- 1, '08- 1, '12- 6; WCh: '01-03-05-07-09-11-13: dnq 26/11/2/2/1/2/6; EC: '02-06-10-12: dnq 15/1/1/4; WJ: '00- 2; EU23: '03- 4; EJ: '99- 7, '01- 2; EY: '97- 1; WCp: '06- 1; CCp: '10- 1; ET: '10- 2. Won DL 2010, WAF 2006, 2009; NOR 2001-06, 2009-11, 2013.
World junior javelin record 2001, seven Norwegian records 2005-06.
Progress at JT: 1996- 53.82, 1998- 61.57, 1999- 72.11, 2000- 77.48, 2001- 83.87, 2002- 83.43, 2003- 85.72, 2004- 86.50, 2005- 89.60, 2006- 91.59, 2007- 89.51, 2008- 90.57, 2009- 91.28, 2010- 90.37, 2011- 90.61, 2012- 84.72, 2013- 84.64, 2014- 80.79. pbs: SP 9.96 '01, DT 38.02 '01.
His mother Bente Amundsen was a Norwegian champion at 100mh (pb 14.6), father Tomm was a junior international with bests of 100m 10.9 and javelin 71.64.

PANAMA

Governing body: Federación Panameña de Atletismo, Apartado 0860-00684, Villa Lucre, Ciudad de Panamá. Founded 1945.

Alonso EDWARD b. 8 Dec 1989 Ciudad de Panamá 1.83m 73kg. Was at Barton County CC.
At (100m)/200m: OG: '12- h; WCh: '09- 2, '11- dnf, '13- sf; WJ: '08-; SAG: '14- (1); SACh: '09- 1/1, SAm-J: '07- (1), SAm-Y: '06- 1/1; CCp: '14- 1. Won DL 2014, C.American 2012, C.AmG 100m 2010, 200m 2013; SAmG 100m 2014.
Records: S.American 200m 2009, Panama 100m (2) 2009-14, 200m (5) 2007-09; South American Junior 100m 2007.
Progress at 100m, 200m: 2006- 10.60, 21.18; 2007-

10.28/10.25w, 20.62; 2008- 10.63, 20.96; 2009- 10.09/9.97w, 19.81; 2010- 10.24/10.08w, 2011- 20.28, 2012- 21.23A, 2013- 10.13, 20.37/20.32w; 2014- 10.02, 19.84. pb 400m 47.40i '10.
World age-19 best 19.81 in World final 2009. Injured in April 2010; did not compete for the rest of the season, and then suffered a 10cm career-threatening hamstring tear in the 2011 World 200m final. Younger brother Mateo (b. 1 May 1993): 60m 6.73i PAN record, 100m 10.29, and 200m 21.48 in 2014.

Women

Yvette LEWIS b. 16 Mar 1985 Germany 1.73m 62kg. Norfolk Read Deal. Was at Hampton University, where now an assistant coach.
At 100mh(/TJ): PAm: '07- 8/6, '11- 1/7; WJ: '04- (dnq); won SAmG 2014, NCAA TJ 2007.
South American records: 100mh and six 60mh indoors 2013.
Progress at 100mh: 2005- 13.53, 2006- 13.14, 2007- 13.06, 2008- 12.85, 2009- 12.85, 2010- 13.19, 2011- 12.76/12.74w, 2012- 12.84/12.74w, 2013- 12.67, 2014- 12.86A/12.95. pbs: 55m 6.96i '07, 60m 7.40i '06, 100m 11.56 '07, 200m 23.50 '06, 400m 56.63i '09, 50mh 7.06+i '09, 60mh 7.84i '13, HJ 1.78i '05, 1.78 '07; LJ 6.29i '09, 6.24 '07, 6.46w '12; TJ 13.84 '08, Hep 5378 '12, Pen 3852i '07.
Switched from USA to Panama 25 Oct 2012.

POLAND

Governing body: Polski Zwiazek Lekkiej Atletyki (PZLA), ul. Myslowicka 4, 01-612 Warszawa. Founded 1919.
National Championships first held in 1920 (men), 1922 (women). **2014 Champions**: **Men**: 100m/200m: Karol Zalewski 10.29/20.80, 400m: Jakub Krzewina 45.11, 800m: Adam Kszczot 1:47.07, 1500m: Marcin Lewandowski 3:41.57, 5000m: Krystian Zalewski 14:16.48, 10000m: Yared Shegumo 30:18.77, HMar: Adam Nowicki 66:17, Mar: Henryk Szost 2:08:55, 3000mSt: Mateusz Demczyszak 8:26.30, 110mh: Artur Noga 13.51, 400mh: Patryk Dobek 49.65, HJ: Sylwester Bednarek 2.25, PV: Robert Sobera 5.60, LJ: Tomasz Jaszczuk 8.15, TJ: Karol Hoffmann 16.64, SP: Tomasz Majewski 20.29, DT: Piotr Malachowski 64.15, HT: Pawel Fajdek 78.80, JT: Lukasz Grzeszczuk 81.40, Dec: Pawel Wiesiolek 7593, 20kW: Lukasz Nowak 1:22:10, 50kW: Rafal Augustyn 3:45:32. **Women**: 100m: Anna Kielbasinska 11.50, 200m: Ewelina Ptak 23.68, 400m: Malgorzata Holub 51.95, 800m: Joanna Józwik 2:02.27, 1500m: Angelika Cichocka 4:09.19, 5000m: Justyna Korytkowska 16:13.98, 10000m: Marta Krawczynska 34:31.81, HMar: Sylwia Ejdys-Tomaszewska 76:41, Mar: Arleta Meloch 2:43:02, 3000mSt: Katarzyna Kowalska 9:51.84, 100mh: Karolina Koleczek 13.09, 400mh: Joanna Linkiewicz 55.98, HJ: Justyna Kasprzycka 1.95, PV: Anna Rogowska 4.30, LJ: Teresa Dobija 6.63w, TJ: Anna Jagaciak 14.06w, SP: Paulina Guba 16.70, DT: Zaneta Glanc 60.15, HT: Anna Wlodarczyk 75.85, JT: Urszula Jakimowicz 55.77, Hep: Agnieszka Borowska 5471, 20kW: Agnieszka Dygacz 1:32:42.

Konrad BUKOWIECKI b. 17 Mar 1997 Olsztyn 1.89m 119kg. PKS Gwardia Szczytno.
At SP: WJ: '14- 1; WY: '13- 5; Yth OG: '14- 1. At 60m: EI: '15- 2.
Shot records: World junior indoor 6kg 22.38i '15, World youth 5kg 2 out to 22.24 & 5 indoor to 24.24 in 2014; European junior (5) 2015.
Progress at SP: 2014- 17.29i, 2015- 20.46i.

Pawel FAJDEK b. 4 Jun 1989 Swiebodzice 1.86m 118kg. KS Agros Zamosc.
At HT: OG: '12- dnq; WCh: '11- 11, '13- 1; EC: 14- 2; WJ: '08- 4; EU23: '09- 8, '11- 1; WUG: '11- 1, '13- 1; CCp: '14- 3; ET: '11-13-14: 2/1/2. Won POL 2012, 2014; Franc G 2013, World HT challenge 2013.
Polish hammer record 2014.
Progress at HT: 2008- 64.58, 2009- 72.36, 2010- 76.07, 2011- 78.54, 2012- 81.39, 2013- 82.27, 2014- 83.48. pb Wt 23.22i '14.

Adam KSZCZOT b. 2 Sep 1989 Opoczno 1.78m 64kg. RKS Lódz. Studied organisation and management.
At 800m: OG: '12- sf; WCh: '09/13- sf, '11- 6; EC: '10- 3, '14- 1; WJ: '08- 4; EU23: '09/11- 1; EJ: '07- 3; WI: '10- 3, '14- 2; EI: '09-11-13: 4/1/1; CCp: '14- 3; ET: '11-13-14: 1/1/2. Polish champion 2009-10, 2012, 2014.
Polish 1000m record 2011 and 2014.
Progress at 800m: 2005- 1:59.57, 2006- 1:51.09, 2007- 1:48.10, 2008- 1:47.16, 2009- 1:45.72, 2010- 1:45.07, 2011- 1:43.30, 2012- 1:43.83, 2013- 1:44.76, 2014- 1:44.02. pbs: 400m 46.51 '11, 600m 1:14.55 '10, 1000m 2:15.72 '14, 1500m 3:46.53 '10.

Marcin LEWANDOWSKI b. 13 Jun 1987 Szczecin 1.80m 64kg. SL WKS Zawisza Bydgoszcz. PE student.
At 800m: OG: '08/12- sf; WCh: '09- 8, '11- 4, '13- 4; EC: '10- 1, '14- 5; WJ: '06- 4; EU23: '07- 1, '09- 2; WI: '14- dq; EI: '09-11-15: 6/2/1; CCp: '10- 2; ECp: '08- 2, '10- 3; won World Military 2011. At 1500m: EJ: '05- 7; EI: '13- 4; ET: '13- 3, '14- 3. Won Polish 800m 2011, 1500m 2008, 2010, 2014.
Polish 1000m record 2011.
Progress at 800m: 2002- 1:57.86, 2003- 1:53.31, 2004- 1:51.73, 2005- 1:48.86, 2006- 1:46.69, 2007- 1:45.52, 2008- 1:45.84, 2009- 1:43.84, 2010- 1:44.10, 2011- 1:44.53, 2012- 1:44.34, 2013- 1:43.79, 2014- 1:44.03. pbs: 400m 47.76 '09, 600m 1:15.17 '14, 1000m 2:15.76 '11, 1500m 3:37.37i, 3:38.19 '14.
Coached by brother Tomasz (1:51.00 '03).

Piotr LISEK b. 16 Aug 1992 Duszniki, Poznan 1.88m 85kg. OSOT Szczecin.
At PV: EC: '14- 6; EU23: '13- dnq 17; EI: '15- 3.
Polish indoor pole vault record 2015.
Progress at PV: 2006- 3.20, 2007- 3.30, 2008- 4.10,

2009- 4.42, 2010- 4.70, 2011- 5.10i/5.00, 2012- 5.20, 2013- 5.60, 2014- 5.82, 2015- 5.87i.
6-months drugs ban in 2012.

Tomasz MAJEWSKI b. 30 Aug 1981 Nasielsk 2.04m 140kg. AZS-AWF Warszawa. Graduated in political science from Cardinal Wyszynski University.
At SP: OG: '04- dnq 17, '08- 1, '12- 1; WCh: '05-07-09-11-13: 7/4/2/8/6; EC: '06-10-14: 6/1/3; EU23: '03- 4; WI: '04-06-08-10-12-14: 4/6/3/4/3/4; EI: '09- 1; WUG: '03- 5, '05- 1; CCp: '10- 2, '14- 5; ECp: '07-08-09-10-11-13-14: 3/2/1/1/2/2/2. Won WAF 2008, Polish 2002-05, 2007-14; Franc G 2013.
Polish shot record 2009.
Progress at SP: 1998- 12.91, 1999- 15.77, 2000- 17.77, 2001- 18.34, 2002- 19.33, 2003- 20.09, 2004- 20.83i/20.52, 2005- 20.64, 2006- 20.66, 2007- 20.87, 2008- 21.51, 2009- 21.95, 2010- 21.44, 2011- 21.60, 2012- 21.89, 2013- 20.98, 2014- 21.04. pb DT 51.79 '07.
Improved pb every year of his career to 2009. Went from 20.97 to 21.04 in qualifying and 21.21 and 21.51 in final to win Olympic gold in 2008.

Piotr MALACHOWSKI b. 7 Jun 1983 Zuromin 1.94m 135kg. WKS Slask Wroclaw. Army corporal.
At DT: OG: '08- 2, '12- 5; WCh: '07-09-11-13: 12,/2/9/2; EC: '06-10-14: 6/1/4; WJ: '02- 6; EU23: '03- 9, '05- 2; EJ: '01- 5; CCp: '10- 4; ECp: '06-07-08-09-10-11-14: 1/1/3/1/2/3/2. Won DL 2010, 2014; POL 2005-10, 2012-14.
Nine Polish discus records 2006-13.
Progress at DT: 1999- 39.48, 2000- 52.04, 2001- 54.19, 2002- 56.84, 2003- 57.83, 2004- 62.04, 2005- 64.74, 2006- 66.21, 2007- 66.61, 2008- 68.65, 2009- 69.15, 2010- 69.83, 2011- 68.49, 2012- 68.94, 2013- 71.84, 2014- 69.28.

Lukasz NOWAK b. 18 Dec 1988 Poznan 1.94m 77kg. AZS Poznan.
At 50kW: OG: '12- 8; WCh: '13- 8; EC: '10- 8, 14- dnf. At 20kW: EU23: '09- 13. Won POL 20kW 2014, 50kW 2012.
Progress at 50kW: 2009- 3:58:57, 2010- 3:50:30, 2011- 3:46:40, 2012- 3:42:47, 2013- 3:43:38, 2015- 3:44:53. pbs: 3000mW 11:41.30 '11; 5000mW 19:13.08i '14, 19:24.57 '11; 10kW 40:30 '13; 20kW 1:20:48 '13; 30kW 2:13:07 '13; 35kW 2:35:17 '13.

Robert SOBERA b. 19 Jan 1991 Wroclaw 1.90m 77kg. KS AZS AWF Wroclaw.
At PV: EC: '14- nh; WJ: '10- 4; EU23: '11- 11, '13- 2; EJ: '09- nh; WI: '14- 6; EI: '13- 6=, '15- 4. Polish champion 2014.
Progress at PV: 2005- 2.80, 2006- 4.12, 2007- 4.60, 2008- 5.00, 2009- 5.30, 2010- 5.30, 2011- 5.40, 2012- 5.42, 2013- 5.71i/5.61, 2014- 5.75i/5.70/5.80exh, 2015- 5.81i.

Grzegorz SUDOL b. 28 Aug 1978 Nowa Deba 1.75m 64kg. KS AZS-AWF Kraków. PE graduate.
At 50kW: OG: '04- 7, '08- 9; WCh: '03-05-07-09-11-13: dq/dq/21/4/dnf/6; EC: '02-06-10-14: 10/10/2/dnf; ECp: '13- 5. At 20kW: OG: '12- 24. At 10000mW: WJ: '96- 7, EJ: '97- 10. Won POL 20kW 2008-09, 2012; 50kW 2002, 2007-08.
Unratified Polish 30,000m record 2011.
Progress at 50kW: 2002- 3:50:37, 2003- 3:55:40, 2004- 3:49:09, 2006- 3:50:24, 2007- 3:55:22, 2008- 3:45:47, 2009- 3:42:34, 2010- 3:42:24, 2012- 3:46:01, 2013- 3:41:20, 2014- 3:52:53A. pbs: 3000mW 11:21.90 '12, 5000mW 18:55.01i '05, 19:03.94 '14; 10kW 39:01 '05, 20kW 1:20:46 '13, 30kW 2:11:12.0t '11, 35kW 2:33:53 '13.
Three times Polish 50k champion – each event held in different countries (CZE, AUT, SVK).

Wojciech THEINER b. 25 Jun 1986 Ruda Slaska 1.87m 74kg. AZS-AWF Katowice.
At HJ: EC: '10- dnq 13, '14- 10; WY: '03- 5; WUG: '11- 2, '13- 6; Polish champion 2010.
Progress at HJ: 2001- 1.87, 2002- 2.00, 2003- 2.12, 2004- 2.15, 2005- 2.24, 2006- 2.28, 2009- 2.18, 2010- 2.30, 2011- 2.26, 2012- 2.25, 2013- 2.28, 2014- 2.32. pbs: LJ 7.45 '05; TJ 14.38 '08.

Robert URBANEK b. 29 Apr 1987 Leczyca 2.00m 120kg. MKS Aleksandrów Lódzki.
At DT: OG: '12- dnq 32; WCh: '13- 6; EC: '12- 6, '14- 3; CCp: '14- 6.
Progress at PV: 2004- 47.09, 2005- 47.83, 2006- 50.84, 2007- 56.18, 2008- 62.22, 2009- 60.54, 2010- 60.74, 2011- 64.37, 2012- 66.93, 2013- 65.30, 2014- 65.75. pb SP 16.21 '07.

Pawel WOJCIECHOWSKI b. 6 Jun 1989 Bydgoszcz 1.90m 81kg. SL WKS Zawisza Bydgoszcz. PE student.
At PV: OG: '12- dnq; WCh: '11- 1; EC: '14- 2; WJ: '08- 2; EU23: '11- 1; EJ: '07- dnq 16; EI: '11- 4; CCp: '14- 5. Won W.Military 2011.
Polish pole vault record 2011.
Progress at PV: 2001- 2.50, 2002- 2.70, 2003- 3.10, 2004- 3.50, 2005- 4.10, 2006- 4.70, 2007- 5.00, 2008- 5.51, 2009- 5.40i/5.22, 2010- 5.60, 2011- 5.91, 2012- 5.62, 2014- 5.80.

Szymon ZIÓLKOWSKI b. 1 Jul 1976 Poznan 1.88m 120kg. OS AZS Poznan.
At HT: OG: '96-00-04-08-12: 10/1/dnq 12/7/7; WCh: '95-99-01-05-07-09-11-13: dnq 22/dnq 23/1/2/7/2/7/9; EC: '98-02-06-10-12-14: 5/dnq 15/4/5/3/5; WJ: '94- 1; EJ: '93- 7, '95- 1; EU23: '97- 2; ECp: '96-99-01-04-05-06-07-08-09: 2/2/1/1/1/1/1/1/2. Polish champion 1996-7, 1999-2002, 2004-09, 2011, 2013.
Six Polish hammer records 2000-01.
Progress at HT: 1991- 55.96, 1992- 63.84, 1993- 67.34, 1994- 72.48, 1995- 75.42, 1996- 79.52, 1997- 79.14, 1998- 79.58, 1999- 79.01, 2000- 81.42, 2001- 83.38, 2002- 79.78, 2003- 76.97, 2004- 79.41, 2005- 79.35, 2006- 82.31, 2007- 80.70, 2008- 79.55, 2009- 79.30, 2010- 77.99, 2011- 79.02, 2012- 78.51, 2013- 78.79, 2014- 78.41. pbs: SP 15.25 '95, DT 49.58 '00, Wt 21.10i '14.
His sister Michalina (b. 1983) was second in the

2000 Polish U18 Championships, pb 58.33 '04. Married javelin thrower (50.90 '98 (old), 50.64 '99) Joanna Domagala in December 2000 and after divorce Iwona Dorobisz (100m 11.47 '09) in 2008.

Women

Joanna FIODOROW b. 4 Mar 1989 Augustów 1.69m 89kg. OS AZS Poznan.
At HT: OG: '12- 10; WCh: '11- dnq 21; EC: '14- 3; WJ: '08- dnq 19; EU23: '09- 4, '11- 2; ET: '14- 2.
Progress at HT: 2005- 40.96, 2006- 50.18, 2007- 55.93, 2008- 61.22, 2009- 62.80, 2010- 64.66, 2011- 70.06, 2012- 74.18, 2013- 68.92, 2014- 74.39. pbs: SP 12.87 '10, JT 35.56 '09.

Zaneta GLANC b. 11 Mar 1983 Poznan 1.86m 93kg. OS AZS Poznan. Studied sociology.
At DT: OG: '08/12- dnq nt/23; WCh: '09- 4, '11- 4, '13- 7; EC: '10- dnq 13; EJ: '05- dnq; WUG: '09- 2, '11- 1; ET: '11- 3, '13- 3. Won POL 2009, 2013-14.
Progress at DT: 2001- 39.97, 2002- 46.25, 2003- 47.03, 2004- 51.30, 2005- 56.15, 2006- 56.00, 2007- 59.36, 2008- 61.42, 2009- 63.96, 2010- 62.16, 2011- 63.99, 2012- 65.34, 2013- 62.90, 2014- 60.95.

Joanna JÓZWIK b. 30 Jan 1991 Walbrzych 1.68m 53kg. AZS-AWF Warszawa.
At HJ: EC: '14- 3; WJ: '10- sf; EU23: '11- h, '13- 8; EI: '15- 4. Polish champion 2014.
Progress at 800m: 2007- 2:12.90, 2008- 2:11.55, 2009- 2:07.31, 2010- 2:05.09, 2011- 2:03.15, 2012- 2:05.87, 2013- 2:02.39, 2014- 1:59.63. pbs: 200m 24.16 '14, 300m 39.83 '11, 400m 53.08 '14, 600m 1:26.80 '14, 1000m 2:38.26 '13.

Justyna KASPRZYCKA b. 20 Aug 1987 Glubczyce 1.83m 62kg. AZS-AWF Wroclaw
At HJ: WCh: '13- 6; EC: '14- 4; EU23: '07- 9=, '09- 9; WI: '12- 4; EI: '15- 6; Polish champion 2013-14.
Polish high jump record 2014
Progress at HJ: 2001- 1.58, 2002- 1.67, 2003- 1.77, 2004- 1.76i/1.72, 2005- 1.74, 2006- 1.78, 2007- 1.86, 2008- 1.79i/1.74, 2009- 1.87, 2010- 1.88, 2011- 1.84i, 2012- 1.84, 2013- 1.97, 2014- 1.99.

Kamila LICWINKO b. 22 Mar 1986 Bielsk Podlaski 1.83m 66kg. née Stepaniuk. KS Podlasie Bialystok.
At HJ: WCh: '09- dnq 16, '13- 7=; EC: '14- 9=; EU23: '07- 4; EJ: '05- 7; WI: '14- 1=, EI: '09- 8, '15- 2; ET: '13- 2; WUG: '13- 1. Won POL 2007-09.
Polish high jump records 2013 & 2014, three indoor 2015.
Progress at HJ: 1999- 1.46, 2000- 1.61, 2001- 1.66, 2002- 1.75, 2003- 1.75, 2004- 1.84, 2005- 1.86, 2006- 1.85i/1.84, 2007- 1.90, 2008- 1.91, 2009- 1.93, 2010- 1.92i/1.89, 2011- 1.88i, 2012- 1.89, 2013- 1.99, 2014- 2.00i/1.97, 2015- 2.02i.
Married her trainer Michal Licwinko in 2013.

Anna ROGOWSKA b. 21 May 1981 Gdynia 1.71m 57kg. SKLA Sopot. PE student.
At PV: OG: '04- 3, '08- 10=, '12- nh; WCh: '03-05-07-09-11-13: 7/6=/8/1/10=/dnq; EC: '02- 7=; EU23: '03- 3; WI: '03-04-06-08-10-14: 6=/7/2/6/3/5=; EI: '05-07-11-13: 2/3/1/2; ECp: '05-08-10-11-13: 1/2/3/1/3. Won POL 2009, 2011, 2013-14.
Nine Polish pole vault records 2004-05, indoors (2) 2010-11.
Progress at PV: 1997- 2.60, 1998- 2.90, 1999- 3.40, 2000- 3.60, 2001- 3.90, 2002- 4.40, 2003- 4.47i/4.45, 2004- 4.71, 2005- 4.83, 2006- 4.80i/4.70, 2007- 4.72i/4.60, 2008- 4.66, 2009- 4.80, 2010- 4.81i/4.71, 2011- 4.85i/4.75, 2012- 4.71i/4.70, 2013- 4.67i/4.60, 2014- 4.76i/4.50.
Coached by husband Jacek Torlinski (PV 4.85 '97).

Karolina TYMINSKA b. 4 Oct 1984 Swiebodzin 1.75m 69kg. SKLA Sopot.
At Hep: OG: '08- 7, '12- dnf; WCh: '07-09-11-13: 15/dnf/4/9; EC: '06- dnf (dnq LJ), '10- 4, '14- 11; EU23: '05- dnf (LJ dnq 17); ECp: '06-09-13: 2/3/1. At Pen: WI: '08-10-12-14: 6/5/4/8; EI: '05-07-09-11: 8/7/5/4. Won POL 100mh 2011, Hep 2006-07, 2011.
Progress at Hep: 2002- 5147, 2004- 5787, 2005- 6026, 2006- 6402, 2007- 6200, 2008- 6428, 2009- 6191, 2010- 6230, 2011- 6544, 2012- dnf, 2013- 6360, 2014- 6266. pbs: 60m 7.55i '14, 100m 11.88 '14, 200m 23.32 '06, 400m 55.11 '14, 800m 2:05.21 '11, 60mh 8.34i '10, 100mh 13.12 '11, HJ 1.78 '11, LJ 6.63 '08, SP 15.11i/14.82 '08, JT 42.40 '13, Pen 4769i '08.

Anita WLODARCZYK b. 8 Aug 1985 Rawicz 1.78m 95kg. RKS Skra Warszawa. PE student.
At HT: OG: '08- 6, '12- 2; WCh: '09- 1, '11- 5, '13- 2; EC: '10- 3, '12- 1, '14- 1; EU23: '07- 9; CCp: '14- 1; ET: '09- 1, '13- 2. Won POL 2009, 2011-12, 2014; Franc G 2013, World HT challenge 2013-14.
Three world hammer records 2009-14, six Polish records 2009-14.
Progress at HT: 2002- 33.83, 2003- 43.24, 2004- 54.74, 2005- 60.51, 2006- 65.53, 2007- 69.07, 2008- 72.80, 2009- 77.96, 2010- 78.30, 2011- 75.33, 2012- 77.60, 2013- 78.46, 2014- 79.58. pbs: SP 13.25 '06, DT 52.26 '08, Wt 20.09i '14.

PORTUGAL

Governing body: Federação Portuguesa de Atletismo, Largo da Lagoa, 1799-538 Linda-a-Velha. Founded in 1921.

National Championships first held in 1910 (men), 1937 (women). **2014 Champions: Men**: 100m/200m: Yazaldes Nascimento 10.39/21.20, 400m: Ricardo dos Santos 46.68, 800m: Sandy Martins 1:48.74, 1500m: Miguel Moreira 3:52.46, 5000m: Rui Pinto 14:22.71, 10000m: Manuel Damião 28:50.70, Mar: Carlos Silva 2:24:29, 3000mSt: Alberto Paulo 8:50.58, 110mh: João Almeida 13.91, 400mh: João Ferreira 51.32, HJ: Paulo Conceição 2.11, PV: Diogo Ferreira 5.67, LJ: Marcos Chuva 7.66w, TJ: Nelson Évora 16.41, SP: Marco Fortes 20.62, DT: Filipe Vital e Silva 56.65, HT: Dário Manso 70.25, JT: Tiago Aperta

69.36, Dec:, 10,000mW: Sérgio Vieira 41:09.75, 20kW: João Vieira 1:26:02, 50kW: Luís Gil 4:11:40. **Women**: 100m: Carla Tavares 11.71, 200m: Filipa Martins 24.80, 400m/400mh: Vera Barbosa 53.72/57.01, 800m: Micaela Lopes 2:11.09, 1500m: Marta Freitas 4:16.68, 5000m: Sara Moreira 15:31.11, 10000m: Jéssica Augusto 31:57.02, Mar: Rosa Madureira 2:48:03, 3000mSt: Catarina Carvalho 10:22.74, 100mh/LJ: Lecabela Quaresma 14.30/5.82, HJ: Anabela Neto 1.82, PV: Maria Eleonor Tavares 4.23, TJ: Patricia Mamona 14.05, SP/ JT: Sílvia Cruz 14.09/55.19, DT: Irina Rodrigues 60.53, HT: Vânia Silva 60.44, Hep: Cláudia Rodrigues 5127, 10000mW/20kW: Ana Cabecinha 43:47.84/1:30:36.

Nelson ÉVORA b. 20 Apr 1984 Abidjan, Côte d'Ivoire 1.81m 64kg. Sport Lisboa e Benfica.
At (LJ/)TJ: OG: '04- dnq 40, '08- 1; WCh: '05-07-09-11: dnq 14/1/2/5; EC: '06- 6/4, '14- 6; WJ: '02- dnq 18/6; EU23: '05- 3; EJ: '03- 1/1; WUG: '09- 1, '11- 1; WI: '06- 6, '08- 3; EI: '07- 5, '15- 1; ECp: '09- 2/1; Won WAF TJ 2008, POR LJ 2006-07, TJ 2003-04, 2006-07, 2009-11, 2013-14.
Six Portuguese triple jump records 2006-07, Cape Verde LJ & TJ records 2001-02.
Progress at TJ: 1999- 14.35, 2000- 14.93i, 2001- 16.15, 2002- 15.87, 2003- 16.43, 2004- 16.85i/16.04, 2005- 16.89, 2006- 17.23, 2007- 17.74, 2008- 17.67, 2009- 17.66/17.82w, 2010- 16.36, 2011- 17.35, 2013- 16.68, 2014- 16.97, 2015- 17.19i. pbs: HJ 2.07i '05, 1.98 '99; LJ 8.10 '07.
Portugal's first male world champion in 2007. He suffered a serious injury in right tibia (in same place where he had an operation in February 2010) in January 2012 and missed season. Father from Cape Verde, mother from Côte d'Ivoire, relocating to Portugal when he was five. Switched nationality in 2002. Sister Dorothé (b. 28 May 1991) 400m pb 55.11 '13.

Marco FORTES b. 26 Sep 1982 Lisboa 1.89m 139kg. Sport Lisboa e Benfica.
At SP: OG: '08/12: dnq 37/15; WCh: '09-13: dnq 17/16, '11- 5; EC: '10-12-14: dnq 12/5/7; WJ: '00- dnq 18 (dnq 26 DT); EU23: '03- 12; EJ: '01- 3; EI: '11- 8, '13- 5; Won IbAm 2010, POR SP 2002-14 (& 12 indoor), DT 2009, 2011
Five Portuguese shot records 2008-12.
Progress at SP: 2000- 17.31, 2001- 18.02, 2002- 18.76, 2003- 18.57, 2004- 18.19, 2005- 17.89, 2006- 18.74, 2007- 19.18, 2008- 20.13, 2009- 20.52, 2010- 20.69, 2011- 20.89, 2012- 21.02, 2013- 20.22, 2014- 21.01. pb DT 58.32 '09.

João VIEIRA b. 20 Feb 1976 Portimão 1.74m 58kg. Sporting Clube de Portugal.
At 20kW: OG: '04- 10, '08- 32, '12- 11 (dnf 50k); WCh: '99-01-03-05-07-09-11-13: dq/dq/17/dnf/25/10/14/4; EC: '98-02-06-10-14: 20/12/3/2/dnf; WCp: '02- 11, '06- 8; ECp: '03-07-13: 4/7/7. At 10000mW: WJ: '94- 11; Won POR 10000mW 2011-13, 20kW 1996, 1999-2007, 2009, 2011-14; 50kW 2004, 2008, 2012.
Portuguese records: 5000mW 2000, 10000mW 2011, 20kW (3) 2002-06, 50kW 2004 & 2012.
Progress at 20kW: 1995- 1:33:51, 1996- 1:23:49, 1997- 1:20:59, 1998- 1:22:50, 1999- 1:22:46, 2000- 1:22:53, 2001- 1:22:52, 2002- 1:20:44, 2003- 1:20:30, 2004- 1:20:48, 2005- 1:21:56, 2006- 1:20:09, 2007- 1:20:42, 2008- 1:21:13, 2009- 1:21:43, 2010- 1:20:49, 2011- 1:22:44, 2012- 1:20:41, 2013- 1:21:08, 2014- 1:23:20. pbs: 5000m 18:33.16 '00, 10000mW 39:44.91 '11, 39:06R '10; 30kW 2:09:49 '04, 50kW 3:45:17 '12.
Partner of Vera Santos. Twin brother Sergio has 20kW pb 1:20:58 '97.

Women

Jéssica AUGUSTO b. 8 Nov 1981 Paris, France 1.65m 46kg. Nike.
At Mar: OG: '12- 7; EC: '14- 3. At 3000mSt: OG: '08- h (h 5000); WCh: '09- 11. At 5000m/(10000m): WCh: '05- h, '07- 15, '11- (10); EC: '10- 3/2; EU23: '03- dnf; WUG: '07- 1; CCp: '10- 7; ECp: '14- (2). At 3000m (1500m): WJ: '00- 8; EU23: '01- (10); EJ: '99- 6 (12); WI: '08- 8, '10- 7; EI: '09- 10. World CC: '07- 12, '10- 21; Eur CC: '98-99-00-02-04-05-06-07-08-09-10: 12J/8J/1J/16/18/30/9/11/2/4/1. Won POR 1500m 2007, 2011; 5000m 2006, 10000m 2014; IbAm 3000m 2004, 2006, 2010.
Two Portuguese 3000m steeplechase records 2008-10, European indoor 2M best 2010.
Progress at 5000m, 10000m, Mar, 3000mSt: 2003- 15:51.63, 2004- 15:15.76, 2005- 15:20.45, 2006- 15:37.55, 2007- 14:56.39, 2008- 15:19.67, 9:22.50; 2009- 9:25.25, 2010- 14:37.07, 31:19.15, 9:18.54; 2011- 15:19.60, 32:06.68, 2:24:33; 2012- 2:24:59, 2013- 15:38.73, 2:29:11; 2014- 31:55.56, 2:24:25. pbs: 800m 2:07.97i '02, 1500m 4:07.89i/4:08.32 '10, 1M 4:32.58i '09, 4:42.15 '99, 2000m 5:45.6i '09, 3000m 8:41.53 '07, 2M 9:19.39i '10, 9:22.89 '07; road 15k 48:40 '08, 10M 53:15 '08, HMar 69:08 '09, 30k 1:41:37 '11.
Won Great North Run 2009.

Ana CABECINHA b. 29 Apr 1984 Beja 1.68m 52kg. CO Pechão.
At 20kW: OG: '08- 8, '12- 9; WCh: '11- 7, '13- 8; EC: '10- 8, '14- 6; EU23: '05- 4; WCp '08-10-12-14: 11/8/9/8; ECp: '13- 5. At 5000mW: WY: '01- 10. At 10000mW: WJ: '02- 12; EJ: '03- 3; won IbAm 2006, 2010; 2nd RWC 2012; POR 10000mW 2005, 2008, 2010, 2012, 2014; 20kW 2012-14.
POR records 10,000m and 20km walk 2008.
Progress at 20kW: 2004- 1:37:39, 2005- 1:34:13, 2006- 1:31:02, 2007- 1:32:46, 2008- 1:27:46, 2009- 1:33:05, 2010- 1:31:14, 2011- 1:31:08, 2012- 1:28:03, 2013- 1:29:17, 2014- 1:27:49. pbs: 3000mW 12:17.50 '14, 5000mW 21:31.06 '14, 21:21R '12; 10000mW 43:08.17 '08; running 1500m 4:31.73 '07, 3000m 9:46.08 '13, 5000m 17:57.34 '12.

Inês HENRIQUES b 1 May 1980 Santarém 1.56m 48kg. CN Rio Maior.
At 20kW: OG: '04- 25, '12- 15; WCh: '01-05-07-09-11-13: dq/27/7/11/10/11; EC: '02-06-10-14:

15/12/9/13; EU23: '01- 10; WCp: '06-10-12: 13/3/10; ECp: '07- 7, '13- 8; Won POR 10000mW 2006, 2009, 2011, 2013; 20kmW 2009, 2011. At 5000mW: EJ: '99- 12.
Progress at 20kW: 2000- 1:41:09, 2001- 1:34:49, 2002- 1:34:46.5t, 2003- 1:36:03, 2004- 1:31:23.7t, 2005- 1:33:24, 2006- 1:30:28, 2007- 1:30:24, 2008- 1:31:06, 2009- 1:30:34, 2010- 1:29:36, 2011- 1:30:29, 2012- 1:29:54, 2013- 1:29:30, 2014- 1:29:33. pbs: 3000mW 12:25.36i '13, 12:38.75 '07; 5000mW 21:32.08 '14, 10000mW 43:22.05 '08, 43:09R '10.

Patrícia MAMONA b. 21 Nov 1988 Lisbon 1.68m 53kg. Sporting CP. Was at Clemson University, USA.
At TJ: OG: '12- dnq 13; WCh: '11- dnq 27; WJ: '06- 6; WY: '05- 7; EC: '10-12-14: 8/2/dnq 13; EU23: '09- 5; EJ: '07- dnq 15; WI: '14- 4; EI: '13- 8, '15- 5; WUG: '11- 2. POR champion 2008-14, NCAA 2010-11.
Seven Portuguese triple jump records 2009-12.
Progress at TJ: 2004- 12.71, 2005- 12.87, 2006- 13.37/13.38w, 2007- 13.24, 2008- 13.51, 2009- 13.83, 2010- 14.12, 2011- 14.42, 2012- 14.52, 2013- 14.02/14.07w, 2014- 14.36/14.49w. pbs: 200m 24.42 '10, 800m 2:19.70i '09, 60mh 8.41i '09, 100mh 13.53/13.49w '10, HJ 1.69i '09, 1.69 '11; LJ 6.21i '09, 6.16 '05; Pen 4081i '09, Hep 5293 '11.

Vera SANTOS b. 3 Dec 1981 Santarém 1.64m 57kg. Sporting Clube de Portugal.
At 20kW: OG: '08- 9, '12- 49; WCh: '03-05-07-09-13: 15/15/11/5/17; EC: '02- 17, '06- 8, '10- 6; EU23: '01- 12, '03- 2; WUG: '05- 2; WCp '08-10-14: 3/2/11; ECp: '05- 7, '13- 10. At 10000mW: WJ: '00- 5. Won POR 20kW 2005, 2010.
Progress at 20kW: 2000- 1:39:20.5t, 2001- 1:35:51, 2002- 1:34:46.6t, 2003- 1:32:43, 2004- 1:33:00, 2005- 1:31:30, 2006- 1:30:41, 2007- 1:32:53, 2008- 1:28:14, 2009- 1:29:27, 2010- 1:28:29, 2011- 1:29:55, 2012- 1:32:48, 2013- 1:31:00, 2014- 1:28:02. pbs: 3000mW 12:17.59 '10, 5000mW 21:01.43 '10, 10000mW 43:52.73 '10.

PUERTO RICO

Governing body: Federación de Atletismo Amateur de Puerto Rico, 90, Ave. Río Hondo, Bayamón, PR 00961-3113. Founded 1947.
National Champions 2014: Men: 100m/200m: Pedro Cruz 10.60/21.01, 400m: Héctor Carrasquillo 46.46, 800m: Andres González 1:54.45, 1500m: Erick Estrada 3:55.72, 5000m: Luis Rivera 15:27.46, 3000mSt: Luis López 9:29.94, 110mh: Héctor Cotto 14.10, 400mh: Derrick Diaz 52.38, HJ: George Rivera 2.10, PV: Kevin Sánchez 4.50, LJ: Jeffrey Burgos 6.98, TJ: Manuel Montano 15.31w, SP: Julio Camacho 16.25, DT: Alfredo Romero 51.82, HT: Alexis Figueroa 63.25, JT: Kevin Ortíz 64.71, Dec: Marcos Sánchez 7299. **Women**: 100m: Celiangeli Morales 11.50, 200m: Genoiska Cancel 23.84w, 400m: Grace Claxton 53.61, 1500m: Beverly Ramos 4:16.66, 100mh: Litzi Vázquez 13.40, 400mh: Janice Machuca 61.35, HJ: Darlene Mercado 1.63, PV: Alexandra González 3.80, LJ: Jasmine Simmons 6.00, TJ: Brianna Santiago 12.17 ?, SP: Neidaliz Flores 12.45, DT: Ashley Arroyo 45.18, HT: Keishla Luna 57.11, JT: Coralys Ortiz 52.49, Hep: Alysbeth Félix 5434.

Javier CULSON b. 25 Jul 1984 Ponce 1.98m 79kg.
At 400mh: OG: '08- sf, '12- 3; WCh: '07-09-11-13: sf/2/2/6; PAm: '07- 6; CAG: '06- 5, '10- 2; PAm-J: '03- 3; WUG: '07- 3; CCp: '10- 2, '14- 3/3R; won DL 2012-13, IbAm 2006, CAC 2009.
Seven Puerto Rican 400mh records 2007-10.
Progress at 400mh: 2002- 54.47, 2003- 51.10, 2004- 50.77, 2005- 50.62, 2006- 49.48, 2007- 49.07, 2008- 48.87, 2009- 48.09, 2010- 47.72. 2011- 48.32, 2012- 47.78, 2013- 48.14, 2014- 48.03. pbs: 200m 21.64w '07, 400m 45.99 '12, 800m 1:49.83 '14, 110mh 13.84 '07.

QATAR

Governing body: Qatar Association of Athletics Federation, PO Box 8139, Doha. Founded 1963.

Mutaz Essa BARSHIM b. 24 Jun 1991 Doha 1.92m 70kg. Team Aspire.
At HJ: OG: '12- 3=; WCh: '11- 7, '13- 2; WJ: '10- 1; AsiG: '10- 1, '14- 1; AsiC: '11- 1; WI: '12- 9=, '14- 1; CCp: '14- 3; won DL 2014, Asian indoors (3) 2012-15; Asi-J 2010, W.Mil G 2011, Arab 2011, 2013; Gulf 2013.
Five Asian high jump records 2012-14 and indoors (3) 2013-15, 14 Qatar records 2010-13.
Progress at HJ: 2008- 2.07, 2009- 2.14, 2010- 2.31, 2011- 2.35, 2012- 2.39, 2013- 2.40, 2014- 2.43, 2015- 2.41i.
His 2.43 at Brussels in 2014 was the world's best since 1993, second only to Javier Sotomayor. Qatari father (who was a race walker), Sudanese mother. Younger brother Muamer Aissa Barshim (b. 3 Jan 1994) has HJ pb 2.28 '14 and was 3rd 2014 Asian Games.

Femi Seun **OGUNODE** b. 15 May 1991 Nigeria 1.83m 79kg.
At (100m)/200m: WCh: '11- sf (8 400m); AsiG: '10- 1 (1 400m), 14- 1/1; AsiC: '11- 1; CCp: '14- 3/3; Arab champion 2011, W.Asian 1000m/200m 2010, W.Military 100m/200m 2011. At 60m: WI: '14- 3.
Asian 100m record 2014, 2 Qatar 200m 2011-14.
Progress at 100m, 200m: 2010- 10.25, 20.43; 2011- 10.07, 20.30; 2014- 9.93, 20.06. pbs: 60m 6.51Ai/6.52i '14, 400m 45.12 '10.
Two-year drugs ban 2012-14. Switched allegiance from Nigeria to Qatar from 31 Oct 2009. Younger brother Tosin suddenly emerged with 6.50i for 60m in 2014.

ROMANIA

Governing body: Federatia Romana de Atletism, 2 Primo Nebiolo Str, 011349 Bucuresti. Founded 1912.

National Championships first held in 1914 (men), 1925 (women). **2014 Champions**: **Men**: 100m/200m: Catalin Câmpeanu 10.36/21.20, 400m: Tiberiu Benesau 48.18, 800m: Valentin Voicu 1:50.35, 1500m: Cristian Vorovenci 3:58.33, 5000m: Nicolae Soare 14:26.41, 10000m/HMar: Marius Ionescu 29:45.81/65:30, Mar: Sorin Mineran 2:30:47, 3000mSt: Alexandru Ghinea 8:47.51, 110mh: Cornel Bananau 14.31, 400mh: Attila Nagy 51.90, HJ: Mihai Donisan 2.22, PV: Andrei Deliu 4.90, LJ: Marian Oprea 7.71, TJ: Alexandru Baciu 16.30w, SP/DT: Andrei Gag 18.78/59.17, HT: Cosmin Sorescu 61.79, JT: Toma Pop 73.74, Dec: Razvan Roman 6852, 20kW/50kW: Marius Cocioran 1:30:57/1:32:36/4:07:37. **Women**: 100m/200m: Andreea Ograzeanu 11.32/23.61, 400m: Bianca Razor 52.29, 800m: Elena Lavric 2:02.36, 1500m: Florina Pierdevara 4:21.08, 5000m/10000m: Monica Florea 16:47.51/34:09.12, HMar/Mar: Paula Todoran 75:19/2:41:23, 3000mSt: Cristian Casandra 9:56.47, 100mh: Anamaria Nesteriuc 13.58, 400mh: Angela Morosanu 57.64, HJ: Daniela Stanciu 1.90, PV: Ionela Pistool 3.30, LJ: Alina Rotaru 6.74, TJ: Cristina Bujin 14.07, SP: Andreea Huzum-Vitan 15.47, DT: Ileana Solrescu 48.92, HT: Bianca Perie 68.60, JT: Nicoleta Anghelescu 54.92, Hep: Beatrice Puiu 5808, 10kW: Ana Rodean 46:09, 20kW: Claudia Stef 1:41:36/1:40:38.

Marian OPREA b. 6 Jun 1982 Pitesti 1.90m 80kg. Rapid Bucuresti & Dinamo Bucuresti. Sports teacher.
At TJ: OG: '04- 2, '08- 5; WCh: '01-03-13: dnq 13/17/15, '05- 3, '13- 6; EC: '02-06-10-12-14: dnq 14/3/2/dnq 21/5; WJ: '00- 1; WY: '99- 4; EU23: '03- 2; EJ: '99- 3, '01- 1; WI: '03-04-06-14: 8/5/4/4; EI: '02-11-15: 2/3/3; WUG: '01- 2; WCp: '06- 3, '10- 1. Won Balkan LJ 2014, TJ 2001-03, 2013-14; ROU LJ 2014, TJ 2001, 2003-08, 2013.
Romanian TJ records 2003 and 2005.
Progress at TJ: 1997- 14.37, 1998- 14.78, 1999- 15.98, 2000- 16.49, 2001- 17.11/17.13w, 2002- 17.29i/17.11/17.39w, 2003- 17.63, 2004- 17.55, 2005- 17.81, 2006- 17.74i/17.56, 2007- 17.32, 2008- 17.28, 2010- 17.51, 2011- 17.62i/17.19, 2012- 16.97i/16.56/16.68w, 2013- 17.24/17.32w, 2014- 17.30i/16.94. pb LJ 7.78 '14, 8.06w '11.
Silver medal in 2004 was best ever Olympic placing by a Romanian male. Major surgery on his left knee in October 2008 meant that he did not compete in 2009.

Women

Cristina-Ioana **BUJIN** b. 12 Apr 1988 Constanta 1.71m 52kg. Farul Constanta. Student
At (LJ)/TJ: WCh: '09- 7; EC: '14- dnq 14; WJ: '04- dnq/10, '06- 6; WY: '03- (5), '05- 3; EU23: '09- 2; EJ: '05- dnq/2, '07- 3; WUG: '11- 3; EI: '11- 5, '15- 6. Won Balkan 2014, ROU 2009, 2012-14.
Progress at TJ: 2004- 13.46, 2005- 13.72, 2006- 14.06i/13.68, 2007- 13.99i/13.57, 2008- 14.07i/13.94, 2009- 14.42, 2010- 13.62, 2011- 14.30, 2012- 14.14i/14.13/14.25w, 2013- 14.24i/13.91, 2014- 14.11. pb LJ 6.38 '09.

Florentina MARINCU b. 8 Apr 1996 Deva 1.78m 60kg. CN Sp.Cetate Deva,
At LJ(/TJ): WY: '13- 1/1; EJ: '13- dnq 15/4; EI: '15- 3.
Progress at LJ: 2011- 6.07, 2013- 6.54, 2014- 6.71/6.73w, 2015- 6.79i. pbs: 60m 7.40i '14, 100m 11.85 '14, TJ 13.81 '13.

Bianca-Florentina **PERIE** b. 1 Jun 1990 Roman, Neamt district 1.70m 70kg. S.C.M. Bacau. Student.
At HT: OG: '08/12- dnq 18/21; WCh: '07/09- dnq 26/19, '11-13- 6/11; EC: '10-12-14: 4/9/7; WJ: '06/08- 1; WY: '05/07- 1; EU23: '11- 1; EJ: '07/09- 1; WUG: '11- 2, '13- 4; ROU champion 2009-14, Balkan 2013-14.
Progress at HT: 2003- 47.14, 2004- 57.67, 2005- 65.13, 2006- 67.38, 2007- 67.24, 2008- 69.59, 2009- 69.63, 2010- 73.52, 2011- 72.04, 2012- 70.05, 2013- 71.57, 2014- 71.93. pb SP 13.04i '07.
World age 14 best of 65.13 in 2005. Her younger sister Roxana won the bronze medal in the 2011 World Youth hammer.

Alina ROTARU b. 5 Jun 1993 Bucharest 1.75m 54kg. CSA Steaua Bucharest.
At LJ: EC: '12- dnq 20, '14- 7; WJ: '10- dnq 19, '12- 5; WY: '09- 2 (4 HJ); Yth OG: '10- 2; EJ: '11- 2; EI: '15- 4. ROU champion 2014.
Progress at LJ: 2008- 6.08i/5.99, 2009- 6.26, 2010- 6.40, 2011- 6.46, 2012- 6.57/6.58w, 2013- 6.63, 2014- 6.74, 2015- 6.74i. pbs: 60m 7.63i '15, 60mh 8.86i '14, HJ 1.85i '12, 1.82 '09; TJ 13.24i/13.21 '12, Pen 4111i '12.

RUSSIA

Governing body: All-Russia Athletic Federation, Luzhnetskaya Nab. 8, Moscow 119992. Founded 1911.
National Championships first held 1908, USSR women from 1922. **2014 Champions**: **Men**: 100m: Mikhail Idrisov 10.34, 200m: Konstantin Petryashov 21.22, 400m: Vladimir Krasnov 45.45, 800m: Ivan Nesterov 1:50.76, 1500m: Valentin Smirnov 3:43.65, 5000m: Yegor Nikolayev 13:42.84, 10000m: Yevgeniy Rybakov 28:02.79, HMar: Fyodor Shutov 64:02, Mar: Sergey Rybin 2:16:43, 3000mSt: Nikolay Chavkin 8:25.59, 110mh: Konstantin Shabanov 13.67, 400mh: Tomofey Chalyy 49.15, HJ: Daniyil Tsyplakov 2.32, PV: Ilya Mudrov & Sergey Kucheryanu 5.70, LJ: Aleksandr Petrov 8.02w, TJ: Aleksey Fyodorov 17.07, SP: Aleksandr Lesnoy 20.57, DT: Gleb Sidorchenko 62.47, HT: Aleksey Korolyov 74.28, JT: Valeriy Iordan 78.20, Dec: Sergey Sviridov 8193, 20kW: Denis Strelkov 1:19:47, 50kW: Aleksandr Yargunkin 3:42:26. **Women**: 100m: Kristina Sivkova 11.31, 200m: Yelizaveta Savlinis 23.25, 400m: Tatyana Veshkurova 51.48, 800m: Svetlana Rogozina

1:59.54, 1500m: Svetlana Karamasheva 4:04.45, 5000m: Yelena Korobkina 15:20.98, 10000m: Yelena Nagovitsyna 32:11.63, HMar: Tatyana Arkhipova 73:33, Mar: Natalya Starkova 2:35:16, 3000mSt: Natalya Aristarkova 9:32.98, 100mh: Svetlana Topylina 13.03, 400mh: Irina Davydova 55.44, HJ: Mariya Kuchina 1.92, PV: Anzhelika Sidorova 4.70, LJ: Darya Klishina 6.90, TJ: Yekaterina Koneva 14.84w, SP: Yevgeniya Kolodko 19.29, DT: Yuliya Maltseva 58.42, HT: Anna Bulgakova 73.31, JT: Viktoriya Sudarushkina 58.53, Hep: Anna Butvina 6068, 20kW: Vera Sokolova 1:28:05.

Lyukman ADAMS b. 24 Sep 1988 St. Petersburg 1.94m 87kg.
At TJ: OG: '12- 9; EC: '10- 6, '14- 2; EJ: '07- 1; CCp: '14- 6; WI: '12- 3, '14- 1. Russian champion 2012.
Progress at TJ: 2005- 15.97, 2006- 15.16, 2007- 16.75, 2008- 16.86i/16.78, 2009- 16.22i/16.20, 2010- 17.17/17.21w, 2011- 17.32i/15.60, 2012- 17.53, 2013- 16.82, 2014- 17.37i/17.29. pb LJ 7.47i '05, 7.42 '07.
Married Yevgeniya Polyakova (60m 7.09 '08, 1 EI '09; 100m 11.09 '07; 4x100m 1 OG '08) on 5 Apr 2014.

Viktor BUTENKO b. 10 Mar 1993 Stavropol 1.96m 116kg. Stavropolskiy.
At DT: WCh: '13- 8; EC: '14- 5; WJ: '12- 4; EU23: '13- 2; EJ: '11- 6; ET: '14- 3.
Progress at DT: 2011- 51.89, 2012- 57.32, 2013- 65.97, 2014- 65.89.

Aleksey DMITRIK b. 12 Apr 1984 Slantsy. Leningrad reg, 1.91m 69kg. St Petersburg YR.
At HJ: WCh: '11- 2, "13- dnq 25=; EC: '10- 7, '14- dnq 23; WJ: '02- 14; WY: '01- 1; EJ: '03- 2; EU23: '05- 6; EI: '09- 2=, '13- 2; ECp: '05- 1, '11- 2. Russian champion 2011.
Progress at HJ: 2000- 2.08, 2001- 2.23, 2002- 2.26, 2003- 2.28, 2004- 2.30, 2005- 2.34i/2.30, 2006- 2.28, 2007- 2.30, 2008- 2.33i/2.27, 2009- 2.33, 2010- 2.32i/2.31, 2011- 2.36, 2012- 2.35i/2.33, 2013- 2.36i/2.30, 2014- 2.40i/2.30.
Mother Yelana was a 1.75m high jumper.

Aleksey FYODOROV b. 25 May 1991 Smolensk 1.84m 73kg. Mosoovskaya Smolenskaya.
At TJ: WCh: '11- dnq 18, 13- 5; EC: '12- 4, '14- 3; WY: '07- 2; EU23: '11-2, '13- 1; EJ: '09- 1; EI: '13- 3, '15- 4; WUG: '13- 2; ET: '13- 1, '14- 1. Russian champion 2011, 2013-14.
Progress at TJ: 2007- 15.59, 2008- 16.08, 2009- 16.62, 2010- 17.12/17.18w, 2011- 17.05i/17.01, 2012- 17.19, 2013- 17.13, 2014- 17.07/17.12w.
Parents Leonid and Tatyana were triple jumpers.

Aleksandr GRIPICH b. 21 Sep 1986 Slavyabsk-n-Kubani 1.90m 80kg. Krasnodar VS. Kuban State University.
At PV: WCh: '09- 5, '13- dnq 24=; EC: '10- dnq, '14- 5; EI: '15- 2; WUG: '09- 1, '11- 2=; ET: '11- 3, '14- 2=.
Progress at PV: 2003- 4.95, 2004- 5.30, 2005- 5.40, 2006- 5.45i/5.20, 2007- 5.65i/5.50, 2008- 5.55, 2009- 5.75, 2010- 5.70i/5.60, 2011- 5.75, 2012- 5.47i/5.00, 2013- 5.60, 2014- 5.70, 2015- 5.85i.

Aleksandr IVANOV b. 26 Jun 1994 Nizhny Tagiul, Sverdlovsk reg. 1.82m 68kg. Mordoviya VS.
At 20kW: WCh: '13- 1; EC: '14- 2; EU23: '13- 2; ECp: '13- 4. At 10000mW: WJ: '12- 2; WCp: 'EJ: '11- 6; 12- 2J.
Progress at 20kW: 2013- 1:20:58, 2014- 1:19:45, 2015- 1:20:06. pbs: 5000mW 19:35.0 '12, 10000mW: 40:12.90 '12, 39:29R '13.
At 20 in 2013 he became the youngest ever World walking champion.

Andrey KRIVOV b. 14 Nov 1985 Komsomolsky, Mordovia 1.85m 72kg. Mordovia. Sports student.
At 20kW: OG: '12- 37; WCh: '09- 17; EC: '10- 5; EU23: '07- 2; WCp: '08-10-12: 5/3/2; ECp: '11- 7; WUG: '11- 1, '13- 1. Russian champion 2009, 2011.
Progress at 20kW: 2005- 1:22:21, 2007- 1:20:12, 2008- 1:19:06, 2009- 1:19:55, 2010- 1:22:20, 2011- 1:20:16, 2012- 1:18:25, 2013- 1:20:47, 2015- 1:20:43. pbs: 10000mW: 40:35.2 '05, 35kW 2:29:44 '06.

Aleksandr LESNOY b. 28 Jul 1988 Krasnodar 1.94m 116kg.
At SP: WCh: '13: dnq 21; EC: '14- 10; WUG: '13- 1; WI: '14- 8; ET: '14- 3. RUS champion 2014.
Progress at SP: 2008- 16.46, 2009- 16.80, 2010- 19.09, 2011- 19.60, 2012- 20.05, 2013- 20.60, 2014- 21.40. pb DT 58.80 '12.

Sergey LITVINOV b. 27 Jan 1986 Rostov-on-Don, Russia 1.85m 105kg.
At HT: WCh: '09- 5, '11- dnq 15, '13- 11; EC: '14- 3; WJ: '04- 9; EU23: '07- 11; EJ: '05- 9; WUG: '13- 3; ET: '14- 1. German champion 2009, Russian 2013.
Progress at HT: 2004- 60.00, 2005- 73.98, 2006- 66.46, 2007- 74.80, 2008- 75.35, 2009- 77.88, 2010- 78.98, 2011- 78.90, 2012- 80.98, 2013- 80.89, 2014- 79.35.
Switched from Belarus to Germany 15 Jul 2008 and from 1 Jan 2011 to Russia. His father Sergey Litvinov (USSR) set three world records at hammer 1980-3 with a pb of 86.04 '86; he was Olympic champion 1988 (2nd 1980) and World champion 1983 and 1987. His mother was born in Germany.

Aleksandr MENKOV b. 7 Dec 1990 Minusinsk, Krasnoyarsk reg. 1.78m 74kg. Krasnoyarsk VS. Krasnoyarsk State University.
At LJ: OG: '12- 11; WCh: '09- dnq 32, '11- 6, '13- 1; EC: '14- dnq 13; WI: '12- 3, '14- 5; EU23: '11- 1; EJ: '09- 1; EI: '13- 1; WUG: '13- 2; ET: '11- 1, '13- 1. Won DL 2012-13, Russian 2012.
Two Russian records 2013.
Progress at LJ: 2008- 6.98, 2009- 8.16, 2010- 8.10, 2011- 8.28, 2012- 8.29, 2013- 8.56, 2014- 8.30i/8.02. pbs: HJ 2.15 '10, TJ 15.20 '09.

Sergey MORGUNOV b. 9 Feb 1993 Shakhty, Rostov 1.78m 70kg.
At LJ: OG: '12- dnq 16; WJ: '12- 1; EU23: '13- 2; EJ: '11- 1. Russian champion 2013.
World junior long jump record 2012.
Progress at LJ: 2010- 7.66, 2011- 8.10/8.18w, 2012- 8.35, 2013- 8.06.

Sergey MUDROV b. 8 Sep 1990 Kineshma, Ivanova reg. 1.88m 79kg. Luch Moskva Reg
At HJ: EC: '12- 4; WJ: '08- 4; WY: '07- 2; EU23: '11- 2; EJ: '09- 1; EI: '13- 1; WUG: '11- 3, '13- 1.
Progress at HJ: 2006- 2.10, 2007- 2.22, 2008- 2.18, 2009- 2.25, 2010- 2.30i/2.27, 2011- 2.30, 2012- 2.31, 2013- 2.35i/2.31, 2014- 2.32i/2.20.

Ivan NOSKOV b. 17 Jul 1988 Perm 1.77m 62kg. Army.
At 50kW: WCh: '13- 7; EC: '14- 3WCp: '14- 2; ECp: '13- 3.
Progress at 50kW: 2012- 3:55:16, 2013- 3:41:36, 2014- 3:37:41. pbs: 20kW: 1:23:49 '11, 30kW 2:05:56 '12, 35kW 2:26:33 '12.

Mikhail RYZHOV b. 17 Dec 1991 1.80m 65kg. Mordoviya.
At 50kW: WCh: '13- 2; EC: '14- 4; WCp: '14- 1; ECp: '13- 2, At 20kW: WUG: '11- 2.
Progress at 50kW: 2012- 3:53:49, 2013- 3:38:58, 2014- 3:39.05. pbs: 5000mW 19:09.86i '14, 10kmW 39:11 '12, 20kW: 1:21:49 '11, 30kW 2:05:39 '12, 35kW 2:25:54 '15.

Ilya SHKURENYOV b. 11 Jan 1991 Linevo, Volgograd reg. 1.91m 82kg. Volgograd Dyn.
At Dec: OG: '12- 16; WCh: '13- 8; EC: '12- 3, '14- 3; WJ: '10- 2; EU23: '11- 5. Russian champion 2013. At Hep: WI: '12- 4; EI: '13- 5, '15- 1.
Progress at Dec: 2011- 7894, 2012- 8219, 2013- 8370, 2014- 8498. pbs: 60m 6.98i '15, 100m 10.91 '13, 400m 48.39 '13, 1000m 2:41.65i '13, 1500m 4:30.41 '12, 60mh 7.86i '15, 110mh 14.13 '13, HJ 2.11i '15, 2.10 '14; PV 5.40 '13, LJ 7.78i '15, 7.54 '13; SP 14.84i '11, 14.20 '14; DT 46.04 '14, JT 63.58 '14, Hep 6353i '15.

Sergey SHUBENKOV b. 4 Oct 1990 Barnaul, Altay Kray 1.90m 75kg. Tyumen State University.
At 110mh: OG: '12- sf; WCh: '11- h, '13- 3; EC: '12- 1, '14- 1; EU23: '11- 1; EJ: '09- 2, WUG: '13- 3; CCp: '14- 1; ET: '13- 1, '14- 1. Russian champion 2013. At 60mh: EI: '13- 1.
Four Russian 110mh records 2012.
Progress at 110mh: 2010- 13.54, 2011- 13.46, 2012- 13.09, 2013- 13.16/13.10w, 2014- 13.13. pb 60mh 7.49i '13.
Mother Natalya Shubenkova had heptathlon pb 6859 '04; 4th 1988 OG and 3rd 1986 EC.

Aleksandr SHUSTOV b. 29 Jun 1984 Karaganda, Kazakhstan 1.99m 85kg. Moskva VS.
At HJ: OG: '12- dnq 15; WCh: '11- 8, '13- 7; EC: '10- 1; EU23: '05- 12; WUG: '07- 1; EI: '09-11-15: 4=/3/4; ET: '09-10: 3/1. Russian champion 2010.
Progress at HJ: 2002- 2.10, 2003- 2.11, 2004- 2.15, 2005- 2.23, 2006- 2.28, 2007- 2.31, 2008- 2.30, 2009- 2.32i, 2010- 2.33, 2011- 2.36, 2012- 2.35, 2013- 2.32, 2014- 2.26i/2.25. pbs: LJ 7.18i '12, Hep 4564i '12.
Married to Yekaterina Kondratyeva (200m 22.64 '04, 2 WUG '03, 6 EC '06).

Maksim SIDOROV b. 13 May 1986 Moskva 1.90m 126kg. Moskva Reg. Dyn.
At SP: OG: '12- 11; WCh: '09-11-13: dnq 30/14/13; EU23: '07- 8; EJ: '05- 3; WUG: '07- 1; WI: '12- 5; EI: '11- 3. Russian champion 2009, 2011-13.
Progress at SP: 2006- 18.52, 2007- 20.01, 2008- 19.98, 2009- 20.92, 2010- 20.50, 2011- 21.45, 2012- 21.51, 2013- 20.98, 2014- 20.78i/20.37. pb DT 50.71 '06.

Andrey SILNOV b. 9 Sep 1984 Shakhty, Rostov region 1.98m 83kg. Moskva Reg. VS.
At HJ: OG: '08- 1, '12- 12; WCh: '07- 11=; EC: '06- 1; EU23: '05- 9; WI: '12- 2; WCp: '06- 2; ECp: '06-08-14: 1/1/2. Won WAF 2008, Russian 2006.
Progress at HJ: 2002- 2.10, 2003- 2.10, 2004- 2.15, 2005- 2.28, 2006- 2.37, 2007- 2.36i/2.30, 2008- 2.38, 2009- 2.21, 2010- 2.33, 2011- 2.36, 2012- 2.37, 2013- 2.32i/2.18, 2014- 2.29i/2.28.

Dmitriy STARODUBTSEV b. 3 Jan 1986 Chelyabinsk 1.91m 79kg. Moskva TU.
At PV: OG: '08- 5, '10- 4; WCh: '11- 12=; EC: '06- dnq 21=, '10- nh; WJ: '04- 1; WY: '03- 2; EU23: '07- 4; EJ: '05- 1; WI: '10- 6=, '12- 9; EI: '07- 6=; WUG: '07- 3; WCp: '06- 9. Won RUS 2010.
Progress at PV: 2003- 5.10, 2004- 5.50, 2005- 5.50, 2006- 5.65i/5.61, 2007- 5.70, 2008- 5.75, 2009- 5.70, 2010- 5.70i/5.65, 2011- 5.90i/5.72, 2012- 5.80i/5.75, 2013- 5.70i/5.30, 2014- 5.70. pb Dec 7412 '07.

Denis STRELKOV b. 26 Oct 1990. Saransk 1.85m 75kg. Mordovian State Pedagocical Instutute in Saransk.
At 20kW: WCh: '13- 5; EC: '14- 3; EU23: '11- 3; ECp: '13- 1; WUG: '13- 3. RUS champion 2014. At 10000m/10kW: WY: '07- 8; EJ: '09- 2; WCp: '08- 3J; ECp: '09- 10J.
Progress at 20kW: 2010- 1:20:19, 2011- 1:24:25, 2012- 1:20:31, 2013- 1:19:53, 2014- 1:19:46, 2015- 1:21:04. pbs: 10000mW 40:24.97 '09, 10kW 39:16 '08, 50kW 4:04:36 '11.

Sergey SVIRIDOV b. 20 Oct 1990 Yekaterinburg 1.92m 85kg. Moskva YU.
At Dec: OG: '12- 8; WCh: '13- 20; EC: '14- dnf; EJ: '09- 15; WG: '13- 2. Russian champion 2012.
Progress at Dec: 2010- 7449, 2011- 8102A/7832, 2012- 8365, 2013- 7939, 2014- 8193. pbs: 60m 6.98i '12, 100m 10.78 '12, 400m 48.28 '12, 1000m 2:43.52i '12, 1500m 4:25.15 '12, 60mh 8.26i '12, 110mh 14.75 '14, HJ 2.04i '13, 1.99 '12; PV 4.60 '12, LJ 7.60 '14, SP 15.03 '12, DT 50.02 '12, JT 69.38 '13, Hep 5855i '12.

Dmitriy TARABIN b. 29 Oct 1991 Berlin, Germany 1.76m 85kg. Student at Russian State University of Physical Education, Moscow
At JT: WCh: '11- 10, '13- 3; EC: '14- 5; WJ: '09- 3;

WY: '07- dnq 23; EU23: '11- 3; EJ: '09- dnq 13; WUG: '13- 1; ET: '13- 1, '14- 2. Won RUS 2013.
Progress at JT: 2007- 55.18, 2008- 67.39, 2009- 69.63, 2010- 77.65, 2011- 85.10, 2012- 82.75; 2013- 88.84, 2014- 85.92.
Switched from Moldova to Russia 9 June 2010. Married Mariya Abakumova on 12 Oct 2012.

Daniyil TSYPLAKOV b. 29 Jul 1992 Khabarovsk reg.1.78m 70kg. Khabarovskiy.
At HJ: EC: '14- 5; WY: '09- 3; EU23: '13- 2; EJ: '11- 4; WI: '14- 5; EI: '15- 1. RUS champion 2014.
Progress at HJ: 2008- 2.11, 2009- 2.21, 2010- 2.21, 2011- 2.26, 2012- 2.31, 2013- 2.30, 2014- 2.34i/2.33.

Ivan UKHOV b. 29 Mar 1986 Chelyabinsk 1.92m 83kg. Sverdlovsk TU.
At HJ: OG: '12- 1; WCh: '09- 10, '11- 5=, '13- 4; EC: '06-10-14: 12=/2/3; WJ: '04- dnq 13; EJ: '05- 1; CCp: '14- 2; WUG: '05- 4; WI: '10-12-14: 1/3/2; EI: '09- 1, '11- 1. Won DL 2010, Russian 2009, 2012-13.
Russian high jump record 2014 (& 2 indoors).
Progress at HJ: 2004- 2.15, 2005- 2.30, 2006- 2.37i/2.33, 2007- 2.39i/2.20, 2008- 2.36i/2.30, 2009- 2.40i/2.35, 2010- 2.38i/2.36, 2011- 2.38i/ 2.34, 2012- 2.39, 2013- 2.35, 2014- 2.42i/2.41.
Former discus thrower.

Women

Mariya ABAKUMOVA b. 15 Jan 1986 Stavropol 1.78m 85kg. Krasnodar VS.
At JT: OG: '08- 2, '12- 10; WCh: '07- 09-11-13: 7/3/1/3; EC: '10- 5; WJ: '04- dnq 25; WY: '03- 4; EU23: '07- 6; EJ: '05- 1; WUG: '13- 1; CCp: '10- 1; ECp: '08-09-10: 2/3/3. Won WAF 2009, Russian 2008, 2011-13.
European javelin record 2008, four Russian 2008-11.
Progress at JT: 2002- 51.81, 2003- 51.41, 2004- 58.26, 2005- 59.53, 2006- 60.12, 2007- 64.28, 2008- 70.78, 2009- 68.92, 2010- 68.89, 2011- 71.99, 2012- 66.86, 2013- 70.53.
Married Dmitriy Tarabin on 12 Oct 2012, twin daughters Kira and Milana born 17 Jun 2014.

Elmira ALEMBEKOVA b. 30 Jun 1990 Saransk. Mordoviya.
At 20kW: EC: '14- 1; WCp: '14- 3. At 10000m/10k-mW: WJ: '08- 2; EJ: '09- 1; WCp: '08- 3J, At 5000mW: WY: '05- 2.
World best for 20k walk 2015.
Progress at 20kW: 2010- 1:35:53, 2011- 1:27:35, 2012- 1:25:27, 2014- 1:27:02, 2015- 1:24:47. pbs: 10000mW: 43:45.26 '08.

Natalya ANTYUKH b. 26 Jun 1981 Leningrad 1.82m 73kg. Moskva VS.
At 400m/4x400mR: OG: '04- 3/2R; WCh: '01- h, '05- sf/1R, '07- 6; EC: '02- 2R; WI: '03-04-06: 1R/ res1R/1R; EI: '02- 1, '07- 2R, '09- 4/1R; WCp: '02- 3R; ECp: '01- 3/1R, '05- 1/1R, '06- 1R. At 200m: ECp: '04- 2. At 400mh: OG: '12- 1/2R; WCh: '09- 6/res 3R, '11- 3/3R, '13- sf/res1R; EC: '10- 1; CCp: '10- 4; ET: '10- 1&1R, '11- 2. Won Russian 400m 2007, 400mh 2010-12.
Progress at 400m: 2000- 54.79, 2001- 51.19, 2002- 51.17i/51.24, 2003- 51.73i/52.28, 2004- 49.85, 2005- 50.67, 2006- 50.37i/50.47, 2007- 49.93, 2008- 51.19, 2009- 50.90, 2011- 50.73, 2012- 51.27. At 400mh: 1996- 60.11, 1997- 59.75, 1998- 59.94, 2000- 58.30, 2009- 54.11, 2010- 52.92, 2011- 53.75, 2012- 52.70, 2013- 55.20, 2014- 58.06. pbs: 200m 22.73 '12, 300m 36.0+ '04, 200mhSt 26.23 '13.

Mariya BESPALOVA b. 21 May 1986 Leningrad 1.83m 85kg. Mordovia VS.
At HT: OG: '12- 10; WJ: '04- dnq; WY: '03- 2; WUG: '13- 3.
Progress at HT: 2002- 52.62, 2003- 58.47, 2004- 59.72, 2005- 61.73, 2006- 62.58, 2007- 63.50, 2008- 67.08, 2009- 69.02, 2010- 64.92, 2011- 71.93, 2012- 76.72, 2013- 71.70, 2014- 71.89. pb DT 44.19 '06.

Lina BIKULOVA b. 1 Oct 1988. Moskva
At 20kmW: WCp: '14- 12; WUG: '13- 3; Russian champion 2013.
World junior 20km walk best 2008.
Progress at 20kW: 2005- 1:48:36, 2008- 1:42:59, 2009- 1:32:39, 2010- 1:35:33, 2011- 1:32:45, 2012- 1:31:01, 2013- 1:28:42, 2014- 1:28:12. pbs: 5000mW 22:09.8i '13, 10kW 42:03 '14.

Anna BULGAKOVA b. 17 Jan 1988 Stavropol 1.73m 90kg. Stavropol VS.
At HT: OG: '08- dnq 20; WCh: '13- 5; EC: '12- 3, '14- nt; WJ: '04- 4, '06- 2; WY: '05- 2; EJ: '07- 4; ET: '14- 3. RUS champion 2014.
Progress at HT: 2003- 57.24, 2004- 63.83, 2005- 64.43, 2006- 67.79, 2007- 68.49, 2008- 73.79, 2010- 66.29, 2011- 69.10, 2012- 74.02, 2013- 76.17, 2014- 74.16. pb DT 44.19 '06.

Tatyana CHERNOVA b. 29 Jan 1988 Krasnodar 1.90m 70kg. Krasnodar VS.
At Hep: OG: '08- 3, '12- 3; WCh: '07- dnf, '09- 8, '11- 1; EC: '10- dq4; WJ: '06- 1; WY: '05- 1; WUG: '13- 1. At Pen: WI: '08-10-12: 7/dq3/5.
Progress at Hep: 2006- 6227, 2007- 6768w, 2008- 6618, 2009- 6386, 2010- 6572, 2011- 6880, 2012- 6774, 2013- 6623. pbs: 200m 23.49 '12, 23.32wdq '11; 800m 2:06.50 '08, 60mh 8.02i '12, 100mh 13.32 '11, 13.04w '07, 400mh 56.14 '07, HJ 1.87 '07, LJ 6.78 '08, 6.82dq '11; SP 14.54i '10, 14.17 '11, JT 54.49 '06, Pen 4855i '10.
She was given a 2 years ban backdated from 22 July 2013 with results also annulled between 15 Aug 2009 and 14 Aug 2011. Won at Talence 2010-11 and IAAF Combined Events Challenge 2010-12. Married to Vitaliy Smirnov UZB (Dec: 17 OG 2004, 10 WC 2003, 4/2 AsG 2002/06, pb 8021 '03), daughter Anna born 10 Jul 2014. Her mother Lyudmila (née Zenina) won a 4x400m Olympic gold medal (ran in heats) for 4x400m in 1980, pbs: 200m 22.9 '82, 400m 50.91 '83.

Anna CHICHEROVA b. 22 Jul 1982 Yerevan, Armenia 1.80m 57kg. Moskva VS. Physical culture graduate.
At HJ: OG: '04- 6, '08- 3, '12- 1; WCh: '03-05-07-

09-11-13: 6/4/2=/2/1/3=; EC: '06- 7=; WJ: '00- 4; WY: '99- 1; EJ: '01- 2; WUG: '05- 1; WI: '03-04-12: 3/2/2=; EI: '05- 1, '07- 5=; ECp: '06- 3. Russian champion 2004, 2007-09, 2011-12.

Progress at HJ: 1998- 1.80, 1999- 1.89, 2000- 1.90, 2001- 1.92, 2002- 2.00i/1.89, 2003- 2.04i/2.00, 2004- 2.04i/1.98, 2005- 2.01i/1.99, 2006- 1.96i/ 1.95, 2007- 2.03, 2008- 2.04, 2009- 2.02, 2011- 2.07, 2012- 2.06i/2.05, 2013- 2.02, 2014- 2.01.

Moved with family to Russia at the beginning of the 1990s. Married to Gennadiy Chernoval KAZ, pbs 100m 10.18, 200m 20.44 (both 2002), 2 WUG 100m & 200m 2001, 2 AsiG 2002 2002; their daughter Nika born on 7 Sep 2010.

Irina DAVYDOVA b. 27 May 1988 Alexandrov, Vladimir reg. 1.70m 65kg. Moskva SC.

At 400mh: OG: '12- sf; WCh: '13- sf; EC: '12- 1, '14- 3; EU23: '09- 5; WUG: '11- 2, '13- 3; ET: '14- 3. Russian champion 2013-14.

Progress at 400mh: 2006- 60.27, 2007- 58.55, 2008- 58.62, 2009- 56.14, 2010- 55.74, 2011- 55.48, 2012- 53.77, 2013- 54.79, 2014- 54.60. pbs: 200m 24.53i '11, 400m 51.94i '12, 53.12 '11; 500m 1:10.54i '12.

Aleksandra FEDORIVA-SHPAYER b. 13 Sep 1988 Moskva 1.75m 60kg. SC Luch Moskva. Student of advertising at Moscow University of Humanitarian Studies.

At 400m/4x400m: WI: '12- 2/3R. At 200m/4x-100mR: OG: '08- sf/1R, '12- sf; EC: '10- 3; EU23: '09- 1; CCp: '10- 1; ECp: '10- 1R, '11- 3/2R. At 100m: WCh: '11- sf; ET: '11- 3. At 100mh: WJ: '06- 4; WY: '05- sf; EJ: '07- 1. Won RUS 200m 2011-12.

Progress at 200m: 2007- 23.29, 2008- 22.56, 2009- 22.97, 2010- 22.41, 2011- 23.17, 2012- 22.19, 2014- 23.45/23.38w. pbs: 60m 7.24i '10, 100m 11.28, 11.09w '11; 300m 36.54i '12, 400m 51.18i '12, 60mh 7.91i '10, 100mh 12.90 '08, 400mh 58.24 '14.

Her mother Lyudmila Belova/Fedoriva had 400m best 50.63 '84, father Andrey Fedoriv 200m 3rd EC and best 20.53 '86; ran at five Worlds and two Olympics. Married Aleksandr Shpayer (RUS 60m indoor champion 6.63 '11) in 2012; daughter Varvara born 31 July 2013.

Svetlana FEOFANOVA b. 16 Jul 1980 Moskva 1.64m 53kg. Moskva TU.

At PV: OG: '00- dnq, '04- 2, '08- 3, '12- dnq; WCh: '01-03-07-11: 2/1/3/3; EC: '02- 1, '06- 4, '10- 1; WI: '01-03-04-06-08-10: 2=/1/3/3/5/2; EI: '02- 1, '07- 1; WCp: '02- 2, '10- 1; ECp: '00-01-02-10: 1/1/1/1; 2nd GP 2001. Won RUS 2001, 2006, 2008, 2011-12.

Pole vault records: World 2004, 9 European 2001-04, 11 Russian 2000-04, 9 world indoor 2002-04 (4.71-4.85), 13 European indoor 2001-04.

Progress at PV: 1998- 3.90, 1999- 4.10, 2000- 4.50, 2001- 4.75, 2002- 4.78, 2003- 4.80i/4.75, 2004- 4.88, 2005- 4.70i, 2006- 4.70, 2007- 4.82, 2008- 4.75, 2009- 4.70, 2010- 4.80i/4.75, 2011- 4.75, 2012- 4.65, 2013- 4.60.

Was a top gymnast, winning Russian titles at youth, junior and U23 level at asymmetric bars and floor exercises. Set five indoor world records in a month in 2002.

Tatyana FIROVA b. 10 Oct 1982 Sarov, Nizhegorodskaya region 1.78m 68kg. Moskva Reg. Dyn.

At 400m/4x400m: OG: '04- res 2R, 08- 6/2R, '12- 2R; WCh: '05- res 1R, '09- 3R, '13- 1R; EC: '06- res 1R, '10- 1/1R; EU23: '03- 3/1R; EJ: '01- 1; WI: '10- 2/2R; WUG: '03- 1; CCp: '10- 3/2R; ECp: '03- 1R, '13- 2R.

Progress at 400m: 2000- 53.69, 2001- 52.94, 2002- 53.72, 2003- 51.43, 2004- 50.44, 2005- 50.41, 2006- 50.08, 2007- 50.98, 2008- 50.11, 2009- 50.59, 2010- 49.89, 2011- 50.84, 2012- 49.72, 2013- 50.71, 2014- 52.08. pbs: 200m 23.27 '11, 500m 1:09.41i '08, 600m 1:25.23i '08.

Irina GORDEYEVA b. 9 Oct 1986 Leningrad 1.85m 55kg. Yunost Rossii.

At HJ: OG: '12- 10; WCh: '13- 9=; EC: '10- dnq 13=, '12- 3=; WJ: '04- 9; WY: '03- 7=; EJ: '05- 4; EI: '09- 5=.

Progress at HJ: 2001- 1.75, 2002- 1.82, 2003- 1.84, 2004- 1.88, 2005- 1.88, 2006- 1.88, 2007- 1.87i/1.83, 2008- 1.95, 2009- 2.02, 2010- 1.97, 2011- 1.94, 2012- 2.04, 2013- 1.99, 2014- 1.95.

Irina GUMENYUK b. 6 Jan 1988 Sankt-Peterburg 1.76m 59kg. St.Petersburg.

At TJ: WCh: '13- 8; EC: '14- 3; EJ: '07- 9; EI: '13- 2. Russian champion 2013.

Progress at TJ: 2006- 13.06, 2007- 13.52, 2008- 13.65, 2009- 13.49i, 2010- 13.33, 2011- 14.14, 2012- 14.24i/14.03, 2013- 14.58, 2014- 14.46. pb LJ 6.38 '11.

Yuliya GUSHCHINA b. 4 Mar 1983 Novocherkask 1.75m 63kg. Moskva reg. VS.

At 200m(/100m)/4x100mR: OG: '08- 1R; WCh: '05- 6, '07- 5R, '09/11- sf; EC: '06- 2/5/1R, '10- 4R; EU23: '03- 5; WCp: '06- 4/5/1R; ECp: '05-06-07-10-11: 1R/(1)&1R/1R/1R/2R. At 400m/4x-400mR: OG: '08- 4/2R, '12- sf/2R; WCh: '13- 1R; WI: '06-08-12: res1R/1R/3R; ECp: '05/07/08- 1R. Won Russian 100m 2011, 200m 2005, 2009; 400m 2008. World indoor records 4x200m 2005, 4x400m 2006.

Progress at 200m, 400m: 1997- 25.96, 1998- 25.32, 1999- 58.18, 2000- 25.01, 55.85; 2001- 24.24, 55.91; 2002- 23.92/23.88w, 53.26; 2003- 23.58, 51.94; 2004- 23.06, 2005- 22.53, 53.81i; 2006- 22.69/22.52w, 51.26i; 2007- 22.75, 2008- 22.58, 50.01; 2009- 22.63, 51.06; 2010- 22.80/22.79w, 52.04i; 2011- 22.88/22.69w, 52.18; 2012- 22.95, 49.28; 2013- 23.32, 51.06. pbs: 60m 7.24i '07, 7.2i '03; 100m 11.13 '06, 300m 36.93i '10.

Married Ivan Buzolin (400m 46.24 '08, 2R EI '07) on 12 Sep 2010. Son born 3 Jul 2014.

Anastasiya KAPACHINSKAYA b. 21 Nov 1979 Moskva 1.76m 65kg. Luch Moskva. Married to Aleksandr Belov.

At 200m/4x400mR: OG: '12- res(2)R; WCh: '03- 1; EC: '10- 4/1R; WI: '03- 2, '04- dq (1); ECp: '03- 1. At 400m: OG: '08- 5/2R; WCh: '01- sf/3R, '03- 2R, '09- 7/3R, '11- 3/3R; EC: '02- 5/2R. Won Russian 200m 2008, 400m 2011.
Progress at 200m, 400m: 1999- 23.85, 2000- 23.66, 53.32; 2001- 23.24i/22.6, 50.97; 2002- 23.41, 51.39; 2003- 22.38, 50.59; 2004- 22.71i, 2006- 22.80, 51.16; 2007- 23.73, 52.14; 2008- 22.48, 50.02; 2009- 22.92, 49.97; 2010- 22.47, 50.16; 2011- 22.55, 49.35; 2012- 50.37, 2013- 22.39, 50.91 pbs: 100m 11.79 '99, 300m 36.61 '02, 800m 2:09.75i '07.
Son Fyodor born 23 Nov 2014. She served a 2-year drugs ban after finishing first in the World Indoor 200m in 2004.

Anisya KIRDYAPKINA b. 23 Oct 1989 Saransk, Mordoviya 1.65m 51kg. née Kornikova. Mordovia TU.
At 20kmW: OG: '12- 5; WCh: '09- 4. '11- 3, '13- 2; EC: '10- 2; WCp: '10-12-14: 6/6/1; ECp: '09-11-13: 2/2/1; WUG: '13- 1; RUS champion 2010, 2012. At 10000mW: EJ: '07- 1; ECp: '07- 1J.
World junior 20km walk best 2008.
Progress at 20kW: 2007- 1:28:00, 2008- 1:25:30, 2009- 1:25:26, 2010- 1:25:11, 2011- 1:25:09, 2012- 1:26:26. 2013- 1:25:59, 2014- 1:26:31. pbs: 3000mW 11:44.10i '12, 5000mW 21:06.3 '06, 10000mW 43:27.30 '07, 42:04R '11.
Married to Sergey Kirdyapkin (50kW: 1 OG 08, 1 WCh 05/09, 1 WCp 12, pb 3:35:59 '12).

Darya KLISHINA b. 15 Jan 1991 Tver 1.80m 57kg. Moskva. Model.
At LJ: WCh: '11- 7, '13- 7; EC: '14- 3; WY: '07- 1; EU23: '11- 1; EJ: '09- 1; WI: '10- 5, '12- 4; EI: '11- 1, '13- 1, WUG: '13- 1; ET: '11- 1, '13- 2. RUS champion 2014.
Progress at LJ: 2005- 5.83, 2006- 6.33/6.47w, 2007- 6.49, 2008- 6.52i/6.20, 2009- 6.80, 2010- 7.03, 2011- 7.05, 2012- 6.93, 2013- 7.01i/6.90/6.98w, 2014- 6.90.

Anna KLYASHTORNAYA b. 3 Feb 1986 Sankt-Petersburg 1.72m 58kg. née Nazarova.
At LJ: OG: '12- 5; EC: '12- 10; WJ: '04- dnq; EJ: '05- 3; EU23: '07- 1; WUG: '11- 1; WI: '10- 6.
Progress at LJ: 2003- 6.00/6.12w, 2004- 6.48, 2005- 6.50i/6.31, 2006- 6.66, 2007- 6.81, 2008- 6.71/6.75w, 2009- 6.60, 2010- 6.75i/6.54, 2011- 6.89i/6.88, 2012- 7.11, 2014- 6.93. pb TJ 13.80i '07, 13.39 '10. Daughter born April 2013.

Yevgeniya KOLODKO b. 2 Jul 1990 Neryungi, Yakutia 1.88m 85kg. Luch Moskva.
At SP: OG: '12- 2; WCh: '11- 5, '13- 5; EC: '14- 2; WI: '12- 7, '14- 4; EU23: '11- 1; EJ: '09- 9; CCp: '14- 4; EI: '13- 2. Russian champion 2012-14.
Progress at SP: 2007- 14.26, 2008- 15.04i/14.87, 2009- 15.38, 2010- 16.73, 2011- 19.78, 2012- 20.48, 2013- 19.97i/19.86, 2014- 19.52.

Oksana KONDRATYEVA b. 22 Nov 1985 Moskva 1.80m 80kg. Moscow State University of PE.
At HT: WCh: '13- 7; WUG: '13- 2.
Progress at HT: 2004- 57.36, 2005- 62.24, 2006- 61.81, 2007- 64.09, 2008- 66.08, 2009- 67.84, 2010- 71.90, 2011- 69.87, 2012- 73.31, 2013- 77.13, 2014- 72.17.
Mother Lydmila Kondratyeva (1980 Olympic 100m champion) and father Yuriy Sedykh (hammer world record holder).

Yekaterina KONEVA b. 25 Sep 1988 Khabarovsk 1.69m 55kg. Khabarovskiy.
At TJ: WCh: '13-2; EC: '14- 2; WI: '14- 1; WUG: '11- 1, '13- 1; CCp: '14- 2; ET: '13- 2, '14- 1. RUS champion 2014.
Progress at TJ: 2010- 13.93/14.00w, 2011- 14.46, 2012- 14.60i/14.36, 2013- 14.82, 2014- 14.89. pbs: 60m 7.39i '07, 100m 11.76 '09, 200m 23.89 '09, LJ 6.82i '15, 6.70/6.80w '11.
Two-year drugs ban 2007-09.

Mariya KONOVALOVA b. 14 Aug 1974 Angarsk 1.78m 62kg. née Pantyukhova. Moskva VS.
At 10000m: OG: '08- 5; WCh: '09- 11. At 5000m: WCh: '95- 6, '99- 7, '07- 11; EC: '10- 4. At 3000m: WI: '95- 12; EI: '96- 5. Eur CC: '05-06-08: 10/2/4. Won RUS 5000m 2009-10.
Progress at 5000m, 10000m, Mar: 1995- 15:01.23, 1997- 16:10.4/32:53.69; 1998- 15:13.22, 1999- 14:58.60, 2000- 15:49.04, 2007- 15:02.96, 2008- 14:38.09, 30:35.84; 2009- 14:42.06, 30:31.03; 2010- 14:49.68, 2:23:50; 2011- 2:25:18, 2012- 15:27.54, 2:25:38; 2013- 15:27.16, 2:22:46; 2014- 2:23:43. pbs: 1500m 4:05.10 '98, 2000m 5:38.98i '10, 3000m 8:30.18 '99, 15km 49:58+ '10, HMar 69:56 '12, 30km 1:41:18+ '10.
Won Nagoya Marathon 2014, 3rd Chicago 2010 & 2013

Angelina KRASNOVA b. 7 Feb 1991 Moskva 1.68m 55kg. née Zhuk. Irkutskaya.
At PV: WCh: '13- 7; EC: '14- 3; EU23: '13- 1; CCp: '14- 2; EI: '13- 5.
Progress at PV: 2007- 3.60i, 2008- 3.80, 2010- 4.10, 2011- 4.30i/4.25, 2012- 4.40, 2013- 4.70, 2014- 4.65, 2015- 4.67i.

Antonina KRIVOSHAPKA b. 21 Jul 1987 Volgograd 1.68m 60kg. Rostov-na-Donu VS.
At 400m/4x400m: OG: '12- 6/2R; WCh: '09- 3/3R, '11- 5/3R, '13- 3/1R; EC: '10- 3/1R; WJ: '04- h; WY: '03- 2; EI: '09- 1/1R; CCp: '10- 2R. Won RUS 2009, 2012.
Progress at 400m: 2002- 54.35, 2003- 53.09, 2004- 53.67, 2005- 55.03i/55.63, 2006- 55.40i, 2007- 52.32, 2008- 51.24, 2009- 49.29, 2010- 50.10, 2011- 49.92, 2012- 49.16, 2013- 49.57. pbs: 200m 23.01 '13, 300m 36.38i '09.
Daughter Sofia born on 26 July 2014.

Anna KRYLOVA b. 3 Oct 1985Bolshoi Kamen, Primorsky. née Kuropatkina. Luch Moskva.
At TJ: WCh: '11- 7; WI: '12- 6; EU23: '07- 4.
Progress at TJ: 2001- 12.85, 2002- 12.75, 2003- 12.86, 2004- 13.34/13.62w, 2005- 13.25, 2006- 14.13, 2007- 14.20, 2008- 13.84i/13.32, 2009-

14.14i/13.27, 2010- 14.02i/13.69/13.77w, 2011- 14.35, 2012- 14.40, 2013- 14.27, 2014- 13.58. pb LJ 6.45 '06.
Cousin of Denis Kapustin, TJ 1 EC 94, 3 OG 00.

Olga KUCHERENKO b. 5 Nov 1985 Sidory, Volgograd region 1.72m 59kg. Lokomotiv Penza.
At LJ: WCh: '09- 5, '11- 2, '13- 5; EC: '10- 3; EU23: '07- 12; EI: '09-3, '13- 6; ET: '09-10: 2/2.
Progress at LJ: 2002- 6.08, 2004- 6.30, 2005- 6.34, 2006- 6.72/6.80w, 2007- 6.41/6.70w, 2008- 6.87i/ 6.70, 2009- 6.91, 2010- 7.13, 2011- 6.86, 2012- 7.03, 2013- 7.00i/6.81, 2014- 6.70.

Mariya KUCHINA b. 14 Jan 1993 Prokhladny, Kabardino-Balkar 1.82m 60kg. Moskovskaya.
At HJ: EC: '14- 2; WJ: '12- 3; WY: '09- 2; EJ: '11- 1; WI: '14- 1=; WUG: '13- 2; CCp: '14- 1; ET: '13- 1, '14- 1. Won DL 2014, Yth Oly 2010, RUS champion 2014.
World junior indoor high jump record 2011.
Progress at HJ: 2009- 1.87, 2010- 1.91, 2011- 1.97i/1.95, 2012- 1.96i/1.89, 2013- 1.98i/1.96, 2014- 2.01i/2.00.

Alyona LUTKOVSKAYA b. 15 Mar 1996. Irkutsk.
At PV: EC: '14- 7=; WJ: '14- 1; WY: '13- 2; EJ: '13- 1.
Progress at PV: 2012- 4.20, 2013- 4.30, 2014- 4.50.

Tatyana LYSENKO b. 9 Oct 1983 Bataisk, Rostov region 1.86m 81kg. Bataisk VS.
At HT: OG: '04- dnq 19, '12- 1; WCh: '05-09-11-13: 2/6/1/1; EC: '06- 1, '10- 2; EU23: '03- 5; WUG: '03- 5; WCp: '06- 2, '10- 1; ECp: '06-07-10-11: 1/ dq1/2/2. Won RUS 2005, 2009-13.
Three world hammer records, nine Russian records 2005-13.
Progress at HT: 2000- 49.08, 2001- 55.73, 2002- 61.85, 2003- 67.19, 2004- 71.54, 2005- 77.06, 2006- 77.80, 2007- 77.30/78.61dq, 2009- 76.41, 2010- 76.03, 2011- 77.13, 2012- 78.51, 2013- 78.80, 2014- 70.62.
Two-year drugs ban after positive test on 9 May 2007. Son Makariy born 14 Feb 2015.

Marina PANDAKOVA 1 Mar 1989. Churvashkaya Region.
At 20kW: WCp: '14- 10. ECp: 13- 3.
Progress at 20kW: 2008- 1:38:19, 2011- 1:33:00, 2012- 1:28:29, 2013- 1:27:39, 2014- 1:27:54, 2015- 1:25:03. pbs: 3000mW: 11:57.89i '14, 5000mW 21:40.41i '13, 10kW 43:29 '12.

Yekaterina POISTOGOVA b. 1 Mar 1991 Arzamas, Nizhny Novgorod 1.75m 65kg. née Zavyalova. Student at Ural State Forestry University.
At 800m: OG: '12- 3; WCh: '13- 5; EC: '14- 4; WJ: '08- sf, '10- 8; WY: '07- sf; EJ: '09- 3 (10 1500m); EI: 15- 2; ET: '14- 1. Russian champion 2012.
Progress at 800m, 1500m: 2007- 2:06.96, 2008- 2:04.96, 2009- 2:02.11, 4:18.82; 2010- 2:04.33, 4:27.68; 2011- 2:02.2, 4:17.9; 2012- 1:57.53, 4:00.11; 2013- 1:58.05, 4:14.63; 2014- 1:58.55. pbs: 400m 52.96 '14, 600m 1:26.6+ '12, 1000m 2:36.97i '13.
Husband Stepan Poistogov 800m pb 1:46.02 '12.

Anna PYATYKH b. 4 Apr 1981 Moskva 1.76m 64kg. Moskva VS.
At TJ: OG: '04- 8, '08- 8; WCh: '03-05-07-09-13: 4/3/4/3/7; EC: '02- 8, '06- 3; WJ: '00- 2; EJ: '99- 3; WI: '03-06-10: 4/2/3; ECp: '02-03-04-05-09: 1/1/1/1/2. Won WAF 2008, Russian 2004, 2006.
Progress at TJ: 1998- 12.98, 1999- 13.59, 2000- 14.19, 2001- 14.21/14.22w, 2002- 14.67, 2003- 14.79, 2004- 14.85, 2005- 14.88, 2006- 15.02/15.17w, 2007- 14.88, 2008- 14.91, 2009- 14.67/14.84w, 2010- 14.68, 2011- 14.24, 2013- 14.40, 2014- 14.27. pb LJ 6.72 '07.
Married to Yuriy Abramov (won Russian marathon 2010 in pb 2:11:39); twin daughters born January 2011.

Kseniya RYZHOVA b. 19 Apr 1987 Lipetsk 1.72m 62kg. née Vdovina. Moskva Dyn.
At 400m/4x400m: WCh: '11- res 3R, '13- 7/1R; WJ: '06- sf; EU23: '07- sf (1 4x100mR), '09- 1R; WI: '10-2R; EI: '11- 1R.
Progress at 400m: 2009- 52.22, 2010- 51.41, 2011- 50.67, 2012- 50.43, 2013- 49.80, 2014- 51.03i. pbs: 60m 7.30i '15, 100m 11.55 '08, 200m 22.91/22.85w '10, 300m 36.3+ '13, TJ 13.18 '04.
Married Yevgeniy Ryzhov (5000m 14:16.67 '09) in January 2013. Ran brilliant final leg in 49.83 for 4th place in WI 4x400m 2014.

Anastasiya SAVCHENKO b. 15 Nov 1989 Omsk 1.75m 65kg. Luch Moskva.
At PV: OG: '12- dnq 26-; WCh: '13- 5=; EC: '12- 4; EU23: '09- 8, '11- 6; WUG: '13- 1; WI: '14- 11; EI: '13- 5=.
Progress at PV: 2005- 3.80, 2006- 3.80i/3.70, 2007- 3.90, 2008- 4.20i/4.10, 2009- 4.30i/4.20, 2010- 4.30, 2011- 4.40, 2012- 4.60, 2013- 4.73, 2014- 4.50, 2015- 4.60i.

Mariya SAVINOVA b. 13 Aug 1985 Chelyabinsk 1.72m 60kg. Sverdlovsk Dyn.
At 800m: OG: '12- 1; WCh: '09- 5, '11- 1, '13- 2; EC: '10- 1; WI: '10- 1; EI: '09- 1; CCp: '10- 3; ET: '11- 1. Won Russian 800m 2009, 2011.
World indoor 4x800m record 2008.
Progress at 800m: 2002- 2:09.68, 2003- 2:08.38, 2004- 2:07.43, 2005- 2:07.03, 2006- 2:05.91, 2007- 2:00.78, 2008- 2:01.07, 2009- 1:57.90, 2010- 1:57.56, 2011- 1:55.87, 2012- 1:56.19, 2013- 1:57.80. pbs: 400m 51.43 '12, 600m 1:26.11i '09, 1:26.6+ '12; 1000m 2:34.56i '09, 1500m 4:08.2i, 4:10.25 '10.
Married Aleksey Farnosov (1500m 3:41.69i '11) on 10 Sep 2010.

Kristina SAVITSKAYA b. 10 Jun 1991 Krasnoyarsk 1.80m 72kg. Student at the Krasnoyarsk Academy of Summer Sports.
At Hep: OG: '12- 7; WCh: '13- dnf; WY: '07- 16; EU23: '11- 7, EJ: '09- 6; WUG: '13- 5; Russian champion 2012-13.
Progress at Hep: 2009- 5642, 2011- 5989, 2012- 6681, 2013- 6210. pbs: 200m 24.46 '12, 800m

2:12.27 '12, 60mh 8.37i '12, 100mh 13.37 '12, HJ 1.88 '12, LJ 6.65 '12, SP 15.27 '12, JT 46.83 '12, Pen 4590i '12.

Yekaterina SHARMINA b. 6 Aug 1986 Bryansk 1.72m 59kg. née Martynova. Sverdlovsk Dyn.
At 1500m: OG: '12- h; WCh: '11- sf, '13- 6; EJ: '05- 2; EI: '11- 3; WUG: '13- 1; ET: '11- 2, '13- 1 (2 800m). At 800m: WJ: '04- sf; WY: '03- 4; EU23: '07- 7. Won Russian 1500m 2011, short CC 2010. World indoor 4x800m record 2011.
Progress at 1500m: 2004- 4:24.71i, 2005- 4:15.46, 2006- 4:15.09, 2007- 4:15.81, 2008- 4:03.68i/4:05.06, 2009- 4:05.40, 2010- 4:09.46, 2011- 4:01.68, 2012- 3:59.49, 2013- 4:04.55, 2014- 4:07.45. pbs: 400m 55.97i '08, 56.59 '06; 800m 1:59.17 '11, 1000m 2:37.63i '08.
Married Yevgeniy Sharmin (800m 1:47.40 '12) in September 2011.

Svetlana SHKOLINA b. 9 Mar 1986 Yartsevo, Smolensk reg. 1.87m 66kg. Luch Moskva.
At HJ: OG: '08- 14, '12- 3; WCh: '09- 6, '11- 5, 13- 1; EC: '10- 4; WJ: '04- 2; WY: '03- 2=; EU23: '07- 1; EJ: '05- 1; WI: '10- 4; EI: '09- 4=, '11- 4=; WUG: '05-4, '07- 4; ECp: '10: 2. Won DL 2013, Russian 2010, 2013.
Progress at HJ: 2001- 1.75, 2002- 1.84, 2003- 1.88, 2004- 1.91, 2005- 1.92, 2006- 1.92, 2007- 1.96, 2008- 1.98, 2009- 1.98, 2010- 2.00i/1.98, 2011- 2.00i/1.99, 2012- 2.03, 2013- 2.03, 2015- 1.95i.
Missed 2014 season due to a take-off foot injury.

Anzhelika SIDOROVA b. 28 Jun 1991 Moskva 1.70m 52kg. Moskva Youth.
At PV: EC: '14- 1; WJ: '10- 4; EU23: '13- 2; WI: '14- 2=; EI: '13- 3, '15- 1; ; ET: '13- 2, '14- 1. RUS champion 2014.
Progress at PV: 2007- 3.80, 2008- 4.00, 2009- 4.10i/4.00, 2010- 4.30, 2011- 4.40i/4.30, 2012- 4.50, 2013- 4.62i/4.60, 2014- 4.72i/4.70, 2015- 4.80i.

Vera SOKOLOVA b. 8 Jun 1987 Solianoy, Chuvashiya 1.51m 51kg. Mordovia VS.
At 20kmW: WCh: '09- 14, '11- 11, '13- dq; EC: '10- 3, '14- 4; WCp: '10- 4, '14- 4; ECp: '09-11-13: 10/1/2; Russian champion 2009, 2014. At 10000mW: WJ: '02-04-06: 9/3/4; EJ: '05- 1; WCp: '04/06- 1J; ECp: '03- 2J, '05- 1J. At 5000mW: WY: '03- 1.
Walks records: World 20km 2011, world junior 10,000m and 5000m indoors 2005.
Progress at 20kW: 2006- 1:40:03, 2007- 1:32:56, 2008- 1:30:11, 2009- 1:25:26, 2010- 1:25:35, 2011- 1:25:08, 2012- 1:28:06. 2013- 1:26:00, 2014- 1:27:03, 2015- 1:25:38. pbs: 3000m 11:58.44i '14, 12:51.96 '04, 5000mW 20:10.3i '10, 10kW 42:04+ '11, 43:11.34t '05.

Yelena SOKOLOVA b. 23 Jul 1986 Staryi Oskol, Belgorod reg. 1.70m 61kg. née Kremneva. Krasnodarsk krai.
At LJ: OG: '12- 2; WCh: '09- dnq 13, '13- 9; EU23: '07- 3; EI: '07- 5, '09- 2; WUG: '07- 2, '13- 2. Won DL 2012, Russian 2009, 2012.
Progress at LJ: 2002- 6.33, 2003- 6.39i?/6.31, 2006- 6.53, 2007- 6.71, 2008- 6.74, 2009- 6.92, 2010- 6.72/6.90w, 2011- 6.76, 2012- 7.07, 2013- 6.91. pbs: 60m 7.34i '12, 100m 11.61 '12, TJ 13.15i/12.93 '03. Son born on 23 Aug 2014.

Irina TARASOVA b. 15 Apr 1987 Kovrov 1.83m 110kg. Army.
At SP: OG: '12- 8; WCh: '13- 7; ECh: '12- 2, '14- 6; WI: '12- 8; WJ: '04- 5, '06- 3; WY: '03- 5; EU23: '07- 1; EJ: '05- 2; EI: '13- 5; WUG: '07- 1, '13- 1; ET: '14- 2.
Progress at SP: 2002- 14.01, 2003- 15.04, 2004- 16.16, 2005- 16.79i/16.53, 2006- 17.11, 2007- 18.27, 2008- 18.45, 2009- 18.21, 2010- 18.18, 2011- 18.72, 2012- 19.35, 2013- 19.20, 2014- 18.38.

Kseniya USTALOVA now AKSYONOVA b. 14 Jan 1988 Sverdlovsk 1.77m 65kg. Sverdlovsk. Engineering student.
At 400m/4x400m: EC: '10- 2/1R; EU23: '09- 1/1R; EJ: '07- 2/1R; WUG: '11- 1R, '13- 1/1R; CCp: '10- 2R; WI: '12- 3R; ET: '10- 1/1R. Russian champion 2010.
Progress at 400m: 2005- 55.51, 2006- 54.00i. 2007- 52.90, 2008- 54.57, 2009- 51.45, 2010- 49.92, 2011- 52.03, 2012- 50.48, 2013- 50.60. pbs: 200m 24.09 '10, 300m 36.76i '13.
Married to Aleksey Aksyonov (400m pb 46.27 '09, 1R EC 2010). Daughter born 27 Jun 2014.

Viktoriya VALYUKEVICH b. 22 May 1982 Sochi 1.78m 63kg. née Gurova. Krasnodar TU.
At TJ: OG: '04- dnq 21, '08- 7, '12- 8; WCh: '05- 10; EU23: '03- 1; EJ: '01- 3; WUG: '03- 2; EI: '05- 1; ECp: '06- 2, '07- 3.
Progress at TJ: 1998- 12.56, 1999- 13.02, 2000- 13.44, 2001- 13.75/13.92w, 2002- 14.22, 2003- 14.37, 2004- 14.65, 2005- 14.74i/14.38, 2006- 14.60, 2007- 14.46, 2008- 14.85, 2009- 14.40, 2012- 14.64, 2013- 14.36, 2014- 14.05. pb LJ 6.72 '07.
Married Dmitrij Valukevic (BLR/SVK triple jumper) in September 2008. Son Georgiy born in June 2010.

Kseniya ZADORINA b. 2 Mar 1987 Moskva 1.73m 59kg. Moskva Dyn.
At 400m/4x400m: WCh: '11- res (3)R; EC: '10- res1R, '12- 2, '14- sf; WJ: '06- 4; EU23: '07- 3/1R, 09- 2/1R; EJ: '05- 2/1R; WUG: '07- 3/2R; EI: '11- 3/1R, '13- 2R; ET: '10- 1R, '13- 2/2R. Russian champion 2013.
Progress at 400m: 2005- 52.64, 2006- 51.81, 2007- 51.06, 2008- 51.48, 2009- 51.41, 2010- 50.87, 2011- 50.92, 2012- 51.16, 2013- 50.55, 2014- 51.69. pbs: 200m 23.66i '11, 24.15 '08; 500m 1:08.94i '06 (WJR).

Yuliya ZARIPOVA b. 26 Apr 1986 Sbetlyi Yar, Volgograd reg. née Zarudneva. 1.72m 54kg. Volgograd Dyn.
At 3000mSt: OG: '12- dq1; WCh: '09- 2, '11- 1; EC: '10- 1; WUG: '13- 1; CCp: '10- 1; ET: '10- 1. At 800m: EJ: '05- h. At 3000m: EI: '09- 7. Eur CC: '05- 8J, '08- 3 U23. Won Russian 3000mSt 2009.

Progress at 3000mSt: 2008- 9:54.9, 2009- 9:08.39, 2010- 9:17.57, 2011- 9:07.03, 2012- 9:05.02dq, 2013- 9:28.00. pbs: 800m 2:05.44 '05, 1500m 4:04.59 '09, 4:01.70dq '12, 3000m 8:54.50i '09, 5000m 16:02.81i '10.

Daughter Yelena born 2007 and second daughter on 22 Jun 2014. Married Ildar Zaripov TJK in 2010. She was given a 2 years 6 months ban backdated from 25 July 2013 with results also annulled between 20 Jun 2011 and 20 Aug 2011 and 3 Jul to 3 Sep 2012, thus losing her 2012 Olympic title and pb of 9:05.02.

SAINT KITTS & NEVIS

Governing body: Saint Kitts Amateur Athletic Association, PO Box 932, Basseterre, St Kitts. Founded 1961.

Kim COLLINS. b. 5 Apr 1976 Ogees, Saint-Peter 1.75m 64kg. Studied sociology at Texas Christian University, USA.

At 100m (/200m): OG: '96- qf, 00- 7/sf, '04- 6, '08- sf/6; WCh: '97- h, 99- h/h, '01- 5/3=, '03- 1, '05- 3, '07- sf, '09- qf/qf, '11- 3/sf/3R; CG: '02- 1; PAm: '07- 5, '11- 2; PAm-J: '95- 2; CAC: '99- 2, '01- 1/1, '03- 1; WCp: '02- 2/2R, '14- 1R/3 4x400mR. At 60m: WI: '03- 2, '08- 2=. Won NCAA indoor 60m & 200m 2001.

SKN records: 100m from 1996 to 2014, 200m from 1998, 400m 2000. CAC indoor 60m 2015. M35 world records: 100m 2013 & 2014, indoor 60m (3) 2014-15.

Progress at 100m, 200m: 1995- 10.63, 21.85; 1996- 10.27, 21.06; 1998- 10.18/10.16w, 20.88/20.78w; 1999- 10.21, 20.43, 2000- 10.13A/10.15/10.02w, 20.31A/20.18w; 2001- 10.04A/10.00?/9.99w, 20.20/20.08w; 2002- 9.98, 20.49; 2003- 9.99/9.92w, 20.40w; 2004- 10.00, 20.98; 2005- 10.00, 2006- 10.33, 21.53; 2007- 10.14, 2008- 10.05, 20.25; 2009- 10.15/10.08w, 20.45; 2010- 10.20, 21.35/20.76w; 2011- 10.00A/10.01, 20.52; 2012- 10.01/9.96w, 2013- 9.97, 21.37i, 2014- 9.96. pbs: 60m 6.47i '15, 400m 46.93 '00.

The first athlete from his country to make Olympic and World finals and in 2003 the first to win a World Indoor medal and a World title; won a further medal in his 8th World Champs. There is a 'Kim Collins Highway' in St Kitts.

ST LUCIA

Governing body: Saint Lucia Athletics Association, Olympic House, Barnard Hill P.O.GM 697 Gable Woods Mall, Castries.

Levern SPENCER b. 23 Jun 1984 Cacao Babonneau 1.80m 54kg. Was at University of Georgia.

At HJ: OG: '08/12- dnq 27/19; WCh: '05-07-09-11-13: dnq 22/15=/dnq 24=/dnq 13/11; CG: '02-06-10-14: 12=/5/3/3; WJ: '02- 8; WY: '01- 3; PAm: '03- 5, '07- 3; CAG: '06-10-14: 3/1/1; WI: '14- 7; CCp: '10- 3=, '14- 5. CAC champion 2001, 2005, 2008-09, 2011.

Nine St. Lucia high jump records 2004-10.

Progress at HJ: 2000- 1.80, 2001- 1.81, 2002- 1.83, 2003- 1.86, 2004- 1.88, 2005- 1.94, 2006- 1.90, 2007- 1.94, 2008- 1.93, 2009- 1.95, 2010- 1.98, 2011- 1.94, 2012- 1.91, 2013- 1.95A, 2014- 1.96. pbs: 200m 24.22 '05, LJ 6.08 '14.

SAUDI ARABIA

Governing body: Saudi Arabian Athletics Federation, PO Box 5802, Riyadh 11432. Founded 1963.

Youssef Ahmed **AL-MASRAHI** b. 31 Dec 1987 Njaran 1.76m 76kg.

At 400m: OG: 12- sf; WCh: '09- h, '13- 6; AsiG: '10- 3/1R, '14- 1; AsiC: '11- 1, '13- 1/1R; CCp: '14- 3; Gulf champion 2009, Arab 2011, 2013- 1.

400m records: Asian 2014, KSA (2) 2013-14.

Progress at 400m/4x400mR: 2007- 48.89, 2008- 46.45, 2009- 45.84, 2010- 45.48, 2011- 45.44, 2012- 45.43, 2013- 44.61, 2014- 44.43. pbs: 200m 21.09 '14, 800m 1:54.14 '07.

Lived in the USA from 2011.

SERBIA

Governing body: Athletic Federation of Serbia, Strahinjica Bana 73a, 11000 Beograd. Founded in 1921 (as Yugoslav Athletic Federation).

National Championships (Yugoslav) first held in 1920 (men) and 1923 (women). **2014 Champions**: **Men**: 100m: Goran Podunavac 10.86, 200/400m: Milos Raovic 21.57/45.96, 800m: Nemanja Kojic 1:52.39, 1500m: Goran Nava 3:48.38, 3000m/3000mSt: Muamer Hasanovic 8:28.78/9:32.34, 5000m: Jasmim Ljajic 14:54.57, 10000m/HMar: Darko Zivanovic 31:43.98/69:00, Mar: Ivan Miskeljin 2:41:13, 110mh: Milan Ristic 14.26, 400mh: Emir Bekric 49.73, HJ: Jovan Vukicevic 2.12, PV: Dino Dogic 4.10, LJ: Strahinja Jovancevic 7.38, TJ: Petar Djuric 15.35, SP: Asmir Kolasinac 20.66, DT: Milos Markovic 50.95, HT: Stevan Veselinovic 57.34, JT: Vedran Samac 75.08; Dec: Marko Milovanovic 5263, 10kW/10000mW: Predrag Filipovic 40:49/42:47.6, **Women**: 100m: Milana Tirnanic 11.97, 200m: Katarina Sirmic 24.40, 400m: Tamara Markovic 53.75, 800m/1500m: Amela Terzic 2:08.11/4:13.53, 3000m/5000m: Teodora Simovic 9:46.66/16:47.95, 10000m/HMar: Olivera Jevtic 34:50.29/79:21, Mar: Dragana Spehar 3:38:01, 3000mSt: Biljana Cvijanovic 10:23.47, 100mh: Ivana Petkovic 14.09, 400mh: Jelena Grujic 61.15, HJ: Zorana Bukvic 1.70, PV: Tamara Moravcevic 3.20, LJ: Milica Kovacevic 5.52, TJ: Ivana Ognjanovic 12.51, SP: Dijana Sefcic 13.88, DT: Dragana Tomasevic 60.96, HT: Sara Savatovic 60.70, JT: Tatjana Jelaca 55.27, Hep: *not held*, 5kW: Jelena Kostic 27:49, 5000W: Dusica Topic 25:38.2.

Emir BEKRIC b. 14 Mar 1991 Belgrade 1.96m 85kg. AC Partizan, Belgrade.

At 400mh: OG: '12- sf; WCh: '11- sf, '13- 3; EC:

'14- 6; WJ: '10- 7; EC: '12- 2; EU23: '11- 3, '13- 1; EJ: '09- sf. Won MedG 2013, Balkan 2011, 2013-14; SRB 400m 2012-13, 400mh 2009, 2012-14.
Eight Serbian 400mh records 2011-13.
Progress at 400mh: 2007- 57.10, 2008- 53.46, 2009- 52.85, 2010- 50.67, 2011- 49.55, 2012- 49.21, 2013- 48.05, 2014- 49.21. pbs; 200m 21.85 '13, 400m 46.49 '13.

Asmir KOLASINAC b. 15 Oct 1984 Skopje, Macedonia 1.85m 130kg. AC Partizan, Belgrade.
At SP: OG: '08- dnq 32, '12- 7; WCh: '09- dnq 21, '11- 10, '13- 10; EC: '10-12-14: 8/3/5; EU23: '05- dnq; EI: '13- 1, '15- 2; Won Balkan 2011; SRB 2008, 2010-14.
Progress at SP: 2004- 15.50, 2005- 17.88, 2006- 17.85, 2007- 19.30, 2008- 19.99, 2009- 20.41, 2010- 20.52i/20.38, 2011- 20.50, 2012- 20.85, 2013- 20.80, 2014- 20.79, 2015- 20.91i.

Women

Tatjana JELACA b. 10 Aug 1990 Sremska Mitrovica 1.78m 76kg. AC Crvena Zvezda, Belgrade.
At JT: OG: '12- dnq 26; WCh: '11- dnq 24, 13- 9; EC: '10-12-14: 12/7/2; WJ: '08- 3; WY: '07- 6; EU23: '11- 7; EJ: '09- 1; Serbian champion 2008-14, Balkan 2013.
Four Serbian javelin records 2009-14.
Progress at JT: 2004- 39.86, 2005- 42.46, 2006- 42.25, 2007- 51.80, 2008- 58.77, 2009- 60.35, 2010- 58.54, 2011- 56.68, 2012- 60.89, 2013- 62.68, 2014- 64.21. pbs: SP 11.45 '09, DT 40.38 '09.

Ivana SPANOVIC b. 10 May 1990 Zrenjanin 1.76m 65kg. AC Vojvodina, Novi Sad.
At LJ: OG: '08- dnq 30, '12- 11; WCh: '13- 3; EC: '10- 8, '12- dnq 14, '14- 2; WJ: '06- 7, '08- 1; WY: '05- dnq, '07- 2; EU23: '11- 2; EJ: '07- 5, '09- 2; WUG: '09- 1; CCp: '14- 2; WI: '14- 3; EI: '13- 5, '15- 1. Serbian champion 2006, 2008, 2011-13, Balkan 2011, 2013.
Five Serbian long jump records 2009-14.
Progress at LJ: 2003- 5.36, 2004- 5.91, 2005- 6.43, 2006- 6.48i/6.38, 2007- 6.53i/6.41, 2008- 6.65, 2009- 6.71, 2010- 6.78, 2011- 6.71/6.74w, 2012- 6.64, 2013- 6.82, 2014- 6.92i/6.88, 2015- 6.98i. pbs: 60m 7.31i '15, 100m 11.90 '13, 60mh 8.49i '13, HJ 1.78i '13, 1.65 '05; TJ 13.78 '14, SP 12.40i '13, Pen 4240i '13.
Won first medal for Serbia at World Champs.

SLOVAKIA

Governing body: Slovak Athletic Federation, Junácka 6, 832 80 Bratislava. Founded 1939.
National Championships first held in 1939.
2014 Champions: **Men**: 100m: Adam Zavacky 10.48, 200m: Roman Turcáni 21.83, 400m: Lukás Privalinec 48.36, 800m: Tomás Timoransky 1:51.55, 1500m: Peter Durec 3:54.73, 5000m: Bálint Magyar 15:30.10, 10000m/HMar: Jozef Urban 32:06.67/67:23, Mar: Boris Csiba 2:29:03, 3000mSt: Jakub Valachovic 9:31.27, 110mh: Viliam Papso 13.94, 400mh: Roman Olejník 54.65, HJ: Matús Bubeník 2.23, PV: Ján Zmoray 5.00, LJ/TJ: Martin Koch 7.31/15.41, SP: Matús Olej 17.78, DT: Matej Gasaj 56.04, HT: Marcel Lomnicky 76.49, JT: Martin Benák 74.56, Dec: Branislav Puvák 5953, 20000mW: Patrik Spevák 1:28:53.6, 50kW: Dusan Majdán 4:07:48. **Women**: 100m: Lenka Krsáková 11.53, 200m: Alexandra Bezeková 23.96, 400m: Iveta Putalová 53.96, 800m: Alexandra Stuková 2:14.54, 1500m: Adriana Vitková 4:43.11, 5000m: Lubomíra Maníková 17:46.37, 10000m: Katarína Beresová 33:47.22, HMar: Adriana Vitková 1:21:50, Mar: Ingrid Petnuchová 2:51:15, 3000mSt: Katarína Pokorná 11:24.57, 100mh: Lucia Mokrásová 13.83, 400mh: Andrea Holleyová 59.92, HJ: Zuzana Karaffová 1.73, PV: Anna Mária Hrvolová 3.50, LJ: Jana Veldáková 6.50, TJ: Dana Veldáková 13.75w, SP: Patrícia Slosárová 13.44, DT: Ivona Tomanová 48.38, HT: Martina Hrasnová 75.27, JT: Jana Licáková 43.03, Hep: Stanislava Lajcáková 4924, 20000mW: María Galíková 1:38:23.3.

Marcel LOMNICKY b. 6 Jul 1987 Nitra 1.77m 106kg. TJ Stavbár Nitra. Was at Virginia Tech University, USA.
At HT: OG: '12- dnq 15; WCh: '11- dnq 21, '13- 8; WJ: '04- dnq 17, '06- 3; EC: '10-12-14: dnq 24/11/7; EU23: '07- 3, '09- 6; EJ: '05- 8; WUG: '11- 2, '13- 2. SVK champion 2012-14, won NCAA HT 2009, indoor Wt 2012.
Progress at HT: 2005- 64.27, 2006- 69.53, 2007- 72.17, 2008- 72.66, 2009- 71.78, 2010- 74.83, 2011- 75.84, 2012- 77.43, 2013- 78.73, 2014- 79.16. pbs: SP 15.73 '07, DT 43.82 '08, Wt 23.05i '12.
Sister Nikola Lomnická (b. 16 Sep 1988) has hammer best 71.58 '14, won NCAA 2010 and was 8th EC 2014.

Matej TÓTH b. 10 Feb 1983 Nitra 1.85m 73kg. Dukla Banská Bystrica.
At 20kW/(50kW): OG: '04- 32, '08- 26, '12- (7); WCh: '05- 21, 07- 14, '09- 9/10, '11- 12/dnf, '13- (5); EC: '06- 6, '10- 6, '14- (2); EU23: '03- 6; WCp: '10- (1); ECp: '09-11-13: 9/1/3. At 10000mW: WJ: '02- 16, WY: '99- 8; EJ: '01- 6. Won SVK 20kW 2005-08, 2010-12; 50kW 2011.
Four SVK 50k walk records 2009-15.
Progress at 20kW, 50kW: 1999- 1:34:29, 2000- 1:30:28, 2001- 1:29:33, 2003- 1:13:17, 2004- 1:23:18, 2005- 1:21:38, 2006- 1:21:39, 2007- 1:25:10, 2008- 1:21:24, 2009- 1:20:53, 3:41:32; 2010- 1:22:04, 3:53:30; 2011- 1:20:16, 3:39:46; 2012- 1:20:25, 3:41:24; 2013- 1:20:14, 3:41:07; 2014- 1:19:48, 3:36:21; 2015- 3:34:38. pbs: 3000mW 10:57.32i '11, 11:05.95 '12; 5000mW 18:34.56i '12, 18:54.39 '11; 10000W 39:45.03 '06, 39:07R '10; 30kW 2:12:44 '13, 35kW 2:34:23 '13.

Women

Martina HRASNOVÁ b. 21 Mar 1983 Bratislava 1.77m 88kg. née Danisová. Dukla Banská Bystrica.

At HT: OG: '08- 8, '12- dnq 19; WCh: '01-07-13: dnq 23/12/21, '09- 3; EC: '02 & '06- dnq 26, '12- 2, '14- 2; WJ: '00- 5, '02- 2; EJ: '99- 4, '01- 2; CCp: '14- 3; WUG: '07- 5, '09- 2. Won SVK SP 2003, 2006; HT 2000-01, 2006, 2008-09, 2011-14.
14 Slovakian hammer records 2001-09.
Progress at HT: 1999- 58.61, 2000- 61.62, 2001- 68.50, 2002- 68.22, 2003- 66.36, 2005- 69.24, 2006- 73.84, 2007- 69.22, 2008- 76.82, 2009- 76.90, 2011- 72.47, 2012- 73.34, 2013- 72.41, 2014- 75.27. pbs: 60m 7.96i '12, SP 15.60i '15, 15.02 '06; DT 43.15 '06, Wt 21.74i '11.
Two-year drugs ban (nandrolone) from July 2003. Daughter Rebeka born on 4 July 2010. Brother of Branislav Danis (HT 69.20 '06).

Dana VELDÁKOVÁ b. 3 Jun 1981 Roznava 1.79m 60kg. Dukla Banská Bystrica.
At (LJ/)TJ: OG: '08- dnq, '12- 12; WCh: '05- dnq 17, '07-09-11-13: 12/8/11/11; EC: '02/06- dnq 15/24, '10-12-14: 7/5/6; WJ: '98- 6, '00- 4/3; EU23: '01- 5, '03- 4; EJ: '99- 8; WI: '06-10-12-14: 8/6/8/8; EI: '07-09-11: 6/3/3; WUG: '03- 5, '07- 2. Won SVK 100mh 2003, TJ 2002-05, 2007-14, Hep 2001, 2004.
Two SVK triple jump records 2007-08.
Progress at TJ: 1998- 13.12, 1999- 13.13/13.19w, 2000- 13.92, 2001- 13.73, 2002- 13.99, 2003- 14.02, 2004- 13.96A, 2005- 14.16, 2006- 14.19, 2007- 14.41, 2008- 14.51, 2009- 14.43, 2010- 14.32/14.59w, 2011- 14.48, 2012- 14.36, 2013- 14.31, 2014- 14.10i/13.91. pbs: 60m 7.73i '06, 100m 11.99 '14, 60mh 8.82i '03, 100mh 14.38 '01, HJ 1.75 '01, LJ 6.56 '08, SP 11.56i '04, Hep 5191 '01, Pen 3746i '03.
Twin **Jana** LJ 6.72 '08, 6.88w '10; TJ 13.40 '04.

SLOVENIA

Governing body: Atletska Zveza Slovenije, Letaliska cesta 33c, 1122 Ljubljana. Current organisation founded 1948.

2014 National Champions: Men: 100m/200m: Gregor Kokalovic 10.71/21.00, 400m/800m: Zan Rudolf 47.37/1:50.25, 1500m: Jan Petrac 3:47.35, 3000m: Mitja Krevs 8:29.70, 5000m: Vid Zevnik 14:54.34, 10000m/HMar: Rok Puhar 31:00.18/ 67:41, Mar: Anton Kosmac 2:22:19, 3000mSt: Blaz Grad 9:05.87, 110mh: Damjan Zlatnar 14.66, 400mh: Peter Hribarsek 54.79, HJ: Rozle Prezelj 2.14, PV: Andrej Poljanec 5.20, LJ: Urban Cehovin 7.37w, TJ: Andrej Batagelj 15.67, SP: Luka Gorjup 17.58, DT: Tadej Hribar 49.48, HT: Primoz Kozmus 77.44, JT: Matija Kranjc 79.46, Dec: Urban Cehovin 6038. **Women**: 100m: Maja Mihalinec 11.84, 200m: Sabina Veit 23.44, 400m: Maja Pogorevc 55.15, 800m: Dorotea Rebernik 2:16.04, 1500m/3000m: Marusa Mismas 4:36.87/ 9:23.20, 5000m: Lucija Krkoc 17:35.15, 10000m: Petra Race 37:55.48, HMar: Neja Krsinar 79:23, Mar: Maja Peperko 3:17:36, 3000mSt: *not held*, 100mh: Joni Tomicic Prezelj 14.33, 400mh: Neza Grkman 65.36, HJ: Monika Podlogar 1.60, PV: Tina Sutej 4.40, LJ: Nina Djordjevic 6.49w, TJ: Snezana Vukmirovic 13.90, SP/DT: Veronika Domjan 13.93/53.03, HT: Barbara Spiler 66.72, JT: Martina Ratej 64.15, Hep: Brina Mljac 3681.

Primoz KOZMUS b. 30 Sep 1979 Novo mesto 1.88m 106kg. AK Brezice.
At HT: OG: '00- dnq 38, '04- 6, '08- 1, '12- 2; WCh: '03-07-09-11-13: 5/2/1/3/4; EC: '02-06-14: dnq 25/7/6; EU23: '99- 12, '01- 14; WJ: '98- dnq. SLO champion 1999-2004, 2006, 2008-09, 2011, 2013-14; WAF 2008-09.
Ten SLO hammer records 2000-09.
Progress at HT: 1995- 45.82, 1996- 54.10, 1997- 61.08, 1998- 66.28, 1999- 70.11, 2000- 76.84, 2001- 71.17, 2002- 75.87, 2003- 81.21, 2004- 79.34, 2006- 80.38, 2007- 82.30, 2008- 82.02, 2009- 82.58, 2011- 80.28, 2012- 79.36, 2013- 79.70. 2014- 77.46.
First Slovenian Olympic champion. Older sister Simona set Slovenian women's hammer record (58.60 '01).

Women

Martina RATEJ b. 2 Nov 1981 Celje 1.78m 69kg. AD Kladivar Celje.
At JT: OG: '08- dnq 37, '12- 7; WCh: '09- 11, '11- 7, '13- dnq 20; EC: '06-10-12-14: dnq 21/7/dnq 21/6; WJ: '00- dnq 15. SLO champion 2005-14, MedG 2013.
Five SLO javelin records 2008-10.
Progress at JT: 1999- 48.74, 2000- 46.83, 2005- 50.86, 2006- 57.49, 2007- 58.49, 2008- 63.44, 2009- 63.42, 2010- 67.16, 2011- 65.89, 2012- 65.24, 2013- 62.60, 2014- 66.13.

Tina SUTEJ b. 7 Nov 1988 Ljubljana 1.73m 58kg. Mass Ljubljana. Biology student at University of Arkansas, USA.
At PV: OG: '12- dnq 19=; WCh: '11= dnq 12; EC: '10-12-14: 10/dnq 24/10=; WJ: '06- 2; WY: '05- 8; EU23: '09- 5; WUG: '11- 2; WI: '14- 10. SLO champion 2006, 2008-14.
Nine SLO pole vault records 2010-11.
Progress at PV: 2004- 3.81, 2005- 4.10, 2006- 4.25, 2007- 4.17i/4.10, 2008- 4.20, 2009- 4.25, 2010- 4.50, 2011- 4.61, 2012- 4.55, 2013- 4.35, 2014- 4.71i/4.50.

Snezana VUKMIROVIC b. 19 Aug 1982 Koper 1.80m 66kg. Former married name Rodic. AD MASS Ljubljana.
At TJ: WCh: '05/09- dnq 16/19, '13- 9; EC: '10- 6, '12- dnq 15, 14- 7; EU23: '03- 11 (dq LJ); EI: '09- 6, '11- 4. SLO champion LJ 2004, 2013; TJ 2003-04, 2008, 2010, 2014.
Progress at TJ: 2003- 13.47, 2004- 13.97, 2005- 14.18, 2007- 14.03, 2008- 14.06/14.29w, 2009- 14.18i/14.10, 2010- 14.47/14.52w, 2011- 14.35i/14.23, 2012- 14.20, 2013- 14.58, 2014- 13.90. pbs: 60m 7.92i '03, 60mh 8.27i '05, 100mh 14.27 '03, LJ 6.53 '13, Hep 4897 '00.
Was married to international footballer Aleksander Rodic, divorced in February 2014.

SOUTH AFRICA

Governing body: Athletics South Africa, PO

Box 2712, Houghton 2041. Original body founded 1894.

National Championships first held in 1894 (men), 1929 (women). **2014 Champions**: **Men**: 100m: Simon Magakwe 9.98, 200m: Ncincihli Titi 20.41, 400m: Wade van Niekerk 44.92, 800m: André Olivier 1:48.38, 1500m: Jerry Motsau 3:47.91, 5000m: Gladwin Mzazi 14:05.5, 10000m: Vuyisle Tshoba 29:40.33, HMar: Lesiba Precious Mashele 65:42, Mar: Desmond Mokgobu 2:16:17, 3000mSt: Rantso Mokopane 8:48.36, 110mh: Ruan de Vries 13.62, 400mh: Cornel Fredericks 49.21, HJ: Mpho Links 2.10, PV: Cheyne Rahme 5.40, LJ: Zarck Visser 8.31, TJ: Khotso Mokoena 16.68, SP: Orazio Cremona 20.29, DT: Victor Hogan 63.45, HT: Chris Harmse 70.56 (20th successive title), JT: Robert Oosthuizen 78.80, Dec: Willem Coertzen 8199, 20kW: Lebogang Shange 1:26:17. **Women**: 100m: Nabeela Parker 11.78, 200m/400m: Justine Palframan 23.11/52.48, 800m: Caster Semenya 2:03.05, 1500m: Mapaseka Makhanya 4:20.42, 5000m: Dina Lebo Phalula 16:16.96, 10000m: Cornelia Joubert 35:49.60, HMar: Makhosazane Mhlongo 78:56, Mar: Zintle Xiniwe 2:41:52, 3000mSt: Thembi Baloyi 10:35.91, 100mh: Rikenette Steenkamp 13.17, 400mh: Wenda Nel 54.92, HJ: Julia du Plessis 1.75, PV: Deoné Joubert 3.90, LJ: Lynique Prinsloo 6.45, TJ: Matsi Dikotla 12.77w, SP: Lezaan Jordaan 16.07, DT: Maryke Oberholzer 56.95, HT: Karin le Roux 54.67, JT: Sunette Viljoen 64.77, Hep: Bianca Erwee 5456, 20kW: Anél Oosthuizen 1:42:40.

Johan CRONJE b. 13 Apr 1982 Bloemfontein 1.82m 69kg.
At 1500m: OG: '04- sf; WCh: '05-09-13: sf/h/3; CG: '14- 3; WJ: '00- 5; WY: '99- 5; AfCh: '04-06-10-12-14: 5/6/9/5/7; RSA champion 2002, 2004, 2008-09, 2012-13.
South African records 1500m (2) 2013, 1M 2014.
Progress at 1500m: 1998- 3:53.5A, 1999- 3:46.45, 2000- 3:41.21, 2001- 3:40.29, 2002- 3:37.28, 2003- 3:43.85, 2004- 3:37.83, 2005- 3:35.58, 2006- 3:36.73, 2007- 3:37.67, 2008- 3:38.37, 2009- 3:33.63, 2010- 3:35.24, 2012- 3:35.23, 2013- 3:31.93, 2014- 3:33.31. pbs: 800m 1:45.64 '13, 1000m 2:18.48i '08, 2:18.56 '10; 1M 3:50.70 '14, 3000m 7:52.33i '15, 8:02.14 '04; 5000m 13:59.52 '09.
Mother Sarina had pbs 1500m 4:08.6 and 1M 4:28.4 (1980), 3000m 8:49.3 (1981), father Danie 1500m 3:44.8 (1979), 1M 4:00.5 (1980).

Cornel FREDERICKS b. 3 Mar 1990 Caledon 1.78m 70kg.
At 400mh/4x400mR: OG: '12- h; WCh: '11- 5, '13- sf; CG: '14- 1; WJ: '08- 4; WY: '07- 5; AfCh: '10- 2, '14- 1; CCp: '14- 1; Won RSA 2010, 2012-14; Af-J 110mh & 400mh 2009.
Progress at 400mh: 2008- 50.39, 2009- 49.92, 2010- 48.79A/48.99, 2011- 48.14, 2012- 48.91, 2013- 48.78, 2014- 48.25. pbs: 400m 46.90 '10, 300mh 35.15 '10.

Victor HOGAN b. 25 Jul 1989 Vredenburg, Western Cape 1.98m 108kg.
At DT: WCh: '13- 5; CG: '14-10; WJ: '08- 4; AfG: '11- 2; AfCh: '10-12-14: 3/1/1; CCp: '10- 8, '14- 4; Af-J: '07- 1; RSA champion 2010-14.
Progress at DT: 2008- 59.21, 2009- 57.67A, 2010- 58.30, 2011- 62.60, 2012- 62.76, 2013- 65.33, 2014- 64.16.

Anaso JOBODWANA b. 30 Jul 1992 Aberdeen, Eastern Cape 1.87m 71kg. Student at Jacksonville State University, USA.
At (100m)/200m: OG: '12- 8; WCh: '13- sf/6; WUG: '13- 1/1.
Progress at 100m, 200m: 2009- 21.68A, 2010- 20.95A, 2012- 10.34/10.24w, 20.27; 2013- 10.10, 20.13/20.00w; 2015- 19.87w. pb 60m 6.60Ai '15, 6.66i '13. Missed 2014 season through injury.

Godfrey Khotso MOKOENA b. 6 Mar 1985 Heidelberg, Gauteng 1.90m 73kg. Tuks AC, Pretoria.
At LJ/(TJ): OG: '04- (dnq 29), '08- 2, '12- 8; WCh: '05-07-09-11-13: 7/5/2/dnq 15=/7; CG: '06- 4/2, '14- (1); WJ: '02- 12, '04- 2/1; AfG: '03- 3/2, '07- 3; AfCh: '06- 2/2, '10- 1, '14- 2/1; CCp: '14- (2); WI: '06-08-10: 5/1/2. At HJ: WY: '01- 5. Won DL LJ 2014, RSA LJ 2005-07, 2009-11; TJ 2004-06, 2014.
Records: African LJ (3) 2009, RSA LJ (5) 2005-09, TJ (3) 2004-14, African junior TJ 2004.
Progress at LJ, TJ: 2001- 7.17A, 2002- 7.82A, 16.03A; 2003- 7.84A/7.83, 16.28; 2004- 8.09, 16.96A/16.77; 2005- 8.37A/8.22, 17.25; 2006- 8.39/8.45w, 16.95; 2007- 8.34A/8.28/8.32w, 16.75; 2008- 8.25/8.35w, 2009- 8.50, 2010- 8.23A/8.15/8.22w, 2011- 8.25/8.31w, 2012- 8.29A/8.24, 2013- 8.30, 15.68i; 2014- 8.19, 17.35. pbs: 100m 10.7A '09, HJ 2.10 '01.
Returned to triple jumping in 2014.

André OLIVIER b. 29 Dec 1989 Pietermaritzburg 1.92m 72kg.
At 800m: OG: '12- sf; CG: '14- 3; WJ: '08- 3; WI: '14- 4; AfCh: '12- 3; Af-J: '07- 4; RSA champion 2013-14. At 1500m: WY: '05- 11. At 4x400m: WUG: '11- 3. RSA 600m best 2014.
Progress at 800m: 2004- 1:57.7A, 2005- 1:52.2A, 2006- 1:49.58A, 2007- 1:47.92, 2008- 1:46.85, 2009- 1:45.41, 2011- 1:46.84, 2012- 1:44.29, 2013- 1:44.37, 2014- 1:44.42. pbs: 400m 46.81A '14, 600m 1:15.03 '14, 1000m 2:18.11 '14, 1500m 3:39.40 '09.

Wayde van NIEKERK b. 15 Jul 1992 Cape Town 1.83m 73kg. University of the Free State, Bloemfontein.
At (200m)/400m: WCh: '13- h; CG: '14- sf/2; AfCh: '14- 2; WJ: '10- (4); CCp: '14- 4/1R. Won RSA 200m 2011, 400m 2013-14.
RSA 400m record 2014
Progress at 200m, 400m: 2010- 21.02, 2011- 20.57, 2012- 20.91, 46.43; 2013- 20.84A, 45.09; 2014- 20.19, 44.38. pb 100m 10.45A '11, 10.15 '10.

Louis J. van ZYL b. 20 Jul 1985 Bloemfontein 1.86m 75kg. Tuks AC, Pretoria.
At 400mh/4x400mR: OG: '08- 5, '12- h; WCh:

'05-07-09-11-13: 6/h/sf/3&2R/h; CG: '06- 1/2R, '10- 2, '14- h; AfG: '07- 1; AfCh: '06-08-10-14: 1/1&1R/1/4; WJ: '02- 1, '04- 4/2R; WY: '01- 3; WCp: '06- 2, '10- 5; RSA champion 2003, 2005-06, 2008, 2011.
Two RSA 400m hurdles records 2011.
Progress at 400mh: 2001- 51.14A, 2002- 48.89, 2003- 49.22, 2004- 49.06, 2005- 48.11, 2006- 48.05, 2007- 48.24, 2008- 48.22, 2009- 47.94, 2010-48.51A/48.63, 2011- 47.66, 2012- 49,42A, 2013-49.11, 2014- 48.96A/48.97. pbs: 100m 10.62 '07, 10.3Aw '03, 10.5A '01; 200m 21.02A '09, 21.0A '03; 300m 32.32 '09, 400m 44.86A '11, 46.02 '08; 200mhSt 22.63 '13, 300mh 35.76 '04.
Ran world U18 record of 48.89 to win World Junior title in 2002 after world age record at 15 in 2001. Commonwealth Games record to win 400mh gold and ran brilliant final leg in 4x400m to take RSA from fifth to second in 2006. Married Irvette van Blerk (pbs HMar 70:56 '11, Mar 2:33:41 '12) on 29 Sep 2012.

Zarck VISSER b. 15 Sep 1989 Welkom 1.78m 70kg.
At LJ: WCh: 13- dnq 13; CG: '14- 2; AfCh: '12- 2, '14- 1; CCp: '14- 3; RSA champion 2012-14.
Progress at LJ: 2007- 7.21A, 2008- 7.62A, 2009-7.77, 2010- 7.76A/7.79Aw, 2011- 7.85, 2012-8.15A/8.07/8.21w, 2013- 8.32, 2014- 8.31A/8.18. pb TJ 15.66A '08.

Women

Wenda NEL b. 27 May 1988 Worcester, Western Cape 1.69m 52kg. née Theron. TUKS.
At 400mh: WCh: '11- sf; CG: '14- h; AfG: '11- 2; AfCh: '10-12-14: 7/5/1; CCp: '14- 5. RSA champion 2011-2. At 100m/200m: WJ: '06- h/h; WY: '05: h/-.
Progress at 400mh: 2008- 60.23A, 2009- 56.45, 2010- 56.97, 2011- 56.13, 2012- 55.36A/55.79, 2013-55.80, 2014- 54.82. pbs: 100m 11.88A '06, 200m 24.05A '11, 400m 52.53A '14, 600: 1:28.05A 15, 100mh 14.23 '07.

Sunette VILJOEN b. 6 Oct 1983 Johannesburg 1.70m 70kg. University of North West, Potchefstroom.
At JT: OG: '04/08- dnq 35/33, '12- 4; WCh: '03/09- dnq 16/18, '11- 3, '13- 6; CG: '06-10-14: 1/1/2; AfG: '03- 3, '07- 3; AfCh: '04-06-08-10-14: 1/2/1/1/1; WUG: '07- 5, '09- 1, '11- 1; CCp: '10- 2, '14- 2. Won Afro-Asian Games 2003, RSA 2003-04, 2006, 2009-14.
Four African javelin records 2009-12, two Commonwealth 2011-12.
Progress at JT: 1999- 43.89A, 2000- 45.50A, 2001-50.70A, 2002- 58.33A, 2003- 61.59, 2004- 61.15A, 2005- 57.31, 2006- 60.72, 2007- 58.39, 2008-62.24A, 2009- 65.43, 2010- 66.38, 2011- 68.38, 2012- 69.35, 2013- 64.51, 2014- 65.32, 2015- 66.62.
Son Hervé born in 2005.

SPAIN

Governing body: Real Federación Española de Atletismo (RFEA), Avda. Valladolid, 81 - 1°, 28008 Madrid, Spain. Founded 1918.
National Championships first held in 1917 (men), 1931 (women). **2014 Champions**: **Men**: 100m: Adrià Burriel 10.34, 200m: Iván Jesús Ramos 20.84, 400m: Samuel García 45.50, 800m: Kevin López 1:47.15, 1500m: Manuel Olmedo 3:42.06, 5000m: Antonio Abadía 13:48.69, 10000m: Alemayehu Bezabeh 28:12.85, HMar: Ayad Lamdassem 62:57, Mar: Carles Castillejo 2:12:43, 3000mSt: Víctor Garcia 8:37.10, 110mh: Javier Colomo 13.74, 400mh: Sergio Fernández 49.90, HJ: Miguel Ángel Sancho 2.22, PV: Igor Bychkov 5.45, LJ: Eusebio Cáceres 8.08, TJ: Pablo Torrijos 16.87, SP: Borja Vivas 21.07, DT: Frank Casañas 61.15, HT: Javier Cienfuegos 70.59, JT: Jordi Sánchez 73.88, Dec: Javier Pérez 7396, 10000mW: Miguel Ángel López 38:54.87, 20kW: Benjamin Sánchez 1:25:45, 35kW: Marc Tur 2:36:34, 50kW: *not held*. **Women**: 100m: Estela García 11.72, 200m: Alba Fernández 24.04, 400m: Indira Terrero 51.77, 800m: Khadija Rahmouni 2:03.42, 1500m: Nuria Fernández 4:20.26, 5000m/10000m: Dolores Checa 15:51.24/32:22.21, HMar: Alessandra Aguilar 71:16, Mar: Estela Navascués 2:32:38, 3000mSt: Diana Martín 10:03.97, 100mh: Caridad Jerez 13.09, 400mh: Laura Natali Sotomayor 57.17, HJ: Ruth Beitia 1.95, PV: Naroa Agirre 4.42, LJ: María del Mar Jover 6.59, TJ: Ruth Marie Ndoumbe 14.15, SP: Úrsula Ruiz 17.15, DT: Sabina Asenjo 57.62, HT: Berta Castells 68.10 (12th successive title), JT: Mercedes Chilla 55.94, Hep: Carmen Romero 5427, 10000mW/20kW: Julia Takacs 42:23.37/ 1:29:08.

Eusebio CÁCERES b. 10 Sep 1991 Onil, Alicante 1.76m 69kg. CD Nike Running.
At LJ: OG: '12- dnq 14; WCh: '11- dnq 19, '13- 4; EC: '10-12-14: 8/5/4; WJ: '08- '3, '10- 2; EJ: '09- 6; EU23: '11- 8, '13- 1; ET: '09- 1, '14- 3. Spanish champion 2012, 2014.
European junior long jump record 2010. World junior indoor heptathlon best 5984 '10.
Progress at LJ: 2002- 4.39, 2003- 4.93, 2004-5.57/5.60w, 2005- 6.77, 2006- 7.36, 2007- 7.57, 2008- 7.86, 2009- 8.00/8.17w, 2010- 8.27, 2011-8.23, 2012- 8.06/8.31w, 2013- 8.37, 2014- 8.11/ 8.16w. pbs: 60m 6.77i '12, 100m 10.43 '11, 10.34w '09; 200m 21.43 '13, 60mh 8.29i '11, 110mh 14.93w '11, HJ 1.96i '10, 1.93 '09; PV 4.60i '10, 4.30 '09; JT 53.32 '11, Hep 5667i '11, Dec 7273w '11.

Frank Yennifer **CASAÑAS** b. 18 Oct 1978 La Habana, Cuba 1.87m 115kg. Playas de Castellón.
At DT: OG: '00/04- dnq 24/17, '08- 5, '12- 7; WCh: '03-05-09-13: dnq 21/21/16;/9 EC: '10-13-14: 11/5/8; WJ: '96- 3; PAm: '99- 4, '03- 2; CAG: '98- 2; PAm-J: '97- 1; ET: '11- 2; won IbAm 2000, Cuban 2003-05, MedG 2009, Spanish 2014.
Progress at DT: 1995- 50.08, 1996- 54.86, 1997-57.36, 1998- 60.52, 1999- 63.90, 2000- 63.32, 2002-64.04, 2003- 65.08, 2004- 64.20, 2005- 65.32, 2006-

67.14, 2007- 64.68, 2008- 67.91, 2009- 67.17, 2010- 66.95, 2010- 66.62, 2011- 67.18, 2012- 67.74, 2013- 66.16, 2014- 65.48. pb SP 17.68 '07.
Spanish citizen from 27 May 2008. Married to Dolores Pedrares (HT pb 67.14 '04).

Jesús Ángel GARCÍA b. 17 Oct 1969 Madrid 1.72m 64kg. CA Diputación BCN.
At 50kW: OG: '92-96-00-04-08-12: 10/dnf/12/5/4/19; WCh: '93-5-7-9-01-03-05-07-09-11-13: 1/5/2/dnf/2/6/dq/dq/3/dq/12; EC: '94-98-02-06-10-14: 4/dq/3/2/5/8; WCp: '93-5-7-9-02-04-06-08-10-12-14: 2/2/1/4/dq/6/6/14/5/6/20; ECp: '96-8-00-01-09: 1/2/1/1/2. At 20kW: WUG: '91- 5. Won Spanish 50kW 1997, 2000, 2007, 2012. World M40 50km walk record 2010.
Progress at 50kW: 1991- 4:05:10, 1992- 3:48:24, 1993- 3:41:41, 1994- 3:41:28, 1995- 3:41:54, 1996- 3:46:59, 1997- 3:39.54, 1998- 3:43:17, 1999- 3:40:40, 2000- 3:42:51, 2001- 3:43:07, 2002- 3:44:33, 2003- 3:43:56, 2004- 3:44:42, 2005- 3:48:19, 2006- 3:42:48, 2007- 3:46:08, 2008- 3:44:08, 2009- 3:41:37, 2010- 3:47:56, 2011- 3:48:11, 2012- 3:48.15, 2013- 3:46:44, 2014- 3:45:41. pbs: 5000mW 19:33.3 '01, 10000mW 40:38.86 '09, road: 5kW 20:07 '04, 10kW 40:25 '99, 20kW 1:23:00 '09, 30kW 2:08:47 '01, 35km 2:31:06 '94; running Mar 2:47:43 '09.
Competed in all major champs 1992-2014, inc. tying men's record of six Olympic Games and six European Champs and setting men's record of 11 World Champs; has 57 races under 4 hours and 42 sub 3:50 for 50km and 23 years walking sub 3:50. In 1997 he married Carmen Acedo, who won a rhythmic gymnastics world title in 1993.

Miguel Ángel LÓPEZ b. 3 Jul 1988 Murcia 1.81m 70kg. UCAM Athleo Cieza.
At 20kW: OG: '12- 5; WCh: '11- 15, '13- 3; EC: '10- 13, '14- 1; EU23: '09- 1; WCp: '10- 12, '14- 5; ECp: '11- 6, '13- 2. At 10kW: WJ: '06- 14; WY: '05- 6; EJ: '05- 9, '07- 8; WCp: '06- 2J; ECp: '07- 2J. Won Spanish 10000mW 2010, 2012-14; 20kW 2010, 2012, 2015.
Progress at 20kW: 2008- 1:23:44, 2009- 1:22:23, 2010- 1:23:08, 2011- 1:21:41, 2012- 1:19:49, 2013- 1:21:21, 2014- 1:19:21, 2015- 1:19:52. pbs: 3000mW 11:39.92 '13, 5000mW 19:20.50 '13, 10000mW 38:54.87 '14.

Mario PESTANO b. 8 Apr 1978 Santa Cruz de Tenerife 1.95m 120kg. Unicaja Jaén.
At DT: OG: '04- dnq 12, '08- 9, '12- dnq 14; WCh: '99-01-03-05-07-09-11-13: dnq 30/dnq 22/8/11/10/10/11/12; EC: '02-06-10-12-14: 4/4/6/4/6; EU23: '99- 3; EJ: '97- 11; WCp: '02- 3; ECp: '01-05-06-08-09-13: 2/1/3/1/3/2. Won WAF 2004, IbAm 2004, 2010; MedG 2005, Spanish 2001-13. Eight Spanish discus records 2001-08.
Progress at DT: 1995- 49.36, 1996- 50.56, 1997- 53.68, 1998- 54.96, 1999- 61.73, 2000- 61.63, 2001- 67.92, 2002- 67.46, 2003- 64.99, 2004- 68.00, 2005- 66.57, 2006- 66.31, 2007- 68.26, 2008- 69.50, 2009- 66.63, 2010- 66.90, 2011- 67.97, 2012- 67.15, 2013- 65.79, 2014- 65.74. pb SP 18.75i '00, 18.64 '02.

Borja VIVAS b. 267 May 1984 Málaga 2.03m 140kg. At. Málaga.
At SP: OG: '12- dnq 30; WCh: '09-11-13: dnq 32/25/23; EC: '10-12-14: 10/7/2; EU23: '05- 8; EJ: '03- 10; EI: '15- 4. Spanish champion 2010-14 (indoor 2009-14), MedG 2013.
Progress at SP: 2003- 16.09, 2004- 18.03, 2005- 18.60, 2006- 18.66, 2007- 18.90, 2008- 19.50i/19.46, 2009- 20.01, 2010- 19.91, 2011- 20.18i/20.01, 2012- 20.06, 2013- 20.63, 2014- 21.07. pb DT 50.57 '08.

Women

Ruth BEITIA b. 1 Apr 1979 Santander 1.92m 71kg. Piélagos Inelecma. Graduate of physical therapy at University of Santander.
At HJ: OG: '04- dnq 16=, '08- 7=, '12- 4; WCh: '03-05-07-09-11-13: 11=/dnq 19=/6/5/dnq 16/3=; EC: '02-06-10-12-14: 11/9/6=/1/1; WJ: '96- dnq, '98- 8, EU23: '01- 1; EJ: '97- 9; WI: '01-03-06-08-10-12-14: 7/5=/3/4/2/6/3; EI: '05-07-09-11-13-15: 2/3/2/2/1/5; WCp: '02- 6=; ECp: '03-06-07-09-11-14: 2/2/2/2/3/3; Won IbAm 2010, Med G 2005, Spanish 2003, 2006-14 (and 14 indoors 2002-15).
Nine Spanish HJ records 1998-2007 (and eight indoors 2001-07). Equal world W35 record 2014.
Progress at HJ: 1989- 1.29, 1990- 1.39, 1991- 1.50, 1992- 1.55, 1993- 1.66, 1994- 1.74, 1995- 1.80, 1996- 1.85, 1997- 1.87i/1.86, 1998- 1.89, 1999- 1.83, 2000- 1.86i/1.85, 2001- 1.94i/1.91, 2002- 1.94, 2003- 2.00, 2004- 2.00i/1.96, 2005- 1.99i/1.97, 2006- 1.98i/1.97; 2007- 2.02, 2008- 2.01, 2009- 2.01, 2010- 2.00, 2011- 1.96i/1.95, 2012- 2.00, 2013- 1.99i/1.97, 2014- 2.01. pbs: 200m 25.26 '02, 100mh 14.95 '97, 14.93w '00; LJ 6.04 '03, TJ 12.43/12.73w '11.
She is a deputy of the Parliament of Cantabria, her autonomous community. Her sister Inmaculada (b. 8 Sep 1975) had TJ pb 13.43 '00.

Beatriz PASCUAL b. 9 May 1982 Barcelona 1.63m 64kg. Valencia Terra i Mar.
At 20kW: OG: '08- 6, '12- 8; WCh: '07-09-11-13: 13/6/9/6; EC: '02-06-10-14: 12/20/5/8; EU23: '03- 4; WCp: '10- 11, '12- 5; ECp: '09- 6, '13- 9. At 10kW: WJ: '00- 6; EJ: '01- 3. Won Spanish 10000mW 2008, 2010, 2012; 20kW 2006, 2008-09, 2011. Spanish walk records 5000m (3) 2008-12, 10000m 2010.
Progress at 20kW: 2002- 1:32:38, 2003- 1:31:31, 2004- 1:30:22, 2005- 1:32:49, 2006- 1:33:55, 2007- 1:30:37, 2008- 1:27:44, 2009- 1:29:54, 2010- 1:28:05, 2011- 1:28:51, 2012- 1:27:56, 2013- 1:29:00, 2014- 1:29:02. pbs: 3000mW 13:06.48 '04, 5000mW 20:45:11 '12, 10000mW 42:40.33 '10; HMar (run) 82:43 '08.

Julia TAKACS b. 29 Jun 1989 Budapest, Hungary 1.71m 53kg. Playas de Castellón.
At 20kW: WCh: '13: 9; EU23: '09- 5, '11- 2; WCp: '12- 11; ECp: '09- 11, '11- 10; WUG: '11- 1. At 10000mW: WJ: '08- 6. Won Spanish 10000mW 2009, 2011, 2013-14; 20kW 2013-14.

Spanish walk records: 3000m & 5000m 2014, 10000m (2) 2013-14.
Progress at 20kW: 2006- 1:43:49, 2007- 1:38:57, 2008- 1:39:12, 2009- 1:35:04, 2010- 1:30:14, 2011- 1:31:32, 2012- 1:30:37, 2013- 1:28:44, 2014- 1:29:08. pbs: 3000mW 12:11.27 '14, 5000mW 20:30.04 '14, 10000mW 42:23.37 '14.
She has lived in Spain from the age of 14 and switched from Hungary to Spain 19 June 2008.

SRI LANKA

Governing body: Athletic Association of Sri Lanka, n°33 Torrington Avenue, Colombo 7. Founded 1922.

National Champions 2014: Men: 100m: Himasha Eashan 10.54, 200m: Mohamad Rajaskan 21.43, 400m: Udaya Viraj Weerasinghe 47.37, 800m: Indunil Herath 1:48.69, 1500m: R.K.C.S. Somawardana 3:49.56, 5000m: Lionel Samarajeewa 14:52.99, 10000m: N.M.C.C. Nawasinghe 30:55.49, 3000mSt: R.M.S.Pushpakumara 9:00.40, 110mh: Hasitha Nirmal 14.49, 400mh: Aravinda Chathuranga 51.64, HJ: Manjula Wijesekara 2.13, PV: Ishara Sandaruwan 4.80, LJ: Amila Jayasiri 7.86, TJ: Dulan Niranjan Thilakarathne 15.93, SP: Joy Perera 15.40, DT: Gayan Jayawardana 49.00, HT: Chjarith Kapukotuwa 51.54, JT: Waruna Lakshan Dayarathne 75.48, Dec: Ajith Kumara Karunathilaka 6274. **Women**: 100m: N.C.D. Priyadharshani 11.89, 200m: Heela P. Sujani Buddika 24.81, 400m: Chandrika Rasnayake 52.76, 800m: Gayanthika Abeyrathne 2:04.46, 1500m/3000mSt: Eranga Rasika Dulakshi 4:25.25/10:28.13, 5000m/10000m: Chaturika Hemamali 16:38.09/34:46.37, 100mh: Ireshani Sachiprabha Rajasinghe 14.85, 400mh: T.G.N.D. Wickramesinghe 59.88, HJ: Priyangika Madumanthi 1.79, PV: Anoma Karunawansa 3.32, LJ: N.C.D.P riyadharshani 6.11w, TJ: Dinusha Erandi Rathnasiri 12.33, SP: Kumudumali Fernando 14.40, DT: Sonali Weerasekara 40.87, HT: P.K.A.A. Maduwanthi 39.54, JT: Dilhani Lekamge 55.87, Hep: W.V.L.Sugandi 4029.

SUDAN

Governing body: Sudan Athletic Association, PO Box 13274, 11 111 Khartoum. Founded 1959.

Abubaker KAKI Khamis b. 21 Jun 1989 Elmuglad 1.76m 63kg.
At 800m: OG: '08- sf, '12- 7; WCh: '07- h, '09- sf, '11- 2; WJ: '06- 6, '08- 1; WI: '08- 1, '10- 1; AfG: '07- 1. At 1500m: WY: '05- 3. At 4x400m: AfCh: '08- 2R. Won Pan Arab G 800m & 1500m 2007.
World junior records 800m & 1000m (& indoor 1000m) 2008. SUD records 800m (3), 1000m (2) 2008-10, 1500m 2011.
Progress at 800m, 1500m: 2005- 1:48.43, 3:45.06; 2006- 1:45.78, 3:47.58; 2007- 1:43.90, 3:47.92; 2008- 1:42.69, 3:39.71; 2009- 1:43.09, 3:39.89; 2010- 1:42.23, 2011- 1:43.13, 3:31.76; 2012- 1:43.32, 3:34.34; 2013- 1:46.57i, 2014- 1:44.09. pbs: 1000m 2:13.62 '10, 10k Rd 30:18 '07.
Ran world's fastest 800m (WJR) for five years at Oslo 2008.

SWEDEN

Governing body: Svenska Friidrottsförbundet, Heliosgaten 3, 120 30 Stockholm. Founded 1895.

National Championships first held in 1896 (men), 1927 (women). **2014 Champions**: **Men**: 100m: Odain Rose 10.52, 200m: Nil de Oliveira 20.82, 400m: Johan Wissman 46.89, 800m: Andreas Almgren 1:50.24, 1500m: Rickard Gunnarsson 3:55.94, 5000m/HMar: Ababa Lama 14:24.30/64:47, 10000m: Adil Bouafif 29:15.88, Mar: Daniel Woldu 2:25:50, 3000mSt: Daniel Lundgren 8:51.50, 110mh: Alexander Brorsson 13.86, 400mh: Petter Olson 51.81, HJ: Mehdi Alkhatib 2.16, PV: Alhaji Jeng 5.52, LJ: Michel Tornéus 8.01, TJ: Erik Ehrlin 16.15w, SP: Leif Arrhenius 19.98, DT: Daniel Ståhl 63.69, HT: Markus Johansson 69.80, JT: Gabriel Wallin 76.83, Dec: Fabian Rosenquist 7246, 10,000mW: Anatole Ibáñez 41:54.4, 20kW: Perseus Karlström 1:28:45, 50kW: Anders Hansson 4:06:31. **Women**: 100m: Isabelle Eurenius 12.00, 200m: Irene Ekelund 23.38, 400m: Elin Moraiti 54.01, 800m: Charlotte Schönbeck 2:06.37, 1500m: Viktoria Tegenfeldt 4:30.73, 5000m: Elin Borglund 16:37.37, 10000m: Madeleine Larsson 34:02.68, HMar: Lena Eliasson 75:18, Mar: Isabellah Andersson 2:32:28, 3000mSt: Klara Bodinson 10:08.78, 100mh: Ellinore Hallin 13.35w, 400mh: Frida Persson 58.47, HJ: Emma Green 1.90, PV: Angelica Bengtsson 4.50, LJ: Erica Jarder 6.65, TJ: Jasmin Sabir 13.28, SP: Fanny Roos 16.21, DT: Sofia Larsson 57.58, HT: Tracey Andersson 67.44, JT: Elisabeth Höglund 51.36, Hep: Emma Stenlöf 5519, 5000mW/10kW: Mari Olsson 22:53.8/48:45.

Kim AMB b. 31 Jul 1990 Solna 1.80m 85kg. F Bålsta IK.
At JT: OG: '12- dnq 18; WCh: '13- 10; EC: '12- 7, '14- dnq; WJ: '08- dnq 13; EU23: '11- 4. Swedish champion 2011-13.
Progress at JT: 2007- 55.01, 2008- 69.34, 2009- 66.06, 2010- 77.81, 2011- 80.09, 2012- 81.84, 2013- 84.61, 2014- 84.14. pb PV 3.45 '06.
His father Björn had a best with the old javelin of 62.60 '79 and ssiset Emilia has JT best of 49.34 '12.

Michel TORNÉUS b. 26 May 1986 Botkyrka 1.84m 70kg. Hammarby IF.
At LJ: OG: '12- 4; WCh: '09-11-13: dnq 28/27/19; EC: '10-12-14: 9/3/5; EU23: '07- 10; EJ: '05- 4; WI: '14- 3; EI: '11-13-15: 7/2/1; ET: '11- 2. Won Swedish LJ 2005, 2007-10, 2012-14; TJ 2012.
Swedish long jump record 2012.
Progress at LJ: 2001- 6.48, 2002- 6.74/6.86w, 2003- 7.07, 2004- 7.41, 2005- 7.94, 2006- 7.68, 2007-

7.85, 2008- 7.86, 2009- 8.11, 2010- 8.12/8.21w, 2011- 8.19, 2012- 8.22, 2013- 8.29i/8.00/8.12w, 2014- 8.21i/8.09/8.10w, 2015- 8.30i. pbs: 60m 6.93i '12, 100m 10.71/10.63w '11, 400mh 55.48 '04, HJ 1.99i '05, 1.92 '04; TJ 15.90 '12, Dec 6115 '04. Father came from DR of Congo.

Women

Abeba AREGAWI Gebretsadik b. 5 Jul 1990 Adigrat, Tigray 1.69m 48kg. Hammarby IF.
At 1500m: OG: '12- 5; WCh: '13- 1; EC: '14- 2; WI: 14- 1; EI: '13- 1; ET: '14- 1; won DL 2012-13. At 800m: Af-J: '09- 3. Won ETH 800m 2009.
Records: Swedish 800m 2013, 1500m: Ethiopian 2012, Swedish 2013, European indoor 2014.
Progress at 1500m: 2010- 4:01.96, 2011- 4:01.47i/ 4:10.30, 2012- 3:56.54, 2013- 3:56.60, 2014- 3:57.57. pbs: 800m 1:59.20 '13.
Lived in Stockholm from 2009; granted Swedish citizenship on 28 Jun 2012 and accepted by the IAAF to compete for Sweden from 10 Dec 2012 but from then has lived in Ethiopia and divorced from her husband and coach Henok Weldegebriel. Unbeaten at 1500m in 2013.

Meraf BAHTA Ogbagaber b. 24 Jun 1989 Dekashinay, Eritrea 1.77m 51kg. Hälle IF.
At 5000m: EC: '14- 1; ET: '14- 1. At 3000m: CCp: '14- 2. At 1500m: WJ: '06- 5. World CC: '06- 12J, '07- 6J; Eur CC: '14-3. Won SWE 5000m 2011, 4k & 8k CC 2013-14.
Swedish 5000m record 2014.
Progress at 1500m, 5000m: 2007- 15:56.30, 2008- 4:12.52, 2009- 4:28.93, 2010- 4:22.86, 16:28.77; 2011- 4:19.82, 16:29.08; 2012- 4:14.09, 2013- 4:05.11, 2014- 4:01.34, 14:59.49. pbs: 800m 2:07.19 '08, 3000m 8:57.06 '14, 10k road 32:40 '14.
Came from Eritrea to Sweden as a refugee in 2009; received Swedish citizenship on 23 Dec 2013.

Angelica BENGTSSON b. 8 July 1993 Väckelsång 1.64m 51kg. Hässelby SK.
At PV: OG: '12- dnq 19=, WCh: '13- dnq 16; EC: '12- 10, '14- 5; WJ: '10- 1, '12- 1; WY: '09- 1; EU23: '13- 3; EJ: '11- 1; YthOG: '10- 1; EI: '15- 3. SWE champion 2014.
Pole vault records: Two world youth 2010; four world junior indoors 2011, two world junior outdoor bests, three Swedish 2011-12.
Progress at PV: 2005- 3.10, 2006- 3.40, 2007- 3.90, 2008- 4.12, 2009- 4.37, 2010- 4.47, 2011- 4.63i/4.57. 2012- 4.58, 2013- 4.55, 2014- 4.62i/4.50, 2015- 4.70i. pbs: LJ 5.22i '13, JT 34.67 '14.
Rising Star Awards: IAAF 2010, European Athletics 2012. Her father Glenn had JT pb 67.08 '82, sister Victoria PV 4.00 '09.

Charlotta FOUGBERG b. 19 Jun 1985 Lerum 1.65m 51kg. Ullevi FK.
At 3000mSt: WCh: '13- h; EC: '14- 2; CCp: '14- 5; ET: '14- 1. Won Swedish 5000m 2013; 3000mSt 2010-13, CC 2011.
Two Swedish 3000mSt records 2014.
Progress at 3000mSt: 2007- 10:48.04, 2008- 11:18.68, 2009- 10:59.69, 2010- 10:23.23, 2011- 10:09.05, 2012- 10:22.03, 2013- 9:39.00, 2014- 9:23.96. pbs: 800m 2:08.56 '11, 1500m 4:11.89 '14, 3000m 8:58.56 '14, 5000m 16:04.21 '13, 10k Rd 33:42 '14.

Emma GREEN b. 8 Dec 1984 Bergsjön Göteborg 1.80m 62kg. Örgryte IS.
At HJ: OG: '08- 9, '12- 8; WCh: '05-07-09-11-13: 3/7=/7=/11/5; EC: '06-10-12-14: 11/2/3=/9=; WJ: '02- 9; EU23: '05- 2; EJ: '03- 3; WI: '10- 5=, '14- 5; EI: '05- 8, '13- 3; CCp: '10- 2; ET: '09- 5, '11- 1. At 200m: ECp: '06- 5. Won Swedish HJ 2005, 2007-11, 2013-14 (& 9 indoors); LJ 2005.
Progress at HJ: 1998- 1.66i, 1999- 1.71, 2000- 1.75i/1.73, 2001- 1.82, 2002- 1.82, 2003- 1.86, 2004- 1.90, 2005- 1.97, 2006- 1.96i/1.92, 2007- 1.95, 2008- 1.98i/1.96, 2009- 1.96, 2010- 2.01, 2011- 1.95, 2012- 1.95i/1.93, 2013- 1.97, 2014- 1.97i/1.93. pbs: 60m 7.42i '06, 100m 11.58 '06, 200m 23.02 '06, 400m 54.95 '06, LJ 6.41 '05, TJ 13.69i '06, 13.39 '07.
Her uncle Göte Green ran 47.9 for 400m in 1977. Married coach Yannick Tregaro in March 2011, but divorced in 2014.

Eruca JARDER b. 2 Apr 1986 Stockholm 1.73m 59 kg. Spårvägens FK. Law student
At LJ: WCh: '13- 10; EC: '14 - 8; EU23: '07- dnq 18; WI: '14- 8; EI: ' 13- 3. SWE champion 2007, 2012-14.
Progress at LJ: 2000- 5.12i, 2005- 5.52/5.59w, 2006- 6.04, 2007- 6.18, 2008- 6.26, 2009- 6.21i/6.15, 2010- 6.33, 2011- 6.42/6.43w, 2012- 6.48, 2013- 6.71i/6.66, 2014- 6.68/6.84w. pbs: 60m 7.46i '14, 100m 11.75 '11, 200m 25.20/25.19w '07, HJ 1.78i '07, 1.76 '96; TJ 12.90 '14.

Ebba JUNGMARK b. 10 Mar 1987 Onsala 1.79m 57 kg. Mölndals AIK. Was at Washington State University, USA.
At HJ: OG: '12- dnq 20=; WCh: '07/11- dnq 23/17; EC: '10- dnq 17, '12- 10; WJ: '06- 5; EU23: '07- 3; EJ: '05- 12; WI: '12- 2=; EI: '11- 3, '13- 2. Won NCAA indoors 2008.
Progress at HJ: 2000- 1.50, 2001- 1.60, 2002- 1.73, 2003- 1.78, 2004- 1.77i/1.75, 2005- 1.80, 2006- 1.85i/1.84, 2007- 1.92, 2008- 1.89i/1.84, 2009- 1.86, 2010- 1.90, 2011- 1.96i/1.94, 2012- 1.95i/1.91, 2013- 1.96i/1.89, 2014- 1.84. pbs: LJ 5.59i '09, TJ 12.98 '12, Pen 3642i '09.

SWITZERLAND

Governing body: Schweizerischer Leichtathletikverband (SLV), Haus des Sports, Postfach 606, 3000 Bern 22. Formed 1905 as Athletischer Ausschuss des Schweizerischen Fussball-Verbandes.

National Championships first held in 1906 (men), 1934 (women). **2014 Champions**: **Men**: 100m: Pascal Mancini 10.30, 200m: Alex Wilson 20.96, 400m: Silvan Lutz 47.20, 800m: Hugo Santacruz 1:52.87, 1500m: Christoph Graf 3:57.86,

5000m: Andreas Kempf 14:28.41, 10000m: Tadesse Abraham 29:05.62, HMar: Adrian Lehmann 67:41, Mar: Patrick Wieser 2:18:14, 3000mSt: Marco Kern 9:25.10, 110mh: Tobias Furer 13.82, 400mh: Kariem Hussein 49.24, HJ: Roman Sieber 2.06, PV: Marquis Richards 5.40, LJ: Yves Zellweger 7.49, TJ: Andreas Graber 16.21, SP: Gregori Ott 17.33, DT: Lukas Jost 52.28, HT: Martim Bingisser 65.10, JT: Roland Thalmann 65.80, Dec: Christian Loosli 7317, 20kW: Roby Ponzio 1:58:52. **Women**: 100m/200m: Mujinga Kambundji 11.33/23.26, 400m: Léa Sprunger 54.12, 800m: Pamela Märzendorfer 2:12.57, 1500m: Fabienne Schlumpf 4:22.89, 5000m/10000m: Nicola Spirig 16:18.96/34:01.32, HMar: Martina Tresch 79:14, Mar: Ursula Spielmann-Jeitziner 2:41:55., 3000mSt: Martina Tresch 10:35.19, 100mh: Noemi Zbären 12.92, 400mh: Valentina Arrieta 57.39, HJ: Salome Lang 1.83, PV: Anna Katharina Schmid 4.20, LJ: Irène Pusterla 6.52, TJ: Barbara Leuthard 12.99, SP: Jasmin Lukas 13.91, DT: Elisabeth Graf 47.66, HT: Nicole Zihlmann 61.62, JT: Nathalie Meier 52.47, Hep: Elodie Jakob 5357, 5000mW/10kW/20kW: Laura Polli 22:56.9/48:21/1:39:35.

Kariem HUSSEIN b. 1 Apr 1989 Münsterlingen 1.90m 77kg. TV Amriswil
At 400mh: EC: '12- sf, '14- 1; EU23: '11- sf; CCp: '14- 2; Swiss champion 2011-14.
Swiss 300mh record 2014.
Progress at 400mh: 2009- 52.33, 2010- 51.64, 2011- 51.09, 2012- 49.61, 2013- 49.78, 2014- 48.47. pbs: 60mh 8.14i '11, 110mh 14.51 '11, 300mh 35.61 '14.
Successive pbs at end of 2014 from 49.08 to 48.96 EC, 48.70 WK, 48.47 CCp. Father Ehab came from Egypt to Switzerland in the early 1980s.

TADJIKISTAN

Governing body: Athletics Federation of Tadjikistan, Rudski Avenue 62, Dushanbe 734025. Founded 1932.

Dilshod NAZAROV b. 6 May 1982 Dushanbe 1.87m 115kg.
At HT: OG: '08- 11, '12- 10; WCh: '05-07-09-11-13: dnq 15/dnq 21/11/10/5; WJ: '98- dnq 15, '00- 5, AsiG: '98-02-06-10-14: 7/9/1/1/1; AsiC: '03-05-07-09-13: 3/2/2/1/1; CCp: '10- 2, '14- 4. Won Asi-J 1999, 2001, C.Asian 2003.
Progress at HT: 1998- 63.91, 1999- 63,56, 2000- 66.50, 2001- 68.08, 2002- 69.86, 2003- 75.56, 2004- 76.58, 2005- 77.63, 2006- 74.43, 2007- 78.89, 2008- 79.05, 2009- 79.28, 2010- 80.11, 2011- 80.30, 2012- 77.70, 2013- 80.71, 2014- 80.62.
President of national federation.

TRINIDAD & TOBAGO

Governing body: National Association of Athletics Administrations of Trinidad & Tobago, PO Box 605, Port of Spain, Trinidad. Founded 1945, reformed 1971.

National Champions 2014: **Men**: 100m: Richard Thompson 9.82, 200m: Lalonde Gordon 20.38, 400m: Renny Quow 45.08, 800m: Jamaal James 1:48.57, 1500m: George Smith 4:00.64, 5000m: Jules LaRode 15:59.05, 110mh: Wayne Davis 13.21; 400m: Emanuel Mayers 49.57, HJ: Omari Benoit 2.00, PV: Mickey Ruben 2.60, LJ: Kyron Blaise 7.28, TJ: Elton Walcott 15.75, SP: Akeem Stewart 17.76, DT: Quincy Wilson 54.93, HT: Gabriel Guerra 20.09, JT: Shakiel Waithe 72.75. **Women**: 100m/200m: Michelle-Lee Ahye 10.88/22.95, 400m: Janeil Bellille 51.83, 800m: Alena Brooks 2:08.32, 1500m: Dawnel Collymore 4:48.31, 5000m: April Francis 19:46.26, 100mh: Deborah John 13.36, HJ: Deandra Daniel 1.75, LJ/TJ: Ayanna Alexander 5.87/12.86, SP: Cleopatra Borel 18.63, DT: Chelsea James 41.43, HT: Tamara Louis 29.89, JT: Darlene Lewis 40.54, Hep: Ayana Glasgow 4062.

Keston BLEDMAN b. 8 Mar 1988 San Fernando 1.83m 75kg. Simplex.
At 100m/4x100mR: OG: '08- 2R, '12- sf/3R; WCh: '07- qf, '09- res(2)R, '11/13- sf; CG: '14- sf/3R; WJ: '06- 7 (h 200m); WY: '05- 3; PAm: '07- sf; CAG: '10- 7/1R. Won PAm-J 2007, CAC 2011, TTO 2012-13.
Progress at 100m: 2005- 10.48, 2006- 10.32, 2007- 10.14/10.05w, 2008- 10.18, 2009- 10.10/10.0, 2010- 10.01/9.93w, 2011- 9.93, 2012- 9.86/9.85w, 2013- 10.02/9.86w, 2014- 10.00. pbs: 60m 6.62i '12, 200m 20.73 '08.

Jehue GORDON b. 15 Dec 1991 Port of Spain 1.90m 80kg. adidas. Sports management student at University of West Indies, Trinidad.
At 400mh: OG: '12- 6; WCh: '09- 4, '11- sf, '13- 1; CG: '14- 2/res 3R; WJ: '08- sf, '10- 1; PAm-J: '09- 2. TTO champion 2008-11, 2013.
Three TTO 400mh records 2009-13.
Progress at 400mh: 2008- 51.39, 2009- 48.26, 2010- 48.47, 2011- 48.66, 2012- 47.96, 2013- 47.69, 2014- 48.75. pbs: 200m 21.26 '14, 400m 46.43 '10, 600m 1:20.65 '14, 800m 1:53.32 '10, 110mh 13.82 '12, 200mhSt 23.00 '12.

Lalonde GORDON b. 25 Nov 1988 Lowlands, Tobago 1.88m 83kg. Tigers. Studied at Mohawk Valley CC.
At 400m/4x400mR: OG: '12- 3/3R; CG: '10- sf, '14- 3/3R; CAG: '10- 3R; WI: '12- 3R, '14- 5. At 200m: WCh: '13- sf. Won TTO 200m 2013-14, 400m 2012.
Progress at 400m: 2009- 49.47, 2010- 46.33, 2011- 45.51, 2012- 44.52, 2013- 45.67, 2014- 44.78. pbs: 100m 10.45 '12, 200m 20.26 '13, 300m 32.47i '14 (CAC record), 32.5+ '12.
Moved with his family to New York at the age of seven, and still lives there.

Deon LENDORE b. 28 Oct 1992 Arima 1.79m 75kg. Student at Texas A&M University, USA.
At 400m/4x400mR: OG: '12- h/3R; WCh: '13- sf; WJ: '10- sf; WY: '09- sf. TTO champion 2013,

NCAA 2014.
Progress at 400m: 2009- 47.61, 2010- 46.59, 2011- 46.50, 2012- 45.13, 2013- 44.94, 2014- 44.36. pb 200m 20.68i '14, 21.20 '11.

Renny QUOW b. 25 Aug 1987 Morvant 1.70m 66kg. Zenith. Was at Florida State University and South Plains College (Texas).
At 400m/4x400mR: OG: '08- 7; WCh: '05-07-09-11-13: hR/h/3/sf/6R; CG: '14- dnf/3R; WJ: '04- sf, '06- 1; PAm: '07- sf; CAG: '06- sf/2R; WI: '12- 3R. Won CAC 2008, 2011; CAC-J 2004, 2006; TTO 2007-09, 2011, 2014.
Progress at 400m: 2004- 46.60, 2005- 45.82, 2006- 45.74, 2007- 45.35, 2008- 44.82, 2009- 44.53, 2010- 45.10, 2011- 44.84, 2012- 45.48, 2013- 45.65, 2014- 45.08. pbs: 200m 20.39 '14, 300m 32.36 '14, 500m 1:01.90i '14, 600y 1:08.04i '14.
One of triplets with Ronald and Ryan.

Richard THOMPSON b. 7 Jun 1985 Cascade 1.87m 79kg. Memphis. Was at Louisiana State University.
At 100m: OG: '08- 2/2R, '12- 6/3R; WCh: '07- qf, '09- 5/2R, '11/13- sf; CG: '14- sf/3R; PAm: '07- h; CCp: '14- 8/1R. Won TTO 100m 2009-11, 2014; 200m 2010; NCAC 100m 2007, NCAA 100m & 60m indoor 2008.
Progress at 100m, 200m: 2004- 10.65, 2005- 10.47, 21.73; 2006- 10.27/10.26w, 21.24; 2007- 10.09/ 9.95w, 20.90; 2008- 9.89, 20.18; 2009- 9.93, 20.65; 2010- 10.01/9.89w, 20.37; 2011- 9.85, 20.85; 2012- 9.96, 20.80; 2013- 10.14/9.91w, 21.06; 2014- 9.82/ 9.74w, 20.81/20.63w. pbs: 60m 6.45+ '09, 6.51i '08.

Keshorn WALCOTT b. 2 Apr 1993 Toco 1.88m 90kg. Toco tafac.
At JT: OG: '12- 1; WCh: '13- dnq 19; CG: '14- 2; WJ: '10- dnq, '12- 1; WY: '09- dnq 13; PAm: '11- 7; CCp: '14- 3. Won CAC-J 2010, 2012; TTO 2012.
Six TTO javelin records 2012-14, eight CAC junior 2011-12.
Progress at JT: 2009- 60.02, 2010- 67.01, 2011- 75.77A, 2012- 84.58, 2013- 84.39, 2014- 85.77. pb TJ 14.28 '10.
First Caribbean Olympic champion and youngest ever Olympic champion in throwing events. Won IAAF Rising Star Award 2012. Elder brother Elton TJ pb 16.43/16.51w '11 & 4 WY '09, aunt Anna Lee Walcott Hep pb 5224 '00.

Women

Michelle-Lee AHYE b. 10 Apr 1992 Port of Spain 1.68m 59kg.
At 100m/(200m): OG: '12- sf; WCh: '11- sf, '13- sf/h; CG: '14- sf; WY: '07- qf; CCp: '14- 2/1R; PAm-J: '11- 1. At 60m: WI: '14- 6. TTO champion 100m & 200m 2014.
Progress at 100m: 2006- 11.94, 2007- 11.76/11.63w, 2008- 11.48, 2009- 11.69, 2010- 11.32, 2011- 11.20/11.15w, 2012- 11.19, 2013- 11.06, 2014- 10.85. pbs: 50m 6.33i '13, 60m 7.10i '14, 200m 22.77 '14.
Unbeaten Outdoors in 2014 up to an injury in Luzern in July.

Kelly-Ann BAPTISTE b. 14 Oct 1986 Plymouth, Tobago 1.60m 54kg. Zenith. Studied psychology at Louisiana State University.
At 100m/(200m): OG: '08- qf, '12- 6; WCh: '05- qf, '09: sf/sf, '11- 3; WJ: '02- sf, '04- (4); WY: '03- 3; PAm: '03- h; CCp: '10- 1/1R. Won NCAA 100m & indoor 60m 2008, TTO 100m 2005-06, 2008-10, 2012-13; 200m 2005, 2013.
TTO records: 100m (6) 2005-14, 200m (5) 2005-13.
Progress at 100m, 200m: 2002- 11.71, 24.03; 2003- 11.48, 23.22; 2004- 11.40, 23.41/22.99w; 2005- 11.17/11.04w, 22.93; 2006- 11.08, 22.73; 2007- 11.22, 22.90i/22.95; 2008- 11.06/10.97w, 22.67; 2009- 10.94/10.91w, 22.60; 2010- 10.84, 22.78/ 22.58w; 2011- 10.90, 2012- 10.86, 22.33w; 2013- 10.83, 22.36. pbs: 55m 6.73i '06, 60m 7.13i '08.
She was withdrawn from 2013 World Champs team after failing a drugs test and was given a 2-year ban by the IAAF, but that was withdrawn by her governing body in August 2014 and after the IAAF appealed this to the CAS the suspension was lifted.

Cleopatra BOREL b. 3 Oct 1979 Port of Spain 1.68m 93kg. Was at University of Maryland; assistant coach at Virginia Tech University.
At SP: OG: '04- 9, '08- dnq 17, '12- 12; WCh: '05-07-09-13: dnq 17/18/13/14, '11- 13; CG: '02-06-10-14: 4/3/2/2; PAm: '03- 6, '07- 3, '11- 2; CAG: '06-10-14: 3/1/1; CCp: '14- 5; WI: '04-06-08: dnq 11/8/7. Won CAC 2008, 2011; TTO 2002, 2004, 2006-10, 2012, 2014.
Eight TTO records at shot 2004-11.
Progress at SP: 2000- 14.64i, 2001- 16.44, 2002- 17.50i/16.90, 2003- 17.95i/17.79, 2004- 19.48i/ 18.90, 2005- 18.44, 2006- 18.81, 2007- 18.91, 2008- 18.87, 2009- 18.52, 2010- 19.30, 2011- 19.42, 2012- 18.82, 2013- 17.84, 2014- 19.13. pb HT 51.28 '01.
Formerly competed under married name Borel-Brown.

TUNISIA

Governing body: Fédération Tunisienne d'Athlétisme, B.P. 264, Cité Mahrajane 1082, Tunis. Founded 1957.

Women

Habiba GHRIBI–Boudraa b. 9 Apr 1984 Kairouan 1.70m 57kg. Entente Franconville Cesame Va, FRA.
At 3000mSt: OG: '08- 13, '12- 1; WCh: '05- h, '09- 6, '11- 2; AfCh: '06- 2, '14- 6 (6 1500m). At 5000m: AfCh: '02- 11. Won FRA 1500m 2014
Tunisian records: 1500m 2014, 3000m (3) 2008-13, 3000mSt (9) 2005-12.
Progress at 3000mSt: 2005- 9:51.49, 2006- 10:14.36, 2007- 9:50.04, 2008- 9:25.50, 2009- 9:12.52, 2011- 9:11.97, 2012- 9:08.37, 2014- 9:15.23. pbs: 1500m 4:06.38 '14, 3000m 8:49.5+ '13, 5000m 16:12.9 '03, 10000m 35:03.83 '05, 10kRd 33:30 '04.
Missed 2010 season after toe surgery. Won first Olympic medal for a woman from Tunisia.

TURKEY

Governing body: Türkiye Atletizm Federasyonu, 19 Mayis Spor Kompleksi, Ulus-Ankara. Founded 1922.

National Champions 2014: **Men**: 100m/200m: Izzet Safer 10.54/21.32, 400m: Yavuz Can 46.56, 800m: Levent Ates 1:48.79, 1500m/3000m: Kemal Koyuncu 3:45.96/8:01.18, 5000m: Cihat Ulus 14:04.41, 10000m: Halil Akkas 28:44.49, Mar: Fatih Bilgic 2:19:57, 3000mSt: Hakan Duvar 8:35.66, 110mh: Oben Mumcuoglu 15.86, 400mh: Yasmani Copello 50.95, HJ: Furkan Göksoy 1.95, PV: Burak Yilmaz 4.80, LJ: Alper Kulaksiz 7.84, TJ: Musa Tüzen 15.93, SP: Hüseyin Atici 18.90, DT: Talat Erdogan 50.92, HT: Özkan Baltaci 68.59, JT: Aykut Tanriverdi 65.51, Dec: Ramazan Can 6338, 10kW: Sahin Senduncu 42:11, 20kW: Serkan Dogan 1:30:48. **Women**: 100m/200m: Nimet Karakus 11.96/24.68, 400m: Meryem Kasap 54.65, 800m: Demet Dinc 2:11.06, 1500m: Gamze Bulut 4:07.79, 3000m/5000m: Fatma Haciköylü 9:47.00/17:07.23, 10000m: Ümmü Kiraz 33:44.87, Mar: Elvan Abeylegeeese 2:32:15, 3000mSt: Elif Karabulut 9:58.28, 100mh: Ilkay Avci 14.19, 400mh: Emel Sanli 58.28, HJ: Burcu Yüksel 1.82, PV: Buse Arikasan 3.90, LJ/TJ: Sevim Serbest-Sinmez 6.20w/13.19, SP: Dilek Özada 14.39, DT: Elcin Kaya 49.73, HT: Göksunur Cömertoglu 47.16, JT: Selema Durna 46.12, Hep: Beyza Tilki 4444, 10kW: Hülya Fansa 59:47, 20kW: Semiha Özdemir-Mutlu 1:44:14.

Tarik Langat AKDAG (ex Patrick Kipkurui LANGAT) b. 16 Jun 1988 Nandi, Kenya 1.76m 60kg. ENKA.
At 3000mSt: OG: '12- 9; WCh: '13- h; EC: '12- 2, '14- 8; ET: '13- 1.
Turkish 3000m steeplechase record 2012.
Progress at 3000mSt: 2004- 8:53.6A, 2005- 8:40.3A, 2006- 8:37.4A, 2007- 8:46.8A, 2008- 8:19.13, 2009- 8:21.38, 2010- 8:09.12, 2011- 8:08.59, 2012- 8:17.85, 2013- 8:20.08, 2014- 8:26.45. pbs: 3000m 7:47.68 '10, 2M 8:26.96 '10, 5000m 13:45.21A '06, 10000m 29:03.1 '06.
Switched from Kenya to Turkey 22 Jun 2011.

Polat Kemboi ARIKAN (ex Paul KEMBOI) b. 12 Dec 1990 Cheptirte, Kenya 1.73m 62kg.
At (5000m)/10000m: OG: '12- h/9; WCh: '13- dnf; EC: '12- 3/1, '14- 4; ECp: '12- 1, '14- 1; won Med G 2013. At 3000m: EI: '13- 10. Eur CC: '12-13-14: 7/2/1. World HMar: 14- 16, CC: '15- 22.
Turkish records 3000m 2012, 5000m 2011, HMar 2014.
Progress at 5000m, 10000m: 2006- 14:23.4A, 2009- 13:24.25, 2010- 13:18.12, 2011- 13:05.98, 2012- 13:12.55i/13:27.21, 27:38.81; 2013- 28:17.26, 2014- 28:11.11. pbs: 1500m 3:47.05 '12, 3000m 7:42.31 '12, HMar 61:22 '14.
Became a Turkish citizen 9 Jun 2011, originally with 2-year wait for international eligibility, but waiting period ended in February 2012.

Ali KAYA b. 20 Apr 1994 Eldoret, Kenya. Ex Stanley Kiprotich KEN.
At 5000m/(10000m): EC: '14- 9/3; ECp: '14- 3/2; EJ: '13- 1/1; CCp: '14- 5. At 3000m: EI: '15- 1. Eur CC: '13-1J, '14: 2.
Turkish half marathon record 2015.
Progress at 5000m, 10000m: 2013- 13:31.39, 28:31.16; 2014- 13:34.83, 28:08.72. pbs: 3000m 7:38.42i '15, 7:58.76 '13; HMar 61:21 '15.
Became a Turkish citizen on 6 Jun 2013.

Ilham Tanui ÖZBILEN (formerly William Biwott Tanui KEN) b. 5 Mar 1990 Kocholwo, Keiyo, Kenya 1.77m 61kg. ENKA.
At 1500m: OG: '12- 8; WCh: '13- sf; EC: '12- 6, '14- h; WI: '12- 2, '14- 4; EI: '13- 2, '15- 2; ET: '13- 1 (2 800m); won WAF 2009, MedG 2013 (& 800m).
Records: World 4x1500m & world junior 1M 2009; Turkish 800m (6), 1000m, 1500m (2), 1M (2) 2011-14.
Progress at 800m, 1500m: 2008- 3:42.5A, 2009- 3:31.70, 2010- 3:33.67, 2011- 1:44.25, 3:31.37; 2012- 3:33.32, 2013- 1:44.00, 3:31.30 ; 2014- 1:47.38, 3:32.09. pbs: 1000m 2:15.08 '14, 1M 3:49.29 '09, 3000m 7:50.61i '12.
Became a Turkish citizen on 9 Jun 2011.

Women

Elvan ABEYLEGESSE b. 11 Sep 1982 Addis Ababa, Ethiopia 1.59m 40kg. ENKA.
At 5000m/(10000m): OG: '04- 12 (8 1500m), '08- 2/2; WCh: '01- h, '03- 5, '07- 5/2, '09- (dnf); EC: '02- 7, '06- 3/dnf, '10- 1/1; WJ: '00- 6 (6 1500m); WY: '99- (5 3000m); EU23: '03- 1; EJ: '99- 2, '01- 1 (1 3000m); CCp: '10- 4; ECp: '06-07-08: (1/1/1). At Mar: EC: '14- 5. Won WAF 5000m 2003-04, Med G 10000m 2009. World CC: '99- 9J; Eur CC: '00-01-02-03: 3J/1J/3/2. Won TUR Mar 2013-14.
Records: World 5000m 2004, European 10000m 2008. Turkish 2000m 2003, 3000m 2002, 5000m 2004, 10000m 2006 & 2008, HMar 2010.
Progress at 1500m, 5000m, 10000m: 1999- 4:24.1, 16:06.40; 2000- 4:18.7, 16:33.77; 2001- 4:11.31, 15:21.12, 33:29.20; 2002- 4:11.00, 15:00.49; 2003- 4:07.25, 14:53.56; 2004- 3:58.28, 14:24.68; 2005- 15:08.59; 2006- 4:11.61, 14:59.29, 30:21.67; 2007- 15:00.88, 31:25.15; 2008- 14:58.79, 29:56.34; 2009- 15:30.47, 31:51.98; 2010- 4:15.23, 14:31.52, 31:10.23; 2013- 32:59.30. pbs: 800m 2:07.10 '04, 2000m 5:33.83 '03, 3000m 8:31.94 '02; Rd: 15k 49:29 '12, HMar 67:07 '10, Mar 2:29:30 '13.
Known as Hewan Abeye ETH, then Elvan Can on move to Turkey. She became the first Turkish athlete to set a world record in 2004 and the first Turkish woman to win an Olympic medal in 2008. Married Semeneh Debelie ETH on 25 Feb 2011, their daughter Arsema was born on 28 July 2011.

UGANDA

Governing body: Uganda Athletics Federation,

PO Box 22726, Kampala. Founded 1925.

Jacob ARAPTANY b. 11 Feb 1992 Kaproron 1.68m 58kg.
At 3000mSt: OG: '12- h; WCh: '11- 6, '13- 12; WJ: '10- 3; AfG: '11- 5; AfCh: '12- 8; Af-J: '11- 3. World CC: '11- 9J.
Progress at 3000mSt: 2009- 8:26.4A, 2010- 8:28.14, 2011- 8:15.72A, 2012- 8:14.48, 2013- 8:16.43, 2014- 8:20.84. pbs: 800m 1:49.95A '11, 1500m 3:36.16A '11, 2000mSt 5:28.48 '11.

Benjamin KIPLAGAT b. 4 Mar 1989 Magoro 1.86m 61kg.
At 3000mSt: OG: '08- 9, '12- dq; WCh: '07-09-11-13: h/11/10/14; CG: '10- 4; WJ: '06- 6, '08- 2; AfG: '07- 7; AfCh: '10- 5, '12- 3; CCp: '10- 4. World CC: '07- 5J, '08- 4J.
Six Ugandan 3000mSt records 2007-10.
Progress at 3000mSt: 2005- 8:39.1A, 2006- 8:34.14, 2007- 8:21.73, 2008- 8:14.29, 2009- 8:12.98, 2010- 8:03.81, 2011- 8:08.43, 2012- 8:17.55, 2013- 8:13.07, 2014- 8:26.05. pbs: 1500m 3:38.86 '09, 3000m 7:46.50 '10, 5000m 13:22.67 '07, 10000m 29:03.1 '06.

Stephen KIPROTICH b. 27 Feb 1989 Kapchorwa 1.72m 56kg.
At Mar: OG: '12- 1; WCh: '11- 9, '13- 1. At 5000m: WCh: '07- h. At 10000m: WJ: '08- 5, AfCh: '10- 6, World CC: '08- 12J, '11- 6; AfrCC: '11- 2.
Ugandan marathon records 2011 & 2015.
Progress at Mar: 2011- 2:07:20, 2012- 2:07:50, 2013- 2:08:05, 2014- 2:11:37, 2015- 2:06:33. Pbs: 5000m 13:23.70 '08, 10000m 27:58.03 '10, HMar 61:15 '13, 3000mSt 8:26.66 '10.
Won Enschede marathon on debut 2011. Became the second man ever to win Olympic and World titles at marathon. 2nd Tokyo 2015.

Moses KIPSIRO b. 2 Sep 1986 Chesimat 1.74m 59kg.
At 5000m(/10000m): OG: '08- 4, '12- 15/10; WCh: '05- h, '07- 3, '09- 4, '13- (13); CG: '06- 7, '10- 1/1, '14- 8/1; AfG: '07- 1, '11- 1; Af Ch: '06- 3/1, '10- 4/2; CCp: '10- 2 (2 3000m). At 3000m: WI: '12- 7. World CC: '03-05-08-09-10-11-13: 18J/20J/13/2/3/11/4.
Ugandan records: 3000m (4) 2005-09, 5000m 2007.
Progress at 5000m: 2005- 13:13.81, 2006- 13:01.88, 28:03.46; 2007- 12:50.72, 2008- 12:54.70, 2009- 12:59.27, 2010- 13:00.15, 27:33.37A; 2011- 13:09.17, 2012- 13:00.68, 27:04.48; 2013- 13:11.56, 27:44.53; 2014- 13:28.23, 27:56.11. pbs: 1500m 3:37.6 '08, 2000m 5:00.66+ '11, 3000m 7:30.95 '09, 2M 8:08.16i '12, HMar 63:15A '14.
Sealed brilliant 5k/10k double at 2010 CG with last laps of 53.01 and 53.96.

UKRAINE

Governing body: Ukrainian Athletic Federation, P.O. Box 607, Kiev 01019. Founded 1991. **National Champions 2014**: **Men**: 100m: Igor Bodrov 10.30, 200m: Sergiy Smelyk 20.35, 400m: Vitaliy Butrym 46.23, 800m: Viktor Tyumentsev 1:48.10, 1500m: Stanislav Maslov 3:38.61, 3000m/5000m: Ivan Strebkov 7:59.51/ 14:08.73, 10000m: Dmytro Lashin 28:59.20, HMar/ Mar: Roman Romanenko 65:50/2:14:50, 3000mSt: Vadym Slobodenyuk 8:29.82, 110mh: Artem Shamatryn 14.38, 400mh: Denys Nechyporenko 50.08, HJ: Dmytro Yakovenko 2.20, PV: Vladyslav Revenko 5.50, LJ: Taras Neledva 7.63, TJ: Viktor Yastrebov 16.18, SP: Viktor Samolyuk 18.23, DT: Oleksiy Semenov 62.49, HT: Yevgen Vynogradov 72.43, JT: Dmytro Kosynskyy 78.04, Dec: Vasyl Ivanytskyy 7525, 20kW: Andriy Kovenko 1:22:00, 50kW: Sergiy Budza 3:48:50. **Women**: 100m/200m: Nataliya Pogrebnyak 11.27/23.02, 400m: Hrystyna Stuy 51.58, 800m: Olena Sidorska 2:03.44, 1500m: Anna Mishchenko 4:11.25, 3000m: Yuliya Kutah 9:18.74, 5000m: Anna Nosenko 15:58.21, 10000m: Olha Skrypak 33:09.56, HMar: Viktoriya Pogoryelska 72:38, Mar: Olena Biloshchuk-Popova 2:40:07, 3000mSt: Mariya Shatalova 10:03.01, 100mh: Anna Plotitsyna 13.13, 400mh: Anna Titimets 56.30, HJ: Oksana Okunyeva 1.89, PV: Hanna Sheleh 4.20, LJ: Oksana Zubkovska 6.61, TJ: Ruslana Tsyhotska 14.20w, SP: Olga Holodnaya 17.51, DT: Natalya Semenova 63.33, HT: Anna Skydan 70.11, JT: Hanna Hatsko-Fedusova 67.29, Hep: Daryna Sloboda 5259, 20kW: Inna Kashyna 1:34:51.

Ivan BANZERUK b. 9 Feb 1990 1.77m 65kg. Volinskaya, Volgu.
At 50kW: EC: '14- 5; WCp: '14- 5; WCp: '14- 9; ECp: '13- 6.
Progress at 50kW: 2010- 4:21:57, 2011- 4:06:52, 2012- 3:56:20, 2013- 3:47:35, 2014- 3:44:49. pbs: 5000mW 19:39.05 '14, 10000mW 40:37.5 '14, 20kW: 1:23:42 '13, 35kW 2:30:58 '14.

Bohdan BONDARENKO b. 30 Aug 1989 Kharkiv 1.97m 80kg.
At HJ: OG: '12- 7; WCh: '11- dnq 15=, '13- 1; EC: '12- 11, '14- 1; WJ: '06- 3, '08- 1; EU23: '11- 1; EJ: '07- 9; WUG: '11- 1, CCp: '14- 1; ET: '13- 1. Won DL 2013.
Two UKR high jump records 2013-14.
Progress at HJ: 2005- 2.15, 2006- 2.26, 2007- 2.25i/2.19, 2008- 2.26, 2009- 2.27/2.15, 2010- 2.10, 2011- 2.30, 2012- 2.31, 2013- 2.41, 2014- 2.42.
His father Viktor had decathlon pb of 7480 '87.

Ruslan DMYTRENKO b. 22 Mar 1986 Kyiv 1.80m 62kg. Donetsk.
At 20kW: WCh: '09-11-13: 33/6/7; EC: '10- 11, '14- 4; WCp: '12- 4, '14- 1; EU23: '07- 6; ECp: '13- 5; WUG: '13- 2; Won IAAF Race Walking Challenge 2014; UKR champion 2009, 2011. At 10000m/10kW: EJ: '05- 11; ECp: '05- 6J.
UKR 20k walk record 2014 (and uofficial 10,000mW).
Progress at 20kW: 2006- 1:27:16, 2007- 1:23:31, 2008- 1:25:26, 2009- 1:21:21, 2010- 1:21:54, 2011- 1:21:31, 2012- 1:20:17, 2013- 1:20:38, 2014- 1:18:37.

pbs: 5000mW 18:21.76i '14, 10000mW 39:26.90i '12, 39:33.91 '10, 38:50R '14.

Igor HLAVAN b. 25 Sep 1990 Nazarivka, Kirovograd 1.72m 62kg.
At 20kW: WCp: '14- 7. At 50kW: OG: '12- 18; WCh: '13- 4; EC: '14- 6; WCp: '12- 12; ECp: '13- 4. Won UKR 35kW 2013.
UKR 50km walk record 2013.
Progress at 50kW: 2010- 4:08:08, 2011- 4:03:18, 2012- 3:48:07, 2013- 3:40:39, 2014- 3:45:08. pbs: 5000mW 19:11.87 '14, 10000mW 39:15.1 '14, 20kW 1:19:59 '14, 35k 2:31:15 '13.

Oleksiy KASYANOV b. 26 Aug 1985 Stakhanov, Lugansk 1.91m 84kg. Spartak Zaporozhye.
At Dec: OG: '08- 7, '12- 7; WCh: '09- 4, '11- 12, '13- dnf; EC: '10-12-14: dnf/2/8; EU23: '07- 4; WUG: '07- 4; ECp: '09- 3. UKR champion 2008. At Hep: WI: '10-12-14: 6/2/5; EI: '09- 2.
Progress at Dec: 2006- 7599, 2007- 7964, 2008- 8238, 2009- 8479, 2010- 8381, 2011- 8251, 2012- 8312, 2014- 8231. pbs: 60m 6.83i '09, 100m 10.50 '11, 400m 47.46 '08, 1000m 2:39.44i '14, 1500m 4:22.27 '08, 60mh 7.85i '13, 110mh 14.01 '12, HJ 2.08i 14, 2.05 '09; PV 4.82 '09, LJ 8.04i/7.97 '10, SP 15.72 '09, DT 51.95 '10, JT 55.84 '07, Hep 6254i '10.
Won Talence decathlon 2009. Married Hanna Melnychenko (qv) on 18 Oct 2014

Andriy PROTSENKO b. 20 May 1988 Kherson 1.94m 65kg. Khersonskaya. Biotechnology graduate.
At HJ: OG: '12- 9; WCh: '09/11/13- dnq 25/27/23=; EC: '10-12: dnq 17/13=, '14- 2; EU23: '09- 3; EJ: '07- 2; EI: '15- 6; WUG: '13- 2; ET: '10- 3, '14- 1. UKR champion 2012.
Progress at HJ: 2005- 2.10, 2006- 2.18i/2.10, 2007- 2.21, 2008- 2.30, 2009- 2.25, 2010- 2.25, 2011- 2.31, 2012- 2.31, 2013- 2.32, 2014- 2.40.

Oleksandr PYATNYTSYA b. 14 Jul 1985 Dnipropetrovsk 1.86m 90kg.
At JT: OG: '12- 2; WCh: '09/11- dnq 25/27/29; EC: '10-12-14: 4/5/dnq 21; EU23: '07- 3. UKR champion 2009, 2011.
UKR javelin records 2010 & 2012.
Progress at JT: 2005- 65.63, 2006- 72.20, 2007- 76.28, 2008- 78.54, 2009- 81.96, 2010- 84.11, 2011- 82.61, 2012- 86.12, 2013- 77.46, 2014- 81.10.

Oleksiy SOKYRSKYY b. 16 Mar 1985 Gorlivka 1.85m 108kg. Krim Sakhi.
At HT: OG: '12- 4; WCh: '09-11: dnq 22/17; EC: '10- 6, '12- nt; WJ: '04- 8, EU23: '07- 6; WUG: '09- 3; ET: '11- 3. UKR champion 2010-11.
Progress at HT: 2005- 70.23, 2006- 71.95, 2007- 73.44, 2008- 75.54, 2009- 76.50, 2010- 76.62, 2011- 78.33, 2012- 78.91, 2013- 77.38, 2014- 77.86.

Women

Alina FYODOROVA b. 13 Jul 1989 Kniazhychi 1.74m 63kg.
At Hep: WCh: '11- 21; WJ: '08- 18; EU23: '11- 6; ECp: 11- 5. At Pen: WI: '14- 3; WI: '13- 8.
Progress at Hep: 2006- 5193, 2007- 5437, 2008- 5475, 2009- 5742, 2010- 5760, 2011- 6008, 2012- 6126, 2013- 5792, 2014- 6090. pbs: 200m 25.12 '12, 800m 2:15.31i '14, 2:15.78 '12; 60mh 8.52i '14, 100mh 13.91 '14, HJ 1.90 '13, LJ 6.34i '15, 6.33 '12; SP 15.76i '15, 14.92 '14; JT 40.60 '11, Pen 4724i '14.

Tetyana HAMERA b. 1 Jun 1983 Hrada, Ternopil 1.65m 52kg. Married name Hamera-Shmyrko. Graduate of Lviv State University of Physical Culture.
At Mar: OG: '12- 5; WCh: '11- 15.
Three UKR marathon records 2012-15.
Progression at marathon: 2011- 2:28:14, 2012- 2:24:32, 2013- 2:23:58, 2014- 2:24:37, 2015- 2:22:09. Pbs: 800m 2:08.81 '04, 1500m 4:26.61 '08, 3000m 9:32.06 '09, 5000m 16:16.55 '10, 10000m 32:50.13 '12, HMar 71:15+ '15, 30k 1:41:08 '15.
Won Kraków marathon on debut 2011, won Osaka 2013-15 (2nd 2012).

Hanna KASYANOVA b. 24 Apr 1983 Tbilisi, Georgia 1.78m 59kg. née Melnychenko.
At Hep: OG: '08- 14, '12- 9; WCh: '07- dnf, '09- 6, '13- 1; EC: '06- 16, '10- dnf; EU23: '05- 13; WUG: '07- 3; ECp: '07-08-09-10-13: 3/1/1/1/2. UKR champion 2003, 2012. At Pen: WI: '14- 7; EI: '13- 3.
Progress at Hep: 2001- 4907, 2002- 5083, 2003- 5523, 2004- 5720, 2005- 5809, 2006- 6055w, 2007- 6143, 2008- 6306/6349u, 2009- 6445, 2010- 6098, 2012- 6407, 2013- 6586, 2014- 5937. pbs: 200m 23.85 '13, 800m 2:09.85 '13, 60mh 8.18i '14, 100mh 13.26 '13, HJ 1.86 '07, LJ 6.74 '12, TJ 13.21/13.40w '03, SP 14.19i '14, 14.09 '13, JT 45.11 '09, Pen 4748i '12.
Won IAAF Combined Events Challenge 2013. Formerly married to William Frullani ITA (Dec 7984 '02, Hep 5972 rec 6th EI '09), married Oleksiy Kasyanov (qv) on 18 Oct 2014.

Nataliya LUPU b. 4 Nov 1987 Marshyntsi 1.70m 50kg. Cherniyetskya.
At 800m: OG: '12- sf; WCh: '09- h, '13- 7; EC: '10- h; WI: '12- 2, '14- dq5; EU23: '07- h, '09- 2; WJ: '06- 4; EJ: '05- 1/3R; EI: '13- 1, '15- 3; ET: '10- 1. Won UKR 2012.
Progress at 800m: 2002- 2:10.99, 2003- 2:07.75, 2004- 2:05.08, 2005- 2:02.66, 2006- 2:03.24, 2007- 2:04.62, 2008- 2:00.96, 2009- 2:00.32, 2010- 1:59.59, 2011- 1:59.12, 2012- 1:58.46, 2013- 1:59.43, 2014- 2:01.33i. pbs: 400m 52.91 '11, 1000m 2:42.58i '13, 1500m 4:20.93 '03.
9-month ban for use of stimulant at World Indoors 7 Mar 2014.

Anna MISHCHENKO b. 25 Aug 1983 Sumy 1.66m 51kg. Kharkov Dynamo.
At 1500m: OG: '08- 9, '12- h; WCh: '09/11- sf; EC: '10-12-14: 11/3/h; WUG: '11- 2; ET: '10- 1, '11- 3; UKR champion 2010, 2014.
Progress at 1500m: 2003- 4:21.41, 2004- 4:14.09, 2005- 4:19.74, 2006- 4:12.17, 2007- 4:14.57, 2008- 4:05.13, 2009- 4:06.45, 2010- 4:03.14, 2011- 4:01.73, 2012- 4:01.16, 2014- 4:05.54. pbs: 800m 2:00.92 '12,

1000m 2:39.00 '08, 2000m 5:46.36 '09, 3000m 9:11.09i '11, 9:17.99 '07.
Daughter Alexandra born 25 Aug 2013.

Oksana OKUNYEVA b. 14 Mar 1990 Mykolaiv 1.75m 61kg. Mykolaivska.
At HJ: WCh: '11/13- dnq 19/15; EC: '14- 6; WY: '07- 6; EU23: '11- 2; EJ: '09- 6; ET: '14- 2. UKR champion 2011, 2013-14.
Progress at HJ: 2005- 1.60, 2006- 1.75, 2007- 1.78, 2008- 1.80, 2009- 1.90, 2010- 1.92, 2011- 1.94, 2012- 1.93i/1.87, 2013- 1.92, 2014- 1.98.

Lyudmyla OLYANOVSKA b. 20 Feb 1993 Solobkivtsi, Khmelnitskya 1.72m 57kg. Khmelnitskya.
At 20kW: WCh: '13- 12; EC: '14- 2; WCp: '14- 7; EU23: '13- 2; ECp: '13- 7.At 10000m/10kW: WJ: '12- 4; EJ: '11- 7; WCp: '12- 5J.
UKR 20k road walk record 2014 (and unofficial 5000m & 10,000m (2)).
Progress at 20kW: 2013- 1:30:26, 2014- 1:27:27. 2015- 1:28:18. pbs: 3000mW 12:38.43i '13, 5000mW 20:15.71 '14, 10000mW 41:42.5 '14.

Vira REBRYK b. 25 Feb 1989 Yalta 1.76m 65kg.
At JT: OG: '08/12- dnq 16/19; WCh: '09- 9, '11- dnq 16, '13- 11; EC: '10- dnq 17, '12- 1; WJ: '06- 2, '08- 1; WY: '05- 2; EU23: '09- 2, '11- 2; EJ: '07- 1; WUG: '09- 2. '11- 4; ET: '13- 3. Won UKR 2010-12.
World junior javelin record 2008; three UKR records 2012.
Progress at JT: 2003- 44.94, 2004- 52.47, 2005- 57.48, 2006- 59.64, 2007- 58.48, 2008- 63.01, 2009- 62.26, 2010- 63.36, 2011- 61.60, 2012- 66.86, 2013- 64.30, 2014- 61.57.
Crimean athlete, looking to transfer to Russia.

Anna RYZHYKOVA b. 24 Nov 1989 Dnipropetrovsk 1.76m 67kg. née Yaroshchuk.
At 400mh/4x400mR: OG: '12- sf; WCh: '11- sf, '13- 6; EC: '10- sf, '12- 3, '14- h/2R; WJ: '08- 6/2R; EU23: '09- 8, '11- 1/2R; WUG: '11- 1, '13- 2; ET: '13- 2, '14- 1. At 200m: EJ: '07- h/2 4x100m.
Progress at 400mh: 2006- 57.52, 2007- 56.46, 2008- 56.09, 2009- 57.23, 2010- 55.60, 2011- 54.77, 2012- 54.35, 2013- 54.77, 2014- 55.00. pbs: 60m 7.74i '06, 200m 23.49 '10, 400m 52.11 '14, LJ 6.05 '13.

Olga SALADUKHA b. 4 Jun 1983 Donetsk 1.75m 55kg.
At TJ: OG: '08- 9, '12- 3; WCh: '07- 7, '11- 1, '13- 3; EC: '06-10-12-14: 4/1/1/1; WJ: '02- 5; EU23: '05- 4; EJ: '01- 9; WI: '08- 6, '14- 2; EI: '13- 1; WUG: '05- 2, '07- 1; WCp: '06-10-14: 6/2/3; ECp: '06-08-10-11-13-14: 1/1/1/1/1/2. Won DL 2011, UKR 2007-08.
Progress at TJ: 1998- 13.32, 1999- 12.86, 2000- 13.26, 2001- 13.48, 2002- 13.66i/13.63, 2003- 13.26i/13.03, 2004- 13.22, 2005- 14.04, 2006- 14.41/14.50w, 2007- 14.79, 2008- 14.84, 2010- 14.81, 2011- 14.98/15.06w, 2012- 14.99, 2013- 14.88i/14.85, 2014- 14.73. pb LJ 6.37 '06.
Married to professional road cyclist Denys Kostyuk with a daughter Diana.

Hanna TITIMETS b. 5 Mar 1989 Pavlograd, Dnipropetrovsk 1.73m 62kg. Dnipropetrovsk.
At 400mh: OG: '12- sf; WCh: '09- h, '11- sf, '13- 4; EC: '10/12- sf, '14- 1; WJ: '08- 4; EU23: '09- 4, '11- 2; EJ: '07- 8 (2 4x100m); CCp: '14- 4; WUG: '11- 1 4x100m, '13- 1. UKR champion 2010, 2012-14.
Progress at 400mh: 2006- 59.79, 2007- 58.35, 2008- 57.22, 2009- 55.95, 2010- 55.58, 2011- 54.69, 2012- 54.98, 2013- 54.63, 2014- 54.56. pbs: 60m 7.46i '11, 200m 23.60 '09, 400m 52.73 '11, 60mh 8.50i '13.

Olga ZEMLYAK b. 16 Jan 1990 Rivne 1.65m 55kg. Rivnenska.
At 400mh: OG: '12- 4R; WCh: '13- hR; EC: '12- 4/1R, '14- 2/2R; WJ: '08- sf/2R; WY: '07- 4/2R; EJ: '09- dq1R; CCp: '14- 5/2R; ET: '14- 3/1R.
Progress at 400mh: 2006- 55.95, 2007- 54.05, 2008- 53.69, 2009- 53.40, 2012- 51.82, 2013- 51.95, 2014- 51.00. pbs: 60m 7.72i '09, 100m 11.68 '14, 200m 23.49 '14.
Two-year drugs ban from positive test on 26 Jul 2009 after running 4x400m first leg at European Juniors.

UNITED KINGDOM

Governing body: UK Athletics, Alexander Stadium, Walsall, Perry Barr, Birmingham B42 2LR. Founded 1999 (replacing British Athletics, founded 1991, which succeeded BAAB, founded 1932). The Amateur Athletic Association was founded in 1880 and the Women's Amateur Athletic Association in 1922.

National Championships (first were English Championships 1866-79, then AAA 1880-2006, WAAA from 1922). **2014 UK Champions**: **Men**: Dwain Chambers 10.12, 200m: Danny Talbot 20.42, 400m: Martyn Rooney 45.78, 800m: Michael Rimmer 1:48.00, 1500m: Charlie Grice 3:46.97, 5000m: Tom Farrell 13:51.43, 10000m: Andy Vernon 28:26.59, HMar: Ryan McLeod 65:00, Mar: Mo Farah 2:08:21, 3000mSt: James Wilkinson 8:37.36, 110mh: William Sharman 13.18w, 400mh: Niall Flannery 49.54, HJ: Allan Smith 2.24, PV: Steven Lewis 5.55, LJ: J.J.Jegede 7.83, TJ: Julian Reid 16.82, SP: Scott Rider 18.34, DT: Zane Duquemin 60.38, HT: Nick Miller 73.96, JT: Lee Doran 70.71, Dec: Curtis Matthews 7005, 5000mW: Tom Bosworth 19:61.82, 20kW: Ben Wears 1:33:33, 50kW: Dominic King 4:12:41.
Women: 100m: Asha Philip 11.11w, 200m: Jodie Williams 22.79, 400m: Kelly Massey 52.42, 800m: Lynsey Sharp 2:01.40, 1500m: Laura Weightman 4:09.77, 5000m: Emily Gorecka 15:40.65, 10000m: Jo Pavey 32:11.04, HMar: Emma Stepto 72:29, Mar: Amy Whitehead 2:34:20, 3000mSt: Eilish McColgan 9:50.06, 100mh: Tiffany Porter 12.85, 400mh: Eilidh Child 55.58, HJ: Isobel Pooley 1.90, PV: Sally Peake 4.30, LJ: Katrina Johnson-Thompson 6.81, TJ: Yamilé Aldama 13.60, SP/DT: Eden Francis 16.66/55.93, HT: Sophie Hitchon 65.56, JT:

Goldie Sayers 62.75, Hep: Devon Byrne 5004, 5000mW: Heather Lewis 22:09.87, 20kW: Michelle Turner 1:50:37.

Lawrence CLARKE b. 13 Jan 1990 London 1.86m 75kg. Windsor, Slough, Eton & Hounslow. Graduate of Bristol University.
At 110mh: OG: '12- 4; WCh: '11- h; EC: '14- dns; CG: '10- 3, '14- 8; E23: '11- 3; EJ: '09- 1. UK champion 2011. At 60mh: EI: '15- 5.
Progress at 110mh: 2008- 15.3, 2009- 13.91/13.82w, 2010- 13.69/13.51w, 2011- 13.58, 2012- 13.31/ 13.14w, 2013- 13.81, 2014- 13.41. Pbs: 100m 10.64 '12, 60mh 7.59i '15.

James DASAOLU b. 5 Sep 1987 Dulwich, London 1.80m 75kg. Croydon H. Graduate of Loughborough University.
At 100m: OG: '12- sf; WCh: '13- 8; EC: '10- sf, '14- 1; CCp: '14- 1; ET: '13- 1R. At 60m: EI: '13- 2.
Progress at 100m: 2006- 10.75/10.7/10.61w, 2007- 10.33, 2008- 10.26, 2009- 10.09, 2010- 10.23/10.06w, 2011- 10.11, 2012- 10.13, 2013- 9.91, 2014- 10.00. pbs: 60m 6.47i '14, 200m 21.9 '07.

Mohamed FARAH b. 23 March 1983 Mogadishu, Somalia 1.71m 65kg. Newham & Essex Beagles.
At 5000m (/10000m): OG: '08- h, '12- 1/1; WCh: '07- 6, '09- 7, '11- 1/2, '13- 1/1; EC: '06- 2, '10- 1/1, '12- 1, '14- 1/1; CG: '06- 9; WJ: '00- 10; EJ: '01- 1; EU23: '03 & '05- 2; ECp: '08-09-10-13: 1/1/1 &(1)/1. At 3000m: WY: '99- 6; WI: '08- 6, '12- 4; EI: '05-07-09-11: 6/5/1/1; ECp: '05-06: 2/2. World CC: '07- 11, '10- 20; Eur CC: '99-00-01-04-05-06-08-09: 5J/7J/2J/15/21/1/2/2. Won UK 5000m 2007, 2011; Mar 2014.
Records: World indoor 2M 2015, European 10000m & indoor 5000m 2011, 1500m 2013; indoor 2M 2012, 20k and half marathon 2015; UK 2M 2014, 5000m 2010 & 2011, half marathon (3) 2011-15.
Progress at 1500m, 5000m, 10000m: 1996- 4:43.9, 1997- 4:06.41, 1998- 3:57.67, 1999- 3:55.78, 2000- 3:49.60, 14:05.72; 2001- 3:46.1, 13:56.31; 2002- 3:47.78, 14:00.5; 2003-3:43.17, 13:38.41; 2004- 3:43.4, c.14:25; 2005- 3:38.62, 13:30.53; 2006- 3:38.02, 13:09.40; 2007- 3:45.2i+, 3:46.50, 13:07.00; 2008- 3:39.66, 13:08.11, 27:44.54; 2009- 3:33.98, 13:09.14; 2010- 12:57.94, 27:28.86; 2011- 12:53.11, 26:46.57; 2012- 3:34.66, 12:56.98, 27:30.42; 2013- 3:28.81, 13:05.88, 27:21.71; 2014- 13:23.42, 28:08.11. pbs: 800m 1:48.69 '03, 1M 3:56.49 '05, 2000m 5:06.34 '06, 3000m 7:34.47i '09, 7:36.8 '14; 2M 8:03.40i '15, 8:07.85 '14. 2000mSt 5:55.72 '00; road 15k 43:13 '09, 10M 45:35 '14, 20k 56:27 '15. HMar 59:32 '15, Mar 2:08:21 '14.
Joined his father in England in 1993. Sixth man ever to win Olympic 5000m/10,000m double at same Games; first British athlete to win either title. In 2013 became third man to win World 5000m/10000m double. Won in New York on half marathon debut 2011.

Adam GEMILI b. 6 Oct 1993 London 1.78m 73kg. Blackheath & Bromley.
At 100m/(200m).4x100mR: OG: '12- sf; WCh: '13- (5); EC: (5)/1RCG: '14- 2; WJ: '12- 1; EU23: '13- 1/4/1R; EJ: '11- 2/2R; ET: '13- 1R.
Progress at 100m, 200m: 2009- 11.2, 2010- 10.80/10.72w, 21.87w; 2011- 10.35/10.23w, 20.98; 2012- 10.05, 20.38; 2013- 10.06, 19.98; 2014- 10.04, 19.98. Pb 60m 6.68i '12.
Sixth equal all-time junior list 10.05 to win World Junior 100m in 2012, improved 200m best from 20.30 to 20.17 and 19.98 at 2013 Worlds before 5th in final in 20.08. As a footballer he was a member of the youth academy at Chelsea before playing for Dagenham & Redbridge and then making a huge impact as a sprinter from 2011. Won European Athletics Rising Star award 2014.

Robbie GRABARZ b. 3 Oct 1987 Enfield 1.92m 87kg. Newham & Essex Beagles.
At HJ: OG: '12- 3=; WCh: '13- 8; EC: '12- 1; WJ: '06- 12; EU23: '09- 11; WI: '12- 6=; EI: '13- 6; won DL 2012, UK 2012-13. UK high jump record 2012.
Progress at HJ: 2002- 1.75, 2004- 2.00, 2005- 2.22, 2006- 2.20i/2.14, 2007- 2.21, 2008- 2.27, 2009- 2.23i/2.22, 2010- 2.28, 2011- 2.28, 2012- 2.37, 2013- 2.31,2014- 2.27i. pb TJ 14.40 '09.

David 'Dai' GREENE b. 11 Apr 1986 Llanelli 1.83m 75kg. Swansea Harriers.
At 400mh: OG: '12- 4; WCh: '09- 7 (res (2)R), '11- 1, '13- sf; EC: '06- h, '10- 1; CG: '10- 1, '14- h; EU23: '07- 1; EJ: '05- 2; CCp: '10- 1; ET: '09-10-11-13: 1/1/1/2. Won DL 2011 UK 2009-10, 2012-13; .
Progress at 400mh: 2003- 55.0/55.06, 2004- 53.42, 2005- 51.14, 2006- 49.91, 2007- 49.58, 2008- 49.53, 2009- 48.27, 2010- 47.88, 2011- 48.20, 2012- 47.84, 2013- 48.66, 2014- 49.89. pbs: 100m 11.1 '06, 200m 22.1 '05, 21.73w '08; 400m 45.82 '11, 600m 1:16.22i '13.

Matthew HUDSON-SMITH b. 26 Oct 1994 Wolverhampton 1.96m. Birchfield H.
At 400m/4x400mR: EC: 2014- 2/1R; CG: '14- 1R. At 200m: EJ: '13- 3/3R.
Progress at 400m: 2009- 52.09, 2011- 50.61, 2013- 48.76i, 2014- 44.75. pbs: 60m 6.96i '12, 100m 10.9 '13, 10.8w '12; 200m 20.88 '13.

Richard KILTY b. 2 Sep 1989 Middlesbrough 1.84m 80kg. Gateshead H.
At 200m/4x100mR: WCh: '13- hR; EC: '14- 1R; CG: '14- sf/2R; EU23: '09- 7, '11- 2R; WJ: '08- sf; CCp: '14- 2R. At 60m: WI: '14- 1; EI: 15- 1.
Progress at 100m, 200m: 2004- 11.43/11.3w, 2005- 10.96/10.90w, 22.60; 2006- 10.76/10.75w, 21.96; 2007- 10.61, 21.37; 2008- 10.60/10.5/10.51w, 21.19; 2009- 10.43, 20.80; 2010- 10.44, 21.41i; 2011- 10.32, 20.53; 2012- 10.23/10.15w, 20.50; 2013- 10.10, 20.34; 2014- 10.12, 20.73. pbs: 60m 6.49i '14, 400m 48.58 '13.

Steve LEWIS b. 20 May 1986 Stoke-on-Trent 1.91m 83kg. Newham & Essex Beagles. Studied

sports science at Loughborough University.
At PV: OG: '08- dnq, '12- 5=; WCh: '07- dnq, '09- 7=, '11- 9=, '13- dnq; EC: '14- 11; CG: '06- 3, '10- 2, '14- 1; WJ: '04- 9; WY: '03- 3; EU23: '07- 7; EJ: '05- 5; WI: '10- 6=, '12- 5=; EI: '09- 4, '13- 6=; ECp: '08- 3. Won AAA 2006, UK 2007-08, 2011-12, 2014. UK pole vault record 2012.
Progress at PV: 1999- 3.20, 2000- 3.70, 2001- 4.30i/4.20, 2002- 4.65, 2003- 5.05, 2004- 5.20, 2005- 5.35, 2006- 5.50, 2007- 5.61, 2008- 5.71, 2009- 5.75i/5.72, 2010- 5.72i/5.65, 2011- 5.65, 2012- 5.82, 2013- 5.71i/5.70, 2014- 5.71i/5.70.

Andrew POZZI b. 15 May 1992 Leamington Spa 1.86m 79kg. Stratford-upon-Avon. Bristol University.
At 110mh: OG: '12- h; EJ: '11- 2. UK champion 2012. At 60mh: WI: '12- 4, '14- 4.
Progress at 110mh: 2009- 14.8, 2011- 13.73/13.66w, 2012- 13.34. pbs: 100m 10.9 '11, 60mh 7.53i '14, LJ 6.73 '09.

Martyn ROONEY b. 3 Apr 1987 Croydon 1.98m 78kg. Croydon H. Was at Loughborough University.
At 400m/4x400mR: OG: '08- 6, '12- sf; WCh: '07- h, '09- sf/2R, '11- sf, '13- 4R; EC: '10- 3/2R, 2014- 1/1R; CG: '06- 5, '14- 4; WJ: '06- 3/3R; EJ: '05- 2/1R; CCp: '10- 2R,'14- 7/2R; ECp: '07-08-10: 3/1&2R/1. Won UK 2008, 2010-12, 2014.
Progress at 400m: 2003- 49.4, 2004- 47.46, 2005- 46.44, 2006- 45.35, 2007- 45.47, 2008- 44.60, 2009- 45.35, 2010- 44.99, 2011- 45.30, 2012- 44.92, 2013- 45.05, 2014- 44.71. pbs: 60m 7.12i '09, 200m 21.08 '13, 20.87w '11; 600m 1:16.9 '05, 800m 1:50.55 '05.
Ran anchor leg in 43.73 on 4x400m at 2008 Olympics. Married Kate Dennison (six UK PV records to 4.60 '09, 3= CG 2010) on 19 Sep 2014.

Greg RUTHERFORD b. 17 Nov 1986 Milton Keynes 1.88m 84kg. Marshall Milton Keynes.
At LJ: OG: '08- 10, '12- 1; WCh: '09- 5, '07-11-13- dnq 21/15=/14; EC: '06- 2, '14- 1; CG: '06-10-14: 8/2/1; EJ: '05- 1; EI: '09- 6; ET: '13- 3, '14- 2. Won AAA 2005-06, UK 2008, 2012.
Three UK Long jump records 2009-14.
Progress at LJ: 1999- 5.04, 2001- 6.16, 2003- 7.04, 2004- 7.28, 2005- 8.14, 2006- 8.26, 2007- 7.96, 2008- 8.20, 2009- 8.30, 2010- 8.22, 2011- 8.27/8.32w, 2012- 8.35, 2013- 8.22, 2014- 8.51. pbs: 60m 6.68i '09, 100m 10.26 '10.
Great-grandfather Jock Rutherford played 11 internationals for England at football 1904-08.

William SHARMAN b. 12 Sep 1984 Lagos, Nigeria 1.88m 82kg. Belgrave Harriers. Economics graduate of University of Leicester.
At 110mh: WCh: '09- 4, '11- 5=, '13- 5; EC: '06-10-12-14: h/sf/sf/2; CG: '10- 2, '14- 2; EU23: '05- 4; EJ: '03- 5; CCp: '14- 3; ET: '14- 2. Won UK 2010, 2013-14. At 60mh: WI: '14- 7.
Progress at 110mh: 2003- 14.31, 2004- 13.94/13.86w, 2005- 13.88/13.72w, 2006- 13.49/13.45w, 2007- 13.68, 2008- 13.67/13.6/13.59w, 2009- 13.30, 2010- 13.39/13.35w/12.9w, 2011- 13.47, 2012- 13.50, 2013- 13.26, 2014- 13.16. pbs: 60m 6.89i '07, 100m 10.86 '05, 10.66w '13; 200m 21.59 '06, 400m 48.53 '05, 1500m 4:45.25 '05, 60mh 7.53i '14, HJ 2.08 '05, PV 4.00 '05, LJ 7.14 '04, 7.15w '05; SP 12.99 '05, DT 33.99 '03, JT 43.45 '05, Dec 7384 '05, Hep 5278i '05.
National junior decathlon champion 2003. Improved pb from 13.44 to 13.38 and 13.30 at 2009 Worlds.

Chris TOMLINSON b. 15 Sep 1981 Middlesbrough 1.97m 84kg. Newham & Essex Beagles.
At LJ: OG: '04- 5, '08- dnq 27, '12- 6; WCh: '03- 9, '05/07- dnq 14/16, '09- 8, '11- 11; EC: '02-06-10-12-14: 6/9/3/dnq 13/11; CG: '02-06-10-14: 6/6/nj/5; WJ: '00- 12; WI: '04- 6, '08- 2; EI: '07- 5, '13- 7; WCp: '02- 6; ECp: '01-02-04-10-11: 2/1/1/3/3; AAA champion 2004, UK 2009-10, 2013.
Three British long jump records 2002-2011.
Progress at LJ: 1996- 5.91/6.09w, 1997- 6.82w/6.44, 1998- 7.23i, 1999- 7.44i/7.40, 2000- 7.62, 2001- 7.75, 2002- 8.27, 2003- 8.16, 2004- 8.25/8.28w, 2005- 7.95i/7.82/7.83w, 2006- 8.09, 2007- 8.29, 2008- 8.18i/7.95/8.09w, 2009- 8.23, 2010- 8.23, 2011- 8.35, 2012- 8.26, 2013- 8.21, 2014- 8.23. pbs: 60m 6.84i '09, 100m 10.69 '02, 10.61w/10.6 '01; 200m 21.73 '02, 21.43w '10; TJ 15.35 '01.
Jumped 8.27 at Tallahassee in April 2002, from a previous best of 7.87 (and 8.19w), to break the 34-year-old British record set by Lynn Davies.

Women

Dina ASHER-SMITH b. 4 Dec 1995 1.65m 55kg. Blackheath & Bromley. King's College.
At 200m/4x100mR (100m): WCh: '13- 3R; EC: '14- dnf; WJ: '12- 7, '14- (1); EJ: '13- 1/1R. At 60m: EI: '15- 2.
Progress at 100m, 200m: 2009- 12.10, 24.83; 2010- 12.00/24.50; 2011- 11.96, 24.16/24.11w; 2012- 11.54, 23.49; 2013- 11.38/11.30w, 23.14; 2014- 11.14/11.93w, 22.61. pbs: 60m 7.08i '15, 400m 53.49 '14.

Holly BRADSHAW b. 2 Nov 1991 Preston 1.75m 68kg. née Bleasdale. Blackburn Harriers.
At PV: OG: '12- 6=; WCh: '11- dnq; WI: '12- 3, '14- 9; WJ: '10- 3; EU23: '11- 1; EI: '13- 1. UK champion 2011-12.
Three UK pole vault records 2011-12, five indoors 2011-12.
Progress at PV: 2007- 2.30, 2008- 3.10i, 2009- 4.05, 2010- 4.35, 2011- 4.71i/4.70, 2012- 4.87i/4.71, 2013- 4.77i/4.60, 2014- 4.73i. pbs: SP 11.32 '11, JT 37.60 '11.
World age-19 best 2011, age-20 best 2012. Married 800m runner Paul Bradshaw (1:47.37 '09) on 25 Oct 2014.

Eilidh CHILD b. 20 Feb 1987 Perth 1.72m 59kg. Pitreavie.
At 400mh/4x400mR: OG: '12- sf; WCh: '09/11- sf, '13- 5/3R; EC: '10- 8, '12- 4R, '14- 1/3R; CG: '10- 2; EU23: '07- 5, '09- 2; CCp: '14- 2; ET: '09-10-

13-14: 3R/2/1&1R/2; UK champion 2014. At 400m: WI: '14- 3R; EI: '13- 2/1R.
Progress at 400mh: 2003- 59.8mx, 2004- 59.53, 2005- 59.78, 2006- 59.7/60.05, 2007- 57.11, 2008- 56.84, 2009- 55.32, 2010- 55.16, 2011- 55.67, 2012- 54.96, 2013- 54.22, 2014- 54.39. pbs: 200m 24.51i '13, 24.56 '08; 300m 37.1i '13, 400m 51.45i/51.83 '13, 800m 2:24.2 '04, 60mh 8.89i '06, 100mh 14.51 '04, 14.38w '07, 200mhSt 25.84 '14.

Jessica ENNIS-HILL b. 28 Jan 1986 Sheffield 1.64m 57kg. Sheffield. Studied psychology at University of Sheffield.
At Hep: OG: '12- 1; WCh: '07- 4, '09- 1, '11- 2; EC: '06- 8, '10- 1; CG: '06- 3; WJ: '04- 8; WY: '03- 5; EJ: '05- 1; WUG: '05- 3; ECp: '07- 1. At Pen: WI: '10- 1, '12- 2; EI: '07- 6. At 100mh: EU23: '07- 3. Won UK 100mh 2007, 2009, 2012; HJ 2007, 2009, 2011-12.
Records: Commonwealth heptathlon (2) 2012, indoor pentathlon 2010 & 2012, UK high jump 2007, 100mh 2012, indoor 60mh 2010.
Progress at Hep: 2001- 4801, 2002- 5194, 2003- 5116, 2004- 5542, 2005- 5910, 2006- 6287, 2007- 6469, 2009- 6731, 2010- 6823, 2011- 6790, 2012- 6955. pbs: 60m 7.36i '10, 100m 11.39+ '10, 150mStr 16.99 '10, 200m 22.83 '12, 800m 2:07.81 '11, 60mh 7.87i '12, 100mh 12.54 '12, HJ 1.95 '07, LJ 6.51 '10, 6.54w '07; SP 14.79i '12, 14.67 '11; JT 48.33 '13, Pen 4965i '12.
Set four pbs in adding 359 points to best score for third at 2006 Commonwealth Games. Stress fracture ended 2008 season in May. Set SP pb when winning 2009 World title and three indoor bests when winning 2010 World Indoor gold. Three pbs en route to Olympic gold 2012. Won Götzis heptathlon 2010-12. Laureus World Sportswoman of the Year 2013. Married Andy Hill on 18 May 2013. Son Reggie born 17 July 2014.

Katarina JOHNSON-THOMPSON b. 9 Jan 1993 Liverpool 1.83m 70kg. Liverpool H.
At Hep: OG: '12- 14; WCh: '13- 5; WY: '09- 1; EU23: '13- 1; EJ: '09- 8, '11- 6. At LJ: WJ: '12- 1 (sf 100mh); WI: '14- 2. At Hep: EI: '15- 1. Won UK LJ 2014.
UK indoor records: high jump (2) 2014-15, long jump & pentathlon 2015.
Progress at LJ, Hep: 2006- 5.11, 2007- 5.77i/5.65, 2008- 6.11i/5.90/6.07w, 5343; 2009- 6.31, 5481; 2010- 6.25i/5.58, 2011- 6.44, 5787; 2012- 6.51/ 6.81w, 6267; 2013- 6449, 6.56; 2014- 6.92, 6682; 2015- 6.93i. pbs: 60m 7.50i '14, 100m 12.35 '08, 12.2 '09, 11.30w '14; 200m 22.89 '14, 300m 38.56i '08, 400m 53.7 '14, 800m 2:07.64 '13, 60mh 8.18i '15, 100mh 13.41 '14, 400mh 58.3 '14, HJ 1.97i '15, 1.90 '14; TJ 12.83, 13.35w '14; SP 12.49i '14, 11.92 '13; JT 41.44 '14, Pen 5000i '12.
Set pbs in the each of the last four events when adding 182 points to her pb for 5th at the 2013 Worlds and 474 points to pentathlon best to win 2015 European Indoors, including a 6.89 long jump, the best ever in a pentathlon. Has all all-time record 27 English age-group titles U15 to U23 at various events.

Morgan LAKE b. 12 May 1997 1.78m 64kg. Windsor, Slough, Eton & Honslow.
At Hep/(HJ): EC: '14- (dnq 17=); WJ: '14- 1/1; WY: '13- dnf. At Pen: EI: '15- 9.
World youth indoor pentathlon record 2014.
Progress at Hep: 2014- 6148. pbs: 60m 7.98i '13, 200m 24.59 '14, 800m 2:21.06 '14, 60mh 8.81i '15, 100mh 14.25 '14, HJ 1.94 '14, LJ 6.32 '14, TJ 12.35, 12.45w '13; SP 14.85 '14, JT 41.66 '14, Pen 4527i '15.
18 English age-group titles 2010-14. Father Eldon had a TJ pb of 15.43 (1989).

Jennifer MEADOWS b. 17 Apr 1981 Billinge, Wigan 1.56m 48kg. Wigan.
At 800m/4x400mR: OG: '08- sf; WCh: '03- 6R, '07- sf, '09- 3, '11- sf; EC: '10- 3; CG: '02- res 2R, '14- 6; WI: '08- 5, '10- 2; EI: '07-09-11-13-15: 5/4/1&2R/4/dns; CCp: '10- 4; ECp: '07-08-09-11: 1R/1/3R/2. At 400m: WJ: '00- sf/1R; EU23: '01- 6/1R, '03- 7/2R; WUG: '01- 2R. Won DL 800m 2011, UK 800m 2011.
Progress at 800m: 1994- 2:16.80, 1995- 2:14.88, 1996- 2:16.4, 1997- 2:16.03, 1999- 2:11.5, 2000- 2:10.7, 2001- 2:05.8, 2002- 2:04.46/2:03.35i, 2003- 2:06.82mx/2:08.0, 2004- 2:06.84i, 2005- 2:02.05, 2006- 2:00.16, 2007- 1:59.39, 2008- 1:59.11, 2009- 1:57.93, 2010- 1:58.43i/1:58.88, 2011- 1:58.60, 2013- 2:01.02i, 2014- 1:59.34mx/2:00.32 , 2015- 1:59.21i. pbs: 100m 11.94/11.8w '01, 11.9 '02; 200m 24.32 '00, 24.0 '02, 23.90w '01; 400m 52.50mx '05, 52.67 '03; 600m 1:25.81i '07, 1000m 2:39.84 '07, 1500m 4:19.36 '06.

Christine OHURUOGU b. 17 May 1984 Forest Gate, London 1.75m 70kg. Newham & Essex Beagles. Studied linguistics at University College, London.
At 400m/4x400mR: OG: '04- sf/4R, '08- 1, '12- 2; WCh: '05- sf/3R, '07- 1/3R, '09- 5, '11- h, '13- 1/3R; EC: '14- 4; CG: '06- 1, '14- 3R; EU23: '05- 2/2R; EJ: '03- 3/3R; WI: '12- 1R, '14- 3R; EI: '13- 1R; ET: '13- 1R. At 200m: ECp: '08- 2, '09- 3. Won AAA 400m 2004, UK 2009, 2012-13.
UK 400m record 2013.
Progress at 400m: 2000- 59.0, 2001- 55.29, 2003- 54.21, 2004- 50.50, 2005- 50.73, 2006- 50.28, 2007- 49.61, 2008- 49.62, 2009- 50.21, 2010- 50.88, 2011- 50.85, 2012- 49.70, 2013- 49.41, 2014- 51.38. pbs: 60m 7.39i '06, 100m 11.35 '08, 150mStr 16.94 '09, 200m 22.85 '09, 300m 36.76+ '09.
Played for England U17 and U19 at netball. Withdrawn from GB European Champs team in 2006 after missing three drugs tests, receiving a one-year ban. Younger sister Victoria (b. 28 Feb 1993) 400m pb 52.62 '13; res 3R WI '14.

Joanne PAVEY b. 20 Sep 1973 Honiton 1.62m 51kg. née Davis. Bristol.
At 5000m/(10000m): OG: '00- 12, '04- 5 (h 1500m), '08- (12), '12- 7/7; WCh: '01- 11, 05- 15,

'07- 9 (4); EC: '02- 5, '06- 4, '12- (2), '14- 7/1R; CG: '02- 5, '06- 2, '14- 3; WCp: '02- 3, '14- 3; ECp: '02-03-10-12: 2/2/2/(2). At 3000m: WI: '04- 5; EI: '07- 6, ECp: '06- 1. At 1500m: WCh: '97- sf, '03-10. Eur CC: '04- 3, '06- 8. Won UK 1500m 1997, AAA 5000m 2001, 2006; UK 5000m 2007-08, 2012; 10000m 2007-08, 2010, 2014.
2 Commonwealth indoor 3000m records 2004-07.
Progress at 1500m, 3000m, 5000m, 10000m: 1988- 4:27.9, 1989- 4:30.91, 1990- 4:26.7, 1993- 9:56.1, 1994-4:23.36, 1995- 4:28.46, 1996- 4:21.14, 9:37.6; 1997- 4:07.28, 9:05.87; 1998- 8:58.2, 2000- 8:36.70, 14:58.27; 2001- 8:36.58, 15:00.56; 2002- 4:11.16, 8:31.27, 14:48.66; 2003- 4:01.79, 8:37.89, 15:09.04; 2004- 4:12.50, 8:34.55i/8:40.22, 14:49.11; 2005- 4:16.3i, 8:33.79, 14:40.71; 2006- 4:05.91, 8:38.80, 14:39.96; 2007- 8:31.50i/8:44.13, 15:04.77, 31:26.94; 2008- 14:58.62, 31:12.30; 2010- 15:02.31, 31:51.91; 2012- 15:02.84, 30:53.20; 2014- 9:01.1+, 15:04.87, 32:11.04. pbs: 800m 2:09.68 '90, 1M 4:30.77 '97, 2000m 5:41.2i '07, 5:41.6 '05; 2M 9:32.00i '07, Road: 15k 48:43 '08, 10M 52:46 '06, 20k 65:30 '08, HMar 68:53 '08, Mar 2:28:24 '11.
Set British under-15 record at 1500m with 4:27.9 in 1988 and won four national titles at U15/U17 level, but did not compete much in the early 1990s, also missing two years through injury 1998-2000. Married to middle-distance runner Gavin Pavey. Son Jacob born on 14 Sep 2009 and daughter Emily on 4 Sep 2013. First non-East African at both 5000m and 10,000m at 2012 Olympics, taking 19.1 secs of 10,000m pb at age of 38. First major gold medal at age 40 in 2014.

Tiffany PORTER b. 13 Nov 1987 Ypsilanti, USA 1.72m 62kg. née Ofili. Doctorate in pharmacy from University of Michigan.
At 100mh: OG: '12- sf; WCh: '11- 4, '13- 3; EC: '14- 1; WJ: '06- 3 (for USA); ET: '13- 1. At 60mh: WI: '12- 2, '14- 3; EI: '11- 2. Won UK 100mh 2011, 2013-14; NCAA 100mh & 60mh indoors 2009.
Four British 100mh records 2011-14, world best 4x100mh 2014.
Progress at 100mh: 2005- 14.19, 2006- 13.37/13.15w, 2007- 12.80, 2008- 12.73, 2009- 12.77/12.57w, 2010- 12.85, 2011- 12.56, 2012- 12.65/12.47w, 2013- 12.55, 2014- 12.51. pbs: 60m 7.41i '11, 100m 11.70 '09, 11.63w '08; 200m 23.90 '08, 400mh 61.96 '06, LJ 6.48 '09; UK records: 50mh 6.83i '12, 55mh 7.38i '12, 60mh 7.80i '11.
Opted for British nationality in September 2010 through her mother being born in London (father born in Nigeria). Married US hurdler Jeff Porter (qv) in May 2011. Sister Cindy Ofili (b. 5 Aug 1994) USA has pbs: 60mh 8.07Ai/8.08i '14, 100mh 12.93 '14.

Shara PROCTOR b. 16 Sep 1988 The Valley, Anguilla 1.74m 56kg. Birchfield H. Was at University of Florida, USA.
At LJ: OG: '12- 9; WCh: '07-09-11-13: dnq 29/6/ dnq 20/6; WI: '12- 3, '14- 4; CG: '06- dnq 13; WJ: '06- dnq 16; WY: '05- 6; EI: '13- 4; ET: '13- 3. Won DL 2013, CAC 2009, UK 2011-13.
Records: Anguilla: LJ 2005-09, TJ 2007-09; UK LJ 2012.
Progress at LJ: 2003- 5.64, 2004- 5.99A. 2005- 6.24, 2006- 6.17, 2007- 6.17, 2008- 6.54A/6.52/6.61w, 2009- 6.71, 2010- 6.69, 2011- 6.81, 2012- 6.95, 2013- 6.92, 2014- 6.82. pbs: 60m 7.49i '13, 100m 12.27 '08, 12.10w '10; TJ 13.88i '10, 13.74 '09.
Switched from Anguilla (a British Dependent Territory without a National Olympic Committee) to Britain from 16 Nov 2010. Younger sister Shinelle (b. 27 Jun 91) set Anguillan high jump records at 1.70 in 2009 and 2010 and 1.72i in 2014.

Lynsey SHARP b. 11 Jul 1990 Dumfries 1.75m 60kg. Edinburgh AC. Law graduate of Edinburgh Napier University.
At 800m: OG: '12- sf; EC: '12- 1, '14- 2; CG: '14- 2; WJ: '08- sf; WY: '07- sf; EU23: '11- 2; CCp: '14- 5. Won UK 2012, 2014.
Progress at 800m: 2000- 2:38.2, 2002- 2:25.97, 2003- 2:16.57, 2004- 2:09.98, 2005- 2:10.44, 2006- 2:10.91i, 2007- 2:06.92, 2008- 2:04.44, 2011- 2:00.65, 2012- 2:00.52, 2013- 2:02.63, 2014- 1:58.80. pbs: 400m 54.74 '14, 600m 1:27.51 '14, 1500m 4:36.27 '11.
Father Cameron (1982: 4th 100m, 2nd 200m EC; 3rd 100m, 200m, 4x100m CG; pbs: 100m 10.20 '83, 200m 20.47 '82); mother Carol Lightfoot (800m 2:02.91 '82).

Gemma STEEL b. 12 Nov 1985. Charnwood.
At 10000m: EC: '12- 9. World HMar: '12- 7; CC: '15- 18. Eur CC: '11-13-14: 3/2/1.
Progress at HMar: 2009- 79:02, 2011- 72:21, 2012- 70:46, 2013- 70:19, 2014- 68:13. pbs: 800m 2:17.5 '10, 1500m 4:44.8 '10, 3000m 9:01.86i '12, 9:29.28 '11; 5000m 15:47.21 '11, 10000m 32:34.81 '12; Road: 10k 31:27 '14, 15k 48:15 '14, 10M 52:43 '14.

Laura WEIGHTMAN b. 1 Jul 1991 Alnwick 1.72m 58kg. Morpeth H. Leeds Met University.
At 1500m: OG: '12- 9; WCh: '13- h; EC: '14- 3; CG: '14- 2; WJ: '10- 6. Won UK 2012, 2014. At 3000m: ET: '13- 2. Eur U23 CC: '13- 8.
Progress at 1500m: 2004- 4:50.5, 2005- 4:44.0, 2006- 4:37.20, 2007- 4:26.02, 2008- 4:22.20, 2009- 4:14.9mx/4:19.9, 2010- 4:09.60mx/4:12.82, 2011- 4:07.94mx/4:15.51, 2012- 4:02.99, 2013- 4:05.36, 2014- 4:00.17. pbs: 400m 58.43 '09, 800m 2:02.52 '12, 1000m 2:38.49 '13, 1M 4:52.7 '09, 2000m 5:44.22 '13, 3000m 8:43.46mx '13, 9:02.62 '12; 5k Rd 16:43b '12.

Jodie WILLIAMS b. 28 Sep 1993 Welwyn Garden City 1.74m 65kg. Herts Phoenix.
At (100m)/200m.4x100mR: WCh: '13- sf; EC: '14- 2/1R; CG: '14- 2/2R; WJ: '10- 1/2; WY: '09- 1/1; EU23: '12- 2/1/2R; EJ: '11- 1/1/3R. At 60m: WI: '11- 4. Won UK 200m 2014.
Progress at 100m, 200m: 2005- 13.1, 27.22/27.07w; 2006- 13.05/12.8, 26.88; 2007- 12.01/11.85w, 24.77/ 24.57w; 2008- 11.56, 24.14; 2009- 11.39, 23.08; 2010- 11.24, 22.79; 2011- 11.18, 22.94, 2012- 11.66, 2013-

11.32/11.23w, 22.92; 2014- 11.20/11.13w, 22.46. pbs: 60m 7.21i '11, 300m 38.00 '11. 400m 52.55 '14, LJ 5.33 '07. Unbeaten in 151 races to 2nd in World Juniors 200m 2010.

USA

Governing body: USA Track and Field, One RCA Dome, Suite #140, Indianapolis, IN 46225. Founded 1979 as The Athletics Congress, when it replaced the AAU (founded 1888) as the governing body.

National Championships first held in 1876 (men), 1923 (women). **2014 Champions**: **Men**: 100m: Mike Rodgers 10.09, 200m: Curtis Mitchell 20.13, 400m: Gil Roberts 44.53, 800m: Duane Solomon 1:44.30, 1500m: Leo Manzano 3:38.63, 5000m: Bernard Lagat 13:31.41, 10000m: Galen Rupp 28:12.07, HMar: Mohamed Trafeh 61:17, Mar: Tyler Pennel 2:13:32, 3000mSt: Evan Jager 8:18.83, 110mh: Devon Allen 13.16w, 400mh: Johnny Dutch 48.93, HJ: Erik Kynard 2.35, PV: Sam Kendricks 5.75, LJ: Jeffery Henderson 8.52w, TJ: Will Claye 17.75, SP: Joe Kovacs 22.02, DT: Hayden Reed 62.19, HT: Kibwe Johnson 74.16, JT: Sean Furey 81.10, Dec: Trey Hardee 8599, 20000mW: John Nunn 1:27:56.39, 50kW: Patrick Stroupe 4:25:06. **Women**: 100m: Tianna Bartoletta 11.15, 200m: Jeneba Tarmoh 22.06w, 400m: Francena McCorory 49.48, 800m: Ajee' Wilson 1:59.70, 1500m: Jenny Simpson 4:04.96, 5000m: Molly Huddle 15:01.56, 10000m: Kim Conley 32:02.07, HMar: Serena Burla 70:48, Mar: Esther Erb 2:34:00, 3000mSt: Emma Coburn 9:19.72, 100mh: Dawn Harper Nelson 12.55, 400mh: Kori Carter 53.84, HJ: Chaunté Lowe 1.94, PV: Jenn Suhr 4.60, LJ: Brittney Reese 6.92, TJ: Amanda Smock 13.77w, SP: Michelle Carter 19.45, DT: Gia Lewis-Smallwood 65.96, HT: Amanda Bingson 75.73, JT: Kara Patterson 62.43, Hep: Sharon Day-Monroe 6470, 20,000mW: Marie Michta 1:35:54.37.

NCAA Championships first held in 1921 (men), 1982 (women). **2014 Champions**: **Men**: 100m: Trayvon Brommell 9.97, 200m: Dedric Dukes 19.91w, 400m: Deon Lendore TTO 45.02, 800m: Brandon McBride CAN 1:46.26, 1500m: Mac Fleet 3:39.09, 5000m: Lawi Lalang KEN 13:18.36, 10000m: Edward Cheserek KEN 28:30.18, 3000mSt: Anthony Rotich KEN 8:32.21, 110mh: Devon Allen 13.16, 400mh: Miles Ukaoma 49.23, HJ: Bryan McBride 2.28, PV: Sam Kendricks 5.70, LJ/TJ: Marquis Dendy 8.00/ 17.05w, SP: Ryan Crouser 21.12, DT: Hayden Reed 62.74, HT: Matthias Tayala 73.57, JT: Sam Crouser 76.98, Dec: Maicel Uibo EST 8182. **Women**: 100m: Remona Burchell JAM 11.25, 200m: Kamaria Brown 22.63w, 400m: Courtney Okolo 50.23, 800m: Laura Roesler 2:01.22, 1500m: Shelby Houlihan 4:18.10, 5000m: Marielle Hall 15:35.11, 10000m: Emma Bates 32:32.35, 3000mSt: Leah O'Connor 9:36.43, 100mh: Sharika Nelvis 12.52w, 400mh: Shamier Little 55.07, HJ: Leontia Kallenou CYP 1.89, PV: Annika Roloff GER 4.40, LJ: Jenna Prandini 6.55, TJ: Shenieka Thomas JAM 14.00, SP: Christina Hillman 17.73, DT: Shelbi Vaughan 60.02, HT: Julia Ratcliffe NZL 66.88, JT: Fawn Miller 58.13, Hep: Kendell Williams 5854.

Devon ALLEN b. 12 Dec 1994 Phoenix, Arizona 1.90m 86kg. Student at University of Oregon.
At 110mh: Won US & NCAA 2014.
Progress at 110mh: 2014- 13.16. pbs: 60m 6.85Ai '14, 100m 10.56/10.48w '13, 200m 20.98 '13, 60mh 7.83Ai '14, 400mh 51.19 '14.
On a football scholarship, wide receiver. Suffered a knee injury on the opening kickoff of the Rose Bowl at the end of 2014.

Ronnie ASH b. 2 Jul 1988 Raleigh NC 1.88m 86kg. Nike. Was at University of Oklahoma.
At 110mh: CCp: '14- 2; won NACAC 2010, NCAA 2009.
Progress at 110mh: 2008- 13.44, 2009- 13.27, 2010- 13.19/12.98w, 2011- 13.25/13.24w, 2012- 13.20/ 13.10w, 2014- 12.99. pbs: 200m 22.08 '08, 60mh 7.55i '10.

Ryan BAILEY b. 13 Apr 1989 Portland, Oregon 1.93m 98kg. Nike.
At 100m/4x100mR: OG: '12- 4/2R. At 4x400m: WJ: '08- res (1)R.
N.American 4x100m record 2012.
Progress at 100m, 200m: 2007- 10.48/10.45w, 21.13/21.11w; 2008- 10.28, 20.69; 2009- 10.05, 20.45; 2010- 9.88, 20.10; 2012- 9.88, 20.43; 2013- 10.10/ 10.00w, 2014- 10.12/10.03w, 20.37. pbs: 55m 6.20i '09, 60m 6.50i '15, 300m 33.50 '07, 400m 47.05 '08, 60mh 7.97i '08, 110mh 14.13 '08.
His nephew Eric Bailey 400mh pb 50.04 '11.

Marvin BRACY b. 15 Dec 1993 Orlando, Florida 1.88m 74kg. adidas. Was at Florida State University.
At 100m/4x100mR: WJ: '10- res 1R; PAm-J: 11-1. At 60m: WI: '14- 2.
Progress at 100m: 2009- 48.72, 2010- 10.42/10.19w, 2011- 10.28/10.05w, 2012- 10.25/10.06w, 2013- 10.09, 2014- 10.08. pbs: 60m 6.48Ai/6.51i '14, 200m 20.55 '14.
Wide receiver at American Football.

Trayvon BROMELL b 10 Jul 1995 St. Petersburg, Florida 1.75m 71kg. Student at Baylor University.
At 100m/4x100mR: WJ: '14- 2/1R; PAm-J: 13- 3/1R. Two world junior 100m records 2014.
Progress at 100m: 2012- 10.40, 2013- 10.27/9.99Aw, 2014- 9.97/9.77w. pbs: 60m 6.54i '15, 200m 20.19i '15, 20.59/20.23w '14.

Christian CANTWELL b. 30 Sep 1980 Jefferson City, Missouri 1.93m 154kg. Nike. Studied hotel and restaurant management at University of Missouri.
At SP: OG: '08- 2, '12- 4; WCh: '05- 4, '09- 1, '11- 3; WI: '04-08-10: 1/1/1; CCp: '10- 1; won DL 2010, WAF 2003, 2009; US 2005, 2009-10. At DT: PAm-J: '99- 2.

Progress at SP: 1999- 15.85, 2000- 19.67, 2001- 19.71, 2002- 21.45, 2003- 21.62, 2004- 22.54, 2005- 21.67, 2006- 22.45, 2007- 21.96, 2008- 22.18i/21.76, 2009- 22.16, 2010- 22.41, 2011- 22.07, 2012- 22.31, 2013- 20.13i/19.86, 2014- 21.85. pbs: DT 59.32 '01, HT 57.18 '01, Wt 22.04i '03.
Three competitions over 22m in 2004, then 4th in US Olympic Trials. Married Teri Steer (b. 3 Oct 1975, SP pb 19.21 '01, 3 WI 1999) 29 Oct 2005.

Matthew CENTROWITZ b. 18 Nov 1989 Beltsville, Maryland 1.76m 61kg. Nike Oregon Project. Studied sociology at the University of Oregon.
At 1500m: OG: '12- 4; WCh: '11- 3, '12- 2; WI: '12- 7. At 5000m WJ: '08- 11. Won US 2011, 2013; NCAA 2011, PAm-J 2007.
Progress at 1500m: 2007- 3:49.54, 2008- 3:44.98, 2009- 3:36.92, 2010- 3:40.14, 2011- 3:34.46, 2012- 3:31.96, 2013- 3:33.58, 2014- 3:31.09. pbs: 800m 1:45.86 '13, 1000m 2:17.00i '15, 1M 3:50.53 '14, 3000m 7:46.19i '12, 2M 8:40.55 '07, 5000m 13:20.06 '14.
Father Matt pbs: 1500m 3:36.60 '76, 3:54.94 '82, 5000m US record 13:12.91 '82, 10000m 28:32.7 '83; h OG 1500m 1976; 1 PAm 5000m 1979. Sister Lauren (b. 25 Sep 1986) 1500m pb 4:10.23 '09.

Will CLAYE b. 13 Jun 1991 Phoenix 1.80m 68kg. Nike. Was at University of Oklahoma, then Florida.
At (LJ)/TJ: OG: '12- 3/2; WCh: '11- 9/3, '13- 3; WI: '12- 4/1; CCp: '14- 2/3; won US 2014, PAm-J and NCAA 2009.
Progress at LJ, TJ: 2007- 14.91/15.19w, 2008- 7.39/7.48w, 15.97; 2009- 7.89/8.00w, 17.19/17.24w; 2010- 7.30w, 16.30; 2011- 8.29, 17.50/17.62w; 2012- 8.25, 17.70i/17.62; 2013- 8.10, 17.52; 2014- 8.19/ 8.29w, 17.75. pb 100m 10.64/10.53w '12.
Possibly youngest ever NCAA champion – he won 2009 title on his 18th birthday with 17.24w (and US junior record 17.19). First athlete to win Olympic medals at both LJ and TJ since 1936.

Kerron CLEMENT b. 31 Oct 1985 Port of Spain, Trinidad 1.88m 84kg. Nike. Was at University of Florida.
At 400mh/4x400mR: OG: '08- 2/res1R, '12- 8; WCh: '05- 4, '07- 1/res 1R, '09- 1/1R, '11- sf, '13- 8; WJ: '04- 1/1R; WI: '10- res 1R; WCp: '06- 1. Won WAF 2008-09, US 2005-06, NCAA 2004-05. World junior 4x400m record 2004, world indoor records: 400m 2005, 4x400m 2006.
Progress at 400m, 400mh: 2002- 49.77H, 2003- 50.13H, 2004- 45.90, 48.51; 2005- 44.57i, 47.24; 2006- 44.71, 47.39; 2007- 44.48, 47.61; 2008- 45.10, 47.79; 2009- 45.08, 47.91; 2010- 46.01, 47.86; 2011- 45.42, 48.74; 2012- 46.49, 48.12; 2013- 45.74, 48.06; 2014- 46.08, -. pbs: 60m 6.89i '10, 100m 10.23 '07, 200m 20.40i '05, 20.49 '07; 300m 31.94i '06, 55mh 7.28i '05, 60mh 7.80i '04, 110mh 13.78 '04.
Born in Trinidad, moved to Texas in 1998, US citizenship confirmed in 2005. Ran 47.24, the world's fastest time since 1998, to win 2005 US 400mh title.

Ryan CROUSER b. 18 Dec 1992 Portland 2.01m 109kg. Student at University of Texas.
At SP/DT: WY: '09- 1/2. Won NCAA shot 2013-14, indoors 2014.
Progress at SP: 2011- 19.48i, 2012- 20.29i/19.32, 2013- 21.09, 2014- 21.39. pbs: DT 63.90 '14, JT 61.16 '09.
Set High School 1.62kg DT record 72.40 '11. His father Mitch SP 20.04i '83, 19.94 '82, DT 67.22 '85; uncle Dean SP 21.07 '82, DT 65.88 '83, won NCAA SP 1982 & DT 1982-3; uncle Brian JT 83.00 '87, old JT 95.10 '85, won NCAA 1982 & 1985, dnq OG 1988 & 1992; Dean's children: Sam SP 17.62 '13, JT 80.80 '12, US junior & HS record '10, won NCAA 2014; Haley US junior JT record 55.22 '12, 4 WY '11.

Marquis DENDY b. 17 Nov 1992 Middleton, Delaware 1.90m 75kg. University of Florida.
At LJ: WCh: '13- dnq 27; At TJ: WJ: '10- 8; won NACAC LJ 2012, NCAA TJ 2014, indoor LJ 2013, 2015; TJ 2015..
Progress at LJ, TJ: 2009- 7.20, 15.40; 2010- 7.45, 16.03; 2011- 7.47/7.56w, 15.62; 2012- 8.06i/7.81, 15.55; 2013- 8.28i/8.10/8.29w, 16.25i/16.03; 2014- 8.00, 16.52/17.05w; 2015- 8.28i, 17.37i. pbs: 60m 6.88i '14. 100m 10.63/10.62w '11.

Walter DIX b. 31 Jan 1986 Coral Springs, Florida 1.78m 84kg. Nike. Studied social science at Florida State University.
At 100m/200m: OG: '08- 3/3; WCh: '11- 2/2; won US 100m 2010-11, 200m 2008, 2011; NCAA 100m 2005, 2007; 200m 2006-08; DL 200m 2011. World junior 200m indoor record (20.37) 2005.
Progress at 100m, 200m: 2002- 10.72/10.67w, 2003- 10.41/10.29w, 21.04/20.94w; 2004- 10.28, 20.62/20.54w; 2005- 10.06/9.96w, 20.18; 2006- 10.12, 20.25; 2007- 9.93, 19.69; 2008- 9.91/9.80w, 19.86; 2009- 10.00, 2010- 9.88, 19.72; 2011- 9.94, 19.53; 2012- 10.03/9.85w, 20.02; 2013- 9.99, 20.12; 2014- 10.17, 20.32/20.21w. pbs: 55m 6.19i '07, 60m 6.59i '06, 150mSt 14.65 '11, 400m 46.75 '10, LJ 7.39 '04.

Dedric DUKES b. 4 Feb 1992 Miami 1.80m 70kg. Student at University of Florida.
At 200m: WY: '09- 4/1 MedR. Won NCAA 2014.
Progress at 200m: 2007- 21.88/21.79w, 2008- 21.19/21.12w, 2009- 20.94, 2011- 20.88w, 2012- 20.47, 2013- 20.45/20.34w, 2014- 19.97/19.91w. pbs: 60m 6.77i '14, 100m 10.27/10.24w '14, 400m 45.66 '14.
Football wide receiver in high school.

Johnny DUTCH b. 20 Jan 1989 Clayton NC 1.80m 82kg. Nike. Studied media arts at University of South Carolina.
At 400mh: WCh: '09- sf; WJ: '08- 2; PAm-J: '07- 1/2R. Won US 2014, NCAA 2010.
Progress at 400mh: 2005- 52.06, 2006- 52.37, 2007- 50.07, 2008- 48.52, 2009- 48.18, 2010- 47.63, 2011- 48.47, 2012- 48.90, 2013- 48.02, 2014- 48.93. pbs: 400m 46.75 '13, 500m 1:03.25i '15, 55mh 7.31i '10, 60mh 7.71i '09, 110mh 13.50/13.30w '10.

Ashton EATON b. 21 Jan 1988 Portland, Oregon 1.86m 86kg. Oregon TC Elite. Graduate of University of Oregon.
At Dec: OG: '12- 1; WCh: '09- 18, '11- 2; won US 2012-13, NCAA 2008-10. At Hep: WI: '12- 1, 14- 1. World decathlon record 2012, indoor heptathlon records 2010 (6499), 2011 (6568) and 2012.
Progress at Dec: 2007- 7123, 2008- 8122, 2009- 8241w/8091, 2010- 8457, 2011- 8729, 2012- 9039, 2013- 8809. At 400mh: 2014- 48.69. pbs: 60m 6.66i '11, 100m 10.21 '12, 10.19w '10; 200m 20.76 '13, 400m 45.64 '13, 800m 1:55.90i '10, 1000m 2:32.67i '10, 1500m 4:14.48 '12, 60mh 7.51i '15, 110mh 13.35 '11, 13.34w '12; HJ 2.11i '10, 2.11 '12; PV 5.35i '14, 5.30 '12; LJ 8.23 '12, SP 15.40 '13, DT 47.36 '11, JT 66.64 '13, Hep 6645i '12.
Set best ever marks in decathlons with 100m 10.21 and LJ 8.23 in WR in Eugene 22/23 June 2012. Married Brianne Theisen CAN on 15 July 2013.

Justin GATLIN b. 10 Feb 1982 Brooklyn, NY 1.85m 79kg. XTEP. Was at University of Tennessee.
At 100m/(200m)/4x100mR: OG: '04- 1/3/2R, '12- 3/2R; WCh: '05- 1/1, '11- sf, '13- 2/2R. At 60m: WI: '03- 1, '12- 1. Won DL 100m 2013-14, US 100m 2005-06, 2012; 200m 2005 (indoor 60m 2003), NCAA 100m & 200m 2001-02 (& indoor 60m/200m 2002).
N.American 4x100m record 2012.
Progress at 100m, 200m: 2000- 10.36, 2001- 10.08, 20.29/19.86w; 2002: under international suspension 10.05/10.00w, 19.86; 2003- 9.97, 20.04; 2004- 9.85, 20.01; 2005- 9.88/9.84w, 20.00; 2006- 9.77dq, 2010- 10.09, 20.63; 2011- 9.95, 20.20; 2012- 9.79, 20.11; 2013- 9.85, 20.21; 2014- 9.77/9.76w, 19.68. pbs: 60m 6.45i '03, 100y 9.10 '14, 55mh 7.39i '02, 60mh 7.86i '01, 110mh 13.41dq '02, 13.78/13.74w '01; LJ 7.34i '01, 7.21 '00.
Top hurdler in high school (110mh 13.66 and 300mh 36.74 on junior hurdles). Retained NCAA sprint titles while ineligible for international competition in 2002 after failing a drugs test in 2001 (when he won 100m, 200m and 110mh at the US Juniors) for a prescribed medication to treat Attention Deficit Disorder. Reinstated by IAAF in July 2002. Won 2005 World 100m title by biggest ever winning margin of 0.17. Won all five 100m competitions in 2006, including tying the world record with 9.77 in Doha and taking the US title, but had tested positive for testosterone before these performances. He received a four-year drugs ban but returned to competition in August 2010. In 2014 he was unbeaten at 100m and 200m (the first man to do so since Usain Bolt in 2009) and in Brussels on 5 Sep recorded the best-ever one-day sprint double with 9.77 and 19.71.

Tyson GAY b. 9 Aug 1982 Lexington 1.83m 73kg. adidas. Studied marketing at University of Arkansas.
At 100m/(200m)/4x100mR: OG: '08- sf, '12- dq4/2R; WCh: '05- (4), '07- 1/1/1R, '09- 2; WCp: '06- 1/1R, '10- 1R. Won DL 2010, WAF 100m 2009, 200m 2005-06, US 100m 2007-08, 2013; 200m 2007, 2013; NCAA 100m 2004.
Five N.American 100m records 2008-12.
Progress at 100m, 200m: 2000- 10.56, 21.27; 2001- 10.28, 21.23; 2002- 10.27/10.08w, 20.88/20.21w; 2003- 10.01Aw/10.14w, 21.15/20.31w; 2004- 10.06/10.10w, 20.07; 2005- 10.08, 19.93; 2006- 9.84, 19.68; 2007- 9.84/9.76w, 19.62; 2008- 9.77/9.68w, 20.00; 2009- 9.69, 19.58; 2010- 9.78, 19.76; 2011- 9.79, 2012- 9.86/9.80dq, 20.21dq; 2013- 9.75dq, 19.74dq; 2014- 9.93, 20.22. pbs: 60m 6.39+ '09, 6.55i '05; 150mSt 14.51 '11, 200m/220ySt 19.41/ 19.54 '10, 400m 44.89 '10.
Ran four 200m races in under 19.85 in 2006. Then greatest ever sprint double (9.84 and 19.62) at 2007 US Champs and ran fastest ever 100m 9.68w/+4.1 (after US record in qf) to win US Olympic Trials in 2008 but pulled hamstring in 200m qf and unable to compete again until Olympics, where he was not back to top form. IAAF Athlete of the Year 2006. He tested positive for a banned substance (later reported as a steroid) in May 2013 and he withdrew from the World Championships; case resolved with a 1-year ban and annulment of results from 15 Jul 2012, thus including his Olympic 2012 results.

Justin GAYMON b. 13 Dec 1986 Stewartsville, New Jersey 1.75m 70kg. Graduate in advertising from University of Georgia.
At 400mh: won NACAC 2008.
Progress at 400mh: 2004- 52.87, 2005- 50.84, 2006- 50.20, 2007- 49.25, 2008- 48.46, 2009- 48.86, 2010- 48.65, 2011- 48.58, 2012- 48.97, 2013- 48.46, 2014- 49.53. pbs: 200m 21.28 '08, 400m 45.94i/ 46.17 '08, 55mh 7.47i '07, 60mh 7.86i '09, 110mh 13.90 '06, 13.85w '07.

Arman HALL b. 12 Feb 1994 Pembroke Pines, Florida 1.88m 77kg. Student at University of Florida.
At 400m/4x400mR: WCh: '13- sf/1R; WJ: '12- 2/1R; WY: '11- 1/1 medley R.
Progress at 400m: 2009- 48.72, 2010- 47.43, 2011- 46.01, 2012- 45.39, 2013- 44.82, 2014- 45.19. pb 200m 20.40 '14.

James Edward '**Trey**' **HARDEE** b. 7 Feb 1984 Birmingham, Alabama 1.96m 95kg. Nike. Was at Mississippi State University and University of Texas.
At Dec: OG: '08- dnf, '12- 2; WCh: '09- 1, '11- 1, '13- dnf; won NCAA 2005, US 2009, 2014. At Hep: WI: '10- 2.
Progress at Dec: 2003- 7544, 2004- 8041, 2005- 7881, 2006- 8465, 2008- 8534, 2009- 8790, 2011- 8689, 2012- 8671, 2013- dnf, 2014- 8599. pbs: 55m 6.30i '06, 60m 6.71i '06, 100m 10.39 '10, 10.28w '06; 200m 20.98 '06, 300m 33.69 '14, 400m 47.51 '06, 1000m 2:45.67i '12, 1500m 4:40.94 '12, 60mh

7.70i '10, 110mh 13.54 '12; HJ 2.06i '10, 2.05 '08; PV 5.30Ai '06, 5.25 '08; LJ 7.88 '11, SP 15.94i '09, 15.72 '12; DT 52.68 '08, JT 68.99 '11, Hep 6208Ai '06.
Won IAAF Combined Events Challenge 2009 and in Götzis 2014. Married Chelsea Johnson (PV 4.73 '08, 2= WCh 2009) in 2014; her father Jan Johnson set a world indoor PV best 5.36 '70, won at the 1971 Pan-Ams and was the 1972 Olympic bronze medallist.

Aleec HARRIS b. 31 Oct 1990 Lawrenceville, Georgia 1.85m 77kg. Was at University of Southern California.
Progress at 110mh: 2010- 14.15/13.88w, 2011- 13.65/13.55w, 2012- 13.69/13.55w, 2014- 13.14. pbs: 55mh 7.18i '11, 60mh 7.50i '15.

Mike HARTFIELD b. 29 Mar 1990 Manchester, Connecticut 1.90m 77kg. adidas. Was at Ohio State University.
Progress at LJ: 2007- 7.19w, 2008- 7.52w, 2009- 7.57, 2010- 7.61i, 2011- 7.91/7.95w, 2012- 7.96, 2013- 8.15, 2014- 8.15/8.17w. pb TJ 15.84 '13.
Broke 77 year-old Ohio State University record set by Jesse Owens.

Jeffery HENDERSON b. 16 Feb 1989 Sherwood, Arkansas 1.78m 82kg. Was at Florida Memorial University and Stillman College.
At LJ: WCh: '09- h; US champion 2014, indoors 2012.
Progress at LJ: 2006- 7.14i, 2007- 7.51i/7.41, 2008- 7.74/7.77w, 2009- 8.15u/7.88/8.19w, 2010- 7.94Ai/ 7.90i, 2011- 7.78, 2012- 7.91w, 2013- 8.22, 2014- 8.43/8.52w. pbs: 55m 6.31i '09, 60m 6.58Ai/6.69i '14. 100m 10.18A/10.20w '13, 10.25 '11; 200m 20.65A '13, TJ 14.90i '08.

Reese HOFFA b. 8 Oct 1977 Evans, Georgia 1.81m 133kg. New York AC. Was at University of Georgia.
At SP: OG: '04- dnq 21, '08- 6, '12- 3; WCh: '03-07-09-11-13: dnq/1/4/4/4; PAm: '03- 1; WI: '04-06-08-12: 2/1/2/4; WUG: '01- 9; WCp: '06- 2; won WAF 2006-07, DL 2012, 2014; USA 2007-08, 2012.
Progress at SP: 1998- 19.08, 1999- 19.35, 2000- 19.79, 2001- 20.22, 2002- 20.47, 2003- 20.95, 2004- 21.67, 2005- 21.74i/21.29, 2006- 22.11i/21.96, 2007- 22.43, 2008- 22.10, 2009- 21.89, 2010- 22.16, 2011- 22.09, 2012- 22.00, 2013- 21.71, 2014- 21.88. pbs: DT 58.46 '99, HT 60.05 '02.
Added 37cm to his best to win World Indoor gold 2006. Married Renata Foerst (HT 55.49 '04) in 2005.

Mark HOLLIS b. 1 Dec 1984 Freeport, Illinois 1.90m 86kg. Nike. Sports management graduate of Olivet Nazarene University.
At PV: WCh: '11- dnq 22=; CCp: '14- 3 US champion 2010 & indoors 2011.
Progress at PV: 2002- 4.42; 2005- 5.10, 2006- 5.25, 2007- 5.34i/5.33, 2008- 5.75, 2009- 5.70, 2010- 5.75, 2011- 5.63i/5.62, 2012- 5.60, 2013- 5.50Ai/ 5.42, 2014- 5.83.

Daniel **HULING** b. 16 Jul 1983 Denver 1.85m 70kg. Nike. Was at Miami University (Ohio).
At 3000mSt: WCh: '09/11/13- h; CCp: '10- 8; US champion 2010.
Progress at 3000mSt: 2004- 8:58.88, 2005- 8:43.59, 2006- 8:27.41, 2008- 8:20.84, 2009- 8:14.69, 2010- 8:13.29, 2011- 8:25.95, 2012- 8:20.81, 2013- 8:21.92, 2014- 8:15.61. pbs: 1500m 3:37.53 '12, 1M 3:58.24i '12, 2000m 5:02.41i '14, 3000m 7:44.42 '13, 5000m 13:18.42 '13, 10000m 30:37.25 '06.

Bershawn JACKSON b. 8 May 1983 Miami 1.73m 69kg. Nike. Studied accountancy at St Augustine's University, Florida.
At 400mh/4x400mR: OG: '08- 3; WCh: '03- h (dq), '05- 1, '07- sf/res 1R, '09- 3/res 1R, '11- 6/1R, '13- sf; WJ: '02- 3/1R; CCp: '10- 3/1R; won DL 2010, WAF 2004-05, US 2003, 2008-10. At 400m: WI: '10- 5/1R; won US indoor 2005, 2010.
Progress at 400mh: 2000- 52.17, 2001- 50.86, 2002- 50.00, 2003- 48.23, 2004- 47.86, 2005- 47.30, 2006- 47.48, 2007- 48.13, 2008- 48.02, 2009- 47.98, 2010- 47.32, 2011- 47.93, 2012- 48.20, 2013- 48.09, 2014- 48.76. pbs: 200m 21.03/20.46w '04, 400m 45.06 '07, 500m 1:00.70i '15, 600m 1:18.65i '06, 800m 1:53.40 '11, 200mhSt 22.26 '11.

Evan JAGER b. 8 Mar 1989 Algonquin, Illinois 1.86m 66kg. Bowerman TC. Was at University of Wisconsin.
At 3000mSt: OG: '12- 6; WCh: '13- 5; CCp: '14- 2; US champion 2012-14. At 1500m: WJ: '08- 8. At 5000m: WCh: '09- h.
N.American 3000m steeplechase record 2012 & 2014.
Progress at 5000m, 3000mSt: 2009- 13:22.18, 2012- 8:06.81, 2013- 13:02.40, 8:08.60; 2014- 13:08.63, 8:04.71. pbs: 800m 1:50.10i '10, 1:51.04 '08; 1000m 2:20.29i '15, 1500m 3:36.34 '13, 1M 3:53.33 '14, 2000m 4:57.56 '14, 3000m 7:35.16 '12, 2M 8:14.95i '13.
Set US record in only his fifth steeplechase race, improving pb by 10.59 secs. In 2009 he had come 3rd in the US Champs in only his second race at 5000m.

Brandon JOHNSON b. 6 Mar 1985 Mannheim, Germany 1.75m 68kg. Nike. Was at UCLA.
At 800m: WCh: '13. At 400mh: WJ: 04- 2/1 4x400mR.
Progress at 400mh, 800m: 2004- 48.62, 2005- 48.59, 2006- 50.12, 2007- 49.02, 1:50.85; 2008- 48.68, 2009- 50.12, 2012- 1:46.73, 2013- 1:43.84, 2014- 1:46.67. pbs: 60m 6.82i '06, 100m 10.60/ 10.44w '03, 10.2w '02; 200m 21.29 '05, 20.9w '03; 400m 46.34 '05, 1500m 3:45.12 '14.

Dustin **'Dusty' JONAS** b. 19 Apr 1986 Floresville, Texas 1.98m 84kg. Was at University of Nebraska.
At HJ: OG: '08- dnq 26=; WCh: '11/13- dnq 30/16=; WI: '10- 3; PAm-J: '05- 1; CCp: '10- 6. Won NCAA indoor 2008.
Progress at HJ: 2002- 2.16, 2003- 2.22, 2004- 2.13,

2005- 2.24, 2006- 2.28, 2007- 2.25i/2.24, 2008- 2.36A, 2009- 2.26i/2.24, 2010- 2.33, 2011- 2.31, 2012- 2.25i, 2013- 2.34i/2.31, 2014- 2.35. pb LJ 7.47/7.76w '07; TJ 15.15i '12, 15.07 '07.

Sam KENDRICKS b. 7 Sep 1992 Mississippi 1.89m 79kg. Was at University of Mississippi.
At PV: WUG: '13- 1; US champion 2014, NCAA 2013-4.
Progress at PV: 2011- 5.18, 2012- 5.50, 2013- 5.81, 2014- 5.75, 2015- 5.86Ai/5.80.

Joe KOVACS b. 28 Jun 1989 Nazareth, Pennsylvania 1.85m 114kg. Nike. Was at Penn State University.
At SP: CCp: '14- 3; US champion 2014.
Progress at SP: 2007- 16.49, 2008- 16.86i, 2009- 18.53, 2010- 19.36i/18.73, 2011- 19.84i/19.15, 2012- 21.08, 2013- 20.82, 2014- 22.03. pbs: DT 56.08 '11, HT 61.50 '11, Wt 19.07i '11.

Erik KYNARD b. 3 Feb 1991 Toledo, Ohio 1.93m 86kg. Nike. Was at Kansas State University.
At HJ: OG: '12- 2; WCh: '11- dnq 14, '13- 5; WJ: '08- dnq 19=; CCp: '14- 5; WI: '14- 4; Won US 2013-14, NCAA 2011-12.
Progress at HJ: 2007- 2.13i, 2008- 2.23i/2.15, 2009- 2.24i/2.22, 2010- 2.25, 2011- 2.33i/2.31, 2012- 2.34, 2013- 2.37, 2014- 2.37. pb LJ 7.15i '09.

Bernard LAGAT b. 12 Dec 1974 Kapsabet, Kenya 1.75m 61kg. Nike. Studied business management at Washington State University, USA.
At 1500m (/5000m): OG: '00- 3, '04- 2, '08- sf/9, '12- (4); WCh: '01- 2, '05- sf, '07- 1/1, '09- 3/2, '11- (2), '13- (6); WI: '03- 2; AfCh: '02- 1; WUG: '99- 1; WCp: '02- 1; 2nd GP 1999-2000-02, WAF 2005-06. At 3000m: WI: '01-04-10-12-14: 6/1/1/1/2; CCp: '10- 1/(1), '14- 3. Won WAF 3000m 2005, 2008; KEN 1500m 2002, US 1500m 2006, 2008; 5000m 2006-08, 2010-11, 2013-14; NCAA 5000m 1999 (and indoor 1M/3000m).
Records: Commonwealth and KEN 1500m 2001, N.American 1500m 2005, 3000m 2010, 5000m 2010 & 2011, indoor 2000m 2014, 3000m 2007, 2M 2011 & 2013, 5000m 2010, 2012. World M35 3000m & 5000m 2010, 1M and 5000m 2011, 2000m 2014; M40 indoor 1500m, 1M, 3000m (3), 2M 2015.
Progress at 1500m, 5000m: 1996- 3:37.7A, 1997- 3:41.19, 13:50.33; 1998- 3:34.48, 13:42.73; 1999- 3:30.56, 13:36.12; 2000- 3:28.51, 13:23.46; 2001- 3:26.34, 13:30.54; 2002- 3:27.91, 13:19.14; 2003- 3:30.55, 2004- 3:27.40, 2005- 3:29.30, 12:59.29; 2006- 3:29.68, 12:59.22; 2007- 3:33.85, 13:30.73; 2008- 3:32.75, 13:16.29; 2009- 3:32.56, 13:03.06; 2010- 3:32.51, 12:54.12; 2011- 3:33.11, 12:53.60; 2012- 3:34.63, 12:59.92; 2013- 3:36.36, 12:58.99; 2014- 13:06.68. pbs: 800m 1:46.00 '03, 1000m 2:16.18 '08, 1M 3:47.28 '01, 2000m 4:54.74i '14, 4:55.49 '99; 3000m 7:29.00 '10, 2M 8:09.49i '13, 8:12.45 '08, HMar 62:33 '13.
Gave up his final year of scholastic eligibility (as under NCAA rules no payments can be received) at his university in order to compete (for money) in the 1999 GP Final, in which he was 2nd. He was 2nd to Hicham El Guerrouj six times in 2001, including his 3:26.34 at Brussels for 2nd on the world all-time list, and six times in 2002. Withdrew from 2003 Worlds after testing positive for EPO, but this was later repudiated. Lives in Tucson, Arizona, gained US citizenship 2005. First man ever to win 1500m/5000m double at the US Champs in 2006 and at World Champs in 2007. Oldest ever male World Indoor champion at 37y 89d in 2012 and medallist at 39y 87d in 2014.
A sister **Mary Chepkemboi** competed at the 1982 Commonwealth Games and won African 3000m in 1984, and another **Evelyne Jerotich Langat** has 71:35 half marathon pb. Of his brothers **William Cheseret** has a marathon pb of 2:12:09 '04 and **Robert Cheseret** won NCAA 5000m in 2004 and 10000m in 2005, pbs 5000m 13:13.23 & 10000m 28:20.11 '05.

Tony McQUAY b. 16 Apr 1990 West Palm Beach, Florida 1.80m 70kg. adidas. Was at University of Florida.
At 400m: OG: '12- sf/2R; WCh: '11- h, '13- 2/1R; US champion 2011, NCAA 2012.
Progress at 400m: 2008- 48.09, 2009- 46.84, 2010- 45.37, 2011- 44.68, 2012- 44.49, 2013- 44.40, 2014- 44.92. pbs: 100m 10.22 '13, 10.13w '14; 200m 20.60 '12, 300m 32.40 '13.

Josh MANCE b. 21 Mar 1992 Los Angeles 1.91m 82kg. Was at University of Southern California.
At 400m/4x400mR: OG: '12- res 2R; WCh: '13- res 1R; WJ: '10- 5/1R; WY: '09- 2/1 Med R; PAm-J: '11- 1/1R; US champion 2011, NCAA 2012.
Progress at 400m: 2007- 48.36, 2008- 46.61, 2009- 46.22, 2010- 45.90, 2011- 45.29, 2012- 44.83, 2013- 45.08, 2014- 44.89. pbs: 200m 21.20 '11, 21.18w '10; 800m 1:51.16 '12.

Leonel MANZANO b. 12 Sep 1984 Dolores Hidalgo, Guanajuato, Mexico 1.65m 57kg. Hoka One One. Was at the University of Texas.
At 1500m: OG: '08- sf,'12- 2; WCh: '07- h, '09- 12, '11/13- sf; CCp: '10- 3, '14- 7. Won US 2012, 2014; NCAA 2005, 2008.
N.American 4x1500m record 2014.
Progress at 1500m: 2003- 4:07.83M, 2005- 3:37.13, 2006- 3:39.49, 2007- 3:35.29, 2008- 3:36.67, 2009- 3:33.33, 2010- 3:32.37, 2011- 3:33.66, 2012- 3:34.08, 2013- 3:33.14, 2014- 3:30.98. pbs: 800m 1:44.56 '10, 1000m 2:19.73 '09, 1M 3:50.64 '10, 3000m 8:14.59i '06.
Has lived in the USA from the age of 4.

Cory MARTIN b. 22 May 1985 Bloomington, Indiana 1.96m 125kg. Nike. Was at Auburn University.
At SP: WCh: '13- 9; WJ: '04- 11 (dnq 15 HT); Won NCAA SP & HT 2008.

Progress at SP: 2004- 17.95i/17.60, 2005- 18.85, 2006- 18.42i, 2007- 19.63, 2008- 20.35, 2009- 20.43, 2010- 22.10, 2011- 20.72, 2012- 21.31, 2013- 20.67, 2014- 20.73. pbs: DT 58.59 '08, HT 75.06 '09, 35lbWt 24.38i '10.

Aries MERRITT b. 24 Jul 1985 Marietta, Georgia 1.83m 74kg. Nike. Studied sports management at University of Tennessee.
At 110mh: OG: '12- 1; WCh: '09- h, '11- 5=, '13- 6; WJ: '04- 1. At 60mh: WI: '12-1, Won DL 110mh 2012, NCAA 60mh indoors & 110mh 2006, US indoor 60mh & 110mh 2012.
World 110mh record 2012.
Progress at 110mh: 2004- 13.47, 2005- 13.38/ 13.34w, 2006- 13.12, 2007- 13.09, 2008- 13.24, 2009- 13.15, 2010- 13.61, 2011- 13.12, 2012- 12.80, 2013- 13.09, 2014- 13.27. pbs: 55m 6.43i '05, 60m 6.90i '10, 200m 21.31 '05, 50mh 6.54i '12, 55mh 7.02+i '12, 60mh 7.43Ai/7.44i '12, 400mh 51.94 '04.
Record 8 (and 2w) sub-13 second times in 2012.

LaShawn MERRITT b. 27 Jun 1986 Portsmouth, Virginia 1.88m 82kg. Nike. Studied sports management at Old Dominion University, Norfolk, Virginia.
At 400m/4x400mR: OG: '08- 1/1R, '12- dnf ht; WCh: '05- res(1)R, '07- 2/1R, '09- 1/1R, '11- 2/1R. '13- 1/1R; WJ: '04- 1/1R (1 at 4x100); WI: '06- 1R; WCp: '06- 1/1R, '14- 1/3R; won WAF 2007-09, DL 2013-14; US 2008-09, 2012-13.
World junior records 4x100m and 4x400m 2004, World indoor 400m junior best (44.93) 2005.
Progress at 200m, 400m: 2002- 21.46, 2003- 21.33, 47.9?; 2004- 20.72/20.69w, 45.25; 2005- 20.38, 44.66; 2006- 20.10, 44.14; 2007- 19.98, 43.96; 2008- 20.08/19.80w, 43.75; 2009- 20.07, 44.06; 2011- 20.13, 44.63; 2012- 20.16, 44.12; 2013- 20.26, 43.74; 2014- 20.42, 43.92. pbs: 55m 6.33i '04, 60m 6.68i '06, 100m 10.47/10.38w '04, 300m 31.30 '09, 500m 1:01.39i '12.
World age-18 400m record with 44.66 in 2005 and world low-altitude 300m best 2006 and 2009. Spent a year at East Carolina University before signing for Nike and returning home to Portsmouth. Two-year drugs ban for three positive tests from October 2009, reduced by three months after US arbitration panel declared that he had taken the steroid accidentally in buying a product intended for sexual enhancement; successfully challenged IOC rule preventing anyone serving 6 months or more from a drugs offence from competing in the next Games. Injured, he had to pull up in 2012 Olympic heat.

Curtis MITCHELL b. 11 Mar 1989 Daytona Beach 1.88m 79kg. adidas. Was at Texas A&M University.
At 200m: WCh: '13- 3; WJ: '08- 4; Won US 2014, NCAA indoors 2010, NACC 2010.
Progress at 200m: 2007- 21.62, 2008- 20.74, 2009- 20.58, 2010- 19.99, 2011- 20.98, 2012- 20.89/20.24w, 2013- 19.97, 2014- 20.13/19.99w. pbs: 60m 6.85i '10, 100m 10.25 '10, 10.23w '08.

Maurice MITCHELL b. 22 Dec 1989 Kansas City, Missouri 1.78m 73kg. Nike. Studied social sciences at Florida State University.
At 200m: OG: '12- sf; Won NCAA 2011-12. At 4x100m: WCh: '11- h.
Progress at 200m: 2007- 20.77, 2008- 21.40/ 21.23w/20.5w, 2009- 20.64, 2010- 20.24, 2011- 20.19/19.99w, 2012- 20.13/20.08w, 2013- 20.32, 2014- 20.30. pbs: 60m 6.55i '11, 100m 10.00 '11, 400m 47.60.

Gunnar NIXON b. 13 Jan 1993 Weatherford, Oklahoma 1.90m 77kg.
At Dec: WCh: '13- 13; WJ: '12- 1; PAm-J '11- 2.
Unratified world heptathlon indoor record & N.American junior decathlon record 2012.
Progress at Dec: 2007- 7245, 2008- 7721 2009- 8146, 2012- 7892, 2013- 8312, 2014- dnf. pbs: 60m 6.86A '13. 100m 10.80 '13, 10.74w '13; 400m 48.56 '13, 1500m 4:22.36 '12, 160mh 7.93Ai '13, 10mh 14.51 '12, HJ 2.17 '12, PV 4.80A '13, 4.70 '14; LJ 7.80 '13. SP 15.03 '114, DT 43.32 '14, JT 60.44 '13., Hep 6232A '13.

David OLIVER b. 24 Apr 1982 Orlando 1.88m 93kg. Nike. Marketing graduate of Howard University.
At 110mh: OG: '08- 3; WCh: '07- sf, '11- 4, '13- 1; CCp: '10- 1. Won DL 2010, 2013; WAF 2008, US 2008, 2010-11. At 60mh: WI: '10- 3.
Two North American 110mh records 2010.
Progress at 110mh: 2001- 14.04, 2002- 13.92/13.88w, 2003- 13.60, 2004- 13.55, 2005- 13.29/13.23w, 2006- 13.20, 2007- 13.14, 2008- 12.95/12.89w, 2009- 13.09, 2010- 12.89, 2011- 12.94, 2012- 13.07, 2013- 13.00, 2014- 13.21. pbs: 60m 6.88i '04, 50mh 6.50i '12, 55mh 7.01+i '12, 60mh 7.37i '11.
Mother, Brenda Chambers, 400mh pb 58.54 '80.

Omoghan **OSAGHAE** b. 18 May 1988 Lubbock 1.84m 75kg. adidas. Was at Texas Tech University.
At 60mh: WI: '14- 1; US indoor champion 2011, 2013-14.
Progress at 110mh: 2007- 13.99, 2008- 13.65, 2009- 13.51/13.42w, 2011- 13.23/13.18w, 2012- 13.24, 2013- 13.35/13.31w, 2014- 13.41/13.40w. pbs: 100m 10.62 '11, 60m 7.01i '08, 100m 10.64 '11, 200m 21.13 '09, 50mh 6.52i '12, 55mh 7.05i '14. 60mh 7.45i '14.
His father played soccer for Nigeria.

Jeff PORTER b. 27 Nov 1985 Summit, New Jersey 1.83m 84kg. Sports management degree from University of Michigan.
At 110mh: OG: '12- sf; PAm: '11- 4. Won NCAA indoor 60mh 2007.
Progress at 110mh: 2004- 14.08, 2005- 14.12, 2006- 13.93/13.92w, 2007- 13.57, 2008- 13.47, 2009- 13.37, 2010- 13.45, 2011- 13.26, 2012- 13.08, 2013- 13.35, 2014- 13.27/13.12w. pbs: 60m 6.77i '14, 100m 10.56 '11, 50mh 6.50i '12, 60mh 7.46i '14.
Married to Tiffany Porter (see UK). His twin brother Joe played in the NFL.

Jason RICHARDSON b. 4 Apr 1986 Houston 1.86m 73kg. Nike. Was at University of South Carolina.
At 110mh: OG: '12- 2; WCh: '11- 1, '13- 4; WY: '03- 1 (1 400mh); won NCAA 2008.
Progress at 110mh: 2004- 13.76, 2005- 13.50, 2006- 13.43/13.36w, 2008- 13.21, 2009- 13.29, 2010- 13.34, 2011- 13.04, 2012- 12.98, 2013- 13.20/13.17w, 2014- 13.29/13.27w. pbs: 100m 10.90 '03, 200m 21.13 '03, 400m 46.96 '12, 60mh 7.53i '08, 400mh 49.79 '04.

Gil ROBERTS b. 15 Mar 1989 Oklahoma City 1.88m 81kg. Nike. Was at Texas Tech University.
At 400m: WCh: '09- h; US champion 2014, indoors 2012.
Progress at 400m: 2005- 47.47, 2006- 47.72A, 2007- 46.16, 2008- 46.14, 2009- 44.86, 2011- 45.22, 2012- 44.84, 2013- 45.73, 2014- 44.53. pbs: 55m 6.26i '12, 100m 10.12/9.92w '14, 200m 20.22 '14, 300m 32.8+ '14.

Kurt ROBERTS b. 20 Feb 1988 Lancaster, Ohio 1.91m 127kg. Nike, Was at Ashland University.
Progress at SP: 2007- 16.39, 2008- 17.81, 2009- 18.78, 2010- 19.80i/18.76, 2011- 19.55, 2012- 21.14, 2013- 20.98, 2014- 21.50i/21.47.

Michael RODGERS b. 24 Apr 1985 Brenham, Texas 1.78m 73kg. Nike. Studied kinesiology at Oklahoma Baptist University.
At 100m/4x100mR: WCh: '09- sf, '13- 6/2R; CCp: '14- 2/1R. At 60m: WI: '08- 4, '10- 2. Won US 100m 2009, 2014; indoor 60m 2008.
Progress at 100m: 2004- 10.55/10.31w, 2005- 10.30/10.25w, 2006- 10.29/10.18w, 2007- 10.10, 10.07w, 2008- 10.06/10.01w, 2009- 9.94/9.9/9.85w, 2010- 10.00/9.99w, 2011- 9.85, 2012- 9.94, 2013- 9.90, 2014- 9.91/9.80w. pbs: 60m 6.48Ai/6.50i '11, 150mSt 15.33 '14, 200m 20.24 '09.
Dropped out of US World Champs team after positive test for stimulant on 19 July 2011, for which he subsequently received a 9-month suspension. Younger sister Alishea Usery won US junior 400m 2009, pb 53.27 '09.

Galen RUPP b. 8 May 1986 Portland 1.80m 62kg. Nike Oregon Project. Studied business at University of Oregon.
At (5000/)10000m: OG: '08- 13, '12- 7/2; WCh: '07- 11, '09- 8, '11- 9/7, '13- 8/4. At 5000m: WJ: '04- 9; PAm-J: '03- 1. At 3000m: WI: '10- 5, '14- 4; WY: '03- 7. Won US 5000m 2012, 10000m 2009-14, NCAA 5000m & 10000m (& indoor 3000m & 5000m) 2009, CC 2008.
N.American records: 10000m 2011 & 2014, junior 5000m 2004, 10000m 2005; indoor 5000m (13:11.44) 2011 & 2014, 3000m 2013, 2M 2012, 2014.
Progress at 5000m, 10000m: 2002- 14:34.05, 2003- 14:20.29, 2004- 13:37.91, 29:09.56; 2005- 13:44.72. 28:15.52; 2006- 13:47.04, 30:42.10; 2007- 13:30.49, 27:33.48; 2008- 13:59.14, 27:36.99; 2009- 13:18.12i/13:42.59+, 27:37.99; 2010- 13:07.35, 27:10.74; 2011- 13:06.86, 26:48.00; 2012- 12:58.90, 27:25.33; 2013- 13:01.37, 27:24.39; 2014- 13:00.99, 26:44.36. pbs: 800m 1:49.87i/1:50.00 '09, 1500m 3:34.15 '14, 1M 3:50.92i/3:52.11 '13, 3000m 7:30.16i '13, 7:43.24 '10, 2M 8:07.41i '14, HMar 60:30 '11.

Charles SILMON b. 4 Jul 1991 Waco, Texas 1.75m 72kg. adidas. Was at Texas Christian University.
At 100m/4x100mR: WCh: '13- h/2R; WJ: 2/1R; won NCAA 2013.
Progress at 100m, 200m: 2007- 10.60, 21.53; 2008- 10.56/10.47w, 21.02; 2009- 10.41/10.24w, 2010- 10.23, 20.65A/20.58w; 2011- 10.20A/10.24/10.18w, 20.56A/20.60; 2012- 10.05/10.04w, 20.65; 2013- 9.98/9.85w, 20.23; 2014- 10.07/9.98w, 20.39w 2015- 9.91w. pbs: 60m 6.60i '13.

Duane SOLOMON b. 28 Dec 1984 Lompoc, California 1.91m 77kg. Saucony. Sociology graduate of University of Southern California.
At 800m: OG: '12- 4; WCh: '07- h, '13- 6; PAm: '07- h; CCp: '14- 6. Won US 2013-14, US indoor 2011. World indoor 4x800m record 2014.
Progress at 800m: 2002- 1:51.76, 2003- 1:49.79, 2005- 1:47.84, 2006- 1:47.45, 2007- 1:45.69, 2008- 1:45.71, 2009- 1:46.82, 2010- 1:45.23, 2011- 1:45.86, 2012- 1:42.82, 2013- 1:43.27, 2014- 1:43.88. pbs: 400m 45.98 '12, 600m 1:13.28 '13, 1000m 2:17.84 '10, 1500m 3:48.29 '08, 1M 4:03.26 '10.

Wallace SPEARMON b. 24 Dec 1984 Chicago 1.90m 80kg. Was at University of Arkansas.
At 200m/4x100mR: OG: '08- dq, '12- 4; WCh: '05-07-09-13: 2/3&1R/3/sf; WCp: '06- 1/1R, '10- 1/1R. Won DL 2010, US 2006, 2010, 2012; NCAA 2004-05. At 4x400m: WI: '06- 1R.
WIR 4x400m and world indoor best 300m 2006. Two US indoor 200m records 2005.
Progress at 100m, 200m: 2003- 21.05, 2004- 10.38, 20.25/20.12w; 2005- 10.35/10.21w, 19.89; 2006- 10.11, 19.65; 2007- 9.96, 19.82; 2008- 10.07, 19.90; 2009- 10.18, 19.85; 2010- 10.15, 19.79/19.77w; 2011- 20.18; 2012- 10.26/10.06w, 19.90/19.82w; 2013- 10.29/9.92w, 20.10; 2014- 20.19. pbs: 60m 6.66i '12, 100m 9.96 '07, 150mSt 14.87 '12, 300m 31.88i '06, 32.14 '09; 400m 45.22 '06.
Disqualified for running out of his lane after crossing the line in 3rd place at the 2008 Olympics. 3-month doping ban for use of a stimulant on 6 Jul 2014. His father (also Wallace, b. 3 Sep 1962) had pbs: of 100m 10.19 '87, 10.05w '86, 10.0w '81; 200m 20.27/20.20w '87; 1 WUG 200/4x100m, 3 PAm 200m 1987.

Nick SYMMONDS b. 30 Dec 1983 Blytheville, Arkansas 1.78m 73kg. Brooks Beasts TC. Biochemistry graduate of Willamette University.
At 800m: OG: '08- sf, '12- 5; WCh: '07-09-11-13: sf/6/5/2; WI: '08- 6; CCp: '10- 5. US champion 2008-12.
Progress at 800m: 2003- 1:49.51, 2004- 1:50.87, 2005- 1:48.82, 2006- 1:45.83, 2007- 1:44.54, 2008- 1:44.10, 2009- 1:43.83, 2010- 1:43.76, 2011- 1:43.83, 2012- 1:42.95, 2013- 1:43.03, 2014- 1:47.29i. pbs:

400m 48.84 '04, 600m 1:14.47 '08, 1000m 2:16.35 '10, 1500m 3:34.55 '13, 1M 3:56.72i '07, 4:00.21 '13.

Christian TAYLOR b. 18 Jun 1990 Fayetteville 1.90m 75kg. Li Ning. Studied at the University of Florida.
At (LJ/)TJ: OG: '12- 1; WCh: '11- 1, '13- 4; WI: '12- 2; WJ: '08- 7/8 (res 1 4x400m); WY: '07- 3/1. Won DL 2012-14, NACAC 2010-11, US 2011-12, NCAA indoor 2009-10.
Progress at Lj, TJ: 2007- 7.29, 15.98; 2008- 7.79i/7.68/7.77w, 16.05; 2009- 8.02i/7.72, 16.98i/16.65/16.91w; 2010- 8.19, 17.18i/17.02/17.09w; 2011- 8.00/8.07w/17.96; 2012- 8.12, 17.81; 2013- 8.01/8.07w, 17.66; 2014- 8.09, 17.51. pbs: 60m 6.79i '11, 200m 20.70 '13, 400m 45.17 '14.
Both parents came from Barbados.

Michael TINSLEY b. 21 Apr 1984 Little Rock, Arkansas 1.85m 74kg. adidas. Studied criminal justice at Jackson State University.
At 400mh: OG: '12- 2; WCh: '13- 2; CCp: '14- 7; won DL 2014, NCAA 2008, US 2012-13.
Progress at 400mh: 2002- 52.5, 2004- 50.87, 2005- 48.55, 2006- 48.25, 2007- 48.02, 2008- 48.84, 2009- 48.53, 2010- 48.46, 2011- 48.45, 2012- 47.91, 2013- 47.70, 2014- 48.25. pbs: 60m 6.92i '05, 200m 20.66 '09, 20.34w '13; 400m 46.02i '06, 46.05 '07; 55mh 7.39i '04, 60mh 7.84i '06, 110mh 13.86 '04.

Brad WALKER b. 21 Jun 1981 Aberdeen, South Dakota 1.88m 86kg. New York AC. Graduated in business administration from University of Washington
At PV: OG: '08- dnq nh, '12- nh; WCh: '05- 2, '07- 1, '13- 4; WI: '06-08-12: 1/2/3; Won WAF 2005, 2007; US 2005, 2007, 2009, 2012-13; indoors 2005-06, NCAA indoor 2003-04.
North American pole vault record 2008.
Progress at PV: 1999- 4.80, 2000- 5.12, 2001- 5.48i/5.36, 2002- 5.64, 2003- 5.80i/5.65, 2004- 5.82, 2005- 5.96, 2006- 6.00, 2007- 5.95, 2008- 6.04, 2009- 5.80, 2010- 5.61, 2011- 5.84, 2012- 5.90, 2013- 5.83, 2014- 5.62.

Ryan WHITING b. 24 Nov 1986 Harrisburg, Pennsylvania 1.91m 134kg. Nike. Studied civil engineering at Arizona State University.
At SP: OG: '12- 9; WCh: '11- 6, '13- 2; WI: '12- 1, '14- 1; PAm-J: '05- 1 (1 DT); Won DL 2013, US 2013, NACAC 2009, NCAA 2009-10, indoor 2008-10, DT 2010.
Progress at SP: 2006- 19.75, 2007- 20.35, 2008- 21.73i/20.60, 2009- 20.99, 2010- 21.97, 2011- 21.76, 2012- 22.00i/21.66, 2013- 22.28, 2014- 22.23i/21.31. pb DT 61.11 '08, Wt 18.94i '10.

Jesse WILLIAMS b. 27 Dec 1983 Modesto 1.84m 75kg. Oregon TC Elite. Graduate of University of Southern California, formerly at North Carolina State.
At HJ: OG: '08- dnq 19=, '12- 9=; WCh: '05/07- dnq 15/26, '11- 1, '13- dnq 23=; WJ: '02- 4=; WI: '08-10-12: 6=/5/6=; Won US 2008, 2010-11; NCAA indoors and out 2005-06; DL 2011.
Progress at HJ: 2001- 2.16, 2002- 2.21, 2003- 2.24, 2004- 2.24, 2005- 2.30, 2006- 2.32, 2007- 2.33, 2008- 2.32i/2.30, 2009- 2.36i/2.34, 2010- 2.34Ai/2.30, 2011- 2.37, 2012- 2.36, 2013- 2.31, 2014- 2.29. pb LJ 7.53 '06. Also a wrestler in high school.

Ryan WILSON b. 19 Dec 1980 Columbus, Ohio 1.88m 81kg. Nike. Graduate (art) of University of Southern California.
At 110mh: WCh: '13- 2; won NCAA 2003.
Progress at 110mh: 2000- 14.00/13.79w, 2001- 13.69, 2002- 13.55, 2003- 13.35, 2004- 13.65/13.58w, 2005- 13.99, 2006- 13.22, 2007- 13.02, 2008- 13.28, 2009- 13.21, 2010- 13.12, 2011- 13.36/13.35w, 2012- 13.18, 2013- 13.08, 2014- 13.18/13.16w. pbs: 400m 48.52 '01, 50mh 6.78i '02, 55mh 7.18+i '12, 60mh 7.75i '12, 400mh 49.33 '03, LJ 7.29 '02.

Isiah YOUNG b. 5 Jan 1990 Manhattan, Kansas 1.83m 75kg. Was at University of Mississippi.
At 200m: OG: '12- sf; WCh: '13- sf.
Progress at 100m, 200m: 2008- 10.96; 2009- 10.44, 21.50/21.33w; 2010- 10.32, 20.98; 2011- 10.31, 20.81; 2012- 10.09/10.08w, 20.33/20.16w; 2013- 9.99/9.93w, 19.86; 2014- 10.23, 20.58/20.55w. pbs: 60m 6.61i '12.

Women

Nia ALI b. 23 Oct 1988 Philadelphia 1.70m 64kg. Nike. Was at University of Southern California.
At 100mh: WCh: '13- sf; WUG: '11- 1. Won NCAA 2011. At 60mh: WI: '14- 1, won US indoor 2013-14.
Progress at 100mh: 2005- 14.20, 2006- 13.63/13.55w, 2007- 13.25, 2008- 13.14, 2009- 13.17, 2011- 12.73/12.63w, 2012- 12.78, 2013- 12.48, 2014- 12.75. pbs: 60m 7.43i '14, 200m 23.90 '09, 800m 2:24.55 '07, 60mh 7.80i '14, HJ 1.86 '11, LJ 5.89 '09, SP 13.61 '09, JT 39.24 '09, Hep 5824 '09.

Alexandria ANDERSON b. 28 Jan 1987 Chicago 1.75m 60kg. Nike. Was at University of Texas.
At 100m/4x100mR: WCh: '11- res (1)R, '13- 7/2R; WJ: '04- 1R, '06- 5/1R. At 200m: PAm-J: '05- 2. Won NCAA 100m 2009.
Progress at 100m, 200m: 2002- 11.81, 24.10w; 2003- 11.62, 23.48; 2004- 11.41, 23.45; 2005- 11.39/11.38w, 22.96; 2006- 11.12/11.10w, 23.16/23.14w; 2007- 11.21/11.11w, 22.67; 2008- 11.07/10.98w, 22.75; 2009- 11.02/10.92w, 22.60; 2010- 11.04, 22.83; 2011- 11.01/10.91w, 22.87; 2012- 11.12/10.88w, 22.98/22.84w; 2013- 10.91, 22.67w; 2014- 11.11. pbs: 50m 6.28i '12, 55m 6.88i '06, 60m 7.12Ai '11, 7.17i '08; 400m 52.63 '05, 60mh 8.83Ai '06, LJ 6.32 '05, TJ 11.68 '07.

Joanna ATKINS b. 31 Jan 1989 Stone Mountain, Georgia 1.75m 61kg. Nike. Was at Auburn University.
At 200m: CCp: '14- 2. At 400m: WCh: '13- res2R; WI: '14- 6/1R; Won NCAA 400m 2009.
Progress at 200m, 400m: 2004- 24.25w, 56.12; 2005- 24.02, 54.32; 2006- 23.82, 55.42; 2007- 24.35i/23.69w, 53.93; 2008- 23.30, 52.94; 2009-

22.89, 50.39; 2010- 23.32, 51.52; 2011- 22.68, 51.50; 2012- 23.10/22.83w, 51.12; 2013- 23.27, 50.77; 2014- 22.27/22.19w, 50.74. pbs: 55m 6.91i '09, 600m 7.28i '09, 100m 11.02 '14.

Brigetta BARRETT b. 24 Dec 1990 Valhalla, New York 1.83m 64kg. Was at University of Arizona.
At HJ: OG: '12- 2; WCh: '11- 10, '13- 2; WUG: '11- 1. Won US 2011, 2013; NCAA 2011-13.
Progress at HJ: 2007- 1.72, 2008- 1.83A, 2009- 1.83, 2010- 1.91, 2011- 1.96, 2012- 2.03, 2013- 2.04, 2014- 1.95. pb 400m 55.04 '13.

Tianna BARTOLETTA b. 30 Aug 1985 Elyria, Ohio 1.68m 60kg. née Madison. Nike. Studied biology at University of Central Florida, formerly at University of Tennessee.
At 100m/4x100mR: OG: '12- 4/1R; won DL 2014, US 2014. At LJ: WCh: '05- 1, '07- 10; CCp: '14- 3/1R; WI: '06- 1; PAm-J: '03- 4, NCAA champion indoors and out 2005. At 60m: WI: '12- 3, '14- 3; won US indoor 2012.
Progress at 100m, LJ: 2000- 5.73, 2001- 6.07, 2002- 11.98/11.91w, 6.20; 2003- 11.68, 6.28; 2004- 11.50/11.35w, 6.60; 2005- 11.41, 6.89/6.92w; 2006- 11.52/11.50w, 6.80i/6.60; 2007- 6.60/6.61w; 2008- 11.54, 6.53/6.58w; 2009- 11.05, 6.48; 2010- 11.20, 6.44; 2011- 11.29, 6.21/6.58w; 2012- 10.85, 6.48; 2013- 11.41; 2014- 10.92, 7.02. pbs: 55m 6.69i '09, 60m 7.02i '12, 200m 22.37/22.33w '12.
Set long jump pbs in qualifying and final of 2005 Worlds. Now concentrating on sprinting, but also competed on the US bobsled team in 2012/13. Married John Bartoletta in 2012.

Jessica BEARD b. 8 Jan 1989 Euclid, Ohio 1.68m 57kg. adidas. Studied psychology at Texas A&M University.
At 400m/4x400mR: WCh: '09- sf/res (1)R, '11- sf/1R, '13- 2R; WJ: '06- 5/1R, '08- 2/1R; PAm-J: '07- 3; won NCAA 2011.
Progress at 400m: 2004- 55.22, 2005- 52.39, 2006- 51.89, 2007- 51.63, 2008- 51.09A/51.47, 2009- 50.56, 2010- 51.02, 2011- 51.06, 2012- 51.19, 2013- 51.05, 2014- 50.81. pbs: 60m 7.52i '11, 100m 11.86 '09, 11.49w '11; 200m 22.81 '13, 300m 36.65i '15.

Amanda BINGSON b. 20 Feb 1990 Victorville, California 1.70m 89kg. New York AC. Sports psychology graduate of University of Nevada, Las Vegas.
At HT: OG: '12- dnq 27; WCh: '13- 10.; CCp: '14- 2; US champion 2013-14, NACAC 2012.
North American hammer record 2013.
Progress at SP: 2009- 55.19, 2010- 64.07, 2011- 69.79, 2012- 71.78, 2013- 75.73, 2014- 75.12. Pbs: DT 46.08A '11, Wt 22.42i '14. Former gymnast.

Tori BOWIE b. 27 Aug 1990 Sandhill, Mississippi 1.75m 61kg. adidas. Studied psychology at University of Southern Mississippi.
At LJ: NCAA 2011.
Progress at 100m, 200m, LJ: 2008- 12.21w, 6.03w; 2009- 11.82, 23.99, 6.30/6.60w; 2010- 11.76/11.72w, 24.55/23.98w, 6.43/6.50w; 2011- 6.64, 2012- 11.28, 24.06, 6.78; 2013- 11.14/11.04w, 6.91, 2014- 10.80, 22.18, 6.95i/6.82. pbs: 60m 7.14i '14, TJ 13.09i/ 12.65 '14.

Tia BROOKS b. 2 Aug 1990 Saginaw, Michigan 1.83m 109kg. Nike. Was at University of Oklahoma.
At SP: OG: '12- dnq 19, WCh: '13- 8. NCAA champion indoors and out 2012-13.
Progress at SP: 2008- 14.64, 2009- 14.13i/14.09, 2010- 17.37, 2011- 18.00, 2012- 19.00i/18.47, 2013- 19.22i/18.96, 2014- 18.83. pb DT 43.71 '08.

Stephanie BROWN TRAFTON b. 1 Dec 1979 San Luis Obispo, California 1.93m 102kg. née Brown. Nike. Engineering graduate of Cal Poly San Luis Obispo.
At DT: OG: '04- dnq 21, '08- 1, '12- 7; WCh: '09- 12, '11- 5. US champion 2009, 2011-12.
US discus record 2012.
Progress at DT: 1997- 45.78, 1998- 55.24, 1999- 52.79, 2001- 51.46, 2002- 54.11, 2003- 57.78, 2004- 61.90, 2005- 55.35, 2006- 59.03, 2007- 61.40, 2008- 66.17, 2009- 66.21, 2010- 61.51, 2011- 64.13, 2012- 67.74, 2013- 55.11, 2014- 59.33. pb SP 17.86 '04.
Former basketball player. Married Jerry Trafton March 2005, daughter Juliana b. September 2013.

Mary CAIN b. 3 May 1996 New York 1.70m 50kg. Nike Oregon Project. Student at University of Portland.
At 1500m: WCh: '13- 10; WJ: '12- 6. At 3000m: WJ: '14- 1.
Two world junior indoor 1000m records 2014; North American junior records: 800m, 1500m, indoor 1500m 2013-14, 1M 2014.
Progress at 1500m: 2011- 4:23.59, 2012- 4:11.01, 2013- 4:04.62, 2014- 4:06.34. pbs: 500m 1:21.43i '14, 800m 1:59.51 '13, 1000m 2:35.80i '14, 1M 4:24.11i '14, 4:39.28 '12; 3000m 8:58.48 '14, 2M 9:38.68i '13, 5000m 15:45.46 '13.

Amber CAMPBELL b. 5 Jun 1981 Indianapolis 1.70m 91kg. Nike. Was at Coastal Carolina University.
At HT: OG: '08/12- dnq 21/12; WCh: '05-11-13: dnq 18/13/13, '09- 11; PAm: '11- 3. Won US HT 2012, indoor Wt 2007-11.
Progress at HT: 2000- 49.16, 2001- 62.08, 2002- 63.76, 2003- 64.58, 2004- 67.23, 2005- 69.52, 2006- 67.52, 2007- 70.33, 2008- 70.19, 2009- 70.61, 2010- 71.94, 2011- 72.59, 2012- 71.80, 2013- 73.03, 2014- 73.61. pbs: SP 14.81i '02, 14.42 '04; 20lb Wt 24.70i '10.

Kori CARTER b. 6 Mar 1992 Pasadena, California 1.65m 57kg. Nike. Human biology student at Stanford University.
At 400mh: WJ: '08- h; CCp: '14- 7; Won US 2014, NCAA 2013. At 100mh: WY: '09- 2.
Progress at 400mh: 2007- 62.21, 2008- 60.22, 2009- 59.89, 2010- 60.47, 2011- 57.10, 2012- 57.60, 2013- 53.21, 2014- 53.84. pbs: 100m 11.57 '11, 200m 23.67 '12, 60mh 8.17Ai '13, 100mh 12.76 '13.

Michelle CARTER b. 12 Oct 1985 San Jose 1.75m 110kg. Nike. Liberal arts graduate from University of Texas.
At SP: OG: '08- 15, '12- 5; WCh: '09- 6, '11- 9, '13- 4; WI: '12- 3, '14- 5; WJ: '04- 1; WY: '01- 2; PAm: '11- 3; PAm-J: '03- 1; CCp: '14- 2. US champion 2008-09, 2011, 2013-14; NCAA indoor 2006.
North American shot record 2013.
Progress at SP: 2000- 14.76, 2001- 15.23, 2002- 16.25, 2003- 16.73, 2004- 17.55, 2005- 18.26, 2006- 17.98, 2007- 17.57, 2008- 18.85, 2009- 19.13, 2010- 18.80, 2011- 19.86, 2012- 19.60, 2013- 20.24, 2014- 19.84. pbs: DT 54.06 '07.
Her father Mike set a world junior shot record in 1979 and won the Olympic silver in 1984, seven NCAA titles (4 in, 3 out) (for a unique father-daughter double) and WUG gold in 1981 and 1983, pb 21.76 '84. Her younger sister D'Andra (b. 17 Jun 1987) won the NCAA discus in 2009, pb 57.73 '08.

Kristi CASTLIN b. 7 Jul 1988 Douglasville, Georgia 1.70m 79kg. adidas. Political science graduate of Virginia Tech University.
At 100mh: Won PAm-J 2007. At 60mh: WI: '12- dq/false start ht; won US indoors 2012.
World best 4x100mh 2014.
Progress at 100mh: 2005- 13.85, 2006- 13.73, 2007- 12.91/12.82w, 2008- 12.81, 2009- 12.89, 2010- 12.83/12.59w, 2011- 12.83/12.68w, 2012- 12.56/12.48w, 2013- 12.61, 2014- 12.58. pbs: 55m 7.04i '08, 60m 7.47i '08, 100m 11.60 '12, 11.49w '11; 200m 23.46 '12, 50mh 6.81+i '12, 55mh 7.37i '12, 60mh 7.84Ai/7.91i '12. 400mh 60.44 '07.

Emma COBURN b. 19 Oct 1990 Boulder 1.73m 55kg. New Balance. Marketing graduate of University of Colorado.
At 3000mSt: OG: '12- 8; WCh: '11- 11; CCp: '14- 1; US champion 2011-12, 2014; NCAA 2011, 2013.
North American 3000m steeple record 2014.
Progress at 3000mSt: 2009- 10:06.21, 2010- 9:51.86, 2011- 9:37.16, 2012- 9:23.54, 2013- 9:28.26, 2014- 9:11.42. pbs: 800m 2:09.81 '10, 1500m 4:05.29 '14, 1M 4:29.86i '13, 4:33.24 '12; 2000m 5:41.11i '15.

Jessica COSBY TORUGA b. 31 May 1982 Reseda, California 1.73m 77kg. Nike. Was at UCLA (now strength coach there).
At HT: OG: '08/12- dnq nt/13; WCh: '07: dnq 14, '09- 7, '11- 10; won NACAC 2007, US 2006, 2008-09, 2011. At SP: WJ: '00- 9, won NCAA 2002.
US hammer record 2012.
Progress at HT: 2001- 55.73, 2002- 59.54, 2003- 61.15, 2005- 66.88, 2006- 70.78, 2007- 68.34, 2008- 70.72, 2009- 72.21, 2010- 71.24, 2011- 72.65, 2012- 74.19, 2013- 73.58, 2014- 74.20. pbs: SP 17.63 '05, 20lb Wt 20.40i '04.
4 months drugs ban from August 2009. Left-handed thrower. Married David Toruga on 25 Aug 2012.

Sharon DAY-MONROE b. 9 Jun 1985 Brooklyn, New York 1.75m 70kg. née Day. Asics. Was at Cal Poly San Luis Obispo.
At Hep: OG: '12- 15; WCh: '09- 10, '11- 17, '13- 6. US champion 2011, 2013-14. At Hep: WI: '14- 4. At HJ: OG: '08- dnq 24=; WCh: '09- dnq 17=; WJ: '04- 3; PAm: '07- 6; won PAm-J 2003, USA 2014, NCAA 2005.
US indoor heptathlon record 2014.
Progress at Hep: 2007- 5244, 2008- 5642, 2009- 6177, 2010- 6006(w), 2011- 6058, 2012- 6343, 2013- 6550, 2014- 6470. pbs: 200m 24.02 '13, 400m 56.54 '07, 800m 2:08.94 '13, 55mh 7.98i '12, 60mh 8.43i '14, 100mh 13.42 '14, HJ 1.95 '08, LJ 6.15 '12, 6.16w '13; SP 15.59i/15.45 '14, JT 47.38 '13, Pen 4805Ai '14. Married Dan Monroe on 1 Sep 2014.

Cynthia **'Janay' DeLOACH** b. 12 Oct 1985 Panama City, Florida 1.65m 59kg. Nike. Psychology graduate of Colorado State University.
At LJ: OG: '12- 3; WCh: '11- 6, '13- 11; WI: '12- 2; PAm: '07- 10. Won US 2013, US indoor 2011-13. At 60mh: WI: '14- 5.
Progress at LJ: 2004- 6.14Ai/6.05/6.14w, 2005- 6.27A/6.43w, 2006- 6.21Ai, 2007- 6.42Ai/6.41/ 6.45w, 2008- 6.48/6.51w, 2009- 6.33i/6.04, 2010- 6.61, 2011- 6.99Ai/6.97, 2012- 7.03/7.15w, 2013- 6.99/7.08w, 2014- 6.53Ai/6.41. pb 55m 6.85Ai '05, 60m 7.31Ai '06, 100m 11.45 '08, 200m 24.60 '07, 24.26Aw '08; 60mh 7.82Ai/7.90i '14, 100mh 12.97 '13, HJ 1.73i '11, SP 13.44i '14, Pen 4289i '11.
Married Patrick Soukup in September 2012.

Lashinda DEMUS b. 10 Mar 1983 Palmdale, California 1.70m 62kg. Nike. Was at University of South Carolina.
At 400mh/4x400mR: OG: '04- sf, '12- 2; WCh: '05- 2, '09- 2/1R, '11- 1, '13- 3; WJ: '02- 1/1R; WCp: '06- 2/2R. Won WAF 2005-06, PAm-J 1999, US 2005-06, 2009, 2011; NCAA 2002.
Two world junior records 400mh 2002.
Progress at 400mh: 1998- 64.61, 1999- 57.04, 2001- 55.76, 2002- 54.70, 2003- 55.65, 2004- 53.43, 2005- 53.27, 2006- 53.02, 2008- 53.99, 2009- 52.63, 2010- 52.82, 2011- 52.47, 2012- 52.77, 2013- 54.22, 2014- 55.17. pbs: 50m 6.64i '01, 60m 7.73i '01, 100m 11.5 '01, 200m 23.35 '08. 400m 51.09 '10, 500y 1:05.8i '01, 800m 2:07.49 '12, 55mh 7.65i '04, 60mh 8.11i '04, 100mh 12.96 '11, 12.93w '05.
Twin sons Duane and Donte born 5 Jun 2007. Her mother, Yolanda Rich, had a 400m best of 52.19 in 1980.

Kimberlyn DUNCAN b. 2 Aug 1991 Katy, Texas 1.73m 59kg. Nike, Was at Louisiana State University.
At 200m: WCh: '13- sf; won US 2013, NCAA 2011-13 (and indoors).
Progress at 100m, 200m: 2007- 24.54, 2008- 24.33, 2009- 23.46, 2010- 11.84, 23.08/22.96w; 2011- 11.09/11.02w, 22.24/22.18w, 2012- 10.96/10.94, 22.22; 2013- 11.08/11.02w, 22.35/21.80w; 2014- 11.20, 22.53/22.10w. pb 60m 7.16i '13.

Allyson FELIX b. 18 Nov 1985 Los Angeles 1.68m 57kg. Nike. Elementary education graduate of University of Southern California.
At 200m/4x400mR: OG: '04- 2, '08- 2/1R, '12- 1/1R (1 4x400m); WCh: '03- qf, '05- 1, '07- 1/1 4x100mR/1R, '09- 1/1R, '11- 3/1R (2 400m, 1 4x100m), '13- dnf; WJ: '02- 5; PAm: '03- 3; WI: '10- 1R. At 100m: OG: '12- 5; WY: '01- 1 (1 Medley R). Won DL 200m & 400m 2010, WAF 200m 2005-06, 2009; US 100m 2010, 200m 2004-05, 2007-09, 2012; 400m 2011.
World junior record 200m 2004 after unratified (no doping test) at age 17 in 2003.
Progress at 100m, 200m, 400m: 2000- 12.19/11.99w, 23.90; 2001- 11.53, 23.31/23.27w; 2002- 11.40, 22.83/22.69w, 55.01; 2003- 11.29/11.12w, 22.11A/22.51, 52.26; 2004- 11.16, 22.18, 51.83A; 2005- 11.05, 22.13, 51.12; 2006- 11.04, 22.11; 2007- 11.01, 21.81, 49.70; 2008- 10.93, 21.93/21.82w, 49.83; 2009- 11.08, 21.88, 49.83; 2010- 11.27, 22.03, 50.15; 2011- 11.26+, 22.32, 49.59; 2012- 10.89, 21.69; 2013- 11.06+, 22.30, 50.19; 2014- 11.01, 22.02, 50.81. pbs: 50m 6.43i '02, 60m 7.10i '12, 150mSt 16.36 '13 (world best), 300m 36.33i '07.
First teenager to won a World sprint title. Unbeaten in ten 200m competitions 2005 and in five 2007. Has women's record eight world gold medals including three in 2007 when she had a record 0.53 winning margin at 200m and ran a 48.0 400m relay leg, and four Olympic gold medals. IAAF female Athlete of the Year 2012. Older brother Wes Felix won World Junior bronze at 200m and gold in WJR at 4x100m in 2002, pbs: 100m 10.23 '05, 200m 20.43 '04.

Shalane FLANAGAN b. 8 Jul 1981 Boulder 1.65m 50kg. Bowerman TC. Was at University of North Carolina.
At 5000m/(10000m): OG: '04- h, '08- 10/3; WCh: '05- h, '07- 8, '09- (14), '11- (7), '13- (8). At Mar: OG: '10. World CC: '10- 12, '11-3; 4k: '04- 14, 05- 20. Won US 5000m 2005, 10000m 2008, 2011, 2013; HMar 2010, Mar 2012, CC 2008, 2010-11, 2013; 4km CC 2004-05, indoor 3000m 2007, NCAA CC 2002-03, indoor 3000m 2003.
N.American records: 5000m and indoor 3000m 2007, 10000m (2) 2008, 15km & 25km road 2014.
Progress at 5000m, 10000m, Mar: 2001- 16:29.68, 2003- 15:20.54, 2004- 15:05.08, 2005- 15:10.96, 2007- 14:44.80, 2008- 14:59.69, 30:22.22; 2009- 14:47.62i/15:10.86, 31:23.43; 2010- 14:49.08, 2:28:40; 2011- 14:45.20, 30:39.57; 2012- 31:59.69, 2:25:38; 2013- 31:04.85, 2:27:08; 2014- 2:21:14. pbs: 800m 2:09.28 '02, 1500m 4:05.86 '07, 1M 4:33.81i '11, 4:48.47 '00; 3000m 8:33.25i/8:35.34 '07, Road: 15k 47:03 '14, 10M 51:45 '10, HMar 68:31 '13, 25k 1:22:36 '14, 30k 1:39:15 '14.
2nd New York 2010 on marathon debut and won Olympic Trials 2012. Married to Steve Edwards. Mother, Cheryl Bridges, set marathon world best with 2:49:40 in 1971 and was 4th in 1969 International CC, father Steve ran in World Cross 1976-7, 1979.

Phyllis FRANCIS b. 4 May 1992 New York 1.78m 61kg. Was at University of Oregon.
At 400m/4x400mR: PAm-J: '11- 3/1R. Won NCAA indoors 2014.
Progress at 400m: 2010- 55.82i, 2011- 52.93, 2012- 51.22, 2013- 50.86, 2014- 50.46Ai/50.59. pbs: 60m 7.41i '14, 200m 22.77 '13, 600m 1:27.38i '11, 800m 2:04.83 '08.

Octavious FREEMAN b. 20 Apr 1992 Lake Wales, Florida 1.69m 57kg. adidas, Was at University of Central Florida.
At 100m/4x100mR: WCh: '13- 8/2R.
Progress at 100m, 200m: 2008- 11.64/11.59w, 23.95/23.71w; 2009- 11.48/11.20Aw, 23.20; 2010- 11.18/11.11Aw, 23.24/23.19Aw; 2011- 11.21, 22.96; 2012- 11.09, 22.74; 2013- 10.87, 22.55; 2014- 11.35. pbs: 60m 7.15i '12, LJ 6.05 '12.

English GARDNER b. 22 Apr 1992 Philadelphia 1.62m 50kg. Nike. Was at University of Oregon.
At 100m/4x100mR: WCh: '13- 4/2R; Won NCAA 100m 2013, indoor 60m 2012.
Progress at 100m, 200m: 2005- 11.99, 24.53; 2007- 11.61, 24.01; 2008- 11.82/11.49w, 24.27/24.19w; 2011- 11.03, 23.02; 2012- 11.10/11.00w, 22.82; 2013- 10.85, 22.62; 2014- 11.01, 22.81. pbs: 60m 7.12i '12, 400m 53.73 '12.

Dawn HARPER NELSON b. 13 May 1984 Norman, Oklahoma 1.68m 61kg. Nike. Studied psychology at UCLA.
At 100mh: OG: '08- 1, '12- 2; WCh: '09- 7, '11- 3, '13- 4; CCp: '14- 1; won DL 2012-14, PAm-J 2003, US 2009.
Progress at 100mh: 2002- 13.63, 2003- 13.33/13.21w, 2004- 13.16/12.91w, 2005- 12.91, 2006- 12.80A/12.86, 2007- 12.67, 2008- 12.54, 2009- 12.48/12.36w, 2010- 12.77w, 2011- 12.47, 2012- 12.37, 2013- 12.48, 2014- 12.44. pbs: 60m 7.70i '05, 100m 11.66 '07, 200m 23.97 '06, 50mh 6.96i '12, 60mh 7.98i '06.
Married Craig Everhart (b. 13 Sep 1983, 400m 44.89 '04) in October 2007, and then Alonzo Nelson on 27 March 2013.

Queen HARRISON b. 10 Sep 1988 Loch Sheldrake, New York 1.70m 60kg. Studied of business marketing at Virginia Tech.
At 100mh: WCh: '13- 5; At 400mh: OG: '08- sf; WCh: '11- sf; PAm-J: '07- 1 (2 100mh); won NCAA 100mh, 400mh & 60mh indoors 2010.
World best 4x100mh 2014.
Progress at 100mh, 400mh: 2007- 12.98, 55.81; 2008- 12.70, 54.60; 2009- 13.14/12.98w, 56.03; 2010- 12.61/12.44w, 54.55; 2011- 12.88, 54.78; 2012- 12.62, 55.32; 2013- 12.43, 2014- 12.46. pbs: 400m 52.88 '08, 60mh 7.94i '10, LJ 5.82i '06.

Natasha HASTINGS b. 23 Jul 1986 Brooklyn, New York 1.73m 63kg. Under Armour. Studied exercise science at University of South Carolina.
At 400m/4x400m: OG: '08- res 1R; WCh: '07- sf/

res 1R, '09/11- res 1R, '13- 5/2R; WJ: '04- 1/1R; WY: '03- 1; WI: '10- 1R, '12- 3/2R; PAm-J: '03- 1R, '05- 1/1R. Won US 2013, NCAA indoors and out 2007.
World junior 500m indoor best 2005, North American indoor 4x400m record 2014.
Progress at 400m: 2000- 54.21, 2001- 55.06, 2002- 53.42, 2003- 52.09, 2004- 52.04, 2005- 51.34, 2006- 51.45, 2007- 49.84, 2008- 50.80, 2009- 50.89, 2010- 50.53, 2011- 50.83Ai/50.97, 2012- 50.72, 2013- 49.94, 2014- 50.53. pbs: 55m 7.08i '02, 60m 7.26i '13, 100m 11.24 '13, 11.08w '14; 200m 22.61 '07, 22.55w '14; 300m 35.9+ '07, 500m 1:10.05i '05.
Father from Jamaica, mother Joanne Gardner was British (ran 11.89 to win WAAA U15 100m at 14 in 1977).

Molly HUDDLE b. 31 Aug 1984 Elmira, New York 1.63m 48kg. Saucony. Was at University of Notre Dame.
At 5000m: OG: '12- 11; WCh: '11- h, '13- 6; CCp: '10- 3; won US 2011, 2014. World CC: '10-11: 19/ 17.
Two North American 5000m records 2010-14.
Progress at 5000m, 10000m: 2003- 15:36.95, 2004- 15:32.55, 2005- 16:12.17i, 2006- 15:40.41, 32:37.87; 2007- 15:17.13, 33:09.27; 2008- 15:25.47, 31:27.12; 2009- 15:53.91, 32:42.11; 2010- 14:44.76, 31:27.12; 2011- 15:10.01, 31:28.66; 2012- 15:01.32, 2013- 14:58.15, 2014- 14:42.64, 30:47.59. pbs: 1000m 4:08.09 '13, 1M 4:26.84 '14, 3000m 8:42.99 '13, Rd: 15k 48:52 '14, 10M 52:15 '14, 20k 65:22 '14, HMar 68:31 '15.
Married Kurt Benninger CAN (pbs 1500m 3:38.03 '08, 1M 3:56.99 '08, 5000m 13:30.27 '09) in 2009. Won US road running titles in 2014 at a women's record four distances.

Kylie HUTSON b. 27 Nov 1987 Terre Haute, Indiana 1.65m 57kg. Nike. Was at Indiana State University.
At PV: WCh: '11/13- dnq 15/nh; won US 2011, NCAA 2009, 2011.
Progress at PV: 2006- 3.58, 2007- 4.10i/3.96, 2008- 4.30, 2009- 4.40, 2010- 4.51, 2011- 4.70i/4.65, 2012- 4.52Ai/4.40, 2013- 4.75Ai/4.70, 2014- 4.68i/4.55.

Carmelita JETER b. 24 Nov 1979 Los Angeles 1.63m 63kg. Nike. Was at California State University, Dominguez Hills.
At 100m/(200m)/4x100mR: OG: '12- 2/3/1R; WCh: '07- 3/res 1R, '09- 3, '11- 1/2/1R, '13- 3; won DL 100m 2010-11, 200m 2011; WAF 100m 2007, 2009; US 100m 2009, 2011-12. At 60m: WI: '10- 2.
Progress at 100m, 200m: 1998- 11.88, 2000- 11.69, 23.65/23.99w; 2001- 11.82, 24.20; 2002- 11.77/ 11.46w, 24.10; 2003- 11.61/11.43w, 23.67; 2004- 11.56, 23.98; 2005- 12.00/11.72w, 2006- 11.48, 23.54; 2007- 11.02, 22.82; 2008- 10.97, 22.47/22.35w; 2009- 10.64, 22.59; 2010- 10.82, 22.54; 2011- 10.70, 22.20; 2012- 10.78, 22.11; 2013- 10.93, 22.77; 2014- 11.24. pbs: 60m 7.02Ai/7.05i '10, 300m 37.52 '13, 400m 53.08 '09.
Second fastest woman of all-time at 100m.

Oluwafunmilayo '**Funmi**' **JIMOH** b. 29 May 1984 Seattle 1.73m 64kg. Nike. Was at Rice University.
At LJ: OG: '08- 12; WCh: '09/11/13- dnq 21/nj/ dnq 13; won US 2008-09, NCAA 2008.
Progress at LJ: 2004- 6.14, 2005- 6.31, 2006- 6.44, 2007- 6.46/6.62w, 2008- 6.91, 2009- 6.96, 2010- 6.81/6.87w, 2011- 6.88, 2012- 6.82, 2013- 6.92, 2014- 6.81. pbs: 60m 7.67i '04, 100m 12.03 '08, 11.65w '11; 200m 23.91A '11, 24.28 '08, 23.65w '06; 400m 59.57i '09, 60mh 8.32i '07, 100mh 13.51 '05, 13.39w '07; HJ 1.75i '05, 1.66 '07; SP 10.68i '06, Pen 3937i '06, Hep 5335 '07.

Lori '**Lolo**' **JONES** b. 5 Aug 1982 Des Moines 1.75m 60kg. Asics. Spanish & economics graduate of Louisiana State University.
At 100mh: OG: '08- 7, '12- 4; WCh: '07- 6; CCp: '10- 2; Won US 2008, 2010; NACAC 2004. At 60mh: WI: '08- 1, '10- 1; won NCAA indoor 2003, US indoor 2007-09.
N.American indoor 60m hurdles record 2010.
Progress at 100mh: 2000- 14.04, 2001- 13.31/ 13.17w/12.7w, 2002- 12.84, 2003- 12.90, 2004- 12.77, 2005- 12.76, 2006- 12.56, 2007- 12.57, 2008- 12.43/12.29w, 2009- 12.47, 2010- 12.55, 2011- 12.67, 2012- 12.58, 2013- 12.50/12.44w, 2014- 12.55. pbs: 55m 6.87i '03, 60m 7.27i '03, 100m 11.24 '06, 200m 23.76 '04, 23.50w '03; 50mh 6.78i '12, 55mh 7.57i '03, 60mh 7.72i '10, 400mh 59.95 '00.
Crashed into 9th hurdle when leading Olympic final after pb 12.43 in semi in 2008. Won gold in the 2-man bobsled as brakeman on the US team at the 2013 World Championships and was 11th at the 2014 Winter Olympics.

Gia LEWIS-SMALLWOOD b. 1 Apr 1979 Urbana, Illinois 1.83m 93kg. Nike. Was at University of Illinois.
At DT: OG: '12- dnq 15; WCh: '11- dnq 15, '13- 5; PAm: '11- 4; CCp: '14- 1. US champion 2013-14.
North American discus record 2014.
Progress at DT: 2000- 53.52, 2001- 57.76, 2002- 52.28, 2003- 54.95, 2004- 57.88, 2005- 50.85, 2006- 49.95, 2007- 52.02, 2008- 59.96, 2009- 60.32, 2010- 65.58, 2011- 62.26, 2012- 63.97, 2013- 66.29, 2014- 69.17. pb Wt 18.91i '02.

Chaunté LOWE b. 12 Jan 1984 Templeton, California 1.75m 59kg. née Howard. Nike. Economics graduate of Georgia Tech University.
At HJ: OG: '04- dnq 26=, '08- 6, '12- 6; WCh: '05- 2, '09- 7=; PAm-J: '03- 3; CCp: '14- 2; WI: '06-10-12: 8/3/1; Won DL 2012, US 2006, 2008-10, 2012, 2014; NCAA 2004, indoors 2004-05.
3 N.American HJ records 2010, indoors 2012.
Progress at HJ: 2000- 1.75, 2001- 1.84, 2002- 1.87, 2003- 1.89, 2004- 1.98A, 2005- 2.00, 2006- 2.01, 2008- 2.00, 2009- 1.98, 2010- 2.05, 2011- 1.78, 2012- 2.02Ai/2.01, 2014- 1.97. pbs: 100m 11.83 '05, 100mh 13.78 '04, LJ 6.90 '10, TJ 12.93 '04, 12.98w '05.
Married Mario Lowe (b. 20 Apr 1980, TJ pb 16.15 '02) in 2005, daughters Jasmine born 30 Jul

2007 and Aurora in 4 Apr 2011 and son Mario Josiah in August 2013.

Brenda MARTINEZ b. 8 Sep 1987 Upland, California 1.63m 52kg. New Balance. Studied sociology and law at University of California - Riverside.
At 800m: WCh: '13- 3; CCp: '14- 1.
N.American 4x800m & 4x1500m records 2014.
Progress at 800m, 1500m: 2007- 2:04.22, 4:21.18; 2008- 2:02.34, 4:17.09; 2009- 2:00.85, 4;09.52; 2010- 2:04.76, 4:18.17; 2011- 2:01.07, 4:10.77; 2012- 1:59.14, 4:06.96; 2013- 1:57.91, 4:00.94; 2014- 1:58.84, 4:01.36. pbs: 1000m 2:38.48 '12, 1M 4:26.76 '12, 3000m 9:07.99+i '13, 2M 9:51.91i '13, 5000m 15:30.89mx '13, 15:41.50 '14; 5km Rd 15:24 '14.
Married Carlos Handler in October 2012.

Francena McCORORY b. 20 Oct 1988 Hampton, Virginia 1.70m 60kg. adidas. Psychology graduate of Hampton University.
At 400m/4x400mR: OG: '12- 7/1R; WCh: '11- 4/1R, '13- 6/2R; CCp: '14- 1/1R; WI: '14- 1/1R; won US 2014, NCAA indoors 2009-10, out 2010.
World junior indoor 300m best 2007, North American indoor 4x400m record 2014.
Progress at 400m: 2004- 54.54, 2006- 51.93i, 2008- 51.54, 2009- 50.58, 2010- 50.52, 2011- 50.24, 2012- 50.06, 2013- 49.86, 2014- 49.48. pbs: 55m 6.86i '06, 60m 7.43i '07, 100m 11.68 '05, 11.56w '10; 200m 22.92 '10, 300m 35.7+ '13, 500m 1:09.01i '12, 600m 1:29.07i '13, 800m 2:20.25i '07.

Inika McPHERSON b. 29 Sep 1986 Galveston, Texas 1.63m 55kg. Was at University of California.
At HJ: WCh: '11/13- dnq 26/18; WJ: '04- 11; PAm: '07- 11.
Progress at HJ: 2002- 1.83, 2004- 1.83, 2005- 1.88, 2006- 1.80i/1.78, 2007- 1.84, 2008- 1.78, 2009- 1.83, 2011- 1.86, 2012- 1.95, 2013- 1.92, 2014- 2.00dq/1.94. pb LJ 5.69 '04.
Set women's high jump world record for height differential of 37cm to 'win' US title 2014, but then tested positive for a banned substance at this meeting and received 21-month ban..

Georganne MOLINE b. 6 Mar 1990 Phoenix, Arizona 1.78m 59kg. Nike Psychology and communications student at University of Arizona.
At 400mh: OG: '12- 5; WCh: '13- h.
Progress at 400mh: 2010- 57.88, 2011- 57.41, 2012- 53.92, 2013- 53.72, 2014- 54.00. pbs: 200m 23.37 '13, 400m 52.09i '13, 52.92 '12; 500m 1:08.84i '15, 600m 1:27.15i '15, 800m 2:08.67i '13. 2:09.58 '14.
53.92 in Olympic final was seventh 400mh pb of her 2012 season.

Alysia MONTAÑO b. 26 Apr 1986 Queens, New York 1.70m 61kg. née Johnson. Nike. Was at University of California.
At 800m: OG: '12- 5; WCh: '07- h, '11- 4, '13- 4; PAm: '07- 6; WI: '10- 3; CCp: '10- 8; won US 2007, 2010-13; NCAA 2007.
North American indoor 600m record 2013.
Progress at 800m: 2004- 2:08.97, 2005- 2:05.49, 2006- 2:01.80, 2007- 1:59.29, 2008- 2:00.57, 2009- 2:01.09, 2010- 1:57.34, 2011- 1:57.48, 2012- 1:57.37, 2013- 1:57.75. pbs: 200m 24.41iA '13, 400m 52.09 '10, 600m 1:23.59i '13, 1:26.7+ '12; 1500m 4:28.43 '09.
Always runs with a flower in her hair. Married Louis Montaño on 19 Mar 2011, daughter Linnea Dori born 15 Aug 2014.

LaShaunte'a MOORE b. 31 Jul 1983 Akron, Ohio 1.70m 62kg. adidas. Was at University of Arkansas. Training to be a nurse.
At 200m: OG: '04- sf, WCh: '07- 7; WY: '99- 4/1 MedR; won NCAA 2004.
Progress at 100m, 200m: 1997- 11.93, 1998- 11.67w, 23.86w; 1999- 11.66, 23.26; 2001- 11.64/11.57w, 23.59/23.40w; 2002- 11.47, 23.13/22.89w; 2003- 11.33/11.27w, 23.09/22.81Aw; 2004- 11.26, 22.63/22.37w; 2005- 11.39/11.25w, 22.93; 2006- 11.40, 22.89/22.64w; 2007- 11.26/11.10w, 22.46; 2008- 11.03, 22.70; 2009- 11.21, 22.57; 2010- 10.97, 22.46; 2011- 11.17/11.04w, 22.58; 2012- 11.11/10.93w, 22.71; 2013- 11.26/10.98w, 22.40; 2014- 11.39/11.12w. pbs: 60m 7.36i '03, 400m 54.92 '07.

Dalilah MUHAMMAD b. 7 Feb 1990 Jamaica, Queens, New York 1.70m 62kg. Nike, Business graduate of University of Southern Califormia.
At 400mh: WCh: '13- 2; WY: '07- 1; PAm-J: '09- 2; US champion 2013.
Progress at 400mh: 2005- 61.25, 2006- 59.82, 2007- 57.09, 2008- 57.81, 2009- 56.49, 2010- 57.14, 2011- 56.04, 2012- 56.19, 2013- 53.83, 2014- 58.02. pbs: 60m 7.64i '10, 100m 11.42 '13, 200m 23.62 '09, 400m 52.75 '13, 60mh 8.23i '12, 100mh 13.33 '12, 200mhSt 25.90 '14, HJ 1.75 '10.

Sharika NELVIS b. 10 May 1990 Memphis 1.78m 64kg. Sociology student at Arkansas State University.
Won NCAA 100mh & indoor 60mh 2014.
Progress at 100mh: 2008- 14.23, 2009- 14.03, 2011- 13.45, 2012- 13.22/12.99w, 2013- 12.84, 2014- 12.71/12.52w. pbs: 60m 7.28i '14, 100m 11.27/11.17w '14, 200m 23.35 '12, 22.70w '14; 400m 54.62 '13, 60mh 7.83i '15, LJ 6.32i '13, 6.27 '14.

Courtney OKOLO b. 15 Mar 1994 Carrolltown, Texas 1.68m 54kg. Student at University of Texas.
At 400m/4x400mR: PAm-J: '13- 1/1R. Won NCAA 2014.
Progress at 400m: 2009- 56.50, 2010- 54.35, 2011- 53.03, 2012- 52.40, 2013- 51.04, 2014- 50.03. pbs: 60m 7.52i '14, 200m 23.17/23.04w '14, 600y 1:18.24 '15.

Demi PAYNE b. 30 Sep 1991 New Braunfels, Texas 1.83m. Studeent at Stephen F.Austin University, formerly University of Kansas.
Progress at PV: 2008- 3.81, 2009- 3.94, 2010- 3.92i/3.86, 2011- 4.06, 2012- 4.22i/4.20, 2013- 4.25i, 2014- 4.29, 2015- 4.75i.
Big improvement to three US collegiate records indoors in January 2015. Her father Bill Payne (b. 21 Dec 1967) in 1991 had pb best of 5.86 (US

collegiate best) and was 2nd WUG. Daughter Carlee born October 2013.

Barbara PIERRE b. 28 Apr 1987 Port-au-Prince, Haiti 1.75m 60kg. Nike. Was at St. Augustine's College.
At 100m/4x100mR: OG: '08- qf; PAm: '11- 2/2R. At 60m: WI: '12-4.
Haiti records at 100m 2009, 200m 2008-09.
Progress at 100m: 2003- 11.98, 2005- 11.78, 2006- 11.66, 2007- 11.30, 2008- 11.40A, 2009- 11.18, 2010- 11.35, 2011- 11.14, 2012- 11.34, 2013- 10.85, 2014- 11.05. pbs: 50m 6.22+i '12, 55m 6.89i '07, 60m 7.06Ai '12, 7.09 '13; 100y 10.38y '11, 200m 23.23 '10, 400m 57.04 '08.
With dual citizenship, she switched from US to Haiti 31 Dec 2007, and back to US 24 Mar 2010.

Chanelle PRICE b. 22 Aug 1990 Livingston, NJ 1.66m 53kg. Nike. Studied journalism at University of Tennessee.
At 800m: WY: '07- 6; WI: '14- 1; won US indoor 2013-14.
North American 4x800m record 2014.
Progress at 800m: 2004- 2:13.54, 2005- 2:08.72, 2006- 2:06.23, 2007- 2:02.38, 2008- 2:01.61, 2009- 2:03.30, 2010- 2:03.12i, 2011- 2:02.84, 2012- 2:00.15, 2013- 2:00.88, 2014- 1:59.75. pbs: 400m 54.26 '13, 500m 1:10.30i 08, 1000m 2:36.63i '14, 1500m 4:16.52 '14, 1M 4:31.68 '14.

Brittney REESE b. 9 Sep 1986 Gulfport, Mississippi 1.73m 64kg. Nike. English graduate of University of Mississippi.
At LJ: OG: '08- 5, '12- 1; WCh: '07-09-11-13: 8/1/1/1; WI: '10- 1, '12- 1; won DL 2010-11, WAF 2009, US 2008-12, 2014; NCAA 2007-08.
North American indoor long jump record 2012.
Progress at LJ: 2004- 6.31, 2006- 5.94, 2007- 6.83, 2008- 6.95, 2009- 7.10, 2010- 6.94/7.05w, 2011- 7.19, 2012- 7.23i/7.15, 2013- 7.25, 2014- 6.92. pbs: 50m 6.23i '12, 60m 7.24i '11, 100m 11.63 '09, 11.20w '11; HJ 1.88i/1.84 '08, TJ 13.16 '08.
Concentrated on basketball at Gulf Coast Community College in 2005-06. Has won six successive global titles

Sanya RICHARDS-ROSS b. 26 Feb 1985 Kingston, Jamaica 1.73m 61kg. Nike. University of Texas.
At (200m)/400m/4x400m: OG: '04- 6/1R, '08- 3/1R, '12- 5/1/1R; WCh: '03- sf/1R, '05- 2, '07- (5)/1R, '09- 1/1R, '11- 7/1R; WJ: '02- 3/2; WCp: '06- 1/1; WI: '12- 1/2R. Won WAF 200m 2008, 400m 2005-09, US 2003, 2005-06, 2008-09, 2012; NCAA 2003.
US & North American 400m record 2006, world junior indoor bests 200m, 400m (2) 2004.
Progress at 200m, 400m: 1999- 23.84, 2000- 23.57, 54.34; 2001- 23.09, 53.49; 2002- 23.01, 50.69; 2003- 22.80i/22.86, 50.58; 2004- 22.49i/22.73, 49.89; 2005- 22.53, 48.92; 2006- 22.17, 48.70; 2007- 22.31, 49.27; 2008- 22.49, 49.74; 2009- 22.29, 48.83; 2010- 51.82; 2011- 22.63, 49.66; 2012- 22.09, 49.28; 2013- 51.43, 2014- 49.66. pbs: 60m 7.21i '04, 100m 10.97 '07, 10.89w '12; 300m 35.6 '05, 800m 2:10.74 '10, LJ 6.08 '01.
Left Jamaica at the age of 12 and gained US citizenship on 20 May 2002. Her 48.92 at Zürich in 2005 and then 48.70 at the World Cup in 2006 (to beat 22 year-old US record) were the world's fastest 400m times since 1996. Unbeaten in 13 finals outdoors at 400m in 2006 and after WAF win scored 200m/400m double at World Cup. Record 46 times sub-50 secs for 400m. Shared Golden League jackpot 2006, 2007 and 2009. IAAF female Athlete of the Year 2006 & 2009. Married US pro football cornerback Aaron Ross on 26 Feb 2010.

Brianna ROLLINS b. 18 Aug 1991 Miami 1.64m 55kg. Nike. Was at Clemson University.
At 100mh: WCh: '13- 1; Won US 2013, NACAC 2012. Won NCAA 100mh 2013, indoor 60mh 2011 & 2013.
North American 100m hurdles record 2013, world best 4x100mh 2014.
Progress at 100mh: 2007- 14.48, 2008- 13.93, 2009- 13.83, 2011- 12.99/12.88w, 2012- 12.70/ 12.60Aw, 2013- 12.26, 2014- 12.53. pbs: 200m 23.04/23.02w '13, 300m 37.90i '10, 400m 53.93 '13, 60mh 7.78i '13, 400mh 60.58 '09.
Undefeated in 2013: inc. heats 200m- 7, 400m- 1, 60mh- 8, 100mh- 18.

Shannon ROWBURY b. 19 Sep 1984 San Francisco 1.65m 52kg. Nike Oregon Project. Was at Duke University.
At 1500m: OG: '08- 7, '12- 6; WCh: '09- 3, '11- sf; CCp: '14- 2; Won US 2008-09, NCAA indoor mile 2007. At 3000m: WI: '14- 8; CCp: '10- 2. At 5000m: WCh: '13- 7.
North American 2M record 2014.
Progress at 1500m, 5000m: 2004- 4:17.41, 2005- 4:14.81, 2006- 4:12.31, 15:38.42; 2007- 16:59.97i, 2008- 4:00.33, 2009- 4:00.81, 15:12.95; 2010- 4:01.30, 15:00.51; 2011- 4:05.73, 2012- 4:03.15, 2013- 4:01.28, 15:06.10, 2014- 3:59.49, 14:48.68. pbs: 800m 2:00.47 '10, 1000m 2:40.25i '15, 1M 4:20.34 '08, 2000m 5:46.2 '14, 3000m 8:29.93 '14, 2M 9:20.25 '14, 3000mSt 9:59.4 '06.
Former ballet and Irish dancer. Due to marry Pablo Solares (Mexican 1500m record 3:36.67 '09) in April 2015.

Mary SAXER b. 21 Jun 1987 Buffalo, NY 1.66m 57kg. Nike. Marketing graduate of University of Notre Dame.
At PV: WI: '12- 4, 14- 8.
Progress at PV: 2004- 3.81, 2005- 4.32i/4.19, 2006- 4.05i/3.90, 2007- 3.86i/3.80, 2008- 4.06, 2009- 4.30, 2010- 4.50, 2011- 4.60, 2012- 4.62Ai/4.53, 2013- 4.70, 2014- 4.71Ai/4.58.

Jennifer SIMPSON b. 23 Aug 1986 Webster City, Iowa 1.65m 50kg. née Barringer. New Balance. Studied political science at University of Colorado.

At 1500m: OG: '12- sf; WCh: '11- 1, '13- 2; won DL 2014. At 3000mSt: OG: '08- 9; WCh: '07- h, '09- 5; won NCAA 2006, 2008-09. Won US 1500m 2014, 5000m 2013, 3000mSt 2009.
North American records: 3000m steeplechase (3) 2008-09, indoor 2 miles 2015.
Progress at 1500m, 5000m, 3000mSt: 2006- 16:15.23, 9:53.04, 2007- 4:21.53, 15:48.24, 9:33.95; 2008- 4:11.36, 9:22.26; 2009- 3:59.90, 15:01.70i/ 15:05.25, 9:12.50; 2010- 4:03.63, 15:33.33; 2011- 4:03.54, 15:11.49; 2012- 4:04.07, 2013- 4:00.48, 14:56.26; 2014- 3:57.22. pbs: 800m 2:00.45 '13, 1M 4:25.91i '09, 2000m 5:45.7 '14, 3000m 8:29.58 '14, 2M 9:18.35i '15.
Married Jason Simpson on 8 Oct 2010. Won 5th Avenue Mile 2011.

Shalonda SOLOMON b. 19 Dec 1985 Inglewood, California 1.69m 56kg. Reebok. Was at University of South Carolina.
At (100m)/200m/4x100m: WCh: '11- 4/res (1)R; WJ: '04- 1/1R; PAm-J: '03- 1/1/1R; CCp: '10- (2)/1R. Won NCAA 200m 2006, NCAAC 100m & 200m 2006.
Progress at 100m, 200m: 2001- 11.57/11.37w, 23.65/23.22w; 2002- 11.51/11.46w, 23.31; 2003- 11.35/11.25w, 22.93; 2004- 11.41/11.32w, 22.82; 2005- 11.29, 22.74/22.72w; 2006- 11.09/11.07w, 22.36/22.30w; 2007- 11.33, 22.77; 2008- 11.16, 22.48/22.36w; 2009- 11.04/11.00w, 22.41; 2010- 10.90, 22.47; 2011- 11.08/10.90w, 22.15; 2012- 11.26, 22.82; 2013- 11.04/10.97w, 22.41/22.33w; 2014- 11.12, 22.64/22.54w. pbs: 55m 6.72i '09, 60m 7.15Ai '11, 7.21i '06; 300m 36.45i '09, 400m 53.47 '08.

Ashley SPENCER b. 8 Jun 1993 Indianapolis 1.68m 54kg. Student at University of Texas, formerly Illinois.
At 400m/4x400mR: WCh: '13- sf/2R; WJ: '12- 1/1R. Won NCAA 2012-13.
Progress at 400m: 2012- 50.50, 2013- 50.28, 2014- 51.38. pbs: 60m 7.42i '13, 100m 11.34/11.27w '14, 200m 22.92/22.69w '14, 100mh 14.40/14.28w '11, 400mh 56.32 '13.

Jeneva STEVENS b. 28 Oct 1989 Dolton, Illinois 1.78m 102kg. née McCall. Was at Southern Illinois University.
At HT: WCh: '11- dnq 14, '13- 9; WUG: '13- 1. At SP: WI: '14- 8. Won NCAA DT 2010, HT 2012.
Progress at HT: 2009- 55.83, 2010- 64.17, 2011- 69.55, 2012- 69.38, 2013- 74.77, 2014- 70.78. Pbs: SP 19.10i '12, 18.47 '13, DT 59.45 '12, Wt 23.94i '13.
Daughter of 1994-5 WBC world heavyweight boxing champion Oliver McCall.

Jasmin STOWERS b. 23 Sep 1991 Pendleton, SC 1.75m 64kg. Degree in nutrition from Louisiana State University.
At 100mh: WY: '07- 4; won NCAA indoor 60mh 2013, US 2015.
Progress at 100mh: 2005- 14.27w, 2006- 14.05/13.82Aw, 2007- 13.69/13.68w, 2008- 13.66/13.46w, 2009- 13.59/13.32Aw, 2010- 14.47, 2011- 12.88/12.86w, 2012- 12.92, 2013- 13.00/ 12.88w, 2014- 12.71/12.54w. pbs: 60m 7.51i '12, 100m 11.82 '11, 60mh 7.84i '15, 400mh 61.17 '08.

Jennifer SUHR b. 6 Feb 1982 Fredonia, New York 1.80m 64kg. adidas. née Stuczynski. Graduate of Roberts Wesleyan University, now studying child psychology.
At PV: OG: '08- 2, '12- 1; WCh: '07- 10, '11- 4, '13- 2; WI: '08- 2, '14- 5=; WCp: '06- nh; US champion 2006-10, 2012-14; indoors 2005, 2007-09, 2011-13.
Records: world indoors 2013, four N.American PV records 2007-08, four indoors 2009-13.
Progress at PV: 2002- 2.75, 2004- 3.49, 2005- 4.57i/4.26, 2006- 4.68i/4.66, 2007- 4.88, 2008- 4.92, 2009- 4.83i/4.81, 2010- 4.89, 2011- 4.91, 2012- 4.88i/4.81, 2013- 5.02Ai/4.91, 2014- 4.73i/4.71. pbs: 55mh 8.07i '05, JT 46.82 '05.
All-time top scorer at basketball at her university, then very rapid progress at vaulting.

Jeneba TARMOH b. 27 Sep 1989 San Jose CA 1.67m 59kg. Nike. Was at Texas A&M University.
At (100m)/200m/4x100m: OG: '12- res (1)R; WCh: '11- h, '13- 5/2R; WJ: '06- 7/1R, '08- (1)/1R. Won NCAAC 100m 2010.
Progress at 100m, 200m: 2004- 12.07w, 2005- 11.81/11.61w, 24.04/23.56w; 2006- 11.24, 23.14; 2007- 11.27, 23.34/23.20w; 2008- 11.21, 22.94; 2009- 11.31, 23.31i/23.43/23.16w; 2010- 11.19/ 11.00w, 22.65; 2011- 11.23/10.94w, 22.28; 2012- 11.07, 22.35/22.30w; 2013- 10.93, 22.70/22.15w; 2014- 11.11, 22.41. pbs: 50m 6.14+i '12. 55m 6.86Ai '06, 60m 7.22i '12.
Her parents came from Sierra Leone.

Cassandra TATE b. 11 Sep 1990 Hammond, Louisiana 1.74m 64kg. Management graduate of Louisiana State University.
At 400m/4x400m: WI: '14- 1R; won NCAA & NACAC 2012.
Progress at 400mh: 2010- 56.87, 2011- 55.99, 2012- 55.22, 2013- 55.45, 2014- 54.70. pbs: 60m 7.49i '11, 100m 11.79 '08, 11.47w '10; 200m 23.37i '10, 23.68 '09; 400m 52.40Ai, 52.77 '14, 60mh 8.61i '09, 100mh 14.21 '08, 14.08w '07.
Progress at 400m: 1998- 58.61, 1999- 59.12, 2000- 56.82, 2001- 56.02, 2002- 53.66, 2003- 50.66, 2004- 50.00, 2005- 49.88, 2006- 49.80, 2007- 49.64, 2008- 50.88, 2009- 52.00, 2010- 51.23Ai/51.52, 2011- 51.17, 2012- 49.72, 2013- 51.67, 2014- 50.98. pbs: 55m 6.93i '04, 60m 7.46i '05, 100m 11.65 '02, 200m 22.85/22.54w '13, 300m 35.8+ '07, LJ 6.00 '02.

Kellie WELLS b. 16 Jul 1982 Richmond, Virginia 1.63m 57kg. Nike. Was at Hampton University.
At 100mh: OG: '12- 3; WCh: '11- dnf. US champion 2011.
Progress at 100mh: 2003- 13.96, 2004- 13.25, 2005- 13.57/13.29w, 2006- 13.25/13.17w, 2007- 12.93, 2008- 12.58, 2009- 13.01, 2010- 12.68, 2011- 12.50/12.35w, 2012- 12.48, 2013- 12.54/12.47w,

2014- 12.68. pbs: 60m 7.33i '06, 100m 11.50 '08, 200m 23.53 '06, 50mh 6.84i '12, 55mh 7.37i '11, 60mh 7.79Ai/7.82i '11.

Charonda WILLIAMS b. 27 Mar 1987 Richmond, California 1.67m 55kg. adidas. Was at Arizona State University.
At 200m: WCh: '09- sf, '13- 6. Won DL 2012.
Progress at 200m: 2006- 24.19/24.08w, 2007- 23.53, 2008- 23.09, 2009- 22.55/22.39w, 2010- 22.97, 2011- 22.85/22.78w, 2012- 22.52, 2013- 22.71, 2014- 23.41. pbs: 55m 6.99Ai '08, 60m 7.29Ai '09, 7.36i '11; 100m 11.07 '13, 10.95w '12; 300m 37.04i '11, 400m 52.71 '11, LJ 5.91 '07, 6.03w '00.

Tiffany WILLIAMS b. 5 Feb 1983 Miami 1.58m 57kg. née Ross. Reebok. Retail management graduate of University of Southern Carolina.
At 400mh: OG: '08- 8; WCh: '07- 7, '09- 5; WJ: '02- 4/1R. Won US 2007-08.
Progress at 400mh: 2000- 58.50, 2001- 57.91, 2002- 55.22, 2003- 55.89, 2005- 54.56, 2006- 53.79, 2007- 53.28, 2008- 53.54, 2009- 53.83, 2011- 55.77, 2012- 55.01, 2013- 55.04, 2014- 54.74. pbs: 200m 24.40 '08, 24.35i '06; 300m 37.36 '12, 400m 52.43i '05, 52.45 '06; 55mh 7.63i '03, 60mh 8.29i '05, 100mh 12.99 '05, 12.8 '08; TJ 12.49.
Married to Steven Williams, they have a daughter, Samya, born in 2004.

Ajee' WILSON b. 8 May 1994 Neptune, New Jersey 1.69m 55kg. adidas. Student of kinesiology at Temple University, Philadelphia.
At 800m: WCh: '13- 6; WJ: '10- 5, '12- 1; WY: 11- 1; CCp: '14- 2; won US 2014, indoor 2013.
Records: North American 4x800m 2014, world junior 600m & N.American junior 800m 2013.
Progress at 800m: 2008- 2:11.43, 2009- 2:07.08, 2010- 2:04.18, 2011- 2:02.64, 2012- 2:00.91, 2013- 1:58.21, 2014- 1:57.67. pbs: 400m 53.63 '14, 500m 1:10.27i '15, 600m 1:26.45 '13, 1000m 2:48.88i '14, 1500m 4:12.10 '14, 3000m 10:13.41 '07.
Elder sister Jade has 400mh pb 59.90 '12.

Kara WINGER b. 10 Apr 1986 Seattle 1.83m 84kg. née Patterson. Studied interior design at Purdue University.
At JT: OG: '08/12- dnq 41/31; WCh: '09/11- dnq 29/21; PAm-J: '05- 2; CCp: '10- 6, '14- 7. US Champion 2008-11, 2014.
North American javelin record 2010.
Progress at JT: 2003- 44.75, 2004- 48.51. 2005- 52.09, 2006- 567.19, 2008- 61.56, 2009- 63.95, 2010- 66.67, 2011- 62.76, 2012- 60.49, 2013- 57.12, 2014- 62.90. Pb DT 35.17 '11.
Married Russ Winger (pbs SP 21.29i '08, 21.25 '10; DT 66.04 '11) on 28 Sep 2014.

UZBEKISTAN

Governing body: Athletic Federation of Uzbekistan, Navoi str. 30, 100129 Tashkent.

Svetlana RADZIVIL b. 17 Jan 1987 Tashkent 1.84m 61kg
At HJ: OG: '08- dnq 18, '12- 7; WCh: '09- dnq 21=, '11- 8=; AsiG: '06-10-14: 7/1/1; AsiC: '09-11-13: 3/2/2; WJ: '02- dnq, '04- 13, '06- 1; WY: '03- dnq; CCp: '14- 4; WI: '12- 8. Won Asi-J 2006, Asian indoor 2014.
Progress at HJ: 2002- 1.84, 2003- 1.78, 2004- 1.88, 2005- 1.85, 2006- 1.91, 2007- 1.91, 2008- 1.93, 2009- 1.91, 2010- 1.95, 2011- 1.95, 2012- 1.97, 2013- 1.94, 2014- 1.96.

VENEZUELA

Governing body: Federación Venezolana de Atletismo, Apartado Postal 29059, Caracas. Founded 1948.
National Champions 2014: **Men** 100m: Dubeiker Cedeño 10.53, 200m: Arturo Ramírez 21.22, 400m: José Daniel Meléndez 46.22, 800m: Roiman Ramítrez 1:51.09, 1500m: Whinton Palma 3:56.22, 3000mSt: William Díaz 9:28.67, 110mh: Andrés Toro 14.54, 400mh: Lucirio Garrido 50.91, HJ: Eure Yáñez 2.25, PV: Johny Caibe 4.60, LJ: Santiago Luis Cova 7.60, TJ: Ángel Delgado 15.75, SP/DT: Jesús Parejo 16.14/52.73, HT: Prinston Quailey 60.14, JT: William Valor 64.10, Dec: Gerson Izaguirre 6690, 20000mW: Richard Vargas 1:27:39.5. **Women**: 100m: Andrea Purica 11.55, 200m/400m: Nercely Soto 23.45/53.47, 800m: María Garrido 2:14.05, 1500m/5000m: María Osorio 4:32.18/17:14.32, 10000m: Yolimar Pineda 36:34.46, 100mh: Génesis Romero 13.63, 400mh: Magdalena Mendoza 59.05, HJ: Verónica Davis 1.70, PV: Robeilys Peinado 4.00, LJ/TJ: Yulimar Rojas 6.40/13.65, SP: Giohanny Rojas 14.94, DT: Elizabeth Álvarez 47.94, HT: Génesis Olivera 65.23, JT: Mariana Romero 44.51, Hep: Guillercy González 5153, 20000mW: Cheskaya Rosales 1:53:41.

ZIMBABWE

Governing body: Amateur Athletic Association of Zimbabwe, PO Box MP 187, Mount Pleasant, Harare. Founded in 1912.

Ngonidzashe MAKUSHA b. 11 Mar 1987 Chitungwiza, Harare 1.78m 73kg. Student at Florida State University, USA.
At LJ (100m): OG: '08- 4; WCh: '11- 3 (sf); WJ: '06- 12 (sf); AfG: '07- 3R (sf). Won NCAA 100m 2011, LJ 2008-09, 2011; ZIM LJ 2006-07.
Zimbabwe records 100 (2) 2011, long jump (5) 2006-11.
Progress at 100m. LJ: 2005- 7.34?, 2006- 10.64Aw, 7.87A; 2007- 10.52, 7.69; 2008- 8.30, 2009- 8.21i/7.73/8.11w, 2010- 7.71i/7.54, 2011- 9.89, 8.40; 2012- 7.86, 2013- 8.04/8.20w, 2014- 8.18i. pbs: 55m 6.30i '08, 60m 6.60i '09, 200m 21.38A '06, TJ 14.90A '06.
Superb unique treble at 2011 NCAAs with 100m 9.89 and LJ 8.40 plus 4x100m leg. Suffered ruptured Achilles in May 2012.

INTRODUCTION TO WORLD LISTS AND INDEX

Records

World, World U20 and U18, Olympic, Area and Continental records are listed for standard events. In running events up to and including 400 metres, only fully automatic times are shown. Marks listed are those which are considered statistically acceptable by the ATFS, and thus may differ from official records. These are followed by 'odd events', road bests and bests by over 35/40 masters.

World All-time and Year Lists

Lists are presented in the following format: Mark, Wind reading (where appropriate), Name, Nationality (abbreviated), Date of birth, Position in competition, Meeting name (if significant), Venue, Date of performance.

In standard events the best 30 or so performances are listed followed by the best marks for other athletes. Position, meet and venue details have been omitted beyond 100th in year lists.

In the all-time lists performances which have been world records (or world bests, thus including some unratified marks) are shown with WR against them (or WIR for world indoor records).

Juniors (U20) are shown with-J after date of birth, and Youths (U18) with -Y.

Indexes

These contain the names of all athletes ranked with full details in the world year lists for standard events (and others such as half marathon). The format of the index is as follows:

Family name, First name, Nationality, Birthdate, Height (cm) and Weight (kg), 2014 best mark, Lifetime best (with year) as at the end of 2013.

* indicates an athlete who is profiled in the Biographies section, and ^ one who has been profiled in previous editions.

General Notes

Altitude aid

Marks set at an altitude of 1000m or higher have been suffixed by the letter "A" in events where altitude may be of significance.

Although there are no separate world records for altitude assisted events, it is understood by experts that in all events up to 400m in length (with the possible exclusion of the 110m hurdles), and in the horizontal jumps, altitude gives a material benefit to performances. For events beyond 800m, however, the thinner air of high altitude has a detrimental effect.

Supplementary lists are included in relevant events for athletes with seasonal bests at altitude who have low altitude marks qualifying for the main list.

Some leading venues over 1000m

Addis Ababa ETH	2365m
Air Force Academy USA	2194
Albuquerque USA	1555
Antananarivo MAD	1350
Ávila ESP	1128
Bloemfontein RSA	1392
Bogotá COL	2644
Boulder USA	1655
Bozeman USA	1467
Calgary CAN	1045
Cali COL	1046
Ciudad de Guatemala GUA	1402
Ciudad de México MEX	2247
Cochabamba BOL	2558
Colorado Springs USA	1823
Cuenca ECU	2561
Denver USA	1609
El Paso USA	1187
Flagstaff USA	2107
Fort Collins USA	1521
Gabarone BOT	1006
Germiston RSA	1661
Guadalajara MEX	1567
Harare ZIM	1473
Johannesburg RSA	1748
Kampala UGA	1189
Krugersdorp RSA	1740
La Paz BOL	3630
Levelland USA	1069
Logan USA	1372
Medellín COL	1541
Monachil ESP	2302
Nairobi KEN	1675
Oren USA	1455
Pietersburg RSA	1230
Pocatello USA	1361
Potchefstroom RSA	1351
Pretoria RSA	1400
Provo USA	1380
Pueblo USA	1487
Reno USA	1369
Roodepoort RSA	1623
Rustenburg RSA	1215
Salt Lake City USA	1321
Sasoilberg RSA	1488
Secunda RSA	1628
Sestriere ITA	2050
Soría ESP	1056
South Lake Tahoe USA	1909
Sucre BOL	2750
Toluca MEX	2680
Windhoek NAM	1725
Xalapa MEX	1356
Some others over 500m	
Albertville FRA	550
Almaty KZK	847
Ankara TUR	902
Bangalore, IND	949
Bern SUI	555
Blacksburg USA	634
Boise USA	818

Canberra AUS	581
La Chaux de Fonds SUI	997
Caracas VEN	922
Edmonton CAN	652
Jablonec CZE	598
Las Vegas USA	619
Lausanne SUI	597
Lubbock USA	988
Madrid ESP	640
Magglingen SUI	751
Malles ITA	980
Moscow, Idaho USA	787
München GER	520
Nampa, Idaho USA	760
Salamanca ESP	806
Santiago de Chile CHI	520
São Paulo BRA	725
Sofia BUL	564
Spokane USA	576
Trípoli GRE	655
Tucson USA	728
Uberlândia BRA	852
350m-500m	
Banská Bystrica SVK	362
Fayetteville USA	407
Genève SUI	385
Götzis AUS	448
Johnson City USA	499
Rieti ITA	402
Sindelfingen GER	440
Stuttgart GER	415
Tashkent UZB	477
Zürich SUI	410

Automatic timing

In the main lists for sprints and hurdles, only times recorded by fully automatic timing devices are included.

Hand timing

In the sprints and hurdles supplementary lists are included for races which are hand timed. Athletes with a hand timed best 0.01 seconds or more better than his or her automatically timed best has been included, but hand timed lists have been terminated close to the differential levels considered by the IAAF to be equivalent to automatic times, i.e. 0.24 sec. for 100m, 200m, 100mh, 110mh, and 0.14 sec. for 400m and 400mh. It should be noted that this effectively recognises bad hand timekeeping, for there should be no material difference between hand and auto times, but badly trained timekeepers anticipate the finish, having reacted to the flash at the start.

In events beyond 400m, auto times are integrated with hand timed marks, the latter identifiable by times being shown to tenths. All-time lists also include some auto times in tenths of a second, identified with '.

Indoor marks

Indoor marks are included in the main lists for field events and straightway track events, but not for other track events as track sizes vary in circumference (200m is the international standard) and banking, while outdoor tracks are standardised at 400m. Outdoor marks for athletes with indoor bests are shown in a supplemental list.

Mixed races

For record purposes athletes may not, except in road races, compete in mixed sex races. Statistically there would not appear to be any particular logic in this, and women's marks set in such races are shown in our lists – annotated with mx. In such cases the athlete's best mark in single sex competition is appended.

Field event series

Field event series are given (where known) for marks in the top 30 performances lists.

Tracks and Courses

As well as climatic conditions, the type and composition of tracks and runways will affect standards of performance, as will the variations in road race courses.

Wind assistance

Anemometer readings have been shown for sprints and horizontal jumps in metres per second to one decimal place. If the figure was given to two decimal places, it has been rounded to the next tenth upwards, e.g. a wind reading of +2.01m/s, beyond the IAAF legal limit of 2.0, is rounded to +2.1; or -1.22m/s is rounded up to -1.2.

For multi-events a wind-assisted mark is one in which the average of the three wind-measured events is > 2m/s.

Drugs bans

The IAAF Council may decertify an athlete's records, titles and results if he or she is found to have used a banned substance before those performances. Performances at or after such a positive finding are shown in footnotes. Such athletes are shown with ¶ after their name in year lists, and in all-time lists if at any stage of their career they have served a drugs suspension of a year or more (thus not including athletes receiving public warnings or 3 month bans for stimulants etc., which for that year only are indicated with a #). This should not be taken as implying that the athlete was using drugs at that time. Nor have those athletes who have subsequently unofficially admitted to using banned substances been indicated; the ¶ is used only for those who have been caught.

Venues

Place names occasionally change. Our policy is to use names in force at the time that the performance was set. Thus Leningrad prior to 1991, Sankt-Peterburg from its re-naming.

Amendments

Keen observers may spot errors in the lists. They are invited to send corrections as well as news and results for 2015.

Peter Matthews
Email p.matthews121@btinternet.com

WORLD & CONTINENTAL RECORDS

As at 1 April 2015. **Key**: W = World, Afr = Africa, Asi = Asia, CAC = Central America & Caribbean, Eur = Europe, NAm = North America, Oce = Oceania, SAm = South America, Com = Commonwealth, W20 = World Junior (U20), W18 = World Youth (U18, not officially ratified by IAAF). h hand timed.
Successive columns show: World or Continent, performance, name, nationality, venue, date.
A altitude over 1000m, + timing by photo-electric-cell, # awaiting ratification, § not officially ratified

100 METRES

W,CAC,Com	9.58	Usain BOLT	JAM	Berlin	16 Aug 2009
NAm	9.69	Tyson GAY	USA	Shanghai	20 Sep 2009
Afr	9.85	Olusoji FASUBA	NGR	Doha	12 May 2006
Eur	9.86	Francis OBIKWELU	POR	Athína	22 Aug 2004
Oce	9.93	Patrick JOHNSON	AUS	Mito	5 May 2003
Asi	9.93	Femi OGUNODE	QAT	Incheon	28 Sep 2014
SAm	10.00A	Róbson da SILVA	BRA	Ciudad de México	22 Jul 1988
W20	9.97	Trayvon BROMELL	USA	Eugene	13 Jun 2014
W18	10.19	Yoshihide KIRYU	JPN	Fukuroi	3 Nov 2012

200 METRES

W,CAC,Com	19.19	Usain BOLT	JAM	Berlin	20 Aug 2009
NAm	19.32	Michael JOHNSON	USA	Atlanta	1 Aug 1996
Afr	19.68	Frank FREDERICKS	NAM	Atlanta	1 Aug 1996
Eur	19.72A	Pietro MENNEA	ITA	Ciudad de México	12 Sep 1979
SAm	19.81	Alonso EDWARD	PAN	Berlin	20 Aug 2009
Asi	20.03	Shingo SUETSUGU	JPN	Yokohama	7 Jun 2003
Oce	20.06A	Peter NORMAN	AUS	Ciudad de México	16 Oct 1968
W20	19.93	Usain BOLT	JAM	Hamilton, BER	11 Apr 2004
W18	20.13	Usain BOLT	JAM	Bridgetown	20 Jul 2003

400 METRES

W, NAm	43.18	Michael JOHNSON	USA	Sevilla	26 Aug 1999
Com, CAC	43.74	Kirani JAMES	GRN	Lausanne	3 Jul 2014
Afr	44.01	Isaac MAKWALA	BOT	La Chaux-de-Fonds	6 Jul 2014
SAm	44.29	Sanderlei PARRELA	BRA	Sevilla	26 Aug 1999
Eur	44.33	Thomas SCHÖNLEBE	GER	Roma	3 Sep 1987
Oce	44.38	Darren CLARK	AUS	Seoul	26 Sep 1988
Asi	44.43	Yousef Ahmed AL-MASRAHI	KSA	Lausanne	3 Jul 2014
W20	43.87	Steve LEWIS	USA	Seoul	28 Sep 1988
W18	45.14	Obea MOORE	USA	Santiago de Chile	2 Sep 1995

800 METRES

W, Afr, Com	1:40.91	David RUDISHA	KEN	London (OS)	9 Aug 2012
Eur	1:41.11	Wilson KIPKETER	DEN	Köln	24 Aug 1997
SAm	1:41.77	Joaquim CRUZ	BRA	Köln	26 Aug 1984
NAm	1:42.60	Johnny GRAY	USA	Koblenz	28 Aug 1985
Asi	1:42.79	Youssef Saad KAMEL	BRN	Monaco	29 Jul 2008
CAC	1:42.85	Norberto TELLEZ	CUB	Atlanta	31 Jul 1996
Oce	1:44.3+ h	Peter SNELL	NZL	Christchurch	3 Feb 1962
W20	1:41.73	Nijel AMOS	BOT	London (OS)	9 Aug 2012
W18	1:43.37	Mohamed AMAN	ETH	Rieti	10 Sep 2011

1000 METRES

W, Afr, Com	2:11.96	Noah NGENY	KEN	Rieti	5 Sep 1999
Eur	2:12.18	Sebastian COE	GBR	Oslo	11 Jul 1981
NAm	2:13.9	Rick WOHLHUTER	USA	Oslo	30 Jul 1974
SAm	2:14.09	Joaquim CRUZ	BRA	Nice	20 Aug 1984
Asi	2:14.72	Youssef Saad KAMEL	BRN	Stockholm	22 Jul 2008
Oce	2:16.09	Jeff RISELEY	AUS	Ostrava	17 Jun 2014
CAC	2:17.0	Byron DYCE	JAM	København	15 Aug 1973
W20	2:13.93 §	Abubaker KAKI	SUD	Stockholm	22 Jul 2008
W18	2:17.44	Hamza DRIOUCH	QAT	Sollentuna	9 Aug 2011

1500 METRES

W, Afr	3:26.00	Hicham EL GUERROUJ	MAR	Roma	14 Jul 1998
Com	3:26.34	Bernard LAGAT	KEN	Bruxelles	24 Aug 2001
Eur	3:28.81	Mo FARAH	GBR	Monaco	19 Jul 2013
Asi	3:29.14	Rashid RAMZI	BRN	Roma	14 Jul 2006
NAm	3:29.30	Bernard LAGAT	USA	Rieti	28 Aug 2005
Oce	3:29.91	Nick WILLIS	NZL	Monaco	18 Jul 2014

SAm	3:33.25	Hudson Santos de SOUZA	BRA	Rieti	28 Aug 2005
CAC	3:35.03	Maurys CASTILLO	CUB	Huelva	7 Jun 2012
W20	3:30.24	Cornelius CHIRCHIR	KEN	Monaco	19 Jul 2002
W18	3:33.72	Nicholas KEMBOI	KEN	Zürich	18 Aug 2006

1 MILE

W, Afr	3:43.13	Hicham El GUERROUJ	MAR	Roma	7 Jul 1999
Com	3:43.40	Noah NGENY	KEN	Roma	7 Jul 1999
Eur	3:46.32	Steve CRAM	GBR	Oslo	27 Jul 1985
NAm	3:46.91	Alan WEBB	USA	Brasschaat	21 Jul 2007
Asi	3:47.97	Daham Najim BASHIR	QAT	Oslo	29 Jul 2005
Oce	3:48.98	Craig MOTTRAM	AUS	Oslo	29 Jul 2005
SAm	3:51.05	Hudson de SOUZA	BRA	Oslo	29 Jul 2005
CAC	3:57.34	Byron DYCE	JAM	Stockholm	1 Jul 1974
	3:57.34	Juan Luis BARRIOS	MEX	Dublin	17 Jul 2013
W20	3:28.81	Ronald KWEMOI	KEN	Monaco	18 Jul 2014
W18	3:54.56	Isaac SONGOK	KEN	Linz	20 Aug 2001

2000 METRES

W, Afr	4:44.79	Hicham EL GUERROUJ	MAR	Berlin	7 Sep 1999
Com	4:48.74	John KIBOWEN	KEN	Hechtel	1 Aug 1998
Oce	4:50.76	Craig MOTTRAM	AUS	Melbourne	9 Mar 2006
Eur	4:51.39	Steve CRAM	GBR	Budapest	4 Aug 1985
NAm	4:52.44	Jim SPIVEY	USA	Lausanne	15 Sep 1987
Asi	4:55.57	Mohammed SULEIMAN	QAT	Roma	8 Jun 1995
SAm	5:03.34	Hudson Santos de SOUZA	BRA	Manaus	6 Apr 2002
CAC	5:03.4	Arturo BARRIOS	MEX	Nice	10 Jul 1989
W20	4:56.25	Tesfaye CHERU	ETH	Reims	5 Jul 2011
W18	4:56.86	Isaac SONGOK	KEN	Berlin	31 Aug 2001

3000 METRES

W, Afr, Com	7:20.67	Daniel KOMEN	KEN	Rieti	1 Sep 1996
Eur	7:26.62	Mohammed MOURHIT	BEL	Monaco	18 Aug 2000
NAm	7:29.00	Bernard LAGAT	USA	Rieti	29 Aug 2010
Asi	7:30.76	Jamal Bilal SALEM	QAT	Doha	13 May 2005
Oce	7:32.19	Craig MOTTRAM	AUS	Athína	17 Sep 2006
CAC	7:35.71	Arturo BARRIOS	MEX	Nice	10 Jul 1989
SAm	7:39.70	Hudson Santos de SOUZA	BRA	Lausanne	2 Jul 2002
W20	7:28.78	Augustine CHOGE	KEN	Doha	13 May 2005
W18	7:32.37	Abreham CHERKOS Feleke	ETH	Lausanne	11 Jul 2006

5000 METRES

W, Afr	12:37.35	Kenenisa BEKELE	ETH	Hengelo	31 May 2004
Com	12:39.74	Daniel KOMEN	KEN	Bruxelles	22 Aug 1997
Eur	12:49.71	Mohammed MOURHIT	BEL	Bruxelles	25 Aug 2000
Asi	12:51.96	Albert ROP	BRN	Monaco	19 Jul 2013
NAm	12:53.60	Bernard LAGAT	USA	Monaco	22 Jul 2011
Oce	12:55.76	Craig MOTTRAM	AUS	London	30 Jul 2004
CAC	13:07.79	Arturo BARRIOS	MEX	London (CP)	14 Jul 1989
SAm	13:19.43	Marilson dos SANTOS	BRA	Kassel	8 Jun 2006
W20	12:47.53	Hagos GEBRHIWET	ETH	Saint-Denis	6 Jul 2012
W18	12:54.19	Abreham CHERKOS Feleke	ETH	Roma	14 Jul 2006

10,000 METRES

W, Afr	26:17.53	Kenenisa BEKELE	ETH	Bruxelles	26 Aug 2005
Com	26:27.85	Paul TERGAT	KEN	Bruxelles	22 Aug 1997
Asi	26:38.76	Abdullah Ahmad HASSAN	QAT	Bruxelles	5 Sep 2003
NAm	26:44.36	Galen RUPP	USA	Eugene	30 May 2014
Eur	26:46.57	Mohamed FARAH	GBR	Eugene	3 Jun 2011
CAC	27:08.23	Arturo BARRIOS	MEX	Berlin	18 Aug 1989
Oce	27:24.95	Ben ST LAWRENCE	AUS	Stanford	1 May 2011
SAm	27:28.12	Marilson dos SANTOS	BRA	Neerpelt	2 Jun 2007
W20	26:41.75	Samuel WANJIRU	KEN	Bruxelles	26 Aug 2005
W18	27:02.81	Ibrahim JAYLAN Gashu	ETH	Bruxelles	25 Aug 2006

HALF MARATHON

W, Afr	58:23	Zersenay TADESE	ERI	Lisboa	21 Mar 2010
Com	58:33	Samuel WANJIRU	KEN	Den Haag	17 Mar 2007
Eur	59:32	Mohamed FARAH	GBR	Lisboa	21 Mar 2015
SAm	59:33	Marilson dos SANTOS	BRA	Udine	14 Oct 2007
NAm	59:43	Ryan HALL	USA	Houston	14 Jan 2007

Oce	59:47	Zane ROBERTSON	NZL	Marugame	1 Feb 2015
CAC	60:14	Armando QUINTANILLA	MEX	Tokyo	21 Jan 1996
Asi	60:25	Atsushi SATO	JPN	Udine	14 Oct 2007
W20	59:16	Samuel WANJIRU	KEN	Rotterdam	11 Sep 2005
W18	60:38	Faustin BAHA Sulle	TAN	Lille	4 Sep 1999

MARATHON

W, Afr, Com	2:02:57	Dennis KIMETTO	KEN	Berlin	28 Sep 2014
NAm	2:05:38	Khalid KHANNOUCHI (ex MAR)	USA	London	14 Apr 2002
SAm	2:06:05	Ronaldo da COSTA	BRA	Berlin	20 Sep 1998
Asi	2:06:16	Toshinari TAKAOKA	JPN	Chicago	13 Oct 2002
Eur	2:06:36 §	António PINTO	POR	London	16 Apr 2000
	2:06:36	Benoît ZWIERZCHIEWSKI	FRA	Paris	6 Apr 2003
Oce	2:08:16	Steve MONEGHETTI	AUS	Berlin	30 Sep 1990
CAC	2:08:30	Dionicio CERÓN	MEX	London	2 Apr 1995
W20	2:04:32	Tsegaye MEKONNEN	ETH	Dubai	24 Jan 2014
W18	2:11:43	LI He	CHN	Beijing	14 Oct 2001

3000 METRES STEEPLECHASE

W, Asi	7:53.63	Saïf Saaeed SHAHEEN	QAT	Bruxelles	3 Sep 2004
Afr, Com	7:53.64	Brimin KIPRUTO	KEN	Monaco	22 Jul 2011
Eur	8:00.09	Mahiedine MEKHISSI-BENABBAD	FRA	Saint-Denis	6 Jul 2013
NAm	8:04.71	Evan JAGER	USA	Bruxelles	5 Sep 2014
Oce	8:14.05	Peter RENNER	NZL	Koblenz	29 Aug 1984
SAm	8:14.41	Wander MOURA	BRA	Mar del Plata	22 Mar 1995
CAC	8:25.69	Salvador MIRANDA	MEX	Barakaldo	9 Jul 2000
W20	7:58.66	Stephen CHERONO (now Shaheen)	KEN	Bruxelles	24 Aug 2001
W18	8:17.28 §	Jonathan NDIKU	KEN	Bydgoszcz	13 Jul 2008

110 METRES HURDLES

W, NAm	12.80	Aries MERRITT	USA	Bruxelles	7 Sep 2012
CAC	12.87	Dayron ROBLES	CUB	Ostrava	12 Jun 2008
Asi	12.88	LIU Xiang	CHN	Lausanne	11 Jul 2006
Eur, Com	12.91	Colin JACKSON	GBR/Wal	Stuttgart	20 Aug 1993
Afr	13.24	Lehann FOURIE	RSA	Bruxelles	7 Sep 2012
SAm	13.27A	Paulo César VILLAR	COL	Guadalajara	28 Oct 2011
Oce	13.29	Kyle VANDER-KUYP	AUS	Göteborg	11 Aug 1995
W20	13.12	LIU Xiang (with 3'6" hurdles)	CHN	Lausanne	2 Jul 2002
W20 99cm h	12.99	Wilhem BELOCIAN	FRA	Eugene	24 Jul 2014
W18	13.43	SHI Dongpeng	CHN	Shanghai	6 May 2001
W18 91cm h	12.96	Jaheel HYDE	JAM	Nanjing	23 Aug 2014

400 METRES HURDLES

W, NAm	46.78	Kevin YOUNG	USA	Barcelona	6 Aug 1992
Afr, Com	47.10	Samuel MATETE	ZAM	Zürich	7 Aug 1991
CAC	47.25	Felix SÁNCHEZ	DOM	Saint-Denis	29 Aug 2003
Eur	47.37	Stéphane DIAGANA	FRA	Lausanne	5 Jul 1995
Asi	47.53	Hadi Soua'an AL-SOMAILY	KSA	Sydney	27 Sep 2000
SAm	47.84	Bayano KAMANI	PAN	Helsinki	7 Aug 2005
Oce	48.28	Rohan ROBINSON	AUS	Atlanta	31 Jul 1996
W20	48.02	Danny HARRIS	USA	Los Angeles	17 Jun 1984
W18	48.89	L.J. VAN ZYL	RSA	Kingston	19 Jul 2002

HIGH JUMP

W, CAC	2.45	Javier SOTOMAYOR	CUB	Salamanca	27 Jul 1993
Asi	2.43	Mutaz Essa BARSHIM	QAT	Bruxelles	5 Sep 2014
Eur	2.42	Patrik SJÖBERG	SWE	Stockholm	30 Jun 1987
	2.42 i§	Carlo THRÄNHARDT	FRG	Berlin	26 Feb 1988
	2.42i	Ivan UKHOV	RUS	Praha	25 Feb 2014
	2.42	Bogdan BONDARENKO	UKR	New York	14 Jun 2014
NAm	2.40 i§	Hollis CONWAY	USA	Sevilla	10 Mar 1991
	2.40	Charles AUSTIN	USA	Zürich	7 Aug 1991
NAm=, Com	2.40	Derek DROUIN	CAN	Des Moines	25 Apr 2014
Afr	2.38	Jacques FREITAG	RSA	Oudtshoorn	5 Mar 2005
Oce	2.36	Tim FORSYTH	AUS	Melbourne	2 Mar 1997
SAm	2.33	Gilmar MAYO	COL	Pereira	17 Oct 1994
W20	2.37	Dragutin TOPIC	YUG	Plovdiv	12 Aug 1990
		Steve SMITH	GBR	Seoul	20 Sep 1992
W18	2.33	Javier SOTOMAYOR	CUB	La Habana	19 May 1984

POLE VAULT

W, Eur	6.16 i	Renaud LAVILLENIE	FRA	Donetsk	15 Feb 2014
	6.14 A	Sergey BUBKA (best outdoor mark)	UKR	Sestriere	31 Jul 1994
Oce, Com	6.05	Dmitriy MARKOV	AUS	Edmonton	9 Aug 2001
NAm	6.04	Brad WALKER	USA	Eugene	8 Jun 2008
Afr	6.03	Okkert BRITS	RSA	Köln	18 Aug 1995
Asi	5.92i	Igor POTAPOVICH	KAZ	Stockholm	19 Feb 1998
	5.90	Grigoriy YEGOROV	KAZ	Stuttgart	19 Aug 1993
	5.90	Grigoriy YEGOROV	KAZ	London (CP)	10 Sep 1993
	5.90	Igor POTAPOVICH	KAZ	Nice	10 Jul 1996
CAC	5.90	Lázaro BORGES	CUB	Daegu	29 Aug 2011
SAm	5.83	Thiago BRAZ da SILVA	BRA	Cartagena	5 Jul 2013
W20	5.80	Maksim TARASOV	RUS	Bryansk	14 Jul 1989
	5.80	Raphael HOLZDEPPE	GER	Biberach	28 Jun 2008
W18	5.51	Germán CHIARAVIGLIO	ARG	Pôrto Alegre	1 May 2004

LONG JUMP

W, NAm	8.95	Mike POWELL	USA	Tokyo	30 Aug 1991
Eur	8.86 A	Robert EMMIYAN	ARM	Tsakhkadzor	22 May 1987
SAm	8.73	Irving SALADINO	PAN	Hengelo	24 May 2008
CAC	8.71	Iván PEDROSO	CUB	Salamanca	18 Jul 1995
Com	8.62	James BECKFORD	JAM	Orlando	5 Apr 1997
Oce	8.54	Mitchell WATT	AUS	Stockholm	29 Jul 2011
Afr	8.50	Khotso MOKOENA	RSA	Madrid	4 Jul 2009
Asi	8.48	Mohamed Salim AL-KHUWALIDI	KSA	Sotteville	2 Jul 2006
W20	8.35	Sergey MORGUNOV	RUS	Cheboksary	20 Jun 2012
W18	8.25	Luis Alberto BUENO	CUB	La Habana	28 Sep 1986

TRIPLE JUMP

W, Eur, Com	18.29	Jonathan EDWARDS	GBR/Eng	Göteborg	7 Aug 1995
NAm	18.09	Kenny HARRISON	USA	Atlanta	27 Jul 1996
CAC	17.92	James BECKFORD	JAM	Odessa, Texas	20 May 1995
SAm	17.90	Jadel GREGÓRIO	BRA	Belém	20 May 2007
Asi	17.59	LI Yanxi	CHN	Jinan	26 Oct 2009
Oce	17.46	Ken LORRAWAY	AUS	London (CP)	7 Aug 1982
Afr	17.37	Tareq BOUGTAÏB	MAR	Khémisset	14 Jul 2007
W20	17.50	Volker MAI	GDR	Erfurt	23 Jun 1985
W18	17.24	Lazaro MARTÍNEZ	CUB	La Habana	1 Feb 2014

SHOT

W, NAm	23.12	Randy BARNES	USA	Westwood	20 May 1990
Eur	23.06	Ulf TIMMERMANN	GER	Haniá	22 May 1988
Com	22.21	Dylan ARMSTRONG	CAN	Calgary	25 Jun 2011
Afr	21.97	Janus ROBBERTS	RSA	Eugene	2 Jun 2001
CAC	21.61	O'Dayne RICHARDS	JAM	Glasgow	28 Jul 2014
Oce	21.37	Tomas WALSH	NZL	Melbourne	21 Mar 2015
SAm	21.26	Germán LAURO	ARG	Doha	10 May 2013
Asi	21.13	Sultan Abdulmajeed AL-HEBSHI	KSA	Doha	8 May 2009
W20	21.05 i§	Terry ALBRITTON	USA	New York	22 Feb 1974
	20.65 §	Mike CARTER	USA	Boston	4 Jul 1979
	20.46i	Konrad BUKOWIECKI	POL	Praha (O2)	5 Mar 1015
	20.43	David STORL	GER	Gerlingen	6 Jul 2009
W18	20.38	Jacko GILL	NZL	Auckland (North Shore)	5 Dec 2011
W20 6kg	23.00	Jacko GILL	NZL	Auckland (North Shore)	18 Aug 2013
W18 5kg	24.45	Jacko GILL	NZL	Auckland (North Shore)	19 Dec 2011

DISCUS

W, Eur	74.08	Jürgen SCHULT	GDR	Neubrandenburg	6 Jun 1986
NAm	72.34 ¶	Ben PLUCKNETT	USA	Stockholm	7 Jul 1981
	71.32 §	Ben PLUCKNETT	USA	Eugene	4 Jun 1983
CAC	71.06	Luis DELIS	CUB	La Habana	21 May 1983
Afr, Com	70.32	Frantz KRUGER	RSA	Salon-de-Provence	26 May 2002
Asi	69.32	Ehsan HADADI	IRI	Tallinn	3 Jun 2008
Oce	68.20	Benn HARRADINE	AUS	Townsville	10 May 2013
SAm	66.32	Jorge BALLIENGO	ARG	Rosario	15 Apr 2006
W20	65.62 §	Werner REITERER	AUS	Melbourne	15 Dec 1987
W18/20	65.31	Mykyta NESTERENKO	UKR	Tallinn	3 Jun 2008
W20 1.75kg	70.13	Mykyta NESTERENKO	UKR	Halle	24 May 2008
W18 1.5kg	77.50	Mykyta NESTERNKO	UKR	Koncha Zaspa	19 May 2008

¶ Disallowed by the IAAF following retrospective disqualification for drug abuse, but ratified by the AAU/TAC

HAMMER

W, Eur	86.74	Yuriy SEDYKH	UKR/RUS	Stuttgart	30 Aug 1986
Asi	84.86	Koji MUROFUSHI	JPN	Praha	29 Jun 2003
NAm	82.52	Lance DEAL	USA	Milano	7 Sep 1996
Afr	81.27	Mostafa Hicham AL-GAMAL	EGY	Al-Qáhira	21 Mar 2014
Com	80.63	Chris HARMSE	RSA	Durban	15 Apr 2005
Oce	79.29	Stuart RENDELL	AUS	Varazdin	6 Jul 2002
CAC	77.78	Alberto SANCHEZ	CUB	La Habana	15 May 1998
SAm	76.42	Juan CERRA	ARG	Trieste	25 Jul 2001
W20	78.33	Olli-Pekka KARJALAINEN	FIN	Seinäjoki	5 Aug 1999
W18	73.66	Vladislav PISKUNOV	UKR	Kyiv	11 Jun 1994
W20 6kg	85.57	Ashraf Amgad EL-SEIFY	QAT	Barcelona	14 Jul 2012
W18 5kg	87.16	Bence HALÁSZ	HUN	Baku	31 May 2014

JAVELIN

W, Eur	98.48	Jan ZELEZNY	CZE	Jena	25 May 1996
Com	91.46	Steve BACKLEY	GBR/Eng	Auckland (NS)	25 Jan 1992
NAm	91.29	Breaux GREER	USA	Indianapolis	21 Jun 2007
Afr	89.21	Ihab ABDELRAHMAN El-Sayed	EGY	Shanghai	18 May 2014
Asi	89.15	ZHAO Qinggang	CHN	Incheon	2 Oct 2014
Oce	89.02	Jarrod BANNISTER	AUS	Brisbane	29 Feb 2008
CAC	87.20A	Guillermo MARTÍNEZ	CUB	Guadalajara	28 Oct 2011
SAm	84.70	Edgar BAUMANN	PAR	San Marcos	17 Oct 1999
W20	84.69	Zigismunds SIRMAIS	LAT	Bauska	22 Jun 2011
W18 700g	89.34	Braian Ezequiel TOLEDO	ARG	Mar del Plata	6 Mar 2010

DECATHLON

W, NAm	9039	Ashton EATON	USA	Eugene	23 Jun 2012
Eur	9026	Roman SEBRLE	CZE	Götzis	27 May 2001
Com	8847	Daley THOMPSON	GBR/Eng	Los Angeles	9 Aug 1984
Asi	8725	Dmitriy KARPOV	KAZ	Athína	24 Aug 2004
CAC	8654	Leonel SUÁREZ	CUB	La Habana	4 Jul 2009
Oce	8490	Jagan HAMES	AUS	Kuala Lumpur	18 Sep 1998
SAm	8393	Carlos Eduardo CHININ	BRA	São Paulo	8 Jun 2013
Afr	8343	Willem COERTZEN	RSA	Moskva	11 Aug 2013
W20	8397	Torsten VOSS (with 3'6" hurdles)	GDR	Erfurt	7 Jul 1982
W18	8104h	Valter KÜLVET	EST	Viimsi	23 Aug 1981
	7829	Valter KÜLVET	EST	Stockholm	13 Sep 1981

4 X 100 METRES RELAY

W, CAC, Com	36.84	JAM (Carter, M Frater, Blake, Bolt)	London (OS)	11 Aug 2012
NAm	37.04	USA (Kimmons, Gatlin, Gay, R Bailey)	London (OS)	11 Aug 2012
Eur	37.73	GBR (Gardener, Campbell, Devonish, Chambers)	Sevilla	29 Aug 1999
SAm	37.90	BRA (V Lima, Ribeiro, A da Silva, Cl da Silva)	Sydney	30 Sep 2000
Afr	37.94	NGR (O Ezinwa, Adeniken, Obikwelu, D Ezinwa)	Athína	9 Aug 1997
Asi	37.99	CHN (Chen S, Xie Z, Su B, Zhang Peimeng)	Incheon	2 Oct 2014
Oce	38.17	AUS (Henderson, Jackson, Brimacombe, Marsh)	Göteborg	12 Aug 1995
W20	38.66	USA (Kimmons, Omole, Williams, Merritt)	Grosseto	18 Jul 2004
W18	40.03	JAM (W Smith, M Frater, Spence, O Brown)	Bydgoszcz	18 Jul 1999

4 X 400 METRES RELAY

W, NAm	2:54.29	USA (Valmon, Watts, Reynolds, Johnson)	Stuttgart	22 Aug1993
Eur	2:56.60	GBR (Thomas, Baulch, Richardson, Black)	Atlanta	3 Aug 1996
CAC, Com	2:56.72	BAH (Brown, Pinder, Mathieu, Miller)	London (OS)	10 Aug 2012
SAm	2:58.56	BRA (C da Silva, A J dosSantos, de Araújo, Parrela)	Winnipeg	30 Jul 1999
Afr	2:58.68	NGR (Chukwu, Monye, Nada, Udo-Obong)	Sydney	30 Sep 2000
Oce	2:59.70	AUS (Frayne, Clark, Minihan, Mitchell)	Los Angeles	11 Aug 1984
Asi	3:00.76	JPN (Karube, K Ito, Osakada, Omori)	Atlanta	3 Aug 1996
W20	3:01.09	USA (Johnson, Merritt, Craig, Clement)	Grosseto	18 Jul 2004
W18	3:12.05	POL (Zrada, Kedzia, Grzegorczyk, Kowalski)	Kaunas	5 Aug 2001

20 KILOMETRES WALK

W, Asi	1:16:36	Yusuke SUZUKI	JPN	Nomi	15 Mar 2015
Eur	1:17:02	Yohann DINIZ	FRA	Arles	8 Mar 2015
	1:16:43 §	Sergey MOROZOV	RUS	Saransk	8 Jun 2008
SAm	1:17:21	Jefferson PÉREZ	ECU	Saint-Denis	23 Aug 2003
CAC	1:17:25.6 t	Bernardo SEGURA	MEX	Bergen (Fana)	7 May 1994
Oce, Com	1:17:33	Nathan DEAKES	AUS	Cixi	23 Apr 2005
Afr	1:19:02	Hatem GHOULA	TUN	Eisenhüttenstadt	10 May 1997
NAm	1:20:13	Evan DUNFEE	CAN	Taicang	4 May 2014

W20	1:18:06 §	Viktor BURAYEV	RUS	Adler	4 Mar 2001
W18	1:18:07	LI Gaobo	CHN	Cixi	23 Apr 2005

20,000 METRES TRACK WALK

W, CAC	1:17:25.6	Bernardo SEGURA	MEX	Bergen (Fana)	7 May 1994
Asi	1:18:03.3	BU Lingtang	CHN	Beijing	7 Apr 1994
Eur	1:18:35.2	Stefan JOHANSSON	SWE	Bergen (Fana)	15 May 1992
Oce, Com	1:19:48.1	Nathan DEAKES	AUS	Brisbane	4 Sep 2001
SAm	1:20:23.8	Andrés CHOCHO	ECU	Buenos Aires	5 Jun 2011
NAm	1:21:57.0	Evan DUNFEE	CAN	Moncton	27 Jun 2014
Afr	1:22:51.84	Hatem GHOULA	TUN	Leutkirch	8 Sep 1994
W20	1:20:11.72	LI Gaobo	CHN	Wuhan	2 Nov 2007
W18	1:24:28.3	ZHU Hongjun	CHN	Xian	15 Sep 1999

50 KILOMETRES WALK

W, Eur	3:32:33	Yohann DINIZ	FRA	Zürich	15 Aug 2014
Oce, Com	3:35:47	Nathan DEAKES	AUS	Geelong	2 Dec 2006
Asi	3:36:06	YU Chaohong	CHN	Nanjing	22 Oct 2005
CAC	3:41:09	Erick BARRONDO	GUA	Dudince	23 Mar 2013
SAm	3:47:41	James RENDÓN	COL	Valley Cottage	14 Sep 2014
NAm	3:47:48	Marcel JOBIN	CAN	Québec	20 Jun 1981
Afr	3:55:32	Marc MUNDELL	RSA	London	11 Aug 2012
W20	3:41:10	ZHAO Jianguo	CHN	Wajima	16 Apr 2006
W18	3:45:46	YU Guoping	CHN	Guangzhou	23 Nov 2001

50,000 METRES TRACK WALK

W, Eur	3:35:27.2	Yoahnn DINIZ	FRA	Reims	12 Mar 2011
CAC	3:41:38.4	Raúl GONZÁLEZ	MEX	Bergen (Fana)	25 May 1979
Oce, Com	3:43:50.0	Simon BAKER	AUS	Melbourne	9 Sep 1990
Asi	3:48:13.7	ZHAO Yongshen	CHN	Bergen (Fana)	7 May 1994
NAm	3:56:13.0	Tim BERRETT	CAN	Saskatoon	21 Jul 1991
SAm	3:57:58.0	Claudio dos SANTOS	BRA	Blumenau	20 Sep 2008
Afr	4:21:44.5	Abdelwahab FERGUÈNE	ALG	Toulouse	25 Mar 1984

World Records at other men's events recognised by the IAAF

20,000m	56:25.98+	Haile GEBRSELASSIE	ETH	Ostrava	27 Jun 2007
1 Hour	21,285 m	Haile GEBRSELASSIE	ETH	Ostrava	27 Jun 2007
25,000m	1:12:25.4	Moses MOSOP	KEN	Eugene	3 Jun 2011
30,000m	1:26:47.4	Moses MOSOP	KEN	Eugene	3 Jun 2011
U18 Octathlon	6491	Jake STEIN	AUS	Villeneuve d'Ascq	7 Jul 2011
4 x 200m	1:18.63	National team	JAM	Nassau	24 May 2014
		(Nickel Ashmeade, Warren Weir, Jermaine Brown, Yohan Blake)			
4 x 800m	7:02.43	National Team	KEN	Bruxelles	25 Aug 2006
		(Joseph Mutua, William Yiampoy, Ismael Kombich, Wilfred Bungei)			
4 x 1500m	14:22.22	C Cheboi, A Kiplagat, Magut, A Kiprop	KEN	Nassau	25 May 2014

Walking

2 Hours track	29,572m+	Maurizio DAMILANO	ITA	Cuneo	3 Oct 1992
30km track	2:01:44.1	Maurizio DAMILANO	ITA	Cuneo	3 Oct 1992
U20 10,000m track	38:46.4	Viktor BURAYEV	RUS	Moskva	20 May 2000
U20 10km road	37:44	WANG Zhen	CHN	Beijing	18 Sep 2010
W18 10km road	38:57	LI Tianlei	CHN	Beijing	18 Sep 2010

WOMEN

100 METRES

W, NAm	10.49	Florence GRIFFITH JOYNER	USA	Indianapolis	16 Jul 1988
CAC, Com	10.70	Shelly-Ann FRASER	JAM	Kingstobn	29 Jun 2012
Eur	10.73	Christine ARRON	FRA	Budapest	19 Aug 1998
Asi	10.79	LI Xuemei	CHN	Shanghai	18 Oct 1997
Afr	10.79	Blessing OKAGBARE	NGR	London (OS)	27 Jul 2013
SAm	11.05	Ana Claúdia SILVA	BRA	Belém	12 May 2013
Oce	11.11	Melissa BREEN	AUS	Canberra	9 Feb 2014
W20	10.88	Marlies OELSNER/GÖHR	GDR	Dresden	1 Jul 1977
W18	11.10	Kaylin WHITNEY	USA	Eugene	5 Jul 2014

200 METRES

W, NAm	21.34	Florence GRIFFITH JOYNER	USA	Seoul	29 Sep 1988
CAC, Com	21.64	Merlene OTTEY	JAM	Bruxelles	13 Sep 1991
Eur	21.71	Marita KOCH	GDR	Chemnitz	10 Jun 1979
	21.71 §	Marita KOCH	GDR	Potsdam	21 Jul 1984
	21.71	Heike DRECHSLER	GDR	Jena	29 Jun 1986
	21.71 §	Heike DRECHSLER	GDR	Stuttgart	29 Aug 1986

Asi	22.01	LI Xuemei	CHN	Shanghai	22 Oct 1997
Afr	22.06 A§	Evette DE KLERK	RSA	Pietersburg	8 Apr 1989
	22.07	Mary ONYALI	NGR	Zürich	14 Aug 1996
Oce	22.23	Melinda GAINSFORD-TAYLOR	AUS	Stuttgart	13 Jul 1997
SAm	22.48	Ana Cláudia da SILVA	BRA	São Paulo	6 Aug 2011
W20	22.18	Allyson FELIX	USA	Athína	25 Aug 2004
	22.11A §	Allyson FELIX (no doping control)	USA	Ciudad de México	3 May 2003
W18	22.49	Kaylin WHITNEY	USA	Eugene	6 Jul 2014

400 METRES

W, Eur	47.60	Marita KOCH	GDR	Canberra	6 Oct 1985
Oce, Com	48.63	Cathy FREEMAN	AUS	Atlanta	29 Jul 1996
NAm	48.70	Sanya RICHARDS	USA	Athína	16 Sep 2006
CAC	48.89	Ana GUEVARA	MEX	Saint-Denis	27 Aug 2003
Afr	49.10	Falilat OGUNKOYA	NGR	Atlanta	29 Jul 1996
SAm	49.64	Ximena RESTREPO	COL	Barcelona	5 Aug 1992
Asi	49.81	MA Yuqin	CHN	Beijing	11 Sep 1993
W20	49.42	Grit BREUER	GER	Tokyo	27 Aug 1991
W18	50.01	LI Jing	CHN	Shanghai	18 Oct 1997

800 METRES

W, Eur	1:53.28	Jarmila KRATOCHVÍLOVÁ	CZE	München	26 Jul 1983
Afr,W20,Com	1:54.01	Pamela JELIMO	KEN	Zürich	29 Aug 2008
CAC	1:54.44	Ana Fidelia QUIROT	CUB	Barcelona	9 Sep 1989
Asi	1:55.54	LIU Dong	CHN	Beijing	9 Sep 1993
NAm	1:56.40	Jearl MILES CLARK	USA	Zürich	11 Aug 1999
SAm	1:56.68	Letitia VRIESDE	SUR	Göteborg	13 Aug 1995
Oce	1:58.25	Toni HODGKINSON	NZL	Atlanta	27 Jul 1996
W18	1:57.18	WANG Yuan	CHN	Beijing	8 Sep 1993

1000 METRES

W, Eur	2:28.98	Svetlana MASTERKOVA	RUS	Bruxelles	23 Aug 1996
Afr	2:29.34	Maria Lurdes MUTOLA	MOZ	Bruxelles	25 Aug 1995
Com	2:29.66	Maria Lurdes MUTOLA	MOZ	Bruxelles	23 Aug 1996
NAm	2:31.80	Regina JACOBS	USA	Brunswick	3 Jul 1999
SAm	2:32.25	Letitia VRIESDE	SUR	Berlin	10 Sep 1991
CAC	2:33.21	Ana Fidelia QUIROT	CUB	Jerez de la Frontera	13 Sep 1989
Asi	2:33.6 §	Svetlana ULMASOVA	UZB	Podolsk	5 Aug 1979
	2:40.53	ZHAO Jing	CHN	Changbaishan	2 Sep 2014
Oce	2:37.84	Zoe BUCKMAN	AUS	Oslo	24 May 2012
W20	2:35.4a	Irina NIKITINA	RUS	Podolsk	5 Aug 1979
	2:35.4	Katrin WÜHN	GDR	Potsdam	12 Jul 1984
W18	2:38.58	Jo WHITE	GBR	London (CP)	9 Sep 1977

1500 METRES

W, Asi	3:50.46	QU Yunxia	CHN	Beijing	11 Sep 1993
Eur	3:52.47	Tatyana KAZANKINA	RUS	Zürich	13 Aug 1980
Afr	3:55.30	Hassiba BOULMERKA	ALG	Barcelona	8 Aug 1992
Com	3:56.98	Faith KIPYEGON	KEN	Doha	10 May 2013
NAm	3:57.12	Mary DECKER/SLANEY	USA	Stockholm	26 Jul 1983
Oce	4:00.93	Sarah JAMIESON	AUS	Stockholm	25 Jul 2006
CAC	4:01.84	Yvonne GRAHAM	JAM	Monaco	25 Jul 1995
SAm	4:05.67	Letitia VRIESDE	SUR	Tokyo	31 Aug 1991
W20	3:51.34	LANG Yinglai	CHN	Shanghai	18 Oct 1997
W18	3:54.52	ZHANG Ling	CHN	Shanghai	18 Oct 1997

1 MILE

W, Eur	4:12.56	Svetlana MASTERKOVA	RUS	Zürich	14 Aug 1996
NAm	4:16.71	Mary SLANEY	USA	Zürich	21 Aug 1985
Com	4:17.57	Zola BUDD	GBR/Eng	Zürich	21 Aug 1985
Asi	4:17.75	Maryam Yusuf JAMAL	BRN	Bruxelles	14 Sep 2007
Afr	4:18.23	Gelete BURKA	ETH	Rieti	7 Sep 2008
Oce	4:22.66	Lisa CORRIGAN	AUS	Melbourne	2 Mar 2007
CAC	4:24.64	Yvonne GRAHAM	JAM	Zürich	17 Aug 1994
SAm	4:30.05	Soraya TELLES	BRA	Praha	9 Jun 1988
W20	4:17.57	Zola BUDD	GBR	Zürich	21 Aug 1985
W18	4:30.81	Gelete BURKA	ETH	Heusden	2 Aug 2003

2000 METRES

W, Eur	5:25.36	Sonia O'SULLIVAN	IRL	Edinburgh	8 Jul 1994
Com	5:26.93	Yvonne MURRAY	GBR/Sco	Edinburgh	8 Jul 1994

Afr	5:27.50	Genzebe DIBABA	ETH	Ostrava	17 Jun 2014
Asi	5:29.43+§	WANG Junxia	CHN	Beijing	12 Sep 1993
	5:31.88	Maryam Yusuf JAMAL	BRN	Eugene	7 Jun 2009
NAm	5:32.7	Mary SLANEY	USA	Eugene	3 Aug 1984
Oce	5:37.71	Benita JOHNSON	AUS	Ostrava	12 Jun 2003
W20	5:33.15	Zola BUDD	GBR	London (CP)	13 Jul 1984
W18	5:46.5+	Sally BARSOSIO	KEN	Zürich	16 Aug 1995

3000 METRES

W, Asi	8:06.11	WANG Junxia	CHN	Beijing	13 Sep 1993
Afr, Com	8:20.68	Hellen OBIRI	KEN	Doha	9 May 2014
Eur	8:21.42	Gabriela SZABO	ROU	Monaco	19 Jul 2002
NAm	8:25.83	Mary SLANEY	USA	Roma	7 Sep 1985
Oce	8:35.31	Kimberley SMITH	NZL	Monaco	25 Jul 2007
CAC	8:37.07	Yvonne GRAHAM	JAM	Zürich	16 Aug 1995
SAm	9:02.37	Delirde BERNARDI	BRA	Linz	4 Jul 1994
W20	8:28.83	Zola BUDD	GBR	Roma	7 Sep 1985
W18	8:36.45	MA Ningning	CHN	Jinan	6 Jun 1993

5000 METRES

W, Afr	14:11.15	Tirunesh DIBABA	ETH	Oslo	6 Jun 2008
Com	14:20.87	Vivian CHERUIYOT	KEN	Stockho;lm	29 Jul 2011
Eur	14:23.75	Liliya SHOBUKHOVA	RUS	Kazan	19 Jul 2008
Asi	14:28.09	JIANG Bo	CHN	Shanghai	23 Oct 1997
NAm	14:42.64	Molly HUDDLE	USA	Monaco	18 Jul 2014
Oce	14:45.93	Kimberley SMITH	NZL	Roma	11 Jul 2008
CAC	15:04.32	Adriana FERNÁNDEZ	MEX	Gresham	17 May 2003
SAm	15:18.85	Simone Alves da SILVA	BRA	São Paulo	20 May 2011
W20	14:30.88	Tirunesh DIBABA	ETH	Bergen (Fana)	11 Jun 2004
W18	14:45.71	SONG Liqing	CHN	Shanghai	21 Oct 1997

10,000 METRES

W, Asi	29:31.78	WANG Junxia	CHN	Beijing	8 Sep 1993
Afr	29:53.80	Meselech MELKAMU	ETH	Utrecht	14 Jun 2009
Eur	29:56.34	Elvan ABEYLEGESSE	TUR	Beijing	15 Aug 2008
Com	30:01.09	Paula RADCLIFFE	GBR/Eng	München	6 Aug 2002
NAm	30:22.22	Shalane FLANAGAN	USA	Beijing	15 Aug 2008
Oce	30:35.54	Kimberley SMITH	NZL	Stanford	4 May 2008
CAC	31:10.12	Adriana FERNANDEZ	MEX	Brunswick	1 Jul 2000
SAm	31:47.76	Carmen de OLIVEIRA	BRA	Stuttgart	21 Aug 1993
W20	30:26.50	Linet MASAI	KEN	Beijing	15 Aug 2008
W18	31:11.26	SONG Liqing	CHN	Shanghai	19 Oct 1997

HALF MARATHON

W, Afr, Com	65:09	Florence KIPLAGAT	KEN	Barcelona	15 Feb 2015
Eur	66:25	Lornah KIPLAGAT	NED	Udine	14 Oct 2007
Oce	67:11	Kimberley SMITH	NZL	Philadelphia	18 Sep 2011
Asi	67:26	Kayoko FUKUSHI	JPN	Marugame	5 Feb 2006
NAm	67:34	Deena KASTOR	USA	Berlin	2 Apr 2006
CAC	68:34 dh	Olga APPELL	MEX	Tokyo	24 Jan 1993
	69:28	Adrian FERNÁNDEZ	MEX	Kyoto	9 Mar 2003
SAm	70:30	Yolanda CABALLERO	COL	New York	17 Mar 2013
W20	67:57	Abebu GELAN	ETH	Ra's Al Khaymah	20 Feb 2009
W18	72:31	LIU Zhuang	CHN	Yangzhou	24 Apr 2011

MARATHON

W, Eur, Com	2:15:25	Paula RADCLIFFE	GBR/Eng	London	13 Apr 2003
Afr	2:18:37	Mary KEITANY	KEN	London	22 Apr 2012
Asi	2:19:12	Mizuki NOGUCHI	JPN	Berlin	25 Sep 2005
NAm	2:19:36	Deena KASTOR	USA	London	23 Apr 2006
Oce	2:22:36	Benita JOHNSON	AUS	Chicago	22 Oct 2006
CAC	2:22:59	Madai PÉREZ	MEX	Chicago	22 Oct 2006
SAm	2:26:48	Inés MELCHOR	PER	Berlin	28 Sep 2014
W20	2:20:59	Shure DEMISE	ETH	Dubai	23 Jan 2015

3000 METRES STEEPLECHASE

W, Eur	8:58.81	Gulnara GALKINA	RUS	Beijing	17 Aug 2008
Afr, Com	9:07.14	Milcah CHEMOS Cheywa	KEN	Oslo	7 Jun 2012
NAm	9:11.42	Emma COBURN	USA	Glasgow	12 Jul 2014
Oce	9:18.35	Donna MacFARLANE	AUS	Oslo	6 Jun 2008

Asi	9:20.55	Ruth CHEBET	BRN	Zürich	28 Aug 2014
CAC	9:27.21	Mardrea HYMAN	JAM	Monaco	9 Sep 2005
SAm	9:41.22	Sabine HEITLING	BRA	London	25 Jul 2009
W20	9:20.37	Birtukan ADAMU	ETH	Roma	26 May 2011
W18	9:28.36	Tigist MEKONEN	ETH	Glasgow	12 Jul 2014

100 METRES HURDLES

W, Eur	12.21	Yordanka DONKOVA	BUL	Stara Zagora	20 Aug 1988
NAm	12.26	Brianna ROLLINS	USA	Des Moines	22 Jun 2013
Oce, Com	12.28	Sally PEARSON	AUS	Daegu	3 Sep 2011
Asi	12.44	Olga SHISHIGINA	KAZ	Luzern	27 Jun 1995
Afr	12.44	Glory ALOZIE	NGR	Monaco	8 Aug 1998
	12.44	Glory ALOZIE	NGR	Bruxelles	28 Aug 1998
	12.44	Glory ALOZIE	NGR	Sevilla	28 Aug 1999
CAC	12.45	Brigitte FOSTER	JAM	Eugene	24 May 2003
SAm	12.67	Yvette LEWIS	PAN	Lahti	17 Jul 2013
W20	12.84	Aliuska LÓPEZ	CUB	Zagreb	16 Jul 1987
W18	12.95	Candy YOUNG	USA	Walnut	16 Jun 1979

400 METRES HURDLES

Eur, W	52.34	Yuliya PECHONKINA	RUS	Tula	8 Aug 2003
CAC, Com	52.42	Melaine WALKER	JAM	Berlin	20 Aug 2009
NAm	52.47	Lashinda DEMUS	USA	Daegu	1 Sep 2011
Afr	52.90	Nezha BIDOUANE	MAR	Sevilla	25 Aug 1999
Oce	53.17	Debbie FLINTOFF-KING	AUS	Seoul	28 Sep 1988
Asi	53.96	HAN Qing	CHN	Beijing	9 Sep 1993
	53.96	SONG Yinglan	CHN	Guangzhou	22 Nov 2001
SAm	55.84	Lucimar TEODORO	BRA	Belém	24 May 2009
W20	54.40	WANG Xing	CHN	Nanjing	21 Oct 2005
W18	55.20	Leslie MAXIE	USA	San Jose	9 Jun 1984

HIGH JUMP

W, Eur	2.09	Stefka KOSTADINOVA	BUL	Roma	30 Aug 1987
Afr, Com	2.06	Hestrie CLOETE	RSA	Saint-Denis	31 Aug 2003
NAm	2.05	Chaunté HOWARD-LOWE	USA	Des Moines	26 Jun 2010
CAC	2.04	Silvia COSTA	CUB	Barcelona	9 Sep 1989
Asi	1.99	Marina AITOVA	KAZ	Athína	13 Jul 2009
Oce	1 98	Vanessa WARD	AUS	Perth	12 Feb 1989
	1.98	Alison INVERARITY	AUS	Ingolstadt	17 Jul 1994
SAm	1.96	Solange WITTEVEEN	ARG	Oristano	8 Sep 1997
W20	2.01	Olga TURCHAK	KAZ	Moskva	7 Jul 1986
	2.01	Heike BALCK	GDR	Chemnitz	18 Jun 1989
W18	1.96A	Charmaine GALE	RSA	Bloemfontein	4 Apr 1981
	1.96	Olga TURCHAK	UKR	Donetsk	7 Sep 1984
	1.96	Eleanor PATTERSON	AUS	Townsville	7 Dec 2013

POLE VAULT

W, Eur	5.06	Yelena ISINBAYEVA	RUS	Zürich	28 Aug 2009
NAm	4.92	Jennifer STUCZYNSKI/SUHR	USA	Eugene	6 Jul 2008
CAC	4.90	Yarisley SILVA	CUB	Hengelo	8 Jun 2013
Com	4.87i	Holly BLEASDALE	GBR	Villeurbanne	21 Jan 2012
SAm	4.85	Fabiana MURER	BRA	San Fernando	4 Jun 2010
	4.85	Fabiana MURER	BRA	Daegu	30 Aug 2011
Oce, Com	4.76	Alana BOYD	AUS	Perth	24 Feb 2012
Asi	4.65	LI Ling	CHN	Shenyang	8 Sep 2013
Afr	4.42	Elmarie GERRYTS	RSA	Wesel	12 Jun 2000
W20	4.63i	Angelica BENGTSSON	SWE	Stockholm	25 Feb 2011
	4.59	Nina KENNEDY	AUS	Perth	14 Feb 2015
W18	4.47	Angelica BENGTSSON	SWE	Moskva	22 May 2010

LONG JUMP

W, Eur	7.52	Galina CHISTYAKOVA	RUS	Sankt-Peterburg	11 Jun 1988
NAm	7.49	Jackie JOYNER-KERSEE	USA	New York	22 May 1994
	7.49A §	Jackie JOYNER-KERSEE	USA	Sestriere	31 Jul 1994
SAm	7.26A	Maurren MAGGI	BRA	Bogotá	26 Jun 1999
CAC, Com	7.16A	Elva GOULBOURNE	JAM	Ciudad de México	22 May 2004
Afr	7.12	Chioma AJUNWA	NGR	Atlanta	1 Aug 1996
Asi	7.01	YAO Weili	CHN	Jinan	5 Jun 1993
Oce	7.00	Bronwyn THOMPSON	AUS	Melbourne	7 Mar 2002
W20	7.14	Heike DAUTE/Drechsler	GDR	Bratislava	4 Jun 1983
W18	6.91	Heike DAUTE/Drechsler	GDR	Jena	9 Aug 1981

TRIPLE JUMP

W, Eur	15.50	Inessa KRAVETS	UKR	Göteborg	10 Aug 1995
Afr, Com	15.39	Françoise MBANGO Etone	CMR	Beijing	17 Aug 2008
SAm	15.31	Caterine IBARGÜEN	COL	Monaco	18 Jul 2014
CAC	15.29	Yamilé ALDAMA	CUB	Roma	11 Jul 2003
Asi	15.25	Olga RYPAKOVA	KAZ	Split	4 Sep 2010
NAm	14.45	Tiombé HURD	USA	Sacramento	11 Jul 2004
Oce	14.04	Nicole MLADENIS	AUS	Hobart	9 Mar 2002
	14.04	Nicole MLADENIS	AUS	Perth	7 Dec 2003
W20	14.62	Tereza MARINOVA	BUL	Sydney	25 Aug 1996
W18	14.57	HUANG Qiuyan	CHN	Shanghai	19 Oct 1997

SHOT

W, Eur	22.63	Natalya LISOVSKAYA	RUS	Moskva	7 Jun 1987
Asi	21.76	LI Meisu	CHN	Shijiazhuang	23 Apr 1988
Oce, Com	21.24	Valerie ADAMS	NZL	Daegu	29 Aug 2011
CAC	20.96	Belsy LAZA	CUB	Ciudad de México	2 May 1992
NAm	20.24	Michelle CARTER	USA	Des Moines	22 Jun 2013
SAm	19.30	Elisângela ADRIANO	BRA	Tunja	14 Jul 2001
Afr	18.43	Vivian CHUKWUEMEKA	NGR	Walnut	19 Apr 2003
W20	20.54	Astrid KUMBERNUSS	GDR	Orimattila	1 Jul 1989
W18	19.08	Ilke WYLUDDA	GDR	Karl-Marx-Stadt	9 Aug 1986

DISCUS

W, Eur	76.80	Gabriele REINSCH	GDR	Neubrandenburg	9 Jul 1988
Asi	71.68	XIAO Yanling	CHN	Beijing	14 Mar 1992
CAC	70.88	Hilda RAMOS	CUB	La Habana	8 May 1992
NAm	69.17	Gia LEWIS-SMALWOOD	USA	Angers	30 Aug 2014
Oce, Com	68.72	Daniela COSTIAN	AUS	Auckland	22 Jan 1994
Afr	64.87	Elizna NAUDE	RSA	Stellenbosch	2 Mar 2007
SAm	64.21	Andressa de MORAIS	BRA	Barquisimeto	10 Jun 2012
W20	74.40	Ilke WYLUDDA	GDR	Berlin	13 Sep 1988
W18	65.86	Ilke WYLUDDA	GDR	Neubrandenburg	1 Aug 1986

HAMMER

W, Eur	79.58	Anita WLODARCZYK	POL	Berlin	31 Aug 2014
Asi	77.68	WANG Zheng	CHN	Chengdu	29 Mar 2014
CAC	76.62	Yipsi MORENO	CUB	Zagreb	9 Sep 2008
NAm, Com	75.73	Sultana FRIZELL	CAN	Tucson	22 May 2014
SAm	73.74	Jennifer DAHLGREN	ARG	Buenos Aires	10 Apr 2010
Oce	71.12	Bronwyn EAGLES	AUS	Adelaide	6 Feb 2003
Afr	69.70	Amy SÈNE	SEN	Forbach	25 May 2014
W20	73.24	ZHANG Wenxiu	CHN	Changsha	24 Jun 2005
W18	70.60	ZHANG Wenxiu	CHN	Nanning	5 Apr 2003
W18 3kg	76.04	Réka GYURÁTZ	HUN	Zalaegerszeg	23 Jun 2013

JAVELIN

W, Eur	72.28	Barbora SPOTÁKOVÁ	CZE	Stuttgart	13 Sep 2008
CAC	71.70	Osleidys MENÉNDEZ	CUB	Helsinki	14 Aug 2005
Afr, Com	69.35	Sunette VILJOEN	RSA	New York	9 Jun 2012
Oce	66.83	Kimberley MICKLE	AUS	Melbourne	22 Mar 2014
NAm	66.67	Kara PATTERSON	USA	Des Moines	25 Jun 2010
Asi	65.62	LU Huihui	CHN	Zhaoqing	27 Apr 2013
SAm	63.80A	Flor Dennis RUIZ	COL	Xalapa	27 Nov 2014
W20	63.01	Vira REBRYK	UKR	Bydgoszcz	10 Jul 2008
W18	62.93	XUE Juan	CHN	Changsha	27 Oct 2003

HEPTATHLON

W, NAm	7291	Jackie JOYNER-KERSEE	USA	Seoul	24 Sep 1988
Eur	7032	Carolina KLÜFT	RUS	Osaka	26 Aug 2007
Com	6955	Jessica ENNIS	GBR/Eng	London (OS)	4 Aug 2012
Asi	6942	Ghada SHOUAA	SYR	Götzis	26 May 1996
Oce	6695	Jane FLEMMING	AUS	Auckland	28 Jan 1990
CAC	6527	Diane GUTHRIE-GRESHAM	JAM	Knoxville	3 Jun 1995
Afr	6423	Margaret SIMPSON	GHA	Götzis	29 May 2005
SAm	6160	Lucimara DA SILVA	BRA	Barquisimeto	10 Jun 2012
W20	6542	Carolina KLÜFT	SWE	München	10 Aug 2002
W18	6185	SHEN Shengfei	CHN	Shanghai	18 Oct 1997

DECATHLON

W, Eur	8358	Austra SKUJYTE	LTU	Columbia, MO	15 Apr 2005
Asi	7798 §	Irina NAUMENKO	KAZ	Talence	26 Sep 2004
NAm	7577 §	Tiffany LOTT-HOGAN	USA	Lage	10 Sep 2000
CAC	7245 §	Magalys GARCÍA	CUB	Wien	29 Jun 2002
Afr, Com	6915	Margaret SIMPSON	GHA	Réduit	19 Apr 2007
SAm	6570	Andrea BORDALEJO	ARG	Rosario	28 Nov 2004
Oce	5740	Preya CAREY	AUS	Brisbane	6 Sep 2001

4 X 100 METRES RELAY

W, NAm	40.82	USA (Madison, Felix, Knight, Jeter)	London (OS)	10 Aug 2012
CAC, Com	41.29	JAM (Russell, Stewart, Calvert, Fraser-Pryce)	Moskva	18 Aug 2013
Eur	41.37	GDR (Gladisch, Rieger, Auerswald, Göhr)	Canberra	6 Oct 1985
Asi	42.23	Sichuan CHN (Xiao Lin, Li Yali, Liu Xiaomei, Li Xuemei)	Shanghai	23 Oct 1997
SAm	42.29	BRA (E dos Santos, Silva, Krasucki, R Santos)	Moskva	18 Aug 2013
Afr	42.39	NGR (Utondu, Idehen, Opara-Thompson, Onyali)	Barcelona	7 Aug 1992
Oce	42.99A	AUS (Massey, Broadrick, Lambert, Gainsford-Taylor)	Pietersburg	18 Mar 2000
W20	43.29	USA (Knight, Tarmoh, Olear, Mayo)	Eugene	8 Aug 2006
W18	44.05	GDR (Koppetsch, Oelsner, Sinzel, Brehmer)	Athína	24 Aug 1975

4 X 400 METRES RELAY

W, Eur	3:15.17	URS (Ledovskaya, Nazarova, Pinigina, Bryzgina)	Seoul	1 Oct 1988
NAm	3:15.51	USA (D.Howard, Dixon, Brisco, Griffith Joyner)	Seoul	1 Oct 1988
CAC, Com	3:18.71	JAM (Whyte, Prendergast, N Williams-Mills, S Williams)	Daegu	3 Sep 2011
Afr	3:21.04	NGR (Bisi Afolabi, Yusuf, Opara, Ogunkoya)	Atlanta	3 Aug 1996
Oce	3:23.81	AUS (Peris, Lewis, Gainsford-Taylor, Freeman)	Sydney	30 Sep 2000
Asi	3:24.28	Hebei CHN (An X, Bai X, Cao C, Ma Y)	Beijing	13 Sep 1993
SAm	3:26.68	BRA (Coutinho, de Oliveira, Souza, de Lima)	São Paulo	7 Aug 2011
W20	3:27.60	USA (Anderson, Kidd, Smith, Hastings)	Grosseto	18 Jul 2004
W18	3:36.98	GBR (Ravenscroft, E McMeekin, Kennedy, Pettett)	Duisburg	26 Aug 1973

10 KILOMETRES WALK

W, Eur	41:04	Yelena NIKOLAYEVA	RUS	Sochi	20 Apr 1996
Asi	41:16	WANG Yan	CHN	Eisenhüttenstadt	8 May 1999
Oce, Com	41:30	Kerry SAXBY-JUNNA	AUS	Canberra	27 Aug 1988
CAC	42:42	Graciela MENDOZA	MEX	Naumburg	25 May 1997
NAm	44:17	Michelle ROHL	USA	Göteborg	7 Aug 1995
SAm	44:22+	Erica de SEÑA	BRA	Dudince	21 Mar 2015
Afr	45:06A	Susan VERMEULEN	RSA	Bloemfontein	17 Apr 1999
W20	41:52 §	Tatyana MINEYEVA	RUS	Penza	5 Sep 2009
	41:57 §	GAO Hongmiao	CHN	Beijing	8 Sep 1993
W18	43:28	Aleksandra KUDRYASHOVA	RUS	Adler	19 Feb 2006

10,000 METRES TRACK WALK

W, Asi	41:37.9 §	GAO Hongmiao	CHN	Beijing	7 Apr 1994
W, Eur	41:56.23	Nadyezhda RYASHKINA	RUS	Seattle	24 Jul 1990
Oce, Com	41:57.22	Kerry SAXBY-JUNNA	AUS	Seattle	24 Jul 1990
SAm	43:41.30	Erica de SEÑA	BRA	São Paulo	1 Aug 2014
NAm	44:30.1 m	Alison BAKER	CAN	Bergen (Fana)	15 May 1992
	44:06 no kerb	Michelle ROHL	USA	Kenosha	2 Jun 1996
CAC	44:16.21	Cristina LÓPEZ	ESA	San Salvador	13 Jul 2007
Afr	47:30.28	Chahinez AL-NASRI	TUN	Amman	16 May 2012
W20	42:47.25	Anezka DRAHOTOVÁ	CZE	Eugene	23 Jul 2014
W18	42:56.09	GAO Hongmiao	CHN	Tangshan	27 Sep 1991

20,000 METRES TRACK WALK

W, Eur	1:26:52.3	Olimpiada IVANOVA	RUS	Brisbane	6 Sep 2001
Asi, W20	1:29:32.4 §	SONG Hongjuan	CHN	Changsha	24 Oct 2003
SAm	1:31:46.9	Sandra Lorena ARENAS	COL	Santiago de Chile	13 Mar 2014
CAC	1:31:53.8A	Mirna ORTIZ	GUA	Ciudad de Guatemala	9 Aug 2014
NAm, Com	1:32:54.0	Rachel SEAMAN	CAN	Moncton	27 Jun 2014
Oce	1:33:40.2	Kerry SAXBY-JUNNA	AUS	Brisbane	6 Sep 2001
Afr	1:36:43.43A	Nicolene CRONJE	RSA	Germiston	20 Mar 2004
W18	1:34:21.56	WANG Xue	CHN	Wuhan	1 Nov 2007

20 KILOMETRES WALK

W, Eur	1:24:47 §	Elmira ALEMBEKOVA	RUS	Sochi	27 Feb 2015
	1:25:02	Yeoena LASHMANOVA	RUS	London	11 Aug 2012
Asi	1:25:12	LU Xiuzhi	CHN	Beijing	20 Mar 2015
Oce, Com	1:27:44	Jane SAVILLE	AUS	Naumburg	2 May 2004

CAC	1:28:31	Mima ORTIZ	GUA	Rio Maior	6 Apr 2013
SAm	1:29:37	Erica de SEÑA	BRA	Dudince	21 Mar 2015
NAm	1:29:54	Rachel SEAMAN	CAN	Nomi	15 Mar 2015
Afr	1:34:19 §	Grace WANJIRU NJUE	KEN	Nairobi	1 Aug 2010
W20	1:25:30	Anisya KIRDYAPKINA	RUS	Adler	23 Feb 2008
W18	1:30:28	ZHOU Tongmei	CHN	Cixi	23 Apr 2005

World Records at other track & field events recognised by the IAAF

1 Hour	18,517 m	Dire TUNE	ETH	Ostrava	12 Jun 2008
20,000m	1:05:26.6	Tegla LOROUPE	KEN	Borgholzhausen	3 Sep 2000
25,000m	1:27:05.84	Tegla LOROUPE	KEN	Mengerskirchen	21 Sep 2002
30,000m	1:45:50.0	Tegla LOROUPE	KEN	Warstein	6 Jun 2003
4x200m	1:27.46	L Jenkins, L Colander, N Perry, M Jones	USA	Philadelphia	29 Apr 2000
4x800m	7:50.17	Olizarenko, Gurina, Borisova, Podyalovskaya	USSR	Moskva	5 Aug 1984
4x1500m	16:33.58	M Cherono, Kipyegon, I Jelagat, Obiri	KEN	Nassau	24 May 2014

WORLD BESTS AT NON-STANDARD EVENTS

Men

50m	5.47+e	Usain Bolt	JAM	Berlin (in 100m)	16 Aug 2009
60m	6.31+	Usain Bolt	JAM	Berlin (in 100m)	16 Aug 2009
100 yards	9.07	Asafa Powell	JAM	Ostrava	27 May 2010
150m turn	14.44+	Usain Bolt	JAM	Berlin (in 200m)	20 Aug 2009
150m straight	14.35	Usain Bolt	JAM	Manchester	17 May 2009
300m	30.85A	Michael Johnson	USA	Pretoria	24 Mar 2000
	30.97	Usain Bolt	JAM	Ostrava	27 May 2010
500m	59.32	Orestes Rodríguez	CUB	La Habana	15 Feb 2013
600m	1:12.81	Johnny Gray	USA	Santa Monica	24 May 1986
2 miles	7:58.61	Daniel Komen	KEN	Hechtel	19 Jul 1997
2000m Steeple	5:10.68	Mahiedine Mekhissi	FRA	Reims	30 Jun 2010
200mh	22.55	Laurent Ottoz	ITA	Milano	31 May 1995
(hand time)	22.5	Martin Lauer	FRG	Zürich	7 Jul 1959
200mh straight	22.10	Andrew Turner	GBR	Manchester	15 May 2011
220yh straight	21.9	Don Styron	USA	Baton Rouge	2 Apr 1960
300mh	34.48	Chris Rawlinson	GBR	Sheffield	30 Jun 2002
35lb weight	25.41	Lance Deal	USA	Azusa	20 Feb 1993
Pentathlon	4282 points	Bill Toomey	USA	London (CP)	16 Aug 1969
(1985 tables)		(7.58, 66.18, 21.3, 44.52, 4:20.3)			
Double decathlon	14,571	Joe Detmer	USA	Lynchburg	24/25 Sep 2010
	10.93w, 7.30, 200mh 24.25w, 12.27, 5k 18:25.32, 2:02.23, 1.98, 400m 50.43, HT 31.82, 3kSt 11:22.47				
	15.01, DT 40.73, 200m 22.58, 4.85, 3k 10:25.99, 400mh 53.83, 51.95, 4:26.66, TJ 13.67, 10k 40:27.26				
4x110mh	53.31y	USA Red Oliver, Herring, Brown, Merritt		Philadelphia	25 Apr 2008
3000m track walk	10:47.11	Giovanni De Benedictis	ITA	San Giovanni Valdarno	19 May 1990
5000m track walk	18:05.49	Hatem Ghoula	TUN	Tunis	1 May 1997
10,000m track walk	37:53.09	Francisco Javier Fernández	ESP	Santa Cruz de Tenerife	27 Jul 2008
10 km road walk	37:11	Roman Rasskazov	RUS	Saransk	28 May 2000
30 km road walk	2:01:13+	Vladimir Kanaykin	RUS	Adler	19 Feb 2006
35 km road walk	2:21:31	Vladimir Kanaykin	RUS	Adler	19 Feb 2006
100 km road walk	8:38:07	Viktor Ginko	BLR	Scanzorosciate	27 Oct 2002

Women

50m	5.93+	Marion Jones	USA	Sevilla (in 100m)	22 Aug 1999
60m	6.85+	Marion Jones	USA	Sevilla (in 100m)	22 Aug 1999
100 yards	9.91	Veronica-Campbell-Brown	JAM	Ostrava	31 May 2011
150m	16.10+	Florence Griffith-Joyner	USA	Seoul (in 200m)	29 Sep 1988
300m	34.1+	Marita Koch	GDR	Canberra (in 400m)	6 Oct 1985
500m	1:05.9	Tatána Kocembová	CZE	Ostrava	2 Aug 1984
600m	1:22.63	Ana Fidelia Quirot	CUB	Guadalajara, ESP	25 Jul 1997
2 miles	8:58.58	Meseret Defar	ETH	Bruxelles	14 Sep 2007
2000m Steeple	6:03.38	Wioletta Janowska	POL	Gdansk	15 Jul 2006
200mh	24.8	Yadisleidis Pedroso	ITA	Caserta	6 Apr 2013
	25.79	Noemi Zbären	SUI	Basel	17 May 2014
300mh	38.16	Zuzana Hejnová	CZE	Cheb	2 Aug 2013
Double heptathlon	10,798	Milla Kelo	FIN	Turku	7/8 Sep 2002
	100mh 14.89, HJ 1.51, 1500m 5:03.74, 400mh 62.18, SP 12.73, 200m 25.16, 100m 12.59				
	LJ 5.73w, 400m 56.10, JT 32.69, 800m 2:23.94, 200mh 28.72, DT 47.86, 3000m 11:48.68				
4x100mh	50.66	Castlin USA, Rollins USA, Q Harrison USA, T Porter GBR		Gainesville	5 Apr 2014
3000m track walk	11:48.24	Ileana Salvador	ITA	Padova	29 Aug 1993
5000m track walk	20:01.80	Eleonora Giorgi	ITA	Misterbianco	17 May 2014
50 km road walk	4:10:59	Monica Svensson	SWE	Scanzorosciate	21 Oct 2007
100 km road walk	10:04:50	Jolanta Dukure	LAT	Scanzorosciate	21 Oct 2007

LONG DISTANCE WORLD BESTS – MEN TRACK

	hr:min:sec	*Name*	*Nat*	*Venue*	*Date*
15,000m	0:42:18.7+	Haile Gebrselassie	ETH	Ostrava	27 Jun 2007
10 miles	0:45:23.8+	Haile Gebrselassie	ETH	Ostrava	27 Jun 2007
15 miles	1:11:43.1	Bill Rodgers	USA	Saratoga, Cal.	21 Feb 1979
20 miles	1:39:14.4	Jack Foster	NZL	Hamilton, NZ	15 Aug 1971
30 miles	2:42:00+	Jeff Norman	GBR	Timperley, Cheshire	7 Jun 1980
50 km	2:48:06	Jeff Norman	GBR	Timperley, Cheshire	7 Jun 1980
40 miles	3:48:35	Don Ritchie	GBR	London (Hendon)	16 Oct 1982
50 miles	4:51:49	Don Ritchie	GBR	London (Hendon)	12 Mar 1983
100 km	6:10:20	Don Ritchie	GBR	London (CP)	28 Oct 1978
150 km	10:34:30	Denis Zhalybin	RUS	London (CP)	20 Oct 2002
100 miles	11:28:03	Oleg Kharitonov	RUS	London (CP)	20 Oct 2002
200 km	15:10:27+	Yiannis Kouros	AUS	Adelaide	4-5 Oct 1997
200 miles	27:48:35	Yiannis Kouros	GRE	Montauban	15-16 Mar 1985
500 km	60:23.00+ ??	Yiannis Kouros	GRE	Colac, Aus	26-29 Nov 1984
500 miles	105:42:09+	Yiannis Kouros	GRE	Colac, Aus	26-30 Nov 1984
1000 km	136:17:00	Yiannis Kouros	GRE	Colac, Aus	26-31 Nov 1984
1500 km	10d 17:28:26	Petrus Silkinas	LTU	Nanango, Qld	11-21 Mar 1998
1000 mile	11d 13:54:58+	Petrus Silkinas	LTU	Nanango, Qld	11-22 Mar 1998
2 hrs	37.994 km	Jim Alder	GBR	Walton-on-Thames	17 Oct 1964
12 hrs	162.400 km +	Yiannis Kouros	GRE	Montauban	15 Mar 1985
24 hrs	303.506 km	Yiannis Kouros	AUS	Adelaide	4-5 Oct 1997
48 hrs	473.797 km	Yiannis Kouros	AUS	Surgères	3-5 May 1996
6 days	1036.8 km	Yiannis Kouros	GRE	Colac, Aus	20-26 Nov 2005

LONG DISTANCE ROAD RECORDS & BESTS – MEN

Where superior to track bests (over 10km) and run on properly measured road courses. (I) IAAF recognition.

10 km (I)	0:26:44	Leonard Patrick Komon	KEN	Utrecht	26 Sep 2010
15 km (I)	0:41:13	Leonard Patrick Komon	KEN	Nijmegen	21 Nov 2010
10 miles	0:44:24 §	Haile Gebrselassie	ETH	Tilburg	4 Sep 2005
	0:44:45	Paul Koech	KEN	Amsterdam-Zaandam	21 Sep 1997
20 km (I)	0:55:21+	Zersenay Tadese	ERI	Lisboa	21 Mar 2010
25 km (I)	1:11:18	Dennis Kimetto	KEN	Berlin	6 May 2012
30 km (I)	1:27:37 Emmanuel Mutai KEN, Geoffrey Kamworor KEN §			Berlin	28 Sep 2014
	1:27:36+ §	Wilfred KIRWA	KEN	Berlin (dnf)	28 Sep 2014
20 miles	1:35:22+	Steve Jones	GBR	Chicago	10 Oct 1985
30 miles	2:37:31+	Thompson Magawana	RSA	Claremont-Kirstenbosch	2 Apr 1988
50km	2:43:38+	Thompson Magawana	RSA	Claremont-Kirstenbosch	2 Apr 1988
40 miles	3:45:39	Andy Jones	CAN	Houston	23 Feb 1991
50 miles	4:50:21	Bruce Fordyce	RSA	London-Brighton	25 Sep 1983
100 km (I)	6:13:33	Takahiro Sunada	JPN	Yubetsu	21 Jun 1998
1000 miles	10d:10:30:35	Yiannis Kouros	GRE	New York	21-30 May 1988
12 hrs	162.543 km	Yiannis Kouros	GRE	Queen's, New York	7 Nov 1984

LONG DISTANCE WORLD BESTS – WOMEN TRACK

15 km	0:48:54.91+	Dire Tune	ETH	Ostrava	12 Jun 2008
10 miles	0:54:21.8	Lorraine Moller	NZL	Auckland	9 Jan 1993
20 miles	1:59:09 !	Chantal Langlacé	FRA	Amiens	3 Sep 1983
30 miles	3:12:25+	Carolyn Hunter-Rowe	GBR	Barry, Wales	3 Mar 1996
50 km	3:18:52+	Carolyn Hunter-Rowe	GBR	Barry, Wales	3 Mar 1996
40 miles	4:26:43	Carolyn Hunter-Rowe	GBR	Barry, Wales	7 Mar 1993
50 miles	5:48:12.0+	Norimi Sakurai	JPN	San Giovanni Lupatoto	27 Sep 2003
100 km	7:14:05.8	Norimi Sakurai	JPN	San Giovanni Lupatoto	27 Sep 2003
150 km	13:45:54	Hilary Walker	GBR	Blackpool	5-6 Nov 1988
100 miles	13:52.02+	Mami Kudo	JPN	Soochow	10-11 Dec 2011
200 km	17:52.18+	Mami Kudo	JPN	Soochow	10-11 Dec 2011
200 miles	39:09:03	Hilary Walker	GBR	Blackpool	5-7 Nov 1988
500 km	77:53:46	Eleanor Adams	GBR	Colac, Aus.	13-16 Nov 1989
500 miles	130:59:58+	Sandra Barwick	NZL	Campbelltown, AUS	18-23 Nov 1990
1000 km	8d 00:27:06+	Eleanor Robinson	GBR	Nanango, Qld	11-19 Mar 1998
1500 km	12d 06:52:12+	Eleanor Robinson	GBR	Nanango, Qld	11-23 Mar 1998
1000 miles	13d 02:16:49	Eleanor Robinson	GBR	Nanango, Qld	11-24 Mar 1998
2 hrs	32.652 km	Chantal Langlacé	FRA	Amiens	3 Sep 1983
12 hrs	147.600 km	Ann Trason	USA	Hayward, Cal	3-4 Aug 1991
24 hours	255.303 km	Mami Kudo	JPN	Soochow	10-11 Dec 2011
48 hrs	385.130 km	Mami Kudo	JPN	Surgères	22-24 May 2010
6 days	883.631 km	Sandra Barwick	NZL	Campbelltown, AUS	18-24 Nov 1990

! Timed on one running watch only

LONG DISTANCE ROAD RECORDS & BESTS - WOMEN

	hr:min:sec	*Name*	*Nat*	*Venue*	*Date*
10 km (l)	0:30:21	Paula Radcliffe	GBR	San Juan	23 Feb 2003
15 km (l)	46:14+	Florence Kiplaget	KEN	Barcelona	15 Feb 2015
10 miles	0:50:05+	Mary Keitany	KEN	Ra's Al-Khaymah	18 Feb 2011
	0:50:01+ dh	Paula Radcliffe	GBR	Newcastle	21 Sep 2003
20 km (l)	1:01:54+	Florence Kiplaget	KEN	Barcelona	15 Feb 2015
25 km (l)	1:19:53	Mary Keitany	KEN	Berlin	9 May 2010
30 km (l)	1:38:23+ §	Liliya Shobukhova	RUS	Chicago	9 Oct 2011
	1:36:36+ dh	Paula Radcliffe	GBR	London	13 Apr 2003
20 miles	1:43:33+	Paula Radcliffe	GBR	London	13 Apr 2003
30 miles	3:01:16+	Frith van der Merwe	RSA	Claremont-Kirstenbosch	25 Mar 1989
50 km	3:08:39	Frith van der Merwe	RSA	Claremont-Kirstenbosch	25 Mar 1989
40 miles	4:26:13+	Ann Trason	USA	Houston	23 Feb 1991
50 miles	5:40:18	Ann Trason	USA	Houston	23 Feb 1991
100 km (l)	6:33:11	Tomoe Abe	JPN	Yubetsu	25 Jun 2000
100 miles	13:47:41	Ann Trason	USA	Queen's, New York	4 May 1991
200 km	18:45:51	Mami Kudo	JPN	Steenbergen	11-12 May 2013
1000 km	7d 01:11:00+	Sandra Barwick	NZL	New York	16-23 Sep 1991
1000 miles	12d 14:38:40	Sandra Barwick	NZL	New York	16-29 Sep 1991
Ekiden (6 stages)	2:11:22	(l)	ETH	Chiba	24 Nov 2003
Berhane Adere, Tirunesh Dibaba, Eyerusalem Kuma, Ejegayou Dibaba, Meseret Defar, Werknesh Kidane					
12 hours	144.840 km	Ann Trason	USA	Queen's, New York	4 May 1991
24 hours	252.205 km	Mami Kudo	JPN	Steenbergen	12 May 2013

100 KILOMETRES CONTINENTAL RECORDS

Men

W, Asi	6:13:33	Takahiro SUNADA	JPN	Yubetsu	21 Jun 1998
Eur	6:16:41	Jean-Paul PRAET	BEL	Torhout	24 Jun 1989
SAm	6:18:09	Valmir NUNES	BRA	Winschoten	16 Sep 1995
Afr	6:25:07	Bruce FORDYCE	RSA	Stellenbosch	4 Feb 1989
NAm	6:27:43	Maxwell KING	USA	Doha	21 Nov 2014
Oce	6:29:23	Tim SLOAN	AUS	Ross-Richmond	23 Apr 1995

Women

W, Asi	6:33:11	Tomoe ABE	JPN	Yubetsu	25 Jun 2000
NAm	7:00:48	Ann TRASON	USA	Winschoten	16 Sep 1995
Eur	7:10:32	Tatyana ZHYRKOVA	RUS	Winschoten	11 Sep 2004
SAm	7:20:22	Maria VENÂNCIO	BRA	Cubatão	8 Aug 1998
Afr	7:31:47	Helena JOUBERT	RSA	Winschoten	16 Sep 1995
Oce	7:40:58	Linda MEADOWS	AUS	North Otago	18 Nov 1995

WORLD INDOOR RECORDS

Men to March 2015

50 metres	5.56A	Donovan Bailey	CAN	Reno	9 Feb 1996
60 metres	6.39	Maurice Greene	USA	Madrid	3 Feb 1998
	6.39	Maurice Greene	USA	Atlanta	3 Mar 2001
100 metres	9.98	Usain Bolt	JAM	Warszawa	23 Aug 2014
200 metres	19.92	Frank Fredericks	NAM	Liévin	18 Feb 1996
400 metres	44.57	Kerron Clement	USA	Fayetteville	12 Mar 2005
800 metres	1:42.67	Wilson Kipketer	KEN	Paris (Bercy)	9 Mar 1997
1000 metres	2:14.96	Wilson Kipketer	KEN	Birmingham	20 Feb 2000
1500 metres	3:31.18	Hicham El Guerrouj	MAR	Stuttgart	2 Feb 1997
1 mile	3:48.45	Hicham El Guerrouj	MAR	Gent	12 Feb 1997
2000 metres #	4:49.99	Kenenisa Bekele	ETH	Birmingham	17 Feb 2007
3000 metres	7:24.90	Daniel Komen	KEN	Budapest	6 Feb 1998
2 miles #	8:04.35	Kenenisa Bekele	ETH	Birmingham	16 Feb 2008
5000 metres	12:49.60	Kenenisa Bekele	ETH	Birmingham	20 Feb 2004
10000 metres #	27:50.29	Mark Bett	KEN	Gent	10 Feb 2002
50 m hurdles	6.25	Mark McKoy	CAN	Kobe	5 Mar 1986
60 m hurdles	7.30	Colin Jackson	GBR	Sindelfingen	6 Mar 1994
110 m hurdles	13.03	Orlando Ortega	CUB	Warszawa	23 Aug 2014
High jump	2.43	Javier Sotomayor	CUB	Budapest	4 Mar 1989
Pole vault	6.16	Renaud Lavillenie	FRA	Donetsk	15 Feb 2014
Long jump	8.79	Carl Lewis	USA	New York	27 Jan 1984
Triple jump	17.92	Teddy Tamgho	FRA	Paris (Bercy)	6 Mar 2011
Shot	22.66	Randy Barnes	USA	Los Angeles	20 Jan 1989
Javelin #	85.78	Matti Närhi	FIN	Kajaani	3 Mar 1996
35 lb weight #	25.86	Lance Deal	USA	Atlanta	4 Mar 1995
3000m walk #	10:31.42	Andreas Erm	GER	Halle	4 Feb 2001

5000m walk	18:07.08	Mikhail Shchennikov	RUS	Moskva	14 Feb 1995
10000m walk #	38:31.4	Werner Heyer	GDR	Berlin	12 Jan 1980
4 x 200m	1:22.11	United Kingdom		Glasgow	3 Mar 1991
		(Linford Christie, Darren Braithwaite, Ade Mafe, John Regis)			
4 x 400m	3:02.13	USA		Sopot	9 Mar 2014
		(Kyle Clemons, David Verburg, Kind Butler, Calvin Smith)			
	3:01.96 §	USA (not ratified – no EPO analysis)		Fayetteville	11 Feb 2006
		(Kerron Clement, Wallace Spearmon, Darold Williamson, Jeremy Wariner)			
4 x 800m	7:13.11	USA All-Stars		Boston (Roxbury)	8 Feb 2014
		(Richard Jones, David Torrence, Duane Solomon, Erik Sowinski)			
Heptathlon	6645 points	Ashton Eaton	USA	Istanbul	9/10 Mar 2012
		(6.79 60m, 8.16 LJ, 14.56 SP, 2.03 HJ, 7.68 60mh, 5.20 PV, 2:32.77 1000m)			

Women

50 metres	5.96+	Irina Privalova	RUS	Madrid	9 Feb 1995
60 metres	6.92	Irina Privalova	RUS	Madrid	11 Feb 1993 & 9 Feb 1995
200 metres	21.87	Merlene Ottey	JAM	Liévin	13 Feb 1993
400 metres	49.59	Jarmila Kratochvílová	CZE	Milano	7 Mar 1982
800 metres	1:55.82	Jolanda Ceplak	SLO	Wien	3 Mar 2002
1000 metres	2:30.94	Maria Lurdes Mutola	MOZ	Stockholm	25 Feb 1999
1500 metres	3:55.17	Genzebe Dibaba	ETH	Karlsruhe	1 Feb 2014
1 mile	4:17.14	Doina Melinte	ROU	East Rutherford	9 Feb 1990
2000 metres #	5:30.53	Gabriela Szabo	ROU	Sindelfingen	8 Mar 1998
3000 metres	8:16.60	Genzebe Dibaba	ETH	Stockholm	6 Feb 2014
2 miles #	9:00.48	Genzebe Dibaba	ETH	Birmingham	15 Feb 2014
5000 metres	14:18.86	Genzebe Dibaba	ETH	Stockholm	19 Feb 2015
50 m hurdles	6.58	Cornelia Oschkenat	GDR	Berlin	20 Feb 1988
60 m hurdles	7.68	Susanna Kallur	SWE	Karlsruhe	10 Feb 2008
100 m hurdles	12.64	Ludmila Engquist	SWE	Tampere	10 Feb 1997
High jump	2.08	Kajsa Bergqvist	SWE	Arnstadt	4 Feb 2006
Pole vault	5.02A	Jenn Suhr	USA	Albuquerque	2 Mar 2013
Long jump	7.37	Heike Drechsler	GDR	Wien	13 Feb 1988
Triple jump	15.36	Tatyana Lebedeva	RUS	Budapest	5 Mar 2004
Shot	22.50	Helena Fibingerová	CZE	Jablonec	19 Feb 1977
Javelin #	61.29	Taina Uppa/Kolkkala	FIN	Mustasaari	28 Feb 1999
20 lb weight #	25.56	Brittany Riley	USA	Fayetteville	10 Mar 2007
3000m walk	11:35.34 un	Gillian O'Sullivan	IRL	Belfast	15 Feb 2003
	11:40.33	Claudia Iovan/Stef	ROU	Bucuresti	30 Jan 1999
5000m walk #	20:37.77	Margarita Turova	BLR	Minsk	13 Feb 2005
10000m walk	43:54.63	Yelena Ginko	BLR	Mogilyov	22 Feb 2008
4 x 200m	1:32.41	Russia		Glasgow	29 Jan 2005
		(Yekaterina Kondratyeva, Irina Khabarova, Yuliya Pechonkina, Yuliya Gushchina)			
4 x 400m	3:23.37	Russia		Glasgow	28 Jan 2006
		(Yuliya Gushchina, Olga Kotlyarova, Olga Zaytseva, Olesya Krasnomovets)			
4 x 800m	8:06.24	Moskva	RUS	Moskva	18 Feb 2011
		(Aleksandra Bulanova, Yekaterina Martynova, Yelena Kofanova , Anna Balakshina)			
Pentathlon	5013 points	Nataliya Dobrynska	UKR	Istanbul	9 Mar 2012
		(8.38 60mh, 1.84 HJ, 16.51 SP, 6.57 LJ, 2:11.15 800m)			

events not officially recognised by the IAAF

WORLD INDOOR JUNIOR (U20) RECORDS

First approved by IAAF Council in 2011. **Men**

60 metres	6.51	Mark Lewis-Francis	GBR	Lisboa	11 Mar 2001
200 metres	20.37	Walter Dix	USA	Fayetteville	11 Mar 2005
400 metres	44.80	Kirani James	GRN	Fayetteville	27 Feb 2011
800 metres	1:44.35	Yuriy Borzakovskiy	RUS	Dortmund	30 Jan 2000
1000 metres	2:15.77	Abubaker Kaki	SUD	Stockholm	21 Feb 2008
1500 metres	3:36.28	Belal Mansoor Ali (overage!)	BRN	Stockholm	20 Feb 2007
One mile	3:55.02	German Fernandez	USA	College Station	28 Feb 2009
3000 metres	7:32.87	Hagos Gebrhiwet	ETH	Boston (Roxbury)	2 Feb 2013
5000 metres	12:53.29	Isiah Koech	KEN	Düsseldorf	11 Feb 2011
60mh (99cm)	7.48 §	Wilhem Belocian	FRA	Val-de-Reuil	9 Mar 2014
	7.50	Konstadínos Douvalidís	GRE	Athína	11 Feb 2006
	7.50 #	David Omoregie	GBR	Cardiff	9 Mar 2014
High jump	2.35	Volodymyr Yashchenko	URS	Milano	12 Mar 1978
Pole vault	5.68	Raphael Holzdeppe	GER	Halle	1 Mar 2008
Long jump	8.22	Viktor Kuznetsov	UKR	Brovary	22 Jan 2005
Triple jump	17.14	Volker Mai	GDR	Piréas	2 Mar 1985
Shot (6kg)	22.38	Konrad Bukowiecki	POL	Torun	24 Jan 2015
Heptathlon	6022	Gunnar Nixon	USA	Fayetteville	27/28 Jan 2012
(jnr imps)		(6.94, 7.96, 13.19, 1.96, 7.90, 4.60, 2:51.42)			

Women

60 metres	7.09	Joan Uduak Ekah	NGR	Maebashi	7 Mar 1999
200 metres	22.40	Bianca Knight	USA	Fayetteville	14 Mar 2008
400 metres	50.82	Sanya Richards	USA	Fayetteville	13 Mar 2004
800 metres	2:01.03	Meskerem Legesse	ETH	Fayetteville	14 Feb 2004
1000 metres	2:35.80	Mary Cain	USA	Boston (Roxbury)	8 Feb 2014
1500 metres	4:03.28	Kalkidan Gezahegne	ETH	Stockholm	10 Feb 2010
One mile	4:24.10	Kalkidan Gezahegne	ETH	Birmingham	20 Feb 2010
3000 metres	8:33.56	Tirunesh Dibaba	ETH	Birmingham	20 Feb 2004
5000 metres	14:53.99	Tirunesh Dibaba	ETH	Boston	31 Jan 2004
60m hurdles	8.01	Dior Hall	USA	Fayetteville	13 Mar 2015
High jump	1.97	Mariya Kuchina	RUS	Trinec	26 Jan 2011
Pole vault	4.63	Angelica Bengtsson	SWE	Stockholm	22 Feb 2011
Long jump	6.88	Heike Daute	GDR	Berlin	1 Feb 1983
Triple jump	14.37	Ren Ruiping	CHN	Barcelona	11 Mar 1995
Shot	20.51	Heidi Krieger	GDR	Budapest	8 Feb 1984
Pentathlon	4635A	Kendell Williams	USA	Albuquerque	15 Mar 2014
		(8.21, 1.88, 12.05, 6.32, 2:17.31)			

WORLD VETERANS/MASTERS RECORDS

MEN – aged 35 or over

100 metres	9.96	Kim Collins (5.4.76)	SKN	London (HG)	20 Jul 2014
200 metres	20.11	Linford Christie (2.4.60)	GBR	Villeneuve d'Ascq	25 Jun 1995
400 metres	44.59	Chris Brown (15.10.78)	BAH	Lausanne	3 Jul 2014
800 metres	1:43.36	Johnny Gray (19.6.60)	USA	Zürich	16 Aug 1995
1000 metres	2:18.8+	William Tanui (22.2.64)	KEN	Rome	7 Jul 1999
1500 metres	3:32.45	William Tanui (22.2.64)	KEN	Athína	16 Jun 1999
1 mile	3:51.38	Bernard Lagat (12.12.74)	USA	London (CP)	6 Aug 2011
2000 metres	4:58.3+ e	William Tanui (22.2.64	KEN	Monaco	4 Aug 1999
	4:54.74i	Bernard Lagat (12.12.74)	USA	New York	15 Feb 2014
3000 metres	7:29.00	Bernard Lagat (12.12.74)	USA	Rieti	29 Aug 2010
5000 metres	12:53.60	Bernard Lagat (12.12.74)	USA	Monaco	22 Jul 2011
10000 metres	26:51.20	Haile Gebrselassie (18.4.73)	ETH	Hengelo	24 May 2008
20000 metres	57:44.4+	Gaston Roelants (5.2.37)	BEL	Bruxelles	20 Sep 1972
1 Hour	20,822m	Haile Gebrselassie (18.4.73)	ETH	Hengelo	1 Jun 2009
Half Marathon	59:10 dh	Paul Tergat (17.6.69)	KEN	Lisboa	13 Mar 2005
	59:50	Haile Gebrselassie (18.4.73)	ETH	Den Haag	14 Mar 2009
Marathon	2:03:59	Haile Gebrselassie (18.4.73)	ETH	Berlin	28 Sep 2008
3000m steeple	8:04.95	Simon Vroemen (11.5.69)	NED	Bruxelles	26 Aug 2005
110m hurdles	12.96	Allen Johnson (1.3.71)	USA	Athína	17 Sep 2006
400m hurdles	48.10	Felix Sánchez (30.8.77)	DOM	Moskva	13 Aug 2013
High jump	2.31	Dragutin Topic (12.3.71)	SRB	Kragujevac	28 Jul 2009
	2.31	Jamie Nieto (2.11.76)	USA	New York	9 Jun 2012
Pole vault	5.90i	Björn Otto (16.10.77)	GER	Cottbus	30 Jan 2013
	5.90i	Björn Otto		Düsseldorf	8 Feb 2013
	5.90	Björn Otto		Eugene	1 Jun 2013
Long jump	8.50	Larry Myricks (10.3.56)	USA	New York	15 Jun 1991
	8.50	Carl Lewis (1.7.61)	USA	Atlanta	29 Jul 1996
Triple jump	17.92	Jonathan Edwards (10.5.66)	GBR	Edmonton	6 Aug 2001
Shot	22.67	Kevin Toth ¶ (29.12.67)	USA	Lawrence	19 Apr 2003
Discus	71.56	Virgilijus Alekna (13.2.72)	LTU	Kaunas	25 Jul 2007
Hammer	83.62	Igor Astapkovich (4.1.63)	BLR	Staiki	20 Jun 1998
Javelin	92.80	Jan Zelezny (16.6.66)	CZE	Edmonton	12 Aug 2001
Decathlon	8241	Kip Janvrin (8.7.65)	USA	Eugene	22 Jun 2001
		(10.98, 7.01, 14.21, 1.89, 48.41, 14.72, 45.59, 5.20, 60.41, 4:14.96)			
20 km walk	1:18:44	Vladimir Andreyev (7.9.66)	RUS	Cheboksary	12 Jun 2004
20000m t walk	1:20:55.4+	Maurizio Damilano (6.4.57)	ITA	Cuneo	3 Oct 1992
50 km walk	3:32:33	Yohann Diniz (1.1.78)	FRA	Zürich	15 Aug 2014
50000m t walk	3:49:29.7	Alain Lemercier (11.1.57)	FRA	Franconville	3 Apr 1994

MEN – aged 40 or over

100 metres	10.29	Troy Douglas (30.11.62)	NED	Leiden	7 Jun 2003
200 metres	20.64	Troy Douglas (30.11.62)	NED	Utrecht	9 Aug 2003
400 metres	47.82	Enrico Saraceni (19.5.64)	ITA	Århus	25 Jul 2004
	47.5u	Lee Evans (25.2.47)	USA		Apr 1989
800 metres	1:48.05	Anthony Whiteman (13.11.71)	GBR	Manchester (Stretford)	12 Jul 2014
1000 metres	2:24.93i	Vyacheslav Shabunin (27.9.69)	RUS	Moskva	10 Jan 2010
1500 metres	3:40.20i+	Bernard Lagat (12.12.74)	USA	New York (Armory)	14 Feb 2015
	3:42.02	Anthony Whiteman (13.11.71)	GBR	Manchester (Stretford)	7 Jul 2012
1 mile	3:54.91i+	Bernard Lagat (12.12.74)	USA	New York (Armory)	14 Feb 2015
	3:58.79	Anthony Whiteman (13.11.71)	GBR	Nashville	2 Jun 2012

3000 metres	7:37.92i+	Bernard Lagat (12.12.74)	USA	Metz	25 Feb 2015
	8:02.54	Vyacheslav Shabunin (27.9.69)	RUS	Moskva	7 Jun 2010
5000 metres	13:43.15	Mohamed Ezzher (26.4.60)	FRA	Sotteville	3 Jul 2000
10000 metres	28:30.88	Martti Vainio (30.12.50)	FIN	Hengelo	25 Jun 1991
10 km road	28:00	Haile Gebrselassie (18.4.73)	ETH	Manchester	25 May 2013
1 Hour	19.710k	Steve Moneghetti (26.9.62)	AUS	Geelong	17 Dec 2005
Half marathon	60:41 dh	Haile Gebrselassie (18.4.73)	ETH	South Shields	15 Sep 2013
	61:09	Haile Gebrselassie		Glasgow	6 Oct 2013
Marathon	2:08:46	Andrés Espinosa (4.2.63)	MEX	Berlin	28 Sep 2003
3000m steeple	8:38.40	Angelo Carosi (20.1.64)	ITA	Firenze	11 Jul 2004
110m hurdles	13.97	David Ashford (24.1.63)	USA	Indianapolis	3 Jul 2004
	13.79 ?	Roger Kingdom (26.8.62)	USA	Slippery Rock	23 Jun 2004
400m hurdles	49.69	Danny McFarlane (14.2.72)	JAM	Kingston	29 Jun 2012
High jump	2.28	Dragutin Topic (12.3.71)	SRB	Beograd	20 May 2012
Pole vault	5.71i	Jeff Hartwig (25.9.67)	USA	Jonesboro	31 May 2008
	5.70	Jeff Hartwig		Eugene	29 Jun 2008
Long jump	7.68A	Aaron Sampson (20.9.61)	USA	Cedar City, UT	21 Jun 2002
	7.59i	Mattias Sunneborn (27.9.70)	SWE	Sätra	3 Feb 2013
	7.57	Hans Schicker (3.10.47)	FRG	Kitzingen	16 Jul 1989
Triple jump	16.58	Ray Kimble (19.4.53)	USA	Edinburgh	2 Jul 1993
Shot	21.41	Brian Oldfield USA (1.6.45)	USA	Innsbruck	22 Aug 1985
Discus	70.28	Virgilijus Alekna (13.2.72)	LTU	Klaipeda	23 Jun 2012
Hammer	82.23	Igor Astapkovich (4.1.63)	BLR	Minsk	10 Jul 2004
Javelin	85.92	Jan Zelezny (16.6.66)	CZE	Göteborg	9 Aug 2006
Pentathlon	3510	Werner Schallau (8.9.38)	FRG	Gelsenkirchen	24 Sep 1978
		6.74, 59.20, 23.0, 43.76, 5:05.7			
Decathlon	7525	Kip Janvrin (8.7.65)	USA	San Sebastián	24 Aug 2005
		11.56, 6.78, 14.01, 1.80, 49.46, 15.40, 42.70, 4.70, 58.43, 4:25.87			
20 km walk	1:20:20	Andriy Kovenko (25.11.73)	UKR	Alushta	28 Feb 2o14
20000m t walk	1:24:58.8	Marcel Jobin (3.1.42)	CAN	Sept Isles	12 May 1984
50 km walk	3:40:46	Yuriy Andronov (6.11.71)	RUS	Moskva	11 Jun 2012
50000m t walk	3:51:54.5	José Marín (21.1.50)	ESP	Manresa	7 Apr 1990
4x100m	42.20	SpeedWest TC	USA	Irvine	2 May 2004
		(Frank Strong, Cornell Stephenson, Kettrell Berry, Willie Gault)			
4x400m	3:20.83	S Allah, K Morning, E Gonera, R Blackwell	USA	Philadelphia	27 Apr 2001

WOMEN – aged 35 or over

100 metres	10.74	Merlene Ottey (10.5.60)	JAM	Milano	7 Sep 1996
200 metres	21.93	Merlene Ottey (10.5.60)	JAM	Bruxelles	25 Aug 1995
400 metres	50.27	Jearl Miles Clark (4.9.66)	USA	Madrid	20 Sep 2002
800 metres	1:56.53	Lyubov Gurina (6.8.57)	RUS	Hechtel	30 Jul 1994
1000 metres	2:31.5	Maricica Puica (29.7.50)	ROU	Poiana Brasov	1 Jun 1986
1500 metres	3:57.73	Maricica Puica (29.7.50)	ROU	Bruxelles	30 Aug 1985
1 mile	4:17.33	Maricica Puica (29.7.50)	ROU	Zürich	21 Aug 1985
2000 metres	5:28.69	Maricica Puica (29.7.50)	ROU	London (CP)	11 Jul 1986
3000 metres	8:23.23	Edith Masai (4.4.67)	KEN	Monaco	19 Jul 2002
5000 metres	14:33.84	Edith Masai (4.4.67)	KEN	Oslo	2 Jun 2006
10000 metres	30:30.26	Edith Masai (4.4.67)	KEN	Helsinki	6 Aug 2005
Half Marathon	67:16	Edith Masai (4.4.67)	KEN	Berlin	2 Apr 2006
Marathon	2:19:19	Irina Mikitenko (23.8.72)	GER	Berlin	28 Sep 2008
3000m steeple	9:24.26	Marta Domínguez (3.11.75)	ESP	Huelva	7 Jun 2012
100m hurdles	12.40	Gail Devers (19.11.66)	USA	Lausanne	2 Jul 2002
400m hurdles	52.94	Marina Styepanova (1.5.50)	RUS	Tashkent	17 Sep 1986
High jump	2.01	Inga Babakova (27.6.67)	UKR	Oslo	27 Jun 2003
	2.01	Ruth Beitia (1.4.79)	ESP	Zürich	17 Aug 2014
Pole vault	4.70	Stacy Dragila (25.3.71)	USA	Chula Vista	22 Jun 2008
Long jump	6.99	Heike Drechsler (16.12.64)	GER	Sydney	29 Sep 2000
Triple jump	14.68	Tatyana Lebedeva (21.7.76)	RUS	Cheboksary	3 Jul 2012
	14.82i	Yamilé Aldama (14.8.72)	GBR	Istanbul	19 Mar 2012
Shot	21.46	Larisa Peleshenko (29.2.64)	RUS	Moskva	26 Aug 2000
	21.47i	Helena Fibingerová (13.7.49)	CZE	Jablonec	9 Feb 1985
Discus	69.60	Faina Melnik (9.7.45)	RUS	Donetsk	9 Sep 1980
Hammer	72.42	Iryna Sekyachova (21.7.76)	UKR	Yalta	4 Jun 2012
Javelin	68.34	Steffi Nerius (1.7.72)	GER	Berlin (Elstal)	31 Aug 2008
Heptathlon	6533	Jane Frederick (7.4.52)	USA	Talence	27 Sep 1987
		13.60, 1.82, 15.50, 24.73; 6.29, 49.70, 2:14.88			
5000m walk	20:12.41	Elisabetta Perrone (9.7.68)	ITA	Rieti	2 Aug 2003
10km walk	41:41	Kjersti Tysse Plätzer (18.1.72)	NOR	Kraków	30 May 2009
10000m t walk	43:26.5	Elisabetta Perrone (9.7.68)	ITA	Saluzzo	4 Aug 2004
20km walk	1:25:59	Tamara Kovalenko (5.6.64)	RUS	Moskva	19 May 2000
20000m t walk	1:27:49.3	Yelena Nikolayeva (1.2.66)	RUS	Brisbane	6 Sep 2001

4x100m	48.63	Desmier, Sulter, Andreas, Apavou	FRA	Eugene	8 Jun 1989
4x400m	3:50.80	Mitchell, Mathews, Beadnall, Gabriel	GBR	Gateshead	8 Aug 1999

WOMEN – aged 40 or over

100 metres	10.99	Merlene Ottey (10.5.60)	JAM	Thessaloniki	30 Aug 2000
200 metres	22.72	Merlene Ottey (10.5.60)	SLO	Athína	23 Aug 2004
400 metres	53.05A	María Figueirêdo (11.11.63)	BRA	Bogotá	10 Jul 2004
	53.14	María Figueirêdo (11.11.63)	BRA	San Carlos, VEN	19 Jun 2004
800 metres	1:59.25	Yekaterina Podkopayeva (11.6.52)	RUS	Luxembourg	30 Jun 1994
1000 metres	2:36.16	Yekaterina Podkopayeva (11.6.52)	RUS	Nancy	14 Sep 1994
	2:36.08i	Yekaterina Podkopayeva	RUS	Liévin	13 Feb 1993
1500 metres	3:59.78	Yekaterina Podkopayeva (11.6.52)	RUS	Nice	18 Jul 1994
1 mile	4:23.78	Yekaterina Podkopayeva (11.6.52)	RUS	Roma	9 Jun 1993
3000 metres	9:01.1+	Jo Pavey (20.9.73)	GBR	Roma	5 Jun 2014
5000 metres	15:04.87	Jo Pavey (20.9.73)	GBR	Roma	5 Jun 2014
10000 metres	31:31.18	Edith Masai (4.4.67)	KEN	Alger	21 Jul 2007
1 hour	16.056k	Jackie Fairweather (10.11.67)	AUS	Canberra	24 Jan 2008
Half Marathon	69:37	Deena Kastor (14.2.73)	USA	Philadelphia	21 Sep 2014
Marathon	2:24:54	Irina Mikitenko (23.8.2)	GER	Berlin	29 Sep 2013
3000m steeple	10:00.75	Minori Hayakari (29.11.72)	JPN	Kumagaya	22 Sep 2013
100 m hurdles	13.20	Patricia Girard (8.4.68)	FRA	Paris	14 Jul 2008
400 m hurdles	58.35	Barbara Gähling (20.3.65)	GER	Erfurt	21 Jul 2007
	58.3 h	Gowry Retchakan (21.6.60)	GBR	Hoo	3 Sep 2000
High jump	1.94i	Venelina Veneva-Mateeva (13.6.74)	BUL	Dobrich 15 Feb & Praha	6 Mar 2015
	1.90	Venelina Veneva-Mateeva	BUL	Plovdiv 12 Jul & Pitesti	27 Jul 2014
Pole vault	4.10	Doris Auer (10.5.71)	AUT	Innsbruck	6 Aug 2011
	4.11 §	Doris Auer	AUT	Wien	5 Jul 2011
Long jump	6.64	Tatyana Ter-Mesrobian (12.5.68)	RUS	Sankt-Peterburg	31 May 2008
	6.64i	Tatyana Ter-Mesrobian	RUS	Sankt-Peterburg	5 Jan 2010
Triple jump	14.06	Yamilé Aldama (14.8.72)	GBR	Eugene	1 Jun 2013
Shot	19.05	Antonina Ivanova (25.12.32)	RUS	Oryol	28 Aug 1973
	19.16i	Antonina Ivanova	RUS	Moskva	24 Feb 1974
Discus	67.89	Iryna Yatchenko (31.10.65)	BLR	Staiki	29 Jun 2008
Hammer	59.29	Oneithea Lewis (11.6.60)	USA	Princeton	10 May 2003
Javelin	61.96	Laverne Eve (16.6.65)	BAH	Monaco	9 Sep 2005
Heptathlon	5449	Tatyana Alisevich (22.1.69)	BLR	Staiki	3 Jun 2010
		14.80, 1.62, 13.92, 26.18, 5.55, 45.44, 2:24.39			
5000m walk	21:46.68	Kelly Ruddick (19.4.73)	AUS	Brisbane	29 Mar 2014
10km walk	45:09+	Kerry Saxby-Junna (2.6.61)	AUS	Edmonton	9 Aug 2001
10000m t walk	45:25.90	Kelly Ruddick (19.4.73)	AUS	Melbourne	4 Apr 2014
20km walk	1:33:04	Graciela Mendoza (23.3.63)	MEX	Lima	7 May 2005
20000m t walk	1:33:28.15t	Teresa Vaill (20.11.62)	USA	Carson	25 Jun 2005
4x100m	48.22	Cadinot, Barilly, Valouvin, Lapierre	FRA	Le Touquet	24 Jun 2006
4x400m	3:57.28	Loizou, Kay, Smithe, Cearns	AUS	Brisbane	14 Jul 2001

WORLD AND CONTINENTAL RECORDS SET IN 2014

OUTDOORS – MEN

§ Not ratified

100	W20=	10.01	Trayvon BROMELL	USA	Austin	29 Mar 14
	W20	9.97	Trayvon BROMELL	USA	Eugene	13 Jun 14
	W35	9.96	Kim COLLINS	SKN	London (HG)	20 Jul 14
	Asi	9.93	Femi OGUNODE	QAT	Incheon	28 Sep 14
400	CAC,Com	43.74	Kirani JAMES	GRN	Lausanne	3 Jul 14
	Asi	44.43	Yousef Ahmed AL-MASRAHI	KSA	Lausanne	3 Jul 14
	W35	44.59	Chris BROWN	BAH	Lausanne	3 Jul 14
	Afr	44.01	Isaac MAKWALA	BOT	La Chaux-de-Fonds	6 Jul 14
800	W40	1:48.05	Anthony WHITEMAN	GBR	Manchester (Stretford)	12 Jul 14
1000	Oce	2:16.09	Jeff RISELEY	AUS	Ostrava	17 Jun 14
1500	W20	3:28.81	Ronald KWEMOI	KEN	Monaco	18 Jul 14
	Oce	3:29.91	Nick WILLIS	NZL	Monaco	18 Jul 14
2 Miles	Eur	8:07.85	Mo FARAH	GBR	Birmingham	24 Aug 14
10000	NAm	26:44.36	Galen RUPP	USA	Eugene	30 May 14
30k	W,Afr,Com	1:27:37+	Emmanuel MUTAI	KEN	Berlin	28 Sep 14
	W,Afr,Com	1:27:37+ §	Geoffrey KAMWOROR	KEN	Berlin	28 Sep 14
	W,Afr,Com	1:27:36+ §	Wilfred KIRWA	KEN	Berlin (dnf)	28 Sep 14
Mar	W20	2:04:32	Tsegaye MEKONNEN	ETH	Dubai	24 Jan 14
	W,Afr,Com	2:02:57	Dennis KIMETTO	KEN	Berlin	28 Sep 14
100k	NAm	6:27:43	Maxwell KING	USA	Doha	21 Nov 14
24Hr track	Asi	285.366k	Yoshikazu HARA	JPN	Taipei	7 Dec 14
3000SC	NAm	8:04.71	Evan JAGER	USA	Bruxelles	5 Sep 14
110H 91cm	W18	12.96	Jaheel HYDE	JAM	Nanjing	23 Aug 14

110H 99cm	W20	12.99	Wilhem BELOCIAN	FRA	Eugene	24 Jul 14
HJ	NAm=,Com	2.40	Derek DROUIN	CAN	Des Moines	25 Apr 14
	Asi	2.41	Mutaz Essa BARSHIM	QAT	Roma	5 Jun 14
	Eur=	2.42	Bogdan BONDARENKO	UKR	New York	14 Jun 14
	Asi	2.42	Mutaz Essa BARSHIM	QAT	New York	14 Jun 14
	Asi	2.43	Mutaz Essa BARSHIM	QAT	Bruxelles	5 Sep 14
TJ	W18	17.24	Lázaro MARTÍNEZ	CUB	La Habana	1 Feb 14
SP	CAC	21.61	O'Dayne RICHARDS	JAM	Glasgow	28 Jul 14
HT/5kg	W18	87.16	Bence HALÁSZ	HUN	Baku	31 May 14
HT	Afr	81.27	Mostafa Hicham AL-GAMAL	EGY	Cairo	21 Mar 14
JT	Afr	89.21	Ihab ABDELRAHMAN El-Sayed	EGY	Shanghai	18 May 14
	Asi	89.15	ZHAO Qinggang	CHN	Incheon	2 Oct 14
4x100 R	Asi	37.99	Chen Shiwei, Xie Zhenye, Su Bingtian, Zhang Peimeng	CHN	Incheon	2 Oct 14
4x200 R	CAC, Com	1:20.15	Dwyer, Brown, Livermore, Weir	JAM	Nassau	24 May 14
	W,CAC,Com	1:18.63	Ashmeade, Weir, Brown, Blake	JAM	Nassau	24 May 14
	Eur	1:20.66	Lemaitre, Fonsat, Bassaw, Romain	FRA	Nassau	24 May 14
4x800 R	Oce	7:11.48	Ralph, Gregson, Williamsz, West	AUS	Nassau	24 May 14
4x1500 R	W,Afr,Com	14:22.22	Cheboi, Kiplagat, Magut, Kiprop	KEN	Nassau	25 May 14
	NAm	14:40.80	Casey, Torrence, Leer, Manzano	USA	Nassau	25 May 14
	Asi	15:10.77	Al-Garni, Salah, Balla, Kamal	QAT	Nassau	25 May 14
5000W	CAC	18:35.36	Éder SANCHEZ	MEX	Katowice	2 Jul 14
10000W	W35	38:08.13	Yohann DINIZ	FRA	Reims	12 Jul 14
	Asi	38:27.09	Yusuke SUZUKI	JPN	Yamaguchi	11 Oct 14
	Asi	38:18.51	Eiki TAKAHASHI	JPN	Nagasaki	14 Dec 14
20000W	NAm	1:21:57.0	Evan DUNFEE	CAN	Moncton	27 Jun 14
20kW	W40	1:20:20	Andriy KOVENKO	UKR	Alushta	28 Feb 14
	NAm	1:20:13	Evan DUNFEE	CAN	Taicang	4 May 14
50kW	W,Eur,W35	3:32:33	Yohann DINIZ	FRA	Zürich	15 Aug 14
	SAm	3:47:41	James RENDÓN	COL	Valley Cottage	14 Sep 14

OUTDOORS – WOMEN

100	Oce	11.11	Melissa BREEN	AUS	Canberra	9 Feb 14
	W18	11.10	Kaylin WHITNEY	USA	Eugene	5 Jul 14
200	W18	22.49	Kaylin WHITNEY	USA	Eugene	6 Jul 14
1000	Asi	2:40.53	ZHAO Jing	CHN	Changbaishan	2 Sep 14
2000	Afr	5:27.50	Genzebe DIBABA	ETH	Ostrava	17 Jun 14
3000	Afr, Com	8:20.68	Hellen OBIRI	KEN	Doha	9 May 14
	W40	9:01.1+	Jo PAVEY	GBR	Roma	5 Jun 14
2 Miles	Asi	9:13.85	Mimi BELETE	BRN	Eugene	31 May 14
	NAm	9:20.25	Shannon ROWBURY	USA	Eugene	31 May 14
	W20	9:20.81	Alemitu HAROYE	ETH	Birmingham	24 Aug 14
5000	W40	15:11.52	Jo PAVEY	GBR	Watford	17 May 14
	W40	15:04.87	Jo PAVEY	GBR	Roma	5 Jun 14
	NAm	14:42.64	Molly HUDDLE	USA	Monaco	18 Jul 14
15k	NAm	47:00	Shalane FLANAGAN	USA	Jacksonville	15 Mar 14
	W40	49:03+	Deena KASTOR	USA	Philadelphia	21 Sep 14
10 Miles	W40	52:41+	Deena KASTOR	USA	Philadelphia	21 Sep 14
20k	W,Afr,Com	61:56+	Florence KIPLAGAT	KEN	Barcelona	16 Feb 14
	SAm	67:02+	Yolanda CABALLERO	COL	Marugame	2 Feb 14
	W40	65:52+	Deena KASTOR	USA	Philadelphia	21 Sep 14
HMar	W,Afr,Com	65:12	Florence KIPLAGAT	KEN	Barcelona	16 Feb 14
	W40	69:37	Deena KASTOR	USA	Philadelphia	21 Sep 14
25k	NAm	1:22:36+	Shalane FLANAGAN	USA	Berlin	28 Sep 14
	SAm	1:26:04+	Inés MELCHOR	PER	Berlin	28 Sep 14
30k	NAm	1:39:15+	Shalane FLANAGAN	USA	Berlin	28 Sep 14
	SAm	1:43:30+	Inés MELCHOR	PER	Berlin	28 Sep 14
Mar	SAm	2:26:48	Inés MELCHOR	PER	Berlin	28 Sep 14
2000SC	NAm	6:14.66	Stephanie GARCIA	USA	Greenville	31 May 14
3000SC	NAm	9:11.42	Emma COBURN	USA	Glasgow	12 Jul 14
	W18	9:28.36	Tigist MEKONEN	ETH	Glasgow	12 Jul 14
	Asi	9:20.55	Ruth CHEBET	BRN	Zürich	28 Aug 14
200H	WR, Eur	25.79	Noemi ZBÄREN	SUI	Basel	17 May 14
HJ	W40	1.90	Venelina VENEVA-MATEEVA	BUL	Plovdiv	12 Jul 14
	W40=	1.90	Venelina VENEVA-MATEEVA	BUL	Pitesti	27 Jul 14
	W35=	2.01	Ruth BEITIA	ESP	Zürich	17 Aug 14
TJ	SAm	15.31	Caterine IBARGÜEN	COL	Monaco	18 Jul 14
DT	NAm	69.17	Gia LEWIS-SMALWOOD	USA	Angers	30 Aug 14
HT	Afr	69.20	Amy SÈNE	SEN	Chateauroux	9 Mar 14
	Asi	77.68	WANG Zheng	CHN	Chengdu	29 Mar 14
	NAm=,Com	75.73	Sultana FRIZELL	CAN	Tucson	22 May 14

	Afr	69.70	Amy SÈNE	SEN	Forbach	25 May 14
	W, Eur	79.58	Anita WLODARCZYK	POL	Berlin	31 Aug 14
JT	Oce	66.83	Kimberley MICKLE	AUS	Melbourne	22 Mar 14
	SAm	62.89	Jucilene de LIMA	BRA	São Paulo	11 Oct 14
	SAm	63.80A	Flor Dennis RUIZ	COL	Xalapa	27 Nov 14
4x200 R	Com	1:29.61	Henry, Onuora, J Williams, Philip	GBR	Nassau	25 May 14
	CAC	1:30.04	Facey, Brooks, McLoughlin, Fraser-Pryce	JAM	Nassau	25 May 14
4x800 R	NAm	8:01.58	Price, Lara, Wilson, Martinez	USA	Nassau	25 May 14
	Afr, Com	8:04.28	Kimaswai, Chesebe, Jepkosgei, Sum	KEN	Nassau	25 May 14
	Oce	8:13.26	McGowan, Buckman, Kajan, Duncan	AUS	Nassau	25 May 14
4x1500 R	W,Afr,Com	17:08.17A	Karindi, Chelimo, Sum, Obiri	KEN	Nairobi	5 Apr 14
	W,Afr,Com	17:05.72A	Jelagat, Karindi, Nenkampi, M Cherono	KEN	Nairobi	26 Apr 14
	W,Afr,Com	16:33.58	M Cherono, Kipyegon, Jelagat, Obiri	KEN	Nassau	24 May 14
	NAm	16:55.33	Kampf, Mackey, Grace, Martinez	USA	Nassau	24 May 14
	Oce	17:08.65	Buckman,Delaney,McGowan,Duncan	AUS	Nassau	24 May 14
4x100H	W	50.66	Castlin/USA, Rollins/USA, Q Harrison/USA, T Porter/GBR	USA/GBR	Gainesville	5 Apr 14
5000W	W, Eur	20:01.80	Eleonora GIORGI	ITA	Misterbianco	17 May 14
	W40	21:46.68	Kelly RUDDICK	AUS	Brisbane	29 Mar 14
10000W	SAm	45:19.80	Kimberly GARCIA	PER	Lima	31 May 14
	W40	45:25.90	Kelly RUDDICK	AUS	Melbourne	4 Apr 14
	W20	42:47.25	Anezka DRAHOTOVÁ	CZE	Eugene	23 Jul 14
	SAm	43:41.30	Erica de SEÑA	BRA	São Paulo	1 Aug 14
10kW	SAm	44:34+	Kimberly GARCIA	PER	Taicang	3 May 14
	SAm	44:34+	Sandra Lorena ARENAS	COL	Taicang	3 May 14
20000W	SAm	1:31:46.9	Sandra Lorena ARENAS	COL	Santiago de Chile	13 Mar 14
	NAm, Com	1:32:54.0	Rachel SEAMAN	CAN	Moncton	27 Jun 14
	CAC	1:31:53.8A	Mirna ORTIZ	GUA	Ciudad de Guatemala	9 Aug 14
20kW	NAm	1:31:40	Rachel SEAMAN	CAN	Lugano	16 Mar 14
	NAm	1:30:43	Rachel SEAMAN	CAN	Manchester, NJ	30 Mar 14
	SAm	1:31:22	Erica de SEÑA	BRA	Rio Maior	5 Apr 14
	SAm	1:30:43	Erica de SEÑA	BRA	Podebrady	12 Apr 14
	SAm	1:29:44	Kimberly GARCIA	PER	Taicang	3 May 14

See ATHLETICS 2014 for Indoor Records set in January - March 2014 – and add/amend

INDOORS – MEN

3000	Asi	7:39.24	Albert ROP	BRN	Düsseldorf	30 Jan 14
	Asi	7:38.77	Albert ROP	BRN	Gent	9 Feb 14
60H 99 cm	W20	7.48 §	Wilhem BELOCIAN	FRA	Val-de-Reuil	9 Mar 14
	W20=	7.50	David OMOREGIE	GBR	Cardiff	9 Mar 14
HJ	W18=	2.24	Danyil LYSENKO	RUS	Kineshma	6 Dec 14
PV	W18	5.46	Adam HAGUE	GBR	Manchester	21 Dec 14
SP 5kg	W18	22.41 & 22.93	Konrad BUKOWIECKI	POL	Alexandrów Lódzki	13 Dec 14
	W18	22.95 & 22.97	Konrad BUKOWIECKI	POL	Alexandrów Lódzki	20 Dec 14
	W18	24.24	Konrad BUKOWIECKI	POL	Spala	30 Dec 14
5000W	W35	18:16.76	Yohann DINIZ	FRA	Reims	7 Dec 14

INDOORS – WOMEN

60H	SAm	7.91	Yvette LEWIS	PAN	Sopot	7 Mar 14
Wt	Eur	21.79A & 21.90A	Ida STORM	SWE	Albuquerque	14 Mar 14
4x200 R	W35	1:43.74	Owusu, Young, McLoughlin, Ruddock	GBR	Budapest	30 Mar 14

WORLD AND CONTINENTAL RECORDS SET IN JAN–MAR 2015

INDOORS – MEN # on oversized track

60	W35	6.48	Kim COLLINS	SKN	Moskva	1 Feb 15
	W35=	6.48	Kim COLLINS	SKN	Torun	3 Feb 15
	W35	6.47	Kim COLLINS	SKN	Lódz	17 Feb 15
400	Asi	45.39	Abdelilah HAROUN	QAT	Stockholm	19 Feb 15
500	W, NAm	1:00.06	Brycen SPRATLING	USA	New York (Armory)	14 Feb 15
600	NAm	1:15.58A	Casimir LOXSOM	USA	Albuquerque	24 Jan 15
	CAC	1:16.01	Luguelin SANTOS	DOM	Montréal	21 Feb 15
	NAm	1:15.33	Casimir LOXSOM	USA	Boston (Roxbury)	1 Mar 15
1500	W40	3:40.20+	Bernard LAGAT	USA	New York (Armory)	14 Feb 15
1M	Oce, Com	3:51.61	Nick WILLIS	NZL	Boston (Roxbury)	7 Feb 15
	Oce, Com	3:51.46	Nick WILLIS	NZL	New York (Armory)	14 Feb 15
	W35,W40	3:54.91	Bernard LAGAT	USA	New York (Armory)	14 Feb 15
3000	W40	7:48.33	Bernard LAGAT	USA	Boston (Roxbury)	7 Feb 15
	W40	7:41.3+	Bernard LAGAT	USA	Birmingham	21 Feb 15
	W40	7:37.92	Bernard LAGAT	USA	Metz	25 Feb 15
2 Miles	Asi	8:16.47	Suguru OSAKO	JPN	New York (Armory)	31 Jan 15

	W,Eur,Com	8:03.40	Mo FARAH	GBR	Birmingham	21 Feb 15
	W40	8:17.05	Bernard LAGAT	USA	Birmingham	21 Feb 15
2000SC	Eur	5:21.59	Ilgizar SAFIULIN	RUS	Moskva	8 Feb 15
HJ	Asi	2.40	Mutaz Essa BARSHIM	QAT	Banská Bystrica	4 Feb 15
	Asi	2.41	Mutaz Essa BARSHIM	QAT	Athlone	18 Feb 15
SP/6kg	W20	22.38	Konrad BUKOWIECKI	POL	Torun	24 Jan 15
Hep (U18)	W18	5873	Hans-Christian HAUSENBERG	EST	Tallinn	1 Mar 15
			(6.97, 7.52, 16.02, 1.92 / 8.11, 4.65, 2:56.46)			
4x400 R	Eur	3:02.87	Watrin, D.Borlée, J.Borlée, K.Borlée	BEL	Praha	8 Mar 15
4x800 R	W20	7:42.19	S.Smith, Brianchard, Ward, McKay	USA	New York (Armory)	14 Mar 15
Dist.Med.R	W, NAm	9:19.93	Centrowicz, Berry, Sowinski, Casey	USA	New York (Armory)	31 Jan 15
	Eur	9:25.37	Murray, Gregan, English, O'Lionaird	IRL	New York (Armory)	31 Jan 15

INDOORS – WOMEN

2000	W20	5:35.46	Dawit SEYAUM	ETH	Boston (Roxbury)	7 Feb 15
2 Miles	NAm	9:18.35	Jenny SIMPSON	USA	Boston (Roxbury)	7 Feb 15
5000	W, Afr	14:18.86	Genzebe DIBABA	ETH	Stockholm	19 Feb 15
	Asi	15:34.70	Alia Mohamed SAEED	UAE	Stockholm	19 Feb 15
	W18	16:10.79	Anna ROHRER	USA	New York (Armory)	13 Mar 15
60H	W20	8.01	Dior HALL	USA	Fayetteville	13 Mar 15
	W18=	8.17	Sydney McLAUGHLIN	USA	New York (Armory)	15 Mar 15
HJ	W40	1.80=, 1.85, 1.90	Venelina VENEVA-MATEEVA	BUL	Moskva	1 Feb 15
	W40=	1.90	Venelina VENEVA-MATEEVA	BUL	Dobrich	12 Feb 15
	W40	1.92 & 1.94	Venelina VENEVA-MATEEVA	BUL	Dobrich	15 Feb 15
	W40=	1.94	Venelina VENEVA-MATEEVA	BUL	Praha	6 Mar 15
PV	SAm	4.83	Fabiana de Almeida MURER	BRA	Nevers	7 Feb 15
	Asi=	4.50	LI Ling	CHN	Shanghai	2 Mar 15
	Asi	4.51	LI Ling	CHN	Xianlin	8 Mar 15
LJ	Com	6.99	Christabel NETTEY	CAN	Stockholm	19 Feb 15
Wt	Eur	22.05 & 22.40	Ida STORM	SWE	Seattle	27 Feb 15
	Eur	22.56	Ida STORM	SWE	Fayetteville	13 Mar 15
Pen	Com	5000	Katarina JOHNSON-THOMPSON	GBR	Praha	6 Mar 15
			(8.18, 1.95, 12.32, 6.89, 2:12.78)			
Pen/LJ	W	6.89	Katarina JOHNSON-THOMPSON	GBR	Praha	6 Mar 15
Dist.Med.R	W, NAm	10:42.57	Brown, Jones, Krumpoch, Martinez	USA	Boston (Roxbury)	7 Feb 15
	Eur	11:03.07	Tarplee, McMahon, Kirk, Mageean	IRL	Boston (Roxbury)	7 Feb 15

OUTDOORS – MEN

20k	Eur	56:27+	Mohamed FARAH	GBR	Lisboa	21 Mar 15
HMar	Oce	59:47	Zane ROBERTSON	NZL	Marugame	1 Feb 15
	Eur	59:32	Mohamed FARAH	GBR	Lisboa	21 Mar 15
SP	Oce	21.37	Tomas WALSH	NZL	Melbourne	21 Mar 15
10000W	Asi	38:23.73	WANG Zhen	CHN	Genova	8 Feb 15
20kW	W, W35, Eur	1:17:02	Yohann DINIZ	FRA	Arles	8 Mar 15
	W,Asi	1:16:36	Yusuke SUZUKI	JPN	Nomi	15 Mar 15

OUTDOORS – WOMEN

15k	W,Afr, Com	46:14+	Florence KIPLAGAT	KEN	Barcelona	15 Feb 15
20k	W,Afr, Com	61:54+	Florence KIPLAGAT	KEN	Barcelona	15 Feb 15
HMar	W,Afr, Com	65:09	Florence KIPLAGAT	KEN	Barcelona	15 Feb 15
Mar	W20	2:20:59	Shure DEMISE	ETH	Dubai	23 Jan 15
	W40	2:22:27	Mariya KONOVALOVA	RUS	Nagoya	08 Mar 15
PV	W20 out	4.59	Nina KENNEDY	AUS	Perth	14 Feb 15
10kW	SAm	44:22+	Erica de SEÑA	BRA	Dudince	21 Mar 15
20kW	W, Eur	1:24:47 §	Elmira ALEMBEKOVA	RUS	Sochi	27 Feb 15
	NAm	1:29:54	Rachel SEAMAN	CAN	Nomi	15 Mar 15
	Asi	1:25:12	LU Xiuzhi	CHN	Beijing	20 Mar 15
	SAm	1:29:37	Erica de SEÑA	BRA	Dudince	21 Mar 15

Most World Records: Sergey Bubka USR/UKR set a total of 35 at pole vault: 17 outdoors from 5.85 (1984) to 6.14 (1994) and 18 indoors (9 ratified by IAAF) from 5.81 (1844) to 6.15 (1993). Paavi Nurmi FIN set 22 official and 13 unofficial world records at distances from 1500m to 20,000m between 1921 and 1931.
The most world records by a woman at one event is 28 at pole vault (15 outdoors, 13 indoors) by Yelena Isinbayeva RUS 2003-09.

Oldest: 41y 238d Yekaterina Podkopayeva RUS women's 4x800m indoor 8:18.71 Moskva 4 Feb 1994.

Youngest: 14y 334d Wang Yan CHN 5000m walk 21:33.8 Jian 9 Mar 1986 (unratified).

Youngest male: 17y 198d Thomas Ray PV 3.42m Ulverston 19 Sep 1879 (prior to IAAF jurisdiction (from 1913).

Most world records set in one day: 6 Jesse Owens USA at Ann Arbor 25 May 1935: 100y 9.4, LJ 8.13m, 220y straight (& 200m) 20.3, 220y hurdles straight (& 220yh) 22.6.

Record span of setting world records: Men: 15 years Haile Gebrselassie ETH 1994-2009

WORLD MEN'S ALL-TIME LISTS

100 METRES

Mark	Wind	Name		Nat	Born	Pos	Meet	Venue	Date
9.58 WR	0.9	Usain	Bolt	JAM	21.8.86	1	WCh	Berlin	16 Aug 09
9.63	1.5		Bolt			1	OG	London (OS)	5 Aug 12
9.69 WR	0.0		Bolt			1	OG	Beijing	16 Aug 08
9.69	2.0	Tyson	Gay ¶	USA	9.8.82	1		Shanghai	20 Sep 09
9.69	-0.1	Yohan	Blake	JAM	26.12.89	1	Athl	Lausanne	23 Aug 12
9.71	0.9		Gay			2	WCh	Berlin	16 Aug 09
9.72 WR	1.7		Bolt			1	Reebok	New York (RI)	31 May 08
9.72	0.2	Asafa	Powell	JAM	23.11.82	1rA	Athl	Lausanne	2 Sep 08
9.74 WR	1.7		Powell			1h2	GP	Rieti	9 Sep 07
9.75	1.1		Blake			1	NC	Kingston	29 Jun 12
9.75	1.5		Blake			2	OG	London (OS)	5 Aug 12
9.76	1.8		Bolt			1		Kingston	3 May 08
9.76	1.3		Bolt			1	VD	Bruxelles	16 Sep 11
9.76	-0.1		Bolt			1	GGala	Roma	31 May 12
9.76	1.4		Blake			1	WK	Zürich	30 Aug 12
9.77 WR	1.6		Powell			1	Tsik	Athína	14 Jun 05
9.77 WR	1.5		Powell			1	BrGP	Gateshead	11 Jun 06
9.77 WR	1.0		Powell			1rA	WK	Zürich	18 Aug 06
9.77	1.6		Gay			1q1	NC/OT	Eugene	28 Jun 08
9.77	-1.3		Bolt			1	VD	Bruxelles	5 Sep 08
9.77	0.9		Powell			1h1	GP	Rieti	7 Sep 08
9.77	0.4		Gay			1	GGala	Roma	10 Jul 09
9.77	-0.3		Bolt			1	WCh	Moskva	11 Aug 13
9.77	0.6	Justin	Gatlin ¶	USA	10.2.82	1	VD	Bruxelles	5 Sep 14
9.78	0.0		Powell			1	GP	Rieti	9 Sep 07
9.78	-0.4		Gay			1	LGP	London (CP)	13 Aug 10
9.78	0.9	Nesta	Carter	JAM	10.11.85	1		Rieti	29 Aug 10
9.78	1.0		Powell			1	Athl	Lausanne	30 Jun 11
9.79 WR	0.1	Maurice	Greene	USA	23.7.74	1rA	Tsik	Athína	16 Jun 99
9.79	-0.2		Bolt			1	GL	Saint-Denis	17 Jul 09
9.79	0.1		Gay			1	VD	Bruxelles	27 Aug 10
9.79	1.1		Gay			1h1		Clermont	4 Jun 11
9.79	0.6		Bolt			1	Bisl	Oslo	7 Jun 12
9.79	1.5		Gatlin			3	OG	London (OS)	5 Aug 12
		(34 performances by 7 athletes)							
9.80	0.4	Steve	Mullings ¶	JAM	29.11.82	1	Pre	Eugene	4 Jun 11
9.82	1.7	Richard	Thompson	TTO	7.6.85	1	NC	Port of Spain	21 Jun 14
9.84 WR	0.7	Donovan	Bailey	CAN	16.12.67	1	OG	Atlanta	27 Jul 96
		(10)							
9.84	0.2	Bruny	Surin	CAN	12.7.67	2	WCh	Sevilla	22 Aug 99
9.85 WR	1.2	Leroy	Burrell	USA	21.2.67	1rA	Athl	Lausanne	6 Jul 94
9.85	1.7	Olusoji	Fasuba	NGR	9.7.84	2	SGP	Doha	12 May 06
9.85	1.3	Michael	Rodgers	USA	24.4.85	2	Pre	Eugene	4 Jun 11
9.86 WR	1.2	Carl	Lewis	USA	1.7.61	1	WCh	Tokyo	25 Aug 91
9.86	-0.4	Frank	Fredericks	NAM	2.10.67	1rA	Athl	Lausanne	3 Jul 96
9.86	1.8	Ato	Boldon	TTO	30.12.73	1rA	MSR	Walnut	19 Apr 98
9.86	1.4	Keston	Bledman	TTO	8.3.88	1	NC	Port-of-Spain	23 Jun 12
9.86	0.6	Francis	Obikwelu	NGR/POR	22.11.78	2	OG	Athína	22 Aug 04
9.87	0.3	Linford	Christie ¶	GBR	2.4.60	1	WCh	Stuttgart	15 Aug 93
		(20)							
9.87A	-0.2	Obadele	Thompson	BAR	30.3.76	1	WCp	Johannesburg	11 Sep 98
9.88	1.8	Shawn	Crawford ¶	USA	14.1.78	1	Pre	Eugene	19 Jun 04
9.88	0.6	Walter	Dix	USA	31.1.86	2		Nottwil	8 Aug 10
9.88	0.9	Ryan	Bailey	USA	13.4.89	2		Rieti	29 Aug 10
9.88	1.0	Michael	Frater	JAM	6.10.82	2	Athl	Lausanne	30 Jun 11
9.89	1.6	Travis	Padgett	USA	13.12.86	1q2	NC/OT	Eugene	28 Jun 08
9.89	1.6	Darvis	Patton	USA	4.12.77	1q3	NC/OT	Eugene	28 Jun 08
9.89	1.3	Ngonidzashe	Makusha	ZIM	11.3.87	1	NCAA	Des Moines	10 Jun 11
9.90	0.4	Nickel	Ashmeade	JAM	7.4.90	1s2	WCh	Moskva	11 Aug 13
9.91	1.2	Dennis	Mitchell ¶	USA	20.2.66	3	WCh	Tokyo	25 Aug 91
		(30)							
9.91	0.9	Leonard	Scott	USA	19.1.80	2	WAF	Stuttgart	9 Sep 06
9.91	-0.5	Derrick	Atkins	BAH	5.1.84	2	WCh	Osaka	26 Aug 07
9.91	-0.2	Daniel	Bailey	ANT	9.9.86	2	GL	Saint-Denis	17 Jul 09
9.91	0.7	Churandy	Martina	NED	3.7.84	2s1	OG	London (OS)	5 Aug 12
9.91	1.1	James	Dasaolu	GBR	5.9.87	1s2	NC	Birmingham	13 Jul 13

Mark	Wind	Name		Nat	Born	Pos	Meet	Venue	Date
9.92	0.3	Andre	Cason	USA	20.1.69	2	WCh	Stuttgart	15 Aug 93
9.92	0.8	Jon	Drummond	USA	9.9.68	1h3	NC	Indianapolis	12 Jun 97
9.92	0.2	Tim	Montgomery ¶	USA	28.1.75	2	NC	Indianapolis	13 Jun 97
9.92A	-0.2	Seun	Ogunkoya	NGR	28.12.77	2	WCp	Johannesburg	11 Sep 98
9.92	1.0	Tim	Harden	USA	27.1.74	1	Spitzen	Luzern	5 Jul 99
		(40)							
9.92	2.0	Christophe	Lemaitre	FRA	11.6.90	1	NC	Albi	29 Jul 11
9.93A	WR1.4	Calvin	Smith	USA	8.1.61	1	USOF	USAF Academy	3 Jul 83
9.93	-0.6	Michael	Marsh	USA	4.8.67	1	MSR	Walnut	18 Apr 92
9.93	1.8	Patrick	Johnson	AUS	26.9.72	1		Mito	5 May 03
9.93	1.1	Ivory	Williams #	USA	2.5.85	1rA		Réthimno	20 Jul 09
9.93	0.4	Kemar	Bailey-Cole	JAM	10.1.92	2s2	WCh	Moskva	11 Aug 13
9.93	1.8	Kemarley	Brown	JAM	20.7.92	1		Walnut	17 May 14
9.93	0.4	Femi Seun	Ogunode ¶	QAT	15.5.91	1	AsiG	Incheon	28 Sep 14
9.94	0.2	Davidson	Ezinwa ¶	NGR	22.11.71	1	Gugl	Linz	4 Jul 94
9.94	-0.2	Bernard	Williams	USA	19.1.78	2	WCh	Edmonton	5 Aug 01
		(50)	100th man 10.00, 200th 10.07, 300th 10.11, 400th 10.15, 500th 10.17						
Doubtful wind reading									
9.91	-2.3	Davidson	Ezinwa ¶	NGR	22.11.71	1		Azusa	11 Apr 92
Low altitude best 9.94	0.1		Ogunkoya			1	AfCh	Dakar	19 Aug 98
Wind-assisted – performances to 9.78, performers listed to 9.90									
9.68	4.1	Tyson	Gay ¶	USA	9.8.82	1	NC/OT	Eugene	29 Jun 08
9.69A	5+	Obadele	Thompson	BAR	30.3.76	1		El Paso	13 Apr 96
9.72	2.1		Powell			1	Bisl	Oslo	4 Jun 10
9.74	w	Richard	Thompson	TTO	7.6.85	1		Clermont	31 May 14
9.75	3.4		Gay			1h1	NC	Eugene	25 Jun 09
9.75	2.6		Powell			1h2	DL	Doha	14 May 10
9.75	4.3	Darvis	Patton	USA	4.12.77	1rA	TexR	Austin	30 Mar 13
9.76A	6.1	Churandy	Martina	AHO	3.7.84	1		El Paso	13 May 06
9.76	2.2		Gay			1	GP	New York	2 Jun 07
9.76	2.7	Justin	Gatlin ¶	USA	10.2.82	1	Pre	Eugene	31 May 14
9.77	2.1		Bolt			1	GS	Ostrava	17 Jun 09
9.77	4.2	Trayvon	Bromell	USA	10.7.95	1	Big 12	Lubbock	18 May 14
9.78	5.2	Carl	Lewis	USA	1.7.61	1	NC/OT	Indianapolis	16 Jul 88
9.78	3.7	Maurice	Greene	USA	23.7.74	1	GP II	Stanford	31 May 04
9.79	5.3	Andre	Cason	USA	20.1.69	1h4	NC	Eugene	16 Jun 93
9.80	4.1	Walter	Dix	USA	31.1.86	2	NC/OT	Eugene	29 Jun 08
9.80	2.7	Michael	Rodgers	USA	24.4.85	2	Pre	Eugene	31 May 14
9.83	7.1	Leonard	Scott	USA	19.1.80	1r1	Sea Ray	Knoxville	9 Apr 99
9.83	2.2	Derrick	Atkins	BAH	5.1.84	2	GP	New York	2 Jun 07
9.84	5.4	Francis	Obikwelu	NGR/POR	22.11.78	1		Zaragoza	3 Jun 06
9.85	4.8	Dennis	Mitchell ¶	USA	20.2.66	2	NC	Eugene	17 Jun 93
9.85A	3.0	Frank	Fredericks	NAM	2.10.67	1		Nairobi	18 May 02
9.85	4.1	Travis	Padgett	USA	13.12.86	4	NC/OT	Eugene	29 Jun 08
9.85	3.6	Keston	Bledman	TTO	8.3.88	1rA		Clermont	2 Jun 12
9.85	3.2	Charles	Silmon	USA	4.7.91	1s1	NC	Des Moines	21 Jun 13
9.86	2.6	Shawn	Crawford ¶	USA	14.1.78	1	GP	Doha	14 May 04
9.86	3.6	Michael	Frater	JAM	6.10.82	2h4	NC	Kingston	23 Jun 11
9.86	3.2	Rakieem "Mookie"	Salaam	USA	5.4.90	2s1	NC	Des Moines	21 Jun 13
9.87	11.2	William	Snoddy	USA	6.12.57	1		Dallas	1 Apr 78
9.87	4.9	Calvin	Smith	USA	8.1.61	1s2	NC/OT	Indianapolis	16 Jul 88
9.87	2.4	Michael	Marsh	USA	4.8.67	1rA	MSR	Walnut	20 Apr 97
9.88	2.3	James	Sanford	USA	27.12.57	1		Los Angeles (Ww)	3 May 80
9.88	5.2	Albert	Robinson	USA	28.11.64	4	NC/OT	Indianapolis	16 Jul 88
9.88	4.9	Tim	Harden	USA	27.1.74	1	NC	New Orleans	20 Jun 98
9.88	4.5	Coby	Miller	USA	19.10.76	1		Auburn	1 Apr 00
9.88	3.6	Patrick	Johnson	AUS	26.9.72	1		Perth	8 Feb 03
9.88	3.0	Darrel	Brown	TTO	11.10.84	1	NC	Port of Spain	23 Jun 07
9.88	3.7	Ivory	Williams #	USA	2.5.85	1	TexR	Austin	3 Apr 10
9.89	4.2	Ray	Stewart	JAM	18.3.65	1s1	PAm	Indianapolis	9 Aug 87
9.89	2.7	Jimmy	Vicaut	FRA	27.2.92	3	Pre	Eugene	31 May 14
9.90	5.2	Joe	DeLoach	USA	5.6.67	5	NC/OT	Indianapolis	16 Jul 88
9.90	7.1	Kenny	Brokenburr	USA	29.10.68	2r1	Sea Ray	Knoxville	9 Apr 99
9.90A	7.8	Teddy	Williams	USA	3.7.88	1		El Paso	11 Apr 09
9.90	2.8	Lerone	Clarke	JAM	2.10.81	1		Clermont	11 Jun 11
9.90	4.2	Senoj-Jay	Givans	JAM	30.12.93	2	Big 12	Lubbock	18 May 14
9.90	w	Adam	Harris	GUY	21.7.87	2		Clermont	31 May 14
Rolling start: 9.89w	3.7	Patrick	Jarrett ¶	JAM	2.10.77	1	Pre	Eugene	27 May 01
Hand timing and three men at 9.7w									
9.7	1.9	Donovan	Powell ¶	JAM	31.10.71	1rA		Houston	19 May 95

MEN All-time

Mark	Wind	Name		Nat	Born	Pos	Meet	Venue	Date
9.7	1.9	Carl	Lewis	USA	1.7.61	2rA		Houston	19 May 95
9.7	1.9	Olapade	Adeniken	NGR	19.8.69	3rA		Houston	19 May 95
Drugs disqualification									
9.75	1.1		Gay ¶			(1)	NC	Des Moines	21 Jun 13
9.77	1.7	Justin	Gatlin ¶	USA	10.2.82	(1)	SGP	Doha	12 May 06
9.78	2.0	Tim	Montgomery ¶	USA	28.1.75	(1)	GPF	Paris (C)	14 Sep 02
9.79	1.1	Ben	Johnson ¶	CAN	30.12.61	(1)	OG	Seoul	24 Sep 88
9.87	2.0	Dwain	Chambers ¶	GBR	5.4.78	(2)	GPF	Paris (C)	14 Sep 02
9.7w ht	3.5		Johnson	CAN	30.12.61	(1)		Perth	24 Jan 87
9.75w	2.4		Gay			(1s2)	NC	Des Moines	21 Jun 13

200 METRES

Mark	Wind	Name		Nat	Born	Pos	Meet	Venue	Date
19.19	WR-0.3	Usain	Bolt	JAM	21.8.86	1	WCh	Berlin	20 Aug 09
19.26	0.7	Yohan	Blake	JAM	26.12.89	1	VD	Bruxelles	16 Sep 11
19.30	WR-0.9		Bolt			1	OG	Beijing	20 Aug 08
19.32	WR0.4	Michael	Johnson	USA	13.9.67	1	OG	Atlanta	1 Aug 96
19.32	0.4		Bolt			1	OG	London (OS)	9 Aug 12
19.40	0.8		Bolt			1	WCh	Daegu	3 Sep 11
19.44	0.4		Blake			2	OG	London (OS)	9 Aug 12
19.53	0.7	Walter	Dix	USA	31.1.86	2	VD	Bruxelles	16 Sep 11
19.54	0.0		Blake			1	VD	Bruxelles	7 Sep 12
19.56	-0.8		Bolt			1		Kingston	1 May 10
19.57	0.0		Bolt			1	VD	Bruxelles	4 Sep 09
19.58	1.3	Tyson	Gay ¶	USA	9.8.82	1	Reebok	New York	30 May 09
19.58	1.4		Bolt			1	Athl	Lausanne	23 Aug 12
19.59	-0.9		Bolt			1	Athl	Lausanne	7 Jul 09
19.62	-0.3		Gay			1	NC	Indianapolis	24 Jun 07
19.63	0.4	Xavier	Carter	USA	8.12.85	1	Athl	Lausanne	11 Jul 06
19.63	-0.9		Bolt			1	Athl	Lausanne	2 Sep 08
19.65	0.0	Wallace	Spearmon	USA	24.12.84	1		Daegu	28 Sep 06
19.66	WR1.7		M Johnson			1	NC	Atlanta	23 Jun 96
19.66	0.0		Bolt			1	WK	Zürich	30 Aug 12
19.66	0.0		Bolt			1	WCh	Moskva	17 Aug 13
19.67	-0.5		Bolt			1	GP	Athína	13 Jul 08
19.68	0.4	Frank	Fredericks	NAM	2.10.67	2	OG	Atlanta	1 Aug 96
19.68	-0.1		Gay			1	WAF	Stuttgart	10 Sep 06
19.68	-0.1		Bolt			1	WAF	Thessaloníki	13 Sep 09
19.68	-0.5	Justin	Gatlin ¶	USA	10.2.82	1	Herc	Monaco	18 Jul 14
19.69	0.9		Dix			1	NCAA-r	Gainesville	26 May 07
19.70	0.4		Gay			2	Athl	Lausanne	11 Jul 06
19.70	0.8		Dix			2	WCh	Daegu	3 Sep 11
19.71A	1.8		M Johnson			1rA		Pietersburg	18 Mar 00
19.71	0.0		Gatlin			1	VD	Bruxelles	5 Sep 14
		(31/9)							
19.72A	WR 1.8	Pietro	Mennea (10)	ITA	28.6.52	1	WUG	Ciudad de México	12 Sep 79
19.73	-0.2	Michael	Marsh	USA	4.8.67	1s1	OG	Barcelona	5 Aug 92
19.75	1.5	Carl	Lewis	USA	1.7.61	1	NC	Indianapolis	19 Jun 83
19.75	1.7	Joe	DeLoach	USA	5.6.67	1	OG	Seoul	28 Sep 88
19.77	0.7	Ato	Boldon	TTO	30.12.73	1rA		Stuttgart	13 Jul 97
19.79	1.2	Shawn	Crawford ¶	USA	14.1.78	1	OG	Athína	26 Aug 04
19.79	0.9	Warren	Weir	JAM	31.10.89	1	NC	Kingston	23 Jun 13
19.80	0.8	Christophe	Lemaitre	FRA	11.6.90	3	WCh	Daegu	3 Sep 11
19.81	-0.3	Alonso	Edward	PAN	8.12.89	2	WCh	Berlin	20 Aug 09
19.83A	WR 0.9	Tommie	Smith	USA	6.6.44	1	OG	Ciudad de México	16 Oct 68
19.84	1.7	Francis	Obikwelu	NGR/POR	22.11.78	1s2	WCh	Sevilla	25 Aug 99
		(20)							
19.85	-0.3	John	Capel ¶	USA	27.10.78	1	NC	Sacramento	23 Jul 00
19.85	-0.5	Konstadínos	Kedéris ¶	GRE	11.7.73	1	EC	München	9 Aug 02
19.85	1.4	Churandy	Martina	NED	3.7.84	2	Athl	Lausanne	23 Aug 12
19.85	0.0	Nickel	Ashmeade	JAM	4.7.90	2	WK	Zürich	30 Aug 12
19.86A	1.0	Don	Quarrie	JAM	25.2.51	1	PAm	Cali	3 Aug 71
19.86	1.6	Maurice	Greene	USA	23.7.74	2rA	DNG	Stockholm	7 Jul 97
19.86	1.5	Jason	Young	JAM	21.3.91	1	Spitzen	Luzern	17 Jul 12
19.86	1.6	Isiah	Young	USA	5.1.90	1	NC	Des Moines	23 Jun 13
19.87	0.8	Lorenzo	Daniel	USA	23.3.66	1	NCAA	Eugene	3 Jun 88
19.87A	1.8	John	Regis	GBR	13.10.66	1		Sestriere	31 Jul 94
		(30)							
19.87	1.2	Jeff	Williams	USA	31.12.65	1		Fresno	13 Apr 96
19.88	-0.3	Floyd	Heard	USA	24.3.66	2	NC	Sacramento	23 Jul 00
19.88	0.1	Joshua 'J.J'	Johnson	USA	10.5.76	1	VD	Bruxelles	24 Aug 01

Mark	Wind	Name		Nat	Born	Pos	Meet	Venue	Date
19.89	-0.8	Claudinei	da Silva	BRA	19.11.70	1	GPF	München	11 Sep 99
19.89	1.3	Jaysuma	Saidy Ndure	NOR	1.1.84	1	WAF	Stuttgart	23 Sep 07
19.90	1.3	Asafa	Powell	JAM	23.11.82	1	NC	Kingston	25 Jun 06
19.92A	WR1.9	John	Carlos	USA	5.6.45	1	FOT	Echo Summit	12 Sep 68
19.96	-0.9	Kirk	Baptiste	USA	20.6.63	2	OG	Los Angeles	8 Aug 84
19.96	0.4	Robson	da Silva	BRA	4.9.64	1	VD	Bruxelles	25 Aug 89
19.96	-0.3	Coby	Miller	USA	19.10.76	3	NC	Sacramento	23 Jul 00
		(40)							
19.96	-0.4	Isaac	Makwala	BOT	29.9.86	1		La Chaux-de-Fonds	6 Jul 14
19.97	-0.9	Obadele	Thompson	BAR	30.3.76	1	Super	Yokohama	9 Sep 00
19.97	0.0	Curtis	Mitchell	USA	11.3.89	1s1	WCh	Moskva	16 Aug 13
19.97	-0.6	Dedric	Dukes	USA	2.4.92	1	FlaR	Gainesville	4 Apr 14
19.98	1.7	Marcin	Urbas	POL	17.9.76	2s2	WCh	Sevilla	25 Aug 99
19.98	0.3	Jordan	Vaden ¶	USA	15.9.78	2	NC	Indianapolis	25 Jun 06
19.98	1.4	LaShawn	Merritt ¶	USA	27.6.86	2	adidas	Carson	20 May 07
19.98	-0.3	Steve	Mullings ¶	JAM	29.11.82	5	WCh	Berlin	20 Aug 09
19.99	0.6	Calvin	Smith	USA	8.1.61	1	WK	Zürich	24 Aug 83
19.98	-0.3	Adam	Gemili	GBR	6.10.93	1s3	WCh	Moskva	16 Aug 13
19.98	0.2	Rasheed	Dwyer	JAM	29.1.89	2	C.Cup	Marrakech	14 Sep 14
		(50)	100th man 20.13, 200th 20.27, 300th 20.34, 400th 20.40, 500th 20.44						

Wind-assisted 2 performances to 19.70, performers listed to 19.96

Mark	Wind	Name		Nat	Born	Pos	Meet	Venue	Date
19.61	>4.0	Leroy	Burrell	USA	21.2.67	1	SWC	College Station	19 May 90
19.70	2.7		Johnson			1s1	NC	Atlanta	22 Jun 96
19.73	3.3	Shawn	Crawford ¶	USA	14.1.78	1	NC	Eugene	28 Jun 09
19.80	3.2	LaShawn	Merritt ¶	USA	27.6.86	1		Greensboro	19 Apr 08
19.83	9.2	Bobby	Cruse	USA	20.3.78	1r2	Sea Ray	Knoxville	9 Apr 99
19.86	4.6	Roy	Martin	USA	25.12.66	1	SWC	Houston	18 May 86
19.90	3.8	Steve	Mullings ¶	JAM	29.11.82	1		Fort Worth	17 Apr 04
19.91	2.1	Dedric	Dukes	USA	2.4.92	1	NCAA	Eugene	14 Jun 14
19.91		James	Jett	USA	28.12.70	1		Morgantown	18 Apr 92
19.93	2.4	Sebastián	Keitel	CHI	14.2.73	1		São Leopoldo	26 Apr 98
19.94	4.0	James	Sanford	USA	27.12.57	1s1	NCAA	Austin	7 Jun 80
19.94	3.7	Chris	Nelloms	USA	14.8.71	1	Big 10	Minneapolis	23 May 92
19.94	2.3	Kevin	Little	USA	3.4.68	1s3	NC	Sacramento	17 Jun 95
19.95	3.4	Mike	Roberson	USA	25.3.56	1h3	NCAA	Austin	5 Jun 80
19.96	2.2	Rohsaan	Griffin	USA	21.2.74	1s1	NC	Eugene	26 Jun 99

Low altitude mark for athletes with lifetime bests at high altitude

19.94 0.3 Regis 2 WCh Stuttgart 20 Aug 93 19.96 0.0 Mennea 1 Barletta 17 Aug 80

Hand timing

Mark	Wind	Name		Nat	Born	Pos	Meet	Venue	Date
19.7A		James	Sanford	USA	27.12.57	1		El Paso	19 Apr 80
19.7A	0.2	Robson C.	da Silva	BRA	4.9.64	1	AmCp	Bogotá	13 Aug 89

300 METRES

In 300m races only, not including intermediate times in 400m races

Mark	Name		Nat	Born	Pos	Meet	Venue	Date
30.85A	Michael	Johnson	USA	13.9.67	1		Pretoria	24 Mar 00
30.97	Usain	Bolt	JAM	21.8.86	1	GS	Ostrava	27 May 10
31.30	LaShawn	Merritt	USA	27.6.86	1	Pre	Eugene	7 Jun 09
31.31		Merritt			1		Eugene	8 Aug 06
31.48	Danny	Everett	USA	1.11.66	1		Jerez de la Frontera	3 Sep 90
31.48	Roberto	Hernández	CUB	6.3.67	2		Jerez de la Frontera	3 Sep 90
31.56	Doug	Walker ¶	GBR	28.7.73	1		Gateshead	19 Jul 98
31.61	Anthuan	Maybank	USA	30.12.69	1		Durham	13 Jul 96
31.67	John	Regis	GBR	13.10.66	1	Vaux	Gateshead	17 Jul 92
31.70	Kirk	Baptiste	USA	20.6.63	1	Nike	London (CP)	18 Aug 84
31.72	Jeremy	Wariner (10)	USA	31.1.84	1	GS	Ostrava	12 Jun 08
31.73	Thomas	Jefferson	USA	8.6.62	1	DCG	London (CP)	22 Aug 87
31.74	Gabriel	Tiacoh	CIV	10.9.63	1		La Coruña	6 Aug 86

400 METRES

Mark	Name		Nat	Born	Pos	Meet	Venue	Date
43.18 WR	Michael	Johnson	USA	13.9.67	1	WCh	Sevilla	26 Aug 99
43.29 WR	Butch	Reynolds ¶	USA	8.6.64	1	WK	Zürich	17 Aug 88
43.39		Johnson			1	WCh	Göteborg	9 Aug 95
43.44		Johnson			1	NC	Atlanta	19 Jun 96
43.45	Jeremy	Wariner	USA	31.1.84	1	WCh	Osaka	31 Aug 07
43.49		Johnson			1	OG	Atlanta	29 Jul 96
43.50	Quincy	Watts	USA	19.6.70	1	OG	Barcelona	5 Aug 92
43.50		Wariner			1	DNG	Stockholm	7 Aug 07
43.62		Wariner			1rA	GGala	Roma	14 Jul 06
43.65		Johnson			1	WCh	Stuttgart	17 Aug 93
43.66		Johnson			1	NC	Sacramento	16 Jun 95
43.66		Johnson			1rA	Athl	Lausanne	3 Jul 96
43.68		Johnson			1	WK	Zürich	12 Aug 98

Mark	Wind	Name		Nat	Born	Pos	Meet	Venue	Date
43.68			Johnson			1	NC	Sacramento	16 Jul 00
43.71			Watts			1s2	OG	Barcelona	3 Aug 92
43.74			Johnson			1	NC	Eugene	19 Jun 93
43.74		LaShawn	Merritt ¶	USA	27.6.86	1	WCh	Moskva	13 Aug 13
43.74		Kirani	James	GRN	1.9.92	1	Athl	Lausanne	3 Jul 14
43.75			Johnson			1		Waco	19 Apr 97
43.75			Merritt			1	OG	Beijing	21 Aug 08
43.76			Johnson			1	GWG	Uniondale, NY	22 Jul 98
43.81		Danny	Everett	USA	1.11.66	1	NC/OT	New Orleans	26 Jun 92
43.82			Wariner			1	WK	Zürich	29 Aug 08
43.83			Watts			1	WK	Zürich	19 Aug 92
43.84			Johnson			1	OG	Sydney	25 Sep 00
43.86A	WR	Lee	Evans	USA	25.2.47	1	OG	Ciudad de México	18 Oct 68
43.86			Johnson			1	Bisl	Oslo	21 Jul 95
43.86			Wariner			1	Gaz	Saint-Denis	18 Jul 08
43.87		Steve	Lewis	USA	16.5.69	1	OG	Seoul	28 Sep 88
43.88			Johnson			1	WK	Zürich	16 Aug 95
		(30/9)							
43.97A		Larry	James (10)	USA	6.11.47	2	OG	Ciudad de México	18 Oct 68
44.01		Isaac	Makwala	BOT	29.9.86	1		La Chaux de Fonds	6 Jul 14
44.05		Angelo	Taylor	USA	29.12.78	1	NC	Indianapolis	23 Jun 07
44.09		Alvin	Harrison ¶	USA/DOM	20.1.74	3	NC	Atlanta	19 Jun 96
44.09		Jerome	Young ¶	USA	14.8.76	1	NC	New Orleans	21 Jun 98
44.10		Gary	Kikaya	COD	4.2.78	2	WAF	Stuttgart	9 Sep 06
44.13		Derek	Mills	USA	9.7.72	1	Pre	Eugene	4 Jun 95
44.14		Roberto	Hernández	CUB	6.3.67	2		Sevilla	30 May 90
44.15		Anthuan	Maybank	USA	30.12.69	1rB	Athl	Lausanne	3 Jul 96
44.16		Otis	Harris	USA	30.6.82	2	OG	Athína	23 Aug 04
44.17		Innocent	Egbunike	NGR	30.11.61	1rA	WK	Zürich	19 Aug 87
		(20)							
44.18		Samson	Kitur	KEN	25.2.66	2s2	OG	Barcelona	3 Aug 92
44.20A		Charles	Gitonga	KEN	5.10.71	1	NC	Nairobi	29 Jun 96
44.21		Ian	Morris	TTO	30.11.61	3s2	OG	Barcelona	3 Aug 92
44.26		Alberto	Juantorena	CUB	21.11.50	1	OG	Montreal	29 Jul 76
44.27		Alonzo	Babers	USA	31.10.61	1	OG	Los Angeles	8 Aug 84
44.27		Antonio	Pettigrew ¶	USA	3.11.67	1	NC	Houston	17 Jun 89
44.27		Darold	Williamson	USA	19.2.83	1s1	NCAA	Sacramento	10 Jun 05
44.28		Andrew	Valmon	USA	1.1.65	4	NC	Eugene	19 Jun 93
44.28		Tyree	Washington	USA	28.8.76	1		Los Angeles (ER)	12 May 01
44.29		Derrick	Brew	USA	28.12.77	1	SEC	Athens, GA	16 May 99
		(30)							
44.29		Sanderlei	Parrela	BRA	7.10.74	2	WCh	Sevilla	26 Aug 99
44.30		Gabriel	Tiacoh	CIV	10.9.63	1	NCAA	Indianapolis	7 Jun 86
44.30		Lamont	Smith	USA	11.12.72	4	NC	Atlanta	19 Jun 96
44.31		Alejandro	Cárdenas	MEX	4.10.74	3	WCh	Sevilla	26 Aug 99
44.33		Thomas	Schönlebe	GDR	6.8.65	1	WCh	Roma	3 Sep 87
44.34		Darnell	Hall	USA	26.9.71	1	Athl	Lausanne	5 Jul 95
44.35		Andrew	Rock	USA	23.1.82	2	WCh	Helsinki	12 Aug 05
44.36		Iwan	Thomas	GBR	5.1.74	1	NC	Birmingham	13 Jul 97
44.36		Deon	Lendore	TTO	28.10.92	1	SEC	Lexington	18 May 14
44.37		Roger	Black	GBR	31.3.66	2rA	Athl	Lausanne	3 Jul 96
		(40)							
44.37		Davis	Kamoga	UGA	17.7.68	2	WCh	Athína	5 Aug 97
44.37		Mark	Richardson	GBR	26.7.72	1	Bisl	Oslo	9 Jul 98
44.38		Darren	Clark	AUS	6.9.65	3s1	OG	Seoul	26 Sep 88
44.38		Wayde	van Niekerk	RSA	15.7.92	2	DL	New York	14 Jun 14
44.40		Fred	Newhouse	USA	8.11.48	2	OG	Montreal	29 Jul 76
44.40		Chris	Brown	BAH	15.10.78	2	Bisl	Oslo	6 Jun 08
44.40		Jermaine	Gonzales	JAM	26.11.84	1	Herc	Monaco	22 Jul 10
44.40		Tony	McQuay	USA	16.4.90	2	WCh	Moskva	13 Aug 13
44.41A		Ron	Freeman	USA	12.6.47	3	OG	Ciudad de México	18 Oct 68
44.43A		Ezra	Sambu	KEN	4.9.78	1	WCT	Nairobi	26 Jul 03
44.43		Jonathan	Borlée	BEL	22.2.88	1h3	OG	London (OS)	4 Aug 12
		(51)	100th man 44.63, 200th 44.88, 300th 45.08, 400th 45.26, 500th 45.38						
Drugs disqualification									
44.21		Antonio	Pettigrew ¶	USA	3.11.67	1		Nassau	26 May 99
Hand timing			** 440 yards time less 0.3 secs*						
44.1		Wayne	Collett	USA	20.10.49	1	OT	Eugene	9 Jul 72
44.2*		John	Smith	USA	5.8.50	1	AAU	Eugene	26 Jun 71
44.2		Fred	Newhouse	USA	8.11.48	1s1	OT	Eugene	7 Jul 72

Mark Wind	Name		Nat	Born	Pos	Meet	Venue	Date
							600 METRES	
1:12.81	Johnny	Gray	USA	19.6.60	1		Santa Monica	24 May 86
1:13.2 + ?	John	Kipkurgat	KEN	16.3.44	1		Pointe-à-Pierre	23 Mar 74
1:13.28	Duane	Solomon	USA	28.12.84	1		Burnaby	1 Jul 13
1:13.49	Joseph	Mutua	KEN	10.12.78	1		Liège (NX)	27 Aug 02
1:13.71	David	Rudisha	KEN	17.12.88	1	DL	Birmingham	24 Aug 14
1:13.80	Earl	Jones	USA	17.7.64	2		Santa Monica	24 May 86
1:13.9	Raidel	Acea	CUB	31.10.90	1		La Habana	20 Apr 13
							800 METRES	
1:40.91 WR	David	Rudisha	KEN	17.12.88	1	OG	London (OS)	9 Aug 12
1:41.01 WR		Rudisha			1rA		Rieti	29 Aug 10
1:41.09 WR		Rudisha			1	ISTAF	Berlin	22 Aug 10
1:41.11 WR	Wilson	Kipketer	DEN	12.12.70	1	ASV	Köln	24 Aug 97
1:41.24 WR		Kipketer			1rA	WK	Zürich	13 Aug 97
1:41.33		Rudisha			1		Rieti	10 Sep 11
1:41.51		Rudisha			1	NA	Heusden-Zolder	10 Jul 10
1:41.54		Rudisha			1	DL	Saint-Denis	6 Jul 12
1:41.73! WR	Sebastian	Coe	GBR	29.9.56	1		Firenze	10 Jun 81
1:41.73 WR		Kipketer			1rA	DNG	Stockholm	7 Jul 97
1:41.73	Nijel	Amos	BOT	15.3.94	2	OG	London (OS)	9 Aug 12
1:41.74		Rudisha			1	adidas	New York	9 Jun 12
1:41.77	Joaquim	Cruz	BRA	12.3.63	1	ASV	Köln	26 Aug 84
1:41.83		Kipketer			1	GP II	Rieti	1 Sep 96
1:42.01		Rudisha			1	GP	Rieti	6 Sep 09
1:42.04		Rudisha			1	Bisl	Oslo	4 Jun 10
1:42.12A		Rudisha			1	OT	Nairobi	23 Jun 12
1:42.17		Kipketer			1	TOTO	Tokyo	16 Sep 96
1:42.20		Kipketer			1	VD	Bruxelles	22 Aug 97
1:42.23	Abubaker	Kaki	SUD	21.6.89	2	Bisl	Oslo	4 Jun 10
1:42.27		Kipketer			1	VD	Bruxelles	3 Sep 99
1:42.28	Sammy	Koskei	KEN	14.5.61	2	ASV	Köln	26 Aug 84
1:42.32		Kipketer			1	GP II	Rieti	8 Sep 02
1:42.33 WR		Coe			1	Bisl	Oslo	5 Jul 79
1:42.34		Cruz			1r1	WK	Zürich	22 Aug 84
1:42.34	Wilfred	Bungei	KEN	24.7.80	2	GP II	Rieti	8 Sep 02
1:42.37	Mohammed	Aman	ETH	10.1.94	1	VD	Bruxelles	6 Sep 13
1:42.41		Cruz			1	VD	Bruxelles	24 Aug 84
1:42.45		Amos			1	Herc	Monaco	18 Jul 14
1:42.47	Yuriy	Borzakovskiy	RUS	12.4.81	1	VD	Bruxelles	24 Aug 01
	(30/10)		*! photo-electric cell time*					
1:42.53	Timothy	Kitum	KEN	20.11.94	3	OG	London (OS)	9 Aug 12
1:42.53	Pierre-Ambroise	Bosse	FRA	11.5.92	2	Herc	Monaco	18 Jul 14
1:42.55	André	Bucher	SUI	19.10.76	1rA	WK	Zürich	17 Aug 01
1:42.58	Vebjørn	Rodal	NOR	16.9.72	1	OG	Atlanta	31 Jul 96
1:42.60	Johnny	Gray	USA	19.6.60	2r1		Koblenz	28 Aug 85
1:42.62	Patrick	Ndururi	KEN	12.1.69	2rA	WK	Zürich	13 Aug 97
1:42.67	Alfred	Kirwa Yego	KEN	28.11.86	2	GP	Rieti	6 Sep 09
1:42.69	Hezekiél	Sepeng ¶	RSA	30.6.74	2	VD	Bruxelles	3 Sep 99
1:42.69	Japheth	Kimutai	KEN	20.12.78	3	VD	Bruxelles	3 Sep 99
1:42.79	Fred	Onyancha	KEN	25.12.69	3	OG	Atlanta	31 Jul 96
	(20)							
1:42.79	Youssef Saad	Kamel	KEN/BRN	29.3.83	2	Herc	Monaco	29 Jul 08
1:42.81	Jean-Patrick	Nduwimana	BDI	9.5.78	2rA	WK	Zürich	17 Aug 01
1:42.82	Duane	Solomon	USA	28.12.84	4	OG	London (OS)	9 Aug 12
1:42.84	Ferguson	Cheruiyot	KEN	30.11.89	4	Herc	Monaco	18 Jul 14
1:42.85	Norberto	Téllez	CUB	22.1.72	4	OG	Atlanta	31 Jul 96
1:42.86	Mbulaeni	Mulaudzi	RSA	8.9.80	3	GP	Rieti	6 Sep 09
1:42.88	Steve	Cram	GBR	14.10.60	1rA	WK	Zürich	21 Aug 85
1:42.91	William	Yiampoy	KEN	17.5.74	3	GP II	Rieti	8 Sep 02
1:42.95	Boaz	Lalang	KEN	8.2.89	2rA		Rieti	29 Aug 10
1:42.95	Nick	Symmonds	USA	30.12.83	5	OG	London (OS)	9 Aug 12
	(30)							
1:42.97	Peter	Elliott	GBR	9.10.62	1		Sevilla	30 May 90
1:42.98	Patrick	Konchellah	KEN	20.4.68	2	ASV	Köln	24 Aug 97
1:43.03	Kennedy/Kenneth	Kimwetich	KEN	1.1.73	2		Stuttgart	19 Jul 98
1:43.06	Billy	Konchellah	KEN	20.10.62	1	WCh	Roma	1 Sep 87
1:43.07	Yeimer	López	CUB	20.8.82	1		Jerez de la Frontera	24 Jun 08
1:43.08	José Luiz	Barbosa	BRA	27.5.61	1		Rieti	6 Sep 91

Mark	Wind	Name		Nat	Born	Pos	Meet	Venue	Date
1:43.09		Djabir	Saïd-Guerni	ALG	29.3.77	5	VD	Bruxelles	3 Sep 99
1:43.13		Abraham Kipchirchir	Rotich	KEN	26.6.93	1	Herc	Monaco	20 Jul 12
1:43.15		Mehdi	Baala	FRA	17.8.78	5	GP II	Rieti	8 Sep 02
1:43.15		Asbel	Kiprop	KEN	30.6.89	2	Herc	Monaco	22 Jul 11
		(40)							
1:43.16		Paul	Ereng	KEN	22.8.67	1	WK	Zürich	16 Aug 89
1:43.17		Benson	Koech	KEN	10.11.74	1		Rieti	28 Aug 94
1:43.20		Mark	Everett	USA	2.9.68	1rA	Gugl	Linz	9 Jul 97
1:43.22		Pawel	Czapiewski	POL	30.3.78	5rA	WK	Zürich	17 Aug 01
1:43.25		Amine	Laâlou ¶	MAR	13.5.82	1	GGala	Roma	14 Jul 06
1:43.26		Sammy	Langat (Kibet)	KEN	24.1.70	1rB	WK	Zürich	14 Aug 96
1:43.30		William	Tanui	KEN	22.2.64	2		Rieti	6 Sep 91
1:43.30		Adam	Kszczot	POL	2.9.89	2		Rieti	10 Sep 11
1:43.31		Nixon	Kiprotich	KEN	4.12.62	1		Rieti	6 Sep 92
1:43.33		Robert	Chirchir	KEN	26.11.72	3		Stuttgart	19 Jul 98
1:43.33		William	Chirchir	KEN	6.2.79	6	VD	Bruxelles	3 Sep 99
1:43.33		Joseph Mwengi	Mutua	KEN	10.12.78	1rA	WK	Zürich	16 Aug 02
		(52)	100th man 1:43.88, 200th 1:44.64, 300th 1:45.05, 400th 1:45.4, 500th 1:45.70						

1000 METRES

Mark	Wind	Name		Nat	Born	Pos	Meet	Venue	Date
2:11.96	WR	Noah	Ngeny	KEN	2.11.78	1	GP II	Rieti	5 Sep 99
2:12.18	WR	Sebastian	Coe	GBR	29.9.56	1	OsloG	Oslo	11 Jul 81
2:12.66			Ngeny			1	Nik	Nice	17 Jul 99
2:12.88		Steve	Cram	GBR	14.10.60	1		Gateshead	9 Aug 85
2:13.40	WR		Coe			1	Bisl	Oslo	1 Jul 80
2:13.56		Kennedy/Kenneth	Kimwetich	KEN	1.1.73	2	Nik	Nice	17 Jul 99
2:13.62		Abubaker	Kaki	SUD	21.6.89	1	Pre	Eugene	3 Jul 10
2:13.73		Noureddine	Morceli	ALG	28.2.70	1	BNP	Villeneuve d'Ascq	2 Jul 93
2:13.9	WR	Rick	Wohlhuter	USA	23.12.48	1	King	Oslo	30 Jul 74
2:13.96		Mehdi	Baala	FRA	17.8.78	1		Strasbourg	26 Jun 03
2:14.09		Joaquim	Cruz	BRA	12.3.63	1	Nik	Nice	20 Aug 84
2:14.28		Japheth	Kimutai	KEN	20.12.78	1	DNG	Stockholm	1 Aug 00
		(10)	50th man 2:15.83, 100th 2:16.64, 200th 2:17.58						

1500 METRES

Mark	Wind	Name		Nat	Born	Pos	Meet	Venue	Date
3:26.00	WR	Hicham	El Guerrouj	MAR	14.9.74	1	GGala	Roma	14 Jul 98
3:26.12			El Guerrouj			1	VD	Bruxelles	24 Aug 01
3:26.34		Bernard	Lagat	KEN/USA	12.12.74	2	VD	Bruxelles	24 Aug 01
3:26.45			El Guerrouj			1 rA	WK	Zürich	12 Aug 98
3:26.89			El Guerrouj			1	WK	Zürich	16 Aug 02
3:26.96			El Guerrouj			1	GP II	Rieti	8 Sep 02
3:27.21			El Guerrouj			1	WK	Zürich	11 Aug 00
3:27.34			El Guerrouj			1	Herc	Monaco	19 Jul 02
3:27.37	WR	Noureddine	Morceli	ALG	28.2.70	1	Nik	Nice	12 Jul 95
3:27.40			Lagat			1rA	WK	Zürich	6 Aug 04
3.27.52			Morceli			1	Herc	Monaco	25 Jul 95
3:27.64			El Guerrouj			2rA	WK	Zürich	6 Aug 04
3:27.64		Silas	Kiplagat	KEN	20.8.89	1	Herc	Monaco	18 Jul 14
3:27.65			El Guerrouj			1	WCh	Sevilla	24 Aug 99
3:27.72		Asbel	Kiprop	KEN	30.6.89	1	Herc	Monaco	19 Jul 13
3:27.91			Lagat			2	Herc	Monaco	19 Jul 02
3:28.12		Noah	Ngeny	KEN	2.11.78	2	WK	Zürich	11 Aug 00
3:28.21+			El Guerrouj			1	in 1M	Roma	7 Jul 99
3.28.37			Morceli			1	GPF	Monaco	9 Sep 95
3:28.37			El Guerrouj			1	Herc	Monaco	8 Aug 98
3:28.38			El Guerrouj			1	GP	Saint-Denis	6 Jul 01
3:28.40			El Guerrouj			1	VD	Bruxelles	5 Sep 03
3:28.45			Kiprop			2	Herc	Monaco	18 Jul 14
3:28.51			Lagat			3	WK	Zürich	11 Aug 00
3:28.57			El Guerrouj			1rA	WK	Zürich	11 Aug 99
3:28.6+			Ngeny			2	in 1M	Roma	7 Jul 99
3:28.73			Ngeny			2	WCh	Sevilla	24 Aug 99
3:28.81		Mohamed	Farah	GBR	23.3.83	2	Herc	Monaco	19 Jul 13
3:28.81		Ronald	Kwemoi	KEN	19.9.95	3	Herc	Monaco	18 Jul 14
3:28.84			Ngeny			1	GP	Paris (C)	21 Jul 99
		(30/8)							
3:28.95		Fermín	Cacho	ESP	16.2.69	2rA	WK	Zürich	13 Aug 97
3:28.98		Mehdi	Baala (10)	FRA	17.8.78	2	VD	Bruxelles	5 Sep 03
3:29.02		Daniel Kipchirchir	Komen	KEN	27.11.84	1	GGala	Roma	14 Jul 06
3:29.14		Rashid	Ramzi ¶	MAR/BRN	17.7.80	2	GGala	Roma	14 Jul 06

Mark	Wind	Name		Nat	Born	Pos	Meet	Venue	Date
3:29.18		Vénuste	Niyongabo	BDI	9.12.73	2	VD	Bruxelles	22 Aug 97
3:29.29		William	Chirchir	KEN	6.2.79	3	VD	Bruxelles	24 Aug 01
3:29.46	WR	Saïd	Aouita	MAR	2.11.59	1	ISTAF	Berlin	23 Aug 85
3:29.46		Daniel	Komen	KEN	17.5.76	1	Herc	Monaco	16 Aug 97
3:29.47		Augustine	Choge	KEN	21.1.87	1	ISTAF	Berlin	14 Jun 09
3:29.50		Caleb	Ndiku	KEN	9.10.92	3	Herc	Monaco	19 Jul 13
3:29.51		Ali	Saïdi-Sief ¶	ALG	15.3.78	1	Athl	Lausanne	4 Jul 01
3:29.53		Amine	Laâlou	MAR	13.5.82	2	Herc	Monaco	22 Jul 10
		(20)							
3:29.58		Ayanleh	Souleiman	DJI	3.12.92	4	Herc	Monaco	18 Jul 14
3:29.67	WR	Steve	Cram	GBR	14.10.60	1	Nik	Nice	16 Jul 85
3:29.77		Sydney	Maree	USA	9.9.56	1	ASV	Köln	25 Aug 85
3:29.77		Sebastian	Coe	GBR	29.9.56	1		Rieti	7 Sep 86
3:29.77		Nixon	Chepseba	KEN	12.12.90	2	Herc	Monaco	20 Jul 12
3:29.83		Abdelaati	Iguider	MAR	25.3.87	5	Herc	Monaco	14 Jul 14
3:29.91		Laban	Rotich	KEN	20.1.69	2rA	WK	Zürich	12 Aug 98
3:29.91		Aman	Wote	ETH	18.4.84	6	Herc	Monaco	14 Jul 14
3:29.91		Nick	Willis	NZL	25.4.83	7	Herc	Monaco	18 Jul 14
3:30.04		Timothy	Kiptanui	KEN	5.1.80	2	GP	Saint-Denis	23 Jul 04
		(30)							
3:30.07		Rui	Silva	POR	3.8.77	3	Herc	Monaco	19 Jul 02
3:30.18		John	Kibowen	KEN	21.4.69	3rA	WK	Zürich	12 Aug 98
3:30.20		Haron	Keitany	KEN	17.12.83	2	ISTAF	Berlin	14 Jun 09
3:30.24		Cornelius	Chirchir	KEN	5.6.83	4	Herc	Monaco	19 Jul 02
3:30.33		Ivan	Heshko	UKR	19.8.79	2	VD	Bruxelles	3 Sep 04
3:30.40		Taoufik	Makhloufi	ALG	29.4.88	4	DL	Doha	9 May 14
3:30.46		Alex	Kipchirchir	KEN	26.11.84	3	VD	Bruxelles	3 Sep 04
3:30.54		Alan	Webb	USA	13.1.83	1	Gaz	Saint-Denis	6 Jul 07
3:30.55		Abdi	Bile	SOM	28.12.62	1		Rieti	3 Sep 89
3:30.57		Reyes	Estévez	ESP	2.8.76	3	WCh	Sevilla	24 Aug 99
		(40)							
3:30.58		William	Tanui	KEN	22.2.64	3	Herc	Monaco	16 Aug 97
3:30.61		James	Magut	KEN	20.7.90	5	DL	Doha	9 May 14
3:30.67		Benjamin	Kipkurui	KEN	28.12.80	2	Herc	Monaco	20 Jul 01
3:30.72		Paul	Korir	KEN	15.7.77	3	VD	Bruxelles	5 Sep 03
3:30.77	WR	Steve	Ovett	GBR	9.10.55	1		Rieti	4 Sep 83
3:30.77		Bethwel	Birgen	KEN	6.8.88	4	Herc	Monaco	19 Jul 13
3:30.83		Fouad	Chouki ¶	FRA	15.10.78	3	WK	Zürich	15 Aug 03
3:30.90		Andrew	Wheating	USA	21.11.87	4	Herc	Monaco	22 Jul 10
3:30.92		José Luis	González	ESP	8.12.57	3	Nik	Nice	16 Jul 85
3:30.92		Tarek	Boukensa	ALG	19.11.81	1	GGala	Roma	13 Jul 07
		(50)	100th man 3:31.96, 200th 3:33.89, 300th 3:34.93, 400th 3:35.75, 500th 3:36.35						
Drugs disqualification: 3:30.77			Adil Kaouch ¶	MAR	1.1.79	1	GGala	Roma	13 Jul 07

1 MILE

Mark	Wind	Name		Nat	Born	Pos	Meet	Venue	Date
3:43.13	WR	Hicham	El Guerrouj	MAR	14.9.74	1	GGala	Roma	7 Jul 99
3:43.40		Noah	Ngeny	KEN	2.11.78	2	GGala	Roma	7 Jul 99
3:44.39	WR	Noureddine	Morceli	ALG	28.2.70	1		Rieti	5 Sep 93
3:44.60			El Guerrouj			1	Nik	Nice	16 Jul 98
3:44.90			El Guerrouj			1	Bisl	Oslo	4 Jul 97
3:44.95			El Guerrouj			1	GGala	Roma	29 Jun 01
3:45.19			Morceli			1	WK	Zürich	16 Aug 95
3:45.64			El Guerrouj			1	ISTAF	Berlin	26 Aug 97
3:45.96			El Guerrouj			1	BrGP	London (CP)	5 Aug 00
3:46.24			El Guerrouj			1	Bisl	Oslo	28 Jul 00
3:46.32	WR	Steve	Cram	GBR	14.10.60	1	Bisl	Oslo	27 Jul 85
3:46.38		Daniel	Komen	KEN	17.5.76	2	ISTAF	Berlin	26 Aug 97
3:46.70		Vénuste	Niyongabo	BDI	9.12.73	3	ISTAF	Berlin	26 Aug 97
3:46.76		Saïd	Aouita	MAR	2.11.59	1	WG	Helsinki	2 Jul 87
3:46.78			Morceli			1	ISTAF	Berlin	27 Aug 93
3:46.91		Alan	Webb	USA	13.1.83	1		Brasschaat	21 Jul 07
3:46.92			Aouita			1	WK	Zürich	21 Aug 85
3:47.10			El Guerrouj			1	BrGP	London (CP)	7 Aug 99
3:47.28		Bernard	Lagat	KEN/USA	12.12.74	2	GGala	Roma	29 Jun 01
3:47.30			Morceli			1	VD	Bruxelles	3 Sep 93
3:47.32		Ayanleh	Souleiman (10)	DJI	3.12.92	1	Pre	Eugene	31 May 14
3:47.33	WR	Sebastian	Coe	GBR	29.9.56	1	VD	Bruxelles	28 Aug 81
		(22/11)							
3:47.65		Laban	Rotich	KEN	20.1.69	2	Bisl	Oslo	4 Jul 97
3:47.69		Steve	Scott	USA	5.5.56	1	OsloG	Oslo	7 Jul 82

Mark	Wind	Name		Nat	Born	Pos	Meet	Venue	Date
3:47.79		José Luis	González	ESP	8.12.57	2	Bisl	Oslo	27 Jul 85
3:47.88		John	Kibowen	KEN	21.4.69	3	Bisl	Oslo	4 Jul 97
3:47.88		Silas	Kiplagat	KEN	20.8.89	2	Pre	Eugene	31 May 14
3:47.94		William	Chirchir	KEN	6.2.79	2	Bisl	Oslo	28 Jul 00
3:47.97		Daham Najim	Bashir	KEN/QAT	8.11.78	1	Bisl	Oslo	29 Jul 05
3:48.17		Paul	Korir	KEN	15.7.77	1	GP	London (CP)	8 Aug 03
3:48.23		Ali	Saïdi-Sief ¶	ALG	15.3.78	1	Bisl	Oslo	13 Jul 01
		(20)							
3:48.28		Daniel Kipchirchir	Komen	KEN	27.11.84	1	Pre	Eugene	10 Jun 07
3:48.38		Andrés Manuel	Díaz	ESP	12.7.69	3	GGala	Roma	29 Jun 01
3:48.40	WR	Steve	Ovett	GBR	9.10.55	1	R-W	Koblenz	26 Aug 81
3:48.50		Asbel	Kiprop	KEN	30.6.89	1	Pre	Eugene	7 Jun 09
3:48.60		Aman	Wote	ETH	18.4.84	3	Pre	Eugene	31 May 14
3:48.78		Haron	Keitany	KEN	17.12.83	2	Pre	Eugene	7 Jun 09
3:48.80		William	Kemei	KEN	22.2.69	1	ISTAF	Berlin	21 Aug 92
3:48.83		Sydney	Maree	USA	9.9.56	1		Rieti	9 Sep 81
3:48.95		Deresse	Mekonnen	ETH	20.10.87	1	Bisl	Oslo	3 Jul 09
3:48.98		Craig	Mottram	AUS	18.6.80	5	Bisl	Oslo	29 Jul 05
		(30)							
3:49.08		John	Walker	NZL	12.1.52	2	OsloG	Oslo	7 Jul 82
3:49.09		Abdelaati	Iguider	MAR	25.3.87	4	Pre	Eugene	31 May 14
3:49.20		Peter	Elliott	GBR	9.10.62	2	Bisl	Oslo	2 Jul 88
3:49.22		Jens-Peter	Herold	GDR	2.6.65	3	Bisl	Oslo	2 Jul 88
3:49.29		William	Biwott/Özbilen	KEN/TUR	5.3.90	2	Bisl	Oslo	3 Jul 09
3:49.31		Joe	Falcon	USA	23.6.66	1	Bisl	Oslo	14 Jul 90
3:49.34		David	Moorcroft	GBR	10.4.53	3	Bisl	Oslo	26 Jun 82
3:49.34		Benjamin	Kipkurui	KEN	28.12.80	3	VD	Bruxelles	25 Aug 00
3:49.38		Andrew	Baddeley	GBR	20.6.82	1	Bisl	Oslo	6 Jun 08
3:49.40		Abdi	Bile	SOM	28.12.62	4	Bisl	Oslo	2 Jul 88
		(40)							
3:49.43		James	Magut	KEN	20.7.90	5	Pre	Eugene	31 May 14
3:49.45		Mike	Boit	KEN	6.1.49	2	VD	Bruxelles	28 Aug 81
3:49.50		Rui	Silva	POR	3.8.77	3	GGala	Roma	12 Jul 02
3:49.56		Fermín	Cacho	ESP	16.2.69	2	Bisl	Oslo	5 Jul 96
3:49.56		Collins	Cheboi	KEN	25.9.87	6	Pre	Eugene	31 May 14
3:49.60		José Antonio	Redolat	ESP	17.2.76	4	GGala	Roma	29 Jun 01
3:49.70		Mekonnen	Gebremedhin	ETH	11.10.88	4	Pre	Eugene	4 Jun 11
3:49.75		Leonard	Mucheru	KEN/BRN	13.6.78	5	GGala	Roma	29 Jun 01
3:49.77		Ray	Flynn	IRL	22.1.57	3	OsloG	Oslo	7 Jul 82
3:49.77		Wilfred	Kirochi	KEN	12.12.69	2	Bisl	Oslo	6 Jul 91
3:49.77		Caleb	Ndiku	KEN	9.10.92	5	Pre	Eugene	4 Jun 11
		(51)	100th 3:51.05, 200th 3:53.29, 300th 3:54.86						

2000 METRES

Mark	Wind	Name		Nat	Born	Pos	Meet	Venue	Date
4:44.79	WR	Hicham	El Guerrouj	MAR	14.9.74	1	ISTAF	Berlin	7 Sep 99
4:46.88		Ali	Saïdi-Sief ¶	ALG	15.3.78	1		Strasbourg	19 Jun 01
4:47.88	WR	Noureddine	Morceli	ALG	28.2.70	1		Paris (JB)	3 Jul 95
4:48.36			El Guerrouj			1		Gateshead	19 Jul 98
4:48.69		Vénuste	Niyongabo	BDI	9.12.73	1	Nik	Nice	12 Jul 95
4:48.74		John	Kibowen	KEN	21.4.69	1		Hechtel	1 Aug 98
4:49.00			Niyongabo			1		Rieti	3 Sep 97
4:49.55			Morceli			1	Nik	Nice	10 Jul 96
4:50.08		Noah	Ngeny	KEN	2.11.78	1	DNG	Stockholm	30 Jul 99
4:50.76		Craig	Mottram	AUS	18.6.80	1		Melbourne (OP)	9 Mar 06
4:50.81	WR	Saïd	Aouita	MAR	2.11.59	1	BNP	Paris (JB)	16 Jul 87
4:51.30		Daniel	Komen	KEN	17.5.76	1		Milano	5 Jun 98
4:51.39	WR	Steve	Cram (10)	GBR	14.10.60	1	BGP	Budapest	4 Aug 85
Indoors									
4:49.99		Kenenisa	Bekele	ETH	13.6.82	1		Birmingham	17 Feb 07

3000 METRES

Mark	Wind	Name		Nat	Born	Pos	Meet	Venue	Date
7:20.67	WR	Daniel	Komen	KEN	17.5.76	1		Rieti	1 Sep 96
7:23.09		Hicham	El Guerrouj	MAR	14.9.74	1	VD	Bruxelles	3 Sep 99
7:25.02		Ali	Saïdi-Sief ¶	ALG	15.3.78	1	Herc	Monaco	18 Aug 00
7:25.09		Haile	Gebrselassie	ETH	18.4.73	1	VD	Bruxelles	28 Aug 98
7:25.11	WR	Noureddine	Morceli	ALG	28.2.70	1	Herc	Monaco	2 Aug 94
7:25.16			Komen			1	Herc	Monaco	10 Aug 96
7:25.54			Gebrselassie			1	Herc	Monaco	8 Aug 98
7:25.79		Kenenisa	Bekele	ETH	13.6.82	1	DNG	Stockholm	7 Aug 07
7:25.87			Komen			1	VD	Bruxelles	23 Aug 96
7:26.02			Gebrselassie			1	VD	Bruxelles	22 Aug 97

Mark Wind	Name		Nat	Born	Pos	Meet	Venue	Date
7:26.03		Gebrselassie			1	GP II	Helsinki	10 Jun 99
7:26.5 e		Komen			1	in 2M	Sydney	28 Feb 98
7:26.62	Mohammed	Mourhit ¶	BEL	10.10.70	2	Herc	Monaco	18 Aug 00
7:26.69		K Bekele			1	BrGP	Sheffield	15 Jul 07
7:27.18	Moses	Kiptanui	KEN	1.10.70	1	Herc	Monaco	25 Jul 95
7:27.26	Yenew	Alamirew	ETH	27.5.90	1	DL	Doha	6 May 11
7:27.3+		Komen			1	in 2M	Hechtel	19 Jul 97
7:27.42		Gebrselassie			1	Bisl	Oslo	9 Jul 98
7:27.50		Morceli			1	VD	Bruxelles	25 Aug 95
7:27.55	Edwin	Soi (10)	KEN	3.3.86	2	DL	Doha	6 May 11
7:27.59	Luke	Kipkosgei	KEN	27.11.75	2	Herc	Monaco	8 Aug 98
7:27.66	Eliud	Kipchoge	KEN	5.11.84	3	DL	Doha	6 May 11
7:27.67		Saïdi-Sief			1	Gaz	Saint-Denis	23 Jun 00
7:27.72		Kipchoge			1	VD	Bruxelles	3 Sep 04
7:27.75	Thomas	Nyariki	KEN	27.9.71	2	Herc	Monaco	10 Aug 96
7.28.04		Kiptanui			1	ASV	Köln	18 Aug 95
7:28.28		Kipkosgei			2	Bisl	Oslo	9 Jul 98
7:28.28	James	Kwalia	KEN/QAT	12.6.84	2	VD	Bruxelles	3 Sep 04
7:28.37		Kipchoge			1	SGP	Doha	8 May 09
7:28.41	Paul	Bitok	KEN	26.6.70	3	Herc	Monaco	10 Aug 96
	(30/15)							
7:28.45	Assefa	Mezegebu	ETH	19.6.78	3	Herc	Monaco	8 Aug 98
7:28.67	Benjamin	Limo	KEN	23.8.74	1	Herc	Monaco	4 Aug 99
7:28.70	Paul	Tergat	KEN	17.6.69	4	Herc	Monaco	10 Aug 96
7:28.70	Tariku	Bekele	ETH	21.1.87	1		Rieti	29 Aug 10
7:28.72	Isaac K.	Songok	KEN	25.4.84	1	GP	Rieti	27 Aug 06
	(20)							
7:28.76	Augustine	Choge	KEN	21.1.87	4	DL	Doha	6 May 11
7:28.93	Salah	Hissou	MAR	16.1.72	2	Herc	Monaco	4 Aug 99
7:28.94	Brahim	Lahlafi	FRA/MAR	15.4.68	3	Herc	Monaco	4 Aug 99
7:29.00	Bernard	Lagat	USA	12.12.74	2		Rieti	29 Aug 10
7:29.09	John	Kibowen	KEN	21.4.69	3	Bisl	Oslo	9 Jul 98
7:29.34	Isaac	Viciosa	ESP	26.12.69	4	Bisl	Oslo	9 Jul 98
7:29.45 WR	Saïd	Aouita	MAR	2.11.59	1	ASV	Köln	20 Aug 89
7:29.92	Sileshi	Sihine	ETH	29.1.83	1	GP	Rieti	28 Aug 05
7:30.09	Ismaïl	Sghyr	MAR/FRA	16.3.72	2	Herc	Monaco	25 Jul 95
7:30.09	Thomas	Longosiwa	KEN	14.1.82	2	SGP	Doha	8 May 09
	(30)							
7:30.15	Vincent	Chepkok	KEN	5.7.88	5	DL	Doha	6 May 11
7:30.36	Mark	Carroll	IRL	15.1.72	5	Herc	Monaco	4 Aug 99
7:30.36	Hagos	Gebrhiwet	ETH	11.5.94	1	DL	Doha	10 May 13
7:30.43	Isiah	Koech	KEN	19.12.93	1	DNG	Stockholm	17 Aug 12
7:30.50	Dieter	Baumann ¶	GER	9.2.65	6	Herc	Monaco	8 Aug 98
7:30.53	El Hassan	Lahssini	MAR/FRA	1.1.75	6	Herc	Monaco	10 Aug 96
7:30.53	Hailu	Mekonnen	ETH	4.4.80	1	VD	Bruxelles	24 Aug 01
7:30.62	Boniface	Songok	KEN	25.12.80	3	VD	Bruxelles	3 Sep 04
7:30.76	Jamal Bilal	Salem	KEN/QAT	12.9.78	4	SGP	Doha	13 May 05
7:30.78	Mustapha	Essaïd	FRA	20.1.70	7	Herc	Monaco	8 Aug 98
	(40)							
7:30.84	Bob	Kennedy	USA	18.8.70	8	Herc	Monaco	8 Aug 98
7:30.95	Moses	Kipsiro	UGA	2.9.86	1	Herc	Monaco	28 Jul 09
7:30.99	Khalid	Boulami	MAR	7.8.69	1	Nik	Nice	16 Jul 97
7:30.99	Caleb	Ndiku	KEN	9.10.92	2	DNG	Stockholm	17 Aug 12
7:31.13	Julius	Gitahi	KEN	29.4.78	6	Bisl	Oslo	9 Jul 98
7:31.14	William	Kalya	KEN	4.8.74	3	Herc	Monaco	16 Aug 97
7:31.20	Joseph	Kiplimo	KEN	20.7.88	1	GP	Rieti	6 Sep 09
7:31.41	Sammy Alex	Mutahi	KEN	1.6.89	2	GP	Rieti	6 Sep 09
7:31.41	Daniel Kipchirchir	Komen	KEN	27.11.84	6	DL	Doha	6 May 11
7:31.59	Manuel	Pancorbo	ESP	7.7.66	7	Bisl	Oslo	9 Jul 98
	(50)	100th man 7:35.1, 200th man 7:39.41, 300th 7:42.02, 400th 7:43.82, 500th 7:45.43						
Indoors								
7:24.90		Komen			1		Budapest	6 Feb 98
7:26.15		Gebrselassie			1		Karlsruhe	25 Jan 98
7:26.80		Gebrselassie			1		Karlsruhe	24 Jan 99
7:27.80		Alamirew			1	Spark	Stuttgart	5 Feb 11
7:27.93		Komen			1	Spark	Stuttgart	1 Feb 98
7:28.00	Augustine	Choge	KEN	21.1.87	2	Spark	Stuttgart	5 Feb 11
7:30.16	Galen	Rupp	USA	8.5.86	1		Stockholm	21 Feb 13

2 MILES

Mark	Wind	Name		Nat	Born	Pos	Meet	Venue	Date
7:58.61	WR	Daniel	Komen	KEN	17.5.76	1		Hechtel	19 Jul 97
7:58.91			Komen			1		Sydney	28 Feb 98
8:01.08	WR	Haile	Gebrselassie	ETH	18.4.73	1	APM	Hengelo	31 May 97
8:01.72			Gebrselassie			1	BrGP	London (CP)	7 Aug 99
8:01.86			Gebrselassie			1	APM	Hengelo	30 May 99
8:03.50		Craig	Mottram	AUS	18.6.80	1	Pre	Eugene	10 Jun 07
8:03.54	WR		Komen			1		Lappeenranta	14 Jul 96
8:04.83		Tariku	Bekele	ETH	21.1.87	2	Pre	Eugene	10 Jun 07
Indoors									
8:04.35		Kenenisa	Bekele	ETH	13.6.82	1	GP	Birmingham	16 Feb 08
8:04.69			Gebrselassie			1	GP	Birmingham	21 Feb 03
8:06.48		Paul Kipsiele	Koech	KEN	10.11.81	2	GP	Birmingham	16 Feb 08
8:06.61		Hicham	El Guerrouj	MAR	14.9.74	1		Liévin	23 Feb 03

5000 METRES

Mark	Wind	Name		Nat	Born	Pos	Meet	Venue	Date
12:37.35	WR	Kenenisa	Bekele	ETH	13.6.82	1	FBK	Hengelo	31 May 04
12:39.36	WR	Haile	Gebrselassie	ETH	18.4.73	1	GP II	Helsinki	13 Jun 98
12:39.74	WR	Daniel	Komen	KEN	17.5.76	1	VD	Bruxelles	22 Aug 97
12:40.18			K Bekele			1	Gaz	Saint-Denis	1 Jul 05
12:41.86	WR		Gebrselassie			1	WK	Zürich	13 Aug 97
12:44.39	WR		Gebrselassie			1	WK	Zürich	16 Aug 95
12:44.90			Komen			2	WK	Zürich	13 Aug 97
12:45.09			Komen			1	WK	Zürich	14 Aug 96
12:46.53		Eliud	Kipchoge	KEN	5.11.84	1	GGala	Roma	2 Jul 04
12:46.81		Dejen	Gebremeskel	ETH	24.11.89	1	DL	Saint-Denis	6 Jul 12
12:47.04		Sileshi	Sihine	ETH	29.9.83	2	GGala	Roma	2 Jul 04
12:47.53		Hagos	Gebrhiwet	ETH	11.5.94	2	DL	Saint-Denis	6 Jul 12
12:48.09			K Bekele			1	VD	Bruxelles	25 Aug 06
12:48.25			K Bekele			1	WK	Zürich	18 Aug 06
12:48.64		Isiah	Koech	KEN	19.12.93	3	DL	Saint-Denis	6 Jul 12
12:48.66		Isaac K.	Songok	KEN	25.4.84	2	WK	Zürich	18 Aug 06
12:48.77		Yenew	Alamirew (10)	ETH	27.5.90	4	DL	Saint-Denis	6 Jul 12
12:48.81		Stephen	Cherono/Shaheen	KEN/QAT	15.10.82	1	GS	Ostrava	12 Jun 03
12:48.98			Komen			1	GGala	Roma	5 Jun 97
12:49.04		Thomas	Longosiwa	KEN	14.1.82	5	DL	Saint-Denis	6 Jul 12
12:49.28		Brahim	Lahlafi	MAR	15.4.68	1	VD	Bruxelles	25 Aug 00
12:49.50		John	Kipkoech	KEN	29.12.91	6	DL	Saint-Denis	6 Jul 12
12:49.53			K Bekele			1	Aragón	Zaragoza	28 Jul 07
12:49.64			Gebrselassie			1	WK	Zürich	11 Aug 99
12:49.71		Mohammed	Mourhit ¶	BEL	10.10.70	2	VD	Bruxelles	25 Aug 00
12:49.87		Paul	Tergat	KEN	17.6.69	3	WK	Zürich	13 Aug 97
12:50.16			Sihine			1	VD	Bruxelles	14 Sep 07
12:50.18			K Bekele			1	WK	Zürich	29 Aug 08
12:50.22			Kipchoge			1	VD	Bruxelles	26 Aug 05
12:50.24		Hicham	El Guerrouj	MAR	14.9.74	2	GS	Ostrava	12 Jun 03
		(30/17)							
12:50.25		Abderrahim	Goumri ¶	MAR	21.5.76	2	VD	Bruxelles	26 Aug 05
12:50.55		Moses	Masai	KEN	1.6.86	1	ISTAF	Berlin	1 Jun 08
12:50.72		Moses	Kipsiro	UGA	2.9.86	3	VD	Bruxelles	14 Sep 07
		(20)							
12:50.80		Salah	Hissou	MAR	16.1.72	1	GGala	Roma	5 Jun 96
12:50.86		Ali	Saïdi-Sief ¶	ALG	15.3.78	1	GGala	Roma	30 Jun 00
12:51.00		Joseph	Ebuya	KEN	20.6.87	4	VD	Bruxelles	14 Sep 07
12:51.34		Edwin	Soi	KEN	3.3.86	1	Herc	Monaco	19 Jul 13
12:51.45		Vincent	Chepkok	KEN	5.7.88	2	DL	Doha	14 May 10
12:51.96		Albert	Rop	KEN/BRN	17.7.92	2	Herc	Monaco	19 Jul 13
12:52.33		Sammy	Kipketer	KEN	29.9.81	2	Bisl	Oslo	27 Jun 03
12:52.45		Tariku	Bekele	ETH	21.1.87	2	ISTAF	Berlin	1 Jun 08
12:52.80		Gebre-egziabher	Gebremariam	ETH	10.9.84	3	GGala	Roma	8 Jul 05
12:52.99		Abraham	Chebii	KEN	23.12.79	4	Bisl	Oslo	27 Jun 03
		(30)							
12:53.11		Mohamed	Farah	GBR	23.3.83	1	Herc	Monaco	22 Jul 11
12:53.41		Khalid	Boulami	MAR	7.8.69	4	WK	Zürich	13 Aug 97
12:53.46		Mark	Kiptoo	KEN	21.6.76	1	DNG	Stockholm	6 Aug 10
12:53.58		Imane	Merga	ETH	15.10.88	3	DNG	Stockholm	6 Aug 10
12:53.60		Bernard	Lagat	USA	12.12.74	2	Herc	Monaco	22 Jul 11
12:53.66		Augustine	Choge	KEN	21.1.87	4	GGala	Roma	8 Jul 05
12:53.72		Philip	Mosima	KEN	2.1.77	2	GGala	Roma	5 Jun 96

Mark	Wind	Name		Nat	Born	Pos	Meet	Venue	Date
12:53.84		Assefa	Mezegebu	ETH	19.6.78	1	VD	Bruxelles	28 Aug 98
12:54.07		John	Kibowen	KEN	21.4.69	4	WCh	Saint-Denis	31 Aug 03
12:54.15		Dejene	Berhanu	ETH	12.12.80	3	GGala	Roma	2 Jul 04
		(40)							
12:54.19		Abreham	Cherkos	ETH	23.9.89	5	GGala	Roma	14 Jul 06
12:54.46		Moses	Mosop	KEN	17.7.85	3	Gaz	Saint-Denis	8 Jul 06
12:54.58		James	Kwalia	KEN/QAT	12.6.84	5	Bisl	Oslo	27 Jun 03
12:54.70		Dieter	Baumann ¶	GER	9.2.65	5	WK	Zürich	13 Aug 97
12:54.83		Muktar	Edris	ETH	14.1.94	1	DNG	Stockholm	21 Aug 14
12:54.85		Moses	Kiptanui	KEN	1.10.70	3	GGala	Roma	5 Jun 96
12:54.99		Benjamin	Limo	KEN	23.8.74	3	Gaz	Saint-Denis	4 Jul 03
12:55.06		Lucas	Rotich	KEN	16.4.90	4	Bisl	Oslo	4 Jun 10
12:55.52		Hicham	Bellani	MAR	15.9.79	7	GGala	Roma	14 Jul 06
12:55.53		Chris	Solinsky	USA	5.12.84	5	DNG	Stockholm	6 Aug 10
		(50)	100th man 13:01.15, 200th 13:09.50, 300th 13:13.02, 400th 13:16.73, 500th 13:19.04						
Indoors: 12:49.60			K Bekele			1		Birmingham	20 Feb 04

10,000 METRES

Mark	Wind	Name		Nat	Born	Pos	Meet	Venue	Date
26:17.53	WR	Kenenisa	Bekele	ETH	13.6.82	1	VD	Bruxelles	26 Aug 05
26:20.31	WR		K Bekele			1	GS	Ostrava	8 Jun 04
26:22.75	WR	Haile	Gebrselassie	ETH	18.4.73	1	APM	Hengelo	1 Jun 98
26:25.97			K Bekele			1	Pre	Eugene	8 Jun 08
26:27.85	WR	Paul	Tergat	KEN	17.6.69	1	VD	Bruxelles	22 Aug 97
26:28.72			K Bekele			1	FBK	Hengelo	29 May 05
26:29.22			Gebrselassie			1	VD	Bruxelles	5 Sep 03
26:30.03		Nicholas	Kemboi	KEN/QAT	25.11.83	2	VD	Bruxelles	5 Sep 03
26:30.74		Abebe	Dinkesa	ETH	6.3.84	2	FBK	Hengelo	29 May 05
26:31.32	WR		Gebrselassie			1	Bisl	Oslo	4 Jul 97
26:35.63		Micah	Kogo	KEN	3.6.86	1	VD	Bruxelles	25 Aug 06
26:36.26		Paul	Koech	KEN	25.6.69	2	VD	Bruxelles	22 Aug 97
26:37.25		Zersenay	Tadese	ERI	8.2.82	2	VD	Bruxelles	25 Aug 06
26:38.08	WR	Salah	Hissou	MAR	16.1.72	1	VD	Bruxelles	23 Aug 96
26:38.76		Abdullah Ahmad	Hassan (10)	QAT	4.4.81	3	VD	Bruxelles	5 Sep 03
		(Formerly Albert Chepkurui KEN)							
26:39.69		Sileshi	Sihine	ETH	29.9.83	1	FBK	Hengelo	31 May 04
26:39.77		Boniface	Kiprop	UGA	12.10.85	2	VD	Bruxelles	26 Aug 05
26:41.58			Gebrselassie			2	FBK	Hengelo	31 May 04
26:41.75		Samuel	Wanjiru	KEN	10.11.86	3	VD	Bruxelles	26 Aug 05
26:41.95			Kiprop			3	VD	Bruxelles	25 Aug 06
26:43.16			K Bekele			1	VD	Bruxelles	16 Sep 11
26:43.53	WR		Gebrselassie			1	APM	Hengelo	5 Jun 95
26:43.98		Lucas	Rotich	KEN	16.4.90	2	VD	Bruxelles	16 Sep 11
26:44.36		Galen	Rupp	USA	8.5.86	1	Pre	Eugene	30 May 14
26:46.19			K Bekele			1	VD	Bruxelles	14 Sep 07
26:46.31			K Bekele			1	WCh	Berlin	17 Aug 09
26:46.44			Tergat			1	VD	Bruxelles	28 Aug 98
26:46.57		Mohamed	Farah	GBR	23.3.83	1	Pre	Eugene	3 Jun 11
26:47.89			Koech			2	VD	Bruxelles	28 Aug 98
26:48.00			Rupp			3	VD	Bruxelles	16 Sep 11
		(30/16)							
26:48.35		Imane	Merga	ETH	15.10.88	2	Pre	Eugene	3 Jun 11
26:48.99		Josphat	Bett	KEN	12.6.90	3	Pre	Eugene	3 Jun 11
26:49.02		Eliud	Kipchoge	KEN	5.11.84	2	FBK	Hengelo	26 May 07
26:49.20		Moses	Masai	KEN	1.6.86	2	VD	Bruxelles	14 Sep 07
		(20)							
26:49.38		Sammy	Kipketer	KEN	29.9.81	1	VD	Bruxelles	30 Aug 02
26:49.41		Paul	Tanui	KEN	22.12.90	2	Pre	Eugene	30 May 14
26:49.55		Moses	Mosop	KEN	17.7.85	3	FBK	Hengelo	26 May 07
26:49.90		Assefa	Mezegebu	ETH	19.6.78	2	VD	Bruxelles	30 Aug 02
26:50.20		Richard	Limo	KEN	18.11.80	3	VD	Bruxelles	30 Aug 02
26:51.02		Dejen	Gebremeskel	ETH	24.11.89	1		Sollentuna	27 Jun 13
26:51.16		Emmanuel	Bett	KEN	30.3.83	1	VD	Bruxelles	7 Sep 12
26:51.49		Charles	Kamathi	KEN	18.5.78	1	VD	Bruxelles	3 Sep 99
26:51.68		Vincent	Chepkok	KEN	5.7.88	2	VD	Bruxelles	7 Sep 12
26:52.23	WR	William	Sigei	KEN	14.10.69	1	Bisl	Oslo	22 Jul 94
		(30)							
26:52.30		Mohammed	Mourhit ¶	BEL	10.10.70	2	VD	Bruxelles	3 Sep 99
26:52.33		Gebre-egziabher	Gebremariam	ETH	10.9.84	4	FBK	Hengelo	26 May 07
26:52.36		Bidan	Karoki	KEN	21.8.90	3	Pre	Eugene	30 May 14
26:52.65		Kenneth	Kipkemoi	KEN	2.8.84	3	VD	Bruxelles	7 Sep 12

Mark	Wind	Name		Nat	Born	Pos	Meet	Venue	Date
26:52.85		Abera	Kuma	ETH	31.8.90	2		Sollentuna	27 Jun 13
26:52.87		John Cheruiyot	Korir	KEN	13.12.81	5	VD	Bruxelles	30 Aug 02
26:52.93		Mark	Bett	KEN	22.12.76	6	VD	Bruxelles	26 Aug 05
26:54.25		Mathew	Kisorio ¶	KEN	16.5.89	7	Pre	Eugene	3 Jun 11
26:54.61		Stephen	Sambu	KEN	7.7.88	4	Pre	Eugene	30 May 14
26:54.64		Mark	Kiptoo	KEN	21.6.76	8	Pre	Eugene	3 Jun 11
		(40)							
26:55.29		Leonard Patrick	Komon	KEN	10.1.88	9	Pre	Eugene	3 Jun 11
26:55.73		Geoffrey	Kirui	KEN	16.2.93	6	VD	Bruxelles	16 Sep 11
26:56.74		Josphat	Menjo	KEN	20.8.79	1		Turku	29 Aug 10
26:57.36		Josphat	Muchiri Ndambiri	KEN	12.2.85	1		Fukuroi	3 May 09
26:57.56		Yigrem	Demelash	ETH	28.1.94	4	VD	Bruxelles	7 Sep 12
26:58.38	WR	Yobes	Ondieki	KEN	21.2.61	1	Bisl	Oslo	10 Jul 93
26:59.51		Bernard	Kipyego	KEN	16.7.86	4	VD	Bruxelles	14 Sep 07
26:59.60		Chris	Solinsky	USA	5.12.84	1		Stanford	1 May 10
26:59.81		Titus	Mbishei	KEN	28.10.90	7	VD	Bruxelles	16 Sep 11
26:59.88		Martin Irungu	Mathathi	KEN	25.12.85	2		Fukuroi	3 May 09
		(50)	100th man 27:15.68, 200th 27:31.00, 300th 27:39.55, 400th 27:45.46, 500th 27:51.07						

20,000 METRES & 1 HOUR

Mark	Distance	Name		Nat	Born	Pos	Meet	Venue	Date
56:25.98+	21 285m	Haile	Gebrselassie	ETH	18.4.73	1	GS	Ostrava	27 Jun 07
56:55.6+	21 101	Arturo	Barrios	MEX	12.12.63	1		La Flèche	30 Mar 91
57:24.19+	20 944	Jos	Hermens	NED	8.1.50	1		Papendal	1 May 76
57:18.4+	20 943	Dionísio	Castro	POR	22.11.63	1		La Flèche	31 Mar 90

HALF MARATHON

Included are the slightly downhill courses: Newcastle to South Shields 30.5m, Tokyo 33m, Lisboa (Spring to 2008) 69m

Mark	Wind	Name		Nat	Born	Pos	Meet	Venue	Date
58:23	WR	Zersenay	Tadese	ERI	8.2.82	1		Lisboa	21 Mar 10
58:30			Z Tadese			1		Lisboa	20 Mar 11
58:33	WR	Samuel	Wanjiru	KEN	10.11.86	1		Den Haag	17 Mar 07
58:46		Mathew	Kisorio ¶	KEN	16.5.89	1		Philadelphia	18 Sep 11
58:47		Atsedu	Tsegay	ETH	17.12.91	1		Praha	31 Mar 12
58:48		Sammy	Kitwara	KEN	26.11.86	2		Philadelphia	18 Sep 11
58:48		Abreham	Cheroben	KEN	10.11.92	1		Valencia	19 Oct 14
58:52		Patrick	Makau	KEN	2.3.85	1		Ra's Al Khaymah	20 Feb 09
58:53	WR		Wanjiru			1		Ra's Al Khaymah	9 Feb 07
58:54		Stephen	Kibet	KEN	9.11.86	1		Den Haag	11 Mar 12
58:54		Geoffrey	Kamworor	KEN	28.11.92	1		Ra's Al-Khaymah	15 Feb 13
58:55	WR	Haile	Gebrselassie (10)	ETH	18.4.73	1		Tempe	15 Jan 06
58:56			Makau			1		Berlin	1 Apr 07
58:56	dh	Martin	Mathathi	KEN	25.12.85	1	GNR	South Shields	18 Sep 11
58:56		Stanley	Biwott	KEN	21.4.86	2		Ra's Al-Khaymah	15 Feb 13
58:58			Kitwara			1		Rotterdam	13 Sep 09
58:58		Geoffrey	Mutai	KEN	7.10.81	3		Ra's Al-Khaymah	15 Feb 13
58:59			Z Tadese			1	WCh	Udine	14 Oct 07
58:59		Wilson	Kipsang	KEN	15.3.82	2		Ra's Al Khaymah	20 Feb 09
59:01		Kenneth	Kipkemoi	KEN	2.8.84	2		Valencia	19 Oct 14
59:02			Makau			2	WCh	Udine	14 Oct 07
59:02		Jonathan	Maiyo	KEN	5.5.88	2		Den Haag	11 Mar 12
59:05	dh		Tadese			1	GNR	South Shields	18 Sep 05
59:05		Evans	Cheruiyot	KEN	10.5.82	3	WCh	Udine	14 Oct 07
59:05		Ezekiel	Chebii	KEN	3.1.91	1		Lille	1 Sep 12
59:06	dh	Paul	Tergat	KEN	17.6.69	1		Lisboa	26 Mar 00
59:06	dh		Kipsang			1	GNR	South Shields	16 Sep 12
59:06			G Mutai			1		Udine	22 Sep 13
59:06		Guye	Adola (20)	ETH	20.10.90	1		New Delhi	23 Nov 14
59:07		Paul	Kosgei	KEN	22.4.78	1		Berlin	2 Apr 06
59:07	dh	Micah	Kogo	KEN	3.6.86	2	GNR	South Shields	16 Sep 12
59:07			Kamworor			2		New Delhi	23 Nov 14
(32/22)									
59:09		James Kipsang	Kwambai	KEN	28.2.83	3		Rotterdam	13 Sep 09
59:10		Bernard	Kipyego	KEN	16.7.86	4		Rotterdam	13 Sep 09
59:10		Bernard	Koech	KEN	31.1.88	2		Lille	1 Sep 12
59:11		Kenneth	Kipkemoi	KEN	2.8.84	3		Den Haag	11 Mar 12
59:11		Mosinet	Geremew	ETH	12.2.92	3		New Delhi	23 Nov 14
59:12		Cyprian	Kotut	KEN	.92	4		New Delhi	23 Nov 14
59:14		Dennis	Kimetto	KEN	22.1.84	1		Berlin	1 Apr 12
59:15		Deriba	Merga	ETH	26.10.80	1		New Delhi	9 Nov 08
		(30)							
59:15		Wilson	Chebet	KEN	12.7.85	5		Rotterdam	13 Sep 09
59:15		Wilson	Kiprop	KEN	14.4.87	2		Berlin	1 Apr 12

Mark	Wind	Name		Nat	Born	Pos	Meet	Venue	Date
59:19		Tilahun	Regassa	ETH	18.1.90	1		Abu Dhabi	7 Jan 10
59:19		Robert	Chemosin	KEN	1.2.89	2		Ostia	3 Mar 13
59:20	dh	Hendrick	Ramaala	RSA	2.2.72	2		Lisboa	26 Mar 00
59:20		Moses	Mosop	KEN	17.7.85	1	Stra	Milano	21 Mar 10
59:20		Simon	Cheprot	KEN	2.7.93	3		Ostia	3 Mar 13
59:21	dh	Robert Kipkoech	Cheruiyot	KEN	26.9.78	2		Lisboa	13 Mar 05
59:21		Samuel	Tsegay	ERI	24.2.88	2	WCh	København	29 Mar 14
59:22		Feyisa	Lilesa	ETH	1.2.90	1		Houston	15 Jan 12
		(40)							
59:22		Peter Cheruiyot	Kirui	KEN	2.1.88	1		Praha	5 Apr 14
59:23		John Kiprotich	Chemisto	KEN	5.6.83	6		Rotterdam	13 Sep 09
59:23		Bidan	Karoki	KEN	21.8.90	1		Philadelphia	21 Sep 14
59:25		Pius	Kirop	KEN	8.1.90	4		Berlin	1 Apr 12
59:25		Eliud	Kipchoge	KEN	5.11.84	3		Lille	1 Sep 12
59:25		Aziz	Lahbabi	MAR	3.2.91	1		Ostia	2 Mar 14
59:26		Francis	Kibiwott	KEN	15.9.78	2		Berlin	1 Apr 07
59:27	dh	Wilson	Kiprotich Kebenei	KEN	20.7.80	3		Lisboa	13 Mar 05
59:27		Patrick	Ivuti	KEN	30.6.78	4		Rotterdam	9 Sep 07
59:28		Robert	Kipchumba	KEN	24.2.84	2		Rotterdam	10 Sep 06
		(50)	100th man 59:53, 200th man 60:26, 300th 60:50, 400th 61:03, 500th 61:14						
Short course:		58:51	Paul Tergat	KEN	17.6.69	1	Stra	Milano 49m sh	30 Mar 96
Excessively downhill:		58:42	Bernard Koech	KEN	31.1.88	1		San Diego (dh 86m)	2 Jun 13

MARATHON

In second column: P = point-to-point or start/finish more than 30% apart, D = point-to-point and downhill over 1/1000

Mark		Name		Nat	Born	Pos	Meet	Venue	Date
2:02:57	WR	Dennis	Kimetto	KEN	22.1.84	1		Berlin	28 Sep 14
2:03:13		Emmanuel	Mutai	KEN	12.10.84	2		Berlin	28 Sep 14
2:03:23	WR	Wilson	Kipsang	KEN	15.3.82	1		Berlin	29 Sep 13
2:03:38	WR	Patrick	Makau	KEN	2.3.85	1		Berlin	25 Sep 11
2:03:42			W Kipsang			1		Frankfurt	30 Oct 11
2:03:45			Kimetto			1		Chicago	13 Oct 13
2:03:52			Mutai			2		Chicago	13 Oct 13
2:03:59	WR	Haile	Gebrselassie	ETH	18.4.73	1		Berlin	28 Sep 08
2:04:05		Eliud	Kipchoge	KEN	5.11.84	2		Berlin	29 Sep 13
2:04:11			Kipchoge			1		Chicago	12 Oct 14
2:04:15		Geoffrey	Mutai	KEN	7.10.81	1		Berlin	30 Sep 12
2:04:16			Kimetto			2		Berlin	30 Sep 12
2:04:23		Ayele	Abshero	ETH	28.12.90	1		Dubai	27 Jan 12
2:04:26	WR		Gebrselassie			1		Berlin	30 Sep 07
2:04:27		Duncan	Kibet	KEN	25.4.78	1		Rotterdam	5 Apr 09
2:04:27		James Kipsang	Kwambai (10)	KEN	28.2.83	2		Rotterdam	5 Apr 09
2:04:28		Sammy	Kitwara	KEN	26.11.86	2		Chicago	12 Oct 14
2:04:29			Kipsang			1		London	13 Apr 14
2:04:32		Tsegaye	Mekonnen	ETH	15.6.95	1		Dubai	24 Jan 14
2:04:32		Dickson	Chumba	KEN	27.10.86	3		Chicago	12 Oct 14
2:04:38		Tsegaye	Kebede	ETH	15.1.87	1		Chicago	7 Oct 12
2:04:40			E Mutai			1		London	17 Apr 11
2:04:44			W Kipsang			1		London	22 Apr 12
2:04:45		Lelisa	Desisa	ETH	14.1.90	1		Dubai	25 Jan 13
2:04:48			Makau			1		Rotterdam	11 Apr 10
2:04:48		Yemane	Tsegay	ETH	8.4.85	1		Rotterdam	15 Apr 12
2:04:48		Berhanu	Shiferaw	ETH	31.5.93	2		Dubai	25 Jan 13
2:04:49		Tadesse	Tola	ETH	31.10.87	3		Dubai	25 Jan 13
2:04:50		Dino	Sefir	ETH	28.5.88	2		Dubai	27 Jan 12
2:04:50		Getu	Feleke	ETH	28.11.86	2		Rotterdam	15 Apr 12
		(30/20)							
2:04:52		Feyisa	Lilesa	ETH	1.2.90	2		Chicago	7 Oct 12
2:04:52		Endeshaw	Negesse	ETH	13.3.88	4		Dubai	25 Jan 13
2:04:53		Bernard	Koech	KEN	31.1.88	5		Dubai	25 Jan 13
2:04:54		Markos	Geneti	ETH	30.5.84	3		Dubai	27 Jan 12
2:04:55	WR	Paul	Tergat	KEN	17.6.69	1		Berlin	28 Sep 03
2:04:55		Stanley	Biwott	KEN	21.4.86	2		London	13 Apr 14
2:04:56		Sammy	Korir	KEN	12.12.71	2		Berlin	28 Sep 03
2:04:56		Jonathan	Maiyo	KEN	5.5.88	4		Dubai	27 Jan 12
2:05:03		Moses	Mosop	KEN	17.7.85	3		Rotterdam	15 Apr 12
2:05:04		Abel	Kirui	KEN	4.6.82	3		Rotterdam	5 Apr 09
		(30)							
2:05:04		Kenenisa	Bekele	ETH	13.6.82	1		Paris	6 Apr 14
2:05:10		Samuel	Wanjiru	KEN	10.11.86	1		London	26 Apr 09
2:05:13		Vincent	Kipruto	KEN	13.9.87	3		Rotterdam	11 Apr 10

Mark	Wind	Name		Nat	Born	Pos	Meet	Venue	Date
2:05:15		Martin	Lel	KEN	29.10.78	1		London	13 Apr 08
2:05:16		Levi	Matebo Omari	KEN	3.11.89	2		Frankfurt	30 Oct 11
2:05:25		Bazu	Worku	ETH	15.9.90	3		Berlin	26 Sep 10
2:05:25		Albert	Matebor	KEN	20.12.80	3		Frankfurt	30 Oct 11
2:05:27		Jaouad	Gharib	MAR	22.5.72	3		London	26 Apr 09
2:05:27		Wilson	Chebet	KEN	12.7.85	1		Rotterdam	10 Apr 11
2:05:27		Tilahun	Regassa	ETH	18.1.90	3		Chicago	7 Oct 12
		(40)							
2:05:30		Abderrahim	Goumri ¶	MAR	21.5.76	3		London	13 Apr 08
2:05:37	P	Wilson	Loyanae ¶	KEN	20.11.88	1		Seoul	18 Mar 12
2:05:38	WR	Khalid	Khannouchi	MAR/USA	22.12.71	1		London	14 Apr 02
2:05:38		Peter	Some	KEN	5.6.90	1		Paris	7 Apr 13
2:05:39		Eliud	Kiptanui	KEN	6.6.89	1		Praha	9 May 10
2:05:41		Yami	Dadi	ETH	.82	6		Dubai	27 Jan 12
2:05:42		Abdullah Dawit	Shami	ETH	16.7.84	7		Dubai	27 Jan 12
2:05:42		Deresse	Chimsa	ETH	21.11.76	8		Dubai	27 Jan 12
2:05:48		Jafred	Kipchumba	KEN	8.8.83	1		Eindhoven	9 Oct 11
2:05:49		William	Kipsang	KEN	26.6.77	1		Rotterdam	13 Apr 08
		(50)	100th man 2:06:44, 200th 2:07:33, 300th 2:08:07, 400th 2:08:38, 500th 2:09:03						

Downhill point-to-point course – Boston marathon is downhill overall (139m) and sometimes strongly wind-aided.

Mark	Wind	Name		Nat	Born	Pos	Meet	Venue	Date
2:03:02		Geoffrey	Mutai	KEN	7.10.81	1		Boston	18 Apr 11
2:03:06		Moses	Mosop	KEN	17.7.85	2		Boston	18 Apr 11
2:04:53		Gebre-egziabher	Gebremariam	ETH	10.9.84	3		Boston	18 Apr 11
2:04:58		Ryan	Hall	USA	14.10.82	4		Boston	18 Apr 11

2000 METRES STEEPLECHASE

Mark	Wind	Name		Nat	Born	Pos	Meet	Venue	Date
5:10.68		Mahiedine	Mekhissi-Benabbad	FRA	15.3.85	1		Reims	30 Jun 10
5:13.47		Bouabdellah	Tahri	FRA	20.12.78	1		Tomblaine	25 Jun 10
5:14.43		Julius	Kariuki	KEN	12.6.61	1		Rovereto	21 Aug 90
5:14.53		Saïf Saaeed	Shaheen	QAT	15.10.82	1	SGP	Doha	13 May 05
5:16.22		Phillip	Barkutwo	KEN	6.10.66	2		Rovereto	21 Aug 90
5:16.46		Wesley	Kiprotich	KEN	31.7.79	2	SGP	Doha	13 May 05
5:16.85		Eliud	Barngetuny	KEN	20.5.73	1		Parma	13 Jun 95

3000 METRES STEEPLECHASE

Mark	Wind	Name		Nat	Born	Pos	Meet	Venue	Date
7:53.63	WR	Saïf Saaeed	Shaheen	KEN/QAT	15.10.82	1	VD	Bruxelles	3 Sep 04
7:53.64		Brimin	Kipruto	KEN	31.7.85	1	Herc	Monaco	22 Jul 11
7:54.31		Paul Kipsiele	Koech	KEN	10.11.81	1	GGala	Roma	31 May 12
7:55.28	WR	Brahim	Boulami ¶	MAR	20.4.72	1	VD	Bruxelles	24 Aug 01
7:55.51			Shaheen			1	VD	Bruxelles	26 Aug 05
7:55.72	WR	Bernard	Barmasai	KEN	6.5.74	1	ASV	Köln	24 Aug 97
7:55.76		Ezekiel	Kemboi	KEN	25.5.82	2	Herc	Monaco	22 Jul 11
7:56.16		Moses	Kiptanui	KEN	1.10.70	2	ASV	Köln	24 Aug 97
7:56.32			Shaheen			1	Tsik	Athína	3 Jul 06
7:56.34			Shaheen			1	GGala	Roma	8 Jul 05
7:56.37			P K Koech			2	GGala	Roma	8 Jul 05
7:56.54			Shaheen			1	WK	Zürich	18 Aug 06
7:56.58			P K Koech			1	DL	Doha	11 May 12
7:56.81		Richard	Mateelong	KEN	14.10.83	2	DL	Doha	11 May 12
7:56.94			Shaheen			1	WAF	Monaco	19 Sep 04
7:57.28			Shaheen			1	Tsik	Athína	14 Jun 05
7:57.29		Reuben	Kosgei	KEN	2.8.79	2	VD	Bruxelles	24 Aug 01
7:57.32			P K Koech			3	Herc	Monaco	22 Jul 11
7:57.38			Shaheen			1	WAF	Monaco	14 Sep 03
7:57.42			P K Koech			2	WAF	Monaco	14 Sep 03
7:58.09			Boulami			1	Herc	Monaco	19 Jul 02
7:58.10			S Cherono			2	Herc	Monaco	19 Jul 02
7:58.41		Jairus	Birech (10)	KEN	14.12.92	1	VD	Bruxelles	5 Sep 14
7:58.50			Boulami			1	WK	Zürich	17 Aug 01
7:58.66			S Cherono			3	VD	Bruxelles	24 Aug 01
7:58.80			P K Koech			1	VD	Bruxelles	14 Sep 07
7:58.85			Kemboi			1	SGP	Doha	8 May 09
7:58.98			Barmasai			1	Herc	Monaco	4 Aug 99
7:59.03			Kemboi			1	DL	Saint-Denis	6 Jul 13
7:59.08	WR	Wilson	Boit Kipketer	KEN	6.10.73	1	WK	Zürich	13 Aug 97
		(30/11)							
8:00.09		Mahiedine	Mekhissi-Benabbad	FRA	15.3.85	2	DL	Saint-Denis	6 Jul 13
8:01.16		Conseslus	Kipruto	KEN	8.12.94	1	DL	Shanghai	18 May 13
8:01.18		Bouabdellah	Tahri	FRA	20.12.78	3	WCh	Berlin	18 Aug 09
8:01.67		Abel	Mutai	KEN	2.10.88	2	GGala	Roma	31 May 12

Mark	Wind	Name		Nat	Born	Pos	Meet	Venue	Date
8:01.69		Kipkirui	Misoi	KEN	23.12.78	4	VD	Bruxelles	24 Aug 01
8:03.41		Patrick	Sang	KEN	11.4.64	3	ASV	Köln	24 Aug 97
8:03.57		Ali	Ezzine	MAR	3.9.78	1	Gaz	Saint-Denis	23 Jun 00
8:03.57		Hillary	Yego	KEN	2.4.92	3	DL	Shanghai	18 May 13
8:03.74		Raymond	Yator	KEN	7.4.81	3	Herc	Monaco	18 Aug 00
		(20)							
8:03.81		Benjamin	Kiplagat	UGA	4.3.89	2	Athl	Lausanne	8 Jul 10
8:03.89		John	Kosgei	KEN	13.7.73	3	Herc	Monaco	16 Aug 97
8:04.71		Evan	Jager	USA	8.3.89	3	VD	Bruxelles	5 Sep 14
8:04.95		Simon	Vroemen ¶	NED	11.5.69	2	VD	Bruxelles	26 Aug 05
8:05.01		Eliud	Barngetuny	KEN	20.5.73	1	Herc	Monaco	25 Jul 95
8:05.35 WR		Peter	Koech	KEN	18.2.58	1	DNG	Stockholm	3 Jul 89
8:05.37		Philip	Barkutwo	KEN	6.10.66	2		Rieti	6 Sep 92
8:05.4 WR		Henry	Rono	KEN	12.2.52	1		Seattle	13 May 78
8:05.43		Christopher	Kosgei	KEN	14.8.74	2	WK	Zürich	11 Aug 99
8:05.51		Julius	Kariuki	KEN	12.6.61	1	OG	Seoul	30 Sep 88
		(30)							
8:05.68		Wesley	Kiprotich	KEN	1.8.79	4	VD	Bruxelles	3 Sep 04
8:05.75		Mustafa	Mohamed	SWE	1.3.79	1	NA	Heusden-Zolder	28 Jul 07
8:05.88		Bernard	Mbugua Nganga	KEN	17.1.85	2	ISTAF	Berlin	11 Sep 11
8:05.99		Joseph	Keter	KEN	13.6.69	1	Herc	Monaco	10 Aug 96
8:06.13		Tareq Mubarak	Taher	BRN	24.3.84	3	Tsik	Athína	13 Jul 09
8:06.16		Roba	Gari	ETH	12.4.82	3	DL	Doha	11 May 12
8:06.77		Gideon	Chirchir	KEN	24.2.66	2	WK	Zürich	16 Aug 95
8:06.88		Richard	Kosgei	KEN	29.12.70	2	GPF	Monaco	9 Sep 95
8:06.96		Gilbert	Kirui	KEN	22.1.94	2	DL	London (OS)	27 Jul 13
8:07.02		Brahim	Taleb	MAR	16.2.85	2	NA	Heusden-Zolder	28 Jul 07
		(40)							
8:07.13		Paul	Kosgei	KEN	22.4.78	2	GP II	Saint-Denis	3 Jul 99
8:07.18		Obaid Moussa	Amer ¶	KEN/QAT	18.4.85	4	OG	Athína	24 Aug 04
8:07.44		Luis Miguel	Martín	ESP	11.1.72	2	VD	Bruxelles	30 Aug 02
8:07.59		Julius	Nyamu	KEN	1.12.77	5	VD	Bruxelles	24 Aug 01
8:07.62		Joseph	Mahmoud	FRA	13.12.55	1	VD	Bruxelles	24 Aug 84
8:07.75		Jonathan	Ndiku Muia	KEN	18.9.91	6	Herc	Monaco	22 Jul 11
8:07.96		Mark	Rowland	GBR	7.3.63	3	OG	Seoul	30 Sep 88
8:08.02 WR		Anders	Gärderud	SWE	28.8.46	1	OG	Montreal	28 Jul 76
8:08.12		Matthew	Birir	KEN	5.7.72	3	GGala	Roma	8 Jun 95
8:08.14		Sa'ad Shaddad	Al-Asmari	KSA	24.9.68	4	DNG	Stockholm	16 Jul 02
		(50)	100th man 8:12.25, 200th 8:18.04, 300th 8:21.72, 400th 8:23.96, 500th 8:26.2						

7:53.63 Shaheen formerly Stephen Cherono KEN

Drugs disqualification: 7:53.17 Brahim Boulami ¶ MAR 20.4.72 1 WK Zürich 16 Aug 02

110 METRES HURDLES

Mark	Wind	Name		Nat	Born	Pos	Meet	Venue	Date
12.80 WR	0.3	Aries	Merritt	USA	24.7.85	1	VD	Bruxelles	7 Sep 12
12.87 WR	0.9	Dayron	Robles	CUB	19.11.86	1	GS	Ostrava	12 Jun 08
12.88 WR	1.1		Liu Xiang	CHN	13.7.83	1rA	Athl	Lausanne	11 Jul 06
12.88	0.5		Robles			1	Gaz	Saint-Denis	18 Jul 08
12.89	0.5	David	Oliver	USA	24.4.82	1	DL	Saint-Denis	16 Jul 10
12.90	1.1	Dominique	Arnold	USA	14.9.73	2rA	Athl	Lausanne	11 Jul 06
12.90	1.6		Oliver			1	Pre	Eugene	3 Jul 10
12.91 WR	0.5	Colin	Jackson	GBR	18.2.67	1	WCh	Stuttgart	20 Aug 93
12.91 WR	0.3		Liu Xiang			1	OG	Athína	27 Aug 04
12.91	0.2		Robles			1	DNG	Stockholm	22 Jul 08
12.92 WR	-0.1	Roger	Kingdom	USA	26.8.62	1	WK	Zürich	16 Aug 89
12.92	0.9	Allen	Johnson	USA	1.3.71	1	NC	Atlanta	23 Jun 96
12.92	0.2		Johnson			1	VD	Bruxelles	23 Aug 96
12.92	1.5		Liu Xiang			1	GP	New York	2 Jun 07
12.92	0.0		Robles			1	WAF	Stuttgart	23 Sep 07
12.92	-0.3		Merritt			1	OG	London (OS)	8 Aug 12
12.93 WR	-0.2	Renaldo	Nehemiah	USA	24.3.59	1	WK	Zürich	19 Aug 81
12.93	0.0		Johnson			1	WCh	Athína	7 Aug 97
12.93	-0.6		Liu Xiang			1	WAF	Stuttgart	9 Sep 06
12.93	0.1		Robles			1	OG	Beijing	21 Aug 08
12.93	1.7		Oliver			1	NC	Des Moines	27 Jun 10
12.93	-0.3		Oliver			1	WK	Zürich	19 Aug 10
12.93	1.2		Merritt			1	NC/OT	Eugene	30 Jun 12
12.93	0.6		Merritt			1	LGP	London (CP)	13 Jul 12
12.93	0.0		Merritt			1	Herc	Monaco	20 Jul 12
12.94	1.6	Jack	Pierce (10)	USA	23.9.62	1s2	NC	Atlanta	22 Jun 96
12.94	1.8		Oliver			1	Pre	Eugene	4 Jun 11

Mark	Wind		Name	Nat	Born	Pos	Meet	Venue	Date
12.94	0.1		Merritt			1s2	OG	London (OS)	8 Aug 12
12.94	0.8	Hansle	Parchment	JAM	17.6.90	1	DL	Saint-Denis	5 Jul 14
12.95	0.6		Johnson			1	OG	Atlanta	29 Jul 96
12.95	1.5	Terrence	Trammell	USA	23.11.78	2	GP	New York	2 Jun 07
12.95	1.7		Liu Xiang			1	WCh	Osaka	31 Aug 07
12.95	2.0		Oliver			1	SGP	Doha	9 May 08
12.95	-1.7		Robles			1		Dubnica nad Váhom	7 Sep 08
12.95	-0.9		Merritt			1	DL	Birmingham	26 Aug 12
12.95	0.2	Pascal	Martinot-Lagarde	FRA	22.9.91	1	Herc	Monaco	18 Jul 14
		(36/13)							
12.97	1.0	Ladji	Doucouré	FRA	28.3.83	1	NC	Angers	15 Jul 05
12.98	0.6	Mark	Crear	USA	2.10.68	1		Zagreb	5 Jul 99
12.98	1.5	Jason	Richardson	USA	4.4.86	1s3	NC/OT	Eugene	30 Jun 12
12.99	1.2	Ronnie	Ash	USA	2.7.88	1s1	NC	Sacramento	29 Jun 14
13.00	0.5	Anthony	Jarrett	GBR	13.8.68	2	WCh	Stuttgart	20 Aug 93
13.00	0.6	Anier	García	CUB	9.3.76	1	OG	Sydney	25 Sep 00
13.01	0.3	Larry	Wade ¶	USA	22.11.74	1rA	Athl	Lausanne	2 Jul 99
		(20)							
13.01	0.2	Orlando	Ortega	CUB	29.7.91	2	Herc	Monaco	18 Jul 14
13.02	1.5	Ryan	Wilson	USA	19.12.80	3	GP	New York	2 Jun 07
13.02	1.7	David	Payne	USA	24.7.82	3	WCh	Osaka	31 Aug 07
13.03	-0.2	Greg	Foster	USA	4.8.58	2	WK	Zürich	19 Aug 81
13.03	1.0	Reggie	Torian	USA	22.4.75	1	NC	New Orleans	21 Jun 98
13.05	1.4	Tony	Dees ¶	USA	6.8.63	1		Vigo	23 Jul 91
13.05	-0.8	Florian	Schwarthoff	GER	7.5.68	1	NC	Bremen	2 Jul 95
13.08	1.2	Mark	McKoy	CAN	10.12.61	1	BNP	Villeneuve-d'Ascq	2 Jul 93
13.08	0.0	Stanislav	Olijar	LAT	22.3.79	2	Athl	Lausanne	1 Jul 03
13.08	1.2	Jeff	Porter	USA	27.11.85	3	NC/OT	Eugene	30 Jun 12
		(30)							
13.09	2.0	Antwon	Hicks	USA	12.3.83	2s2	NC/OT	Eugene	6 Jul 08
13.09	-1.1	Sergey	Shubenkov	RUS	4.10.90	1s2	EC	Helsinki	1 Jul 12
13.12	1.5	Falk	Balzer ¶	GER	14.12.73	2	EC	Budapest	22 Aug 98
13.12	1.0	Duane	Ross ¶	USA	5.12.72	3	WCh	Sevilla	25 Aug 99
13.12	1.9	Anwar	Moore	USA	5.3.79	1	ModR	Modesto	5 May 07
13.13	1.6	Igor	Kovác	SVK	12.5.69	1	DNG	Stockholm	7 Jul 97
13.13	2.0	Dexter	Faulk	USA	14.4.84	2	GS	Ostrava	17 Jun 09
13.14	0.1	Ryan	Brathwaite	BAR	6.6.88	1	WCh	Berlin	20 Aug 09
13.14	0.0	Andrew	Riley	JAM	6.9.88	4	DL	Saint-Denis	6 Jul 13
13.14	1.1	Aleec	Harris	USA	31.10.90	1		Eugene	26 Jul 14
		(40)							
13.15	0.3	Robin	Korving	NED	29.7.74	5rA	Athl	Lausanne	2 Jul 99
13.15	0.1	Dwight	Thomas	JAM	23.9.80	2	Bisl	Oslo	9 Jun 11
13.15	-0.3	Garfield	Darien	FRA	22.12.87	1s3	EC	Helsinki	1 Jul 12
13.16	1.3	Devon	Allen	USA	12.12.94	1	NCAA	Eugene	14 Jun 14
13.16	0.4	William	Sharman	GBR	12.9.84	1s1	EC	Zürich	14 Aug 14
13.17	-0.4	Sam	Turner	USA	17.6.57	2	Pepsi	Los Angeles (Ww)	15 May 83
13.17	0.0	Tonie	Campbell	USA	14.6.60	3	WK	Zürich	17 Aug 88
13.17	0.5	Courtney	Hawkins	USA	11.7.67	1		Ingolstadt	26 Jul 98
13.17	0.4	Mike	Fenner	GER	24.4.71	1		Leverkusen	9 Aug 98
13.17	-0.1	Maurice	Wignall	JAM	17.4.76	1s1	OG	Athína	26 Aug 04
		(50)	100th man 13.28, 200th 13.42, 300th 13.49, 400th 13.56, 500th 13.62						

Rolling start but accepted by race officials

Mark	Wind		Name	Nat	Born	Pos	Meet	Venue	Date
13.10A	2.0	Falk	Balzer ¶	GER	14.12.73	1	WCp	Johannesburg	13 Sep 98

Doubtful timing: Scheessel 4 Jun 95 +1.3 1. Mike Fenner GER 24.4.71 13.06, 2. Eric Kaiser ¶ GER 7.3.71 13.08

Wind-assisted marks *Performances to 12.94, performers to 13.17*

Mark	Wind		Name	Nat	Born	Pos	Meet	Venue	Date
12.87	2.6	Roger	Kingdom	USA	26.8.62	1	WCp	Barcelona	10 Sep 89
12.87	2.4		Liu Xiang	CHN	13.7.83	1	Pre	Eugene	2 Jun 12
12.89	3.2	David	Oliver	USA	24.4.82	1s1	NC/OT	Eugene	6 Jul 08
12.91	3.5	Renaldo	Nehemiah	USA	24.3.59	1	NCAA	Champaign	1 Jun 79
12.94A	2.8		Jackson			1rA		Sestriere	31 Jul 94
12.98	3.1	Ronnie	Ash	USA	2.7.88	1	NACAC	Miramar	9 Jul 10
13.00	2.6	Anwar	Moore	USA	5.3.79	1	DrakeR	Des Moines	28 Apr 07
13.05	3.6	Ryan	Brathwaite	BAR	6.6.88	1		Austin	2 May 09
13.06	2.1	Mark	McKoy	CAN	10.12.61	1	Gugl	Linz	13 Aug 92
13.12	2.4	Dexter	Faulk	USA	14.4.84	4	Pre	Eugene	2 Jun 12
13.14	2.9	Igor	Kazanov	LAT	24.9.63	1r1	Znam	Leningrad	8 Jun 86
13.14	4.7	Lawrence	Clarke	GBR	12.3.90	1h1		Madrid	7 Jul 12
13.14	3.8	Wayne	Davis	TTO	22.8.91	1	NCAA	Eugene	8 Jun 13
13.15	2.1	Courtney	Hawkins	USA	11.7.67	1		Salamanca	10 Jul 98

Hand timing

Mark	Wind	Name		Nat	Born	Pos	Meet	Venue	Date
12.8	1.0	Renaldo	Nehemiah	USA	24.3.59	1		Kingston	11 May 79
12.9	0.0	Yordan	O'Farrill	CUB	9.2.93	1	Barr	La Habana	23 May 14
Wind-assisted									
12.8	2.4	Colin	Jackson	GBR	18.2.67	1		Sydney	10 Jan 90
12.9	4.1	Mark	Crear	USA	2.10.68	1rA	S&W	Modesto	8 May 93
12.9	3.1	William	Sharman	GBR	12.9.84	1r2		Madrid	2 Jul 10

400 METRES HURDLES

Mark	Wind	Name		Nat	Born	Pos	Meet	Venue	Date
46.78 WR		Kevin	Young	USA	16.9.66	1	OG	Barcelona	6 Aug 92
47.02 WR		Edwin	Moses	USA	31.8.55	1		Koblenz	31 Aug 83
47.03		Bryan	Bronson ¶	USA	9.9.72	1	NC	New Orleans	21 Jun 98
47.10		Samuel	Matete	ZAM	27.7.68	1rA	WK	Zürich	7 Aug 91
47.13 WR			Moses			1		Milano	3 Jul 80
47.14			Moses			1	Athl	Lausanne	14 Jul 81
47.17			Moses			1	ISTAF	Berlin	8 Aug 80
47.18			Young			1	WCh	Stuttgart	19 Aug 93
47.19		Andre	Phillips	USA	5.9.59	1	OG	Seoul	25 Sep 88
47.23		Amadou	Dia Bâ	SEN	22.9.58	2	OG	Seoul	25 Sep 88
47.24		Kerron	Clement	USA	31.10.85	1	NC	Carson	26 Jun 05
47.25		Félix	Sánchez	DOM	30.8.77	1	WCh	Saint-Denis	29 Aug 03
47.25		Angelo	Taylor	USA	29.12.78	1	OG	Beijing	18 Aug 08
47.27			Moses			1	ISTAF	Berlin	21 Aug 81
47.30		Bershawn	Jackson (10)	USA	8.5.83	1	WCh	Helsinki	9 Aug 05
47.32			Moses			1		Koblenz	29 Aug 84
47.32			Jackson			1	NC	Des Moines	26 Jun 10
47.35			Sánchez			1rA	WK	Zürich	16 Aug 02
47.37			Moses			1	WCp	Roma	4 Sep 81
47.37			Moses			1	WK	Zürich	24 Aug 83
47.37			Moses			1	NC/OT	Indianapolis	17 Jul 88
47.37			Young			1	Athl	Lausanne	7 Jul 93
47.37		Stéphane	Diagana	FRA	23.7.69	1	Athl	Lausanne	5 Jul 95
47.38			Moses			1	Athl	Lausanne	2 Sep 86
47.38		Danny	Harris ¶	USA	7.9.65	1	Athl	Lausanne	10 Jul 91
47.38			Sánchez			1rA	WK	Zürich	17 Aug 01
47.39			Clement			1	NC	Indianapolis	24 Jun 06
47.40			Young			1	WK	Zürich	19 Aug 92
47.42			Young			1	ASV	Köln	16 Aug 92
47.43			Moses			1	ASV	Köln	28 Aug 83
47.43		James	Carter	USA	7.5.78	2	WCh	Helsinki	9 Aug 05
		(31/13)							
47.48		Harald	Schmid	FRG	29.9.57	1	EC	Athína	8 Sep 82
47.53		Hadi Soua'an	Al-Somaily	KSA	21.8.76	2	OG	Sydney	27 Sep 00
47.54		Derrick	Adkins	USA	2.7.70	2	Athl	Lausanne	5 Jul 95
47.54		Fabrizio	Mori	ITA	28.6.69	2	WCh	Edmonton	10 Aug 01
47.60		Winthrop	Graham	JAM	17.11.65	1	WK	Zürich	4 Aug 93
47.63		Johnny	Dutch	USA	20.1.89	2	NC	Des Moines	26 Jun 10
47.66A		L.J. 'Louis'	van Zyl	RSA	20.7.85	1		Pretoria	25 Feb 11
		(20)							
47.67		Bennie	Brazell	USA	2.6.82	2	NCAA	Sacramento	11 Jun 05
47.69		Jehue	Gordon	TTO	15.12.91	1	WCh	Moskva	15 Aug 13
47.70		Michael	Tinsley	USA	21.4.84	2	WCh	Moskva	15 Aug 13
47.72		Javier	Culson	PUR	25.7.84	1		Ponce	8 May 10
47.75		David	Patrick	USA	12.6.60	4	NC/OT	Indianapolis	17 Jul 88
47.81		Llewellyn	Herbert	RSA	21.7.77	3	OG	Sydney	27 Sep 00
47.82 WR		John	Akii-Bua	UGA	3.12.49	1	OG	München	2 Sep 72
47.82		Kriss	Akabusi	GBR	28.11.58	3	OG	Barcelona	6 Aug 92
47.82		Periklis	Iakovákis	GRE	24.3.79	2	GP	Osaka	6 May 06
47.84		Bayano	Kamani	PAN	17.4.80	2s1	WCh	Helsinki	7 Aug 05
		(30)							
47.84		David	Greene	GBR	11.4.86	2	DL	Saint Denis	6 Jul 12
47.89		Dai	Tamesue	JPN	3.5.78	3	WCh	Edmonton	10 Aug 01
47.91		Calvin	Davis	USA	2.4.72	1s2	OG	Atlanta	31 Jul 96
47.92		Aleksandr	Vasilyev	BLR	26.7.61	2	ECp	Moskva	17 Aug 85
47.93		Kenji	Narisako	JPN	25.7.84	3	GP	Osaka	6 May 06
47.93		Jeshua	Anderson	USA	22.6.89	1	NC	Eugene	26 Jun 11
47.93		Omar	Cisneros	CUB	19.11.89	1s3	WCh	Moskva	13 Aug 13
47.94		Eric	Thomas	USA	1.12.73	1	GGala	Roma	30 Jun 00
47.97		Maurice	Mitchell	USA	14.5.71	2rA	WK	Zürich	14 Aug 96
47.97		Joey	Woody	USA	22.5.73	3	NC	New Orleans	21 Jun 98
		(40)							

Mark	Wind	Name		Nat	Born	Pos	Meet	Venue	Date
47.98		Sven	Nylander	SWE	1.1.62	4	OG	Atlanta	1 Aug 96
48.00		Danny	McFarlane	JAM	14.2.72	1s2	OG	Athína	24 Aug 04
48.02A		Ockert	Cilliers	RSA	21.4.81	1		Pretoria	20 Feb 04
48.04		Eronilde	de Araújo	BRA	31.12.70	2	Nik	Nice	12 Jul 95
48.05		Ken	Harnden	ZIM	31.3.73	1	GP	Paris (C)	29 Jul 98
48.05		Kemel	Thompson	JAM	25.9.74	1	GP	London (CP)	8 Aug 03
48.05		Isa	Phillips	JAM	22.4.84	1	NC	Kingston	27 Jun 09
48.05		Emir	Bekric	SRB	14.3.91	3	WCh	Moskva	15 Aug 13
48.06		Oleg	Tverdokhleb	UKR	3.11.69	1	EC	Helsinki	10 Aug 94
48.06		Ruslan	Mashchenko	RUS	11.11.71	1	GP II	Helsinki	13 Jun 98
		(50)	100th man 48.50, 200th man 49.00, 300th man 49.25, 400th 49.47, 500th 49.64						

Best at low altitude: 47.66 van Zyl 1 GS Ostrava 31 May 11

Drugs disqualification 47.15 Bronson ¶ 1 GWG Uniondale, NY 19 Jul 98

HIGH JUMP

Mark	Wind	Name		Nat	Born	Pos	Meet	Venue	Date
2.45 WR		Javier	Sotomayor ¶	CUB	13.10.67	1		Salamanca	27 Jul 93
2.44 WR			Sotomayor			1	CAC	San Juan	29 Jul 89
2.43 WR			Sotomayor			1		Salamanca	8 Sep 88
2.43i			Sotomayor			1	WI	Budapest	4 Mar 89
2.43		Mutaz Essa	Barshim	QAT	24.6.91	1	VD	Bruxelles	5 Sep 14
2.42 WR		Patrik	Sjöberg	SWE	5.1.65	1	DNG	Stockholm	30 Jun 87
2.42i WR		Carlo	Thränhardt	FRG	5.7.57	1		Berlin	26 Feb 88
2.42			Sotomayor			1		Sevilla	5 Jun 94
2.42i		Ivan	Ukhov	RUS	29.3.86	1		Praha	25 Feb 14
2.42		Bohdan	Bondarenko	UKR	30.8.89	1	adidas	New York	14 Jun 14
2.42			Barshim			2	adidas	New York	14 Jun 14
2.41 WR		Igor	Paklin	KGZ	15.6.63	1	WUG	Kobe	4 Sep 85
2.41i			Sjöberg			1		Pireás	1 Feb 87
2.41i			Sotomayor			1	WI	Toronto	14 Mar 93
2.41			Sotomayor			1	NC	La Habana	25 Jun 94
2.41			Sotomayor			1	TSB	London (CP)	15 Jul 94
2.41			Bondarenko			1	Athl	Lausanne	4 Jul 13
2.41			Bondarenko			1	WCh	Moskva	15 Aug 13
2.41i			Ukhov			1		Chelyabinsk	16 Jan 14
2.41			Ukhov			1	DL	Doha	9 May 14
2.41			Barshim			1	GGala	Roma	5 Jun 14
2.41			Barshim			1		Eberstadt	22 Aug 14
		(23/7)							
2.40 WR		Rudolf	Povarnitsyn	UKR	13.6.62	1		Donetsk	11 Aug 85
2.40		Sorin	Matei	ROU	6.7.63	1	PTS	Bratislava	20 Jun 90
2.40i		Hollis	Conway (10)	USA	8.1.67	1	WI	Sevilla	10 Mar 91
2.40		Charles	Austin	USA	19.12.67	1	WK	Zürich	7 Aug 91
2.40		Vyacheslav	Voronin	RUS	5.4.74	1	BrGP	London (CP)	5 Aug 00
2.40i		Stefan	Holm	SWE	25.5.76	1	EI	Madrid	6 Mar 05
2.40i		Aleksey	Dmitrik	RUS	12.4.84	1		Arnstadt	8 Feb 14
2.40		Derek	Drouin	CAN	6.3.90	1	DrakeR	Des Moines	25 Apr 14
2.40		Andriy	Protsenko	UKR	20.5.88	2	Athl	Lausanne	3 Jul 14
2.40	26 more performances: Sotomayor 13, Bondarenko 4, Sjöberg, Ukhov 2, Thränhardt, Barshim 1 for (55/16)								
2.39 WR			Zhu Jianhua	CHN	29.5.63	1		Eberstadt	10 Jun 84
2.39i		Dietmar	Mögenburg	FRG	15.8.61	1		Köln	24 Feb 85
2.39i		Ralf	Sonn	GER	17.1.67	1		Berlin	1 Mar 91
2.38i		Gennadiy	Avdeyenko	UKR	4.11.63	2	WI	Indianapolis	7 Mar 87
		(20)							
2.38		Sergey	Malchenko	RUS	2.11.63	1		Banská Bystrica	4 Sep 88
2.38		Dragutin	Topic ¶	YUG	12.3.71	1		Beograd	1 Aug 93
2.38i		Steve	Smith	GBR	29.3.73	2		Wuppertal	4 Feb 94
2.38i		Wolf-Hendrik	Beyer	GER	14.2.72	1		Weinheim	18 Mar 94
2.38		Troy	Kemp	BAH	18.6.66	1	Nik	Nice	12 Jul 95
2.38		Artur	Partyka	POL	25.7.69	1		Eberstadt	18 Aug 96
2.38i		Matt	Hemingway	USA	24.10.72	1	NC	Atlanta	4 Mar 00
2.38i		Yaroslav	Rybakov	RUS	22.11.80	1		Stockholm	15 Feb 05
2.38		Jacques	Freitag	RSA	11.6.82	1		Oudtshoorn	5 Mar 05
2.38		Andriy	Sokolovskyy	UKR	16.7.78	1	GGala	Roma	8 Jul 05
		(30)							
2.38i		Linus	Thörnblad	SWE	6.3.85	2	NC	Göteborg	25 Feb 07
2.38		Andrey	Silnov	RUS	9.9.84	1	LGP	London (CP)	25 Jul 08
2.37		Valeriy	Sereda	RUS	30.6.59	1		Rieti	2 Sep 84
2.37		Tom	McCants	USA	27.11.62	1	Owens	Columbus	8 May 88
2.37		Jerome	Carter	USA	25.3.63	2	Owens	Columbus	8 May 88
2.37		Sergey	Dymchenko	UKR	23.8.67	1		Kyiv	16 Sep 90

Mark	Wind	Name		Nat	Born	Pos	Meet	Venue	Date
2.37i		Dalton	Grant	GBR	8.4.66	1	EI	Paris	13 Mar 94
2.37i		Jaroslav	Bába	CZE	2.9.84	2		Arnstadt	5 Feb 05
2.37		Jesse	Williams	USA	27.12.83	1	NC	Eugene	26 Jun 11
2.37		Robbie	Grabarz	GBR	3.10.87	3	Athl	Lausanne	23 Aug 12
		(40)							
2.37		Eric	Kynard	USA	3.2.91	2	Athl	Lausanne	4 Jul 13
2.36	WR	Gerd	Wessig	GDR	16.7.59	1	OG	Moskva	1 Aug 80
2.36		Sergey	Zasimovich	KZK	6.9.62	1		Tashkent	5 May 84
2.36		Eddy	Annys	BEL	15.12.58	1		Gent	26 May 85
2.36i		Jim	Howard	USA	11.9.59	1		Albuquerque	25 Jan 86
2.36i		Jan	Zvara	CZE	12.2.63	1	vGDR	Jablonec	14 Feb 87
2.36i		Gerd	Nagel	FRG	22.10.57	1		Sulingen	17 Mar 89
2.36		Nick	Saunders	BER	14.9.63	1	CG	Auckland	1 Feb 90
2.36		Doug	Nordquist	USA	20.12.58	2	NC	Norwalk	15 Jun 90
2.36		Georgi	Dakov	BUL	21.10.67	2	VD	Bruxelles	10 Aug 90
		(50)							
2.36		Lábros	Papakóstas	GRE	20.10.69	1	NC	Athína	21 Jun 92
2.36i		Steinar	Hoen	NOR	8.2.71	1		Balingen	12 Feb 94
2.36		Tim	Forsyth	AUS	17.8.73	1	NC	Melbourne	2 Mar 97
2.36		Sergey	Klyugin	RUS	24.3.74	1	WK	Zürich	12 Aug 98
2.36		Konstantin	Matusevich	ISR	25.2.71	1		Perth	5 Feb 00
2.36		Martin	Buss	GER	7.4.76	1	WCh	Edmonton	8 Aug 01
2.36		Aleksander	Walerianczyk	POL	1.9.82	1	EU23	Bydgoszcz	20 Jul 03
2.36		Michal	Bieniek	POL	17.5.84	1		Biala Podlaska	28 May 05
2.36i		Andrey	Tereshin	RUS	15.12.82	1	NC	Moskva	17 Feb 06
2.36A		Dusty	Jonas	USA	19.4.86	1	Big 12	Boulder	18 May 08
2.36		Aleksandr	Shustov	RUS	29.6.84	2	NC	Cheboksary	23 Jul 11
		(61)	100th man 2.34, 200th 2.31, 300th 2.30, 400th 2.28, 500th 2.27						

Best outdoor marks for athletes with indoor bests

2.41	Ukhov	1	DL	Doha	9 May 14
2.39	Conway	1	USOF	Norman	30 Jul 89
2.39	Ukhov	1	NC	Cheboksary	5 Jul 12
2.38	Avdeyenko	2=	WCh	Roma	6 Sep 87
2.37	Thränhardt	2		Rieti	2 Sep 84
2.37	Smith	1	WJ	Seoul	20 Sep 92
2.37	Holm	1		Athína	13 Jul 08
2.36	Mögenburg	3		Eberstadt	10 Jun 84
2.36	Howard	1		Rehlingen	8 Jun 87
2.36	Zvara	1		Praha	23 Aug 87
2.36	Grant	4	WCh	Tokyo	1 Sep 91
2.36	Hoen	1		Oslo	1 Jul 97
2.36	Bába	2=	GGala	Roma	8 Jul 05
2.36	Dmitrik	1	NC	Chelyabinsk	23 Jul 11

Ancillary jumps – en route to final marks

2.40	Sotomayor	8 Sep 88
2.30	Bondarenko	14 Jun 14
2.40	Sotomayor	29 Jul 89
2.40	Barshim	14 Jun 14
2.40	Sotomayor	5 Jun 94
2.40	Barshim	5 Sep 14

POLE VAULT

Mark	Wind	Name		Nat	Born	Pos	Meet	Venue	Date
6.16i		Renaud	Lavillenie	FRA	18.9.86	1		Donetsk	15 Feb 14
6.15i		Sergey	Bubka	UKR	4.12.63	1		Donetsk	21 Feb 93
6.14i			Bubka			1		Liévin	13 Feb 93
6.14A	WR		Bubka			1		Sestriere	31 Jul 94
6.13i			Bubka			1		Berlin	21 Feb 92
6.13	WR		Bubka			1	TOTO	Tokyo	19 Sep 92
6.12i			Bubka			1	Mast	Grenoble	23 Mar 91
6.12	WR		Bubka			1		Padova	30 Aug 92
6.11i			Bubka			1		Donetsk	19 Mar 91
6.11	WR		Bubka			1		Dijon	13 Jun 92
6.10i			Bubka			1		San Sebastián	15 Mar 91
6.10	WR		Bubka			1	MAI	Malmö	5 Aug 91
6.09	WR		Bubka			1		Formia	8 Jul 91
6.08i			Bubka			1	NC	Volgograd	9 Feb 91
6.08	WR		Bubka			1	Znam	Moskva	9 Jun 91
6.08i			Lavillenie			1		Bydgoszcz	31 Jan 14
6.07	WR		Bubka			1	Super	Shizuoka	6 May 91
6.06	WR		Bubka			1	Nik	Nice	10 Jul 88
6.06i		Steve	Hooker	AUS	16.7.82	1		Boston (R)	7 Feb 09
6.05	WR		Bubka			1	PTS	Bratislava	9 Jun 88
6.05i			Bubka			1		Donetsk	17 Mar 90
6.05i			Bubka			1		Berlin	5 Mar 93
6.05			Bubka			1	GPF	London (CP)	10 Sep 93
6.05i			Bubka			1	Mast	Grenoble	6 Feb 94
6.05			Bubka			1	ISTAF	Berlin	30 Aug 94
6.05			Bubka			1	GPF	Fukuoka	13 Sep 97
6.05		Maksim	Tarasov	RUS	2.12.70	1	GP II	Athína	16 Jun 99
6.05		Dmitriy	Markov	BLR/AUS	14.3.75	1	WCh	Edmonton	9 Aug 01
6.04		Brad	Walker	USA	21.6.81	1	Pre	Eugene	8 Jun 08

MEN All-time

Mark	Wind	Name		Nat	Born	Pos	Meet	Venue	Date
6.04i			Lavillenie			1		Rouen	25 Jan 14
		(30/6)							
6.03		Okkert	Brits	RSA	22.8.73	1	ASV	Köln	18 Aug 95
6.03		Jeff	Hartwig	USA	25.9.67	1		Jonesboro	14 Jun 00
6.02i		Rodion	Gataullin	RUS	23.11.65	1	NC	Gomel	4 Feb 89
6.01		Igor	Trandenkov	RUS	17.8.66	1	NC	Sankt Peterburg	4 Jul 96
		Hit bar hard, but kept it on with his hand illegally. Next best 5.95 1						Dijon	26 May 96
		(10)							
6.01		Tim	Mack	USA	15.9.72	1	WAF	Monaco	18 Sep 04
6.01		Yevgeniy	Lukyanenko	RUS	23.1.85	1	EAF	Bydgoszcz	1 Jul 08
6.01	sq	Björn	Otto	GER	16.10.77	1		Aachen	5 Sep 12
6.00		Tim	Lobinger	GER	3.9.72	1	ASV	Köln	24 Aug 97
6.00i		Jean	Galfione	FRA	9.6.71	1	WI	Maebashi	6 Mar 99
6.00i		Danny	Ecker	GER	21.7.77	1		Dortmund	11 Feb 01
6.00		Toby	Stevenson	USA	19.11.76	1eA	CalR	Modesto	8 May 04
6.00		Paul	Burgess	AUS	14.8.79	1		Perth	25 Feb 05
5.98		Lawrence	Johnson	USA	7.5.74	1		Knoxville	25 May 96
5.97		Scott	Huffman	USA	30.11.64	1	NC	Knoxville	18 Jun 94
		(20)							
5.96		Joe	Dial	USA	26.10.62	1		Norman	18 Jun 87
5.95		Andrei	Tivontchik	GER	13.7.70	1	ASV	Köln	16 Aug 96
5.95		Michael	Stolle	GER	17.12.74	1	Herc	Monaco	18 Aug 00
5.95		Romain	Mesnil	FRA	13.6.77	1		Castres	6 Aug 03
5.94i		Philippe	Collet	FRA	13.12.63	1	Mast	Grenoble	10 Mar 90
5.93i	WIR	Billy	Olson	USA	19.7.58	1		East Rutherford	8 Feb 86
5.93i		Tye	Harvey	USA	25.9.74	2	NC	Atlanta	3 Mar 01
5.93		Alex	Averbukh	ISR	1.10.74	1	GP	Madrid (C)	19 Jul 03
5.92		István	Bagyula	HUN	2.1.69	1	Gugl	Linz	5 Jul 91
5.92		Igor	Potapovich	KAZ	6.9.67	2		Dijon	13 Jun 92
		(30)							
5.92		Dean	Starkey	USA	27.3.67	1	Banes	São Paulo	21 May 94
5.91	WR	Thierry	Vigneron	FRA	9.3.60	2	GGala	Roma	31 Aug 84
5.91i		Viktor	Ryzhenkov	UZB	25.8.66	2		San Sebastián	15 Mar 91
5.91A		Riaan	Botha	RSA	8.11.70	1		Pretoria	2 Apr 97
5.91		Pawel	Wojciechowski	POL	6.6.89	1		Szczecin	15 Aug 11
5.91		Malte	Mohr	GER	24.7.86	1		Ingolstadt	22 Jun 12
5.91		Raphael	Holzdeppe	GER	28.9.89	3	OG	London (OS)	10 Aug 12
5.90		Pierre	Quinon	FRA	20.2.62	2	Nik	Nice	16 Jul 85
5.90i		Ferenc	Salbert	HUN/FRA	5.8.60	1	Mast	Grenoble	14 Mar 87
5.90		Miroslaw	Chmara	POL	9.5.64	1	BNP	Villeneuve d'Ascq	27 Jun 88
		(40)							
5.90i		Grigoriy	Yegorov	KAZ	12.1.67	1		Yokohama	11 Mar 90
5.90		Denis	Petushinskiy ¶	RUS	28.6.67	1	Znam	Moskva	13 Jun 93
5.90i		Pyotr	Bochkaryov	RUS	3.11.67	1	EI	Paris (B)	12 Mar 94
5.90		Jacob	Davis	USA	29.4.78	1	TexR	Austin	4 Apr 98
5.90		Viktor	Chistyakov	RUS/AUS	9.2.75	1		Salamanca	15 Jul 99
5.90		Pavel	Gerasimov	RUS	29.5.79	1		Rüdlingen	12 Aug 00
5.90		Nick	Hysong	USA	9.12.71	1	OG	Sydney	29 Sep 00
5.90		Giuseppe	Gibilisco	ITA	5.1.79	1	WCh	Saint-Denis	28 Aug 03
5.90i		Igor	Pavlov	RUS	18.7.79	1	EI	Madrid	5 Mar 05
5.90		Lázaro	Borges	CUB	19.6.86	2	WCh	Daegu	29 Aug 11
5.90i		Dmitriy	Starodubtsev	RUS	3.1.86	1		Chelyabinsk	18 Dec 11
		(51)	100th man 5.81, 200th 5.72, 300th 5.65, 400th 5.60, 500th 5.55						

Best outdoor marks for athletes with lifetime bests indoors

Mark	Name	Pos	Meet	Venue	Date	Mark	Name	Pos	Meet	Venue	Date
6.02	Lavillenie	1	DL	London (OS)	27 Jul 13	5.98	Galfione	1		Amiens	23 Jul 99
6.00	Gataullin	1		Tokyo	16 Sep 89	5.93	Ecker	1		Ingolstadt	26 Jul 98
6.00	Hooker	1		Perth	27 Jan 08	5.90	Yegorov	2	WCh	Stuttgart	19 Aug 93

Ancillary jump: 6.05i Bubka 13 Feb 93

Exhibition or Market Square competitions

Mark	Name		Nat	Born	Pos	Venue	Date
6.00	Jean	Galfione	FRA	9.6.71	1	Besançon	23 May 97
5.95	Viktor	Chistiakov	RUS/AUS	9.2.75	1	Chiari	8 Sep 99
5.90	Pyotr	Bochkaryov	RUS	3.11.67	1	Karlskrona	28 Jun 96

LONG JUMP

Mark	Wind	Name		Nat	Born	Pos	Meet	Venue	Date
8.95 WR	0.3	Mike	Powell	USA	10.11.63	1	WCh	Tokyo	30 Aug 91
8.90A WR	2.0	Bob	Beamon	USA	29.8.46	1	OG	Ciudad de México	18 Oct 68
8.87	-0.2	Carl	Lewis	USA	1.7.61	*	WCh	Tokyo	30 Aug 91
8.86A	1.9	Robert	Emmiyan	ARM	16.2.65	1		Tsakhkadzor	22 May 87
8.79	1.9		Lewis			1	TAC	Indianapolis	19 Jun 83
8.79i	-		Lewis			1		New York	27 Jan 84
8.76	1.0		Lewis			1	USOF	Indianapolis	24 Jul 82

Mark	Wind	Name		Nat	Born	Pos	Meet	Venue	Date
8.76	0.8		Lewis			1	NC/OT	Indianapolis	18 Jul 88
8.75	1.7		Lewis			1	PAm	Indianapolis	16 Aug 87
8.74	1.4	Larry	Myricks ¶	USA	10.3.56	2	NC/OT	Indianapolis	18 Jul 88
8.74A	2.0	Erick	Walder	USA	5.11.71	1		El Paso	2 Apr 94
8.74	1.2	Dwight	Phillips	USA	1.10.77	1	Pre	Eugene	7 Jun 09
8.73	1.2	Irving	Saladino	PAN	23.1.83	1	FBK	Hengelo	24 May 08
8.72	-0.2		Lewis			1	OG	Seoul	26 Sep 88
8.71	-0.4		Lewis			1	Pepsi	Los Angeles (Ww)	13 May 84
8.71	0.1		Lewis			1	OT	Los Angeles	19 Jun 84
8.71	1.9	Iván	Pedroso	CUB	17.12.72	1		Salamanca	18 Jul 95
8.71i		Sebastian	Bayer (10)	GER	11.6.86	1	EI	Torino	8 Mar 09
8.70	0.8		Myricks			1	NC	Houston	17 Jun 89
8.70	0.7		Powell			1		Salamanca	27 Jul 93
8.70	1.6		Pedroso			1	WCh	Göteborg	12 Aug 95
8.68	1.0		Lewis			Q	OG	Barcelona	5 Aug 92
8.68	1.6		Pedroso			1		Lisboa	17 Jun 95
8.67	0.4		Lewis			1	WCh	Roma	5 Sep 87
8.67	-0.7		Lewis			1	OG	Barcelona	6 Aug 92
8.66	0.8		Lewis			*	MSR	Walnut	26 Apr 87
8.66	1.0		Myricks			1		Tokyo	23 Sep 87
8.66	0.9		Powell			1	BNP	Villeneuve d'Ascq	29 Jun 90
8.66A	1.4		Lewis			*		Sestriere	31 Jul 94
8.66	0.3		Pedroso			1		Linz	22 Aug 95
8.66	1.6	Loúis	Tsátoumas	GRE	12.2.82	1		Kalamáta	2 Jun 07
		(31/11)							
8.63	0.5	Kareem	Streete-Thompson	CAY/USA	30.3.73	1	GP II	Linz	4 Jul 94
8.62	0.7	James	Beckford	JAM	9.1.75	1		Orlando	5 Apr 97
8.59i		Miguel	Pate	USA	13.6.79	1	NC	New York	1 Mar 02
8.56i	-	Yago	Lamela	ESP	24.7.77	2	WI	Maebashi	7 Mar 99
8.56	0.2	Aleksandr	Menkov	RUS	7.12.90	1	WCh	Moskva	16 Aug 13
8.54	0.9	Lutz	Dombrowski	GDR	25.6.59	1	OG	Moskva	28 Jul 80
8.54	1.7	Mitchell	Watt	AUS	25.3.88	1	DNG	Stockholm	29 Jul 11
8.53	1.2	Jaime	Jefferson	CUB	17.1.62	1	Barr	La Habana	12 May 90
8.52	0.7	Savanté	Stringfellow	USA	6.11.78	1	NC	Stanford	21 Jun 02
		(20)							
8.51	1.7	Roland	McGhee	USA	15.10.71	2		São Paulo	14 May 95
8.51	1.7	Greg	Rutherford	GBR	17.11.86	1		Chula Vista	24 Apr 14
8.50	0.2	Llewellyn	Starks	USA	10.2.67	2		Rhede	7 Jul 91
8.50	1.3	Godfrey Khotso	Mokoena	RSA	6.3.85	2	GP	Madrid	4 Jul 09
8.49	2.0	Melvin	Lister	USA	29.8.77	1	SEC	Baton Rouge	13 May 00
8.49	0.6	Jai	Taurima	AUS	26.6.72	2	OG	Sydney	28 Sep 00
8.49	0.7	Christian	Reif	GER	24.10.84	1		Weinheim	31 May 14
8.48	0.8	Joe	Greene	USA	17.2.67	3		São Paulo	14 May 95
8.48	0.6	Mohamed Salim	Al-Khuwalidi	KSA	19.6.81	1		Sotteville-lès-Rouen	2 Jul 06
8.47	1.9	Kevin	Dilworth	USA	14.2.74	1		Abilene	9 May 96
		(30)							
8.47	0.9	John	Moffitt	USA	12.12.80	2	OG	Athína	26 Aug 04
8.47	-0.2	Andrew	Howe	ITA	12.5.85	2	WCh	Osaka	30 Aug 07
8.47	0.0		Li Jinzhe	CHN	1.9.89	1		Bad Langensalza	28 Jun 14
8.46	1.2	Leonid	Voloshin	RUS	30.3.66	1	NC	Tallinn	5 Jul 88
8.46	1.6	Mike	Conley	USA	5.10.62	2		Springfield	4 May 96
8.46	1.8	Cheikh Tidiane	Touré	SEN/FRA	25.1.70	1		Bad Langensalza	15 Jun 97
8.46	0.3	Ibrahin	Camejo	CUB	28.6.82	1		Bilbao	21 Jun 08
8.46	1.3	Luis	Rivera	MEX	21.6.87	1	WUG	Kazan	12 Jul 13
8.45	2.0	Nenad	Stekic	YUG	7.3.51	1	PO	Montreal	25 Jul 75
8.44	1.7	Eric	Metcalf	USA	23.1.68	1	NC	Tampa	17 Jun 88
		(40)							
8.43	0.8	Jason	Grimes	USA	10.9.59	*	NC	Indianapolis	16 Jun 85
8.43	1.8	Giovanni	Evangelisti	ITA	11.9.61	1		San Giovanni Valdarno	16 May 87
8.43i	-	Stanislav	Tarasenko	RUS	23.7.66	1		Moskva	26 Jan 94
8.43	0.1	Luis Felipe	Méliz	CUB/ESP	11.8.79	2	OD	Jena	3 Jun 00
8.43	-0.2	Ignisious	Gaisah	GHA/NED	20.6.83	2	GGala	Roma	14 Jul 06
8.43	1.8	Jeff	Henderson	USA	19.2.89	*	NC	Sacramento	29 Jun 14
8.42	0.4	Salim	Sdiri	FRA	26.10.78	1		Pierre-Bénite	12 Jun 09
8.41	1.5	Craig	Hepburn	BAH	10.12.69	1	NC	Nassau	17 Jun 93
8.41i	-	Kirill	Sosunov	RUS	1.11.75	2	WI	Paris (B)	8 Mar 97
8.40	1.4	Douglas de	Souza	BRA	6.8.72	1		São Paulo	15 Feb 95
		(50)							
8.40	0.4	Robert	Howard	USA	26.11.75	1	SEC	Auburn	17 May 97
8.40	2.0	Gregor	Cankar	SLO	25.1.75	1		Celje	18 May 97

Mark	Wind	Name		Nat	Born	Pos	Meet	Venue	Date
8.40	0.0		Lao Jianfeng	CHN	24.5.75	1	NC	Zhaoqing	28 May 97
8.40	1.0	Yahya	Berrabah	MAR	13.10.81	1	Franc	Beirut	2 Oct 09
8.40	0.5	Fabrice	Lapierre	AUS	17.10.83	1		Nuoro	14 Jul 10
8.40	0.0	Ngonidzashe	Makusha	ZIM	11.3.87	1	NCAA	Des Moines	9 Jun 11
		(56)	100th man 8.33, 200th 8.23, 300th 8.17, 400th 8.12, 500th 8.09						

Best at low altitude: 8.61 1.3 Emmiyan 1 GWG Moskva 6 Jul 86 8.58 1.8 Walder 1 Springfield 4 May 86

Wind-assisted marks performances to 8.70, performers to 8.42

Mark	Wind	Name		Nat	Born	Pos	Meet	Venue	Date
8.99A	4.4	Mike	Powell	USA	10.11.63	1		Sestriere	21 Jul 92
8.96A	1.2+	Iván	Pedroso	CUB	17.12.72	1		Sestriere	29 Jul 95
8.95A	3.9		Powell			1		Sestriere	31 Jul 94
8.91	2.9	Carl	Lewis	USA	1.7.61	2	WCh	Tokyo	30 Aug 91
8.90	3.7		Powell			1	S&W	Modesto	16 May 92
8.79	3.0		Pedroso			1	Barr	La Habana	21 May 92
8.78	3.1	Fabrice	Lapierre	AUS	17.10.83	1	NC	Perth	18 Apr 10
8.77	3.9		Lewis			1	Pepsi	Los Angeles (Ww)	18 May 85
8.77	3.4		Lewis			1	MSR	Walnut	26 Apr 87
8.73	4.6		Lewis			Q	NC	Sacramento	19 Jun 81
8.73	3.2		Lewis			Q	NC	Indianapolis	17 Jun 83
8.73A	2.6		Powell			1		Sestriere	31 Jul 91
8.73	4.8		Pedroso			1		Madrid	20 Jun 95
8.72	2.2		Lewis			1	NYG	New York	24 May 92
8.72A	3.9		Lewis			2		Sestriere	31 Jul 94
8.70	2.5		Pedroso			1		Padova	16 Jul 95
8.68	4.9	James	Beckford	JAM	9.1.75	1	JUCO	Odessa, Tx	19 May 95
8.66A	4.0	Joe	Greene	USA	17.2.67	2		Sestriere	21 Jul 92
8.64	3.5	Kareem	Streete-Thompson	CAY/USA	30.3.73	2	NC	Knoxville	18 Jun 94
8.63	3.9	Mike	Conley	USA	5.10.62	2	NC	Eugene	20 Jun 86
8.57	5.2	Jason	Grimes	USA	10.9.59	1	vFRG,AFR	Durham	27 Jun 82
8.53	4.9	Kevin	Dilworth	USA	14.2.74	1		Fort-de-France	27 Apr 02
8.52	3.5	Jeff	Henderson	USA	19.2.89	1	NC	Sacramento	29 Jun 14
8.51	3.7	Ignisious	Gaisah	GHA	20.6.83	1	AfCh	Bambous	9 Aug 06
8.49	2.6	Ralph	Boston	USA	9.5.39	1	OT	Los Angeles	12 Sep 64
8.49	4.5	Stanislav	Tarasenko	RUS	23.7.66	2		Madrid	20 Jun 95
8.48	2.8	Kirill	Sosunov	RUS	1.11.75	1		Oristano	18 Sep 95
8.48	3.4	Peter	Burge	AUS	3.7.74	1		Gold Coast (RB)	10 Sep 00
8.48	2.1	Brian	Johnson	USA	25.3.80	1	Conseil	Fort-de-France	8 May 08
8.46	3.4	Randy	Williams	USA	23.8.53	1		Eugene	18 May 73
8.46		Vernon	George	USA	6.10.64	1		Houston	21 May 89
8.44		Keith	Talley	USA	28.1.64	Q		Odessa, Tx	16 May 85
8.42		Anthony	Bailous	USA	6.4.65	Q		Odessa, Tx	16 May 85
8.42A	4.5	Milan	Gombala	CZE	29.1.68	3		Sestriere	21 Jul 92
Exhibition:	8.46	Yuriy	Naumkin	RUS	4.11.68	1		Iglesias	6 Sep 96

Best outdoors

8.56 1.3 Lamela 1 Torino 24 Jun 99 8.49 1.6 Bayer 1 NC Ulm 4 Jul 09

8.46A 0.0 Pate 1 Cd. de México 3 May 03 and 8.45 1.5 2 NC Stanford 21 Jun 02, 8.48w 5.6 1 Fort Worth 21 Apr 01

Ancillary marks – other marks during series (to 8.67/8.70w)

8.84	1.7	Lewis	30 Aug 91	8.89Aw	2.4	Pedroso	29 Jul 95	8.75w	2.1	Lewis	16 Aug 87
8.71	0.6	Lewis	19 Jun 83	8.84Aw	3.8	Powell	21 Jul 92	8.75Aw	3.4	Powell	21 Jul 92
8.68	0.3	Lewis	18 Jul 88	8.83w	2.3	Lewis	30 Aug 91	8.73w	2.4	Lewis	18 May 85
8.68	0.0	Lewis	30 Aug 91	8.80Aw	4.0	Powell	21 Jul 92	8.73w		Powell	16 May 92
8.67	-0.2	Lewis	5 Sep 87	8.78Aw		Powell	21 Jul 92	8.71Aw		Powell	31 Jul 91

TRIPLE JUMP

Mark	Wind	Name		Nat	Born	Pos	Meet	Venue	Date
18.29 WR	1.3	Jonathan	Edwards	GBR	10.5.66	1	WCh	Göteborg	7 Aug 95
18.09	-0.4	Kenny	Harrison	USA	13.2.65	1	OG	Atlanta	27 Jul 96
18.04	0.3	Teddy	Tamgho	FRA	15.6.89	1	WCh	Moskva	18 Aug 13
18.01	0.4		Edwards			1	Bisl	Oslo	9 Jul 98
18.00	1.3		Edwards			1	McD	London (CP)	27 Aug 95
17.99	0.5		Edwards			1	EC	Budapest	23 Aug 98
17.98 WR	1.8		Edwards			1		Salamanca	18 Jul 95
17.98	1.2		Tamgho			1	DL	New York	12 Jun 10
17.97 WR	1.5	Willie	Banks	USA	11.3.56	1	TAC	Indianapolis	16 Jun 85
17.96	0.1	Christian	Taylor	USA	18.6.90	1	WCh	Daegu	4 Sep 11
17.93	1.6		Harrison			1	DNG	Stockholm	2 Jul 90
17.92	1.6	Khristo	Markov	BUL	27.1.65	1	WCh	Roma	31 Aug 87
17.92	1.9	James	Beckford	JAM	9.1.75	1	JUCO	Odessa, TX	20 May 95
17.92i WIR	-		Tamgho			1	EI	Paris (Bercy)	6 Mar 11
17.92	0.7		Edwards			1	WCh	Edmonton	6 Aug 01
17.91i WIR	-		Tamgho			1	NC	Aubière	20 Feb 11
17.91	1.4		Tamgho			1	Athl	Lausanne	30 Jun 11

Mark	Wind	Name		Nat	Born	Pos	Meet	Venue	Date
17.90	1.0	Vladimir	Inozemtsev	UKR	25.5.64	1	PTS	Bratislava	20 Jun 90
17.90	0.4	Jadel	Gregório	BRA	16.9.80	1	GP	Belém	20 May 07
17.90i			Tamgho			1	WI	Doha	14 Mar 10
17.89A	WR 0.0	João Carlos	de Oliveira (10)	BRA	28.5.54	1	PAm	Ciudad de México	15 Oct 75
17.88	0.9		Edwards			2	OG	Atlanta	27 Jul 96
17.87	1.7	Mike	Conley	USA	5.10.62	1	NC	San José	27 Jun 87
17.86	1.3	Charles	Simpkins	USA	19.10.63	1	WUG	Kobe	2 Sep 85
17.86	0.3		Conley			1	WCh	Stuttgart	16 Aug 93
17.86	0.7		Edwards			1	CG	Manchester	28 Jul 02
17.85	0.9	Yoelbi	Quesada	CUB	4.8.73	1	WCh	Athína	8 Aug 97
17.84	0.7		Conley			1		Bad Cannstatt	4 Jul 93
17.83i	WIR -	Aliecer	Urrutia	CUB	22.9.74	1		Sindelfingen	1 Mar 97
17.83i	WIR -	Christian	Olsson	SWE	25.1.80	1	WI	Budapest	7 Mar 04
		(30/15)							
17.81	1.0	Marian	Oprea	ROU	6.6.82	1	Athl	Lausanne	5 Jul 05
17.81	0.1	Phillips	Idowu	GBR	30.12.78	1	EC	Barcelona	29 Jul 10
17.78	1.0	Nikolay	Musiyenko	UKR	16.12.59	1	Znam	Leningrad	7 Jun 86
17.78	0.6	Lázaro	Betancourt ¶	CUB	18.3.63	1	Barr	La Habana	15 Jun 86
17.78	0.8	Melvin	Lister	USA	29.8.77	1	NC/OT	Sacramento	17 Jul 04
		(20)							
17.77	1.0	Aleksandr	Kovalenko	RUS	8.5.63	1	NC	Bryansk	18 Jul 87
17.77i	-	Leonid	Voloshin	RUS	30.3.66	1		Grenoble	6 Feb 94
17.76	-0.2	Pedro Pablo	Pichardo	CUB	30.6.93	1		La Habana	7 Feb 14
17.75	0.3	Oleg	Protsenko	RUS	11.8.63	1	Znam	Moskva	10 Jun 90
17.75	0.8	Will	Claye	USA	13.6.91	1	NC	Sacramento	27 Jun 14
17.74	1.4	Nelson	Évora	POR	20.4.84	1	WCh	Osaka	27 Aug 07
17.73i		Walter	Davis	USA	2.7.79	1	WI	Moskva	12 Mar 06
17.73i	-	Fabrizio	Donato	ITA	14.8.76	2	EI	Paris (Bercy)	6 Mar 11
17.72i		Brian	Wellman	BER	8.9.67	1	WI	Barcelona	12 Mar 95
17.72	1.3	Sheryf	El-Sheryf	UKR	2.1.89	1	EU23	Ostrava	17 Jul 11
		(30)							
17.70i		Daniele	Greco	ITA	1.3.89	1	EI	Göteborg	2 Mar 13
17.69	1.5	Igor	Lapshin	BLR	8.8.63	1		Stayki	31 Jul 88
17.69i		Yoandri	Betanzos	CUB	15.2.82	2	WI	Doha	14 Mar 10
17.68	0.4	Danil	Burkenya	RUS	20.7.78	1	NC	Tula	31 Jul 04
17.68A	1.6	Alexis	Copello	CUB	12.8.85	1		Ávila	17 Jul 11
17.66	1.7	Ralf	Jaros	GER	13.12.65	1	ECp	Frankfurt-am-Main	30 Jun 91
17.65	1.0	Aleksandr	Yakovlev	UKR	8.9.57	1	Znam	Moskva	6 Jun 87
17.65	0.8	Denis	Kapustin	RUS	5.10.70	2	Bisl	Oslo	9 Jul 98
17.64	1.4	Nathan	Douglas	GBR	4.12.82	1	NC	Manchester (SC)	10 Jul 05
17.63	0.9	Kenta	Bell	USA	16.3.77	1c2	MSR	Walnut	21 Apr 02
		(40)							
17.62i	-	Yoel	García	CUB	25.11.73	2		Sindelfingen	1 Mar 97
17.62	-0.2	Arne David	Girat	CUB	26.8.84	3	ALBA	La Habana	25 Apr 09
17.60	0.6	Vladimir	Plekhanov	RUS	11.4.58	2	NC	Leningrad	4 Aug 85
17.59i	-	Pierre	Camara	FRA	10.9.65	1	WI	Toronto	13 Mar 93
17.59	0.3	Vasiliy	Sokov	RUS	7.4.68	1	NC	Moskva	19 Jun 93
17.59	0.8	Charles	Friedek	GER	26.8.71	1		Hamburg	23 Jul 97
17.59	0.9	Leevan	Sands	BAH	16.8.81	3	OG	Beijing	21 Aug 08
17.59	0.0		Li Yanxi	CHN	26.6.84	1	NG	Jinan	26 Oct 09
17.58	1.5	Oleg	Sakirkin	KZK	23.1.66	2	NC	Gorkiy	23 Jul 89
17.58	1.6	Aarik	Wilson	USA	25.10.82	1	LGP	London (CP)	3 Aug 07
17.58	-1.7	Ernesto	Revé	CUB	26.2.92	2		La Habana	7 Feb 14
		(51)	100th man 17.38, 200th 17.18, 300th 17.01, 400th 16.88, 500th 16.77						

Wind-assisted marks – performances to 17.86, performers to 17.59

Mark	Wind	Name		Nat	Born	Pos	Meet	Venue	Date
18.43	2.4	Jonathan	Edwards	GBR	10.5.66	1	ECp	Villeneuve d'Ascq	25 Jun 95
18.20	5.2	Willie	Banks	USA	11.3.56	1	NC/OT	Indianapolis	16 Jul 88
18.17	2.1	Mike	Conley	USA	5.10.62	1	OG	Barcelona	3 Aug 92
18.08	2.5		Edwards			1	BrGP	Sheffield	23 Jul 95
18.03	2.9		Edwards			1	GhG	Gateshead	2 Jul 95
18.01	3.7		Harrison			1	NC	Atlanta	15 Jun 96
17.97	7.5	Yoelbi	Quesada	CUB	4.8.73	1		Madrid	20 Jun 95
17.93	5.2	Charles	Simpkins	USA	19.10.63	2	NC/OT	Indianapolis	16 Jul 88
17.92	3.4	Christian	Olsson	SWE	25.1.80	1	GP	Gateshead	13 Jul 03
17.91	3.2		Simpkins			1	NC	Eugene	21 Jun 86
17.86	3.9		Simpkins			1	NC/OT	New Orleans	21 Jun 92
17.86	5.7	Denis	Kapustin	RUS	5.10.70	1		Sevilla	5 Jun 94
17.82	2.5	Nelson	Évora	POR	20.4.84	1	NC	Seixal	26 Jul 09
17.81	4.6	Keith	Connor	GBR	16.9.57	1	CG	Brisbane	9 Oct 82
17.76A	2.2	Kenta	Bell	USA	16.3.77	1		El Paso	10 Apr 04

Mark	Wind		Name	Nat	Born	Pos	Meet	Venue	Date
17.75		Gennadiy	Valyukevich	BLR	1.6.58	1		Uzhgorod	27 Apr 86
17.75	7.1	Brian	Wellman	BER	8.9.67	2		Madrid	20 Jun 95
17.73	4.1	Vasiliy	Sokov	RUS	7.4.68	1		Riga	3 Jun 89
17.69	3.9	Alexis	Copello	CUB	12.8.85	1	ALBA	La Habana	25 Apr 09
17.63	4.3	Robert	Cannon	USA	9.7.58	3	NC/OT	Indianapolis	16 Jul 88
17.59	2.1	Jerome	Romain	DMA/FRA	12.6.71	3	WCh	Göteborg	7 Aug 95

Best outdoor marks for athletes with indoor bests

Mark	Wind	Name	Pos	Meet	Venue	Date
17.79	1.4	Olsson	1	OG	Athína	22 Aug 04
17.75	1.0	Voloshin	2	WCh	Tokyo	26 Aug 91
17.71	-0.7	Davis	1	NC	Indianapolis	25 Jun 06
17.70	1.7	Urrutia	1	GP II	Sevilla	6 Jun 96
17.67w	3.4	Greco	1	NC	Bressanone	8 Jul 12
17.65	1.4	Betanzos	2	ALBA	La Habana	25 Apr 09
17.67w	5.4		1		Bilbao	1 Jul 06
17.62A	0.1	Wellman	1		El Paso	15 Apr 95
17.60	1.9	Donato	1		Milano	7 Jun 00
17.63w	2.8		1	EC	Helsinki	30 Jun 12

Low altitude best: 17.65 0.1 Copello 1 Barr La Habana 30 May 09

Ancillary marks – other marks during series (to 17.78/17.84w)

Mark	Wind	Name	Date
18.16 WR	1.3	Edwards	7 Aug 95
17.99	0.1	Harrison	27 Jul 96
17.84	1.7	Tamgho	12 Jun 10
18.39w	3.7	Edwards	25 Jun 95
18.06w	4.9	Banks	16 Jul 88
17.90w	2.5	Edwards	25 Jun 95
17.84w	2.1	Edwards	23 Aug 98

SHOT

Mark		Name	Nat	Born	Pos	Meet	Venue	Date
23.12 WR	Randy	Barnes ¶	USA	16.6.66	1		Los Angeles (Ww)	20 May 90
23.10		Barnes			1	Jenner	San José	26 May 90
23.06 WR	Ulf	Timmermann	GDR	1.11.62	1	Veniz	Haniá	22 May 88
22.91 WR	Alessandro	Andrei	ITA	3.1.59	1		Viareggio	12 Aug 87
22.86	Brian	Oldfield	USA	1.6.45	1	ITA	El Paso	10 May 75
22.75	Werner	Günthör	SUI	1.6.61	1		Bern	23 Aug 88
22.67	Kevin	Toth ¶	USA	29.12.67	1	KansR	Lawrence	19 Apr 03
22.66i		Barnes			1	Sunkist	Los Angeles	20 Jan 89
22.64 WR	Udo	Beyer	GDR	9.8.55	1		Berlin	20 Aug 86
22.62 WR		Timmermann			1		Berlin	22 Sep 85
22.61		Timmermann			1		Potsdam	8 Sep 88
22.60		Timmermann			1	vURS	Tallinn	21 Jun 86
22.56		Timmermann			1		Berlin	13 Sep 88
22.55i		Timmermann			1	NC	Senftenberg	11 Feb 89
22.54	Christian	Cantwell	USA	30.9.80	1	GP II	Gresham	5 Jun 04
22.52	John	Brenner	USA	4.1.61	1	MSR	Walnut	26 Apr 87
22.51		Timmermann			1		Erfurt	1 Jun 86
22.51	Adam	Nelson (10)	USA	7.7.75	1		Gresham	18 May 02
22.47		Timmermann			1		Dresden	17 Aug 86
22.47		Günthör			1	WG	Helsinki	2 Jul 87
22.47		Timmermann			1	OG	Seoul	23 Sep 88
22.45		Oldfield			1	ITA	El Paso	22 May 76
22.45		Cantwell			1	GP	Gateshead	11 Jun 06
22.43		Günthör			1	v3-N	Lüdenscheid	18 Jun 87
22.43	Reese	Hoffa	USA	8.10.77	1	LGP	London (CP)	3 Aug 07
22.42		Barnes			1	WK	Zürich	17 Aug 88
22.41		Cantwell			1	Pre	Eugene	3 Jul 10
22.40		Barnes			1		Rüdlingen	13 Jul 96
22.40i		Nelson			1		Fayetteville	15 Feb 08
22.39		Barnes			2	OG	Seoul	23 Sep 88
	(30/11)							
22.28	Ryan	Whiting	USA	24.11.86	1	DL	Doha	10 May 13
22.24	Sergey	Smirnov	RUS	17.9.60	2	vGDR	Tallinn	21 Jun 86
22.21	Dylan	Armstrong	CAN	15.1.81	1	NC	Calgary	25 Jun 11
22.20	John	Godina	USA	31.5.72	1		Carson	22 May 05
22.10	Sergey	Gavryushin	RUS	27.6.59	1		Tbilisi	31 Aug 86
22.10	Cory	Martin	USA	22.5.85	1		Tucson	22 May 10
22.09	Sergey	Kasnauskas	BLR	20.4.61	1		Stayki	23 Aug 84
22.09i	Mika	Halvari	FIN	13.2.70	1		Tampere	7 Feb 00
22.03	Joe	Kovacs	USA	28.6.89	1	NC	Sacramento	25 Jun 14
	(20)							
22.02i	George	Woods	USA	11.2.43	1	LAT	Inglewood	8 Feb 74
22.02	Dave	Laut	USA	21.12.56	1		Koblenz	25 Aug 82
22.00 WR	Aleksandr	Baryshnikov	RUS	11.11.48	1	vFRA	Colombes	10 Jul 76
21.98	Gregg	Tafralis ¶	USA	9.4.58	1		Los Gatos	13 Jun 92
21.97	Janus	Robberts	RSA	10.3.79	1	NCAA	Eugene	2 Jun 01
21.97	David	Storl	GER	27.7.90	1		London	20 Jul 14
21.96	Mikhail	Kostin	RUS	10.5.59	1		Vitebsk	20 Jul 86
21.95	Tomasz	Majewski	POL	30.8.81	1	DNG	Stockholm	30 Jul 09
21.93	Remigius	Machura ¶	CZE	3.7.60	1		Praha	23 Aug 87
21.92	Carl	Myerscough ¶	GBR	21.10.79	1	NCAA	Sacramento	13 Jun 03
	(30)							

Mark Wind	Name		Nat	Born	Pos	Meet	Venue	Date
21.87	C.J.	Hunter ¶	USA	14.12.68	2	NC	Sacramento	15 Jul 00
21.85 WR	Terry	Albritton	USA	14.1.55	1		Honolulu	21 Feb 76
21.83i	Aleksandr	Bagach ¶	UKR	21.11.66	1		Brovary	21 Feb 99
21.82 WR	Al	Feuerbach	USA	14.1.48	1		San José	5 May 73
21.82	Andy	Bloom	USA	11.8.73	1	GPF	Doha	5 Oct 00
21.81	Yuriy	Bilonog ¶	UKR	9.3.74	1	NC	Kiev	3 Jul 03
21.78 WR	Randy	Matson	USA	5.3.45	1		College Station	22 Apr 67
21.78	Dan	Taylor	USA	12.5.82	1		Tucson	23 May 09
21.77i	Mike	Stulce ¶	USA	21.7.69	1	v GBR	Birmingham	13 Feb 93
21.77	Dragan	Peric	YUG	8.5.64	1		Bar	25 Apr 98
	(40)							
21.76	Michael	Carter	USA	29.10.60	2	NCAA	Eugene	2 Jun 84
21.74	Janis	Bojars	LAT	12.5.56	1		Riga	14 Jul 84
21.73	Augie	Wolf ¶	USA	3.9.61	1		Leverkusen	12 Apr 84
21.69	Reijo	Ståhlberg	FIN	21.9.52	1	WCR	Fresno	5 May 79
21.69	Andrey	Mikhnevich ¶	BLR	12.7.76	1	WCh	Saint-Denis	23 Aug 03
21.68	Geoff	Capes	GBR	23.8.49	1	4-N	Cwmbrân	18 May 80
21.68	Edward	Sarul	POL	16.11.58	1		Sopot	31 Jul 83
21.67	Hartmut	Briesenick	GDR	17.3.49	1		Potsdam	1 Sep 73
21.63i	Joachim	Olsen	DEN	31.5.77	1		Tallinn	25 Feb 04
21.63	Maris	Urtans	LAT	9.2.81	1	ET-2	Beograd	19 Jun 10
	(50)	100th man 21.16, 200th 20.73, 300th 20.38, 400th 20.10, 500th 19.88						

Not recognised by GDR authorities: 22.11 Rolf Oesterreich GDR 24.8.49 1 Zschopau 12 Sep 76

Drugs disqualification

Mark	Name		Nat	Born	Pos	Meet	Venue	Date
22.84		Barnes			1		Malmö	7 Aug 90
22.10	Andrey	Mikhnevich ¶	BLR	12.7.76	1		Minsk	11 Aug 11
21.82	Mike	Stulce ¶	USA	21.7.69	1		Brenham	9 May 90

Best outdoor marks for athletes with lifetime bests indoors

21.70 Stulce ¶ 1 OG Barcelona 31 Jul 92 | 21.63 Woods 2 CalR Modesto 22 May 76

Ancillary marks – other marks during series (to 22.45)

22.84 WR	Andrei	12 Aug 87	22.72 WR	Andrei	12 Aug 87	22.55	Barnes	20 May 90
22.76	Barnes	20 May 90	22.70	Günthör	23 Aug 88	22.49	Nelson	18 May 02
22.74	Andrei	12 Aug 87	22.58	Beyer	20 Aug 86	22.45	Timmermann	22 May 88

DISCUS

Mark Wind	Name		Nat	Born	Pos	Meet	Venue	Date
74.08 WR	Jürgen	Schult	GDR	11.5.60	1		Neubrandenburg	6 Jun 86
73.88	Virgilijus	Alekna	LTU	13.2.72	1	NC	Kaunas	3 Aug 00
73.38	Gerd	Kanter	EST	6.5.79	1		Helsingborg	4 Sep 06
72.02		Kanter			1eA		Salinas	3 May 07
71.88		Kanter			1eA		Salinas	8 May 08
71.86 WR	Yuriy	Dumchev	RUS	5.8.58	1		Moskva	29 May 83
71.84	Piotr	Malachowski	POL	7.6.83	1	FBK	Hengelo	8 Jun 13
71.70	Róbert	Fazekas ¶	HUN	18.8.75	1		Szombathely	14 Jul 02
71.64		Kanter			1		Kohila	25 Jun 09
71.56		Alekna			1		Kaunas	25 Jul 07
71.50	Lars	Riedel	GER	28.6.67	1		Wiesbaden	3 May 97
71.45		Kanter			1		Chula Vista	29 Apr 10
71.32	Ben	Plucknett ¶	USA	13.4.54	1	Pre	Eugene	4 Jun 83
71.26	John	Powell	USA	25.6.47	1	NC	San José	9 Jun 84
71.26	Rickard	Bruch	SWE	2.7.46	1		Malmö	15 Nov 84
71.26	Imrich	Bugár (10)	CZE	14.4.55	1	Jenner	San José	25 May 85
71.25		Fazekas			1	WCp	Madrid (C)	21 Sep 02
71.25		Alekna			1	Danek	Turnov	20 May 08
71.18	Art	Burns	USA	19.7.54	1		San José	19 Jul 83
71.16 WR	Wolfgang	Schmidt	GDR	16.1.54	1		Berlin	9 Aug 78
71.14		Plucknett			1		Berkeley	12 Jun 83
71.14	Anthony	Washington	USA	16.1.66	1eA		Salinas	22 May 96
71.12		Alekna			1	WK	Zürich	11 Aug 00
71.08		Alekna			1		Réthimno	21 Jul 06
71.06	Luis Mariano	Delís ¶	CUB	12.12.57	1	Barr	La Habana	21 May 83
71.06		Riedel			1	WK	Zürich	14 Aug 96
71.00		Bruch			1		Malmö	14 Oct 84
70.99		Alekna			1		Stellenbosch	30 Mar 01
70.98	Mac	Wilkins	USA	15.11.50	1	WG	Helsinki	9 Jul 80
70.98		Burns			1	Pre	Eugene	21 Jul 84
	(30/16)							
70.82	Aleksander	Tammert	EST	2.2.73	1		Denton	15 Apr 06
70.66	Robert	Harting	GER	18.10.84	1	Danek	Turnov	22 May 12
70.54	Dmitriy	Shevchenko ¶	RUS	13.5.68	1		Krasnodar	7 May 02

Mark	Wind	Name		Nat	Born	Pos	Meet	Venue	Date
70.38	WR u	Jay	Silvester	USA	27.8.37	1		Lancaster	16 May 71
		(20)							
70.32		Frantz	Kruger	RSA/FIN	22.5.75	1		Salon-de-Provence	26 May 02
70.06		Romas	Ubartas ¶	LTU	26.5.60	1		Smalininkay	8 May 88
70.00		Juan	Martínez ¶	CUB	17.5.58	2	Barr	La Habana	21 May 83
69.95		Zoltán	Kövágó	HUN	10.4.79	1		Salon-de-Provence	25 May 06
69.91		John	Godina	USA	31.5.72	1		Salinas	19 May 98
69.90		Jason	Young	USA	27.5.81	1		Lubbock	26 Mar 10
69.70		Géjza	Valent	CZE	3.10.53	2		Nitra	26 Aug 84
69.62		Knut	Hjeltnes ¶	NOR	8.12.51	2	Jen	San José	25 May 85
69.62		Timo	Tompuri	FIN	9.6.69	1		Helsingborg	8 Jul 01
69.50		Mario	Pestano	ESP	8.4.78	1	NC	Santa Cruz de Tenerife	27 Jul 08
		(30)							
69.46		Al	Oerter	USA	19.9.36	1	TFA	Wichita	31 May 80
69.44		Georgiy	Kolnootchenko	BLR	7.5.59	1	vUSA	Indianapolis	3 Jul 82
69.40		Art	Swarts ¶	USA	14.2.45	1		Scotch Plains	8 Dec 79
69.36		Mike	Buncic	USA	25.7.62	1		Fresno	6 Apr 91
69.32		Ehsan	Hadadi	IRI	21.1.85	1		Tallinn	3 Jun 08
69.28		Vladimir	Dubrovshchik	BLR	7.1.72	1	NC	Staiki	3 Jun 00
69.26		Ken	Stadel	USA	19.2.52	2	AAU	Walnut	16 Jun 79
68.94		Adam	Setliff	USA	15.12.69	1		Atascadero	25 Jul 01
68.91		Ian	Waltz	USA	15.4.77	1		Salinas	24 May 06
68.90		Jean-Claude	Retel	FRA	11.2.68	1		Salon-de-Provence	17 Jul 02
		(40)							
68.88		Vladimir	Zinchenko	UKR	25.7.59	1		Dnepropetrovsk	16 Jul 88
68.76		Jarred	Rome	USA	21.12.76	2cA		Chula Vista	6 Aug 11
68.64		Dmitriy	Kovtsun ¶	UKR	29.9.55	1		Riga	6 Jul 84
68.58		Attila	Horváth	HUN	28.7.67	1		Budapest	24 Jun 94
68.52		Igor	Duginyets	UKR	20.5.56	1	NC	Kyiv	21 Aug 82
68.50		Armin	Lemme	GDR	28.10.55	1	vUSA	Karl-Marx-Stadt	10 Jul 82
68.49A		Casey	Malone	USA	6.4.77	1		Fort Collins	20 Jun 09
68.48	WR	John	van Reenen	RSA	26.3.47	1		Stellenbosch	14 Mar 75
68.44		Vaclovas	Kidykas	LTU	17.10.61	1		Sochi	1 Jun 88
68.33		Martin	Wierig	GER	10.6.87	1		Schönebeck	26 Jul 12
		(50)	100th man 67.08, 200th 65.24, 300th 64.28, 400th 63.14, 500th 62.16						
Subsequent to or at drugs disqualification				! recognised as US record					
72.34!		Ben	Plucknett ¶	USA	13.4.54	(1)	DNG	Stockholm	7 Jul 81
71.20			Plucknett			(1)	CalR	Modesto	16 May 81
70.84		Kamy	Keshmiri ¶	USA	23.1.69	(1)		Salinas	27 May 92
Sloping ground									
72.08		John	Powell	USA	25.6.47	1		Klagshamn	11 Sep 87
69.80		Stefan	Fernholm	SWE	2.7.59	1		Klagshamn	13 Aug 87
69.44		Adam	Setliff	USA	15.12.69	1		La Jolla	21 Jul 01
68.46		Andy	Bloom	USA	11.8.73	2cA		La Jolla	25 Mar 00

Ancillary marks – other marks during series (to 70.98)

72.35 Alekna 3 Aug 00 72.30 Kanter 4 Sep 06 71.08 Plucknett 4 Jun 83

HAMMER

Mark	Wind	Name		Nat	Born	Pos	Meet	Venue	Date
86.74	WR	Yuriy	Sedykh	RUS	11.6.55	1	EC	Stuttgart	30 Aug 86
86.66	WR		Sedykh			1	vGDR	Tallinn	22 Jun 86
86.34	WR		Sedykh			1		Cork	3 Jul 84
86.04		Sergey	Litvinov	RUS	23.1.58	1	OD	Dresden	3 Jul 86
85.74			Litvinov			2	EC	Stuttgart	30 Aug 86
85.68			Sedykh			1	BGP	Budapest	11 Aug 86
85.60			Sedykh			1	PTG	London (CP)	13 Jul 84
85.60			Sedykh			1	Drz	Moskva	17 Aug 84
85.20			Litvinov			2		Cork	3 Jul 84
85.14			Litvinov			1	PTG	London	11 Jul 86
85.14			Sedykh			1	Kuts	Moskva	4 Sep 88
85.02			Sedykh			1	BGP	Budapest	20 Aug 84
84.92			Sedykh			2	OD	Dresden	3 Jul 86
84.90		Vadim	Devyatovskiy ¶	BLR	20.3.77	1		Staiki	21 Jul 05
84.88			Litvinov			1	GP-GG	Roma	10 Sep 86
84.86		Koji	Murofushi	JPN	8.10.74	1	Odlozil	Praha	29 Jun 03
84.80			Litvinov			1	OG	Seoul	26 Sep 88
84.72			Sedykh			1	GWG	Moskva	9 Jul 86
84.64			Litvinov			2	GWG	Moskva	9 Jul 86
84.62		Igor	Astapkovich	BLR	4.1.63	1	Expo	Sevilla	6 Jun 92
84.60			Sedykh			1	8-N	Tokyo	14 Sep 84

Mark	Wind	Name		Nat	Born	Pos	Meet	Venue	Date
84.58			Sedykh			1	Znam	Leningrad	8 Jun 86
84.51		Ivan	Tikhon ¶	BLR	24.7.76	1	NC	Grodno	9 Jul 08
84.48		Igor	Nikulin	RUS	14.8.60	1	Athl	Lausanne	12 Jul 90
84.46			Sedykh			1		Vladivostok	14 Sep 88
84.46			Tikhon			1		Minsk	7 May 04
84.40		Jüri	Tamm	EST	5.2.57	1		Banská Bystrica	9 Sep 84
84.36			Litvinov			2	vGDR	Tallinn	22 Jun 86
84.32			Tikhon			1		Staiki	8 Aug 03
84.26			Sedykh			1	Nik	Nice	15 Jul 86
		(30/8)							
84.19		Adrián	Annus ¶	HUN	28.6.73	1		Szombathely	10 Aug 03
83.68		Tibor	Gécsek ¶	HUN	22.9.64	1		Zalaegerszeg	19 Sep 98
		(10)							
83.48		Pawel	Fajdek	POL	4.6.89	1		Warszawa	23 Aug 14
83.46		Andrey	Abduvaliyev	TJK/UZB	30.6.66	1		Adler	26 May 90
83.43		Aleksey	Zagornyi	RUS	31.5.78	1		Adler	10 Feb 02
83.40 @		Ralf	Haber	GDR	18.8.62	1		Athína	16 May 88
		82.54				1		Potsdam	9 Sep 88
83.38		Szymon	Ziólkowski	POL	1.7.76	1	WCh	Edmonton	5 Aug 01
83.30		Olli-Pekka	Karjalainen	FIN	7.3.80	1		Lahti	14 Jul 04
83.04		Heinz	Weis	GER	14.7.63	1	NC	Frankfurt	29 Jun 97
83.00		Balázs	Kiss	HUN	21.3.72	1	GP II	Saint-Denis	4 Jun 98
82.78		Karsten	Kobs	GER	16.9.71	1		Dortmund	26 Jun 99
82.69		Krisztián	Pars	HUN	18.2.82	1	EC	Zürich	16 Aug 14
		(20)		*@ competitive meeting but unsanctioned by GDR federation*					
82.64		Günther	Rodehau	GDR	6.7.59	1		Dresden	3 Aug 85
82.62		Sergey	Kirmasov ¶	RUS	25.3.70	1		Bryansk	30 May 98
82.62		Andrey	Skvaruk	UKR	9.3.67	1		Koncha-Zaspa	27 Apr 02
82.58		Primoz	Kozmus	SLO	30.9.79	1		Celje	2 Sep 09
82.54		Vasiliy	Sidorenko	RUS	1.5.61	1		Krasnodar	13 May 92
82.52		Lance	Deal	USA	21.8.61	1	GPF	Milano	7 Sep 96
82.40		Plamen	Minev	BUL	28.4.65	1	NM	Plovdiv	1 Jun 91
82.38		Gilles	Dupray	FRA	2.1.70	1		Chelles	21 Jun 00
82.28		Ilya	Konovalov ¶	RUS	4.3.71	1	NC	Tula	10 Aug 03
82.24		Benjaminas	Viluckis	LIT	20.3.61	1		Klaipeda	24 Aug 86
		(30)							
82.24		Vyacheslav	Korovin	RUS	8.9.62	1		Chelyabinsk	20 Jun 87
82.23		Vladislav	Piskunov ¶	UKR	7.6.78	2		Koncha-Zaspa	27 Apr 02
82.22		Holger	Klose	GER	5.12.72	1		Dortmund	2 May 98
82.16		Vitaliy	Alisevich	BLR	15.6.67	1		Parnu	13 Jul 88
82.08		Ivan	Tanev	BUL	1.5.57	1	NC	Sofia	3 Sep 88
82.00		Sergey	Alay ¶	BLR	11.6.65	1		Stayki	12 May 92
81.88		Jud	Logan ¶	USA	19.7.59	1		State College	22 Apr 88
81.81		Libor	Charfreitag	SVK	11.9.77	3	Odlozil	Praha	29 Jun 03
81.79		Christophe	Épalle	FRA	23.1.69	1		Clermont-Ferrand	30 Jun 00
81.78		Christoph	Sahner	FRG	23.9.63	1		Wemmetsweiler	11 Sep 88
		(40)							
81.70		Aleksandr	Seleznyov	RUS	25.1.63	2		Sochi	22 May 93
81.66		Aleksandr	Krykun	UKR	1.3.68	1		Kiev	29 May 04
81.64		Enrico	Sgrulletti	ITA	24.4.65	1		Ostia	9 Mar 97
81.56		Sergey	Gavrilov	RUS	22.5.70	1	Army	Rostov	16 Jun 96
81.56		Zsolt	Németh	HUN	9.11.71	1		Veszprém	14 Aug 99
81.52		Juha	Tiainen	FIN	5.12.55	1		Tampere	11 Jun 84
81.49		Valeriy	Svyatokho	BLR	20.7.81	1	NCp	Brest	27 May 06
81.45		Esref	Apak ¶	TUR	3.1.82	1	Cezmi	Istanbul	4 Jun 05
81.44		Yuriy	Tarasyuk	BLR	11.4.57	1		Minsk	10 Aug 84
81.35		Wojciech	Kondratowicz	POL	18.4.80	1		Bydgosczcz	13 Jul 03
		(50)	100th man 80.08, 200th 77.56, 300th 75.68, 400th 74.36, 500th 73.06						

Drugs disqualification

Mark	Wind	Name		Nat	Born	Pos	Meet	Venue	Date
86.73		Ivan	Tikhon ¶	BLR	24.7.76	1	NC	Brest	3 Jul 05

Ancillary marks – other marks during series (to 84.85)

86.68	Sedykh	30 Aug 86	85.82	Sedykh	22 Jun 86	85.42	Litvinov	3 Jul 86	85.20	Sedykh	3 Jul 84
86.62	Sedykh	30 Aug 86	85.52	Sedykh	13 Jul 84	85.28	Sedykh	30 Aug 86	85.04	Sedykh	13 Jul 84
86.00	Sedykh	3 Jul 84	85.46	Sedykh	30 Aug 86	85.26	Sedykh	11 Aug 86	84.98	Sedykh	4 Sep 88
86.00	Sedykh	22 Jun 86	85.42	Sedykh	11 Aug 86	85.24	Sedykh	11 Aug 86	84.92	Litvinov	3 Jul 86

JAVELIN

Mark	Wind	Name		Nat	Born	Pos	Meet	Venue	Date
98.48 WR		Jan	Zelezny	CZE	16.6.66	1		Jena	25 May 96
95.66 WR			Zelezny			1	McD	Sheffield	29 Aug 93
95.54A WR			Zelezny			1		Pietersburg	6 Apr 93
94.64			Zelezny			1	GS	Ostrava	31 May 96

Mark	Wind	Name		Nat	Born	Pos	Meet	Venue	Date
94.02			Zelezny			1		Stellenbosch	26 Mar 97
93.09		Aki	Parviainen	FIN	26.10.74	1		Kuortane	26 Jun 99
92.80			Zelezny			1	WCh	Edmonton	12 Aug 01
92.61		Sergey	Makarov	RUS	19.3.73	1		Sheffield	30 Jun 02
92.60		Raymond	Hecht	GER	11.11.68	1	Bisl	Oslo	21 Jul 95
92.42			Zelezny			1	GS	Ostrava	28 May 97
92.41			Parviainen			1	ECp-1A	Vaasa	24 Jun 01
92.28			Zelezny			1	GPF	Monaco	9 Sep 95
92.28			Hecht			1	WK	Zürich	14 Aug 96
92.12			Zelezny			1	McD	London (CP)	27 Aug 95
92.12			Zelezny			1	TOTO	Tokyo	15 Sep 95
91.82			Zelezny			1	McD	Sheffield	4 Sep 94
91.69		Kostadínos	Gatsioúdis	GRE	17.12.73	1		Kuortane	24 Jun 00
91.68			Zelezny			1	GP	Gateshead	1 Jul 94
91.59		Andreas	Thorkildsen	NOR	1.4.82	1	Bisl	Oslo	2 Jun 06
91.53		Tero	Pitkämäki	FIN	19.12.82	1		Kuortane	26 Jun 05
91.50			Zelezny			1	Kuso	Lublin	4 Jun 94
91.50A			Zelezny			1		Pretoria	8 Apr 96
91.50			Hecht			1		Gengenbach	1 Sep 96
91.46	WR	Steve	Backley	GBR	12.2.69	1		Auckland (NS)	25 Jan 92
91.40			Zelezny			1	BNP	Villeneuve d'Ascq	2 Jul 93
91.34			Zelezny			1		Cape Town	8 Apr 97
91.33			Pitkämäki			1	WAF	Monaco	10 Sep 05
91.31			Parviainen			2	WCh	Edmonton	12 Aug 01
91.30			Zelezny			1	ISTAF	Berlin	1 Sep 95
91.29		Breaux	Greer	USA	19.10.76	1	NC	Indianapolis	21 Jun 07
		(30/9) 79 over 90m (most: Zelezny 34, Parviainen 8, Thorkildsen 8, Hecht & Pitkämäki 6, Makarov 5)							
90.73		Vadims	Vasilevskis	LAT	5.1.82	1		Tallinn	22 Jul 07
		(10)							
90.60		Seppo	Räty	FIN	27.4.62	1		Nurmijärvi	20 Jul 92
90.44		Boris	Henry	GER	14.12.73	1	Gugl	Linz	9 Jul 97
89.21		Ihab	Abdelrahman	EGY	1.5.89	1	DL	Shanghai	18 May 14
89.16A		Tom	Petranoff	USA	8.4.58	1		Potchefstroom	1 Mar 91
89.15			Zhao Qinggang	CHN	24.7.85	1	AsiG	Incheon	2 Oct 14
89.10	WR	Patrik	Bodén	SWE	30.6.67	1		Austin	24 Mar 90
89.02		Jarrod	Bannister	AUS	3.10.84	1	NC	Brisbane	29 Feb 08
88.90		Aleksandr	Ivanov	RUS	25.5.82	1	Znam	Tula	7 Jun 03
88.84		Dmitriy	Tarabin	RUS	29.10.91	1	NC	Moskva	24 Jul 13
88.75		Marius	Corbett	RSA	26.9.75	1	CG	Kuala Lumpur	21 Sep 98
		(20)							
88.70		Peter	Blank	GER	10.4.62	1	NC	Stuttgart	30 Jun 01
88.36		Matthias	de Zordo	GER	21.2.88	1	VD	Bruxelles	16 Sep 11
88.34		Vitezslav	Vesely	CZE	27.2.83	Q	OG	London (OS)	8 Aug 12
88.24		Matti	Närhi	FIN	17.8.75	1		Soini	27 Jul 97
88.23		Petr	Frydrych	CZE	13.1.88	1	GS	Ostrava	27 May 10
88.22		Juha	Laukkanen	FIN	6.1.69	1		Kuortane	20 Jun 92
88.20		Gavin	Lovegrove	NZL	21.10.67	1	Bisl	Oslo	5 Jul 96
88.01		Antti	Ruuskanen	FIN	21.2.84	1	EC	Zürich	17 Aug 14
88.00		Vladimir	Ovchinnikov	RUS	2.8.70	1		Tolyatti	14 May 95
87.83		Andrus	Värnik	EST	27.9.77	1		Valga	19 Aug 03
		(30)							
87.82		Harri	Hakkarainen	FIN	16.10.69	1		Kuortane	24 Jun 95
87.63		Thomas	Röhler	GER	30.9.91	1	WK	Zürich	28 Aug 14
87.60		Kazuhiro	Mizoguchi	JPN	18.3.62	1	Jenner	San José	27 May 89
87.40		Vladimir	Sasimovich ¶	BLR	14.9.68	2		Kuortane	24 Jun 95
87.34		Andrey	Moruyev	RUS	6.5.70	1	ECp	Birmingham	25 Jun 94
87.23		Teemu	Wirkkala	FIN	14.1.84	1		Joensuu	22 Jul 09
87.20		Viktor	Zaytsev	UZB	6.6.66	1	OT	Moskva	23 Jun 92
87.20		Peter	Esenwein	GER	7.12.67	1		Rehlingen	31 May 04
87.20A		Guillermo	Martínez	CUB	28.6.81	1	PAm	Guadalajara	28 Oct 11
87.17		Dariusz	Trafas	POL	16.5.72	1		Gold Coast (RB)	17 Sep 00
		(40)							
87.12		Tom	Pukstys	USA	28.5.68	2	OD	Jena	25 May 97
87.12		Emeterio	González	CUB	11.4.73	1	OD	Jena	3 Jun 00
86.98		Yuriy	Rybin	RUS	5.3.63	1		Nitra	26 Aug 95
86.94		Mick	Hill	GBR	22.10.64	1	NC	London (CP)	13 Jun 93
86.83		Ryohei	Arai	JPN	23.6.91	1		Isahaya	21 Oct 14
86.80		Einar	Vihljálmsson	ISL	1.6.60	1		Reykjavik	29 Aug 92
86.80		Robert	Oosthuizen	RSA	23.1.87	1		Oudtshoorn	1 Mar 08
86.74		Pål Arne	Fagernes	NOR	8.6.74	Q	OG	Sydney	22 Sep 00

Mark	Wind	Name		Nat	Born	Pos	Meet	Venue	Date
86.68		Tero	Järvenpää	FIN	2.10.84	1	NC	Tampere	27 Jul 08
86.67		Andrew	Currey	AUS	7.2.71	1		Wollongong	22 Jul 01

(50) 100th man 84.50, 200th 81.88, 300th 80.18, 400th 79.00 new javelin introduced in 1986

Ancillary marks – other marks during series (to 91.40)

95.34	Zelezny	29 Aug 93	92.26	Zelezny	26 Mar 97	91.44	Zelezny	25 May 96
92.88	Zelezny	25 May 96	91.88	Zelezny	27 Aug 95	91.44	Zelezny	26 Mar 97
92.30	Zelezny	26 Mar 97	91.48	Zelezny	15 Sep 95			

Javelins with roughened tails, now banned by the IAAF

Mark	Wind	Name		Nat	Born	Pos	Meet	Venue	Date
96.96	WR	Seppo	Räty	FIN	27.4.62	1		Punkalaidun	2 Jun 91
94.74	Irreg		Zelezny			1	Bisl	Oslo	4 Jul 92
91.98	WR		Räty			1	Super	Shizuoka	6 May 91
90.82		Kimmo	Kinnunen	FIN	31.3.68	1	WCh	Tokyo	26 Aug 91
87.00		Peter	Borglund	SWE	29.1.64	1	vFIN	Stockholm	13 Aug 91

DECATHLON

Mark	Wind	Name		Nat	Born	Pos	Meet	Venue	Date
9039	WR	Ashton	Eaton	USA	21.1.88	1	NC/OT	Eugene	23 Jun 12
10.21/0.4	8.23/0.8	14.20	2.05	46.70	13.70/-0.8	42.81	5.30	58.87	4:14.48
9026	WR	Roman	Sebrle	CZE	26.11.74	1		Götzis	27 May 01
10.64/0.0	8.11/1.9	15.33	2.12	47.79	13.92/-0.2	47.92	4.80	70.16	4:21.98
8994	WR	Tomás	Dvorák	CZE	11.5.72	1	ECp	Praha	4 Jul 99
10.54/-0.1	7.90/1.1	16.78	2.04	48.08	13.73/0.0	48.33	4.90	72.32	4:37.20
8902			Dvorák			1	WCh	Edmonton	7 Aug 01
10.62/1.5	8.07/0.9	16.57	2.00	47.74	13.80/-0.4	45.51	5.00	68.53	4:35.13
8900			Dvorák			1		Götzis	4 Jun 00
10.54/1.3	8.03/0.0	16.68	2.09	48.36	13.89/-1.0	47.89	4.85	67.21	4:42.33
8893			Sebrle			1	OG	Athína	24 Aug 04
10.85/1.5	7.84/0.3	16.36	2.12	48.36	14.05/1.5	48.72	5.00	70.52	4:40.01
8891	WR	Dan	O'Brien	USA	18.7.66	1		Talence	5 Sep 92
10.43w/2.1	8.08/1.8	16.69	2.07	48.51	13.98/-0.5	48.56	5.00	62.58	4:42.10
8869			Eaton			1	OG	London (OS)	9 Aug 12
10.35/0.4	8.03/0.8	14.66	2.05	46.90	13.56/0.1	42.53	5.20	61.96	4:33.59
8847	WR	Daley	Thompson	GBR	30.7.58	1	OG	Los Angeles	9 Aug 84
10.44/-1.0	8.01/0.4	15.72	2.03	46.97	14.33/-1.1	46.56	5.00	65.24	4:35.00
8844w			O'Brien			1	TAC	New York	13 Jun 91
10.23	7.96	16.06	2.08	47.70	13.95W/4.2	48.08	5.10	57.40	4:45.54
8842			Sebrle			1		Götzis	30 May 04
10.92/0.5	7.86w/3.3	16.22	2.09	48.59	14.15/0.3	47.44	5.00	71.10	4:34.09
8837			Dvorák			1	WCh	Athína	6 Aug 97
10.60/0.8	7.64/-0.7	16.32	2.00	47.56	13.61/0.8	45.16	5.00	70.34	4:35.40
8832	WR	Jürgen	Hingsen	FRG	25.1.58	1	OT	Mannheim	9 Jun 84
10.70w/2.9	7.76/-1.6	16.42	2.07	48.05	14.07/0.2	49.36	4.90	59.86	4:19.75
8832		Bryan	Clay	USA	3.1.80	1	NC/OT	Eugene	30 Jun 08
10.39/-0.4	7.39/-1.6	15.17	2.08	48.41	13.75/1.9	52.74	5.00	70.55	4:50.97
8825	WR		Hingsen			1		Bernhausen	5 Jun 83
10.92/0.0	7.74	15.94	2.15	47.89	14.10	46.80	4.70	67.26	4:19.74
8824			O'Brien			1	OG	Atlanta	1 Aug 96
10.50/0.7	7.57/1.4	15.66	2.07	46.82	13.87/0.3	48.78	5.00	66.90	4:45.89
8820			Clay			2	OG	Athína	24 Aug 04
10.44w/2.2	7.96/0.2	15.23	2.06	49.19	14.13/1.5	50.11	4.90	69.71	4:41.65
8817			O'Brien			1	WCh	Stuttgart	20 Aug 93
10.57/0.9	7.99/0.4	15.41	2.03	47.46	14.08/0.0	47.92	5.20	62.56	4:40.08
8815		Erki	Nool	EST	25.6.70	2	WCh	Edmonton	7 Aug 01
10.60/1.5	7.63/2.0	14.90	2.03	46.23	14.40/0.0	43.40	5.40	67.01	4:29.58
8812			O'Brien			1	WCh	Tokyo	30 Aug 91
10.41/-1.6	7.90/0.8	16.24	1.91	46.53	13.94/-1.2	47.20	5.20	60.66	4:37.50
8811			Thompson			1	EC	Stuttgart	28 Aug 86
10.26/2.0	7.72/1.0	15.73	2.00	47.02	14.04/-0.3	43.38	5.10	62.78	4:26.16
8809			Eaton			1	WCh	Moskva	11 Aug 13
10.35/-0.5	7.73/0.3	14.39	1.93	46.02	13.72/0.4	45.00	5.20	64.83	4:29.80
8807			Sebrle			1		Götzis	1 Jun 03
10.78/-0.2	7.86/1.2	15.41	2.12	47.83	13.96/0.0	43.42	4.90	69.22	4:28.63
8800			Sebrle			1		Götzis	2 Jun 02
10.95/0.5	7.79/1.8	15.50	2.12	48.35	13.89/1.6	48.02	5.00	68.97	4:38.16
8800			Sebrle			1	EC	München	8 Aug 02
10.83/1.3	7.92/0.8	15.41	2.12	48.48	14.04/0.0	46.88	5.10	68.51	4:42.94
8792		Uwe	Freimuth	GDR	10.9.61	1	OD	Potsdam	21 Jul 84
11.06/	7.79/	16.30	2.03	48.43	14.66/	46.58	5.15	72.42	4:25.19
8791			Clay			1	OG	Beijing	22 Aug 08
10.44/0.3	7.78/0.0	16.27	1.99	48.92	13.93/-0.5	53.79	5.00	70.97	5:06.59

Mark Wind	Name			Nat	Born	Pos	Meet	Venue			Date
8790	Trey	Hardee (10)		USA	7.2.84	1	WCh	Berlin			20 Aug 09
	10.45/0.2	7.83/1.9	15.33	1.99	48.13	13.86/0.3		48.08	5.20	68.00	4:48.91
8784	Tom	Pappas		USA	6.9.76	1	NC	Stanford			22 Jun 03
	10.78/0.2	7.96/1.4	16.28	2.17	48.22	14.13/1.7		45.84	5.20	60.77	4:48.12
8774 WR		Thompson				1	EC	Athína			8 Sep 82
	10.51/0.3	7.80/0.8	15.44	2.03	47.11	14.39/0.9		45.48	5.00	63.56	4:23.71
	(30/11)										
8762	Siegfried	Wentz		FRG	7.3.60	2		Bernhausen			5 Jun 83
	10.89	7.49/	15.35	2.09	47.38	14.00		46.90	4.80	70.68	4:24.90
8735	Eduard	Hämäläinen		FIN/BLR	21.1.69	1		Götzis			29 May 94
	10.50w/2.1	7.26/1.0	16.05	2.11	47.63	13.82/-3.0		49.70	4.90	60.32	4:35.09
8727	Dave	Johnson		USA	7.4.63	1		Azusa			24 Apr 92
	10.96/0.4	7.52w/4.5	14.61	2.04	48.19	14.17/0.3		49.88	5.28	66.96	4:29.38
8725	Dmitriy	Karpov		KAZ	23.7.81	3	OG	Athína			24 Aug 04
	10.50w/2.2	7.81/-0.9	15.93	2.09	46.81	13.97/1.5		51.65	4.60	55.54	4:38.11
8709	Aleksandr	Apaychev		UKR	6.5.61	1	vGDR	Neubrandenburg			3 Jun 84
	10.96/	7.57/	16.00	1.97	48.72	13.93/		48.00	4.90	72.24	4:26.51
8706	Frank	Busemann		GER	26.2.75	2	OG	Atlanta			1 Aug 96
	10.60/0.7	8.07/0.8	13.60	2.04	48.34	13.47/0.3		45.04	4.80	66.86	4:31.41
8698	Grigoriy	Degtyaryov		RUS	16.8.58	1	NC	Kiyev			22 Jun 84
	10.87/0.7	7.42/0.1	16.03	2.10	49.75	14.53/0.3		51.20	4.90	67.08	4:23.09
8694	Chris	Huffins		USA	15.4.70	1	NC	New Orleans			20 Jun 98
	10.31w/3.5	7.76w/2.5	15.43	2.18	49.02	14.02/1.0		53.22	4.60	61.59	4:59.43
8680	Torsten	Voss		GDR	24.3.63	1	WCh	Roma			4 Sep 87
	10.69/-0.3	7.88/1.2	14.98	2.10	47.96	14.13/0.1		43.96	5.10	58.02	4:25.93
	(20)										
8670	Michael	Schrader		GER	1.7.87	2	WCh	Moskva			11 Aug 13
	10.73/-0.5	7.85/0.2	14.56	1.99	47.66	14.29/0.4		46.44	5.00	65.67	4:25.38
8667 WR	Guido	Kratschmer		FRG	10.1.53	1		Bernhausen			14 Jun 80
	10.58w/2.4	7.80/	15.47	2.00	48.04	13.92/		45.52	4.60	66.50	4:24.15
8654	Leonel	Suárez		CUB	1.9.87	1	CAC	La Habana			4 Jul 09
	11.07/0.7	7.42/0.8	14.39	2.09	47.65	14.15/-0.6		46.07	4.70	77.47	4:27.29
8644	Steve	Fritz		USA	1.11.67	4	OG	Atlanta			1 Aug 96
	10.90/0.8	7.77/0.9	15.31	2.04	50.13	13.97/0.3		49.84	5.10	65.70	4:38.26
8644	Maurice	Smith		JAM	28.9.80	2	WCh	Osaka			1 Sep 07
	10.62/0.7	7.50/0.0	17.32	1.97	47.48	13.91/-0.2		52.36	4.80	53.61	4:33.52
8634 WR	Bruce	Jenner		USA	28.10.49	1	OG	Montreal			30 Jul 76
	10.94/0.0	7.22/0.0	15.35	2.03	47.51	14.84/0.0		50.04	4.80	68.52	4:12.61
8627	Robert	Zmelík		CZE	18.4.69	1		Götzis			31 May 92
	10.62w/2.1	8.02/0.2	13.93	2.05	48.73	13.84/1.2		44.44	4.90	61.26	4:24.83
8626	Michael	Smith		CAN	16.9.67	1		Götzis			26 May 96
	11.23/-0.6	7.72/0.6	16.94	1.97	48.69	14.77/-2.4		52.90	4.90	71.22	4:41.95
8617	Andrey	Kravchenko		BLR	4.1.86	1		Götzis			27 May 07
	10.86/0.2	7.90/0.9	13.89	2.15	47.46	14.05/-0.1		39.63	5.00	64.35	4:29.10
8603	Dean	Macey		GBR	12.12.77	3	WCh	Edmonton			7 Aug 01
	10.72/-0.7	7.59/0.4	15.41	2.15	46.21	14.34/0.0		46.96	4.70	54.61	4:29.05
	(30)										
8583w	Jón Arnar	Magnússon		ISL	28.7.69	1	ECp-2	Reykjavik			5 Jul 98
	10.68/2.0	7.63/2.0	15.57	2.07	47.78	14.33W/5.2		44.53	5.00	64.16	4:41.60
	8573					3		Götzis			31 May 98
	10.74/0.5	7.60/-0.2	16.03	2.03	47.66	14.24/0.7		47.82	5.10	59.77	4:46.43
8574	Christian	Plaziat		FRA	28.10.63	1	EC	Split			29 Aug 90
	10.72/-0.6	7.77/1.1	14.19	2.10	47.10	13.98/0.7		44.36	5.00	54.72	4:27.83
8574	Aleksandr	Yurkov		UKR	21.7.75	4		Götzis			4 Jun 00
	10.69/0.9	7.93/1.8	15.26	2.03	49.74	14.56/-0.9		47.85	5.15	58.92	4:32.49
8571	Lev	Lobodin		RUS	1.4.69	3	EC	Budapest			20 Aug 98
	10.66w/2.2	7.42/0.2	15.67	2.03	48.65	13.97/0.9		46.55	5.20	56.55	4:30.27
8566	Sebastian	Chmara		POL	21.11.71	1		Alhama de Murcia			17 May 98
	10.97w/2.9	7.56/1.2	16.03	2.10	48.27	14.32/1.8		44.39	5.20	57.25	4:29.66
8558	Pascal	Behrenbruch		GER	19.1.85	1	EC	Helsinki			28 Jun 12
	10.93/0.8	7.15/-0.8	16.89	1.97	48.54	14.16/0.2		48.24	5.00	67.45	4:34.02
8554	Attila	Zsivoczky		HUN	29.4.77	5		Götzis			4 Jun 00
	10.64w/2.1	7.24/-1.0	15.72	2.18	48.13	14.87/-0.9		45.64	4.65	63.57	4:23.13
8548	Paul	Meier		GER	27.7.71	3	WCh	Stuttgart			20 Aug 93
	10.57/0.9	7.57/1.1	15.45	2.15	47.73	14.63/0.0		45.72	4.60	61.22	4:32.05
8547	Igor	Sobolevskiy		UKR	4.5.62	2	NC	Kiyev			22 Jun 84
	10.64/0.7	7.71/0.2	15.93	2.01	48.24	14.82/0.3		50.54	4.40	67.40	4:32.84
8534	Siegfried	Stark		GDR	12.6.55	1	OT	Halle			4 May 80
	11.10w	7.64	15.81	2.03	49.53	14.86w		47.20	5.00	68.70	4:27.7
	(40)	Peñalver below (7.19w/4.0)									

Mark Wind	Name		Nat	Born	Pos	Meet	Venue	Date
8534w/8478	Antonio	Peñalver	ESP	1.12.68	1		Alhama de Murcia	24 May 92
	10.76w/3.9 7.42W/6.2	16.50	2.12	49.50	14.32/0.8		47.38 5.00 59.32	4:39.94
8528	Aleksandr	Pogorelov	RUS	10.1.80	3	WCh	Berlin	20 Aug 09
	10.95/-0.3 7.49/-0.4	16.65	2.08	50.27	14.19/0.3		48.46 5.10 63.95	4:48.70
8526	Francisco Javier	Benet	ESP	25.3.68	2		Alhama de Murcia	17 May 98
	10.72w/2.9 7.45/-1.2	14.57	1.92	48.10	13.83/1.8		46.12 5.00 65.37	4:26.81
8526	Kristjan	Rahnu	EST	29.8.79	1		Arles	5 Jun 05
	10.52w/2.2 7.58/1.6	15.51	1.99	48.60	14.04w/3.1		50.81 4.95 60.71	4:52.18
8524	Sébastien	Levicq	FRA	25.6.71	4	WCh	Sevilla	25 Aug 99
	11.05/0.2 7.52/-0.4	14.22	2.00	50.13	14.48/0.6		44.65 5.50 69.01	4:26.81
8521	Kevin	Mayer	FRA	10.2.92	2	EC	Zürich	13 Aug 14
	11.10/-0.9 7.65/0.2	15.14	2.01	49.23	14.28/0.5		44.53 5.20 64.03	4:24.16
8519	Yuriy	Kutsenko	RUS	5.3.52	3	NC	Kiyev	22 Jun 84
	11.07/0.5 7.54/-0.1	15.11	2.13	49.07	14.94/0.3		50.38 4.60 61.70	4:12.68
8519	Hans	Van Alphen	BEL	12.1.82	1		Götzis	27 May 12
	10.96/1.0 7.62/1.1	15.23	2.06	49.54	14.55/0.4		45.45 4.96 64.15	4:20.87
8512	Damian	Warner	CAN	4.11.89	3	WCh	Moskva	11 Aug 13
	10.43/-0.5 7.39/0.3	14.23	2.05	48.41	13.96/0.4		44.13 4.80 64.67	4:29.97
8506	Valter	Külvet	EST	19.2.64	1		Staiki	3 Jul 88
	11.05/-1.4 7.35/0.4	15.78	2.00	48.08	14.55/-0.8		52.04 4.60 61.72	4:15.93
8506	Eelco	Sintnicolaas	NED	7.4.87	2		Götzis	27 May 12
	10.77/-0.7 7.27/-1.6	14.20	2.00	48.02	14.10/0.8		42.81 5.36 63.59	4:30.08
	(51)	100th man 8330, 200th 8175, 300th 8068, 400th 7977, 500th 7902						

4 x 100 METRES RELAY

Mark	Nat	Team	Pos	Meet	Venue	Date
36.84 WR	JAM	N Carter 10.1, Frater 8.9, Blake 9.0, Bolt 8.8	1	OG	London (OS)	11 Aug 12
37.04 WR	JAM	N Carter, Frater, Blake, Bolt	1	WCh	Daegu	4 Sep 11
37.04	USA	Kimmons 10.1, Gatlin 8.9, Gay 9.0, Bailey 9.0	2	OG	London (OS)	11 Aug 12
37.10 WR	JAM	N Carter, Frater, Bolt, Powell	1	OG	Beijing	22 Aug 08
37.31	JAM	Mullings, Frater, Bolt, Powell	1	WCh	Berlin	22 Aug 09
37.36	JAM	Carter, Bailey Cole, Ashmeade, Bolt	1	WCh	Moskva	18 Aug 13
37.38	USA	Demps, Patton, Kimmons, Gatlin	1h2	OG	London (OS)	10 Aug 12
37.39	JAM	Carter, Frater, Blake, Bailey-Cole	1h1	OG	London (OS)	10 Aug 12
37.40 WR	USA	Marsh, Burrell, Mitchell, C Lewis	1	OG	Barcelona	8 Aug 92
37.40 WR	USA	Drummond, Cason, D Mitchell, L Burrell	1s1	WCh	Stuttgart	21 Aug 93
37.45	USA	Kimmons, Spearmon, Gay, Rodgers	1	WK	Zürich	19 Aug 10
37.48	USA	Drummond, Cason, D Mitchell, L Burrell	1	WCh	Stuttgart	22 Aug 93
37.50 WR	USA	Cason, Burrell, Mitchell, C Lewis	1	WCh	Tokyo	1 Sep 91
37.58	USA	'Red' Silmon, Rodgers, Salaam, Gatlin	1	Herc	Monaco	19 Jul 13
37.58	JAM	Livermore, Bailey-Cole, Ashmeade, Bolt	1	CG	Glasgow	2 Aug 14
37.59	USA	Drummond, Montgomery, B Lewis, Greene	1	WCh	Sevilla	29 Aug 99
37.59	USA	Conwright, Spearmon, Gay, Smoots	1	WCp	Athína	16 Sep 06
37.61	USA	Drummond, Williams, B Lewis, Greene	1	OG	Sydney	30 Sep 00
37.61	USA	Kimmons, Gatlin, Gay, Bailey	1	Herc	Monaco	20 Jul 12
37.62	TTO	Brown, Burns, Callander, Thompson	2	WCh	Berlin	22 Aug 09
37.65	USA	Drummond, Williams, C Johnson, Greene	1	ISTAF	Berlin	1 Sep 00
37.66	USA	Silmon, Rodgers, Salaam, Gatlin	2	WCh	Moskva	18 Aug 13
37.67 WR	USA	Marsh, Burrell, Mitchell, C Lewis	1	WK	Zürich	7 Aug 91
37.69	CAN	Esmie 10.47, Gilbert 9.02, Surin 9.25, Bailey 8.95	1	OG	Atlanta	3 Aug 96
37.70	JAM	Clarke, Frater, Mullins, Bolt	1	WK	Zürich	28 Aug 09
37.71	JAM	Carter, Bailey-Cole, Forte, Fisher	1h2	WRly	Nassau	25 May 14
37.73	GBR	Gardener, Campbell, Devonish, Chambers	2	WCh	Sevilla	29 Aug 99
37.73	USA	Trammell, Rodgers, Patton, Spearmon	2	WK	Zürich	28 Aug 09
37.75	USA	Cason, Burrell, Mitchell, Marsh	1h2	WCh	Tokyo	31 Aug 91
37.75	JAM	Forsythe, Bailey-Cole, Weir, Bolt	1	DL	London (OS)	27 Jul 13
	(30 performances by teams from 5 nations)	Further bests by nations:				
37.79 WR	FRA	Morinière, Sangouma 8.90, Trouabal, Marie-Rose	1	EC	Split	1 Sep 90
37.90	BRA	de Lima, Ribeiro, A da Silva, Cl da Silva	2	OG	Sydney	30 Sep 00
37.94	NGR	O Ezinwa, Adeniken, Obikwelu, D Ezinwa	1s2	WCh	Athína	9 Aug 97
37.99	CHN	Chen Shiwei, Xie Zhenye, Su Bingtian, Zhang Peimeng	1	AsiG	Incheon	2 Oct 14
38.00	CUB	Simón, Lamela, Isasi, Aguilera	3	OG	Barcelona	8 Aug 92
	(10)					
38.02	URS	Yevgenyev, Bryzgin, Muravyov, Krylov	2	WCh	Roma	6 Sep 87
38.02	GER	Reus, Unger, Kosenkow, Jakubczyk	1		Weinheim	27 Jul 12
38.03	JPN	Tsukahara, Suetsugu 9.08, Takahira, Asahara	5	WCh	Osaka	1 Sep 07
38.12	GHA	Duah, Nkansah, Zakari, Tuffour	1s1	WCh	Athína	9 Aug 97
38.17	AUS	Henderson, Jackson, Brimacombe, Marsh	1s2	WCh	Göteborg	12 Aug 95
38.17	ITA	Donati, Collio, Di Gregorio, Checcucci	2	EC	Barcelona	1 Aug 10
38.29	NED	Mariano, Martina, Codrington, van Luijk	3h1	OG	London (OS)	10 Aug 12
38.31	POL	Masztak, Kuc, Kubaczyk, Krynski	6h2	OG	London (OS)	10 Aug 12

Mark	Wind	Name	Nat	Born	Pos	Meet	Venue	Date
38.35	RSA	Bruintjies, Magakwe, Titi, Simbine			4	CG	Glasgow	2 Aug 14
38.41	SKN	Lestrod, Rogers, Adams, Lawrence			6h1	OG	London (OS)	10 Aug 12
	(20)							
38.45	AHO	Goeloe, Raffaela, Duzant, Martina			6	WCh	Helsinki	13 Aug 05
38.46	URS/RUS	Zharov, Krylov, Fatun, Goremykin			4	EC	Split	1 Sep 90
38.46	ESP	Viles, Ruiz, Hortelano, Rodríguez			4h1	WCh	Moskva	18 Aug 13
38.47	HKG	Tang Yik Chun, Lai Chun Ho, Ng Ka Fung, Tsui Chi Ho			1		Taipei	26 May 12
38.52	BAH	Griffith, Fraser, Hart, T.Smith			3h1	CG	Glasgow	1 Aug 14
38.53	UKR	Rurak, Osovich, Kramarenko, Dologodin			1	ECp	Madrid	1 Jun 96
38.54	SUI	Mancini, Schenkel, Somasundaran, Wilson			2h1	EC	Zürich	18 Aug 14
38.60	CIV	Meité, Douhou, Sonan, N'Dri			3s1	WCh	Edmonton	12 Aug 01
38.61	GRE	Séggos, Alexópoulos, Panayiotópoulos, Hoídis			2	ECp	Paris (C)	19 Jun 99
38.62	SUI	Mancini, Schenkel, Wilson, Schneeberger			3	WK	Zürich	8 Sep 11
38.63	SWE	Karlsson, Mårtensson, Hedner, Strenius (30)			3s2	OG	Atlanta	2 Aug 96
Multi-nation team								
37.46	Racers TC	Bailey/ANT, Blake JAM, Forsythe JAM, Bolt JAM			1	LGP	London (CP)	25 Jul 09
One man disqualified for drugs								
37.91	NGR	Asonze ¶, Obikwelu, Effiong, Aliu			(3)	WCh	Sevilla	29 Aug 99

4 x 200 METRES RELAY

Mark	Team	Name	Pos	Meet	Venue	Date
1:18.63	JAM	Ashmeade, Weir, J Brown, Y Blake	1	WRly	Nassau	24 May 14
1:18.68 WR	USA - Santa Monica Track Cluc	Marsh 20.0, Burrell 19.6, Heard 19.7, C Lewis 19.4	1	MSR	Walnut	17 Apr 94
1:19.10	World All-Stars	Drummond USA 20.4, Mitchell USA 19.3, Bridgewater USA 20.3, Regis GBR 19.1	2	MSR	Walnut	17 Apr 94
1:19.11 WR	Santa Monica TC/USA	M.Marsh, L Burrell, Heard, C Lewis	1	Penn	Philadelphia	25 Apr 92
1:19.16	USA Red Team	Crawford, Clay, Patton, Gatlin	1	PennR	Philadelphia	26 Apr 03
1:19.38 WR	Santa Monica TC/USA	Everett, Burrell, Heard, C Lewis	1	R-W	Koblenz	23 Aug 89
1:19.39	USA Blue	Drummond, Crawford, B Williams, Greene	1	PennR	Philadelphia	28 Apr 01
1:19.45	Santa Monica TC/USA	DeLoach, Burrell, C.Lewis, Heard	1	Penn	Philadelphia	27 Apr 91
1:19.47	Nike Int./USA	Brokenburr, A Harrison, Greene, M Johnson	1	Penn	Philadelphia	24 Apr 99
Best non-US nations						
1:20.51	SKN	A Adams, L Roland, BJ Lawrence, A Clarke	2	WRly	Nassau	24 May 14
1:20.66	FRA	Lemaitre, Fonsat, Bassaw, Romain	3	WRly	Nassau	25 May 14
1:21.10	ITA	Tilli, Simionato, Bongiorno, Mennea	1		Cagliari	29 Sep 83
1:21.22	POL	Tulin, Balcerzak, Pilarczyk, Urbas	2		Gdansk	14 Jul 01
1:21.29	GBR	Adam, Mafe, Christie, Regis	1	vURS	Birmingham	23 Jun 89

4 x 400 METRES RELAY

Mark	Team	Name	Pos	Meet	Venue	Date
2:54.29 WR	USA	Valmon 44.5, Watts 43.6, Reynolds 43.23, Johnson 42.94	1	WCh	Stuttgart	22 Aug 93
2:55.39	USA	Merritt 44.4, Taylor 43.7, Neville 44.16, Wariner 43.18	1	OG	Beijing	23 Aug 08
2:55.56	USA	Merritt 44.4, Taylor 43.7, Williamson 44.32, Wariner 43.10	1	WCh	Osaka	2 Sep 07
2:55.74 WR	USA	Valmon 44.6, Watts 43.00, M Johnson 44.73, S Lewis 43.41	1	OG	Barcelona	8 Aug 92
2:55.91	USA	O Harris 44.5, Brew 43.6, Wariner 43.98, Williamson 43.83	1	OG	Athína	28 Aug 04
2:55.99	USA	L Smith 44.62, A Harrison 43.84, Mills 43.66, Maybank 43.87	1	OG	Atlanta	3 Aug 96
2:56.16A WR	USA	Matthews 45.0, Freeman 43.2, James 43.9, Evans 44.1	1	OG	Ciud. México	20 Oct 68
2:56.16 WR	USA	Everett 43.79, S Lewis 43.69, Robinzine 44.74, Reynolds 43.94	1	OG	Seoul	1 Oct 88
2:56.60	GBR	I Thomas 44.92, Baulch 44.19, Richardson 43.62, Black 43.87	2	OG	Atlanta	3 Aug 96
2:56.65	GBR	Thomas 44.8, Black 44.2, Baulch 44.08, Richardson 43.57	2	WCh	Athína	10 Aug 97
2:56.72	BAH	Brown 44.9, Pinder 43.5, Mathieu 44.25, Miller 44.01	1	OG	London (OS)	10 Aug 12
2:56.75	JAM	McDonald 44.5, Haughton 44.4, McFarlane 44.37, Clarke 43.51	3	WCh	Athína	10 Aug 97
2:56.91	USA	Rock 44.7, Brew 44.3, Williamson 44.40, Wariner 43.49	1	WCh	Helsinki	14 Aug 05
2:57.05	USA	Nellum 45.2, Mance 43.5, McQuay 43.41, Taylor 44.85	2	OG	London (OS)	10 Aug 12
2:57.25	USA	Verburg 44.8, McQuay 44.1, C Taylor 44.6, L Merritt 43.8	1	WRly	Nassau	25 May 14
2:57.29	USA	Everett 45.1, Haley 44.0, McKay 44.20, Reynolds 44.00	1	WCh	Roma	6 Sep 87
2:57.32	USA	Ramsey 44.9, Mills 44.6, Reynolds 43.74, Johnson 44.11	1	WCh	Göteborg	13 Aug 95
2:57.32	BAH	McKinney 44.9, Moncur 44.6, A Williams 44.43, Brown 43.42	2	WCh	Helsinki	14 Aug 05
2:57.53	GBR	Black 44.7, Redmond 44.0, Regis 44.22, Akabusi 44.59	1	WCh	Tokyo	1 Sep 91
2:57.57	USA	Valmon 44.9, Watts 43.4, D.Everett 44.31, Pettigrew 44.93	2	WCh	Tokyo	1 Sep 91
2:57.59	BAH	L Williams 45.0, Pinder 43.8, C Brown 44.2, Mathieu 44.6	2	WRly	Nassau	25 May 14
2:57.86	USA	Taylor 45.4, Wariner 43.6, Clement 44.72, Merritt 44.16	1	WCh	Berlin	23 Aug 09
2:57.87	USA	L Smith 44.59, Rouser 44.33, Mills 44.32, Maybank 44.63	1s2	OG	Atlanta	2 Aug 96
2:57.91	USA	Nix 45.59, Armstead 43.97, Babers 43.75, McKay 44.60	1	OG	Los Angeles	11 Aug 84
2:57.97	JAM	McDonald , Haughton , McFarlane, D Clarke	1	PAm	Winnipeg	30 Jul 99
2:58.00	POL	Rysiukiewicz 45.6, Czubak 44.2, Haczek 44.0, Mackowiak 44.2	2	GWG	Uniondale, NY	22 Jul 98
2:58.03	BAH	Bain 45.9, Mathieu 44.1, A Williams 44.02, Brown 44.05	2	OG	Beijing	23 Aug 08
2:58.06	RUS	Dyldin 45.5, Frolov 44.6, Kokorin 44.34, Alekseyev 43.56	3	OG	Beijing	23 Aug 08
2:58.07	JAM	Ayre 44.9, Simpson 44.9, Spence 44.48, Clarke 43.81	3	WCh	Helsinki	14 Aug 05
2:58.19	BAH	Moncur 45.1, C Brown 44.5, McIntosh 44.42, Munnings 44.13	2	WCh	Edmonton	12 Aug 01

(30/6) plus six times for teams that contained an athlete who was subsequently banned for drugs abuse

Mark	Wind	Name	Pos	Meet	Venue	Date
2:58.34	TTO	L Gordon 45.3, Quow 43.6, Cedenio 44.5, Solomon 44.9	3	WRly	Nassau	25 May 14
2:58.56	BRA	Cl. da Silva 44.6, A dos Santos 45.1, de Araújo 45.0, Parrela 43.9	2	PAm	Winnipeg	30 Jul 99
2:58.68	NGR	Chukwu 45.18, Monye 44.49, Bada 44.70, Udo-Obong 44.31	1	OG	Sydney	30 Sep 00
2:58.96	FRA	Djhone 45.4, Keita 44.7, Diagana 44.69, Raquil 44.15	2	WCh	Saint-Denis	31 Aug 03
	(10)					
2:59.13	CUB	Martínez 45.6, Herrera 44.38, Tellez 44.81, Hernández 44.34	1h2	OG	Barcelona	7 Aug 92
2:59.21	RSA	Pistorius 45.58, Mogawane 43.97, de Beer 44.46, Victor 45.20	3h1	WCh	Daegu	1 Sep 11
2:59.37	BEL	K Borlée 45.4, J Borlée 43.6, Van Branteghem 44.44, Ghislain 45.88	5	OG	Beijing	23 Aug 08
2:59.63	KEN	D Kitur 45.4, S Kitur 45.13, Kipkemboi 44.76, Kemboi 44.34	3h2	OG	Barcelona	7 Aug 92
2:59.70	AUS	Frayne 45.38, Clark 43.86, Minihan 45.07, Mitchell 45.39	4	OG	Los Angeles	11 Aug 84
2:59.86	GDR	Möller 45.8, Schersing 44.8, Carlowitz 45.3, Schönlebe 44.1	1	vURS	Erfurt	23 Jun 85
2:59.95	YUG	Jovkovic, Djurovic, Macev, Brankovic 44.3	2h3	WCh	Tokyo	31 Aug 91
2:59.96	FRG	Dobeleit 45.7, Henrich 44.3, Itt 45.12, Schmid 44.93	4	WCh	Roma	6 Sep 87
3:00.44A	DOM	Cuesta 46.2, Peguero 44.6, Tapia 45.2, L Santos 44.5	2	PAm	Guadalajara	28 Oct 11
		3:02.02 Peguero, Santa, Vidal, Sánchez	3	PAm	Santo Domingo	9 Aug 03
3:00.64	SEN	Diarra 46.53, Dia 44.94, Ndiaye 44.70, Faye 44.47	4	OG	Atlanta	3 Aug 96
	(20)					
3:00.76	JPN	Karube 45.88, Ito 44.86, Osakada 45.08, Omori 44.94	5	OG	Atlanta	3 Aug 96
3:00.79	ZIM	Chiwira 46.2, Mukomana 44.6, Ngidhi 45.79, Harnden 44.20	2h3	WCh	Athína	9 Aug 97
3:00.82A	VEN	A Ramírez 45.7, Aguilar 45.3, Acevedo 44.7, Longart 45.2	3	PAm	Guadalajara	28 Oct 11
		3:01.44 Ramirez 46.0, Bravo 45.0, Meléndez 45.6, Mezones 44.8	6	W.Rly	Nassau	25 May 14
3:01.12	FIN	Lönnqvist 46.7, Salin 45.1, Karttunen 44.8, Kukkoaho 44.5	6	OG	München	10 Sep 72
3:01.37	ITA	Bongiorni 46.2, Zuliani 45.0, Petrella 45.3, Ribaud 44.9	4	EC	Stuttgart	31 Aug 86
3:01.42	ESP	I Rodríguez 46.0, Canal 44.1, Andrés 45.88, Reina 45.48	4h1	WCh	Edmonton	11 Aug 01
3:01.60	BAR	Louis 46.67, Peltier 44.97, Edwards 45.04, Forde 44.92	6	OG	Los Angeles	11 Aug 84
3:01.61	BUL	Georgiev 45.9, Stankulov 46.0, Raykov 45.07, Ivanov 44.66	2h1	WCh	Stuttgart	21 Aug 93
3:01.67	IRL	Gregan 45.7, English 45.0, Morrissey 45.55, Barr 45.31	5	EC	Zürich	17 Aug 14
3:01.89	BOT	Seribe 46.4, Amos 44.6, Maotoanong 46.46, Makwala 44.47	1	AfrC	Marrakech	14 Aug 14
	(30)					

Including subsequently banned athlete

Mark	Nat	Name	Pos	Meet	Venue	Date
2:54.20(WR)	USA	Young 44.3, Pettigrew ¶ 43.2, Washington 43.5, Johnson 43.2	(1)	GWG	Uniondale, NY	22 Jul 98
2:56.35	USA	A Harrison 44.36, Pettigrew 44.17, C Harrison 43.53, Johnson 44.29	(1)	OG	Sydney	30 Sep 00
2:56.45	USA	J Davis 45.2, Pettigrew 43.9, Taylor 43.92, M Johnson 43.49	(1)	WCh	Sevilla	29 Aug 99
2:56.47	USA	Young 44.6, Pettigrew 43.1, Jones 44.80, Washington 44.80	(1)	WCh	Athína	10 Aug 97
2:56.60	USA Red	Taylor 45.0, Pettigrew 44.2, Washington 43.7, Johnson 43.7	(1)	PennR	Philadelphia	29 Apr 00
2:57.54	USA	Byrd 45.9, Pettigrew 43.9, Brew 44.03, Taylor 43.71	1	WCh	Edmonton	12 Aug 01

4 x 800 METRES RELAY

Mark	Nat	Name	Pos	Meet	Venue	Date
7:02.43	KEN	Mutua 1:46.73, Yiampoy 1:44.38, Kombich 1:45.92, Bungei 1:45.40	1	VD	Bruxelles	25 Aug 06
7:02.82	USA	J Harris 1:47.05, Robinson 1:44.03, Burley 1:46.05, Krummenacker 1:45.69	2	VD	Bruxelles	25 Aug 06
7:03.89 WR	GBR	Elliott 1:49.14, Cook 1:46.20, Cram 1:44.54, Coe 1:44.01	1		London (CP)	30 Aug 82
7:04.70	RSA	van Oudtshoorn 1:46.9, Sepeng 1:45.2, Kotze 1:48.3, J Botha 1:44.3	1		Stuttgart	6 Jun 99
7:06.66	QAT	Sultan 1:45.81, Al-Badri 1:46.71, Suleiman 1:45.89, Ali Kamal 1:48.25	4	VD	Bruxelles	25 Aug 06
7:07.40	URS	Masunov, Kostetskiy, Matvetev, Kalinkin	1		Moskva	5 Aug 84
7:08.5 WR	FRG	Kinder 1:46.9, Adams 1:47.5, Bogatzki 1:47.9, Kemper 1:46.2	1		Wiesbaden	13 Aug 66
7:08.89	POL	Konieczny 1:48.9, Krawczyk 1:49.1, Lewandowski 1:45.9, Kszczot 1:44.8	2	WRly	Nassau	24 May 14

4 x 1500 METRES RELAY

Mark	Nat	Name	Pos	Meet	Venue	Date
14:22.22 WR	KEN	C Cheboi 3:38.5, S Kiplagat 3:32.4, Magut 3:39.0, A Kiprop 3:32.3	1	WRly	Nassau	25 May 14
14:36.23 WR	KEN	W Biwott 3:38.5, Gathimba 3:39.5, G Rono 3:41.4, Choge 3:36.9	1	VD	Bruxelles	4 Sep 09
14:38.8 WR	FRG	Wessinghage 3:38.8, Hudak 3:39.1, Lederer 3:44.6, Fleschen 3:36.3	1		Köln	16 Aug 77
14:40.4 WR	NZL	Polhill 3:42.9, Walker 3:40.4, Dixon 3:41.2, Quax 3:35.9	1		Oslo	22 Aug 73
14:40.80	USA	Casey 3:38.2, Torrence 3:36.6, Leer 3:39.3, Manzano 3:46.7	2	WRly	Nassau	25 May 14
14:41.22	ETH	Gebremedhin 3:39.9, Fida 3:37.5, Z Alemayehu 3:46.5, Wote 3:37.3	3	WRly	Nassau	25 May 14
14:45.63	URS	Kalutskiy, Yakovlev, Legeda, Lotarev	1		Leningrad	4 Aug 85
14:46.04	AUS	Gregson 3:39.1, McEntee 3:44.9, Birmingham 3:38.3, Williamsz 3:43.7	4	WRly	Nassau	25 May 14
14:46.16		Larios, ESP Jiménez 3:40.9, Pancorbo 3:41.2, A García 3:43.9, Viciosa 3:40.2	1		Madrid	5 Sep 97
14:48.2	FRA	Bégouin 3:44.5, Lequement 3:44.3, Philippe 3:42.2, Dien 3:37.2	2		Bourges	23 Jun 79
Mixed Team: 14:44.31		Ali BRN, Birgen KEN, N Kemboi KEN, Campbell IRL	2	VD	Bruxelles	4 Sep 09

4 x 1 MILE RELAY

Mark	Nat	Name	Pos	Meet	Venue	Date
15:49.08	IRL	Coghlan 4:00.2, O'Sullivan 3:55.3, O'Mara 3:56.6, Flynn 3:56.98	1		Dublin	17 Aug 85
15:59.57	NZL	Rogers 3:57.2, Bowden 4:02.5, Gilchrist 4:02.8, Walker 3:57.07	1		Auckland	2 Mar 83

4 x 110m/120y HURDLES

Mark	Nat	Name	Pos	Meet	Venue	Date
53.31y	USA Red	Oliver, Herring, Brown, Merritt	1	PennR	Philadelphia	25 Apr 08
53.36	USA	Bramlett, Moore, Payne, Merritt	1	DNG	Stockholm	7 Aug 07
53.62	USA	(ACC All-Stars) A Johnson, Reese, Brown, Ross	1		Clemson	16 May 98
53.77	USA	Porter, Berger, A Merritt, Akins	1	DrakeR	Des Moines	26 Apr 14
53.83	JAM	Riley, D Carter, Parchment, Fennell)	2	DrakeR	Des Moines	26 Apr 14

Mark Wind	Name		Nat	Born	Pos	Meet	Venue	Date

3000 METRES TRACK WALK

Mark	First name	Name	Nat	Born	Pos	Meet	Venue	Date
10:47.11	Giovanni	De Benedictis	ITA	8.1.68	1		S.Giovanni Valdarno	19 May 90
10:52.44+	Yohann	Diniz	FRA	1.1.78	1	in 5k	Villeneuve d'Ascq	27 Jun 08
10:56.22	Andrew	Jachno	AUS	13.4.62	1		Melbourne	7 Feb 91
10:56.23	Dane	Bird-Smith	AUS	15.7.92	1		Cork	8 Jul 14
10:56.34+	Roman	Mrázek	SVK	21.1.62	1	in 5k	Bratislava	14 Jun 89
10:58.16	Kevin	Campion	FRA	23.5.88	2		Cork	8 Jul 14
10:58.47	Alex	Wright	IRL	19.12.90	3		Cork	8 Jul 14
10:59.04	Luke	Adams	AUS	22.10.76	1		Cork	3 Jul 10
11:00.2+	Jozef	Pribilinec	SVK	6.7.60	1	in 10k	Banská Bystrica	30 Aug 85
11:00.50+	Francisco Javier	Fernández ¶	ESP	6.3.77	1	in 5k	Villeneuve d'Ascq	8 Jun 07
11:00.56	David	Smith	AUS	24.7.55	1		Perth	24 Jan 87
11:00.68	Antón	Kucmin	SVK	7.6.84	1		Dubnica nad Váhom	21 Aug 13
Indoors								
10:31.42	Andreas	Erm	GER	12.3.76	1		Halle	4 Feb 01
10:54.61	Carlo	Mattioli	ITA	23.10.54	1		Milano	6 Feb 80
10:56.77+	Ivano	Brugnetti	ITA	1.9.76	1	in 5k	Torino	21 Feb 09
10:56.88	Reima	Salonen	FIN	19.11.55	1		Turku	5 Feb 84
10:57.32	Matej	Tóth	SVK	10.2.83	1		Wien	12 Feb 11
11:00.86+	Frants	Kostyukevich	BLR	4.4.63	1	in 5k	Genova	28 Feb 92

5000 METRES TRACK WALK

Mark	First name	Name	Nat	Born	Pos	Meet	Venue	Date
18:05.49	Hatem	Ghoula	TUN	7.6.73	1		Tunis	1 May 97
18:17.22	Robert	Korzeniowski	POL	30.7.68	1		Reims	3 Jul 92
18:18.01	Yohann	Diniz	FRA	1.1.78	1		Villeneuve d'Ascq	27 Jun 08
18:27.34	Francisco Javier	Fernández ¶	ESP	6.3.77	1		Villeneuve d'Ascq	8 Jun 07
18:28.80	Roman	Mrázek	SVK	21.1.62	1	PTS	Bratislava	14 Jun 89
18:30.43	Maurizio	Damilano	ITA	6.4.57	1		Caserta	11 Jun 92
Indoors								
18:07.08	Mikhail	Shchennikov	RUS	24.12.67	1		Moskva	14 Feb 95
18:08.86	Ivano	Brugnetti	ITA	1.9.76	1	NC	Ancona	17 Feb 07
18:11.41	Ronald	Weigel	GDR	8.8.59	1mx		Wien	13 Feb 88
18:11.8	Valeriy	Borchin ¶	RUS	11.9.86	1		Saransk	30 Dec 10
18:15.25	Grigoriy	Kornev	RUS	14.3.61	1		Moskva	7 Feb 92
18:15.54	Andrey	Ruzavin	RUS	28.3.86	1		Samara	30 Jan 14
18:16.54 ?	Frants	Kostyukevich	BLR	4.4.63	2	NC	Gomel	4 Feb 89
18:16.76	Yohann	Diniz	FRA	1.1.78	1		Reims	7 Dec 14
18:17.13	Vladimir	Kanaykin ¶	RUS	21.3.85	2	Winter	Moskva	5 Feb 12
18:19.97	Giovanni	De Benedictis	ITA	8.1.68	1	EI	Genova	28 Feb 92
18:21.76	Ruslan	Dmytrenko	UKR	22.3.86	2		Samara	30 Jan 14
18:22.25	Andreas	Erm	GER	12.3.76	1	NC	Dortmund	25 Feb 01
18:23.18	Rishat	Shafikov	RUS	23.1.70	1		Samara	1 Mar 97
18:24.13	Francisco Javier	Fernández ¶	ESP	6.3.77	1		Belfast	17 Feb 07
18:26.82	Sergey	Bakulin	RUS	13.11.86	3	Winter	Moskva	5 Feb 12
18:27.15	Alessandro	Gandellini	ITA	30.4.73	1	NC	Genova	12 Feb 00
18:27.80	Jozef	Pribilinec	SVK	6.7.60	2	WI	Indianapolis	7 Mar 87
18:27.95	Stefan	Johansson	SWE	11.4.67	3	EI	Genova	28 Feb 92
18:28.54	Igor	Yerokhin	RUS	4.9.85	1		Samara	31 Jan 13

10,000 METRES TRACK WALK

Mark	First name	Name	Nat	Born	Pos	Meet	Venue	Date
37:53.09	Francisco Javier	Fernández ¶	ESP	6.3.77	1	NC	Santa Cruz de Tenerife	27 Jul 08
37:58.6	Ivano	Brugnetti	ITA	1.9.76	1		Sesto San Gioavnni	23 Jul 05
38:02.60	Jozef	Pribilinec	SVK	6.7.60	1		Banská Bystrica	30 Aug 85
38:06.6	David	Smith	AUS	24.7.55	1		Sydney	25 Sep 86
38:08.13	Yohann	Diniz	FRA	1.1.78	1	NC	Reims	12 Jul 14
38:12.13	Ronald	Weigel	GDR	8.8.59	1		Potsdam	10 May 86
38:18.0+	Valdas	Kazlauskas	LTU	23.2.58	1		Moskva	18 Sep 83
38:18.51	Eiki	Takahashi	JPN	19.11.92	1		Isahaya	14 Dec 14
38:20.0	Moacir	Zimmermann	BRA	30.12.83	1		Blumenau	7 Jun 08
38:24 0+	Bernardo	Segura	MEX	11.2.70	1	SGP	Fana	7 May 94
38:24.31	Hatem	Ghoula	TUN	7.6.73	1		Tunis	30 May 98
38:26.4	Daniel	García	MEX	28.10.71	1		Sdr Omme	17 May 97
38:26.53	Robert	Korzeniowski	POL	30.7.68	1		Riga	31 May 02
38:27.09	Yusuke	Suzuki	JPN	2.1.88	1		Yamaguchi	11 Oct 14
38:27.57	Robert	Heffernan	IRL	20.2.78	1	NC	Dublin	20 Jul 08
38:30.38		Wang Zhen	CHN	24.8.91	1		Tianjin	16 Sep 12
38:32.0	Erik	Tysse	NOR	4.12.80	1	NC	Bergen (Fana)	13 Jun 08
38:37.02	Kevin	Campion	FRA	23.5.88	1	NC	Paris (C)	13 Jul 13
38:37.6+	Jefferson	Pérez	ECU	1.7.74	1	in 20k	Fana	9 May 98
Indoors								
38:31.4	Werner	Heyer	GDR	14.11.56	1		Berlin	12 Jan 80

20 KILOMETRES WALK

Mark Wind	Name		Nat	Born	Pos	Meet	Venue	Date
1:16:43	Sergey	Morozov ¶	RUS	21.3.88	1	NC	Saransk	8 Jun 08
1:17:16WR	Vladimir	Kanaykin ¶	RUS	21.3.85	1	RWC	Saransk	29 Sep 07
1:17:21WR	Jefferson	Pérez	ECU	1.7.74	1	WCh	Saint-Denis	23 Aug 03
1:17:22WR	Francisco Javier	Fernández ¶	ESP	6.3.77	1		Turku	28 Apr 02
1:17:23	Vladimir	Stankin	RUS	2.1.74	1	NC-w	Adler	8 Feb 04
1:17:25.6t	Bernardo	Segura	MEX	11.2.70	1	SGP	Bergen (Fana)	7 May 94
1:17:30	Alex	Schwazer ¶	ITA	26.12.84	1		Lugano	18 Mar 12
1:17:33	Nathan	Deakes	AUS	17.8.77	1		Cixi	23 Apr 05
1:17:36		Kanaykin			1	NC	Cheboksary	17 Jun 07
1:17:36		Wang Zhen	CHN	24.8.91	1		Taicang	30 Mar 12
1:17:38	Valeriy	Borchin ¶ (10)	RUS	11.9.86	1	NC-w	Adler	28 Feb 09
1:17:40		Chen Ding	CHN	5.8.92	2		Taicang	30 Mar 12
1:17:41		Zhu Hongjun	CHN	18.8.83	2		Cixi	23 Apr 05
1:17:43	Yohann	Diniz	FRA	1.1.78	2		Lugano	18 Mar 12
1:17:46	Julio	Martínez	GUA	27.9.73	1		Eisenhüttenstadt	8 May 99
1:17:46	Roman	Rasskazov	RUS	28.4.79	1	NC	Moskva	19 May 00
1:17:47	Andrey	Ruzavin ¶	RUS	28.3.86	1	NC-w	Sochi	18 Feb 12
1:17:52		Fernández			1		La Coruña	4 Jun 05
1:17:53		Cui Zhide	CHN	11.1.83	3		Cixi	23 Apr 05
1:17:55		Borchin			1	NC-w	Adler	23 Feb 08
1:17:56	Alejandro	López	MEX	9.2.75	2		Eisenhüttenstadt	8 May 99
1:18:00		Fernández			2	WCh	Saint-Denis	23 Aug 03
1:18:03.3tWR		Bo Lingtang	CHN	12.8.70	1	NC	Beijing	7 Apr 94
1:18:05	Dmitriy	Yesipchuk (20)	RUS	17.11.74	1	NC-w	Adler	4 Mar 01
1:18:06	Viktor	Burayev ¶	RUS	23.8.82	2	NC-w	Adler	4 Mar 01
1:18:06	Vladimir	Parvatkin	RUS	10.10.84	1	NC-w	Adler	12 Mar 05
1:18:07		Rasskazov			1	NC-w	Adler	20 Feb 00
1:18:07		Rasskazov			3	WCh	Saint-Denis	23 Aug 03
1:18:07		Li Gaobo	CHN	4.5.89	4		Cixi	23 Apr 05
1:18:12	Artur	Meleshkevich	BLR	11.4.75	1		Brest	10 Mar 01
	(30/24)							
1:18:13WR	Pavol	Blazek	SVK	9.7.58	1		Hildesheim	16 Sep 90
1:18:13		Wang Hao	CHN	16.8.89	1	NG	Jinan	22 Oct 09
1:18:14	Mikhail	Khmelnitskiy	BLR	24.7.69	1	NC	Soligorsk	13 May 00
1:18:14	Noé	Hernández	MEX	15.3.78	4	WCh	Saint-Denis	23 Aug 03
1:18:16	Vladimir	Andreyev	RUS	7.9.66	2	NC	Moskva	19 May 00
1:18:17	Ilya	Markov	RUS	19.6.72	2	NC-w	Adler	12 Mar 05
	(30)							
1:18:17	Yusuke	Suzuki	JPN	2.1.88	1	NC	Kobe	16 Feb 14
1:18:18	Yevgeniy	Misyulya	BLR	13.3.64	1		Eisenhüttenstadt	11 May 96
1:18:18	Sergey	Bakulin ¶	RUS	13.11.86	2	NC-w	Adler	23 Feb 08
1:18:20WR	Andrey	Perlov	RUS	12.12.61	1	NC	Moskva	26 May 90
1:18:20	Denis	Nizhegorodov	RUS	26.7.80	3	NC-w	Adler	4 Mar 01
1:18:22	Robert	Korzeniowski	POL	30.7.68	1		Hildesheim	9 Jul 00
1:18:23	Andrey	Makarov	BLR	2.1.71	2	NC	Soligorsk	13 May 00
1:18:25	Andrey	Krivov	RUS	14.11.85	3	NC-w	Sochi	18 Feb 12
1:18:25	Erick	Barrondo	GUA	14.6.91	3		Lugano	18 Mar 12
1:18:27	Daniel	García	MEX	28.10.71	2	WCp	Podebrady	19 Apr 97
	(40)							
1:18:27		Xing Shucai	CHN	4.8.84	5		Cixi	23 Apr 05
1:18:28	Pyotr	Trofimov	RUS	28.11.83	1	NC-w	Sochi	23 Feb 13
1:18:30		Yu Chaohong	CHN	12.12.76	6		Cixi	23 Apr 05
1:18:31		Han Yucheng	CHN	16.12.78	7		Cixi	23 Apr 05
1:18:32		Li Zewen	CHN	5.12.73	4	WCp	Podebrady	19 Apr 97
1:18:33		Liu Yunfeng ¶	CHN	3.8.79	8		Cixi	23 Apr 05
1:18:34	Eder	Sánchez	MEX	21.5.86	3	WCp	Cheboksary	10 May 08
1:18:35.2t	Stefan	Johansson	SWE	11.4.67	1	SGP	Bergen (Fana)	15 May 92
1:18:36	Mikhail	Shchennikov	RUS	24.12.67	1	NC	Sochi	20 Apr 96
1:18:37	Aleksandr	Pershin	RUS	4.9.68	2	NC	Moskva	26 May 90
	(50)	100th man 1:19:29, 200th 1:20:31, 300th 1:21:18, 400th 1:21:53, 500th 1:22:19						

Probable short course

Mark Wind	Name		Nat	Born	Pos	Meet	Venue	Date
1:18:33	Mikhail	Shchennikov	RUS	24.12.67	1	4-N	Livorno	10 Jul 93

Drugs disqualification

Mark Wind	Name		Nat	Born	Pos	Meet	Venue	Date
1:16:53	Vladimir	Kanaykin ¶	RUS	21.3.85	(2)	NC	Saransk	8 Jun 08
1:17:52		Morozov ¶			(2)	NC-w	Sochi	18 Feb 12
1:18:29	Stanislav	Yemelyanov ¶	RUS	23.10.90	(4)	NC-w	Sochi	18 Feb 12

Note that the fiull effects of recently announced bans on some Russian walkers inc. Sergey Bakulin, Valeriy Borchin, Vladimir Kanaykin and Andrey Ruzavin have yet to be fully determined.

Mark Wind	Name		Nat	Born	Pos	Meet	Venue	Date

30 KILOMETRES WALK

Mark		Name	Nat	Born	Pos	Meet	Venue	Date
2:01:13+	Vladimir	Kanaykin ¶	RUS	21.3.85	1	in 35k	Adler	19 Feb 06
2:01:44.1t	Maurizio	Damilano	ITA	6.4.57	1		Cuneo	3 Oct 92
2:01:47+		Kanaykin			1	in 35k	Adler	13 Mar 05
2:02:27+		Kanaykin			1	in 35k	Adler	8 Feb 04
2:02:41	Andrey	Perlov	RUS	12.12.61	1	NC-w	Sochi	19 Feb 89
2:02:45	Yevgeniy	Misyulya	BLR	13.3.64	1		Mogilyov	28 Apr 91
2:03:06	Daniel	Bautista	MEX	4.8.52	1		Cherkassy	27 Apr 80
2:03:50+	Vladimir	Parvatkin	RUS	10.10.84	2	in 35k	Adler	19 Feb 06
2:03:56.5t	Thierry	Toutain	FRA	14.2.62	1		Héricourt	24 Mar 91
2:04:00	Aleksandr	Potashov	BLR	12.3.62	1		Adler	14 Feb 93
2:04:24	Valeriy	Spitsyn	RUS	5.12.65	1	NC-w	Sochi	22 Feb 92
2:04:30	Vitaliy	Matsko (10)	RUS	8.6.60	2	NC-w	Sochi	19 Feb 89
2:04:49+	Semyon	Lovkin	RUS	14.7.77	1=	in 35k	Adler	1 Mar 03
2:04:49+	Stepan	Yudin	RUS	3.4.80	1=	in 35k	Adler	1 Mar 03
2:04:50+	Sergey	Kirdyapkin ¶	RUS	16.1.80	2	in 35k	Adler	13 Mar 05
2:04:55.5t	Guillaume	Leblanc	CAN	14.4.62	1		Sept-Iles	16 Jun 90
2:05:01	Sergey	Katureyev	RUS	29.9.67	2	NC-w	Sochi	22 Feb 92
2:05:05	Pyotr	Pochenchuk	UKR	26.7.54	2		Cherkassy	27 Apr 80
2:05:06	Nathan	Deakes	AUS	17.8.77	1	NC	Hobart	27 Aug 06
2:05:08+	Denis	Nizhegorodov	RUS	26.7.80	3	in 35k	Adler	19 Feb 06
2:05:09	Mikhail	Shchennikov	RUS	24.12.67	1	NC-w	Adler	11 Feb 96
2:05:12	Valeriy	Suntsov (20)	RUS	10.7.55	3		Cherkassy	27 Apr 80

35 KILOMETRES WALK

Mark		Name	Nat	Born	Pos	Meet	Venue	Date
2:21:31	Vladimir	Kanaykin ¶	RUS	21.3.85	1	NC-w	Adler	19 Feb 06
2:23:17		Kanaykin			1	NC-w	Adler	8 Feb 04
2:23:17		Kanaykin			1	NC-w	Adler	13 Mar 05
2:24:25	Semyon	Lovkin	RUS	14.7.77	1	NC-w	Adler	1 Mar 03
2:24:25	Sergey	Bakulin ¶	RUS	13.11.86	1	NC-w	Adler	1 Mar 09
2:24:50	Denis	Nizhegorodov	RUS	26.7.80	2	NC-w	Adler	19 Feb 06
2:24:56		Nizhegorodov			2	NC-w	Adler	1 Mar 09
2:25:19	Andrey	Ruzavin ¶	RUS	28.3.86	3	NC-w	Adler	1 Mar 09
2:25:38	Stepan	Yudin	RUS	3.4.80	2	NC-w	Adler	1 Mar 03
2:25:42	Sergey	Kirdyapkin ¶	RUS	18.6.80	1	NC-w	Sochi	18 Feb 12
2:25:57		Kirdyapkin			2	NC-w	Adler	13 Mar 05
2:25:58	German	Skurygin ¶	RUS	15.9.63	1	NC-w	Adler	20 Feb 98
2:25:59		Kanaykin ¶			1	NC-w	Adler	23 Feb 08
2:25:59	Mikhail	Ryzhov	RUS	17.12.91	2	NC-w	Sochi	26 Feb 12
	(14/9)							
2:26:16	Alex	Schwazer ¶ (10)	ITA	26.12.84	1		Montalto Di Castro	24 Jan 10
2:26:25	Aleksey	Voyevodin ¶	RUS	9.8.70	2	NC-w	Adler	8 Feb 04
2:26:29	Yuriy	Andronov	RUS	6.11.71	4	NC-w	Adler	1 Mar 09
2:26:33	Ivan	Noskov	RUS	16.7.88	3	NC-w	Sochi	26 Feb 12
2:26:36	Igor	Yerokhin ¶	RUS	4.9.85	1	NC-w	Sochi	26 Feb 11
2:26:46	Oleg	Ishutkin	RUS	22.7.75	1	NC-w	Adler	9 Feb 97
2:27:02	Yevgeniy	Shmalyuk	RUS	14.1.76	1	NC-w	Adler	20 Feb 00
2:27:07	Dmitriy	Dolnikov	RUS	19.11.72	2	NC-w	Adler	20 Feb 98
2:27:21	Pavel	Nikolayev	RUS	18.12.77	3	NC-w	Adler	20 Feb 98
2:27:29	Nikolay	Matyukhin	RUS	13.12.68	2	NC-w	Adler	9 Feb 97
2:27:42	Aleksey	Bartsaykin (20)	RUS	22.3.89	2	NC-w	Sochi	23 Feb 13

50 KILOMETRES WALK

Mark		Name	Nat	Born	Pos	Meet	Venue	Date
3:32:33 WR	Yohann	Diniz	FRA	1.1.78	1	EC	Zürich	15 Aug 14
3:34:14 WR	Denis	Nizhegorodov	RUS	26.7.80	1	WCp	Cheboksary	11 May 08
3:35:27.2t WR		Diniz		8	1		Reims	12 Mar 11
3:35:29		Nizhegorodov			1	NC	Cheboksary	13 Jun 04
3:35:47	Nathan	Deakes	AUS	17.8.77	1	NC	Geelong	2 Dec 06
3:35:59	Sergey	Kirdyapkin ¶	RUS	16.1.80	1	OG	London	11 Aug 12
3:36:03 WR	Robert	Korzeniowski	POL	30.7.68	1	WCh	Saint-Denis	27 Aug 03
3:36:04	Alex	Schwazer ¶	ITA	26.12.84	1	NC	Rosignano Solvay	11 Feb 07
3:36:06		Yu Chaohong	CHN	12.12.76	1	NG	Nanjing	22 Oct 05
3:36:13		Zhao Chengliang	CHN	1.6.84	2	NG	Nanjing	22 Oct 05
3:36:20		Han Yucheng	CHN	16.12.78	1	NC	Nanning	27 Feb 05
3:36:21	Matej	Tóth (10)	SVK	10.2.83	2	EC	Zürich	15 Aug 14
3:36:39 WR		Korzeniowski			1	EC	München	8 Aug 02
3:36:42	German	Skurygin ¶	RUS	15.9.63	2	WCh	Saint-Denis	27 Aug 03
3:36:53	Jared	Tallent	AUS	17.10.84	2	OG	London	11 Aug 12
3:37:04		Schwazer			2	WCp	Cheboksary	11 May 08
3:37:09		Schwazer			1	OG	Beijing	22 Aug 08

Mark	Wind	Name		Nat	Born	Pos	Meet	Venue	Date
3:37:16			Si Tianfeng	CHN	17.6.84	3	OG	London	11 Aug 12
3:37:26	WR	Valeriy	Spitsyn	RUS	5.12.65	1	NC	Moskva	21 May 00
3:37:41	WR	Andrey	Perlov	RUS	12.12.61	1	NC	Leningrad	5 Aug 89
3:37:41		Ivan	Noskov	RUS	16.7.88	3	EC	Zürich	15 Aug 14
3:37:46		Andreas	Erm	GER	12.3.76	3	WCh	Saint-Denis	27 Aug 03
3:37:54		Robert	Heffernan	IRL	20.2.78	4	OG	London	11 Aug 12
3:37:56			Heffernan			1	WCh	Moskva	14 Aug 13
3:37:58			Xing Shucai	CHN	4.8.84	2	NC	Nanning	27 Feb 05
3:38:01		Aleksey	Voyevodin ¶	RUS	9.8.70	4	WCh	Saint-Denis	27 Aug 03
3:38:02			Nizhegorodov			1	WCp	La Coruña	14 May 06
3:38:08			Kirdyapkin			1	WCh	Helsinki	12 Aug 05
3:38:08		Igor	Yerokhin ¶	RUS	4.9.85	1	NC	Saransk	8 Jun 08
3:38:08			Kirdyapkin			1	WCp	Saransk	13 May 12
		(30/21)							
3:38:17	WR	Ronald	Weigel	GDR	8.8.59	1	IM	Potsdam	25 May 86
3:38:29		Vyacheslav	Ivanenko	RUS	3.3.61	1	OG	Seoul	30 Sep 88
3:38:43		Valentí	Massana	ESP	5.7.70	1	NC	Orense	20 Mar 94
3:38:46		Sergey	Bakulin ¶	RUS	13.11.86	1	NC	Saransk	12 Jun 11
3:38:58		Mikhail	Ryzhov	RUS	17.12.91	2	WCh	Moskva	14 Aug 13
3:39:01			Li Jianbo	CHN	14.11.86	7	OG	London	11 Aug 12
3:39:17			Dong Jimin	CHN	10.10.83	4	NC	Nanning	27 Feb 05
3:39:21		Vladimir	Potemin	RUS	15.1.80	2	NC	Moskva	21 May 00
3:39:22		Sergey	Korepanov	KAZ	9.5.64	1	WCp	Mézidon-Canon	2 May 99
		(30)							
3:39:34		Valentin	Kononen	FIN	7.3.69	1		Dudince	25 Mar 00
3:39:45		Hartwig	Gauder	GDR	10.11.54	3	OG	Seoul	30 Sep 88
3:39:54		Jesús Angel	García	ESP	17.10.69	1	WCp	Podebrady	20 Apr 97
3:40:02		Aleksandr	Potashov	BLR	12.3.62	1	NC	Moskva	27 May 90
3:40:07		Andrey	Plotnikov	RUS	12.8.67	2	NC	Moskva	27 May 90
3:40:08		Tomasz	Lipiec ¶	POL	10.5.71	2	WCp	Mézidon-Canon	2 May 99
3:40:12		Oleg	Ishutkin	RUS	22.7.75	2	WCp	Podebrady	20 Apr 97
3:40:12		Yuki	Yamazaki	JPN	16.1.84	1		Wajima	12 Apr 09
3:40:13		Nikolay	Matyukhin	RUS	13.12.68	3	WCp	Mézidon-Canon	2 May 99
3:40:19		Takayuki	Tanii	JPN	14.2.83	2	AsiG	Incheon	1 Oct 14
		(40)							
3:40:23			Gadasu Alatan	CHN	27.1.84	3	NG	Nanjing	22 Oct 05
3:40:34		Hiroki	Arai	JPN	18.5.88	1		Takahata	26 Oct 14
3:40:39		Igor	Hlavan	UKR	25.9.90	4	WCh	Moskva	14 Aug 13
3:40:40		Vladimir	Kanaykin ¶	RUS	21.3.85	1	NC	Saransk	12 Jun 05
3:40:46	WR	José	Marin	ESP	21.1.50	1	NC	Valencia	13 Mar 83
3:40:46		Yuriy	Andronov ¶	RUS	6.11.71	1		Moskva	11 Jun 12
3:40:57.9t		Thierry	Toutain	FRA	14.2.62	1		Héricourt	29 Sep 96
3:41:02		Francisco Javier	Fernández ¶	ESP	6.3.77	1	NC	San Pedro del Pinatar	1 Mar 09
3:41:09		Érick	Barrondo	GUA	14.6.91	1		Dudince	23 Mar 13
3:41:10			Zhao Jianguo	CHN	19.1.88	1	AsiC	Wajima	16 Apr 06
		(51)	100th man 3:44:49, 200th 3:49:30, 300th 3:52:03, 400th 3:54:42, 500th 3:57:22						
Drugs disqualification									
3:36:55		Vladimir	Kanaykin ¶	RUS	21.3.85	(2)	WCp	Cheboksary	11 May 08
3:37:54		Igor	Yerokhin ¶	RUS	4.9.85	(5)	OG	London	11 Aug 12

100 KILOMETRES WALK

Mark	Wind	Name		Nat	Born	Pos	Meet	Venue	Date
8:38.07		Viktor	Ginko	BLR	7.12.65	1		Scanzorosciate	27 Oct 02
8:43:30			Ginko			1		Scanzorosciate	29 Oct 00
8:44:28			Ginko			1		Scanzorosciate	19 Oct 03
8:48:28		Modris	Liepins	LAT	30.8.66	1		Scanzorosciate	28 Oct 01
8:54:35		Aleksey	Rodionov	RUS	5.3.57	1		Scanzorosciate	15 Nov 98
8:55:12		Pascal	Kieffer	FRA	6.5.61	1		Besançon	18 Oct 92
8:55:40		Vitaliy	Popovich	UKR	22.10.62	1		Scanzorosciate	31 Oct 99
8:58:12		Gérard	Lelièvre	FRA	13.11.49	1		Laval	7 Oct 84
8:58:47		Zóltan	Czukor	HUN	18.12.62	2		Scanzorosciate	27 Oct 02

Deep all-time lists (generally 100 performances and 500 performers for all standard men's and women's events) have been compiled by Richard Hymans and Peter Matthews in a book published this spring by Jonas Hedman; this also includes the authors' selections of the all-time top ten greats for each event. Contact jonas.hedman@textograf.com

Oldest mark in top 50 World Lists: Men: in wind assisted sections: LJ 8.49w Ralph Boston USA 2 Sep 1964, 100m 9.91w Bob Hayes USA 15 Oct 1964; in main lists: SP: 37= 21.78 Randy Matson USA 22 Apr 1967. Women: by an individual – just outside: 100mh 52= 12.59 Anneliese Ehrhardt GDR 8 Sep 1972.

Oldest marks in top 500s: LJ : 372= 8.13 Jesse Owens 25 May 35, then 800m: 499= 1:45.7 Roger Moens 3 Aug 1955

Mark	Wind	Name		Nat	Born	Pos	Meet	Venue	Date

WOMEN'S ALL-TIME WORLD LISTS

100 METRES

Mark	Wind	Name		Nat	Born	Pos	Meet	Venue	Date
10.49WR	0.0	Florence	Griffith-Joyner	USA	21.12.59	1q1	NC/OT	Indianapolis	16 Jul 88
		@ Probably strongly wind-assisted, but recognised as a US and world record							
10.61	1.2		Griffith-Joyner			1	NC/OT	Indianapolis	17 Jul 88
10.62	1.0		Griffith-Joyner			1q3	OG	Seoul	24 Sep 88
10.64	1.2	Carmelita	Jeter	USA	24.11.79	1		Shanghai	20 Sep 09
10.65A	1.1	Marion	Jones ¶	USA	12.10.75	1	WCp	Johannesburg	12 Sep 98
10.67	-0.1		Jeter			1	WAF	Thessaloníki	13 Sep 09
10.70 (WR)	1.6		Griffith-Joyner			1s1	NC/OT	Indianapolis	17 Jul 88
10.70	-0.1		Jones			1	WCh	Sevilla	22 Aug 99
10.70	2.0		Jeter			1	Pre	Eugene	4 Jun 11
10.70	0.6	Shelly-Ann	Fraser-Pryce	JAM	27.12.86	1	NC	Kingston	29 Jun 12
10.71	0.1		Jones			1		Chengdu	12 May 98
10.71	2.0		Jones			1s2	NC	New Orleans	19 Jun 98
10.71	-0.3		Fraser-Pryce			1	WCh	Moskva	12 Aug 13
10.72	2.0		Jones			1	NC	New Orleans	20 Jun 98
10.72	0.0		Jones			1	Herc	Monaco	8 Aug 98
10.72	0.0		Jones			1	Athl	Lausanne	25 Aug 98
10.72	-0.3		Fraser-Pryce			1	VD	Bruxelles	6 Sep 13
10.73	2.0	Christine	Arron	FRA	13.9.73	1	EC	Budapest	19 Aug 98
10.73	0.1		Fraser-Pryce			1	WCh	Berlin	17 Aug 09
10.74	1.3	Merlene	Ottey	JAM/SLO	10.5.60	1	GPF	Milano	7 Sep 96
10.75	0.6		Jones			1	GGala	Roma	14 Jul 98
10.75	0.4	Kerron	Stewart	JAM	16.4.84	1	GGala	Roma	10 Jul 09
10.75	0.1		Stewart			2	WCh	Berlin	17 Aug 09
10.75	1.5		Fraser-Pryce			1	OG	London (OS)	4 Aug 12
10.76 WR	1.7	Evelyn	Ashford	USA	15.4.57	1	WK	Zürich	22 Aug 84
10.76	0.9		Jones			1	VD	Bruxelles	22 Aug 97
10.76	0.3		Jones			1q4	WCh	Sevilla	21 Aug 99
10.76	1.1	Veronica	Campbell-Brown	JAM	15.5.82	1	GS	Ostrava	31 May 11
10.77	0.9	Irina	Privalova (10)	RUS	22.11.68	1rA	Athl	Lausanne	6 Jul 94
10.77	-0.9		Jones			1rA	WK	Zürich	12 Aug 98
10.77	0.7	Ivet	Lalova	BUL	18.5.84	1	ECp-1A	Plovdiv	19 Jun 04
		(31 performances by 11 athletes)							
10.78A	1.0	Dawn	Sowell	USA	27.3.66	1	NCAA	Provo	3 Jun 89
10.78	1.8	Torri	Edwards ¶	USA	31.1.77	1s2	OT	Eugene	28 Jun 08
10.79	0.0		Li Xuemei	CHN	5.1.77	1	NG	Shanghai	18 Oct 97
10.79	-0.1	Inger	Miller	USA	12.6.72	2	WCh	Sevilla	22 Aug 99
10.79	1.1	Blessing	Okagbare	NGR	9.10.88	1	DL	London (OS)	27 Jul 13
10.80	0.8	Tori	Bowie	USA	27.8.90	21	Herc	Monaco	18 Jul 14
10.81 WR	1.7	Marlies	Göhr'	GDR	21.3.58	1	OD	Berlin	8 Jun 83
10.82	-1.0	Gail	Devers	USA	19.11.66	1	OG	Barcelona	1 Aug 92
10.82	0.4	Gwen	Torrence	USA	12.6.65	2	GPF	Paris	3 Sep 94
		(20)							
10.82	-0.3	Zhanna	Pintusevich-Block ¶	UKR	6.7.72	1	WCh	Edmonton	6 Aug 01
10.82	-0.7	Sherone	Simpson	JAM	12.8.84	1	NC	Kingston	24 Jun 06
10.83	1.7	Marita	Koch	GDR	18.2.57	2	OD	Berlin	8 Jun 83
10.83	-1.0	Juliet	Cuthbert	JAM	9.4.64	2	OG	Barcelona	1 Aug 92
10.83	0.1	Ekateríni	Thánou ¶	GRE	1.2.75	2s1	WCh	Sevilla	22 Aug 99
10.83	1.6	Kelly-Ann	Baptiste	TTO	14.10.86	1	NC	Port of Spain	22 Jun 13
10.84	1.3	Chioma	Ajunwa ¶	NGR	25.12.70	1		Lagos	11 Apr 92
10.84	1.9	Chandra	Sturrup	BAH	12.9.71	1	Athl	Lausanne	5 Jul 05
10.85	2.0	Anelia	Nuneva	BUL	30.6.62	1h1	NC	Sofia	2 Sep 88
10.85	1.0	Muna	Lee	USA	30.10.81	1	OT	Eugene	28 Jun 08
		(30)							
10.85	1.5	Tianna	Madison'	USA	30.8.85	4	OG	London (OS)	4 Aug 12
10.85	2.0	Barbara	Pierre	HAI/USA	28.4.87	1s1	NC	Des Moines	21 Jun 13
10.85	1.8	English	Gardner	USA	22.4.92	1	NC	Des Moines	21 Jun 13
10.85	1.6	Michelle-Lee	Ahye	TTO	10.4.92	1	NC	Port of Spain	21 Jun 14
10.86	0.6	Silke	Gladisch'	GDR	20.6.64	1	NC	Potsdam	20 Aug 87
10.86	1.2	Chryste	Gaines ¶	USA	14.9.70	1	WAF	Monaco	14 Sep 03
10.86	2.0	Marshevet	Hooker/Myers	USA	25.9.84	2	Pre	Eugene	4 Jun 11
10.87	1.8	Octavious	Freeman	USA	20.4.92	2	NC	Des Moines	21 Jun 13
10.88	0.4	Lauryn	Williams	USA	11.9.83	2	WK	Zürich	19 Aug 05
10.89	1.8	Katrin	Krabbe ¶	GDR	22.11.69	1		Berlin	20 Jul 88
		(40)							
10.89	0.0		Liu Xiaomei	CHN	11.1.72	2	NG	Shanghai	18 Oct 97

Mark	Wind	Name		Nat	Born	Pos	Meet	Venue	Date
10.89	1.5	Allyson	Felix	USA	18.11.85	5	OG	London (OS)	4 Aug 12
10.90	1.4	Glory	Alozie	NGR/ESP	30.12.77	1		La Laguna	5 Jun 99
10.90	1.8	Shalonda	Solomon	USA	19.12.85	2		Clermont	5 Jun 10
10.91	0.2	Heike	Drechsler'	GDR/GER	16.12.64	2	GWG	Moskva	6 Jul 86
10.91	1.1	Savatheda	Fynes	BAH	17.10.74	2	Athl	Lausanne	2 Jul 99
10.91	1.5	Debbie	Ferguson McKenzie	BAH	16.1.76	1	CG	Manchester	27 Jul 02
10.91	1.7	Alexandria	Anderson	USA	28.1.87	3s2	NC	Des Moines	21 Jun 13
10.91	1.5	Murielle	Ahouré	CIV	23.8.87	1		Sotteville-lès-Rouen	8 Jul 13
10.92	0.0	Alice	Brown	USA	20.9.60	2q2	NC/OT	Indianapolis	16 Jul 88
10.92	1.1	D'Andre	Hill	USA	19.4.73	3	NC	Atlanta	15 Jun 96
10.92	0.1	Yuliya	Nesterenko	BLR	15.6.79	1s1	OG	Athína	21 Aug 04
		(52)	100th women 11.03, 200th 11.12, 300th 11.19, 400th 11.24, 500th 11.28						
Doubtful wind reading									
10.83	0.0	Sheila	Echols	USA	2.10.64	1q2	NC/OT	Indianapolis	16 Jul 88
10.86	0.0	Diane	Williams	USA	14.12.60	2q1	NC/OT	Indianapolis	16 Jul 88
Probably semi-automatic timing									
10.87	1.9	Lyudmila	Kondratyeva	RUS	11.4.58	1		Leningrad	3 Jun 80
Low altitude best: 10.91	1.6		Sowell			1	NC	Houston	16 Jun 89
Wind-assisted to 10.76 performances and performers to 10.89									
10.54	3.0		Griffith-Joyner			1	OG	Seoul	25 Sep 88
10.60	3.2		Griffith-Joyner			1h1	NC/OT	Indianapolis	16 Jul 88
10.68	2.2		Jones			1	DNG	Stockholm	1 Aug 00
10.70	2.6		Griffith-Joyner			1s2	OG	Seoul	25 Sep 88
10.71	2.2		Fraser-Pryce			1	Pre	Eugene	1 Jun 13
10.72	3.0		Jeter			1s1	NC	Eugene	26 Jun 09
10.74	2.7		Jeter			1	NC	Eugene	24 Jun 11
10.75	4.1		Jones			1h3	NC	New Orleans	19 Jun 98
10.75	2.2	Blessing	Okagbare	NGR	9.10.88	2	Pre	Eugene	1 Jun 13
10.76	3.4	Marshevet	Hooker/Myers	USA	25.9.84	1q1	NC/OT	Eugene	27 Jun 08
10.77	2.3	Gail	Devers	USA	19.11.66	1	Jen	San José	28 May 94
10.77	2.3	Ekateríni	Thánou ¶	GRE	1.2.75	1		Rethymno	28 May 99
10.78	5.0	Gwen	Torrence	USA	12.6.65	1q3	NC/OT	Indianapolis	16 Jul 88
10.78	3.3	Muna	Lee	USA	30.10.81	2	NC	Eugene	26 Jun 09
10.79	3.3	Marlies	Göhr'	GDR	21.3.58	1	NC	Cottbus	16 Jul 80
10.80	2.9	Pam	Marshall	USA	16.8.60	1	NC	Eugene	20 Jun 86
10.80	2.8	Heike	Drechsler'	GDR	16.12.64	1	Bisl	Oslo	5 Jul 86
10.82	2.2	Silke	Gladisch/Möller	GDR	20.6.64	1s1	WCh	Roma	30 Aug 87
10.83	3.9	Sheila	Echols	USA	2.10.84	1h2	NC/OT	Indianapolis	16 Jul 88
10.84	2.9	Alice	Brown	USA	20.9.60	2	NC	Eugene	20 Jun 86
10.86	3.4	Lauryn	Williams	USA	11.9.83	2q1	NC/OT	Eugene	27 Jun 08
10.86	2.9	Murielle	Ahouré	CIV	23.8.87	1		Clermont	4 Jun 11
10.87	3.0	Me'Lisa	Barber	USA	4.10.80	1s1	NC	Carson	25 Jun 05
10.88	5.9	Alexandria	Anderson	USA	28.1.87	1		Austin	14 Apr 12
10.89	3.1	Kerstin	Behrendt	GDR	2.9.67	2		Berlin	13 Sep 88
10.89	2.9	Sanya	Richards-Ross	USA	26.2.85	1	TexR	Austin	31 Mar 12
Hand timing									
10.6	0.1	Zhanna	Pintusevich ¶	UKR	6.7.72	1		Kiev	12 Jun 97
10.7		Merlene	Ottey	JAM	10.5.60	1h	NC	Kingston	15 Jul 88
10.7	1.1	Juliet	Cuthbert	JAM	9.4.64	1	NC	Kingston	4 Jul 92
10.7		Mary	Onyali	NGR	3.2.68	1	NC	Lagos	22 Jun 96
10.7	-0.2	Svetlana	Goncharenko	RUS	28.5.71	1		Rostov-na-Donu	30 May 98
10.7A	1.3	Blessing	Okagbare	NGR	9.10.86	1		El Paso	10 Apr 10
10.7w	2.6	Savatheda	Fynes	BAH	17.10.74	1	NC	Nassau	22 Jun 95
Drugs disqualification									
10.75	-0.4		Jones			(1)	OG	Sydney	23 Sep 00
10.78	0.1		Jones			(1)	ISTAF	Berlin	1 Sep 00
10.85	0.9	Kelli	White ¶	USA	1.4.77	(1)	WCh	Saint-Denis	24 Aug 03
10.79w	2.3	Kelli	White ¶	USA	1.4.77	(1)		Carson	1 Jun 03
10.89w	4.6	Tahesia	Harrigan-Scott	IVB	15.2.82	(1h1)		Clernont	4 Jun 11

200 METRES

Mark	Wind	Name		Nat	Born	Pos	Meet	Venue	Date
21.34WR	1.3	Florence	Griffith-Joyner	USA	21.12.59	1	OG	Seoul	29 Sep 88
21.56WR	1.7		Griffith-Joyner			1s1	OG	Seoul	29 Sep 88
21.62A	-0.6	Marion	Jones ¶	USA	12.10.75	1	WCp	Johannesburg	11 Sep 98
21.64	0.8	Merlene	Ottey	JAM	10.5.60	1	VD	Bruxelles	13 Sep 91
21.66	-1.0		Ottey			1	WK	Zürich	15 Aug 90
21.69	1.0	Allyson	Felix	USA	18.11.85	1	NC/OT	Eugene	30 Jun 12
21.71WR	0.7	Marita	Koch	GDR	18.2.57	1	v CAN	Karl-Marx-Stadt	10 Jun 79
21.71WR	0.3		Koch			1	OD	Potsdam	21 Jul 84
21.71WR	1.2	Heike	Drechsler'	GDR	16.12.64	1	NC	Jena	29 Jun 86
21.71WR	-0.8		Drechsler			1	EC	Stuttgart	29 Aug 86

WOMEN All-time

Mark	Wind	Name		Nat	Born	Pos	Meet	Venue	Date
21.72	1.3	Grace	Jackson	JAM	14.6.61	2	OG	Seoul	29 Sep 88
21.72	-0.1	Gwen	Torrence	USA	12.6.65	1s2	OG	Barcelona	5 Aug 92
21.74	0.4	Marlies	Göhr'	GDR	21.3.58	1	NC	Erfurt	3 Jun 84
21.74	1.2	Silke	Gladisch' (10)	GDR	20.6.64	1	WCh	Roma	3 Sep 87
21.74	0.6	Veronica	Campbell-Brown	JAM	15.5.82	1	OG	Beijing	21 Aug 08
21.75	-0.1	Juliet	Cuthbert	JAM	9.4.64	2s2	OG	Barcelona	5 Aug 92
21.76	0.3		Koch			1	NC	Dresden	3 Jul 82
21.76	0.7		Griffith-Joyner			1q1	OG	Seoul	28 Sep 88
21.76	-0.8		Jones			1	WK	Zürich	13 Aug 97
21.77	-0.1		Griffith-Joyner			1q2	NC/OT	Indianapolis	22 Jul 88
21.77	1.0		Ottey			1	Herc	Monaco	7 Aug 93
21.77	-0.3		Torrence			1	ASV	Köln	18 Aug 95
21.77	0.6	Inger	Miller	USA	12.6.72	1	WCh	Sevilla	27 Aug 99
21.78	-1.3		Koch			1	NC	Leipzig	11 Aug 85
21.79	1.7		Gladisch			1	NC	Potsdam	22 Aug 87
21.80	-1.1		Ottey			1	Nik	Nice	10 Jul 90
21.80	0.4		Jones			1	GWG	Uniondale, NY	20 Jul 98
21.81	-0.1	Valerie	Brisco	USA	6.7.60	1	OG	Los Angeles	9 Aug 84
21.81	0.4		Ottey			1	ASV	Köln	19 Aug 90
21.81	-0.6		Torrence			1	OG	Barcelona	6 Aug 92
21.81	0.0		Torrence			1	Herc	Monaco	25 Jul 95
21.81	1.6		Jones			1	Pre	Eugene	30 May 99
21.81	1.7		Felix			1	WCh	Osaka	31 Aug 07
		(33/14)							
21.83	-0.2	Evelyn	Ashford	USA	15.4.57	1	WCp	Montreal	24 Aug 79
21.85	0.3	Bärbel	Wöckel'	GDR	21.3.55	2	OD	Potsdam	21 Jul 84
21.87	0.0	Irina	Privalova	RUS	22.11.68	2	Herc	Monaco	25 Jul 95
21.93	1.3	Pam	Marshall	USA	16.8.60	2	NC/OT	Indianapolis	23 Jul 88
21.95	0.3	Katrin	Krabbe ¶	GDR	22.11.69	1	EC	Split	30 Aug 90
21.97	1.9	Jarmila	Kratochvílová	CZE	26.1.51	1	PTS	Bratislava	6 Jun 81
		(20)							
21.99	0.9	Chandra	Cheeseborough	USA	10.1.59	2	NC	Indianapolis	19 Jun 83
21.99	1.1	Marie-José	Pérec	FRA	9.5.68	1	BNP	Villeneuve d'Ascq	2 Jul 93
21.99	1.1	Kerron	Stewart	JAM	16.4.84	2	NC	Kingston	29 Jun 08
22.00	1.3	Sherone	Simpson	JAM	12.8.84	1	NC	Kingston	25 Jun 06
22.01	-0.5	Anelia	Nuneva'	BUL	30.6.62	1	NC	Sofia	16 Aug 87
22.01	0.0		Li Xuemei	CHN	5.1.77	1	NG	Shanghai	22 Oct 97
22.01	0.6	Muna	Lee	USA	30.10.81	4	OG	Beijing	21 Aug 08
22.03	-0.5	Dafne	Schippers	NED	15.6.92	1	EC	Zürich	15 Aug 14
22.04A	0.7	Dawn	Sowell	USA	27.3.66	1	NCAA	Provo	2 Jun 89
22.06A	0.7	Evette	de Klerk'	RSA	21.8.65	1		Pietersburg	8 Apr 89
		(30)							
22.07	-0.1	Mary	Onyali	NGR	3.2.68	1	WK	Zürich	14 Aug 96
22.09	-0.3	Sanya	Richards-Ross	USA	26.2.85	1	DL	New York	9 Jun 12
22.09	-0.2	Shelly-Ann	Fraser-Pryce	JAM	27.12.86	2	OG	London (OS)	8 Aug 12
22.10	-0.1	Kathy	Cook'	GBR	3.5.60	4	OG	Los Angeles	9 Aug 84
22.11	1.0	Carmelita	Jeter	USA	24.11.79	2	NC/OT	Eugene	30 Jun 12
22.11	0.1	Myriam	Soumaré	FRA	29.10.86	2	VD	Bruxelles	5 Sep 14
22.13	1.2	Ewa	Kasprzyk	POL	7.9.57	2	GWG	Moskva	8 Jul 86
22.14	-0.6	Carlette	Guidry	USA	4.9.68	1	NC	Atlanta	23 Jun 96
22.15	1.0	Shalonda	Solomon	USA	19.12.85	1	NC	Eugene	26 Jun 11
22.17A	-2.3	Zhanna	Pintusevich-Block ¶	UKR	6.7.72	1		Monachil	9 Jul 97
		22.24	-0.3			2	VD	Bruxelles	30 Aug 02
		(40)							
22.18	-0.6	Dannette	Young-Stone	USA	6.10.64	2	NC	Atlanta	23 Jun 96
22.18	0.9	Galina	Malchugina	RUS	17.12.62	1s2	NC	Sankt Peterburg	4 Jul 96
22.18	0.5	Merlene	Frazer	JAM	27.12.73	1s2	WCh	Sevilla	25 Aug 99
22.18	1.5	Tori	Bowie	USA	27.8.90	1	Pre	Eugene	31 May 14
22.19	1.5	Natalya	Bochina	RUS	4.1.62	2	OG	Moskva	30 Jul 80
22.19	0.0	Debbie	Ferguson McKenzie	BAH	16.1.76	1	GP II	Saint-Denis	3 Jul 99
22.19	1.9	Kimberlyn	Duncan	USA	2.8.91	1s2	NCAA	Des Moines	7 Jun 12
22.19	1.0	Aleksandra	Fedoriva	RUS	13.9.88	1	NC	Cheboksary	6 Jul 12
22.20	2.0	Kim	Gevaert	BEL	5.8.78	1	NC	Bruxelles	9 Jul 06
22.21 WR	1.9	Irena	Szewinska'	POL	24.5.46	1		Potsdam	13 Jun 74
		(50)	100th woman 22.36, 200th 22.60, 300th 22.74, 4th 22.85, 500th 22.93						
Wind-assisted			*Performers listed to 22.18*						
21.80	3.2	Kimberlyn	Duncan	USA	2.8.91	1	NC	Des Moines	23 Jun 13
21.82	3.1	Irina	Privalova	RUS	22.11.68	1	Athl	Lausanne	6 Jul 94
21.91	2.8	Muna	Lee	USA	30.10.81	1		Fort-de-France	10 May 08
22.15	3.2	Jeneba	Tarmoh	USA	27.9.89	3	NC	Des Moines	23 Jun 13

Mark	Wind	Name		Nat	Born	Pos	Meet	Venue	Date
22.16	3.1	Dannette	Young-Stone	USA	6.10.64	2	Athl	Lausanne	6 Jul 94
22.16	3.2	Nanceen	Perry	USA	19.4.77	1		Austin	6 May 00
22.16	3.2	Kamaria	Brown	USA	21.12.92	4	NC	Des Moines	23 Jun 13
22.17	4.3	Morolake	Akinosun	USA	17.5.94	1	Big 12	Lubbock	18 May 14
22.18A	2.8	Melinda	Gainsford-Taylor	AUS	1.10.71	1		Pietersburg	18 Mar 00
Hand timing									
21.9	-0.1	Svetlana	Goncharenko	RUS	28.5.71	1		Rostov-na-Donu	31 May 98
21.6w	2.5	Pam	Marshall	USA	16.8.60	1	NC	San José	26 Jun 87
Drugs disqualification									
22.05	-0.3	Kelli	White ¶	USA	1.4.77	1	WCh	Saint-Denis	28 Aug 03
22.18i		Michelle	Collins ¶	USA	12.2.71	1	WI	Birmingham	15 Mar 03

300 METRES

Times in 300m races only

Mark	Wind	Name		Nat	Born	Pos	Meet	Venue	Date
35.30A		Ana Gabriela	Guevara	MEX	4.3.77	1		Ciudad de México	3 May 03
35.46		Kathy	Cook'	GBR	3.5.60	1	Nike	London (CP)	18 Aug 84
35.46		Chandra	Cheeseborough	USA	10.1.59	2	Nike	London (CP)	18 Aug 84
Indoors									
35.45		Irina	Privalova	RUS	22.11.68	1		Moskva	17 Jan 93
35.48	#	Svetlana	Goncharenko	RUS	28.5.71	1		Tampere	4 Feb 98

400 METRES

Mark	Wind	Name		Nat	Born	Pos	Meet	Venue	Date
47.60 WR		Marita	Koch	GDR	18.2.57	1	WCp	Canberra	6 Oct 85
47.99 WR		Jarmila	Kratochvílová	CZE	26.1.51	1	WCh	Helsinki	10 Aug 83
48.16 WR			Koch			1	EC	Athína	8 Sep 82
48.16			Koch			1	Drz	Praha	16 Aug 84
48.22			Koch			1	EC	Stuttgart	28 Aug 86
48.25		Marie-José	Pérec	FRA	9.5.68	1	OG	Atlanta	29 Jul 96
48.26			Koch			1	GO	Dresden	27 Jul 84
48.27		Olga	Vladykina'	UKR	30.6.63	2	WCp	Canberra	6 Oct 85
48.45			Kratochvílová			1	NC	Praha	23 Jul 83
48.59		Tatána	Kocembová'	CZE	2.5.62	2	WCh	Helsinki	10 Aug 83
48.60 WR			Koch			1	ECp	Torino	4 Aug 79
48.60			Vladykina			1	ECp	Moskva	17 Aug 85
48.61			Kratochvílová			1	WCp	Roma	6 Sep 81
48.63		Cathy	Freeman	AUS	16.2.73	2	OG	Atlanta	29 Jul 96
48.65			Bryzgina'			1	OG	Seoul	26 Sep 88
48.70		Sanya	Richards	USA	26.2.85	1	WCp	Athína	16 Sep 06
48.73			Kocembová			2	Drz	Praha	16 Aug 84
48.77			Koch			1	v USA	Karl-Marx-Stadt	9 Jul 82
48.82			Kratochvílová			1	Ros	Praha	23 Jun 83
48.83		Valerie	Brisco	USA	6.7.60	1	OG	Los Angeles	6 Aug 84
48.83			Pérec			1	OG	Barcelona	5 Aug 92
48.83			Richards			1	VD	Bruxelles	4 Sep 09
48.85			Kratochvílová			2	EC	Athína	8 Sep 82
48.86			Kratochvílová			1	WK	Zürich	18 Aug 82
48.86			Koch			1	NC	Erfurt	2 Jun 84
48.87			Koch			1	VD	Bruxelles	27 Aug 82
48.88			Koch			1	OG	Moskva	28 Jul 80
48.89 WR			Koch			1		Potsdam	29 Jul 79
48.89			Koch			1		Berlin	15 Jul 84
48.89		Ana Gabriela (30/9)	Guevara	MEX	4.3.77	1	WCh	Saint-Denis	27 Aug 03
49.05		Chandra (10)	Cheeseborough	USA	10.1.59	2	OG	Los Angeles	6 Aug 84
49.07		Tonique	Williams-Darling	BAH	17.1.76	1	ISTAF	Berlin	12 Sep 04
49.10		Falilat	Ogunkoya	NGR	12.5.68	3	OG	Atlanta	29 Jul 96
49.11		Olga	Nazarova ¶	RUS	1.6.65	1s1	OG	Seoul	25 Sep 88
49.16		Antonina	Krivoshapka	RUS	21.7.87	1	NC	Cheboksary	5 Jul 12
49.19		Mariya	Pinigina'	UKR	9.2.58	3	WCh	Helsinki	10 Aug 83
49.24		Sabine	Busch	GDR	21.11.62	2	NC	Erfurt	2 Jun 84
49.28 WR		Irena	Szewinska'	POL	24.5.46	1	OG	Montreal	29 Jul 76
49.28		Pauline	Davis-Thompson	BAH	9.7.66	4	OG	Atlanta	29 Jul 96
49.28		Yuliya	Gushchina	RUS	4.3.83	2	NC	Cheboksary	5 Jul 12
49.29		Charity (20)	Opara ¶	NGR	20.5.72	1	GGala	Roma	14 Jul 98
49.30		Petra	Müller'	GDR	18.7.65	1		Jena	3 Jun 88
49.30		Lorraine	Fenton'	JAM	8.9.73	2	Herc	Monaco	19 Jul 02
49.32		Shericka	Williams	JAM	17.9.85	2	WCh	Berlin	18 Aug 09
49.33		Amantle	Montsho ¶	BOT	4.7.83	1	Herc	Monaco	19 Jul 13
49.35		Anastasiya	Kapachinskaya ¶	RUS	21.11.79	1	NC	Cheboksary	22 Jul 11
49.40		Jearl	Miles-Clark	USA	4.9.66	1	NC	Indianapolis	14 Jun 97

Mark	Wind	Name		Nat	Born	Pos	Meet	Venue	Date
49.41		Christine	Ohuruogu	GBR	17.5.84	1	WCh	Moskva	12 Aug 13
49.42		Grit	Breuer ¶	GER	16.2.72	2	WCh	Tokyo	27 Aug 91
49.43		Kathy	Cook'	GBR	3.5.60	3	OG	Los Angeles	6 Aug 84
49.43A		Fatima	Yusuf	NGR	2.5.71	1	AfG	Harare	15 Sep 95
		(30)							
49.47		Aelita	Yurchenko	UKR	1.1.65	2	Kuts	Moskva	4 Sep 88
49.48		Francena	McCorory	USA	20.10.88	1	NC	Sacramento	28 Jun 14
49.49		Olga	Zaytseva	RUS	10.11.84	1	NCp	Tula	16 Jul 06
49.53		Vanya	Stambolova ¶	BUL	28.11.83	1	GP	Rieti	27 Aug 06
49.56		Bärbel	Wöckel'	GDR	21.3.55	1		Erfurt	30 May 82
49.56		Monique	Hennagan	USA	26.5.76	1	NC/OT	Sacramento	17 Jul 04
49.57		Grace	Jackson	JAM	14.6.61	1	Nik	Nice	10 Jul 88
49.58		Dagmar	Rübsam'	GDR	3.6.62	3	NC	Erfurt	2 Jun 84
49.59		Marion	Jones ¶	USA	12.10.75	1r6	MSR	Walnut	16 Apr 00
49.59		Katharine	Merry	GBR	21.9.74	1	GP	Athína	11 Jun 01
		(40)							
49.59		Allyson	Felix	USA	18.11.85	2	WCh	Daegu	29 Aug 11
49.61		Ana Fidelia	Quirot	CUB	23.3.63	1	PAm	La Habana	5 Aug 91
49.63		Novlene	Williams-Mills	JAM	26.4.82	1		Shanghai	23 Sep 06
49.64		Gwen	Torrence	USA	12.6.65	2	Nik	Nice	15 Jul 92
49.64		Ximena	Restrepo	COL	10.3.69	3	OG	Barcelona	5 Aug 92
49.64		Deedee	Trotter	USA	8.12.82	1	NC	Indianapolis	23 Jun 07
49.64		Debbie	Dunn ¶	USA	26.3.78	1	NC	Des Moines	26 Jun 10
49.65		Natalya	Nazarova	RUS	26.5.79	1	NC	Tula	31 Jul 04
49.65		Nicola	Sanders	GBR	23.6.82	2	WCh	Osaka	29 Aug 07
49.66		Christina	Brehmer/Lathan	GDR	28.2.58	3	OG	Moskva	28 Jul 80
49.66		Lillie	Leatherwood	USA	6.7.64	1	NC	New York	15 Jun 91
		(51)	100th woman 50.19, 200th 50.83, 300th 51.17, 400th 51.42, 500th 51.65						

Hand timing

Mark	Wind	Name		Nat	Born	Pos	Meet	Venue	Date
48.9		Olga	Nazarova ¶	RUS	1.6.65	1	NP	Vladivostok	13 Sep 88
49.2A		Ana Fidelia	Quirot	CUB	23.3.63	1	AmCp	Bogotá	13 Aug 89

600 METRES

Mark	Name		Nat	Born	Pos	Meet	Venue	Date
1:22.63	Ana Fidelia	Quirot	CUB	23.3.63	1		Guadalajara, ESP	25 Jul 97
1:22.87	Maria Lurdes	Mutola	MOZ	27.10.72	1		Liège (NX)	27 Aug 02
1:23.35	Pamela	Jelimo	KEN	5.12.89	1		Liège (NX)	5 Jul 12

800 METRES

Mark	Name		Nat	Born	Pos	Meet	Venue	Date
1:53.28 WR	Jarmila	Kratochvílová	CZE	26.1.51	1		München	26 Jul 83
1:53.43 WR	Nadezhda	Olizarenko'	UKR	28.11.53	1	OG	Moskva	27 Jul 80
1:54.01	Pamela	Jelimo	KEN	5.12.89	1	WK	Zürich	29 Aug 08
1:54.44	Ana Fidelia	Quirot	CUB	23.3.63	1	WCp	Barcelona	9 Sep 89
1:54.68		Kratochvílová			1	WCh	Helsinki	9 Aug 83
1:54.81	Olga	Mineyeva	RUS	1.9.52	2	OG	Moskva	27 Jul 80
1:54.82		Quirot			1	ASV	Köln	24 Aug 97
1:54.85 WR		Olizarenko			1	Prav	Moskva	12 Jun 80
1:54.87		Jelimo			1	OG	Beijing	18 Aug 08
1:54.94 WR	Tatyana	Kazankina ¶	RUS	17.12.51	1	OG	Montreal	26 Jul 76
1:54.97		Jelimo			1	Gaz	Saint-Denis	18 Jul 08
1:54.99		Jelimo			1	ISTAF	Berlin	1 Jun 08
1:55.04		Kratochvílová			1	OsloG	Oslo	23 Aug 83
1:55.05	Doina	Melinte	ROU	27.12.56	1	NC	Bucuresti	1 Aug 82
1:55.1 '		Mineyeva			1	Znam	Moskva	6 Jul 80
1:55.16		Jelimo			1	VD	Bruxelles	5 Sep 08
1:55.19	Maria Lurdes	Mutola	MOZ	27.10.72	1	WK	Zürich	17 Aug 94
1:55.19	Jolanda	Ceplak ¶	SLO	12.9.76	1rA	NA	Heusden	20 Jul 02
1:55.26	Sigrun	Wodars/Grau (10)	GDR	7.11.65	1	WCh	Roma	31 Aug 87
1:55.29		Mutola			2	ASV	Köln	24 Aug 97
1:55.32	Christine	Wachtel	GDR	6.1.65	2	WCh	Roma	31 Aug 87
1:55.41		Mineyeva			1	EC	Athína	8 Sep 82
1:55.41		Jelimo			1	Bisl	Oslo	6 Jun 08
1:55.42	Nikolina	Shtereva	BUL	25.1.55	2	OG	Montreal	26 Jul 76
1:55.43		Mutola			1	WCh	Stuttgart	17 Aug 93
1:55.45	Caster	Semenya	RSA	7.1.91	1	WCh	Berlin	19 Aug 09
1:55.46	Tatyana	Providokhina	RUS	26.3.53	3	OG	Moskva	27 Jul 80
1:55.5		Mineyeva			1	Kuts	Podolsk	21 Aug 82
1:55.54	Ellen	van Langen	NED	9.2.66	1	OG	Barcelona	3 Aug 92
1:55.54		Liu Dong	CHN	24.12.73	1	NG	Beijing	9 Sep 93
	(30/16)							
1:55.56	Lyubov	Gurina	RUS	6.8.57	3	WCh	Roma	31 Aug 87

Mark Wind	Name		Nat	Born	Pos	Meet	Venue	Date
1:55.60	Elfi	Zinn	GDR	24.8.53	3	OG	Montreal	26 Jul 76
1:55.68	Ella	Kovacs	ROU	11.12.64	1	RomIC	Bucuresti	2 Jun 85
1:55.69	Irina	Podyalovskaya	RUS	19.10.59	1	Izv	Kyiv	22 Jun 84
	(20)							
1:55.74	Anita	Weiss'	GDR	16.7.55	4	OG	Montreal	26 Jul 76
1:55.87	Svetlana	Masterkova	RUS	17.1.68	1	Kuts	Moskva	18 Jun 99
1:55.87	Mariya	Savinova	RUS	13.8.85	1	WCh	Daegu	4 Sep 11
1:55.96	Lyudmila	Veselkova	RUS	25.10.50	2	EC	Athína	8 Sep 82
1:55.96	Yekaterina	Podkopayeva'	RUS	11.6.52	1		Leningrad	27 Jul 83
1:55.99	Liliya	Nurutdinova ¶	RUS	15.12.63	2	OG	Barcelona	3 Aug 92
1:56.00	Tatyana	Andrianova	RUS	10.12.79	1	NC	Kazan	18 Jul 08
1:56.0 WR	Valentina	Gerasimova	KAZ	15.5.48	1	NC	Kyiv	12 Jun 76
1:56.0	Inna	Yevseyeva	UKR	14.8.64	1		Kyiv	25 Jun 88
1:56.04	Janeth	Jepkosgei	KEN	13.12.83	1	WCh	Osaka	28 Aug 07
	(30)							
1:56.09	Zulia	Calatayud	CUB	9.11.79	1	Herc	Monaco	19 Jul 02
1:56.1	Ravilya	Agletdinova'	BLR	10.2.60	2	Kuts	Podolsk	21 Aug 82
1:56.2 '	Totka	Petrova ¶	BUL	17.12.56	1		Paris (C)	6 Jul 79
1:56.2	Tatyana	Mishkel	UKR	10.6.52	3	Kuts	Podolsk	21 Aug 82
1:56.21	Martina	Kämpfert'	GDR	11.11.59	4	OG	Moskva	27 Jul 80
1:56.21	Zamira	Zaytseva	UZB	16.2.53	2		Leningrad	27 Jul 83
1:56.21	Kelly	Holmes	GBR	19.4.70	2	GPF	Monaco	9 Sep 95
1:56.24		Qu Yunxia	CHN	8.12.72	2	NG	Beijing	9 Sep 93
1:56.40	Jearl	Miles-Clark	USA	4.9.66	3	WK	Zürich	11 Aug 99
1:56.42	Paula	Ivan	ROU	20.7.63	1	Balk	Ankara	16 Jul 88
	(40)							
1:56.43	Hasna	Benhassi	MAR	1.6.78	2	OG	Athína	23 Aug 04
1:56.44	Svetlana	Styrkina	RUS	1.1.49	5	OG	Montreal	26 Jul 76
1:56.51	Slobodanka	Colovic	YUG	10.1.65	1		Beograd	17 Jun 87
1:56.53	Patricia	Djaté	FRA	3.1.71	3	GPF	Monaco	9 Sep 95
1:56.56	Ludmila	Formanová	CZE	2.1.74	4	WK	Zürich	11 Aug 99
1:56.57	Zoya	Rigel	RUS	15.10.52	3	EC	Praha	31 Aug 78
1:56.59	Natalya	Khrushchelyova	RUS	30.5.73	2	NC	Tula	31 Jul 04
1:56.59	Francine	Niyonsaba	BDI	5.5.93	1	VD	Bruxelles	7 Sep 12
1:56.60	Natalya	Tsyganova	RUS	7.2.71	1	NC	Tula	25 Jul 00
1:56.6	Tamara	Sorokina'	RUS	15.8.50	5	Kuts	Podolsk	21 Aug 82
	(50)	100th woman 1:57.5, 200th 1:58.58, 300th 1:59.37, 400th 1:59.82, 500th 2:00.23						
Indoors: 1:55.85	Stephanie	Graf	AUT	26.4.73	2	EI	Wien	3 Mar 02
Drugs disqualification								
1:54.85	Yelena	Soboleva ¶	RUS	3.10.82	(1)	NC	Kazan	18 Jul 08

1000 METRES

Mark Wind	Name		Nat	Born	Pos	Meet	Venue	Date
2:28.98 WR	Svetlana	Masterkova	RUS	17.1.68	1	VD	Bruxelles	23 Aug 96
2:29.34 WR	Maria Lurdes	Mutola	MOZ	27.10.72	1	VD	Bruxelles	25 Aug 95
2:30.6 WR	Tatyana	Providokhina	RUS	26.3.53	1		Podolsk	20 Aug 78
2:30.67 WR	Christine	Wachtel	GDR	6.1.65	1	ISTAF	Berlin	17 Aug 90
2:30.85	Martina	Kämpfert'	GDR	11.11.59	1		Berlin	9 Jul 80
2:31.50	Natalya	Artyomova ¶	RUS	5.1.63	1	ISTAF	Berlin	10 Sep 91
2:31.5 A	Maricica	Puica	ROU	29.7.50	1		Poiana Brasov	1 Jun 86
2:31.51	Sandra	Gasser ¶	SUI	27.7.62	1		Jerez de la Frontera	13 Sep 89

1500 METRES

Mark Wind	Name		Nat	Born	Pos	Meet	Venue	Date
3:50.46 WR		Qu Yunxia	CHN	8.12.72	1	NG	Beijing	11 Sep 93
3:50.98		Jiang Bo	CHN	13.3.77	1	NG	Shanghai	18 Oct 97
3:51.34		Lang Yinglai	CHN	22.8.79	2	NG	Shanghai	18 Oct 97
3:51.92		Wang Junxia	CHN	9.1.73	2	NG	Beijing	11 Sep 93
3:52.47 WR	Tatyana	Kazankina ¶	RUS	17.12.51	1	WK	Zürich	13 Aug 80
3:53.91		Yin Lili ¶	CHN	11.11.79	3	NG	Shanghai	18 Oct 97
3:53.96	Paula	Ivan'	ROU	20.7.63	1	OG	Seoul	1 Oct 88
3:53.97		Lan Lixin	CHN	14.2.79	4	NG	Shanghai	18 Oct 97
3:54.23	Olga	Dvirna	RUS	11.2.53	1	NC	Kyiv	27 Jul 82
3:54.52		Zhang Ling (10)	CHN	13.4.80	5	NG	Shanghai	18 Oct 97
3:55.0 ' WR		Kazankina ¶			1	Znam	Moskva	6 Jul 80
3:55.01		Lan Lixin			1h2	NG	Shanghai	17 Oct 97
3:55.07		Dong Yanmei	CHN	16.2.77	6	NG	Shanghai	18 Oct 97
3:55.30	Hassiba	Boulmerka	ALG	10.7.68	1	OG	Barcelona	8 Aug 92
3:55.33	Süreyya	Ayhan ¶	TUR	6.9.78	1	VD	Bruxelles	5 Sep 03
3:55.38		Qu Yunxia			2h2	NG	Shanghai	17 Oct 97
3:55.47		Zhang Ling			3h2	NG	Shanghai	17 Oct 97
3:55.60		Ayhan			1	WK	Zürich	15 Aug 03
3:55.68	Yuliya	Chizhenko ¶	RUS	30.8.79	1	Gaz	Saint-Denis	8 Jul 06

Mark Wind		Name	Nat	Born	Pos	Meet	Venue	Date
3:55.82		Dong Yanmei			4h2	NG	Shanghai	17 Oct 97
3:56.0 WR		Kazankina ¶			1		Podolsk	28 Jun 76
3:56.14	Zamira	Zaytseva	UZB	16.2.53	2	NC	Kyiv	27 Jul 82
3:56.18	Maryam	Jamal	BRN	16.9.84	1	GP	Rieti	27 Aug 06
3:56.22		Ivan			1	WK	Zürich	17 Aug 88
3:56.31		Liu Dong	CHN	24.12.73	5h2	NG	Shanghai	17 Oct 97
3:56.43	Yelena	Soboleva ¶	RUS	3.10.82	2	Gaz	Saint-Denis	8 Jul 06
3:56.50	Tatyana	Pozdnyakova	RUS	4.3.56	3	NC	Kyiv	27 Jul 82
3:56.54	Abeba	Aregawi	ETH	5.7.90	1	GGala	Roma	31 May 12
3:56.55		Jamal			1	GGala	Roma	10 Jul 09
3:56.56		Kazankina ¶			1	OG	Moskva	1 Aug 80
	(30/20)							
3:56.62	Asli	Çakir Alptekin ¶	TUR	20.8.85	1	DL	Saint-Denis	6 Jul 12
3:56.63	Nadezhda	Ralldugina	UKR	15.11.57	1	Drz	Praha	18 Aug 84
3:56.65	Yekaterina	Podkopayeva'	RUS	11.6.52	1		Rieti	2 Sep 84
3:56.7 '	Lyubov	Smolka	UKR	29.11.52	2	Znam	Moskva	6 Jul 80
3:56.7	Doina	Melinte	ROU	27.12.56	1		Bucuresti	12 Jul 86
3:56.77+	Svetlana	Masterkova	RUS	17.1.68	1	WK	Zürich	14 Aug 96
3:56.8 '	Nadezhda	Olizarenko'	UKR	28.11.53	3	Znam	Moskva	6 Jul 80
3:56.91	Lyudmila	Rogachova	RUS	30.10.66	2	OG	Barcelona	8 Aug 92
3:56.91	Tatyana	Tomashova ¶	RUS	1.7.75	1	EC	Göteborg	13 Aug 06
3:56.97	Gabriela	Szabo	ROU	14.11.75	1	Herc	Monaco	8 Aug 98
	(30)							
3:56.98	Faith	Kipyegon	KEN	10.1.94	2	DL	Doha	10 May 13
3:57.00	Sifan	Hassan	ETH/NED	.93	1	DL	Saint-Denis	5 Jul 14
3:57.03		Liu Jing	CHN	3.2.71	6h2	NG	Shanghai	17 Oct 97
3:57.05	Svetlana	Guskova	MDA	19.8.59	4	NC	Kyiv	27 Jul 82
3:57.05	Hellen	Obiri	KEN	13.12.89	1	Pre	Eugene	31 May 14
3:57.12	Mary	Decker/Slaney	USA	4.8.58	1	vNord	Stockholm	26 Jul 83
3:57.22	Maricica	Puica	ROU	29.7.50	1		Bucuresti	1 Jul 84
3:57.22	Jennifer	Simpson	USA	23.8.86	2	DL	Saint-Denis	5 Jul 14
3:57.40	Suzy	Favor Hamilton	USA	8.8.68	1	Bisl	Oslo	28 Jul 00
3:57.4 '	Totka	Petrova ¶	BUL	17.12.56	1	Balk	Athína	11 Aug 79
	(40)							
3:57.41	Jackline	Maranga	KEN	16.12.77	3	Herc	Monaco	8 Aug 98
3:57.46		Zhang Linli	CHN	6.3.73	3	NG	Beijing	11 Sep 93
3:57.54	Genzebe	Dibaba	ETH	8.2.91	3	DL	Doha	10 May 13
3:57.71	Christiane	Wartenberg'	GDR	27.10.56	2	OG	Moskva	1 Aug 80
3:57.71	Carla	Sacramento	POR	10.12.71	4	Herc	Monaco	8 Aug 98
3:57.72	Galina	Zakharova	RUS	7.9.56	1	NP	Baku	14 Sep 84
3:57.73	Natalya	Yevdokimova	RUS	17.3.78	2	GP	Rieti	28 Aug 05
3:57.90	Kelly	Holmes	GBR	19.4.70	1	OG	Athína	28 Aug 04
3:57.92	Tatyana	Samolenko/Dorovskikh ¶	UKR	12.8.61	4	OG	Barcelona	8 Aug 92
3:58.12	Naomi	Mugo	KEN	2.1.77	5	Herc	Monaco	8 Aug 98
	(50)	100th woman 3:59.94, 200th 4:02.32, 300th 4:04.42, 400th 4:05.73, 500th 4:06.71						
Indoors								
3:55.17 WIR	Genzebe	Dibaba	ETH	8.2.91	1		Karlsruhe	1 Feb 14
Drugs disqualification: 3:56.15		Mariem Alaoui Selsouli ¶	MAR	8.4.84	(1)	DL	Saint-Denis	6 Jul 12
3:57.65	Anna	Alminova ¶	RUS	17.1.85	(1)	DL	Saint-Denis	16 Jul 10

1 MILE

Mark Wind		Name	Nat	Born	Pos	Meet	Venue	Date
4:12.56 WR	Svetlana	Masterkova	RUS	17.1.68	1	WK	Zürich	14 Aug 96
4:15.61 WR	Paula	Ivan'	ROU	20.7.63	1	Nik	Nice	10 Jul 89
4:15.8	Natalya	Artyomova ¶	RUS	5.1.63	1		Leningrad	5 Aug 84
4:16.71 WR	Mary	Slaney (Decker)	USA	4.8.58	1	WK	Zürich	21 Aug 85
4:17.25	Sonia	O'Sullivan	IRL	28.11.69	1	Bisl	Oslo	22 Jul 94
4:17.33	Maricica	Puica	ROU	29.7.50	2	WK	Zürich	21 Aug 85
4:17.57	Zola	Budd'	GBR	26.5.66	3	WK	Zürich	21 Aug 85
4:17.14 **indoor**	Doina	Melinte	ROU	27.12.56	1		East Rutherford	9 Feb 90
Drugs dq: 4:15.63	Yelena	Soboleva ¶	RUS	3.10.82	1		Moskva	29 Jun 07

2000 METRES

Mark Wind		Name	Nat	Born	Pos	Meet	Venue	Date
5:25.36 WR	Sonia	O'Sullivan	IRL	28.11.69	1	TSB	Edinburgh	8 Jul 94
5:26.93	Yvonne	Murray	GBR	4.10.64	2	TSB	Edinburgh	8 Jul 94
5:27.50	Genzebe	Dibaba	ETH	8.2.91	1	GS	Ostrava	17 Jun 14
5:28.69 WR	Maricica	Puica	ROU	29.7.50	1	PTG	London (CP)	11 Jul 86
5:28.72 WR	Tatyana	Kazankina ¶	RUS	17.12.51	1		Moskva	4 Aug 84
5:29.43+		Wang Junxia	CHN	9.1.73	1h2	NG	Beijing	12 Sep 93
5:29.64	Tatyana	Pozdnyakova	UKR	4.3.56	2		Moskva	4 Aug 84
5:30.19	Zola	Budd'	GBR	26.5.66	3	PTG	London (CP)	11 Jul 86
5:30.19	Gelete	Burka	ETH	15.2.86	1	VD	Bruxelles	4 Sep 09

Mark	Wind	Name		Nat	Born	Pos	Meet	Venue	Date
5:30.92		Galina	Zakharova	RUS	7.9.56	3		Moskva	4 Aug 84
5:31.03		Gulnara	Samitova/Galkina	RUS	9.7.78	1		Sochi	27 May 07
Indoors: 5:30.53		Gabriela	Szabo	ROU	14.11.75	1		Sindelfingen	8 Mar 98

3000 METRES

Mark	Wind	Name		Nat	Born	Pos	Meet	Venue	Date
8:06.11	WR		Wang Junxia	CHN	9.1.73	1	NG	Beijing	13 Sep 93
8:12.18			Qu Yunxia	CHN	8.12.72	2	NG	Beijing	13 Sep 93
8:12.19	WR		Wang Junxia			1h2	NG	Beijing	12 Sep 93
8:12.27			Qu Yunxia			2h2	NG	Beijing	12 Sep 93
8:16.50			Zhang Linli	CHN	6.3.73	3	NG	Beijing	13 Sep 93
8:19.78			Ma Liyan	CHN	6.9.68	3h2	NG	Beijing	12 Sep 93
8:20.68		Hellen	Obiri	KEN	13.12.89	1	DL	Doha	9 May 14
8:21.14		Mercy	Cherono	KEN	7.5.91	2	DL	Doha	9 May 14
8:21.26			Ma Liyan			4	NG	Beijing	13 Sep 93
8:21.42		Gabriela	Szabo	ROU	14.11.75	1	Herc	Monaco	19 Jul 02
8:21.64		Sonia	O'Sullivan	IRL	28.11.69	1	TSB	London (CP)	15 Jul 94
8:21.84			Zhang Lirong	CHN	3.3.73	5	NG	Beijing	13 Sep 93
8:22.06	WR		Zhang Linli			1h1	NG	Beijing	12 Sep 93
8:22.20		Paula	Radcliffe (10)	GBR	17.12.73	2	Herc	Monaco	19 Jul 02
8:22.44			Zhang Lirong			2h1	NG	Beijing	12 Sep 93
8:22.62	WR	Tatyana	Kazankina ¶	RUS	17.12.51	1		Leningrad	26 Aug 84
8:23.23		Edith	Masai	KEN	4.4.67	3	Herc	Monaco	19 Jul 02
8:23.26		Olga	Yegorova ¶	RUS	28.3.72	1	WK	Zürich	17 Aug 01
8:23.55		Faith	Kipyegon	KEN	10.1.94	3	DL	Doha	9 May 14
8:23.75			Yegorova			1	GP	Saint-Denis	6 Jul 01
8:23.96			Yegorova			1	GGala	Roma	29 Jun 01
8:24.19			Szabo			2	WK	Zürich	17 Aug 01
8:24.31			Szabo			1	GP	Paris (C)	29 Jul 98
8:24.41		Viola	Kibiwot	KEN	22.12.83	4	DL	Doha	9 May 14
8:24.51+		Meseret	Defar	ETH	19.11.83	1	in 2M	Bruxelles	14 Sep 07
8:24.58		Almaz	Ayana	ETH	21.10.91	5	DL	Doha	9 May 14
8:24.66			Defar			1	DNG	Stockholm	25 Jul 06
8:25.03			Szabo			1	WK	Zürich	11 Aug 99
8:25.40		Yelena	Zadorozhnaya	RUS	3.12.77	2	GGala	Roma	29 Jun 01
8:25.56		Tatyana	Tomashova ¶	RUS	1.7.75	3	GGala	Roma	29 Jun 01
		(30/19)							
8:25.62		Berhane	Adere (20)	ETH	21.7.73	3	WK	Zürich	17 Aug 01
8:25.83		Mary	Slaney	USA	4.8.58	1	GGala	Roma	7 Sep 85
8:25.92		Gelete	Burka	ETH	15.2.86	2	DNG	Stockholm	25 Jul 06
8:26.21		Genzebe	Dibaba	ETH	8.2.91	6	DL	Doha	9 May 14
8:26.48		Zahra	Ouaziz	MAR	20.12.69	2	WK	Zürich	11 Aug 99
8:26.53		Tatyana	Samolenko' ¶	UKR	12.8.61	1	OG	Seoul	25 Sep 88
8:26.78	WR	Svetlana	Ulmasova	UZB	4.2.53	1	NC	Kyiv	25 Jul 82
8:27.12	WR	Lyudmila	Bragina	RUS	24.7.43	1	v USA	College Park	7 Aug 76
8:27.15		Paula	Ivan'	ROU	20.7.63	2	OG	Seoul	25 Sep 88
8:27.62		Getenesh	Wami	ETH	11.12.74	4	WK	Zürich	17 Aug 01
8:27.83		Maricica	Puica	ROU	29.7.50	2	GGala	Roma	7 Sep 85
		(30)							
8:28.41		Sentayehu	Ejigu	ETH	21.6.85	1	Herc	Monaco	22 Jul 10
8:28.51		Irene	Jelagat	KEN	10.12.88	7	DL	Doha	9 May 14
8:28.66		Vivian	Cheruiyot	KEN	11.9.83	2	WAF	Stuttgart	23 Sep 07
8:28.80		Marta	Domínguez	ESP	3.11.75	3	WK	Zürich	11 Aug 00
8:28.83		Zola	Budd'	GBR	26.5.66	3	GGala	Roma	7 Sep 85
8:28.87		Maryam	Jamal	BRN	16.9.84	1	Bisl	Oslo	29 Jul 05
8:29.02		Yvonne	Murray	GBR	4.10.64	3	OG	Seoul	25 Sep 88
8:29.06		Priscah	Cherono	KEN	27.6.80	3	WAF	Stuttgart	23 Sep 07
8:29.14		Lydia	Cheromei ¶	KEN	11.5.77	5	WK	Zürich	11 Aug 00
8:29.36		Svetlana	Guskova	MDA	19.8.59	2	NC	Kyiv	25 Jul 82
		(40)							
8:29.38		Sifan	Hassan	NED	.93	2	VD	Bruxelles	5 Sep 14
8:29.52		Mariem Alaoui	Selsouli ¶	MAR	8.4.84	1	Herc	Monaco	25 Jul 07
8:29.55		Tirunesh	Dibaba	ETH	1.10.85	1	LGP	London (CP)	28 Jul 06
8:29.58		Jennifer	Simpson'	USA	23.8.86	4	VD	Bruxelles	5 Sep 14
8:29.93		Shannon	Rowbury	USA	19.9.84	5	VD	Bruxelles	5 Sep 14
8:30.00		Mimi	Belete	BRN	9.6.88	8	DL	Doha	9 May 14
8:30.18		Mariya	Pantyukhova	RUS	14.8.74	4	WK	Zürich	11 Aug 99
8:30.22		Carla	Sacramento	POR	10.12.71	2	Herc	Monaco	4 Aug 99
8:30.39		Irina	Mikitenko	GER	23.8.72	6	WK	Zürich	11 Aug 00
8:30.45		Yelena	Romanova	RUS	20.3.63	4	OG	Seoul	25 Sep 88
		(50)	100th woman 8:35.94, 200th 8:43.08, 300th 8:47.46						

Mark	Wind	Name		Nat	Born	Pos	Meet	Venue	Date
Indoors:									
8:16.60	WIR	Genzebe	Dibaba	ETH	8.2.91	1		Stockholm	6 Feb 14
8:23.72	WIR	Meseret	Defar	ETH	19.11.83	1	Spark	Stuttgart	3 Feb 07
8:23.74		Meselech	Melkamu	ETH	27.4.85	2	Spark	Stuttgart	3 Feb 07
8:25.27		Sentayehu	Ejigu	ETH	21.6.85	2	Spark	Stuttgart	6 Feb 10
8:27.86	WIR	Liliya	Shobukhova ¶	RUS	13.11.77	1	NC	Moskva	17 Feb 06
8:28.49		Anna	Alminova	RUS	17.1.85	2	Spark	Stuttgart	7 Feb 09
8:29.00		Olesya	Syreva ¶	RUS	25.11.83	2	NC	Moskva	17 Feb 06

5000 METRES

Mark	Wind	Name		Nat	Born	Pos	Meet	Venue	Date
14:11.15	WR	Tirunesh	Dibaba	ETH	1.10.85	1	Bisl	Oslo	6 Jun 08
14:12.88		Meseret	Defar	ETH	19.11.83	1	DNG	Stockholm	22 Jul 08
14:16.63	WR		Defar			1	Bisl	Oslo	15 Jun 07
14:20.87		Vivian	Cheruiyot	KEN	11.9.83	1	DNG	Stockholm	29 Jul 11
14:22.51			Cheruiyot			2	Bisl	Oslo	15 Jun 07
14:23.46			T Dibaba			1	GP	Rieti	7 Sep 08
14:23.68			T Dibaba			1	DL	Saint-Denis	6 Jul 13
14:23.75		Liliya	Shobukhova ¶	RUS	13.11.77	1	NC	Kazan	19 Jul 08
14:24.53	WR		Defar			1		New York (RI)	3 Jun 06
14:24.68	WR	Elvan	Abeylegesse	TUR	11.9.82	1	Bisl	Bergen (Fana)	11 Jun 04
14:25.43			Cheruiyot			1	VD	Bruxelles	5 Sep 08
14:25.52			Defar			2	VD	Bruxelles	5 Sep 08
14:25.84		Almaz	Ayana	ETH	21.11.91	2	DL	Saint-Denis	6 Jul 13
14:26.90			Defar			1	Bisl	Oslo	13 Jun 13
14:27.41			Cheruiyot			1	DL	Saint-Denis	16 Jul 10
14:28.09	WR		Jiang Bo	CHN	13.3.77	1	NG	Shanghai	23 Oct 97
14:28.39		Sentayehu	Ejigu	ETH	21.6.85	2	DL	Saint-Denis	16 Jul 10
14:28.88		Genzebe	Dibaba	ETH	8.2.91	1	Herc	Monaco	18 Jul 14
14:28.98			Defar			1	VD	Bruxelles	26 Aug 05
14:29.11		Paula	Radcliffe (10)	GBR	17.12.73	1	ECpS	Bydgoszcz	20 Jun 04
14:29.19			Ayana			2	Herc	Monaco	18 Jul 14
14:29.32		Olga	Yegorova	RUS	28.3.72	1	ISTAF	Berlin	31 Aug 01
14:29.32		Berhane	Adere	ETH	21.7.73	1	Bisl	Oslo	27 Jun 03
14:29.52			Defar			1	DL	Saint-Denis	8 Jul 11
14:29.82			Dong Yanmei	CHN	16.2.77	2	NG	Shanghai	23 Oct 97
14:30.10			Cheruiyot			1	WK	Zürich	8 Sep 11
14:30.18			Defar			1	GS	Ostrava	27 Jun 07
14:30.40			T Dibaba			1	Bisl	Oslo	2 Jun 06
14:30.42		Sally	Kipyego	KEN	19.12.85	2	WK	Zürich	8 Sep 11
14:30.63			T Dibaba			1	VD	Bruxelles	25 Aug 06
		(30/14)							
14:30.88		Getenesh	Wami	ETH	11.12.74	1	NA	Heusden-Zolder	5 Aug 00
14:31.14		Linet	Masai	KEN	5.12.89	2	DL	Shanghai	23 May 10
14:31.20		Gelete	Burka	ETH	15.2.86	2	GS	Ostrava	27 Jun 07
14:31.48		Gabriela	Szabo	ROU	14.11.75	1	ISTAF	Berlin	1 Sep 98
14:31.91		Meselech	Melkamu	ETH	27.4.85	3	DL	Shanghai	23 May 10
14:31.91		Sylvia	Kibet	KEN	28.3.84	4	DL	Shanghai	23 May 10
		(20)							
14:32.08		Zahra	Ouaziz	MAR	20.12.69	2	ISTAF	Berlin	1 Sep 98
14:32.33			Liu Shixiang ¶	CHN	13.1.71	3h1	NG	Shanghai	21 Oct 97
14:32.74		Ejagayehu	Dibaba	ETH	25.6.82	3	Bisl	Bergen (Fana)	11 Jun 04
14:33.04		Werknesh	Kidane	ETH	21.11.81	2	Bisl	Oslo	27 Jun 03
14:33.13		Gulnara	Galkina'	RUS	9.7.78	2	NC	Kazan	19 Jul 08
14:33.48		Viola	Kibiwot	KEN	22.12.83	2	Bisl	Oslo	13 Jun 13
14:33.49		Lucy Wangui	Kabuu	KEN	24.3.84	2	Bisl	Oslo	6 Jun 08
14:33.84		Edith	Masai	KEN	4.4.67	3	Bisl	Oslo	2 Jun 06
14:35.13		Mercy	Cherono	KEN	7.5.91	3	DL	Saint-Denis	8 Jul 11
14:35.30		Priscah	Jepleting/Cherono	KEN	27.6.80	4	Bisl	Oslo	2 Jun 06
		(30)							
14:36.45	WR	Fernanda	Ribeiro	POR	23.6.69	1		Hechtel	22 Jul 95
14:36.52		Mariem Alaoui	Selsouli ¶	MAR	8.4.84	1	G Gala	Roma	13 Jul 07
14:37.07		Jéssica	Augusto	POR	8.11.81	5	DL	Saint-Denis	16 Jul 10
14:37.33	WR	Ingrid	Kristiansen'	NOR	21.3.56	1		Stockholm	5 Aug 86
14:38.09		Mariya	Konovalova	RUS	14.8.74	3	NC	Kazan	19 Jul 08
14:38.21		Isabella	Ochichi	KEN	28.10.79	4	VD	Bruxelles	26 Aug 05
14:38.44		Wude	Ayalew	ETH	4.7.87	5	Bisl	Oslo	3 Jul 09
14:39.19		Ines	Chenonge	KEN	1.2.82	6	DL	Saint-Denis	16 Jul 10
14:39.22		Tatyana	Tomashova ¶	RUS	1.7.75	4	ISTAF	Berlin	31 Aug 01
14:39.49		Betsy	Saina	KEN	30.6.88	5	Herc	Monaco	18 Jul 14
	(40)								

Mark Wind		Name	Nat	Born	Pos	Meet	Venue	Date
14:39.83	Leah	Malot	KEN	7.6.72	1	ISTAF	Berlin	1 Sep 00
14:39.96		Yin Lili ¶	CHN	11.11.79	4	NG	Shanghai	23 Oct 97
14:39.96	Jo	Pavey	GBR	20.9.73	3	VD	Bruxelles	25 Aug 06
14:40.14	Florence	Kiplagat	KEN	27.2.87	6	Bisl	Oslo	3 Jul 09
14:40.41		Sun Yingjie ¶	CHN	3.10.77	1	AsiG	Busan	12 Oct 02
14:40.47	Yelena	Zadorozhnaya	RUS	3.12.77	1	ECp-S	Bremen	24 Jun 01
14:40.48	Margaret	Muriuki	KEN	21.3.86	4	Bisl	Oslo	13 Jun 13
14:41.02	Sonia	O'Sullivan	IRL	28.11.69	2	OG	Sydney	25 Sep 00
14:41.23	Ayelech	Worku	ETH	12.6.79	1	BrGP	London (CP)	5 Aug 00
14:41.28	Pauline	Korikwiang	KEN	1.3.88	7	DL	Shanghai	15 May 11
	(50)	100th woman 14:50.99, 200th 15:05.37, 300th 15:11.78, 400th 15:17.53, 500th 15:22.01						
Indoors: 14:24.37 WIR		Defar			1		Stockholm	18 Feb 09
14:24.79		Defar			1	GE Galan	Stockholm	10 Feb 10
14:27.42 WIR		T Dibaba			1	BIG	Boston (R)	27 Jan 07
14:39.89	Kimberley	Smith	NZL	19.11.73	1		New York (Armory)	27 Feb 09
Drugs disqualification: 14:36.79	Alemitu	Bekele ¶	TUR	17.9.77	4	VD	Bruxelles	27 Aug 10

10,000 METRES

Mark Wind		Name	Nat	Born	Pos	Meet	Venue	Date
29:31.78 WR		Wang Junxia	CHN	9.1.73	1	NG	Beijing	8 Sep 93
29:53.80	Meselech	Melkamu	ETH	27.4.85	1		Utrecht	14 Jun 09
29:54.66	Tirunesh	Dibaba	ETH	1.10.85	1	OG	Beijing	15 Aug 08
29:56.34	Elvan	Abeylegesse	TUR	11.9.82	2	OG	Beijing	15 Aug 08
29:59.20	Meseret	Defar	ETH	19.11.83	1	NC	Birmingham	11 Jul 09
30:01.09	Paula	Radcliffe	GBR	17.12.73	1	EC	München	6 Aug 02
30:04.18	Berhane	Adere	ETH	21.7.73	1	WCh	Saint-Denis	23 Aug 03
30:07.15	Werknesh	Kidane	ETH	21.11.81	2	WCh	Saint-Denis	23 Aug 03
30:07.20		Sun Yingjie ¶	CHN	3.10.77	3	WCh	Saint-Denis	23 Aug 03
30:08.06		Defar			1		Sollentuna	27 Jun 13
30:11.53	Florence	Kiplagat (10)	KEN	27.2.87	2		Utrecht	14 Jun 09
30:11.87	Wude	Ayalew	ETH	4.7.87	3		Utrecht	14 Jun 09
30:12.53	Lornah	Kiplagat (KEN)	NED	1.5.74	4	WCh	Saint-Denis	23 Aug 03
30:13.37		Zhong Huandi	CHN	28.6.67	2	NG	Beijing	8 Sep 93
30:13.74 WR	Ingrid	Kristiansen'	NOR	21.3.56	1	Bisl	Oslo	5 Jul 86
30:15.67		T Dibaba			1		Sollentuna	28 Jun 05
30:17.15		Radcliffe			1	GP	Gateshead	27 Jun 04
30:17.49	Derartu	Tulu	ETH	21.3.72	1	OG	Sydney	30 Sep 00
30:18.39	Ejegayehu	Dibaba	ETH	25.6.82	2		Sollentuna	28 Jun 05
30:19.39		Kidane			1	GP II	Stanford	29 May 05
30:20.75		T Dibaba			1	OG	London (OS)	3 Aug 12
30:21.67		Abeylegesse			1	ECp	Antalya	15 Apr 06
30:22.22	Shalane	Flanagan	USA	8.7.81	3	OG	Beijing	15 Aug 08
30:22.48	Getenesh	Wami	ETH	11.12.74	2	OG	Sydney	30 Sep 00
30:22.88	Fernanda	Ribeiro	POR	23.6.69	3	OG	Sydney	30 Sep 00
30:23.07	Alla	Zhilyayeva (20)	RUS	5.2.69	5	WCh	Saint-Denis	23 Aug 03
30:23.25		Kristiansen			1	EC	Stuttgart	30 Aug 86
30:24.02		T Dibaba			1	WCh	Helsinki	6 Aug 05
30:24.36		Xing Huina	CHN	25.2.84	1	OG	Athína	27 Aug 04
30:24.39		T Dibaba			1	Pre	Eugene	1 Jun 12
	(30/21)							
30:26.20	Galina	Bogomolova	RUS	15.10.77	6	WCh	Saint-Denis	23 Aug 03
30:26.37	Sally	Kipyego	KEN	19.12.85	2	OG	London (OS)	3 Aug 12
30:26.50	Linet	Masai	KEN	5.12.89	4	OG	Beijing	15 Aug 08
30:26.70	Belaynesh	Oljira	ETH	26.6.90	3	Pre	Eugene	1 Jun 12
30:29.21mx	Philes	Ongori	KEN	19.7.86	1mx		Yokohama	23 Nov 08
30:29.23	Gladys	Cherono	KEN	12.5.83	2	GS	Ostrava	27 Jun 13
30:29.36	Liliya	Shobukhova ¶	RUS	13.11.77	1	NC	Cheboksary	23 Jul 09
30:30.26	Edith	Masai	KEN	4.4.67	5	WCh	Helsinki	6 Aug 05
30:30.44	Vivian	Cheruiyot	KEN	11.9.83	3	OG	London (OS)	3 Aug 12
	(30)							
30:31.03	Mariya	Konovalova	RUS	14.8.74	2	NC	Cheboksary	23 Jul 09
30:31.42	Inga	Abitova ¶	RUS	6.3.82	1	EC	Göteborg	7 Aug 06
30:32.03	Tegla	Loroupe	KEN	9.5.73	3	WCh	Sevilla	26 Aug 99
30:32.36	Susanne	Wigene	NOR	12.2.78	2	EC	Göteborg	7 Aug 06
30:32.72	Lidiya	Grigoryeva	RUS	21.1.74	3	EC	Göteborg	7 Aug 06
30:35.54	Kimberley	Smith	NZL	19.11.81	2		Stanford	4 May 08
30:35.91	Birhane	Ababel	ETH	10.6.90	4	GS	Ostrava	27 Jun 13
30:37.68	Benita	Johnson	AUS	6.5.79	8	WCh	Saint-Denis	23 Aug 03
30:38.09		Dong Yanmei	CHN	16.2.77	1	NG	Shanghai	19 Oct 97
30:38.33	Mestawat	Tufa	ETH	14.9.83	1		Nijmegen	25 Jun 08
	(40)							

Mark	Wind	Name		Nat	Born	Pos	Meet	Venue	Date
30:38.78		Jelena	Prokopcuka	LAT	21.9.76	6	EC	Göteborg	7 Aug 06
30:39.41			Lan Lixin	CHN	14.2.79	2	NG	Shanghai	19 Oct 97
30:39.96		Lucy Wangui	Kabuu	KEN	24.3.84	7	OG	Beijing	15 Aug 08
30:39.98			Yin Lili ¶	CHN	11.11.79	3	NG	Shanghai	19 Oct 97
30:47.02		Emily	Chebet	KEN	18.2.86	4	WCh	Moskva	11 Aug 13
30:47.20		Sylvia	Kibet	KEN	28.3.84	4		Utrecht	14 Jun 09
30:47.22			Dong Zhaoxia	CHN	13.11.74	4	NG	Shanghai	19 Oct 97
30:47.25		Shitaye	Eshete	BRN	21.5.90	6	OG	London (OS)	3 Aug 12
30:47.59		Sonia	O'Sullivan	IRL	28.11.69	2	EC	München	6 Aug 02
30:47.59		Molly	Huddle	USA	31.8.84	2	Jordan	Stanford	4 May 14
		(50)	100th woman 31:11.26, 200th 31:34.01, 300th 31:49.71, 400th 32:00.11, 500th 32:10.57						

HALF MARATHON

Slightly downhill courses included: Newcastle-South Shields 30.5m, Tokyo 33m (to 1998), Lisboa (Spring to 2008) 69m

Mark	Wind	Name		Nat	Born	Pos	Meet	Venue	Date
65:12	WR	Florence	Kiplagat	KEN	27.2.87	1		Barcelona	16 Feb 14
65:39	dh	Mary	Keitany	KEN	18.1.82	1	GNR	South Shields	7 Sep 14
65:40	dh	Paula	Radcliffe	GBR	17.12.73	1	GNR	South Shields	21 Sep 03
65:44	dh	Susan	Chepkemei	KEN	25.6.75	1		Lisboa	1 Apr 01
65:45	dh	Priscah	Jeptoo	KEN	26.6.84	1	GNR	South Shields	15 Sep 13
65:50	WR		Keitany			1		Ra's Al Khaymah	18 Feb 11
66:09		Lucy Wangui	Kabuu	KEN	24.3.84	1		Ra's Al-Khaymah	15 Feb 13
66:09	dh	Meseret	Defar	ETH	19.11.83	2	GNR	South Shields	15 Sep 13
66:11			P Jeptoo			2		Ra's Al-Khaymah	15 Feb 13
66:19		Joyce	Chepkirui	KEN	20.8.88	1		Praha	5 Apr 14
66:25		Lornah	Kiplagat	NED	1.5.74	1	WCh	Udine	14 Oct 07
66:27		Rita	Jeptoo ¶ (10)	KEN	15.2.81	3		Ra's Al-Khaymah	15 Feb 13
66:34	dh		Kiplagat			2		Lisboa	1 Apr 01
66:36			Keitany			1	WCh	Birmingham	11 Oct 09
66:38			F Kiplagat			1		Ostia	26 Feb 12
66:40*		Ingrid	Kristiansen	NOR	21.3.56	1	NC	Sandnes	5 Apr 87
66:43	dh	Masako	Chiba	JPN	18.7.76	1		Tokyo	19 Jan 97
66:44		Elana	Meyer	RSA	10.10.66	1		Tokyo	15 Jan 99
66:47			Radcliffe			1	WCh	Bristol	7 Oct 01
66:48			Keitany			2	WCh	Udine	14 Oct 07
66:48		Gladys	Cherono	KEN	12.5.83	1		Praha	6 Apr 13
66:49		Esther	Wanjiru	KEN	27.3.77	2		Tokyo	15 Jan 99
66:49			Keitany			1		Ra's Al-Khaymah	17 Feb 12
66:54			Keitany			1		New Delhi	1 Nov 09
66:56			L Kiplagat			1	City-Pier	Den Haag	25 Mar 00
66:56		Meseret	Hailu	ETH	12.9.90	4		Ra's Al-Khaymah	15 Feb 13
66:56	dh	Tirunesh	Dibaba	ETH	1.10.85	3	GNR	South Shields	15 Sep 13
66:57	dh	Kara	Goucher	USA	9.7.78	1	GNR	South Shields	30 Sep 07
67:00			Keitany			1		Lille	5 Sep 09
67:02			P Jeptoo			1		Ra's Al-Khaymah	14 Feb 14
		(30/18)	* uncertain course measurement						
67:03	dh	Derartu	Tulu	ETH	21.3.72	3		Lisboa	1 Apr 01
67:07		Elvan	Abeylegesse	TUR	11.9.82	1		Ra's Al Khaymah	19 Feb 10
		(20)							
67:08		Sharon	Cherop	KEN	16.3.84	2		New Delhi	21 Nov 11
67:11	dh	Liz	McColgan	GBR	24.5.64	1		Tokyo	26 Jan 92
67:11		Kimberley	Smith	NZL	19.11.81	1		Philadelphia	18 Sep 11
67:12	dh	Tegla	Loroupe	KEN	9.5.73	1		Lisboa	10 Mar 96
67:13		Mare	Dibaba	ETH	20.10.89	2		Ra's Al Khaymah	19 Feb 10
67:16		Edith	Masai	KEN	4.4.67	1		Berlin	2 Apr 06
67:17		Pasalia	Kipkoech	KEN	22.12.88	1		Rio de Janeiro	19 Aug 12
67:18		Dire	Tune	ETH	19.6.85	1		R'as Al Khaymah	20 Feb 09
67:19	dh	Sonia	O'Sullivan	IRL	28.11.69	1	GNR	South Shields	6 Oct 02
67:21		Aselefech	Mergia	ETH	23.1.85	3		New Delhi	21 Nov 11
		(30)							
67:22		Agnes	Kiprop	KEN	12.12.79	2		Ostia	26 Feb 12
67:23		Margaret	Okayo	KEN	30.5.76	1		Udine	28 Sep 03
67:26		Kayoko	Fukushi	JPN	25.3.82	1		Marugame	5 Feb 06
67:26		Lydia	Cheromei ¶	KEN	11.5.77	2		Praha	31 Mar 12
67:27		Belaynesh	Oljira	ETH	26.6.90	4		New Delhi	27 Nov 11
67:28		Worknesh	Kidane	ETH	21.11.81	2		Philadelphia	18 Sep 11
67:32	dh	Berhane	Adere	ETH	21.7.73	2	GNR	South Shields	21 Sep 03
67:34		Deena	Kastor	USA	14.2.73	2		Berlin	2 Apr 06
67:34		Atsede	Baysa	ETH	16.4.87	1		Barcelona	17 Feb 13
67:38		Philes	Ongori	KEN	19.7.86	2	WCh	Birmingham	11 Oct 09
		(40)							

Mark	Wind	Name		Nat	Born	Pos	Meet	Venue	Date
67:39		Aberu	Kebede	ETH	12.9.89	3	WCh	Birmingham	11 Oct 09
67:39		Helah	Kiprop	KEN	7.4.85	6		Ra's Al-Khaymah	15 Feb 13
67:39		Filomena	Cheyech	KEN	5.7.82	1		Ostia	3 Mar 13
67:41		Teyiba	Erkesso	ETH	30.10.82	4		Ra's Al Khaymah	19 Feb 10
67:41dh		Edna	Kiplagat	KEN	15.9.79	2	GNR	South Shields	16 Sep 12
67:42		Tirfi	Tsegaye	ETH	25.11.84	3		Ostia	26 Feb 12
67:43		Mizuki	Noguchi	JPN	3.7.78	2		Marugame	5 Feb 06
67:44		Mary	Wacera	KEN	17.12.88	2	WCh	København	29 Mar 14
67:46		Valeria	Straneo	ITA	5.4.76	4		Ostia	26 Feb 12
67:47		Lineth	Chepkurui	KEN	23.2.88	2		Philadelphia	19 Sep 10
		(50)	100th woman 68:31, 200th 69:16, 300th 69:46, 400th 70:13, 500th 70:34						

MARATHON

L = loop course or start and finish within 30%, P = point-to-point or start and finish more than 30% apart, D + point-to-point and downhil over 1/1000. 2nd column: M mixed marathon (men and women), W women only race

Mark	Wind	Name		Nat	Born	Pos	Meet	Venue	Date
2:15:25	LM	Paula	Radcliffe	GBR	17.12.73	1		London	13 Apr 03
2:17:18	LM		Radcliffe			1		Chicago	13 Oct 02
2:17:42	LW		Radcliffe			1		London	17 Apr 05
2:18:37	LW	Mary	Keitany	KEN	18.1.82	1		London	22 Apr 12
2:18:47	LM	Catherine	Ndereba	KEN	21.7.72	1		Chicago	7 Oct 01
2:18:56	LW		Radcliffe			1		London	14 Apr 02
2:18:58	LW	Tiki	Gelana	ETH	22.10.87	1		Rotterdam	15 Apr 12
2:19:12	LM	Mizuki	Noguchi	JPN	3.7.78	1		Berlin	25 Sep 05
2:19:19	LM	Irina	Mikitenko	GER	23.8.72	1		Berlin	28 Sep 08
2:19:19	LW		Keitany			1		London	17 Apr 11
2:19:26	LM		Ndereba			2		Chicago	13 Oct 02
2:19:31	LM	Aselefech	Mergia	ETH	23.1.85	1		Dubai	27 Jan 12
2:19:34	LM	Lucy Wangui	Kabuu	KEN	24.3.84	2		Dubai	27 Jan 12
2:19:36	LW	Deena	Kastor	USA	14.2.73	1		London	23 Apr 06
2:19:39	LM		Sun Yingjie ¶ (10)	CHN	3.10.77	1		Beijing	19 Oct 03
2:19:41	LM	Yoko	Shibui	JPN	14.3.79	1		Berlin	26 Sep 04
2:19:44	LM	Florence	Kiplagat	KEN	27.2.87	1		Berlin	25 Sep 11
2:19:46	LM	Naoko	Takahashi	JPN	6.5.72	1		Berlin	30 Sep 01
2:19:50	LW	Edna	Kiplagat	KEN	15.11.79	2		London	22 Apr 12
2:19:51	PM		Zhou Chunxiu	CHN	15.11.78	1	Dong-A	Seoul	12 Mar 06
2:19:52	LM	Mare	Dibaba	ETH	20.10.89	3		Dubai	27 Jan 12
2:19:55	LM		Ndereba			2		London	13 Apr 03
2:19:57	L	Rita	Jeptoo ¶	KEN	15.2.81	1		Chicago	13 Oct 13
2:20:14	LW	Priscah	Jeptoo	KEN	26.6.84	3		London	22 Apr 12
2:20:15	LW		P Jeptoo			1		London	21 Apr 13
2:20:18	LM	Tirfi	Tsegaye	ETH	25.11.84	2		Berlin	28 Sep 14
2:20:21	LW		E Kiplagat			1		London	13 Apr 14
2:20:24	LW		F Kiplagat			2		London	13 Apr 14
2:20:27	LM	Feyse	Tadesse (20)	ETH	19.11.88	2		Berlin	28 Sep 14
2:20:30	LM	Bezunesh	Bekele	ETH	29.1.83	4		Dubai	27 Jan 12
		(30/21)							
2:20:30	LM	Aberu	Kebede	ETH	12.9.89	1		Berlin	30 Sep 12
2:20:35	LW	Tirunesh	Dibaba	ETH	1.10.85	3		London	13 Apr 14
2:20:42	LM	Berhane	Adere	ETH	21.7.73	1		Chicago	22 Oct 06
2:20:43	LM	Tegla	Loroupe	KEN	9.5.73	1		Berlin	26 Sep 99
2:20:47	LM	Galina	Bogomolova	RUS	15.10.77	2		Chicago	22 Oct 06
2:20:48	L	Jemima	Jelagat	KEN	21.12.84	2		Chicago	13 Oct 13
2:21:01	LM	Meselech	Melkamu	ETH	27.4.85	1		Frankfurt	28 Oct 12
2:21:06	LM	Ingrid	Kristiansen	NOR	21.3.56	1		London	21 Apr 85
2:21:09	LM	Meseret	Hailu	ETH	12.9.90	1		Amsterdam	21 Oct 12
		(30)							
2:21:14	LM	Shalane	Flanagan	USA	8.7.81	3		Berlin	28 Sep 14
2:21:21	LM	Joan	Benoit'	USA	16.5.57	1		Chicago	20 Oct 85
2:21:29	LW	Lyudmila	Petrova	RUS	7.10.68	2		London	23 Apr 06
2:21:30	LM	Constantina	Dita	ROU	23.1.70	2		Chicago	9 Oct 05
2:21:30	LM	Lydia	Cheromei ¶	KEN	11.5.77	6		Dubai	27 Jan 12
2:21:31	LM	Svetlana	Zakharova	RUS	15.9.70	4		Chicago	13 Oct 02
2:21:31	LM	Askale	Tafa	ETH	27.9.84	2		Berlin	28 Sep 08
2:21:34	LM	Getenesh	Wami	ETH	11.12.74	1		Berlin	25 Sep 06
2:21:39	LM	Georgina	Rono	KEN	19.5.84	2		Frankfurt	28 Oct 12
2:21:41	LM	Eunice	Jepkirui	KEN	20.5.84	2		Amsterdam	21 Oct 12
		(40)							
2:21:45	LW	Masako	Chiba	JPN	18.7.76	2		Osaka	26 Jan 03
2:21:46	LW	Susan	Chepkemei ¶	KEN	25.6.75	3		London	23 Apr 06
2:21:51	LW	Naoko	Sakamoto	JPN	14.11.80	3		Osaka	26 Jan 03

Mark	Wind	Name		Nat	Born	Pos	Meet	Venue	Date
2:21:52	LM	Tigist	Tufa	ETH	26.1.87	1		Shanghai	2 Nov 14
2:21:59	LM	Mamitu	Daska	ETH	16.10.83	1		Frankfurt	30 Oct 11
2:22:03		Atsede	Baysa	ETH	16.4.87	1		Chicago	7 Oct 12
2:22:09	LM	Ejegayehu	Dibaba	ETH	25.6.82	2		Chicago	9 Oct 11
2:22:12	LW	Eri	Yamaguchi	JPN	14.1.73	1		Tokyo	21 Nov 99
2:22:22	LW	Lornah	Kiplagat	KEN/NED	1.5.74	4		Osaka	26 Jan 03
2:22:23	LM	Catherina	McKiernan	IRL	30.11.69	1		Amsterdam	1 Nov 98
		(50)	100th woman 2:23:44, 200th 2:25:49, 300th 2:26:51, 400th 2:27:55, 500th 2:28:47						
Drugs disqualification									
2:18:20	LM	Liliya	Shobukhova	RUS	13.11.77	1		Chicago	9 Oct 11
2:20:15	LW		Shobukhova			2		London	17 Apr 11
2:20:23	LM		Wei Yanan ¶	CHN	6.12.81	1		Beijing	20 Oct 02
2:20:25	LM		Shobukhova			1		Chicago	10 Oct 10
2:22:19	LW	Inga	Abitova ¶	RUS	6.3.82	2		London	25 Apr 10
Downhill point-to-point course – Boston marathon is downhill overall (139m) and sometimes strongly wind-aided.									
2:18:57	DM	Rita	Jeptoo ¶	KEN	15.2.81	1		Boston	21 Apr 14
2:19:59	DM	Buzunesh	Deba	ETH	8.9.87	2		Boston	21 Apr 14
2:20:41	DM	Jemima	Jelagat	KEN	21.12.84	4		Boston	21 Apr 14
2:20:43	DM	Margaret	Okayo	KEN	30.5.76	1		Boston	15 Apr 02
2:21:29	DM	Aleksandra	Duliba	BLR	9.1.88	6		Boston	21 Apr 14
2:21:45	DM	Uta	Pippig ¶	GER	7.9.65	1		Boston	18 Apr 94

2000 METRES STEEPLECHASE

Mark		Name		Nat	Born	Pos	Meet	Venue	Date
6:03.38		Wioletta	Janowska	POL	9.6.77	1		Gdansk	15 Jul 06
6:04.46		Dorcus	Inzikuru	UGA	2.2.82	1	GP II	Milano	1 Jun 05
6:11.63		Livia	Tóth	HUN	7.1.80	2		Gdansk	15 Jul 06
6:11.83		Korahubish	Itaa	KEN	28.2.92	1	WY	Bressanone	10 Jul 09
6:11.84		Marina	Pluzhnikova	RUS	25.2.63	1	GWG	Sankt-Peterburg	25 Jul 94

3000 METRES STEEPLECHASE

Mark		Name		Nat	Born	Pos	Meet	Venue	Date
8:58.81	WR	Gulnara	Samitova/Galkina	RUS	9.7.78	1	OG	Beijing	17 Aug 08
9:01.59	WR		Samitova/Galkina			1		Iráklio	4 Jul 04
9:06.57		Yekaterina	Volkova	RUS	16.2.78	1	WCh	Osaka	27 Aug 07
9:07.03		Yuliya	Zaripova' ¶	RUS	26.4.86	1	WCh	Daegu	30 Aug 11
9:07.14		Milcah	Chemos Cheywa	KEN	24.2.86	1	Bisl	Oslo	7 Jun 12
9:07.32		Marta	Dominguez	ESP	3.11.75	1	WCh	Berlin	17 Aug 09
9:07.41		Eunice	Jepkorir	KEN	17.2.82	2	OG	Beijing	17 Aug 08
9:07.64			Volkova			3	OG	Beijing	17 Aug 08
9:08.21			Galkina			1	NC	Kazan	18 Jul 08
9:08.33	WR		Samitova			1	NC	Tula	10 Aug 03
9:08.37		Habiba	Ghribi	TUN	9.4.84	2	OG	London (OS)	6 Aug 12
9:08.39			Zarudneva/Zaripova			2	WCh	Berlin	17 Aug 09
9:08.57			Chemos			3	WCh	Berlin	17 Aug 09
9:09.00		Sofia	Assefa	ETH	14.11.87	2	Bisl	Oslo	7 Jun 12
9:09.19		Tatyana	Petrova	RUS	8.4.83	2	WCh	Osaka	27 Aug 07
9:09.39			Domínguez			1		Barcelona	25 Jul 09
9:09.61		Hiwot	Ayalew (10)	ETH	6.3.90	3	Bisl	Oslo	7 Jun 12
9:09.84			Samitova			1		Réthimno	23 Jun 04
9:09.84			Assefa			3	OG	London (OS)	6 Aug 12
9:09.88			Chemos			4	OG	London (OS)	6 Aug 12
9:10.36			Ghribi			2	DNG	Stockholm	17 Aug 12
9:10.64			Ayalew			1	DL	Glasgow	12 Jul 14
9:11.09			Galkina			4	WCh	Berlin	17 Aug 09
9:11.18			Jepkorir			1		Huelva	13 Jun 08
9:11.39			Assefa			1	Pre	Eugene	31 May 14
9:11.42		Emma	Coburn	USA	19.10.90	2	DL	Glasgow	12 Jul 14
9:11.58			Galkina			1	GGala	Roma	10 Jul 09
9:11.65			Chemos			1	WCh	Moskva	13 Aug 13
9:11.65			Ayalew			1	DL	Saint-Denis	5 Jul 14
9:11.68			Galkina			1	GP	Athína	2 Jul 07
		(30/11)							
9:12.50		Jennifer	Barringer/Simpson	USA	23.8.86	5	WCh	Berlin	17 Aug 09
9:12.55		Lydia	Chepkurui	KEN	23.8.84	2	WCh	Moskva	13 Aug 13
9:13.16		Ruth	Bisibori	KEN	2.1.88	7	WCh	Berlin	17 Aug 09
9:13.22		Gladys	Kipkemboi	KEN	15.10.86	2	GGala	Roma	10 Jun 10
9:13.53		Gülcan	Mingir	TUR	21.5.89	1	Pavlov	Sofia	9 Jun 12
9:14.07		Etenesh	Diro	ETH	10.5.91	3	DNG	Stockholm	17 Aug 12
9:15.04		Dorcus	Inzikuru	UGA	2.2.82	1	SGP	Athína	14 Jun 05
9:16.51	WR	Alesya	Turova	BLR	6.12.79	1		Gdansk	27 Jul 02
9:16.85		Cristina	Casandra	ROU	21.10.77	5	OG	Beijing	17 Aug 08
		(20)							

Mark	Wind	Name		Nat	Born	Pos	Meet	Venue	Date
9:16.94		Mercy	Njoroge	KEN	10.6.86	2	DL	Doha	6 May 11
9:17.15		Wioletta	Frankiewicz/Janowska	POL	9.6.77	1	SGP	Athína	3 Jul 06
9:17.85		Zemzem	Ahmed	ETH	27.12.84	7	OG	Beijing	17 Aug 08
9:18.03		Lydia	Rotich	KEN	8.8.88	3	Bisl	Oslo	4 Jun 10
9:18.35		Donna	MacFarlane	AUS	18.6.77	3	Bisl	Oslo	6 Jun 08
9:18.54		Antje	Möldner-Schmidt	GER	13.6.84	9	WCh	Berlin	17 Aug 09
9:18.54		Jéssica	Augusto	POR	8.11.81	2		Huelva	9 Jun 10
9:19.42		Purity	Kirui	KEN	13.8.91	6	DL	Doha	10 May 13
9:20.23		Mekdes	Bekele	ETH	20.1.87	2		Huelva	13 Jun 08
9:20.37		Birtukan	Adamu	ETH	29.4.92	4	GGala	Roma	26 May 11
		(30)							
9:20.55		Ruth	Chebet	KEN/BRN	17.11.96	4	WK	Zürich	28 Aug 14
9:21.24		Salima	Alami El Ouali	MAR	29.12.83	5	DL	Saint-Denis	5 Jul 14
9:21.94		Lyubov	Ivanova' ¶	RUS	2.3.81	2	Tsik	Athína	3 Jul 06
9:22.05		Hyvin	Jepkemoi	KEN	13.1.92	6	WCh	Moskva	13 Aug 13
9:22.12		Hanane	Ouhaddou	MAR	.82	1	NA	Heusden-Zolder	18 Jul 09
9:22.15		Yelena	Sidorchenkova	RUS	30.5.80	2	NC	Cheboksary	23 Jul 09
9:22.29 WR		Justyna	Bak	POL	1.8.74	1		Milano	5 Jun 02
9:22.51		Almaz	Ayana	ETH	21.11.91	3	VD	Bruxelles	27 Aug 10
9:22.76		Anna	Willard/Pierce	USA	31.3.84	2	NA	Heusden-Zolder	20 Jul 08
9:23.35		Jeruto	Kiptum	KEN	12.12.81	2	GP	Rieti	27 Aug 06
		(40)							
9:23.52		Gesa-Felicitas	Krause	GER	3.8.92	8	OG	London (OS)	6 Aug 12
9:23.96		Charlotta	Fougberg	SWE	19.6.85	4	DL	Glasgow	12 Jul 14
9:24.24		Barbara	Parker	GBR	8.11.82	4	Pre	Eugene	2 Jun 12
9:24.28		Stephanie	Garcia	USA	3.5.88	5	DL	Glasgow	12 Jul 14
9:24.29		Melissa	Rollison	AUS	13.4.83	2	CG	Melbourne	22 Mar 06
9:24.59		Nicole	Bush	USA	4.4.86	1	NA	Heusden-Zolder	19 Jul 14
9:24.70		Sandra	Eriksson	FIN	4.5.89	6	DL	Glasgow	12 Jul 14
9:24.84		Lisa	Aguilera	USA	30.11.79	5	VD	Bruxelles	27 Aug 10
9:25.14		Eva	Arias	ESP	8.10.80	5h1	WCh	Berlin	15 Aug 09
9:25.62		Sophie	Duarte	FRA	31.7.81	6	GGala	Roma	10 Jul 09
		(50)	100th woman 9:33.34, 200th 9:45.21, 300th 9:53.95						

Drugs disqualification

Mark	Wind	Name		Nat	Born	Pos	Meet	Venue	Date
9:05.02		Yuliya	Zaripova	RUS	26.4.86	(1)	DNG	Stockholm	17 Aug 12
9:06.72			Zaripova			(1)	OG	London (OS)	6 Aug 12
9:09.99			Zaripova			(1)	NC	Cheboksary	3 Jul 12
9:24.06		Binnaz	Uslu ¶	TUR	12.3.85	(1h1)	WCh	Daegu	27 Aug 11

100 METRES HURDLES

Mark	Wind	Name		Nat	Born	Pos	Meet	Venue	Date
12.21 WR	0.7	Yordanka	Donkova	BUL	28.9.61	1		Stara Zagora	20 Aug 88
12.24	0.9		Donkova			1h		Stara Zagora	28 Aug 88
12.25 WR	1.4	Ginka	Zagorcheva	BUL	12.4.58	1	v TCH,GRE	Drama	8 Aug 87
12.26 WR	1.5		Donkova			1	Balk	Ljubljana	7 Sep 86
12.26	1.7	Lyudmila	Narozhilenko ¶	RUS	21.4.64	1rB		Sevilla	6 Jun 92
		(now Ludmila Engquist SWE)							
12.26	1.2	Brianna	Rollins	USA	18.8.91	1	NC	Des Moines	22 Jun 13
12.27	-1.2		Donkova			1		Stara Zagora	28 Aug 88
12.28	1.8		Narozhilenko			1	NC	Kyiv	11 Jul 91
12.28	0.9		Narozhilenko			1rA		Sevilla	6 Jun 92
12.28	1.1	Sally	Pearson'	AUS	19.9.86	1	WCh	Daegu	3 Sep 11
12.29 WR	-0.4		Donkova			1	ASV	Köln	17 Aug 86
12.32	1.6		Narozhilenko			1		Saint-Denis	4 Jun 92
12.33	1.4		Donkova			1		Fürth	14 Jun 87
12.33	-0.3	Gail	Devers	USA	19.11.66	1	NC	Sacramento	23 Jul 00
12.34	-0.5		Zagorcheva			1	WCh	Roma	4 Sep 87
12.35 WR	0.1		Donkova			1h2	ASV	Köln	17 Aug 86
12.35	-0.2		Pearson			1	OG	London (OS)	7 Aug 12
12.36 WR	1.9	Grazyna	Rabsztyn	POL	20.9.52	1	Kuso	Warszawa	13 Jun 80
12.36 WR	-0.6		Donkova			1	NC	Sofia	13 Aug 86
12.36	1.1		Donkova			1		Schwechat	15 Jun 88
12.36	0.3		Pearson			1s2	WCh	Daegu	3 Sep 11
12.37	1.4		Donkova			1	ISTAF	Berlin	15 Aug 86
12.37	0.7		Devers			1	WCh	Sevilla	28 Aug 99
12.37	1.5	Joanna	Hayes	USA	23.12.76	1	OG	Athína	24 Aug 04
12.37	-0.2	Dawn	Harper-Nelson	USA	13.5.84	2	OG	London (OS)	7 Aug 12
12.38	0.0		Donkova			1	BGP	Budapest	11 Aug 86
12.38	-0.7		Donkova			1	EC	Stuttgart	29 Aug 86
12.38	0.2		Donkova			1	OG	Seoul	30 Sep 88
12.39	1.5	Vera	Komisova' (10)	RUS	11.6.53	1	GGala	Roma	5 Aug 80

Mark	Wind	Name		Nat	Born	Pos	Meet	Venue	Date
12.39	1.5		Zagorcheva			2	Balk	Ljubljana	7 Sep 86
12.39	1.8	Natalya	Grigoryeva ¶	UKR	3.12.62	2	NC	Kyiv	11 Jul 91
12.39	-0.7		Devers			1	WK	Zürich	11 Aug 00
12.39	1.3		Pearson			1s2	OG	London (OS)	7 Aug 12
12.39	1.7		Rollins			1	NCAA	Eugene	8 Jun 13
		(34/11)							
12.42	1.8	Bettine	Jahn	GDR	3.8.58	1	OD	Berlin	8 Jun 83
12.42	2.0	Anjanette	Kirkland	USA	24.2.74	1	WCh	Edmonton	11 Aug 01
12.43	-0.9	Lucyna	Kalek (Langer)	POL	9.1.56	1		Hannover	19 Aug 84
12.43	-0.3	Michelle	Perry	USA	1.5.79	1s1	NC	Carson	26 Jun 05
12.43	0.2	Lolo	Jones	USA	5.8.82	1s1	OG	Beijing	18 Aug 08
12.43	1.2	Queen	Harrison	USA	10.9.88	2	NC	Des Moines	22 Jun 13
12.44	-0.5	Gloria	Uibel (-Siebert)	GDR	13.1.64	2	WCh	Roma	4 Sep 87
12.44	-0.8	Olga	Shishigina ¶	KAZ	23.12.68	1	Spitzen	Luzern	27 Jun 95
12.44	0.4	Glory	Alozie	NGR/ESP	30.12.77	1	Herc	Monaco	8 Aug 98
		(20)							
12.44	0.6	Damu	Cherry ¶	USA	29.11.77	2rA	Athl	Lausanne	11 Jul 06
12.45	1.3	Cornelia	Oschkenat'	GDR	29.10.61	1		Neubrandenburg	11 Jun 87
12.45	1.4	Brigitte	Foster-Hylton	JAM	7.11.74	1	Pre	Eugene	24 May 03
12.45	1.5	Olena	Krasovska	UKR	17.8.76	2	OG	Athína	24 Aug 04
12.45	1.4	Virginia	Powell/Crawford	USA	7.9.83	1	GP	New York	2 Jun 07
12.46	0.7	Perdita	Felicien	CAN	29.8.80	1	Pre	Eugene	19 Jun 04
12.47	1.1	Marina	Azyabina	RUS	15.6.63	1s2	NC	Moskva	19 Jun 93
12.47	1.1	Danielle	Carruthers	USA	22.12.79	2	WCh	Daegu	3 Sep 11
12.48	-0.2	Kellie	Wells	USA	16.7.82	3	OG	London (OS)	7 Aug 12
12.48	1.2	Nia	Ali	USA	23.10.88	3	NC	Des Moines	22 Jun 13
		(30)							
12.49	0.9	Susanna	Kallur	SWE	16.2.81	1	ISTAF	Berlin	16 Sep 07
12.49	1.0	Priscilla	Lopes-Schliep	CAN	26.8.82	2	VD	Bruxelles	4 Sep 09
12.50	0.0	Vera	Akimova'	RUS	5.6.59	1		Sochi	19 May 84
12.50	-0.1	Delloreen	Ennis-London	JAM	5.3.75	3	WCh	Osaka	29 Aug 07
12.50	0.8	Josephine	Onyia ¶	NGR/ESP	15.7.86	1	ISTAF	Berlin	1 Jun 08
12.51	1.4	Miesha	McKelvy	USA	26.7.76	2	Pre	Eugene	24 May 03
12.51	0.7	Tiffany	Porter'	USA/GBR	13.11.87	2	C.Cup	Marrakech	14 Sep 14
12.52	-0.4	Michelle	Freeman	JAM	5.5.69	1s1	WCh	Athína	10 Aug 97
12.53	0.2	Tatyana	Reshetnikova	RUS	14.10.66	1rA	GP II	Linz	4 Jul 94
12.53	-0.4	Svetla	Dimitrova ¶	BUL	27.1.70	1	Herc	Stara Zagora	16 Jul 94
		(40)							
12.53	1.0	Melissa	Morrison	USA	9.7.71	1	DNG	Stockholm	5 Aug 98
12.54	0.4	Kerstin	Knabe	GDR	7.7.59	3	EC	Athína	9 Sep 82
12.54	0.9	Sabine	Paetz/John'	GDR	16.10.57	1		Berlin	15 Jul 84
12.54	1.7	Nichole	Denby	USA	10.10.82	2s2	OT	Eugene	6 Jul 08
12.54	1.3	Jessica	Ennis	GBR	28.1.86	1H5	OG	London (OS)	3 Aug 12
12.56	1.2	Johanna	Klier'	GDR	13.9.52	1r2		Cottbus	17 Jul 80
12.56	1.2	Monique	Ewanjé-Epée	FRA	11.7.67	1	BNP	Villeneuve d'Ascq	29 Jun 90
12.56	0.7	Kristi	Castlin	USA	7.7.88	2	Bisl	Oslo	7 Jun 12
12.56	1.2	Cindy	Billaud	FRA	11.3.86	1h1	NC	Reims	12 Jul 14
12.57	0.3	Carolin	Nytra	GER	26.2.85	2	Athl	Lausanne	8 Jul 10
		(50)	100th woman 12.69, 200th 12.84, 300th 12.94, 400th 13.03, 500th 13.11						

Wind assisted performances to 12.37, performers to 12.54

Mark	Wind	Name		Nat	Born	Pos	Meet	Venue	Date
12.28	2.7	Cornelia	Oschkenat'	GDR	29.10.61	1		Berlin	25 Aug 87
12.29	3.5		Donkova			1	Athl	Lausanne	24 Jun 88
12.29	2.7	Gail	Devers	USA	19.11.66	1	Pre	Eugene	26 May 02
12.29	3.8	Lolo	Jones	USA	5.8.82	1	NC/OT	Eugene	6 Jul 08
12.30	2.8		Rollins			1s1	NC	Des Moines	22 Jun 13
12.33	2.3		Rollins			1h3	NC	Des Moines	21 Jun 13
12.35	2.4	Bettine	Jahn	GDR	3.8.58	1	WCh	Helsinki	13 Aug 83
12.35	3.7	Kellie	Wells	USA	16.7.82	1		Gainesville	16 Apr 11
12.36	2.2	Dawn	Harper	USA	13.5.84	1	NC	Eugene	28 Jun 09
12.37	2.7	Gloria	Uibel/Siebert'	GDR	13.1.64	2		Berlin	25 Aug 87
12.37	3.4	Danielle	Carruthers	USA	22.12.79	1s1	NC	Eugene	26 Jun 11
12.40	2.1	Michelle	Freeman	JAM	5.5.69	1	GPF	Fukuoka	13 Sep 97
12.41	2.2	Olga	Shishigina ¶	KAZ	23.12.68	1rA	Athl	Lausanne	5 Jul 95
12.42	2.4	Kerstin	Knabe	GDR	7.7.59	2	WCh	Helsinki	13 Aug 83
12.43	2.7	Yvette	Lewis	USA/PAN	16.3.85	1	MSR	Walnut	20 Apr 13
12.44	2.6	Melissa	Morrison	USA	9.7.71	1		Carson	22 May 04
12.45	2.1	Perdita	Felicien	CAN	29.8.80	1	NC	Victoria	10 Jul 04
12.47	3.0	Tiffany	Porter	USA/GBR	13.11.87	1		Gainesville	21 Apr 12
12.48	3.8	Kristi	Castlin	USA	7.7.88	1		Clermont	2 Jun 12
12.50	2.7	Svetla	Dimitrova ¶	BUL	27.1.70	1		Saint-Denis	10 Jun 94

Mark	Wind	Name		Nat	Born	Pos	Meet	Venue	Date
12.51	3.2	Johanna	Klier'	GDR	13.9.52	1	NC	Cottbus	17 Jul 80
12.51	3.6	Sabine	Paetz/John'	GDR	16.10.57	1		Dresden	27 Jul 84
12.51A	3.3	Yuliya	Graudyn	RUS	13.11.70	1		Sestriere	31 Jul 94
12.52	3.1	Angela	Whyte	CAN	22.5.80	2		Edmonton	29 Jun 13
12.53	2.2	Mihaela	Pogacian	ROU	27.1.58	1	IAC	Edinburgh	6 Jul 90
12.54	2.8	Jasmin	Stowers	USA	23.9.91	2	NCAA	Eugene	14 Jun 14
Probably hand timed Officially 12.36, but subsequent investigations showed this unlikely to have been auto-timed									
12.4	0.7	Svetla	Dimitrova ¶	BUL	27.1.70	1		Stara Zagora	9 Jul 97
Hand timed									
12.3 WR	1.5	Anneliese	Ehrhardt	GDR	18.6.50	1	NC	Dresden	22 Jul 73
12.3		Marina	Azyabina	RUS	15.6.63	1		Yekaterinburg	30 May 93
12.0w	2.1	Yordanka	Donkova	BUL	28.9.61	1		Sofia	3 Aug 86
12.1w	2.1	Ginka	Zagorcheva	BUL	12.4.58	2		Sofia	3 Aug 86

400 METRES HURDLES

Mark	Name		Nat	Born	Pos	Meet	Venue	Date
52.34 WR	Yuliya	Nosova-Pechonkina'	RUS	21.4.78	1	NC	Tula	8 Aug 03
52.42	Melaine	Walker	JAM	1.1.83	1	WCh	Berlin	20 Aug 09
52.47	Lashinda	Demus	USA	10.3.83	1	WCh	Daegu	1 Sep 11
52.61 WR	Kim	Batten	USA	29.3.69	1	WCh	Göteborg	11 Aug 95
52.62	Tonja	Buford-Bailey	USA	13.12.70	2	WCh	Göteborg	11 Aug 95
52.63		Demus			1	Herc	Monaco	28 Jul 09
52.64		Walker			1	OG	Beijing	20 Aug 08
52.70	Natalya	Antyukh	RUS	26.6.81	1	OG	London (OS)	8 Aug 12
52.73		Walker			2	WCh	Daegu	1 Sep 11
52.74 WR	Sally	Gunnell	GBR	29.7.66	1	WCh	Stuttgart	19 Aug 93
52.74		Batten			1	Herc	Monaco	8 Aug 98
52.77	Faní	Halkiá	GRE	2.2.79	1s2	OG	Athína	22 Aug 04
52.77		Demus			2	OG	London (OS)	8 Aug 12
52.79	Sandra	Farmer-Patrick	USA	18.8.62	2	WCh	Stuttgart	19 Aug 93
52.79	Kaliese	Spencer (10)	JAM	6.5.87	1	LGP	London (CP)	5 Aug 11
52.82	Deon	Hemmings	JAM	9.10.68	1	OG	Atlanta	31 Jul 96
52.82		Halkiá			1	OG	Athína	25 Aug 04
52.82		Demus			1	GGala	Roma	10 Jun 10
52.83	Zuzana	Hejnová	CZE	19.12.86	1	WCh	Moskva	15 Aug 13
52.84		Batten			1	WK	Zürich	12 Aug 98
52.89	Daimí	Pernía	CUB	27.12.76	1	WCh	Sevilla	25 Aug 99
52.90		Buford			1	WK	Zürich	16 Aug 95
52.90	Nezha	Bidouane	MAR	18.9.69	2	WCh	Sevilla	25 Aug 99
52.90		Pechonkina			1	WCh	Helsinki	13 Aug 05
52.92		Antyukh			1	EC	Barcelona	30 Jul 10
52.94 WR	Marina	Styepanova'	RUS	1.5.50	1s	Spart	Tashkent	17 Sep 86
52.95	Sheena	Johnson/Tosta	USA	1.10.82	1	NC/OT	Sacramento	11 Jul 04
52.96A		Bidouane			1	WCp	Johannesburg	11 Sep 98
52.96		Demus			2	WCh	Berlin	20 Aug 09
52.97		Batten			1	NC	Indianapolis	14 Jun 97
52.97		Bidouane			1	WCh	Athína	8 Aug 97
	(31/16)							
53.02	Irina	Privalova	RUS	22.11.68	1	OG	Sydney	27 Sep 00
53.11	Tatyana	Ledovskaya	BLR	21.5.66	1	WCh	Tokyo	29 Aug 91
53.17	Debbie	Flintoff-King	AUS	20.4.60	1	OG	Seoul	28 Sep 88
53.20	Josanne	Lucas	TTO	14.5.84	3	WCh	Berlin	20 Aug 09
	(20)							
53.21	Marie-José	Pérec	FRA	9.5.68	2	WK	Zürich	16 Aug 95
53.21	Kori	Carter	USA	6.3.92	1	NCAA	Eugene	7 Jun 13
53.22	Jana	Pittman/Rawlinson	AUS	9.11.82	1	WCh	Saint-Denis	28 Aug 03
53.24	Sabine	Busch	GDR	21.11.62	1	NC	Potsdam	21 Aug 87
53.25	Ionela	Târlea-Manolache	ROU	9.2.76	2	GGala	Roma	7 Jul 99
53.28	Tiffany	Ross-Williams	USA	5.2.83	1	NC	Indianapolis	24 Jun 07
53.32	Sandra	Glover	USA	30.12.68	3	WCh	Helsinki	13 Aug 05
53.36	Andrea	Blackett	BAR	24.1.76	4	WCh	Sevilla	25 Aug 99
53.36	Brenda	Taylor	USA	9.2.79	2	NC/OT	Sacramento	11 Jul 04
53.37	Tetyana	Tereshchuk	UKR	11.10.69	3s2	OG	Athína	22 Aug 04
	(30)							
53.47	Janeene	Vickers	USA	3.10.68	3	WCh	Tokyo	29 Aug 91
53.48	Margarita	Ponomaryova'	RUS	19.6.63	3	WCh	Stuttgart	19 Aug 93
53.58	Cornelia	Ullrich'	GDR	26.4.63	2	NC	Potsdam	21 Aug 87
53.63	Ellen	Fiedler'	GDR	26.11.58	3	OG	Seoul	28 Sep 88
53.65A mx	Myrtle	Bothma'	RSA	18.2.64	mx		Pretoria	12 Mar 90
	53.74A				1		Johannesburg	18 Apr 86
53.67	Perri	Shakes-Drayton	GBR	21.12.88	2	DL	London (OS)	26 Jul 13

Mark	Wind	Name		Nat	Born	Pos	Meet	Venue	Date
53.68		Vania	Stambolova ¶	BUL	28.11.83	1		Rabat	5 Jun 11
53.72		Yekaterina	Bikert	RUS	13.5.80	2	NC	Tula	30 Jul 04
53.72		Georgeanne	Moline	USA	6.3.90	2	NCAA	Eugene	7 Jun 13
53.77		Irina	Davydova	RUS	27.5.88	1	EC	Helsinki	29 Jun 12
		(40)							
53.83		Dalilah	Muhammad	USA	7.2.90	1	NC	Des Moines	23 Jun 13
53.84		Natasha	Danvers	GBR	19.9.77	3	OG	Beijing	20 Aug 08
53.85		Angela	Morosanu	ROU	26.7.86	2	DL	Shanghai	18 May 13
53.86		Anna	Jesien	POL	10.12.78	1s3	WCh	Osaka	28 Aug 07
53.88		Debbie-Ann	Parris	JAM	24.3.73	3s1	WCh	Edmonton	6 Aug 01
53.93		Yevgeniya	Isakova	RUS	27.11.78	1	EC	Göteborg	9 Aug 06
53.96			Han Qing ¶	CHN	4.3.70	1	NG	Beijing	9 Sep 93
53.96			Song Yinglan	CHN	14.9.75	1	NG	Guangzhou	22 Nov 01
53.96		Anastasiya	Rabchenyuk	UKR	14.9.83	4	OG	Beijing	20 Aug 08
53.97		Nickiesha	Wilson	JAM	28.7.86	2s3	WCh	Osaka	28 Aug 07
		(50)	100th woman 54.57, 200th 55.44, 300th 55.85, 400th 56.24, 500th 56.53						
Drugs disqualification: 53.38			Jiang Limei ¶	CHN	.3.70	(1)	89	Shanghai	22 Oct 97

HIGH JUMP

Mark	Wind	Name		Nat	Born	Pos	Meet	Venue	Date
2.09 WR		Stefka	Kostadinova	BUL	25.3.65	1	WCh	Roma	30 Aug 87
2.08 WR			Kostadinova			1	NM	Sofia	31 May 86
2.08i		Kajsa	Bergqvist	SWE	12.10.76	1		Arnstadt	4 Feb 06
2.08		Blanka	Vlasic	CRO	8.11.83	1	Hanz	Zagreb	31 Aug 09
2.07 WR		Lyudmila	Andonova ¶	BUL	6.5.60	1	OD	Berlin	20 Jul 84
2.07 WR			Kostadinova			1		Sofia	25 May 86
2.07			Kostadinova			1		Cagliari	16 Sep 87
2.07			Kostadinova			1	NC	Sofia	3 Sep 88
2.07i		Heike	Henkel'	GER	5.5.64	1	NC	Karlsruhe	8 Feb 92
2.07			Vlasic			1	DNG	Stockholm	7 Aug 07
2.07		Anna	Chicherova	RUS	22.7.82	1	NC	Cheboksary	22 Jul 11
2.06			Kostadinova			1	ECp	Moskva	18 Aug 85
2.06			Kostadinova			1		Fürth	15 Jun 86
2.06			Kostadinova			1		Cagliari	14 Sep 86
2.06			Kostadinova			1		Wörrstadt	6 Jun 87
2.06			Kostadinova			1		Rieti	8 Sep 87
2.06i			Kostadinova			1		Pireás	20 Feb 88
2.06			Bergqvist			1		Eberstadt	26 Jul 03
2.06		Hestrie	Cloete	RSA	26.8.78	1	WCh	Saint-Denis	31 Aug 03
2.06		Yelena	Slesarenko	RUS	28.2.82	1	OG	Athína	28 Aug 04
2.06			Vlasic			1		Thessaloníki	30 Jul 07
2.06			Vlasic			1	ECp-1B	Istanbul	22 Jun 08
2.06			Vlasic			1	GP	Madrid	5 Jul 08
2.06		Ariane	Friedrich	GER	10.1.84	1	ISTAF	Berlin	14 Jun 09
2.06i			Vlasic			1		Arnstadt	6 Feb 10
2.06i			Chicherova			1		Arnstadt	4 Feb 12
2.05 WR		Tamara	Bykova (10)	RUS	21.12.58	1	Izv	Kyiv	22 Jun 84
2.05		Inga	Babakova	UKR	27.6.67	1		Tokyo	15 Sep 95
2.05i		Tia	Hellebaut	BEL	16.2.78	1	EI	Birmingham	3 Mar 07
2.05			Hellebaut			1	OG	Beijing	23 Aug 08
2.05		Chaunté	Lowe'	USA	12.1.84	1	NC	Des Moines	26 Jun 10
Further 2.05 performances: Kostadinova 10, Vlasic 10, Bergqvist, Chicherova 2, Henkel, Cloete, Friedrich 1									
		(58/13)							
2.04		Silvia	Costa	CUB	4.5.64	1	WCp	Barcelona	9 Sep 89
2.04i		Alina	Astafei	GER	7.6.69	1		Berlin	3 Mar 95
2.04		Venelina	Veneva ¶	BUL	13.6.74	1		Kalamáta	2 Jun 01
2.04i		Antonietta	Di Martino	ITA	1.6.78	1		Banská Bystrica	9 Feb 11
2.04		Irina	Gordeyeva	RUS	9.10.86	1		Eberstadt	19 Aug 12
2.04		Brigetta	Barrett	USA	24.12.90	1	NC	Des Moines	22 Jun 13
2.03 WR		Ulrike	Meyfarth	FRG	4.5.56	1	ECp	London (CP)	21 Aug 83
		(20)							
2.03		Louise	Ritter	USA	18.2.58	1		Austin	8 Jul 88
2.03		Tatyana	Motkova	RUS	23.11.68	2		Bratislava	30 May 95
2.03		Níki	Bakoyiánni	GRE	9.6.68	2	OG	Atlanta	3 Aug 96
2.03i		Monica	Iagar/Dinescu	ROU	2.4.73	1		Bucuresti	23 Jan 99
2.03i		Marina	Kuptsova	RUS	22.12.81	1	EI	Wien	2 Mar 02
2.03		Svetlana	Shkolina	RUS	9.3.86	3	OG	London (OS)	11 Aug 12
2.02i		Susanne	Beyer'	GDR	24.6.61	2	WI	Indianapolis	8 Mar 87
2.02		Yelena	Yelesina	RUS	4.4.70	1	GWG	Seattle	23 Jul 90
2.02		Viktoriya	Styopina	UKR	21.2.76	3	OG	Athína	28 Aug 04
2.02		Ruth	Beitia	ESP	1.4.79	1	NC	San Sebastián	4 Aug 07
		(30)							

Mark Wind	Name		Nat	Born	Pos	Meet	Venue	Date
2.01 WR	Sara	Simeoni	ITA	19.4.53	1	v Pol	Brescia	4 Aug 78
2.01	Olga	Turchak	UKR	5.3.67	2	GWG	Moskva	7 Jul 86
2.01	Desiré	du Plessis	RSA	20.5.65	1		Johannesburg	16 Sep 86
2.01i	Gabriele	Günz	GDR	8.9.61	2		Stuttgart	31 Jan 88
2.01	Heike	Balck	GDR	19.8.70	1	vUSSR-j	Karl-Marx-Stadt	18 Jun 89
2.01i	Ioamnet	Quintero	CUB	8.9.72	1		Berlin	5 Mar 93
2.01	Hanne	Haugland	NOR	14.12.67	1	WK	Zürich	13 Aug 97
2.01i	Tisha	Waller	USA	1.12.70	1	NC	Atlanta	28 Feb 98
2.01	Yelena	Gulyayeva	RUS	14.8.67	2		Kalamáta	23 May 98
2.01	Vita	Palamar	UKR	12.10.77	2=	WK	Zürich	15 Aug 03
	(40)							
2.01	Amy	Acuff	USA	14.7.75	4	WK	Zürich	15 Aug 03
2.01	Iryna	Myhalchenko	UKR	20.1.72	1		Eberstadt	18 Jul 04
2.01	Emma	Green Tregaro	SWE	8.12.84	2	EC	Barcelona	1 Aug 10
2.01i	Mariya	Kuchina	RUS	14.1.93	1		Stockholm	6 Feb 14
2.00 WR	Rosemarie	Ackermann'	GDR	4.4.52	1	ISTAF	Berlin	26 Aug 77
2.00	by 23 other women							
	(67)	100th woman 1.98, 200th 1.95, 300th 1.95, 400th 1.95, 500th 1.90						

Best outdoor marks

2.05	Henkel	1	WCh	Tokyo	31 Aug 91
2.05	Hellebaut	1	OG	Beijing	23 Aug 08
2.03	Di Martino	1	ECp-1B	Milano	24 Jun 07
2.02	Iagar/Dinescu	1		Budapest	6 Jun 98
2.02	Kuptsova	1	FBK	Hengelo	1 Jun 03
2.01	Astafei	2		Wörrstadt	27 May 95
2.00	five women				

Ancillary jumps: 2.06 Kostadinova 30 Aug 87, 2.05i Henkel 8 Feb 92, 2.05i Bergqvist 4 Feb 06, 2.05 Vlasic 31 Aug 09

POLE VAULT

Mark Wind	Name		Nat	Born	Pos	Meet	Venue	Date
5.06 WR	Yelena	Isinbayeva	RUS	3.6.82	1	WK	Zürich	28 Aug 09
5.05 WR		Isinbayeva			1	OG	Beijing	18 Aug 08
5.04 WR		Isinbayeva			1	Herc	Monaco	29 Jul 08
5.03 WR		Isinbayeva			1	GGala	Roma	11 Jul 08
5.02Ai	Jennifer	Suhr	USA	5.2.82	1	NC	Albuquerque	2 Mar 13
5.01 WR		Isinbayeva		2	1	WCh	Helsinki	12 Aug 05
5.01i		Isinbayeva			1	XL Galan	Stockholm	23 Feb 12
5.00 WR		Isinbayeva			1	LGP	London (CP)	22 Jul 05
5.00i		Isinbayeva			1		Donetsk	15 Feb 09
4.95 WR		Isinbayeva			1	GP	Madrid	16 Jul 05
4.95i		Isinbayeva			1		Donetsk	16 Feb 08
4.93 WR		Isinbayeva			1	Athl	Lausanne	5 Jul 05
4.93		Isinbayeva			1	VD	Bruxelles	26 Aug 05
4.93i		Isinbayeva			1		Donetsk	10 Feb 07
4.93		Isinbayeva			1	LGP	London (CP)	25 Jul 08
4.92 WR		Isinbayeva			1	VD	Bruxelles	3 Sep 04
4.92		Stuczynski/Suhr			1	NC/OT	Eugene	6 Jul 08
4.91 WR		Isinbayeva (this jump on 25 Aug)			1	OG	Athína	25 Aug 04
4.91i		Isinbayeva			1		Donetsk	12 Feb 06
4.91		Isinbayeva			1	LGP	London (CP)	28 Jul 06
4.91		Isinbayeva			1	Gaz	Saint-Denis	6 Jul 07
4.91		Suhr			1		Rochester, NY	26 Jul 11
4.91		Suhr			1		Lyndonville	14 Jun 13
4.90 WR		Isinbayeva			1	GP	London (CP)	30 Jul 04
4.90i		Isinbayeva			1	EI	Madrid	6 Mar 05
4.90		Isinbayeva			1	Athl	Lausanne	11 Jul 06
4.90		Isinbayeva			1	GGala	Roma	13 Jul 07
4.90		Stuczynski			1	adidas	Carson	18 May 08
4.90i		Isinbayeva			1		Praha (O2)	26 Feb 09
4.90	Yarisley	Silva	CUB	1.6.87	1	FBK	Hengelo	8 Jun 13
	(30/3)							
4.88 WR	Svetlana	Feofanova	RUS	16.7.80	1		Iráklio	4 Jul 04
4.87i	Holly	Bleasdale	GBR	2.11.91	1		Villeurbanne	20 Jan 12
4.85	Fabiana	Murer	BRA	16.3.81	1	IbAm	San Fernando	4 Jun 10
4.85i	Anna	Rogowska	POL	21.5.81	1	EI	Paris (Bercy)	6 Mar 11
4.83	Stacy	Dragila	USA	25.3.71	1	GS	Ostrava	8 Jun 04
4.82	Monika	Pyrek	POL	11.8.80	2	WAF	Stuttgart	22 Sep 07
4.82	Silke	Spiegelburg	GER	17.3.86	1	Herc	Monaco	20 Jul 12
	(10)							
4.80	Martina	Strutz	GER	4.11.81	2	WCh	Daegu	30 Aug 11
4.78	Tatyana	Polnova	RUS	20.4.79	2	WAF	Monaco	19 Sep 04
4.77	Annika	Becker	GER	12.11.81	1	NC	Wattenscheid	7 Jul 02
4.76	Alana	Boyd	AUS	10.5.84	1		Perth	24 Feb 12
4.76	Jirina	Ptácníková'	CZE	20.5.86	1		Plzen	4 Sep 13
4.75	Katerina	Badurová	CZE	18.12.82	2	WCh	Osaka	28 Aug 07

Mark	Wind	Name		Nat	Born	Pos	Meet	Venue	Date
4.75i		Yuliya	Golubchikova	RUS	27.3.83	1		Athína (P)	13 Feb 08
4.75Ai		Kylie	Hutson	USA	27.11.87	2	NC	Albuquerque	2 Mar 13
4.73		Chelsea	Johnson	USA	20.12.83	1		Los Gatos	26 Jun 08
4.73		Anastasiya	Savchenko	RUS	15.11.89	1	NCp	Yerino	15 Jun 13
		(20)							
4.72i		Kym	Howe	AUS	12.6.80	2		Donetsk	10 Feb 07
4.72i		Jillian	Schwartz	USA/ISR	19.9.79	1		Jonesboro	15 Jun 08
4.72		Carolin	Hingst	GER	18.9.80	1		Biberach	9 Jul 10
4.71		Nikolía	Kiriakopoúlou	GRE	21.3.86	4	LGP	London (CP)	5 Aug 11
4.72i		Anzhelika	Sidorova	RUS	28.6.91	3	NC	Moskva	17 Feb 14
4.71i		Tina	Sutej	SLO	7.11.88	1		Moskva	2 Feb 14
4.71Ai		Mary	Saxer	USA	21.6.87	1	NC	Albuquerque	23 Feb 14
4.71		Lisa	Ryzih	GER	27.9.88	1	adidas	New York	14 Jun 14
4.71		Ekateríni	Stefanídi	GRE	4.2.90	3	Herc	Monaco	18 Jul 14
4.70		Yvonne	Buschbaum	GER	14.7.80	1	NC	Ulm	29 Jun 03
		(30)							
4.70		Vanessa	Boslak	FRA	11.6.82	2	ECp-S	Málaga	28 Jun 06
4.70		Angelina	Zhuk/Krasnova	RUS	7.2.91	1	EU23	Tampere	13 Jul 13
4.68		Anna	Battke	GER	3.1.85	5	ISTAF	Berlin	14 Jun 09
4.67i		Kellie	Suttle	USA	9.5.73	1		Jonesboro	16 Jun 04
4.67		Nicole	Büchler	SUI	17.12.83	5	WK	Zürich	28 Aug 14
4.66i		Christine	Adams	GER	28.2.74	1	IHS	Sindelfingen	10 Mar 02
4.66i		Lacy	Janson	USA	20.2.83	1		Fayetteville	12 Feb 10
4.66i		Kristina	Gadschiew	GER	3.7.84	1		Potsdam	18 Feb 11
4.65		Mary	Sauer/Vincent	USA	31.10.75	2		Madrid (C)	3 Jul 02
4.65		Anastasiya	Ivanova/Shvedova	RUS/BLR	3.5.79	1	Odlozil	Praha	13 Jun 07
		(40)							
4.65		Aleksandra	Kiryashova	RUS	21.8.85	1	NCp	Tula	1 Aug 09
4.65			Li Ling	CHN	6.7.89	1	NG	Shenyang	8 Sep 13
4.64i		Pavla	Hamácková/Rybová	CZE	20.5.78	4		Bydgoszcz	14 Feb 07
4.64			Gao Shuying	CHN	28.10.79	2	GP	New York	2 Jun 07
4.63		Nastja	Ryshich	GER	19.9.77	1		Nürnberg	29 Jul 06
4.63		April	Steiner-Bennett	USA	22.4.80	1		Norman	12 Apr 08
4.63i		Angelica	Bengtsson	SWE	8.7.93	2		Stockholm	22 Feb 11
4.62b		Melissa	Mueller	USA	16.11.72	1		Clovis	4 Aug 01
4.61		Kate	Dennison	GBR	7.5.84	2		Barcelona	22 Jul 11
4.61i		Marion	Fiack	FRA	13.10.92	1		Orléans	18 Jan 14
		(50)	100th woman 4.50, 200th 4.40, 300th 4.20, 400th 4.22, 500th 4.19						

Outdoor bests

Mark	Name	Pos	Meet	Venue	Date
4.75	Golubchikova	4	OG	Beijing	18 Aug 08
4.71	Bleasdale	1	NC	Birmingham	24 Jun 12
4.71	Kiriakopoúlou	4	GP	London	5 Aug 11
4.70	Hutson	1		Terre Haute	15 Jun 13
4.70	Saxer	1		Chula Vista	6 Jun 13
4.70	Sidorova	1	NC	Kazan	24 Jul 13
4.65	Howe	1		Saulheim	30 Jun 07
4.61	Sutej	1	SEC	Athens, GA	14 May 11
4.61	Gadschiew	1		Rovereto	3 Sep 13

Ancillary jumps: Isinbayeva: 4.97 15 Feb 09, 4.96 WR 22 Jul 05, 4.95 18 Aug 08, 4.93 29 Jul 08, 4.92i 23 Feb 12

Exhibition: 4.72 Anastasiya Shvedova RUS 3.5.79 1 Aosta 5 Jul 08

LONG JUMP

Mark	Wind	Name		Nat	Born	Pos	Meet	Venue	Date
7.52 WR	1.4	Galina	Chistyakova	RUS	26.7.62	1	Znam	Leningrad	11 Jun 88
7.49	1.3	Jackie	Joyner-Kersee	USA	3.3.62	1	NYG	New York	22 May 94
7.49A	1.7		Joyner-Kersee			1		Sestriere	31 Jul 94
7.48	1.2	Heike	Drechsler	GER	16.12.64	1	v ITA	Neubrandenburg	9 Jul 88
7.48	0.4		Drechsler			1	Athl	Lausanne	8 Jul 92
7.45 WR	0.9		Drechsler'			1	v USSR	Tallinn	21 Jun 86
7.45 WR	1.1		Drechsler			1	OD	Dresden	3 Jul 86
7.45 WR	0.6		Joyner-Kersee			1	PAm	Indianapolis	13 Aug 87
7.45	1.6		Chistyakova			1	BGP	Budapest	12 Aug 88
7.44 WR	2.0		Drechsler			1		Berlin	22 Sep 85
7.43 WR	1.4	Anisoara	Cusmir/Stanciu	ROU	28.6.62	1	RomIC	Bucuresti	4 Jun 83
7.42	2.0	Tatyana	Kotova ¶	RUS	11.12.76	1	ECp-S	Annecy	23 Jun 02
7.40	1.8		Daute' (Drechsler)			1		Dresden	26 Jul 84
7.40	0.7		Drechsler			1	NC	Potsdam	21 Aug 87
7.40	0.9		Joyner-Kersee			1	OG	Seoul	29 Sep 88
7.39	0.3		Drechsler			1	WK	Zürich	21 Aug 85
7.39	0.5	Yelena	Byelevskaya'	BLR	11.10.63	1	NC	Bryansk	18 Jul 87
7.39			Joyner-Kersee			1		San Diego	25 Jun 88
7.37i	-		Drechsler			1	v2N	Wien	13 Feb 88
7.37A	1.8		Drechsler			1		Sestriere	31 Jul 91
7.37		Inessa	Kravets ¶	UKR	5.10.66	1		Kyiv	13 Jun 92
7.36	0.4		Joyner			1	WCh	Roma	4 Sep 87
7.36	1.8		Byelevskaya			2	Znam	Leningrad	11 Jun 88

Mark	Wind	Name		Nat	Born	Pos	Meet	Venue	Date
7.36	1.8		Drechsler			1		Jena	28 May 92
7.35	1.9		Chistyakova			1	GPB	Bratislava	20 Jun 90
7.34	1.6		Daute'			1		Dresden	19 May 84
7.34	1.4		Chistyakova			2	v GDR	Tallinn	21 Jun 86
7.34			Byelevskaya			1		Sukhumi	17 May 87
7.34	0.7		Drechsler			1	v USSR	Karl-Marx-Stadt	20 Jun 87
7.33	0.4		Drechsler			1	v USSR	Erfurt	22 Jun 85
7.33	2.0		Drechsler			1		Dresden	2 Aug 85
7.33	-0.3		Drechsler			1	Herc	Monaco	11 Aug 92
7.33	0.4	Tatyana	Lebedeva	RUS	21.7.76	1	NC	Tula	31 Jul 04
		(33/8)							
7.31	1.5	Yelena	Kokonova'	UKR	4.8.63	1	NP	Alma-Ata	12 Sep 85
7.31	1.9	Marion	Jones ¶	USA	12.10.75	1	Pre	Eugene	31 May 98
		(10)							
7.27	-0.4	Irina	Simagina/Meleshina	RUS	25.5.82	2	NC	Tula	31 Jul 04
7.26A	1.8	Maurren	Maggi ¶	BRA	25.6.76	1	SACh	Bogotá	26 Jun 99
7.25	1.6	Brittney	Reese	USA	9.9.86	1	DL	Doha	10 May 13
7.24	1.0	Larisa	Berezhnaya	UKR	28.2.61	1		Granada	25 May 91
7.21	1.6	Helga	Radtke	GDR	16.5.62	2		Dresden	26 Jul 84
7.21	1.9	Lyudmila	Kolchanova	RUS	1.10.79	1		Sochi	27 May 07
7.20 WR	-0.5	Valy	Ionescu	ROU	31.8.60	1	NC	Bucuresti	1 Aug 82
7.20	2.0	Irena	Ozhenko'	LTU	13.11.62	1		Budapest	12 Sep 86
7.20	0.8	Yelena	Sinchukova'	RUS	23.1.61	1	BGP	Budapest	20 Jun 91
7.20	0.7	Irina	Mushayilova	RUS	6.1.67	1	NC	Sankt-Peterburg	14 Jul 94
		(20)							
7.17	1.8	Irina	Valyukevich	BLR	19.11.59	2	NC	Bryansk	18 Jul 87
7.16		Iolanda	Chen	RUS	26.7.61	1		Moskva	30 Jul 88
7.16A	-0.1	Elva	Goulbourne	JAM	21.1.80	1		Ciudad de México	22 May 04
7.14	1.8	Nijole	Medvedeva ¶	LTU	20.10.60	1		Riga	4 Jun 88
7.14	1.2	Mirela	Dulgheru	ROU	5.10.66	1	Balk G	Sofia	5 Jul 92
7.13	2.0	Olga	Kucherenko	RUS	5.11.85	1		Sochi	27 May 10
7.12	1.6	Sabine	Paetz/John'	GDR	16.10.57	2		Dresden	19 May 84
7.12	0.9	Chioma	Ajunwa ¶	NGR	25.12.70	1	OG	Atlanta	2 Aug 96
7.12	1.3	Naide	Gomes	CPV/POR	10.11.79	1	Herc	Monaco	29 Jul 08
7.11	0.8	Fiona	May	GBR/ITA	12.12.69	2	EC	Budapest	22 Aug 98
		(30)							
7.11	1.3	Anna	Nazarova	RUS	3.2.86	1	Mosc Ch	Moskva	20 Jun 12
7.10	1.6	Chelsea	Hayes	USA	9.2.88	2	NC/OT	Eugene	1 Jul 12
7.09 WR	0.0	Vilhelmina	Bardauskiené	LTU	15.6.53	Q	EC	Praha	29 Aug 78
7.09	1.5	Ljudmila	Ninova	AUT	25.6.60	1	GP II	Sevilla	5 Jun 94
7.08	0.5	Marieta	Ilcu ¶	ROU	16.10.62	1	RumIC	Pitesti	25 Jun 89
7.08	1.9	Anastasiya	Mironchik-Ivanova	BLR	13.4.89	1		Minsk	12 Jun 12
7.07	0.0	Svetlana	Zorina	RUS	2.2.60	1		Krasnodar	15 Aug 87
7.07	0.5	Yelena	Sokolova	RUS	23.7.86	2	OG	London (OS)	8 Aug 12
7.06	0.4	Tatyana	Kolpakova	KGZ	18.10.59	1	OG	Moskva	31 Jul 80
7.06	-0.1	Niurka	Montalvo	CUB/ESP	4.6.68	1	WCh	Sevilla	23 Aug 99
		(40)							
7.06		Tatyana	Ter-Mesrobyan	RUS	12.5.68	1		Sankt Peterburg	22 May 02
7.05	0.6	Lyudmila	Galkina	RUS	20.1.72	1	WCh	Athína	9 Aug 97
7.05	-0.4	Eunice	Barber	FRA	17.11.74	1	WAF	Monaco	14 Sep 03
7.05	1.1	Darya	Klishina	RUS	15.1.91	1	EU23	Ostrava	17 Jul 11
7.04	0.5	Brigitte	Wujak'	GDR	6.3.55	2	OG	Moskva	31 Jul 80
7.04	0.9	Tatyana	Proskuryakova'	RUS	13.1.56	1		Kyiv	25 Aug 83
7.04	2.0	Yelena	Yatsuk	UKR	16.3.61	1	Znam	Moskva	8 Jun 85
7.04	0.3	Carol	Lewis	USA	8.8.63	5	WK	Zürich	21 Aug 85
7.04	1.5	Sosthene	Moguenara	GER	17.10.89	1		Weinheim	2 Aug 13
7.03	0.6	Níki	Xánthou	GRE	11.10.73	1		Bellinzona	18 Aug 97
7.03i	-	Dawn	Burrell	USA	1.11.73	1	WI	Lisboa	10 Mar 01
7.03	1.7	Janay	DeLoach-Soukup	USA	12.10.85	*	NC/OT	Eugene	1 Jul 12
		(52)	100th woman 6.92, 200th 6.81, 300th 6.75, 400th 6.69, 500th 6.64						
Drugs disquailification									
7.03	0.1		Xiong Qiying ¶	CHN	14.10.67	Q	NG	Shanghai	21 Oct 97
Wind assisted			*Performances to 7.35, performers to 7.05*						
7.63A	2.1	Heike	Drechsler	GER	16.12.64	1		Sestriere	21 Jul 92
7.45	2.6		Joyner-Kersee			1	NC/OT	Indianapolis	23 Jul 88
7.39	2.6		Drechsler			1		Padova	15 Sep 91
7.39	2.9		Drechsler			1	Expo	Sevilla	6 Jun 92
7.39A	3.3		Drechsler			2		Sestriere	31 Jul 94
7.36	2.2		Chistyakova			1	Znam	Volgograd	11 Jun 89
7.35	3.4		Drechsler			1	NC	Jena	29 Jun 86
7.23A	4.3	Fiona	May	ITA	12.12.69	1		Sestriere	29 Jul 95

Mark	Wind	Name		Nat	Born	Pos	Meet	Venue	Date
7.22	4.3	Anastasiya	Mironchik-Ivanova	BLR	13.4.89	1	NC	Grodno	6 Jul 12
7.19A	3.7	Susen	Tiedtke ¶	GER	23.1.69	1		Sestriere	28 Jul 93
7.17	3.6	Eva	Murková	SVK	29.5.62	1		Nitra	26 Aug 84
7.15	2.8	Janay	DeLoach-Soukup	USA	12.10.85	Q	NC/OT	Eugene	29 Jun 12
7.14A	4.5	Marieke	Veltman	USA	18.9.71	2		Sestriere	29 Jul 95
7.14	2.2	Blessing	Okagbare	NGR	9.10.88	2	DL	Doha	10 May 13
7.12A	5.8	Níki	Xánthou	GRE	11.10.73	3		Sestriere	29 Jul 95
7.12A	4.3	Nicole	Boegman	AUS	5.3.67	4		Sestriere	29 Jul 95
7.09	2.9	Renata	Nielsen	DEN	18.5.66	2		Sevilla	5 Jun 94
7.08	2.2	Lyudmila	Galkina	RUS	20.1.72	1		Thessaloniki	23 Jun 99
7.07A	5.6	Valentina	Uccheddu	ITA	26.10.66	5		Sestriere	29 Jul 95
7.07A	2.7	Sharon	Couch	USA	13.9.67	1		El Paso	12 Apr 97
7.07A	w	Erica	Johansson	SWE	5.2.74	1		Vygieskraal	15 Jan 00
7.06	3.4		Ma Miaolan	CHN	18.1.70	1	NG	Beijing	10 Sep 93

Best at low altitude:
7.06 0.8 Maggi ¶ 1 Milano 3 Jun 03 | 7.12w 3.4 May 1 NC Bologna 25 May 96
7.17w 2.6 1 São Paulo 13 Apr 02

Ancillary marks – other marks during series (to 7.34/7.36w)
7.45 1.0 Chistyakova 11 Jun 88 | 7.47Aw 3.1 Drechsler 21 Jul 92 | 7.38w 2.2 Chistyakova 11 Jun 88
7.37 Drechsler 9 Jul 88 | 7.39Aw 3.1 Drechsler 21 Jul 92 | 7.36w Joyner-Kersee 31 Jul 94

TRIPLE JUMP

Mark	Wind	Name		Nat	Born	Pos	Meet	Venue	Date
15.50 WR	0.9	Inessa	Kravets ¶	UKR	5.10.66	1	WCh	Göteborg	10 Aug 95
15.39	0.5	Françoise	Mbango	CMR	14.4.76	1	OG	Beijing	17 Aug 08
15.36i		Tatyana	Lebedeva	RUS	21.7.76	1	WI	Budapest	6 Mar 04
15.34	-0.5		Lebedeva			1		Iráklio	4 Jul 04
15.33	-0.1		Kravets			1	OG	Atlanta	31 Jul 96
15.33	1.2		Lebedeva			1	Athl	Lausanne	6 Jul 04
15.32	0.5		Lebedeva			1	Super	Yokohama	9 Sep 00
15.32	0.9	Hrisopiyi	Devetzí ¶	GRE	2.1.76	Q	OG	Athína	21 Aug 04
15.32	0.5		Lebedeva			2	OG	Beijing	17 Aug 08
15.31	0.0	Caterine	Ibargüen	COL	12.2.84	1	Herc	Monaco	18 Jul 14
15.30	0.6		Mbango			1	OG	Athína	23 Aug 04
15.29	0.3	Yamilé	Aldama	CUB/SUD/GBR	14.8.72	1	GGala	Roma	11 Jul 03
15.28	0.3		Aldama			1	GP	Linz	2 Aug 04
15.28	0.9	Yargelis	Savigne	CUB	13.11.84	1	WCh	Osaka	31 Aug 07
15.27	1.3		Aldama			1	GP	London (CP)	8 Aug 03
15.25	-0.8		Lebedeva			1	WCh	Edmonton	10 Aug 01
15.25	-0.1		Devetzí			2	OG	Athína	23 Aug 04
15.25	1.7	Olga	Rypakova	KAZ	30.11.84	1	C.Cup	Split	4 Sep 10
15.23	0.8		Lebedeva			1		Réthimno	23 Jun 04
15.23	0.6		Lebedeva			1	Tsik	Athína	3 Jul 06
15.23	1.6		Devetzí			3	OG	Beijing	17 Aug 08
15.22	1.5		Devetzí			1		Thessaloníki	9 Jul 08
15.21	1.2		Aldama			2		Réthimno	23 Jun 04
15.20	0.0	Sarka	Kaspárková	CZE	20.5.71	1	WCh	Athína	4 Aug 97
15.20	-0.3	Tereza	Marinova (10)	BUL	5.9.77	1	OG	Sydney	24 Sep 00
15.20	1.3		Savigne			1	Vard	Réthimno	14 Jul 08
15.19	0.5		Lebedeva			1	Athl	Lausanne	11 Jul 06
15.18	0.3	Iva	Prandzheva ¶	BUL	15.2.72	2	WCh	Göteborg	10 Aug 95
15.18	-0.2		Lebedeva			1	WCh	Saint-Denis	26 Aug 03
15.16	0.1	Rodica	Mateescu ¶	ROU	13.3.71	2	WCh	Athína	4 Aug 97
15.16i WIR	-	Ashia	Hansen	GBR	5.12.71	1	EI	Valencia	28 Feb 98
15.16	0.7	Trecia	Smith	JAM	5.11.75	2	GP	Linz	2 Aug 04
		(32/14)							
15.14	1.9	Nadezhda	Alekhina	RUS	22.9.78	1	NC	Cheboksary	26 Jul 09
15.09 WR	0.5	Anna	Biryukova	RUS	27.9.67	1	WCh	Stuttgart	21 Aug 93
15.09	-0.5	Inna	Lasovskaya	RUS	17.12.69	1	ECCp-A	Valencia	31 May 97
15.08i		Marija	Sestak	SLO	17.4.79	1		Athína (P)	13 Feb 08
15.07	-0.6	Paraskeví	Tsiamíta	GRE	10.3.72	Q	WCh	Sevilla	22 Aug 99
15.03i		Iolanda	Chen	RUS	26.7.61	1	WI	Barcelona	11 Mar 95
		(20)							
15.03	1.9	Magdelin	Martinez	ITA	10.2.76	1		Roma	26 Jun 04
15.02	0.9	Anna	Pyatykh	RUS	4.4.81	3	EC	Göteborg	8 Sep 06
15.00	1.2	Kène	Ndoye	SEN	20.11.78	2		Iráklio	4 Jul 04
14.99	0.2	Olha	Saladukha	UKR	4.6.83	1	EC	Helsinki	29 Jun 12
14.98	1.8	Sofia	Bozhanova ¶	BUL	4.10.67	1		Stara Zagora	16 Jul 94
14.98	0.2	Baya	Rahouli	ALG	27.7.79	1	MedG	Almeria	1 Jul 05
14.96	0.7	Yelena	Hovorova	UKR	18.9.73	4	OG	Sydney	24 Sep 00
14.94i	–	Cristina	Nicolau	ROU	9.8.77	1	NC	Bucuresti	5 Feb 00

Mark	Wind	Name		Nat	Born	Pos	Meet	Venue	Date
14.94i		Oksana	Udmurtova	RUS	1.2.82	1		Tartu	20 Feb 08
14.90	1.0		Xie Limei	CHN	27.6.86	1		Urumqi	20 Sep 07
		(30)							
14.89	0.6	Yekaterina	Koneva	RUS	25.9.88	2	Herc	Monaco	18 Jul 14
14.85	1.2	Viktoriya	Gurova	RUS	22.5.82	3	NC	Kazan	19 Jul 08
14.83i	-	Yelena	Lebedenko	RUS	16.1.71	1		Samara	1 Feb 01
14.83	0.5	Yelena	Oleynikova	RUS	9.12.76	1	Odlozil	Praha	17 Jun 02
14.79	1.7	Irina	Mushayilova	RUS	6.1.67	1	DNG	Stockholm	5 Jul 93
14.78i		Adelina	Gavrila	ROU	26.11.78	1		Bucuresti	3 Feb 08
14.76	0.9	Galina	Chistyakova	RUS	26.7.62	1	Spitzen	Luzern	27 Jun 95
14.76	1.1	Gundega	Sproge ¶	LAT	12.12.72	3		Sheffield	29 Jun 97
14.76	0.4	Kseniya	Detsuk	BLR	23.4.86	*	NCp	Brest	26 May 12
14.72	1.8		Huang Qiuyan	CHN	25.1.80	1	NG	Guangzhou	22 Nov 01
		(40)							
14.72		Paraskeví	Papahrístou	GRE	17.4.89	1	Veniz	Haniá	11 Jun 11
14.71	2.0	Hanna	Knyazyeva-Minenko	UKR/ISR	25.9.89	1	NC	Yalta	15 Jun 12
14.71	1.4	Athanasía	Pérra	GRE	2.2.83	1	NC	Athína	16 Jun 12
14.70i		Oksana	Rogova	RUS	7.10.78	1		Volgograd	6 Feb 02
14.69	1.2	Anja	Valant	SLO	8.9.77	3		Kalamáta	4 Jun 00
14.69	1.2	Simona	La Mantia	ITA	14.4.83	1		Palermo	22 May 05
14.69	2.0	Teresa	N'zola Meso	ANG/FRA	30.11.83	1	ECp-S	München	23 Jun 07
14.68i		Anastasiya	Taranova-Potapova	RUS	6.9.85	1	EI	Torino	8 Mar 09
14.67	1.2	Ólga	Vasdéki	GRE	26.9.73	1	Veniz	Haniá	28 Jul 99
14.67	1.5	Natalya	Kutyakova	RUS	28.11.86	1		Huelva	2 Jun 11
14.67	0.4	Mabel	Gay	CUB	5.5.83	4	WCh	Daegu	1 Sep 11
		(51)	100th woman 14.43, 200th 14.13, 300th 13.95, 400th 13.79, 500th 13.67						

Wind assisted *Performances to 15.14, performers to 14.68*

Mark	Wind	Name		Nat	Born	Pos	Meet	Venue	Date
15.24A	4.2	Magdelin	Martinez	ITA	10.2.76	1		Sestriere	1 Aug 04
15.17	2.4	Anna	Pyatykh	RUS	4.4.81	2	SGP	Athína	3 Jul 06
15.10	2.7	Keila	Costa	BRA	6.2.83	1		Uberlandia	6 May 07
15.06	2.6	Olga	Saladukha	UKR	4.6.83	1	DNG	Stockholm	29 Jul 11
14.99	6.8	Yelena	Hovorova	UKR	18.9.73	1	WUG	Palma de Mallorca	11 Jul 99
14.84	4.1	Galina	Chistyakova	RUS	26.7.62	1		Innsbruck	28 Jun 95
14.83	8.3		Ren Ruiping	CHN	1.2.76	1	NC	Taiyuan	21 May 95
14.83	2.2	Heli	Koivula-Kruger	FIN	27.6.75	2	EC	München	10 Aug 02
14.81	2.4	Kseniya	Detsuk	BLR	23.4.86	1	NCp	Brest	26 May 12
14.78	2.7	Kimberly	Williams	JAM	3.11.88	3	Pre	Eugene	1 Jun 13
14.77	2.3	Paraskeví	Papahrístou	GRE	17.4.89	1		Ankara	5 Jun 12
14.75	4.2	Jelena	Blazevica	LAT	11.5.70	1	v2N	Kaunas	23 Aug 97
14.71	2.5	Simona	La Mantia	ITA	14.4.83	1		Roma	25 Jun 04

Best outdoor mark for athlete with all-time best indoors

Mark	Wind	Name	Pos	Meet	Venue	Date	Mark	Wind	Name	Pos	Meet	Venue	Date
15.15	1.7	Hansen	1	GPF	Fukuoka	13 Sep 97	14.85	1.4	Udmurtova	1		Padova	31 Aug 08
15.03	1.1	Sestak	6	OG	Beijing	17 Aug 08	14.75	1.1	Gavrila	3	GP II	Rieti	7 Sep 03
14.97WR	0.9	Chen	1	NC	Moskva	18 Jun 93	14.70	1.3	Nicolau	1	EU23	Göteborg	1 Aug 99

Ancillary marks – other marks during series (to 15.19)

Mark	Wind	Name	Date	Mark	Wind	Name	Date	Mark	Wind	Name	Date
15.30	0.5	Mbango	23 Aug 04	15.28	-0.3	Ledebeva	4 Jul 04	15.25i		Ledebeva	6 Mar 04
15.21	-0.2	Mbango	23 Aug 04	15.19	1.0	Lebedeva	3 Jul 06	15.19	1.3	Mbango	17 Aug 08

SHOT

Mark	Name		Nat	Born	Pos	Meet	Venue	Date
22.63 WR	Natalya	Lisovskaya	RUS	16.7.62	1	Znam	Moskva	7 Jun 87
22.55		Lisovskaya			1	NC	Tallinn	5 Jul 88
22.53 WR		Lisovskaya			1		Sochi	27 May 84
22.53		Lisovskaya			1		Kyiv	14 Aug 88
22.50i	Helena	Fibingerová	CZE	13.7.49	1		Jablonec	19 Feb 77
22.45 WR	Ilona	Slupianek' ¶	GDR	24.9.56	1		Potsdam	11 May 80
22.41		Slupianek			1	OG	Moskva	24 Jul 80
22.40		Slupianek			1		Berlin	3 Jun 83
22.38		Slupianek			1		Karl-Marx-Stadt	25 May 80
22.36 WR		Slupianek			1		Celje	2 May 80
22.34		Slupianek			1		Berlin	7 May 80
22.34		Slupianek			1	NC	Cottbus	18 Jul 80
22.32 WR		Fibingerová			1		Nitra	20 Aug 77
22.24		Lisovskaya			1	OG	Seoul	1 Oct 88
22.22		Slupianek			1		Potsdam	13 Jul 80
22.19	Claudia	Losch	FRG	10.1.60	1		Hainfeld	23 Aug 87
22.14i		Lisovskaya			1	NC	Penza	7 Feb 87
22.13		Slupianek			1		Split	29 Apr 80
22.06		Slupianek			1		Berlin	15 Aug 78
22.06		Lisovskaya			1		Moskva	6 Aug 88
22.05		Slupianek			1	OD	Berlin	28 May 80

Mark	Wind	Name		Nat	Born	Pos	Meet	Venue	Date
22.05			Slupianek			1		Potsdam	31 May 80
22.04			Slupianek			1		Potsdam	4 Jul 79
22.04			Slupianek			1		Potsdam	29 Jul 79
21.99 WR			Fibingerová			1		Opava	26 Sep 76
21.98			Slupianek			1		Berlin	17 Jul 79
21.96			Fibingerová			1	GS	Ostrava	8 Jun 77
21.96			Lisovskaya			1	Drz	Praha	16 Aug 84
21.96			Lisovskaya			1		Vilnius	28 Aug 88
21.95			Lisovskaya			1	IAC	Edinburgh	29 Jul 88
		(30/4)							
21.89 WR		Ivanka	Khristova	BUL	19.11.41	1		Belmeken	4 Jul 76
21.86		Marianne	Adam	GDR	19.9.51	1	v URS	Leipzig	23 Jun 79
21.76			Li Meisu	CHN	17.4.59	1		Shijiazhuang	23 Apr 88
21.73		Natalya	Akhrimenko	RUS	12.5.55	1		Leselidze	21 May 88
21.70i		Nadezhda	Ostapchuk ¶	BLR	12.10.80	1	NC	Mogilyov	12 Feb 10
21.69		Viktoriya	Pavlysh ¶	UKR	15.1.69	1	EC	Budapest	20 Aug 98
		(10)							
21.66			Sui Xinmei ¶	CHN	29.1.65	1		Beijing	9 Jun 90
21.61		Verzhinia	Veselinova	BUL	18.11.57	1		Sofia	21 Aug 82
21.60i		Valentina	Fedyushina	UKR	18.2.65	1		Simferopol	28 Dec 91
21.58		Margitta	Droese/Pufe	GDR	10.9.52	1		Erfurt	28 May 78
21.57 @		Ines	Müller'	GDR	2.1.59	1		Athína	16 May 88
		21.45				1		Schwerin	4 Jun 86
21.53		Nunu	Abashidze ¶	UKR	27.3.55	2	Izv	Kyiv	20 Jun 84
21.52			Huang Zhihong	CHN	7.5.65	1	NC	Beijing	27 Jun 90
21.46		Larisa	Peleshenko ¶	RUS	29.2.64	1	Kuts	Moskva	26 Aug 00
21.45 WR		Nadezhda	Chizhova	RUS	29.9.45	1		Varna	29 Sep 73
21.43		Eva	Wilms	FRG	28.7.52	2	HB	München	17 Jun 77
		(20)	*@ competitive meeting, but unsanctioned by GDR federation*						
21.42		Svetlana	Krachevskaya'	RUS	23.11.44	2	OG	Moskva	24 Jul 80
21.31 @		Heike	Hartwig'	GDR	30.12.62	2		Athína	16 May 88
		21.27				1		Haniá	22 May 88
21.27		Liane	Schmuhl	GDR	29.6.61	1		Cottbus	26 Jun 82
21.24		Valerie	Adams	NZL	6.10.84	1	WCh	Daegu	29 Aug 11
21.22		Astrid	Kumbernuss	GDR/GER	5.2.70	1	WCh	Göteborg	5 Aug 95
21.21		Kathrin	Neimke	GDR	18.7.66	2	WCh	Roma	5 Sep 87
21.19		Helma	Knorscheidt	GDR	31.12.56	1		Berlin	24 May 84
21.15i		Irina	Korzhanenko ¶	RUS	16.5.74	1	NC	Moskva	18 Feb 99
21.10		Heidi	Krieger	GDR	20.7.65	1	EC	Stuttgart	26 Aug 86
21.06		Svetlana	Krivelyova ¶	RUS	13.6.69	1	OG	Barcelona	7 Aug 92
		(30)							
21.05		Zdenka	Silhavá' ¶	CZE	15.6.54	2	NC	Praha	23 Jul 83
21.01		Ivanka	Petrova-Stoycheva	BUL	3.2.51	1	NC	Sofia	28 Jul 79
21.00		Mihaela	Loghin	ROU	1.6.52	1		Formia	30 Jun 84
21.00		Cordula	Schulze	GDR	11.9.59	4	OD	Potsdam	21 Jul 84
20.96		Belsy	Laza	CUB	5.6.67	1		Ciudad de México	2 May 92
20.95		Elena	Stoyanova ¶	BUL	23.1.52	2	Balk	Sofia	14 Jun 80
20.91		Svetla	Mitkova	BUL	17.6.64	1		Sofia	24 May 87
20.80		Sona	Vasícková	CZE	14.3.62	1		Praha	2 Jun 88
20.72		Grit	Haupt/Hammer	GDR	4.6.66	3		Neubrandenburg	11 Jun 87
20.70		Natalya	Mikhnevich' ¶	BLR	25.5.82	2	NC	Grodno	8 Jul 08
		(40)							
20.61		María Elena	Sarría	CUB	14.9.54	1		La Habana	22 Jul 82
20.61		Yanina	Korolchik' ¶	BLR	26.12.76	1	WCh	Edmonton	5 Aug 01
20.60		Marina	Antonyuk	RUS	12.5.62	1		Chelyabinsk	10 Aug 86
20.54			Zhang Liuhong	CHN	16.1.69	1	NC	Beijing	5 Jun 94
20.53		Iris	Plotzitzka	FRG	7.1.66	1	ASV	Köln	21 Aug 88
20.50i		Christa	Wiese	GDR	25.12.67	2	NC	Senftenberg	12 Feb 89
20.48		Yevgeniya	Kolodko	RUS	2.7.90	2	OG	London (OS)	6 Aug 12
20.47		Nina	Isayeva	RUS	6.7.50	1		Bryansk	28 Aug 82
20.47			Cong Yuzhen	CHN	22.1.63	2	IntC	Tianjin	3 Sep 88
20.44		Tatyana	Orlova	BLR	19.7.55	1		Staiki	28 May 83
		(50)	100th woman 19.69, 200th 18.81, 300th 18.16, 400th 17.74, 500th 17.45						

Best outdoor marks

21.58	Ostapchuk ¶	1	Minsk	18 Jul 12
21.08	Fedyushina	1	Leselidze	15 May 88
20.82	Korzhanenko ¶	1	Rostov na Donu	30 May 98
	21.06 drugs dq	(1) OG	Athína	18 Aug 04

Ancillary marks – other marks during series (to 22.09)

22.60	Lisovskaya (WR)	7 Jun 87
22.40	Lisovskaya	14 Aug 88
22.34	Slupianek	11 May 80
22.33	Slupianek	2 May 80
22.20	Slupianek	13 Jul 80
22.19	Lisovskaya	5 Jul 88
22.14	Slupianek	25 May 80
22.14	Slupianek	13 Jul 80
22.12	Slupianek	13 Jul 80
22.11	Slupianek	7 May 80
22.10	Slupianek	25 May 80
22.09	Slupianek	7 May 80

Mark Wind		Name	Nat	Born	Pos	Meet	Venue	Date
DISCUS								
76.80 WR	Gabriele	Reinsch	GDR	23.9.63	1	v ITA	Neubrandenburg	9 Jul 88
74.56 WR	Zdenka	Silhavá' ¶	CZE	15.6.54	1		Nitra	26 Aug 84
74.56	Ilke	Wyludda	GDR	28.3.69	1	NC	Neubrandenburg	23 Jul 89
74.44		Reinsch			1		Berlin	13 Sep 88
74.40		Wyludda			2		Berlin	13 Sep 88
74.08	Diana	Gansky'	GDR	14.12.63	1	v USSR	Karl-Marx-Stadt	20 Jun 87
73.90		Gansky			1	ECp	Praha	27 Jun 87
73.84	Daniela	Costian ¶	ROU	30.4.65	1		Bucuresti	30 Apr 88
73.78		Costian			1		Bucuresti	24 Apr 88
73.42		Reinsch			1		Karl-Marx-Stadt	12 Jun 88
73.36 WR	Irina	Meszynski	GDR	24.3.62	1	Drz	Praha	17 Aug 84
73.32		Gansky			1		Neubrandenburg	11 Jun 87
73.28	Galina	Savinkova'	RUS	15.7.53	1	NC	Donetsk	8 Sep 84
73.26 WR		Savinkova			1		Leselidze	21 May 83
73.26		Sachse/Gansky			1		Neubrandenburg	6 Jun 86
73.24		Gansky			1		Leipzig	29 May 87
73.22	Tsvetanka	Khristova ¶	BUL	14.3.62	1		Kazanlak	19 Apr 87
73.10	Gisela	Beyer	GDR	16.7.60	1	OD	Berlin	20 Jul 84
73.04		Gansky			1		Potsdam	6 Jun 87
73.04		Wyludda			1	ECp	Gateshead	5 Aug 89
72.96		Savinkova			1	v GDR	Erfurt	23 Jun 85
72.94		Gansky			2	v ITA	Neubrandenburg	9 Jul 88
72.92	Martina	Opitz/Hellmann	GDR	12.12.60	1	NC	Potsdam	20 Aug 87
72.90		Costian			1		Bucuresti	14 May 88
72.78		Hellmann			2		Neubrandenburg	11 Jun 87
72.78		Reinsch			1	OD	Berlin	29 Jun 88
72.72		Wyludda			1		Neubrandenburg	23 Jun 89
72.70		Wyludda			1	NC-j	Karl-Marx-Stadt	15 Jul 88
72.54		Gansky			1	NC	Rostock	25 Jun 88
72.52		Hellmann			1		Frohburg	15 Jun 86
72.52		Khristova			1	BGP	Budapest	11 Aug 86
	(31/10)							
72.14	Galina	Murashova	LTU	22.12.55	2	Drz	Praha	17 Aug 84
71.80 WR	Maria	Vergova/Petkova	BUL	3.11.50	1	NC	Sofia	13 Jul 80
71.68		Xiao Yanling ¶	CHN	27.3.68	1		Beijing	14 Mar 92
71.58	Ellina	Zvereva' ¶	BLR	16.11.60	1	Znam	Leningrad	12 Jun 88
71.50 WR	Evelin	Schlaak/Jahl	GDR	28.3.56	1		Potsdam	10 May 80
71.30	Larisa	Korotkevich	RUS	3.1.67	1	RusCp	Sochi	29 May 92
71.22	Ria	Stalman	NED	11.12.51	1		Walnut	15 Jul 84
71.08	Sandra	Perkovic	CRO	21.6.90	1	EC	Zürich	16 Aug 14
70.88	Hilda Elia	Ramos ¶	CUB	1.9.64	1		La Habana	8 May 92
70.80	Larisa	Mikhalchenko	UKR	16.5.63	1		Kharkov	18 Jun 88
	(20)							
70.68	Maritza	Martén	CUB	16.8.63	1	Ib Am	Sevilla	18 Jul 92
70.50 WR	Faina	Melnik	RUS	9.6.45	1	Znam	Sochi	24 Apr 76
70.34 @	Silvia	Madetzky	GDR	24.6.62	3		Athína	16 May 88
	69.34				1		Halle	26 Jun 87
70.02	Natalya	Sadova ¶	RUS	15.7.72	1		Thessaloniki	23 Jun 99
69.86	Valentina	Kharchenko	RUS	.49	1		Feodosiya	16 May 81
69.72	Svetla	Mitkova	BUL	17.6.64	2	NC	Sofia	15 Aug 87
69.68	Mette	Bergmann	NOR	9.11.62	1		Florø	27 May 95
69.51	Franka	Dietzsch	GER	22.1.68	1		Wiesbaden	8 May 99
69.50	Florenta	Craciunescu'	ROU	7.5.55	1	Balk	Stara Zagora	2 Aug 85
69.17	Gia	Lewis-Smallwood	USA	1.4.79	1	Déca	Angers	30 Aug 14
	(30)							
69.14	Irina	Yatchenko ¶	BLR	31.10.65	1		Staiki	31 Jul 04
69.08	Carmen	Romero	CUB	6.10.50	1	NC	La Habana	17 Apr 76
69.08	Mariana	Ionescu/Lengyel	ROU	14.4.53	1		Constanta	19 Apr 86
68.92	Sabine	Engel	GDR	21.4.54	1	v URS,POL	Karl-Marx-Stadt	25 Jun 77
68.89	Nadine	Müller	GER	21.11.85	1	ECp-w	Bar	18 Mar 12
68.80A	Nicoleta	Grasu	ROU	11.9.71	1		Poiana Brasov	7 Aug 99
68.64	Margitta	Pufe'	GDR	10.9.52	1	ISTAF	Berlin	17 Aug 79
68.62		Yu Hourun	CHN	9.7.64	1		Beijing	6 May 88
68.62		Hou Xuemei	CHN	27.2.62	1	IntC	Tianjin	4 Sep 88
68.60	Nadezhda	Kugayevskikh	RUS	19.4.60	1		Oryol	30 Aug 83
	(40)							
68.58	Lyubov	Zverkova	RUS	14.6.55	1	Izv	Kyiv	22 Jun 84
68.52	Beatrice	Faumuiná	NZL	23.10.74	1	Bisl	Oslo	4 Jul 97

Mark	Wind	Name		Nat	Born	Pos	Meet	Venue	Date
68.38		Olga	Burova'	RUS	17.9.63	2	RusCp	Sochi	29 May 92
68.18		Tatyana	Lesovaya	KAZ	24.4.56	1		Alma-Ata	23 Sep 82
68.18		Irina	Khval	RUS	17.5.62	1		Moskva	8 Jul 88
68.18		Barbara	Hechevarría	CUB	6.8.66	2		La Habana	17 Feb 89
68.03		Yarelis	Barrios	CUB	12.7.83	1	NC	La Habana	22 Mar 12
67.99		Dani	Samuels	AUS	26.5.88	1	Werfer	Wiesbaden	10 May 14
67.98			Li Yanfeng	CHN	15.5.79	1		Schönebeck	5 Jun 11
67.96		Argentina	Menis	ROU	19.7.48	1	RomIC	Bucuresti	15 May 76
		(50)	100th woman 65.90, 200th 63.66, 300th 61.80, 400th 59.92, 500th 58.88						

Unofficial meeting: Berlin 6 Sep 88: 1. Martina Hellmann 78.14, 2. Ilke Wyludda 75.36

Downhill: 69.44		Suzy	Powell	USA	3.9.76	1		La Jolla	27 Apr 02

Drugs disqualification:

70.69		Darya	Pishchalnikova ¶	RUS	19.7.85	(1)	NC	Cheboksary	5 Jul 12

Ancillary marks – other marks during series (to 72.92)

73.32	Reinsch	13 Sep 88	73.28	Gansky	27 Jun 87	73.10	Reinsch	9 Jul 88
73.28	Gansky	11 Jun 87	73.16	Wyludda	13 Sep 88	73.06	Gansky	27 Jun 87
						72.92	Hellmann	20 Aug 87

HAMMER

Mark	Wind	Name		Nat	Born	Pos	Meet	Venue	Date
79.58	WR	Anita	Wlodarczyk	POL	8.8.85	1	ISTAF	Berlin	31 Aug 14
79.42	WR	Betty	Heidler	GER	14.10.83	1		Halle	21 May 11
78.80		Tatyana	Lysenko ¶	RUS	9.10.83	1	WCh	Moskva	16 Aug 13
78.76			Wlodarczyk			1	EC	Zürich	15 Aug 14
78.69		Oksana	Menkova	BLR	28.3.82	1		Minsk	18 Jul 12
78.51			Lysenko			1	NC	Cheboksary	5 Jul 12
78.46			Wlodarczyk			2	WCh	Moskva	16 Aug 13
78.30	WR		Wlodarczyk			1	EAF	Bydgoszcz	6 Jun 10
78.22			Wlodarczyk			1		Dubnica nad Vahom	21 Aug 13
78.19			Menkova			1		Brest	28 Apr 12
78.19			Menkova			1		Minsk	12 Jun 12
78.18			Lysenko			1	OG	London (OS)	10 Aug 12
78.17			Wlodarczyk			1		Cetniewo	26 Jul 14
78.15			Lysenko			1	NC	Moskva	24 Jul 13
78.07			Heidler			1	GS	Ostrava	24 May 12
78.00			Heidler			1	GS	Ostrava	16 Jun 14
77.96	WR		Wlodarczyk			1	WCh	Berlin	22 Aug 09
77.80	WR		Lysenko			1		Tallinn	15 Aug 06
77.68			Wang Zheng	CHN	14.12.87	1		Chengdu	29 Mar 14
77.66			Wlodarczyk			1		Warszawa	23 Aug 14
77.60			Włodarczyk			2	OG	London (OS)	10 Aug 12
77.53			Heidler			1		Fränkisch-Crumbach	12 Jun 11
77.53			Heidler			1		Elstal	9 Sep 11
77.41	WR		Lysenko			1	Znam	Zhukovskiy	24 Jun 06
77.40			Heidler			1	ISTAF	Berlin	11 Sep 11
77.32			Menkova			1		Staiki	29 Jun 08
77.30			Lysenko			1		Adler	22 Apr 07
77.26	WR	Gulfiya	Khanafeyeva ¶	RUS	4.6.82	1	NC	Tula	12 Jun 06
77.24			Heidler			1	Colorful	Daegu	16 May 12
77.22			Heidler			1	GS	Ostrava	30 May 11
		(30/6)							
77.13		Oksana	Kondratyeva	RUS	22.11.85	1	Znam	Zhukovskiy	30 Jun 13
76.99			Zhang Wenxiu ¶	CHN	22.3.86	2	GS	Ostrava	24 May 12
76.90		Martina	Hrasnová' ¶	SVK	21.3.83	1		Trnava	16 May 09
76.83		Kamila	Skolimowska	POL	4.11.82	1	SGP	Doha	11 May 07
		(10)							
76.72		Mariya	Bespalova	RUS	21.5.86	2		Zhukovskiy	23 Jun 12
76.66		Olga	Tsander	BLR	18.5.76	1		Staiki	21 Jul 05
76.63		Yekaterina	Khoroshikh ¶	RUS	21.1.83	2	Znam	Moskva	24 Jun 06
76.62		Yipsi	Moreno	CUB	19.11.80	1	GP	Zagreb	9 Sep 08
76.56		Alena	Matoshko	BLR	23.6.82	2		Minsk	12 Jun 12
76.33		Darya	Pchelnik	BLR	20.12.81	2		Staiki	29 Jun 08
76.21		Yelena	Konevtsova	RUS	11.3.81	3		Sochi	26 May 07
76.17		Anna	Bulgakova	RUS	17.1.88	2	NC	Moskva	24 Jul 13
76.07	WR	Mihaela	Melinte ¶	ROU	27.3.75	1		Rüdlingen	29 Aug 99
76.05		Kathrin	Klaas	GER	6.2.84	5	OG	London (OS)	10 Aug 12
		(20)							
75.73		Amanda	Bingson	USA	20.2.90	1	NC	Des Moines	22 Jun 13
75.73		Sultana	Frizell	CAN	24.10.84	1		Tucson	22 May 14
75.68		Olga	Kuzenkova ¶	RUS	4.10.70	1	NCp	Tula	4 Jun 00
75.09		Yelena	Rigert'	RUS	2.12.83	1	Kuts	Moskva	15 Jul 13

Mark	Wind	Name		Nat	Born	Pos	Meet	Venue	Date
75.08		Ivana	Brkljacic	CRO	25.1.83	2	Kuso	Waszawa	17 Jun 07
75.04		Sultana	Frizell	CAN	24.10.84	1		Tucson	16 Mar 12
74.90			Wang Zheng	CHN	14.12.87	4	WCh	Moskva	16 Aug 13
74.77		Jeneva	McCall/Stevens	USA	28.10.89	2		Dubnica nad Vahom	21 Aug 13
74.66		Manuèla	Montebrun	FRA	13.11.79	1	GP II	Zagreb	11 Jul 05
74.65		Mariya	Smolyachkova	BLR	10.2.85	2		Staiki	19 Jul 08
74.52		Iryna	Sekachova	UKR	21.7.76	1	NC	Kyiv	2 Jul 08
74.39		Joanna	Fiodorow	POL	4.3.89	2	Werfer	Halle	17 May 14
		(30)							
74.21		Hanna	Skydan	UKR	14.5.92	1	NC	Yalta	14 Jun 12
74.20		Jessica	Cosby Toruga	USA	31.5.82	3		Tucson	22 May 14
74.17		Tugçe	Sahutoglu ¶	TUR	1.5.88	1		Izmir	19 May 12
74.10		Iryna	Novozhylova	UKR	7.1.86	1		Kyiv	19 May 12
73.90		Arasay	Thondike	CUB	28.5.86	1		La Habana	18 Jun 09
73.87		Erin	Gilreath	USA	11.10.80	1	NC	Carson	25 Jun 05
73.81		Gwen	Berry	USA	29.6.89	1		Lisle	8 Jun 13
73.74		Jennifer	Dahlgren	ARG	21.4.84	1		Buenos Aires	10 Apr 10
73.64		Rosa	Rodríguez	VEN	2.7.86	1		Barquisimeto	16 May 13
73.61		Amber	Campbell	USA	5.6.81	1		Edmonton	6 Jul 14
		(40)							
73.59		Ester	Balassini	ITA	20.10.77	1	NC	Bressanone	25 Jun 05
73.52		Bianca	Perie	ROU	1.6.90	1	NC	Bucuresti	16 Jul 10
73.44		Éva	Orbán	HUN	29.11.84	2	Werfer	Halle	25 May 13
73.40		Stéphanie	Falzon	FRA	7.1.83	1	NC	Albi	26 Jul 08
73.21		Eileen	O'Keeffe	IRL	31.5.81	1	NC	Dublin	21 Jul 07
73.16		Yunaika	Crawford	CUB	2.11.82	3	OG	Athína	25 Aug 04
73.06			Liu Tingting	CHN	29.10.90	4	Werfer	Halle	17 May 14
72.97		Sophie	Hitchon	GBR	11.7.91	3	ET	Gateshead	23 Jun 13
72.74		Susanne	Keil	GER	18.5.78	1		Nikiti	15 Jul 05
72.55		Kivilcim	Salman-Kaya ¶	TUR	27.3.92	1	NC	Izmir	5 Jul 12
		(50)	100th woman 69.92, 200th 66.80, 300th 64.26, 400th 63.07, 500th 61.84						
Downhill: 75.20		Manuéla	Montebrun	FRA	13.11.79	1		Vineuil	18 May 03

Ancillary marks – other marks during series to 77.56

Mark	Name	Date	Mark	Name	Date	Mark	Name	Date
79.04	Wlodarczyk	31 Aug 14	77.94	Wlodarczyk	31 Aug 14	77.67	Wlodarczyk	6 Jun 10
78.64	Wlodarczyk	31 Aug 14	77.84	Wlodarczyk	26 Jul 14	77.58	Lysenko	16 Aug 13
78.46	Wlodarczyk	31 Aug 14	77.79	Wlodarczyk	16 Aug 13	77.56	Lysenko	10 Aug 12

Drugs disqualification

Mark	Wind	Name		Nat	Born	Pos	Meet	Venue	Date
78.61			Lysenko			(1)		Sochi	26 May 07
77.71			Lysenko			(1)	GS	Ostrava	27 Jun 07
77.36		Gulfiya	Khanafeyeva ¶	RUS	4.6.82	(2)		Sochi	26 May 07
77.33			Zhang Wenxiu ¶	CHN	22.3.86	(1)	AsiG	Incheon	28 Sep 14
74.47		Zalina	Marghieva ¶	MDA	5.2.88	1	Univ Ch	Chisinau	7 May 12

JAVELIN

Mark	Wind	Name		Nat	Born	Pos	Meet	Venue	Date
72.28	WR	Barbora	Spotáková	CZE	30.6.81	1	WAF	Stuttgart	13 Sep 08
71.99		Mariya	Abakumova	RUS	15.1.86	1	WCh	Daegu	2 Sep 11
71.70	WR	Osleidys	Menéndez	CUB	14.11.79	1	WCh	Helsinki	14 Aug 05
71.58			Spotáková			2	WCh	Daegu	2 Sep 11
71.54	WR		Menéndez			1		Réthimno	1 Jul 01
71.53			Menéndez			1	OG	Athína	27 Aug 04
71.42			Spotáková			1	OG	Beijing	21 Aug 08
70.78			Abakumova			2	OG	Beijing	21 Aug 08
70.53			Abakumova			1	ISTAF	Berlin	1 Sep 13
70.20		Christina	Obergföll	GER	22.8.81	1	ECp-S	München	23 Jun 07
70.03			Obergföll			2	WCh	Helsinki	14 Aug 05
69.82			Menéndez			1	WUG	Beijing	29 Aug 01
69.81			Obergföll			1		Berlin (Elstal)	31 Aug 08
69.75			Abakumova			1		Berlin (Elstal)	25 Aug 13
69.57			Obergföll			1	WK	Zürich	8 Sep 11
69.55			Spotáková			1	OG	London (OS)	9 Aug 12
69.53			Menéndez			1	WCh	Edmonton	7 Aug 01
69.48	WR	Trine	Hattestad	NOR	18.4.66	1	Bisl	Oslo	28 Jul 00
69.45			Spotáková			1	Herc	Monaco	22 Jul 11
69.35		Sunette	Viljoen	RSA	6.1.83	1	DL	New York	9 Jun 12
69.34			Abakumova			1	ECp-w	Castellón	16 Mar 13
69.15			Spotáková			1		Zaragoza	31 May 08
69.09			Abakumova			Q	WCh	Moskva	16 Aug 13
69.05			Obergföll			1	WCh	Moskva	18 Aug 13
68.94			Abakumova			1	WK	Zürich	29 Aug 13
68.92			Abakumova			Q	WCh	Berlin	16 Aug 09

Mark	Wind	Name		Nat	Born	Pos	Meet	Venue	Date
68.91			Hattestad			1	OG	Sydney	30 Sep 00
68.89			Abakumova			1	DL	Doha	14 May 10
68.86			Obergföll			1	NC	Kassel	24 Jul 11
68.81		(30/6)	Spotáková			1	Odlozil	Praha	16 Jun 08
68.34		Steffi	Nerius	GER	1.7.72	2		Berlin (Elstal)	31 Aug 08
67.67		Sonia	Bisset	CUB	1.4.71	1		Salamanca	6 Jul 05
67.51		Miréla	Manjani/Tzelíli	GRE	21.12.76	2	OG	Sydney	30 Sep 00
67.32		Linda	Stahl	GER	2.10.85	1	adidas	New York	14 Jun 14
		(10)							
67.29		Hanna	Hatsko-Fedusova	UKR	3.10.90	1	NC	Kirovohrad	26 Jul 14
67.20		Tatyana	Shikolenko	RUS	10.5.68	1	Herc	Monaco	18 Aug 00
67.16		Martina	Ratej	SLO	2.11.81	3	DL	Doha	14 May 10
66.91		Tanja	Damaske	GER	16.11.71	1	NC	Erfurt	4 Jul 99
66.86		Vira	Rebryk	UKR	25.2.89	1	EC	Helsinki	29 Jun 12
66.83		Kimberley	Mickle	AUS	28.12.84	1		Melbourne	22 Mar 14
66.80		Louise	McPaul/Currey	AUS	24.1.69	1		Gold Coast (RB)	5 Aug 00
66.67		Kara	Patterson/Winger	USA	10.4.86	1	NC	Des Moines	25 Jun 10
66.17		Goldie	Sayers	GBR	16.7.82	1	LGP	London (CP)	14 Jul 12
66.15		Madara	Palameika	LAT	18.6.87	1		Jelgava	26 Jun 14
		(20)							
66.10		Kathryn	Mitchell	AUS	10.7.82	2		Adelaide	15 Feb 14
65.91		Nikola	Brejchová'	CZE	25.6.74	1	GP	Linz	2 Aug 04
65.62			Lu Huihui	CHN	26.6.89	1		Zhaoqing	27 Apr 13
65.47			Zhang Li	CHN	17.1.89	1	AsiG	Incheon	1 Oct 14
65.30		Claudia	Coslovich	ITA	26.4.72	1		Ljubljana	10 Jun 00
65.29		Xiomara	Rivero	CUB	22.11.68	1		Santiago de Cuba	17 Mar 01
65.17		Karen	Forkel	GER	24.9.70	2	NC	Erfurt	4 Jul 99
65.11			Li Lingwei	CHN	26.1.89	1		Fuzhou	23 Jun 1210
65.08		Ana Mirela	Termure ¶	ROU	13.1.75	1	NC	Bucuresti	10 Jun 01
64.90		Paula	Huhtaniemi'	FIN	17.2.73	1	NC	Helsinki	10 Aug 03
		(30)							
64.89		Yekaterina	Ivakina	RUS	4.12.64	4	Bisl	Oslo	28 Jul 00
64.87		Kelly	Morgan	GBR	17.6.80	1	NC	Birmingham	14 Jul 02
64.83		Christina	Scherwin	DEN	11.7.76	3	WAF	Stuttgart	9 Sep 06
64.67		Katharina	Molitor	GER	8.11.83	2	NC	Kassel	24 Jul 11
64.62		Joanna	Stone	AUS	4.10.72	2		Gold Coast (RB)	5 Aug 00
64.62		Nikolett	Szabó	HUN	3.3.80	1		Pátra	22 Jul 01
64.61		Oksana	Makarova	RUS	21.7.71	2	ECp	Paris (C)	19 Jun 99
64.51		Monica	Stoian	ROU	25.8.82	4	WCh	Berlin	18 Aug 09
64.50		Liz	Gleadle	CAN	5.12.88	1		Lethbridge	16 May 14
64.49		Valeriya	Zabruskova	RUS	29.7.75	1	Znam	Tula	7 Jun 03
		(40)							
64.46		Dörthe	Friedrich	GER	21.6.73	1	NC	Wattenscheid	7 Jul 02
64.38		Sinta	Ozolina-Kovale	LAT	26.2.88	1		Riga	30 May 13
64.21		Tatjana	Jelaca	SRB	10.8.90	2	EC	Zürich	14 Aug 14
64.19		Kim	Kreiner	USA	26.7.77	1		Fortaleza	16 May 07
64.08		Barbara	Madejczyk	POL	30.9.76	1	ECp-S	Málaga	28 Jun 06
64.07		Mercedes	Chilla	ESP	19.1.80	1		Valencia	12 Jun 10
64.06		Taina	Uppa/Kolkkala	FIN	24.10.76	1		Pihtipudas	23 Jul 00
64.03		Mikaela	Ingberg	FIN	29.7.74	6	ISTAF	Berlin	1 Sep 00
63.92			Wei Jianhua	CHN	23.3.79	1		Beijing	18 Aug 00
63.92		Kelsey-Lee	Roberts	AUS	21.9.91	1		Canberra	8 Feb 14
		(50)	100th woman 61.66, 200th 58.36, 300th 56.56						

Ancillary marks – other marks during series (to 68.80)

71.25	Abakumova	2 Sep 11	69.32	Abakumova	21 Aug 08	68.95	Obergföll	8 Sep 11
69.42	Menéndez	7 Aug 01	69.22	Spotáková	21 Aug 08	68.82	Abakumova	1 Sep 13
69.35	Abakumova	25 Aug 13	69.08	Abakumova	21 Aug 08			

Specification changed from 1 May 1999. See ATHLETICS 2000 for Old specification all-time list.

80.00	WR	Petra	Felke	GDR	30.7.59	1		Potsdam	9 Sep 88

HEPTATHLON

Mark		Name		Nat	Born	Pos	Meet	Venue	Date
7291	WR	Jackie	Joyner-Kersee	USA	3.3.62	1	OG	Seoul	24 Sep 88
		12.69/0.5	1.86 15.80		22.56/1.6		7.27/0.7	45.66 2:08.51	
7215	WR		Joyner-Kersee			1	NC/OT	Indianapolis	16 Jul 88
		12.71/-0.9	1.93 15.65		22.30/ 0.0		7.00/-1.3	50.08 2:20.70	
7158	WR		Joyner-Kersee			1	USOF	Houston	2 Aug 86
		13.18/-0.5	1.88 15.20		22.85/1.2		7.03w/2.9	50.12 2:09.69	
7148	WR		Joyner-Kersee			1	GWG	Moskva	7 Jul 86
		12.85/0.2	1.88 14.76		23.00/0.3		7.01/-0.5	49.86 2:10.02	
7128			Joyner-Kersee			1	WCh	Roma	1 Sep 87
		12.91/0.2	1.90 16.00		22.95/1.2		7.14/0.9	45.68 2:16.29	

Mark Wind	Name			Nat	Born	Pos	Meet	Venue		Date
7044		Joyner-Kersee				1	OG	Barcelona		2 Aug 92
	12.85/-0.9	1.91	14.13		23.12/0.7	7.10/1.3		44.98	2:11.78	
7032	Carolina	Klüft		SWE	2.2.83	1	WCh	Osaka		26 Aug 07
	13.15/0.1	1.95	14.81		23.38/0.3	6.85/1.0		47.98	2:12.56	
7007	Larisa	Nikitina ¶		RUS	29.4.65	1	NC	Bryansk		11 Jun 89
	13.40/1.4	1.89	16.45		23.97/1.1	6.73w/4.0		53.94	2:15.31	
7001		Klüft				1	WCh	Saint-Denis		24 Aug 03
	13.18/-0.4	1.94	14.19		22.98/1.1	6.68/1.0		49.90	2:12.12	
6985	Sabine	Braun		GER	19.6.65	1		Götzis		31 May 92
	13.11/-0.4	1.93	14.84		23.65/2.0	6.63w/2.9		51.62	2:12.67	
6979		Joyner-Kersee				1	NC	San José		24 Jun 87
	12.90/2.0	1.85	15.17		23.02/0.4	7.25/2.3		40.24	2:13.07	
6955	Jessica	Ennis		GBR	28.1.86	1	OG	London (OS)		4 Aug 12
	12.54/1.3	1.86	14.28		22.83/-0.3	6.48/-0.6		47.49	2:08.65	
6952		Klüft				1	OG	Athína		21 Aug 04
	13.21/0.2	1.91	14.77		23.27/-0.1	6.78/0.4		48.89	2:14.15	
6946 WR	Sabine	Paetz'		GDR	16.10.57	1	NC	Potsdam		6 May 84
	12.64/0.3	1.80	15.37		23.37/0.7	6.86/-0.2		44.62	2:08.93	
6942	Ghada	Shouaa		SYR	10.9.72	1		Götzis		26 May 96
	13.78/0.3	1.87	15.64		23.78/0.6	6.77/0.6		54.74	2:13.61	
6935 WR	Ramona	Neubert		GDR	26.7.58	1	v USSR	Moskva		19 Jun 83
	13.42/1.7	1.82	15.25		23.49/0.5	6.79/0.7		49.94	2:07.51	
6910		Joyner				1	MSR	Walnut		25 Apr 86
	12.9/0.0	1.86	14.75		23.24w/2.8	6.85/2.1		48.30	2:14.11	
6906		Ennis				1		Götzis		27 May 12
	12.81/0.0	1.85	14.51		22.88/1.9	6.51/0.8		47.11	2:09.00	
6897		John'				2	wOG	Seoul		24 Sep 88
	12.85/0.5	1.80	16.23		23.65/1.6	6.71/ 0.0		42.56	2:06.14	
6889	Eunice	Barber		FRA	17.11.74	1		Arles		5 Jun 05
	12.62w/2.9	1.91	12.61		24.12/1.2	6.78w/3.4		53.07	2:14.66	
6887		Klüft				1	WCh	Helsinki		7 Aug 05
	13.19/-0.4	1.82	15.02		23.70/-2.5	6.87/0.2		47.20	2:08.89	
6880	Tatyana	Chernova ¶ (10)		RUS	29.1.88	1	WCh	Daegu		30 Aug 11
	13.32/0.9	1.83	14.17		23.50/-1.5	6.61/-0.7		52.95	2:08.04	
6878		Joyner-Kersee				1	NC	New York		13 Jun 91
	12.77	1.89	15.62		23.42	6.97/0.4		43.28	2:22.12	
6875		Nikitina				1	ECp-A	Helmond		16 Jul 89
	13.55/-2.1	1.84	15.99		24.29/-2.1	6.75/-2.5		56.78	2:18.67	
6861		Barber				1	WCh	Sevilla		22 Aug 99
	12.89/-0.5	1.93	12.37		23.57/0.5	6.86/-0.3		49.88	2:15.65	
6859	Natalya	Shubenkova		RUS	25.9.57	1	NC	Kyiv		21 Jun 84
	12.93/1.0	1.83	13.66		23.57/-0.3	6.73/0.4		46.26	2:04.60	
6858	Anke	Vater/Behmer		GDR	5.6.61	3	OG	Seoul		24 Sep 88
	13.20/0.5	1.83	14.20		23.10/1.6	6.68/0.1		44.54	2:04.20	
6847		Nikitina				1	WUG	Duisburg		29 Aug 89
	13.47	1.81	16.12		24.12	6.66		59.28	2:22.07	
6845 WR		Neubert				1	v URS	Halle		20 Jun 82
	13.58/1.8	1.83	15.10		23.14/1.4	6.84w/2.3		42.54	2:06.16	
6845	Irina	Belova ¶		RUS	27.3.68	2	OG	Barcelona		2 Aug 92
	13.25/-0.1	1.88	13.77		23.34/0.2	6.82/0.0		41.90	2:05.08	
	(30/13)									
6832	Lyudmila	Blonska ¶		UKR	9.11.77	2	WCh	Osaka		26 Aug 07
	13.25/0.1	1.92	14.44		24.09/0.3	6.88/1.0		47.77	2:16.68	
6831	Denise	Lewis		GBR	27.8.72	1		Talence		30 Jul 00
	13.13/1.0	1.84	15.07		24.01w/3.6	6.69/-0.4		49.42	2:12.20	
6803	Jane	Frederick		USA	7.4.52	1		Talence		16 Sep 84
	13.27/1.2	1.87	15.49		24.15/1.6	6.43/0.2		51.74	2:13.55	
6778	Nataliya	Dobrynska		UKR	29.5.82	2	EC	Barcelona		31 Jul 10
	13.59/-1.6	1.86	15.88		24.23/-0.2	6.56/0.3		49.25	2:12.06	
6765	Yelena	Prokhorova		RUS	16.4.78	1	NC	Tula		23 Jul 00
	13.54/-2.8	1.82	14.30		23.37/-0.2	6.72/1.0		43.40	2:04.27	
6750		Ma Miaolan		CHN	18.1.70	1	NG	Beijing		12 Sep 93
	13.28/1.5	1.89	14.98		23.86/	6.64/		45.82	2:15.33	
6741	Heike	Drechsler		GER	16.12.64	1		Talence		11 Sep 94
	13.34/-0.3	1.84	13.58		22.84/-1.1	6.95/1.0		40.64	2:11.53	
	(20)									
6735(w)	Hyleas	Fountain		USA	14.1.81	1	NC	Des Moines		26 Jun 10
	12.93w/2.6	1.90	13.73		23.28w/3.3	6.79w/2.7		42.26	2:17.80	
6703	Tatyana	Blokhina		RUS	12.3.70	1		Talence		11 Sep 93
	13.69/-0.6	1.91	14.94		23.95/-0.4	5.99/-0.3		52.16	2:09.65	

Mark	Wind	Name		Nat	Born	Pos	Meet	Venue	Date
6702		Chantal	Beaugeant ¶	FRA	16.2.61	2		Götzis	19 Jun 88
		13.10/1.6 1.78 13.74 23.96w/3.5 6.45/0.2 50.96 2:07.09							
6695		Jane	Flemming	AUS	14.4.65	1	CG	Auckland	28 Jan 90
		13.21/1.4 1.82 13.76 23.62w/2.4 6.57/1.6 49.28 2:12.53							
6683		Jennifer	Oeser	GER	29.11.83	3	EC	Barcelona	31 Jul 10
		13.37/-1.0 1.83 13.82 24.07/-0.3 6.68/-0.3 49.17 2:12.28							
6682		Katarina	Johnson-Thompson	GBR	9.1.93	1		Götzis	1 Jun 14
		13.47/-1.2 1.90 12.17 22.89/1.5 6.70/-0.1 41.44 2:08.16							
6681		Kristina	Savitskaya	RUS	10.6.91	1	NC	Cheboksary	3 Jun 12
		13.52/0.0 1.88 15.27 24.61/0.0 6.65/0.0 46.83 2:14.73							
6660		Ines	Schulz	GDR	10.7.65	3		Götzis	19 Jun 88
		13.56/0.4 1.84 13.95 23.93w/2.8 6.70/0.7 42.82 2:06.31							
6658		Svetla	Dimitrova ¶	BUL	27.1.70	2		Götzis	31 May 92
		13.41/-0.7 1.75 14.72 23.06w/2.4 6.64/1.9 43.84 2:09.60							
6649		Lilli	Schwarzkopf	GER	28.8.83	2	OG	London (OS)	4 Aug 12
		13.26/0.9 1.83 14.77 24.77/0.9 6.30/-0.7 51.73 2:10.50							
6646		Natalya	Grachova	UKR	21.2.52	1	NC	Moskva	2 Aug 82
		(30)							
		13.80 1.80 16.18 23.86 6.65w/3.5 39.42 2:06.59							
6641		Brianne	Theisen-Eaton	CAN	18,12.88	2		Götzis	1 Jun 14
		13.18/-1.2 1.87 13.29 23.52/1.5 6.59/1.3 42.78 2:11.31							
6635		Sibylle	Thiele	GDR	6.3.65	2	GWG	Moskva	7 Jul 86
		13.14/0.6 1.76 16.00 24.18 6.62/1.0 45.74 2:15.30							
6635		Svetlana	Buraga	BLR	4.9.65	3	WCh	Stuttgart	17 Aug 93
		12.95/0.1 1.84 14.55 23.69/0.0 6.58/-0.2 41.04 2:13.65							
6633		Natalya	Roshchupkina	RUS	13.1.78	2	NC	Tula	23 Jul 00
		14.05/-2.8 1.88 14.28 23.47/-0.2 6.45/0.4 44.34 2:07.93							
6623		Judy	Simpson'	GBR	14.11.60	3	EC	Stuttgart	30 Aug 86
		13.05/0.8 1.92 14.73 25.09/0.0 6.56w/2.5 40.92 2:11.70							
6619		Liliana	Nastase	ROU	1.8.62	4	OG	Barcelona	2 Aug 92
		12.86/-0.9 1.82 14.34 23.70/0.2 6.49/-0.3 41.30 2:11.22							
6616		Malgorzata	Nowak'	POL	9.2.59	1	WUG	Kobe	31 Aug 85
		13.27w/4.0 1.95 15.35 24.20/0.0 6.37w/3.9 43.36 2:20.39							
6604		Remigija	Nazaroviene'	LTU	2.6.67	2	URSCh	Bryansk	11 Jun 89
		13.26/1.4 1.86 14.27 24.12/0.7 6.58/0.9 40.94 2:09.98							
6604		Irina	Tyukhay	RUS	14.1.67	3		Götzis	28 May 95
		13.20/-0.7 1.84 14.97 24.33/1.7 6.71/0.5 43.84 2:17.64							
		(40)							
6599A		Jessica	Zelinka	CAN	3.9.81	1	NC	Calgary	28 Jun 12
		12.76/-0.6 1.77 14.74 23.42w/2.1 5.98w/2.9 46.60 2:08.95							
6599		Austra	Skujyté	LTU	12.8.79	5	OG	London (OS)	4 Aug 12
		14.00/0.7 1.92 17.31 25.43/0.9 6.25/-0.6 51.13 2:20.59							
6598		Svetlana	Moskalets	RUS	22.1.69	1	NC	Vladimir	17 Jun 94
		13.20/0.8 1.82 13.78 23.56/0.1 6.74/0.8 42.48 2:14.54							
6591		Svetlana	Sokolova	RUS	9.1.81	1	NC	Tula	23 Jun 04
		13.56/1.1 1.82 15.09 24.02/0.6 6.26/0.3 45.07 2:07.23							
6586		Anna	Melnychenko	UKR	24.4.83	1	WCh	Moskva	13 Aug 13
		13.29/-0.6 1.86 13.85 23.87/0.0 6.49/0.2 41.87 2:09.85							
6577		DeDee	Nathan	USA	20.4.68	1		Götzis	30 May 99
		13.28/-0.1 1.76 14.74 24.23/0.2 6.59/1.6 50.08 2:16.92							
6576		Antoinette	Nana Djimou	FRA	2.8.85	5	OG	London (OS)	4 Aug 12
		12.96/1.3 1.80 14.26 24.72/0.3 6.13/-0.2 55.87 2:15.94							
6573		Rita	Ináncsi	HUN	6.1.71	3		Götzis	29 May 94
		13.66/2.0 1.84 13.94 24.20w/2.5 6.78/1.4 46.28 2:16.02							
6572		Heike	Tischler	GDR	4.2.64	2	EC	Split	31 Aug 90
		14.08/-0.9 1.82 13.73 24.29/0.9 6.22/-0.7 53.24 2:05.50							
6563		Natalya	Sazanovich	BLR	15.8.73	2	OG	Atlanta	28 Jul 96
		13.56/-1.6 1.80 14.52 23.72/-0.3 6.70/1.1 46.00 2:17.92							
		(50) 100th woman 6399, 200th 6200, 300th 6085, 400th 5989, 500th 5895							

Drugs disqualification

Mark	Wind	Name		Nat	Born	Pos	Meet	Venue	Date
6618		Lyudmyla	Yosypenko ¶	UKR	24.9.84	4	OG	London (OS)	4 Aug 12
		13.25/0.9 1.83 13.90 23.68/0.6 6.31/-0.6 49.63 2:13.28							

DECATHLON

Mark	Wind	Name		Nat	Born	Pos	Meet	Venue	Date
8358	WR	Austra	Skujyte	LTU	12.8.79	1		Columbia, MO	15 Apr 05
		12.49/1.6 46.19 3.10 48.78 57.19 14.22w/2.4 6.12/1.6 16.42 1.78 5:15.86							
8150		Marie	Collonvillé	FRA	23.11.73	1		Talence	26 Sep 04
		12.48/0.4 34.69 3.50 47.19 56.15 13.96/0.4 6.18/1.0 11.90 1.80 5:06.09							
7885		Mona	Steigauf	GER	17.1.70	1		Ahlen	21 Sep 97
		12.15/1.2 5.93 12.49 1.73 55.34 13.75/0.2 34.68 3.10 42.24 5:07.95							

IAAF approved order: 100m, DT, PV, JT, 400m / 100mh, LJ, SP, HJ, 1500m. 1997 above was men's order

Mark	Wind	Name	Nat	Born	Pos	Meet	Venue	Date

4 x 100 METRES RELAY

Mark	Nat	Name	Pos	Meet	Venue	Date
40.82	USA	Madison, Felix, Knight, Jeter	1	OG	London (OS)	10 Aug 12
41.29	JAM	Russell, Stewart, Calvert, Fraser-Pryce	1	WCh	Moskva	18 Aug 13
41.37 WR	GDR	Gladisch, Rieger, Auerswald, Göhr	1	WCp	Canberra	6 Oct 85
41.41	JAM	Fraser-Pryce, Simpson, Campbell-Brown, Stewart	2	OG	London (OS)	10 Aug 12
41.47	USA	Gaines, Jones, Miller, Devers	1	WCh	Athína	9 Aug 97
41.49	RUS	Bogoslovskaya, Malchugina, Voronova, Privalova	1	WCh	Stuttgart	22 Aug 93
41.49	USA	Finn, Torrence, Vereen, Devers	2	WCh	Stuttgart	22 Aug 93
41.52	USA	Gaines, Jones, Miller, Devers	1h1	WCh	Athína	8 Aug 97
41.53 WR	GDR	Gladisch, Koch, Auerswald, Göhr	1		Berlin	31 Jul 83
41.55	USA	Brown, Williams, Griffith, Marshall	1	ISTAF	Berlin	21 Aug 87
41.56	USA	B Knight, Felix, Myers, Jeter	1	WCh	Daegu	4 Sep 11
41.58	USA	Brown, Williams, Griffith, Marshall	1	WCh	Roma	6 Sep 87
41.58	USA	L.Williams, Felix, Lee, Jeter	1		Cottbus	8 Aug 09
41.60 WR	GDR	Müller, Wöckel, Auerswald, Göhr	1	OG	Moskva	1 Aug 80
41.61A	USA	Brown, Williams, Cheeseborough, Ashford	1	USOF	USAF Academy	3 Jul 83
41.63	USA	Brown, Williams, Cheeseborough, Ashford	1	v GDR	Los Angeles	25 Jun 83
41.64	USA	Madison, Tarmoh, Knight, L Williams	1h1	OG	London (OS)	9 Aug 12
41.65	USA	Brown, Bolden, Cheeseborough, Ashford	1	OG	Los Angeles	11 Aug 84
41.65	GDR	Gladisch, Koch, Auerswald, Göhr	1	ECp	Moskva	17 Aug 85
41.67	USA	Pierre, Anderson, Townsend, C Williams	1	WK	Zürich	29 Aug 13
		(20 performances by 4 nations) from here just best by nation				
41.78	FRA	Girard, Hurtis, Félix, Arron	1	WCh	Saint-Denis	30 Aug 03
41.92	BAH	Fynes, Sturrup, Davis-Thompson, Ferguson	1	WCh	Sevilla	29 Aug 99
42.04	UKR	Povh, Stuy, Ryemyen, Bryzgina	3	OG	London (OS)	10 Aug 12
42.08mx	BUL	Pavlova, Nuneva, Georgieva, Ivanova	mx		Sofia	8 Aug 84
		42.29 Pencheva, Nuneva, Georgieva, Donkova	1		Sofia	26 Jun 88
42.21	GBR	Philip, Nelson, Onuora, Henry	1	WK	Zürich	28 Aug 14
42.23	CHN	(Sichuan) Xiao Lin, Li Yali, Liu Xiaomei, Li Xuemei (10)	1	NG	Shanghai	23 Oct 97
42.29	BRA	E dos Santos, Silva, Krasucki, R Santos	2h3	WCh	Moskva	18 Aug 13
42.39	NGR	Utondu, Idehen, Opara-Thompson, Onyali	2h2	OG	Barcelona	7 Aug 92
42.40	NED	Ghafoor, Schippers, Van Schagen, Samuel	1	Athl	Lausanne	3 Jul 14
42.54	BEL	Borlée, Mariën, Ouédraogo, Gevaert	2	OG	Beijing	22 Aug 08
42.56	BLR	Nesterenko, Sologub, Nevmerzhitskaya, Dragun	3	WCh	Helsinki	13 Aug 05
42.59	FRG	Possekel, Helten, Richter, Kroniger	2	OG	Montreal	31 Jul 76
42.59	TTO	Durant, Ayhe, R Thomas, Selvon	2h1	WRly	Nassau	24 May 14
42.68	POL	Popowicz, Korczynska, Jeschke, Wedler	3	EC	Barcelona	1 Aug 10
42.89	CUB	Ferrer, López, Duporty, Allen	6	WCh	Stuttgart	22 Aug 93
42.94	SUI	Kambundji, Lavanchy, E.Sprunger, L.Sprunger (20)	3	Athl	Lausanne	3 Jul 14
42.98	CZE/TCH	Sokolová, Soborová, Kocembová, Kratochvilová	1	WK	Zürich	18 Aug 82
42.99A	AUS	Massey, Broadrick, Lambert, Gainsford-Taylor	1		Pietersburg	18 Mar 00
42.99	CAN	Emmanuel, Hyacinthe, S Davis, Bingham	2h2	WCh	Moskva	18 Aug 13
43.03A	COL	M.Murillo, Palacios, Obregón, D Murillo	2	SAm-r	Bogotá	10 Jul 04
43.04	ITA	Pistone, Calí, Arcioni, Alloh	3	ECp-S	Annecy	21 Jun 08
43.07	GRE	Tsóni, Kóffa, Vasarmídou, Thánou	2	MedG	Bari	18 Jun 97
43.19	GHA	Akoto, Twum, Anim, Nsiah	5s1	OG	Sydney	29 Sep 00
43.25A	RSA	Hartman, Moropane, Holtshausen, Seyerling	2		Pietersburg	18 Mar 00
43.28	DOM	M Sánchez, Chala, Mejía, Manzueta	5h1	WCh	Moskva	18 Aug 13
43.35	KAZ	Aleksandrova, Kvast, Miljauskiene, Sevalnikova (30)	2	SPART	Taskent	16 Sep 86
Best at low altitude						
43.03	COL	M.Murillo, Palacios, Obregón, N.González	3h2	WCh	Helsinki	12 Aug 05
43.18	AUS	Wilson, Wells, Robertson, Boyle	5	OG	Montreal	31 Jul 76
One or more athlete susbsequently drugs dq						
41.67	USA	A Williams, Jones ¶, L Williams, Colander	(1)	3-N	München	8 Aug 04
41.67	USA	A Williams, Jones ¶, L Williams, Colander	(1h1)	OG	Athína	26 Aug 04
42.31	TTO	Ahye, Baptiste, Selvon, Hackett #	2h1	OG	London (OS)	9 Aug 12
42.77	CAN	Bailey ¶, Payne, Taylor, Gareau	2	OG	Los Angeles	11 Aug 84

4 x 200 METRES RELAY

Mark	Nat	Name	Pos	Meet	Venue	Date
1:27.46 WR	USA Blue	Jenkins, Colander-Richardson, Perry, M Jones	1	PennR	Philadelphia	29 Apr 00
1:28.15 WR	GDR	Göhr, R.Müller, Wöckel, Koch	1		Jena	9 Aug 80
1:29.42	Texas A & M (USA)	Tarmoh, Mayo, Beard, Lucas	1	Penn R	Philadelphia	24 Apr 10
1:29.45	USA	Solomon, Meadows, Knight, K Duncan	1	WRly	Nassau	25 May 14
1:29.61	GBR	Henry, A Onuora, B Williams, A Philip	2	WRly	Nassau	25 May 14
Drugs dq: 1:29.40	USA Red	Colander, Gaines, Miller, M Jones ¶	1	Penn	Philadelphia	24 Apr 04

4 x 400 METRES RELAY

Mark	Nat	Name	Pos	Meet	Venue	Date
3:15.17 WR	URS	Ledovskaya 50.12, O.Nazarova 47.82, Pinigina 49.43, Bryzgina 47.80	1	OG	Seoul	1 Oct 88

Mark	Wind	Nat	Name	Pos	Meet	Venue	Date
3:15.51		USA		2	OG	Seoul	1 Oct 88
			D.Howard 49.82, Dixon 49.17, Brisco 48.44, Griffith-Joyner 48.08				
3:15.92	WR	GDR	G.Walther 49.8, Busch 48.9, Rübsam 49.4, Koch 47.8	1	NC	Erfurt	3 Jun 84
3:16.71		USA	Torrence 49.0, Malone 49.4, Kaiser-Brown 49.48, Miles 48.78	1	WCh	Stuttgart	22 Aug 93
3:16.87		GDR	Emmelmann 50.9, Busch 48.8, Müller 48.9, Koch 48.21	1	EC	Stuttgart	31 Aug 86
3:16.87		USA	Trotter 50.3, Felix 48.1, McCorory 49.39, Richards-Ross 49.10	1	OG	London (OS)	11 Aug 12
3:17.83		USA	Dunn 50.5, Felix 48.8, Demus 50.14, Richards 48.44	1	WCh	Berlin	23 Aug 09
3:18.09		USA	Richards-Ross 49.3, Felix 49.4, Beard 49.84, McCorory 49.52	1	WCh	Daegu	3 Sep 11
3:18.29		USA		1	OG	Los Angeles	11 Aug 84
			Leatherwood 50.50, S.Howard 48.83, Brisco-Hooks 49.23, Cheeseborough 49.73				
3:18.29		GDR	Neubauer 50.58, Emmelmann 49.89, Busch 48.81, Müller 48.99	3	OG	Seoul	1 Oct 88
3:18.38		RUS		2	WCh	Stuttgart	22 Aug 93
			Ruzina 50.8, Alekseyeva 49.3, Ponomaryova 49.78, Privalova 48.47				
3:18.43		URS	Ledovskaya 51.7, Dzhigalova 49.2, Nazarova 48.87, Bryzgina 48.67	1	WCh	Tokyo	1 Sep 91
3:18.54		USA	Wineberg 51.0, Felix 48.6, Henderson 50.06, Richards 48.93	1	OG	Beijing	23 Aug 08
3:18.55		USA	Trotter 51.2, Felix 48.0, Wineberg 50.24, Richards 49.07	1	WCh	Osaka	2 Sep 07
3:18.58		URS	I.Nazarova, Olizarenko, Pinigina, Vladykina	1	ECp	Moskva	18 Aug 85
3:18.63		GDR	Neubauer 51.4, Emmelmann 49.1, Müller 48.64, Busch 49.48	1	WCh	Roma	6 Sep 87
3:18.71		JAM	Whyte 50.0, Prendergast 49.6, Williams-Mills 49.84, Williams 49.22	2	WCh	Daegu	3 Sep 11
3:18.82		RUS	Gushchina 50.6, Litvinova 49.2, Firova 49.20, Kapachinskaya 49.82	2	OG	Beijing	23 Aug 08
3:19.01		USA	Trotter 49.8, Henderson 49.7, Richards 49.81, Hennagan 49.73	(1)	OG	Athína	28 Aug 04
			Note team was disqualified as Crystal Cox (subject of retrospective drugs ban) ran for them in the heat				
3:19.04	WR	GDR	Siemon' 51.0, Busch 50.0, Rübsam 50.2, Koch 47.9	1	EC	Athína	11 Sep 82
3:19.12		URS	Baskakova, I.Nazarova, Pinigina, Vladykina	1	Drz	Praha	18 Aug 84
3:19.23	WR	GDR	Maletzki 50.05, Rohde 49.00, Streidt 49.51, Brehmer 49.79	1	OG	Montreal	31 Jul 76
3:19.36		RUS		3	WCh	Daegu	3 Sep 11
			Krivoshapka 50.3, Antyukh 50.0, Litvinova 49.96, Kapachinskaya 49.22				
3:19.49		GDR	Emmelmann, Busch, Neubauer, Koch 47.9	1	WCp	Canberra	4 Oct 85
3:19.50		URS	Yurchenko 51.2, O.Nazarova 50.2, Pinigina 49.09, Bryzgina 49.03	2	WCh	Roma	6 Sep 87
3:19.60		USA	Leatherwood 50.7 , S.Howard 50.0, Brisco-Hooks 48.7, Cheeseborough 50.2	1		Walnut	25 Jul 84
3:19.62		GDR	Kotte, Brehmer, Köhn, Koch 48.3	1	ECp	Torino	5 Aug 79
			(27/5 with USSR and Russia counted separately)				
3:20.04		GBR	Ohuruogu 50.6, Okoro 50.9, McConnell 49.79, Sanders 48.76	3	WCh	Osaka	2 Sep 07
3:20.32		CZE/TCH		2	WCh	Helsinki	14 Aug 83
			Kocembová 48.93, Matejkovicová 52.13, Moravcíková 51.51, Kratochvílová 47.75				
3:21.04		NGR	Afolabi 51.13, Yusuf 49.72, Opara 51.29, Ogunkoya 48.90	2	OG	Atlanta	3 Aug 96
3:21.21		CAN	Crooks 50.30, Richardson 50.22, Killingbeck ¶ 50.62, Payne 50.07	2	OG	Los Angeles	11 Aug 84
3:21.85		BLR	Kozak 52.0, Khlyustova 50.3, I Usovich 49.85, S Usovich 49.69	4	OG	Beijing	23 Aug 08
			(10)				
3:21.94		UKR	Dzhigalova, Olizarenko, Pinigina, Vladykina	1	URS Ch	Kyiv	17 Jul 86
3:22.34		FRA	Landre 51.3, Dorsile 51.1, Elien 50.54, Pérec 49.36	1	EC	Helsinki	14 Aug 94
3:22.49		FRG	Thimm 50.81, Arendt 49.95, Thomas 51.50, Abt 50.23	4	OG	Seoul	1 Oct 88
3:23.21		CUB	Díaz 51.1, Calatayud 51.2, Clement 50.47, Terrero 50.46	6	OG	Beijing	23 Aug 08
3:23.81		AUS	Peris-K 51.71, Lewis 51.69, Gainsford-T 51.06, Freeman 49.35	4	OG	Sydney	30 Sep 00
3:24.28		CHN	(Hebei) An X, Bai X, Cao C, Ma Y	1	NG	Beijing	13 Sep 93
3:24.49		POL	Guzowska 52.2, Bejnar 50.2, Prokopek 50.47, Jesien 51.59	4	WCh	Helsinki	14 Aug 05
3:25.68		ROU	Ruicu 52.69, Rîpanu 51.09, Barbu 52.64, Tîrlea 49.26	2	ECp	Paris (C)	20 Jun 99
3:25.7a		FIN	Eklund 53.6, Pursiainen 50.6, Wilmi 51.6, Salin 49.9	2	EC	Roma	8 Sep 74
3:25.71		ITA	Bazzoni 53.7, Milani 50.8, Spacca 51.64, Grenot 49.61	4	EC	Barcelona	1 Aug 10
			(20)				
3:25.81		BUL	Ilieva, Stamenova, Penkova, Damyanova	1	v Hun,Pol	Sofia	24 Jul 83
3:26.33		GRE	Kaidantzi 53.2, Goudenoúdi 51.6, Boudá 51.76, Halkiá 49.75	3	ECpS	Bydgoszcz	20 Jun 04
3:26.68		BRA	(Bovespa) Coutinho, de Oliveira, Sousa, de Lima	1	NC	São Paulo	7 Aug 11
3:26.89		IND	R Kaur 53.1, Beenamol 51.4, Soman 52.51, M Kaur 49.85	3h2	OG	Athína	27 Aug 04
3:27.08		CMR	Nguimgo 51.7, Kaboud 52.1, Atangana 51.98, Béwouda 51.35	7	WCh	Saint-Denis	31 Aug 03
3:27.14		MEX	Rodríguez 53.3, Medina 51.2, Vela 52.94, Guevara 49.70	4h2	WCh	Osaka	1 Sep 07
3:27.48		IRL	Andrews 53.4, Cuddihy 49.9, Bergin 52.60, Carey 51.54	4h3	WCh	Daegu	2 Sep 11
3:27.54		LTU	Navickaite, Valiuliene, Mendzoryte, Ambraziene	3	SPART	Moskva	22 Jun 83
3:27.57		ESP	Merino 52.2, Lacambra 52.0, Myers 50.85, Ferrer 52.56	7	WCh	Tokyo	1 Sep 91
3:27.86		HUN	Orosz, Forgács, Tóth, Pál (30)	5	OG	Moskva	1 Aug 80

4 x 800 METRES RELAY

Mark	Wind	Nat	Name	Pos	Meet	Venue	Date
7:50.17	WR	USSR	Olizarenko, Gurina, Borisova, Podyalovskaya	1		Moskva	5 Aug 84
7:54.10	WR	GDR	Zinn, Hoffmeister, Weiss, Klapezynski	1	NC	Karl-Marx-Stadt	6 Aug 76
8:01.58		USA	Price 2:01.0, Lara 2:02.8, A Wilson 1:59.1, Martinez 1:58.7	1	WRly	Nassau	25 May 14

4 x 1500 METRES RELAY

Mark	Wind	Nat	Name	Pos	Meet	Venue	Date
16:33.58	WR	KEN	M Cherono 4:07.5, Kipyegon 4:08.5, Jelagat 4:10.5, Obiri 4:07.1	1	WRly	Nassau	24 May 14
16:55.33		USA	Kampf 4:09.2, Mackey, Grace, Martinez 4:10.2	2	WRly	Nassau	24 May 14
17:08.65		AUS	Buckman 4:08.1, Delaney 4:15.5, McGowan, Duncan 4:16.0	3	WRly	Nassau	25 May 14

Mark	Wind	Name		Nat	Born	Pos	Meet	Venue	Date

5000 METRES WALK (TRACK)

Mark	Name		Nat	Born	Pos	Meet	Venue	Date
20:01.80 WR	Eleonora	Giorgi	ITA	14.9.89	1		Misterbianco	18 May 14
20:02.60 WR	Gillian	O'Sullivan	IRL	21.8.76	1	NC	Dublin (S)	13 Jul 02
20:03.0 WR	Kerry	Saxby-Junna	AUS	2.6.61	1		Sydney	11 Feb 96
20:07.52 WR	Beate	Anders/Gummelt	GDR	4.2.68	1	vURS	Rostock	23 Jun 90
20:11.45	Sabine	Zimmer/Krantz	GER	6.2.81	1	NC	Wattenscheid	2 Jul 05
20:12.41	Elisabetta	Perrone	ITA	9.7.68	1	NC	Rieti	2 Aug 03
20:15.71	Lyudmyla	Olyanovska	UKR	20.2.93	1		Kyiv	4 Jun 14
20:18.87	Melanie	Seeger	GER	8.1.77	1	NC	Braunschweig	10 Jul 04
20:21.69	Annarita	Sidoti	ITA	25.7.69	1	NC	Cesenatico	1 Jul 95
20:27.59 WR	Ileana	Salvador	ITA	16.1.62	1		Trento	3 Jun 89

10 KILOMETRES WALK

WOMEN All-time

Mark	Name		Nat	Born	Pos	Meet	Venue	Date
41:04 WR	Yelena	Nikolayeva	RUS	1.2.66	1	NC	Sochi	20 Apr 96
41:16		Wang Yan	CHN	3.5.71	1		Eisenhüttenstadt	8 May 99
41:16	Kjersti	Plätzer (Tysse)	NOR	18.1.72	1	NC	Os	11 May 02
41:17	Irina	Stankina	RUS	25.3.77	1	NC-w	Adler	9 Feb 97
41:24	Olimpiada	Ivanova ¶	RUS	26.8.70	2	NC-w	Adler	9 Feb 97
41:29 WR	Larisa	Ramazanova	RUS	23.9.71	1	NC	Izhevsk	4 Jun 95
41:30 WR	Kerry	Saxby-Junna	AUS	2.6.61	1	NC	Canberra	27 Aug 88
41:30		O Ivanova			2	NC	Izhevsk	4 Jun 95
41:31	Yelena	Gruzinova	RUS	24.12.67	2	NC	Sochi	20 Apr 96
41:37.9t		Gao Hongmiao	CHN	17.3.74	1	NC	Beijing	7 Apr 94
41:38	Rossella	Giordano (10)	ITA	1.12.72	1		Naumburg	25 May 97
41:41		Nikolayeva			2		Naumburg	25 May 97
41:41		Tysse Plätzer			1		Kraków	30 May 09
41:42	Olga	Kaniskina ¶	RUS	19.1.85	2		Kraków	30 May 09
41:42.5t	Lyudmyla	Olyanovska	UKR	20.2.93	1		Mukachevo	1 Nov 14
41:45		Liu Hongyu	CHN	11.1.75	2		Eisenhüttenstadt	8 May 99
41:46	Annarita	Sidoti	ITA	25.7.69	1		Livorno	12 Jun 94
41:46		O Ivanova			1	NC/w	Adler	11 Feb 96
41:47		Saxby-Junna			1		Eisenhüttenstadt	11 May 96
41:48		Li Chunxiu	CHN	13.8.69	1	NG	Beijing	8 Sep 93
	(20/15)							
41:50	Yelena	Arshintseva	RUS	5.4.71	1	NC-w	Adler	11 Feb 95
41:51	Beate	Anders/Gummelt	GER	4.2.68	2		Eisenhüttenstadt	11 May 96
41:52	Tatyana	Mineyeva ¶	RUS	10.8.90	1	NCp-j	Penza	5 Sep 09
41:52	Tatyana	Korotkova	RUS	24.4.80	1		Buy	19 Sep 10
41:53	Tatyana	Sibileva	RUS	17.5.80	1	RWC-F	Beijing	18 Sep 10
	(20)							
41:56	Yelena	Sayko	RUS	24.12.67	2	NC/w	Adler	11 Feb 96
41:56.23t	Nadezhda	Ryashkina	RUS	22.1.67	1	GWG	Seattle	24 Jul 90
42:01	Tamara	Kovalenko	RUS	5.6.64	3	NC-w	Adler	11 Feb 95
42:01	Olga	Panfyorova	RUS	21.8.77	1	NC-23	Izhevsk	16 May 98
42:03	Lina	Bikulova	RUS	1.10.88	1		Bui	13 Sep 14
42:04+	Vera	Sokolova	RUS	8.6.87	1=	in 20k	Sochi	26 Feb 11
42:04+	Anisya	Kirdyapkina	RUS	23.10.89	1=	in 20k	Sochi	26 Feb 11
42:04+	Tatyana	Shemyakina	RUS	3.9.87	1=	in 20k	Sochi	26 Feb 11
42:05+	Margarita	Turova	BLR	28.12.80	1+	in 20k	Adler	12 Mar 05
42:06	Valentina	Tsybulskaya	BLR	19.2.68	4		Eisenhüttenstadt	8 May 99
	(30)							
42:07	Ileana	Salvador	ITA	16.1.62	1		Sesto San Giovanni	1 May 92
42:09	Elisabetta	Perrone	ITA	9.7.68	4		Eisenhüttenstadt	11 May 96
42:11	Nina	Alyushenko	RUS	29.5.68	3	NC	Izhevsk	4 Jun 95
42:13	Natalya	Misyulya	BLR	16.4.66	5		Eisenhüttenstadt	8 May 99
42:13.7t	Madelein	Svensson	SWE	20.7.69	2	SGP	Fana	15 May 92
42:15		Gu Yan	CHN	17.3.74	3	WCp	Podebrady	19 Apr 97
42:15	Erica	Alfridi	ITA	22.2.68	5		Naumburg	25 May 97
42:15	Jane	Saville	AUS	5.11.74	6		Eisenhüttenstadt	8 May 99
42:16	Alina	Ivanova	RUS	16.3.69	1		Novopolotsk	27 May 89
42:16	Norica	Cîmpean	ROU	22.3.72	1		Calella	9 May 99
	(40)	50th woman 42:31, 100th 43:10, 200th 43:58, 300th 44:38						

Probable short course: Livorno 10 Jul 93: 1. Ileana Salvador ITA 16.1.62 41:30, 2. Elisabeta Perrone 9.7.68 41:56

Best track times

Mark	Name		Nat	Born	Pos	Meet	Venue	Date
41:57.22	Kerry	Saxby-Junna	AUS	2.6.61	2	GWG	Seattle	24 Jul 90
42:11.5	Beate	Anders/Gummelt	GER	4.2.68	1	SGP	Fana	15 May 92

20 KILOMETRES WALK

Mark	Name		Nat	Born	Pos	Meet	Venue	Date
1:24:50	Olimpiada	Ivanova ¶	RUS	26.8.70	1	NC-w	Adler	4 Mar 01
1:24:56	Olga	Kaniskina ¶	RUS	19.1.85	1	NC-w	Adler	28 Feb 09

Mark	Wind	Name		Nat	Born	Pos	Meet	Venue	Date
1:25:02	WR	Yelena	Lashmanova ¶	RUS	9.4.92	1	OG	London	11 Aug 12
1:25:08	WR	Vera	Sokolova	RUS	8.6.87	1	NC-w	Sochi	26 Feb 11
1:25:09		Anisya	Kirdyapkina	RUS	23.10.89	2	NC-w	Sochi	26 Feb 11
1:25:09			Kaniskina			2	OG	London	11 Aug 12
1:25:11			Kaniskina			1	NC-w	Adler	23 Feb 08
1:25:11			Kirdyapkina			1	NC-w	Sochi	20 Feb 10
1:25:16			Qieyang Shenjie	CHN	11.11.90	3	OG	London	11 Aug 12
1:25:18		Tatyana	Gudkova	RUS	23.1.78	1	NC	Moskva	19 May 00
1:25:20		Olga	Polyakova	RUS	23.9.80	2	NC	Moskva	19 May 00
1:25:26			Sokolova			2	NC-w	Adler	28 Feb 09
1:25:26			Kirdyapkina			3	NC-w	Adler	28 Feb 09
1:25:27		Elmira	Alembekova	RUS	30.6.90	1	NC-w	Sochi	18 Feb 12
1:25:29		Irina	Stankina (10)	RUS	25.3.77	3	NC	Moskva	19 May 00
1:25:30			Kirdyapkina			2	NC-w	Adler	23 Feb 08
1:25:32		Yelena	Shumkina	RUS	24.1.88	4	NC-w	Adler	28 Feb 09
1:25:35			Sokolova			2	NC-w	Sochi	20 Feb 10
1:25:41	WR		O Ivanova			1	WCh	Helsinki	7 Aug 05
1:25:42			Kaniskina			1	WCp	Cheboksary	11 May 08
1:25:46		Tatyana	Shemyakina	RUS	3.9.87	3	NC-w	Adler	23 Feb 08
1:25:46			Liu Hong	CHN	12.5.87	1		Taicang	30 Mar 12
1:25:49			Lashmanova			1	NC-w	Sochi	23 Feb 13
1:25:52		Larisa	Yemelyanova	RUS	6.1.80	5	NC-w	Adler	28 Feb 09
1:25:52		Tatyana	Sibileva	RUS	17.5.80	3	NC-w	Sochi	20 Feb 10
1:25:59		Tamara	Kovalenko	RUS	5.6.64	4	NC	Moskva	19 May 00
1:25:59			Kirdyapkina			2	NC-w	Sochi	23 Feb 13
1:26:00			Liu Hong			4	OG	London	11 Aug 12
1:26:00			Sokolova			3	NC-w	Sochi	23 Feb 13
1:26:02			Kaniskina			1	NC-w	Adler	19 Feb 06
		(30/16)							
1:26:11		Margarita	Turova	BLR	28.12.80	1	NC	Nesvizh	15 Apr 06
1:26:14		Irina	Petrova	RUS	26.5.85	2	NC-w	Adler	19 Feb 06
1:26:16		Lyudmila	Arkhipova	RUS	25.11.78	5	NC-w	Adler	23 Feb 08
1:26:22	WR		Wang Yan (20)	CHN	3.5.71	1	NG	Guangzhou	19 Nov 01
1:26:22	WR	Yelena	Nikolayeva	RUS	1.2.66	1	ECp	Cheboksary	18 May 03
1:26:23			Wang Liping	CHN	8.7.76	2	NG	Guangzhou	19 Nov 01
1:26:28		Iraida	Pudovkina	RUS	2.11.80	1	NC-w	Adler	12 Mar 05
1:26:34		Tatyana	Kalmykova	RUS	10.1.90	1	NC	Saransk	8 Jun 08
1:26:35			Liu Hongyu	CHN	11.1.75	3	NG	Guangzhou	19 Nov 01
1:26:46			Song Hongjuan	CHN	4.7.84	1	NC	Guangzhou	20 Mar 04
1:26:47		Irina	Yumanova ¶	RUS	6.11.90	3	NC-w	Sochi	18 Feb 12
1:26:50		Natalya	Fedoskina	RUS	25.6.80	2	ECp	Dudince	19 May 01
1:26:57		Lyudmila	Yefimkina	RUS	22.8.81	3	NC-w	Adler	19 Feb 06
1:27:01			Lu Xiuzhi	CHN	26.10.93	2		Taicang	30 Mar 12
		(30)							
1:27:05		Eleonora	Giorgi	ITA	14.9.89	5	WCp	Taicang	3 May 14
1:27:07		Kjersti	Tysse Plätzer	NOR	18.1.72	2	OG	Beijing	21 Aug 08
1:27:08		Anna	Lukyanova	RUS	23.4.91	5	NC-w	Sochi	18 Feb 12
1:27:09		Elisabetta	Perrone	ITA	9.7.68	3	ECp	Dudince	19 May 01
1:27:12		Elisa	Rigaudo	ITA	17.6.80	3	OG	Beijing	21 Aug 08
1:27:14		Antonina	Petrova	RUS	1.5.77	1	NC-w	Adler	1 Mar 03
1:27:18		Alena	Nartova	RUS	1.1.82	6	NC-w	Adler	23 Feb 08
1:27:19			Jiang Jing	CHN	23.10.85	1	NC	Nanning	25 Feb 05
1:27:22		Gillian	O'Sullivan	IRL	21.8.76	1		Sesto San Giovanni	1 May 03
1:27:25		María	Vasco	ESP	26.12.75	5	OG	Beijing	21 Aug 08
		(40)							
1:27:27		Vira	Zozulya	UKR	31.8.70	1	NC	Sumy	7 Jun 08
1:27:27		Lyudmyla	Olyanovska	UKR	20.2.93	7	WCp	Taicang	3 May 14
1:27:29		Erica	Alfridi	ITA	22.2.68	4	ECp	Dudince	19 May 01
1:27:30	WB	Nadezhda	Ryashkina	RUS	22.1.67	1	NC-w	Adler	7 Feb 99
1:27:30		Tatyana	Kozlova	RUS	2.9.83	2	NC-w	Adler	12 Mar 05
1:27:35		Tatyana	Korotkova	RUS	24.4.80	2	NC	Cheboksary	12 Jun 04
1:27:36			Sun Huanhuan	CHN	15.3.90	1	NC	Taicang	1 Mar 13
1:27:37			Bo Yanmin	CHN	29.6.87	1	NG	Nanjing	20 Oct 05
1:27:39		Marina	Pandakova	RUS	1.3.89	5	NC-w	Sochi	23 Feb 13
1:27:40			Li Yanfei	CHN	12.1.90	2	NC	Taicang	1 Mar 13
		(50)	100th best woman 1:28:56, 200th 1:30:52, 300th 1:32:23, 400th 1:34:13						

50 KILOMETRES WALK

Mark	Wind	Name		Nat	Born	Pos	Meet	Venue	Date
4:10:59		Monica	Svensson	SWE	26.12.78	1		Scanzorosciate	21 Oct 07
4:12:16		Yelena	Ginko	BLR	30.7.76	1		Scanzorosciate	17 Oct 04

JUNIOR MEN'S ALL-TIME LISTS

100 METRES

Mark	Wind	Name		Nat	Born	Pos	Meet	Venue	Date
9.97	1.8	Trayvon	Bromell	USA	10.7.95	1	NCAA	Eugene	13 Jun 14
10.00	1.6	Trentavis	Friday	USA	5.6.95	1h1	NC-j	Eugene	5 Jul 14
10.01	0.0	Darrel	Brown	TTO	11.10.84	1q3	WCh	Saint-Denis	24 Aug 03
10.01	1.6	Jeffery	Demps	USA	8.1.90	2q1	NC/OT	Eugene	28 Jun 08
10.01	0.9	Yoshihide	Kiryu	JPN	15.12.95	1h3	Oda	Hiroshima	29 Apr 13
10.03	0.7	Marcus	Rowland	USA	11.3.90	1	PAm-J	Port of Spain	31 Jul 09
10.04	1.7	DeAngelo	Cherry	USA	1.8.90	1h4	NCAA	Fayetteville	10 Jun 09
10.04	0.2	Christoph	Lemaitre	FRA	11.6.90	1	EJ	Novi Sad	24 Jul 09
10.05		Davidson	Ezinwa	NGR	22.11.71	1		Bauchi	4 Jan 90
10.05	0.1	Adam	Gemili	GBR	6.10.93	1	WJ	Barcelona	11 Jul 12
Wind assisted to 10.03									
9.77	4.2	Trayvon	Bromell	USA	10.7.95	1	Big 12	Lubbock	18 May 14
9.83	7.1	Leonard	Scott	USA	19.1.80	1		Knoxville	9 Apr 99
9.96	4.5	Walter	Dix	USA	31.1.86	1rA	TexR	Austin	9 Apr 05
9.97	??	Mark	Lewis-Francis	GBR	4.9.82	1q3	WCh	Edmonton	4 Aug 01
9.96	5.0	André	De Grasse	CAN	10.11.94	1	JUCO	Hutchinson, KS	18 May 13
9.98	5.0	Tyreek	Hill	USA	1.3.94	2	JUCO	Hutchinson, KS	18 May 13
10.02	2.8	DeAngelo	Cherry	USA	1.8.90	1h2	NC-j	Eugene	26 Jun 09
10.02	2.4	Marcus	Rowland	USA	11.3.90	1	NC-j	Eugene	26 Jun 09
10.03	4.9	Christoph	Lemaitre	FRA-	11.6.90	1		Forbach	31 May 09

200 METRES

Mark	Wind	Name		Nat	Born	Pos	Meet	Venue	Date
19.93	1.4	Usain	Bolt	JAM	21.8.86	1		Hamilton, BER	11 Apr 04
20.04	0.1	Ramil	Guliyev	AZE	29.5.90	1	WUG	Beograd	10 Jul 09
20.07	1.5	Lorenzo	Daniel	USA	23.3.66	1	SEC	Starkville	18 May 85
20.13	1.7	Roy	Martin	USA	25.12.66	1		Austin	11 May 85
20.14	1.8	Tyreek	Hill	USA	1.3.94	1		Orlando	26 May 12
20.16A	-0.2	Riaan	Dempers	RSA	4.3.77	1	NC-j	Germiston	7 Apr 95
20.18	1.0	Walter	Dix	USA	31.1.86	1s2	NCAA	Sacramento	9 Jun 05
20.22	1.7	Dwayne	Evans	USA	13.10.58	2	OT	Eugene	22 Jun 76
20.23	0.5	Michael	Timpson	USA	6.6.67	1		State College	16 May 86
20.24	0.2	Joe	DeLoach	USA	5.6.67	3		Los Angeles	8 Jun 85
20.24	0.2	Francis	Obikwelu	NGR	22.11.78	2rB		Granada	29 May 96
20.24	1.4	Roberto	Skyers	CUB	12.11.91	1h5		Camagüey	14 Mar 09
Wind assisted									
19.86	4.0	Justin	Gatlin	USA	10.2.82	1h2	NCAA	Eugene	30 May 01
20.01	2.5	Derald	Harris	USA	5.4.58	1		San José	9 Apr 77
20.03	2.9	Trentavis	Friday	USA	5.6.95	1	NC-j	Eugene	6 Jul 14
20.08	9.2	Leonard	Scott	USA	19.1.80	2r2		Knoxville	9 Apr 99
20.10	4.6	Stanley	Kerr	USA	19.6.67	2r2	SWC	Houston	18 May 86
20.16	5.2	Nickel	Ashmeade	JAM	4.7.90	1	Carifta	Basseterre	24 Mar 08
Hand timing: 19.9		Davidson	Ezinwa	NGR	22.11.71	1		Bauchi	18 Mar 89

400 METRES

Mark	Name		Nat	Born	Pos	Meet	Venue	Date
43.87	Steve	Lewis	USA	16.5.69	1	OG	Seoul	28 Sep 88
44.36	Kirani	James	GRN	1.9.92	1	WK	Zürich	8 Sep 11
44.45	Luguelín	Santos	DOM	12.11.93	1	FBK	Hengelo	27 May 12
44.66	Hamdam Odha	Al-Bishi	KSA	5.5.81	1	WJ	Santiago de Chile	20 Oct 00
44.66	LaShawn	Merritt	USA	27.6.86	1		Kingston	7 May 05
44.69	Darrell	Robinson	USA	23.12.63	2	USOF	Indianapolis	24 Jul 82
44.73A	James	Rolle	USA	2.2.64	1	USOF	USAF Academy	2 Jul 83
44.75	Darren	Clark	AUS	6.9.65	4	OG	Los Angeles	8 Aug 84
44.75	Deon	Minor	USA	22.1.73	1s1	NCAA	Austin	5 Jun 92
44.82	Arman	Hall	USA	14.2.94	4s1	NC	Des Moines	21 Jun 13
44.93	Nagmeldin	El Abubakr	SUD	22.2.86	1	Is.Sol	Makkah	14 Apr 05

800 METRES

Mark	Name		Nat	Born	Pos	Meet	Venue	Date
1:41.73	Nijel	Amos	BOT	15.3.94	2	OG	London (OS)	9 Aug 12
1:42.37	Mohammed	Aman	ETH	10.1.94	1	VD	Bruxelles	6 Sep 13
1:42.53	Timothy	Kitum	KEN	20.11.94	3	OG	London (OS)	9 Aug 12
1:42.69	Abubaker	Kaki	SUD	21.6.89	1	Bisl	Oslo	6 Jun 08
1:43.13	Abraham Kipchirchir	Rotich	KEN	26.6.93	1	Herc	Monaco	20 Jul 12
1:43.40	Leonard	Kosencha	KEN	21.8.94	2	Herc	Monaco	20 Jul 12
1:43.64	Japheth	Kimutai	KEN	20.12.78	3rB	WK	Zürich	13 Aug 97
1:43.81	Edwin	Melly	KEN	24.3.94	2		Rieti	9 Sep 12
1:43.95	Alfred	Kipketer	KEN	26.12.96	1	WJ	Eugene	27 Jul 14
1:43.99	David	Mutua	KEN	20.4.92	4	Herc	Monaco	22 Jul 11
1:44.15	David	Rudisha	KEN	17.12.88	1	VD	Bruxelles	14 Sep 07

Mark	Wind	Name		Nat	Born	Pos	Meet	Venue	Date
1000 METRES									
2:13.93		Abubaker	Kaki	SUD	21.6.89	1	DNG	Stockholm	22 Jul 08
2:15.00		Benjamin	Kipkurui	KEN	28.12.80	5	Nik	Nice	17 Jul 99
1500 METRES									
3:28.81		Ronald	Kwemoi	KEN	19.9.95	3	Herc	Monaco	18 Jul 14
3:30.24		Cornelius	Chirchir	KEN	5.6.83	4	Herc	Monaco	19 Jul 02
3:31.13		Mulugueta	Wondimu	ETH	28.2.85	2rA	NA	Heusden	31 Jul 04
3:31.42		Alex	Kipchirchir	KEN	26.11.84	5	VD	Bruxelles	5 Sep 03
3:31.54		Isaac	Songok	KEN	25.4.84	1	NA	Heusden	2 Aug 03
3:31.64		Asbel	Kiprop	KEN	30.6.89	1	GGala	Roma	11 Jul 08
3:31.70		William	Biwott	KEN	5.3.90	3	GGala	Roma	10 Jul 09
3:32.02		Caleb	Ndiku	KEN	9.10.92	4	FBK	Hengelo	29 May 11
3:32.48		Augustine	Choge	KEN	21.1.87	1	ISTAF	Berlin	3 Sep 06
3:32.68		Abdelaati	Iguider	MAR	25.3.87	5	VD	Bruxelles	25 Aug 06
3:32.91		Noah	Ngeny	KEN	2.11.78	9	Herc	Monaco	16 Aug 97
1 MILE									
3:49.29		William	Biwott	KEN	5.3.90	2	Bisl	Oslo	3 Jul 09
3:49.77		Caleb	Ndiku	KEN	9.10.92	5	Pre	Eugene	4 Jun 11
3:50.25		Alex	Kipchirchir	KEN	26.11.84	2	GP II	Rieti	7 Sep 03
3:50.39		James	Kwalia	KEN	12.6.84	1	FBK	Hengelo	1 Jun 03
3:50.41		Noah	Ngeny	KEN	2.11.78	2	Nik	Nice	16 Jul 97
3:50.69		Cornelius	Chirchir	KEN	5.6.83	5	GGala	Roma	12 Jul 02
3:50.83		Nicholas	Kemboi	KEN	18.12.89	6	Bisl	Oslo	6 Jun 08
2000 METRES									
4:56.25		Tesfaye	Cheru	ETH	2.3.93	1		Reims	5 Jul 11
4:56.86		Isaac	Songok	KEN	25.4.84	6	ISTAF	Berlin	31 Aug 01
4:58.18		Soresa	Fida	ETH	27.5.93	4		Reims	5 Jul 11
4:58.76		Jairus	Kipchoge	KEN	15.12.92	7		Reims	5 Jul 11
3000 METRES									
7:28.78		Augustine	Choge	KEN	21.1.87	2	SGP	Doha	13 May 05
7:29.11		Tariku	Bekele	ETH	21.1.87	2	GP	Rieti	27 Aug 06
7:30.36		Hagos	Gebrhiwet	ETH	11.5.94	1	DL	Doha	10 May 13
7:30.43		Isiah	Koech	KEN	19.12.93	1	DNG	Stockholm	17 Aug 12
7:30.67		Kenenisa	Bekele	ETH	13.6.82	2	VD	Bruxelles	24 Aug 01
7:30.91		Eliud	Kipchoge	KEN	5.11.84	2	VD	Bruxelles	5 Sep 03
7:32.37		Abreham	Cherkos	ETH	23.9.89	2	Athl	Lausanne	11 Jul 06
7:32.72		John	Kipkoech	KEN	29.12.91	4		Rieti	29 Aug 10
7:33.00		Hailu	Mekonnen	ETH	4.4.80	2		Stuttgart	6 Jun 99
7:33.01		Levy	Matebo	KEN	3.11.89	2	GP	Rieti	7 Sep 08
7:34.32		Richard	Limo	KEN	18.11.80	4	VD	Bruxelles	3 Sep 99
5000 METRES									
12:47.53		Hagos	Gebrhiwet	ETH	11.5.94	2	DL	Saint-Denis	6 Jul 12
12:48.64		Isiah	Koech	KEN	19.12.93	3	DL	Saint-Denis	6 Jul 12
12:52.61		Eliud	Kipchoge	KEN	5.11.84	3	Bisl	Oslo	27 Jun 03
12:53.66		Augustine	Choge	KEN	21.1.87	4	GGala	Roma	8 Jul 05
12:53.72		Philip	Mosima	KEN	2.1.77	2	GGala	Roma	5 Jun 96
12:53.81		Tariku	Bekele	ETH	21.1.87	4	GGala	Roma	14 Jul 06
12:54.07		Sammy	Kipketer	KEN	29.9.81	2	GGala	Roma	30 Jun 00
12:54.19		Abreham	Cherkos	ETH	23.9.89	5	GGala	Roma	14 Jul 06
12:54.58		James	Kwalia	KEN	12.6.84	5	Bisl	Oslo	27 Jun 03
12:56.15		Daniel	Komen	KEN	17.5.76	2	GG	Roma	8 Jun 95
12:57.05		Mulugueta	Wondimu	ETH	28.2.85	2	ISTAF	Berlin	12 Sep 04
10,000 METRES									
26:41.75		Samuel	Wanjiru	KEN	10.11.86	3	VD	Bruxelles	26 Aug 05
26:55.73		Geoffrey	Kirui	KEN	16.2.93	6	VD	Bruxelles	16 Sep 11
26:57.56		Yigrem	Demelash	ETH	28.1.94	4	VD	Bruxelles	7 Sep 12
27:02.81		Ibrahim	Jeylan	ETH	12.6.89	4	VD	Bruxelles	25 Aug 06
27:04.00		Boniface	Kiprop	UGA	12.10.85	5	VD	Bruxelles	3 Sep 04
27:04.45		Bernard	Kipyego	KEN	16.7.86	4	FBK	Hengelo	29 May 05
27:06.35		Geoffrey	Kipsang	KEN	28.11.92	10	Pre	Eugene	3 Jun 11
27:06.47		Habtanu	Fikadu	ETH	13.3.88	8	FBK	Hengelo	26 May 07
27:07.29		Moses	Masai	KEN	1.6.86	7	VD	Bruxelles	3 Sep 04
27:11.18		Richard	Chelimo	KEN	21.4.72	1	APM	Hengelo	25 Jun 91
27:12.42		Sammy Alex	Mutahi	KEN	1.6.89	1		Tokamchi	29 Sep 07
27:13.66		Moses	Mosop	KEN	17.7.85	7	VD	Bruxelles	5 Sep 03

Mark	Wind	Name		Nat	Born	Pos	Meet	Venue	Date

3000 METRES STEEPLECHASE

Mark	Wind	Name		Nat	Born	Pos	Meet	Venue	Date
7:58.66		Stephen	Cherono	KEN	15.10.82	3	VD	Bruxelles	24 Aug 01
8:01.16		Conseslus	Kipruto	KEN	8.12.94	1	DL	Shanghai	18 May 13
8:03.74		Raymond	Yator	KEN	7.4.81	3	Herc	Monaco	18 Aug 00
8:05.52		Brimin	Kipruto	KEN	31.7.85	1	FBK	Hengelo	31 May 04
8:06.96		Gilbert	Kirui	KEN	22.1.94	2	DL	London (OS)	27 Jul 13
8:07.18		Moussa	Omar Obaid	QAT	18.4.85	4	OG	Athína	24 Aug 04
8:07.69		Paul	Kosgei	KEN	22.4.78	5	DNG	Stockholm	7 Jul 97
8:07.71		Hillary	Yego	KEN	2.4.92	3	DL	Shanghai	15 May 11
8:09.37		Abel	Cheruiyot/Yugut	KEN	26.12.84	2	NA	Heusden	2 Aug 03
8:11.31		Jairus	Birech	KEN	15.12.92	5	DL	Saint Denis	8 Jul 11
8:12.91		Thomas	Kiplitan	KEN	15.6.83	7	GP	Doha	15 May 02

110 METRES HURDLES (106cm)

Mark	Wind	Name		Nat	Born	Pos	Meet	Venue	Date
13.12	1.6		Liu Xiang	CHN	13.7.83	1rB	Athl	Lausanne	2 Jul 02
13.23	0.0	Renaldo	Nehemiah	USA	24.3.59	1r2	WK	Zürich	16 Aug 78
13.40	-1.0		Shi Dongpeng	CHN	6.1.84	1	NC	Shanghai	14 Sep 03
13.44	-0.8	Colin	Jackson	GBR	18.2.67	1	WJ	Athína	19 Jul 86
13.46	1.8	Jon	Ridgeon	GBR	14.2.67	1	EJ	Cottbus	23 Aug 85
13.46	-1.6	Dayron	Robles	CUB	19.11.86	1	PAm-J	Windsor	29 Jul 05
13.47	1.9	Holger	Pohland	GDR	5.4.63	2	vUSA	Karl-Marx-Stadt	10 Jul 82
13.47	1.2	Aries	Merritt	USA	24.7.85	4	NCAA	Austin	12 Jun 04
13.47	0.2		Xie Wenjun	CHN	11.7.90	2	GP	Shanghai	20 Sep 08
13.49	0.6	Stanislav	Olijar	LAT	22.3.79	1		Valmiera	11 Jul 98
13.49	1.2	Booker	Nunley	USA	2.7.90	2	SEC	Gainesville	17 May 09
Wind assisted									
13.41	2.6	Dayron	Robles	CUB	19.11.86	2	CAC	Nassau	10 Jul 05
13.42	4.5	Colin	Jackson	GBR	18.2.67	2	CG	Edinburgh	27 Jul 86
13.42	2.6	Antwon	Hicks	USA	12.3.83	1	WJ	Kingston	21 Jul 02
13.47	2.1	Frank	Busemann	GER	26.2.75	1	WJ	Lisboa	22 Jul 94

99 cm Hurdles

Mark	Wind	Name		Nat	Born	Pos	Meet	Venue	Date
12.99	0.5	Wilhem	Belocian	FRA	22.6.95	1	WJ	Eugene	24 Jul 14
13.06	0.5	Tyler	Mason	JAM	15.1.95	2	WJ	Eugene	24 Jul 14
13.08	2.0	Wayne	Davis	USA	2.7.90	1	PAm-J	Port of Spain	31 Jul 09
13.14	1.6	Eddie	Lovett	USA	25.6.92	1	PAm-J	Miramar	23 Jul 11
13.17	-0.7	David	Omoregie	GBR	1.11.95	1	NC-j	Bedford	22 Jun 14
13.18	1.0	Yordan	O'Farrill	CUB	9.2.93	1	WJ	Barcelona	12 Jul 12
13.23	1.5	Artur	Noga	POL	2.5.88	1	WJ	Beijing	20 Aug 06
13.24	1.6	Roy	Smith	USA	12.4.92	2	PAm-J	Miramar	23 Jul 11
Wind assisted to 13.20									
13.03	2.9	Eddie	Lovett	USA	25.6.92	1h1	PAm-J	Miramar	23 Jul 11
13.15	2.7	Brendan	Ames	USA	6.10.88	1	NC-j	Indianapolis	21 Jun 07
13.18		Arthur	Blake	USA	19.8.66	1	GWest	Sacramento	9 Jun 84
Hand timed: 12.9y		Renaldo	Nehemiah	USA	24.3.59	1		Jamaica, NY	30 May 77

400 METRES HURDLES

Mark	Wind	Name		Nat	Born	Pos	Meet	Venue	Date
48.02		Danny	Harris	USA	7.9.65	2s1	OT	Los Angeles	17 Jun 84
48.26		Jehue	Gordon	TTO	15.12.91	4	WCh	Berlin	18 Aug 09
48.51		Kerron	Clement	USA	31.10.85	1	WJ	Grosseto	16 Jul 04
48.52		Johnny	Dutch	USA	20.1.89	5	NC/OT	Eugene	29 Jun 08
48.62		Brandon	Johnson	USA	6.3.85	2	WJ	Grosseto	16 Jul 04
48.68		Bayano	Kamani	USA	17.4.80	1	NCAA	Boise	4 Jun 99
48.68		Jeshua	Anderson	USA	22.6.89	1	WJ	Bydgoszcz	11 Jul 08
48.72		Angelo	Taylor	USA	29.12.78	2	NCAA	Bloomington	6 Jun 97
48.74		Vladimir	Budko	BLR	4.2.65	2	DRZ	Moskva	18 Aug 84
48.76A		Llewellyn	Herbert	RSA	21.7.77	1		Pretoria	7 Apr 96
48.79		Kenneth	Ferguson	USA	22.3.84	1	SEC	Knoxville	18 May 03

HIGH JUMP

Mark	Wind	Name		Nat	Born	Pos	Meet	Venue	Date
2.37		Dragutin	Topic	YUG	12.3.71	1	WJ	Plovdiv	12 Aug 90
2.37		Steve	Smith	GBR	29.3.73	1	WJ	Seoul	20 Sep 92
2.36		Javier	Sotomayor	CUB	13.10.67	1		Santiago de Cuba	23 Feb 86
2.35i		Vladimir	Yashchenko	UKR	12.1.59	1	EI	Milano	12 Mar 78
		2.34				1	Prv	Tbilisi	16 Jun 78
2.35		Dietmar	Mögenburg	FRG	15.8.61	1		Rehlingen	26 May 80
2.34		Tim	Forsyth	AUS	17.8.73	1	Bisl	Oslo	4 Jul 92
2.33			Zhu Jianhua	CHN	29.5.63	1	AsiG	New Delhi	1 Dec 82
2.33		Patrik	Sjöberg	SWE	5.1.65	1	OsloG	Oslo	9 Jul 83
2.32i		Jaroslav	Bába	CZE	2.9.84	3		Arnstadt	8 Feb 03
2.32			Huang Haiqiang	CHN	8.2.88	1	WJ	Beijing	17 Aug 06

Mark	Wind	Name		Nat	Born	Pos	Meet	Venue	Date
POLE VAULT									
5.80		Maksim	Tarasov	RUS	2.12.70	1	vGDR-j	Bryansk	14 Jul 89
5.80		Raphael	Holzdeppe	GER	28.9.89	2		Biberach	28 Jun 08
5.75		Konstadínos	Filippídis	GRE	26.11.86	2	WUG	Izmir	18 Aug 05
5.72		Andrew	Irwin	USA	23.1.93	1	SEC	Baton Rouge	13 May 12
5.71		Lawrence	Johnson	USA	7.5.74	1		Knoxville	12 Jun 93
5.71		Germán	Chiaraviglio	ARG	16.4.87	1	WJ	Beijing	19 Aug 06
5.71		Shawn	Barber	CAN	27.5.94	2	TexR	Austin	29 Mar 13
5.70		Viktor	Chistyakov	RUS	9.2.75	1		Leppävirta	7 Jun 94
5.70		Artyom	Kuptsov	RUS	22.4.84	1	Znam	Tula	7 Jun 03
5.67i		Leonid	Kivalov	RUS	1.4.88	1	NC-j	Penza	1 Feb 07
LONG JUMP									
8.35	1.1	Sergey	Morgunov	RUS	9.2.93	1	NC-j	Cheboksary	19 Jun 12
8.34	0.0	Randy	Williams	USA	23.8.53	Q	OG	München	8 Sep 72
8.28	0.8	Luis Alberto	Bueno	CUB	22.5.69	1		La Habana	16 Jul 88
8.27	1.7	Eusebio	Cáceres	ESP	10.9.91	Q	EC	Barcelona	30 Jul 10
8.24	0.2	Eric	Metcalf	USA	23.1.68	1	NCAA	Indianapolis	6 Jun 86
8.24	1.8	Vladimir	Ochkan	UKR	13.1.68	1	vGDR-j	Leningrad	21 Jun 87
8.22		Larry	Doubley	USA	15.3.58	1	NCAA	Champaign	3 Jun 77
8.22		Iván	Pedroso	CUB	17.12.72	1		Santiago de Cuba	3 May 91
8.22i		Viktor	Kuznetsov	UKR	14.7.86	1		Brovary	22 Jan 05
8.21A	2.0	Vance	Johnson	USA	13.3.63	1	NCAA	Provo	4 Jun 82
8.20	1.5	James	Stallworth	USA	29.4.71	Q	WJ	Plovdiv	9 Aug 90
Wind assisted to 8.23									
8.40	3.2	Kareem	Streete-Thompson	CAY	30.3.73	1		Houston	5 May 91
8.35	2.2	Carl	Lewis	USA	1.7.61	1	NCAA	Austin	6 Jun 80
8.29	2.3	James	Beckford	JAM	9.1.75	1		Tempe	2 Apr 94
8.23	4.4	Peller	Phillips	USA	23.6.70	1		Sacramento	11 Jun 88
TRIPLE JUMP									
17.50	0.4	Volker	Mai	GDR	3.5.66	1	vURS	Erfurt	23 Jun 85
17.42	1.3	Khristo	Markov	BUL	27.1.65	1	Nar	Sofiya	19 May 84
17.40A	0.4	Pedro	Pérez	CUB	23.2.52	1	PAm	Cali	5 Aug 71
17.40	0.8	Ernesto	Revé	CUB	26.2.92	1		La Habana	10 Jun 11
17.31	-0.2	David	Girat Jr.	CUB	26.8.84	Q	WCh	Saint-Denis	23 Aug 03
17.29	1.3	James	Beckford	JAM	9.1.75	1		Tempe	2 Apr 94
17.27		Aliecer	Urrutia	CUB	22.9.74	1		Artemisa	23 Apr 93
17.24	0.7	Lázaro	Martínez	CUB	3.11.97	2		La Habana	1 Feb 14
17.23	0.2	Yoelbi	Quesada	CUB	4.8.73	1	NC	La Habana	13 May 92
17.19	-0.4	Teddy	Tamgho	FRA	15.6.89	4	Herc	Monaco	29 Jul 08
17.19	2.0	Will	Claye	USA	13.6.91	*	NCAA	Fayetteville	13 Jun 09
Wind assisted									
17.33	2.1	Teddy	Tamgho	FRA	15.6.89	1	WJ	Bydgoszcz	11 Jul 08
17.24	2.5	Will	Claye	USA	13.6.91	1	NCAA	Fayetteville	13 Jun 09
SHOT									
21.05i		Terry	Albritton	USA	14.1.55	1	AAU	New York	22 Feb 74
		20.38				2	MSR	Walnut	27 Apr 74
20.65		Mike	Carter	USA	29.10.60	1	vSU-j	Boston	4 Jul 79
20.43		David	Storl	GER	27.7.90	2		Gerlingen	6 Jul 09
20.39		Janus	Robberts	RSA	10.3.79	1	NC	Germiston	7 Mar 98
20.38		Jacko	Gill	NZL	10.12.94	1		Auckland (NS)	5 Dec 11
20.20		Randy	Matson	USA	5.3.45	2	OG	Tokyo	17 Oct 64
20.20		Udo	Beyer	GDR	9.8.55	2	NC	Leipzig	6 Jul 74
20.13		Jeff	Chakouian	USA	20.4.82	2		Atlanta	18 May 01
19.99		Karl	Salb	USA	19.5.49	4	OT	Echo Summit	10 Sep 68
19.95		Edis	Elkasevic	CRO	18.2.83	1		Velenje	15 Jun 02
6 kg Shot									
23.00		Jacko	Gill	NZL	10.12.94	1		Auckland	18 Aug 13
22.73		David	Storl	GER	27.7.90	1		Osterode	14 Jul 09
22.06		Konrad	Bukowiecki	POL	17.3.97	1	WJ	Eugene	24 Jul 14
21.96		Edis	Elkasevic	CRO	18.2.83	1	NC-j	Zagreb	29 Jun 02
21.79		Mustafa Amer	Ahmed	EGY	16.12.95	1	Arab	Cairo	23 Feb 14
21.78		Krzysztof	Brzozowski	POL	15.7.93	2	WJ	Barcelona	11 Jul 12
21.68		Marin	Premeru	CRO	29.8.90	1		Rijeka	19 May 09
21.24		Georgi	Ivanov	BUL	13.3.85	1	NC-j	Sofia	12 Jun 04
DISCUS									
65.62		Werner	Reiterer	AUS	27.1.68	1		Melbourne	15 Dec 87
65.31		Mykyta	Nesterenko	UKR	15.4.91	3		Tallinn	3 Jun 08

Mark	Wind	Name		Nat	Born	Pos	Meet	Venue	Date
63.64		Werner	Hartmann	FRG	20.4.59	1	vFRA	Strasbourg	25 Jun 78
63.26		Sergey	Pachin	UKR	24.5.68	2		Moskva	25 Jul 87
63.22		Brian	Milne	USA	7.1.73	1		State College	28 Mar 92
62.52		John	Nichols	USA	23.8.69	1		Baton Rouge	23 Apr 88
62.36		Tulake	Nuermaimaiti	CHN	8.3.82	2	NG	Guangzhou	21 Nov 01
62.16		Zoltán	Kövágó	HUN	10.4.79	1		Budapest	9 May 97
62.04		Kenth	Gardenkrans	SWE	2.10.55	2		Helsingborg	11 Aug 74
62.04			Wu Tao	CHN	3.10.83	1	NGP	Shanghai	18 May 02
1.75kg Discus									
70.13		Mykyta	Nesterenko	UKR	15.4.91	1		Halle	24 May 08
67.32		Margus	Hunt	EST	14.7.87	1	WJ	Beijing	16 Aug 06
66.94		Martin	Markovic	CRO	13.1.96	1	WJ	Eugene	26 Jul 14
66.88		Traves	Smikle	JAM	7.5.92	1		Kingston	31 Mar 11
66.81		Matthew	Denny	AUS	2.6.96	1		Brisbane	23 Nov 14
66.45		Gordon	Wolf	GER	17.1.90	1		Halle	23 May 09
65.88		Omar	El-Ghazaly	EGY	9.2.84	1		Cairo	7 Nov 03
65.71		Marin	Premeru	CRO	29.8.90	1		Split	31 May 09
65.66		Sven Martin	Skagestad	NOR	13.1.95	1		Oslo	12 Jun 14
65.55		Mihai	Grasu	ROM	21.4.87	1	NC	Bucuresti	23 Jul 06

HAMMER

Mark	Name		Nat	Born	Pos	Meet	Venue	Date
78.33	Olli-Pekka	Karjalainen	FIN	7.3.80	1	NC	Seinäjoki	5 Aug 99
78.14	Roland	Steuk	GDR	5.3.59	1	NC	Leipzig	30 Jun 78
78.00	Sergey	Dorozhon	UKR	17.2.64	1		Moskva	7 Aug 83
76.54	Valeriy	Gubkin	BLR	3.9.67	2		Minsk	27 Jun 86
76.42	Ruslan	Dikiy	TJK	18.1.72	1		Togliatti	7 Sep 91
76.37	Ashraf Amjad	El-Seify	QAT	20.2.95	1		Doha	10 Apr 13
75.52	Sergey	Kirmasov	RUS	25.3.70	1		Kharkov	4 Jun 89
75.42	Szymon	Ziolkowski	POL	1.7.76	1	EJ	Nyíregyhazá	30 Jul 95
75.24	Christoph	Sahner	FRG	23.9.63	1	vPOL-j	Göttingen	26 Jun 82
6kg Hammer								
85.57	Ashraf Amgad	El-Seify	QAT-Y	20.2.95	1	WJ	Barcelona	14 Jul 12
82.97	Javier	Cienfuegos	ESP	15.7.90	1		Madrid	17 Jun 09
82.84	Quentin	Bigot	FRA	1.12.92	1		Bondoufle	16 Oct 11
82.62	Yevgeniy	Aydamirov	RUS	11.5.87	1	NC-j	Tula	22 Jul 06
81.34	Krisztián	Pars	HUN	18.2.82	1		Szombathely	2 Sep 01
81.16	Özkan	Baltaci	TUR	13.2.94	1		Ankara	31 Jul 13
81.15	Ákos	Hudi	HUN	10.8.91	1		Veszprém	7 Jul 10
81.04	Werner	Smit	RSA	14.9.84	1		Bellville	29 Mar 03

JAVELIN

Mark	Name		Nat	Born	Pos	Meet	Venue	Date
84.69	Zigismunds	Sirmais	LAT	6.5.92	2		Bauska	22 Jun 11
84.58	Keshorn	Walcott	TTO	2.4.93	1	OG	London (OS)	11 Aug 12
83.87	Andreas	Thorkildsen	NOR	1.4.82	1		Fana	7 Jun 01
83.55	Aleksandr	Ivanov	RUS	25.5.82	2	NC	Tula	14 Jul 01
83.07	Robert	Oosthuizen	RSA	23.1.87	1	WJ	Beijing	19 Aug 06
82.52	Harri	Haatainen	FIN	5.1.78	4		Leppävirta	25 May 96
82.52	Till	Wöschler	GER	9.6.91	1	WJ	Moncton	23 Jul 10
81.95	Jakub	Vadlejch	CZE	10.10.90	1		Domazlice	26 Sep 09
81.80	Sergey	Voynov	UZB	26.2.77	1		Tashkent	6 Jun 96
80.94	Aki	Parviainen	FIN	26.10.74	4	NC	Jyväskylä	5 Jul 92

DECATHLON

Mark	Name			Nat	Born	Pos	Meet	Venue			Date
8397	Torsten	Voss		GDR	24.3.63	1	NC	Erfurt			7 Jul 82
	10.76	7.66	14.41	2.09	48.37	14.37		41.76	4.80	62.90	4:34.04
8257	Yordani	Garcia		CUB	21.11.88	8	WCh	Osaka			1 Sep 07
	10.73/0.7	7.15/0.2	14.94	2.09	49.25	14.08/-0.2		42.91	4.70	68.74	4:55.42
8114	Michael	Kohnle		FRG	3.5.70	1	EJ	Varazdin			26 Aug 89
	10.95	7.09/0.1	15.27	2.02	49.91	14.40		45.82	4.90	60.82	4:49.43
8104	Valter	Külvet		EST	19.2.64	1		Viimsi			23 Aug 81
	10.7	7.26	13.86	2.09	48.5	14.8		47.92	4.50	60.34	4:37.8
8082	Daley	Thompson		GBR	30.7.58	1	ECp/s	Sittard			31 Jul 77
	10.70/0.8	7.54/0.7	13.84	2.01	47.31	15.26/2.0		41.70	4.70	54.48	4:30.4
8041		Qi Haifeng		CHN	7.8.83	1	AsiG	Busan			10 Oct 02
	11.09/0.2	7.22/0.0	13.05	2.06	49.09	14.54/0.0		43.16	4.80	61.04	4:35.17
8036	Christian	Schenk		GDR	9.2.65	5		Potsdam			21 Jul 84
	11.54	7.18	14.26	2.16	49.23	15.06		44.74	4.20	65.98	4:24.11
7992	Kevin	Mayer		FRA	10.2.92	8		Kladno			16 Jun 11
	11.23/0.1	7.34/0.2	12.44	2.01	48.66	14.74/-2.0		38.64	4.90	60.96	4:19.79
7938	Frank	Busemann		GER	26.2.75	1		Zeven			2 Oct 94
	10.68/1.6	7.37/1.1	13.08	2.03	50.41	14.34/-1.1		39.84	4.40	63.00	4:37.31

Mark	Wind	Name		Nat	Born	Pos	Meet	Venue	Date
7927		Jiri	Sykora	CZE	20.1.95	2	ECp-1	Ribeira Brava	6 Jul
		10.85w/3.8 7.34/0.1 13.87		2.01	48.80	15.08/-1.3		44.84 4.60 59.91	4:52.61

IAAF Junior specification with 99cm 110mh, 6kg shot, 1.75kg Discus

Mark	Wind	Name		Nat	Born	Pos	Meet	Venue	Date
8135		Jiri	Sykora	CZE	20.1.95	1	WJ	Eugene	23 Jul
		10.92/0.5 7.35/2.0 15.50		1.94	49.00	14.23/-0.1		48.55 4.40 60.56	4:42.10
8131		Arkadiy	Vasilyev	RUS	19.1.87	1		Sochi	27 May
		11.28/-0.8 7.70/2.0 14.59		2.00	49.17	14.67/0.6		46.30 4.70 56.96	4:32.10
8126		Andrey	Kravchenko	BLR	4.1.86	1	WJ	Grosseto	15 Jul
		11.09/-0.5 7.46-0.2 14.51		2.16	48.98	14.55*/0.4		43.41 4.50 52.84	4:28.46
8124		Kévin	Mayer	FRA	10.2.92	1	EJ	Tallin	24 Jul
		11.40/-1.7 7.52/1.5 14.65		2.04	49.41	14.09/0.7		41.00 4.80 56.60	4:25.23

10,000 METRES WAL

Mark	Name		Nat	Born	Pos	Meet	Venue	Date
38:46.4	Viktor	Burayev	RUS	23.8.82	1	NC-j	Moskva	20 May
38:54.75	Ralf	Kowalsky	GDR	22.3.62	1		Cottbus	24 Jun
39:08.23	Daisuke	Matsunaga	JPN	24.3.95	1		Tama	14 Dec
39:28.45	Andrey	Ruzavin	RUS	28.3.86	1	EJ	Kaunas	23 Jul
39:35.01	Stanislav	Yemelyanov	RUS	23.10.90	1	WJ	Bydgoszcz	11 Jul
39:44.71	Giovanni	De Benedictis	ITA	8.1.68	1	EJ	Birmingham	7 Aug
39:47.20		Chen Ding	CHN	5.8.92	2	WJ	Bydgoszcz	11 Jul
39:49.22		Pei Chuang	CHN	5.12.81	2	NSG	Chengdu	8 Sep

20 KILOMETRES WAL

Mark	Name		Nat	Born	Pos	Meet	Venue	Date
1:18:06	Viktor	Burayev	RUS	23.8.82	2	NC-w	Adler	4 Mar
1:18:07		Li Gaobo	CHN	23.7.89	4		Cixi	23 Apr
1:18:44		Chu Yafei	CHN	5.9.88	5		Yangzhou	22 Apr
1:18:52		Chen Ding	CHN	5.8.92	3		Taicang	22 Apr
1:18:57		Bai Xuejin	CHN	6.6.87	7		Yangzhou	22 Apr
1:19:02	Éder	Sánchez	MEX	21.5.86	11		Cixi	23 Apr
1:19:14		Xu Xingde	CHN	12.6.84	3	NC	Yangzhou	12 Apr
1:19:34		Li Jianbo	CHN	14.11.86	16		Cixi	23 Apr

4 x 100 METRES RELA

Mark	Nat	Team	Pos	Meet	Venue	Date
38.66	USA	Kimmons, Omole, I Williams, L Merritt	1	WJ	Grosseto	18 Jun
38.97	JAM	Tracey, Skeen, Minzie, Murphy	2	WJ	Barcelona	14 Jul
39.01	JPN	Oseto, Hashimoto, Cambridge, Kanamori	1h1	WJ	Barcelona	13 Jul
39.05	GBR	Edgar, Grant, Benjamin, Lewis-Francis	1	WJ	Santiago de Chile	22 Oct
39.17	TTO	Simpson, Burns, Holder, Brown	3	WJ	Kingston	21 Jul
39.25	FRG	Dobeleit, Klameth, Evers, Lübke	1	EJ	Schwechat	28 Aug
39.29	BRA	de Araújo, Monteiro, R dos Santos Jnr, Rocha	2h1	WJ	Barcelona	13 Jul
39.31	POL	Bijowski, Slowikowski, Zalewski, Jabłonski	3h1	WJ	Barcelona	13 Jul

4 x 400 METRES RELA

Mark	Nat	Team	Pos	Meet	Venue	Date
3:01.09	USA	B Johnson, L Merritt, Craig, Clement	1	WJ	Grosseto	18 Jul
3:03.80	GBR	Grindley, Patrick, Winrow, Richardson	2	WJ	Plovdiv	12 Aug
3:04.06	JAM	S Clarke, Bolt, Myers, Gonzales	2	WJ	Kingston	21 Jul
3:04.11	JPN	Walsh, Yui, Kitagawa, Kato	2	WJ	Eugene	27 Jul
3:04.22	CUB	Cadogan, Mordoche, González, Hernández	2	WJ	Athína	20 Jul
3:04.50	RSA	le Roux, Gebhardt, Julius, van Zyl	2	WJ	Grosseto	18 Jul
3:04.58	GDR	Preusche, Löper, Trylus, Carlowitz	1	EJ	Utrecht	23 Aug
3:04.74	AUS	McFarlane, Batman, Thom, Vincent	1	WJ	Annecy	2 Aug

JUNIOR WOMEN'S ALL-TIME LISTS

100 METRE

Mark	Wind	Name		Nat	Born	Pos	Meet	Venue	Date
10.88	2.0	Marlies	Oelsner	GDR	21.3.58	1	NC	Dresden	1 Jul
10.89	1.8	Katrin	Krabbe	GDR	22.11.69	1rB		Berlin	20 Jul
11.03	1.7	Silke	Gladisch	GDR	20.6.64	3	OD	Berlin	8 Jun
11.03	0.6	English	Gardner	USA	22.4.92	1	Pac10	Tucson	14 May
11.04	1.4	Angela	Williams	USA	30.1.80	1	NCAA	Boise	5 Jun
11.07	0.7	Bianca	Knight	USA	2.1.89	4q2	NC/OT	Eugene	27 Jun
11.08	2.0	Brenda	Morehead	USA	5.10.57	1	OT	Eugene	21 Jun
11.10	0.9	Kaylin	Whitney	USA	9.3.98	1	NC-j	Eugene	5 Jul
11.11	0.2	Shakedia	Jones	USA	15.3.79	1		Los Angeles (Ww)	2 May
11.11	1.1	Joan Uduak	Ekah	NGR	16.12.80	5	Athl	Lausanne	2 Jul
Uncertain timing: 10.99	1.9	Natalya	Bochina	RUS	4.1.62	2		Leningrad	3 Jun
Wind assisted to 11.08									
10.96	3.7	Angela	Williams	USA	30.1.80	1		Las Vegas	3 Apr
10.97	3.3	Gesine	Walther	GDR	6.10.62	4	NC	Cottbus	16 Jul
11.02	2.1	Nikole	Mitchell	JAM	5.6.74	1	Mutual	Kingston	1 May
11.03	2.2	Dina	Asher-Smith	GBR	4.12.95	1		Mannheim	5 Jul

Mark	Wind	Name		Nat	Born	Pos	Meet	Venue	Date
11.04	5.6	Kelly-Ann	Baptiste	TTO	14.10.86	1rB	TexR	Austin	9 Apr 05
11.04	3.1	Desiree	Henry	GBR	26.8.95	1		Clermont	26 Apr 14
11.06	2.2	Brenda	Morehead	USA	5.10.57	1s2	OT	Eugene	21 Jun 76

200 METRES

Mark	Wind	Name		Nat	Born	Pos	Meet	Venue	Date
22.11A	-0.5	Allyson	Felix	USA	18.11.85	1		Ciudad de México	3 May 03
		22.18	0.8			2	OG	Athína	25 Aug 04
22.19	1.5	Natalya	Bochina	RUS	4.1.62	2	OG	Moskva	30 Jul 80
22.37	1.3	Sabine	Rieger	GDR	6.11.63	2	vURS	Cottbus	26 Jun 82
22.42	0.4	Gesine	Walther	GDR	6.10.62	1		Potsdam	29 Aug 81
22.43	0.8	Bianca	Knight	USA	2.1.89	1	Reebok	New York (RI)	31 May 08
22.45	0.5	Grit	Breuer	GER	16.2.72	2	ASV	Köln	8 Sep 91
22.45	0.9	Shaunae	Miller	BAH	15.4.94	2	NC	Freeport	22 Jun 13
22.49	1.3	Kaylin	Whitney	USA	9.3.98	1	NC-j	Eugene	6 Jul 14
22.51	2.0	Katrin	Krabbe	GDR	22.11.69	3		Berlin	13 Sep 88
22.52	1.2	Mary	Onyali	NGR	3.2.68	6	WCh	Roma	3 Sep 87
22.53	0.2	Anthonique	Strachan	BAH	22.8.93	1	WJ	Barcelona	13 Jul 12
Indoors									
22.40		Bianca	Knight	USA	2.1.89	1r2	NCAA	Fayetteville	15 Mar 08
22.49		Sanya	Richards	USA	26.2.85	2rA	NCAA	Fayetteville	12 Mar 04
Wind assisted									
22.25	5.6	Bianca	Knight	USA	2.1.89	5	NC/OT	Eugene	6 Jul 08
22.34	2.3	Katrin	Krabbe	GDR	22.11.69	1	WJ	Sudbury	30 Jul 88
22.41	3.1	Shaunae	Miller	BAH	15.4.94	1		Athens, GA	13 Apr 13
22.49	2.3	Brenda	Morehead	USA	5.10.57	1	OT	Eugene	24 Jun 76
22.53	2.5	Valerie	Brisco	USA	6.7.60	2	AAU	Walnut	17 Jun 79

400 METRES

Mark	Wind	Name		Nat	Born	Pos	Meet	Venue	Date
49.42		Grit	Breuer	GER	16.2.72	2	WCh	Tokyo	27 Aug 91
49.77		Christina	Brehmer	GDR	28.2.58	1		Dresden	9 May 76
49.89		Sanya	Richards	USA	26.2.85	2	NC/OT	Sacramento	17 Jul 04
50.01			Li Jing	CHN	14.2.80	1	NG	Shanghai	18 Oct 97
50.19		Marita	Koch	GDR	18.2.57	3	OD	Berlin	10 Jul 76
50.46		Kendall	Baisden	USA	5.3.95	2	Big 12	Lubbock	18 May 14
50.50		Ashley	Spencer	USA	8.6.93	1	WJ	Barcelona	13 Jul 12
50.59		Fatima	Yusuf	NGR	2.5.71	1	HGP	Budapest	5 Aug 90
50.70		Shaunae	Miller	BAH	15.4.94	2	NCAA	Eugene	7 Jun 13
50.74		Monique	Henderson	USA	18.2.83	1		Norwalk	3 Jun 00
50.78		Danijela	Grgic	CRO	28.9.88	1	WJ	Beijing	17 Aug 06

800 METRES

Mark	Wind	Name		Nat	Born	Pos	Meet	Venue	Date
1:54.01		Pamela	Jelimo	KEN	5.12.89	1	WK	Zürich	29 Aug 08
1:55.45		Caster	Semenya	RSA	7.1.91	1	WCh	Berlin	19 Aug 09
1:56.59		Francine	Niyonsaba	BDI	5.5.93	1	VD	Bruxelles	7 Sep 12
1:57.18			Wang Yuan	CHN	8.4.76	2h2	NG	Beijing	8 Sep 93
1:57.45		Hildegard	Ullrich	GDR	20.12.59	5	EC	Praha	31 Aug 78
1:57.62			Lang Yinglai	CHN	22.8.79	1	NG	Shanghai	22 Oct 97
1:57.63		Maria	Mutola	MOZ	27.10.72	4	WCh	Tokyo	26 Aug 91
1:57.74		Sahily	Diago	CUB	26.8.95	1	Barr	La Habana	25 Jul 14
1:57.77			Lu Yi	CHN	10.4.74	4	NG	Beijing	9 Sep 93
1:57.86		Katrin	Wühn	GDR	19.11.65	1		Celje	5 May 84
1:58.16			Lin Nuo	CHN	18.1.80	3	NG	Shanghai	22 Oct 97

1000 METRES

Mark	Wind	Name		Nat	Born	Pos	Meet	Venue	Date
2:35.4		Irina	Nikitina	RUS	16.1.61	5	Kuts	Podolsk	5 Aug 79
2:35.4		Katrin	Wühn	GDR	19.11.65	3		Potsdam	12 Jul 84

1500 METRES

Mark	Wind	Name		Nat	Born	Pos	Meet	Venue	Date
3:51.34			Lang Yinglai	CHN	22.8.79	2	NG	Shanghai	18 Oct 97
3:53.91			Yin Lili	CHN	11.11.79	3	NG	Shanghai	18 Oct 97
3:53.97			Lan Lixin	CHN	14.2.79	4	NG	Shanghai	18 Oct 97
3:54.52			Zhang Ling	CHN	13.4.80	5	NG	Shanghai	18 Oct 97
3:56.98		Faith	Kipyegon	KEN	10.1.94	2	DL	Doha	10 May 13
3:59.53		Dawit	Seyaum	ETH	27.7.96	1		Marrakech	8 Jun 14
3:59.60		Gelete	Burka	ETH	15.2.86	5	GP	Rieti	28 Aug 05
3:59.81			Wang Yuan	CHN	8.4.76	7	NG	Beijing	11 Sep 93
3:59.96		Zola	Budd	GBR	26.5.66	3	VD	Bruxelles	30 Aug 85
4:00.05			Lu Yi	CHN	10.4.74	8	NG	Beijing	11 Sep 93
4:01.71			Li Ying	CHN	24.6.75	4h2	NG	Beijing	10 Sep 93
1 MILE: 4:17.57 Zola			Budd	GBR	26.5.66	3	WK	Zürich	21 Aug 85
2000 METRES: 5:33.15 Zola			Budd	GBR	26.5.66	1		London	13 Jul 84

3000 METRES

Mark	Wind	Name		Nat	Born	Pos	Meet	Venue	Date
8:28.83		Zola	Budd	GBR	26.5.66	3	GG	Roma	7 Sep 85
8:35.89		Sally	Barsosio	KEN	21.3.78	2	Herc	Monaco	16 Aug 97
8:36.45			Ma Ningning	CHN	1.6.76	4	NC	Jinan	6 Jun 93
8:36.87		Alemitu	Haroye	ETH	9.5.95	14	VD	Bruxelles	5 Sep 14
8:38.61		Kalkedan	Gezahegn	ETH	8.5.91	5	WAF	Thessaloníki	13 Sep 09
8:38.97		Linet	Masai	KEN	5.12.89	5	GP	Rieti	9 Sep 07
8:39.13		Agnes	Tirop	KEN	23.10.95	3		Rieti	8 Sep 13
8:39.65		Buze	Diriba	ETH	9.2.94	3	Herc	Monaco	20 Jul 12
8:39.90		Gelete	Burka	ETH	15.2.86	3	SGP	Doha	13 May 05
8:40.08		Gabriela	Szabo	ROM	14.11.75	3	EC	Helsinki	10 Aug 94
8:40.28		Meseret	Defar	ETH	19.11.83	10	VD	Bruxelles	30 Aug 02

5000 METRES

Mark	Wind	Name		Nat	Born	Pos	Meet	Venue	Date
14:30.88		Tirunesh	Dibaba	ETH	1.10.85	2	Bisl	Bergen (Fana)	11 Jun 04
14:35.18		Sentayehu	Ejigu	ETH	21.6.85	4	Bisl	Bergen (Fana)	11 Jun 04
14:39.96			Yin Lili	CHN	11.11.79	4	NG	Shanghai	23 Oct 97
14:43.29		Emebet	Anteneh	ETH	13.1.92	5	Bisl	Oslo	9 Jun 11
14:45.33			Lan Lixin	CHN	14.2.79	2h2	NG	Shanghai	21 Oct 97
14:45.71			Song Liqing	CHN	20.1.80	3h2	NG	Shanghai	21 Oct 97
14:45.90			Jiang Bo	CHN	13.3.77	1		Nanjing	24 Oct 95
14:45.98		Pauline	Korikwiang	KEN	1.3.88	7	Bisl	Oslo	2 Jun 06
14:46.71		Sally	Barsosio	KEN	21.3.78	3	VD	Bruxelles	22 Aug 97
14:47.13		Mercy	Cherono	KEN	7.5.91	7	DL	Shanghai	23 May 10
14:47.14		Linet	Masai	KEN	5.12.89	4	FBK	Hengelo	24 May 08

10,000 METRES

Mark	Wind	Name		Nat	Born	Pos	Meet	Venue	Date
30:26.50		Linet	Masai	KEN	5.12.89	4	OG	Beijing	15 Aug 08
30:31.55			Xing Huina	CHN	25.2.84	7	WCh	Saint-Denis	23 Aug 03
30:39.41			Lan Lixin	CHN	14.2.79	2	NG	Shanghai	19 Oct 97
30:39.98			Yin Lili	CHN	11.11.79	3	NG	Shanghai	19 Oct 97
30:59.92		Merima	Hashim	ETH	.81	3	NA	Heusden-Zolder	5 Aug 00
31:06.20		Lucy	Wangui	KEN	24.3.84	1rA		Okayama	27 Sep 03
31:11.26			Song Liqing	CHN	20.1.80	7	NG	Shanghai	19 Oct 97
31:15.38		Sally	Barsosio	KEN	21.3.78	3	WCh	Stuttgart	21 Aug 93
31:16.50		Evelyne	Kimwei	KEN	25.8.87	1		Kobe	21 Oct 06
31:17.30			Zhang Yingying	CHN	4.1.90	1		Wuhan	2 Nov 07
31:20.38		Tigist	Kiros	ETH	8.6.92	4	GS	Ostrava	31 May 11

MARATHON

Mark	Wind	Name		Nat	Born	Pos	Meet	Venue	Date
2:22:38			Zhang Yingying	CHN	4.1.90	1	NC	Xiamen	5 Jan 08
2:23:06		Merima	Mohamed	ETH	10.6.92	3		Toronto	26 Sep 10
2:23:37			Liu Min	CHN	29.11.83	1		Beijing	14 Oct 01
2:23:57			Zhu Xiaolin	CHN	20.4.84	4		Beijing	20 Oct 02
2:25:48			Jin Li	CHN	29.5.83	6		Beijing	14 Oct 01
2:26:34			Wei Yanan	CHN	6.12.81	1		Beijing	15 Oct 00
2:27:05			Chen Rong	CHN	18.5.88	1		Beijing	21 Oct 07
2:27:30			Ai Dongmei	CHN	15.10.79	3	NG	Beijing	4 Oct 97

3000 METRES STEEPLECHASE

Mark	Wind	Name		Nat	Born	Pos	Meet	Venue	Date
9:20.37		Birtukan	Adamu	ETH	29.4.92	4	GGala	Roma	26 May 11
9:20.55		Ruth	Chebet	KEN/BRN	17.11.96	4	WK	Zürich	28 Aug 14
9:22.51		Almaz	Ayana	ETH	21.11.91	3	VD	Bruxelles	27 Aug 10
9:24.51		Ruth	Bisibori	KEN	2.1.88	1		Daegu	3 Oct 07
9:26.25			Liu Nian	CHN	26.4.88	1		Wuhan	2 Nov 07
9:28.36		Tigist Getnet	Mekonen	ETH	7.7.97	7	DL	Glasgow	12 Jul 14
9:29.52		Korahubish	Itaa	ETH	28.2.92	1		Huelva	10 Jun 09
9:30.70		Melissa	Rollison	AUS	13.4.83	1	GWG	Brisbane	4 Sep 01
9:31.35		Christine	Muyanga	KEN	21.3.91	1	WJ	Bydgoszcz	10 Jul 08
9:32.74		Gesa-Felicitas	Krause	GER	3.8.92	9	WCh	Daegu	30 Aug 11

100 METRES HURDLES

Mark	Wind	Name		Nat	Born	Pos	Meet	Venue	Date
12.84	1.5	Aliuska	López	CUB	29.8.69	2	WUG	Zagreb	16 Jul 87
12.87	2.0	Kendell	Williams	USA	14.6.95	1	NC-j	Eugene	6 Jul 14
12.88	1.5	Yelena	Ovcharova	UKR	17.6.76	2	ECp	Villeneuve d'Ascq	25 Jun 95
12.89	1.3	Anay	Tejeda	CUB	3.4.83	1		Padova	1 Sep 02
12.91	1.8	Kristina	Castlin	USA	7.7.88	1	NCAA-r	Gainesville	26 May 07
12.92	0.0		Sun Hongwei	CHN	24.11.79	6	NG	Shanghai	18 Oct 97
12.92	1.9	Dior	Hall	USA	2.1.96	2	WJ	Eugene	27 Jul 14
12.95	1.5	Candy	Young	USA	21.5.62	2	AAU	Walnut	16 Jun 79
12.95A	1.5	Cinnamon	Sheffield	USA	8.3.70	2	NCAA	Provo	3 Jun 89

Mark	Wind	Name		Nat	Born	Pos	Meet	Venue	Date
12.98	1.8	Queen	Harrison	USA	10.9.88	5	NCAA	Sacramento	8 Jun 07
12.99	1.9	Nadine	Visser	NED	9.2.95	3	WJ	Eugene	27 Jul 14
Wind assisted									
12.81	3.4	Anay	Tejeda	CUB	3.4.83	1	WJ	Kingston	21 Jul 02
12.82	2.1	Kristina	Castlin	USA	7.7.88	1		College Park	21 Apr 07
12.90	3.0	Adrianna	Lamalle	FRA	27.9.82	1		Fort-de-France	28 Apr 01
12.95	2.4	Shermaine	Williams	JAM	4.2.90	1	NCAA II	San Angelo	23 May 09

400 METRES HURDLES

Mark	Wind	Name		Nat	Born	Pos	Meet	Venue	Date
54.40			Wang Xing	CHN	30.11.86	2	NG	Nanjing	21 Oct 05
54.58		Ristananna	Tracey	JAM	5.9.92	2	NC	Kingston	24 Jun 11
54.70		Lashinda	Demus	USA	10.3.83	1	WJ	Kingston	19 Jul 02
54.93			Li Rui	CHN	22.11.79	1	NG	Shanghai	22 Oct 97
55.07		Shamier	Little	USA	20.3.95	1	NCAA	Eugene	13 Jun 14
55.11		Kaliese	Spencer	JAM	6.4.87	1	WJ	Beijing	17 Aug 06
55.15			Huang Xiaoxiao	CHN	3.3.83	2	NG	Guangzhou	22 Nov 01
55.20		Lesley	Maxie	USA	4.1.67	2	TAC	San Jose	9 Jun 84
55.20A		Jana	Pittman	AUS	9.11.82	1		Pietersburg	18 Mar 00
55.22		Tiffany	Ross	USA	5.2.83	2	NCAA	Baton Rouge	31 May 02
55.26		Ionela	Tîrlea	ROM	9.2.76	1	Nik	Nice	12 Jul 95
Drugs disqualification: 54.54			Peng Yinghua ¶	CHN	21.2.79	(2)	NG	Shanghai	22 Oct 97

HIGH JUMP

Mark	Wind	Name		Nat	Born	Pos	Meet	Venue	Date
2.01		Olga	Turchak	UKR	5.3.67	2	GWG	Moskva	7 Jul 86
2.01		Heike	Balck	GDR	19.8.70	1	vURS-j	Karl-Marx-Stadt	18 Jun 89
2.00		Stefka	Kostadinova	BUL	25.3.65	1		Sofia	25 Aug 84
2.00		Alina	Astafei	ROM	7.6.69	1	WJ	Sudbury	29 Jul 88
1.98		Silvia	Costa	CUB	4.5.64	2	WUG	Edmonton	11 Jul 83
1.98		Yelena	Yelesina	RUS	5.4.70	1	Druzh	Nyiregyháza	13 Aug 88
1.97		Svetlana	Isaeva	BUL	18.3.67	2		Sofia	25 May 86
1.97i		Mariya	Kuchina	RUS	14.1.93	1		Trinec	26 Jan 11
1.96A		Charmaine	Gale	RSA	27.2.64	1	NC-j	Bloemfontein	4 Apr 81
1.96i		Desislava	Aleksandrova	BUL	27.10.75	2	EI	Paris (B)	12 Mar 94
1.96		Marina	Kuptsova	RUS	22.12.81	1	NC	Tula	26 Jul 00
1.96		Blanka	Vlasic	CRO	8.11.83	1	WJ	Kingston	20 Jul 02
1.96		Airine	Palsyte	LTU	13.7.92	2	WUG	Shenzhen	21 Aug 11
1.96		Eleanor	Patterson	AUS	22.5.96	1	N.Sch	Townsville	7 Dec 13

POLE VAULT

Mark	Wind	Name		Nat	Born	Pos	Meet	Venue	Date
4.63i		Angelica	Bengtsson	SWE	8.7.93	2		Stockholm	22 Feb 11
		4.58				1		Sollentuna	5 Jul 12
4.60i		Hanna	Sheleh	UKR	14.7.93	3		Donetsk	11 Feb 12
4.60i		Roberta	Bruni	ITA	8.3.94	1	NC	Ancona	17 Feb 13
4.52i		Katie	Byres	GBR	11.9.93	2		Nevers	18 Feb 12
4.50		Valeriya	Volik	RUS	11.5.89	1		Krasnodar	4 Jun 08
4.50		Liz	Parnov	AUS	9.5.94	1		Perth	17 Feb 12
4.50i		Alyona	Lutkovskaya	RUS	15.3.96	3	NC	Moskva	17 Feb 14
		4.50				1	WJ	Eugene	24 Jul 14
4.48i		Silke	Spiegelburg	GER	17.3.86	2		Münster	25 Aug 05
4.47i		Yelena	Isinbayeva	RUS	3.6.82	1		Budapest	10 Feb 01
		4.46				2	ISTAF	Berlin	31 Aug 01
4.46i			Zhang Yingning	CHN	6.1.90	1		Shanghai	15 Mar 07

LONG JUMP

Mark	Wind	Name		Nat	Born	Pos	Meet	Venue	Date
7.14	1.1	Heike	Daute	GDR	16.12.64	1	PTS	Bratislava	4 Jun 83
7.03	1.3	Darya	Klishina	RUS	15.1.91	1	Znam	Zhukovskiy	26 Jun 10
7.00	-0.2	Birgit	Grosshennig	GDR	21.2.65	2		Berlin	9 Jun 84
6.94	-0.5	Magdalena	Khristova	BUL	25.2.77	2		Kalamáta	22 Jun 96
6.91	0.0	Anisoara	Cusmir	ROM	28.6.62	1		Bucuresti	23 May 81
6.90	1.4	Beverly	Kinch	GBR	14.1.64	*	WCh	Helsinki	14 Aug 83
6.88	0.6	Natalya	Shevchenko	RUS	28.12.66	2		Sochi	26 May 84
6.84		Larisa	Baluta	UKR	13.8.65	2		Krasnodar	6 Aug 83
6.82	1.8	Fiona	May	GBR	12.12.69	*	WJ	Sudbury	30 Jul 88
6.81	1.6	Carol	Lewis	USA	8.8.63	1	TAC	Knoxville	20 Jun 82
6.81	1.4	Yelena	Davydova	KZK	16.11.67	1	NC-j	Krasnodar	17 Jul 85
Wind assisted									
7.27	2.2	Heike	Daute	GDR	16.12.64	1	WCh	Helsinki	14 Aug 83
6.93	4.6	Beverly	Kinch	GBR	14.1.64	5	WCh	Helsinki	14 Aug 83
6.88	2.1	Fiona	May	GBR	12.12.69	1	WJ	Sudbury	30 Jul 88
6.84	2.8	Anu	Kaljurand	EST	16.4.69	2		Riga	4 Jun 88
6.81	2.5	Katarina	Johnson-Thompson	GBR	9.1.93	1	WJ	Barcelona	13 Jul 12

Mark	Wind	Name		Nat	Born	Pos	Meet	Venue	Date

TRIPLE JUMP

Mark	Wind	Name		Nat	Born	Pos	Meet	Venue	Date
14.62	1.0	Tereza	Marinova	BUL	5.9.77	1	WC	Sydney	25 Aug 96
14.57	0.2		Huang Qiuyan	CHN	25.1.80	1	NG	Shanghai	19 Oct 97
14.52	0.6	Anastasiya	Ilyina	RUS	16.1.82	q	WJ	Santiago de Chile	20 Oct 00
14.46	1.0		Peng Fengmei	CHN	2.7.79	1		Chengdu	18 Apr 98
14.43	0.6	Kaire	Leibak	EST	21.5.88	1	WJ	Beijing	17 Aug 06
14.38	-0.7		Xie Limei	CHN	27.6.86	1	AsiC	Inchon	1 Sep 05
14.37i	-		Ren Ruiping	CHN	1.2.76	3	WI	Barcelona	11 Mar 95
		14.36	0.0			1	NC	Beijing	1 Jun 94
14.36	0.0	Dailenys	Alcántara	CUB	10.8.91	3	Barr/NC	La Habana	29 May 09
14.35		Yana	Borodina	RUS	21.4.92	1J	Mosc Ch	Moskva	15 Jun 11
14.32	-0.1	Yelena	Lysak ¶	RUS	19.10.75	1		Voronezh	18 Jun 94
Wind assisted									
14.83	8.3		Ren Ruiping	CHN	1.2.76	1	NC	Taiyuan	21 May 95
14.55	3.7	Dailenis	Alcántara	CUB	10.8.91	1	Barr/NC	La Habana	21 Mar 10
14.43	2.7	Yelena	Lysak ¶	RUS	19.10.75	1	WJ	Lisboa	21 Jul 94

SHOT

Mark	Wind	Name		Nat	Born	Pos	Meet	Venue	Date
20.54		Astrid	Kumbernuss	GDR	5.2.70	1	vFIN-j	Orimattila	1 Jul 89
20.51i		Heidi	Krieger	GDR	20.7.65	2		Budapest	8 Feb 84
		20.24				5		Split	30 Apr 84
20.23		Ilke	Wyludda	GDR	28.3.69	1	NC-j	Karl-Marx-Stadt	16 Jul 88
20.12		Ilona	Schoknecht	GDR	24.9.56	2	NC	Erfurt	23 Aug 75
20.02			Cheng Xiaoyan	CHN	30.11.75	3	NC	Beijing	5 Jun 94
19.90		Stephanie	Storp	FRG	28.11.68	1		Hamburg	16 Aug 87
19.63			Wang Yawen	CHN	23.8.73	1		Shijiazhuang	25 Apr 92
19.57		Grit	Haupt	GDR	4.6.66	1		Gera	7 Jul 84
19.48		Ines	Wittich	GDR	14.11.69	5		Leipzig	29 Jul 87
19.46			Gong Lijiao	CHN	24.1.89	Q	OG	Beijing	16 Aug 08
19.42		Simone	Michel	GDR	18.12.60	3	vSU	Leipzig	23 Jun 79

DISCUS

Mark	Wind	Name		Nat	Born	Pos	Meet	Venue	Date
74.40		Ilke	Wyludda	GDR	28.3.69	2		Berlin	13 Sep 88
		75.36 unofficial meeting				2		Berlin	6 Sep 88
67.38		Irina	Meszynski	GDR	24.3.62	1		Berlin	14 Aug 81
67.00		Jana	Günther	GDR	7.1.68	6	NC	Potsdam	20 Aug 87
66.80		Svetla	Mitkova	BUL	17.6.64	1		Sofia	2 Aug 83
66.60		Astrid	Kumbernuss	GDR	5.2.70	1		Berlin	20 Jul 88
66.34		Franka	Dietzsch	GDR	22.1.68	2		Saint-Denis	11 Jun 87
66.30		Jana	Lauren	GDR	28.6.70	1	vURS-j	Karl-Marx-Stadt	18 Jun 89
66.08			Cao Qi	CHN	15.1.74	1	NG	Beijing	12 Sep 93
65.96		Grit	Haupt	GDR	4.6.66	3		Leipzig	13 Jul 84
65.22		Daniela	Costian	ROM	30.4.65	3		Nitra	26 Aug 84

HAMMER

Mark	Wind	Name		Nat	Born	Pos	Meet	Venue	Date
73.24			Zhang Wenxiu	CHN	22.3.86	1	NC	Changsha	24 Jun 05
71.71		Kamila	Skolimowska	POL	4.11.82	1	GPF	Melbourne	9 Sep 01
70.62		Alexandra	Tavernier	FRA	13.12.93	1	WJ	Barcelona	14 Jul 12
70.39		Mariya	Smolyachkova	BLR	10.2.85	1		Staiki	26 Jun 04
69.73		Natalya	Zolotukhina	UKR	4.1.85	1		Kiev	24 Jul 04
69.63		Bianca	Perie	ROU	1.6.90	1	NC-j	Bucuresti	14 Aug 09
68.74		Arasay	Thondike	CUB	28.5.86	2	Barr	La Habana	2 May 05
68.50		Martina	Danisová	SVK	21.3.83	1		Kladno	16 Jun 01
68.49		Anna	Bulgakova	RUS	17.1.88	6		Sochi	26 May 07
68.43		Alyona	Shamotina	UKR	27.12.95	1	NC-j	Kyiv	13 Jun 14
68.40		Bianca	Achilles	GER	17.4.81	1		Dortmund	25 Sep 99

JAVELIN

Mark	Wind	Name		Nat	Born	Pos	Meet	Venue	Date
63.01		Vira	Rebryk	UKR	25.2.89	1	WJ	Bydgoszcz	10 Jul 08
62.93			Xue Juan	CHN	10.2.86	1	NG	Changsha	27 Oct 03
62.09			Zhang Li	CHN	17.1.89	1		Beijing	25 May 08
61.99			Wang Yaning	CHN	4.1.80	1	NC	Huizhou	14 Oct 99
61.96		Sofi	Flink	SWE	8.7.95	Q	WCh	Moskva	16 Aug 13
61.79		Nikolett	Szabó	HUN	3.3.80	1		Schwechat	23 May 99
61.61			Chang Chunfeng	CHN	4.5.88	1	NC-j	Chengdu	4 Jun 07
61.49			Liang Lili	CHN	16.11.83	1	NC	Benxi	1 Jun 02
61.38		Annika	Suthe	GER	15.10.85	1-j		Halle	23 May 04
61.24		Marcelina	Witek	POL	2.6.95	1		Białogard	6 Sep 14
Pre 1999 specification									
71.88		Antoaneta	Todorova	BUL	8.6.63	1	ECp	Zagreb	15 Aug 81
71.82		Ivonne	Leal	CUB	27.2.66	1	WUG	Kobe	30 Aug 85

Mark	Wind	Name		Nat	Born	Pos	Meet	Venue	Date
70.12		Karen	Forkel	GDR	24.9.70	1	EJ	Varazdin	26 Aug 89
68.94		Trine	Solberg	NOR	18.4.66	1	vURS	Oslo	16 Jul 85

HEPTATHLON

Mark	Name		Nat	Born	Pos	Meet	Venue	Date
6768w	Tatyana	Chernova	RUS	29.1.88	1		Arles	3 Jun 07
	13.04w/6.1 1.82	13.57 23.59w/5.2			6.61/1.2		53.43 2:15.05	
	6227				1	WJ	Beijing	19 Aug 06
	13.70/1.6 1.80	12.18 24.05/0.3			6.35/-0.4		50.51 2:25.49	
6542	Carolina	Klüft	SWE	2.2.83	1	EC	München	10 Aug 02
	13.33/-0.3 1.89	13.16 23.71/-0.3			6.36/1.1		47.61 2:17.99	
6465	Sibylle	Thiele	GDR	6.3.65	1	EJ	Schwechat	28 Aug 83
	13.49 1.90	14.63 24.07			6.65		36.22 2:18.36	
6436	Sabine	Braun	FRG	19.6.65	1	vBUL	Mannheim	9 Jun 84
	13.68 1.78	13.09 23.88			6.03		52.14 2:09.41	
6428	Svetla	Dimitrova ¶	BUL	27.1.70	1	NC	Sofia	18 Jun 89
	13.49/-0.7 1.77	13.98 23.59/-0.2			6.49/0.7		40.10 2:11.10	
6403	Emilia	Dimitrova	BUL	13.11.67	6	GWG	Moskva	7 Jul 86
	13.73 1.76	13.46 23.17			6.29		43.30 2:09.85	
6298	Nafissatou	Thiam	BEL	19.8.94	1	EJ	Rieti	19 Jul 13
	13.87/1.2 1.89	14.26 25.15/-0.6			6.37/0.1		46.94 2:24.89	
6276	Larisa	Nikitina	RUS	29.4.65	8	URS Ch	Kiyev	21 Jun 84
	13.87/1.6 1.86	14.04 25.26/-0.7			6.31/0.1		48.62 2:22.76	
6267	Katarina	Johnson-Thompson	GBR	9.1.93	15	OG	London (OS)	4 Aug 12
	13.48/0.9 1.89	11.32 23.73/-0.3			6.19/-0.4		38.37 2:10.76	
6231	Yorgelis	Rodríguez	CUB	25.1.95	1		La Habana	22 Feb 14
	14.01/0.0 1.84	14.21 24.93/0.0			6.03/0.0		47.58 2:17.93	
Drugs disqualification: 6534	Svetla	Dimitrova	BUL	27.1.70	(3)	ECp	Helmond	16 Jul 89
	13.30/1.0 1.84	14.35 23.33/-2.2			6.47/-1.4		39.20 2:13.56	

10 KILOMETRES WALK

Mark	Wind	Name		Nat	Born	Pos	Meet	Venue	Date
41:52		Tatyana	Mineyeva	RUS	10.8.90	1	NCp-j	Penza	5 Sep 09
41:55		Irina	Stankina	RUS	25.3.77	1	NC-wj	Adler	11 Feb 95
41:57			Gao Hongmiao	CHN	17.3.74	2	NG	Beijing	8 Sep 93
42:15+		Anisya	Kirdyapkina	RUS	23.10.89	1=	in 20k	Adler	23 Feb 08
42:29		Tatyana	Kalmykova	RUS	10.1.90	1	NC-wj	Adler	23 Feb 08
42:31		Irina	Yumanova	RUS	17.6.90	2	NC-wj	Adler	23 Feb 08
42:43.0	t	Svetlana	Vasilyeva	RUS	24.7.92	1	NC-wj	Sochi	27 Feb 11
42:44			Long Yuwen	CHN	1.8.75	3	NC	Shenzen	18 Feb 93
42:45			Li Yuxin	CHN	4.12.74	4		Shenzhen	18 Feb 93
42:45		Kseniya	Trifonova	RUS	7.5.90	2	NC-wj	Adler	28 Feb 09

20 KILOMETRES WALK

Mark	Name		Nat	Born	Pos	Meet	Venue	Date
1:25:30	Anisya	Kirdyapkina	RUS	23.10.89	2	NC-w	Adler	23 Feb 08
1:26:36	Tatyana	Kalmykova	RUS	10.1.90	1	NC	Saransk	8 Jun 08
1:27:01		Lu Xiuzhi	CHN	26.10.93	2		Taicang	30 Mar 12
1:27:16		Song Hongjuan	CHN	4.7.84	1	NC	Yangzhou	14 Apr 03
1:27:34		Jiang Jing	CHN	23.10.85	2	WCp	Naumburg	2 May 04
1:27:35	Natalya	Fedoskina	RUS	25.6.80	2	WCp	Mézidon-Canon	2 May 99
1:28:08	Anezka	Drahotová	CZE	22.7.95	3	EC	Zürich	14 Aug 14

4 X 100 METRES RELAY

Mark	Nat	Team	Pos	Meet	Venue	Date
43.29	USA (Blue)	Knight, Tarmoh, Olear, Mayo	1		Eugene	8 Aug 06
43.40	JAM	Simpson, Stewart, McLaughlin, Facey	1	WJ	Kingston	20 Jul 02
43.42	GER	Burghardt, Grompe, Pinto, Frese	1	EJ	Tallinn	24 Jul 11
43.44A	NGR	Utondu, Iheagwam, Onyali, Ogunkoya	1	AfrG	Nairobi	9 Aug 87
43.68	FRA	Vouaux, Jacques-Sebastien, Kamga, Banco	3	WJ	Grosseto	18 Jul 04
43.81	GBR	Miller, Asher-Smith, S Wilson, Henry	1	EJ	Rieti	21 Jul 13
43.87	URS	Lapshina, Doronina, Bulatova, Kovalyova	1	vGDR-j	Leningrad	20 Jun 87
43.98	BRA	Silva, Leoncio, Krasucki, Santos	2	PAm-J	São Paulo	7 Jul 07
44.04	CUB	Riquelme, Allen, López, Valdivia	2	WJ	Sudbury	31 Jul 88

4 X 400 METRES RELAY

Mark	Nat	Team	Pos	Meet	Venue	Date
3:27.60	USA	Anderson, Kidd, Smith, Hastings	1	WJ	Grosseto	18 Jul 04
3:28.39	GDR	Derr, Fabert, Wöhlk, Breuer	1	WJ	Sudbury	31 Jul 88
3:29.66	JAM	Stewart, Morgan, Walker, Hall	1	PennR	Philadelphia	28 Apr 01
3:30.03	RUS	Talko, Shapayeva, Soldatova, Kostetskaya	2	WJ	Grosseto	18 Jul 04
3:30.38	AUS	Scamps, R Poetschka, Hanigan, Andrews	1	WJ	Plovdiv	12 Aug 90
3:30.46	GBR	Wall, Spencer, James, Miller	2	WJ	Kingston	21 Jul 02
3:30.72	BUL	Kireva, Angelova, Rashova, Dimitrova	3	v2N	Sofia	24 Jul 83
3:30.84	NGR	Abugan, Odumosu, Eze, Adesanya	2	WJ	Beijing	20 Aug 06
3:31.57	ROU	Petrea, Florea, Tîrlea, Nedelcu	1	WJ	Seoul	20 Sep 92

Mark	Name		Nat	Born	Pos	Meet	Venue	Date

MEN'S WORLD LISTS 2014

60 METRES INDOORS

Mark	Name		Nat	Born	Pos	Meet	Venue	Date
6.47	James	Dasaolu	GBR	5.9.87	1h2	GP	Birmingham	15 Feb
6.48	Jimmy	Vicaut	FRA	27.2.92	1h1	GP	Birmingham	15 Feb
6.48A	Marvin	Bracy	USA	15.12.93	1	NC	Albuquerque	23 Feb
6.49	Yunier	Pérez	CUB/TUR	16.2.85	1	Winter	Moskva	2 Feb
6.49A	Trell	Kimmons	USA	13.7.85	2	NC	Albuquerque	23 Feb
6.49	Kim	Collins	SKN	5.4.76	1		Praha (O2)	25 Feb
6.49	Richard	Kilty	GBR	2.9.89	1	WI	Sopot	8 Mar
6.50A	Tosin	Ogunode	NGR	2.3.94	1		Flagstaff	25 Jan
6.50		Dasaolu			1	v3N	Glasgow	25 Jan
6.50		Pérez			1		Düsseldorf	30 Jan
6.50		Dasaolu			1	NC	Sheffield	8 Feb
6.50		Dasaolu			1	GP	Birmingham	15 Feb
6.50		Bracy			1	Mill	New York (Arm)	15 Feb
6.50	Nesta	Carter	JAM	11.10.85	1s1	WI	Sopot	8 Mar
	(15/9)							
6.51A	Femi	Ogunode (10)	QAT	15.5.91	2		Flagstaff	25 Jan
6.51A	Mike	Rodgers	USA	24.4.85	1h4	NC	Albuquerque	22 Feb
6.52	Jason	Rogers	SKN	31.8.91	1		Toronto	15 Feb
6.52A	D'Angelo	Cherry	USA	1.8.90	1s2	NC	Albuquerque	23 Feb
6.52A	Joe	Morris	USA	4.10.89	3	NC	Albuquerque	23 Feb
6.52	Dwain	Chambers	GBR	5.4.78	2		Praha (O2)	25 Feb
6.52		Su Bingtian	CHN	29.8.89	4	WI	Sopot	8 Mar
6.52	Gerald	Phiri	ZAM	6.10.88	5	WI	Sopot	8 Mar
6.52A	Dentarius	Locke	USA	12.12.89	1	NCAA	Albuquerque	15 Mar
6.54	Warren	Fraser	BAH	8.7.91	1		Birmingham AL	18 Jan
6.54A	Diondre	Batson	USA	13.7.92	1h1	NCAA	Albuquerque	14 Mar
	(20)							
6.54A	Cameron	Burrell	USA	11.9.94	1h2	NCAA	Albuquerque	14 Mar
6.55	Clayton	Vaughn	USA	15.5.92	1		Lincoln NE	8 Feb
6.55A	Aaron	Brown	CAN	27.5.92	1		Albuquerque	15 Feb
6.55	Adam	Harris	GUY	21.7.87	1		Allendale	21 Feb
6.55A	Sean	McLean	USA	23.3.92	4	NC	Albuquerque	23 Feb
6.55	Kimmari	Roach	JAM	21.9.90	2s2	WI	Sopot	8 Mar
6.56	Prezel	Hardy	USA	1.6.92	1		College Station	18 Jan
6.56A	Keith	Ricks	USA	9.10.90	2s1	NC	Albuquerque	23 Feb
6.56	Lucas	Jakubczyk	GER	28.4.85	2	ISTAF	Berlin	1 Mar
6.57A	Ryan	Milus	USA	19.9.90	2	NCAA	Albuquerque	15 Mar
	(30)							
6.58	Sam	Effah	CAN	29.12.88	1		Edmonton	18 Jan
6.58A	Mark	Jelks	USA	10.4.84	1		Air Force Academy	15 Feb
6.58A	Jeffrey	Henderson	USA	19.2.89	2h3	NC	Albuquerque	22 Feb
6.58	Reza	Ghasemi	IRI	24.7.87	2h4	WI	Sopot	7 Mar
6.58	Dariusz	Kuc	POL	24.4.86	2h5	WI	Sopot	7 Mar
6.59	Sean	Safo-Antwi	GBR	31.10.90	1		London (LV)	18 Jan
6.59A	Tatum	Benard-Taylor	USA	8.9.94	1rB		Flagstaff	25 Jan
6.59	Alex	Schaf	GER	28.4.87	1		Sindelfingen	8 Feb
6.59	Chijindu	Ujah	GBR	5.3.94	2s1	NC	Sheffield	8 Feb
6.59	Yoshihide	Kiryu	JPN-J	15.12.95	1		Osaka	9 Feb
	(40)							
6.60	LeShon	Collins	USA	11.12.93	1		Houston	11 Jan
6.60	Rion	Pierre	GBR	24.11.87	1r2		London (LV)	26 Jan
6.60A	Raymond	Bozmans	USA	16.12.94	1		Albuquerque	1 Feb
6.60	Tevin	Hester	USA	10.1.94	1		New York (Arm)	7 Feb
6.60	Markesh	Woodson	USA	6.9.93	2		New York (Arm)	7 Feb
6.60A	Gavin	Smellie	CAN	26.6.86	1		Flagstaff	8 Feb
6.60	T.J.	Lawrence	CAN	26.2.91	2		Toronto	15 Feb
6.60A	Cordero	Gray	USA	9.5.89	3h4	NC	Albuquerque	22 Feb
6.60A	Jeremy	Dodson	USA	30.8.87	4h4	NC	Albuquerque	22 Feb
6.60A	Ryan	Bailey	USA	13.4.89	6	NC	Albuquerque	23 Feb
	(50)							
6.60	Gabriel	Mvumvure	ZIM	23.4.88	3s1	WI	Sopot	8 Mar
6.60A	Antwan	Wright	USA	17.11.93	4h2	NCAA	Albuquerque	14 Mar
6.61	Christophe	Lemaitre	FRA	11.6.90	1h3		Mondeville	1 Feb
6.61	Devin	Jenkins	USA	16.2.94	3		Houston	1 Feb
6.61	Samuel	Francis	QAT	27.3.87	1	AsiC	Hangzhou	15 Feb
6.61	Christian	Blum	GER	10.3.87	1	NC	Leipzig	22 Feb
6.61A	Nic	Bowens	USA	28.6.93	1	MWC	Air Force Academy	1 Mar

Mark	Wind	Name		Nat	Born	Pos	Meet	Venue	Date
6.61		Dontae	Richards-Kwok	CAN	1.3.89	1		Edmonton	6 Mar
6.62		Marcus	Rowland	USA	11.3.90	2		Birmingham AL	18 Jan
6.62A		Jermaine (60)	Brown	JAM	4.7.91	1h2		Albuquerque	24 Jan
6.62		Dominique	Hubert	USA	4.11.90	2		Bloomington	1 Feb
6.62		Jalen	Miller	USA-J	17.6.95	3		New York (Arm)	7 Feb
6.62A		B.J.	Lawrence	SKN	27.12.89	1		Albuquerque	8 Feb
6.62		Danny	Talbot	GBR	1.5.91	2s3	NC	Sheffield	8 Feb
6.62		Nickel	Ashmeade	JAM	7.4.90	6		Boston (R)	8 Feb
6.62		Hugh	Graham	USA	10.10.92	1h1	SEC	College Station	28 Feb
6.62		Bolade	Ajomale	CAN-J	31.8.95	1		Toronto	1 Mar

Low altitude bests

Mark	Name	Pos	Meet	Venue	Date
6.50	Bracy	1	Mill	New York (Arm)	15 Feb
6.52	F Ogunode	3	WI	Sopot	8 Mar
6.54	Rodgers	1		Houston	1 Feb
6.54	Cherry	2	Mill	New York (Arm)	15 Feb
6.55	Morris	2		Boston (R)	8 Feb
6.57	Burrell	1	Tyson	Fayetteville	14 Feb
6.59	A Brown	1		Seattle	18 Jan
6.59	Ricks	3		Düsseldorf	30 Jan
6.61	Batson	1		Bloomington	1 Feb
6.61	Locke	2	Tyson	Fayetteville	14 Feb
6.62	Kimmons	2		Houston	11 Jan
6.62	R Bailey	1		Seattle	1 Feb
6.62	Milus	1		Seattle	1 Mar

100 METRES

Mark	Wind	Name		Nat	Born	Pos	Meet	Venue	Date
9.77	0.6	Justin	Gatlin	USA	10.2.82	1	VD	Bruxelles	5 Sep
9.80	0.1		Gatlin			1	Athl	Lausanne	3 Jul
9.82	1.7	Richard	Thompson	TTO	7.6.85	1	NC	Port of Spain	21 Jun
9.82	-0.1		Gatlin			1	Gugl	Linz	14 Jul
9.83	0.7		Gatlin			1rA	WCM	Rieti	7 Sep
9.86	-0.4		Gatlin (100y 9.10)			1	GS	Ostrava	17 Jun
9.87	0.0		Gatlin			1	WCM	Beijing	21 May
9.87	1.8	Asafa	Powell	JAM	23.11.82	1		Austin	23 Aug
9.90	0.7		Powell			1rB	WCM	Rieti	7 Sep
9.91	0.4		Gatlin			1	GGala	Roma	5 Jun
9.91	1.0	Michael	Rodgers	USA	24.4.85	1	Anniv	London (HG)	20 Jul
9.92	0.0		Gatlin			1	DL	Shanghai	18 May
9.92	-0.1		Rodgers			2	Gugl	Linz	14 Jul
9.93	1.8	Kemarley	Brown	JAM	20.7.92	1		Walnut	17 May
9.93	0.1	Tyson	Gay	USA	9.8.82	2	Athl	Lausanne	3 Jul
9.93	0.6		Rodgers			2	VD	Bruxelles	5 Sep
9.93	0.4	Femi Seun	Ogunode	QAT	15.5.91	1	AsiG	Incheon	28 Sep
9.95	1.7	Jimmy	Vicaut	FRA	27.2.92	1		Aix-les-Bains	18 May
9.95	1.4		Thompson			1	FBK	Hengelo	8 Jun
9.95	0.6		Powell			3	VD	Bruxelles	5 Sep
9.96	1.4	Chijindu	Ujah	GBR	5.3.94	2	FBK	Hengelo	8 Jun
9.96	1.0	Kim	Collins (10)	SKN	5.4.76	2	Anniv	London (HG)	20 Jul
9.96	2.0	Nesta	Carter	JAM	10.11.85	1	DNG	Stockholm	21 Aug
9.96	-0.3	Kemar	Bailey-Cole	JAM	10.1.92	1	WK	Zürich	28 Aug
9.96	0.6		Bailey-Cole			4	VD	Bruxelles	5 Sep
9.97	1.8	Trayvon	Bromell	USA-J	10.7.95	1	NCAA	Eugene	13 Jun
9.97	0.3	Nickel	Ashmeade	JAM	7.4.90	1rA	DL	Glasgow	11 Jul
9.97	0.3		Rodgers			2rA	DL	Glasgow	11 Jul
9.98A	1.4	Simon	Magakwe	RSA	25.5.86	1	NC	Pretoria	12 Apr
9.98	0.1		Rodgers			3	Athl	Lausanne	3 Jul
9.98	0.3		Carter			3rA	DL	Glasgow	11 Jul
9.98 (i)	-0.6	Usain (32/16)	Bolt	JAM	21.8.86	1		Warszawa	23 Aug
10.00	1.7	Keston	Bledman	TTO	8.3.88	2	NC	Port of Spain	21 Jun
10.00	1.6	Trentavis	Friday	USA-J	5.6.95	1h1	NC-j	Eugene	5 Jul
10.00	0.6	James	Dasaolu	GBR	5.9.87	5	VD	Bruxelles	5 Sep
10.01	0.0	Antoine (20)	Adams	SKN	31.8.88	1	NC	Basseterre	22 Jun
10.02A	1.4	Akani	Simbine	RSA	21.9.93	2	NC	Pretoria	12 Apr
10.02	1.0	Alonso	Edward	PAN	8.12.89	1h8		Clermont	26 Apr
10.02	0.6	Yohan	Blake	JAM	26.12.89	1		Kingston	7 Jun
10.02	1.8	Dentarius	Locke	USA	12.12.89	2	NCAA	Eugene	13 Jun
10.03	1.5	Gerald	Phiri	ZAM	6.10.88	1		Clermont	10 May
10.03	1.5	Julian	Forte	JAM	1.7.93	1		Kingston	17 May
10.04	2.0	Diondre	Batson	USA	13.7.92	1		Starkville	3 May
10.04	0.0	Jason	Rogers	SKN	31.8.91	2	NC	Basseterre	22 Jun
10.04	1.6	Adam	Gemili	GBR	6.10.93	1h1		Mannheim	5 Jul
10.05	1.6	Yoshihide (30)	Kiryu	JPN-J	15.12.95	1		Kumagaya	17 May

Mark	Wind	Name		Nat	Born	Pos	Meet	Venue	Date
10.05	1.7	Darrell	Brown	TTO	11.10.84	3	NC	Port of Spain	21 Jun
10.05	-0.4	Jason	Livermore	JAM	25.4.88	1s2	NC	Kingston	27 Jun
10.05	1.8	Julian	Reus	GER	29.4.88	1s2	NC	Ulm	26 Jul
10.05	0.4	Wilfried	Koffi Hua	CIV	24.9.89	1	AfCh	Marrakech	11 Aug
10.06	0.9	Ramon	Gittens	BAR	20.7.87	1		Regensburg	7 Jun
10.07	1.6	Gabriel	Mvumuvre	ZIM	23.4.88	1		Baton Rouge	19 Apr
10.07	1.5	Lucas	Jakubczyk	GER	28.4.85	2		Clermont	10 May
10.07	1.8	Aaron	Brown	CAN	27.5.92	3	NCAA	Eugene	13 Jun
10.07	1.7	Charles	Silmon	USA	4.7.91	1s2	NC	Sacramento	27 Jun
10.07	0.4	Mark	Jelks	NGR	10.4.84	2	AfCh	Marrakech	11 Aug
		(40)							
10.08	1.7	Maurice	Mitchell	USA	22.12.89	1		Joplin, MO	25 Apr
10.08	1.5	Marvin	Bracy	USA	15.12.93	1		Clermont	26 Apr
10.08	1.4	Harry	Aikines-Aryeetey	GBR	29.8.88	5	FBK	Hengelo	8 Jun
10.08	1.7	Rakieem "Mookie"	Salaam	USA	5.4.90	2s2	NC	Sacramento	27 Jun
10.09	0.5	Rondell	Sorrillo	TTO	21.1.86	1s1	NC	Port of Spain	21 Jun
10.09	0.3	Andrew	Fisher	JAM	15.12.91	1h3	NC	Kingston	26 Jun
10.10	0.1	Senoj-Jay	Givans	JAM	30.12.93	2h2	Big 12	Lubbock	17 May
10.10	0.6	Christophe	Lemaitre	FRA	11.6.90	2s2	EC	Zürich	13 Aug
10.10A	-1.3	Daniel	Bailey	ANT	9.9.86	2		Ciudad de México	15 Aug
10.10	1.9	Andrew	Robertson	GBR	17.12.90	1s1	CAU	Bedford	23 Aug
		(50)							
10.10	0.4		Su Bingtian	CHN	29.8.89	2	AsiG	Incheon	28 Sep
10.11	0.7	Shavez	Hart	BAH	9.6.92	1	NC	Nassau	27 Jun
10.11	1.0	Jaysuma	Saidy Ndure	NOR	1.7.84	1h2		Mannheim	5 Jul
10.12	1.3	Zharnel	Hughes	AIA-J	13.7.95	1		Kingston	28 Mar
10.12	1.0	Gil	Roberts	USA	15.3.89	1		Lubbock	3 May
10.12	1.5	Richard	Kilty	GBR	2.9.89	3		Clermont	10 May
10.12	0.4	Adam	Harris	GUY	21.7.87	1		Port of Spain	17 May
10.12	1.4	Kimmari	Roach	JAM	21.9.90	6	FBK	Hengelo	8 Jun
10.12	1.8	Justin	Walker	USA	30.11.90	4	NCAA	Eugene	13 Jun
10.12	0.3	Dwain	Chambers	GBR	5.4.78	1	NC	Birmingham	29 Jun
		(60)							
10.12	-0.1	Ryan	Bailey	USA	13.4.89	3	Gugl	Linz	14 Jul
10.13	0.8	Clayton	Vaughn	USA	15.5.92	1		San Marcos, TX	26 Apr
10.13	1.5	James	Ellington	GBR	6.9.85	2		Clermont	26 Apr
10.13	0.7	Kei	Takase	JPN	25.11.88	1	Oda	Hiroshima	29 Apr
10.13	-0.3	Harry	Adams	USA	27.11.89	1		Houston	6 Jun
10.13	1.3	Mosito	Lehata	LES	8.4.89	1		Tomblaine	27 Jun
10.13	1.7	Sean	McLean	USA	23.3.92	4s2	NC	Sacramento	27 Jun
10.13	1.3	Churandy	Martina	NED	3.7.84	2	NC	Amsterdam	26 Jul
10.14	1.9	John	Teeters	USA	19.5.93	1	MSR	Walnut	18 Apr
10.14	1.5	Adrian	Griffith	BAH	11.11.84	3		Clermont	10 May
		(70)							
10.14	0.9	Odean	Skeen	JAM	28.8.94	1	JUCO	Mesa	17 May
10.14	1.5	Danny	Talbot	GBR	1.5.91	2	BIG	Bedford	31 May
10.14	0.6	Oshane	Bailey	JAM	9.8.89	2		Kingston	7 Jun
10.14	0.9	Sean	Safo-Antwi	GBR	31.10.90	2		Regensburg	7 Jun
10.14	0.6	Remontay	McClain	USA	21.9.92	1		Chula Vista	14 Jun
10.14	0.7	Warren	Fraser	BAH	8.7.91	2	NC	Nassau	27 Jun
10.14	0.1	Ryota	Yamagata	JPN	10.6.92	1s2		Kumagaya	5 Sep
10.15	1.5	Reggie	Lewis	USA	18.8.93	2rA	TexR	Austin	29 Mar
10.15	0.9	André	De Grasse	CAN	10.11.94	2	JUCO	Mesa	17 May
10.15	1.7	Kemar	Hyman	CAY	11.10.89	1		Cork	8 Jul
		(80)							
10.15A	2.0	Isidro	Montoya	COL	3.11.90	1		Cali	29 Aug
10.16	1.3	Jevaughn	Minzie	JAM-J	20.7.95	2		Kingston	28 Mar
10.16	1.4	Cordero	Gray	USA	9.5.89	1rB	TexR	Austin	29 Mar
10.16	1.5	Tevin	Hester	USA	10.1.94	3rA	TexR	Austin	29 Mar
10.16	1.3	David	Winters	USA	19.2.94	1		Wichita	12 Apr
10.16	1.4	Keith	Ricks	USA	9.10.90	1		Radford, VA	26 Apr
10.16		Brijesh "BJ"	Lawrence	SKN	27.12.89	2		Arima	10 May
10.16	1.0	Devin	Jenkins	USA	16.2.94	2		Atlanta	16 May
10.16	0.4	Rae	Edwards	NGR	7.5.81	3	AfCh	Marrakech	11 Aug
10.16	1.9	Ojie	Edoburun	GBR-J	2.6.96	2s1	CAU	Bedford	23 Aug
		(90)							
10.17A	1.8	Henricho	Bruintjies	RSA	16.7.93	2s3	NC	Pretoria	11 Apr
10.17	1.8	Winston	Barnes	JAM	7.11.88	1		Kingston	24 May
10.17	-0.4	Walter	Dix	USA	31.1.86	1		Charlotte	13 Jun
10.17	1.8	Yadier	Luis	CUB	1.3.89	1		La Habana	27 Jun
10.17	0.7	Jacques	Harvey	JAM/TUR	5.4.89	4rA	WCM	Rieti	7 Sep

Mark	Wind	Name		Nat	Born	Pos	Meet	Venue	Date
10.17	0.2		Zhang Peimeng	CHN	13.3.87	3s2	AsiG	Incheon	28 Sep
10.18	1.8	Justin	Thymes	USA	24.1.94	1		Riverside	8 Mar
10.18A	0.8	Nic	Bowens	USA	28.6.93	1		Laramie	17 May
10.18	0.8	Bryce	Robinson	USA	13.11.93	3q1	NCAA-W	Fayetteville	30 May
10.18	0.9	Deji	Tobais	GBR	31.10.91	3		Regensburg	7 Jun
		(100)							
10.18	-0.8	Egweru	Ogho-Oghene	NGR	26.11.88	1		Warri	13 Jun
10.18	1.4	Kieran	Daly	GBR	28.9.92	1	NC-23	Bedford	21 Jun

Mark	Wind	Name		Nat	Born	Date
10.19	1.4	Aleixo Platini Menga		GER	29.9.87	26 Apr
10.19	1.8	Michael	O'Hara	JAM-J	29.9.96	24 May
10.19	1.5	Aaron	Ernest	USA	8.11.93	30 May
10.19	1.1	Ángel David Rodríguez		ESP	25.4.80	12 Jun
10.19	0.0	Andrew	Hinds	BAR	25.4.84	21 Jun
10.19	1.6	Jalen	Miller	USA-J	17.6.95	5 Jul
10.19	1.2	Sheldon	Mitchell	JAM	19.7.90	24 Jul
10.20	1.5	Antwan	Wright	USA	17.11.93	29 Mar
10.20	0.2	Johnathan	Smith	USA	15.9.92	12 Apr
10.20	1.5	Gavin	Smellie	CAN	26.6.86	26 Apr
10.20	1.9	Martin	Keller	GER	26.9.86	26 Apr
10.20A	0.9	Isaac	Makwala	BOT	29.9.86	3 May
10.20	1.0	Everett	Walker	USA	3.10.90	17 May
10.20	1.1	Chris	Royster	USA	26.1.92	30 May
10.20	1.5	Christian	Blum	GER	10.3.87	31 May
10.20	1.2	Ramil	Guliyev	TUR	29.5.90	12 Jun
10.20	1.4	Darryl	Haraway	USA-Y	20.3.97	14 Jun
10.21	1.0	Trevorvano	Mackey ¶	BAH	5.1.92	3 May
10.21	1.6	Asuka	Cambridge	JPN	31.5.93	17 May
10.21	0.7	Ronnie	Baker	USA	15.10.93	29 May
10.21	0.6	Jared	Ware	USA	12.5.86	14 Jun
10.21	1.7	Marc	Burns	TTO	7.6.83	21 Jun
10.21	-0.6	Kendal	Williams	USA-J	23.9.95	23 Jul
10.21	0.2	Tyquendo	Tracey	JAM	10.6.93	8 Aug
10.21A	0.8	José Carlos	Herrera	MEX	5.2.86	29 Aug
10.21	0.7	Rasheed	Dwyer	JAM	29.1.89	7 Sep
10.21	0.7	Yazaldes	Nascimento	POR	17.4.86	7 Sep
10.22	1.3	Kenneth	Combs	USA	94	12 Apr
10.22	1.4	Sven	Knipphals	GER	20.9.85	26 Apr
10.22	1.9	DeAngelo	Cherry	USA	1.8.90	9 May
10.22	-0.4	Calesio	Newman	USA	20.8.86	13 Jun
10.22	1.1	Hassan	Taftian	IRI	4.5.93	14 Jun
10.22	1.8	Yusuke	Kotani	JPN	23.9.89	29 Jun
10.22	1.0		Pan Xinyue	CHN	17.1.93	6 Jul
10.22	1.3	Efthímios	Steryioúlis	GRE	9.2.85	19 Jul
10.23A	1.8	Gideon	Trotter	RSA	3.3.92	11 Apr
10.23A	1.4	Emile	Erasmus	RSA	3.4.92	12 Apr
10.23	1.6	Isiah	Young	USA	5.1.90	26 Apr
10.23	1.4	Darrell	Wesh	USA	21.1.92	26 Apr
10.23	1.9	Seye	Ogunlewe	NGR	30.8.91	26 Apr
10.23	1.0	Kolby	Listenbee	USA	25.1.94	17 May
10.23	1.5	Jared	Connaughton	CAN	20.7.85	31 May
10.23	1.3	Peter	Emelieze	NGR	19.4.88	19 Jun
10.23A	0.8	Rolando	Palacios	HON	3.5.87	29 Aug
10.24	1.5	Prezel	Hardy	USA	1.6.92	29 Mar
10.24	2.0	Masashi	Eriguchi	JPN	17.12.88	29 Apr
10.24	1.8	Desmond	Lawrence	USA	19.12.91	13 Jun
10.24	1.0	Adolphus	Nevers	JAM	19.3.90	26 Jun
10.24	1.0		Kim Kuk-young	KOR	19.4.91	6 Jul
10.25	1.7	Levi	Cadogan	BAR-J	8.11.95	19 Apr
10.25	0.7	Takumi	Kuki	JPN	18.5.92	29 Apr
10.25	0.7	Kazuma	Oseto	JPN	5.8.94	29 Apr
10.25	0.7	Beejay	Lee	USA	5.3.93	4 May
10.25	1.9	Jonathan	Farinha	TTO-J	16.5.96	31 May
10.25	1.1	Obinna	Metu	NGR	12.7.88	19 Jun
10.25	1.3	Jorén	Tromp	NED	1.11.88	17 Jul
10.25	0.5	Yu	Onabuta	JPN	5.2.94	5 Sep
10.25	0.7	Sergiy	Smelyk	UKR	19.4.87	7 Sep
10.25	0.4	Reza	Ghasemi	IRI	24.7.87	28 Sep
10.25	1.2	Samuel	Francis	QAT	27.3.87	28 Sep
10.26	2.0	Benjamin	Martin	USA	4.8.93	26 Apr
10.26	1.2	Marcus	Rowland	USA	11.3.90	9 May
10.26+	1.3	Chris	Brown	BAH	15.10.78	17 May
10.26	1.0	Alex	Wilson	SUI	19.9.90	21 May
10.26	1.5	Joel	Fearon	GBR	11.10.88	31 May
10.26	1.7	Emmanuel	Callender	TTO	10.5.84	21 Jun
10.26	1.7		Yang Yang	CHN	13.10.93	5 Jul
10.26	1.7	Joe	Morris	USA	4.10.89	8 Jul
10.26	1.4	Hensley	Paulina	NED	26.6.93	19 Jul
10.26	1.2	Amaru 'Reto' Schenkel		SUI	28.4.88	25 Jul
10.26	0.8	Alexander	Kosenkow	GER	14.3.77	26 Jul
10.26	0.7	Michael	Tumi	ITA	12.2.90	7 Sep
10.26	1.5	Reynier	Mena	CUB-J	21.11.96	12 Sep
10.27	2.0	Jefferson	Lucindo	BRA	17.10.90	8 Mar
10.27	-1.8	Dedric	Dukes	USA	2.4.92	4 Apr
10.27	0.6	Akeem	Haynes	CAN	3.11.92	19 Apr
10.27	1.9	Raheem	Chambers	JAM-Y	6.10.97	20 Apr
10.27	0.9	Chris	Belcher	USA	29.1.94	17 May
10.27	1.4	Fabio	Cerutti	ITA	26.9.85	18 May
10.27	-0.2	Terry	Jernigan	USA-J	6.6.96	24 May
10.27	1.6	Ramone	McKenzie	JAM	15.11.90	31 May
10.27	1.9	Idrissa	Adam	CMR	28.12.84	21 Jun
10.27	-0.3	Bernardo	Brady	JAM	14.6.91	27 Jun
10.27	1.7	Tim	Abeyie	GHA	7.11.82	5 Jul
10.27	0.4	Cejhae	Greene	ANT-J	6.10.95	22 Jul
10.27	2.0	Hayato	Suda	JPN	23.10.94	5 Sep
10.28	1.6	Jorge Henrique Vides		BRA	24.11.92	8 Mar
10.28	2.0	Broderick	Snoddy	USA	3.1.93	29 Mar
10.28	0.2	Thurgood	Dennis	USA	30.9.92	12 Apr
10.28	1.0	Lestrod	Roland	SKN	5.9.92	3 May
10.28	0.0	Raheem	Mostert	USA	9.4.92	17 May
10.28	1.4	Enrico	Demonte	ITA	25.9.88	18 May
10.28		Dmitriy	Khomutov ¶	RUS	4.1.92	6 Jun
10.28	0.7	Naoki	Tsukahara	JPN	10.5.85	7 Jun
10.28	1.3	Pascal	Mancini ¶	SUI	18.4.89	9 Jun
10.28	0.2	Kenroy	Anderson	JAM	27.6.87	26 Jun
10.28	2.0	Kenji	Fujimitsu	JPN	1.5.86	29 Jun
10.28	1.0	Mikhail	Idrisov	RUS	21.6.88	24 Jul
10.28	1.1	Antônio César Rodrigues		BRA	12.1.93	23 Aug
10.28	2.0	Tatsuya	Yamaguchi	JPN	4.12.93	5 Sep
10.28	0.0	Aldemir	da Silva	BRA	8.6.92	6 Sep
10.28A	0.9	Yaniel	Carrero	CUB-J	17.8.95	25 Nov
		(203)				

Wind assisted to 10.15

Mark	Wind	Name		Nat	Born	Pos	Meet	Venue	Date
9.74		Richard	Thompson	TTO	7.6.85	1		Clermont	31 May
9.76	2.7	Justin	Gatlin	USA	10.2.82	1	Pre	Eugene	31 May
9.77	4.2	Trayvon	Bromell	USA-J	10.7.95	1	Big 12	Lubbock	18 May
9.80	2.7	Michael	Rodgers	USA	24.4.85	2	Pre	Eugene	31 May
9.80	2.4		Rodgers			1s1	NC	Sacramento	27 Jun
9.89	2.7	Jimmy	Vicaut	FRA	27.2.92	3	Pre	Eugene	31 May
9.89	2.7	Nesta	Carter	JAM	10.11.85	4	Pre	Eugene	31 May
9.90	4.2	Senoj-Jay	Givans	JAM	30.12.93	2	Big 12	Lubbock	18 May
9.90		Adam	Harris	GUY	21.7.87	2		Clermont	31 May
9.91	4.2	John	Teeters	USA	19.5.93	3	Big 12	Lubbock	18 May
9.92		Gil	Roberts	USA	15.3.89	3		Clermont	31 May
9.92	2.3	Jaysuma	Saidy Ndure	NOR	1.7.84	1h1		Florø	7 Jun
9.92	2.2		Bromell			1s1	NCAA	Eugene	11 Jun
9.95	2.5	Justin	Walker	USA	30.11.90	1		Conway, AR	11 May
9.95	2.7	Nickel	Ashmeade	JAM	7.4.90	5	Pre	Eugene	31 May
9.95	2.5	Kemar	Bailey-Cole	JAM	10.1.92	1h1	NC	Kingston	26 Jun
9.96		Calesio	Newman	USA	20.8.86	4		Clermont	31 May

Mark	Wind	Name		Nat	Born	Pos	Meet	Venue	Date
9.98	3.0	Charles	Silmon	USA	4.7.91	1		Austin	3 May
9.98	4.2	Everett	Walker	USA	3.10.90	4	Big 12	Lubbock	18 May
10.01	2.3	Diondre	Batson	USA	13.7.92	1		Tuscaloosa	11 Apr
10.01	2.2	Julian	Reus	GER	29.4.88	1	NC	Ulm	26 Jul
10.01	2.2	Lucas	Jakubczyk	GER	28.4.85	2	NC	Ulm	26 Jul
10.03	4.4	Cordero	Gray	USA	9.5.89	2rD		Fort Worth	21 Mar
10.03	4.0	André	De Grasse	CAN	10.11.94	1	KansR	Lawrence	19 Apr
10.03		Adrian	Griffith	BAH	11.11.84	5		Clermont	31 May
10.03	2.4	Ryan	Bailey	USA	13.4.89	2s1	NC	Sacramento	27 Jun
10.04	2.7	Maurice	Mitchell	USA	22.12.89	6	Pre	Eugene	31 May
10.04	2.6	Deji	Tobais	GBR	31.10.91	1s2	CAU	Bedford	23 Aug
10.05	8.6	Mark	Jelks	USA/NGR	10.4.84	1h9		Wichita	12 Apr
10.06	3.0	Harry	Adams	USA	27.11.89	1		Coral Gables	29 Mar
10.06	5.2	Devin	Jenkins	USA	16.2.94	1		New Orleans	27 Apr
10.06		Dwain	Chambers	GBR	5.4.78	6		Clermont	31 May
10.06	4.1	Kemar	Hyman	CAY	11.10.89	1		Bruxelles	6 Jul
10.07	4.4	Clayton	Vaughn	USA	15.5.92	1		Austin	12 Apr
10.07		Emmanuel	Callender	TTO	10.5.84	7		Clermont	31 May
10.07	3.6	Sean	Safo-Antwi	GBR	31.10.90	1	CAU	Bedford	23 Aug
10.08	2.7		Zhang Peimeng	CHN	13.3.87	7	Pre	Eugene	31 May
10.08	2.4	Antwan	Wright	USA	17.11.93	4s1	NC	Sacramento	27 Jun
10.10	3.4	Sota	Kawatsura	JPN	19.6.89	1	TexR	Austin	29 Mar
10.10		DeAngelo	Cherry	USA	1.8.90	1r2		Clermont	31 May
10.11	3.9	Benjamin	Martin	USA	4.8.93	1		San Marcos, TX	11 May
10.11	3.4	Brijesh "BJ"	Lawrence	SKN	27.12.89	2h2	NC	Basseterre	22 Jun
10.12	4.2	Kolby	Listenbee	USA	25.1.94	5	Big 12	Lubbock	18 May
10.12	2.2	Desmond	Lawrence	USA	19.12.91	3s1	NCAA	Eugene	11 Jun
10.12	2.5	Odean	Skeen	JAM	28.8.94	2h1	NC	Kingston	26 Jun
10.13	2.4	Tony	McQuay	USA	16.4.90	1rB	FlaR	Gainesville	4 Apr
10.13	4.1	Ahmed	Ali	USA	15.11.93	1		Lubbock	5 Apr
10.13	2.8	Nic	Bowens	USA	28.6.93	1h3		Laramie	16 May
10.13	2.3	Aaron	Ernest	USA	8.11.93	4s2	NCAA	Eugene	11 Jun
10.13	2.5	Oshane	Bailey	JAM	9.8.89	3h1	NC	Kingston	26 Jun
10.13	3.4	Jack	Hale	AUS-Y	22.5.98	1	N.Sch	Adelaide	6 Dec
10.14	3.4	Jared	Connaughton	CAN	20.7.85	2	TexR	Austin	29 Mar
10.14	2.2	Isaac	Makwala	BOT	29.9.86	1		Gaborone	19 Apr
10.14	3.1	Jevaughn	Minzie	JAM-J	20.7.95	1h3	Carifta	Fort-de-France	19 Apr
10.14	2.7	Ronnie	Baker	USA	15.10.93	2q2	NCAA-W	Fayetteville	30 May
10.15	3.9	Bryce	Robinson	USA	13.11.93	1		Fayetteville	12 Apr
10.15	2.6	Raheem	Mostert	USA	9.4.92	2q3	NCAA-E	Jacksonville	30 May
10.15	3.5	Ojie	Edoburun	GBR-J	2.6.96	2	CAU	Bedford	23 Aug

Mark	Wind	Name		Nat	Born	Date
10.16	2.7	Beejay	Lee	USA	5.3.93	30 May
10.16		Leroy	Dixon	USA	20.6.83	31 May
10.17	2.2	Roscoe	Engel	RSA	6.3.89	11 Apr
10.17	4.2	DeMario	Johnson	USA	11.9.90	18 May
10.18	2.2	Jonathan	Farinha	TTO-J	16.5.96	15 Mar
10.18	6.9	Kenneth	Combs	USA	.94	12 Apr
10.18	2.6	Mickey	Grimes	USA	10.10.76	15 May
10.18	3.4	Rohan	Browning	AUS-Y	31.12.97	6 Dec
10.19	2.3	Prezel	Hardy	USA	1.6.92	28 Mar
10.19	3.8	Tim	Price	USA	26.12.87	3 May
10.19	3.1	Taffawee	Johnson	JAM	10.3.88	22 May
10.19		Vitaliy	Korzh	UKR	5.10.87	7 Jun
10.19	3.0	Takuya	Kawakami	JPN-J	8.6.95	12 Jun
10.20	3.3	Joshua	Clarke	AUS-J	19.5.95	8 Feb
10.20	3.0	Tremayne	Acy	USA-J	21.1.95	5 Apr
10.20	2.3	Akeem	Haynes	CAN	3.11.92	11 Apr
10.20	3.1	Cejhae	Greene	ANT-J	6.10.95	19 Apr
10.20	3.9	Kazuma	Oseto	JPN	5.8.94	3 May
10.20	3.6	Justin	Whitfield	USA	.92	10 May
10.20	4.2	Trevorvano	Mackey ¶	BAH	5.1.92	18 May
10.20	2.2	Alexander	Kosenkow	GER	14.3.77	7 Jun
10.20	3.0	Mikel	Thomas	TTO	23.11.87	7 Jun
10.20	2.2	Reza	Ghasemi	IRI	24.7.87	5 Jul
10.21	3.4	Yuki	Koike	JPN-J	13.5.95	29 Mar
10.21	3.1	Romel	Lewis	JAM	28.1.88	22 May
10.21	2.3	Darrell	Wesh	USA	21.1.92	11 Jun
10.21	2.2	Sven	Knipphals	GER	20.9.85	26 Jul
10.22	3.3	Wayne	Gordon	USA	20.12.93	4 Apr
10.22	2.6	Kirk	Wilson	USA	27.5.91	11 Apr
10.22	2.9	Segun	Makinde	CAN	6.7.91	1 May
10.22		Tre	Houston	BER	12.1.87	31 May
10.22	3.2	Likoúrgos-Stéfanos	Tsákonas	GRE	8.3.90	21 Jun
10.22	2.6	Samuel	Francis	QAT	27.3.87	12 Jul
10.23	4.4	Akeem	Forde	BAR	3.6.87	21 Mar
10.23	4.1	Jamil	Hubbard	USA	12.5.86	5 Apr
10.23	3.9	Nílson	André	BRA	30.1.86	26 Apr
10.23	3.2	Rytis	Sakalauskas	LTU	27.6.87	21 Jun
10.24	4.4	Steve	Slowly	JAM	18.4.79	21 Mar
10.24	3.9	Marek	Niit	EST	9.8.87	12 Apr
10.24	4.2	Levi	Cadogan	BAR-J	8.11.95	19 Apr
10.24	2.6	Takumi	Kuki	JPN	18.5.92	29 Apr
10.24	2.1	Dedric	Dukes	USA	2.4.92	17 May
10.24		James	Law	USA	8.10.80	31 May
10.24	2.3	Patrick	Domogala	GER	14.3.93	5 Jul
10.24	2.2		Xie Zhenye	CHN	17.8.93	5 Jul

(199 legal and windy to 10.24)

Low altitude bests

Mark	Wind	Name	Pos	Meet	Venue	Date
10.17	0.8	D Bailey	1		St. John's	28 Jun
		10.15w	1		Kingston	8 Feb
10.18	0.1	Simbine	6	Athl	Lausanne	3 Jul
10.19	0.4	Magakwe	4	AfCh	Marrakech	11 Aug
	2.7	10.13w	8	Pre	Eugene	31 May
10.24	0.0	Trotter				21 Mar
10.28	0.7	Bowens				29 May
10.26	1.7	Bruintjies				8 Jul

Hand Timing

Mark	Name		Nat	Born	Pos	Meet	Venue	Date
10.0	Mohamed Hassan	Juma	IRQ	16.12.89	1	NC	Baghdad	27 Mar
10.0	Yoandry	Andujar	DOM	5.7.90	1h2		Santo Domingo	10 May

31 Oct Kaduna, all NGR +1.8: 1. Nicholas Imhoaperamhe 18.4.92 9.8, 2. Obinna Metu 12.7.88 9.9

Doubtful wind reading: 9.95 1.9? Jaysuma Saidy Ndure NOR 1.7.84 1 Florø 7 Jun

Questionable auto-timing: 10.08 1.7 Jirapong Meenapra THA 11.5.93 1h3 NG Nakhon Ratchasima 11 Dec

Mark	Wind	Name		Nat	Born	Pos	Meet	Venue	Date

JUNIORS

See main list for top 6 juniors. 16 performances by 6 men to 10.16. Additional marks and further juniors:

Bromell 10.01 1.5 1 TexR Austin 29 Mar 10.09 0.1 1h2 Big12 Lubbock 17 May
10.02 0.9 1h1 TexR Austin 28 Mar 10.13 0.7 1h6 WJ Eugene 22 Jul
10.07 1.2 1 NC-j Eugene 5 Jul 10.16 -0.1 1r3 FlaR Gainesville 4 Apr
10.08 1.4 1h2 NC-j Eugene 5 Jul 10.16 2.0 1h4 DrakeR Des Moines 25 Apr
Kiryu 10.10 2.0 1h1 Oda Hiroshima 29 Apr 10.15 1.4 1h4 NC Fuykushima 7 Jun

Mark	Wind	Name		Nat	Born	Pos	Meet	Venue	Date
10.19	1.8	Michael	O'Hara	JAM	29.9.96	2		Kingston	24 May
10.19	1.6	Jalen	Miller	USA	17.6.95	2h1	NC-j	Eugene	5 Jul
10.20	1.4	Darryl	Haraway	USA-Y	20.3.97	1	N.Sch	Greensboro	14 Jun
10.21	-0.6	Kendal	Williams (10)	USA	23.9.95	1	WJ	Eugene	23 Jul
10.25	1.7	Levi	Cadogan	BAR	8.11.95	2		Fort-de-France	19 Apr
10.25	1.9	Jonathan	Farinha	TTO-	16.5.96	1		Port of Spain	31 May
10.26	1.5	Reynier	Mena	CUB	21.11.96	1		La Habana	12 Sep
10.27	1.9	Raheem	Chambers	JAM-Y	6.10.97	1		Fort-de-France	20 Apr
10.27	-0.2	Terry	Jernigan	USA	6.6.96	1		Orlando	24 May
10.27	0.4	Cejhae	Greene	ANT-	6.10.95	1h1	WJ	Eugene	22 Jul
10.28A	0.9	Yaniel	Carrero	CUB	17.8.95	3	CAG	Xalapa	25 Nov
10.30A	1.4	Thando	Ruto	RSA	26.9.95	6	NC	Pretoria	12 Apr
10.30	0.9	Christian	Coleman	USA	6.3.96	1h1	N.Sch	Greensboro	14 Jun
10.31	1.9	Andre	Ewers (20)	USA	7.6.95	1		Miramar	24 Apr

Wind assisted to 10.25

See main list for top 6 juniors. 5 performances by 4 men to 10.15. Additional mark:

Bromell 9.92 2.2 1s1 NCAA Eugene 11 Jun

Mark	Wind	Name		Nat	Born	Pos	Meet	Venue	Date
10.18	2.2	Jonathan	Farinha	TTO	16.5.96	1		Port of Spain	15 Mar
10.18	3.4	Rohan	Browning	AUS-Y	31.12.97	2	N.Sch	Adelaide	6 Dec
10.19	3.0	Takuya	Kawakami	JPN	8.6.95	1h3	Asi-J	Taipei	12 Jun
10.20	3.3	Joshua	Clarke	AUS	19.5.95	1		Sydney	8 Feb
10.20	3.0	Tremayne	Acy	USA	21.1.95	1		Baton Rouge	5 Apr
10.20	3.1	Cejhae	Greene	ANT	6.10.95	2h3		Fort-de-France	19 Apr
10.21	3.4	Yuki	Koike	JPN	13.5.95	3	TexR	Austin	29 Mar
10.24	4.2	Levi	Cadogan	BAR	8.11.95	1h2		Fort-de-France	19 Apr
10.25	3.6	Emmanuel	Dasor	GHA	14.9.95	2h2		San Marcos	10 May

150 METRES STRAIGHT

Manchester 17 May: (1.3) 1. Yohan Blake JAM 26.12.89 14.71; 2. Kemar Bailey-Cole JAM 10.1.92 15.00

200 METRES

Mark	Wind	Name		Nat	Born	Pos	Meet	Venue	Date
19.68	-0.5	Justin	Gatlin	USA	10.2.82	1	Herc	Monaco	18 Jul
19.71	0.0		Gatlin			1	VD	Bruxelles	5 Sep
19.82	-0.2	Warren	Weir	JAM	31.10.89	1	DL	New York	14 Jun
19.84	1.2	Alonso	Edward	PAN	8.12.89	1	Athl	Lausanne	3 Jul
19.95	-0.2	Nickel	Ashmeade	JAM	7.4.90	2	adidas	New York	14 Jun
19.95	-0.9		Edward			1	WK	Zürich	28 Aug
19.96	-0.4	Isaac	Makwala	BOT	29.9.86	1		La Chaux de Fonds	6 Jul
19.97	-0.6	Dedric	Dukes	USA	2.4.92	1	FlaR	Gainesville	4 Apr
19.98	-1.6	Adam	Gemili	GBR	6.10.93	1	EC	Zürich	15 Aug
19.98	0.2		Edward			1	C.Cup	Marrakech	14 Sep
19.98	0.2	Rasheed	Dwyer	JAM	29.1.89	2	C.Cup	Marrakech	14 Sep
19.99	-0.5		Ashmeade			2	Herc	Monaco	18 Jul
20.00	0.3		Edward			1		George Town	7 May
20.01	-0.9		Ashmeade			2	WK	Zürich	28 Aug
20.04	0.5		Dwyer			1	NC	Kingston	29 Jun
20.06	-0.2		Edward			3	adidas	New York	14 Jun
20.06	1.7	Femi	Ogunode	QAT	15.5.91	1		Sofia	28 Jun
20.06	1.2		Ashmeade			2	Athl	Lausanne	3 Jul
20.07	1.4		Edward			1		Clermont	26 Apr
20.08	1.6	Antoine	Adams (10)	SKN	31.8.88	1	NC	Basseterre	22 Jun
20.08	-0.5	Christophe	Lemaitre	FRA	11.6.90	3	Herc	Monaco	18 Jul
20.11	1.2		Lemaitre			3	Athl	Lausanne	3 Jul
20.13	-0.2		Ashmeade			1	DL	Doha	9 May
20.13	1.3	Curtis	Mitchell	USA	11.3.89	1	NC	Sacramento	29 Jun
20.14	1.7	Aaron	Ernest	USA	8.11.93	1		Baton Rouge	3 May
20.14	0.5		Dwyer			1	CG	Glasgow	31 Jul
20.14A	0.6	Sheldon	Mitchell	JAM	19.7.90	1	PAm SF	Ciudad de México	16 Aug
20.14	0.3		Ogunode			1	AsiG	Incheon	1 Oct
20.15	-1.6		Lemaitre			2	EC	Zürich	15 Aug
20.15	0.0		Ogunode			2	VD	Bruxelles	5 Sep

(30/14)

Mark	Wind	Name		Nat	Born	Pos	Meet	Venue	Date
20.16	-0.5	Prezel	Hardy	USA	1.6.92	1	SEC	Lexington	18 May
20.16	0.5	Aaron	Brown	CAN	27.5.92	1q1	NCAA-W	Fayetteville	31 May
20.17	2.0	Carvin	Nkanata	USA/KEN	6.5.91	1		Knoxville	12 Apr
20.19	-0.2	Wallace	Spearmon	USA	24.12.84	4	DL	New York	14 Jun
20.19	1.2	Wayde	van Niekerk	RSA	15.7.92	4	Athl	Lausanne	3 Jul
20.22	1.8	Rondell	Sorrillo	TTO	21.1.86	1		Montverde	7 Jun
		(20)							
20.22	0.6	Gil	Roberts	USA	15.3.89	1		Chula Vista	14 Jun
20.22	-0.5	Tyson	Gay	USA	9.8.82	4	Herc	Monaco	18 Jul
20.25	0.5	Jason	Livermore	JAM	25.4.88	3	NC	Kingston	29 Jun
20.25	-0.8	Hua Wilfried	Koffi	CIV	24.9.89	1	AfCh	Marrakech	14 Aug
20.25	-0.9	Churandy	Martina	NED	3.7.84	5	WK	Zürich	28 Aug
20.27	-0.1	Brandon	Byram	USA	11.9.88	1rB	FlaR	Gainesville	4 Apr
20.27A	1.6	Jeremy	Dodson	USA	30.8.87	1		Greenwood Village	1 Jun
20.27	0.6	Remontay	McClain	USA	21.9.92	2		Chula Vista	14 Jun
20.28A	0.6	Roberto	Skyers	CUB	12.11.91	2	PAm SF	Ciudad de México	16 Aug
20.28A	0.6	Jermaine	Brown	JAM	4.7.91	3	PAm SF	Ciudad de México	16 Aug
		(30)							
20.30	1.3	Maurice	Mitchell	USA	22.12.89	3	NC	Sacramento	29 Jun
20.30	-1.6	Sergiy	Smelyk	UKR	19.4.87	3	EC	Zürich	15 Aug
20.32	-1.0	Aldemir	da Silva	BRA	8.6.92	1	SAmG	Santiago de Chile	15 Mar
20.32	1.3	Zharnel	Hughes	AIA-J	13.7.95	1s2		Kingston	27 Mar
20.32	-0.6	Walter	Dix	USA	31.1.86	1		Charlotte	13 Jun
20.33	0.0	Trentavis	Friday	USA-J	5.6.95	1		Kernersville	31 May
20.33	-0.6	Calesio	Newman	USA	20.8.86	2		Charlotte	13 Jun
20.34	1.1	Brijesh "BJ"	Lawrence	SKN	27.12.89	1rB	MSR	Walnut	19 Apr
20.34	1.7	Kei	Takase	JPN	25.11.88	1h3		Fukuroi	3 May
20.35	-0.5	Shavez	Hart	BAH	9.6.92	2	SEC	Lexington	18 May
		(40)							
20.35	-0.7	José Carlos	Herrera	MEX	5.2.86	1		Ninove	2 Aug
20.36	0.3	Danny	Talbot	GBR	1.5.91	1	Odlozil	Praha	9 Jun
20.36	0.5	Mosito	Lehata	LES	8.4.89	4	CG	Glasgow	31 Jul
20.36	-0.4	Diego	Marani	ITA	27.4.90	3s1	EC	Zürich	14 Aug
20.37	0.6	Jevaughn	Minzie	JAM-J	20.7.95	1s1		Kingston	27 Mar
20.37	-0.5	Ryan	Bailey	USA	13.4.89	6	Herc	Monaco	18 Jul
20.37	1.9	Thomas	Somers	GBR-Y	28.4.97	1s1	WJ	Eugene	24 Jul
20.37	0.5	Akani	Simbine	RSA	21.9.93	5	CG	Glasgow	31 Jul
20.38	1.2	Ameer	Webb	USA	19.3.91	1	TexR	Austin	29 Mar
20.38	1.6	Kemarley	Brown	JAM	20.7.92	1	MSR	Walnut	18 Apr
		(50)							
20.38	1.8	Jorge Henrique	Vides	BRA	24.11.92	1		São Paulo	4 May
20.38	0.5	André	De Grasse	CAN	10.11.94	1	JUCO	Mesa	17 May
20.38	-2.2	Lalonde	Gordon	TTO	25.11.88	1	NC	Port of Spain	22 Jun
20.38	-0.4	Ramil	Guliyev	TUR	29.5.90	4s1	EC	Zürich	14 Aug
20.39	0.8	Shota	Izuka	JPN	25.6.91	1		Fukuroi	3 May
20.39	1.4	Renny	Quow	TTO	25.8.87	1		Lubbock	3 May
20.40	1.7	Arman	Hall	USA	14.2.94	2		Baton Rouge	3 May
20.40	0.4	Likoúrgos-Stéfanos	Tsákonas	GRE	8.3.90	3s2	EC	Zürich	14 Aug
20.40A	0.6	Daniel	Bailey	ANT	9.9.86	5	PAm SF	Ciudad de México	16 Aug
20.41A	1.9	Ncincihli	Titi	RSA	15.12.93	1s2	NC	Pretoria	11 Apr
		(60)							
20.41	1.3	Brendon	Rodney	CAN	9.4.92	1		Moon Township	4 May
20.41	0.0	Shota	Hara	JPN	18.7.92	1		Yokohama	25 May
20.41	0.6	Edino	Steele	JAM	6.1.87	1		Kingston	31 May
20.41	1.3	Sean	McLean	USA	23.3.92	4	NC	Sacramento	29 Jun
20.42	0.2	LaShawn	Merritt	USA	27.6.86	1		Sydney	15 Mar
20.42	0.3	Karol	Zalewski	POL	7.8.93	2	Odlozil	Praha	9 Jun
20.43	-0.2	Jaysuma	Saidy Ndure	NOR	1.7.84	4	DL	Doha	9 May
20.43	1.1	Aleixo Platini	Menga	GER	29.9.87	1rB		Clermont	10 May
20.43	1.0	Ben	Bassaw	FRA	9.7.89	1		La Roche-sur-Yon	23 Jul
20.43	0.7	Bernardo	Baloyes	COL	6.1.94	2	IbAmC	São Paulo	3 Aug
		(70)							
20.44	-0.3	James	Ellington	GBR	6.9.85	1rB		Clermont	26 Apr
20.44	1.8	Masafumi	Naoki	JPN	19.11.93	1h2		Fukuroi	3 May
20.44		Ramon	Gittens	BAR	20.7.87	2		Arima	10 May
20.44	0.6	Julian	Reus	GER	29.4.88	1		Rehlingen	9 Jun
20.44	-0.3		Xie Zhenye	CHN	17.8.93	1	NC	Suzhou	11 Oct
20.45	0.0	Joe	Morris	USA	4.10.89	2		Tempe	12 Apr
20.45	1.1	Gavin	Smellie	CAN	26.6.86	1rC		Clermont	26 Apr
20.45	0.6	Kotaro	Taniguchi	JPN	3.11.94	1rB		Fukuroi	3 May
20.45	1.3	Michael	O'Hara	JAM-J	29.9.96	1s2	WJ	Eugene	24 Jul

Mark	Wind	Name		Nat	Born	Pos	Meet	Venue	Date
20.46	1.7	Robin	Erewa	GER	24.6.91	1rC		Mannheim	5 Jul
		(80)							
20.46	1.5	Trevorvano	Mackey ¶	BAH	5.1.92	2	NACAC	Kamloops	10 Aug
20.46	-0.1	Enrico	Demonte	ITA	25.9.88	1		Fossano	13 Sep
20.46	1.6	Bruno	de Barros	BRA	7.1.87	2	NC	São Paulo	12 Oct
20.47	1.6	Justin	Walker	USA	30.11.90	1		Conway, AR	11 May
20.48	-0.3	Bryce	Robinson	USA	13.11.93	1h2	NCAA-W	Fayetteville	30 May
20.48	1.2	Yohan	Blake	JAM	26.12.89	6	Athl	Lausanne	3 Jul
20.48	1.7	Sven	Knipphals	GER	20.9.85	2rC		Mannheim	5 Jul
20.49	-0.4	Diondre	Batson	USA	13.7.92	1		Tuscaloosa	5 Apr
20.49	1.7	Nery	Brenes	CRC	25.9.85	1		San José	11 May
20.49	1.0	Everett	Walker	USA	3.10.90	1q3	NCAA-W	Fayetteville	31 May
		(90)							
20.49	0.9	Julian	Forte	JAM	1.7.93	4	GGala	Roma	5 Jun
20.49	0.0	Kenji	Fujimutsu	JPN	1.5.86	1		Yamaguchi	11 Oct
20.50	0.6	Shinji	Takahira	JPN	18.7.84	2rB		Fukuroi	3 May
20.50	0.3	Michael	Mathieu	BAH	24.6.83	3	Odlozil	Praha	9 Jun
20.50	0.0	Chris	Clarke	GBR	25.1.90	1		Manchester	9 Aug
20.50A	0.6	Roland	Palacios	HON	3.5.87	7	PAm SF	Ciudad de México	16 Aug
20.50A	-0.4	Reynier	Mena	CUB-J	21.11.96	1s1	CAG	Xalapa	26 Nov
20.51	1.4	David	Winters	USA	19.2.94	1		Amarillo	26 Apr
20.51	1.7	Oluwasegun	Makinde	CAN	6.7.91	1		Lynchburg	1 May
20.51	0.8	Michael	Rodgers	USA	24.4.85	3		Fukuroi	3 May
		(100)							
20.51	1.3	Keith	Ricks	USA	9.10.90	5	NC	Sacramento	29 Jun
20.51	1.5	Everton	Clarke	JAM	24.12.92	3	NACAC	Kamloops	10 Aug

Mark	Wind	First	Last	Nat	Born	Date
20.52A	0.9	Simon	Magakwe	RSA	25.5.86	11 Apr
20.52	0.5	Arthur	Delaney	USA	23.6.93	31 May
20.52	1.5	Julius	Morris	MNT	14.4.94	10 Aug
20.53	1.9	Omar	Johnson	JAM	25.11.88	12 Apr
20.53	0.5	Ceolamar	Ways	USA	22.11.94	19 Apr
20.54	0.1	Nesta	Carter	JAM	10.11.85	12 Apr
20.54	1.8	Jefferson	Lucindo	BRA	17.10.90	4 May
20.54	1.1	Adrian	Griffith	BAH	11.11.84	10 May
20.54	0.6	Pierre	Vincent	FRA	20.2.92	28 Aug
20.55	-0.3	Marvin	Bracy	USA	15.12.93	26 Apr
20.55	0.0	Kendal	Williams	USA-J	23.9.95	24 May
20.55	-0.2	Eseosa	Desalu	ITA	19.2.94	14 Aug
20.57A		Pako	Seribe	BOT	7.4.91	22 Feb
20.57	1.4	Martin	Manley	JAM-Y	10.3.97	27 Mar
20.57	2.0	Wayne	Gordon	USA	20.12.93	12 Apr
20.57	1.0	Teray	Smith	BAH	28.9.94	3 May
20.58	0.6	Javon	Francis	JAM	14.12.94	27 Mar
20.58	2.0	Jereem	Richards	TTO	13.1.94	14 Jun
20.58	0.9	Jimmy	Vicaut	FRA	27.2.92	14 Jun
20.58	-0.8	Isiah	Young	USA	5.1.90	15 Jul
20.59	1.1	Jarrod	Geddes	AUS	24.2.94	22 Feb
20.59	1.4	Ramon	Miller	BAH	17.2.87	12 Apr
20.59	0.4	Trayvon	Bromell	USA-J	10.7.95	19 Apr
20.59	1.8	Andrew	Hinds	BAR	25.4.84	4 May
20.59	0.0	Joel	Redhead	GRN	3.7.86	6 Jun
20.59	-2.2	Kyle	Greaux	TTO	26.4.88	22 Jun
20.59	1.0	Yannick	Fonsat	FRA	16.6.88	23 Jul
20.59	-0.5	Adama	Jammeh	GAM	10.6.93	13 Aug
20.59	-0.1	Yoshihide	Kiryu	JPN-J	15.12.95	6 Sep
20.60	0.8	Kirk	Wilson	USA	27.5.91	28 Jun
20.60	0.2	Igor	Bodrov	UKR	9.7.87	25 Jul
20.61	0.6	Yuki	Koike	JPN-J	13.5.95	3 May
20.61	0.6	Just'n	Thymes	USA	24.1.94	14 Jun
20.61	0.4	Alex	Wilson	SUI	19.9.90	14 Aug
20.62	1.3	Renard	Howell	USA-J	3.3.95	3 May
20.62	0.0	Ryota	Yamagata	JPN	10.6.92	25 May
20.63	-1.2	Kirani	James	GRN	1.9.92	11 May
20.63	-1.7	Pavel	Maslák	CZE	21.2.91	25 May
20.63	1.1	Khalil	Henderson	USA	18.11.94	31 May
20.63	1.0	Mohamed	Hussein Abaraghi	IRI-J	5.1.95	14 Jun
20.63	0.2	Jeffrey	John	FRA	6.6.92	15 Jun
20.63	-0.1	Chijindu	Ujah	GBR	5.3.94	6 Aug
20.64A	0.9	Roscoe	Engel	RSA	6.3.89	11 Apr
20.64	2.0	Brycen	Spratling	USA	10.3.92	12 Apr
20.64	1.7	Jermaine	Jones	USA	24.5.91	1 May
20.64	0.3	Delano	Williams	GBR	23.12.93	7 May
20.64	1.3	Elvyonn	Bailey	USA	28.9.91	10 May
20.64	0.6	Tim	Faust	USA	11.8.92	30 May
20.64	1.8	Kazuma	Oseto	JPN	5.8.94	21 Jun
20.64	1.8	Patrick	Domogala	GER	14.3.93	5 Jul
20.64	1.6	Andrew	Hudson	USA-J	14.12.96	12 Jul
20.64	-0.5	Idrissa	Adam	CMR	28.12.84	13 Aug
20.65	0.7	Raheem	Mostert	USA	9.4.92	30 May
20.65	1.3	Bryshon	Nellum	USA	1.5.89	29 Jun
20.65	0.2	Vitaliy	Korzh	UKR	5.10.87	25 Jul
20.65	1.2	Alexander	Kosenkow	GER	14.3.77	27 Jul
20.65A	0.9	Akeem	Williams	JAM	7.11.90	16 Aug
20.66	-1.0	Alex	Quiñónez	ECU	11.8.89	15 Mar
20.66	0.0	Clayton	Parros	USA	11.12.90	4 Apr
20.66	1.9	Steven	Gardiner	BAH-J	12.9.95	5 Apr
20.66	1.2	Charles	Clark	USA	10.8.87	2 May
20.66	-0.1	Ahmed	Ali	USA	15.11.93	16 May
20.66	0.9	Oshane	Bailey	JAM	9.8.89	17 May
20.66	0.7	Trey	Hadnot	USA	7.3.92	30 May
20.66	1.0	Clayton	Vaughn	USA	15.5.92	31 May
20.66	0.7	Brandon	Stryganek	USA	7.1.93	31 May
20.66	0.2	Henricho	Bruintjies	RSA	16.7.93	11 Jul
20.66	1.3	Ejowvokoghene	Oduduru	NGR-J	7.10.96	24 Jul
20.67	-1.0	Arturo	Ramírez	VEN	19.4.91	15 Mar
20.67	1.3	Levi	Cadogan	BAR-J	8.11.95	21 Apr
20.67	2.0	Yusuke	Kotani	JPN	23.9.89	3 May
20.67	0.5	Senoj-Jay	Givans	JAM	30.12.93	31 May
20.67	1.1	Johan	Wissman	SWE	2.11.82	20 Jul
20.67	0.3	Sebastian	Ernst	GER	11.10.84	27 Jul
20.68	0.1	Davonte	Stewart	USA	11.6.93	4 Apr
20.68	1.1	Michael	Tinsley	USA	21.4.84	19 Apr
20.68	-0.2	Jamil	Hubbard	USA	12.5.86	18 May
20.68	0.6	Jonathan	Farinha	TTO-J	16.5.96	1 Jun
20.68	1.4	Kai	Yoshida	JPN	31.7.90	29 Jun
20.69	1.7	Kento	Terada	JPN	11.11.93	3 May
20.69	0.4	Yuichi	Kobayashi	JPN	25.8.89	3 May
20.69	0.1	Marcus	Rowland	USA	11.3.90	9 May
20.69	1.2	Nethaneel	Mitchell-Blake	GBR	2.4.94	31 May
20.69	-0.5	Aziz	Ouhadi	MAR	24.7.84	8 Jun
20.69	-0.1	Antonio	Infantino	GBR	22.3.91	6 Aug
20.70	-0.5	Gideon	Trotter	RSA	3.3.92	5 Apr
20.70	0.2	Ricco	Hall	USA	24.11.92	12 Apr
20.70	1.5	Jonathan	McCants	USA	10.3.91	12 Apr
20.70	-0.1	Teddy	Tinmar	FRA	30.5.87	19 Jul
20.71A	0.2	Jon	Seeliger	RSA-J	27.4.95	26 Apr
20.71	0.3	Miguel	Francis	ANT-J	28.2.95	29 Jun
20.71	0.3	Matteo	Galvan	ITA	24.8.88	20 Jul
20.71	1.9	Masaharu	Mori	JPN-J	27.1.95	24 Jul
20.71	-0.4	Noah	Lyles	USA-Y	18.7.97	22 Aug
20.71	-0.3		Zhang Peimeng	CHN	13.3.87	11 Oct
20.72	-0.1	Torrin	Lawrence	USA	11.4.89	4 Apr
20.72	0.1	Johnathan	Smith	USA	15.9.92	4 Apr
20.72	1.6	Manteo	Mitchell	USA	6.7.87	19 Apr
20.72A	0.4	Nic	Bowens	USA	28.6.93	17 May
20.72	-0.9	Devin	Jenkins	USA	16.2.94	17 May

Mark	Wind	Name		Nat	Born	Pos	Meet	Venue	Date

Mark	Wind	Name		Nat	Born	Date
20.72	-0.6	Jefferey	Pendergrass	USA	25.3.89	13 Jun
20.72	1.6	Lestrod	Roland	SKN	5.9.92	22 Jun
20.72	0.5	Mario	Forsythe	JAM	30.10.85	29 Jun

(205)

Wind assisted

Mark	Wind	Name		Nat	Born	Pos	Meet	Venue	Date
19.91	2.1	Dedric	Dukes	USA	2.4.92	1	NCAA	Eugene	14 Jun
19.99	2.7	Curtis	Mitchell	USA	11.3.89	1s2	NC	Sacramento	29 Jun
20.02	2.1	Aaron	Brown	CAN	27.5.92	2	NCAA	Eugene	14 Jun
20.03	2.9	Trentavis	Friday	USA-J	5.6.95	1	NC-j	Eugene	6 Jul
20.04	2.3		Friday			1	WJ	Eugene	25 Jul
20.13	5.7	Devin	Jenkins	USA	16.2.94	1		New Orleans	27 Apr
20.13	2.1	Justin	Walker	USA	30.11.90	3	NCAA	Eugene	14 Jun
20.14	3.2	Prezel	Hardy	USA	1.6.92	1		Baton Rouge	19 Apr
20.15	3.4	Elvyonn	Bailey	USA	28.9.91	1		San Marcos	11 May
20.19	3.6	Lestrod	Roland	SKN	5.9.92	1		Abilene	12 Apr
20.21	5.6	Walter	Dix	USA	31.1.86	1		Clermont	31 May
20.23	3.3	Trayvon	Bromell	USA-J	10.7.95	1		Fort Worth	21 Mar
20.23	2.6	Chris	Clarke	GBR	25.1.90	1r2		Mannheim	5 Jul
20.25	2.3	Ejowvokoghene	Oduduru	NGR-J	7.10.96	2	WJ	Eugene	25 Jul
20.28	4.2	Senoj-Jay	Givans	JAM	30.12.93	1	Big 12	Lubbock	18 May
20.29	2.6	Kemarley	Brown	JAM	20.7.92	1		Walnut	17 May
20.30	5.1	Bryce	Robinson	USA	13.11.93	1		Fayetteville	12 Apr
20.31	2.3	Michael	O'Hara	JAM-J	29.9.96	3	WJ	Eugene	25 Jul
20.32	4.2	Everett	Walker	USA	3.10.90	2	Big 12	Lubbock	18 May
20.33	2.1	Gavin	Smellie	CAN	26.6.86	1		Clermont	10 May
20.34	2.3	Yuki	Koike	JPN-J	13.5.95	4	WJ	Eugene	25 Jul
20.35A	4.5	Bernardo	Baloyes	COL	6.1.94	1	NC	Medellín	28 Jun
20.36	3.7	Bryshon	Nellum	USA	1.5.89	2s1	NC	Sacramento	29 Jun
20.38	3.7	Sean	McLean	USA	23.3.92	3s1	NC	Sacramento	29 Jun
20.39	3.0	Charles	Silmon	USA	4.7.91	1		Austin	3 May
20.39	2.1	Keith	Ricks	USA	9.10.90	3s2	NC	Sacramento	29 Jun
20.40	2.7	Jamil	Hubbard	USA	12.5.86	1rE		Fort Worth	21 Mar
20.40	2.1	Manteo	Mitchell	USA	6.7.87	1		Charlotte, NC	22 Mar
20.42	2.6	Julian	Reus	GER	29.4.88	2r2		Mannheim	5 Jul
20.43	2.9	Trey	Hadnot	USA	7.3.92	1		San Marcos	26 Apr
20.44	4.1	Kirk	Wilson	USA	27.5.91	1rB		Clermont	31 May
20.45	3.3	Blake	Heriot	USA	26.9.91	2		Fort Worth	21 Mar
20.46	3.2	Michael	Mathieu	BAH	24.6.83	4		Baton Rouge	19 Apr
20.46	2.9	Kendal	Williams	USA-J	23.9.95	2	NC-j	Eugene	6 Jul
20.47	3.4	Clayton	Vaughn	USA	15.5.92	2		San Marcos	11 May
20.47	2.1	Pierre	Vincent	FRA	20.2.92	1	Med-23	Aubagne	13 Jun
20.49	5.1	Akheem	Gauntlett	JAM	26.8.90	2		Fayetteville	12 Apr
20.50	3.3	Sam	Watts	GBR	14.2.92	3		Fort Worth	21 Mar

Mark	Wind	Name		Nat	Born	Date
20.52	2.6	Just'n	Thymes	USA	24.1.94	17 May
20.54	2.5	Johnathan	Smith	USA	15.9.92	29 Mar
20.54	2.4	Harry	Aikines-Aryeetey	GBR	29.8.88	10 May
20.55	2.1	Isiah	Young	USA	5.1.90	29 Jun
20.58	3.4	Ventavius	Sears	USA-J	14.5.95	11 May
20.60	3.4	Emmanuel	Dasor	GHA-J	14.9.95	11 May
20.60	3.2	Andrew	Howe	ITA	12.5.85	25 May
20.61	3.5	Cameron	Echols-Luper	USA-J	9.4.95	21 Mar
20.61	4.9	Zack	Bilderback	USA	15.7.94	12 Apr
20.61	2.1	Khalil	Henderson	USA	18.11.94	14 Jun
20.62	4.9	Errol	Nolan	JAM	18.8.91	12 Apr
20.62	4.1	Emmanuel	Callender	TTO	10.5.84	31 May
20.63	3.2	Richard	Thompson	TTO	7.6.85	19 Apr
20.63	2.1	Luke	Fagan	GBR	31.7.88	29 May
20.63	2.6	Sebastian	Ernst	GER	11.10.84	5 Jul
20.64	2.2	Jonathan	McCants	USA	10.3.91	26 Apr
20.65	5.7	Cameron	Burrell	USA	11.9.94	12 Apr
20.65	4.2	Kolby	Listenbee	USA	25.1.94	18 May
20.66	2.6	Kyree	King	USA	9.7.94	17 May
20.66	3.0	James	Law	USA	8.10.80	31 May

(200 legal and windy to 20.67)

Low altitude bests

Mark	Wind	Name	Pos	Meet	Venue	Date
20.29	0.0	J Brown	1		Tempe	12 Apr
20.37	1.2	Skyers	1		Port of Spain	2 May
20.43	0.5	D Bailey	6	CG	Glasgow	31 Jul
20.48	0.5	S Mitchell	4	NC	Kingston	29 Jun
20.48	-0.5	Titi	1s1	AfCh	Marrakech	13 Aug
20.56	-0.5	Magakwe				8 Jun
20.57	-0.1	Palacios				5 Jul

Indoors

Mark	Name		Nat	Born	Date
20.52	Pavel	Maslák	CZE	21.2.91	16 Feb
20.57A	Tyreek	Hill	USA	1.3.94	14 Mar
20.62	Sebastian	Ernst	GER	11.10.84	23 Feb
20.63	Marek	Niit	EST	9.8.87	15 Feb
20.66A	Aldrich	Bailey	USA	6.2.94	14 Mar
20.68	Deon	Lendore	TTO	28.10.92	8 Feb
20.75A	Bruno	Hortelano	ESP	18.9.91	14 Mar

Hand Timing

Mark	Wind	Name		Nat	Born	Pos	Venue	Date
19.7A	-1.4	Isaac	Makwala	BOT	29.9.86	1	Germiston	15 Mar
20.0A	-1.4	Danie	van Blerk	RSA	11.11.91	2	Germiston	15 Mar
20.4A	-1.4	Waide	Jooste	RSA	24.7.91			15 Mar
20.4		Winston	George	GUY	19.5.87			15 Oct

31 Oct Kaduna, all NGR +2.4: 1. Noah Akwu 23.9.90 20.0w, 2. Obinna Metu 12.7.88 20.1w, 3. Tosin Ogunmakinju 3.3.94 20.4w

JUNIORS

See main list for top 6 juniors. 11 performances by 5 men to 20.48. Additional marks and further juniors:

Name	Mark	Wind	Pos	Meet	Venue	Date
Hughes	20.33A	0.8	1	CAC-J	Morelia	5 Jul
	20.38	1.9	2s1	WJ	Eugene	24 Jul
Friday	20.35	1.8	1s3	WJ	Eugene	24 Jul
	20.39	0.6	1h1	NC-j	Eugene	6 Jul
	20.41	-0.2	1	N.Sch	Greensboro	13 Jun
	20.48	0.6	1h3	N.Sch	Greensboro	13 Jun

Mark	Wind	Name		Nat	Born	Pos	Venue	Date
20.55	0.0	Kendal	Williams	USA	23.9.95	1	Orlando	24 May
20.57	1.4	Martin	Manley	JAM-Y	10.3.97	1s3	Kingston	27 Mar

Mark	Wind	Name		Nat	Born	Pos	Meet	Venue	Date
20.59	0.4	Trayvon	Bromell	USA	10.7.95	1		Waco	19 Apr
20.59	-0.1	Yoshihide	Kiryu (10)	JPN	15.12.95	1		Kumagaya	6 Sep
20.61	0.6	Yuki	Koike	JPN	13.5.95	3rB		Fukuroi	3 May
20.62	1.3	Renard	Howell	USA	3.3.95	1rB		Lubbock	3 May
20.63	1.0	Mohamed Hussein	Abaraghi	IRI	5.1.95	1h3	AsC-j	Taipei	14 Jun
20.64	1.6	Andrew	Hudson	USA	14.12.96	1		San Marcos	12 Jul
20.66	1.9	Steven	Gardiner	BAH	12.9.95	1		Nassau	5 Apr
20.66	1.3	Ejowvokoghene	Oduduru	NGR	7.10.96	2s2	WJ	Eugene	24 Jul
20.67	1.3	Levi	Cadogan	BAR	8.11.95	3	Carifta	Fort-de-France	21 Apr
20.68	0.6	Jonathan	Farinha	TTO	16.5.96	1		Port of Spain	1 Jun
20.71A	0.2	Jon	Seeliger	RSA	27.4.95	2s1	Univ Ch	Pretoria	26 Apr
20.71	0.3	Miguel	Francis (20)	ANT	28.2.95	2	NC	St John's	29 Jun
20.71	1.9	Masaharu	Mori	JPN	27.1.95	3s1	WJ	Eugene	24 Jul
20.71	-0.4	Noah	Lyles	USA-Y	18.7.97	1h1	YOG	Beijing	22 Aug
Wind assisted. See main list for top 6 juniors. 7 performances by 6 men to 20.48. Additional marks and further juniors:									
20.58	3.4	Ventavius	Sears	USA-J	14.5.95	3		San Marcos	11 May
20.60	3.4	Emmanuel	Dasor	GHA-J	14.9.95	4		San Marcos	11 May
20.61	3.5	Cameron	Echols-Luper	USA-J	9.4.95	1rB		Fort Worth	21 Mar
20.68	6.5	Kevin	Harris	USA-J	4.12.95	1		Arlington	26 Apr

300 METRES

Mark	Name		Nat	Born	Pos	Meet	Venue	Date
31.93	Karol	Zalewski	POL	7.8.93	1	WCM	Rieti	7 Sep
32.01	Matteo	Galvan	ITA	24.8.88	2	WCM	Rieti	7 Sep
32.05	Demetrius	Pinder	BAH	13.2.89	1rA		Liège (NX)	16 Jul
32.24	Marek	Niit	EST	9.8.87	3	WCM	Rieti	7 Sep
32.28	Eseosa	Desalu	ITA	19.2.94	4	WCM	Rieti	7 Sep
32.31	Rafal	Omelko	POL	16.1.89	1rA		Pliezhausen	18 May
32.31	Rabah	Yousif	GBR	11.12.86	5	WCM	Rieti	7 Sep
32.33	James	Harris	USA	18.9.91	1rB		Liège (NX)	16 Jul
32.35	Kenji	Fujimitsu	JPN	1.5.86	1		Izumo	20 Apr
32.36	Rennie	Quow (10)	TTO	25.8.87	2rB		Liège (NX)	16 Jul
32.38	Manteo	Mitchell	USA	6.7.87	2rA		Liège (NX)	16 Jul
32.39	Kei	Takase	JPN	25.11.88	2		Izumo	20 Apr
32.40	José Carlos	Herrera	MEX	5.2.86	3rB		Liège (NX)	16 Jul
32.41	Jonathan	Borlée	BEL	22.2.88	3rA		Liège (NX)	16 Jul
32.47	Julien	Watrin	BEL	27.6.92	4rA		Liège (NX)	16 Jul
32.51	Marcus	Boyd	USA	3.3.89	2		San Marcos	24 May
32.53	Yuzo	Kanemaru	JPN	18.9.87	3		Izumo	20 Apr
32.59	Edino	Steele	JAM	6.1.87	4rB		Liège (NX)	16 Jul
32.68	Pako	Seribe	BOT	7.4.91	5rA		Liège (NX)	16 Jul
Indoors								
32.15	Pavel	Maslák	CZE	21.2.91	1	Flanders	Gent	9 Feb
32.47	Lalonde	Gordon	TTO	25.11.88	1	Mill	New York (Arm)	15 Feb

400 METRES

Mark	Name		Nat	Born	Pos	Meet	Venue	Date
43.74	Kirani	James	GRN	1.9.92	1	Athl	Lausanne	3 Jul
43.92	LaShawn	Merritt	USA	27.6.86	2	Athl	Lausanne	3 Jul
43.97		James			1	Pre	Eugene	31 May
43.97		Merritt			2	Pre	Eugene	31 May
44.01	Isaac	Makwala	BOT	29.9.86	1		La Chaux de Fonds	6 Jul
44.14		Merritt			1	GP	Ponce	17 May
44.16		Merritt			1	GS	Ostrava	17 Jun
44.19		Merritt			1	adidas	New York	14 Jun
44.23		Makwala			1	AfCh	Marrakech	12 Aug
44.24		James			1	CG	Glasgow	30 Jul
44.30		Merritt			1		Edmonton	6 Jul
44.30		Merritt			1	Herc	Monaco	18 Jul
44.36	Deon	Lendore	TTO	28.10.92	1	SEC	Lexington	18 May
44.36		Merritt			1	WK	Zürich	28 Aug
44.38	Wayde	van Niekerk	RSA	15.7.92	2	DL	New York	14 Jun
44.43	Youssef	Al-Masrahi	KSA	31.12.87	3	Athl	Lausanne	3 Jul
44.44		Merritt			1	Drake	Des Moines	25 Apr
44.44		Merritt			1	DL	Doha	9 May
44.46		Al-Masrahi			1	AsiG	Incheon	28 Sep
44.48		Merritt			1	GGala	Roma	5 Jun
44.53	Luguelín	Santos	DOM	12.11.93	2	GP	Ponce	17 May
44.53	Gil	Roberts	USA	15.3.89	1	NC	Sacramento	28 Jun
44.55		Al-Masrahi			1		Montreuil-sous-Bois	7 Jul
44.59	Chris	Brown	BAH	15.10.78	4	Athl	Lausanne	3 Jul

Mark	Wind	Name		Nat	Born	Pos	Meet	Venue	Date
44.59			James			1	DL	Birmingham	24 Aug
44.60			James			2	Drake	Des Moines	25 Apr
44.60			Merritt			1	C.Cup	Marrakech	13 Sep
44.61			Brown			3	adidas	New York	14 Jun
44.62			Roberts			2	Herc	Monaco	18 Jul
44.68			van Niekerk			2	CG	Glasgow	30 Jul
		(30/9)							
44.71		Martyn	Rooney (10)	GBR	3.4.87	1	EC	Zürich	15 Aug
44.75		Matthew	Hudson-Smith	GBR	26.10.94	2	EC	Zürich	15 Aug
44.78		Lalonde	Gordon	TTO	25.11.88	3	CG	Glasgow	30 Jul
44.79		Pavel	Maslák	CZE	21.2.91	3	DL	Doha	9 May
44.89		Josh	Mance	USA	21.3.92	2	NC	Sacramento	28 Jun
44.92		Tony	McQuay	USA	16.4.90	4	DL	Doha	9 May
44.97		LaToy	Williams	BAH	28.5.88	1	NC	Nassau	28 Jun
44.98		Jarrin	Solomon	TTO	11.1.86	1	NA	Heusden-Zolder	19 Jul
45.00		Javon	Francis	JAM	14.12.94	1		Kingston	29 Mar
45.00		Kyle	Clemons	USA	27.8.90	3	NC	Sacramento	28 Jun
45.00		Akheem	Gauntlett	JAM	26.8.90	1	NC	Kingston	29 Jun
		(20)							
45.02		Vernon	Norwood	USA	10.4.92	4	NC	Sacramento	28 Jun
45.03		Anderson	Henriques	BRA	3.3.92	1	SAmG	Santiago de Chile	14 Mar
45.03		David	Verburg	USA	14.5.91	3	GP	Ponce	17 May
45.04A		Pako	Seribe	BOT	7.4.91	2		Potchefstroom	10 May
45.05		Michael	Berry	USA	10.12.91	1	Pac-12	Pullman	18 May
45.07		Boniface	Mucheru	KEN	2.5.92	3	AfCh	Marrakech	12 Aug
45.08		Renny	Quow	TTO	25.8.87	1	NC	Port of Spain	21 Jun
45.09		Hugo	Sousa	BRA	5.3.87	2	SAmG	Santiago de Chile	14 Mar
45.09		Brycen	Spratling	USA	10.3.92	1q1	NCAA-E	Jacksonville	30 May
45.09		Manteo	Mitchell	USA	6.7.87	5	NC	Sacramento	28 Jun
		(30)							
45.11		Michael	Mathieu	BAH	24.6.83	1		Clermont	31 May
45.11		Jacob	Krzewina	POL	10.10.89	1		Wroclaw	14 Jul
45.13		Michael	Bingham	GBR	13.4.86	1rB	DL	New York	14 Jun
45.13		Machel	Cedenio	TTO-J	6.9.95	1	WJ	Eugene	24 Jul
45.17		Christian	Taylor	USA	18.6.90	5	Drake	Des Moines	25 Apr
45.17		Abbas	Abubaker	BRN-J	17.5.96	1s1	AsiG	Incheon	27 Sep
45.18		Bralon	Taplin	GRN	8.5.92	1q1	NCAA-W	Fayetteville	30 May
45.19		Arman	Hall	USA	12.2.94	1	FlaR	Gainesville	4 Apr
45.21		Ramon	Miller	BAH	17.2.87	2		Baie Mahault	10 May
45.21A		Alberth	Bravo	VEN	29.8.87	1h1	CAG	Xalapa	25 Nov
		(40)							
45.22		Akeem	Alexander	USA	9.9.94	3s2	NC	Sacramento	27 Jun
45.25		Rusheen	McDonald	JAM	17.8.92	2	NC	Kingston	29 Jun
45.27		Saviour	Kombe	ZAM	3.8.91	4	AfCh	Marrakech	12 Aug
45.27		Donald	Sanford	ISR	5.2.87	3	EC	Zürich	15 Aug
45.28		Kévin	Borlée	BEL	22.2.88	1	NC	Bruxelles	27 Jul
45.29		Hugh	Graham	JAM	10.10.92	1q2	NCAA-E	Jacksonville	30 May
45.30		Demetrius	Pinder	BAH	13.2.89	4	GS	Ostrava	17 Jun
45.32		Torrin	Lawrence	USA	11.4.89	1		Kortrijk	12 Jul
45.33		James	Harris	USA	18.9.91	1	Gugl	Linz	14 Jul
45.36		Steven	Solomon	AUS	16.5.93	1	NC	Melbourne	5 Apr
		(50)							
45.36A		Raidel	Acea	CUB	31.10.90	1	CAG	Xalapa	26 Nov
45.37		Michael	Cherry	USA-J	23.3.95	2q2	NCAA-E	Jacksonville	30 May
45.37		Jonathan	Borlée	BEL	22.2.88	3	NA	Heusden-Zolder	19 Jul
45.40		Najee	Glass	USA	12.6.94	3	SEC	Lexington	18 May
45.40		Mohamed	Khwaja	LBA	1.11.87	5	AfCh	Marrakech	12 Aug
45.41		Rabah	Yousif	GBR	11.12.86	1		London (He)	5 Jul
45.41		Liemarvin	Bonevacia	CUR/NED	5.4.89	1	NC	Amsterdam	27 Jul
45.42		Clayton	Parros	USA	11.12.90	2		Gainesville	19 Apr
45.42		Omar	Johnson	JAM	25.11.88	1		Lubbock	3 May
45.44		Edino	Steele	JAM	6.1.87	1		Kingston	8 Feb
		(60)							
45.44		Mame-Ibra	Anne	FRA	7.11.89	1		Genève	14 Jun
45.45		Vladimir	Krasnov	RUS	19.8.90	1	NC	Kazan	24 Jul
45.45		Maksim	Dyldin	RUS	19.5.87	1h2	EC	Zürich	12 Aug
45.46		Yuzo	Kanemaru	JPN	18.9.87	1		Fukuroi	3 May
45.46		Pavel	Ivashko	RUS	16.11.94	1		Moskva	12 Jun
45.46		Calvin	Smith	USA	10.12.87	1		Charlotte	13 Jun
45.46		Conrad	Williams	GBR	20.3.82	6	DL	Glasgow	12 Jul
45.47		Nery	Brenes	CRC	25.9.85	1		Rehlingen	9 Jun

Mark	Wind	Name		Nat	Born	Pos	Meet	Venue	Date
45.47A		Allodin	Fothergill	JAM	7.2.87	2	PAm SF	Ciudad de México	16 Aug
45.50		Samuel	García	ESP	4.12.91	1	NC	Alcobendas	27 Jul
		(70)							
45.52		Elvyonn	Bailey	USA	28.9.91	1h2		San Marcos	10 May
45.53		Chris	Giesting	USA	10.12.92	2		Charlottesville	9 May
45.53		Nikita	Uglov	RUS	11.10.93	2	NC	Kazan	24 Jul
45.54A		Yoandys	Lescay	CUB	5.1.94	3	PAm SF	Ciudad de México	16 Aug
45.55		Freddy	Mezones	VEN	24.9.87	1		Uberlândia	7 May
45.55		Daundre	Barnaby	CAN	9.12.90	3	Jerome	Burnaby	10 Jul
45.56		Patrick	Feeney	USA	29.12.91	1		Stanford	4 Apr
45.56		Nijel	Amos	BOT	15.3.94	1		Abidjan	26 Apr
45.56		Kind	Butler	USA	8.4.89	5	GP	Ponce	17 May
45.56A		Chumaine	Fitten	JAM	15.3.85	4	PAm SF	Ciudad de México	16 Aug
		(80)							
45.57		Winston	George	GUY	19.5.87	3rB	DL	New York	14 Jun
45.58		Matteo	Galvan	ITA	24.8.88	1	NC	Rovereto	19 Jul
45.59A		Anas	Beshr	EGY	19.7.93	1		Sasolburg	25 Mar
45.62		Tabarie	Henry	ISV	1.12.87	4rB	DL	New York	14 Jun
45.62		Hederson	Estefani	BRA	11.9.91	2	NC	São Paulo	10 Oct
45.63		Kamghe	Gaba	GER	13.1.84	1rB	Athl	Lausanne	3 Jul
45.64		Julien	Watrin	BEL	27.6.92	1h3	NC	Bruxelles	26 Jul
45.65		Lukasz	Krawczuk	POL	15.6.89	2	NC	Szczecin	2 Aug
45.66		Dedric	Dukes	USA	2.4.92	4		Gainesville	19 Apr
45.66A		Shaun	de Jager	RSA	28.6.91	1s1	Univ Ch	Pretoria	25 Apr
		(90)							
45.66		Zack	Bilderback	USA	15.7.94	1	Big 12	Lubbock	18 May
45.66		Carlyle	Roudette	TTO	6.9.91	2q3	NCAA-W	Fayetteville	30 May
45.66		Rafal	Omelko	POL	16.1.89	3	NC	Szczecin	2 Aug
45.68		Nigel	Levine	GBR	30.4.89	2		Genève	14 Jun
45.68A		Bernardo	Baloyes	COL	6.1.94	1	NC	Medellín	28 Jun
45.69		Emmanuel	Tugumisirize	UGA	30.11.88	5q2	NCAA-E	Jacksonville	30 May
45.69		D.J.	Zahn	USA	31.1.93	2q3	NCAA-W	Fayetteville	30 May
45.69		Andrew	Steele	GBR	19.9.84	2h3	BEL Ch	Bruxelles	26 Jul
45.69A		Pedro	de Oliveira	BRA	17.2.92	5	PAm SF	Ciudad de México	16 Aug
45.69		Wágner	Cardoso	BRA	20.3.89	3	NC	São Paulo	10 Oct
		(100)							

Mark	Name		Nat	Born	Date
45.70	Dane	Hyatt	JAM	22.1.84	7 May
45.70	Lev	Mosin	RUS	7.12.92	29 May
45.71	Alberto	Aguilar	VEN	9.3.85	15 May
45.71	Je'Von	Hutchison	USA	4.5.92	30 May
45.71A	Carlos Andrés	Lemos	COL	3.6.88	16 Aug
45.72	Pavel	Trenikhin	RUS	24.3.86	24 Jul
45.73	Yannick	Fonsat	FRA	16.6.88	22 Jun
45.74	Abdelilah	Haroun	SUD/QAT-Y	.97	29 Apr
45.74	Aldrich	Bailey	USA	6.2.94	30 May
45.74	Tyler	Brown	USA-J	24.3.95	6 Jul
45.74	Marek	Niit		9.8.87	12 Aug
45.74	Vítor Ricardo	dos Santos	POR	18.12.94	13 Aug
45.76	Clinton	Collins	USA	14.12.91	18 May
45.76A	Héctor	Carrasquillo	PUR	30.9.87	28 Jun
45.77A	Dennis	Opio	UGA	1.6.94	11 Jul
45.79	Naoki	Kobayashi	JPN	20.12.90	6 Jul
45.80	Alfred	Larry	USA	.93	17 May
45.80	Joseph	Richards	USA	14.10.93	18 May
45.81	Nick	Ekelund-Arenander	DEN	23.1.89	5 Jul
45.81	Brian	Gregan	IRL	31.12.89	13 Aug
45.84	Daniel	Awde	GBR	22.6.88	17 Jul
45.84A	Alex	Sampao	KEN-J	31.12.96	25 Jun
45.84	Teddy	Atine-Venel	FRA	16.3.85	2 Aug
45.86	Ashton	Eaton	USA	21.1.88	4 Apr
45.86	Noah	Akwu	NGR	23.9.90	11 Aug
45.88	Nobuya	Kato	JPN-J	16.4.95	5 Sep
45.90	Peterson	dos Santos	BRA	31.3.91	10 Oct
45.91	Stephon	Pamilton	USA	18.9.91	18 May
45.91	Rabea	Al-Kowari	QAT-Y	2.8.98	8 Jun
45.92	Arokia	Rajiv	IND	22.5.91	28 Sep
45.93	Ceolamar	Ways	USA	22.11.94	4 Apr
45.93	Johan	Wissman	SWE	2.11.82	26 Jul
45.93A	Juander	Santos	DOM-J	7.5.95	26 Nov
45.94	Terrence	Agard	NED	16.4.90	5 Jul
45.95	William	Collazo	CUB	31.8.86	17 May
45.95	Cass	Brown-Stewart	USA	2.8.92	30 May
45.96i	Neal	Braddy	USA	18.12.91	14 Feb
45.96	Alejandro	Perlaza	COL	30.6.93	29 Mar
45.96	Milos	Raovic	SRB	12.5.94	12 Jul
45.97A	Barend	Koekemoer	RSA-J	12.6.95	10 May
45.98	Yusuke	Ishitsuka	JPN	19.6.87	3 May
45.98		Park Bong-ko	KOR	8.5.91	25 Jun
45.99	Jordan	Edwards	USA	4.2.91	22 May
46.00	Errol	Nolan	JAM	18.8.91	4 May
46.00	Josh	Edmonds	USA	23.7.91	21 May
46.00	Thomas	Jordier	FRA	12.8.94	13 Jul
46.00	Davide	Re	ITA	16.3.93	19 Jul
46.00	Mehdi	Zamani	IRI	20.12.89	21 Aug
46.01	Jeremy	Wariner	USA	31.1.84	17 May
46.01	Kacper	Kozlowski	POL	7.12.86	2 Aug
46.02	Lamar	Bruton	USA-J	26.5.95	30 May
46.03A	Willem	de Beer	RSA	14.3.88	10 May
46.05	Karol	Zalewski	POL	7.8.93	6 Aug
46.05	José Daniel	Meléndez	VEN	19.5.93	3 Oct
46.05A	Manuel	Soriano	DOM	5.1.87	25 Nov
46.06	Burkheart	Ellis	BAR	18.9.92	22 May
46.06	Sadam	Koumi	SUD	6.4.94	23 Jul
46.06	Sajad	Hashemi	IRI	22.8.91	7 Aug
46.07	Quentin	Iglehart-Summers	USA	15.6.87	18 Apr
46.08	Kerron	Clement	USA	31.10.85	31 May
46.08	Zwede	Hewitt	TTO	10.6.89	21 Jun
46.08	Thomas	Schneider	GER	7.11.88	27 Jul
46.08	P.P.Kunhu	Muhammed	IND	5.3.87	27 Sep
46.09	Daniel	Nemecek	CZE	11.8.91	3 Aug
46.10	Marqueze	Washington	USA	.94	18 Apr
46.10	Devante	Lacy	USA-J	8.11.95	10 May
46.10	Mamadou-Elimane	Hanne	FRA	6.3.88	13 Jul
46.10	Tomoya	Tamura	JPN	20.8.92	5 Sep
46.11	Nathon	Allen	JAM-J	28.10.95	9 Mar
46.11A	Sonwabisi	Skhosana	RSA-J	4.7.95	10 May
46.11	Yegor	Kibakin	RUS	17.4.92	6 Jun
46.12	Byron	Robinson	USA-J	16.2.95	12 Apr
46.12	Payton	Hazzard	USA	6.9.93	9 May
46.12	Cody	Rush	USA	11.11.93	30 May
46.13	Mamadou	Kassé Hann	SEN	10.10.86	28 May
46.13	Braxton	Klavins	USA	.92	30 May
46.13	Miguel	Rigau	GER	22.7.85	7 Jun
46.13	Ali Khamis	Abbas	BRN-J	30.6.95	12 Jul

Mark	Wind	Name		Nat	Born	Pos	Meet	Venue	Date
46.14		Marcus	Boyd	USA	3.3.89				3 May
46.14		Rashard	Clark	USA	4.11.94				16 May
46.14		Miguel	Barton	JAM	4.12.88				17 May
46.14		William	Shell	USA	12.6.91				24 May
46.14		Alvin	Green	JAM	26.8.89				7 Jun
46.15		Jereem	Richards	TTO	13.1.94				12 Apr
46.15		Michael	Courtney	USA	12.6.86				3 May
46.15		Ismail	Al-Sabyani	KSA	25.4.89				9 May
46.15		Stephan	James	GUY	23.6.93				17 May
46.15		Mark	Ujakpor	ESP	18.1.87				12 Jun
46.15		Isah	Salihu	NGR	2.11.91				21 Jun
46.15		Alexander	Russo	BRA	26.7.94				19 Jul
46.15		Aleksandr	Khyutte	RUS	29.9.88				24 Jul
46.15		Osmaidel	Pellicier	CUB	30.3.92				8 Oct
46.16		Yeimer	López	ex-CUB	20.8.82				7 Jun
46.17A		Gideon Ernst	Narib	NAM	27.5.90				10 May
46.18		Gustavo	Cuesta	DOM	14.11.88				15 Feb
46.18		Akino	Ming	JAM	29.11.90				10 May
46.18		Richard	Buck	GBR	14.11.86				14 Jun
46.18		Jarryd	Dunn	GBR	30.1.92				28 Jun
46.18		Quintaveon	Poole #	USA-J	12.10.96				7 Jul
46.18		Jamie	Bowie	GBR	1.4.89				19 Jul
46.19A		Solomon	Buoga	KEN	20.11.85				7 Jun
46.19		Nicholas (203)	Maitland	JAM	27.11.89				7 Jun

Indoors

Mark	Name		Nat	Born	Date
45.95i	Gustavo	Cuesta	DOM	14.11.88	8 Feb
46.09i	Richard	Buck	GBR	14.11.86	15 Feb
46.16i	Luke	Lennon-Ford	GBR	5.5.89	15 Feb

Low altitude bests

Mark	Name	Pos	Meet	Venue	Date
45.21	Seribe	2		La Chaux de Fonds	6 Jul
45.57	Lescay	1		Dessau	11 Jun
45.60	Beshr	5	GS	Ostrava	17 Jun
45.62	Fitten	5	NC	Kingston	29 Jun
45.70	Fothergill				29 Jun
45.73	de Oliveira				2 Aug
45.74	de Jager				14 Mar
46.03	Acea				8 Oct
46.11	Baloyes				3 Oct
46.18	Bravo				15 May

JUNIORS

See main list for top 3 juniors. 10 performances by 5 men to 45.88. Additional marks and further juniors:

	Mark	Pos	Meet	Venue	Date	Mark	Pos	Meet	Venue	Date
Cedenio	45.23	1		George Town	7 May	45.48	1		Amsterdam	22 Aug
	45.28A	1	CAC-J	Morelia	6 Jul					
Abubaker	45.61	1h2	AsiG	Incheon	27 Sep	45.62	2	AsiG	Incheon	28 Sep

Mark	Name		Nat	Born	Pos	Meet	Venue	Date
45.74	Abdeliah	Haroun	SUD/QAT-Y	.97	1		Doha	29 Apr
45.74	Tyler	Brown	USA	24.3.95	1	NC-j	Eugene	6 Jul
45.84A	Alex	Sampao	KEN	31.12.96	1		Nairobi	25 Jun
45.88	Nobuya	Kato	JPN	16.4.95	1		Kumagaya	5 Sep
45.91	Rabea	Al-Kowari	QAT-Y	2.8.98	1		Istanbul	8 Jun
45.93A	Juander	Santos	DOM	7.5.95	4	CAG	Xalapa	26 Nov
45.97A	Barend	Koekemoer (10)	RSA	12.6.95	1		Potchefstroom	10 May
46.02	Lamar	Bruton	USA	26.5.95	3q3	NCAA-E	Jacksonville	30 May
46.10	Devante	Lacy	USA	8.11.95	1		Austin	10 May
46.11	Nathon	Allen	JAM	28.10.95	1		Kingston	9 Mar
46.11A	Sonwabisi	Skhosana	RSA	4.7.95	2		Potchefstroom	10 May
46.12	Byron	Robinson	USA	16.2.95	3		Tempe	12 Apr
46.13	Ali Khamis	Abbas	BRN	30.6.95	2		Plovdiv	12 Jul
46.18	Quintaveon	Poole #	USA	12.10.96	1		Rock Hill	7 Jul
46.23	Josephus	Lyles	USA-Y	22.7.98	1	N.Sch	Greensboro	13 Jun
46.24	Martin	Manley	JAM-Y	10.3.97	1	NC-j	Kingston	15 Jun
46.25A	Jon	Seeliger (20)	RSA	27.4.95	3		Potchefstroom	10 May

600 METRES

Mark	Name		Nat	Born	Pos	Meet	Venue	Date
1:13.71	David	Rudisha	KEN	17.12.88	1	DL	Birmingham	24 Aug
1:14.43	Duane	Solomon	USA	28.12.84	1		Orlando	29 Mar
1:14.69	Adam	Kszczot	POL	2.9.89	2	DL	Birmingham	24 Aug
1:14.92	Wesley	Vázquez	PUR	27.3.94	2		Orlando	29 Mar
1:15.03	André	Olivier	RSA	29.12.89	3	DL	Birmingham	24 Aug
1:15.17	Marcin	Lewandowski	POL	13.6.87	4	DL	Birmingham	24 Aug
1:15.78	Patryk	Dobek	POL	13.2.94	1		Pliezhausen	18 May
1:15.79	Erik	Sowinski	USA	21.12.89	5	DL	Birmingham	24 Aug
1:16.0+	Nijel	Amos	BOT	15.3.94				18 Jul
1:16.1+	Pierre-Ambroise	Bosse	FRA	11.5.92				18 Jul
1:16.15	Andreas	Bube	DEN	13.7.87				24 Aug
1:16.28	Artur	Kuciapski	POL	26.12.93				24 May
1:16.30	Kyle	Langford	GBR-J	2.2.96				24 Aug
1:16.46	Abdulrahman Musaeb	Balla	QAT	19.3.89				5 Aug

Indoors

Mark	Name		Nat	Born	Pos	Meet	Venue	Date
1:15.31	Mohamed	Aman	ETH	10.1.94	1	Winter	Moskva	2 Feb
1:15.83	Abdulrahman Musaeb	Balla	QAT	19.3.89				2 Feb
1:16.08	Stepan	Poistogov	RUS	14.12.86				2 Feb
1:16.11	Erik	Sowinski	USA	21.12.89				2 Feb
1:16.48	Guy	Learmonth	GBR	24.4.92				25 Jan

800 METRES

Mark	Name		Nat	Born	Pos	Meet	Venue	Date
1:42.45	Nijel	Amos	BOT	15.3.94	1	Herc	Monaco	18 Jul
1:42.53	Pierre-Ambroise	Bosse	FRA	11.5.92	2	Herc	Monaco	18 Jul
1:42.83	Mohammed	Aman	ETH	10.1.94	3	Herc	Monaco	18 Jul
1:42.84	Ferguson	Cheruiyot	KEN	30.11.89	4	Herc	Monaco	18 Jul
1:42.98	David	Rudisha	KEN	17.12.88	5	Herc	Monaco	18 Jul
1:43.34	Asbel	Kiprop	KEN	30.6.89	1	DL	Saint-Denis	5 Jul
1:43.34		Rudisha			1	DL	Glasgow	12 Jul
1:43.52		Aman			1	ISTAF	Berlin	31 Aug
1:43.53	Taoufik	Makhloufi	ALG	29.4.88	2	ISTAF	Berlin	31 Aug
1:43.63		Amos			1	Pre	Eugene	31 May
1:43.65	Timothy	Kitum	KEN	20.11.94	1rA	NA	Heusden-Zolder	19 Jul

Mark Wind	Name		Nat	Born	Pos	Meet	Venue	Date
1:43.69	Ayanleh	Souleiman	DJI	3.12.92	1		Huddinge	25 Jul
1:43.70		Amos			2	DL	Saint-Denis	5 Jul
1:43.71	Yeimer	López (10)	ex-CUB	20.8.82	3	DL	Saint-Denis	5 Jul
1:43.77		Amos			1	WK	Zürich	28 Aug
1:43.83		Makhloufi			1rA	WCM	Rieti	7 Sep
1:43.88	Duane	Solomon	USA	28.12.84	1	MSR	Walnut	19 Apr
1:43.93		Souleiman			2	WK	Zürich	28 Aug
1:43.95	Alfred	Kipketer	KEN-J	26.12.96	1	WJ	Eugene	27 Jul
1:43.96		Rudisha			3	WK	Zürich	28 Aug
1:43.98		López			1		Göteborg	14 Jun
1:43.99		Aman			2	Pre	Eugene	31 May
1:44.01		López			1		Oslo	22 May
1:44.02	Adam	Kszczot	POL	2.9.89	3	ISTAF	Berlin	31 Aug
1:44.03	Marcin	Lewandowski	POL	13.6.87	4	ISTAF	Berlin	31 Aug
1:44.03	Abdulrahman Musaeb Balla		QAT	19.3.89	2rA	WCM	Rieti	7 Sep
1:44.09	Abubaker	Kaki	SUD	21.6.89	3	Pre	Eugene	31 May
1:44.12		Balla			2rA	NA	Heusden-Zolder	19 Jul
1:44.15		Kszczot			1	EC	Zürich	15 Aug
1:44.2A		Kipketer			1		Nairobi	26 Apr
	(30/16)							
1:44.30	Abdulaziz Ladan	Mohamed	KSA	7.1.91	3rA	WCM	Rieti	7 Sep
1:44.40	Alex	Rowe	AUS	8.7.92	7	Herc	Monaco	18 Jul
1:44.42	André	Olivier	RSA	29.12.89	6	DL	Saint-Denis	5 Jul
1:44.55	Job	Kinyor	KEN	2.9.90	5rA	WCM	Rieti	7 Sep
	(20)							
1:44.58	Erik	Sowinski	USA	21.12.89	2	MSR	Walnut	19 Apr
1:44.64	Wesley	Vázquez	PUR	27.3.94	3	MSR	Walnut	19 Apr
1:44.69	Robert	Biwott	KEN-J	28.1.96	1	DL	Shanghai	18 May
1:44.72	Anthony	Chemut	KEN	17.12.92	3rA	NA	Heusden-Zolder	19 Jul
1:44.77	Rafith	Rodríguez	COL	1.6.89	1	IbAmC	São Paulo	2 Aug
1:44.85	Jeremiah	Mutai	KEN	27.12.92	4	DL	Shanghai	18 May
1:44.89	Artur	Kuciapski	POL	26.12.93	2	EC	Zürich	15 Aug
1:44.91	Elijah	Greer	USA	24.10.90	4rA	NA	Heusden-Zolder	19 Jul
1:45.03	Mark	English	IRL	18.3.93	2	adidas	New York	14 Jun
1:45.14	Joshua	Masikonde	KEN-J	16.8.96	2	WJ	Eugene	27 Jul
	(30)							
1:45.21	Andreas	Bube	DEN	13.7.87	4	EC	Zürich	15 Aug
1:45.27	Ronald	Musagala	UGA	16.12.92	2	FBK	Hengelo	8 Jun
1:45.30	Kléberson	Davide	BRA	20.7.85	1	SAmG	Santiago de Chile	16 Mar
1:45.3A	Sammy	Kirongo	KEN	4.2.94	4		Nairobi	26 Apr
1:45.35	Brandon	McBride	CAN	15.6.94	4	MSR	Walnut	19 Apr
1:45.37	Eliud	Rutto	KEN	4.6.88	1	Jordan	Stanford	4 May
1:45.37	Andrew	Osagie	GBR	19.2.88	8	Pre	Eugene	31 May
1:45.37	Nader	Belhanbel	MAR	1.7.94	7	GGala	Roma	5 Jun
1:45.37	Jozef	Repcík	SVK	3.8.86	6	ISTAF	Berlin	31 Aug
1:45.5A	Edwin	Kemboi	KEN	22.8.86	1	Army Ch	Nairobi	17 May
	(40)							
1:45.50A	Evans	Kipkorir	KEN	4.4.94	2	NC	Nairobi	7 Jun
1:45.55	Harun	Abda	USA	1.1.90	3	GP	Ponce	17 May
1:45.59	Cleiton	Abrão	BRA	8.9.89	1	NC	São Paulo	12 Oct
1:45.65	Ryan	Martin	USA	23.3.89	5rA	NA	Heusden-Zolder	19 Jul
1:45.65	Andreas	Almgren	SWE-J	12.6.95	3	WJ	Eugene	27 Jul
1:45.68	Thijmen	Kupers	NED	4.10.91	3	FBK	Hengelo	8 Jun
1:45.7A	Nicholas	Kipkoech	KEN	22.10.92	5		Nairobi	26 Apr
1:45.7A	Cornelius	Kiplangat	KEN	21.12.92	2	Army Ch	Nairobi	17 May
1:45.73A	Andy	González	CUB	17.10.87	1	CAG	Xalapa	28 Nov
1:45.75	Sho	Kawamoto	JPN	1.3.93	1		Tokyo	11 May
	(50)							
1:45.79	Dennis	Krüger	GER	24.4.93	1		Mannheim	17 Jul
1:45.80	Casimir	Loxsom	USA	17.3.91	2s1	NC	Sacramento	27 Jun
1:45.81	Joshua	Ralph	AUS	27.10.91	2		Melbourne	22 Mar
1:45.81	Jeff	Riseley	AUS	11.11.86	1		Padova	6 Jul
1:45.87	Edwin	Melly	KEN	23.4.94	3	WCM	Beijing	21 May
1:45.89	Michael	Rimmer	GBR	3.2.86	3	DL	Glasgow	12 Jul
1:45.89	Johan	Rogestedt	SWE	27.1.93	1rB	WCM	Rieti	7 Sep
1:45.90	Charles	Jock	USA	23.11.89	4	GP	Ponce	17 May
1:45.92A	Timothy	Cheruiyot	KEN-J	20.11.95	3	NC-j	Nairobi	25 Jun
1:45.94	Sofiane	Selmouni	FRA	22.9.89	2		Montreuil-sous-Bois	7 Jul
	(60)							
1:45.99	Giordano	Benedetti	ITA	22.5.89	8	GGala	Roma	5 Jun

Mark	Wind	Name		Nat	Born	Pos	Meet	Venue	Date
1:45.99		Thiago	André	BRA-J	4.8.95	2	IbAmC	São Paulo	2 Aug
1:46.01		Amine	El Manaoui	MAR	20.11.91	2h1	AfCh	Marrakech	11 Aug
1:46.04		Michael	Rutt	USA	28.10.87	2rB	NA	Heusden-Zolder	19 Jul
1:46.05		Paul	Renaudie	FRA	2.4.90	3		Montreuil-sous-Bois	7 Jul
1:46.09		Felix	Kitur	KEN	17.4.87	2		Los Angeles (ER)	15 May
1:46.12		Matthew	Centrowitz	USA	18.10.89	4	DL	Glasgow	12 Jul
1:46.12		Amel	Tuka	BIH	9.1.91	6	EC	Zürich	15 Aug
1:46.12		Leonel	Manzano	USA	12.9.84	2rB	WCM	Rieti	7 Sep
1:46.13		Abraham	Kiplagat	KEN	8.9.84	4	FBK	Hengelo	8 Jun
		(70)							
1:46.14		Edward	Kemboi	KEN	12.12.91	5	MSR	Walnut	19 Apr
1:46.15		Thomas	Roth	NOR	11.2.91	3rB	NA	Heusden-Zolder	19 Jul
1:46.16		Jan	Van Den Broeck	BEL	11.3.89	6rA	NA	Heusden-Zolder	19 Jul
1:46.17		Aaron	Botterman	BEL	1.5.94	4rB	NA	Heusden-Zolder	19 Jul
1:46.21		Jorge Félix	Liranzo	CUB	3.2.94	1	NC	La Habana	20 Mar
1:46.23		Jena	Umar	ETH-J	24.12.95	5	WJ	Eugene	27 Jul
1:46.23		Lutimar	Paes	BRA	14.12.88	2	NC	São Paulo	12 Oct
1:46.24		Timo	Benitz	GER	24.12.91	1	ET	Braunschweig	22 Jun
1:46.24		Antoine	Gakeme	BDI	24.12.91	3h1	AfCh	Marrakech	11 Aug
1:46.27		Ryan	Gregson	AUS	26.4.90	3		Dublin	11 Jul
		(80)							
1:46.28		Robby	Andrews	USA	29.3.91	8	adidas	New York	14 Jun
1:46.29		Ryan	Schnulle	USA	8.9.93	2	NCAA	Eugene	13 Jun
1:46.3A		Patrick Kiprotich	Rono	KEN-J	9.4.96	1		Nairobi	4 Apr
1:46.3A		Moses	Kipchirchir	KEN	.86	4	Army	Nairobi	15 May
1:46.32			Teng Haining	CHN	25.6.93	4	WCM	Beijing	21 May
1:46.33		Robin	Schembera	GER	1.10.88	6	FBK	Hengelo	8 Jun
1:46.33		Maurys Surel	Castillo	ex-CUB	19.10.84	1h2	ESP Ch	Alcobendas	26 Jul
1:46.39		Keffri	Neal	CAN	26.10.93	3	NCAA	Eugene	13 Jun
1:46.40		Paul	Robinson	IRL	24.5.91	4		Dublin	11 Jul
1:46.46		Patrick	Rono	KEN	8.4.92	4	NCAA	Eugene	13 Jun
		(90)							
1:46.47		Redouane	Baaziri	MAR	23.7.93	1		Montbéliard	6 Jun
1:46.50		Lucas Gabriel	Rodrigues	BRA-J	2.10.95	3	NC	São Paulo	12 Oct
1:46.5A		Fredrick	Korir	KEN	17.4.87	5	Army	Nairobi	15 May
1:46.52		Yassine	Hathat	ALG	30.7.91	1	NC	Algiers	25 Jun
1:46.55		Sadik	Mikhou	MAR	25.7.90	1		Rabat	31 May
1:46.55		Mor	Seck	SEN	24.9.85	1		Conegliano	20 Jun
1:46.55		Reuben	Bett	KEN	6.11.84	6		Liège (NX)	16 Jul
1:46.56		Mukhtar	Mohammed	GBR	1.12.90	7	DL	Glasgow	12 Jul
1:46.58		Stepan	Poistogov	RUS	14.12.86	4	Kuso	Szczecin	7 Jun
1:46.60		Lucirio Antonio	Garrido	VEN	8.4.92	3	IbAmC	São Paulo	2 Aug
		(100)							

Mark	Name		Nat	Born	Date
1:46.61	James	Eichberger	MEX	4.8.90	19 Jul
1:46.62	Brian	Gagnon	USA	8.5.87	5 Jun
1:46.64	Kevin	López	ESP	12.6.90	19 Jul
1:46.67	Brandon	Johnson	USA	6.3.85	18 May
1:46.68	Sean	Obinwa	USA/NGR	4.1.91	4 Apr
1:46.68A	Reinhardt	van Rensburg	RSA	23.3.92	14 Apr
1:46.68	Alberto	Mamba	MOZ	9.10.94	11 Aug
1:46.69	Patrick	Zwicker	GER	13.7.94	17 Jul
1:46.69	Guy	Learmonth	GBR	24.4.92	31 Jul
1:46.7A	Isaac	Chirchir	KEN-J	20.10.96	4 Apr
1:46.71	Andreas	Lange	GER	29.1.91	5 Jul
1:46.71	David	Torrence	USA	26.11.85	15 Jul
1:46.71	Vincent	Kibet	KEN	6.5.91	16 Aug
1:46.77	David	Mutua	KEN	20.4.92	9 Jun
1:46.77	Jordan	Williamsz	AUS	21.8.92	11 Jul
1:46.78	Nikolaus	Franzmair	AUT-J	18.2.95	7 Jun
1:46.78	Daniel	Andújar	ESP	14.5.94	6 Jul
1:46.78	Samir	Jamaa	MAR	9.2.90	30 Jul
1:46.8A	Anthony	Kiptoo	KEN-Y	19.8.97	4 Apr
1:46.80	Tyler	Mulder	USA	15.2.87	21 May
1:46.80	Anthony	Romaniw	CAN	15.9.91	10 Jul
1:46.81	Mark	Wieczorek	USA	25.12.84	5 Jun
1:46.81	Sajeesh	Joseph	IND	14.1.87	17 Aug
1:46.83	Declan	Murray	USA/IRL	4.6.91	15 May
1:46.83	Tamás	Kazi	HUN	16.5.85	29 Jul
1:46.87	Salah	Echchibani	MAR	1.7.91	30 Jul
1:46.88	Mamush	Lencho	ETH-J	24.3.96	9 Jun
1:46.88	Brice	Leroy	FRA	26.6.89	2 Aug
1:46.91	Drew	Windle	USA	22.7.92	12 Apr
1:46.93	Andreas	Vojta	AUT	9.6.89	7 Jun
1:46.94	Leonard	Kosencha	KEN	21.8.94	21 May
1:46.95	Hugo	Santacruz	SUI	6.5.88	15 Jul
1:46.97	Tarik	Moukrime	BEL	3.3.92	16 Jul
1:46.98	Léo	Morgana	FRA	23.9.94	6 Jun
1:47.00	Charlie	Grice	GBR	7.11.93	11 Jun
1:47.02	Ali Saad	Al-Daran	KSA	17.4.90	10 May
1:47.02	Thomas	Riva	CAN	31.1.92	8 Jul
1:47.03	Joe	Thomas	GBR	29.1.88	5 Jul
1:47.04	Jared	West	AUS	14.7.88	15 Mar
1:47.04	Gareth	Warburton #	GBR	23.4.83	12 Jun
1:47.06	Jamaal	James	TTO	4.9.88	11 Jul
1:47.09	Benson	Scheetz	USA	5.6.90	27 Jun
1:47.09	Zan	Rudolf	SLO	9.5.93	2 Sep
1:47.10	Andreas	Roth	NOR	29.4.93	11 Jul
1:47.1A	Bacha	Morka	ETH-Y	6.6.97	12 May
1:47.13	Tre	Kinnaird	USA-J	13.1.95	27 Jul
1:47.14	Mouhcine	El Amine	MAR	8.1.82	26 Apr
1:47.14	Stanislav	Maslov	UKR	19.1.89	20 Jul
1:47.14	Moussa	Camara	MLI	12.2.88	11 Aug
1:47.15	Aaron	Evans	BER	31.1.90	4 May
1:47.16	Jordan	McNamara	USA	7.3.87	15 Jun
1:47.17	Roald Hagbart	Frøskeland	NOR	28.3.94	31 May
1:47.17	Abednego	Chesebe	KEN	20.6.82	16 Jul
1:47.18	Mohamed	Belbachir	ALG	11.1.94	10 May
1:47.19	Brandon	Lasater	USA	9.10.92	4 Apr
1:47.19	Rabie	Doukkana	MAR	6.12.87	87 Jun
1:47.20	Rickard	Gunnarsson	SWE	19.9.91	26 Jun
1:47.20	Fouad	El Kaam	MAR	27.5.88	16 Jul
1:47.20	Benedikt	Huber	GER	13.10.89	19 Jul
1:47.22	Charel	Grethen	LUX	22.6.92	4 Apr
1:47.22	Khaled	Benmahdi	ALG	22.10.88	25 Jun
1:47.25	Gabe	Hilbert	USA	24.10.91	10 May
1:47.26	Hamid	Oualich	FRA	26.4.88	9 Jun
1:47.26	Mohamed Amine	Belferrar	ALG	6.2.91	6 Jul

Mark	Wind	Name		Nat	Born	Pos	Meet	Venue	Date

Mark	Name		Nat	Born	Date
1:47.28	Denis	Bäuerle	GER	27.10.89	17 Jul
1:47.29	Karol	Konieczny	POL	5.5.93	20 Jul
1:47.3A	Bernard	Koros	KEN	7.5.94	24 May
1:47.3A	Mengistu	Terecha	ETH		12 May
1:47.31	Yassine	Bensghir	MAR	3.1.83	31 May
1:47.31	Alejandro	Rodríguez	ESP	1.5.89	12 Jun
1:47.31	Kalle	Berglund	SWE-J	11.3.96	27 Jul
1:47.35	Ján	Kubista	CZE	23.9.90	1 Jul
1:47.35	Danyil	Strelnikov	RUS	3.5.92	15 Jul
1:47.35	Jan	Riedel	GER	14.10.89	17 Jul
1:47.36	Jesse	Garn	USA	4.6.93	2 May
1:47.38	Ilham	Tanui Özbilen	TUR	5.3.90	25 May
1:47.4A	Jimmy	Cheruiyot	KEN-J	.96	4 Apr
1:47.4	Musa	Hajdari	KOS	11.10.87	31 Aug
1:47.41	Kyle	Langford	GBR-J	2.2.96	17 May
1:47.41	Florian	Orth	GER	24.7.89	19 Jul
1:47.42	Álvaro	de Arriba	ESP	2.6.94	27 Jul
1:47.43	David	Verbrugghe	FRA	16.7.87	25 Jun
1:47.44	Raidel	Acea	CUB	31.10.90	28 Jun
1:47.44	Karl	Griffin	IRL-J	5.6.95	11 Jul
1:47.46A	Charles	Simotwo	KEN-J	6.5.95	25 Jun
1:47.48	Homiyu	Tesfaye	GER	23.6.93	29 Aug
1:47.48	Bob	van der Ham	NED	6.7.90	22 Aug
1:47.48	Adrian Taees	Akkar	IRQ	24.3.80	1 Oct
1:47.49	Bryan Antonio	Martínez	MEX	1.8.94	31 Aug
(189)					

Disqualified: 1:46.94 Abraham Rotich BRN 26.6.93 1 Oct

Indoors

Mark	Name		Nat	Born	Pos	Meet	Venue	Date
1:45.22	Andrew	Osagie	GBR	19.2.88	4	GP	Birmingham	15 Feb
1:45.69	Kevin	López	ESP	12.6.90	3	XLG	Stockholm	6 Feb
1:45.98	Edward	Kemboi	KEN	12.12.91	1		Ames	15 Feb
1:46.30	Abraham	Rotich	BRN	26.6.93	1		Karlsruhe	1 Feb
1:46.52	Drew	Windle	USA	22.7.92	1		Allendale	14 Feb
1:46.53	Stepan	Poistogov	RUS	14.12.86	1	NC	Moskva	18 Feb

Mark	Name		Nat	Born	Date
1:47.18	Ivan	Nesterov	RUS	10.2.85	18 Feb
1:47.29	Nick	Symmonds	USA	30.12.83	7 Mar
1:47.45	Brannon	Kidder	USA	18.11.93	18 Feb

Drugs disqualification: 1:46.75 Gareth Warburton # GBR 23.4.83 5 Padova 6 Jul

JUNIORS

See main list for top 9 juniors. 11 performances by 6 men to 1:45.99. Additional marks and further juniors:

Kipketer 2+	1:45.67A	1	NC-j	Nairobi	25 Jun				
Biwott	1:44.75	1	FBK	Hengelo	7 Jun	1:45.21	9	DL Saint-Denis	5 Jul
Masikonde	1:45.85A	2	NC-j	Nairobi	25 Jun				

Mark	Name		Nat	Born	Pos	Meet	Venue	Date
1:46.7A	Isaac	Chirchir (10)	KEN	20.10.96	2		Nairobi	4 Apr
1:46.78	Nikolaus	Franzmair	AUT	18.2.95	2		Regensburg	7 Jun
1:46.8A	Anthony	Kiptoo	KEN-Y	19.8.97	3		Nairobi	4 Apr
1:46.88	Mamush	Lencho	ETH	24.3.96	3		Rehlingen	9 Jun
1:47.1A	Bacha	Morka	ETH-Y	6.6.97	2	NC	Addis Ababa	12 May
1:47.13	Tre	Kinnaird	USA	13.1.95	6	WJ	Eugene	27 Jul
1:47.31	Kalle	Berglund	SWE	11.3.96	7	WJ	Eugene	27 Jul
1:47.4A	Jimmy	Cheruiyot	KEN	.96	4		Nairobi	4 Apr
1:47.41	Kyle	Langford	GBR	2.2.96	2		Watford	17 May
1:47.44	Karl	Griffin	IRL	5.6.95	10		Dublin	11 Jul
1:47.46A	Charles	Simotwo (20)	KEN	6.5.95	5	NC-j	Nairobi	25 Jun

1000 METRES

Mark	Name		Nat	Born	Pos	Meet	Venue	Date
2:15.08	Ilham Tanui	Özbilen	TUR	5.3.90	1	GS	Ostrava	17 Jun
2:15.31	Pierre-Ambroise	Bosse	FRA	11.5.92	2	GS	Ostrava	17 Jun
2:15.72	Adam	Kszczot	POL	2.9.89	1	VD	Bruxelles	5 Sep
2:15.75	Mohammed	Aman	ETH	10.1.94	2	VD	Bruxelles	5 Sep
2:15.79	Marcin	Lewandowski	POL	13.6.87	3	VD	Bruxelles	5 Sep
2:16.09	Jeff	Riseley	AUS	11.11.86	3	GS	Ostrava	17 Jun
2:16.33		Aman			4	GS	Ostrava	17 Jun
2:16.52	Sammy	Kirongo	KEN	4.2.94	1		Tomblaine	27 Jun
2:16.76	Yassine	Hathat	MAR	30.7.91	2		Tomblaine	27 Jun
2:16.79	Jakub	Holusa	CZE	20.2.88	5	GS	Ostrava	17 Jun
2:16.88	Ferguson	Cheruiyot	KEN	30.11.89	4	VD	Bruxelles	5 Sep
2:16.90	Timo	Benitz	GER	1.12.91	1		Pliezhausen	18 May
2:17.11	Ronald	Musagala	UGA	16.12.92	5	VD	Bruxelles	5 Sep
2:17.18	Mahiedine	Mekhissi-Benabbad	FRA	15.3.85	3		Tomblaine	27 Jun
2:17.38	Tamás	Kazi	HUN	16.5.85	8	GS	Ostrava	17 Jun
2:17.56	Homiyu	Tesfaye	GER	23.6.93	2		Pliezhausen	18 May
2:17.76	Jozef	Repcík	SVK	3.8.86	9	GS	Ostrava	17 Jun

Mark	Name		Nat	Born	Date
2:17.91	Amine	El Manaoui	MAR	20.11.91	27 Jun
2:17.93	Paul	Robinson	IRL	24.5.91	17 Jun
2:17.98	Reuben	Bett	KEN	6.11.84	5 Sep
2:18.06	Andreas	Vojta	AUT	9.6.89	17 Jun
2:18.11	André	Olivier	RSA	29.12.89	5 Sep
2:18.17	Jeremiah	Mutai	KEN	27.12.92	27 Jun
2:18.20	Anthony	Chemut	KEN	17.12.92	14 Jul
2:18.33	Timothy	Kitum	KEN	20.11.94	5 Sep
2:18.41	Mohamed	Al-Garni	QAT	2.7.92	14 Jul
2:18.46	Ryan	Gregson	AUS	26.4.90	14 Jul

Indoors

Mark	Name		Nat	Born	Pos	Venue	Date
2:15.96		Özbilen			1	Istanbul	20 Feb
2:16.76	David	Torrence	USA	26.11.85	1	Boston (A)	2 Mar
2:16.87	Nathan	Brannen	CAN	8.9.82	2	Boston (A)	2 Mar

Mark	Name		Nat	Born	Date
2:18.55	Richard	Peters	GBR	18.2.90	2 Mar
2:18.63	Erik	Sowinski	USA	21.12.89	15 Feb
2:18.87	Nick	Symmonds	USA	30.12.83	15 Feb

+ intermediate time in longer race, A made at an altitude of 1000m or higher, D made in a decathlon, h made in a heat, qf quarter-final, sf semi-final, i indoors, Q qualifying round, r race number, -J juniors, -Y youths (b. 1997 or later)

1500 METRES

Mark	Wind	Name		Nat	Born	Pos	Meet	Venue	Date
3:27.64		Silas	Kiplagat	KEN	20.8.89	1	Herc	Monaco	18 Jul
3:28.45		Asbel	Kiprop	KEN	30.6.89	2	Herc	Monaco	18 Jul
3:28.81		Ronald	Kwemoi	KEN-J	19.9.95	3	Herc	Monaco	18 Jul
3:29.18			Kiprop			1	DL	Doha	9 May
3:29.58		Ayanleh	Souleiman	DJI	3.12.92	4	Herc	Monaco	18 Jul
3:29.70			Kiplagat			2	DL	Doha	9 May
3:29.83		Abdelati	Iguider	MAR	25.3.87	5	Herc	Monaco	18 Jul
3:29.91		Aman	Wote	ETH	18.4.84	6	Herc	Monaco	18 Jul
3:29.91		Nick	Willis	NZL	25.4.83	7	Herc	Monaco	18 Jul
3:30.16			Souleiman			3	DL	Doha	9 May
3:30.40		Taoufik	Makhloufi	ALG	29.4.88	4	DL	Doha	9 May
3:30.44			Kiplagat			1	GGala	Roma	5 Jun
3:30.61		James	Magut	KEN	20.7.90	5	DL	Doha	9 May
3:30.86			Wote			6	DL	Doha	9 May
3:30.98		Leonel	Manzano (10)	USA	12.9.84	8	Herc	Monaco	18 Jul
3:31.09		Matthew	Centrowitz	USA	18.10.89	9	Herc	Monaco	18 Jul
3:31.19			Souleiman			2	GGala	Roma	5 Jun
3:31.22		Bethwel	Birgen	KEN	6.8.88	7	DL	Doha	9 May
3:31.44			Kiplagat			1	WCM	Rieti	7 Sep
3:31.46		Henrik	Ingebrigtsen	NOR	24.2.91	10	Herc	Monaco	18 Jul
3:31.48			Kwemoi			1	Athl	Lausanne	3 Jul
3:31.78			Makhloufi			1	VD	Bruxelles	5 Sep
3:31.80			Kiplagat			2	VD	Bruxelles	5 Sep
3:31.81			Kiplagat			2	Athl	Lausanne	3 Jul
3:31.89			Kiprop			3	GGala	Roma	5 Jun
3:31.91			Magut			3	Athl	Lausanne	3 Jul
3:31.96			Wote			4	Athl	Lausanne	3 Jul
3:31.96		Vincent	Kibet	KEN	6.5.91	2	WCM	Rieti	7 Sep
3:31.98		Homiyu	Tesfaye	GER	23.6.93	4	GGala	Roma	5 Jun
3:32.00		Collins	Cheboi	KEN	25.9.87	3	WCM	Rieti	7 Sep
		(30/16)							
3:32.09		Ilham Tanui	Özbilen	TUR	5.3.90	8	DL	Doha	9 May
3:32.79		Mekonnen	Gebremedhin	ETH	11.10.88	4	WCM	Rieti	7 Sep
3:33.31		Johan	Cronje	RSA	13.4.82	10	DL	Doha	9 May
3:33.47		Sadik	Mikhou	MAR	25.7.90	1		Oordegem	5 Jul
		(20)							
3:34.15		Galen	Rupp	USA	8.5.86	11	VD	Bruxelles	5 Sep
3:34.19		Zane	Robertson	NZL	14.11.89	5	WCM	Rieti	7 Sep
3:34.24		Benson	Seurei	BRN	27.3.84	12	DL	Doha	9 May
3:34.26		Will	Leer	USA	15.4.85	1rA	NA	Heusden-Zolder	19 Jul
3:34.49		Pieter-Jan	Hannes	BEL	30.10.92	2rA	NA	Heusden-Zolder	19 Jul
3:34.54		Florian	Orth	GER	24.7.89	2		Oordegem	5 Jul
3:34.64		Nixon	Chepseba	KEN	12.12.90	13	DL	Doha	9 May
3:34.69		Fouad	El Kaam	MAR	27.5.88	3rA	NA	Heusden-Zolder	19 Jul
3:34.80		Yassine	Bensghir	MAR	3.1.83	3=		Marrakech	8 Jun
3:34.94		Timo	Benitz	GER	1.12.91	1		Dessau	11 Jun
		(30)							
3:34.97		Abiyot	Abinet	ETH	10.5.89	1		Carquefou	20 Jun
3:35.0A		Elijah	Manangoi	KEN	5.1.93	2	NC	Nairobi	7 Jun
3:35.06		Chris	O'Hare	GBR	23.11.90	5	DL	Glasgow	12 Jul
3:35.12		Tesfaye	Cheru	ETH	2.3.93	4rA	NA	Heusden-Zolder	19 Jul
3:35.21		Mohamed	Moustaoui	MAR	2.4.85	8	ISTAF	Berlin	31 Aug
3:35.26		Jakub	Holusa	CZE	20.2.88	1	Bisl	Oslo	11 Jun
3:35.32		Patrick	Casey	USA	23.5.90	3		Oordegem	5 Jul
3:35.34		Mahiedine	Mekhissi-Benabbad	FRA	15.3.85	2		Montreuil-sous-Bois	7 Jul
3:35.49		Jake	Wightman	GBR	11.7.94	6	DL	Glasgow	12 Jul
3:35.5A		Augustine	Choge	KEN	21.1.87	1		Nairobi	17 May
		(40)							
3:35.51		Florian	Carvalho	FRA	9.3.89	10	GGala	Roma	5 Jun
3:35.59		Charlie	Grice	GBR	7.11.93	9	DL	Glasgow	12 Jul
3:35.59		David	Bustos	ESP	25.8.90	5rA	NA	Heusden-Zolder	19 Jul
3:35.63		Vincent	Mutai	KEN	3.11.94	6rA	NA	Heusden-Zolder	19 Jul
3:35.68		Yassine	Hathat	MAR	30.7.91	5		Oordegem	5 Jul
3:35.8A		Caleb	Ndiku	KEN	9.10.92	2		Nairobi	17 May
3:35.81		Elijah	Kiptoo	KEN	9.6.86	1		Bellinzona	3 Jun
3:35.81		Zakaria	Maazouzi	MAR	15.6.85	11	GGala	Roma	5 Jun
3:35.89		Garrett	Heath	USA	3.11.85	10	DL	Glasgow	12 Jul
3:35.96		Tarik	Moukrime	BEL	3.3.92	7rA	NA	Heusden-Zolder	19 Jul
		(50)							

Mark	Wind	Name		Nat	Born	Pos	Meet	Venue	Date
3:36.08		Bryan	Cantero	FRA	28.4.91	8rA	NA	Heusden-Zolder	19 Jul
3:36.11		Andreas	Vojta	AUT	9.6.89	11	DL	Glasgow	12 Jul
3:36.17		Ryan	Gregson	AUS	26.4.90	3		Los Angeles (ER)	15 May
3:36.21		Hillary	Maiyo	KEN	2.10.93	1	Odlozil	Praha	9 Jun
3:36.21		Abednego	Chesebe	KEN	20.6.82	5		Montreuil-sous-Bois	7 Jul
3:36.34		Lawi	Lalang	KEN	15.6.91	1	Pac-12	Pullman	18 May
3:36.36		David	Torrence	USA	26.11.85	6	WCM	Rieti	7 Sep
3:36.45		Paul	Robinson	IRL	24.5.91	12	GGala	Roma	5 Jun
3:36.50		Edward	Cheserek	KEN	2.2.94	2	Pac-12	Pullman	18 May
3:36.55		Bashir	Abdi	BEL	10.2.89	7		Oordegem	5 Jul
		(60)							
3:36.71		John	Bolas	USA	1.11.87	8		Oordegem	5 Jul
3:36.74		Jerry	Motsau	RSA	12.3.90	7	WCM	Rieti	7 Sep
3:36.96		Imad	Touil	ALG	11.2.89	5		Marrakech	8 Jun
3:37.10		Ryan	Hill	USA	31.1.90	6		Los Angeles (ER)	15 May
3:37.21		Othmane	Belharbazi	FRA	3.11.88	9		Oordegem	5 Jul
3:37.27+		John	Travers	IRL	16.3.91	2	in 1M	Dublin	11 Jul
3:37.30		Maurys Surel	Castillo	ex-CUB	19.10.84	3		Huelva	12 Jun
3:37.34		Ismael	Kombich	KEN	16.10.85	4		Huelva	12 Jun
3:37.36		Younès	Essalhi	MAR	20.2.93	1		Fès	24 May
3:37.39		Jordan	McNamara	USA	7.3.87	1rB		Los Angeles (ER)	15 May
		(70)							
3:37.52		Abdelhadi	Labali	MAR	26.4.93	8		Marrakech	8 Jun
3:37.54		Bouabdellah	Tahri	FRA	20.12.78	1		Metz	26 Jun
3:37.64+		Cory	Leslie	USA	24.10.89	4	in 1M	Dublin	11 Jul
3:37.72		Ciarán	O'Lionáird	IRL	11.4.88	1		Watford	16 Jul
3:37.75		Ronald	Musagala	UGA	16.12.94	1		Nijmegen	11 Jun
3:37.78		Carsten	Schlangen	GER	31.12.80	3		Dessau	11 Jun
3:37.81		Rabie	Doukkana	MAR	6.12.87	2		Amiens	21 Jun
3:37.84		Manuel	Olmedo	ESP	17.5.83	1		Lignano	8 Jul
3:37.88		Michael	Hammond	USA	7.11.89	1		Greenville, SC	31 May
3:37.90		Thomas	Farrell	GBR	23.3.91	14	DL	Glasgow	12 Jul
		(80)							
3:37.99		Jeff	See	USA	6.6.86	2		Greenville, SC	31 May
3:38.00		Riley	Masters	USA	5.4.90	2		Watford	16 Jul
3:38.04		Teklit	Teweldebrhan	ERI	1.10.93	3		Carquefou	20 Jun
3:38.06		Bernard	Koros	KEN	7.5.94	2		Nijmegen	11 Jun
3:38.06		Chala	Regassa	ETH	.90	3		Nijmegen	11 Jun
3:38.10+		Evan	Jager	USA	8.3.89	3	in 1M	Eugene	31 May
3:38.11		German	Fernandez	USA	2.11.90	10		Oordegem	5 Jul
3:38.16+		Nathan	Brannen	CAN	8.9.82	1	in 1M	Nashville	8 Jun
3:38.18		Jamal	Hitrane	MAR	1.9.89	2		Marrakech	3 May
3:38.19		Marcin	Lewandowski	POL	13.6.87	3	ET	Braunschweig	21 Jun
		(90)							
3:38.20		Julian	Matthews	NZL	21.7.88	3rB		Los Angeles (ER)	15 May
3:38.20		Geoffrey	Barusei	KEN	.94	2		Bellinzona	3 Jun
3:38.27		Steve	Mitchell	GBR	24.5.88	11		Oordegem	5 Jul
3:38.33		Charles	Philibert-Thiboutot	CAN	31.12.90	1		Indianapolis	15 Jun
3:38.37		Valentin	Smirnov	RUS	13.2.86	1		Adler	29 May
3:38.41		Guillaume	Adam	FRA	15.1.90	1		Montbéliard	6 Jun
3:38.41		Jeff	Riseley	AUS	11.11.86	1		Lignano	8 Jul
3:38.44		Andreas	Bueno	DEN	7.7.88	3		Watford	16 Jul
3:38.46		Cameron	Levins	CAN	28.3.89	5rB		Los Angeles (ER)	15 May
3:38.47+		Lopez	Lomong	USA	1.1.85	6	in 1M	Eugene	31 May
		(100)							

Mark	Name		Nat	Born	Date
3:38.48	Brahim	Kaazouzi	MAR	15.6.90	24 May
3:38.53	Andrew	Wheating	USA	21.11.87	15 Jun
3:38.54	Kyle	Merber	USA	19.11.90	19 Jul
3:38.56	Iván	López	CHI	10.3.90	21 Jun
3:38.56	Hassan	Ghachoui	MAR-J	1.1.95	5 Jul
3:38.57	Abdullah Obaid Al-Salhi		KSA	.94	7 Sep
3:38.58	Ford	Palmer	USA	6.10.90	15 May
3:38.58	Álvaro	Rodríguez	ESP	25.5.87	12 Jun
3:38.61	Jeroen	D'Hoedt	BEL	10.1.90	31 May
3:38.61	Stanislav	Maslov	UKR	19.1.89	25 Jul
3:38.62	Mac	Fleet	USA	17.10.90	19 Jul
3:38.66	Emanuel	Rolim	POR	30.1.93	15 Jul
3:38.7+	Collis	Birmingham	AUS	27.12.84	22 Feb
3:38.7A	Bernard	Muia	KEN-J	26.5.95	7 Jun
3:38.70	Alex	Kibet	KEN/QAT	20.10.90	8 Jun
3:38.70	Youssouf Hiss Bachir		DJI	.87	15 Jul
3:38.72	Hassan	Mead	USA	28.8.89	15 May
3:38.73	Dorian	Ulrey	USA	11.7.87	15 Jun
3:38.82	Brandon	Kidder	USA	18.11.93	4 May
3:38.83	Richard	Peters	GBR	18.2.90	15 May
3:38.83	Mohammed Ayoub Tiouali		MAR	26.5.91	27 Jun
3:38.87	Vyacheslav	Sokolov	RUS	20.5.84	17 Jul
3:38.88	Mor	Seck	SEN	24.9.85	15 Jul
3:38.92	Soufiyan	Bouqantar	MAR	30.8.93	27 Jun
3:38.96	David	Vuste	FRA	20.4.88	20 Jun
3:38.99	Bekele	Gutema	ETH	.94	19 Jul
3:39.01	Enoch	Omwamba	KEN	4.4.93	5 Sep
3:39.08	Chris	Gowell	GBR	26.9.85	15 May
3:39.09	Víctor José	Corrales	ESP	12.3.89	15 Jul
3:39.13	Luc	Bruchet	CAN	23.2.91	31 May
3:39.17	Soufiane	El Kabbouri	ITA	5.3.93	15 Jul
3:39.21	Alberto	Imedio	ESP	24.5.91	15 Jul
3:39.23	Oleksandr	Borysyuk	UKR	9.12.85	25 Jul
3:39.27	David	Bishop	GBR	9.5.87	15 May
3:39.27	Peter	Callahan	USA	1.6.91	19 Jul
3:39.27	Hamish	Carson	NZL	1.11.88	19 Jul

Mark	Name		Nat	Born	Date
3:39.3A	Robert	Kaptingei	KEN	8.12.86	17 May
3:39.33	Ben	Blankenship	USA	15.12.88	9 May
3:39.37	Jonas	Leanderson	SWE	26.1.91	11 Jun
3:39.39	Simon	Denissel	FRA	22.5.90	5 Jul
3:39.43	Mohad	Abdikadar	ITA	12.6.93	15 Jul
3:39.46	Ivan	Tukhtachev	RUS	12.7.89	29 May
3:39.46	Yoann	Kowal	FRA	28.5.87	7 Jul
3:39.46	Ross	Proudfoot	CAN	4.7.92	19 Jul
3:39.47	Joe	Stilin	USA	5.12.89	12 Jul
3:39.49	David	Palacio	ESP	8.6.88	15 Jul
3:39.51	Sami	Lafi	ALG	25.4.90	24 May
3:39.53	Carlos	Alonso	ESP	15.9.89	15 Jul
3:39.54	Jan	Hochstrasser	SUI	23.10.88	19 Jul
3:39.56	Mohamed	Al-Garni	QAT	2.7.92	19 Jul
3:39.56	Kota	Murayama	JPN	23.2.93	5 Sep
3:39.59	David	McCarthy	IRL	3.8.88	11 Jun
3:39.60	Adel	Mechaal	ESP	5.12.90	15 Jul
3:39.61	Tommy	Schmitz	USA	16.7.83	15 May
3:39.64+	Eoin	Everard	IRL	23.4.86	11 Jul
3:39.77	Sam	Penzenstadler	USA	11.9.92	14 Jun
3:39.78	Amine	Khadiri	CYP	20.11.88	31 May
3:39.79	Dan	Stockberger	USA	23.6.88	15 May
3:39.79	Mounir	Akbache	FRA	14.3.86	7 Jul
3:39.83	Oleksandr	Osmolovych	UKR	8.10.85	21 Jun
3:39.84	Mohamed	Hajjaj	MAR	22.3.83	24 May
3:39.84	Matt	Hillenbrand	USA	8.5.92	15 Jun
3:39.86	Aleksey	Kharitonov	RUS	5.1.91	29 May
3:39.86	Volodomyr	Kyts	UKR	15.1.87	25 Jul
3:39.92	Yegor	Nikolayev	RUS	12.2.88	3 Jun
3:39.93	Bilal	Tabti	ALG	7.6.93	21 Jun
3:39.94	Lutimar	Paes	BRA	14.12.88	11 Jun
3:39.95	Timofey	Petrov	RUS	25.8.88	29 May
3:39.96	Federico	Bruno	ARG	18.6.93	14 Mar
3:39.97	Andrew "AJ"	Acosta	USA	13.4.88	28 Jun
3:39.98	Goran	Nava	SRB	15.4.81	15 Jul
3:40.0	Tamás	Kazi	HUN	16.5.85	7 Sep
3:40.01	Llorenc	Sales	ESP	14.7.88	10 Jul
3:40.02	Abdi Waiss	Mouhyadin	DJI-J	3.7.96	5 Jun
3:40.02	Aregawi	Birhanu	ETH-Y	30.6.97	21 Jun
3:40.02	Jonathan	Sawe	KEN-J	22.5.95	24 Jul
3:40.05	Mark	Nouws	NED	20.8.90	2 Aug
3:40.06	Chad	Noelle	USA	12.4.93	19 Apr
3:40.07	Nabil	Oussama	MAR	18.2.96	24 May
3:40.07	Conseslus	Kipruto	KEN	8.12.94	12 Jul
3:40.07	Trevor	Dunbar	USA	29.4.91	26 Jul
3:40.10	Andy	Bayer	USA	3.2.90	12 Jul
3:40.16	Austin	Mudd	USA	13.5.93	4 May
3:40.21	Tyler	Stutzman	USA	24.3.91	4 May
	(184)				

Indoors

Mark	Name		Nat	Born	Pos	Meet	Venue	Date
3:35.0i	Mohamed	Moustaoui	MAR	2.4.85	1	XLG	Stockholm	6 Feb
3:37.37i	Marcin	Lewandowski	POL	13.6.87	2	GP	Birmingham	15 Feb

Mark	Name		Nat	Born	Date
3:38.88+	Craig	Miller	USA	3.8.87	15 Feb
3:38.99+	Lee	Emanuel	GBR	24.1.85	25 Jan
3:39.14	David	McCarthy	IRL	3.8.88	2 Feb
3:39.36	Adel	Mechaal	ESP	5.12.90	15 Feb

JUNIORS

Mark	Name		Nat	Born	Pos	Meet	Venue	Date
3:28.81	Ronald	Kwemoi	KEN-J	19.9.95	3	Herc	Monaco	18 Jul

Kwemoi 2+ 3:34.6A 1 NC Nairobi 7 Jun 3:39.90 1h2 CG Glasgow 1 Aug

10 performances by 6 men to 3:40.07

Mark	Name		Nat	Born	Pos	Meet	Venue	Date
3:38.56	Hassan	Ghachoui	MAR-J	1.1.95	12		Oordegem	5 Jul
3:38.7A	Bernard	Muia	KEN-J	26.5.95	6	NC	Nairobi	7 Jun
3:40.02	Abdi Waiss	Mouhyadin	DJI	3.7.96	2		Riyadh	5 Jun
3:40.02	Aregawi	Birhanu	ETH-Y	30.6.97	5		Bilbao	21 Jun
3:40.02	Jonathan	Sawe	KEN	22.5.95	1	WJ	Eugene	24 Jul
3:40.07	Nabil	Oussama	MAR	18.2.96	6		Fès	24 May
3:40.26i	Hillary	Ngetich	KEN	15.9.95	3		Gent	9 Feb
	3:41.61				3	WJ	Eugene	24 Jul
3:40.59	Thiago	André	BRA	4.8.95	1		São Paulo	14 Jun
3:40.6A	Jonathan	Kiplimo (10)	KEN	.95	2		Mumias	3 May
3:40.69	Mohammed	Abid	MAR	18.3.95	7		Fès	24 May
3:41.4A	Titus	Kibiego	KEN	3.5.96	4		Mumias	3 May
3:41.43	Shaun	Wyllie	GBR	27.2.95	3		Regensburg	7 Jun
3:41.54	Ben	Saarel	USA	8.3.95	1		Azusa	18 Apr
3:41.95i	Chalachew	Shimelis	ETH	17.9.96	5		Gent	9 Feb
3:41.99	Gilbert	Kwemboi	KEN-Y	3.10.97	1	Yth Oly	Nanjing	24 Aug
3:42.09	Jawad	Douhri	MAR	10.4.96	8		Carquefou	20 Jun
3:42.23	Adam Ali	Musaab	QAT	17.4.95	4		Palafrugell	31 May
3:42.39	Zach	Perrin	USA	25.1.95	2rB		Azusa	18 Apr
3:42.4A	Hosea	Cheromei (20)	KEN	11.11.96	1		Nairobi	4 Apr

1 MILE

Mark	Name		Nat	Born	Pos	Meet	Venue	Date
3:47.32	Ayanleh	Souleiman	DJI	3.12.92	1	Pre	Eugene	31 May
3:47.88	Silas	Kiplagat	KEN	20.8.89	2	Pre	Eugene	31 May
3:48.60	Aman	Wote	ETH	18.4.84	3	Pre	Eugene	31 May
3:49.09	Abdelati	Iguider	MAR	25.3.87	4	Pre	Eugene	31 May
3:49.43	James	Magut	KEN	20.7.90	5	Pre	Eugene	31 May
3:49.49		Souleiman			1	Bisl	Oslo	11 Jun
3:49.56	Collins	Cheboi	KEN	25.9.87	6	Pre	Eugene	31 May
3:49.83	Nick	Willis	NZL	25.4.83	2	Bisl	Oslo	11 Jun
3:49.86	Homiyu	Tesfaye	GER	23.6.93	3	Bisl	Oslo	11 Jun
3:50.26	Asbel	Kiprop	KEN	30.6.89	7	Pre	Eugene	31 May
3:50.53	Matthew	Centrowitz (10)	USA	18.10.89	8	Pre	Eugene	31 May
3:50.70	Johan	Cronje	RSA	13.4.82	9	Pre	Eugene	31 May
3:50.72	Henrik	Ingebrigtsen	NOR	24.2.91	4	Bisl	Oslo	11 Jun
	(13/12)							
3:51.12	Bethwel	Birgen	KEN	6.8.88	10	Pre	Eugene	31 May
3:51.55	Mahiedine	Mekhissi-Benabbad	FRA	15.3.85	5	Bisl	Oslo	11 Jun
3:51.59	Mekonnen	Gebremedhin	ETH	11.10.88	6	Bisl	Oslo	11 Jun
3:51.71	Ilham Tanui	Özbilen	TUR	5.3.90	7	Bisl	Oslo	11 Jun

Mark	Wind	Name		Nat	Born	Pos	Meet	Venue	Date
3:51.82		Will	Leer	USA	15.4.85	1		Dublin	11 Jul
3:52.15		Vincent	Kibet	KEN	6.5.91	3	DL	Birmingham	24 Aug
3:52.16		Taoufik	Makhloufi	ALG	29.4.88	11	Pre	Eugene	31 May
3:52.41		Leonel	Manzano	USA	12.9.84	1rB	Pre	Eugene	31 May
		(20)							
3:52.62		Patrick	Casey	USA	23.5.90	2		Dublin	11 Jul
3:52.89		Jordan	McNamara	USA	7.3.87	2rB	Pre	Eugene	31 May
3:53.33		Evan	Jager	USA	8.3.89	3rB	Pre	Eugene	31 May
3:53.44		Cory	Leslie	USA	24.10.89	3		Dublin	11 Jul
3:53.61		Garrett	Heath	USA	3.11.85	2		Saline	9 Aug
3:53.72		Zane	Robertson	NZL	14.11.89	4		Dublin	11 Jul
3:53.85		Ryan	Gregson	AUS	26.4.90	6rB	Pre	Eugene	31 May
3:53.95		David	Torrence	USA	26.11.85	7rB	Pre	Eugene	31 May
3:54.21		Fouad	El Kaam	MAR	27.5.88	8rB	Pre	Eugene	31 May
3:54.28		Lopez	Lomong	USA	1.1.85	9rB	Pre	Eugene	31 May
		(30)							
3:54.76		Kyle	Merber	USA	19.11.90	5		Dublin	11 Jul
3:54.77		Paul	Robinson	IRL	24.5.91	11	Bisl	Oslo	11 Jun
3:54.92		Collis	Birmingham	AUS	27.12.84	2		Perth	22 Feb
3:54.92		Nixon	Chepseba	KEN	12.12.90	12	DL	Birmingham	24 Aug
3:55.33		Pieter Jan	Hannes	BEL	30.10.92	12	Bisl	Oslo	11 Jun
3:55.44		John	Travers	IRL	16.3.91	6		Dublin	11 Jul
3:55.65		Nathan	Brannen	CAN	8.9.82	1		Nashville	7 Jun

Mark	Name		Nat	Born	Date
3:56.10	Duncan	Phillips	USA	7.6.89	5 Jun
3:56.45	Tommy	Schmitz	USA	16.7.83	5 Jun
3:56.75	Riley	Masters	USA	5.4.90	8 Jul
3:56.77	Mac	Fleet	USA	17.10.90	9 Aug
3:56.89	Eric	Avila	USA	3.10.89	5 Jun
3:56.94	Charlie	Grice	GBR	7.11.93	31 May
3:56.96	David	Bishop	GBR	9.5.87	11 Jul
3:57.05	Andrew "AJ"	Acosta	USA	13.4.88	5 Jun
3:57.19	Trevor	Dunbar	USA	29.4.91	5 Jul
3:57.39	John	Bolas	USA	1.11.87	9 Aug
3:57.44	Vincent	Letting	KEN	16.6.93	11 Jul
3:57.52	Dorian	Ulrey	USA	11.7.87	9 Aug
3:57.61	Ford	Palmer	USA	6.10.90	1 Aug
3:57.70	Michael	Hammond	USA	7.11.89	12 Apr
3:57.79	Hamish	Carson	NZL	1.11.88	11 Jul
3:57.85	Charles	Philibert-Thiboutot	CAN	31.12.90	10 Jul
3:57.99	Ciarán	O'Lionáird	IRL	11.4.88	31 May

Indoors

Mark	Wind	Name		Nat	Born	Pos	Meet	Venue	Date
3:52.88		Lawi	Lalang	KEN	15.6.91	2	Mill	New York (Arm)	15 Feb
3:54.30		Lee	Emanuel	GBR	24.1.85	1		New York (Arm)	25 Jan
3:54.32		Nathan	Brannen	CAN	8.9.82	4	Mill	New York (Arm)	15 Feb
3:54.66		Chris	O'Hare	GBR	23.11.90	5	Mill	New York (Arm)	15 Feb
3:55.09		Craig	Miller	USA	3.8.87	6	Mill	New York (Arm)	15 Feb

Mark	Name		Nat	Born	Date
3:56.84	Jordan	Williamsz	AUS	21.8.92	15 Feb
3:57.00	Matt	Hillenbrand	USA	8.5.92	15 Feb
3:57.27	Richard	Peters	GBR	18.2.90	8 Feb
3:57.29	Chris	Gowell	GBR	26.9.85	8 Feb
3:57.48	Frezer	Legesse	USA	4.6.90	15 Feb
3:57.71	Luc	Bruchet	CAN	23.2.91	1 Feb

2000 METRES

Indoors

Mark	Wind	Name		Nat	Born	Pos	Meet	Venue	Date
4:54.74		Bernard	Lagat	USA	12.12.74	1	Mill	New York (Arm)	15 Feb
4:55.35		Cameron	Levins	CAN	28.3.89	2	Mill	New York (Arm)	15 Feb
4:56.99		David	Torrence	USA	26.11.85	3	Mill	New York (Arm)	15 Feb
4:57.17		Abiyot	Abinet	ETH	10.5.89	1		Metz	28 Feb
4:57.35		Andrew	Bumbalough	USA	14.3.87	4	Mill	New York (Arm)	15 Feb
4:57.56		Evan	Jager	USA	8.3.89	5	Mill	New York (Arm)	15 Feb
4:57.74		Yomif	Kejelcha	ETH-Y	1.8.97	2		Metz	28 Feb
5:00.18		Donn	Cabral	USA	12.12.89	6	Mill	New York (Arm)	15 Feb
5:00.84		Soufiyan	Bouqantar	MAR	30.8.93	3		Metz	28 Feb
5:01.84		Paul Kipsiele	Koech (10)	KEN	10.11.81	4		Metz	28 Feb
5:02.41		Dan	Huling	USA	16.7.83	7	Mill	New York (Arm)	15 Feb

3000 METRES

Mark	Wind	Name		Nat	Born	Pos	Meet	Venue	Date
7:31.66		Caleb	Ndiku	KEN	9.10.92	1	GS	Ostrava	17 Jun
7:34.99		Abdelati	Iguider	MAR	25.3.87	1	WCM	Rieti	7 Sep
7:35.28		Thomas	Longosiwa	KEN	14.1.82	2	WCM	Rieti	7 Sep
7:36.28		Yomif	Kejelcha	ETH-Y	1.8.97	2	GS	Ostrava	17 Jun
7:36.44		Lawi	Lalang	KEN	15.6.91	3	WCM	Rieti	7 Sep
7:36.8+		Mohamed	Farah	GBR	23.3.83	1	in 2M	Birmingham	24 Aug
7:36.91		Nick	Willis	NZL	25.4.83	3	GS	Ostrava	17 Jun
7:38.30		Bernard	Lagat	USA	12.12.74	4	GS	Ostrava	17 Jun
7:38.64		Ryan	Hill	USA	31.1.90	4	WCM	Rieti	7 Sep
7:38.97		John	Kipkoech	KEN	29.12.91	5	GS	Ostrava	17 Jun
		(10)							
7:39.63		Jonathan	Ndiku	KEN	18.9.91	6	GS	Ostrava	17 Jun
7:39.81		Lopez	Lomong	USA	1.1.85	5	WCM	Rieti	7 Sep
7:40.09		Suguru	Osako	JPN	23.5.91	6	WCM	Rieti	7 Sep
7:41.27		Cornelius	Kangogo	KEN	31.12.93	1	FBK	Hengelo	8 Jun

Mark Wind	Name		Nat	Born	Pos	Meet	Venue	Date
7:41.37	Zane	Robertson	NZL	14.11.89	1		Cork	8 Jul
7:41.41	Arne	Gabius	GER	22.3.81	7	GS	Ostrava	17 Jun
7:41.57	Augustine	Choge	KEN	21.1.87	2	FBK	Hengelo	8 Jun
7:41.79	Joseph	Kiplimo	KEN	20.7.88	8	GS	Ostrava	17 Jun
7:42.89	Collis	Birmingham	AUS	27.12.84	9	GS	Ostrava	17 Jun
7:42.90	Mekonnen	Gebremedhin	ETH	11.10.88	4	FBK	Hengelo	8 Jun
	(20)							
7:43.33	Soufiyan	Bouqantar	MAR	30.8.93	5	FBK	Hengelo	8 Jun
7:43.59	Imane	Merga	ETH	15.10.88	7	WCM	Rieti	7 Sep
7:43.90	Juan Luis	Barrios	MEX	24.6.83	10	GS	Ostrava	17 Jun
7:44.12	Bashir	Abdi	BEL	10.2.89	6	FBK	Hengelo	8 Jun
7:44.14	Phillip	Kipyeko	UGA-J	10.1.95	7	FBK	Hengelo	8 Jun
7:44.20	Elroy	Gelant	RSA	25.8.86	8	FBK	Hengelo	8 Jun
7:44.65	Florian	Orth	GER	24.7.89	9	WCM	Rieti	7 Sep
7:45.06	Jesús	España	ESP	21.8.78	10	WCM	Rieti	7 Sep
7:45.09	Trevor	Dunbar	USA	29.4.91	2		Dublin	11 Jul
7:45.33+	Vincent	Rono	KEN	11.11.90	1	DNG	Stockholm	21 Aug
	(30)							
7:45.6+	Galen	Rupp	USA	8.5.86	2	DNG	Stockholm	21 Aug
7:45.8+	Hagos	Gebrhiwet	ETH	11.5.94	3	DNG	Stockholm	21 Aug
7:45.82	Moses	Kipsiro	UGA	2.9.86	12	GS	Ostrava	17 Jun
7:45.95	Eric	Tirop	KEN	.87	1		Celle Ligure	26 Jun
7:46.0+	Muktar	Edris	ETH	14.1.94	4	DNG	Stockholm	21 Aug
7:46.5+	Edwin	Soi	KEN	3.3.86	6=	DNG	Stockholm	21 Aug
7:46.57	Joílson	da Silva	BRA	29.8.87	9	FBK	Hengelo	8 Jun
7:46.84	Maverick	Darling	USA	9.6.89	11	WCM	Rieti	7 Sep
7:46.92	Teshome	Dirirsa	ETH	25.4.94	10	FBK	Hengelo	8 Jun
7:47.34	Abdellah	Haidane	ITA	28.3.89	12	WCM	Rieti	7 Sep
	(40)							
7:47.71	Geoffrey	Barusei	KEN	.94	3	Gyulai	Székesfehérvár	8 Jul
7:48.12	Abdallah	Mande	UGA-J	10.5.95	11	FBK	Hengelo	8 Jun

Mark	Name		Nat	Born	Date
7:48.20	Yohan	Durand	FRA	14.5.85	17 Jun
7:48.24	Tiidrek	Nurme		18.11.85	11 Jul
7:48.7+	Ben	True	USA	29.12.85	21 Aug
7:48.8+	Emmanuel	Bett	KEN	30.3.83	24 Aug
7:49.09	Aweke	Ayalew	BRN	23.2.93	8 Jul
7:49.13	Illias	Fifa	MAR	16.5.89	17 May
7:49.21	Younès	Essalhi	MAR	20.2.93	8 Jul
7:49.4+	Isiah	Koech	KEN	19.12.93	21 Aug
7:49.51	Dmitrijs	Jurkevics	LAT	7.1.87	8 Jun
7:49.64	William Malel	Sitonik	KEN	1.3.94	26 Jun
7:49.65	Titus	Kibiego	KEN-J	3.5.96	7 Sep
7:50.1+	Hassan	Mead	USA	28.8.89	21 Aug
7:50.99	Richard	Ringer	GER	27.2.89	22 Jun
7:51.09	Berhanu	Legesse	ETH	93	8 Jun
7:51.28	Roberto	Alaiz	ESP	20.7.90	24 May
7:51.43	Jakub	Holusa	CZE	20.2.88	22 Jun
7:51.65	Daniel Kipchirchir	Komen	KEN	27.11.84	8 Jul

Indoors

Mark Wind	Name		Nat	Born	Pos	Meet	Venue	Date
7:34.13	Hagos	Gebrhiwet	ETH	11.5.94	1		Boston (R)	8 Feb
7:34.68+	Galen	Rupp	USA	8.5.86	1	in 2M	Boston (A)	25 Jan
7:34.70	Dejen	Gebremeskel	ETH	24.11.89	2		Boston (R)	8 Feb
7:34.87	Ryan	Hill	USA	31.1.90	3		Boston (R)	8 Feb
7:35.73		Gebrhiwet			1	GP	Birmingham	15 Feb
7:36.27		C Ndiku			1		Karlsruhe	1 Feb
7:36.53		Gebremeskel			2	GP	Birmingham	15 Feb
7:37.10	Yenew	Alamirew	ETH	27.5.90	3	GP	Birmingham	15 Feb
7:37.11	Augustine	Choge	KEN	21.1.87	4	GP	Birmingham	15 Feb
7:37.17+	Bethwell	Birgen	KEN	6.8.88	2		Boston (A)	25 Jan
7:37.22	Paul K.	Koech	KEN	10.11.81	5	GP	Birmingham	15 Feb
	(11/9)							
7:37.40	Garrett	Heath	USA	3.11.85	4		Boston (R)	8 Feb
7:37.62	Andrew	Bumbalough	USA	14.3.87	5		Boston (R)	8 Feb
7:38.77	Albert	Rop	BRN	17.7.92	1		Gent	9 Feb
7:39.14	Isiah	Koech	KEN	19.12.93	3		Gent	9 Feb
7:39.55	Elroy	Gelant	RSA	25.8.86	4		Gent	9 Feb
7:39.73	Hayle	Ibrahimov	AZE	18.1.90	6		Boston (R)	8 Feb
7:40.00	Mohamed	Moustaoui	MAR	2.4.85	1		Düsseldorf	30 Jan
7:40.85	Ayanleh	Souleiman	DJI	3.12.92	2		Düsseldorf	30 Jan
7:41.59	Cameron	Levins	CAN	28.3.89	7		Boston (R)	8 Feb
7:42.95	Will	Leer	USA	15.4.85	8		Boston (R)	8 Feb
7:43.61	Ali	Kaya	TUR	20.4.94	6		Düsseldorf	30 Jan
7:44.73	Othmane	El Goumri	MAR	28.5.92	2		Bordeaux	26 Jan
7:44.78	Edwin	Soi	KEN	3.3.86	7		Düsseldorf	30 Jan
7:44.88	Hassan	Mead	USA	28.8.89	9		Boston (R)	8 Feb
7:45.12	Lee	Emanuel	GBR	24.1.85	7	GP	Birmingham	15 Feb
7:45.21	Samuel	Chelanga	KEN	23.2.85	10		Boston (R)	8 Feb
7:45.49	Andrew	Vernon	GBR	7.1.86	4h1	WI	Sopot	7 Mar
7:45.62	Abdelhadi	Labali	MAR	26.4.93	3		Mondeville	1 Feb
7:46.36	Antonio	Abadia	ESP	2.7.90	7h2	WI	Sopot	7 Mar
7:46.55	Ben	Blankenship	USA	15.12.88	11		Boston (R)	8 Feb

Mark	Wind	Name		Nat	Born	Pos	Meet	Venue	Date
7:46.73		Jonathan	Mellor	GBR	27.12.86	8	GP	Birmingham	15 Feb
7:47.20		Edward	Cheserek	KEN	2.2.94	1		Seattle	1 Mar
7:47.50		Younès	Essalhi	MAR	20.2.93	3		Bordeaux	26 Jan
7:47.54		Thomas	Farrell	GBR	23.3.91	9	GP	Birmingham	15 Feb

Mark	Name		Nat	Born	Date
7:48.32	Youssouf	Hiss Bachir	DJI	.87	1 Feb
7:49.05	Craig	Miller	USA	3.8.87	8 Feb
7:49.26	Lukasz	Parszczynski	POL	4.5.85	23 Feb
7:49.36	Yoann	Kowal	FRA	28.5.87	26 Jan
7:49.99	Yegor	Nikolayev	RUS	12.2.88	25 Feb
7:50.31	Andrew	Poore	USA	3.12.88	15 Feb
7:50.50	Jake	Hurysz	USA	15.7.92	1 Mar
7:50.58	De'Sean	Turner	USA	16.9.88	15 Feb
7:50.81	Erik	Olson	USA	15.3.92	1 Mar
7:50.86	Joe	Bosshard	USA	30.10.89	1 Mar
7:51.06	Parker	Stinson	USA	3.3.92	1 Mar
7:51.47	Donn	Cabral	USA	12.12.89	8 Feb
7:51.52	Maksim	Korolev	USA	15.7.92	8 Feb
7:51.57	Will	Geoghegan	USA	15.7.92	8 Feb
7:51.78	Reed	Connor	USA	25.9.90	28 Feb

98 at 7:51.78 or better in total

JUNIORS

See main list for top 3 juniors. 9 performances by 7 men to 7:48.0. Additional marks and further juniors:

Kejelcha 7:42.05i 1 Bordeaux 26 Jan 7:50.24 5 Mondeville 1 Feb

Mark	Name		Nat	Born	Pos	Meet	Venue	Date
7:49.65	Titus	Kibiego	KEN	3.5.96	13	WCM	Rieti	7 Sep
7:59.02	Thiago	André	BRA	4.8.95	1		Uberlândia	7 May
7:59.41	Nftalem	Librab	ERI-Y	9.5.97	3		Oslo	22 May
7:59.53	Meresa	Kassaye	ETH	23.5.96	15	FBK	Hengelo	8 Jun
Indoors								
7:52.61	Ben	Saarel	USA	8.3.95	2		Seattle	15 Feb
7:53.04	Debeli	Gezmu	ETH	14.4.96	4		Praha	25 Feb
7:57.52	Chartt	Miller	AUS	7.5.95	1		Boston (A)	15 Feb

2 MILES

Mark	Name		Nat	Born	Pos	Meet	Venue	Date
8:07.85	Mohamed	Farah	GBR	23.3.83	1	DL	Birmingham	24 Aug
8:22.82	Zane	Robertson	NZL	14.11.89	2	DL	Birmingham	24 Aug

Mark	Name		Nat	Born	Date
8:25.55	Emmanuel	Bett	KEN	30.3.83	24 Aug
8:26.50	Jordan	McNamara	USA	7.3.87	24 Aug
8:27.15	Will	Leer	USA	15.4.85	24 Aug
8:27.55	Andrew	Vernon	GBR	7.1.86	24 Aug
8:28.30	Suguru	Osako	JPN	23.5.91	24 Aug

Mark	Name		Nat	Born	Pos	Meet	Venue	Date
Indoors								
8:07.41	Galen	Rupp	USA	8.5.86	1		Boston (A)	25 Jan

5000 METRES

Mark	Name		Nat	Born	Pos	Meet	Venue	Date
12:54.83	Muktar	Edris	ETH	14.1.94	1	DNG	Stockholm	21 Aug
12:56.16	Thomas	Longosiwa	KEN	14.1.82	2	DNG	Stockholm	21 Aug
12:59.17	Caleb	Ndiku	KEN	9.10.92	3	DNG	Stockholm	21 Aug
12:59.82	Edwin	Soi	KEN	3.3.86	1	DL	Saint-Denis	5 Jul
13:00.21	Yenew	Alamirew	ETH	27.5.90	2	DL	Saint-Denis	5 Jul
13:00.53	Paul	Tanui	KEN	22.12.90	3	DL	Saint-Denis	5 Jul
13:00.99	Galen	Rupp	USA	8.5.86	4	DL	Saint-Denis	5 Jul
13:01.57		Alamirew			1	Bisl	Oslo	11 Jun
13:01.71		Ndiku			1	Pre	Eugene	31 May
13:01.74		Longosiwa			5	DL	Saint-Denis	5 Jul
13:02.15		Ndiku			2	Bisl	Oslo	11 Jun
13:02.74	Ben	True	USA	29.12.85	1	Jordan	Stanford	4 May
13:02.80	Hassan	Mead	USA	28.8.89	2	Jordan	Stanford	4 May
13:02.91		Alamirew			2	Pre	Eugene	31 May
13:03.35		Rupp			3	Bisl	Oslo	11 Jun
13:03.85	Lawi	Lalang (10)	KEN	15.6.91	6	DL	Saint-Denis	5 Jul
13:04.68		Longosiwa			4	Bisl	Oslo	11 Jun
13:04.83		Alamirew			1	DL	Shanghai	18 May
13:04.92		Soi			3	Pre	Eugene	31 May
13:05.44		Longosiwa			2	DL	Shanghai	18 May
13:05.97		Rupp			4	DNG	Stockholm	21 Aug
13:06.12	Albert	Rop	BRN	17.7.92	4	Pre	Eugene	31 May
13:06.12	Augustine	Choge	KEN	21.1.87	1	ISTAF	Berlin	31 Aug
13:06.68	Bernard	Lagat	USA	12.12.74	2	ISTAF	Berlin	31 Aug
13:06.71		Choge			1	NA	Heusden-Zolder	19 Jul
13:06.88	Hagos	Gebrhiwet	ETH	11.5.94	3	DL	Shanghai	18 May
13:07.01		Ndiku			1	WK	Zürich	28 Aug
13:07.32		Edris			2	WK	Zürich	28 Aug
13:07.55	Isiah	Koech	KEN	19.12.92	5	Pre	Eugene	31 May
13:07.60	John	Kipkoech	KEN	29.12.91	3	ISTAF	Berlin	31 Aug
	(30/16)							
13:07.95	Lopez	Lomong	USA	1.1.85	3	Jordan	Stanford	4 May
13:08.18	Chris	Derrick	USA	17.10.90	4	Jordan	Stanford	4 May
13:08.63	Evan	Jager	USA	8.3.89	5	Jordan	Stanford	4 May
13:08.88	Berhanu	Legesse	ETH	.93	6	DL	Shanghai	18 May
	(20)							
13:09.17	Hayle	Ibrahimov	AZE	18.1.90	5	WK	Zürich	28 Aug

Mark	Wind	Name		Nat	Born	Pos	Meet	Venue	Date
13:09.67		Ibrahim	Jeylan	ETH	12.6.89	9	DL	Saint-Denis	5 Jul
13:09.73		Dejen	Gebremeskel	ETH	24.11.89	7	Bisl	Oslo	11 Jun
13:11.14		Cornelius	Kangogo	KEN	31.12.93	8	DL	Shanghai	18 May
13:11.50		Andrew	Vernon	GBR	7.1.86	6	Jordan	Stanford	4 May
13:11.80		Yigrem	Demelash	ETH	28.1.94	6	ISTAF	Berlin	31 Aug
13:11.94		Imane	Merga	ETH	15.10.88	10	DL	Saint-Denis	5 Jul
13:12.22		Bouabdellah	Tahri	FRA	20.12.78	9	DL	Shanghai	18 May
13:12.41		Kinde	Atanaw	ETH	15.4.93	1		Carquefou	20 Jun
13:12.72		Wilfred	Kimitei	KEN	11.3.85	2		Carquefou	20 Jun
		(30)							
13:12.94		Jonathan	Ndiku	KEN	18.9.91	10	DL	Shanghai	18 May
13:13.04		Getaneh	Tamire	ETH	.94	3		Carquefou	20 Jun
13:13.16		Kenneth	Kipkemoi	KEN	2.8.84	4	NA	Heusden-Zolder	19 Jul
13:13.67		Andrew	Bumbalough	USA	14.3.87	9	Bisl	Oslo	11 Jun
13:14.31		Ryan	Hill	USA	31.1.90	7	Jordan	Stanford	4 May
13:14.59		Leul	Gebrselassie	ETH	20.9.93	4		Carquefou	20 Jun
13:14.64		Bernard	Kimani	KEN	10.9.93	1		Nobeoka	10 May
13:14.69		Zane	Robertson	NZL	14.11.89	7	ISTAF	Berlin	31 Aug
13:14.89		Illias	Fifa	MAR	16.5.89	2		Marrakech	8 Jun
13:14.91		Emmanuel	Bett	KEN	30.3.83	5	DL	Glasgow	11 Jul
		(40)							
13:15.25		Bidan	Karoki	KEN	21.8.90	1		Kitami	2 Jul
13:15.38		Cameron	Levins	CAN	28.3.89	6	DL	Glasgow	11 Jul
13:16.06		James	Mwangi	KEN	23.6.84	2		Nobeoka	10 May
13:16.24		Samuel	Chelanga	KEN	23.2.85	9	ISTAF	Berlin	31 Aug
13:16.42		Vincent	Rono	KEN	11.11.90	3		Marrakech	8 Jun
13:16.45		Abrar	Osman	ERI	1.1.94	11	DL	Shanghai	18 May
13:16.65		Garrett	Heath	USA	4.2.89	8	Jordan	Stanford	4 May
13:17.04		Dawit	Wolde	ETH	19.5.91	7	NA	Heusden-Zolder	19 Jul
13:17.49		Joseph	Kiplimo	KEN	20.7.88	4	CG	Glasgow	27 Jul
13:18.10		Aweke	Ayalew	BRN	23.2.93	13	DL	Shanghai	18 May
		(50)							
13:18.57		Collis	Birmingham	AUS	27.12.84	1		Los Angeles (ER)	15 May
13:18.71		Edward	Cheserek	KEN	2.2.94	2	NCAA	Eugene	13 Jun
13:18.88		Mohammed	Ahmed	CAN	5.1.91	5	CG	Glasgow	27 Jul
13:19.26		Moses	Mukuno	KEN-J	27.11.95	14	DL	Shanghai	18 May
13:20.06		Matthew	Centrowitz	USA	18.10.89	9	Jordan	Stanford	4 May
13:20.33		Nick	Willis	NZL	25.4.83	3		Los Angeles (ER)	15 May
13:20.61		Bashir	Abdi	BEL	10.2.89	4		Los Angeles (ER)	15 May
13:21.44		Leonard	Barsoton	KEN	21.10.94	3		Nobeoka	10 May
13:21.53		Ronald	Kwemoi	KEN-J	19.9.95	4		Nobeoka	10 May
13:22.08		Hiram	Ngatia	KEN-J	1.1.96	1		Toyota	30 May
		(60)							
13:22.19		Donn	Cabral	USA	12.12.89	10	Jordan	Stanford	4 May
13:22.27		Thomas	Farrell	GBR	23.3.91	11	Jordan	Stanford	4 May
13:22.72		Hicham	Bellani	MAR	15.9.79	4		Marrakech	8 Jun
13:22.75		David	Bett	KEN	18.10.92	1		Velenje	1 Jul
13:23.42		Mohamed	Farah	GBR	23.3.83	1		Portland	15 Jun
13:23.44		Olivier	Irabaruta	BDI	25.8.90	2		Velenje	1 Jul
13:23.89		David	Njuguna	KEN	6.9.89	2		Yokohama	27 Apr
13:23.94		Will	Leer	USA	15.4.85	5		Los Angeles (ER)	15 May
13:23.94		Patrick	Mutunga	KEN	20.11.94	2		Toyota	30 May
13:24.74		Leonard	Korir	KEN	10.12.86	12	Jordan	Stanford	4 May
		(70)							
13:25.09		Jamal	Hitrane	MAR	1.9.89	1		Rabat	31 May
13:25.19		Yomif	Kejelcha	ETH-Y	1.8.97	1	WJ	Eugene	25 Jul
13:25.24		Richard	Ringer	GER	27.2.89	10	ISTAF	Berlin	31 Aug
13:25.33		Tesfaye	Cheru	ETH	2.3.93	5		Marrakech	8 Jun
13:25.50		Arne	Gabius	GER	22.3.81	13	DL	Saint-Denis	5 Jul
13:25.51		Ali Abubaker	Kamal	QAT	8.11.83	2		Ninove	2 Aug
13:25.68		Ben	St. Lawrence	AUS	7.11.81	10	DL	Glasgow	11 Jul
13:26.07		Kassa	Mekashaw	ETH	19.3.84	1r1		Yamaguchi	12 Oct
13:26.13		Mohamed	Al-Garni	QAT	2.7.92	1	AsiG	Incheon	27 Sep
13:26.15		Suguru	Osako	JPN	23.5.91	9	NA	Heusden-Zolder	19 Jul
		(80)							
13:26.21		Yasin	Haji	ETH-J	22.1.96	2	WJ	Eugene	25 Jul
13:26.28		Nixon	Chepseba	KEN	12.12.90	11	ISTAF	Berlin	31 Aug
13:26.44+		Stephen	Sambu	KEN	3.7.88	1	Pre	Eugene	30 May
13:26.53		Elroy	Gelant	RSA	25.8.86	1		Oordegem	31 May
13:26.6+		Mike	Kigen	KEN	15.1.86	2	Pre	Eugene	31 May
13:26.67		Dejene	Debela	ETH	.94	12	ISTAF	Berlin	31 Aug

Mark Wind	Name		Nat	Born	Pos	Meet	Venue	Date
13:26.90	Trevor	Dunbar	USA	29.4.91	3	NCAA	Eugene	13 Jun
13:26.98	Kennedy	Kithuka	KEN	4.6.89	1	MSR	Walnut	18 Apr
13:27.13	William Malel	Sitonik	KEN	1.3.94	3		Velenje	1 Jul
13:27.27	James (90)	Wilkinson	GBR	13.7.90	2		Oordegem	31 May
13:27.41	Eric	Jenkins	USA	24.11.91	4	NCAA	Eugene	13 Jun
13:27.55	Kirubel	Erassa	USA	17.6.93	13	Jordan	Stanford	4 May
13:27.98	Alemu	Bekele	BRN	23.3.90	2	AsiG	Incheon	27 Sep
13:28.11	Ryan	Vail	USA	19.3.86	3		Ninove	2 Aug
13:28.13	David	McNeill	AUS	6.10.86	2		Portland	15 Jun
13:28.23	Moses	Kipsiro	UGA	2.9.86	8	CG	Glasgow	27 Jul
13:28.31	Mustapha	El Aziz	MAR	.85	2		Rabat	31 May
13:28.36	Matt	Hughes	CAN	3.8.89	16	Jordan	Stanford	4 May
13:28.41	Tariku	Bekele	ETH	21.1.87	13	DL	Glasgow	11 Jul
13:28.60	Karemi Jeremiah (100)	Thuku	KEN	7.7.94	1		Kitakyushu	31 May

Mark	Name		Nat	Born	Date
13:28.61	Joseph	Kamathi	KEN-J	23.11.96	11 May
13:28.81	Zewdie	Milion	ETH	24.1.89	13 Apr
13:29.03	Tetsuya	Yoroizaka	JPN	20.3.90	19 Jul
13:29.54	Phillip	Kipyeko	UGA-J	10.1.95	11 Jun
13:29.64	Mulaku	Abera	ETH	20.4.94	31 May
13:29.69	Jake	Robertson	NZL	14.11.89	27 Jul
13:29.81	Debele	Gezmu	ETH-J	14.4.96	11 Jun
13:30.00	George	Alex	USA	20.1.90	4 May
13:30.41	Jesús	España	ESP	21.8.78	31 Aug
13:30.83	Daniel	Kipkemoi	KEN-J	5.7.96	25 Jun
13:30.91	Antonio	Abadia	ESP	2.7.90	31 May
13:31.01	Joílson	da Silva	BRA	29.8.87	31 May
13:31.13	Tariq	Al-Amri	KSA	23.12.90	31 May
13:31.16	Abdallah	Mande	UGA-J	10.5.95	11 Jun
13:31.21	Jonathan	Mellor	GBR	27.12.86	11 Jul
13:31.25	Patrick	Tiernan	AUS	11.9.94	13 Jun
13:31.31	Nguse	Tesfaldet	ERI	10.11.86	13 Sep
13:31.55	Macharia	Ndirangu	KEN	9.9.94	12 Oct
13:31.64	Ambrose	Bore	KEN-J	8.8.95	31 May
13:31.69	Joe	Rosa	PUR	10.4.93	13 Jun
13:32.14	Soufiyan	Bouqantar	MAR	30.8.93	18 May
13:32.27	Agato	Yashin Hasen	ETH	19.1.86	2 Jul
13:32.83	Koen	Naert	BEL	3.9.89	31 May
13:32.84	Joshua	Cheptegei	UGA-J	12.9.96	25 Jul
13:33.12	Aaron	Braun	USA	28.5.87	15 May
13:33.20	Luc	Bruchet	CAN	23.2.91	4 May
13:33.28	Luke	Caldwell	GBR	2.8.91	18 Apr
13:33.28	Alberto	Sánchez	ESP	19.10.88	31 May
13:33.4A	Spencer	Maiyo	KEN-J	.96	4 Apr
13:33.51A	Timothy	Kiptoo	KEN	2.8.84	7 Jun
13:33.53	Liam	Adams	AUS	4.9.86	18 Apr
13:33.6A	Fredrick	Kipkosgei	KEN-J	13.11.96	4 Apr
13:33.67	Daniel Kipchirchir Komen		KEN	27.11.84	9 Jun
13:33.82	Othmane	El Goumri	MAR	28.5.92	2 Aug
13:33.95	El Hassan	El Abbassi	BRN	15.7.79	8 Jun
13:34.0A	Moses	Koech	KEN-Y	5.4.97	4 Apr
13:34.08A	Franklin	Ngelel	KEN	.86	7 Jun
13:34.48	Isaac	Kimeli	BEL	9.3.94	2 Aug
13:34.53	Kenta	Murayama	JPN	23.2.93	10 May
13:34.54	Abayneh	Ayele	ETH	4.11.87	11 Jun
13:34.57	Kota	Murayama	JPN	23.2.93	27 Sep
13:34.60	Paul	Kuira	KEN	25.1.90	28 Sep
13:34.74	Jared	Ward	USA	9.9.88	18 Apr
13:34.83	Ali	Kaya	TUR	20.4.94	18 May
13:34.90	Jeroen	D'Hoedt	BEL	10.1.90	4 May
13:34.92A	Douglas	Kipserem	KEN	.87	7 Jun
13:34.95	David	Torrence	USA	26.11.85	27 Jun
13:34.97	Yuichiro	Ueno	JPN	29.7.85	29 Apr
13:34.97	Yuki	Sato	JPN	26.11.86	27 Sep
13:35.02	Timothy	Toroitich	UGA	10.10.91	27 Jul
13:35.18	Masato	Kikuchi	JPN	18.9.90	10 May
13:35.49	Mumin	Gala	DJI	6.9.86	26 Jun
13:35.55	Charles	Ndungu	KEN-J	20.2.96	2 Jul
13:35.63	Edward	Waweru	KEN	3.10.90	5 Apr
13:35.78	Juan Luis	Barrios	MEX	24.6.83	19 Jul
13:35.80	Aron	Rono	USA	1.11.82	15 Jun
13:35.81	Daniel	Kitonyi	KEN	12.1.94	26 Oct
13:35.86	Edwin	Mokua	KEN	31.12.93	28 Sep
13:35.91	Patrick	Mwaka	KEN	2.11.92	12 Oct
13:36.10	Maverick	Darling	USA	9.6.89	18 Apr
13:36.21	Joe	Stilin	USA	5.12.89	15 Jun
13:36.40	Minato	Oishi	JPN	19.5.88	2 Jul
13:36.48	Tony	Okello	UGA	26.12.83	18 Apr
13:36.67	Craig	Forys	USA	13.7.89	4 May
13:36.83	Daniele	Meucci	ITA	7.10.85	1 Jul
13:36.91	Erik	Olson	USA	15.3.92	4 May
13:36.94	Abraham	Niyonkuru	BDI	26.12.89	20 Jun
13:36.96	Enoch	Omwamba	KEN	4.4.93	25 May
13:36.98	Diego Alberto	Borrego	MEX	9.1.88	18 Apr
13:37.16	Soufiane	Bouchiki	BEL	22.3.90	2 Aug
13:37.25	Yuki	Yagi	JPN	17.9.89	10 May
13:37.32	Abdellah	Haidane	ITA	28.3.89	2 Sep
13:37.40	Kheta	Ram	IND	20.9.86	27 Sep
13:37.64	Sean	McGorty	USA-J	7.3.95	4 May
13:37.68	Shadrack	Kipchirchir	KEN	22.2.89	18 Apr
13:37.71	Eric	Finan	USA	9.6.87	19 Jul
13:37.80	Marouan	Razine	ITA	9.4.91	31 May
13:37.86	Steffen (178)	Uliczka	GER	17.7.84	31 May

Indoors

Mark	Name		Nat	Born	Pos	Meet	Venue	Date
13:01.26		Rupp			1		Boston (A)	16 Jan
13:04.35	Samuel	Chelanga	KEN	23.2.85	2		Boston (A)	16 Jan
13:37.42	Reed	Connor	USA	25.9.90	1		Ames	14 Feb

Drugs disqualification: 13:37.12 Mohammed El Hachimi ¶ BEL 15.12.74 14 NA Heusden-Zolder 19 Jul

JUNIORS

See main list for top 5 juniors. 11 performances by 9 men to 13:31.0. Additional marks and further juniors:

Mukono 13:28.11 3 WJ Eugene 25 Jul

Ngatia 13:29.29 2 Yokohama 12 Apr 13:30.06 2 Gifu 11 May

Mark	Name		Nat	Born	Pos	Meet	Venue	Date
13:28.61	Joseph	Kamathi	KEN	23.11.96	1rB		Gifu	11 May
13:29.54	Phillip	Kipyeko	UGA	10.1.95	2		Nijmegen	11 Jun
13:29.81	Debele	Gezmu	ETH	14.4.96	15	Bisl	Oslo	11 Jun
13:30.83	Daniel	Kipkemoi	KEN	5.7.96	2		Fukagawa	25 Jun
13:31.16	Abdallah	Mande (10)	UGA	10.5.95	3		Nijmegen	11 Jun
13:31.64	Ambrose	Bore	KEN	8.8.95	5		Oordegem	31 May
13:32.84	Joshua	Cheptegei	UGA	12.9.96	4	WJ	Eugene	25 Jul
13:33.4A	Spencer	Maiyo	KEN	.96	1		Nairobi	4 Apr
13:33.6A	Fredrick	Kipkosgei	KEN	13.11.96	2		Nairobi	4 Apr
13:34.0A	Moses	Koech	KEN-Y	5.4.97	3		Nairobi	4 Apr
13:35.55	Charles	Ndungu	KEN	20.2.96	3		Kitami	2 Jul

Mark	Wind	Name		Nat	Born	Pos	Meet	Venue	Date
13:37.64		Sean	McGorty	USA	7.3.95	6rB	Jordan	Stanford	4 May
13:38.08		Keisuke	Nakatani	JPN	12.1.95	3rB		Nobeoka	10 May
13:38.13		Yihunilign	Adane	ETH	29.2.96	6		Carquefou	20 Jun
13:38.94		Moses	Letoyie (20	KEN	27.1.95	7		Rovereto	2 Sep
Best European: 13:53.29		Amanal	Petros	GER	17.5.95	4		Oordegem	5 Jul

10,000 METRES

Mark	Wind	Name		Nat	Born	Pos	Meet	Venue	Date
26:44.36		Galen	Rupp	USA	8.5.86	1	Pre	Eugene	30 May
26:49.41		Paul	Tanui	KEN	22.12.90	2	Pre	Eugene	30 May
26:52.36		Bidan	Karoki	KEN	21.8.90	3	Pre	Eugene	30 May
26:54.61		Stephen	Sambu	KEN	3.7.88	4	Pre	Eugene	30 May
27:16.75			Tanui			1		Kitakyushu	17 May
27:17.82			Tanui			1		Yamaguchi	10 Oct
27:20.74		Leonard	Barsoton	KEN	21.10.94	2		Yamaguchi	10 Oct
27:21.61		Emmanuel	Bett	KEN	30.3.83	5	Pre	Eugene	30 May
27:23.66		James	Mwangi	KEN	23.6.84	1		Abashiri	6 Jul
27:25.56		William Malel	Sitonik	KEN	1.3.94	1		Kobe	20 Apr
27:26.92		Edward	Waweru	KEN	3.10.90	2		Kobe	20 Apr
27:28.27		Karemi Jeremiah	Thuku (10)	KEN	7.7.94	2		Abashiri	6 Jul
27:30.94		Kenneth	Kipkemoi	KEN	2.8.84	6	Pre	Eugene	30 May
27:31.76			Waweru			3		Abashiri	6 Jul
27:32.83			Karoki			3		Kobe	20 Apr
27:32.96		El Hassan	El Abbassi	BRN	15.7.79	7	Pre	Eugene	30 May
27:34.40		Juan Luis	Barrios	MEX	24.6.83	1	Jordan	Stanford	4 May
27:36.00		Cameron	Levins	CAN	28.3.89	2	Jordan	Stanford	4 May
27:36.35		Zewdie	Milion	ETH	24.1.89	1		Machida	29 Nov
27:36.40		Bashir	Abdi	BEL	10.2.89	3	Jordan	Stanford	4 May
27:36.53		Daniele	Meucci	ITA	7.10.85	4	Jordan	Stanford	4 May
27:36.60		Bernard	Kimani	KEN	10.9.93	2		Machida	29 Nov
27:36.79		Shadrack	Kipchirchir	KEN	22.2.89	5	Jordan	Stanford	4 May
27:37.67		Patrick	Mwaka (20)	KEN	2.11.92	3		Yamaguchi	10 Oct
27:38.18		Joseph	Kamathi	KEN-J	23.11.96	4		Yamaguchi	10 Oct
27:38.83		Teklemariam	Medhin	ERI	24.6.89	8	Pre	Eugene	30 May
27:38.93		Kassa	Mekashaw	ETH	19.3.84	3		Machida	29 Nov
27:38.99		Tetsuya	Yoroizaka	JPN	20.3.90	4		Machida	29 Nov
27:40.43		Paul	Kuira	KEN	25.1.90	5		Yamaguchi	10 Oct
27:40.95			Mwangi			5		Machida	29 Nov
		(30/25)							
27:41.73		Kennedy	Kithuka	KEN	4.6.89	6	Jordan	Stanford	4 May
27:42.35		Melaku	Abera	ETH	20.4.94	3		Kitakyushu	17 May
27:42.89		Birhan	Nebebew	ETH	14.8.94	9	Pre	Eugene	30 May
27:43.27		Timothy	Toroitich	UGA	10.10.91	10	Pre	Eugene	30 May
27:43.30		Goitom	Kifle	ERI	3.12.93	11	Pre	Eugene	30 May
		(30)							
27:46.30		Bobby	Curtis	USA	28.11.84	7	Jordan	Stanford	4 May
27:46.59		Yuki	Sato	JPN	26.11.86	8	Jordan	Stanford	4 May
27:49.94		Kenta	Murayama	JPN	23.2.93	4		Kobe	20 Apr
27:51.72		Agato	Yashin Hasen	ETH	19.1.86	6		Yamaguchi	10 Oct
27:54.25		Shinobu	Kubota	JPN	12.12.91	8		Machida	29 Nov
27:55.21		Tasama	Dame	ETH	12.10.87	9	Jordan	Stanford	4 May
27:55.35		Arne	Gabius	GER	22.3.81	10	Jordan	Stanford	4 May
27:56.11		Moses	Kipsiro	UGA	2.9.86	1	CG	Glasgow	1 Aug
27:56.14		Josphat	Bett	KEN	12.6.90	2	CG	Glasgow	1 Aug
27:56.26		Joshua	Cheptegei	UGA-J	12.9.96	1		Leiden	14 Jun
		(40)							
27:56.60		Keita	Shitara	JPN	18.12.91	10		Machida	29 Nov
27:57.52		Bouabdellah	Tahri	FRA	20.12.78	12	Pre	Eugene	30 May
27:58.24		Peter	Kirui	KEN	2.1.88	4	CG	Glasgow	1 Aug
27:58.91		Yuta	Shitara	JPN	18.12.91	11		Machida	29 Nov
27:59.74		Samuel	Chelanga	KEN	23.2.85	13	Pre	Eugene	30 May
27:59.91		Charles	Cheruiyot	KEN	4.8.88	5	CG	Glasgow	1 Aug
28:00.05		Daniel	Gitau	KEN	1.10.87	12		Machida	29 Nov
28:00.33		Enoch	Omwamba	KEN	4.4.93	1		Fukagawa	25 Jun
28:01.09		Macharia	Ndirangu	KEN	9.9.94	5		Abashiri	6 Jul
28:01.71		Yuichiro	Ueno	JPN	29.7.85	5		Kobe	20 Apr
		(50)							
28:01.85		Leonard	Korir	KEN	10.12.86	14	Pre	Eugene	30 May
28:02.79		Yevgeniy	Rybakov	RUS	27.2.85	1	NC	Yerino	9 Jul
28:02.87		Jonathan	Maina	KEN	24.12.90	3		Fukagawa	25 Jun

Mark	Wind	Name		Nat	Born	Pos	Meet	Venue	Date
28:02.96		Mohammed	Ahmed	CAN	5.1.91	6	CG	Glasgow	1 Aug
28:03.21		Wilson	Too	KEN	.91	15	Pre	Eugene	30 May
28:03.45		Lewis	Korir	KEN	11.6.86	1		Jämsä	28 Jun
28:03.51		Aron	Rono	USA	1.11.82	11	Jordan	Stanford	4 May
28:03.59		Anatoliy	Rybakov	RUS	27.2.85	2	NC	Yerino	9 Jul
28:03.70		Jake	Robertson	NZL	14.11.89	7	CG	Glasgow	1 Aug
28:03.81		Muryo	Takase	JPN	31.1.89	6		Abashiri	6 Jul
		(60)							
28:03.88		Eric	Sebahire	RWA	6.1.85	9	CG	Glasgow	1 Aug
28:04.16		Abayneh	Ayele	ETH	4.11,87	13		Machida	29 Nov
28:04.25		Masato	Kikuchi	JPN	18.9.90	14		Machida	29 Nov
28:05.71		Moses	Kibet	KEN	23.3.91	1	Ita Ch	Ferrara	17 May
28:08.11		Mohamed	Farah	GBR	23.3.83	1	EC	Zürich	13 Aug
28:08.5A		Peter	Mwololo	KEN	.92	4	NC	Nairobi	7 Jun
28:08.66		Andrew	Vernon	GBR	7.1.86	2	EC	Zürich	13 Aug
28:08.72		Ali	Kaya	TUR	20.4.94	3	EC	Zürich	13 Aug
28:10.0A		Hosea	Macharinyang	KEN	12.6.85	6	NC	Nairobi	7 Jun
28:11.07		Nguse	Tesfaldet	ERI	10.11.86	1	AfCh	Marrakech	10 Aug
		(70)							
28:11.11		Polat Kemboi	Arikan	TUR	12.12.90	4	EC	Zürich	13 Aug
28:11.33		Alex	Mwangi	KEN	14.6.90	8		Abashiri	6 Jul
28:11.36		Mustapha	El Aziz	MAR	.85	2	AfCh	Marrakech	10 Aug
28:11.94		Suguru	Osako	JPN	23.5.91	2	AsiG	Incheon	2 Oct
28:12.27		Adugna	Tekele	ETH	26.2.89	4	AfCh	Marrakech	10 Aug
28:12.85		Alemayehu	Bezabeh	ESP	22.9.86	1		Lisboa	29 Mar
28:12.87		Aimeru	Almeya	ISR	8.6.90	1		Tel Aviv	8 May
28:14.87		Jamel	Chatbi	ITA	30.4.84	2	NC	Ferrara	17 May
28:15.36		Tsubasa	Hayakawa	JPN	2.7.90	15		Machida	29 Nov
28:15.45		Kenta	Murozuka	JPN	12.2.86	9		Abashiri	6 Jul
		(80)							
28:15.6A		Peter	Kurui	KEN	.90	9	NC	Nairobi	7 Jun
28:15.99		Daniel	Kitonyi	KEN	12.1.94	1		Tokyo	29 Jun
28:16.10		Noahiro	Yamada	JPN	18.12.84	10		Abashiri	6 Jul
28:16.2A		Hosea	Nailel	KEN	.88	10	NC	Nairobi	7 Jun
28:16.72		Josephat	Onsarigo	KEN	.93	2		Yokohama	27 Sep
28:17.07		Felicien	Muhitira	RWA	4.11.94	10	CG	Glasgow	1 Aug
28:17.74		Takuya	Ishikawa	JPN	29.10.87	2		Nobeoka	10 May
28:17.75		Imane	Merga	ETH	15.10.88	5	AfCh	Marrakech	10 Aug
28:17.8A		Thomas	Ayeko	UGA	10.2.92	1	NC	Kampala	11 Jul
28:17.94		Girmaw	Amare	ISR	26.10.87	2		Tel Aviv	8 May
		(90)							
28:18.18		Chris	Derrick	USA	17.10.90	2	NC	Sacramento	26 Jun
28:18.54		Charles	Ndirangu	KEN	8.2.93	1		Kobe	19 Apr
28:18.78		Dmitriy	Safronov	RUS	9.10.81	3	NC	Yerino	9 Jul
28:18.87		Tsuyoshi	Ugachi	JPN	27.4.87	11		Abashiri	6 Jul
28:19.11		Edwin	Mokua	KEN	31.12.93	12		Abashiri	6 Jul
28:19.28		Hiroto	Inoue	JPN	6.1.93	1		Yokohama	23 Nov
28:19.35		Maru	Kebede	ETH		3		Tel Aviv	8 May
28:19.36		Stefano	La Rosa	ITA	22.9.85	14	Jordan	Stanford	4 May
28:20.31		Takuya	Fujikawa	JPN	17.12.92	2		Yokohama	23 Nov
28:20.77		Chihiro	Miyawaki	JPN	28.8.91	6		Fukagawa	25 Jun
		(100)							

Mark	Name		Nat	Born	Date
28:20.96	Taku	Fujimoto	JPN	11.9.89	29 Nov
28:20.98	Christopher	Landry	USA	29.4.86	4 May
28:22.30	Yassine	Mandour	FRA	21.1.85	7 Jun
28:22.73	Maina	Karukawa	KEN	19.6.91	27 Sep
28:22.74	Minato	Oishi	JPN	19.5.88	20 Apr
28:22.8A	Daniel	Muindi	KEN	.94	7 Jun
28:23.40	Tadashi	Isshiki	JPN	5.6.94	6 Jul
28:23.66	William	Kibor	KEN	10.1.85	16 Mar
28:23.93	Keita	Baba	JPN	28.4.86	6 Jul
28:23.99	Daniel	Kipkemoi	KEN-J	5.7.96	6 Jul
28:24.93	Hiroyuki	Yamamoto	JPN	30.4.86	6 Jul
28:24.97	Naohiro	Domoto	JPN	23.7.89	29 Nov
28:25.07	Atsushi	Yamazaki	JPN	7.10.86	20 Apr
28:25.25	Hiram	Ngatia	KEN-J	1.1.96	25 Jun
28:25.47	Kazuya	Deguchi	JPN	14.8.88	25 Oct
28:26.02	Ryan	Vail	USA	19.3.86	26 Jun
28:27.3A	John	Elimlim	KEN		7 Jun
28:27.54	Luke	Puskedra	USA	8.2.90	4 May
28:27.73	Kensuke	Takezawa	JPN	11.10.86	20 Apr
28:27.73	Yusuke	Ogura	JPN	16.4.93	6 Jul
28:27.76	Roberto	Alaiz	ESP	20.7.90	29 Mar
28:28.22	Mohamed	Marhoum	ESP	8.3.91	29 Mar
28:28.4A	Caleb	Ndiku	KEN	9.10.92	9 May
28:28.54	Brendan	Gregg	USA	15.5.89	4 May
28:28.96	Richard	Ringer	GER	27.2.89	3 May
28:29.30	Shota	Hattori	JPN	28.10.91	29 Nov
28:29.49	El Hassane	Ben Lkhainouch	FRA	1.6.81	30 Apr
28:29.50	Shintaro	Miwa	JPN	4.1.92	29 Nov
28:29.56	Mitsunori	Asaoka	JPN	11.1.93	29 Nov
28:29.69	Amos	Kibitok	KEN	4.4.94	9 Jul
28:29.69	Benjamin	Ngandu	KEN	21.5.90	10 Oct
28:29.84	Sean	Quigley	USA	8.2.85	26 Jun
28:30.18	Edward	Cheserek	KEN	2.2.94	11 Jun
28:30.52	Keisuke	Nakatani	JPN-J	12.1.95	25 Jun
28:30.78	Kazuma	Kubota	JPN	24.9.93	23 Nov
28:30.9	Dickson	Marwa	TAN	6.3.82	13 Jul
28:31.12	Stanley	Siteki	KEN-J		15 Nov
28:32.01	Rinas	Akhmadiyev	RUS	25.5.89	9 Jul
28:32.18	Paul	Pollock	IRL	25.6.86	4 May
28:32.4	Joseph	Theophil	TAN		13 Jul

Mark	Wind	Name		Nat	Born	Pos	Meet	Venue	Date

Mark	First	Last	Nat	Born	Date
28:32.59	Jake	Riley	USA	11.2.88	4 May
28:32.67	Satoru	Kitamura	JPN	4.2.86	15 Nov
28:32.75	Masato	Imai	JPN	2.4.84	20 Apr
28:32.80	Keigo	Yano	JPN	3.12.91	19 Apr
28:33.20	Evans	Kiplagat	KEN	5.3.88	9 Jul
28:33.73A	Elvis	Cheboi	KEN-J	29.9.95	24 Jun
28:33.74	Tom	Wiggers	NED	10.8.87	14 Jun
28:33.8A	Josephat	Kiprono Menjo	KEN	20.8.79	7 Jun
28:34.43	Aaron	Braun	USA	28.5.87	26 Jun
28:34.45	Ryotaro	Matoba	JPN	16.6.89	17 May
28:34.49	Koen	Naert	BEL	3.9.89	4 May
28:35.0A	Eliud (152)	Mwangi	KEN	.89	7 Jun

JUNIORS

See main list for top 2 juniors. 11 performances by 8 men to 28:00.0. Additional marks and further juniors:

Kamathi	28:03.40	1		Fukagawa	25 Jun
Cheptegei	28:32.76	1	WJ	Eugene	22 Jul
Cheboi	28:35.20	2	WJ	Eugene	22 Jul

Mark	First	Last	Nat	Born	Pos	Meet	Venue	Date
28:23.99	Daniel	Kipkemoi	KEN	5.7.96	15		Abashiri	6 Jul
28:25.25	Hiram	Ngatia	KEN	1.1.96	7		Fukagawa	25 Jun
28:30.52	Keisuke	Nakatani	JPN	12.1.95	10		Fukagawa	25 Jun
28:31.12	Stanley	Siteki	KEN		2		Yokohama	15 Nov
28:33.73A	Elvis	Cheboi	KEN	29.9.95	1	NC-j	Nairobi	24 Jun
28:36.77	Charles	Ndungu	KEN	20.2.96	4		Yokohama	15 Nov
28:37.58A	Nicholas	Kosimbei	KEN	10.1.96	2	NC-j	Nairobi	24 Jun
28:45.83	Berhane	Afewerki (10)	ERI	6.5.96	4	WJ	Eugene	22 Jul
28:47.51A	Emmanuel	Bett	KEN	14.7.95	3	NC-j	Nairobi	24 Jun
28:52.41A	Geoffrey	Korir	KEN	2.5.96	4	NC-j	Nairobi	24 Jun
28:53.20	Kazuto	Kawabata	JPN	20.12.95	7		Yokohama	6 Dec
28:53.77	Abdallah	Mande	UGA	10.5.95	5	WJ	Eugene	22 Jul
28:54.84	Yihunilign	Adane	ETH	29.2.96	6	WJ	Eugene	22 Jul
28:55.31	Hazuma	Hattori	JPN	7.2.95	1r3		Konosu	29 Apr
28:56.17A	Silas	Laikong	KEN	29.11.95	5	NC-j	Nairobi	24 Jun
28:59.64A	Elvis	Kipkoech	KEN	20.10.95	6	NC-j	Nairobi	24 Jun
29:03.56	Jinnosuke	Matsumara	JPN	22.3.95	6		Yokohama	23 Nov
29:03.8A	Reuben	Kemboi (20)	KEN	27.8.95	3		Mumias	3 May

10 KILOMETRES ROAD

Mark	First	Last	Nat	Born	Pos	Meet	Venue	Date
27:25	Stephen	Sambu	KEN	3.7.88	1		Boston	22 Jun
27:28	Geoffrey	Ronoh	KEN	29.11.82	1		Praha	6 Sep
27:32	Geoffrey	Mutai	KEN	7.10.81	2		Praha	6 Sep
27:35		G Mutai			2		Boston	22 Jun
27:37	Bidan	Karoki	KEN	21.8.90	1		Cape Elizabeth	2 Aug
27:38	Nicholas	Bor	KEN	.88	3		Praha	6 Sep
27:39		Sambu			1		New York	10 May
27:40	Wilson	Too	KEN	.91	1		Laredo	22 Mar
27:40+	Leonard Patrick	Komon	KEN	10.1.88	1=	in HMar	Berlin	30 Mar
27:40+	Vincent	Rono	KEN	11.11.90	1=	in HMar	Berlin	30 Mar
27:41+	Abreham	Cheroben	KEN	10.11.92	3=	in HMar	Berlin	30 Mar
27:41+	Daniel	Chebii	KEN	28.5.85	3=	in HMar	Berlin	30 Mar
27:41	Daniel	Salel	KEN	11.12.90	3		Boston	22 Jun
27:41	Simon	Cheprot	KEN	2.7.93	4		Praha	6 Sep
Where superior to track bests								
27:42+	Matthew	Kisorio	KEN	16.5.89		in HMar	Valencia	19 Oct
27:43+	Bernard	Koech	KEN	31.1.88		in 10M	Tilburg	7 Sep
27:43+	Titus	Mbishei	KEN	28.10.90		in HMar	Valencia	19 Oct
27:44	Geoffrey	Kamworor	KEN	28.11.92	1		Bangalore	18 May
27:44	Stephen	Kibet	KEN	9.11.86	2		Cape Elizabeth	2 Aug
27:46+	Cyprian	Kotut	KEN	.92	1=	in HMar	Philadelphia	21 Sep
27:48+	Sylas	Chebogel	KEN	.83		in HMar	Berlin	30 Mar
27:48+	Richard	Mengich	KEN	3.4.89		in HMar	Berlin	30 Mar
	27:48				5		Praha	6 Sep
27:49	Kinde	Atanaw	ETH	15.4.93	1		Berlin	12 Oct
27:51	Ben	True	USA	29.12.85	3		Cape Elizabeth	2 Aug
27:52+	Edwin	Kiptoo	KEN			in 10M	Tilburg	7 Sep
27:52+	Eliud	Tarus	KEN			in 10M	Tilburg	7 Sep
27:56+	Geoffrey	Bundi	KEN	.87	3	in HMar	Philadelphia	21 Sep
27:57+	John	Kipkoech	KEN	29.12.91		in HMar	Berlin	30 Mar
27:57	Patrick	Makau	KEN	2.3.85	4		Cape Elizabeth	2 Aug
27:58	Julius	Kogo	KEN	12.8.85	1		Mobile	22 Mar
28:01	Wilson	Kiprop	KEN	14.4.87	1		Ottawa	24 May
28:02+	Victor	Chumo	KEN	.87		in HMar	Rome-Ostia	2 Mar
28:02	Cleophas	Ngetich	KEN	.90	2		Mobile	22 Mar
28:04	Reuben	Maiyo	KEN		2		Berlin	12 Oct
28:05+	Titus	Masai	KEN	9.10.89		in HMar	Rome-Ostia	2 Mar
28:05+	Aziz	Lahbadi	MAR	3.2.91		in HMar	Rome-Ostia	2 Mar
28:05	Abrar	Osman	ERI	1.1.94	2		Houilles	28 Dec

Mark	Wind	Name		Nat	Born	Pos	Meet	Venue	Date
28:06+		Robert	Chemosin	KEN	1.2.89		in HMar	Rome-Ostia	2 Mar
28:06+		Hunegnaw	Mesfin	ETH	31.1.89		in HMar	Rome-Ostia	2 Mar
28:07+		Nicholas	Kipkemboi	KEN	5.7.86		in HMar	Praha	5 Apr
28:07+		Hillary	Kipchumba	KEN	25.11.92		in HMar	Praha	5 Apr
28:07		Isiah	Koech	KEN	19.12.92	2		New Orleans	19 Apr
28:07		David	Kosgei	KEN	.85	2		Ottawa	24 May
28:08+		Daniel	Wanjiru	KEN	26.5.92		in HMar	Praha	5 Apr
28:08+		Henry	Kiplagat	KEN	16.12.82		in HMar	Praha	5 Apr
28:08+		Mosinet	Geremew	ETH	12.2.92		in HMar	Praha	5 Apr
28:08+		Bernard	Bett	KEN	.93		in HMar	Praha	5 Apr
28:08+		Evans	Kiplagat	KEN	5.3.88		in HMar	Praha	5 Apr
28:09+		Eric	Ndiema	KEN	28.12.92		in HMar	Rome-Ostia	2 Mar
28:09+		Andrew	Mangata	KEN			in 10M	Tilburg	7 Sep
28:09+		Tsegay	Tuemay	ERI-J	20.12.95		in 10M	Tilburg	7 Sep
28:10+		Million	Feyisa	ETH	.88		in HMar	Praha	5 Apr
28:10		Philip	Langat	KEN	23.4.90	1		Appingedam	28 Jun
28:12		Alphonse Felix	Simbu	TAN		1	NC	Dar es Salaam	2 Feb
28:12+		Jacob	Kendagor	KEN	19.9.84		in HMar	Valencia	19 Oct
28:13		Edwin	Rotich	KEN		1		Casablanca	15 Jun
28:13		Ayele	Abshero	ETH	28.12.90	2		Appingedam	28 Jun
28:13		Geoffrey	Kusuro	UGA	12.2.89	7		Praha	6 Sep
28:13+		Dawit	Weldesilasie	ERI	10.12.94		in HMar	Valencia	19 Oct
28:13+		Nuguse	Hirsuato	ETH	13.2.82		in HMar	Valencia	19 Oct
28:14		Ahmed	Tamri	MAR	8.2.85	1		Casablanca	15 Jun
28:14		Mule	Wasihun	ETH	.93	2		Rennes	12 Oct
28:15		Cornelius	Kangogo	KEN	31.12.93	1		Donglo	21 Apr
28:15		Eliud	Mwangi	KEN	.89	3		Appingedam	28 Jun
28:15		Micah	Kogo	KEN	3.6.86	5		Cape Elizabeth	2 Aug
28:16+		Wilson	Kipsang	KEN	15.3.82		in HMar	Olomouc	21 Jun
28:16		Hillary	Langat	KEN-J	14.8.95	4		Appingedam	28 Jun
28:16		Yasin	Haji	ETH-J	22.1.96	3		Rennes	12 Oct
28:17		Joseph	Aperumoi	KEN	.90	1		Santos	18 May
28:17		John	Mwangangi	KEN	1.11.90	5		Appingedam	28 Jun
28:18+		Mule	Wasehun	ETH	.93	1	in HMar	Paris	2 Mar
28:18		Thomas	Longosiwa	KEN	14.1.82	2		Donglo	21 Apr
28:18		Mark	Korir	KEN	10.1.85	2		Languex	14 Jun
28:19		Simon	Ndirangu	KEN	1.11.85	3		Mobile	22 Mar
28:19		Japheth	Korir	KEN	30.6.93	3		New Orleans	19 Apr

Mark	Name		Nat	Born	Date
28:20+	Henry	Kiplagat	KEN	16.12.82	30 Mar
28:20+	Abraham	Kiplimo	UGA	14.4.89	18 May
28:20+	Zelalem	Mengistu	ETH		7 Sep
28:21+	Ghirmay	Gebrselassie	ERI-J	14.11.95	18 May
28:21	Dawit	Fikadu	ETH-J	.95	14 Jun
28:22	Berhanu	Legesse	ETH	.93	9 Mar
28:22	Getaneh	Tamire	ETH	.94	9 Mar
28:22	Guye	Adola	ETH	20.10.90	21 Apr
28:22	Collis	Birmingham	AUS	27.12.84	10 May
28:22	Edwin	Kipyego	KEN	16.11.90	24 May
28:22	Bernard	Kipkemoi	KEN	.94	28 Jun
28:22	Gladwin	Mzazi	RSA	29.8.88	12 Oct
28:22	Teshome	Mekonnen	ETH-J	.95	12 Oct
28:23	Charles	Maina	KEN	11.11.82	6 Apr
28:23	Emmanuel	Bor	KEN	14.4.88	27 Apr
28:23	Kenenisa	Bekele	ETH	13.6.82	18 May
28:23	Salaheddine	Bounasser	MAR	27.9.90	28 Sep
28:24	Eliya	Daudi	TAN	29.6.84	2 Feb
28:24	Tesfaye	Abera	ETH	31.3.92	14 Jun
28:24	Andrew	Kimutai	KEN	12.8.89	7 Sep
28:24	Anis	Selmouini	MAR	15.3.79	28 Sep
28:25+	Zersenay	Tadese	ERI	8.2.82	18 May
28:25	Abraham	Kipyatich	KEN	.93	12 Oct
28:25	Azmeraw	Mengistu	ETH	15.9.92	12 Oct
28:26	Josphat Kiptanui Too		KEN	.86	7 Jun
28:26	Moussaab	Hadout	MAR	11.3.88	15 Jun
28:26+	Asefa	Mengistu	ETH-J	19.1.95	19 Oct
28:27	Alfgred	Cherop	KEN	2.3.86	14 Jun
28:27	Abdelmajid	El Hissouf	MAR	23.9.92	28 Sep
28:28	Frederick	Ngeny	KEN	.88	19 Apr
28:28	Lucky	Mohale	RSA	21.8.85	12 Apr
28:28+	Kende	Atanaw	KEN	.94	21 Sep
28:28+	Abera	Kuma	ETH	31.8.90	16 Nov
28:29+	Dejen	Gebremeskel	ETH	24.11.89	21 Sep
28:29+	Wilfred Kimeli	Kimitei	KEN	11.3.85	21 Sep
28:29+	Yenew	Alamirew	ETH	27.5.90	16 Nov

Drugs dq

Mark	Name		Nat	Born	Date
28:26	Ahmed	Baday ¶	MAR	12.1.74	28 Sep

Dec 31, Madrid (55m dh): 1. Mike Kigen KEN 15.1.86 27:51; 2. Jesús España ESP 21.8.78 28:29

Aug 17, Nairobi (A): distance?: 1, Amos Mitei 27:42; 2, Edwin Kiptoo 27:44; 3, Vincent Yator 27:45; 4, Leonard Kipkoech 27:46; 5, Timothy Kiptoo 27:53, 6. Franklin Ngelel 28:04, 7. Julius Kalekem 28:07, 8. James Rungaru 28:10, 9. Lani Kiplagat 28:13, 10. Francis Kipkeoch 28:17

Jan 31, Abu Dhabi: distance?: 1. Taoufik Al Allam MAR 27:45; 2. Birhanu Shumi ETH 27:45; 3. Mumin Gala DJI 27:51; 4, Abdalla Gadana ETH ? 27:52; 5. Deriba Merga ETH 28:04; 6. Tesfaye Girma ETH 28:09

15/20 KILOMETRES ROAD

See also Half Marathon lists

20k	15k	Name		Nat	Born	Pos	Meet	Venue	Date
	42:18	Abera	Kuma	ETH	31.8.90	1		Nijmegen	16 Nov
	42:22	Wilson	Too	KEN	.91	1		Bursa	13 Apr
	42:26	Yigrem	Demelash	ETH	28.1.94	2		Nijmegen	16 Nov
	42:27+	Nguse	Tesfaldet	ERI	10.11.86		In HMar	København	29 Mar
	42:28+	Nicholas	Bor	KEN	.88		in HMar	Praha	5 Apr
	42:30	Yenew	Alamirew	ETH	27.5.90	3		Nijmegen	16 Nov
	42:31	Tesfaye	Abera	ETH	31.3.92	4		Nijmegen	16 Nov

Mark	Wind	Name		Nat	Born	Pos	Meet	Venue	Date
56:57	42:32+	Wilson	Kiprop	KEN	14.4.87		In HMar	København	29 Mar
57:01	42:27+	Geoffrey	Ronoh	KEN	29.11.82		in HMar	Breda	5 Oct
	42:43+	Ghirmay	Ghebrselassie	ERI-J	14.11.95		in HMar	Göteborg	18 May
57:44	42:59+	Ezekiel	Chebii	KEN	3.1.91		in HMar	Den Haag	8 Mar
	42:59+	Edwin	Kipyego	KEN	16.11.90		in HMar	Den Haag	8 Mar
	43:04	Ben	True	USA	29.12.85	1		Jacksonville	15 Mar
	43:08+	Dawit	Weldesilasie	ERI	10.12.94		in HMar	Praha	5 Apr
	43:08+	Abayneh	Ayele	ETH	4.11.87		in HMar	Gifu	18 May
	43:08+	Azmeraw	Bekele	ETH	22.1.86		in HMar	Ústi nad Labem	14 Sep
	43:10+	Tebalu	Zawude	ETH	2.11.87		In HMar	København	29 Mar
	43:10	Gadisa	Birhanu	ETH	.92	6		Nijmegen	16 Nov
	43:13	Thomas	Lokomwa	KEN	.87	1		Kerzers	15 Mar

10 MILES ROAD

10M	15k	Name		Nat	Born	Pos	Meet	Venue	Date
45:03+	42:01	Bidan	Karoki	KEN	21.8.90	1	in HMar	Philadelphia	21 Sep
45:09+		Cyprian	Kotut	KEN	.92	2	in HMar	Philadelphia	21 Sep
45:12	42:05	Bernard	Koech	KEN	31.1.88	1		Tilburg	7 Sep
45:29		Stephen	Sambu	KEN	3.7.88	1		Washington	6 Apr
45:29		Daniel	Salel	KEN	11.12.90	2		Washington	6 Apr
45:34+		Mike	Kigen	KEN	15.1.86	1	in HMar	Newcastle	7 Sep
45:35+		Mohamed	Farah	GBR	23.3.83	2	in HMar	Newcastle	7 Sep
45:45	42:42	John	Mwangangi	KEN	1.11.90	1		Zaandam	21 Sep
45:47		Allan	Kiprono	KEN	15.2.90	3		Washington	6 Apr
45:47	42:42	Nguse	Tesfaldet	ERI	10.11.86	2		Zaandam	21 Sep
45:51	42:39	Edwin	Kiptoo	KEN	.93	2		Tilburg	7 Sep
45:51		Karemi Jeremiah	Thuku	KEN	7.7.94	1		Kosa	7 Dec
45:52	42:42	Kinde	Atanaw	ETH	15.4.93	3		Zaandam	21 Sep
45:59	42:47	Eliud	Tarus	KEN	3.3.93	3		Tilburg	7 Sep
46:00	42:50	Andrew	Mangata	KEN		4		Tilburg	7 Sep
46:13+		Geoffrey	Bundi	KEN	.87	3	in HMar	Philadelphia	21 Sep
46:19		Edwin	Kipyego	KEN	16.11.90	4		Washington	6 Apr
46:22	43:07	Josphat	Bett	KEN	12.6.90	4		Zaandam	21 Sep
46:25	43:07	Tsegay	Tuemay	ERI-J	20.12.95	5		Tilburg	7 Sep
46:29	43:21	Zelalem	Mengistu	ETH		6		Tilburg	7 Sep
46:31	43:15	James	Rungaru	KEN	14.1.93	1	Gt.South	Portsmouth	26 Oct
46:32		Nicholas	Togom	KEN	17.2.92	1		Schortens	16 Aug
46:33	43:08	Peter	Kirui	KEN	2.1.88	5		Zaandam	21 Sep
46:33		Natsuki	Terada	JPN	30.8.91	2		Kosa	7 Dec

Mark	Name		Nat	Born	Date
46:35	Yuya	Konishi	JPN	22.8.90	7 Dec
46:36	Julius	Kogo	KEN	12.8.85	24 Aug
46:36	Gideon	Kipketer	KEN	10.11.92	21 Sep
46:36	Aritaka	Kajiwara	JPN	16.6.88	7 Dec
46:37	Fentahun	Hunegnaw	ETH		21 Sep
46:37	Masato	Imai	JPN	2.4.84	7 Dec
46:37	Kensuke	Takezawa	JPN	11.10.86	7 Dec
46:37	Shintaro	Miwa	JPN	4.1.92	7 Dec
46:38	Tolossa	Gedefa	ETH	.92	6 Apr
46:38	Abraham	Kiplimo	UGA	14.4.89	26 Oct
46:38	Yo	Yazawa	JPN	29.1.90	7 Dec

HALF MARATHON

Slighly downhill race: 30.5m South Shields

HMar	20k	15k	Name		Nat	Born	Pos	Meet	Venue	Date
58:48	55:50	41:55	Abreham	Cheroben	KEN	10.11.92	1		Valencia	19 Oct
59:01	55:58	41:57	Kenneth	Kipkemoi	KEN	2.8.84	2		Valencia	19 Oct
59:06			Guye	Adola	ETH	20.10.90	1		New Delhi	23 Nov
59:07			Geoffrey	Kamworor	KEN	28.11.92	2		New Delhi	23 Nov
59:08	56:13	42:26		Kamworor			1	WCh	København	29 Mar
59:11			Mosinet	Geremew	ETH	12.2.92	3		New Delhi	23 Nov
59:12			Cyprian	Kotut	KEN	.92	4		New Delhi	23 Nov
59:14		41:44	Leonard Patrick	Komon	KEN	10.1.88	1		Berlin	30 Mar
59:14				Cheroben			2		Berlin	30 Mar
59:18			Stanley	Biwott	KEN	21.4.86	5		New Delhi	23 Nov
59:21	56:21	42:26	Samuel	Tsegay	ERI	24.10.88	2	WCh	København	29 Mar
59:21	56:20	42:27		Adola			3	WCh	København	29 Mar
59:21			Stephen	Kibet (10)	KEN	9.11.86	6		New Delhi	23 Nov
59:21				Cheroben			7		New Delhi	23 Nov
59:22	56:19	42:01	Peter	Kirui	KEN	2.1.88	1		Praha	5 Apr
59:23		42:01	Bidan	Karoki	KEN	21.8.90	1		Philadelphia	21 Sep
59:25		42:25	Aziz	Lahbabi	MAR	3.2.91	1		Ostia	2 Mar
59:28			Jonathan	Maiyo	KEN	5.5.88	8		New Delhi	23 Nov
59:36	56:41	42:39	Lelisa	Desisa	ETH	14.1.90	1		Ra's Al-Khaymah	14 Feb
59:38	56:28	42:29	Zersenay	Tadese	ERI	8.2.82	4	WCh	København	29 Mar
59:39	56:41	42:39	Nguse	Tesfaldet	ERI	10.11.86	2		Ra's Al-Khaymah	14 Feb
59:39		42:25	Hunegnaw	Mesfin	ETH	31.1.89	2		Ostia	2 Mar
59:41		42:24	Titus	Masai	KEN	9.10.89	3		Ostia	2 Mar

Mark	Wind		Name		Nat	Born	Pos	Meet	Venue	Date
59:43				Kipkemoi			9		New Delhi	23 Nov
59:45	56:45	42:38	Wilson	Kiprop (20)	KEN	14.4.87	3		Ra's Al-Khaymah	14 Feb
59:45	56:59		Geoffrey	Ronoh	KEN	29.11.82	1		Klagenfurt	24 Aug
59:46	56:43	42:38	Bernard	Koech	KEN	31.1.88	4		Ra's Al-Khaymah	14 Feb
59:47	56:46	42:39	Bernard	Kipyego	KEN	16.7.86	5		Ra's Al-Khaymah	14 Feb
59:49	56:45	42:40	Micah	Kogo	KEN	3.6.86	6		Ra's Al-Khaymah	14 Feb
59:50	56:38	41:57	Matthew	Kisorio	KEN	16.5.89	3		Valencia	19 Oct
59:51	56:45	42:39	Feyisa	Lilesa	ETH	1.2.90	7		Ra's Al-Khaymah	14 Feb
59:54	56:45	42:40	Paul	Lonyangata	KEN	12.12.92	8		Ra's Al-Khaymah	14 Feb
59:54	56:55	42:16		Geremew			2		Praha	5 Apr
59:55	56:39	41:59	Titus	Mbishei	KEN	28.10.90	4		Valencia	19 Oct
59:58	56:46			Karoki			1		Lisboa	16 Mar
59:58			Alex	Oleitiptip	KEN	22.9.82	1		Azkoitia	22 Mar
59:58	56:55	42:16	Daniel	Wanjiru (30)	KEN	26.5.92	3		Praha	5 Apr
59:59			Edwin	Rotich	KEN		2		Azkoitia	22 Mar
59:59				Kotut			2		Philadelphia	21 Sep
			(39/31)							
60:00dh			Mohamed	Farah	GBR	23.3.83	1	GNR	South Shields	7 Sep
60:00dh			Mike	Kigen	KEN	15.1.86	2	GNR	South Shields	7 Sep
60:05		42:25	Simon	Cheprot	KEN	2.7.93	4		Ostia	2 Mar
60:08			Mule	Wasehun	ETH	.93	1		Paris	2 Mar
60:10	57:07	42:46	Ghirmay	Ghebrselassie	ERI-J	14.11.95	7	WCh	København	29 Mar
60:11	57:06	42:48	Martin	Mathathi	KEN	25.12.85	1		Marugame	2 Feb
60:11	56:56	42:16	Nicholas	Kipkemboi	KEN	5.7.86	4		Praha	5 Apr
60:11	57:02	42:30	Richard	Mengich	KEN	3.4.89	1		Breda	5 Oct
60:13	57:08	42:46	Samson	Gebreyohanes	ERI	7.2.92	8	WCh	København	29 Mar
			(40)							
60:13			Edwin	Koech	KEN	.87	1		Sarnen	7 Sep
60:15	57:09	42:46	Adugna	Tekele	ETH	26.2.89	9	WCh	København	29 Mar
60:17	57:09		Silas	Kipruto	KEN	26.9.84	2		Lisboa	16 Mar
60:17			Sylas	Chebogei	KEN	.83	4		Berlin	30 Mar
60:17			Kinde	Atanaw	ETH	15.4.93	10		New Delhi	23 Nov
60:20			Goitom	Kifle	ERI	3.12.93	3		Azkoitia	22 Mar
60:24		42:30	Robert	Chemosin	KEN	1.2.89	5		Ostia	2 Mar
60:24	57:08	42:16	Henry	Kiplagat	KEN	16.12.82	5		Praha	5 Apr
60:24			Sammy	Kitwara	KEN	26.11.86	1		Luanda	7 Sep
60:25		42:43	Wilson	Kipsang	KEN	15.3.82	2		Olomouc	21 Jun
			(50)							
60:26	57:18	42:59	John	Mwangangi	KEN	1.11.90	1		Den Haag	9 Mar
60:29			Feyera	Gemeda	ETH	.82	4		Yangzhou	20 Apr
60:32	57:24	42:59	Jacob	Kendagor	KEN	19.9.84	2		Den Haag	9 Mar
60:32			John Kipsang	Loitang	KEN	.91	5		Yangzhou	20 Apr
60:40			Daniel	Chebii	KEN	28.5.85	5		Berlin	30 Mar
60:41	57:24	42:46	Geoffrey	Kusuro	UGA	12.2.89	11	WCh	København	29 Mar
60:46	57:33	42:22	Bernard	Bett	KEN	.93	6		Praha	5 Apr
60:47	57:42	42:49	Stephen	Mokoka	RSA	31.1.85	12	WCh	København	29 Mar
60:48			Victor	Kipchirchir	KEN	5.12.87	1		Warszawa	30 Mar
60:49			Mark	Korir	KEN	10.1.85	1		Lille	6 Sep
			(60)							
60:50	57:44	42:48	Kenta	Murayama	JPN	23.2.93	2		Marugame	2 Feb
60:50	57:35		Ezekiel	Chebii	KEN	3.1.91	3		Lisboa	16 Mar
60:50			Geoffrey	Mutai	KEN	7.10.81	1		New York	16 Mar
60:51		43:02	William	Kibor	KEN	10.1.85	1		Verona	16 Feb
60:51			Geoffrey	Kirui	KEN	16.2.93	2		Lille	6 Sep
60:52	57:47	43:16	Eliud	Kipchoge	KEN	5.11.84	1		Barcelona	16 Feb
60:52			Philemon	Rono	KEN	8.2.91	3		Lille	6 Sep
60:53			Amos	Mitei	KEN	.92	4		Luanda	7 Sep
60:53			Vincent	Chepkok	KEN	5.7.88	2		Porto	14 Sep
60:54	57:41	42:45	Evans	Kiplagat	KEN	5.3.88	7		Praha	5 Apr
			(70)							
60:55			Azmeraw	Bekele	ETH	22.1.86	4		Paris	2 Mar
60:55			Moses	Too	KEN	.82	1		Izmir	7 Sep
60:56			Thomas	Lokomwa	KEN	.87	2		Klagenfurt	24 Aug
60:57		43:05	Philip Sanga	Kimutai	KEN	10.9.83	6		Ostia	2 Mar
60:57			Tesfaye	Abera	ETH	31.3.92	7		Yangzhou	20 Apr
60:58			Ketema	Behailu	ETH	19.3.94	5		Paris	2 Mar
60:58			Abera	Kuma	ETH	31.8.90	3		Klagenfurt	24 Aug
60:59	57:55	43:21	Daniel	Gitau	KEN	1.10.87	1		Yamaguchi	16 Feb
61:00			Leul	Gebrselassie	ETH	20.9.93	9		Yangzhou	20 Apr
61:03	57:49	43:00	Ezra	Sang	KEN	8.6.94	5		Den Haag	9 Mar
			(80)							

Mark	Wind	Name		Nat	Born	Pos	Meet	Venue	Date
61:03		Yitayal	Atnafu	ETH	20.1.93	1		Boulogne-Billancourt	16 Nov
61:03		Nicholas	Bor	KEN	.88	11		New Delhi	23 Nov
61:04		James	Rungaru	KEN	14.1.93	2		Boulogne-Billancourt	16 Nov
61:07	43:08	Nuguse	Hirsuato	ETH	13.2.82	5		Valencia	19 Oct
61:08		Stephen	Sambu	KEN	3.7.88	3		New York	16 Mar
61:08		Berhanu	Girma	ETH	22.11.86	4		Lille	6 Sep
61:09		Eliud Macharia	Mwangi	KEN	.89	5		Lille	6 Sep
61:10	42:53	Joseph	Kiptum	KEN	25.9.87	7		Ostia	2 Mar
61:10	43:08	Elroy	Gelant	RSA	25.8.86	13	WCh	København	29 Mar
61:10		John (90)	Cheruiyot	KEN	5.7.90	6		Lille	6 Sep
61:11		Hillary	Kipchumba	KEN	25.11.92	2		Verbania	9 Mar
61:12	43:06	Bonse	Dida	ETH-J	21.1.95	14	WCh	København	29 Mar
61:13	57:57	Edwin	Kiptoo	KEN	.93	7		Valencia	19 Oct
61:16	43:08	Lusapho	April	RSA	24.5.82	15	WCh	København	29 Mar
61:16		John	Mwangi	KEN	.85	1		Szczecin	31 Aug
61:17		Masato	Kikuchi	JPN	18.9.90	2		Yamaguchi	16 Feb
61:17		David	Kosgei	KEN	.85	3		Breda	5 Oct
61:18		Sota	Hoshi	JPN	6.1.88	3		Yamaguchi	16 Feb
61:18		Robert	Kwambai	KEN	22.11.85	6		Paris	2 Mar
61:18		James (100)	Emuria	KEN	.81	2		Szczecin	31 Aug

Mark	Wind	Name		Nat	Born	Date
61:19		Laban	Mutai	KEN	.85	16 Feb
61:21	42:53	Eric	Ndiema	KEN	28.12.92	2 Mar
61:21		Teshome	Mekonen	ETH-J	15.6.95	24 May
61:22	43:05	Polat Kemboi Arikan		TUR	12.12.90	29 Mar
61:22		Ayad	Lamdassem	ESP	11.10.81	29 Mar
61:22		Charles	Ogari	KEN	.92	13 Apr
61:22	43:02	Philip Sanga Langat		KEN	23.4.90	5 Oct
61:23		Meb	Keflezighi	USA	5.5.75	19 Jan
61:23		Stephen	Ogari	KEN	.92	13 Apr
61:26	43:00	Million	Feyisa	ETH	.88	5 Apr
61:26		Geoffrey	Bundi	KEN	.87	21 Sep
61:27		Abraham	Kasongor	KEN	.93	22 Mar
61:30		Richard	Kiprotich	KEN	11.5.84	26 Jan
61:30		Fikre	Assefa	ETH	18.1.89	29 Mar
61:31		El Hassan	Ben Lkhainouch	FRA	1.6.81	29 Mar
61:31		Kennedy	Kipyego	KEN	.91	27 Apr
61:32		Jacob	Wanjuki	KEN	16.1.86	16 Feb
61:32		Stephen	Chemlany	KEN	9.8.82	5 Oct
61:33		Hicham	Laqouahi	MAR	13.6.89	26 Jan
61:33		Josphat	Boit	USA	26.11.83	29 Mar
61:33		Nigussie	Sahlesilassie	ETH-J	.95	6 Sep
61:34		Salaheddine Bounasser		MAR	27.9.90	26 Jan
61:34A		Tebalu	Zawude	ETH	2.11.87	23 Feb
61:34		Isaac	Birir	KEN	.79	27 Apr
61:34		Mark	Kiptoo	KEN	21.6.76	5 Oct
61:34		Yihunilign	Adane	ETH-J	29.2.96	16 Nov
61:35A		Fentahun	Hunegnaw	ETH		23 Feb
61:35	dh	Stephen	Kiprotich	UGA	27.2.89	7 Sep
61:36		Daniel Kiprop Limo		KEN	10.12.83	27 Apr
61:36		Lawi	Kiptui	KEN	.93	27 Apr
61:36		Asefa	Mengistu	ETH-J	19.1.95	19 Oct
61:36		Isaac	Langat	KEN	18.12.94	19 Nov
61:37+		Abera	Chane	ETH	10.5.95	24 Jan
61:37		Yuki	Yagi	JPN	17.9.89	16 Feb
61:37		Dawit	Weldesilasie	ERI	10.12.94	19 Oct
61:38		Aaron	Braun	USA	28.5.87	19 Jan
61:38+		Shumi	Dechasa	BRN	28.5.89	24 Jan
61:38+		Markos	Geneti	ETH	30.5.84	24 Jan
61:38+		Edwin	Kipyego	KEN	16.11.90	24 Jan
61:38		John	Kipkoech	KEN	29.12.91	30 Mar
61:39		Franklin	Chepkwony	KEN	15.6.84	19 Jan
61:39+		Tsegaye	Mekonnen	ETH-J	15.6.95	24 Jan
61:39+		Jonathan	Maina	KEN	24.12.90	24 Jan
61:39+		Sisay	Lemma	ETH	12.12.90	24 Jan
61:39+		Abere	Kassaw	ETH	8.12.94	24 Jan
61:39+		Abrha	Milaw	ETH	3.1.88	24 Jan
61:39+		Tamirat	Tola	ETH	11.8.91	24 Jan
61:39+		Atsedu	Tsegay	ETH	17.12.91	24 Jan
61:39		Hirohito	Inoue	JPN	6.1.93	2 Feb
61:39	dh	Tariku	Bekele	ETH	21.1.87	7 Sep
61:39		Joel	Kimutai	KEN	5.10.??	19 Oct
61:40		Isaac	Korir	KEN	26.8.90	29 Mar
61:41		Charles	Maina	KEN	11.10.82	29 Jun
61:42		Daniel	Salel	KEN	11.12.90	2 Mar
61:42		Eliud	Barngetuny	KEN	.87	20 Apr
61:42	43:10	Dennis	Kimetto	KEN	22.1.84	21 Jun
61:43	43:08	Abayneh	Ayele	ETH	4.11.87	18 May
61:43		Vincent	Rono	KEN	22.12.90	19 Oct
61:44		Tyler	Pennel	USA	21.12.87	19 Jan
61:44		Daniel	Kitonyi	KEN	12.1.94	2 Feb
61:44		Silas	Ngetich	KEN	.88	14 Sep
61:45+		Wilfred	Kirwa	KEN	21.1.86	28 Sep
61:45		Jackson	Limo	KEN	.88	2 Mar
61:45		Daniel	Rotich	KEN	1.1.92	14 Jun
61:45+		Bernard	Kitur	KEN	.90	28 Sep
61:45A		Nicholas	Kipkemboi	KEN	.82	30 Nov
61:46		Juan Luis	Barrios	MEX	24.6.83	16 Mar
61:46		Alemu	Bekele	BRN	23.3.90	29 Mar
61:46+		Emmanuel	Mutai	KEN	12.10.84	28 Sep
61:47		Matt	Llano	USA	1.8.88	19 Jan
61:47		Ibrahim	Jeylan	ETH	12.6.89	14 Feb
61:47		Kenji	Yamamoto	JPN	17.11.89	16 Feb
61:47		Teklemariam Medhin		ERI	24.6.89	16 Mar
61:47		Ascealew	Meketa	ETH	.92	16 Mar
61:47	43:09	Festus	Talam	KEN		14 Sep
61:48		Luke	Puskedra	USA	8.2.90	19 Jan
61:48+		Eliud	Kiptanui	KEN	6.6.89	28 Sep
61:50		Fikadu	Haftu	ETH	21.2.94	20 Apr
61:51		Leonard	Korir	KEN	10.12.86	12 Oct
61:52+		Chala	Sufa	ETH		24 Jan
61:52		Nicholas	Togom	KEN	17.2.92	30 Mar
61:53		Nelson	Oyugi	KEN	.93	3 May
61:54		Abderrahim	El Asri	MAR	10.7.82	26 Jan
61:55		Alem	Anyew	ETH		26 Jan
61:55		Takuya	Fukatsu	JPN	10.11.87	16 Feb
61:55		Moses	Bowen	KEN	.91	30 Mar
61:55		Gladwin	Mzazi	RSA	28.8.88	5 Apr
61:55	43:05	Abraham	Kiplimo	UGA	14.4.89	18 May
61:56		Shadrack	Biwott	USA	19.2.85	19 Mar
61:56		Patrick	Mwaka	KEN	2.11.92	18 May
61:56		Wilfred	Kigen	KEN	21.1.86	21 Jun
61:56+		Levy	Matebo	KEN	3.11.89	28 Sep
61:56		Charles	Cheruiyot	KEN	4.8.88	5 Oct
61:57		Daniele	Meucci	ITA	7.10.85	29 Mar
61:57		Shogo	Nakamura	JPN	16.9.92	29 Mar
61:57		Peter	Matelong	KEN	26.11.89	30 Mar
61:57		Lucas	Rotich	KEN	16.4.90	30 Mar
61:58		Kenta	Murozuka	JPN	12.2.86	16 Feb
61:59		Solomon (199)	Yego	KEN	.87	25 May

Excessively downhill

Mark	Wind	Name		Nat	Born	Pos	Meet	Venue	Date
60:12		Solomon	Deksisa	ETH	11.3.94	1		San Diego (86.5m)	1 Jun
60:28		Geoffrey	Bundi	KEN	.87	2		San Diego	1 Jun
60:39		Dickson	Chumba	KEN	27.10.86	3		San Diego	1 Jun

Mark Wind	Name		Nat	Born	Pos	Meet	Venue	Date
61:03A	Josphat	Kiprop	KEN	16.11.93	1		Kabarnet	1 Nov
61:11	Tilahun	Regassa	ETH	18.1.90	5		San Diego	1 Jun

Also at San Diego: 6. Shadrack Biwott USA 19.2.85 61:25, 8. Kevin Kochei KEN 2.12.89 61:39, 9. Gabe Proctor USA 29.4.90 61:40

Short by 97m: Jan 5, Keren (1390mA): ERI HMar Champs: 1, S Tsegay 59:42; 2, G Ghebresilassie 60:01; 3, N Tesfaldet 60:18; 4, S Gebreyohannes 61:02; 5, Esayas Habtemichael 61:05; 6, Goitom Kifle 61:08; 7,Tsegay Tuemay 61:14; 8, Yohannes Ghebremichael 61:17. Short?: Dieudonné Disi RWA 24.11.80 1 Brazzaville 14 Aug

Drugs disqualification and probably short course

Mark	Name		Nat	Born	Pos	Meet	Venue	Date
61:02	Abraham	Kiprotich ¶	FRA	17.8.85	(1)		Brazzaville	14 Aug

JUNIORS

See main list for top 2 juniors. 9 performances by 5 men to 62:10. Additional marks and further juniors:

Ghebreslassie 60:36 1 Göteborg 18 May 61:37 10 Yangzhou 20 Apr

Dida 61:47A 3 NC Addis Ababa 23 Feb

Mark	Name		Nat	Born	Pos	Meet	Venue	Date
61:21	Teshome	Mekonen	ETH	15.6.95	1		Karlovy Vary	24 May
61:33	Nigussie	Sahlesilassie	ETH	.95	7		Lille	6 Sep
61:34	Yihunilign	Adane	ETH	29.2.96	3		Boulogne-Billancourt	16 Nov
61:36	Asefa	Mengistu	ETH	19.1.95	9		Valencia	19 Oct
61:39+	Tsegaye	Mekonnen	ETH	15.6.95		in Mar	Dubai	24 Jan
62:02	Ayana	Tsedat	ETH	18.2.96	4		Verbania	9 Mar
62:31	Hazuma	Hattori	JPN	7.2.95	5		Ageo	16 Nov
63:05	Elvis	Kipkoech (10)	KEN	20.10.95	2		Cremona	19 Oct
63:22	Samuel	Rutto	KEN	.95	2		Tarsus	16 Mar
62:12dh	Berhane	Afewerki	ETH	6.5.96	10		San Diego	1 Jun

25 – 30 KILOMETRES ROAD

25k	30k	Name		Nat	Born	Pos	Meet	Venue	Date
1:11:47		Abreham	Cheroben	KEN	10.11.92	1		Berlin	4 May
1:12:32		Kenneth	Kipkemoi	KEN	2.8.84	2		Berlin	4 May
1:13:08	1:27:36+	Wilfred	Kirwa	KEN	21.1.86		in Mar	Berlin	28 Sep
1:13:08	1:27:37+	Geoffrey	Ronoh	KEN	29.11.82		in Mar	Berlin	28 Sep
1:13:09		Tebalu	Zawude	ETH	2.11.87	3		Berlin	4 May
1:13:11		Richard	Kiprotich	KEN	.85	4		Berlin	4 May
	1:28:15	Shumi	Dechasa	BRN	28.5.89		in Mar	Dubai	24 Jan
	1:28:15	Edwin	Koech	KEN	.87		in Mar	Dubai	24 Jan
	1:28:30	Atsedu	Tsegay	ETH	17.12.91		in Mar	Dubai	24 Jan
1:13:39	1:29:18	Eliud	Kiptanui	KEN	6.6.89		in Mar	Berlin	28 Sep
1:13:42	1:28:46	Ghirmay	Gebrselassie	ERI-J	14.11.95		in Mar	Chicago	12 Oct
1:13:42	1:28:47	Bernard	Koech	KEN	31.1.88		in Mar	Chicago	12 Oct
1:13:42	1:28:48	Geoffrey	Kirui	KEN	16.2.93		in Mar	Chicago	12 Oct
1:13:43	1:28:47	Tadesse	Tola	ETH	31.10.87		in Mar	Chicago	12 Oct
1:13:43	1:28:46	Lani	Rutto	KEN			in Mar	Chicago	12 Oct
1:13:44	1:28:49	Feyisa	Lilesa	ETH	1.2.90		in Mar	Chicago	12 Oct
1:13:55	1:28:51	Gideon	Kipketer	KEN	10.11.92		in Mar	Paris	6 Apr
1:13:54	1:28:52	Yuma	Hattori	JPN	13.11.93	1		Kumamoto	16 Feb
1:14:11	1:28:56	Bernard	Kipyego	KEN	16.7.86		in Mar	Rotterdam	13 Apr
1:14:11	1:29:04	Deribe	Robi	ETH	26.9.84		in Mar	Rotterdam	13 Apr
1:13:56	1:29:18	Levi	Matebo	KEN	3.11.89		in Mar	Berlin	28 Sep
1:13:58	1:29:01	Tsegaye	Mekonnen	ETH-J	15.6.95		in Mar	London	13 Apr
1:13:55	1:29:08	Jackson	Limo	KEN	88		in Mar	Paris	6 Apr
1:14:15	1:29:15	Richard	Mengich	KEN	3.4.89		in Mar	Frankfurt	26 Oct
1:14:16	1:29:15	Vincent	Kipruto	KEN	13.9.87		in Mar	Frankfurt	26 Oct
1:14:16	1:29:16	Solomon	Deksisa	ETH	11.3.94		in Mar	Frankfurt	26 Oct
1:14:17	1:29:16	Vincent	Chepkok	KEN	5.7.88		in Mar	Frankfurt	26 Oct
1:14:17	1:29:16	Allan	Kiprono	KEN	15.2.90		in Mar	Frankfurt	26 Oct
1:14:13	1:29:55	Jonathan	Maina	KEN	24.12.90	2		Kumamoto	16 Feb
1:13:08	(1:32:15)+	Bernard	Kitur	KEN	.90		in Mar	Berlin	28 Sep
1:13:54	(1:30:11)	Shogo	Nakamura	JPN	16.9.92	2		Kumamoto	16 Feb
1:14:06		Mark	Korir	KEN	10.1.85	5		Berlin	4 May
1:14:08		Samson	Gebreyohanes	ERI	7.2.92	1	US Ch	Grand Rapids	10 May

MARATHON

Mark	25k	30k	Name		Nat	Born	Pos	Venue	Date
2:02:57	1:13:08	1:27:38	Dennis	Kimetto	KEN	22.1.84	1	Berlin	28 Sep
2:03:13	1:13:08	1:27:37	Emmanuel	Mutai	KEN	12.10.84	2	Berlin	28 Sep
2:04:11	1:13:42	1:28:46	Eliud	Kipchoge	KEN	5.11.84	1	Chicago	12 Oct
2:04:28	1:13:42	1:28:46	Sammy	Kitwara	KEN	26.11.86	2	Chicago	12 Oct
2:04:29	1:13:59	1:29:02	Wilson	Kipsang	KEN	15.3.82	1	London	13 Apr
2:04:32		1:28:15	Tsegaye	Mekonnen	ETH-J	15.6.95	1	Dubai	24 Jan
2:04:32	1:13:43	1:28:49	Dickson	Chumba	KEN	27.10.86	3	Chicago	12 Oct
2:04:55	1:14:00	1:29:02	Stanley	Biwott	KEN	21.4.86	2	London	13 Apr
2:05:00	1:14:11	1:28:56		Kipchoge			1	Rotterdam	13 Apr
2:05:04	1:13:55	1:28:40	Kenenisa	Bekele	ETH	13.6.82	1	Paris	6 Apr

Mark	Wind		Name		Nat	Born	Pos Meet	Venue	Date
2:05:13		1:28:15	Markos	Geneti (10)	ETH	30.5.84	2	Dubai	24 Jan
2:05:41		1:28:48	Getu	Feleke	ETH	28.11.86	1	Wien	13 Apr
2:05:42	1:15:15	1:30:11		Chumba			1	Tokyo	23 Feb
2:05:49		1:28:16	Berhanu	Girma	ETH	22.11.86	3	Dubai	24 Jan
2:05:51	1:13:43	1:28:47		Bekele			4	Chicago	12 Oct
2:05:56	1:13:08	1:27:38	Abera	Kuma	ETH	31.8.90	3	Berlin	28 Sep
2:05:57			Tadesse	Tola	ETH	31.10.87	2	Tokyo	23 Feb
2:06:08	1:14:11	1:28:56	Bernard	Koech	KEN	31.1.88	2	Rotterdam	13 Apr
2:06:17		1:28:16	Tamirat	Tola	ETH	11.8.91	4	Dubai	24 Jan
2:06:17			Yakob	Jarso	ETH	5.2.88	1	Seoul	16 Mar
2:06:21	1:14:25	1:29:23	Tilahun	Regassa	ETH	18.1.90	1	Eindhoven	12 Oct
2:06:22		1:29:51	Bernard	Kipyego	KEN	16.7.86	1	Amsterdam	19 Oct
2:06:24			Stephen	Chemlany (20)	KEN	9.8.82	2	Seoul	16 Mar
2:06:30				Kitwara			3	Tokyo	23 Feb
2:06:30	1:13:58	1:29:01	Tsegaye	Kebede	ETH	15.1.87	3	London	13 Apr
2:06:31	1:14:00	1:29:02	Ayele	Abshero	ETH	28.12.90	4	London	13 Apr
2:06:39	1:13:08	1:27:37	Geoffrey	Kamworor	KEN	28.11.92	4	Berlin	28 Sep
2:06:43			Shumi	Dechasa	BRN	28.5.89	1	Hamburg	4 May
2:06:44			Gilbert	Kirwa	KEN	20.12.85	3	Seoul	16 Mar
2:06:47	1:14:25	1:29:23	Jonathan	Maiyo	KEN	5.5.88	2	Eindhoven	12 Oct
2:06:49	1:13:55	1:28:50	Limenih	Getachew	ETH	30.4.90	2	Paris	6 Apr
2:06:49	1:14:17	1:29:15	Mark	Kiptoo	KEN	21.6.76	1	Frankfurt	26 Oct
2:06:51			Yemane Tsegay	Adhane	ETH	8.4.85	1	Daegu	6 Apr
2:06:54	1:14:08	1:29:21		Adhane			1	Ottawa	25 May
2:06:55		1:29:25		Tad. Tola			1	Warszawa	13 Apr
2:06:58			Michael	Kipyego (30)	KEN	2.10.83	4	Tokyo	23 Feb
2:06:59	1:14:17	1:29:15	Mike	Kigen	KEN	15.1.86	2	Frankfurt	26 Oct
			(37/31)						
2:07:00			Eric	Ndiema	KEN	28.12.92	2	Hamburg	4 May
2:07:02			Tariku	Jufar	ETH	18.7.84	4	Seoul	16 Mar
2:07:05			Peter	Some	KEN	5.6.90	5	Tokyo	23 Feb
2:07:06			Gebretsadik	Adhana	ETH	16.7.92	2	Daegu	6 Apr
2:07:07			Philemon	Rono	KEN	8.2.91	3	Hamburg	4 May
2:07:08			Abreham	Cherkos	ETH	23.9.89	5	Seoul	16 Mar
2:07:08	1:14:16	1:29:15	Gilbert Yegon	Koech	KEN	.81	3	Frankfurt	26 Oct
2:07:10			Belay	Asefa	ETH	17.6.92	4	Hamburg	4 May
2:07:10	1:14:17	1:29:15	Tebalu	Zawude	ETH	2.11.87	4	Frankfurt	26 Oct
			(40)						
2:07:11	1:14:24	1:29:22	Alfers	Lagat	KEN	7.8.86	3	Eindhoven	12 Oct
2:07:11			Nixson	Kurgat	KEN	7.11.87	1	Chunchon	26 Oct
2:07:12		1:28:16	Azmeraw	Bekele	ETH	22.1.86	5	Dubai	24 Jan
2:07:15			Silas	Cheboit	KEN	.92	1	Gyeongju	19 Oct
2:07:16	1:14:16	1:29:06?	Deribe	Robi	ETH	26.9.84	5	Frankfurt	26 Oct
2:07:18		1:29:51	Lucas	Rotich	KEN	16.4.90	2	Amsterdam	19 Oct
2:07:28		1:29:18	Eliud	Kiptanui	KEN	6.6.89	5	Berlin	28 Sep
2:07:28		1:29:51	John	Mwangangi	KEN	1.11.90	3	Amsterdam	19 Oct
2:07:29	1:14:15	1:29:14	Ronald	Korir	KEN	.91	6	Frankfurt	26 Oct
2:07:32		1:30:04	Bazu	Worku	ETH	15.9.90	1	Houston	19 Jan
			(50)						
2:07:35	1:13:08	1:27:39	Franklin	Chepkwony	KEN	15.6.84	6	Berlin	28 Sep
2:07:38			James	Kwambai	KEN	28.2.83	6	Seoul	16 Mar
2:07:40			Deressa	Chimsa	ETH	21.11.86	7	Tokyo	23 Feb
2:07:43			Elijah	Kemboi	KEN	10.9.84	4	Daegu	6 Apr
2:07:43			Feyisa	Bekele	ETH	4.8.83	1	Seoul	9 Nov
2:07:46		1:29:08	Abrha	Milaw	ETH	3.1.88	7	Dubai	24 Jan
2:07:46			Evans Kiplagat	Chebet	KEN	5.3.88	2	Seoul	9 Nov
2:07:52			Thomas	Kiplagat	KEN		3	Seoul	9 Nov
2:07:53			Jacob	Kendagor	KEN	19.9.84	5	Daegu	6 Apr
2:07:53			Joel	Kimurer Kemboi	KEN	21.1.88	2	Gyeongju	19 Oct
			(60)						
2:07:54		1:30:04	Negari	Terfa	ETH	12.6.83	2	Houston	19 Jan
2:07:54		1:29:51	Essa Ismail	Rashed	QAT	14.12.86	4	Amsterdam	19 Oct
2:08:02			Lukas	Kanda	KEN	.87	3	Paris	6 Apr
2:08:03			Laban	Mutai	KEN	.85	1	Linz	6 Apr
2:08:04			Laban	Korir	KEN	30.12.85	5	Hamburg	4 May
2:08:05	1:14:25	1:29:23	Sammy	Kigen	KEN	29.9.85	4	Eindhoven	12 Oct
2:08:05			Felix	Kiprotich	KEN	.88	1	Rennes	26 Oct
2:08:06			Mariko	Kiplagat	KEN	10.1.82	1	Xiamen	2 Jan
2:08:07			Patrick	Terer	KEN	6.7.89	1	Praha	11 May
2:08:09			Kohei	Matsumura	JPN	25.11.86	8	Tokyo	23 Feb
			(70)						

Mark	Wind		Name		Nat	Born	Pos	Meet	Venue	Date
2:08:09		1:29:45	Levi	Matebo	KEN	3.11.89	2		Warszawa	13 Apr
2:08:17			Dereje	Tesfaye	ETH	30.9.85	3		Gyeongju	19 Oct
2:08:18		1:28:16	Abere	Kassaw	ETH	8.12.94	8		Dubai	24 Jan
2:08:18	1:13:59	1:29:02	Geoffrey	Mutai	KEN	7.10.81	6		London	13 Apr
2:08:18			Mulugeta	Wami	ETH	12.7.82	2		Ottawa	25 May
2:08:18	1:14:16	1:29:15	Daniel	Wanjiru	KEN	26.5.92	7		Frankfurt	26 Oct
2:08:21			Mohamed	Farah	GBR	23.3.83	8		London	13 Apr
2:08:21			Samuel	Ndungu	KEN	4.4.88	1		Lisboa	5 Oct
2:08:22			Patrick	Makau	KEN	2.3.85	1		Fukuoka	7 Dec
2:08:25			Ishmael (80)	Busendich	KEN	7.7.91	1		Ljubljana	26 Oct
2:08:26			Feyisa	Lilesa	ETH	1.2.90	9		London	13 Apr
2:08:26			Gilbert	Chepkwony	KEN	.85	1		Kosice	5 Oct
2:08:27			Berraki	Beyene	ERI	6.2.80	2		Hengshui	20 Sep
2:08:28		1:29:08	Alfred	Kering	KEN	.80	2		Wien	13 Apr
2:08:31	1:14:16	1:29:16	Adugna	Tekele	ETH	26.2.89	8		Frankfurt	26 Oct
2:08:32			Endeshaw	Negesse	ETH	13.3.88	2		Düsseldorf	27 Apr
2:08:32			Sergey	Lebid	UKR	15.7.75	4		Seoul	9 Nov
2:08:33			Cosmas	Lagat	KEN-J	.95	1		Sevilla	23 Feb
2:08:37			Elijah	Keitany	KEN	18.10.83	2		Ljubljana	26 Oct
2:08:41			Abdullah Dawit (90)	Shami	ETH	16.7.84	3		Toronto	19 Oct
2:08:43			Stephen	Mokoka	RSA	31.1.85	1		Shanghai	2 Nov
2:08:48			Robert	Kwambai	KEN	22.11.85	4		Paris	6 Apr
2:08:48			Luka	Rotich	KEN	7.8.88	5		Seoul	9 Nov
2:08:48			Raji	Assefa	ETH	18.2.86	2		Fukuoka	7 Dec
2:08:50			Serod	Bat-Ochir	MGL	7.10.81	3		Fukuoka	7 Dec
2:08:51			Koji	Kobayashi	JPN	16.1.89	9		Tokyo	23 Feb
2:08:53			Francis	Kiprop	KEN	4.6.82	1		Milano	6 Apr
2:08:55			José Antonio	Uribe	MEX	3.1.86	3		Houston	19 Jan
2:08:55			Henryk	Szost	POL	20.1.82	3	NC	Warszawa	13 Apr
2:08:58			Philip Sanga (100)	Kimutai	KEN	10.9.83	3		Wien	13 Apr

Mark	Name		Nat	Born	Date
2:09:00	Julius	Chepkwony	KEN	.88	6 Apr
2:09:04	Abel	Kirui	KEN	4.6.82	23 Feb
2:09:04	Felix	Keny	KEN	25.12.85	4 May
2:09:04	Edwin	Koech	KEN	.87	26 Oct
2:09:05	Charles	Cheruiyot	KEN	4.6.88	13 Apr
2:09:06	Jackson	Limo	KEN	.88	6 Apr
2:09:06	Dominic	Ondoro	KEN	.88	21 Jun
2:09:06	Masakazu	Fujiwara	JPN	6.3.81	7 Dec
2:09:07	Daniel	Rono	KEN	13.7.78	26 Jan
2:09:07	Hirokatsu	Kurosaki	JPN	8.8.85	23 Feb
2:09:08	Ghirmay	Gebrselassie	ERI-J	14.11.95	12 Oct
2:09:10	Masanori	Sakai	JPN	30.6.86	23 Feb
2:09:10	Samuel Kiplimo Kosgei		KEN	20.1.86	16 Nov
2:09:14	Weldu	Negash	ETH	12.11.86	13 Apr
2:09:14	Silah	Limo	KEN	.92	6 Jul
2:09:15	Ezekiel	Chebii	KEN	3.1.91	27 Apr
2:09:17	Duncan	Koech	KEN	28.12.81	13 Apr
2:09:17	Wesley	Korir	KEN	15.11.82	25 May
2:09:23	Abraham	Kiplimo	UGA	14.4.89	2 Feb
2:09:25	William	Chebor	KEN	22.12.82	6 Apr
2:09:25	Laban	Kipkemboi	KEN	30.12.77	19 Oct
2:09:27	Shume	Hailu	ETH	27.10.87	9 Nov
2:09:28	Julius	Muriuki	KEN	3.7.85	2 Jan
2:09:29	Suehiro	Ishikawa	JPN	27.9.79	23 Feb
2:09:29	Mutai	Kipkemei	KEN	.86	20 Sep
2:09:30	Masato	Imai	JPN	2.4.84	2 Feb
2:09:32	Arne	Gabius	GER	22.3.81	26 Oct
2:09:33	Evans	Ruto	KEN	14.1.84	19 Jan
2:09:34	Fikadu	Girma	ETH	.93	27 Apr
2:09:35	Dereje	Debele	ETH	26.7.86	2 Jan
2:09:35	Cyrus	Njui	KEN	11.2.86	23 Feb
2:09:35	Megersa	Bacha	ETH	18.1.85	13 Apr
2:09:36	Dominic	Kimwetich	KEN	20.7.89	6 Apr
2:09:36	Yuki	Kawauchi	JPN	5.3.87	4 May
2:09:38	Allan	Kiprono	KEN	15.2.90	26 Oct
2:09:45	Lawrence	Kimaiyo	KEN	2.9.90	19 Jan
2:09:46	Kipkemoi	Kipsang	KEN	.90	6 Apr
2:09:47	Satoru	Sasaki	JPN	16.10.85	2 Mar
2:09:50	Belachew	Alemayehu	ETH	.85	24 Jan
2:09:52	Edeo	Mamo	ETH	.90	13 Apr
2:09:52	Cuthbert	Nyasango	ZIM	17.9.82	11 May
2:09:53	Vitaliy	Shafar	UKR	27.1.82	19 Oct
2:09:54	Vincent	Kipruto	KEN	13.9.87	2 Mar
2:09:55	Asbel	Kipsang	KEN	10.9.93	30 Nov
2:09:57	Cosmas	Kyeva	KEN	25.6.85	6 Apr
2:09:58	Philemon	Baaru	KEN	20.5.81	19 Jan
2:09:58	Megersa	Gosa	ETH	.82	26 Jan
2:09:59	Victor	Kipchirchir	KEN	5.12.87	28 Sep
2:09:59	Tomoya	Adachi	JPN	18.12.85	7 Dec
2:10:00	Ghebrezghiabhuer Kibrom		ERI	.87	20 Sep
2:10:00	Samuel	Rutto	KEN-J	.95	16 Nov
2:10:01	Ernest	Ngeno	KEN-J	20.5.95	16 Nov
2:10:03	Chiharu	Takada	JPN	9.7.81	7 Dec
2:10:05	Peter	Kamais	KEN	7.11.76	2 Jan
2:10:09	Daniel	Aschenik	ETH		9 Nov
2:10:09	Yared	Asmerom	ETH	2.2.80	7 Dec
2:10:13	Daniel	Kosgei	KEN	19.6.86	7 Dec
2:10:14	Yekeber	Bayabel	ETH	10.11.91	24 Jan
2:10:14	Shengo	Kebede	ETH		27 Apr
2:10:17	Augustine	Rono	KEN	.81	26 Oct
2:10:18	Samuel Kiptanui Maswai		KEN	29.3.88	28 Sep
2:10:19	Philemon	Rotich	KEN	.84	26 Oct
2:10:20	Birhanu	Addisie	ETH-J	.95	26 Oct
2:10:21	Benedict	Moeng	RSA	25.1.83	2 Jan
2:10:21	Mark	Korir	KEN	10.1.85	16 Mar
2:10:22	Abraraw	Misganaw	ETH	.90	24 Jan
2:10:22	Elijah	Sang	KEN	.83	27 Apr
2:10:22	William Kiprono Yegon		KEN	10.1.83	16 Nov
2:10:26	Anthony	Maritim	KEN	.86	14 Sep
2:10:26	Wilfred	Kirwa	KEN	21.1.86	26 Oct
2:10:28	Barnabas	Kiptum	KEN	.86	9 Nov
2:10:30	Hillary	Kipchumba	KEN	25.11.92	16 Nov
2:10:36	Ken-ichi	Shiraishi	JPN	6.4.82	2 Feb
2:10:36	Gideon	Kipketer	KEN	10.11.92	6 Apr
2:10:36	Moses	Masai	KEN	1.6.86	27 Apr
2:10:37	Felix	Kandie	KEN	.86	9 Nov
2:10:38	Edwin	Kemboi	KEN	.84	9 Nov
2:10:40	Hayle	Lemi	ETH	13.9.94	6 Apr
2:10:40	Albert	Matebor	KEN	20.12.80	13 Apr
2:10:40	Josphat	Kiprono	KEN	.88	14 Sep
2:10:41	Stephen	Tum	KEN	12.7.86	6 Apr
2:10:41	Yared	Shegumo	POL	11.1.83	13 Apr
2:10:41	Benjamin	Bitok	KEN	.82	26 Oct
2:10:42	Simon	Mukun	KEN	5.8.84	26 Jan
2:10:42	Dawit	Wolde	ETH	19.5.91	27 Apr
2:10:42	Lani	Rutto	KEN		12 Oct

Mark	Name		Nat	Born	Date
2:10:44	Oleksandr	Sitkovskiy	UKR	9.6.78	13 Apr
2:10:45	Getachew	Abayu	ETH		16 Mar
2:10:45	William	Kibor	KEN	10.1.85	21 Sep
2:10:47	Hassan	Mokaya	KEN		13 Apr
2:10:48	Milton	Rotich	KEN	.84	25 Ma
2:10:49	Hussan	Adelo	ETH	18.5.82	9 Nov
2:10:50	Tsuyoshi	Ugachi	JPN	27.4.87	7 Dec
2:10:51	Solomon	Molla	ETH	20.1.87	2 Jan
2:10:52	Khalid	Choukoud	NED	23.3.86	13 Apr
2:10:52	Jeff	Eggleston	USA	1.10.84	6 Jul
2:10:53	Gelgelo	Tona	ETH		13 Apr
2:10:54	Rachid	Kisri	MAR	1.3.75	25 Ma
2:10:54	Abebe	Degefa	ETH	20.5.84	19 Oct
2:10:54	Amanuel	Mesel	ERI	29.12.90	23 Nov
2:10:56	Stephen	Chebogut	KEN	.84	19 Jan
2:10:56	Marius	Kipserem	KEN	.88	25 Ma
2:10:57	Ryan	Vail	USA	19.3.86	13 Apr
2:10:57	Lazarus	Too	KEN	.88	26 Oct
2:10:58	Jonathan	Kiptoo	KEN	.75	28 Sep
2:10:59	Ryo	Yamamoto	JPN	18.5.84	13 Apr
2:10:59	Raymond	Kemboi	KEN	.86	26 Oct
	(207)				

Excessively downhill (Los Angeles 122.22m, Boston 136.29m)

Mark	Name		Nat	Born	Pos	Venue	Date
2:08:37	Mebrahtom	Keflezighi	USA	5.5.75	1	Boston	21 Apr
2:08:48	Wilson	Chebet	KEN	12.7.85	2	Boston	21 Apr
2:09:38	Vitaliy	Shafar	UKR	27.1.82			21 Apr
2:10:37	Gebo	Burka	ETH	27.9.87			9 Mar

JUNIORS

See main list for top 2 juniors. 10 performances by 6 men to 62:10. Additional marks and further juniors:

Mekonnen 2:08:06 5 London 13 Apr

Mark	Name		Nat	Born	Pos	Venue	Date
2:09:08	Ghirmay	Gebrselassie	ERI	14.11.95	6	Chicago	12 Oct
2:10:00	Samuel	Rutto	KEN	.95	1	Torino	16 Nov
2:10:01	Ernest	Ngeno	KEN	20.5.95	2	Torino	16 Nov
2:10:20	Birhanu	Addisie	ETH	.95	2	Rennes	26 Oct
2:12:33	Bonsa	Dida	ETH	21.1.95	10	Hamburg	4 May

100 KILOMETRES

Mark	Name		Nat	Born	Pos	Meet	Venue	Date
6:19:20	Steven	Way	GBR	6.7.74	1		Gravesend	6 May
6:27:43	Maxwell	King	USA	24.2.80	1	WCh	Doha	21 Nov
6:32:04	Jonas	Buud	SWE	28.3.74	2	WCh	Doha	21 Nov
6:37:01	José Antonio	Requejo	ESP	12.12.82	3	WCh	Doha	21 Nov
6:39:21	Hideo	Nojo	JPN	24.12.76	4	WCh	Doha	21 Nov
6:40:15		Nojo			1		Yubetsu	29 Jun
6:43:24	Yoshikazu	Hara	JPN	13.8.72	1		Shimanto	19 Oct
6:44:04	Zach	Bitter	USA	21.1.86	1		Madison	13 Apr
6:45:28	Koji	Hayasaka	JPN	5.12.83	2		Yubetsu	29 Jun
6:46:47	Yoshiki	Takada	JPN	18.7.83	5	WCh	Doha	21 Nov
6:47:43	Alberico	Di Cecco	ITA	19.4.74	1		Seregno	30 Mar
6:48:53		Bitter			6	WCh	Doha	21 Nov
6:49:56	Yu	Yasuda	JPN	28.12.84	3		Yubetsu	29 Jun

Mark	Name		Nat	Born	Date
6:50:38	Vasiliy	Larkin	RUS	19.8.91	21 Nov
6:51:30	Zach	Miller	USA	30.10.88	21 Nov
6:54:42	Wouter	Decock	BEL	23.9.83	28 Jun
6:55:31	Fritjof	Fagerlund	SWE	27.6.74	21 Nov
6:55:59	Yoshifumi	Kiyomoto	JPN	27.11.78	29 Jun
6:56:12	Paul	Giblin	GBR	30.10.69	21 Nov
6:56:26	Ryo	Mitsui	JPN	.85	19 Oct
6:56:41	Joseph	Binder	USA	16.8.83	13 Apr
6:56:45	Brendan	Davies	AUS	3.1.77	21 Nov
6:57:22	Paul	Martelletti	GBR	1.8.79	19 Jul
Indoors					
6:56:52	Vadim	Sharkov	RUS	20.7.87	15 Feb

24 HOURS

Mark		Name		Nat	Born	Pos	Meet	Venue	Date
285.366	t	Yoshikazu	Hara	JPN	13.8.72	1		Taipei	7 Dec
265.000	t	Barry	Loveday	GBR/AUS	5.10.77	1		Coburg	6 Apr
258.687		Toshiro	Naraki	JPN	10.8.76	1		Tokyo	9 Nov
255.499	t	Ivan	Cudin	ITA	15.2.75	2		Taipei	7 Dec
253.899	t	Florian	Reus	GER	2.3.84	3		Taipei	7 Dec
253.697	t	Vadim	Sharkov	RUS	20.7.87	1		Moskva	10 May
253.567		Pawel	Szynal	POL	20.11.73	1	NC	Katowice	28 Sep
252.271	t	Stéphane	Ruel	FRA	21.1.66	1		Barcelona	21 Dec
252.230		Yasuhisa	Oshima	JPN	23.4.76	2		Tokyo	9 Nov
250.466		Christian	Dilmi	FRA	15.6.66	1	NC	Portet-sur-Garonne	6 Apr

Mark	Name		Nat	Born	Date
248.784	Isaiah	Janzen	USA	9.5.86	24 Sep
248.784 t	John	Cash	USA	22.6.73	14 Dec
246.161 t	Anders	Tysk	SWE	1.8.72	14 Dec
246.128	Allain	David	FRA	18.12.65	14 Sep
245.975	Lajkó	Csaba	HUN	26.10.66	27 Apr
245.012 t	Ewan	Horsburgh	AUS	22.10.77	6 Apr

Indoors: 253.041t Elov Olsson SWE .89 1 Växjö 14 Dec

2000 METRES STEEPLECHASE

Mark	Name		Nat	Born	Pos	Meet	Venue	Date
5:26.85	Nikolay	Chavkin	RUS	24.4.84	1	Kuts	Moskva	17 Jul
5:27.06	Ildar	Minshin	RUS	5..2.85	2	Kuts	Moskva	17 Jul
5:31.56	Hailemariyam	Amare	ETH-Y	22.2.97	1		Poitiers	13 Sep

JUNIORS: 5:39.60 Hicham Chemlal MAR-Y 2.12.97 2h Yth Oly Nanjing 21 Aug

3000 METRES STEEPLECHASE

Mark	Name		Nat	Born	Pos	Meet	Venue	Date
7:58.41	Jairus	Birech	KEN	15.12.92	1	VD	Bruxelles	5 Sep
8:02.37		Birech			1	Bisl	Oslo	11 Jun
8:03.23	Mahiedine	Mekhissi-Benabbad	FRA	15.3.85	2	VD	Bruxelles	5 Sep
8:03.33		Birech			1	Herc	Monaco	18 Jul

Mark	Wind	Name		Nat	Born	Pos	Meet	Venue	Date
8:03.34			Birech			1	Athl	Lausanne	3 Jul
8:04.12		Ezekiel	Kemboi	KEN	25.5.82	1	DL	Doha	9 May
8:04.64		Brimin	Kipruto	KEN	31.7.85	2	DL	Doha	9 May
8:04.71		Evan	Jager	USA	8.3.89	3	VD	Bruxelles	5 Sep
8:05.47		Paul K.	Koech	KEN	10.11.81	3	DL	Doha	9 May
8:06.04			Koech			1	WCM	Beijing	21 May
8:06.20			Birech			1	GGala	Roma	5 Jun
8:06.55			Birech			2	WCM	Beijing	21 May
8:06.97			Jager			2	Bisl	Oslo	11 Jun
8:07.37			Birech			4	DL	Doha	9 May
8:07.45			Mekhissi-Benabbad			1		Sotteville-lès-Rouen	14 Jun
8:07.80			Birech			1	DL	Birmingham	24 Aug
8:09.07		Hillary	Yego	KEN	2.4.92	5	DL	Doha	9 May
8:09.81		Conseslus	Kipruto	KEN	8.12.94	2	Herc	Monaco	18 Jul
8:10.23			Yego			3	Herc	Monaco	18 Jul
8:10.44		Jonathan	Ndiku	KEN	18.9.91	1	CG	Glasgow	1 Aug
8:10.53			Koech			2	GGala	Roma	5 Jun
8:10.72			Ndiku			3	WCM	Beijing	21 May
8:10.93			Yego			3	Bisl	Oslo	11 Jun
8:11.39			B Kipruto			3	GGala	Roma	5 Jun
8:11.86		Gilbert	Kirui (10)	KEN	22.1.94	6	DL	Doha	9 May
8:11.93			C Kipruto			2	Athl	Lausanne	3 Jul
8:12.68			Birech			2	CG	Glasgow	1 Aug
8:12.81		Matt	Hughes	CAN	3.8.89	4	Herc	Monaco	18 Jul
8:12.95			Ndiku			3	Athl	Lausanne	3 Jul
8:13.18			Birech			1	C.Cup	Marrakech	14 Sep
		(30/11)							
8:14.33		Hamid	Ezzine	MAR	5.10.83	2		Sotteville-lès-Rouen	14 Jun
8:15.01		Bernard Mbugua	Nganga	KEN	17.1.85	5	Herc	Monaco	18 Jul
8:15.48		Brahim	Taleb	MAR	16.2.85	6	Bisl	Oslo	11 Jun
8:15.61		Dan	Huling	USA	16.7.83	4	VD	Bruxelles	5 Sep
8:15.83		Abel	Mutai	KEN	2.10.88	4	GGala	Roma	5 Jun
8:16.20		Krystian	Zalewski	POL	11.4.89	5	GGala	Roma	5 Jun
8:16.96		Clement	Kemboi	KEN	1.2.92	6	GGala	Roma	5 Jun
8:17.03		Barnabas	Kipyego	KEN-J	12.6.95	3	DL	Birmingham	24 Aug
8:17.27		Ali Abubaker	Kamal	QAT	8.11.83	3	C.Cup	Marrakech	14 Sep
		(20)							
8:17.40		Víctor	García	ESP	13.3.85	7	GGala	Roma	5 Jun
8:18.31		Sebastián	Martos	ESP	20.6.89	2		Huelva	12 Jun
8:19.00		Haron	Lagat	KEN	15.8.83	6	DL	Birmingham	24 Aug
8:19.59		Lawrence	Kemboi	KEN	15.6.93	1	Hanz	Zagreb	2 Sep
8:19.99		John	Koech	BRN-J	23.8.95	2	EAF	Bydgoszcz	2 Jun
8:20.04		Donn	Cabral	USA	12.12.89	3	NC	Sacramento	29 Jun
8:20.29		Ilgizar	Safiulin	RUS	9.12.92	7	VD	Bruxelles	5 Sep
8:20.84		Jacob	Araptany	UGA	11.2.92	1		Tokyo	11 May
8:20.87		Mitko	Tsenov	BUL	13.6.93	4		Huelva	12 Jun
8:20.92		Jaouad	Chemlal	MAR	11.4.94	11	GGala	Roma	5 Jun
		(30)							
8:21.78		Marvin	Blanco	VEN	15.6.88	5		Huelva	12 Jun
8:22.26		Hillary	Kemboi	KEN	.86	1		Bilbao	21 Jun
8:22.38		Mateusz	Demczyszak	POL	18.1.86	12	GGala	Roma	5 Jun
8:22.46A		Titus	Kibiego	KEN-J	3.5.96	1	NC-j	Nairobi	25 Jun
8:22.76		James	Wilkinson	GBR	13.7.90	6		Huelva	12 Jun
8:24.09		Craig	Forys	USA	13.7.89	5	Spitzen	Luzern	15 Jul
8:24.29		Martin	Grau	GER	26.3.92	2		Dessau	11 Jun
8:24.45		Nelson	Kipkosgei	KEN	9.3.93	3	EAF	Bydgoszcz	2 Jun
8:25.20		Hicham	Sigueni	MAR	30.1.93	2		Bilbao	21 Jun
8:25.38		Jamal	Chatbi	ITA	30.4.84	7		Huelva	12 Jun
		(40)							
8:25.45		Chala	Beyo	ETH		4	C.Cup	Marrakech	14 Sep
8:25.50		Yoann	Kowal	FRA	28.5.87	1	ET	Braunschweig	22 Jun
8:25.59		Nikolay	Chavkin	RUS	24.4.84	1	NC	Kazan	24 Jul
8:25.71		Andrew	Bayer	USA	3.2.90	6	Spitzen	Luzern	15 Jul
8:26.05		Benjamin	Kiplagat	UGA	4.3.89	3		Tokyo	11 May
8:26.08		Meresa	Kassaye	ETH-J	23.5.96	11	DL	Doha	9 May
8:26.19		Ivan	Lukyanov	RUS	31.1.81	2	NC	Kazan	24 Jul
8:26.30		Cory	Leslie	USA	24.10.89	4	NC	Sacramento	29 Jun
8:26.34		Yuri	Floriani	ITA	25.12.81	13	GGala	Roma	5 Jun
8:26.45		Tarik Langat	Akdag	TUR	16.6.88	5		Marrakech	8 Jun
		(50)							

Mark	Wind	Name		Nat	Born	Pos	Meet	Venue	Date
8:26.61		José Gregorio	Peña	VEN	12.1.87	4		Sotteville-lès-Rouen	14 Jun
8:26.79		Steffen	Uliczka	GER	17.7.84	7	Spitzen	Luzern	15 Jul
8:26.85		Birhan	Getahun	ETH	5.9.91	1		Montbéliard	6 Jun
8:27.00		Roberto	Alaiz	ESP	20.7.90	3		Padova	6 Jul
8:27.0A		Peter	Lagat	KEN	26.5.92	1		Nairobi	24 May
8:27.0A		Joash	Kiplimo	KEN	.91	4	NC	Nairobi	7 Jun
8:27.53		Abdelaziz	Merzougui	MAR	30.8.91	9		Huelva	12 Jun
8:27.81		Taylor	Milne	CAN	14.6.81	1		Guelph	31 May
8:28.03		Yuriy	Kloptsov	RUS	22.12.89	2		Adler	29 May
8:28.03		Lukasz	Parszczynski	POL	4.5.85	1		Joensuu	24 Jul
		(60)							
8:28.12		Patrick	Nasti	ITA	30.8.89	10		Huelva	12 Jun
8:28.17		Chris	Winter	CAN	22.7.86	9	Spitzen	Luzern	15 Jul
8:28.42		Billy	Nelson	USA	11.9.84	5		Tokyo	11 May
8:28.73		Andrey	Farnosov	RUS	9.7.80	3	NC	Kazan	24 Jul
8:28.83		Nicholas	Bett	KEN-J	20.12.96	3		Dessau	11 Jun
8:28.97		Tolossa	Nurgi	ETH	29.3.90	2		Montbéliard	6 Jun
8:29.08		Donnie	Cowart	USA	24.10.85	2		Joensuu	24 Jul
8:29.16		Ángel	Mullera	ESP	20.4.84	3	EC	Zürich	14 Aug
8:29.28A		Dominic	Kiptarus	KEN-J	3.8.96	3	NC-j	Nairobi	25 Jun
8:29.41		Abdelhakim	Zilali	FRA	20.6.83	5		Sotteville-lès-Rouen	14 Jun
		(70)							
8:29.48		Halil	Akkas	TUR	1.7.83	1		Fès	24 May
8:29.82		Vadym	Slobodenyuk	UKR	17.3.81	1	NC	Kirovohrad	25 Jul
8:29.89		Jukka	Keskisalo	FIN	27.3.81	3		Joensuu	24 Jul
8:29.97		Habtamu	Jaleta	ETH	19.4.93	3		Montbéliard	6 Jun
8:29.99		Romain	Collenot-Spriet	FRA	9.1.92	6		Sotteville-lès-Rouen	11 Jun
8:30.0A		Willy	Komen	KEN	22.12.87	1		Iten	31 May
8:30.0A		Abraham	Chirchir	KEN	1.8.80	5	NC	Nairobi	7 Jun
8:30.54		Anthony	Rotich	KEN	.93	2		Stanford	4 May
8:30.7A		Wilson	Maraba	KEN	2.12.86	6	NC	Nairobi	7 Jun
8:32.0A		Edwin	Kirwa	KEN	.80	7	NC	Nairobi	7 Jun
		(80)							
8:32.03		Hichem	Bouchicha	ALG	19.5.89	8		Marrakech	8 Jun
8:32.23		Abdelhamid	Zerrifi	ALG	20.6.86	7		Sotteville-lès-Rouen	14 Jun
8:32.61		Evans	Chematot	BRN-J	19.3.96	3	WJ	Eugene	27 Jul
8:32.66		Soufiane	El Bakkali	MAR-J	7.1.96	3		Fès	24 May
8:32.69		Ilya	Sukharyev	UKR	17.6.86	2	NC	Kirovohrad	25 Jul
8:32.82		Tomás	Tajadura	ESP	25.6.85	11		Huelva	12 Jun
8:32.92		Aric	Van Halen	USA	6.10.89	3	Jordan	Stanford	4 May
8:33.09		Janne	Ukonmaanaho	FIN	13.3.84	8	WCM	Beijing	21 May
8:33.40		Dejene	Regassa	BRN	18.4.89	9		Marrakech	8 Jun
8:33.53		Mounatcer	Zaghou	MAR	1.1.89	8	WCM	Beijing	21 May
		(90)							
8:33.79		De'Sean	Turner	USA	16.9.88	1		Bloomington	2 May
8:33.84		Aoi	Matsumoto	JPN	7.9.87	4		Joensuu	24 Jul
8:34.1A		Kennedy	Mureithi	KEN		9	NC	Nairobi	7 Jun
8:34.37		Mohammed	Boulama	MAR	31.12.93	6		Tokyo	11 May
8:34.37		Jun	Shinoto	JPN	2.4.85	1		Yamaguchi	11 Oct
8:34.64		James	Nipperess	AUS	21.5.90	7		Tokyo	11 May
8:34.71		Alexandre	Genest	CAN	30.6.86	3		Guelph	31 May
8:34.8A		Kennedy	Kosgei	KEN	.85	3h1	NC	Nairobi	7 Jun
8:35.0A		Silas	Too	KEN	.89	2		Iten	31 May
8:35.05		Tabor	Stevens	USA	21.6.91	1	NCAA-2	Allendale	23 May
		(100)							

Mark	First name	Name	Nat	Born	Date
8:35.2	Amor	Benyahia	TUN	1.7.85	24 Jun
8:35.27	Stanley	Kebenei	KEN	6.11.89	14 Jun
8:35.45	Luke	Gunn	GBR	22.3.85	15 May
8:35.66	Mustapha	Houdadi	MAR	5.8..86	24 May
8:35.66	Hakan	Duvar	TUR	21.8.90	19 Jul
8:35.67	Maksim	Yakushev	RUS	15.3.92	24 Jul
8:35.84	Bilal	Tabti	ALG	7.6.93	24 Jun
8:36.29	Boris	Zakharov	RUS	1.4.84	24 Jul
8:36.42	Artur	Burtsev	RUS	23.4.88	29 May
8:36.81	Fernando	Carro	ESP	1.4.92	6 Jul
8:37.1A	Silas	Kitum	KEN	25.5.90	24 May
8:37.26	Viktor	Bakharev	RUS	5.5.94	24 Jul
8:37.5A	Isaac	Yego	KEN	.89	24 May
8:37.54	Curtis	Carr	USA	24.5.89	18 Apr
8:37.6A	Hannington	Kirui	KEN-J	29.6.95	4 Apr
8:37.65	Ryan	Brockerville	CAN	29.7.89	15 May
8:38.15	Noam	Ne'eman	ISR	26.6.87	11 Jun
8:38.32	Ildar	Minshin	RUS	5.2.85	29 May
8:38.42	Hillary	Bor	KEN	22.11.89	15 May
8:38.59	Minato	Yamashita	JPN	15.11.88	11 Oct
8:38.68	Stephen	Lisgo	GBR	29.3.87	31 May
8:38.70	Tumisang	Monnatlala	RSA-J	31.1.95	4 Apr
8:38.74	Mason	Ferlic	USA	5.8.93	30 May
8:38.75	Ole	Hesselbjerg	DEN	23.4.90	14 Jun
8:38.75	Daniel	Lundgren	SWE	4.7.85	12 Jul
8:38.76	Hiroyoshi	Umegae	JPN	5.1.84	11 Oct
8:38.78	Radhouane	Majdoub	MAR	9.10.91	24 May
8:39.02	Mauricio	Valdivia	CHI	11.10.89	6 Jun
8:39.12	Mouname	Sassoui	MAR-J	20.3.95	24 May
8:39.27	Ibrahim	Ezzaydouny	MAR	28.4.91	18 Jun
8:39.32	Salim	Keddar	ALG	23.11.93	24 Jun
8:39.33	Diego	Tamayo	ESP	6.12.83	12 Jul
8:39.44	Benjamin	Bruce	USA	10.9.82	27 Jun
8:39.53	Kaur	Kivistik	EST	29.4.91	4 May
8:39.54	Tom Erling	Kårbø	NOR	4.2.89	31 May
8:39.54	Hironori	Tsuetaki	JPN	8.5.93	6 Jun

Mark	Wind	Name		Nat	Born	Pos	Meet	Venue	Date
8:39.62		Tareq MubarakTaher		BRN	24.3.84				29 Sep
8:39.83		Adrico (138)	Williams	RSA-J	.96				4 Apr

JUNIORS

See main list for top 8 juniors. 10 performances by 4 men to 8:26.10. Additional marks and further juniors:

B Kipyego	8:24.10A	2	NC-j	Nairobi	25 Jun	8:25.64	5	Hanz Zagreb	2 Sep
	8:25.57	1	WJ	Eugene	27 Jul				
Koech	8:22.55	2		Tokyo	11 May	8:23.33	4	Marrakech	8 Jun
	8:26.02	10	Athl	Lausanne	3 Jul				

Mark	Name		Nat	Born	Pos	Meet	Venue	Date
8:37.6A	Hannington	Kirui	KEN	29.6.95	1		Nairobi	4 Apr
8:38.70	Tumisang	Monnatlala (10)	RSA	31.1.95	1	NC-j	Stellenbosch	4 Apr
8:39.12	Mouname	Sassoui	MAR	20.3.95	7		Fès	24 May
8:39.83	Adrico	Williams	RSA	.96	2	NC-j	Stellenbosch	4 Apr
8:40.68	Molemo	Maqeba	RSA		3	NC-j	Stellenbosch	4 Apr
8:41.0A	Hicham	Chemlal	MAR-Y	2.12.97	5	NC	Rabat	22 Jun
8:41.41A	Edwin	Melly	KEN	10.8.96	4	NC-j	Nairobi	25 Jun
8:42.00	Hailemariyam	Amare	ETH-Y	22.2.97	5	WJ	Eugene	27 Jul
8:43.18	Yohanes	Chiappinelli	ITA-Y	18.8.97	6	WJ	Eugene	27 Jul
8:43.87	Ali	Messaoui	ALG	13.10.95	4	NC	Alger	24 Jun
8:45.66	Kazuya	Shiojiri	JPN	8.11.96	9	WJ	Eugene	27 Jul
8:47.04	Bailey	Roth (20)	USA	17.1.96	10	WJ	Eugene	27 Jul
8:47.20	Patrick	Kari	GER	3.5.96	6h1	WJ	Eugene	25 Jul
8:47.2A	Edwin	Kibet	KEN	7.7.96	3		Nairobi	4 Apr

60 METRES HURDLES INDOORS

Mark	Name		Nat	Born	Pos	Meet	Venue	Date
7.45	Pascal	Martinot-Lagarde	FRA	22.9.91	1		Mondeville	1 Feb
7.45	Omo	Osaghae	USA	18.5.88	1	WI	Sopot	9 Mar
7.46	Jeff	Porter	USA	27.11.85	2		Mondeville	1 Feb
7.46		Martinot-Lagarde			2	WI	Sopot	9 Mar
7.47	Garfield	Darien	FRA	22.12.87	3	WI	Sopot	9 Mar
7.49		Martinot-Lagarde			1h2		Mondeville	1 Feb
7.49		Martinot-Lagarde			1	NC	Bordeaux	22 Feb
7.50		Osaghae			1s1	WI	Sopot	9 Mar
7.50		Martinot-Lagarde			2s1	WI	Sopot	9 Mar
7.51	Dayron (10/5)	Robles	CUB	19.11.86	1		Praha (O2)	25 Feb
7.53	William	Sharman	GBR	12.9.84	3s1	WI	Sopot	9 Mar
7.53	Andy	Pozzi	GBR	15.5.92	4	WI	Sopot	9 Mar
7.54	Jarret	Eaton	USA	24.6.89	1		Karlsruhe	1 Feb
7.54	Erik	Balnuweit	GER	21.9.88	4s1	WI	Sopot	9 Mar
7.55	Sergey (10)	Shubenkov	RUS	4.10.90	1h2	Winter	Moskva	2 Feb
7.56	Konstantin	Shabanov	RUS	17.11.89	3	Winter	Moskva	2 Feb
7.56A	Dominic	Berger	USA	19.5.86	2	NC	Albuquerque	23 Feb
7.56A	Terrence	Trammell	USA	23.11.78	3	NC	Albuquerque	23 Feb
7.56	Gregor	Traber	GER	2.12.92	5	WI	Sopot	9 Mar
7.57A	Omar	McLeod	JAM	25.4.94	1h1	NCAA	Albuquerque	14 Mar
7.57A	Eddie	Lovett	ISV	25.6.92	1h2	NCAA	Albuquerque	14 Mar
7.58	Kevin	Craddock	USA	25.6.87	2		Karlsruhe	1 Feb
7.59	Andrew	Riley	JAM	6.9.88	4s2	WI	Sopot	9 Mar
7.60A	Aleec	Harris	USA	31.10.90	1		Albuquerque	15 Feb
7.60	Paolo (20)	Dal Molin	ITA	31.7.87	1	NC	Ancona	22 Feb
7.60A	Terence	Somerville	USA	5.11.89	5	NC	Albuquerque	23 Feb
7.60	Konstadínos	Douvalídis	GRE	10.3.87	2=		Praha (O2)	25 Feb
7.61	Ashton	Eaton	USA	21.1.88	1		Seattle	1 Feb
7.61	Dapo	Akinmoladun	USA	28.2.94	1	Big 10	Geneva	1 Mar
7.61A	Wayne	Davis II	TTO	22.8.91	3	NCAA	Albuquerque	15 Mar
7.62	Ladji	Doucouré	FRA	28.3.83	1h2		Karlsruhe	1 Feb
7.63	Dominik	Bochenek	POL	14.5.87	1		Spala	8 Feb
7.63A	Andrew	Brunson	USA	4.4.86	6	NC	Albuquerque	23 Feb
7.63	Balázs	Baji	HUN	9.6.89	3h4	WI	Sopot	8 Mar
7.64	Greggmar (30)	Swift	BAR	16.2.91	1		Bloomington	1 Feb
7.64	Martin	Mazác	CZE	6.5.90	1	NC	Praha (Strom)	15 Feb
7.65	Demoye	Bogle	USA	8.11.91	1		Columbus	10 Jan
7.65	Donovan	Robertson	USA	8.11.93	2	Big 10	Geneva	1 Mar
7.65A	Johnathan	Cabral	USA	31.12.92	4	NCAA	Albuquerque	15 Mar
7.66A	Brendan	Ames	USA	6.10.88	1		Air Force Academy	11 Jan
7.66	Rasul	Dabo	POR	14.2.89	2		Metz	28 Feb
7.67	Gregory	Sedoc	NED	16.10.81	1		Luxembourg (K)	1 Feb
7.67	Simon	Krauss	FRA	12.2.92	1		Reims	12 Feb

Mark	Wind	Name		Nat	Born	Pos	Meet	Venue	Date
7.67			Xie Wenjun	CHN	11.7.90	4h1	GP	Birmingham	15 Feb
7.67		Koen	Smet	NED	9.8.92	1	NC	Apeldoorn	23 Feb
		(40)							
7.67A		Milan	Ristic	SRB	8.8.91	4h1	NCAA	Albuquerque	14 Mar
7.68		Chris	Caldwell	USA	6.4.94	1	Tyson	Fayetteville	14 Feb
7.68A		Artie	Burns	USA-J	1.5.95	3		Albuquerque	15 Feb
7.69		Thomas	Martinot-Lagarde	FRA	7.2.88	1		Nantes	18 Jan
7.69		Dimitri	Bascou	FRA	20.7.87	1h1		Bordeaux	26 Jan
7.69		Damian	Warner	CAN	4.11.89	1		Geneva OH	15 Feb
7.69A		Ray	Stewart	USA	5.4.89	8	NC	Albuquerque	23 Feb
7.70		Jordan	Moore	USA	13.12.93	2	Tyson	Fayetteville	14 Feb
7.70		Aleksey	Dryomin	RUS	10.5.89	3	NC	Moskva	18 Feb
7.70		Maksim	Lynsha	BLR	6.4.85	1h2	NC	Mogilyov	22 Feb
		(50)							
7.71A		Héctor	Cotto	PUR	8.8.84	1		Flagstaff	8 Feb
7.72		Nick	Gayle	GBR	4.1.85	1A2		London (LV)	26 Jan
7.73		Kemar	Clarke	USA	20.5.88	1		Birmingham	30 Jan
7.73		Andy	Turner	GBR	19.9.80	3	Flanders	Gent	9 Feb
7.73		Aurel	Manga	FRA	24.7.92	1s2		Lyon	13 Feb
7.73		David	Oliver	USA	24.4.82	6h1	GP	Birmingham	15 Feb
7.73		Thomas	Delmestre	FRA	31.3.91	2h1	NC	Bordeaux	22 Feb
7.73		Damian	Czykier	POL	10.8.92	1h2	NC	Sopot	23 Feb
7.73A		Trevor	Brown	USA	24.3.92	1	MWC	Air Force Academy	1 Mar
		(59)							

Best at low altitude

7.57	Trammell	1	Mill	New York (Arm)	15 Feb
7.57	Berger	2	Mill	New York (Arm)	15 Feb
7.64	Harris	2		Notre Dame	22 Feb
7.65	Lovett	1h3	SEC	College Station	28 Feb
7.66	Somerville	1		Bloomington	15 Feb
7.70	Davis	2		College Station	15 Feb
7.70	McLeod	2	SEC	College Station	1 Mar

110 METRES HURDLES

Mark	Wind	Name		Nat	Born	Pos	Meet	Venue	Date
12.94	0.8	Hansle	Parchment	JAM	17.6.90	1	DL	Saint-Denis	5 Jul
12.95	0.2	Pascal	Martinot-Lagarde	FRA	22.9.91	1	Herc	Monaco	18 Jul
12.99	1.2	Ronnie	Ash	USA	2.7.88	1s1	NC	Sacramento	29 Jun
13.01	0.2	Orlando	Ortega	ex-CUB	29.7.91	2	Herc	Monaco	18 Jul
13.03	-0.5		Ortega			1	Skol	Warszawa	23 Aug
13.05	0.8		Martinot-Lagarde			2	DL	Saint-Denis	5 Jul
13.06	0.4		Martinot-Lagarde			1	Athl	Lausanne	3 Jul
13.06	-0.5		Martinot-Lagarde			2	Skol	Warszawa	23 Aug
13.08	-0.1		Martinot-Lagarde			1	Déca	Angers	30 Aug
13.08	0.3		Ortega			1	ISTAF	Berlin	31 Aug
13.08	-0.1		Martinot-Lagarde			1	VD	Bruxelles	5 Sep
13.10	0.8		Ortega			3	DL	Saint-Denis	5 Jul
13.10	0.3		Martinot-Lagarde			1	NC	Reims	13 Jul
13.10	-0.5		Ortega			1h2	Skol	Warszawa	23 Aug
13.12	-0.6		Martinot-Lagarde			1	Bisl	Oslo	11 Jun
13.12	1.1		Ortega			1		Tomblaine	27 Jun
13.13	0.8		Martinot-Lagarde			1	Pre	Eugene	31 May
13.13	0.4	Sergey	Shubenkov	RUS	4.10.90	2	Athl	Lausanne	3 Jul
13.13	-0.1		Ortega			2	VD	Bruxelles	5 Sep
13.14	1.0		Parchment			1	Drake	Des Moines	25 Apr
13.14	0.2		Shubenkov			3	Herc	Monaco	18 Jul
13.14	1.1	Aleec	Harris	USA	31.10.90	1		Eugene	26 Jul
13.16	1.3	Devon	Allen	USA	12.12.94	1	NCAA	Eugene	14 Jun
13.16	0.4	William	Sharman	GBR	12.9.84	1s1	EC	Zürich	14 Aug
13.16	0.4		Shubenkov			2s1	EC	Zürich	14 Aug
13.17	-0.3		Martinot-Lagarde			1s2	EC	Zürich	14 Aug
13.18	1.8		Harris			1q2	NCAA-W	Fayetteville	31 May
13.18	1.3		Harris			2	NCAA	Eugene	14 Jun
13.18	-0.8		Parchment			1	GS	Ostrava	17 Jun
13.18	0.8	Ryan	Wilson	USA	19.12.80	4	DL	Saint-Denis	5 Jul
13.18	0.2		Wilson			4	Herc	Monaco	18 Jul
		(31/9)							
13.19	0.0	Yordan	O'Farrill (10)	CUB	9.2.93	1	Odlozil	Praha	9 Jun
13.19	0.2	Andrew	Riley	JAM	6.9.88	5	Herc	Monaco	18 Jul
13.20	1.9	Wayne	Davis	TTO	22.8.91	1q1	NCAA-W	Fayetteville	31 May
13.21	0.8	David	Oliver	USA	24.4.82	3	Pre	Eugene	31 May
13.23	-0.3		Xie Wenjun	CHN	11.7.90	1	DL	Shanghai	18 May
13.24	-0.4	Shane	Brathwaite	BAR	8.2.90	2=	Anniv	London (HG)	20 Jul
13.25	1.1	Dimitri	Bascou	FRA	20.7.87	3		Tomblaine	27 Jun
13.27	0.7	Jeff	Porter	USA	27.11.85	2	DL	Glasgow	11 Jul

Mark	Wind	Name		Nat	Born	Pos	Meet	Venue	Date
13.27	0.7	Jeff	Porter	USA	27.11.85	2	DL	Glasgow	11 Jul
13.27	1.2	Aries	Merritt	USA	24.7.85	2		Eugene	26 Jul
13.29	0.4	Jason	Richardson	USA	4.4.86	7	Athl	Lausanne	3 Jul
13.29	0.5	Balázs	Baji	HUN	9.6.89	4	EC	Zürich	14 Aug
		(20)							
13.29	1.2	Dayron	Robles	CUB	19.11.86	1		Rovereto	2 Sep
13.32	1.2	Dominic	Berger	USA	19.5.86	4s1	NC	Sacramento	29 Jun
13.33	1.2	Spencer	Adams	USA	10.9.89	5s1	NC	Sacramento	29 Jun
13.35	0.8	Ashton	Eaton	USA	21.1.88	6	Pre	Eugene	31 May
13.35	1.3	Greggmar	Swift	BAR	16.2.91	4	NCAA	Eugene	14 Jun
13.35	1.2	Ray	Stewart	USA	5.4.89	6s1	NC	Sacramento	29 Jun
13.38	-0.3	Thomas	Martinot-Lagarde	FRA	7.2.88	3		Montreuil-sous-Bois	7 Jul
13.39	1.2	Matthias	Bühler	GER	2.9.86	1h3		Weinheim	31 May
13.39	-0.3	Petr	Svoboda	CZE	10.10.84	4s2	EC	Zürich	14 Aug
13.39	-0.3	Artur	Noga	POL	2.5.88	5s2	EC	Zürich	14 Aug
		(30)							
13.39	1.2	Konstadínos	Douvalídis	GRE	10.3.87	2		Rovereto	2 Sep
13.41	0.1	Omo	Osaghae	USA	18.5.88	2	MSR	Walnut	19 Apr
13.41	1.6	Lawrence	Clarke	GBR	12.3.90	3	FBK	Hengelo	8 Jun
13.41	0.0	Jhoanis	Portilla	CUB	24.7.90	1		La Habana	14 Jun
13.41A	-0.1	Ryan	Brathwaite	BAR	6.6.88	2	PAm SF	Ciudad de México	16 Aug
13.42	2.0	Mikel	Thomas	TTO	23.11.87	1		Clermont	26 Apr
13.43	0.2	Eddie	Lovett	ISV	25.6.92	1h2	NCAA-E	Jacksonville	30 May
13.43	0.4	Gregor	Traber	GER	2.12.92	2h2	EC	Zürich	13 Aug
13.43	0.4		Kim Byung-jun	KOR	15.8.91	2	AsiG	Incheon	30 Sep
13.44	1.9	Omar	McLeod	JAM	25.4.94	2q3	NCAA-W	Fayetteville	31 May
		(40)							
13.44	1.6	Ladji	Doucouré	FRA	28.3.83	1		La Roche-sur-Yon	23 Jul
13.45	0.1	Ronald	Brookins	USA	5.7.89	3	MSR	Walnut	19 Apr
13.46	0.0	Erik	Balnuweit	GER	21.9.88	4	Odlozil	Praha	9 Jun
13.46	0.6	Kevin	Craddock	USA	25.6.87	3h1	NC	Sacramento	28 Jun
13.47	2.0	Andrew	Turner	GBR	19.9.80	2		Clermont	26 Apr
13.47	0.7	Paolo	Dal Molin	ITA	31.7.87	1h2	NC	Rovereto	19 Jul
13.48	0.0	Lyès	Mokdel	ALG	20.6.90	2		Forbach	25 May
13.48	0.1	Tyrone	Akins	USA/NGR	6.1.86	5	C.Cup	Marrakech	14 Sep
13.49	0.6	Dominik	Bochenek	POL	14.5.87	1h1	NC	Szczecin	31 Jul
13.49	0.1	Abdulaziz	Al-Mandeel	KUW	22.5.89	6	C.Cup	Marrakech	14 Sep
		(50)							
13.50	0.7	Fred	Townsend	USA	19.2.82	2		Liège (NX)	16 Jul
13.50	0.5	Damian	Warner	CAN	4.11.89	1D	CG	Glasgow	29 Jul
13.51	-0.3	Simon	Krauss	FRA	12.2.92	6		Montreuil-sous-Bois	7 Jul
13.51	0.3	Konstantin	Shabanov	RUS	17.11.89	4h3	EC	Zürich	13 Aug
13.51A	-0.1	Deuce	Carter	JAM	28.9.90	2	PAm SF	Ciudad de México	16 Aug
13.53	1.2	David	Omoregie	GBR-J	1.11.95	6		Eugene	26 Jul
13.53	-0.3	Jorge	McFarlane	PER	20.2.88	1	IbAmC	São Paulo	2 Aug
13.53	0.4	Jonatha	Mendes	BRA	14.4.90	1	NC	São Paulo	12 Oct
13.54	2.0	Alex	Al-Ameen	GBR/NGR	2.3.89	3		Clermont	26 Apr
13.54	0.7	Johnathan	Cabral	USA	31.12.92	2h2	NCAA-W	Fayetteville	30 May
		(60)							
13.54	1.9	Wilhem	Belocian	FRA-J	22.6.95	6		Sotteville-lès-Rouen	14 Jun
13.55	1.1	Devon	Hill	USA	26.10.89	1		Coral Gables	12 Apr
13.55	1.8	Trevor	Brown	USA	24.3.92	2q2	NCAA-W	Fayetteville	31 May
13.55	0.9	Gregory	Sedoc	NED	16.10.81	1		Mannheim	17 Jul
13.55	0.7	Hassane	Fofana	ITA	28.4.92	5h4	EC	Zürich	13 Aug
13.55	0.5	Arthur	Abele	GER	30.7.86	1D	EC	Zürich	13 Aug
13.56	0.7	Othman	Hadj Lazib	ALG	10.5.83	2	NC	Alger	24 Jun
13.56	1.2	Ignacio	Morales	CUB	28.1.87	1		La Habana	8 Aug
13.56	1.0		Jiang Fan	CHN	16.9.89	1h1	AsiG	Incheon	28 Sep
13.57	-0.3	Nick	Hough	AUS	20.10.93	4	CG	Glasgow	29 Jul
		(70)							
13.57	-1.5	Javier	McFarlane	PER	21.10.91	1h1	IbAmC	São Paulo	2 Aug
13.58	0.4	Genta	Masuno	JPN	24.5.93	1	NC	Fukushima	8 Jun
13.58	0.4	João	Almeida	POR	5.4.88	5h2	EC	Zürich	13 Aug
13.59	0.4	Wataru	Yazawa	JPN	26.7.91	2	NC	Fukushima	8 Jun
13.60	0.5	Vincent	Wyatt	USA	18.10.92	1q3	NCAA-E	Jacksonville	31 May
13.61	0.8	Brandon	Winters	USA	11.12.91	1h1	Big 10	West Lafayette	17 May
13.61	0.4	Jamras	Rittidet	THA	1.2.89	3	AsiG	Incheon	30 Sep
13.62A	1.2	Ruan	de Vries	RSA	1.2.86	1	NC	Pretoria	12 Apr
13.62		Andrew	Brunson	USA	4.4.86	1		Arima	10 May
13.62	1.2	Jarret	Eaton	USA	24.6.89	8		Eugene	26 Jul
		(80)							

Mark	Wind	Name		Nat	Born	Pos	Meet	Venue	Date
13.62	1.2	Éder Antônio	de Souza	BRA	15.10.86	1h2	IbAmC	São Paulo	2 Aug
13.63	1.9	Milan	Ristic	SRB	8.8.91	3q3	NCAA-W	Fayetteville	31 May
13.63	0.5	Rico	Freimuth	GER	14.3.88	2D	EC	Zürich	13 Aug
13.64	1.0	Gerkenz	Senesca	USA/HAI	6.4.90	1		Greensboro	12 Apr
13.64	1.8	Richard	Phillips	JAM	26.1.83	2		Clermont	31 May
13.64	0.4	Durrell	Busby	TTO	23.12.89	3	NC	Port of Spain	21 Jun
13.64	0.7	Helge	Schwarzer	GER	26.11.85	1r3		Mannheim	6 Jul
13.64	0.7	Dániel	Kiss	HUN	12.2.82	6h4	EC	Zürich	13 Aug
13.64	0.7	Yaqoub	Al-Yoha	KUW	31.1.93	4h2	AsiG	Incheon	28 Sep
13.65	-0.4	Logan (90)	Taylor	USA	3.4.86	2		Irvine	3 May
13.65	1.8	Jermaine	Collier	USA	5.7.93	2h3	SEC	Lexington	17 May
13.65	1.2	Milan	Trajkovic	CYP	17.9.92	1	NC	Nicosia	7 Jun
13.65	1.6		Lee Jung-joon	KOR	26.3.84	1		Yeosu	16 Jul
13.65	0.6	Thingalaya	Siddhanth	IND	1.3.91	1		Patiala	19 Aug
13.66	0.4	Tobias	Furer	SUI	13.8.87	1h2	NC	Frauenfeld	26 Jul
13.67	-1.0	Keith	Hayes	USA	16.2.90	3r2	FlaR	Gainesville	4 Apr
13.67	1.8	Torrey	Campbell	USA	27.11.92	3h3	SEC	Lexington	17 May
13.67	1.4	Ogierakhi	Martins	NGR	30.6.91	2h1	NC	Calabar	19 Jun
13.67	0.4	Adrien	Deghelt	BEL	10.5.85	1		Bruxelles	6 Jul
13.67	1.0	Julian (100)	Marquardt	GER	2.4.91	1r1		Mannheim	6 Jul

Mark	Wind	Name		Nat	Born	Date
13.68	-1.6	Vanier	Joseph	USA	9.9.91	26 Apr
13.68	0.5	Tremayne	Banks	USA	29.7.92	31 May
13.68	1.1	Damian	Czykier	POL	10.8.92	20 Jun
13.68	0.6	Sekou	Kaba	CAN	25.8.90	19 Jul
13.69	1.0	Samuel	Baines	AUS	8.2.91	15 Mar
13.69	1.5	Hideki	Omuro	JPN	25.7.90	6 May
13.69	-2.1		Park Tae-kyong	KOR	30.7.80	23 May
13.69	1.8	Sean	Pille	USA	28.6.93	31 May
13.69	0.0	Trey	Hardee	USA	7.2.84	1 Jun
13.69	1.7	Aurel	Manga	FRA	24.7.92	1 Jun
13.69	2.0	Ronald	Forbes	CAY	5.4.85	19 Jul
13.69	1.1		Zhang Honglin	CHN	12.1.94	11 Oct
13.70	0.5	Donovan	Robertson	USA	8.11.93	31 May
13.70	0.0	Trey	Holloway	USA	7.7.94	12 Jun
13.70	0.0	Lorenzo	Perini	ITA	22.7.94	19 Jul
13.70	0.9	Alexander	John	GER	3.5.86	26 Jul
13.71	-0.1	Yidiel	Contreras	CUB	27.11.91	28 May
13.71	0.2	Hiroyuki	Sato	JPN	6.8.90	8 Jun
13.71	1.4	Vladimir	Vukicevic	NOR	6.5.91	13 Jun
13.71	0.6	Gregory	MacNeill	CAN	15.4.92	19 Jul
13.72	1.9	Jordan	Moore	USA	13.12.93	31 May
13.72A	-0.8	Genaro	Rodríguez	MEX	10.12.90	30 Aug
13.73	0.8	Don	Pollitt	USA	1.10.91	26 Apr
13.73	0.2	Freddie	Crittenden	USA	3.8.94	31 May
13.73	0.7	Damien	Broothaerts	BEL	12.11.84	16 Jul
13.73	0.4	Jonathas	Brito	BRA	30.11.92	12 Oct
13.74	1.8	Agustín	Carrera	ARG	13.6.88	25 Jan
13.74	0.4	Adarius	Washington	USA	19.10.92	30 May
13.74	0.5	Max	Hairston	USA	8.5.94	31 May
13.74	1.6	Koen	Smet	NED	9.8.92	8 Jun
13.74	-1.0	Javier	Colomo	ESP	26.3.94	27 Jul
13.75	-0.2	Kemar	Clarke	USA/JAM	20.5.88	28 Jun
13.76	-0.3		Huang Hao	CHN	7.10.87	13 Jul
13.76	1.4	Ramón	Sosa	DOM	11.1.86	16 Jul
13.77	0.3	Michael	Stigler	USA	5.4.92	17 May
13.77	-1.1	Philip	Nossmy	SWE	6.12.82	22 Jun
13.77	2.0	Edirin	Okoro	GBR	4.4.89	29 Jun
13.78	0.2	Randy	McCoy	USA	23.12.89	31 May
13.78	0.4	Yutaro	Furukawa	JPN	3.6.85	8 Jun
13.78	0.7	Andreas	Martinsen	DEN	17.7.90	6 Jul
13.78	0.2	Nicolas	Borome	FRA	7.10.93	16 Jul
13.79	-0.8	Ben	Reynolds	IRL	26.9.90	18 May
13.80	0.5	Robert	Semien	USA	15.4.93	31 May
13.80	1.8	Bryce	Grace	USA	18.7.94	31 May
13.80	0.5	Christian	Lupica	USA	17.5.93	31 May
13.80	0.9	Kiril	Nevdakh	RUS	26.7.93	22 Jun
13.80	-1.0	David	King	GBR	13.6.94	6 Jul
13.80	0.4	Fábio dos	Santos	BRA	11.10.83	12 Oct
13.81	0.7	Terence	Somerville	USA	5.11.89	19 Apr
13.81	1.9	Isaac	Williams	USA	30.11.93	31 May
13.81	0.8	Antwon	Hicks	USA/NGR	12.3.83	19 Jun
13.81	-0.2	Jackson	Quiñónez	ESP	12.6.80	12 Jul
13.81	1.6	Maximilian	Bayer	GER	5.12.90	26 Jul
13.82	0.9	Dondre	Echols	USA	6.7.93	17 May
13.82	-0.2	Luke	Campbell	USA	22.11.94	24 May
13.82	1.8	Sebastian	Barth	GER	1.2.93	31 May
13.82		Carrington	Queen	USA	21.9.87	7 Jun
13.82	0.3	Mikolay	Justynski	POL	19.7.92	15 Jun
13.82	0.0	Maksim	Lynsha	BLR	6.4.85	24 Jul
13.83	1.0	Dennis	Bain	BAH	15.12.90	12 Apr
13.83	1.2	Viliam	Papso	SVK	23.5.89	17 May
13.83	0.7	Spencer	Dunkerley-Offor	USA-J	6.1.95	30 May
13.83	1.8	Filipp	Shabanov	RUS	29.1.91	9 Jul
13.83	0.3	Thomas	Ravon	FRA	1.5.84	13 Jul
13.83	0.4	Ingvar	Moseley	CAN	24.11.91	19 Jul
13.83	0.7	Takumu	Furuya	JPN-Y	12.3.97	3 Oct
13.84	-0.7	Dapo	Akinmoladun	USA	28.2.94	5 Apr
13.84	0.1	Héctor	Cotto	PUR	8.8.84	19 Apr
13.84	-0.4		Lei Yiwen	CHN	11.12.93	20 Apr
13.84	0.9	Yuta	Notoya	JPN	8.7.89	6 May
13.84	0.6	Chris	Caldwell	USA	5.4.94	17 May
13.84	-1.5	Kazuaki	Ota	JPN	6.5.92	17 May
13.84	1.8	Teivaskie	Lewin	JAM	27.12.91	31 May
13.85	0.4	Miles	Ukaoma	USA	21.7.92	17 May
13.85	0.9	Francisco Javier	López	ESP	29.12.89	30 May
13.85	-0.6	David	Ilariani	GEO	20.1.81	14 Jun
13.85	-0.3		Ma Lei	CHN	29.6.89	13 Jul
13.85	0.1	Eduardo	de Deus	BRA-J	8.10.95	6 Sep
13.86	1.3	Tatsuya	Wado	JPN	4.10.90	29 Apr
13.86	1.8	Kendall	Parks	USA	28.7.89	9 May
13.86	0.9	Will	Barnes	USA	17.3.94	17 May
13.86	-0.4		Chen Kuei-Ju	TPE	22.9.93	19 May
13.86	0.6	Josh	Thompson	USA	16.1.93	30 May
13.86	1.9	Aaron	Mallett	USA	26.9.94	31 May
13.86	1.3	Alexander	Brorsson	SWE	29.5.90	2 Aug
13.87	0.7	Keyunta	Hayes	USA	15.2.92	22 Mar
13.87	1.8	Hironori	Murao	JPN	10.4.86	4 May
13.87	-0.8	Yannick	Budd	GBR	5.9.91	18 May
13.87	1.9	Michael	Prejean	USA	.93	31 May
13.87	1.1	Masato	Yamane	JPN	24.12.92	4 Jul
13.87	-0.7	Arttu	Hirvonen	FIN	21.1.89	13 Aug
13.88	0.2	Matheus	Inocêncio	BRA	17.5.81	9 Mar
13.88	0.4		Ko Wen-Ting	TPE	17.4.89	12 Apr
13.88	0.6	Trae	Proctor	USA	10.2.91	12 Apr
13.88	-0.1	Norihiro	Kiriyama	JPN	29.10.92	8 May
13.88	0.9	Tramaine	Maloney	BAR	1.6.94	17 May
13.88	1.8	Joseph	Hylton	GBR	17.11.89	18 May
13.88	0.6	Jussi	Kanervo	FIN	1.2.93	30 May
13.88	0.4	Amadou	Guèye	USA	12.10.90	30 May
13.88	0.0	Samuele (200)	Devarti	ITA	8.7.90	19 Jul

Wind assisted

Mark	Wind	Name		Nat	Born	Pos	Meet	Venue	Date
13.12	2.6	Jeff	Porter	USA	27.11.85	1s2	NC	Sacramento	29 Jun
13.16	2.1		D Allen			1	NC	Sacramento	29 Jun
13.16	2.1	Ryan	Wilson	USA	19.12.80	2	NC	Sacramento	29 Jun

Mark	Wind	Name		Nat	Born	Pos	Meet	Venue	Date
13.20	3.4	Matthias	Bühler	GER	2.9.86	1	NC	Ulm	26 Jul
13.23	3.4	Gregor	Traber	GER	2.12.92	2	NC	Ulm	26 Jul
13.27	2.1	Jason	Richardson	USA	4.4.86	5	NC	Sacramento	29 Jun
13.38	2.8	Mikel	Thomas	TTO	23.11.87	1		Montverde	7 Jun
13.38	2.6	Ladji	Doucouré	FRA	28.3.83	1h1		Castres	30 Jul
13.39	2.1	Eddie	Lovett	ISV	25.6.92	1	NACAC	Kamloops	9 Aug
13.40	3.3	Omo	Osaghae	USA	18.5.88	1		Lubbock	5 Apr
13.41	2.6	Vanier	Joseph	USA	9.9.91	1		Champaign	12 Apr
13.41	2.8	Konstantin	Shabanov	RUS	17.11.89	2		Göteborg	14 Jun
13.44	2.9	Isaac	Williams	USA	30.11.93	1rB	MSR	Walnut	19 Apr
13.45	2.4	Erik	Balnuweit	GER	21.9.88	2		Clermont	10 May
13.48	2.9	Logan	Taylor	USA	3.4.86	2rB	MSR	Walnut	19 Apr
13.51A	3.7	Javier	McFarlane	PER	21.10.91	1	NC	Medellín	27 Jun
13.55	2.1	Vincent	Wyatt	USA	18.10.92	2	NACAC	Kamloops	10 Aug
13.56	2.8	Durrell	Busby	TTO	23.12.89	1		Charleston, IL	9 May
13.58	2.7		Park Tae-kyong	KOR	30.7.80	1		Redlands	15 May
13.59	2.1	Milan	Ristic	SRB	8.8.91	3	TexR	Austin	29 Mar
13.59	2.8	Jarret	Eaton	USA	24.6.89	3	FlaR	Gainesville	4 Apr
13.59	2.4	Kemar	Clarke	USA/JAM	20.5.88	1		Miramar	28 Apr
13.59	2.8	Ben	Reynolds	IRL	26.9.90	4		Göteborg	14 Jun
13.59	3.4	Helge	Schwarzer	GER	26.11.85	3	NC	Ulm	26 Jul
13.60	3.4	Julian	Marquardt	GER	2.4.91	4	NC	Ulm	26 Jul
13.61	3.4	Alexander	John	GER	3.5.86	5	NC	Ulm	26 Jul
13.63	3.5	Keith	Hayes	USA	16.2.90	1		Knoxville	11 Apr
13.63	3.4	Maximilian	Bayer	GER	5.12.90	6	NC	Ulm	26 Jul
13.64	2.2	Bryce	Grace	USA	18.7.94	1		Austin	3 May
13.64	3.9	Jordan	Moore	USA	13.12.93	1	Big 12	Lubbock	18 May
13.64A	3.7	Agustin	Carrera	ARG	13.6.88	2	COL Ch	Medellín	27 Jun
13.64	2.7	Takumu	Furuya	JPN-Y	12.3.97	1		Sagamihara	6 Jul
13.65	4.1	Calvin	Arsenault	CAN	29.9.93	1		Louisville	12 Apr

Mark	Wind	Name		Nat	Born	Date
13.69	4.9	Chris	Caldwell	USA	5.4.94	12 Apr
13.69	4.4	Dexter	Faulk	USA	14.4.84	19 Apr
13.69	2.4	Yannick	Budd	GBR	5.9.91	29 Jun
13.69	2.2	Jonathas	Brito	BRA	30.11.92	4 Oct
13.70	3.5	Francisco	Javier López	ESP	29.12.89	28 Jun
13.70	2.5	Yutaro	Furukawa	JPN	3.6.85	6 Jul
13.70	3.4	David	King	GBR	13.6.94	19 Jul
13.71	3.5	Jackson	Quiñónez	ESP	12.6.80	28 Jun
13.72	2.5		Huang Hao	CHN	7.10.87	6 Jul
13.77	2.3	Jussi	Kanervo	FIN	1.2.93	29 Mar
13.77	2.2	Andreas	Martinsen	DEN	17.7.90	20 Jul
13.79	4.4	Angelo	Goss	USA	.94	19 Apr
13.80	2.5	Roger	Iribarne	CUB-J	2.1.96	18 Mar
13.80	2.4	Jarvis	Harris	USA	28.1.93	19 Apr
13.80	2.3	Cherif	Banda	FRA	29.1.92	22 Jun
13.81	2.5	Kevin	Baxter	USA	.93	5 Apr
13.81	2.2	Sabiel	Anderson	JAM	21.6.88	7 Jun
13.82	2.1	Yuta	Notoya	JPN	8.7.89	29 Apr
13.82	2.2	Nick	Anderson	USA-J	28.4.95	3 May
13.82	3.0	Denis	Hanjoul	BEL	17.1.91	17 May
13.82	2.2	Tjendo	Samuel	NED	19.12.89	27 Jul
13.83	3.5		Chen Kuei-Ju	TPE	22.9.93	21 Jun
13.83	3.5		Huang Kun-Yu	TPE	24.10.94	21 Jun
13.84	2.7	Joseph	Hylton	GBR	17.11.89	29 Jun
13.84	2.5	Felipe	dos Santos	BRA	30.7.94	18 Oct
13.85	3.6	Shujaa	Benson	DEN	26.7.90	12 Apr
13.85	4.2	Tibor	Koroknai	HUN	24.1.90	23 Apr
13.85	4.0	Joshua	Lamers	USA	4.2.94	3 May
13.85	4.3	Thaddeus	Curtis	USA	13.10.91	11 May

(199 to 13.85 legal and windy)

Low altitude bests

13.44 -0.5 R Brathwaite 2 Edmonton 6 Jul

13.57 0.3 D Carter 3 George Town 7 May

13.82 0.5 de Vries 4 AfCh Marrakech 13 Aug

Hand timing: 12.9 0.0 Yordan O'Farrill CUB 9.2.93 1 Barr La Habana 23 May

JUNIORS

See main list for top 2 juniors. 6 performances by 4 men to 13.78. Additional marks and further juniors:

Omoregie 13.61 1 Welsh Cardiff 1 Jun 13.71 0.8 1 Oxford (H) 28 May

Belocian 13.62 -1.6 4rB GS Ostrava 17 Jun 13.78 -0.5 2 Baie Mahault 10 May

Mark	Wind	Name		Nat	Born	Pos	Meet	Venue	Date
13.83	0.7	Spencer	Dunkerley-Offor	USA	6.1.95	3h2	NCAA-W	Fayetteville	30 May
13.83	0.7	Takumu	Furuya	JPN-Y	12.3.97	1s1		Nagoya	3 Oct
13.85	0.1	Eduardo	de Deus	BRA	8.10.95	1	NC-23	São Paulo	6 Sep
13.91	1.1	Nick	Anderson	USA	28.4.95	1	FlaR	Gainesville	4 Apr
13.92	0.4	Gabriel	Constantino	BRA	9.2.95	5	NC	São Paulo	12 Oct
13.96	0.9	Myles	Hunter	USA	16.8.95	2	NCAA-II	Allendale	24 May
14.00	-0.5	Wellington	Zaza	LBR	20.1.95	1h2	JUCO	Mesa	16 May
14.01	1.9	William	Gibbs (10)	USA	25.5.95	2h4	TexR	Austin	28 Mar
14.01	1.4	Lloyd	Sicard	USA	31.5.95	2		Davis	17 May
14.04	1.9	Daniel	Zmuda	USA	1.1.95	7s1	NCAA-w	Fayetteville	31 May
14.04	0.3	Seanie	Selvin	JAM	6.9.96	1		Kingston	7 Jun

Wind assisted

Mark	Wind	Name		Nat	Born	Pos	Meet	Venue	Date
13.64	2.7	Takumu	Furuya	JPN-Y	12.3.97	1		Sagamihara	6 Jul
13.80	2.5	Roger	Iribarne	CUB	2.1.96	3	NC	La Habana	18 Mar
13.82	2.2	Nick	Anderson	USA	28.4.95	2		Austin	3 May
13.87	2.2	Jaron	Thomas	USA	8.1.95	3		Austin	3 May
13.87	2.7	Naoya	Kawamura	JPN	10.6.96	2		Nagoya	3 Oct
13.88	2.7	Taio	Kanai	JPN	28.9.85	3		Nagoya	3 Oct
13.93	4.9	William	Gibbs	USA	25.5.95	4		Austin	12 Apr
14.03	2.5	Marcel	Jastrzemski	GER	24.9.95	1		Berlin	22 May

110 Metres Hurdles – 99 cm hurdles

Mark	Wind	Name		Nat	Born	Pos	Meet	Venue	Date
12.99	0.5	Wilhem	Belocian	FRA	22.6.95	1	WJ	Eugene	24 Jul
		13.15 1.8 1 Mannheim 5 Jul			13.23 -1.6 1s1 WJ Eugene 23 Jul				
		13.23 1.6 1 Carifta Fort-de-France 21 Apr			13.33w 2.2 1h3 Mannheim 5 Jul				
13.06	0.5	Tyler	Mason	JAM	15.1.95	2	WJ	Eugene	24 Jul
		13.25 1.6 2 Carifta Fort-de-France 21 Apr							
13.17	-0.7	David	Omoregie	GBR	1.11.95	1	NC-j	Bedford	22 Jun
		13.23 1.4 1 LI Loughborough 18 May			13.36 -0.3 1s2 WJ Eugene 22 Jul				
		13.24 0.7 1h6 WJ Eugene 22 Jul			13.38 -0.4 1h3 NC-j Bedford 22 Jun				
		13.35 0.5 3 WJ Eugene 23 Jul			14 performances (+1w) by 5 men to 13.38				
13.33	0.5	Taio	Kanai	JPN	28.9.95	1	Asi-J	Taipei	14 Jun
13.37	1.7	Nick	Anderson	USA	28.4.95	1	NC-j	Eugene	6 Jul
13.38	0.5	Wellington	Zaza	LBR	20.1.95	4	WJ	Eugene	24 Jul
13.40	1.0	Isaiah	Moore	USA	12.6.96	1	N.Jnr	Greensboro	14 Jun
13.40	1.8	Benjamin	Sedecias	FRA	18.1.95	2		Mannheim	5 Jul
13.42	1.7	Misana	Viltz	USA	21.2.96	2	NC-j	Eugene	6 Jul
13.46	1.6	Patrick	Elger (10)	GER	25.1.96	1h2		Mannheim	5 Jul
13.47	1.5	Roger	Iribarne	CUB	2.1.96	1		La Habana	20 Jun
13.51	0.5	Masahiro	Kagimoto	JPN	29.9.95	2	Asi-J	Taipei	14 Jun
13.52A	1.0	Marvin	Williams	JAM	13.6.96	1	CAC-J	Morelia	6 Jul
13.52	0.5	Ruebin	Walters	TTO	2.4.95	6	WJ	Eugene	24 Jul
13.53	-3.5	Jaheel	Hyde	JAM-Y	2.2.97	1	NC	Kingston	29 Mar
13.55	-0.3	Francisco	López	ESP	16.4.95	3s2	WJ	Eugene	23 Jul
13.56	0.5	Mohammed Amin	Ghamsari	IRI	26.9.95	3	Asi-J	Taipei	14 Jun
13.58	1.1	Julio César	de Oliveira	BRA	15.5.96	1	NC-j	Maringá	28 Jun
13.58	1.7	Spencer	Dunkerley-Offor	USA	6.1.95	4	NC-j	Eugene	6 Jul
13.59	0.5	(20)	Huang Shih-Wei	TPE	11.10.95	4	Asi-J	Taipei	14 Jun

Wind assisted

Mark	Wind	Name		Nat	Born	Pos	Meet	Venue	Date
13.52	4.2	Christopher	Grinley	USA	18.7.95	1h3	NC-j	Eugene	5 Jul
13.55	4.2	Spencer	Dunkerley-Offor	USA	6.1.95	2h3	NC-j	Eugene	5 Jul

200 METRES HURDLES STRAIGHT

Mark	Wind	Name		Nat	Born	Pos	Meet	Venue	Date
22.58	1.4	Andrew	Turner	GBR	19.9.80	1		Manchester	17 May
22.61	1.4	Félix	Sánchez	DOM	30.8.77	2		Manchester	17 May

400 METRES HURDLES

Mark	Name		Nat	Born	Pos	Meet	Venue	Date
48.03	Javier	Culson	PUR	25.7.84	1	adidas	New York	14 Jun
48.25	Michael	Tinsley	USA	21.4.84	1	DL	Saint-Denis	5 Jul
48.25	Cornel	Fredericks	RSA	3.3.90	1	WK	Zürich	28 Aug
48.31		Tinsley			2	WK	Zürich	28 Aug
48.32		Culson			1	Athl	Lausanne	3 Jul
48.34		Fredericks			1	C.Cup	Marrakech	13 Sep
48.35		Culson			1	DL	Glasgow	11 Jul
48.40		Tinsley			2	Athl	Lausanne	3 Jul
48.41		Culson			1		Cork	8 Jul
48.42		Fredericks			2	DL	Saint-Denis	5 Jul
48.45		Culson			3	DL	Saint-Denis	5 Jul
48.47	Kariem	Hussein	SUI	1.4.89	2	C.Cup	Marrakech	13 Sep
48.48	Roxroy	Cato	JAM	1.5.88	1	NC	Kingston	27 Jun
48.50		Fredericks			1	CG	Glasgow	31 Jul
48.53		Culson			3	WK	Zürich	28 Aug
48.54	Rasmus	Mägi	EST	4.5.92	1s3	EC	Zürich	13 Aug
48.56		Tinsley			2	adidas	New York	14 Jun
48.57		Tinsley			1	Drake	Des Moines	25 Apr
48.58		Fredericks			3	adidas	New York	14 Jun
48.58	Annsert	Whyte	JAM	10.4.87	2	NC	Kingston	27 Jun
48.65	Andrés	Silva	URU	27.3.86	1	IbAmC	São Paulo	2 Aug
48.66		Culson			1	FBK	Hengelo	8 Jun
48.67		Cato			1	FlaR	Gainesville	4 Apr
48.68		Culson			2	Drake	Des Moines	25 Apr
48.69		Culson			1	GP	Ponce	17 May
48.69		Whyte			1h2	NC	Kingston	26 Jun
48.69	Ashton	Eaton	USA	21.1.88	2	DL	Glasgow	11 Jul
48.69	Timothy	Chalyy (10)	RUS	7.4.94	2s3	EC	Zürich	13 Aug
48.70		Hussein			4	WK	Zürich	28 Aug
48.75	Jehue	Gordon	TTO	15.12.91	2	CG	Glasgow	31 Jul
	(30/11)							
48.76	Bershawn	Jackson	USA	8.5.83	1		Charlottesville	9 May

Mark	Wind	Name		Nat	Born	Pos	Meet	Venue	Date
48.78		Jeffrey	Gibson	BAH	15.8.90	3	CG	Glasgow	31 Jul
48.80		Niall	Flannery	GBR	26.4.91	1	GS	Ostrava	17 Jun
48.86		Mamadou Kassé	Hann	SEN	10.10.86	2	DL	Shanghai	18 May
48.90		Thomas	Barr	IRL	24.7.92	1		Genève	14 Jun
48.91		Félix	Sánchez	DOM	30.8.77	4	DL	Saint-Denis	5 Jul
48.92		Amaechi	Morton	NGR	30.10.89	2	AfCh	Marrakech	12 Aug
48.93		Johnny	Dutch	USA	20.1.89	1	NC	Sacramento	29 Jun
48.95		Denis	Kudryavtsev	RUS	13.4.92	1		Adler	30 May
		(20)							
48.95		Rhys	Williams #	GBR	27.2.84	2		Genève	14 Jun
48.96A		Louis 'L.J'	van Zyl	RSA	20.7.85	1		Sasolburg	25 Mar
48.96		Felix	Franz	GER	6.5.93	3s3	EC	Zürich	13 Aug
49.00		Leford	Green	JAM	14.11.86	3	NC	Kingston	27 Jun
49.03		Nicholas	Bett	KEN	14.6.92	3	AfCh	Marrakech	12 Aug
49.04A		Josef	Robertson	JAM	14.5.87	2	PAm SF	Ciudad de México	16 Aug
49.07		Eric	Alejandro	PUR	15.4.86	2	IbAmC	São Paulo	2 Aug
49.08		Oskari	Mörö	FIN	31.1.93	4s3	EC	Zürich	13 Aug
49.09		Mahau	Suguimati	BRA	13.11.84	1		Belém	10 Aug
49.10		Jeshua	Anderson	USA	22.6.89	1		Los Angeles (Ww)	7 Jun
		(30)							
49.12		Varg	Königsmark	GER	28.4.92	2s1	EC	Zürich	13 Aug
49.13		Michaël	Bultheel	BEL	30.6.86	1	NC	Bruxelles	27 Jul
49.13		Patryk	Dobek	POL	13.2.94	3s1	EC	Zürich	13 Aug
49.21		Emir	Bekric	SRB	14.3.91	2s2	EC	Zürich	13 Aug
49.23		Miles	Ukaoma	USA/NGR	21.7.92	1	NCAA	Eugene	13 Jun
49.25A		Boniface	Mucheru	KEN	2.5.92	1	NC	Nairobi	7 Jun
49.29		Jaheel	Hyde	JAM-Y	2.2.97	1	WJ	Eugene	25 Jul
49.32		Reggie	Wyatt	USA	17.9.90	1		Huelva	12 Jun
49.34		Michael	Stigler	USA	5.4.92	1s2	NCAA	Eugene	11 Jun
49.40		Dmitriy	Koblov	KAZ	30.11.92	1	NC	Almaty	28 Jun
		(40)							
49.45		Kazuaki	Yoshida	JPN	31.8.87	1		Osaka	29 Jun
49.46		Richard	Yates	GBR	26.1.86	1		Salzburg	24 May
49.47		Sebastian	Rodger	GBR	29.6.91	4s1	EC	Zürich	13 Aug
49.48		Yuta	Konishi	JPN	31.7.90	2		Osaka	29 Jun
49.49		Takayuki	Kishimoto	JPN	6.5.90	1	NC	Fukushima	8 Jun
49.52		Ian	Dewhurst	AUS	13.11.90	1	NC	Melbourne	6 Apr
49.53		Justin	Gaymon	USA	13.12.86	3		Belém	10 Aug
49.54		Wouter	le Roux	RSA	17.1.86	5		Genève	14 Jun
49.55		Ali Khamis	Abbas	BRN-J	30.6.95	2	WJ	Eugene	25 Jul
49.56A		Kurt	Couto	MOZ	14.5.85	1		Potchefstroom	10 May
		(50)							
49.56A		Omar	Cisneros	CUB	19.11.89	1	CAG	Xalapa	27 Nov
49.57		Emanuel	Mayers	TTO	9.3.89	1	NC	Port of Spain	22 Jun
49.59		Keyunta	Hayes	USA	15.2.92	1rB	FlaR	Gainesville	4 Apr
49.59		Hederson	Estefani	BRA	11.9.91	1	NC	São Paulo	12 Oct
49.60		Greg	Coleman	USA	24.7.93	1q3	NCAA-W	Fayetteville	30 May
49.60		Yoan	Décimus	FRA	30.11.87	3h1	EC	Zürich	12 Aug
49.61		Amadou	Ndiaye	SEN	6.12.92	1	FRA Ch	Reims	13 Jul
49.64A		Trevor	Brown	USA	24.3.92	1		Laramie	3 May
49.66		Lucirio Francisco	Garrido	VEN	4.10.88	2	SAmG	Santiago de Chile	15 Mar
49.66		Silvio	Schirrmeister	GER	7.12.88	2		Salzburg	24 May
		(60)							
49.66		Tom	Burton	GBR	29.10.88	1rB		Genève	14 Jun
49.69		Takatoshi	Abe	JPN	12.11.91	2		Fukushima	18 May
49.71		Mohamed	Sghaier	TUN	18.7.88	2	FRA Ch	Reims	13 Jul
49.72		Michael	Cochrane	NZL	13.8.91	1		Perth	22 Feb
49.83		Stef	Vanhaeren	BEL	15.1.92	2	NC	Bruxelles	27 Jul
49.83		Artur	Langowski	BRA	8.5.91	2	NC	São Paulo	12 Oct
49.85		Tristan	Thomas	AUS	23.5.86	2		Melbourne	22 Mar
49.88		José Luis	Gaspar	CUB-J	25.8.95	1		La Habana	4 Oct
49.89		Isa	Phillips	JAM	22.4.84	4		Kingston	3 May
49.89		David	Greene	GBR	11.4.86	1	Gyulai	Székesfehérvár	8 Jul
		(70)							
49.89			Cheng Wen	CHN	18.3.92	1h3	AsiG	Incheon	29 Sep
49.90		Timothy	Holmes	USA-J	2.7.95	1q1	NCAA-W	Fayetteville	30 May
49.90		Tim	Rummens	BEL	16.12.87	1rB		Oordegem	31 May
49.90		Saber	Boukamouche	ALG	20.4.92	1		Alger	23 Jul
49.90		Sergio	Fernández	ESP	1.4.93	1	NC	Alcobendas	27 Jul
49.90		Michal	Broz	CZE	16.6.92	4h1	EC	Zürich	12 Aug
49.94		Demar	Murray	JAM	31.8.91	6	NC	Kingston	27 Jun

Mark	Name		Nat	Born	Pos	Meet	Venue	Date
49.95	Vladimir	Antmanis	RUS	12.3.84	3		Adler	30 May
49.95	Akihiko	Nakamura	JPN	23.10.90	2	NC	Fukushima	8 Jun
49.97	Quincy	Downing	USA	16.1.93	3	NCAA	Eugene	13 Jun
	(80)							
49.98	Tatsuya	Tateno	JPN	5.8.91	4	NC	Fukushima	8 Jun
49.98	Adam	Durham	USA	30.8.85	2s1	NC	Sacramento	28 Jun
50.00	Eric	Cray	PHI	6.11.88	2h3	AsiG	Incheon	29 Sep
50.01	Oleg	Mironov	RUS	5.3.93	1		Moskva	3 Jul
50.03	Jordin	Andrade	USA	5.5.92	1		Boise	2 May
50.05	Adrian	Clémenceau	FRA	25.5.88	3	NC	Reims	13 Jul
50.05	Leonardo	Capotosti	ITA	24.7.88	3	WCM	Rieti	7 Sep
50.07	Reuben	McCoy	USA	16.3.86	2		Clermont	7 Jun
50.07	Yuki	Matsushita	JPN	9.9.91	3	NA	Heusden-Zolder	19 Jul
50.08	Denys	Nechyporenko	UKR	7.1.90	1	NC	Kirovohrad	25 Jul
	(90)							
50.09	Cam	Viney	USA	6.9.93	3	Drake	Des Moines	26 Apr
50.09		Chen Chieh	TPE	8.5.92	1		Yunlin	21 May
50.11	Rilwan	Alowonle	NGR	12.12.93	1q1	NCAA-E	Jacksonville	30 May
50.12	Seth	Mbow	SEN	2.4.85	5	FlaR	Gainesville	4 Apr
50.13	Kenny	Selmon	USA-J	27.8.96	2	NC-j	Eugene	6 Jul
50.15	Abdelmadik	Lahoulou	ALG	7.5.92	2		Marseille	31 May
50.16	Cameron	French	NZL	17.5.92	1	NC	Wellington	30 Mar
50.17	Joshua	Taylor	USA	19.6.92	2q1	NCAA-W	Fayetteville	30 May
50.17	Arnaud	Ghislain	BEL	2.12.88	1h1	NC	Bruxelles	26 Jul
50.21A	Leslie	Murray	ISV	24.1.91	3	CAG	Xalapa	27 Nov
	(100)							

Mark	First	Last	Nat	Born	Date
50.22	Ben	Sumner	GBR	16.8.83	31 May
50.23	Tobias	Giehl	GER	25.7.91	27 Jul
50.24	Yasuhiro	Fueki	JPN	20.12.85	29 Jun
50.25	Tibor	Koroknai	HUN	24.1.90	30 May
50.26	Stéphane	Yato	FRA	11.9.92	19 Apr
50.26	Keisuke	Nozawa	JPN	7.6.91	7 Jun
50.26	Rafal	Omelko	POL	16.1.89	6 Sep
50.27	Sergio	Rios	MEX	30.8.91	19 Apr
50.29A	Le Roux	Hamman	RSA	6.1.92	11 Apr
50.29	Mohammed Amine	Gouneiber	ALG	25.2.88	19 Jul
50.30	Mickaël	François	FRA	12.3.88	31 May
50.33	Maté	Koroknai	HUN	13.1.93	12 Aug
50.34	Seiya	Kato	JPN	22.11.92	6 Sep
50.35	Jussi	Kanervo	FIN	1.2.93	12 Aug
50.36	Luke	Campbell	USA	22.11.94	24 May
50.37	Georg	Fleischhauer	GER	21.10.88	14 Jun
50.37	Robert	Díez	ESP	22.11.88	27 Jul
50.38	Takaoki	Hashimoto	JPN	18.7.92	25 May
50.38	Hardus	Maritz	NAM	10.5.90	12 Aug
50.38	Thiago	Sales	BRA	12.8.86	12 Oct
50.38A	Gerber	Blanco	GUA	6.9.93	27 Nov
50.39	Nikita	Andriyanov	RUS	7.2.90	30 May
50.39	Miloud	Rahmani	ALG	13.12.83	23 Jul
50.41	Drew	Branch	USA	13.5.93	18 May
50.41	Jithin	Paul	IND	13.3.90	6 Jun
50.41A	Kiprono	Kosgei	KEN		7 Jun
50.41	Naohiro	Kawakita	JPN	10.7.80	29 Jun
50.41	Gerald	Drummond	CRC	5.9.94	2 Aug
50.44	Fernando	Martínez	MEX	5.9.93	2 May
50.45	Anthony Tyrell	Kuriki	JPN-J	.96	19 Oct
50.47	Jodi-Rae	Blackwood	JAM	6.3.91	30 May
50.47	Robert	Brylinski	POL	2.4.91	30 Jul
50.49		Yu Chia-Hsuan	TPE-J	22.1.95	15 Jun
50.49	James	Forman	GBR	12.12.91	28 Jun
50.50	Kenji	Matsumoto	JPN	.93	29 Jun
50.50	Jassem Waleed	Al-Mass	KUW	5.2.90	29 Sep
50.52	Atsushi	Yamada	JPN	3.7.91	7 Jun
50.54	Andre	Peart	JAM	14.9.89	19 Apr
50.55	Charles	Lewis	USA	5.9.92	30 May
50.56	Mehdi	Omara Besson	FRA	8.4.88	14 Jun
50.56		Wang Guozhong	CHN-J	31.1.95	10 Oct
50.56	Kotaro	Miyao	JPN	12.7.91	11 Oct
50.57	Eusebio	Haliti	ITA	1.1.91	24 May
50.58	Daniel	O'Shea	NZL	11.2.89	22 Mar
50.58	Ryan	Newtoff	USA	7.3.90	18 May
50.58	Emerson	Chalá	ECU	2.8.91	2 Aug
50.59	Noriuki	Ideura	JPN	29.10.87	3 May
50.59	Øyvind	Kjerpeset	NOR	12.12.91	2 Aug
50.60	Víctor	Solarte	VEN	6.1.86	15 May
50.60	Stanislav	Melnikov	UKR	26.2.87	13 Aug
50.61	Durgesh	Kumar Pal	IND	20.4.94	5 Nov
50.62	Konstantin	Andreyev	RUS	10.8.90	8 Jun
50.62	Yuta	Imazeki	JPN	6.11.87	29 Jun
50.62	Khallifah	Rosser	USA-J	13.7.95	6 Jul
50.62	Shotaro	Tanabe	JPN	23.4.94	21 Jul
50.62	Yasmani	Copello	TUR	15.4.87	26 Jul
50.62	Jakub	Smolinski	POL	21.7.92	30 Jul
50.63	Ignacio	Sarmiento	ESP	28.12.86	27 Jul
50.64		Chen Ke	CHN	14.9.89	20 Apr
50.64	Joshua	Smith	USA	.92	18 May
50.64	Jason	Harvey	IRL	9.8.91	11 Jul
50.64	Ivan	Shablyuyev	RUS	17.4.88	25 Jul
50.65	Javonte	Lipsey	USA	17.10.92	19 Apr
50.65	Winder	Cuevas	DOM	1.8.88	2 Aug
50.66	Amaurys	Valle	CUB	18.1.90	20 Mar
50.66	Scottie	Hearn	USA	3.1.94	18 May
50.66		Lee Seung-Yun	KOR	28.2.89	26 Jun
50.68	David	Gollnow	GER	8.4.89	31 May
50.68	Takayoshi	Shinohara	JPN	4.6.92	29 Jun
50.68	Jonas	Hanßen	GER-J	15.7.95	6 Jul
50.68	Kei	Maeno	JPN	10.5.91	11 Oct
50.69	Ludovic	Dubois	FRA	13.4.86	13 Jul
50.69	Jaak-Heinrich	Jagor	EST	11.5.90	3 Aug
50.71A	Ruan	Mentz	RSA-J	12.1.95	26 Apr
50.71	Márcio	Teles	BRA	27.1.94	12 Oct
50.73	Kenneth	Medwood	BIZ	14.12.87	10 May
50.73	Desmond	Palmer	USA-J	30.7.95	30 May
50.74A	Dijan	Johnson	USA	18.7.91	17 May
50.74	Christian	Heimann	GER	15.11.91	29 May
50.75	Byron	Robinson	USA-J	16.2.95	5 Apr
50.75	Shawn	Rowe	JAM	7.12.92	12 Apr
50.75	Jermel	Kindred	USA	.91	24 May
50.75	Calvin	Arsenault	CAN	29.9.93	30 May
50.75	Joseph G.	Abraham	IND	11.9.81	17 Aug
50.76A	Vincent	Kosgei	KEN	11.11.85	7 Jun
50.76	Yusuke	Sakanashi	JPN-J	26.4.95	15 Jun
50.77	LaRon	Bennett	USA	25.11.82	12 Apr
50.77A	Jefferson	Valencia	COL	20.10.94	31 May
50.77	Takahiro	Matsumoto	JPN	19.9.94	6 Sep
50.78	Mica-Jonathan	Petit-Homme	USA	9.4.94	30 May
50.78	Vyacheslav	Sakayev	RUS	12.1.88	25 Jul
	(191)				

Low altitude bests

Mark	Name	Pos	Meet	Venue	Date
48.97	van Zyl	4	DL	Shanghai	18 May
49.54	Robertson	4	NC	Kingston	27 Jun
49.67	Mucheru	1h3	CG	Glasgow	30 Jul
49.89	Brown	1s1	NCAA	Eugene	11 Jun

Mark Name Nat Born Pos Meet Venue Date

JUNIORS

See main list for top 5 juniors. 11 performances by 4 men to 50.10. Additional marks and further juniors:

Hyde 49.49 1 N.Sch Kingston 28 Mar
Abbas 49.71 1 AsiG Incheon 1 Aug 49.93 1s3 WJ Eugene 24 Jul
Holmes 49.98 2 Big12 Lubbock 18 May 50.07 4 NCAA Eugene 13 Jun
50.02 1 NC-j Eugene 6 Jul 50.07 3 WJ Eugene 25 Jul

Mark		Name	Nat	Born	Pos	Meet	Venue	Date
50.45	Anthony Tyrell	Kuriki	JPN	.96	1J		Isahaya	19 Oct
50.49		Yu Chia-Hsuan	TPE	22.1.95	1	AsC-j	Taipei	15 Jun
50.56		Wang Guozhong	CHN	31.1.95	2	NC	Suzhou	10 Oct
50.62	Khallifah	Rosser	USA	13.7.95	3	NC-j	Eugene	6 Jul
50.68	Jonas	Hanßen (10)	GER	15.7.95	1		Mannheim	6 Jul
50.71A	Ruan	Mentz	RSA	12.1.95	3	Univ Ch	Pretoria	26 Apr
50.73	Desmond	Palmer	USA	30.7.95	2q1	NCAA-E	Jacksonville	30 May
50.75	Byron	Robinson	USA	16.2.95	1		Tuscaloosa	5 Apr
50.76	Yusuke	Sakanashi	JPN	26.4.95	3	AsC-j	Taipei	15 Jun
50.88	Okeem	Williams	JAM	1.1.96	2	NC-j	Kingston	14 Jun
51.01	Marvin	Williams	JAM	13.6.96	3	NC-j	Kingston	14 Jun
51.02	Derek	Jones	USA	9.5.95	3	Big12	Lubbock	18 May
51.04		Wang Yang	CHN	20.9.96	2		Jinan	12 Jul
51.07	Leandro	Zamora	CUB	11.3.96	1		La Habana	10 May
51.08	J.W.	Smith (20)	USA	1.1.95	4	Big12	Lubbock	18 May

HIGH JUMP

2.43 Mutaz Essa Barshim QAT 24.6.91 1 VD Bruxelles 5 Sep
2.25/1 2.28/2 2.31/1 2.34/1 2.37/2 2.40/1 2.43/1 2.46/xxx
2.42 2 adidas New York 14 Jun 2.20/1 2.25/1 2.29/1 2.32/1 2.35/3 2.38/1 2.40/2 2.42/1
2.44/x 2.46/xx
2.41 1 GGala Roma 5 Jun 2.20/1 2.24/1 2.28/2 2.31/1 2.34/1 2.37/1 2.41/1 2.43/xxx
2.41 1 Eberstadt 22 Aug 2.24/1 2.30/2 2.33/1 2.35/1 2.37/1 2.39/1 2.41/2 2.43/xxx
2.38i 1 WI Sopot 9 Mar 2.20/1 2.25/1 2.29/1 2.32/1 2.34/1 2.36/1 2.38/1 2.40/xxx
2.38 4 Athl Lausanne 3 Jul 2.20/1 2.25/1 2.29/3 2.35/1 2.38/1 2.40/xxx
2.38 1 DL Birmingham 24 Aug 2.24/1 2.28/1 2.32/1 2.35/1 2.38/3 2.41/xxx
2.37 4 DL Doha 9 May 2.19/1 2.24/1 2.27/1 2.30/1 2.33/1 2.35/3 2.37/3
2.37 2 Herc Monaco 18 Jul 2.20/1 2.25/1 2.30/1 2.34/1 2.37/1 2.40/xx 2.43/x
2.42i Ivan Ukhov RUS 29.3.86 1 Praha 25 Feb
2.15/1 2.25/1 2.33/1 2.42/1 2.44/xxx
2.41i 1 Chelyabinsk 16 Jan 2.15/1 2.23/1 2.32/1 2.36/1 2.41/3
2.41 1 DL Doha 9 May 2.19/1 2.27/x 2.30/1 2.35/x 2.39/1 2.41/1 2.43/x
2.40i 1 Arnstadt 8 Feb 2.24/1 2.30/1 2.36/1 2.40/1 2.44/xxx
2.38i 1 Novocheboksarsk 11 Jan 2.15/1 2.24/1 2.30/1 2.35/1 2.38/3 2.41/xxx
2.38i 1 NC Moskva 18 Feb 2.15/1 2.24/1 2.30/2 2.34/1 2.38/1 2.44/xx
2.38i 2 WI Sopot 9 Mar 2.20/1 2.29/1 2.34/1 2.38/3 2.40/xxx
2.38 3 Athl Lausanne 3 Jul 2.20/1 2.29/2 2.35/1 2.38/1 2.42/xxx
2.42 Bogdan Bondarenko UKR 30.8.89 1 adidas New York 14 Jun
2.25/1 2.35/1 2.40/2 2.42/1 2.46/xxx
2.40 1 Tokyo 11 May 2.20/1 2.31/3 2.34/3 2.40/3 2.46/x
2.40 1 Athl Lausanne 3 Jul 2.29/3 2.35/1 2.40/2 2.46/xxx
2.40 1 Herc Monaco 18 Jul 2.25/2 2.34/1 2.40/1 2.43/xxx
2.40 2 VD Bruxelles 5 Sep 2.28/1 2.34/1 2.37/1 2.40/1 2.43/x 2.46/xx
2.39 1 Marrakech 8 Jun 2.25/1 2.33/1 2.39/2 2.46/xxx
2.38 1 Gyulai Székesfehérvár 8 Jul 2.26/2 2.32/1 2.38/3 2.43/x
2.38 2 DL Birmingham 24 Aug 2.28/2 2.35/1 2.38/3 2.41/xxx
2.37 1 C.Cup Marrakech 13 Sep 2.27/1 2.34/3 2.37/1 2.43/xxx
2.40i Aleksey Dmitrik RUS 12.4.84 2 Arnstadt 8 Feb
2.10/2 2.15/1 2.20/1 2.24/1 2.27/1 2.30/1 2.33/3 2.36/1 2.40/2 2.42/xxx
2.40 Derek Drouin CAN 6.3.90 1 Drake Des Moines 25 Apr
2.11/1 2.16/1 2.21/1 2.25/1 2.29/1 2.32/1 2.35/1 2.38/1 2.40/3
2.37 2= DL Doha 9 May 2.19/1 2.24/2 2.30/1 2.33/2 2.35/1 2.37/1 2.39/xxx
2.40 Andriy Protsenko UKR 20.5.88 2 Athl Lausanne 3 Jul
2.20/1 2.25/1 2.29/x 2.32/1 2.35/1 2.38/1 2.40/3 2.42/x
2.37 Eric Kynard USA 3.2.91 2= DL Doha 9 May
(31/7) 2.19/2 2.24/1 2.27/1 2.30/1 2.33/1 2.35/2 2.37/1 2.39/xx 2.41/x

Mark		Name	Nat	Born	Pos	Meet	Venue	Date
2.35	Dusty	Jonas	USA	19.4.86	3	Drake	Des Moines	25 Apr
2.34i	Daniyil	Tsyplakov	RUS	12.7.92	2	NC	Moskva	18 Feb
2.34i	Marco (10)	Fassinotti	ITA	29.4.89	1	NC	Ancona	23 Feb
2.34A	Mickaël	Hanany	FRA	25.3.83	1		El Paso	22 Mar
2.34		Zhang Guowei	CHN	4.6.91	1		Oordegem	5 Jul
2.33i	Lev	Missirov	RUS	4.8.90	3		Arnstadt	8 Feb
2.33i	Donald	Thomas	BAH	1.7.84	4		Arnstadt	8 Feb
2.32i	Mihai	Donisan	ROU	24.7.88	1	NC	Bucuresti	15 Feb

Mark	Name		Nat	Born	Pos	Meet	Venue	Date
2.32i	Sergey	Mudrov	RUS	8.9.90	3	NC	Moskva	18 Feb
2.32iA	James	Harris	USA	18.9.91	1	NCAA	Albuquerque	14 Mar
2.32	Wojciech	Theiner	POL	25.6.86	1		Katowice	2 Jul
2.31Ai	Nick	Ross	USA	8.8.91	1		Albuquerque	24 Jan
2.31	Naoto	Tobe	JPN	31.3.92	3		Tokyo	11 Ma
	(20)							
2.31		Wang Yu	CHN	18.8.91	1		Bruay-Le-Buissière	27 Jun
2.31	Jaroslav	Bába	CZE	2.9.84	1	NC	Ostrava	2 Aug
2.30i	Ivan	Ilyichev	RUS	14.10.86	1		Moskva	12 Jan
2.30i	Tom	Parsons	GBR	5.5.84	1		Solihull	19 Jan
2.30i	Ricky	Robertson	USA	19.9.90	1		Nashville	24 Jan
2.30i	Michael	Mason	CAN	30.9.86	1	Mill	New York (Arm)	15 Feb
2.30	Jeron	Robinson	USA	30.4.91	1	NCAA-2	Allendale	23 May
2.30	Adónios	Mástoras	GRE	6.1.91	2	GS	Ostrava	17 Jun
2.30	Andrey	Churylo	BLR	19.5.93	1		Minsk	18 Jul
2.29i	Andrey	Silnov	RUS	9.9.84	2		Chelyabinsk	16 Jan
	(30)							
2.29i	Yevgeniy	Korshunov	RUS	11.4.86	3		Chelyabinsk	16 Jan
2.29iA	Marcus	Jackson	USA	8.7.91	3	NCAA	Albuquerque	14 Mar
2.29	Jesse	Williams	USA	27.12.83	5	adidas	New York	14 Jun
2.29	Gianmarco	Tamberi	ITA	1.6.92	1		Ancona	27 Aug
2.29	Joel	Baden	AUS-J	1.2.96	1		Melbourne	18 Oct
2.28i	Martin	Günther	GER	8.10.86	1	NC	Leipzig	23 Feb
2.28i	Ali Mohamed	Younes Idriss	SUD	15.9.89	1	FRA Ch	Bordeaux	23 Feb
2.28A	Kabelo Mmono	Kgosiemang	BOT	7.1.86	1		Germiston	15 Mar
2.28	Takashi	Eto	JPN	5.2.91	4		Tokyo	11 May
2.28	Dmitriy	Semyonov	RUS	2.8.92	2		Cluj-Napoca	6 Jun
	(40)							
2.28i	Chris	Baker	GBR	2.2.91	1		Birmingham	7 Jun
2.28	Bryan	McBride	USA	10.12.91	1	NCAA	Eugene	13 Jun
2.28	Fernand	Djoumessi	CMR	5.9.89	1		Bühl	19 Jun
2.28	Yuriy	Dergachev	KAZ	8.11.94	1	NC	Almaty	28 Jun
2.28	Ryan	Ingraham	BAH	2.11.93	1	NC	Nassau	28 Jun
2.28	Yuriy	Krymarenko	UKR	11.8.83	1		Berdychev	28 Jun
2.28	Konstadínos	Baniótis	GRE	6.11.86	1		Argos Orestikó	9 Jul
2.28	Ray	Bobrownicki	GBR	3.3.84	1		Grangemouth	13 Jul
2.28	Arseniy	Rasov	RUS	23.6.92	2	NC-23	Saransk	16 Jul
2.28	Muamer Aissa	Barshim	QAT	3.1.94	1	Sidlo	Sopot	20 Jul
	(50)							
2.28	Kyriakos	Ioannou	CYP	26.7.84	2	CG	Glasgow	30 Jul
2.28	Tihomir Ivaylo	Ivanov	BUL	11.7.94	1		Kragujevac	3 Aug
2.28	Edgar	Rivera	MEX	13.2.91	1	IbAmC	São Paulo	3 Aug
2.27i	Robbie	Grabarz	GBR	3.10.87	3	GP	Birmingham	15 Feb
2.27Ai	Darius	Purcell	USA	10.1.89	2	NC	Albuquerque	22 Feb
2.27	Jacorian	Duffield	USA	2.9.92	1		Lubbock	3 May
2.27	Eure	Yáñez	VEN	20.5.93	1		São Paulo	4 May
2.27	Matús	Bubeník	SVK	14.11.89	2		Tábor	8 Jul
2.26i	Aleksandr	Shustov	RUS	29.6.84	4		Chelyabinsk	16 Jan
2.26i	Donte	Nall	USA	27.1.88	1		Chapel Hill	22 Feb
	(60)							
2.26		Yoon Sung-hyun	KOR	1.6.94	1		Andong	12 Apr
2.26	Edward	Dudley	USA	21.6.92	1		Akron	10 May
2.26	Luis Joel	Castro	PUR	28.1.91	1		Garbsen	18 May
2.26	Andrey	Skobeyko	BLR-J	11.6.95	2		Brest	31 May
2.26	Viktor	Ninov	BUL	19.6.88	1	NC	Sliven	4 Jun
2.26	Lukás	Beer	SVK	23.8.89	1		Banská Bystrica	7 Jun
2.26	Majed El Dein	Ghazal	SYR	21.4.87	1		Kangar	25 Jun
2.26	Raivydas	Stanys	LTU	3.2.87	1	NC	Kaunas	27 Jul
2.26	Jussi	Viita	FIN	26.9.85	1	NC	Kuopio	3 Aug
2.26A	Jamal	Wilson	BAH	1.9.88	2	PAm SF	Ciudad de México	16 Aug
	(70)							
2.26A	Sergio	Mestre	CUB	30.8.91	1	CAG	Xalapa	27 Nov
2.25i	Trevor	Barry	BAH	14.6.83	5		Hustopece	1 Feb
2.25	Talles	Silva	BRA	20.8.91	1		Campinas	29 Mar
2.25	Garrett	Huyler	USA	15.1.87	1		St Louis	12 Apr
2.25	Maalik	Reynolds	USA	26.4.92	1		New Haven	10 May
2.25		Wang Chen	CHN	27.2.90	1		Manhattan, KS	10 May
2.25	Brandon	Starc	AUS	24.11.93	5		Tokyo	11 May
2.25	David	Smith	GBR	14.7.91	1		Loughborough	24 May
2.25	Sylwester	Bednarek	POL	28.4.89	1		Mikolow	25 May
2.25	Allan	Smith	GBR	6.11.92	2=	BIG	Bedford	1 Jun
	(80)							

Mark	Name		Nat	Born	Pos	Meet	Venue	Date
2.25	Wally	Ellenson	USA	4.5.94	2	NCAA	Eugene	13 Jun
2.25i	Dmytro	Yakovenko	UKR	17.9.92	1		Kyiv	11 Jul
2.25i	Andriy	Kovalyov	UKR	11.6.92	2		Kyiv	11 Jul
2.25	Vadim	Vrublevskiy	RUS	18.3.93	2		Saransk	3 Aug
2.25	Mohammad Reza	Vazifehdoost	IRI	13.10.93	1		Tehran	22 Aug
2.25	Hiromi	Takahari	JPN	13.11.87	1		Yokohama	21 Sep
2.25i	Mikhail	Veryovkin	RUS	28.6.91	1		Kineshma	7 Dec
2.25i	Ilya	Ivanyuk	RUS	9.3.93	1		Moskva	21 Dec
2.24i	Andrey	Patrakov	RUS	7.11.89	4		Moskva	28 Jan
2.24i	Mikhail	Andreyev	RUS	4.4.91	2		Samara	30 Jan
	(90)							
2.24i	Giulio	Ciotti	ITA	5.10.76	1		Pordenone	1 Feb
2.24i	Nikita	Anishchenkov	RUS	25.7.92	8		Moskva	2 Feb
2.24i	Mikhail	Akimenko	RUS-J	6.12.95	1	NC-j	Volgograd	8 Feb
2.24i	Raul	Spank	GER	13.7.88	7		Arnstadt	8 Feb
2.24i	Montez	Blair	USA	23.10.90	1		Ithaca	22 Feb
2.24i	Peter	Horák	SVK	7.12.83	2	NC	Bratislava	23 Feb
2.24i	Mateusz	Przybylko	GER	9.3.92	2	NC	Leipzig	23 Feb
2.24i		Guo Jinqi	CHN	21.9.92	1		Nanjing	8 Mar
2.24i		Sun Zhao	CHN	8.2.90	2		Nanjing	8 Mar
2.24	Danyil	Lysenko	RUS-Y	19.5.97	1	EYOT	Baku	1 Jun
	(100)							
2.24	Vladyslav	Dorofyeyev	UKR	22.4.94	1		Kyiv	3 Jun
2.24	Eugenio	Rossi	SMR	6.3.92	1	ETC-3	Tbilisi	21 Jun
2.24	Chris	Kandu	GBR-J	10.9.95	1	NC-J	Bedford	22 Jun
2.24		Chen Ji	CHN	27.1.90	2		Jinan	11 Jul
2.24	Dakarai	Hightower	USA	15.7.94	1		Tacoma	12 Jul
2.24	Guilherme	Cobbo	BRA	1.10.87	1		Buenos Aires	19 Jul
2.24	Dmitriy	Nabokov	BLR-J	20.1.96	2	WJ	Eugene	25 Jul
2.24		Woo Sang-hyeok	KOR-J	23.4.96	3	WJ	Eugene	25 Jul
2.24	Christoffe	Bryan	JAM-J	26.4.96	4	WJ	Eugene	25 Jul
2.24	Osku	Torro	FIN	21.8.79	2	NC	Kuopio	3 Aug
2.24	Bram	Ghuys	BEL	14.2.93	1	NC-23	Mouscron	14 Sep
2.24	Fernando	Ferreira	BRA	13.12.94	1	SAm-23	Montevideo	5 Oct

Mark	Name		Nat	Born	Date
2.23i	Jeffery	Herron	USA	22.4.90	1 Feb
2.23	Chris	Dodd	AUS	28.2.89	22 Feb
2.23i	Andre	Dorsey	USA	11.3.93	22 Feb
2.23i	Cameron	Ostrowski	USA	15.6.92	1 Mar
2.23i	Bradley	Adkins	USA	30.12.93	1 Mar
2.23i	Dávid	Fajoyomi	HUN	3.9.89	8 Mar
2.23	Nik	Bojic	AUS	18.1.92	5 Apr
2.23	Deante	Kemper	USA	27.3.93	19 Apr
2.23	Anthony	May	USA	19.9.90	26 Apr
2.23	Miguel Ángel	Sancho	ESP	24.4.90	9 May
2.23	Xavier	McAllister	USA	4.11.93	17 May
2.23	Artyom	Naumovich	BLR	19.2.91	31 May
2.23	Péter	Bakosi	HUN	23.6.93	14 Jun
2.23	Florian	Labourel	FRA	28.1.90	24 Jun
2.23	Douwe	Amels	NED	16.9.91	20 Jul
2.23	Tobias	Potye	GER-J	16.3.95	24 Aug
2.23	Falk	Wendrich	GER-J	12.6.95	24 Aug
2.23i	Hoova	Taylor	USA	11.6.87	6 Dec
2.22i	Viktor	Shapoval	UKR	17.10.79	9 Jan
2.22i	Mike	Edwards	GBR	11.7.90	1 Feb
2.22i	Andrea	Lemmi	ITA	12.5.84	23 Feb
2.22i	Sebastién	Deschamps	FRA	12.4.87	23 Feb
2.22	Raudelis	Rodríguez	CUB	27.9.92	19 Mar
2.22	Martyn	Bernard	GBR	15.12.84	26 Apr
2.22	Matthew	Roberts	GBR	22.12.84	1 Jun
2.22	Kirill	Rudov	RUS	23.10.92	6 Jun
2.22	Keyvan	Ghanbarzadeh	IRI	26.5.90	15 Jun
2.22	Sergey	Zasimovich	KAZ	11.3.86	15 Jun
2.22	Vitaliy	Tsykunov	KAZ	22.1.87	28 Jun
2.22	Andrey	Kravchenko	BLR	4.1.86	12 Aug
2.21i	Ignacio	Vigo	ESP	11.5.94	18 Jan
2.21i	Kristoffer	Nilsen	NOR	28.3.89	8 Feb
2.21i	Isaiah	Harris	USA	.92	21 Feb
2.21i	Kris	Kornegay-Gober	USA	6.10.91	22 Feb
2.21i	Milos	Todosijevic	SRB	8.3.86	22 Feb
2.21i	David	Bolado	ESP	10.9.92	23 Feb
2.21i	Tanner	Anderson	USA	4.5.92	28 Feb
2.21	Ronnie	Black	USA	2.8.90	22 Mar
2.21	Justin	Fondren	USA	2.2.94	5 Apr
2.21	Domanique	Missick	TKS	9.1.92	10 Apr
2.21	Gemikal	Prude	USA	.92	12 Apr
2.21	Ferrante	Grasselli	ITA	4.4.91	25 Apr
2.21	Josué	da Costa	BRA	15.3.93	4 May
2.21A	Gobe	Takobana	BOT	7.9.91	10 May
2.21	Avion	Jones	USA	31.1.94	11 May
2.21	Manjula Kumara	Wijesekara	SRI	30.1.84	18 May
2.21	Viktor	Brumel	RUS	8.10.92	24 May
2.21	Nauraj Singh	Randhawa	MAS	27.1.92	25 Jun
2.21	Dmitriy	Kroyter	ISR	18.2.93	16 Jul
2.21	Carlos	Layoy	ARG	26.2.91	19 Jul
2.21	David	Nopper	GER-J	25.1.95	27 Jul
2.21	Brendon	Rivera	USA-Y	10.3.97	3 Aug
2.21	Nichil	Chittarasu	IND	24.8.90	18 Aug
2.20i	Alexander	Bowen	USA	3.4.93	11 Jan
2.20i	Dmytro	Demyanyuk	UKR	30.6.83	17 Jan
2.20i	Piotr	Sleboda	POL	22.1.87	27 Jan
2.20i	Szymon	Kiecana	POL	26.3.89	27 Jan
2.20i	Vitaliy	Samoylenko	UKR	22.5.84	28 Jan
2.20i	Martin	Heindl	CZE	2.6.92	29 Jan
2.20i	Jon	Hendershot	USA	12.11.91	1 Feb
2.20i	Mohamed	Koita	FRA	8.1.90	15 Feb
2.20	Niki	Palli	ISR	28.5.87	27 Feb
2.20iA	Django	Lovett	CAN	6.7.92	28 Feb
2.20	Liam	Zamel-Paez	IRL	4.8.88	15 Mar
2.20i		Bi Xiaoliang	CHN	26.12.92	21 Mar
2.20	Cody	Crampton	USA	5.11.93	22 Mar
2.20	Enrique	Esquer	MEX	2.12.91	22 Mar
2.20	Arturo Joaquín	Abascal	MEX-J	19.6.95	22 Mar
2.20A	Jorge Ignacio	Rouco	MEX	15.11.87	30 Mar
2.20		Bai Jiaxu	CHN-Y	1.11.97	3 Apr
2.20	Kyle	Landon	USA	16.10.94	19 Apr
2.20		Yi Shisuo	CHN	20.2.90	19 Apr
2.20	Trevor	James	USA	4.5.92	26 Apr
2.20	Kevin	Spejcher	USA	17.12.93	3 May
2.20A	Justin	Bethea	USA	28.3.91	6 May
2.20	Jamario	Taylor	USA	18.12.90	16 May
2.20	Justin	Frick	USA	3.8.88	17 May
2.20	Batyrkhan	Baimukhambetov	KAZ	7.9.92	29 May
2.20		Pai Long	CHN	8.10.89	31 May
2.20	Daisuke	Nakajima	JPN-J	18.4.95	1 Jun
2.20	Mihai	Anastasiu	ROU	11.3.93	6 Jun
2.20	Andrei	Miticov	MDA	15.11.86	6 Jun
2.20	David	Smith	USA	2.5.92	13 Jun
2.20	Andy	Gilmore	USA	16.8.80	21 Jun

Mark	Name		Nat	Born	Pos Meet	Venue	Date
2.20	Anton	Bodnar	KAZ	12.4.92			28 Jun
2.20	Hikaru	Tsuchiya	JPN	1.2.86			29 Jun
2.20	Vasilios	Constantinou	CYP	13.9.92			9 Jul
2.20		Hsiang Chun-Hsieng	TPE	4.9.93			11 Jul
2.20	Tairo	Omata	JPN	12.9.89			12 Jul
2.20	Paulo César	Conceição	POR	29.12.93			16 Jul
2.20	Artyom	Zaytsev	BLR	7.12.84			18 Jul
2.20	Janick	Klausen	DEN	3.4.93			26 Jul
2.20	Javier	Bermejo	ESP	23.12.78			26 Jul
2.20	Sreenith	Mohan	IND-J	24.3.95			9 Aug
2.20	Tiago	Portela	BRA	31.7.91			14 Sep
2.20	Yuji	Hiramatsu	JPN-Y	11.1.97			20 Oct
2.20	Rafael	dos Santos	BRA	10.10.91			21 Nov
2.20i	Ilya	Spitsyn	RUS-J	28.7.96			27 Dec
	(210)						

Best outdoor marks

Mark	Name	Pos	Meet	Venue	Date
2.33	Tsyplakov	1		Saransk	3 Aug
2.30	Ross	1		Tucson	3 May
2.30	Fassinotti	7	Herc	Monaco	18 Jul
2.30	Dmitrik	10	Herc	Monaco	18 Jul
2.29	Robertson	1	TexR	Austin	29 Mar
2.29	Parsons	1		Birmingham	20 Jul
2.28	Mason	1	MSR	Walnut	19 Apr
2.28	Silnov	5=	GGala	Roma	5 Jun
2.28	Donisan	1		Cluj-Napoca	6 Jun
2.27	Baker	1	LI	Loughborough	18 May
2.26	Younes Idriss	1		Abidjan	26 Apr
2.25	Barry	4	Drake	Des Moines	25 Apr
2.25	Missirov	6	WCM	Beijing	21 May
2.25	Shustov	1		Adler	30 May
2.25	D Thomas	4		Marrakech	8 Jun
2.25	Günther	1	NC	Ulm	27 Jul
2.24	Guo Jinqi	1		Zhaoqing	19 Apr
2.24	Yakovenko	2		Berdychiv	28 Jun
2.24	Akimenko (J)	1	WJ	Eugene	25 Jul

Mark	Name	Date	Mark	Name	Date
2.23	Veryovkin	5 Jun	2.22	Ilyichev	15 Jun
2.23	Ivanyuk	6 Jul	2.22	Lemmi	28 Sep
2.23	Korshunov	26 Jul	2.21	Harris	8 Apr
2.22	Blair	10 May	2.21	Adkins	5 Apr
2.22	Przybylko	17 May	2.21	Purcell	26 Apr
2.20	Kornegay-Gober	19 Apr	2.20	Herron	28 Jun
2.20	Jackson	3 May	2.20	Deschamps	6 Jul
2.20	Bi Xiaoliang	31 May	2.20	Nall	6 Jul
2.20	Mudrov	8 Jun	2.20	Horák	13 Jul
2.20	Kovalyov	20 Jun	2.20	Todosijevic	9 Aug
2.20	Patrakov	25 Jun	2.20	Sun Zhao	9 Oct

JUNIORS

See main list for top 8 juniors. 10 performances (inc. 1 indoors) by 8 men to 2.24. Additional marks and further juniors:

	Mark	Pos	Meet	Venue	Date
Baden	2.26	1		Melbourne	9 Nov
Lysenko	2.24	1	NC-j	Cheboksary	17 Jun

Mark	Name		Nat	Born	Pos	Meet	Venue	Date
2.23	Tobias	Potye	GER-J	16.3.95	1-u23		Eberstadt	24 Aug
2.23	Falk	Wendrich (10)	GER-J	12.6.95	2-u23		Eberstadt	24 Aug
2.21	David	Nopper	GER	25.1.95	2	NC	Ulm	27 Jul
2.21	Brendon	Rivera	USA-Y	10.3.97	1		College Station	3 Aug
2.20	Arturo Joaquín	Abascal	MEX	19.6.95	3		Monterrey	22 Mar
2.20		Bai Jiaxu	CHN-Y	1.11.97	1	NC-y	Chongqing	3 Apr
2.20	Daisuke	Nakajima	JPN	18.4.95	1		Utsunomiya	1 Jun
2.20	Sreenith	Mohan	IND	24.3.95	1		Kochi	9 Aug
2.20	Yuji	Hiramatsu	JPN-Y	11.1.97	1-Y		Isahaya	20 Oct
2.20i	Ilya	Spitsyn	RUS	28.7.96	1		Sankt-Peterburg	27 Dec
2.19	Bryant	O'Georgia	USA	11.6.96	1		Mesa	10 May
2.19	Daniel	Cortéz (20)	COL	9.10.95	1		Cartagena	10 Oct

POLE VAULT

Mark	Name		Nat	Born	Pos Meet	Venue	Date
6.16i	Renaud	Lavillenie	FRA	18.9.86	1	Donetsk	15 Feb

5.76/1 5.91/1 6.01/3 6.16/1 6.21/x

Mark	Pos	Meet	Venue	Date	Series
6.08i	1		Bydgoszcz	31 Jan	5.68/1 5.81/2 5.92/1 6.00/1 6.08/1 6.16/xxx
6.04i	1		Rouen	25 Jan	5.67/1 5.83/2 5.93/1 6.04/1 6.16/x
5.93	1	VD	Bruxelles	5 Sep	5.65/2 5.83/1 5.93/2 6.03/xxx
5.92	1	DL	Shanghai	18 May	5.52/2 5.72/2 5.82/1 5.92/1 6.03/xxx
5.90	1	EC	Zürich	16 Aug	5.65/1 5.80/1 5.90/2 6.01/xxx
5.90	1	Déca	Angers	30 Aug	5.65/1 5.80/2 5.90/3 6.00/xxx
5.87	1	Athl	Lausanne	3 Jul	5.72/2 5.82/x 5.87/1 5.93/xxx
5.84i	1		Aubière	11 Jan	5.66/2 5.84/1 5.94/xxx
5.83	1	GS	Ostrava	17 Jun	5.73/2 5.83/1 5.93/xxx
5.80	1	Pre	Eugene	31 May	5.63/2 5.80/2 5.90/xxx
5.80	1	FBK	Hengelo	8 Jun	5.65/1 5.80/3 5.91/xxx
5.80	1	NC	Reims	13 Jul	5.65/1 5.80/1 5.90/xxx
5.80	1	C.Cup	Marrakech	14 Sep	5.65/1 5.80/3 5.90/xxx
5.77	1	Bisl	Oslo	11 Jun	5.60/1 5.70/1 5.77/1 5.83/xxx

Mark	Name		Nat	Born	Pos Meet	Venue	Date
5.90i	Malte	Mohr	GER	24.7.86	1 ISTAF	Berlin	1 Mar

5.50/1 5.70/1 5.80/1 5.90/3 6.01/xxx

Mark	Pos	Meet	Venue	Date	Series
5.84i	1	NC	Leipzig	23 Feb	5.40/1 5.60/1 5.76/1 5.84/2 6.01/xxx
5.80i	2	WI	Sopot	8 Mar	5.55/1 5.65/1 5.75/1 5.80/2 5.85/xxx

Mark	Name		Nat	Born	Pos Meet	Venue	Date
5.83i	Luke	Cutts	GBR	13.2.88	2	Rouen	25 Jan

5.28/1 5.43/1 5.58/2 5.67/1 5.75/2 5.83/1 5.88/xxx

Mark	Pos	Meet	Venue	Date	Series
5.81i	2		Donetsk	15 Feb	5.31/2 5.46/1 5.56/1 5.66/1 5.76/2 5.81/2 5.91/x 5.96/xx

Mark	Name		Nat	Born	Pos Meet	Venue	Date
5.83	Mark	Hollis	USA	1.12.84	1	Landau	19 Aug

5.32/1 5.52/1 5.62/2 5.72/1 5.83/2

Mark	Pos	Meet	Venue	Date	Series
5.80	1		Aachen	3 Sep	5.40/1 5.50/1 5.60/1 5.70/3 5.80/1 5.85/xxx
5.80	1		Liège (NX)	16 Jul	5.30/1 5.45/1 5.59/1 5.71/1 5.80/1 5.85/x

Mark	Name		Nat	Born	Pos Meet	Venue	Date
5.82	Piotr	Lisek	POL	16.8.92	1 Odlozil	Praha	9 Jun

5.42/1 5.52/1 5.60/2 5.72/3 5.82/1

Mark	Pos	Meet	Venue	Date	Series
5.77i	1		Bad Oeynhausen	1 Mar	5.44/1 5.64/1 5.77/1 5.87/xxx

Mark		Name		Nat	Born	Pos	Meet	Venue	Date
5.80i		Konstadinos	Filippídis	GRE	26.11.86	1	WI	Sopot	8 Mar
					5.40/1	5.55/1	5.65/1	5.75/1	5.80/1 5.85/xxx
	5.77i	1 NC	Pireás	8 Feb	5.40/1	5.50/1	5.60/1	5.77/2	5.84/xxx
5.80i		Jan	Kudlicka	CZE	29.4.88	3	WI	Sopot	8 Mar
					5.40/1	5.65/1	5.75/3	5.80/3	5.85/xxx
5.80			Xue Changrui	CHN	31.5.91	1	WCM	Beijing	21 May
					5.40/1	5.60/1	5.70/3	5.80/2	5.94/xxx
5.80		Pawel	Wojciechowski	POL	6.6.89	1	ISTAF	Berlin	31 Aug
		(30/9)			5.40/1	5.60/1	5.70/3	5.80/1	5.92/xxx
5.76i		Jérôme	Clavier (10)	FRA	3.5.83	2		Nice	8 Feb
5.76i		Thiago	Braz da Silva	BRA	16.12.93	3		Donetsk	15 Feb
5.75i		Kévin	Menaldo	FRA	12.7.92	2		Aubière	11 Jan
5.75i		Robert	Sobera	POL	19.1.91	2	Pedros	Bydgoszcz	31 Jan
5.75Ai		Shawn	Barber	CAN	27.5.94	1	NCAA	Albuquerque	15 Mar
5.75		Sam	Kendricks	USA	7.9.92	1	NC	Sacramento	29 Jun
5.73		Tobias	Scherbarth	GER	17.8.85	1		Phoenix	24 May
5.71i		Alhaji	Jeng	SWE	13.12.81	3		Dessau	27 Feb
5.71i		Steve	Lewis	GBR	20.5.86	2	Drake	Des Moines	23 Apr
5.71		Karsten	Dilla	GER	17.7.89	1		Hof	21 Jun
5.71		Michal	Balner	CZE	12.9.82	1		Kolín	7 Sep
		(20)							
5.71		Fábio Gomes	da Silva	BRA	4.8.83	1	NC	São Paulo	10 Oct
5.70i		Edi	Maia	POR	10.11.87	3		Orléans	18 Jan
5.70		Logan	Cunningham	USA	30.5.91	1	TexR	Austin	29 Mar
5.70		Daichi	Sawano	JPN	16.9.80	1	MSR	Walnut	19 Apr
5.70		Colton	Ross	USA	4.6.92	1		Austin	3 May
5.70		Aleksandr	Gripich	RUS	21.9.86	1		Adler	29 May
5.70		Jack	Whitt	USA	12.4.90	2		Rottach-Egern	5 Jul
5.70		Augusto	Dutra de Oliveira	BRA	16.7.90	2=	DL	Saint-Denis	5 Jul
5.70		Giuseppe	Gibilisco	ITA	5.1.79	1		Rieti	12 Jul
5.70		Sergey	Kucheranyu	RUS	30.6.85	1=	NC	Kazan	25 Jul
		(30)							
5.70		Ilya	Mudrov	RUS	17.11.91	1=	NC	Kazan	25 Jul
5.70		Dmitriy	Starodubtsev	RUS	3.1.86	3	NC	Kazan	25 Jul
5.67		Diogo	Ferreira	POR	30.7.90	1	NC	Lisboa (U)	26 Jul
5.66i			Yang Yancheng	CHN	5.1.88	1eB		Aubière	11 Jan
5.66i		Valentin	Lavillenie	FRA	16.7.91	3		Nice	8 Feb
5.66i		Damiel	Dossévi	FRA	3.2.83	4		Nice	8 Feb
5.65i		Melker	Svärd Jacobsson	SWE	8.1.94	3		Potsdam	15 Feb
5.65			Jin Min-sup	KOR	2.9.92	1		Busan	17 May
5.65		Anton	Ivakin	RUS	3.2.91	2		Adler	29 May
5.65	sq	Lukasz	Michalski	POL	2.8.88	1		Pila	13 Jun
		(40)							
5.64		Jacob	Blankenship	USA	15.3.94	2	SEC	Lexington	18 May
5.62		Mike	Woepse	USA	29.5.91	1		Los Angeles (Ww)	4 May
5.62		Dimítrios	Patsoukákis	GRE	18.3.87	1		Athina	10 May
5.62		Seito	Yamamoto	JPN	11.3.92	5	DL	Shanghai	18 May
5.62		Brad	Walker	USA	21.6.81	4=	Athl	Lausanne	3 Jul
5.62		Max	Eaves	GBR	31.5.88	1	LEAP	Loughborough	19 Jul
5.61		Hiroki	Ogita	JPN	30.12.87	1		Fukushima	17 May
5.61i		Jax	Thoirs	GBR	7.4.93	1		Grangemouth	2 Jul
5.61		Artem	Burya	RUS	11.4.86	5	NC	Kazan	25 Jul
5.61		Leonid	Kivalov	RUS	1.4.88	6	NC	Kazan	25 Jul
		(50)							
5.60i		Anatoliy	Bednyuk	RUS	30.1.89	1		Chelyabinsk	16 Jan
5.60iA		Mike	Arnold	USA	13.8.90	3		Reno	17 Jan
5.60i		Björn	Otto	GER	16.10.77	1		Cottbus	22 Jan
5.60i		Andrew	Irwin	USA	23.1.93	1		Fayetteville	15 Feb
5.60i		Igor	Bychkov	ESP	7.3.87	1		Madrid	1 Mar
5.60		Dmitry	Zhelyabin	RUS	20.5.90	3		Adler	29 May
5.60			Zhang Wei	CHN	22.3.94	1		Kunshan	30 May
5.60		Dídac	Salas	ESP	19.5.93	1		Palafrugell	31 May
5.60	sq	Przemyslaw	Czerwinski	POL	28.7.83	3		Pila	13 Jun
5.60		Victor	Weirich	USA	25.10.87	3	NC	Sacramento	29 Jun
		(60)							
5.60			Yao Jie	CHN	21.9.90	2	3-N	Jinhua	6 Jul
5.60		Alexandre	Feger	FRA	22.1.90	1		La Roche-sur-Yon	23 Jul
5.60		Mareks	Arents	LAT	6.8.86	2		Szczecin	3 Aug
5.56		Peter	Geraghty	USA	11.6.91	1		Charleton, IL	22 Apr
5.56		Chase	Wolfle	USA	9.10.92	3	SEC	Lexington	18 May
5.55i		Stanley	Joseph	FRA	24.10.91	7		Orléans	18 Jan

Mark	Name		Nat	Born	Pos	Meet	Venue	Date
5.55i	Eemeli	Salomäki	FIN	11.10.87	1		Lempäälä	25 Jan
5.55i	Japeth	Cato	USA	25.12.90	2		Fayetteville	15 Feb
5.55Ai	Shawn	Francis	USA	16.12.85	2	NC	Albuquerque	22 Feb
5.55Ai	Nicholas	Frawley	USA	21.6.88	3	NC	Albuquerque	22 Feb
	(70)							
5.55i	Theo	Chapelle	FRA	16.3.92	2		Nantes	16 Mar
5.55	Giorgio	Piantella	ITA	6.7.81	1		Modena	21 Jun
5.55	Alexandre	Marchand	FRA	23.2.90	3	NC	Reims	13 Jul
5.55	Axel	Chapelle	FRA-J	24.4.95	1	WJ	Eugene	26 Jul
5.55	Arnaud	Art	BEL	28.1.93	3		Castres	30 Jul
5.55	Marquis	Richards	SUI	29.7.91	1		Arlesheim	24 Aug
5.54	Pauls	Pujats	LAT	6.8.91	1		Memphis	29 Mar
5.54	Jeff	Coover	USA	1.12.87	1		Cedar Falls	21 Jun
5.53	Dustin	DeLeo	USA	3.1.86	2		Phoenix	24 May
5.53	Nick	Mossberg	USA	5.4.86	3		Phoenix	24 May
	(80)							
5.53	Raphael	Holzdeppe	GER	28.9.89	4	Pre	Eugene	31 May
5.53	Marco	Boni	ITA	21.5.84	1		Modena	30 Aug
5.52	Nikandros	Stylianou	CYP	22.8.89	4		Athina	10 May
5.52	Stanislav	Tivonchik	BLR	5.3.85	1		Brest	31 May
5.51i	Daniel	Clemens	GER	28.4.92	3		Zweibrücken	7 Feb
5.51i	Max	Babits	USA	30.5.92	1		Hillsdale	22 Feb
5.51	Reese	Watson	USA	8.10.93	1		Austin	12 Apr
5.51	Jacob	Winder	USA	12.11.87	1	KansR	Lawrence	19 Apr
5.51	Zachary	Siegmeier	USA	8.1.91	1		Iowa City	3 May
5.51	Germán	Chiaraviglio	ARG	16.4.87	3		Hof	21 Jun
	(90)							
5.50i	Oleksandr	Korchmid	UKR	22.1.82	1		Kyiv	10 Jan
5.50i	Brayden	Bringhurst	USA	89	1		Albuquerque	18 Jan
5.50i	Vincent	Favretto	FRA	5.4.84	1		Lyon	18 Jan
5.50i	Dmitriy	Sokolov	RUS	16.1.93	1		Chelyabinsk	19 Jan
5.50i	Grigoriy	Gorokhov	RUS	20.4.93	1		Moskva	4 Feb
5.50i	Gayk	Kazaryan	RUS	19.5.90	?		Moskva	4 Feb
5.50	Lázaro	Borges	CUB	19.6.86	1		La Habana	8 Feb
5.50i	Nicolas	Homo	FRA	24.11.88	1		Eaubonne	8 Feb
5.50i	Adam	Pasiak	CZE	18.7.90	2	NC	Praha	16 Feb
5.50i	Florian	Gaul	GER	21.9.91	2	NC	Leipzig	23 Feb
	(100)							
5.50	Casey	Bowen	USA	11.1.93	1	TexR	Austin	27 Mar
5.50	Chris	Pillow	USA	8.7.93	2	TexR	Austin	27 Mar
5.50	Michael	Viken	USA	21.9.90	4	TexR	Austin	28 Mar
5.50		Kim Yoo-suk	KOR	19.1.82	4		Chula Vista	8 May
5.50	Vladislav	Revenko	UKR	15.11.84	1		Kyiv	3 Jun
5.50	Sergey	Grigoryev	KAZ	24.6.92	1		Almaty	15 Jun
5.50	Nikita	Filippov	KAZ	7.10.91	1	NC	Almaty	27 Jun
5.50	Jason	Wurster	CAN	23.9.84	2	NC	Moncton	29 Jun
5.50	Danyil	Kotov	RUS-J	14.11.95	2	WJ	Eugene	26 Jul
5.50	Oleg	Zernikel	GER-J	16.4.95	3	WJ	Eugene	26 Jul
5.50	Devin	King	USA-J	12.3.96	4	WJ	Eugene	26 Jul
5.50	Shota	Doi	JPN	10.4.90	2		Marugame	11 Aug
5.50iA	Dylan	Bell	USA	21.7.93	1		Air Force Academy	12 Dec
5.50iA	Joseph	Uhle	USA	25.4.89	2		Air Force Academy	12 Dec

Mark	Name		Nat	Born	Date
5.46i	Denys	Yurchenko	UKR	27.1.78	15 Feb
5.46	Heorhiy	Bykov	UKR	31.1.94	25 Jun
5.46	Baptiste	Boirie	FRA	26.12.92	2 Jul
5.46i	Adam	Hague	GBR-Y	29.8.97	21 Dec
5.45i	Hendrik	Gruber	GER	28.9.86	5 Jan
5.45i	Levi	Keller	USA	30.1.86	18 Jan
5.45	João Gabriel	Sousa	BRA	6.11.84	25 Jan
5.45iA	Sam	Pierson	USA	7.4.88	25 Jan
5.45i	Alex	Bishop	USA	17.5.91	8 Feb
5.45iA	Jordan	Scott	USA	22.2.88	15 Feb
5.45i	Mikkel	Nielsen	DEN	13.9.88	15 Feb
5.45i	Noël	Ost	FRA	15.11.89	23 Feb
5.45i	Kyle	Wait	USA	20.2.92	28 Feb
5.45i	Torben	Laidig	GER	13.3.94	1 Mar
5.45i	Paul	Walker	GBR	15.8.85	2 Mar
5.45iA	Alex	McCune	USA	7.4.93	15 Mar
5.45	Stephan	Munz	GER	19.10.88	19 Apr
5.45	Gregor	MacLean	GBR	17.10.91	10 May
5.45		Han Do-hyun	KOR	28.7.94	17 May
5.45	Scott	Roth	USA	25.6.88	14 Jun
5.45	Marvin	Caspari	GER	9.8.91	14 Jul

Mark	Name		Nat	Born	Date
5.45	Tom	Konrad	GER	30.3.91	14 Jul
5.45		Huang Bokai	CHN-J	26.9.96	26 Jul
5.45	Leonid	Kobelev	RUS-J	24.6.95	26 Jul
5.45	Mickaël	Guillaume	FRA	8.9.89	30 Jul
5.45	Per Magne	Florvaag	NOR	21.2.93	8 Aug
5.44	Josh	Dangel	USA	21.1.91	11 Apr
5.43i	Chase	Brannon	USA	8.2.91	22 Feb
5.42i	Michael	Morrison	USA	18.3.88	1 Feb
5.42i	Seth	Arnold	USA	29.7.92	15 Feb
5.42	Mitch	Greeley	USA	5.5.86	24 May
5.42	Ivan	Horvat	CRO	17.8.93	14 Jun
5.41	Joel	Pocklington	AUS	12.4.86	18 Jan
5.41	Nikita	Kirillov	USA	5.6.93	12 Apr
5.41	Hiroki	Sasase	JPN	17.8.89	29 Apr
5.41	Rens	Blom	NED	1.3.77	21 Jun
5.41	Cheyne	Rahme	RSA	23.1.91	13 Aug
5.41	Lukás	Posekany	CZE	30.12.92	30 Aug
5.41	Menno	Vloon	NED	11.5.94	15 Aug
5.41	Hayato	Hotta	JPN	17.11.94	25 Oct
5.40i	Andrew	Sutcliffe	GBR	10.7.91	18 Jan
5.40i	Viktor	Kozlitin	RUS	12.6.88	24 Jan

Mark		Name	Nat	Born	Pos	Meet	Venue	Date
5.40iA	Gonzalo	Barroilhet	CHI	19.3.86				24 Jan
5.40i	Alessandro	Sinno	ITA	17.7.94				9 Feb
5.40i	Eelco	Sintnicolaas	NED	7.4.87				16 Feb
5.40i	Aleksey	Kovalchuk	RUS	22.7.88				19 Feb
5.40i	Nick	Cruchley	GBR	1.1.90				22 Feb
5.40i	Daniel	Gardner	GBR	26.3.94				22 Feb
5.40i	Mitsuru	Tanaka	JPN	22.11.89				2 Mar
5.40	Derick	Hinch	USA	2.2.91				18 Apr
5.40	Steven	Cahoy	USA	30.7.94				25 Apr
5.40	Jun-ya	Nagata	JPN	15.4.88				6 May
5.40	Brandon	Bray	USA-Y	24.4.97				10 May
5.40	Ryo	Tanaka	JPN	11.12.91				17 May
5.40	Nariharu	Matsuzawa	JPN	6.1.92				31 May
5.40	Mikhail	Gelmanov	RUS	18.3.90				4 Jun
5.40	Adam	Bragg	USA	18.4.93				11 Jun
5.40	Thomas	Van Der Plaetsen	BEL	24.12.90				14 Jun
5.40	Harry	Coppell	GBR-J	11.7.96				6 Jul
5.40	Maksym	Mazuryk	UKR	2.4.83				25 Jul
5.40	Jack	Hicking	AUS-J	22.2.95				26 Jul
5.40	Oscar	Janson	SWE	22.7.75				23 Aug
5.40i	Dmitriy	Lyubushkin	RUS	23.3.94				13 Dec
5.38	Joseph	Caraway	USA	13.10.90				5 Apr
5.38	Austin	Crenshaw	USA	22.1.82				4 May
5.37iA	Justin	Estala	USA					15 Feb
5.37i	Cyriel	Verberne	NED	4.12.84				23 Feb
5.37A	Matt	Sullivan	USA	.93				16 May
5.36	Michael	Frauen	GER	19.1.86				1 Jun
5.36	Mikkel Marek	Nielsen	DEN	13.9.88				3 Aug

(184)

Best outdoors

Mark	Name	Pos	Meet	Venue	Date
5.73	Braz da Silva	2	GS	Ostrava	17 Jun
5.72	Menaldo	1	Med23	Aubagne	14 Jun
5.72	Kudlicka	1	NC	Ostrava	3 Aug
	5.76 dh	1		Praha	2 Jul
5.70	Lewis	2	Drake	Des Moines	26 Apr
5.70	Mohr	2	Bisl	Oslo	11 Jun
5.70	Filippídis	2	ISTAF	Berlin	31 Aug
5.70	Sobera	3	ISTAF	Berlin	31 Aug
5.65	Barber	2	NCAA	Eugene	11 Jun
5.60	Thoirs	1		Seattle	10 May
5.60	Yang Yancheng	3	WCM	Beijing	21 May
5.60	Svärd Jacobsson	1		Soest	31 May
5.60	Maia	1		Hérouville	12 Jun
5.60	Dossévi	1		Castres	22 Jun
5.60	Cutts	2	Anniv	London (HG)	20 Jul
5.55	Jeng	3	FBK	Hengelo	8 Jun
5.52	Clavier	1		Aulnay-sous-Bois	25 Jun
5.50	Francis	4	Drake	Des Moines	25 Apr
5.50	Irwin	2	Drake	Des Moines	25 Apr
5.50	Homo	1		Conflans-St-Honorine	17 May
5.50	Kazaryan	1		Moskva	10 Jun
5.50	V Lavillenie	1		Bron	3 Jul

Mark	Name	Date
5.46	Pasiak	2 Sep
5.45	Scott	29 Mar
5.45	Bringhurst	14 Jun
5.45	S Joseph	22 Jun
5.45	Bychkov	27 Jul
5.44	Wait	18 May
5.42	Laidig	18 May
5.42	Korchmid	9 Jun
5.42	Gaul	1 Aug
5.42	Clemens	19 Aug
5.41	Gorokhov	25 Jul
5.41	Sokolov	25 Jul
5.40	M Arnold	6 May
5.40	R Tanaka	17 May
5.40	Bednyuk	29 May
5.40	Kovalchuk	29 May
5.40	Kozlitin	6 Jun
5.40	Frawley	29 Jun
5.40	Sintnicolaas	13 Aug
5.38	Ost	6 Jul
5.36	Nielsen	3 Aug

Exhibition

Mark		Name		Nat	Born	Pos	Venue	Date
5.80	sq	Robert	Sobera	POL	19.1.91	1	Chiari	2 Sep
5.75	sq	Michal	Balner	CZE	12.9.82	3	Chiari	2 Sep
5.65		Przemyslaw	Czerwinski	POL	28.7.83	3	Chiari	2 Sep

Drugs disqualification: 5.55 Rutger Koppelaar NED 1.5.93 1 Leiden 14 Jun

JUNIORS

See main list for top 4 juniors. 13 performances by 4 men to 5.43. Additional marks and further juniors:

Name	Mark	Pos	Meet/Venue	Date	Mark	Pos	Meet/Venue	Date
Chapelle	5.52	1	Ternier	29 May	5.45i	9	Orléans	18 Jan
	5.50	2	Bonneuil-sur-Marne	5 Jun	5.43i	10	Rouen	25 Jan
King	5.44i	1	N.Sch New York (A)	15 Mar	5.43	1	N.Jnr Greensboro	15 Jun

Mark		Name	Nat	Born	Pos	Meet	Venue	Date
5.46i	Adam	Hague	GBR-Y	29.8.97	2		Manchester	21 Dec
	5.35				3		Mannheim	6 Jul
5.45		Huang Bokai	CHN	26.9.96	5=	WJ	Eugene	26 Jul
5.45	Leonid	Kobelev	RUS	24.6.95	5=	WJ	Eugene	26 Jul
5.40	Brandon	Bray	USA-Y	24.4.97	1		Austin	10 May
5.40	Harry	Coppell	GBR	11.7.96	1		Mannheim	6 Jul
5.40	Jack	Hicking (10)	AUS	22.2.95	7	WJ	Eugene	26 Jul
5.35	Dylan	Duvio	USA	6.4.95	5		Austin	3 May
5.35	Eirik Greibrokk	Dolve	NOR	5.5.95	1		Göteborg	27 Jun
5.35	Cole	Walsh	USA	14.6.95	1	NC-j	Eugene	5 Jul
5.35	Kurtis	Marschall	AUS-Y	25.4.97	1		Adelaide	13 Dec
5.32	Hussain Asim	Al-Hizam	KSA-Y	4.1.98	1	Arab	Cairo	24 Apr
5.31	Kuke	Winder	USA	2.8.95	1		Romeoville	22 Mar
5.31	Adrián	Valles	ESP	16.3.95	1	NC-j	Castellón	5 Jul
5.30	Sergey	Safonov	RUS	18.2.95	2		Chelyabinsk	26 Jun
5.30	Grant	Sisserson	USA	4.2.95	3	NC-j	Eugene	5 Jul
5.30	Tomas	Wecksten (20)	FIN	2.11.96	4		Mannheim	6 Jul

LONG JUMP

Mark	Wind	Name		Nat	Born	Pos	Meet	Venue	Date
8.51	1.7	Greg	Rutherford	GBR	17.11.86	1		Chula Vista	24 Apr
					x	x	8.18w	8.51	p	p
8.29	-0.4	1 EC	Zürich	17 Aug	7.95	8.27/-0.2	8.18/-0.3	8.29	p	p
8.24	1.1	2 FBK	Hengelo	8 Jun	8.09	7.91	8.02	8.05	8.10	8.24
8.20	-0.7	1 CG	Glasgow	30 Jul	8.12	x	8.20	x	8.10	x
8.19	1.1	2 Athl	Lausanne	3 Jul	8.11	8.19	8.07	8.14	7.99	8.12
8.49	0.7	Christian	Reif	GER	24.10.84	1		Weinheim	31 May
					8.02w	x	8.49	p	p	p
8.20	0.0	2 NC	Ulm	26 Jul	8.09	8.10	8.05w	8.18	8.17	8.20
8.47	0.0		Li Jinzhe	CHN	1.9.89	1		Bad Langensalza	28 Jun
					7.64	8.00	8.15	8.13	8.13	8.47
8.23i		2 WI	Sopot	8 Mar	8.19	8.07	8.23	7.52	x	x

MEN 2014

Mark	Wind	Name		Nat	Born	Pos	Meet	Venue	Date
8.43	1.8	Jeff	Henderson	USA	19.2.89	*	NC	Sacramento	29 Jun
					x 8.43 8.35w/3.1 p p 8.52w/3.5				
		8.33 1.6 1 adidas	New York	14 Jun	8.00 x x 8.33 p p				
		8.31 1.3 1 Athl	Lausanne	3 Jul	8.00 8.04 8.00 8.31 7.96 8.06				
		8.25 0.9 1	Baie Mahault	10 May	8.19 8.25 x p p p				
		8.21 0.8 1 DL	Glasgow	12 Jul	x x 7.95 p 8.21 p				
8.39iA		Jarrion	Lawson	USA	6.5.94	1	NCAA	Albuquerque	14 Mar
					x 7.68 x x 8.01 8.39				
8.39	2.0	Tyron	Stewart	USA	8.7.89	2		Chula Vista	24 Apr
					8.15 x 8.22w/3.2 8.39 p p				
		8.22A 1 NC	Albuquerque	22 Feb	7.81 x 7.68 8.04 8.07 8.22				
8.35	1.0	Salim	Sdiri	FRA	26.10.78	1		Pierre-Bénite	13 Jun
					x 8.08 x 8.13 8.10w 8.35				
8.31A	0.4	Zarck	Visser	RSA	15.9.89	1	NC	Pretoria	11 Apr
					8.31 ??				
		8.28A 0.2 1	Johannesburg	26 Feb					
8.30i		Aleksandr	Menkov	RUS	7.12.90	1		Moskva	2 Feb
					7.89 7.93 8.30 p				
8.28i		Mauro Vinícius	da Silva (10)	BRA	26.12.86	1	WI	Sopot	8 Mar
					8.06 7.94 x 8.04 x 8.28				
8.25	0.5	Loúis	Tsátoumas	GRE	12.2.82	1	FBK	Hengelo	8 Jun
					7.98 x x 8.23 p p				
		8.23i 1 NC	Pireás	8 Feb	7.98 x x 8.23 p p				
		8.22 1.4 1	Kalamata	31 May	x x 8.17 8.22 p p				
		8.19 -0.5 Q EC	Zürich	15 Aug	7.94 8.19				
8.24	0.1	Luis	Rivera	MEX	21.6.87	1	IbAmC	São Paulo	2 Aug
					8.24 x p p p p				
8.23	1.8	Chris	Tomlinson	GBR	15.9.81	1		Bottrop	1 Jun
					7.99 x 8.23 7.74 p 7.81				
8.22i		Corey	Crawford	USA	12.12.91	1		New York (Arm)	28 Feb
					8.07 7.69 x 8.18 x 8.22				
8.21i		Michel	Tornéus	SWE	26.5.86	3	WI	Sopot	7 Mar
					x 8.13 x 8.21 x 8.10				
8.19	1.9	Kafétien	Gomis	FRA	23.3.80	2		Pierre-Bénite	13 Jun
8.19	0.5	Will	Claye	USA	13.6.91	1	Gugl	Linz	14 Jul
8.19	-0.3	Khotso	Mokoena	RSA	6.3.85	1	VD	Bruxelles	5 Sep
		(33/18)							
8.18i		Ngonidzashe	Makusha	ZIM	11.3.87	1	XLG	Stockholm	6 Feb
8.18i		Adrian	Strzalkowski	POL	28.3.90	Q	WI	Sopot	7 Mar
		(20)							
8.18	1.4		Gao Xinglong	CHN	12.3.94	1	vJPN,KOR	Jinhua	6 Jul
8.18	0.6	Higor	Alves	BRA	23.2.94	1	NC	São Paulo	12 Oct
8.16	-0.5	Irving	Saladino	PAN	23.1.83	1	SAmG	Santiago de Chile	14 Mar
8.16		Bradley	Pickup	GBR	4.4.89	1		Bournemouth	2 Aug
8.15	1.9	Mike	Hartfield	USA	29.3.90	*		Kingston	3 May
8.15	1.2	Tomasz	Jaszczuk	POL	9.3.92	1	NC	Szczecin	31 Jul
8.14	0.5		Zhang Yu	CHN	17.7.92	1		Beijing	27 Aug
8.13A	-1.2	Rushwal	Samaai	RSA	25.9.91	1		Germiston	15 Mar
8.13		Kirill	Sukharev	RUS	24.5.92	1		Moskva	9 Jun
8.13	0.5	Ignisious	Gaisah	NED	20.6.83	1	ISTAF	Berlin	31 Aug
		(30)							
8.13	1.2	Paulo Sérgio	Oliveira	BRA	1.6.93	1		São Paulo	27 Sep
8.12	0.9		Huang Changzhou	CHN	20.8.94	2		Beijing	27 Aug
8.11	-0.7	Eusebio	Cáceres	ESP	10.9.91	4	EC	Zürich	17 Aug
8.10Ai		Chris	Benard	USA	4.4.90	1		Albuquerque	14 Feb
8.10	0.1	Henry	Frayne	AUS	14.4.90	1		Melbourne	22 Mar
8.10	-0.1		Wang Jianan	CHN-J	27.8.96	2		Beijing	24 Apr
8.10	1.6	Damar	Forbes	JAM	18.9.90	1	NC	Kingston	28 Jun
8.09	0.5		Tang Gongchen	CHN	24.4.89	2		Kunshan	30 May
8.09	1.4	Tiago	da Silva	BRA	23.10.93	1		Osasco	21 Jun
8.09	0.6	Christian	Taylor	USA	18.6.90	1	DL	Birmingham	24 Aug
		(40)							
8.08i		Pavel	Shalin	RUS	15.3.87	1		Moskva	23 Jan
8.07	1.4		Jie Lei	CHN	8.5.89	3		Beijing	24 Apr
8.07	1.1	Mathias	Broothaerts	BEL	12.7.94	1	NC	Bruxelles	27 Jul
8.06iA		Jeremy	Hicks ¶	USA	19.9.86	3	NC	Albuquerque	22 Feb
8.06i		Stefano	Tremigliozzi	ITA	7.5.85	1	NC	Ancona	23 Feb
8.06A	1.8	David	Registe	DMA	2.5.88	1	PAm SF	Ciudad de México	15 Aug
8.05	0.3	J.J.	Jegede	GBR	3.10.85	4		Baie Mahault	10 May
8.05	1.2	Aleksandr	Petrov	RUS	9.8.86	2		Kalamáta	31 May
8.05	1.4	Sebastian	Bayer	GER	11.6.86	1		Regensburg	7 Jun

Mark	Wind	Name		Nat	Born	Pos	Meet	Venue	Date
8.05	1.4	Elvijs	Misans	LAT	8.4.89	1	ETC-2	Riga	21 Jun
		(50)							
8.04	1.0	Julian	Howard	GER	3.4.89	1		Weinheim	31 May
8.04	0.5	Denis	Bogdanov	RUS	2.4.91	1		Krasnodar	6 Jun
8.04	1.7	Marcos	Chuva	POR	8.8.89	1		Salamanca	12 Jun
8.04	1.7	Travonn	White	USA-J	3.6.95	1	NC-j	Eugene	5 Jul
8.04	1.8		Kim Duk-hyung	KOR	8.12.85	1		Jeju	30 Oct
8.04i		Cal	Lane	USA		1		Bloomington	12 Dec
8.03	-1.2	Robert	Crowther	AUS	2.8.87	1	NC	Melbourne	6 Apr
8.02	1.8	Ron	Taylor	USA	13.8.90	*		Chula Vista	24 Apr
8.01	0.1	Dmitriy	Bobkov	RUS	20.3.88	2		Krasnodar	6 Jun
8.01	1.7	Jean Marie	Okutu	ESP	4.8.88	1		Pontevedra	15 Jun
		(60)							
8.01A	1.0	Jorge	McFarlane	PER	20.2.88	2	PAm SF	Ciudad de México	15 Aug
8.00	1.9	Laderrick	Ward	USA	28.12.92	1		Edwardsville	19 Apr
8.00	-0.9	Marquis	Dendy	USA	17.11.92	1	NCAA	Eugene	12 Jun
8.00	0.9	Fabrice	Lapierre	AUS	17.10.83	4	CG	Glasgow	30 Jul
8.00	1.8	Yohei	Sugai	JPN	30.8.85	1		Odawara	21 Sep
7.99i		Dino	Pervan	CRO	12.1.91	1	NC	Zagreb	15 Feb
7.99	1.1		Zhang Yaoguang	CHN	21.6.93	4		Beijing	24 Apr
7.99	0.5	Wilfredo	Martínez	ex-CUB	9.1.85	2		Bottrop	1 Jun
7.99	0.6		Lin Qing	CHN-J	5.4.95	1	Asi-J	Taipei	12 Jun
7.99	1.0	Nikólaos	Xenikákis	GRE	23.12.94	1	NC-23	Trikala	15 Jun
		(70)							
7.99i		Raymond	Higgs	BAH	24.1.91	1	Tyson	Fayetteville	14 Feb
7.98	1.0	Yves	Zellweger	SUI	27.3.87	1		Zofingen	7 Jun
7.98	1.3	Emanuele	Catania	ITA	3.10.88	1	NC	Rovereto	19 Jul
7.97	1.6	Junior	Díaz	CUB	28.4.87	*		La Habana	7 Feb
7.96	0.0	Raihau	Maiau	PYF	1.8.92	1		Limoges	18 May
7.96A		Tera	Langat	KEN	26.12.85	1	NC	Nairobi	6 Jun
7.94	0.4	Tim	McGuire	AUS	29.4.92	1		Adelaide	11 Jan
7.94i		Vasiliy	Kopeykin	RUS	9.3.88	1		Sankt-Peterburg	8 Feb
7.94i		Saleh Abdelaziz	Al-Haddad	KUW	7.4.86	1	AsCh	Hangzhou	15 Feb
7.94	0.5	Emiliano	Lasa	URU	25.1.90	2	SAmG	Santiago de Chile	14 Mar
		(80)							
7.94	0.6	Kota	Minemura	JPN	22.12.92	1	NC	Fukushima	8 Jun
7.94	-0.7	Radek	Juska	CZE	8.3.93	1		Praha	9 Jun
7.94	1.5		Li Chengbin	CHN	22.2.90	1		Hong Kong	28 Jun
7.93	1.2	Samson	Idiata	NGR	28.2.82	1		Castellón	22 May
7.93A		Elijah	Kimitei	KEN	25.12.86	2	NC	Nairobi	6 Jun
7.92	1.6	Robert	Martey	GHA	27.12.84	1		Novo Mesto	11 Jul
7.92	2.0	Artty	Halmela	FIN	25.9.91	6	DNG	Stockholm	21 Aug
7.91i		Guillaume	Victorin	FRA	26.5.90	2		New York (Arm)	28 Feb
7.90	0.8	Ahmad Fayez	Al-Dosari	KSA	6.9.79	1		Qatif	7 Mar
7.90	1.3	M	Vigneshwar	IND	15.10.91	1		Lucknow	6 Jun
		(90)							
7.90	1.0	Konstantin	Safronov	KAZ	2.9.87	1	NC	Almaty	28 Jun
7.90	0.2	Yuhi	Oiwa	JPN	17.2.91	1		Tokyo	6 Jul
7.90A	0.2	Luis Felipe	Méliz	ESP	11.8.79	1		Ávila	13 Jul
7.90	1.0	Konstantin	Borichevskiy	BLR	29.5.90	1		Minsk	18 Jul
7.89	0.7	Duwayne	Boer	RSA-J	6.1.95	1	NC-j	Stellenbosch	3 Apr
7.89	1.8	Mikese	Morse	USA	30.10.87	1		Tampa	23 May
7.89	1.5	Alyn	Camara	GER	31.3.89	3		Weinheim	31 May
7.89	0.1	Eero	Haapala	FIN	10.7.89	1		Ikaalinen	3 Jun
7.89	1.2	Cedric	Nolf	BEL	18.6.89	1		Kortrijk	12 Jul
7.89	1.5	Kristian	Pulli	FIN	2.9.94	1		København	27 Jul
		(100)							
7.89		Mohammad	Arzandeh	IRI	30.10.87	1		Tehran	21 Aug

Mark	Wind	Name		Nat	Born	Date
7.88i		Norris	Frederick	USA	17.2.86	18 Jan
7.88	0.4	Ted	Hooper	USA	31.1.91	3 May
7.88	1.6	Vladimir	Kolindenkov	RUS	6.12.89	9 Jul
7.88	1.3	Danylo	Martins	BRA	21.11.92	12 Oct
7.87	1.2		Ge Xiaodong	CHN	1.9.92	19 Apr
7.87	1.9		Kim Sang-su	KOR	5.6.84	24 Apr
7.87	0.0	Paulo Sérgio	Madzivire	ZIM	28.5.91	9 May
7.87	0.9	Tomas	Vitonis	LTU	19.9.91	31 May
7.87	0.8	Sergey	Mikhailovskiy	RUS	11.5.87	6 Jun
7.87	1.3	Matthew	Burton	GBR	18.12.87	9 Jun
7.87	0.1	Ashton	Eaton	USA	21.1.88	20 Jul
7.87	0.5	Tyrone	Smith	BER	7.8.86	29 Jul
7.87	0.0	Ankit	Sharma	IND	20.7.92	3 Nov
7.86i		Mihaíl	Mertzanídis-Despotéris	GRE	21.8.87	8 Feb
7.86i		Patrick	Rädler	GER	23.9.90	14 Feb
7.86i		Valentin	Toboc	ROU	17.3.92	16 Feb
7.86	-0.2	DeJon	Wilkinson	USA	10.8.92	25 Apr
7.86A		John	Kariuki	KEN		6 Jun
7.86	0.3	Alain	Sotolongo	CUB	19.10.91	7 Jun
7.86	0.2	Ndiss Kaba	Badji	SEN	21.9.83	28 Jun
7.86	0.0	Julian	Reid	GBR	23.9.88	19 Jul
7.86	0.3	Povilas	Mykolaitis	LTU	23.2.83	26 Jul
7.86	1.6	W.P. Amila	Jayasiri	SRI	.94	14 Aug
7.85i		Mantas	Silkauskas	LTU	10.4.88	1 Feb
7.85i		Henri	Väyrynen	FIN	16.10.91	8 Feb
7.85A		Larona	Koosimile	BOT	14.10.85	22 Feb
7.85iA		Kendall	Spencer	USA	24.7.91	28 Feb
7.85	2.0	Ronni	Ollikainen	FIN	27.8.90	12 Apr
7.85	0.1	Abdelhakim	Mlaab	MAR	22.9.88	10 May
7.85	1.5	Stephan	Hartmann	GER	13.1.94	31 May

Mark	Wind	Name		Nat	Born	Pos	Meet	Venue	Date

Mark	Wind	First	Last	Nat	Born	Date
7.85	0.6	Andrey	Ovcharenko	RUS	21.4.94	6 Jun
7.84	1.7	Shujaa	Benson	TAN	26.7.90	17 May
7.84	-0.8	Yasuhiro	Moro	JPN	21.12.94	24 May
7.84	0.0	Artem	Shpytko	UKR	26.4.92	3 Jun
7.84	0.9	Viktor	Sirotkin	RUS	27.3.87	6 Jun
7.84	0.6	Nate	Moore	USA-J	28.5.96	7 Jun
7.84		Shamar	Rock	BAR-J	20.4.95	21 Jun
7.84	1.1	Alper	Kulaksiz	TUR	6.4.92	19 Jul
7.84	0.8	Tomonori	Kimura	JPN	17.9.84	2 Aug
7.84	0.8		Gao Chao	CHN	1.6.92	27 Aug
7.83i		Yevgeniy	Antonov	RUS	26.4.92	8 Feb
7.83i		Alessio	Guarini	ITA	5.4.85	23 Feb
7.83i		Jerry	Westerfield	USA	18.6.94	7 Mar
7.83	1.5	Jarvis	Gotch	USA	25.3.92	19 Apr
7.83	1.5	Clice	Chafausipo	ZIM	2.6.88	19 Apr
7.83	0.6	Roelf	Pienaar	RSA	23.12.93	26 Apr
7.83	2.0	Nicolas	Gomont	FRA	15.9.86	29 May
7.82i		Keenan	Soles	USA	16.4.92	31 Jan
7.82	1.5	Bryce	Lamb	USA	9.11.90	10 May
7.82	1.2	Naohiro	Shinada	JPN	10.2.86	11 May
7.82	-1.3	Cameron	Hudson	USA	5.3.94	17 May
7.82	1.1	Jerome	Wilson	JAM	10.9.91	17 May
7.82A		Kiplagat	Ruto	KEN	1.11.94	6 Jun
7.82		Semen	Popov	RUS	26.5.94	9 Jun
7.82		Sobhan	Taherkhani	IRI	21.9.92	26 Jun
7.82	0.7	Michal	Rejmus	POL	8.9.91	5 Jul
7.82	1.1	Sergey	Polyanskiy	RUS	29.10.89	17 Jul
7.82	2.0	Yeóryios	Tsákonas	GRE	22.1.88	23 Jul
7.82	0.3	Darius	Aucyna	LTU	7.5.89	26 Jul
7.81	-1.1	Lucas M.	dos Santos	BRA-J	4.1.95	25 Jan
7.81i		Kamal	Fuller	JAM	20.1.91	14 Feb
7.81	0.3	Devin	Field	USA	9.10.93	17 May
7.81	1.7	Allan	Hamilton	GBR	14.7.92	7 Jun
7.81	1.8	Adrian	Vasile	ROM	9.4.86	21 Jun
7.81		Vladimir	Golovin	RUS	22.6.91	23 Jul
7.81	1.3	Vitaliy	Muravyov	RUS	1.10.93	2 Aug
7.81	0.4	Suphanara	Ayudhaya	THA	11.6.92	30 Sep
7.81	1.2	Felipe	Maximiano	BRA	29.12.91	12 Oct
7.80	0.2	Angus	Gould	AUS	8.1.94	9 Jan
7.80		Jairo	Guibert	CUB	22.2.84	31 Jan
7.80i		Daniel	Bramble	GBR	14.10.90	8 Feb
7.80i		Henrik	Kutberg	EST	2.11.92	11 Feb
7.80iA		Emmanuel	Williams	USA	27.2.93	14 Mar
7.80	0.0	Aubrey	Smith	CAN	30.6.88	17 May
7.80	0.3	Mizuki	Matsubara	JPN	9.9.92	31 May
7.80	0.0	Michal	Lukasiak	POL	7.3.84	7 Jun
7.80	1.5	Melvin	Echard	USA	29.8.89	29 Jun
7.80	1.7	Milan	Pírek	CZE	17.7.87	2 Aug
7.80	2.0	Kodai	Sakuma	JPN-J	29.4.96	1 Aug
7.80	-0.4		Ju Eun-jae	KOR	12.6.93	30 Oct

(181)

Wind assisted

Mark	Wind		Name		Nat	Born	Pos	Meet	Venue	Date
8.52	3.5	(see 8.43)	Jeff	Henderson	USA	19.2.89	1	NC	Sacramento	29 Jun
8.29	4.1		Will	Claye	USA	13.6.91	3		Chula Vista	24 Apr
						x	8.01	8.29w	x x 8.12	
8.25	3.2			Tsátoumas			1	ET-1	Tallinn	21 Jun
						8.03w	8.25w	8.12	p	
8.21	2.3			Gao Xinglong	CHN	12.3.94	1	NC	Suzhou	10 Oct
8.17	2.7		Mike	Hartfield	USA	29.3.90	2		Kingston	3 May
8.16	2.5		Yohei	Sugai	JPN	30.8.85	1		Fukushima	18 May
8.16	4.1		Eusebio	Cáceres	ESP	10.9.91	1	WCM	Madrid	19 Jul
8.10	3.3		Junior	Díaz	CUB	28.4.87	1		La Habana	8 Feb
8.08	3.2		Mikese	Morse	USA	30.10.87	3		Kingston	3 May
8.08	6.1		Carlton	Lavong	USA	18.6.92	1		Alamosa	5 May
8.06	2.4		J.J.	Jegede	GBR	3.10.85	1		St .Pölten	14 Jun
8.05	2.7		Ron	Taylor	USA	13.8.90	4		Chula Vista	24 Apr
8.05	2.3		Henri	Väyrynen	FIN	16.10.91	1		Jämsä	28 Jun
8.05	3.6		Sergey	Polyanskiy	RUS	29.10.89	1	Kuts	Moskva	17 Jul
8.05	2.9		Jean Marie	Okutu	ESP	4.8.88	2	WCM	Madrid	19 Jul
8.02	4.4		Samson	Idiata	NGR	28.2.82	1		Valencia	7 Jun
8.01	3.3		Wilfredo	Martínez	ex-CUB	9.1.85	1		Zaragoza	28 Jun
8.01	3.2		Yeóryios	Tsákonas	GRE	22.1.88	1		Thíva	23 Jul
7.99	2.2		Ronni	Ollikainen	FIN	27.8.90	1		Coral Gables	12 Apr
7.99	2.3		Tomas	Vitonis	LTU	19.9.91	2	ETC-1	Tallinn	21 Jun
7.97	3.4		Roelf	Pienaar	RSA	23.12.93	1		San Marcos	11 May
7.96	2.5		Adrian	Vasile	ROM	9.4.86	1		Cluj-Napoca	6 Jun
7.96	5.2		Mizuki	Matsubara	JPN	9.9.92	1		Hiratsuka	21 Jun
7.95A	2.1		Kendall	Spencer	USA	24.7.91	1		Albuquerque	2 May
7.95	4.5			Lin Hung-Min	TPE	7.9.90	2		Hiratsuka	21 Jun
7.93A	3.5		Jarvis	Gotch	USA	25.3.92	1		El Paso	12 Apr
7.93	2.5		Nick	Gordon	JAM	17.9.88	1		Port of Spain	13 Apr
7.93	4.8		Hamed	Suleman	USA	14.7.90	1	Pac 12	Pullman	17 May
7.92			Artyom	Bondarenko	BLR	19.6.91	1		Brest	17 May
7.90	3.1		Sobhan	Taherkhani	IRI	21.9.92	1		Tehran	8 Aug

Mark	Wind	First	Last	Nat	Born	Date
7.89	2.4	Tyrone	Smith	BER	7.8.86	16 Jul
7.89	4.8	Alper	Kulaksiz	TUR	6.4.92	6 Aug
7.88	2.3	DeJon	Wilkinson	USA	10.8.92	25 Apr
7.88	3.2	Corey	Wesley	USA	8.4.94	10 May
7.88	2.2	Mihaíl	Mertzanídis-Despotéris	GRE	21.8.87	20 Jul
7.87	2.3	Nate	Moore	USA-J	28.5.96	19 Apr
7.86	3.7	Daniel	Bramble	GBR	14.10.90	5 Jul
7.85	2.7	Melvin	Echard	USA	29.8.89	29 Jun
7.85	2.3	Tomonori	Kimura	JPN	17.9.84	19 Jul
7.84	2.6	Kenneth	Fisher	USA-J	28.2.95	5 Jul
7.83	2.7	Matthew	Wyatt	NZL	7.10.90	8 Mar
7.83	2.7	Anthony	May	USA	19.9.90	17 May
7.83	6.3	Kodai	Sakuma	JPN	29.4.96	20 Jun
7.83	2.5	Tommy	Evilä	FIN	6.4.80	21 Jun
7.83	2.4	Shontaro	Shiroyama	JPN-J	6.3.95	24 Jul
7.82	2.3	Rikiya	Saruyama	JPN	15.2.84	29 Apr
7.81	3.5	Jamal	Peden	USA	22.6.92	28 Mar
7.81	2.3	Walter	Jones	USA-J	6.7.95	14 Jun
7.81	4.4		Chan Ming Tai	HKG-J	30.1.95	7 Sep
7.80	2.2	Olabanji	Asekun	USA	15.7.92	4 Apr
7.80	3.3	Joey	Souza	USA-J	18.3.96	19 Apr
7.80		Daniel	Gardiner	GBR	25.6.90	18 May
7.80	2.1	Yuriy	Yeramich	BLR-J	24.4.95	22 Jul

Low altitude bests

Mark	Wind	Name	Pos	Meet	Venue	Date
8.18	1.3	Visser	1		Kuortane	13 Jul
8.08	-0.1	Samaai	3	CG	Glasgow	30 Jul
7.84	-1.6	Registe				18 Apr
7.81	0.8	Méliz				10 May

Best outdoors

Mark	Wind	Name	Pos	Meet	Venue	Date
8.09	0.1	Tornéus	5	EC	Zürich	17 Aug
		8.10w 2.5	1		Karlstad	16 Jul
8.05	1.7	Tremigliozzi	1		Marano	11 May
8.02	0.5	Menkov	6	Athl	Lausanne	3 Jul

Mark Wind Name Nat Born Pos Meet Venue Date

8.02 1.7 Strzalkowski 2 NC Szczecin 31 Jul
7.99 0.0 Shalin 1 Innsbruck 7 Jun
7.92 1.3 Lawson 2 SEC Lexington 17 May
8.13w 2.6 2 NC Sacramento 29 Jun
7.92 1.4 Pervan 1 Zagreb 31 May
7.88 1.1 Kopeykin 25 Jul
7.85 0.9 Al-Haddad 14 Jun
7.90 1.8 Crawford 1 PennR Philadelphia 25 Apr
7.91w 2.7 1 IC4A Princeton 17 May
7.88 0.7 M da Silva 3 SAmG Santiago 14 Mar
8.08w 4.5 1 Rovereto 2 Sep
7.88 0.8 Higgs 1 NC Nassau 28 Jun
7.94w 2.5 1 SEC Lexington 17 May
7.81 1.0 Benard 10 May
Benard 7.95w 2.1 3 May

Drugs disqualification: 7.87 0.5 Daniel Pineda ¶ CHI 19.9.95 (2) Montevideo 4 Apr
8.23w 2.5 Jeremy Hicks ¶ USA 19.9.86 (1) Baton Rouge 19 Apr
With prosthetics: 8.24 1.8 Markus Rehm GER 22.8.88 1 NC Ulm 26 Jul

JUNIORS

See main list for top 4 juniors. 10 performances by 4 men to 7.89. Additional marks and further juniors:

Wang 8.09 0.0 1 WCM Beijing 21 May
8.08 1.5 1 WJ Eugene 24 Jul
8.02i 2 Nanjing 8 Mar
7.93 -0.6 Q WJ Eugene 24 Jul
7.91 0.1 3 DL Glasgow 12 Jul
Lin 7.94 1.6 2 WJ Eugene 24 Jul

Mark	Wind	Name		Nat	Born	Pos	Meet	Venue	Date
7.84	0.6	Nate	Moore	USA	28.5.96	1		Clovis, CA	7 Jun
7.84		Shamar	Rock	BAR	20.4.95	1	NC	Bridgetown	21 Jun
7.81	-1.1	Lucas M.	dos Santos	BRA	4.1.95	2		São Paulo	25 Jan
7.80	2.0	Kodai	Sakuma	JPN	29.4.96	1		Kofu	1 Aug
7.79	0.5	Anatoliy	Ryapolov	RUS-Y	31.1.97	1	EYOT	Baku	31 May
7.78	0.9	Kenneth	Fisher (10)	USA	28.2.95	1		Greensboro	2 May
7.77i		Will	Williams	USA	31.1.95	2	JUCO	New York (A)	7 Mar
7.77	1.2	Daiki	Oda	JPN	15.1.96	1		Tokyo	6 Aug
7.76	0.5		Li Zhipeng	CHN	1.5.95	6	NC	Suzhou	10 Oct
7.75	0.0	Adorée	Jackson	USA	18.9.95	1		Chandler	22 Mar
7.74	0.3	Jonathan	Addison	USA	27.2.95	3q	NCAA-w	Jacksonville	29 May
7.74	1.2	Cedric	Dubbler	AUS	13.1.95	1D	WJ	Eugene	22 Jul
7.73	0.7		Chan Ming Tai	HKG	30.1.95	5	AsiG	Incheon	30 Sep
7.72	0.2	Bruno Valerio	de Souza	BRA	29.9.95	2		São Bernardo do Campo	11 Apr
7.72	2.0	Yevgeniy	Likhanov	RUS	10.1.95	1D	WJ	Eugene	22 Jul
7.72	1.1	Shotaro	Saruyama (20)	JPN	5.3.95	*	WJ	Eugene	24 Jul
Wind assisted									
7.87	2.3	Nate	Moore	USA	28.5.96	1-HS	MSR	Walnut	19 Apr
7.84	2.6	Kenneth	Fisher	USA	28.2.95	2	NC-j	Eugene	5 Jul
7.83	2.4	Shontaro	Shiroyama	JPN-	6.3.95	3	WJ	Eugene	24 Jul
7.81	2.3	Walter	Jones	USA	6.7.95	1		Chula Vista	14 Jun
7.81	4.4		Chan Ming Tai	HKG	30.1.95	1		Hong Kong	7 Sep
7.80	3.3	Joey	Souza	USA	18.3.96	2-HS	MSR	Walnut	19 Apr
7.80	2.1	Yuriy	Yeramich	BLR	24.4.95	1D	WJ	Eugene	22 Jul
7.79A	2.2	JaMari	Ward	USA-Y	21.7.98	1		Albuquerque	7 Jun
7.77	5.1	Kaito	Akiyama	JPN	28.7.95	1		Hakodate	19 Jul

TRIPLE JUMP

17.76 -0.2 Pedro Pablo Pichardo CUB 30.6.93 1 La Habana 7 Feb
17.76 x 17.42/0.0 p p p
17.71 0.5 1 NC La Habana 20 Mar 17.28/0.0 17.71 16.85 p p p
17.32i 1 Praha 25 Feb 16.90 16.33 16.68 17.32 p p
17.24i 3 WI Sopot 9 Mar 16.73 x 16.73 16.81 17.18 17.24
17.75 0.8 Will Claye USA 13.6.91 1 NC Sacramento 27 Jun
16.95w 17.16 17.64/-0.3 17.16 17.65/1.7 17.75
17.66 0.8 1 Pre Eugene 31 May x 17.42w/2.2 17.66 p p p
17.41 0.3 1 Bisl Oslo 11 Jun 16.64 16.71 16.66 17.12 16.60 17.41
17.39 -1.1 3 WK Zürich 28 Aug 16.90 16.81 17.24/-0.5 16.85 17.22/-0.3 17.39
17.27 1.1 2 DL Glasgow 12 Jul 16.58 16.83 16.75 17.27 17.09 17.15
17.21 0.5 3 C.Cup Marrakech 14 Sep 16.87 17.20/-0.4 17.21 17.18
17.58 -1.7 Ernesto Revé CUB 26.2.92 2 La Habana 7 Feb
17.17 17.58 17.55/-0.1 x p p
17.50 -0.4 1 La Habana 1 Feb 17.29 17.32/-0.1 17.50 17.34/0.0 p x
17.33i 2 WI Sopot 9 Mar 15.78 17.33 x p p p
17.30w 3.3 1 Sotteville-lès-Rouen 14 Jun x 17.07w 17.30w p p p
17.51 -0.6 Christian Taylor USA 18.6.90 1 WK Zürich 28 Aug
16.88 17.17 17.17 17.07 17.13 17.51
17.37 1.1 2 NC Sacramento 27 Jun 16.92 17.10 17.37 17.07 x 17.31/0.8
17.36 1.5 1 DL Glasgow 12 Jul 16.33 16.54 16.86 17.00 17.08 17.36
17.42w 2.6 2 Pre Eugene 31 May 16.46 16.45 16.96w 16.80 17.25w/3.9 17.42w
17.48 -0.1 Benjamin Compaoré FRA 5.8.87 1 C.Cup Marrakech 14 Sep
17.26/1.0 17.48 17.23/-0.1 x
17.46 -0.1 1 EC Zürich 14 Aug 17.46 17.18 x p x p
17.45 -0.8 2 WK Zürich 28 Aug 16.70 17.45 16.90 p x 16.49

Mark	Wind	Name		Nat	Born	Pos	Meet	Venue	Date
17.37i		Lyukman	Adams	RUS	24.9.88	1	WI	Sopot	9 Mar
					x	17.21	x	x 17.17	17.37
17.29	1.4	3 Pre	Eugene	31 May	17.29	x	x	x x	x
17.35	0.2	Khotso	Mokoena	RSA	6.3.85	2	C.Cup	Marrakech	14 Sep
					17.13	17.35	x	16.72	
17.20	-0.1	1 CG	Glasgow	2 Aug	x	17.20	16.99	p p	x
17.30i		Marian	Oprea	ROU	6.6.82	1	NC	Bucuresti	15 Feb
					16.88	17.30	x	p p	p
17.21i		4 WI	Sopot	9 Mar	17.02	16.34	x	x 16.46	17.21
17.30	-0.2		Cao Shuo	CHN	8.10.91	1	AsiG	Incheon	2 Oct
					16.99	x	17.30	p p	16.57
17.27	-0.5	Samyr	Laine	HAI	17.7.84	1		Alexandria, VA	31 Aug
17.24	0.7	Lázaro	Martínez (10)	CUB-Y	3.11.97	2		La Habana	1 Feb
					x	17.24	16.56	13.68 p	p
17.20A	-1.0	Yordanys	Durañona	DMA	16.6.88	3	PAm SF	Ciudad de México	16 Aug
		(29/11)							
17.17	0.0	Arpinder	Singh	IND	30.12.92	1		Lucknow	8 Jun
17.16	1.0	Yoann	Rapinier	FRA	29.9.89	1	NC	Reims	12 Jul
17.15iA		Chris	Carter	USA	11.3.89	1	NC	Albuquerque	23 Feb
17.10	0.0	Chris	Benard	USA	4.4.90	3	NC	Sacramento	27 Jun
17.07	0.9	Aleksey	Fyodorov	RUS	25.5.91	1	NC	Kazan	26 Jul
17.05	0.0	Alexis	Copello	ex-CUB	12.8.85	1		Cluj-Napoca	6 Jun
16.99	0.0	Phillips	Idowu	GBR	30.12.78	1		Brisbane	31 May
16.98	1.4	Omar	Craddock	USA	26.4.91	1	TexR	Austin	28 Mar
16.97	0.0	Nelson	Évora	POR	20.4.84	4	DL	Saint-Denis	5 Jul
		(20)							
16.97	1.9	Tosin	Oke	NGR	1.10.80	2	AfCh	Marrakech	13 Aug
16.96	0.8	Dmitriy	Sorokin	RUS	27.9.92	1		Adler	30 May
16.95	0.9		Dong Bin	CHN	22.11.88	2	AsiG	Incheon	2 Oct
16.94	0.2	Jonathan	Silva	BRA	21.7.91	1		Uberlândia	7 May
16.93	1.4		Kim Duk-hyung	KOR	8.12.85	3	AsiG	Incheon	2 Oct
16.91	0.3	Latario	Collie-Minns	BAH	10.3.94	1	KansR	Lawrence	18 Apr
16.89i		Karol	Hoffmann	POL	1.6.89	5	WI	Sopot	9 Mar
16.89	-0.5	Fabrizio	Donato	ITA	14.8.76	4	GGala	Roma	5 Jun
16.89	-0.7	Kaual Kamal	Bento	BRA	10.1.93	1		São Paulo	14 Jun
16.87i		Julian	Reid	GBR	23.9.88	1	NC	Sheffield	8 Feb
		(30)							
16.87	0.2	Pablo	Torrijos	ESP	12.5.92	1	NC	Alcobendas	27 Jul
16.85	1.8	Troy	Doris	USA	12.4.89	1		Padova	6 Jul
16.84	-0.6	Daniele	Greco	ITA	1.3.89	7	GGala	Roma	5 Jun
16.83	0.8	Josh	Honeycutt	USA	7.3.89	1		Emporia	10 May
16.82	-0.3	Osviel	Hernández	CUB	31.5.89	1		La Habana	15 Feb
16.82	-0.4		Xu Xiaolong	CHN	20.12.92	1	NC	Suzhou	12 Oct
16.80i		Gaetan	Saku-Bafuanga	FRA	22.7.91	1		Eaubonne	9 Feb
16.78i		Fabrizio	Schembri	ITA	27.1.81	1	NC	Ancona	22 Feb
16.75	1.2	Dimítrios	Tsiámis	GRE	12.1.82	1	Veniz	Haniá	7 Jun
16.73	1.2	Olu	Olamigoke	NGR	19.9.90	1		Charlottesville	9 May
		(40)							
16.73	0.0	Adrian	Swiderski	POL	26.9.86	1		Opava	19 Jul
16.69i		Aboubacar	Bamba	FRA	20.6.91	2		Eaubonne	9 Feb
16.69	0.3	Nathan	Fox	GBR	21.10.90	1	BIG	Bedford	1 Jun
16.69	1.4	Rumen	Dimitrov	BUL	19.9.86	1		Stara Zagora	19 Jul
16.67	0.0	Issam	Nima	ALG	8.4.79	1		Alger	27 Jun
16.65	0.2	Nathan	Douglas	GBR	4.12.82	2	BIG	Bedford	1 Jun
16.63i		Igor	Spasovkhodskiy	RUS	1.8.79	3	NC	Moskva	18 Feb
16.63	-0.1	Alberto	Álvarez	MEX	8.3.91	1		Monterrey	22 Mar
16.63	-1.6	Viktor	Kuznetsov	UKR	17.7.86	3	ET	Braunschweig	22 Jun
16.63	1.8	Louhab	Kafia	ALG	24.2.87	1	NC	Alger	25 Jun
		(50)							
16.63	1.1	Yuriy	Kovalyov	RUS	18.6.91	2	NC	Kazan	26 Jul
16.62	1.9	Andreas	Pohle	GER	6.4.81	1		Rehlingen	9 Jun
16.62	2.0	Yevgeniy	Ektov	KAZ	1.9.86	4	AsiG	Incheon	2 Oct
16.61	0.0	Kola	Adedoyin	GBR	8.4.91	1		Clermont	26 Apr
16.61	1.6	Jorge	Gimeno	ESP	16.2.90	1		Cartagena	9 May
16.61	1.2	Vladimir	Letnicov	MDA	7.10.81	1		Tiraspol	19 Jun
16.61	1.6	Aleksi	Tammentie	FIN	6.8.86	1		Jämsä	28 Jun
16.61		Aleksey	Tsapik	BLR	4.8.88	1		Minsk	18 Jul
16.61		Renjith	Maheswary	IND	30.1.86	1		Patiala	18 Sep
16.60	0.5	Dmitriy	Plotnitskiy	BLR	26.8.88	1	NC	Grodno	25 Jul
		(60)							
16.59iA		Felix	Obi	USA	15.6.94	1	NCAA	Albuquerque	15 Mar

Mark	Wind	Name		Nat	Born	Pos	Meet	Venue	Date
16.57A	-1.1	Roger	Haitengi	NAM	12.9.83	1		Sasolburg	25 Mar
16.57	0.6	Danylo	Martins	BRA	21.11.92	2		São Paulo	15 Jun
16.56	0.0	Kevin	Luron	FRA	8.11.91	1		Saint-Denis	6 Jun
16.55	1.8	Darius	Aucyna	LTU	7.5.89	1	NC	Kaunas	27 Jul
16.55	1.4	Max	Hess	GER-J	13.7.96	2	WJ	Eugene	27 Jul
16.54	-1.9	Karl	Taillepierre	FRA	13.8.76	3	NC	Reims	12 Jul
16.54	1.8	Manuel	Ziegler	GER	28.7.90	1	NC	Ulm	26 Jul
16.52A	-0.9	Tumelo	Thagane	RSA	3.7.84	2		Sasolburg	25 Mar
16.52	0.0	Ryan	Grinnell	USA	4.2.87	1		Atlanta	17 May
		(70)							
16.52	1.3	Marquis	Dendy	USA	17.11.92	1	SEC	Lexington	18 May
16.52	0.1	Daniele	Cavazzani	ITA	4.12.92	2	NC	Rovereto	20 Jul
16.52	1.1	Kazuyoshi	Ishikawa	JPN	6.11.82	1		Yamaguchi	12 Oct
16.51	1.4	Dmitriy	Chizhikov	RUS	6.12.93	1		Moskva	3 Jul
16.51	0.7	Jean-Noël	Cretinoir	FRA	28.12.94	2		La Roche-sur-Yon	23 Jul
16.50	1.9	José Emilio	Bellido	ESP	25.5.87	1		Valencia	7 Jun
16.50	1.7	Sief el Islem	Temacini	ALG	5.3.88	2	NC	Alger	25 Jun
16.49	0.3	Jean	Rosa	BRA	1.2.90	2	NC	São Paulo	10 Oct
16.48i		Jean-Marc	Pontvianne	FRA	6.8.94	1	NC-23	Nantes	15 Mar
16.47i		Dmitriy	Kolosov	RUS	19.5.86	4	NC	Moskva	18 Feb
		(80)							
16.47A	-0.5	Jhon Freddy	Murillo	COL	13.6.84	1	NC	Medellín	29 Jun
16.47	1.5	Mateus Daniel	de Sá	BRA-J	21.11.95	3	WJ	Eugene	27 Jul
16.46i		Maksim	Nesterenko	BLR	1.9.92	2	NC	Mogilyov	21 Feb
16.46	1.3	Ben	Williams	GBR	25.1.92	*	NC	Birmingham	29 Jun
16.45	1.7	Timothy	White-Edwards	USA	15.7.94	5	MSR	Walnut	19 Apr
16.45	-1.4	Ricky	Robertson	USA	19.9.90	2	SEC	Lexington	18 May
16.45	1.3	Dimitrios	Baltadoúros	GRE	1.10.89	2	NC	Athina	19 Jul
16.45	0.9	Ilya	Potapstev	RUS	19.4.93	4	NC	Kazan	26 Jul
16.44	0.7	Jefferson	Dias Sabino	BRA	4.11.82	2	SAmG	Santiago de Chile	16 Mar
16.44	0.5	DeJon	Wilkinson	USA	10.8.92	1	FlaR	Gainesville	5 Apr
		(90)							
16.44			Li Pangshuai	CHN	9.4.92	1		Beijing	18 May
16.42	-0.6	Jadel	Gregório	BRA	16.9.80	3	NC	São Paulo	10 Oct
16.41	1.0	Harold	Correa	FRA	26.6.88	2		Tokyo	11 May
16.41	0.0	Muhammad Hakimi	Ismail	MAS	8.4.91	1	NC	Kangar	25 Jun
16.40A		Elijah	Kimitei	KEN	25.12.86	1	NC	Nairobi	7 Jun
16.39	1.5	Alexandru George	Baciu	ROM	25.2.91	4	Balk Ch	Pitesti	27 Jul
16.38iA		Mark	Jackson	USA	12.10.91	2	NCAA	Albuquerque	15 Mar
16.38A	1.0	Boipele	Mothlahlego	RSA	27.11.90	1	Univ Ch	Pretoria	26 Apr
16.38	1.8	Andy	Diaz	CUB-J	25.12.95	Q	WJ	Eugene	25 Jul
16.38	-0.2	Thiago	Dias	BRA	2.3.84	1		São Paulo	14 Sep
		(100)							

Mark	Wind	Name		Nat	Born	Date
16.37	-0.5	Fabien	Florant	NED	1.2.83	28 Jun
16.37	0.9	Martin	Jasper	GER	6.1.89	26 Jul
16.37	1.0	Mamadou	Guèye	SEN	1.4.86	26 Jul
16.35	0.0	Vladimir	Kozlov	RUS	15.3.94	16 Jul
16.35	-1.3	Georgi	Tsonov	BUL	2.5.93	12 Aug
16.34	1.4	Warunyu	Kongnil	THA	9.7.88	9 May
16.34		Nguyen	Van Hung	VIE	4.3.89	26 Jul
16.33	2.0	Miguel	van Assen	SUR-Y	30.7.97	19 Apr
16.33	0.3	Zlatozar	Atanasov	BUL	12.12.89	21 May
16.33	-1.2	Paulo Sérgio	Oliveira	BRA	1.6.93	10 Oct
16.32i		Jonathan	Reid	JAM	9.5.92	15 Feb
16.32i		Vicente	Docavo	ESP	13.2.92	22 Feb
16.32	0.2	Adrian	Daianu	ROU	27.11.87	6 Jun
16.32	0.9	Cordairo	Golden	USA	3.9.92	14 Jun
16.32	0.1		Fang Yaoqing	CHN-J	20.4.96	15 Jun
16.32A	2.0	Carlos	Veiga	POR	22.2.89	13 Jul
16.31i		Aleksandr	Yurchenko	RUS	30.7.92	30 Jan
16.31i		Daniel	Lewis	GBR/JAM	8.11.89	8 Feb
16.31	1.4	Eric	Sloan	USA	20.6.94	17 May
16.31 ?	0.6	Louis-Grégory	Occin	FRA	2.6.89	6 Jun
16.30		Hugo	Mamba-Schlick	CMR	1.2.82	24 May
16.30	0.8	Devin	Field	USA	9.10.93	31 May
16.30	-2.0	Martin	Seiler	GER	3.4.89	9 Jun
16.30	1.7	Roman	Valiyev	KAZ	27.3.84	22 Aug
16.29i		Jeremiah	Green	USA	9.2.94	1 Mar
16.29A	0.4	Levon	Aghasyan	ARM-J	19.1.95	25 May
16.29	1.8	Alexander	Hochuli	SUI	19.1.84	2 Aug
16.28i		Viktor	Yastrebov	UKR	13.1.82	30 Jan
16.28	1.8	Adil	Gandou	FRA	18.8.93	25 May
16.28	1.0	Okba	Ramoul	ALG	24.1.86	25 Jun
16.28	1.2		Li Li	CHN	6.8.87	13 Jul
16.28	1.5	Artyom	Primak	RUS	14.1.93	16 Jul
16.28	1.7	Erik	Ehrlin	SWE	16.8.90	20 Jul
16.28	0.0	Ryuma	Yamamoto	JPN-J	14.7.95	5 Sep
16.27i		Andre	Dorsey	USA	11.3.93	8 Feb
16.27i		Yevgen	Semenenko	UKR/RUS	17.7.84	21 Feb
16.27i		Daniel	Lennartsson	SWE	12.2.88	22 Feb
16.27	1.5	Pratchaya	Tepparak	THA	1.9.93	29 Jun
16.26	0.0		Wu Lianglin	CHN-J	15.11.95	22 Jun
16.26	0.8	Ruslan	Samitov	RUS	11.2.91	26 Jul
16.25A		Isaac	Yego	KEN	23.11.94	7 Jun
16.25	1.1	Ruslan	Kurbanov	UZB	10.2.93	2 Oct
		(142)				

Wind assisted

Mark	Wind	Name		Nat	Born	Pos	Meet	Venue	Date
17.26	2.3	Omar	Craddock	USA	26.4.91	1	MSR	Walnut	19 Apr
				16.61	16.74	16.83	x	16.75	17.26w
17.24	2.3	Fabrizio	Donato	ITA	14.8.76	1	ECCp	Vila Real	25 May
17.21	2.4	Tosin	Oke	NGR	1.10.80	1	NC	Calabar	20 Jun
17.12	4.7	Latario	Collie-Minns	BAH	10.3.94	1		Wichita	12 Apr
17.12	2.2	Aleksey	Fyodorov	RUS	25.5.91	1		Tomblaine	27 Jun
17.05	3.1	Marquis	Dendy	USA	17.11.92	1	NCAA	Eugene	14 Jun
16.93	2.2	Osviel	Hernández	CUB	31.5.89	2		La Habana	22 Feb

Mark	Wind	Name		Nat	Born	Pos	Meet	Venue	Date
16.79	3.3	Artyom	Primak	RUS	14.1.93	1		Saransk	3 Aug
16.77	3.1	Rumen	Dimitrov	BUL	19.9.86	1	ETC-2	Riga	22 Jun
16.75	7.4	Lathone	Collie-Minns	BAH	10.3.94	2		Wichita	12 Apr
16.74	2.3	Jadel	Gregório	BRA	16.9.80	1		São Paulo	22 Feb
16.73	2.3	Ben	Williams	GBR	25.1.92	2	NC	Birmingham	29 Jun
16.72	2.8	Roger	Haitengi	NAM	12.9.83	3	AfCh	Marrakech	13 Aug
16.67A	2.6	Carlos	Veiga	POR	22.2.89	2		Ávila	13 Jul
16.61	2.3	Dmitriy	Plotnitskiy	BLR	26.8.88	1		Brest	31 May
16.60	4.2	Ruslan	Samitov	RUS	11.2.91	1		Yerino	9 Jul
16.58	2.6	Zlatozar	Atanasov	BUL	12.12.89	4		Marrakech	8 Jun
16.55	4.6	Ryan	Grinnell	USA	4.2.87	5	NC	Sacramento	27 Jun
16.53	3.1	Martin	Seiler	GER	3.4.89	2		Rehlingen	9 Jun
16.52	2.1	Pratchaya	Tepparak	THA	1.9.93	1		Hong Kong	29 Jun
16.50	3.2	Vicente	Docavo	ESP	13.2.92	1		Castellón	16 May
16.48	2.3	Andrew	Issaka	FRA	15.9.92	1		Toulouse	1 Jun
16.46	2.7	Devin	Field	USA	9.10.93	2	NCAA	Eugene	14 Jun
16.43	2.1	Andy	Diaz	CUB-J	25.12.95	4	WJ	Eugene	27 Jul

Mark	Wind	Name		Nat	Born	Date
16.38	3.1	Yevgeniy	Ognev	RUS	25.2.94	3 Aug
16.37	0.7	Alwyn	Jones	AUS	28.2.85	5 Apr
16.37	2.6	Marius	Vadeikis	LTU	2.8.89	27 Jul
16.36	2.4	Hugo	Mamba-Schlick	CMR	1.2.82	13 Aug
16.36		Warunyu	Kongnil	THA	9.7.88	13 Dec
16.34	2.5	Donald	Scott	USA	23.2.92	3 May
16.33A	4.2	Mark	Jackson	USA	12.10.91	2 May
16.33	3.0	Nate	Moore	USA-J	28.5.96	6 Jul
16.32	2.4	Kristian	Pulli	FIN	2.9.94	28 Jun
16.31	4.0	Mathias	Ström	SWE	30.12.87	14 Jun
16.30	4.5	Sho	Sawaki	JPN	7.11.91	20 Jun
16.29	2.4	Peder	Nielsen	DEN	13.9.88	22 Jun
16.25	2.1	Jonathan	Drack	MRI	6.11.88	28 Jun

Best outdoors

Mark	Wind	Name	Pos	Meet	Venue	Date
17.29	1.4	Adams	3	Pre	Eugene	31 May
17.09	1.7	Carter	1		Austin	3 May
16.94	0.9	Oprea	5	EC	Zürich	14 Aug
16.82	0.0	Reid	1	NC	Birmingham	29 Jun
16.64	1.1	Hoffmann	1	NC	Szczecin	29 Jul
16.61	-0.1	Schembri	1	NC	Rovereto	20 Jul
16.57	0.5	Spasovkhodskiy	3	NC	Kazan	26 Jul
16.58w	2.3		2		Yerino	9 Jul
16.29	1.6	Bamba	5	NC	Reims	12 Jul
16.66w	2.2		1		Albi	21 Jun
16.26	-0.4	Nesterenko				21 May
16.40w						16 May
16.26	2.0	Lewis				21 Jun
16.24	2.0	Yurchenko				3 Aug
16.33A	4.2	M Jackson				2 May

Low altitude bests 16.27 0.4 Murillo 16 Mar 16.25 -0.9 Durañona 22 Jun

JUNIORS

See main list for top 4 juniors. 11 performances by 2 men to 16.53. Additional marks and further juniors:

	Mark	Wind	Pos	Meet	Venue	Date	Mark	Wind	Pos	Meet	Venue	Date
Martínez	17.13	0.7	1	WJ	Eugene	27 Jul	16.82	0.4	4	Bisl	Oslo	11 Jun
	17.07	-0.2	3	GGala	Roma	5 Jul	16.76	-0.3	2	DL	Shanghai	18 May
	17.06	-1.1	1		La Habana	10 May	16.63	1.9	Q	WJ	Eugene	25 Jul
	16.91A	-0.6	2	CAG	Xalapa	28 Nov	16.53A	-0.1	3	PAmSF	Ciudad de México	16Aug
	16.89	1.9	*		La Habana	21 Feb	(& 17.16w 2.7 1)					
	17.11w	3.1	2	NC	La Habana	20 Mar	16.70w	2.5	4		Sotteville-lès-Rouen	14 Jun

Mark	Wind	Name		Nat	Born	Pos	Meet	Venue	Date
16.33	2.0	Miguel	van Assen	SUR-Y	30.7.97	1		Fort-de-France	19 Apr
16.32	0.1		Fang Yaoqing	CHN	20.4.96	1	AsCh-j	Taipei	15 Jun
16.29A	0.4	Levon	Aghasyan	ARM	19.1.95	1	NC	Artashat	25 May
	16.17	1.0				*	WJ	Eugene	27 Jul
16.28	0.0	Ryuma	Yamamoto	JPN	14.7.95	1		Kumagaya	5 Sep
16.26	0.0		Wu Lianglin	CHN	15.11.95	1	NC-j	Lishui	22 Jun
16.21	0.5	Yugo	Takahashi (10)	JPN	8.2.96	1		Nagoya	4 Oct
16.18	1.7	Nazim	Babayev	AZE-Y	8.10.97	1	NC	Baku	13 Jun
16.18		Marouane	Aissaoui	MAR	12.8.96	1	NC-j	Benslimane	26 Jun
16.13	-0.4	Bruno Valerio	de Souza	BRA	29.9.95	1		São Paulo	23 Mar
16.04	1.2	Tobia	Bocchi	ITA-Y	7.4.97	1	NC-y	Rieti	22 Jun
16.02i		Simone	Forte	ITA	20.1.96	4	NC	Ancona	22 Feb
16.00i		Vitaliy	Pavlov	RUS-Y	12.1.97	1	NC-j	Volgograd	9 Feb
15.99	1.2	Tobias	Hell	GER	23.10.95	1		Rostock	22 Jun
15.97		Konstantin	Smal	BLR	1.12.95	5		Minsk	18 Jul
15.93	-0.1		Huang Jianjie	CHN	17.1.95	3		Kunshan	31 May
15.90			Liu Mingxuan (20)	CHN		1		Shanghai	1 Aug

Wind assisted

Mark	Wind	Name		Nat	Born	Pos	Meet	Venue	Date
16.43	2.1	Andy	Diaz	CUB	25.12.95	4	WJ	Eugene	27 Jul
16.33	3.0	Nate	Moore	USA	28.5.96	1	NC-j	Eugene	6 Jul
15.99	2.4	Lorenzo	Dallavalle	ITA	26.4.95	Q	WJ	Eugene	25 Jul
15.97	3.6	Alvaro	Cortéz	CHI	27.10.95	Q	WJ	Eugene	25 Jul
15.96	2.7	Jan	Luxa	SLO	11.2.96	1	v4N	Slovenj Gradec	5 Jul

SHOT

Mark		Name		Nat	Born	Pos	Meet	Venue			Date
22.23i		Ryan	Whiting	USA	24.11.86	1	NC	Albuquerque			23 Feb
					19.90	21.33	20.72	x	22.23		20.71
	22.05i	1 WI	Sopot	7 Mar	20.89	21.47	x	22.05	21.95		21.11
22.03		Joe	Kovacs	USA	28.6.89	1	NC	Sacramento			25 Jun
					20.38	20.59	20.49	20.75	22.03		21.17
	21.52	2 DL	Shanghai	18 May	20.64	20.50	x	20.94	21.52		20.85

Mark	Wind	Name			Nat	Born	Pos	Meet	Venue		Date
	21.47	1		Chula Vista	24 Apr	21.32	21.11	21.14	21.46	21.47	21.34
	21.46i	3	NC	Albuquerque	23 Feb	19.11	20.62	20.44	21.09	21.46	x
	21.46	2	Pre	Eugene	30 May	20.97	x	x	20.30	20.37	21.46
	21.44	2	Anniv	London (HG)	20 Jul	20.35	21.44	20.55	20.12		
	21.43	3	WK	Zürich	28 Aug	21.07	20.69	21.43	21.18	21.00	21.38
21.97		David		Storl	GER	27.7.90	1	Anniv	London (HG)		20 Jul
						21.88	21.86-	21.20	21.35	21.97	21.68
	21.90	1		Schönebeck	27 Jun	x	21.14	21.90	x	x	x
	21.87	1	NC	Ulm	25 Jul	21.32	21.32	21.36	x	21.58	21.87
	21.84	1		Biberach	14 Jul	21.61	x	21.84	x	x	x
	21.79i	2	WI	Sopot	7 Mar	21.35	21.79	x	x	x	21.19
	21.55	1	C.Cup	Marrakech	13 Sep	20.43	21.19	x	21.55		
	21.52	1		Gotha	19 Jul	x	21.38	x	x	21.26	21.52
	21.47	2	WK	Zürich	28 Aug	20.56	20.87	x	x	21.47	21.22
	21.42	1		Thum	29 Aug	20.97	21.17	21.37	x	21.42	x
	21.41	1	DL	Saint-Denis	5 Jul	21.17	x	21.41	x	x	x
	21.41	1	EC	Zürich	12 Aug	21.41	x	x	20.75	x	20.98
	21.41	1	ISTAF	Berlin	31 Aug	20.56	21.41	x	21.23	20.96	21.07
21.88		Reese		Hoffa	USA	8.10.77	1	WK	Zürich		28 Aug
						21.05	20.95	21.05	21.37	21.58	21.88
	21.67	1	DL	Glasgow	11 Jul	20.27	20.55	21.67	21.01	21.31	21.55
	21.64	1	Pre	Eugene	30 May	20.58	20.79	21.00	20.98	21.64	x
	21.48	1		Tucson	22 May	20.53	21.23	21.19	x	21.48	21.40
21.85		Christian		Cantwell	USA	30.9.80	1		Kingston		3 May
						21.45	21.43	21.85	x		
	21.73	1	DL	Shanghai	18 May	21.06	x	20.56	21.18	21.73	x
21.61		O'Dayne		Richards	JAM	14.12.88	1	CG	Glasgow		28 Jul
						20.94	20.83	20.70	21.61	x	20.20
21.50i		Kurt		Roberts	USA	20.2.88	2	NC	Albuquerque		23 Feb
						x	20.57	21.50	20.97	x	x
	21.47	2	NC	Sacramento	25 Jun	20.56	21.03	21.47	20.27	20.82	21.34
	21.41	1		Coeur d'Alene	14 Jun	21.27	21.41	x	x	21.16	20.82
21.40		Aleksandr		Lesnoy	RUS	28.7.88	1		Adler		30 May
		(32/8)				21.27	x	20.86	x	21.40	21.04
21.39		Ryan		Crouser	USA	18.12.92	1	Big 12	Lubbock		17 May
21.37		Jordan		Clarke	USA	10.7.90	2		Coeur d'Alene		14 Jun
		(10)									
21.26i		Tomas		Walsh	NZL	1.3.92	3	WI	Sopot		7 Mar
21.10		Anton		Tikhomirov	RUS	29.4.88	2		Adler		30 May
21.07		Borja		Vivas	ESP	26.5.84	1	NC	Alcobendas		27 Jul
21.04i		Germán		Lauro	ARG	2.4.84	1		Praha		25 Feb
21.04i		Tomasz		Majewski	POL	30.8.81	4	WI	Sopot		7 Mar
21.02i		Georgi		Ivanov	BUL	13.3.85	5	WI	Sopot		7 Mar
21.01		Marco		Fortes	POR	26.9.82	2	ECp-w	Leiria		16 Mar
20.98		Tim		Nedow	CAN	16.10.90	1		La Jolla		26 Apr
20.93		Tomás		Stanek	CZE	13.6.91	3	Kuso	Szczecin		7 Jun
20.93		Jan		Marcell	CZE	4.6.85	1		Ústi nad Labem		16 Jul
		(20)									
20.84		Darlan		Romani	BRA	9.4.91	1	NC	São Paulo		10 Oct
20.82i		Ladislav		Prásil	CZE	17.5.90	1		Jablonec		22 Jan
20.79i		Stephen		Mozia	NGR	16.8.93	1		Hanover, NH		1 Mar
20.79		Asmir		Kolasinac	SRB	15.10.84	1		Prijepolje		7 Aug
20.78i		Maksim		Sidorov	RUS	13.5.86	1	NC	Moskva		18 Feb
20.75		Jonathan		Jones	USA	23.4.91	4	NC	Sacramento		25 Jun
20.75		Pavel		Lyzhin	BLR	24.3.81	3		Ústi nad Labem		16 Jul
20.73		Cory		Martin	USA	22.5.85	2		Tokyo		11 May
20.70		Jacko		Gill	NZL	20.12.94	1		Rarotonga		25 Jun
20.68		Stipe		Zunic	CRO	13.12.90	4	EC	Zürich		12 Aug
		(30)									
20.67		Nedzad		Mulabegovic	CRO	4.2.81	1	NC	Varazdin		12 Jul
20.63		Orazio		Cremona	RSA	1.7.89	1		Port Elizabeth		21 Mar
20.61		Zach		Lloyd	USA	10.10.84	3		Coeur d'Alene		14 Jun
20.58i		Valeriy		Kokoyev	RUS	25.7.88	1		Moskva		23 Jan
20.58		Soslan		Tsirikhov	RUS	24.11.84	3		Adler		30 May
20.57		Darrell		Hill	USA	17.8.93	1	Big 10	West Lafayette		18 May
20.54		Konstantin		Lyadusov	RUS	2.3.88	1		Krasnodar		6 Jun
20.39		Nick		Vena	USA	16.4.93	2	NCAA-E	Jacksonville		29 May
20.35		Raymond		Brown	JAM	15.1.88	1		Kingston		5 Apr
20.35		Stephen		Sáenz	MEX	23.8.90	2		La Jolla		26 Apr
		(40)									
20.35		Richard		Garrett	USA	21.12.90	5	NC	Sacramento		25 Jun

Mark	Wind	Name		Nat	Born	Pos	Meet	Venue	Date
20.35		Martin	Stasek	CZE	8.4.89	1		Joensuu	24 Jul
20.33		Curtis	Jensen	USA	1.11.90	1		Normal	3 May
20.32		Carlos	Tobalina	ESP	2.8.85	1		Leiria	2 Aug
20.32			Chang Ming-Huang	TPE	7.8.82	1		Athens, GA	19 Sep
20.25		Yoiser	Toledo	ESP	24.4.83	2	NC	Alcobendas	27 Jul
20.21		Gaëtan	Bucki	FRA	9.5.80	Q	EC	Zürich	12 Aug
20.20i		Mason	Finley	USA	7.10.90	1		Laramie	21 Feb
20.19		Justin	Rodhe	CAN	17.10.84	6	KansR	Lawrence	18 Apr
20.18		Kemal	Mesic	BIH	4.8.85	2		Slovenska Bistrica	24 May
		(50)							
20.17i		Andrei	Gag	ROU	7.4.91	2	Balk C	Istanbul	22 Feb
20.13		Willy	Irwin	USA	2.6.92	2		Chula Vista	24 Apr
20.13		Eric	Werskey	USA	17.7.87	4		Tucson	24 May
20.11i		Kole	Weldon	USA	25.3.92	2		Albuquerque	8 Feb
20.09		Albert	Fournette	USA	21.10.91	1		San Marcos	11 May
20.08		Jakub	Szyszkowski	POL	21.8.91	1		Radom	21 Jun
20.07i		Chris	Reed	USA	22.7.92	1		Mankato	1 Feb
20.06		Hayden	Baillio	USA	22.7.91	1		San Antonio	2 May
20.06		Mihaíl	Stamatóyiannis ¶	GRE	20.5.82	1		Pátra	21 May
19.99		Sultan	Al-Hebshi	KSA	23.2.83	1	AsiG	Incheon	2 Oct
		(60)							
19.98i		Richard	Chavez	USA	30.7.92	1		Jonesboro	24 Jan
19.98		Leif	Arrhenius	SWE	15.7.86	1	NC	Umeå	1 Aug
19.96		Tobias	Dahm	GER	23.5.87	3		Biberach	14 Jul
19.95		Michael	Haratyk	POL	10.4.92	1	NC-23	Wroclaw	30 Aug
19.93i		Antonio	James	USA	7.4.92	1	Big 10	Geneva, OH	28 Feb
19.92		Hamza	Alic	BIH	20.1.79	1		Zenica	4 Jun
19.90i		Bobby	Grace	USA	10.10.90	3	NCAA	Albuquerque	15 Mar
19.90		Andriy	Borodkin ¶	UKR	18.4.78	1		Kosice	3 May
19.89i		Paul	Davis	USA	11.9.90	1		Lubbock	31 Jan
19.89		Inderjeet	Singh	IND	19.4.88	1		Patiala	17 Aug
		(70)							
19.88		Mikhal	Abramchuk	BLR	15.11.92	2		Brest	15 May
19.86		Jaco	Engelbrecht	RSA	8.3.87	1		Potchefstroom	9 May
19.86		Josh	Freeman	USA	22.8.94	1		Carbondale	17 May
19.85		Brad	Szypka	USA	13.2.93	1		Knoxville	3 May
19.83		Caleb	Whitener	USA	29.5.92	2	MSR	Walnut	19 Apr
19.81		Anatoliy	Garmashov	RUS	5.7.88	1		St Petersburg	4 Jul
19.80i		Rafal	Kownatke	POL	24.3.85	2	NC	Sopot	22 Feb
19.80		Wesley	Lavong	USA	27.1.91	1		Alamosa	6 May
19.79		Maris	Urtans	LAT	9.2.81	1		Tallinn	6 Aug
19.75i		Aleksandr	Bulanov	RUS	26.12.89	1		Volgograd	25 Jan
		(80)							
19.74		Christian	Jagusch	GER	13.7.92	1		Leipzig	7 Jun
19.74		Om Prakash	Singh	IND	11.1.87	1		Princeton	17 Jun
19.74		Antonin	Zalsky	CZE	7.8.80	2		Pacov	5 Jul
19.74		Arttu	Kangas	FIN	13.7.93	1		Hämeenkyrö	6 Jul
19.72i		Luke	Pinkelman	USA	5.5.88	1		Lincoln	8 Feb
19.72		Amin	Nikfar	IRI	2.1.81	1	Jordan	Stanford	4 May
19.72		Marin	Premeru	CRO	29.8.90	2		Kragujevac	3 Aug
19.72		Frank	Elemba	CGO	21.7.90	7	C.Cup	Marrakech	13 Sep
19.70		Tumatai	Dauphin	FRA	12.1.88	1		Vineuil	11 Oct
19.69		Damien	Birkinhead	AUS	8.4.93	1		Melbourne (Frankston)	1 Jun
		(90)							
19.69		Martin	Novák	CZE	5.10.92	1		Praha	3 Jun
19.67			Wang Like	CHN	2.4.89	1		Jinan	13 Jul
19.65		Filip	Mihaljevic	CRO	31.7.94	2		Split	20 Jul
19.63i		Luka	Rujevic	SRB	14.10.85	2		Novi Sad	1 Mar
19.62		Nicholas	Scarvelis	USA	2.2.93	1		Los Angeles (Ww)	4 May
19.60			Wang Guangfu	CHN	15.11.87	2		Jinan	13 Jul
19.55i		Hüseyin	Atici	TUR	3.5.86	1		Izmir	8 Feb
19.55i		Dan	Block	USA	8.1.91	1		Madison, WO	21 Feb
19.54		Ashinia	Miller	JAM	6.6.93	5	SEC	Lexington	18 May
19.47		Damian	Kusiak	POL	14.4.88	1		Katowice	2 Jul
		(100)							

Mark	Name		Nat	Born	Date
19.45i	Bob	Bertemes	LUX	24.5.93	20 Dec
19.43i	Marco	Schmidt	GER	5.9.83	12 Jan
19.43i	Matt	Babicz	USA	92	1 Feb
19.41	Patrick	Cronie	NED	5.11.89	2 Aug
19.40i	Andy	Novak	USA	24.4.90	14 Feb
19.39	Niklas	Arrhenius	SWE	10.9.82	1 Aug

Mark	Name		Nat	Born	Date
19.38	Chukwuebuka	Enekwechi	USA	28.1.93	18 May
19.37	Mesud	Pezer	BIH	27.8.94	27 Aug
19.36	David	Nichols	USA	13.1.85	15 Mar
19.36	Dominik	Witczak	POL	10.3.92	26 Jul
19.34	Robert	Dippl	GER	21.10.83	19 Jun
19.33	Sylwester	Zielinski	POL	13.8.89	4 May

Mark	Wind	Name		Nat	Born	Pos	Meet	Venue	Date
19.32i		Anton	Lyuboslavskiy	RUS	26.6.84				18 Jan
19.32		Coy	Blair	USA	10.6.94				3 May
19.31		Darien	Moore	USA	10.6.91				10 May
19.30i		Nick	Baatz	USA	4.1.90				23 Feb
19.30		Mario	Cota	MEX	11.9.90				25 Nov
19.29		Tavis	Bailey	USA	1.6.92				12 Apr
19.29		Ryan	Hershberger	USA	26.2.91				11 Jun
19.28		Jacob	Thormaehlen	USA	13.2.90				12 Apr
19.28i		Daniele	Secci	ITA	9.3.92				18 Dec
19.27		Tomás	Kozák	CZE	1.5.90				5 Sep
19.25i		Kim	Christensen	DEN	1.4.84				18 Jan
19.25		Will	Spence	USA	.92				19 Apr
19.24		Kyle	McKelvey	USA	15.7.92				16 May
19.23i		Kyle	Felpel	USA	26.7.93				1 Jan
19.22i		Sarunas	Banevicius	LTU	20.11.91				8 Feb
19.19		Mustafa Amer	Ahmed	EGY-J	16.12.95				5 Jun
19.17		Daniel	Ståhl	SWE	27.8.92				1 Aug
19.16			Liu Yang	CHN	29.10.86				19 Apr
19.15		Chad	Wright	JAM	25.3.91				11 Jun
19.15		Kristo	Galeta	EST	9.4.83				27 Jul
19.13		JC	Murasky	USA	.93				18 May
19.13			Tian Zhizhong	CHN	15.12.92				13 Jul
19.11		Will	Lohman	USA	31.3.91				26 Apr
19.09i		Derrick	Vicars	USA	8.5.89				11 Jan
19.09i		Donald "DJ"	Duke	USA	23.12.90				14 Feb
19.06i		Ivan	Emelianov	MDA	19.2.77				8 Feb
19.05		Frédéric	Dagée	FRA	11.12.92				16 Mar
19.05		Sergey	Dementyev	UZB	1.6.90				20 Aug
19.00		Chase	Sammons	USA	9.12.92				29 Mar
19.00		Marko	Spiler	SLO	8.1.90				4 Jun
18.99		Fedrick	Dacres	JAM	28.2.94				1 May
18.99		Braheme	Days	USA-J	18.1.95				7 Jun
18.99		Hendrik	Müller	GER	28.8.90				25 Jul
18.98i		Matt	DeChant	USA	31.5.89				25 Jan
18.98i		Andriy	Semenov	UKR	4.7.84				19 Feb
18.98		Willian	Braido	BRA	18.3.92				5 Oct
18.97		Errol	Jeffrey	USA	.90				12 Apr
18.97		Krzysztof	Brzozowski	POL	15.7.93				17 May
18.96		Rimantas	Martisauskas	LTU	18.9.86				13 Jul
18.92		Emanuele	Fuamatu	SAM	27.10.89				8 Mar
18.91i		Mateusz	Mikos	POL	10.4.87				18 Jan
18.91		Isaiah	Simmons	USA	3.12.92				18 Apr
18.90i		Aaron	Castle	USA	7.10.93				1 Mar
18.90		Zane	Duquemin	GBR	23.9.91				27 Jul
18.87		Nélson	Fernandes	BRA	9.7.94				7 May
18.86i		Tobias	Hepperle	GER	8.5.87				22 Feb
18.86		Russ	Winger	USA	2.8.84				29 Mar
18.86		Matt	Hoty	USA	21.10.91				18 May
18.85i		Nate	Hunter	USA	4.10.86				2 Mar
18.85		Derek	Sievers	USA	18.10.92				29 May
18.84		Jasdeep	Singh	IND	6.10.90				17 Aug
18.82i		Dennis	Lewke	GER	23.7.93				22 Feb
18.81i		Dillon	Simon	DMA	5.3.92				1 Feb
18.80		David	Pless	USA	.91				1 Jun
18.80		Dmytro	Savytskyy	UKR	14.12.90				3 Jun
18.80		Grigoriy	Kamulya ¶	UZB	31.1.89				8 Jun
18.80		Tsanko	Arnaudov	POR	14.3.92				19 Jul
18.80		Ali Reza	Mehrsafooti	IRI	21.2.91				22 Aug
18.77		Darian	Brown	USA	30.7.93				2 May
18.77		Bodo	Göder	GER	27.6.93				25 Jul
18.76		Vladislav	Tulácek	CZE	9.7.88				27 Apr
18.75		Mykola	Bahach	UKR	24.6.93				3 Jun
18.75		Jan Josef	Jeuschede	GER	23.4.93				11 Jun
18.75		Jacek	Wisniewski	POL	29.1.91				21 Jun
18.73i		Lukas	Weißhaidinger	AUT	20.2.92				30 Dec
18.71i		Michael	King	USA	.93				1 Mar
18.71		Ahmed Hassan	Gholoum	KUW	31.5.80				2 Oct
18.70			Wu Jiaxing	CHN	29.3.90				9 Oct
18.69		Mihai	Grasu	ROU	21.4.87				20 Jul
18.68i		Raigo	Toompuu	EST	17.7.81				1 Feb
18.68i		Zach	Coniglio	USA	31.3.92				15 Feb
18.68		Hayden	Reed	USA	4.4.94				11 Apr
18.68		Andrew	Akens	USA	9.12.92				18 May
18.67			Guo Yanxiang	CHN	29.1.87				13 Jul
18.66		Tomas	Söderlund	FIN	14.5.89				20 Jul
18.65		Alejandro	Noguera	ESP	11.3.93				21 Jun
18.64		Meshari Suroor	Saad	KUW	2.7.87				2 Oct
18.61			Feng Jie	CHN	18.1.86				9 Oct
18.60i		Austin	Perry	USA	8.5.92				31 Jan
18.60		Taylor	Miller	USA	23.8.91				9 May
18.60		Zeljko	Milovanovic	SRB	3.5.80				3 Aug
		(193)							

Best outdoor marks

Mark	Name	Pos	Meet	Venue	Date
21.47	Roberts	2	NC	Sacramento	25 Jun
21.31	Whiting	3	DL	Shanghai	18 May
21.24	Walsh	Q	CG	Glasgow	27 Jul
21.04	Majewski	2	Kuso	Szczecin	7 Jun
20.91	Ivanov	1		Sofia	21 May
20.70	Lauro	1		Santiago de Chile	15 Mar
20.56	Prásil	1		Olomouc	8 May
20.46	Mozia	2	NCAA	Eugene	11 Jun
20.37	Sidorov	4	ECp-w	Leiria	16 Mar
20.23	Kokoyev	8	EC	Zürich	12 Aug
19.93	C Reed	1	NCAA-2	Allendale	24 May
19.71	Bulanov	2		Moskva	12 Jun
19.67	Weldon	2	TexR	Austin	28 Mar
19.64	Gag	2	ETC-1	Tallinn	21 Jun
19.56	Grace	2	Owens	Columbus	19 Apr
19.55	Atici	1		Ankara	2 Sep

Mark	Name	Date	Mark	Name	Date	Mark	Name	Date	Mark	Name	Date
19.36	Bertemes	29 Jun	19.24	Kownatke	18 Jun	19.04	Banevicius	15 Jul	18.71	Novak	15 May
19.35	James	3 May	19.18	Felpel	11 Jun	19.03	Secci	10 May	18.66	Simon	28 Jul
19.27	Babicz	11 May	19.11	Lyuboslavskiy	30 May	18.90	Block	26 Apr	18.65	Davis	12 Apr
						18.79	Duke	12 Apr	18.60	DeChant	5 Apr

Drugs disqualification: 19.17 Eder Moreno ¶ COL 4.2.89 16 Feb

JUNIORS

Mark	Name		Nat	Born	Pos	Meet	Venue	Date
19.19	Mustafa Amer	Ahmed	EGY	16.12.95	1		Riyadh	5 Jun
18.99	Braheme	Days	USA	18.1.95	6		Los Angeles (Ww)	7 Jun
18.47	Nick	Ponzio	USA	4.1.95	1		Chula Vista	14 Jun
18.25	Denzel	Comenentia	NED	25.11.95	2		Lisse	10 May
18.10	Patrick	Müller	GER	4.2.96	1		Neubrandenburg	24 May
18.09	Mathijs	Damsteegt	NED	26.8.95	2		Hoorn	17 May

6 kg Shot

Mark	Name		Nat	Born	Pos	Meet	Venue	Date
22.06	Konrad	Bukowiecki	POL-Y	17.3.97	1	WJ	Eugene	24 Jul
	21.60 1 Lódz 13 Sep						20.61 1 Aleksandrów	22 Jun
	21.39 1 Lidzbark Warminski 14 Jun						20.54 1 Lomza	11 Jun
	21.31 1 NC-j Torun 28 Jun							
21.79	Mustafa Amer	Ahmed	EGY	16.12.95	1	Arab	Cairo	23 Apr
21.16	Braheme	Days	USA	18.1.95	1		Chula Vista	14 Jun
20.63i	Patrick	Müller	GER	4.2.96	1	NC-j	Sindelfingen	16 Feb
	20.51				1		Halle	17 May
	20.55i 2 Rochlitz 2 Feb						12 performances by 5 men over 20.50	
20.60i	Henning	Prüfer	GER	7.3.96	1		Rochlitz	2 Feb
	19.89				2		Osterode	17 Jun
20.17	Denzel	Comenentia	NED	25.11.95	2	WJ	Eugene	24 Jul

Mark	Wind	Name		Nat	Born	Pos	Meet	Venue	Date
20.01		Merten	Howe	GER-Y	7.1.97	1		Gotha	19 Jul
19.91		Siomon	Bayer	GER	23.11.95	1		Biberach	14 Jul
19.85		Hamza	Mohammed	EGY	30.8.96	4	WJ	Eugene	24 Jul
19.83		Andrei	Toader	ROU-Y	26.5.97	1		Bucuresti	25 May
19.70		Osman	Can Özdeveci	TUR	23.8.95	1		Ankara	5 Jul
19.63		Ahmed Sherif	Adel	EGY	25.1.96	2	Arab	Cairo	23 Apr
19.57		Martin	Markovic	CRO	13.1.96	6	WJ	Eugene	24 Jul
19.54		Nicolai	Ceban	MDA	4.2.95	1	NC-j	Chisinau	1 Jun
19.51		Mathijs	Damsteegt	NED	26.8.95	12		Hilversum	13 Jul
19.46		Nace	Plesko	SLO	21.8.96	1		Slovenska Bistrica	24 May
19.27		Amir Ali	Patterson	USA	30.1.96	2	NC-j	Eugene	6 Jul
19.20i		Sebastiano	Bianchetti	ITA	20.1.96	3	v2N	Halle	1 Mar
19.20		Valdivino	Nunes	BRA	9.1.95	1		São Bernardo do Campo	11 Apr
19.17		Willy	Vicaut	FRA	27.11.95	1		Conflans-St-Honorine	28 Jun
19.17		Josh	Awotunde	USA	12.6.95	3	NC-j	Eugene	6 Jul

DISCUS

Mark				Name		Nat	Born	Pos	Meet	Venue		Date
69.28				Piotr	Malachowski	POL	7.6.83	1		Halle		17 May
							x	67.20	69.28	x	65.14	x
	67.35	2	VD	Bruxelles		5 Sep	64.08	66.34	67.35	x	65.66	x
	67.26	1	Danek	Turnov		27 May	61.70	61.07	63.60	x	66.37	67.26
	67.07	2	FBK	Hengelo		8 Jun	62.97	x	61.86	67.07	63.55	63.77
	66.72	1	DL	Doha		9 May	65.33	66.72	65.19	65.38	66.14	65.82
	66.63	1	Athl	Lausanne		3 Jul	64.05	66.63	62.60	x	66.05	x
68.47				Robert	Harting	GER	18.10.84	1	FBK	Hengelo		8 Jun
							63.62	66.99	67.14	67.84	x	68.47
	68.36	1	GGala	Roma		5 Jun	62.07	66.64	66.61	66.21	68.36	x
	68.28	2		Halle		17 May	x	x	67.00	68.28	x	x
	68.24	1	adidas	New York		14 Jun	64.63	66.49	67.02	66.79	x	68.24
	68.21	1	ISTAF	Berlin		31 Aug	65.62	67.68	68.21	x	67.56	x
	67.57	1	DL	Birmingham		24 Aug	x	63.18	66.27	x	x	67.57
	67.57	1	VD	Bruxelles		5 Sep	64.33	67.57	x	x	x	x
	67.46	1		Wiesbaden		10 May	x	66.97	67.46	x	66.41	x
	67.42	1	ET	Braunschweig		22 Jun	66.72	67.42	65.82	65.52		
	67.40	1		Warszawa		23 Aug	63.28	66.08	67.40	x	x	x
	67.29	1		Schönebeck		27 Jun	x	65.07	x	66.53	x	67.29
	67.01	Q	EC	Zürich		12 Aug	67.01					
	66.67	1	NC	Ulm		27 Jul	65.51	65.90	x	66.67	p	p
	66.10	1		Dessau		11 Jun	64.16	65.98	65.34	65.61	x	66.10
	66.07	1	EC	Zürich		13 Aug	63.94	x	66.07	p	x	x
67.92				Martin	Maric ¶	CRO	19.4.84	1		Chula Vista		17 May
							58.63	65.18	67.92	x	62.95	p
66.89				Daniel	Ståhl	SWE	27.8.92	1		Irvine		3 May
							63.48	66.89	x	x	59.54	61.00
66.75				Fedrick	Dacres	JAM	28.2.94	1	TexR	Austin		29 Mar
							63.30	59.91	61.95	65.12	66.75	65.94
66.59				Martin	Wierig	GER	10.6.87	2		Wiesbaden		10 May
							x	x	61.72	66.59	x	63.37
	66.13	2	ISTAF	Berlin		31 Aug	65.44	x	x	65.00	x	66.13
66.50				Jorge	Fernández	CUB	2.10.87	2	Athl	Lausanne		3 Jul
							62.72	x	66.50	x	x	x
66.37				Andrew	Evans	USA	25.1.91	1		Knoxville		3 May
							60.22	66.37	62.14	66.06	x	59.20
66.28				Gerd	Kanter	EST	6.5.79	1		Pärnu		24 Sep
							66.28	64.62	x	62.57	x	65.91
	66.26	1		Türi		20 Sep	x	x	65.65	66.26	64.36	64.33
66.11				Andrius	Gudzius	LTU	14.2.91	1	NCp	Kaunas		31 May
				(31/10)			63.75	66.11	x	x	x	x
66.02				Philip	Milanov	BEL	6.7.91	3	FBK	Hengelo		8 Jun
65.98				Daniel	Jasinski	GER	5.8.89	3		Wiesbaden		10 May
65.94				Benn	Harradine	AUS	14.10.82	1		Brisbane		29 Mar
65.89				Viktor	Butenko	RUS	10.3.93	1		Adler		29 May
65.82				Zoltán	Kövágó	HUN	10.4.79	1	Gugl	Linz		14 Jul
65.76				Virgilijus	Alekna	LTU	13.2.72	4		Halle		17 May
65.75				Robert	Urbanek	POL	29.4.87	5		Halle		17 May
65.74				Mario	Pestano	ESP	8.4.78	1		Leiria		3 Aug
65.62				Vikas	Gowda	IND	5.7.83	1		Tucson		24 May
65.54				Julian	Wruck	AUS	6.7.91	1		Brisbane		23 Nov
				(20)								
65.48				Frank	Casañas	ESP	18.10.78	2		Leiria		3 Aug

Mark	Wind	Name		Nat	Born	Pos	Meet	Venue	Date
65.46		Mohammed	Samimi	IRI	29.3.87	1		Szombathely	23 Jul
65.24		Erik	Cadée	NED	15.2.84	3		Leiria	3 Aug
65.23		Ehsan	Hadadi	IRI	21.1.85	3	adidas	New York	14 Jun
65.13		Lois Maikel	Martínez	ex-CUB	3.6.81	1		Málaga	22 Feb
64.98		Martin	Kupper	EST	31.5.89	2		Tallinn	17 Sep
64.72		Jason	Morgan	JAM	6.10.82	1		Hattiesburg	3 May
64.68		Rodney	Brown	USA	21.5.93	1		Chula Vista	31 Jul
64.54		Markus	Münch	GER	13.6.86	5		Wiesbaden	10 May
64.54		Russ	Winger	USA	2.8.84	1		Claremont	7 Jun
		(30)							
64.51		Tavis	Bailey	USA	6.1.92	2		Knoxville	3 May
64.44		Oleksiy	Semenov	UKR	27.6.82	1		Kyiv	4 Jun
64.42		Jared	Schuurmans	USA	20.8.87	2		Chula Vista	24 Apr
64.40		Märt	Israel	EST	23.9.83	1		Malmö	18 Jun
64.36		Jason	Young	USA	27.5.81	1		Abilene	12 Apr
64.17A		Mason	Finley	USA	7.10.90	1		Laramie	3 May
64.16		Przemyslaw	Czajkowski	POL	26.10.88	9		Halle	17 May
64.16		Victor	Hogan	RSA	25.7.89	Q	CG	Glasgow	30 Jul
64.11		Ronald	Julião	BRA	16.6.85	4		Chula Vista	24 Apr
63.96		Chad	Wright	JAM	25.3.91	1	Big 10	West Lafayette	17 May
		(40)							
63.94		Mykyta	Nesterenko	UKR	15.4.91	2		Kyiv	4 Jun
63.90		Ryan	Crouser	USA	18.12.92	1	Big 12	Lubbock	18 May
63.89		Apostolos	Parellis	CYP	24.7.85	1		Nicosia	17 May
63.78		Christoph	Harting	GER	4.10.90	10		Halle	17 May
63.76		Luke	Bryant	USA	5.12.88	1		Emporia	23 Apr
63.74		Hayden	Reed	USA	4.4.94	2	SEC	Lexington	17 May
63.59		Nikolay	Sedyuk	RUS	29.4.88	2		Adler	29 May
63.43		Roland	Varga	CRO	22.10.77	2		Szombathely	23 Jul
63.39		Ivan	Panasyuk	UKR	8.10.91	1		Novo Mesto	11 Jul
63.34		Brett	Morse	GBR	11.2.89	1		Cardiff	12 Jul
		(50)							
63.33		Hannes	Kirchler	ITA	22.12.78	5		Chula Vista	24 Apr
63.20		Robert	Szikszai	HUN	30.9.94	1		Antony	14 May
63.11		Gabe	Hull	USA	1.12.93	1		Iowa City	3 May
63.00		Yeóryios	Trémos	GRE	21.3.89	1		Thessaloníki	23 May
62.90		Mahmoud	Samimi	IRI	18.9.88	3		Szombathely	23 Jul
62.83A		Niklas	Arrhenius	SWE	10.9.82	1		Provo	30 Jun
62.81		Bryan	Powlen	USA	3.12.87	2		Tucson	22 May
62.80		Stephen	Mozia	NGR	16.8.93	2	NCAA-E	Jacksonville	31 May
62.72		David	Wrobel	GER	13.2.91	4	NC	Ulm	27 Jul
62.58		Aleksas	Abromavicius	LTU	6.12.84	1		Klaipeda	15 Jul
		(60)							
62.51		Carl	Myerscough	GBR	21.10.79	1		Claremont	28 Jun
62.47		Gleb	Sidorchenko	RUS	15.5.86	1	NC	Kazan	26 Jul
62.43		Sergiu	Ursu ¶	ROU	26.4.80	1	NC-w	Bucuresti	4 Mar
62.43		Axel	Härstedt	SWE	28.2.87	2eB		Halle	17 May
62.30A		Mauricio	Ortega	COL	4.8.94	1	NC	Medellín	28 Jun
62.27		András	Seres	HUN	31.1.89	2		Abbeville	10 May
62.19		Danijel	Furtula	MNE	31.7.92	1	ECp-w23	Leiria	15 Mar
62.15		Russel	Tucker	RSA	4.11.90	2	AfCh	Marrakech	11 Aug
62.13		Sam	Mattis	USA	19.3.94	4	NCAA-E	Jacksonville	31 May
62.10		Tomás	Vonavka	CZE	4.6.90	1		Domazlice	19 Sep
		(70)							
62.07		Giovanni	Faloci	ITA	13.10.85	1		Donnas	13 Jul
62.05		Kole	Weldon	USA	25.3.92	1		Lubbock	3 May
61.95		Jouni	Waldén	FIN	9.1.82	1		Viitasaari	13 Jun
61.91		Jan	Marcell	CZE	4.6.85	6	ET	Braunschweig	22 Jun
61.90		Eldred	Henry	IVB	18.9.94	6		La Jolla	26 Apr
61.82		Gordon	Wolf	GER	17.1.90	1eB		Wiesbaden	10 May
61.81		Nathaniel	Moses	USA	1.4.90	1		Gulf Shores	23 May
61.77		Orestis	Antoniades	CYP	10.7.85	2		Thessaloniki	23 May
61.65		Stanislav	Nesterovskiy	UKR	31.7.80	2	NC	Kirovohrad	25 Jul
61.63		Mario	Cota	MEX	11.9.90	3		Tucson	22 May
		(80)							
61.62		Germán	Lauro	ARG	2.4.84	1	IbAmC	São Paulo	3 Aug
61.61		Mike	Torie	USA	12.3.86	1		Chula Vista	29 May
61.58		Lance	Brooks	USA	1.1.84	2		Coeur d'Alene	14 Jun
61.50		Chase	Madison	USA	13.9.85	3		Iowa City	3 May
61.45		Gerhard	Mayer	AUT	20.5.80	1		Hainfeld	14 May
61.38		Aleksandr	Tammert	EST	2.2.73	2		Paunküla	29 Aug

Mark	Wind	Name		Nat	Born	Pos	Meet	Venue	Date
61.27		Andrei	Gag	ROU	7.4.91	2	NC-w	Bucuresti	4 Mar
61.25		Ahmed Mohamed	Dheeb	QAT	29.9.85	3	AsiG	Incheon	30 Sep
61.19A		Leif	Arrhenius	SWE	15.7.86	1		Park City, UT	31 May
61.18		Ercüment	Olgundeniz	TUR	7.7.76	1		Izmir	8 Feb
		(90)							
61.15		Zane	Duquemin	GBR	23.9.91	2		London (He)	5 Jul
61.12		Nick	Jones	USA	22.6.89	1		Abilene	12 Apr
60.89		Magomed	Magomedov	RUS	26.7.91	1eB	ECp-w	Leiria	15 Mar
60.87		Wojciech	Praczyk	POL	10.1.93	1		Szprotawa	10 May
60.85		Maximiliano	Alonso	CHI	10.10.86	1		Hays	18 May
60.82		Stéphane	Marthély	FRA	9.9.79	1		Vannes	14 Jun
60.71		Pyry	Niskala	FIN	6.11.90	1	NC	Kuopio	3 Aug
60.68		Lukas	Weißhaidinger	AUT	20.2.92	2		Hainfeld	14 May
60.67		Roman	Ryzhyy	UKR	17.1.85	3	NC	Kirovohrad	25 Jul
60.64		Federico	Apolloni	ITA	14.3.87	1		Tarquinia	11 Jun
		(100)							

Mark	Name		Nat	Born	Date
60.61	Carter	Comito	USA	26.10.90	7 May
60.51	Pedro José	Cuesta	ESP	22.8.83	14 Jun
60.45	Eligijus	Ruskys	LTU	1.12.90	10 Jun
60.41	Filip	Mihaljevic	CRO	31.7.94	29 Mar
60.40	Dmitriy	Chebotaryov	RUS	9.10.88	24 Apr
60.39	Mikhail	Dvornikov	RUS	15.8.89	8 Jun
60.38	Andrés	Rossini	ARG	4.12.88	26 Jan
60.38	Pawel	Pasinski	POL	6.3.93	30 Jul
60.19	Pavel	Lyzhin	BLR	24.3.81	25 Jul
60.17	Cody	Snyder	USA	27.4.92	3 May
60.15	Antonio	James	USA	7.4.92	26 Apr
60.09	Mike	Guidry	USA	29.10.79	10 May
60.07	Fredrik	Amundgård	NOR	12.1.89	12 Jun
60.05	Yuji	Tsutsumi	JPN	22.12.89	21 Sep
60.04	Maarten	Persoon	NED	15.3.87	3 Aug
59.95	Matthew	Kosecki	USA	1.7.91	18 Apr
59.93	Jorge	Grave	POR	5.9.82	1 Jul
59.90	Priidu	Niit	EST	27.1.90	28 Jul
59.85	Felipe	Lorenzon	BRA	11.11.93	3 Aug
59.81	Dominique	Howard	USA	3.12.91	17 May
59.80	Yunior	Lastre	CUB	26.10.81	27 Jun
59.76	Ivan	Krasnoshenkov	RUS	26.3.87	29 May
59.73	Ulf	Ankarling	SWE	12.4.88	29 Jun
59.71	Aleksandr	Kirya	RUS	23.3.92	29 May
59.60	Mário Luis	David Jr	BRA	9.7.92	25 Oct
59.58	Irfan	Yildirum	TUR	26.7.88	1 Mar
59.54	Lolassonn	Djouhan	FRA	18.5.91	31 May
59.46	Igor	Gondor	CZE	10.3.79	5 May
59.42	Derek	White	USA	19.11.90	12 Apr
59.37	Macklin	Tudor	USA	13.6.94	16 May
59.36	Carlos	Valle	BRA	11.4.87	27 Sep
59.35	Caleb	Fricke	USA	2.12.93	3 Mar
59.30	Tom	Norman	GBR	15.9.82	5 May
59.27	James	Plummer	USA	19.8.90	14 Jun
59.26	Michael	Salzer	GER	25.10.91	4 May
59.24		Wu Jian	CHN	25.5.86	13 Jul
59.23	Dylan	Banagis	USA	.94	10 May
59.19	Reggie	Jagers	USA	13.8.94	10 May
59.19	Eric	Masington	USA	23.6.92	13 Jun
59.15	Sultan M.	Al-Dawoodi	KSA	16.6.77	5 Jun
59.11	Jared	Thomas	USA	17.2.90	26 Apr
59.10	Filipe Vital e	Silva	POR	27.1.83	10 Jun
59.09	Mihai	Grasu	ROU	21.4.87	27 Jul
59.04	Matt	Denny	AUS-J	2.6.96	29 Mar
59.03	Brian	Bishop	USA	16.4.89	11 Apr
59.01	János	Huszák	HUN	5.2.92	23 Jul
58.97	Marin	Premeru	CRO	29.8.90	8 Jun
58.92	Nazzareno	Di Marco	ITA	30.4.85	2 Aug
58.84	Dan	Block	USA	8.1.91	24 Apr
58.80	Clint	Harris	USA	.92	3 May
58.76	Bartosz	Roch	POL	27.3.90	1 Jun
58.70	Sebastian	Scheffel	GER	17.11.93	10 May
58.68	Courtland	Clavette	USA	4.7.93	10 May
58.61	Will	Spence	USA	.92	3 May
58.61	Nick	Percy	GBR	5.12.94	29 Jun
58.46	Jason	Harrell	USA	.92	15 Mar
58.41	Jan-Louw	Kotze	RSA	18.3.94	7 Mar
58.40	János	Káplar	HUN	8.2.94	27 Sep
58.31	Stipe	Zunic	CRO	13.12.90	3 Aug
58.29	Aleksey	Sysoyev	RUS	8.3.85	11 Feb
58.27i	Jordan	Williams	USA	22.5.90	17 Jan
58.27	Zach	Duncavage	USA	.91	26 Apr
58.26	Marek	Bárta	CZE	8.12.92	27 May
58.25	Marshall	Hall	NZL	7.10.88	28 Mar
58.19	Dmitriy	Kalmykov	RUS	28.2.93	24 Apr
58.19	Paul	Thomas	USA	.93	3 May
58.17	Damian	Kaminski	POL	15.12.93	4 May
58.16	Benedikt	Stienen	GER	12.1.92	9 Aug
58.15	Matthias	Tayala	USA	27.4.93	17 May
58.12	Jorge	Balliengo	ARG	5.1.78	24 May
58.10i	Darian	Brown	USA	30.7.93	31 May
58.02	Luke	Vaughn	USA	24.8.94	31 May
58.00	Stefano	Petrei	ITA	27.12.93	25 Apr
	(173)				

Drugs disqualification: 62.73 Sergiu Ursu ¶ ROU 26.4.80 (1) Bacau 27 Apr

JUNIORS

Mark	Name		Nat	Born	Pos	Meet	Venue	Date
59.04	Matt	Denny	AUS	2.6.96	2		Brisbane	29 Mar
57.54	Martin	Markovic	CRO	13.1.96	4		Zagreb	31 May
57.40	Henning	Prüfer	GER	7.3.96	2	NC-23	Wesel	15 Jun
57.36	Domantas	Poska	LTU	10.1.96	4		Kaunas	31 May
57.36	Sven Martin	Skagestad	NOR	13.1.95	7		Bottnaryd	28 Jun
	57.19 1	Oslo		2 May	6 performances by 5 men to 57.00			
56.99	Mitch	Cooper	AUS	2.6.95	2		La Jolla	26 Apr
56.45	Alin Alexandru	Firfirica	ROU	3.11.95	3	NC-w	Bucuresti	4 Mar
56.01		Wei Zidong	CHN	18.2.95	4	NC	Suzhou	9 Oct
55.64	Aleksey	Khudyakov	RUS	31.3.95	3		Adler	24 Apr
55.57	Ola Stunes	Isene (10)	NOR	29.1.95	1		Spikkestad	21 Sep
55.50	Brenden	Song	USA	29.3.95	1		San Diego	18 Jun
55.47	Gian Piero	Ragonesi	ITA	19.4.95	17q	NCAA-w	Jacksonville	31 May
55.21	Mustafa Kazem	Dagher	IRQ	29.11.95	10	AsiG	Incheon	30 Sep
54.98	Bryan	Bjerk	USA	10.3.95	8		Iowa City	3 May
54.88		Cheng Yulong	CHN-Y	1.2.97	7		Jinan	13 Jul
54.85	Nicolai	Ceban	MDA	4.2.95	3	ET-3	Tbilisi	22 Jun
54.70	Cullen	Prena	USA	17.3.95	2		Eugene	22 Mar
54.62	Braheme	Days	USA	18.1.95	5		La Jolla	26 Apr

1.75kg Discus

Mark	Wind	Name		Nat	Born	Pos	Meet	Venue		Date
66.94		Martin	Markovic	CRO	13.1.96	1	WJ	Eugene		26 Jul
		65.35	1 NC-j Varazdin	29 Jun		63.71	Q	WJ Eugene		25 Jul
66.81		Matthew	Denny	AUS	2.6.96	1		Brisbane		23 Nov
		63.66	1 Brisbane	1 Mar						
65.66		Sven Martin	Skagestad	NOR	13.1.95	1		Oslo		12 Jun
		63.21	3 WJ Eugene	26 Jul						
64.18		Henning	Prüfer	GER	7.3.96	2	WJ	Eugene		26 Jul
		63.15	1 Osterode	27 Jun		10 performances by 5 men to 63.00				
63.83		Domantas	Poska	LTU	10.1.96	1		Vilnius		10 Jun
63.07		Ola Stunes	Isene	NOR	29.1.95	1		Bergen		30 May
62.35		Valeriy	Golubkovich	BLR	21.1.95	Q	WJ	Eugene		25 Jul
61.77		Mitch	Cooper	AUS	2.6.95	6	WJ	Eugene		26 Jul
61.67		Aleksey	Khudyakov	RUS	31.3.95	1		Adler		24 Apr
61.35		Maximilian	Klaus	GER-Y	7.2.98	2	Werfer	Wiesbaden		10 May
61.28		Kord	Ferguson	USA	19.6.95	1	NC-j	Eugene		5 Jul
61.06		Alin Alexandru	Firfirica	ROU	3.11.95	1	NC-w	Bucuresti		5 Mar
60.59		Tony	Zeuke	GER	14.8.96	3		Osterode		27 Jun
60.47		Gian Piero	Ragonesi	ITA	19.4.95	7	WJ	Eugene		26 Jul
60.14		Bartlomiej	Stój	POL	15.5.96	1		Mielec		11 May
59.89		Ryan	Njegovan	USA	27.6.95	Q	WJ	Eugene		25 Jul
59.89		Denzel	Comenentia	NED	25.11.95	1		Breda		12 Oct
59.56		Mustafa Kazem	Dagher	IRQ	29.11.95	1		Baghdad		24 Oct
59.17		Nicolai	Ceban	MDA	4.2.95	Q	WJ	Eugene		25 Jul
58.87		Clemens	Prüfer	GER	13.8.97	6	Werfer	Halle		17 May

HAMMER

Mark	Wind	Name		Nat	Born	Pos	Meet	Venue		Date
83.48		Pawel	Fajdek	POL	4.6.89	1		Warszawa		23 Aug
					80.19	83.48	83.37	82.16	81.57	81.46
	82.37	1	Velenje	1 Jul	78.73	78.50	82.37	76.48	80.65	81.63
	82.05	2 EC	Zürich	16 Aug	x	78.48	x	x	82.05	x
	81.11	1 WCM	Rieti	6 Sep	73.08	81.11	78.35	x	x	x
	80.79	1 Skol	Cetniewo	26 Jul	x	79.53	79.27	79.33	80.79	78.02
	80.73	2 Gyulai	Székesfehérvár	8 Jul	76.84	80.73	x	x	x	x
	79.65	3 GS	Ostrava	16 Jun	x	x	x	x	79.65	x
	79.59	1	Halle	17 May	79.05	x	77.90	79.59	77.22	
82.69		Krisztián	Pars	HUN	18.2.82	1	EC	Zürich		16 Aug
					78.11	78.45	82.18	78.36	81.69	82.69
	82.49	1 Gyulai	Székesfehérvár	8 Jul	79.84	81.65	x	x	81.35	82.49
	81.57	1 GS	Ostrava	16 Jun	78.19	81.57	78.47	p	x	x
	81.38	1 NC	Székesfehérvár	2 Aug	78.84	78.79	81.38	p	p	p
	81.31	1	Veszprém	8 Jun						
	81.08	2	Velenje	1 Jul	78.38	81.08	p	p	p	p
	80.78	2 WCM	Rieti	6 Sep	77.45	79.82	80.03	80.78	80.70	80.04
	80.69	2 Skol	Cetniewo	26 Jul	78.66	78.81	80.40	80.47	80.69	x
	80.61	1	Debrecen	30 Aug	77.63	x	79.80	80.61	p	p
	79.83	1 PNG	Turku	25 Jun	77.83	76.70	79.83	78.37	77.71	77.89
	79.35	1 Kuso	Szczecin	7 Jun	73.69	75.45	78.63	78.32	79.35	77.72
	79.31	1 GP	Ponce	17 May	x	78.08	77.73	77.40	79.31	78.87
	79.30	1	Nyiregyháza	20 Sep						
81.27		Mostafa	Al-Gamal	EGY	1.10.88	1		Cairo		21 Mar
					x	x	79.29	77.96	81.27	x
	79.85	1 NC	Cairo	7 May						
80.62		Dilshod	Nazarov	TJK	6.5.82	2	GS	Ostrava		16 Jun
					77.39	79.37	x	78.67	80.62	78.16
	80.51	1 WCM	Madrid	19 Jul	x	77.61	80.51	78.48	78.57	78.36
	80.24	3 Gyulai	Székesfehérvár	8 Jul	76.63	77.96	76.95	78.93	79.74	80.24
	79.62	1	Karlstad	16 Jul	75.54	79.62	77.73	77.34	75.72	78.05
	79.49	2	Halle	17 May	x	76.27	77.33	79.49	78.42	79.29
79.39		Pavel	Krivitskiy	BLR	17.4.84	1		Jablonec		30 Apr
79.35		Sergey	Litvinov	RUS	27.1.86	3	EC	Zürich		16 Aug
		(30/6)			77.33	77.09	x	x	79.35	x
79.16		Marcel	Lomnicky	SVK	6.7.87	1		Nové Zámky		2 Aug
78.58		Quentin	Bigot ¶	FRA	1.12.92	1	NCw-23	Chateauroux		8 Mar
78.41		Szymon	Ziólkowski	POL	1.7.76	5	EC	Zürich		16 Aug
78.27		Sergey	Marghiev	MDA	7.11.92	1	NC	Chisinau		31 May
		(10)								
77.86		Oleksiy	Sokyrskyy	UKR/RUS	16.3.85	1		Kyiv		3 Jun
77.57		David	Söderberg	FIN	11.8.79	3		Karlstad		16 Jul
77.46		Primoz	Kozmus	SLO	30.9.79	6	EC	Zürich		16 Aug
77.20		Conor	McCullough	IRL/USA	31.1.91	1		Edmonton		6 Jul

Mark	Wind	Name		Nat	Born	Pos	Meet	Venue	Date
77.03		Denis	Lukyanov	RUS	11.7.89	3		Moskva	11 Jun
77.01		Yevgen	Vynogradov	UKR	30.4.84	2		Kyiv	3 Jun
76.86		Pavel	Boreysha	BLR	16.2.91	1	Klim	Minsk	18 Jun
76.86		Yuriy	Shayunov	BLR	22.10.87	1		Novopolotsk	28 Nov
76.64		Markus	Esser	GER	3.2.80	4	EAF	Bydgoszcz	2 Jun
76.55		Sergey	Kolomoyets	BLR	11.8.89	2	NC-w	Staiki	13 Feb
		(20)							
76.46		Aleksey	Korolyov	RUS	5.4.82	2		Adler	29 May
76.29		Alexander	Ziegler	GER	7.7.87	1		Schönebeck	27 Jun
76.25		A.G.	Kruger	USA	18.2.79	1		Columbia, SC	28 Mar
76.16		Markus	Johansson	SWE	8.5.90	1		Göteborg	22 May
76.14		Wojciech	Nowicki	POL	22.2.89	2	NC	Szczecin	30 Jul
75.99		Roberto	Janet	CUB	29.8.86	1	Barr	La Habana	24 May
75.99		Nicola	Vizzoni	ITA	4.11.73	1	NC	Rovereto	20 Jul
75.89		Lukás	Melich	CZE	16.9.80	5		Halle	17 May
75.73		Ali Mohamed	Al-Zankawi	KUW	27.2.84	1	NC	Doha	28 Apr
75.71		Anatoliy	Pozdnyakov	RUS	1.2.87	3	NC-w	Krasnodar	23 Feb
		(30)							
75.70		Jérôme	Bortoluzzi	FRA	20.5.82	2		Forbach	25 May
75.56		Zakhar	Makhrosenko	BLR	10.10.91	1		Brest	31 May
75.56		Oleg	Dubitskiy	BLR	14.10.90	2		Brest	31 May
75.55		Valeriy	Svyatokho	BLR	20.7.81	1		Minsk	7 Jun
75.54		James	Steacy	CAN	29.5.84	1		Sherwood Park	13 Jul
75.47		Wágner	Domingos	BRA	23.6.83	1	NC	São Paulo	9 Oct
75.26		Chris	Cralle	USA	13.6.88	1		Tucson	22 May
75.22		Tuomas	Seppänen	FIN	16.5.86	2	NC	Kuopio	1 Aug
75.15		Igors	Sokolovs	LAT	17.8.74	1	NC-w	Salaspils	8 Mar
75.03		Javier	Cienfuegos	ESP	15.7.90	1		Alcorcón	12 Jul
		(40)							
74.86		Kibwé	Johnson	USA	17.7.81	1		Coeur d'Alene	14 Jun
74.63		Mark	Dry	GBR	11.10.87	1	SCO Ch	Kilmarnock	17 Aug
74.58		Reinier	Mejias	CUB	22.9.90	1		La Habana	15 Feb
74.38		Nick	Miller	GBR	1.5.93	1	Big 12	Lubbock	16 May
74.17		Ákos	Hudi	HUN	10.8.91	1		Budapest	15 Jun
74.04		Kristóf	Németh	HUN	17.9.87	1		Szombathely	2 Jul
74.04		András	Haklits	CRO	23.9.77	1		Tapolca	9 Aug
74.00		Marco	Lingua	ITA	4.6.78	1		Marano	13 Sep
73.93		Koji	Murofushi	JPN	8.10.74	1	NC	Fukushima	7 Jun
73.90		Andy	Fryman	USA	3.2.85	1		Knoxville	3 May
		(50)							
73.90		Chris	Harmse	RSA	31.5.73	2	AfCh	Marrakech	13 Aug
73.85		Roberto	Sawyers	CRC	17.10.86	2	PAm SF	Ciudad de México	16 Aug
73.80		Mohsen	Anani	EGY	25.5.85	1		Radès	9 Apr
73.65			Wang Shizhu	CHN	20.2.89	2	AsiG	Incheon	27 Sep
73.57		Matthias	Tayala	USA	27.4.93	1	NCAA	Eugene	12 Jun
73.52		Alex	Smith	GBR	6.3.88	2	NC	Birmingham	28 Jun
73.43			Wan Yong	CHN	22.7.87	3	AsiG	Incheon	27 Sep
72.94		Dmitriy	Velikopolskiy	RUS	27.11.84	4		Yerino	9 Jul
72.93		Justin	Welch	USA	29.9.91	1		Toledo	9 May
72.89		Õzkan	Baltaci	TUR	13.2.94	1		Mersin	2 Mar
		(60)							
72.76		Remy	Conatser	USA	20.7.90	1		Los Angeles	21 Mar
72.70		Eivind	Henriksen	NOR	14.9.90	1	NC	Jessheim	24 Aug
72.60		Konstadínos	Stathelakos	CYP	30.12.87	2		Nikiti	11 Jul
72.58		Chris	Bennett	GBR	17.12.89	4	NC	Birmingham	28 Jun
72.26		Mergen	Mamedov	TKM	24.12.90	1		Ashkhabad	10 Oct
72.24			Lee Yun-chul	KOR	28.3.82	1		Kimchun	3 May
72.24		Frédérick	Pouzy	FRA	18.2.83	2	NC	Reims	11 Jul
72.21		Arkadiusz	Rogowski	POL	30.3.93	1		Torun	10 Sep
72.16		Yevgeniy	Korotovskiy	RUS	21.6.92	1		Vladimir	5 May
72.11		Arno	Laitinen	FIN	9.3.88	1		Turku	13 Aug
		(70)							
72.01		Libor	Charfreitag	SVK	11.9.77	1		Banská Bystrica	7 Jun
71.93		Allan	Wolski	BRA	18.1.90	2		São Bernardo do Campo	24 Aug
71.83		Andriy	Martynyuk	UKR	25.9.90	1eB	ECw	Leiria	15 Mar
71.81		Ashraf Amjad	El-Seify	QAT-J	20.2.95	2	NC	Doha	27 Apr
71.81		Jesse	Lehto	FIN	12.2.93	4		Kaustinen	27 Jun
71.80		Juha	Kauppinen	FIN	16.8.86	1		Albuquerque	2 May
71.72		Reza	Moghaddam	IRI	17.11.88	1		Tehran	2 May
71.67		Joachim	Koivu	FIN	5.9.88	1		El Paso	12 Apr
71.61		Nikolay	Bashan	BLR	18.11.92	2		Adler	23 Feb

Mark	Wind	Name		Nat	Born	Pos	Meet	Venue	Date
71.60		Sven	Möhsner	GER	30.1.86	2		Rhede	11 Jul
		(80)							
71.56		Kaveh	Mousavi	IRI	27.5.85	1		Tehran	23 May
71.52		Juho	Saarikoski	FIN	19.5.93	5		Kaustinen	27 Jun
71.50		Bence	Pásztor	HUN-J	5.2.95	4		Veszprém	8 Jun
71.43		Jacob	Freeman	USA	5.11.80	1		Princeton	2 May
71.43		Sukhrob	Khodjayev	UZB	21.5.93	5	AsiG	Incheon	27 Sep
71.42		Dmitriy	Marshin	AZE	24.2.72	19q	EC	Zürich	14 Aug
71.38		Elias	Håkansson	SWE	29.2.92	1		Tuscaloosa	20 Mar
71.34		Valeriy	Pronkin	RUS	15.6.94	2	NC-w23	Krasnodar	23 Feb
71.24		Michael	Lihrman	USA	6.12.91	3	NCAA	Eugene	12 Jun
71.19		Andrew	Frost	GBR	17.4.81	1		Loughborough	1 Mar
		(90)							
70.92		Aurélien	Boisrond	FRA	17.2.85	1		Talence	30 Apr
70.77		Isaac	Vicente	ESP	30.4.87	1		Vila Nova de Cerveira	23 Jul
70.73		Peyman	Ghalenouei	IRI	29.1.92	1		Tehran	21 Aug
70.65		Nicolas	Figère	FRA	19.5.79	1		Gagny	4 May
70.63		Mihaíl	Anastasákis	GRE	3.12.94	2		Trípoli	26 May
70.57		Greg	Skipper	USA	26.3.93	1		Eugene	5 Apr
70.55		Andreas	Sahner	GER	27.1.85	1		Sarreguemines	29 May
70.50		Dmytro	Mykolaychuk ¶	UKR	30.1.87	2	NC-w	Yalta	21 Feb
70.48		Pedro José	Martín	ESP	12.8.92	1		Barcelona	26 Jan
70.45		Hiroshi	Noguchi	JPN	3.5.83	1		Sagamihara	30 Aug
		(100)							

Mark	Name		Nat	Born	Date
70.39	Johannes	Bichler	GER	3.7.90	12 Jul
70.37	Kamalpreet	Singh	IND	3.11.87	24 May
70.35	Dário	Manso	POR	1.7.82	25 Jun
70.32	Garland	Porter	USA	10.2.82	27 Jul
70.30	Mirko	Micuda	CRO	22.12.89	13 Jul
70.23	Simone	Falloni	ITA	26.9.91	15 Mar
70.17	Noleisis	Bicet	CUB	6.2.81	27 Jun
70.15	Marco	Bortolato	ITA	11.2.94	22 Feb
70.13	Paul	Hützen	GER	7.3.91	17 May
70.07	Amir	Williamson	GBR	10.4.87	24 May
69.97	Sebastian	Nowicki	POL	26.8.94	12 Jul
69.94	Tim	Driesen	AUS	27.3.84	29 Jul
69.84	Alan Diego	del Real	MEX	6.3.94	26 Nov
69.82	Bruno	Boccalatte	FRA	10.11.88	22 Feb
69.72	James	Bedford	GBR	29.12.88	24 May
69.70	Yevgeniy	Chetverikov	RUS	17.1.93	29 May
69.67	Nejc	Plesko	SLO	9.10.92	22 Jun
69.55	Igor	Buryi	RUS	8.4.93	15 Jul
69.51	Yuriy	Vasilchenko	BLR	4.1.94	8 Jun
69.47	Tomás	Kruzliak	SVK	9.2.92	12 Jun
69.38	Chandrodaya	Narayan Singh	IND	14.7.91	8 Jun
69.28		Park Young-Sik	KOR	1.8.89	23 Apr
69.28	Alexandros	Poursanides	CYP	23.1.93	30 May
69.26	Islam Saad	Abou Seri	EGY	20.2.91	30 Sep
69.18	Ryan	Loughney	USA	21.8.89	26 Jun
69.10	Michael	Bomba	GBR	10.10.86	26 Aug
69.08	Nils	Lindner	GER	25.5.93	30 Jul
68.96	Hiroki	Ako	JPN	5.1.90	26 Apr
68.89		Qi Dakai	CHN	23.5.87	10 Apr
68.86	Neeraj	Kumar	IND	17.9.90	5 Nov
68.75	Adonson	Shallow	VIN	17.8.86	18 Apr
68.67	Tristan	Schwandke	GER	23.5.92	8 Jun
68.65	Fabián	Di Paolo	ARG	25.11.83	15 Jan
68.65	Hilmar Örn	Jonsson	ISL-J	6.5.96	27 Jun
68.59	Toru	Tanaka	JPN	17.5.86	26 Apr
68.55	Bence	Halász	HUN-Y	4.8.97	10 May
68.54	Pedro Luis	Muñoz	VEN	24.4.82	21 Feb
68.53	Chukwuebuka	Enekwechi	USA	28.1.93	27 Apr
68.52	Konstadínos	Kostoglídis	GRE	10.8.90	26 Jul
68.49	Adam	Keenan	CAN	26.3.93	29 Jun
68.38	Juan Ignacio	Cerra	ARG	16.10.76	19 Jul
68.31	Anders	Eriksson	SWE	22.3.94	20 Aug
68.30	Dan	Raithel	USA	3.6.84	18 Apr
68.28	Jordan	Young	CAN	21.6.93	19 Apr
68.18	Kyle	Strawn	USA	28.4.93	19 Apr
68.18	Aykhan	Apti	BUL	25.4.93	26 Jul
68.18	Yevgeniy	Ivanov	BLR	.92	28 Nov
	(147)				

Downhill

Mark	Name		Nat	Born	Date
70.71	Ryan	Loughney	USA	21.8.89	12 Apr

JUNIORS

Mark	Name		Nat	Born	Pos	Meet	Venue	Date
71.81	Ashraf Amjad	El-Seify	QAT	20.2.95	2	NC	Doha	28 Apr
	69.40 1	Doha		9 Apr	7 performances by 2 men over 69.20			
71.50	Bence	Pásztor	HUN	5.2.95	4		Veszprém	8 Jun
	70.93 4 NC	Székesfehérvár		2 Aug	69.58	3	Tapolca	9 Aug
	70.88 3	Budapest		15 Jun	69.20	3	Zalaegerszeg	10 May
68.65	Hilmar Örn	Jonsson	ISL	6.5.96	1		Hafnafjördur	27 Jun
68.55	Bence	Halász	HUN-Y	4.8.97	4		Zalaegerszeg	10 May
67.98	Joaquín	Gómez	ARG	14.10.96	1	SAm-23	Montevideo	3 Oct
67.60	Matija	Greguric	CRO	17.9.96	4	ECp-23	Leiria	15 Mar
67.23	Matthew	Denny	AUS	2.6.96	2		Hobart	1 Feb
66.91	Humberto	Mansilla	CHI	22.5.96	1		Temuco	1 Mar
66.37	Matt	Bloxham	NZL	16.11.96	1		Auckland	1 Nov
66.17	Miguel Alberto	Blanco (10)	ESP	22.2.96	1		Palafrugell	31 May
65.60	Yshepang	Makhethe	RSA	9.2.96	2	NC	Pretoria	12 Apr
65.20	Ivan	Aksyonov	RUS	16.8.95	2		Penza	29 Jun
65.00	Taylor	Campbell	GBR	30.6.96	7	NC	Birmingham	28 Jun

6kg Hammer

Mark	Name		Nat	Born	Pos	Meet	Venue	Date
84.71	Ashraf Amjad	El-Seify	QAT	20.2.95	1	WJ	Eugene	25 Jul
	84.66 1	Rhede		11 Jul	79.71	1 Asi-J	Taipeh	12 Jun
80.29	Bence	Pásztor	HUN	5.2.95	1		Budapest	15 Jun
	80.25 1 Werfer	Halle		17 May	79.26	Q WJ	Eugene	24 Jul
	80.23 1 v4N	Slovenj Gradec		5 Jul	78.72	1 NC-j	Debrecen	29 Jun
	79.99 2 WJ	Eugene		25 Jul	78.51	1	Veszprém	26 Apr

Mark	Wind	Name		Nat	Born	Pos	Meet	Venue		Date
78.23		Ilya	Terentyev	RUS	23.1.95	1	NC-j	Cheboksary		17 Jun
		11 performances by 3 men over 78.00								
77.85		Igor	Yevseyev	RUS	27.3.96	1		Krasnodar		19 May
77.54		Hilmar Örn	Jónsson	ISL	6.5.96	1		Selfoss		12 Aug
76.59		Joaquín	Gómez	ARG	14.10.96	1		Buenos Aires		11 Oct
76.50		Matija	Greguric	CRO	17.9.96	1		Bar		1 May
75.88		Alexej	Mikhailov	GER	12.4.96	4	WJ	Eugene		25 Jul
75.87		Matthew	Denny	AUS	2.6.96	1		Gold Coast		28 Jun
75.67		Bence	Halász (10)	HUN-Y	4.8.97	1		Veszprém		8 Jun
75.00		Tareq Ismael	Ahmed	EGY	18.10.97	1		Cairo		18 Sep
74.94		Miguel Alberto	Blanco	ESP	22.2.96	1		Manresa		17 Jul
74.82		Maksim	Mitskov	BLR	1.12.95	1j	Klim	Minsk		18 Jun
74.81		Artem	Poleshko	UKR	13.2.95	1	NC-j	Kyiv		13 Jun
74.81		Waltteri	Lahtinen	FIN	3.3.95	1		Pori		21 Aug
74.76		Ivan	Aksyonov	RUS	16.8.95	1	NC-wj	Krasnodar		22 Feb
74.70		Humberto	Mansilla	CHI	22.5.96	1		Temuco		29 Mar
74.45		Yasmani	Fernández	CUB	7.4.96	1		La Habana		7 Feb
74.42		Taylor	Campbell	GBR	30.6.96	1	N.Sch	Birmingham		28 Jun
74.13		Yshepang	Makhethe (20)	RSA	9.2.96	1	NC-j	Stellenbosch		3 Apr

JAVELIN

Mark	Wind	Name		Nat	Born	Pos	Meet	Venue		Date
89.21		Ihab	Abdelrahman	EGY	1.5.89	1	DL	Shanghai		18 May
					89.21	86.01	x	p	p	p
	87.10	1 DL	Saint-Denis	5 Jul	81.48	x	79.84	79.31	87.10	x
	85.44	1 C.Cup	Marrakech	14 Sep	81.77	85.44	79.28	83.33		
	84.79	1	Kuortane	13 Jul	83.11	84.79	x	x	x	x
89.15			Zhao Qinggang	CHN	24.7.85	1	AsiG	Incheon		2 Oct
					75.14	81.96	85.29	x	86.50	89.15
88.01		Antti	Ruuskanen	FIN	21.2.84	1	EC	Zürich		17 Aug
					83.81	86.85	88.01	83.69	84.62	83.67
	87.24	1 DNG	Stockholm	21 Aug	83.76	87.24	84.56	p	p	p
	85.28	2 PNG	Turku	25 Jun	83.54	x	85.28	x	80.66	80.67
87.63		Thomas	Röhler	GER	30.9.91	1	WK	Zürich		28 Aug
					87.63	81.57	83.03	81.25	84.38	84.73
	86.99	1 DL	Glasgow	12 Jul	80.87	x	83.51	82.59	x	86.99
	86.74	1	Bad Köstritz	24 Aug	86.74	x	79.76	79.06	84.74	x
	85.12	2 DNG	Stockholm	21 Aug	85.12	x	83.03	81.53	78.28	81.78
87.38		Vitezslav	Vesely	CZE	27.2.83	1	GS	Ostrava		17 Jun
					87.38	84.21	87.04	x	87.01	86.57
	85.23	2 DL	Glasgow	12 Jul	85.23	82.10	x	x	78.04	80.45
	84.79	2 EC	Zürich	17 Aug	76.04	81.98	81.68	82.68	84.79	79.16
86.83		Ryohei	Arai	JPN	23.6.91	1		Isahaya		21 Oct
					78.33	77.32	78.71	81.30	81.46	86.83
	85.48	1 Oda	Hiroshima	29 Apr	79.27	84.08	85.48	82.30	82.24	84.35
86.63		Tero	Pitkämaki	FIN	19.12.82	2	DL	Saint-Denis		5 Jul
					86.63	83.57	x	79.62	79.69	82.71
	85.89	1 PNG	Turku	25 Jun	x	85.89	80.62	x	x	84.75
	85.48	1	Lahti	15 Jun	x	83.19	83.20	85.48	81.12	p
	85.12	1	Pihtipudas	29 Jun	78.40	78.34	80.60	84.55	82.68	85.12
	85.12	3 WK	Zürich	28 Aug	83.05	79.80	85.12	x	80.52	x
	84.95	3 DL	Glasgow	12 Jul	79.03	79.63	x	79.41	82.69	84.95
86.61		Zigismunds	Sirmais	LAT	6.5.92	2	GS	Ostrava		17 Jun
					79.72	x	86.61	79.34	76.00	80.72
86.13		Andreas	Hoffman	GER	16.12.91	1	ET	Braunschweig		22 Jun
					86.13	x	75.39	77.40		
85.92		Dmitriy	Tarabin (10)	RUS	29.10.91	3	GS	Ostrava		17 Jun
					80.93	85.92	x	x	x	x
85.77		Keshorn	Walcott	TTO	2.4.93	2	WK	Zürich		28 Aug
					85.77	x	81.11	77.38	83.99	x
	85.28	Q CG	Glasgow	1 Aug	85.28					
85.07		Petr	Frydrych	CZE	13.1.88	1	Odlozil	Praha		9 Jun
					80.22	80.23	81.67	85.07	82.10	x
84.98		Lassi	Etelätalo	FIN	30.4.88	1		Joensuu		24 Jul
					79.96	x	84.98	81.49	p	80.65
84.83		Patrik	Zenúch	SVK	30.12.90	1		Košice		3 May
		(31/14)			73.80	84.83	p	p	p	p
84.77		Lukasz	Grzeszczuk	POL	3.3.90	1		Riga		29 May
84.72		Julius	Yego	KEN	4.1.89	1	AfCh	Marrakech		14 Aug
84.14		Kim	Amb	SWE	31.7.90	2	DL	Shanghai		18 May
84.01		Tim	Glover	USA	1.11.90	1		Knoxville		12 Apr
83.70		Ari	Mannio	FIN	23.7.87	2		Lapinlahti		20 Jul

Mark	Wind	Name		Nat	Born	Pos	Meet	Venue	Date
83.68		Ivan	Zaytsev	UZB	7.11.88	3	AsiG	Incheon	2 Oct
		(20)							
83.41		Maksym	Bohdan	UKR	27.2.94	1	ECp-w23	Leiria	16 Mar
83.10		Rolands	Strobinders	LAT	14.4.92	1		Valmiera	18 Jul
83.05		Fatih	Avan	TUR	1.1.89	1		Yerino	8 Jun
82.97		Jakub	Vadlejch	CZE	10.10.90	2		Kuortane	13 Jul
82.58		Hubert	Chmielak	POL	19.6.89	1		Kolobrzeg	19 Sep
82.48		Joshua	Robinson	AUS	4.10.85	1	NC	Melbourne	6 Apr
82.30		Sean	Furey	USA	31.8.82	1		Chula Vista	4 Oct
82.28		Dmytro	Kosynskyy	UKR	31.3.89	1	NC-w	Yalta	21 Feb
82.24		Hamish	Peacock	AUS	15.10.90	1		Sollentuna	26 Jun
82.05		Valeriy	Iordan	RUS	14.2.92	2	WCM	Beijing	21 May
		(30)							
81.75		Ainars	Kovals	LAT	21.11.81	1	NC	Ogre	1 Aug
81.66		Yukifumi	Murakami	JPN	23.12.79	4	AsiG	Incheon	2 Oct
81.61			Cheng Chao-Tsun	TPE	17.10.93	5	AsiG	Incheon	2 Oct
81.53			Huang Shih-Feng	TPE	2.3.92	1		Tokyo	11 May
81.51		Sam	Humphreys	USA	12.9.90	1		Tucson	24 May
81.35		Craig	Kinsley	USA	19.1.89	1		Victoria, BC	8 Jul
81.28		Ansis	Bruns	LAT	30.3.89	2	NC	Ogre	1 Aug
81.22		Oleksandr	Nychyporchuk	UKR	14.4.92	3	Sule	Tartu	15 Jun
81.16		Tanel	Laanmäe	EST	29.9.89	1		Bellinzona	3 Jun
81.10		Oleksandr	Pyatnytsya	UKR	14.7.85	2		Kyiv	4 Jun
		(40)							
80.79		Andreas	Thorkildsen	NOR	1.4.82	7	DL	Saint-Denis	5 Jul
80.73		Risto	Mätas	EST	30.4.84	6	EC	Zürich	17 Aug
80.72		Julian	Weber	GER	29.8.94	2	NC	Ulm	26 Jul
80.68		Pavel	Meleshko	BLR	24.11.92	2		Brest	25 Apr
80.66		Marcin	Krukowski	POL	14.6.92	1		Katowice	2 Jul
80.64		Spiridon	Lebésis	GRE	30.5.87	2		Bellinzona	3 Jun
80.46		Matija	Kranjc	SLO	12.6.84	Q	EC	Zürich	14 Aug
80.40		Dejan	Mileusnic	BIH	16.11.91	4	ECp-w	Leiria	16 Mar
80.37		Norbert	Bonvecchio	ITA	14.8.85	4	ET	Braunschweig	22 Jun
80.36		Sami	Peltomäki	FIN	11.1.91	2		Pihtipudas	29 Jun
		(50)							
80.32		David	Golling	GER	13.3.90	1		Neukieritzsch	1 Aug
80.28		Aleksandr	Ashomko	BLR	18.2.84	5	ECp-w	Leiria	16 Mar
80.28		Cyrus	Hostetler	USA	8.8.86	1		Eugene	9 May
80.10		Rocco	van Rooyen	RSA	23.12.92	1		Bellville	29 Mar
79.90		Toni	Sirviö	FIN	8.1.92	1		Joensuu	18 Sep
79.83		Bobur	Shokirjanov	UZB	5.12.90	5		Riga	29 May
79.75		Johannes	Vetter	GER	26.3.93	1		Haldensleben	21 Jun
79.70		Magnus	Kirt	EST	10.4.90	1		Tallinn	16 May
79.69		Stuart	Farquhar	NZL	15.3.82	4		Lahti	15 Jun
79.65		Lars	Hamann	GER	4.4.89	6	ECp-w	Leiria	16 Mar
		(60)							
79.57A		Robert	Oosthuizen	RSA	23.1.87	1	Univ Ch	Pretoria	26 Apr
79.36		Luke	Cann	AUS	17.7.94	Q	CG	Glasgow	1 Aug
79.34		Ilya	Korotkov	RUS	6.12.83	2		Yerino	8 Jun
79.32		Rajender	Singh Dalvir	IND	5.4.89	1		Patiala	17 Aug
79.27		Riley	Dolezal	USA	16.11.85	2	NC	Sacramento	29 Jun
79.27A		Guillermo	Martínez	CUB	28.6.81	1	CAG	Xalapa	28 Nov
79.22		Vedran	Samac	SRB	22.1.90	1		Sremska Mitrovica	16 Jul
79.17		Martin	Benák	SVK	27.5.88	1		Banská Bystrica	7 Jun
79.10A		Júlio César	de Oliveira	BRA	4.2.86	1	PAm SF	Ciudad de México	16 Aug
79.00		Pawel	Rozinski	POL	11.7.87	1		Postomino	24 May
		(70)							
78.82A		Dayron	Márquez	COL	19.11.83	1	NC	Medellín	27 Jun
78.69			Park Jae-myong	KOR	15.12.81	1		Kimchun	4 May
78.58		Raymond	Dykstra	CAN	18.6.92	1	NC	Moncton	28 Jun
78.57		Devender	Singh	IND	18.12.88	2		Patiala	17 Aug
78.39			Song Bin	CHN	30.9.90	1		Kunshan	31 May
78.29		Gudmundur	Sverrisson	ISL	24.5.90	1		Selfoss	17 May
78.28		Kyle	Quinn	USA	28.4.93	2		Knoxville	12 Apr
78.17			Kim Ye-ram	KOR	2.3.94	1	NC	Kimchun	26 Jun
78.05		Matthew	Outzen	AUS	12.10.87	2		Newcastle	18 Jan
78.03		Ben	Woodruff	USA	9.5.89	6		Tucson	24 May
		(80)							
78.02		Aleksandr	Kharitonov	RUS	19.7.90	2		Liepaja	10 May
78.02		Ravinder	Singh Kharia	IND	19.3.86	1		Lucknow	6 Jun
78.02		Bernhard	Seifert	GER	15.2.93	2		Jena	13 Jul

Mark	Wind	Name		Nat	Born	Pos	Meet	Venue	Date
77.88		Gabriel	Wallin	SWE	14.10.81	4		Saarijärvi	21 Jun
77.83		Jani	Kiiskilä	FIN	28.12.89	1		Rovaniemi	13 Sep
77.75		Braian	Toledo	ARG	8.9.93	1	SAm23	Montevideo	5 Oct
77.72			Dai Li	CHN	20.5.91	2		Zhaoqing	20 Apr
77.69		Timothy	Herman	BEL	19.10.90	2		Domazlice	19 Sep
77.61		Harri	Haatainen	FIN	5.1.78	1		Sastamalä	21 Jul
77.58		Yeóryios	Íltsios	GRE	28.11.81	1		Haniá	1 Jun
		(90)							
77.54		Viktor	Goncharov	RUS	9.5.91	3		Yerino	8 Jun
77.46		Kacper	Oleszczuk	POL	15.5.94	2		Postomino	24 May
77.45		Teemu	Wirkkala	FIN	14.1.84	Q	NC	Kuopio	2 Aug
77.32		Roderick Genki	Dean	JPN	30.12.91	6		Tokyo	11 May
77.28		Sindri Hrafn	Gudmundsson	ISL-J	21.11.95	1	NC	Hafnarfjördur	12 Jul
77.26		Oleksandr	Chehlatyy	UKR	27.9.89	3	NC	Kirovohrad	26 Jul
77.26		Gatis	Cakss	LAT-J	13.6.95	1		Ventspils	27 Sep
77.24A		David	Ocampo	MEX	14.2.92	1		Xalapa	17 May
77.23		Roberto	Bertolini	ITA	9.10.85	1		Milano	27 Sep
77.16		Jurriaan	Wouters	NED	18.4.93	1	NC	Amsterdam	26 Jul
		(100)							

Mark	Name		Nat	Born	Date
77.08	Waruna Lakshan	Dayarathne	SRI	14.5.88	5 Nov
76.98	Sam	Crouser	USA	31.12.91	14 Jun
76.96	Ranno	Koorep	EST	24.1.90	18 Sep
76.92		Park Won-kil	KOR	24.2.90	5 Aug
76.80A	Juan José	Méndez	MEX	27.4.88	28 Nov
76.75	Kohei	Hasegawa	JPN	1.1.90	29 Apr
76.71A	Tobie	Holthausen	RSA	25.5.87	22 Feb
76.66	Caleb	Jones	CAN	17.5.91	20 Jul
76.63	Erki	Leppik	EST	18.3.88	21 Jul
76.61	Lee	Doran	GBR	5.3.85	1 Jun
76.61	Rohit	Kumar	IND	15.7.94	17 Aug
76.59	Bartosz	Osewski	POL	20.3.91	24 May
76.57	Arley	Ibargüen	COL	4.12.82	11 Oct
76.52	Adriaan	Beukes	BOT	14.7.94	14 Aug
76.42	Vadims	Vasilevskis	LAT	5.1.82	1 Aug
76.41		Ma Qun	CHN	8.2.94	13 Jul
76.28A	Osmani	Laffita	CUB	14.8.94	28 Nov
76.18	Yuya	Koriki	JPN	19.10.89	8 Jun
76.15	Jan	Kubes	CZE	19.6.94	16 Mar
76.15A	Phil-Mar	van Rensburg	RSA	23.6.89	11 Apr
76.13	Joe	Dunderdale	GBR	4.9.92	18 May
76.11		Li Yingchang	CHN	22.6.91	29 Mar
76.10	Leslie	Copeland	FIJ	23.4.88	31 May
76.09	Víctor	Fatecha	PAR	10.3.88	13 Mar
76.08	Marcin	Plener	POL	22.8.90	17 May
76.04	Igor	Sukhomlinov	RUS	13.2.77	16 Mar
76.02	Michael	Shuey	USA	2.2.94	9 Aug
75.99	Antonio	Fent	ITA	31.3.88	13 Apr
75.99	John	Ampomah	GHA	11.7.90	14 Aug
75.92	Tuomas	Laaksonen	FIN	9.3.90	8 Jun
75.89	Amit	Kumar	IND	18.9.92	3 Nov
75.88	Robert	Robbins	USA	16.11.92	13 Apr
75.80	Konstadínos	Vertoúdos	GRE	5.1.86	26 May
75.80	Jiannis	Smaliós	SWE	17.2.87	16 Jul
75.74	Takashi	Minami	JPN	7.8.92	21 Oct
75.73	Hubert	Treciakowski	POL	29.10.88	20 Jul
75.70	Barry	Krammes	USA	1.9.81	10 May
75.59	Homare	Mori	JPN	8.8.94	5 Sep
75.57	Vipin	Kasana	IND	4.8.89	6 Jun
75.57	Leonardo	Gottardo	ITA	21.3.88	20 Jun
75.50	Samarjeet	Singh	IND	7.11.88	17 Aug
75.48	Tiago	Aperta	POR	15.1.92	18 Jun
75.38	Matija	Muhar	SLO-J	23.7.96	10 May
75.38	Borja	Barbeito	ESP	27.3.91	17 May
75.24	Jonni	Karvinen	FIN	7.2.94	27 Aug
75.12	Nick	Howe	USA	17.11.89	26 Apr
75.09		Jiang Xingyu	CHN	16.3.87	10 Oct
75.04	Tomoya	Era	JPN	19.6.93	19 Apr
74.97	Killian	Duréchou	FRA	15.8.92	19 Apr
74.92	Hikaru	Takahashi	JPN	28.8.93	10 May
74.88	Yasuo	Ikeda	JPN	28.7.77	21 Oct
74.86	Paraskevás	Batzávalis	GRE	25.11.94	23 May
74.84		Jung Sang-jin	KOR	16.4.84	4 May
74.84	Kyle	Nielsen	CAN	22.4.89	16 May
74.75	Aleksandr	Ivanov	RUS	25.5.82	8 Jun
74.73	Ryan	Young	USA	3.1.87	29 Jun
74.71	Yegor	Yermoshin	RUS	6.7.93	16 Mar
74.71	Benjamin	Pearson	GBR	23.5.94	26 Apr
74.69	Ben	Langton-Burnell	NZL	10.7.92	29 Mar
74.67A	Chad	Herman	RSA	25.5.92	26 Apr
74.64	Bonne	Buwembo	GBR	24.12.89	24 Aug
74.59	Håkon	Løvenskiold Kveseth	NOR	19.4.93	10 Jul
74.56	Takuma	Nakanishi	JPN	8.4.94	21 Oct
74.47	Fumitaka	Saito	JPN	10.2.93	27 Jul
74.46	Adrian	Mardare	MDA-J	20.6.95	25 Jul
74.45	Amit	Majumder	IND	4.5.87	17 Aug
74.42		Deng Shen	CHN	14.11.92	20 Apr
74.42	Toma	Pop	ROU	11.3.92	6 Jun
74.41	Aleksey	Tovarnov	RUS	21.1.85	18 Jan
74.41	Jérémy	Nicollin	FRA	8.4.91	12 Jul
74.38	Billy	Stanley	USA	6.2.94	28 Mar
74.38	Naoya	Imada	JPN	21.5.90	21 Oct
74.32	Toni	Kuusela	FIN	21.1.94	12 Jun
74.29	Pawel	Rakoczy	POL	15.5.87	16 Mar
74.26	Pieter	Kriel	RSA-J	23.1.95	3 Apr
74.25	Fabián	Dohmann (Jara)	PAR	8.1.93	16 May
74.25	Yervásios	Filippídis	GRE	24.7.87	9 Jul
74.23	Kenta	Sonoda	JPN	.93	17 May
74.21	Jarne	Duchateau	BEL-J	12.11.96	12 Oct
74.20	Daan	Meijer	NED	17.2.83	14 Jun
74.20	Shu	Mori	JPN-J	1.11.96	4 May
74.18	German	Komarov	RUS	14.12.94	2 Aug
74.14	Timo	Moorast	EST	26.3.86	9 May
74.11	Tim	Van Liew	USA	25.5.90	24 May
74.10	Ben	Baker	AUS	19.1.83	29 Mar
74.07	Rustem	Dremdzhy	UKR	3.6.91	30 May
74.01	Simon	Litzell	SWE-Y	11.2.97	3 Aug
	(187)				

JUNIORS

See main list for top 2 juniors. 10 performances by 6 men over 76.50. Additional marks and further juniors:

Gudmundsson 78.17 1 Reykjavik 8 Aug

Cakss 74.04 1 WJ Eugene 27 Jul

Mark	Name		Nat	Born	Pos	Meet	Venue	Date
75.38	Matija	Muhar	SLO	23.7.96	2		Split	10 May
	75.16				2	NCp	Nova Gorica	14 Jun
74.46	Adrian	Mardare	MDA	20.6.95	Q	WJ	Eugene	25 Jul
74.26	Pieter	Kriel	RSA	23.1.95	1	NC-j	Stellenbosch	3 Apr
74.21	Jarne	Duchateau	BEL	12.11.96	1		Vineuil	12 Oct
74.20	Shu	Mori	JPN	1.11.96	1		Saijo	4 May
74.01	Simon	Litzell	SWE-Y	11.2.97	4	NC	Umeå	3 Aug
73.73	Norbert	Rivasz-Tóth	HUN	6.5.96	1		Debrecen	30 Aug

Mark	Name		Nat	Born	Pos	Meet	Venue	Date
73.66	Raul	Russu (10)	ROU	20.7.95	1	NC-j	Bucuresti	20 Jun
73.66	Ioannís	Kiriázos	GRE	19.1.96	1	Balk-J	Sérres	6 Jul
72.93	Emin	Önsel	TUR-Y	1.5.97	1		Samsun	7 Aug
72.75	Shakiel	Waithe	TTO	10.6.95	1	NC	Port of Spain	22 Jun
72.74	Mateusz	Kwasniewski	POL	16.7.95	1J	Werfer	Halle	17 May
72.69	Quincy	Andersson	SWE	20.2.95	5		Göteborg	14 Jun
72.59A	Leon	Laubsher	RSA-Y	29.4.97	5	NC	Pretoria	11 Apr
72.45	George	Zaharia	ROU	.95	2	Balk-J	Sérres	6 Jul
72.38		Xu Jiajie	CHN-Y	8.10.97	1		Shanghai	31 Jul
72.37		Kim Woo-jung	KOR-Y	6.1.97	1	NG-HS	Jeju	2 Nov
72.09	Kensei	Hanada (20)	JPN	.96	2		Isahaya	21 Oct

DECATHLON

Mark	Name		Nat	Born	Pos	Meet	Venue			Date
8616	Andrey	Kravchenko	BLR	4.1.86	1	EC	Zürich			13 Aug
	11.31/-1.1	7.63/-0.7	15.19	2.22	50.53	14.20/0.1	47.46	5.10	68.11	4:39.39
8599	Trey	Hardee	USA	7.2.84	1	NC	Sacramento			27 Jun
	10.38W/4.2	7.22w/3.6	15.38	2.05	48.02	13.69/1.5	50.65	5.00	56.91	4:43.63
8521	Kevin	Mayer	FRA	10.2.92	2	EC	Zürich			13 Aug
	11.10/-0.9	7.65/0.2	15.14	2.01	49.23	14.28/0.5	44.53	5.20	64.03	4:24.16
8518		Hardee			1		Götzis			13 Aug
	10.50/-0.2	7.49w/2.2	15.15	1.97	48.63	13.69/0.0	49.09	5.06	58.20	4:44.75
8498	Ilya	Shkurenyov	RUS	11.1.91	3	EC	Zürich			13 Aug
	11.05/-0.9	7.50/-0.7	14.20	2.10	49.00	14.14/0.6	46.04	5.20	63.58	4:35.89
8478	Eelco	Sintnicolaas	NED	7.4.87	4	EC	Zürich			13 Aug
	10.90/-0.9	7.65/0.0	14.28	2.01	48.44	14.12/0.5	42.56	5.40	59.37	4:30.95
8477	Arthur	Abele	GER	30.7.86	5	EC	Zürich			13 Aug
	10.90/-1.9	7.55/-0.2	15.39	1.98	48.59	13.55/0.5	43.25	4.70	62.45	4:20.37
8471	Kai	Kazmirek	GER	28.1.91	2		Götzis			1 Jun
	10.76/0.0	7.45/0.1	14.20	2.15	47.04	14.15/1.7	43.59	4.96	56.31	4:33.78
8458		Kazmirek			6	EC	Zürich			13 Aug
	10.75/-1.9	7.68/0.0	14.01	2.13	47.34	14.05/0.5	43.37	4.60	63.17	4:38.67
8356	Rico	Freimuth	GER	14.3.88	1		Ratingen			29 Jun
	10.40/1.1	7.34/1.4	14.54	1.92	48.23	13.78/0.0	49.61	4.70	60.08	4:45.12
8337	Yordani	García	CUB	21.11.88	1		La Habana			22 Feb
	10.80/0.0	7.22w/2.6	15.75	2.07	49.07	14.07/0.0	42.54	4.60	64.69	4:33.36
8323		Mayer			2		Ratingen			29 Jun
	11.08/1.1	7.33/0.0	14.67	2.07	49.63	14.28/0.0	38.41	5.20	64.01	4:25.18
8317		Freimuth			3		Götzis			1 Jun
	10.52/-0.2	7.19/0.6	14.54	1.94	48.42	13.95/0.0	49.41	4.86	59.87	4:45.56
8311	Larbi	Bouraada (10)	ALG	10.5.88	1	AfCh	Marrakech			11 Aug
	10.90/1.0	7.45/1.1	13.20	2.04	48.33	14.33/0.2	39.99	4.90	64.60	4:20.05
8308	Keisuke	Ushiro	JPN	24.7.86	1	NC	Nagano			1 Jun
	11.24/-0.6	7.15/-0.5	15.19	2.03	49.66	14.90/0.1	50.17	4.80	69.11	4:32.62
8308		Freimuth			7	EC	Zürich			13 Aug
	10.71/-1.9	7.36/0.5	14.39	1.98	48.53	13.63/0.5	48.81	4.80	62.74	4:59.27
8299		García			4		Götzis			1 Jun
	10.69/-0.2	6.91w/2.2	15.27	2.03	48.18	13.92/0.0	39.54	4.76	66.48	4:32.86
8282	Damian	Warner	CAN	4.11.89	1	CG	Glasgow			29 Jul
	10.29/1.1	7.50/-0.6	14.04	1.96	47.78	13.50/0.5	41.31	4.50	61.96	4:45.43
8231	Oleksiy	Kasyanov	UKR	26.8.85	8	EC	Zürich			13 Aug
	10.92/-1.9	7.64/0.3	14.66	1.98	48.88	13.95/0.5	47.96	4.60	52.33	4:30.76
8204	Pelle	Rietveld	NED	4.2.85	5		Götzis			1 Jun
	10.93/-0.2	7.15/-0.4	13.92	1.91	48.47	14.14/0.0	39.89	5.06	68.38	4:31.83
8199A	Willem	Coertzen	RSA	30.12.82	1	NC	Pretoria			12 Apr
	10.99/1.0	7.47	14.11	2.00	49.65	14.38/-0.2	44.50	4.50	69.40	4:34.21
8194	Gaël	Quérin	FRA	26.6.87	9	EC	Zürich			13 Aug
	11.11/-1.1	7.59/-0.8	14.02	1.98	48.76	14.23/0.5	43.08	4.90	51.67	4:14.73
8193	Sergey	Sviridov	RUS	20.10.90	1	NC	Cheboksary			10 Jun
	10.85/0.2	7.60/0.8	14.50	1.94	49.12	14.75/0.6	48.22	4.60	62.45	4:37.42
8184	Thomas	Van Der Plaetsen	BEL	24.12.90	6		Götzis			1 Jun
	11.04/0.6	7.68/0.7	13.65	2.03	49.16	14.76/0.7	39.63	5.16	60.92	4:35.09
8182	Maicel	Uibo	EST	27.12.92	1	NCAA	Eugene			12 Jun
	11.05w/2.2	7.33/1.0	13.56	2.14	50.64	15.04/0.3	46.05	5.00	59.15	4:29.00
8179		García			1		Ottawa			18 Jul
	10.71/1.1	6.92/1.6	15.19	2.05	48.20	14.32/1.5	38.18	4.60	67.90	4:36.98
8169	Garrett	Scantling (20)	USA	19.5.93	1		Athens, GA			11 Apr
	11.02w/2.9	7.02/0.0	14.05	2.07	49.84	14.43w/2.2	46.09	4.95	66.69	4:48.02
8168	Dominik	Distelberger	AUT	16.3.90	7		Götzis			1 Jun
	10.73/-0.2	7.57/0.0	13.02	2.00	48.53	14.34/0.9	40.55	4.86	59.80	4:32.44

Mark	Wind	Name		Nat	Born	Pos	Meet	Venue		Date
8164		Florian	Geffrouais	FRA	5.12.88	1	NC	Reims		12 Jul
	11.07/1.2	7.23/1.9	15.11	1.93	48.91	14.86/1.1	44.55	4.60	63.75	4:16.02
8161			Sintnicolaas			1		Firenze		3 May
	10.94/-0.1	7.27/-0.3	13.98	1.86	48.81	14.31/0.1	43.38	5.25	61.82	4:35.23
	(30/22)									
8141		Ashley	Bryant	GBR	17.5.91	8		Götzis		1 Jun
	11.09/-0.2	7.52/0.7	13.77	1.94	49.10	14.38/0.9	43.31	4.56	69.65	4:33.83
8123		Yevgeniy	Sarantsev	RUS	5.8.88	1		Adler		16 May
	11.20/0.8	7.19/0.0	15.34	2.03	50.57	15.07/0.1	42.60	5.00	66.44	4:35.09
8112		Ivan	Grigoryev	RUS	27.10.89	2		Adler		16 May
	10.84/0.8	7.28/0.0	13.67	2.00	49.70	14.72/0.1	43.02	5.00	61.81	4:35.28
8104		Romain	Martin	FRA	12.7.88	1		Oyonnax		15 Jun
	10.84/1.3	7.33w/2.6	14.15	2.03	48.99	14.26/0.9	36.25	4.77	65.72	4:38.57
8092		Johannes	Hock	GER	24.3.92	2	NCAA	Eugene		12 Jun
	10.69w/2.4	7.41/1.3	15.06	1.96	49.48	14.77/0.2	48.94	4.40	61.08	4:46.83
8077		Mikk	Pahapill	EST	18.7.83	1		Talence		21 Sep
	11.34/-1.6	6.96/0.0	14.80	2.11	51.56	14.68/1.5	48.44	4.90	60.64	4:35.91
8070		Kurt	Felix	GRN	4.7.88	3	CG	Glasgow		29 Jul
	11.02/0.8	7.43/0.2	13.26	2.11	48.93	15.06/0.4	45.30	4.50	66.33	4:47.66
8068		Dakotah	Keys	USA	27.9.91	3	NCAA	Eugene		12 Jun
	11.12w/2.3	7.31/2.0	13.74	2.02	50.00	14.78/0.2	37.93	4.90	68.18	4:28.29
	(30)									
8055		Pascal	Behrenbruch	GER	19.1.85	4		Ratingen		29 Jun
	11.00/1.1	6.94/-0.1	15.07	1.98	49.22	14.32/0.0	43.16	4.90	64.83	4:51.30
8035		Akihiko	Nakamura	JPN	23.10.90	2	NC	Nagano		1 Jun
	10.80/-1.3	7.35/2.0	12.44	2.03	47.48	14.21/0.1	35.01	4.90	50.40	4:15.03
8004		Eduard	Mikhan	BLR	7.6.89	2	ECp	Torun		6 Jul
	11.11/-0.7	7.32w/2.1	13.95	1.95	48.81	14.82/0.6	46.38	4.90	52.33	4:28.44
8001		Adam	Helcelet	CZE	27.10.91	9		Götzis		1 Jun
	11.06/-0.2	7.22/0.0	14.82	2.00	49.67	14.36/1.7	40.92	4.76	60.68	4:40.19
8000		Niels	Pittomvils	BEL	18.7.92	1	ECp-1	Ribeira Brava		6 Jul
	11.36/-0.9	7.35/0.5	13.38	1.98	48.94	14.59/-1.3	44.67	5.00	57.75	4:35.72
7981		Zach	Ziemek	USA	23.2.93	5	NCAA	Eugene		12 Jun
	10.81w/2.3	7.73/1.7	12.63	2.08	50.21	15.00/0.3	43.95	5.10	53.90	4:57.29
7980		Mathias	Prey	GER	9.8.88	10		Götzis		1 Jun
	11.19/-0.2	7.37/0.6	15.44	1.88	50.32	14.55/1.7	47.56	4.26	63.58	4:31.14
7959		Ingmar	Vos	NED	28.5.86	3	ECp	Torun		6 Jul
	11.23/-4.8	7.44w/3.6	14.34	2.07	50.64	14.36/0.5	42.52	4.40	62.73	4:41.27
7955		Norman	Müller	GER	7.8.85	5		Ratingen		29 Jun
	10.85/1.1	7.15/0.0	14.88	1.92	49.12	15.00/0.0	42.15	4.80	58.97	4:34.91
7952		Felipe	dos Santos	BRA	30.7.94	1	NC	São Paulo		11 Oct
	10.48/0.3	7.55/0.8	13.27	1.91	47.73	14.03w/2.4	41.50	4.30	54.98	4:42.50
	(40)									
7927		Jiri	Sykora	CZE-J	20.1.95	2	ECp-1	Ribeira Brava		6 Jul
	10.85w/3.8	7.34/0.1	13.87	2.01	48.80	15.08/-1.3	44.84	4.60	59.91	4:52.61
7922		John	Lane	GBR	29.1.89	4	CG	Glasgow		29 Jul
	10.71/1.1	7.50/0.8	14.12	1.99	48.13	14.64/0.5	38.96	4.90	52.25	4:54.95
7918		Lars Vikan	Rise	NOR	23.11.88	4		Kladno		15 Jun
	11.32/0.8	7.03/-1.4	16.05	2.06	51.15	15.69/0.3	44.30	4.55	68.03	4:40.52
7892		Pieter	Braun	NED	21.1.93	11		Götzis		1 Jun
	11.20/0.6	7.22/-0.5	13.79	2.03	48.76	14.48/0.7	37.23	4.76	57.29	4:31.53
7882		Artem	Lukyanenko	RUS	30.1.90	4	NC	Cheboksary		10 Jun
	11.29/0.2	7.01/0.8	14.03	1.94	50.16	14.31/0.5	42.10	5.00	58.78	4:35.21
7879		Leonid	Andreyev	UZB	6.10.83	2	AsiG	Incheon		1 Oct
	10.96w/2.1	7.28/0.1	15.75	1.99	49.59	14.95/0.2	43.85	5.00	60.05	5:26.72
7862		Wesley	Bray	USA	11.4.88	1	vGER	Marburg		27 Jul
	11.05/-0.6	7.37/0.1	12.37	1.93	49.55	14.62/1.7	40.26	4.81	57.49	4:23.63
7849		Attila	Zsivoczky	HUN	29.4.77	1		Budapest		6 Jul
	11.27/2.0	6.75/2.0	15.03	2.11	50.38	15.26/-1.6	44.10	4.50	61.78	4:35.86
7847		Bastien	Auzeil	FRA	22.10.89	7	ECp	Torun		6 Jul
	11.58/-4.8	7.26w/3.2	14.87	1.95	49.93	14.45/0.5	42.80	4.90	58.12	4:45.15
7844		Fabian	Rosenquist	SWE	1.4.91	3	ECp-1	Ribeira Brava		6 Jul
	11.01/1.7	7.35/0.5	12.29	2.01	49.20	14.94/1.5	40.90	4.80	52.34	4:23.63
	(50)									
7829		Marek	Lukás	CZE	16.7.91	4	ECp-1	Ribeira Brava		6 Jul
	10.98/1.9	6.85/0.8	14.07	1.86	49.74	14.48/-1.5	40.28	4.60	66.76	4:31.63
7829		Matthias	Brugger	GER	6.8.92	2	vUSA	Marburg		27 Jul
	11.17/-1.3	7.06/-1.7	14.23	2.05	49.28	14.65/1.6	43.01	4.81	52.81	4:46.79
7822		Liam	Ramsay	GBR	18.11.92	1		Woerden		25 Aug
	10.92w/3.3	7.11/1.7	13.03	2.00	47.97	14.67/0.8	38.25	4.54	54.33	4:25.07

Mark	Wind	Name		Nat	Born	Pos	Meet	Venue	Date
7819		René	Stauß	GER	17.9.87	3	vUSA	Marburg	27 Jul
11.15/-0.6	7.01/-0.1	14.41	2.14	50.57	15.24/0.8	44.43	4.71	55.72	4:48.53
7815		Janek	Oiglane	EST	25.4.94	1	3-N	Tampere	15 Jun
11.56w/3.0	7.06w/2.4	13.74	2.03	51.13	14.90/0.0	40.26	4.73	71.11	4:40.88
7806		Alex	McCune	USA	7.4.93	6	NCAA	Eugene	12 Jun
11.00w/2.4	7.48/1.6	13.04	1.90	50.63	14.56/1.5	41.28	4.80	60.51	4:43.86
7804			Guo Qi	CHN	28.12.90	1		Zhaoqing	20 Apr
11.32/0.3	7.11/-0.2	13.18	2.07	50.00	14.34/0.5	42.28	5.00	48.65	4:38.25
7801		Petter	Olson	SWE	14.2.91	5	ECp-1	Ribeira Brava	6 Jul
10.70/1.9	7.19/0.4	13.35	1.95	48.50	14.39/-1.5	33.36	5.00	49.84	4:32.40
7794		Sergey	Timshin	RUS	25.11.92	2		Adler	5 Sep
11.11/1.2	6.98/0.6	12.90	2.12	49.16	14.66/0.7	40.15	4.80	51.52	4:36.83
7792		Devin	Dick	USA	12.1.90	1	Big 12	Lubbock	17 May
11.29/0.0	7.21/-0.3	14.67	2.05	49.41	14.75/0.5	35.96	4.79	52.77	4:32.07
		(60)							
7787		Stephen	Cain	AUS	23.7.84	5	CG	Glasgow	29 Jul
11.33/0.8	6.73/0.9	13.87	1.99	51.07	14.85/0.0	44.87	4.90	62.68	4:40.29
7764		Aleksey	Kravtsov	RUS	8.5.93	5	NC	Cheboksary	10 Jun
10.80/0.2	7.49/0.8	14.23	2.00	49.15	14.87/0.6	39.39	4.60	50.28	4:48.65
7764		Maxime	Maugein	FRA	27.9.92	4	NC	Reims	12 Jul
11.01/1.2	7.17/1.5	13.25	1.96	50.19	14.51/1.1	40.00	4.80	51.07	4:26.30
7756		Dmitriy	Karpov	KAZ	23.7.81	1		Asikkala	16 Aug
11.15/0.1	6.72/0.0	15.98	2.02	50.21	14.64/0.1	47.48	4.80	47.42	4:54.44
7742		Manuel	González	CUB	23.3.93	2		La Habana	22 Feb
11.58/0.0	7.25/0.1	14.06	2.01	51.24	14.85/0.0	38.72	5.00	54.90	4:28.99
7733		Luiz Alberto	de Araújo	BRA	27.9.87	1	SAmG	Santiago de Chile	15 Mar
10.88/0.3	7.31/0.3	15.07	1.82	50.42	14.45/0.6	43.37	4.80	54.35	4:57.83
7730A		Friedrich	Pretorius	RSA-J	4.8.95	1		Pretoria	16 Mar
11.17/0.5	7.22/1.2	13.64	1.96	49.40	14.18/1.1	40.38	4.50	53.63	4:36.70
7725		Ben	Gregory	GBR	21.11.90	6	CG	Glasgow	29 Jul
11.26/1.1	7.42/0.1	13.03	1.90	50.49	14.70/0.5	40.40	5.00	54.05	4:34.89
7712		Viktor	Fajoyomi	HUN	27.3.91	7	NCAA	Eugene	12 Jun
11.12w/2.3	7.56/1.6	12.72	2.11	49.75	14.62/0.2	37.54	4.50	50.04	4:39.11
7703		Jérémy	Lelièvre	FRA	8.2.91	2		Oyonnax	15 Jun
10.88/1.3	7.16/1.4	14.35	1.88	49.48	14.90/1.0	41.93	4.27	53.91	4:25.89
		(70)							
7699		Mike	Morgan	USA	19.6.94	1		Athens, OH	16 May
11.12/0.2	7.23/0.0	13.01	2.08	49.11	15.21/-1.6	38.00	4.90	47.79	4:35.38
7672		Kaarel	Jõeväli	EST	8.1.90	1	NC	Rakvere	10 Aug
11.07/-0.9	7.36/1.1	13.71	2.04	49.08	15.05/0.8	39.62	4.40	54.09	4:46.75
7666		Robert	Cardina	USA	29.11.93	8	NCAA	Eugene	12 Jun
10.87w/2.4	7.08w/2.2	13.14	2.05	49.49	14.77/0.2	40.67	4.20	61.00	4:53.63
7656		Jorge	Ureña	ESP	8.10.93	7	ECp-1	Ribeira Brava	6 Jul
10.86/1.9	7.14/1.3	11.95	2.04	49.48	14.07/-1.5	33.45	4.50	51.03	4:25.77
7656		Marcus	Nilsson	SWE	3.5.91	8	ECp-1	Ribeira Brava	6 Jul
11.18w/2.5	6.67/-1.0	13.90	1.92	50.09	14.90/-1.3	43.51	4.60	55.44	4:24.79
7651		Vasyl	Ivanytskyy	UKR	29.1.91	9	ECp-1	Ribeira Brava	6 Jul
11.11/1.9	7.39/0.2	13.00	2.07	50.99	15.59/-1.5	38.96	4.60	57.80	4:39.49
7645		J Patrick	Smith	USA	28.4.91	1	NCAA-2	Allendale	23 May
10.78/1.7	7.59w/2.2	12.92	1.92	49.64	14.78w/2.1	38.92	4.40	51.25	4:37.33
7645		Tom	Fitzsimons	USA	8.3.89	3	NC	Sacramento	27 Jun
11.19/1.9	6.84w/2.1	11.98	1.93	49.02	15.19/1.5	39.47	4.60	61.20	4:19.01
7642		Chase	Dalton	USA	1.2.89	1	TexR	Austin	27 Mar
11.13w/3.6	7.09w/3.5	13.55	1.93	52.33	15.10w/2.7	44.07	4.50	64.17	4:40.44
7618		Reinis	Kregers	LAT	22.1.92	2	Big 12	Lubbock	17 May
11.34/0.0	7.09/1.2	13.19	1.96	49.96	15.31/0.5	45.84	4.39	60.70	4:42.71
		(80)							
7618		Felix	Hepperle	GER	23.11.89	1		Heidenheim	13 Jul
11.14/1.0	7.07/-0.8	12.08	2.00	49.54	15.58/-0.1	38.41	5.20	54.48	4:41.97
7617		Gonzalo	Barroilhet	CHI	19.8.86	2	SAmG	Santiago de Chile	15 Mar
11.34/0.6	6.86/1.8	13.86	2.00	52.94	14.22/0.6	47.63	5.10	52.35	5:08.50
7609		Tommy	Barrineau	FIN	28.8.88	1	NC	Kuopio	3 Aug
11.16/1.3	6.59/1.3	13.68	1.93	49.99	14.80/0.1	37.16	4.95	58.28	4:34.77
7605		Lars-Niklas	Heinke	GER	7.11.89	1		Wesel	24 May
11.09/1.2	6.96/0.3	12.45	1.92	50.25	15.26/0.7	43.51	4.80	57.88	4:39.56
7604		Takumi	Otobe	JPN	22.4.89	3	NC	Nagano	1 Jun
10.67/-1.3	7.42w/2.5	12.49	1.91	48.49	14.87/0.1	36.63	4.80	48.13	4:46.79
7603h	??	Kurtis	Brondyke	USA	24.1.89	1		Worthington	14 Jun
10.9	6.98	13.68	1.95	51.7	14.7	44.27	4.50	60.65	4:45.2
7602		Wolf	Mahler	USA	26.9.94	3	Big 12	Lubbock	17 May
10.86/0.0	6.93/1.0	11.98	1.84	47.27	14.84/0.5	40.09	4.79	49.44	4:30.50

Mark Wind Name Nat Born Pos Meet Venue Date

7601 Jake Stein AUS 17.1.94 1 Canberra 2 Feb
11.56/-0.8 7.29/0.3 13.81 1.91 51.38 15.04/0.5 47.26 4.50 66.88 5:05.99
7597 Koki Someya JPN 18.8.88 4 NC Nagano 1 Jun
11.24/-0.6 7.05/0.4 12.30 1.91 49.55 14.81/0.1 37.76 4.80 57.45 4:30.78
7594 Darko Pesic MNE 30.11.92 1 Novi Sad 25 May
11.55/-1.3 6.97/0.4 14.51 1.92 51.14 14.90/-1.1 42.06 4.60 54.55 4:25.28
(90)
7593 Pawel Wiesiolek POL 13.8.91 1 NC Zgorzelec 8 Jun
11.44/-3.3 7.15/-0.3 13.88 1.95 50.25 14.81/-2.3 43.17 4.80 55.70 4:57.95
7592 Kevin Lazas USA 25.1.92 2 TexR Austin 27 Mar
10.99w/2.9 6.94/1.2 13.54 1.87 52.41 15.17w/2.8 38.95 5.30 59.79 4:48.92
7582 Hu Yufei CHN 9.11.93 2 Zhaoqing 20 Apr
11.24/0.5 7.17/0.8 13.50 2.01 50.27 14.56/0.5 41.89 4.60 49.22 4:47.43
7580 Andres Raja EST 2.6.82 18 EC Zürich 13 Aug
11.12/-1.1 7.28/-1.0 14.22 2.04 51.28 14.35/0.5 41.89 4.30 52.51 4:59.08
7574 Max Wannemacher GER 10.3.91 5 vUSA Marburg 27 Jul
11.23/-1.3 7.20/1.1 12.55 2.05 49.91 14.74/1.7 39.69 4.91 50.70 4:57.93
7572 Hadi Sepehrzad IRI 19.1.83 5 AsiG Incheon 1 Oct
11.14/1.7 6.75/0.9 15.78 1.90 50.85 14.95/1.9 50.88 4.40 54.35 5:05.30
7569 Jouko Hassi FIN 4.4.93 2 NC Kuopio 3 Aug
11.01/1.3 7.08/1.7 13.42 1.93 49.55 15.35/0.1 40.65 4.35 59.31 4:39.96
7565 Osman Muskwe GBR 24.11.85 10 ECp Torun 6 Jul
11.15/-0.6 6.46/1.0 14.42 2.04 51.24 15.33/-0.8 46.86 4.60 58.14 4:55.98
7562 Benjamin Fenrich FRA 11.6.90 5 NC Reims 12 Jul
11.35/2.0 7.08/1.3 12.69 1.93 50.36 15.41/0.9 37.28 4.60 57.78 4:13.70
7559 José Angel Mendieta CUB 16.10.91 2 Ottawa 18 Jul
11.23/1.1 7.20/1.8 14.99 1.90 50.16 14.69/1.5 38.67 4.30 59.61 4:50.12
(100)

Mark	First	Last	Nat	Born	Date
7546	Frédéric	Xhonneux	BEL	11.5.83	18 May
7537	Guillaume	Thierry	MRI	15.9.86	27 Apr
7536	James	Turner	CAN	4.8.93	10 Aug
7535		Kim Kun-woo	KOR	29.2.80	1 Nov
7533	Jeff	Mohl	USA	28.3.91	12 Jun
7530	Yaroslav	Novitskiy	RUS	4.4.88	16 May
7521	Nikolay	Shubyanok	BLR	4.5.85	6 Jul
7516	David	Guest	GBR	8.11.91	29 Jul
7515	Kazuya	Kawasaki	JPN	2.9.92	1 Jun
7514	Bas	Markies	NED	24.7.84	9 Jun
7512	Austin	Bahner	USA	7.7.91	27 Jun
7510w	Nadir	El Fassi	FRA	23.9.83	1 Jun
7506	Brent	Newdick	NZL	31.1.85	15 Jun
7504	Aleksandr	Dergachev	BLR	17.6.90	25 Jul
7498	Hans	Van Alphen	BEL	12.1.82	21 Sep
7496	Martin	Brockman	GBR	13.11.87	25 May
7496	Nils	Merten	GER	20.2.91	13 Jul
7495	Patrick	Spinner	GER	28.11.85	25 May
7493	Martin	Roe	NOR	1.4.92	3 May
7493	Michele	Calvi	ITA	7.6.90	6 Jul
7487	Taavi	Tsernjavski	EST-J	4.3.95	18 Sep
7486	Ramo	Kask	EST	13.7.89	6 Jul
7485	Mitch	Modin	USA-J	12.4.95	12 Jun
7480	Patrick	Scherfose	GER	28.11.91	27 Jul
7471	Karl-Robert	Saluri	EST	6.8.93	27 Mar
7471	Luis	Hanßler	GER	15.3.92	3 May
7459	Javier	Pérez	ESP	9.1.88	6 Jul
7451	Fredrick	Ekholm	SWE	15.6.94	6 Jul
7448		Bae Sang-hwa	KOR	21.7.90	1 Nov
7444	Ben	Hazell	GBR	1.10.84	1 Jun
7444	Maksim	Fayzulin	RUS	18.1.92	10 Jun
7442	Martin	Sisas	EST	11.2.89	14 Jul
7438	Theodore	Elsenbaumer	USA	6.2.91	23 May
7431	Kurt	Schneider	USA	28.8.90	17 May
7430	Dominik	Siedlaczek	AUT	10.3.92	1 Jun
7429	Einar Dadi	Lárusson	ISL	10.5.90	19 Jul
7429	Lindon	Victor	GRN	28.2.93	29 Jul
7426	Julius	Sommer	GER	23.2.93	29 Jun
7425	Juan Carlos	de la Cruz	DOM	16.5.90	30 May
7423	Derek	Masterson	USA	30.1.90	27 Jun
7422	Curtis	Mathews	GBR	22.1.92	29 Jul
7418	Anatoliy	Koshar	BLR	11.6.89	25 Jul
7416	Kale	Wolken	USA	.93	23 May
7413	Payson	Maydew	USA	24.2.94	23 May
7412	Joshua	Weirich	USA	27.7.89	21 Mar
7411	Danilo	Bastida	CUB	5.4.92	28 Jun
7402	Samuli	Bryggare	FIN	10.3.91	15 Jun
7401A	Michael	McPherson	USA	25.12.89	15 May
7400	Otto	Ylöstalo	FIN	4.2.91	3 Aug
7400	Aleksandr	Frolov	RUS	5.3.87	5 Sep
	(150)				

Best al low altitude

7639 Friedrich Pretorius RSA 4.8.95 7 CG Glasgow 29 Jul
11.29/1.1 7.13/1.8 11.86 1.90 49.31 14.62/0.5 40.61 4.60 58.76 4:28.33

JUNIORS

See main list for top 2 juniors.

Pretorius 7639 7 CG Glasgow 29 Jul 7572 1 Bambous 27 Apr
7487 Taavi Tsernjavski EST 4.3.95 1 Rakvere 18 Sep
11.33/0.9 6.77/0.5 13.06 1.91 49.94 15.26/1.1 45.16 4.30 57.47 4:31.23
7485 Mitch Modin USA 12.4.95 13 NCAA Eugene 12 Jun
10.84w/2.2 7.20w/3.2 13.43 1.96 49.76 15.24w/2.4 34.27 4.60 54.04 4:47.JUNI
7383 Wang Qunhao CHN 3.2.95 3 NGP Zhaoqing 20 Apr
11.30/1.8 7.04/0.8 10.79 1.98 48.77 14.45/0.1 35.82 4.30 56.04 4:37.19
7315 Jefferson Santos BRA 30.8.95 4 NC São Paulo 11 Oct
11.21/0.9 7.06/-0.4 13.35 1.94 51.76 15.33w/2.4 46.44 4.40 50.49 4:58.98
7237 Yuriy Yeramich BLR 24.4.95 2 Brest 17 May
10.88 6.98 11.54 1.99 50.52 14.89 33.35 4.60 51.41 4:56.06
7175 Thomas Cheval USA 21.4.95 1 Walnut 17 May
11.01w/3.2 7.29/1.8 11.56 2.01 49.41 14.98/1.2 35.12 3.85 44.29 4:36.90
7114 Qin Guoyuan CHN 20.1.96 5 NC Suzhou 12 Oct
11.24/1.5 6.87/0.0 11.69 1.92 49.79 15.18/1.0 35.80 4.40 48.48 4:40.90

Mark	Wind	Name		Nat	Born	Pos	Meet	Venue	Date
7111		(10)	Chen Xiaohong	CHN	9.2.97	6	NC	Suzhou	12 Oct
		10.97/-0.3 7.24/-0.1 12.86		1.83 49.21		16.02/0.4		37.21 4.10 56.80	5:03.99
7106		Alex	Soares	BRA	2.2.95	5	NC	São Paulo	11 Oct
		11.28/0.3 7.13/-0.4 13.43		1.91 50.39		15.24w/2.4		37.04 4.20 56.14	5:16.20
7045		Scott	Filip	USA	28.1.95	10	TexR	Austin	27 Mar
		10.82w/2.9 7.10w/2.8 11.92		1.93 50.50		15.76w/3.7		33.80 4.40 50.06	5:01.31
7027		Hunter	Veith	USA	14.1.95	1		Houston	20 Mar
		11.15/0.4 7.22/0.0 11.29		2.08 51.13		15.73/0.0		33.53 3.80 55.00	4:51.85
7021		Steven	Nuytinck	NED	16.9.96	6		Woerden	31 Aug
		11.19w/3.3 7.14w/2.1 11.56		1.88 51.55		14.93/0.8		33.48 3.84 54.22	4:34.00
		IAAF Junior Specification – with 99cm 110mh, 6kg SP, 1.75kg DT							
8135		Jiri	Sykora	CZE	20.1.95	1	WJ	Eugene	23 Jul
		10.92/0.5 7.35/2.0 15.50		1.94 49.00		14.23/-0.1		48.55 4.40 60.56	4:42.10
8094		Cedric	Dubler	AUS	13.1.95	2	WJ	Eugene	23 Jul
		10.80/0.6 7.74/1.2 13.02		2.09 48.75		14.08/-0.5		38.25 4.80 53.63	4:39.81
8047			Sykora			1	NC-j	Praha	25 May
		10.90/0.3 7.26/0.6 15.66		2.02 48.82		14.76/0.0		45.81 4.50 59.87	4:51.97
7980		Tim	Nowak	GER	13.8.95	3	WJ	Eugene	23 Jul
		11.09/1.4 7.16/1.4 14.47		2.03 49.60		14.14/-0.6		42.42 4.70 59.74	4:46.19
		7802 1	Ulm 25	May					
7791		Friedrich	Pretorius	RSA	4.8.95	1	NC-j	Pretoria	11 Apr
		11.26/-0.3 7.25/0.0 13.33		1.96 49.72		13.96/1.0		43.34 4.40 55.02	4:33.14
7788		Yevgeniy	Likhanov	RUS	10.1.95	4	WJ	Eugene	23 Jul
		11.01/1.4 7.72/2.0 14.19		2.09 50.18		14.87/-0.1		34.64 4.60 54.83	4:47.12
7780		Roman	Kondratyev	RUS	15.5.95	5	WJ	Eugene	23 Jul
		10.88/0.5 7.29w/2.4 14.93		2.03 49.25		14.04/-0.5		37.56 4.60 47.66	4:50.39
7760		Harrison	Williams	USA	6.3.96	6	WJ	Eugene	23 Jul
		10.75/2.0 6.80/0.7 13.53		1.94 48.21		14.37/-0.9		35.09 4.90 56.31	4:41.01
		7734w 1 NC-j	Sacramento	25 Jun		10 performances by 8 men over 7734			
7704		Yuri	Yaremich	BLR	24.4.95	1		Brest	25 Jun
		11.00/-1.2 7.36/1.2 14.19		2.00 49.89		14.29/0.4		36.15 4.70 52.91	4:52.22
7691		Santiago	Ford	CUB	25.8.97	1		La Habana	22 Feb
		11.27/0.0 6.83/0.0 14.16		2.16 49.14		14.34/0.0		48.95/3.40 55.35	4:42.50
7619		Gabriel	Moore (10)	USA	10.1.96	8	WJ	Eugene	23 Jul
		10.98/2.0 7.01/1.8 13.41		1.97 49.01		14.82/-0.6		45.09 4.30 52.25	4:45.68
7579		Taavi	Tsernjavski	EST	4.3.95	9	WJ	Eugene	23 Jul
		11.19/1.4 6.85/-0.1 14.73		1.91 50.48		15.23/-0.6		46.16 4.30 56.63	4:38.35
7574		Fabian	Christ	GER	18.9.95	1		Bernhausen	15 Jun
		10.87/1.4 6.69/0.0 12.08		1.97 48.15		14.05/1.5		36.84 5.00 50.57	4:56.89
7551		Karsten	Warholm	NOR	28.2.96	10	WJ	Eugene	23 Jul
		10.55/0.5 7.53w/2.6 11.60		2.00 47.21		14.14/-0.5		36.05 4.20 43.77	4:52.94
7537		Mathias	Ako Bienes	FRA	28.7.95	11	WJ	Eugene	23 Jul
		11.01/2.0 7.27/1.8 13.98		1.85 51.72		14.47/-0.1		46.49 5.00 44.68	5:04.50
7532		Elmo	Savola	FIN	10.3.95	1	Nord-j	Kopavogur	8 Jun
		11.33/-0.8 6.94/1.5 13.59		1.97 50.07		14.74/0.0		43.54 4.70 56.55	5:05.08
7527		Jefferson	Santos	BRA	30.8.95	1		São Bernardo	1 Jun
		11.32/0.0 6.81/0.9 15.03		2.01 51.42		14.67/0.0		50.53 4.40 47.71	5:00.74
7516		Mitch	Modin	USA	12.4.95	3	NC-j	Sacramento	26 Jun
		10.82w/2.7 6.87/0.1 13.96		1.96 48.78		14.77/0.5		36.61 4.30 53.88	4:45.68
7513		Frederik	Samuelsson	SWE	16.2.95	12	WJ	Eugene	23 Jul
		11.20/1.0 7.03/1.7 14.62		1.94 50.74		14.90/-0.6		40.02 4.40 52.64	4:37.96
7511		Simon	Hosten	GER	23.3.95	2		Ulm	25 May
		11.11/0.7 7.18/2.0 14.02		1.90 50.15		14.63/0.0		38.06 4.70 55.49	5:00.47
7501		(20)	Wang Qunhao	CHN	3.2.95	1	NC-j	Lishui	21 Jun
		11.59/-0.2 6.75/-0.2 13.10		1.93 49.09		14.44/-0.5		43.59 4.50 52.77	4:37.51

Wind assisted marks: w against a score shows that as per the IAAF rules up to 2009 the wind velocity in an event exceeded 4m/s and the average of the winds in the three measured events exceeded 2 m/s; (w) as per the current IAAF rules the average of the three events exceeded 2m/s but not necessarily any event over 4m/s.

4 X 100 METRES RELAY

Mark	Nat	Team	Pos	Meet	Venue	Date
37.58	JAM	Livermore, Bailey Cole, Ashmeade, Bolt	1	CG	Glasgow	2 Aug
37.71	JAM	Carter, Bailey Cole, Forte, Fisher	1h2	W.Rly	Nassau	25 May
37.77	JAM	Carter, Ashmeade, Forte, Blake	1	W.Rly	Nassau	25 May
37.93	GBR	Kilty, Aikines-Aryeetey, Ellington, Talbot	1h1	W.Rly	Nassau	25 May
37.93	GBR	Ellington, Aikines-Aryeetey, Kilty, Gemili	1	EC	Zürich	17 Aug
37.99	CHN	Chen Shiwei, Xie Zhenye, Su Bingtian, Zhang Peimeng	1	AsiG	Incheon	2 Oct
38.02	GBR-ENG	Gemili, Aikines-Aryeetey, Kilty, Talbot	2	CG	Glasgow	2 Aug
38.04	TTO	Bledman, Burns, Sorrillo, Thompson	2	W.Rly	Nassau	25 May
38.09	TTO	Bledman, Burns, Sorrillo, Thompson	2h1	W.Rly	Nassau	25 May
38.09	GER	Reus, Knipphals, Kosenkow, Jakubczyk	2	EC	Zürich	17 Aug

MEN 2014

Mark	Nat	Name	Pos	Meet	Venue	Date
38.10	BRA	de Barros, Lucindo, A da Silva, Vides	2h2	W.Rly	Nassau	25 May
38.10	TTO	Bledman, Burns, Sorrillo, Thompson	3	CG	Glasgow	2 Aug
38.13	JAM	Racers TC K.Anderson, Frater, Weir, Blake	1		Kingston	22 Feb
38.15	GER	Reus, Knipphals, Kosenkow, Jakubczyk	1h2	EC	Zürich	16 Aug
38.19	GBR	Kilty, Aikines-Aryeetey, Ellington, Chambers	3	W.Rly	Nassau	25 May
38.26	GBR	Ellington, Aikines-Aryeetey, Kilty, Talbot	1h1	EC	Zürich	16 Aug
38.29	USA	Un. of Florida A.Wright, H.Graham, Hall, Dukes	1	TexR	Austin	29 Mar
38.33	FRA	Rémy, Vicaut, Bassaw, Lemaitre	3h2	W.Rly	Nassau	25 May
38.33	TTO	Bledman, Burns, Sorrillo, Thompson	1h1	CG	Glasgow	1 Aug
38.34	JPN	Oseto, Takase, Kiryu, Iizuka	3h1	W.Rly	Nassau	25 May
38.35	RSA	Bruintjies, Magakwe, Titi, Simbine	4	CG	Glasgow	2 Aug
38.39	GBR-ENG	Kilty, Aikines-Aryeetey, Ellington, Talbot	1	DL	Glasgow	11 Jul
		(22 performances by teams from 10 nations)				
38.41	CAN	Smellie, Brown, Richards-Kwok, De Grasse	2h1	CG	Glasgow	1 Aug
38.44	CUB	Carrero, Skyers, Mena, Luis	4h1	W.Rly	Nassau	25 May
38.52	NED	Codrington, Martina, Tromp, Paulina	5h1	W.Rly	Nassau	25 May
38.52	BAH	Griffith, Fraser, Hart, T.Smith	3h1	CG	Glasgow	1 Aug
38.53	UKR	Ibrahimov, Smelyk, Bodrov, Korzh	1rB	W.Rly	Nassau	25 May
38.54	SUI	Mancini, Schenkel, Somasundaran, Wilson	2h1	EC	Zürich	16 Aug
38.60	POL	Olszewski, Kuc, Maszlak, Zalewski	4h2	W.Rly	Nassau	25 May
38.71	ITA	Cerutti, Desalu, Marani, Obou	3h2	EC	Zürich	16 Aug
38.74	KOR	Oh, Cho, Kim, Yeo	1	3-N	Jinhua	6 Jul
38.76	SKN	Rogers, Adams, Roland, Lawrence	3h3	W.Rly	Nassau	25 May
	(20)					
38.79	POR	Antunes, Obikwelu, Abrantes, Nascimento	5h2	EC	Zürich	16 Aug
38.80	NGR	Ogho-Ogene, Edwards, Metu, Jelks	1	AfCh	Marrakech	12 Aug
38.98	HKG	Tang, So, Ng, Tsui	3	AsiG	Incheon	2 Oct
39.01A	DOM	Cuesta, Andujar, Del Carmen, Martinez	2	CAG	Xalapa	28 Nov
39.08	THA	Sowan, Promkaew, Meenapra, Namsuwan	4	AsiG	Incheon	2 Oct
39.20	TPE	Yang, Liu, Wang, Lo	5	AsiG	Incheon	2 Oct
39.21	AUS	Jung, Geddes, Hammond, Hartmann	6h1	W.Rly	Nassau	25 May
39.22A	VEN	Aguilar, Cedeño, Cassiani, Ramírez	3	CAG	Xalapa	28 Nov
39.27	BAR	Hinds, Cadogan, Forde, Gittens	6h2	W.Rly	Nassau	25 May
39.27	SWE	Kling-Baptiste, Tärnhuvud, Brorsson, Hagberg	5h1	EC	Zürich	16 Aug
	(30)					

39.28	GHA	12 Aug	39.38	QAT	26 Apr	39.52	EST	16 Aug	39.74A	GUY	28 Nov	39.85	ESP	21 Jun
39.33	FIN	30 Aug	39.47	SIN	2 Oct	39.65A	COL	28 Jun	39.76	CAY	25 May	39.88	IRL	14 Jun
39.35	RUS	21 Jun	39.48	ANT	1 Aug	39.67	ROU	16 Aug	39.83	TUR	16 Aug	Best at low altitude		
												39.29	VEN	25 May

Mixed nationality teams

Mark	Team	Pos	Meet	Venue	Date
37.97	Americas Collins SKN, Rodgers USA, Carter JAM, Thompson TTO	1	C.Cup	Marrakech	13 Sep
38.30	Texas A&M Hardy USA, Hart BAH, Bryan USA, Lendore TTO	2	TexR	Austin	29 Mar

JUNIORS

Mark	Nat	Name	Pos	Meet	Venue	Date
38.70	USA	J Miller, T Bromell, K Williams, T Friday	1	WJ	Eugene	26 Jul
39.02	JPN	T Kawakami, Y Kiryu, Y Koike, M Mori	2	WJ	Eugene	26 Jul
39.12	JAM	R Robinson, M O'Hara, E Clarke, J Minzie	3	WJ	Eugene	26 Jul
39.23	JPN	T Kawakami, Y Kiryu, Y Koike, M Mori	1h2	WJ	Eugene	25 Jul
39.51	CHN	Mo Youxue, Liang Jinsheng, Lin Renkeng, Li Zhe	4	WJ	Eugene	26 Jul
39.66	NGR	Akerele, Tega, Oye, Oduduru	5	WJ	Eugene	26 Jul
39.74	THA	Sunthanon, Sawangyen, Chuchuai, Kaijun	2	Asi-J	Taipei	14 Jun
39.91	TPE	Cheng Po-Yu, Li Hsiang, Huang Shu-Wei, Yang Chun-Han	3	Asi-J	Taipei	14 Jun
39.92	TTO	Cabara, Farinha, Ballantyne, Constantine	6	WJ	Eugene	26 Jul
39.97	GBR	Arthur, Sinclair, Stone, Popoola	1		Mannheim	6 Jul
40.09	AUS	Clarke, Usoali, Despard, Collum	7	WJ	Eugene	26 Jul

4 X 200 METRES RELAY

Mark	Nat	Name	Pos	Meet	Venue	Date
1:18.63	JAM	Ashmeade, Weir, J.Brown, Blake	1	W.Rly	Nassau	24 May
1:20.07	JAM-	U.Tech Dantago, Forte, Fisher, Levy	1	PennR	Philadelphia	26 Apr
1:20.15	JAM	Dwyer, J.Brown, Livermore, Weir	1h1	W.Rly	Nassau	24 May
1:20.51	SKN	Adams, Roland, Lawrence, Clarke	2	W.Rly	Nassau	24 May
1:20.66	FRA	Lemaitre, Fonsat, Bassaw, Romain	3	W.Rly	Nassau	24 May

1:21.35	USA	24 May	1:21.88	BAR	24 May	1:22.18	BAH	24 May	1:22.35	KEN	24 May

Mixed nationality teams

Mark	Team	Pos	Meet	Venue	Date
1:20.29	Texas A&M Roudette TTO, Hardy USA, Hart BAH, Lendore TTO	2	PennR	Philadelphia	26 Apr
1:20.67	Texas A&M Roudette TTO, Hardy USA, Hart BAH, Lendore TTO	1h1	PennR	Philadelphia	25 Apr
1:20.78	Texas A&M Bryan, USA, Hardy USA, Hart BAH, Roudette TTO	1	TexR	Astin	29 Mar

4 X 400 METRES RELAY

Mark	Nat	Name	Pos	Meet	Venue	Date
2:57.25	USA	Verburg 44.8, McQuay 44.1, C.Taylor 44.6, Merritt 43.8	1	W.Rly	Nassau	25 May
2:57.59	BAH	L.Williams 45.0, Pinder 43.8, Brown 44.2, Mathieu 44.6	2	W.Rly	Nassau	25 May
2:58.34	TTO	Gordon 45.3, Quow 43.6, Cedenio 44.5, Solomon 44.9	3	W.Rly	Nassau	25 May

Mark	Nat	Name	Pos	Meet	Venue	Date
2:58.79	GBR	C.Williams 44.8, Hudson-Smith 44.5, Bingham 45.61, Rooney 43.93	1	EC	Zürich	17 Aug
2:59.38	RUS	Dyldin 45.1, Ivashko 44.1, Uglov 45.28, Krasnov 44.83	2	EC	Zürich	17 Aug
2:59.73	USA- Un of Florida	Glass 45.9, H Graham 45.3, Dukes 44.7, Hall 43.8	1	FlaR	Gainesville	5 Apr
2:59.76	USA-Gainesville Elite	Verburg 45.6, Lawrence 44.8, C.Taylor 44.5, Clement 44.9	2	FlaR	Gainesville	5 Apr
2:59.85	POL	Omelko 45.4, Kozlowski 44.5, Krawczuk 45.63 , Krzewina 44.31	3	EC	Zürich	17 Aug
2:59.89	FRA	Anne 45.3, Atine-Venel 44.7, Hanne 45.22, Jordier 44.59	4	EC	Zürich	17 Aug
3:00.30	BAH	Pinder 45.5, Miller 44.5, Brown 44.8, Mathieu 45.5	1h3	W.Rly	Nassau	24 May
3:00.32	GBR	Bingham 45.4, C Williams 44.7, Levine 46.0, Rooney 44.2	4	W.Rly	Nassau	25 May
3:00.42	USA	Un of Florida Glass 46.1, Graham 45.0, Dukes 44.59, Hall 44.73	2	NCAA	Eugene	14 Jun
3:00.46	GBR-ENG	C Williams 45.2, Bingham 45.3, Awde 45.38, Hudson-Smith 44.56	1	CG	Glasgow	2 Aug
3:00.51	BAH	L Williams 45.7, Mathieu 45.1, Russell 45.16, Brown 44.39	2	CG	Glasgow	2 Aug
3:00.61	CUB	Collazo 45.5, Acea 44.5, Chacón 46.2, Lescay 44.4	5	W.Rly	Nassau	25 May
3:00.65	GBR	Levine 45.7, Bingham 44.9, Yousif 45.40, Rooney 44.50	1h1	EC	Zürich	16 Aug
3:00.70A	CUB	Collazo, Acea, Pellicier, Lescay	1	CAG	Xalapa	28 Nov
3:00.74	GBR	Bingham 45.8, C.Williams 45.4, Levine 45.2, Rooney 44.4	1h1	W.Rly	Nassau	24 May
3:00.78	BAH	Mathieu 45.7, Pinder 44.7, Brown 45.09, Miller 45.32	1	Penn R	Philadelphia	26 Apr
3:00.80	FRA	Anne 45.6, Atine-Venel 45.3, Hanne 45.31, Jordier 44.56	2h1	EC	Zürich	16 Aug
3:01.06	TTO	L Gordon, Quow, Cedenio 45.2, J Solomon 45.3	2h3	W.Rly	Nassau	24 May
3:01.09	USA	Verburg 45.5, Parros 45.8, T Lawrence 44.9, C Taylor 44.9	1h2	W.Rly	Nassau	24 May
3:01.17	JAM	Bell 45.6, Steele 44.8, Hyatt 45.0, McDonald 45.8	2h2	W.Rly	Nassau	24 May
3:01.44	VEN	Ramirez 46.0, Bravo 45.0, Meléndez 45.6, Mezones 44.8	6	W.Rly	Nassau	25 May
	(24 performances by teams from 10 nations)					
3:01.67	IRL	Gregan 45.7, English 45.0, Morrisey 45.55, Barr 45.31	5	EC	Zürich	17 Aug
3:01.70	GER	Gaba 45.4, Rigau 44.8, Gollnow 45.72, Plass 45.68	6	EC	Zürich	17 Aug
3:01.88	JPN	Kanemaru 45.7, Fujimitsu 44.6, Iizuka 45.7, Kato 45.9	1	AsiG	Incheon	2 Oct
3:01.89	BOT	Seribe 46.4, Amos 44.6, Maotoanong 46.46, Makwala 44.47	1	AfCh	Marrakech	14 Aug
3:02.52A	COL	Baloyes, Lemos, Palomeque, R Rodriguez	3	CAG	Xalapa	28 Nov
3:02.60	BEL	Watrin 46.2, K.Borlée 43.6, Bultheel 46.91, Vanhaeren 45.80	7	EC	Zürich	17 Aug
3:02.73	DOM	Cuevas, Soriano, J Santos, L Santos	1	IbAmC	São Paulo	3 Aug
3:02.78	BRA	P de Oliveira 45.9, Cardoso 45.4, Henriques 45.0, H Sousa 46.5	3h1	W.Rly	Nassau	24 May
3:03.09	NGR	Akwu 45.8, Simmons 45.5, Ukaoma 46.39, Morton 45.40	2	AfCh	Marrakech	14 Aug
3:03.6A	KEN		1	NC	Nairobi	7 Jun
	(20)					
3:04.03	KOR	Park Se-jung 46.7, Park Bong-ko 45.6, Sung 46.7, Yeo 45.0	2	AsiG	Incheon	2 Oct
3:04.03	KSA	Al-Sabani 46.2 , Al Khayri 46.2 , Al-Bishi 46.7, Al-Masrahi 44.9	3	AsiG	Incheon	2 Oct
3:04.07	CZE	Tesar 46.4, Nemecek 45.1, Desensky 46.84, Sorm 45.68	4h1	EC	Zürich	16 Aug
3:04.19	AUS	Burns 46.2, Beck 46.1, Geddes 46.20, Steffensen 45.67	6	CG	Glasgow	2 Aug
3:04.61	IND	Kunhu 45.6, Abraham 47.2, Paul 46.8, Rajiv 45.1	4	AsiG	Incheon	2 Oct
3:04.67	CAN	Harper 47.2, Barnaby 45.0, Harris 47.0, Osei 45.5	6rB	W.Rly	Nassau	25 May
3:04.68	ESP	Fradera 47.5, Ujakpor 45.7, Bua 46.37, Garcia 45.09	5h2	EC	Zürich	16 Aug
3:04.72	NED	Blauwhof 46.9, Agard 47.2, Martis 45.56, Bonevacia 44.97	5h1	EC	Zürich	16 Aug
3:04.74	ITA	Valentini 46.9, Tricca 45.5, Juarez 46.96, Galvan 45.30	6h1	EC	Zürich	16 Aug
3:05.00	PUR	Carrasquillo 46.7, Culson 45.1, Vázquez 46.4, Rodríguez 46.8	6h3	W.Rly	Nassau	24 May
	(30)					

3:05.41	CHN	13 Jul	3:07.00	UKR	22 Jun	3:07.43	ZAM	1 Aug	3:07.71	OMA	2 Oct	3:08.00	KAZ	15 Jun
3:05.6A	ETH	15 May	3:07.41	TUR	27 Jul	3:07.57	DEN	22 Jun	3:07.91A	RSA	12 Apr			

Mixed nationality teams

Mark	Team	Name	Pos	Meet	Venue	Date
2:59.60	Texas A&M	A.Bailey USA 46.5, Roudette TTO 44.7, Taplin GRN 44.30, Lendore TTO 44.10	1	NCAA		14 Jun
3:00.02	Africa	Mucheru KEN 45.7, Makwala BOT 43.9, Kombe ZAM 45.56, van Niekerk RSA 44.74	1	C.Cup		14 Sep
3:00.10	Europe	Williams GBR 45.7, Krzewina POL 45.3, Sanford ISR 44.33, Rooney GBR 44.82	2	C.Cup		14 Sep
3:00.76	Texas A&M	A Bailey USA, Roudette TTO, Taplin GRN 45.07, Lendore TTO 44.08	1h1	NCAA	Eugene	12 Jun
3:01.41	IMG Academy	Re ITA, L Merritt, Pinder BAH, Jobodwana RSA	3	FlaR	Gainesville	5 Apr

JUNIORS

Mark	Nat	Name	Pos	Meet	Venue	Date
3:03.31	USA	Lyles 46.6, T Brown 45.9, R Morgan 45.9, M Cherry 44.9	1	WJ	Eugene	27 Jul
3:03.97	USA	Lyles, Morgan, Parish, Cherry	1h1	WJ	Eugene	26 Jul
3:04.11	JPN	J Walsh 46.7, K Yui 46.5, T Kitagawa 45.9, N Kato 45.0	2	WJ	Eugene	27 Jul
3:04.47	JAM	T Crooks 47.7, M Manley 45.3, N Allen 46.5, J Hyde 46.0	3	WJ	Eugene	27 Jul
3:06.02	TTO	Guevara, Farinha, T Lewis, Cedenio	1	Carifta	Fort-de-France	21 Apr
3:06.42	GBR	Snaith 47.8, Somers 47.1, Rutter 45.58, Crosby 46.02	4	WJ	Eugene	27 Jul
3:06.80	AUS	Kermond, Reiser, Robinson, Forsyth	5	WJ	Eugene	27 Jul
3:07.03	BAH	Delauze, Rolle, Cartwright, Gardiner	3h2	WJ	Eugene	26 Jul
3:07.74	GER	Schattner, Krempin, C Schmidt, Walter	1		Mannheim	6 Jul
3:08.89	THA	Chimruang, Thumcha, Krittanukulwong, Phosri	1	Asi-J	Taipei	15 Jun

4 X 800 METRES RELAY

Mark	Nat	Name	Pos	Meet	Venue	Date
7:08.30A	KEN- A	R.Biwott, Kemboi, C.Kiplagat, A.Kiplagat	1		Nairobi	26 Apr
7:08.40	KEN	Cheruiyot 1:46.0, Kirongo 1:45.7, Kinyor 1:47.9, Kipketer 1:48.8	1	W.Rly	Nassau	24 May
7:08.69	POL	Kocieczny 1:48.9, Krawczyk 1:49.1, Lewandowski 1:45.9, Kszczot 1:44.8	2	W.Rly	Nassau	24 May
7:09.06	USA	Rutt 1:48.6, Andrews 1:47.2, Johnson 1:48.1, Solomon 1:45.2	3	W.Rly	Nassau	24 May
7:09.21	KEN- B	Kinyor, Cheruiyot, Kirongo, Kipketer	2		Nairobi	26 Apr

Mark	Wind	Name	Nat	Born	Pos	Meet	Venue	Date
7:11.3A	KEN	Biwott, Rono, Chemut, Kosencha			1		Nairobi	22 Mar
7:11.48	AUS	Ralph 1:49.6, Gregson 1:48.3, Williamsz 1:46.3, West 1:47.3			4	W.Rly	Nassau	24 May
7:16.22	USA- NJ NYTC	Scheetz 1:49.4, Gagnon 1:47.3, Rutt 1:48.2, Andrews 1:51.3			1		Eugene	26 Jul
7:16.41	USA- Oregon TC	Abda 1:48.0, Jock 1:48.4, Mulder 1:49.9, Greer 1:50.1			2		Eugene	26 Jul

Indoors at Boston (R) 8 Feb

Mark	Team	Result
7:13.11	USA All-Stars	1. R Jones 1:51.01, D Torrence 1:47.46, D Solomon 1:47.98, E Sowinski 1:46.66
7:13.22	New Jersey-New York TC	2. Merber 1:49.68, Gagnon 1:48.59, Andrews 1:48.29, Rutt 1:48.66

4 X 1500 METRES RELAY

Mark	Nat	Name	Pos	Meet	Venue	Date
14:22.22	KEN	Cheboi 3:38.5, Kiplagat 3:32.4, Magut 3:39.0, Kiprop 3:32.3	1	W.Rly	Nassau	25 May
14:40.80	USA	Casey 3:38.2, Torrence 3:36.6, Leer 3:39.3, Manzano 3:46.7	2	W.Rly	Nassau	25 May
14:41.22	ETH	Gebremedhin 3:39.9, Fida 3:37.5, Alemayehu 3:46.5, Wote 3:37.3	3	W.Rly	Nassau	25 May
14:46.04	AUS	Gregson 3:39.3, McEntee 3:44.9, Birmingham 3:38.3, Williamsz 3:43.7	4	W.Rly	Nassau	25 May
15:00.69	ESP	Mechaal 3:44.4, Rodriguez 3:44.8, Alsonso 3:47.2, Imedio 3:44.3	5	W.Rly	Nassau	25 May
15:05.70	POL	Krawczyk 3:49.8, Demczyzsak 3:46.1, Lewandowski 3:43.1, Kszczot 3:46.7	6	W.Rly	Nassau	25 May
15:10.77	QAT	Al-Garni 3:43.0, Mohamed 3:51.2, Shagag 3:49.5, Kamal 3:47.1	7	W.Rly	Nassau	25 May

4 X 1 MILE RELAY

Mark	Team	Name	Pos	Meet	Venue	Date
16:09.67	Oregon Un USA	Prakel, Chesarek KEN 3:56.4, Jenkins, Fleet 4:00.4	1	Penn	Philadelphia	26 Apr

4 X 110 METRES HURDLES

Mark	Nat	Name	Pos	Meet	Venue	Date
53.77	USA	Porter, Berger, A Merritt, Akins	1	DrakeR	Des Moines	26 Apr
53.83	JAM	Riley, D Carter, Parchment, Fennell)	2	DrakeR	Des Moines	26 Apr
54.97	Star Athletics		1	FlaR	Gainesville	5 Apr

3000 METRES WALK

Mark	First name	Name	Nat	Born	Pos	Meet	Venue	Date
10:56.23	Dane	Bird-Smith	AUS	15.7.92	1		Cork	8 Jul
10:58.16	Kévin	Campion	FRA	23.5.88	2		Cork	8 Jul
10:58.47	Alex	Wright	IRL	19.12.90	3		Cork	8 Jul
11:08.65	Andreas	Gustafsson	SWE	10.8.81	1		San Diego	25 Jan
11:09.08	Robert	Heffernan	IRL	20.2.78	4		Cork	8 Jul
11:11.14	Antón	Kucmin	SVK	7.6.84	1		Dubnica nad Váhom	30 Aug
11:17.78+	Eder	Sánchez	MEX	21.5.86	1	in 5k	Katowice	2 Jul
11:20.80	Erik	Tysse	NOR	4.12.80	1		Bergen (Fana)	2 Sep
11:22.36	Ivan	Losev	UKR	26.1.86	2		Dubnica nad Váhom	30 Aug
11:23.2+		Wang Zhen	CHN	24.8.91	1	in 5k	Fossano	13 Sep
11:27.81	Liam	Hickey	IRL	24.10.94	5		Cork	8 Jul
11:30.19	Dawid	Tomala	POL	27.8.89	1		Mikolów	25 May

Mark	First name	Name	Nat	Born	Date	Mark	First name	Name	Nat	Born	Date
11:32.45	Rafal	Fedaczynski	POL	3.12.80	25 May	11:35.92	Brendan	Boyce	IRL	15.10.86	8 Jul
11:34.70	Dudan	Majdan	SVK	8.9.87	30 Aug	11:38.37	Rafal	Augustyn	POL	14.5.84	25 May
11:35.78	Petrik	Sopevák	SVK	30.7.94	30 Aug	11:38.9	Chris	Erickson	AUS	1.12.81	22 Feb

Indoors

Mark	First name	Name	Nat	Born	Pos	Meet	Venue	Date
11:15.0+	Matej	Tóth	SVK	10.2.83	1	in 5k	Wien	8 Feb
11:17.66	Quentin	Rew	NZL	16.7.84	1		Sheffield	5 Jan
11:19.0+	Anatole	Ibáñez	SWE	14.11.85	2	in 5k	Wien	8 Feb
11:20.48	Erik	Tysse	NOR	4.12.80	1		Bergen	18 Jan
11:25.0+	Perseus	Karlström	SWE	2.5.90	3	in 5k	Wien	8 Feb

5000 METRES WALK

Mark	First name	Name	Nat	Born	Pos	Meet	Venue	Date
18:35.36	Eder	Sánchez	MEX	21.5.86	1		Katowice	2 Jul
18:39.28	Ever	Palma	MEX	18.3.92	2		Katowice	2 Jul
18:49.10		Wang Zhen	CHN	24.8.91	1		Fossano	13 Sep
18:53.06	Evan	Dunfee	CAN	28.9.90	1		Vancouver	5 Apr
18:59.51	Dane	Bird-Smith	AUS	15.7.92	1		Brisbane	29 Mar
19:00.91		Bird-Smith			1		Brisbane (Nathan)	9 Mar
19:00.92	Benjamin	Thorne	CAN	19.3.93	2		Vancouver	5 Apr
19:03.53	Iñaki	Gómez	CAN	16.1.86	1		Vancouver	30 Mar
19:03.94	Grzegorz (9/8)	Sudol	POL	28.8.78	1		Mielec	6 Jun
19:07.64	Yohann	Diniz	FRA	1.1.78	1		Dijon	18 May
19:11.86	Pedro	Gómez (10)	MEX	31.12.90	3		Katowice	2 Jul
19:11.87	Igor	Hlavan	UKR	25.9.90	1		Kyiv	3 Jun
19:15.08	Álvaro	Martín	ESP	18.6.94	1		Cáceres	2 Jul
19:16.82	Tom	Bosworth	GBR	17.1.90	2	NC	Birminghma	29 Jun
19:18.1	Quentin	Rew	NZL	16.7.84	1		Melbourne (W'town)	6 Dec
19:18.27	Isamu	Fujisawa	JPN	12.10.87	1		Fukushima	17 May
19:18.35	Mark	Tur	ESP	30.11.94	2		Cáceres	2 Jul
19:20.10	Hiroki	Arai	JPN	18.5.88	2		Fukushima	17 May
19:20.31	Kévin	Campion	FRA	23.5.88	1		Amiens	21 Jun
19:22.01	Rafal	Fedaczynski	POL	3.12.80	2		Mielec	6 Jun
19:24.08	Erik	Tysse	NOR	4.12.80	1	NC	Jessheim	24 Aug
19:24.13	Diego	García	ESP-J	19.1.96	3		Cáceres	2 Jul

Mark Wind		Name	Nat	Born	Pos	Meet	Venue	Date
19:28.91	Daisuke	Matsunaga	JPN-J	24.3.95	1		Konosu	12 Apr

Mark		Name	Nat	Born	Date
19:29.16	Lukasz	Nowak	POL	18.12.88	14 Jun
19:30.28	Adrian	Blocki	POL	11.4.90	14 Jun
19:30.86	Rafal	Augustyn	POL	14.5.84	6 Jun
19:31.24	Marius	Ziukas	LTU	29.6.85	20 Sep
19:31.63	Dawid	Tomala	POL	27.8.89	24 May
19:32.89	Federico	Tontodonati	ITA	30.10.89	24 May
19:35.00		Cai Zelin	CHN	11.4.91	13 Sep
19:35.51	Chris	Erickson	AUS	1.12.81	2 Mar
19:38.24	Kai	Kobayashi	JPN	28.2.93	6 Jul
19:38.77	Máté	Helebrandt	HUN	12.1.89	14 Jun
19:39.05	Ivan	Banzeruk	UKR	9.2.90	3 Jun

Indoors

Mark		Name	Nat	Born	Pos	Meet	Venue	Date
18:15.54	Andrey	Ruzavin ¶	RUS	28.3.86	1		Samara	30 Jan
18:16.76	Yohann	Diniz	FRA	1.1.78	1		Reims	7 Dec
18:21.76	Ruslan	Dmytrenko	UKR	22.3.86	2		Samara	30 Jan
18:26.51		Ruzavin			1		Novocheboksarsk	11 Jan
18:29.44		Diniz			1		Reims	26 Jan
18:46.02	Matej	Tóth	SVK	10.2.83	1		Wien	8 Feb
18:57.37	Aleksandr	Yargunkin	RUS	6.1.81	2		Novocheboksarsk	11 Jan
18:57.08		Tóth			1	NC	Bratislava	22 Feb
19:00.48	Pyotr (9/6)	Trofimov	RUS	28.12.83	3		Novocheboksarsk	11 Jan
19:03.05	Anatole	Ibáñez	SWE	14.11.85	2		Wien	8 Feb
19:08.27	Marius	Ziukas	LTU	29.6.85	1	NCp	Vilnius	1 Feb
19:09.86	Mikhail	Ryzhov	RUS	17.12.91	3		Samara	30 Jan
19:13.08	Lukasz	Nowak	POL	18.12.88	1	NC	Sopot	23 Feb
19:13.25	Aléxandros	Papamihaíl	GRE	18.9.88	1		Pireás	2 Feb
19:13.77	Rafal	Sikora	POL	17.2.87	2	NC	Sopot	23 Feb
19:14.06	Erik	Tysse	NOR	4.12.80	1		Bergen	5 Feb
19:16.06	Perseus	Karlström	SWE	2.5.90	3		Wien	8 Feb
19:16.51	Rafal	Augustyn	POL	14.5.84	3	NC	Sopot	23 Feb
19:21.07	João	Vieira	POR	20.2.76	1	NC	Pombal	15 Feb
19:24.59	Sérgio	Vieira	POR	20.2.76	2	NC	Pombal	15 Feb
19:25.48	Alex	Wright	IRL	19.12.90	1	NC	Athlone	15 Feb

Mark		Name	Nat	Born	Date
19:28.30	Kirill	Frolov	RUS	29.9.93	11 Jan
19:36.5	Perseus	Karlström	SWE	2.5.90	29 Nov
19:37.1	Antón	Kucmín	SVK	7.6.84	7 Jan
19:37.90	Tadas	Suskevicius	LTU	22.5.85	1 Feb

JUNIORS García and Marinaga in main list and

Mark		Name	Nat	Born	Pos	Meet	Venue	Date
19:46.23	Jesse	Osborne	AUS	21.1.95	2		Melbourne	2 Mar

10,000 METRES WALK

Mark		Name	Nat	Born	Pos	Meet	Venue	Date
38:08.13	Yohann	Diniz	FRA	1.1.78	1	NC	Reims	12 Jul
38:18.51	Eiki	Takahashi	JPN	19.11.92	1		Isahaya	14 Dec
38:27.09	Yusuke	Suzuki	JPN	2.1.88	1		Yamaguchi	11 Oct
38:54.87	Miguel Ángel	López	ESP	3.7.88	1	NC	Alcobendas	27 Jul
38:57.16	Dane	Bird-Smith	AUS	15.7.92	1	NC	Melbourne	4 Apr
39:06.43		Suzuki			1		Isahaya	21 Oct
39:17.66	Hiroki	Arai	JPN	18.5.88	2		Yamaguchi	11 Oct
39:18.60	Perseus	Karlström	SWE	2.5.90	1	vFIN	Helsinki	30 Aug
39:18.71	Daisuke	Matsunaga	JPN-J	24.3.95	1		Kumagaya	17 May
39:23.58	Takumi	Saito	JPN	23.3.93	2		Kumagaya	17 May
39:25.70	Isamu	Fujisawa (10)	JPN	12.10.87	3		Yamaguchi	11 Oct
39:27.90	Kai	Kobayashi	JPN	28.2.94	3		Kumagaya	17 May
39:32.08	Andreas	Gustafsson	SWE	10.8.81	2	vFIN	Helsinki	30 Aug
39:42.12	Christopher	Linke	GER	24.10.88	1	NC	Bühlertal	21 Jun
39:51.59	Diego	García	ESP-J	19.1.96	2	WJ	Eugene	25 Jul
39:58.8	Pedro	Gómez	MEX	31.12.90	2		Göteborg	28 Jul
40:01.50	Kévin	Campion	FRA	23.5.88	2	NC	Reims	12 Jul
40:02.07	Paulo	Yurivilca	PER-J	23.4.96	3	WJ	Eugene	25 Jul
40:05.03	Juan Manuel	Cano	ARG	21.12.87	1	NC	Rosario	20 Jun
40:05.84	Fumitaka	Oikawa	JPN-J	5.4.95	1		Tama	13 Dec
40:05.99	Álvaro	Martín	ESP	18.6.94	1	NC-23	Durango	6 Jul
40:06.23	Hagen	Pohle	GER	5.3.92	2	NC	Bühlertal	21 Jun
40:08.92	Satoshi	Maruo	JPN	28.11.91	2		Tama	13 Dec
40:15.27	Yuga	Yamashita	JPN-J	6.2.96	4	WJ	Eugene	25 Jul
40:19.53	Tomohiro	Noda	JPN-J	.96	2		Tama	13 Dec

Mark		Name	Nat	Born	Date
40:19.85	Mark	Tur	ESP	30.11.94	6 Jul
40:21.50A	Jesús Tadeo	Vega	MEX	23.5.94	17 May
40:22.48	Nikolay	Markov	RUS-J	1.2.95	25 Jul
40:25.6	Erik	Tysse	NOR	4.12.80	28 Jul
40:27.37	Koichiro	Morioka	JPN	2.4.85	21 Oct
40:31.12A	Erwin	González	MEX	7.2.94	17 May
40:33.11	Takayuki	Tanii	JPN	14.2.83	21 Oct
40:34.88	Luis Alberto	Amezcua	ESP	1.5.92	6 Jul
40:35.89	Zaharías	Tsamoudákis	GRE-J	14.1.96	25 Jul

Indoors

Mark		Name	Nat	Born	Pos	Meet	Venue	Date
39:06.06	Igor	Hlavan	UKR	25.9.90	1		Sumy	24 Dec
39:47.97	Aleksandr	Lyakhovich	BLR	4.7.89	1	NC	Mogilyov	21 Feb
39:53.70	Ivan	Trotskiy	BLR	27.5.76	2	NC	Mogilyov	21 Feb

JUNIORS

See main list for top 6 juniors. 11 performances by 10 men to 40:45.0. Additional marks and further juniors:

Matsunaga 39:27.19 1 WJ Eugene 25 Jul

MEN 2014

Mark	Wind	Name		Nat	Born	Pos	Meet	Venue	Date
40:22.48		Nikolay	Markov	RUS-J	1.2.95	5	WJ	Eugene	25 Jul
40:35.89		Zaharías	Tsamoudákis	GRE-J	14.1.96	6	WJ	Eugene	25 Jul
40:40.31		Ricardo	Ortiz	MEX	7.2.95	7	WJ	Eugene	25 Jul
40:40.96		Toshikazu	Yamanishi	JPN	15.2.96	7		Isahaya	21 Oct
40:48.62			Wang Rui	CHN	6.1.96	8	WJ	Eugene	25 Jul
40:49.71		José Luis	Doctor	MEX	14.6.96	9	WJ	Eugene	25 Jul

10 KILOMETRES ROAD WALK

Where better than track times above. See also intermediate times in 20k lists below.

Mark	Name		Nat	Born	Pos	Meet	Venue	Date
38:01	Pyotr	Trofimov	RUS	28.11.83	1		Voronovo	13 Sep
38:50	Ruslan	Dmytrenko	UKR	22.3.86	1		Voronovo	30 Aug
39:08	Bertrand	Moulinet	FRA	6.1.87	2		Voronovo	30 Aug
39:08	Aleksandr	Yargunkin	RUS	6.1.81	2		Voronovo	13 Sep
39:34	Aleksandr	Pichkalov	RUS	16.6.93	3		Voronovo	13 Sep
39:38+		Matsunaga J			5	in 20k	Kobe	16 Feb
39:40		Gao Wenkui	CHN-J	28.7.95	1	WCp-J	Taicang	3 May
39:45		Matsunaga J			2	WCp-J	Taicang	3 May
39:46	Koichiro	Morioka	JPN	2.4.85	1		Wajima	19 Apr
39:46	Kirill	Frolov	RUS	29.9.93	1		Podolsk	9 May
39:47	Marius	Ziukas	LTU	29.6.85	1	NC	Druskininkai	8 Sep
39:51	Quentin	Rew	NZL	16.7.84	1		Coventry	1 Mar
39:55	Nikolay	Markov	RUS-J	1.2.95	3	WCp-J	Taicang	3 May
39:56+	Takaki	Matsuzaki	JPN	12.8.82		in 20k	Kobe	16 Feb
40:05+	Andriy	Kovenko	UKR	25.11.73		in 20k	Podebrady	12 Apr
40:05	Érick	Barrondo	GUA	14.6.91	1		Katowice	13 Sep
40:11	Giorgio	Rubino	ITA	15.4.86				18 Jul
40:11	Eider	Arévalo	COL	9.3.93				14 Sep
40:21	Federico	Tontodonati	ITA	30.10.89				18 Jul
40:23	Máté	Helebrandt	HUN	12.1.89				24 May
40:25+	Jared	Tallent	AUS	17.10.84				22 Mar
40:31+		Yu Wei	CHN	11.9.87				16 Mar
40:34		Xu Gang	CHN-J	24.3.96				12 Apr
40:34	Andriy	Kovenko	UKR	25.11.73				13 Sep
40:36		Wang Rui	CHN-J	6.1.96				12 Apr

JUNIORS

See main list for top 2 juniors. 8 performances by 6 men to 40:35. Additional marks and further juniors:

García 40:10 4 WCp-J Taicang 3 May
Gao 40:25 1 NC-j Huangshan 27 Feb

Mark	Name		Nat	Born	Pos	Meet	Venue	Date
40:34		Xu Gang	CHN	24.3.96	1		Xintai	12 Apr
40:36		Wang Rui	CHN	6.1.96	2		Xintai	12 Apr
40:46		Jie Jinzhu	CHN	25.7.95	5	WCp-J	Taicang	3 May
40:51	Yuga	Yamashita	JPN	6.2.96	1rB		Wajima	19 Apr
40:55		Tong Dongliang	CHN-Y	3.4.97	1	NC-y	Huangshan	27 Feb
41:03		Sun Song	CHN	15.12.96	1		Taicang	5 May
41:07	Nathan	Brill	AUS	24.5.96	7	WCp-J	Taicang	3 May
41:20	Yuko	Kurumisawa (10)	JPN	.95	1	NC-j	Kobe	16 Feb
41:20		Zhang Rongjin	CHN	24.4.96	3	NC-y	Huangshan	27 Feb
41:22		Zhang Jun	CHN-Y	20.7.98	1y		Taicang	5 May
41:25	Zhang	Wanxin	CHN	25.10.96	2		Changbaishan	12 Sep
41:27	Jesse	Osborne	AUS	21.1.95	1		Hobart	2 Feb
41:27		Leng Xiao	CHN	26.1.96	8	WCp-J	Taicang	3 May

20 KILOMETRES WALK

10k split in 2nd column

Mark	10k	Name		Nat	Born	Pos	Meet	Venue	Date
1:18:17	39:02	Yusuke	Suzuki	JPN	2.1.88	1	NC	Kobe	16 Feb
1:18:37	40:10	Ruslan	Dmytrenko	UKR	22.3.86	1	WCp	Taicang	4 May
1:18:41	39:02	Eiki	Takahashi	JPN	19.11.92	2	NC	Kobe	16 Feb
1:18:52	40:10		Cai Zelin	CHN	11.4.91	2	WCp	Taicang	4 May
1:18:59	40:10	Andrey	Ruzavin ¶	RUS	28.3.86	3	WCp	Taicang	4 May
1:19:19	40:10		Suzuki			4	WCp	Taicang	4 May
1:19:21	40:10	Miguel Ángel	López	ESP	3.7.88	5	WCp	Taicang	4 May
1:19:24	40:00		Kim Hyun-sub	KOR	31.5.85	1	AsCh	Nomi	16 Mar
1:19:33		Ivan	Losyev	UKR	26.1.86	1	NC	Alushta	28 Feb
1:19:40	40:10		Wang Zhen	CHN	24.8.91	6	WCp	Taicang	4 May
1:19:42.1 t		Yohann	Diniz (10)	FRA	1.1.78	1		Bogny-sur-Meuse	25 May
1:19:44	40:43		López			1	EC	Zürich	13 Aug
1:19:45	40:43	Aleksandr	Ivanov	RUS	25.4.93	2	EC	Zürich	13 Aug
1:19:45	40:43		Wang Zhen			1	AsiG	Incheon	28 Sep
1:19:46		Nazar	Kovalenko	UKR	9.2.89	2	NC	Alushta	28 Feb
1:19:46	40:43	Denis	Strelkov	RUS	26.10.90	3	EC	Zürich	13 Aug
1:19:46	40:43		Dmytrenko			4	EC	Zürich	13 Aug
1:19:47	39:44		Strelkov			1	NC	Cheboksary	6 Jun
1:19:48	40:06	Matej	Tóth	SVK	10.2.83	1		Dudince	22 Mar
1:19:59	40:13	Igor	Hlavan	UKR	25.9.90	7	WCp	Taicang	4 May

Mark	Wind	Name		Nat	Born	Pos	Meet	Venue	Date
1:20:00	39:59		Tóth			1		Podebrady	12 Apr
1:20:01		Ihor	Lyashchenko	UKR	24.8.93	3	NC	Alushta	28 Feb
1:20:03	39:02	Isamu	Fujisawa	JPN	12.10.87	3	NC	Kobe	16 Feb
1:20:03	40:11	Omar	Segura	MEX	24.3.81	8	WCp	Taicang	4 May
1:20:04	40:10		Takahashi			9	WCp	Taicang	4 May
1:20:08	40:30		Dmytrenko			1		Lugano	16 Mar
1:20:11	40:11		Kovalenko			10	WCp	Taicang	4 May
1:20:12		Kostyantyn	Puzanov	UKR	19.5.91	4	NC	Alushta	28 Feb
1:20:13	40:18	Evan	Dunfee (20)	CAN	28.9.90	11	WCp	Taicang	4 May
1:20:18	39:59	Rafal	Fedaczynski	POL	3.12.80	2		Podebrady	12 Apr
1:20:18	40:11	Iñaki	Gómez	CAN	16.1.88	12	WCp	Taicang	4 May
		(31/22)							
1:20:19	40:12	Benjamin	Thorne	CAN	19.3.93	13	WCp	Taicang	4 May
1:20:20		Andriy	Kovenko	UKR	25.11.73	5	NC	Alushta	28 Feb
1:20:21	39:22	Takumi	Saito	JPN	23.3.93	4	NC	Kobe	16 Feb
1:20:27	40:10	Dane	Bird-Smith	AUS	15.7.92	14	WCp	Taicang	4 May
1:20:28	40:10		Chen Ding	CHN	5.8.92	15	WCp	Taicang	4 May
1:20:28	40:11	Caio	Bonfim	BRA	19.3.91	16	WCp	Taicang	4 May
1:20:30	39:56	Koichiro	Morioka	JPN	2.4.85	5	NC	Kobe	16 Feb
1:20:33	40:11	Pyotr	Trofimov	RUS	28.11.83	17	WCp	Taicang	4 May
		(30)							
1:20:38	39:55	Hiroki	Arai	JPN	18.5.88	6	NC	Kobe	16 Feb
1:20:39	40:02	Kévin	Campion	FRA	23.5.88	4		Podebrady	12 Apr
1:20:39	40:41	Álvaro	Martín	ESP	18.6.94	19	WCp	Taicang	4 May
1:20:44	40:12	Giorgio	Rubino	ITA	15.4.86	20	WCp	Taicang	4 May
1:20:45	40:29		Bian Fongda	CHN	1.4.91	1	NC	Huangshan	27 Feb
1:20:47	39:56	Takayuki	Tanii	JPN	14.2.83	7	NC	Kobe	16 Feb
1:20:47	40:36		Yu Wei	CHN	11.9.87	21	WCp	Taicang	4 May
1:20:50	40:05	Erik	Tysse	NOR	4.12.80	5		Podebrady	12 Apr
1:20:51	40:29		Liu Jianmin	CHN	9.3.88	2	NC	Huangshan	27 Feb
1:20:55	40:30	Jared	Tallent	AUS	17.10.84	4		Lugano	16 Mar
		(40)							
1:20:57	40:31	Robert	Heffernan	IRL	20.2.78	5		Lugano	16 Mar
1:20:57	40:40	Lukasz	Nowak	POL	18.12.88	1		Zaniemysl	5 Apr
1:21:00	40:43	Christopher	Linke	GER	24.10.88	5	EC	Zürich	13 Aug
1:21:04		Ivan	Trotskiy	BLR	27.5.76	1		Grodno	4 Oct
1:21:08	40:04	Aleksandr	Yargunkin	RUS	6.1.81	6		Podebrady	12 Apr
1:21:09	40:11	Kolothum Thodi	Irfan	IND	8.2.90	26	WCp	Taicang	4 May
1:21:09		Dmitriy	Dziubin	BLR	12.7.90	2		Grodno	4 Oct
1:21:13	40:18	Rafal	Augustyn	POL	14.5.84	7		Podebrady	12 Apr
1:21:13		Sergiy	Budza	UKR	6.12.84	3		Grodno	4 Oct
1:21:13		Kai	Kobayashi	JPN	28.2.93	1		Takahata	26 Oct
		(50)							
1:21:14		Érick	Barrondo	GUA	14.6.91	1		La Coruña	31 May
1:21:17	40:30	Daisuke	Matsunaga	JPN-J	24.3.95	6		Lugano	16 Mar
1:21:20			Choi Byung-kwang	KOR	7.4.91	9	JPN Ch	Kobe	16 Feb
1:21:20	40:15	Gurmeet	Singh	IND	1.7.85	27	WCp	Taicang	4 May
1:21:28		Eider	Arévalo	COL	9.3.93	4		La Coruña	31 May
1:21:29		Basant Bahadur	Rana	IND	18.1.84	4		Nomi	16 Mar
1:21:29		Hagen	Pohle	GER	5.3.92	2	NC	Naumburg	18 May
1:21:42		Carl	Dohmann	GER	18.5.90	3	NC	Naumburg	18 May
1:21:44		Georgiy	Sheyko	KAZ	24.8.89	7		Nomi	16 Mar
1:21:46		Mauricio	Arteaga	ECU	8.8.88	29	WCp	Taicang	4 May
		(60)							
1:21:49		Devender	Singh	IND	5.12.83	8		Nomi	16 Mar
1:21:49		Nils Christopher	Gloger	GER	6.8.90	4	NC	Naumburg	18 May
1:21:54	40:29		Sun Chengang	CHN	11.3.91	3	NC	Huangshan	27 Feb
1:21:54		Perseus	Karlström	SWE	2.5.90	8		Podebrady	12 Apr
1:21:55		Pavel	Parshin	RUS	2.1.94	5	NC-w	Sochi	22 Mar
1:21:58		Julio César	Salazar	MEX	8.7.93	31	WCp	Taicang	4 May
1:21:59		Antón	Kucmín	SVK	7.6.84	9		Podebrady	12 Apr
1:22:03		José Leonardo	Montaña	COL	21.3.92	32	WCp	Taicang	4 May
1:22:06		Aleksey	Golovin	RUS	24.12.88	6	NC-w	Sochi	22 Mar
1:22:06		Fumitaka	Oikawa	JPN-J	5.4.95	3		Takahata	26 Oct
		(70)							
1:22:09		Marius	Ziukas	LTU	29.6.85	34	WCp	Taicang	4 May
1:22:10A		Jesús Tadeo	Vega	MEX	23.5.94	1		Xalapa	8 Mar
1:22:11		Quentin	Rew	NZL	16.7.84	2		Melbourne	14 Dec
1:22:13.74t		Iván	Garrido	COL	25.1.94	1	IbAm	São Paulo	2 Aug
1:22:16			Park Chil-sung	KOR	8.7.82	9		Nomi	16 Mar
1:22:17	40:09	Takuya	Yoshida	JPN	10.8.90	10	NC	Kobe	16 Feb

Mark	Wind	Name		Nat	Born	Pos	Meet	Venue	Date
1:22:18.5 t		Juan Manuel	Cano	ARG	21.12.87	1		Buenos Aires	25 Jan
1:22:19		Chris	Erickson	AUS	1.12.81	10		Nomi	16 Mar
1:22:19		Rafal	Sikora	POL	17.2.87	2		Zaniemysl	5 Apr
1:22:19		Luis Alberto	Amezcua	ESP	1.5.82	37	WCp	Taicang	4 May
		(80)							
1:22:20		Tom	Bosworth	GBR	17.1.90	10		Podebrady	12 Apr
1:22:21		Antonin	Boyez	FRA	9.11.84	39	WCp	Taicang	4 May
1:22:25A		Diego	Flores	MEX	23.3.87	2		Xalapa	8 Mar
1:22:32			Ma Haijun	CHN	24.11.92	1		Taicang	5 May
1:22:36		Erwin	González	MEX	7.2.94	11		Podebrady	12 Apr
1:22:37		Tomohiro	Noda	JPN-J	24.1.96	4		Takahata	26 Oct
1:22:41		Yosuke	Kimura	JPN	5.2.93	2		Nomi	16 Mar
1:22:41	40:12	Krishnan	Ganapathi	IND	29.6.89	41	WCp	Taicang	4 May
1:22:44		Denis	Simanovich	BLR	20.4.87	1	NC	Brest	24 Jun
1:22:46		Mark	Tur	ESP	30.11.94	42	WCp	Taicang	4 May
		(90)							
1:22:50			Wang Qin	CHN	8.5.94	2		Taicang	5 May
1:22:50		Aleksandr	Lyakhovich	BLR	4.7.89	2	NC	Brest	24 Jun
1:23:00		Moacir	Zimmerman	BRA	30.12.83	1		Blumenáu	13 Apr
1:23:01		Massimo	Stano	ITA	27.2.92	46	WCp	Taicang	4 May
1:23:01A		Horacio	Nava	MEX	20.1.82	1	NC	Xalapa	31 Aug
1:23:02	40:32	Dawid	Tomala	POL	27.8.89	8		Lugano	16 Mar
1:23:04		Aléxandros	Papamihaíl	GRE	18.9.88	9		Lugano	16 Mar
1:23:06			Chen Zongliang	CHN	9.1.92	3		Taicang	5 May
1:23:06		Yuga	Yamashita	JPN-J	6.2.96	5		Takahata	26 Oct
1:23:07		Grzegorz	Sudol	POL	28.8.78	4		Szczecin	30 Jul
		(100)							

Mark	Name		Nat	Born	Date
1:23:11		Byun Young-jun	KOR	20.3.84	16 Mar
1:23:12	Yuriy	Andronov ¶	RUS	6.11.71	22 Mar
1:23:20		Kim Dae-ro	KOR	30.4.88	16 Mar
1:23:20	João	Vieira	POR	20.2.76	5 Apr
1:23:20	José Alessandro	Bagio	BRA	16.4.81	13 Apr
1:23:22.7t	Esteban	Soto	COL	28.1.94	4 Oct
1:23:24	Marco	De Luca	ITA	12.5.81	16 Mar
1:23:24		Li Tianlei	CHN-J	13.1.95	5 May
1:23:25	Francisco	Arcilla	ESP	14.1.84	31 May
1:23:25.6t	Richard	Vargas	VEN	28.12.94	4 Oct
1:23:28.09t	Alex	Wright	IRL	19.12.90	13 Sep
1:23:31	Yerko	Araya	CHI	14.2.86	31 May
1:23:33		Su Guanyu	CHN	26.6.94	5 May
1:23:35	Máté	Helebrandt	HUN	12.1.89	16 Mar
1:23:40A	Eder	Sánchez	MEX	21.5.86	8 Mar
1:23:43	Anatole	Ibáñez	SWE	14.11.85	4 May
1:23:43	Federico	Tontodonati	ITA	30.10.89	31 May
1:23:44	Nils	Brembach	GER	23.2.93	31 May
1:23:45		Dong Guozhu	CHN	2.8.92	5 May
1:23:45		Yin Jiaxing	CHN	16.3.94	5 May
1:23:50	Sergey	Sharipov	RUS	14.4.92	6 Sep
1:23:55	Hitoshi	Warita	JPN	26.9.91	1 Jan
1:23:55	Andrey	Talashko	BLR	31.5.82	29 Mar
1:23:55		Men Fuqiang	CHN	22.6.92	5 May
1:23:56		Yan Dexiang	CHN	18.6.93	5 May
1:23:58	Rhydian	Cowley	AUS	4.1.91	4 May
1:23:58A	David	Kimutai	KEN	18.8.69	7 Jun
1:23:59	Kuldeep	Singh	IND	20.12.94	8 Feb
1:23:59A	Samuel	Gathimba	KEN		7 Jun
1:24:00	Bruno	Fidelis	BRA	8.11.94	13 Apr
1:24:02A	Isaac	Palma	MEX	26.10.90	22 Feb
1:24:04	Kirill	Frolov	RUS	29.9.93	22 Mar
1:24:08	Aníbal	Paau	GUA	12.1.87	16 Mar
1:24:09	Lebogang	Shange	RSA	1.8.90	22 Mar
1:24:13	Sérgio	Vieira	POR	20.2.76	4 May
1:24:16		Li Shijia	CHN	14.1.92	27 Feb
1:24:25	Jarkko	Kinnunen	FIN	19.1.84	31 May
1:24:25	Hironari	Tomatsu	JPN	23.9.93	26 Oct
1:24:29	Igor	Saharuk	UKR	3.6.88	14 Jun
1:24:29	Yuki	Kurumisawa	JPN-J	11.2.95	26 Oct
1:24:38	Cédric	Houssaye	FRA	13.12.79	31 May
1:24:39A	Daniel	Gómez	MEX	31.12.90	31 Aug
1:24:44	Adam	Rutter	AUS	24.12.86	4 May
1:24:47	Masaki	Yamamoto	JPN	10.2.93	26 Oct
1:24:48	Jonathan	Cáceres	ECU	20.1.90	12 Apr
1:24:52	Tadas	Suskevicius	LTU	22.5.85	13 Jun
1:24:54	Tomofumi	Kanno	JPN	25.4.93	16 Mar
1:24:54	Marius	Savelskis	LTU	30.7.94	13 Aug
1:24:54A	Omar	Pineda	MEX	2.12.94	8 Mar
1:24:55	Viktor	Sokolov	RUS	7.1.94	6 Jun
1:24:57	Satoshi	Maruo	JPN	28.11.91	26 Oct
	(151)				

Best track times

Mark	Name		Nat	Born	Pos	Meet	Venue	Date
1:22:11.1	Eider	Arévalo	COL	9.3.93	1	SAmG	Santiago de Chile	15 Mar
1:22:14.1	José Leonardo	Montaña	COL	21.3.92	2	SAmG	Santiago de Chile	15 Mar

Mark	Name		Nat	Born	Date
1:23:19.3	Mauricio	Arteaga	ECU	8.8.88	15 Mar
1:23:22.19	Mark	Tur	ESP	30.11.94	2 Aug
1:23:34.68	Yerko	Araya	CHI	14.2.86	2 Aug
1:24:49.52	Caio	Bonfim	BRA	19.3.91	2 Aug
1:24:53.20	Anatole	Ibáñez	SWE	14.11.85	13 Sep

JUNIORS

See main list for top 4 juniors. 7 performances by 6 men to 1:24:30. Additional marks and further juniors:

Matsunaga 1:21:18 8 NC Kobe 16 Feb

Mark	Name		Nat	Born	Pos	Meet	Venue	Date
1:23:24		Li Tianlei	CHN	13.1.95	4		Taicang	5 May
1:24:29	Yuki	Kurumisawa	JPN	11.2.95	7		Takahata	26 Oct
1:25:19		Gao Wenkui	CHN	28.7.95	25		La Coruña	31 May
1:28:24	Bence	Venyercsán	HUN	8.1.96	4	NC	Békéscsaba	13 Apr
1:28:40	Brian	Pentado	ECU	29.7.95	27		Podebrady	12 Apr
1:28:56A	Brayan	Fuentes (10)	COL	1.8.96	3	NC-23	Calí	31 Aug

30-35 KILOMETRES WALK

Mark	Name		Nat	Born	Pos	Meet	Venue	Date
2:28:11	Mikhail	Ryzhov	RUS	17.12.91	1	NC-w	Sochi	22 Mar
2:30:00	Roman	Yecstifeyev	RUS	19.9.92	1	NCp	Cheboksary	6 Sep
2:30:14	Ivan	Noskov	RUS	16.7.88	2	NC-w	Sochi	22 Mar
2:30:17	Igor	Saharuk	UKR	3.6.88	1	NC	Alushta	28 Feb

Mark	Wind	Name		Nat	Born	Pos	Meet	Venue	Date
	2:30:20	Oleksiy	Kazanin	UKR	22.5.82	2	NC	Alushta	28 Feb
	2:30:58	Ivan	Banzeruk	UKR	9.2.90	3	NC	Alushta	28 Feb
	2:32:10	Aleksey	Bartsaykin	RUS	22.3.89	3	NC-w	Sochi	22 Mar
	2:32:14	Denis	Asanov	RUS	23.9.92	4	NC-w	Sochi	22 Mar
2:11:01+		Robert	Heffernan	IRL	20.2.78	5	in 50k	Zürich	15 Aug
2:11:44	2:33:42	Koichiro	Morioka	JPN	2.4.85	1	in 50k	Takahata	26 Oct
	2:33:57	Aleksandr	Yargunkin	RUS	6.1.81	6	NC-w	Sochi	22 Mar
2:11:54		Evan	Dunfee	CAN	28.9.90	1		Richmond	18 Aug
2:12:08			Sun Song	CHN-J	15.12.96	1	NC-j	Huangshan	28 Feb
	2:34:11	Sergiy	Budza	UKR	6.12.84	4	NC	Alushta	28 Feb
2:13:33+		Aleksandr	Yargunkin	RUS	6.1.81		in 50k	Zürich	15 Aug
2:13:35+		Lukasz	Nowak	POL	18.12.88	8	in 50k	Zürich	15 Aug
2:13:45+		Oleksiy	Kazanin	UKR	22.5.82		in 50k	Zürich	15 Aug
2:13:47+		Clemente	García	MEX	21.8.89		in 50k	Cheboksary	7 Jun
	2:36:34	Marc	Tur	ESP	30.11.94	1	NC	Murcia	16 Feb
	2:27:17	Álvaro	Martín	ESP	19.6.94	2	NC	Murcia	16 Feb
	2:37:17	Andrey	Hrechkovskyy	UKR	30.8.93	5	NC	Alushta	28 Feb
	2:37:27	Oleksandr	Venglovskyy	UKR	5.8.85	6	NC	Alushta	28 Feb

50 KILOMETRES WALK

50k	30k	35k	Name		Nat	Born	Pos	Meet	Venue	Date
3:32:33	2:09:20		Yohann	Diniz	FRA	1.1.78	1	EC	Zürich	15 Aug
3:36:21	2:10:51		Matej	Tóth	SVK	10.2.83	2	EC	Zürich	15 Aug
3:37:41	2:10:48		Ivan	Noskov	RUS	16.7.88	3	EC	Zürich	15 Aug
3:39:05	2:12:31	2:34:27	Mikhail	Ryzhov	RUS	17.12.91	1	WCp	Taicang	3 May
3:39:07	2:09:14			Ryzhov			4	EC	Zürich	15 Aug
3:39:38	2:12:31	2:34:27		Noskov			2	WCp	Taicang	3 May
3:40:19			Takayuki	Tanii	JPN	14.2.83	1	AsiG	Incheon	1 Oct
3:40:34	2:13:08	2:35:03	Hiroki	Arai	JPN	18.5.88	1		Takahata	26 Oct
3:41:32	2:11:34	2:33:37		Tanii			1	NC	Wajima	20 Apr
3:42:26			Aleksandr	Yargunkin	RUS	6.1.81	1	NC	Cheboksary	7 Jun
3:42:48	2:12:34	2:34:46	Jared	Tallent	AUS	17.10.84	3	WCp	Taicang	3 May
3:42:51	2:13:47		Horacio	Nava	MEX	20.1.82	2	RUS Ch	Cheboksary	7 Jun
3:43:02	2:13:08	2:35:04	Takuya	Yoshida (10)	JPN	10.8.90	2		Takahata	26 Oct
3:44:23	2:11:31	2:33:27	Yuki	Yamazaki	JPN	16.1.84	2	NC	Wajima	20 Apr
3:44:49	2:15:40		Ivan	Banzeruk	UKR	9.2.90	5	EC	Zürich	15 Aug
3:45:08	2:11:15		Igor	Hlavan	UKR	25.9.90	6	EC	Zürich	15 Aug
3:45:25	2:15:13		Marco	De Luca	ITA	12.5.81	7	EC	Zürich	15 Aug
3:45:32			Rafal	Augustyn	POL	14.5.84	1	NC	Dudince	22 Mar
3:45:41			Roman	Yevstifeyev	RUS	19.9.92	3	NC	Cheboksary	7 Jun
3:45:41			Jesús Ángel	García	ESP	17.10.69	8	EC	Zürich	15 Aug
3:46:34	2:15:45	2:37:41	Aleksey	Bartsaykin	RUS	22.3.89	4	WCp	Taicang	3 May
3:47:01			Oleksiy	Kazanin	UKR	22.5.82	5	WCp	Taicang	3 May
3:47:18			(20)	Wang Zhendong	CHN	11.1.91	2		Dudince	22 Mar
3:47:35	2:15:42	2:37:37	Omar	Zepeda	MEX	8.6.77	6	WCp	Taicang	3 May
3:47:41			James	Rendón	COL	7.4.85	1		Valley Cottage	14 Sep
3:48:15	2:13:36			Augustyn			9	EC	Zürich	15 Aug
3:48:42			Anatole	Ibáñez	SWE	14.11.85	10	EC	Zürich	15 Aug
3:48:49				Zhang Lin	CHN	11.11.93	7	WCp	Taicang	3 May
3:48:49			Jarkko	Kinnunen	FIN	19.1.84	11	EC	Zürich	15 Aug
3:48:50			Sergiy (30/26)	Budza	UKR	6.12.84	1	NC	Ivano-Frankivsk	19 Oct
3:49:06			Andrey	Hrechkovskyy	UKR	30.8.93	2	NC	Ivano-Frankivsk	19 Oct
3:49:15	2:13:09	2:36:40		Park Chil-sung	KOR	8.7.82	2	AsiG	Incheon	1 Oct
3:49:33			Chris	Erickson	AUS	1.12.81	10	WCp	Taicang	3 May
3:49:40A			Érick (30)	Barrondo	GUA	14.6.91	1	CAG	Xalapa	29 Nov
3:49:58			Aléxandros	Papamihaíl	GRE	18.9.88	13	EC	Zürich	15 Aug
3:50:19			Rolando	Saquipay	ECU	21.7.79	11	WCp	Taicang	3 May
3:50:22			Quentin	Rew	NZL	16.7.84	12	WCp	Taicang	3 May
3:50:42A			José	Leyver	MEX	12.11.85	1		Chihuahua	22 Feb
3:50:49			Igor	Saharuk	UKR	3.6.88	13	WCp	Taicang	3 May
3:50:51				Wu Qianlong	CHN	30.1.90	14	WCp	Taicang	3 May
3:50:52			Jonathan	Cáceres	ECU	20.1.90	15	WCp	Taicang	3 May
3:51:16			Andreas	Gustafsson	SWE	10.8.81	1		Santee	14 Dec
3:51:27			Carl	Dohmann	GER	18.5.90	15	EC	Zürich	15 Aug
3:51:28			Alex (40)	Wright	IRL	19.12.90	1		Gleina	11 Oct
3:51:34			Brendan	Boyce	IRL	15.10.86	16	EC	Zürich	15 Aug
3:51:47				Zhao Qi	CHN	14.1.93	16	WCp	Taicang	3 May

Mark	Wind	Name		Nat	Born	Pos	Meet	Venue	Date
3:51:49		Matteo	Giupponi	ITA	8.10.88	1		Latina	26 Jan
3:51:58		Tadas	Suskevicius	LTU	22.5.85	4	1 NC	Dudince	22 Mar
3:52:07		Adrian	Blocki	POL	11.4.90	5	2 NC	Dudince	22 Mar
3:52:53A		Grzegorz	Sudol	POL	28.8.78	3		Chihuahua	22 Feb
3:52:58		Veli-Matti	Partanen	FIN	28.10.91	18	EC	Zürich	15 Aug
3:53:26		Dusan	Majdán	SVK	8.9.87	19	EC	Zürich	15 Aug
3:53:39A		Cristian	Berdeja	MEX	21.6.81	3	CAG	Xalapa	29 Nov
3:53:44		Jean-Jacques (50)	Nkouloukidi	ITA	15.4.82	19	WCp	Taicang	3 May
3:54:00A		Luis	Bustamante	MEX	10.6.84	5		Chihuahua	22 Feb
3:54:17		Sergey	Stepanov	RUS	28.7.86	4	NC	Cheboksary	7 Jun
3:54:47		Nils	Brembach	GER	23.2.93	2		Gleina	11 Oct
3:55:09		Konstantin	Kulagov	RUS	14.10.91	5	NC	Cheboksary	7 Jun
3:55:11		Rafal	Sikora	POL	17.2.87	7	3 NC	Dudince	22 Mar
3:55:42A		Jaime	Quiyuch	GUA	24.4.88	4	CAG	Xalapa	29 Nov
3:56:15		Pedro	Isidro	POR	17.7.85	21	WCp	Taicang	3 May
3:56:22		Sandeep	Kumar	IND	1.5.86	22	WCp	Taicang	3 May
3:56:35		Pavel	Chihuán	PER	19.1.86	23	WCp	Taicang	3 May
3:57:00		Andrés (60)	Chocho	ECU	4.11.83	2		Santee	14 Dec
3:57:29		Mário José	dos Santos	BRA	10.9.79	8		Dudince	22 Mar
3:58:00		Francisco	Arcilla	ESP	14.1.84	25	WCp	Taicang	3 May
3:58:23		Teodorico	Caporaso	ITA	14.9.87	20	EC	Zürich	15 Aug
3:58:34		Evan	Dunfee	CAN	28.9.90	2		Melbourne	14 Dec
3:58:54		Cédric	Houssaye	FRA	13.12.79	1	NC	Fontenay-le-Comte	9 Mar
3:58:58		Jorge	Ruiz	COL	17.5.89	27	WCp	Taicang	3 May
3:59:02		Mikel	Odriozola	ESP	25.5.73	1		Hayes, GBR	5 Oct
3:59:08		Omar	Sierra	COL	10.9.88	29	WCp	Taicang	3 May
3:59:25		Ivan	Losyev	UKR	26.1.86	4	NC	Ivano-Frankivsk	19 Oct
3:59:48		Mathieu (70)	Bilodeau	CAN	.88	3		Santee	14 Dec
3:59:50		Maciej	Rosiewicz	GEO	31.7.77	1	NC	Wien	4 Oct
4:00:48			Cheng Min	CHN	6.7.91	1	NC	Huangshan	28 Feb
4:00:57			Yu Wei	CHN	11.9.87	1		Changbaishan	14 Sep
4:01:10		Yuki	Ito	JPN	12.4.92	3		Takahata	26 Oct
4:01:21		Xavier	Le Coz	FRA	30.12.79	2	NC	Fontenay-le-Comte	9 Mar
4:01:22		Lukasz	Augustyn	POL	29.11.90	9		Dudince	22 Mar
4:01:52		Lukás	Gdula	CZE	6.12.91	10	1 NC	Dudince	22 Mar
4:01:54			He Yongqiang	CHN	27.11.93	30	WCp	Taicang	3 May
4:01:55		Federico	Tontodonati	ITA	30.10.89	2		Latina	26 Jan
4:02:06		Jorge (80)	Díaz	COL	2.3.87	2		Valley Cottage	14 Sep
4:02:08		Manish Singh	Rawat	IND	5.5.91	31	WCp	Taicang	3 May
4:02:09		Ferney	Rojas	COL	30.9.87	3		Valley Cottage	14 Sep
4:02:19		Marc	Mundell	RSA	7.7.83	32	WCp	Taicang	3 May
4:03:04		Sergey	Korepanov	RUS	15.7.84	6	NC	Cheboksary	7 Jun
4:03:17		Oleksandr	Romanenko	UKR	26.6.81	5	NC	Ivano-Frankivsk	19 Oct
4:03:25		Marius	Cocioran	ROU	10.7.83	23	EC	Zürich	15 Aug
4:04:05			Hu Wanli	CHN	27.5.92	1		Taicang	6 May
4:04:08		John	Nunn	USA	3.2.78	4	1 NC	Santee	14 Dec
4:04:26			Luo Yadong	CHN	15.1.92	4		Changbaishan	14 Sep
4:05:14		Luis Fernando (90)	López	COL	3.6.79	33	WCp	Taicang	3 May
4:05:16		Luis Manuel	Corchete	ESP	14.5.84	2		Hayes, GBR	5 Oct
4:05:20		Oleksiy	Bilorus	UKR	11.9.92	6	NC	Ivano-Frankivsk	19 Oct
4:05:30		Clemente	García	MEX	21.8.89	7	Rus C	Cheboksary	7 Jun
4:05:39		Ivan	Trotskiy	BLR	27.5.76	1	NC	Brest	25 Jun
4:05:41			Pei Lianyou	CHN	27.1.90	2		Taicang	6 May
4:06:04A		Jorge	Martínez	MEX	25.10.90	4	NC	Xalapa	31 Aug
4:06:10		Takafumi	Higuma	JPN	3.9.82	5	NC	Wajima	20 Apr
4:06:11		Martin	Tistan	SVK	12.11.92	24	EC	Zürich	15 Aug
4:06:16		Pavel	Schrom	CZE	17.3.91	11	2 NC	Dudince	22 Mar
4:06:22		Aleksey	Arkhipov (100)	RUS	7.12.88	8	NC	Cheboksary	7 Jun

Mark	Name		Nat	Born	Date
4:06:31	Anders	Hansson	SWE	10.3.92	4 Oct
4:06:40		Liu Rusi	CHN	6.8.91	28 Feb
4:06:53	Hideto	Goto	JPN	26.2.94	26 Oct
4:07:06	Basant Bahadur Rana		IND	18.1.84	1 Oct
4:07:08	Maryan	Zakalnytskyy	UKR	19.8.94	19 Oct
4:07:10		Jiang Je	CHN	25.10.94	3 May
4:07:26		Yin Jiaxing	CHN	16.3.94	22 Mar
4:08:00		Han Jijiang	CHN	20.7.93	6 May
4:08:21	Volodymyr	Hontsovskyy	UKR	23.8.91	19 Oct
4:09:17	Surender	Singh	IND	4.7.88	3 May
4:09:18	Xavier	Moreno	ECU	15.11.79	22 Mar
4:09:30	Ricardas	Rekst	LTU	10.10.87	22 Mar
4:09:39	(113)	Guo Xiaoxin	CHN	18.1.86	14 Sep

Drugs disqualification

Mark			Name		Nat	Born	Pos	Meet	Venue	Date
3:43:52	2:13:22	2:35:31	Yuriy	Andronov ¶	RUS	6.11.71	(4)	WCp	Taicang	3 May

WOMEN'S WORLD LISTS 2014

60 METRES INDOORS

Mark	Wind	Name		Nat	Born	Pos	Meet	Venue	Date
6.98		Shelly-Ann	Fraser-Pryce	JAM	27.12.86	1	WI	Sopot	9 Mar
7.01		Murielle	Ahouré	CIV	23.8.87	2	WI	Sopot	9 Mar
7.03			Ahouré			1		Houston	1 Feb
7.05			Ahouré			1		Houston	17 Jan
7.06			Ahouré			1s1	WI	Sopot	9 Mar
7.06		Tianna	Bartoletta	USA	30.8.85	3	WI	Sopot	9 Mar
7.08A			Bartoletta			1	NC	Albuquerque	23 Feb
7.08			Fraser-Pryce			1s3	WI	Sopot	9 Mar
7.09		Asha	Philip	GBR	25.10.90	1	NC	Sheffield	8 Feb
7.09A		LaKeisha	Lawson	USA	3.6.87	2	NC	Albuquerque	23 Feb
7.09			Ahouré			1h6	WI	Sopot	8 Mar
7.09			Philip			2s3	WI	Sopot	9 Mar
		(12/5)							
7.10A		Barbara	Pierre	USA	28.4.87	3	NC	Albuquerque	23 Feb
7.10		Michelle-Lee	Ahye	TTO	10.4.92	3s3	WI	Sopot	9 Mar
7.11A		Kya	Brookins	USA	28.7.89	4	NC	Albuquerque	23 Feb
7.11		Gloria	Asumnu	NGR	22.5.85	2s1	WI	Sopot	9 Mar
7.11A		Remona	Burchell	JAM	15.9.91	1	NCAA	Albuquerque	15 Mar
		(10)							
7.12		Verena	Sailer	GER	16.10.85	1	ISTAF	Berlin	1 Mar
7.12A		Dezerea	Bryant	USA	27.4.93	2	NCAA	Albuquerque	15 Mar
7.13		Veronica	Campbell-Brown	JAM	15.5.82	5	WI	Sopot	9 Mar
7.14		Tori	Bowie	USA	27.8.90	2	Mill	New York (Arm)	15 Feb
7.16A		Chauntae	Bayne	USA	4.4.84	5	NC	Albuquerque	23 Feb
7.16A		Jasmine	Todd	USA	23.12.93	3	NCAA	Albuquerque	15 Mar
7.17		Dafne	Schippers	NED	15.6.92	4	GP	Birmingham	15 Feb
7.17		Ruddy	Zang Milama #	GAB	6.6.87	1		Praha (O2)	25 Feb
7.17		Tahesia	Harrigan-Scott	IVB	15.2.82	2	ISTAF	Berlin	1 Mar
7.18		Ezinne	Okparaebo	NOR	3.3.88	3		Karlsruhe	1 Feb
		(20)							
7.18A		Shayla	Sanders	USA	6.1.94	2h1	NCAA	Albuquerque	14 Mar
7.19		Franciela	Krasucki	BRA	26.4.88	1r2		São Caetano do Sul	16 Feb
7.21A		Kenyanna	Wilson	USA	27.10.88	2h2	NC	Albuquerque	22 Feb
7.22		Muna	Lee	USA	30.10.81	4		Houston	1 Feb
7.22		Dina	Asher-Smith	GBR-J	4.12.95	1s2	NC	Sheffield	8 Feb
7.22		Bianca	Knight	USA	2.1.89	2		Boston (R)	8 Feb
7.22		Sophie	Papps	GBR	6.10.94	2h2	GP	Birmingham	15 Feb
7.22		Aleen	Bailey	JAM	25.11.80	2		Praha (O2)	25 Feb
7.22		Desiree	Henry	GBR-J	26.8.95	3		Praha (O2)	25 Feb
7.23A		Morolake	Akinosun	USA	17.5.94	1		Albuquerque	8 Feb
		(30)							
7.23		Flings	Owusu-Agyapong	GHA	16.10.88	1		Toronto	15 Feb
7.23		Khamica	Bingham	CAN	15.6.94	1		Toronto	22 Feb
7.24		Jenna	Prandini	USA	20.11.92	2		Seattle	18 Jan
7.24		Nataliya	Pogrebnyak	UKR	19.2.88	1		Mondeville	1 Feb
7.24		Takeia	Pinckney	USA	24.7.91	5		Houston	1 Feb
7.25		Samantha	Henry-Robinson	JAM	25.9.88	6		Houston	1 Feb
7.25		Jessica	Young	USA	6.4.87	3		Boston (R)	8 Feb
7.25		Olivia	Ekponé	USA	5.1.93	1h4	SEC	College Station	28 Feb
7.25		Jennifer	Madu	USA	23.9.94	2h5	SEC	College Station	28 Feb
7.25		Sheniqua	Ferguson	BAH	24.11.89	5s1	WI	Sopot	9 Mar
		(40)							
7.25A		Katie	Wise	USA	15.10.93	5h1	NCAA	Albuquerque	14 Mar
7.26		Mahagony	Jones	USA	20.12.90	2		University Park	31 Jan
7.26		Tawanna	Meadows	USA	4.8.86	1		Houston	14 Feb
7.26		Yasmin	Kwadwo	GER	9.11.90	1h3	NC	Leipzig	22 Feb
7.26A		Shalonda	Solomon	USA	19.12.85	5s2	NC	Albuquerque	23 Feb
7.26		Mikiah	Brisco	USA-J	14.7.96	1		New York	16 Mar
7.26			Wei Yongli	CHN	11.10.91	1	NGP	Beijing	21 Mar
7.27		Jeneba	Tarmoh	USA	27.9.89	6	Mill	New York (Arm)	15 Feb
7.27A		Shayla	Mahan	USA	18.1.89	4s1	NC	Albuquerque	23 Feb
7.28		Tatjana	Pinto	GER	2.7.92	1		Dortmund	18 Jan
		(50)							
7.28		Carina	Horn	RSA	9.3.89	1		Wien	28 Jan
7.28		Sharika	Nelvis	USA	10.5.90	1		Birmingham	25 Feb
7.28		Stephanie	Kalu	NGR	5.8.93	1h1		New York (Arm)	1 Mar
7.29		Kimberley	Hyacinthe	CAN	28.3.89	1		Montréal	24 Jan

Mark	Wind	Name		Nat	Born	Pos	Meet	Venue	Date
7.29		Nadine	Hildebrand	GER	20.9.87	1		Karlsruhe	25 Jan
7.29		Ashlee	Abraham	USA	24.9.91	1		New York (Arm)	7 Feb
7.29		Montell	Douglas	GBR	24.1.86	1s3	NC	Sheffield	8 Feb
7.29		María	Gátou (58)	GRE	16.8.89	1h1	NC	Pireás	8 Feb

Hand timed: 6.9 Nataliya Pogrebnyak UKR 19.2.88 1 Kharkiv 24 Dec

Best at low altitude

Mark	Name	Pos	Meet	Venue	Date
7.16	Bryant	1		Fayetteville	14 Feb
7.18	Bayne	2		Karlsruhe	1 Feb
7.19	Lawson	1h5	WI	Sopot	8 Mar
7.20	Todd	1		Seattle	18 Jan
7.24	Sanders	1h5	SEC	College Station	28 Feb
7.24	Burchell	2	SEC	College Station	1 Mar
7.25	Brookins	1		Birmingham AL	18 Jan
7.25	Akinosun	2		Fayetteville	14 Feb
7.26	Pierre	6h1	GP	Birmingham	15 Feb

Outdoors

Mark	Wind	Name		Nat	Born	Pos	Meet	Venue	Date
7.11	0.4	Shelly-Ann	Fraser-Pryce	JAM	27.12.86	1		Kingston	25 Jan
7.26		Ruddy	Zang Milama #	GAB	6.6.87	1		Eaubonne	11 Feb
7.28	0.4	Carrie	Russell	JAM	18.10.90	2		Kingston	25 Jan

100 METRES

Mark	Wind	Name		Nat	Born	Pos	Meet	Venue	Date
10.80	0.8	Tori	Bowie	USA	27.8.90	1	Herc	Monaco	18 Jul
10.85	1.6	Michelle-Lee	Ahye	TTO	10.4.92	1s2	NC	Port of Spain	21 Jun
10.85	0.3	Blessing	Okagbare	NGR	9.10.88	1	CG	Glasgow	28 Jul
10.86	2.0	Veronica	Campbell-Brown	JAM	15.5.82	1h1		Montverde	7 Jun
10.88	1.2		Ahye			1	NC	Port of Spain	21 Jun
10.91	2.0		Bowie			1s2	NC	Sacramento	27 Jun
10.92	2.0	Tianna	Bartoletta	USA	30.8.85	1s1	NC	Sacramento	27 Jun
10.93	-0.7		Okagbare			1s3	CG	Glasgow	28 Jul
10.96	-0.4		Campbell-Brown			1	NC	Kingston	27 Jun
10.96	0.8		Campbell-Brown			2	Herc	Monaco	18 Jul
10.97	1.1		Campbell-Brown			1h1	NC	Kingston	27 Jun
10.97	0.8	Murielle	Ahouré	CIV	23.8.87	3	Herc	Monaco	18 Jul
10.97	0.8		Okagbare			4	Herc	Monaco	18 Jul
10.98	-0.3		Ahye			1	Athl	Lausanne	3 Jul
10.98	-0.3		Ahouré			2	Athl	Lausanne	3 Jul
11.00	1.5	Samantha	Henry-Robinson	JAM	25.9.88	1h4		Clermont	26 Apr
11.00	-1.4		Okagbare			1	AfCh	Marrakech	11 Aug
11.01	1.2		Henry-Robinson			1		Clermont	31 May
11.01	2.0	English	Gardner	USA	22.4.92	2s1	NC	Sacramento	27 Jun
11.01	0.3		Ahye			1	DL	Glasgow	12 Jul
11.01	0.8	Allyson	Felix	USA	18.11.85	5	Herc	Monaco	18 Jul
11.01	0.8	Shelly-Ann	Fraser-Pryce (10)	JAM	27.12.86	6	Herc	Monaco	18 Jul
11.02	-0.4	Kerron	Stewart	JAM	16.4.84	2	NC	Kingston	27 Jun
11.02	2.0	Joanna	Atkins	USA	31.1.89	3s1	NC	Sacramento	27 Jun
11.02	0.5		Campbell-Brown			1s2	CG	Glasgow	28 Jul
11.03	1.7	Remona	Burchell	JAM	15.9.91	1q2	NCAA-E	Jacksonville	30 May
11.03	0.9	Dafne	Schippers	NED	15.6.92	1rB	DL	Glasgow	12 Jul
11.03	0.8	Myriam	Soumaré	FRA	29.10.86	7	Herc	Monaco	18 Jul
11.03	0.3		Campbell-Brown			2	CG	Glasgow	28 Jul
11.03	-1.4		Ahouré			2	AfCh	Marrakech	11 Aug
11.03	-0.4		Soumaré			1h4	EC	Zürich	12 Aug
		(31/15)							
11.04	0.6	Morolake	Akinosun	USA	17.5.94	1s2	NCAA	Eugene	11 Jun
11.05	2.0	Barbara	Pierre	USA	28.4.87	2s2	NC	Sacramento	27 Jun
11.06	1.1	Natasha	Morrison	JAM	17.11.92	2h1	NC	Kingston	27 Jun
11.07	2.0	LaKeisha	Lawson	USA	3.6.87	3s2	NC	Sacramento	27 Jun
11.08	1.1	Schillonie	Calvert	JAM	27.7.88	3h1	NC	Kingston	27 Jun
		(20)							
11.09	1.3	Simone	Facey	JAM	7.5.85	1		Clermont	10 May
11.10	1.1	Ivet	Lalova	BUL	18.5.84	1		Gavardo	18 May
11.10	0.9	Kaylin	Whitney	USA-Y	9.3.98	1	NC-j	Eugene	5 Jul
11.10	0.5	Carrie	Russell	JAM	18.10.90	1	WCM	Rieti	7 Sep
11.11	1.9	Melissa	Breen	AUS	17.9.90	1h1		Canberra	9 Feb
11.11	0.8	Jenna	Prandini	USA	20.11.92	1	MSR	Walnut	19 Apr
11.11	1.0	Tawanna	Meadows	USA	4.8.86	1		San Marcos	26 Apr
11.11	1.3	Olivia	Ekponé	USA	5.1.93	1	SEC	Lexington	18 May
11.11	1.2	Alex	Anderson	USA	28.1.87	2		Clermont	31 May
11.11	-1.0	Jeneba	Tarmoh	USA	27.9.89	1		Edmonton	6 Jul
		(30)							
11.12	1.0	Jamile	Samuel	NED	24.4.92	1		Genève	14 Jun
11.12	2.0	Shalonda	Solomon	USA	19.12.85	4s2	NC	Sacramento	27 Jun
11.13	0.0	Ana Cláudia	Silva	BRA	6.11.88	1	IbAmC	São Paulo	1 Aug
11.13	0.5	Jessica	Young	USA	6.4.87	2	WCM	Rieti	7 Sep

Mark	Wind	Name		Nat	Born	Pos	Meet	Venue	Date
11.14	1.5	Dina	Asher-Smith	GBR-J	4.12.95	1h1		Mannheim	5 Jul
11.14	1.7	Verena	Sailer	GER	16.10.85	1		Mannheim	5 Jul
11.15	0.0	Gloria	Asumnu	NGR	22.5.85	1h3	NC	Calabar	19 Jun
11.16	1.2	Aleen	Bailey	JAM	25.11.80	3		Clermont	31 May
11.17	1.1	Elaine	Thompson	JAM	28.6.92	1		Kingston	31 May
11.17	1.0	Carina	Horn	RSA	9.3.89	1h1		St. Pölten	14 Jun
		(40)							
11.17	1.0	Bianca	Williams	GBR	18.12.93	2=		Genève	14 Jun
11.18	0.3	Asha	Philip	GBR	25.10.90	4	CG	Glasgow	28 Jul
11.19	-0.6	Christania	Williams	JAM	17.10.94	1	N.Sch	Kingston	28 Mar
11.19	0.8	Ashleigh	Nelson	GBR	20.2.91	2h5	EC	Zürich	12 Aug
11.20	1.9	Shayla	Sanders	USA	6.1.94	1h1	TexR	Austin	28 Mar
11.20	0.8	Kimberlyn	Duncan	USA	2.8.91	1		Baton Rouge	19 Apr
11.20	1.3	Jodie	Williams	GBR	28.9.93	3		Gainesville	19 Apr
11.20	1.3	Cierra	White	USA	29.4.93	1h1	Big 12	Lubbock	17 May
11.20	2.0	Bianca	Knight	USA	2.1.89	5s2	NC	Sacramento	27 Jun
11.20	0.0	Tatjana	Pinto	GER	2.7.92	1	NC	Ulm	26 Jul
		(50)							
11.20	-1.4	Marie Josée	Lou Gonerie	CIV	18.11.88	3	AfCh	Marrakech	11 Aug
11.20	0.0	Mujinga	Kambundji	SUI	17.6.92	2s3	EC	Zürich	13 Aug
11.21	-0.4	Desiree	Henry	GBR-J	26.8.95	2h2	EC	Zürich	12 Aug
11.22	0.6	Ariana	Washington	USA-J	4.9.96	1		Clovis	7 Jun
11.22	1.0	Nataliya	Pogrebnyak	UKR	19.2.88	2h1		St. Pölten	14 Jun
11.22	0.0	Ayodelé	Ikuesan	FRA	15.5.85	3s3	EC	Zürich	13 Aug
11.23	1.7	Katie	Wise	USA	15.10.93	1		Carbondale	18 May
11.23	0.1	Trisha-Ann	Hawthorne	JAM	8.11.89	3	WCM	Beijing	21 May
11.23	0.6	Jennifer	Madu	USA	23.9.94	3s3	NCAA	Eugene	11 Jun
11.23	1.3	Olga	Safronova	KAZ	5.11.91	1h1	Kozanov	Almaty	14 Jun
		(60)							
11.24	-1.1	Franciela	Krasucki	BRA	26.4.88	1		São Paulo	5 Apr
11.24	1.3	Dezerea	Bryant	USA	27.4.93	3	SEC	Lexington	18 May
11.24	1.4	Hrystyna	Stuy	UKR	3.2.88	1		Izmir	3 Jun
11.24	1.5	Céline	Distel-Bonnet	FRA	25.7.87	2h1	NC	Reims	12 Jul
11.24	1.1	Stella	Akakpo	FRA	28.2.94	1h2	NC	Reims	12 Jul
11.24	-0.4	Ezinne	Okparaebo	NOR	3.3.88	2h4	EC	Zürich	12 Aug
11.24	0.0	Carmelita	Jeter	USA	24.11.79	2h1	DL	Birmingham	24 Aug
11.25	0.0	Jasmine	Todd	USA	23.12.93	1rB	MSR	Walnut	19 Apr
11.25A	0.3	Ángela	Tenorio	ECU-J	27.1.96	1		Medellín	31 May
11.26	1.2	Candyce	McGrone	USA	24.3.89	3	FlaR	Gainesville	4 Apr
		(70)							
11.26	0.3	Muna	Lee	USA	30.10.81	1r2		Kuortane	13 Jul
11.27	1.8	Sally	Pearson	AUS	19.9.86	2		Canberra	9 Feb
11.27	1.5	Sharika	Nelvis	USA	10.5.90	1		Jonesboro	26 Apr
11.28	1.5	Ruddy	Zang Milama #	GAB	6.6.87	1h5		Greensboro	11 May
11.28	1.0	Jura	Levy	JAM	4.11.90	1	NAIA	Gulf Shores	24 May
11.28	1.8	Margaret	Adeoye	GBR	27.4.85	1h2		Genève	14 Jun
11.29	1.3	Tahesia	Harrigan-Scott	IVB	15.2.82	4		Gainesville	19 Apr
11.29	0.9	Tristie	Johnson	USA	20.11.93	1	MEAC	Greensboro	3 May
11.29	2.0	Kai	Selvon	TTO	13.4.92	1		Tallahassee	9 May
11.29	1.4	Mikele	Barber	USA	4.10.80	1		Los Angeles (Ww)	7 Jun
		(80)							
11.29	0.6	Mahagony	Jones	USA	20.12.90	2s2	NCAA	Eugene	11 Jun
11.29	2.0	Kenyanna	Wilson	USA	27.10.88	7s1	NC	Sacramento	27 Jun
11.29A	1.5	Andrea	Purica	VEN-J	21.11.95	1	CAG	Xalapa	25 Nov
11.30	0.0	Jessica	Davis	USA	31.10.92	2rB	MSR	Walnut	19 Apr
11.30	0.2	Hanna-Maari	Latvala	FIN	30.10.87	3h3	EC	Zürich	12 Aug
11.30	0.0	Ewa	Swoboda	POL-Y	26.7.97	1h3	Yth OG	Nanjing	21 Aug
11.30 (i)	-0.5	Tiffany	Townsend	USA	14.6.89	2	Skol	Warszawa	23 Aug
11.30	0.3	Chisato	Fukushima	JPN	27.6.88	1h1		Isahaya	20 Oct
11.31	0.9	Sheniqua	Ferguson	BAH	24.11.89	1		Auburn AL	5 Apr
11.31	0.8	Aaliyah	Brown	USA-J	6.1.95	2		Baton Rouge	19 Apr
		(90)							
11.31	0.7	Andreea	Ogrâzeanu	ROU	24.3.90	2		Weinheim	31 May
11.31	1.7	Teahna	Daniels	USA-Y	25.3.97	2	adidas	New York	14 Jun
11.31	1.0	Kristina	Sivkova	RUS-Y	28.2.97	1	NC	Kazan	24 Jul
11.32	-0.6	Jonielle	Smith	JAM-J	30.1.96	2	N.Sch	Kingston	28 Mar
11.32	0.0	Chelsea	Hayes	USA	9.2.88	3rB	MSR	Walnut	19 Apr
11.32	1.3	Tiffani	McReynolds	USA	4.12.91	2h1	Big 12	Lubbock	17 May
11.32	1.3	Keilah	Tyson	USA	6.11.92	4	SEC	Lexington	18 May
11.32	1.0	Rebekka	Haase	GER	2.1.93	1h2	NC	Ulm	26 Jul
11.32	0.5	Khamica	Bingham	CAN	15.6.94	3s2	CG	Glasgow	28 Jul

Mark	Wind	Name		Nat	Born	Pos	Meet	Venue	Date
11.32	-0.5	Rosângela	Santos (100)	BRA	20.12.90	1		São Bernardo do Campo	23 Aug

Mark	Wind	Name		Nat	Born	Date
11.33A	1.8	Shavine	Hodges	JAM	22.10.91	17 May
11.33	1.6	Reyare	Thomas	TTO	23.11.87	21 Jun
11.33	0.0	Anthonique	Strachan	BAH	22.8.93	27 Jun
11.33	-0.5	Anneisha	McLaughlin	JAM	6.1.86	27 Jun
11.33	1.7	Josefina	Elsler	GER	7.6.91	5 Jul
11.34	1.1	Krystal	Sparling	USA-Y	.97	24 Apr
11.34	1.0	Ashley	Spencer	USA	8.6.93	17 May
11.34	-0.5	Sherone	Simpson	JAM	12.8.84	27 Jun
11.34	2.0	Léa	Sprunger	SUI	5.3.90	12 Jul
11.35	1.5	Jada	Martin	USA-J	8.6.95	5 Apr
11.35	0.8	Natasha	Hastings	USA	23.7.86	19 Apr
11.35	0.7	Ashton	Purvis	USA	12.7.92	29 May
11.35	-0.1	Octavious	Freeman	USA	20.4.92	14 Jun
11.35	1.3	Ksenija	Balta	EST	11.1.86	15 Jun
11.35	0.8	Inna	Eftimova	BUL	19.6.88	28 Jun
11.36	1.3	Sheri-Ann	Brooks	JAM	11.2.83	10 May
11.36	1.0	Janet	Amponsah	GHA	12.4.93	17 May
11.36	0.4	Ashley	Marshall	USA	10.9.93	17 May
11.37	1.7	Jade	Bailey	BAR	10.6.83	2 May
11.37	0.6	Chesna	Sykes	USA	28.8.92	11 Jun
11.37	1.6	Kamara	Durant	TTO	24.2.91	21 Jun
11.37	1.7	Montell	Douglas	GBR	24.1.86	20 Jul
11.38	1.5	Ashlee	Abraham	USA	24.9.91	5 Apr
11.38	1.7	Kiara	Porter	USA	22.10.93	12 Apr
11.38	1.4	Briana	Vaughn	USA	28.4.94	17 Apr
11.38	0.6	Anna	Yegorova	RUS	25.2.87	27 Apr
11.38	2.0	Marecia	Pemberton	SKN	7.1.90	9 May
11.39	0.1	LaShauntea	Moore	USA	31.7.83	19 Apr
11.39	1.7	Inna	Weit	GER	5.8.88	10 May
11.39	-1.0	Viktoriya	Yarushkina	RUS	4.4.91	29 May
11.39	0.0	Celiangeli	Morales	PUR	2.11.85	6 Jun
11.39	1.4	Sharadha	Narayanan	IND	22.8.86	8 Jun
11.39	-1.1	Fanny	Appes Ekanga	CMR	9.6.89	21 Jul
11.40	-0.8	Shaunae	Miller	BAH	15.4.94	12 Apr
11.40	1.0		Wei Yongli	CHN	11.10.91	19 Apr
11.40	0.9	Nakia	Linson	USA	2.8.92	3 May
11.40	1.7	Amy	Foster	IRL	2.10.88	10 May
11.40	1.0	Tianna	Valentine	USA	15.5.94	17 May
11.40	1.8	Jennifer	Galais	FRA	7.3.92	25 May
11.40	1.4	Destiny	Smith-Barnett	USA-J	26.7.96	6 Jun
11.40	0.0	Eliecit	Palacios	COL	15.8.87	1 Aug
11.41	0.5	Tynia	Gaither	BAH	16.3.93	4 Apr
11.41	0.4	Kimberly	Hyacinthe	CAN	28.3.89	26 Apr
11.41	1.0	Diamond	Gause	USA	4.4.94	17 May
11.41	0.9	Zakiya	Denoon	TTO-J	23.1.95	31 May
11.41	1.2	Natalya	Shishkova	RUS	28.8.90	9 Jul
11.41	0.7	Yeoryía	Koklóni	GRE	7.5.81	19 Jul
11.41	1.1	Nataliya	Strohova	UKR	26.12.92	24 Aug
11.42	0.7	Takeia	Pinckney	USA	24.7.91	28 Mar
11.42	0.5	Olga	Lenskiy #	ISR	24.12.92	19 Apr
11.42	1.1	Audrey	Alloh	ITA	21.7.87	18 May
11.42	0.7	Véronique	Mang	FRA	15.12.84	5 Jul
11.42	2.0	Joëlle	Golay	SUI	15.10.87	12 Jul
11.42	0.0	Olesya	Povh	UKR	18.10.87	13 Aug
11.43	0.2	Katharina	Grompe	GER	1.9.93	7 Jun
11.43	0.9	Ky	Westbrook	USA-J	25.2.96	5 Jul
11.43	0.9	Irene	Siragusa	ITA	23.6.93	19 Jul
11.43	0.1	Crystal	Emmanuel	CAN	27.11.91	28 Jul
11.43	-0.5	Evelyn	dos Santos	BRA	11.4.85	23 Aug
11.43A	1.5	Nediam	Vargas	VEN	5.9.94	25 Nov
11.44	1.8	Candace	Hill	USA-Y	11.2.99	3 May
11.44	2.0	Anne	Zagré	BEL	13.3.90	9 May
11.44	1.5	Audrea	Segree	JAM	5.10.90	17 May
11.44	1.7	Alyssa	McClure	USA	21.1.92	30 May
11.44	0.7	Esther	Cremer	GER	29.3.88	31 May
11.44	0.3	Cleo	VanBuren	USA	1.5.86	7 Jun
11.44	0.0	Katerina	Cechová	CZE	21.3.88	9 Jun
11.44	1.2	María	Gátou	GRE	16.8.89	19 Jul
11.44	0.1	Toea	Wisil	PNG	1.1.88	28 Jul
11.45	0.8	Peace	Uko	NGR-J	26.12.95	12 Apr
11.45	-0.9	Alexis	Faulknor	USA	22.9.94	4 May
11.45	1.4	Shai-Anne	Davis	CAN	4.12.93	10 May
11.45	1.6	Maryam	Toosi	IRI	5.12.88	15 May
11.45	1.8	Carima	Louami	FRA	12.5.79	25 May
11.45	1.7	Rachel	Johncock	GBR	4.10.93	31 May
11.45	2.0	Flings	Owusu-Agyapong	GHA	16.10.88	7 Jun
11.45	1.2	Deborah	Odeyemi	NGR-J	21.2.95	19 Jun
11.45	1.3	Ramona-Anna	Papaioannou	CYP	15.6.89	21 Jun
11.45	1.0	Natalya	Rusakova	RUS	12.12.80	24 Jul
11.45	1.0	Viktoriya	Zyabkina	KAZ	4.9.92	22 Aug
11.46	-0.6	Monique	Spencer	JAM	20.10.94	28 Mar
11.46	1.9	Regine	Williams	USA-J	5.9.95	28 Mar
11.46	0.6	MaryBeth	Sant	USA-J	6.4.95	17 May
11.46		Natalya	Rakacheva	RUS	16.4.88	6 Jun
11.46	0.0	Vanusa	dos Santos	BRA	22.1.90	14 Jun
11.46	1.1	Brittany	Brown	USA-J	18.4.95	5 Jul
11.46	1.0	Marina	Panteleyeva	RUS	16.5.89	24 Jul
11.46	2.0	Marta	Jeschke	POL	2.6.86	29 Jul
11.46	1.3	Thaíssa	Presti	BRA	7.11.85	9 Oct
11.47	1.2	Kedisha	Dallas	JAM-J	3.11.95	8 Mar
11.47	1.2	Dianna	Johnson	JAM	12.11.95	8 Mar
11.47	1.7	Cambrya	Jones	USA	20.9.90	12 Apr
11.47	0.9	Loudia	Laarman	CAN	4.10.91	18 Apr
11.47	1.7	Hayley	Jones	GBR	14.9.88	10 May
11.47	2.0	Tyshonda	Hawkins	USA		17 May
11.47	0.6	Gayon	Evans	JAM	15.1.90	11 Jun
11.47	1.2	Aaliyah	Telesford	TTO-J	10.3.95	21 Jun
11.47	2.0	Marisa	Lavanchy	SUI	4.1.90	12 Jul
11.47	-0.6	Kseniya	Karandyuk	UKR	21.6.86	24 Jul

(200) plus 20 at 11.48-11.49

Wind assisted

Mark	Wind	Name		Nat	Born	Pos	Meet	Venue	Date
10.95	2.3	Remona	Burchell	JAM	15.9.91	1s1	NCAA	Eugene	11 Jun
10.96	4.0	Dezerea	Bryant	USA	27.4.93	1		Austin	3 May
10.96	3.8	Morolake	Akinosun	USA	17.5.94	1	Big12	Lubbock	18 May
10.99	4.5	Franciela	Krasucki	BRA	26.4.88	1h1		São Paulo	5 Apr
11.02	3.4	Verena	Sailer	GER	16.10.85	1h1	NC	Ulm	26 Jul
11.03	2.2	Dina	Asher-Smith	GBR-J	4.12.95	1		Mannheim	5 Jul
11.04	3.1	Desiree	Henry	GBR-J	26.8.95	1		Clermont	26 Apr
11.08	4.0	Natasha	Hastings	USA	23.7.86	3		Austin	3 May
11.09	4.8	Janet	Amponsah	GHA	12.4.93	1		Lubbock	3 May
11.09	4.8	Cierra	White	USA	29.4.93	2		Lubbock	3 May
11.11	3.6	Asha	Philip	GBR	25.10.90	1	NC	Birmingham	29 Jun
11.11	2.5	Tatjana	Pinto	GER	2.7.92	1h3	NC	Ulm	26 Jul
11.12	2.6	LaShauntea	Moore	USA	31.7.83	1		Austin	12 Apr
11.12	2.3	Shayla	Sanders	USA	6.1.94	2s1	NCAA	Eugene	11 Jun
11.12	2.8	Ezinne	Okparaebo	NOR	3.3.88	1		Oslo	2 Aug
11.13	3.1	Jodie	Williams	GBR	28.9.93	2		Clermont	26 Apr
11.14	4.0	Keilah	Tyson	USA	6.11.92	4		Austin	3 May
11.15	4.5	Stephanie	Kalu	NGR	5.8.93	1		Fort Worth	21 Mar
11.15	3.6	Ashleigh	Nelson	GBR	20.2.91	2	NC	Birmingham	29 Jun
11.16	3.9	Reyare	Thomas	TTO	23.11.87	1		Abilene	12 Apr
11.16	4.7	Danielle	Williams	JAM	14.9.92	1h3	NCAA-II	Allendale	22 May
11.16	2.1	Ayodelé	Ikuesan	FRA	15.5.85	2	NC	Reims	12 Jul
11.16	2.6	Carina	Horn	RSA	9.3.89	4	WCM	Madrid	19 Jul
11.17	5.1	Jonielle	Smith	JAM-J	30.1.96	1	Carifta	Fort-de-France	19 Apr

Mark	Wind	Name		Nat	Born	Pos	Meet	Venue	Date
11.17	2.9	Tahesia	Harrigan-Scott	IVB	15.2.82	1		Coral Springs	28 Apr
11.17	3.5	Sharika	Nelvis	USA	10.5.90	1		San Marcos	11 May
11.18	2.5	Katie	Wise	USA	15.10.93	1q1	NCAA-E	Jacksonville	30 May
11.18	2.1	Céline	Distel-Bonnet	FRA	25.7.87	3	NC	Reims	12 Jul
11.20	4.0	Chelsea	Hayes	USA	9.2.88	1rC		Fort Worth	21 Mar
11.20	2.7	Aaliyah	Brown	USA-J	6.1.95	3	TexR	Austin	29 Mar
11.20	2.9	Candyce	McGrone	USA	24.3.89	1h2		Montverde	7 Jun
11.21	3.8	Tiffani	McReynolds	USA	4.12.91	3	Big 12	Lubbock	18 May
11.21	2.5	Rebekka	Haase	GER	2.1.93	1h2		Mannheim	5 Jul
11.21	2.1	Stella	Akakpo	FRA	28.2.94	4	NC	Reims	12 Jul
11.22	3.4	Ashley	Marshall	USA	10.9.93	1		Sacramento	2 May
11.23	2.2	Jessica	Davis	USA	31.10.92	1h1	Pac 12	Pullman	17 May
11.23	2.2	Hanna-Maari	Latvala	FIN	30.10.87	1r2		Florø	7 Jun
11.23	2.3	Tynia	Gaither	BAH	16.3.93	3s1	NCAA	Eugene	11 Jun
11.24	2.3	Sally	Pearson	AUS	19.9.86	1h2		Canberra	9 Feb
11.24	3.2	Kenyanna	Wilson	USA	27.10.88	1		Redlands	15 May
11.25	4.0	Porscha	Lucas	USA	18.6.88	2rC		Fort Worth	21 Mar
11.27	2.6	Ashley	Spencer	USA	8.6.93	3		Austin	12 Apr
11.27	3.0	Andreea	Ogrâzeanu	ROU	24.3.90	1h1	NC	Pitesti	19 Jul
11.28	2.9	Tiffany	Townsend	USA	14.6.89	1h3		Clermont	26 Apr
11.28	3.1	Shai-Anne	Davis	CAN	4.12.93	4		Clermont	26 Apr

Mark	Wind	Name		Nat	Born	Date
11.29	2.2	Regine	Williams	USA-J	5.9.95	12 Apr
11.29	4.6	Audrey	Alloh	ITA	21.7.87	25 May
11.30	2.4	Ashlee	Abraham	USA	24.9.91	30 May
11.30	2.3	Ashton	Purvis	USA	12.7.92	11 Jun
11.30	3.5	Katarina	Johnson-Thompson	GBR	9.1.93	21 Jun
11.31	4.0	Laverne	Jones-Ferrette	ISV	16.9.81	3 May
11.31	3.8	Tianna	Valentine	USA	15.5.94	18 May
11.33	3.4	Evelyn	dos Santos	BRA	11.4.85	29 Mar
11.33	3.1	Kimberly	Hyacinthe	CAN	28.3.89	26 Apr
11.33	2.8	Kendall	Baisden	USA-J	5.3.95	3 May
11.33	2.6	Montell	Douglas	GBR	24.1.86	5 Jul
11.34	4.3	V'Alonee	Robinson	BAH	6.5.92	19 Apr
11.34	2.1	Cambrya	Jones	USA	20.9.90	19 Apr
11.34	3.0	Ada	Udaya	LBR	28.6.92	10 May
11.34	2.7	Candace	Hill	USA-Y	11.2.99	14 Jun
11.34	2.7	Brenessa	Thompson	GUY-J	22.7.96	14 Jun
11.34	2.7	Gina	Lückenkemper	GER-J	21.11.96	5 Jul
11.35	3.0	Cleo	VanBuren	USA	1.5.86	8 Jul
11.36	2.1	Sherry	Fletcher	GRN	17.1.86	19 Apr
11.36	3.9	Antoinette	Goodman	USA	29.7.90	3 May
11.36	3.2	Janae	Johnson	USA	.82	22 May
11.36	4.6	Irene	Siragusa	ITA	23.6.93	25 May
11.36	3.0	Phil	Healy	IRL	19.11.94	8 Jul
11.37		Kortnei	Johnson	USA-Y	.97	25 Apr
11.37	3.5	Carrol	Hardy	USA-J		10 May
11.37	3.5	Marika	Brown	USA-J	18.7.95	11 May
11.37A	2.1	Eliecít	Palacios	COL	15.8.87	27 Jun
11.38	2.8	Alexis	Faulknor	USA	22.9.94	4 Apr
11.38	2.3	Amy	Foster	IRL	2.10.88	26 Apr
11.38	3.8	Ashley	Fields	USA	13.4.93	18 May
11.38	3.5	Annie	Tagoe	GBR	4.6.93	21 Jun
11.39	3.4	Karene	King	IVB	24.10.87	29 Mar
11.39	4.3	Destiny	Carter	USA		17 Apr
11.39	2.3	Hayley	Jones	GBR	14.9.88	26 Apr
11.40	2.4	Hannah	Cunliffe	USA-J	9.1.96	29 Mar
11.40	4.7	Yanique	Ellington	JAM	3.9.92	22 May
11.40	2.8	Yasmin	Kwadwo	GER	9.11.90	7 Jun
11.40	2.6	Olesya	Povh	UKR	18.10.87	19 Jul
11.41	2.4	Aline	Torres	BRA	12.5.82	8 Mar
11.41A	2.1	Narcisa	Landázuri	ECU	14.7.93	27 Jun
11.42	2.5	Tayla	Carter	BAH	29.1.94	4 Apr
11.42	3.3	Kimonme	Shaw	JAM-Y	28.9.99	19 Apr
11.42	5.1	Aaliyah	Telesford	TTO-J	10.3.95	19 Apr
11.42A	2.1	María Alejandra	Idrobo	COL	8.4.88	27 Jun
11.42	2.1	Sarah	Goujon	FRA	11.9.90	12 Jul

(191 legal and windy to 11.42)

Best at low altitude

11.27	1.2	Tenorio	1h8	WJ	Eugene	22 Jul
11.48	1.6	Tavares				30 Jul
11.40w	0.0	Palacios				1 Aug

Hand timing

11.0		Olesya	Povh	UKR	18.10.87	1		Kharkiv	27 May
11.0	2.4	Arialis	Gandulla	CUB-J	22.6.95	1	Barr	La Habana	23 May
11.1	1.2	Agnes	Osazuwa	NGR	21.6.90	1		Kaduna	31 Oct

Drugs disqualification

11.24		Ruddy	Zang Milama #	GAB	6.6.87	(1rB)		Clermont	31 May

JUNIORS

See main list for top 11 juniors (& 4 wa). 12 performances by 4 women to 11.23. Additional marks and further juniors:

Whitney	11.17	0.8	1h1	NC-j	Eugene	5 Jul							
Asher-Smith	11.18	0.3	1h5	WJ	Eugene	22 Jul	11.21	1.5	1s1	NC-j	Bedford	21 Jun
	11.20	0.7	1	LI	Loughborough	18 May	11.23	-1.0	1	WJ	Eugene	23 Jul
	11.21	1.6	1r2	BIG	Bedford	31 May						
Henry	11.21	0.6	2s2	EC	Zürich	13 Aug	11.23	1.2	2	F!aR	Gainesville	4 Apr

11.34	1.1	Krystal	Sparling	USA-Y	.97	1		Miramar	24 Apr
11.35	1.5	Jada	Martin	USA	8.6.95	1		Baton Rouge	5 Apr
11.40	1.4	Destiny	Smith-Barnett	USA	26.7.96	1h3		Clovis	6 Jun
11.41	0.9	Zakiya	Denoon	TTO	23.1.95	1	NC-j	Port of Spain	31 May
11.43	0.9	Ky	Westbrook	USA	25.2.96	5	Jul		
11.44	1.8	Candace	Hill	USA-Y	11.2.99	1		Albany	3 May
11.45	0.8	Peace	Uko	NGR	26.12.95	1		Abuja	12 Apr
11.45	1.2	Deborah	Odeyemi	NGR	21.2.95	2h2	NC	Calabar	19 Jun
11.46	1.9	Regine	Williams (20)	USA	5.9.95	4h1	TexR	Austin	28 Mar
11.46	0.6	MaryBeth	Sant	USA	6.4.95	3h3	Pac 12	Pullman	17 May
11.46	1.1	Brittany	Brown	USA	18.4.95	4h2	NC-j	Eugene	5 Jul

Wind assisted: 5 performances by 4 women to 11.20w. To 11.36w.

Asher-Smith	11.11w	3.0	1	NC-j	Bedford	21 Jun	11.17w	3.5	1h3	NC-j	Bedford	21 Jun

11.29	2.2	Regine	Williams	USA	5.9.95	1		Fayetteville	12 Apr
11.33	2.8	Kendall	Baisden	USA	5.3.95	1rB		Austin	3 May

Mark	Wind	Name		Nat	Born	Pos	Meet	Venue	Date
11.34	2.7	Candace	Hill	USA-Y	11.2.99	1	J.Nat	Greensboro	14 Jun
11.34	2.7	Brenessa	Thompson	GUY	22.7.96	2	J.Nat	Greensboro	14 Jun
11.34	2.7	Gina	Lückenkemper	GER	21.11.96	1h2		Mannheim	5 Jul
11.37		Kortnei	Johnson	USA-Y	.97	1h2		Abilene	25 Apr
11.37	3.5	Carrol	Hardy	USA		1h3		San Marcos	10 May
11.37	3.5	Marika	Brown	USA	18.7.95	2		San Marcos	11 May

150 METRES STRAIGHT

6 Sep Gateshead: (-0.9) 1. Asha Philip GBR 16.69, 2. Jodie Williams GBR 16.84; 3. Allyson Felix USA 16.92

200 METRES

Mark	Wind	Name		Nat	Born	Pos	Meet	Venue	Date
22.02	0.1	Allyson	Felix	USA	18.11.85	1	VD	Bruxelles	5 Sep
22.03	-0.5	Dafne	Schippers	NED	15.6.92	1	EC	Zürich	15 Aug
22.11	0.1	Myriam	Soumaré	FRA	29.10.86	2	VD	Bruxelles	5 Sep
22.18	1.5	Tori	Bowie	USA	27.8.90	1	Pre	Eugene	31 May
22.23	-0.8	Olivia	Ekponé	USA	5.1.93	1	SEC	Lexington	18 May
22.23	1.5	Blessing	Okagbare	NGR	9.10.88	2	Pre	Eugene	31 May
22.25	0.4		Okagbare			1	CG	Glasgow	31 Jul
22.27	1.3	Joanna	Atkins	USA	31.1.89	1	FlaR	Gainesville	4 Apr
22.28	0.3		Schippers			1	C.Cup	Marrakech	14 Sep
22.30	0.3		Schippers			1	C.Cup	Marrakech	14 Sep
22.32	0.4		Okagbare			1	DL	Saint-Denis	5 Jul
22.34	0.4		Felix			2	DL	Saint-Denis	5 Jul
22.34	0.2		Schippers			1	DL	Glasgow	12 Jul
22.35	1.5		Schippers			1H		Götzis	31 May
22.35	0.2		Felix			2	DL	Glasgow	12 Jul
22.36	0.0		Okagbare			1	DL	Shanghai	18 May
22.36	-0.1	Murielle	Ahouré	CIV	23.8.87	1	AfCh	Marrakech	14 Aug
22.41	1.9	Jeneba	Tarmoh	USA	27.9.89	1h2	NC	Sacramento	29 Jun
22.41	0.2		Okagbare			3	DL	Glasgow	12 Jul
22.43	-1.1		Okagbare			1s1	CG	Glasgow	31 Jul
22.44	1.5		Felix			3	Pre	Eugene	31 May
22.46	-0.5	Jodie	Williams (10)	GBR	28.9.93	2	EC	Zürich	15 Aug
22.48	-0.6		Schippers			1s2	EC	Zürich	14 Aug
22.49	1.3	Kaylin	Whitney	USA-Y	9.3.98	1	NC-j	Eugene	6 Jul
22.50	0.0	Anthonique	Strachan	BAH	22.8.93	2	DL	Shanghai	18 May
22.50	0.4		J Williams			2	CG	Glasgow	31 Jul
22.53	1.3	Kimberlyn	Duncan	USA	2.8.91	1		Coral Gables	12 Apr
22.53	0.2	Shelly-Ann	Fraser-Pryce	JAM	27.12.86	1		Kingston	3 May
22.53	0.3		Atkins			2	C.Cup	Marrakech	14 Sep
22.54	0.4		Strachan			3	DL	Saint-Denis	5 Jul
		(30/14)							
22.58	0.4	Bianca	Williams	GBR	18.12.93	3	CG	Glasgow	31 Jul
22.60	-1.6	Jenna	Prandini	USA	20.11.92	1	Pac 12	Pullman	18 May
22.61	1.6	Yekaterina	Renzhina	RUS	18.10.94	1	NCp	Yerino	10 Jul
22.61	0.3	Dina	Asher-Smith	GBR-J	4.12.95	2s1	EC	Zürich	14 Aug
22.64	1.8	Shalonda	Solomon	USA	19.12.85	2h3	NC	Sacramento	29 Jun
22.64	0.4	Anyika	Onuora	GBR	28.10.84	4	CG	Glasgow	31 Jul
		(20)							
22.66	0.9	Kamaria	Brown	USA	21.12.92	2q1	NCAA-W	Fayetteville	31 May
22.67	0.0	Simone	Facey	JAM	7.5.85	1	WCM	Beijing	21 May
22.68	-0.8	Dezerea	Bryant	USA	27.4.93	2	SEC	Lexington	18 May
22.68	1.4	Morolake	Akinosun	USA	17.5.94	1q2	NCAA-W	Fayetteville	31 May
22.68	-0.5	Tianna	Bartoletta	USA	30.8.85	1	adidas	New York	14 Jun
22.68	0.4	Anneisha	McLaughlin	JAM	6.1.86	5	CG	Glasgow	31 Jul
22.72	-1.0	Jamile	Samuel	NED	24.4.92	1		Genève	14 Jun
22.72	0.3	Tiffany	Townsend	USA	14.6.89	2	NA	Heusden-Zolder	19 Jul
22.77	-1.1	Michelle-Lee	Ahye	TTO	10.4.92	1h2	NC	Port of Spain	22 Jun
22.78	-0.6	Kyra	Jefferson	USA	23.9.94	1rD	FlaR	Gainesville	4 Apr
		(30)							
22.78	0.3	Marie Josée	Lou Gonerie	CIV	18.11.88	5	C.Cup	Marrakech	14 Sep
22.80	1.6	Yekaterina	Vukolova	RUS	10.8.87	2	NCp	Yerino	10 Jul
22.81	1.5	English	Gardner	USA	22.4.92	6	Pre	Eugene	31 May
22.81	0.1	Ana Cláudia	Silva	BRA	6.11.88	1	NC	São Paulo	12 Oct
22.82	0.4	Dominique	Duncan	USA/NGR	7.5.90	1		San Marcos	5 Apr
22.82	1.5	Franciela	Krasucki	BRA	26.4.88	1		São Paulo	4 May
22.83	-0.5	Mujinga	Kambundji	SUI	17.6.92	5	EC	Zürich	15 Aug
22.85	0.1	Samantha	Henry-Robinson	JAM	25.9.88	4		Clermont	26 Apr
22.85	0.1	Olga	Safronova	KAZ	5.11.91	1	NC	Almaty	28 Jun

Mark	Wind	Name		Nat	Born	Pos	Meet	Venue	Date
22.87	0.1	Shaunae	Miller	BAH	15.4.94	1	Towns	Athens GA	12 Apr
		(40)							
22.88	1.5	Tynia	Gaither	BAH	16.3.93	2q3	NCAA-W	Fayetteville	31 May
22.88	1.6	Allison	Peter	ISV	14.7.92	1	NC	St. John's	29 Jun
22.88	-0.6	Schillonie	Calvert	JAM	27.7.88	2	NC	Kingston	29 Jun
22.89	1.3	Nataliya	Pogrebnyak	UKR	19.2.88	1		Kalamáta	31 May
22.89	1.5	Katarina	Johnson-Thompson	GBR	9.1.93	2H		Götzis	31 May
22.89	-1.0	Aleen	Bailey	JAM	25.11.80	2		Marrakech	8 Jun
22.90	1.9	Mahagony	Jones	USA	20.12.90	2h2	NC	Sacramento	29 Jun
22.91	1.8	Tawanna	Meadows	USA	4.8.86	1		San Marcos	26 Apr
22.92	0.1	Ashley	Spencer	USA	8.6.93	1	Johnson	Waco	19 Apr
22.92	-1.6	Phyllis	Francis	USA	4.5.92	1h4	Pac 12	Pullman	17 May
		(50)							
22.93	-0.5	Stephenie Ann	McPherson	JAM	25.11.88	1		Kingston	12 Apr
22.94	1.9	Veronica	Campbell-Brown	JAM	15.5.82	1		Clermont	10 May
22.95	0.1	Ashton	Purvis	USA	12.7.92	1	Sun Angel	Tempe	12 Apr
22.95	0.9	Brittany	Brown	USA-J	18.4.95	3q1	NCAA-W	Fayetteville	31 May
22.96	0.2	Ariana	Washington	USA-J	4.9.96	1		Clovis	7 Jun
22.97	1.5	Sheniqua	Ferguson	BAH	24.11.89	2		São Paulo	4 May
22.97	1.5	Ashley	Fields	USA	13.4.93	3q3	NCAA-W	Fayetteville	31 May
22.98	0.3	Hanna-Maari	Latvala	FIN	30.10.87	3s1	EC	Zürich	14 Aug
23.01	0.6	Cierra	White	USA	29.4.93	2s2	NCAA	Eugene	12 Jun
23.01	1.8	Rebekka	Haase	GER	2.1.93	1		Mannheim	6 Jul
		(60)							
23.01	1.6	Yelizaveta	Savlinis	RUS	14.8.87	3	NCp	Yerino	10 Jul
23.02A	1.3	Justine	Palframan	RSA	4.11.93	1	Univ Ch	Pretoria	26 Apr
23.02	1.9	Bianca	Knight	USA	2.1.89	3h2	NC	Sacramento	29 Jun
23.02	1.3	Jada	Martin	USA-J	8.6.95	2	NC-j	Eugene	6 Jul
23.03	0.9	Paris	Daniels	USA	25.1.90	1	TexR	Austin	29 Mar
23.03	1.3	Deedee	Trotter	USA	8.12.82	4	FlaR	Gainesville	4 Apr
23.03	1.6	Kimberly	Hyacinthe	CAN	28.3.89	2rB		Clermont	26 Apr
23.04	1.2	Crystal	Emmanuel	CAN	27.11.91	1		Ottawa	31 May
23.05	1.0	Janet	Amponsah	GHA	12.4.93	1		Amarillo	12 Apr
23.05	0.7	Marie	Gayot	FRA	18.12.89	1		La Roche-sur-Yon	23 Jul
		(70)							
23.06	-0.3	Amantle	Montsho ¶	BOT	4.7.83	1h1		Fukuroi	3 May
23.06	1.2	Katie	Wise	USA	15.10.93	1		Carbondale	18 May
23.06	-0.5	Natasha	Hastings	USA	23.7.86	2	adidas	New York	14 Jun
23.06	0.0	Jennifer	Galais	FRA	7.3.92	1	Med-23	Aubagne	15 Jun
23.06	1.6	Yelena	Bolsun	RUS	25.6.82	4	NCp	Yerino	10 Jul
23.06	-0.9	Muna	Lee	USA	30.10.81	1		Lapinlahti	20 Jul
23.08	-0.3	Jessica	Beard	USA	8.1.89	1		Houston	6 Jun
23.09	2.0	LaKeisha	Lawson	USA	3.6.87	1		Azusa	18 Apr
23.09	-0.6	Gloria	Asumnu	NGR	22.5.85	1s1	AfCh	Marrakech	13 Aug
23.10	1.8	Kai	Selvon	TTO	13.4.92	2		Auburn	5 Apr
		(80)							
23.10	2.0	Shapri	Romero	USA	13.11.91	1		Tucson	12 Apr
23.12	0.9	Cambrya	Jones	USA	20.9.90	1		Fairfax	12 Apr
23.12	0.4	Shakima	Wimbley	USA-J	23.4.95	1	ACC	Chapel Hill	19 Apr
23.12	-0.8	Aaliyah	Brown	USA-J	6.1.95	3	SEC	Lexington	18 May
23.12	-0.6	Maria	Belibasáki	GRE	19.6.91	1	ET-1	Tallinn	22 Jun
23.12	1.2	Candace	Hill	USA-Y	11.2.99	1		Rock Hill	6 Jul
23.12	1.6	Anastasiya	Kocherzhova	RUS	16.10.90	5	NCp	Yerino	10 Jul
23.12	0.7	Nataliya	Strohova	UKR	26.12.92	2	NC	Kirovohrad	25 Jul
23.12	0.3	Léa	Sprunger	SUI	5.3.90	4s1	EC	Zürich	14 Aug
23.14A	0.1	Nercely	Soto	VEN	26.8.90	1h1	CAG	Xalapa	26 Nov
		(90)							
23.15	1.2	Kendall	Baisden	USA-J	5.3.95	2h2	Big 12	Lubbock	17 May
23.15	1.8	Esther	Cremer	GER	29.3.88	1		Weinheim	31 May
23.15	0.3	Kelly	Proper	IRL	1.5.88	5s1	EC	Zürich	14 Aug
23.16	1.8	Lyudmila	Litvinova	RUS	8.6.85	2		San Marcos	26 Apr
23.16	1.7	Jura	Levy	JAM	4.11.90	1	NAIA	Gulf Shores	24 May
23.16	1.2	Ángela	Tenorio	ECU-J	27.1.96	1s2	WJ	Eugene	24 Jul
23.17	0.1	Courtney	Okolo	USA	15.3.94	3	Johnson	Waco	19 Apr
23.17	-1.3	Reyare	Thomas	TTO	23.11.87	2	NC	Port of Spain	22 Jun
23.17	1.6	Kineke	Alexander	VIN	21.2.86	2	NC	St. John's	29 Jun
23.17	-0.4	Ivet	Lalova	BUL	18.5.84	3h4	EC	Zürich	14 Aug
		(100)							

Mark	Wind	Name		Nat	Born	Date
23.18	1.3	Sally	Pearson	AUS	19.9.86	15 Feb
23.18	-0.6	Jessica	Davis	USA	31.10.92	4 Apr
23.18	1.8	Inna	Weit	GER	5.8.88	6 Jul
23.19	1.7	Arialis	Gandulla	CUB-J	22.6.95	8 Mar
23.19A	1.3	Melissa	Hewitt	RSA	20.5.91	26 Apr
23.19	0.0	Jade	Bailey	BAR	10.6.83	22 Jun
23.20	-0.8	Felicia	Brown	USA	27.10.93	18 May
23.21	0.5	Porscha	Lucas	USA	18.6.88	7 May

Mark	Wind	Name		Nat	Born	Pos	Meet	Venue	Date

Mark	Wind	Name		Nat	Born	Date
23.22	0.4	Margaret	Adeoye	GBR	27.4.85	12 Jun
23.22	0.1	Viktoriya	Zyabkina	KAZ	4.9.92	28 Jun
23.22	-1.1	Nivea	Smith	BAH	18.2.90	31 Jul
23.23	0.7	Gayon	Evans	JAM	15.1.90	18 May
23.23	0.2	Elaine	Thompson	JAM	28.6.92	12 Jul
23.23	-0.6	Marzia	Caravelli	ITA	23.10.81	14 Aug
23.24	0.4	Marika	Brown	USA-J	18.7.95	5 Apr
23.24	2.0	Agne	Serksniene	LTU	18.2.88	12 Jul
23.25	0.1	Anastasia	Le-Roy	JAM	11.9.87	22 Mar
23.25	0.2	Shayla	Sanders	USA	6.1.94	4 Apr
23.25	0.0		Wei Yongli	CHN	11.10.91	21 May
23.26	0.4	Ella	Nelson	AUS	10.5.94	15 Mar
23.26	1.6	Shai-Anne	Davis	CAN	4.12.93	26 Apr
23.26	1.5	Ellen	Sprunger	SUI	5.8.86	31 May
23.26	-0.4	Hrystyna	Stuy	UKR	3.2.88	4 Jun
23.26	0.6	Gina	Lückenkemper	GER-J	21.11.96	15 Jun
23.26	0.3	Irene	Ekelund	SWE-Y	8.3.97	14 Aug
23.27	-0.3	Irene	Siragusa	ITA	23.6.93	20 Jul
23.27	0.7	Kseniya	Karandyuk	UKR	21.6.86	25 Jul
23.27	-0.1	Nadine	Gonska	GER	23.1.90	27 Jul
23.27	0.3	Inna	Eftimova	BUL	19.6.88	14 Aug
23.28	1.8	Jessica	Young	USA	6.4.87	7 Jun
23.28	0.8	Andriána	Férra	GRE	11.2.88	7 Jun
23.29		Shericka	Jackson	JAM	15.7.94	25 Jan
23.29	-1.6	Destinee	Gause	USA	4.4.94	4 Apr
23.29	0.0	Desiree	Henry	GBR-J	26.8.95	19 Apr
23.29	-1.6	Tyshonda	Hawkins	USA		18 May
23.29	0.8	Ksenija	Balta	EST	11.1.86	15 Jun
23.29	1.6	Natalya	Rakacheva	RUS	16.4.88	10 Jul
23.29	0.1	Kauiza	Venâncio	BRA	11.6.87	12 Oct
23.30	0.9	Stacey Anne	Smith	USA	8.1.91	29 Mar
23.30	1.3	Lénora	Guion-Firmin	FRA	7.8.91	4 Apr
23.30	-1.3	Sophie	Papps	GBR	6.10.94	19 Apr
23.30	2.0	Jernail	Hayes	USA	8.7.88	1 May
23.30	0.9	Shannon	Hylton	GBR-J	19.12.96	18 May
23.31	-0.5	Natasha	Morrison	JAM	17.11.92	12 Apr
23.31	1.5	Antoinette	Goodman	USA	29.7.90	31 May
23.32	1.1	Barbara	Pierre	USA	28.4.87	5 Apr
23.32	0.7	Brittany	Johnson	USA	20.7.92	18 May
23.32	0.0	Trisha-Ann	Hawthorne	JAM	8.11.89	21 May
23.33	1.3	Tahesia	Harrigan-Scott	IVB	15.2.82	4 Apr
23.33	0.5	Sheri-Ann	Brooks	JAM	11.2.83	7 May
23.33	0.9	Janae	Johnson	USA	.82	23 May
23.33	0.7	Josefina	Elsler	GER	7.6.91	6 Jul
23.34	2.0	Krystal	Sparling	USA-Y	.97	24 Apr
23.35		Krisztina	Khorosheva	RUS	5.4.93	3 Jun
23.35	0.3	Kabange	Mpopo	ZAM	21.9.92	27 Sep
23.35	1.2	Chisato	Fukushima	JPN	27.6.88	30 Sep
23.35	0.9		Lin Huijun	CHN	1.2.93	30 Sep
23.36	0.4	Jonielle	Smith	JAM-J	30.1.96	27 Mar
23.36	0.1	Christy	Udoh	NGR	30.9.91	19 Apr
23.36	0.9	Natalliah	Whyte	JAM-Y	9.8.97	21 Apr
23.36	-0.3	Tessa	van Schagen	NED	2.2.94	31 May
23.36	0.7	Ashlee	Abraham	USA	24.9.91	31 May
23.36	0.9	Regine	Williams	USA-J	5.9.95	31 May
23.36	1.2	Diamond	Spaulding	USA-J	29.9.96	13 Jun
23.37	-2.8	Keilah	Tyson	USA	6.11.92	4 Apr
23.37	1.5	Marie	Veale	USA	17.11.94	26 Apr
23.37	1.8	Melissa	Breen	AUS	17.9.90	3 May
23.37	0.9	Ahty	Johnson	USA	9.2.93	30 May
23.37	1.2	Farah	Jacques	CAN	8.2.90	31 May
23.37	0.1	Vanda	Gomes	BRA	7.11.88	12 Oct
23.38	0.4	J'Nea	Bellamy	USA	.94	4 May
23.38	0.2	Marina	Panteleyeva	RUS	16.5.89	30 May
23.38	0.9	Emily	Yarnell	USA		30 May
23.38	-0.6	Sherone	Simpson	JAM	12.8.84	29 Jun
23.38	0.0	Sabina	Veit	SLO	2.12.85	1 Jul
		(175)				

Indoors

Mark	Name		Nat	Born	Pos	Meet	Venue	Date
22.50	Kamaria	Brown	USA	21.12.92	1r1	SEC	College Station	1 Mar
22.51		K Brown			1h6	SEC	College Station	28 Feb
23.06	Regine	Williams	USA-J	5.9.95	1		Fayetteville	31 Jan
23.11	Patricia	Hall	JAM	16.10.82	1		College Station	8 Feb

Mark	Name		Nat	Born	Date
23.21	Felecia	Majors	USA	11.2.95	28 Feb
23.22A	Destinee	Gause	USA	4.4.94	14 Mar
23.24	Shannon	Hylton	GBR-J	19.12.96	9 Feb
23.24	Anna	Kielbasinska	POL	26.6.90	23 Feb
23.26	Maike	Dix	GER	2.7.86	8 Feb
23.33	Robin	Reynolds	USA	22.2.94	28 Feb
23.39	Floria	Guei	FRA	2.5.90	13 Feb

Wind assisted

Mark	Wind	Name		Nat	Born	Pos	Meet	Venue	Date
22.06	3.8	Jeneba	Tarmoh	USA	27.9.89	1	NC	Sacramento	29 Jun
22.10	3.8	Kimberlyn	Duncan	USA	2.8.91	2	NC	Sacramento	29 Jun
22.17	4.3	Morolake	Akinosun	USA	17.5.94	1	Big12	Lubbock	18 May
22.19	3.8	Joanna	Atkins	USA	31.1.89	3	NC	Sacramento	29 Jun
22.30	2.1	Veronica	Campbell-Brown	JAM	15.5.82	1		Montverde	7 Jun
22.39	2.1		Duncan			1		Baton Rouge	19 Apr
		(6/5)							
22.54	3.8	Shalonda	Solomon	USA	19.12.85	4	NC	Sacramento	29 Jun
22.55	3.1	Natasha	Hastings	USA	23.7.86	1		Austin	3 May
22.57	3.7	Reyare	Thomas	TTO	23.11.87	1		Abilene	12 Apr
22.61	4.3	Cierra	White	USA	29.4.93	2	Big 12	Lubbock	18 May
22.63	4.3	Ashley	Fields	USA	13.4.93	3	Big 12	Lubbock	18 May
22.63	2.2	Kamaria	Brown	USA	21.12.92	1	NCAA	Eugene	14 Jun
22.64	3.1	Mahagony	Jones	USA	20.12.90	5	NC	Sacramento	29 Jun
22.69	0.1	Ashley	Spencer	USA	8.6.93	2		Austin	3 May
22.70	3.0	Sharika	Nelvis	USA	10.5.90	1		San Marcos	11 May
22.80	3.0	Tynia	Gaither	BAH	16.3.93	1rB	MSR	Walnut	19 Apr
22.82	2.5	Phyllis	Francis	USA	4.5.92	1		Eugene	5 Apr
22.82A	2.1	Ángela	Tenorio	ECU-J	27.1.96	1	PAm SF	Ciudad de México	16 Aug
22.83	4.8	Antoinette	Goodman	USA	29.7.90	1		Sioux Falls	3 May
22.86	3.0	Jessica	Davis	USA	31.10.92	2rB	MSR	Walnut	19 Apr
22.87	3.5	Jessica	Beard	USA	8.1.89	2	MSR	Walnut	19 Apr
22.90	3.8	Tawanna	Meadows	USA	4.8.86	6	NC	Sacramento	29 Jun
22.92	3.5	Bianca	Knight	USA	2.1.89	3	MSR	Walnut	19 Apr
22.92	2.1	Ivet	Lalova	BUL	18.5.84	1	ET-2	Riga	22 Jun
22.93	4.3	Chelsea	Hayes	USA	9.2.88	1		Fort Worth	21 Mar
22.94	5.9	Marika	Brown	USA-J	18.7.95	2		San Marcos	11 May
22.96	2.4	Jada	Martin	USA-J	8.6.95	1rB		Coral Gables	12 Apr
22.97	4.0	Muna	Lee	USA	30.10.81	1		Göteborg	14 Jun
22.97	2.6	Kineke	Alexander	VIN	21.2.86	1		Basseterre	5 Jul
22.97	2.5	Irene	Ekelund	SWE-Y	8.3.97	1s1	WJ	Eugene	24 Jul
22.98	3.1	Laverne	Jones-Ferrette	ISV	16.9.81	4		Austin	3 May

Mark	Wind	Name		Nat	Born	Pos	Meet	Venue	Date
22.99	4.0	Kendall	Baisden	USA-J	5.3.95	1rB		Austin	3 May
23.00A	2.2	Diamond	Spaulding	USA-J	29.9.96	1		Albuquerque	7 Jun
23.02	5.9	Carrol	Hardy	USA-J		3		San Marcos	11 May
23.03	2.1	Lénora	Guion-Firmin	FRA	7.8.91	3		Montverde	7 Jun
23.04	3.1	Courtney	Okolo	USA	15.3.94	5		Austin	3 May
23.08	2.3	Gayon	Evans	JAM	15.1.90	1		Greensboro	3 May
23.08	2.3	Nivea	Smith	BAH	18.2.90	1	NC	Nassau	29 Jun
23.09	2.8	Nadine	Gonska	GER	23.1.90	1h2	NC	Ulm	27 Jul
23.10	4.4	Ella	Nelson	AUS	10.5.94	1		Sydney (C'tonn)	5 Jan
23.10	2.8	Felicia	Brown	USA	27.10.93	2		Knoxville	12 Apr
23.10	2.3	Kayelle	Clarke	TTO-J	28.2.96	1	Carifta	Fort-de-France	21 Apr
23.11	3.0	Kamara	Durant	TTO	24.2.91	1		Port of Spain	12 Apr
23.13	2.3	Kadecia	Baird	GUY-J	24.2.95	2	Carifta	Fort-de-France	21 Apr
23.14	2.8	Arialis	Gandulla	CUB-J	22.6.95	1	Barr	La Habana	24 May

Mark	Wind	Name		Nat	Born	Date
23.15A	2.1	Audrea	Segree	JAM	5.10.90	16 Aug
23.16	3.3	Desiree	Henry	GBR-J	26.8.95	31 May
23.17	2.3	Nakia	Linson	USA	2.8.92	3 May
23.18	2.1	Tristie	Johnson	USA	20.11.93	26 Apr
23.19	4.5	Christy	Udoh	NGR	30.9.91	12 Apr
23.21	4.3	Stephanie	Kalu	NGR	5.8.93	21 Mar
23.21	2.1	Hrystyna	Stuy	UKR	3.2.88	27 Jun
23.22	2.1	Ada	Udaya	LBR	28.6.92	22 Mar
23.22mx	3.4	Ashleigh	Nelson	GBR	20.2.91	9 Jul
23.22	2.7	Christania	Williams	JAM	17.1.94	20 Jul
23.23	3.0	Stacey Anne	Smith	USA	8.1.91	19 Apr
23.23	2.5	Zakiya	Denoon	TTO-J	23.1.95	1 Jun
23.24	3.0	Natasha	Morrison	JAM	17.11.92	5 Apr
23.24	6.7	Destiny	Carter	USA		19 Apr
23.24	2.9	Briana	Nelson	USA	18.7.92	3 May
23.25	2.4	Shannon	Hylton	GBR-J	19.12.96	25 Jul
23.26	2.8	Shawna	Fermin	TTO	17.8.91	15 Mar
23.26	4.8	Ashley	Tingelstad	USA	29.9.90	3 May
23.26	3.9	Hayley	Jones	GBR	14.9.88	31 May
23.28	2.3	Melissa	Breen	AUS	17.9.90	3 May
23.28	2.3	Le'Quisha	Parker	USA	26.5.93	3 May
23.31	3.1	Saqukine	Cameron	JAM-J	21.8.96	9 Mar
23.31	3.2	Anne	Zagré	BEL	13.3.90	12 Apr
23.31	2.4	A'Keyla	Mitchell	USA-J	11.11.95	10 May
23.32	2.8	Alicia	Evans	USA	27.3.92	26 Apr
23.33	2.1	Ashlee	Abraham	USA	24.9.91	5 Apr
23.33	3.8	Ashley	Marshall	USA	10.9.93	2 May
23.33	2.6	Erica	Bougard	USA	26.7.93	27 Jun

(194 legal and windy to 23.33)

Best at low altitude

23.25 -0.4 Soto 15 Mar | 23.27 -0.1 Palframan 14 Aug | 23.15w 2.4 Tenorio 25 Jul

Hand timed: 23.1 Anna Golovina RUS 28.6.89 4 Jul

Drugs disqualification: 23.27 1.3 Grigoria-Emmanouéla Keramidá GRE 25.8.90 31 May

JUNIORS

See main list for top 10 juniors (& 1 wa). 10 performances by 3 women to 23.08 (+ 1 ind). Additional and further juniors

Name	Mark	Wind	Pos	Meet	Venue	Date	Mark	Wind	Pos	Venue	Date
Whitney	23.05	1.4	1s3	WJ	Eugene	24 Jul					
Asher-S	22.74	0.0	1	NC-j	Bedford	22 Jun	22.98		1	Birmingham	7 Jun
	22.75	0.1	1h5	EC	Zürich	14 Aug	23.08	-0.6	1	Norwich	27 Apr

Mark	Wind	Name		Nat	Born	Pos	Meet	Venue	Date
23.19	1.7	Arialis	Gandulla	CUB	22.6.95	1		Camagüey	8 Mar
23.24	0.4	Marika	Brown	USA	18.7.95	2		San Marcos	5 Apr
23.26	0.6	Gina	Lückenkemper	GER	21.11.96	1	NC-23	Wesel	15 Jun
23.26	0.3	Irene	Ekelund	SWE-Y	8.3.97	3=s3	EC	Zürich	14 Aug
23.29	0.0	Desiree	Henry	GBR	26.8.95	3		Gainesville	19 Apr
23.30	0.9	Shannon	Hylton	GBR	19.12.96	2	LI	Loughborough	18 May
23.34	2.0	Krystal	Sparling	USA-Y	.97	1		Miramar	24 Apr
23.36	0.4	Jonielle	Smith	JAM	30.1.96	1s2	N.Sch	Kingston	27 Mar
23.36	0.9	Natalliah	Whyte	JAM-Y	9.8.97	1	Carifta-Y	Fort-de-France	21 Apr
23.36	0.9	Regine	Williams (20)	USA	5.9.95	5q1	NCAA-W	Fayetteville	31 May
23.36	1.2	Diamond	Spaulding	USA	29.9.96	2	N.Jnr	Greensboro	13 Jun
23.24 i		Shannon	Hylton	GBR	19.12.96	2	NC	Sheffield	9 Feb

Wind assisted

Name	Mark	Wind	Pos	Meet	Venue	Date	Mark	Wind	Pos	Meet	Venue	Date
Whitney	22.80w	2.1	2		Montverde	7 Jun	22.82w	2.4	1	WJ	Eugene	25 Jul
Ekelund	22.97w	2.4	2	WJ	Eugene	25 Jul	9 performances to 23.00 by 6 women					

Mark	Wind	Name		Nat	Born	Pos	Meet	Venue	Date
23.16	3.3	Desiree	Henry	GBR	26.8.95	1r2		Clermont	31 May
23.23	2.5	Zakiya	Denoon	TTO	23.1.95	1	NC-j	Port of Spain	1 Jun
23.25	2.4	Shannon	Hylton	GBR	19.12.96	4	WJ	Eugene	25 Jul
23.31	3.1	Saqukine	Cameron	JAM	21.8.96	1h3		Kingston	9 Mar
23.31	2.4	A'Keyla	Mitchell	USA	11.11.95	1		Austin	10 May

300 METRES

Mark	Name		Nat	Born	Pos	Meet	Venue	Date
36.29	Deedee	Trotter	USA	8.12.82	1		Atlanta	16 May
36.58	Denisa	Rosolová	CZE	21.8.86	1		Praha	25 Jul
36.63	Paris	Daniels	USA	25.1.90	2		Atlanta	16 May
36.74	Anyika	Onuora	GBR	28.10.84	3		Atlanta	16 May
36.82	Libania	Grenot	ITA	12.7.83	4		Atlanta	16 May
36.90	Agne	Serksniene	LTU	18.2.88	1		Fribourg	10 May
37.25	Cambrya	Jones	USA	20.9.90				16 May
37.40	Monica	Hargrove	USA	30.12.82				16 May

In 400m: Sacramento 29 Jun: Francema McCorory 36.2, Sanya Richards-Ross 36.5, Natasha Hastings 36.6

Indoors

Mark	Name		Nat	Born	Pos	Meet	Venue	Date
36.10	Shaunae	Miller	BAH	15.4.94	1	Mill	New York (Arm)	15 Feb
36.50	Francena	McCorory	USA	20.10.88	2	Mill	New York (Arm)	15 Feb
36.70	Dezerea	Bryant	USA	27.4.93	1		Bloomington	12 Dec

Mark	Name		Nat	Born	Pos	Meet	Venue	Date
37.23	Kseniya	Ryzhova #	RUS	19.4.87				12 Jan
37.26	Kadecia	Baird	GUY-J	24.2.95				25 Jan
37.27	Marina	Chernova	RUS	17.4.91				7 Jan
37.40	Alena	Tamkova	RUS	30.5.90				7 Jan

400 METRES

Mark	Name		Nat	Born	Pos	Meet	Venue	Date
49.48	Francena	McCorory	USA	20.10.88	1	NC	Sacramento	28 Jun
49.66	Sanya	Richards-Ross	USA	26.2.85	2	NC	Sacramento	28 Jun
49.93		McCorory			1	DL	Glasgow	11 Jul
49.94		McCorory			1	C.Cup	Marrakech	13 Sep
49.98		Richards-Ross			1	VD	Bruxelles	5 Sep
50.03	Courtney	Okolo	USA	15.3.94	1	Big 12	Lubbock	18 May
50.03		Richards-Ross			1s1	NC	Sacramento	27 Jun
50.05		McCorory			2s1	NC	Sacramento	27 Jun
50.05	Novlene	Williams-Mills	JAM	26.4.82	1	NC	Kingston	29 Jun
50.06		Williams-Mills			1	Bisl	Oslo	11 Jun
50.08		Williams-Mills			2	C.Cup	Marrakech	13 Sep
50.09		Williams-Mills			1	DNG	Stockholm	21 Aug
50.10		Richards-Ross			1	DL	Saint-Denis	5 Jul
50.12	Stephenie Ann	McPherson	JAM	25.11.88	2	VD	Bruxelles	5 Sep
50.15		McCorory			1	adidas	New York	14 Jun
50.16	Christine	Day	JAM	23.8.86	2	NC	Kingston	29 Jun
50.23		Okolo			1	NCAA	Eugene	13 Jun
50.24		McCorory			1		Kingston	3 May
50.26		Williams-Mills			1		George Town	7 May
50.27		Richards-Ross			2	DNG	Stockholm	21 Aug
50.31		Williams-Mills			1	DL	Shanghai	18 May
50.37	Amantle	Montsho ¶	BOT	4.7.83	2	DL	Shanghai	18 May
50.38		McPherson			1	WCM	Rieti	7 Sep
50.39		Richards-Ross			2	DL	Glasgow	11 Jul
50.40		Williams-Mills			1	Pre	Eugene	31 May
50.40		McPherson			2	DL	Saint-Denis	5 Jul
50.42		Williams-Mills			3	VD	Bruxelles	5 Sep
50.43		McCorory			1		Edmonton	6 Jul
50.45		McPherson			1	WCM	Madrid	19 Jul
50.46	Kendall	Baisden	USA-J	5.3.95	2	Big 12	Lubbock	18 May
50.50		McPherson			3	NC	Kingston	29 Jun
	(31/8)							
50.53	Natasha	Hastings	USA	23.7.86	3	NC	Sacramento	28 Jun
50.55	Libania	Grenot	ITA	12.7.83	1	NC	Rovereto	19 Jul
	(10)							
50.59	Phyllis	Francis	USA	4.5.92	2	NCAA	Eugene	13 Jun
50.74	Joanna	Atkins	USA	31.1.89	2		Edmonton	6 Jul
50.81	Allyson	Felix	USA	18.11.85	5	DL	Shanghai	18 May
50.81	Jessica	Beard	USA	8.1.89	4	NC	Sacramento	28 Jun
50.84	Anastasia	LeRoy	JAM	11.9.87	4	NC	Kingston	29 Jun
50.87	Kabange	Mpopo	ZAM	21.9.92	4	C.Cup	Marrakech	13 Sep
50.98	Deedee	Trotter	USA	8.12.82	1s2	NC	Sacramento	27 Jun
51.00	Kaliese	Spencer	JAM	6.5.87	7	DL	Shanghai	18 May
51.00	Olha	Zemlyak	UKR	16.1.90	5	C.Cup	Marrakech	13 Sep
51.05	Briana	Nelson	USA	18.7.92	4s1	NC	Sacramento	27 Jun
	(20)							
51.06	Shamier	Little	USA-J	20.3.95	1	SEC	Lexington	18 May
51.11	Kemi	Adekoya	BRN	16.1.93	1h3	AsiG	Incheon	27 Sep
51.21	Sade	Abugan	NGR	17.12.90	1	LEAP	Loughborough	19 Jul
51.23	Kineke	Alexander	VIN	21.2.86	1		San Marcos	26 Apr
51.23	Shericka	Williams	JAM	17.9.85	5	NC	Kingston	29 Jun
51.29	Patience	George	NGR	25.11.91	1		Warri	13 Jun
51.30	Regina	George	NGR	17.2.91	1h2	NC	Calabar	19 Jun
51.30	Floria	Guei	FRA	2.5.90	4	WCM	Rieti	7 Sep
51.32	Shericka	Jackson	JAM	15.7.94	6	NC	Kingston	29 Jun
51.33	Alena	Tamkova	RUS	30.5.90	1	NCp	Yerino	9 Jul
	(30)							
51.36	Robin	Reynolds	USA	22.2.94	1s1	NCAA	Eugene	11 Jun
51.38	Ashley	Spencer	USA	8.6.93	1s2	NCAA-W	Fayetteville	30 May
51.38	Indira	Terrero	ESP	29.11.85	3	EC	Zürich	15 Aug
51.38	Christine	Ohuruogu	GBR	17.5.84	4	EC	Zürich	15 Aug
51.39	Chris-Ann	Gordon	JAM	18.9.94	7	NC	Kingston	29 Jun
51.41	Tatyana	Veshkurova	RUS	23.9.81	1		Adler	29 May
51.44	Geisa	Coutinho	BRA	1.6.80	1	NC	São Paulo	10 Oct
51.49	Janeive	Russell	JAM	14.11.93	1		Kingston	7 Jun

Mark	Wind	Name		Nat	Born	Pos	Meet	Venue	Date
51.55		Patricia	Hall	JAM	16.10.82	1	GP	Ponce	17 May
51.56		Omolara	Omotosho	NGR	25.5.93	2	NC	Calabar	20 Jun
		(40)							
51.58		Hrystyna	Stuy	UKR	3.2.88	1	NC	Kirovohrad	25 Jul
51.58		Shaunae	Miller	BAH	15.4.94	2s2	CG	Glasgow	28 Jul
51.62		Agne	Serksniene	LTU	18.2.88	1		La Chaux-de-Fonds	6 Jul
51.66		Aauri Lorena	Bokesa	ESP	14.12.88	1		Alcorcón	12 Jul
51.67		Yekaterina	Renzhina	RUS	18.10.94	2	NC	Kazan	24 Jul
51.68		Shakima	Wimbley	USA-J	23.4.95	1		Atlanta	17 May
51.68		Ada	Benjamin	NGR	18.5.94	2h3	AfCh	Marrakech	11 Aug
51.69		Kseniya	Zadorina	RUS	2.3.87	2	NCp	Yerino	9 Jul
51.70		Michelle	Brown	USA	24.1.92	5	NCAA	Eugene	13 Jun
51.72		Kiara	Porter	USA	22.10.93	2q1	NCAA-E	Jacksonville	30 May
		(50)							
51.72		Margaret	Bamgbose	USA	19.10.93	6	NCAA	Eugene	13 Jun
51.72		Joelma	Souza	BRA	13.7.84	2	NC	São Paulo	10 Oct
51.72A		Lisneidy	Veitia	CUB	29.4.94	1	CAG	Xalapa	26 Nov
51.73		Machettira Raju	Poovamma	IND	5.6.90	1	I-S	Lucknow	8 Jun
51.73		Daysurami	Bonne	CUB	9.3.88	1		La Habana	20 Jun
51.76		Anyika	Onuora	GBR	28.10.84	5	WCM	Rieti	7 Sep
51.77		Bianca	Râzor	ROU	8.8.94	2h1	EC	Zürich	12 Aug
51.78A		Maureen	Maiyo	KEN	28.5.85	1	NC	Nairobi	7 Jun
51.78		Taylor	Ellis-Watson	USA	6.5.93	7	NC	Sacramento	28 Jun
51.80		Marie	Gayot	FRA	18.12.89	3h1	EC	Zürich	12 Aug
		(60)							
51.83		Janeil	Bellille	TTO	18.6.89	1	NC	Port of Spain	21 Jun
51.84		Malgorzata	Holub	POL	30.10.92	5	EC	Zürich	15 Aug
51.84A		Bobby-Gaye	Wilkins-Gooden	JAM	10.9.88	3	PAm SF	Ciudad de México	16 Aug
51.87		Esther	Cremer	GER	29.3.88	2	FBK	Hengelo	8 Jun
51.87		Kala	Funderburk	USA	14.9.92	4h1	NC	Sacramento	26 Jun
51.91		Quanera	Hayes	USA	7.3.92	1	NCAA-II	Allendale	24 May
51.92		Allison	Peter	ISV	14.7.92	1	NACAC	Kamloops	9 Aug
51.94A		Florence	Uwakwe	NGR	28.7.94	1		Albuquerque	2 May
51.95		Emily	Diamond	GBR	11.6.91	1		Rhede	11 Jul
51.95		Nataliya	Pygyda	UKR	30.1.81	1h3	EC	Zürich	12 Aug
		(70)							
51.96		Shapri	Romero	USA	13.11.91	1		Tucson	3 May
51.96		Kelly	Massey	GBR	11.1.85	5	DL	Birmingham	24 Aug
52.06		Lyudmila	Litvinova	RUS	8.6.85	2	Johnson	Waco	19 Apr
52.06			Quach Thi Lan	VIE-J	18.10.95	2	AsiG	Incheon	28 Sep
52.08		Tatyana	Firova	RUS	10.10.82	3	NCp	Yerino	9 Jul
52.10		Olga	Tovarnova	RUS	11.4.85	1		Krasnodar	6 Jun
52.11		Shana	Cox	GBR	22.1.85	6	adidas	New York	14 Jun
52.11		Hanna	Ryzhykova	UKR	24.11.89	3	NC	Kirovohrad	25 Jul
52.13		Carline	Muir	CAN	1.10.87	1	NC	Moncton	28 Jun
52.14		Patrycja	Wyciszkiewicz	POL	8.1.94	2		Huelva	12 Jun
		(80)							
52.15		Vanessa	Jones	USA	1.1.93	2h3	NCAA-W	Fayetteville	29 May
52.16		Rosemarie	Whyte-Robinson	JAM	8.9.86	8	NC	Kingston	29 Jun
52.17		Muriel	Hurtis	FRA	25.3.79	2		Castres	30 Jul
52.19		Chiara	Bazzoni	ITA	5.7.84	5h1	EC	Zürich	12 Aug
52.20		Chizoba	Okodogbe	NGR	3.11.92	2	Pac 12	Pullman	18 May
52.20		Kristina	Malvinova	RUS	16.7.89	4	NCp	Yerino	9 Jul
52.21		Mariya	Mikhailyuk	RUS	29.1.91	1		Yerino	8 Jun
52.22		Anneisha	McLaughlin	JAM	6.1.86	3		Kingston	22 Feb
52.22		Morgan	Mitchell	AUS	3.10.94	1	NC	Melbourne	5 Apr
52.22		Justyna	Swiety	POL	3.12.92	1	Sidło	Sopot	20 Jul
		(90)							
52.25		Monica	Hargrove	USA	30.12.82	4		Houston	6 Jun
52.26		Ebony	Eutsey	USA	3.5.92	3s1	NCAA	Eugene	11 Jun
52.28		Gilda	Casanova	CUB-J	19.12.95	1		Port of Spain	2 May
52.30		Nercely	Soto	VEN	26.8.90	2	SAmG	Santiago de Chile	14 Mar
52.30		Jéssica	dos Santos	BRA	21.3.91	3	NC	São Paulo	10 Oct
52.32		Brianna	Tate	USA	1.1.93	2		Tucson	3 May
52.32		Darya	Prystupa	UKR	26.11.87	2		Kyiv	4 Jun
52.35		Anneliese	Rubie	AUS	22.4.92	2	NC	Melbourne	5 Apr
52.36		Destinee	Gause	USA	4.4.94	2q2	NCAA-E	Jacksonville	30 May
52.36		Madiea	Ghafoor	NED	9.9.92	1		Genève	14 Jun
		(100)							

Mark	Name		Nat	Born	Date
52.37	Yekaterina	Vukolova	RUS	10.8.87	17 Jul
52.39	Maria Benedict	Chigboglu	ITA	27.7.89	7 Sep
52.40	Eilidh	Child	GBR	20.2.87	18 May
52.42	Liliya	Molgacheva	RUS	2.3.90	6 Jun

WOMEN 2014

Mark	Wind	Name		Nat	Born	Pos	Meet	Venue	Date

Mark	First name	Surname	Nat	Born	Date
52.42	Natalia	da Silva	BRA	25.12.92	10 Oct
52.43	Chrishuna	Williams	USA	31.3.93	17 May
52.43	Laniece	Clarke	BAH	4.11.87	28 Jun
52.44	Marlena	Wesh	HAI	16.2.91	9 May
52.44	Estelle	Perrossier	FRA	12.1.90	12 Jul
52.45	Diamond	Dixon	USA	29.6.92	3 May
52.46	Olivia	Baker	USA-J	12.6.96	6 Jul
52.47	Lashinda	Demus	USA	10.3.83	14 Mar
52.47	Svetlana	Rogozina	RUS	26.12.92	2 Jul
52.47	Chandrika	Subashini	SRI	20.6.87	28 Sep
52.48A	Justine	Palframan	RSA	4.11.93	12 Apr
52.48	Jordan	Lavender	USA	23.7.93	19 Apr
52.48	Nadia	Cummins	BAR	28.4.91	17 May
52.48	Margaret	Adeoye	GBR	27.4.85	28 Jul
52.48	Agnès	Raharolahy	FRA	7.11.92	30 Jul
52.50	Ristananna	Tracey	JAM	5.9.92	22 Mar
52.50	Seren	Bundy-Davies	GBR	30.12.94	30 Jul
52.50	Jessica	Thornton	AUS-Y	12.4.98	23 Aug
52.51	Bukola	Abogunloko	NGR	18.8.94	13 Jun
52.52	Kaelin	Roberts	USA-Y	6.1.99	7 Jun
52.53A	Wenda	Nel	RSA	30.7.88	10 May
52.53	Déborah	Rodríguez	URU	2.12.92	3 Oct
52.55	Funke	Oladoye	NGR	12.5.93	13 Jun
52.55	Jodie	Williams	GBR	28.9.93	27 Aug
52.56	Danielle	Dowie	JAM	5.5.92	3 May
52.56	Maria Enrica	Spacca	ITA	20.3.86	19 Jul
52.57	Raena	Rhone	USA	27.9.93	30 May
52.58	Agata	Bednarek	POL	28.6.88	7 Jun
52.60		Yang Huizhen	CHN	13.8.92	12 Jul
52.61	Cátia	Azevedo	POR	9.3.94	24 May
52.62	Anilda	Thomas	IND	6.5.92	18 Dec
52.65	Breigh	Jones	USA	12.7.94	30 May
52.66	Yaneisi	Borlot	CUB	18.2.91	13 Jun
52.67	Montenae	Roye-Speight	USA	5.11.92	18 May
52.67	Felicia	Majors	USA-J	2.12.95	30 May
52.69	Ruth Sophia	Spelmeyer	GER	19.9.90	7 Jun
52.70	Kristyn	Williams	USA	27.1.94	4 Apr
52.70	Aaliyah	Barnes	USA-J	17.2.95	30 May
52.71	Victoria	Ohuruogu	GBR	28.2.93	1 Jun
52.72	Sonia	Gaskin	BAR	4.10.94	18 May
52.72	Elena	Bonfanti	ITA	9.7.88	19 Jul
52.72	Yenifer	Padilla	COL	1.1.90	2 Aug
52.73	Laura	Maddox	GBR	13.5.90	14 Jun
52.73	Nadezhda	Kotlyarova	RUS	12.6.89	23 Jul
52.74	Caitlin	Sargent	AUS	14.6.92	28 Jun
52.74	Salwa Eid	Nasser	BRN-Y	23.5.98	23 Aug
52.76		Nguyen Thi Huyen	VIE	19.8.93	11 Dec
52.77	Afia	Charles	ANT	22.7.92	4 May
52.77	Elexis	Guster	USA	7.7.94	18 May
52.77	Cassandra	Tate	USA	11.9.90	6 Jun
52.77	Rita	Ossai	NGR-J	21.10.95	13 Jun
52.78	Lena	Schmidt	GER	4.8.89	7 Jun
52.79	Celina	Emerson	USA	13.2.92	30 May
52.79	Yana	Glotova	RUS-J	8.4.95	16 Jun
52.80A	Kayan	Robinson	JAM	27.3.89	5 May
52.81	Christian	Brennan	CAN-J	27.3.95	19 Apr
52.81	Lydia	Mashila	BOT	22.6.90	3 May
52.81	Vania	Stambolova	BUL	28.11.83	28 Jun
52.82	Maggie	Vessey	USA	23.12.81	10 May
52.82	Zola	Golden	USA-Y	20.6.97	10 May
52.82	Ilona	Usovich	BLR	14.11.82	24 Jul
52.83	Myriam	Soumaré	FRA	29.10.86	19 Apr
52.83	Amy	Allcock	GBR	24.8.93	14 Jun
52.85	Natoya	Goule	JAM	30.3.91	5 Apr
52.86	Briyanni	Thomas	USA	13.3.91	17 May
52.86	Phara	Anacharsis	FRA	17.12.83	25 May
52.87	Dawnalee	Loney	JAM-J	15.5.96	9 Mar
52.87	Ashley	Tingelstad	USA	29.9.90	18 Apr
52.87	Madison	Reynolds	USA	14.7.94	11 Jun
52.88	Yanique	McNeil	JAM-J	28.7.96	29 Mar
52.89	Precious	Holmes	USA-J	27.11.95	22 Mar
52.89	Mary	Iheke	GBR	19.11.90	29 Jun
52.91	Yuliya	Rakhmanova	KAZ	25.10.91	7 Jun
52.91	Laura	Müller	GER-J	11.12.95	5 Jul
52.93	Yuliya	Terekhova	RUS	20.2.90	9 Jul
52.93	Marina	Konovalova	RUS	17.9.90	24 Jul
52.94	Elina	Mikhina	KAZ	16.7.94	14 Jun
52.94	Christine	Amertil	BAH	18.8.79	28 Jun
52.95	Kendall	Ellis	USA-J	8.3.96	3 May
52.95	Domonique	Williams	TTO	8.8.94	3 May
52.96	Keshia	Baker-Kirtz	USA	30.1.88	19 Apr
52.96	Yekaterina	Poistogova	RUS	1.3.91	29 May
52.97	Kamaria	Brown	USA	21.12.92	12 Apr
52.98	Laura	Wake	GBR	3.5.91	26 Apr
52.99	Christiane	Klopsch	GER	21.8.90	5 Jul
52.99	Seika (190)	Aoyama	JPN-J	1.5.96	27 Sep

Indoors

Mark	First name	Surname	Nat	Born	Pos	Meet	Venue	Date
50.46A	Phyllis	Francis	USA	4.5.92	1r2	NCAA	Albuquerque	15 Mar
50.94	Kamaria	Brown	USA	21.12.92	1r1	SEC	College Station	1 Mar
51.03	Kseniya	Ryzhova #	RUS	19.4.87	1	NC	Moskva	18 Feb
52.13	Justyna	Swiety	POL	3.12.92	2h1	WI	Sopot	7 Mar

Mark	First name	Surname	Nat	Born	Date
52.37	Denisa	Rosolová	CZE	21.8.86	7 Mar
52.39	Irina	Davydova	RUS	27.5.88	2 Feb
52.40A	Cassandra	Tate	USA	11.9.90	23 Feb
52.47A	Akawkaw	Ndipagbor	USA	30.4.93	14 Mar
52.49	Nicky	van Leuveren	NED	20.5.90	23 Feb
52.58A	Kiah	Seymour	USA	11.1.94	14 Mar
52.61	Lisanne	de Witte	NED	10.9.92	7 Mar
52.65	Felecia	Majors	USA-J	11.2.95	1 Mar
52.68	Yuliya	Terekhova	RUS	20.2.90	17 Feb
52.81	Marina	Chernova	RUS	17.4.91	18 Jan
52.83A	Jernail	Hayes	USA	8.7.88	23 Feb
52.91	Sophia	Smellie	JAM	6.11.79	7 Feb
52.93	Brittany	Wallace	USA	13.7.91	1 Mar

Best at low altitude

52.56 Uwakwe 18 May | 52.62 Maiyo 11 Aug | 52.67 Wilkins-Gooden 12 Apr

Hand timing

Mark	First name	Surname	Nat	Born	Pos	Meet	Venue	Date
50.8	Kineke	Alexander	VIN	21.2.86	1		Clermont	31 May
51.1	Carline	Muir	CAN	1.10.87	2		Clermont	31 May
51.5A	Genet	Lire	ETH-Y	23.1.97	1	NC	Addis Ababa	13 May
51.9	Lénora	Guion-Firmin	FRA	7.8.91	3		Clermont	31 May
52.7	Samantha	Edwards	ANT	14.1.90	4		Clermont	31 May

JUNIORS

See main list for top 5 juniors. 10 performances (+2 indoors) by 4 women to 52.06. Additional marks and further juniors:

Name	Mark	Pos	Meet	Venue	Date	Mark	Pos	Meet	Venue	Date
Baisden	51.32	3	NCAA	Eugene	13 Jun	51.85	1	WJ	Eugene	25 Jul
	51.67	2s3	NCAA	Eugene	11 Jun	51.96	2q3	NCAA-W	Fayetteville	30 May
	51.72	1		Waco	19 Apr					
Wibley	51.81	1q3	NCAA-E	Jacksonville	30 May					
Little	51.86i	3	SEC	College Station	1 Mar	51.96Ai	1A	NCAA	Albuquerque	15 Mar

Mark	First name	Surname	Nat	Born	Pos	Meet	Venue	Date
52.46	Olivia	Baker	USA	12.6.96	2	NC-j	Eugene	6 Jul
52.50	Jessica	Thornton	AUS-Y	12.4.98	1	Yth OG	Nanjing	23 Aug
52.52	Kaelin	Roberts	USA-Y	6.1.99	1		Clovis	7 Jun
52.67	Felicia	Majors	USA	2.12.95	3q2	NCAA-E	Jacksonville	30 May
52.70	Aaliyah	Barnes (10)	USA	17.2.95	4q2	NCAA-E	Jacksonville	30 May
52.74	Salwa Eid	Nasser	BRN-Y	23.5.98	2	Yth OG	Nanjing	23 Aug
52.77	Rita	Ossai	NGR	21.10.95	2rB		Warri	13 Jun

Mark Wind	Name		Nat	Born	Pos	Meet	Venue	Date
52.79	Yana	Glotova	RUS	8.4.95	1	NC-j	Cheboksary	16 Jun
52.81	Christian	Brennan	CAN	27.3.95	3	MSR	Walnut	19 Apr
52.82	Zola	Golden	USA-Y	20.6.97	1		White Plains	10 May
52.87	Dawnalee	Loney	JAM	15.5.96	1J		Kingston	9 Mar
52.88	Yanique	McNeil	JAM	28.7.96	1	N.Sch-19	Kingston	29 Mar
52.89	Precious	Holmes	USA	27.11.95	1		Myrtle Beach	22 Mar
52.91	Laura	Müller	GER	11.12.95	1		Mannheim	5 Jul
52.95	Kendall	Ellis (20)	USA	8.3.96	1		Jacksonville	3 May
52.65 i	Felecia	Majors	USA	11.2.95	2r2	SEC	College Station	1 Mar

500 METRES

Mark	Name		Nat	Born	Pos	Meet	Venue	Date
1:07.9	Sahily	Diago	CUB-J	26.8.95	1		La Habana	22 Apr
1:08.8	Yaneisi	Borlot	CUB	18.2.91	2		La Habana	22 Apr
1:09.1	Daysurami	Bonne	CUB	9.3.88	1		La Habana	31 Jan
1:09.9	Lisneidy	Veitia	CUB	29.4.94	3		La Habana	22 Apr

600 METRES

Mark	Name		Nat	Born	Pos	Meet	Venue	Date
1:26.10	Fabienne	Kohlmann	GER	6.11.89	1		Pliezhausen	18 May
1:26.33mx	Rose Mary	Almanza	CUB	13.7.92	1		La Habana	15 Feb
1:26.5+	Sahily	Diago	CUB-J	26.8.95	1	in 800	La Habana	10 May
1:26.68	Justyna	Swiety	POL	3.12.92				10 May
1:26.80	Joanna	Józwik	POL	30.1.91				18 May
1:27.12	Christina	Hering	GER	9.10.94				18 May
1:27.56	Omolara	Omotoso	NGR	25.5.93				15 Feb

Indoors

Mark	Name		Nat	Born	Pos	Meet	Venue	Date
1:25.76	Regina	George	NGR	17.2.91	1		Fayetteville	10 Jan
1:26.73	Aleena	Brooks	TTO	14.11.91				1 Mar
1:26.98	Shawnice	Williams	USA	18.3.92				1 Mar

800 METRES

Mark	Name		Nat	Born	Pos	Meet	Venue	Date
1:57.67	Ajee'	Wilson	USA	8.5.94	1	Herc	Monaco	18 Jul
1:57.74	Sahily	Diago	CUB-J	26.8.95	1	Barr	La Habana	25 May
1:57.92	Eunice	Sum	KEN	2.9.88	2	Herc	Monaco	18 Jul
1:58.14		Diago			1		La Habana	9 May
1:58.15	Marina	Arzamasova	BLR	17.12.87	1	EC	Zürich	16 Aug
1:58.21		Sum			1	C.Cup	Marrakech	13 Sep
1:58.48		Sum			1	Athl	Lausanne	3 Jul
1:58.55	Yekaterina	Poistogova	RUS	1.3.91	1		Adler	30 May
1:58.63	Winnie	Nanyondo	UGA	23.8.93	3	Herc	Monaco	18 Jul
1:58.70		Wilson			1	NC	Sacramento	29 Jun
1:58.70	Svetlana	Karamasheva	RUS	24.5.88	1	Kuts	Moskva	17 Jul
1:58.70	Janeth	Jepkosgei	KEN	13.12.83	4	Herc	Monaco	18 Jul
1:58.79		Poistogova			2	Athl	Lausanne	3 Jul
1:58.80	Lynsey	Sharp	GBR	11.7.90	2	EC	Zürich	16 Aug
1:58.84	Brenda	Martinez (10)	USA	8.9.87	1	VD	Bruxelles	5 Sep
1:58.94		Sharp			2	VD	Bruxelles	5 Sep
1:58.94		Sum			3	VD	Bruxelles	5 Sep
1:59.02		Sum			1	Bisl	Oslo	11 Jun
1:59.02	Margarita	Mukasheva	KAZ	4.1.86	1	AsiG	Incheon	1 Oct
1:59.04	Laura	Roesler	USA	19.12.91	2	NC	Sacramento	29 Jun
1:59.13		Poistogova			1	Mosc Ch	Moskva	12 Jun
1:59.14		Sharp			1	DL	Birmingham	24 Aug
1:59.19	Tintu	Luka	IND	26.4.89	2	AsiG	Incheon	1 Oct
1:59.19mx		Diago			1mx		La Habana	29 Oct
1:59.24		Martinez			1	FBK	Hengelo	8 Jun
1:59.24	Tigist	Assefa	ETH-J	3.12.96	3	Athl	Lausanne	3 Jul
1:59.27		Nanyondo			1	GS	Ostrava	17 Jun
1:59.30	Molly	Beckwith-Ludlow	USA	4.8.87	4	Athl	Lausanne	3 Jul
1:59.31		Poistogova			5	Herc	Monaco	18 Jul
1:59.32		Beckwith-Ludlow			6	Herc	Monaco	18 Jul
1:59.33		Sum			1	DL	Doha	9 May
	(31/15)							
1:59.34mx	Jenny	Meadows	GBR	17.4.81	1		Manchester (Str)	26 Aug
	2:00.32				7		Glasgow	12 Jul
1:59.48	Rose Mary	Almanza	CUB	13.7.92	1		Tomblaine	27 Jun
1:59.48		Zhao Jing	CHN	9.7.88	3	AsiG	Incheon	1 Oct
1:59.51	Agatha	Kimaswai	KEN	2.4.94	1	WCM	Rieti	7 Sep
1:59.54	Svetlana	Rogozina	RUS	26.12.92	1	NC	Kazan	24 Jul
	(20)							
1:59.63	Joanna	Józwik	POL	30.1.91	3	EC	Zürich	16 Aug
1:59.70	Melissa	Bishop	CAN	5.8.88	1		Victoria	8 Jul
1:59.75	Chanelle	Price	USA	22.8.90	2	DL	Doha	9 May
1:59.77	Jessica	Judd	GBR-J	7.1.95	3	Bisl	Oslo	11 Jun

Mark	Wind	Name		Nat	Born	Pos	Meet	Venue	Date
1:59.86		Olga	Lvova	RUS	21.9.89	3	Mosc Ch	Moskva	12 Jun
1:59.92		Olha	Lyakhova	UKR	18.3.92	2	WCM	Rieti	7 Sep
1:59.93		Lenka	Masná	CZE	22.4.85	4	GS	Ostrava	17 Jun
1:59.95		Sifan	Hassan	NED	.93	5	GS	Ostrava	17 Jun
1:59.96		Maggie	Vessey	USA	23.12.81	2		Los Angeles (ER)	15 May
2:00.06		Renelle	Lamote	FRA	26.12.93	9	Herc	Monaco	18 Jul
		(30)							
2:00.08		Alison	Leonard	GBR	17.3.90	5	DL	Glasgow	12 Jul
2:00.12		Yekaterina	Kupina	RUS	2.2.86	2		Adler	30 May
2:00.28		Natoya	Goule	JAM	30.3.91	1	adidas	New York	14 Jun
2:00.29mx		Morgan	Uceny	USA	10.3.85	1		Waltham	31 May
		2:02.74				6	Gugl	Linz	14 Jul
2:00.30		Angelika	Cichocka	POL	15.3.88	4	GGala	Roma	5 Jun
2:00.41		Justine	Fédronic	FRA	11.5.91	10	Herc	Monaco	18 Jul
2:00.49		Margaret	Wambui	KEN-J	15.9.95	1	WJ	Eugene	24 Jul
2:00.50		Hannah	England	GBR	6.3.87	1	BMC	Oxford	19 Jul
2:00.51		Noélie	Yarigo	BEN	26.12.85	1		Ninove	2 Aug
2:00.55		Sanne	Verstegen	NED	10.11.85	2	NA	Heusden-Zolder	19 Jul
		(40)							
2:00.58		Malika	Akkaoui	MAR	25.12.87	6	GGala	Roma	5 Jun
2:00.58		Federica	Del Buono	ITA	12.12.94	5	WCM	Rieti	7 Sep
2:00.59		Angela	Smit	NZL	16.8.91	1		Manchester (Str)	12 Jul
2:00.6A		Hellen	Obiri	KEN	13.12.89	1	Army Ch	Nairobi	15 May
2:00.65		Heather	Kampf	USA	19.1.87	4r2	Pre	Eugene	30 May
2:00.67		Yevgeniya	Zinurova	RUS	16.11.82	3		Adler	30 May
2:00.67		Laura	Muir	GBR	9.5.93	4	DL	Birmingham	24 Aug
2:00.90		Anastasiya	Bazdyreva	RUS	6.3.92	1-23		Chelyabinsk	6 Jun
2:00.9		Anna	Musina	RUS	3.11.84	2h3	NC	Kazan	23 Jul
2:00.91		Charlene	Lipsey	USA	16.7.91	2	WCM	Madrid	19 Jul
		(50)							
2:00.91		Vania	Stambolova	BUL	28.11.83	6	EC	Zürich	16 Aug
2:00.92		Marina	Pospelova	RUS	23.7.90	5	Mosc Ch	Moskva	12 Jun
2:00.92		Jessica	Smith	CAN	11.10.89	3	NA	Heusden-Zolder	19 Jul
2:00.95		LaTavia	Thomas	USA	17.12.88	3	WCM	Madrid	19 Jul
2:01.05		Yevgeniya	Subbotina	RUS	30.10.89	3	NC	Kazan	24 Jul
2:01.10		Geena	Lara	USA	18.1.87	2	MSR	Walnut	19 Apr
2:01.1		Yelena	Zhilkina	RUS	4.5.90	3h3	NC	Kazan	23 Jul
2:01.12		Shelby	Houlihan	USA	8.2.93	7	NC	Sacramento	29 Jun
2:01.22		Kate	Grace	USA	24.10.88	3		Saline	10 Aug
2:01.23		Anita	Hinriksdóttir	ISL-J	13.1.96	2-22	WK	Zürich	28 Aug
		(60)							
2:01.24		Mirela	Lavric	ROU	17.2.91	4s1	EC	Zürich	14 Aug
2:01.25		Christina	Hering	GER	9.10.94	8	ISTAF	Berlin	31 Aug
2:01.26		Brittany	McGowan	AUS	24.4.91	1		Brisbane	29 Mar
2:01.31		Luiza	Gega	ALB	5.11.88	1	ET-3	Tbilisi	21 Jun
2:01.35		Svetlana	Uloga	RUS	23.11.86	1		Montbéliard	6 Jun
2:01.38		Diane	Cummins	CAN	19.1.74	2		Victoria	8 Jul
2:01.42		Selina	Büchel	SUI	26.7.91	1		Oslo	2 Aug
2:01.45		Anastasiya	Tkachuk	UKR	20.4.93	2		Kyiv	4 Jun
2:01.46		Karine	Belleau-Béliveau	CAN	29.12.83	1	Jordan	Stanford	4 May
2:01.50		Jemma	Simpson	GBR	10.2.84	7r2	Pre	Eugene	30 May
		(70)							
2:01.53		Kelly	Hetherington	AUS	10.3.89	2		Brisbane	29 Mar
2:01.54		Helen	Crofts	CAN	28.5.90	3		Ninove	2 Aug
2:01.57		Marilyn	Okoro	GBR	23.9.84	3	adidas	New York	14 Jun
2:01.6A		Zeytuna	Mohammed	ETH-J	2.2.96	1	NC	Addis Ababa	12 May
2:01.61		Yekaterina	Sharmina	RUS	6.8.86	2	Kuts	Moskva	17 Jul
2:01.67		Mary	Cain	USA-J	3.5.96	4	adidas	New York	14 Jun
2:01.68A		Cristina	Guevara	MEX	11.12.87	2	CAG	Xalapa	25 Nov
2:01.70		Fabienne	Kohlmann	GER	6.11.89	1	Spark	Regensburg	7 Jun
2:01.73		Lovisa	Lindh	SWE	9.7.91	3h1	EC	Zürich	13 Aug
2:01.74		Anna	Shchagina	RUS	7.12.91	4		Bellinzona	3 Jun
		(80)							
2:01.75		Christina	Rodgers	USA	8.4.88	2rB		Los Angeles (ER)	15 May
2:01.75		Katherine	Katsanevakis	AUS	11.6.88	3		San Marcos	23 May
2:01.76		Marta	Milani	ITA	9.3.87	1rB	WCM	Rieti	7 Sep
2:01.78		Georgia	Wassall	AUS-J	30.3.96	2		Sydney	15 Mar
2:01.79		Treniere	Moser	USA	27.10.81	2	Jordan	Stanford	4 May
2:01.82		Hanna	Tarver	GBR	22.10.93	4		Ninove	2 Aug
2:01.85		Sylivia	Chesebe	KEN	17.5.87	5		Tomblaine	27 Jun
2:01.89		Emily	Dudgeon	GBR	3.3.93	1		Watford	18 Jun

Mark	Wind	Name		Nat	Born	Pos	Meet	Venue	Date
2:01.9A		Mantegbosh	Melese	ETH	20.1.88	2	NC	Addis Ababa	12 May
2:01.91		Phoebe (90)	Wright	USA	30.8.88	1		Dublin	11 Jul
2:01.92		Sushma	Devi	IND	7.5.84	4	AsiG	Incheon	1 Oct
2:01.94		Shelayna	Oskan-Clarke	GBR	20.1.90	9	DL	Doha	9 May
2:01.96		Selma	Kajan	AUS	30.7.91	2		Dublin	11 Jul
2:01.97		Yusneysi	Santiusti	CUB	24.12.84	7	WCM	Rieti	7 Sep
2:02.01		Adele	Tracey	GBR	27.5.93	5		Los Angeles (ER)	15 May
2:02.01		Shannon	Leinert	USA	30.6.87	2		Portland	15 Jun
2:02.01		Gabe	Grunewald	USA	25.6.86	2rB	WCM	Rieti	7 Sep
2:02.02		Nicole	Sifuentes	CAN	30.6.86	4	NA	Heusden-Zolder	19 Jul
2:02.04A		Dorcus (100)	Ajok	UGA	12.7.94	1		Kampala	1 Jun

Mark	Name		Nat	Born	Date
2:02.05	Rachel	Aubry	CAN	18.5.90	2 Aug
2:02.07	Rose-Anne	Galligan	IRL	9.12.87	31 May
2:02.07	Clarisse	Moh	FRA	6.12.86	19 Jul
2:02.14	Cecilia	Barowski	USA	7.12.92	26 Jun
2:02.14	Erica	Moore	USA	25.3.88	10 Jul
2:02.15	Maureen	Koster	NED	3.7.92	2 Aug
2:02.16	Lauren	Wallace	USA	19.12.88	26 Jun
2:02.18	Rachel	François	CAN	14.11.92	23 May
2:02.18	Ayvika	Malanova	RUS	28.11.92	3 Jul
2:02.19	Lauren	Johnson	USA	4.5.87	15 Jun
2:02.2	Irina	Maracheva	RUS	29.9.84	23 Jul
2:02.21	Zoe	Buckman	AUS	21.12.88	29 Mar
2:02.21	Ingvill	Måkestad Bovim	NOR	7.8.81	2 Aug
2:02.24	Laura	Crowe	IRL	5.9.87	15 May
2:02.24	Hedda	Hynne	NOR	13.3.90	19 Jul
2:02.30	Natalya	Peryakova	RUS	4.3.83	6 Jun
2:02.31	Megan	Malasarte	USA	1.8.92	30 May
2:02.36	Paulina	Mikiewicz	POL	13.7.92	20 Jul
2:02.36A	Gabriela	Medina	MEX	3.3.85	25 Nov
2:02.37	Kseniya	Savina	UKR	4.6.89	2 Aug
2:02.40	Yelena	Murashova	RUS	5.10.87	3 Jul
2:02.40	Trine	Mjåland	NOR	30.6.90	19 Jul
2:02.43	Simoya	Campbell	JAM	1.3.94	28 Jun
2:02.43	Nikki	Hamblin	NZL	20.5.88	1 Aug
2:02.49	Katie	Mackey	USA	12.11.87	15 Jun
2:02.50	Corinna	Harrer	GER	19.1.91	7 Jun
2:02.50	Gilda	Casanova	CUB-J	19.12.95	13 Jun
2:02.50	Jenna	Westaway	CAN	19.6.94	10 Jul
2:02.51	Kimarra	McDonald	JAM	14.8.87	28 Jun
2:02.53	Florina	Pierdevarâ	ROU	29.3.90	29 Jun
2:02.53	Charline	Mathias	LUX	23.5.92	19 Jul
2:02.53	Victoria	Sauleda	ESP	28.8.92	2 Aug
2:02.57	Mihaela	Nunu	ROU	10.5.89	11 May
2:02.58	Shannon	Rowbury	USA	19.9.84	4 May
2:02.58	Sarah	Brown	USA	15.10.86	8 Jul
2:02.58	Oksana	Spasovkhodskaya	RUS	4.9.84	17 Jul
2:02.60	Amy	Weissenbach	USA	16.6.94	4 May
2:02.6A	Baso	Sado	ETH	.91	12 May
2:02.61	Samantha	Murphy	CAN	18.3.92	19 Apr
2:02.61	Violah	Lagat	KEN	1.3.89	7 Sep
2:02.62	Natalya	Danilova	RUS	28.8.91	30 May
2:02.62	Kate	Van Buskirk	CAN	9.6.87	31 May
2:02.63	Katie	Kirk	GBR	5.11.93	31 Jul
2:02.64	Selam	Abrhaley	ETH	9.11.94	13 Aug
2:02.66	Caster	Semenya	RSA	7.1.91	5 Jun
2:02.68	Alena	Glazkova	RUS	6.5.88	30 May
2:02.68	Claudia	Saunders	USA	19.5.94	11 Jun
2:02.69	Diana	Mezuliániková	CZE	10.4.92	28 Aug
2:02.83	Bethany	Praska	USA	10.6.89	15 May
2:02.84	Savannah	Camacho	USA	29.3.94	19 Apr
2:02.85	Dana	Mecke	USA	20.9.87	5 Jun
2:02.86	Mariya	Bykova	RUS	7.11.89	17 Jul
2:02.87	Khadija	Rahmouni	ESP	30.11.86	29 May
2:02.92	Stephanie	Charnigo	USA	25.7.88	5 Jun
2:02.95	Christy	Cazzola	USA	18.6.85	26 Jun
2:02.95	Katy	Brown	GBR	18.11.93	12 Jul
2:02.97	Lauren	Paquette	USA	27.6.86	31 May
2:02.97	Hsifa	Tarchoun	TUN	18.2.89	5 Jul
2:03.00	Sofia	Ennaoui	POL-J	30.8.95	2 Jun
2:03.02	Tatyana	Markelova	RUS	19.12.88	30 May
2:03.03	Lydia	Wafula	KEN	15.2.88	27 Jun
2:03.11	Carolin	Walter	GER	29.2.88	27 Jul
2:03.12	Thea	Heim	GER	26.7.92	14 Jul
2:03.12	Danuta	Urbanik	POL	24.12.89	20 Jul
2:03.13	Margherita	Magnani	ITA	26.2.87	7 Sep
2:03.16	Alexandra	Bell	GBR	4.11.92	12 Jul
2:03.21	Caroline	King	USA	21.9.88	30 May
2:03.23	Laura	Weightman	GBR	1.7.91	14 Jun
2:03.24	Maren	Kock	GER	22.6.90	7 Jun
2:03.26	Alexa	Efraimson	USA-Y	20.2.97	21 Jun
2:03.27	Rosalie	Waller	USA	18.12.91	26 Jun
2:03.28	Yanique	Malcolm	JAM	8.8.91	18 May
2:03.30A	Dina Lebo	Phalula	RSA	9.12.83	12 Apr
2:03.31	Lea	Wallace	USA	19.12.88	14 Jun
2:03.36	Manal	Bahraoui	MAR	6.1.94	6 Jun
2:03.36mx	Denise	Krebs	GER	27.6.87	6 Aug
2:03.37	Ejiro	Okoro	GBR	4.7.90	13 Jun
2:03.38	Georgia	Bell	GBR	17.10.93	22 Jun
2:03.42	Marta	Pen Freitas	POR	31.7.93	23 Jul
2:03.44	Olena	Sidorska	UKR	30.7.94	26 Jul
2:03.46	Katie	Snowden	GBR	9.3.94	18 Jun
2:03.46	Dorina	Korozsi	ROU	22.5.82	20 Jul
2:03.47	Sinimole (183)	Markose	IND	24.6.83	6 Jun

Indoors

Mark	Name		Nat	Born	Pos	Meet	Venue	Date
2:00.93	Selina	Büchel	SUI	26.7.91	1h3	WI	Sopot	7 Mar
2:01.29	Anna	Shchagina	RUS	7.12.91	1	NC	Moskva	18 Feb
2:01.33	Nataliya	Lupu #	UKR	4.11.87	2		Moskva	2 Feb
2:01.89	Jenna	Westaway	CAN	19.6.94	2	Mill	New York (Arm)	15 Feb

Mark	Name		Nat	Born	Date
2:02.15	Stephanie	Charnigo	USA	25.7.88	7 Feb
2:02.29	Tatyana	Myazina	RUS	18.3.88	17 Feb
2:02.89	Yelena	Kobeleva	RUS	12.6.88	18 Feb
2:02.95	Stina	Troest	DEN	17.1.94	7 Mar
2:03.16	Yekaterina	Brodovaya	RUS	28.6.91	17 Feb
2:03.18	Rabab	Arrafi	MAR	12.1.91	28 Feb
2:03.19	Anna	Balakshina	RUS	22.11.86	24 Jan
2:03.21	Stephanie	Brown	USA	29.7.91	1 Mar
2:03.29	Katarzyna	Broniatowska	POL	22.2.90	22 Feb

Drugs disqualification

Mark	Name		Nat	Born	Pos	Meet	Venue	Date
2:00.65i	Nataliya	Lupu #	UKR	4.11.87	(1h2)	WI	Sopot	7 Mar

JUNIORS

See main list for top 8 juniors. 15 performances by 4 women to 2:00.80. Additional mark and further juniors:

Diago 3+	2:00.01	2	GGala	Roma	6 Jun	2:00.96	6	CCp	Marrakech	23 Sep
Assefa	1:59.97	2		Tomblaine	27 Jun	2:00.57	4	CCp	Marrakech	23 Sep
	2:00.16	1	ISTAF	Berlin	31 Aug	2:00.94	1h3	AfCh	Mrrakech	13 Aug
	2:00.43	4	AfCh	Marrakech	14 Aug					
Judd	1:59.99	8	Herc	Monaco	18 Jul	2:00.01	3	DL	Glasgow	12 Jul

Mark	Name		Nat	Born	Pos	Meet	Venue	Date
2:02.50	Gilda	Casanova	CUB	19.12.95	1		La Habana	13 Jun
2:03.00	Sofia	Ennaoui (10)	POL	30.8.95	1	EAF	Bydgoszcz	2 Jun

Mark	Wind	Name		Nat	Born	Pos	Meet	Venue	Date
2:03.26		Alexa	Efraimson	USA-Y	20.2.97	1		Seattle	21 Jun
2:04.00		Georgia	Griffith	AUS	5.12.96	3s1	WJ	Eugene	23 Jul
2:04.13		Dureti	Edao	ETH	8.4.96	8		Marrakeh	8 Jun
2:04.20A		Maximila	Imali	KEN	8.2.96	1	NC-j	Nairobi	25 Jun
2:04.21		Sabrina	Southerland	USA	18.12.95	1h2	Big East	Villanova	10 May
2:04.40		Raevyn	Rogers	USA	7.9.96	1	NC-j	Eugene	6 Jul
2:04.47		Mohammed	Zeyituna	ETH	2.2.96	1h3	WJ	Eugene	22 Jul
2:04.58A		Monique	Stander	USA	10.3.95	1		Sasolburg	25 Mar
2:04.58A		Melissa	Torres	COL	29.4.95	4	CAG	Xalapa	25 Nov
2:04.66		Charlotte	Mouchet (20)	FRA	5.6.96	6		Montbéliard	6 Jun

1000 METRES

Mark	Wind	Name		Nat	Born	Pos	Meet	Venue	Date
2:37.5		Sahily	Diago	CUB-J	26.8.95	1		La Habana	25 Apr
2:38.01		Susan	Kuijken	NED	8.7.86	1	Flame	Amsterdam	22 Aug
2:38.1		Rose Mary	Almanza	CUB	13.7.92	2		La Habana	25 Apr
2:38.53		Sanne	Verstegen	NED	10.11.85	2	Flame	Amsterdam	22 Aug
2:38.67		Olha	Lyakhova	UKR	18.3.92	3	Flame	Amsterdam	22 Aug
2:38.75		Melissa	Bishop	CAN	5.8.88	4	Flame	Amsterdam	22 Aug

Mark	Name		Nat	Born	Date	Mark	Name		Nat	Born	Date
2:40.07	Diana	Sujew	GER	2.11.90	18 May	2:40.74	Cherono	Koech	KEN	8.12.92	22 Aug
2:40.09	Maureen	Koster	NED	3.7.92	22 Aug	2:40.74	Selma	Kajan	AUS	30.7.91	22 Aug
2:40.53		Zhao Jing	CHN	9.7.88	2 Sep	2:40.88	Kerstin	Marxen	GER	21.6.85	18 May
2:40.70	Yekaterina	Kupina	RUS	2.2.86	12 Aug	2:40.89	Paulina	Mikiewicz	POL	13.7.92	12 Aug

Indoors

Mark	Wind	Name		Nat	Born	Pos	Meet	Venue	Date
2:35.80		Mary	Cain	USA-J	3.5.96	1		Boston (R)	8 Feb
2:36.63		Chanelle	Price	USA	22.8.90	2		Boston (R)	8 Feb
2:36.90		Sarah	Brown	USA	15.10.86	3		Boston (R)	8 Feb
2:37.19		Molly	Beckwith-Ludlow	USA	4.8.87	4		Boston (R)	8 Feb
2:37.88		Treniere	Moser	USA	27.10.81	5		Boston (R)	8 Feb

Mark	Name		Nat	Born	Date	Mark	Name		Nat	Born	Date
2:39.16	Svetlana	Karamasheva	RUS	24.5.88	12 Jan	2:40.72	Violah	Lagat	KEN	1.3.89	8 Feb
2:39.94	Margherita	Magnani	ITA	26.2.87	26 Jan	2:40.90	Heather	Kampf	USA	19.1.87	8 Feb

1500 METRES

Mark	Wind	Name		Nat	Born	Pos	Meet	Venue	Date
3:57.00		Sifan	Hassan	NED	.93	1	DL	Saint-Denis	5 Jul
3:57.05		Hellen	Obiri	KEN	13.12.89	1	Pre	Eugene	31 May
3:57.22		Jennifer	Simpson	USA	23.8.86	2	DL	Saint-Denis	5 Jul
3:57.57		Abeba	Aregawi	SWE	5.7.90	2	Pre	Eugene	31 May
3:58.01		Faith	Kipyegon	KEN	10.1.94	3	Pre	Eugene	31 May
3:58.28			Simpson			4	Pre	Eugene	31 May
3:58.72			Aregawi			1	DL	Shanghai	18 May
3:58.89			Obiri			3	DL	Saint-Denis	5 Jul
3:59.21			Kipyegon			5	DL	Saint-Denis	5 Jul
3:59.38			Hassan			5	Pre	Eugene	31 May
3:59.49		Shannon	Rowbury	USA	19.9.84	5	DL	Saint-Denis	5 Jul
3:59.53		Dawit	Seyaum	ETH-J	27.7.96	1		Marrakech	8 Jun
3:59.92			Simpson			1	WK	Zürich	28 Aug
3:59.93			Rowbury			2	WK	Zürich	28 Aug
4:00.07		Laura	Muir	GBR	9.5.93	6	DL	Saint-Denis	5 Jul
4:00.08		Mimi	Belete	BRN	9.6.88	7	DL	Saint-Denis	5 Jul
4:00.13			Aregawi			1	adidas	New York	14 Jun
4:00.17		Laura	Weightman (10)	GBR	1.7.91	8	DL	Saint-Denis	5 Jul
4:00.38			Simpson			1	DNG	Stockholm	21 Aug
4:00.42			Simpson			2	DL	Shanghai	18 May
4:00.46		Viola	Kibiwot	KEN	22.12.83	3	WK	Zürich	28 Aug
4:00.66			Seyaum			2	adidas	New York	14 Jun
4:00.67			Hassan			1	DL	Glasgow	11 Jul
4:00.72			Hassan			4	WK	Zürich	28 Aug
4:00.94			Aregawi			2	DL	Glasgow	11 Jul
4:01.00		Genzebe	Dibaba	ETH	8.2.91	2	DNG	Stockholm	21 Aug
4:01.19			Hassan			3	DL	Shanghai	18 May
4:01.31			Kibiwot			4	DL	Shanghai	18 May
4:01.34		Meraf	Bahta	SWE	24.6.89	5	WK	Zürich	28 Aug
4:01.36		Brenda	Martinez	USA	8.9.87	6	WK	Zürich	28 Aug
		(30/14)							
4:01.54		Eunice	Sum	KEN	2.9.88	6	Pre	Eugene	31 May
4:02.35		Axumawit	Embaye	ETH	18.10.94	9	DL	Saint-Denis	5 Jul
4:02.71		Rabab	Arrafi	MAR	12.1.91	1	WCM	Beijing	21 May
4:02.83		Gudaf	Tsegay	ETH-Y	23.1.97	2	WCM	Beijing	21 May
4:03.12		Luiza	Gega	ALB	5.11.88	3	WCM	Beijing	21 May
4:03.98		Perine	Nengampi	KEN	1.1.89	2	NA	Heusden-Zolder	19 Jul
		(20)							

Mark	Wind	Name		Nat	Born	Pos	Meet	Venue	Date
4:04.07		Irene	Jelagat	KEN	10.12.88	5	adidas	New York	14 Jun
4:04.09		Zoe	Buckman	AUS	21.12.88	9	Pre	Eugene	31 May
4:04.10		Maryam	Jamal	BRN	16.9.84	6	FBK	Hengelo	8 Jun
4:04.11		Ingvill	Måkestad Bovim	NOR	7.8.81	3	NA	Heusden-Zolder	19 Jul
4:04.18		Treniere	Moser	USA	27.10.81	5	DL	Glasgow	11 Jul
4:04.45		Svetlana	Karamasheva	RUS	24.5.88	1	NC	Kazan	26 Jul
4:04.67		Nuria	Fernández	ESP	16.8.76	5	NA	Heusden-Zolder	19 Jul
4:04.76		Morgan	Uceny	USA	10.3.85	12	DL	Saint-Denis	5 Jul
4:04.87		Nicole	Sifuentes	CAN	30.6.86	13	DL	Saint-Denis	5 Jul
4:04.92		Maureen	Koster	NED	3.7.92	8	FBK	Hengelo	8 Jun
		(30)							
4:05.08		Nikki	Hamblin	NZL	20.5.88	2h1	CG	Glasgow	28 Jul
4:05.22		Gabe	Grunewald	USA	25.6.86	1		Lignano	8 Jul
4:05.23		Ann	Mwangi	KEN	8.12.88	6	NA	Heusden-Zolder	19 Jul
4:05.27		Hannah	England	GBR	6.3.87	9	FBK	Hengelo	8 Jun
4:05.29		Emma	Coburn	USA	19.10.90	7	NA	Heusden-Zolder	19 Jul
4:05.32		Federica	Del Buono	ITA	12.12.94	1		Rovereto	2 Sep
4:05.38		Kate	Van Buskirk	CAN	9.6.87	8	NA	Heusden-Zolder	19 Jul
4:05.40		Renata	Plis	POL	5.2.85	9	DL	Glasgow	11 Jul
4:05.46		Siham	Hilali	MAR	2.5.86	11	Pre	Eugene	31 May
4:05.54		Anna	Mishchenko	UKR	25.8.83	1		Kyiv	3 Jun
		(40)							
4:05.58		Anna	Shchagina	RUS	7.12.91	2		Marrakech	8 Jun
4:05.72		Diana	Sujew	GER	2.11.90	10	FBK	Hengelo	8 Jun
4:05.74		Katie	Mackey	USA	12.11.87	1		Seattle	6 Aug
4:05.76		Melissa	Duncan	AUS	30.1.90	5h1	CG	Glasgow	28 Jul
4:06.05		Margherita	Magnani	ITA	26.2.87	9	NA	Heusden-Zolder	19 Jul
4:06.06		Kaila	McKnight	AUS	5.5.86	6h1	CG	Glasgow	28 Jul
4:06.10		Stacy	Ndiwa	KEN	6.12.92	2		Rovereto	2 Sep
4:06.16		Heather	Kampf	USA	19.1.87	10	NA	Heusden-Zolder	19 Jul
4:06.34		Mary	Cain	USA-J	3.5.96	2	NC	Sacramento	29 Jun
4:06.38		Habiba	Ghribi	TUN	9.4.84	3	Hanz	Zagreb	2 Sep
		(50)							
4:06.77		Tatyana	Tomashova	RUS	1.7.75	2	NC	Kazan	26 Jul
4:07.05		Alexa	Efraimson	USA-Y	20.2.97	10	adidas	New York	14 Jun
4:07.05		Betlhem	Desalegn	UAE	13.11.91	11	NA	Heusden-Zolder	19 Jul
4:07.11		Violah	Lagat	KEN	1.3.89	3		Los Angeles (ER)	15 May
4:07.21		Susan	Kuijken	NED	8.7.86	1		Perth	22 Feb
4:07.34		Sofia	Ennaoui	POL-J	30.8.95	1	Kuso	Szczecin	7 Jun
4:07.34		Amela	Terzic	SRB	2.1.93	1		Velenje	1 Jul
4:07.34		Kokebe	Tesfaye	ETH-Y	5.5.97	1		Montreuil	7 Jul
4:07.35		Kate	Grace	USA	24.10.88	1	Jordan	Stanford	4 May
4:07.37		Jemma	Simpson	GBR	10.2.84	5		Los Angeles (ER)	15 May
		(60)							
4:07.42		Brie	Felnagle	USA	9.12.86	6		Los Angeles (ER)	15 May
4:07.45		Yekaterina	Sharmina	RUS	6.8.86	3	NC	Kazan	26 Jul
4:07.47		Heather	Wilson	USA	13.6.90	7		Los Angeles (ER)	15 May
4:07.50		Viktoriya	Pohoryelska	UKR	4.8.90	2		Kyiv	3 Jun
4:07.55		Angelika	Cichocka	POL	15.3.88	2	Kuso	Szczecin	7 Jun
4:07.59		Baso	Sado	ETH	.91	2		Montreuil	7 Jul
4:07.62		Yelena	Korobkina	RUS	25.11.90	1-22	Mosc Ch	Moskva	9 Jun
4:07.67		Giulia	Viola	ITA	24.4.91	5		Rovereto	2 Sep
4:07.70		Jordan	Hasay	USA	21.9.91	13	DL	Glasgow	11 Jul
4:07.77		Gemeda	Feyne	ETH	28.6.92	1		Sotteville-lès-Rouen	14 Jun
		(70)							
4:07.79		Gamze	Bulut	TUR	3.8.92	1	NC	Izmir	19 Jul
4:07.82		Elina	Sujew	GER	2.11.90	13	FBK	Hengelo	8 Jun
4:07.88		Molly	Beckwith-Ludlow	USA	4.8.87	3		Lignano	8 Jul
4:07.95		Danuta	Urbanik	POL	24.12.89	3	Kuso	Szczecin	7 Jun
4:08.08		Amanda	Eccleston	USA	18.6.90	2		Seattle	6 Aug
4:08.16		Tamara	Tverdostup	UKR	17.7.79	4	WCM	Beijing	21 May
4:08.16		Denise	Krebs	GER	27.6.87	13	NA	Heusden-Zolder	19 Jul
4:08.24		Kristina	Ugarova	RUS	22.10.87	4	NC	Kazan	26 Jul
4:08.49		Senbera	Teferi	ETH-J	3.5.95	3	Seiko	Tokyo	11 May
4:08.57		Sarah	Brown	USA	15.10.86	4	NC	Sacramento	29 Jun
		(80)							
4:08.58		Mercy	Cherono	KEN	7.5.91	1	WCM	Melbourne	22 Mar
4:08.62		Tigist	Gashaw	ETH-J	25.12.96	1		Montbéliard	6 Jun
4:08.62+		Molly	Huddle	USA	31.8.84	1		Dublin	11 Jul
4:08.79		Katarzyna	Broniatowska	POL	22.2.90	4	Kuso	Szczecin	7 Jun
4:08.85A		Selah	Busienei	KEN	27.12.91	3	NC	Nairobi	7 Jun

Mark Wind	Name		Nat	Born	Pos	Meet	Venue	Date
4:08.88	Malika	Akkaoui	MAR	25.12.87	1		Fès	24 May
4:08.89	Nataliya	Pryshchepa	UKR	11.9.94	10	EC	Zürich	15 Aug
4:08.92+	Aisha	Praught	USA	14.12.89	2		Dublin	11 Jul
4:09.00	Stephanie	Charnigo	USA	25.7.88	2h2	NC	Sacramento	27 Jun
4:09.14	Orchatteri P. (90)	Jaisha	IND	23.5.83	1	Fed Cup	Patiala	19 Aug
4:09.23	Sanae	El Otmani	MAR	20.12.86	2		Fès	24 May
4:09.34	Lea	Wallace	USA	19.12.88	8	Drake	Des Moines	25 Apr
4:09.42+	Lauren	Penney	USA	1.5.90	4		Dublin	11 Jul
4:09.48	Kim	Conley	USA	14.3.86	4		Kortrijk	12 Jul
4:09.73mx	Alison	Leonard	GBR	17.3.90	1		Manchester (Str)	26 Aug
4:09.87	Nicole	Schappert	USA	30.10.86	10		Los Angeles (ER)	15 May
4:09.88	Yuliya	Vasilyeva	RUS	23.3.87	3h2	NC	Kazan	25 Jul
4:09.99	Kerri	Gallagher	USA	31.5.89	1		Victoria	8 Jul
4:10.05	Sara	Vaughn	USA	16.5.86	1	MSR	Walnut	18 Apr
4:10.09	Corinna (100)	Harrer	GER	19.1.91	3		Dessau	11 Jun
4:10.09	Marina	Pospelova	RUS	23.7.90	2	Znam	Zhukovskiy	27 Jun

Mark	Name		Nat	Born	Date
4:10.11	Jip	Vastenburg	NED	21.3.94	19 Jul
4:10.14	Olga	Nitsina	RUS	11.2.89	29 May
4:10.28	Maren	Kock	GER	22.6.90	11 Jun
4:10.36	Bridey	Delaney	AUS	16.7.89	22 Mar
4:10.38	Sultana	Aït Hammou	MAR	10.5.80	22 Jun
4:10.41	Genzebe	Shumi Regasa	BRN	29.1.91	8 Jun
4:10.45	Sofie	Van Accom	BEL	7.6.89	2 Aug
4:10.51	Katie	Wright	NZL	17.2.88	2 Aug
4:10.55	Laura	Thweatt	USA	17.12.88	18 Apr
4:10.67	Lauren	Johnson	USA	4.5.87	5 Jul
4:10.76	Svetlana	Kudzelich	BLR	7.5.87	24 Jul
4:10.88	Cory	McGee	USA	29.5.92	27 Jun
4:10.89	Shelby	Houlihan	USA	8.2.93	8 Jul
4:10.95	Elise	Cranny	USA-J	9.5.96	4 May
4:10.95	Lucy	Van Dalen	NZL	18.11.88	8 Jul
4:10.98	Lauren	Paquette	USA	27.6.86	15 Jun
4:11.05	Sandra	Eriksson	FIN	4.6.89	31 Aug
4:11.06	Stephanie	Brown	USA	29.7.91	27 Jun
4:11.21	Sheila	Keter	KEN-J	27.6.95	27 Jul
4:11.27	Isabel	Macias	ESP	11.8.84	19 Jul
4:11.33	Solange Andreia	Pereira	ESP	12.12.89	21 Jun
4:11.38	Charlene	Thomas	GBR	6.5.82	31 May
4:11.41	Melissa	Courtney	GBR	30.8.93	31 May
4:11.43	Anna	Konovalova	RUS	4.7.88	25 Jul
4:11.46	Aleksandra	Pavlyutenkova	RUS	21.3.90	4 Jun
4:11.49	Laura	Crowe	IRL	5.9.87	18 Jan
4:11.63	Angela	Bizzarri	USA	15.2.88	14 Jun
4:11.66	Heidi	Gregson	AUS	8.9.89	5 Apr
4:11.78	Sonja	Roman	SLO	11.3.79	11 Jun
4:11.84	Diana	Mezuliáníková	CZE	10.4.92	24 May
4:11.84	Jessica	O'Connell	CAN	10.2.89	14 Jun
4:11.87	Marusa	Mismas	SLO	24.10.94	2 Sep
4:11.89	Charlotta	Fougberg	SWE	19.6.85	16 Jul
4:12.00	Jenny	Blundell	AUS	9.5.94	5 Apr
4:12.02	Anne	Kesselring	GER	4.12.89	14 Jun
4:12.10	Ajee'	Wilson	USA	8.5.94	12 May
4:12.12	Tizita	Bogale	ETH	13.7.93	7 Jul
4:12.17	Geena	Lara	USA	18.1.87	15 May
4:12.21	Claire	Perraux	FRA	6.10.87	2 Aug
4:12.23	Svetlana	Kireyeva	RUS	12.6.87	6 Jun
4:12.25	Olena	Zhushman	UKR	30.12.85	3 Jun
4:12.25	Amanda	Mergaert	USA	4.9.91	27 Jun
4:12.33	Josephine	Moultrie	GBR	19.11.90	18 Apr
4:12.33	Amanda	Winslow	USA	10.12.90	15 May
4:12.35	Melissa	Salerno	USA	22.11.86	12 May
4:12.37	Rebecca	Tracy	USA	20.2.91	18 Apr
4:12.37A	Beatrice	Chepkoech	KEN	.91	7 Jun
4:12.41	Ayako	Jinnouchi	JPN	21.1.87	2 Jul
4:12.44	Annett	Horna	GER	4.2.87	11 Jun
4:12.47	Darya	Barysevich	BLR	6.4.90	24 Jul
4:12.54	Agata	Strausa	LAT	2.12.89	4 May
4:12.61	Ayvika	Malanova	RUS	28.11.92	9 Jul
4:12.73	Liina	Tsernov	EST	28.12.87	7 Jun
4:12.86	Kristiina	Mäki	CZE	22.9.91	24 May
4:12.89	Tatyana	Markelova	RUS	19.12.88	29 May
4:12.94	Thea	Heim	GER	26.7.92	19 Jul
4:12.99	Yuliya	Kutah	UKR	18.8.91	25 Jul
4:13.04	Sinimole	Markose	IND	24.6.83	5 Jul
4:13.09	Kristine Eikrem	Engeset	NOR	15.11.88	2 Aug
4:13.13	Hillary	Holt	USA	24.4.92	18 Apr
4:13.15	Morag	MacLarty	GBR	10.2.86	7 Jun
4:13.16	Selma	Kajan	AUS	30.7.91	20 Jul
4:13.25	Caterina	Granz	GER	14.3.94	5 Jul
4:13.27	Anastasiya	Kalina	RUS	16.2.94	29 May
4:13.27	Jessica	Tebo	USA	8.4.88	8 Jul
4:13.29	Shannon	Morton	USA	10.7.93	14 Jun
4:13.47	Florina	Pierdevarâ	ROU	29.3.90	28 Jun
4:13.48	Yevgeniya	Zinurova	RUS	16.11.82	9 Jul
4:13.51	Laura	Méndez	ESP	6.11.88	5 Jul
4:13.51	Svetlana	Uloga	RUS	23.11.86	26 Jul
4:13.53	Genevieve	LaCaze	AUS	4.8.89	8 Jul
4:13.59A	Caroline	Chepkemoi	KEN	.93	7 Jun
4:13.63	Sarah (174)	Gollish	CAN	27.12.81	12 Jul

Indoors

Mark	Name		Nat	Born	Pos	Meet	Venue	Date
3:55.17	Genzebe	Dibaba	ETH	8.2.91	1		Karlsruhe	1 Feb
3:57.91		Aregawi			1	XLG	Stockholm	6 Feb
4:00.61		Aregawi			1	WI	Sopot	8 Mar
4:05.70+	Kim	Conley	USA	14.3.86	1	in 1M	New York (Arm)	25 Jan
4:05.78	Yelena	Korobkina	RUS	25.11.90	3	GP	Birmingham	15 Feb
4:09.22	Isabel	Macías	ESP	11.8.84	6	GP	Birmingham	15 Feb
4:09.77+	Abbey	D'Agostino	USA	25.5.92	3	in 1M	Boston (A)	24 Jan

Mark	Name		Nat	Born	Date
4:12.51	Natalya	Aristarkhova	RUS	31.10.89	19 Feb
4:12.76	Gabe	Grunewald	USA	25.6.86	25 Jan
4:13.23	Ophélie	Claude-Boxberger	FRA	18.10.88	1 Feb
4:13.42	Yelena	Kobeleva	RUS	12.6.88	1 Feb

JUNIORS

See main list for top 8 juniors. 14 performances (2 indoors) by 6 women to 4:08.4. Additional marks and further juniors:

Name	Mark	Pos	Meet	Venue	Date	Mark	Pos	Meet	Venue	Date
Seyaum 2+	4:07.61	3	CCp	Marrakech	14 Sep					
Tsegaye	4:03.21	4	FBK	Hengelo	8 Jun	4:07.02	5	Hanz	Zagreb	2 Sep
	4:05.13	7	DL	Shanghai	18 May	4:08.34	12	DNG	Stockholm	21 Aug
Cain	4:06.63+i	1		Boston (A)	24 Jan	4:07.05Ai	12	NC	Albuquerque	23 Feb

Mark	Name		Nat	Born	Pos	Meet	Venue	Date
4:10.95	Elise	Cranny	USA	9.5.96	6	Jordan	Stanford	4 May
4:11.21	Sheila	Keter (10)	KEN	27.6.95	3	WJ	Eugene	27 Jul
4:13.80	Winfredah	Nzisa	KEN-Y	30.5.97	7	WJ	Eugene	27 Jul

Mark	Wind	Name		Nat	Born	Pos	Meet	Venue	Date
4:14.66		Anastasía-Panayióta	Marinákou	GRE	12.6.96	5	ET-1	Tallinn	22 Jun
4:14.73		Sahily	Diago	CUB	26.8.95	2		La Habana	9 Oct
4:15.08		Amy	Griffiths	GBR	22.3.96	1	N.Sch	Birmingham	12 Jul
4:15.14		Anita	Hinriksdóttir	ISL	13.1.96	1	ECCp-B	Amsterdam	24 May
4:15.23		Anna	Laman	AUS	25.5.95	8		Perth	22 Feb
4:15.32mx		Rosie	Johnson	GBR-Y	17.9.97	1mx		Manchester (Str)	1 Jul
4:16.47		Bobby	Clay	GBR-Y	19.5.97	8	WJ	Eugene	27 Jul
4:16.65		Rosa	Flanahan	NZL	28.2.96	9		Victoria	8 Jul
4:17.00		Gabriella	Stafford (20)	CAN	13.9.95	1		Charlottesville	10 May

1 MILE

Mark	Name		Nat	Born	Pos	Meet	Venue	Date
4:22.22e+	Genzebe	Dibaba	ETH	8.2.91	1	in 2000	Ostrava	17 Jun
4:26.67	Sarah	Brown	USA	15.10.86	1	Jerome	Burnaby	10 Jul
4:26.84	Molly	Huddle	USA	31.8.84	1		Dublin	11 Jul
4:26.90	Melissa	Duncan	AUS	30.1.90	2		Dublin	11 Jul
4:27.61	Aisha	Praught	USA	14.12.89	3		Dublin	11 Jul
4:27.78	Katie	Mackey	USA	12.11.87	1		Falmouth	16 Aug
4:28.02	Lauren	Penney	USA	1.5.90	4		Dublin	11 Jul
4:28.08	Kate	Van Buskirk	CAN	9.6.87	2	Jerome	Burnaby	10 Jul
4:29.43	Violah	Lagat	KEN	1.3.89	1		Concord	5 Jun
4:29.61	Morgan	Uceny	USA	10.3.85	3		Falmouth	16 Aug
4:29.83	Brie	Felnagle	USA	9.12.86	4		Falmouth	16 Aug

Mark	Name		Nat	Born	Date	Mark	Name		Nat	Born	Date
4:30.42	Amanda	Eccleston	USA	18.6.90	16 Aug	4:31.68	Chanelle	Price	USA	22.8.90	26 Apr
4:30.73	Lauren	Paquette	USA	27.6.86	10 Jul	4:32.35	Racheal	Bamford	GBR	4.8.89	11 Jul
4:30.75	Jessica	O'Connell	CAN	10.2.89	10 Jul	4:32.57	Angela	Bizzarri	USA	15.2.88	10 Jul
4:31.25	Stephanie	Garcia	USA	3.5.88	16 Aug	4:33.00	Lauren	Johnson	USA	4.5.87	5 Jun
4:31.66	Amanda	Winslow	USA	10.12.90	5 Jun	4:33.00	Katrina	Coogan	USA	15.11.93	5 Jun

Indoors

Mark	Name		Nat	Born	Pos	Meet	Venue	Date
4:24.11	Mary	Cain	USA-J	3.5.96	1		Boston (A)	24 Jan
4:24.54	Kim	Conley	USA	14.3.86	1		New York (Arm)	25 Jan
4:26.28	Amanda	Winslow	USA	10.12.90	1		Boston (A)	7 Feb
4:28.31	Abbey	D'Agostino	USA	25.5.92	2		Boston (A)	24 Jan
4:28.37	Jordan	Hasay	USA	21.9.91	3		Boston (A)	24 Jan
4:28.86	Treniere	Moser	USA	27.10.81	2	Mill	New York (Arm)	15 Feb
4:28.97	Nicole	Sifuentes	CAN	30.6.86	3	Mill	New York (Arm)	15 Feb

Mark	Name		Nat	Born	Date	Mark	Name		Nat	Born	Date
4:30.14	Heather	Kampf	USA	19.1.87	25 Jan	4:32.20	Yelena	Korobkina	RUS	25.11.90	8 Feb
4:32.01	Emma	Coburn	USA	19.10.90	15 Feb	4:32.37	Nicole	Schappert	USA	30.10.86	7 Feb
4:32.15	Alexa	Efraimson	USA-Y	20.2.97	15 Feb	4:32.61	Lucy	Van Dalen	NZL	18.11.88	25 Jan

JUNIORS

Cain 4:27.73i 1 Mill New York (Arm) 15 Feb

Mark	Name		Nat	Born	Pos	Meet	Venue	Date
4:38.32	Rosa	Flanagan	NZL	28.2.96	1	Jerome	Burnaby	10 Jul
4:36.14i	Elinor	Purrier	USA	20.2.95	3		Boston (A)	2 Mar
At 1600m: 4:33.29	Alexa	Efraimson	USA-Y	20.2.97	1		Tacoma	30 May

2000 METRES

Mark	Name		Nat	Born	Pos	Meet	Venue	Date
5:27.50	Genzebe	Dibaba	ETH	8.2.91	1	GS	Ostrava	17 Jun
5:29.42		G Dibaba			1		Sollentuna	26 Jun
5:34.27	Senbera	Teferi	ETH-J	3.5.95	2	GS	Ostrava	17 Jun
5:37.32+		G Dibaba			1	in 3000	Doha	9 May
5:37.5+	Almaz	Ayana	ETH	21.11.91	2	in 3000	Doha	9 May
5:37.6+	Mercy	Cherono	KEN	7.5.91	3	in 3000	Doha	9 May
5:37.7+	Hellen	Obiri	KEN	13.12.89	4	in 3000	Doha	9 May
5:37.8+	Faith	Kipyegon	KEN	10.1.94	5	in 3000	Doha	9 May
5:38.0+	Mimi	Belete	BRN	9.6.88	6	in 3000	Doha	9 May
5:38.2+	Viola	Kibiwot	KEN	22.12.83	7	in 3000	Doha	9 May
5:39.96	Gemeda	Feyne	ETH	28.6.92	3	GS	Ostrava	17 Jun
5:41.98	Renata	Plis	POL	5.2.85	4	GS	Ostrava	17 Jun
5:42.71	Kristiina	Mäki	CZE	22.9.91	5	GS	Ostrava	17 Jun

Mark	Name		Nat	Born	Date	Mark	Name		Nat	Born	Date
5:43.8+	Luiza	Gega	ALB	5.11.88	5 Sep	5:46.0+	Perine	Nengampi	KEN	1.1.89	5 Sep
5:45.7+	Betsy	Saina	KEN	30.6.88	5 Sep	5:46.1+	Sifan	Hassan	NED	.93	5 Sep
5:45.7+	Stacy	Ndiwa	KEN	6.12.92	5 Sep	5:46.2+	Shannon	Rowbury	USA	19.9.84	5 Sep
5:45.7+	Jennifer	Simpson	USA	23.8.86	5 Sep	5:46.4+	Irene	Jelagat	KEN	10.12.88	5 Sep
5:45.9+	Alemitu	Haroye	ETH-J	9.5.95	5 Sep	5:46.4+	Sally	Kipyego	KEN	19.12.85	5 Sep
5:45.9+	Janet	Kisa	KEN	5.3.92	5 Sep	5:46.70	Etagegne	Woldu	ETH-J	10.5.96	17 Jun
5:45.9+	Mimi	Belete	BRN	9.6.88	5 Sep	5:46.7+	Susan	Kuijken	NED	8.7.86	5 Sep
						5:46.78	Katarzyna	Broniatowska	POL	22.2.90	17 Jun

Indoors

Mark	Name		Nat	Born	Pos	Meet	Venue	Date
5:34.24+		G Dibaba			1	in 3000	Stockholm	6 Feb
5:41.10	Kim	Conley	USA	14.3.86	1		Boston (R)	8 Feb

3000 METRES

Mark	Name		Nat	Born	Pos	Meet	Venue	Date
8:20.68	Hellen	Obiri	KEN	13.12.89	1	DL	Doha	9 May

Mark	Wind	Name		Nat	Born	Pos	Meet	Venue	Date
8:21.14		Mercy	Cherono	KEN	7.5.91	2	DL	Doha	9 May
8:23.55		Faith	Kipyegon	KEN	10.1.94	3	DL	Doha	9 May
8:24.41		Viola	Kibiwot	KEN	22.12.83	4	DL	Doha	9 May
8:24.58		Almaz	Ayana	ETH	21.11.91	5	DL	Doha	9 May
8:26.21		Genzebe	Dibaba	ETH	8.2.91	6	DL	Doha	9 May
8:28.51		Irene	Jelagat	KEN	10.12.88	7	DL	Doha	9 May
8:28.95			Cherono			1	VD	Bruxelles	5 Sep
8:29.38		Sifan	Hassan	NED	.93	2	VD	Bruxelles	5 Sep
8:29.41			G Dibaba			3	VD	Bruxelles	5 Sep
8:29.58		Jennifer	Simpson	USA	23.8.86	4	VD	Bruxelles	5 Sep
8:29.93		Shannon	Rowbury (10)	USA	19.9.84	5	VD	Bruxelles	5 Sep
8:30.00		Mimi	Belete	BRN	9.6.88	8	DL	Doha	9 May
8:30.14			Kibiwot			6	VD	Bruxelles	5 Sep
8:30.54		Stacy	Ndiwa	KEN	6.12.92	7	VD	Bruxelles	5 Sep
8:32.66		Janet	Kisa	KEN	5.3.92	8	VD	Bruxelles	5 Sep
8:33.43			Ayana			9	VD	Bruxelles	5 Sep
8:34.18		Sally	Kipyego	KEN	19.12.85	10	VD	Bruxelles	5 Sep
8:34.67			Jelagat			11	VD	Bruxelles	5 Sep
8:34.73			Belete			12	VD	Bruxelles	5 Sep
8:36.08		Susan	Kuijken	NED	8.7.86	13	VD	Bruxelles	5 Sep
8:36.87		Alemitu	Haroye	ETH-J	9.5.95	14	VD	Bruxelles	5 Sep
8:36.9+			Cherono			1	in 2M	Eugene	31 May
8:37.1+			Kibiwot			2	in 2M	Eugene	31 May
8:37.3+			Rowbury			3	in 2M	Eugene	31 May
8:38.0+			Belete			4	in 2M	Eugene	31 May
		(26/16)							
8:38.01		Betsy	Saina	KEN	30.6.88	15	VD	Bruxelles	5 Sep
8:39.18		Renata	Plis	POL	5.2.85	16	VD	Bruxelles	5 Sep
8:41.54		Senbera	Teferi	ETH-J	3.5.95	9	DL	Doha	9 May
8:42.54		Kalkidan	Gezahegne	BRN	8.5.91	3	adidas	New York	14 Jun
		(20)							
8:44.11		Kim	Conley	USA	14.3.86	5	adidas	New York	14 Jun
8:44.2+		Belaynesh	Oljira	ETH	26.6.90	6	in 2M	Eugene	31 May
8:45.15		Perine	Nengampi	KEN	1.1.89	17	VD	Bruxelles	5 Sep
8:46.6+		Margaret	Muriuki	KEN	21.3.86	8	in 2M	Eugene	31 May
8:47.26		Agnes	Tirop	KEN-J	23.10.95	11	DL	Doha	9 May
8:47.74		Maryam	Jamal	BRN	16.9.84	12	DL	Doha	9 May
8:48.44		Rosemary	Wanjiru	KEN	9.12.94	1		Yamaguchi	11 Oct
8:48.7+		Molly	Huddle	USA	31.8.84	6	in 5000	Monaco	18 Jul
8:48.90		Julia	Bleasdale	GBR	9.9.81	6	adidas	New York	14 Jun
8:49.45		Yeshaneh	Ababel	ETH	10.6.90	13	DL	Doha	9 May
		(30)							
8:49.94		Purity	Rionoripo	KEN	10.6.93	2	WCM	Madrid	19 Jul
8:50.12mx		Maren	Kock	GER	22.6.90	1		Osterode	27 Jun
8:50.80mx		Fionnuala	Britton	IRL	24.9.84	1		Dublin	15 Jun
8:51.00		Yelena	Korobkina	RUS	25.11.90	2	ET	Braunschweig	21 Jun
8:51.46		Buze	Diriba	ETH	9.2.94	7	adidas	New York	14 Jun
8:51.48		Nikki	Hamblin	NZL	20.5.88	8	adidas	New York	14 Jun
8:51.54		Nuria	Fernández	ESP	16.8.76	3	ET	Braunschweig	21 Jun
8:51.69		Kristiina	Mäki	CZE	22.9.91	4	ET	Braunschweig	21 Jun
8:51.82		Margherita	Magnani	ITA	26.2.87	5	ET	Braunschweig	21 Jun
8:52.23		Chelsea	Reilly	USA	9.5.89	9	adidas	New York	14 Jun
		(40)							
8:52.24		Tejitu	Daba	BRN	20.8.91	1		Bilbao	21 Jun
8:52.39		Gabe	Grunewald	USA	25.6.86	3	WCM	Madrid	19 Jul
8:52.63		Gladys	Chesire	KEN	20.2.93	2		Bilbao	21 Jun
8:52.68mx		Diana	Sujew	GER	2.11.90	1		Berlin	11 May
		8:54.50				8	ET	Braunschweig	21 Jun
8:53.1+		Clémence	Calvin	FRA	17.5.90	8	in 2M	Birmingham	24 Aug
8:53.41		Lilian	Rengeruk	KEN-Y	3.5.97	14	DL	Doha	9 May
8:53.55		Alice	Nawowuna	KEN	11.3.94	15	DL	Doha	9 May
8:54.11		Eloise	Wellings	AUS	9.11.82	18	VD	Bruxelles	5 Sep
8:54.48		Marielle	Hall	USA	28.1.92	1		Cork	8 Jul
8:54.87		Jessica	O'Connell	CAN	10.2.89	1	Flanders	Gent	21 Jul
		(50)							
8:55.13		Sandra	Eriksson	FIN	4.6.89	1	PNG	Turku	25 Jun
8:55.48		Nicole	Schappert	USA	30.10.86	10	adidas	New York	14 Jun
8:55.55		Lauren	Penney	USA	1.5.90	11	adidas	New York	14 Jun

Mark	Name		Nat	Born	Date
8:56.24	Kate	Avery	GBR	10.10.91	21 Jun
8:56.67	Ashley	Higginson	USA	17.3.89	14 Jun
8:57.06	Meraf	Bahta	SWE	24.6.89	3 Jul
8:57.23	Gotytom	Gebreslase	ETH-J	15.1.95	14 Jun

Mark	Wind	Name		Nat	Born	Pos	Meet	Venue	Date

Mark	Name		Nat	Born	Pos	Date
8:57.31	Belaynesh	Oljira	ETH	26.6.90	3	Jul
8:57.52	Gemeda	Feyne	ETH	28.6.92	19	Jul
8:57.68	Beverly	Ramos	PUR	24.8.87	17	May
8:57.8+	Hiwot	Ayalew	ETH	6.3.90	5	Jun
8:58.01mx	Beth	Potter	GBR	27.12.91	2	Jul
8:58.01mx	Stevie	Stockton	GBR	23.8.89	30	Jul
8:58.08	Ayuko	Suzuki	JPN	8.10.91	27	Sep
8:58.09	Stephanie	Garcia	USA	3.5.88	17	May
8:58.14	Melissa	Duncan	AUS	30.1.90	8	Jul
8:58.48	Mary	Cain	USA-J	3.5.96	24	Jul
8:58.56	Charlotta	Fougberg	SWE	19.6.85	22	May
8:58.6+	Etagegne	Woldu	ETH-J	10.5.96	5	Jun
8:59.44	Sofia	Ennaoui	POL-J	30.8.95	14	Jun
8:59.52	Yuka	Miyazaki	JPN	21.8.92	30	Aug
8:59.57mx	Laura	Whittle	GBR	27.6.85	11	Jun
9:00.67	Aisha	Praught	USA	14.12.89	17	May
9:00.79	Valentine	Mateiko	KEN-J	6.9.96	24	Jul
9:00.89	Azusa	Sumi	JPN-J	12.8.96	11	Oct
9:00.91	Harumi	Okamoto	JPN-Y	7.2.98	11	Oct
9:01.1+	Jo	Pavey	GBR	20.9.73	5	Jun
9:01.25	Jessica	Tebo	USA	8.4.88	14	Jun
9:01.29	Susan	Wairimu	KEN	11.10.92	2	Jul
9:01.33	Giulia	Viola	ITA	24.4.91	6	Jul
9:01.38	Federica	Del Buono	ITA	12.12.94	18	May
9:01.58	Nozomi	Takamatsu	JPN-Y	31.8.97	24	Aug
9:02.23	Azmera	Gebru	ETH	5.5.92	6	Jul
9:02.50	Habiba	Ghribi	TUN	9.4.84	4	May
9:02.61	Sabrina	Mockenhaupt	GER	6.12.80	21	May
9:02.73	Irene	Cheptai	KEN	4.2.92	3	Jul
9:03.06	Ruti	Aga	ETH	16.1.94	6	Jul
9:03.61	Christelle	Daunay	FRA	5.12.74	18	Jun
9:03.89	Eilish	McColgan	GBR	25.11.90	21	Jun
9:03.95	Helen	Clitheroe	GBR	2.1.74	8	Jul
9:04.10	Sara	Moreira	POR	17.10.85	19	Jul
9:04.30mx	Elina	Sujew	GER	2.11.90	18	May
9:04.40	Yekaterina	Doseykina	RUS	30.3.90	12	Jun
9:04.66	Linah	Cheruto	KEN-J	18.3.95	18	May
9:04.79	Marta	Silvestre	ESP	4.4.82	21	Jun
9:04.6+	Emelia	Gorecka	GBR	29.1.94	24	Aug
9:05.07	Alina	Reh	GER-Y	23.5.97	24	Aug
9:05.45	Misaki	Onishi	JPN	24.2.85	2	Jul
9:05.54	Gema	Barrachina	ESP	10.4.86	21	Jun
9:05.57	Yuika	Mori (100)	JPN	25.1.88	8	Jul
9:05.66	Maria	McCambridge	IRL	10.7.75	8	Jul

Indoors

Mark	Name		Nat	Born	Pos	Meet	Venue	Date
8:16.60	Genzebe	Dibaba	ETH	8.2.91	1	XLG	Stockholm	6 Feb
8:24.85+		G Dibaba			1	in 2M	Birmingham	15 Feb
8:29.99		Obiri			2	XLG	Stockholm	6 Feb
8:43.16	Maryam	Jamal	BRN	16.9.84	1	AsiC	Hangzhou	16 Feb
8:43.29+	Hiwot	Ayalew	ETH	6.3.90	2	in 2M	Birmingham	15 Feb
8:46.54	Betlhem	Desalegn	UAE	13.11.91	2	AsiC	Hangzhou	16 Feb
8:48.27	Alia Mohamed	Saeed	UAE	18.5.91	7	XLG	Stockholm	6 Feb
8:51.81	Margherita	Magnani	ITA	26.2.87	3	Mill	New York (Arm)	15 Feb
8:51.91	Abbey	D'Agostino	USA	25.5.92	4	Mill	New York (Arm)	15 Feb
8:53.95	Lucy	Van Dalen	NZL	18.11.88	6	Mill	New York (Arm)	15 Feb
8:54.30+	Jordan	Hasay	USA	21.9.91	3	in 2M	Boston (R)	8 Feb
8:55.21	Lydia	Chepkurui	KEN	23.8.84	8	XLG	Stockholm	6 Feb

Mark	Name		Nat	Born	Pos	Date
8:56.20	Kate	Avery	GBR	10.10.91	15	Feb
8:56.37	Amanda	Winslow	USA	10.12.90	1	Feb
8:57.03	Natalya	Aristarkhova	RUS	31.10.89	17	Feb
8:58.79	Yelena	Nagovitsyna	RUS	7.12.82	11	Jan
9:00.16	Alexa	Efraimson	USA-Y	20.2.97	1	Feb
9:00.47	Haftamnesh	Tesfay	ETH	28.4.94	11	Feb
9:00.76	Emily	Sisson	USA	12.10.91	7	Feb
9:00.88+	Stephanie	Twell	GBR	17.8.89	15	Feb
9:01.30	Svitlana	Shmidt	UKR	20.3.90	11	Feb
9:01.35	Laura	Nagel	NZL	11.2.92	7	Feb
9:01.57	Brie	Felnagle	USA	9.12.86	15	Feb
9:01.58	Laura	Thweatt	USA	17.12.88	15	Feb
9:02.33	Dominique	Scott	RSA	24.6.92	15	Feb
9:02.79	Deborah	Maier	USA	17.8.90	1	Feb
9:03.99	Alena	Kudashkina	RUS	10.4.94	11	Jan
9:04.31	Kelsey	Smith	USA	5.11.91	1	Feb
9:04.57	Aisling	Cuffe	USA	12.9.93	1	Mar
9:04.63+	Josephine	Moultrie	GBR	19.11.90	15	Feb
9:04.96	Megan	Patrignelli	USA	22.6.92	15	Feb
9:05.16	Grace	Heymsfield	USA	24.3.92	15	Feb
9:05.86	Shelby	Houlihan	USA	8.2.93	15	Feb
9:05.93	Charlene	Thomas	GBR	6.5.82	9	Feb

Best in women's only race

Mark	Name	Date
9:00.60	Kock	24 May
9:01.01	Britton	8 Jul
9:04.62	Whittle	18 May
9:04.96i	Sujew	23 Feb

JUNIORS

See main list for top 4 juniors. 10 performances (2 indoors) by 5 women to 8:58.0. Additional marks and further juniors:

Name	Mark	Pos	Meet	Venue	Date	Mark	Pos	Meet	Venue	Date
Haroye	8:43.2+	6	in 2M	Birmingham	24 Aug	8:45.93	10	DL	Doha	9 May
Tirop	8:57.00	8	Athl	Lausanne	3 Jul					
Teferi	8:47.94i	6	XLG	Stockhoilm	6 Feb	8:57.93i	1		Eaubonne	11 Feb

Mark	Name		Nat	Born	Pos	Meet	Venue	Date
8:57.23	Gotytom	Gebreslase	ETH	15.1.95	13	adidas	New York	14 Jun
8:58.48	Mary	Cain	USA	3.5.96	1	WJ	Eugene	24 Jul
8:58.6+	Etagegne	Woldu	ETH	10.5.96	12	in 5000	Roma	5 Jun
8:59.44	Sofia	Ennaoui	POL	30.8.95	2		Sotteville-lès-Rouen	14 Jun
9:00.79	Valentine	Mateiko	KEN	6.9.96	3	WJ	Eugene	24 Jul
9:00.89	Azusa	Sumi (10)	JPN	12.8.96	1		Fukuroi	11 Oct
9:00.91	Harumi	Okamoto	JPN-Y	7.2.98	2		Fukuroi	11 Oct
9:01.58	Nozomi	Takamatsu	JPN-Y	31.8.97	1	Yth OG	Nanjing	24 Aug
9:04.66	Linah	Cheruto	KEN	18.3.95	3		Gavardo	18 May
9:05.07	Alina	Reh	GER-Y	23.5.97	2	Yth OG	Nanjing	24 Aug
9:06.10	Berhan	Demisse	ETH-Y	3.1.97	3	Yth OG	Nanjing	24 Aug
9:06.85	Emine Hatun	Tuna	TUR	7.12.95	6	WJ	Eugene	24 Jul
9:06.87	Fatuma	Jawaro	BRN-Y	11.8.98	1h1	Yth OG	Nanjing	20 Aug
9:07.23	Cavaline	Nahimana	BDI-Y	14.1.97	2h1	Yth Oly	Nanjing	20 Aug
9:07.43	Sakiho	Tsutsui	JPN	19.1.96	2		Yamaguchi	11 Oct
9:07.75A	Mariam	Waithera	KEN	23.12.96	1		Kofu	3 Aug
9:00.16 i	Alexa	Efraimson	USA-Y	20.2.97	4		Seattle	1 Feb

2 MILES

Mark	Name		Nat	Born	Pos	Meet	Venue	Date
9:11.49	Mercy	Cherono	KEN	7.5.91	1	DL	Birmingham	24 Aug
9:12.59	Viola	Kibiwot	KEN	22.12.83	2	DL	Birmingham	24 Aug

WOMEN 2014

Mark Wind	Name		Nat	Born	Pos	Meet	Venue	Date
9:12.90	Irene	Jelagat	KEN	10.12.88	3	DL	Birmingham	24 Aug
9:13.27		Cherono			1	Pre	Eugene	31 May
9:13.48		Kibiwot			2	Pre	Eugene	31 May
9:13.85	Mimi	Belete	BRN	9.6.88	3	Pre	Eugene	31 May
9:14.28	Genzebe	Dibaba	ETH	8.2.91	4	DL	Birmingham	24 Aug
9:16.95	Betsy	Saina	KEN	30.6.88	5	DL	Birmingham	24 Aug
	(8/6)							
9:20.25	Shannon	Rowbury	USA	19.9.84	4	Pre	Eugene	31 May
9:20.81	Alemitu	Haroye	ETH-J	9.5.95	6	DL	Birmingham	24 Aug
9:22.10	Sally	Kipyego	KEN	19.12.85	5	Pre	Eugene	31 May
9:23.32	Belaynesh	Oljira	ETH	26.6.90	6	Pre	Eugene	31 May
9:23.52	Susan	Kuijken	NED	8.7.86	7	DL	Birmingham	24 Aug
9:24.89	Margaret	Muriuki	KEN	21.3.86	7	Pre	Eugene	31 May
9:28.80	Renata	Plis	POL	5.2.85	8	DL	Birmingham	24 Aug
9:30.39	Clémence	Calvin	FRA	17.5.90	9	DL	Birmingham	24 Aug
9:33.47	Maryam	Jamal	BRN	16.9.84	10	DL	Birmingham	24 Aug
9:35.05	Jordan	Hasay	USA	21.9.91	9	Pre	Eugene	31 May

Mark	Name		Nat	Born	Date
9:40.01	Buze	Diriba	ETH	9.2.94	31 May
9:41.76	Gabe	Grunewald	USA	25.6.86	24 Aug
9:42.51	Chelsea	Reilly	USA	9.5.89	31 May
9:43.22	Emelia	Gorecka	GBR	29.1.94	24 Aug
9:44.46	Laura	Thweatt	USA	17.12.88	31 May

Indoors

Mark	Name		Nat	Born	Pos	Meet	Venue	Date
9:00.48	Genzebe	Dibaba	ETH	8.2.91	1	GP	Birmingham	15 Feb
9:21.04	Sally	Kipyego	KEN	19.12.85	1		Boston (R)	8 Feb
9:21.59	Hiwot	Ayalew	ETH	6.3.90	2	GP	Birmingham	15 Feb
9:26.19	Jennifer	Simpson	USA	23.8.86	2		Boston (R)	8 Feb

Mark	Name		Nat	Born	Date
9:42.41	Stephanie	Twell	GBR	17.8.89	15 Feb
9:45.97	Lydia	Chepkurui	KEN	23.8.84	15 Feb
9:46.77	Josephine	Moultrie	GBR	19.11.90	15 Feb

JUNIORS: 9:49.08i Gotytom Gebreslase ETH 15.1.95 4 Boston (R) 8 Feb

5000 METRES

Mark Wind	Name		Nat	Born	Pos	Meet	Venue	Date
14:28.88	Genzebe	Dibaba	ETH	8.2.91	1	Herc	Monaco	18 Jul
14:29.19	Almaz	Ayana	ETH	21.11.91	2	Herc	Monaco	18 Jul
14:33.73	Viola	Kibiwot	KEN	22.12.83	3	Herc	Monaco	18 Jul
14:34.99		G Dibaba			1	GGala	Roma	5 Jun
14:37.16		Ayana			2	GGala	Roma	5 Jun
14:37.18	Sally	Kipyego	KEN	19.12.85	4	Herc	Monaco	18 Jul
14:39.49	Betsy	Saina	KEN	30.6.88	5	Herc	Monaco	18 Jul
14:40.05		Kibiwot			3	GGala	Roma	5 Jun
14:42.64	Molly	Huddle	USA	31.8.84	6	Herc	Monaco	18 Jul
14:43.11	Mercy	Cherono	KEN	7.5.91	4	GGala	Roma	5 Jun
14:44.56		Cherono			7	Herc	Monaco	18 Jul
14:48.68	Shannon	Rowbury	USA	19.9.84	8	Herc	Monaco	18 Jul
14:52.59	Janet	Kisa	KEN	5.3.92	5	GGala	Roma	5 Jun
14:52.67	Alemitu	Haroye (10)	ETH-J	9.5.95	6	GGala	Roma	5 Jun
14:55.90		Huddle			7	GGala	Roma	5 Jun
14:59.23	Sifan	Hassan	NED	.93	1	Jordan	Stanford	4 May
14:59.49	Meraf	Bahta	SWE	24.6.89	2	Jordan	Stanford	4 May
14:59.69	Maryam	Jamal	BRN	16.9.84	1	AsiG	Incheon	2 Oct
14:59.93		Kisa			9	GGala	Roma	5 Jun
15:00.19	Agnes	Tirop	KEN-J	23.10.95	8	GGala	Roma	5 Jun
15:00.87	Mimi	Belete	BRN	9.6.88	2	AsiG	Incheon	2 Oct
15:01.56		Huddle			1	NC	Sacramento	27 Jun
15:01.71		Rowbury			2	NC	Sacramento	27 Jun
15:01.73	Irene	Jelagat	KEN	10.12.88	9	GGala	Roma	5 Jun
	(24/16)							
15:04.74	Katie	Mackey	USA	12.11.87	3	Jordan	Stanford	4 May
15:04.87	Jo	Pavey	GBR	20.9.73	10	GGala	Roma	5 Jun
15:04.98	Laura	Thweatt	USA	17.12.88	4	Jordan	Stanford	4 May
15:07.45	Emelia	Gorecka	GBR	29.1.94	5	Jordan	Stanford	4 May
	(20)							
15:07.58mx	Clémence	Calvin	FRA	17.5.90	1		Le Mans	25 May
15:08.31	Selly	Chepyego	KEN	3.10.85	1		Isahaya	29 Nov
15:08.61	Kim	Conley	USA	14.3.86	11	GGala	Roma	5 Jun
15:09.64	Hiwot	Ayalew	ETH	6.3.90	12	GGala	Roma	5 Jun
15:10.38	Margaret	Muriuki	KEN	21.3.86	4	CG	Glasgow	2 Aug
15:10.46	Alemitu	Hawi	ETH-J	14.11.96	2	WJ	Eugene	23 Jul
15:11.13	Aisling	Cuffe	USA	12.9.93	6	Jordan	Stanford	4 May
15:11.42	Etagegne	Woldu	ETH-J	10.5.96	13	GGala	Roma	5 Jun
15:11.68	Julia	Bleasdale	GBR	9.9.81	14	GGala	Roma	5 Jun
15:12.51		Ding Changqin	CHN	27.11.91	3	AsiG	Incheon	2 Oct
	(30)							

Mark	Wind	Name		Nat	Born	Pos	Meet	Venue	Date
15:12.79		Marielle	Hall	USA	28.1.92	3	NC	Sacramento	27 Jun
15:13.21		Jessica	O'Connell	CAN	10.2.89	7	Jordan	Stanford	4 May
15:14.67		Yelena	Korobkina	RUS	25.11.90	1		Adler	30 May
15:14.96		Ayuko	Suzuki	JPN	8.10.91	2		Yamaguchi	12 Oct
15:14.99		Eloise	Wellings	AUS	9.11.82	5	CG	Glasgow	2 Aug
15:15.14		Stacy	Ndiwa	KEN	6.12.92	1	Spitzen	Luzern	15 Jul
15:15.74		Tejitu	Daba	BRN	20.8.91	1		Nijmegen	11 Jun
15:16.01mx		Christine	Bardelle	FRA	16.8.74	1		Ninove	2 Aug
15:16.50		Perine	Nengampi	KEN	1.1.89	1		Liège (NX)	16 Jul
15:16.83		Buze	Diriba	ETH	9.2.94	2		Liège (NX)	16 Jul
		(40)							
15:17.76		Irene	Cheptai	KEN	4.2.92	4		Liège (NX)	16 Jul
15:18.17		Jessica	Tebo	USA	8.4.88	8	Jordan	Stanford	4 May
15:18.30		Orchatteri P.	Jaisha	IND	23.5.83	4	AsiG	Incheon	2 Oct
15:18.53mx		Sabrina	Mockenhaupt	GER	6.12.80	1		Koblenz	28 May
15:18.75		Renata	Plis	POL	5.2.85	5		Liège (NX)	16 Jul
15:18.95		Riko	Matsuzaki	JPN	24.12.92	5	AsiG	Incheon	2 Oct
15:19.00		Rosemary	Wanjiru	KEN	9.12.94	1	JPN Ch	Fukushima	8 Jun
15:19.79		Alisha	Williams	USA	5.2.82	2		Stanford	4 Apr
15:19.93		Gladys	Chesire	KEN	20.2.93	2		Nijmegen	11 Jun
15:20.01		Sara	Moreira	POR	17.10.85	2		Huelva	12 Jun
		(50)							
15:20.92		Laura	Whittle	GBR	27.6.85	2	Spitzen	Luzern	15 Jul
15:20.93		Dolores	Checa	ESP	27.12.82	3		Huelva	12 Jun
15:21.32		Dulce	Félix	POR	23.10.82	1	ET-1	Tallinn	22 Jun
15:21.93		Kellyn	Johnson	USA	22.7.86	9	Jordan	Stanford	4 May
15:22.75mx		Maren	Kock	GER	22.6.90	2		Koblenz	28 May
15:22.95		Lucy	Van Dalen	NZL	18.11.88	11	Jordan	Stanford	4 May
15:22.98		Amy	Van Alstine	USA	11.11.87	12	Jordan	Stanford	4 May
15:23.37		Fionnuala	Britton	IRL	24.9.84	2	ET-1	Tallinn	22 Jun
15:24.40		Helen	Clitheroe	GBR	2.1.74	1		Manchester	31 May
15:24.56		Ayumi	Hagiwara	JPN	1.6.92	3		Yamaguchi	12 Oct
		(60)							
15:24.94		Alia Mohamed	Saeed	UAE	18.5.91	6		Liège (NX)	16 Jul
15:24.96		Misaki	Onishi	JPN	24.2.85	4		Yamaguchi	12 Oct
15:25.58		Yuika	Mori	JPN	25.1.88	3	Spitzen	Luzern	15 Jul
15:25.85		Rochelle	Kanuho	USA	4.7.90	6	NC	Sacramento	27 Jun
15:25.88		Gema	Barrachina	ESP	10.4.86	7		Liège (NX)	16 Jul
15:25.94		Amy	Hastings	USA	21.1.84	1		Concord	5 Jun
15:26.08		Erin	Finn	USA	19.11.94	13	Jordan	Stanford	4 May
15:26.71		Grace	Kimanzi	KEN	1.3.92	5		Yamaguchi	12 Oct
15:27.26		Alla	Kulyatina	RUS	9.6.90	2		Adler	30 May
15:27.30		Jip	Vastenburg	NED	21.3.94	3		Nijmegen	11 Jun
		(70)							
15:27.49		Yuka	Miyazaki	JPN	21.8.92	6		Yamaguchi	12 Oct
15:27.75		Madeline	Heiner	AUS	5.3.88	2		Sydney	15 Mar
15:27.90		Kate	Avery	GBR	10.10.91	4		Stanford	4 Apr
15:28.38		Alexi	Pappas	USA	28.3.90	7	NC	Sacramento	27 Jun
15:28.56		Jordan	Hasay	USA	21.9.91	1		Portland	15 Jun
15:29.02		Kasumi	Nishihara	JPN	1.3.89	1		Isahaya	18 Oct
15:29.55		Pauline	Kamulu	KEN-J	16.4.95	1		Nobeoka	10 May
15:29.94		Katie	Brough	GBR	27.4.82	5		Stanford	4 Apr
15:30.33		Lauren	Penney	USA	1.5.90	15	Jordan	Stanford	4 May
15:30.50		Nicole	Sifuentes	CAN	30.6.86	6		Stanford	4 Apr
		(80)							
15:30.61A		Purity	Rionoripo	KEN	10.6.93	4	NC	Nairobi	7 Jun
15:30.87		Brenda	Flores	MEX	4.9.91	2	MSR	Walnut	18 Apr
15:30.93		Abbey	D'Agostino	USA	25.5.92	3	MSR	Walnut	18 Apr
15:31.02		Nuria	Fernández	ESP	16.8.76	4		Huelva	12 Jun
15:31.03		Sarah	Collins	IRL	15.9.94	7		Stanford	4 Apr
15:31.27		Natalya	Popkova	RUS	21.9.88	2	NC	Kazan	25 Jul
15:31.43		Nicole	Bush	USA	4.4.86	16	Jordan	Stanford	4 May
15:31.49		Emily	Brichacek	AUS	7.7.90	3		Sydney	15 Mar
15:31.66		Yuka	Takashima	JPN	12.5.88	1		Yokohama	15 Nov
15:31.85		Rina	Nabeshima	JPN	16.12.93	1		Oita	18 Oct
		(90)							
15:31.97		Karolina	Jarzynska	POL	6.9.81	5		Huelva	12 Jun
15:32.07		Gulshat	Fazlitdinova	RUS	28.8.92	3		Adler	30 May
15:32.20		Shiho	Takechi	JPN	18.8.90	2		Isahaya	18 Oct
15:32.26		Jessica	Tonn	USA	15.2.92	18	Jordan	Stanford	4 May
15:32.29		Kate	Spencer	AUS-J	23.6.95	4		Sydney	15 Mar

Mark	Wind	Name		Nat	Born	Pos	Meet	Venue	Date
15:32.41		Michi	Numata	JPN	6.5.89	1		Yokohama	27 Sep
15:32.82		Susan	Kuijken	NED	8.7.86	3	EC	Zürich	16 Aug
15:33.16		Emily	Sisson	USA	12.10.91	1		Princeton	18 Apr
15:33.21		Felista	Wanjugu	KEN	18.2.90	2		Fukushima	18 May
15:33.42		Emma (100)	Bates	USA	8.7.92	5	MSR	Walnut	18 Apr

Mark	Name		Nat	Born	Date
15:33.64	Gabe	Grunewald	USA	25.6.86	15 Jul
15:33.74	Kotona	Ota	JPN-J	25.9.95	15 Nov
15:33.77	Mao	Kiyota	JPN	12.9.93	89 Oct
15:34.22	Miho	Shimizu	JPN	13.5.90	15 Nov
15:34.25	Mary	Waithera	KEN	12.12.94	15 Nov
15:34.34	Katrina	Coogan	USA	15.11.93	4 May
15:34.57	Toshika	Tamura	JPN	6.6.90	6 Jul
15:34.73	Mai	Shoji	JPN	9.12.93	15 Nov
15:34.85	Ashley	Higginson	USA	17.3.89	4 May
15:35.12	Violah	Lagat	KEN	1.3.89	4 Apr
15:35.38	Yuki	Hidaka	JPN	22.7.92	27 Sep
15:35.44	Olga	Mazuronak	BLR	14.4.89	22 Jun
15:35.62	Kristiina	Mäki	CZE	22.9.91	12 Jun
15:35.97	Nicol	Traynor	USA	6.5.89	4 May
15:36.72	Haruna	Maekawa	JPN	17.2.94	18 Oct
15:36.74A	Mary	Munanu	KEN		7 Jun
15:36.78	Angela	Bizzarri	USA	15.2.88	4 May
15:36.96mx	Jennifer	Wenth	AUT	24.7.91	28 May
15:37.14	Marta	Silvestre	ESP	4.4.82	16 Jul
15:37.42	Risa	Kikuchi	JPN	5.2.90	12 Oct
15:37.62	Paula	González	ESP	2.5.85	16 Jul
15:37.63	Kaori	Morita	JPN-J	19.9.95	6 Jul
15:37.70	Gamze	Bulut	TUR	3.8.92	22 Jun
15:37.74	Saori	Noda	JPN	30.3.93	6 Jul
15:37.85	Waverly	Neer	USA	12.7.92	4 Apr
15:37.92	Lyudmila	Lebedeva	RUS	23.5.90	25 Jul
15:37.94	Hanami	Sekine	JPN-J	26.2.96	6 Jul
15:38.74mx	Camille	Buscomb	NZL	11.7.90	12 Mar
15:38.76	Giulia	Viola	ITA	24.4.91	16 Aug
15:38.77	Akari	Ota	JPN	26.1.94	18 Oct
15:38.88	Rina	Yamazaki	JPN	6.5.88	2 Jul
15:38.92	Chiaki	Morikawa	JPN	22.9.87	12 Oct
15:39.04	Kanako	Shimada	JPN	11.10.88	6 Jul
15:39.10	Haftamnesh	Tesfay	ETH	28.4.94	5 Jun
15:39.42	Eri	Makikawa	JPN	22.4.93	29 Apr
15:39.42	Rachel	Johnson	USA	30.4.93	4 May
15:39.52	Preeja	Sreedharan	IND	13.3.82	2 Oct
15:39.53	Yuko	Kikuchi	JPN	8.6.92	6 Jul
15:39.96	Natsuki	Omori	JPN	22.6.94	15 Jul
15:40.07	Yuka	Ando	JPN	16.3.94	6 Jul
15:40.21	Naoko	Koizumi	JPN	14.12.92	12 Oct
15:40.41	Sonja	Roman	SLO	11.3.79	22 Jun
15:40.60	Elizeba	Cherono	KEN	6.6.88	11 Jun
15:40.79	Beth	Potter	GBR	27.12.91	17 May
15:40.89	Alina	Prokopyeva	RUS	16.8.85	25 Jul
15:41.21	Kotomi	Takayama	JPN	18.2.93	6 Jul
15:41.50	Brenda	Martinez	USA	8.9.87	18 Apr
15:41.67	Miho	Ihara	JPN	4.2.88	6 Jul
15:41.73mx	Corinna	Harrer	GER	19.1.91	28 May
15:42.11	Yuki	Mitsunobu	JPN	9.11.92	15 Nov
15:42.13	Elinor	Kirk	GBR	26.4.89	18 Apr
15:42.23	Sakiho	Tsutsui	JPN-J	19.1.96	6 Jul
15:42.40	Fuyuka	Kimura	JPN-J	13.1.95	18 Oct
15:42.42	Dominique	Scott	RSA	24.6.92	18 Apr
15:42.95	Katie	Matthews	USA	19.11.90	4 Apr
15:43.11	Doricah	Obare	KEN	10.1.90	27 Sep
15:43.14	Sakurako	Fukuuchi	JPN	30.8.93	24 May
15:43.47	Stephanie	Garcia	USA	3.5.88	4 May
15:43.47	Juliet	Chekwel	UGA	25.5.90	20 Jun
15:43.60	Yukari	Abe	JPN	21.8.89	10 May
15:43.77	Svetlana	Kireyeva	RUS	12.6.87	25 Jul
15:43.84	Treniere	Moser	USA	27.10.81	27 Jun
15:44.02	Rina	Koeda	JPN	29.8.94	15 Nov
15:44.04	Sakie	Arai	JPN	3.6.94	15 Nov
15:44.07	Ai	Inoue	JPN	13.1.90	15 Nov
15:44.32	Almensch	Belete	BEL	26.7.89	22 Jun
15:44.53	Alfiya	Muryasova	RUS	3.10.88	25 Jul
15:44.78	Chikako	Mori	JPN	25.11.92	15 Nov
15:44.85	Jessica	Coulson	GBR	18.4.90	16 Aug
15:44.89mx	Natasha	LaBeaud Anzures	CAN	5.8.87	4 Jun
15:44.93	Lindsey	Drake	USA	23.11.89	15 Jun
15:44.97	Yelena (172)	Nagovitsyna	RUS	7.12.82	30 May

Indoors

Mark	Name		Nat	Born	Pos	Venue	Date
15:20.57	Sarah	Disanza	USA-J	25.8.95	1	Boston (A)	6 Dec
15:21.84	Emily	Sisson	USA	12.10.91	2	Boston (A)	6 Dec
15:31.62	Liv	Westphal	FRA	22.12.93	3	Boston (A)	6 Dec
15:33.68	Yelena	Nagovitsyna	RUS	7.12.82			19 Feb
15:37.76	Yuliya	Chizhenko	RUS	30.8.79			19 Feb
15:43.69	Emily	Stites	USA	2.6.94			2 Mar

Best in women's only race

Mark	Name	Pos	Meet	Venue	Date
15:12.83	Calvin	12	Herc	Monaco	18 Jul
15:27.30	Bardelle	1		Carquefou	20 Jun
15:39.88	Kock	5			Jul
15:45.50	Wenth	12			Jun

JUNIORS

See main list for top 6 juniors. 7 performances 1 indooors) by 6 women to 15:30.0. Additional marks and further juniors:

Haroye 15:10.08 1 WJ Eugene 23 Jul

Mark	Name		Nat	Born	Pos	Meet	Venue	Date
15:33.74	Kotona	Ota	JPN	25.9.95	3		Yokohama	15 Nov
15:37.63	Kaori	Morita	JPN	19.9.95	5		Abashiri	6 Jul
15:37.94	Hanami	Sekine	JPN	26.2.96	7		Abashiri	6 Jul
15:42.23	Sakiho	Tsutsui (10)	JPN	19.1.96	14		Abashiri	6 Jul
15:42.40	Fuyuka	Kimura	JPN	13.1.95	7		Isahaya	18 Oct
15:45.12	Misaki	Hayashida	JPN	31.1.96	5		Yokohama	27 Sep
15:45.66	Mai	Takahashi	JPN	.96	12		Yokohama	15 Nov
15:46.77	Ayaka	Nakagawa	JPN	26.9.96	6		Yokohama	27 Sep
15:47.17	Daria	Maslova	KGZ	6.5.95	9	AsiG	Incheon	2 Oct

10,000 METRES

Mark	Name		Nat	Born	Pos	Meet	Venue	Date
30:42.26	Sally	Kipyego	KEN	19.12.85	1	Jordan	Stanford	4 May
30:47.59	Molly	Huddle	USA	31.8.84	2	Jordan	Stanford	4 May
30:57.30	Betsy	Saina	KEN	30.6.88	3	Jordan	Stanford	4 May
31:28.07	Selly	Chepyego	KEN	3.10.85	1		Kobe	20 Apr
31:38.54		Chepyego			1		Yamaguchi	10 Oct
31:39.67	Jordan	Hasay	USA	21.9.91	4	Jordan	Stanford	4 May
31:41.80	Ayumi	Hagiwara	JPN	1.6.92	2		Yamaguchi	10 Oct
31:42.02	Julia	Bleasdale	GBR	9.9.81	5	Jordan	Stanford	4 May
31:43.05	Almensch	Belete	BEL	26.7.89	6	Jordan	Stanford	4 May
31:45.24	Doricah	Obare	KEN	10.1.90	7	Jordan	Stanford	4 May

Mark	Wind	Name		Nat	Born	Pos	Meet	Venue	Date
31:48.6A		Florence	Kiplagat (10)	KEN	27.2.87	1		Iten	31 May
31:48.71		Kim	Conley	USA	14.3.86	8	Jordan	Stanford	4 May
31:50.85			Hagiwara			2		Kobe	20 Apr
31:51.86		Alia Mohamed	Saeed	UAE	18.5.91	1	AsiG	Incheon	27 Sep
31:52.86		Clémence	Calvin	FRA	17.5.90	1	ECp	Skopje	7 Jun
31:53.09			Ding Changqin	CHN	27.11.91	2	AsiG	Incheon	27 Sep
31:53.69		Kasumi	Nishihara	JPN	1.3.89	3		Kobe	20 Apr
31:55.56		Jéssica	Augusto	POR	8.11.81	2	ECp	Skopje	7 Jun
31:55.67			Hagiwara			3	AsiG	Incheon	27 Sep
31:55.81		Yuka	Takashima	JPN	12.5.88	1		Abashiri	6 Jul
		(20/17)							
31:56.11		Rina	Yamazaki	JPN	6.5.88	3		Yamaguchi	10 Oct
32:00.15		Hanae	Tanaka	JPN	12.2.90	5		Yamaguchi	10 Oct
32:00.25		Eri	Makikawa	JPN	22.4.93	4		Kobe	20 Apr
		(20)							
32:01.42		Sara	Moreira	POR	17.10.85	3	ECp	Skopje	7 Jun
32:03.43		Sairi	Maeda	JPN	7.11.91	6		Yamaguchi	10 Oct
32:03.57		Karolina	Jarzynska	POL	6.9.81	4	ECp	Skopje	7 Jun
32:05.87		Misaki	Kato	JPN	15.6.91	7		Yamaguchi	10 Oct
32:07.08		Risa	Takenaka	JPN	6.1.90	3		Abashiri	6 Jul
32:09.35		Joyce	Chepkirui	KEN	10.8.88	1	CG	Glasgow	29 Jul
32:10.82		Emily	Chebet	KEN	18.2.86	3	CG	Glasgow	29 Jul
32:11.04		Jo	Pavey	GBR	20.9.73	1	Eng Ch	London (PH)	10 May
32:11.21		Chieko	Kido	JPN	14.3.90	5		Kobe	20 Apr
32:11.63		Yelena	Nagovitsyna	RUS	7.12.82	1	NC	Yerino	9 Jul
		(30)							
32:11.90		Jip	Vastenburg	NED	21.3.94	1		Stanford	4 Apr
32:12.27		Mao	Kiyota	JPN	12.9.93	6		Kobe	20 Apr
32:12.54		Sitora	Khamidova	UZB	12.5.89	4	AsiG	Incheon	27 Sep
32:14.44		Miho	Shimizu	JPN	13.5.90	6		Abashiri	6 Jul
32:14.82		Valentina	Galimova	RUS	11.5.86	2	NC	Yerino	9 Jul
32:15.20		Kotomi	Takayama	JPN	18.2.93	10	Jordan	Stanford	4 May
32:15.42		Miho	Ihara	JPN	4.2.88	11	Jordan	Stanford	4 May
32:15.85		Rachel	Ward	USA	11.10.89	12	Jordan	Stanford	4 May
32:17.05		Elinor	Kirk	GBR	26.4.89	2		Stanford	4 Apr
32:17.24		Yuki	Mitsunobu	JPN	9.11.92	7		Abashiri	6 Jul
		(40)							
32:18.81		Amy	Hastings	USA	21.1.84	3	NC	Sacramento	26 Jun
32:19.98		Carla Salomé	Rocha	POR	25.4.90	2	NC	Lisboa (I)	29 Mar
32:20.83		Emma	Bates	USA	8.7.92	13	Jordan	Stanford	4 May
32:21.74			Jia Chaofeng	CHN	16.11.88	5	AsiG	Incheon	27 Sep
32:22.06		Kaoru	Nagao	JPN	26.9.89	7		Kobe	19 Apr
32:22.14		Grace	Kimanzi	KEN	1.3.92	3		Fukagawa	25 Jun
32:22.21		Dolores	Checa	ESP	27.12.82	3		Lisboa	29 Mar
32:22.22		Veronica	Nyaruai	KEN	29.10.89	1	Zátopek	Melbourne	10 Dec
32:24+		Beatrice	Mutai	KEN	19.4.87	1	in 20,000	Ostrava	17 Jun
32:24.38		Reia	Iwade	JPN	8.12.94	8		Kobe	19 Apr
		(50)							
32:24.50		Yuka	Ando	JPN	16.3.94	2		Fukuroi	16 Nov
32:24.54		Gema	Barrachina	ESP	10.4.86	4		Lisboa	29 Mar
32:24.55		Ayumi	Sakaida	JPN	7.11.85	8		Abashiri	6 Jul
32:24.73		Kaho	Tanaka	JPN	24.6.91	4		Fukagawa	25 Jun
32:25.69		Juliet	Bottorff	USA	21.1.91	14	Jordan	Stanford	4 May
32:25.76		Veronica	Inglese	ITA	22.11.90	1	NC	Ferrara	17 May
32:26.03		Laïla	Traby	FRA	26.3.79	3	EC	Zürich	12 Aug
32:26.32		Asahi	Takeuchi	JPN-J	9.1.95	9		Abashiri	6 Jul
32:26.53		Shiho	Takechi	JPN	18.8.90	10		Kobe	19 Apr
32:26.59		Eloise	Wellings	AUS	9.11.82	2	1 NC	Melbourne	10 Dec
		(60)							
32:27.36		Mai	Shoji	JPN	9.12.93	1		Toyota	30 Nov
32:27.69		Eunice	Chumba	BRN	23.5.93	6	AsiG	Incheon	27 Sep
32:27.75		Corinna	Harrer	GER	19.1.91	1	NC	Aichach	3 May
32:28.88		Rei	Ohara	JPN	10.8.90	9		Yamaguchi	10 Oct
32:29.17		Preeja	Sreedharan	IND	13.3.82	7	AsiG	Incheon	27 Sep
32:29.26		Sabrina	Mockenhaupt	GER	6.12.80	2	NC	Aichach	3 May
32:29.61		Lanni	Marchant	CAN	11.4.84	3		Stanford	4 Apr
32:29.62		Albina	Mayorova	RUS	16.5.77	3	NC	Yerino	9 Jul
32:31.06		Emily	Sisson	USA	12.10.91	15	Jordan	Stanford	4 May
32:31.15		Olga	Mazuronak	BLR	14.4.89	7	EC	Zürich	12 Aug
		(70)							
32:31.37		Yuko	Mizuguchi	JPN	24.5.85	10		Yamaguchi	10 Oct

Mark Wind	Name		Nat	Born	Pos	Meet	Venue	Date
32:32.45	Fionnuala	Britton	IRL	24.9.84	8	EC	Zürich	12 Aug
32:32.62	Krisztina	Papp	HUN	17.12.82	9	EC	Zürich	12 Aug
32:33.35	Kate	Avery	GBR	10.10.91	4	CG	Glasgow	29 Jul
32:33.36	Beth	Potter	GBR	27.12.91	5	CG	Glasgow	29 Jul
32:34.03	Jelena	Prokopcuka	LAT	21.9.76	11	EC	Zürich	12 Aug
32:35.90	Dulce	Félix	POR	23.10.82	12	EC	Zürich	12 Aug
32:36.32	Sophie	Duarte	FRA	31.7.81	2		London (PH)	10 May
32:37.19	Kara	Foster	USA	20.2.90	16	Jordan	Stanford	4 May
32:37.50	Yurie	Doi	JPN	8.12.88	13		Yamaguchi	10 Oct
	(80)							
32:37.60	Sakiko	Matsumi	JPN	7.8.88	14		Yamaguchi	10 Oct
32:38.25	Lidia	Rodriguez	ESP	26.5.86	5		Lisboa	29 Mar
32:38.77	Kara	Lubieniecki	USA	25.3.89	17	Jordan	Stanford	4 May
32:38.85mx	Annie	Bersagel	USA	30.3.83	1		Oslo	2 Aug
32:39.13	Carolina	Tabares	COL	18.7.86	18	Jordan	Stanford	4 May
32:39.36	Sonia	Samuels	GBR	16.5.79	19	Jordan	Stanford	4 May
32:39.76	Megumi	Hirai	JPN	14.2.90	12		Kobe	19 Apr
32:40.22	Elvin	Kibet	KEN	4.2.90	1	MSR	Walnut	17 Apr
32:40.66	Kristen	Swisher	USA	16.6.83	20	Jordan	Stanford	4 May
32:40.82	Misato	Horie	JPN	10.3.87	14		Kobe	19 Apr
	(90)							
32:40.89	Eri	Hayakawa	JPN	15.11.81	10		Abashiri	6 Jul
32:41.38	Yukari	Abe	JPN	21.8.89	11		Abashiri	6 Jul
32:41.55	Emily	Stites	USA	2.6.94	2	MSR	Walnut	17 Apr
32:41.65	Erin	Finn	USA	19.11.94	1	Big 10	West Lafayette	16 May
32:41.92	Mao	Kuroda	JPN	1.11.89	21	Jordan	Stanford	4 May
32:41.95	Linet	Chebet	UGA	4.11.92	6	CG	Glasgow	29 Jul
32:42.53	Souad	Aït Salem	ALG	6.1.79	1		Tlemcen	18 Jun
32:42.93	Sayuri	Oka	JPN	19.9.90	5	NC	Fukushima	6 Jun
32:43.14	Natasha	LaBeaud Anzures	CAN	5.8.87	23	Jordan	Stanford	4 May
32:43.90	Mai	Ito	JPN	23.5.84	6	NC	Fukushima	6 Jun
	(100)							

Mark	Name		Nat	Born	Date
32:44.71	Madeline	Heiner	AUS	5.3.88	10 Dec
32:45.1A	Genet	Ayalew	ETH	31.12.92	11 May
32:46.29	Gulshat	Fazlitdinova	RUS	28.8.92	9 Jul
32:46.30	Natalya	Pendyukhova	RUS	9.10.88	9 Jul
32:46.57	Elaina	Balouris	USA	.92	12 Jun
32:46.68	Susan	Wairimu	KEN	11.10.92	6 Jul
32:47.37	Meghan	Peyton	USA	6.1.86	4 May
32:48.29	Yukari	Ishizawa	JPN	16.4.88	10 Oct
32:48.87	Kayoko	Fukushi	JPN	25.3.82	6 Jul
32:49.09	Brenda	Flores	MEX	4.9.91	14 Jun
32:49.24	Alena	Kudashkina	RUS	10.4.94	9 Jul
32:49.39	Belaynesh	Oljira	ETH	26.6.90	13 Aug
32:50.06	Diana	Martín	ESP	1.4.81	29 Mar
32:50.37	Kathya	García	MEX	3.12.87	4 May
32:50.37A	Lucy	Kabuu	KEN	24.3.84	6 Jun
32:51.26	Lily	Partridge	GBR	9.3.91	29 Mar
32:51.40	Carrie	Dimoff	USA	31.5.83	4 May
32:51.76	Kanayo	Miyata	JPN-J	.95	20 Dec
32:51.92	Asami	Kato	JPN	12.10.90	10 Oct
32:53.48	Michi	Numata	JPN	6.5.89	25 Jun
32:54.08	Keiko	Nogami	JPN	6.12.85	17 May
32:54.60	Catarina	Ribeiro	POR	31.5.90	29 Mar
32:54.78	Ayaka	Inoue	JPN	19.6.91	16 May
32:55.89	Natsuko	Goto	JPN	4.8.87	19 Apr
32:56.13	Paula	González	ESP	2.5.85	29 Mar
32:56.14	Stephanie	Dinius	USA	25.8.89	26 Jun
32:56.33	Natalya	Popkova	RUS	21.9.88	9 Jul
32:56.38	Ayumi	Uehara	JPN	23.11.94	23 Nov
32:56.90	Hannah	Walker	GBR	9.8.91	17 Apr
32:57.38	Lyudmila	Lebedeva	RUS	23.5.90	9 Jul
32:57.45	Rika	Shintaku	JPN	19.10.85	10 Oct
32:57.82	Mami	Onuki	JPN	9.10.91	10 Oct
32:57.85	Alia	Gray	USA	12.11.88	4 May
32:58.67	Yuko	Aoki	JPN	27.9.92	10 Oct
33:00.01	Katie	Kellner	USA	4.8.91	4 May
33:00.17	Haruna	Takada	JPN	17.2.90	6 Jul
33:00.35	Yuka	Hakoyama	JPN	9.3.90	10 Oct
33:00.46	Sarah	Pagano	USA	23.7.91	12 Jun
33:00.79	Yuki	Hidaka	JPN	22.7.92	6 Jul
33:01.99	Gladys	Tejeda	PER	30.9.85	4 May
33:02.02	Jana	Soethout	GER	28.12.89	12 Jun
33:02.54	Fuyuka	Kimura	JPN-J	13.1.95	23 Nov
33:03.25	Yuri	Karasawa	JPN-J	.95	23 Nov
33:05.33	Anna	Matsuda	JPN	18.4.94	6 Jul
33:05.77	Megan	Goethals	USA	8.7.92	4 Apr
33:05.88	Mai	Tsuda	JPN	21.2.93	7 May
33:05.89	Celia	Sullohern	AUS	5.7.92	10 Dec
33:06.10	Olha	Skrypak	UKR	2.12.90	7 Jun
33:06.21	Ayako	Mitsui	JPN	17.1.92	6 Jul
33:06.42	Tetyana	Holovchenko	UKR	13.2.80	7 Jun
33:06.48	Jessica	Trengrove	AUS	15.8.87	10 Dec
33:06.8A	Tigist	Abayechew	ETH		11 May
33:08.0mx	Rina	Nabeshima	JPN	16.12.93	19 Jul
33:08.95	Iwona	Lewandowska	POL	19.2.85	10 May
33:09.58	Rhona	Auckland	GBR	11.5.93	10 May
33:09.61	Hanami	Sekine	JPN-J	26.2.96	20 Dec
	(156)				

JUNIORS

Mark	Name		Nat	Born	Pos	Meet	Venue	Date
32:26.32	Asahi	Takeuchi	JPN	9.1.95	9		Abashiri	6 Jul
32:51.76	Kanayo	Miyata	JPN	.95	1		Yokohama	20 Dec
	32:57.76 1rB	Abashiri	6 Jul	8 performances by 7 women to 33:15.0.0				
33:02.54	Fuyuka	Kimura	JPN	13.1.95	2		Yokohama	23 Nov
33:03.25	Yuri	Karasawa	JPN	.95	3		Yokohama	23 Nov
33:09.61	Hanami	Sekine	JPN	26.2.96	3		Yokohama	20 Dec
33:15.18	Maki	Izumida	JPN	22.1.96	4		Yokohama	23 Nov
33:24.73	Kotona	Ona	JPN	25.9.95	1		Kyoto	29 Nov
33:32.21		Li Dan	CHN	1.5.95	3	NC	Suzhou	10 Oct
33:39.52	Miki	Muraoka	JPN	4.2.95	11rB		Abashiri	6 Jul
33:40.48		Ma Yugui (10)	CHN	4.3.95	6	NC	Suzhou	10 Oct

10 KILOMETRES ROAD

Mark	Wind	Name		Nat	Born	Pos	Meet	Venue	Date
30:46		Betsy	Saina	KEN	30.6.88	1		Tilburg	7 Sep
30:56+		Joyce	Chepkirui	KEN	10.8.88	1	in HMar	Praha	5 Apr
31:02			Chepkirui			1		Berlin	12 Oct
31:02		Emily	Chebet	KEN	18.2.86	2		Berlin	12 Oct
31:04		Mamitu	Daska	ETH	16.10.83	1		Boston	22 Jun
31:05		Goreti	Chepkoech	KEN	7.3.94	1		Praha	6 Sep
31:05			Chebet			2		Tilburg	7 Sep
31:06		Margaret	Muriuki	KEN	21.3.86	3		Berlin	12 Oct
31:09+		Florence	Kiplagat	KEN	27.2.87	1	in HMar	Barcelona	16 Feb
31:09		Tirunesh	Dibaba	ETH	1.10.85	1		Manchester	18 May
31:10			Saina			2		Boston	22 Jun
31:16			Muriuki			1		Würzburg	13 Apr
31:17			Chepkirui			1		New York	10 May
31:22		Mary	Keitany	KEN	18.1.82	1		Ottawa	24 May
31:27		Gemma	Steel	GBR	12.11.85	1		Cape Elizabeth	3 Aug
31:27		Shalane	Flanagan	USA	8.7.81	2		Cape Elizabeth	3 Aug
31:28+		Priscah	Jeptoo	KEN	26.6.84	1	in 15k	Nijmegen	16 Nov
31:34			Muriuki			3		Tilburg	7 Sep
31:34		Peris	Jepchirchir	KEN	.93	1		Houilles	28 Dec
31:37		Molly	Huddle	USA	31.8.84	1		New York	14 Jun
31:39		Jordan	Hasay	USA	21.9.91	1		Boston	13 Oct
		(21/15)							
Where better than 10,000m track times									
31:41		Caroline	Rotich	KEN	13.5.84	2		Boston	13 Oct
31:43		Risper	Gesabwa	KEN	10.2.89	1		New Orleans	19 Apr
31:46		Lucy	Kabuu	KEN	24.3.84	1		Bangalore	18 May
31:47		Hiwot	Ayalew	ETH	6.3.90	2		New Orleans	19 Apr
31:48+		Wude	Ayalew	ETH	4.7.87		in HMar	Praha	5 Apr
31:50		Azmera	Gebru	ETH	5.5.92	4		Boston	13 Oct
31:51		Angela	Tanui	KEN	.92	1		Languex	14 Jun
31:51		Esther	Chemtai Ndiema	KEN	4.6.88	2		Praha	6 Sep
31:52		Mercy	Wacera	KEN	17.12.88	3		New York	10 May
31:52		Aliphine	Tuliamuk-Bolton	KEN	5.4.89	3		Boston	22 Jun
31:52		Diane	Nukuri	BDI	1.12.84	3		Cape Elizabeth	3 Aug
31:53		Sophie	Duarte	FRA	31.7.81	1		Auch	16 Mar
31:53+		Beatrice	Mutai	KEN	19.4.87		in HMar	Valencia	19 Oct
31:57		Emily	Sisson	USA	12.10.91	5		Boston	13 Oct
31:58		Bekelech	Daba	ETH	.81	2		Languex	14 Jun
31:58		Malika	Asahssah	MAR	24.9.82	2		Marrakech	28 Sep
32:01		Gelete	Burka	ETH	15.2.86	4		New York	10 May
32:03		Janet	Bawcom	USA	22.8.78	1		Mobile	22 Mar
32:03		Caroline	Kilel	KEN	21.3.81	1		Appingedam	28 Jun
32:03		Emily	Infeld	USA	21.3.90	6		Boston	13 Oct
32:04		Edith	Chelimo	KEN	16.7.86	1		Brunssum	6 Apr
32:05		Rose	Chelimo	KEN	12.7.89	1		Hamburg	7 Sep
32:05		Grace	Kimanzi	KEN	1.3.92	1		Okayama	16 Nov
32:07		Rkia	El Moukim	MAR	22.2.88	3		New Orleans	19 Apr
32:08		Leonida	Mosop	KEN	.91	2		Appingedam	28 Jun
32:09		Gladys	Cherono	KEN	12.5.83	2		San Juan	23 Feb
32:10		Pauline	Njeru	KEN	.88	3		Manchester	18 May
32:11		Parendis	Lekapana	KEN	4.8.91	3		Marrakech	28 Sep
32:13		Linet	Masai	KEN	5.12.89	3		San Juan	23 Feb
32:13		Nancy	Kipron	KEN		1		Santos	18 May
32:13		Worknesh	Kidane	ETH	21.11.81	5		Boston	22 Jun
32:14+		Mercy	Kibarus	KEN	25.2.84		in HMar	København	29 Mar
32:14		Sara	Hall	USA	15.4.83	8		Boston	13 Oct
32:14		Aster	Demissie	CAN	.83	1		Lausanne	26 Oct
32:15+		Netsanet	Gudeta	ETH	12.2.91		in HMar	København	29 Mar
32:15+		Tsehay	Desalegn	ETH	28.10.91		in HMar	København	29 Mar
32:15+		Genet	Ayalew	ETH	31.12.92		in HMar	København	29 Mar
32:15+		Mame	Feysa	ETH	.89		in HMar	København	29 Mar
32:16	dh	Amy	Hastings	USA	21.1.84	1	NC	Atlanta	4 Jul
32:16		Dulce	Félix	POR	23.10.82	1		Lisboa	27 Dec
32:17+		Edna	Kiplagat	KEN	1511.79		in HMar	Olomouc	21 Jun
32:18+		Christelle	Daunay	FRA	5.12.74		in HMar	København	29 Mar
32:18+		Alice	Kimutai	KEN	7.9.92		in HMar	Valencia	19 Oct
32:18		Ruth	Chebet	BRN	17.11.96	2		Houilles	28 Dec
32:20+		Valeria	Straneo	ITA	5.4.76		in HMar	København	29 Mar
32:20+		Esther	Chemtai	KEN	4.6.88		in HMar	Praha	5 Apr

Mark	Wind	Name		Nat	Born	Pos	Meet	Venue	Date
32:20+		Afera	Godfay	ETH	25.9.91		in HMar	Praha	5 Apr
32:20+		Waganesh	Mekasha	ETH	16.1.92		in HMar	Praha	5 Apr
32:20		Etalemahu	Habtewold	ETH	.90	2		Charleston SC	5 Apr
32:20		Helah	Kiprop	KEN	7.4.85	1		Oelde	6 Jun
32:20		Buzunesh	Deba	ETH	8.9.87	5		New York	14 Jun
32:20+		Gladys	Chesire	KEN	20.2.93	3	in 15k	Nijmegen	16 Nov
32:20		Yemenu	Tewabech	ETH		3		Houilles	28 Dec
32:20		Josephine	Chepkoech	KEN	.89	1		Luanda	31 Dec
32:20		Stacy	Ndiwa	KEN	6.12.92	2		Luanda	31 Dec
32:21		Violah	Jepchumba	KEN	.90	2		Brunssum	6 Apr
32:21		Gwen	Jorgensen	USA	25.4.86	1		Sydney	3 May
32:21		Delvin	Meringor	KEN	1.8.92	2		Santos	18 May
32:21		Ruti	Aga	ETH	16.1.94	2		Ottawa	24 May
32:21		Karoline	Bjerkeli Grøvdal	NOR	14.6.90	1		Hole	18 Oct
32:21		Irene	Cheptai	KEN	4.2.92	3		Luanda	31 Dec
32:22		Sophy	Jepchirchir	KEN	.93	2		Mobile	22 Mar
32:22+		Deena	Kastor	USA	14.2.73		in HMar	Philadelphia	21 Sep
32:22		Linet	Chebet	UGA	4.11.92	4		Houilles	28 Dec
32:23		Hiwot	Gebrekidan	ETH-J	11.5.95	3		Languex	14 Jun
32:23		Khadija	Sammah	MAR	9.7.83	1		Casablanca	15 Jun
32:23		Katie	Matthews	USA	19.11.90	9		Boston	13 Oct
32:24		Belaynesh	Oljira	ETH	26.6.90	4		San Juan	23 Feb
32:25		Maryanne	Wanjiru	KEN	.86	3		Brunssum	6 Apr

Mark	Name		Nat	Born	Date
32:26+	Worknesh	Degefa	ETH	28.10.90	18 May
32:26	Lucy	Macharia	KEN	.91	28 Sep
32:27	Dina Lebo	Phalula	RSA	9.12.83	3 May
32:29	Sabrina	Mockenhaupt	GER	6.12.80	15 Mar
32:29+	Hirut	Alemayehu	ETH	19.12.93	29 Mar
32:30	Gotytom	Gebreslase	ETH-J	15.1.95	13 Oct
32:30	Steph	Twell	GBR	17.8.89	16 Nov
32:31	Asmae	Leghzaoui	MAR	30.8.76	9 Mar
32:31	Aselefech	Mergia	ETH	23.1.85	3 Aug
32:32	Yuiki	Mori	JPN	25.1.88	16 Feb
32:32	Megumi	Hirai	JPN	14.2.90	16 Feb
32:32	Bouchra	Ben Thami	FRA	18.5.79	15 Jun
32:32	Alexi	Pappas	USA	28.3.90	3 Aug
32:33	Lindsey	Scherf	USA	18.9.86	22 Mar
32:33	Makida	Abdela	ETH	.89	5 Apr
32:33+	Faith	Kipsum	KEN	11.5.93	21 Jun
32:33+	Bethlehem	Moges	ETH	3.5.91	21 Jun
32:33	Jen	Rhines	USA	1.7.74	13 Oct
32:34	Mai	Ito	JPN	23.5.84	16 Feb
32:35	Alyson	Dixon	GBR	24.9.78	6 Apr
32:35	Beatrice	Chepkoech	KEN	.91	31 Aug
32:36	Paula	González	ESP	2.5.85	22 Mar
32:36	Julia	Mombi ¶	KEN	25.9.85	28 Jun
32:36	Christine	Bardelle	FRA	16.8.74	9 Nov
32:37+	Tadelech	Bekele	ETH	11.4.91	18 May
32:37	Laura	Thweatt	USA	17.12.88	14 Jun
32:40	Iwona	Lewandowska	POL	19.2.85	22 Mar
32:40	Risper	Chebet	KEN	.92	31 Aug
32:40	Meraf	Bahta	SWE	24.6.89	6 Sep
32:40	Elaina	Balouris	USA		13 Oct
32:41	Guteni	Shone	ETH	17.11.91	18 May
32:41	Sharon	Cherop	KEN	16.3.84	8 Jun
32:42	Zewdnesh	Ayele	ETH	21.11.93	19 Apr
32:42+	Emebet	Anteneh	ETH	13.1.92	16 Nov
32:43	Zhang Yingying		CHN	4.1.90	13 Apr
32:45	Risa	Kikuchi	JPN	5.2.90	16 Feb
32:45	Helen	Clitheroe	GBR	2.1.74	2 Nov
32:46+	Filomena	Cheyech	KEN	5.7.82	14 Feb
32:46+	Jane	Onyangi	KEN	.92	5 Oct
32:47	Akari	Ota	JPN	26.1.94	16 Feb
32:47	Felista	Wanjugu	KEN	18.2.90	16 Nov
32:47	Sylvia	Kibet	KEN	28.3.84	31 Dec
32:49+	Caroline	Chepkwony	KEN	18.4.84	2 Mar
32:49+	Shure	Demise	ETH-J	21.1.96	2 Mar
32:49	Viola	Jelagat	KEN	.93	13 Apr
32:49dh	Kellyn	Johnson	USA	22.7.86	4 Jul
32:50	Helen	Jepkurgat	KEN	21.2.89	30 Mar
32:51+	Vicoty	Chepokimoi	KEN	.87	2 Mar
32:51+	Lisa	Nemec	CRO	18.5.84	29 Mar
32:51	Natalya	Popkova	RUS	21.9.88	14 Sep
32:52+	Rita	Jeptoo ¶	KEN	15.2.81	14 Feb
32:52+	Anna	Incerti	ITA	19.1.80	16 Feb
32:52+	Letekidan	Gebreaham	ERI	16.1.94	29 Mar
32:52+	Lauren	Kleppin	USA	22.11.88	29 Mar
32:52	Saïda	El Mehdi	MAR	21.9.81	15 Jun
32:53	Olha	Kotovska	UKR	5.12.83	21 Sep
32:53	Genet	Abdukadir	ETH-Y	.97	28 Sep
32:53	Alice	Kamunya	KEN		13 Oct
32:54	Nazha	Machrouh	MAR	13.7.85	15 Jun
32:56+	Firehiwot	Dado	ETH	9.1.84	5 Apr
32:56	Susan	Kuijken	NED	8.7.86	19 Oct
32:56+	Doris	Changeiywo	KEN	12.12.84	26 Oct
32:57	Mattie	Suver	USA	10.9.87	4 Jul
32:58	Joan	Chelimo	KEN	10.11.88	9 Mar
32:58	Agnes	Mutune	KEN	26.6.86	6 Jun
32:59+	Mare	Dibaba	ETH	20.10.89	14 Feb
32:59	Winnie	Jepkorir	KEN	.90	9 Mar
32:59	Birhane	Dibaba	ETH	11.9.93	3 May

Downhill

Mark	Name		Nat	Born	Pos	Venue	Date
31:42	Malika	Asahssah	MAR	24.9.82	1	Madrid (55m)	23 Nov
32:25	Iwona	Lewandowska	POL	19.2.85	1	Madrid	31 Dec

Mark	Name		Nat	Born	Date
32:33	Rachel	Hannah	USA	2.10.86	13 Apr
32:41	Krista	Duchene	CAN	9.1.77	13 Apr
32:48	Marta	Tigabea	ETH	4.10.90	23 Nov

Uncertain measurement

Mark	Name		Nat	Born	Pos	Venue	Date
31:44	Amane	Gobena	ETH	1.9.82	1	Abu Dhabi	31 Jan
31:45A	Irene	Cheptai	KEN	4.2.92	2	Nairobi	17 Aug
31:46A	Alice	Aprot	KEN	11.3.94	3	Nairobi	17 Aug
31:51	Makida	Wordofa	ETH	.89	2	Abu Dhabi	31 Jan
31:54A	Peris	Chepkirui	KEN		1	Eldoret	2 Feb
31:56	Laïla	Traby	FRA	26.3.79	3	Abu Dhabi	31 Jan
32:24A	Jackline	Chepngeno	KEN	16.1.93	4	Nairobi	17 Aug

Mark	Name		Nat	Born	Date
32:36A	Doris	Changeiywo	KEN	12.12.84	17 Aug
32:38A	Emily	Chemutai	KEN	.84	17 Aug
32:40A	Visiline	Jepkesho	KEN	.88	17 Aug
32:56A	Lineth	Chepkurui	KEN	23.2.88	2 Feb

Drugs disqualification

Mark	Name		Nat	Born	Pos	Venue	Date
32:30	Filomena	Chepchirchir #	KEN	1.12.81	(3)	Praha	6 Sep

+ intermediate time in longer race, A made at altitude of 1000m or higher, H made in a heptathlon, h made in a heat, qf quarter-final, sf semi-final, i **Indoors**, Q qualifying round, r race number, -J juniors, -Y youths (born 1997 or later)

15/20 KILOMETRES ROAD

And see splits in 10 Miles, 20 Km and Half Marathon lists

20k	15k	Name		Nat	Born	Pos	Meet	Venue	Date
	46:59	Priscah	Jeptoo	KEN	26.6.84	1		Nijmegen	16 Nov
	47:03	Shalane	Flanagan	USA	8.7.81	1	NC	Jacksonville	15 Mar
	47:32	Emily	Chebet	KEN	18.2.86	2		Nijmegen	16 Nov
65:28	48:17	Wude	Ayalew	ETH	4.7.87	3	in HMar	Praha	5 Apr
	48:16	Goreti	Chepkoech	KEN	7.3.94	1		Bursa	13 Apr
	48:27	Caroline	Kilel	KEN	21.3.81		in HMar	Newcastle	7 Sep
	48:43	Gladys	Chesire	KEN	20.2.93	3		Nijmegen	16 Nov
65:54	49:09+	Aberu	Kebede	ETH	12.9.89		in HMar	R'as Al-Khaymah	14 Feb
65:55	49:08+	Worknesh	Degefa	ETH	28.10.90		in HMar	R'as Al-Khaymah	14 Feb
66:35	49:17+	Waganesh	Mekasha	ETH	16.1.92		ih HMar	Praha	5 Apr
	49:20	Emebet	Anteneh	ETH	13.1.92	4		Nijmegen	16 Nov
	49:24	Janet	Bawcom	USA	22.8.78	2	NC	Jacksonville	15 Mar
65:58	49:25	Lisa	Nemec	CRO	18.5.84		in HMar	New York	16 Mar
	49:28	Lucy	Murigi	KEN	7.7.85	1		Kerzers	15 Mar
	49:35+	Tadelech	Bekele	ETH	11.4.91		in HMar	Göteborg	18 May
66:54+	(49:59)	Caroline	Kilel	KEN	21.3.81		in HMar	R'as Al-Khaymah	14 Feb
66:58+		Sharon	Cherop	KEN	16.3.84		in Mar	Frankfurt	26 Oct
67:00	49:36+	Alice	Kimutai	KEN	7.9.92		in HMar	Valencia	19 Oct

Mark	Name		Nat	Born	Date
49:39+	Risa	Takenaka	JPN	6.1.90	29 Mar
49:41+	Filomena	Chepchirchir #	KEN	1.12.81	14 Sep
49:47+	Faith	Kipsum	KEN	11.5.93	21 Jun
49:47	Jane	Onyangi (67:01)	KEN	.92	5 Oct
49:49	Amy	Van Alstine	USA	11.11.87	15 Mar

10 MILES ROAD

Times at 15km in 2nd column

10M	15k	Name		Nat	Born	Pos	Meet	Venue	Date
51:54+		Mamitu	Daska	ETH	16.10.83		in HMar	Boston	12 Oct
51:55+		Cynthia	Limo	KEN	18.12.89		in HMar	Boston	12 Oct
51:55+		Betsy	Saina	KEN	30.6.88		in HMar	Boston	12 Oct
52:05			Daska			1		Washington	6 Apr
52:12		Janet	Bawcom	USA	22.8.78	2		Washington	6 Apr
52:15+		Molly	Huddle	USA	31.8.84		in HMar	Boston	12 Oct
52:16		Aliphine	Tuliamuk-Bolton	KEN	5.4.89	3		Washington	6 Apr
52:29+		Aberu	Kebede	ETH	12.9.89	1	in HMar	Philadelphia	21 Sep
52:34+		Caroline	Rotich	KEN	13.5.84	2	in HMar	Philadelphia	21 Sep
52:40	49:08	Belaynesh	Oljira	ETH	26.6.90	1	Gt.South	Portsmouth	26 Oct
52:41+		Deena	Kastor	USA	14.2.73	3	in HMar	Philadelphia	21 Sep
52:43	49:08	Gemma	Steel	GBR	12.11.85	2	Gt.South	Portsmouth	26 Oct
52:54		Sara	Hall	USA	15.4.83	4		Washington	6 Apr
53:09	49:31	Linet	Masai	KEN	5.12.89	1		Zaandam	21 Sep
Downhill 30.5m									
50:04+	46:38	Mary	Keitany	KEN	18.1.82	1	in HMar	South Shields	7 Sep
52:00+e	48:15	Gemma	Steel	GBR	12.11.85	2	in HMar	South Shields	7 Sep

20 KILOMETRES

Mark	Name		Nat	Born	Pos	Meet	Venue	Date
65:01	Rose	Chelimo	KEN	12.7.89	1		Paris	12 Oct
67:25	Leonida	Mosop	KEN	.91	2		Paris	12 Oct
1:08:32.2 track	Alice	Kimutai	KEN	7.9.92	1	GS	Ostrava	17 Jun

HALF MARATHON

HMar	20k	15k	Name		Nat	Born	Pos	Meet	Venue	Date
65:12	61:56	46:36	Florence	Kiplagat	KEN	27.2.87	1		Barcelona	16 Feb
65:39dh		46:38	Mary	Keitany	KEN	18.1.82	1	GNR	South Shields	7 Sep
66:19	62:55	46:49	Joyce	Chepkirui	KEN	10.8.88	1		Praha	5 Apr
67:02	63:43	48:06	Priscah	Jeptoo	KEN	26.6.84	1		R'as Al-Khaymah	14 Feb
67:29	64:04	48:08	Gladys	Cherono	KEN	12.5.83	1	WCh	København	29 Mar
67:44	64:15	48:08	Mercy	Wacera	KEN	17.12.88	2	WCh	København	29 Mar
67:52	64:16	48:08	Selly	Chepyego	KEN	3.10.85	3	WCh	København	29 Mar
67:57		48:35	Edna	Kiplagat	KEN	15.11.79	1	GSR	Glasgow	5 Oct
68:01	64:38		Emily	Chebet	KEN	18.2.86	1		Valencia	19 Oct
68:13	64:46	48:42	Filomena	Cheyech (10)	KEN	5.7.82	2		R'as Al-Khaymah	14 Feb
68:13dh		48:16	Gemma	Steel	GBR	12.11.85	2	GNR	South Shields	7 Sep
68:16				G Cherono			1		Yangzhou	20 Apr
68:20			Mamitu	Daska	ETH	16.10.83	1		Boston	12 Oct
68:24			Cynthia	Limo	KEN	18.12.89	2		Boston	12 Oct
68:26	64:59	48:16		Chebet			2		Praha	5 Apr
68:31	65:04	48:48	Guteni	Shone	ETH	17.11.91	3		R'as Al-Khaymah	14 Feb
68:31	64:54	48:51	Sally	Kipyego	KEN	19.12.85	1		New York	16 Mar
68:31			Eunice	Jepkirui	BRN	20.5.84	1		Luanda	7 Sep
68:32			Jemima	Jelagat	KEN	21.12.84	2		Luanda	7 Sep
68:36	65:07	48:46	Helah	Kiprop	KEN	7.4.85	4		R'as Al-Khaymah	14 Feb

Mark	Wind		Name		Nat	Born	Pos	Meet	Venue	Date
68:36			Wude	Ayalew	ETH	4.7.87	3		Luanda	7 Sep
68:37	64:48	48:08	Lucy	Kabuu (20)	KEN	24.3.84	4	WCh	København	29 Mar
68:40		49:09	Rose	Chelimo	KEN	12.7.89	1		Breda	5 Oct
68:41			Aberu	Kebede	ETH	12.9.89	1		Philadelphia	21 Sep
68:42	65:06	48:30	Mercy	Kibarus	KEN	25.2.84	5	WCh	København	29 Mar
68:45dh		48:19	Tiki	Gelana	ETH	22.10.87	3	GNR	South Shields	7 Sep
68:46			Worknesh	Degefa	ETH	28.10.90	1		Lisboa	16 Mar
68:46	65:05	48:23	Netsanet	Gudeta	ETH	12.2.91	6	WCh	København	29 Mar
68:48		49:21	Caroline	Chepkwony	KEN	18.4.84	1		Ostia	2 Mar
68:48				Jelagat			2		Lisboa	16 Mar
68:48	65:15	48:38	Christelle	Daunay	FRA	5.12.74	7	WCh	København	29 Mar
			(31/28)							
68:49	65:10	48:59	Rita	Jeptoo ¶	KEN	15.2.81	5		R'as Al-Khaymah	14 Feb
68:51		49:22	Sharon	Cherop	KEN	16.3.84	2		Ostia	2 Mar
			(30)							
68:51			Filomena	Chepchirchir #	KEN	1.12.81	3		Lisboa	16 Mar
68:53		49:22	Shure	Demise	ETH-J	21.1.96	4		Ostia	2 Mar
68:53		48:51	Caroline	Kilel	KEN	21.3.81	2	GSR	Glasgow	5 Oct
68:55	65:19	48:43	Valeria	Straneo	ITA	5.4.76	8	WCh	København	29 Mar
68:56	65:20	49:06	Mare	Dibaba	ETH	20.10.89	6		R'as Al-Khaymah	14 Feb
68:59	65:21	49:05	Buzunesh	Deba	ETH	8.9.87	2		New York	16 Mar
69:02	65:35	48:39	Margaret	Muriuki	KEN	21.3.86	2		Valencia	19 Oct
69:04	65:22	48:52	Molly	Huddle	USA	31.8.84	3		New York	16 Mar
69:04	65:25	48:38	Tsehay	Desalegn	ETH	28.10.91	9	WCh	København	29 Mar
69:06			Pauline Wanjiku	Njeru	KEN	.88	1		Warszawa	30 Mar
			(40)							
69:10			Meskerem	Assefa	ETH	20.9.85	3		Yangzhou	20 Apr
69:12			Peris	Jepchirchir	KEN	.93	1		Montbéliard	28 Sep
69:15	65:25	48:19	Genet	Ayalew	ETH	31.12.92	10	WCh	København	29 Mar
69:15+			Josephine	Chepkoech	KEN	.89	1	in Mar	London	13 Apr
69:16			Lisa	Nemec	CRO	18.5.84	1		Zagreb	16 Nov
69:17+			Tirunesh	Dibaba	ETH	1.10.85		in Mar	London	13 Apr
69:19	65:54	49:25	Feyse	Tadese	ETH	19.11.88	7		R'as Al-Khaymah	14 Feb
69:22			Caroline	Rotich	KEN	13.5.84	2		Philadelphia	21 Sep
69:23			Yebrqual	Melese	ETH	18.4.90	1		Paris	2 Mar
69:23	66:47	49:12	Bethlehem	Moges	ETH	3.5.91	2		Olomouc	21 Jun
			(50)							
69:24	65:50	49:35	Tomomi	Tanaka	JPN	25.1.88	1		Yamaguchi	16 Feb
69:27			Betsy	Saina	KEN	30.6.88	4		Boston	12 Oct
69:28			Gulume	Tollesa	ETH	.92	4		Yangzhou	20 Apr
69:29			Rael	Kiyara	KEN	4.4.84	1		Lille	6 Sep
69:30			Waganesh	Mekasha	ETH	16.1.92	5		Yangzhou	20 Apr
69:30	65:51	49:01	Beatrice	Mutai	KEN	19.4.87	3		Valencia	19 Oct
69:31			Georgina	Rono	KEN	19.5.84	2		Paris	2 Mar
69:35		48:43	Goreti	Chepkoech	KEN	7.3.94	1		Ústí Nad Labem	14 Sep
69:37	65:52	49:03	Deena	Kastor	USA	14.2.73	3		Philadelphia	21 Sep
69:38			Sarah	Chepchirchir	KEN	27.7.84	3		Paris	2 Mar
			(60)							
69:38+	65:59	49:26	Shalane	Flanagan	USA	8.7.81		in Mar	Berlin	28 Sep
69:44			Monica	Jepkoech	KEN	.85	5		Paris	2 Mar
69:45			Letebrhan	Gebreslasea	ETH	29.10.90	1		Paderborn	19 Apr
69:49	66:14	49:17	Esther	Chemtai	KEN	4.6.88	4		Praha	5 Apr
69:50	66:35	49:26	Krisztina	Papp	HUN	17.12.82	5		Ostia	2 Mar
69:52	66:11	49:18	Afera	Godfay	ETH	25.9.91	5		Praha	5 Apr
69:53			Jane	Kiptoo	KEN	8.8.82	7		Lisboa	16 Mar
69:56+	66:17	49:48+	Tirfi	Tsegaye	ETH	25.11.84		in Mar	Berlin	28 Sep
69:56+	66:17+		Tadelech	Bekele	ETH	11.4.91		in Mar	Berlin	28 Sep
69:57+	66:17	49:49+	Abebech	Afework	ETH	11.12.90		in Mar	Berlin	28 Sep
			(70)							
70:03			Rkia	El Moukim	MAR	22.2.88	1		Marrakech	26 Jan
70:04+	66:19	49:33+	Kayoko	Fukushi	JPN	25.3.82		in Mar	Berlin	28 Sep
70:08	66:34	48:59	Mame	Feysa	ETH	.89	12	WCh	København	29 Mar
70:08			Belaynesh	Oljira	ETH	26.6.90	4		New Delhi	23 Nov
70:09		49:35	Vicoty	Chepokimoi	KEN	.87	6		Ostia	2 Mar
70:09			Diane	Nukuri	BDI	1.12.84	6		New York	16 Mar
70:10	66:28	49:42	Risa	Takenaka	JPN	6.1.90	2		Yamaguchi	16 Feb
70:10		49:40	Anna	Incerti	ITA	19.1.80	2		Verona	16 Feb
70:10	66:34	49:49	Annie	Bersagel	USA	30.3.83	13	WCh	København	29 Mar
70:11			Leonida	Mosop	KEN	.91	2		Paderborn	19 Apr
			(80)							
70:13			Agnes	Mutune	KEN	26.6.86	2		Berlin	30 Mar

Mark	Wind		Name		Nat	Born	Pos	Meet	Venue	Date
70:15			Elizeba	Cherono	KEN	6.6.88	1		Venlo	30 Mar
70:15			Alice	Kimutai	KEN	7.9.92	1		Bejaia	2 May
70:16	66:35	49:41	Lauren	Kleppin	USA	22.11.88	14	WCh	København	29 Mar
70:17	66:42	49:35	Ayumi	Hagiwara	JPN	1.6.92	1		Matsue	16 Mar
70:18	66:43	49:47	Sayo	Nomura	JPN	18.4.89	15	WCh	København	29 Mar
70:25	66:35	49:39	Hirut	Alemayehu	ETH	19.12.93	16	WCh	København	29 Mar
70:27	66:54	(50:03)	Eri	Makikawa	JPN	22.4.93	1		Marugame	2 Feb
70:29			Philes	Ongori	KEN	19.7.86	8		Lisboa	16 Mar
70:32			Marta (90)	Tigabea	ETH	4.10.90	1		Azkoitia	22 Mar
70:32			Bornes	Kitur	KEN	.88	2		Azkoitia	22 Mar
70:36			Souad	Aït Salem	ALG	6.1.79	8		Ostia	2 Mar
70:36+	66:58		Meselech	Melkamu	ETH	27.4.85		in Mar	Frankfurt	26 Oct
70:37			Peninah	Kigen	KEN	.86	6		Yangzhou	20 Apr
70:38	66:52	49:47	Alyson	Dixon	GBR	24.9.78	18	WCh	København	29 Mar
70:38			Aliphine	Tuliamuk-Bolton	KEN	5.4.89	5		Boston	12 Oct
70:40			Purity	Rionoripo	KEN	10.6.93	1		Porto	14 Sep
70:41	66:39	49:09	Lucy	Macharia	KEN	.91	2		Breda	5 Oct
70:42			Helen	Jepkurgat	KEN	21.2.89	1		Prato	21 Apr
70:45	67:02		Yolanda (100)	Caballero	COL	19.3.82	2		Marugame	2 Feb
70:45	67:12		Chieko	Kido	JPN	14.3.90	3		Yamaguchi	16 Feb
70:45	67:12		Rina	Yamazaki	JPN	6.5.88	4		Yamaguchi	16 Feb
70:45	67:07	49:46	Reia	Iwade	JPN	8.12.94	19	WCh	København	29 Mar

Mark		Name		Nat	Born	Date
70:46		Eunice	Chumba	BRN	23.5.93	26 Jan
70:47		Lanni	Marchant	CAN	11.4.84	8 Mar
70:48		Serena	Burla	USA	29.7.82	19 Jan
70:50		Sara	Moreira	POR	17.10.85	14 Sep
70:51		Nazret	Weldu	ERI	.90	20 Apr
70:52		Lucy	Murigi	KEN	7.7.85	23 Mar
70:53		Souad	Kanbouchia	MAR	12.8.82	26 Jan
70:53		Parendis	Lekapana	KEN	4.8.91	2 Mar
70:53	67:21	Karoline	Bjerkeli Grøvdal	NOR	14.6.90	29 Mar
70:53	67:26	Visiline	Jepkesho	KEN	.88	18 May
70:55	49:47	Jane	Onyangi	KEN	.92	5 Oct
70:55+		Amane	Gobena	ETH	1.9.82	19 Oct
70:55+		Mulu	Seboka	ETH	13.1.84	19 Oct
70:56	67:21	Alessandra	Aguilar	ESP	1.7.78	29 Mar
70:56		Kumeshi	Sichala	ETH-J	.95	24 May
70:57	67:21	Veronica	Inglese	ITA	22.11.90	29 Mar
71:01		Janet	Kisa	KEN	5.3.92	27 Apr
71:02	67:19	Miho	Ihara	JPN	4.2.88	16 Feb
71:02		Laura	Thweatt	USA	17.12.88	21 Sep
71:04	67:20	Bouchra	BenThami	FRA	18.5.79	5 Apr
71:07		Kotomi	Takayama	JPN	18.2.93	16 Feb
71:07		Mao	Kuroda	JPN	1.11.89	16 Feb
71:09		Kimberley	Smith	NZL	19.11.81	16 Mar
71:09		Nancy	Wambua	KEN-J	29.12.95	7 Dec
71:10		Konjit	Tilahun	ETH	22.9.87	23 Mar
71:10		Faith	Kipsum	KEN	11.5.93	5 Oct
71:10		Bekelech	Daba	ETH	29.12.91	16 Nov
71:15	49:37	Firehiwot	Dado	ETH	9.1.84	5 Apr
71:18		Ashete	Bekele	ETH	17.4.88	19 Jan
71:18		Yukari	Abe	JPN	21.8.89	16 Feb
71:19		Hilda	Kibet	NED	27.3.81	18 May
71:21		Maryanne	Wanjiru	KEN	.86	19 Apr
71:24		Gladys	Tejeda	PER	30.9.85	29 Mar
71:24		Nikki	Chapple	AUS	9.2.81	18 May
71:24		Zintle	Xiniwe	RSA	23.10.86	27 Sep
71:24+		Melkam	Gisaw	ETH	17.9.90	19 Oct
71:27		Yui	Okada	JPN	15.3.94	11 May
71:28		Lilian	Mariita	KEN	4.3.88	16 Aug
71:29		Doris	Changeiywo	KEN	12.12.84	19 Oct
71:30+		Karolina	Jarzynska	POL	6.9.81	26 Jan
71:31+		Yukiko	Akaba	JPN	18.10.79	26 Jan
71:33		Shiho	Takechi	JPN	18.8.90	16 Feb
71:34			He Yinli	CHN	20.9.88	9 Mar
71:34+		Fantu	Jimma Eticha	ETH	11.9.87	19 Oct
71:34+		Emily	Ngetich	KEN	.84	26 Oct
71:35			Jia Chaofeng	CHN	16.11.88	2 Mar
71:35+		Winnie	Jepkorir	KEN	.90	26 Oct
71:36		Sophy	Jepchirchir	KEN	.93	16 Aug
71:37		Desiree	Linden	USA	26.7.83	16 Mar
71:37		Zewdnesh	Ayele	ETH	21.11.93	16 Nov
71:40		Risper	Chebet	KEN	.92	6 Sep
71:41		Risper	Gesabwa	KEN	10.2.89	27 Apr
71:41		Kara	Goucher	USA	9.7.78	21 Sep
71:42		Gladys	Kipsoi	KEN	.86	16 Mar
71:42		Alice	Serser	KEN	.82	5 Oct
71:43		Sabrina	Mockenhaupt	GER	6.12.80	30 Mar
71:43	dh	Charlotte	Purdue	GBR	10.6.91	7 Sep
71:45		Gladys	Tarus	KEN		20 Apr
71:45		Linet	Masai	KEN	5.12.89	19 Oct
71:46		Haruna	Takada	JPN	17.2.90	16 Feb
71:46+		Aleksandra	Duliba	BLR	9.1.88	19 Oct
71:48		Valentine	Kibet	KEN	.89	19 Apr
71:49+dh		Mai	Ito	JPN	23.5.84	23 Feb
71:49		Svetlana	Kudzelich	BLR	7.5.87	30 Mar
71:49		Zakya	Mrisho	TAN	19.2.84	19 Oct
71:50+dh		Birhane	Dibaba	ETH	11.9.93	23 Feb
71:50+dh		Janet	Rono	KEN	8.12.88	23 Feb
71:50		Adriana	Nelson	USA	31.1.80	16 Mar
71:50		Etaferahu	Temesgen	ETH	.89	16 Mar
71:50		Caroline	Kimosop	KEN		23 Mar
71:50		Kellyn	Johnson	USA	22.7.86	6 Apr
71:50		Sachi	Tanaka	JPN	28.3.88	11 May
71:50		Dot	McMahan	USA	6.11.76	21 Jun
71:50		Mao	Kiyota	JPN	12.9.93	14 Dec
71:51		Amane	Beriso	ETH		14 Sep
71:52		Joan	Chelimo	KEN	10.11.88	14 Sep
71:53		René	Kalmer	RSA	3.11.80	29 Mar
71:54		Lucy	Liavoga	KEN	.89	24 May
71:55		Angela	Tanui	KEN	.92	14 Sep
71:55+		Azalech	Masresha	ETH	4.5.88	5 Oct
71:56		Jéssica	Augusto	POR	8.11.81	2 Feb
71:56		Doricah	Obare	KEN	10.1.90	16 Mar
71:56		Hellen	Musyoka	KEN	3.1.87	30 Mar
71:56+		Azusa	Nojiri	JPN	6.6.82	16 Nov
71:57		Misato	Horie	JPN	10.3.87	2 Feb
71:57		Misaki	Kato	JPN	15.6.91	16 Feb
71:59+		Risa	Shigemoto	JPN	29.8.87	26 Jan
71:59		Malika (191)	Asahssah	MAR	24.9.82	22 Mar

Excessively downhill

San Diego 1 Jun: 1. Birhane Dibaba ETH 11.9.93 69:34, 3. Eri Hayakawa JPN 15.11.81 71:37, 4. Lindsey Scherf USA 18.9.86 71:46

Probably short course: Brazzaville 14 Aug: 1. Agnes Barsosio KEN 5.8.82 70:56, 2. Linah Chirchir KEN 71:48

Drugs disqualification

Mark	Name		Nat	Born	Pos	Venue	Date
70:21	Joyce	Kiplimo ¶	KEN	28.9.88	(6)	Yangzhou	20 Apr

Mark	Name		Nat	Born	Pos	Meet	Venue	Date

JUNIORS

See main list for top 1 junior. 6 performances by 4 women to 72:30. Additional marks and further juniors:

Mark		Name	Nat	Born	Pos	Meet	Venue	Date
68:53	Shure	Demise	ETH	21.1.96	4		Ostia	2 Mar
	71:22				2		Warszawa	30 Mar
70:56	Kumeshi	Sichala	ETH	.95	2		Karlovy Vary	24 May
	72:06				3	Stra	Milano	23 Mar
71:09	Nancy	Wambua	KEN-J	29.12.95	1		Pune	7 Dec
72:08A	Linah	Cheruto	KEN-J	18.3.95	4		Baringo	1 Nov
72:44	Asahi	Takeuchi	JPN	9.1.95	6		Matsue	16 Mar
73:03		Ma Yugui	CHN	4.3.95	14		Yangzhou	20 Apr
73:47	Damaris	Areba	KEN	.95	7		Paderborn	19 Apr

25 – 30 KILOMETRES ROAD

25k	30k	Name		Nat	Born	Pos	Meet	Venue	Date
1:23:28	1:41:13	Meselech	Melkamu	ETH	27.4.85		in Mar	Frankfurt	26 Oct
1:24:17	1:41:14	Amane	Gobena	ETH	1.9.82		in Mar	Toronto	19 Oct
1:24:33	1:41:31	Tsehay	Desalegn	ETH	28.10.91		in Mar	Praha	11 May
1:24:17	1:41:32	Tetyana	Hamera-Shmyrko	UKR	1.6.83		in Mar	London	13 Apr
1:24:37		Janet	Rono	KEN	8.12.88	1		Berlin	4 May
1:24:47	1:42:06	Winnie	Jepkorir	KEN	.90		in Mar	Frankfurt	26 Oct
1:25:01	1:42:01	Guteni	Shone	ETH	17.11.91		in Mar	Rotterdam	13 Apr
	1:42:16	Azalech	Masresha	ETH	4.5.88		in Mar	Lisboa	5 Oct
1:25:26		Kellyn	Johnson	USA	22.7.86	1	NC	Grand Rapids	10 May
1:25:42	1:42:48	Meseret	Legesse	ETH	28.8.87		in Mar	Daegu	6 Apr
	1:42:58	Agnes	Kiprop	KEN	12.12.79		in Mar	Nagoya	9 Mar
1:24:59	1:43:02	Melkam	Gisaw	ETH	17.9.90		in Mar	Toronto	19 Oct
1:25:08+		Marta	Tigabea	ETH	4.10.90		in Mar	Frankfurt	26 Oct
1:25:09+		Emebet	Etea	ETH	11.1.90		in Mar	Daegu	6 Apr

MARATHON

Mark	25k	30k	Name		Nat	Born	Pos	Meet	Venue	Date
2:20:18	1:22:58	1:39:17	Tirfi	Tsegaye	ETH	25.11.84	1		Berlin	28 Sep
2:20:21	1:22:20	1:39:11	Edna	Kiplagat	KEN	1511.79	1		London	13 Apr
2:20:24	1:22:19	1:39:11	Florence	Kiplagat	KEN	27.2.87	2		London	13 Apr
2:20:27	1:22:58	1:39:18	Feyse	Tadese	ETH	19.11.88	2		Berlin	28 Sep
2:20:35	1:22:19	1:39:14	Tirunesh	Dibaba	ETH	1.10.85	3		London	13 Apr
2:21:14	1:22:36	1:39:15	Shalane	Flanagan	USA	8.7.81	3		Berlin	28 Sep
2:21:36	1:22:41	1:39:19	Mare	Dibaba	ETH	20.10.89	1		Xiamen	2 Jan
2:21:42	1:23:08	1:40:09		Tadese			4		London	13 Apr
2:21:52			Tigist	Tufa	ETH	26.1.87	1		Shanghai	2 Nov
2:22:21	1:23:21	1:39:50	Aberu	Kebede	ETH	12.9.89	1		Frankfurt	26 Oct
2:22:23	1:24:45	1:41:27		Tsegaye			1		Tokyo	23 Feb
2:22:30	1:24:45	1:41:27	Birhane	Dibaba (10)	ETH	11.9.93	2		Tokyo	23 Feb
2:22:44	1:24:03	1:40:33	Filomena	Cheyech	KEN	5.7.82	1		Paris	6 Apr
2:23:02	1:22:58	1:39:17	Tadelech	Bekele	ETH	11.4.91	4		Berlin	28 Sep
2:23:15		1:41:13	Mulu	Seboka	ETH	13.1.84	1		Toronto	19 Oct
2:23:21	1:23:09	1:40:09		Kebede			5		London	13 Apr
2:23:34	1:24:33	1:41:37	Firehiwot	Dado	ETH	9.1.84	1		Praha	11 May
2:23:43	1:25:52	1:42:58	Mariya	Konovalova	RUS	14.8.74	1		Nagoya	9 Mar
2:23:44	1:23:26	1:40:04	Sharon	Cherop	KEN	16.3.84	2		Frankfurt	26 Oct
2:24:07		1:42:59	Jelena	Prokopcuka	LAT	21.9.76	2		Nagoya	9 Mar
2:24:16	1:24:46	1:41:28	Lucy	Kabuu	KEN	24.3.84	3		Tokyo	23 Feb
2:24:25	1:25:34	1:42:33	Jéssica	Augusto	POR	8.11.81	6		London	13 Apr
2:24:31				Tufa			1		Ottawa	25 May
2:24:35	1:24:46	1:41:28	Caroline	Rotich (20)	KEN	13.5.84	4		Tokyo	23 Feb
2:24:37	1:25:32	1:42:37	Tetyana	Hamera-Shmyrko	UKR	1.6.83	1		Osaka	26 Jan
2:24:43	1:24:58	1:42:06	Aleksandra	Duliba	BLR	9.1.88	2		Toronto	19 Oct
2:24:59	1:24:46	1:41:56	Ashete	Bekele	ETH	17.4.88	3		Frankfurt	26 Oct
2:25:01				Seboka			1		Dubai	24 Jan
2:25:02	1:22:58	1:40:10	Abebech	Afework	ETH	11.12.90	5		Berlin	28 Sep
2:25:07			Mary (30/25)	Keitany	KEN	18.1.82	1		New York	2 Nov
2:25:10			Jemima	Jelagat Sumgong	KEN	21.12.84	2		New York	2 Nov
2:25:14			Christelle	Daunay	FRA	5.12.74	1	EC	Zürich	16 Aug
2:25:14	1:24:46	1:41:56	Emily	Ngetich	KEN	.84	4		Frankfurt	26 Oct
2:25:22			Caroline	Kilel	KEN	21.3.81	2		Shanghai	2 Nov
2:25:23			Meselech (30)	Melkamu	ETH	27.4.85	2		Dubai	24 Jan
2:25:26		1:42:59	Ryoko	Kizaki	JPN	21.6.85	3		Nagoya	9 Mar
2:25:27			Valeria	Straneo	ITA	5.4.76	2	EC	Zürich	16 Aug
2:25:31		1:42:59	Eri	Hayakawa	JPN	15.11.81	4		Nagoya	9 Mar

Mark	Wind		Name		Nat	Born	Pos	Meet	Venue	Date
2:25:37			Eunice	Jepkirui	BRN	20.5.84	1	AsiG	Incheon	2 Oct
2:25:59	1:25:39	1:43:02	Meskerem	Assefa	ETH	20.9.85	2		Houston	19 Jan
2:26:00	1:25:00	1:42:34	Yukiko	Akaba	JPN	18.10.79	2		Osaka	26 Jan
2:26:00			Sara	Moreira	POR	17.10.85	3		New York	2 Nov
2:26:03	1:25:39	1:43:03	Gelete	Burka	ETH	15.2.86	3		Houston	19 Jan
2:26:03		1:42:18	Janet	Rono	KEN	8.12.88	5		Tokyo	23 Feb
2:26:05		1:42:59	Tomomi	Tanaka	JPN	25.1.88	5		Nagoya	9 Mar
			(40)							
2:26:20			Meseret	Hailu	ETH	12.9.90	4		Dubai	24 Jan
2:26:21	1:24:05	1:41:45	Yebrqual	Melese	ETH	18.4.90	2		Paris	6 Apr
2:26:22	1:25:39	1:43:02	Biruktayit	Degefa	ETH	29.9.90	4		Houston	19 Jan
2:26:25	1:24:00	1:42:01	Kayoko	Fukushi	JPN	25.3.82	6		Berlin	28 Sep
2:26:31	1:25:00	1:42:22	Karolina	Jarzynska	POL	6.9.81	3		Osaka	26 Jan
2:26:36			Meseret	Legesse	ETH	28.8.87	2		Xiamen	2 Jan
2:26:42			Bethlehem	Moges	ETH	3.5.91	5		Dubai	24 Jan
2:26:44		1:44:27	Anna	Hahner	GER	20.11.89	7		Berlin	28 Sep
2:26:46			Sairi	Maeda	JPN	7.11.91	4		Osaka	26 Jan
2:26:46	1:26:08	1:43:30	Dulce	Félix	POR	23.10.82	8		London	13 Apr
			(50)							
2:26:47			Georgina	Rono	KEN	19.5.84	1		Hamburg	4 May
2:26:47		1:42:03	Visiline	Jepkesho	KEN	.88	1		Lisboa	5 Oct
2:26:48			Inés	Melchor	PER	30.8.86	8		Berlin	28 Sep
2:26:58	1:25:05	1:43:09	Tiki	Gelana	ETH	22.10.87	9		London	13 Apr
2:26:59			Philes	Ongori	KEN	19.7.86	2		Yokohama	16 Nov
2:27:03		1:43:30	Amy	Hastings	USA	21.1.84	5		Chicago	12 Oct
2:27:05			Amane	Gobena	ETH	1.9.82	6		Dubai	24 Jan
2:27:05				Kim Hye-gyong	PRK	9.3.93	1		Pyongyang	13 Apr
2:27:10	1:24:58	1:42:43	Rael	Kiyara	KEN	4.4.84	3		Toronto	19 Oct
2:27:14	1:24:46	1:41:57	Helah	Kiprop	KEN	7.4.85	5		Frankfurt	26 Oct
				(60)						
2:27:16			Rebecca	Kangogo	KEN	.92	1		Hengshui	20 Sep
2:27:21			Reia	Iwade	JPN	8.12.94	3		Yokohama	16 Nov
2:27:26			Meseret	Kitata	ETH	8.11.93	2		Ottawa	25 May
2:27:29			Dinknesh	Mekasha	ETH	.85	2		Hamburg	4 May
2:27:31			Fantu	Jimma Eticha	ETH	11.9.87	2		Praha	11 May
2:27:37			Makda	Harun	ETH	.88	5		Houston	19 Jan
2:27:44			Goitetom	Haftu	ETH	.87	8		Dubai	24 Jan
2:27:45			Ashu	Kasim	ETH	20.10.84	2	Dong-A	Seoul	16 Mar
2:27:47			Sechale	Delasa	ETH	20.9.91	9		Dubai	24 Jan
2:27:51			Agnes	Kiprop	KEN	12.12.79	6		Nagoya	9 Mar
			(70)							
2:27:54			Sultan	Haydar	TUR	23.5.87	10		Dubai	24 Jan
2:27:57			Misato	Horie	JPN	10.3.87	7		Nagoya	9 Mar
2:27:57			Winnie	Jepkorir	KEN	.90	3		Hamburg	4 May
2:27:58				Kim Hye-song	PRK	9.3.93	2		Pyongyang	13 Apr
2:28:06			Marta	Lema	ETH	.90	5		Osaka	26 Jan
2:28:11			Konjit	Tilahun	ETH	22.9.87	11		Dubai	24 Jan
2:28:11			Desiree	Linden	USA	26.7.83	5		New York	2 Nov
2:28:12			Rkia	El Moukim	MAR	22.2.88	6		New York	2 Nov
2:28:14			Melkam	Gisaw	ETH	17.9.90	4		Hamburg	4 May
2:28:18			Albina	Mayorova	RUS	16.5.77	6		Tokyo	23 Feb
			(80)							
2:28:18			Sardana	Trofimova	RUS	28.3.88	1		Toulouse	26 Oct
2:28:20			Miriam	Wangari	KEN	22.2.79	2		Hengshui	20 Sep
2:28:27			Helaria	Johannes	NAM	13.8.80	3	Dong-A	Seoul	16 Mar
2:28:27			Mestawat	Tufa	ETH	14.9.83	1		Dongying	1 May
2:28:33			Iwona	Lewandowska	POL	19.2.85	1		Eindhoven	12 Oct
2:28:36			Mai	Ito	JPN	23.5.84	7		Tokyo	23 Feb
2:28:36			Lisa	Nemec	CRO	18.5.84	4	EC	Zürich	16 Aug
2:28:41			Esther	Chemtai Ndiema	KEN	4,6.88	1		Torino	16 Nov
2:28:44			Natalya	Puchkova	RUS	28.1.87	6		Osaka	26 Jan
2:28:47			Olha	Kotovska	UKR	5.12.83	1		Rennes	26 Oct
			(90)							
2:28:48			Lydia	Rutto	KEN	.94	1		Kosice	5 Oct
2:28:51			Asami	Kato	JPN	12.10.90	1		Brisbane	6 Jul
2:28:54			Azusa	Nojiri	JPN	6.6.82	5		Yokohama	16 Nov
2:28:56				He Yinli	CHN	20.9.88	5		Hamburg	4 May
2:28:58			Anna	Incerti	ITA	19.1.80	2		Torino	16 Nov
2:28:59			Annie	Bersagel	USA	30.3.83	1		Düsseldorf	27 Apr
2:29:00			Etalemahu	Kidane	ETH	14.2.83	4		Ottawa	25 May
2:29:03			Misiker	Mekonnin	ETH	23.7.86	3		Shanghai	2 Nov

Mark	Wind	Name		Nat	Born	Pos	Meet	Venue	Date
2:29:15		Olga	Kimaiyo	KEN	24.7.88	2		Amsterdam	19 Oct
2:29:17		Muluhabt (100)	Tsega	ETH	11.9.89	1		Beirut	9 Nov

Mark	First name	Surname	Nat	Born	Date
2:29:18	Caroline	Chepkwony	KEN	18.4.84	13 Apr
2:29:18	Alina	Prokopyeva	RUS	16.8.85	16 Nov
2:29:26	Olena	Shurhno	UKR	8.1.78	16 Nov
2:29:27	René	Kalmer	RSA	3.11.80	28 Sep
2:29:31		Kim Sung-eun	KOR	24.2.89	16 Mar
2:29:35	Zemzem	Ahmed	ETH	27.12.84	6 Apr
2:29:35	Diane	Nukuri	BDI	1.12.84	19 Oct
2:29:35	Mamitu	Daska	ETH	16.10.83	2 Nov
2:29:42	Worknesh	Kidane	ETH	21.11.81	24 Jan
2:29:43	Makida	Wordofa	ETH	.89	25 May
2:29:43	Azalech	Masresha	ETH	4.5.88	5 Oct
2:29:44		Liu Ruihuan	CHN	29.6.92	20 Sep
2:29:46	Elvan	Abeylegesse	TUR	11.9.82	16 Aug
2:29:48		Zhang Jingxia	CHN	15.7.91	22 Mar
2:29:51	Judith	Toribio	PER	9.1.82	6 Apr
2:29:51		Kim Mi-kyong	PRK	17.10.90	13 Apr
2:29:53	Gladys	Kipsoi	KEN	.86	19 Jan
2:29:54	Agnes	Barsosio	KEN	5.8.82	20 Dec
2:30:00	Bizunesh	Urgesa	ETH	18.6.89	19 Jan
2:30:03	Fatuma	Sado	ETH	11.10.91	19 Oct
2:30:12	Jessica	Trengove	AUS	15.8.87	27 Jul
2:30:19	Valary	Aiyabei	KEN	.91	26 Oct
2:30:23	Guteni	Shone	ETH	17.11.91	13 Apr
2:30:23	Joyce	Chepkirui	KEN	10.8.88	14 Dec
2:30:26	Eshetu	Degefa	ETH	.82	9 Nov
2:30:29	Selomie	Getnet	ETH	10.4.86	27 Apr
2:30:30	Bizuayehu	Ehitu	ETH	.91	13 Apr
2:30:32	Rasa	Drazdauskaite	LTU	20.3.81	16 Aug
2:30:37	Rika	Shintaku	JPN	19.10.85	6 Jul
2:30:48	Yuka	Hakoyama	JPN	9.3.90	9 Mar
2:30:53	Jess	Draskau-Petersson	DEN	8.9.77	16 Aug
2:30:53	Mona	Jaber Salem	BRN	.83	9 Nov
2:30:54	Beata	Naigambo	NAM	11.3.80	16 Nov
2:30:56	Meseret	Mengistu	ETH	6.3.90	21 Sep
2:30:58	Kateryna	Stetsenko	UKR	22.1.82	5 Oct
2:31:02	Yuka	Yano	JPN	11.6.86	9 Feb
2:31:05	Nikki	Chapple	AUS	9.2.81	12 Oct
2:31:06	Lanni	Marchant	CAN	11.4.84	19 Oct
2:31:08	Filomena	Costa	POR	22.2.85	4 May
2:31:08	Maja	Neuenschwander	SUI	13.2.80	16 Aug
2:31:09	Shuko	Genemo	ETH		26 Jan
2:31:09	Sarah	Chebet	KEN		26 Oct
2:31:10	Abeba	Gebremeskel	ETH	.89	24 Jan
2:31:10		Yue Chao	CHN	5.1.91	4 May
2:31:17	Mari	Ozaki	JPN	16.7.75	26 Jan
2:31:17	Lemlem	Berha	ETH	.92	5 Oct
2:31:20	Alem	Mokonnin	ETH	19.6.94	24 Jan
2:31:20	Pamela	Rotich	KEN		16 Nov
2:31:21	Jane	Kiptoo	KEN	8.8.82	27 Apr
2:31:23	Chaltu	Chimdesa	ETH-J	.95	26 Jan
2:31:25	Tsehay	Desalegn	ETH	28.10.91	11 May
2:31:30	Olena	Burkovska	UKR	9.8.81	16 Nov
2:31:31	Lyudmyla	Kovalenko	UKR	26.6.89	13 Apr
2:31:31	Askale	Alemaheyu	ETH	.93	26 Oct
2:31:34	Manami	Kamitanida	JPN	21.12.89	23 Feb
2:31:34	Helena	Kiprop	KEN	9.9.76	9 Mar
2:31:35	Ednah	Kimaiyo	KEN	.88	16 Nov
2:31:35	Deborah	Toniolo	ITA	24.4.77	16 Nov
2:31:39	Yuko	Mizuguchi	JPN	24.5.85	9 Mar
2:31:39	Ruth	Wanjiru	KEN	11.9.81	25 May
2:31:40	Buzunesh	Deba	ETH	8.9.87	2 Nov
2:31:41	Adhane	Tsehay	ETH	8.4.85	6 Jul
2:31:42	Mercy	Kibarus	KEN	25.2.84	4 May
2:31:44	Atsede	Baysa	ETH	16.4.87	2 Nov
2:31:46	Fionnuala	Britton	IRL	24.9.84	16 Aug
2:31:47	Tatyana	Arkhipova	RUS	8.4.83	16 Nov
2:31:50	Serkalem	Taye	ETH	.93	26 Jan
2:31:54	Marta	Tigabea	ETH	4.10.90	2 Nov
2:31:55	Irene	Chepkirui	KEN	.82	12 Oct
2:31:59	Faith	Chemaoi	KEN	.79	6 Apr
2:32:00	Yuko	Shimizu	JPN	13.7.85	13 Apr
2:32:01		Kim Kum-ok	PRK	9.12.85	13 Apr
2:32:02A	Edith	Irungu	KEN		26 Oct
2:32:06	Olga	Ochal	POL	15.7.85	12 Oct
2:32:11	Alem	Fikre	ETH	22.10.88	27 Apr
2:32:16	Diane	Chepkemoi	KEN	.87	13 Apr
2:32:18	Susan	Partridge	GBR	4.1.80	27 Jul
2:32:21	Louise	Damen	GBR	12.10.82	26 Jan
2:32:21	Clara	Santucci	USA	24.3.87	12 Oct
2:32:22	Azucena	Díaz	ESP	19.12.82	13 Apr
2:32:22	Isabellah	Ochichi	KEN	10.8.88	14 Dec
2:32:23		Gong Lihua	CHN	10.5.93	19 Oct
2:32:25	Monika	Stefanowicz	POL	15.5.80	12 Oct
2:32:26	Frashiah	Waithaka	KEN	.80	16 Mar
2:32:26	Valentina	Galimova	RUS	11.5.86	14 Dec
2:32:28	Isabellah	Andersson	SWE	12.11.80	31 May
2:32:28	Abnet	Simegn	ETH	.86	19 Oct
2:32:29	Sayo	Nomura	JPN	18.4.89	26 Jan
2:32:29	Rehima	Kedir	ETH	11.12.85	26 Oct
2:32:31	Megertu	Ifa	ETH	.91	19 Oct
2:32:34	Milka	Cherotich	KEN	24.2.78	4 May
2:32:34	Nadia	Ejjafini	ITA	8.11.77	16 Aug
2:32:38	Hiroko	Yoshitomi	JPN	26.12.83	23 Feb
2:32:39	Winfrida	Kwamboka	KEN	4.3.82	27 Apr
2:32:39	Andrea	Deelstra	NED	6.3.85	16 Aug
2:32:40	Emma	Stepto	GBR	4.4.70	26 Oct
2:32:42	Asnakech	Mengistu	ETH	9.5.86	19 Jan
2:32:43		Choi Bo-ra	KOR	15.7.91	16 Mar
2:32:44	Sarah	Crouch	USA	22.8.89	12 Oct
2:32:45	Emma	Quaglia	ITA	15.8.80	16 Aug
2:32:46	Alice	Chelagat	KEN	27.12.76	13 Apr
2:32:46	Catherine	Bertone	ITA	6.5.72	16 Nov
2:32:50	Deribe	Godana	ETH	13.3.88	2 Nov
2:32:52	Ümmü	Kiraz	TUR	27.9.82	16 Nov
2:32:58	Chika (205)	Horie	JPN	15.2.81	9 Mar

Excessively Downhill (Boston 136.29m, Los Angeles - Santa Monica 122.22m, Sacramento 104m)

Mark			Name		Nat	Born	Pos	Venue	Date
2:18:57	1:22:26	1:39:21	Rita	Jeptoo ¶	KEN	15.2.81	1	Boston	21 Apr
2:19:59	1:22:26	1:39:21	Buzunesh	Deba	ETH	8.9.87	2	Boston	21 Apr
2:20:35	1:22:26	1:39:20	Mare	Dibaba	ETH	20.10.89	3	Boston	21 Apr
2:20:41	1:22:27	1:39:20	Jemima	Jelagat	KEN	21.12.84	4	Boston	21 Apr
2:21:28	1:22:27	1:39:21	Meselech	Melkamu	ETH	27.4.85	5	Boston	21 Apr
2:21:29	1:23:24	1:40:35	Aleksandra	Duliba	BLR	9.1.88	6	Boston	21 Apr
2:22:02	1:22:26	1:39:20		Flanagan			7	Boston	21 Apr
2:23:00	1:22:27	1:39:21	Sharon	Cherop	KEN	16.3.84	8	Boston	21 Apr
2:23:22			Philes	Ongori	KEN	19.7.86	9	Boston	21 Apr
2:23:54			Desiree	Linden	USA	26.7.83	10	Boston	21 Apr
2:24:21	1:22:26	1:39:33	Belaynesh	Oljira	ETH	26.6.90	11	Boston	21 Apr
2:27:33			Olga	Mazuronak	BLR	14.4.89	1	Sacramento	7 Dec
2:27:40			Yeshi	Esayias	ETH	28.12.85	12	Boston	21 Apr
2:28:48			Lauren	Kleppin	USA	22.11.88	3	Santa Monica	9 Mar

Mark	First name	Surname	Nat	Born	Date
2:30:29	Tatyana	Arkhipova	RUS	8.4.83	21 Apr
2:30:34	Lanni	Marchant	CAN	11.4.84	21 Apr
2:31:15	Adriana	Nelson	USA	31.1.80	21 Apr
2:31:18	Adriana	da Silva	BRA	22.7.81	21 Apr
2:32:24	Jane	Kibii	KEN	10.3.85	7 Dec
2:32:27dh	Serena	Burla	USA	29.7.82	21 Apr
2:32:48	Kristen	Zaitz	USA	3.12.80	7 Dec
2:32:49	Wendy	Thomas	USA	19.1.79	21 Apr

Drugs disqualification

Mark			Name		Nat	Born	Pos	Venue	Date
2:24:35	1:25:54	1:43:28	Rita	Jeptoo ¶	KEN	15.2.81	1	Chicago	12 Oct
2:28:00			Julia	Mombi ¶	KEN	25.9.85	1	Köln	14 Sep

Mark	Wind	Name		Nat	Born	Pos	Meet	Venue	Date

JUNIORS

Mark	Wind	Name		Nat	Born	Pos	Meet	Venue	Date
2:34:52			Kim Ji-hyang	PRK-J	26.9.95	1		Taipei	2 Mar
2:38:34		Alana	Hadley	USA-Y	8.1.97	1		Indianapolis	1 Nov
2:39:30		Fasila	Mateferika	ETH	.96	2		La Rochelle	30 Nov
2:39:52		Abebech	Tsegaye	ETH	.96	1		Lyon	5 Oct

100 KILOMETRES

Mark	Wind	Name		Nat	Born	Pos	Meet	Venue	Date
7:30:48		Ellie	Greenwood	GBR	14.3.79	1	WCh	Doha	21 Nov
7:38:23		Chiyuki	Mochizuki	JPN	29.9.86	2	WCh	Doha	21 Nov
7:42:02		Joasia	Zakrzewski	GBR	19.1.76	3	WCh	Doha	21 Nov
7:43:37		Jo	Meek	GBR	20.5.77	4	WCh	Doha	21 Nov
7:44:26		Irina	Antropova	RUS	2.6.82	5	WCh	Doha	21 Nov
7:47:52		Pam	Smith	USA	22.9.74	1		Madison	12 Apr
7:49:41		Shiho	Katayama	JPN	18.12.77	6	WCh	Doha	21 Nov
7:51:08		Veronika	Jurisic	CRO	6.4.77	7	WCh	Doha	21 Nov
7:51:43		Marija	Vrajic	CRO	23.9.76	1		Firenze	25 May
7:52:12		Meghan	Arbogast	USA	14.4.61	8	WCh	Doha	21 Nov
7:54:28		Mai	Fujisawa	JPN	21.9.74	9	WCh	Doha	21 Nov
7:55:09		Chiyuki	Michizuki	JPN	29.9.86	1		Yubetsu	29 Jun
8:00:46		Yukiya	Khazova	RUS	7.10.83	11	WCh	Doha	21 Nov
8:02:12		Sophia	Sundberg	SWE	5.9.84	13	WCh	Doha	21 Nov
8:03:40		Nikolina	Sustic	CRO	24.7.87	1		Stockholm	9 Aug

Mark	Name		Nat	Born	Date	Mark	Name		Nat	Born	Date
8:06:48	Rita	Nordsveen	NOR	21.7.71	21 Nov	8:12:59	Oksana	Teplykh	RUS	17.8.83	21 Nov
8:08:19	Oksana	Akimenkova	RUS	28.9.86	21 Nov	8:13:03	Barbara	Cimmarusti	ITA	18.12.71	30 Mar
8:09:34	Marita	Eisler	AUS	7.3.80	8 Jun	8:14:02	Amy	Sproston	USA	5.2.74	21 Nov
8:11:40	Neza	Mravlje	SLO	27.7.79	21 Nov	8:14:44	Cristina	González	ESP	19.2.84	21 Jun

Indoors: 7:56:49 Nadezhda Shikhanova RUS 14.5.84 1 Moskva 15 Feb

24 HOURS

Mark	Wind	Name		Nat	Born	Pos	Meet	Venue	Date
243.725	t	Katalin	Nagy	USA	5.5.79	1		Phoenix	14 Dec
238.261	t	Bernadette	Benson	AUS	25.3.69	1		Coburg	6 Apr
237.662	t	Traci	Falbo	USA	12.11.71	2		Phoenix	14 Dec
233.018	t	Fiona	Ross	GBR	28.1.90	1		London (TB)	21 Sep
230.134	t	Isobel	Wykes	GBR	24.4.78	2		London (TB)	21 Sep
228.526		Maggie	Guterl	USA	20.8.80	1		Augusta	9 Nov
226.763		Alyson	Venti	USA	24.6.82	1		Fort Lauderdale	16 Nov
223.989		Mizuki	Aotani	JPN	5.12.73	1		Tokyo	9 Nov
222.431	t	Mami	Kudo	JPN	17.7.64	1		Taipei	7 Dec
221.560	t	Karen	Hathaway	GBR	9.5.77	1		Barcelona	21 Dec
221.446		Leonie	van den Haak	NED	14.3.81	1		Berlin	13 Jul
221.055		Anne-Marie	Vernet	FRA	15.12.67	1		Grenoble	5 Oct
219.000		Anne Marie	Andersen	DEN	15.4.81	1		Kladno	27 Jul
218.870		Nina Sky	Canaves	USA	13.10.74	2		Augusta	9 Nov
218.473		Sandrine	Gard	FRA	2.9.67	1	NC	Portet-sur-Garonne	6 Apr

Mark	Name		Nat	Born	Date	Mark	Name		Nat	Born	Date
217.409 t	Natasha	Farid-Doyle	GBR	24.3.77	21 Dec	216.146	Christine	Zanconato-Bianchi	FRA	23.10.62	5 Oct
217.300	Edit	Máté-Varjú	HUN	3.10.71	8 Mar	215.326	Anita	Vajda	HUN	21.10.76	15 Jun
216.447	Antje	Krause	GER	1.5.72	13 Jul	215.248	Sadako	Fujiwara	JPN	3.4.61	9 Nov

Indoors

Mark	Wind	Name		Nat	Born	Pos	Meet	Venue	Date
228.432		Maria	Jansson	SWE	10.7.85	1		Oslo	23 Nov
213.575		Laila	Öjefelt	SWE	1.5.68	2		Oslo	23 Nov

2000 METRES STEEPLECHASE

Mark	Wind	Name		Nat	Born	Pos	Meet	Venue	Date
6:13.97		Yekaterina	Doseykina	RUS	30.3.90	1	Kuts	Moskva	17 Jul
6:14.66		Stephanie	Garcia	USA	3.5.88	1		Greenville	31 May
6:18.63		Viktoriya	Ivanova	RUS	21.11.91	2	Kuts	Moskva	17 Jul
6:20.10		Roseline	Chepngetich	KEN-Y	17.6.97	1	Yth OG	Nanjing	21 Aug
6:24.59A		Zeddinesh	Mamo	ETH-Y	14.1.97	2	Afr-Y	Gaborone	31 May

Mark	Name		Nat	Born	Date	Mark	Name		Nat	Born	Date
6:26.72	Aisha	Praught	USA	14.12.89	22 Mar	6:30.80	Klara	Bodinson	SWE	11.6.90	22 Jul
6:27.98A	Mihret	Tefera	ETH-Y		29 May	6:31.92	Lili Anna	Tóth	HUN-Y	17.9.98	25 Aug
6:30.69	Natalya	Tarantinova	RUS	28.11.87	17 Jul	6:33.19	Astrid	Leutert	SUI	12.9.87	18 May

JUNIORS

See main list for top 2 juniors. 5 performances by 3 women to 6:28.0. Additional marks and further juniors

Chepngetich	6:21.81A	1	Afr-Y	Gaborone	31 May
Mamo	6:26.02	2	Yth OG	Nanjing	25 Aug

Mark	Wind	Name		Nat	Born	Pos	Meet	Venue	Date
6:27.98A		Mihret	Tefera	ETH-Y		1B		Gaborone	29 May
6:31.92		Lili Anna	Tóth	HUN-Y	17.9.98	3	Yth OG	Nanjing	25 Aug

3000 METRES STEEPLECHASE

Mark	Wind	Name		Nat	Born	Pos	Meet	Venue	Date
9:10.64		Hiwot	Ayalew	ETH	6.3.90	1	DL	Glasgow	12 Jul
9:11.39		Sofia	Assefa	ETH	14.11.87	1	Pre	Eugene	31 May

WOMEN 2014

Mark Wind	Name		Nat	Born	Pos	Meet	Venue	Date
9:11.42	Emma	Coburn	USA	19.10.90	2	DL	Glasgow	12 Jul
9:11.65		Ayalew			1	DL	Saint-Denis	5 Jul
9:12.89		Ayalew			2	Pre	Eugene	31 May
9:14.12		Coburn			2	DL	Saint-Denis	5 Jul
9:15.23	Habiba	Ghribi	TUN	9.4.84	1	WK	Zürich	28 Aug
9:17.04		Ayalew			1	DNG	Stockholm	21 Aug
9:17.84		Coburn			3	Pre	Eugene	31 May
9:18.58		Assefa			1	adidas	New York	14 Jun
9:18.71		Assefa			3	DL	Saint-Denis	5 Jul
9:19.29		Ayalew			2	WK	Zürich	28 Aug
9:19.39		Ghribi			2	DNG	Stockholm	21 Aug
9:19.71	Etenesh	Diro	ETH	10.5.91	4	DL	Saint-Denis	5 Jul
9:19.72		Coburn			1	NC	Sacramento	28 Jun
9:19.79		Assefa			3	WK	Zürich	28 Aug
9:19.80		Coburn			1	DL	Shanghai	18 May
9:20.31		Coburn			3	DNG	Stockholm	21 Aug
9:20.55	Ruth	Chebet	BRN-J	17.11.96	4	WK	Zürich	28 Aug
9:21.24	Salima	Alami El Ouali	MAR	29.12.83	5	DL	Saint-Denis	5 Jul
9:21.73		Ghribi			1	WCM	Rieti	7 Sep
9:21.91	Milcah	Chemos	KEN	24.2.86	3	DL	Glasgow	12 Jul
9:22.02		Assefa			4	DNG	Stockholm	21 Aug
9:22.58	Hyvin	Jepkemoi	KEN	13.1.92	1	GS	Ostrava	17 Jun
9:23.27		Alami El Ouali			2	GS	Ostrava	17 Jun
9:23.43	Purity	Kirui (10)	KEN	13.8.91	2	adidas	New York	14 Jun
9:23.89		Coburn			5	WK	Zürich	28 Aug
9:23.96	Charlotta	Fougberg	SWE	19.6.85	4	DL	Glasgow	12 Jul
9:24.03		Jepkemoi			5	DNG	Stockholm	21 Aug
9:24.07	Lydia	Chepkurui	KEN	23.8.84	6	DL	Saint-Denis	5 Jul
	(30/12)							
9:24.28	Stephanie	Garcia	USA	3.5.88	5	DL	Glasgow	12 Jul
9:24.59	Nicole	Bush	USA	4.4.86	1	NA	Heusden-Zolder	19 Jul
9:24.70	Sandra	Eriksson	FIN	4.6.89	6	DL	Glasgow	12 Jul
9:27.29	Birtukan	Adamu	ETH	29.4.92	3	GS	Ostrava	17 Jun
9:27.59	Ashley	Higginson	USA	17.3.89	2	NC	Sacramento	28 Jun
9:27.95	Svetlana	Kudzelich	BLR	7.5.87	2	ISTAF	Berlin	31 Aug
9:28.36	Tigist Getnet	Mekonen	ETH-Y	7.7.97	7	DL	Glasgow	12 Jul
9:29.20	Amina	Bettiche	ALG	14.12.87	4	GS	Ostrava	17 Jun
	(20)							
9:29.43	Antje	Möldner-Schmidt	GER	13.6.84	1	EC	Zürich	17 Aug
9:30.70	Diana	Martín	ESP	1.4.81	3	EC	Zürich	17 Aug
9:30.75	Birtukan	Fente	ETH	18.6.89	5	GS	Ostrava	17 Jun
9:32.98	Natalya	Aristarkhova	RUS	31.10.89	1	NC	Kazan	23 Jul
9:33.19	Genevieve	LaCaze	AUS	4.8.89	9	DL	Glasgow	12 Jul
9:33.34	Joan	Rotich	KEN	27.11.93	3	CG	Glasgow	30 Jul
9:33.45	Jessica	Furlan	CAN	15.3.90	4	NA	Heusden-Zolder	19 Jul
9:34.01	Madeline	Heiner	AUS	5.3.88	4	CG	Glasgow	30 Jul
9:34.12	Yekaterina	Sokolenko	RUS	13.9.92	2	NC	Kazan	23 Jul
9:34.16	Natalya	Vlasova	RUS	19.7.88	1	Déca	Angers	30 Aug
	(30)							
9:34.69	Aisha	Praught	USA	14.12.89	4	NC	Sacramento	28 Jun
9:35.23		Li Zhenzhu	CHN	13.12.85	2	AsiG	Incheon	27 Sep
9:35.28	Yekaterina	Doseykina	RUS	30.3.90	1		Adler	29 May
9:35.37	Lalita	Babar	IND	2.6.89	3	AsiG	Incheon	27 Sep
9:35.46	Gesa-Felicitas	Krause	GER	3.8.92	5	EC	Zürich	17 Aug
9:35.64	Sudha	Singh	IND	25.6.86	4	AsiG	Incheon	27 Sep
9:36.43	Leah	O'Connor	USA	30.8.92	1	NCAA	Eugene	13 Jun
9:36.56	Katarzyna	Kowalska	POL	7.4.85	2	WCM	Rieti	7 Sep
9:37.81	Fabienne	Schlumpf	SUI	17.11.90	3		Oordegem	31 May
9:39.12	Shalaya	Kipp	USA	19.8.90	1	Jordan	Stanford	4 May
	(40)							
9:39.56	Bridget	Franek	USA	8.11.87	1h1	NC	Sacramento	26 Jun
9:40.01	Lyudmila	Lebedeva	RUS	23.5.90	4	NC	Kazan	23 Jul
9:40.26	Bezuayehu	Mohamed	ETH-J	4.1.96	7	GS	Ostrava	17 Jun
9:40.28	Roseline	Chepngetich	KEN-Y	17.6.97	2	WJ	Eugene	26 Jul
9:40.49	Marusa	Mismas	SLO	24.10.94	2	ET-1	Tallinn	21 Jun
9:40.50		Yin Anna	CHN	23.3.92	1	NGPF	Jinan	11 Jul
9:40.77	Olga	Dereveva	RUS	5.4.85	4		Adler	29 May
9:40.78	Viktoriya	Ivanova	RUS	21.11.91	6	NC	Kazan	23 Jul
9:41.02	Fancy	Cherotich	KEN	10.8.90	7	Pre	Eugene	31 May
9:41.55	Sara	Vaughn	USA	16.5.86	5h1	NC	Sacramento	26 Jun
	(50)							

Mark	Wind	Name		Nat	Born	Pos	Meet	Venue	Date
9:41.56		Rachel	Johnson	USA	30.4.93	5	NC	Sacramento	28 Jun
9:42.01		Victoria	Mitchell	AUS	25.4.82	1	NC	Melbourne	5 Apr
9:42.10		Sara	Hall	USA	15.4.83	3	Jordan	Stanford	4 May
9:42.13		Nicol	Traynor	USA	6.5.89	2		Princeton	18 Apr
9:42.23		Mekdes	Bekele	ETH	20.1.87	3		Montbéliard	6 Jun
9:42.38		Natalya	Gorchakova	RUS	17.4.83	7	NC	Kazan	23 Jul
9:42.88		Gladys	Kipkemboi	KEN	15.10.86	4	WCM	Beijing	21 May
9:43.07		Courtney	Frerichs	USA	18.1.93	4h2	NC	Sacramento	26 Jun
9:43.13		Silvia	Danekova	BUL	7.2.83	1	ET-2	Riga	21 Jun
9:43.48		Rachel	Sorna	USA	15.4.92	3		Princeton	18 Apr
		(60)							
9:43.52		Jana	Sussmann	GER	12.10.90	6	NA	Heusden-Zolder	19 Jul
9:43.82		Marisa	Howard	USA	9.8.92	2	NCAA	Eugene	13 Jun
9:44.65		Eilish	McColgan	GBR	25.11.90	6	CG	Glasgow	30 Jul
9:45.42		Chantelle	Groenewoud	CAN	3.3.89	7	NA	Heusden-Zolder	19 Jul
9:45.50		Claire	Perraux	FRA	6.10.87	8	NA	Heusden-Zolder	19 Jul
9:45.51		Racheal	Bamford	GBR	4.8.89	7	CG	Glasgow	30 Jul
9:45.84		Maria	Mancebo	DOM	29.8.93	1	IbAmC	São Paulo	1 Aug
9:46.4A		Agnes	Chesang	KEN	1.4.86	1	Army Ch	Nairobi	14 May
9:47.28		Carmen	Graves	USA	27.1.91	6h1	NC	Sacramento	26 Jun
9:47.34		Özlem	Kaya	TUR	20.4.90	2	BalkC	Pitesti	26 Jul
		(70)							
9:47.60		Beverly	Ramos	PUR	24.8.87	6	adidas	New York	14 Jun
9:47.65		Daisy	Jepkemei	KEN-J	13.2.96	3	WJ	Eugene	26 Jul
9:47.76		Yelena	Orlova	RUS	30.5.80	1	Mosc Ch	Moskva	2 Jul
9:47.92		Sara	Treacy	IRL	22.6.89	1		Kessel-Lo	9 Aug
9:47.97		Pippa	Woolven	GBR	26.7.93	8	CG	Glasgow	30 Jul
9:48.10		Grace	Heymsfield	USA	24.3.92	9	NC	Sacramento	28 Jun
9:48.17		Lennie	Waite	GBR	4.5.86	1		Stanford	4 Apr
9:48.41		Matylda	Kowal	POL	11.1.89	3		Joensuu	24 Jul
9:48.50		Johanna	Lehtinen	FIN	21.2.79	4		Joensuu	24 Jul
9:48.75		Sanaa	Koubaa	GER	6.1.85	2		Kessel-Lo	9 Aug
		(80)							
9:48.91		Alicia	Nelson	USA	20.10.90	6h2	NC	Sacramento	26 Jun
9:48.94		Sarah	Pease	USA	9.11.87	7h2	NC	Sacramento	26 Jun
9:49.25		Jessica	Kamilos	USA	3.8.93	7	NCAA	Eugene	13 Jun
9:49.35		María Teresa	Urbina	ESP	20.3.85	10	NA	Heusden-Zolder	19 Jul
9:49.46		Rini	Budiarti	INA	22.1.83	5	AsiG	Incheon	27 Sep
9:49.85		Misaki	Sango	JPN	21.4.89	1	NC	Fukushima	8 Jun
9:50.10		Yekaterina	Rogozina	RUS	21.12.89	5		Adler	29 May
9:50.15		Jekaterina	Patjuk	EST	6.4.83	3	ET-1	Tallinn	21 Jun
9:50.35		Astrid	Leutert	SUI	12.9.87	4		Oordegem	31 May
9:50.42		Zewdnesh	Ayele	ETH	.93	11	NA	Heusden-Zolder	19 Jul
		(90)							
9:50.79		Geneviève	Lalonde	CAN	5.9.91	1		Ninove	2 Aug
9:51.29		Kimber	Mattox	USA	27.11.88	9h2	NC	Sacramento	26 Jun
9:51.40		Cristina	Casandra	ROU	1.2.77	3	BalkC	Pitesti	26 Jul
9:52.2A		Nancy	Kimaiyo	KEN	.84	1		Nairobi	23 May
9:52.58		Polina	Jelizarova	LAT	1.5.89	4h2	EC	Zürich	15 Aug
9:52.94		Kerry	O'Flaherty	IRL	15.7.81	5		Oordegem	31 May
9:52.97		Magdalene	Masai	KEN	12.11.93	12	DL	Shanghai	18 May
9:53.15		Kate	Spencer	AUS-J	23.6.95	1		Sydney	2 Mar
9:53.18		Rebeka	Stowe	USA	9.3.90	10h2	NC	Sacramento	26 Jun
9:53.19		Betlhem	Desalegn	UAE	13.11.91	13	DNG	Stockholm	21 Aug
		(100)							

Mark	Name		Nat	Born	Date
9:53.23	Klara	Bodinson	SWE	11.6.90	30 Aug
9:53.42	Zulema	Arenas	PER-J	15.11.95	1 Aug
9:53.60	Addie	Bracy	USA	4.8.86	4 May
9:53.82	Valeria	Roffino	ITA	9.4.90	20 Jul
9:53.87	Mayuko	Nakamura	JPN	20.11.90	8 Jun
9:54.27	Alexa	Aragon	USA	1.7.94	13 Jun
9:54.91	Maeva	Danois	FRA	10.3.93	6 Jun
9:54.94	Mary	Goldkamp	USA	4.10.88	14 Jun
9:55.69	Maria	Bernard	CAN	6.4.93	9 Aug
9:55.73	Maya	Rehberg	GER	28.4.94	13 Jun
9:55.77	Justyna	Korytkowska	POL	12.3.86	31 Jul
9:55.79	Carla Salomé	Rocha	POR	25.4.90	21 Jun
9:55.83	Jamie	Cheever	USA	28.2.87	4 May
9:56.06	Woynshet	Ansa	ETH-J	9.4.96	24 Jul
9:56.25	Ophélie	Claude-Boxberger	FRA	18.10.88	2 Aug
9:56.44	Camilla	Richardsson	FIN	14.9.93	28 Jun
9:56.51	Minttu	Hukka	FIN-J	31.3.95	28 Jun
9:56.96	Colleen	Quigley	USA	20.11.92	5 Apr
9:56.98	Rosa	Flanagan	NZL-J	28.2.96	22 Mar
9:56.98	Megan	Rolland	USA	30.8.88	14 Jun
9:57.33	Urszula	Necka	POL	28.6.84	24 Jul
9:57.70	Gulnara	Galkina	RUS	9.7.78	23 Jul
9:57.83	Rolanda	Bell	PAN	27.10.87	15 May
9:57.89	Michele	Finn	IRL	16.12.89	14 Jun
9:58.19	Oona	Kettunen	FIN	10.2.94	30 Aug
9:58.28	Elif	Karabulut	TUR	8.8.91	20 Jul
9:58.42	Amber	Schulz	USA	27.12.90	19 Apr
9:58.42	Aleksandra	Pavlyutenkova	RUS	21.3.90	23 Jul
9:58.56	Julie-Ann	Staehli	CAN	1.12.93	9 May
9:58.65	Jordan	Hamric	USA	4.10.89	26 Jun
9:58.98	Chikako	Mori	JPN	25.11.92	24 May
9:59.43	Eliane	Sahalinirina	MAD	20.3.82	6 Jun
10:00.02	Muriel	Coneo	COL	15.3.87	10 Aug
10:00.05	Viktória	Gyürkés	HUN	15.10.92	21 Jun
10:00.48	Kara	DeWalt	USA	27.7.88	19 Apr
10:00.58	Cornelia	Griesche	GER	28.8.93	17 May

Mark	Wind	Name		Nat	Born	Pos	Meet	Venue	Date

Mark	Name		Nat	Born	Date
10:00.73	Ingeborg	Løvnes	NOR	5.9.92	2 Aug
10:00.74	Sarah	Benson	GBR	9.6.82	19 Apr
10:00.79	Lauren	Johnson	USA	4.5.87	4 May
10:00.87	Maria	Pardaloú	GRE	21.4.84	21 Jun
10:00.99	Anju	Takamizawa	JPN-J	6.3.96	7 Sep
10:01.00		Zhang Xinyan	CHN	9.2.94	11 Jul
10:01.37	Anastasiya	Puzakova	BLR	12.12.93	25 Jul
10:01.71A	Norah	Tanui	KEN-J	2.10.95	7 Jun
10:02.0A	Elizabeth	Mueni	KEN	28.12.91	14 May
10:02.18	Virginia	Nyambura	KEN	20.7.93	9 Jun
10:02.26	Liberty	Miller	USA	4.7.92	26 Jun
10:02.61	Betsy	Graney	USA	23.10.89	19 Apr
10:02.64	Julia	Webb	USA	14.2.83	14 Jun
10:03.01	Mariya	Shatalova	UKR	3.3.89	25 Jul
10:03.07	Maggie	Callahan	USA	28.9.88	4 May
10:03.32	Cinthya	Paucar	PER	10.6.90	25 Jun
10:03.43	Alex	Leptich	USA	3.2.92	30 May
10:03.52	Olga	Vovk	RUS	13.2.93	29 May
10:03.55	Tori	Gerlach	USA	2.6.94	30 May
10:03.65	Jennifer	Agnew	USA		15 Jun
10:03.82	Megan	Patrignelli	USA	22.6.92	4 May
10:04.36	Zita	Kácser	HUN	2.10.88	13 Sep
10:04.74	Olga	Tarantinova	RUS	28.11.87	2 Jul
10:04.89	Viktoriya	Voronko	RUS	15.5.91	30 May
10:05.25A	Ángela	Figueroa	COL	28.6.84	28 Nov
10:05.27	Sarah	Martinelli	USA	25.9.90	11 Jun
10:05.80	Misato	Horie	JPN	10.3.87	8 Jun
10:06.06	Türkan	Özata	TUR	5.1.84	3 Aug
10:06.08	Kristine Eikrem	Engeset	NOR	15.11.88	21 Jun
10:06.78	Maria José	Pérez	ESP	12.6.92	15 Jun
10:07.03	Janica	Mäkelä	FIN	24.6.86	24 Jul
10:07.1A	Lucia	Muangi	KEN	26.6.92	14 May
10:07.18	Rosemary	Katua	BRN-J	10.8.96	24 Jul
10:07.37	Diana	Martín Hidalgo	ESP	31.7.90	31 May
10:07.42	Maria	Larsson	SWE	24.3.94	30 Aug
10:07.54	Aïssé	Sow	FRA	19.8.91	11 Jul
10:07.63	Sabahat	Akpinar	TUR	20.7.93	15 Jun
10:07.87	Mackenzie	Chojnacky	USA	7.10.92	30 May
10:07.98	Tova	Eurén	SWE	11.2.94	11 Jun
10:08.09	Jovana	de la Cruz	PER	12.7.92	25 Jun
10:08.17	Ann	Detmer	USA	1.11.85	15 May
10:08.20	Krista	Moylan	USA		4 May
10:08.21	Madelin	Talbert	USA	23.4.94	30 May
10:08.23	Blair	Doney	USA	21.4.92	26 Apr
10:08.33	Elinor	Purrier	USA-J	20.2.95	24 Jul
10:08.4	Kaltoum	Bouaasayriya	MAR	23.8.82	21 Jun
10:08.64	Alycia	Butterworth	CAN	1.10.92	4 May
10:09.06	Dana Elena	Loghin	ROU	23.10.94	26 Jul
10:09.38	Allix	Potratz-Lee	USA	3.5.86	14 Jun
10:09.39	Iona	Lake	GBR	15.1.93	31 May
10:09.74	Jannika	John	GER	26.12.92	15 Jun
10:09.84	Nawal	Yahi	ALG	9.12.91	24 Jun
10:09.86	Andrea	Harrison	USA	25.10.91	4 Apr
10:09.87	Katie	Landwehr	USA	23.1.93	18 Apr
10:09.87	Heather	Olson	USA	23.4.91	17 May
(191)					

JUNIORS

See main list for top 6 juniors. 13 performances by 5 women to 9:50.0. Additional marks and further juniors:

Name	Mark	Pos	Meet	Venue	Date	Mark	Pos	Meet	Venue	Date
Chebet	9:26.94	1	ISTAF	Berlin	31 Aug	9:31.36	1	AsiG	Incheon	27 Sep
	9:27.90	2		Marrakech	18 Jun	9:36.74	1	WJ	Eugene	26 Jul
Mekonen	9:31.16	3	ISTAF	Berlin	31 Aug	9:36.73	10	WK	Zürich	28 Aug
Chepngetich	9:43.25A	1	NC-j	Nairobi	25 Jun					
Mohamed	9:48.66	4	WJ	Eugene	26 Jul					

Mark	Name		Nat	Born	Pos	Meet	Venue	Date
9:53.42	Zulema	Arenas	PER	15.11.95	2	IbAmC	São Paulo	1 Aug
9:56.06	Woynshet	Ansa	ETH	9.4.96	1h1	WJ	Eugene	24 Jul
9:56.51	Minttu	Hukka	FIN	31.3.95	2		Jämsä	28 Jun
9:56.98	Rosa	Flanagan (10)	NZL	28.2.96	2	WCM	Melbourne	22 Mar
10:00.99	Anju	Takamizawa	JPN	6.3.96	2	Univ Ch	Kumagaya	7 Sep
10:01.71A	Norah	Tanui	KEN	2.10.95	8	NC	Nairobi	7 Jun
10:07.18	Rosemary	Katua	BRN	10.8.96	4h2	WJ	Eugene	24 Jul
10:08.33	Elinor	Purrier	USA	20.2.95	6h2	WJ	Eugene	24 Jul
10:10.59A	Stella	Jepkosgei	KEN	12.12.96	3	NC-j	Nairobi	25 Jun
10:11.62A	Dorcas	Nzembi	KEN-Y	22.12.97	4	NC-j	Nairobi	25 Jun
10:12.69	Emma	Oudiou	FRA	2.10.95	7h2	WJ	Eugene	24 Jul
10:12.91	Nicole	Reina	ITA-Y	25.9.97	2	NC	Rovereto	20 Jul
10:13.75	Anezka	Drahotová	CZE	22.7.95	3	ECCp	VR de Santo António	24 May
10:13.99	Katie	Ingle (20)	GBR	4.3.95	3		Manchester	31 May

60 METRES HURDLES INDOORS

Mark	Name		Nat	Born	Pos	Meet	Venue	Date
7.79	Sally	Pearson	AUS	19.9.86	1h1	ISTAF	Berlin	1 Mar
7.79		Pearson			1h1	WI	Sopot	7 Mar
7.80A	Nia	Ali	USA	23.10.88	1	NC	Albuquerque	23 Feb
7.80		Pearson			1	ISTAF	Berlin	1 Mar
7.80		Ali			1	WI	Sopot	8 Mar
7.81		Pearson			1s1	WI	Sopot	8 Mar
7.82A	Janay	DeLoach Soukup	USA	12.10.85	2	NC	Albuquerque	23 Feb
7.85		Pearson			2	WI	Sopot	8 Mar
7.86	Tiffany	Porter	GBR	13.11.87	3	WI	Sopot	8 Mar
7.87	Cindy	Billaud	FRA	11.3.86	1h3	WI	Sopot	7 Mar
7.87		Ali			1h2	WI	Sopot	7 Mar
	(11/5)							
7.88A	Kristi	Castlin	USA	7.7.88	3	NC	Albuquerque	23 Feb
7.91	Nadine	Hildebrand	GER	20.9.87	1		Karlsruhe	1 Feb
7.91	Yvette	Lewis	PAN	16.3.85	2h2	WI	Sopot	7 Mar
7.93	Yekaterina	Galitskaya	RUS	24.2.87	1	NC	Moskva	18 Feb
7.93A	Sharika	Nelvis	USA	10.5.90	1	NCAA	Albuquerque	15 Mar
	(10)							
7.93A	Tiffani	McReynolds	USA	4.12.91	2	NCAA	Albuquerque	15 Mar
7.94	Kendra	Harrison	USA	18.9.92	1	SEC	College Station	1 Mar
7.94A	Jasmin	Stowers	USA	23.9.91	3	NCAA	Albuquerque	15 Mar
7.95	Cindy	Roleder	GER	21.8.89	2	NC	Leipzig	22 Feb

Mark	Wind	Name		Nat	Born	Pos	Meet	Venue	Date
7.95		Eline	Berings	BEL	28.5.86	2h1	WI	Sopot	7 Mar
7.97		Marzia	Caravelli	ITA	23.10.81	3h2	WI	Sopot	7 Mar
7.98A		Janice	Jackson	USA	30.10.91	2h1	NCAA	Albuquerque	14 Mar
8.00A		Candice	Price	USA	26.10.85	1		Flagstaff	8 Feb
8.02A		Jessica	Zelinka	CAN	3.9.81	2		Albuquerque	8 Feb
8.02			Wu Shujiao	CHN	19.6.92	1	AsiC	Hangzhou	15 Feb
		(20)							
8.02		Alina	Talay	BLR	14.5.89	1	NC	Mogilyov	22 Feb
8.02A		Vashti	Thomas	USA	21.4.90	3s1	NC	Albuquerque	23 Feb
8.03		Yuliya	Kondakova	RUS	4.12.81	4s2	WI	Sopot	8 Mar
8.04		Giulia	Pennella	ITA	27.10.89	1	NC	Ancona	22 Feb
8.05		Marina	Tomic	SLO	30.4.83	3h2		Karlsruhe	1 Feb
8.05		Sara	Aerts	BEL	25.1.84	4h3	WI	Sopot	7 Mar
8.06		Jacqueline	Coward	USA	5.11.89	1h1		Houston	14 Feb
8.07A		LeTristan	Pledger	USA	27.8.93	1h3		Albuquerque	8 Feb
8.07		Rosina	Hodde	NED	10.2.83	4h1	WI	Sopot	7 Mar
8.07A		Cindy	Ofili	USA	5.8.94	6	NCAA	Albuquerque	15 Mar
		(30)							
8.08		Kellie	Wells	USA	16.7.82	1h1		Karlsruhe	1 Feb
8.08		Angela	Whyte	CAN	22.5.80	1		Moscow ID	7 Feb
8.08A		Sasha	Wallace	USA-J	21.9.95	3h2	NCAA	Albuquerque	14 Mar
8.09A		Jade	Barber	USA	4.4.93	1h2		Albuquerque	1 Feb
8.09		Nooralotta	Neziri	FIN	9.11.92	1	NC	Rovaniemi	23 Feb
8.09		Andrea	Ivancevic	CRO	21.8.84	7s1	WI	Sopot	8 Mar
8.10		Evonne	Britton	USA	10.10.91	2	Big 10	Geneva	1 Mar
8.10		Monique	Morgan	JAM	14.10.85	5h1	WI	Sopot	7 Mar
8.11		Dior	Hall	USA-J	2.1.96	1	N.Sch	New York (Arm)	16 Mar
8.12A		Indira	Spence	JAM	8.9.86	4		Albuquerque	8 Feb
		(40)							
8.12		Matilda	Bogdanoff	FIN	8.10.90	6h3	WI	Sopot	7 Mar
8.12		Danielle	Williams	JAM	14.9.92	1	NCAA-II	Winston-Salem	15 Mar
8.13		Eva	Vital	POR	8.7.92	1		Jamor	21 Jan
8.13		Natalya	Ivoninskaya	KAZ	22.2.85	1	NC	Shymkent	30 Jan
8.13		Aïsseta	Diawara	FRA	29.6.89	1		Mondeville	1 Feb
8.13A		Lindsay	Lindley	USA	6.10.89	2		Flagstaff	8 Feb
8.13		Brianne	Theisen-Eaton	CAN	18.12.88	1P	WI	Sopot	7 Mar
8.14		Sharona	Bakker	NED	12.4.90	2h1		Karlsruhe	1 Feb
8.14		Alice	Decaux	FRA	10.4.85	1		Eaubonne	11 Feb
8.14		Lisa	Urech	SUI	27.7.89	1	NC	Magglingen	15 Feb
		(50)							
8.14		Chelsea	Carrier-Eades	USA	21.8.89	1h2		Geneva OH	15 Feb
8.14		Yekaterina	Voronkova	RUS	24.11.88	2h1	NC	Moskva	18 Feb
8.15		Cassandra	Lloyd	USA	27.1.90	2		Lexington	18 Jan
8.15		Shermaine	Williams	JAM	4.2.90	2		University Park	31 Jan
8.15		Hanna	Plotitsyna	UKR	1.1.87	1	NC	Sumy	21 Feb
8.15		Gnima	Faye	SEN	17.11.84	5h2	WI	Sopot	7 Mar

Best at low altitude

Mark	Name	Pos	Meet	Venue	Date
7.90	DeLoach Soukup	5	WI	Sopot	8 Mar
7.93	Castlin	2	Mill	New York (Arm)	15 Feb
8.01	Stowers	2	SEC	College Station	1 Mar
8.03	Nelvis	1h3		Birmingham AL	25 Feb
8.05	McReynolds	2		Lexington	25 Jan
8.08	Ofili	1	Big 10	Geneva	1 Mar
8.10	Wallace	3		Lexington	25 Jan
8.10	Pledger	1h2	Big 12	Ames	1 Mar
8.12	Jackson	2		College Station	8 Feb
8.13	Thomas	1		Geneva OH	8 Feb
8.13	Zelinka	1		Montreal	15 Mat
8.14	Spence	4h2	WI	Sopot	7 Mar

100 METRES HURDLES

Mark	Wind	Name		Nat	Born	Pos	Meet	Venue	Date
12.44	0.0	Dawn	Harper Nelson	USA	13.5.84	1	DL	Saint-Denis	5 Jul
12.46	0.0	Queen	Harrison	USA	10.9.88	2	DL	Saint-Denis	5 Jul
12.47	0.7		Harper Nelson			1	C.Cup	Marrakech	14 Sep
12.51	0.7	Tiffany	Porter	GBR	13.11.87	2	C.Cup	Marrakech	14 Sep
12.53	0.5	Brianna	Rollins	USA	18.8.91	1	GGala	Roma	5 Jun
12.54	0.5		Harper Nelson			2	GGala	Roma	5 Jun
12.54	-1.6		Harper Nelson			1s1	NC	Sacramento	28 Jun
12.55	-1.6	Lolo	Jones	USA	5.8.82	2s1	NC	Sacramento	28 Jun
12.55	-1.6		Harper Nelson			1	NC	Sacramento	28 Jun
12.56	0.9		Harrison			1	FBK	Hengelo	8 Jun
12.56	1.0		Harrison			1h3	NC	Sacramento	27 Jun
12.56	-1.6		Harrison			2	NC	Sacramento	28 Jun
12.56	1.2	Cindy	Billaud	FRA	11.3.86	1h1	NC	Reims	12 Jul
12.58	0.2	Kristi	Castlin	USA	7.7.88	1	Drake	Des Moines	26 Apr
12.58	0.2		Rollins			2	Drake	Des Moines	26 Apr
12.58	0.0		Rollins			1	WCM	Beijing	21 May

Mark	Wind	Name		Nat	Born	Pos	Meet	Venue	Date
12.58	0.2		Harrison			1	DL	Glasgow	12 Jul
12.58	1.4		Billaud			1	NC	Reims	12 Jul
12.58	-0.5		Harper Nelson			1	WK	Zürich	28 Aug
12.59	-0.2	Sally	Pearson	AUS	19.9.86	1		Perth	22 Feb
12.61	0.5		Harrison			3	GGala	Roma	5 Jun
12.62	-1.9		Rollins			1		Tokyo	11 May
12.62	-2.1		Harrison			1	adidas	New York	14 Jun
12.62	1.9		Jones			1h1	NC	Sacramento	27 Jun
12.63	-2.1		Harper Nelson			2	adidas	New York	14 Jun
12.63	1.4		Harper Nelson			1h2	NC	Sacramento	27 Jun
12.63	-0.1		Porter			1s2	EC	Zürich	12 Aug
12.64	0.0		Porter			1	ISTAF	Berlin	31 Aug
12.65	1.7		Porter			1		Manchester	17 May
12.65	-1.6		Jones			3	NC	Sacramento	28 Jun
		(30/8)							
12.68	0.2	Kellie	Wells	USA	16.7.82	3	Drake	Des Moines	26 Apr
12.71	1.3	Sharika	Nelvis (10)	USA	10.5.90	1	MSR	Walnut	19 Apr
12.71	1.0	Jasmin	Stowers	USA	23.9.91	2h3	NC	Sacramento	27 Jun
12.71	1.9	Kendra	Harrison	USA	18.9.92	2h1	NC	Sacramento	27 Jun
12.71	2.0	Nadine	Hildebrand	GER	20.9.87	1	NC	Ulm	26 Jul
12.72	0.0		Wu Shuijiao	CHN	19.6.91	1	AsiG	Incheon	1 Oct
12.73	0.2	Jackie	Coward	USA	5.11.89	6	Drake	Des Moines	26 Apr
12.75	0.9	Tenaya	Jones	USA	22.3.89	1		Clermont	31 May
12.75	0.2	Nia	Ali	USA	23.10.88	1	NA	Heusden-Zolder	19 Jul
12.77	1.4	Tiffani	McReynolds	USA	4.12.91	2h2	NC	Sacramento	27 Jun
12.80	1.4	Bridgette	Owens	USA	14.3.92	1q2	NCAA-E	Jacksonville	31 May
12.80	2.0	Cindy	Roleder	GER	21.8.89	2	NC	Ulm	26 Jul
		(20)							
12.81	0.7	Lavonne	Idlette	DOM	31.10.85	1		Montverde	7 Jun
12.83	0.5	Anne	Zagré	BEL	13.3.90	2		Liège (NX)	16 Jul
12.83	1.5	Jessica	Zelinka	CAN	3.9.81	1H	CG	Glasgow	29 Jul
12.84	-0.1	Vashti	Thomas	USA	21.4.90	1	Odlozil	Praha	9 Jun
12.85	0.0	Sharona	Bakker	NED	12.4.90	2h3	EC	Zürich	12 Aug
12.86	1.8	Yuliya	Kondakova	RUS	4.12.81	3	ET	Braunschweig	22 Jun
12.86A	0.9	Yvette	Lewis	PAN	16.3.85	1	PAm SF	Ciudad de México	16 Aug
12.87	2.0	Kendell	Williams	USA-J	14.6.95	1	NC-j	Eugene	6 Jul
12.87	2.0	Franziska	Hofmann	GER	27.3.94	3	NC	Ulm	26 Jul
12.87	0.1	Eline	Berings	BEL	28.5.86	1	NC	Bruxelles	27 Jul
		(30)							
12.88	1.3	Yekaterina	Galitskaya	RUS	24.2.87	1	NCp	Yerino	9 Jul
12.89	1.3	Angela	Whyte	CAN	22.5.80	2	MSR	Walnut	19 Apr
12.89	0.1	Rosina	Hodde	NED	10.2.83	3	VD	Bruxelles	5 Sep
12.89	0.1	Alina	Talay	BLR	14.5.89	3	VD	Bruxelles	5 Sep
12.91	0.5	Morgan	Snow	USA	26.7.93	1h2	Big 12	Lubbock	17 May
12.91A	0.9	Shermaine	Williams	JAM	4.2.90	2	PAm SF	Ciudad de México	16 Aug
12.92	1.5	Noemi	Zbären	SUI	12.3.94	1	NC	Frauenfeld	26 Jul
12.92	1.9	Dior	Hall	USA-J	2.1.96	2	WJ	Eugene	27 Jul
12.93	1.3	Candice	Price	USA	26.10.85	3	MSR	Walnut	19 Apr
12.93	0.5	LeTristan	Pledger	USA	27.8.93	2h2	Big 12	Lubbock	17 May
		(40)							
12.93	1.4	Cindy	Ofili	USA	5.8.94	1	Big 10	West Lafayette	18 May
12.93		Yekaterina	Gubina	RUS	27.11.85	1		Cheboksary	3 Jun
12.93	1.8	Anna	Plotitsyna	UKR	1.1.87	4	ET	Braunschweig	22 Jun
12.93	0.9	Anastasiya	Pilipenko	KAZ	13.9.86	1	NC	Almaty	28 Jun
12.94	0.6	Monique	Morgan	JAM	14.10.85	1h1	NC	Kingston	29 Jun
12.94	1.7	Karolina	Koleczek	POL	15.1.93	1h2	NC	Szczecin	31 Jul
12.95	0.9	Marina	Tomic	SLO	30.4.83	1r1		Sundsvall	20 Jul
12.95	2.0	Pamela	Dutkiewicz	GER	28.9.91	4	NC	Ulm	26 Jul
12.97	-0.3	Jade	Barber	USA	4.4.93	1h1	Drake	Des Moines	25 Apr
12.97A	0.3	Lina	Florez	COL	1.11.84	1		Medellín	31 May
		(50)							
12.98	1.2	Fabiana	Moraes	BRA	5.6.86	1		São Paulo	5 Apr
12.98	1.3	Indira	Spence	JAM	8.9.86	4	MSR	Walnut	19 Apr
12.98	0.9	Janice	Jackson	JAM	30.10.91	1q2	NCAA-W	Fayetteville	31 May
12.98	0.9	Kierre	Beckles	BAR	21.5.90	4		Clermont	31 May
12.98	1.5	Nooralotta	Neziri	FIN	9.11.92	1h2		Kuortane	13 Jul
12.98	-1.1	Marzia	Caravelli	ITA	23.10.81	3h2	EC	Zürich	12 Aug
12.99	0.9	Danielle	Williams	JAM	14.9.92	2	NC	Kingston	29 Jun
12.99	1.3	Svetlana	Topylina	RUS	6.1.85	2	NCp	Yerino	9 Jul
12.99	1.9	Nadine	Visser	NED-J	9.2.95	3	WJ	Eugene	27 Jul

Mark	Wind	Name		Nat	Born	Pos	Meet	Venue	Date
12.99	0.4	Lucie	Skrobáková	CZE	4.1.82	1	NC	Ostrava	2 Aug
		(60)							
13.00	1.4	Janay	DeLoach	USA	12.10.85	4h2	NC	Sacramento	27 Jun
13.00	-0.6	Brianne	Theisen-Eaton	CAN	18.12.88	1rB	AnnivG	London (HG)	20 Jul
13.01	0.6	Samantha	Scarlett	JAM	7.4.93	2q1	NCAA-E	Jacksonville	31 May
13.01	1.3	Kayla	Parker	USA	12.3.92	2q3	NCAA-E	Jacksonville	31 May
13.01	1.4	Reina-Flor	Okori	FRA	2.5.80	2	NC	Reims	12 Jul
13.01	1.6		Sun Yawei	CHN	17.10.87	1	NC	Suzhou	11 Oct
13.02	1.9	Kim	Francis	USA	6.1.92	2		Baton Rouge	19 Apr
13.02	1.5	Lisa	Urech	SUI	27.7.89	2	NC	Frauenfeld	26 Jul
13.03	1.9	Evonne	Britton	USA	10.10.91	5h1	NC	Sacramento	27 Jun
13.03	2.0	Giulia	Pennella	ITA	27.10.89	1		Savona	2 Jul
		(70)							
13.05	0.4	Samantha	Elliott	JAM	3.2.92	1	NCAA-II	Allendale	24 May
13.05A	0.3	Briggit	Merlano	COL	29.4.82	2		Medellín	31 May
13.05	0.6	Antoinette	Nana Djimou	FRA	2.8.85	1H2	EC	Zürich	14 Aug
13.06	2.0	Nickiesha	Wilson	JAM	28.7.86	2		Baltimore	11 Apr
13.06	1.4	Ebony	Morrison	USA	28.12.94	3q2	NCAA-E	Jacksonville	31 May
13.07	1.9	Yvana	Hepburn-Bailey	USA	9.11.87	3		Baton Rouge	19 Apr
13.07	0.1	Isabelle	Pedersen	NOR	27.1.92	2	Spark	Regensburg	7 Jun
13.07	0.9	Megan	Simmonds	JAM	18.3.94	2		Sundsvall	20 Jul
13.08	0.4	Lauren	Blackburn	USA	18.11.91	1	Pac 12	Pullman	18 May
13.08	1.0	Phylicia	George	CAN	16.11.87	1r2		Toronto	11 Jun
		(80)							
13.08	1.0	Ida	Aidanpää	FIN	25.11.88	1r2		Joensuu	24 Jul
13.08	0.2	Anastasiya	Mokhnyuk	UKR	1.1.91	1H3	EC	Zürich	14 Aug
13.09	-0.3	Caridad	Jerez	ESP	23.1.91	1	NC	Alcobendas	27 Jul
13.10	1.9	Cassandra	Lloyd	USA	27.1.90	6h1	NC	Sacramento	27 Jun
13.11	0.4	Nina	Argunova	RUS	15.9.89	1h1	NC	Kazan	24 Jul
13.11	1.2	Belkis	Milanés	CUB	16.1.90	1		La Habana	8 Aug
13.12	-0.4	Elexis	Fuller-Stewart	USA	11.10.93	1h1	JUCO	Mesa	16 May
13.12	0.9	Kendra	Newton	USA	3.8.87	5		Clermont	31 May
13.12	0.9	Valentina	Kibalnikova	UZB	16.10.90	1		Krasnodar	6 Jun
13.12	0.2	Kimberley	Laing	JAM	8.1.89	3h3	NC	Kingston	29 Jun
		(90)							
13.12	0.9	Matilda	Bogdanoff	FIN	8.10.90	3		Lapinlahti	20 Jul
13.13	0.5	Chelsea	Eades	USA	21.8.89	1		Princeton	19 Apr
13.13	-1.9	Ayako	Kimura	JPN	11.6.88	6		Tokyo	11 May
13.13	-1.2	Dafne	Schippers	NED	15.6.92	1H		Götzis	31 May
13.13	1.4	Aisseta	Diawara	FRA	29.6.89	3	NC	Reims	12 Jul
13.13	0.3		Kang Ya	CHN	16.3.90	1	NGPF	Jinan	13 Jul
13.13	1.9	Yasmin	Miller	GBR-J	24.5.95	4	WJ	Eugene	27 Jul
13.14	1.6	Gabby	Mayo	USA	26.1.89	1		San Marcos	26 Apr
13.14	-0.3	Beate	Schrott	AUT	15.4.88	1		Rif	24 May
13.14	1.4	Rosvitha	Okou	CIV	5.9.86	4	NC	Reims	12 Jul
		(100)							

Mark	Wind	Name		Nat	Born	Date
13.15	-0.2	Shannon	McCann	AUS	20.12.88	22 Feb
13.15	0.5	Andrea	Bliss	JAM	5.10.80	7 May
13.15	0.4	Lucie	Koudelová	CZE	6.7.94	2 Aug
13.16	1.1	LaToya	Greaves	JAM	31.5.86	24 May
13.16	0.7	Rikenette	Steenkamp	RSA	16.10.92	14 Sep
13.17	0.6	Veronica	Borsi	ITA	13.6.87	1 Jun
13.17	0.2	Tatyana	Dektyareva ¶	RUS	8.5.81	23 Aug
13.17	0.7		Jung Hye-lim	KOR	1.7.87	30 Sep
13.18A	0.3	Eliecít	Palacios	COL	15.8.87	31 May
13.18	1.6	Ivana	Loncarek	CRO	8.4.91	22 Jun
13.20	1.6	Chanice	Taylor-Chase	CAN	6.8.93	30 May
13.20	0.5	Lucy	Hatton	GBR	8.11.94	28 Jun
13.20	-1.2	Nichole	Denby	NGR	10.10.82	10 Aug
13.20	0.2	Carolin	Schäfer	GER	5.12.91	14 Aug
13.21	1.2	Yariatou	Touré	FRA	27.12.90	18 May
13.21	0.6	Lindsay	Lindley	NGR	6.10.89	14 Jun
13.21	0.2	Yuliya	Zhuk	RUS	25.11.91	28 Jun
13.21	1.6	Josanne	Lucas	TTO	14.5.84	24 Aug
13.22	1.0	Hayley	Warren	CAN	4.1.91	11 Jun
13.22	-0.4	Serita	Solomon	GBR	1.3.90	22 Jun
13.23	0.8	Michelle	Jenneke	AUS	23.6.93	29 Mar
13.23	0.3	Solène	Hamelin	FRA	9.12.88	4 May
13.23	0.4	Dinesha	Bean	USA	20.4.91	24 May
13.23	1.8	Sasha	Wallace	USA-J	21.9.95	31 May
13.23	0.7	Natasha	Ruddock	JAM	25.12.89	7 Jun
13.23	-3.3	Sarah	Lavin	IRL	28.5.94	14 Jun
13.23	1.6		Wang Dou	CHN	18.5.93	11 Oct
13.24	0.9	Alexis	Perry	USA	8.8.94	19 Apr
13.24	1.3	Sade-Mariah	Greenidge	BAR	14.10.93	19 Apr
13.24	0.2	Yekaterina	Poplavskaya	BLR	7.5.87	24 Jul
13.25	0.6	Keisha	Wallace	JAM	25.1.90	30 May
13.25	0.0	Anastasiya	Soprunova	KAZ	14.1.86	7 Jun
13.26	0.4	LaQue	Moen-Davis	USA	14.8.93	3 May
13.26	1.9	Génesis	Romero	VEN-J	6.11.95	27 Jul
13.27	0.8	Rojaine	Coto	CUB	18.7.88	14 Feb
13.27	0.6	Sirena	Williams	USA	.87	29 Jun
13.27	0.3	Tatyana	Degtyarova	RUS	4.6.84	9 Jul
13.27	1.3	Yekaterina	Voronkova	RUS	24.11.88	9 Jul
13.27	2.0	Sabrina	Lindenmayer	GER	24.4.89	26 Jul
13.27	-2.0	Elisávet	Pesiridou	GRE	12.2.92	12 Aug
13.28	0.6	Alexis	Franklin	USA	9.10.93	31 May
13.28	1.4	Shanique	Walker	USA	20.11.93	31 May
13.28	0.9	Erica	Bougard	USA	26.7.93	27 Jun
13.28	0.9	Sandra	Gomis	FRA	21.11.83	16 Jul
13.28	0.2	Grit	Sadeiko	EST	29.7.89	14 Aug
13.29	-0.3	Leah	Nugent	USA	23.11.92	26 Apr
13.29	-0.6	Alina	Antipova	RUS	11.1.91	24 Jul
13.29	1.9	Sarah	Missinne	BEL-J	16.5.95	27 Jul
13.30	1.2	Gnima	Faye	SEN	17.11.84	11 May
13.30	1.4	Ann-Marie	Duffus	JAM	18.12.90	17 May
13.30	0.2	Mulern	Jean	USA	25.9.92	30 May
13.30	1.3	Aleksandra	Antonova	RUS	24.3.80	9 Jul
13.31	1.0	Ugonna	Ndu	NGR	27.6.91	19 Apr
13.31		Irina	Reshetkina	RUS	30.1.89	7 Jun
13.31	0.4	Sonata	Tamosaityte	LTU	26.6.87	26 Jul
13.32	0.4	Ladonna	Richards	JAM	.92	24 May

Mark	Wind	Name		Nat	Born	Pos	Meet	Venue	Date

Mark	Wind	Name		Nat	Born	Date
13.32	0.9	Brea	Buchanan	USA	8.1.93	31 May
13.32	1.8	Elin	Westerlund	SWE	4.2.90	6 Jun
13.32	0.7	Kori	Carter	USA	3.6.92	7 Jun
13.32	1.7	Eva	Strogies	GER	21.3.91	2 Jul
13.32	0.2	Josephine	Onyia	ESP	15.7.86	27 Jul
13.33	0.9	Eva	Vital	POR	8.7.92	1 Jun
13.33		Anna	Kostina	RUS	16.12.86	6 Jun
13.33	0.5	Alexis	Duncan	USA-Y	16.8.98	14 Jun
13.34	1.4	Ciana	Tabb	USA	9.3.92	18 May
13.34	1.3	Erin	Tucker	USA	24.11.92	31 May
13.34	0.5	Sydney	McLaughlin	USA-Y	7.8.99	14 Jun
13.34	-1.6	Ashlea	Maddex	CAN	16.12.92	29 Jun
13.34	1.6	Giselle	de Albuquerque	BRA	11.7.88	13 Sep
13.35	0.9	Akela	Jones	BAR-J	21.4.95	24 May
13.35	1.6	Breana	Norman	USA	14.9.92	30 May
13.35	1.9	Masumi	Aoki	JPN	16.4.94	20 Jun
13.36	2.0	Danielle	Demas	USA	.93	3 May
13.36	-0.6	Deborah	John	TTO	10.4.90	21 Jun
13.36	-0.1	María	Pinní	GRE	18.8.90	19 Jul
13.36	1.0	Elisa	Leinonen	FIN	27.1.87	24 Jul
13.37	1.2	Erica	Twiss	USA	17.6.92	3 May
13.37	1.3	Lutisha	Bowen	USA	9.7.90	16 May
13.37A	0.8	Kristen	Brown	USA	26.5.92	17 May
13.37	0.5	Chene	Townsend	JAM	12.12.90	17 May
13.37	1.4	Alexandria	Johnson	USA	16.5.94	18 May
13.37	1.4	Jesica	Ejesieme	USA	20.5.92	18 May
13.37	0.9	Jasmine	Quinn	USA-J	21.8.96	21 Jun
13.38	-0.3	Chrisdale	McCarthy	JAM	12.4.94	26 Apr
13.38	0.7	Miku	Fujiwara	JPN	7.12.92	29 Apr
13.38A	1.6	Ashley	Miller	USA-Y	17.2.98	17 May
13.38	1.1	Michelle	Young	CAN	6.12.92	27 May
13.38	1.8	Allison	Reaser	USA	9.9.92	12 Jun
13.39	0.8	Christine	Spence	USA	25.11.81	22 Mar
13.39	1.1	Mariah	Georgetown	USA	14.3.92	28 Mar
13.39	0.4	Trinity	Wilson	USA	4.9.94	18 May
13.39	0.0	Nadine	Broersen	NED	29.4.90	31 May
13.39	0.1	Yuliya	Dolzhkova	UKR	3.7.93	3 Jun
13.39	1.8	Adja	N'Diaye	SEN	26.2.84	22 Jun
13.39	1.4	Edith	Doekoe	FRA	16.9.92	28 Jun
		(195)				

Wind assisted to 13.35

Mark	Wind	Name		Nat	Born	Pos	Meet	Venue	Date
12.52	2.8	Sharika	Nelvis	USA	10.5.90	1	NCAA	Eugene	14 Jun
12.54	2.8	Jasmin	Stowers	USA	23.9.91	2	NCAA	Eugene	14 Jun
12.59	2.6	Tiffani	McReynolds	USA	4.12.91	1	Big 12	Lubbock	18 May
12.62	2.8	Bridgette	Owens	USA	14.3.92	3	NCAA	Eugene	14 Jun
12.68	2.1	Kendra	Harrison	USA	18.9.92	1	TexR	Austin	29 Mar
12.80	2.8	Anne	Zagré	BEL	13.3.90	6	NCAA	Eugene	14 Jun
12.81	2.8	Morgan	Snow	USA	26.7.93	7	NCAA	Eugene	14 Jun
12.85	2.6	LeTristan	Pledger	USA	27.8.93	3	Big 12	Lubbock	18 May
12.94	2.1	Yvana	Hepburn-Bailey	USA	9.11.87	1		Tuscaloosa	11 Apr
12.99	3.1	Kimberley	Laing	JAM	8.1.89	1		Auburn	19 Apr
12.99	2.7	Lauren	Blackburn	USA	18.11.91	1rB	MSR	Walnut	19 Apr
13.01A	2.4	Briggit	Merlano	COL	29.4.82	1	NC	Medellín	27 Jun
13.06	2.7	Sasha	Wallace	USA-J	21.9.95	2rB	MSR	Walnut	19 Apr
13.06	2.2	Megan	Simmonds	JAM	18.3.94	2	NACAC	Kamloops	9 Aug
13.08A	2.4	Eliecít	Palacios	COL	15.8.87	2	NC	Medellín	27 Jun
13.10	2.4	Lutisha	Bowen	USA	9.7.90	1		Jacksonville	26 Apr
13.10	2.2	Alina	Antipova	RUS	11.1.91	3	Znam	Zhukovskiy	27 Jun
13.11	2.7	Lindsay	Lindley	NGR	6.10.89	3rB	MSR	Walnut	19 Apr
13.11	2.7	Shanique	Walker	USA	20.11.93	2		Tallahassee	9 May
13.13	2.7	Sirena	Williams	USA/JAM	.87	4rB	MSR	Walnut	19 Apr

Mark	Wind	Name		Nat	Born	Date
13.14	2.1	Keisha	Wallace	JAM	25.1.90	11 Apr
13.16	4.0	Nichole	Denby	NGR	10.10.82	3 May
13.16	3.1	Yekaterina	Poplavskaya	BLR	7.5.87	24 Jul
13.17	3.9	Sade-Mariah	Greenidge	BAR	14.10.93	12 Apr
13.17	2.5	Hayley	Warren	CAN	.91	11 Jun
13.17	3.1	Sarah	Missinne	BEL-J	16.5.95	26 Jul
13.17	2.5	Lucy	Hatton	GBR	8.11.94	23 Aug
13.19	2.6	Sabrina	Starr	USA		11 May
13.19	2.2	Ashlea	Maddex	CAN	16.12.92	9 Aug
13.20	2.6	Erica	Twiss	USA	17.6.92	18 May
13.22	4.0	Taije	Jordan	USA	18.8.94	3 May
13.22	2.3	Trinity	Wilson	USA	4.9.94	31 May
13.23	2.2	Mathilde	Raibaut	FRA	18.4.92	14 Jun
13.25	2.5	Clémence	Vifquin	FRA	9.6.86	22 Jun
13.25	2.5	Adja	N'Diaye	SEN	26.2.84	22 Jun
13.26A	3.7	Jazmin	Ratcliff	USA	6.7.93	16 May
13.27	3.5	Leah	Nugent	USA	23.11.92	4 Apr
13.28	6.0	Fiona	Morrison	NZL	24.10.88	22 Nov
13.30	2.3	Deborah	John	TTO	10.4.90	31 May
13.30	3.9	Masumi	Aoki	JPN	16.4.94	21 Jun
13.30	3.1	Reetta	Hurske	FIN-J	15.5.95	26 Jul
13.31	2.4	Jenna	Pletsch	GER	11.9.91	6 Jul
13.32	4.9	Karla	Drew	GBR	22.3.89	12 Apr
13.33		Jasmine	Quinn	USA-J	21.8.96	5 Apr
13.35	3.3	Elisa	Girard-Mondoloni	FRA-J	13.6.95	26 Jul
13.35	3.1	Ellinore	Hallin	SWE	12.8.87	2 Aug

(192 legal and windy to 13.35)

Best at low altitude

Mark	Wind	Name	Pos	Meet	Venue	Date
12.95	0.9	Lewis	3		Clermont	31 May
12.95	0.6	Williams	2h1	NC	Kingston	29 Jun
13.13	1.5	Merlano	1		São Paulo	4 May
13.18	0.1	Florez	3	IbAmC	São Paulo	3 Aug

Unconfirmed: 13.09 5.5 Darya Sharova RUS-J 21.7.95 3h2 Moskva 2 Jul

JUNIORS

See main list for top 4 juniors.11 performances by 4 women to 13.13. Additional marks and further juniors:

Name	Mark	Wind	Pos	Meet	Venue	Date	Mark	Wind	Pos	Meet	Venue	Date
Williams	12.89	1.9	1	WJ	Eugene	27 Jul	13.00	1.6	1h1	WJ	Eugene	25 Jul
	12.99	1.8	1H	NCAA	Eugene	12 Jun						
Hall	13.00	2.0	2	NC-j	Eugene	6 Jul	13.09A	1.6	1		Lakewood	17 May
Visser	13.11	0.1	1	WK-23	Zürich	28 Aug	13.12	-2.0	4h4	EC	Zürich	12 Aug

Mark	Wind	Name		Nat	Born	Pos	Meet	Venue	Date
13.23	1.8	Sasha	Wallace	USA	21.9.95	3q3	NCAA-W	Fayetteville	31 May
13.26	1.9	Génesis	Romero	VEN	6.11.95	5	WJ	Eugene	27 Jul
13.29	1.9	Sarah	Missinne	BEL	16.5.95	6	WJ	Eugene	27 Jul
13.33	0.5	Alexis	Duncan	USA-Y	16.8.98	1	N.Jnr	Greensboro	14 Jun
13.34	0.5	Sydney	McLaughlin	USA-Y	7.8.99	2	N.Jnr	Greensboro	14 Jun
13.35	0.9	Akela	Jones (10)	BAR	21.4.95	1	NAIA	Gulf Shores	24 May
13.37	0.9	Jasmine	Quinn	USA	21.8.96	2		Renton	21 Jun
13.38A	1.6	Ashley	Miller	USA-Y	17.2.98	2		Lakewood	17 May
13.40	1.4	Chrystie	Lange	FRA	8.6.95	5	NC	Reims	12 Jul

Mark	Wind	Name		Nat	Born	Pos	Meet	Venue	Date
13.42	1.0	Chantel	Ray	USA	3.1.96	1		Newport News	7 Jun
13.42	1.7	Elisa	Girard-Mondoloni	FRA	13.6.95	2h3	WJ	Eugene	25 Jul
13.43	1.2	Nicole	Setterington	CAN	18.4.95	3		Tallahassee	12 Apr
13.43	1.7	Reetta	Hurske	FIN	15.5.95	3h3	WJ	Eugene	25 Jul
13.46	0.5	Anna	Cockrell	USA-Y	28.8.97	3	N.Jnr	Greensboro	14 Jun
13.47	1.1	Peta Gaye	Williams	JAM	13.9.95	3		Kingston	24 May
13.47	1.6	Megumi	Hemphill (20)	JPN	23.5.96	3	NC	Fukushima	7 Jun

Wind assisted see main lists for 1 junior. 6 performances by 4 women to 13.10. To 13.45.

Williams 12.98 2.4 1h2 NC-j Eugene 5 Jul 13.06 2.2 1 Athens, GA 10 May
12.98 3.3 1s2 WJ Eugene 26 Jul
Visser 13.01 3.1 1s3 WJ Eugene 26 Jul
Hall 13.09 2.2 1s1 WJ Eugene 26 Jul

Mark	Wind	Name		Nat	Born	Pos	Meet	Venue	Date
13.17	3.1	Sarah	Missinne	BEL-J	16.5.95	2s3	WJ	Eugene	26 Jul
13.30	3.1	Reetta	Hurske	FIN-J	15.5.95	3s3	WJ	Eugene	26 Jul
13.33		Jasmine	Quinn	USA-J	21.8.96	1		Charleston	5 Apr
13.35	3.3	Elisa	Girard-Mondoloni	FRA-J	13.6.95	3s2	WJ	Eugene	26 Jul
13.36	3.1	Devynne	Charlton	BAH-J	26.11.95	4s3	WJ	Eugene	26 Jul
13.41	2.5	Shamier	Little	USA-J	20.3.95	1h7	TexR	Austin	28 Mar
13.42	2.2	Yanique	Thompson	JAM-J	12.3.96	3s1	WJ	Eugene	26 Jul

200 METRES HURDLES

Mark	Wind	Name		Nat	Born	Pos	Meet	Venue	Date
25.79	0.5	Noemi	Zbären	SUI	12.3.94	1		Basel	17 May

Straight at Manchester 17 May: (1.0) 1. 25.05 Meghan Beesley GBR 15.11.89, 2. 25.84 Eilidh Child GBR 20.2.87, 3. 25.86 Denisa Rosolová CZE 21.8.86. 4. 25.90 Dalilah Muhammad USA 7.2.90

300 METRES HURDLES

Mark	Wind	Name		Nat	Born	Pos	Meet	Venue	Date
39.00		Marzia	Caravelli	ITA	23.10.81	1		Roma	25 Apr
39.98		Zuzana	Hejnová	CZE	19.12.86	1		Cheb	29 Jul

400 METRES HURDLES

Mark	Name		Nat	Born	Pos	Meet	Venue	Date
53.41	Kaliese	Spencer	JAM	6.5.87	1	NC	Kingston	27 Jun
53.80		Spencer			1	DL	Birmingham	24 Aug
53.81		Spencer			1	C.Cup	Marrakech	13 Sep
53.84	Kori	Carter	USA	3.6.92	1	NC	Sacramento	29 Jun
53.97		Spencer			1	GGala	Roma	5 Jun
54.00	Georganne	Moline	USA	6.3.90	2	NC	Sacramento	29 Jun
54.09		Spencer			1	Herc	Moinaco	18 Jul
54.10		Spencer			1	CG	Glasgow	31 Jul
54.12		Spencer			1	VD	Bruxelles	5 Sep
54.29		Spencer			1	Pre	Eugene	31 May
54.39	Eilidh	Child	GBR	20.2.87	1	DL	Glasgow	11 Jul
54.42		Child			2	C.Cup	Marrakech	13 Sep
54.48		Child			1	EC	Zürich	16 Aug
54.54	Denisa	Rosolová	CZE	21.8.86	2	VD	Bruxelles	5 Sep
54.56		Moline			2	GGala	Roma	5 Jun
54.56	Anna	Titimets	UKR	5.3.89	2	EC	Zürich	16 Aug
54.59	Kemi	Adekoya	BRN	16.1.93	1	DL	Doha	9 May
54.60	Irina	Davydova	RUS	27.5.88	3	EC	Zürich	16 Aug
54.63		Spencer			1h1	NC	Kingston	26 Jun
54.63		Rosolová			1	NC	Ostrava	3 Aug
54.67		Moline			1	GP	Ponce	17 May
54.70	Cassandra	Tate	USA	11.9.90	3	NC	Sacramento	29 Jun
54.70		Rosolová			4	EC	Zürich	16 Aug
54.70		Adekoya			3	C.Cup	Marrakech	13 Sep
54.71		Child			1s2	EC	Zürich	14 Aug
54.73		Moline			2	Herc	Moinaco	18 Jul
54.74	Tiffany	Williams (10)	USA	5.2.83	1s1	NC	Sacramento	28 Jun
54.75	Janeive	Russell	JAM	14.11.93	2	NC	Kingston	27 Jun
54.76	Kendra	Harrison	USA	18.9.92	1	SEC	Lexington	18 May
54.76		Child			3	VD	Bruxelles	5 Sep
	(30/12)							
54.82	Wenda	Nel	RSA	30.7.88	1		Marrakech	8 Jun
55.00	Anna	Ryzhykova	UKR	24.11.89	1	ET	Braunschweig	21 Jun
55.07	Shamier	Little	USA-J	20.3.95	1	NCAA	Eugene	13 Jun
55.12	Ristananna	Tracey	JAM	5.9.92	2		Kingston	3 May
55.17	Lashinda	Demus	USA	10.3.83	5	NC	Sacramento	29 Jun
55.18	Nikita	Tracey	JAM	18.9.90	3	NC	Kingston	27 Jun
55.22	Nickiesha	Wilson	JAM	28.7.86	1	GS	Ostrava	17 Jun
55.37	Vera	Barbosa	POR	13.1.89	1		Genève	14 Jun
	(20)							

Mark	Name		Nat	Born	Pos	Meet	Venue	Date
55.41	Janeil	Bellille	TTO	18.6.89	1q3	NCAA-W	Fayetteville	30 May
55.42	Yadisleidis	Pedroso	ITA	28.1.87	3		Tomblaine	27 Jun
55.46	Amaka	Ogoebune	NGR	3.3.90	2	AfCh	Marrakech	14 Aug
55.55	Meghan	Beesley	GBR	15.11.89	1		Namur	28 May
55.56	Shevon	Stoddart	JAM	21.11.82	4	NC	Kingston	27 Jun
55.56	Axelle	Dauwens	BEL	1.12.90	7	VD	Bruxelles	5 Sep
55.60	Jernail	Hayes	USA	8.7.88	3		San Marcos	23 May
55.63	Sydney	McLaughlin	USA-Y	7.8.99	2	NC-j	Eugene	6 Jul
55.69	Lauren	Wells	AUS	3.8.88	1		Oordegem	5 Jul
55.78A	Zudikey	Rodríguez	MEX	14.3.87	1	PAm SF	Ciudad de México	16 Aug
	(30)							
55.79	Tatyana	Veshkurova	RUS	23.9.81	1rB		Adler	30 May
55.80	Valeriya	Khramova	RUS	13.8.92	1	NC-23	Saransk	14 Jul
55.81	Noelle	Montcalm	CAN	3.4.88	1		København	6 Aug
55.84	Francisca	Koki	KEN	30.10.93	3	AfCh	Marrakech	14 Aug
55.86	Zuzana	Hejnová	CZE	19.12.86	7	Herc	Monaco	18 Jul
55.88	Kiah	Seymour	USA	11.1.94	1		College Park	2 May
55.89	Joanna	Linkiewicz	POL	2.5.90	4s2	EC	Zürich	14 Aug
55.93	Vera	Rudakova	RUS	20.3.92	2	NC-23	Saransk	14 Jul
55.93	Hayat	Lambarki	MAR	18.5.88	4	AfCh	Marrakech	14 Aug
55.98	Christine	Spence	USA	25.11.81	3s1	NC	Sacramento	28 Jun
	(40)							
56.02	Christiane	Klopsch	GER	21.8.90	1	Spark	Regensburg	7 Jun
56.09	Turquoise	Thompson	USA	31.7.91	4		George Town	7 May
56.16	Shona	Richards	GBR-J	1.9.95	2	WJ	Eugene	26 Jul
56.21	Petra	Fontanive	SUI	10.10.88	1rB		Genève	14 Jun
56.21	Satomi	Kubokura	JPN	27.4.82	2	AsiG	Incheon	1 Oct
56.22	Jade	Miller	USA-J	13.1.95	3	WY	Eugene	26 Jul
56.25	MacKenzie	Hill	USA	5.1.86	5	Drake	Des Moines	26 Apr
56.26	Phara	Anacharsis	FRA	17.12.83	1		Chambéry	6 Jul
56.27	Chanice	Taylor-Chase	CAN	6.8.93	5	SEC	Lexington	18 May
56.39	Egle	Staisiunaite	LTU	30.9.88	6s2	EC	Zürich	14 Aug
	(50)							
56.41	Rushell	Clayton	JAM	18.10.92	1		Kingston	4 Apr
56.43	Hayley	McLean	GBR	9.9.94	3	NC	Birmingham	29 Jun
56.44	Sara	Petersen	DEN	9.4.87	2		København	6 Aug
56.49		Nguyen Thi Huyen	VIE	19.8.93	1	NG	Nam Dinh	9 Dec
56.53	Aurélie	Chaboudez	FRA	9.5.93	2	LEAP	Loughborough	19 Jul
56.54A	Zurián	Hechavarría	CUB-J	10.8.95	2	PAm SF	Ciudad de México	16 Aug
56.55	Stina	Troest	DEN	17.1.94	1rB		Namur	28 May
56.55	Alexis	Franklin	USA	9.10.93	2s1	NCAA-E	Jacksonville	30 May
56.55	Olena	Kolesnychenko	UKR	3.6.93	2	NC	Kirovohrad	25 Jul
56.56	Annerie	Ebersohn	RSA	9.8.90	2		Genève	14 Jun
	(60)							
56.58	Angela	Morosanu	ROU	26.7.86	1	RomIC	Cluj-Napoca	6 Jun
56.59		Xiao Xia	CHN	6.6.91	3	AsiG	Incheon	1 Oct
56.60	Déborah	Rodríguez	URU	2.12.92	1	SAmG	Santiago de Chile	15 Mar
56.60	Valentine	Arrieta	SUI	29.4.90	2rB		Genève	14 Jun
56.62	Danielle	Dowie	JAM	5.5.92	1	Big 12	Lubbock	18 May
56.63	Samantha	Elliott	JAM	3.2.92	1	PennR	Philadelphia	24 Apr
56.63	Manami	Kira	JPN	23.10.91	2		Osaka	11 May
56.63	Yekaterina	Artyukh	BLR	14.1.91	2		Yerino	8 Jun
56.65	Yekaterina	Brodovaya	RUS	28.6.91	3r1		Sochi	30 May
56.65	Autumne	Franklin	USA	20.7.94	3s2	NCAA-E	Jacksonville	30 May
	(70)							
56.65	Tyler	Brockington	USA	6.2.94	4s2	NCAA-E	Jacksonville	30 May
56.67	Eseroghene	Okoro	GBR	4.7.90	3s1	NCAA	Eugene	11 Jun
56.73	Emilia	Ankiewicz	POL	22.11.90	2	NC	Szczecin	30 Jul
56.86	Jennifer	Cotten	CAN	14.10.87	2	NC	Moncton	29 Jun
56.87	Jessica	Gelibert	HAI	8.11.94	1h4	NCAA-E	Jacksonville	29 May
56.87	Evann	Thompson	USA	9.10.94	2s3	NCAA-E	Jacksonville	30 May
56.87	Fabienne	Kohlmann	GER	6.11.89	3		Rehlingen	9 Jun
56.87	Liga	Velvere	LAT	10.2.90	7s1	EC	Zürich	14 Aug
56.87A	Magdalena	Mendoza	VEN	20.10.90	2h1	CAG	Xalapa	24 Nov
56.92	Landria	Buckley	USA	2.7.88	2		Norcross	16 May
	(80)							
56.96	Kaila	Barber	USA	4.4.93	3q3	NCAA-E	Jacksonville	30 May
56.96	Lucie	Slanicková	SVK	8.11.88	2h1	NC	Ostrava	2 Aug
56.97	Leah	Nugent	USA	23.11.92	2h1	SEC	Lexington	16 May
56.97	Christine	McMahon	IRL	6.7.92	2		Nivelles	28 Jun
56.99	Jaide	Stepter	USA	25.4.94	1	Pac 12	Pullman	18 May

Mark		Name	Nat	Born	Pos	Meet	Venue	Date
56.99	Nnenya	Hailey	USA	23.2.94	1q1	NCAA-W	Fayetteville	30 May
57.06	Laura	Sotomayor	ESP	22.4.86	5		Huelva	12 Jun
57.11	Lyndsay	Pekin	AUS	13.6.86	2	NC	Melbourne	6 Apr
57.14	Sayaka	Aoki	JPN	15.12.86	2		Yamaguchi	11 Oct
57.16		Wang Huan	CHN	21.9.94	1	NC	Suzhou	10 Oct
	(90)							
57.17	Laura	Wake	GBR	3.5.91	2		Sint-Niklaas	29 May
57.17	Ellen	Wortham	USA	5.1.90	5s1	NC	Sacramento	28 Jun
57.18	Irina	Takuncheva	RUS	14.11.90	5	NC	Kazan	25 Jul
57.20	Claudia	Wehrsen	GER	18.10.84	2	NC	Ulm	27 Jul
57.21	Jesica	Ejesieme	USA	20.5.92	2q1	NCAA-W	Fayetteville	30 May
57.23	Viktoriya	Nikolenko	UKR	15.6.91	3	NC	Kirovohrad	25 Jul
57.24	Lamia	Lhabz	MAR	19.5.84	6	AfCh	Marrakech	14 Aug
57.30	Jess	Gulli	AUS	19.3.88	2	WCM	Melbourne	22 Mar
57.30	Hanne	Claes	BEL	4.8.91	1	Univ Ch	Liège	1 May
57.34A	Sharolyn	Scott	CRC	27.10.84	3h1	CAG	Xalapa	24 Nov
	(100)							

Mark		Name	Nat	Born	Date
57.36	Joanna	Banach	POL	28.8.92	29 Jul
57.38	Sarah	Wells	CAN	10.11.89	7 Jun
57.41	Evonne	Britton	USA	10.10.91	30 May
57.41	Darya	Korableva	RUS	23.5.88	8 Jun
57.42	Anna	Simone	USA		18 May
57.42	Nadezhda	Alekseyeva	RUS	16.7.88	10 Jul
57.42	Mariam	Abdul-Rashid	CAN-Y	21.9.97	26 Jul
57.43	Akkunji C.	Ashwini	IND	7.10.87	6 Jun
57.43	Jaílma	de Lima	BRA	31.12.86	12 Oct
57.44		Huang Yan	CHN-J	12.1.96	10 Oct
57.48		Quach Thi Lan	VIE-J	18.10.95	9 Dec
57.49	Yekaterina	Khairullina	BLR	13.10.92	17 May
57.50	Jamika	Glades	USA	27.10.93	3 May
57.51	Robine	Schürmann	SUI	31.1.89	14 Jun
57.52	Francesca	Doveri	ITA	21.12.82	20 Jul
57.54	Anastasiya	Lebid	UKR	30.10.93	4 Jun
57.55	Christine	Salterberg	GER	9.6.94	27 Jul
57.58	Tia Adana	Belle	BAR-J	16.6.96	24 May
57.58	Marina	Zayko	KAZ	17.1.93	23 Aug
57.59	Yanique	Haye-Smith	JAM	22.3.90	13 Jun
57.62	Ellie	Grooters	USA	21.9.91	3 May
57.66	Liliane Cristina	Barbosa	BRA	8.10.87	11 Oct
57.68	Javiera	Errázuriz	CHI	5.6.90	22 Feb
57.68	Maeva	Contion	FRA	31.5.92	12 Jul
57.69	Joan	Medjid	FRA-J	29.9.95	31 May
57.69	Anna	Raukuc	GER	7.1.90	27 Jul
57.70	Tetyana	Melnyk	UKR-J	2.4.95	3 Jun
57.71	Olga	Samylova	RUS	4.1.86	23 Jul
57.72	Tameka	Jameson	NGR	11.8.89	4 Apr
57.72	Gianna	Woodruff	USA	18.11.93	3 May
57.72	Kayla	Stueckle	USA	19.1.92	30 May
57.74	Chastity	Stewart	USA		30 May
57.80	Allison	Reaser	USA	9.9.92	29 May
57.81A	Stephanie	Jolley	USA	1.11.90	25 Apr
57.81	Montayla	Holder	USA	7.2.94	18 May
57.81	Maya	Williamson	USA	26.2.93	30 May
57.82	Haruka	Shibata	JPN	13.1.91	13 Jul
57.84	Josanne	Lucas	TTO	14.5.84	18 Apr
57.84	Svetlana	Karmalita	RUS	11.12.85	27 Jun
57.85	Anastasiya	Fedyayeva	RUS	19.12.88	17 Jul
57.87	Sandy	Jean-Claude	USA	4.9.91	4 May
57.89	Polina	Bordyugova	RUS	18.8.91	6 Jun
57.90	Zoe	Ballantyne	NZL	28.3.92	21 Mar
57.90	Sade-Mariah	Greenidge	BAR	14.10.93	4 May
57.91	Gezelle	Magerman	RSA-Y	21.4.97	25 Aug
57.92	Anna	Punich	RUS	28.8.87	30 May
57.93A	Taylor	Gardner	USA		3 May
57.94	Melissa	Gonzalez	USA	24.6.94	30 May
57.94	Aleksandra	Romanova	KAZ	26.12.90	23 Aug
57.95	Erica	Twiss	USA	17.6.92	30 May
57.95	Tina	Matusinska	POL	12.7.88	21 Jun
57.95		Deng Xiaoqing	CHN	13.6.89	6 Jul
58.02	Dalilah	Muhammad	USA	7.2.90	9 May
58.05A	Jean-Marie	Senekal	RSA	11.12.92	12 Apr
58.05	Consuela	Lindsay	USA	22.11.91	11 May
58.05	Genekee	Leith	JAM-J	25.10.95	25 Jul
58.06	Natalya	Antyukh	RUS	26.6.81	11 Jun
58.06	Anniina	Laitinen	FIN	18.11.89	27 Jul
58.07	Donna	Jeanty	USA	20.5.92	2 May
58.07	Alicia	Noel	USA	13.2.91	11 May
58.08	Yelizaveta	Anikiyenko	RUS	30.6.94	14 Jul
58.09A	Kourtney	Danreuther	USA	6.9.90	3 May
58.10	Amalie	Iuel	NOR/DEN	17.4.94	30 May
58.11	Alena	Klimentyova	RUS	12.11.94	14 Jul
58.14	Andreia	Crespo	POR	9.4.93	19 Jul
58.15	Frida	Persson	SWE	14.12.89	14 Jun
58.17	Klaudia	Zurek	POL	22.9.91	21 Jun
58.19	Ari	Curtis	USA	3.7.89	18 Apr
58.20	Lisa	Meneau	USA		30 May
58.20		Cai Minjia	CHN	2.4.93	12 Jul
58.21	Nisha	Desai	GBR	5.8.84	5 Jul
58.23	Ugonna	Ndu	NGR	27.6.91	26 Apr
58.24	Aleksandra	Fedoriva-Shpayer	RUS	13.9.88	12 Jun
58.25	Christine	Merrill	SRI	20.8.87	19 Apr
58.25	Viktoriya	Tkachuk	UKR	8.11.94	4 Jun
58.26	Vilde	Svortevik	NOR	18.5.94	13 Aug
58.26	Michaela	Pesková	SVK-Y	22.10.97	25 Aug
58.27	Svetlana	Gogoleva	RUS	11.12.86	17 Aug
58.28	Emel	Sanli	TUR	7.7.93	20 Jul
	(179)				

Hand timed: 57.9 Anna Berghii MDA 19.2.93 31 May

Best at low altitude

56.64	Rodríguez	1	IbAmC	São Paulo	2 Aug
56.89	Hechavarria	4	WJ	Eugene	26 Jul
58.10	S Scott				2 Aug
58.16	Jolley				22 Mar

JUNIORS

See main list for top 5 juniors.10 performances by 4 women to 56.50. Additional marks and further juniors:

Little	55.43	1	NC-j	Eugene	6 Jul	55.98	1q2	NCAAw	Fayetteville	30 May
	55.58	1s1	NCAA	Eugene	11 Jun	56.01	3	SEC	Lexington	18 May
	55.66	1	WJ	Eugene	26 Jul	56.34	1h1	SEC	Lexington	16 May

57.42	Mariam	Abdul-Rashid	CAN-Y	21.9.97	5	WJ	Eugene	26 Jul
57.44		Huang Yan	CHN	12.1.96	3	NC	Suzhou	10 Oct
57.48		Quach Thi Lan	VIE	18.10.95	2	NG	Nam Dinh	9 Dec
57.58	Tia Adana	Belle	BAR	16.6.96	2	NCAA-II	Allendale	24 May
57.69	Joan	Medjid (10)	FRA	29.9.95	4		Oordegem	31 May
57.70	Tetyana	Melnyk	UKR	2.4.95	3h1		Kyiv	3 Jun
57.91	Gezelle	Magerman	RSA-Y	21.4.97	1	Yth OG	Nanjing	25 Aug
58.05	Genekee	Leith	JAM	25.10.95	2s1	WJ	Eugene	25 Jul
58.26	Michaela	Pesková	SVK-Y	22.10.97	2	Yth OG	Nanjing	25 Aug
58.34	Ayomide	Folorunso	ITA	17.10.96	7	WJ	Eugene	26 Jul

Mark	Name		Nat	Born	Pos	Meet	Venue	Date
58.42	Jackie	Baumann	GER	24.8.95	1		Braunschweig	24 May
58.42	Elise	Malmberg	SWE	13.7.95	1	vFIN	Helsinki	30 Aug
58.43	Haruko	Ishizuka	JPN-Y	2.6.97	1		Kyoto	21 Jun
58.44	Jessica	Turner	GBR	8.8.95	1rB		Tarare	5 Jul
58.53	Ilaria	Verderio (20)	ITA-Y	22.4.98	1	NC-y	Rieti	21 Jun

HIGH JUMP

2.01i Mariya Kuchina RUS 14.1.93 1 XLG Stockholm 6 Feb
1.83/1 1.88/1 1.92/1 1.94/2 1.96/1 1.98/1 2.01/3
2.00i 1 Chelyabinsk 16 Jan 1.75/1 1.80/1 1.86/1 1.89/1 1.91/1 1.95/1 2.00/3
2.00i 1= WI Sopot 8 Mar 1.85/1 1.90/1 1.94/1 1.97/2 2.00/1 2.02/xxx
2.00 2 DL Saint-Denis 5 Jul 1.80/1 1.85/1 1.89/1 1.92/1 1.94/1 1.96/1 1.98/2 2.00/3
2.02/xxx
2.00 1 WK Zürich 28 Aug 1.85/2 1.89/2 1.93/1 1.96/2 1.98/x 2.00/1
1.99 2 EC Zürich 17 Aug 1.85/1 1.90/1 1.94/1 1.97/1 1.99/1 2.01/xxx
1.99 1 C.Cup Marrakech 14 Sep 1.69/1 1.79/1 1.83/1 1.87/1 1.90/1 1.93/1 1.95/1 1.97/1
1.99/2 2.01/xxx
1.98 1 Bisl Oslo 11 Jun 1.80/1 1.85/1 1.90/3 1.95/3 1.98/2 2.01/xxx
2.01 Anna Chicherova RUS 22.7.82 1 Pre Eugene 31 May
1.88/1 1.92/1 1.95/1 1.97/3 1.99/2 2.01/1
2.01 Ruth Beitia ESP 1.4.79 1 EC Zürich 17 Aug
1.85/1 1.90/2 1.94/1 1.97/1 1.99/2 2.01/1 2.03/xxx
2.00i 1 NC Sabadell 22 Feb 1.82/1 1.87/1 1.91/1 1.95/2 1.98/3 2.00/2 2.02/xxx
2.00i 3 WI Sopot 8 Mar 1.85/1 1.90/1 1.94/1 1.97/1 2.00/2 2.02/xxx
1.99 3 Pre Eugene 31 May 1.80/1 1.84/1 1.88/1 1.92/2 1.95/2 1.97/1 1.99/3 2.01/xxx
1.98i 1 Cottbus 22 Jan 1.85/1 1.90/1 1.94/2 1.97/1 2.00/3 2.02/xxx
2.00i Kamila Licwinko POL 22.3.86 1 Arnstadt 8 Feb
1.80/1 1.85/1 1.88/1 1.91/1 1.94/2 1.97/1 2.00/3
2.00i 1 NC Sopot 22 Feb 1.79/1 1.84/1 1.88/1 1.92/1 1.96/1 2.00/1
2.00i 1= WI Sopot 8 Mar 1.85/1 1.90/1 1.94/1 1.97/2 2.00/1 2.02/xxx
2.00i Blanka Vlasic CRO 8.11.83 1 Praha (O2) 25 Feb
1.84/1 1.88/1 1.92/3 1.94/2 1.96/xx1.98/1 2.02/xx
2.00 1 DL Saint-Denis 5 Jul 1.85/1 1.89/1 1.92/ 1 1.94/1 1.96/1 1.98/2 2.00/1 2.02/xxx
2.00 1 Anniv London (HG) 20 Jul 1.84/1 1.90/1 1.93/1 1.96/1 1.98/1 2.00/1 2.02/xxx
1.98 2 Bisl Oslo 11 Jun 1.80/1 1.85/1 1.90/1 1.95/3 1.98/3 2.01/xxx
1.99 Justyna Kasprzycka POL 20.8.87 2 Pre Eugene 31 May
1.80/1 1.84/1 1.88/2 1.92/1 1.95/1 1.97/2 1.99/1 2.01/xxx
1.99 4 EC Zürich 17 Aug 1.85/2 1.90/1 1.94/1 1.97/2 1.99/1 2.01/xxx
1.99 Ana Simic CRO 5.5.90 3 EC Zürich 17 Aug
1.85/1 1.90/1 1.94/1 1.97/2 1.99/1 2.01/xxx
1.98 1 WCM Beijing 21 May 1.80/1 1.85/1 1.89/1 1.92/1 1.95/2 1.98/3 2.00/xxx
1.98 2 WK Zürich 28 Aug 1.85/1 1.89/1 1.93/1 1.96/1 1.98/1 2.00/xx
1.98 Oksana Okunyeva UKR 14.3.90 1 Berdychiv 28 Jun
1.75/11.80/1 1.84/1 1.87/1 1.90/1 1.93/1 1.96/2 1.98/3 2.00/x
1.98 Airine Palsyte LTU 13.7.92 1 NC Kaunas 27 Jul
1.80/1 1.85/1 1.90/1 1.98/3
1.98 1 Eberstadt 24 Aug 1.80/1 1.85/1 1.88/1 1.91/1 1.94/2 1.96/1 1.98/1 2.00/xxx
(29/9)

Mark	Name		Nat	Born	Pos	Meet	Venue	Date
1.97i	Emma	Green Tregaro (10)	SWE	8.12.84	1		Trinec	29 Jan
1.97i	Marie-Laurence	Jungfleisch	GER	7.10.90	2		Arnstadt	8 Feb
1.97	Nafissatou	Thiam	BEL	19.8.94	1H	EC	Zürich	14 Aug
1.97	Chaunté	Lowe	USA	12.1.84	2	C.Cup	Marrakech	14 Sep
1.96i	Alessia	Trost	ITA	8.3.93	1P		Padova	11 Jan
1.96i	Katarina	Johnson-Thompson	GBR	9.1.93	1	NC	Sheffield	8 Feb
1.96i	Svetlana	Radzivil	UZB	17.1.87	1	AsiC	Hangzhou	16 Feb
1.96	Levern	Spencer	LCA	23.6.84	1	Towns	Athens GA	12 Apr
1.96	Inika	McPherson ¶	USA	29.9.86	2	Drake	Des Moines	26 Apr
1.96	Isobel	Pooley	GBR	21.12.92	5		Eberstadt	24 Aug
1.96		Zheng Xingjuan	CHN	20.3.89	1	NC	Suzhou	12 Oct
	(20)							
1.95i	Iryna	Herashchenko	UKR-J	10.3.95	1	NC	Sumy	21 Feb
1.95	Irina	Gordeyeva	RUS	9.10.86	6	Pre	Eugene	31 May
1.95	Brigetta	Barrett	USA	24.12.90	1		Houston	6 Jun
1.94i	Nadezhda	Dusanova	UZB	17.11.87	3		Arnstadt	8 Feb
1.94	Eleanor	Patterson	AUS-J	22.5.96	1		Gold Coast	12 Jul
1.94	Morgan	Lake	GBR-Y	12.5.97	1H	WJ	Eugene	22 Jul
1.94	Nadine	Broersen	NED	29.4.90	2H	EC	Zürich	14 Aug
1.94	Eleriin	Haas	EST	4.7.92	7	EC	Zürich	17 Aug
1.94	Daniela	Stanciu	ROU	15.10.87	8	EC	Zürich	17 Aug
1.93i	Yana	Maksimova	BLR	9.1.89	1	NC	Mogilyov	21 Feb
	(30)							

Mark	Name		Nat	Born	Pos	Meet	Venue	Date
1.93	Vita	Palamar	UKR	12.10.77	2		Kyiv	3 Jun
1.93	Tonje	Angelsen	NOR	17.1.90	1		Stjørdal	7 Jun
1.92i	Anna	Iljustsenko	EST	12.10.85	1	NC	Tartu	22 Feb
1.92	Leontia	Kallenou	CYP	5.10.94	1	SEC	Lexington	17 May
1.92	Venelina	Veneva-Mateeva	BUL	13.6.74	1		Izmir	3 Jun
1.91i	Adonía	Steryíou	GRE	7.7.85	1		Pátra	25 Jan
1.91i	Barbara	Szabó	HUN	17.2.90	1		Seattle	15 Feb
1.91	Tynita	Butts	USA	10.6.90	1	Conf USA	Houston	17 May
1.91	Susan	Jackson	USA	26.7.89	2	NCAA-II	Allendale	24 May
1.91	Valentyna	Lyashenko	UKR	30.1.81	1		Argentan	7 Jun
	(40)							
1.91	Jeannelle	Scheper	LCA	21.11.94	1		Basseterre	5 Jul
1.91	Michaela	Hrubá	CZE-Y	21.2.98	2	WJ	Eugene	27 Jul
1.90i	Oksana	Krasnokutskaya	RUS	24.9.93	1		Sankt-Peterburg	4 Jan
1.90i	Yekaterina	Kuntsevich	RUS	13.7.84	1		Wien	28 Jan
1.90i	Mariya	Nesterchuk	BLR	14.8.89	2	NC	Mogilyov	21 Feb
1.90i	Urszula	Domel	POL	21.7.88	3	NC	Sopot	22 Feb
1.90	Vashti	Cunningham	USA-Y	18.1.98	1		Las Vegas	17 May
1.90	Irina	Iliyeva	RUS-J	22.12.95	1		Moskva	29 May
1.90	Burcu	Yüksel-Ayhan	TUR	3.5.90	2		Izmir	4 Jun
1.90	Ma'ayan	Shahaf	ISR	9.11.86	1		Tel Aviv	7 Jun
	(50)							
1.90	Eliska	Klucinová	CZE	14.4.88	1H		Kladno	14 Jun
1.90	Viktoriya	Styopina	UKR	21.2.76	3=		Berdychiv	28 Jun
1.90	Iryna	Kovalenko	UKR	17.6.86	3=		Berdychiv	28 Jun
1.90	Yekaterina	Fedotova	RUS	3.7.92	1	NC-23	Saransk	15 Jul
1.90	Mirela	Demireva	BUL	28.9.89	2	NA	Heusden-Zolder	19 Jul
1.90	Tatyana	Mnatsakanova	RUS	25.5.83	2	NC	Kazan	25 Jul
1.89i	Yuliya	Kostrova	RUS	20.8.91	1		Novocheboksarsk	11 Jan
1.89i	Oksana	Starostina	RUS	1.4.88	2		Chelyabinsk	16 Jan
1.89i	Olena	Holosha	UKR	26.1.82	3	NC	Sumy	21 Feb
1.89	Sarah	Cowley	NZL	3.2.84	2	NC	Melbourne	6 Apr
	(60)							
1.89	Allison	Barwise	USA	21.7.91	1H		Annapolis	3 May
1.89	Sahana	Kumari	IND	6.3.81	1	I-S	Lucknow	6 Jun
1.89	Alyx	Treasure	CAN	15.5.92	1	NC	Moncton	27 Jun
1.89	Hannah	Joye	AUS-J	4.1.96	2		Gold Coast	28 Jun
1.89	Yuliya	Levchenko	UKR-Y	28.11.97	1	Yth OG	Nanjing	24 Aug
1.88i	Alesya	Paklina	KGZ	22.6.88	1		Volgograd	25 Jan
1.88i	Erika	Wiklund	SWE	10.3.88	1		Joplin	1 Feb
1.88i	Sofie	Skoog	SWE	7.6.90	5	XLG	Stockholm	6 Feb
1.88i	Grete	Udras	EST	11.3.88	2		Tartu	11 Feb
1.88i	Tatyana	Kivimyagi	RUS	23.6.84	5	NC	Moskva	19 Feb
	(70)							
1.88Ai	Sharon	Day-Monroe	USA	9.6.85	1P	NC	Albuquerque	21 Feb
1.88Ai	Tiana	Wills	USA		2	NC	Albuquerque	23 Feb
1.88i	Emma	Nuttall	GBR	23.4.92	1		Edmonton	8 Mar
1.88Ai	Kendell	Williams	USA-J	14.6.95	1P	NCAA	Albuquerque	15 Mar
1.88	Kimberly	Williamson	JAM	2.10.93	1	Sun Angel	Tempe	12 Apr
1.88	Oldriska	Maresová	CZE	14.10.86	1		Olomouc	8 May
1.88	Taisa	Roslova	BLR	7.2.92	1	NCp	Brest	31 May
1.88		Wang Lin	CHN-J	8.1.95	1	Asi-J	Taipei	13 Jun
1.88	Desirée	Rossit	ITA	19.3.94	2	NC	Rovereto	19 Jul
1.88	Hanna	Gorodskaya	BLR	31.1.93	2	NC	Grodno	24 Jul
	(80)							
1.88	Rachel	McCoy	USA-J	1.8.95	4	WJ	Eugene	27 Jul
1.88		Wang Yang	CHN	14.2.89	2	NC	Suzhou	12 Oct
1.88		Zhang Luyu	CHN	18.8.94	3	NC	Suzhou	12 Oct
1.87i	Saniel	Atkinson Grier	BAH	2.7.91	1		Nashville	24 Jan
1.87i	Jayne	Nisbet	GBR	17.7.88	2	NC	Sheffield	8 Feb
1.87i	Akela	Jones	BAR-J	31.12.95	1		Lincoln NE	21 Feb
1.87i	Taylor	Burke	USA	4.6.93	3	SEC	College Station	1 Mar
1.87	Amy	Pejkovic	AUS	1.2.93	1		Brisbane	7 Mar
1.87	Amina	Smith	USA	10.1.92	1		Chapel Hill	19 Apr
1.87	Erika	Furlani	ITA-J	2.1.96	1		Pontedera	10 May
	(90)							
1.87	Brianne	Theisen-Eaton	CAN	18.12.88	5H		Götzis	31 May
1.87	Patricia	Bihari	HUN	6.2.92	1	NC-23	Debrecen	28 Jun
1.87	Alina	Fyodorova	UKR	31.7.89	1H	ECp-1	Ribeira Brava	5 Jul
1.87	Jillian	Drouin	CAN	30.9.86	1H	PAmCp	Ottawa	17 Jul
1.87	Alexandra	Plaza	GER	10.8.94	2	NC	Ulm	26 Jul

Mark	Name		Nat	Born	Pos	Meet	Venue	Date
1.87	Nawal	Meniker	FRA-Y	9.12.97	2	Yth OG	Nanjing	24 Aug
1.87	Agnieszka	Borowska	POL	21.10.91	1H		Woerden	30 Aug

Mark	Name		Nat	Born	Date
1.86i	Nataliya	Hapchuk	UKR	15.11.88	11 Jan
1.86i	Anastasiya	Muzankova	RUS	11.1.92	23 Jan
1.86i	Natalya	Aksenova (100)	RUS-Y	6.6.97	2 Feb
1.86i	Madara	Onuzane	LAT	7.6.89	22 Feb
1.86i	Amber	Melville	USA	20.12.92	28 Feb
1.86	Nicola	McDermott	AUS-J	28.12.96	1 Mar
1.86	Zoe	Timmers	AUS	25.5.89	14 Mar
1.86	Enrica	Cipolloni	ITA	19.10.90	17 May
1.86	Gintare	Nesteckyte	LTU-J	30.12.95	23 May
1.86	Dainellys	Dutil	CUB-J	12.2.95	24 May
1.86	Monika	Gollner	AUT	23.10.74	7 Jun
1.86	Linda	Rainwater	USA	1.8.88	14 Jun
1.86	Maya	Pressley	USA	1.2.91	14 Jun
1.86	Shanay	Briscoe	USA	7.8.92	14 Jun
1.86	Tatiána	Goúsin	GRE	26.1.94	9 Jul
1.86	Sietske	Noorman	NED	16.7.91	13 Jul
1.86	Elina	Smolander	FIN	11.10.89	1 Aug
1.86	My	Nordström	SWE	27.4.90	2 Aug
1.86	Laura	Rautanen	FIN	13.2.88	24 Aug
1.86	Gyorgyi	Zsivoczky-Farkas	HUN	13.2.85	30 Aug
1.86	Mônica	Freitas	BRA	21.6.84	11 Oct
1.86	Cassie	Purdon	AUS-J	24.10.96	24 Oct
1.86		Pham Thi Diem	VIE	24.1.90	16 Dec
1.86i	Erika	Hurd	USA	8.4.94	12 Dec
1.855	Kelsey	Herman	USA-J	.96	1 May
1.85i	Yekaterina	Stepanova	RUS	24.7.94	18 Jan
1.85i	Elena	Brambilla	ITA	23.4.83	26 Jan
1.85i	Marina	Aitova	KAZ	13.9.82	8 Feb
1.85i	Elina	Kakko	FIN-Y	12.1.97	9 Feb
1.85i	Megan	Glisar	USA	30.3.91	14 Feb
1.85	Lesyaní	Mayor	CUB	8.7.89	14 Feb
1.85Ai	Barbara	Nwaba	USA	18.1.89	21 Feb
1.85i	Dior	Delophont	FRA	19.10.94	22 Feb
1.85i	Thea	Lafond	DMA	5.4.94	27 Feb
1.85A	Ximena	Esquivel	MEX-Y	22.8.97	2 Mar
1.85	Elizabeth	Lamb	NZL	12.5.91	1 Mar
1.85	Hanne	Van Hessche	BEL	5.7.91	17 May
1.85	Yelena	Slesarenko	RUS	28.2.82	21 May
1.85	Margarita	Mazina	RUS-J	7.7.95	29 May
1.85	Viktoriya	Dobrynska	UKR	18.1.80	3 Jun
1.85	Doreen	Amata	NGR	6.5.88	13 Jun
1.85	Tamara	de Souza	BRA	8.9.93	14 Jun
1.85	Aneta	Rydz	POL	30.3.94	5 Jul
1.85	Mélanie	Skotnik	FRA	8.11.82	12 Jul
1.85	Mari	Sepänmaa	FIN	17.9.85	13 Jul
1.85	Linda	Sandblom	FIN	18.10.89	13 Jul
1.85	Heta	Tuuri	FIN-J	14.1.95	13 Jul
1.85	Lilli	Schwarzkopf	GER	28.8.83	14 Aug
1.85	Wanida	Boonwan	THA	30.8.86	2 Oct
1.85A	Yorgelis	Rodríguez	CUB-J	25.1.95	26 Nov
1.85i	Aleksandra	Yaryshkina	RUS	10.6.94	7 Dec
1.84i	Sofiya	Voronina	RUS-Y	22.10.97	9 Feb
1.84	Kristina	Korolyova	RUS	6.11.90	14 Feb
1.84i	Alina	Rotaru	ROU	5.6.93	16 Feb
1.84Ai	Mimi	Land	USA	27.1.94	15 Mar
1.84i		Zhao Jian	CHN	24.3.91	22 Mar
1.84	Lauren	Crockett	USA	12.4.92	22 Mar
1.84	Vanessa	Jules	USA	21.3.91	12 Apr
1.84	Eliska	Buchlovská	CZE-Y	27.8.98	10 May
1.84	Carolin	Schäfer	GER	5.12.91	31 May
1.84	Nadja	Kampschulte	GER	5.9.92	15 Jun
1.84	Eleonora	Omoregie	ITA-J	22.5.96	28 Jun
1.84	Darya	Kuchina	UKR	14.6.93	28 Jun
1.84	Miyuki	Fukumoto	JPN	4.1.77	11 Jul
1.84		Liu Jingyi	CHN	27.10.94	13 Jul
1.84	Rachel	Machin	CAN	14.3.92	17 Jul
1.84	Katarina	Mögenburg	NOR	16.6.91	26 Jul
1.84	Laura	Ikauniece-Admidina	LAT	31.5.92	2 Aug
1.84	Ebba	Jungmark	SWE	10.3.87	2 Aug
1.84	Elena	Vallortigara	ITA	21.9.91	29 Aug
1.84	Anna	Blank	RUS	12.1.90	4 Sep
1.84	Valdiléia	Martins	BRA	19.9.89	14 Sep
1.84		Shen Xin	CHN	5.11.92	12 Oct
1.84		Zhang Xiyao	CHN-J	20.12.95	12 Oct

(171)

Best outdoors

Mark	Name	Pos	Meet	Venue	Date
2.00	Vlasic	1	DL	Saint-Denis	5 Jul
2.00	Kuchina	2	DL	Saint-Denis	5 Jul
1.97	Licwinko	1c		Płock	4 Jun
1.97	Jungfleisch	5	EC	Zürich	17 Aug
1.96	Radzivil	1		Opole	15 Jun
1.94	Dusanova	1	WCM	Rieti	7 Sep
1.93	Green	4	AnnivG	London (HG)	20 Jul
1.92	Herashchenko	2		Athína (Filothéi)	28 May
1.91	Szabó	1	NCAA-II	Allendale	24 May
1.91	Trost	2		Rovereto	2 Sep
1.90	Johnson-Thompson	2H		Götzis	31 May
1.90	Maksimova	1H	ECp	Torun	5 Jul
1.90	Krasnokutskaya	2	NC-23	Saransk	15 Jul
1.89	Domel	3	NC	Szczecin	30 Jul
1.88	Wiklund	1		Columbia MO	12 Apr
1.88	Steryiou	3		Athína (Filothéi)	28 May
1.87	Holosha	5		Berdychiv	28 Jun
1.87	Kivimyagi	1	NCp	Yerino	10 Jul
1.87	Starostina	2	NCp	Yerino	10 Jul
1.87	Skoog	1=		Joensuu	24 Jul

Mark	Name	Date
1.86	Onuzane	7 Jun
1.86	Kuntsevich	7 Jun
1.86	Atkinson Grier	1 Aug
1.85	Wills	4 Apr
1.85	Paklina	7 Jun
1.85	Aitova	14 Jun
1.85	Jones	25 Jul
1.85	Nisbet	30 Jul
1.85	Udras	3 Aug
1.84	Hurd	25 Apr
1.84	Delophont	25 Apr
1.84	Zhao Jian	30 May
1.84	Iljustsenko	15 Jun
1.84	Day-Monroe	27 Jun
1.84	Brambilla	10 Jul
1.84	Muzankova	10 Jul
1.84	Yaryshkina	2 Aug

Drugs disqualification

Mark	Name		Nat	Born	Pos	Meet	Venue	Date
2.00	Inika	McPherson ¶	USA	29.9.86	(1)	NC	Sacramento	29 Jun

1.85/1 1.88/1 1.91/1 1.94/3 1.97/1 2.00/1

JUNIORS

See main list for top 14 juniors. 14 performances (inc. 3 indoors) by 3 women to 1.92. Additional marks and further juniors:

Name	Mark	Pos	Meet	Venue	Date	Mark	Pos	Meet	Venue	Date
Herashchenko	1.92i	1		Kyiv	11 Jan	1.92i	10q	WI	Sopot	10 Mar
Patterson	1.94	1	CG	Glasgow	1 Aug	1.92	1	WCM	Melbourne	22 Mar
	1.94	1		Melbourne	14 Dec	1.92	1	NC	Melbourne	6 Apr
	1.93	1		Brisbane (Nathan)	14 Jun	1.92	1		Gold Coast	28 Jun
Lake	1.93	1	LI	Loughborough	18 May	1.93	1	WJ	Eugene	27 Jul

Mark	Name		Nat	Born	Pos	Meet	Venue	Date
1.86i	Natalya	Aksenova	RUS-Y	6.6.97	1	NC-y	Novocheboksarsk	2 Feb
1.86	Nicola	McDermott	AUS	28.12.96	1		Sydney	1 Mar
1.86	Gintare	Nesteckyte	LTU	30.12.95	1		Vidukle	23 May
1.86	Dainellys	Dutil	CUB	12.2.95	1	Barr	La Habana	24 May
1.86	Cassie	Purdon	AUS	24.10.96	1		Brisbane	24 Oct
1.855	Kelsey	Herman (20)	USA	.96	1		Crossett	1 May

Symbols/Abbreviations

+ intermediate time in longer race, A made at an altitude of 1000m or higher, D made in a decathlon, h made in a heat, qf quarter-final, sf semi-final, i indoors, Q qualifying round, r race number, -J juniors, -Y youths (b. 1997 or later)

Mark	Name		Nat	Born	Pos	Meet	Venue	Date

POLE VAULT

4.80 Fabiana Murer BRA 16.3.81 1 adidas New York 14 Jun
4.50/1 4.60/1 4.70/1 4.80/1 4.90/xxx
4.76 1 Herc Monaco 18 Jul 4.55/1 4.65/2 4.76/1 4.86/xxx
4.72 1 WK Zürich 28 Aug 4.47/1 4.57/1 4.67/1 4.72/1 4.82/xxx
4.70i 4 WI Sopot 9 Mar 4.45/1 4.55/1 4.65/1 4.70/3 4.75/xxx
4.76i Anna Rogowska POL 21.5.81 1 Flanders Gent 9 Feb
4.41/3 4.51/1 4.61/1 4.71/3 4.76/2 4.81/xxx
4.73i Holly Bleasdale GBR 2.11.91 1 NC Sheffield 8 Feb
4.46/1 4.60/1 4.73/1 4.81/xxx
4.71i 1= Dresden 31 Jan 4.42/1 4.52/1 4.61/xxx 4.61/1 4.66/1 4.71/1 4.76/x
4.71i 1 GP Birmingham 15 Feb 4.46/1 4.61/2 4.71/1 4.77/xxx
4.73i Jenn Suhr USA 5.2.82 1 Jonesboro 27 Feb
4.60/3 4.73/2 4.78/xxx
4.71Ai 1 Albuquerque 15 Feb 4.61/2 4.71/1 4.78/xxx
4.71 1 London ON 1 Jun ??
4.71 2 Herc Monaco 18 Jul 4.55/1 4.65/2 4.71/1 4.76/x 4.81/xx
4.70i 1 Boston (R) 8 Feb 4.60/1 4.70/3 4.75/x 4.76/x
4.70 2 adidas New York 14 Jun 4.60/1 4.70/1 4.80/xxx
4.72i Silke Spiegelburg GER 17.3.86 1 XLG Stockholm 6 Feb
4.42/1 4.64/1 4.72/1 4.81/xxx
4.71i 1 Leverkusen 19 Jan 4.50/1 4.71/1 4.81/xxx
4.72i Nikoléta Kiriakopoúlou GRE 21.3.86 2 XLG Stockholm 6 Feb
4.30/2 4.42 1 4.53/1 4.64/2 4.72/2 4.78/xxx
4.72i Anzhelika Sidorova RUS 28.6.91 1 NC Moskva 17 Feb
4.30/1 4.50/1 4.61/1 4.72/1
4.71i 1 Eaubonne 11 Feb 4.36/2 4.46/1 4.56/2 4.66/xx4.71/1
4.70i 2= WI Sopot 9 Mar 4.30/1 4.45/1 4.55/1 4.65/1 4.70/2 4.75/xxx
4.70 1 NC Kazan 24 Jul 4.35/1 4.50/1 4.60/1. 4.70/3
4.71i Jirina Svobodová CZE 20.5.86 1= Dresden 31 Jan
4.32/1 4.52/1 4.61/xxx 4.61/1 4.66/1 4.71/1 4.76/x
4.70i 2= WI Sopot 9 Mar 4.45/1 4.55/1 4.65/1 4.70/2 4.75/xxx
4.71i Tina Sutej SLO 7.11.88 1 Winter Moskva 2 Feb
4.36/1 4.46/1 4.56/2 4.61/1 4.66/1 4.71/2 4.76/xxx
4.71Ai Mary Saxer (10) USA 21.6.87 1 NC Albuquerque 23 Feb
4.41/1 4.61/1 4.71/1 4.76/xxx
4.71 Lisa Ryzih GER 27.9.88 1 Rottach-Egern 5 Jul
4.43/2 4.53/1 4.63/2 4.68/1 4.71/2
4.71 Ekaterini Stefanidi GRE 4.2.90 3 Herc Monaco 18 Jul
4.40/1 4.55/1 4.65/3 4.71/1 4.76/xxx
4.70i Yarisley Silva CUB 1.6.87 1 WI Sopot 9 Mar
4.45/1 4.55/1 4.65/2 4.70/1 4.75/xxx
4.70 1 GGala Roma 5 Jun 4.40/1 4.50/2 4.60/1 4.70/3 4.80/xxx
4.70 3 adidas New York 14 Jun 4.50/2 4.60/1 4.70/2 4.80/xxx
(30/13)

Mark	Name		Nat	Born	Pos	Meet	Venue	Date
4.68i	Kylie	Hutson	USA	27.11.87	2	Drake	Des Moines	23 Apr
4.67	Nicole	Büchler	SUI	17.12.83	5	WK	Zürich	28 Aug
4.65	Angelina	Krasnova	RUS	7.2.91	1		Adler	29 May
4.65	Alana	Boyd	AUS	10.5.84	1		Mannheim	5 Jul
4.62i	Angelica	Bengtsson	SWE	8.7.93	1		Nice	8 Feb
4.61i	Marion	Fiack	FRA	13.10.92	1		Orléans	18 Jan
4.61i	Kristina	Gadschiew	GER	3.7.84	2	NC	Leipzig	22 Feb
	(20)							
4.61		Li Ling	CHN	6.7.89	1	NGPF	Jinan	12 Jul
4.60Ai	Kaitlin	Petrillose	USA	10.12.92	1	NCAA	Albuquerque	14 Mar
4.58i	Becky	Holliday	USA	12.3.80	3	Drake	Des Moines	23 Apr
4.56i	Lyudmila	Yeryomina	RUS	8.8.91	2	NC	Moskva	17 Feb
4.56i	Marion	Lotout	FRA	19.11.89	1	NC	Bordeaux	22 Feb
4.55i	Minna	Nikkanen	FIN	9.4.88	1	v3N	Tampere	8 Feb
4.55	Katharina	Bauer	GER	12.6.90	1		Bönnigheim	29 May
4.55	Yuliya	Golubchikova	RUS	27.3.83	3		Adler	29 May
4.55	Sandi	Morris	USA	8.7.92	2	NC	Sacramento	27 Jun
4.55	Vanessa	Boslak	FRA	11.6.82	1		Blois	2 Jul
	(30)							
4.52i	Malin	Dahlström	SWE	26.8.89	3		Dresden	31 Jan
4.52i	Hanna	Shelekh	UKR	14.7.93	6	Stars	Donetsk	15 Feb
4.51Ai	Kat	Majester	USA	22.5.87	5	NC	Albuquerque	23 Feb
4.51Ai	Emily	Grove	USA	22.5.93	6	NC	Albuquerque	23 Feb
4.51	Naroa	Agirre	ESP	15.5.79	1		Valladolid	10 May
4.50i	Alyona	Lutkovskaya	RUS-J	15.3.96	3	NC	Moskva	17 Feb
4.50i	Anastasiya	Savchenko	RUS	15.11.89	4	NC	Moskva	17 Feb

Mark	Name		Nat	Born	Pos	Meet	Venue	Date
4.50	Kristen	Hixson	USA	1.7.92	1	NCAA-II	Allendale	22 May
4.50	Romana	Malácová	CZE	15.5.87	1		Praha	3 Jun
4.50	Carolin	Hingst	GER	18.9.80	2		Hof	21 Jun
	(40)							
4.48	Katie	Nageotte	USA	30.6.91	3	GP	Ponce	17 May
4.46i	Joana	Kraft	GER	27.7.91	1		Sindelfingen	8 Feb
4.46i	Martina	Strutz	GER	4.11.81	5	NC	Leipzig	22 Feb
4.45Ai	April	Steiner Bennett	USA	22.4.80	2		Air Force Academy	11 Jan
4.45Ai	Annika	Roloff	GER	10.3.91	3	NCAA	Albuquerque	14 Mar
4.45	Megan	Clark	USA	10.6.94	1		Chapel Hill	22 Mar
4.45	Tori	Pena	IRL	30.7.87	1		Chula Vista	17 May
4.45	Zoë	Brown	IRL	15.9.83	1		Cardiff	15 Jul
4.45	Desiree	Freier	USA-J	24.7.96	2	WJ	Eugene	24 Jul
4.45	Eliza	McCartney	NZL-J	11.12.96	3	WJ	Eugene	24 Jul
	(50)							
4.45	Yekaterina	Kazeka	RUS	7.10.90	4	NC	Kazan	24 Jul
4.45	Roberta	Bruni	ITA	8.3.94	1		Rieti	31 Jul
4.45	Kira	Grünberg	AUT	13.8.93	Q	EC	Zürich	12 Aug
4.44i	Maria Eleonor	Tavares	POR	24.9.85	1	NC	Pombal	16 Feb
4.43i	Caroline Bonde	Holm	DEN	19.7.90	5		Bad Oeynhausen	28 Feb
4.41	Alysha	Newman	CAN	29.6.94	1		Atlanta	17 May
4.41	Melinda	Withrow	USA	30.10.84	1		Chula Vista	14 Jun
4.41	Chloë	Henry	BEL	5.3.87	1		Seraing	15 Aug
4.40i	Tatyana	Stetsyuk	RUS	27.8.92	2		Moskva	12 Jan
4.40i	Kayla	Caldwell	USA	19.6.91	2		Jonesboro	3 Feb
	(60)							
4.40i	Aleksandra	Kiryashova	RUS	21.8.85	1		Sankt-Peterburg	8 Feb
4.40i	Tatyana	Shvydkina	RUS	8.5.90	6	NC	Moskva	17 Feb
4.40i	Martina	Schultze	GER	12.9.90	1	ACC	Clemson	1 Mar
4.40Ai	Bethany	Firsick	USA	4.12.91	4	NCAA	Albuquerque	14 Mar
4.40		Xu Huiqin	CHN	4.9.93	1		Beijing	24 Apr
4.40	Megan	Jamerson	USA	4.5.86	1		Chula Vista	8 May
4.40	Elizabeth	Parnov	AUS	9.5.94	1		Perth	30 May
4.40	Kelsie	Ahbe	USA	6.7.91	2	NCAA	Eugene	13 Jun
4.40	Sally	Peake	GBR	8.2.86	8	DL	Glasgow	12 Jul
4.40	Olga	Chigirintseva	RUS	29.6.87	1		Kuortane	13 Jul
	(70)							
4.40	Olga	Mullina	RUS	1.8.92	1	NC-23	Saransk	14 Jul
4.40	Nina	Kennedy	AUS-Y	5.4.97	4	WJ	Eugene	24 Jul
4.38i	Morgann	LeLeux	USA	14.11.92	1	SEC	College Station	28 Feb
4.36i	Loréla	Mánou	GRE	20.12.90	1	BalkC	Istanbul	22 Feb
4.36	Patrícia	dos Santos	BRA	13.6.84	1		Campinas	17 May
4.36	Desiree	Singh	GER	17.8.94	1		Wipperfürth	19 Jul
4.36	Angelica	Moser	SUI-Y	9.10.97	1	Yth OG	Nanjing	23 Aug
4.35i	Alexis	Paine	USA	12.10.90	1		Birmingham AL	8 Feb
4.35A	Marta	Onofre	POR	28.1.91	1		Ávila	13 Jul
4.35	Karla	da Silva	BRA	12.11.84	1		São Paulo	22 Feb
	(80)							
4.35	Vera	Schmitz	USA	3.12.87	2		Chula Vista	31 May
4.35	Rebeka	Silhanová	CZE-J	22.3.95	1	Odlozil	Praha	9 Jun
4.35	Lucy	Bryan	GBR-J	22.5.95	1		Genève	14 Jun
4.35	Sonia	Malavisi	ITA	31.10.94	2		Rieti	29 Jun
4.35	Cátia	Pereira	POR	5.7.89	1		Faro	19 Jul
4.35	Anastasiya	Sadovnikova	RUS-J	22.6.95	1		Irkutsk	2 Aug
4.35	Anna Katharina	Schmid	SUI	2.12.89	15q	EC	Zürich	12 Aug
4.32i	Natalya	Bartnovskaya	RUS	7.1.89	1		Wichita	31 Jan
4.32i	Mandissa	Marshall	USA	2.4.91	1		Fairfax	2 Mar
4.31Ai	Sarah	Pappas/Sheppard	USA	30.3.87	7=		Reno	17 Jan
	(90)							
4.31i	Fanny	Smets	BEL	21.4.86	4	Flanders	Gent	9 Feb
4.31A	Robeilys	Peinado	VEN-Y	26.11.97	1		Cali	18 May
4.30i	Victoria	von Eynatten	GER	6.10.91	2		Leverkusen	5 Jan
4.30i	Jade	Riebold	USA	14.4.91	2		Champaign	11 Jan
4.30i	Anna	Felzmann	GER	18.1.92	2		Ludwigshafen	18 Jan
4.30i	Alina	Kakoshinskaya	RUS	16.11.86	2		Sankt-Peterburg	8 Feb
4.30i	Cathrine	Larsåsen	NOR	5.12.86	1		Göteborg	15 Feb
4.30i	Tomomi	Abiko	JPN	17.3.88	1	AsiC	Hangzhou	16 Feb
4.30i	Natalya	Demidenko	RUS	7.8.93	9	NC	Moskva	17 Feb
4.30i	Giorgia	Benecchi	ITA	9.7.89	1	NC	Ancona	23 Feb
	(100)							
4.30i	Ariel	Voskamp	USA	3.8.92	2	SEC	College Station	28 Feb

Mark	Name		Nat	Born	Pos	Meet	Venue	Date
4.30i	Danielle	Nowell	USA	25.3.92	3	SEC	College Station	28 Feb
4.30i		Ren Mengqian	CHN	4.10.93	1	NGP	Nanjing	8 Mar
4.30	Vicky	Parnov	AUS	24.10.90	3		Sydney	15 Mar
4.30	Sophie	Gutermuth	USA	2.11.92	3	TexR	Austin	28 Mar
4.30	Allison	Koressel	USA	2.3.91	1		Chula Vista	24 Apr
4.30	Janice	Keppler	USA	22.3.87	2		Charlottesville	9 May
4.30	Angie	Rummans	USA	23.3.92	1		Atlanta	16 May
4.30	Melissa	Gergel	USA	24.4.89	1		Los Angeles (Ww)	7 Jun
4.30	Henrietta	Paxton	GBR	19.9.83	1		Loughborough	11 Jun
4.30	Kristina	Bondarenko	RUS-J	10.8.95	1		Chelyabinsk	4 Jul
4.30	Stélla-Iró	Ledáki	GRE	18.7.88	3	NC	Athína	20 Jul
4.30	Femke	Pluim	NED	10.5.94	1		Alphen aan den Rijn	14 Sep

Mark	Name		Nat	Born	Date
4.28	Diamara	Planell	PUR	16.2.93	18 May
4.28	Neal	Tisher	USA	3.7.91	18 May
4.28	Michaela	Meijer	SWE	30.7.93	29 Jun
4.27Ai	Merritt	Van Meter	USA	8.1.92	27 Jan
4.27	Annie	Rhodes	USA-J	13.5.95	12 Apr
4.26i	Leslie	Brost	USA	28.9.89	24 Jan
4.26i	Anais	Poumarat	FRA	25.2.89	25 Jan
4.26i	Robin	Wingbermühle	NED	20.5.92	25 Jan
4.26i	Anjuli	Knäsche	GER	18.10.93	22 Feb
4.26	Petra	Olsen	SWE	2.10.90	29 Mar
4.26irreg	Lexi	Weeks	USA-J	20.11.96	17 May
4.26	Lilli	Schnitzerling	GER	5.12.93	19 Jul
4.26	Regine	Kramer	GER	5.4.93	22 Jul
4.25i	Kiley	Tobel	USA	7.7.91	18 Jan
4.25i	Heather	Hamilton	CAN	31.3.88	26 Jan
4.25	Emma	Philippe	AUS-Y	6.6.97	21 Mar
4.25	Bonnie	Draxler	USA-J	13.10.95	6 Jul
4.25	Aneta	Morysková	CZE	19.9.92	12 Jul
4.25	Rianna	Galiart	NED	22.11.85	20 Jul
4.25	Lindsey	Bergevin	CAN	14.1.89	20 Jul
4.23i	Sirine	Ebondo	TUN	31.10.83	8 Feb
4.23i	Kimyanna	Rudolph	USA	27.5.94	2 Mar
4.23	Natasha	Kolbo	USA	5.4.92	18 May
4.21i	Anna	Khitrova	RUS	14.3.93	1 Feb
4.21Ai	Heather	Arseneau	USA	10.4.92	15 Feb
4.21	Karley	King	USA	29.10.90	26 Apr
4.21	Demi	Payne	USA	30.9.91	26 Apr
4.21	McKenzie	Johnson	USA	26.9.94	26 Apr
4.21	Joana	Costa	BRA	15.8.81	13 Sep
4.20i	Yekaterina	Kulikova	RUS	11.9.88	4 Jan
4.20i	Franziska	Kappes	GER	6.5.94	10 Jan
4.20i	Reena	Koll	EST-J	15.11.96	18 Jan
4.20i	Sophie	Dangla	FRA	19.10.87	18 Jan
4.20i	Ninon	Guillon-Romarin	FRA-J	15.4.95	18 Jan
4.20i	Katie	Tannehill	USA	9.9.87	24 Jan
4.20Ai	Rachel	Fisher	USA	9.1.91	25 Jan
4.20i	Gina	Reuland	LUX	28.8.92	5 Feb
4.20i	Valeriya	Novikova	RUS	25.8.94	13 Feb
4.20i	Giulia	Cargnelli	ITA	18.3.88	23 Feb
4.20i	Claire	Lucas	USA	.93	1 Mar
4.20	Lakan	Taylor	USA-J	21.6.95	11 Apr
4.20	Catherine	Street	USA	9.5.90	18 Apr
4.20	Madison	Mills	USA	18.1.94	26 Apr
4.20	Paula	Andrie	USA	26.1.93	26 Apr
4.20	Bryson	Stately	USA	22.11.86	2 May
4.20	Rebeca	Yagüe	ESP	8.8.89	10 May
4.20	Carla	Franch	ESP	25.10.89	10 May
4.20	Olga	Lapina	KAZ	6.7.90	17 May
4.20	Megumi	Hamana	JPN	10.7.84	17 May
4.20	Sukanya	Chomchuendee	THA	9.9.88	17 May
4.20	Elena	Scarpellini	ITA	14.1.87	24 May
4.20	Carolina	Carmichael	USA	28.4.94	30 May
4.20	Sydney	Clute	USA	15.11.93	30 May
4.20	Sydney	White	USA	22.6.94	30 May
4.20	Kateryna	Kozlova	UKR	14.9.89	3 Jun
4.20	Katrine	Haarklau	NOR	21.2.91	13 Jun
4.20	Elienor	Werner	SWE-Y	5.5.98	29 Jun
4.20	Tatyana	Shakhlenkova	BLR	29.6.85	20 Jul
4.19	Kaitlyn	Merritt	USA-Y	27.3.97	3 Apr
4.18i	Alyssa	McBride	USA	2.2.94	28 Feb
4.18	Cameron	Overstreet	USA	30.9.92	18 Apr
4.18	Lauren	Chorny	USA	22.6.93	18 May
4.17	Kristen	Brown	USA	26.5.92	15 Mar
4.15i	Erica	Hjerpe	FIN	20.8.93	11 Jan
4.15i	Robin	Bone	CAN	13.2.94	1 Feb
4.15i	Kristine	Felix	USA	1.5.94	7 Feb
4.15i	Lembi	Vaher	EST	11.2.87	11 Feb
4.15i	Gabriella	Duclos-Lasnier	CAN	1.3.88	14 Mar
4.15	Valeria	Chiaraviglio	ARG	9.4.89	15 Feb
4.15	Brittany	Wooten	USA		28 Mar
4.15	Samantha	Clark	USA	19.2.92	29 Mar
4.15	Sarah	Birkmeier	USA	9.11.91	5 Apr
4.15	Hunter	Wilkes	USA	17.8.94	18 Apr
4.15	Shaylah	Simpson	USA	16.3.92	18 Apr
4.15	Sabrina	Hochreuther	GER	2.8.90	18 Apr
4.15		Sun Sinan	CHN	15.12.93	20 Apr
4.15	Chanel	Krause	USA	31.10.94	26 Apr
4.15	Caroline	Hasse	GER	8.3.91	3 May
4.15	Miho	Imano	JPN	25.1.90	5 May
4.15	Sally	Scott	GBR	12.4.91	18 May
4.15	Anna	Etherington	USA		22 May
4.15	Alexandra	Wasik	USA	6.12.92	30 May
4.15	Miriam	Galli	ITA	30.10.91	8 Jun
4.15	Aino	Siitonen	FIN	29.9.94	11 Jun
4.15	Leanna	Carriere	CAN	3.4.85	6 Jul
4.15		Choi Yea-eun	KOR	22.12.94	24 Aug
4.15		Lim Eun-ji	KOR	2.4.89	24 Aug
4.15	Aleksandra	Wisnik	POL	7.5.92	31 Aug
4.15	Vazhipali	Suresh Surekha	IND	14.8.84	4 Nov
4.15	Jamie	Scroop	AUS	29.3.88	29 Nov
	(203)				

Best outdoor marks

Mark	Name	Pos	Meet	Venue	Date
4.71	Suhr	1		London ON	1 Jun
4.70	Silva	1	GGala	Roma	5 Jun
4.70	Sidorova	1	NC	Kazan	24 Jul
4.67	Kiriakopoúlou	3	WK	Zürich	28 Aug
4.60	Svobodová	2	ET	Braunschweig	21 Jun
4.58	Saxer	1	GP	Ponce	17 May
4.55	Hutson	2	MSR	Walnut	19 Apr
4.55	Fiack	1		Pézenas	24 May
4.52	Nikkanen	1	vSWE	Helsinki	29 Aug
4.50	Petrillose	1	TexR	Austin	28 Mar
4.50	Lotout	2		Pézenas	24 May
4.50	Rogowska	1		Sopot	30 Mar
4.50	Gadschiew	1		Rechberghausen	1 Jul
4.50	Spiegelburg	3	GGala	Roma	5 Jun
4.50	Shelekh	4	GGala	Roma	5 Jun
4.50	Sutej	1	NCp	Nova Gorica	15 Jun
4.50	Savchenko	2	NC	Kazan	24 Jul
4.50	Lutkovskaya	1	WJ	Eugene	24 Jul
4.50	Bengtsson	1	NC	Umeå	1 Aug
4.45	Holliday	3	NC	Sacramento	27 Jun
4.41	Roloff	1		Akron OH	10 May
4.41	Strutz	1		Recklinghausen	23 May
4.40	Schultze	2	TexR	Austin	28 Mar
4.40	Stetsyuk	3=	Kuts	Moskva	17 Jul
4.40	Shvydkina	3=	Kuts	Moskva	17 Jul
4.36	Steiner Bennett	7	Drake	Des Moines	25 Apr
4.35	Kraft	3		Bönnigheim	29 May
4.35	Caldwell	2=		Louisville	7 Jun
4.35	Holm	1	ET-2	Riga	21 Jun
4.35	Tavares	4	FRA Ch	Reims	12 Jul
4.35	Mánou	2	NC	Athína	20 Jul
4.35	Kiryashova	6	NC	Kazan	24 Jul
4.30	Bartnovskaya	4	TexR	Austin	28 Mar
4.30	Marshall	3	PennR	Philadelphia	24 Apr
4.30	Majester	1		Atlanta	16 May
4.30	Yeryomina	6		Adler	29 May

Mark	Wind	Name		Nat	Born	Pos	Meet	Venue	Date

4.30 Felzmann 1 NC-23 Wesel 14 Jun
4.30 Ren Mengqian 3 NGPF Jinan 12 Jul
4.28 Nowell 2 May
4.26 Knäsche 22 Jul
4.25 Brost 19 Apr
4.25 Voskamp 17 May
4.25 Benecchi 8 Jun
4.25 Demidenko 21 Jun
4.25 Abiko 30 Sep
4.20 Sheppard 22 Mar
4.20 Rudolph 5 Apr
4.20 Paine 2 May
4.30 Smets 1 NA Heusden-Zolder 19 Jul
4.20 Guillon-Romarin 24 May
4.20 Cargnelli 29 Jun
4.20 Poumarat 2 Jul
4.20 Wingbermühle 19 Jul
4.20 Reuland 19 Jul
4.20 Koll 24 Jul
4.20 Galiart 26 Jul
4.20 Kappes 23 Aug
4.16 Hamilton 24 Jun
4.15 Lucas 30 May
4.15 Larsåsen 7 Jun
4.15 Dangla 12 Jul

Unsurveyed runway, possibly downhill

4.50dh?	Katie	Nageotte	USA	30.6.91	1	Henderson	9 Aug
4.40dh?	Melissa	Gergel	USA	24.4.89	2	Henderson	9 Aug
4.29 irreg	Demi	Payne	USA	30.9.91	1	Port Aransas	28 Jun

JUNIORS

See main list for top 10 juniors. 11 performances (inc. 3 indoors) by 6 women to 4.40. Additional marks and further juniors:

Lukovskaya 4.46 3 Tomblaine 27 Jun 4.43 5 Rottach-Egern 5 Jul
2+ 4.45 Q EC Zürich 12 Aug 4.41i 1 Zweibrücken 7 Feb
Freier 4.42 1 irreg? Coppell 18 Apr
Parnov 4.40 2 Perth 16 Mar
Malavisi 4.41 1 NC-j Rieti 15 Jun

4.27	Annie	Rhodes	USA	13.5.95	2		Austin	12 Apr
4.26 irreg	Lexi	Weeks	USA	20.11.96	1		Heber Springs	17 May
4.25	Emma	Philippe	AUS-Y	6.6.97	1		Perth	21 Mar
4.25	Bonnie	Draxler	USA	13.10.95	2	NC-j	Eugene	6 Jul
4.20i	Reena	Koll	EST-	15.11.96	1		Kuldiga	18 Jan
	4.20				8	WJ	Eugene	24 Jul
4.20i	Ninon	Guillon-Romarin	FRA	15.4.95	5		Orléans	18 Jan
	4.20				3		Pézenas	24 May
4.20	Lakan	Taylor	USA	21.6.95	1		Tuscaloosa	11 Apr
4.20	Elienor	Werner	SWE-Y	5.5.98	2		Göteborg	29 Jun
4.19	Kaitlyn	Merritt	USA-Y	27.3.97	1		Rancho Santa Margarita	3 Apr
4.14	Kally	Long (20)	USA	28.8.95	1		College Station	2 Aug

LONG JUMP

7.02 0.1 Tianna Bartoletta USA 30.8.85 1 Bisl Oslo 11 Jun
6.69 7.02 p p p p
6.98 1.2 1 DL Glasgow 11 Jul 4.31 6.72 6.97/0.3 6.98 6.69 6.89/-0.6
6.94 0.9 1 Gyulai Székesfehérvár 8 Jul x 6.70 6.89/1.9 6.80 6.94 6.61
6.93 0.2 1 Marrakech 8 Jun x 6.93 6.80 4.47 6.59 p
6.86 -1.2 2 NC Sacramento 28 Jun x 6.86/-1.2 6.85/1.0 6.86/-2.3 6.85/0.4 6.80/-2.4
6.98i Svetlana Biryukova ¶ RUS 1.4.91 1 Moskva 12 Jan
6.98 6.51 6.83 6.58 p p
6.98i 1 Volgograd 25 Jan ??
6.87i 1 NC Moskva 18 Feb x 6.87 5.23 6.75 6.59 6.71
6.95i Tori Bowie USA 27.8.90 1 Naperville 25 Jan
6.30 6.80 x 6.95
6.93 1.2 Anna Klyashtornaya RUS 3.2.86 Q NC Kazan 23 Jul
6.93 only jump
6.92i Ivana Spanovic SRB 10.5.90 1 BalkC Istanbul 22 Feb
6.92 x x p p p
6.88 1.5 1 Pre Eugene 30 May 6.77 6.75 6.62 6.86/1.9 6.77 6.88
6.85 0.3 2 DL Shanghai 18 May 6.85 6.71 6.64 6.61 6.59 p
6.92 1.9 Brittney Reese USA 9.9.86 1 NC Sacramento 28 Jun
x 6.66 x x 6.92 6.44
6.87 -0.2 2 DL Saint-Denis 5 Jul 6.82/0.0 6.87/-0.2 6.74 6.65 6.50 6.87/1.4
6.86 1.6 4 Pre Eugene 30 May 6.86 x x x 6.69 6.80w
6.92 0.4 Éloyse Lesueur FRA 15.7.88 1 DL Saint-Denis 5 Jul
6.66 6.56 6.92 x x x
6.87 1.0 3 Pre Eugene 30 May x x 6.87 x x x
6.86i 1 Mill New York (Arm) 15 Feb 6.68 x 6.49 6.76 x 6.86
6.86 0.0 1 NC Reims 13 Jul x 6.53 6.86 p p p
6.85i 1 WI Sopot 9 Mar 6.72 x 6.74 6.85 x 6.70
6.85 -0.3 1 EC Zürich 13 Aug 6.65 x x 6.85 x x
6.92 0.6 Katarina Johnson-Thompson GBR 9.1.93 2 DL Glasgow 11 Jul
6.44 x 6.92 x x 6.85/1.7
6.90 1.5 Malaika Mihambo GER 3.2.94 1 ET Braunschweig 22 Jun
6.90 6.71 6.90w/2.4 6.53
6.88 1 Regensburg 7 Jun 6.44 x 6.57 6.71 6.46 6.88
6.90 0.1 Darya Klishina (10) RUS 15.1.91 1 NC Kazan 24 Jul
6.70/0.4 6.70 6.67 x 6.90 p
6.88 2.0 1 Tokyo 11 May 6.77w 6.72 6.83/-1.1 6.88 6.41 6.68
6.88 0.6 2 Pre Eugene 30 May 6.74 x 6.88 x 6.81w 6.67

Mark	Wind	Name		Nat	Born	Pos	Meet	Venue	Date
6.88	1.3	Lena	Malkus	GER	6.8.93	1		Weinheim	31 May
				6.54	6.56	6.59	6.20	6.56 6.88	
6.86	0.1	Blessing	Okagbare	NGR	9.10.88	1	DL	Shanghai	18 May
		(30/12)			6.86	6.70	x	p p	p
6.82	1.2	Sosthene	Moguenara	GER	17.10.89	1		Bad Langensalza	28 Jun
6.82	1.2	Shara	Proctor	GBR	16.9.88	3	DL	Glasgow	11 Jul
6.81	-0.2	Funmi	Jimoh	USA	29.5.84	3	NC	Sacramento	28 Jun
6.80		Yuliya	Pidluzhnaya	RUS	1.10.88	1		Chelyabinsk	6 Jun
6.78A	0.2	Maria del Mar	Jover	ESP	21.4.88	1		Monachil	9 Jul
6.78	0.0	Dafne	Schippers	NED	15.6.92	1	NC	Amsterdam	26 Jul
6.75	0.8	Irène	Pusterla	SUI	21.6.88	2		Rovereto	2 Sep
6.74	1.4	Alina	Rotaru	ROU	5.6.93	1	NC	Pitesti	20 Jul
		(20)							
6.73	1.1	Christabel	Nettey	CAN	2.6.91	4	DL	Glasgow	11 Jul
6.73Ai		Lorraine	Ugen	GBR	22.8.91	1	NCAA	Albuquerque	14 Mar
6.72	1.3	Melanie	Bauschke	GER	14.7.88	1		Weinheim	31 May
6.71	1.5	Florentina	Marincu	ROU-J	8.4.96	*		Bucuresti	29 Jun
6.70Ai		Tori	Polk	USA	21.9.83	1	NC	Albuquerque	22 Feb
6.70	1.4	Brooke	Stratton	AUS	12.7.93	1	NC	Melbourne	6 Apr
6.70		Yekaterina	Levitskaya	RUS	2.1.87	1		Krasnodar	6 Jun
6.70	0.1	Olga	Kucherenko	RUS	5.11.85	3		Marrakech	8 Jun
6.69	0.0	Aiga	Grabuste	LAT	24.3.88	1	Odlozil	Praha	9 Jun
6.68i		Nadja	Käther	GER	29.9.88	1		Hamburg	26 Jan
		(30)							
6.68i		Teresa	Dobija	POL	9.10.82	1	Pedros	Bydgoszcz	31 Jan
6.68	1.8	Ese	Brume	NGR-J	20.1.96	1	NC	Calabar	21 Jun
6.68	0.8	Olga	Balayeva	RUS	31.7.84	1	Kuts	Moskva	17 Jul
6.68	-0.6	Erica	Jarder	SWE	2.4.86	1	v FIN	Helsinki	30 Aug
6.67	1.2	Olga	Sudareva	BLR	22.2.84	1	NC	Grodno	24 Jul
6.67	?	Bianca	Stuart	BAH	17.5.88	Q	CG	Glasgow	30 Jul
6.66	0.5	Michelle	Weitzel	GER	18.6.87	3		Weinheim	31 May
6.66	1.2	Jéssica Carolina	dos Reis	BRA	17.3.93	1		São Paulo	27 Sep
6.65	0.5	Tania	Vicenzino	ITA	1.4.86	1		Gavardo	18 May
6.64	0.0	Juliet	Itoya	ESP	17.8.86	1	IbAmC	São Paulo	1 Aug
		(40)							
6.63	0.0	Keila	Costa	BRA	6.2.83	1	NC	São Paulo	10 Oct
6.62	1.8	Margaret	Gayen	AUS	10.7.94	1		Adelaide	18 Jan
6.61	2.0	Efthimía	Kolokithá	GRE	9.7.87	1		Thíva	23 Jul
6.61	0.2	Oksana	Zubkovska	UKR	15.7.81	1	NC	Kirovohrad	25 Jul
6.61Ai		Andrea	Geubelle	USA	21.6.91	3	NC	Albuquerque	22 Feb
6.60	2.0	Cornelia	Deiac	ROU	20.3.88	2		Bucuresti	29 Jun
6.59	1.3	Brianne	Theisen-Eaton	CAN	18.12.88	2H		Götzis	1 Jun
6.59	1.4	Anna	Jagaciak	POL	10.2.90	2	NC	Szczecin	31 Jul
6.58	1.0	Anna	Yermakova	UKR	1.10.91	2		Kyiv	20 Jun
6.58	1.0	Nina	Djordjevic	SLO	15.5.88	1		Kapfenberg	20 Jul
		(50)							
6.57	0.5		Jiang Yanfei	CHN	5.7.92	1	NGP	Zhaoqing	19 Apr
6.57	1.2	Vanessa	Seles	BRA	26.10.81	1		São Paulo	4 May
6.57	1.9		Lu Minjia	CHN	29.12.92	1		Oordegem	5 Jul
6.56i		Yekaterina	Koneva	RUS	25.9.88	3		Volgograd	25 Jan
6.56Ai		Chelsea	Hayes	USA	9.2.88	5	NC	Albuquerque	22 Feb
6.56	1.5	Alitta	Boyd	USA	7.12.91	1		Los Angeles	21 Mar
6.56	1.9	Fanni	Schmelcz	HUN	19.4.92	1	Univ Ch	Budapest	24 Ma
6.56		Mayookha	Johny	IND	9.4.88	1	I-S	Lucknow	5 Jun
6.56	1.3	Maiko	Gogoladze	GEO	9.9.91	1	Kozanov	Almaty	14 Jun
6.56	1.5	Ulyana	Aleksandrova	RUS	1.1.91	2	Kuts	Moskva	17 Jul
		(60)							
6.56	0.4	Irisdaymi	Herrera	CUB	18.4.92	1		La Habana	1 Aug
6.55	1.9	Jessie	Gaines	USA	12.8.90	3		Baie Mahault	10 May
6.55	1.0	Akela	Jones	BAR-J	21.4.95	1	NAIA	Gulf Shores	22 May
6.55	1.7	Karolina	Zawila	POL	21.11.86	1		Rzeszów	24 May
6.55	1.4	Marharyta	Tverdohlib	UKR	2.6.91	5		Marrakech	8 Jun
6.55	1.2	Jenna	Prandini	USA	20.11.92	1	NCAA	Eugene	11 Jun
6.55		Chantel	Malone	IVB	2.12.91	Q	CG	Glasgow	30 Jul
6.55	1.3	Khaddi	Sagnia	SWE	20.4.94	1		Kalmar	12 Aug
6.55	0.3	Maria Natalia	Londa	INA	29.10.90	1	AsiG	Incheon	29 Sep
6.54	1.4	Jessica	Penney	AUS	21.12.87	1		Canberra	8 Feb
		(70)							
6.54	1.9	Jazmin	Sawyers	GBR	21.5.94	2	CG	Glasgow	31 Jul
6.53Ai		Janay	DeLoach	USA	12.10.85	1		Air Force Academy	24 Jan
6.53i		Anna	Kornuta	UKR	10.11.88	1	NC	Sumy	21 Feb

Mark	Wind	Name		Nat	Born	Pos	Meet	Venue	Date
6.53	1.0	Chanice	Porter	JAM	25.5.94	1		Tuscaloosa AL	22 Mar
6.53	1.4	Whitney	Gipson	USA	20.9.90	4		Baie Mahault	10 May
6.53	0.3	Lauma	Griva	LAT	27.10.84	1		Valmiera	19 Jul
6.52	0.8	Cristina	Sandu	ROU	4.3.90	2	RomIC	Cluj-Napoca	6 Jun
6.52	0.8	Teresa	Carvalho	POR-J	30.1.95	1	Med-23	Aubagne	15 Jun
6.52	0.4	Hanna	Minenko	ISR	25.9.89	1	NC	Tel Aviv	17 Jul
6.52	1.2	Sarah	Ngo Ngoa	CMR	7.7.83	Q	CG	Glasgow	30 Jul
		(80)							
6.52	0.6	Tânia	da Silva	BRA	17.12.86	3		São Paulo	27 Sep
6.51	-1.2	Anastasiya	Mokhnyuk	UKR	1.1.91	3H		Götzis	1 Jun
6.50i		Anna	Misochenko	RUS	15.4.92	1		Krasnodar	9 Feb
6.50Ai		Jasmine	Todd	USA	23.12.93	2		Albuquerque	14 Feb
6.50	0.3	Jana	Veldáková	SVK	3.6.81	1	NC	Banská Bystrica	13 Jul
6.49i		Kelly	Proper	IRL	1.5.88	1		Athlone	26 Feb
6.49	0.5	Irina	Ilyina	RUS	25.5.85	2		Adler	29 May
6.49		Yuliya	Tarasova	UZB	13.3.86	1H	NC	Tashkent	22 Aug
6.49	1.9	Renata	Medgyesová	SVK	28.1.83	1		Bratislava	3 Sep
6.49	1.8	Corinna	Minko	AUS	13.12.89	1		Melbourne (D)	6 Dec
		(90)							
6.48	1.6	Rochelle	Farquharson	JAM	16.1.93	1		Baton Rouge	19 Apr
6.48	-0.1	Yulimar	Rojas	VEN-J	21.10.95	1	NC-j	Barquisimeto	27 Jun
6.47A	-2.8	Carla	Marais	RSA	10.12.87	1		Pretoria	22 Feb
6.47	0.4	Eliane	Martins	BRA	26.5.86	1		Campinas	17 May
6.46	2.0	Arantxa	King	BER	27.11.89	3	MSR	Walnut	19 Apr
6.46	2.0	Claudia	Rath	GER	25.4.86	1		Salzburg	24 May
6.46	0.3		Zhou Xiaoxue	CHN	19.6.92	1	NGP	Kunshan	30 May
6.46			Bui Thi Thu Thao	VIE	29.4.92	1		Ho Chi Minh	25 Jul

Mark	Wind	Name		Nat	Born	Date
6.45Ai		Kylie	Price (100)	USA	1.10.93	1 Feb
6.45i		Lisa	Steinkamp	GER	17.8.90	23 Feb
6.45	1.4	Alexis	Perry	USA	8.8.94	28 Mar
6.45	0.8	Claudette	Allen	JAM-J	4.4.95	29 Mar
6.45A	0.7	Lynique	Prinsloo	RSA	30.3.91	11 Apr
6.45	0.4		Xu Xiaoling	CHN	13.5.92	11 Jul
6.45	0.4	Tatyana	Tarasova	RUS	2.10.90	5 Sep
6.44	1.9	Chinazor	Amadi	NGR	9.12.87	24 May
6.44	1.1	Xenia	Atschkinadze	GER	14.1.89	31 May
6.43	0.1	Sha'Keela	Saunders	USA	18.12.93	29 May
6.43	1.5	Eliska	Klucinová	CZE	14.4.88	15 Jun
6.43	0.3	Iryna	Nikolayeva	UKR	20.1.84	20 Jun
6.43Ai		Stachia	Reuwsaat	USA	.94	13 Dec
6.42i		Oksana	Aydamirova	RUS	24.9.94	23 Jan
6.42i		Daria	Derkach	ITA	27.3.93	8 Feb
6.42	0.0		Wang Wupin	CHN	18.1.91	19 Apr
6.42	-0.1	Jennifer	Clayton	PAN	5.10.92	26 Apr
6.42	0.9	Lisa	Kurschilgen	GER	27.3.91	31 May
6.42	1.7	Sarah	Warnock	GBR	5.6.91	29 Jun
6.41i		Stefanie	Voss	GER	9.9.89	18 Jan
6.41i		Anastasiya	Juravlyeva	UZB	9.10.81	23 Jan
6.41	0.6	Abigail	Irozuru	GBR	3.1.90	26 Apr
6.41	0.5	Alesha	Walker	USA	9.4.88	23 May
6.41	0.5	Rebecca	Camilleri	MLT	6.7.85	1 Jun
6.41	0.0	Hafdís	Sigurdjardóttir	ISL	12.2.87	22 Jun
6.40i		Kristin	Gierisch	GER	20.8.90	18 Jan
6.40i		Shaina	Mags	POR	11.4.92	22 Feb
6.40	1.1	Toni	Smith	USA	13.10.84	23 May
6.40	0.8	Yana	Nikulina	RUS	2.7.90	29 May
6.40	0.9	Paula Catarina	Neves	BRA	1.3.93	7 Sep
6.40i		Harua	Kessely	FRA	1.2.88	19 Dec
6.39i		Veronika	Mosina	RUS	17.10.90	5 Jan
6.39i		Amy	Woodman	GBR	1.11.84	15 Feb
6.39	1.0	Keturah	Orji	USA-J	5.3.96	13 Jun
6.39	0.0	Nadine	Broersen	NED	29.4.90	28 Jun
6.39	0.2	Tamara	Myers	BAH	27.7.93	28 Jun
6.39	1.9	Evaggelía	Galéni	GRE	29.12.88	9 Jul
6.39	1.3	Nadia	Akpana Assa	NOR-J	22.12.95	22 Jul
6.39	1.4	Gabriela	dos Santos	BRA-J	23.2.95	10 Oct
6.38i		Robin	Reynolds	USA	22.2.94	11 Jan
6.38i		Erica	Bougard	USA	26.7.93	24 Jan
6.38i		DeRanae	Freeman	USA	15.4.94	28 Feb
6.38	1.8	Janae	Gennette	USA	.83	24 Apr
6.38	1.7	Bernadett	Berecz	HUN	27.7.88	8 Jun
6.38	1.8	April	Sinkler	USA	1.9.89	14 Jun
6.38	0.8	Shana	Woods	USA	7.7.88	14 Jun
6.38	0.1	Jovanee	Jarrett	JAM	15.1.83	27 Jun
6.38	1.4	Yekaterina	Kropivko	RUS-Y	13.6.97	4 Jul
6.38	1.8	Quanesha	Burks	USA-J	15.3.95	6 Jul
6.38		Darya	Reznichenko	UZB	3.4.91	21 Aug
6.37	0.6	Chelsea	Jaensch	AUS	6.1.85	6 Apr
6.37	1.6	Erica	Twiss	USA	17.6.92	10 May
6.37	-1.8	Charla	Craddock	USA	31.10.92	17 May
6.37	0.4	Brittney	Howell	USA	1.9.92	29 May
6.37	0.3	Jung	Soon-ook	KOR	23.4.83	5 Jun
6.37	1.7	Chyna	Ries	USA-J	5.9.96	6 Jul
6.37	0.8	Lucie	Slanicková	SVK	8.11.88	13 Jul
6.36i		Annika	Gärtz	GER	24.8.94	1 Feb
6.36i		Amy	Harris	GBR/ANT	14.9.87	9 Feb
6.36i		Karolina	Tyminska	POL	4.10.84	22 Feb
6.36A	1.0	Samantha	Pretorius	RSA	3.2.92	9 May
6.36		Yekaterina	Voloshina	RUS	16.4.88	6 Jun
6.36	0.0	Maryna	Bekh	UKR-J	18.7.95	13 Jun
6.36		Nektaria	Panayi	CYP	20.3.90	30 Jul
6.36	0.1	Yoshimi	Kai	JPN	10.7.93	16 Nov
6.35	1.6	Macarena	Reyes	CHI	30.3.84	1 Feb
6.35		Joelle	Mbumi Nkouindjin	CMR	25.5.86	24 May
6.35	1.9	Yorgelis	Rodríguez	CUB-J	25.1.95	28 Jun
6.35	-0.1		Wang Rong	CHN-J	1.7.96	9 Oct
		(168)				

Wind assisted

Mark	Wind	Name		Nat	Born	Pos	Meet	Venue	Date
6.98	2.3		Bartoletta			1	DNG	Stockholm	21 Aug
					6.62	6.70w	x	6.66 6.67	6.98w
6.94	2.6	Éloyse	Lesueur	FRA	15.7.88	2	DNG	Stockholm	21 Aug
					6.59	6.94w	6.56	x 6.50w	p
	6.87	2.3 2 ET	Braunschweig	22 Jun	6.48	6.87w	x	6.68	
6.88	2.6	Chelsea	Hayes	USA	9.2.88	1		Fort Worth	21 Mar
					6.82w	x	6.88w	p p	p
Reese	6.87	2.6 1	Chula Vista	24 Apr	6.44w	x	6.56	6.62 x	6.87w
6.84	2.3	Erica	Jarder	SWE	2.4.86	1		Göteborg	14 Jun
					6.84w	6.61w	6.67w	6.63w x	6.52w
6.75	2.6	Aiga	Grabuste	LAT	24.3.88	1		Rovereto	2 Sep

Mark	Wind	Name		Nat	Born	Pos	Meet	Venue	Date
6.73	2.4	Florentina	Marincu	ROU-J	8.4.96	1		Bucuresti	29 Jun
6.72	2.8	Hafdis	Sigurdjardóttir	ISL	12.2.87	1		Saudárkrókur	2 Aug
6.67	3.2	Crystal	Walker	USA	23.6.91	1		Bowling Green	12 Apr
6.64	2.6	Abigail	Irozuru	GBR	3.1.90	1		Baie Mahault	10 May
6.63	2.6	Alesha	Walker	USA	9.4.88	1		Austin	3 May
6.62	3.2	Iryna	Nikolayeva	UKR	20.1.84	1		Kyiv	20 Jun
6.58	3.2	Toni	Smith	USA	13.10.84	3		Chula Vista	24 Apr
6.57	2.6	Whitney	Gipson	USA	20.9.90	3		San Marcos	23 May
6.55	2.1	Eliane	Martins	BRA	26.5.86	2		São Paulo	4 May
6.53A	2.1	Yulimar	Rojas	VEN-J	21.10.95	1	PAm SF	Ciudad de México	15 Aug
6.50	3.5	Sydney	Conley	USA	11.12.93	1	KansR	Lawrence KS	19 Apr
6.50	3.1	Chyna	Ries	USA-J	5.9.96	1		Aurora	15 Jun

Mark	Wind	Name		Nat	Born	Date
6.48	2.8	Vanessa	Jules	USA		12 Apr
6.46	2.7	Chinazor	Amadi	NGR	9.12.87	21 Jun
6.45	2.1	Shameka	Marshall	USA	9.9.83	19 Apr
6.45	2.4	Marestella	Torres	PHI	20.2.81	23 Aug
6.43	3.9	Fátima	Diama	ESP-J	22.9.96	26 Apr
6.42	2.2	Jaana	Sieviläinen	FIN	18.8.82	28 Jun
6.42	2.6	Concepción	Montaner	ESP	14.1.81	17 Jul
6.41	3.4	Amy	Woodman	GBR	1.11.84	10 May
6.41	2.1	Polina	Yurchenko	RUS	20.8.93	15 Jul
6.40	4.2	Malaina	Payton	USA	16.10.91	5 Apr
6.40	3.6	LaToya	Powell	JAM		11 Apr
6.38	4.3	Jazmin	McCoy	USA-J	22.1.95	6 Jul
6.38	3.3	Háido	Alexoúli	GRE	29.3.91	9 Jul
6.37A	3.1	Yosiri	Urrutia	COL	26.6.86	28 Jun
6.36	2.1	Bianca	Kappler	GER	8.8.77	6 Jul

Best outdoor marks

Mark	Wind	Name	Pos	Meet	Venue	Date
6.88	1.5	Spanovic	1	Pre	Eugene	30 May
6.82	0.7	Bowie	5	Pre	Eugene	30 May
6.59	1.3	Käther	3		Bad Langensalza	28 Jun
6.58	0.7	Polk	4	NC	Sacramento	28 Jun
6.54	0.7	Dobija	2	EAF	Bydgoszcz	2 Jun
			1	NC	Szczecin	31 Jul
6.51	0.0	Kornuta	2	NC	Kirovohrad	25 Jul
6.50	1.5	Geubelle	5		Baie Mahault	10 May
6.48	0.5	Hayes	6	NC	Sacramento	28 Jun

6.45 1.7 Proper 14 Jun
6.43 1.2 Price 12 Apr
6.42 0.2 Derkach 19 Jul
6.42 0.1 Koneva 26 Sep
6.41 1.5 DeLoach 30 May
6.39 0.1 Voss 9 Jun
6.39 -0.8 Ugen 31 Jul
Ugen 6.40w 2.2 11 Jun
6.37 Juravlyeva 22 Aug
6.36 1.3 Reynolds 19 Apr

Best at low altitude

Mark	Wind	Name	Pos	Meet	Venue	Date
6.62i		Polk	2	Mill	New York (Arm)	15 Feb
6.59i		Ugen	1		Ames	28 Feb
6.59	0.5	Jover	1	NC	Alcobendas	27 Jul
6.40i		Todd				24 Jan
6.40	2.0	Prinsloo				28 Jun

Unknown irregularity: 6.56 1.0 Keri Emanuel USA 30.6.92 1 TexR Austin 28 Mar

JUNIORS

See main list for top 5 juniors. 10 performances by 5 women to 6.48. Additional marks and further juniors:

Name	Mark	Wind	Pos	Meet	Venue	Date	Mark	Wind	Pos	Meet	Venue	Date
Marincu	6.67i		2	NC	Bucuresti	16 Feb	6.63i		1	NC-j	Bucharest	22 Feb
Brume	6.60	0.1	1		Warri	13 Jun	6.50	0.9	1	AfCh	Marrakech	12 Aug
	6.56	0.4	1	CG	Glasgow	31 Jul						

Mark	Wind	Name		Nat	Born	Pos	Meet	Venue	Date
6.45	0.8	Claudette	Allen	JAM	4.4.95	1	N.Sch	Kingston	29 Mar
6.39	1.0	Keturah	Orji	USA	5.3.96	1	N.Jnr	Greensboro	13 Jun
6.39	1.3	Nadia	Akpana Assa	NOR	22.12.95	Q	WJ	Eugene	22 Jul
6.39	1.4	Gabriela	dos Santos	BRA	23.2.95	3	NC	São Paulo	10 Oct
6.38	1.4	Yekaterina	Kropivko (10)	RUS-Y	13.6.97	1	NC-Y-j	Chelyabinsk	4 Jul
6.38	1.8	Quanesha	Burks	USA-J	15.3.95	2	NC-j	Eugene	6 Jul
6.37	1.7	Chyna	Ries	USA	5.9.96	3	NC-j	Eugene	6 Jul
6.36	0.0	Maryna	Bekh	UKR	18.7.95	1	NC-j	Kyiv	13 Jun
6.35	1.9	Yorgelis	Rodríguez	CUB	25.1.95	1		La Habana	28 Jun
6.35	-0.1		Wang Rong	CHN	1.7.96	2	NC	Suzhou	9 Oct
6.34	2.0	Alysha	Burnett	AUS-Y	4.1.97	1		Sydney	2 Mar
6.33	0.5	Jogaile	Petrokaite	LTU	30.9.95	1	NC-j	Alytus	3 Jul
6.32Ai		Kendell	Williams	USA	14.6.95	1P	NCAA	Albuquerque	15 Mar
6.32	0.4	Celina	Leffler	GER	9.4.96	1		Weinheim	31 May
6.32	-1.9	Anastasiya	Yeremina (20)	RUS	14.7.95	2		Omsk	21 Jun
6.32	1,6	Morgan	Lake	GBR-Y	12.5.97	5	NC	Birmingham	29 Jun
6.32	1,9	Jazmin	McCoy	USA	22.1.95	*	NC-j	Eugene	6 Jul

Wind assisted to 6.33 2 performances to 6.48

Mark	Wind	Name		Nat	Born	Pos	Meet	Venue	Date
6.43	3.9	Fátima	Diama	ESP	22.9.86	1		Elche	26 Apr
6.38	4.3	Jazmin	McCoy	USA	22.1.95	1	NC-j	Eugene	6 Jul
6.33	3.6	Cora	Salas	ESP	27.9.95	1		Palafrugell	31 May

TRIPLE JUMP

15.31 0.0 Caterine Ibargüen COL 12.2.84 1 Herc Monaco 18 Jul
14.78/0.5 14.77/1.3 14.81/0.4 x x 15.31

Mark	Wind	Pos	Meet	Venue	Date	Series					
14.98	-0.6	1	VD	Bruxelles	5 Sep	14.45/0.2	14.75/0.3	14.52/-0.1	14.63/0.4	x	14.98
14.87	1.5	1	GP	Ponce	17 May	14.87	14.60/1.1	14.60/0.1	14.72/0.6	14.34	14.43
14.87	1.5	1	Athl	Lausanne	3 Jul	14.41	14.51/0.4	14.75/1.2	14.87	14.74/0.8	14.46w
14.63	1.7	1	FBK	Hengelo	8 Jun	13.23	14.20	14.24	p	14.31	14.63
14.57A	-0.4	1	CAG	Xalapa	28 Nov	14.37	14.57	p	14.21	14.11	p
14.52A	0.0	*	NC	Medellín	27 Jun	14.37w	x	14.52	14.77w/2.5	14.98w	p
14.52	0.0	1	DL	Birmingham	24 Aug	14.52	14.34	14.33	p	14.33	14.39
14.52	-0.5	1	C.Cup	Marrakech	13 Sep	14.30/-0.2	14.43/0.1	14.52	p		
14.48	0.0	1	GGala	Roma	5 Jun	14.06	14.48	p	p	p	p

WOMEN 2014

Mark	Wind	Name		Nat	Born	Pos	Meet	Venue	Date	Series
14.89	0.6	Yekaterina	Koneva	RUS	25.9.88	2	Herc	Monaco	18 Jul	14.20 14.89 14.41 p 14.16 14.50
14.83	0.4					1		Adler	30 May	14.47/-0.2 14.83 14.49/0.8 x x x
14.69	1.1					2	EC	Zürich	16 Aug	14.40 14.69 14.01 14.16 14.54/0.3 14.31
14.67	0.3					2	Athl	Lausanne	3 Jul	14.40 x 14.60/1.1 14.42/0.2 14.67 13.54
14.65i						1		Samara	30 Jan	14.65 p 13.84 x p p
14.64	1.3					*	NC	Kazan	26 Jul	14.84w 14.30 14.40 x 14.64/1.3 14.58/-0.1
14.55	-0.9					1	ET	Braunschweig	21 Jun	13.77 14.55 14.29/-0.7 14.20
14.46i						1	WI	Sopot	8 Mar	13.96 14.46 14.07 x 14.30 x
14.73	-0.4	Olha	Saladukha	UKR	4.6.83	1	EC	Zürich	16 Aug	14.12 14.73 14.68/-0.4 x 14.59/0.4 14.63/0.0
14.65i						1	NC	Sumy	21 Feb	14.28 14.54 14.36 14.65 14.47 x
14.60i						1		Eaubonne	11 Feb	13.53 14.54 14.60 14.52 x 14.19
14.53	0.4					2	VD	Bruxelles	5 Sep	14.18 14.53 x x 14.34 14.10
14.59	1.2	Kimberly	Williams	JAM	3.11.88	3	Herc	Monaco	18 Jul	14.07 14.28 14.59 14.26 14.25 14.11
14.56	0.6					2	FBK	Hengelo	8 Jun	13.75 14.08 x 13.83 14.28 14.56
14.58	0.7	Yosiri	Urrutia	COL	26.6.86	4	Herc	Monaco	18 Jul	13.95 14.13 14.58 14.39 14.24 x
14.52A	1.8					2	NC	Medellín	27 Jun	14.21 14.29 14.29 14.26 14.52 13.97w
14.47	1.0					2	GP	Ponce	17 May	14.10 13.74 x 14.03 14.47 x
14.47A	1.8					1		Medellín	31 May	13.49 13.89 14.47 14.10 x 13.02w
14.53A	-0.1	Mabel	Gay	CUB	5.5.83	1	PAm SF	Ciudad de México	16 Aug	
14.50	1.9	Alsu	Murtazina	RUS	12.12.87	2	NC	Kazan	26 Jul	14.50 13.96 14.36 x p p
14.46	-0.2	Irina	Gumenyuk	RUS	6.1.88	3	EC	Zürich	16 Aug	14.30 x x 14.00 14.46 x
		(31/8)								
14.45	1.9	Dailenis	Alcántara	CUB	10.8.91	1		La Habana	27 Jun	
14.40	0.0	Ayanna	Alexander	TTO	20.7.82	1		Alexandria VA	31 Aug	
		(10)								
14.37	0.0	Olga	Rypakova	KAZ	30.11.84	2	DL	Birmingham	24 Aug	
14.36i		Patrícia	Mamona	POR	21.11.88	1		Pombal	23 Feb	
14.36	0.0	Yarianna	Martínez	CUB	20.9.84	1		La Habana	7 Feb	
14.35	0.1	Natalya	Vyatkina	BLR	10.2.87	1	NC	Grodno	25 Jul	
14.34i		Kseniya	Detsuk	BLR	23.4.86	1	NCp	Gomel	8 Feb	
14.32	0.1	Andriana	Bânova	BUL	1.5.87	1		Kragujevac	3 Aug	
14.31	1.4	Kristin	Gierisch	GER	20.8.90	*	NC	Ulm	27 Jul	
14.29	2.0	Hanna	Minenko	ISR	25.9.89	1	NC	Lisboa	27 Jul	
14.27	1.9	Anna	Pyatykh	RUS	4.4.81	5	Athl	Lausanne	3 Jul	
14.24	1.6	Katja	Demut	GER	21.12.83	1		Jena	13 Jul	
		(20)								
14.22	1.0	Núbia	Soares	BRA-J	26.3.96	1	NC	São Paulo	12 Oct	
14.20	-0.1	Jenny	Elbe	GER	18.4.90	*		Ingolstadt	24 May	
14.20	0.8	Anna	Jagaciak	POL	10.2.90	3	FBK	Hengelo	8 Jun	
14.20	1.8	Rouguy	Diallo	FRA-J	5.2.95	*	WJ	Eugene	26 Jul	
14.19i			Li Yanmei	CHN	6.2.90	5	WI	Sopot	8 Mar	
14.15	1.6	Ruth Marie	Ndoumbe	ESP	1.1.87	1	NC	Alcobendas	26 Jul	
14.13	0.2	Keila	Costa	BRA	6.2.83	2		Belém	10 Aug	
14.13	0.1	Gabriela	Petrova	BUL	29.6.92	5	EC	Zürich	16 Aug	
14.12	0.0	Yosleivis	Ribalta	CUB	2.5.90	1		La Habana	15 Feb	
14.12	0.0	Liuba M.	Zaldívar	CUB	5.4.93	4		La Habana	21 Feb	
		(30)								
14.11	-0.7	Susana	Costa	POR	22.9.84	5	FBK	Hengelo	8 Jun	
14.11	1.1	Cristina	Bujin	ROU	12.4.88	1	BalkC	Pitesti	26 Jul	
14.11	1.9	Irina	Kosko	RUS	1.3.90	4	NC	Kazan	26 Jul	
14.10i		Dana	Veldáková	SVK	3.6.81	Q	WI	Sopot	7 Mar	
14.09i		Veronika	Mosina	RUS	17.10.90	1		Sankt-Peterburg	8 Feb	
14.09	0.2	Olesya	Zabara	RUS	6.10.82	Q	NC	Kazan	25 Jul	
14.09	1.5	Laura	Samuel	GBR	19.2.91	2	CG	Glasgow	29 Jul	
14.07	0.0	Ana	Peleteiro	ESP-J	2.12.95	1		Salamanca	12 Jun	
14.05		Viktoriya	Valyukevich	RUS	22.5.82	1		Moskva	11 May	
14.05	0.2	Aleksandra	Kotlyarova	UZB	10.10.88	2	AsiG	Incheon	1 Oct	
		(40)								
14.04	0.0	Tânia	da Silva	BRA	17.12.86	3		Belém	10 Aug	
14.02	2.0	Liadagmis	Povea	CUB-J	6.2.96	*	WJ	Eugene	26 Jul	
14.02	1.0	Joelle	Mbumi Nkouindjin	CMR	25.5.86	1	AfCh	Marrakech	14 Aug	
14.01	0.0	Yargelis	Savigne	CUB	13.11.84	3		La Habana	1 Feb	
14.00	1.9	Shanieka	Thomas	JAM	2.2.92	1	NCAA	Eugene	13 Jun	
13.99	0.4	Cristina	Sandu	ROU	4.3.90	2	RomIC	Cluj-Napoca	6 Jun	
13.98i		Dovilé	Dzindzaletaite	LTU	14.7.93	1	NC	Klaipeda	22 Feb	
13.98	-0.3		Wang Rong	CHN-J	1.7.96	2	NGP	Kunshan	31 May	

Mark	Wind	Name		Nat	Born	Pos	Meet	Venue	Date
13.97			Tran Hue Hoa	VIE	8.8.91	1	NG	Nam Dinh	12 Dec
13.96A	2.0	Patricia	Sarrapio	ESP	16.11.82	2		Ávila	13 Jul
		(50)							
13.95	0.8	Jeanine	Assani Issouf	FRA	17.8.92	1	Med-23	Aubagne	14 Jun
13.94i		Nataliya	Yastrebova	UKR	12.10.84	1		Kyiv	11 Jan
13.94	0.8	Simona	La Mantia	ITA	14.4.83	1		Palermo	10 May
13.93i		Elena Andreea	Panturoiu	ROU-J	24.2.95	1	NC	Bucuresti	15 Feb
13.93	2.0	Linda	Leverton	AUS	22.3.87	1	NC	Melbourne	5 Apr
13.93	1.8	Iryna	Nikolayeva	UKR	20.1.84	*		Kyiv	20 Jun
13.92	0.8	Irina	Ektova	KAZ	8.1.87	1	NC	Almaty	27 Jun
13.91	-0.7	Ciarra	Brewer	USA	12.3.93	1	SEC	Lexington	18 May
13.91	1.6	Nathalie	Marie-Nély	FRA	24.11.86	1	NC	Reims	11 Jul
13.90	0.7	Snezana	Rodic/Vukmirovic	SLO	19.8.82	7	GGala	Roma	5 Jun
		(60)							
13.87	0.0	Ruslana	Tsyhotska	UKR	23.3.86	*	NC	Kirovohrad	26 Jul
13.87	1.8	Anastasiya	Potapova	RUS	6.9.85	7	NC	Kazan	26 Jul
13.85	2.0	Yamilé	Aldama	GBR	14.8.72	7	FBK	Hengelo	8 Jun
13.82	1.8		Deng Lina	CHN	16.3.92	1	vJPN,KOR	Jinhua	6 Jul
13.81Ai		Amanda	Smock	USA	27.7.82	1	NC	Albuquerque	23 Feb
13.81	0.1	Gisele	de Oliveira	BRA	1.8.80	1		Campinas	17 May
13.79	1.2	Irina	Vaskovskaya	BLR	2.4.91	1		Minsk	11 Jul
13.79	1.4	Yelena	Sidorkina	RUS	27.9.88	8	NC	Kazan	26 Jul
13.78	0.2	Ivana	Spanovic	SRB	10.5.90	1	NCp	Beograd	14 Jun
13.78	1.2	Alisa	Vlasova	RUS	16.9.90	1	Mosc Ch	Moskva	3 Jul
		(70)							
13.78	0.0	Déborah	Calveras	ESP	26.12.88	2		Alcorcón	12 Jul
13.78	-0.4	Maria Natalia	Londa	INA	29.10.90	1	Asi Univs	Palembang	17 Dec
13.77i		Anastasiya	Juravlyeva	UZB	9.10.81	1	NCp	Tashkent	24 Jan
13.75	2.0		Li Xiaohong	CHN-J	8.1.95	*	WJ	Eugene	26 Jul
13.74	2.0	Malgorzata	Trybanska	POL	21.6.81	2	NC	Szczecin	29 Jul
13.73			Sun Yan	CHN	30.3.91	1		Beijing	18 May
13.72	0.8		Hu Guanlian	CHN	18.7.90	3	NGP	Zhaoqing	20 Apr
13.72		Mayookha	Johny	IND	9.4.88	1	I-S	Lucknow	7 Jun
13.72		Thitima	Muangjan	THA	13.4.83	2		Ho Chi Minh	26 Jul
13.71	1.7	Lucie	Májková	CZE	9.7.88	1		Brno	11 Jun
		(80)							
13.71	0.9	Olga	Salomatina	RUS	15.8.92	1	NC-23	Saransk	16 Jul
13.71	1.8	Vasylyna	Bovanko	UKR	11.12.94	3	NC	Kirovohrad	26 Jul
13.70	1.4	Darya	Nelovko	RUS	9.2.94	4		Adler	30 May
13.70	0.4		Chen Mudan	CHN	4.10.93	3	NGP	Kunshan	31 May
13.70	0.0	Tetyana	Ptashkina	UKR	10.1.93	4	NC	Kirovohrad	26 Jul
13.70	-0.5	Kristiina	Mäkelä	FIN	20.11.92	1	vSWE	Helsinki	31 Aug
13.69	1.0	Andrea	Geubelle	USA	21.6.91	4	GP	Ponce	17 May
13.69	0.2	Valeriya	Fyodorova	RUS-J	9.4.96	1	NC-j	Cheboksary	17 Jun
13.68	1.5	Amy	Zongo-Filet	FRA	4.10.80	1		Marseille	8 Jun
13.68	1.5	Teresa	N'Zola Meso	FRA	30.11.83	2		Pierre-Bénite	13 Jun
		(90)							
13.68	1.8	Jolanta	Verseckaite	LTU	9.2.88	2	NC	Kaunas	27 Jul
13.67	1.1	Neele	Eckhardt	GER	2.7.92	1		Hamburg	12 Jul
13.67	-0.5		Wang Wupin	CHN	18.1.91	1	Univ Ch	Beijing	27 Aug
13.65	0.1		Bae Chan-mi	KOR	24.3.91	1		Kimchun	6 May
13.65	1.1	Carmen	Toma	ROU	28.3.89	3	NC	Pitesti	19 Jul
13.65	1.7	Martyna	Bielawska	POL	15.11.90	3	NC	Szczecin	29 Jul
13.65	0.2	Yulimar	Rojas	VEN-J	21.10.95	1	NC	Barquisimeto	27 Sep
13.64	-0.2	Ottavia	Cestonaro	ITA-J	12.1.95	3	Med-23	Aubagne	14 Jun
13.61	0.0	Hanna	Krasutska	UKR-J	20.7.95	1	NC-j	Kyiv	14 Jun
13.60	1.8	Andrea	Calleja	ESP	3.10.92	3	NC	Alcobendas	26 Jul
		(100)							
13.60	1.0	Marshay	Ryan	USA-J	4.2.95	7	WJ	Eugene	26 Jul
13.60i		Haoua	Kessely	FRA	2.2.88	1		Lyon	19 Dec

Mark	Wind	Name		Nat	Born	Date
13.59	1.6	Blessing	Ibrahim	NGR	4.4.90	24 May
13.58	-1.5	LaQue	Moen-Davis	USA	14.8.93	18 May
13.58	1.5	Anna	Krylova	RUS	3.10.85	26 Jul
13.57Ai		Toni	Smith	USA	13.10.84	23 Feb
13.57		Jamaa	Chnaïk	MAR	28.7.84	22 Jun
13.57			Vu Thi Men	VIE	10.7.90	12 Dec
13.56i		Tori	Franklin	USA	7.10.92	1 Mar
13.56	1.8	Daria	Derkach	ITA	27.3.93	25 May
13.56	0.1	Nadja	Käther	GER	29.9.88	12 Jul
13.55	2.0	Nneka	Okpala	NZL	27.4.88	5 Apr
13.54	1.7	Eva	Linnenbaum	GER	3.6.89	27 Jul
13.54	1.1	Ellen	Pettitt	AUS	13.5.86	29 Jul
13.52	0.4	Mariya	Kostusyeva	UKR	14.11.90	26 Jul
13.51	0.9	Tamara	Moncrieffe	JAM-J	16.5.96	28 Mar
13.51	2.0	Sanna	Nygård	FIN	22.3.88	13 Jul
13.51	0.8	Olesya	Tikhonova	RUS	22.1.90	26 Jul
13.50A	0.1	Liliana	Hernández	MEX	22.8.90	27 Nov
13.49	1.7	Silvana	Segura	PER	6.11.90	22 Jun
13.49	1.9	Anna	Zych	POL	15.5.88	20 Jun
13.48i		Mathilde	Boateng	GHA	24.7.89	22 Feb
13.48	1.0	Gabriela	dos Santos	BRA-J	23.2.95	12 Oct
13.47A	-1.0	Pascale	Delaunay	HAI	21.9.82	27 Nov
13.46i		Cecilia	Pacchetti	ITA	18.5.89	22 Feb
13.46i		Keturah	Orji	USA-J	5.3.96	16 Mar

Mark	Wind	Name		Nat	Born	Date
13.46	1.4	Blessing	Ufodiama	USA	28.11.81	19 Apr
13.46			Wang Huiqin	CHN	7.2.90	18 May
13.46	1.9	Darya	Kucharova	BLR	14.11.93	25 Jul
13.46	0.8	Chioma	Matthews	GBR	12.3.81	29 Jul
13.45	1.1	Inger-Anne	Frøysedal	NOR	25.4.89	22 Aug
13.44	1.0	Ellie	Ewere	USA	27.6.93	26 Apr
13.44	0.0	Lynnika	Pitts	USA	19.5.92	13 Jun
13.44	1.1	Violetta	Maksimchuk	RUS	1.12.90	3 Jul
13.43	1.2	Georgiana	Anitei	ROU-Y	26.3.99	15 May
13.43	-0.2	Maria	Dimitrova	BUL	7.8.76	4 Jun
13.43	0.6	Angelica	Ström	SWE	15.9.81	21 Jun
13.42	1.0	Aleksandra	Nikitsina	BLR	12.9.93	31 May
13.42	1.4	Elina	Torro	FIN	22.7.86	13 Jul
13.41	-1.0		Rao Fan	CHN-J	1.1.96	20 Apr
13.41	-1.3	Petia	Dacheva	BUL	10.3.85	19 Jul
13.40	0.1	Christina	Epps	USA	20.6.91	31 May
13.40	0.3	Kristina	Marukhlenko	RUS	8.9.89	17 Jul
13.40	0.6	Yekaterina	Chernenko	RUS	9.10.86	26 Jul
13.40	0.0	Noor Amira	Mohd Nafiah	MAS	16.7.89	17 Dec
13.39i		Andreea	Lefcenco	ROU-J	10.5.95	22 Feb
13.39	0.9	Mara	Griva	LAT	4.8.89	18 Jul
13.39	0.0	Maliakhal	Prajusha	IND	20.5.87	18 Aug
13.38	1.1	Natalya	Yevdokimova	RUS	7.9.93	26 Jul
13.37		Anastasia	Foutsitzidou	GRE	25.10.91	6 Jun
13.37	0.0		Fu Luna	CHN-J	3.5.95	21 Jun
13.37	1.5	Linda	Onana	CMR	20.8.89	28 Jun
13.36i			Lai Mengqin	CHN	21.1.91	22 Mar
13.36	0.5	Florentina	Marincu	ROU-J	8.4.96	10 May
13.36	1.4	Anastasiya	Leonova	BLR	6.4.94	7 Jun
13.36	0.0	Lisanne	Rieker	GER	8.8.92	14 Jun
13.35i		Darya	Nelovko	RUS	9.2.94	19 Jan
13.35	0.0	Alitta	Boyd	USA	7.12.91	7 Jun
13.35	1.9	Oda Utsi	Onstad	NOR	12.5.90	8 Jun
13.35A		Ivonne	Rangel	MEX	24.8.93	12 Jul
13.34i		Kristina	Poletayeva	RUS	24.2.91	19 Feb
13.34	1.9	Claudine	de Jesus	BRA	9.9.94	22 Feb
13.34	0.3	Tatyana	Blagoveshkaya	RUS-Y	25.1.97	31 May
13.34	1.0	Athanasía	Pérra	GRE	2.2.83	20 Jul
13.34	0.0	Narayanan	Neena	IND	2.5.91	18 Aug
13.34	0.6		Tang Pingping	CHN	16.2.89	27 Aug
13.33	0.2	Yanis	David	FRA-Y	12.12.97	25 Aug
13.32	-0.6	Mariya	Suntsova	RUS-J	20.1.95	29 May
13.32	0.2		Liu Yanan	CHN	18.1.87	31 May
13.32	0.4	Eva	Mustar	SLO-J	30.9.96	5 Jul
13.30	-0.3	Essi	Lindgren	FIN	10.4.90	15 Jun
13.30	1.6		Wei Mingchen	CHN	4.1.91	12 Jul

(172)

Wind assisted

Mark	Wind	Name		Nat	Born	Pos	Meet	Venue	Date
14.98A	3.8		Ibargüen	see 14.52A		1	NC	Medellín	27 Jun
14.84	2.1		Koneva	see 14.64		1	NC	Kazan	26 Jul
14.49	2.6	Patricia	Mamona	POR	21.11.88	3	Athl	Lausanne	3 Jul
						14.12	x	14.36 14.35	14.49w x
14.44	3.3	Rouguy	Diallo	FRA-J	5.2.95	1	WJ	Eugene	26 Jul
14.39	2.8	Yarianna	Martínez	CUB	20.9.84	1		La Habana	21 Feb
14.34	2.5	Kristin	Gierisch	GER	20.8.90	1	NC	Ulm	27 Jul
14.26	2.6	Dovile	Dzindzaletaite	LTU	14.7.93	1	NC	Kaunas	27 Jul
14.24	2.1	Jenny	Elbe	GER	18.4.90	1		Ingolstadt	24 May
14.20	2.2	Elena Andreea	Panturoiu	ROU-J	24.2.95	1	RomIC	Cluj-Napoca	6 Jun
14.20	2.3	Ruslana	Tsyhotska	UKR	23.3.86	1	NC	Kirovohrad	26 Jul
14.18	2.3	Yosleivis	Ribalta	CUB	2.5.90	3		La Habana	21 Feb
14.11	4.5	Olesya	Tikhonova	RUS	22.1.90	1	NCp	Yerino	10 Jul
14.07	3.3	Liadagmis	Povea	CUB-J	6.2.96	2	WJ	Eugene	26 Jul
14.05A	4.3	Yamilé	Aldama	GBR	14.8.72	1		Ávila	13 Jul
14.03	2.6		Li Xiaohong	CHN-J	8.1.95	3	WJ	Eugene	26 Jul
13.98	2.3	Neele	Eckhardt	GER	2.7.92	3	NC	Ulm	27 Jul
13.97	3.2	Iryna	Nikolayeva	UKR	20.1.84	1		Kyiv	20 Jun
13.96	3.5	Valeriya	Fyodorova	RUS-J	9.4.96	4	WJ	Eugene	26 Jul
13.88	3.2	Olga	Salomatina	RUS	15.8.92	1-22		Saransk	3 Aug
13.85	3.1	Lucie	Májková	CZE	9.7.88	1		Brno	21 May
13.85	2.2	Yelena	Sidorkina	RUS	27.9.88	4q	NC	Kazan	25 Jul
13.81	2.8	Daria	Derkach	ITA	27.3.93	2	Med-23	Aubagne	14 Jun
13.81	3.1	Kristiina	Mäkelä	FIN	20.11.92	1		Hämeenlinna	20 Aug
13.72	3.5	Yekaterina	Chernenko	RUS	9.10.86	3	NCp	Yerino	10 Jul
13.72	2.7	Eva	Linnenbaum	GER	3.6.89	5	NC	Ulm	27 Jul
13.64A	3.0	Keturah	Orji	USA-J	5.3.96	1		Albuquerque	7 Jun

Mark	Wind	Name		Nat	Born	Date
13.63	4.1	Alitta	Boyd	USA	7.12.91	14 Jun
13.59	2.2		Fu Luna	CHN-J	3.5.95	20 Apr
13.57	3.0	Lynnika	Pitts	USA	19.5.92	26 Jun
13.56	4.0	Jasia	Richardson	USA	.91	12 Apr
13.53	2.8	Santa	Matule	LAT	13.12.92	19 Jun
13.53	2.8	Petia	Dacheva	BUL	10.3.85	28 Jun
13.51	3.2	Silvana	Segura	PER	6.11.90	22 Jun
13.47	2.3	Blessing	Ufodiama	USA	28.11.81	19 Apr
13.46	3.2	April	Sinkler	USA	1.9.89	17 May
13.40	2.3	Nadia	Eke	GHA	11.1.93	14 Aug
13.39	2.6	Sevim	Serbest-Sinmez	TUR	20.4.87	15 Jun
13.38	2.1	Nickevea	Wilson	JAM	11.5.92	18 May
13.38	2.1	Asta	Dauksaite	LTU	3.4.88	27 Jul
13.35	4.0	Viktoriya	Sadokhina	RUS	18.7.94	18 May
13.35	4.9	Katarina	Johnson-Thompson	GBR	9.1.93	6 Jul
13.33	4.2	Brianna	Richardson	USA	9.9.94	18 May
13.33	3.2	Antqunita	Reed	USA	20.4.91	23 May

Best outdoor marks

Mark	Wind	Name		Meet	Venue	Date
14.36	-0.2	Mamona	*	Athl	Lausanne	3 Jul
14.16	0.5	Detsuk	*	NCp	Brest	31 May
14.27	2.8		1	NCp	Brest	31 May
14.14	1.4	Li Yanmei	4	FBK	Hengelo	8 Jun
13.96	1.2	Dzindzaletaite	*	NC	Kaunas	27 Jul
13.91	1.5	Veldáková	4	GS	Ostrava	17 Jun
13.81	-0.3	Panturoiu	*	RomIC	Cluj-Napoca	6 Jun
13.66	0.4	Smock	6	adidas	New York	14 Jun
13.77w	2.2		1	NC	Sacramento	26 Jun
13.64	1.0	Juravlyeva	7	AsiG	Incheon	1 Oct

Mark	Wind	Name	Date
13.49	1.0	Franklin	31 May
13.46	0.9	Orji	24 Jul
13.45	1.2	Kessely	30 Jul
13.44	1.1	T Smith	14 Jun
13.47w	2.6		17 May
13.37	1.3	Boateng	11 Jul
13.32	0.5	Lefcenco	1 Jun
13.30	0.3	Mosina	30 May

Best at low altitude: 14.42 1.5 Gay 3 GP Ponce 17 May 13.91 1.7 Sarrapio 2 Padova 6 Jul

JUNIORS

See main list for top 12 juniors (5 wa). 12 performances (2 Ind) by 7 women to 13.75. Additional marks and further juniors:

Name	Mark	Wind	Pos	Meet	Venue	Date
Soares	13.76	0.6	2		São Paulo	14 Sep
Diallo	13.77	0.0	Q	WJ	Eugene	24 Jul

Mark	Wind	Name		Nat	Born	Pos	Meet	Venue		Date
Peleteiro		13.91i	1 NC Sabadell	23 Feb						
Panturoiu 2+		13.75 0.0	* ET-1 Tallinn	21 Jun		13.93w 5.2 3		ET-1 Tallinn		21 Jun
13.51	0.9	Tamara	Moncrieffe	JAM	16.5.96	1	N.Sch	Kingston		28 Mar
13.48	1.0	Gabriela	dos Santos	BRA	23.2.95	4	NC	São Paulo		12 Oct
13.46i		Keturah	Orji	USA	5.3.96	1		New York		16 Mar
		13.46 0.9				Q	WJ	Eugene		24 Jul
13.43	1.2	Georgiana	Anitei	ROU-Y	26.3.99	1	Balk-Y	Sliven		15 May
13.41	-1.0		Rao Fan	CHN	1.1.96	7	NGP	Zhaoqing		20 Apr
13.39i		Andreea	Lefcenco	ROU	10.5.95	2	NC-j	Bucuresti		22 Feb
		13.32 0.5				1		Bucuresti		1 Jun
13.37	0.0		Fu Luna	CHN	3.5.95	2	NC-j	Lishui		21 Jun
13.36	0.5	Florentina	Marincu (20)	ROU	8.4.96	1		Bucuresti		10 May
Wind assisted				6 performances by 5 women to 13.75						
13.59	2.2		Fu Luna	CHN	3.5.95	6	NGP	Zhaoqing		20 Apr

SHOT

Mark		Name		Nat	Born	Pos	Meet	Venue		Date
20.67i		Valerie	Adams	NZL	6.10.84	1	WI	Sopot		8 Mar
					20.06	20.41	x	20.10	20.67	20.16
20.59	1 VD	Bruxelles		5 Sep	19.66	20.59	x	19.93	x	19.89
20.46	1 NC	Wellington		29 Mar	20.46	20.38	20.43	x	20.29	x
20.42	1 Athl	Lausanne		3 Jul	20.42	20.42	x	20.24		
20.42	1 Spitzen	Luzern		15 Jul	19.65	20.24	20.18	20.30	x	20.42
20.38	1 Herc	Monaco		19 Jul	19.71	20.38	20.30	x	x	20.34
20.20	1 DL	Doha		9 May	20.20	x	x	x	19.51	x
20.19	1	Christchurch		22 Feb	18.89	20.04	20.16	20.19	x	20.10
20.11i	Q WI	Sopot		8 Mar	20.11		only throw			
20.01	1 GGala	Roma		5 Jul	x	20.01	19.85	x	19.35	19.66
19.96	1 DL	Birmingham		24 Aug	19.96	19.92	19.95	x	x	19.73
19.88	1 CG	Glasgow		30 Jul	x	19.88	19.58	x	19.76	19.79
20.22		Christina	Schwanitz	GER	24.12.85	1	Werfer	Halle		17 May
					20.22	x	19.59	19.03	18.82	19.96
20.22	1 WCM	Beijing		21 May	19.19	19.29	19.22	20.22	19.45	18.82
20.10	1	Binz		7 Sep	19.26	19.51	19.26	20.00	20.05	20.10
20.08	1	Thum		29 Aug	19.14	19.54	19.71	x	20.08	x
20.05i	1	Rochlitz		2 Feb	x	19.04	x	19.98	x	20.05
20.02	1 C.Cup	Marrakech		14 Sep	19.94	20.02	19.92	x		
19.94i	2 WI	Sopot		8 Mar	19.69	x	19.54	19.36	19.94	19.51
19.93i	1	Düsseldorf		30 Jan	19.93	x	19.75	19,63	x	19.63
19.92	1 Anniv	London (HG)		20 Jul	18.38	19.04	19.92	19.43		
19.90	1	Rehlingen		9 Jun	19.06	x	18.95	x	19.67	19.90
19.90	1 EC	Zürich		17 Aug	18.87	19.90	19.66	19.79	19.66	x
19.89i	1 NC	Leipzig		22 Feb	19.26	x	19.48	19.89	19.66	x
19.86	2 VD	Bruxelles		5 Sep	19.66	19.08	19.69	19.58	x	19.86
19.79i	1	Saßnitz		18 Jan	x	17.17	19.37	19.25	19.21	19.79
19.73i	Q WI	Sopot		8 Mar	18.58	19.73				
19.84		Michelle	Carter	USA	12.10.85	2	C.Cup	Marrakech		14 Sep
					18.76	19.84	19.74	19.21		
19.80	2 Anniv	London (HG)		20 Jul	19.80	x	18.14	18.61		
19.73	3 VD	Bruxelles		5 Sep	18.85	19.69	x	19.73	x	x
	(30/3)									
19.65			Gong Lijiao	CHN	24.1.89	2	Athl	Lausanne		3 Jul
19.52		Yevgeniya	Kolodko	RUS	2.7.90	1	Déca	Angers		30 Aug
19.40		Halyna	Obleshchuk	UKR	23.2.89	1		Kyiv		21 May
19.18		Felisha	Johnson	USA	24.7.89	2	NC	Sacramento		25 Jun
19.13		Cleopatra	Borel	TTO	3.10.79	4	VD	Bruxelles		5 Sep
19.04		Anita	Márton	HUN	15.1.89	3	EC	Zürich		17 Aug
19.03		Alyona (10)	Dubitskaya #	BLR	25.1.90	1	NC	Grodno		24 Jul
18.87		Yuliya	Leontyuk	BLR	31.1.84	1	NCp	Brest		31 May
18.83		Tia	Brooks	USA	2.8.90	3	NC	Sacramento		25 Jun
18.81		Alena	Kopets	BLR	14.2.88	2	NCp	Brest		31 May
18.57		Brittany	Smith	USA	25.3.91	1		Tucson		24 May
18.54		Olga	Holodna	UKR	14.11.91	2		Kyiv		21 May
18.49		Chiara	Rosa	ITA	28.1.83	2		Padova		6 Jul
18.45i		Jeneva	McCall	USA	28.10.89	1		New York		14 Feb
18.38		Irina	Tarasova	RUS	15.4.87	4	adidas	New York		14 Jun
18.22i		Vera	Yepimashko	BLR	10.7.76	1		Minsk		17 Jan
18.15i		Christina (20)	Hillman	USA	6.10.93	1	NCAA	Albuquerque		15 Mar
18.11		Yaniuvis	López	CUB	1.2.86	1		La Habana		1 Aug
18.08			Guo Tianqian	CHN-J	1.6.95	1	NGPF	Jinan		13 Jul

Mark	Name		Nat	Born	Pos	Meet	Venue	Date
18.07	Natalia	Ducó	CHI	31.1.89	1	SAmG	Santiago de Chile	16 Mar
18.05	Radoslava	Mavrodieva	BUL	13.3.87	1		Burgas	5 Jul
17.93	Leyla	Rajabi	IRI	18.4.83	2		Minsk	18 Jul
17.90	Kearsten	Peoples	USA	20.12.91	3		La Jolla	26 Apr
17.89i	Valentina	Muzaric	CRO	23.7.92	2	NCAA	Albuquerque	15 Mar
17.86	Melissa	Boekelman	NED	11.5.89	1		Sint-Niklaas	29 May
17.85	Rebecca	O'Brien	USA	30.4.90	4		Chula Vista	31 Jul
17.84	Lena	Urbaniak	GER	31.10.92	2	NC	Ulm	25 Jul
	(30)							
17.77	Kelsey	Card	USA	20.8.92	4	NC	Sacramento	25 Jun
17.75	Shanice	Craft	GER	15.5.93	3	NC	Ulm	25 Jul
17.73	Geisa	Arcanjo	BRA	19.9.91	1		São Bernardo do Campo	23 Aug
17.71	Anastasiya	Bessoltseva	RUS	18.8.90	2		Yerino	8 Jun
17.71		Bian Ka	CHN	5.1.93	3	NC	Suzhou	12 Oct
17.70	Úrsula	Ruiz	ESP	11.8.83	1		Salamanca	12 Jun
17.69i	Josephine	Terlecki	GER	17.2.86	2		Rochlitz	2 Feb
17.66		Meng Qianqian	CHN	6.1.91	3	NGP	Kunshan	30 May
17.63	Ahymara	Espinoza	VEN	28.5.85	2	SAmG	Santiago de Chile	16 Mar
17.62	Jill	Rushin	USA	18.7.91	2		Columbia MO	3 May
	(40)							
17.60	Tremanisha	Taylor	USA	10.3.92	1	PennR	Philadelphia	24 Apr
17.58	Julie	Labonté	CAN	12.1.90	3	CG	Glasgow	30 Jul
17.58	Keely	Medeiros	BRA	30.4.87	1	NC	São Paulo	12 Oct
17.52		Gao Yang	CHN	1.3.93	3	NGPF	Jinan	13 Jul
17.52		Lee Mi-young	KOR	19.8.79	1		Yeosu	15 Jul
17.50	Sandra	Lemus	COL	1.1.89	3	CAG	Xalapa	27 Nov
17.49	Jessica	Ramsey	USA	26.7.91	1		Bowling Green	12 Apr
17.48	Irina	Kirichenko	RUS	18.5.87	1		Adler	30 May
17.48	Tori	Bliss	USA	1.12.92	2	NCAA	Eugene	14 Jun
17.48		Lin Chia-Ying	TPE	5.11.82	4	AsiG	Incheon	27 Sep
	(50)							
17.45	Kyla	Buckley	USA	22.3.91	Q	NC	Sacramento	25 Jun
17.40i	Emel	Dereli	TUR-J	25.2.96	1	NC-j	Istanbul	1 Feb
17.39	Dani	Bunch	USA	16.5.91	1q	NCAA-E	Jacksonville	31 May
17.33	Jessica	Cérival	FRA	20.1.82	5	ET	Braunschweig	22 Jun
17.32	Assunta	Legnante	ITA	14.5.78	4		Padova	6 Jul
17.30i	Mary	Theisen	USA	3.11.90	2		Bloomington	1 Feb
17.30	Valeriya	Zyryanova	RUS	12.8.90	2	NCp	Yerino	10 Jul
17.29	Anna	Omarova	RUS	3.10.81	1		Krasnodar	6 Jun
17.28	Raven	Saunders	USA-J	15.5.96	1		Columbia SC	12 Apr
17.26	Casandra	Wertman	USA	14.6.93	2q	NCAA-E	Jacksonville	31 May
	(60)							
17.22i	Whitney	Ashley	USA	18.2.89	2		Seattle	1 Feb
17.21	Saily	Viart	CUB-J	10.9.95	4	CAG	Xalapa	27 Nov
17.20	Agnieszka	Maluskiewicz	POL	18.3.89	1		Leszno	28 Aug
17.18i	Amber	Monroe	USA	14.10.93	1	ACC	Clemson	1 Mar
17.18	Claire	Uke	USA	31.12.92	1	Conf USA	Houston	18 May
17.18	Ányela	Rivas	COL	13.8.89	2		Medellín	31 May
17.17i	Alyssa	Hasslen	USA	13.5.91	1		Seattle	1 Mar
17.17	Yanina	Provalinskaya-Korolchyk	BLR	26.12.76	3		Min	
17.15	Annie	Alexander	TTO	28.8.87	1		Myrtle Beach	22 Mar
17.10	Olesya	Sviridova	RUS	28.10.89	3	NCp	Yerino	10 Jul
	(70)							
17.09	Jana	Kárníková	CZE	14.2.81	1		Kolín	7 Sep
17.07	Eden	Francis	GBR	19.10.88	1		Nuneaton	17 May
17.07	Brittany	Mann	USA	16.4.94	7	NCAA	Eugene	14 Jun
17.06i	Anna	Wloka	POL	14.3.93	1		Spala	2 Feb
17.05	Dani	Samuels	AUS	26.5.88	1		Sydney	2 Mar
17.03i	Kayla	Kovar	USA	11.8.91	1		Albuquerque	15 Feb
17.01	Nia	Henderson	USA	21.10.86	1		Adrian	12 Apr
16.98i	Sarah	Howard	USA	11.10.93	1		Chapel Hill	22 Feb
16.97i	Danniel	Thomas	JAM	11.11.92	1		Kent	22 Feb
16.96	Olga	Sidorina	RUS	23.8.92	1	Mosc-23	Moskva	9 Jun
	(80)							
16.95	Sofiya	Burkhanova	UZB	1.12.89	5	AsiG	Incheon	27 Sep
16.94	Alyona	Bugakova	RUS-Y	24.4.97	1	Kuts	Moskva	17 Jul
16.92i	Natalya	Troneva	RUS	24.2.93	6	NC	Moskva	18 Feb
16.92i	Joh'vonnie	Mosley	USA	24.5.92	2		Kent	22 Feb
16.92i	Anna	Jelmini	USA	15.7.90	2		Seattle	1 Mar
16.91i	Viktoriya	Kolb	BLR	26.10.93	6	NC	Mogilyov	21 Feb
16.84	Auriole	Dongmo	CMR	3.8.90	1	AfCh	Marrakech	14 Aug

Mark	Wind	Name		Nat	Born	Pos	Meet	Venue	Date
16.83		Sara	Gambetta	GER	18.2.93	4	Werfer	Halle	17 May
16.83		Rachel	Wallader	GBR	1.9.89	4	CG	Glasgow	30 Jul
16.78i		Paulina	Guba	POL	14.5.91	2	NC	Sopot	23 Feb
		(90)							
16.76		Annie	Jackson	USA	11.3.90	3	Big 10	West Lafayette	17 May
16.75i		Agnieszka	Dudzinska	POL	16.3.88	1		Spala	8 Feb
16.73i		Jessica	Maroszek	USA	26.2.92	1		Lawrence	6 Dec
16.72		Frida	Åkerström	SWE	29.11.90	1		Ashland	14 Jun
16.70i		Danielle	Frere	USA	27.4.90	1		Nampa	15 Feb
16.69i		Trine	Mulbjerg	DEN	23.4.90	1	NC	Skive	23 Feb
16.68		Yevgeniya	Smirnova	RUS	16.3.91	2		Adler	24 Apr
16.68		Aaliyah	Pete	USA-J	15.3.95	6q	NCAA-W	Fayetteville	29 May
16.64i		Monique	Riddick	USA	8.11.89	1		West Long Branch	8 Feb
16.60			Geng Shuang	CHN	9.7.93	5	NGPF	Jinan	13 Jul
		(100)							

Mark	Name		Nat	Born	Date
16.59	Sophie	McKinna	GBR	31.8.94	30 Jul
16.59	Brittany	Crew	CAN	3.6.94	9 Aug
16.57i	Maggie	Ewen	USA	23.9.94	23 Feb
16.57	Fabienne	Digard	FRA	2.2.91	11 Jun
16.56		Dong Yangzi	CHN	22.10.92	12 Oct
16.55	Denise	Hinrichs	GER	7.6.87	17 May
16.53	Emily	Morris	USA		31 May
16.53	Maria	Sløk Hansen	DEN	8.6.83	8 Jun
16.51	Yiliena	Otamendi	CUB-J	12.4.96	7 Mar
16.51	Rachel	Dincoff	USA	24.12.93	17 May
16.51	Yekaterina	Burmistrova	RUS	18.8.90	30 May
16.50		Xu Jiaqi	CHN-J	3.2.95	12 Jun
16.48	Taryn	Suttie	CAN	7.12.90	27 Jun
16.46	Kätlin	Piirimäe	EST-J	8.11.95	16 May
16.46	Jamie	Sindelar	USA		24 May
16.44	Megan	Smith	USA	31.3.93	17 May
16.42	Yana	Pogodicheva	RUS	28.1.93	14 Jul
16.42	Kirsty	Yates	GBR	14.5.93	30 Jul
16.41i	Ashlie	Blake	USA-J	7.6.96	15 Mar
16.40	Chelsea	Whalen	CAN	18.10.92	28 Mar
16.40	Chinwe	Okoro	NGR	20.6.89	14 Aug
16.39	Stamatia	Scarvelis	USA-J	17.8.95	1 May
16.39	Manpreet	Kaur	IND	6.7.90	2 Nov
16.38	Itohan	Aikhonbare	USA	29.3.94	3 May
16.38	Izabela	da Silva	BRA-J	2.8.95	29 Jun
16.35i	Tiffany	Okieme	USA	8.1.94	2 Mar
16.33	Yelena	Smolyanova	UZB	16.2.86	8 Jun
16.32i	Vera	Kunova	RUS	2.4.90	18 Feb
16.30	Renata	Severiano	BRA	2.6.90	23 Aug
16.30	Julaika	Nicoletti	ITA	20.3.88	2 Sep
16.29i	DeAnna	Price	USA	8.6.93	11 Jan
16.29i	Mychelle	Cumings	USA	11.5.93	1 Mar
16.29	Klaudia	Kardasz	POL-J	2.5.96	25 Jul
16.29	Fanny	Roos	SWE-J	2.1.95	25 Jul
16.25	Evaggelía	Sofáni	GRE	28.1.85	17 May
16.24	Yelena	Bezruchenko	RUS-J	23.7.96	25 Jul
16.22	Ashley	Gaston	USA	1.1.93	26 Apr
16.22	Carlie	Pinkelman	USA	21.11.91	29 May
16.21	Magdalena	Zebrowska	POL	11.1.91	28 Aug
16.20i	Alexis	Cooks	USA	11.9.93	15 Feb
16.20		Wang Xiaoyun	CHN	7.12.93	13 Jul
16.20	Claire	Fitzgerald	IRL	12.9.91	20 Jul
16.20		Cai Yilin	CHN	27.11.90	27 Aug
16.20	Ivanna	Gallardo	CHI	20.7.93	4 Oct
16.19i	Chioma	Amaechi	USA	2.3.92	1 Mar
16.16	Jessica	Sharbono	USA	14.2.92	5 Apr
16.15	Lezaan	Jordaan	RSA-J	17.10.95	25 Jul
16.14i		Xu Yang	CHN	22.4.91	9 Mar
16.13	Chioma	Onyekwere	USA	28.6.94	31 May
16.12	Michelle	Anumba	USA	18.9.91	18 Apr
16.12	Jolien	Boumkwo	BEL	27.8.93	29 May
16.11i	Kim	Fortney	USA	15.8.91	1 Feb
16.11	Candicea	Bernard	JAM	8.11.91	31 May
16.10i	Anika	Nehls	GER-Y	15.4.97	15 Feb
16.10	Annastasia	Muchkaev	ISR	18.7.91	17 May
16.10	Rachel	Fatherly	USA	20.4.94	31 May
16.10	Laura	Jokeit	GER-J	16.8.95	5 Jul
16.07	Margo	Britton	USA	21.9.93	4 May
16.05	Rachel	Roberts	USA	25.5.91	16 May
16.05	Nikki	Okwelogu	NGR-J	5.5.95	31 May
16.04	Lakitta	Johnson	USA	26.11.91	28 Mar
16.03		Wei Linying	CHN-Y	.97	30 Jul
16.02i	Baillie	Gibson	USA	18.11.91	25 Jan
16.01i	Kellion	Knibb	JAM	25.12.93	25 Jan
16.01	Jasmine	Burrell	USA	27.2.92	29 Mar
16.01	Florentia	Kappa	CYP	29.5.88	18 May
16.00	Liberty	Slinden	USA	26.8.90	4 May
16.00	Hayli	Bozarth	USA	10.6.91	17 May
15.99i	Rayann	Chin	CAN	3.4.93	1 Mar
15.99	Aslynn	Halvorson	USA	15.3.91	17 May
15.98	Omotayo	Talabi	NGR	11.8.92	24 May
15.97	Andreea	Huzum-Vitan	ROU	15.4.93	27 Apr
15.97	Hélèna	Perez	FRA	13.9.91	4 May
15.96	Katie	Evans	USA	7.9.90	17 May
15.96	Shaunagh	Brown	GBR	15.3.90	18 May
15.95	Sara	Wells	USA	11.8.92	12 Apr
15.93i	Megan	Patterson	USA	14.1.94	1 Mar
15.93	Alex	Hartig	USA	5.9.91	26 Apr
15.93	Eleanor	Gatrell	GBR	5.10.76	17 May
15.93	Dani	Winters	USA	18.2.93	17 May
15.93i	Chase	Ealey	USA	20.7.94	13 Dec
15.91	Sonia	Smuts	RSA	5.10.91	12 Apr
15.91	Alexus	Scott	USA	18.11.93	29 May
15.91		Lee Su-jung	KOR	15.2.93	30 Oct
15.90	Raqurra	Ishmar	USA	3.2.93	18 May
15.90	Sophie	Kleeberg	GER	30.5.90	25 Jul
	(186)				

Best outdoor marks

Mark	Name	Pos	Meet	Venue	Date
17.86	McCall	7		Marrakech	8 Jun
17.73	Hillman	1	NCAA	Eugene	14 Jun
17.72	Yepimashko	1		Minsk	7 Jun
17.54	Terlecki	2		Schönebeck	27 Jun
17.33	Dereli	1	ECp-w23	Leiria	15 Mar
17.20	Theisen	6	NCAA	Eugene	14 Jun
17.16	Hasslen	5		La Jolla	26 Apr
17.08	Muzaric	6		La Jolla	26 Apr
17.00	Ashley	5	Spitzen	Luzern	15 Jul
16.88	Troneva	2		Krasnodar	6 Jun
16.82	D Thomas	1		Athens OH	16 May
16.81	Kolb	3	ECp-w23	Leiria	15 Mar
16.79	Mosley	1		Akron	10 May
16.70	Guba	1	NC	Szczecin	29 Jul

Mark	Name	Date
16.51	Riddick	24 May
16.49	S Howard	31 May
16.43	Wloka	23 Aug
16.37	Mulbjerg	29 Jun
16.32	Kovar	8 Mar
16.31	Kunova	30 May
16.25	Frere	2 May
16.23	Maroszek	28 Mar
16.14	Monroe	18 Apr
16.13	Amaechi	12 Apr
16.12	Xu Yang	12 Oct
15.98	Jelmini	26 Apr
15.96	Cooks	10 May
15.93	Cumings	1 May
15.90	Ewen	24 May

Drugs disqualification: 18.88 Anca Heltne ¶ ROU 1.1.78 1 NC Bucuresti 15 Feb

JUNIORS

See main list for top 6 juniors. 12 performances (2 indoors) by 2 women to 17.30. Additional marks and further juniors:

Name	Mark	Pos	Meet	Venue	Date	Mark	Pos	Meet	Venue	Date
Guo Tianqian	17.84	2		Kunshan	30 May	17.52	3	AsiG	Incheon	27 Sep
	17.79	2	NC	Suzghou	12 Oct	17.51	1	NC-j	Lishui	22 Jun

WOMEN 2014

Mark	Wind			Name	Nat	Born	Pos	Meet	Venue		Date
Gao	17.71	1	WJ	Eugene	25 Jul	17.40	2		Zhaoqing		19 Apr
	17.58	6	WCM	Beijing	21 May	17.35	1		Juinan		10 May
Dereli 2+	17.40i	1	NC-j	Istanbul	1 Feb						
16.51	Yiliena			Otamendi	CUB	12.4.96	3		La Habana		7 Mar
16.50				Xu Jiaqi	CHN	3.2.95	1	Asi-J	Taipei		12 Jun
16.46	Kätlin			Piirimäe	EST	8.11.95	1J		Tallinn		16 May
16.41i	Ashlie			Blake (10)	USA	7.6.96	2	N.Sch	New York (Arm)		15 Mar
16.39	Stamatia			Scarvelis	USA	17.8.95	1		Goleta		1 May
16.38	Izabela			da Silva	BRA	2.8.95	1	NC-j	Maringá		29 Jun
16.29	Klaudia			Kardasz	POL	2.5.96	5	WJ	Eugene		25 Jul
16.29	Fanny			Roos	SWE	2.1.95	6	WJ	Eugene		25 Jul
16.24	Yelena			Bezruchenko	RUS	23.7.96	7	WJ	Eugene		25 Jul
16.15	Lezaan			Jordaan	RSA	17.10.95	8	WJ	Eugene		25 Jul
16.10i	Anika			Nehls	GER-Y	15.4.97	1	NC-j	Sindelfingen		15 Feb
16.10	Laura			Jokeit	GER	16.8.95	1		Mannheim		5 Jul
16.05	Nikki			Okwelogu	NGR	5.5.95	16q	NCAA-E	Jacksonville		31 May
16.03				Wei Linying (20)	CHN-Y	.97	1		Shanghai		30 Jul

DISCUS

Mark	Wind			Name	Nat	Born	Pos	Meet	Venue		Date
71.08	Sandra			Perkovic	CRO	21.6.90	1	EC	Zürich		16 Aug
						64.58	67.37	68.78	x	71.08	x
	70.52	1	DL	Shanghai	18 May	x	69.93	66.32	69.89	70.52	x
	70.51	1		Split	1 Mar	69.96	x	65.19	70.51	x	x
	69.32	1	Pre	Eugene	30 May	65.77	63.33	x	x	67.07	69.32
	68.48	1	DL	Saint-Denis	5 Jul	x	63.93	x	x	63.43	68.48
	68.36	1	WK	Zürich	28 Aug	65.57	x	67.32	67.54	x	68.36
	67.17	1	Bisl	Oslo	11 Jun	x	67.17	63.59	67.14	66.64	65.80
	66.74	1	DNG	Stockholm	21 Aug	58.54	x	66.27	66.74	65.60	x
	66.30	2	DL	Glasgow	11 Jul	62.31	64.14	64.32	65.63	60.79	66.30
69.17	Gia			Lewis-Smallwood	USA	1.4.79	1	Déca	Angers		30 Aug
						63.80	x	69.17	x		
	67.59	1	DL	Glasgow	11 Jul	61.59	65.24	64.20	67.59	64.69	64.44
	67.32	2	WK	Zürich	28 Aug	64.25	67.32	62.18	63.41	66.52	64.54
	65.96	1	NC	Sacramento	29 Jun	58.24	61.55	65.96	65.42	x	64.19
	65.77	2	Bisl	Oslo	11 Jun	59.49	x	63.97	x	65.77	x
	65.59	3	DL	Saint-Denis	5 Jul	65.59	60.53	63.70	63.17	60.16	x
67.99	Dani			Samuels	AUS	26.5.88	1	Werfer	Wiesbaden		10 May
						x	x	67.41	67.71	67.99	62.51
	67.89	2	DL	Shanghai	18 May	63.42	63.93	64.21	67.89	x	67.88
	67.40	2	DL	Saint-Denis	5 Jul	63.77	66.74	65.38	64.43	x	67.40
	66.81	1	NC	Melbourne	6 Apr	61.23	x	65.15	x	63.03	66.81
	65.70	2	DNG	Stockholm	21 Aug	63.15	63.46	63.50	65.70	x	64.70
	65.59	1		Sydney	1 Mar	65.59	59.61	61.00	60.03	x	x
67.30	Nadine			Müller	GER	21.11.85	1	Werfer	Halle		17 May
						67.30	x	61.76	61.73	67.26	x
66.46	Julia			Fischer	GER	1.4.90	2	Werfer	Wiesbaden		10 May
						63.71	66.46	63.74	64.70	x	63.21
66.03	Yaimi			Pérez	CUB	29.5.91	1	Barr	La Habana		23 May
						66.03	62.15	x	61.26	65.68	x
65.88	Shanice			Craft	GER	15.5.93	1	NC	Ulm		26 Jul
						64.43	x	61.75	61.74	x	65.88
	65.38	2	Pre	Eugene	30 May	x	65.38	x	x	64.98	62.15
65.83	Zinaida			Sendriute	LTU	20.12.84	1	ET-1	Tallinn		21 Jun
						56.12	x	56.32	65.83		
65.78	Yekaterina			Strokova	RUS	17.12.89	1		Moskva		10 May
						x	x	60.54	62.84	65.78	62.43
65.51	Mélina			Robert-Michon	FRA	18.7.79	1	ET	Braunschweig		21 Jun
						x	65.51	61.71	63.65		
	65.33	2	WK	Zürich	28 Aug	55.08	62.96	59.05	65.33	x	62.18
	(30/10)										
64.89	Denia			Caballero	CUB	13.1.90	3	Bisl	Oslo		11 Jun
64.17	Anna			Rüh	GER	17.6.93	4		Wiesbaden		10 May
64.01	Fernanda Raquel			Borges	BRA	26.7.88	1		Chula Vista		15 May
63.78	Whitney			Ashley	USA	18.2.89	1		La Jolla		25 Apr
63.60	Shelbi			Vaughan	USA	24.8.94	1	SEC	Lexington		18 May
63.39	Yuliya			Maltseva	RUS	30.11.90	1	Mosc Ch	Moskva		3 Jul
63.33	Nataliya			Semenova	UKR	7.7.82	1	NC	Kirovohrad		25 Jul
63.31				Yang Yanbo	CHN	9.3.90	1	MSR	Walnut		18 Apr
62.23	Irina			Rodrigues	POR	5.2.91	1		Leiria		25 Jun
62.21	Rocío			Comba	ARG	14.7.87	1		Buenos Aires		8 Feb
	(20)										

Mark	Wind	Name		Nat	Born	Pos	Meet	Venue	Date
62.12		Yarisley	Collado	CUB	30.4.85	2		La Habana	8 Mar
61.61		Seema	Punia	IND	27.7.83	2	CG	Glasgow	1 Aug
61.38		Liz	Podominick	USA	5.12.84	2		Chula Vista	17 May
61.34		Kellion	Knibb	JAM	25.12.93	1q	NCAA-E	Jacksonville	30 May
61.31			Su Xinyue	CHN	8.11.91	1	NGP	Zhaoqing	19 Apr
61.07			Tan Jian	CHN	20.1.88	1	NC	Suzhou	11 Oct
60.96		Dragana	Tomasevic	SRB	4.6.82	1	NC	Novi Sad	12 Jul
60.95		Zaneta	Glanc	POL	11.3.83	1	Sidlo	Sopot	20 Jul
60.94		Sanna	Kämäräinen	FIN	8.2.86	1	vSWE	Helsinki	31 Aug
60.89		Kristin	Pudenz	GER	9.2.93	5	Werfer	Halle	17 May
		(30)							
60.78			Gu Siyu	CHN	11.2.93	1		Jinan	11 May
60.68			Lu Xiaoxin	CHN	22.2.89	2		Zeulenroda	30 May
60.48		Jade	Lally	GBR	30.3.87	3	CG	Glasgow	1 Aug
60.39		Beth	Rohl	USA	7.11.90	3		Mesa	11 Apr
60.35		Sabine	Rumpf	GER	18.3.83	5		Wiesbaden	10 May
60.18		Jessica	Maroszek	USA	26.2.92	1	Big 12	Lubbock	18 May
59.89		Karen	Gallardo	CHI	6.3.84	2	SAmGP	Buenos Aires	18 Jul
59.88		Joanna	Wisniewska	POL	24.5.72	2		Cetniewo	26 Jul
59.79		Chinwe	Okoro	NGR	20.6.89	1	AfCh	Marrakech	12 Aug
59.73			Feng Bin	CHN	3.4.94	1	NGPF	Jinan	12 Jul
		(40)							
59.67		Rachel	Longfors	USA	6.6.83	1		Tucson	22 May
59.65		Siositina	Hakeai	NZL	1.3.94	1		Hamilton	8 Feb
59.65		Andressa	de Morais	BRA	21.12.90	1		São Paulo	14 Jun
59.61		Suzanne	Kragbé	CIV	22.12.81	6		Tomblaine	27 Jun
59.38		Danniel	Thomas	JAM	11.11.92	1		Akron	10 May
59.34		Eliska	Stanková	CZE	11.11.84	1		Kladno	22 Jul
59.33		Stephanie	Brown Trafton	USA	1.12.79	3		Tucson	22 May
59.32		Heike	Koderisch	GER	27.5.85	5		Rehlingen	9 Jun
59.27		Anita	Márton	HUN	15.1.89	1		Szeged	7 Sep
59.20			Yang Fei	CHN	20.7.87	4	NC	Suzhou	11 Oct
		(50)							
59.17		Krishna	Poonia	IND	5.5.82	2		Lisle	12 Jul
59.06		Rachel	Varner	USA	20.7.83	1		Claremont	11 May
59.03		Anastasiya	Kashtonova	BLR	14.1.89	1	NCp	Brest	31 May
58.94		Kelsey	Card	USA	20.8.92	1		Madison	10 May
58.92		Karolina	Makul	POL	23.8.94	3	NC	Szczecin	31 Jul
58.89			Weng Chunxia	CHN	29.8.92	4	NGP	Zhaoqing	19 Apr
58.86A		Jessica	Sharbono	USA	14.2.92	1		Laramie	16 May
58.74		Alexis	Cooks	USA	11.9.93	2q	NCAA-E	Jacksonville	30 May
58.70		Izabela	da Silva	BRA-J	2.8.95	1	SAm23	Montevideo	3 Oct
58.62		Summer	Pierson	USA	3.9.78	4		Tucson	24 May
		(60)							
58.53			Chen Yang	CHN	10.7.91	6	NC	Suzhou	11 Oct
58.38		Jitka	Kubelová	CZE	2.10.91	1		Praha	9 May
58.31		Sabina	Asenjo	ESP	3.8.86	1		León	9 Jul
58.25			Jiang Fengjing	CHN	28.8.87	7	NC	Suzhou	11 Oct
58.24		Taryn	Gollshewsky	AUS	18.5.93	3q	CG	Glasgow	31 Jul
58.13		Svetlana	Saykina	RUS	10.7.85	2	NC	Kazan	24 Jul
57.97		Jaleesa	Williams	USA	6.4.91	3q	NCAA-E	Jacksonville	30 May
57.76		Jeré	Summers	USA	21.5.87	1	Jordan	Stanford	4 May
57.64A		Elizna	Naude	RSA	14.9.78	1		Sasolburg	25 Mar
57.58		Sofia	Larsson	SWE	22.7.88	1	NC	Umeå	1 Aug
		(70)							
57.54			Liang Yan	CHN-J	2.1.95	1	Univ Ch	Beijing	26 Aug
57.45		Valarie	Allman	USA-J	23.2.95	1	NC-j	Eugene	6 Jul
57.44		Katri	Hirvonen	FIN	25.6.90	1		Faro	10 May
57.37			Li Tsai-Yi	TPE	3.12.89	8		Tucson	22 May
57.36		Marike	Steinacker	GER	4.3.92	2cB		Wiesbaden	10 May
57.32		Tera	Novy	USA	10.2.94	1		Claremont	7 Jun
57.32		Valentina	Aniballi	ITA	19.4.84	1		Tarquinia	11 Jun
57.31		Kearsten	Peoples	USA	20.12.91	1		Emporia	23 Apr
57.20		Hrisoúla	Anagnostopoúlou	GRE	27.8.91	1	Veniz	Haniá	7 Jun
57.17		Viktoriya	Klochko	UKR	2.9.92	2	NC	Kirovohrad	25 Jul
		(80)							
57.15		Alex	Collatz	USA	25.5.93	1		Los Angeles	8 Mar
57.15		Kirsty	Law	GBR	11.10.86	1		Loughborough	12 Apr
57.15		Pauline	Pousse	FRA	17.9.87	1		Marseille	31 May
56.98		Claudine	Vita	GER-J	19.9.96	1-J		Wiesbaden	10 May
56.95A		Maryke	Oberholzer	RSA	27.11.89	1	NC	Pretoria	12 Apr

Mark	Wind	Name		Nat	Born	Pos	Meet	Venue	Date
56.85		Subenrat	Insaeng	THA	10.2.94	1		Palembang	15 Dec
56.84		Julie	Labonté	CAN	12.1.90	1		Tempe	29 Mar
56.80		Julia	Bremser	GER	27.4.82	1		Frankenberg	20 Jul
56.79		Christie	Chamberlain	AUS	9.6.89	1		Adelaide	15 Feb
56.77		Lidia Milena	Cansian	BRA	8.1.92	2	SAm23	Montevideo	3 Oct
		(90)							
56.69		Androniki	Lada	CYP	19.4.91	1		Limassol	25 Mar
56.55		Olha	Abramchuk	UKR	12.4.91	2		Kyiv	4 Jun
56.54		Laura	Bordignon	ITA	26.3.81	2		Tarquinia	11 Jun
56.54		Andzelika	Przybylska	POL	14.10.92	4	NC	Szczecin	31 Jul
56.37		Annie	Alexander	TTO	28.8.87	2		Tempe	29 Mar
56.37		Julia	Viberg	SWE	8.1.92	2	NC	Umeå	1 Aug
56.36		Navjeet	Kaur Dhillon	IND-J	6.3.95	3	WJ	Eugene	25 Jul
56.29		Eden	Francis	GBR	19.10.88	1		Nuneaton	17 May
56.29		Laura	Bobek	USA	16.2.91	3	NCAA	Eugene	12 Jun
56.27		Anna	Jelmini	USA	15.7.90	8		La Jolla	25 Apr
		(100)							

Mark	Name		Nat	Born	Date
56.27A	Johana	Martínez	COL	9.9.86	26 Nov
56.24	Becky	Famurewa	USA	24.2.94	30 May
56.23	Sam	Lockhart	USA	25.8.91	10 May
56.10	Tatyana	Zhuravlyova	RUS	27.5.89	23 May
56.10	Grete	Etholm	NOR	25.1.76	30 Jul
56.09	Annelies	Peetroons	BEL	4.5.87	13 Jul
55.87	Mélanie	Pingeon	FRA	4.11.86	18 May
55.84	Rachel	Andres	CAN	21.4.87	13 Jul
55.79		Xie Yuchen	CHN-J	12.5.96	12 Jul
55.66	June	Kintana	ESP-J	12.4.95	14 Jun
55.42	Megan	Smith	USA	31.3.93	30 May
55.35	Jasmine	Burrell	USA	27.2.92	7 Jun
55.31	Heidi	Schmidt	SWE	13.11.93	31 Aug
55.29	Emily	Pendleton	USA	16.4.89	26 Apr
55.29	Ulrike	Giesa	GER	16.8.84	26 Jul
55.26	Anna	Salvini	ITA	9.7.78	4 May
55.15	Alix	Kennedy	AUS	22.1.92	15 Feb
55.07	Maggie	Ewen	USA	23.9.94	24 May
55.07	Stefania	Strumillo	ITA	14.10.89	11 Jun
54.98	Sequoia	Watkins	USA	12.9.92	30 May
54.91A	Tara-Sue	Barnett	JAM	9.10.93	16 Aug
54.90	Hannah	Carson	USA	26.1.93	12 Apr
54.84	Alex	Hartig	USA	5.9.91	18 May
54.82	Malgorzata	Raciborska	POL	23.9.91	31 May
54.80	Tetyana	Yuryeva	UKR-J	21.1.95	4 Jun
54.79	Amber	Monroe	USA	14.10.93	30 May
54.74	Kiana	Phelps	USA-Y	22.7.97	8 May
54.74	Te Rina	Keenan	NZL	29.9.90	3 Dec
54.71A	Kiah	Hicks	USA	21.2.93	12 Apr
54.64	Devene	Brown	JAM	16.3.93	5 Apr
54.58	Daria	Zabawska	POL-J	16.4.95	21 Sep
54.57	Alena	Kopets	BLR	14.2.88	26 Apr
54.56	Tremanisha	Taylor	USA	10.3.92	28 Mar
54.44	Ieva	Zarankaite	LTU	23.11.94	18 May
54.41	Madison	Jacobs	USA-J	2.8.95	30 May
54.38	Salla	Sipponen	FIN-J	13.3.95	12 Jul
54.35	Mary	Theisen	USA	3.11.90	30 May
54.30	Julie	Hartwig	GER	30.6.94	10 May
54.27	Kayla	Kovar	USA	11.8.91	29 Mar
54.22	Ayumi	Takahashi	JPN	31.8.89	1 Jun
54.10	Rebecca	Hammar	USA	28.1.93	18 May
54.10	Yekaterina	Burmistrova	RUS	18.8.90	3 Jul
53.95	Ashley	Gaston	USA	1.1.93	18 May
53.92	Filoi	Aokuso	AUS-J	26.12.95	25 Jul
53.91	Rachel	Polk	USA	19.10.92	15 Mar
53.89	Andrea	Hiler	USA		30 May
53.89	Katrine	Bebe	DEN	27.1.91	6 Sep
53.84	Jessica	Ramsey	USA	26.7.91	26 Apr
53.78A	Aaliyah	Pete	USA-J	15.3.95	16 May
53.74	Viktoriya	Savytska	UKR	18.6.94	25 Jul
53.66	Natalina	Capoferri	ITA	6.11.92	6 Apr
53.66	Irène	Donzelot	FRA	8.12.88	2 Jul
53.63		Kim Min	KOR	9.4.86	15 Jul
53.63	Tanja	Komulainen	FIN	2.3.80	24 Jul
53.58	Skylar	White	USA	15.9.91	3 May
53.54	Veronika	Domjan	SLO-J	3.9.96	1 Mar
53.54	Annastasia	Muchkaev	ISR	18.7.91	3 May
	(157)				

JUNIORS

See main list for top 5 juniors. 10 performances by 4 women to 56.46. Additional marks and further juniors:

Name	Mark	Pos	Meet	Venue	Date	Mark	Pos	Meet	Venue	Date
da Silva	58.03	1	WJ	Eugene	25 Jul					
Liang Jan	56.51	2		Kunshan	30 May					
Allman	57.17	1		Berkeley	8 Mar	56.75	2	WJ	Eugene	25 Jul
Vita	56.80	1J	Werfer	Halle	17 May	56.46	1	NC-j	Wattenscheid	9 Aug

Mark	Name		Nat	Born	Pos	Meet	Venue	Date
55.79		Xie Yuchen	CHN	12.5.96	9	NGPF	Jinan	12 Jul
55.66	June	Kintana	ESP	12.4.95	2		León	14 Jun
54.80	Tetyana	Yuryeva	UKR	21.1.95	4		Kyiv	4 Jun
54.74	Kiana	Phelps	USA-Y	22.7.97	1		Kingsley	8 May
54.58	Daria	Zabawska (10)	POL	16.4.95	1		Białystok	21 Sep
54.41	Madison	Jacobs	USA	2.8.95	8q	NCAA-E	Jacksonville	30 May
54.38	Salla	Sipponen	FIN	13.3.95	1		Joensuu	12 Jul
53.92	Filoi	Aokuso	AUS	26.12.95	7	WJ	Eugene	25 Jul
53.78A	Aaliyah	Pete	USA	15.3.95	3		Laramie	16 May
53.54	Veronika	Domjan	SLO	3.9.96	1	NC-wJ	Ptuj	1 Mar
53.39	Gleneve	Grange	JAM	6.7.95	1		Kingston	31 May
53.31	Nikki	Okwelogu	NGR	5.5.95	2	NC	Calabar	19 Jun
53.26	Katelyn	Daniels	USA	11.4.95	2	NC-j	Eugene	6 Jul
53.10		Liang Xingyun	CHN	4.6.96	3	NC-j	Lishui	21 Jun
53.04	Geraldine	Duvenage (20)	RSA	17.8.95	1		Stellenbosch	21 Apr

HAMMER

Mark	Name		Nat	Born	Pos	Meet	Venue	Date
79.58	Anita	Wlodarczyk	POL	8.8.85	1	ISTAF	Berlin	31 Aug

75.29 79.58 78.46 79.04 78.64 77.94

Mark	Pos	Meet	Venue	Date	Series					
78.76	1	EC	Zürich	15 Aug	x	x	75.88	76.18	78.76	x
78.17	1		Cetniewo	26 Jul	75.93	77.84	75.56	74.99	78.17	x

Mark	Wind	Name			Nat	Born	Pos	Meet	Venue		Date
A.WI	77.66	1	Skol	Warszawa	23 Aug	76.11	77.52	77.11	77.66	76.51	72.04
	76.41	2	GS	Ostrava	16 Jun	x	74.73	76.16	76.41	x	70.56
	75.85	1	NC	Szczecin	31 Jul	70.01	75.42	75.85	75.49	x	x
	75.73	Q	EC	Zürich	13 Aug	75.73		only throw			
	75.53	1	Gyulai	Székesfehérvár	8 Jul	62.35	68.97	x	73.62	74.70	75.53
	75.21	1	C.Cup	Marrakech	14 Sep	72.83	74.26	75.21	72.33		
78.00		Betty		Heidler	GER	14.10.83	1	GS	Ostrava		16 Jun
						72.80	75.97	x	75.27	78.00	73.09
	76.91	1		Fränkisch-Crumbach	8 Jun	72.31	73.86	74.53	75.10	72.90	76.91
	76.26	2	Skol	Warszawa	23 Aug	73.18	75.19	75.61	74.04	76.26	74.39
	75.34	2	Gyulai	Székesfehérvár	8 Jul	69.52	x	68.89	75.34	x	x
	75.20	2	ISTAF	Berlin	31 Aug	72.00	75.20	71.88	x	x	68.92
	74.63	1	ET	Braunschweig	22 Jun	72.22	73.80	74.63	73.94		
77.68				Wang Zheng	CHN	14.12.87	1		Chengdu		29 Mar
						71.03	75.93	77.68	x	76.33	74.28
	75.73	2		Fränkisch-Crumbach	8 Jun	71.07	73.21	75.73	x	72.85	73.86
	75.23	1	WCM	Beijing	21 May	69.74	72.40	75.23	74.71	67.22	72.85
	74.59	1		Xi'an	10 Apr						
75.73		Sultana		Frizell	CAN	24.10.84	1		Tucson		22 May
						69.96	67.78	x	71.89	74.10	75.73
	74.98	1	MSR	Walnut	19 Apr	71.00	73.23	74.98	72.00	71.72	72.14
75.50				Zhang Wenxiu ¶	CHN	22.3.86	3		Fränkisch-Crumbach		8 Jun
						75.30	74.25	x	71.64	71.25	75.50
	75.06	1	Werfer	Halle	17 May	73.45	71.63	74.55	75.06	74.69	73.52
	74.77	2		Chengdu	29 Mar	73.39	72.28	x	74.77	73.02	71.40
75.27		Martina		Hrasnová	SVK	21.3.83	1	NC	Banská Bystrica		12 Jul
						71.08	70.52	75.27	70.98	69.44	73.61
	74.66	2	EC	Zürich	15 Aug	71.66	x	73.03	69.72	74.66	73.21
75.12		Amanda		Bingson	USA	20.2.90	1		Las Vegas		21 Mar
						72.09	72.45	x	75.12	73.54	x
	75.07	1	NC	Sacramento	28 Jun	74.41	75.07	x	70.83	73.64	x
74.62		Kathrin		Klaas	GER	6.2.84	3	Gyulai	Székesfehérvár		8 Jul
						68.51	69.31	x	72.22	x	74.62
	74.61	3	GS	Ostrava	16 Jun	74.61	73.36	70.80	x	x	x
		(30/8)									
74.39		Joanna		Fiodorow	POL	4.3.89	2	Werfer	Halle		17 May
74.20		Jessica		Cosby Toruga	USA	31.5.82	3		Tucson		22 May
		(10)									
74.16		Anna		Bulgakova	RUS	17.1.88	1	NC-w	Krasnodar		23 Feb
73.65		Iryna		Novozhylova	UKR	7.1.86	1		Kyiv		21 May
73.61		Amber		Campbell	USA	5.6.81	1		Edmonton		6 Jul
73.06				Liu Tingting	CHN	29.10.90	4	Werfer	Halle		17 May
72.49		Éva		Orbán	HUN	29.11.84	2	ECp-w	Leiria		16 Mar
72.20		Rosa		Rodríguez	VEN	2.7.86	1		Barquisimeto		15 May
72.17		Oksana		Kondratyeva	RUS	22.11.85	1	Kuts	Moskva		17 Jul
72.04		Gwen		Berry	USA	29.6.89	1	PAm SF	Ciudad de México		15 Aug
71.93		Bianca		Perie	ROU	1.6.90	1	ET-1	Tallinn		22 Jun
71.89		Mariya		Bespalova	RUS	21.5.86	2	Mosc Ch	Moskva		11 Jun
		(20)									
71.66		Jenny		Dahlgren	ARG	27.8.84	1		Buenos Aires		1 Mar
71.58		Nikola		Lomnická	SVK	16.9.88	1		Marietta		8 Jun
71.56		Oksana		Menkova	BLR	28.3.82	1		Minsk		7 Jun
71.53		Sophie		Hitchon	GBR	11.7.91	5	Werfer	Halle		17 May
71.35		Yipsi		Moreno	CUB	19.11.80	1	CAG	Xalapa		24 Nov
71.17		Alexandra		Tavernier	FRA	13.12.93	1		Oyonnax		6 Jul
71.14		Anna		Skydan	UKR	14.5.92	1		Kyiv		7 May
71.07		Ariannis		Vichy	CUB	18.5.89	1	NC	La Habana		20 Mar
70.79		Katerina		Safránková	CZE	8.6.89	1		Kladno		17 May
70.78		Jeneva		McCall	USA	28.10.89	3	GP	Ponce		17 May
		(30)									
70.76		Carolin		Paesler	GER	16.12.90	2		Schönebeck		27 Jun
70.62		Tatyana		Lysenko	RUS	9.10.83	1		Adler		29 May
70.51		Tracey		Andersson	SWE	5.12.84	1		Göteborg		14 Jun
70.48		Silvia		Salis	ITA	17.9.85	1	NC-w	Lucca		22 Feb
70.46		Yurisleydi		Ford	CUB	18.8.91	1		La Habana		8 Oct
70.28		Julia		Ratcliffe	NZL	14.7.93	1		Princeton		19 Apr
70.27		Brittany		Smith	USA	25.3.91	1		Normal		3 May
70.18		Tereza		Králová	CZE	22.10.89	1		Lovosice		3 May
70.04		Natalya		Polyakova	RUS	9.12.90	2	Kuts	Moskva		17 Jul
69.92		Alena		Krechyk	BLR	20.7.87	2		Minsk		7 Jun
		(40)									

Mark	Wind	Name		Nat	Born	Pos	Meet	Venue	Date
69.81			Luo Na	CHN	8.10.93	4	WCM	Beijing	21 May
69.70		Britney	Henry	USA	17.10.84	4		Tucson	24 May
69.70		Amy	Sène	SEN	6.4.85	3		Forbach	25 May
69.33		Berta	Castells	ESP	24.1.84	1		Manresa	17 Jul
69.30		Malwina	Kopron	POL	16.11.94	1	ECp-w23	Leiria	16 Mar
69.23		Jessika	Guéhaseim	FRA	23.8.89	1		Taverny	25 Jun
69.13		Ida	Storm	SWE	26.12.91	1		Halmstad	12 Jul
69.10		Iryna	Sekachyova	UKR	21.7.76	6	WCM	Beijing	21 May
69.08		Barbara	Spiler	SLO	2.1.92	1	NC	Varazdin	12 Jul
69.01		Alena	Lysenko	RUS	3.2.88	4		Adler	29 May
		(50)							
68.96		Alena	Novogrodskaya	BLR	11.5.93	2		Brest	25 Apr
68.76		Yelena	Rigert	RUS	2.12.83	5	NCp	Yerino	9 Jul
68.44		Merja	Korpela	FIN	15.5.81	1		Kuortane	13 Jul
68.43		Alyona	Shamotina	UKR-J	27.12.95	1	NC-j	Kyiv	13 Jun
68.40		Kristin	Smith	USA	23.12.87	8	NC	Sacramento	28 Jun
68.30		Nina	Volkova	RUS	26.8.84	6	ECp-w	Leiria	16 Mar
68.14		Yelizaveta	Tsareva	RUS	15.3.93	9	Mosc Ch	Moskva	11 Jun
68.02		Taylor	Bush	USA	26.11.89	1		Tucson	12 Apr
67.97		Brooke	Pleger	USA	21.6.92	1		Toledo OH	9 May
67.77		Eli Johana	Moreno	COL	15.4.85	3	CAG	Xalapa	24 Nov
		(60)							
67.73		Alina	Kostrova	BLR	2.3.90	1		Minsk	12 Jun
67.67		Chelsea	Cassulo	USA	10.6.90	1		Tempe	22 Mar
67.57		Laura	Redondo	ESP	3.7.88	1	NC-w	León	1 Mar
67.53		Hanna	Zinchuk	BLR	4.2.94	2	NC	Grodno	24 Jul
67.46		Amy	Haapanen	USA	23.3.84	6		Tucson	22 May
67.43		Jillian	Weir	CAN	9.2.93	1	Pac 12	Pullman	18 May
67.32		Réka	Gyurátz	HUN-J	31.5.96	2	NC-w	Budapest	22 Feb
67.23		Anastasiya	Shatybelko	BLR	20.5.94	1		Minsk	18 Jul
67.04		Mariya	Smolyachkova	BLR	10.2.85	2		Minsk	18 Jul
66.93		Vânia	Silva	POR	8.6.80	1		Quinto do Anjo	8 Mar
		(70)							
66.92		Jolien	Boumkwo	BEL	27.8.93	1	NC	Nivelles	27 Jul
66.85		Shaunagh	Brown	GBR	15.3.90	2		Göteborg	14 Jun
66.80		Carys	Parry	GBR	24.7.81	2		Cardiff	15 Jul
66.73		Heather	Steacy	CAN	14.4.88	1		Calgary	31 May
66.65		Fruzsina	Fertig	HUN	2.9.93	1	Univ Ch	Budapest	24 May
66.46		Denise	Hinton	USA	17.12.91	1		Baton Rouge	3 May
66.42		Daniela	Manz	GER	19.9.86	1		Hamm	13 Jul
66.33		Brittany	Funk	USA	13.5.92	1		San Marcos	29 Mar
66.30		Rachel	Hunter	GBR	30.8.93	2	LI	Loughborough	18 May
66.29		Paraskevi	Theodorou	CYP	15.3.86	1		Athína (Kipséli)	1 Jun
		(80)							
66.24		Micaela	Mariani	ITA	11.2.88	1	NC	Rovereto	19 Jul
66.12		Jenni	Penttilä	FIN	9.3.91	1		Pudasjärvi	19 Jun
66.08		Kayla	Kovar	USA	11.8.91	8	MSR	Walnut	19 Apr
66.03		Elisa	Palmieri	ITA	18.9.83	2	NC	Rovereto	19 Jul
65.93		Sarah	Bensaad	TUN	27.1.87	1		Bobigny	27 Apr
65.92		Charlene	Woitha	GER	21.8.93	3		Schönebeck	27 Jun
65.77		Laëtitia	Bambara	BUR	30.3.84	3		Eaubonne	2 Jul
65.67		Sarah	Holt	GBR	17.4.87	4	CG	Glasgow	28 Jul
65.64		Eleni	Larsson	SWE	4.4.93	1	NC-23	Gävle	9 Aug
65.55		Karolina	Pedersen	SWE	16.4.87	3		Bottnaryd	29 May
		(90)							
65.34		Iliána	Korosídou	GRE-J	14.1.95	1		Thessaloníki	7 Jun
65.23		Génesis	Olivera	VEN	21.5.93	1	NC	Barquisimeto	26 Sep
65.19		Sara	Savatovic	SRB	5.1.93	1	TexR	Austin	27 Mar
65.16		Alexia	Sedykh	FRA	13.9.93	2	NC-23	Albi	28 Jun
65.07		Kati	Ojaloo	EST	31.1.90	1		Tallinn	20 May
65.05		Lauren	Stuart	CAN	16.11.91	2	NC	Moncton	29 Jun
65.00			Wang Lu	CHN	22.12.91	3	NGP	Zhaoqing	19 Apr
64.91		Emily	Hunsucker	USA	20.4.91	1		Boulder	21 Mar
64.80		Megann	Rodhe	CAN	27.8.85	1		Kamloops	20 Oct
64.79		Hayli	Bozarth	USA	10.6.91	1		Laramie	16 May
		(100)							
64.79		Zsófia	Bácskay	HUN-Y	18.3.97	2		Veszprém	8 Jun
64.79		Cintia	Gergelics	HUN	16.11.91	1		Szombathely	1 Oct

Mark	Name		Nat	Born	Date
64.45	Aline	Salut	FRA	30.7.92	4 Jun
64.44	Johanna	Salmela	FIN	6.11.90	12 Jun
64.42	Josefin	Berg	SWE	27.12.85	18 Jul
64.40		Dan Dongxue	CHN	23.3.92	11 Oct
64.36	Viktoriya	Sadova	RUS	18.3.93	16 Jul
64.28	Lisa	Wilson	USA	29.3.88	10 May

Mark	Wind	Name		Nat	Born	Pos	Meet	Venue	Date

Mark	First name	Name	Nat	Born	Date
64.24		Yan Ni	CHN	7.2.93	11 Jul
64.21	Susan	McKelvie	GBR	15.6.85	16 Aug
64.20	Lenka	Ledvinová	CZE	11.8.85	26 Jul
64.18	Elizabeth	Tepe	USA	31.10.87	15 May
64.14	Zlata	Tarasova	RUS	2.12.86	23 Apr
64.14	Crystal	Bourque	USA	7.1.89	13 Jul
64.12	Veronika	Kanuchová	SVK	19.4.93	1 Jun
64.11	Masumi	Aya	JPN	1.1.80	27 Apr
64.05	Heavin	Warner	USA	4.3.93	18 Apr
63.98	Gabrielle	Neighbour	AUS	22.11.83	11 Jul
63.94	Katarzyna	Furmanek	POL-J	19.2.96	18 Jun
63.79	Nicole	Zihlmann	SUI	30.7.86	15 Jul
63.78	Laura	Igaune	LAT	2.10.88	26 Apr
63.67	Beatrice	Nedberge Llano	NOR-Y	14.12.97	22 Jul
63.50	Kayla	Padgett	USA	.93	11 Apr
63.44	Mona	Holm Solberg	NOR	5.8.83	12 Jun
63.30	Audrey	Ciofani	FRA-J	13.3.96	23 Jul
63.27	Susen	Küster	GER	27.7.94	27 Jun
63.22	Annabelle	Rolnin	FRA	28.12.87	14 Jun
63.16	Carla	Michel	BRA	18.1.88	14 Sep
63.11	Lara	Nielsen	AUS	19.12.92	4 Apr
63.11	Myra	Perkins	GBR	21.1.92	18 May
63.05	Marte	Rygg Årdal	NOR	5.7.92	27 Jul
63.04	Galina	Mityaeva	TJK/CAN	29.4.91	27 Jul
63.01	Erin	Atkinson	USA	30.1.92	11 Jun
62.99	Rachel	Peña	USA/PUR	1.12.91	19 Apr
62.85	Kiah	Hicks	USA	21.2.93	16 May
62.84	Zuleima	Mina	ECU	5.6.90	1 Aug
62.82	Shelby	Ashe	USA	13.3.93	18 May
62.78	Zeliha	Uzunbilek	TUR	10.6.91	2 Mar
62.78	Daina	Levy	JAM	27.5.93	5 Apr
62.74	Carly	Fehringer	USA	9.11.91	12 Apr
62.74	Manju	Bala Singh	IND	1.7.89	7 Jun
62.65	Melissa	Kurzdorfer	USA	30.12.91	11 Jun
62.58		Xia Youlian	CHN	4.8.93	29 Mar
62.57	Valeria	Chiliquinga	ECU	27.2.92	1 Aug
62.55	Agápi	Proskinitopoúlou	GRE	3.9.93	10 May
62.49	Lauren	Chambers	USA	3.2.91	18 May
62.44	Wendy	Koolhaas	NED	2.1.80	27 Jul
62.43	Bianca	Lazar	ROU	24.2.93	19 Jul
62.39	Gabi	Wolfarth	GER	6.9.89	31 May
62.35	Odette	Palma	CHI	7.8.82	8 Mar
	63.21 ?				6 Jul
62.34	Sanni	Saarinen	FIN	29.12.94	24 Aug
62.30	Louisa	James	GBR	5.7.94	29 Jun
62.29	Veronica	Grizzle	USA	8.8.91	3 May
62.28	Jonna	Miettinen	FIN	7.12.90	2 Aug
62.25	Darya	Pchelnik	BLR	20.12.81	13 Feb
62.25	Chandra	Andrews	USA	4.9.83	10 May
62.24	Jade	Grace	USA	22.9.88	7 Jun
62.17	Irina	Sarvilova	RUS	11.11.91	17 Jul
62.16	Cynthia	Watt	USA	8.12.93	19 Apr
62.16	Gulfiya	Agafonova	RUS	4.6.82	23 Apr
62.16	Trude	Raad	NOR	27.4.90	13 Jun
62.11	Nia	Barnes	USA	25.9.93	29 May
62.05	Mariana	Marcelino	BRA	16.7.92	7 Sep
62.00	Francesca	Massobrio	ITA	9.7.93	6 Jun
61.97	Emma	Johannesson	SWE	16.1.84	22 May
61.97	Marinda	Petersson	SWE-J	3.2.95	22 Jul
61.83	Dagmara	Stala	POL	9.12.91	18 May
61.77	Kimberley	Reed	GBR-J	18.2.95	3 May
61.72		Wang Yingying	CHN	16.5.93	29 Mar
61.72	Venessa	Pfeifer	GER	26.7.94	8 Jun
61.69	Christina	Jones	GBR	5.4.90	7 Jun
61.63	Vanessa	Sterckendries	BEL-J	15.9.95	23 Jul
61.62	Jackie	Leppelmeier	USA	13.10.92	26 Apr
61.62	Victoria	Flowers	USA	17.1.90	27 Apr
61.57	Zouina	Bouzebra	ALG	3.10.90	10 May
61.55	Annie	Larose	CAN	16.2.89	27 Jul
61.52	Haruno	Chinen	JPN	14.4.90	19 Jul
61.51	Daramola	Feyisayo	NGR	19.1.80	12 Apr
61.45	Jessica	Ramsey	USA	26.7.91	9 May
61.43	Ami	Schimanski	CAN	23.8.90	17 May
61.41	Hassana	Divó	CUB-J	15.8.95	1 Mar
61.40	Meiken	Greve	DEN	7.11.80	1 Jul
61.39	Mélanie	Fromentin	FRA	10.10.81	1 Jun
61.38	Brea	Garrett	USA	27.6.93	31 May
61.37	Lea	Johnson	USA		17 Apr
61.34	Helena	Perez	FRA	13.9.91	18 Apr
61.28	Akane	Watanabe	JPN	13.8.91	12 Oct
61.19	Gunjan	Singh	IND	20.11.85	7 Jun
61.15	Magdalena	Szewa	POL	20.9.90	17 May
61.10	Jessika	Byrd	USA	15.3.93	22 Mar
61.05	Tatyana	Kachegina	RUS	6.2.89	5 May
61.03		Li Yumao	CHN	28.3.93	10 Apr
61.02	E'Lana	Lemon	USA	3.2.91	25 Apr
	(193)				

Drugs disqualification

Mark	Name	Nat	Born	Pos	Meet	Venue	Date
77.33	Zhang Wenxiu ¶	CHN	22.3.86	(1)	AsiG	Incheon	28 Sep

JUNIORS

See main list for top 4 juniors. 11 performances by 4 women to 64.80. Additional marks and further juniors:

Name	Mark	Pos	Meet	Venue	Date	Mark	Pos	Meet	Venue	Date
Shamotina	67.87	2	ECp-23	Leiria	16 Mar	64.95	1	NC-w	Yalta	21 Feb
	66.05	1	WJ	Eugene	23 Jul					
Gyurátz	65.45	3		Potchefstroom	8 Feb	64.99	1	NC-w	Budapest	1 Mar
	65.16	1		Debrecen	29 Aug	64.95	10	Gyulai	Székesfehérvár	8 Jul

Mark	First name	Name	Nat	Born	Pos	Meet	Venue	Date
63.94	Katarzyna	Furmanek	POL	19.2.96	2		Torun	18 Jun
63.67	Beatrice	Nedberge Llano	NOR-Y	14.12.97	Q	WJ	Eugene	22 Jul
63.30	Audrey	Ciofani	FRA	13.3.96	4	WJ	Eugene	23 Jul
61.97	Marinda	Petersson	SWE	3.2.95	Q	WJ	Eugene	22 Jul
61.77	Kimberley	Reed	GBR	18.2.95	2	Univ Ch	Bedford	3 May
61.63	Vanessa	Sterckendries (10)	BEL	15.9.95	8	WJ	Eugene	23 Jul
61.41	Hassana	Divó	CUB-J	15.8.95	3		La Habana	1 Mar
60.80	Alex	Hulley	AUS-Y	24.7.97	1		Sydney	13 Dec
60.63	Inga	Linna	FIN-J	21.2.95	2		Kotka	24 May
59.98	Elaine	Despaigne	CUB-Y	11.1.97	3	Barr	La Habana	25 May
59.95	Krista	Terva	FIN-Y	15.11.97	4		Kuopio	1 Aug
59.94	Petra	Jakeljic	CRO	2.5.95	1		Split	10 May
59.90		Xi Yaru	CHN-Y	2.5.97	1		Lishui	28 Jun
59.89	Sofiya	Palkina	RUS-Y	9.6.98	1	NC-j	Cheboksary	17 Jun
59.76	Anastasiya	Maslova	BLR-Y	16.10.97	7	NC	Grodno	24 Jul
59.74	Alessandra	Wall (20)	SWE	11.2.95	8		Göteborg	14 Jun

JAVELIN

Mark	First name	Name	Nat	Born	Pos	Meet	Venue	Date
67.99	Barbora	Spotáková	CZE	30.6.81	1	VD	Bruxelles	5 Sep

Mark	Pos	Meet	Venue	Date	1	2	3	4	5	6
67.99					60.00	60.01	66.22	67.99	65.04	64.38
66.96	1	Herc	Monaco	18 Jul	64.84	66.96	x	66.66	65.72	65.20
66.72	1	Athl	Lausanne	3 Jul	65.10	x	66.72	65.39	65.72	x
66.43	1	GGala	Roma	5 Jul	x	66.43	66.38	64.65	65.06	66.05

WOMEN 2014

Mark	Wind	Name		Nat	Born	Pos	Meet	Venue		Date
	65.57	1 ET	Braunschweig	21 Jun	62.26	63.27	x	65.57		
	65.52	1 C.Cup	Marrakech	13 Sep	62.06	62.17	65.52	62.23		
	64.41	1 EC	Zürich	14 Aug	62.86	59.67	58.83	57.24	64.41	61.59
67.32		Linda	Stahl	GER	2.10.85	1	adidas	New York		14 Jun
					64.09	65.72	67.32	63.35	64.56	66.00
67.29		Hanna	Hatsko-Fedusova	UKR	3.10.90	1	NC	Kirovohrad		26 Jul
					62.86	62.31	60.01	67.29	p	p
66.83		Kimberley	Mickle	AUS	28.12.84	1	WCM	Melbourne		22 Mar
					62.34	61.66	66.83	x	x	65.54
	66.12	1	Adelaide	15 Feb	x	61.73	66.12	x	64.23	61.73
	65.96	1 CG	Glasgow	30 Jul	62.97	65.96	61.45	x	x	x
	65.36	2 DL	Doha	9 May	60.33	64.05	x	62.20	63.67	65.36
	64.28	1 NC	Melbourne	5 Apr	61.14	x	59.96	62.82	64.28	62.30
66.15		Madara	Palameika	LAT	18.6.87	1	Lusis	Jelgava		26 Jun
					59.27	58.62	66.15	61.44	59.95	59.93
	64.86	3 adidas	New York	14 Jun	57.53	60.58	59.40	62.51	58.92	64.86
66.13		Martina	Ratej	SLO	2.11.81	1		Velenje		1 Jul
					58.26	x	60.54	59.92	66.13	60.49
	65.48	1 DL	Doha	9 May	64.78	60.19	65.48	65.45	x	62.04
	64.63	2 Athl	Lausanne	3 Jul	x	64.63	x	59.73	62.00	x
	64.58	2 Herc	Monaco	18 Jul	59.30	64.58	61.62	x	x	x
	64.45	1 GS	Ostrava	17 Jun	61.20	61.73	62.52	61.49	x	64.45
66.10		Kathryn	Mitchell	AUS	10.7.82	2		Adelaide		15 Feb
					66.10	63.83	x	x	x	x
	66.08	2 adidas	New York	14 Jun	66.08	62.55	61.43	61.06	x	61.12
65.47			Zhang Li	CHN	17.1.89	1	AsiG	Incheon		1 Oct
					53.76	58.84	58.51	62.42	63.98	65.47
65.32		Sunette	Viljoen	RSA	6.1.83	1	AfCh	Marrakech		13 Aug
					63.39	65.32	57.87	57.27	62.23	65.21
	64.77A	1 NC	Pretoria	11 Apr	??					
	64.30	2 VD	Bruxelles	5 Sep	56.51	57.33	63.48	60.59	58.46	64.30
	64.23	3 DL	Doha	9 May	x	54.20	59.32	64.23	58.24	58.29
64.50		Liz	Gleadle	CAN	5.12.88	1		Lethbridge		16 May
					x	64.50	60.08	x	p	p
	64.49	1 DL	Birmingham	24 Aug	60.55	64.49	x	x	62.37	60.40
		(30/10)								
64.21		Tatjana	Jelaca	SRB	10.8.90	2	EC	Zürich		14 Aug
63.92		Kelsey-Lee	Roberts	AUS	21.9.91	1		Canberra		8 Feb
63.80A		Flor Denis	Ruiz	COL	24.1.91	1	CAG	Xalapa		27 Nov
63.61		Tatyana	Kholodovich	BLR	21.6.91	1	NC	Grodno		25 Jul
63.40		Katharina	Molitor	GER	8.11.83	2	NC	Ulm		27 Jul
63.34		Christin	Hussong	GER	17.4.94	1	Spitzen	Luzern		15 Jul
63.17		Liina	Laasma	EST	13.1.92	1	ECp-w23	Leiria		15 Mar
62.90		Kara	Patterson	USA	10.4.86	1		Chula Vista		31 Jul
62.89		Jucilene	de Lima	BRA	14.9.90	1	NC	São Paulo		11 Oct
62.75		Goldie	Sayers	GBR	16.7.82	1	NC	Birmingham		29 Jun
		(20)								
62.72			Liu Shiying	CHN	24.9.93	1		Chengdu		29 Mar
62.56			Li Lingwei	CHN	26.1.89	1	NC	Suzhou		10 Oct
62.05		Brittany	Borman	USA	1.7.89	2	NC	Sacramento		26 Jun
61.61		Sinta	Ozolina-Kovale	LAT	26.2.88	2	Lusis	Jelgava		26 Jun
61.57		Vira	Rebryk	UKR/RUS	25.2.89	1		Adler		30 May
61.34		Marharyta	Dorozhon	UKR	4.9.87	1	NC	Tel Aviv		17 Jul
61.24		Marcelina	Witek	POL-J	2.6.95	1		Białogard		6 Sep
60.33		Laila	Ferrer e Silva	BRA	30.7.82	2	NC	São Paulo		11 Oct
60.32		Kateryna	Derun	UKR	24.9.93	2	NC	Kirovohrad		26 Jul
60.30			Yang Xinli	CHN	7.2.88	3	NC	Suzhou		10 Oct
		(30)								
60.25		Yuki	Ebihara	JPN	28.10.85	1		Isahaya		20 Oct
60.15		Viktoriya	Sudarushkina	RUS	2.9.90	2		Bottrop		1 Jun
60.04		Nikola	Ogrodníková	CZE	18.8.90	1		Kolín		7 Sep
60.03		Asdis	Hjálmsdóttir	ISL	28.10.85	3	Odlozil	Praha		9 Jun
59.95		Olga	Shestakova	RUS	4.12.93	1	NC-w23	Krasnodar		21 Feb
59.80		Matilde	Andraud	FRA	28.4.89	6	Herc	Monaco		18 Jul
59.53		Annu	Rani	IND	29.8.92	3	AsiG	Incheon		1 Oct
59.42		Susanne	Siebert	GER	2.8.84	5	Spitzen	Luzern		15 Jul
59.34		Lyubov	Zhatkina	RUS	30.3.90	1	NC-w	Krasnodar		21 Feb
59.10			Song Xiaodan	CHN	23.1.93	2	NGP	Zhaoqing		20 Apr
		(40)								
59.04		Nadeeka	Lakmali	SRI	18.9.81	6	CG	Glasgow		30 Jul
58.63		Izzy	Jeffs	GBR	3.2.92	1		Loughborough		26 Apr

Mark	Wind	Name		Nat	Born	Pos	Meet	Venue	Date
58.47		Lismania	Muñoz	CUB	28.2.93	1	NC	La Habana	19 Mar
58.44		Sofi	Flink	SWE-J	8.7.95	1		Pihtipudas	29 Jun
58.43		Oona	Sormunen	FIN	2.8.89	3		Kuortane	13 Jul
58.37		Leigh	Petranoff	USA	16.5.89	1		Tucson	22 May
58.33		Risa	Miyashita	JPN	26.4.84	2		Isahaya	20 Oct
58.20A		Coralys	Ortiz	PUR	16.4.85	3	PAm SF	Ciudad de México	15 Aug
58.13		Fawn	Miller	USA	10.5.92	1	NCAA	Eugene	11 Jun
58.06		Mercedes	Chilla	ESP	19.1.80	1		Zaragoza	28 Jun
		(50)							
58.02		Lina	Müze	LAT	4.12.92	1		Valmiera	18 Jul
57.97		Kiho	Kuze	JPN-J	28.3.95	1	Univ Ch	Kumagaya	5 Sep
57.90		Ariana	Ince	USA	14.3.89	1	Sun Angel	Tempe	12 Apr
57.79		Sara	Kolak	CRO-J	22.6.95	2	ECp-w23	Leiria	15 Mar
57.73		Elizabeth	Herrs	USA	20.12.93	1	Big 12	Lubbock	16 May
57.63		Avione	Allgood	USA	14.12.93	2	Big 12	Lubbock	16 May
57.60		Mackenzie	Little	AUS-J	22.12.96	Q	NC	Melbourne	4 Apr
57.59		Kim	Hamilton	USA	28.11.85	4	NC	Sacramento	26 Jun
57.54		Elisabeth	Eberl	AUT	25.3.88	1		Wien	4 Jul
57.48		Petra	Andrejsková	CZE	25.6.92	1	NC	Ostrava	2 Aug
		(60)							
57.44		Marie-Therese	Obst	NOR-J	7.1.96	1		Mannheim	5 Jul
57.31		Indre	Jakubaityte	LTU	24.1.76	1	NCp	Kaunas	1 Jun
57.28		Heidi	Nokelainen	FIN	30.9.90	1		Joensuu	24 Jul
57.28A		Abigail	Gómez	MEX	30.6.91	2	CAG	Xalapa	27 Nov
57.23			Kim Kyung-ae	KOR	5.3.88	1	NG	Jeju	1 Nov
57.12			Chang Chunfeng	CHN	4.5.88	4	NC	Suzhou	10 Oct
56.99		Marina	Maksimova	RUS	20.5.85	1		Cheboksary	4 Jun
56.94		Jarmila	Jurkovicová	CZE	9.2.81	2	NC	Ostrava	2 Aug
56.92		Suman	Devi	IND	15.7.85	2	I-S	Lucknow	7 Jun
56.91		Prescilla	Lecurieux	FRA	1.12.92	3	ECp-w23	Leiria	15 Mar
		(70)							
56.85		Yekaterina	Starygina	RUS	26.8.95	1	WJ	Eugene	24 Jul
56.80		Eva	Vivod	SLO	7.8.94	1	FlaR	Gainesville	4 Apr
56.76			Du Xiaowei	CHN	11.8.87	5	NC	Suzhou	10 Oct
56.73		Marija	Vucenovic	SRB	3.4.93	2	TexR	Austin	28 Mar
56.71A		María Lucelly	Murillo	COL	5.5.91	2	NC	Medellín	29 Jun
56.60		Rafaela	Gonçalves	BRA	27.11.91	2		Belém	10 Aug
56.57		Dilhani	Lekamge	SRI	14.1.87	1		Colombo	15 Jul
56.55		Sara	Jemai	ITA	12.4.92	2		Padova	5 Jul
56.55		Ai	Yamauchi	JPN	6.12.94	2	Univ Ch	Kumagaya	5 Sep
56.53		Maria	Andrejczyk	POL-J	9.3.96	1J		Torun	4 May
		(80)							
56.44		Yevgeniya	Ananchenko	RUS	7.11.92	1-22		Krasnodar	6 Jun
56.43		Hannah	Carson	USA	26.1.93	7	NC	Sacramento	26 Jun
56.39		Nora Aida	Bicet	ESP	29.10.77	1		Linz	19 Jul
56.30		Alexie	Alais	FRA	9.10.94	1	Med-23	Aubagne	15 Jun
56.26		Tereza	Vytlacilová	CZE-J	25.9.95	1	NC-j	Trinec	28 Jun
56.15		Barbara	Madejczyk	POL	30.9.76	7	ECp-w	Leiria	15 Mar
56.14		Karolina	Boldysz	POL	21.4.93	1	Univ Ch	Białystok	1 Jun
56.05		Sarah	Mayer	GER	20.5.91	5	NC	Ulm	27 Jul
56.02		Marta	Kakol	POL	25.2.92	1		Gdans	31 May
56.02		Suh	Hae-an	KOR	1.7.85	2	NC	Kimchun	26 Jun
		(90)							
56.01		Irena	Sedivá	CZE	19.1.92	1		Praha	3 Jun
55.98		Marina	Saito	JPN-J	15.10.95	3		Isahaya	20 Oct
55.97		Nicoleta	Anghelescu	ROU	13.1.92	1	Univ Ch	Bucuresti	25 May
55.96		Yainelis	Ribeaux	CUB	30.12.87	2	NC	La Habana	19 Mar
55.95		Gundega	Griva	LAT	8.4.91	5		Leverkusen	6 Jun
55.91		Victoria	Paterra	USA	7.7.92	1		Athens OH	15 May
55.89		Orie	Ushiro	JPN	24.8.90	1		Hiratsuka	20 Jun
55.89		Urszula	Jakimowicz	POL	11.6.88	1		Kołobrzeg	19 Sep
55.87		Katrina	Sirma	LAT	31.3.94	1	NC-w	Riga	8 Mar
55.78		Sarah	Leidl	GER	5.3.87	1		München	31 May
		(100)							

Mark	Name		Nat	Born	Date
55.75	Shiori	Toma	JPN-J	7.2.96	13 Jun
55.72		Liu Beibei	CHN	5.10.90	29 Mar
55.62	Sofia	Ifantídou	GRE	5.1.85	7 Jun
55.56	Anete	Kocina	LAT-J	5.2.96	26 Jun
55.51	Liveta	Jasiunaite	LTU	26.7.94	1 Jun
55.46	Oksana	Gromova	RUS	3.9.80	21 Feb
55.45	Lilian	Seibert	BRA	23.7.89	11 Oct
55.40	Jelena	Jaakkola	FIN	7.3.89	4 Jun
55.37	Maggie	Malone	USA	30.12.93	17 May
55.36	Freya	Jones	GBR	13.11.93	12 Apr
55.36	Helina	Karvak	EST	28.11.90	3 Aug
55.28	Jenni	Kangas	FIN	3.7.92	2 Aug
55.22	Séphora	Bissoly	FRA	6.11.81	11 Jul
55.19	Silvia	Cruz	POR	29.12.80	27 Jul
55.18	Karlee	McQuillen	USA	31.5.89	26 Jun
55.17	Tetyana	Fetiskina	UKR	11.9.94	26 Jul

Mark	Wind	Name		Nat	Born	Pos	Meet	Venue	Date

Mark	Name		Nat	Born	Date
55.14	Hitomi	Sukenaga	JPN	4.5.88	20 Oct
55.00	Brianna	Bain	USA	23.6.93	4 Apr
54.98		Kang Qiyan	CHN-J	4.9.96	30 Mar
54.87	Daniella	Mieko Nisimura	BRA	26.3.94	6 Sep
54.86	Mareike	Rittweg	GER	1.6.84	6 Jun
54.77	Alexia	Kogut Kubiak	FRA	22.1.88	11 Jul
54.71	Kike	Oniwinde	GBR	6.10.92	14 Jun
54.67A	Megan	Wilke	RSA-J	23.8.95	25 Mar
54.65	Janice	Waldvogel	GER	7.4.93	1 Mar
54.65	Haruka	Matoba	JPN	24.4.87	12 Oct
54.50A	Yulenmis	Aguilar	CUB-J	3.8.96	27 Nov
54.45	Tori	Peeters	NZL	17.5.94	30 Mar
54.42	Yuka	Sato	JPN	21.7.92	3 Apr
54.41	Laura	Loht	USA	30.6.92	11 Jun
54.40	Laura	Whittingham	GBR	6.6.86	31 Aug
54.37	Mihaela	Tacu	MDA-J	29.6.95	21 Jun
54.34	Marissa	Tschida	USA	7.7.89	26 Apr
54.26	Antoinette	Nana Djimou	FRA	2.8.85	11 Jul
54.21	Charlotte	Müller	GER	14.9.93	6 Jun
54.21		Heo Hyo-jung	KOR	19.12.94	26 Jun
54.14	Edivania	Araújo	BRA-J	27.8.95	10 Aug
54.14	Mizuki	Kato	JPN	27.10.93	13 Aug
54.13	Melissa	Dupré	BEL	5.11.86	27 Jul
54.10		Xue Juan	CHN	10.2.86	30 May
54.10	Marte	Aaltvedt	NOR	15.2.89	23 Aug
54.03	Simona	Dobilaite	LTU-J	23.5.95	19 Jun
54.01	Annabella	Bogdán	HUN	7.4.92	7 Sep
53.95	Franziska	Krebs	GER	11.10.85	27 Jul
53.94	Jessie	Merckle	USA	13.7.94	18 Apr
53.92	Kseniya	Zybina	RUS	1.2.89	26 Jul
53.85	Tatyana	Korzh	BLR	17.3.93	25 Apr
53.74	Lidia	Parada	ESP	11.6.93	15 Mar
53.74	Christine	Winkler	GER-J	4.5.95	17 May
53.72	María Paz	Rios	CHI	13.10.89	29 Mar
53.68	Hiroko	Takigawa	JPN	25.7.94	20 Jun
53.58	Nicolle	Murphy	USA	19.10.94	17 May
53.53	Lisanne	Schol	NED	22.6.91	27 Jul
53.50	Sigrid	Borge	NOR-J	3.12.95	17 Aug
53.49	Linda	Treiel	EST	8.5.91	10 Aug
53.49		He Daixian	CHN	1.9.94	10 Oct
53.48		Park Ju-hyun	KOR	22.6.94	1 Nov
53.44	Margaux	Nicollin	FRA-J	1.5.95	1 Mar
53.38	Arantxa	Moreno	ESP-J	16.1.95	16 Jul
53.35	Megan	Glasmann	USA-J	3.1.95	6 Jul
53.34	Lee	Hye-rim	KOR	6.3.89	5 May
53.33	Andrea	Lindenthaler	AUT	7.9.87	9 Jun
53.33	Fabienne	Schönig	GER-Y	27.7.97	14 Sep
53.27	Anastasiya	Svechnikova	UZB	20.9.92	29 May
53.26	Anna	Sakakura	JPN-J	29.8.95	3 Oct
53.18	Mariya	Safonova	RUS	28.10.94	16 Jul
53.15	Nathalie	Meier	SUI	30.3.93	7 Sep
53.15	Haruka	Kitaguchi	JPN-Y	16.3.98	20 Oct
53.13		Su Lingdan	CHN-J		1 Aug
53.09	Sabine	Kopplin	GER	23.11.90	29 May
53.06	Maddalena	Purgato	ITA	6.7.89	20 Jul
53.01	Elia	Pascual	ESP	4.7.89	2 Aug
	(172)				

JUNIORS

See main list for top 9 juniors. 10 performances by 6 women to 57.30. Additional marks and further juniors:

Witek	57.31	1	NC-j	Torun	29 Jun				
Flink	58.34	7	DL	Doha	9 May	57.53	Q	EC Zürich	12 Aug
Kolak	57.41	1	NC-w	Solit	1 Mar				

Mark	Name		Nat	Born	Pos	Meet	Venue	Date
55.75	Shiori	Toma (10)	JPN	7.2.96	1	Asi-J	Taipei	13 Jun
55.56	Anete	Kocina	LAT	5.2.96	4		Jelgava	26 Jun
54.98		Kang Qiyan	CHN	4.9.96	1J		Chengdu	30 Mar
54.67A	Megan	Wilke	RSA	23.8.95	2		Sasolburg	25 Mar
54.50A	Yulenmis	Aguilar	CUB	3.8.96	4	CAG	Xalapa	27 Nov
54.37	Mihaela	Tacu	MDA	29.6.95	1	ET-3	Tbilisi	21 Jun
54.14	Edivania	Araújo	BRA	27.8.95	4		Belém	10 Aug
54.03	Simona	Dobilaite	LTU	23.5.95	2		Marijampole	19 Jun
53.74	Christine	Winkler	GER	4.5.95	1J	Werfer	Halle	17 May
53.50	Sigrid	Borge	NOR	3.12.95	1	v3N-J	Kristiansand	17 Aug
53.44	Margaux	Nicollin (20)	FRA	1.5.95	1	v2N-J	Halle	1 Mar

INDOOR PENTATHLON

Mark	Name		Nat	Born	Pos	Meet	Venue	Date
4830	Nadine	Broersen	NED	29.4.90	1	WI	Sopot	7 Mar
	8.32 1.93 14.59 6.17 2:14.97							
4805A	Sharon	Day-Monroe	USA	9.6.85	1	NC	Albuquerque	21 Feb
	8.44 1.88 15.59 6.09 2:13.19							
4768	Brianne	Theisen-Eaton	CAN	18.12.88	2	WI	Sopot	7 Mar
	8.13 1.84 13.86 6.13 2:10.07							
4724	Alina	Fyodorova	UKR	31.7.89	3	WI	Sopot	7 Mar
	8.52 1.84 15.05 6.26 2:15.31							
4718		Day-Monroe			4	WI	Sopot	7 Mar
	8.43 1.84 14.95 5.94 2:09.80							
4686	Yana	Maksimova	BLR	9.1.89	1	NC	Gomel	8 Feb
	8.51 1.86 14.43 6.14 2:12.86							
4681	Claudia	Rath	GER	25.4.86	5	WI	Sopot	7 Mar
	8.43 1.78 13.66 6.37 2:10.29							

And see Indoor lists in ATHLETICS 2014

HEPTATHLON

Mark	Name		Nat	Born	Pos	Meet	Venue	Date
6682	Katarina	Johnson-Thompson	GBR	9.1.93	1		Götzis	1 Jun
	13.47/-1.2 1.90 12.17 22.89/1.5			6.70/-0.1		41.44	2:08.16	
6641	Brianne	Theisen-Eaton	CAN	18.12.88	2		Götzis	1 Jun
	13.18/-1.2 1.87 13.29 23.52/1.5			6.59/1.3		42.78	2:11.31	
6597		Theisen-Eaton			1	CG	Glasgow	30 Jul
	13.18/1.5 1.84 13.71 23.41/0.2			6.44/1.7		43.13	2:11.46	
6551	Antoinette	Nana Djimou	FRA	2.8.85	1	EC	Zürich	15 Aug
	13.05/0.6 1.76 14.35 24.52/-0.2			6.25/-0.1		54.18	2:15.22	
6545	Dafne	Schippers	NED	15.6.92	3		Götzis	1 Jun
	13.13/-1.2 1.69 13.69 22.35/1.5			6.48/-0.2		41.39	2:08.59	

Mark	Wind	Name		Nat	Born	Pos	Meet	Venue	Date
6539	Nadine	Broersen		NED	29.4.90	1	ECp	Torun	6 Jul
	13.57/-0.2	1.87 13.89 25.09/-1.6			6.31/0.4		51.96	2:12.94	
6536		Broersen				4		Götzis	1 Jun
	13.39/0.0	1.87 13.72 24.57/1.9			6.21/-0.3		48.87	2:11.11	
6508	Nafissatou	Thiam		BEL	19.8.94	5		Götzis	1 Jun
	13.81/1.4	1.93 15.03 24.78/1.2			6.19/0.0		51.90	2:22.98	
6498		Broersen				2	EC	Zürich	15 Aug
	13.48/0.2	1.94 13.35 25.08/-0.2			6.16/0.6		52.18	2:17.66	
6470	Sharon	Day-Monroe		USA	9.6.85	1	NC	Sacramento	28 Jun
	13.42/0.9	1.84 15.45 24.40w/2.6			5.85/1.8		46.84	2:11.54	
6460	Eliska	Klucinová		CZE	14.4.88	1		Kladno	15 Jun
	13.81/1.8	1.90 14.10 24.67/0.8			6.43/1.5		45.53	2:16.47	
6426	Lilli	Schwarzkopf		GER	28.8.83	1		Ratingen	29 Jun
	13.82/1.2	1.84 14.45 25.68/0.5			6.20/0.4		52.50	2:12.85	
6423		Thiam				3	EC	Zürich	15 Aug
	14.05/0.6	1.97 14.29 25.19/-0.2			6.18/-0.9		49.69	2:20.79	
6395	Carolin	Schäfer (10)		GER	5.12.91	4	EC	Zürich	15 Aug
	13.20/0.2	1.82 13.37 23.84/-0.5			6.30/-0.3		44.19	2:17.39	
6386		Schäfer				6		Götzis	1 Jun
	13.52/-1.4	1.84 13.13 23.53w/3.1			6.23/1.5		48.76	2:22.44	
6383		Schäfer				1		Talence	21 Sep
	13.42/-0.7	1.80 13.12 23.78/0.4			6.13/-0.1		48.49	2:15.55	
6332		Schwarzkopf				5	EC	Zürich	15 Aug
	13.87/0.4	1.85 14.44 25.86/-0.8			6.18/-0.3		52.17	2:17.67	
6320	Laura	Ikauniece-Admidina		LAT	31.5.92	7		Götzis	1 Jun
	13.75/-1.2	1.78 13.00 24.06w/3.1			5.97/0.3		50.65	2:11.83	
6317(w)	Xénia	Krizsán		HUN	13.1.93	8		Götzis	1 Jun
	13.77/1.4	1.81 14.04 24.98w/3.4			6.14w/2.2		47.71	2:13.05	6267 with LJ 5.98/0.4
6316	Anouk	Vetter		NED	4.2.93	9		Götzis	1 Jun
	13.56/0.2	1.78 14.63 23.91/1.9			5.90/-1.0		52.18	2:23.53	
6314	Claudia	Rath		GER	25.4.86	2		Ratingen	29 Jun
	13.47/1.2	1.75 13.08 24.20/0.5			6.41/0.9		41.39	2:09.20	
6310		Ikauniece-Admidina				6	EC	Zürich	15 Aug
	13.61/0.2	1.82 12.58 24.75/-0.5			6.20/0.8		51.30	2:16.90	
6307	Barbara	Nwaba		USA	18.1.89	2	NC	Sacramento	28 Jun
	13.63/1.8	1.78 14.54 23.92w/2.6			6.02/0.6		43.74	2:13.76	
6270	Jessica	Zelinka		CAN	3.9.81	2	CG	Glasgow	30 Jul
	12.83/1.5	1.69 13.65 24.00/0.2			5.91/-2.2		44.90	2:11.54	
6266	Karolina	Tyminska		POL	4.10.84	3		Ratingen	29 Jun
	13.70/1.2	1.72 14.81 24.26/0.9			6.10/1.0		41.72	2:08.81	
6281		Vetter				7	EC	Zürich	15 Aug
	13.68/0.2	1.79 14.16 24.61/-0.5			6.04/0.3		52.49	2:22.27	
6231	Yorgelis	Rodríguez		CUB-J	25.1.95	1		La Habana	22 Feb
	14.01/0.0	1.84 14.21 24.93/0.0			6.03/0.0		47.58	2:17.93	
6225		Rath				8	EC	Zürich	15 Aug
	13.54/0.2	1.79 12.88 24.43/-0.5			6.32/0.5		43.45	2:16.43	
6220	Anastasiya	Mokhnyuk		UKR	1.1.91	2		Talence	21 Sep
	13.31/-0.7	1.80 13.46 24.36/0.4			6.38/0.8		36.82	2:15.52	
6215		Schwarzkopf				10		Götzis	1 Jun
	13.96/1.4	1.81 14.09 25.71.1.9			6.02/1.4		51.74	2:16.86	
	(30/19)								
6189	Yana	Maksimova (20)		BLR	9.1.89	3		Talence	21 Sep
	14.32/-0.7	1.89 14.46 26.11/0.3			5.81/1.6		47.17	2:10.84	
6180	Györgyi	Farkas-Zsivoczky		HUN	13.2.85	4		Talence	21 Sep
	14.31/-1.1	1.86 13.33 25.67/0.3			6.11/0.9		47.11	2:12.49	
6148	Morgan	Lake		GBR-Y	12.5.97	1	WJ	Eugene	23 Jul
	14.29/0.3	1.94 14.17 24.64/-0.5			5.90/-0.4		41.66	2:21.06	
6128	Grit	Sadeiko		EST	29.7.89	4	ECp	Torun	6 Jul
	13.45/-0.2	1.78 12.76 24.33/-1.6			6.05/0.5		42.83	2:16.60	
6121	Yekaterina	Netsvetayeva		BLR	26.6.89	1	NC	Grodno	25 Jul
	13.78/0.6	1.77 14.81 24.97/1.1			5.73/-0.6		43.83	2:12.88	
6118	Erica	Bougard		USA	26.7.93	3	NC	Sacramento	28 Jun
	13.28/0.9	1.78 11.32 23.33w/2.6			6.21/2.0		33.05	2:09.64	
6110	Nadine	Visser		NED-J	9.2.95	14		Götzis	1 Jun
	13.40/0.0	1.78 12.50 23.90/2.0			6.16/-0.1		39.52	2:18.01	
6106	Julia	Mächtig		GER	1.1.86	15		Götzis	1 Jun
	14.31/0.2	1.72 15.52 24.94/1.9			6.23/-0.2		43.07	2:17.57	
6100	Heather	Miller Koch		USA	30.3.87	4	NC	Sacramento	28 Jun
	13.65/1.8	1.78 11.94 23.89/0.6			5.94/1.9		40.16	2:09.65	

Mark	Wind	Name		Nat	Born	Pos	Meet	Venue	Date
6091		Valérie	Reggel	SUI	3.1.87	12	EC	Zürich	15 Aug
		13.79/0.6	1.70 13.70 25.05/-0.5		6.14/-0.3		44.46	2:12.68	
6090		Alina	Fyodorova	UKR	31.7.89	2	ECp-1	Ribeira Brava	6 Jul
		13.88w/2.3	1.87 14.92 25.47/-1.0		6.15/0.6		37.48	2:20.74	
		(30)							
6083		Ida	Marcussen	NOR	1.11.87	4		Ratingen	29 Jun
		14.25/1.0	1.72 13.64 25.41/0.9		6.12/0.5		46.82	2:10.65	
6082		Ellen	Sprunger	SUI	5.8.86	13	EC	Zürich	15 Aug
		13.65/0.6	1.73 13.42 24.17/-0.5		5.95/0.8		41.06	2:12.93	
6072		Kiani	Profit	USA	18.2.90	5	NC	Sacramento	28 Jun
		13.51/0.9	1.69 12.80 24.12w/2.6		5.94w/2.2		40.92	2:08.85	
6068		Aleksandra	Butvina	RUS	14.2.86	1	NC	Cheboksary	10 Jun
		14.05/0.3	1.80 14.08 24.74/1.1		6.00/0.0		39.67	2:14.63	
6067		Anna	Blank	RUS	12.1.90	1	NCp	Adler	16 May
		14.41/0.6	1.77 12.66 25.43/1.0		6.13/0.0		48.00	2:11.63	
6038		Maren	Schwerdtner	GER	3.10.85	1		Ulm	25 May
		13.61/1.4	1.73 14.11 24.33w/2.1		6.13/-0.6		42.90	2:25.51	
6018		Kendell	Williams	USA-J	14.6.95	1		Athens GA	12 Apr
		13.32/1.0	1.83 12.59 24.58/-0.5		5.93/0.0		38.15	2:18.86	
6018		Angela	Whyte	CAN	22.5.80	2	MSR	Azusa	17 Apr
		13.12/1.3	1.69 13.26 24.20w/3.7		6.23/1.9		40.02	2:23.68	
6013		Yusleidys	Mendieta	CUB	17.2.94	1	NC	La Habana	19 Mar
		13.91/-1.2	1.73 14.22 24.25/0.0		5.95/0.0		43.24	2:21.67	
6003		Sami	Spenner	USA	21.3.91	3	MSR	Azusa	17 Apr
		14.00/1.3	1.72 11.99 23.54/1.5		6.20/2.0		37.11	2:11.93	
		(40)							
5981		Jessica	Samuelsson	SWE	14.3.85	5		Ratingen	29 Jun
		14.36/1.0	1.72 14.27 25.07/0.5		6.10/1.0		39.95	2:11.98	
5972		Jillian	Drouin	CAN	30.9.86	1	PAmCp	Ottawa	18 Jul
		13.82/1.2	1.87 12.85 25.26/1.9		5.83/1.8		42.44	2:21.09	
5962		Tamara	de Souza	BRA	8.9.93	1	NC	São Paulo	10 Oct
		13.88w/2.2	1.77 14.50 24.91/0.7		6.04/-0.3		44.42	2:30.26	
5945		Vanessa	Spínola	BRA	5.3.90	2	NC	São Paulo	10 Oct
		14.21w/2.2	1.74 13.70 24.20/0.7		5.65/-1.2		43.70	2:16.28	
5942		Lindsay	Schwartz	USA	23.4.90	1		Santa Barbara	5 Apr
		13.90/0.3	1.75 12.67 24.20/1.9		5.95/0.0		39.75	2:16.71	
5937		Hanna	Melnychenko	UKR	24.4.83	4	ECp-1	Ribeira Brava	6 Jul
		13.70/2.0	1.72 13.05 24.64/-1.5		6.23/1.0		36.41	2:16.90	
5932		Ulyana	Aleksandrova	RUS	1.1.91	2	NCp	Adler	5 Sep
		14.38/0.3	1.78 13.00 25.53w/2.3		6.45/0.8		44.14	2:25.53	
5928		Natasha	Jackson	CAN	10.6.89	2	PAmCp	Ottawa	18 Jul
		13.43w/2.5	1.81 11.01 24.36/2.0		6.09w/2.3		33.30	2:13.15	
5918		Annett	Fleming	GER	4.5.84	4	MSR	Azusa	17 Apr
		14.06/0.3	1.72 14.01 25.46w/3.7		5.77/1.5		45.86	2:16.68	
5917		Allison	Reaser	USA	9.9.92	7	NC	Sacramento	28 Jun
		13.49/0.9	1.60 11.94 23.86w/2.6		6.21/1.8		37.20	2:11.10	
		(50)							
5914		Marisa	De Aniceto	FRA	11.11.86	1		Arona	25 May
		14.13/-0.5	1.77 12.90 25.80/0.0		5.95/-1.1		50.39	2:23.61	
5912		Yekaterina	Voronina	UZB	16.2.92	1	AsiG	Incheon	29 Sep
		15.19/-0.5	1.83 12.91 25.51/0.6		6.03/-0.6		49.53	2:21.21	
5903		Lyubov	Tkach	RUS	18.2.93	2	NC	Cheboksary	10 Jun
		14.59/0.2	1.71 14.42 24.52/1.1		5.89/0.0		44.31	2:20.28	
5894		Anna	Maiwald	GER	21.7.90	2		Ulm	25 May
		14.00/1.4	1.70 13.32 24.03w/2.1		5.64/0.9		42.38	2:15.92	
5893		Breanna	Leslie	USA	11.8.91	5	MSR	Azusa	17 Apr
		13.83/1.3	1.69 11.35 24.05/1.5		5.94/1.7		41.29	2:12.33	
5873			Wang Qingling	CHN	14.1.93	1	NC	Suzhou	10 Oct
		13.76/-0.2	1.78 12.56 24.41/0.2		6.10/1.8		34.89	2:20.47	
5859		Lindsay	Lettow	USA	6.6.90	2		Dallas	25 May
		13.85/0.1	1.74 12.43 24.64w/3.2		5.86/0.3		38.40	2:14.38	
5846		Celina	Leffler	GER-J	9.4.96	1J		Ulm	25 May
		13.87/1.1	1.67 12.48 23.96/1.3		5.93/-1.8		40.39	2:18.03	
5835		Brittany	Harrell	USA	.91	3	NCAA	Eugene	13 Jun
		13.84/0.9	1.75 10.97 24.67/1.3		5.92/-2.1		40.44	2:13.96	
5833A		Salsa	Slack	JAM	10.12.89	1		Alamosa	5 May
		14.05/-1.1	1.65 14.00 24.11w/3.3		5.87w/2.2		44.87	2:26.95	
		(60)							
5826		Jessica	Taylor	GBR	27.6.88	3	CG	Glasgow	30 Jul
		13.81/1.5	1.75 11.95 24.42/0.2		6.16/2.0		33.89	2:17.59	

Mark	Wind	Name	Nat	Born	Pos	Meet	Venue	Date
5826	Yuliya	Tarasova	UZB	13.3.86	1	NC	Tashkent	22 Aug
	14.40	1.70 12.62 24.44		6.49		43.42	2:31.82	
5818	Lisa	Linnell	SWE	30.4.91	6	ECp-1	Ribeira Brava	6 Jul
	14.07/1.7	1.78 11.66 25.03/-1.6		6.01/2.0		37.23	2:13.99	
5817	Anaëlle	Nyabeu Djapa	FRA	15.9.92	2		Arona	25 May
	13.64/-0.5	1.65 13.79 25.31/0.0		5.78/-0.9		41.86	2:16.81	
5817	Linda	Züblin	SUI	21.3.86	7	ECp	Torun	6 Jul
	14.31/-2.0	1.63 12.92 25.34/-2.2		6.14/-0.3		45.31	2:16.53	
5812	Laura	Arteil	FRA	9.10.93	4		Arona	25 May
	14.56/0.0	1.65 13.36 25.26/0.0		6.07/-0.7		43.81	2:15.19	
5808	Beatrice	Puiu	ROU	1.1.86	1	NC	Bucuresti	14 Jul
	13.92/0.2	1.80 13.89 26.05/-0.7		5.98/0.8		36.31	2:20.23	
5807	Yilian	Durruthy	CUB	30.1.90	2	NC	La Habana	19 Mar
	13.74/-1.2	1.73 14.18 24.30/0.0		5.95/-1.3		33.44	2:24.22	
5806	Sofía	Ifantídou	GRE	5.1.85	1	ECp-2	Ribeira Brava	6 Jul
	14.42/-0.9	1.69 12.65 26.13/-1.1		5.77/1.1		54.53	2:19.84	
5797	Kristina	Korolyova	RUS	6.11.90	3	NCp	Adler	16 May
	14.46/0.6	1.83 11.92 25.76/1.0		5.88/0.0		41.61	2:15.73	
	(70)							
5795	Emma	Stenlöf	SWE-J	25.6.96	1	v2N	Tampere	15 Jun
	13.98/1.2	1.76 12.77 25.12/1.0		5.87/0.0		41.56	2:22.45	
5791	Anna	Petrich	RUS	10.2.92	4	NCp	Adler	16 May
	14.32/0.6	1.77 11.32 25.60/0.7		6.32/0.0		35.65	2:12.13	
5789	Rachael	McIntosh	CAN	17.1.91	6	MSR	Azusa	17 Apr
	14.33/1.1	1.69 12.62 24.91w/2.7		6.07/1.2		38.10	2:13.34	
5789	Lucia	Mokrásová	SVK	27.3.94	2	ECp-2	Ribeira Brava	6 Jul
	14.04/-0.5	1.78 12.60 24.41/-1.5		5.78/1.3		36.73	2:19.40	
5786	Lindsay	Vollmer	USA	10.9.92	1	Big 12	Lubbock	17 May
	13.57/0.3	1.73 12.95 24.41/-0.4		5.80/0.9		44.12	2:33.21	
5776	Myrte	Goor	NED	3.4.89	1	NC	Apeldoorn	9 Jun
	14.29/0.3	1.70 13.12 24.80/1.8		5.77/-0.3		40.23	2:15.09	
5770	Jess	Tappin	GBR	17.5.90	1		Málaga	1 Jun
	13.93/-1.7	1.71 11.95 24.38/-0.4		5.75/0.0		36.59	2:11.98	
5765	Mari	Klaup	EST	27.2.90	19	EC	Zürich	15 Aug
	14.17/0.4	1.76 13.16 25.83/-0.8		5.73/0.6		47.52	2:25.30	
5762	Yelena	Molodchinina	RUS	16.4.91	4	NC	Cheboksary	10 Jun
	14.14/0.3	1.77 12.33 25.41/1.1		5.74/0.0		40.49	2:15.83	
5754	Sophie	Stanwell	AUS	8.6.91	4	CG	Glasgow	30 Jul
	14.18/-1.4	1.69 11.96 24.35/0.2		5.99/-1.0		36.77	2:14.28	
	(80)							
5745	Deanna	Latham	USA	23.2.92	2		Athens GA	12 Apr
	13.73/1.0	1.62 12.39 24.57/-0.5		5.81/0.5		41.59	2:17.01	
5744	Lecabela	Quaresma	POR	26.12.89	7	ECp-1	Ribeira Brava	6 Jul
	13.86/1.7	1.72 12.67 25.30/-1.6		5.95/1.1		36.80	2:17.17	
5740	Yelizaveta	Kolokolchikova	RUS-J	7.6.96	5	NCp	Adler	16 May
	14.33/0.0	1.74 12.14 24.73/1.0		6.14/0.0		39.48	2:23.80	
5728	Cindy	Roleder	GER	21.8.89	6		Ratingen	29 Jun
	12.96/1.2	1.60 11.99 23.97/0.5		6.12/0.9		31.08	2:19.22	
5723	Sveinbjörg	Zophoníasdóttir	ISL	27.4.92	1	Nord-23	Kópavogur	8 Jun
	14.46/-0.1	1.74 13.85 25.74/0.0		5.99w/2.2		38.55	2:20.50	
5721	Niki	Oudenaarden	CAN	14.1.94	8	MSR	Azusa	17 Apr
	15.37/0.3	1.69 14.15 25.10w/2.7		6.04/0.8		44.58	2:22.72	
5721A	Alysbeth	Félix	PUR	7.3.93	3	CAG	Xalapa	27 Nov
	14.27/-0.2	1.79 10.32 24.79/0.2		6.33/-0.4		37.93	2:23.45	
5711	Agnieszka	Borowska	POL	21.10.91	2		Woerden	31 Aug
	14.13/-0.7	1.87 11.28 26.07w/2.7		6.09/-0.1		38.12	2:23.96	
5710	Grace	Clements	GBR	2.5.84	6		Arona	25 May
	14.54/-0.5	1.74 13.29 26.60/0.0		5.81/0.0		44.61	2:17.08	
5709	Mareike	Arndt	GER	29.1.92	3		Ulm	25 May
	13.93/1.3	1.61 12.96 24.38w/2.1		5.79/-1.8		39.30	2:17.08	
	(90)							
5707A	Evelys	Aguilar	COL	3.1.93	1	NC	Medellín	29 Jun
	14.74/0.6	1.69 12.61 23.93/2.6		5.67/0.0		37.50	2:12.35	
5706	Grete	Sadeiko	EST	29.5.93	1	ACC	Chapel Hill	18 Apr
	14.09/1.5	1.76 12.55 25.36/0.3		5.89/0.9		45.24	2:31.33	
5702	Lucie	Ondraschková	CZE	12.10.89	3		Athens GA	12 Apr
	14.22/1.0	1.74 11.80 25.11/-0.5		5.93/0.0		36.36	2:14.42	
5701	Sofia	Linde	SWE-J	12.1.95	25		Götzis	1 Jun
	14.37/-1.4	1.78 13.79 25.74/1.4		5.70/0.0		37.00	2:17.93	
5695	Portia	Bing	NZL	17.4.93	1	NC	Waitakere	16 Feb
	13.91/-2.4	1.73 12.07 24.52/-0.6		5.76w/2.1		35.37	2:17.37	

Mark	Wind	Name		Nat	Born	Pos	Meet	Venue	Date
5681		Paige	Knodle	USA	15.8.93	4	NCAA	Eugene	13 Jun
		13.54/0.9	1.63 10.07	24.83/-1.2	5.70/0.0		45.48	2:14.65	
5678		Amanda	Spiljard	NED	18.9.89	2	NC	Apeldoorn	9 Jun
		14.56/0.3	1.73 14.40	25.30/1.8	5.90/0.0		35.68	2:21.60	
5674		Shanice	Stewart	USA	2.12.93	2	Big 12	Lubbock	17 May
		13.70/0.3	1.70 13.54	25.04/-0.2	6.25/1.4		36.05	2:34.91	
5669		Ana Camila	Pirelli	PAR	10.1.89	1	SAmG	Santiago de Chile	15 Mar
		13.66/0.1	1.63 12.79	24.92/-1.5	5.51/0.6		41.30	2:16.67	
5668		Shana	Woods	USA	7.7.88	3		Santa Barbara	5 Apr
		13.64/0.3	1.72 11.85	23.98/1.9	6.26/-0.9		32.01	2:31.02	
		(100)							

Mark	Name		Nat	Born	Date
5662	Laura	Ginés	ESP	11.6.86	25 May
5660	Estefanía	Fortes	ESP	25.4.87	6 Jul
5659	Quintunya	Chapman	USA	7.1.93	12 Apr
5642	Ryann	Krais	USA	21.3.90	27 Jul
5638	Sarah	Chauchard	FRA	13.3.91	13 Jun
5629	Yasmina	Omrani	ALG	1.1.88	12 Jul
5628	Allison	Barwise	USA	21.7.91	3 May
5627	Noemi	Zbären	SUI	12.3.94	25 May
5625	Brittney	Howell	USA	1.9.92	27 Mar
5621	Louisa	Grauvogel	GER-J	28.9.96	23 Jul
5606A	Jessamyn	Sauceda	MEX	22.5.89	27 Nov
5603	Lindsey	Hall	USA	25.3.91	13 Jun
5594	Georgia	Ellenwood	CAN-J	5.8.95	23 Jul
5576	Jallycia	Pearson	USA	1.5.93	16 May
5568	Fiorella	Chiappe	ARG-J	1.1.96	15 Mar
5562	Tiffeny	Parker	USA	8.6.88	17 Apr
5562	Victoria	Joäng	SWE	17.10.89	6 Jul
5558	Ashleigh	Hamilton	AUS	11.10.90	2 Mar
5558	Xenia	Rahn	GER	9.3.91	13 Jun
5552	Chari	Hawkins	USA	21.5.91	13 Jun
5542	Agustina	Zerboni	ARG	24.8.88	26 Jan
5542	Tatum	Souza	USA	20.4.92	17 Apr
5540	Caroline	Agnou	SUI-J	26.5.96	24 Aug
5537	Mariya	Pavlova	RUS-J	21.5.96	11 Jun
5534	Madelaine	Buttinger	CAN	3.11.89	5 Apr
5534	Lucija	Cvitanovic	CRO	17.9.91	4 May
5530	Verena	Preiner	AUT-J	1.2.95	23 Jul
5523	Alexandra	Wester	GER	21.3.94	25 May
5522	Alex	Gochenour	USA	17.2.93	27 Mar
5521	Anne	Martin	USA	16.4.91	17 Apr
5519		Chu Chia-Ling	TPE	11.1.91	21 May
5519	Megu	Hemphill	JPN-J	23.5.96	2 Aug
5516	Tatyana	Tarasova	RUS	2.10.90	5 Sep
5510	Enrica	Cipolloni	ITA	19.10.90	6 Jul
5509	Guillercy	González	VEN	7.5.88	15 Mar
5504	Hanna	Gorodskaya	BLR	31.1.93	5 Jun
5500w	Chie	Kiriyama	JPN	2.8.91	1 Jun
5490	Jess	Herauf	USA	17.1.93	17 May
5489	Kristella	Jurkatamm	EST-J	9.4.96	25 May
5489	Rimma	Hordiyenko	UKR-J	19.6.95	14 Jun
5477	Giovana	Cavaleti	BRA	13.1.89	10 Oct
5476	Alysha	Burnett	AUS-Y	4.1.97	5 Jan
5471	Jena	Hemann	USA	16.10.92	16 May
5471	Yelena	Yermolina	RUS	2.2.89	10 Jun
5469	Linda	Treiel	EST	8.5.91	10 Aug
5468	Henna	Palosaari	FIN	9.9.93	15 Jun
5468	Flavia	Nasella	ITA	18.6.94	19 Jul
5466	Sandra	Jacmaire	FRA	4.1.91	12 Jul
5466	Ashlee	Moore	USA-J	21.5.95	23 Jul
5459	Casidhe	Simmons	AUS-J	6.2.95	23 Jul
5456A	Bianca	Erwee	RSA	4.3.90	12 Apr
5455	Bianca	Broda	GER	13.2.86	6 Jul
5454	Shaye	Springall	USA		28 Mar
5454	Marthe Yasmine Koala		BUR	8.3.94	13 Aug
5451	Milagros	Montes de Oca	DOM	4.4.92	9 Aug
5450	Carolina	Bianchi	ITA	7.2.88	19 Jul
5446	Marjolein	Lindemans	BEL	17.2.94	3 Aug
5444	Liksy	Joseph	IND	17.2.90	5 Nov
5439	Noor	Vidts	BEL-J	30.5.96	25 May
5437	Darya	Khramtsova	RUS	7.1.90	16 May
5436	Yelena	Aksamitova	RUS	20.8.92	10 Jun
5433	Anastasiya	Belyakova	RUS	4.12.90	5 Sep
5429	Frida	Thorsås	NOR	31.1.94	6 Jul
5427	Carmen	Romero	ESP	4.3.91	27 Jul
5424	Kotchakorn	Khamrueangsri	THA-J	13.3.95	7 May
5419	Fumie	Takehara	JPN	14.7.87	1 Jun
5416	Aaron	Howell	USA-J	3.10.95	17 Apr
5411		Li Weijian	CHN	19.10.93	29 Aug
5409	Alexis	Walker	USA	26.10.92	17 Apr
5404A	Rachel	Machin	CAN	14.3.92	11 May
5402	Sushmita	Singha Roy	IND	26.3.84	19 Aug
5400	Swapana	Barman	IND-J	29.10.96	19 Aug
	(172)				

Best at low altitude

5718 Slack 5 CG Glasgow 30 Jul
14.34/1.5 1.63 12.82 24.67/0.2 5.87/-1.5 44.48 2:20.21

5528 Sauceda 23 Mar
5518 Aguilar 3 Aug

JUNIORS

See main list for top 8 juniors. 12 performances by 4 women to 5850. Additional marks and further juniors:

Name	Mark	Pos	Meet	Venue	Date	Mark	Pos	Meet	Venue	Date
Rodríguez	6092	16		Götzis	1 Jun	5984A	1	CAG	Xalapa	27 Nov
	6006	2	WJ	Eugene	23 Jul					
Lake	6081	17		Götzis	1 Jun	5896	1		Firenze	3 May
Visser	5948	3	WJ	Eugene	23 Jul					
Williams	5877	1	SEC	Lexington	16 May	5854	1	NCAA	Eugene	13 Jun

Mark	Name		Nat	Born	Pos	Meet	Venue	Date
5621	Louisa	Grauvogel	GER	28.9.96	5	WJ	Eugene	23 Jul
	14.02/1.1	1.67 12.12 24.85/-0.5		5.70/-0.6		40.49	2:20.18	
5594	Georgia	Ellenwood (10)	CAN	5.8.95	7	WJ	Eugene	23 Jul
	14.36/1.1	1.73 10.90 24.86/1.2		5.70/-0.9		39.81	2:17.10	
5568	Fiorella	Chiappe	ARG	1.1.96	2	SAmG	Santiago de Chile	15 Mar
	14.33/0.1	1.69 10.66 25.36/-1.5		6.05/0.2		35.98	2:13.63	
5540	Caroline	Agnou	SUI	26.5.96	1	NC-j	Winterthur	24 Aug
	14.30/0.0	1.63 13.00 25.50/-1.1		5.94/0.8		40.41	2:24.82	
5537	Mariya	Pavlova	RUS	21.5.96	1	NC-j	Cheboksary	11 Jun
	14.65/0.3	1.77 11.89 25.63/-0.4		5.98/1.0		36.85	2:23.69	
5534	Madelaine	Buttinger	CAN	3.11.89	5		Santa Barbara	5 Apr
	14.94/0.2	1.75 13.44 25.51/1.7		5.64/-3.0		34.43	2:16.78	
5534	Lucija	Cvitanovic	CRO	17.9.91	1		Tampa	4 May
	14.60/0.8	1.73 12.05 26.84/0.7		5.53/-0.7		46.67	2:17.80	
5530	Verena	Preiner	AUT	1.2.95	9	WJ	Eugene	23 Jul
	14.71/-0.8	1.58 13.65 25.69/0.5		5.56/-0.3		43.04	2:14.46	

Mark	Wind	Name		Nat	Born	Pos	Meet	Venue	Date
5519		Megu	Hemphill	JPN	23.5.96	1		Kofu	2 Aug
		13.57/0.6	1.62 10.46	25.39/-2.3	5.81/1.5		39.84	2:17.87	
5489		Kristella	Jurkatamm	EST	9.4.96	1j		Valga	25 May
		14.41/0.1	1.71 11.50	25.66/-0.8	6.02/0.9		38.98	2:26.18	
5489		Rimma	Hordiyenko	UKR	19.6.95	1	NC-j	Kyiv	14 Jun
		14.37/-0.6	1.76 13.06	25.86/0.4	5.86/0.0		35.10	2:28.41	
5476		Alysha	Burnett (20)	AUS-Y	4.1.97	2		Sydney (C'town)	5 Jan
		14.75/0.0	1.78 11.34	25.69/-2.7	6.04w/2.9		38.45	2:28.93	

4 X 100 METRES RELAY

Mark	Nat	Team	Pos	Meet	Venue	Date
41.83	JAM	Stewart, Campbell-Brown, Calvert, Fraser-Pryce	1	CG	Glasgow	2 Aug
41.88	USA	Bartoletta, Anderson, Tarmoh, Lawson	1	W.Rly	Nassau	24 May
42.21	GBR	Philip, Nelson, Onuora, Henry	1	WK	Zürich	28 Aug
42.24	GBR	Philip, Nelson, J Williams, Henry	1	EC	Zürich	17 Aug
42.28	JAM	Russell, Stewart, Calvert, Henry-Robinson	2	W.Rly	Nassau	24 May
42.29	JAM	Russell, Stewart, Calvert, Henry-Robinson	1h2	W.Rly	Nassau	24 May
42.29	USA	Bartoletta, Anderson, Tarmoh, Lawson	1h1	W.Rly	Nassau	24 May
42.29	FRA	Distel-Bonnet, Ikuesan, Soumaré, Akakpo	1h1	EC	Zürich	16 Aug
42.33	JAM	Russell, Stewart, Calvert, Henry-Robinson	2	WK	Zürich	28 Aug
42.40	NED	Ghafoor, Schippers, van Schagen, Samuel	1	Athl	Lausanne	3 Jul
42.44	JAM	Stewart, Campbell-Brown, Thompson, Fraser-Pryce	1h2	CG	Glasgow	1 Aug
42.45	FRA	Distel-Bonnet, Ikuesan, Soumaré, Akakpo	2	EC	Zürich	17 Aug
42.48	USA	Bartoletta, Felix, Tarmoh, Gardner	3	WK	Zürich	28 Aug
42.59	TTO	Durant, Ahye, Thomas, Selvon	2h1	W.Rly	Nassau	24 May
42.62	GBR	Philip, Nelson, Onuora, Henry	1h2	EC	Zürich	16 Aug
42.63	GER	Weit, Haase, Pinto, Sailer	2	Athl	Lausanne	3 Jul
42.66	TTO	Durant, Ahye, Thomas, Selvon	3	W.Rly	Nassau	24 May
42.67	NGR	Asumnu, Okagbare, D Duncan, Okwara	4	W.Rly	Nassau	24 May
42.74	GBR	Philip, Nelson, J Williams, Henry	1	DL	Glasgow	11 Jul
42.75	GBR	Philip, B Williams, J Williams, Henry	5	W.Rly	Nassau	24 May
42.77	NGR	Asumnu, Okagbare, D Duncan, Okwara	2h2	W.Rly	Nassau	24 May
42.77	NED	Ghafoor, Schippers, van Schagen, Samuel	2h1	EC	Zürich	16 Aug
	(22 performances by teams from 8 nations)					
42.83	CHN	Tao Yujia, Kong Lingwei, Lin Huijun, Wei Yongli	1	AsiG	Incheon	2 Oct
42.92	BRA	V.dos Santos, Silva, Krasucki, R.Santos	1	IbAm	São Paulo	3 Aug
	(10)					
42.94	SUI	Kambundji, Lavanchy, E.Sprunger, L.Sprunger	3	Athl	Lausanne	3 Jul
43.22	RUS	Panteleyeva, Rusakova, Savlinis, Sivkova	3	EC	Zürich	17 Aug
43.26	ITA	Caravelli, Siragusa, Amidei, Alloh	4	EC	Zürich	17 Aug
43.33	CAN	Bingham, Hyacinthe, Emmanuel, Davis	1rB	W.Rly	Nassau	24 May
43.37	UKR	Karandyuk, Strohova, Povh, Pohrebnyak	2h2	EC	Zürich	16 Aug
43.46	BAH	Robinson, Ferguson, Armbrister, Strachan	2rB	W.Rly	Nassau	24 May
43.53A	VEN	Vargas, Purica, Villalobos, Soto	1	CAG	Xalapa	28 Nov
43.74	JPN	Kitakaze, Doi, Watanabe, Ichikawa	1		Tokyo	11 May
43.76	KAZ	Ivanchukova, Zyabkina, Tulapina, Safronova	1		Almaty	14 Jun
43.80	SWE	Ekelund, Eurenius, Busk, Nilsson	5h1	EC	Zürich	16 Aug
	(20)					
43.81	GRE	Koklóni, Pesirídou, Férra, Belibasáki	6h1	EC	Zürich	16 Aug
43.84	IRL	Foster, Proper, Lavin, Healy	4h2	EC	Zürich	16 Aug
43.97	POL	Kielbasinska, Wedler, Jeschke, Ptak	6	ET	Braunschweig	21 Jun
43.99	PUR	Cruz, Morales, Cancel, Rodriguez	4rB	W.Rly	Nassau	24 May
43.99	CIV	Kouamé, Gaha, Gouenon, Lou Gonerie	2	AfCh	Marrakech	12 Aug
44.02A	COL	Florez, Idrobo, Obregón, Palacios	2	CAG	Xalapa	28 Nov
44.06	GHA	Owusu-Agyapong, Acheampong, Gyaman, Amponsah	3	AfCh	Marrakech	12 Aug
44.19A	CUB	Montes, Gandulla, Guillén, Odelín	3	CAG	Xalapa	28 Nov
44.21	AUS	Breen, Whittaker, Nelson, Gayen	5	CG	Glasgow	2 Aug
44.22	FIN	Thureson, Latvala, Laukka, Neziri	7h1	EC	Zürich	16 Aug
	(30)					

44.29	NOR	16 Aug	44.53	BUL	16 Aug	44.74	BEL	21 Jun	45.09	CHI	15 Mar	**Best at low altitude**		
44.30	DOM	24 May	44.60	KOR	2 Oct	44.75	EST	21 Jun	45.10	ROU	21 Jun	44.64	VEN	24 May
44.39	THA	2 Oct	44.63	CZE	21 Jun	44.81	IND	1 Aug	45.11	CYP	21 Jun	45.13	COL	15 Mar
44.53	IVB	24 May	44.68	ESP	16 Aug	44.99	TPE	2 Oct	45.12	CUB	20 Mar			

Mixed nationality team

Mark	Team	Pos	Meet	Venue	Date
42.44	Americas	1	C.Cup	Marrakech	13 Sep
	Bartoletta USA, Ayhe TTO, Henry-Robinson JAM, Campbell-Brown JAM				

JUNIORS

Mark	Nat	Team	Pos	Meet	Venue	Date
43.46	USA	T Daniels, A Washington, J Martin, K Whitney	1	WJ	Eugene	26 Jul
43.97	JAM	S Forbes, K Dallas, S Cameron, N Whyte	2	WJ	Eugene	26 Jul
44.24A	TTO	A Telesford, K McShine, Z Denoon, K Clarke	1	CAC-J	Morelia	4 Jul
44.61	BRA	L de Souza, V Rosa, M da Silva, T Liuz	2h1	WJ	Eugene	25 Jul

Mark	Wind	Name	Nat	Born	Pos	Meet	Venue	Date
44.65	GER	Kwaiye, Mayer, Lückenkemper, Butzek			3	WJ	Eugene	26 Jul
44.66	GBR	Pipi, C Hylton, Lansiquot, Asher-Smith			1		Mannheim	6 Jul
45.17	SUI	KHauiri, Del Ponte, Atcho, Strebel			2h2	WJ	Eugene	25 Jul
45.21	NED	Runier, Hovenkamp, Klaver, van Hunenstijn			1		Lier	21 Jun
45.22	BAH	Cox, Ambrose, Bethel, Albury			4h1	WJ	Eugene	25 Jul
45.32	FRA	Kané, Berger, Compper, Gnafoua			2		Bonneuil-sur-Marne	5 Jun

4 X 200 METRES RELAY

1:29.45	USA	Solomon, Meadows, Knight, K Duncan	1 W.Rly	Nassau	25 May
1:29.61	GBR	Henry, Onuora, B.Williams, Philip	2 W.Rly	Nassau	25 May
1:30.04	JAM	Facey, Brooks, McLaughlin, Fraser-Pryce	3 W.Rly	Nassau	25 May
1:30.21	USA	Texas A&M Univ. Ash. Purvis, Little, Ekponé, K.Brown	1 PennR	Philadelphia	26 Apr
1:30.26	USA	Texas Un Akinosun, Udoh, Nelson, Spencer	2 PennR	Philadelphia	26 Apr
1:30.61	USA	Texas A&M Univ. A.Brown, Little, Ekponé, K.Brown	1h1 PennR	Philadelphia	25 Apr
Additional nations					
1:31:31	BAH	Ferguson, Strachan, Smith, Armbrister	4 W.Rly	Nassau	25 May
1:31.75	SUI	Kambundji, L.Sprunger, Golay, Humair	5 W.Rly	Nassau	25 May
1:32:23	FRA	Lagui, Distel-Bonnet, Gaydu, Goujon	6 W.Rly	Nassau	25 May

4 X 400 METRES RELAY

3:21.73	USA	Trotter 50.7, Richards-Ross 50.4, Hastings 50.0, Atkins 50.6	1	W.Rly	Nassau	25 May
3:23.26	JAM	Spencer 51.2, Williams-Mills 49.7, Le-Roy 51.2, Jackson 51.2	2	W.Rly	Nassau	25 May
3:23.41	NGR	Abugan 52.1, R George 49.6, Omotoso 50.9, P George50.8	3	W.Rly	Nassau	25 May
3:23.82	JAM	Day 51.3, Williams-Mills 50.6, Le-Roy 51.52, McPherson 50.33	1	CG	Glasgow	2 Aug
3:23.84	USA	Trotter 51.5, Richards-Ross 50.0, Hargrove 51.9, Beard 50.5	1h2	W.Rly	Nassau	24 May
3:24.21	USA	Texas Un B Nelson 52.8, Baisden 50.5, Akinosun 51.37, Okolo 49.57	1	NCAA	Eugene	14 Jun
3:24.27	FRA	Gayot 52.0, Hurtis 50.7, Raharolahy 51.78, Guei 49.71	1	EC	Zürich	17 Aug
3:24.32	UKR	Pygyda 51.6, Stuy 51.2, Ryzhykova 50.82, Zemlyak 50.62	2	EC	Zürich	17 Aug
3:24.34	GBR	Child 51.3, Massey 50.9, Cox 51.26, Adeoye 50.74	3	EC	Zürich	17 Aug
3:24.71	NGR	P.George 51.7, R.George 50.8, Benjamin 51.06, Abugan 51.07	2	CG	Glasgow	2 Aug
3:24.95	JAM	Day 51.8, Le-Roy 51.1, Jackson 50.9, Spencer 51.2	2h2	W.Rly	Nassau	25 May
3:25.02	RUS	Tamkova 51.5, Veshkurova 51.2, Firova 50.5, Renzhina 51.43	4	EC	Zürich	17 Aug
3:25.05	USA	Texas Un B Nelson 52.1, Okolo 49.7, Baisden 52.57, Spencer 50.67	1U	PennR	Philadelphia	26 Apr
3:25.62	USA	Kirtz 52.7, Hargrove 51.7, Trotter 50.78, Beard 50.46	1	PennR	Philadelphia	26 Apr
3:25.73	POL	Holub 51.9, Wyciszkiewicz 51.2, Linkiewicz 51.78, Swiety 50.80	5	EC	Zürich	17 Aug
3:25.84	FRA	Gayot 52.2, Guion-Firmin 51.5, Raharolahy 51.8, Guei 50.4	4	W.Rly	Nassau	25 May
3:26.38	USA	Texas Un B Nelson 52.6, Okolo 51.0, Baisden 51.9, Spencer 50.9	1	TexR	Austin	29 Mar
3:27.07	NGR	Abugan 52.3, R George 50.4, Abogunloko 52.5, P George 51.9	1h1	W.Rly	Nassau	24 May
3:27.16	NGR	Abugan 52.8, Omotoso 51.8, Abogunloko 52.09, R George 50.49	2	PennR	Philadelphia	26 Apr
3:27.24	GBR	England C Ohuruogu 52.0, Cox 51.7, Massey 51.83, Onuora 51.72	3	CG	Glasgow	2 Aug
		(20 performances by teams from 8 nations)				
3:27.44	ITA	Bazzoni 52.8, Spacca 51.8, Bonfanti 52.6, Grenot 50.2	6	W.Rly	Nassau	25 May
3:27.69	GER	Cremer 51.4, Klopsch 52.1, Schmidt 52.22, Spelmeyer 51.97	6	EC	Zürich	17 Aug
	(10)					
3:28.68	IND	Panwar, Luka, Kaur, Poovamma	1	AsiG	Incheon	2 Oct
3:29.66	BRA	Coutinho, B de Oliveira, J Souza, de Lima	1	IbAmC	São Paulo	2 Aug
3:29.69A	CUB	Veitía, Casanova, Borlot, Bonne	1	CAG	Xalapa	30 Nov
3:30.27	AUS	Rubie 52.5, Sargent 52.3, Wells 52.49, Mitchell 52.91	4	CG	Glasgow	2 Aug
3:30.80	JPN	Aoyama, Matsumoto, Ichikawa, Chiba	2	AsiG	Incheon	2 Oct
3:30.91	TTO	Fermin 52.9, Williams, Modeste, Brooks	4h1	W.Rly	Nassau	24 May
3:31.02	ROU	Pastor, Lavric, Morosanu, Razor	1		Pitesti	27 Jul
3:31.02	CAN	Jean-Baptiste 53.4, Dorr 52.1, Montcalm 53.73, Chase 51.64	3h2	CG	Glasgow	1 Aug
3:31.71	BAH	Clarke 53.4, Amertil 51.4, Henfield 54.8, Byfield 52.1	2rB	W.Rly	Nassau	25 May
3:31.82	BEL	Libert 53.5, Borlée 51.8, Efonye 52.38, Grillet 53.98	8	EC	Zürich	17 Aug
	(20)					
3:32.02	CHN	Li Manyuan, Wang Huan, Chen Jingwen, Cheng Chong	3	AsiG	Incheon	2 Oct
3:32.26	KEN	Shikanda, Koki, Jepkosgei, Jelagat	2	AfCh	Marrakech	14 Aug
3:32.84	NED	Dopheide, Voskamp, van, Leuveren, Ghafoor	2rB	ET	Braunschweig	22 Jun
3:33.16	THA	Hoenhuk, Engchuan, Srimueng, Yongphan	4	AsiG	Incheon	2 Oct
3:33.16A	MEX	Brito, Medina, Espinoza, Z Rodríguez	2	CAG	Xalapa	28 Nov
3:33.20	VIE	Nguyen Thu Huyen, Ng. Thi Thuy, Ng. Thi Oanh, Quach Thi Lan	5	AsiG	Incheon	2 Oct
3:33.57	LTU	Misiunaite, Staisiunaite, Morauskaite, Serksniene	1rB	ET-1	Tallinn	22 Jun
3:34.14A	COL	González, Torres, Padilla, Aguilar	3	CAG	Xalapa	28 Nov
3:34.23	NOR	Norum, Mjaland, Hauge, Kloster	2rA	ET-1	Tallinn	22 Jun
3:34.29	BLR	Mishyna, Boyko, I.Usovich, Arzamasova (30)	3rA	ET-1	Tallinn	22 Jun

3:34.51	FIN	19 Jul	3:37.04	BUL	22 Jun	3:37.7A	ETH	15 May	3:39.47	GRE	22 Jun
3:34.62	NZL	1 Aug	3:37.16	SVK	19 Jul	3:38.21	SWE	22 Jun	3:39.52	HUN	22 Jun
3:35.38	CZE	22 Jun	3:37.26	BOT	13 Jun	3:38.95	SUI	22 Jun	3:39.90	KOR	2 Oct
3:35.41	POR	16 Aug	3:37.42	CHI	16 Mar	3:39.08A	VEN	28 Nov	3:39.93	SRB	27 Jul
3:36.83	KAZ	2 Oct	3:37.67	CRO	27 Jul	3:39.40	IRL	22 Jun			

Best at low altitude

3:35.96	COL	16 Mar
3:36.12	CUB	20 Mar

Mark	Wind	Name	Nat	Born	Pos	Meet	Venue	Date

Mixed nationality teams

3:20.93 Americas — 1 C.Cup Marrakech 14 Sep
Day JAM 51.3, McCorory USA 50.01, McPherson JAM 49.72, Williams-Mills JAM 49.86

3:24.12 Europe — 2 C.Cup Marrakech 14 Sep
Terrero ESP 52.4, Holub POL 50.1, Zemlyak UKR 50.24, Grenot ITA 51.40

3:25.51 Africa — 3 C.Cup Marrakech 14 Sep
P George NGR 51.7, Abugan NGR 50.5, Benjamin NGR 52.47, Mpopo ZAM 50.84

3:25.63 Texas A&M Un USA — 2 NCAA Eugene 14 Jun
Little 52.1, K Brown 51.1, Bellille TTO 51.68, Ekponé 50.78

Indoors

3:24.83	USA	Hastings 51.89, Atkins 50.91, McCorory 50.33, Tate 51.70	1	WI	Sopot	9 Mar
3:26.54	JAM	Hall 52.80, McLaughlin 51.25. Spencer 51.13, McPherson 51.36	2	WI	Sopot	9 Mar

JUNIORS

3:30.42	USA	S Little 52.7, O Baker 53.0, S Wimbley 52.3, K Baisden 52.4	1	WJ	Eugene	27 Jul
3:32.00	GBR	S Richards 53.4, L Bleaken 53.2, S Bakare 53.0, C Hylton 52.4	2	WJ	Eugene	27 Jul
3:33.02	GER	L Müller 54.7, Mergenthaler 51.4, L Gläsner 54.2, Kopf 52.7	3	WJ	Eugene	27 Jul
3:33.17	CAN	Sharpe, K Clarke, Brennan, M Price	4	WJ	Eugene	27 Jul
3:34.69	JAM	Edwin Allen Sch.	1	PennR	Philadelphia	25 Apr
3:34.99	NGR	Oghenefejiro, Edobi, Ajayi, Odlong	3h2	WJ	Eugene	26 Jul
3:36.13	JPN	(High School select)	1		Fukuroi	8 Nov
3:36.15	CUB	Cipriano, Alvarez, Diago, Casanova	1		Camagüey	9 Mar
3:37.52	POL	Bartosiewicz, Pakula, Szczerbaczewicz, Janowicz	6	WJ	Eugene	27 Jul
3:39.18	AUS	Lawson, Wassall, Griffith, Lind	4h2	WJ	Eugene	26 Jul
3:39.65	BAH	Doirsett, Rolle, Bethe, Anderson	2	Carifta	Fort-de-France	21 Apr

4 X 800 METRES RELAY

8:01.58	USA	Price 2:01.0, Lara 2:02.8, Wilson 1:59.1, Martinez 1:58.7	1	W.Rly	Nassau	25 May
8:04.28	KEN	Kimaswai 2:03.8, Chesebe 2:01.7, Jepkosgei 1:59.6, Sum 1:59.2	2	W.Rly	Nassau	25 May
8:07.65	USA	Eugene All Stars Leinert, Lipsey, Roesler, Wilson	1		Eugene	26 Jul
8:08.19	RUS	Maracheva 2:02.6, Kobeleva 2:01.9, Myazina 2:02.3, Rogozina 2:01.4	3	W.Rly	Nassau	25 May
8:08.39	USA	Pacific Northwest Wallace, Moore, Wright, Grace	2		Eugene	26 Jul
8:13.26	AUS	McGowan 2:03.6, Buckman 2:01.6, Kajan 2:02.2, Duncan 2:05.9	4	W.Rly	Nassau	25 May
8:14.76	USA	New Jersey/New York TC Ross, Donohue, Charnigo, Thomas	3		Eugene	26 Jul
8:17.22	JAM	Malcolm 2:04.8, Campbell 2:07.0, Gordon 2:05.5, Goule 2:00.0	5	W.Rly	Nassau	25 May
8:17.54	FRA	Fedronic 2:02.6, Moh 2:02.8, Blamèble 2:08.5, Lamote 2:03.7	6	W.Rly	Nassau	25 May

4 X 1500 METRES RELAY

16:33.58	KEN	Cherono 4:07.5, Kipyegon 4:08.5, Jelagat 4:10.5, Obiri 4:07.1	1	W.Rly	Nassau	24 May
16:55.33	USA	Kampf 4:09.2, Mackey 4:19.4, Grace 4:16.6, Martinez 4:10.2	2	W.Rly	Nassau	24 May
17:05.72A	KEN	Jelagat, Karindi, Nenkampi, Cherono	1		Nairobi	26 Apr
17:08.17A	KEN	Karingi, Chelimo, Sum, Obiri	1		Nairobi	22 Mar
17:08.65	AUS	Buckman 4:08.0, Delaney 4:15.6, McGowan 4:29.1, Duncan 4:16.0	3	W.Rly	Nassau	24 May

4 X 100 METRES HURDLES

50.66	Boogie Johnson TC, USA	Castlin, Rollins, Q Harrison, Porter GBR	1	FlaR	Gainesville	5 Apr
50.93	USA Red	Rollins, L Jones, Thomas, Harrison	1	Drake	Des Moines	25 Apr
52.01	JAM	S Williams, Bliss, Morgan, Greaves	2	Drake	Des Moines	25 Apr
52.07	Star Athletics	Wells, T Jones, Idlette DOM, Coward	2	FlaR	Gainesville	5 Apr

3000 METRES WALK

12:05.83+	Eleonora	Giorgi	ITA	14.9.89	1	in 5000	Misterbianco	18 May
12:11.27	Julia	Takacs	ESP	29.6.89	1		Huelva	12 Jun
12:17.50	Ana	Cabecinha	POR	29.4.84	2		Huelva	12 Jun
12:21.84	Brigita	Virbalyte	LTU	1.2.85	1		Kaunas	10 May
12:34.20	Viktória	Madarász	HUN	12.5.85	1		Dubnica nad Váhom	30 Aug
Indoors								
11:50.08	Eleonora	Giorgi	ITA	14.9.89	1	NC	Ancona	22 Feb
11:56.59	Irina	Yumanova ¶	RUS	6.11.90	1		Novocheboksarsk	11 Jan
11:57.66	Anisya	Kirdyapkina	RUS	23.10.89	1		Samara	30 Jan
11:57.71	Svetlana	Vasilyeva	RUS	24.7.92	2		Novocheboksarsk	11 Jan
11:57.89	Marina	Pandakova	RUS	1.3.89	3		Novocheboksarsk	11 Jan
11:58.44	Vera	Sokolova	RUS	8.6.87	4		Novocheboksarsk	11 Jan
12:07.19	Brigita	Virbalyte	LTU	1.2.85	1		Wien	8 Feb
12:23.84	Rachel	Seaman	CAN	14.1.86	1		Toronto	9 Feb
12:31.78	Viktória	Madarász	HUN	12.5.85	1	NC	Budapest (Sy)	23 Feb
12:34.46	María José	Poves	ESP	16.3.78	1		Zaragoza	9 Mar
12:35.16	Déspina	Zapounídou	GRE	5.10.85	1	NC	Pireás	8 Feb
12:37.01	Vera	Santos	POR	3.12.81	2	NC	Pombal	15 Feb
Best juniors								
12:44.21	Laura	García-Cano	ESP	16.4.95	3		Huelva	12 Jun
12:52.72i	Svetlana	Broidatskaya	RUS	4.10.95	3		Samara	30 Jan

5000 METRES WALK

Mark Wind	Name		Nat	Born	Pos	Meet	Venue	Date
20:01.80	Eleonora	Giorgi	ITA	14.9.89	1		Misterbianco	18 May
20:15.71	Lyudmyla	Olyanovska	UKR	20.2.93	1		Kyiv	4 Jun
20:30.04	Julia	Takacs	ESP	29.6.89	1		Cáceres	2 Jul
20:41.47		Takacs			1		Alcorcón	12 Jul
21:10.92	Raquel	González	ESP	16.11.89	1		Cartagena	9 May
21:17.8	Brigita	Virbalyte	LTU	1.2.85	1		Valga	17 May
21:20.97	Agnieszka	Dygacz	POL	18.7.85	1		Katowice	2 Jul
21:21.15+	Anezka	Drahotová	CZE-J	22.7.95	1	in 10k	Eugene	23 Jul
21:31.06	Ana	Cabecinha	POR	29.4.84	1		Faro	8 Mar

Mark	Name		Nat	Born	Date
21:32.08	Inês	Henriques	POR	1.5.80	10 Jun
21:36.20mx	Tanya	Holliday	AUS	21.9.88	28 Feb
21:37.32	Rachel	Seaman	CAN	14.1.86	25 Jan
21:42.62		Duan Dandan	CHN-J	23.5.95	28 Aug
21:46.68	Kelly	Ruddick	AUS	19.4.73	29 Mar
21:48.80	Viktória	Madarász	HUN	12.5.85	14 Jun
21:49.3	Laura	Polli	SUI	7.9.83	27 Jul
21:55.64	Paulina	Buziak	POL	16.12.86	14 Jun

10 KILOMETRES WALK

Mark Wind	Name		Nat	Born	Pos	Meet	Venue	Date
41:42.5	Lyudmyla	Olyanovska	UKR	20.2.93	1		Mukachevo	1 Nov
42:03	Lina	Bikulova	RUS	1.10.88	1		Bui	13 Sep
42:23.37 t	Julia	Takacs	ESP	29.6.89	1	NC	Alcobendas	26 Jul
42:30		Olyanovska			1		Moskva	30 Aug
42:47.25 t	Anezka	Drahotová	CZE-J	22.7.95	1	WJ	Eugene	23 Jul
42:50	Antonella	Palmisano	ITA	6.8.91	2		Moskva	30 Aug
43:05		Duan Dandan	CHN-J	23.5.95	1	WCp-J	Taicang	4 May
43:09	Mirna	Ortiz	GUA	28.2.87	1		Katowice	13 Sep
43:10.95 t		Takacs			1	IbAm	São Paulo	1 Aug
43:13	Brigita	Virbalyte	LTU	1.2.85	2		Katowice	13 Sep
43:17	Irina	Shushina	RUS	30.10.86	2		Bui	13 Sep
43:31		Duan Dandan			1J		Huangshan	27 Feb
43:31.21 t	Raquel	González	ESP	16.11.89	2	NC	Alcobendas	26 Jul
43:36		Virbalyte			1		Gdansk	30 Aug
43:37		Yang Jiayu	CHN-J	18.2.96	2	WCp-J	Taicang	4 May
43:40		Drahotová			3	WCp-J	Taicang	4 May
43:41.30 t	Erica	de Sena	BRA	3.5.85	2	IbAm	São Paulo	1 Aug
43:44		Bikulova			3		Moskva	30 Aug
43:44.03 t	Inês	Henriques	POR	1.5.80	1		Cartaxo	22 Mar
43:47.84 t	Ana	Cabecinha	POR	29.4.84	1	NC	Lisboa (U)	26 Jul
43:48	Hanna	Drabenya	BLR	15.8.87	1		Grodno	4 Oct
43:57.13 t	Beatriz	Pascual	ESP	9.5.82	3	NC	Alcobendas	26 Jul
43:57.44t	Kimberley	García	PER	19.10.93	3	IbAm	São Paulo	1 Aug
44:02.64 t		Wang Na	CHN-J	29.5.95	2	WJ	Eugene	23 Jul
44:05		Ji Yefang	CHN-J	4.3.96	3	NGP-J	Changbaishan	12 Sep
44:10.29 t	Kumiko	Okada	JPN	17.10.91	1		Yamaguchi	11 Oct
44:14+	Agnieszka	Dygacz	POL	18.7.85		in 20k	Lugano	16 Mar
44:15	Neringa	Aidietyte	LTU	5.6.83	1		Birstonas	26 Apr
44:15.45 t	Susana	Feitor	POR	28.1.75	4	IbAm	São Paulo	1 Aug
44:16.72 t		Ni Yuanyuan	CHN-J	6.4.95	3	WJ	Eugene	23 Jul
44:27	Sofiya	Brodatskaya	RUS-J	4.10.95	3		Bui	13 Sep
44:32.84 t	Laura	García-Cano	ESP-J	16.4.95	4	WJ	Eugene	23 Jul
44:35+	Mayra Carolina	Herrera	GUA	20.12.88		in 20k	Taicang	3 May
44:38		La Mao	CHN-J	17.12.96	2	NGP-J	Taicang	5 May
44:39.78 t	Viktória	Madarász	HUN	12.5.85	1		Debrecen	29 Aug
44:39.92 t	Natalya	Serezhkina	RUS	7.5.92	1		Saransk	3 Aug
44:49.84 t	Chiaki	Asada	JPN	21.1.91	2		Yamaguchi	11 Oct
44:56		Su Yingqiu	CHN-J	1.2.95	1	NGP-J	Changbaishan	12 Sep
44:57.30 t	Mária	Pérez	ESP-J	29.4.96	5	WJ	Eugene	23 Jul
44:57.6	Inna	Kashyna	UKR	27.9.91	2		Mukahchevo	1 Nov
44:58+	Olha	Yakovenko	UKR	1.6.87		in 20k	Taicang	3 May
44:58.26 t	Lorena	Arenas	COL	17.9.93	5	IbAm	São Paulo	1 Aug
45:02	Johanna	Atkinson	GBR	17.1.85	1		Coventry	1 Mar
45:08+	Alina	Matveyuk	BLR	29.7.90		in 20k	Taicang	3 May
45:08.42 r	Tanya	Holliday	AUS	21.9.88	1	NC	Melbourne	4 Apr
45:09+	Rachel	Seaman	CAN	14.1.86		in 20k	Taicang	3 May
45:09	Mária	Gáliková	SVK	21.8.80	5		Katowice	13 Sep
45:09.33 t	Ai	Michiguchi	JPN	3.6.88	3		Yamaguchi	11 Oct
45:11		Yang Lei	CHN-J	29.11.95	3	NGP-J	Taicang	5 May
45:16	Oksana	Golyatkina	RUS-J	13.3.95	1	NC-wJ	Sochi	23 Mar
45:21.47 t	Nicole	Fagan	AUS	24.7.89	2	NC	Melbourne	4 Apr
45:23	Maritza Rafaela	Poncio	GUA	3.12.94	6		Katowice	13 Sep
45:23.8	Nadiya	Borovska	UKR	25.2.81	3		Mukachevo	1 Nov
45:24.21 t	Kristina	Saltanovic	LTU	20.2.75	2		Cartaxo	22 Mar

Mark	Wind	Name		Nat	Born	Pos	Meet	Venue	Date
45:25.06	t	Ingrid	Hernández	COL	29.11.88	6	IbAm	São Paulo	1 Aug
45:25.90	t	Kelly	Ruddick	AUS	19.4.73	3	NC	Melbourne	4 Apr
45:28+		Sandra	Galvis	COL	28.6.86		in 20k	Taicang	3 May

Mark	First name	Name	Nat	Born	Date
45:31	Klavdiya	Afanasyeva	RUS-J	15.1.96	6 Sep
45:33	Ainhoa	Pinedo	ESP	17.2.83	25 Jan
45:33+	Olga	Dubrovina	RUS	11.6.93	6 Jun
45:34+		Luo Xingcai	CHN	18.7.94	27 Feb
45:34+		Xie Lijuan	CHN	14.5.93	27 Feb
45:36		Cun Hailu	CHN-Y	15.8.97	27 Feb
45:37+	Déspina	Zapounídou	GRE	5.10.85	14 Aug
45:38+	Anastasiya	Yatsevich	BLR	18.1.85	13 Jun
45:38	Yevdokiya	Korotkova	RUS	28.2.79	13 Sep
45:43	Natalya	Kholodilina	RUS	21.7.89	30 Aug
45:43	Mariya	Ponomaryova	RUS-J	18.6.95	6 Sep
45:44.89t	Masumi	Fuchise	JPN	2.9.86	11 Oct
45:54+		Xie Lijuan	CHN	14.5.93	27 Feb
45:54.07t	Rena	Goto	JPN-J	6.9.95	23 Jul
45:51+	Vasylyna	Vitovchuk	UKR	30.4.90	14 Aug
45:58	Olga	Shargina	RUS-J	24.7.96	6 Jun
45:59		Gao Shan	CHN-J	8.4.95	27 Feb
45:59	Anastasiya	Taushkanova	RUS-J	25.3.96	6 Sep
45:59.81		Yang Jianyu	CHN	18.2.86	29 Aug
46:04+	Rei	Inoue	JPN	23.7.91	3 May
46:04+	Olena	Shumkina	UKR	24.1.88	3 May
46:04.91t		Liang Rui	CHN	18.6.94	29 Aug
46:06.7	Halyna	Yakovchuk	UKR	21.2.92	1 Nov
46:07.59t	Sae	Matsumoto	JPN	15.5.93	21 Oct
46:09	Ana	Rodeanu	ROU	23.6.84	30 May
46:10		Zhao Qianyuan	CHN-J	11.3.95	27 Feb
46:12		Jeon Yeong-eun	KOR	24.5.88	24 Apr
46:13.83t	Mari	Olsson	SWE	27.4.86	4 Apr
46:13.83t	Marina	Ignatova	RUS-J	6.6.95	28 Jun
46:16.79t	Tomomi	Maekawa	JPN	28.9.91	11 Oct
46:17		Ma Zhenxia	CHN-Y	1.8.98	27 Feb
46:18		Zhang Rui	CHN-J	16.5.95	27 Feb
46:18	Emilie	Menuet	FRA	27.9.91	15 Jun
46:21	Viktoriya	Roshchupkina	BLR-J	23.5.95	4 May
46:21	Federica	Curiazzi	ITA	14.8.92	18 Jul
46:22		Ma Yiming	CHN-Y	10.9.97	27 Feb
46:22.88t	Kana	Minemura	JPN-J	12.5.96	23 Jul
46:23		Yang Liujing	CHN-Y	22.8.98	5 May
46:23.22t	Cisiane	Lopes	BRA	17.2.83	1 Aug
46:25		Zhang Lili	CHN-J	29.3.95	12 Sep
46:25	Mariya	Losinova	RUS-J		13 Sep
46:26	Kristina	Mikhaylova	RUS	16.10.92	9 May
46:28		Yin Hang	CHN	7.2.97	5 May

Best track performances

44:56.78	Poves	4	NC	Alcobendas	26 Jul
45:33.26	Duan Dandan	1		Beijing	29 Aug

45:43.12A	Caballero	15 May
45:53.76	Gáliková	7 Jun
45:56.43	La Mao	5 Jun
46:08.54	Khramova	3 Aug
46:25.2	Vitovchuk	1 Nov

Indoors

45:51.23	Matveyuk	21 Feb

JUNIORS

See main list for top 13 juniors. 12 performances by 6 women to 44:20. Additional marks and further juniors:

Duan	43:31	1	NC-j	Huangshan	27 Feb	43:52	1	Changbaishan	12 Sep
Yang	44:05	2		Changbaishan	12 Sep	44:16	2	NC-j Huangshan	27 Feb
Wang Na	44:17	1		Taicang	5 May				

Mark		Name		Nat	Born	Pos	Meet	Venue	Date
45:31		Klavdiya	Afanasyeva	RUS	15.1.96	1	NCp	Cheboksary	6 Sep
45:36			Cun Hailu	CHN-Y	15.8.97	1	NC-Y	Huangshan	27 Feb
45:43		Mariya	Ponomaryova	RUS	18.6.95	2	NCp	Cheboksary	6 Sep
45:54.07	t	Rena	Goto	JPN-	6.9.95	6	WJ	Eugene	23 Jul
45:58		Olga	Shargina	RUS	24.7.96	1	NC-j	Cheboksary	6 Jun
45:59			Gao Shan	CHN	8.4.95	4	NC-j	Huangshan	27 Feb
45:59		Anastasiya	Taushkanova	RUS	25.3.96	3	NCp	Cheboksary	6 Sep
45:33.26	t		Duan Dandan	CHN	23.5.95	1		Beijing	29 Aug
45:56.43			La Mao	CHN	17.12.96	1		Huajan	5 Jun

20 KILOMETRES WALK

20k	10k	Name		Nat	Born	Pos	Meet	Venue	Date
1:26:31	44:34	Anisya	Kirdyapkina	RUS	23.10.89	1	WCp	Taicang	3 May
1:26:58	44:33		Liu Hong	CHN	12.5.87	2	WCp	Taicang	3 May
1:27:02	44:34	Elmira	Alembekova	RUS	30.6.90	3	WCp	Taicang	3 May
1:27:03	44:34	Vera	Sokolova	RUS	8.6.87	4	WCp	Taicang	3 May
1:27:05	44:34	Eleonora	Giorgi	ITA	14.9.89	5	WCp	Taicang	3 May
1:27:15	44:34		Lu Xiuzhi	CHN	26.10.93	6	WCp	Taicang	3 May
1:27:25	44:14		Liu Hong			1		Lugano	16 Mar
1:27:27	44:20	Lyudmyla	Olyanovska	UKR	20.2.93	7	WCp	Taicang	3 May
1:27:29	44:14		Giorgi			2		Lugano	16 Mar
1:27:39	44:35		Liu Hong			1		La Coruña	31 May
1:27:49	44:34	Ana	Cabecinha	POR	29.4.84	8	WCp	Taicang	3 May
1:27:51	44:34	Antonella	Palmisano	ITA	6.8.91	9	WCp	Taicang	3 May
1:27:54	44:34	Marina	Pandakova (10)	RUS	1.3.89	10	WCp	Taicang	3 May
1:27:56	45:05		Alembekova			1	EC	Zürich	14 Aug
1:28:02	44:34	Vera	Santos	POR	3.12.81	11	WCp	Taicang	3 May
1:28:05			Kirdyapkina			1	NC-w	Sochi	22 Mar
1:28:05	45:13		Sokolova			1	NC	Cheboksary	6 Jun
1:28:07	45:05		Olyanovska			2	EC	Zürich	14 Aug
1:28:08	45:06	Anezka	Drahotová	CZE-J	22.7.95	3	EC	Zürich	14 Aug
1:28:12	44:34	Lina	Bikulova	RUS	1.10.88	12	WCp	Taicang	3 May
1:28:13	44:14		Drahotová			3		Lugano	16 Mar
1:28:24	45:06		Sokolova			4	EC	Zürich	14 Aug
1:28:28	45:06		Giorgi			5	EC	Zürich	14 Aug
1:28:32			Sokolova			2	NC-w	Sochi	22 Mar
1:28:36	44:44	Raquel	González	ESP	16.11.89	13	WCp	Taicang	3 May
1:28:40	45:06		Cabecinha			6	EC	Zürich	14 Aug
1:28:43	44:34		Nie Jingjing	CHN	1.3.88	14	WCp	Taicang	3 May

Mark	Wind	Name		Nat	Born	Pos	Meet	Venue	Date
1:28:43	45:05		Palmisano			7	EC	Zürich	14 Aug
1:28:46	44:44	María José	Poves	ESP	16.3.78	15	WCp	Taicang	3 May
1:28:48			Pandakova			3	NC-w	Sochi	22 Mar
1:28:48	44:42	María Guadalupe	González	MEX	9.1.89	16	WCp	Taicang	3 May
1:28:49	45:13	Svetlana	Vasilyeva	RUS	24.7.92	2	NC	Cheboksary	6 Jun
1:28:51	44:35	Susana	Feitor	POR	28.1.75	17	WCp	Taicang	3 May
		(33/19)							
1:28:58	44:33	Agnieszka	Dygacz (20)	POL	18.7.85	18	WCp	Taicang	3 May
1:29:01	44:22	Neringa	Aidietyte	LTU	5.6.83	1	NC	Alytus	13 Jun
1:29:02	45:06	Beatriz	Pascual	ESP	9.5.82	8	EC	Zürich	14 Aug
1:29:08	45:40	Julia	Takacs	ESP	29.6.89	1	NC	Murcia	16 Feb
1:29:17	44:34		Ding Huiqin	CHN	5.2.90	19	WCp	Taicang	3 May
1:29:20	44:34		Sun Huanhuan	CHN	15.3.90	20	WCp	Taicang	3 May
1:29:33	44:44	Inês	Henriques	POR	1.5.80	22	WCp	Taicang	3 May
1:29:39	45:07	Hanna	Drabenya	BLR	15.8.87	9	EC	Zürich	14 Aug
1:29:41	44:41	Paulina	Buziak	POL	16.12.86	1		Zaniemysl	5 Apr
1:29:44	44:34	Kimberley	García	PER	19.10.93	24	WCp	Taicang	3 May
1:29:45	45:05	Mirna	Ortiz	GUA	28.2.87	2		Alytus	13 Jun
		(30)							
1:30:17		Inna	Kashyna	UKR	27.9.91	1	NC	Alushta	28 Feb
1:30:18	44:34	Lorena	Arenas	COL	17.9.93	25	WCp	Taicang	3 May
1:30:27	45:33		Hou Yongbo	CHN	15.9.94	4	NC	Huangshan	27 Feb
1:30:41		Olena	Shumkina	UKR	24.1.88	2	NC	Alushta	28 Feb
1:30:41	44:35	Mayra Carolina	Herrera	GUA	20.12.88	28	WCp	Taicang	3 May
1:30:43		Rachel	Seaman	CAN	14.1.86	1		Manchester, NJ	30 Mar
1:30:43	45:15	Érica	de Sena	BRA	3.5.85	2		Podébrady	12 Apr
1:30:44			Wang Di	CHN	30.8.92	1	NGP	Taicang	5 May
1:30:48		Alina	Matveyuk	BLR	29.7.90	1	NC	Brest	24 Jun
1:30:49	45:07	Maria	Michta	USA	23.6.86	30	WCp	Taicang	3 May
		(40)							
1:30:51	45:32		Wang Yingliu	CHN	1.3.92	6	NC	Huangshan	27 Feb
1:30:57	45:26	Viktória	Madarász	HUN	12.5.85	12	EC	Zürich	14 Aug
1:31:00	45:03	Brigita	Virbalyte	LTU	1.2.85	3		Alytus	13 Jun
1:31:02		Ingrid	Hernández	COL	29.11.88	1		Valley Cottage	14 Sep
1:31:06			Ji Yefang	CHN-J	4.3.96	3	NGP	Taicang	5 May
1:31:09	45:33		Zhou Kang	CHN	24.12.89	7	NC	Huangshan	27 Feb
1:31:09			Luo Xingcai	CHN	18.7.94	4	NGP	Taicang	5 May
1:31:14		Olga	Dubrovina	RUS	11.6.93	6	NC-w	Sochi	22 Mar
1:31:15		Sandra	Galvis	COL	28.6.86	2		Valley Cottage	14 Sep
1:31:19			Xie Lijuan	CHN	14.5.93	5	NGP	Taicang	5 May
		(50)							
1:31:23	45:55		Zhao Jing	CHN	18.2.92	9	NC	Huangshan	27 Feb
1:31:30	45:33		Liu Huan	CHN	24.2.93	10	NC	Huangshan	27 Feb
1:31:40	44:42	Khushbir	Kaur	IND	9.7.93	35	WCp	Taicang	3 May
1:31:48	46:38	Rei	Inoue	JPN	23.7.91	1	NC	Kobe	16 Feb
1:31:48	45:15	Katarzyna	Burghardt	POL	29.6.85	4		Podébrady	12 Apr
1:31:53		Anastasiya	Yatsevich	BLR	18.1.85	2	NC	Brest	24 Jun
1:31:55	45:33		Li Maocuo	CHN	20.10.92	12	NC	Huangshan	27 Feb
1:31:57	45:41	Laura	Reynolds	IRL	20.1.89	7		La Coruña	31 May
1:31:58	46:07		Zhou Tongmei	CHN	4.4.88	1		Nomi	16 Mar
1:31:59	45:33		Dong Genmiao	CHN	16.7.94	13	NC	Huangshan	27 Feb
		(60)							
1:32:03	45:37	Mária	Gáliková	SVK	21.8.80	17	EC	Zürich	14 Aug
1:32:07	45:33	Alyona	Khramova	RUS	18.8.93	2	NCp	Cheboksary	6 Sep
1:32:31	46:38	Masumi	Fuchise	JPN	2.9.86	2	NC	Kobe	16 Feb
1:32:36	45:01	Tanya	Holliday	AUS	21.9.88	39	WCp	Taicang	3 May
1:32:41	46:38	Ai	Michiguchi	JPN	3.6.88	3	NC	Kobe	16 Feb
1:32:44	45:33	Natalya	Kholodilina	RUS	21.7.89	5	NC	Cheboksary	6 Jun
1:32:46		Halyna	Yakovchuk	UKR	21.2.92	3	NC	Alushta	28 Feb
1:32:51	45:27	Yanelli	Caballero	MEX	29.5.93	40	WCp	Taicang	3 May
1:32:57	45:50	Irina	Shushina	RUS	30.10.86	6	NC	Cheboksary	6 Jun
1:32:58	45:50	Kristina	Saltanovic	LTU	20.2.75	43	WCp	Taicang	3 May
		(70)							
1:32:59		Ainhoa	Pinedo	ESP	17.2.83	10		La Coruña	31 May
1:33:02	46:02	Déspina	Zapounídou	GRE	5.10.85	11		Lugano	16 Mar
1:33:11		Miranda	Melville	USA	20.3.89	3		Manchester, NJ	30 Mar
1:33:14		Maritza Rafaela	Poncio	GUA	3.12.94	5		Alytus	13 Jun
1:33:18	45:52		Jeon Yeong-eun	KOR	24.5.88	3	AsiG	Incheon	28 Sep
1:33:22	45:52	Laura	Polli	SUI	7.9.83	19	EC	Zürich	14 Aug
1:33:23			Li Leilei	CHN	18.8.89	14	NC	Huangshan	27 Feb
1:33:25	46:38	Kumiko	Okada	JPN	17.10.91	1r2		Nomi	16 Mar

Mark	Wind	Name		Nat	Born	Pos	Meet	Venue	Date
1:33:40	45:15	Paola	Pérez	ECU	21.12.89	5		Podébrady	12 Apr
1:33:43	46:43	Johanna (80)	Atkinson	GBR	17.1.85	12		Lugano	16 Mar
1:34:00	46:30	Kelly	Ruddick	AUS	19.4.73	49	WCp	Taicang	3 May
1:34:13		Mária	Czaková	SVK	2.10.88	51	WCp	Taicang	3 May
1:34:18		Anna	Krakhmaleva	RUS	1.5.92	9	NC-w	Sochi	22 Mar
1:34:18		Kristina	Mikhaylova	RUS	16.10.92	10	NC-w	Sochi	22 Mar
1:34:20	46:35		Chen Zhen	CHN	3.11.94	15	NC	Huangshan	27 Feb
1:34:20		Monika	Kapera	POL	15.2.90	2		Zaniemysl	5 Apr
1:34:26	46:45	Katarzyna	Golba	POL	21.12.89	6		Alytus	13 Jun
1:34:28	46:12		Yang Mingxia	CHN	13.1.90	13		Lugano	16 Mar
1:34:36		Olha	Yakovenko	UKR	1.6.87	4	NC	Alushta	28 Feb
1:34:39		Lucie (90)	Pelantová	CZE	7.5.86	14		Lugano	16 Mar
1:34:39	46:40	Marie	Polli	SUI	28.10.80	21	EC	Zürich	14 Aug
1:34:50		Valentina	Trapletti	ITA	12.7.85	8		Podébrady	12 Apr
1:34:50		Laura	García-Cano	ESP-J	16.4.95	12		La Coruña	31 May
1:34:59			He Qin	CHN	23.3.92	1	NGP	Changbaishan	13 Sep
1:35:05		Chiaki	Asada	JPN	21.1.91	1		Takahata	26 Oct
1:35:07		Nguyen	Thi Thanh Duc	VIE	12.8.90	1	NG	Nam Dinh	13 Dec
1:35:08	46:19	Magaly	Bonilla	ECU	8.2.92	52	WCp	Taicang	3 May
1:35:12	46:37	Tatyana	Akulinushkina	RUS	6.4.94	8	NC	Cheboksary	6 Jun
1:35:16		Emilie	Menuet	FRA	27.11.91	9		Podébrady	12 Apr
1:35:20	46:38	Hiroi (100)	Maeda	JPN	1.6.91	5	NC	Kobe	16 Feb

Mark	Name		Nat	Born	Date
1:35:22	Vasylyna	Vitovshchyk	UKR	30.4.90	12 Apr
1:35:26	Cisiane	Lopes	BRA	17.2.83	3 May
1:35:30		Lee Jung-kyung	KOR	13.9.94	15 Jul
1:35:31	Mónica	Equihua	MEX	23.9.82	31 May
1:35:34	Shiori	Kawase (46:38)	JPN	11.12.93	16 Feb
1:35:36		Xin Shasha	CHN	20.1.92	27 Feb
1:35:37	Beki	Lee	AUS	25.11.86	14 Dec
1:35:38	Antigóni	Drisbióti	GRE	21.3.84	23 Mar
1:35:39	Kaori	Kawazoe	JPN-J	30.5.95	16 Feb
1:35:40A	Grace	Wanjiru	KEN	10.1.79	6 Jun
1:35:46		Wang Yalan	CHN	19.2.93	12 Apr
1:35:48	Federica	Curiazzi	ITA	14.8.92	14 Aug
1:35:55A	Claudia	Balderrama	BOL	13.11.83	22 Feb
1:36:03		Kim Mi-jung	KOR	10.6.79	1 Nov
1:36:07		Li Ping	CHN	7.1.94	27 Feb
1:36:07	Sofiya	Brodatskaya	RUS-J	4.10.95	6 Jun
1:36:11		Ma Faying	CHN	30.8.93	12 Apr
1:36:13	Corinne	Baudoin	FRA	22.2.80	3 May
1:36:20	Sae	Matsumoto	JPN	15.5.93	26 Oct
1:36:22	Tomomi	Maekawa	JPN	28.9.91	16 Mar
1:36:31	Darya	Balkunets	BLR	4.3.93	3 May
1:36:32	Ángela	Castro	BOL	21.2.93	3 May
1:36:38	Olga	Chudayeva	RUS	8.11.88	6 Sep
1:36:41	Fumiko	Okabe	JPN	8.7.90	16 Feb
1:36:45	Valentyna	Myronchuk	UKR	10.8.94	28 Feb
1:36:51		Wang Tingting	CHN	18.1.87	27 Feb
1:36:51	Lorena	Luaces	ESP	29.2.84	31 May
1:36:53	Serena	Pruner	ITA	21.5.86	12 Apr
1:36:57	Yeseida	Carrillo	COL	22.10.93	31 May
1:37:00.0t	Galina	Kichigina	KAZ	14.7.88	27 Jun
1:37:01	Inès	Pastorino	FRA	20.10.92	9 Mar
1:37:02	Nataliya	Kontsevych	UKR	14.4.84	28 Feb
1:37:07		Kang Jinzi	CHN	25.1.90	13 Sep
1:37:08	Mami	Urabe	JPN	18.1.88	16 Mar
1:37:09		Duan Dandan	CHN-J	23.5.95	16 Mar
1:37:11A	Wendy	Cornejo	BOL	7.1.93	15 Feb
1:37:19		Li Qiuye	CHN	2.12.93	27 Feb
1:37:27	Maria	Juarez	ESP	27.9.93	31 May
1:37:28	Oksana	Trofymovych	UKR	26.2.92	28 Feb
1:37:28		Liang Rui	CHN	18.6.94	13 Sep
1:37:39	Stephanie	Stigwood	AUS	21.10.90	2 Feb
1:37:39	Eliska	Drahotová	CZE-J	22.7.95	12 Apr
1:37:39		Mao Yanxue	CHN	15.2.94	5 May
1:37:41		Zhu Chunyan	CHN	3.6.92	27 Feb
1:37:45	Nicole	Fagan	AUS	24.7.89	27 Jul
1:37:51		Weon Aseas-byeol	KOR	8.4.90	3 May
1:37:57	Daniela	Cardoso	POR	15.12.91	31 May
1:38:00	Natalya (148)	Serezhkina	RUS	7.5.92	6 Sep

Best track marks

Mark	Name	Pos	Meet	Venue	Date
1:31:46.9	Arenas	1	SAmG	Santigo de Chile	13 Mar
1:31:53.8A	Ortiz	1	NC	C. de Guatemala	9 Aug
1:33:20.1A	Poncio	2	NC	C. de Guatemala	9 Aug
1:34:04.4	Galvis	2	SAmG	Santigo de Chile	13 Mar
1:36:37.3	de Sena	3	SAmG	Santigo de Chile	13 Mar
1:37:43.1	Cornejo	1	SAm23	Montevideo	4 Oct

Drugs disqualification

Mark	Name		Nat	Born	Pos	Meet	Venue	Date
1:28:44	Irina	Yumanova ¶	RUS	6.11.90	(4)	NC-w	Sochi	22 Mar

JUNIORS

See main list for top 3 juniors. 5 performances by 3 women to 1:35:00. Additional marks and further juniors:

Drahotová 2+ 1:29:43 1 Podebrady 12 Apr

Mark	Name		Nat	Born	Pos	Meet	Venue	Date
1:35:39	Kaori	Kawazoe	JPN-J	30.5.95	7	NC	Kobe	16 Feb
1:36:07	Sofiya	Brodatskaya	RUS-J	4.10.95	9	NC	Cheboksary	6 Jun
1:37:09		Duan Dandan	CHN-J	23.5.95	5		Nomi	16 Mar
1:37:39	Eliska	Drahotová	CZE-J	22.7.95	16		Podébrady	12 Apr
1:38:10	Remi	Okubo	JPN-J	22.2.95	7		Takahata	26 Oct

50 KILOMETRES WALK

Mark	Name		Nat	Born	Pos	Meet	Venue	Date
4:38:11	Erin	Taylor-Talcott	USA	21.5.78	1	NC	Santee	14 Dec
4:39:42	Katie	Burnett	USA	10.7.88	2	NC	Santee	14 Dec
4:42:34	Susan	Randall	USA	6.9.74	3	NC	Santee	14 Dec

MEN'S INDEX 2014

Athletes included are those ranked in the top 100s at standard (World Championships) events (plus shorter lists for 1000m, 1M, 2000m and 3000m). Those with detailed biographical profiles are indicated in first column by:
* in this year's Annual, ^ featured in a previous year's Annual.

Name		Nat	Born	Ht/Wt	Event	2014 Mark	Pre-2014 Best
Abadia	Antonio	ESP	2.7.90	180/72	3000	7:46.36i	7:58.75i- 11, 8:00.78- 13
Abbas	Ali Khamis	BRN-J	30.6.95	178/73	400h	49.55	52.67- 13
Abda	Harun	USA	1.1.90	178/64	800	1:45.55	1:46.38- 13
* Abdelrahman	Ihab	EGY	1.5.89	194/96	JT	89.21	83.62- 13
Abdi	Bashir	BEL	10.2.89	178/64	1500	3:36.55	3:44.31- 13
3000 7:44.12 7:58.80-11	5000 13:20.61 13:29.09- 12				10k	27:36.40	27:43.99- 13
Abe	Takatoshi	JPN	12.11.91	189/82	400h	49.69	49.46- 10
* Abele	Arthur	GER	30.7.86	184/80	110h	13.55	13.90- 08
					Dec	8477	8269- 07
Abera	Melaku	ETH	20.4.94	177/61	10k	27:42.35	27:54.74- 13
Abera	Tesfaye	ETH	31.3.92		HMar	60:57	60:32- 12
Abinet	Abiyot	ETH	10.5.89	168/54	1500	3:34.97	3:34.06- 13
					2000	4:57.17i	
Abramchuk	Mikhal	BLR	15.11.92		SP	19.88	19.45- 13
Abrão	Cleiton	BRA	8.9.89	175/64	800	1:45.59	1:48.16- 12
Abromavicius	Aleksas	LTU	6.12.84	197/115	DT	62.58	63.32- 10
* Abshero	Ayele	ETH	28.12.90	167/52	Mar	2:06:31	2:04:23- 12
Abubaker	Abbas	BRN-J	17.5.96	175/64	400	45.17	46.85- 13
Acea	Raidel	CUB	31.10.90	188/77	400	45.36A, 46.03	45.90- 13, 45.8- 09
Adam	Guillaume	FRA	15.1.90	188/70	1500	3:38.41	3:40.35- 13
Adams	Antoine	SKN	31.8.88	180/79	100	10.01	10.01, 10.00w- 13
					200	20.08	20.43- 12, 20.13A, 20.25w- 13
^ Adams	Harry	USA	27.11.89	182/81	100	10.13, 10.06w	9.96- 12
* Adams	Lyukman	RUS	24.9.88	194/87	TJ	17.37i, 17.29	17.53- 12
Adams	Spencer	USA	10.9.89	188/84	110h	13.33	13.39- 12, 13.24w- 13
Adedoyin	Kola	GBR	8.4.91	188/79	TJ	16.61	16.50i- 13, 16.25- 12
Adhana	Gebretsadik	ETH	16.7.92		Mar	2:07:06	2:06:21- 12
^ Adhane	Yemane Tsegay	ETH	8.4.85		Mar	2:06:51	2:04:48- 12
Adola	Guye	ETH	20.10.90	180/60	HMar	59:06	
Ahmed	Mohammed	CAN	5.1.91	175/61	5000	13:18.88	13:34.23- 11
					10k	28:02.96	27:34.64- 12
Aikines-Aryeetey	Harry	GBR	29.8.88	176/86	100	10.08	10.08- 13
* Akdag	Tarik Langat	TUR	16.6.88	176/60	3kSt	8:26.45	8:08.59- 11
Akimenko	Mikhail	RUS-J	6.12.95		HJ	2.24i, 2.24	2.20i, 2.18- 13
Akins	Tyrone	USA/NGR	6.1.86	180/79	110h	13.48	13.25- 08, 13.2w- 10
^ Akkas	Halil	TUR	1.7.83	174/60	3kSt	8:29.48	8:18.43- 07
Al-Ameen	Alex	GBR/NGR	2.3.89	186/82	110h	13.54	13.67- 12, 13.66w- 10
Al-Dosari	Ahmad Fayez	KSA	6.9.79	180/75	LJ	7.90	8.12- 02
* Al-Gamal	Mostafa	EGY	1.10.88	191/105	HT	81.27	77.73- 13
Al-Garni	Mohamed	QAT	2.7.92	171/62	5000	13:26.13	14:28.34- 13
Al-Haddad	Saleh Abdelaziz	KUW	7.4.86	179/65	LJ	7.94i, 7.85	8.02- 09, 8.05w- 07
Al-Hebshi	Sultan	KSA	23.2.83	185/103	SP	19.99	21.13- 09
Al-Mandeel	Abdulaziz	KUW	22.5.89	175/66	110h	13.49	13.58, 13.50w- 12
* Al-Masrahi	Youssef	KSA	31.12.87	176/76	400	44.43	44.61- 13
Al-Yoha	Yaqoub	KUW	31.1.93	185/70	110h	13.64	14.00- 13
* Al-Zankawi	Ali Mohamed	KUW	27.2.84	186/97	HT	75.73	79.74- 09
Alaiz	Roberto	ESP	20.7.90	182/63	3kSt	8:27.00	8:24.53- 12
* Alamirew	Yenew	ETH	27.5.90	175/57	3000	7:37.10i	7:27.26- 11
					5000	13:00.21	12:48.77- 12
Alejandro	Eric	PUR	15.4.86	180/70	400h	49.07	49.15- 12
* Alekna	Virgilijus	LTU	13.2.72	200/130	DT	65.76	73.88- 00
Alexander	Akeem	USA	9.9.94	175/70	400	45.22	47.08- 13
Ali	Ahmed	USA	15.11.93	180/80	100	10.13w	10.23, 10.12w- 13
Alic	Hamza	BIH	20.1.79	192/108	SP	19.92	20.73- 13
* Allen	Devon	USA	12.12.94	190/86	110h	13.16	-0-
Almeida	João	POR	5.4.88	188/79	110h	13.58	13.47- 12
Almeya	Aimeru	ISR	8.6.90	175/55	10k	28:12.87	29:10.29- 13
Almgren	Andreas	SWE-J	12.6.95	177/66	800	1:45.65	1:49.46- 13
Alonso	Maximiliano	CHI	10.10.86		DT	60.85	60.22- 12
Alowonle	Rilwan	NGR	12.12.93	175/66	400h	50.11	51.03- 13
Álvarez	Alberto	MEX	8.3.91	189/72	TJ	16.63	16.39A- 13, 16.30, 16.52w- 12
Alves	Higor	BRA	23.2.94	181/75	LJ	8.18	8.02- 13
* Aman	Mohammed	ETH	10.1.94	169/55	800	1:42.83	1:42.37- 13
600 1:15.31i	1:15.0+- 12				1000	2:15.75	2:19.54- 10
Amare	Girmaw	ISR	26.10.87	172/60	10k	28:17.94	29:23.70- 12
* Amb	Kim	SWE	31.7.90	180/85	JT	84.14	84.61- 13

Name		Nat	Born	Ht/Wt	Event	2014 Mark	Pre-2014 Best
Amezcua	Luis Alberto	ESP	1.5.82	183/67	20kW	1:22:19	1:24:10- 12
* Amos	Nijel	BOT	15.3.94	179/60	400	45.56	45.66A- 13, 45.94- 12
600	1:16.0+		1:15.0+- 12		800	1:42.45	1:41.73- 12
Anani	Mohsen	EGY	25.5.85	187/117	HT	73.80	77.36- 10
Anastasákis	Mihaíl	GRE	3.12.94	183/92	HT	70.63	68.45- 13
^ Anderson	Jeshua	USA	22.6.89	187/84	400h	49.10	47.93- 11
Andrade	Jordin	USA	5.5.92	183/73	400h	50.03	50.11- 13
André	Thiago	BRA-J	4.8.95	177/62	800	1:45.99	
Andrews	Robby	USA	29.3.91	177/68	800	1:46.28	1:44.71- 11
Andreyev	Leonid	UZB	6.10.83	188/82	Dec	7879	7383- 13
Andreyev	Mikhail	RUS	4.4.91		HJ	2.24i	2.20i- 12, 2.15- 11
^ Andronov	Yuriy	RUS	6.11.71	180/68	50kW	3:43:52 drugs dq	3:40:46- 12
Anishchenkov	Nikita	RUS	25.7.92	188/80	HJ	2.24i	2.30- 11
Anne	Mame-Ibra	FRA	7.11.89	181/73	400	45.44	45.73- 13
Antmanis	Vladimir	RUS	12.3.84	188/77	400h	49.95	49.47- 13
Antoniades	Orestis	CYP	10.7.85	190/98	DT	61.77	60.12- 12
Apolloni	Federico	ITA	14.3.87	187/90	DT	60.64	59.75- 11
April	Lusapho	RSA	24.5.82	172/50	HMar	61:16	61:49- 09
Arai	Hiroki	JPN	18.5.88	179/61	20kW	1:20:38	1:21:10- 12
					50kW	3:40:34	3:45:56- 13
* Arai	Ryohei	JPN	23.6.91	183/92	JT	86.83	78.21- 11
* Araptany	Jacob	UGA	11.2.92	168/58	3kSt	8:20.84	8:14.48- 12
de Araújo	Luiz Alberto	BRA	27.9.87	190/90	Dec	7733	8276- 12
Arcilla	Francisco	ESP	14.1.84	171/62	50kW	3:58:00	-0-
Arents	Mareks	LAT	6.8.86	190/90	PV	5.60	5.62- 13
Arévalo	Eider	COL	9.3.93	165/58	20kW	1:21:28, 1:22:11.1t	1:19:45- 13
* Arikan	Polat Kemboi	TUR	12.12.90	173/62	10k	28:11.11	27:38.81- 12
Arkhipov	Aleksey	RUS	7.12.88		50kW	4:06:22	4:00:37- 13
Arnold	Mike	USA	13.8.90	190/84	PV	5.60iA, 5.40	5.70- 13
Arrhenius	Leif	SWE	15.7.86	192/120	SP	19.98	20.50- 13
					DT	61.19A	64.46- 11
Arrhenius	Niklas	SWE	10.9.82	192/125	DT	62.83A	66.22- 11
Art	Arnaud	BEL	28.1.93	185/83	PV	5.55	5.46i, 5.35- 12
Arteaga	Mauricio	ECU	8.8.88	173/65	20kW	1:21:46, 1:23:19.3t	1:21:56- 12
Arzandeh	Mohammad	IRI	30.10.87	180/76	LJ	7.89	8.17- 12
Asefa	Belay	ETH	17.6.92	167/52	Mar	2:07:10	2:09:31- 13
* Ash	Ronnie	USA	2.7.88	188/86	110h	12.99	13.19, 12.98w- 10
* Ashmeade	Nickel	JAM	7.4.90	184/87	100	9.97, 9.95w	9.90- 13
					200	19.95	19.85- 12
Ashomko	Aleksandr	BLR	18.2.84	186/92	JT	80.28	84.27- 08
Assefa	Raji	ETH	18.2.86		Mar	2:08:48	2:06:24- 12
Atanasov	Zlatozar	BUL	12.12.89	191/77	TJ	16.33, 16.58w	17.09- 13
Atanaw	Kinde	ETH	15.4.93	167/52	5000	13:12.41	
					HMar	60:17	
Atici	Hüseyin	TUR	3.5.86	188/118	SP	19.55i, 19.55	20.42- 12
Atnafu	Yitayal	ETH	20.1.93		HMar	61:03	
Aucyna	Darius	LTU	7.5.89	193/80	TJ	16.55	16.84- 12
Augustyn	Lukasz	POL	29.11.90	180/70	50kW	4:01:22	4:04:42- 13
Augustyn	Rafal	POL	14.5.84	177/71	20kW	1:21:13	1:20:53- 12
					50kW	3:45:32	3:46:56- 11
Auzeil	Bastien	FRA	22.10.89	190/82	Dec	7847	8022- 13
^ Avan	Fatih	TUR	1.1.89	183/90	JT	83.05	85.60- 12
Ayalew	Aweke	BRN	23.2.93	170/54	5000	13:18.10	13:05.00- 13
Ayeko	Thomas	UGA	10.2.92	168/58	10k	28:17.8A	27:40.96- 13
Ayele	Abayneh	ETH	4.11,87	175/57	10k	28:04.16	27:57.51- 13
Baaziri	Redouane	MAR	23.7.93		800	1:46.47	1:46.75- 13
* Bába	Jaroslav	CZE	2.9.84	196/82	HJ	2.31	2.37i, 2.36- 05
Babits	Max	USA	30.5.92	185/70	PV	5.51i	5.33Ai, 5.30- 13
Baciu	Alexandru George	ROM	25.2.91	186/65	TJ	16.39	16.56- 12
Baden	Joel	AUS-J	1.2.96		HJ	2.29	2.16- 13
^ Bailey	Daniel	ANT	9.9.86	173/70	100	10.10A, 10.17, 10.15w	9.91- 09
					200	20.40A, 20.43	20.51- 11
Bailey	Elvyonn	USA	28.9.91	173/75	200	20.64, 20.15w	20.93- 12
					400	45.52	46.17- 13
Bailey	Oshane	JAM	9.8.89	168/64	100	10.14, 10.13w	10.11- 10, 10.06w- 12
* Bailey	Ryan	USA	13.4.89	193/98	100	10.12, 10.03w	9.88- 10
					200	20.37	20.10- 10
Bailey	Tavis	USA	6.1.92	190/134	DT	64.51	59.51- 13
* Bailey-Cole	Kemar	JAM	10.1.92	195/84	100	9.96, 9.95w	9.93- 13
Baillio	Hayden	USA	22.7.91	186/141	SP	20.06	19.92- 12
* Baji	Balázs	HUN	9.6.89	192/84	110h	13.29	13.36- 13

	Name		Nat	Born	Ht/Wt	Event	2014 Mark	Pre-2014 Best
	Baker	Chris	GBR	2.2.91	197/84	HJ	2.28i, 2.27	2.22- 13
	Baker	Ronnie	USA	15.10.93	178/73	100	10.21, 10.14w	10.58, 10.33w- 13
	Balla	Abdulrahman Musaeb	QAT	19.3.89	175/60	800	1:44.03	1:43.93- 13
	Balner	Michal	CZE	12.9.82	193/78	PV	5.71, 5.75ex	5.76i, 5.73- 10
	Balnuweit	Erik	GER	21.9.88	189/75	110h	13.46, 13.45w	13.44, 13.32w-13
	Baloyes	Bernardo	COL	6.1.94	177/66	200	20.43, 20.35Aw	20.46A, 20.71- 13
						400	45.68A, 46.11	45.98A, 46.88- 13
	Baltaci	Õzkan	TUR	13.2.94	187/111	HT	72.89	70.61- 13
	Baltadoúros	Dimitrios	GRE	1.10.89	180/70	TJ	16.45	16.01- 13
	Bamba	Aboubacar	FRA	20.6.91	190/70	TJ	16.69i	16.67- 13
^	Baniótis	Konstadínos	GRE	6.11.86	202/80	HJ	2.28	2.34- 13
*	Banzeruk	Ivan	UKR	9.2.90	177/65	50kW	3:44:49	3:47:35- 13
*	Barber	Shawn	CAN	27.5.94	190/82	PV	5.75Ai, 5.65	5.71- 13
	Barnaby	Daundre	CAN	9.12.90	189/75	400	45.55	45.47- 13
	Barnes	Winston	JAM	7.11.88	178/73	100	10.17	10.14- 13
	Barr	Thomas	IRL	24.7.92	183/73	400h	48.90	49.78- 13
	Barrineau	Tommy	FIN	28.8.88	188/82	Dec	7609	7654- 11
	Barrios	Juan Luis	MEX	24.6.83	175/63	3000	7:43.90	7:37.64- 06
	5000	13:35.78		13:09.81-11		10k	27:34.40	27:28.82- 12
	Barroilhet	Gonzalo	CHI	19.8.86	196/96	Dec	7617	8065- 12
*	Barrondo	Érick	GUA	14.6.91	172/60	20kW	1:21:14	1:18:25- 12
						50kW	3:49:40A	3:41:09- 13
	de Barros	Bruno	BRA	7.1.87	178/70	200	20.46	20.16- 11
^	Barry	Trevor	BAH	14.6.83	190/77	HJ	2.25i, 2.25	2.32- 11
	Barshim	Muamer Aissa	QAT	3.1.94	191/68	HJ	2.28	2.20- 12
*	Barshim	Mutaz Essa	QAT	24.6.91	192/70	HJ	2.43	2.40- 13
*	Barsoton	Leonard	KEN	21.10.94	166/56	5000	13:21.44	13:19.04- 13
						10k	27:20.74	27:33.13- 13
	Bartsaykin	Aleksey	RUS	22.3.89		50kW	3:46:34	4:08:45- 12
	Barusei	Geoffrey	KEN	.94	164/53	1500	3:38.20	3:33.39- 12
						3000	7:47.71	7:44.32+- 13
*	Bascou	Dimitri	FRA	20.7.87	182/79	110h	13.25	13.34- 12, 13.26w- 11
	Bashan	Nikolay	BLR	18.11.92		HT	71.61	68.69- 13
	Bassaw	Ben	FRA	9.7.89	184/80	200	20.43	20.58- 12
	Bat-Ochir	Serod	MGL	7.10.81	169/59	Mar	2:08:50	2:09:00- 13
	Batson	Diondre	USA	13.7.92	188/75	100	10.04, 10.01w	10.06, 10.01w- 13
						200	20.49	20.50- 12, 20.35w- 13
	Bayer	Andrew	USA	3.2.90	180/60	3kSt	8:25.71	-0-
	Bayer	Maximilian	GER	5.12.90	181/73	110h	13.81, 13.63w	13.93- 13
*	Bayer	Sebastian	GER	11.6.86	189/79	LJ	8.05	8.71i, 8.49- 09
^	Bednarek	Sylwester	POL	28.4.89	198/75	HJ	2.25	2.32- 09
	Bednyuk	Anatoliy	RUS	30.1.89		PV	5.60i, 5.40	5.55- 12
	Beer	Lukás	SVK	23.8.89	186/73	HJ	2.26	2.22- 12
	Behailu	Ketema	ETH			HMar	60:58	60:53- 13
*	Behrenbruch	Pascal	GER	19.1.85	196/96	Dec	8055	8558- 12
	Bekele	Alemu	BRN	23.3.90	163/50	5000	13:27.98	13:18.00- 13
	Bekele	Azmeraw	ETH	22.1.86		HMar	60:55	59:39- 11
						Mar	2:07:12	2:10:25- 10
	Bekele	Feyisa	ETH	4.8.83	170/55	Mar	2:07:43	2:06:26- 12
*	Bekele	Kenenisa	ETH	13.6.82	162/54	Mar	2:05:04	-0-
*	Bekele	Tariku	ETH	21.1.87	168/52	5000	13:28.41	12:52.45- 08
*	Bekric	Emir	SRB	14.3.91	196/85	400h	49.21	48.05- 13
	Belhanbel	Nader	MAR	1.7.94	175/61	800	1:45.37	1:45.69- 13
	Belharbazi	Othmane	FRA	3.11.88	174/57	1500	3:37.21	3:35.93- 13
	Bell	Dylan	USA	21.7.93	190/82	PV	5.50iA	5.32Ai- 13, 5.25- 12
	Bellani	Hicham	MAR	15.9.79	180/64	5000	13:22.72	12:55.52- 06
	Bellido	José Emilio	ESP	25.5.87	180/68	TJ	16.50	16.80A, 16.65- 12
*	Belocian	Wilhem	FRA-J	22.6.95	179/70	110h	13.54	-0-
	Benák	Martin	SVK	27.5.88	193/100	JT	79.17	79.90- 10
	Benard	Chris	USA	4.4.90	190/79	LJ	8.10Ai, 7.81, 7.96w	7.75- 12
						TJ	17.10	16.78- 13
	Benedetti	Giordano	ITA	22.5.89	189/67	800	1:45.99	1:44.67- 13
	Benitz	Timo	GER	24.12.91	170/56	800	1:46.24	1:47.56- 13
	1000	2:16.90		2:22.77- 12		1500	3:34.94	3:40.36- 11
	Bennett	Chris	GBR	17.12.89	188/115	HT	72.58	71.24- 13
	Bensghir	Yassine	MAR	3.1.83	170/68	1500	3:34.80	3:33.04- 07
	Bento	Kaual Kamal	BRA	10.1.93	189/75	TJ	16.89	15.90, 15.91w- 12
	Berdeja	Cristian	MEX	21.6.81	169/58	50kW	3:53:39A	3:52:18A- 12
	Berger	Dominic	USA	19.5.86	181/79	110h	13.32	13.32- 11
	Berry	Michael	USA	10.12.91	184/73	400	45.05	44.75- 12
	Bertolini	Roberto	ITA	9.10.85	187/100	JT	77.23	78.10- 08

Name		Nat	Born	Ht/Wt	Event	2014 Mark	Pre-2014 Best
Beshr	Anas	EGY	19.7.93	188/77	400	45.59A, 45.60	45.79- 13
Bett	Bernard	KEN	.93		HMar	60:46	
Bett	David	KEN	18.10.92	160/52	5000	13:22.75	13:06.06- 10
* Bett	Emmanuel	KEN	30.3.83	170/55	3000	7:48.8+	
5000	13:14.91		13:08.35- 12		10k	27:21.61	26:51.16- 12
* Bett	Josphat	KEN	12.6.90	173/60	10k	27:56.14	26:48.99- 11
Bett	Nicholas	KEN-J	20.12.96		3kSt	8:28.83	
Bett	Nicholas	KEN	14.6.92	186/77	400h	49.03	49.70A- 13
Bett	Reuben	KEN	6.11.84	180/70	800	1:46.55	1:44.79- 09
Beyene	Berraki	ERI	6.2.80		Mar	2:08.27	2:09:01- 12
Beyo	Chala	ETH			3kSt	8:25.45	
^ Bezabeh	Alemayehu	ESP	22.9.86	182/53	10k	28:12.85	-0-
Bian Fongda		CHN	1.4.91	170/58	20kW	1:20:45	1:19:34- 13
Bigot ¶	Quentin	FRA	1.12.92	179/95	HT	78.58	78.28- 12
Bilderback	Zack	USA	15.7.94	193/80	400	45.66	46.08- 13
Bilodeau	Mathieu	CAN	.88	185/73	50kW	3:59:48	
Bilorus	Oleksiy	UKR	11.9.92		50kW	4:05:20	4:16:30- 13
Bingham	Michael	GBR	13.4.86	183/75	400	45.13	44.74- 09
Bird-Smith	Dane	AUS	15.7.92	178/66	20kW	1:20:27	1:22:03- 13
* Birech	Jairus	KEN	15.12.92	167/56	3kSt	7:58.41	8:03.43- 12
* Birgen	Bethwel	KEN	6.8.88	178/64	1500	3:31.22	3:30.77- 13
1M	3:51.12		3:50.42- 13		3000	7:37.17+i	7:37.15- 13
Birkinhead	Damien	AUS	8.4.93	190/130	SP	19.69	19.27- 13
Birmingham	Collis	AUS	27.12.84	189/71	1M	3:54.92	3:54.30- 09
3000	7:42.89		7:35.45- 12		5000	13:18.57	13:09.57- 12
Biwott	Robert	KEN-J	28.1.96	180/68	800	1:44.69	1:46.98- 13
* Biwott	Stanley	KEN	21.4.86	176/60	HMar	59:18	58:56- 13
					Mar	2:04:55	2:05:12- 12
Blair	Montez	USA	23.10.90	190/77	HJ	2.24i, 2.22	2.27i, 2.25- 13
* Blake	Yohan	JAM	26.12.89	181/79	100	10.02	9.69- 12
					200	20.48	19.26- 11
Blanco	Marvin	VEN	15.6.88	175/59	3kSt	8:21.78	8:34.27- 12
Blankenship	Ben	USA	15.12.88	173/61	3000	7:46.55i	7:47.07- 13
Blankenship	Jacob	USA	15.3.94	183/79	PV	5.64	5.61- 13
* Bledman	Keston	TTO	8.3.88	183/75	100	10.00	9.86, 9.85w- 12
Block	Dan	USA	8.1.91	193/109	SP	19.55i, 18.90	20.00i, 19.31- 13
Blocki	Adrian	POL	11.4.90	173/63	50kW	3:52:07	3:50:48- 13
Bobkov	Dmitriy	RUS	20.3.88		LJ	8.01	7.79- 09
Bobrownicki	Ray	GBR	3.3.84	186/73	HJ	2.28	2.22i- 11, 2.20- 12
Bochenek	Dominik	POL	14.5.87	182/70	110h	13.49	13.44- 11, 13.3w- 10
Boer	Duwayne	RSA-J	6.1.95		LJ	7.89	7.81- 13
Bogdanov	Denis	RUS	2.4.91	180/73	LJ	8.04	7.91- 13
Bohdan	Maksym	UKR	27.2.94	182/82	JT	83.41	78.77- 13
Boisrond	Aurélien	FRA	17.2.85	187/98	HT	70.92	70.38- 13
Bolas	John	USA	1.11.87	183/72	1500	3:36.71	3:35.54- 13
* Bolt	Usain	JAM	21.8.86	196/88	100	9.98 (i)	9.58- 09
Bondarenko	Artyom	BLR	19.6.91		LJ	7.92	7.70- 13
* Bondarenko	Bogdan	UKR	30.8.89	197/80	HJ	2.42	2.41- 13
Bonevacia	Liemarvin	CUR/NED	5.4.89	190/79	400	45.41	45.60- 12
Bonfim	Caio	BRA	19.3.91	170/58	20kW	1:20:28	1:20:58.5t- 11
Boni	Marco	ITA	21.5.84	182/80	PV	5.53	5.60i- 12, 5.40- 09
Bonvecchio	Norbert	ITA	14.8.85	183/82	JT	80.37	79.22- 12
Bor	Nicholas	KEN	.88		HMar	61:03	62:10- 13
Boreysha	Pavel	BLR	16.2.91	193/105	HT	76.86	75.62- 13
^ Borges	Lázaro	CUB	19.6.86	173/70	PV	5.50	5.90- 11
Borichevskiy	Konstantin	BLR	29.5.90		LJ	7.90	7.68- 13
* Borlée	Jonathan	BEL	22.2.88	180/70	400	45.37	44.43- 12
* Borlée	Kévin	BEL	22.2.88	180/71	400	45.28	44.56- 12
Borodkin ¶	Andriy	UKR	18.4.78	202/135	SP	19.90	20.38- 04
Bortoluzzi	Jérôme	FRA	20.5.82	180/111	HT	75.70	78.26- 12
* Bosse	Pierre-Ambroise	FRA	11.5.92	185/68	800	1:42.53	1:43.76- 13
600	1:16.1+		1:15.63i- 13		1000	2:15.31	2:18.20- 13
Bosworth	Tom	GBR	17.1.90	184/54	20kW	1:22:20	1:24:44- 13
Botterman	Aaron	BEL	1.5.94	188/73	800	1:46.17	1:49.18- 13
Bouchicha	Hichem	ALG	19.5.89		3kSt	8:32.03	8:20.11- 13
Boukamouche	Saber	ALG	20.4.92	189/80	400h	49.90	51.42- 13
Boulama	Mohammed	MAR	31.12.93		3kSt	8:34.37	8:21.62- 13
Bouqantar	Soufiyan	MAR	30.8.93	170/50	3000	7:43.33	7:51.99- 13
* Bouraada	Larbi	ALG	10.5.88	187/84	Dec	8311	8332dq- 12, 8302- 11
Bowen	Casey	USA	11.1.93	188/82	PV	5.50	5.40- 13
Bowens	Nic	USA	28.6.93	170/64	100	10.18A, 10.28, 10.13w	10.47- 12

Name		Nat	Born	Ht/Wt	Event	2014 Mark	Pre-2014 Best
Boyce	Brendan	IRL	15.10.86	183/76	50kW	3:51:34	3:54:24- 13
Boyez	Antonin	FRA	9.11.84	185/72	20kW	1:22:21	1:23:25- 10
* Bracy	Marvin	USA	15.12.93	175/74	100	10.08	10.09- 13, 10.05w- 11
Brannen	Nathan	CAN	8.9.82	175/59	1000	2:16.87i	2:16.52- 12
1500	3:38.16+	3:34.22- 12			1M	3:54.32i, 3:55.65	3:52.63- 09
* Brathwaite	Ryan	BAR	6.6.88	186/75	110h	13.41A, 13.44	13.14, 13.05w- 09
* Brathwaite	Shane	BAR	8.2.90	185/75	110h	13.24	13.44- 13, 13.31A, 13.43w- 12
Braun	Pieter	NED	21.1.93	182/80	Dec	7892	7540- 13
Bravo	Alberth	VEN	29.8.87	198/85	400	45.21A, 46.18	45.61- 12
Bray	Wesley	USA	11.4.88	180/80	Dec	7862	7932(w)- 12, 7718- 13
* Braz da Silva	Thiago	BRA	16.12.93	193/84	PV	5.76i, 5.73	5.83- 13
Brembach	Nils	GER	23.2.93	184/68	50kW	3:54:47	-0-
^ Brenes	Nery	CRC	25.9.85	174/62	200	20.49	20.62-12, 20.3- 08
					400	45.47	44.65A- 11, 44.84- 10
Bringhurst	Brayden	USA	.89	175/73	PV	5.50i, 5.45	5.30- 13
* Bromell	Trayvon	USA-J	10.7.95	175/71	100	9.97, 9.77w	10.27, 9.99Aw- 13
					200	20.59, 20.23w	20.91- 13
Brondyke	Kurtis	USA	24.1.89	198/93	Dec	7613h ?	
Brookins	Ronald	USA	5.7.89	185/75	110h	13.45	13.42- 11
Brooks	Lance	USA	1.1.84	198/123	DT	61.58	65.15- 12
Broothaerts	Mathias	BEL	12.7.94	185/72	LJ	8.07	7.84- 13
Brown	Aaron	CAN	27.5.92	185/79	100	10.07	10.05, 10.01w- 13
					200	20.16, 20.02w	20.42- 12, 20.26w- 13
* Brown	Chris	BAH	15.10.78	178/68	400	44.59	44.40- 08
^ Brown	Darrell	TTO	11.10.84	179/85	100	10.05	9.99- 05, 9.88w- 07
Brown	Jermaine	JAM	4.7.91	183/80	200	20.28A, 20.29	20.49- 13
Brown	Kemarley	JAM	20.7.92	180/72	100	9.93	10.38, 10.34w- 13
					200	20.38, 20.29w	20.94- 13
Brown	Raymond	JAM	15.1.88	193/125	SP	20.35	20.13- 13
Brown	Rodney	USA	21.5.93	183/109	DT	64.68	62.88- 13
Brown	Trevor	USA	24.3.92	183/79	110h	13.55	13.75- 12, 13.55w- 13
					400h	49.64A, 49.89	51.08A- 12, 51.61- 13
Broz	Michal	CZE	16.6.92	186/73	400h	49.90	49.78- 13
Brugger	Matthias	GER	6.8.92	192/93	Dec	7829	7942- 12
Bruintjies	Henricho	RSA	16.7.93	182/73	100	10.17A, 10.26	10.41A, 10.06Aw-dt- 13
Bruns	Ansis	LAT	30.3.89	182/93	JT	81.28	80.40- 11
Brunson	Andrew	USA	4.4.86	182/75	110h	13.62	13.33- 08
Bryan	Christoffe	JAM-J	26.4.96		HJ	2.24	2.20- 12
Bryant	Ashley	GBR	17.5.91	180/82	Dec	8141	8070- 13
Bryant	Luke	USA	5.12.88	188/110	DT	63.76	62.70- 12
Bube	Andreas	DEN	13.7.87	178/65	800	1:45.21	1:44.89- 12
Bubeník	Matús	SVK	14.11.89	196/77	HJ	2.27	2.26i, 2.24- 13
Bucki	Gaëtan	FRA	9.5.80	195/135	SP	20.21	20.39i- 11, 20.10- 13
Budza	Sergiy	UKR	6.12.84	180/72	20kW	1:21:13	1:24:28- 08
					50kW	3:48:50	3:47:36- 13
Bueno	Andreas	DEN	7.7.88	186/73	1500	3:38.44	3:40.08- 12
Bühler	Matthias	GER	2.9.86	189/74	110h	13.39, 13.20w	13.34- 12, 13.2w- 10
Bulanov	Aleksandr	RUS	26.12.89	193/120	SP	19.75i, 19.71	19.92i ,19.81-13
Bultheel	Michaël	BEL	30.6.86	189/81	400h	49.13	49.10- 12
Bumbalough	Andrew	USA	14.3.87		2000	4:57.35i	
3000	7:37.62i	7:40.02- 13			5000	13:13.67	13:12.01- 13
Bundi	Geoffrey	KEN	.87		HMar	60:28dh	61:14- 12
Burton	Tom	GBR	29.10.88	178/68	400h	49.66	50.43- 10
Burya	Artem	RUS	11.4.86	185/82	PV	5.61	5.60- 12
Busby	Durrell	TTO	23.12.89	185/73	110h	13.64, 13.56w	13.67- 12
Busendich	Ishmael	KEN	7.7.91		Mar	2:08:25	2:09:09- 12
Bustamante	Luis	MEX	10.6.84		50kW	3:54:00A	3:59:07A- 13
Bustos	David	ESP	25.8.90	182/65	1500	3:35.59	3:34.77- 12
* Butenko	Viktor	RUS	10.3.93	196/116	DT	65.89	65.97- 13
Butler	Kind	USA	8.4.89	183/75	400	45.56	45.43- 12
Bychkov	Igor	ESP	7.3.87	189/80	PV	5.60i	5.65- 13
Byram	Brandon	USA	11.9.88	188/82	200	20.27	20.31- 10
Byun Young-jun		KOR	20.3.84	175/57	20kW	1:23:11	1:21:42- 12
Cabral	Donn	USA	12.12.89	175/60	2000	5:00.18i	
5000	13:22.19	13:40.62- 11			3kSt	8:20.04	8:19.14- 12
Cabral	Johnathan	USA	31.12.92	193/82	110h	13.54	13.45- 12, 13.33w- 13
* Cáceres	Eusebio	ESP	10.9.91	176/69	LJ	8.11, 8.16w	8.37- 13
Cáceres	Jonathan	ECU	20.1.90		50kW	3:50:52	3:56:58- 13
* Cadée	Erik	NED	15.2.84	201/120	DT	65.24	67.30- 12
* Cai Zelin		CHN	11.4.91	172/55	20kW	1:18:52	1:18:47- 12
Cain	Stephen	AUS	23.7.84	181/81	Dec	7787	7844- 12

	Name		Nat	Born	Ht/Wt	Event	2014 Mark	Pre-2014 Best
	Cakss	Gatis	LAT-J	13.6.95	185/83	JT	77.26	71.47- 13
	Callender	Emmanuel	TTO	10.5.84	184/79	100	10.26, 10.07w	10.05- 09
	Camara	Alyn	GER	31.3.89	195/85	LJ	7.89	8.29- 13
	Campbell	Torrey	USA	27.11.92	180/82	110h	13.67	-0-
	Campion	Kévin	FRA	23.5.88	183/63	20kW	1:20:39	1:21:02- 13
	Cann	Luke	AUS	17.7.94	183/90	JT	79.36	76.58- 13
	Cano	Juan Manuel	ARG	21.12.87	168/57	20kW	1:22:18.5t	1:22:10-12
	Cantero	Bryan	FRA	28.4.91	178/64	1500	3:36.08	3:37.24- 12
*	Cantwell	Christian	USA	30.9.80	193/154	SP	21.85	22.54- 04
	Caporaso	Teodorico	ITA	14.9.87	166/60	50kW	3:58:23	3:56:45- 13
	Capotosti	Leonardo	ITA	24.7.88	192/78	400h	50.05	50.06- 13
	Cardina	Robert	USA	29.11.93	190/86	Dec	7666	-0-
	Cardoso	Wágner	BRA	20.3.89	182/73	400	45.69	45.80- 13
	Carrera	Agustin	ARG	13.6.88	184/77	110h	13.74, 13.64Aw	13.92- 12, 13.90w- 13
	Carter	Chris	USA	11.3.89	186/80	TJ	17.15iA, 17.09	16.86, 16.92w- 11
	Carter	Deuce	JAM	28.9.90	182/75	110h	13.51A, 13.57	13.53- 13
*	Carter	Nesta	JAM	10.11.85	178/70	100	9.96, 9.89w	9.78- 10
	Carvalho	Florian	FRA	9.3.89	182/69	1500	3:35.51	3:33.47- 13
*	Casañas	Frank	ESP	18.10.78	187/115	DT	65.48	67.91- 08
	Casey	Patrick	USA	23.5.90	175/60	1500	3:35.32	3:40.04- 13
						1M	3:52.62	3:56.28i- 13
	Castillo	Maurys Surel	ex-CUB	19.10.84	182/60	800	1:46.33	1:44.89- 12
						1500	3:37.30	3:35.03- 12
	Castro	Luis Joel	PUR	28.1.91	195/72	HJ	2.26	2.25A- 12, 2.25- 13
	Catania	Emanuele	ITA	3.10.88	182/68	LJ	7.98	7.96i- 13, 7.85- 11
	Cato	Japeth	USA	25.12.90	190/82	PV	5.55i	5.33- 13
*	Cato	Roxroy	JAM	1.5.88	183/76	400h	48.48	49.03- 12
	Cavazzani	Daniele	ITA	4.12.92		TJ	16.52	15.98- 13
	Cedenio	Machel	TTO-J	6.9.95	183/70	400	45.13	45.93- 13
*	Centrowitz	Matthew	USA	18.10.89	175/61	800	1:46.12	1:45.86- 13
						1500	3:31.09	3:31.96- 12
						1M	3:50.53	3:51.34i, 3:51.79- 13
						5000	13:20.06	13:47.73- 10
	Chalyy	Timothy	RUS	7.4.94	190/79	400h	48.69	49.23- 13
^	Chambers	Dwain	GBR	5.4.78	180/83	100	10.12, 10.06w	9.97- 99, 9.87dq- 02
	Chang Ming-Huang		TPE	7.8.82	194/130	SP	20.32	20.58- 11
	Chapelle	Axel	FRA-J	24.4.95	179/73	PV	5.55	5.38i, 5.32- 13
	Chapelle	Theo	FRA	16.3.92	186/72	PV	5.55i	5.38i, 5.25- 13
^	Charfreitag	Libor	SVK	11.9.77	191/117	HT	72.01	81.81- 03
	Chatbi	Jamal	ITA	30.4.84	178/62	3kSt	8:25.38	8:08.86- 09
						10k	28:14.87	28:56.27- 13
	Chavez	Richard	USA	30.7.92	178/115	SP	19.98i	20.06i- 13, 18.43- 12
	Chavkin	Nikolay	RUS	24.4.84	183/70	3kSt	8:25.59	8:22.81- 12
	Chebet	Evans Kiplagat	KEN	5.3.88		Mar	2:07:46	2:09:22- 11
^	Chebet	Wilson	KEN	12.7.85	174/59	Mar	2:08:48dh	2:05:27- 11
	Chebii	Daniel	KEN	28.5.85		HMar	60:40	59:49- 12
	Chebii	Ezekiel	KEN	3.1.91		HMar	60:50	59:05- 12
	Chebogei	Sylas	KEN	.83		HMar	60:17	62:57- 13
*	Cheboi	Collins	KEN	25.9.87	175/64	1500	3:32.00	3:31.53- 13
						1M	3:49.56	3:51.44- 12
	Cheboit	Silas	TAN	.92		Mar	2:07:15	2:18:22- 12
	Chehlatyy	Oleksandr	UKR	27.9.89	191/87	JT	77.26	76.97- 13
	Chelanga	Samuel	KEN	23.2.85	168/57	3000	7:45.21i	7:48.24i- 11
						5000	13:04.35i, 13:16.24	13:09.67- 12
						10k	27:59.74	27:08.39- 10
	Chematot	Evans	BRN-J	19.3.96		3kSt	8:32.61	8:55.66- 13
	Chemlal	Jaouad	MAR	11.4.94	175/59	3kSt	8:20.92	8:19.22- 13
	Chemlany	Stephen	KEN	9.8.82	175/64	Mar	2:06:24	2:07:44- 13
	Chemosin	Robert	KEN	1.2.89		HMar	60:24	59:19- 13
	Chemut	Anthony	KEN	17.12.92	170/57	800	1:44.72	1:43.96A- 12
	Chen Chieh		TPE	8.5.92	174/55	400h	50.09	49.68- 12
*	Chen Ding		CHN	5.8.92	180/62	20kW	1:20:28	1:17:40- 12
	Chen Ji		CHN	27.1.90		HJ	2.24	2.24- 10
	Chen Zongliang		CHN	9.1.92		20kW	1:23:06	1:22:30- 12
	Cheng Chao-Tsun		TPE	17.10.93	182/88	JT	81.61	78.68- 10
	Cheng Min		CHN	6.7.91		50kW	4:00:48	4:16:05- 13
	Cheng Wen		CHN	18.3.92	187/77	400h	49.89	49.28- 11
*	Chepkok	Vincent	KEN	5.7.88	174/60	HMar	60:53	
	Chepkwony	Frankline	KEN	15.6.84		Mar	2:07:35	2:06:11- 12
	Chepkwony	Gilbert	KEN	.85		Mar	2:08:26	2:08:16- 12
	Cheprot	Simon	KEN	2.7.93	183/62	HMar	60:05	59:20- 13
*	Chepseba	Nixon	KEN	12.12.90	185/66	1500	3:34.64	3:29.77- 12
						1M	3:54.92	3:50.95- 13
						5000	13:26.28	13:46.2A- 13
	Cheptegei	Joshua	UGA-J	12.9.96	167/52	10k	27:56.26	

Name		Nat	Born	Ht/Wt	Event	2014 Mark	Pre-2014 Best
^ Cherkos	Abreham	ETH	23.9.89	163/52	Mar	2:07:08	2:07:29- 10, 2:06:13wdh- 11
Cheroben	Abreham	KEN	10.11.92	174/58	HMar	58:48	60:38- 13
Cherry	DeAngelo	USA	1.8.90	163/64	100	10.22, 10.10w	10.04, 10.02w- 09
Cherry	Michael	USA-J	23.3.95	186/75	400	45.37	46.02- 13
Cheru	Tesfaye	ETH	2.3.93	171/55	1500	3:35.12	3:35.67- 13
					5000	13:25.33	
Cheruiyot	Charles	KEN	4.8.88	172/54	10k	27:59.91	28:20.6A- 13
* Cheruiyot	Ferguson	KEN	30.11.89	183/73	800	1:42.84	1:43.22- 13
					1000	2:16.88	-0-
Cheruiyot	John	KEN	5.7.90	167/55	HMar	61:10	
Cheruiyot	Timothy	KEN-J	20.11.95		800	1:45.92A	
Chesebe	Abednego	KEN	20.6.82	174/62	1500	3:36.21	3:35.02A- 12
Cheserek	Edward	KEN	2.2.94	168/57	1500	3:36.50	3:48.89- 13
3000	7:47.20i	8:05.46i- 13			5000	13:18.71	14:02.33- 11, 13:57.04i- 12
Chiaraviglio	Germán	ARG	16.4.87	192/77	PV	5.51	5.71- 06
Chihuán	Pavel	PER	19.1.86		50kW	3:56:35	4:08:33- 13
* Chimsa	Deressa	ETH	21.11.86	175/62	Mar	2:07:40	2:05:42- 12
Chirchir	Abraham	KEN	1.8.80	173/59	3kSt	8:30.0A	8:19.81- 08
Chizhikov	Dmitriy	RUS	6.12.93		TJ	16.51	16.16- 13
Chmielak	Hubert	POL	19.6.89	188/88	JT	82.58	80.28- 13
Chocho	Andrés	ECU	4.11.83	167/67	50kW	3:57:00	3:49:32- 11
* Choge	Augustine	KEN	21.1.87	162/53	1500	3:35.5A	3:29.47- 09
3000	7:41.57, 7:37.11i	7:28.00i, 7:28.76- 11			5000	13:06.12	12:53.66- 05
Choi Byung-kwang		KOR	7.4.91	185/70	20kW	1:21:20	1:21:52- 13
* Chumba	Dickson	KEN	27.10.86	167/50	HMar	60:39 very dh	61:34- 12
					Mar	2:04:32	2:05:46- 12
Churylo	Andrey	BLR	19.5.93	190/72	HJ	2.30	2.28- 12
Chuva	Marcos	POR	8.8.89	182/75	LJ	8.04	8.34- 11
Cienfuegos	Javier	ESP	15.7.90	193/134	HT	75.03	76.71- 13
Ciotti	Giulio	ITA	5.10.76	187/75	HJ	2.24i	2.31i- 06, 2.31- 09
* Cisneros	Omar	CUB	19.11.89	186/80	400h	49.56A	47.93- 13
Clarke	Chris	GBR	25.1.90	176/70	200	20.50, 20.23w	20.22- 13
Clarke	Everton	JAM	24.12.92	172/70	200	20.51	21.56- 11
Clarke	Jordan	USA	10.7.90	193/125	SP	21.37	20.86i, 20.40- 12
Clarke	Kemar	USA/JAM	20.5.88	178/70	110h	13.75, 13.59w	13.78- 11, 13.65w- 12
* Clarke	Lawrence	GBR	12.3.90	187/78	110h	13.41	13.31, 13.14w- 12
^ Clavier	Jérôme	FRA	3.5.83	185/73	PV	5.76i, 5.52	5.81i- 11, 5.75- 08
* Claye	Will	USA	13.6.91	180/68	LJ	8.19, 8.29w	8.29- 11
					TJ	17.75	17.70i, 17.62- 12
Clémenceau	Adrian	FRA	25.5.88	186/76	400h	50.05	49.70- 12
Clemens	Daniel	GER	28.4.92	181/74	PV	5.51i, 5.42	5.60- 13
Clemons	Kyle	USA	27.8.90	181/73	400	45.00	45.10- 13
Cobbo	Guilherme	BRA	1.10.87	185/65	HJ	2.24	2.28- 12
Cochrane	Michael	NZL	13.8.91	188/82	400h	49.72	50.07- 13
Cocioran	Marius	ROU	10.7.83	178/66	50kW	4:03:25	3:57:52- 12
Coertzen	Willem	RSA	30.12.82	186/80	Dec	8199A	8343- 13
Coleman	Greg	USA	24.7.93	190/79	400h	49.60	50.50- 13
Collenot-Spriet	Romain	FRA	9.1.92	183/69	3kSt	8:29.99	8:33.23- 12
Collie-Minns	Latario	BAH	10.3.94	173/64	TJ	16.91, 17.12w	16.64, 16.66w- 12
Collie-Minns	Lathone	BAH	10.3.94		TJ	16.22, 16.75w	16.06- 12
Collier	Jermaine	USA	5.7.93	180/75	110h	13.65	14.18, 14.06w- 13
* Collins	Kim	SKN	5.4.76	175/64	100	9.96	9.97- 13, 9.92w- 03
* Compaoré	Benjamin	FRA	5.8.87	189/86	TJ	17.48	17.31- 11
Conatser	Remy	USA	20.7.90	195/109	HT	72.76	68.30- 13
Connaughton	Jared	CAN	20.7.85	175/77	100	10.23, 10.14w	10.15- 08, 10.04w- 11
Coover	Jeff	USA	1.12.87	185/77	PV	5.54	5.60- 13
* Copello	Alexis	ex-CUB	12.8.85	185/80	TJ	17.05	17.68A- 11, 17.65, 17.69w- 09
Corchete	Luis Manuel	ESP	14.5.84	185/74	50kW	4:05:16	3:59:58- 12
Correa	Harold	FRA	26.6.88	190/78	TJ	16.41	16.94i, 16.92- 13
Cota	Mario	MEX	11.9.90	188/115	DT	61.63	60.45- 12
Couto	Kurt	MOZ	14.5.85	180/67	400h	49.56A	49.02- 12
Cowart	Donnie	USA	24.10.85	170/60	3kSt	8:29.08	8:26.38- 11
Craddock	Kevin	USA	25.6.87	193/84	110h	13.46	13.42- 12, 13.41w- 08
Craddock	Omar	USA	26.4.91	178/79	TJ	16.98, 17.26w	16.92, 17.15w- 13
Cralle	Chris	USA	13.6.88	183/109	HT	75.26	74.55- 13
Crawford	Corey	USA	12.12.91	190/86	LJ	8.22i, 7.90, 7.91w	7.79i- 13, 7.60- 12
Cray	Eric	PHI	6.11.88	196/86	400h	50.00	50.46- 12
Cremona	Orazio	RSA	1.7.89	192/130	SP	20.63	20.55- 13
Cretinoir	Jean-Noël	FRA	28.12.94	178/64	TJ	16.51	16.34i, 16.45w- 13
* Cronje	Johan	RSA	13.4.82	182/69	1500	3:33.31	3:31.93- 13
					1M	3:50.70	3:54.84- 09

	Name		Nat	Born	Ht/Wt	Event	2014 Mark	Pre-2014 Best
*	Crouser	Ryan	USA	18.12.92	201/109	SP	21.39	21.09- 13
						DT	63.90	59.91- 12
	Crowther	Robert	AUS	2.8.87	188/77	LJ	8.03	8.12- 11, 8.15w- 07
*	Culson	Javier	PUR	25.7.84	198/79	400h	48.03	47.72- 10
	Cunningham	Logan	USA	30.5.91	183/80	PV	5.70	5.53- 12
	Curtis	Bobby	USA	28.11.84	182/68	10k	27:46.30	27:24.67- 11
^	Cutts	Luke	GBR	13.2.88	192/82	PV	5.83i, 5.60	5.71i, 5.70- 13
	Czajkowski	Przemyslaw	POL	26.10.88	197/108	DT	64.16	65.61- 12
	Czerwinski	Przemyslaw	POL	28.7.83	185/80	PV	5.60, 5.65ex	5.82i- 10, 5.80- 06
	Dacres	Fedrick	JAM	28.2.94	191/77	DT	66.75	59.30- 13
	Dahm	Tobias	GER	23.5.87	203/117	SP	19.96	19.96- 13
	Dai Li		CHN	20.5.91		JT	77.72	74.92- 12
	Dal Molin	Paolo	ITA	31.7.87	179/76	110h	13.47	13.64- 12
	Dalton	Chase	USA	1.2.89	190/89	Dec	7642	7215- 13
	Daly	Kieran	GBR	28.9.92	181/70	100	10.18	10.58- 12
	Dame	Tasama	ETH	12.10.87	173/57	10k	27:55.21	28:58.92- 08
	Darling	Maverick	USA	9.6.89	178/61	3000	7:46.84	7:50.97i- 13, 8:05.89- 12
*	Dasaolu	James	GBR	5.9.87	180/75	100	10.00	9.91- 13
	Dauphin	Tumatai	FRA	12.1.88	188/138	SP	19.70	19.76- 13
	Davide	Kléberson	BRA	20.7.85	175/67	800	1:45.30	1:44.21- 11
	Davis	Paul	USA	11.9.90	190/97	SP	19.89i, 18.65	20.53- 13
	Davis	Wayne	TTO	22.8.91	178/72	110h	13.20	13.37- 12, 13.14w- 13
	De Grasse	André	CAN	10.11.94	180/73	100	10.15, 10.03w	10.25, 9.96w- 13
						200	20.38	20.74A, 20.57w- 13
	de Jager	Shaun	RSA	28.6.91	186/68	400	45.66A, 45.74	45.97- 12
*	De Luca	Marco	ITA	12.5.81	189/72	50kW	3:45:25	3:46:31- 09
	de Sá	Mateus Daniel	BRA-J	21.11.95	183/73	TJ	16.47	16.14- 13
	de Souza	Éder Antônio	BRA	15.10.86	189/85	110h	13.62	13.58- 07
	de Vries	Ruan	RSA	1.2.86	187/80	110h	13.62A, 13.82	13.59A, 13.67- 13
	Dean	Roderick Genki	JPN	30.12.91	182/85	JT	77.32	84.28- 12
	Debela	Dejene	ETH	.94	180/62	5000	13:26.67	
	Dechasa	Shumi	BRN	28.5.89	172/54	Mar	2:06:43	2:07:11- 13
	Décimus	Yoan	FRA	30.11.87	182/62	400h	49.60	49.52- 13
	Deghelt	Adrien	BEL	10.5.85	188/78	110h	13.67	13.42- 12
	Deksisa	Solomon	ETH	11.3.94		HMar	60:12 very dh	62:26- 13
	DeLeo	Dustin	USA	3.1.86	185/82	PV	5.53	5.60- 13
	Demczyszak	Mateusz	POL	18.1.86	176/62	3kSt	8:22.38	8:26.30- 13
*	Demelash	Yigrem	ETH	28.1.94	167/52	5000	13:11.80	13:03.30- 12
	Demonte	Enrico	ITA	25.9.88	180/73	200	20.46	20.45- 13
*	Dendy	Marquis	USA	17.11.92	190/75	LJ	8.00	8.28i, 8.10, 8.29w- 13
						TJ	16.52, 17.05w	16.25i, 16.03- 13
	Dergachev	Yuriy	KAZ	8.11.94	191/66	HJ	2.28	2.21i, 2.20- 12
	Derrick	Chris	USA	17.10.90	180/64	5000	13:08.18	13:08.04- 13
						10k	28:18.18	27:31.38- 12
*	Desisa	Lelisa	ETH	14.1.90	170/52	HMar	59:36	59:30- 11
	Dewhurst	Ian	AUS	13.11.90	185/73	400h	49.52	49.89- 13
	Dheeb	Ahmed Mohamed	QAT	29.9.85	195/113	DT	61.25	63.70. 64.56dq- 10
	Dias	Thiago	BRA	2.3.84	188/71	TJ	16.38	16.59- 09
	Dias Sabino	Jefferson	BRA	4.11.82	192/94	TJ	16.44	17.28- 08
	Diaz	Andy	CUB-J	25.12.95	180/68	TJ	16.38, 16.43w	15.63- 13
	Díaz	Jorge	COL	2.3.87	167/57	50kW	4:02:06	3:59:13- 13
	Díaz	Junior	CUB	28.4.87	193/80	LJ	7.97, 8.10w	8.02- 13
	Dick	Devin	USA	12.1.90	193/89	Dec	7792	7425- 12
	Dida	Bonse	ETH-J	21.1.95		HMar	61:12	61:53- 13
	Dilla	Karsten	GER	17.7.89	188/74	PV	5.71	5.73i, 5.72- 11
	Dimitrov	Rumen	BUL	19.9.86	175/77	TJ	16.69, 16.77w	16.61, 16.74w- 12
*	Diniz	Yohann	FRA	1.1.78	185/69	20kW	1:19:42.1t	1:17:43- 12
						50kW	3:32:33	3:35:27.2t- 11
	Dirirsa	Teshome	ETH	25.4.94	175/56	3000	7:46.92	7:51.76i- 12
	Distelberger	Dominik	AUT	16.3.90	182/77	Dec	8168	7872- 13
*	Dix	Walter	USA	31.1.86	178/84	100	10.17	9.88- 10, 9.80w- 08
						200	20.32, 20.21w	19.53- 11
	Dixon	Leroy	USA	20.6.83	177/72	100	10.16w	10.02, 9.99w- 08
	Djoumessi	Fernand	CMR	5.9.89	189/75	HJ	2.28	2.22- 13
*	Dmitrik	Aleksey	RUS	12.4.84	191/69	HJ	2.40i, 2.30	2.36- 11
*	Dmytrenko	Ruslan	UKR	22.3.86	180/62	20kW	1:18:37	1:20:17- 12
	Dobek	Patryk	POL	13.2.94	183/75	400h	49.13	50.67- 13
	Docavo	Vicente	ESP	13.2.92	182/72	TJ	16.32i, 16.50w	16.72- 12
	Dodson	Jeremy	USA	30.8.87	184/75	200	20.27A	20.33, 20.07w- 11
	Dohmann	Carl	GER	18.5.90	182/60	20kW	1:21:42	1:23:50- 13
						50kW	3:51:27	3:57:58- 13

Name		Nat	Born	Ht/Wt	Event	2014 Mark	Pre-2014 Best
Doi	Shota	JPN	10.4.90		PV	5.50	5.22- 08
Dolezal	Riley	USA	16.11.85	188/100	JT	79.27	83.50- 13
Domingos	Wágner	BRA	23.6.83	183/126	HT	75.47	72.78- 12
* Donato	Fabrizio	ITA	14.8.76	189/82	TJ	16.89, 17.24w	17.73i- 11,17.60- 00,17.63w- 12
Dong Bin		CHN	22.11.88	179/67	TJ	16.95	17.38- 12
Donisan	Mihai	ROU	24.7.88	193/74	HJ	2.32i, 2.28	2.31- 13
Doris	Troy	USA	12.4.89	174/73	TJ	16.85	16.66- 12
Dorofyeyev	Vladyslav	UKR	22.4.94		HJ	2.24	2.18- 13
dos Santos	Felipe	BRA	30.7.94		Dec	7952	-0-
dos Santos	Mário José	BRA	10.9.79	172/59	50kW	3:57:29	3:58:30- 08
^ Dossévi	Damiel	FRA	3.2.83	182/82	PV	5.66i, 5.60	5.75- 05
^ Doucouré	Ladji	FRA	28.3.83	183/75	110h	13.44, 13.38w	12.97- 05
^ Douglas	Nathan	GBR	4.12.82	183/71	TJ	16.65	17.64- 05
Doukkana	Rabie	MAR	6.12.87	168/57	1500	3:37.81	3:40.25- 12
Douvalídis	Konstadínos	GRE	10.3.87	184/78	110h	13.39	13.34- 13
Downing	Quincy	USA	16.1.93	185/75	400h	49.97	52.77- 13
* Drouin	Derek	CAN	6.3.90	195/80	HJ	2.40	2.38- 13
Dry	Mark	GBR	11.10.87	184/110	HT	74.63	74.82- 12
Dubitskiy	Oleg	BLR	14.10.90	184/100	HT	75.56	73.62- 12
Dudley	Edward	USA	21.6.92	194/80	HJ	2.26	2.25- 12
Duffield	Jacorian	USA	2.9.92	190/79	HJ	2.27	2.20- 12
* Dukes	Dedric	USA	2.4.92	180/70	200	19.97, 19.91w	20.45, 20.34w- 13
					400	45.66	46.38- 09
Dunbar	Trevor	USA	29.4.91	180/70	3000	7:45.09	7:51.55i- 12
					5000	13:26.90	13:40.66- 12
Dunfee	Evan	CAN	28.9.90	186/68	20kW	1:20:13	1:23:45- 11
					50kW	3:58:34	3:59:28- 13
Duquemin	Zane	GBR	23.9.91	185/110	DT	61.15	63.46- 12
Durand	Yohan	FRA	14.5.85	174/58	3000	7:48.20	7:44.46i- 12, 7:46.46- 11
Durañona	Yordanys	DMA	16.6.88	188/75	TJ	17.20A, 16.25	17.02, 17.28w- 09
Durham	Adam	USA	30.8.85	186/79	400h	49.98	49.88- 13
* Dutch	Johnny	USA	20.1.89	180/82	400h	48.93	47.63- 10
* Dutra de Oliveira	Augusto	BRA	16.7.90	180/70	PV	5.70	5.82- 13
* Dwyer	Rasheed	JAM	29.1.89	188/80	200	19.98	20.15- 13
Dykstra	Raymond	CAN	18.6.92	188/93	JT	78.58	75.41- 12
Dyldin	Maksim	RUS	19.5.87	185/78	400	45.45	45.01- 12
Dziubin	Dmitriy	BLR	12.7.90		20kW	1:21:09	1:24:30- 13
* Eaton	Ashton	USA	21.1.88	186/86	110h	13.35	13.35- 11, 13.34w- 12
					400h	48.69	-0-
Eaton	Jarret	USA	24.6.89	183/82	110h	13.62, 13.58w	13.44- 12
Eaves	Max	GBR	31.5.88	186/84	PV	5.62	5.61i- 11, 5.40- 10
Edoburun	Ojie	GBR-J	2.6.96	180/68	100	10.16, 10.15w	10.35- 13
* Edris	Muktar	ETH	14.1.94	172/57	3000	7:46.0+	
					5000	12:54.83	13:03.69- 13
* Edward	Alonso	PAN	8.12.89	183/73	100	10.02	10.09, 9.97w- 09
					200	19.84	19.81- 09
Edwards	Rae	NGR	7.5.81	183/77	100	10.16	10.00- 10, 9.98w- 09
Eichberger	James	MEX	4.8.90	175/66	800	1:46.61	1:45.88- 13
Ektov	Yevgeniy	KAZ	1.9.86	187/76	TJ	16.62	17.22- 12
El Abbassi	El Hassan	BRN	15.7.79	171/54	10k	27:32.96	28:12.40- 12
El Aziz	Mustapha	MAR	.85	175/60	5000	13:28.31	13:42.28- 11
					10k	28:11.36	27:26.24- 05
El Bakkali	Soufiane	MAR-J	7.1.96		3kSt	8:32.66	8:52.00- 13
El Goumri	Othmane	MAR	28.5.92	171/57	3000	7:44.73i	7:48.95- 13
El Kaam	Fouad	MAR	27.5.88	177/62	1500	3:34.69	3:33.71- 13
800	1:47.20		1:47.38- 13		1M	3:54.21	-0-
El Manaoui	Amine	MAR	20.11.91	183/65	800	1:46.01	1:44.96- 13
El-Seify	Ashraf Amjad	QAT-J	20.2.95	183/93	HT	71.81	76.37- 13
Elemba	Frank	CGO	21.7.90	200/115	SP	19.72	19.02- 13
Ellenson	Wally	USA	4.5.94	193/91	HJ	2.25	2.20- 13
Ellington	James	GBR	6.9.85	180/75	100	10.13	10.17- 13, 10.12w- 11
					200	20.44	20.42- 13
Emanuel	Lee	GBR	24.1.85	178/64	1M	3:54.30i	3:54.75- 13
1500	3:38.99i		3:36.55- 03		3000	7:45.12i	7:51.20i- 10
Engelbrecht	Jaco	RSA	8.3.87	200/125	SP	19.86	20.31- 13
English	Mark	IRL	18.3.93	184/73	800	1:45.03	1:44.84- 13
Erassa	Kirubel	USA	17.6.93	172/61	5000	13:27.55	13:47.26- 12
Erewa	Robin	GER	24.6.91	184/77	200	20.46	20.75- 13
Erickson	Chris	AUS	1.12.81	175/62	20kW	1:22:19	1:22:20- 12
					50kW	3:49:33	3:49:41- 13
Ernest	Aaron	USA	8.11.93	183/75	100	10.19, 10.13w	10.17- 12, 10.04w- 13
					200	20.14	20.38, 20.36w- 13

Name		Nat	Born	Ht/Wt	Event	2014 Mark	Pre-2014 Best
^ España	Jesús	ESP	21.8.78	173/56	3000	7:45.06	7:38.26- 06
Essalhi	Younès	MAR	20.2.93	181/68	1500	3:37.36	3:35.52- 13
					3000	7:47.50i, 7:49.21	7:53.94- 13
* Esser	Markus	GER	3.2.80	180/105	HT	76.64	81.10- 06
Estefani	Hederson	BRA	11.9.91	184/75	400	45.62	45.25- 12
					400h	49.59	49.71- 12
* Etelätalo	Lassi	FIN	30.4.88	193/90	JT	84.98	84.41- 11
Eto	Takashi	JPN	5.2.91	183/69	HJ	2.28	2.27- 13
Evans	Andrew	USA	25.1.91	198/105	DT	66.37	62.78- 13
* Évora	Nelson	POR	20.4.84	181/64	TJ	16.97	17.74- 07, 17.82w- 09
Ezzine	Hamid	MAR	5.10.83	174/60	3kSt	8:14.33	8:09.72- 07
* Fajdek	Pawel	POL	4.6.89	186/118	HT	83.48	82.27- 13
Fajoyomi	Viktor	HUN	27.3.91	185/82	Dec	7712	7299- 13
Faloci	Giovanni	ITA	13.10.85	193/108	DT	62.07	64.77- 13
* Farah	Mohamed	GBR	23.3.83	171/65	3000	7:36.8+	7:34.47i- 09, 7:36.85- 13
2M	8:07.85	8:08.07i- 12, 8:20.47- 07			HMar	60:00dh	60:23- 11, 60:10dh- 13
5000	13:23.42 12:53.11- 11	10k	28:08.11	26:46.57- 11	Mar	2:08:21	-0-
Farnosov	Andrey	RUS	9.7.80	182/66	3kSt	8:28.73	8:21.95- 11
^ Farquhar	Stuart	NZL	15.3.82	187/98	JT	79.69	86.31- 12
Farrell	Thomas	GBR	23.3.91	174/61	1500	3:37.90	3:41.07- 12
3000	7:47.54i	7:51.77i- 13			5000	13:22.27	13:15.31- 12
* Fassinotti	Marco	ITA	29.4.89	190/71	HJ	2.34i, 2.30	2.29i- 11, 2.28- 10
Favretto	Vincent	FRA	5.4.84	188/73	PV	5.50i	5.65- 06
Fedaczynski	Rafal	POL	3.12.80	168/61	20kW	1:20:18	1:21:21- 12
Feeney	Patrick	USA	29.12.91	188/82	400	45.56	46.19 ,45.92i- 13
Feger	Alexandre	FRA	22.1.90	178/75	PV	5.60	5.55- 12
Feleke	Getu	ETH	28.11.86		Mar	2:05:41	2:04:50- 12
Felix	Kurt	GRN	4.7.88	190/88	Dec	8070	8062- 12
Fenrich	Benjamin	FRA	11.6.90	176/65	Dec	7562	7478- 13
Fernandez	German	USA	2.11.90	183/66	1500	3:38.11	3:34.60- 12
* Fernández	Jorge	CUB	2.10.87	190/100	DT	66.50	66.05- 12
Fernández	Sergio	ESP	1.4.93	181/70	400h	49.90	52.30- 13
Ferreira	Diogo	POR	30.7.90	175/77	PV	5.67	5.41- 12
Ferreira	Fernando	BRA	13.12.94		HJ	2.24	2.15- 13
Field	Devin	USA	9.10.93	175/73	TJ	16.30, 16.46w	15.14i- 12, 15.28w- 1
Fifa	Illias	MAR	16.5.89	174/55	5000	13:14.89	13:25.55- 11
^ Figère	Nicolas	FRA	19.5.79	177/100	HT	70.65	80.88- 01
* Filippídis	Konstadinos	GRE	26.11.86	188/73	PV	5.80i, 5.70	5.83i, 5.82- 13
Filippov	Nikita	KAZ	7.10.91	191/84	PV	5.50	5.60- 12
Finley	Mason	USA	7.10.90	203/150	SP	20.20i	20.71i- 11, 19.89- 12
					DT	64.17A	62.48- 13
Fisher	Andrew	JAM	15.12.91	168/64	100	10.09	10.07A, 10.28- 13
Fitten	Chumaine	JAM	15.3.85	190/75	400	45.56A, 45.62	46.50- 13
Fitzsimons	Tom	USA	8.3.89	188/83	Dec	7645	7547- 12, 7607w- 11
Flannery	Niall	GBR	26.4.91	178/70	400h	48.80	49.62- 13
Flores	Diego	MEX	23.3.87		20kW	1:22:25A	1:21:56- 13
Floriani	Yuri	ITA	25.12.81	180/64	3kSt	8:26.34	8:22.62- 12
Fofana	Hassane	ITA	28.4.92	187/77	110h	13.55	13.81- 13
Forbes	Damar	JAM	18.9.90	185/77	LJ	8.10	8.25, 8.35w- 13
Forte	Julian	JAM	1.7.93	186/73	100	10.03	10.12, 9.98w- 13
					200	20.49	20.38- 12, 20.22w- 13
* Fortes	Marco	POR	26.9.82	189/139	SP	21.01	21.02- 12
Forys	Craig	USA	13.7.89	176/64	3kSt	8:24.09	8:28.90- 12
Fothergill	Allodin	JAM	7.2.87	183/75	400	45.47A, 456.70	45.24- 10
Fournette	Albert	USA	21.10.91	190/127	SP	20.09	19.39- 12
Fox	Nathan	GBR	21.10.90	186/84	TJ	16.69	16.29- 12
Francis	Javon	JAM	14.12.94	183/73	400	45.00	45.24- 13
Francis	Shawn	USA	16.12.85	178/75	PV	5.55Ai, 5.50	5.51i- 13, 5.40- 10
Franz	Felix	GER	6.5.93	193/78	400h	48.96	50.35- 13
Fraser	Warren	BAH	8.7.91	172/73	100	10.14	10.18- 12
Frawley	Nicholas	USA	21.6.88	178/70	PV	5.55Ai, 5.40	5.53- 12
Frayne	Henry	AUS	14.4.90	187/72	LJ	8.10	8.27- 12
* Fredericks	Cornel	RSA	3.3.90	178/70	400h	48.25	48.14- 11
Freeman	Jacob	USA	5.11.80	193/129	HT	71.43	76.86- 09
Freeman	Josh	USA	22.8.94	193/134	SP	19.86	18.48i, 18.09- 13
* Freimuth	Rico	GER	14.3.88	198/93	110h	13.63	13.79- 12
					Dec	8356	8488w, 8382- 13
French	Cameron	NZL	17.5.92	180/73	400h	50.16	50.56- 13
Friday	Trentavis	USA-J	5.6.95	188/75	100	10.00	10.37- 13
					200	20.33, 20.03w	21.29, 21.25w- 13
Frost	Andrew	GBR	17.4.81	189/115	HT	71.19	72.79- 11

	Name		Nat	Born	Ht/Wt	Event	2014 Mark	Pre-2014 Best
	Frydrych	Petr	CZE	13.1.88	198/99	JT	85.07	88.23- 10
	Fryman	Andy	USA	3.2.85	188/130	HT	73.90	73.23- 12
	Fujikawa	Takuya	JPN	17.12.92	161/50	10k	28:20.31	28:35.72- 13
	Fujimoto	Taku	JPN	11.9.89	166/54	10k	28:20.96	28:25.53- 13
	Fujimutsu	Kenji	JPN	1.5.86	185/80	200	20.49	20.38- 10
	Fujisawa	Isamu	JPN	12.10.87	164/56	20kW	1:20:03	1:20:12- 10
	Furer	Tobias	SUI	13.8.87	184/79	110h	13.66	13.87- 12
	Furey	Sean	USA	31.8.82	190/95	JT	82.30	82.73- 12
	Furtula	Danijel	MNE	31.7.92	195/115	DT	62.19	64.60- 13
	Furuya	Takumu	JPN-Y	12.3.97	183.77	110h	13.83, 13.64w	
*	Fyodorov	Aleksey	RUS	25.5.91	184/73	TJ	17.07, 17.12w	17.19- 12
	Gaba	Kamghe	GER	13.1.84	202/94	400	45.63	45.47- 06
	Gabius	Arne	GER	22.3.81	188/68	3000	7:41.41	7:35.43- 12
	5000	13:25.50		13:12.50- 13		10k	27:55.35	-0-
	Gag	Andrei	ROU	7.4.91	195/118	SP	20.17i, 19.64	18.40- 13
						DT	61.27	61.11- 13
*	Gaisah	Ignisious	NED	20.6.83	185/75	LJ	8.13	8.43, 8.51w- 06
	Gakeme	Antoine	BDI	24.12.91	170/57	800	1:46.24	1:45.39- 13
	Galvan	Matteo	ITA	24.8.88	174/73	400	45.58	45.35- 13
	Ganapathi	Krishnan	IND	29.6.89	173/76	20kW	1:22:41	1:26:06- 13
	Gao Xinglong		CHN	12.3.94	181/65	LJ	8.18, 8.21w	8.02i, 7.98- 13
	García	Clemente	MEX	21.8.89		50kW	4:05:30	3:50:57A- 12
*	García	Jesús Ángel	ESP	17.10.69	172/64	50kW	3:45:41	3:39:54- 97
	García	Samuel	ESP	4.12.91	194/84	400	45.50	46.25- 13
	García	Víctor	ESP	13.3.85	173/56	3kSt	8:17.40	8:15.20- 12
*	García	Yordani	CUB	21.11.88	193/88	Dec	8337	8496- 09
	Garmashov	Anatoliy	RUS	5.7.88		SP	19.81	18.53- 13
	Garrett	Richard	USA	21.12.90	186/118	SP	20.35	20.05i, 19.26- 13
	Garrido	Iván	COL	25.1.94		20kW	1:22:13.74t	-0-
	Garrido	Lucirio Antonio	VEN	8.4.92	184/75	800	1:46.60	1:47.32- 13
	Garrido	Lucirio Francisco	VEN	4.10.88	184/75	400h	49.66	49.74- 13
	Gaspar	José Luis	CUB-J	25.8.95	191/79	400h	49.88	-0-
*	Gatlin	Justin	USA	10.2.82	185/79	100	9.77, 9.76w	9.79- 12, 9.77dq- 06
						200	19.68	20.00- 05, 19.86w- 01, 19.86dq- 02
	Gaul	Florian	GER	21.9.91	182/78	PV	5.50i	5.50- 13
	Gauntlett	Akheem	JAM	26.8.90	181/70	400	45.00	45.13- 12
*	Gay	Tyson	USA	9.8.82	180/73	100	9.93	9.69- 09, 9.68w- 08
						200	20.22	19.58- 09
*	Gaymon	Justin	USA	13.12.86	175/70	400h	49.53	48.46- 08
	Gdula	Lukás	CZE	6.12.91		50kW	4:01:52	4:12:55- 13
*	Gebremedhin	Mekonnen	ETH	11.10.88	180/64	1500	3:32.79	3:31.45- 12
	1M	3:51.59		3:49.70- 11		3000	7:42.90	7:41.42- 11
*	Gebremeskel	Dejen	ETH	24.11.89	178/53	3000	7:34.70i	7:34.14i- 12, 7:45.9- 10
						5000	13:09.73	12:46.81- 12
	Gebreyohanes	Samson	ERI	7.2.92		HMar	60:13	62:21- 13
*	Gebrhiwet	Hagos	ETH	11.5.94	167/65	3000	7:45.8+, 7:34.13i	7:30.36- 13
						5000	13:06.88	12:47.53- 12
	Gebrselassie	Leul	ETH	20.9.93	170/55	5000	13:14.59	13:31.19- 13
						HMar	61:00	
	Geffrouais	Florian	FRA	5.12.88	183/78	Dec	8164	8118- 12
	Gelant	Elroy	RSA	25.8.86	174/55	3000	7:44.20, 7:39.55i	7:41.38- 12
	5000	13:26.53		13:15.87- 13		HMar	61:10	62:59- 12
	Gemeda	Feyera	ETH	.82		HMar	60:29	
*	Gemili	Adam	GBR	6.10.93	178/73	100	10.04	10.05- 12
						200	19.98	19.98- 13
	Genest	Alexandre	CAN	30.6.86	175/57	3kSt	8:34.71	8:19.33- 11
*	Geneti	Markos	ETH	30.5.84	175/55	Mar	2:05:13	2:04:54- 12
	George	Winston	GUY	19.5.87	174/66	400	45.57	45.86- 11
	Geraghty	Peter	USA	11.6.91	180/73	PV	5.56	5.40- 12
	Geremew	Mosinet	ETH	12.2.92	168/52	HMar	59:11	
	Getachew	Limenih	ETH	30.4.90		Mar	2:06:49	2:07:35- 13
	Getahun	Birhan	ETH	5.9.91	181/64	3kSt	8:26.85	8:17.36- 11
	Ghalenouei	Peyman	IRI	29.1.92		HT	70.73	66.10- 12, 69.59irr- 13
	Ghazal	Majed El Dein	SYR	21.4.87	193/70	HJ	2.26	2.28- 11
	Ghebrselassie	Ghirmay	ERI-J	14.11.95		HMar	60:10	60:09- 13
	Ghislain	Arnaud	BEL	2.12.88	182/69	400h	50.17	51.58- 13
	Ghuys	Bram	BEL	14.2.93	192/68	HJ	2.24	2.20- 13
^	Gibilisco	Giuseppe	ITA	5.1.79	183/79	PV	5.70	5.90- 03
	Gibson	Jeffrey	BAH	15.8.90	186/79	400h	48.78	49.39- 13
	Giesting	Chris	USA	10.12.92	191/80	400	45.53	45.90- 13
*	Gill	Jacko	NZL	20.12.94	190/118	SP	20.70	20.38- 11

Name		Nat	Born	Ht/Wt	Event	2014 Mark	Pre-2014 Best
Gimeno	Jorge	ESP	16.2.90	179/64	TJ	16.61	16.23- 12
Girma	Berhanu	ETH	22.11.86		HMar	61:08	61:54- 12
					Mar	2:05:49	2:06:06- 13
Gitau	Daniel	KEN	1.10.87	175/57	10k	28:00.05	27:42.91- 12
					HMar	60:59	61:01- 12
Gittens	Ramon	BAR	20.7.87	180/77	100	10.06	10.02- 13
					200	20.44	20.56- 09
Giupponi	Matteo	ITA	8.10.88	190/65	50kW	3:51:49	4:10:49- 08
Givans	Senoj-Jay	JAM	30.12.93	178/73	100	10.10, 9.90w	10.45- 13
					200	20.67, 20.28w	21.03- 13
Glass	Najee	USA	12.6.94	183/73	400	45.40	45.71- 13
Gloger	Nils Christopher	GER	6.8.90	178/66	20kW	1:21:49	1:24:01- 13
Glover	Tim	USA	1.11.90	185/86	JT	84.01	81.69- 12
Golling	David	GER	13.3.90	193/94	JT	80.32	80.67- 13
Golovin	Aleksey	RUS	24.12.88		20kW	1:22:06	1:23:39- 13
Gómez	Iñaki	CAN	16.1.88	172/58	20kW	1:20:18	1:20:58- 12
Gomis	Kafétien	FRA	23.3.80	183/67	LJ	8.19	8.24- 10
Goncharov	Viktor	RUS	9.5.91	178/84	JT	77.54	80.34- 11
González	Andy	CUB	17.10.87	183/70	800	1:45.73A	1:45.3- 08, 1:45.41- 09
González	Erwin	MEX	7.2.94		20kW	1:22:36	-0-
González	Manuel	CUB	23.3.93	187/84	Dec	7742	7854h- 13
* Gordon	Jehue	TTO	15.12.91	190/80	400h	48.75	47.69- 13
* Gordon	Lalonde	TTO	25.11.88	188/83	200	20.38	20.26- 13
					400	44.78	44.52- 12
Gordon	Nick	JAM	17.9.88	174/73	LJ	7.93w	8.11- 09, 8.14w- 11
Gorokhov	Grigoriy	RUS	20.4.93		PV	5.50i	5.40- 12
Gotch	Jarvis	USA	25.3.92	185/73	LJ	7.83, 7.93Aw	8.09A, 8.18Aw- 13
* Gowda	Vikas	IND	5.7.83	196/115	DT	65.62	66.28- 12
* Grabarz	Robbie	GBR	3.10.87	192/87	HJ	2.27i	2.37- 12
Grace	Bobby	USA	10.10.90	193/118	SP	19.90i, 19.56	19.31- 13
Grace	Bryce	USA	18.7.94	188/77	110h	13.64w	13.84, 13.73w- 12
Graham	Hugh	JAM	10.10.92	184/75	400	45.29	45.19- 13
Grau	Martin	GER	26.3.92	176/64	3kSt	8:24.29	8:42.90- 13
Gray	Cordero	USA	9.5.89	173/68	100	10.16, 10.03w	10.11, 10.09w- 12
* Greco	Daniele	ITA	1.3.89	184/75	TJ	16.84	17.70i- 13, 17.47, 17.67w- 12
^ Green	Leford	JAM	14.11.86	186/79	400h	49.00	48.47- 10
* Greene	David	GBR	11.4.86	183/75	400h	49.89	47.84- 12
Greer	Elijah	USA	24.10.90	185/66	800	1:44.91	1:45.04- 13
^ Gregório	Jadel	BRA	16.9.80	202/102	TJ	16.42, 16.74w	17.90- 07
Gregory	Ben	GBR	21.11.90	184/82	Dec	7725	7554w- 12, 7383- 10
^ Gregson	Ryan	AUS	26.4.90	184/68	800	1:46.27	1:46.04- 10
					1500	3:36.17	3:31.06- 10
					1M	3:53.85	3:52.24- 10
Grice	Charlie	GBR	7.11.93	182/68	1500	3:35.59	3:38.13- 13
Griffith	Adrian	BAH	11.11.84	178/75	100	10.14, 10.03w	10.19- 10, 10.09w- 13
Grigoryev	Ivan	RUS	27.10.89		Dec	8112	7828- 12
Grigoryev	Sergey	KAZ	24.6.92	178/65	PV	5.50	5.20- 09
Grinnell	Ryan	USA	4.2.87	188/82	TJ	16.52, 16.55w	17.22- 13
* Gripich	Aleksandr	RUS	21.9.86	190/80	PV	5.70	5.75- 09
Grzeszczuk	Lukasz	POL	3.3.90	189/95	JT	84.77	83.98- 13
Gudmundsson	Sindri Hrafn	ISL-J	21.11.95	178/86	JT	77.28	70.25- 13
Gudzius	Andrius	LTU	14.2.91	198/125	DT	66.11	63.39- 12
^ Guliyev	Ramil	TUR	29.5.90	187/73	200	20.38	20.04- 09
Günther	Martin	GER	8.10.86	188/74	HJ	2.28i, 2.25	2.30i- 10, 2.24- 08
Guo Jinqi		CHN	21.9.92		HJ	2.24i, 2.24	2.24- 12
Guo Qi		CHN	28.12.90	190/80	Dec	7804	7692- 12
Gustafsson	Andreas	SWE	10.8.81	180/67	50kW	3:51:16	3:50:47- 12
Haapala	Eero	FIN	10.7.89	193/87	LJ	7.89	8.11i, 7.90- 13
Haatainen	Harri	FIN	5.1.78	186/85	JT	77.61	86.63- 01
* Hadadi	Ehsan	IRI	21.1.85	193/125	DT	65.23	69.32- 08
Hadj Lazib	Othman	ALG	10.5.83	186/85	110h	13.56	13.46- 11
Hadnot	Trey	USA	7.3.92	173/70	200	20.66, 20.43w	20.48i, 20.49- 13
Haidane	Abdellah	ITA	28.3.89		3000	7:47.34	7:54.73i, 7:56.45- 12
Haitengi	Roger	NAM	12.9.83	184/80	TJ	16.57A, 16.72w	16.46A,16.74w?- 10,16.35- 07
Haji	Yasin	ETH-J	22.1.96	168/52	5000	13:26.21	
Håkansson	Elias	SWE	29.2.92	190/104	HT	71.38	65.69- 11
^ Haklits	András	CRO	23.9.77	189/103	HT	74.04	80.41- 05
Hale	Jack	AUS-Y	22.5.98		100	10.13w	
* Hall	Arman	USA	14.2.94	188/77	200	20.40	20.73, 20.71w- 13
					400	45.19	44.82- 13
Halmela	Artty	FIN	25.9.91	182/75	LJ	7.92	7.84- 12
Hamann	Lars	GER	4.4.89	187/88	JT	79.65	84.20- 13

	Name		Nat	Born	Ht/Wt	Event	2014 Mark	Pre-2014 Best
	Hammond	Michael	USA	7.11.89	182/64	1500	3:37.88	3:39.22- 12
	Hanany	Mickaël	FRA	25.3.83	198/84	HJ	2.34A	2.32- 08
*	Hann	Mamadou Kassé	SEN	10.10.86	190/73	400h	48.86	48.50- 13
	Hannes	Pieter-Jan	BEL	30.10.92	186/72	1500	3:34.49	3:35.97- 13
						1M	3:55.33	
	Hara	Shota	JPN	18.7.92	180/75	200	20.41	20.90, 20.57w- 13
	Haratyk	Michael	POL	10.4.92	187/90	SP	19.95	17.72- 12
*	Hardee	Trey	USA	7.2.84	196/95	Dec	8599	8790- 09
	Hardy	Prezel	USA	1.6.92	168/64	200	20.16, 20.14w	20.33- 12
	Harmse	Chris	RSA	31.5.73	184/118	HT	73.90	80.63- 05
*	Harradine	Benn	AUS	14.10.82	198/115	DT	65.94	68.20- 13
	Harris	Adam	GUY	21.7.87	178/77	100	10.12, 9.90w	10.16- 13, 10.09w- 09
*	Harris	Aleec	USA	31.10.90	185/77	110h	13.14	13.65, 13.55w- 11
	Harris	James	USA	18.9.91	196/88	400	45.33	45.23- 13
						HJ	2.32iA, 2.21	2.27i- 12, 2.24- 13
	Härstedt	Axel	SWE	28.2.87	197/130	DT	62.43	61.66- 13
	Hart	Shavez	BAH	9.6.92	176/70	100	10.11	10.16A, 10.24, 10.08w- 13
						200	20.35	21.02A, 20.24w- 12, 21.12- 11
	Hartfield	Mike	USA	29.3.90	190/77	LJ	8.15, 8.127w	8.15- 13
	Harting	Christoph	GER	4.10.90	205/117	DT	63.78	64.99- 13
*	Harting	Robert	GER	18.10.84	201/126	DT	68.47	70.66- 12
	Harvey	Jacques	JAM/TUR	5.4.89	182/73	100	10.17	10.04- 13, 10.03w- 11
	Hassi	Jouko	FIN	4.4.93	185/79	Dec	7569	7289- 13
	Hathat	Yassine	ALG	30.7.91	180/68	800	1:46.52	1:46.09- 13
	1000	2:16.76				1500	3:35.68	3:46.17- 13
	Hayakawa	Tsubasa	JPN	2.7.90	168/48	10k	28:15.36	28:22.47- 13
	Hayes	Keith	USA	16.2.90	186/77	110h	13.67, 13.63w	13.65- 11, 13.30w- 13
	Hayes	Keyunta	USA	15.2.92	183/73	400h	49.59	49.38- 12
	He Yongqiang		CHN	27.11.93		50kW	4:01:54	4:01:45- 13
	Heath	Garrett	USA	3.11.85	183/65	1500	3:35.89	3:34.12- 13
	1M	3:53.61	3:53.15- 13	3000	7:37.40i	7:45.80i,7:51.34- 12	5000 13:16.65	13:20.01- 13
*	Heffernan	Robert	IRL	20.2.78	173/55	20kW	1:20:57	1:19:22- 08
	Heinke	Lars-Niklas	GER	7.11.89	191/80	Dec	7605	7648- 12
	Helcelet	Adam	CZE	27.10.91	187/86	Dec	8001	8252- 13
*	Henderson	Jeff	USA	19.2.89	178/82	LJ	8.43, 8.25w	8.22- 13
	Henriksen	Eivind	NOR	14.9.90	191/116	HT	72.70	75.57- 12
^	Henriques	Anderson	BRA	3.3.92	187/80	400	45.03	44.95- 13
	Henry	Eldred	IVB	18.9.94	198/125	DT	61.90	-0-
^	Henry	Tabarie	ISV	1.12.87	187/79	400	45.62	44.77- 09
	Hepperle	Felix	GER	23.11.89		Dec	7618	7596- 12
	Heriot	Blake	USA	26.9.91	178/70	200	20.45w	20.52- 13
	Herman	Timothy	BEL	19.10.90		JT	77.69	78.98- 12
	Hernández	Osviel	CUB	31.5.89	179/76	TJ	16.82, 16.93w	17.49- 12
	Herrera	José Carlos	MEX	5.2.86	187/77	200	20.35	20.57A- 12, 21.00- 10
	Hess	Max	GER-J	13.7.96	185/75	TJ	16.55	15.52- 13
	Hester	Tevin	USA	10.1.94	170/66	100	10.16	10.21- 13
	Hicks ¶	Jeremy	USA	19.9.86	178/75	LJ	8.06iA, 8.23w drugs dq	8.11- 12, 8.31w- 13
	Higgs	Raymond	BAH	24.1.91	188/75	LJ	7.99i, 7.88, 7.94w	8.15- 11, 8.36w- 12
	Hightower	Dakarai	USA	15.7.94	183/68	HJ	2.24	2.21- 12
	Higuma	Takafumi	JPN	3.9.82		50kW	4:06:10	3:52:53- 12
	Hill	Darrell	USA	17.8.93	193/135	SP	20.57	19.13- 13
	Hill	Devon	USA	26.10.89	185/75	110h	13.55	13.35- 12, 13.32w- 13
	Hill	Ryan	USA	31.1.90	176/60	1500	3:37.10	3:38.36- 12
	3000	7:38.64, 7:34.87i		7:42.32- 13		5000	13:14.31	13:14.22- 13
	Hirsuato	Nuguse	ETH	13.2.82		HMar	61:07	-0-
	Hiss Bachir	Youssouf	DJI	.87	178/70	3000	7:48.32i	7:50.96- 13
	Hitrane	Jamal	MAR	1.9.89	172/65	1500	3:38.18	3:36.08- 12
						5000	13:25.09	13:22.63- 12
*	Hlavan	Igor	UKR	25.9.90	172/62	20kW	1:19:59	1:22:32- 13
						50kW	3:45:08	3:40:39- 13
	Hock	Johannes	GER	24.3.92	185/86	Dec	8092	8293(w), 8267- 13
*	Hoffa	Reese	USA	8.10.77	181/133	SP	21.88	22.43- 07
	Hoffman	Andreas	GER	16.12.91	195/95	JT	86.13	80.81- 12
	Hoffmann	Karol	POL	1.6.89	197/80	TJ	16.89i, 16.64	17.09- 12
*	Hogan	Victor	RSA	25.7.89	198/108	DT	64.16	65.33- 13
*	Hollis	Mark	USA	1.12.84	190/84	PV	5.83	5.75- 08
	Holmes	Timothy	USA-J	2.7.95	182/73	400h	49.90	50.61- 13
	Holusa	Jakub	CZE	20.2.88	183/72	1000	2:16.79	2:17.08- 11
						1500	3:35.26	3:38.10- 11
*	Holzdeppe	Raphael	GER	28.9.89	181/78	PV	5.53	5.91- 12
	Homo	Nicolas	FRA	24.11.88	186/80	PV	5.50i, 5.50	5.38i- 13, 5.25- 12

	Name		Nat	Born	Ht/Wt	Event	2014 Mark	Pre-2014 Best
	Honeycutt	Josh	USA	7.3.89	182/73	TJ	16.83	16.59Ai, 16.78w- 13
	Horák	Peter	SVK	7.12.83	197/83	HJ	2.24i, 2.20	2.30i- 07, 2.28- 09
	Hostetler	Cyrus	USA	8.8.86	190/95	JT	80.28	83.16- 09
	Hough	Nick	AUS	20.10.93	191/86	110h	13.57	13.98- 12
	Houssaye	Cédric	FRA	13.12.79	178/65	50kW	3:58:54	3:53:24- 11
	Howard	Julian	GER	3.4.89	176/75	LJ	8.04	8.07- 13
	Hrechkovskyy	Andrey	UKR	30.8.93		50kW	3:49:06	3:58:26- 13
	Hu Wanli		CHN	27.5.92		50kW	4:04:05	4:06:57- 12
	Hu Yufei		CHN	9.11.93		Dec	7582	7104- 12
	Huang Shih-Feng		TPE	2.3.92	181/88	JT	81.53	82.11- 13
	Huang Changzhou		CHN	20.8.94		LJ	8.12	7.97- 13
	Hubbard	Jamil	USA	12.5.86	170/64	200	20.40w	20.67- 12, 20.54w- 13
	Hudi	Ákos	HUN	10.8.91	185/95	HT	74.17	76.93- 13
*	Hudson-Smith	Matthew	GBR	26.10.94	192/79	400	44.75	48.76i- 13
	Hughes	Matt	CAN	3.8.89	180/64	5000	13:28.36	13:59.30- 10
						3kSt	8:12.81	8:11.64- 13
	Hughes	Zharnel	AIA-J	13.7.95	190/79	100	10.12	10.23A- 13, 10.42- 12
						200	20.32	20.79, 20.77w- 13
*	Huling	Dan	USA	16.7.83	185/70	3kSt	8:15.61	8:13.29- 10
	Hull	Gabe	USA	1.12.93	203/127	DT	63.11	59.80- 13
	Humphreys	Sam	USA	12.9.90	201/115	JT	81.51	83.14- 13
*	Hussein	Kariem	SUI	1.4.89	190/77	400h	48.47	49.61- 12
	Huyler	Garrett	USA	15.1.87	196/86	HJ	2.25	2.24i- 13, 2.21- 09
	Hyde	Jaheel	JAM-Y	2.2.97	180/73	400h	49.29	51.06LH- 13
	Hyman	Kemar	CAY	11.10.89	178/74	100	10.15, 10.06w	9.95- 12
	Ibáñez	Anatole	SWE	14.11.85	176/67	50kW	3:48:42	3:53:38- 13
*	Ibrahimov	Hayle	AZE	18.1.90	168/58	3000	7:39.73i	7:34.57- 13
						5000	13:09.17	13:11.34- 12
	Idiata	Samson	NGR	28.2.82	186/75	LJ	7.93, 8.02w	8.00- 13, 8.02w- 12
^	Idowu	Phillips	GBR	30.12.78	192/86	TJ	16.99	17.81- 10
*	Iguider	Abdelati	MAR	25.3.87	170/52	1500	3:29.83	3:31.47- 09
	1M	3:49.09		3:51.78- 12		3000	7:34.99	7:34.92i- 13, 7:41.95- 07
	Íltsios	Yeóryios	GRE	28.11.81	187/95	JT	77.58	79.72- 06
	Ilyichev	Ivan	RUS	14.10.86		HJ	2.30i, 2.22	2.28i- 07, 2.26- 08
*	Ingebrigtsen	Henrik	NOR	24.2.91	180/69	1500	3:31.46	3:33.95- 13
						1M	3:50.72	3:54.28- 12
	Ingraham	Ryan	BAH	2.11.93	191/70	HJ	2.28	2.30- 13
	Inoue	Hiroto	JPN	6.1.93	164/53	10k	28:19.28	28:39.08- 13
^	Ioannou	Kyriakos	CYP	26.7.84	193/66	HJ	2.28	2.35- 07
	Iordan	Valeriy	RUS	14.2.92	192/95	JT	82.05	83.23- 12
	Irabaruta	Olivier	BDI	25.8.90	171/61	5000	13:23.44	13:28.80- 11
	Irfan	Kolothum Thodi	IND	8.2.90	172/55	20kW	1:21:09	1:20:21- 12
	Irwin	Andrew	USA	23.1.93	190/84	PV	5.60i, 5.50	5.72- 12
	Irwin	Willy	USA	2.6.92	188/107	SP	20.13	19.49- 13
	Ishikawa	Kazuyoshi	JPN	6.11.82	178/70	TJ	16.52	16.98- 04
	Ishikawa	Takuya	JPN	29.10.87	173/54	10k	28:17.74	28:09.49- 12
	Isidro	Pedro	POR	17.7.85	175/58	50kW	3:56:15	3:57:09- 13
	Ismail	Muhammad Hakimi	MAS	8.4.91	187/75	TJ	16.41	16.44- 13
^	Israel	Märt	EST	23.9.83	190/119	DT	64.40	66.98- 11
	Issaka	Andrew	FRA	15.9.92	194/85	TJ	16.48w	15.91, 16.06w- 13
	Ito	Yuki	JPN	12.4.92		50kW	4:01:10	
	Ivakin	Anton	RUS	3.2.91	178/73	PV	5.65	5.65i, 5.63- 13
*	Ivanov	Aleksandr	RUS	25.4.93	182/68	20kW	1:19:45	1:20:58- 13
*	Ivanov	Georgi	BUL	13.3.85	187/130	SP	21.02i, 20.91	21.09- 13
	Ivanov	Tihomir Ivaylo	BUL	11.7.94	196/73	HJ	2.28	2.18- 13
	Ivanytskyy	Vasyl	UKR	29.1.91		Dec	7651	7558- 13
	Ivanyuk	Ilya	RUS	9.3.93	183/75	HJ	2.25i	2.27i, 2.26- 13
	Ivashko	Pavel	RUS	16.11.94	185/75	400	45.46	45.81- 13
	Izuka	Shota	JPN	25.6.91	185/80	200	20.39	20.21- 13
*	Jackson	Bershawn	USA	8.5.83	173/69	400h	48.76	47.30- 05
	Jackson	Marcus	USA	8.7.91	201/82	HJ	2.29iA	2.29i, 2.27- 13
	Jackson	Mark	USA	12.10.91	175/82	TJ	16.38iA	16.19- 13
*	Jager	Evan	USA	8.3.89	186/66	1500	3:38.10+	3:36.34- 13
	1M	3:53.33		3:54.35- 09		2000	4:57.56i	
	5000	13:08.63		13:02.40- 13		3kSt	8:04.71	8:06.81- 12
	Jagusch	Christian	GER	13.7.92	190/110	SP	19.74	18.49- 13
	Jakubczyk	Lucas	GER	28.4.85	183/73	100	10.07, 10.01w	10.20, 10.16w- 12
	Jaleta	Habtamu	ETH	19.4.93		3kSt	8:29.97	8:24.90- 13
	James	Antonio	USA	7.4.92	190/116	SP	19.93i, 19.35	18.17- 13
*	James	Kirani	GRN	1.9.92	185/74	400	43.74	43.94- 12
	Janet	Roberto	CUB	29.8.86	187/95	HT	75.99	77.08- 12

Name		Nat	Born	Ht/Wt	Event	2014 Mark	Pre-2014 Best
^ Jarso	Yakob	ETH	5.2.88	173/54	Mar	2:06:17	2:11:13- 12
Jasinski	Daniel	GER	5.8.89	207/125	DT	65.98	64.69- 13
Jaszczuk	Tomasz	POL	9.3.92	195/83	LJ	8.15	8.11- 11
Jegede	J.J.	GBR	3.10.85	185/80	LJ	8.05, 8.06w	8.11- 12
* Jelks	Mark	NGR	10.4.84	170/66	100	10.07, 10.05w	9.99- 08, 9.8w- 05
^ Jeng	Alhaji	SWE	13.12.81	185/77	PV	5.71i, 5.55	5.81i- 09, 5.80- 06
Jenkins	Devin	USA	16.2.94	183/75	100	10.16, 10.06w	10.42, 10.38w- 13, 10.1- 12
					200	20.72, 20.13w	20.92- 13
Jenkins	Eric	USA	24.11.91	170/61	5000	13:27.41	13:18.57- 13
Jensen	Curtis	USA	1.11.90	193/130	SP	20.33	20.29i, 19.63- 13
* Jeylan	Ibrahim	ETH	12.6.89	168/57	5000	13:09.67	13:09.16- 13
Jiang Fan		CHN	16.9.89	188/75	110h	13.56	13.47- 11
Jie Lei		CHN	8.5.89		LJ	8.07	7.99- 13
Jin Min-sup		KOR	2.9.92	185/75	PV	5.65	5.64- 13
Jock	Charles	USA	23.11.89	188/73	800	1:45.90	1:44.67- 11
Jöeväli	Kaarel	EST	8.1.90		Dec	7672	7658- 13
Johansson	Markus	SWE	8.5.90	183/110	HT	76.16	76.43- 13
John	Alexander	GER	3.5.86	185/77	110h	13.70, 13.61w	13.35- 09
^ Johnson	Kibwé	USA	17.7.81	189/108	HT	74.86	80.31- 11
Johnson	Omar	JAM	25.11.88	183/74	400	45.42	45.50- 13
* Jonas	Dusty	USA	19.4.86	198/84	HJ	2.35	2.36A- 08, 2.33- 10
Jones	Jonathan	USA	23.4.91	183/127	SP	20.75	19.59i, 19.24- 13
Jones	Nick	USA	22.6.89	188/109	DT	61.12	61.95A- 12
Joseph	Stanley	FRA	24.10.91	181/66	PV	5.55i, 5.45	5.62i- 13, 5.55- 12
Joseph	Vanier	USA	9.9.91	185/79	110h	13.68, 13.41w	13.59- 13
Jufar	Tariku	ETH	18.7.84	173/55	Mar	2:07:02	2:06:51- 12
Julião	Ronald	BRA	16.6.85	194/113	DT	64.11	65.55- 13
Juska	Radek	CZE	8.3.93		LJ	7.94	7.71- 12
Kafia	Louhab	ALG	24.2.87		TJ	16.63	16.47- 13
* Kaki	Abubaker	SUD	21.6.89	176/63	800	1:44.09	1:42.23- 10
^ Kamal	Ali Abubaker	QAT	8.11.83	169/58	5000	13:25.51	13:47.79- 04
					3kSt	8:17.27	8:15.80- 08
Kamathi	Joseph	KEN-J	23.11.96	175/56	10k	27:38.18	28:16.27- 13
* Kamworor	Geoffrey	KEN	28.11.92	168/54	HMar	59:07	58:54- 13
					Mar	2:06:39	2:06:12- 12
Kanda	Lukas	KEN	.87		Mar	2:08:02	2:08:04- 12
Kandu	Chris	GBR-J	10.9.95	197/79	HJ	2.24	2.18- 13
Kanemaru	Yuzo	JPN	18.9.87	177/77	400	45.46	45.16- 09
Kangas	Arttu	FIN	13.7.93	186/108	SP	19.74	19.07- 13
Kangogo	Cornelius	KEN	31.12.93	166/62	3000	7:41.27	7:39.73- 12
					5000	13:11.14	13:15.26- 13
* Kanter	Gerd	EST	6.5.79	196/125	DT	66.28	73.38- 06
Karlström	Perseus	SWE	2.5.90	184/73	20kW	1:21:54	1:23:43- 12
* Karoki	Bidan	KEN	21.8.90	169/53	5000	13:15.25	13:15.75- 13
10k	26:52.36	27:05.50- 12			HMar	59:23	-0-
^ Karpov	Dmitriy	KAZ	23.7.81	198/98	Dec	7756	8725- 04
Kassaw	Abere	ETH	8.12.94		Mar	2:08:18	
Kassaye	Meresa	ETH-J	23.5.96		3kSt	8:26.08	8:29.92- 13
* Kasyanov	Oleksiy	UKR	26.8.85	191/82	Dec	8231	8479- 09
Kauppinen	Juha	FIN	16.8.86	182/103	HT	71.80	74.38- 09
Kawamoto	Sho	JPN	1.3.93	175/68	800	1:45.75	1:46.4A- 12
Kawatsura	Sota	JPN	19.6.89	174/60	100	10.10w	10.22- 11
* Kaya	Ali	TUR	20.4.94		3000	7:43.61i	7:48.20i, 7:58.76- 13
5000	13:34.83	13:31.39- 13			10k	28:08.72	28:31.16- 13
Kazanin	Oleksiy	UKR	22.5.82	170/58	50kW	3:47:01	3:50:17- 12
Kazaryan	Gayk	RUS	19.5.90		PV	5.50i, 5.50	5.50- 13
Kazi	Tamás	HUN	16.5.85	179/70	1000	2:17.38	2:19.06- 10
* Kazmirek	Kai	GER	28.1.91	189/91	Dec	8471	8366- 13
Kebede	Maru	ETH			10k	28:19.35	
* Kebede	Tsegaye	ETH	15.1.87	158/50	Mar	2:06:30	2:04:38- 12
^ Keflezighi	Mebrahtom	USA	5.5.75	170/58	Mar	2:08:37dh	2:09:08- 12
Keitany	Elijah	KEN	18.10.83		Mar	2:08:37	2:06:41- 09
Kejelcha	Yomif	ETH-Y	1.8.97	168/68	2000	4:57.74i	
3000	7:36.28	7:53.56- 13			5000	13:25.19	
Kemboi	Clement	KEN	1.2.92	180/65	3kSt	8:16.96	8:17.18- 13
Kemboi	Edward	KEN	12.12.91	170/57	800	1:46.14, 1:45.98i	1:46.06- 11
Kemboi	Edwin	KEN	22.8.86		800	1:45.5A	1:46.8A- 11
Kemboi	Elijah	KEN	10.9.84		Mar	2:07:43	2:07:34- 13
* Kemboi	Ezekiel	KEN	25.5.82	175/62	3kSt	8:04.12	7:55.76- 11
Kemboi	Hillary	KEN	.86		3kSt	8:22.26	8:29.2A- 13
Kemboi	Lawrence	KEN	15.6.93	170/57	3kSt	8:19.59	8:25.0A- 13

	Name		Nat	Born	Ht/Wt	Event	2014 Mark	Pre-2014 Best
	Kendagor	Jacob	KEN	19.9.84		HMar	60:32	59:36- 13
						Mar	2:07:53	2:09:05- 10
*	Kendricks	Sam	USA	7.9.92	189/79	PV	5.75	5.81- 13
	Kering	Alfred	KEN	.80	172/57	Mar	2:08:28	2:07:11- 10
^	Keskisalo	Jukka	FIN	27.3.81	184/66	3kSt	8:29.89	8:10.67- 09
	Keys	Dakotah	USA	27.9.91	188/79	Dec	8068	8001- 13
	Kgosiemang	Kabelo Mmono	BOT	7.1.86	188/74	HJ	2.28	2.34A- 08, 2.30- 06
	Kharitonov	Aleksandr	RUS	19.7.90	186/88	JT	78.02	77.66- 13
	Khodjayev	Sukhrob	UZB	21.5.93	186/105	HT	71.43	74.20- 12
	Khwaja	Mohamed	LBA	1.11.87	180/70	400	45.40	44.98A- 10, 45.35- 09
	Kibet	Moses	KEN	23.3.91	165/55	10k	28:05.71	
*	Kibet	Stephen	KEN	9.11.86	172/55	HMar	59:21	58:54- 12
*	Kibet	Vincent	KEN	6.5.91	170/57	1500	3:31.96	3:35.62- 13
	800	1:46.71		1:47.8- 13		1M	3:52.15	
	Kibiego	Titus	KEN-J	3.5.96	174/57	3kSt	8:22.46A	
	Kibor	William	KEN	10.1.85		HMar	60:51	63:23- 12
	Kifle	Goitom	ERI	3.12.93	178/60	10k	27:43.30	27:32.00- 13
						HMar	60:20	61:18- 13
*	Kigen	Mike	KEN	15.1.86	170/54	5000	13:26.6+	12:58.58- 06
	HMar	60:00dh		59:58- 11		Mar	2:06:59	2:08:24- 13
	Kigen	Sammy	KEN	29.9.85		Mar	2:08:05	2:12:50- 13
	Kiiskilä	Jani	FIN	28.12.89	180/81	JT	77.83	75.80- 13
	Kikuchi	Masato	JPN	18.9.90	172/56	10k	28:04.25	28:42.61- 13
						HMar	61:17	62:26- 13
*	Kilty	Richard	GBR	2.9.89	184/79	100	10.12	10.10- 13
	Kim Byung-jun		KOR	15.8.91	190/80	110h	13.43	13.61- 13
	Kim Duk-hyung		KOR	8.12.85	180/68	LJ	8.04	8.20, 8.41w- 09
						TJ	16.93	17.10- 09
*	Kim Hyun-sub		KOR	31.5.85	175/53	20kW	1:19:24	1:19:31- 11
	Kim Ye-ram		KOR	2.3.94	178/86	JT	78.17	74.46- 13
	Kim Yoo-suk		KOR	19.1.82	191/87	PV	5.50	5.66- 07
	Kimani	Bernard	KEN	10.9.93	172/54	5000	13:14.64	13:22.15- 13
						10k	27:36.60	29:01.42- 13
*	Kimetto	Dennis	KEN	22.1.84	172/57	Mar	2:02:57	2:03:45- 13
	Kimitei	Elijah	KEN	25.12.86	182/84	LJ	7.93A, (7.50)	8.09A, 7.47- 12
						TJ	16.40A	16.66A, 16.28- 12
	Kimitei	Wilfred	KEN	11.3.85	172/57	5000	13:12.72	13:50.8A- 11
	Kimura	Yosuke	JPN	5.2.93		20kW	1:22:41	1:25:59- 11
	Kimurer Kemboi	Joel	KEN	21.1.88		Mar	2:07:53	2:07:48- 13
	Kimutai	Philip Sanga	KEN	10.9.83	170/60	HMar	60:57	61:09- 11
						Mar	2:08:58	2:06:07- 11
	King	Devin	USA-J	12.3.96	185/75	PV	5.50	5.25- 13
	Kinnunen	Jarkko	FIN	19.1.84	187/69	50kW	3:48:49	3:46:25- 12
	Kinsley	Craig	USA	19.1.89	186/82	JT	81.35	82.31- 12
	Kinyor	Job	KEN	2.9.90	176/68	800	1:44.55	1:43.76- 12
	Kipchirchir	Moses	KEN	.86		800	1:46.3A	1:47.09A- 13
	Kipchirchir	Shadrack	KEN	22.2.89	175/60	10k	27:36.79	29:08.64- 11
	Kipchirchir	Victor	KEN	5.12.87		HMar	60:48	59:31- 12
*	Kipchoge	Eliud	KEN	5.11.84	167/52	HMar	60:52	59:25- 12
						Mar	2:04:11	2:04:05- 13
	Kipchumba	Hillary	KEN	25.11.92		HMar	61:11	61:02- 13
	Kipkemboi	Nicholas	KEN	5.7.86		HMar	60:11	60:15- 12
*	Kipkemoi	Kenneth	KEN	2.8.84	165/52	5000	13:13.16	13:03.37- 12
	10k	27:30.94		26:52.65- 12		HMar	59:01	59:11- 12
*	Kipketer	Alfred	KEN-J	26.12.96	169/61	800	1:43.95	1:46.2A- 13
*	Kipkoech	John	KEN	29.12.91	160/52	3000	7:38.97	7:32.72- 10
	HMar	61:38				5000	13:07.60	12:49.50- 12
	Kipkoech	Nicholas	KEN	22.10.92	168/57	800	1:45.7A	1:45.01- 12
	Kipkorir	Evans	KEN	4.4.94	175/65	800	1:45.50A	1:45.91- 12
	Kipkosgei	Nelson	KEN	9.3.93		3kSt	8:24.45	8:22.24- 12
	Kiplagat	Abraham	KEN	8.9.84	182/72	800	1:46.13	1:43.77- 10
*	Kiplagat	Benjamin	UGA	4.3.89	186/61	3kSt	8:26.05	8:03.81- 10
	Kiplagat	Evans	KEN	5.3.88		HMar	60:54	59:56- 09
	Kiplagat	Henry	KEN	16.12.82		HMar	60:24	60:01- 12
	Kiplagat	Mariko	KEN	10.1.82		Mar	2:08:06	2:06:05- 12
*	Kiplagat	Silas	KEN	20.8.89	170/57	1500	3:27.64	3:29.27- 10
						1M	3:47.88	3:49.39- 11
	Kiplagat	Thomas	KEN			Mar	2:07:52	2:18:19A- 13
	Kiplangat	Cornelius	KEN	21.12.92	168/55	800	1:45.7A	1:45.47A- 13
	Kiplimo	Joash	KEN	.91		3kSt	8:27.0A	8:42.3A- 13
	Kiplimo	Joseph	KEN	20.7.88	173/57	3000	7:41.79	7:31.20- 09
						5000	13:17.49	13:09.34- 09

Name		Nat	Born	Ht/Wt	Event	2014 Mark	Pre-2014 Best
* Kiprop	Asbel	KEN	30.6.89	186/70	800	1:43.34	1:43.15- 11
1500	3:28.45		3:27.72- 13		1M	3:50.26	3:48.50- 09
Kiprop	Francis	KEN	4.6.82	172/54	Mar	2:08:53	2:07:04- 09
Kiprop	Josphat	KEN	16.11.93		HMar	61:03Adh	64:42A- 13
* Kiprop	Wilson	KEN	14.4.87	179/62	HMar	59:45	59:15- 12
Kiprotich	Felix	KEN	.88		Mar	2:08:05	2:09:43- 13
* Kipruto	Brimin	KEN	31.7.85	176/54	3kSt	8:04.64	7:53.64- 11
* Kipruto	Conseslus	KEN	8.12.94	174/55	3kSt	8:09.81	8:01.16- 13
Kipruto	Silas	KEN	26.9.84	184/66	HMar	60:17	59:39- 10
* Kipsang	Wilson	KEN	15.3.82	178/59	HMar	60:25	58:59- 09
					Mar	2:04:29	2:03:23- 13
* Kipsiro	Moses	UGA	2.9.86	174/59	3000	7:45.82	7:30.95- 09
5000	13:28.23		12:50.72- 07		10k	27:56.11	27:04.48- 12
^ Kiptanui	Eliud	KEN	6.6.89		Mar	2:07:28	2:05:39- 10
Kiptarus	Dominic	KEN-J	3.8.96		3kSt	8:29.28A	
Kiptoo	Edwin	KEN	.93		HMar	61:13	
Kiptoo	Elijah	KEN	9.6.86	171/53	1500	3:35.81	3:33.81- 12
* Kiptoo	Mark	KEN	21.6.76	175/64	Mar	2:06:49	2:06:16- 13
Kiptum	Joseph	KEN	25.9.87		HMar	61:10	60:26- 12
Kipyego	Barnabas	KEN-J	12.6.95	176/57	3kSt	8:17.03	
* Kipyego	Bernard	KEN	16.7.86	160/50	HMar	59:47	59:10- 09
					Mar	2:06:22	2:06:29- 11
* Kipyego	Michael	KEN	2.10.83	168/59	Mar	2:06:58	2:06:48- 11
Kipyeko	Phillip	UGA-J	10.1.95	167/52	3000	7:44.14	8:02.33- 11
Kirchler	Hannes	ITA	22.12.78	191/105	DT	63.33	65.01- 07
Kirongo	Sammy	KEN	4.2.94	176/62	800	1:45.3A	1:45.38- 13
					1000	2:16.52	2:20.67- 13
Kirt	Magnus	EST	10.4.90	191/87	JT	79.70	79.82- 13
Kirui	Geoffrey	KEN	16.2.93	158/50	HMar	60:51	
* Kirui	Gilbert	KEN	22.1.94	172/55	3kSt	8:11.86	8:06.96- 13
Kirui	Peter	KEN	2.1.88	182/62	10k	27:58.24	27:25.63- 11
					HMar	59:22	59:39- 12
Kirwa	Edwin	KEN	.80		3kSt	8:32.0A	8:25.2A- 13
Kirwa	Gilbert	KEN	20.12.85	178/59	Mar	2:06:44	2:06:14- 09
Kiryu	Yoshihide	JPN-J	15.12.95	175/69	100	10.05	10.01- 13
Kishimoto	Takayuki	JPN	6.5.90	171/61	400h	49.49	48.41- 12
^ Kisorio	Matthew	KEN	16.5.89	178/62	HMar	59:50	58:46- 11
^ Kiss	Dániel	HUN	12.2.82	195/73	110h	13.64	13.32, 13.20w- 10
Kithuka	Kennedy	KEN	4.6.89	170/57	5000	13:26.98	13:25.38i- 13, 13:28.61- 12
					10k	27:41.73	28:18.97- 12
Kitonyi	Daniel	KEN	12.1.94		10k	28:15.99	28:02.79- 13
* Kitum	Timothy	KEN	20.11.94	172/60	800	1:43.65	1:42.53- 12
Kitur	Felix	KEN	17.4.87	178/66	800	1:46.09	1:45.13- 13
* Kitwara	Sammy	KEN	26.11.86	177/54	HMar	60:24	58:47- 11
					Mar	2:04:28	2:05:16- 13
Kivalov	Leonid	RUS	1.4.88	183/75	PV	5.61	5.71i- 08, 5.60- 07
Kloptsov	Yuriy	RUS	22.12.89	176/64	3kSt	8:28.03	8:35.07- 12
Knipphals	Sven	GER	20.9.85	190/85	200	20.48	20.53- 12
Kobayashi	Kai	JPN	28.2.93		20kW	1:21:13	
Kobayashi	Koji	JPN	16.1.89	171/53	Mar	2:08:51	2:10:40- 12
Koblov	Dmitriy	KAZ	30.11.92	186/78	400h	49.40	50.30- 12
* Koech	Bernard	KEN	31.1.88	165/50	HMar	59:46	59:10- 12, 58:42dh- 13
					Mar	2:06:08	2:04:53- 13
Koech	Edwin	KEN			HMar	60:13	
Koech	Gilbert Yegon	KEN	.81	175/64	Mar	2:07:08	2:06:18- 09
* Koech	Isiah	KEN	19.12.93	178/60	3000	7:39.14i, 7:49.4+	7:30.43- 12
					5000	13:07.55	12:48.64- 12
Koech	John	BRN-J	23.8.95	174/59	3kSt	8:19.99	8:16.96- 13
* Koech	Paul Kipsiele	KEN	10.11.81	168/57	3000	7:37.22i	7:32.78i- 10, 7:33.93- 05
2000	5:01.84		5:00.0i- 08		3kSt	8:05.47	7:54.31- 12
Koffi Hua	Wilfried	CIV	24.9.89	186/80	100	10.05	10.21- 13
					200	20.25	20.57- 13
* Kogo	Micah	KEN	3.6.86	170/60	HMar	59:49	59:07dh- 12
Koike	Yuki	JPN-J	13.5.95	178/72	200	20.61, 20.34w	20.99- 13
Koivu	Joachim	FIN	5.9.88	195/104	HT	71.67	71.22- 11
Kokoyev	Valeriy	RUS	25.7.88	197/118	SP	20.58i, 20.23	20.46- 13
* Kolasinac	Asmir	SRB	15.10.84	185/130	SP	20.79	20.85- 12
Kolomoyets	Sergey	BLR	11.8.89	191/110	HT	76.55	77.52- 11
Kolosov	Dmitriy	RUS	19.5.86		TJ	16.47i	16.89- 11, 17.00w- 08
Kombe	Saviour	ZAM	3.8.91	174/66	400	45.27	46.49- 12
Kombich	Ismael	KEN	16.10.85	183/73	1500	3:37.34	3:33.31- 10

	Name		Nat	Born	Ht/Wt	Event	2014 Mark	Pre-2014 Best
	Komen	Willy	KEN	22.12.87	168/55	3kSt	8:30.0A	8:11.18- 07
*	Komon	Leonard Patrick	KEN	10.1.88	175/52	HMar	59:14	-0-
	Königsmark	Varg	GER	28.4.92	193/84	400h	49.12	49.54- 12
	Konishi	Yuta	JPN	31.7.90	182/70	400h	49.48	49.41- 11
	Kopeykin	Vasiliy	RUS	9.3.88		LJ	7.94i, 7.88	8.00, 8.06w- 13
	Koppelaar ¶	Rutger	NED	1.5.93	187/73	PV	5.55dq	5.42- 13
	Korchmid	Oleksandr	UKR	22.1.82	188/89	PV	5.50i	5.81- 05
	Korepanov	Sergey	RUS	15.7.84		50kW	4:03:04	3:56:16- 08
	Korir	Fredrick	KEN	17.4.87		800	1:46.5A	1:46.30A- 13
	Korir	Laban	KEN	30.12.85		Mar	2:08:04	2:06:05- 11
	Korir	Leonard	KEN	10.12.86	173/61	5000	13:24.74	13:15.45- 13
						10k	28:01.85	27:29.40- 11
	Korir	Lewis	KEN	11.6.86	168/52	10k	28:03.45	27:41.33- 11
	Korir	Mark	KEN	10.1.85		HMar	60:49	60:49- 13
	Korir	Ronald	KEN	.91		Mar	2:07:29	-0-
	Korolyov	Aleksey	RUS	5.4.82	190/118	HT	76.46	79.36- 08
	Koros	Bernard	KEN	7.5.94		1500	3:38.06	3:40.4A- 13
	Korotkov	Ilya	RUS	6.12.83	193/90	JT	79.34	85.47- 10
	Korotovskiy	Yevgeniy	RUS	21.6.92		HT	72.16	72.03- 13
	Korshunov	Yevgeniy	RUS	11.4.86		HJ	2.29i, 2.23	2.22i, 2.22- 13
	Kosgei	David	KEN	.85		HMar	61:17	60:50- 13
	Kosgei	Kennedy	KEN	.85		3kSt	8:34.8A	8:35.0A- 13
	Kosynskyy	Dmytro	UKR	31.3.89	191/95	JT	82.28	83.39- 11
	Kotov	Danyil	RUS-J	14.11.95	183/73	PV	5.50	5.10- 12
	Kotut	Cyprian	KEN	.92		HMar	59:12	59:59- 13
*	Kovacs	Joe	USA	28.6.89	185/114	SP	22.03	21.08- 12
*	Kövágó	Zoltán	HUN	10.4.79	204/127	DT	65.82	69.95- 06
	Kovalenko	Nazar	UKR	9.2.89	177/65	20kW	1:19:46	1:19:55- 12
	Kovals	Ainars	LAT	21.11.81	192/105	JT	81.75	86.64- 08
	Kovalyov	Andriy	UKR	11.6.92	197/78	HJ	2.25i, 2.20	2.24- 13
	Kovalyov	Yuriy	RUS	18.6.91		TJ	16.63	17.06- 11
	Kovenko	Andriy	UKR	25.11.73	174/64	20kW	1:20:20	1:20:22- 13
*	Kowal	Yoann	FRA	28.5.87	174/58	3kSt	8:25.50	8:12.53- 13
	Kownatke	Rafal	POL	24.3.85	189/133	SP	19.80i, 19.24	20.13- 13
*	Kozmus	Primoz	SLO	30.9.79	188/106	HT	77.46	82.58- 09
	Kranjc	Matija	SLO	12.6.84	183/91	JT	80.46	79.72- 11
	Krasnov	Vladimir	RUS	19.8.90	190/70	400	45.45	45.12- 10
	Krauss	Simon	FRA	12.2.92	182/75	110h	13.51	13.55, 13.41w- 13
*	Kravchenko	Andrey	BLR	4.1.86	187/84	Dec	8616	8617- 07
	Kravtsov	Aleksey	RUS	8.5.93		Dec	7764	-0-
	Krawczuk	Lukasz	POL	15.6.89	183/70	400	45.65	46.13- 13
	Kregers	Reinis	LAT	22.1.92	188/82	Dec	7618	7406(w)- 13
*	Krivitskiy	Pavel	BLR	17.4.84	184/110	HT	79.39	80.67- 11
	Kruger	A.G.	USA	18.2.79	193/118	HT	76.25	79.26- 04
	Krüger	Dennis	GER	24.4.93	180/78	800	1:45.79	1:46.92- 12
	Krukowski	Marcin	POL	14.6.92	182/92	JT	80.66	83.04- 13
^	Krymarenko	Yuriy	UKR	11.8.83	187/65	HJ	2.28	2.34i- 07, 2.34- 13
	Krzewina	Jacob	POL	10.10.89	186/72	400	45.11	46.51- 11
*	Kszczot	Adam	POL	2.9.89	178/64	800	1:44.02	1:43.30- 11
						1000	2:15.72	2:16.99- 11
	Kubota	Shinobu	JPN	12.12.91	167/53	10k	27:54.25	28:07.01- 12
^	Kucheranyu	Sergey	RUS	30.6.85	185/75	PV	5.70	5.81- 08
	Kuciapski	Artur	POL	26.12.93	183/65	800	1:44.89	1:48.15- 13
	Kucmín	Antón	SVK	7.6.84	180/64	20kW	1:21:59	1:22:25- 12
*	Kudlicka	Jan	CZE	29.4.88	184/76	PV	5.80i, 5.72, 5.76ex	5.81ex- 11, 5.77i/5.76- 13
	Kudryavtsev	Denis	RUS	13.4.92	187/77	400h	48.95	49.40- 13
	Kuira	Paul	KEN	25.1.90	172/53	10k	27:40.43	27:40.60- 11
	Kulagov	Konstantin	RUS	14.10.91		50kW	3:55:09	4:19:58- 12
*	Kuma	Abera	ETH	31.8.90	160/50	HMar	60:58	60:19- 12
						Mar	2:05:56	-0-
	Kumar	Sandeep	IND	1.5.86	183/68	50kW	3:56:22	4:02:19- 13
	Kupers	Thijmen	NED	4.10.91	180/65	800	1:45.68	1:46.46- 12
	Kupper	Martin	EST	31.5.89	195/108	DT	64.98	65.03- 13
	Kurgat	Nixson	KEN	7.11.87		Mar	2:07:11	2:08:29- 13
	Kurui	Peter	KEN	.90		10k	28:15.6A	28:19.1A- 11
	Kusiak	Damian	POL	14.4.88	190/112	SP	19.47	20.45- 12
	Kusuro	Geoffrey	UGA	12.2.89	169/55	HMar	60:41	62:46A- 13
	Kuznetsov	Viktor	UKR	17.7.86	190/75	TJ	16.63	17.29- 10
*	Kwambai	James	KEN	28.2.83	162/52	Mar	2:07:38	2:05:36- 08
	Kwambai	Robert	KEN	22.11.85		Mar	2:08:48	2:09:14- 12
*	Kwemoi	Ronald	KEN-J	19.9.95	180/68	1500	3:28.81	3:45.39- 13
						5000	13:21.53	13:41.99- 13

Name		Nat	Born	Ht/Wt	Event	2014 Mark	Pre-2014 Best
* Kynard	Eric	USA	3.2.91	193/86	HJ	2.37	2.37- 13
La Rosa	Stefano	ITA	22.9.85	166/55	10k	28:19.36	28:13.62- 12
Laanmäe	Tanel	EST	29.9.89	184/89	JT	81.16	81.96- 09
Labali	Abdelhadi	MAR	26.4.93	174/62	1500	3:37.52	3:35.95- 13
					3000	7:45.62i	
Lagat	Alfers	KEN	7.8.86		Mar	2:07:10	-0-
* Lagat	Bernard	USA	12.12.74		2000	4:54.74i	4:55.49- 99
3000	7:38.30		7:29.00- 10		5000	13:06.68	12:53.60- 11
Lagat	Cosmas	KEN-J	.95		Mar	2:08:33	
Lagat	Haron	KEN	15.8.83	185/72	3kSt	8:19.00	8:15.80- 11
Lagat	Peter	KEN	26.5.92		3kSt	8:27.0A	9:01.0A- 10
Lahbabi	Aziz	MAR	3.2.91	178/62	HMar	59:25	-0-
Lahoulou	Abdelmadik	ALG	7.5.92	180/70	400h	50.15	50.71- 13
Laine	Samyr	HAI	17.7.84	188/82	TJ	17.27	17.39A, 17.45w- 09, 17.36- 13
Laitinen	Arno	FIN	9.3.88	187/95	HT	72.11	72.37- 11
* Lalang	Lawi	KEN	15.6.91	170/58	1500	3:36.34	3:33.20- 13
1M	3:52.88i	3:54.56i- 13	3000	7:36.44	7:41.9+- 13	5000 13:03.85	13:00.95- 13
Lane	Cal	USA			LJ	8.04i	7.77- 13
Lane	John	GBR	29.1.89	186/88	Dec	7922	7916- 13
Langat	Tera	KEN	26.12.85	181/75	LJ	7.96A, (7.74)	7.90A, 7.63- 10
Langowski	Artur	BRA	8.5.91	183/77	400h	49.83	49.77- 13
^ Lapierre	Fabrice	AUS	17.10.83	179/66	LJ	8.00	8.40, 8.78w- 10
Lasa	Emiliano	URU	25.1.90	178/68	LJ	7.94	7.88- 13
* Lauro	Germán	ARG	2.4.84	185/127	SP	21.04i, 20.70	21.26- 13
					DT	61.62	63.55- 12
* Lavillenie	Renaud	FRA	18.9.86	177/69	PV	6.16i, 5.93	6.03i- 11, 6.02- 13
Lavillenie	Valentin	FRA	16.7.91	170/65	PV	5.66i, 5.50	5.70i, 5.65- 13
Lavong	Carlton	USA	18.6.92	178/82	LJ	(7.75), 8.08w	7.77A- 11, , 7.51, 7.61w- 13
Lavong	Wesley	USA	27.1.91	183/118	SP	19.80	18.26- 13
Lawrence	Brijesh "BJ"	SKN	27.12.89	181/75	100	10.16, 10.11w	10.12- 12
					200	20.34	20.59- 11, 20.53w- 13
Lawrence	Desmond	USA	19.12.91	178/77	100	10.12w	10.35- 13
^ Lawrence	Torrin	USA	11.4.89	186/77	400	45.32	45.33- 13
Lawson	Jarrion	USA	6.5.94	188/75	LJ	8.39iA, 7.92, 8.13w	7.93- 13
Lazas	Kevin	USA	25.1.92	178/84	Dec	7592	7955- 12
Le Coz	Xavier	FRA	30.12.79	182/62	50kW	4:01:21	4:05:06- 12
le Roux	Wouter	RSA	17.1.86	186/77	400h	49.54	49.25A- 05, 49.96- 04
Lebésis	Spiridon	GRE	30.5.87	192/94	JT	80.64	83.02- 12
^ Lebid	Sergey	UKR	15.7.75	180/65	Mar	2:08:32	2:11:24- 13
Lee	Beejay	USA	5.3.93	168/72	100	10.16w	10.07- 13
Lee Jung-joon		KOR	26.3.84	186/78	110h	13.65	13.53- 08
Lee Yun-chul		KOR	28.3.82	188/110	HT	72.24	72.98- 13
Leer	Will	USA	15.4.85	184/70	1500	3:34.26	3:35.27- 13
1M	3:51.82	3:55.66i- 10, 3:56.39- 12			3000	7:42.95i	7:39.38- 13
5000	13:23.94		13:21.55- 13				
Legesse	Berhanu	ETH	.93	168/55	5000	13:08.88	13:15.32- 13
Lehata	Mosito	LES	8.4.89	177/69	100	10.13	10.26- 13, 9.8- 11
					200	20.36	20.37- 13
Lehto	Jesse	FIN	12.2.93	180/85	HT	71.81	67.74- 12
Lelièvre	Jérémy	FRA	8.2.91	186/80	Dec	7703	7911- 12
* Lemaitre	Christophe	FRA	11.6.90	189/74	100	10.10	9.92- 11
					200	20.08	19.80- 11
* Lendore	Deon	TTO	28.10.92	179/75	400	44.36	44.94- 13
Lescay	Yoandys	CUB	5.1.94	183/75	400	45.54A, 45.57	45.29- 13
Leslie	Cory	USA	24.10.89	175/60	1500	3:37.64+	3:34.93- 13
1M	3:53.44		3:55.85- 13		3kSt	8:26.30	8:20.08- 13
* Lesnoy	Aleksandr	RUS	28.7.88	194/116	SP	21.40	20.60- 13
Letnicov	Vladimir	MDA	7.10.81	174/68	TJ	16.61	17.06- 02
Levine	Nigel	GBR	30.4.89	175/68	400	45.68	45.11- 12
Levins	Cameron	CAN	28.3.89	181/68	1500	3:38.46	3:36.88- 13
2000	4:55.35i				3000	7:41.59i	7:41.74i- 13, 7:45.75i- 12
5000	13:15.38		13:15.19- 13		10k	27:36.00	27:27.96- 12
* Lewandowski	Marcin	POL	13.6.87	180/64	800	1:44.03	1:43.79- 13
1000	2:15.79		2:15.76- 11		1500	3:38.19, 3:37.37i	3:37.76i- 12, 3:38.98- 13
Lewis	Reggie	USA	18.8.93	180/73	100	10.15	10.22, 10.07w- 13
* Lewis	Steve	GBR	20.5.86	191/83	PV	5.71i, 5.70	5.82- 12
Leyver	José	MEX	12.11.85	164/52	50kW	3:50:42A	3:49:16A- 11
Li Chengbin		CHN	22.2.90		LJ	7.94	7.93i, 7.96w-13
* Li Jinzhe		CHN	1.9.89	188/64	LJ	8.47	8.34- 13
Li Pangshuai		CHN	9.4.92	180/66	TJ	16.44	16.24- 13, 16.44w- 11
Lihrman	Michael	USA	6.12.91	196/114	HT	71.24	67.28- 13

Name		Nat	Born	Ht/Wt	Event	2014 Mark	Pre-2014 Best
* Lilesa	Feyisa	ETH	1.2.90	158/50	HMar	59:51	59:22- 12
					Mar	2:08:26	2:04:52- 12
Lin Hung-Min		TPE	7.9.90		LJ	7.95w	7.86- 12
Lin Qing		CHN-J	5.4.95		LJ	7.99	7.96- 12
^ Lingua	Marco	ITA	4.6.78	179/112	HT	74.00	79.97- 08
Linke	Christopher	GER	24.10.88	191/64	20kW	1:21:00	1:20:41- 12
Liranzo	Jorge Félix	CUB	3.2.94	182/67	800	1:46.21	1:49.92- 12
* Lisek	Piotr	POL	16.8.92	188/85	PV	5.82	5.60- 13
Listenbee	Kolby	USA	25.1.94	186/83	100	10.23, 10.12w	
* Litvinov	Sergey	RUS	27.1.86	185/105	HT	79.35	80.98- 12
Liu Jianmin		CHN	9.3.88	183/68	20kW	1:20:51	1:19:34- 13
* Livermore	Jason	JAM	25.4.88	178/77	100	10.05	10.07- 13
					200	20.25	20.13- 13
Lloyd	Zach	USA	10.10.84	191/141	SP	20.61	21.09- 13
Locke	Dentarius	USA	12.12.89	170/68	100	10.02	9.96, 9.91w- 13
Loitang	John Kipsang	KEN	.91		HMar	60:32	60:16- 13
Lokomwa	Thomas	KEN	.87		HMar	60:56	
* Lomnicky	Marcel	SVK	6.7.87	177/106	HT	79.16	78.73- 13
Lomong	Lopez	USA	1.1.85	178/67	1500	3:38.47+	3:32.20- 10
1M	3:54.28	3:51.21i, 3:51.45- 13			3000	7:39.81	7:44.16i- 12, 7:50.36- 11
					5000	13:07.95	13:07.00i- 13, 13:11.63- 12
* Longosiwa	Thomas	KEN	14.1.82	175/57	3000	7:35.28	7:30.09- 09
					5000	12:56.16	12:49.04- 12
Lonyangata	Paul	KEN	12.12.92	170/55	HMar	59:54	59:53- 12
López	Kevin	ESP	12.6.90	172/60	800	1:45.69i	1:43.74- 12
^ López	Luis Fernando	COL	3.6.79	173/60	50kW	4:05:14	-0-
* López	Miguel Ángel	ESP	3.7.88	181/70	20kW	1:19:21	1:19:49- 12
* López	Yeimer	ex-CUB	20.8.82	184/73	800	1:43.71	1:43.07- 08
Losyev	Ivan	UKR	26.1.86	176/65	20kW	1:19:33	1:20:48- 12
					50kW	3:59:25	4:01:51- 10
Loughney	Ryan	USA	21.8.89	180/120	HT	69.18, 70.71dh	70.74- 12
Lovett	Eddie	ISV	25.6.92	181/73	110h	13.43, 13.39w	13.39, 13.29w- 13
Loxsom	Casimir	USA	17.3.91	183/64	800	1:45.80	1:45.28- 11
Luis	Yadier	CUB	1.3.89	177/77	100	10.17	10.42- 11
Lukás	Marek	CZE	16.7.91	180/75	Dec	7829	7753- 13
Lukyanenko	Artem	RUS	30.1.90	193/84	Dec	7882	8177- 13
Lukyanov	Denis	RUS	11.7.89	190/115	HT	77.03	79.61- 13
Lukyanov	Ivan	RUS	31.1.81	178/67	3kSt	8:26.19	8:18.97- 08
Luo Yadong		CHN	15.1.92		50kW	4:04:26	4:28:12- 12
Luron	Kevin	FRA	8.11.91	184/80	TJ	16.56	16.26- 12, 16.48w- 13
Lyadusov	Konstantin	RUS	2.3.88	190/125	SP	20.54	20.44- 13
Lyakhovich	Aleksandr	BLR	4.7.89	171/65	20kW	1:22:50	1:22:55- 12
Lyashchenko	Ihor	UKR	24.8.93	182/68	20kW	1:20:01	1:21:07- 12
Lysenko	Danyil	RUS-Y	19.5.97		HJ	2.24	2.10- 13
* Lyzhin	Pavel	BLR	24.3.81	189/110	SP	20.75	21.21- 10
Ma Haijun		CHN	24.11.92		20kW	1:22:32	1:23:02- 12
Maazouzi	Zakaria	MAR	15.6.85	171/62	1500	3:35.81	3:31.94- 13
Macharinyang	Hosea	KEN	12.6.85	160/45	10k	28:10.0A	27:58.41- 07
Mackey ¶	Trevorvano	BAH	5.1.92	188/84	200	20.46	20.52A, 20.68- 12, 20.60dq- 13
Madison	Chase	USA	13.9.85	192/130	DT	61.50	62.85- 08
Magakwe	Simon	RSA	25.5.86	177/73	100	9.98A,10.19,10.13Aw	10.06A,10.11- 12,9.9- 13
* Mägi	Rasmus	EST	4.5.92	188/74	400h	48.54	49.19- 13
Magomedov	Magomed	RUS	26.7.91		DT	60.89	56.72- 13
* Magut	James	KEN	20.7.90	180/64	1500	3:30.61	3:33.31- 12
					1M	3:49.43	3:50.68- 12
Maheswary	Renjith	IND	30.1.86	177/72	TJ	16.61	17.07- 10, 17.19w- 07
Mahler	Wolf	USA	26.9.94	180/77	Dec	7602	7065A- 13
Maia	Edi	POR	10.11.87	176/75	PV	5.70i, 5.60	5.70- 13
Maiau	Raihau	PYF	1.8.92		LJ	7.96	7.58- 11, 7.64w- 10
Maina	Jonathan	KEN	24.12.90	170/54	10k	28:02.87	28:04.25- 12
Maiyo	Hillary	KEN	2.10.93	174/61	1500	3:36.21	3:35.43- 11
Maiyo	Jonathan	KEN	5.5.88	175/52	HMar	59:28	59:02- 12
					Mar	2:06:47	2:04:56- 12
Majdán	Dusan	SVK	8.9.87	180/67	50kW	3:53:26	3:57:50- 13
* Majewski	Tomasz	POL	30.8.81	204/140	SP	21.04i, 21.04	21.95- 09
* Makau	Patrick	KEN	2.3.85	173/57	Mar	2:08:22	2:03:38- 11
* Makhloufi	Taoufik	ALG	29.4.88	181/66	800	1:43.53	1:43.71- 12
1500	3:30.40	3:30.80- 12			1M	3:52.16	3:52.94- 13
Makhrosenko	Zakhar	BLR	10.10.91		HT	75.56	76.08- 13
Makinde	Oluwasegun	CAN	6.7.91	180/81	200	20.51	20.62, 20.48w- 13
* Makusha	Ngonidzashe	ZIM	11.3.87	178/73	LJ	8.18i	8.40- 11

Name		Nat	Born	Ht/Wt	Event	2014 Mark	Pre-2014 Best
* Makwala	Isaac	BOT	29.9.86	183/79	100	10.20A, 10.14Aw	10.40- 13
200	19.96, 19,7A		20.21- 13		400	44.01	45.25- 12
* Malachowski	Piotr	POL	7.6.83	194/135	DT	69.28	71.84- 13
Mamedov	Mergen	TKM	24.12.90	187/108	HT	72.26	74.01- 13
Manangoi	Elijah	KEN	5.1.93	181/65	1500	3:35.0A	
* Mance	Josh	USA	21.3.92	191/82	400	44.89	44.83- 12
Mande	Abdallah	UGA-J	10.5.95	166/52	3000	7:48.12	
* Mannio	Ari	FIN	23.7.87	185/104	JT	83.70	85.70- 09
* Manzano	Leonel	USA	12.9.84	165/57	800	1:46.12	1:44.56- 10
1500	3:30.98		3:32.37- 10		1M	3:52.41	3:50.64- 10
Maraba	Wilson	KEN	2.12.86		3kSt	8:30.7A	8:16.96- 12
Marani	Diego	ITA	27.4.90	182/73	200	20.36	20.77- 12
Marcell	Jan	CZE	4.6.85	197/111	SP	20.93	20.76- 11
					DT	61.91	66.00- 11
Marchand	Alexandre	FRA	23.2.90	180/73	PV	5.55	5.40- 12
Marghiev	Sergey	MDA	7.11.92	195/93	HT	78.27	75.20- 12
Maric ¶	Martin	CRO	19.4.84	196/115	DT	67.92	66.53- 12
Marquardt	Julian	GER	2.4.91	196/87	110h	13.67, 13.60w	13.81- 13
Márquez	Dayron	COL	19.11.83	181/93	JT	78.82A	80.61A- 12, 82.20Au- 08
Marshin	Dmitriy	AZE	24.2.72	180/100	HT	71.42	79.56- 12
Martey	Robert	GHA	27.12.84	178/73	LJ	7.92	7.92- 11
Marthély	Stéphane	FRA	9.9.79	193/104	DT	60.82	60.84- 13
Martin	Benjamin	USA	4.8.93		100	10.26, 10.11w	10.44- 13
* Martin	Cory	USA	22.5.85	196/125	SP	20.73	22.10- 10
Martin	Romain	FRA	12.7.88	198/86	Dec	8104	8013- 13
Martin	Ryan	USA	23.3.89	185/68	800	1:45.65	1:44.77- 12
Martín	Álvaro	ESP	18.6.94	181/62	20kW	1:20:39	1:22:12- 12
Martín	Pedro José	ESP	12.8.92	188/100	HT	70.48	71.65- 13
* Martina	Churandy	NED	3.7.84	178/75	100	10.13	9.91- 12, 9.76Aw- 06
					200	20.25	19.85- 12
* Martínez	Guillermo	CUB	28.6.81	185/100	JT	79.27A	87.20A- 11
Martínez	Jorge	MEX	25.10.90		50kW	4:06:04A	
* Martínez	Lázaro	CUB-Y	3.11.97	192/83	TJ	17.24	16.63- 13
Martínez	Lois Maikel	ex-CUB	3.6.81	185/90	DT	65.13	67.45- 05
^ Martínez	Wilfredo	ex-CUB	9.1.85	180/82	LJ	7.99, 8.01w	8.31A- 08, 8.20- 10
* Martinot-Lagarde	Pascal	FRA	22.9.91	190/80	110h	12.95	13.12- 13
Martinot-Lagarde	Thomas	FRA	7.2.88	186/78	110h	13.38	13.26- 13
Martins	Danylo	BRA	21.11.92		TJ	16.57	15.20, 15.60w- 13
Martins	Ogierakhi	NGR	30.6.91	184/75	110h	13.67	13.89- 11
Martos	Sebastián	ESP	20.6.89	178/63	3kSt	8:18.31	8:22.97- 13
Martynyuk	Andriy	UKR	25.9.90	179/86	HT	71.83	77.70- 12
Masai	Titus	KEN	9.10.89	170/55	HMar	59:41	59:51- 10
Masikonde	Joshua	KEN-J	16.8.96	184/73	800	1:45.14	1:46.5A- 13
* Maslák	Pavel	CZE	21.2.91	176/67	400	44.79	44.84- 13
Mason	Michael	CAN	30.9.86	188/67	HJ	2.30i, 2.28	2.31- 12
Masters	Riley	USA	5.4.90	185/73	1500	3:38.00	3:37.19- 12
Mástoras	Adónios	GRE	6.1.91	198/77	HJ	2.30	2.29i, 2.26- 13
Masuno	Genta	JPN	24.5.93	182/76	110h	13.58	13.77, 13.71w- 13
^ Mätas	Risto	EST	30.4.84	189/91	JT	80.73	83.48- 13
Matebo	Levi	KEN	3.11.89	173/55	Mar	2:08:09	2:05:15- 11
* Mathathi	Martin	KEN	25.12.85	167/52	HMar	60:11	59:48- 10, 58:56dh- 11
Mathieu	Michael	BAH	24.6.83	180/78	200	20.50, 20.46w	20.16- 12
					400	45.11	45.06- 12
Matsubara	Mizuki	JPN	9.9.92		LJ	7.80, 7.96w	
Matsumoto	Aoi	JPN	7.9.87	177/60	3kSt	8:33.84	8:30.49- 10
Matsumura	Kohei	JPN	25.11.86	176/59	Mar	2:08:09	2:10:12- 13
Matsunaga	Daisuke	JPN-J	24.3.95	173/56	20kW	1:21:17	1:23:56- 13
Matsushita	Yuki	JPN	9.9.91	175/68	400h	50.07	49.71- 13
Matthews	Julian	NZL	21.7.88	178/66	1500	3:38.20	3:38.59- 13
Mattis	Sam	USA	19.3.94	185/100	DT	62.13	58.34- 13
Maugein	Maxime	FRA	27.9.92	182/80	Dec	7764	7445- 12
Mayer	Gerhard	AUT	20.5.80	191/100	DT	61.45	65.24- 10
* Mayer	Kevin	FRA	10.2.92	186/77	Dec	8521	8447w- 12, 8446- 13
Mayers	Emanuel	TTO	9.3.89	178/70	400h	49.57	49.65- 10
^ Mbishei	Titus	KEN	28.10.90	178/59	HMar	59:55	62:30- 13
Mbow	Seth	SEN	2.4.85	183/74	400h	50.12	49.86A, 50.09- 13
McBride	Brandon	CAN	15.6.94	195/75	800	1:45.35	1:46.07- 12
McBride	Bryan	USA	10.12.91	188/77	HJ	2.28	2.26i, 2.20- 12
McClain	Remontay	USA	21.9.92	188/85	100	10.14	10.27- 13, 10.16w- 12
					200	20.27	20.54, 20.32w- 13
^ McCoy	Reuben	USA	16.3.86	186/75	400h	50.07	48.37- 08

	Name		Nat	Born	Ht/Wt	Event	2014 Mark	Pre-2014 Best
	McCullough	Conor	IRL/USA	31.1.91	186/102	HT	77.20	75.09- 12
	McCune	Alex	USA	7.4.93	188/80	Dec	7806	7411- 13
	McDonald	Rusheen	JAM	17.8.92	175/73	400	45.25	45.10- 12
	McFarlane	Javier	PER	21.10.91	186/78	110h	13.57, 13.51Aw	13.85- 13
	McFarlane	Jorge	PER	20.2.88	176/70	110h	13.53	13.61, 13.53Aw, 13.5- 13
						LJ	8.01A	8.10A- 09, 7.95- 11
	McGuire	Tim	AUS	29.4.92	174/70	LJ	7.94	7.73, 7.74w- 13
	McLean	Sean	USA	23.3.92	185/79	100	10.13	10.31, 10.30w- 11
						200	20.41, 20.38w	20.62- 11
	McLeod	Omar	JAM	25.4.94	183/73	110h	13.44	-0-
	McNamara	Jordan	USA	7.3.87	178/64	1500	3:37.39	3:34.00- 13
	800	1:47.16		1:52.29- 07		1M	3:52.89	3:52.42- 13
	McNeill	David	AUS	6.10.86	175/59	5000	13:28.13	13:18.60- 12
*	McQuay	Tony	USA	16.4.90	180/70	100	10.13w	10.22- 13
						400	44.92	44.40- 13
	Mead	Hassan	USA	28.8.89	174/61	3000	7:44.88i	7:56.15i- 09
						5000	13:02.80	13:11.80- 13
*	Medhin	Teklemariam	ERI	24.6.89	183/62	10k	27:38.83	27:16.69- 12
	Mejias	Reinier	CUB	22.9.90	180/96	HT	74.58	75.98- 13
	Mekashaw	Kassa	ETH	19.3.84	167/54	5000	13:26.07	13:42.07- 13
						10k	27:38.93	28:01.01- 13
*	Mekhissi-Benabbad	Mahiedine	FRA	15.3.85	190/75	1000	2:17.18	2:17.14- 09
	1500	3:35.34	3:33.12- 13			1M	3:51.55	-0-
						3kSt	8:03.23	8:00.09- 13
	Mekonnen	Tsegaye	ETH-J	15.6.95	174/56	Mar	2:04:32	-0-
	Meleshko	Pavel	BLR	24.11.92	187/90	JT	80.68	78.08- 11
*	Melich	Lukás	CZE	16.9.80	186/110	HT	75.89	80.28- 13
^	Méliz	Luis Felipe	ESP	11.8.79	182/80	LJ	7.90A, 7.81	8.43- 00
	Mellor	Jonathan	GBR	27.12.86		3000	7:46.73i	7:51.88- 13
	Melly	Edwin	KEN	23.4.94	178/60	800	1:45.87	1:43.81- 12
	Mena	Reynier	CUB-J	21.11.96	179/72	200	20.50A	20.72, 20.63A- 13
	Menaldo	Kévin	FRA	12.7.92	176/66	PV	5.75i, 5.72	5.65i, 5.60- 13
	Mendes	Jonatha	BRA	14.4.90	187/80	110h	13.53	13.61, 13.55w, 13.5- 13
	Mendieta	José Angel	CUB	16.10.91	187/84	Dec	7559	7967h- 13
	Menga	Aleixo Platini	GER	29.9.87	179/76	200	20.43	20.33- 12
	Mengich	Richard	KEN	3.4.89	187/68	HMar	60:11	60:48- 12
*	Menkov	Aleksandr	RUS	7.12.90	178/74	LJ	8.30i, 8.02	8.56- 13
	Merber	Kyle	USA	19.11.90	180/64	1M	3:54.76	3:58.52i- 10
*	Merga	Imane	ETH	15.10.88	174/61	3000	7:43.59	7:45.8 - 10
	5000	13:11.94		12:53.58- 10		10k	28:17.75	26:48.35- 11
*	Merritt	Aries	USA	24.7.85	182/74	110h	13.27	12.80- 12
*	Merritt	LaShawn	USA	27.6.86	188/82	200	20.42	19.98- 07, 19.80w- 08
						400	43.92	43.74- 13
	Merzougui	Abdelaziz	MAR	30.8.91	177/62	3kSt	8:27.53	8:18.03- 12
	Mesfin	Hunegnaw	ETH	31.1.89	175/55	HMar	59:39	62:00- 11
	Mesic	Kemal	BIH	4.8.85	196/110	SP	20.18	20.71- 12
	Mestre	Sergio	CUB	30.8.91	194/85	HJ	2.26A	2.25- 12
	Meucci	Daniele	ITA	7.10.85	178/62	10k	27:36.53	27:32.86- 12
	Mezones	Freddy	VEN	24.9.87	176/68	400	45.55	45.93- 10
^	Michalski	Lukasz	POL	2.8.88	190/85	PV	5.65	5.85- 11
	Mihaljevic	Filip	CRO	31.7.94	200/115	SP	19.65	17.54- 13
	Mikhan	Eduard	BLR	7.6.89	194/85	Dec	8004	8152- 11
	Mikhou	Sadik	MAR	25.7.90	173/62	800	1:46.55	1:47.01- 11
						1500	3:33.47	3:33.31- 13
	Milanov	Philip	BEL	6.7.91	191/118	DT	66.02	61.81- 13
	Milaw	Abrha	ETH	3.1.88		Mar	2:07:46	2:09:00- 13
	Mileusnic	Dejan	BIH	16.11.91	183/84	JT	80.40	79.62- 13
	Milion	Zewdie	ETH	24.1.89	171/53	10k	27:36.35	27:54.52- 12
	Miller	Ashinia	JAM	6.6.93	189/100	SP	19.54	19.05- 13
	Miller	Craig	USA	3.8.87	185/70	1M	3:55.09i	3:56.41- 12
	Miller	Nick	GBR	1.5.93	185/105	HT	74.38	71.60- 13
	Miller	Ramon	BAH	17.2.87	180/73	400	45.21	44.87- 12
	Milne	Taylor	CAN	14.6.81	180/66	3kSt	8:27.81	8:31.48- 13
	Minemura	Kota	JPN	22.12.92	176/61	LJ	7.94	7.88- 13
	Minzie	Jevaughn	JAM-J	20.7.95	173/66	100	10.16, 10.14w	10.28- 12
						200	20.37	20.85- 12, 20.64w- 13
	Mironov	Oleg	RUS	5.3.93	188/79	400h	50.01	50.58- 13
	Misans	Elvijs	LAT	8.4.89	182/73	LJ	8.05	8.00i- 11, 7.96- 12
	Missirov	Lev	RUS	4.8.90	194/75	HJ	2.33i, 2.25	2.26- 13
*	Mitchell	Curtis	USA	11.3.89	188/79	200	20.13, 19.99w	19.97- 13
	Mitchell	Manteo	USA	6.7.87	178/73	200	20.72, 20.40w	20.47- 12
	100	(10.31), 10.26w		10.39- 12		400	45.09	44.96- 12

MEN'S INDEX

	Name		Nat	Born	Ht/Wt	Event	2014 Mark	Pre-2014 Best
*	Mitchell	Maurice	USA	22.12.89	178/73	100	10.08, 10.04w	10.00- 11
						200	20.30	20.13- 12, 19.99w- 11
	Mitchell	Sheldon	JAM	19.7.90	181/75	200	20.14A, 20.48	20.78, 20.62w- 12
	Mitchell	Steve	GBR	24.5.88	178/61	1500	3:38.27	3:41.90- 12
	Mitei	Amos	KEN	.92		HMar	60:53	64:45- 13
	Miyawaki	Chihiro	JPN	28.8.91	173/55	10k	28:20.77	27:41.57- 11
	Moghaddam	Reza	IRI	17.11.88	197/128	HT	71.72	71.82- 11
	Mohamed	Abdulaziz Ladan	KSA	7.1.91	184/70	800	1:44.30	1:43.86- 13
	Mohammed	Mukhtar	GBR	1.12.90	175/59	800	1:46.56	1:45.67- 13
*	Mohr	Malte	GER	24.7.86	192/84	PV	5.90i, 5.70	5.91- 12
	Möhsner	Sven	GER	30.1.86	190/115	HT	71.60	73.82- 09
	Mokdel	Lyès	ALG	20.6.90	195/84	110h	13.48	13.63- 13, 13.5- 10
*	Mokoena	Khotso	RSA	6.3.85	190/73	LJ	8.19	8.50- 09
						TJ	17.35	17.25- 05
	Mokoka	Stephen	RSA	31.1.85	156/50	HMar	60:47	60:57- 12
						Mar	2:08:43	2:08:33- 10
	Mokua	Edwin	KEN	31.12.93	171/52	10k	28:19.11	28:16.0A- 13
	Montaña	José Leonardo	COL	21.3.92	168/61	20kW	1:22:03, 1:22:14.1t	1:23:41.6t- 12
	Montoya	Isidro	COL	3.11.90	165/64	100	10.15A	10.24- 12
	Moore	Jordan	USA	13.12.93	190/101	110h	13.72, 13.64w	-0-
	Morales	Ignacio	CUB	28.1.87	183/69	110h	13.56	13.48- 13, 13.1- 08
	Morgan	Jason	JAM	6.10.82	186/114	DT	64.72	67.15- 12
	Morgan	Mike	USA	19.6.94	185/75	Dec	7699	6029- 13
^	Morioka	Koichiro	JPN	2.4.85	184/65	20kW	1:20:30	1:20:14- 13
	Mörö	Oskari	FIN	31.1.93	181/66	400h	49.08	50.80- 11
	Morris	Joe	USA	4.10.89	180/68	200	20.45	20.77A,20.82,20.77w- 12, 20.45Aw- 13
	Morse	Brett	GBR	11.2.89	191/114	DT	63.34	66.84- 13
	Morse	Mikese	USA	30.10.87	185/73	LJ	7.89, 8.08w	7.90i- 09, 7.86- 12
	Morton	Amaechi	NGR	30.10.89	187/77	400h	48.92	48.79- 12
	Moses	Nathaniel	USA	1.4.90	183/100	DT	61.81	60.17- 12
	Mossberg	Nick	USA	5.4.86	178/77	PV	5.53	5.60- 13
	Mostert	Raheem	USA	9.4.92	180/83	100	10.28, 10.15w	10.68- 11
	Mothlahlego	Boipele	RSA	27.11.90		TJ	16.38A	16.07A- 09, 16.35Aw- 11
	Motsau	Jerry	RSA	12.3.90	173/57	1500	3:36.74	3:38.82- 12
	Moukrime	Tarik	BEL	3.3.92	179/59	1500	3:35.96	3:39.59- 13
	Mousavi	Kaveh	IRI	27.5.85	196/105	HT	71.56	75.26- 11
*	Moustaoui	Mohamed	MAR	2.4.85	174/60	1500	3:35.21, 3:35.0i	3:31.84- 11
						3000	7:40.00i	7:43.99- 11, 7:43.08i- 08
	Mozia	Stephen	NGR	16.8.93	190/102	SP	20.79i, 20.46	19.89i, 19.20- 13
						DT	62.80	61.13- 13
	Mucheru	Boniface	KEN	2.5.92	175/65	400	45.07	47.10A-10
						400h	49.25A, 49.67	49.45- 12
	Mudrov	Ilya	RUS	17.11.91	190/79	PV	5.70	5.50- 12
*	Mudrov	Sergey	RUS	8.9.90	190/79	HJ	2.32i, 2.20	2.35i- 13, 2.31- 12
	Muhitira	Felicien	RWA	4.11.94		10k	28:17.07	
	Mukuno	Moses	KEN-J	27.11.95	171/55	5000	13:19.26	13:36.5A- 13
^	Mulabegovic	Nedzad	CRO	4.2.81	190/120	SP	20.67	20.66- 12
	Müller	Norman	GER	7.8.85	195/84	Dec	7955	8295- 09
	Mullera	Ángel	ESP	20.4.84	175/62	3kSt	8:29.16	8:13.71- 12
	Münch	Markus	GER	13.6.86	207/117	DT	64.54	66.87- 11
	Mundell	Marc	RSA	7.7.83	189/86	50kW	4:02:19	3:55:32- 12
*	Murakami	Yukifumi	JPN	23.12.79	186/102	JT	81.66	85.96- 13
	Murayama	Kenta	JPN	23.2.93	175/54	10k	27:49.94	28:14.27- 12
						HMar	60:50	61:19- 13
	Mureithi	Kennedy	KEN			3kSt	8:34.1A	
	Murillo	Jhon Freddy	COL	13.6.84	183/84	TJ	16.47A, 16.27	16.58, 16.82Aw- 13
^	Murofushi	Koji	JPN	8.10.74	187/105	HT	73.93	84.86- 03
	Murozuka	Kenta	JPN	12.2.86	173/56	10k	28:15.45	28:04.40- 07
	Murray	Demar	JAM	31.8.91	175/68	400h	49.94	52.75- 13
	Murray	Leslie	ISV	24.1.91	188/77	400h	50.21A	49.83- 09
	Musagala	Ronald	UGA	16.12.92	176/61	800	1:45.27	1:45.71A- 13
	1000	2:17.11		-0-		1500	3:37.75	3:38.89A- 13
	Muskwe	Osman	GBR	24.11.85	192/86	Dec	7565	7326- 13
*	Mutai	Abel	KEN	2.10.88	172/73	3kSt	8:15.83	8:01.67- 12
*	Mutai	Emmanuel	KEN	12.10.84	168/54	Mar	2:03:13	2:03:52- 13
*	Mutai	Geoffrey	KEN	7.10.81	170/54	HMar	60:50	58:58- 13
						Mar	2:08:18	2:04:15- 12, 2:03:02wdh- 11
	Mutai	Jeremiah	KEN	27.12.92	173/60	800	1:44.85	1:43.9A- 13
	Mutai	Laban	KEN	.85		Mar	2:08:03	2:08:01- 12
	Mutai	Vincent	KEN	3.11.94	174/61	1500	3:35.63	3:35.45- 12
	Mutunga	Patrick	KEN	20.11.94	174/57	5000	13:23.94	13:19.13- 11

	Name		Nat	Born	Ht/Wt	Event	2014 Mark	Pre-2014 Best
	Mvumuvre	Gabriel	ZIM	23.4.88	172/75	100	10.07	9.98- 13
	Mwaka	Patrick	KEN	2.11.92	165/45	10k	27:37.67	27:33.14- 11
	Mwangangi	John	KEN	1.11.90		HMar	60:26	59:45- 11
						Mar	2:07:28	2:09:32- 13
	Mwangi	Alex	KEN	14.6.90	158/50	10k	28:11.33	27:42.20- 10
	Mwangi	Eliud Macharia	KEN	.89		HMar	61:09	
	Mwangi	James	KEN	23.6.84	175/58	5000	13:16.06	13:14.00- 05
						10k	27:23.66	27:49.27- 09
	Mwangi	John	KEN	.85		HMar	61:16	
	Mwololo	Peter	KEN	.92	168/57	10k	28:08.5A	
^	Myerscough	Carl	GBR	21.10.79	209/149	DT	62.51	65.24- 12
	Mykolaychuk ¶	Dmytro	UKR	30.1.87	192/89	HT	70.50	75.24- 11
	Nabokov	Dmitriy	BLR-J	20.1.96		HJ	2.24	2.02- 13
	Nailel	Hosea	KEN	.88		10k	28:16.2A	
	Nakamura	Akihiko	JPN	23.10.90	180/73	400h	49.95	49.38- 12
						Dec	8035	7723- 13
	Nall	Donte	USA	27.1.88	188/77	HJ	2.26i, 2.20	2.25- 13
	Naoki	Masafumi	JPN	19.11.93	173/63	200	20.44	20.73- 13
	Nasti	Patrick	ITA	30.8.89	188/73	3kSt	8:28.12	8:29.08- 12
*	Nava	Horacio	MEX	20.1.82	175/62	20kW	1:23:01A	1:22:04- 12
						50kW	3:42:51	3:45:21- 08
*	Nazarov	Dilshod	TJK	6.5.82	187/115	HT	80.62	80.71- 13
	Ndiaye	Amadou	SEN	6.12.92	180/71	400h	49.61	49.74- 13
	Ndiema	Eric	KEN	28.12.92	172/58	Mar	2:07:00	2:06:07- 11
*	Ndiku	Caleb	KEN	9.10.92	183/68	1500	3:35.8A	3:29.50- 13
	3000	7:31.66		7:30.99- 12		5000	12:59.17	13:03.80- 13
*	Ndiku	Jonathan	KEN	18.9.91	170/54	3000	7:39.63	7:52.89- 09
	5000	13:12.94		13:11.99- 09		3kSt	8:10.44	8:07.75- 11
	Ndirangu	Charles	KEN	8.2.93	170/50	10k	28:18.54	27:58.02- 12
	Ndirangu	Macharia	KEN	9.9.94	168/49	10k	28:01.09	27:59.11- 13
	Ndungu	Samuel	KEN	4.4.88		Mar	2:08:21	2:07:04- 12
	Neal	Keffri	CAN	26.10.93	171/60	800	1:46.39	1:49.41- 13
	Nebebew	Birhan	ETH	14.8.94	172/55	10k	27:42.89	27:14.34- 13
	Nechyporenko	Denys	UKR	7.1.90	181/70	400h	50.08	50.51- 12
	Nedow	Tim	CAN	16.10.90	198/125	SP	20.98	20.74- 13
*	Negesse	Endeshaw	ETH	13.3.88		Mar	2:08:32	2:04:54- 13
^	Nellum	Bryshon	USA	1.5.89	183/79	200	20.65, 20.36w	20.23, 19.99w- 13
	Nelson	Billy	USA	11.9.84	167/55	3kSt	8:28.42	8:17.27- 11
	Németh	Kristóf	HUN	17.9.87	190/97	HT	74.04	76.45- 10
	Nesterenko	Maksim	BLR	1.9.92		TJ	16.46i, 16.36, 16.40w	16.40i, 16.35- 13
	Nesterenko	Mykyta	UKR	15.4.91	202/97	DT	63.94	65.31- 08
	Nesterovskiy	Stanislav	UKR	31.7.80	198/120	DT	61.65	64.94- 07
	Newman	Calesio	USA	20.8.86	172/66	100	10.22, 9.96w	10.07- 12, 10.05w- 13
						200	20.33	20.28, 20.17w- 12
*	Nganga	Bernard Mbugua	KEN	17.1.85	170/55	3kSt	8:15.01	8:05.88- 11
	Ngatia	Hiram	KEN-J	1.1.96	170/56	5000	13:22.08	13:26.73- 13
	Nikfar	Amin	IRI	2.1.81	198/130	SP	19.72	20.05- 11
	Nilsson	Marcus	SWE	3.5.91	185/90	Dec	7656	8104(w)- 13, 7823- 12
	Nima	Issam	ALG	8.4.79	187/75	TJ	16.67	16.89, 17.01w- 12
	Ninov	Viktor	BUL	19.6.88	197/82	HJ	2.26	2.30i- 13, 2.29- 11
	Nipperess	James	AUS	21.5.90	183/66	3kSt	8:34.64	8:34.87- 13
	Niskala	Pyry	FIN	6.11.90	191/105	DT	60.71	58.42- 13
	Njuguna	David	KEN	6.9.89	176/60	5000	13:23.89	13:44.21- 13
	Nkanata	Carvin	USA/KEN	6.5.91	183/73	200	20.17	20.32, 20.29w- 13
	Nkouloukidi	Jean-Jacques	ITA	15.4.82	172/56	50kW	3:53:44	3:52:35- 11
	Noda	Tomohiro	JPN-J	24.1.96		20kW	1:22:37	-0-
^	Noga	Artur	POL	2.5.88	196/82	110h	13.39	13.26- 13, 13.20w- 10
	Noguchi	Hiroshi	JPN	3.5.83	176/115	HT	70.45	72.43- 13
	Nolf	Cedric	BEL	18.6.89	182/82	LJ	7.89	7.55- 11
	Norwood	Vernon	USA	10.4.92	187/77	400	45.02	45.56A, 45.67- 13
*	Noskov	Ivan	RUS	16.7.88	177/62	50kW	3:37:41	3:41:36- 13
	Novák	Martin	CZE	5.10.92	196/115	SP	19.69	19.19- 13
*	Nowak	Lukasz	POL	18.12.88	194/77	20kW	1:20:57	1:20:48- 13
	Nowicki	Wojciech	POL	22.2.89	196/112	HT	76.14	75.87- 13
	Nunn	John	USA	3.2.78	190/77	50kW	4:04:08	4:03:28- 12
	Nurgi	Tolossa	ETH	29.3.90		3kSt	8:28.97	8:35.65- 13
	Nurme	Tiidrek	EST	18.11.85	178/71	3000	7:48.24	7:51.49- 13
	Nychyporchuk	Oleksandr	UKR	14.4.92	185/84	JT	81.22	81.65- 12
	O'Farrill	Yordan	CUB	9.2.93	185/77	110h	13.19, 12.9	13.44- 13
	O'Hara	Michael	JAM-J	29.9.96	185/73	200	20.45, 20.31w	20.63- 13
	O'Hare	Chris	GBR	23.11.90	174/60	1500	3:35.06	3:35.37- 13
						1M	3:54.66i	3:52.98i- 13, 3:58.77- 11

Name		Nat	Born	Ht/Wt	Event	2014 Mark	Pre-2014 Best
O'Lionáird	Ciarán	IRL	11.4.88	180/64	1500	3:37.72	3:34.46- 11
Obi	Felix	USA	15.6.94	188/79	TJ	16.59iA	16.18i, 15.82, 16.08w- 13
Ocampo	David	MEX	14.2.92		JT	77.24A	73.51- 13
^ Odriozola	Mikel	ESP	25.5.73	180/62	50kW	3:59:02	3:41:47- 05
Oduduru	Ejowvokoghene	NGR-J	7.10.96	175/70	200	20.66, 20.25w	21.13- 13
Ogho-Oghene	Egweru	NGR	26.11.88	171/66	100	10.18	10.06- 11, 10.0- 08
Ogita	Hiroki	JPN	30.12.87	185/78	PV	5.61	5.70- 13
* Ogunode	Femi Seun	QAT	15.5.91	183/79	100	9.93	10.07- 11
					200	20.06	20.30- 11
Oiglane	Janek	EST	25.4.94	182/78	Dec	7815	-0-
Oikawa	Fumitaka	JPN-J	5.4.95		20kW	1:22:06	-0-
Oiwa	Yuhi	JPN	17.2.91	173/62	LJ	7.90	7.86, 7.87w- 13
* Oke	Tosin	NGR	1.10.80	178/77	TJ	16.97, 17.21w	17.23- 12
Okutu	Jean Marie	ESP	4.8.88	179/68	LJ	8.01, 8.05w	7.94- 09, 8.05w- 12
Olamigoke	Olu	NGR	19.9.90	178/68	TJ	16.73	16.16, 16.25w- 13
Oleitiptip	Alex	KEN	22.9.82	176/58	HMar	59:58	61:34- 13
Oleszczuk	Kacper	POL	15.5.94	182/78	JT	77.46	75.39- 13
Olgundeniz	Ercüment	TUR	7.7.76	203/120	DT	61.18	67.50- 12
de Oliveira	Júlio César	BRA	4.2.86	185/97	JT	79.10A	80.05, 80.29 irreg- 09
Oliveira	Paulo Sérgio	BRA	1.6.93	185/65	LJ	8.13	7.99- 13
de Oliveira	Pedro	BRA	17.2.92	188/85	400	45.69A, 45.73	45.52- 12
* Oliver	David	USA	24.4.82	188/93	110h	13.21	12.89- 10
* Olivier	André	RSA	29.12.89	192/72	800	1:44.42	1:44.29- 12
Ollikainen	Ronni	FIN	27.8.90	188/76	LJ	7.85, 7.99w	8.05, 8.32w- 12
^ Olmedo	Manuel	ESP	17.5.83	173/53	1500	3:37.84	3:34.44- 11
Olson	Petter	SWE	14.2.91	183/81	Dec	7801	7857- 12
Omelko	Rafal	POL	16.1.89	195/75	400	45.66	45.69- 13
Omoregie	David	GBR-J	1.11.95	185/84	110h	13.53	-0-
Omwamba	Enoch	KEN	4.4.93	166/52	10k	28:00.33	28:15.80- 13
Onsarigo	Josephat	KEN	.93	166/56	10k	28:16.72	28:20.43- 13
^ Oosthuizen	Robert	RSA	23.1.87	188/101	JT	79.57A	86.80- 08
* Oprea	Marian	ROU	6.6.82	190/80	TJ	17.30i, 16.94	17.81- 05
Ortega	Mauricio	COL	4.8.94	184/102	DT	62.30A	59.67- 13
* Ortega	Orlando	ex-CUB	29.7.91	185/70	110h	13.01	13.08- 13
Orth	Florian	GER	24.7.89	181/64	1500	3:34.54	3:34.56- 12
					3000	7:44.65	8:11.98- 10
* Osaghae	Omo	USA	18.5.88	184/75	110h	13.41, 13.40w	13.23, 13.18w- 11
^ Osagie	Andrew	GBR	19.2.88	189/72	800	1:45.37, 1:45.22i	1:43.77- 12
3000	7:40.09		7:54.68- 12		5000	13:26.15	13:20.80- 13
Osako	Suguru	JPN	23.5.91	170/53	10k	28:11.94	27:38.31- 13
Osman	Abrar	ERI	1.1.94	173/55	5000	13:16.45	13:17.32- 12
Otobe	Takumi	JPN	22.4.89	183/76	Dec	7604	7600- 11
* Otto	Björn	GER	16.10.77	188/84	PV	5.60i	6.01- 12
Outzen	Matthew	AUS	12.10.87	185/100	JT	78.05	79.41- 10
* Özbilen	Ilham Tanui	TUR	5.3.90	177/60	1000	2:15.08	2:17.08- 11
1500	3:32.09		3:31.30- 13		1M	3:51.71	3:49.29- 09
Paes	Lutimar	BRA	14.12.88	179/70	800	1:46.23	1:45.32- 11
^ Pahapill	Mikk	EST	18.7.83	196/93	Dec	8077	8398- 11
Palacios	Roland	HON	3.5.87	186/78	200	20.50A, 20.57	20.40A- 08, 20.64- 12, 20.4- 10
Panasyuk	Ivan	UKR	8.10.91	190/120	DT	63.39	58.48- 13
Papamihaíl	Aléxandros	GRE	18.9.88	178/63	20kW	1:23:04	1:21:12- 12
					50kW	3:49:58	3:49:56- 12
* Parchment	Hansle	JAM	17.6.90	196/90	110h	12.94	13.05- 13
Parellis	Apostolos	CYP	24.7.85	186/110	DT	63.89	65.36- 12
Park Chil-sung		KOR	8.7.82	173/65	20kW	1:22:16	1:20:17- 08
					50kW	3:49:15	3:45:55- 12
Park Jae-myong		KOR	15.12.81	180/95	JT	78.69	83.99- 04
Park Tae-kyong		KOR	30.7.80	181/75	110h	13.69, 13.58w	13.48- 10
Parros	Clayton	USA	11.12.90	178/70	400	45.42	45.71- 09
* Pars	Krisztián	HUN	18.2.82	188/113	HT	82.69	82.45- 06
Parshin	Pavel	RUS	2.1.94	171/55	20kW	1:21:55	-0-
Parsons	Tom	GBR	5.5.84	192/80	HJ	2.30i, 2.29	2.31i- 11, 2.30- 08
Parszczynski	Lukasz	POL	4.5.85	180/64	3kSt	8:28.03	8:15.47- 11
Partanen	Veli-Matti	FIN	28.10.91	178/62	50kW	3:52:58	3:58:50- 13
Pasiak	Adam	CZE	18.7.90	185/77	PV	5.50i, 5.46	5.45, 5.46ex- 12
Pásztor	Bence	HUN-J	5.2.95	186/84	HT	71.50	66.69- 13
Patrakov	Andrey	RUS	7.11.89	196/80	HJ	2.24i, 2.20	2.30i- 12, 2.24- 13
Patsoukákis	Dimítrios	GRE	18.3.87	180/70	PV	5.62	5.55- 09
Peacock	Hamish	AUS	15.10.90	186/96	JT	82.24	81.14- 13
Pei Lianyou		CHN	27.1.90		50kW	4:05:41	4:10:32- 11
Peltomäki	Sami	FIN	11.1.91	180/87	JT	80.36	77.27- 13

	Name		Nat	Born	Ht/Wt	Event	2014 Mark	Pre-2014 Best
	Peña	José Gregorio	VEN	12.1.87	163/60	3kSt	8:26.61	8:20.87- 13
	Pervan	Dino	CRO	12.1.91	192/75	LJ	7.99i, 7.92	7.95- 11
	Pesic	Darko	MNE	30.11.92	189/89	Dec	7594	7636- 13
*	Pestano	Mario	ESP	8.4.78	195/120	DT	65.74	69.50- 08
	Petrov	Aleksandr	RUS	9.8.86	187/79	LJ	8.05	8.20- 11
	Philibert-Thiboutot	Charles	CAN	31.12.90	176/62	1500	3:38.33	3:40.57- 13
^	Phillips	Isa	JAM	22.4.84	193/84	400h	49.89	48.05- 09
	Phillips	Richard	JAM	26.1.83	188/75	110h	13.64	13.39- 04, 13.33w- 08
	Phiri	Gerald	ZAM	6.10.88	184/80	100	10.03	10.06- 11, 10.00w- 13
	Piantella	Giorgio	ITA	6.7.81	181/75	PV	5.55	5.60- 10
*	Pichardo	Pedro Pablo	CUB	30.6.93	185/71	TJ	17.76	17.69- 13
	Pickup	Bradley	GBR	4.4.89	193/76	LJ	8.16	7.91- 13
	Pienaar	Roelf	RSA	23.12.93	183/76	LJ	7.83, 7.97w	7.87A. 7.71, 7.78w- 11
	Pillow	Chris	USA	8.7.93	190/82	PV	5.50	5.41- 12
*	Pinder	Demetrius	BAH	13.2.89	178/70	400	45.30	44.77- 12
	Pinkelman	Luke	USA	5.5.88	190/114	SP	19.72i	20.07i- 11, 20.02- 12
*	Pitkämaki	Tero	FIN	19.12.82	195/92	JT	86.63	91.53- 05
	Pittomvils	Niels	BEL	18.7.92	198/88	Dec	8000	7644- 13
	Plotnitskiy	Dmitriy	BLR	26.8.88	189/80	TJ	16.60, 16.61w	16.91- 10
	Pohle	Andreas	GER	6.4.81	178/65	TJ	16.62	16.99- 04
	Pohle	Hagen	GER	5.3.92	177/64	20kW	1:21:29	1:22:37- 13
	Poistogov	Stepan	RUS	14.12.86	182/68	800	1:46.58, 1:46.53i	1:46.02- 12
	Polyanskiy	Sergey	RUS	29.10.89	180/75	LJ	7.82, 8.05w	8.16- 13, 8.18w- 11
	Pontvianne	Jean-Marc	FRA	6.8.94	170/60	TJ	16.48i	15.81- 13
*	Porter	Jeff	USA	27.11.85	183/84	110h	13.27, 13.12w	13.08- 12
	Portilla	Jhoanis	CUB	24.7.90	181/70	110h	13.41	13.46- 13, 13.1w- 11, 13.3- 10
	Potapstev	Ilya	RUS	19.4.93		TJ	16.45	16.12- 13, 16.23w- 12
	Pouzy	Frédérick	FRA	18.2.83	184/88	HT	72.24	77.05- 12
*	Powell	Asafa	JAM	23.11.82	190/88	100	9.87	9.72- 08
	Powlen	Bryan	USA	3.12.87	193/120	DT	62.81	61.09- 12
	Pozdnyakov	Anatoliy	RUS	1.2.87	184/101	HT	75.71	79.06- 13
	Praczyk	Wojciech	POL	10.1.93	188/90	DT	60.87	58.49- 12
*	Prásil	Ladislav	CZE	17.5.90	198/125	SP	20.82i, 20.56	21.47- 13
	Premeru	Marin	CRO	29.8.90	186/115	SP	19.72	20.59- 13
	Pretorius	Friedrich	RSA-J	4.8.95	187/84	Dec	7730A, 7639	-0-
	Prey	Mathias	GER	9.8.88	192/89	Dec	7980	8215- 13
	Primak	Artyom	RUS	14.1.93	190/77	TJ	16.28, 16.79w	16.76- 12
	Pronkin	Valeriy	RUS	15.6.94	195/115	HT	71.34	73.50- 13
*	Protsenko	Andriy	UKR	20.5.88	194/65	HJ	2.40	2.32- 13
	Przybylko	Mateusz	GER	9.3.92	194/72	HJ	2.24i, 2.22	2.24- 13
	Pujats	Pauls	LAT	6.8.91	184/73	PV	5.54	5.50- 12
	Pulli	Kristian	FIN	2.9.94	189/71	LJ	7.89	7.69- 13
	Purcell	Darius	USA	10.1.89	183/72	HJ	2.27Ai, 2.21	2.22- 12
	Puzanov	Kostyantyn	UKR	19.5.91		20kW	1:20:12	1:23:44- 13
*	Pyatnytsya	Oleksandr	UKR	14.7.85	186/90	JT	81.10	86.12- 12
	Quérin	Gaël	FRA	26.6.87	182/76	Dec	8194	8146- 13
	Quinn	Kyle	USA	28.4.93	185/86	JT	78.28	70.58- 13
	Quiyuch	Jaime	GUA	24.4.88	178/59	50kW	3:55:42A	3:50:33A- 11
*	Quow	Renny	TTO	25.8.87	170/66	200	20.39	20.61- 09
						400	45.08	44.53- 09
	Raja	Andres	EST	2.6.82	187/80	Dec	7580	8119- 09
	Ralph	Joshua	AUS	27.10.91	185/70	800	1:45.81	1:47.12- 13
	Ramsay	Liam	GBR	18.11.92	188/82	Dec	7822	7403- 13
	Rana	Basant Bahadur	IND	18.1.84	172/76	20kW	1:21:29	1:24:47- 11
*	Rapinier	Yoann	FRA	29.9.89	182/70	TJ	17.16	17.45- 13
	Rashed	Essa Ismail	QAT	14.12.86	176/63	Mar	2:07:54	2:09:22- 12
	Rasov	Arseniy	RUS	23.6.92	192/79	HJ	2.28	2.26- 10
	Rawat	Manish Singh	IND	5.5.91		50kW	4:02:08	4:13:55- 13
	Reed	Chris	USA	22.7.92	193/140	SP	20.07i, 19.93	19.99- 13
	Reed	Hayden	USA	4.4.94	190/102	DT	63.74	56.62- 13
	Regassa	Chala	ETH	.90		1500	3:38.06	
	Regassa	Dejene	BRN	18.4.89	176/68	3kSt	8:33.40	8:25.66- 12
	Regassa	Tilahun	ETH	18.1.90	170/54	Mar	2:06:21	2:05:27- 12
	Registe	David	DMA	2.5.88	180/80	LJ	8.06A, 7.84	7.89, 7.91w- 09
	Rehm	Markus	GER	22.8.88	185/75	LJ	8.24 prosthetics	7.95- 13
	Reid	Julian	GBR	23.9.88	186/77	TJ	16.87i, 16.82	16.98, 17.10w- 09
*	Reif	Christian	GER	24.10.84	196/84	LJ	8.49	8.47- 10
	Renaudie	Paul	FRA	2.4.90	192/78	800	1:46.05	1:45.85- 12
	Rendón	James	COL	7.4.85	155/55	50kW	3:47:41	-0-
	Repcík	Jozef	SVK	3.8.86	186/72	800	1:45.37	1:44.94- 08
	Reus	Julian	GER	29.4.88	177/73	100	10.05, 10.01w	10.08, 10.00w- 13
						200	20.44, 20.42w	20.36- 13

Name		Nat	Born	Ht/Wt	Event	2014 Mark	Pre-2014 Best
* Revé	Ernesto	CUB	26.2.92	181/65	TJ	17.58	17.46- 13
Revenko	Vladislav	UKR	15.11.84	181/71	PV	5.50	5.80- 05
Rew	Quentin	NZL	16.7.84	175/63	20kW	1:22:11	1:22:16- 13
					50kW	3:50:22	3:50:27- 13
Reynolds	Ben	IRL	26.9.90	188/77	110h	13.79, 13.59w	13.49- 13
Reynolds	Maalik	USA	26.4.92	193/73	HJ	2.25	2.28- 11
Richards	Marquis	SUI	29.7.91	174/74	PV	5.55	5.33- 13
Richards	O'Dayne	JAM	14.12.88	178/117	SP	21.61	20.97- 13
* Richardson	Jason	USA	4.4.86	186/73	110h	13.29, 13.27w	12.98- 12
Ricks	Keith	USA	9.10.90	183/75	100	10.16	10.13- 13
					200	20.51, 20.39w	20.45- 12
Rietveld	Pelle	NED	4.2.85	184/75	Dec	8204	8073- 12
* Riley	Andrew	JAM	6.9.88	188/80	110h	13.19	13.14- 13
Rimmer	Michael	GBR	3.2.86	180/71	800	1:45.89	1:43.89- 10
Ringer	Richard	GER	27.2.89	180/64	5000	13:25.24	13:27.29- 13
Rise	Lars Vikan	NOR	23.11.88	184/86	Dec	7918	7942- 11
Riseley	Jeff	AUS	11.11.86	192/74	800	1:45.81	1:44.48- 12
1000	2:16.09		2:16.63- 12		1500	3:38.41	3:32.93- 09
Ristic	Milan	SRB	8.8.91	186/72	110h	13.63, 13.59w	13.88- 12, 13.78w- 13
Rittidet	Jamras	THA	1.2.89	183/75	110h	13.61	13.72, 13.67Aw- 13
Rivera	Edgar	MEX	13.2.91	191/80	HJ	2.28	2.28- 11
* Rivera	Luis	MEX	21.6.87	183/79	LJ	8.24	8.46- 13
Roach	Kimmari	JAM	21.9.90	175/73	100	10.12	10.13- 10
* Roberts	Gil	USA	15.3.89	183/75	100	10.12, 9.92w	10.41- 13, 10.33w- 11
200	20.22	20.54A- 12, 20.62, 20.33w- 13			400	44.53	44.84- 12
* Roberts	Kurt	USA	20.2.88	191/127	SP	21.50i, 21.47	21.14- 12
Robertson	Andrew	GBR	17.12.90	174/72	100	10.10	10.14- 13
Robertson	Jake	NZL	14.11.89	180/65	10k	28:03.70	27:45.46- 13
Robertson	Josef	JAM	14.5.87	176/63	400h	49.04A, 49.54	49.16- 12
Robertson	Ricky	USA	19.9.90	178/70	HJ	2.30i, 2.29	2.32- 12
					TJ	16.45	16.20, 16.21w- 12
* Robertson	Zane	NZL	14.11.89	180/65	1500	3:34.19	3:35.45- 13
1M	3:53.72		3:56.13- 12		3000	7:41.37	
2M	8:22.82				5000	13:14.69	13:13.83- 13
Robi	Deribe	ETH	26.9.84		Mar	2:07:16	2:08:10- 13
Robinson	Bryce	USA	13.11.93	178/75	100	10.18, 10.15w	10.43- 13
					200	20.48, 20.30w	21.22- 13
Robinson	Jeron	USA	30.4.91	193/73	HJ	2.30	2.26- 13
Robinson	Joshua	AUS	4.10.85	187/95	JT	82.48	80.73- 07
Robinson	Paul	IRL	24.5.91	175/64	800	1:46.40	1:45.86- 13
1500	3:36.45		3:35.22- 13		1M	3:54.77	3:56.18- 13
* Robles	Dayron	CUB	19.11.86	191/91	110h	13.29	12.87- 08
Rodger	Sebastian	GBR	29.6.91	181/73	400h	49.47	49.19- 13
* Rodgers	Michael	USA	24.4.85	178/73	100	9.91, 9.80w	9.85- 11
					200	20.51	20.24- 09
Rodhe	Justin	CAN	17.10.84	186/118	SP	20.19	21.29- 13
Rodney	Brendon	CAN	9.4.92	190/84	200	20.41	20.60, 20.58w- 13
Rodrigues	Lucas Gabriel	BRA-J	2.10.95		800	1:46.50	1:50.24- 13
Rodríguez	Rafith	COL	1.6.89	187/73	800	1:44.77	1:44.31- 11
Rogers	Jason	SKN	31.8.91	173/66	100	10.04	10.01- 13
Rogestedt	Johan	SWE	27.1.93	196/72	800	1:45.89	1:47.18- 11
Rogowski	Arkadiusz	POL	30.3.93	182/90	HT	72.21	67.74- 13
* Röhler	Thomas	GER	30.9.91	195/83	JT	87.63	83.95- 13
Rojas	Ferney	COL	30.9.87		50kW	4:02:09	4:04:23- 13
Roland	Lestrod	SKN	5.9.92	173/66	200	20.72, 20.19w	20.60- 13
Romanenko	Oleksandr	UKR	26.6.81	168/60	50kW	4:03:17	3:58:31- 12
Romani	Darlan	BRA	9.4.91	183/127	SP	20.84	20.48- 12
Rono	Aron	USA	1.11.82	173/57	10k	28:03.51	27:31.15- 11
Rono	Patrick	USA	8.4.92	183/70	800	1:46.46	1:46.49- 13
Rono	Patrick Kiprotich	KEN-J	9.4.96	175/68	800	1:46.3A	1:46.6A- 13
Rono	Philemon	KEN	8.2.91		HMar	60:52	60:39- 13
					Mar	2:07:07	
Rono	Vincent	KEN	11.11.90	165/55	3000	7:45.33+	7:41.18- 10, 7:37.87i- 11
					5000	13:16.42	13:21.96- 10
Ronoh	Geoffrey	KEN	29.11.82		HMar	59:45	
* Rooney	Martyn	GBR	3.4.87	198/78	400	44.71	44.60- 08
* Rop	Albert	BRN	17.7.92	176/55	3000	7:38.77i	7:35.53- 13
					5000	13:06.12	12:51.96- 13
Rosa	Jean	BRA	1.2.90		TJ	16.49	16.53- 12, 16.82w- 13
Rosenquist	Fabian	SWE	1.4.91	186/80	Dec	7844	7738- 13
Rosiewicz	Maciej	GEO	31.7.77	173/68	50kW	3:59:50	3:55:48- 10

	Name		Nat	Born	Ht/Wt	Event	2014 Mark	Pre-2014 Best
	Ross	Colton	USA	4.6.92	184/79	PV	5.70	5.51- 13
	Ross	Nick	USA	8.8.91	188/75	HJ	2.31Ai, 2.30	2.28- 12
	Rossi	Eugenio	SMR	6.3.92		HJ	2.24	2.15- 11
	Roth	Thomas	NOR	11.2.91	183/68	800	1:46.15	1:46.88- 12
*	Rotich	Abraham	BRN	26.6.93	183/64	800	1:46.30i, 1:46.94dq	1:43.13- 12
	Rotich	Anthony	KEN	.93	174/60	3kSt	8:30.54	8:21.19- 13
	Rotich	Edwin	KEN		168/50	HMar	59:59	61:25- 13
*	Rotich	Lucas	KEN	16.4.90	171/57	Mar	2:07:18	-0-
	Rotich	Luka	KEN	7.8.88		Mar	2:08:48	2:08:12- 13
	Roudette	Carlyle	TTO	6.9.91	190/84	400	45.66	46.67- 13
	Rowe	Alex	AUS	8.7.92	181/70	800	1:44.40	1:45.44- 13
	Rozinski	Pawel	POL	11.7.87	198/91	JT	79.00	78.90- 13
	Rubino	Giorgio	ITA	15.4.86	174/56	20kW	1:20:44	1:19:37- 09
*	Rudisha	David	KEN	17.12.88	189/73	800	1:42.98	1:40.91- 12
	Ruiz	Jorge	COL	17.5.89	167/57	50kW	3:58:58	3:59:13- 13
	Rujevic	Luka	SRB	14.10.85	200/132	SP	19.63i	20.46- 09
	Rummens	Tim	BEL	16.12.87	182/73	400h	49.90	50.23- 13
	Rungaru	James	KEN	14.1.93		HMar	61:04	61:51- 13
*	Rupp	Galen	USA	8.5.86	180/62	1500	3:34.15	3:34.75- 12
	3000	7:45.6+, 7:34.68i	7:30.16i- 13, 7:43.24- 10			2M	8:07.41i	8:09.72i- 12
	5000	13:00.99		12:58.90- 12		10k	26:44.36	26:48.00- 11
*	Rutherford	Greg	GBR	17.11.86	188/84	LJ	8.51	8.35- 12
	Rutt	Michael	USA	28.10.87	175/64	800	1:46.04	1:45.08- 13
	Rutto	Eliud	KEN	4.6.88	175/64	800	1:45.37	1:46.5 - 11
*	Ruuskanen	Antti	FIN	21.2.84	189/86	JT	88.01	87.79- 12, 87.88dh- 07
*	Ruzavin	Andrey	RUS	28.3.86	175/70	20kW	1:18:59 dq?	1:17:47- 12
	Rybakov	Anatoliy	RUS	27.2.85	160/51	10k	28:03.59	28:06.54- 08
	Rybakov	Yevgeniy	RUS	27.2.85	168/56	10k	28:02.79	28:05.75- 08
*	Ryzhov	Mikhail	RUS	17.12.91	180/65	50kW	3:39:05	3:38:58- 13
	Ryzhyy	Roman	UKR	17.1.85	187/105	DT	60.67	61.48- 08
	Saarikoski	Juho	FIN	19.5.93	180/95	HT	71.52	67.10- 13
	Sáenz	Stephen	MEX	23.8.90	188/116	SP	20.35	20.08i, 19.91- 12
	Safiulin	Ilgizar	RUS	9.12.92	183/64	3kSt	8:20.29	8:28.65- 13
	Safo-Antwi	Sean	GBR	31.10.90	171/69	100	10.14, 10.07w	10.38, 10.10w- 13
	Safronov	Dmitriy	RUS	9.10.81	184/66	10k	28:18.78	28:15.11- 08
	Safronov	Konstantin	KAZ	2.9.87	184/68	LJ	7.90	8.10- 13
	Saharuk	Igor	UKR	3.6.88		50kW	3:50:49	3:54:40- 12
	Sahner	Andreas	GER	27.1.85	175/100	HT	70.55	71.67- 10
*	Saidy Ndure	Jaysuma	NOR	1.7.84	192/72	100	10.11, 9.92w	9.99- 11, 9.95w- 13
						200	20.43	19.89- 07
	Saito	Takumi	JPN	23.3.93	178/61	20kW	1:20:21	1:20:05- 13
	Saku-Bafuanga	Gaetan	FRA	22.7.91	181/75	TJ	16.80i	17.07- 13
	Salaam	Rakieem "Mookie"	USA	5.4.90	180/73	100	10.08	9.97- 11, 9.86w- 13
^	Saladino	Irving	PAN	23.1.83	183/70	LJ	8.16	8.73- 08
	Salas	Dídac	ESP	19.5.93	187/75	PV	5.60	5.55- 12
	Salazar	Julio César	MEX	8.7.93		20kW	1:21:58	1:29:00A- 13
	Salomäki	Eemeli	FIN	11.10.87	182/71	PV	5.55i	5.60- 09
	Samaai	Rushwal	RSA	25.9.91	178/73	LJ	8.13A, 8.08	7.94A- 12, 7.96Aw- 13
	Samac	Vedran	SRB	22.1.90	183/90	JT	79.22	78.20- 13
*	Sambu	Stephen	KEN	3.7.88	169/55	5000	13:26.44+	13:13.74i, 13:31.51- 12
	10k	26:54.61		27:28.64- 11		HMar	61:08	60:41- 13
	Samimi	Mahmoud	IRI	18.9.88	190/105	DT	62.90	64.67- 09
	Samimi	Mohammed	IRI	29.3.87	188/104	DT	65.46	65.41- 10
^	Samitov	Ruslan	RUS	11.2.91	187/77	TJ	16.26, 16.60w	17.30i- 13, 17.25- 12
*	Sánchez	Félix	DOM	30.8.77	178/73	400h	48.91	47.25- 03
	Sanford	Donald	ISR	5.2.87	193/84	400	45.27	45.21- 10
	Sang	Ezra	KEN	8.6.94		HMar	61:03	
*	Santos	Luguelín	DOM	12.11.93	173/61	400	44.53	44.45- 12
	Saquipay	Rolando	ECU	21.7.79	166/57	50kW	3:50:19	4:01:20- 11
	Sarantsev	Yevgeniy	RUS	5.8.88		Dec	8123	7861- 12
	Sato	Yuki	JPN	26.11.86	179/60	10k	27:46.59	27:38.25- 09
^	Sawano	Daichi	JPN	16.9.80	183/75	PV	5.70	5.83- 05
	Sawyers	Roberto	CRC	17.10.86	189/107	HT	73.85	73.60- 13
	Scantling	Garrett	USA	19.5.93	190/86	Dec	8169	7873(w)- 13
	Scarvelis	Nicholas	USA	2.2.93	185/114	SP	19.62	18.69i, 18.19- 13
	Schembera	Robin	GER	1.10.88	186/67	800	1:46.33	1:45.63- 09
	Schembri	Fabrizio	ITA	27.1.81	183/74	TJ	16.78i, 16.61	17.27- 09
	Scherbarth	Tobias	GER	17.8.85	195/84	PV	5.73	5.76i- 09, 5.71- 10
	Schirrmeister	Silvio	GER	7.12.88	195/80	400h	49.66	49.15- 13
	Schlangen	Carsten	GER	31.12.80	189/68	1500	3:37.78	3:33.64- 12
	Schnulle	Ryan	USA	8.9.93	178/70	800	1:46.29	1:49.50- 13

	Name		Nat	Born	Ht/Wt	Event	2014 Mark	Pre-2014 Best
	Schrom	Pavel	CZE	17.3.91		50kW	4:06:16	
	Schuurmans	Jared	USA	20.8.87	198/118	DT	64.42	62.89- 13
	Schwarzer	Helge	GER	26.11.85	185/76	110h	13.64, 13.59w	13.39- 09
^	Sdiri	Salim	FRA	26.10.78	185/80	LJ	8.35	8.42- 09
	Sebahire	Eric	RWA	6.1.85	171/55	10k	28:03.88	28:31.49- 11
	Seck	Mor	SEN	24.9.85	179/64	800	1:46.55	1:45.81- 10
	Sedoc	Gregory	NED	16.10.81	179/74	110h	13.55	13.37- 07, 13.1w- 10
	Sedyuk	Nikolay	RUS	29.4.88	198/115	DT	63.59	64.72- 08
	See	Jeff	USA	6.6.86	186/72	1500	3:37.99	3:35.21- 12
	Segura	Omar	MEX	24.3.81	170/57	20kW	1:20:03	1:20:25- 05
	Seifert	Bernhard	GER	15.2.93	190/88	JT	78.02	82.42- 13
	Seiler	Martin	GER	3.4.89	186/75	TJ	16.30, 16.53w	16.16i- 12, 16.12- 11
	Selmon	Kenny	USA-J	27.8.96	188/82	400h	50.13	51.82- 13
	Selmouni	Sofiane	FRA	22.9.89	190/73	800	1:45.94	1:47.03- 13
	Semenov	Oleksiy	UKR	27.6.82	204/115	DT	64.44	65.96- 12
	Semyonov	Dmitriy	RUS	2.8.92	195/77	HJ	2.28	2.30i- 13, 2.26- 12
	Senesca	Gerkenz	USA/HAI	6.4.90	183/82	110h	13.64	13.65, 13.54w- 13
	Sepehrzad	Hadi	IRI	19.1.83	191/90	Dec	7572	7729- 12
	Seppänen	Tuomas	FIN	16.5.86	180/107	HT	75.22	75.31- 11
	Seres	András	HUN	31.1.89	187/102	DT	62.27	59.09- 11
	Seribe	Pako	BOT	7.4.91	183/68	400	45.04A, 45.21	46.24- 13
	Seurei	Benson	BRN	27.3.84	172/62	1500	3:34.24	3:31.61- 12
	Sghaier	Mohamed	TUN	18.7.88	188/77	400h	49.71	49.82- 13
	Shabanov	Konstantin	RUS	17.11.89	184/75	110h	13.51, 13.41w	13.35- 11
	Shalin	Pavel	RUS	15.3.87	175/73	LJ	8.08i, 7.99	8.25- 10, 8.33w- 11
	Shami	Abdullah Dawit	ETH	16.7.84	176/53	Mar	2:08:41	2:05:42- 12
*	Sharman	William	GBR	12.9.84	188/82	110h	13.16	13.26- 13, 12.9w- 10
*	Shayunov	Yuriy	BLR	22.10.87	189/120	HT	76.86	80.72- 09
	Sheyko	Georgiy	KAZ	24.8.89	183/70	20kW	1:21:44	1:23:52- 12
	Shinoto	Jun	JPN	2.4.85	172/54	3kSt	8:34.37	8:32.89- 03
	Shitara	Keita	JPN	18.12.91	169/50	10k	27:56.60	27:51.54- 13
	Shitara	Yuta	JPN	18.12.91	167/44	10k	27:58.91	27:54.82- 13
*	Shkurenyov	Ilya	RUS	11.1.91	191/82	Dec	8498	8370- 13
	Shokirjanov	Bobur	UZB	5.12.90	190/84	JT	79.83	79.31- 09
*	Shubenkov	Sergey	RUS	4.10.90	190/75	110h	13.13	13.09- 12
*	Shustov	Aleksandr	RUS	29.6.84	188/80	HJ	2.26i, 2.25	2.36- 11
	Siddhanth	Thingalaya	IND	1.3.91	193/87	110h	13.65	13.65- 12
	Sidorchenko	Gleb	RUS	15.5.86	197/110	DT	62.47	62.55- 13
*	Sidorov	Maksim	RUS	13.5.86	190/126	SP	20.78i, 20.37	21.51- 12
	Siegmeier	Zachary	USA	8.1.91	183/77	PV	5.51	5.31- 13
	Sierra	Omar	COL	10.9.88		50kW	3:59:08	4:09:02A- 13
	Sigueni	Hicham	MAR	30.1.93	172/51	3kSt	8:25.20	8:21.78- 12
	Sikora	Rafal	POL	17.2.87	187/76	20kW	1:22:19	1:21:04- 11
						50kW	3:55:11	3:46:16- 11
*	Silmon	Charles	USA	4.7.91	175/72	100	10.07, 9.98w	9.98, 9.85w- 13
						200	20.39w	20.23- 13
*	Silnov	Andrey	RUS	9.9.84	198/83	HJ	2.29i, 2.28	2.38- 08
	da Silva	Aldemir	BRA	8.6.92	186/73	200	20.32	20.38, 20.33w- 12
	Silva	Andrés	URU	27.3.86	180/76	400h	48.65	49.16- 11
	da Silva	Fábio Gomes	BRA	4.8.83	178/74	PV	5.71	5.80- 11
	da Silva	Joílson	BRA	29.8.87	180/66	3000	7:46.57	7:52.71- 10
	Silva	Jonathan	BRA	21.7.91	185/75	TJ	16.94	17.39- 12
*	da Silva	Mauro Vinícius	BRA	26.12.86	183/69	LJ	8.28i, 7.88, 8.08w	8.31- 13
	Silva	Talles	BRA	20.8.91		HJ	2.25	2.23- 10
	da Silva	Tiago	BRA	23.10.93	176/73	LJ	8.09	7.91- 13
	Simanovich	Denis	BLR	20.4.87	179/58	20kW	1:22:44	1:20:42- 12
	Simbine	Akani	RSA	21.9.93	174/67	100	10.02A, 10.18	10.19A- 12, 10.36, 10.24w- 13
						200	20.37	20.68A- 12, 20.90, 20.78w- 13
	Singh	Arpinder	IND	30.12.92	188/80	TJ	17.17	16.84- 13
	Singh	Devender	IND	18.12.88	178/92	JT	78.57	76.77- 13
	Singh	Devender	IND	5.12.83		20kW	1:21:49	1:26:19- 13
	Singh	Gurmeet	IND	1.7.85		20kW	1:21:20	1:20:22.52t- 12
	Singh	Inderjeet	IND	19.4.88	191/125	SP	19.89	19.70- 13
	Singh	Om Prakash	IND	11.1.87	198/130	SP	19.74	20.69- 12
	Singh Dalvir	Rajender	IND	5.4.89	175/89	JT	79.32	76.12- 12
	Singh Kharia	Ravinder	IND	19.3.86	192/109	JT	78.02	75.47- 13
*	Sintnicolaas	Eelco	NED	7.4.87	186/81	Dec	8478	8506- 12
*	Sirmais	Zigismunds	LAT	6.5.92	191/90	JT	86.61	84.69- 11
	Sirviö	Toni	FIN	8.1.92	190/93	JT	79.90	78.62- 13
	Sitonik	William Malel	KEN	1.3.94	165/52	5000	13:27.13	13:19.83- 13
						10k	27:25.56	27:48.55- 13

Name		Nat	Born	Ht/Wt	Event	2014 Mark	Pre-2014 Best
Skeen	Odean	JAM	28.8.94	181/75	100	10.14, 10.12w	10.28, 10.24w- 12
Skipper	Greg	USA	26.3.93	193/105	HT	70.57	67.79- 13
Skobeyko	Andrey	BLR-J	11.6.95		HJ	2.26	2.18- 13
Skyers	Roberto	CUB	12.11.91	187/75	200	20.28A, 20.37	20.24- 09
Slobodenyuk	Vadym	UKR	17.3.81	189/74	3kSt	8:29.82	8:22.19- 12
Smellie	Gavin	CAN	26.6.86	180/75	200	20.45, 20.33w	20.45- 09
Smelyk	Sergiy	UKR	19.4.87	178/72	200	20.30	20.39- 13
Smirnov	Valentin	RUS	13.2.86	177/62	1500	3:38.37	3:36.14- 11
Smith	Alex	GBR	6.3.88	183/115	HT	73.52	75.63- 12
Smith	Allan	GBR	6.11.92	198/84	HJ	2.25	2.26- 13
Smith	Calvin	USA	10.12.87	180/75	400	45.46	44.81- 10
Smith	David	GBR	14.7.91	188	HJ	2.25	2.22- 11
Smith	J. Patrick	USA	28.4.91	185/84	Dec	7645	7612A(w)- 13
* Sobera	Robert	POL	19.1.91	190/77	PV	5.75i, 5.70, 5.80ex	5.71i, 5.61- 13
Söderberg	David	FIN	11.8.79	185/100	HT	77.57	78.83- 03
* Soi	Edwin	KEN	3.3.86	172/55	3000	7:46.5+, 7:44.78i	7:27.55- 11
					5000	12:59.82	12:51.34- 13
Sokolov	Dmitriy	RUS	16.1.93		PV	5.50i, 5.41	5.50- 13
^ Sokolovs	Igors	LAT	17.8.74	187/110	HT	75.15	80.14- 09
* Sokyrskyy	Oleksiy	UKR/RUS	16.3.85	185/108	HT	77.86	78.91- 12
* Solomon	Duane	USA	28.12.84	191/77	800	1:43.88	1:42.82- 12
Solomon	Jarrin	TTO	11.1.86	173/73	400	44.98	45.19- 13
^ Solomon	Steven	AUS	16.5.93	186/73	400	45.36	44.97- 12
Some	Peter	KEN	5.6.90		Mar	2:07:05	2:05:38- 13
Somers	Thomas	GBR-Y	28.4.97	184/75	200	20.37	20.84- 13
Someya	Koki	JPN	18.8.88	180/80	Dec	7597	7520- 10
Song Bin		CHN	30.9.90		JT	78.39	75.35- 12
Sorokin	Dmitriy	RUS	27.9.92	176/73	TJ	16.96	16.38- 11, 16.41w- 10
Sorrillo	Rondell	TTO	21.1.86	178/62	100	10.09	10.03- 12, 9.99w- 13
					200	20.22	20.16- 11
* Souleiman	Ayanleh	DJI	3.12.92	172/60	800	1:43.69	1:43.63- 13
1500 3:29.58 3:30.31- 12 1M 3:47.32 3:50.07- 13 3000 7:40.85i 7:39.81i- 13, 7:42.22- 12							
Sousa	Hugo	BRA	5.3.87	188/77	400	45.09	45.31- 13
Sowinski	Erik	USA	21.12.89	186/70	800	1:44.58	1:45.21- 13
^ Spank	Raul	GER	13.7.88	191/78	HJ	2.24i	2.33- 09
^ Spasovkhodskiy	Igor	RUS	1.8.79	191/91	TJ	16.63i, 16.57, 16.58w	17.44- 01
* Spearmon	Wallace	USA	24.12.84	190/80	200	20.19	19.65- 06
Spencer	Kendall	USA	24.7.91	178/73	LJ	7.85Ai, 7.95Aw	8.16A, 7.76- 12
Spratling	Brycen	USA	10.3.92	175/68	400	45.09	45.71- 13
St. Lawrence	Ben	AUS	7.11.81	176/62	5000	13:25.68	13:10.08- 11
Ståhl	Daniel	SWE	27.8.92	200/135	DT	66.89	62.16- 12
Stamatóyiannis ¶	Mihaíl	GRE	20.5.82	188/112	SP	20.06	20.36i- 10, 20.17- 11
Stanek	Tomás	CZE	13.6.91	190/127	SP	20.93	19.50- 13
Stano	Massimo	ITA	27.2.92	180/60	20kW	1:23:01	1:25:25- 13
Stanys	Raivydas	LTU	3.2.87	184/77	HJ	2.26	2.31- 12
Starc	Brandon	AUS	24.11.93	188/73	HJ	2.25	2.28- 13
* Starodubtsev	Dmitriy	RUS	3.1.86	191/79	PV	5.70	5.90i- 11, 5.75- 08
Stasek	Martin	CZE	8.4.89	190/127	SP	20.35	20.98- 13
Stathelakos	Konstadínos	CYP	30.12.87	182/130	HT	72.60	74.38- 11
Stauß	René	GER	17.9.87	190/75	Dec	7819	7694- 13
Steacy	James	CAN	29.5.84	189/115	HT	75.54	79.13- 08
Steele	Andrew	GBR	19.9.84	190/82	400	45.69	44.94- 08
Steele	Edino	JAM	6.1.87	178/72	200	20.41	20.39- 13
					400	45.44	45.38- 12
Stein	Jake	AUS	17.1.94	186/85	Dec	7601	-0-
Stepanov	Sergey	RUS	28.7.86		50kW	3:54:17	-0-
Stevens	Tabor	USA	21.6.91	196/79	3kSt	8:35.05	8:43.70- 13
Stewart	Ray	USA	5.4.89	183/79	110h	13.35	13.43- 13
Stewart	Tyron	USA	8.7.89	180/70	LJ	8.39	8.21- 12
Stigler	Michael	USA	5.4.92	178/70	400h	49.34	49.19- 13
* Storl	David	GER	27.7.90	199/122	SP	21.97	21.88i, 21.86- 12
* Strelkov	Denis	RUS	26.10.90	185/75	20kW	1:19:46	1:19:53-13
Strobinders	Rolands	LAT	14.4.92	193/90	JT	83.10	81.68- 13
Strzalkowski	Adrian	POL	28.3.90	178/64	LJ	8.18i, 8.02	7.90, 7.99w- 13
Stylianou	Nikandros	CYP	22.8.89	179/72	PV	5.52	5.40- 10
Su Bingtian		CHN	29.8.89	185/65	100	10.10	10.06- 13, 10.04w- 12
* Sudol	Grzegorz	POL	28.8.78	174/64	20kW	1:23:07	1:20:46- 13
					50kW	3:52:53A	3:41:20- 13
Sugai	Yohei	JPN	30.8.85	178/73	LJ	8.00, 8.16w	8.10- 10, 8.13w- 08
Suguimati	Mahau	BRA	13.11.84	184/78	400h	49.09	48.67- 09
Sukharev	Kirill	RUS	24.5.92	183/75	LJ	8.13	8.06- 13

Name		Nat	Born	Ht/Wt	Event	2014 Mark	Pre-2014 Best
Sukharyev	Ilya	UKR	17.6.86	190/68	3kSt	8:32.69	8:33.22- 09
Suleman	Hamed	USA	14.7.90	179/75	LJ	7.93w	7.75- 12, 7.91w- 13
Sun Chengang		CHN	11.3.91		20kW	1:21:54	1:19:55- 13
Sun Zhao		CHN	8.2.90		HJ	2.24i, 2.20	2.25- 12
Suskevicius	Tadas	LTU	22.5.85	175/65	50kW	3:51:58	3:52:31- 10
* Suzuki	Yusuke	JPN	2.1.88	169/56	20kW	1:18:17	1:18:34- 13
Svärd Jacobsson	Melker	SWE	8.1.94	188/78	PV	5.65i, 5.60	5.50i- 13, 5.48- 12
Sverrisson	Gudmundur	ISL	24.5.90	191/89	JT	78.29	80.66- 13
* Sviridov	Sergey	RUS	20.10.90	192/85	Dec	8193	8365- 12
^ Svoboda	Petr	CZE	10.10.84	195/83	110h	13.39	13.27- 10
^ Svyatokho	Valeriy	BLR	20.7.81	186/112	HT	75.55	81.49- 06
Swiderski	Adrian	POL	26.9.86	188/74	TJ	16.73	16.69- 10
Swift	Greggmar	BAR	16.2.91	183/68	110h	13.35	13.48- 13
Sykora	Jiri	CZE-J	20.1.95	184/79	Dec	7927	-0-
Szikszai	Robert	HUN	30.9.94	201/115	DT	63.20	56.85- 13
Szost	Henryk	POL	20.1.82	188/69	Mar	2:08:55	2:07:39- 12
Szypka	Brad	USA	13.2.93	188/111	SP	19.85	18.83i, 18.57- 13
Szyszkowski	Jakub	POL	21.8.91	193/145	SP	20.08	20.32- 13
* Tadese	Zersenay	ERI	8.2.82	158/52	HMar	59:38	58:23- 10
Taherkhani	Sobhan	IRI	21.9.92		LJ	7.90w	7.71- 13
* Tahri	Bouabdellah	FRA	20.12.78	191/68	1500	3:37.54	3:32.73- 13
5000	13:12.22	13:12.29- 07			10k	27:57.52	27:31.46- 11
^ Taillepierre	Karl	FRA	13.8.76	176/64	TJ	16.54	17.45- 05
Tajadura	Tomás	ESP	25.6.85	170/58	3kSt	8:32.82	8:19.00- 11
Takahari	Hiromi	JPN	13.11.87	182/64	HJ	2.25	2.25- 13
* Takahashi	Eiki	JPN	19.11.92	175/58	20kW	1:18:41	1:20:25- 13
Takahira	Shinji	JPN	18.7.84	180/62	200	20.50	20.22- 09
Takase	Kei	JPN	25.11.88	179/62	100	10.13	10.13- 02
					200	20.34	20.42- 12
Takase	Muryo	JPN	31.1.89	171/50	10k	28:03.81	28:27.86- 11
Talbot	Danny	GBR	1.5.91	184/73	100	10.14	10.21- 11
					200	20.36	20.45- 13
Taleb	Brahim	MAR	16.2.85	182/70	3kSt	8:15.48	8:07.02- 07
* Tallent	Jared	AUS	17.10.84	178/60	20kW	1:20:55	1:19:15- 10
					50kW	3:42:48	3:36:53- 12
Tamberi	Gianmarco	ITA	1.6.92	192/77	HJ	2.29	2.31- 12
Tamire	Getaneh	ETH	.94	171/55	5000	13:13.04	
Tammentie	Aleksi	FIN	6.8.86	185/75	TJ	16.61	16.49- 13
^ Tammert	Aleksandr	EST	2.2.73	196/125	DT	61.38	70.82- 06
Tang Gongchen		CHN	24.4.89	185/71	LJ	8.09	8.03i- 12, 7.99- 13
Taniguchi	Kotaro	JPN	3.11.94	182/70	200	20.45	20.63- 13
* Tanii	Takayuki	JPN	14.2.83	167/57	20kW	1:20:47	1:20:39- 04
					50kW	3:40:19	3:43:56- 12
* Tanui	Paul	KEN	22.12.90	172/54	5000	13:00.53	13:04.65- 11
					10k	26:49.41	26:50.63- 11
Taplin	Bralon	GRN	8.5.92	180/73	400	45.18	45.36- 12
* Tarabin	Dmitriy	RUS	29.10.91	176/85	JT	85.92	88.84- 13
Tateno	Tatsuya	JPN	5.8.91	178/73	400h	49.98	49.49- 12
Tayala	Matthias	USA	27.4.93	183/100	HT	73.57	66.37- 13
* Taylor	Christian	USA	18.6.90	190/75	400	45.17	45.34- 09
LJ	8.09		8.19- 10		TJ	17.51	17.96- 11
Taylor	Joshua	USA	19.6.92	183/82	400h	50.17	
Taylor	Logan	USA	3.4.86	183/70	110h	13.65, 13.48w	13.66, 13.60w- 12
Taylor	Ron	USA	13.8.90	182/73	LJ	8.02, 8.05w	8.19- 13
Teeters	John	USA	19.5.93	183/77	100	10.14, 9.91w	10.27- 13
Tekele	Adugna	ETH	26.2.89		10k	28:12.27	
HMar	60:15		60:35- 13		Mar	2:08:31	-0-
Temacini	Sief el Islem	ALG	5.3.88	180/65	TJ	16.50	16.88- 11
Teng Haining		CHN	25.6.93	183/65	800	1:46.32	1:46.56- 12
Tepparak	Pratchaya	THA	1.9.93	176/66	TJ	16.27, 16.52w	16.25- 12
Terer	Patrick	KEN	6.7.89	178/60	Mar	2:08:07	2:08:52- 13
Terfa	Negari	ETH	12.6.83	166/52	Mar	2:07:54	2:07:32- 03
Tesfaldet	Nguse	ERI	10.11.86	180/56	10k	28:11.07	27:28.10- 12
					HMar	59:39	60:46- 13
Tesfaye	Dereje	ETH	30.9.85	167/52	Mar	2:08:17	2:08:36- 09
* Tesfaye	Homiyu	GER	23.6.93	183/66	1000	2:17.56	
1500	3:31.98		3:34.18- 13		1M	3:49.86	-0-
Teweldebrhan	Teklit	ERI	1.10.93	172/65	1500	3:38.04	3:36.50- 12
Thagane	Tumelo	RSA	3.7.84	180/70	TJ	16.52A	17.09- 10
* Theiner	Wojciech	POL	25.6.86	187/74	HJ	2.32	2.30- 10
Thoirs	Jax	GBR	7.4.93	198/88	PV	5.61i, 5.60	5.53i, 5.50- 13

Name		Nat	Born	Ht/Wt	Event	2014 Mark	Pre-2014 Best
* Thomas	Donald	BAH	1.7.84	190/75	HJ	2.33i, 2.25	2.35- 07
Thomas	Mikel	TTO	23.11.87	182/77	110h	13.42, 13.38w	13.19- 13
Thomas	Tristan	AUS	23.5.86	184/70	400h	49.85	48.68- 09
* Thompson	Richard	TTO	7.6.85	187/79	100	9.82, 9.74w	9.85- 11
* Thorkildsen	Andreas	NOR	1.4.82	188/90	JT	80.79	91.59- 06
Thorne	Benjamin	CAN	19.3.93	175/64	20kW	1:20:19	1:21:55- 12
Thuku	Karemi Jeremiah	KEN	7.7.94	176/62	5000	13:28.60	13:24.50- 13
					10k	27:28.27	27:33.38- 13
Thymes	Justin	USA	24.1.94	180/70	100	10.18	10.58- 13
Tikhomirov	Anton	RUS	29.4.88	191/118	SP	21.10	19.74- 13
Timshin	Sergey	RUS	25.11.92		Dec	7794	7261- 13
* Tinsley	Michael	USA	21.4.84	185/74	400h	48.25	47.70- 13
Tirop	Eric	KEN	87	168/55	3000	7:45.95	7:48.03- 13
Tistan	Martin	SVK	12.11.92		50kW	4:06:11	4:30:47- 12
Titi	Ncincihli	RSA	15.12.93	167/61	200	20.41A, 20.48	21.07A- 11
Tivonchik	Stanislav	BLR	5.3.85	183/79	PV	5.52	5.60- 12
Tobais	Deji	GBR	31.10.91	180/73	100	10.18, 10.04w	10.27- 13, 10.21w- 12
Tobalina	Carlos	ESP	2.8.85	187/127	SP	20.32	19.24- 13
Tobe	Naoto	JPN	31.3.92	194/71	HJ	2.31	2.28- 13
* Tola	Tadesse	ETH	31.10.87	178/60	Mar	2:05:57	2:04:49- 13
Tola	Tamirat	ETH	11.8.91	180/58	Mar	2:06:17	-0-
Toledo	Braian	ARG	8.9.93	182/86	JT	77.75	79.87- 12
Toledo	Yoiser	ESP	24.4.83	196/110	SP	20.25	19.41- 13
Tomala	Dawid	POL	27.8.89	182/65	20kW	1:23:02	1:20:30- 13
* Tomlinson	Chris	GBR	15.9.81	197/84	LJ	8.23	8.35- 11
Tontodonati	Federico	ITA	30.10.89	169/55	50kW	4:01:55	3:51:37- 12
Too	Moses	KEN	.82		HMar	60:55	
Too	Silas	KEN	.89		3kSt	8:35.0A	8:35.46- 13
Too	Wilson	KEN	.91	165/52	10k	28:03.21	
Torie	Mike	USA	12.3.86	186/110	DT	61.61	63.12- 13
* Tornéus	Michel	SWE	26.5.86	184/70	LJ	8.21i, 8.09, 8.10w	8.29i- 13, 8.22- 12
Toroitich	Timothy	UGA	10.10.91	169/57	10k	27:43.27	27:31.07- 13
Torrence	David	USA	26.11.85	175/61	1000	2:16.76i	
1500 3:36.36 3:33.23- 13	1M 3:53.95 3:52.01- 12	2000 4:56.99i					
Torrijos	Pablo	ESP	12.5.92	187/78	TJ	16.87	16.28, 16.71w- 13
Torro	Osku	FIN	21.8.79	183/68	HJ	2.24	2.33i- 11, 2.28- 12
* Tóth	Matej	SVK	10.2.83	185/72	20kW	1:19:48	1:20:14- 13
					50kW	3:36:21	3:39:46- 11
Touil	Imad	ALG	11.2.89	172/62	1500	3:36.96	3:35.82- 12
Townsend	Fred	USA	19.2.82	188/82	110h	13.50	13.39- 12
Traber	Gregor	GER	2.12.92	189/77	110h	13.43, 13.23w	13.47- 12
Trajkovic	Milan	CYP	17.9.92	187/72	110h	13.65	13.67, 13.5- 13
Travers	John	IRL	16.3.91	175/60	1500	3:37.27+	3:42.07- 11
					1M	3:55.44	4:04.25- 11
True	Ben	USA	29.12.85	183/70	3000	7:48.7+	7:36.59- 13
					5000	13:02.74	13:11.59- 13
Tremigliozzi	Stefano	ITA	7.5.85	178/68	LJ	8.06i, 8.05	8.01- 10
Trémos	Yeóryios	GRE	21.3.89	197/118	DT	63.00	62.92- 12
Trofimov	Pyotr	RUS	28.11.83	174/63	20kW	1:20:33	1:18:28- 13
^ Trotskiy	Ivan	BLR	27.5.76	171/64	20kW	1:21:04	1:19:40- 03
					50kW	4:05:39	3:46:09- 12
Tsákonas	Likoúrgos-Stéfanos	GRE	8.3.90	184/67	200	20.40	20.45- 13
Tsákonas	Yeóryios	GRE	22.1.88	190/78	LJ	7.82, 8.01w	8.25- 12
Tsapik	Aleksey	BLR	4.8.88		TJ	16.61	16.86i, 16.82, 16.97w- 12
* Tsátoumas	Loúis	GRE	12.2.82	187/76	LJ	8.25	8.66- 07
* Tsegay	Samuel	ERI	24.10.88	178/55	HMar	59:21	60:17- 09
Tsenov	Mitko	BUL	13.6.93	182/64	3kSt	8:20.87	8:27.09- 13
Tsiámis	Dimítrios	GRE	12.1.82	178/67	TJ	16.75	17.55- 06
Tsirikhov	Soslan	RUS	24.11.84	195/125	SP	20.58	20.76- 11
* Tsyplakov	Daniyil	RUS	12.7.92	190/75	HJ	2.34i, 2.33	2.31- 12
Tucker	Russel	RSA	4.11.90	197/115	DT	62.15	59.27A- 13
Tugumisirize	Emmanuel	UGA	30.11.88	174/64	400	45.69	45.82- 13
Tuka	Amel	BIH	9.1.91	183/68	800	1:46.12	1:46.29- 13
Tur	Mark	ESP	30.11.94	190/70	20kW	1:22:46, 1:23:22.19t	1:26:10- 13
^ Turner	Andrew	GBR	19.9.80	183/77	110h	13.47	13.22- 11
Turner	De'Sean	USA	16.9.88	175/62	3kSt	8:33.79	8:25.56- 13
^ Tysse	Erik	NOR	4.12.80	184/59	20kW	1:20:50	1:19:11- 08
Ueno	Yuichiro	JPN	29.7.85	180/60	10k	28:01.71	28:09.56- 13
Ugachi	Tsuyoshi	JPN	27.4.87	163/45	10k	28:18.87	27:40.69- 11
Uglov	Nikita	RUS	11.10.93	188/76	400	45.53	46.01- 11
Uhle	Joseph	USA	25.4.89	185/82	PV	5.50iA	5.51- 13

Name		Nat	Born	Ht/Wt	Event	2014 Mark	Pre-2014 Best
Uibo	Maicel	EST	27.12.92	188/86	Dec	8182	8223- 13
Ujah	Chijindu	GBR	5.3.94	180/75	100	9.96	10.26- 12
Ukaoma	Miles	USA/NGR	21.7.92	183/75	400h	49.23	49.23- 12
* Ukhov	Ivan	RUS	29.3.86	192/83	HJ	2.42i/2.41	2.40i- 09, 2.39- 12
Ukonmaanaho	Janne	FIN	13.3.84	184/71	3kSt	8:33.09	8:27.08- 11
Uliczka	Steffen	GER	17.7.84	179/65	3kSt	8:26.79	8:22.93- 12
Umar	Jena	ETH-J	24.12.95	173/60	800	1:46.23	1:47.1A- 12
* Urbanek	Robert	POL	29.4.87	200/120	DT	65.75	66.93- 12
Ureña	Jorge	ESP	8.10.93	178/75	Dec	7656	7358- 13
Uribe	José Antonio	MEX	3.1.86		Mar	2:08:55	2:12:43- 12
Ursu	Sergiu ¶	ROU	26.4.80	202/127	DT	62.43, 62.73 drugs dq	64.74- 10
^ Urtans	Maris	LAT	9.2.81	188/123	SP	19.79	21.63- 10
Ushiro	Keisuke	JPN	24.7.86	196/86	Dec	8308	8076w, 8073- 11
Vadlejch	Jakub	CZE	10.10.90	190/93	JT	82.97	84.47- 10
Vail	Ryan	USA	19.3.86	173/59	5000	13:28.11	13:32.10- 10
van Blerk	Danie	RSA	11.11.91	188/77	200	20.0A	
Van Den Broeck	Jan	BEL	11.3.89	179/70	800	1:46.16	1:46.44- 13
* Van Der Plaetsen	Thomas	BEL	24.12.90	188/82	Dec	8184	8255- 13
Van Halen	Aric	USA	6.10.89	180/64	3kSt	8:32.92	8:37.45- 12
* van Niekerk	Wayde	RSA	15.7.92	183/73	200	20.19	20.57- 11
					400	44.38	45.09- 13
van Rooyen	Rocco	RSA	23.12.92	188/93	JT	80.10	75.72- 11
* van Zyl	Louis 'L.J'	RSA	20.7.85	186/75	400h	48.96A, 48.97	47.66- 11
Vanhaeren	Stef	BEL	15.1.92	184/60	400h	49.83	50.01- 11
^ Varga	Roland	CRO	22.10.77	196/125	DT	63.43	67.38- 02
Vasile	Adrian	ROM	9.4.86	190/72	LJ	7.81, 7.96w	8.11- 13
Vaughn	Clayton	USA	15.5.92	173/77	100	10.13, 10.07w	10.33- 12, 10.13w- 13
					200	20.66, 20.47w	21.31, 21.14w- 11
Väyrynen	Henri	FIN	16.10.91	185/75	LJ	7.85i, 8.05w	7.52- 13
Vazifehdoost	Mohammad Reza	IRI	13.10.93	190/70	HJ	2.25	2.15- 11
Vázquez	Wesley	PUR	27.3.94	184/73	800	1:44.64	1:45.29- 12
Vega	Jesús Tadeo	MEX	23.5.94	179/61	20kW	1:22:10A	-0-
Veiga	Carlos	POR	22.2.89		TJ	16.32A, 16.67Aw	15.84- 11, 16.24w- 12
Velikopolskiy	Dmitriy	RUS	27.11.84	188/110	HT	72.94	78.76- 08
Vena	Nick	USA	16.4.93	194/120	SP	20.39	19.51- 12
Verburg	David	USA	14.5.91	168/64	400	45.03	44.75- 13
Vernon	Andrew	GBR	7.1.86	175/64	3000	7:45.49i	7:45.75- 13
5000	13:11.50		13:23.20- 12		10k	28:08.66	27:53.65- 12
Veryovkin	Mikhail	RUS	28.6.91		HJ	2.25i	2.25i- 13
* Vesely	Vitezslav	CZE	27.2.83	186/94	JT	87.38	88.34- 12
Vetter	Johannes	GER	26.3.93	187/92	JT	79.75	76.58- 13
* Vicaut	Jimmy	FRA	27.2.92	188/83	100	9.95, 9.89w	9.95- 13
Vicente	Isaac	ESP	30.4.87	184/87	HT	70.77	70.41- 11
Victorin	Guillaume	FRA	26.5.90	183/75	LJ	7.91i	7.86- 11
Vides	Jorge Henrique	BRA	24.11.92	190/77	200	20.38	20.62- 13
Vigneshwar	M	IND	15.10.91		LJ	7.90	
Viita	Jussi	FIN	26.9.85	186/75	HJ	2.26	2.24i, 2.23- 11
Viken	Michael	USA	21.9.90	183/77	PV	5.50	5.45i- 13, 5.40- 12
Vincent	Pierre	FRA	20.2.92	182/74	200	20.54, 20.47w	21.22- 11, 21.17i- 13
Viney	Cam	USA	6.9.93	185/75	400h	50.09	50.54- 13
* Visser	Zarck	RSA	15.9.89	178/70	LJ	8.31A, 8.18	8.32- 13
Vitonis	Tomas	LTU	19.9.91	193/77	LJ	7.87, 7.99w	8.03i- 13, 7.75- 12
* Vivas	Borja	ESP	26.5.84	203/140	SP	21.07	20.63- 13
* Vizzoni	Nicola	ITA	4.11.73	193/126	HT	75.99	80.50- 01
Vojta	Andreas	AUT	9.6.89	184/68	1500	3:36.11	3:36.36- 13
Vonavka	Tomás	CZE	4.6.90	197/109	DT	62.10	61.74- 12
Vos	Ingmar	NED	28.5.86	186/80	Dec	7959	8224- 12
Vrublevskiy	Vadim	RUS	18.3.93		HJ	2.25	2.24- 13
Vynogradov	Yevgen	UKR	30.4.84	195/98	HT	77.01	80.58- 08
* Walcott	Keshorn	TTO	2.4.93	188/90	JT	85.77	84.58- 12
Waldén	Jouni	FIN	9.1.82	195/110	DT	61.95	60.49- 08
* Walker	Brad	USA	21.6.81	188/86	PV	5.62	6.04- 08
Walker	Everett	USA	3.10.90	180/75	100	10.20, 9.98w	10.18, 10.12w- 12, 10.05wdt- 11
					200	20.49, 20.32w	20.54, 20.53w- 12
Walker	Justin	USA	30.11.90	175/70	100	10.12, 9.95w	10.46, 10.13w- 10
					200	20.47, 20.13w	20.49- 10
Wallin	Gabriel	SWE	14.10.81	193/93	JT	77.88	83.23- 13
* Walsh	Tom	NZL	1.3.92	186/123	SP	21.26i, 21.24	20.61- 13
Wami	Mulugeta	ETH	12.7.82		Mar	2:08:18	2:07:11- 12
Wan Yong		CHN	22.7.87	188/97	HT	73.43	73.49- 13
Wang Chen		CHN	27.2.90	193/65	HJ	2.25	2.26- 09

	Name		Nat	Born	Ht/Wt	Event	2014 Mark	Pre-2014 Best
	Wang Guangfu		CHN	15.11.87	192/110	SP	19.60	20.20- 12
	Wang Jianan		CHN-J	27.8.96		LJ	8.10	8.04- 12
	Wang Like		CHN	2.4.89	190/120	SP	19.67	19.61- 11
	Wang Qin		CHN	8.5.94		20kW	1:22:50	-0-
	Wang Shizhu		CHN	20.2.89		HT	73.65	75.20- 13
	Wang Yu		CHN	18.8.91	192/73	HJ	2.31	2.33- 13
*	Wang Zhen		CHN	24.8.91	180/62	20kW	1:19:40	1:17:36- 12
	Wang Zhendong		CHN	11.1.91	180/65	50kW	3:47:18	3:57:47- 12
	Wanjiru	Daniel	KEN	26.5.92		HMar	59:58	61:10- 13
						Mar	2:08:18	-0-
	Wannemacher	Max	GER	10.3.91		Dec	7574	6935- 12
	Ward	Laderrick	USA	28.12.92	173/68	LJ	8.00	7.83- 13
*	Warner	Damian	CAN	4.11.89	185/83	110h	13.50	13.61- 12
						Dec	8282	8512- 13
	Wasehun	Mule	ETH	.93		HMar	60:08	60:35- 13
	Watrin	Julien	BEL	27.6.92	188/75	400	45.64	47.36- 13
	Watson	Reese	USA	8.10.93	188/85	PV	5.51	5.40- 13
	Waweru	Edward	KEN	3.10.90	178/58	10k	27:26.92	27:13.94- 10
	Webb	Ameer	USA	19.3.91	175/75	200	20.38	20.20, 20.05w- 13
	Weber	Julian	GER	29.8.94	190/94	JT	80.72	79.68- 13
*	Weir	Warren	JAM	31.10.89	178/75	200	19.82	19.79- 13
	Weirich	Victor	USA	25.10.87	188/86	PV	5.60	5.55- 13
	Weißhaidinger	Lukas	AUT	20.2.92	192/115	DT	60.68	59.13- 13
	Welch	Justin	USA	29.9.91	185/105	HT	72.93	69.61- 13
	Weldon	Kole	USA	25.3.92	193/114	SP	20.11i, 19.67	20.02i, 19.43- 13
						DT	62.05	59.92- 12
	Werskey	Eric	USA	17.7.87	188/120	SP	20.13	20.13- 13
	White	Travonn	USA-J	3.6.95	178/70	LJ	8.04	7.76A- 13, 7.58- 12
	White-Edwards	Timothy	USA	15.7.94	181/82	TJ	16.45	16.49A- 13
	Whitener	Caleb	USA	29.5.92	190/129	SP	19.83	19.54- 12
*	Whiting	Ryan	USA	24.11.86	191/134	SP	22.23i, 21.31	22.28- 13
	Whitt	Jack	USA	12.4.90	193/84	PV	5.70	5.72i- 12, 5.70- 13
	Whyte	Annsert	JAM	10.4.87	185/75	400h	48.58	49.17- 13
*	Wierig	Martin	GER	10.6.87	202/108	DT	66.59	68.33- 12
	Wiesiolek	Pawel	POL	13.8.91	194/84	Dec	7593	7727- 13
	Wightman	Jake	GBR	11.7.94	173/60	1500	3:35.49	3:43.74- 13
	Wilkinson	DeJon	USA	10.8.92	188/80	TJ	16.44	15.80- 13
	Wilkinson	James	GBR	13.7.90	178/70	5000	13:27.27	13:38.43- 13
						3kSt	8:22.76	8:28.74- 13
	Williams	Ben	GBR	25.1.92	183/73	TJ	16.46, 16.73w	16.09- 09
	Williams	Conrad	GBR	20.3.82	182/76	400	45.46	45.08- 12
	Williams	Isaac	USA	30.11.93	188/80	110h	13.44w	13.86- 13
*	Williams	Jesse	USA	27.12.83	184/75	HJ	2.29	2.37- 11
	Williams	Kendal	USA-J	23.9.95	180/73	200	20.55, 20.46w	20.64 , 20.63w- 13
	Williams	LaToy	BAH	28.5.88	190/77	400	44.97	44.73- 09
^	Williams #	Rhys	GBR	27.2.84	183/73	400h	48.95	48.84- 13
	Willis	Nick	NZL	25.4.83	183/68	1500	3:29.91	3:30.35- 12
	1M 3:49.83 3:50.66- 08		3000 7:36.91		7:40.62- 13	5000	13:20.33	13:27.54- 05
	Wilson	Jamal	BAH	1.9.88	188/68	HJ	2.26A	2.28- 13
	Wilson	Kirk	USA	27.5.91	173/68	200	20.60, 20.44w	20.90- 12
*	Wilson	Ryan	USA	19.12.80	188/81	110h	13.18, 13.16w	13.02- 07
	Winder	Jacob	USA	12.11.87	183/79	PV	5.51	5.55Ai- 13, 5.50- 09
	Windle	Drew	USA	22.7.92	183/73	800	1:46.52i, 1:46.91	1:48.04- 13
	Winger	Russ	USA	2.8.84	191/120	DT	64.54	66.04- 11
	Winter	Chris	CAN	22.7.86	188/75	3kSt	8:28.17	8:28.46- 12
	Winters	Brandon	USA	11.12.91	186/84	110h	13.61	13.69- 13
	Winters	David	USA	19.2.94	175/66	100	10.16	10.56, 10.26w- 13
						200	20.51	20.72- 12, 20.59w- 13
^	Wirkkala	Teemu	FIN	14.1.84	187/85	JT	77.45	87.23- 09
	Woepse	Mike	USA	29.5.91	185/79	PV	5.62	5.60Ai- 13, 5.55- 12
*	Wojciechowski	Pawel	POL	6.6.89	190/81	PV	5.80	5.91- 11
	Wolde	Dawit	ETH	19.5.91	184/64	5000	13:17.04	
	Wolf	Gordon	GER	17.1.90	199/102	DT	61.82	62.16- 10
	Wolfle	Chase	USA	9.10.92	185/84	PV	5.56	5.41- 12
	Wolski	Allan	BRA	18.1.90	185/110	HT	71.93	69.06- 11
	Woo Sang-hyeok		KOR-J	23.4.96	187/66	HJ	2.24	2.20- 13
	Woodruff	Ben	USA	9.5.89	183/91	JT	78.03	74.12- 12
	Worku	Bazu	ETH	15.9.90	170/52	Mar	2:07:32	2:05:25- 10
*	Wote	Aman	ETH	18.4.84	181/64	1500	3:29.91	3:32.65- 13
						1M	3:48.60	3:49.88- 13
	Wouters	Jurriaan	NED	18.4.93	180/79	JT	77.16	68.03- 12

Name		Nat	Born	Ht/Wt	Event	2014 Mark	Pre-2014 Best
Wright	Alex	IRL	19.12.90	173/64	50kW	3:51:28	-0-
Wright	Antwan	USA	17.11.93	175/73	100	10.20, 10.08w	10.48- 13, 10.45Aw- 11
Wright	Chad	JAM	25.3.91	188/110	DT	63.96	63.74- 13
Wrobel	David	GER	13.2.91	195/100	DT	62.72	60.63- 13
* Wruck	Julian	AUS	6.7.91	198/125	DT	65.54	68.16- 13
Wu Qianlong		CHN	30.1.90	176/62	50kW	3:50:51	3:51:35- 13
Wurster	Jason	CAN	23.9.84	185/82	PV	5.50	5.60i- 13, 5.51- 12
Wyatt	Reggie	USA	17.9.90	195/86	400h	49.32	48.58- 13
Wyatt	Vincent	USA	18.10.92	190/84	110h	13.60, 13.55w	13.79- 13
Xenikákis	Nikólaos	GRE	23.12.94	171/68	LJ	7.99	7.75- 13
Xhonneux	Frédéric	BEL	11.5.83	184/79	Dec	7546	8142- 08
* Xie Wenjun		CHN	11.7.90	188/77	110h	13.23	13.28- 13
Xie Zhenye		CHN	17.8.93	183/72	200	20.44	20.54- 12
Xu Xiaolong		CHN	20.12.92		TJ	16.82	16.47- 13
* Xue Changrui		CHN	31.5.91	183/60	PV	5.80	5.75i, 5.65- 13
Yakovenko	Dmytro	UKR	17.9.92	191/72	HJ	2.25i, 2.24	2.24i, 2.21- 13
Yamada	Noahiro	JPN	18.12.84	172/55	10k	28:16.10	28:37.64- 13
Yamagata	Ryota	JPN	10.6.92	176/60	100	10.14	10.07- 12, 10.04w- 13
Yamamoto	Seito	JPN	11.3.92	178/67	PV	5.62	5.75- 13
Yamashita	Yuga	JPN-J	6.2.96		20kW	1:23:06	-0-
* Yamazaki	Yuki	JPN	16.1.84	177/65	50kW	3:44:23	3:40:12- 09
Yáñez	Eure	VEN	20.5.93	194/77	HJ	2.27	2.25- 13
Yang Yancheng		CHN	5.1.88	189/75	PV	5.66i, 5.60	5.80i- 13, 5.75- 10
Yao Jie		CHN	21.9.90	188/85	PV	5.60	5.50i, 5.50- 13
Yargunkin	Aleksandr	RUS	6.1.81	182/68	20kW	1:21:08	1:19:57- 09
					50kW	3:42:26	3:49:47- 13
Yashin Hasen	Agato	ETH	19.1.86	175/58	10k	27:51.72	27:46.35- 13
Yates	Richard	GBR	26.1.86	185/77	400h	49.46	49.06- 08
Yazawa	Wataru	JPN	2 .7.91	179/73	110h	13.59	13.59- 13
* Yego	Hillary	KEN	2.4.92	178/60	3kSt	8:09.07	8:03.57- 13
* Yego	Julius	KEN	4.1.89	175/90	JT	84.72	85.40- 13
Yevstifeyev	Roman	RUS	19.9.92		50kW	3:45:41	-0-
Yoon Sung-hyun		KOR	1.6.94	194/74	HJ	2.26	2.22- 13
Yoroizaka	Tetsuya	JPN	20.3.90	166/52	10k	27:38.99	27:44.30- 11
Yoshida	Kazuaki	JPN	31.8.87	180/73	400h	49.45	49.45- 09
Yoshida	Takuya	JPN	10.8.90		20kW	1:22:17	1:20:47- 13
					50kW	3:43:02	-0-
Younes Idriss	Ali Mohamed	SUD	15.9.89	191/75	HJ	2.28i, 2.26	2.25- 11
* Young	Jason	USA	27.5.81	185/127	DT	64.36	69.90- 10
Yousif	Rabah	GBR	11.12.86	183/73	400	45.41	45.13- 12
Yu Wei		CHN	11.9.87	180/60	20kW	1:20:47	1:19:07- 13
					50kW	4:00:57	3:51:46- 11
Zaghou	Mounatcer	MAR	1.1.89		3kSt	8:33.53	8:23.84- 13
Zahn	D.J.	USA	31.1.93	178/80	400	45.69	46.98- 13
Zalewski	Karol	POL	7.8.93	185/73	200	20.42	20.41- 13
Zalewski	Krystian	POL	11.4.89	185/67	3kSt	8:16.20	8:23.31- 13
Zalsky	Antonin	CZE	7.8.80	200/128	SP	19.74	20.71- 04
Zawude	Tebalu	ETH	2.11.87		Mar	2:07:10	
Zaytsev	Ivan	UZB	7.11.88	190/98	JT	83.68	85.03- 12
Zellweger	Yves	SUI	27.3.87	188/76	LJ	7.98	8.03- 13
Zenúch	Patrik	SVK	30.12.90	184/84	JT	84.83	79.52- 13
Zepeda	Omar	MEX	8.6.77	177/68	50kW	3:47:35	3:48:38A- 12
Zernikel	Oleg	GER-J	16.4.95	184/72	PV	5.50	5.33- 13
Zerrifi	Abdelhamid	ALG	20.6.86		3kSt	8:32.23	8:25.96- 13
* Zhang Guowei		CHN	4.6.91	200/77	HJ	2.34	2.32i- 13, 2.31- 11
Zhang Lin		CHN	11.11.93	175/55	50kW	3:48:49	4:07:28- 13
* Zhang Peimeng		CHN	13.3.87	186/78	100	10.17, 10.08w	10.00- 13
Zhang Wei		CHN	22.3.94	188/77	PV	5.60	5.62i- 13, 5.50- 12
Zhang Yaoguang		CHN	21.6.93		LJ	7.99	7.99- 13
Zhang Yu		CHN	17.7.92		LJ	8.14	7.93- 12
Zhao Qi		CHN	14.1.93		50kW	3:51:47	4:11:58- 13
* Zhao Qinggang		CHN	24.7.85	184/93	JT	89.15	83.14- 13
Zhelyabin	Dmitry	RUS	20.5.90	187/75	PV	5.60	5.65- 12
Ziegler	Alexander	GER	7.7.87	180/98	HT	76.29	75.78- 12
Ziegler	Manuel	GER	28.7.90	183/75	TJ	16.54	16.35, 16.48w- 13
Ziemek	Zach	USA	23.2.93	190/77	Dec	7981	7640(w)- 13
Zilali	Abdelhakim	FRA	20.6.83	190/75	3kSt	8:29.41	8:25.42- 07
Zimmerman	Moacir	BRA	30.12.83	185/62	20kW	1:23:00	1:21:02.5t- 11
* Ziółkowski	Szymon	POL	1.7.76	188/120	HT	78.41	83.38- 01
Ziukas	Marius	LTU	29.6.85	185/70	20kW	1:22:09	1:22:25- 13
^ Zsivoczky	Attila	HUN	29.4.77	193/82	Dec	7849	8554- 00
* Zunic	Stipe	CRO	13.12.90	188/115	SP	20.68	17.39i- 11, 16.83- 09

WOMEN'S INDEX 2014

Athletes included are those ranked in the top 100s at standard (World Champs) events (plus shorter lists for 1000m, 1M, 2000m and 3000m). Those with detailed biographical profiles are indicated in first column by:
* in this year's Annual, ^ featured in a previous year's Annual

Name		Nat	Born	Ht/Wt	Event	2014 Mark	Pre-2014 Best
Ababel	Yeshaneh	ETH	10.6.90		3000	8:49.45	9:23.5- 11
Abe	Yukari	JPN	21.8.89	154/48	10k	32:41.38	32:52.60- 13
Abiko	Tomomi	JPN	17.3.88	175/53	PV	4.30i, 4.25	4.40- 12
Abraham	Ashlee	USA	24.9.91		100	11.38, 11.30w	11.37- 13
Abramchuk	Olha	UKR	12.4.91		DT	56.55	55.18- 13
Abugan	Sade	NGR	17.12.90	150/64	400	51.21	50.89- 08
* Adams	Valerie	NZL	6.10.84	193/123	SP	20.67i, 20.59	21.24- 11
* Adamu	Birtukan	ETH	29.4.92	164/49	3kSt	9:27.29	9:20.37- 11
* Adekoya	Kemi	BRN	16.1.93	168/57	400	51.11	52.57- 13
					400h	54.59	55.30- 13
Adeoye	Margaret	GBR	27.4.85	174/65	100	11.28	11.46- 12
Afework	Abebech	ETH	11.12.90	152/42	HMar	69:57+	70:30- 11
					Mar	2:25:02	2:23:59- 13
^ Agirre	Naroa	ESP	15.5.79	177/64	PV	4.51	4.56i, 4.50- 07
Aguilar	Evelys	COL	3.1.93	170/62	Hep	5707A, 5518	-0-
Ahbe	Kelsie	USA	6.7.91		PV	4.40	4.30- 11
* Ahouré	Murielle	CIV	23.8.87	167/57	100	10.97	10.91- 13, 10.86w- 11
					200	22.36	22.24- 13
* Ahye	Michelle-Lee	TTO	10.4.92	168/59	100	10.85	11.06- 13
					200	22.77	22.98- 13
Aidanpää	Ida	FIN	25.11.88	166/55	100h	13.08	13.58- 10
Aidietyte	Neringa	LTU	5.6.83	177/64	20kW	1:29:01	1:33:05- 12
Aït Salem	Souad	ALG	6.1.79	158/51	10k	32:42.53	32:13.15- 04
					HMar	70:36	69:15- 08
Ajok	Dorcus	UGA	12.7.94	162/65	800	2:02.04A	2:08.78- 13
Akaba	Yukiko	JPN	18.10.79	155/43	Mar	2:26:00	2:24:09- 11
Akakpo	Stella	FRA	28.2.94	158/50	100	11.24, 11.21w	11.26- 13
Åkerström	Frida	SWE	29.11.90	172/88	SP	16.72	15.92- 13
Akinosun	Morolake	USA	17.5.94	165/54	100	11.04, 10.96w	11.41- 12, 11.92w- 13
					200	22.68, 22.17w	23.26. 23.18w- 13
* Akkaoui	Malika	MAR	25.12.87	160/46	800	2:00.58	1:57.64- 13
					1500	4:08.88	4:04.96- 11
Akulinushkina	Tatyana	RUS	6.4.94		20kW	1:35:12	
Alais	Alexie	FRA	9.10.94	168/68	JT	56.30	53.54- 11
* Alami El Ouali	Salima	MAR	29.12.83	167/53	3kSt	9:21.24	9:31.03- 12
Alcántara	Dailenis	CUB	10.8.91	163/56	TJ	14.45	14.58- 12
^ Aldama	Yamilé	GBR	14.8.72	171/63	TJ	13.85, 14.05Aw	15.29- 03
Aleksandrova	Ulyana	RUS	1.1.91	182/63	LJ	6.56	6.42i, 6.27- 13
					Hep	5932	5916- 13
Alemayehu	Hirut	ETH	19.12.93		HMar	70:25	72:31- 12
* Alembekova	Elmira	RUS	30.6.90		20kW	1:27:02	1:25:27- 12
Alexander	Annie	TTO	28.8.87	175/91	SP	17.15	17.70i- 12, 17.66- 11
					DT	56.37	58.58- 11
Alexander	Ayanna	TTO	20.7.82	172/65	TJ	14.40	14.15- 12
Alexander	Kineke	VIN	21.2.86	178/65	200	23.17, 22.97w	23.00A, 23.27- 13
					400	51.23, 50.8	51.35- 06
* Ali	Nia	USA	23.10.88	170/64	100h	12.75	12.48- 13
Allgood	Avione	USA	14.12.93	165/	JT	57.63	53.85- 11
Allman	Valarie	USA-J	23.2.95	183/70	DT	57.45	56.13- 13
Alloh	Audrey	ITA	21.7.87	171/56	100	11.42, 11.29w	11.43- 12
* Almanza	Rose Mary	CUB	13.7.92	166/53	800	1:59.48	1:59.4- 13
					1000	2:38.1	2:39.5- 11
Amponsah	Janet	GHA	12.4.93		100	11.36, 11.09w	11.51- 12
					200	23.05	23.41- 12
Anacharsis	Phara	FRA	17.12.83	177/60	400h	56.26	55.94- 13
Anagnostopoúlou	Hrisoúla	GRE	27.8.91	176/79	DT	57.20	57.10- 12
Ananchenko	Yevgeniya	RUS	7.11.92		JT	56.44	53.91- 12
* Anderson	Alexandria	USA	28.1.87	175/60	100	11.11	10.91- 13, 10.88w- 12
Andersson	Tracey	SWE	5.12.84	167/87	HT	70.51	70.82- 13
Ando	Yuka	JPN	16.3.94	160/42		32:24.50	
Andraud	Matilde	FRA	28.4.89	172/68	JT	59.80	56.96- 12
Andrejczyk	Maria	POL-J	9.3.96	172/71	JT	56.53	44.58- 12
Andrejsková	Petra	CZE	25.6.92		JT	57.48	53.28- 13
^ Angelsen	Tonje	NOR	17.1.90	179/62	HJ	1.93	1.97- 12
Anghelescu	Nicoleta	ROU	13.1.92	160/70	JT	55.97	55.89- 13

Name		Nat	Born	Ht/Wt	Event	2014 Mark	Pre-2014 Best
Aniballi	Valentina	ITA	19.4.84	176/85	DT	57.32	57.73- 13
Ankiewicz	Emilia	POL	22.11.90	178/64	400h	56.73	57.76- 13
Antipova	Alina	RUS	11.1.91		100h	13.29, 13.10w	13.38- 11
Aoki	Sayaka	JPN	15.12.86	163/51	400h	57.14	55.94- 08
Arcanjo	Geisa	BRA	19.9.91	180/92	SP	17.73	19.02- 12
* Aregawi	Abeba	SWE	5.7.90	169/48	1500	3:57.57	3:56.54- 12
Arenas	Lorena	COL	17.9.93	160/50	20kW	1:30:18, 1:31:46.9t	1:32:25- 13
Argunova	Nina	RUS	15.9.89	172/62	100h	13.11	13.01- 13
Aristarkhova	Natalya	RUS	31.10.89	163/46	3000	8:57.03i	8:50.76i- 13, 9:11.55- 12
					3kSt	9:32.98	9:30.64- 13
Arndt	Mareike	GER	29.1.92		Hep	5709	5113- 13
Arrafi	Rabab	MAR	12.1.91	177/64	1500	4:02.71	4:05.22- 13
Arrieta	Valentine	SUI	29.4.90	168/58	400h	56.60	57.37- 11
Arteil	Laura	FRA	9.10.93	171/60	Hep	5812	5735- 13
Artyukh	Yekaterina	BLR	14.1.91		400h	56.63	56.88, 56.16dq- 10
* Arzamasova	Marina	BLR	17.12.87	173/57	800	1:58.15	1:59.30- 11
Asada	Chiaki	JPN	21.1.91		20kW	1:35:05	
Asenjo	Sabina	ESP	3.8.86	181/95	DT	58.31	58.65- 13
* Asher-Smith	Dina	GBR-J	4.12.95	165/56	100	11.14, 11.03w	11.38, 11.30w- 13
					200	22.61	23.14- 13
Ashley	Whitney	USA	18.2.89	178/89	SP	17.22i, 17.00	16.89- 12
					DT	63.78	61.64- 13
Assani Issouf	Jeanine	FRA	17.8.92	169/57	TJ	13.95	13.34- 13
Assefa	Meskerem	ETH	20.9.85	155/43	HMar	69:10	70:56- 13
					Mar	2:25:59	2:25:17- 13
* Assefa	Sofia	ETH	14.11.87	171/58	3kSt	9:11.39	9:09.00- 12
Assefa	Tigist	ETH-J	3.12.96	170/55	800	1:59.24	2:01.25- 13
Asumnu	Gloria	NGR	22.5.85	163/52	100	11.15	11.03- 08
					200	23.09	22.70- 07
* Atkins	Joanna	USA	31.1.89	175/61	100	11.02	11.30- 11
200	22.27, 22.19w		22.68- 11		400	50.74	50.39- 09
Atkinson	Johanna	GBR	17.1.85	168/54	20kW	1:33:43	1:30:41- 10
Atkinson Grier	Saniel	BAH	2.7.91	175/60	HJ	1.87i, 1.86	1.89- 12
Aubry	Rachel	CAN	18.5.90		800	2:02.05	2:02.56- 13
* Augusto	Jéssica	POR	8.11.81	165/46	10k	31:55.56	31:19.15- 10
					Mar	2:24:25	2:24:33- 11
Avery	Kate	GBR	10.10.91		3000	8:56.24, 8:56.20i	8:58.90mx, 9:02.48- 13
5000	15:27.90		15:35.12- 12		10k	32:33.35	33:27.44- 13
Ayalew	Genet	ETH	31.12.92		10k	32:45.1A	32:05.90- 11
					HMar	69:15	
* Ayalew	Hiwot	ETH	6.3.90	173/51	3000	8:57.8+, 8:32.29+i	8:50.?e- 13
2M	9:21.59i		5000	15:09.64	14:49.36- 11	3kSt 9:10.64	9:09.61- 12
* Ayalew	Wude	ETH	4.7.87	150/44	HMar	68:36	67:58- 09
* Ayana	Almaz	ETH	21.11.91	165/50	2000	5:37.5+	
3000	8:24.58		8:40.53- 13		5000	14:29.19	14:25.84- 13
Ayele	Zewdnesh	ETH	.93		3kSt	9:50.42	10:01.9A- 11
Babar	Lalita	IND	2.6.89	162/55	3kSt	9:35.37	10:33.40- 13
Bácskay	Zsófia	HUN-Y	18.3.97		HT	64.79	64.23- 13
Bae Chan-mi		KOR	24.3.91	175/62	TJ	13.65	13.46- 12
* Bahta	Meraf	SWE	24.6.89	177/51	1500	4:01.34	4:05.11- 13
3000	8:57.06		8:58.55- 13		5000	14:59.49	15:56.30- 07
^ Bailey	Aleen	JAM	25.11.80	170/64	100	11.16	11.04- 04
					200	22.89	22.33- 04
Baird	Kadecia	GUY-J	24.2.95		200	23.13w	23.79A- 13, 23.26w- 12
Baisden	Kendall	USA-J	5.3.95	168/54	200	23.15, 22.99w	23.42- 10
					400	50.46	52.03- 13
Bakker	Sharona	NED	12.4.90	170/62	100h	12.85	13.14- 12
Balayeva	Olga	RUS	31.7.84		LJ	6.68	6.89- 11
Bambara	Laëtitia	BUR	30.3.84	180/75	HT	65.77	68.53- 11
Bamford	Racheal	GBR	4.8.89		3kSt	9:45.51	-0-
Bamgbose	Margaret	USA	19.10.93	162/52	400	51.72	52.25- 13
Bânova	Andriana	BUL	1.5.87	178/64	TJ	14.32	14.34- 11
Barber	Jade	USA	4.4.93		100h	12.97	13.00- 13
Barber	Kaila	USA	4.4.93		400h	56.96	57.29- 12
^ Barber	Mikele	USA	4.10.80	159/50	100	11.29	11.02- 07, 10.96w- 11
Barbosa	Vera	POR	13.1.89	168/58	400h	55.37	55.22- 12
Bardelle	Christine	FRA	16.8.74	160/48	5000	15:16.01mx, 15:27.30	15:20.84- 12
Barrachina	Gema	ESP	10.4.86	162/49	5000	15:25.88	15:44.22- 10
					10k	32:24.54	31:54.64- 10
* Barrett	Brigetta	USA	24.12.90	183/64	HJ	1.95	2.04- 13
Bartnovskaya	Natalya	RUS	7.1.89	163	PV	4.32i, 4.30	4.45- 13

Name		Nat	Born	Ht/Wt	Event	2014 Mark	Pre-2014 Best
* Bartoletta	Tianna	USA	30.8.85	168/60	100	10.92	10.85- 12
200	22.68		22.37, 22.33w- 12		LJ	7.02	6.89- 05
Barwise	Allison	USA	21.7.91		HJ	1.89	1.87- 12
Bates	Emma	USA	8.7.92		5000	15:33.42	15:59.35- 13
					10k	32:20.83	33:37.13- 13
Bauer	Katharina	GER	12.6.90	178/66	PV	4.55	4.46i, 4.45- 13
Bauschke	Melanie	GER	14.7.88	179/63	LJ	6.72	6.83- 09
Bazdyreva	Anastasiya	RUS	6.3.92		800	2:00.90	2:02.51- 13
Bazzoni	Chiara	ITA	5.7.84	172/58	400	52.19	52.06- 13
* Beard	Jessica	USA	8.1.89	168/57	200	23.08, 22.87w	22.81- 13
					400	50.81	50.56- 09
Beckles	Kierre	BAR	21.5.90	169/54	100h	12.98	13.01- 11, 12.97w- 12
Beckwith-Ludlow	Molly	USA	4.8.87	173/59	800	1:59.30	1:59.12- 11
1000	2:37.19i		-0-		1500	4:07.88	4:17.22- 11
Beesley	Meghan	GBR	15.11.89	165/63	400h	55.55	54.97- 13
* Beitia	Ruth	ESP	1.4.79	192/71	HJ	2.01	2.02- 07
Bekele	Ashete	ETH	17.4.88		Mar	2:24:59	2:27:47- 13
Bekele	Mekdes	ETH	20.1.87	180/58	3kSt	9:42.23	9:20.23- 08
Bekele	Tadelech	ETH	11.4.91	156/42	HMar	69:56+	68:38- 13
					Mar	2:23:02	
Belete	Almensch	BEL	26.7.89	166/44	10k	31:43.05	-0-
* Belete	Mimi	BRN	9.6.88	164/62	1500	4:00.08	4:00.25- 10
2000	5:38.0+		5:38.53- 13		3000	8:30.00	8:32.18- 10
2M	9:13.85		10:06.60- 07		5000	15:00.87	15:15.59- 10
Belibasáki	Maria	GRE	19.6.91	174/54	200	23.12	23.18- 13
Belleau-Béliveau	Karine	CAN	29.12.83	168/52	800	2:01.46	2:01.13- 13
Bellille	Janeil	TTO	18.6.89	172/60	400	51.83	53.43- 07
					400h	55.41	55.80- 11
Benecchi	Giorgia	ITA	9.7.89	164/55	PV	4.30i, 4.25	4.40i- 13, 4.35- 12
* Bengtsson	Angelica	SWE	8.7.93	164/51	PV	4.62i, 4.50	4.63i- 11, 4.58- 12
Benjamin	Ada	NGR	18.5.94		400	51.68	52.87- 13
Bensaad	Sarah	TUN	27.1.87	180/82	HT	65.93	64.11- 11
Berings	Eline	BEL	28.5.86	162/53	100h	12.87	12.94- 09
Berry	Gwen	USA	29.6.89	165/68	HT	72.04	73.81- 13
Bersagel	Annie	USA	30.3.83		10k	32:38.85mx	32:54.08- 11
HMar	70:10		73:16- 12		Mar	2:28:59	2:30:53- 13
* Bespalova	Mariya	RUS	21.5.86	183/85	HT	71.89	76.72- 12
Bessoltseva	Anastasiya	RUS	18.8.90		SP	17.71	16.68- 11
Bettiche	Amina	ALG	14.12.87	161/44	3kSt	9:29.20	9:40.71- 13
Bian Ka		CHN	5.1.93		SP	17.71	17.50- 13
Bicet	Nora Aida	ESP	29.10.77	178/78	JT	56.39	63.32- 04
Bielawska	Martyna	POL	15.11.90	175/58	TJ	13.65	13.97- 11
Bihari	Patricia	HUN	6.2.92		HJ	1.87	1.82- 13
* Bikulova	Lina	RUS	1.10.88	165/51	20kW	1:28:12	1:28:42- 13
* Billaud	Cindy	FRA	11.3.86	167/59	100h	12.56	12.59- 13
Bing	Portia	NZL	17.4.93	179/65	Hep	5695	5774(w)- 13, 5653- 12
Bingham	Khamica	CAN	15.6.94	163/59	100	11.32	11.46- 12
* Bingson	Amanda	USA	20.2.90	170/89	HT	75.12	75.73- 13
^ Biryukova ¶	Svetlana	RUS	1.4.91	180/72	LJ	6.98i	6.76i- 13, 6.72, 6.85w- 12
Bishop	Melissa	CAN	5.8.88	173/57	800	1:59.70	1:59.76- 13
					1000	2:38.75	
Blackburn	Lauren	USA	18.11.91	173/	100h	13.08, 12.99w	13.06- 11
Blank	Anna	RUS	12.1.90		Hep	6067	5813- 11
* Bleasdale	Holly	GBR	2.11.91	175/68	PV	4.73i	4.87i, 4.71- 12
^ Bleasdale	Julia	GBR	9.9.81	167/46	3000	8:48.90	8:46.38- 12
5000	15:11.68		15:02.00- 12		10k	31:42.02	30:55.63- 12
Bliss	Tori	USA	1.12.92	183/91	SP	17.48	17.04- 13
Bobek	Laura	USA	16.2.91		DT	56.29	52.58- 13
Boekelman	Melissa	NED	11.5.89	177/82	SP	17.86	18.17- 10
Bogdanoff	Matilda	FIN	8.10.90		100h	13.12	13.36- 12
Bokesa	Aauri Lorena	ESP	14.12.88	183/68	400	51.66	51.77- 13
Boldysz	Karolina	POL	21.4.93	167/71	JT	56.14	55.36- 12
Bolsun	Yelena	RUS	25.6.82	168/60	200	23.06	22.64- 04
Bondarenko	Kristina	RUS-J	10.8.95		PV	4.30	4.30- 13
Bonilla	Magaly	ECU	8.2.92		20kW	1:35:08	1:37:07- 13
Bonne	Daysurami	CUB	9.3.88	173/56	400	51.73	51.69A- 11, 51.81- 09, 51.2- 13
Bordignon	Laura	ITA	26.3.81	180/78	DT	56.54	59.21- 08
* Borel	Cleopatra	TTO	3.10.79	168/93	SP	19.13	19.48i- 04, 19.42- 11
Borges	Fernanda Raquel	BRA	26.7.88	165/65	DT	64.01	60.91- 11
Borman	Brittany	USA	1.7.89	180/77	JT	62.05	61.51- 12

	Name		Nat	Born	Ht/Wt	Event	2014 Mark	Pre-2014 Best
	Borowska	Agnieszka	POL	21.10.91	187/64	HJ	1.87	1.87- 13
						Hep	5711	5586- 13
^	Boslak	Vanessa	FRA	11.6.82	170/57	PV	4.55	4.70- 06
	Bottorff	Juliet	USA	21.1.91	158/44	10k	32:25.69	32:58.00- 13
	Bougard	Erica	USA	26.7.93	168/57	Hep	6118	5990w, 5976- 13
	Boumkwo	Jolien	BEL	27.8.93		HT	66.92	61.11- 12
	Bovanko	Vasylyna	UKR	11.12.94		TJ	13.71	13.61- 13
	Bowen	Lutisha	USA	9.7.90	159/52	100h	13.37, 13.10w	13.15- 13
*	Bowie	Tori	USA	27.8.90	175/61	100	10.80	11.14, 11.04w- 13
	200 22.18			23.99- 09		LJ	6.95i, 6.82	6.91- 13
*	Boyd	Alana	AUS	10.5.84	171/60	PV	4.65	4.76- 12
	Boyd	Alitta	USA	7.12.91	178/	LJ	6.56	6.33i- 12, 6.26- 09
	Bozarth	Hayli	USA	10.6.91		HT	64.79	63.29- 13
	Breen	Melissa	AUS	17.9.90	174/66	100	11.11	11.25- 13, 11.22w- 09
	Bremser	Julia	GER	27.4.82	176/78	DT	56.80	59.84- 11
	Brewer	Ciarra	USA	12.3.93	158/52	TJ	13.91	13.85- 13
	Brichacek	Emily	AUS	7.7.90		5000	15:31.49	15:30.00- 12
	Britton	Evonne	USA	10.10.91	167/55	100h	13.03	13.06- 13
^	Britton	Fionnuala	IRL	24.9.84	158/45	3000	8:50.80mx,9:01.01	8:54.37i- 13,8:55.01mx- 12
	5000 15:23.37			15:12.97- 12		10k	32:32.45	31:29.22- 12
	Brockington	Tyler	USA	6.2.94	169/55	400h	56.65	57.40- 13
	Brodovaya	Yekaterina	RUS	28.6.91		400h	56.65	58.21- 12
*	Broersen	Nadine	NED	29.4.90	171/62	HJ	1.94	1.90- 13
						Hep	6539	6345- 13
	Broniatowska	Katarzyna	POL	22.2.90	167/53	1500	4:08.79	4:10.04- 13
*	Brooks	Tia	USA	2.8.90	183/109	SP	18.83	19.22i, 18.96- 13
	Brough	Katie	GBR	27.4.82		5000	15:29.94	15:49.71- 13
	Brown	Aaliyah	USA-J	6.1.95		100	11.31, 11.20w	11.44- 12, 11.42w- 13
						200	23.12	23.72- 10
	Brown	Brittany	USA-J	18.4.95		200	22.95	23.78- 13
	Brown	Felicia	USA	27.10.93	168/57	200	23.20, 23.10w	23.19- 13
	Brown	Kamaria	USA	21.12.92		200	22.66, 22.50i, 22.63w	22.58- 13
						400	50.94i, 52.97	52.10- 13
	Brown	Marika	USA-J	18.7.95		200	23.24, 22.94w	24.41, 24.19w- 12
	Brown	Michelle	USA	24.1.92	170/57	400	51.70	52.19- 13
	Brown	Sarah	USA	15.10.86	170/52	1000	2:36.90i	0-
	1500 4:08.57			4:05.27- 13		1M	4:26.67	4:31.26i- 13, 4:31.40- 12
	Brown	Shaunagh	GBR	15.3.90	182/82	HT	66.85	66.06- 13
	Brown	Zoë	IRL	15.9.83	170/64	PV	4.45	4.30- 12
*	Brown Trafton	Stephanie	USA	1.12.79	193/102	DT	59.33	67.74- 12
	Brume	Ese	NGR-J	20.1.96		LJ	6.68	6.53- 13
	Bruni	Roberta	ITA	8.3.94	170/54	PV	4.45	4.60i, 4.40- 13
	Bryan	Lucy	GBR-J	22.5.95	162/48	PV	4.35	4.40- 13
	Bryant	Dezerea	USA	27.4.93	157/50	100	11.24, 10.96w	11.20- 13
						200	22.68	22.87, 22.54w- 13
	Büchel	Selina	SUI	26.7.91	168/55	800	2:01.42, 2:00.93i	2:01.64i, 2:01.66- 13
	Büchler	Nicole	SUI	17.12.83	162/55	PV	4.67	4.61- 13
	Buckley	Kyla	USA	22.3.91	168/86	SP	17.45	17.28- 13
	Buckley	Landria	USA	2.7.88	166/53	400h	56.92	56.15- 13
^	Buckman	Zoe	AUS	21.12.88	172/55	1500	4:04.09	4:04.82- 13
	Budiarti	Rini	INA	22.1.83		3kSt	9:49.46	10:00.58- 11
	Bugakova	Alyona	RUS-Y	24.4.97		SP	16.94	15.74- 13
	Bui Thi Thu Thao		VIE	29.4.92	160/55	LJ	6.46	6.14- 13
*	Bujin	Cristina	ROU	12.4.88	171/52	TJ	14.11	14.42- 09
*	Bulgakova	Anna	RUS	17.1.88	173/90	HT	74.16	76.17- 13
^	Bulut	Gamze	TUR	3.8.92	166/48	1500	4:07.79	4:01.18- 12
	Bunch	Dani	USA	16.5.91	178/95	SP	17.39	17.13- 13
	Burchell	Remona	JAM	15.9.91	166/52	100	11.03, 10.95w	11.34- 13
	Burghardt	Katarzyna	POL	29.6.85	168/55	20kW	1:31:48	1:29:21- 13
*	Burka	Gelete	ETH	15.2.86	158/45	Mar	2:26:03	2:30:40- 13
	Burke	Taylor	USA	4.6.93		HJ	1.87i	1.86- 11
	Burkhanova	Sofiya	UZB	1.12.89	170/60	SP	16.95	17.44- 12
	Bush	Nicole	USA	4.4.86	159/50	5000	15:31.43	15:55.41- 09
						3kSt	9:24.59	9:39.36- 13
	Bush	Taylor	USA	26.11.89	1.67/	HT	68.02	64.49- 13
	Busienei	Selah	KEN	27.12.91	170/59	1500	4:08.85A	4:13.46- 13
	Butts	Tynita	USA	10.6.90		HJ	1.91	1.90i- 13, 1.87- 12
	Butvina	Aleksandra	RUS	14.2.86	181/71	Hep	6068	6110- 12
	Buziak	Paulina	POL	16.12.86	170/52	20kW	1:29:41	1:29:44- 12
*	Caballero	Denia	CUB	13.1.90	175/73	DT	64.89	65.60- 12
	Caballero	Yanelli	MEX	29.5.93	161/43	20kW	1:32:51	1:30:58- 13

	Name		Nat	Born	Ht/Wt	Event	2014 Mark	Pre-2014 Best
	Caballero	Yolanda	COL	19.3.82	155/46	HMar	70:45	70:30- 13
*	Cabecinha	Ana	POR	29.4.84	168/52	20kW	1:27:49	1:27:46- 08
*	Cain	Mary	USA-J	3.5.96	170/50	800	2:01.67	1:59.51- 13
	1000 2:35.80i 2:47.29i- 12 1500 4:06.34 4:04.62- 13					1M	4:24.11i	4:28.25i- 13, 4:39.28- 12
	Caldwell	Kayla	USA	19.6.91	163/57	PV	4.40i, 4.35	4.40A- 13
	Calleja	Andrea	ESP	3.10.92		TJ	13.60	13.26- 13
	Calveras	Déborah	ESP	26.12.88	174/61	TJ	13.78	13.75- 13
*	Calvert	Schillonie	JAM	27.7.88	166/57	100	11.08	11.05- 11
						200	22.88	22.55- 11
	Calvin	Clémence	FRA	17.5.90	166/55	3000	8:53.1+, 8:53.20	9:09.24- 11
	2M 9:30.39 5000 15:07.58mx, 15:12.83 15:57.85- 12					10k	31:52.86	-0-
*	Campbell	Amber	USA	5.6.81	170/91	HT	73.61	73.03- 13
*	Campbell-Brown	Veronica	JAM	15.5.82	163/61	100	10.86	10.76- 11
						200	22.94, 22.30w	21.74- 08
	Cansian	Lidia Milena	BRA	8.1.92		DT	56.77	53.28- 13
	Caravelli	Marzia	ITA	23.10.81	176/64	100h	12.98	12.85- 12
	Card	Kelsey	USA	20.8.92	173/90	SP	17.77	16.98i- 12, 16.02- 13
						DT	58.94	54.43- 13
	Carson	Hannah	USA	26.1.93	160/66	JT	56.43	52.90- 07
*	Carter	Kori	USA	3.6.92	165/57	400h	53.84	53.21- 13
*	Carter	Michelle	USA	12.10.85	175/110	SP	19.84	20.24- 13
	Carvalho	Teresa	POR-J	30.1.95		LJ	6.52	6.35- 13
^	Casandra	Cristina	ROU	1.2.77	168/50	3kSt	9:51.40	9:16.85- 08
	Casanova	Gilda	CUB-J	19.12.95	167/55	400	52.28	54.08- 13
	Cassulo	Chelsea	USA	10.6.90	173/77	HT	67.67	70.07- 13
	Castells	Berta	ESP	24.1.84	174/73	HT	69.33	69.59- 12
*	Castlin	Kristi	USA	7.7.88	170/79	100h	12.58	12.56, 12.48w- 12
	Cérival	Jessica	FRA	20.1.82	185/120	SP	17.33	17.99i- 11, 17.87- 09
	Cestonaro	Ottavia	ITA-J	12.1.95	162/55	TJ	13.64	13.69- 13
	Chaboudez	Aurélie	FRA	9.5.93	173/60	400h	56.53	56.80- 13
	Chamberlain	Christie	AUS	9.6.89	179/95	DT	56.79	52.79- 13
	Chang Chunfeng		CHN	4.5.88	179/75	JT	57.12	61.61- 07
	Charnigo	Stephanie	USA	25.7.88		1500	4:09.00	4:10.91- 12
*	Chebet	Emily	KEN	18.2.86	157/45	10k	32:10.82	30:47.02- 13
						HMar	68:01	68:20- 13
	Chebet	Linet	UGA	4.11.92		10k	32:41.95	
*	Chebet	Ruth	BRN-J	17.11.96	165/49	3kSt	9:20.55	9:40.84- 13
^	Checa	Dolores	ESP	27.12.82	168/52	5000	15:20.93	14:46.30- 11
						10k	32:22.21	
	Chelimo	Rose	KEN	12.7.89		HMar	68:40	69:45- 11
*	Chemos	Milcah	KEN	24.2.86	163/48	3kSt	9:21.91	9:07.14- 12
	Chemtai Ndiema	Esther	KEN	4.6.88		HMar	69:49	70:04- 13
						Mar	2:28:41	-0-
	Chen Mudan		CHN	4.10.93		TJ	13.70	13.77i, 13.72- 12
	Chen Yang		CHN	10.7.91		DT	58.53	53.10- 12
	Chen Zhen		CHN	3.11.94		20kW	1:34:20	1:32:28- 13
	Chepchirchir	Sarah	KEN	27.7.84		HMar	69:38	68:07- 11
	Chepchirchir #	Filomena	KEN	1.12.81	165/43	HMar	68:51	68:06- 12
*	Chepkirui	Joyce	KEN	10.8.88	152/48	10k	32:09.35	31:26.10- 11
						HMar	66:19	67:03- 12
	Chepkoech	Goreti	KEN	7.3.94		HMar	69:35	72:19- 13
	Chepkoech	Josephine	KEN	.89		HMar	69:15+	68:53- 13
*	Chepkurui	Lydia	KEN	23.8.84	170/53	3000	8:55.21i	
	2M 9:45.97i					3kSt	9:24.07	9:12.55- 13
	Chepkwony	Caroline	KEN	18.4.84		HMar	68:48	68:36- 12
	Chepngetich	Roseline	KEN-Y	17.6.97		3kSt	9:40.28	
	Chepokimoi	Vicoty	KEN	.87		HMar	70:09	71:12- 12
	Cheptai	Irene	KEN	4.2.92	160/45	5000	15:17.76	14:50.99- 13
	Chepyego	Selly	KEN	3.10.85	160/42	5000	15:08.31	15:06.26- 06
	10k 31:28.07 31:22.11- 13					HMar	67:52	68:24- 13
	Chernenko	Yekaterina	RUS	9.10.86	175/61	TJ	13.40, 13.72w	14.64- 09
	Cherono	Elizeba	KEN	6.6.88		HMar	70:15	70:48- 12
*	Cherono	Gladys	KEN	12.5.83	158/46	HMar	67:29	66:48- 13
*	Cherono	Mercy	KEN	7.5.91	168/54	1500	4:08.58	4:02.31- 11
	2000 5:37.6+ 5:35.65- 0					3000	8:21.14	8:31.23- 13
	2M 9:11.49					5000	14:43.11	14:35.13- 11
*	Cherop	Sharon	KEN	16.3.84	157/45	HMar	68:51	67:08- 11
						Mar	2:23:44, 2:23:00dh	2:22:28- 13
	Cherotich	Fancy	KEN	10.8.90	173/54	3kSt	9:41.02	9:28.04- 13
	Chesang	Agnes	KEN	1.4.86		3kSt	9:46.4A	9:34.33- 13
	Chesebe	Sylivia	KEN	17.5.87	167/52	800	2:01.85	2:00.76A- 13

Name		Nat	Born	Ht/Wt	Event	2014 Mark	Pre-2014 Best
Chesire	Gladys	KEN	20.2.93		3000	8:52.63	9:13.58- 10
					5000	15:19.93	16:06.8- 13
* Cheyech	Flomena	KEN	5.7.82	168/49	HMar	68:13	67:39- 13
					Mar	2:22:44	2:24:34- 13
* Chicherova	Anna	RUS	22.7.82	180/57	HJ	2.01	2.07- 11
Chigirintseva	Olga	RUS	29.6.87		PV	4.40	4.20i- 12, 4.10- 13
* Child	Eilidh	GBR	20.2.87	172/59	400h	54.39	54.22- 13
^ Chilla	Mercedes	ESP	19.1.80	170/62	JT	58.06	64.07- 10
Chumba	Eunice	BRN	23.5.93	160/46	10k	32:27.69	
Cichocka	Angelika	POL	15.3.88	169/54	800	2:00.30	2:00.20- 11
					1500	4:07.55	4:06.50- 11
Claes	Hanne	BEL	4.8.91		400h	57.30	62.43- 08
Clark	Megan	USA	10.6.94	167/	PV	4.45	4.15- 13
Clarke	Kayelle	TTO-J	28.2.96		200	23.44, 23.10w	23.76- 13
Clayton	Rushell	JAM	18.10.92		400h	56.41	57.67- 12
Clements	Grace	GBR	2.5.84	170/64	Hep	5710	5819- 10
Clitheroe	Helen	GBR	2.1.74	167/57	5000	15:24.40	15:06.75- 11
* Coburn	Emma	USA	19.10.90	173/55	1500	4:05.29	4:06.87- 13
					3kSt	9:11.42	9:23.54- 12
Collado	Yarisley	CUB	30.4.85	178/74	DT	62.12	64.10- 09
Collatz	Alex	USA	25.5.93	171/77	DT	57.15	55.50- 13
Collins	Sarah	IRL	15.9.94		5000	15:31.03	16:19.80- 13
Comba	Rocío	ARG	14.7.87	175/78	DT	62.21	62.77- 13
Conley	Kim	USA	14.3.86	160/49	1500	4:09.48, 4:05.70i+	4:07.17- 13
1M 4:24.54i 4:27.23- 12		2000	5:41.10i		3000	8:44.11	8:47.95- 13
5000 15:08.61		15:09.57- 13			10k	31:48.71	32:00.94- 12
Conley	Sydney	USA	11.12.93	176/	LJ	6.50w	6.35- 13, 6.45Aw- 12
Cooks	Alexis	USA	11.9.93	178/89	DT	58.74	55.53- 13
* Cosby Toruga	Jessica	USA	31.5.82	173/77	HT	74.20	74.19- 12
^ Costa	Keila	BRA	6.2.83	170/62	LJ	6.63	6.88- 07
					TJ	14.13	14.58- 13, 15.10w- 07
Costa	Susana	POR	22.9.84	178/65	TJ	14.11	14.19- 12
Cotten	Jennifer	CAN	14.10.87	173/60	400h	56.86	61.00- 05
Coutinho	Geisa	BRA	1.6.80	160/53	400	51.44	51.08- 11
Coward	Jackie	USA	5.11.89	167/55	100h	12.73	12.80, 12.67w- 13
Cowley	Sarah	NZL	3.2.84	176/66	HJ	1.89	1.91- 12
Cox	Shana	GBR	22.1.85	171/57	400	52.11	50.84- 08
* Craft	Shanice	GER	15.5.93	185/89	SP	17.75	17.66i, 17.29- 13
					DT	65.88	62.92- 12
Cremer	Esther	GER	29.3.88	170/55	200	23.15	23.10- 10
					400	51.87	51.62- 13
Crofts	Helen	CAN	28.5.90	178/59	800	2:01.54	2:01.35- 13
Cuffe	Aisling	USA	12.9.93		5000	15:11.13	16:15.53- 13
Cummins	Diane	CAN	19.1.74	165/50	800	2:01.38	1:58.39- 01
Cunningham	Vashti	USA-Y	18.1.98		HJ	1.90	1.78- 13
Czaková	Mária	SVK	2.10.88	165/60	20kW	1:34:13	1:35:30- 13
D'Agostino	Abbey	USA	25.5.92	159/48	1500	4:09.77i+	4:11.94- 13
1M 4:28.31i 4:30.03i- 13		3000	8:51.91i		8:55.41i- 13	5000 15:30.93	15:11.35- 13
Daba	Tejitu	BRN	20.8.91	157/56	3000	8:52.24	8:48.37- 13
					5000	15:15.74	15:05.59- 12
* Dado	Firehiwot	ETH	9.1.84		Mar	2:28:36	2:23:15- 11
* Dahlgren	Jenny	ARG	27.8.84	180/115	HT	71.66	73.74- 10
Dahlström	Malin	SWE	26.8.89	171/60	PV	4.52i	4.50i- 11, 4.50- 12
Danekova	Silvia	BUL	7.2.83	165/50	3kSt	9:43.13	9:35.66- 13
Daniels	Paris	USA	25.1.90	163/52	200	23.03	22.73, 22/52w- 13
Daniels	Teahna	USA-Y	25.3.97		100	11.31	11.67- 13
* Daska	Mamitu	ETH	16.10.83	164/45	HMar	68:20	68:07- 09
Daunay	Christelle	FRA	5.12.74	163/43	HMar	68:48	68:34- 10
					Mar	2:25:14	2:24:22- 10
Dauwens	Axelle	BEL	1.12.90	171/62	400h	55.56	55.96- 13
Davis	Jessica	USA	31.10.92	178/	100	11.30, 11.23w	11.19- 11
					200	23.18, 22.86w	22.84- 11
Davis	Shai-Anne	CAN	4.12.93	167/60	100	11.45, 11.28w	11.33, 11.31w- 13
* Davydova	Irina	RUS	27.5.88	170/65	400h	54.60	53.77- 12
* Day	Christine	JAM	23.8.86	168/51	400	50.16	50.85- 12
* Day-Monroe	Sharon	USA	9.6.85	175/70	HJ	1.88Ai, 1.84	1.95- 08
					Hep	6470	6550- 13
De Aniceto	Marisa	FRA	11.11.86	162/57	Hep	5914	6182- 12
* Deba	Buzunesh	ETH	8.9.87	162/45	HMar	68:59	69:53dh, 69:55- 11
					Mar	2:19:59dh, 2:31:40	2:23:19- 11
Degefa	Biruktayit	ETH	29.9.90		Mar	2:26:22	2:27:34- 11

Name		Nat	Born	Ht/Wt	Event	2014 Mark	Pre-2014 Best
Degefa	Worknesh	ETH	28.10.90	159/42	HMar	68:46	67:49- 13
Deiac	Cornelia	ROU	20.3.88	171/55	LJ	6.60	6.70- 10
Del Buono	Federica	ITA	12.12.94	164/48	800	2:00.58	2:06.86- 12
					1500	4:05.32	4:19.61- 13
Delasa	Sechale	ETH	20.9.91		Mar	2:27:47	2:26:27- 12
* DeLoach	Janay	USA	12.10.85	165/59	100h	13.00	12.97- 13
					LJ	6.53Ai, 6.41	7.03, 7.15w- 12
Demidenko	Natalya	RUS	7.8.93		PV	4.30i, 4.25	4.40- 11
Demireva	Mirela	BUL	28.9.89	180/50	HJ	1.90	1.95- 12
Demise	Shure	ETH-J	21.1.96	159/45	HMar	68:53	71:03- 13
* Demus	Lashinda	USA	10.3.83	170/62	400h	55.17	52.47- 11
Demut	Katja	GER	21.12.83	176/55	TJ	14.24	14.57- 11
Deng Lina		CHN	16.3.92	165/44	TJ	13.82	13.92- 13
Dereli	Emel	TUR-J	25.2.96	167/90	SP	17.40i, 17.33	18.04- 13
Dereveva	Olga	RUS	5.4.85	158/54	3kSt	9:40.77	9:43.52- 11
Derkach	Daria	ITA	27.3.93	167/56	TJ	13.56, 13.81w	13.92- 13
Derun	Kateryna	UKR	24.9.93	168/73	JT	60.32	56.31- 11
Desalegn	Betlhem	UAE	13.11.91	164/42	1500	4:07.05	4:05.13- 13
3000 8:46.54i					3kSt	9:53.19	
Desalegn	Tsehay	ETH	28.10.91		HMar	69:04	72:40- 12
Detsuk	Kseniya	BLR	23.4.86	177/56	TJ	14.34i, 14.16, 14.27w	14.76, 14.81w- 12
Devi	Suman	IND	15.7.84		JT	56.92	56.11- 12
Devi	Sushma	IND	7.5.84	167/62	800	2:01.92	2:03.11- 13
Diago	Sahily	CUB-J	26.8.95	168/49	800	1:57.74	2:00.9- 12
					1000	2:37.5	2:42.8- 13
Diallo	Rouguy	FRA-J	5.2.95	168/52	TJ	14.20, 14.44w	13.20- 13
Diamond	Emily	GBR	11.6.91	173/59	400	51.95	52.42- 13
Diawara	Aisseta	FRA	29.6.89	169/54	100h	13.13	12.88- 12
* Dibaba	Birhane	ETH	11.9.93		Mar	2:22:30	2:23:01- 13
* Dibaba	Genzebe	ETH	8.2.91	168/52	1500	4:01.00	3:57.54- 13
1500 3:55.17i 1M 4:22.22e+ 2000 5:27.50							
3000 8:26.21, 8:16.60i 8:37.00- 13 2M 9:14.28, 9:00.48i 5000 14:28.88							14:37.56- 11
* Dibaba	Mare	ETH	20.10.89	160/42	HMar	68:56	67:13- 10
					Mar	2:21:36, 2:20:35dh	2:19:52- 12
* Dibaba	Tirunesh	ETH	1.10.85	155/44	HMar	69:17+	66:56dh- 13
					Mar	2:20:35	-0-
Ding Changqin		CHN	27.11.91	160/50	5000	15:12.51	15:42.23- 12
					10k	31:53.09	32:44.86- 11
Ding Huiqin		CHN	5.2.90		20kW	1:29:17	1:29:42- 13
* Diriba	Buze	ETH	9.2.94	160/43	3000	8:51.46	8:39.65- 12
					5000	15:16.83	14:50.02- 13
* Diro	Etenesh	ETH	10.5.91	169/47	3kSt	9:19.71	9:14.07- 12
Disanza	Sarah	USA-J	25.8.95	158/	5000	15:20.57i	-
Distel-Bonnet	Céline	FRA	25.7.87	170/60	100	11.24, 11.18w	11.31- 13, 11.30w- 11
Dixon	Alyson	GBR	24.9.78		HMar	70:38	71:21- 13
Djordjevic	Nina	SLO	15.5.88		LJ	6.58	6.40- 07
Dobija	Teresa	POL	9.10.82	175/62	LJ	6.68i, 6.54, 6.63w	6.78- 11
Doi	Yurie	JPN	8.12.88	163/47	10k	32:37.50	32:16.05- 13
Domel	Urszula	POL	21.7.88	178/55	HJ	1.90i, 1.89	1.89- 12
Dong Genmiao		CHN	16.7.94		20kW	1:31:59	1:35:03- 13
Dongmo	Auriole	CMR	3.8.90	173/75	SP	16.84	16.03- 11
Dorozhon	Marharyta	UKR	4.9.87	180/75	JT	61.34	62.01- 13
dos Reis	Jéssica Carolina	BRA	17.3.93	160/50	LJ	6.66	6.58- 12
Doseykina	Yekaterina	RUS	30.3.90		3kSt	9:35.28	9:42.10- 13
Dowie	Danielle	JAM	5.5.92	173/60	400h	56.62	54.94- 13
Drabenya	Hanna	BLR	15.8.87	153/46	20kW	1:29:39	1:31:16- 13
* Drahotová	Anezka	CZE-J	22.7.95		20kW	1:28:08	1:29:05- 13
Drouin	Jillian	CAN	30.9.86	180/66	HJ	1.87	1.89- 10
					Hep	5972	5890w, 5822- 07
Du Xiaowei		CHN	11.8.87	180/72	JT	56.76	61.89- 12
^ Duarte	Sophie	FRA	31.7.81	170/54	10k	32:36.32	-0-
Dubitskaya #	Alyona	BLR	25.1.90	182/77	SP	19.03	17.95- 09
Dubrovina	Olga	RUS	11.6.93		20kW	1:31:14	1:34:23- 13
Ducó	Natalia	CHI	31.1.89	177/95	SP	18.07	18.80- 12
Dudgeon	Emily	GBR	3.3.93	174/59	800	2:01.89	2:02.32- 12
Dudzinska	Agnieszka	POL	16.3.88	178/86	SP	16.75i	17.36- 13
Duliba	Aleksandra	BLR	9.1.88	168/54	Mar	2:24:43, 2:21:29dh	2:23:44- 13
Duncan	Dominique	USA/NGR	7.5.90	169/59	200	22.82	22.94, 22.70w- 12
* Duncan	Kimberlyn	USA	2.8.91	173/59	100	11.20	10.96, 10.94w- 12
					200	22.53, 22.10w	22.19- 12, 21.80w- 13

Name		Nat	Born	Ht/Wt	Event	2014 Mark	Pre-2014 Best
Duncan	Melissa	AUS	30.1.90	170/55	1500	4:05.76	4:13.34- 12
					1M	4:26.90	4:40.58- 07
Durant	Kamara	TTO	24.2.91		200	23.11w	23.35- 13
Durruthy	Yilian	CUB	30.1.90	177/77	Hep	5807	5966- 12
Dusanova	Nadezhda	UZB	17.11.87	174/56	HJ	1.94i, 1.94	1.96i, 1.95- 09
Dutkiewicz	Pamela	GER	28.9.91	168/58	100h	12.95	13.37- 10
Dygacz	Agnieszka	POL	18.7.85	160/51	20kW	1:28:58	1:30:56- 11
Dzindzaletaite	Dovilé	LTU	14.7.93	168/58	TJ	13.98i, 13.96, 14.26w	14.17- 12
Eades	Chelsea	USA	21.8.89	168/59	100h	13.13	12.78- 12
Eberl	Elisabeth	AUT	25.3.88	170/63	JT	57.54	60.07- 11
Ebersohn	Annerie	RSA	9.8.90	167/55	400h	56.56	55.87A, 56.03- 13
Ebihara	Yuki	JPN	28.10.85	164/68	JT	60.25	62.83- 13
Eccleston	Amanda	USA	18.6.90		1500	4:08.08	4:14.56- 13
Eckhardt	Neele	GER	2.7.92	166/49	TJ	13.67, 13.98w	13.25- 12
Efraimson	Alexa	USA-Y	20.2.97	170/	1500	4:07.05	4:16.00- 13
Ejesieme	Jesica	USA	20.5.92		400h	57.21	57.30- 12
Ekelund	Irene	SWE-Y	8.3.97	170/57	200	23.26, 22.97w	22.92- 13
Ekponé	Olivia	USA	5.1.93	172/59	100	11.11	11.37, 11.27w- 13
					200	22.23	23.15- 12, 22.91w- 13
Ektova	Irina	KAZ	8.1.87	173/61	TJ	13.92	14.48- 11
El Moukim	Rkia	MAR	22.2.88		HMar	70:03	70:38- 11
					Mar	2:28:12	
El Otmani	Sanae	MAR	20.12.86		1500	4:09.23	4:09.45- 13
Elbe	Jenny	GER	18.4.90	180/60	TJ	14.20, 14.24w	14.12- 13
Elliott	Samantha	JAM	3.2.92	164/52	100h	13.05	13.23, 13.08Aw- 13
					400h	56.63	56.38A, 56.44- 13
Ellis-Watson	Taylor	USA	6.5.93		400	51.78	55.65- 08
* Embaye	Axumawit	ETH	18.10.94	160/50	1500	4:02.35	4:05.16- 13
Emmanuel	Crystal	CAN	27.11.91	170/50	200	23.04	22.89- 13
^ England	Hannah	GBR	6.3.87	177/54	800	2:00.50	1:59.66- 12
					1500	4:05.27	4:01.89- 11
Ennaoui	Sofia	POL-J	30.8.95	152/35	1500	4:07.34	4:12.05- 13
Eriksson	Sandra	FIN	4.6.89	163/48	3000	8:55.13	9:03.28- 13
					3kSt	9:24.70	9:38.38- 13
Esayias	Yeshi	ETH	28.12.85	160/48	Mar	2:27:40dh	2:24:06- 13
Espinoza	Ahymara	VEN	28.5.85	170/80	SP	17.63	18.15- 13
Eticha	Fantu	ETH	11.9.87		Mar	2:27:31	2:28:03- 13
Eutsey	Ebony	USA	3.5.92	166/55	400	52.26	52.07- 12
Evans	Gayon	JAM	15.1.90		200	23.23, 23.08w	23.21- 11
^ Facey	Simone	JAM	7.5.85	162/53	100	11.09	10.95A, 11.11- 08, 11.0- 04
					200	22.67	22.25- 08
Farkas-Zsivoczky	Györgyi	HUN	13.2.85	170/58	Hep	6180	6269- 13
Farquharson	Rochelle	JAM	16.1.93		LJ	6.48	6.48- 11
Fazlitdinova	Gulshat	RUS	28.8.92	165/48	5000	15:32.07	15:43.58- 12
Fedotova	Yekaterina	RUS	3.7.92		HJ	1.90	1.90- 11
Fédronic	Justine	FRA	11.5.91	168/54	800	2:00.41	2:00.97- 13
Feitor	Susana	POR	28.1.75	160/52	20kW	1:28:51	1:27:55- 01
* Felix	Allyson	USA	18.11.85	168/57	100	11.01	10.89- 12
200	22.02		21.69- 12		400	50.81	49.59- 11
Félix	Alysbeth	PUR	7.3.93		Hep	5721A	5065A- 13
Félix	Dulce	POR	23.10.82	165/53	5000	15:21.32	15:08.02- 09
10k	32:35.90		31:30.90- 09		Mar	2:26:46	2:25:40- 11
Felnagle	Brie	USA	9.12.86	170/57	1500	4:07.42	4:05.64- 13
					1M	4:29.83	4:30.44, 4:28.90irr- 13
Felzmann	Anna	GER	18.1.92	166/49	PV	4.30i, 4.30	4.30- 13
Feng Bin		CHN	3.4.94		DT	59.73	58.14- 13
Fente	Birtukan	ETH	18.6.89	167/52	3kSt	9:30.75	9:28.27- 11
Ferguson	Sheniqua	BAH	24.11.89	170/57	100	11.31	11.07- 12
					200	22.97	22.64- 12
^ Fernández	Nuria	ESP	16.8.76	170/57	1500	4:04.67	4:00.20- 10
3000	8:51.54		8:38.05- 10		5000	15:31.02	17:02.78- 12
Ferrer e Silva	Laila	BRA	30.7.82	180/80	JT	60.33	60.21- 12
Fertig	Fruzsina	HUN	2.9.93	175/80	HT	66.65	67.02- 13
Feyne	Gemeda	ETH	28.6.92	159/50	1500	4:07.77	4:06.66- 12
2000	5:39.96				3000	8:57.52	9:07.53- 11
Feysa	Mame	ETH	.89		HMar	70:08	72:49- 13
Fiack	Marion	FRA	13.10.92	170/60	PV	4.61i, 4.55	4.42i- 12, 4.35- 13
Fields	Ashley	USA	13.4.93	175/59	200	22.97, 22.63w	23.22, 22.98w- 13
Finn	Erin	USA	19.11.94		5000	15:26.08	16:17.89- 13
					10k	32:41.65	

Name		Nat	Born	Ht/Wt	Event	2014 Mark	Pre-2014 Best
* Fiodorow	Joanna	POL	4.3.89	169/89	HT	74.39	74.18- 12
* Firova	Tatyana	RUS	10.10.82	174/59	400	52.08	49.72- 12
Firsick	Bethany	USA	4.12.91		PV	4.40Ai	4.46- 13
* Fischer	Julia	GER	1.4.90	192/95	DT	66.46	66.04- 13
* Flanagan	Shalane	USA	8.7.81	165/50	HMar	69:45	68:31- 13
					Mar	2:21:14	2:25:38- 12
Fleming	Annett	GER	4.5.84	178/66	Hep	5918	5851- 12
Flink	Sofi	SWE-J	8.7.95	168/71	JT	58.44	61.96- 13
Flores	Brenda	MEX	4.9.91	160/51	5000	15:30.87	15:53.91- 13
Florez	Lina	COL	1.11.84	165/55	100h	12.97A, 13.18	12.94- 11
Fontanive	Petra	SUI	10.10.88	170/60	400h	56.21	57.61- 13
Ford	Yurisleydi	CUB	18.8.91	168/69	HT	70.46	68.64- 13
Foster	Kara	USA	20.2.90	157/46	10k	32:37.19	32:57.33- 12
* Fougberg	Charlotta	SWE	19.6.85	165/51	3kSt	9:23.96	9:39.00- 13
Francis	Eden	GBR	19.10.88	178/85	SP	17.07	17.24- 12
					DT	56.29	59.78- 11
Francis	Kim	USA	6.1.92	170/50	100h	13.02	13.15, 12.95w- 13
* Francis	Phyllis	USA	4.5.92	178/61	200	22.92, 22.82w	22.77- 13
					400	50.59, 50.46Ai	50.86- 13
Franek	Bridget	USA	8.11.87	160/50	3kSt	9:39.56	9:29.53- 12
Franklin	Alexis	USA	9.10.93		400h	56.55	57.46- 13
Franklin	Autumne	USA	20.7.94	162/54	400h	56.65	57.10- 13
* Fraser-Pryce	Shelly-Ann	JAM	27.12.86	160/52	100	11.01	10.70- 12
					200	22.53	22.09- 12
Freier	Desiree	USA-J	24.7.96	152/	PV	4.45	4.19- 13
Frere	Danielle	USA	27.4.90		SP	16.70i, 16.25	16.88i, 16.76- 13
Frerichs	Courtney	USA	18.1.93	167/52	3kSt	9:43.07	9:55.02- 13
* Frizell	Sultana	CAN	24.10.84	183/110	HT	75.73	75.04- 12
^ Fuchise	Masumi	JPN	2.9.86	161/51	20kW	1:32:31	1:28:03- 09
^ Fukushi	Kayoko	JPN	25.3.82	160/45	HMar	70:04+	67:26- 06
					Mar	2:26:25	2:24:21- 13
Fukushima	Chisato	JPN	27.6.88	166/50	100	11.30	11.21- 10, 11.16w- 11
Fuller-Stewart	Elexis	USA	11.10.93		100h	13.12	13.77- 13
Funderburk	Kala	USA	14.9.92		400	51.87	52.59- 13
Funk	Brittany	USA	13.5.92	172/86	HT	66.33	66.08- 13
Furlan	Jessica	CAN	15.3.90	165/54	3kSt	9:33.45	9:51.23- 13
Furlani	Erika	ITA-J	2.1.96	175/53	HJ	1.87	1.82- 13
* Fyodorova	Alina	UKR	31.7.89	174/63	HJ	1.87	1.90- 13
					Hep	6090	6126- 12
Fyodorova	Valeriya	RUS-J	9.4.96		TJ	13.69, 13.96w	
^ Gadschiew	Kristina	GER	3.7.84	170/62	PV	4.61i, 4.50	4.66i- 11, 4.61- 13
Gaines	Jessie	USA	12.8.90	164/52	LJ	6.55	6.50Ai- 13, 6.48- 12
Gaither	Tynia	BAH	16.3.93	158/50	100	11.41, 11.23w	11.41- 11
					200	22.88, 22.80w	23.17- 11
Galais	Jennifer	FRA	7.3.92	169/69	200	23.06	23.22- 12
Gáliková	Mária	SVK	21.8.80	161/55	20kW	1:32:03	1:33:03- 09
Galimova	Valentina	RUS	11.5.86		10k	32:14.82	32:07.82- 12
Galitskaya	Yekaterina	RUS	24.2.87	174/63	100h	12.88	12.78- 12
Gallagher	Kerri	USA	31.5.89	169/52	1500	4:09.99	4:09.64- 13
Gallardo	Karen	CHI	6.3.84	175/95	DT	59.89	60.48- 11
Galvis	Sandra	COL	28.6.86	165/60	20kW	1:31:15, 1:34:04.4t	1:33:24- 12
Gambetta	Sara	GER	18.2.93	183/70	SP	16.83	16.36- 13
Gandulla	Arialis	CUB-J	22.6.95	170/65	100	11.0	11.48A, 11.32Aw, 11.1- 13
					200	23.19, 23.14w	23.27A, 23.32- 13
Gao Yang		CHN	1.3.93		SP	17.52	17.76- 13
Garcia	Stephanie	USA	3.5.88	168/52	3kSt	9:24.28	9:41.12- 11
García	Kimberley	PER	19.10.93	167/64	20kW	1:29:44	1:33:57- 13
García-Cano	Laura	ESP-J	16.4.95		20kW	1:34:50	
* Gardner	English	USA	22.4.92	162/50	100	11.01	10.85- 13
					200	22.81	22.62- 13
Gashaw	Tigist	ETH-J	25.12.96	172/54	1500	4:08.62	4:10.37- 13
Gause	Destinee	USA	4.4.94		200	23.22Ai, 23.29	
					400	52.36	56.50- 08
* Gay	Mabel	CUB	5.5.83	178/67	TJ	14.53A, 14.42	14.67- 11
Gayen	Margaret	AUS	10.7.94	172/65	LJ	6.62	6.28- 12
Gayot	Marie	FRA	18.12.89	171/58	200	23.05	23.42- 13
					400	51.80	51.54- 13
Gebreslase	Gotytom	ETH-J	15.1.95		3000	8:57.23	8:56.36- 11
Gebreslasea	Letebrhan	ETH	29.10.90		HMar	69:45	71:37- 13
Gega	Luiza	ALB	5.11.88	166/56	800	2:01.31	2:01.96- 13
1500	4:03.12		4:05.11- 13		2000	5:43.8+	

Name		Nat	Born	Ht/Wt	Event	2014 Mark	Pre-2014 Best
* Gelana	Tiki	ETH	22.10.87	165/48	HMar	68:45dh	67:48dh- 12
					Mar	2:26:58	2:18:58- 12
Gelibert	Jessica	HAI	8.11.94	173/57	400h	56.87	57.29- 13
Geng Shuang		CHN	9.7.93		SP	16.60	16.67- 13
George	Patience	NGR	25.11.91	176/61	400	51.29	51.87- 13
George	Phylicia	CAN	16.11.87	178/65	100h	13.08	12.65- 12
George	Regina	NGR	17.2.91	168/53	400	51.30	50.84- 13
Gergel	Melissa	USA	24.4.89	170/62	PV	4.30, 4.40dh?	4.50- 13
Gergelics	Cintia	HUN	16.11.91		HT	64.79	64.83- 12
Geubelle	Andrea	USA	21.6.91	165/57	LJ	6.61Ai, 6.50	6.69i, 6.53- 13
					TJ	13.69	14.18i, 13.85- 13, 14.17w- 12
Gezahegne	Kalkidan	BRN	8.5.91	163/44	3000	8:42.54	8:38.61- 09
Ghafoor	Madiea	NED	9.9.92	169/52	400	52.36	52.46- 13
* Ghribi	Habiba	TUN	9.4.84	170/57	1500	4:06.38	4:12.37- 09
					3kSt	9:15.23	9:08.37- 12
Gierisch	Kristin	GER	20.8.90	177/57	TJ	14.31, 14.34w	14.19i- 12, 14.02- 09
* Giorgi	Eleonora	ITA	14.9.89	163/52	20kW	1:27:05	1:29:48- 12
Gipson	Whitney	USA	20.9.90	168/57	LJ	6.53, 6.57w	6.97- 12
Gisaw	Melkam	ETH	17.9.90		Mar	2:28:14	2:26:24- 13
* Glanc	Zaneta	POL	11.3.83	186/93	DT	60.95	65.34- 12
Gleadle	Liz	CAN	5.12.88	183/95	JT	64.50	61.15- 12
Gobena	Amane	ETH	1.9.82	163/48	Mar	2:27:05	2:23:50- 13
Godfay	Afera	ETH	25.9.91		HMar	69:52	73:19- 13
Gogoladze	Maiko	GEO	9.9.91	166/58	LJ	6.56	6.67- 12
Golba	Katarzyna	POL	21.12.89	160/52	20kW	1:34:26	1:32:37- 13
Gollshewsky	Taryn	AUS	18.5.93	184/80	DT	58.24	54.79- 13
Golubchikova	Yuliya	RUS	27.3.83	175/57	PV	4.55	4.75- 08
Gómez	Abigail	MEX	30.6.91	164/69	JT	57.28A	56.89A- 12
Gonçalves	Rafaela	BRA	27.11.91	168/70	JT	56.60	55.60- 10
* Gong Lijiao		CHN	24.1.89	174/110	SP	19.65	20.35- 09
Gonska	Nadine	GER	23.1.90		200	23.27, 23.09w	23.77- 13
González	María Guadalupe	MEX	9.1.89		20kW	1:28:48	1:37:02- 13
González	Raquel	ESP	16.11.89	176/55	20kW	1:28:36	1:30:11- 13
Goodman	Antoinette	USA	29.7.90		200	23.31, 22.83w	23.74- 11
Goor	Myrte	NED	3.4.89	179/68	Hep	5776	5772- 13
Gorchakova	Natalya	RUS	17.4.83	167/55	3kSt	9:42.38	9:35.55- 12
* Gordeyeva	Irina	RUS	9.10.86	185/55	HJ	1.95	2.04- 12
Gordon	Chris-Ann	JAM	18.9.94	164/52	400	51.39	51.62- 11
Gorecka	Emelia	GBR	29.1.94	172/52	5000	15:07.45	15:34.21- 12
Gorodskaya	Hanna	BLR	31.1.93		HJ	1.88	1.75- 12
Goule	Natoya	JAM	30.3.91	160/50	800	2:00.28	1:59.93- 13
* Grabuste	Aiga	LAT	24.3.88	178/67	LJ	6.69, 6.75w	6.65- 11
Grace	Kate	USA	24.10.88	171/55	800	2:01.22	1:59.47- 13
					1500	4:07.35	4:07.40- 13
Graves	Carmen	USA	27.1.91	165/	3kSt	9:47.28	
* Green (Tregaro)	Emma	SWE	8.12.84	180/62	HJ	1.97i, 1.93	2.01- 10
* Grenot	Libania	ITA	12.7.83	175/61	400	50.55	50.30- 09
Griva	Gundega	LAT	8.4.91	168/62	JT	55.95	57.32A- 13
Griva	Lauma	LAT	27.10.84	180/64	LJ	6.53	6.86- 11
Groenewoud	Chantelle	CAN	3.3.89	172/57	3kSt	9:45.42	9:51.17- 13
Grove	Emily	USA	22.5.93	168/61	PV	4.51Ai	4.32- 12
Grünberg	Kira	AUT	13.8.93	169/56	PV	4.45	4.22- 13
Grunewald	Gabe	USA	25.6.86	168/55	800	2:02.01	2:01.38- 13
1500 4:05.22 4:01.48- 13 3000 8:52.39 8:42.64- 13 5000 15:33.64 15:45.99- 11							
* Gu Siyu		CHN	11.2.93	182/80	DT	60.78	67.86- 13
Guba	Paulina	POL	14.5.91	184/90	SP	16.78i, 16.70	17.79i, 17.47- 12
Gubina	Yekaterina	RUS	27.11.85		100h	12.93	13.26- 12
Gudeta	Netsanet	ETH	12.2.91		HMar	68:46	
Guéhaseim	Jessika	FRA	23.8.89	175/79	HT	69.23	70.44- 12
Guei	Floria	FRA	2.5.90	166/53	400	51.30	51.42- 13
Guevara	Cristina	MEX	11.12.87	158/53	800	2:01.68A	2:04.27- 12
Guion-Firmin	Lénora	FRA	7.8.91	174/66	200	23.30, 23.03w	22.91- 13
					400	51.9	51.68- 13
Gulli	Jessica	AUS	19.3.88	157/50	400h	57.30	57.68- 13
Gumenyuk	Irina	RUS	6.1.88	176/59	TJ	14.46	14.58- 13
Guo Tianqian		CHN-J	1.6.95	180/110	SP	18.08	17.57- 13
Gutermuth	Sophie	USA	2.11.92		PV	4.30	4.10- 13
Gyurátz	Réka	HUN-J	31.5.96	175/70	HT	67.32	65.01- 13
Haapanen	Amy	USA	23.3.84	172/79	HT	67.46	70.63- 12
Haas	Eleriin	EST	4.7.92	180/60	HJ	1.94	1.92- 12

Name		Nat	Born	Ht/Wt	Event	2014 Mark	Pre-2014 Best
Haase	Rebekka	GER	2.1.93	170/57	100	11.32, 11.21w	11.55. 11.48w- 13
					200	23.01	23.80- 13
Hae-an	Suh	KOR	1.7.85	177/77	JT	56.02	57.61- 10
Haftu	Goitetom	ETH	.87		Mar	2:27:44	2:26:21- 11
Hagiwara	Ayumi	JPN	1.6.92	155/41	5000	15:24.56	15:49.19- 13
10k	31:41.80		31:45.29- 13		HMar	70:17	
Hahner	Anna	GER	20.11.89	164/47	Mar	2:26:44	2:27:55- 13
Hailey	Nnenya	USA	23.2.94	165/	400h	56.99	57.93- 11
^ Hailu	Meseret	ETH	12.9.90	170/54	Mar	2:26:20	2:21:09- 12
Hakeai	Siositina	NZL	1.3.94	182/105	DT	59.65	57.91- 13
Hall	Dior	USA-J	2.1.96	168/	100h	12.92	13.18A- 11
Hall	Marielle	USA	28.1.92		3000	8:54.48	9:40.23- 10
					5000	15:12.79	16:22.83- 12
Hall	Patricia	JAM	16.10.82	165/58	200	23.11i, 23.45	22.51- 13
					400	51.55	50.71- 12
Hall	Sara	USA	15.4.83	163/48	3kSt	9:42.10	9:39.48- 11
Hamblin	Nikki	NZL	20.5.88	165/52	1500	4:05.08	4:04.82- 11
					3000	8:51.48	9:18.41- 11
* Hamera-Shmyrko	Tetyana	UKR	1.6.83	165/52	Mar	2:24:37	2:23:58- 13
Hamilton	Kim	USA	28.11.85		JT	57.59	58.04- 12
Hardy	Carrol	USA-J			200	23.02w	
Hargrove	Monica	USA	30.12.82	173/58	400	52.25	50.39- 09
Haroye	Alemitu	ETH-J	9.5.95	160/44	3000	8:36.87	8:50.40- 13
2M	9:20.81				5000	14:52.67	15:05.08- 13
* Harper Nelson	Dawn	USA	13.5.84	168/61	100h	12.44	12.37- 12, 12.36w- 09
Harrell	Brittany	USA	.91	173	Hep	5835	5838- 12
Harrer	Corinna	GER	19.1.91	167/55	1500	4:10.09	4:04.30- 12
					10k	32:27.75	32:30.41- 13
^ Harrigan-Scott	Tahesia	IVB	15.2.82	158/56	100	11.29, 11.17w	11.13,11.02w- 06,10.89wdq- 11
Harrison	Kendra	USA	18.9.92	163/52	100h	12.71, 12.68w	12.88, 12.87w- 13
					400h	54.76	55.75- 13
* Harrison	Queen	USA	10.9.88	168/60	100h	12.46	12.43- 13
Harun	Makda	ETH	.88		Mar	2:27:37	2:26:46- 12
Hasay	Jordan	USA	21.9.91	163/45	1500	4:07.70	4:10.28- 11
1M	4:28.37i	4:33.01i- 11, 4:42.01- 06			3000	8:54.30i+	8:46.89- 13
2M	9:35.05	10:07.65- 07	5000	15:28.56	15:37.29- 11	10k 31:39.67	31:46.42mx- 13
* Hassan	Sifan	NED	.93	166/52	800	1:59.95	2:00.86- 13
1500	3:57.00		4:03.73- 13		3000	8:29.38	8:32.53- 13
Hasslen	Alyssa	USA	13.5.91	180/91	SP	17.17i, 17.16	18.35- 12
Hastings	Amy	USA	21.1.84	163/46	5000	15:25.94	15:09.59- 13
10k	32:18.81		31:10.69- 12		Mar	2:27:03	2:27:03- 11
* Hastings	Natasha	USA	23.7.86	173/63	100	11.08	11.24- 13
200	23.06, 22.55w		22.61- 07		400	50.53	49.84- 07
Hatsko-Fedusova	Hanna	UKR	3.10.90	175/70	JT	67.29	61.46- 12
Hawi	Alemitu	ETH-J	14.11.96		5000	15:10.46	
Hawthorne	Trisha-Ann	JAM	8.11.89	165/57	100	11.23	11.22- 12
Hayakawa	Eri	JPN	15.11.81	153/42	10k	32:40.89	33:13.35- 13
					Mar	2:25:31	2:26:17- 13
Haydar	Sultan	TUR	23.5.87	170/55	Mar	2:27:54	2:25:09- 12
Hayes	Chelsea	USA	9.2.88	168/55	100	11.32, 11.20w	11.15, 11.09w- 12
200	22.93w		23.22, 23.10w- 12		LJ	6.56Ai, 6,48, 6.88w	7.10- 12
Hayes	Jernail	USA	8.7.88	163/55	400h	55.60	55.89- 13
Hayes	Quanera	USA	7.3.92		400	51.91	51.54A- 13
He Qin		CHN	23.3.92		20kW	1:34:59	1:27:42- 13
He Yinli		CHN	20.9.88		Mar	2:28:56	2:28:31- 12
Hechavarría	Zurián	CUB-J	10.8.95	164/58	400h	56.54A	58.37- 11
* Heidler	Betty	GER	14.10.83	175/80	HT	78.00	79.42- 11
Heiner	Madeline	AUS	5.3.88		5000	15:27.75	
10000	32:44.71		-0-		3kSt	9:34.01	9:56.54- 06
* Hejnová	Zuzana	CZE	19.12.86	170/54	400h	55.86	52.83- 13
Heltne ¶	Anca	ROU	1.1.78	175/80	SP	18.88 dq	19.90i- 10, 19.08- 09
Henderson	Nia	USA	21.10.86		SP	17.01	17.38- 13
* Henriques	Inês	POR	1.5.80	156/48	20kW	1:29:33	1:29:30- 13
Henry	Britney	USA	17.10.84	178/84	HT	69.70	71.27- 10
Henry	Chloë	BEL	5.3.87	170/58	PV	4.41	4.33- 13
Henry	Desiree	GBR-J	26.8.95		100	11.21, 11.04w	11.50, 11.43w- 13
Henry-Robinson	Samantha	JAM	25.9.88	160/52	100	11.00	11.11, 10.94w- 12
					200	22.85	22.77, 22.50w- 12
Hepburn-Bailey	Yvana	USA	9.11.87		100h	13.07, 12.94w	13.10- 12
Herashchenko	Iryna	UKR-J	10.3.95	181/60	HJ	1.95i, 1.92	1.92i, 1.91- 13
Hering	Christina	GER	9.10.94	185/62	800	2:01.25	2:03.11- 13

Name		Nat	Born	Ht/Wt	Event	2014 Mark	Pre-2014 Best
Hernández	Ingrid	COL	29.11.88	169/61	20kW	1:31:02	1:33:34- 12
Herrera	Irisdaymi	CUB	18.4.92	167/62	LJ	6.56	6.41- 10
Herrera	Mayra Carolina	GUA	20.12.88	158/55	20kW	1:30:41	1:30:59- 13
Herrs	Elizabeth	USA	20.12.93	176/	JT	57.73	52.97- 13
Hetherington	Kelly	AUS	10.3.89	168/54	800	2:01.53	2:01.22- 13
Heymsfield	Grace	USA	24.3.92	171/52	3kSt	9:48.10	9:57.18- 13
Higginson	Ashley	USA	17.3.89	167/62	3000	8:56.67	8:59.24- 12
					3kSt	9:27.59	9:34.49- 12
Hilali	Siham	MAR	2.5.86	161/58	1500	4:05.46	4:01.33- 11
Hildebrand	Nadine	GER	20.9.87	158/51	100h	12.71	12.85- 13
Hill	Candace	USA-Y	11.2.99		200	23.12	23.85- 13
Hill	MacKenzie	USA	5.1.86	166/54	400h	56.25	56.73- 11
Hillman	Christina	USA	6.10.93	178/84	SP	18.15i, 17.73	17.69i, 17.40- 13
^ Hingst	Carolin	GER	18.9.80	174/60	PV	4.50	4.72- 10
Hinriksdóttir	Anita	ISL-J	13.1.96	161/50	800	2:01.23	2:00.49- 13
Hinton	Denise	USA	17.12.91	173/	HT	66.46	61.58- 13
Hirai	Megumi	JPN	14.2.90	156/42	10k	32:39.76	32:39.41- 12
Hirvonen	Katri	FIN	25.6.90	176/89	DT	57.44	55.83- 13
Hitchon	Sophie	GBR	11.7.91	167/74	HT	71.53	72.97- 13
Hixson	Kristen	USA	1.7.92		PV	4.50	4.25- 13
Hjálmsdóttir	Asdis	ISL	28.10.85	175/65	JT	60.03	62.77- 12
Hodde	Rosina	NED	10.2.83	171/59	100h	12.89	13.00, 12.93w- 13
Hofmann	Franziska	GER	27.3.94	175/69	100h	12.87	13.20- 12
Holliday	Becky	USA	12.3.80	160/52	PV	4.58i, 4.45	4.60- 10, 4.61dh- 11
Holliday	Tanya	AUS	21.9.88		20kW	1:32:36	1:31:28- 12
Holm	Caroline Bonde	DEN	19.7.90	178/68	PV	4.43i, 4.35	4.42i, 4.36- 12
Holodna	Olga	UKR	14.11.91		SP	18.54	18.72- 13
Holosha	Olena	UKR	26.1.82	182/56	HJ	1.89i, 1.87	1.96- 12
Holt	Sarah	GBR	17.4.87	185/80	HT	65.67	68.50- 12
Holub	Malgorzata	POL	30.10.92	168/56	400	51.84	52.28- 13
Horie	Misato	JPN	10.3.87	168/49	10k	32:40.82	32:44.00- 11
					Mar	2:27:57	2:30:52- 13
Horn	Carina	RSA	9.3.89	169/56	100	11.17, 11.16w	11.50- 13, 11.46Aw- 11
Hou Yongbo		CHN	15.9.94		20kW	1:30:27	1:33:25- 13
Houlihan	Shelby	USA	8.2.93	160/	800	2:01.12	2:02.63- 13
Howard	Marisa	USA	9.8.92		3kSt	9:43.82	
Howard	Sarah	USA	11.10.93		SP	16.98i, 16.49	16.17- 13
* Hrasnová	Martina	SVK	21.3.83	177/88	HT	75.27	76.90- 09
Hrubá	Michaela	CZE-Y	21.2.98		HJ	1.91	1.83- 13
Hu Guanlian		CHN	18.7.90		TJ	13.72	13.83- 13
* Huddle	Molly	USA	31.8.84	163/48	1500	4:08.62+	4:08.09- 13
					1M	4:26.84	4:46.70- 07
					3000	8:48.7+	8:42.99- 13
					5000	14:42.64	14:44.76- 10
					10k	30:47.59	31:27.12- 08
					HMar	69:04	-0-
Hunsucker	Emily	USA	20.4.91	168/	HT	64.91	63.35- 13
Hunter	Rachel	GBR	30.8.93	176/100	HT	66.30	60.91- 13
Hurtis	Muriel	FRA	25.3.79	180/68	400	52.17	51.41- 10
Hussong	Christin	GER	17.4.94	187/82	JT	63.34	59.74- 11
* Hutson	Kylie	USA	27.11.87	165/57	PV	4.68i, 4.55	4.75Ai, 4.70- 13
Hyacinthe	Kimberly	CAN	28.3.89	179/62	200	23.03	22.78- 13
* Ibargüen	Caterine	COL	12.2.84	181/65	TJ	15.31	14.99A- 11, 14.85- 12, 14.93w 13
Idlette	Lavonne	DOM	31.10.85	167/54	100h	12.81	12.77- 13
Ifantídou	Sofía	GRE	5.1.85	164/53	Hep	5806	6109- 12
Ihara	Miho	JPN	4.2.88	154/40	10k	32:15.42	32:16.46- 13
* Ikauniece-Admidina	Laura	LAT	31.5.92	179/60	Hep	6320	6414- 12
Ikuesan	Ayodelé	FRA	15.5.85	176/60	100	11.22, 11.16w	11.34- 11
Iliyeva	Irina	RUS-J	22.12.95	180/58	HJ	1.90	1.89i, 1.88- 13
^ Iljustsenko	Anna	EST	12.10.85	168/49	HJ	1.92i	1.96- 11
Ilyina	Irina	RUS	25.5.85		LJ	6.49	6.51- 13
Ince	Ariana	USA	14.3.89	180/75	JT	57.90	56.66- 13
Incerti	Anna	ITA	19.1.80	168/45	HMar	70:10	68:18- 12
					Mar	2:28:58	2:25:32- 11
Inglese	Veronica	ITA	22.11.90	161/45	10k	32:25.76	33:31.20- 12
Inoue	Rei	JPN	23.7.91	155/41	20kW	1:31:48	1:32:43- 12
Insaeng	Subenrat	THA	10.2.94	180/85	DT	56.85	56.77- 13
Irozuru	Abigail	GBR	3.1.90	170/61	LJ	6.41, 6.64w	6.80- 12
Ito	Mai	JPN	23.5.84	156/41	10k	32:43.90	32:07.41- 13
					Mar	2:28:36	2:25:26- 12
Itoya	Juliet	ESP	17.8.86	174/63	LJ	6.64	6.48- 12
Ivanova	Viktoriya	RUS	21.11.91		3kSt	9:40.78	10:15.46- 12
Iwade	Reia	JPN	8.12.94	154/42	10k	32:24.38	33:46.12- 13
					HMar	70:45	69:45- 13
					Mar	2:27:21	

	Name		Nat	Born	Ht/Wt	Event	2014 Mark	Pre-2014 Best
	Jackson	Annie	USA	11.3.90		SP	16.76	16.76- 13
	Jackson	Janice	JAM	30.10.91	173/55	100h	12.98	13.06, 12.99w- 13
	Jackson	Natasha	CAN	10.6.89		Hep	5928	5593- 11
	Jackson	Shericka	JAM	15.7.94	174/59	400	51.32	51.60- 13
	Jackson	Susan	USA	26.7.89		HJ	1.91	1.85A- 13
	Jagaciak	Anna	POL	10.2.90	177/59	LJ	6.59	6.74- 10
						TJ	14.20	14.25- 11
	Jaisha	Orchatteri P.	IND	23.5.83	156/48	1500	4:09.14	4:11.83- 06
						5000	15:18.30	15:41.91- 06
	Jakimowicz	Urszula	POL	11.6.88	172/62	JT	55.89	55.18- 12
	Jakubaityte	Indre	LTU	24.1.76	177/70	JT	57.31	63.65- 07
*	Jamal	Maryam	BRN	16.9.84	170/54	1500	4:04.10	3:56.18- 06
	3000	8:47.74, 8:43.16i		8:28.87- 05		2M	9:33.47	-0-
						5000	14:59.69	14:51.68- 05
	Jamerson	Megan	USA	4.5.86	175/59	PV	4.40	4.41- 13
*	Jarder	Erica	SWE	2.4.86	173/59	LJ	6.68, 6.84w	6.71i, 6.66- 13
	Jarzynska	Karolina	POL	6.9.81	165/54	5000	15:31.97	15:25.52- 13
	10k	32:03.57		31:43.51- 13		Mar	2:26:31	2:26:45- 13
	Jefferson	Kyra	USA	23.9.94		200	22.78	23.53- 11
	Jeffs	Izzy	GBR	3.2.92	178/74	JT	58.63	56.31- 13
*	Jelaca	Tatjana	SRB	10.8.90	178/76	JT	64.21	62.68- 13
*	Jelagat	Irene	KEN	10.12.88	162/45	1500	4:04.07	4:02.59- 11
	3000	8:28.51		2M	9:12.90	5000	15:01.73	16:08.2A- 13
*	Jelagat Sumgong	Jemima	KEN	21.12.84	158/45	HMar	68:32	68:35- 12
					158/45	Mar	2:25:10, 2:20:41dh	2:20:48- 13
	Jelizarova	Polina	LAT	1.5.89	155/47	3kSt	9:52.58	9:27.21- 12
	Jelmini	Anna	USA	15.7.90	176/86	SP	16.92i, 15.98	17.63- 10
						DT	56.27	60.80- 10
	Jemai	Sara	ITA	12.4.92	178/65	JT	56.55	55.35- 13
	Jeon Yeong-eun		KOR	24.5.88	157/43	20kW	1:33:18	1:33:59- 12
	Jepchirchir	Peris	KEN	.93		HMar	69:12	
	Jepkemei	Daisy	KEN-J	13.2.96		3kSt	9:47.65	9:47.22- 12
*	Jepkemoi	Hyvin	KEN	13.1.92	156/45	3kSt	9:22.58	9:22.05- 13
	Jepkesho	Visiline	KEN	.88		Mar	2:26:47	
	Jepkirui	Eunice	BRN	20.5.84	158/45	HMar	68:31	68:39- 12
						Mar	2:25:37	2:21:41- 12
	Jepkoech	Monica	KEN	.85		HMar	69:44	69:12- 12
	Jepkorir	Winnie	KEN	.90		Mar	2:27:57	
*	Jepkosgei	Janeth	KEN	13.12.83	167/47	800	1:58.70	1:56.04- 07
	Jepkurgat	Helen	KEN	21.2.89		HMar	70:42	71:16- 12
*	Jeptoo	Priscah	KEN	26.6.84	165/49	HMar	67:02	65:45dh- 13
*	Jeptoo ¶	Rita	KEN	15.2.81	165.48	Mar	2:18:57dh, 2:24:35 dq	2:19:57- 13
						HMar	68:49	66:27- 13
	Jerez	Caridad	ESP	23.1.91	170/57	100h	13.09	13.18- 13
*	Jeter	Carmelita	USA	24.11.79	163/63	100	11.24	10.64- 09
	Ji Yefang		CHN-J	4.3.96		20kW	1:31:06	1:33:00- 13
	Jia Chaofeng		CHN	16.11.88	164/47	10k	32:21.74	31:45.67- 09
	Jiang Fengjing		CHN	28.8.87	180/75	DT	58.25	62.56- 11
	Jiang Yanfei		CHN	5.7.92	172/54	LJ	6.57	6.45i, 6.36- 13
*	Jimoh	Funmi	USA	29.5.84	173/64	LJ	6.81	6.96- 09
	Johannes	Helaria	NAM	13.8.80	165/48	Mar	2:28:27	2:26:09- 12
	Johnson	Felisha	USA	24.7.89	185/105	SP	19.18	18.27- 13
	Johnson	Kellyn	USA	22.7.86	163/50	5000	15:21.93	15:31.66- 12
	Johnson	Rachel	USA	30.4.93	165/	3kSt	9:41.56	10:29.08- 13
	Johnson	Tristie	USA	20.11.93	163/	100	11.29	11.58- 13
*	Johnson-Thompson	Katarina	GBR	9.1.93	183/70	100	11.30w	12.00- 12
	200	22.89		23.37- 13		HJ	1.96i, 1.90	1.89- 12
	LJ	6.92		6.56- 13, 6.81w- 12		Hep	6682	6449- 13
	Johny	Mayookha	IND	9.4.88	171/55	LJ	6.56	6.64- 10
						TJ	13.72	14.11- 11
	Jones	Akela	BAR-J	31.12.95	184/	HJ	1.87i, 1.85	1.86i- 13, 1.85- 10
						LJ	6.55	6.36- 12
	Jones	Cambrya	USA	20.9.90	171/64	200	23.12	22.72- 12
*	Jones	Lolo	USA	5.8.82	175/60	100h	12.55	12.43, 12.29w- 08
	Jones	Mahagony	USA	20.12.90	167/55	100	11.29	11.33, 11.30w- 13
						200	22.90, 22.64w	23.19, 23.05w- 13
	Jones	Tenaya	USA	22.3.89	162/53	100h	12.75	12.87, 12.65w- 13
	Jones	Vanessa	USA	1.1.93	170/	400	52.15	52.89- 13
^	Jones-Ferrette	Laverne	ISV	16.9.81	173/66	200	22.98w	22.46- 09
	Jover	Maria del Mar	ESP	21.4.88	161/51	LJ	6.78A, 6.59	6.69A- 12, 6.58, 6.73w- 13
	Joye	Hannah	AUS-J	4.1.96	177/63	HJ	1.89	1.80- 13

	Name		Nat	Born	Ht/Wt	Event	2014 Mark	Pre-2014 Best
*	Józwik	Joanna	POL	30.1.91	168/53	800	1:59.63	2:02.39- 13
	Judd	Jessica	GBR-J	7.1.95	178/60	800	1:59.77	1:59.85- 13
	Jungfleisch	Marie-Laurence	GER	7.10.90	181/68	HJ	1.97i, 1.97	1.95- 12
	Juravlyeva	Anastasiya	UZB	9.10.81	172/57	TJ	13.77i, 13.64	14.55- 05
	Jurkovicová	Jarmila	CZE	9.2.81	172/78	JT	56.94	62.60- 06
*	Kabuu	Lucy	KEN	24.3.84	155/41	HMar	68:37	66:09- 13
						Mar	2:24:16	2:19:34- 12
	Kajan	Selma	AUS	30.7.91	169/52	800	2:01.96	2:03.64- 13
	Kakol	Marta	POL	25.2.92	174/68	JT	56.02	54.20- 13
	Kakoshinskaya	Alina	RUS	16.11.86		PV	4.30i	4.30i, 4.25- 13
	Kallenou	Leontia	CYP	5.10.94	183/68	HJ	1.92	1.87- 13
	Kalu	Stephanie	NGR	5.8.93		100	11.15w	11.33- 13
	Kämäräinen	Sanna	FIN	8.2.86	182/82	DT	60.94	57.30- 11
	Kambundji	Mujinga	SUI	17.6.92	168/59	100	11.20	11.50- 13
						200	22.83	23.24- 13
	Kamilos	Jessica	USA	3.8.93	158/	3kSt	9:49.25	10:10.11- 13
	Kampf	Heather	USA	19.1.87	162/53	800	2:00.65	2:00.04- 13
	1500	4:06.16		4:08.37- 13		1M	4:30.14i	4:37.10i- 13
	Kamulu	Pauline	KEN-J	16.4.95	154/40	5000	15:29.55	15:30.46- 13
	Kang Ya		CHN	16.3.90	168/50	100h	13.13	13.19- 13
	Kangogo	Rebecca	KEN	.92		Mar	2:27:16	2:27:52- 13
	Kanuho	Rochelle	USA	4.7.90		5000	15:25.85	16:12.62- 13
	Kapera	Monika	POL	15.2.90	170/52	20kW	1:34:20	1:37:20- 12
	Karamasheva	Svetlana	RUS	24.5.88	167/52	800	1:58.70	2:00.69- 12
						1500	4:04.45	3:59.61- 12
	Kárníková	Jana	CZE	14.2.81	187/85	SP	17.09	17.30i- 10, 17.29- 08
	Kashtonova	Anastasiya	BLR	14.1.89	173/70	DT	59.03	61.13- 13
	Kashyna	Inna	UKR	27.9.91		20kW	1:30:17	1:32:58- 13
	Kasim	Ashu	ETH	20.10.84	172/54	Mar	2:27:45	2:23:09- 12
*	Kasprzycka	Justyna	POL	20.8.87	183/62	HJ	1.99	1.97- 13
^	Kastor	Deena	USA	14.2.73	163/47	HMar	69:37	67:34- 06
	Käther	Nadja	GER	29.9.88	178/62	LJ	6.68i, 6.,59	6.66- 10
	Kato	Asami	JPN	12.10.90	155/38	Mar	2:28:51	2:30:26- 13
	Kato	Misaki	JPN	15.6.91	155/40	10k	32:05.87	32:44.13- 13
	Katsanevakis	Katherine	AUS	11.6.88	165/	800	2:01.75	2:02.60- 11
	Kaur	Khushbir	IND	9.7.93		20kW	1:31:40	1:34:28- 13
	Kaur Dhillon	Navjeet	IND-J	6.3.95		DT	56.36	51.23- 13
	Kaya	Özlem	TUR	20.4.90	165/49	3kSt	9:47.34	9:38.32- 12
	Kazeka	Yekaterina	RUS	7.10.90		PV	4.45	4.40i- 11, 4.40- 13
*	Kebede	Aberu	ETH	12.9.89	163/50	HMar	68:41	67:39- 09
						Mar	2:22:21	2:20:30- 12
*	Keitany	Mary	KEN	18.1.82	168/53	HMar	65:39dh	65:50- 11
						Mar	2:25:07	2:18:37- 12
	Kennedy	Nina	AUS-Y	5.4.97	166/57	PV	4.40	4.31- 13
	Keppler	Janice	USA	22.3.87	178.68	PV	4.30	4.60Ai, 4.43- 13
	Kessely	Haoua	FRA	2.2.88	173/66	TJ	13.60i, 13.45	13.93- 11
	Khamidova	Sitora	UZB	12.5.89	166/50	10k	32:12.54	32:46.52- 13
	Kholodilina	Natalya	RUS	21.7.89		20kW	1:32:44	1:29:49- 13
	Kholodovich	Tatyana	BLR	21.6.91		JT	63.61	59.37- 13
	Khramova	Alyona	RUS	18.8.93		20kW	1:32:07	1:51:47- 13
	Khramova	Valeriya	RUS	13.8.92		400h	55.80	57.06- 13
	Kibalnikova	Valentina	UZB	16.10.90	176/54	100h	13.12	13.22- 12
	Kibarus	Mercy	KEN	25.2.84	155/42	HMar	68:42	68:18- 13
	Kibet	Elvin	KEN	4.2.90		10k	32:40.22	33:02.04- 12
*	Kibiwot	Viola	KEN	22.12.83	157/45	1500	4:00.46	3:59.25- 12
	2000	5:38.2+		5:42.57- 09		3000	8:24.41	8:33.97- 13
	2M	9:12.59		9:18.26- 07		5000	14:33.73	14:33.48- 13
	Kidane	Etalemahu	ETH	14.2.83		Mar	2:29:00	2:25:49- 12
	Kido	Chieko	JPN	14.3.90	161/48	10k	32:11.21	32:48.17- 13
						HMar	70:45	70:11- 13
	Kigen	Peninah	KEN	.86		HMar	70:37	71:25- 11
	Kilel	Caroline	KEN	21.3.81	172/54	HMar	68:53	68:16- 09
						Mar	2:25:22	2:22:34- 13
	Kim Hye-gyong		PRK	9.3.93	153/42	Mar	2:27:05	2:28:32- 13
	Kim Hye-song		PRK	9.3.93	153/42	Mar	2:27:58	2:34:46- 13
	Kim Kyung-ae		KOR	5.3.88	163/62	JT	57.23	58.76- 08
	Kimaiyo	Nancy	KEN	.84		3kSt	9:52.2A	10:02.6A- 13
	Kimaiyo	Olga	KEN	24.7.88		Mar	2:29:15	2:36:57- 13
	Kimanzi	Grace	KEN	1.3.92	161/48	5000	15:26.71	15:17.43- 13
						10k	32:22.14	32:41.69- 13
	Kimaswai	Agatha	KEN	2.4.94		800	1:59.51	2:03.22- 12

Name		Nat	Born	Ht/Wt	Event	2014 Mark	Pre-2014 Best
Kimura	Ayako	JPN	11.6.88	168/53	100h	13.13	13.03, 13.02w- 13
Kimutai	Alice	KEN	7.9.92		HMar	70:15	70:09- 13
King	Arantxa	BER	27.11.89	178/64	LJ	6.46	6.50- 12, 6.57w- 10
Kipkemboi	Gladys	KEN	15.10.86	163/51	3kSt	9:42.88	9:13.22- 10
* Kiplagat	Edna	KEN	15.11.79	171/54	HMar	67:57	67:41- 12
					Mar	2:20:21	2:19:50- 12
* Kiplagat	Florence	KEN	27.2.87	155/42	10k	31:48.6A	30:11.53- 09
HMar	65:12		66:38- 12		Mar	2:20:24	2:19:44- 11
Kiplimo ¶	Joyce	KEN	28.9.88		HMar	70:21 dq	70:24- 13
Kipp	Shalaya	USA	19.8.90	170/58	3kSt	9:39.12	9:35.73- 12
Kiprop	Agnes	KEN	12.12.79	171/51	Mar	2:27:51	2:23:54- 11
Kiprop	Helah	KEN	7.4.85	164/48	HMar	68:36	67:39- 13
					Mar	2:27:14	2:28:02- 13
Kiptoo	Jane	KEN	8.8.82		HMar	69:53	69:07- 09
* Kipyego	Sally	KEN	19.12.85	168/52	3000	8:34.18	8:35.89- 12
2M	9:22.10, 9:21.04i				5000	14:37.18	14:30.42- 11
10k	30:42.26		30:26.37- 12		HMar	68:31	-0-
* Kipyegon	Faith	KEN	10.1.94	157/42	1500	3:58.01	3:56.98- 13
2000	5:37.8+				3000	8:23.55	-0-
Kira	Manami	JPN	23.10.91	174/62	400h	56.63	57.15- 13
* Kirdyapkina	Anisya	RUS	23.10.89	165/51	20kW	1:26:31	1:25:09- 11
* Kiriakopoúlou	Nikoléta	GRE	21.3.86	167/54	PV	4.72i, 4.67	4.71- 11
Kirichenko	Irina	RUS	18.5.87		SP	17.48	17.24- 07
Kirk	Elinor	GBR	26.4.89	172/60	10k	32:17.05	-0-
* Kirui	Purity	KEN	13.8.91	162/47	3kSt	9:23.43	9:19.42- 13
^ Kiryashova	Aleksandra	RUS	21.8.85	166/53	PV	4.40i, 4.35	4.65- 09
* Kisa	Janet	KEN	5.3.92	160/48	3000	8:32.66	8:48.10- 13
					5000	14:52.59	14:57.68- 12
Kitata	Meseret	ETH	.90		Mar	2:27:26	
Kitur	Bornes	KEN	.88		HMar	70:32	
Kiyara	Rael	KEN	4.4.84		HMar	69:29	73:21- 12
					Mar	2:27:10	2:25:23- 11
Kiyota	Mao	JPN	12.9.93		10k	32:12.27	32:34.04- 13
* Kizaki	Ryoko	JPN	21.6.85	157/44	Mar	2:25:26	2:23:34- 13
* Klaas	Kathrin	GER	6.2.84	168/72	HT	74.62	76.05- 12
Klaup	Mari	EST	27.2.90	180/58	Hep	5765	6002- 13
Kleppin	Lauren	USA	22.11.88	160/57	HMar	70:16	75:21- 12
					Mar	2:28:48dh	2:42:17- 13
* Klishina	Darya	RUS	15.1.91	180/57	LJ	6.90	7.05- 11
Klochko	Viktoriya	UKR	2.9.92	187/112	DT	57.17	56.12- 13
Klopsch	Christiane	GER	21.8.90	175/58	400h	56.02	56.83- 13
* Klucinová	Eliska	CZE	14.4.88	177/68	HJ	1.90	1.89- 13
					Hep	6460	6332- 13
* Klyashtornaya	Anna	RUS	3.2.86	172/58	LJ	6.93	7.11- 12
Knäsche	Anjuli	GER	18.10.93		PV	4.26	
Knibb	Kellion	JAM	25.12.93	183/84	DT	61.34	55.68- 13
^ Knight	Bianca	USA	2.1.89	163/60	100	11.20	11.07- 08
					200	23.02, 22.92w	22.35- 11, 22.25w- 08
Knodle	Paige	USA	15.8.93		Hep	5681	5476w- 13, 5392- 12
Kocherzhova	Anastasiya	RUS	16.10.90		200	23.12	23.27- 13
Kock	Maren	GER	22.6.90	173/55	3000	8:50.12mx, 9:00.60	8:55.60- 12
					5000	15:22.75mx, 15:39.88	15:27.65- 12
Koderisch	Heike	GER	27.5.85	188/87	DT	59.32	61.18- 12
Kohlmann	Fabienne	GER	6.11.89	170/57	800	2:01.70	2:00.72- 10
					400h	56.87	55.49- 10
Koki	Francisca	KEN	30.10.93		400h	55.84	58.27- 11
Kolak	Sara	CRO-J	22.6.95	168/70	JT	57.79	57.79- 13
Kolb	Viktoriya	BLR	26.10.93		SP	16.91i, 16.81	15.97- 13
Koleczek	Karolina	POL	15.1.93	169/49	100h	12.94	13.21- 13
Kolesnychenko	Olena	UKR	3.6.93		400h	56.55	57.35- 12
* Kolodko	Yevgeniya	RUS	2.7.90	188/85	SP	19.52	20.48- 12
Kolokithá	Efthimía	GRE	9.7.87	168/55	LJ	6.61	6.48- 12
Kolokolchikova	Yelizaveta	RUS-J	7.6.96		Hep	5740	5359- 13
Kondakova	Yuliya	RUS	4.12.81	170/64	100h	12.86	12.73- 13
* Kondratyeva	Oksana	RUS	22.11.85	180/80	HT	72.17	77.13- 13
* Koneva	Yekaterina	RUS	25.9.88	169/55	LJ	6.56i, 6.42	6.70, 6.80w- 11
					TJ	14.89	14.82- 13
* Konovalova	Mariya	RUS	14.8.74	178/62	Mar	2:23:43	2:22:46- 13
* Kopets	Alena	BLR	14.2.88	178/84	SP	18.81	19.24- 13
Kopron	Malwina	POL	16.11.94	170/63	HT	69.30	66.11- 13
Koressel	Allison	USA	2.3.91	168.57	PV	4.30	4.31- 13

Name		Nat	Born	Ht/Wt	Event	2014 Mark	Pre-2014 Best
Kornuta	Anna	UKR	10.11.88	168/57	LJ	6.53i, 6.51	6.72- 13
Korobkina	Yelena	RUS	25.11.90	163/47	1500	4:07.62, 4:05.78i	4:05.18- 13
3000	8:51.00		8:59.42i- 13, 8:51.41- 10		5000	15:14.67	15:22.14- 11
Korolyova	Kristina	RUS	6.11.90		Hep	5797	5679- 12
Korosídou	Iliána	GRE-J	14.1.95	175/72	HT	65.34	63.88- 13
Korpela	Merja	FIN	15.5.81	170/75	HT	68.44	69.56- 09
Kosko	Irina	RUS	1.3.90		TJ	14.11	13.84i- 13, 13.52- 12
Koster	Maureen	NED	3.7.92	175/56	1500	4:04.92	4:06.50- 13
Kostrova	Alina	BLR	2.3.90	181/79	HT	67.73	70.31- 12
Kostrova	Yuliya	RUS	20.8.91	174/59	HJ	1.89i	1.92- 11
Kotlyarova	Aleksandra	UZB	10.10.88	170/64	TJ	14.05	14.35- 11
Kotovska	Olha	UKR	5.12.83	166/53	Mar	2:28:47	2:30:04- 13
Koubaa	Sanaa	GER	6.1.85	168/58	3kSt	9:48.75	9:43.08- 12
Kovalenko	Iryna	UKR	17.6.86	181/53	HJ	1.90	1.95i- 03, 1.93- 07
Kovar	Kayla	USA	11.8.91	176/	SP	17.03i	16.341i- 13, 15.61- 12
					HT	66.08	58.73- 13
Kowal	Matylda	POL	11.1.89	165/54	3kSt	9:48.41	9:39.87- 12
Kowalska	Katarzyna	POL	7.4.85	177/55	3kSt	9:36.56	9:26.93- 09
Kraft	Joana	GER	27.7.91	173/57	PV	4.46i, 4.35	4.45i- 10, 4.40- 13
Kragbé	Suzanne	CIV	22.12.81	179/92	DT	59.61	59.32- 11
Krakhmaleva	Anna	RUS	1.5.92		20kW	1:34:18	1:35:34- 13
Králová	Tereza	CZE	22.10.89	175/85	HT	70.18	70.21- 13
Krasnokutskaya	Oksana	RUS	24.9.93		HJ	1.90i, 1.90	1.90- 13
* Krasnova	Angelina	RUS	7.2.91	168/55	PV	4.65	4.70- 13
Krasucki	Franciela	BRA	26.4.88	172/59	100	11.24, 10.99w	11.13- 13
					200	22.82	22.76- 13
Krasutska	Hanna	UKR-J	20.7.95		TJ	13.61	13.47, 13.48w- 13
* Krause	Gesa-Felicitas	GER	3.8.92	167/55	3kSt	9:35.46	9:23.52- 12
Krebs	Denise	GER	27.6.87	157/48	1500	4:08.16	4:06.01- 12
Krechyk	Alena	BLR	20.7.87	174/73	HT	69.92	69.02- 12
Krizsán	Xénia	HUN	13.1.93	171/62	Hep	6317(w)	5957- 12
Kubelová	Jitka	CZE	2.10.91	176/82	DT	58.38	58.30- 13
Kubokura	Satomi	JPN	27.4.82	161/52	400h	56.21	55.34- 11
* Kucherenko	Olga	RUS	5.11.85	172/59	LJ	6.70	7.13- 10
* Kuchina	Mariya	RUS	14.1.93	182/60	HJ	2.01i, 2.00	1.98i, 1.96- 13
Kudzelich	Svetlana	BLR	7.5.87	170/52	3kSt	9:27.95	9:39.43- 12
Kuijken	Susan	NED	8.7.86	170/54	1000	2:38.01	
1500	4:07.21		4:05.38- 13		3000	8:36.08	8:39.65- 13
2M	9:23.52				5000	15:32.82	15:04.36- 13
Kulyatina	Alla	RUS	9.6.90		5000	15:27.26	15:48.33- 13
Kumari	Sahana	IND	6.3.81	178/62	HJ	1.89	1.92- 12
Kuntsevich	Yekaterina	RUS	13.7.84	175/60	HJ	1.90i, 1.86	1.94- 06
Kupina	Yekaterina	RUS	2.2.86	172/59	800	2:00.12	1:59.21- 13
Kuroda	Mao	JPN	1.11.89	157/48	10k	32:41.92	32:56.45- 11
Kuze	Kiho	JPN-J	28.3.95	165/58	JT	57.97	58.98- 13
^ La Mantia	Simona	ITA	14.4.83	177/65	TJ	13.94	14.69- 05, 14.71w- 04
Laasma	Liina	EST	13.1.92	178.77	JT	63.17	62.50- 13
LaBeaud Anzures	Natasha	CAN	5.8.87	181/59	10k	32:43.14	32:57.78- 13
Labonté	Julie	CAN	12.1.90	183/91	SP	17.58	18.31- 11
					DT	56.84	56.79- 13
LaCaze	Genevieve	AUS	4.8.89	168/54	3kSt	9:33.19	9:37.62- 13
Lada	Androniki	CYP	19.4.91	184/86	DT	56.69	54.86- 12
Lagat	Violah	KEN	1.3.89	165/49	1500	4:07.11	4:05.66- 13
					1M	4:29.43	4:39.42i- 13
Laing	Kimberley	JAM	8.1.89	167/55	100h	13.12, 12.99w	12.97- 12, 12.92w- 10
* Lake	Morgan	GBR-Y	12.5.97	178/64	HJ	1.94	1.90- 13
					Hep	6148	-0-
Lakmali	Nadeeka	SRI	18.9.81	165/60	JT	59.04	60.64- 13
Lally	Jade	GBR	30.3.87	183/81	DT	60.48	60.76- 11
Lalonde	Geneviève	CAN	5.9.91	167/47	3kSt	9:50.79	9:53.35- 13
* Lalova	Ivet	BUL	18.5.84	168/55	100	11.10	10.77- 04
					200	23.17, 22.92w	22.51, 22.36w- 04
Lambarki	Hayat	MAR	18.5.88	168/62	400h	55.93	55.27- 13
Lamote	Renelle	FRA	26.12.93	168/57	800	2:00.06	2:02.40- 13
Lara	Geena	USA	18.1.87	167/57	800	2:01.10	1:59.24- 12
Larsåsen	Cathrine	NOR	5.12.86	172/59	PV	4.30i, 4.15	4.41i- 12, 4.40- 11
Larsson	Eleni	SWE	4.4.93	186/100	HT	65.64	67.13- 13
Larsson	Sofia	SWE	22.7.88	174/82	DT	57.58	58.65- 09
Latham	Deanna	USA	23.2.92	168/59	Hep	5745	5606- 12
Latvala	Hanna-Maari	FIN	30.10.87	170/59	100	11.30, 11.23w	11.36- 13
					200	22.98	22.98- 13

Name		Nat	Born	Ht/Wt	Event	2014 Mark	Pre-2014 Best
Lavric	Mirela	ROU	17.2.91	162/45	800	2:01.24	1:59.74- 12
Law	Kirsty	GBR	11.10.86		DT	57.15	57.79- 12
Lawson	LaKeisha	USA	3.6.87	168/57	100	11.07	11.14- 13
					200	23.09	23.15- 13
Lebedeva	Lyudmila	RUS	23.5.90	165/48	3kSt	9:40.01	9:39.98- 13
Lecurieux	Prescilla	FRA	1.12.92	180/82	JT	56.91	57.23- 12
Ledáki	Stélla-Iró	GRE	18.7.88	170/58	PV	4.30	4.50- 12
^ Lee	Muna	USA	30.10.81	173/50	100	11.26	10.85- 08, 10.78w- 09
					200	23.06, 22.97w	22.01, 21.91w- 08
Lee Mi-young		KOR	19.8.79	174/81	SP	17.52	17.62- 05
Leffler	Celina	GER-J	9.4.96	174/60	Hep	5846	
Legesse	Meseret	ETH	28.8.87		Mar	2:26:36	2:26:15- 13
^ Legnante	Assunta	ITA	14.5.78	190/125	SP	17.32	19.04- 06
Lehtinen	Johanna	FIN	21.2.79	170/55	3kSt	9:48.50	9:40.28- 06
Leidl	Sarah	GER	5.3.87		JT	55.78	52.86- 11
Leinert	Shannon	USA	30.6.87	170/60	800	2:02.01	2:01.65- 12
Lekamge	Dilhani	SRI	14.1.87		JT	56.57	55.76- 12
LeLeux	Morgann	USA	14.11.92	170/61	PV	4.38i	4.50i- 13, 4.44- 12
Lema	Marta	ETH	.90		Mar	2:28:06	2:28:02- 13
Lemus	Sandra	COL	1.1.89	170/102	SP	17.50	18.03- 13
Leonard	Alison	GBR	17.3.90	168/56	800	2:00.08	2:01.82- 10
					1500	4:09.73mx, 4:14.61	4:13.74- 13
* Leontyuk	Yuliya	BLR	31.1.84	185/80	SP	18.87	19.79- 08
LeRoy	Anastasia	JAM	11.9.87	168/55	400	50.84	51.09- 08
Leslie	Breanna	USA	11.8.91		Hep	5893	5761- 13
* Lesueur	Éloyse	FRA	15.7.88	179/65	LJ	6.92, 6.94w	6.91- 11, 7.04w- 12
Lettow	Lindsay	USA	6.6.90	175/62	Hep	5859	5807- 12
Leutert	Astrid	SUI	12.9.87	167/51	3kSt	9:50.35	9:53.15- 12
Levchenko	Yuliya	UKR-Y	28.11.97		HJ	1.89	1.77- 13
Leverton	Linda	AUS	22.3.87	178/65	TJ	13.93	13.82- 11, 14.07w- 13
Levitskaya	Yekaterina	RUS	2.1.87		LJ	6.70	6.70- 13
Levy	Jura	JAM	4.11.90	157/50	100	11.28	11.10, 11.07w- 11
					200	23.16	22.76- 11
Lewandowska	Iwona	POL	19.2.85	158/47	Mar	2:28:33	2:28:32- 12
* Lewis	Yvette	PAN	16.3.85	173/62	100h	12.86A, 12.95	12.67, 12.43w- 13
* Lewis-Smallwood	Gia	USA	1.4.79	183/93	DT	69.17	66.29- 13
Lhabz	Lamia	MAR	19.5.84	178/59	400h	57.24	55.51- 13
Li Leilei		CHN	18.8.89	160/46	20kW	1:33:23	1:41:24- 07
* Li Ling		CHN	6.7.89	185/70	PV	4.61	4.65- 13
Li Lingwei		CHN	26.1.89	172/75	JT	62.56	65.11- 12
Li Maocuo		CHN	20.10.92		20kW	1:31:55	1:35:40- 11
Li Tsai-Yi		TPE	3.12.89	180/130	DT	57.37	60.23- 12
Li Xiaohong		CHN-J	8.1.95		TJ	13.75, 14.03w	14.06i- 13, 13.85- 12
Li Yanmei		CHN	6.2.90	171/56	TJ	14.19i, 14.14	14.35- 13
Li Zhenzhu		CHN	13.12.85	168/45	3kSt	9:35.23	9:32.35- 07
Liang Yan		CHN-J	2.1.95		DT	57.54	62.01- 13
* Licwinko	Kamila	POL	22.3.86	183/66	HJ	2.00i, 1.97	1.99- 13
de Lima	Jucilene	BRA	14.9.90	172/63	JT	62.89	61.98- 13
Limo	Cynthia	KEN	18.12.89		HMar	68:24	69:59- 13
Lin Chia-Ying		TPE	5.11.82	168/91	SP	17.48	17.43- 12
Linde	Sofia	SWE-J	12.1.95	174/66	Hep	5701	6081- 13
Linden	Desiree	USA	26.7.83	157/	Mar	2:28:11, 2:23:54dh	2:22:38- 11
Lindh	Lovisa	SWE	9.7.91	169/56	800	2:01.73	2:03.51- 13
Lindley	Lindsay	USA	6.10.89		100h	13.21, 13.11w	13.24- 10
Linkiewicz	Joanna	POL	2.5.90	172/55	400h	55.89	56.86- 13
Linnell	Lisa	SWE	30.4.91		Hep	5818	5888- 13
Linnenbaum	Eva	GER	3.6.89	189/61	TJ	13.54, 13.72w	13.50- 10
Lipsey	Charlene	USA	16.7.91	168/57	800	2:00.91	2:01.40- 12
Lire	Genet	ETH-Y	23.1.97		400	51.5A	
Little	Mackenzie	AUS-J	22.12.96		JT	57.60	50.81- 12
Little	Shamier	USA-J	20.3.95		400	51.06	52.59- 13
					400h	55.07	57.44- 12
Litvinova	Lyudmila	RUS	8.6.85	177/60	200	23.16	22.82- 09
					400	52.06	50.27- 09
* Liu Hong		CHN	12.5.87	161/48	20kW	1:26:58	1:25:46- 12
Liu Huan		CHN	24.2.93		20kW	1:31:30	1:30:25- 13
Liu Shiying		CHN	24.9.93		JT	62.72	60.23- 13
Liu Tingting		CHN	29.10.90	174/75	HT	73.06	69.83- 13
Lloyd	Cassandra	USA	27.1.90	163/54	100h	13.10	12.90- 13
Lomnická	Nikola	SVK	16.9.88	166/70	HT	71.58	67.88- 13
Londa	Maria Natalia	INA	29.10.90	163/57	LJ	6.55	6.55- 12

Name		Nat	Born	Ht/Wt	Event	2014 Mark	Pre-2014 Best
					TJ	13.78	14.17- 13
Longfors	Rachel	USA	6.6.83	183/82	DT	59.67	58.10- 13
López	Yaniuvis	CUB	1.2.86	180/71	SP	18.11	18.81- 09
Lotout	Marion	FRA	19.11.89	165/54	PV	4.56i, 4.50	4.60- 13
Lou Gonerie	Marie Josée	CIV	18.11.88	159/57	100	11.20	11.53- 12
					200	22.78	23.26- 12
* Lowe	Chaunté	USA	12.1.84	175/59	HJ	1.97	2.05- 10
Lu Minjia		CHN	29.12.92	172/58	LJ	6.57	6.74- 09
Lu Xiaoxin		CHN	22.2.89	184/90	DT	60.68	63.27- 13
* Lu Xiuzhi		CHN	26.10.93	167/52	20kW	1:27:15	1:27:01- 12
Lubieniecki	Kara	USA	25.3.89		10k	32:38.77	33:36.45- 13
Lucas	Porscha	USA	18.6.88	170/56	100	11.25w	11.12- 09, 11.02w- 12
Luka	Tintu	IND	26.4.89	164/51	800	1:59.19	1:59.17- 10
Luo Na		CHN	8.10.93		HT	69.81	67.09- 13
Luo Xingcai		CHN	18.7.94		20kW	1:31:09	1:31:03- 13
* Lupu #	Nataliya	UKR	4.11.87	170/50	800	2:01.33i, 2:00.65i dq	1:58.46- 12
* Lutkovskaya	Alyona	RUS-J	15.3.96		PV	4.50i, 4.50	4.30- 13
Lvova	Olga	RUS	21.9.89		800	1:59.86	2:01.56i- 13, 2:02.12- 12
Lyakhova	Olha	UKR	18.3.92	170/59	800	1:59.92	2:00.55- 12
					1000	2:38.67	
Lyashenko	Valentyna	UKR	30.1.81		HJ	1.91	1.91- 12
Lysenko	Alena	RUS	3.2.88		HT	69.01	67.96- 12
* Lysenko	Tatyana	RUS	9.10.83	186/81	HT	70.62	78.80- 13
Macharia	Lucy	KEN	.91		HMar	70:41	70:04- 11
Mächtig	Julia	GER	1.1.86	187/80	Hep	6106	6430- 13
Macías	Isabel	ESP	11.8.84	165/52	1500	4:09.22i	4:04.84- 12
Mackey	Katie	USA	12.11.87	165/52	1500	4:05.74	4:04.60- 13
1M 4:27.78	4:34.98i- 10, 4:30.60irr- 13				5000	15:04.74	15:23.65- 13
Madarász	Viktória	HUN	12.5.85	153/46	20kW	1:30:57	1:33:21- 13
^ Madejczyk	Barbara	POL	30.9.76	180/81	JT	56.15	64.08- 06
Madu	Jennifer	USA	23.9.94	160/52	100	11.23	11.31, 11.18w- 13
Maeda	Hiroi	JPN	1.6.91	161/48	20kW	1:35:20	1:32:25- 13
Maeda	Sairi	JPN	7.11.91	158/45	10k	32:03.43	32:51.53- 13
					Mar	2:26:46	
Magnani	Margherita	ITA	26.2.87	161/45	1500	4:06.05	4:06.34- 13
					3000	8:51.82, 8:51.81i	9:00.25- 13
Maiwald	Anna	GER	21.7.90	176/62	Hep	5894	5863- 13
Maiyo	Maureen	KEN	28.5.85	167/59	400	51.78A, 52.62	51.63A- 13
Majester	Kat	USA	22.5.87	173/59	PV	4.51Ai, 4.30	4.40- 12
Májková	Lucie	CZE	9.7.88		TJ	13.71, 13.85w	13.60- 12
Mäkelä	Kristiina	FIN	20.11.92	184/71	TJ	13.70, 13.81w	13.67- 11
Måkestad Bovim	Ingvill	NOR	7.8.81	172/59	1500	4:04.11	4:02.20- 10
Mäki	Kristiina	CZE	22.9.91	170/50	2000	5:42.71	
					3000	8:51.69	9:13.28- 13
Makikawa	Eri	JPN	22.4.93		10k	32:00.25	32:34.38- 13
					HMar	70:27	
Maksimova	Marina	RUS	20.5.85	177/80	JT	56.99	60.73- 11
Maksimova	Yana	BLR	9.1.89	182/70	HJ	1.93i, 1.90	1.91- 12
					Hep	6189	6198- 12
Makul	Karolina	POL	23.8.94	178/82	DT	58.92	54.79- 13
Malácová	Romana	CZE	15.5.87	164/57	PV	4.50	4.42i- 13, 4.41- 10
Malavisi	Sonia	ITA	31.10.94	172/65	PV	4.35	4.42- 13
Malkus	Lena	GER	6.8.93	180/74	LJ	6.88	6.76- 13, 6.80w- 12
Malone	Chantel	IVB	2.12.91	175/62	LJ	6.55	6.65- 13, 6.66w- 12
Maltseva	Yuliya	RUS	30.11.90		DT	63.39	59.50- 13
Maluskiewicz	Agnieszka	POL	18.3.89	175/83	SP	17.20	16.00i, 15.96- 13
Malvinova	Kristina	RUS	16.7.89		400	52.20	51.97- 12
* Mamona	Patricia	POR	21.11.88	168/53	TJ	14.36i, 14.36, 14.49w	14.52- 12
Mancebo	Maria	DOM	29.8.93	150/54	3kSt	9:45.84	10:17.83- 12
Mann	Brittany	USA	16.4.94	173/	SP	17.07	14.75- 13
Mánou	Loréla	GRE	20.12.90	167/52	PV	4.36i, 4.35	4.45- 13
Manz	Daniela	GER	19.9.86	164/72	HT	66.42	63.35- 13
Marais	Carla	RSA	10.12.87	166/55	LJ	6.47A	6.64- 13
Marchant	Lanni	CAN	11.4.84	155/45	10k	32:29.61	34:16.36- 06
Marcussen	Ida	NOR	1.11.87	173/67	Hep	6083	6226- 07
Maresová	Oldriska	CZE	14.10.86	187/67	HJ	1.88	1.92- 12
Mariani	Micaela	ITA	11.2.88	166/70	HT	66.24	64.02- 13
Marie-Nély	Nathalie	FRA	24.11.86	175/66	TJ	13.91	14.03- 12, 14.18w- 11
* Marincu	Florentina	ROU-J	8.4.96	178/60	LJ	6.71, 6.73w	6.54- 13
Maroszek	Jessica	USA	26.2.92	175/91	SP	16.73i, 16.23	15.81- 13
					DT	60.18	58.01- 13

	Name		Nat	Born	Ht/Wt	Event	2014 Mark	Pre-2014 Best
	Marshall	Ashley	USA	10.9.93	160/52	100	11.36, 11.22w	11.34- 13
	Marshall	Mandissa	USA	2.4.91	173/61	PV	4.32i, 4.30	4.35- 13
	Martin	Jada	USA-J	8.6.95		200	23.02, 22/96w	23.75- 13
	Martín	Diana	ESP	1.4.81	162/50	3kSt	9:30.70	9:35.77- 12
*	Martinez	Brenda	USA	8.9.87	163/52	800	1:58.84	1:57.91- 13
						1500	4:01.36	4:00.94- 13
	Martínez	Johana	COL	9.9.86	180/84	DT	56.27A	55.87- 13
	Martínez	Yarianna	CUB	20.9.84	167/56	TJ	14.36, 14.39w	14.42- 11
	Martins	Eliane	BRA	26.5.86		LJ	6.47, 6.55w	6.66A- 07, 6.61- 09
*	Márton	Anita	HUN	15.1.89	171/84	SP	19.04	18.48- 12
						DT	59.27	56.62- 10
	Masai	Magdalyne	KEN	21.11.93		3kSt	9:52.97	
	Masná	Lenka	CZE	22.4.85	170/56	800	1:59.93	1:59.56- 13
	Massey	Kelly	GBR	11.1.85	168/57	400	51.96	52.38- 12
	Matsumi	Sakiko	JPN	7.8.88	159/41	10k	32:37.60	32:44.44- 13
	Matsuzaki	Riko	JPN	24.12.92	157/44	5000	15:18.95	15:26.05- 13
	Mattox	Kimber	USA	27.11.88		3kSt	9:51.29	10:03.93- 13
	Matveyuk	Alina	BLR	29.7.90		20kW	1:30:48	1:32:06- 10
	Mavrodieva	Radoslava	BUL	13.3.87	178/86	SP	18.05	18.67- 13
	Mayer	Sarah	GER	20.5.91	170/60	JT	56.05	59.29- 11
	Mayo	Gabby	USA	26.1.89	168/	100h	13.14	12.81- 10
	Mayorova	Albina	RUS	16.5.77	167/50	10k	32:29.62	32:44.03- 03
						Mar	2:28:18	2:23:52- 12
	Mazuronak	Olga	BLR	14.4.89	166/48	10k	32:31.15	34:19.66- 13
						Mar	2:27:33dh	2:33:33- 13
	Mbumi Nkouindjin	Joëlle	CMR	25.5.86	170/54	TJ	14.02	13.44- 13
*	McCall	Jeneva	USA	28.10.89	178/102	SP	18.45i, 17.86	19.10i- 12, 18.47- 13
	(now Stevens)					HT	70.78	74.77- 13
	McCartney	Eliza	NZL-J	11.12.96		PV	4.45	4.11- 13
	McColgan	Eilish	GBR	25.11.90	176/59	3kSt	9:44.65	9:35.82- 13
*	McCorory	Francena	USA	20.10.88	170/60	400	49.48	49.86- 13
	McCoy	Rachel	USA-J	1.8.95		HJ	1.88	1.85- 13
	McGowan	Brittany	AUS	24.4.91	163/49	800	2:01.26	2:06.03- 13
	McGrone	Candyce	USA	24.3.89	160/59	100	11.26, 11.20w	11.08, 11.07w- 11
	McIntosh	Rachael	CAN	17.1.91	174/62	Hep	5789	5601A- 13
	McKnight	Kaila	AUS	5.5.86	172/52	1500	4:06.06	4:05.61- 12
^	McLaughlin	Anneisha	JAM	6.1.86	163/54	200	22.68	22.54- 10
	(-Wilby)					400	52.22	51.89- 12
	McLaughlin	Sydney	USA-Y	7.8.99		400h	55.63	
	McLean	Hayley	GBR	9.9.94	164/57	400h	56.43	57.26- 13
	McMahon	Christine	IRL	6.7.92	167/55	400h	56.97	59.46- 13
*	McPherson	Stephenie Ann	JAM	25.11.88	168/55	200	22.93	23.04- 10
						400	50.12	49.92- 13
*	McPherson ¶	Inika	USA	29.9.86	167/55	HJ	1.96, 2.00dq	1.95- 12
	McReynolds	Tiffani	USA	4.12.91	153/50	100	11.32, 11.21w	11.42- 12
						100h	12.77, 12.59w	13.04- 12, 12.74w- 11
*	Meadows	Jenny	GBR	17.4.81	156/48	800	1:59.34mx, 2:00.32	1:57.93- 09
	Meadows	Tawanna	USA	4.8.86	168/55	100	11.11	11.24- 13, 11.13w- 08, 11.1w- 10
						200	22.90	23.14- 08
	Medeiros	Keely	BRA	30.4.87	180/100	SP	17.58	17.26- 11
	Medgyesová	Renata	SVK	28.1.83	172/53	LJ	6.49	6.79- 10
	Mekasha	Dinknesh	ETH	.85	160/48	Mar	2:27:29	2:25:09- 13
	Mekasha	Waganesh	ETH	16.1.92	159/45	HMar	69:30	68:48- 13
	Mekonen	Tigist Getnet	ETH-Y	7.7.97		3kSt	9:28.36	10:03.84- 13
	Mekonnin	Misiker	ETH	23.7.86		Mar	2:29:03	2:25:21dh- 11, 2:25:45- 13
	Melchor	Inés	PER	30.8.86	158/55	Mar	2:26:48	2:28:54- 12
	Melese	Mantegbosh	ETH	20.1.88	156/45	800	2:01.9A	2:02.22- 13
	Melese	Yebrqual	ETH	18.4.90	164/55	HMar	69:23	69:02- 13
						Mar	2:26:21	
*	Melkamu	Meselech	ETH	27.4.85	158/48	HMar	70:36+	68:05- 13
						Mar	2:25:23, 2:21:28dh	2:21:01- 12
*	Melnychenko	Hanna	UKR	24.4.83	178/59	Hep	5937	6586- 13
	Melville	Miranda	USA	20.3.89	160/54	20kW	1:33:11	1:38:01- 11
	Mendieta	Yusleidys	CUB	17.2.94	180/66	Hep	6013	6024- 13
	Mendoza	Magdalena	VEN	20.10.90		400h	56.87A	58.86- 13
	Meng Qianqian		CHN	6.1.91	178/85	SP	17.66	18.31- 11
	Meniker	Nawal	FRA-Y	9.12.97	173/55	HJ	1.87	1.84- 13
*	Menkova	Oksana	BLR	28.3.82	183/91	HT	71.56	78.69- 12
	Menuet	Emilie	FRA	27.11.91	155/44	20kW	1:35:16	1:37:56- 12
	Merlano	Briggit	COL	29.4.82	174/65	100h	13.05A, 13.13, 13.01Aw	12.89- 11
	Michiguchi	Ai	JPN	3.6.88	159/53	20kW	1:32:41	1:35:39- 13

Name		Nat	Born	Ht/Wt	Event	2014 Mark	Pre-2014 Best
Michta	Maria	USA	23.6.86	165/51	20kW	1:30:49	1:32:27- 12
* Mickle	Kimberley	AUS	28.12.84	169/69	JT	66.83	66.60- 13
* Mihambo	Malaika	GER	3.2.94	170/52	LJ	6.90	6.70, 6.80w- 13
Mikhailyuk	Mariya	RUS	29.1.91		400	52.21	53.10- 12
Mikhaylova	Kristina	RUS	16.10.92		20kW	1:34:18	1:41:27- 13
Milanés	Belkis	CUB	16.1.90	175/65	100h	13.11	13.17- 10
Milani	Marta	ITA	9.3.87	174/61	800	2:01.76	2:01.35- 12
Miller	Fawn	USA	10.5.92		JT	58.13	52.67- 13
Miller	Jade	USA-J	13.1.95	168/57	400h	56.22	57.21- 13
* Miller	Shaunae	BAH	15.4.94	185/69	200	22.87	22.45, 22.41w- 13
					400	51.58	50.70- 13
Miller	Yasmin	GBR-J	24.5.95		100h	13.13	13.44- 13
Miller Koch	Heather	USA	30.3.87	173/63	Hep	6100	5945(w)- 13
* Minenko	Hanna	ISR	25.9.89	178/61	LJ	6.52	6.40- 12
(née Knyzhyeva)					TJ	14.29	14.71- 12
Minko	Corinna	AUS	13.12.89		LJ	6.49	6.36- 13
* Mishchenko	Anna	UKR	25.8.83	166/51	1500	4:05.54	4:01.16- 12
Mismas	Marusa	SLO	24.10.94	164/52	3kSt	9:40.49	9:51.15- 13
Misochenko	Anna	RUS	15.4.92		LJ	6.50i	6.53- 13
* Mitchell	Kathryn	AUS	10.7.82	168/75	JT	66.10	64.34- 12
Mitchell	Morgan	AUS	3.10.94	177/64	400	52.22	53.88- 12
Mitchell	Victoria	AUS	25.4.82	164/48	3kSt	9:42.01	9:30.84- 06
Mitsunobu	Yuki	JPN	9.11.92	161/47	10k	32:17.24	32:15.45- 13
Miyashita	Risa	JPN	26.4.84	171/71	JT	58.33	60.08- 11
Miyazaki	Yuka	JPN	21.8.92	160/41	5000	15:27.49	15:44.62- 12
Mizuguchi	Yuko	JPN	24.5.85	164/43	10k	32:31.37	32:10.15- 13
Mnatsakanova	Tatyana	RUS	25.5.83		HJ	1.90	1.95- 11
^ Mockenhaupt	Sabrina	GER	6.12.80	156/45	5000	15:18.53mx	14:59.88mx- 09, 15:03.47- 04
					10k	32:29.26	31:14.21- 08
Moges	Bethlehem	ETH	3.5.91		HMar	69:23	70:38- 13
					Mar	2:26:42	
* Moguenara	Sosthene	GER	17.10.89	182/68	LJ	6.82	7.04- 13
Mohamed	Bezuayehu	ETH-J	4.1.96		3kSt	9:40.26	10:45.0- 12
Mohammed	Zeytuna	ETH-J	2.2.96		800	2:01.6A	2:05.05- 13
Mokhnyuk	Anastasiya	UKR	1.1.91	175.67	100h	13.08	13.40- 13
LJ	6.51	6.62i, 6.57- 13			Hep	6220	5941- 13
Mokrásová	Lucia	SVK	27.3.94		Hep	5789	5649- 13
* Möldner-Schmidt	Antje	GER	13.6.84	173/56	3kSt	9:29.43	9:18.54- 09
* Moline	Georganne	USA	6.3.90	178/59	400h	54.00	53.72- 13
* Molitor	Katharina	GER	8.11.83	182/76	JT	63.40	64.67- 11
Molodchinina	Yelena	RUS	16.4.91	174/65	Hep	5762	5796- 13
Mombi ¶	Julia	KEN	25.9.85		Mar	2:28:00dq	2:26:00- 08
Monroe	Amber	USA	14.10.93	183/	SP	17.18i, 16.14	
Montcalm	Noelle	CAN	3.4.88	166/53	400h	55.81	55.96- 13
* Montsho ¶	Amantle	BOT	4.7.83	173/64	200	23.06	22.89- 12
					400	50.37	49.33- 13
* Moore	LaShauntea	USA	31.7.83	170/62	100	11.39, 11.12w	10.97- 10, 10.93w- 12
Moraes	Fabiana	BRA	5.6.86	170/53	100h	12.98	13.14- 09
de Morais	Andressa	BRA	21.12.90	178/100	DT	59.65	64.21- 12
^ Moreira	Sara	POR	17.10.85	168/51	5000	15:20.01	14:54.71- 10
10k	32:01.42	31:16.44- 12			Mar	2:26:00	-0-
Moreno	Eli Johana	COL	15.4.85	175/78	HT	67.77	69.80- 09
* Moreno	Yipsi	CUB	19.11.80	168/80	HT	71.35	76.62- 08
Morgan	Monique	JAM	14.10.85	168/60	100h	12.94	12.97, 12.93w- 13
Mori	Yuika	JPN	25.1.88	158/46	5000	15:25.58	15:26.80- 13
^ Morosanu	Angela	ROU	26.7.86	178/57	400h	56.58	53.85- 13
Morris	Sandi	USA	8.7.92	163/54	PV	4.55	4.43i- 13, 4.30- 11
Morrison	Ebony	USA	28.12.94	165/	100h	13.06	13.88- 11
Morrison	Natasha	JAM	17.11.92	170/57	100	11.06	11.17, 11.12w- 13
Moser	Angelica	SUI-Y	9.10.97		PV	4.36	4.07- 13
Moser	Treniere	USA	27.10.81	159/50	800	2:01.79	1:59.15- 07
1000 2:37.88i 2:41.89i- 10 1500 4:04.18 4:02.85- 13 1M 4:28.86i 4:29.93i- 06, 4:35.07- 07							
Mosina	Veronika	RUS	17.10.90	172/57	TJ	14.09i, 13.30	14.50- 12
Mosley	Joh'vonnie	USA	24.5.92		SP	16.92i, 16.79	16.23i- 13, 16.12- 12
Mosop	Leonida	KEN	.91		HMar	70:11	70:11- 13
Mpopo	Kabange	ZAM	21.9.92	170/	400	50.87	
Muangjan	Thitima	THA	13.4.83	168/53	TJ	13.72	14.16- 13
Muir	Carline	CAN	1.10.87	170/65	400	52.13, 51.1	51.55- 08
Muir	Laura	GBR	9.5.93	162/54	800	2:00.67	2:00.80- 13
					1500	4:00.07	4:07.76- 13
Mukasheva	Margarita	KAZ	4.1.86	165/50	800	1:59.02	1:58.96- 13

Name		Nat	Born	Ht/Wt	Event	2014 Mark	Pre-2014 Best
Mulbjerg	Trine	DEN	23.4.90		SP	16.69i	16.45- 13
* Müller	Nadine	GER	21.11.85	193/90	DT	67.30	68.89- 12
Mullina	Olga	RUS	1.8.92		PV	4.40	4.30i, 4.20- 13
Muñoz	Lismania	CUB	28.2.93	171/63	JT	58.47	59.29- 13
* Murer	Fabiana	BRA	16.3.81	172/64	PV	4.80	4.85- 10
Murillo	María Lucelly	COL	5.5.91	176/65	JT	56.71A	57.16A- 10
* Muriuki	Margaret	KEN	21.3.86	158/45	3000	8:46.6+	
2M	9:24.89		5000	15:10.38	14:40.48- 13	HMar 69:02	69:21- 12
Murtazina	Alsu	RUS	12.12.87	175/59	TJ	14.50	14.55- 11
Musina	Anna	RUS	3.11.84		800	2:00.9	2:05.66- 13
Mutai	Beatrice	KEN	19.4.87		10k	32:24+	
					HMar	69:30	
Mutune	Agnes	KEN	26.6.86		HMar	70:13	70:03- 13
Muzaric	Valentina	CRO	23.7.92	178/86	SP	17.89i, 17.08	17.52- 13
Müze	Lina	LAT	4.12.92	182/75	JT	58.02	61.97- 13
Mwangi	Ann	KEN	8.12.88		1500	4:05.23	4:06.58- 10
Nabeshima	Rina	JPN	16.12.93		5000	15:31.85	15:52.95- 12
Nagao	Kaoru	JPN	26.9.89	160/45	10k	32:22.06	32:10.46- 11
Nageotte	Katie	USA	30.6.91	168/59	PV	4.48, 4.50dh?	4.45- 13
Nagovitsyna	Yelena	RUS	7.12.82	165/55	10k	32:11.63	32:02.99- 13
* Nana Djimou	Antoinette	FRA	2.8.85	174/69	100h	13.05	12.96- 12
					Hep	6551	6576- 12
Nanyondo	Winnie	UGA	23.8.93		800	1:58.63	2:02.38- 12
^ Naude	Elizna	RSA	14.9.78	180/105	DT	57.64A	64.87- 07
Nawowuna	Alice	KEN	11.3.94		3000	8:53.55	
Ndiwa	Stacy	KEN	6.12.92		1500	4:06.10	4:13.0A - 13
3000	8:30.54				5000	15:15.14	16:04.0- 13
Ndoumbe	Ruth Marie	ESP	1.1.87	173/59	TJ	14.15	13.78- 11
* Nel	Wenda	RSA	30.7.88	169/52	400h	54.82	55.36A, 55.79- 12
Nelovko	Darya	RUS	9.2.94		TJ	13.70	13.48- 12
Nelson	Alicia	USA	20.10.90	167/	3kSt	9:48.91	10:03.20- 13
Nelson	Ashleigh	GBR	20.2.91	175/69	100	11.19, 11.15w	11.33- 13
Nelson	Briana	USA	18.7.92	168/57	400	51.05	52.18i- 13, 52.31- 13
Nelson	Ella	AUS	10.5.94	169/56	200	23.26, 23.10w	23.68- 10
* Nelvis	Sharika	USA	10.5.90	178/64	100	11.27, 11.17w	11.36. 11.27w- 12
200	22.70w		23.35- 12		100h	12.71, 12.52w	12.84- 13
Nemec	Lisa	CRO	18.5.84	158/44	HMar	69:16	69:18- 13
(née Stublic)					Mar	2:28:36	2:25:44- 13
Nengampi	Perine	KEN	1.1.89	167/49	1500	4:03.98	4:09.96- 12
3000	8:45.15		8:51.60- 13		5000	15:16.50	
Nesterchuk	Mariya	BLR	14.8.89		HJ	1.90i	1.86- 07
Netsvetayeva	Yekaterina	BLR	26.6.89	174/64	Hep	6121	5989- 13
* Nettey	Christabel	CAN	2.6.91	162/59	LJ	6.73	6.75- 13
Newman	Alysha	CAN	29.6.94	175/63	PV	4.41	4.40A- 13
Newton	Kendra	USA	3.8.87		100h	13.12	13.19, 12.92w- 13
Neziri	Nooralotta	FIN	9.11.92	174/60	100h	12.98	13.04- 13
Ngetich	Emily	KEN	.84		Mar	2:25:14	2:35:23- 13
Ngo Ngoa	Sarah	CMR	7.7.83	159/60	LJ	6.52	6.36- 13
Nguyen Thi Huyen		VIE	19.8.93	162/50	400h	56.49	58.50- 13
Nie Jingjing		CHN	1.3.88	168/45	20kW	1:28:43	1:28:26- 12
Nikkanen	Minna	FIN	9.4.88	169/53	PV	4.55i, 4.52	4.60i- 11, 4.50- 13
Nikolayeva	Iryna	UKR	20.1.84	170/55	LJ	6.43, 6.62w	6.60- 13
					TJ	13.93, 13.97w	13.93- 13
Nikolenko	Viktoriya	UKR	15.6.91		400h	57.23	58.21- 13
Nisbet	Jayne	GBR	17.7.88	173/57	HJ	1.87i	1.86- 11
Nishihara	Kasumi	JPN	1.3.89	162/47	5000	15:29.02	15:23.80- 11
					10k	31:53.69	32:05.88- 13
Njeru	Pauline Wanjiku	KEN	.88		HMar	69:06	70:48- 13
Nojiri	Azusa	JPN	6.6.82	156/43	Mar	2:28:54	2:24:57- 12
Nokelainen	Heidi	FIN	30.9.90	170/68	JT	57.28	54.56- 13
Nomura	Sayo	JPN	18.4.89	157/48	HMar	70:18	70:03- 13
Novogrodskaya	Alena	BLR	11.5.93	180/96	HT	68.96	67.13- 12
Novozhylova	Iryna	UKR	7.1.86	175/71	HT	73.65	74.10- 12
Novy	Tera	USA	10.2.94	183/	DT	57.32	50.81- 13
Nowell	Danielle	USA	25.3.92	160	PV	4.30i, 4.28	4.11- 13
Nugent	Leah	USA	23.11.92		400h	56.97	57.72- 11
Nukuri	Diane	BDI	1.12.84	175/54	HMar	70:09	69:12- 13
Numata	Michi	JPN	6.5.89	155/45	5000	15:32.41	15:41.00- 09
Nuttall	Emma	GBR	23.4.92	184/64	HJ	1.88i	1.87- 13
Nwaba	Barbara	USA	18.1.89	175/64	Hep	6307	5986- 12
Nyabeu Djapa	Anaëlle	FRA	15.9.92	174/63	Hep	5817	5514- 13

Name		Nat	Born	Ht/Wt	Event	2014 Mark	Pre-2014 Best
^ Nyaruai	Veronica	KEN	29.10.89		10k	32:22.22	-0-
N'Zola Meso	Teresa	FRA	30.11.83	169/53	TJ	13.68	14.69- 07
O'Brien	Rebecca	USA	30.4.90	173.86	SP	17.85	17.78- 13
O'Connell	Jessica	CAN	10.2.89	158/48	3000	8:54.87	9:25.92- 08
					5000	15:13.21	15:50.65- 13
O'Connor	Leah	USA	30.8.92	174/81	3kSt	9:36.43	9:53.53- 13
O'Flaherty	Kerry	IRL	15.7.81		3kSt	9:52.94	9:56.73- 12
Obare	Doricah	KEN	10.1.90	162/48	10k	31:45.24	31:37.07- 10
Oberholzer	Maryke	RSA	27.11.89	175/65	DT	56.95A	57.24- 13
* Obiri	Hellen	KEN	13.12.89	155/45	800	2:00.6A	2:00.54- 11
1500 3:57.05 3:58.58- 13			2000 5:37.7+		5:53.58- 11	3000 8:20.68	8:34.25- 13
Obleshchuk	Halyna	UKR	23.2.89	186/88	SP	19.40	19.23- 12
Obst	Marie-Therese	NOR-J	7.1.96		JT	57.44	52.05- 13
Ofili	Cindy	USA	5.8.94		100h	12.93	13.34, 13.30w- 13
Ogoebune	Amaka	NGR	3.3.90		400h	55.46	56.46- 08
Ogrâzeanu	Andreea	ROU	24.3.90	179/62	100	11.31, 11.27w	11.32- 12, 11.29w- 11
Ogrodníková	Nikola	CZE	18.8.90	175/73	JT	60.04	56.20- 13
Ohara	Rei	JPN	10.8.90	165/47	10k	32:28.88	32:08.73- 13
* Ohuruogu	Christine	GBR	17.5.84	175/70	400	51.38	49.41- 13
Ojaloo	Kati	EST	31.1.90		HT	65.07	60.07- 13
Oka	Sayuri	JPN	19.9.90	156/43	10k	32:42.93	32:06.79- 13
Okada	Kumiko	JPN	17.10.91	158/44	20kW	1:33:25	1:32:22- 13
* Okagbare	Blessing	NGR	9.10.88	180/68	100	10.85	10.79, 10.75w- 13, 10.7Aw- 10
200 22.23			22.31- 13		LJ	6.86	7.00, 7.14w- 13
Okodogbe	Chizoba	NGR	3.11.92	170/60	400	52.20	52.22- 13
* Okolo	Courtney	USA	15.3.94	168/54	200	23.17, 23.04w	23.56- 13
					400	50.03	51.04- 13
Okori	Reina-Flor	FRA	2.5.80	165/56	100h	13.01	12.65- 08
Okoro	Chinwe	NGR	20.6.89		DT	59.79	58.25- 12
Okoro	Eseroghene	GBR	4.7.90	170/59	400h	56.67	57.21- 13
Okoro	Marilyn	GBR	23.9.84	165/60	800	2:01.57	1:58.45- 08
Okou	Rosvitha	CIV	5.9.86	165/62	100h	13.14	13.13- 11
Okparaebo	Ezinne	NOR	3.3.88	164/56	100	11.24, 11.12w	11.10- 12
* Okunyeva	Oksana	UKR	14.3.90	175/61	HJ	1.98	1.94- 11
de Oliveira	Gisele	BRA	1.8.80	160/57	TJ	13.81	14.28, 14.31w- 08
Olivera	Génesis	VEN	21.5.93		HT	65.23	60.00- 13
* Oljira	Belaynesh	ETH	26.6.90	165/49	3000	8:44.2+	8:40.73- 10
3000 8:57.31			8:40.73- 10		2M	9:23.32	
HMar 70:08			67:21- 11		Mar	2:24:21dh	2:25:01- 13
* Olyanovska	Lyudmyla	UKR	20.2.93	172/57	20kW	1:27:27	1:30:26- 13
^ Omarova	Anna	RUS	3.10.81	180/108	SP	17.29	19.69- 07
Omotosho	Omolara	NGR	25.5.93	152/50	400	51.56	51.28- 12
Ondraschková	Lucie	CZE	12.10.89	168/59	Hep	5702	5853- 13
* Ongori	Philes	KEN	19.7.86	158/47	HMar	70:29	67:38- 09
					Mar	2:26:59, 2:23:22dh	2:24:20- 11
Onishi	Misaki	JPN	24.2.85	164/46	5000	15:24.96	15:21.73- 13
Onofre	Marta	POR	28.1.91		PV	4.35A	4.22- 13
Onuora	Anyika	GBR	28.10.84	175/69	200	22.64	22.79, 22.71w- 13
					400	51.76	51.38- 13
* Orbán	Éva	HUN	29.11.84	173/75	HT	72.49	73.44- 13
Orji	Keturah	USA	5.3.96	165/	TJ	13.46i, 13.46, 13.64Aw	13.69- 13
Orlova	Yelena	RUS	30.5.80	165/53	3kSt	9:47.76	9:22.15- 09
Ortiz	Coralys	PUR	16.4.85	176/61	JT	58.20A	57.48A- 13
Ortiz	Mirna	GUA	28.2.87	158/44	20kW	1:29:45, 1:31:53.8At	1:28:32- 13
Oskan-Clarke	Shelayna	GBR	20.1.90		800	2:01.94	2:03.52- 13
Oudenaarden	Niki	CAN	14.1.94	178/65	Hep	5721	5774w, 5716- 13
Owens	Bridgette	USA	14.3.92	163/52	100h	12.80, 12.62w	12.71- 12
Ozolina-Kovale	Sinta	LAT	26.2.88	185/72	JT	61.61	64.38- 13
Paesler	Carolin	GER	16.12.90	167/72	HT	70.76	68.63- 13
Paine	Alexis	USA	12.10.90	168/60	PV	4.35i, 4.20	4.45- 13
Paklina	Alesya	KGZ	22.6.88		HJ	1.88i	1.90i- 13, 1.89- 12
Palacios	Eliecít	COL	15.8.87		100h	13.18A, 13.08wA	13.15- 12
^ Palamar	Vita	UKR	12.10.77	187/62	HJ	1.93	2.01- 03
* Palameika	Madara	LAT	18.6.87	185/76	JT	66.15	64.51- 09
Palframan	Justine	RSA	4.11.93	165/64	200	23.02A, 23.27	23.22A- 12, 23.28- 13
Palmieri	Elisa	ITA	18.9.83	169/85	HT	66.03	67.33- 11
Palmisano	Antonella	ITA	6.8.91	166/49	20kW	1:27:51	1:30:50- 13
* Palsyte	Airine	LTU	13.7.92	186/62	HJ	1.98	1.96- 11
* Pandakova	Marina	RUS	1.3.89		20kW	1:27:54	1:27:39- 13
Panturoiu	Elena Andreea	ROU-J	24.2.95		TJ	13.93i, 13.81, 14.20w	13.36- 13

	Name		Nat	Born	Ht/Wt	Event	2014 Mark	Pre-2014 Best
	Papp	Krisztina	HUN	17.12.82	170/54	10k	32:32.62	31:46.47- 10
						HMar	69:50	70:53- 07
	Pappas	Alexi	USA	28.3.90	165/	5000	15:28.38	15:47.13i- 13
	Pappas/Sheppard	Sarah	USA	30.3.87		PV	4.31Ai, 4.20	4.35i- 13. 4.18- 11
	Parker	Kayla	USA	12.3.92	163/52	100h	13.01	13.19, 13.16w- 13
	Parnov	Elizabeth	AUS	9.5.94	175/57	PV	4.40	4.50- 12
	Parnov	Vicky	AUS	24.10.90	175/62	PV	4.30	4.40- 07
	Parry	Carys	GBR	24.7.81	173/72	HT	66.80	66.31- 08
*	Pascual	Beatriz	ESP	9.5.82	163/64	20kW	1:29:02	1:27:44- 08
	Paterra	Victoria	USA	7.7.92		JT	55.91	50.51- 13
	Patjuk	Jekaterina	EST	6.4.83	162/49	3kSt	9:50.15	10:03.04- 11
*	Patterson	Eleanor	AUS-J	22.5.96	182/66	HJ	1.94	1.96- 13
*	Patterson/Winger	Kara	USA	10.4.86	183/86	JT	62.90	66.67- 10
*	Pavey	Jo	GBR	20.9.73	168/48	5000	15:04.87	14:39.96- 06
						10k	32:11.04	30:53.20- 12
	Paxton	Henrietta	GBR	19.9.83	174/59	PV	4.30	4.35- 10
	Peake	Sally	GBR	8.2.86	164/57	PV	4.40	4.42i- 12, 4.35- 11
*	Pearson	Sally	AUS	19.9.86	167/60	100	11.27, 11.24w	11.14- 07
						200	23.18	23.02, 22.66w- 09
						100h	12.59	12.28- 11
	Pease	Sarah	USA	9.11.87		3kSt	9:48.94	9:52.43- 12
	Pedersen	Isabelle	NOR	27.1.92	170/64	100h	13.07	13.04- 13
	Pedersen	Karolina	SWE	16.4.87		HT	65.55	64.66- 12
	Pedroso	Yadisleidis	ITA	28.1.87	168/51	400h	55.42	54.54- 13
	Peinado	Robeilys	VEN-Y	26.11.97	168/62	PV	4.31A	4.40A- 13
	Pejkovic	Amy	AUS	1.2.93		HJ	1.87	1.86- 10
	Pekin	Lyndsay	AUS	13.6.86		400h	57.11	57.41- 12
	Pelantová	Lucie	CZE	7.5.86	168/60	20kW	1:34:39	1:32:07- 13
	Peleteiro	Ana	ESP-J	2.12.95	171/52	TJ	14.07	14.17- 12
	Pena	Tori	IRL	30.7.87	167/57	PV	4.45	4.60- 13
	Pennella	Giulia	ITA	27.10.89	169/53	100h	13.03	13.06- 12
	Penney	Jessica	AUS	21.12.87	179/63	LJ	6.54	6.43- 12
	Penney	Lauren	USA	1.5.90		1500	4:09.42+	4:13.87- 13
						1M	4:28.02	4:37.41i- 13
						3000	8:55.55	
						5000	15:30.33	15:56.80- 13
	Penttilä	Jenni	FIN	9.3.91	183/90	HT	66.12	65.74- 12
	Peoples	Kearsten	USA	20.12.91	181/105	SP	17.90	18.22- 12
						DT	57.31	55.60- 12
	Pereira	Cátia	POR	5.7.89		PV	4.35	4.05- 13
	Pérez	Paola	ECU	21.12.89	148/55	20kW	1:33:40	1:32:01- 12
*	Pérez	Yaimi	CUB	29.5.91	174/78	DT	66.03	66.01- 13
*	Perie	Bianca	ROU	1.6.90	170/70	HT	71.93	73.52- 10
*	Perkovic	Sandra	CRO	21.6.90	183/80	DT	71.08	69.11- 12
	Perraux	Claire	FRA	6.10.87	170/50	3kSt	9:45.50	9:43.70- 13
	Pete	Aaliyah	USA-J	15.3.95		SP	16.68	15.93- 13
	Peter	Allison	ISV	14.7.92	173/59	200	22.88	22.77- 12
						400	51.92	54.42- 10
	Petersen	Sara	DEN	9.4.87	171/57	400h	56.44	55.68- 12
	Petranoff	Leigh	USA	16.5.89	170/65	JT	58.37	54.84- 13
	Petrich	Anna	RUS	10.2.92		Hep	5791	5500- 13
	Petrillose	Kaitlin	USA	10.12.92	168/57	PV	4.60Ai, 4.50	4.50i, 4.36- 13
*	Petrova	Gabriela	BUL	29.6.92	167/61	TJ	14.13	14.14i- 13, 13.92- 13
	Philip	Asha	GBR	25.10.90	163/54	100	11.18, 11.11w	11.20- 13
	Pidluzhnaya	Yuliya	RUS	1.10.88	180/63	LJ	6.80	6.84- 10, 6.85w- 11
*	Pierre	Barbara	USA	28.4.87	175/60	100	11.05	10.85- 13
	Pierson	Summer	USA	3.9.78	180/64	DT	58.62	61.19, 61.25dh- 09
	Pilipenko	Anastasiya	KAZ	13.9.86	174/55	100h	12.93	12.69- 12
	Pinedo	Ainhoa	ESP	17.2.83	171/60	20kW	1:32:59	1:32:20- 13
	Pinto	Tatjana	GER	2.7.92	170/56	100	11.20, 11.11w	11.19- 12
	Pirelli	Ana Camila	PAR	10.1.89	167/62	Hep	5669	5733- 13
	Plaza	Alexandra	GER	10.8.94	176/58	HJ	1.87	1.88- 12
	Pledger	LeTristan	USA	27.8.93		100h	12.93, 12.85w	13.29, 13.21w- 13
	Pleger	Brooke	USA	21.6.92	171/77	HT	67.97	66.99- 13
	Plis	Renata	POL	5.2.85	165/51	1500	4:05.40	4:03.50- 11
						2000	5:41.98	5:44.17- 09
						3000	8:39.18	8:40.42- 13
						2M	9:28.80	9:36.89i- 10
						5000	15:18.75	-0-
	Plotitsyna	Anna	UKR	1.1.87	182/65	100h	12.93	13.03, 12.91w- 13
	Pluim	Femke	NED	10.5.94	180/62	PV	4.30	4.30- 13
	Podominick	Liz	USA	5.12.84	188/86	DT	61.38	62.32- 13
	Pogrebnyak	Nataliya	UKR	19.2.88	171/62	100	11.22	11.17- 11
						200	22.89	23.16- 13
	Pohoryelska	Viktoriya	UKR	4.8.90		1500	4:07.50	4:14.68- 11
*	Poistogova	Yekaterina	RUS	1.3.91	175/65	800	1:58.55	1:57.53- 12

	Name		Nat	Born	Ht/Wt	Event	2014 Mark	Pre-2014 Best
	Polk	Tori	USA	21.9.83	173/62	LJ	6.70Ai, 6.62i, 6.58	6.75, 6.80w- 13
	Polli	Laura	SUI	7.9.83	162/54	20kW	1:33:22	1:34:07- 13
	Polli	Marie	SUI	28.10.80	165/49	20kW	1:34:39	1:32:36- 09
	Polyakova	Natalya	RUS	9.12.90		HT	70.04	68.84- 13
	Poncio	Maritza Rafaela	GUA	3.12.94		20kW	1:33:14, 1:33:20.1At	
	Pooley	Isobel	GBR	21.12.92	192/70	HJ	1.96	1.91- 13
^	Poonia	Krishna	IND	5.5.82	180/86	DT	59.17	64.76- 12
	Poovamma	Machettira Raju	IND	5.6.90	175/59	400	51.73	52.75- 13
	Popkova	Natalya	RUS	21.9.88	165/50	5000	15:31.27	15:05.95- 09
	Porter	Chanice	JAM	25.5.94		LJ	6.53	6.58, 6.78w- 12
	Porter	Kiara	USA	22.10.93	155/	400	51.72	52.33- 13
*	Porter	Tiffany	GBR	13.11.87	172/62	100h	12.51	12.55- 13, 12.47w- 12
	Pospelova	Marina	RUS	23.7.90	164/53	800	2:00.92	1:59.70- 12
						1500	4:10.09	4:11.40- 12
	Potapova	Anastasiya	RUS	6.9.85	178/61	TJ	13.87	14.68i, 14.40- 09
	Potter	Beth	GBR	27.12.91	168/48	10k	32:33.36	34:56.21- 13
	Pousse	Pauline	FRA	17.9.87	184/84	DT	57.15	55.80- 13
	Povea	Liadagmis	CUB-J	6.2.96	165/61	TJ	14.02, 14.07w	13.54- 13
	Poves	María José	ESP	16.3.78	168/52	20kW	1:28:46	1:28:15- 12
^	Povh	Olesya	UKR	18.10.87	169/63	100	11.0	11.08- 12
	Prandini	Jenna	USA	20.11.92	172/59	100	11.11, 22.60	11.31, 11.14w- 13
	200	22.60		23.15- 13		LJ	6.55	6.20- 11
	Praught	Aisha	USA	14.12.89	173/55	1500	4:08.92+	4:16.06- 12
	1M	4:27.61		4:35.70- 13		3kSt	9:34.69	9:50.06- 13
	Price	Candice	USA	26.10.85	170/62	100h	12.93	12.71, 12.66w- 08
*	Price	Chanelle	USA	22.8.90	166/53	800	1:59.75	2:00.15- 12
						1000	2:36.63i	2:42.71i- 10
*	Proctor	Shara	GBR	16.9.88	174/56	LJ	6.82	6.95- 12
	Profit	Kiani	USA	18.2.90	163/55	Hep	6072	6133- 13
^	Prokopcuka	Jelena	LAT	21.9.76	168/51	10k	32:34.03	30:38.78- 06
						Mar	2:24:07	2:22:56- 05
	Proper	Kelly	IRL	1.5.88	164/58	200	23.15	23.49- 13
						LJ	6.49i, 6.45	6.62i, 6.60- 10, 6.68w- 09
^	Provalinskaya-Korolchyk	Yanina	BLR	26.12.76	186/85	SP	17.17	20.61- 01
	Pryshchepa	Nataliya	UKR	11.9.94		1500	4:08.89	4:13.81- 13
	Prystupa	Darya	UKR	26.11.87	162/55	400	52.32	51.70- 12
	Przybylska	Andzelika	POL	14.10.92	183/105	DT	56.54	55.07- 13
	Ptashkina	Tetyana	UKR	10.1.93		TJ	13.70	13.23- 13
	Puchkova	Natalya	RUS	28.1.87	154/47	Mar	2:28:44	2:30:17- 12
	Pudenz	Kristin	GER	9.2.93	190/92	DT	60.89	59.74- 13
	Puiu	Beatrice	ROU	1.1.86		Hep	5808	5814- 13
	Punia	Seema	IND	27.7.83	185/85	DT	61.61	64.84- 04
	Purica	Andrea	VEN-J	21.11.95		100	11.29A	
	Purvis	Ashton	USA	12.7.92	173/60	100	11.35, 11.30w	11.17- 10
						200	22.95	22.90- 10
	Pusterla	Irène	SUI	21.6.88	176/64	LJ	6.75	6.84- 11
*	Pyatykh	Anna	RUS	4.4.81	175/64	TJ	14.27	15.02, 15.17w- 06
	Pygyda	Nataliya	UKR	30.1.81	167/54	400	51.95	50.86- 13
	Quach Thi Lan		VIE-J	18.10.95	173/58	400	52.06	53.25- 12
	Quaresma	Lecabela	POR	26.12.89		Hep	5744	4397- 07
*	Radzivil	Svetlana	UZB	17.1.87	184/61	HJ	1.96i.1.96	1.97- 12
	Rajabi	Leyla	IRI	18.4.83	185/95	SP	17.93	18.18- 13
	Ramos	Beverly	PUR	24.8.87	163/51	3000	8:57.68	8:59.90- 13
						3kSt	9:47.60	9:39.33- 12
	Ramsey	Jessica	USA	26.7.91		SP	17.49	16.18i, 15.96- 13
	Rani	Annu	IND	29.8.92	165/63	JT	59.53	56.04- 13
	Ratcliffe	Julia	NZL	14.7.93	171/66	HT	70.28	68.80- 13
*	Ratej	Martina	SLO	2.11.81	178/69	JT	66.13	67.16- 10
*	Rath	Claudia	GER	25.4.86	175/65	LJ	6.46	6.67- 13
						Hep	6314	6462- 13
	Râzor	Bianca	ROU	8.8.94	169/54	400	51.77	51.49- 13
	Reaser	Allison	USA	9.9.92	171/61	Hep	5917	5813- 13
*	Rebryk	Vira	UKR/RUS	25.2.89	176/65	JT	61.57	66.86- 12
	Redondo	Laura	ESP	3.7.88	165/80	HT	67.57	69.59- 13
*	Reese	Brittney	USA	9.9.86	173/64	LJ	6.92	7.25- 13
	Reggel	Valérie	SUI	3.1.87	174/64	Hep	6091	5794- 12
	Reilly	Chelsea	USA	9.5.89	168/54	3000	8:52.23	8:47.34- 13
	Ren Mengqian		CHN	4.10.93	175/62	PV	4.30i, 4.30	4.40- 13
	Rengeruk	Lilian	KEN-Y	3.5.97		3000	8:53.41	8:58.74- 13
	Renzhina	Yekaterina	RUS	18.10.94	172/57	200	22.61	23.51- 13
						400	51.67	52.16- 13

Name		Nat	Born	Ht/Wt	Event	2014 Mark	Pre-2014 Best
Reynolds	Laura	IRL	20.1.89	173/57	20kW	1:31:57	1:31:02- 12
Reynolds	Robin	USA	22.2.94	162/50	400	51.36	52.13- 13
Ribalta	Yosleivis	CUB	2.5.90	183/74	TJ	14.12, 14.18w	14.61- 11
Ribeaux	Yainelis	CUB	30.12.87	163/57	JT	55.96	63.18- 09
Richards	Shona	GBR-J	1.9.95		400h	56.16	58.33- 13
* Richards-Ross	Sanya	USA	26.2.85	173/61	400	49.66	48.70- 06
Riddick	Monique	USA	8.11.89		SP	16.64i, 16.51	16.39- 11
Riebold	Jade	USA	14.4.91	163/	PV	4.30i	4.45i. 4.40- 13
Ries	Chyna	USA-J	5.9.96		LJ	6.37, 6.50w	6.21- 13
Rigert	Yelena	RUS	2.12.83	167/73	HT	68.76	75.09- 13
Rionoripo	Purity	KEN	10.6.93		3000	8:49.94	8:44.54- 10
5000 15:30.61A 15:20.93- 11					HMar	70:40	
Rivas	Ányela	COL	13.8.89	180/82	SP	17.18	17.53- 12
* Robert-Michon	Mélina	FRA	18.7.79	180/85	DT	65.51	66.28- 13
Roberts	Kelsey-Lee	AUS	21.9.91	175/72	JT	63.92	58.58- 13
Rocha	Carla Salomé	POR	25.4.90	158/48	10k	32:19.98	32:40.03- 13
Rodgers	Christina	USA	8.4.88	173/	800	2:01.75	2:02.65- 13
Rodhe	Megann	CAN	27.8.85	180/90	HT	64.80	67.03- 11
* Rodic/Vukmirovic	Snezana	SLO	19.8.82	180/66	TJ	13.90	14.58- 13
Rodrigues	Irina	POR	5.2.91	182/81	DT	62.23	62.91- 12
Rodriguez	Lidia	ESP	26.5.86	171/59	10k	32:38.25	32:50.34- 13
Rodríguez	Déborah	URU	2.12.92	174/63	400h	56.60	57.04- 12
Rodríguez	Rosa	VEN	2.7.86	179/78	HT	72.20	73.64- 13
Rodríguez	Yorgelis	CUB-J	25.1.95	173/60	Hep	6231	6186- 13
Rodríguez	Zudikey	MEX	14.3.87	168/56	400h	55.78A	56.10- 10
Roesler	Laura	USA	19.12.91	168/54	800	1:59.04	2:00.23- 13
* Rogowska	Anna	POL	21.5.81	171/57	PV	4.76i, 4.50	4.85i- 11, 4.83- 05
Rogozina	Svetlana	RUS	26.12.92	165/52	800	1:59.54	2:01.68- 13
Rogozina	Yekaterina	RUS	21.12.89		3kSt	9:50.10	9:59.16- 13
Rohl	Beth	USA	7.11.90	175/82	DT	60.39	59.66- 13
Rojas	Yolimar	VEN-J	21.10.95	169/50	LJ	6.48, 6.53Aw	6.23- 13
					TJ	13.65	
* Roleder	Cindy	GER	21.8.89	175/62	100h	12.80	12.91- 11
					Hep	5728	-0-
* Rollins	Brianna	USA	18.8.91	164/55	100h	12.53	12.26- 13
Roloff	Annika	GER	10.3.91	166/54	PV	4.45Ai, 4.41	4.42i- 12, 4.41- 13
Romero	Shapri	USA	13.11.91	158/	200	23.10	23.50- 13
					400	51.96	52.37- 13
Rono	Georgina	KEN	19.5.84	165/47	HMar	69:31	67:58- 12
					Mar	2:26:47	2:21:39- 12
Rono	Janet	KEN	8.12.88		Mar	2:26:03	2:28:36- 13
Rosa	Chiara	ITA	28.1.83	178/112	SP	18.49	19.15- 09
Roslova	Taisa	BLR	7.2.92		HJ	1.88	1.86i, 1.84- 13
* Rosolová	Denisa	CZE	21.8.86	175/61	400h	54.54	54.24- 12
Rossit	Desirée	ITA	19.3.94	181/53	HJ	1.88	1.81- 13
* Rotaru	Alina	ROU	5.6.93	175/54	LJ	6.74	6.63- 13
Rotich	Caroline	KEN	13.5.84	161/45	HMar	69:22	68:52- 11
					Mar	2:24:35	2:23:22- 12
Rotich	Joan	KEN	27.11.93		3kSt	9:33.34	
* Rowbury	Shannon	USA	19.9.84	165/52	1500	3:59.49	4:00.33- 08
3000 8:29.93 8:31.38- 10 2M 9:20.25 - 5000 14:48.68 15:00.51- 10							
Rubie	Anneliese	AUS	22.4.92	172/56	400	52.35	52.61- 13
Rudakova	Vera	RUS	20.3.92	175/57	400h	55.93	55.92- 13
Ruddick	Kelly	AUS	19.4.73		20kW	1:34:00	1:33:15- 13
* Rüh	Anna	GER	17.6.93	186/78	DT	64.17	64.33- 13
Ruiz	Flor Denis	COL	24.1.91	171/67	JT	63.80A	60.23- 13
Ruiz	Úrsula	ESP	11.8.83	170/83	SP	17.70	17.99- 12
Rummans	Angie	USA	23.3.92	168/57	PV	4.30	4.40- 12
Rumpf	Sabine	GER	18.3.83	176/95	DT	60.35	62.21- 10
Rushin	Jill	USA	18.7.91		SP	17.62	16.67i, 16.52- 13
* Russell	Carrie	JAM	18.10.90	171/68	100	11.10	10.98- 13
Russell	Janeive	JAM	14.11.93	175/63	400	51.49	53.13- 13
					400h	54.75	56.30- 13
Rutto	Lydia	KEN	.94		Mar	2:28:48	2:28:22- 13
Ryan	Marshay	USA-J	4.2.95	168/	TJ	13.60	12.87- 12
* Rypakova	Olga	KAZ	30.11.84	183/62	TJ	14.37	15.25- 10
Ryzhova #	Kseniya	RUS	19.4.87	172/62	400	51.03i	49.80- 13
* Ryzhykova	Anna	UKR	24.11.89	176/67	400h	55.00	54.35- 12
Ryzhykova	Hanna	UKR	24.11.89	176/67	400	52.11	53.31- 11
* Ryzih	Lisa	GER	27.9.88	179/59	PV	4.71	4.65- 10
Sadeiko	Grete	EST	29.5.93	178/	Hep	5706	5705- 10

	Name		Nat	Born	Ht/Wt	Event	2014 Mark	Pre-2014 Best
	Sadeiko	Grit	EST	29.7.89	172/62	Hep	6128	6221- 13
	Sado	Baso	ETH	.91		1500	4:07.59	
	Sadovnikova	Anastasiya	RUS-J	22.6.95		PV	4.35	4.10- 13
	Saeed	Alia Mohamed	UAE	18.5.91	164/53	3000	8:48.27i	
	5000	15:24.94		15:31.21- 11		10k	31:51.86	32:39.39- 13
	Safránková	Katerina	CZE	8.6.89	191/105	HT	70.79	71.16- 12
	Safronova	Olga	KAZ	5.11.91	171/62	100	11.23	11.12- 12
						200	22.85	23.21- 13
	Sagnia	Khaddi	SWE	20.4.94	173/63	LJ	6.55	6.32- 11
*	Sailer	Verena	GER	16.10.85	166/57	100	11.14, 11.02w	11.02- 13
*	Saina	Betsy	KEN	30.6.88	163/48	3000	8:38.01	
	2M	9:16.95				5000	14:39.49	15:12.05- 13
	Saina 10k	30:57.30		31:15.97- 12		HMar	69:27	
	Saito	Marina	JPN-J	15.10.95	161/61	JT	55.98	56.76- 13
	Sakaida	Ayumi	JPN	7.11.85	157/44	10k	32:24.55	32:24.85- 13
*	Saladukha	Olha	UKR	4.6.83	175/55	TJ	14.73	14.99- 12, 15.06w- 11
	Salis	Silvia	ITA	17.9.85	179/74	HT	70.48	71.93- 11
	Salomatina	Olga	RUS	15.8.92		TJ	13.71, 13.88w	13.41- 10
	Saltanovic	Kristina	LTU	20.2.75	163/54	20kW	1:32:58	1:30:44- 02
	Samuel	Jamile	NED	24.4.92	168/54	100	11.12	11.38- 12
						200	22.72	22.93- 12
	Samuel	Laura	GBR	19.2.91	165/65	TJ	14.09	13.75- 10, 13.77w- 11
*	Samuels	Dani	AUS	26.5.88	182/82	SP	17.05	16.82- 13
						DT	67.99	65.84- 10
	Samuels	Sonia	GBR	16.5.79	162/47	10k	32:39.36	32:57.23- 11
	Samuelsson	Jessica	SWE	14.3.85	176/67	Hep	5981	6300- 12
	Sanders	Shayla	USA	6.1.94	168/55	100	11.20, 11.12w	11.33, 11.32w- 12
	Sandu	Cristina	ROU	4.3.90	172/58	LJ	6.52	6.57, 6.70w- 12
						TJ	13.99	13.71- 13
	Sango	Misaki	JPN	21.4.89	165/46	3kSt	9:49.85	9:54.02- 13
	Santiusti	Yusneysi	CUB	24.12.84	166/60	800	2:01.97	1:58.53- 12
	dos Santos	Jéssica	BRA	21.3.91		400	52.30	54.22- 12
	dos Santos	Patrícia	BRA	13.6.84	168/58	PV	4.36	4.43- 13
	Santos	Rosângela	BRA	20.12.90	165/55	100	11.32	11.17, 11.07w- 12
*	Santos	Vera	POR	3.12.81	164/57	20kW	1:28:02	1:28:14- 08
	Sarrapio	Patricia	ESP	16.11.82	168/58	TJ	13.96A, 13.91	14.10- 10, 14.30w- 12
	Saunders	Raven	USA-J	15.5.96	165/	SP	17.28	
	Savatovic	Sara	SRB	5.1.93	169/87	HT	65.19	64.11- 13
*	Savchenko	Anastasiya	RUS	15.11.89	175/65	PV	4.50i, 4.50	4.73- 13
*	Savigne	Yargelis	CUB	13.11.84	165/55	TJ	14.01	15.28- 07
	Savlinis	Yelizaveta	RUS	14.8.87	178/65	200	23.01	22.62- 12
	Sawyers	Jazmin	GBR	21.5.94	167/52	LJ	6.54	6.67- 12
*	Saxer	Mary	USA	21.6.87	166/57	PV	4.71Ai, 4.58	4.70- 13
^	Sayers	Goldie	GBR	16.7.82	171/70	JT	62.75	66.17- 12
	Saykina	Svetlana	RUS	10.7.85	177/82	DT	58.13	63.42- 08
	Scarlett	Samantha	JAM	7.4.93		100h	13.01	13.62- 12
*	Schäfer	Carolin	GER	5.12.91	176/66	Hep	6395	6072- 12
	Schappert	Nicole	USA	30.10.86		1500	4:09.87	4:06.87- 12
						3000	8:55.48	9:50.80- 07
	Scheper	Jeannelle	LCA	21.11.94	180/58	HJ	1.91	1.92A- 13
*	Schippers	Dafne	NED	15.6.92	179/68	100	11.03	11.09- 13
	200	22.03		22.69- 11		100h	13.13	13.27- 11
	LJ	6.78		6.59- 13		Hep	6545	6477- 13
	Schlumpf	Fabienne	SUI	17.11.90	183/62	3kSt	9:37.81	9:46.98- 13
	Schmelcz	Fanni	HUN	19.4.92	169/56	LJ	6.56	6.25, 6.54w- 13
	Schmid	Anna Katharina	SUI	2.12.89	165/57	PV	4.35	4.45- 11
	Schmitz	Vera	USA	3.12.87	168/57	PV	4.35	4.45- 13
	Schrott	Beate	AUT	15.4.88	177/66	100h	13.14	12.82- 12
	Schultze	Martina	GER	12.9.90	172/59	PV	4.40i, 4.40	4.50- 13
*	Schwanitz	Christina	GER	24.12.85	180/103	SP	20.22	20.41- 13
	Schwartz	Lindsay	USA	23.4.90	178/64	Hep	5942	5980- 13
*	Schwarzkopf	Lilli	GER	28.8.83	174/63	Hep	6426	6649- 12
	Schwerdtner	Maren	GER	3.10.85	182/72	Hep	6038	6167- 10
	Scott	Sharolyn	CRC	27.10.84	167/64	400h	57.34A, 58.10	56.19- 12
	Seaman	Rachel	CAN	14.1.86	173/59	20kW	1:30:43	1:33:05- 12
*	Seboka	Mulu	ETH	13.1.84	158/45	Mar	2:23:15	2:23:43- 13
	Sedivá	Irena	CZE	19.1.92		JT	56.01	57.41- 12
	Sedykh	Alexia	FRA	13.9.93	173/70	HT	65.16	68.35- 13
^	Sekachyova	Iryna	UKR	21.7.76	165/72	HT	69.10	74.52- 08
	Seles	Vanessa	BRA	26.10.81		LJ	6.57	6.60- 11
	Selvon	Kai	TTO	13.4.92	165/59	100	11.29	11.21- 12, 11.19w- 11

Name		Nat	Born	Ht/Wt	Event	2014 Mark	Pre-2014 Best
					200	23.10	22.85- 12, 22.65w- 13
^ Semenova	Nataliya	UKR	7.7.82	178/85	DT	63.33	64.70- 08
de Sena	Érica	BRA	3.5.85	152/52	20kW	1:30:43	1:31:53- 12
* Sendriute	Zinaida	LTU	20.12.84	188/89	DT	65.83	65.97- 13
Sène	Amy	SEN	6.4.85	174/70	HT	69.70	69.10- 12
Serksniene	Agne	LTU	18.2.88	173/60	400	51.62	52.28- 13
* Seyaum	Dawit	ETH-J	27.7.96		1500	3:59.53	4:09.00- 13
Seymour	Kiah	USA	11.1.94		400h	55.88	58.22- 13
Shahaf	Ma'ayan	ISR	9.11.86	184/62	HJ	1.90	1.92- 11
Shamotina	Alyona	UKR-J	27.12.95	178/98	HT	68.43	66.01- 13
Sharbono	Jessica	USA	14.2.92		DT	58.86A	53.21- 13
* Sharmina	Yekaterina	RUS	6.8.86	172/59	800	2:01.61	1:59.17- 11
					1500	4:07.45	3:59.49- 12
* Sharp	Lynsey	GBR	11.7.90	175/60	800	1:58.80	2:00.52- 12
Shatybelko	Anastasiya	BLR	20.5.94		HT	67.23	64.33- 13
Shchagina	Anna	RUS	7.12.91	166/54	800	2:01.74, 2:01.29i	2:01.07- 13
					1500	4:05.58	4:05.91- 13
Shelekh	Hanna	UKR	14.7.93	166/54	PV	4.52i, 4,50	4.60i- 12, 4.30- 10
Shestakova	Olga	RUS	4.12.93		JT	59.95	53.52- 13
Shimizu	Miho	JPN	13.5.90	158/52	10k	32:14.44	
Shoji	Mai	JPN	9.12.93			32:27.36	
Shone	Guteni	ETH	17.11.91		HMar	68:31	68:59- 13
Shumkina	Olena	UKR	24.1.88	153/47	20kW	1:30:41	1:25:32- 09
Shushina	Irina	RUS	30.10.86		20kW	1:32:57	1:32:03- 12
Shvydkina	Tatyana	RUS	8.5.90		PV	4.40i, 4.40	4.20i- 13, 4.10- 12
Sidorina	Olga	RUS	23.8.92	166/89	SP	16.96	16.15- 12
Sidorkina	Yelena	RUS	27.9.88		TJ	13.79, 13.85w	14.11- 12
Sidorova	Anzhelika	RUS	28.6.91	170/52	PV	4.72i, 4.70	4.62i, 4.60- 13
Siebert	Susanne	GER	2.8.84	173/68	JT	59.42	58.83- 09
Sifuentes	Nicole	CAN	30.6.86	173/57	800	2:02.02	2:01.30- 12
1500 4:04.87 4:04.65- 13 1M 4:28.97i 4:29.42i- 10, 4:31.98- 11 5000 15:30.50 15:27.58- 13							
Sigurjardóttir	Hafdís	ISL	12.2.87		LJ	6.41, 6.72w	6.36- 13
Silhanová	Rebeka	CZE-J	22.3.95		PV	4.35	4.05- 13
Silva	Ana Cláudia	BRA	6.11.88	158/55	100	11.13	11.05, 10.93w- 13
					200	22.81	22.48- 11
da Silva	Izabela	BRA-J	2.8.95		DT	58.70	55.88- 13
da Silva	Karla	BRA	12.11.84	168/58	PV	4.35	4.53- 13
da Silva	Tânia	BRA	17.12.86	178/59	LJ	6.52	6.47- 10
					TJ	14.04	14.11- 07
Silva	Vânia	POR	8.6.80	174/78	HT	66.93	69.55- 11
* Silva	Yarisley	CUB	1.6.87	169/68	PV	4.70i, 4.70	4.90- 13
* Simic	Ana	CRO	5.5.90	177/58	HJ	1.99	1.96- 13
Simmonds	Megan	JAM	18.3.94		100h	13.07, 13.06w	13.33, 13.23w- 13
^ Simpson	Jemma	GBR	10.2.84	178/58	800	2:01.50	1:58.74- 10
					1500	4:07.37	4:06.39- 10
* Simpson	Jennifer	USA	23.8.86	165/50	1500	3:57.22	3:59.90- 09
3000 8:29.58			8:48.72- 12		2M	9:26.19i	
Singh	Desiree	GER	17.8.94	166/54	PV	4.36	4.32- 11
Singh	Sudha	IND	25.6.86	163/52	3kSt	9:35.64	9:45.60- 13
Sirma	Katrina	LAT	31.3.94		JT	55.87	51.69- 11
Sisson	Emily	USA	12.10.91	160/48	5000	15:33.16, 15:21.84i	15:34.54- 12
					10k	32:31.06	33:02.88- 13
Sivkova	Kristina	RUS-Y	28.2.97		100	11.31	11.66- 13
Skoog	Sofie	SWE	7.6.90	181/65	HJ	1.88i, 1.87	1.90- 13
Skrobáková	Lucie	CZE	4.1.82	170/62	100h	12.99	12.73- 09
Skydan	Anna	UKR	14.5.92	183/114	HT	71.14	74.21- 12
Slack	Salsa	JAM	10.12.89		Hep	5833A, 5718	5534- 11
Slanicková	Lucie	SVK	8.11.88	179/65	400h	56.96	57.87- 10
Smets	Fanny	BEL	21.4.86	173/59	PV	4.31i, 4.30	4.40- 13
Smirnova	Yevgeniya	RUS	16.3.91		SP	16.68	16.77- 10
Smit	Angela	NZL	16.8.91	164/55	800	2:00.59	2:00.03- 13
Smith	Amina	USA	10.1.92		HJ	1.87	1.79- 13
Smith	Brittany	USA	25.3.91	178/89	SP	18.57	17.92- 12
					HT	70.27	68.51- 13
Smith	Jessica	CAN	11.10.89	172/54	800	2:00.92	1:59.86- 12
Smith	Jonielle	JAM-J	30.1.96		100	11.32, 11.17w	11.58- 13
Smith	Kristin	USA	23.12.87	168/75	HT	68.40	68.25- 12
Smith	Nivea	BAH	18.2.90		200	23.08	22.71- 10
Smith	Toni	USA	13.10.84		LJ	6.40, 6.58w	6.36- 05
Smock	Amanda	USA	27.7.82	170/57	TJ	13.81Ai, 13,66, 13.77w	14.18- 11
^ Smolyachkova	Mariya	BLR	10.2.85	177/78	HT	67.04	74.65- 08

	Name		Nat	Born	Ht/Wt	Event	2014 Mark	Pre-2014 Best
	Snow	Morgan	USA	26.7.93	161/52	100h	12.91, 12.81w	12.88- 13
	Soares	Núbia	BRA-J	26.3.96		TJ	14.22	13.60- 13
	Sokolenko	Yekaterina	RUS	13.9.92		3kSt	9:34.12	9:43.50- 13
*	Sokolova	Vera	RUS	8.6.87	151/42	20kW	1:27:03	1:25:08- 11
*	Solomon	Shalonda	USA	19.12.85	169/56	100	11.12	10.90- 10
						200	22.64, 22.54w	22.15- 11
	Song Xiaodan		CHN	23.1.93		JT	59.10	59.21- 13
	Sormunen	Oona	FIN	2.8.89	168/72	JT	58.43	60.56- 13
	Sorna	Rachel	USA	15.4.92		3kSt	9:43.48	9:50.39- 13
	Soto	Nercely	VEN	26.8.90	169/55	200	23.14A, 23.25	22.53- 12
						400	52.30	51.94- 13
	Sotomayor	Laura	ESP	22.4.86	172/60	400h	57.06	57.57- 13
*	Soumaré	Myriam	FRA	29.10.86	167/57	100	11.03	11.07- 12
						200	22.11	22.32- 10
	Souza	Joelma	BRA	13.7.84	174/51	400	51.72	51.54- 12
	de Souza	Tamara	BRA	8.9.93	185/76	Hep	5962	5900- 12
*	Spanovic	Ivana	SRB	10.5.90	176/65	LJ	6.92i, 6.88	6.82- 13
						TJ	13.78	13.54- 11
	Spaulding	Diamond	USA-J	29.9.96	163/57	200	23.36, 23.00wA	23.59- 13
	Spence	Christine	USA	25.11.81	174/54	400h	55.98	54.21- 08
	Spence	Indira	JAM	8.9.86	178/68	100h	12.98	12.92, 12.80Aw, 12.80w- 12
*	Spencer	Ashley	USA	8.6.93	168/54	100	11.34, 11.27w	11.46- 13
	200	22.92, 22.69w		22.99- 12		400	51.38	50.28- 13
*	Spencer	Kaliese	JAM	6.5.87	173/59	400	51.00	50.19- 13
						400h	53.41	52.79- 11
	Spencer	Kate	AUS-J	23.6.95		5000	15:32.29	16:56.66- 13
						3kSt	9:53.15	10:20.72- 13
*	Spencer	Levern	LCA	23.6.84	180/54	HJ	1.96	1.98- 10
	Spenner	Sami	USA	21.3.91	168/59	Hep	6003	5897- 13
*	Spiegelburg	Silke	GER	17.3.86	173/64	PV	4.72i, 4.50	4.82- 12
	Spiler	Barbara	SLO	2.1.92	184/79	HT	69.08	71.25- 12
	Spiljard	Amanda	NED	18.9.89		Hep	5678	5681- 13
	Spínola	Vanessa	BRA	5.3.90	178/68	Hep	5945	6015- 12
*	Spotáková	Barbora	CZE	30.6.81	182/80	JT	67.99	72.28- 08
	Sprunger	Ellen	SUI	5.8.86	172/62	Hep	6082	6124- 12
	Sprunger	Léa	SUI	5.3.90	183/69	200	23.12	23.08- 12
	Sreedharan	Preeja	IND	13.3.82	155/52	10k	32:29.17	31:50.47- 10
*	Stahl	Linda	GER	2.10.85	174/72	JT	67.32	66.81- 10
	Staisiunaite	Egle	LTU	30.9.88	174/59	400h	56.39	56.58- 12
*	Stambolova	Vania	BUL	28.11.83	175/53	800	2:00.91	2:12.61- 13
	Stanciu	Daniela	ROU	15.10.87	175/57	HJ	1.94	1.91i, 1.90- 13
	Stanková	Eliska	CZE	11.11.84		DT	59.34	58.70- 12
	Stanwell	Sophie	AUS	8.6.91	174/61	Hep	5754	5556- 13
	Starostina	Oksana	RUS	1.4.88		HJ	1.89i, 1.87	1.92- 12
	Starygina	Yekaterina	RUS	26.8.95	177/73	JT	56.85	58.59- 13
	Steacy	Heather	CAN	14.4.88	175/73	HT	66.73	72.16- 12
*	Steel	Gemma	GBR	12.11.85		HMar	68:13dh	70:19- 13
*	Stefanidi	Ekaterini	GRE	4.2.90	172/63	PV	4.71	4.51- 12
	Steinacker	Marike	GER	4.3.92	184/80	DT	57.36	55.75- 12
	Steiner Bennett	April	USA	22.4.80	175/61	PV	4.45Ai, 4.36	4.63- 08
	Stenlöf	Emma	SWE-J	25.6.96	179/68	Hep	5795	-0-
	Stepter	Jaide	USA	25.4.94	173/	400h	56.99	59.54- 11
	Steryíou	Adonía	GRE	7.7.85	180/58	HJ	1.91i, 1.88	1.97- 08
	Stetsyuk	Tatyana	RUS	27.8.92	174	PV	4.40i, 4.40	4.25- 13
*	Stewart	Kerron	JAM	16.4.84	175/61	100	11.02	10.75- 09
	Stewart	Shanice	USA	2.12.93		Hep	5674	
	Stites	Emily	USA	2.6.94	170/55	10k	32:41.55	34:15.49- 13
	Stoddart	Shevon	JAM	21.11.82	165/52	400h	55.56	54.47- 05
	Storm	Ida	SWE	26.12.91	189/90	HT	69.13	68.05- 13
	Stowe	Rebeka	USA	9.3.90		3kSt	9:53.18	9:52.82- 12
	Stowers	Jasmin	USA	23.9.91	175/64	100h	12.71, 12.54w	12.88, 12.86w- 11
*	Strachan	Anthonique	BAH	22.8.93	168/57	200	22.50	22.32- 13
*	Straneo	Valeria	ITA	5.4.76	168/44	HMar	68:55	67:46- 12
						Mar	2:25:27	2:23:44- 12
	Stratton	Brooke	AUS	12.7.93	168/58	LJ	6.70	6.60- 11
	Strohova	Nataliya	UKR	26.12.92		200	23.12	23.28- 12
	Strokova	Yekaterina	RUS	17.12.89	184/80	DT	65.78	63.80- 13
*	Strutz	Martina	GER	4.11.81	160/57	PV	4.46i, 4.41	4.80- 11
	Stuart	Bianca	BAH	17.5.88	168/52	LJ	6.67	6.81, 6.91w- 11
	Stuart	Lauren	CAN	16.11.91		HT	65.05	61.48- 13
	Stuy	Hrystyna	UKR	3.2.88	168/57	100	11.24	11.32- 10

	Name		Nat	Born	Ht/Wt	Event	2014 Mark	Pre-2014 Best
	200	23.26, 23.21w		22.66- 12		400	51.58	
^	Styopina	Viktoriya	UKR	21.2.76	178/58	HJ	1.90	2.02- 04
	Su Xinyue		CHN	8.11.91	179/70	DT	61.31	61.67- 13
	Subbotina	Yevgeniya	RUS	30.10.89		800	2:01.05	2:03.15- 10
*	Sudareva	Olga	BLR	22.2.84	176/63	LJ	6.67	6.85- 12
	Sudarushkina	Viktoriya	RUS	2.9.90	176/76	JT	60.15	62.77- 13
*	Suhr	Jenn	USA	5.2.82	183/63	PV	4.73i, 4.71	5.02Ai- 13, 4.92- 08
	Sujew	Diana	GER	2.11.90	166/52	1500	4:05.72	4:05.62- 13
						3000	8:52.68mx, 8:54.70	8:47.68- 13
	Sujew	Elina	GER	2.11.90	164/51	1500	4:07.82	4:07.36- 12
*	Sum	Eunice	KEN	2.9.88	172/53	800	1:57.92	1:57.38- 13
						1500	4:01.54	4:02.05- 13
	Summers	Jeré	USA	21.5.87	172/84	DT	57.76	59.59- 12
*	Sun Huanhuan		CHN	15.3.90	161/50	20kW	1:29:20	1:27:36- 13
	Sun Yan		CHN	30.3.91		TJ	13.73	14.00- 10
	Sun Yawei		CHN	17.10.87	169/55	100h	13.01	12.94- 11
	Sussmann	Jana	GER	12.10.90	166/47	3kSt	9:43.52	9:43.28- 11
*	Sutej	Tina	SLO	7.11.88	173/58	PV	4.71i, 4.50	4.61- 11
	Suzuki	Ayuko	JPN	8.10.91	154/38	5000	15:14.96	15:31.45- 13
	Sviridova	Olesya	RUS	28.10.89	176/94	SP	17.10	19.72- 12
*	Svobodová	Jirina	CZE	20.5.86	175/69	PV	4.71i, 4.60	4.76- 13
	Swiety	Justyna	POL	3.12.92	170/56	400	52.22, 52.13i	52.22- 13
	Swisher	Kristen	USA	16.6.83	170/52	10k	32:40.66	
	Swoboda	Ewa	POL-Y	26.7.97	164/55	100	11.30	11.54, 11.46w- 13
	Szabó	Barbara	HUN	17.2.90	175/59	HJ	1.91i, 1.91	1.92Ai, 1.89A- 13
	Tabares	Carolina	COL	18.7.86		10k	32:39.13	34:14.5- 13
*	Tadesse	Feyse	ETH	19.11.88	167/53	HMar	69:19	68:35- 13
						Mar	2:20:27	2:21:06- 13
*	Takacs	Julia	ESP	29.6.89	171/53	20kW	1:29:08	1:28:44- 13
	Takashima	Yuka	JPN	12.5.88	153/42	5000	15:31.66	15:43.51- 12
						10k	31:55.81	32:06.70- 13
	Takayama	Kotomi	JPN	18.2.93	155/42	10k	32:15.20	32:49.12- 13
	Takechi	Shiho	JPN	18.8.90	159/44	5000	15:32.20	15:29.85- 13
						10k	32:26.53	32:52.57- 13
	Takenaka	Risa	JPN	6.1.90	159/41	10k	32:07.08	32:10.66- 13
						HMar	70:10	
	Takeuchi	Asahi	JPN-J	9.1.95		10k	32:26.32	
	Takuncheva	Irina	RUS	14.11.90		400h	57.18	57.02- 13
*	Talay	Alina	BLR	14.5.89	164/54	100h	12.89	12.71- 12
	Tamkova	Alena	RUS	30.5.90	168/58	400	51.33	51.17- 13
*	Tan Jian		CHN	20.1.88	179/80	DT	61.07	64.45- 12
	Tanaka	Hanae	JPN	12.2.90	160/48	10k	32:00.15	32:25.05- 13
	Tanaka	Kaho	JPN	24.6.91	161/41	10k	32:24.73	
	Tanaka	Tomomi	JPN	25.1.88	154/40	HMar	69:24	69:47- 12
						Mar	2:26:05	
	Tappin	Jess	GBR	17.5.90	179/64	Hep	5770	5676(w)- 13
*	Tarasova	Irina	RUS	15.4.87	183/110	SP	18.38	19.35- 12
	Tarasova	Yuliya	UZB	13.3.86	177/68	LJ	6.49	6.81- 10
						Hep	5826	5989- 09
*	Tarmoh	Jeneba	USA	27.9.89	167/59	100	11.11	10.93- 13
						200	22.41, 22.06w	22.28- 11, 22.15w- 13
	Tarver	Hanna	GBR	22.10.93		800	2:01.82	2:05.42- 13
	Tate	Brianna	USA	1.1.93	168/	400	52.32	52.65- 13
*	Tate	Cassandra	USA	11.9.90	174/64	400h	54.70	55.22- 12
	Tavares	Maria Eleonor	POR	24.9.85	164/55	PV	4.44i, 4.35	4.50- 11
	Tavernier	Alexandra	FRA	13.12.93	170/75	HT	71.17	70.79- 13
	Taylor	Jessica	GBR	27.6.88		Hep	5826	5369- 13
	Taylor	Tremanisha	USA	10.3.92		SP	17.60	16.77- 12
	Taylor-Chase	Chanice	CAN	6.8.93	172/61	400h	56.27	58.72- 13
	Tebo	Jessica	USA	8.4.88	168/	5000	15:18.17	15:19.43- 12
*	Teferi	Senbera	ETH-J	3.5.95	159/45	1500	4:08.49	4:04.55- 13
	2000	5:34.27				3000	8:41.54	9:13.0- 13
	Tenorio	Ángela	ECU-J	27.1.96	167/59	100	11.25A, 11.17	11.41, 11.24w- 13
						200	22.82A, 23.16, 23.15w	23.13- 13
	Terlecki	Josephine	GER	17.2.86	183/84	SP	17.69i, 17.54	18.87- 12
	Terrero	Indira	ESP	29.11.85	161/52	400	51.38	50.98A, 50.5- 08, 51.00- 07
	Terzic	Amela	SRB	2.1.93	169/50	1500	4:07.34	4:05.69- 13
	Tesfaye	Kokebe	ETH-Y	5.5.97		1500	4:07.34	
	Theisen	Mary	USA	3.11.90	176/	SP	17.30i, 17.20	15.96- 12
*	Theisen-Eaton	Brianne	CAN	18.12.88	180/64	100h	13.00	13.09A- 12, 13.13- 13
	HJ	1.871.88i- 12, 1.86- 10	LJ	6.59		6.37, 6.39w- 13	Hep 6641	6530- 13

	Name		Nat	Born	Ht/Wt	Event	2014 Mark	Pre-2014 Best
	Theodorou	Paraskevi	CYP	15.3.86	167/85	HT	66.29	69.29- 09
	Thi Thanh Duc	Nguyen	VIE	12.8.90	154/45	20kW	1:35:07	1:33:36- 12
*	Thiam	Nafissatou	BEL	19.8.94	184/69	HJ	1.97	1.92- 13
						Hep	6508	6298- 13
	Thomas	Danniel	JAM	11.11.92	166/89	SP	16.97i, 16.82	16.10- 13
						DT	59.38	54.78- 13
	Thomas	LaTavia	USA	17.12.88	173/	800	2:00.95	1:59.67- 11
	Thomas	Reyare	TTO	23.11.87	168/60	100	11.16	11.30A- 12, 11.40- 13, 11.36w- 11
						200	23.17, 22.57w	23.23, 23.04w- 13
	Thomas	Shanieka	JAM	2.2.92	180/64	TJ	14.00	14.15- 13
^	Thomas	Vashti	USA	21.4.90	175/60	100h	12.84	12.61, 12.56w- 13
	Thompson	Elaine	JAM	28.6.92		100	11.17	11.41- 13
	Thompson	Evann	USA	9.10.94		400h	56.87	58.89- 13
	Thompson	Turquoise	USA	31.7.91	178/66	400h	56.09	54.99- 13
	Thweatt	Laura	USA	17.12.88	165/54	5000	15:04.98	15:36.85- 13
	Tigabea	Marta	ETH	4.10.90		HMar	70:32	71:37- 13
	Tikhonova	Olesya	RUS	22.1.90		TJ	13.51, 14.11w	13.89- 12
	Tilahun	Konjit	ETH	22.9.87		Mar	2:28:11	2:34:23- 09
*	Tirop	Agnes	KEN-J	23.10.95	159/44	3000	8:47.26	8:39.13- 13
						5000	15:00.19	14:50.36- 13
*	Titimets	Anna	UKR	5.3.89	173/62	400h	54.56	54.63- 13
	Tkach	Lyubov	RUS	18.2.93		Hep	5903	5380- 12
	Tkachuk	Anastasiya	UKR	20.4.93	168/56	800	2:01.45	2:00.37- 11
	Todd	Jasmine	USA	23.12.93	165/	100	11.25	11.99- 10
						LJ	6.50Ai, 6.40i	6.08i- 12, 6.01- 11, 6.02Aw- 10
	Tollesa	Gulume	ETH	.92		HMar	69:28	72:16- 13
	Toma	Carmen	ROU	28.3.89	168/50	TJ	13.65	14.29- 09, 14.56w- 13
^	Tomasevic	Dragana	SRB	4.6.82	175/80	DT	60.96	63.63- 06
^	Tomashova	Tatyana	RUS	1.7.75	164/50	1500	4:06.77	3:56.91- 06
	Tomic	Marina	SLO	30.4.83	167/55	100h	12.95	12.94- 13
	Tonn	Jessica	USA	15.2.92		5000	15:32.26	15:54.90- 13
	Topylina	Svetlana	RUS	6.1.85	173/62	100h	12.99	13.14- 11
	Tovarnova	Olga	RUS	11.4.85		400	52.10	52.46i, 52.62- 13
	Townsend	Tiffany	USA	14.6.89	163/50	100	11.30 (i), 11,28w	11.13- 09, 11.09w- 11
						200	22.72	22.26- 13
	Traby	Laïla	FRA	26.3.79	160/48	10k	32:26.03	
	Tracey	Adele	GBR	27.5.93		800	2:02.01	2:03.18- 12
	Tracey	Nikita	JAM	18.9.90	173/63	400h	55.18	56.08- 13
	Tracey	Ristananna	JAM	5.9.92	170/61	400h	55.12	54.52- 13
	Tran Hue Hoa		VIE	8.8.91	170/63	TJ	13.97	14.12- 13
	Trapletti	Valentina	ITA	12.7.85	172/56	20kW	1:34:50	1:32:53- 08
	Traynor	Nicol	USA	6.5.89	170/54	3kSt	9:42.13	9:55.91- 13
	Treacy	Sara	IRL	22.6.89		3kSt	9:47.92	-0-
	Treasure	Alyx	CAN	15.5.92	181/	HJ	1.89	1.84- 12
	Troest	Stina	DEN	17.1.94	158/52	400h	56.55	57.41- 13
	Trofimova	Sardana	RUS	28.3.88		Mar	2:28:18	2:35:48- 13
	Troneva	Natalya	RUS	24.2.93	181/84	SP	16.92i, 16.88	17.25- 13
*	Trost	Alessia	ITA	8.3.93	188/66	HJ	1.96i, 1.91	2.00i, 1.98- 13
^	Trotter	Deedee	USA	8.12.82	180/63	200	23.03	22.85, 22.54w- 13
						400	50.98	49.64- 07
	Trybanska	Malgorzata	POL	21.6.81	177/59	TJ	13.74	14.44- 10
	Tsareva	Yelizaveta	RUS	15.3.93		HT	68.14	67.59- 13
	Tsega	Muluhabt	ETH	11.9.89		Mar	2:29:17	
	Tsegay	Gudaf	ETH-Y	23.1.97		1500	4:02.83	4:07.27- 13
*	Tsegaye	Tirfi	ETH	25.11.84	165/54	HMar	69:56+	67:42- 12
						Mar	2:20:18	2:21:19- 12
	Tsyhotska	Ruslana	UKR	23.3.86	166/49	TJ	13.87, 14.20w	14.53- 12
	Tufa	Mestawat	ETH	14.9.83	157/45	Mar	2:28:27	2:26:20- 13
	Tufa	Tigist	ETH	26.1.87		Mar	2:21:52	2:29:24- 13
	Tuliamuk-Bolton	Aliphine	KEN	5.4.89		HMar	70:38	69:16dh- 13
	Tverdohlib	Marharyta	UKR	2.6.91	179/70	LJ	6.55	6.80- 12
	Tverdostup	Tamara	UKR	17.7.79	167/56	1500	4:08.16	4:07.43- 09
*	Tyminska	Karolina	POL	4.10.84	175/69	Hep	6266	6544- 11
	Tyson	Keilah	USA	6.11.92		100	11.32, 11.14w	11.39- 11, 11.37w- 13
^	Uceny	Morgan	USA	10.3.85	168/57	800	2:00.29mx, 2:02.74	1:58.37- 11
	1500	4:04.76		4:00.06- 11		1M	4:29.61	4:38.87i- 08
	Udras	Grete	EST	11.3.88	180/59	HJ	1.88i	1.92i- 11, 1.90- 13
	Ugarova	Kristina	RUS	22.10.87		1500	4:08.24	4:00.53- 12
	Ugen	Lorraine	GBR	22.8.91	178/64	LJ	6.73Ai, 6.59i, 6.39, 6.40w	6.77- 13, 6.83w- 12
	Uke	Claire	USA	31.12.92	179/80	SP	17.18	16.51i, 16.49- 13
	Uloga	Svetlana	RUS	23.11.86		800	2:01.35	2:02.79- 13

Name		Nat	Born	Ht/Wt	Event	2014 Mark	Pre-2014 Best
Urbaniak	Lena	GER	31.10.92	175/95	SP	17.84	17.58- 13
Urbanik	Danuta	POL	24.12.89	167/58	1500	4:07.95	4:08.32- 12
Urbina	María Teresa	ESP	20.3.85	177/53	3kSt	9:49.35	9:41.95- 09
Urech	Lisa	SUI	27.7.89	168/54	100h	13.02	12.62- 11
* Urrutia	Yosiri	COL	26.6.86	175/61	TJ	14.58	14.08- 13
Ushiro	Orie	JPN	24.8.90	174/68	JT	55.89	53.89- 13
Uwakwe	Florence	NGR	28.7.94		400	51.94A, 52.56	52.09- 12
* Valyukevich	Viktoriya	RUS	22.5.82	178/63	TJ	14.05	14.85- 08
Van Alstine	Amy	USA	11.11.87	163/50	5000	15:22.98	15:36.56- 13
Van Buskirk	Kate	CAN	9.6.87	178/60	1500	4:05.38	4:07.36- 13
					1M	4:28.08	4:33.71i- 11
Van Dalen	Lucy	NZL	18.11.88	168/53	3000	8:53.95i	
					5000	15:22.95	15:21.08- 13
Varner	Rachel	USA	20.7.83	176/	DT	59.06	57.93- 04
Vasilyeva	Svetlana	RUS	24.7.92		20kW	1:28:49	1:28:30- 12
Vasilyeva	Yuliya	RUS	23.3.87		1500	4:09.88	4:11.49- 13
Vaskovskaya	Irina	BLR	2.4.91		TJ	13.79	13.76- 13
Vastenburg	Jip	NED	21.3.94	181/59	1500	4:10.11	4:21.98- 13
5000	15:27.30	15:53.24- 13			10k	32:11.90	
Vaughan	Shelbi	USA	24.8.94	185/91	DT	63.60	60.59- 12
Vaughn	Sara	USA	16.5.86	155/48	1500	4:10.05	4:08.34- 12
					3kSt	9:41.55	9:47.58- 13
Veitia	Lisneidy	CUB	29.4.94	167/53	400	51.72A	53.39- 13
* Veldáková	Dana	SVK	3.6.81	182/68	TJ	14.10i, 13.91	14.51- 08, 14.59w- 10
Veldáková	Jana	SVK	3.6.81	177/59	LJ	6.50	6.72- 08, 6.88w- 10
Velvere	Liga	LAT	10.2.90	171/59	400h	56.87	58.40- 13
^ Veneva-Mateeva	Venelina	BUL	13.6.74	179/61	HJ	1.92	2.04- 01
Verseckaite	Jolanta	LTU	9.2.88		TJ	13.68	13.72- 09
Verstegen	Sanne	NED	10.11.85	164/54	800	2:00.55	2:01.15- 13
					1000	2:38.53	2:45.23- 13
^ Veshkurova	Tatyana	RUS	23.9.81	180/70	400	51.41	49.99- 06
					400h	55.79	-0-
^ Vessey	Maggie	USA	23.12.81	170/58	800	1:59.96	1:57.84- 09
Vetter	Anouk	NED	4.2.93	177/62	Hep	6316	5872- 13
Viart	Saily	CUB-J	10.9.95	169/97	SP	17.21	15.74- 13
Viberg	Julia	SWE	8.1.92	175/80	DT	56.37	54.07- 13
Vicenzino	Tania	ITA	1.4.86	167/61	LJ	6.65	6.57, 6.65w- 12
Vichy	Ariannis	CUB	18.5.89	170/70	HT	71.07	71.50- 12
* Viljoen	Sunette	RSA	6.1.83	170/70	JT	65.32	69.35- 12
Viola	Giulia	ITA	24.4.91	162/45	1500	4:07.67	4:10.00- 13
Virbalyte	Brigita	LTU	1.2.85	165/50	20kW	1:31:00	1:30:55- 13
Visser	Nadine	NED-J	9.2.95	173/63	100h	12.99	13.21- 13
					Hep	6110	5774- 13
Vita	Claudine	GER-J	19.9.96	177/66	DT	56.98	52.59- 13
Vivod	Eva	SLO	7.8.94	174/65	JT	56.80	56.98- 13
* Vlasic	Blanka	CRO	8.11.83	192/75	HJ	2.00i, 2.00	2.08- 09
Vlasova	Alisa	RUS	16.9.90		TJ	13.78	13.86i- 10, 13.73- 13
Vlasova	Natalya	RUS	19.7.88	164/48	3kSt	9:34.16	9:37.41- 12
Volkova	Nina	RUS	26.8.84	168/70	HT	68.30	67.82- 12
Vollmer	Lindsay	USA	10.9.92	168/59	Hep	5786	6086- 13
von Eynatten	Victoria	GER	6.10.91	174/54	PV	4.30i	4.40i- 13, 4.30- 11
Voronina	Yekaterina	UZB	16.2.92	175/65	Hep	5912	5599- 13
Voskamp	Ariel	USA	3.8.92	170	PV	4.30i, 4.25	3.95- 12
Vucenovic	Marija	SRB	3.4.93	172/70	JT	56.73	57.12- 12
Vukolova	Yekaterina	RUS	10.8.87		200	22.80	22.79- 10
					400	52.37	52.13- 10
Vyatkina	Natalya	BLR	10.2.87	176/50	TJ	14.35	14.40- 13
Vytlacilová	Tereza	CZE-J	25.9.95		JT	56.26	51.29- 13
Wacera	Mercy	KEN	17.12.88		HMar	67:44	70:32- 13
Waite	Lennie	GBR	4.5.86	173/60	3kSt	9:48.17	9:48.35- 12
Wake	Laura	GBR	3.5.91	165/55	400h	57.17	57.62- 13
Walker	Alesha	USA	9.4.88		LJ	6.41, 6.63w	6.50- 08
Walker	Crystal	USA	23.6.91		LJ	6.67w	6.35, 6.41w- 13
Walker	Shanique	USA	20.11.93		100h	13.28, 13.11w	13.16- 13
Wallace	Lea	USA	19.12.88	163/52	1500	4:09.34	4:09.13- 13
Wallace	Sasha	USA-J	21.9.95		100h	13.23, 13.06w	13.33- 12
Wallader	Rachel	GBR	1.9.89	180/87	SP	16.83	16.41- 13
Wambui	Margaret	KEN-J	15.9.95		800	2:00.49	
Wang Di		CHN	30.8.92		20kW	1:30:44	1:33:48- 13
Wang Huan		CHN	21.9.94	168/54	400h	57.16	
Wang Lin		CHN-J	8.1.95		HJ	1.88	1.84- 13

	Name		Nat	Born	Ht/Wt	Event	2014 Mark	Pre-2014 Best
	Wang Lu		CHN	22.12.91	178/83	HT	65.00	69.39- 13
	Wang Qingling		CHN	14.1.93	170/58	Hep	5873	5785- 13
	Wang Rong		CHN-J	1.7.96		TJ	13.98	14.09i- 13, 13.76- 12
	Wang Wupin		CHN	18.1.91		TJ	13.67	
	Wang Yang		CHN	14.2.89	185/65	HJ	1.88	1.92- 12
	Wang Yingliu		CHN	1.3.92		20kW	1:30:51	1:32:01- 13
*	Wang Zheng		CHN	14.12.87	174/108	HT	77.68	74.90- 13
	Wangari	Miriam	KEN	22.2.79		Mar	2:28:20	2:31:30- 12
	Wanjiru	Rosemary	KEN	9.12.94	159/44	3000	8:48.44	8:49.32- 13
						5000	15:19.00	15:26.07mx- 11, 15:30.41- 13
	Wanjugu	Felista	KEN	18.2.90	158/46	5000	15:33.21	15:02.28mx- 08, 15:21.57- 13
	Ward	Rachel	USA	11.10.89		10k	32:15.85	32:39.53- 12
	Washington	Ariana	USA-J	4.9.96	175/59	100	11.22	11.39, 11.18Aw, 11.20w- 13
						200	22.96	23.18, 23.05Aw- 13
	Wassall	Georgia	AUS-J	30.3.96		800	2:01.78	2:03.37- 13
	Wehrsen	Claudia	GER	18.10.84	177/62	400h	57.20	57.36- 12
*	Weightman	Laura	GBR	1.7.91	172/58	1500	4:00.17	4:02.99- 12
	Weir	Jillian	CAN	9.2.93	177/78	HT	67.43	64.70- 13
	Weitzel	Michelle	GER	18.6.87	181/63	LJ	6.66	6.64- 11, 6.67w- 13
	Wellings	Eloise	AUS	9.11.82	167/44	3000	8:54.11	8:41.78- 06
	5000	15:14.99	14:54.11- 06			10k	32:26.59	31:41.31- 11
*	Wells	Kellie	USA	16.7.82	163/57	100h	12.68	12.48- 12, 12.35w- 11
	Wells	Lauren	AUS	3.8.88	179/66	400h	55.69	55.08- 13
	Weng Chunxia		CHN	29.8.92		DT	58.89	58.64- 12
	Wertman	Casandra	USA	14.6.93	176/	SP	17.26	16.21- 13
	Westaway	Jenna	CAN	19.6.94		800	2:01.89i, 2:02.50	2:05.60- 13
	Westphal	Liv	FRA	22.12.93		5000	15:31.62i	16:03.69mx- 13
	White	Cierra	USA	29.4.93	165/52	100	11.20, 11.09w	11.09- 13
						200	23.01, 22.61w	22.89- 13
	Whitney	Kaylin	USA-Y	9.3.98		100	11.10	11.54, 11.47Aw- 13
						200	22.49	23.28A, 23.40, 23.30w- 13
	Whittle	Laura	GBR	27.6.85	169/55	5000	15:20.92	15:26.96- 08
	Whyte	Angela	CAN	22.5.80	170/56	100h	12.89	12.63, 12.55w- 07
						Hep	6018	5745- 03
*	Whyte-Robinson	Rosemarie	JAM	8.9.86	175/66	400	52.16	49.84- 11
	Wiklund	Erika	SWE	10.3.88		HJ	1.88i, 1.88	1.91- 08
	Wilkins-Gooden	Bobby-Gaye	JAM	10.9.88	160/53	400	51.84A, 52.67	50.87- 08
	Williams	Alisha	USA	5.2.82	167/52	5000	15:19.79	15:09.73- 13
	Williams	Bianca	GBR	18.12.93		100	11.17	11.36- 13
						200	22.58	23.24- 13
	Williams	Christania	JAM	17.10.94		100	11.19	11.39- 11
	Williams	Danielle	JAM	14.9.92	168/59	100	11.16	11.24A, 11.41, 11.35w- 13
						100h	12.99	12.69- 13
	Williams	Jaleesa	USA	6.4.91	170/	DT	57.97	53.12- 13
*	Williams	Jodie	GBR	28.9.93	174/65	100	11.20, 11.13w	11.18- 11
						200	22.46	22.79- 10
	Williams	Kendell	USA-J	14.6.95		100h	12.87	13.23- 13
	HJ	1.88Ai	1.82i- 13, 1.81- 11			Hep	6018	5578- 12
*	Williams	Kimberly	JAM	3.11.88	169/66	TJ	14.59	14.62, 14.78w- 13
	Williams	Regine	USA-J	5.9.95		100	11.46, 11.29w	11.79- 10
						200	23.36, 23.06i	23.80- 13
*	Williams	Shericka	JAM	17.9.85	170/64	400	51.23	49.32- 09
	Williams	Shermaine	JAM	4.2.90	174/62	100h	12.91A, 12.95	12.78, 12.65w- 12
*	Williams	Tiffany	USA	5.2.83	158/57	400h	54.74	53.28- 07
*	Williams-Mills	Novlene	JAM	26.4.82	167/55	400	50.05	49.63- 06
	Williamson	Kimberly	JAM	2.10.93	168/	HJ	1.88	1.88- 11
	Wills	Tiana	USA		186/	HJ	1.88Ai, 1.85	1.84A- 13
*	Wilson	Ajee'	USA	8.5.94	169/55	800	1:57.67	1:58.21- 13
	Wilson	Heather	USA	13.6.90	169/55	1500	4:07.47	4:08.25- 13
	Wilson	Kenyanna	USA	27.10.88	165/	100	11.29, 11.24w	11.19- 11
^	Wilson	Nickiesha	JAM	28.7.86	173/64	100h	13.06	12.79- 09
						400h	55.22	53.97- 07
	Wimbley	Shakima	USA-J	23.4.95		200	23.12	23.73- 13
						400	51.68	55.11- 12
	Winslow	Amanda	USA	10.12.90		1M	4:26.28i, 4:31.66	4:31.08i- 13, 4:50.88- 08
	1500	4:12.33	4:10.79- 13			3000	8:56.37i	9:08.13i- 13
	Wise	Katie	USA	15.10.93	165/54	100	11.23, 11.18w	11.50- 13
						200	23.06	23.92- 13
^	Wisniewska	Joanna	POL	24.5.72	178/84	DT	59.88	63.97- 99
	Witek	Marcelina	POL-J	2.6.95	168/58	JT	61.24	56.20- 13
	Withrow	Melinda	USA	30.10.84	165/52	PV	4.41	4.55Ai- 11, 4.52- 10

	Name		Nat	Born	Ht/Wt	Event	2014 Mark	Pre-2014 Best
*	Wlodarczyk	Anita	POL	8.8.85	178/95	HT	79.58	78.46- 13
	Wloka	Anna	POL	14.3.93	176/80	SP	17.06i, 16.43	16.83- 13
	Woitha	Charlene	GER	21.8.93		HT	65.92	61.79- 13
	Woldu	Etagegne	ETH-J	10.5.96		5000	15:11.42	
	Woods	Shana	USA	7.7.88	1.76/	Hep	5668	5533- 06
	Woolven	Pippa	GBR	26.7.93		3kSt	9:47.97	10:11.86- 12
	Wortham	Ellen	USA	5.1.90	174/61	400h	57.17	55.55- 12
	Wright	Phoebe	USA	30.8.88	170/57	800	2:01.91	1:58.22- 10
	Wu Shuijiao		CHN	19.6.91	159/48	100h	12.72	12.93- 13
	Wyciszkiewicz	Patrycja	POL	8.1.94	164/46	400	52.14	51.56- 13
	Xiao Xia		CHN	6.6.91		400h	56.59	56.25- 13
	Xie Lijuan		CHN	14.5.93		20kW	1:31:19	1:33:25- 12
	Xu Huiqin		CHN	4.9.93	175/55	PV	4.40	4.40- 11
	Yakovchuk	Halyna	UKR	21.2.92		20kW	1:32:46	1:35:58- 13
	Yakovenko	Olha	UKR	1.6.87	159/46	20kW	1:34:36	1:30:38- 13
	Yamauchi	Ai	JPN	6.12.94	167	JT	56.55	55.73- 13
	Yamazaki	Rina	JPN	6.5.88	162/50	10k	31:56.11	32:41.16- 13
						HMar	70:45	73:31- 08
	Yang Fei		CHN	20.7.87	186/90	DT	59.20	60.43- 12
	Yang Mingxia		CHN	13.1.90	163/44	20kW	1:34:28	1:28:56- 08
	Yang Xinli		CHN	7.2.88		JT	60.30	61.37- 13
	Yang Yanbo		CHN	9.3.90		DT	63.31	63.32- 12
	Yarigo	Noélie	BEN	26.12.85		800	2:00.51	2:06.03- 13
	Yastrebova	Nataliya	UKR	12.10.84	175/57	TJ	13.94i	14.50- 11
	Yatsevich	Anastasiya	BLR	18.1.85		20kW	1:31:53	1:29:30- 11
	Yepimashko	Vera	BLR	10.7.76	181/74	SP	18.22i, 17.72	18.95- 10
	Yermakova	Anna	UKR	1.10.91		LJ	6.58	6.39- 12, 6.49w- 13
	Yeryomina	Lyudmila	RUS	8.8.91	171/60	PV	4.56i, 4.30	4.50i, 4.45- 13
	Yin Anna		CHN	23.3.92	168/54	3kSt	9:40.50	9:41.44- 12
	Young	Jessica	USA	6.4.87	160/50	100	11.13	11.14, 11.08w- 11
	Yüksel-Ayhan	Burcu	TUR	3.5.90	182/58	HJ	1.90	1.94- 11
	Yumanova ¶	Irina	RUS	6.11.90		20kW	1:28:44dq	1:26:47- 12
	Zabara	Olesya	RUS	6.10.82	165/56	TJ	14.09	14.54i- 08, 14.50- 06
*	Zadorina	Kseniya	RUS	2.3.87	173/59	400	51.69	50.55- 13
	Zagré	Anne	BEL	13.3.90	178/69	100h	12.83, 12.80w	12.79- 12
	Zaldívar	Liuba M.	CUB	5.4.93	161/54	TJ	14.12	14.20- 13
	Zang Milama #	Ruddy	GAB	6.6.87	156/46	100	11.28, 11.24 dq	11.03- 12
	Zapounídou	Déspina	GRE	5.10.85	166/55	20kW	1:33:02	1:31:08- 12
	Zawila	Karolina	POL	21.11.86	169/50	LJ	6.55	6.49, 6.50w- 13
	Zbären	Noemi	SUI	12.3.94	177/65	100h	12.92	13.04- 13
*	Zelinka	Jessica	CAN	3.9.81	172/62	100h	12.83	12.65- 12
						Hep	6270	6599- 12
*	Zemlyak	Olha	UKR	16.1.90	165/55	400	51.00	51.82- 12
	Zhang Li		CHN	17.1.89	174/65	JT	65.47	64.74- 12
	Zhang Luyu		CHN	18.8.94		HJ	1.88	1.87- 13
*	Zhang Wenxiu ¶		CHN	22.3.86	182/108	HT	75.50, 77.33dq	76.99- 12
	Zhao Jing		CHN	9.7.88	168/55	800	1:59.48	2:01.46- 12
	Zhao Jing		CHN	18.2.92		20kW	1:31:23	1:32:45- 11
	Zhatkina	Lyubov	RUS	30.3.90		JT	59.34	58.52- 12
	Zheng Xingjuan		CHN	20.3.89	184/60	HJ	1.96	1.95- 09
	Zhilkina	Yelena	RUS	4.5.90		800	2:01.1	2:02.64- 09
	Zhou Kang		CHN	24.12.89	165/54	20kW	1:31:09	1:30:58- 13
	Zhou Tongmei		CHN	4.4.88		20kW	1:31:58	1:30:28- 13
	Zhou Xiaoxue		CHN	19.6.92		LJ	6.46	6.38- 11
	Zinchuk	Hanna	BLR	4.2.94		HT	67.53	66.36- 13
	Zinurova	Yevgeniya	RUS	16.11.82		800	2:00.67	1:58.04- 08
	Zongo-Filet	Amy	FRA	4.10.80	165/51	TJ	13.68	14.08i- 09, 14.03- 08, 14.16w- 12
	Zophoníasdóttir	Sveinbjörg	ISL	27.4.92		Hep	5723	5479- 13
	Zubkovska	Oksana	UKR	15.7.81	175/62	LJ	6.61	6.71- 07
	Züblin	Linda	SUI	21.3.86	171/60	Hep	5817	6057- 13
	Zyryanova	Valeriya	RUS	12.8.90		SP	17.30	15.47- 13

WORLD INDOOR LISTS 2015 – MEN

60 METRES

Note: including some marks froim December 2014, # Oversized track

6.47	Kim	Collins	SKN	5.4.76	1	Pedros	Lódz	17 Feb
6.48		Collins			1	Winter	Moskva	1 Feb
6.48		Collins			1		Torun	3 Feb
6.50		Collins			1	ISTAF	Berlin	14 Feb
6.50	Ryan	Bailey	USA	13.4.89	1h5		Seattle	14 Feb
6.50		Collins			1	GP	Birmingham	21 Feb
6.51A	Akeem	Haynes	CAN	3.11.92	1		Flagstaff	31 Jan
6.51	Trell	Kimmons	USA	13.7.85	1	NB GP	Boston (Roxbury)	7 Feb
6.51	Richard	Kilty	GBR	2.9.89	1	EI	Praha (02)	8 Mar
6.52	James	Dasaolu	GBR	5.9.87	2		Düsseldorf	29 Jan
6.52	Michael	Rodgers	USA	24.4.85	1h1	NB GP	Boston (Roxbury)	7 Feb
6.52	Asafa	Powell	JAM	23.11.82	2	NB GP	Boston (Roxbury)	7 Feb
6.52	John	Teeters	USA	19.5.93	1h3	Tyson	Fayetteville	13 Feb
6.52	Ronnie	Baker (10)	USA	15.10.93	1	NCAA	Fayetteville	14 Mar
6.53	Joe	Morris	USA	4.10.89	1		Seattle	31 Jan
6.53	Chijindu	Ujah	GBR	5.3.94	1A2		London (LV	1 Feb
6.53	Marvin	Bracy	USA	15.12.93	1	Mill	New York (Armory)	14 Feb
6.54	Clayton	Vaughn	USA	15.5.92	1		Houston	16 Jan
6.54	Trayvon	Bromell	USA	10.7.95	1		Lexington	24 Jan
6.54	Jalen	Miller	USA	17.6.95	1h2	NCAA	Fayetteville	13 Mar
6.55	Yunier	Pérez	CUB/TUR	16.2.85	4	Pedros	Lódz	17 Feb
6.56	Christian	Blum	GER	10.3.87	1rA		Chemnitz	7 Feb
6.56	Kendal	Williams	USA	23.9.95	1	ACC	Blacksburg	28 Feb
6.56	Tevin	Hester (20)	USA	10.1.94	2	ACC	Blacksburg	28 Feb
6.56A	Odean	Skeen	JAM	28.8.94	1	JUCO	Albuquerque	7 Mar
6.57	Rondell	Sorrillo	TTO	21.1.86	2		Lexington	24 Jan
6.57	Christophe	Lemaitre	FRA	11.6.90	1		Lyon	31 Jan
6.57A	Eric	Cray	PHI	6.11.88	1h1		Albuquerque	14 Feb
6.57	Daniel	Bailey	ANT	9.9.86	2h1	ISTAF	Berlin	14 Feb
6.57	Justyn	Warner	CAN	28.6.87	4	GP	Birmingham	21 Feb
6.57	Senoj-Jay	Givans	JAM	30.12.93	2h2	NCAA	Fayetteville	13 Mar
6.58	Christian	Coleman	USA-J	6.3.96	1		Blacksburg	6 Feb
6.58	Sean	McLean	USA	23.3.92	7	NB GP	Boston (Roxbury)	7 Feb
6.58	Lucas	Jakubczyk (30)	GER	28.4.85	2	NC	Karlsruhe	21 Feb
6.58	Adam	Harris	GUY	21.7.87	1		Metz	25 Feb
6.58	Marquesh	Woodson	USA	6.9.93	2	SEC	Lexington	28 Feb

6.60A	Cameron	Burrell	USA	11.9.94	24 Jan
6.60	Trentavis	Friday	USA	5.6.95	24 Jan
6.60	Darrell	Wesh	USA	21.1.92	6 Feb
6.60	Andre	De Grasse	CAN	10.11.94	7 Feb
6.60	Julian	Reus	GER	29.4.88	7 Feb
6.60A	Anaso	Jobodwana	RSA	30.7.92	14 Feb
6.60	Winston	Barnes	JAM	7.11.88	18 Feb
6.60	Hugh	Graham (40)	JAM	10.10.92	27 Feb
6.60A	Ridge	Jones	USA	25.3.94	28 Feb
6.60		Yang Yang	CHN	13.10.93	1 Mar
6.60	Desmond	Lawrence	USA	19.12.91	1 Mar
6.60		Xie Zhenye	CHN	17.8.93	8 Mar
6.60	Pascal	Mancini	SUI	18.4.89	8 Mar
6.60		Zhang Peimeng	CHN	13.3.87	15 Mar
6.61A	Cameron	Hudson	USA	5.3.94	31 Jan
6.61	Keith	Ricks	USA	9.10.90	3 Feb
6.61	Sean	Safo-Antwi	GBR	31.10.90	3 Feb
6.61	Jaysuma	Saidy Ndure (50)	NOR	1.1.84	7 Feb
6.61	DionDre	Batson	USA	13.7.92	13 Feb
6.61	Catalin	Cîmpeanu	ROU	10.3.85	14 Feb
6.61		Su Bingtian	CHN	29.8.89	14 Feb
6.61	Beejay	Lee	USA	5.3.93	28 Feb
6.61A	Chris	Lewis	USA	6.8.95	7 Mar
6.61	Emmanuel	Biron	FRA	29.7.88	8 Mar
6.61	Michael	Tumi	ITA	12.2.90	8 Mar
6.62	Harry	Adams	USA	27.11.89	29 Jan
6.62	Daveon	Collins	USA	3.10.92	31 Jan
6.62A	Kendrick	Smith (60)	USA	19.5.92	7 Mar

Best at low altitude: 6.56 Haynes 5 NB GP Boston (Roxbury) 7 Feb

55 METRES: 6.09 Marvin Bracy USA 15.12.93 1 Gainesville 23 Jan

200 METRES

20.19	Trayvon	Bromell	USA	10.7.95	1r1	NCAA	Fayetteville	14 Mar
20.23		Bromell			1h1	NCAA	Fayetteville	13 Mar
20.26	Andre	De Grasse	CAN	10.11.94	2r1	NCAA	Fayetteville	14 Mar
20.57	Shavez	Hart	BAH	9.6.92	1r1		College Station	7 Feb

20.66A	Aaron	Ernest	USA	8.11.93	6 Feb
20.66	Karol	Zalewski	POL	7.8.93	22 Feb
20.69	Brendon	Rodney	CAN	9.4.92	14 Feb
20.70	Robin	Erewa	GER	24.6.91	22 Feb
20.70	Bryce	Robinson	USA	13.11.93	13 Mar
20.71	Lalonde	Gordon	TTO	25.11.88	14 Feb
20.74	Dedric	Dukes (10)	USA	2.4.92	13 Mar
20.76A	Jermaine	Brown	JAM	4.7.91	24 Jan
20.76	Lucas	Jakubczyk	GER	28.4.85	22 Feb
20.75#	D.J.	Zahn	USA	31.1.93	28 Feb

300 METRES

32.53	Pavel	Maslák	CZE	21.2.91	1		Praha (Strom)	20 Jan
32.57	Lalonde	Gordon	TTO	25.11.88	1		New York (Armory)	31 Jan

32.81	Manteo	Mitchell	USA	6.7.87	31 Jan
32.91	Jermaine	Brown	JAM	4.7.91	31 Jan

400 METRES

45.27	Pavel	Maslák	CZE	21.2.91	1	NC	Praha (Strom)	22 Feb
45.31	Vernon	Norwood	USA	10.4.92	1r1	NCAA	Fayetteville	14 Mar

45.33 Maslák 1 EI Praha (02) 7 Mar
45.34 Najee Glass USA 12.6.94 1 Fayetteville 31 Jan
45.38 Deon Lendore TTO 28.10.92 1r3 Tyson Fayetteville 13 Feb
45.39 Bralon Taplin GRN 8.5.92 1r4 Tyson Fayetteville 13 Feb
45.39 Abdelilah Haroun QAT .97 1rB XLG Stockholm 19 Feb
45.75 Clayton Parros USA 11.12.90 1r2 College Station 7 Feb
45.96A Aldrich Bailey USA 6.2.94 1 Albuquerque 7 Feb
45.98 Christopher Giesting USA 10.12.92 3 Fayetteville 31 Jan
45.98 Hugh Graham (10) JAM 10.10.92 4 Fayetteville 31 Jan
45.98 Zach Bilderback USA 15.7.94 2r4 Tyson Fayetteville 13 Feb

46.13 Quincy Downing USA 16.1.93 14 Mar
46.18 Arman Hall USA 12.2.94 13 Mar
46.20 D.J. Zahn USA 31.1.93 13 Mar
46.21 Jan Tesar CZE 26.3.90 22 Feb
46.25 Karol Zalewski POL 7.8.93 22 Feb
46.25 Dylan Borlee USA 20.9.92 7 Mar

Oversized track

45.63 D.J. Zahn USA 31.1.93 1 Big Ten Geneva 28 Feb
45.76 Lamar Bruton USA 26.5.95 2 Big Ten Geneva 28 Feb
45.90 Brycen Spratling USA 10.3.92 1 Notre Dame 7 Feb
45.91 Cody Rush USA 11.11.93 3r Big Ten Geneva 28 Feb

45.97 Arman Hall USA 12.2.94 28 Feb
46.13 Patrick Feeney USA 29.12.91 7 Feb

500 METRES

New York (A) 14 Feb: 1. Brycen Spratling 1:00.06; 2. Michael Berry USA 10.12.91 1:00.43; 3. Bershawn Jackson USA 6.5.83 1:00.70; 4, Jonathan Borlée BEL 22.2.88 1:00.76. Spala 1 Feb: 1. Jakub Krzewina POL 10.10.89 1:00.68

600 METRES

1:15.33 Casimir Loxsom USA 17.3.91 1 NC Boston (Roxbury) 1 Mar
1:15.58A Loxsom 1 Albuquerque 24 Jan
1:15.99 Abdulrahman Musaeb Balla QAT 19.3.89 1 Winter Moskva 1 Feb
1:16.01 Luguelin Santos DOM 12.11.93 1 Montreal 21 Feb

1:16.22A Jaymes Dennison USA 7 Mar
1:16.32 Je'Von Hutchison USA 4.5.92 1 Mar
1:16.50 Andrew Osagie GBR 19.2.88 1 Feb
1:16.52 Erik Sowinski USA 21.12.89 1 Mar
1:16.26# Mitch Hechsel USA 15.3.94 28 Feb
1:16.47# Nate Roese USA 19.9.94 28 Feb

800 METRES

1:45.48 Abdulrahman Musaeb Balla QAT 19.3.89 1 XLG Stockholm 19 Feb
1:45.77 Adam Kszczot POL 2.9.89 2 XLG Stockholm 19 Feb
1:45.78 Marcin Lewandowski POL 13.6.87 3 XLG Stockholm 19 Feb
1:45.93 Jeremiah Mutai KEN 27.12.92 1 GP Birmingham 21 Feb
1:46.04 Andre Olivier RSA 29.12.89 4 XLG Stockholm 19 Feb
1:46.05 Edward Kemboi KEN 12.12.91 1 NCAA Fayetteville 14 Mar
1:46.55 Timothy Kitum KEN 20.11.94 5 XLG Stockholm 19 Feb
1:46.56 Andreas Almgren SWE 12.6.95 6 XLG Stockholm 19 Feb
1:46.70 Dylan Capwell USA 1.7.95 2 NCAA Fayetteville 14 Mar

1:46.78# Andres Arroyo (10) PUR 7.6.95 14 Feb
1:46.80# Brandon McBride CAN 15.6.94 14 Feb
1:46.86# Alex Amankwah USA 2.3.92 24 Jan
1:46.92 Erik Sowinski USA 21.12.89 21 Feb
1:46.98# Jesse Garn USA 4.6.93 14 Feb
1:47.06 Clayton Murphy USA 26.2.95 14 Mar
1:47.17 Mark English IRL 18.3.93 21 Feb
1:47.25 Thijmen Kupers NED 4.10.91 8 Mar
1:47.26 Thomas Roth NOR 11.2.91 31 Jan
1:47.29# Ryan Schnulle USA 8.9.93 14 Feb
1:47.34 Ryan Manahan (20) USA 21 Feb
1:47.38# Joe McAsey USA 1.6.93 14 Feb
1:47.38 Guy Learmonth GBR 20.4.92 21 Feb
1:47.44# Shaquille Walker USA 24.6.93 31 Jan
1:47.45 Kevin López ESP 12.6.90 7 Feb

1000 METRES

2:17.00 Matthew Centrowitz USA 18.10.89 1 NB GP Boston (Roxbury) 7 Feb

2:18.30 Patrick Casey USA 23.5.90 7 Feb
2:19.12 Erik Sowinski USA 21.12.89 7 Feb
2:19.24 Andre Olivier RSA 29.12.89 25 Feb
2:19.45 Jakub Holusa CZE 20.2.88 25 Feb

1500 METRES

3:34.13 Homiyu Tesfaye GER 23.6.93 1 XLG Stockholm 19 Feb
3:34.62 Bethwell Birgen KEN 6.8.88 2 XLG Stockholm 19 Feb
3:34.91 Vincent Kibet KEN 6.5.91 1 GP Birmingham 21 Feb
3:34.91 Birgen 2 GP Birmingham 21 Feb
3:35.26 Hillary Ngetich KEN 25.9.95 3 GP Birmingham 21 Feb
3:35.28 Nixon Chepseba KEN 12.12.90 4= GP Birmingham 21 Feb
3:35.28 Ben Blankenship USA 15.12.88 4= GP Birmingham 21 Feb
3:35.66 Lee Emanuel GBR 24.1.85 6 GP Birmingham 21 Feb
3:35.71 Tesfaye 1 Wien 14 Feb
3:35.90 Collins Cheboi KEN 25.9.87 3 XLG Stockholm 19 Feb
3:36.73+ Matthew Centrowitz USA 18.10.89 1= in 1M New York (Armory) 14 Feb
3:36.73+ Nick Willis (10) NZL 25.4.83 1= in 1M New York (Armory) 14 Feb
3:37.30 Pieter-Jan Hannes BEL 30.10.92 7 GP Birmingham 21 Feb
3:37.68 Jakub Holusa CZE 20.2.88 1 EI Praha (02) 8 Mar
3:37.74 Ilham Tanui Özbilen TUR 5.3.90 2 EI Praha (02) 8 Mar
3:38.15 Silas Kiplagat KEN 20.8.89 4 XLG Stockholm 19 Feb

3:38.28+ Patrick Casey USA 23.5.90 14 Feb
3:38.30 Adel Mechaal ESP 5.12.90 13 Feb
3:38.68 Marcin Lewandowski POL 13.6.87 31 Jan
3:38.74 Valentin Smirnov RUS 13.2.86 1 Feb
3:38.86 Teshome Dirirsa ETH 25.4.94 21 Feb
3:38.96 Chris O'Hare (20) GBR 23.11.90 8 Mar

3:39.22 Yoann Kowal FRA 28.5.87 31 Jan
3:39.33 Fouad El Kaam MAR 27.5.88 19 Feb
3:39.43 Charlie Grice GBR 7.11.93 8 Mar
3:39.70 Henrik Ingebrigtsen NOR 24.2.91 8 Mar

1 MILE

3:51.35	Matthew	Centrowitz	USA	18.10.89	1	Mill	New York (Armory)	14 Feb
3:51.46	Nick	Willis	NZL	25.4.83	2	Mill	New York (Armory)	14 Feb
3:51.61		Willis			1	NB GP	Boston (Roxbury)	7 Feb
3:53.13	Ben	Blankenship	USA	15.12.88	2	NB GP	Boston (Roxbury)	7 Feb
3:54.36	Patrick	Casey	USA	23.5.90	3	Mill	New York (Armory)	14 Feb
3:54.41	Abdelaati	Iguider	MAR	25.3.87	3	NB GP	Boston (Roxbury)	7 Feb
3:54.74	Cameron	Levins	CAN	28.3.89	1		New York (Armory)	31 Jan
3:54.91	Bernard	Lagat	USA	12.12.74	4	Mill	New York (Armory)	14 Feb
3:55.25	Evan	Jager	USA	8.3.89	5	Mill	New York (Armory)	14 Feb
3:55.27#	Cristian	Soratos	USA	26.9.92	1		Seattle	14 Feb
3:55.35	Chris	O'Hare (10)	GBR	23.11.90	6	Mill	New York (Armory)	14 Feb

3:56.05 Leonel Manzano USA 12.9.84 14 Feb
3:56.15 Riley Masters USA 5.4.90 7 Feb
3:56.43 Edward Cheserek KEN 2.2.94 14 Feb
3:56.79 Ford Palmer USA 6.10.90 14 Feb
3:56.84# Ryan Hill USA 31.1.90 31 Jan
3:56.86 Pablo Solares MEX 22.12.84 15 Jan
3:56.99 Cory Leslie USA 24.10.89 31 Jan
3:57.13# Brannon Kidder USA 18.11.93 14 Feb
3:57.15 Lawi Lalang KEN 15.6.91 14 Feb
3:57.22 Julian Oakley (20) NZL 23.6.93 14 Feb
3:57.28 Michael Rutt USA 28.10.87 14 Feb

3000 METRES

7:33.1	Mohammed	Farah	GBR	23.3.83	1+	in 2M	Birmingham	21 Feb
7:37.92	Bernard	Lagat	USA	12.12.74	1		Metz	25 Feb
7:38.42	Ali	Kaya	TUR	20.4.94	1	EI	Praha (02)	7 Mar
7:39.68	Paul Kipsiele	Koech	KEN	10.11.81	2		Metz	25 Feb
7:42.65	Nixon	Chepseba	KEN	12.12.90	3		Metz	25 Feb
7:43.77	Bethwell	Birgen	KEN	6.8.88	4		Metz	25 Feb
7:44.48	Lee	Emanuel	GBR	24.1.85	2	EI	Praha (02)	7 Mar
7:44.91	Eric	Jenkins	USA	24.11.91	1	Mill	New York (Armory)	14 Feb
7:44.97+	Galen	Rupp	USA	8.5.86	1	in 2M	New York (Armory)	31 Jan
7:45.21+	Cameron	Levins	CAN	28.3.89	2	in 2M	New York (Armory)	31 Jan
7:45.44+	Ben	Blankenship	USA	15.12.88	3	in 2M	New York (Armory)	31 Jan
7:45.54	Henrik	Ingebrigtsen	NOR	24.2.91	3	EI	Praha (02)	7 Mar
7:45.62+	Suguru	Osako	JPN	23.5.91	4	in 2M	New York (Armory)	31 Jan
7:45.71	Will	Geoghegan	USA	15.7.92	2	Mill	New York (Armory)	14 Feb
7:46.18	Richard	Ringer (10)	GER	27.2.89	2		Karlsruhe	31 Jan
7:46.92	Adel	Mechaal	ESP	5.12.90	2h2	EI	Praha (02)	6 Mar

7:47.12 Jesus España ESP 21.8.78 7 Mar
7:47.55 Pieter-Jan Hannes BEL 30.10.92 6 Mar
7:47.77 Othmane El Goumri MAR 28.4.92 29 Jan
7:48.13# Kemoy Campbell JAM 14.1.91 14 Feb
7:48.17# Garrett Heath USA 3.11.85 14 Feb
7:48.19 Dejen Gebremeskel ETH 24.11.89 7 Feb
7:48.36 Yegor Nikolayev RUS 12.2.88 31 Jan
7:48.48# Jeramy Elkaim USA 28 Feb
7:48.59 Florian Carvalho (20) FRA 9.3.89 6 Mar
7:48.72 Hassan Mead USA 28.8.89 7 Feb
7:48.80 William Leer USA 15.4.85 7 Feb
7:49.25# Colby Gilbert USA 17.3.95 14 Feb
7:49.48 Florian Orth GER 24.7.89 31 Jan
7:49.49 Halil Akkas TUR 1.7.83 7 Feb
7:49.51 Aleksey Popov RUS 17.6.87 17 Feb
7:49.56# Edward Cheserek KEN 2.2.94 24 Jan
7:49.74# Stanley Kebenei KEN 6.11.89 14 Feb

2 MILES

8:03.40	Mohamed	Farah	GBR	23.3.83	1	GP	Birmingham	21 Feb
8:13.46	Paul Kipsiele	Koech (7:41.7+)	KEN	10.11.81	2	GP	Birmingham	21 Feb
8:15.38	Cameron	Levins	CAN	28.3.89	1		New York (Armory)	31 Jan
8:16.47	Suguru	Osako	JPN	23.5.91	2		New York (Armory)	31 Jan
8:16.53	Ben	Blankenship	USA	15.12.88	3		New York (Armory)	31 Jan
8:17.05	Bernard	Lagat (7:41.3+)	USA	12.12.74	4	GP	Birmingham	21 Feb
8:17.24	Galen	Rupp	USA	8.5.86	4		New York (Armory)	31 Jan
8:21.24	Lee	Emanuel	GBR	24.1.85	5		New York (Armory)	31 Jan

5000 METRES

13:27.53	Arne	Gabius	GER	22.3.81	1		Düsseldorf	29 Jan
13:27.60	Lopez	Lomong	USA	1.1.85	1	Mill	New York (Armory)	14 Feb
13:27.80	Ryan	Hill	USA	31.1.90	2	Mill	New York (Armory)	14 Feb
13:28.00	Suguru	Osako	JPN	23.5.91	3	Mill	New York (Armory)	14 Feb

13:28.64 Donn Cabral USA 12.12,89 14 Feb
13:28.64 Andrew Bumbalough USA 14.3.87 14 Feb
13:30.79 Aweke Ayalew BRN 23.2.93 29 Jan
13:31.76# Eric Jenkins USA 24.11.91 23 Jan
13:31.85 Amos Kibitok KEN 4.4.94 19 Feb
13:33.35 Cameron Levins (10) CAN 28.3.89 14 Feb

60 METRES HURDLES

7.45	Orlando	Ortega	ex-CUB	29.7.91	1	Pedros	Lódz	17 Feb
7.45	Omar	McLeod	JAM	25.4.94	1	NCAA	Fayetteville	14 Mar
7.46	Dimitri	Bascou	FRA	20.7.87	1s2	EI	Praha (02)	6 Mar
7.48		Bascou			1	NC	Aubière	21 Feb
7.49		McLeod			1	SEC	Lexington	28 Feb
7.49	Pascal	Martinot-Lagarde	FRA	22.9.91	1	EI	Praha (02)	6 Mar
7.50	Aleec	Harris	USA	31.10.90	1	Mill	New York (Armory)	14 Feb
7.50		Bascou			2	EI	Praha (02)	6 Mar
7.51		Bascou			1		Mondeville	7 Feb
7.51		Ortega			1	ISTAF	Berlin	14 Feb

7.51	David	Oliver	USA	24.4.82	2	Mill	New York (Armory)	14 Feb
7.51	Ashton	Eaton	USA	21.1.88	3	Mill	New York (Armory)	14 Feb
7.51		Harris			1	NC	Boston (Roxbury)	1 Mar
7.52	Aries	Merritt	USA	24.7.85	2		Malmö	25 Feb
7.52	Wilhem	Belocian	FRA	22.6.95	3	EI	Praha (02)	6 Mar
7.53	Dayron	Robles (10)	CUB	19.11.86	2	ISTAF	Berlin	14 Feb
7.54	Greggmar	Swift	BAR	16.2.91	4	Mill	New York (Armory)	14 Feb
7.58	Kevin	Craddock	USA	25.6.87	1	GP	Birmingham	21 Feb
7.59	Lawrence	Clarke	GBR	12.3.90	2		Mondeville	7 Feb
7.59	Jarret	Eaton	USA	24.6.89	2	NC	Boston (Roxbury)	1 Mar
7.59	Erik	Balnuweit	GER	21.9.88	3s2	EI	Praha (02)	6 Mar
7.60	Jeff	Porter	USA	27.11.85	5	Mill	New York (Armory)	14 Feb
7.61	Konstantin	Shabanov	RUS	17.11.89	1h4	EI	Praha (02)	6 Mar
7.61	Petr	Svoboda	CZE	10.10.84	2s1	EI	Praha (02)	6 Mar
7.62	Jason	Richardson	USA	4.4.86	2		Winston-Salem	31 Jan
7.62		Xie Wenjun (20)	CHN	11.7.90	2		Karlsruhe	31 Jan
7.62	Balazs	Baji	HUN	9.6.89	1r2		Budapest (SH)	22 Feb
7.62	Konstadínos	Douvalídis	GRE	10.3.87	3s1	EI	Praha (02)	6 Mar

7.63	Dominik	Bochenek	POL	14.5.87	22 Feb
7.64	Myles	Hunter	USA	16.8.95	13 Feb
7.64	Chris	Caldwell	USA	6.4.94	13 Mar
7.65	Spencer	Adams	USA	10.9.89	10 Jan
7.65	Gregory	Sedoc	NED	16.10.81	6 Mar
7.66	Damian	Warner	CAN	4.11.89	14 Feb
7.66	João	Almeida	POR	5.4.88	6 Mar
7.67	Omo	Osaghae (30)	USA	18.5.88	14 Feb
7.67	Milan	Trajkovic	CYP	17.9.92	15 Feb
7.67	Damian	Czykier	POL	10.8.92	22 Feb
7.67	Wayne	Davis	TTO	22.8.91	25 Feb
7.67	Arthur	Abele	GER	30.7.86	8 Mar
7.68	Damien	Broothaerts	BEL	13.3.83	21 Feb
7.69	Ray	Stewart	USA	5.4.89	29 Jan
7.69	Simon	Krauss	FRA	12.2.92	21 Feb
7.70	Mikel	Thomas	TTO	23.11.87	21 Feb

55mh: 7.09 Omo Osaghae USA 1 Lubbock 20 Feb

HIGH JUMP

2.41	Mutaz Essa	Barshim	QAT	24.6.91	1		Athlone	18 Feb
2.40		Barshim			1		Banská Bystrica	4 Feb
2.34	Marco	Fassinotti	ITA	29.4.89	1		Hustopece	24 Jan
2.34		Barshim			1		Malmö	25 Feb
2.34	Erik	Kynard	USA	3.2.91	1	NC	Boston (Roxbury)	28 Feb
2.33	Andriy	Protsenko	UKR	20.5.88	2		Banská Bystrica	4 Feb
2.32	Dimitrios	Hondrokoúkis	CYP	26.1.88	1	GRE Ch	Athína (Pireás)	14 Feb
2.32		Zhang Guowei	CHN	4.6.91	1		Fresno	16 Feb
2.31	Aleksey	Dmitrik	RUS	12.4.84	1		Volgograd	24 Jan
2.31	Dmitriy	Semyonov	RUS	2.8.92	1	Winter	Moskva	1 Feb
2.31	Daniyil	Tsyplakov	RUS	12.7.92	2	Winter	Moskva	1 Feb
2.31	Ivan	Ukhov (10)	RUS	29.3.86	3		Banská Bystrica	4 Feb
2.31	Donald	Thomas	BAH	1.7.84	5		Banská Bystrica	4 Feb
2.31	Matús	Bubeník	SVK	14.11.89	6		Banská Bystrica	4 Feb
2.31	Jesse	Williams	USA	27.12.83	1	Mill	New York (Armory)	14 Feb
2.31	Michael	Mason	CAN	30.9.86	2	Mill	New York (Armory)	14 Feb
2.31	Richard	Robertson	USA	19.9.90	2	NC	Boston (Roxbury)	28 Feb
2.31	Adonios	Mástoras	GRE	6.1.91	2=	EI	Praha (02)	8 Mar
2.31	Silvano	Chesani	ITA	17.7.88	2=	EI	Praha (02)	8 Mar
2.30	Jaroslav	Bába	CZE	2.9.84	2		Ostrava	27 Jan
2.29A	Nicholas	Ross	USA	8.8.91	1		Albuquerque	24 Jan
2.29	Allan	Smith (20)	GBR	6.11.92	1	NC	Sheffield	15 Feb
2.29	Jacorian	Duffield	USA	2.9.92	1	NCAA	Fayetteville	14 Mar
2.29	Bradley	Adkins	USA	30.12.93	2	NCAA	Fayetteville	14 Mar
2.28	Wally	Ellenson	USA	4.5.94	1		Madison	17 Jan
2.28	Aleksandr	Shustov	RUS	29.6.84	3		Volgograd	24 Jan
2.28	Rauvydas	Stanys	LTU	3.2.87	1		Vilnius	31 Jan
2.28	Konstadínos	Baniótis	GRE	6.11.86	3	Winter	Moskva	1 Feb
2.28	Mihai	Donisan	ROU	24.7.88	7		Banská Bystrica	4 Feb
2.28	Andriy	Kovalyov	UKR	11.6.92	1	NC	Sumy	14 Feb
2.28	Christoffe	Bryan	JAM-J	26.4.96	1	Tyson	Fayetteville	14 Feb
2.28	Sylwester	Bednarek (30)	POL	28.4.89	1	NC	Torun	22 Feb
2.28	Gianmarco	Tamberi	ITA	1.6.92	Q	EI	Praha (02)	7 Mar
2.28	Kyriacos	Ioannou	CYP	26.7.84	Q	EI	Praha (02)	7 Mar

2.26	Lev	Missirov	RUS	4.8.90	17 Jan
2.26	Andrea	Lemmi	ITA	12.5.84	25 Jan
2.26	Andrey	Churylo	BLR	19.5.93	7 Feb
2.26	Yuriy	Krymarenko	UKR	11.8.83	14 Feb
2.26	Chris	Kandu	GBR	10.9.95	21 Feb
2.26	David	Smith	GBR	14.7.91	21 Feb
2.26	Ali Mohamed	Younes Idriss	SUD	15.9.89	22 Feb
2.26	Mateusz	Przybylko (40)	GER	9.3.92	22 Feb
2.26	Bryan	McBride	USA	10.12.91	28 Feb
2.25	Mikhail	Veryovkin	RUS	28.6.91	7 Dec
2.25	Ilya	Ivanyuk	RUS	9.3.93	21 Dec
2.25	Tihomir	Ivanov	BUL	11.7.94	24 Jan
2.25	Hiromi	Takahari	JPN	13.11.87	1 Feb
2.25	Lukás	Beer	SVK	23.8.89	4 Feb
2.25	Naoto	Tobe	JPN	31.3.92	4 Feb
2.25	Muamer Aissa	Barshim	QAT	3.1.94	18 Feb
2.24	Danyil	Lysenko	RUS-J	19.5.97	6 Dec
2.24	Yevgeniy	Korshunov (50)	RUS	11.4.86	7 Jan
2.24	Artyom	Naumovich	BLR	19.2.91	16 Jan
2.24	Miguel Ángel	Sancho	ESP	24.4.90	17 Jan
2.24	Mikhail	Akimenko	RUS	6.12.95	24 Jan
2.24	Abdoulaye	Diarra	FRA	27.8.88	7 Feb
2.24	Avion	Jones	USA	31.1.94	7 Feb
2.24	Vadim	Vrublevskiy	RUS	18.3.93	10 Feb
2.24	Deante	Kemper	USA	27.3.93	14 Feb
2.24		Wang Yu	CHN	18.8.91	8 Mar

POLE VAULT

6.04	Renaud	Lavillenie	FRA	18.9.86	1	EI	Praha (02)	7 Mar
6.02		Lavillenie			1	ISTAF	Berlin	14 Feb
6.01		Lavillenie			1		Nevers	7 Feb
6.01		Lavillenie			1	NC	Aubière	22 Feb
6.00		Lavillenie			1		Rouen	24 Jan
5.92A		Lavillenie			1		Reno	16 Jan
5.92		Lavillenie			1		Malmö	25 Feb
5.91	Shawn	Barber	CAN	27.5.94	1	NCAA	Fayetteville	13 Mar
5.90		Barber			1	Tyson	Fayetteville	14 Feb
5.90	Piotr	Lisek	POL	16.8.92	1		Bad Oeynhausen	28 Feb
5.88		Barber			1		Akron	7 Feb
5.87		Barber			1		Belton	3 Jan
5.87		Lisek			1		Dessau	11 Feb
5.86A	Sam	Kendricks	USA	7.9.92	2		Reno	16 Jan
5.86		Lavillenie			1		Karlsruhe	31 Jan
5.85		Lisek			2		Malmö	25 Feb
5.85	Aleksandr	Gripich	RUS	21.9.86	2	EI	Praha (02)	7 Mar
5.85		Lisek			3	EI	Praha (02)	7 Mar
5.81	Robert	Sobera	POL	19.1.91	2	ISTAF	Berlin	14 Feb
5.80	Valentin	Lavillenie	FRA	16.7.91	2		Nevers	7 Feb
5.80	Jake	Blankenship	USA	15.3.94	2	NCAA	Fayetteville	13 Mar
5.78	Ilya	Mudrov	RUS	17.11.91	3		Malmö	25 Feb
5.75	Andrew	Irwin (10)	USA	23.1.93	2	Tyson	Fayetteville	14 Feb
5.75	Konstadínos	Filippídis	GRE	26.1186	5	EI	Praha (02)	7 Mar
5.71A	Steven	Lewis	GBR	20.5.86	1		Albuquerque	6 Feb
5.70	Anton	Ivakin	RUS	3.2.91	2		Volgograd	24 Jan
5.70	Tobias	Scherbarth	GER	17.8.85	1	NC	Karlsruhe	22 Feb
5.70	Jan	Kudlicka	CZE	29.4.88	Q	EI	Praha (02)	6 Mar
5.68	Jeff	Coover	USA	1.12.87	1		Cedar Falls	20 Feb
5.67	Jack	Whitt	USA	12.4.90	1		Wichita	14 Feb
5.66A	Victor	Weirich	USA	25.10.87	2		Albuquerque	6 Feb
5.66	Kévin	Menaldo	FRA	12.7.92	2	NC	Aubière	22 Feb
5.65	Hiroki	Ogita (20)	JPN	30.12.87	1cB		Orléans	17 Jan
5.65	Michal	Balner	CZE	12.9.82	2		Cottbus	27 Jan
5.65	Carlo	Paech	GER	18.12.92	3		Potsdam	7 Feb
5.65	Augusto	Dutra de Oliveira	BRA	16.7.90	1	Pedros	Lódz	17 Feb
5.61A	Brad	Walker	USA	21.6.81	3		Albuquerque	6 Feb
5.60	Jérôme	Clavier	FRA	3.5.83	2		Aubière	10 Jan
5.60	Damiel	Dossévi	FRA	3.2.83	3		Orléans	17 Jan
5.60	Edi	Maia	POR	10.11.87	5		Orléans	17 Jan
5.60	Artem	Burya	RUS	11.4.86	3		Volgograd	24 Jan
5.60	Raphael	Holzdeppe	GER	28.9.89	5		Rouen	24 Jan
5.60	Georgiy	Gorokhov (30)	RUS	20.4.93	1		Moskva	27 Jan
5.60	Luke	Cutts	GBR	13.2.88	1		Manchester	1 Feb
5.60	Nicolas	Homo	FRA	24.11.88	4		Nevers	7 Feb
5.60	Diogo	Ferreira	POR	30.7.90	4		Potsdam	7 Feb
5.60	Chris	Pillow	USA	8.7.93	2	NC	Boston (Roxbury)	28 Feb
5.60	Didac	Salas	ESP	19.5.93	10q	EI	Praha (02)	6 Mar
5.60	Marek	Arents	LAT	6.8.86	11q	EI	Praha (02)	6 Mar

5.55A	Jordan	Scott	USA	22.2.88	16 Jan
5.55	Daniel	Clemens	GER	28.4.92	17 Jan
5.55A	Joseph	Uhle	USA	25.4.89	24 Jan
5.55	Adam	Hague (40)	GBR-J	29.8.97	31 Jan
5.55A	Sam	Pierson	USA	7.4.88	1 Feb
5.55A	Michael	Woepse	USA	29.5.91	13 Feb
5.55	Oleksandr	Korchmyd	UKR	22.1.82	17 Feb
5.52	Chris	Uhle	USA	14.11.92	24 Jan
5.51	Scott	Houston	USA	11,6,90	31 Jan
5.51A	Reese	Watson	USA	8.10.93	6 Feb
5.51	Stanley	Joseph	FRA	24.10.91	28 Feb
5.50A	Dylan	Bell	USA	21.7.93	12 Dec
5.50	Seito	Yamamoto	JPN	11.3.92	23 Dec
5.50	Max	Eaves (50)	GBR	31.5.88	10 Jan
5.50A	Micke	Arnold	USA	13.8.90	10 Jan
5.50	Alexandre	Feger	FRA	22.1.90	10 Jan
5.50	Josh	Dangel	USA	21.1.91	11 Jan
5.50	Mikhail	Gelmanov	RUS	18.3.90	16 Jan
5.50	Pawel	Wojchiechowski	POL	6.6.89	17 Jan
5.50	Jax	Thoirs	GBR	7.4.93	17 Jan
5.50		Huang Bokai	CHN-J	26.9.96	29 Jan
5.50	Marvin	Caspari	GER	9.8.91	29 Jan
5.50	Ivan	Horvat	CRO	17.8.93	31 Jan
5.50	Baptiste	Boirie (60)	FRA	26.12.92	7 Feb
5.50	Przemyslaw	Czerwinski	POL	28.7.83	7 Feb
5.50A	Derick	Hinch	USA	2.2.91	13 Feb
5.50	Leonid	Kivalov	RUS	1.4.88	19 Feb
5.50A	Zachary	Siegmeier	USA	8.1.91	20 Feb
5.50	Noël	Ost	FRA	15.11.89	22 Feb
5.50	Chase	Wolfle	USA	9.10.92	28 Feb
5.50		Xia Xiang	CHN	28.3.91	1 Mar
5.50		Zhang Wei	CHN	22.3.94	1 Mar

LONG JUMP

8.30	Michel	Tornéus	SWE	26.5.86	1	EI	Praha (02)	6 Mar
8.28	Marquis	Dendy	USA	17.11.92	1	NCAA	Fayetteville	13 Mar
8.27	Jarrion	Lawson	USA	6.5.94	2	NCAA	Fayetteville	13 Mar
8.18	Kafetien	Gomis	FRA	23.3.80	1	NC	Aubière	22 Feb
8.17	Greg	Rutherford	GBR	17.11.86	1	GP	Birmingham	21 Feb
8.16	Eusebio	Cáceres	ESP	10.9.91	1		Karlsruhe	31 Jan

8.14		Huang Changzhou	CHN	20.8.94	1		Xianlin	8 Mar
8.12	Jarvis	Gotch	USA	25.3.92	1		Nashville	24 Jan
8.12		Gao Xinglong	CHN	12.3.94	2	GP	Birmingham	21 Feb
8.10		Li Jinzhe (10)	CHN	1.9.89	1		Mondeville	7 Feb
8.10	Radek	Juska	CZE	8.3.93	2	EI	Praha (02)	6 Mar
8.06	Andreas	Otterling	SWE	25.5.86	3	EI	Praha (02)	6 Mar
8.05	Loúis	Tsátoumas	GRE	12.2.82	1	Winter	Moskva	1 Feb
8.04	Julian	Howard	GER	3.4.89	2		Karlsruhe	31 Jan
8.04!	Cal	Lane	USA		1		Bloomington	12 Dec
8.03	Max	Hess	GER-J	13.7.96	1		Chemnitz	17 Jan
8.03	Damar	Forbes	JAM	18.9.90	1	Mill	New York (Armory)	14 Feb
8.03	Lamont Marcell	Jacobs	ITA	26.9.94	Q	NC	Padova	22 Feb
8.02	Will	Claye	USA	13.6.91	2	Mill	New York (Armory)	14 Feb
8.02	KeAndre	Bates	USA-J	24.5.96	3	NCAA	Fayetteville	13 Mar

8.00	Vasiliy	Kopeykin (20)	RUS	9.3.88	19 Feb
7.98	Kirill	Sukharev	RUS	24.5.92	7 Feb
7.97	Elvijs	Misans	LAT	8.4.89	17 Jan
7.97	Roelf	Pienaar	RSA	23.12.93	31 Jan
7.97	Adrian	Strzalkowski	POL	28.3.90	3 Feb
7.97	Pavel	Shalin	RUS	15.3.87	19 Feb
7.97	Alyn	Camara	GER	31.3.89	21 Feb
7.97	Jalen	Ramsey	USA	24.10.94	13 Mar
7.96	Sergey	Polyanskiy	RUS	29.10.89	19 Feb
7.96	Jean Marie	Okutu	ESP	4.8.88	21 Feb
7.95	Aleksandr	Petrov (30)	RUS	9.8.86	19 Feb
7.94	Konstantin	Borichevskiy	BLR	25.9.90	7 Feb
7.94	Bachana	Khorava	GEO	15.3.93	8 Feb
7.94		Zhang Yaoguang	CHN	21.6.93	8 Mar
7.92		Li Zhipeng	CHN	1.5.95	8 Mar
7.92		Tang Gongchen	CHN	24.4.89	15 Mar
7.91	Julian	Reid	GBR	23.9.88	11 Jan
7.91	Cedric	Nolf	BEL	18.6.89	21 Feb
7.91	Cameron	Echols-Luper	USA	9.4.95	13 Mar
7.90	Dan	Bramble	GBR	14.10.90	14 Feb

TRIPLE JUMP

17.37	Marquis	Dendy	USA	17.11.92	1	NCAA	Fayetteville	14 Mar
17.23		Dendy			1	Tyson	Fayetteville	14 Feb
17.21	Nelson	Évora	POR	20.4.84	1	EI	Praha (02)	7 Mar
17.19		Évora			1		Pombal	22 Feb
17.07	Alexis	Copello	ex-CUB	12.8.85	1		Metz	25 Feb
17.04	Pablo	Torrijos	ESP	12.5.92	2	EI	Praha (02)	7 Mar
17.00	Roman	Valiyev	KAZ	27.3.84	1	NC	Ust-Kamenogorsk	15 Feb
16.94	Dmitriy	Sorokin	RUS	27.9.92	1	NC	Moskva	18 Feb
16.93	Will	Claye	USA	13.6.91	1		New York (Armory)	31 Jan
16.91	Aleksey	Fyodorov	RUS	25.5.91	2	NC	Moskva	18 Feb
16.91	Marian	Oprea	ROU	6.6.82	3	EI	Praha (02)	7 Mar
16.89	Dmitriy	Chizhikov (10)	RUS	6.12.93	3	NC	Moskva	18 Feb
16.87	Omar	Craddock	USA	26.4.91	2		New York (Armory)	31 Jan
16.84	Donald	Scott	USA	23.2.92	2	NCAA	Fayetteville	14 Mar
16.81	Aleksandr	Yurchenko	RUS	30.7.92	1		Orenburg	28 Feb
16.78	Teddy	Tamgho	FRA	15.6.89	1		Eaubonne	21 Mar
16.77	Aleksey	Tsapik	BLR	4.8.88	1		Mogilyov	27 Feb
16.75	Adrian	Swiderski	POL	26.9.86	1	NC	Torun	22 Feb
16.75	Georgi	Tsonov	BUL	2.5.93	5	EI	Praha (02)	7 Mar
16.72		Fu Haitao	CHN	1.11.93	1		Xianlin	9 Mar
16.71	Chris	Carter	USA	11.3.89	1		Houston	31 Jan
16.70	Fabrizio	Donato (20)	ITA	14.8.76	1		Ancona	31 Jan
16.69	Latario	Collie-Minns	BAH	10.3.94	2	Tyson	Fayetteville	14 Feb
16.69	Jean-Marc	Pontvianne	FRA	6.8.94	1		Nogent-sur-Oise	7 Mar
16.67	Jorge	Gimeno	ESP	16.2.90	2	NC	Antequera	22 Feb
16.66	Maksim	Nesterenko	BLR	1.9.92	1		Minsk	16 Jan
16.65	Dmitriy	Plotnitskiy	BLR	26.8.88	1		Mogilyov	20 Feb
16.63	Tosin	Oke	NGR	1.10.80	1		London (LV	31 Jan
16.62		Dong Bin	CHN	22.11.88	2		Xianlin	9 Mar
16.61	Manuel	Ziegler	GER	28.7.90	1	ACC	Blacksburg	28 Feb

16.59	Zlatozar	Atanasov	BUL	12.12.89	14 Feb
16.58	Fabrizio	Schembri (30)	ITA	27.1.81	21 Feb
16.57	Chris	Benard	USA	4.4.90	1 Mar
16.55	Ben	Williams	GBR	25.1.92	6 Feb
16.50	Rumen	Dimitrov	BUL	19.9.86	21 Feb
16.50	Sergio	Solanas	ESP	28.4.87	25 Feb
16.50		Xu Xiaoliang	CHN	20.12.92	9 Mar
16.47	Fabian	Florant	NED	1.2.83	21 Feb
16.46		Wu Ruiting	CHN	29.11.95	16 Mar
16.45	Brandon	Roulhac	USA	13.12.83	23 Jan
16.45	Dimítrios	Tsiámis	GRE	12.1.82	24 Jan
16.45	Jonathan	Gardner (40)	USA	10.12.91	28 Feb

SHOT

21.80	Ryan	Whiting	USA	24.11.86	1	Pedros	Lódz	17 Feb
21.43		Whiting			1	NB GP	Boston (Roxbury)	7 Feb
21.26	David	Storl	GER	27.7.90	1	NC	Karlsruhe	21 Feb
21.23		Storl			Q	EI	Praha (02)	5 Mar
21.23		Storl			1	EI	Praha (02)	6 Mar
21.20		Whiting			1		Potsdam	3 Feb
21.14	Ryan	Crouser	USA	18.12.92	1	Big 12	Ames	28 Feb
21.11	Stipe	Zunic	CRO	13.12.90	1	NCAA	Fayetteville	14 Mar
20.94	Tomas	Stanek	CZE	13.6.91	2	Pedros	Lódz	17 Feb
20.91	Asmir	Kolasinac	SRB	15.10.84	1		Novi Sad	14 Feb
20.83	Christian	Cantwell	USA	30.9.80	2	NB GP	Boston (Roxbury)	7 Feb
20.71	Jan	Marcell	CZE	4.6.85	1		Praha (Strom)	22 Feb

20.70	Aleksandr	Lesnoy	RUS	28.7.88	1		Krasnodar	8 Feb
20.66	Borja	Vivas (10)	ESP	26.5.84	1	NC	Antequera	21 Feb
20.66	Ladislav	Prásil	CZE	17.5.90	3	EI	Praha (02)	6 Mar
20.59	Jonathan	Jones	USA	23.4.91	3	NCAA	Fayetteville	14 Mar
20.56	Maksim	Sidorov	RUS	13.5.86	1		Sankt-Peterburg	10 Feb
20.56	Bob	Bertemes	LUX	24.5.93	Q	EI	Praha (02)	5 Mar
20.55	Jakub	Szyszkowski	POL	21.8.91	1	NC	Torun	21 Feb
20.54	Tim	Nedow	CAN	16.10.90	1		Göteborg	7 Feb
20.51	Darrell	Hill	USA	17.8.93	1		University Park	31 Jan
20.46	Konrad	Bukowiecki	POL-J	17.3.97	Q	EI	Praha (02)	5 Mar
20.41	Georgi	Ivanov	BUL	13.3.85	1		Dobrich	11 Feb
20.37	Maris	Urtans (20)	LAT	9.2.81	1		Vilnius	31 Jan
20.31	Ashinia	Miller	JAM	6.6.93	1		Lexington	24 Jan
20.25	Ivan	Emilianov	MDA	19.2.77	1		IBucuresti	15 Feb
20.20	Konstantin	Lyadusov	RUS	2.3.88	1		Volgograd	18 Jan
20.14	Pavel	Lyzhyn	BLR	24.3.81	1	NCp	Gomel	7 Feb
20.10	Michal	Haratyk	POL	10.4.92	1		Torun	3 Feb
20.10	Tumatai	Dauphin	FRA	12.1.88	1	NC	Aubière	21 Feb
20.09	Gaëtan	Bucki	FRA	9.5.80	2	NC	Aubière	21 Feb
20.09	Arttu	Kangas	FIN	13.7.93	1	NC	Tampere	22 Feb
20.07	Rafal	Kownatke	POL	24.3.85	2	NC	Torun	21 Feb
20.03	Andrei	Gag (30)	ROU	7.4.91	2	NC	Bucuresti	15 Feb

19.99	Nick	Vena	USA	16.4.93	7 Feb
19.99	Justin	Rodhe	CAN	17.10.84	7 Feb
19.97	Leif	Arrhenius	SWE	15.7.86	1 Mar
19.97	Tobias	Dahm	GER	23.5.87	5 Mar
19.96	Matt	Babicz	USA	.92	21 Feb
19.95	Yioser	Toledo	ESP	24.4.83	21 Feb
19.90	Frank	Elemba	CGO	21.7.90	21 Feb
19.89	Carlos	Tobalina	ESP	2.8.85	21 Feb
19.87	Christian	Jagusch	GER	13.7.92	17 Jan
19.80	Kemal	Mesic (40)	BIH	4.8.85	24 Jan
19.74	Vladislav	Tulácek	CZE	9.7.88	28 Jan
19.74	Frédéric	Dagée	FRA	11.12.92	21 Feb
19.68!	Robert	Grace	USA	10.10.90	5 Dec
19.68	Brad	Szypka	USA	13.2.93	24 Jan
19.67	Anton	Tikhomirov	RUS	29.4.88	10 Feb
19.65	Hamza	Alic	BIH	20.1.79	7 Feb
19.65	Aleksandr	Bulanov	RUS	26.12.89	17 Feb
19.63	Sarunas	Banevicius	LTU	23.1.91	23 Jan
19.63	Filip	Mihaljevic	CRO	31.7.94	24 Jan
19.61	Richard	Chavez (50)	USA	30.7.92	31 Jan
19.56	Daniele	Secci	ITA	9.3.92	22 Feb
19.55	Krzysztof	Brzozowski	POL	15.7.93	3 Feb
19.54	Martin	Stasek	CZE	8.4.89	28 Jan
19.54	Nicholas	Scarvelis	USA	2.2.93	28 Feb
19.53	Darian	Brown	USA	30.7.93	13 Feb
19.50	Derek	Sievers	USA	18.10.92	17 Jan
19.45	Anatoliy	Garmashov	RUS	5.7.88	10 Feb
19.45	Mateusz	Mikos	POL	10.4.87	21 Feb
19.40	Damian	Kusiak	POL	14.4.88	1 Feb
19.40	Josh	Freeman (60)	USA	22.8.94	14 Feb
19.36	Kole	Weldon	USA	25.3.92	14 Feb
19.36	Mesud	Pezer	BIH	27.8.94	21 Feb
19.35	Stephen	Mozia	NGR	16.8.93	15 Feb
19.34	Maksim	Afonin	RUS	6.1.92	7 Feb
19.33	Denis	Kurtsev	RUS	21.8.88	3 Mar
19.31	Stephen	Sáenz	MEX	23.8.90	21 Feb
19.30	Dillon	Simon	DMA	5.3.92	1 Mar

DISCUS Berlin 1 Mar ISTAF: 1. Martin Wierig GER 10.6.87 64.24, 2. Viktor Butenko RUS 10.3.93 62.47 3. Philip Milanov BEL 6.7.91 62.06, 4. Christoph Harting GER 4.10.90 61.47.

35 LB WEIGHT

25.58	Michael	Lihrman	USA	6.12.91	1	Big Ten	Geneva	28 Feb
24.91		Lihrman			1		Madison	20 Feb
24.64		Lihrman			1	NCAA	Fayetteville	13 Mar
24.48	Conor	McCullough	USA	31.1.91	2	NCAA	Fayetteville	13 Mar
24.47		Lihrman			1		Madison	24 Jan
24.39	Chukwuebuka	Enekwechi	USA	28.1.93	1		West Lafayette	13 Feb
24.20	James	Lambert	USA	12.4.90	1		Bloomington IN	31 Jan
24.18		Enekwechi			3	NCAA	Fayetteville	13 Mar
24.04		Enekwechi			1		Notre Dame	24 Jan
23.99		Lihrman			1		New York (Armory)	31 Jan
23.97		Lihrman			1		Ames	13 Feb
23.67	A.G.	Kruger	USA	18.2.79	1		Findlay	30 Jan
23.38	Cameron	Brown	USA	15.3.94	1		Blacksburg	6 Feb
22.92	Jordan	Young	CAN	21.6.93	1		Blacksburg	26 Feb
22.90	Matthias	Tayala	USA	27.4.93	1		Mount Pleasant	27 Feb
22.74	Andrew	Fryman	USA	3.2.85	3	NC	Boston (Roxbury)	1 Mar
22.56!	Nicholas	Miller	GBR	1.5.93	1		Manhattan KS	13 Dec
22.54	Kibwé	Johnson	USA	17.7.81	4	NC	Boston (Roxbury)	1 Mar
22.50	Davis	Fraker	USA	26.2.92	3	Big Ten	Geneva	28 Feb
22.43	Gregory	Skipper	USA	26.3.93	2		Seattle	27 Feb
22.41!	Jérôme	Bortoluzzi	FRA	20.5.82	1		College Station	13 Dec

22.15	Justin	Welch	USA	29.9.91	16 Jan
21.98!	Joe	Frye	USA	20.7.88	6 Dec
21.97	Antonio	James	USA	7.4.92	6 Feb
21.93	Tavis	Bailey	USA	1.6.92	13 Feb
21.91	Darien	Thornton	USA	14.7.94	20 Feb
21.89	Zachary	Ball	USA	1.5.92	9 Jan
21.88	Jared	Conklin	USA		28 Feb
21.81!	Matt	Royer	USA		6 Dec

HEPTATHLON

6353	Ilya	Shkurenyov	RUS	11.1.91	1	EI	Praha (02)	8 Mar
	6.98	7.78	13.89	2.10	7.86	5.30	2:44.84	
6344#	Jeremy	Taiwo	USA	15.1.90	1		Seattle	31 Jan
	7.06	7.56	14.77	2.13	8.03	4.90	2:30.85	

6279	Arthur	Abele	GER	30.7.86	2	EI	Praha (02)	8 Mar
	6.93	7.56	15.54	1.92	7.67	4.90	2:35.64	
6273		Taiwo			1	NC	Boston (Roxbury)	28 Feb
	7.09	7.39	14.50	2.16	7.87	4.80	2:34.26	
6185	Eelco	Sintnicolaas	NED	7.4.87	3	EI	Praha (02)	8 Mar
	6.98	7.51	14.03	1.98	7.98	5.20	2:39.00	
6164	Adam Sebastian	Helcelet	CZE	27.10.91	1	NC	Praha (Strom)	8 Feb
	6.98	7.60	14.97	2.06	7.99	4.90	2:46.33	
6115	Gaël	Quérin	FRA	26.6.87	4	EI	Praha (02)	8 Mar
	7.12	7.41	13.81	2.01	7.98	5.00	2:34.54	
6100		Shkurenyov			1		Volgograd	18 Jan
	7.05	7.47	14.03	2.11	8.01	5.00	2:48.35	
6070	Luca	Wieland	GER	.94	1	NCAA	Fayetteville	14 Mar
	7.01	7.61	14.56	2.07	8.13	4.75	2:45.35	
6068	Garrett	Scantling	USA	19.5.93	2	NCAA	Fayetteville	14 Mar
	7.11	6.88	15.39	2.13	8.00	4.95	2:44.57	
6051	Jorge	Ureña	ESP	8.10.93	1	NC	Antequera	22 Feb
	6.95	7.58	13.89	1.98	7.94	4.70	2:40.06	
6049	Kai	Kazmirek (10)	GER	28.1.91	1		Tallinn	7 Feb
	7.01	7.52	13.83	2.08	8.06	5.10	2:53.80	
6011	Bastien	Auzeil	FRA	22.10.89	6	EI	Praha (02)	8 Mar
	7.08	7.08	14.90	2.01	8.10	5.20	2:46.93	
5995	Michael	Morgan	USA	19.6.94	3	NCAA	Fayetteville	14 Mar
	7.12	7.40	13.49	2.13	8.29	4.85	2:42.30	
5988	Artem	Lukyanenko	RUS	30.1.90	1	NC	Sankt-Peterburg	14 Feb
	7.07	7.19	14.84	2.00	8.02	4.90	2:43.88	
5986	Pawel	Wiesiolek	POL	13.8.91	1	NC	Spala	1 Feb
	7.07	7.27	13.83	2.07	8.10	4.80	2:41.39	
5975	Mathias	Brugger	GER	6.8.92	2		Tallinn	7 Feb
	7.06	7.06	15.39	1.96	8.15	5.00	2:41.99	
5957	Niels	Pittomvils	BEL	18.7.92	1	NC	Gent	1 Feb
	7.18	723	199	13.96	8.18	520	2:43.01	
5948	Yevgeniy	Sarantsev	RUS	5.8.88	2	NC	Sankt-Peterburg	14 Feb
	7.20	7.17	15.13	2.03	8.32	5.10	2:46.03	
5941	Bilal	Abdullah	USA		4	NCAA	Fayetteville	14 Mar
	6.90	7.65	10.98	2.13	7.87	4.55	2:47.55	
5909#	Maicel	Uibo	EST	27.12.92	2	SEC	Lexington	28 Feb
	7.33	7.25	13.78	2.13	8.46	5.15	2:46.74	

5883	Marek	Lukás (20)	CZE	16.7.91	8 Feb	5783	Yevgeniy	Teptin	RUS	16.3.90	14 Feb
5869	Petter	Olson	SWE	14.2.91	8 Mar	5779	Mikk	Pahapill	EST	18.7.83	7 Feb
5859	Einar Dadi	Lárusson	ISL	10.5.90	19 Feb	5777!	Yuriy	Yeremich	BLR	24,4,95	18 Dec
5837	Pieter	Braun	NED	21.1.93	15 Feb	5777	Reinis	Kregers	LAT	22.1.92	30 Jan
5835	Devon	Williams	USA	17.1.94	14 Mar	5759	Romain	Martin (30)	FRA	12.7.88	22 Feb
5785	Scott	Filip	USA	28.1.95	26 Feb	5758	Romain	Barras	FRA	1.8.80	25 Jan

3000 METRES WALK

11:17.33	Erik	Tysse	NOR	4.12.80	1		Bergen	24 Jan
11:19.33	Alex	Wright	IRL	19.12.90	1		Athlone	1 Feb

5000 METRES WALK

18:16.76!	Yohann	Diniz	FRA	1.1.78	1		Reims	7 Dec
18:39.92		Diniz			1		Mondeville	7 Feb
19:11.07	Aléxandros	Papamihaíl	GRE	18.9.88	1	NC	Athína (Pireás)	14 Feb
19:14.82	Marius	Ziukas	LTU	29.6.85	1	NC	Klaipeda	21 Feb
19:16.34	Leonardo	Dei Tos	ITA	27.4.92	1	NC	Padova	21 Feb

19:22.62	Massimo	Stano	ITA	27.2.92	21 Feb	19:26.24	Máté	Helebrandt	HUN	12.1.89	21 Feb
19:23.44	Evan	Dunfee	CAN	28.9.90	21 Feb	19:26.92	Rafal	Augustyn	POL	14.5.84	22 Feb
19:25.35	Dawid	Tomala	POL	27.8.89	22 Feb	19:26.94	Federico	Tontodonati (10)	ITA	30.10.89	21 Feb

10,000 METRES WALK

39:06.06!	Ihor	Hlavan	UKR	25.9.90	1		Sumy	24 Dec

WORLD INDOOR LISTS 2015 – WOMEN

60 METRES

7.05	Murielle	Ahouré	CIV	23.8.87	1	Mill	New York (Armory)	14 Feb
7.05	Dafne	Schippers	NED	15.6.92	1	EI	Praha (02)	8 Mar
7.07		Schippers			1h3	EI	Praha (02)	7 Mar
7.08		Ahouré			1		Houston	31 Jan
7.08	Remona	Burchell	JAM	15.9.91	1	SEC	Lexington	28 Feb
7.08	Tianna	Bartoletta	USA	30.8.85	1	NC	Boston (Roxbury)	1 Mar
7.08	Verena	Sailer	GER	16.10.85	1s3	EI	Praha (02)	8 Mar
7.08	Dina	Asher-Smith	GBR	4.12.95	2	EI	Praha (02)	8 Mar
7.09		Schippers			1	ISTAF	Berlin	14 Feb
7.09		Sailer			3	EI	Praha (02)	8 Mar

7.10	Ezinne	Okparaebo	NOR	3.3.88	4	EI	Praha (02)	8 Mar
7.11	Michelle-Lee	Ahye	TTO	10.4.92	2	Mill	New York (Armory)	14 Feb
7.11	Mujinga	Kambundji	SUI	17.6.92	5	EI	Praha (02)	8 Mar
7.11	Olesya	Povh (10)	UKR	18.10.87	6	EI	Praha (02)	8 Mar
7.14	Jessica	Young	USA	6.4.87	2h2	GP	Birmingham	21 Feb
7.15	Jasmine	Todd	USA	23.12.93	1r1		Seattle	17 Jan
7.15	Dezerea	Bryant	USA	27.4.93	1h2	NCAA	Fayetteville	13 Mar
7.15	Jenna	Prandini	USA	20.11.92	1h1	NCAA	Fayetteville	13 Mar
7.18	Flings	Owusu-Agyapong	GHA	16.10.88	1		New York (Armory)	16 Jan
7.18	Ky	Westbrook	USA-J	25.2.96	2r1		Seattle	17 Jan
7.18A	Muna	Lee	USA	30.10.81	1r1		Flagstaff	31 Jan
7.19	Kelly-Ann	Baptiste	TTO	14.10.86	1		Baton Rouge	20 Feb
7.19		Wei Yongli	CHN	11.10.91	1rA		Shanghai	1 Mar
7.19	Jamile	Samuel (20)	NED	24.4.92	7	EI	Praha (02)	8 Mar
7.19	Khamica	Bingham	CAN	15.6.94	1		Windsor	12 Mar

7.20A	Morolake	Akinosun	USA	17.5.94	7 Feb
7.20	Carina	Horn	RSA	9.3.89	14 Feb
7.20	Ewa	Swoboda	POL-J	26.7.97	8 Mar
7.21	Nataliya	Pohrebnyak	UKR	19.2.88	27 Jan
7.21	Tiffany	Townsend	USA	14.6.89	14 Feb
7.21	Shayla	Sanders	USA	6.1.94	27 Feb
7.22A	Cierra	White	USA	29.4.93	7 Feb
7.22	Ivet	Lalova	BUL	18.5.84	17 Feb
7.22	Mikele	Barber (30)	USA	4.10.80	1 Mar
7.23	Tynia	Gaither	BAH	16.3.93	28 Feb
7.23	Alexandra	Burghardt	GER	28.4.94	7 Mar
7.23	Mikiah	Brisco	USA-J	14.7.96	13 Mar
7.24	Rebekka	Haase	GER	2.1.93	31 Jan
7.24	Crystal	Emmanuel	CAN	27.11.91	7 Feb
7.24	Rachel	Johncock	GBR	4.10.93	21 Feb
7.24	Yasmin	Kwadwo	GER	9.11.90	21 Feb
7.24	Céline	Distel-Bonnet	FRA	25.7.87	7 Mar
7.24	Audrey	Alloh	ITA	21.7.87	8 Mar
7.25	Tawanna	Meadows (40)	USA	4.8.86	1 Mar

Best at low altitude

7.21 Akinosun 13 Feb 7.25 Lee 14 Feb

Hand timing

6.9!	Nataliya	Pohrebnyak	UKR	19.2.88	1		Kharkhiv	23 Dec
6.9	Inna	Eftimova	BUL	19.6.88	1		Sofia	1 Feb

200 METRES

22.52	Jenna	Prandini	USA	20.11.92	1h3	NCAA	Fayetteville	13 Mar
22.63	Kyra	Jefferson	USA	23.9.94	1r2	NCAA	Fayetteville	14 Mar
22.64		Jefferson			1h2	NCAA	Fayetteville	13 Mar
22.74	Dezerea	Bryant	USA	27.4.93	2h2	NCAA	Fayetteville	13 Mar
22.74		Prandini			2r2	NCAA	Fayetteville	14 Mar
22.90	Cierra	White	USA	29.4.93	2r1	NCAA	Fayetteville	14 Mar
22.96	A'Keyla	Mitchell	USA	11.11.95	3r2	NCAA	Fayetteville	14 Mar
22.97	Kamaria	Brown	USA	21.12.92	1r3	Tyson	Fayetteville	14 Feb
23.07	Ariana	Washington	USA-J	4.9.96	3r1	NCAA	Fayetteville	14 Mar
23.08	Taylor	Ellis-Watson	USA	6.5.93	1r4	Tyson	Fayetteville	14 Feb
23.08	Shakima	Wimbley	USA	23.4.95	1	ACC	Blacksburg	28 Feb
23.12	Rebekka	Haase (10)	GER	2.1.93	1	NC	Karlsruhe	22 Feb
23.16	Robin	Reynolds	USA	22.2.94	1r6	Tyson	Fayetteville	14 Feb

23.19A	Tynia	Gaither	BAH	16.3.93	13 Feb
23.22	Destinee	Gause	USA	4.4.94	31 Jan
23.24	Kineke	Alexander	VIN	21.2.86	14 Feb
23.27	Anna	Kielbasinska	POL	26.6.90	22 Feb
23.27	Kelly	Proper	IRL	1.5.88	22 Feb
23.27	Ashton	Purvis	USA	12.7.92	14 Mar
23.30	Jada	Martin	USA	8.6.95	14 Feb
23.30	Nadine	Gonska	GER	23.1.90	22 Feb

300 METRES

36.52	Natasha	Hastings	USA	23.7.86	1r2	NC	Boston (Roxbury)	28 Feb
36.65	Jessica	Beard	USA	8.1.89	2r2	NC	Boston (Roxbury)	28 Feb
36.70!	Dezerea	Bryant	USA	27.4.93	1		Bloomington	12 Dec
36.74	Tiffany	Townsend	USA	14.6.89	1	NB GP	Boston (Roxbury)	7 Feb

37.07	Floria	Guei	FRA	2.5.90	25 Feb
37.13	Alena	Mamina	RUS	90	7 Jan
37.29	Yekaterina	Renzhina	RUS	18.10.94	7 Jan
37.36	Kineke	Alexander	VIN	21.2.86	9 Jan

400 METRES

51.12	Courtney	Okolo	USA	15.3.94	1r2	NCAA	Fayetteville	14 Mar
51.35A		Okolo			1		Albuquerque	7 Feb
51.52	Taylor	Ellis-Watson	USA	6.5.93	2r2	NCAA	Fayetteville	14 Mar
51.65		Okolo			1r2	Tyson	Fayetteville	13 Feb
51.70	Francena	McCorory	USA	20.10.88	1		Boston (Allston)	1 Mar
51.72	Seren	Bundy-Davies	GBR	30.12.94	1	GP	Birmingham	21 Feb
51.85	Ashley	Spencer	USA	8.6.93	1r1	NCAA	Fayetteville	14 Mar
51.92	Shamier	Little	USA	20.3.95	1r3	Tyson	Fayetteville	13 Feb
51.96	Nataliya	Pyhyda	UKR	30.1.81	1	EI	Praha (02)	7 Mar
52.06A	Shapri	Romero	USA	13.11.91	1		Albuquerque	14 Feb
52.08	Yekaterina	Renzhina	RUS	18.10.94	1	Winter	Moskva	1 Feb
52.10	Margaret	Bamgbose (10)	USA	19.10.93	1	ACC	Blacksburg	28 Feb
52.14	Marie	Gayot	FRA	18.12.89	1	NC	Aubière	22 Feb
52.15	Shakima	Wimbley	USA	23.4.95	2	ACC	Blacksburg	28 Feb

52.20	Kineke	Alexander	VIN	21.2.86	13 Feb
52.26	Kala	Funderburk	USA	14.9.92	28 Feb
52.27	Robin	Reynolds	USA	22.2.94	31 Jan
52.27	Kiara	Porter	USA	22.10.93	1 Mar
52.28	Kyra	Jefferson	USA	23.9.94	13 Feb
52.28	Kirsten	McAslan	GBR	1.9.93	21 Feb
52.32	Kamaria	Brown	USA	21.12.92	7 Feb
52.32	Laura	Maddox (20)	GBR	13.5.90	21 Feb

52.34 Floria Guei FRA 2.5.90 22 Feb
52.39 Alena Mamina RUS 30.5.90 1 Feb
52.40 Brianna Tate USA 1.1.93 13 Mar
52.41 Chris-Ann Gordon JAM 18.9.94 13 Feb
52.42 Madiea Ghafoor NED 9.9.92 22 Feb
52.48 Denisa Rosolová CZE 21.8.86 6 Mar
52.51 Justyna Swiety POL 3.12.92 22 Feb
52.63 Indira Terrero ESP 29.11.85 7 Mar
52.67 Sparkle McKnight TTO 21.12.91 31 Jan
52.76 Zuzana Hejnová (30) CZE 19.12.86 22 Feb

Oversized track

51.37 Shamier Little USA 20.3.95 1r2 SEC Lexington 28 Feb
51.81 Kendall Baisden USA 5.3.95 1 Lexington 24 Jan
51.82 Shakima Wimbley USA 23.4.95 2 Lexington 24 Jan
52.00 Kyra Jefferson USA 23.9.94 2r2 SEC Lexington 28 Feb
52.69 Morganne Phillips USA 10.11.92 2r1 SEC Lexington 28 Feb

500 METRES

1:08.84 Georganne Moline USA 6.3.90 1 New York (Armory) 30 Jan
1:09.75 Mariya Nikolayeva RUS 14.4.91 1 Moskva 11 Jan

600 METRES

1:26.22 Kirsten McAslan GBR 1.9.93 1 Manchester 4 Jan
1:26.56 Ajee' Wilson USA 8.5.94 1h3 NC Boston (Roxbury) 28 Feb
1:26.59 Alysia Montaño USA 26.4.86 1 NC Boston (Roxbury) 1 Mar
1:26.73 Kendra Chambers USA 9.1.90 2h3 NC Boston (Roxbury) 28 Feb
1:27.15A Georganne Moline USA 6.3.90 1r1 Albuquerque 13 Feb
1:27.47 Montaño 1h2 NC Boston (Roxbury) 28 Feb
1:27.65! Aníta Hinriksdóttir ISL-J 13.1.96 1 Reykjavik 16 Dec

800 METRES

1:59.21 Jennifer Meadows GBR 17.4.81 1 Wien 31 Jan
1:59.85 Meadows 1 Torun 3 Feb
2:00.01 Joanna Józwik POL 30.1.91 2 Torun 3 Feb
2:01.44 Yekaterina Poistogova RUS 1.3.91 1h1 EI Praha (02) 6 Mar
2:01.56 Aníta Hinriksdóttir ISL-J 13.1.96 2h1 EI Praha (02) 6 Mar
2:01.57 Ajee' Wilson USA 8.5.94 1 Mill New York (Armory) 14 Feb
2:01.64 Natoya Goule JAM 30.3.91 1 NCAA Fayetteville 14 Mar
2:01.71 Ayvika Malanova RUS 28.11.92 1r1 Moskva 28 Jan
2:01.79 Treniere Moser USA 27.10.81 2r1 New York (Armory) 31 Jan
2:01.87 Selina Büchel SUI 26.7.91 1 Düsseldorf 29 Jan
2:01.97 Renelle Lamote (10) FRA 26.12.93 1 v3N Glasgow 24 Jan

2:02.01 Noëlie Yarigo BEN 26.12.85 25 Feb
2:02.05 Charlene Lipsey USA 16.7.91 14 Feb
2:02.13 Anastasiya Bazdyreva RUS 6.3.92 18 Feb
2:02.15 Angelika Cichocka POL 15.3.88 22 Feb
2:02.18 Nataliya Lupu UKR 4.11.87 6 Mar
2:02.22 Mariya Nikolayeva RUS 14.4.91 17 Feb
2:02.50 Yekaterina Kupina RUS 2.2.86 18 Feb
2:02.59 Svetlana Rogozina RUS 26.12.92 8 Feb
2:02.64 Rabab Arrafi MAR 12.1.91 25 Feb
2:02.66 Stephanie Charnigo (20) USA 25.7.88 31 Jan
2:02.68 Yuliya Stepanova RUS 3.7.86 25 Feb
2:02.69 Ciara Everard IRL 10.7.90 6 Mar
2:02.71 Irina Maracheva RUS 29.9.84 18 Jan
2:02.75 Mary Cain USA-J 3.5.96 31 Jan
2:02.84 Yekaterina Brodovaya RUS 28.6.91 17 Feb

1000 METRES

2:37.86 Treniere Moser USA 27.10.81 1 NB GP Boston (Roxbury) 7 Feb
2:38.25 Mary Cain USA-J 3.5.96 2 NB GP Boston (Roxbury) 7 Feb

2:39.16 Molly Beckwith-Ludlow USA 4.8.87 7 Feb
2:39.64 Stephanie Brown USA 29.7.91 7 Feb
2:39.66 Sanne Verstegen NED 10.11.85 7 Feb
2:39.70# Sasha Gollish CAN 27.12.81 13 Feb
2:39.72 Yevgeniya Zinurova RUS 16.11.82 25 Jan
2:39.99 Morgan Uceny USA 10.3.85 7 Feb

1500 METRES

4:00.46 Sifan Hassan NED .93 1 XLG Stockholm 19 Feb
4:02.57 Hassan 1 Karlsruhe 31 Jan
4:02.92 Axumawit Embaye ETH 18.10.94 2 Karlsruhe 31 Jan
4:05.08+ Shannon Rowbury USA 19.9.84 1 in 1M New York (Armory) 14 Feb
4:05.61 Bethlem Desalegn UAE 13.11.91 2 XLG Stockholm 19 Feb
4:06.42 Meraf Bahta SWE 24.6.89 3 XLG Stockholm 19 Feb
4:06.42 Angelika Cichocka POL 15.3.88 4 XLG Stockholm 19 Feb
4:07.69 Gudaf Tsegay ETH-J 23.1.97 5 XLG Stockholm 19 Feb
4:07.91 Rabab Arrafi MAR 12.1.91 6 XLG Stockholm 19 Feb
4:07.93+ Jordan Hasay USA 21.9.91 2 in 1M New York (Armory) 14 Feb
4:08.87 Federica Del Buono (10) ITA 12.12.94 1 Ancona 7 Feb
4:08.95 Renata Plis POL 5.2.85 1 Spala 7 Feb
4:09.22 Katarzyna Broniatowska POL 22.2.90 2 Spala 7 Feb
4:09.54+ Treniere Moser USA 27.10.81 3 in 1M New York (Armory) 14 Feb

4:10.15 Basu Sado ETH .91 7 Feb
4:10.4mx Laura Muir GBR 9.5.93 17 Jan
4:12.10 19 Feb
4:10.68+ Stephanie Charnigo USA 25.7.88 14 Feb
4:11.10+ Mary Cain USA-J 3.5.96 14 Feb
4:11.18+ Morgan Uceny USA 10.3.85 14 Feb
4:11.36 Maureen Koster NED 3.7.92 7 Feb
4:11.76+ Heather Kampf (20) USA 19.1.87 14 Feb
4:11.89 Sandra Eriksson FIN 4.6.89 19 Feb
4:11.90+ Shelby Houlihan USA 8.2.93 14 Feb
4:11.95 Sofia Ennaoui POL 30.8.95 7 Feb
4:12.06 Hanna Klein GER 6.4.93 7 Feb
4:12.18 Yelena Zhilkina RUS 4.5.90 18 Jan
4:12.18+ Rosie Clarke GBR 17.11.91 14 Feb
4:12.27 Anna Shchagina RUS 7.12.91 31 Jan
4:12.33+ Nicole Tully USA 30.10.86 14 Feb
4:12.46 Gesa-Felicitas Krause GER 3.8.92 18 Feb
4:13.20 Giulia Alessandra Viola (30) ITA 24.4.91 21 Feb

1 MILE

4:22.66	Shannon	Rowbury	USA	19.9.84	1		Winston-Salem	31 Jan
4:23.50	Axumawit	Embaye	ETH	18.10.94	1	GP	Birmingham	21 Feb
4:24.12		Rowbury			2	GP	Birmingham	21 Feb
4:24.32		Rowbury			1	Mill	New York (Armory)	14 Feb
4:26.84	Gudaf	Tsegay	ETH-J	23.1.97	3	GP	Birmingham	21 Feb
4:27.18	Leah	O'Connor	USA	30.8.92	1	NCAA	Fayetteville	14 Mar
4:27.49	Treniere	Moser	USA	27.10.81	2	Mill	New York (Armory)	14 Feb
4:28.02	Stephanie	Charnigo	USA	25.7.88	3	Mill	New York (Armory)	14 Feb
4:28.27	Jordan	Hasay	USA	21.9.91	4	Mill	New York (Armory)	14 Feb
4:28.71	Shelby	Houlihan	USA	8.2.93	2	NCAA	Fayetteville	14 Mar
4:28.73#	Jordan	Hasay	USA	21.9.91	2		Seattle	17 Jan
4:29.39	Morgan	Uceny (10)	USA	10.3.85	5	Mill	New York (Armory)	14 Feb
4:29.67	Colleen	Quigley	USA	20.11.92	1		Boston (Allston)	13 Feb
4:30.07	Heather	Kampf	USA	19.1.87	6	Mill	New York (Armory)	14 Feb

4:30.62	Rachel	Schneider	USA	18.7.91	13 Feb
4:30.70#	Becca	Addison	USA	28.5.91	21 Feb
4:31.31	Mary	Cain	USA-J	3.5.96	14 Feb
4:31.75	Rosie	Clarke	GBR	17.11.91	14 Mar
4:32.13+	Dawit	Seyaum	ETH	27.7.96	7 Feb
4:32.31	Ashley	Higginson	USA	17.3.89	26 Jan
4:32.35	Erin	Teschuk	CAN	25.10.94	14 Mar
4:32.36#	Nicole	Sifuentes (20)	CAN	30.6.86	21 Feb
4:32.48#	Dominique	Scott	RSA	24.6.92	24 Jan
4:32.74#	Rhianwedd	Price	GBR	11.8.94	28 Feb
4:32.86	Aisha	Praught	USA	14.12.89	21 Feb
4:33.23	Stephanie	Garcia	USA	3.5.88	31 Jan

2000 METRES

5:35.46	Dawit	Seyaum	ETH-J	27.7.96	1	NB GP	Boston (Roxbury)	7 Feb
5:40.35	Sally	Kipyego	KEN	19.12.85	2	NB GP	Boston (Roxbury)	7 Feb
5:41.11	Emma	Coburn	USA	19.10.90	3	NB GP	Boston (Roxbury)	7 Feb
5:43.82	Heidi	See	AUS	8.9.89	4	NB GP	Boston (Roxbury)	7 Feb
5:44.8+	Genzebe	Dibaba	ETH	8.2.91	1	in 5000	Stockholm	19 Feb

3000 METRES

8:37.22+	Genzebe	Dibaba	ETH	8.2.91	1	in 5000	Stockholm	19 Feb
8:41.72	Sally	Kipyego	KEN	19.12.85	1	Mill	New York (Armory)	14 Feb
8:43.19	Betsy	Saina	KEN	30.6.88	2	Mill	New York (Armory)	14 Feb
8:45.05	Gotytom	Gebreslase	ETH	15.1.95	3	Mill	New York (Armory)	14 Feb
8:46.61	Habiba	Ghribi	TUN	9.4.84	1	GP	Birmingham	21 Feb
8:46.84	Senbera	Teferi	ETH	3.5.95	2	GP	Birmingham	21 Feb
8:47.61	Yelena	Korobkina	RUS	25.11.90	1		Karlsruhe	31 Jan
8:48.02	Svetlana	Kudzelich	BLR	7.5.87	2	EI	Praha (02)	7 Mar
8:49.73	Laura	Muir	GBR	9.5.93	2		Karlsruhe	31 Jan
8:50.21	Jordan	Hasay (10)	USA	21.9.91	3	GP	Birmingham	21 Feb
8:51.10	Maureen	Koster	NED	3.7.92	4	GP	Birmingham	21 Feb

8:52.57#	Dominique	Scott	RSA	24.6.92	14 Feb
8:52.60	Emily	Sisson	USA	12.10.91	14 Feb
8:53.09	Jessica	O'Connell	CAN	10.2.89	14 Feb
8:53.12	Kate	Avery	GBR	10.10.91	14 Feb
8:53.22	Sofia	Ennaoui	POL	30.8.95	31 Jan
8:54.06	Sandra	Eriksson	FIN	4.6.89	7 Mar
8:54.77#	Brie	Felnagle	USA	9.12.86	14 Feb
8:55.09	Ciara	Mageean	IRL	12.3.92	14 Feb
8:55.19	Dominique	Scott (20)	RSA	24.6.92	14 Mar
8:55.20	Heidi	See	AUS	8.9.89	13 Feb
8:56.23	Giulia Alessandra	Viola	ITA	24.4.91	22 Feb
8:56.77	Elizabeth	Costello	USA	23.2.88	3 Jan
8:56.83	Sara	Moreira	POR	17.10.85	22 Feb
8:57.86	Ashley	Higginson	USA	17.3.89	14 Feb
8:57.87	Maren	Kock	GER	22.6.90	31 Jan
8:57.96	Marusa	Mismas	SLO	24.10.94	6 Mar
8:58.51#	Angela	Bizzarri	USA	15.2.88	14 Feb
8:58.84	Alla	Kulyatina	RUS	9.6.90	17 Feb
8:58.88	Kristiina	Maki (30)	CZE	22.9.91	31 Jan
8:58.88	Elise	Cranny	USA-J	8.5.96	14 Mar
8:59.84	Jennifer	Wenth	AUT	24.7.91	7 Mar
8:59.88	Marielle	Hall	USA	28.1.92	14 Feb

2 MILES

9:18.35	Jennifer	Simpson	USA	23.6.86	1	NB GP	Boston (Roxbury)	7 Feb
9:27.05	Sentayehu	Ejigu	ETH	21.6.85	2	NB GP	Boston (Roxbury)	7 Feb
9:29.03	Buze	Diriba	ETH	9.2.94	3	NB GP	Boston (Roxbury)	7 Feb

9:31.41	Gotytom	Gebreslase	ETH	15.1.95	7 Feb
9:38.28	Jordan	Hasay	USA	21.9.91	31 Jan
9:39.38	Nicole	Tully	USA	30.10.86	31 Jan
9:39.61	Marielle	Hall	USA	28.1.92	31 Jan

5000 METRES

15:12.22	Emily	Sisson	USA	12.10.91	1		New York (Armory)	28 Feb
15:20.57!	Sarah	Disanza	USA	25.8.95	1		Boston (Allston)	6 Dec
15:22.56	Birtukan	Fente	ETH	18.6.89	2	XLG	Stockholm	19 Feb

15:31.62!	Liv	Westphal	FRA	22.12.93	6 Dec
15:34.15	Birtukan	Adamu	ETH	29.4.92	19 Feb
15:34.70	Alia Saeed	Mohammed	UAE	18.5.91	19 Feb
15:35.71	Dagmawit	Kidane	ETH-J	2.12.96	19 Feb

2000 METRES STEEPLECHASE

6:14.4	Natalya	Tarantinova	RUS	28.11.87	1		Smolensk	18 Jan
6:17.69	Yekaterina	Doseykina	RUS	30.3.90	1		Moskva	8 Feb
6:19.5		Doseykina			2		Smolensk	18 Jan
6:20.97	Viktoriya	Ivanova	RUS	21.11.91	1		Novocheboksarsk	17 Jan
6:22.31	Anastasiya	Puzakova	BLR	12.12.93	1		Minsk	24 Jan
6:23.67	Alina	Sergeyeva	RUS	15.9.94	3		Moskva	8 Feb

55 METRES HURDLES

7.55	Le'Tristan	Pledger	USA	27.8.93	1		Lubbock	20 Feb

60 METRES HURDLES

7.83	Sharika	Nelvis	USA	10.5.90	1		Malmö	25 Feb
7.84	Jasmin	Stowers	USA	23.9.91	1	NC	Boston (Roxbury)	1 Mar
7.85	Alina	Talay	BLR	14.5.89	1	EI	Praha (02)	6 Mar
7.87		Nelvis			1	GP	Birmingham	21 Feb
7.87	Kendra	Harrison	USA	18.9.92	1	NCAA	Fayetteville	14 Mar
7.88		Talay			1		Wien	14 Feb
7.88		Talay			1		Mogilyov	21 Feb
7.88	Bridgette	Owens	USA	14.3.92	2	NCAA	Fayetteville	14 Mar
7.89		Stowers			1h1	NC	Boston (Roxbury)	1 Mar
7.89		Talay			1s1	EI	Praha (02)	6 Mar
7.90	Lucy	Hatton	GBR	8.11.94	2	EI	Praha (02)	6 Mar
7.93	Serita	Solomon	GBR	1.3.90	3	EI	Praha (02)	6 Mar
7.93	Cindy	Roleder	GER	21.8.89	4	EI	Praha (02)	6 Mar
7.95	Eline	Berings	BEL	28.5.86	1	NC	Gent	21 Feb
7.95	Isabelle	Pedersen (10)	NOR	27.1.92	3s1	EI	Praha (02)	6 Mar
7.97	Andrea	Ivancevic	CRO	21.8.84	4s1	EI	Praha (02)	6 Mar
7.97	Nooralotta	Neziri	FIN	9.11.92	6	EI	Praha (02)	6 Mar
7.98	Tiffany	Porter	GBR	13.11.87	2h2		Malmö	25 Feb
7.99	Hanna	Plotitsyna	UKR	1.1.87	1h1	Pedros	Lódz	17 Feb

8.01	Josephine	Onyia	ESP	15.7.86	22 Feb
8.01	Dior	Hall	USA-J	2.1.96	13 Mar
8.02	Danielle	Williams	JAM	14.9.92	30 Jan
8.02	Yvette	Lewis	PAN	16.3.85	10 Feb
8.03	Anne	Zagré	BEL	13.3.90	21 Feb
8.03	Erica	Bougard (20)	USA	26.7.93	27 Feb
8.03	Tenaya	Jones	USA	22.3.89	1 Mar
8.05A	Lindsay	Lindley	NGR	6.10.89	20 Feb
8.05	Nina	Morozova	RUS	15.9.89	6 Mar
8.05	Karolina	Koleczek	POL	15.1.93	6 Mar
8.06	Tiffany	McReynolds	USA	4.12.91	1 Mar
8.07	Morgan	Snow	USA	26.7.93	13 Feb
8.07	Yekaterina	Galitskaya	RUS	24.2.87	18 Feb
8.07	Alice	Decaux	FRA	10.4.85	22 Feb
8.07	Pamela	Dutkiewicz	GER	28.9.91	22 Feb
8.07	Kristi	Castlin (30)	USA	7.7.88	1 Mar
8.08	Kseniya	Medvedeva	BLR	24.10.94	23 Jan
8.08	Nadine	Visser	NED	9.2.95	14 Feb
8.08	Giulia	Pennella	ITA	27.10.89	21 Feb
8.08	Marina	Tomic	SLO	30.4.83	6 Mar
8.09	Yekaterina	Poplavskaya	BLR	7.5.87	23 Jan
8.09	Beate	Schrott	AUT	15.4.88	6 Feb
8.10	Cindy	Ofili	USA	5.8.94	7 Feb
8.10	Brianne	Theisen-Eaton	CAN	18.12.88	14 Feb
8.10	Svetlana	Topylina	RUS	6.1.85	18 Feb
8.10	Sandra	Gomis (40)	FRA	21.11.83	22 Feb
8.10	Le'Tristan	Pledger	USA	27.8.93	13 Mar
8.10	Kendell	Williams	USA	14.6.95	14 Mar

HIGH JUMP

2.02	Kamila	Licwinko	POL	22.3.86	1	NC	Torun	21 Feb
2.01		Licwinko			1	Winter	Moskva	1 Feb
2.00		Licwinko			1		Cottbus	27 Jan
1.99	Mariya	Kuchina	RUS	14.1.93	2	Winter	Moskva	1 Feb
1.98	Airine	Palsyte	LTU	13.7.92	2		Cottbus	27 Jan
1.98		Kuchina			1		Trinec	8 Feb
1.98		Licwinko			1	Pedros	Lódz	17 Feb
1.98		Palsyte			1	NC	Klaipeda	20 Feb
1.97	Katarina	Johnson-Thompson	GBR	9.1. 93	1	NC	Sheffield	14 Feb
1.97	Alessia	Trost	ITA	8.3.93	2	EI	Praha (02)	7 Mar
1.96	Ruth	Beitia	ESP	1.4.79	3		Cottbus	27 Jan
1.96	Irina	Gordeyeva	RUS	9.10.86	1		Sankt-Peterburg	22 Feb
1.95	Svetlana	Shkolina	RUS	9.3.86	1		Novocheboksarsk	16 Jan
1.95	Yana	Maksimova	BLR	9.1..89	1		Minsk	23 Jan
1.95	Ana	Simic (10)	CRO	5.5.90	3		Trinec	8 Feb
1.94	Daniela	Stanciu	ROU	15.10.87	1	NC	Bucuresti	14 Feb
1.94	Morgan	Lake	GBR-J	12.5.97	2	NC	Sheffield	14 Feb
1.94	Venelina	Veneva-Mateeva	BUL	13.6.74	1		Dobrich	15 Feb
1.94	Justyna	Kasprzycka	POL	20.8.87	Q	EI	Praha (02)	6 Mar
1.93	Barbara	Szabó	HUN	17.2.90	1	NC	Budapest (SH)	22 Feb
1.93	Leontia	Kallenou	CYP	5.10.94	1	NCAA	Fayetteville	13 Mar
1.92	Oksana	Okunyeva	UKR	14.3.90	1		Lviv	17 Jan
1.92A		Zheng Xingjuan	CHN	20.3.89	1		Albuquerque	24 Jan
1.92	Isobel	Pooley	GBR	21.12.92	5		Cottbus	27 Jan
1.92	Urszula	Gardzielewska (20)	POL	21.7.88	1=		Torun	3 Feb
1.92	Mirela	Demireva	BUL	28.9.89	1	Flanders	Gent	7 Feb
1.92	Oldriska	Maresová	CZE	14.10.86	1		Valasské Mezirící	14 Mar

1.91	Tatyana	Mnatsakanova	RUS	25.5.83	24 Jan
1.91	Oksana	Krasnokutskaya	RUS	24.9.93	24 Jan
1.91	Desiree	Rossit	ITA	193,94	31 Jan
1.91	Michaela	Hruba	CZE-Y	21.2.98	6 Mar
1.91	Iryna	Herashchenko	UKR	10.3.95	6 Mar
1.90	Taisiya	Roslova	BLR	7.10.92	16 Jan
1.90	Erika	Kinsey	SWE	10.3.88	30 Jan
1.90	Jeannelle	Scheper (30)	LCA	21.11.94	31 Jan
1.90	Claudia	García	ESP	30.9.92	13 Mar
1.89	Nafissatou	Thiam	BEL	19.8.94	6 Mar
1.88	Marina	Smolyakova	RUS	20.6.89	17 Jan
1.88	Katarina	Mögenburg	NOR	16.6.91	27 Jan
1.88	Chaunte	Lowe	USA	12.1.84	7 Feb
1.88	Yevgeniya	Kononova	RUS	28.9.89	10 Feb
1.88	Eliska	Klucinová	CZE	14.4.88	21 Feb
1.87	ten women				

POLE VAULT

4.83	Fabiana	Murer	BRA	16.3.81	1		Nevers	7 Feb
4.80	Nikoleta	Kiriakopoúlou	GRE	21.3.86	1	GP	Birmingham	21 Feb

4.80	Anzhelika	Sidorova	RUS	28.6.91	1	EI	Praha (02)	8 Mar
4.77A	Ekateríni	Stefanídi	GRE	4.2.90	1		Flagstaff	20 Feb
4.76		Kiriakopoúlou			1	XLG	Stockholm	19 Feb
4.75A	Demi	Payne	USA	30.9.91	1		Albuquerque	24 Jan
4.75		Sidorova			1	NC	Moskva	17 Feb
4.75		Stefanídi			2	EI	Praha (02)	8 Mar
4.72	Elizaveta	Ryzih	GER	27.9.88	1		Metz	25 Feb
4.71	Marion	Fiack	FRA	13.10.92	1		Aubière	10 Jan
4.70	Angelica	Bengtsson	SWE	8.7.93	3	EI	Praha (02)	8 Mar
4.67	Angelina	Krasnova	RUS	7.2.91	2		Metz	25 Feb
4.66	Sandi	Morris (10)	USA	8.7.92	1	SEC	Lexington	27 Feb
4.62	Jirina	Ptacníková	CZE	20.5.86	1		Praha (SH)	25 Feb
4.60	Katharina	Bauer	GER	12.6.90	1		Leverkusen	18 Jan
4.60	Anastasiya	Savchenko	RUS	15.11.89	2=	NC	Moskva	17 Feb
4.60	Olga	Mullina	RUS	1.8.92	4	NC	Moskva	17 Feb
4.55	Nicole	Büchler	SUI	17.12.83	1		Potsdam	6 Feb
4.55	Michaela	Meijer	SWE	30.7.93	9q	EI	Praha (02)	6 Mar
4.55	Tina	Sutej	SLO	7.11.88	10q	EI	Praha (02)	6 Mar
4.54	Alayna	Lutkovskaya	RUS-J	15.3.96	1		Zweibrücken	28 Feb
4.54	Marion	Lotout	FRA	19.11.89	2		Zweibrücken	28 Feb
4.53	Melissa	Gergel (20)	USA	14.4.89	2		Lexington	23 Jan
4.51	Victoria	von Eynatten	GER	6.10.91	1		Dortmund	1 Feb
4.51		Li Ling	CHN	6.7.89	1		Xianlin	8 Mar
4.50A	Becky	Holliday	USA	12.3.80	2		Reno	16 Jan
4.50A	Mary	Saxer	USA	21.6.87	3		Reno	16 Jan
4.50	Natalya	Demidenko	RUS	7.8.93	1		Volgograd	18 Jan
4.50	Martina	Strutz	GER	4.11.81	1		Berlin	1 Feb
4.50	Tatyana	Shvydkina	RUS	8.5.90	2		Moskva	7 Feb
4.50	Jennifer	Suhr	USA	5.2.82	3	NB GP	Boston (Roxbury)	7 Feb
4.50	Katie	Nageotte	USA	30.6.91	3	NC	Boston (Roxbury)	1 Mar
4.50	Megan	Clark (30)	USA	10.6.94	2	NCAA	Fayetteville	14 Mar
4.49	April	Steiner-Bennett	USA	22.4.80	2		Fayetteville	21 Feb

4.47	Kelsie	Ahbe	USA	6.7.91	7 Feb
4.47	Femke	Pluim	NED	10.5.94	21 Feb
4.46A	Tori	Pena	IRL	30.7.87	7 Feb
4.45	Anastasiya	Sadovnikova	RUS	22.6.94	14 Feb
4.45	Minna	Nikkanen	FIN	9.4.88	21 Feb
4.45	Kayla	Caldwell	USA	19.6.91	1 Mar
4.45	Malin	Dahlström	SWE	26.8.89	6 Mar
4.45	Kira	Grünberg	AUT	13.8.93	6 Mar
4.45	Stephanie	Richartz (40)	USA	21.1.92	14 Mar
4.43	Kristen	Hixson	USA	1.7.92	13 Feb
4.42	Naroa	Agirre	ESP	15.5.79	25 Feb
4.41	Leslie	Brost	USA	28.9.89	30 Jan
4.40	Yekaterina	Kazeka	RUS	7.10.90	9 Jan
4.40	Lyudmila	Yeryomina	RUS	8.8.91	17 Jan
4.40	Annika	Roloff	GER	10.3.91	1 Feb
4.40	Desiree	Singh	GER	17.8.94	4 Feb
4.40	Stellá-Iró	Ledáki	GRE	18.7.88	15 Feb
4.40	Hanna	Shelekh	UKR	14.7.93	20 Feb
4.40	Wilma	Murto (50)	FIN-Y	11.6.98	21 Feb
4.40	Alexis	Paine	USA	12.10.90	1 Mar
4.39	Kaitlin	Petrillose	USA	10.12.92	27 Feb
4.37	Morgann	LeLeux	USA	14.11.92	7 Feb
4.37	Heather	Hamilton	CAN	31.3.88	14 Feb
4.35	Robin	Bone	CAN	13.2.94	30 Jan
4.35	Caroline Bonde	Holm	DEN	19.7.90	6 Feb
4.35	Anjuli	Knäsche	GER	18.10.93	6 Feb
4.35	Loréla	Mánou	GRE	20.12.90	15 Feb
4.35	Lexi	Weeks	USA-J	20.11.96	21 Feb
4.35	Romana	Malácová (60)	CZE	15.5.87	25 Feb
4.35	Diamara	Planell	PUR	16.2.93	14 Mar

LONG JUMP

6.99	Christabel	Nettey	CAN	2.6.91	1	XLG	Stockholm	19 Feb
6.98	Ivana	Spanovic	SRB	10.5.90	1	EI	Praha (02)	7 Mar
6.93	Katarina	Johnson-Thompson	GBR	9.1.93	1	NC	Birmingham	21 Feb
6.89		Johnson-Thompson			1P	EI	Praha (02)	6 Mar
6.86	Sosthene	Moguenara	GER	17.10.89	1		Saarbrucken	11 Jan
6.84		Nettey			2	GP	Birmingham	21 Feb
6.83		Spanovic			1		Malmö	25 Feb
6.83		Moguenara			2	EI	Praha (02)	7 Mar
6.82	Yekaterina	Koneva	RUS	25.9.88	1	Winter	Moskva	1 Feb
6.82	Aiga	Grabuste	LAT	24.3.88	1		Tbilisi	8 Feb
6.79	Florentina	Marincu	ROU-J	8.4.96	3	EI	Praha (02)	7 Mar
6.75	Funmilayo	Jimoh	USA	29.5.84	4	GP	Birmingham	21 Feb
6.74	Éloyse	Lesueur	FRA	15.7.88	4		Malmö	25 Feb
6.74	Alina	Rotaru (10)	ROU	5.6.93	4	EI	Praha (02)	7 Mar
6.73	Abigail	Irozuru	GBR	3.1.90	1	NC	Sheffield	15 Feb
6.69	Erica	Jarder	SWE	2.4.86	2		Karlsruhe	31 Jan
6.66	Khaddi	Sagnia	SWE	20.4.94	1		Malmö	25 Jan
6.65	Jenna	Prandini	USA	20.11.92	1	NCAA	Fayetteville	13 Mar
6.64	Akela	Jones	BAR	21.4.95	1	Tyson	Fayetteville	13 Feb
6.62	Bianca	Stuart	BAH	17.5.88	2	Tyson	Fayetteville	13 Feb
6.61	Melanie	Bauschke	GER	14.7.88	3	ISTAF	Berlin	14 Feb

6.57	Olga	Balayeva	RUS	31.7.84	17 Jan
6.57	Karin	Melis Mey	TUR	31.5.84	6 Mar
6.56	Amastasiya	Mironchik-Ivanova (20)	BLR	13.4.89	16 Jan
6.56	Yuliy	Pidluzhnaya	RUS	1.10.88	18 Feb
6.55	Jessie	Gaines	USA	12.8.90	13 Feb
6.55	Xenia	Atschkinadze	GER	14.1.89	22 Feb
6.55	Sha'Keela	Saunders	USA	18.12.93	27 Feb
6.54	Nadja	Käther	GER	29.9.88	25 Jan
6.54	Lena	Malkus	GER	6.8.93	1 Feb
6.54	Kendell	Williams	USA	14.6.95	7 Feb

6.53	Anastasiya	Mokhnyuk	UKR	1.1.91	27	Jan
6.53	Laura	Strati	ITA	3.10.90	22	Feb
6.52	Anna	Misochenko (30)	RUS	15.4.92	18	Jan
6.52	Julienne	McKee	USA	6.12.91	13	Feb

TRIPLE JUMP

14.69	Yekaterina	Koneva	RUS	25.9.88	1	EI	Praha (02)	8 Mar
14.68		Koneva			1		Volgograd	24 Jan
14.57		Koneva			Q	NC	Moskva	19 Feb
14.55	Gabriela	Petrova	BUL	29.6.92	1	NC	Dobrich	15 Feb
14.52		Petrova			2	EI	Praha (02)	8 Mar
14.49	Hanna	Minenko	ISR	25.9.89	3	EI	Praha (02)	8 Mar
14.46	Kristin	Gierisch	GER	20.8.90	4	EI	Praha (02)	8 Mar
14.44		Koneva			1	NC	Moskva	19 Feb
14.40		Minenko			Q	EI	Praha (02)	7 Mar
14.32	Patricia	Mamona	POR	21.11.88	5	EI	Praha (02)	8 Mar
14.30		Gierisch			1		Düsseldorf	29 Jan
14.28	Cristina	Bujin	ROU	12.4.88	1		Bucuresti	31 Jan
14.21	Natalya	Vyatkina	BLR	10.2.87	Q	EI	Praha (02)	7 Mar
14.21		Li Yanmei	CHN	6.2.90	1		Xianlin	9 Mar
14.20	Kristiina	Mäkelä	FIN	20.11.92	1		Mustasaari	4 Feb
14.16	Katja	Demut (10)	GER	21.12.83	2		Chemnitz	7 Feb
14.14	Olha	Saladukha	UKR	4.6.83	2		Düsseldorf	29 Jan
14.13	Jeanine	Assani Issouf	FRA	17.8.92	1	NC	Aubière	21 Feb
14.11	Irina	Gumenyuk	RUS	6.1.88	1		Sankt-Peterburg	10 Feb
14.10	Andriana	Bânova	BUL	1.5.87	1		Dobrich	11 Feb
14.08	Natalya	Alekseyeva	RUS	27.5.86	2	NC	Moskva	19 Feb
14.03	Olga	Rypakova	KAZ	30.11.84	1	NC	Ust-Kamenogorsk	15 Feb
14.03	Olesya	Zabara	RUS	6.10.82	3	NC	Moskva	19 Feb
14.01	Ciarra	Brewer	USA	12.3.93	1	NCAA	Fayetteville	14 Mar
13.98	Keturah	Orji	USA-J	5.3.96	1		Lexington	24 Jan
13.98	Kseniya	Detsuk (20)	BLR	23.4.86	2	NCp	Gomel	7 Feb
13.97	Cristina	Sandu	ROU	4.3.90	9q	EI	Praha (02)	7 Mar
13.95	Dovile	Dzindzalietaite	LTU	14.7.93	1		Vilnius	31 Jan
13.94	Patricia	Sarrapio	ESP	16.11.82	1	NC	Antequera	21 Feb

13.89	Dana	Veldáková	SVK	3.6.81	7	Mar
13.86	Elena Andreea	Panturoiu	ROU	24.2.95	31	Jan
13.85	Anna	Jagaciak	POL	10.2.90	14	Feb
13.85	Ruth Marie	Ndoumbe	ESP	1.1.87	21	Feb
13.84	Darya	Derkach	ITA	27.3.93	21	Feb
13.83	Rouguy	Diallo	FRA	5.2.95	8	Feb
13.82	Snezana	Vukmirovic (30)	SLO	19.8.82	24	Jan
13.82	Anastasiya	Potapova	RUS	6.9.85	24	Jan
13.79	Lucie	Majková	CZE	9.7.88	7	Mar
13.78	Susana	Costa	POR	22.9.84	7	Mar
13.75	Simona	La Mantia	ITA	14.4.83	21	Feb
13.70		Wang Wupin	CHN	18.1.91	2	Mar

SHOT

19.45	Michelle	Carter	USA	12.10.85	1	NC	Boston (Roxbury)	1 Mar
19.23	Anita	Márton	HUN	15.1.89	1	EI	Praha (02)	7 Mar
19.01	Brittany	Smith	USA	25.3.91	1		Bloomington IL	17 Jan
19.00	Yuliya	Leontyuk	BLR	31.1.84	1	NC	Mogilyov	20 Feb
18.83	Jeneva	Stevens	USA	28.10.89	1		Bloomington IN	31 Jan
18.62		Leontyuk			1		Minsk	16 Jan
18.62	Raven	Saunders	USA-J	15.5.96	1	NCAA	Fayetteville	14 Mar
18.60		Márton			1		Budapest	7 Feb
18.60		Leontyuk			2	EI	Praha (02)	7 Mar
18.34	Radoslava	Mavrodieva	BUL	13.3.87	1		Dobrich	11 Feb
18.34	Rebecca	O'Brien	USA	30.4.90	2	NC	Boston (Roxbury)	1 Mar
18.32	Felisha	Johnson	USA	24.7.89	1		Bloomington IN	13 Feb
18.31	Elena	Abramchuk (10)	BLR	14.2.88	2	NCp	Gomel	7 Feb
18.21	Chiara	Rosa	ITA	28.1.83	1		Padova	31 Jan
17.97	Julaika	Nicoletti	ITA	20.3.88	1		Ancona	24 Jan
17.97	Anastasiya	Podolskaya	RUS	18.8.90	1		Moskva	7 Feb
17.95	Claire	Uke	USA	30.12.92	1		Birmingham AL	26 Feb
17.94	Halyna	Obleshchuk	UKR	23.2.89	1	NC	Sumy	13 Feb
17.82		Gao Yang	CHN	1.3.93	1		Shanghai	2 Mar
17.79	Lena	Urbaniak	GER	31.10.92	1	NC	Karlsruhe	21 Feb
17.76	Denise	Hinrichs	GER	7.6.87	2	NC	Karlsruhe	21 Feb

17.74	Olha	Holodnaya	UKR	14.11.91	13	Feb
17.73	Paulina	Guba (20)	POL	14.5.90	5	Mar
17.71	Danniel	Thomas	JAM	11.11.92	28	Feb
17.68	Úrsula	Ruíz	ESP	11.8.83	7	Feb
17.61	Jill	Rushin	USA	18.7.91	27	Feb
17.55	Emel	Dereli	TUR-J	25.2.96	21	Feb
17.52	Josephine	Terlecki	GER	17.2.86	1	Feb
17.45	Dani	Winters	USA	18.2.93	7	Feb
17.45		Bian Ka	CHN	5.1.93	16	Mar
17.40	Brittany	Mann	USA	16.4.94	14	Mar
17.37		Meng Qianqian	CHN	6.1.91	2	Mar
17.30	(30)	Guo Tianqian	CHN	1.6.95	2	Mar
17.25	Kelsey	Card	USA	20.8.92	14	Feb
17.22	Nikki	Okwelogu	NGR	5.5.95	14	Mar
17.16	Cassie	Wertman	USA	14.6.93	27	Feb
17.15	Monique	Riddick	USA	8.11.89	1	Mar

20 LB WEIGHT

23.69	Jeneva	Stevens	USA	28.10.89	1		Charleston	20 Feb
23.45	Felisha	Johnson	USA	24.7.89	1	NC	Boston (Roxbury)	28 Feb
23.43		Stevens			2	NC	Boston (Roxbury)	28 Feb
23.41		Stevens			1		Bloomington IN	30 Jan

23.20 Johnson 1 Bloomington IN 13 Feb
23.19! Johnson 1 Bloomington IN 12 Dec
23.15 Amber Campbell USA 5.6.81 1 Chapel Hill 21 Feb
23.09 Campbell 1 Chapel Hill 17 Jan
22.84 Kearsten Peoples USA 20.12.91 1 Columbia MO 20 Feb
22.56 Ida Storm SWE 26.12.91 2 NCAA Fayetteville 13 Mar
22.30 Amanda Bingson USA 20.2.90 4 NC Boston (Roxbury) 28 Feb
22.28 Brea Garrett USA 27.6.93 1 Tyson Fayetteville 13 Feb
22.04 Deanna Price USA 8.6.93 3 NCAA Fayetteville 13 Mar
21.86 Brittany Funk USA 13.5.92 27 Feb
21.82 Kelsey Card (10) USA 20.8.92 13 Feb
21.75 Carly Fehringer USA 9.11.91 31 Jan
21.68 Alexis Cooks USA 11.9.93 16 Jan
21.61 Becky Famurewa USA 24.2.94 23 Jan
21.57! Sophia Lozano USA 26.4.93 6 Dec
21.45 Lea Johnson USA 26 Feb

PENTATHLON

5000 Katarina Johnson-Thompson GBR 9.1.93 1 EI Praha (02) 6 Mar
8.18 1.95 12.32 6.89 2:12.78
4742 Yana Maksimova BLR 9.1.89 1 NC Gomel 6 Feb
8.66 1.92 14.95 6.07 2:14.57
4707 Anastasiya Mokhnyuk UKR 1.1.91 1 Zaporizhzhya 27 Jan
8.13 1.80 13.73 6.53 2:19.05
4696 Nafissatou Thiam BEL 19.8.94 2 EI Praha (02) 6 Mar
8.42 1.89 14.80 6.33 2:24.23
4691 Györgyi Zsivoczky-Farkas HUN 13.2.85 1 NC Budapest (SH) 14 Feb
8.44 1.85 14.34 6.20 2:15.10
4687 Eliska Klucinová CZE 14.4.88 3 EI Praha (02) 6 Mar
8.53 1.86 15.07 6.15 2:17.26
4678 Kendell Williams USA 14.6.95 1 NCAA Fayetteville 14 Mar
8.10 1.83 12.24 6.53 2:17.30
4654 Sharon Day-Monroe USA 9.6.85 1 NC Boston (Roxbury) 27 Feb
8.56 1.83 15.41 5.94 2:13.45
4628 Maksimova 4 EI Praha (02) 6 Mar
8.76 1.89 14.96 5.85 2:13.67
4609 Alina Fyodorova UKR 31.7.89 1 NC Sumy 12 Feb
8.70 1.83 15.76 6.35 2:25.71
4591 Antoinette Nana Djimou (10) FRA 2.8.85 5 EI Praha (02) 6 Mar
8.25 1.80 15.05 6.13 2:22.78
4566 Erica Bougard USA 26.7.93 2 NCAA Fayetteville 14 Mar
8.16 1.83 12.46 6.16 2:16.93
4548 Anouk Vetter NED 4.2.93 8 EI Praha (02) 6 Mar
8.33 1.77 14.80 6.29 2:24.48
4527 Morgan Lake GBR-J 12.5.97 9 EI Praha (02) 6 Mar
8.81 1.92 13.91 6.10 2:23.44
4518 Aleksandra Butvina RUS 14.2.86 10 EI Praha (02) 6 Mar
8.74 1.77 14.96 6.03 2:14.84
4489 Yekaterina Netsvetayeva BLR 26.6.89 2 NC Gomel 6 Feb
8.57 1.77 14.91 5.79 2:14.10
4489 Anna Blank RUS 12.1.90 11 EI Praha (02) 6 Mar
8.73 1.77 14.11 6.03 2:13.04
4478 Xénia Krizsán HUN 13.1.93 2 NC Budapest (SH) 14 Feb
8.38 1.76 14.09 5.95 2:16.51
4450 Xenia Rahn GER 9.3.91 3 NCAA Fayetteville 14 Mar
8.39 1.77 12.98 6.23 2:20.17
4430 Alex Gochenour USA 17.2.93 4 NCAA Fayetteville 14 Mar
8.41 1.80 12.37 6.04 2:16.85
4404# Lindsay Vollmer (20) USA 10.9.92 1 Big 12 Ames 27 Feb
8.35 1.78 13.12 6.09 2:22.56
4402 Akela Jones BAR 31.12.95 1 Lawrence 30 Jan
8.21 1.82 12.78 6.38 2:34.75
4389 Barbara Nwaba USA 18.1.89 27 Feb
4386 Katerina Cachová CZE 26.2.90 7 Feb
4372 Jess Herauf USA 17.1.93 14 Mar
4368 Agnieszka Borowska POL 21.10.91 7 Feb
4368 Lyubov Tkach RUS 18.2.93 14 Feb
4366 Magdalena Sochon POL 25.2.95 1 Feb
4317 Kaylon Eppinger USA 17.9.89 27 Feb
4274 Sofia Linde SWE 12.1.95 8 Feb
4266 Lucia Mokrásová (30) SVK 27.3.94 7 Feb
4261 Yelena Molodchinina RUS 16.4.91 14 Feb
4259 Quintunya Chapman USA 7.1.93 14 Mar
4249 Jessica Taylor GBR 27.6.88 24 Jan
4233 Beatrice Puiu ROU 1.1.86 7 Feb
4230 Anaëlle Nyabeu Djapa FRA 15.9.92 22 Feb
4230 Taliyah Brooks USA 8.2.95 14 Mar
4226 Brittany Harrell USA .91 30 Jan
4226 Anna Petrich RUS 10.2.92 14 Feb
4223# Georgia Ellenwood CAN 5.8.95 27 Feb

3000 METRES WALK

12:05.68 Antonella Palmisano ITA 6.8.91 1 NC Padova 21 Feb
12:17.93 Ana Cabecinha POR 29.4.84 1 NC Pombal 14 Feb

5000 METRES WALK

21:21.13! Lyudmila Olyanovska UKR 20.2.93 1 Sumy 24 Dec
21:34.8 Olga Shargina RUS-J 24.7.96 1 Chelyabinsk 6 Jan

10000m WALK: 43:55.51 Ana Cabecinha POR 29.4.84 1 Vila Real de S.Antonio 11 Jan